CHILTON'S AUTO REPAIR MANUAL 1972-1979

Merry Christmas Todd
With Lots of Love
Jami

When your old & gray please remember
you wanted Chilton book
for Christmas - We rather
would have richer
you something much, much nicer.
Love ya Anyway
Tamera Cheryl.

Christmas "83"
Almost '84'

President	William A. Barbour
Executive Vice President	Richard H. Groves
Vice President & General Manager	John P. Kushnerick
Managing Editor	John H. Weise, S.A.E.
Assistant Managing Editors	Peter J. Meyer, S.A.E.
	Kerry A. Freeman, S.A.E.
Service Editors	John Baxter
	Arthur I. Birney
	Theodore B. Costantino
	Martin J. Gunther
	Robert King
	David H. Lee
	Robert McAnally
	Richard J. Rivele
	Miles Schofield
Graphics Editor	Martin W. Kane
Production Manager	Warren Owens
Assistant Production Manager	Timothy Frelick
Production Assistant	Joseph Rauen
Editorial Production	Dru Brown
	Anne Warner

CHILTON BOOK COMPANY
Chilton Way, Radnor, Pa. 19089

Manufactured in USA
© 1978 by Chilton Book Company
ISBN 0-8019-6914-X
Library of Congress Catalog Card No. 76-648878

CONTENTS

Car Section

AMERICAN MOTORS

CHRYSLER CORPORATION

FORD MOTOR COMPANY

GENERAL MOTORS

Unit Repair Section

American Motors

Index

American Motors

YEAR IDENTIFICATION

SERIES 10, MATADOR

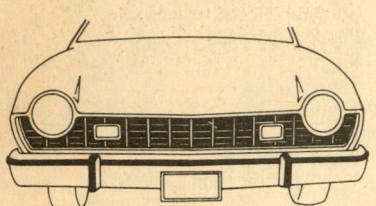

1972 Matador

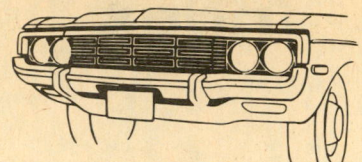

1973 Matador

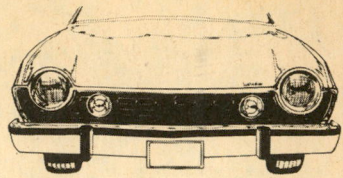

1974-1975 Matador Coupe

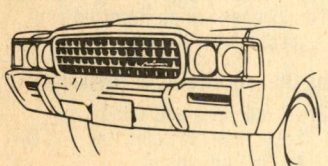

1976 Matador Coupe

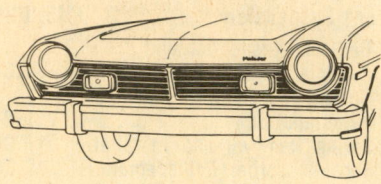

1977 Matador Coupe

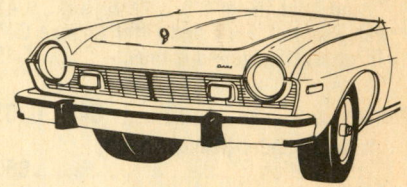

1978 Matador

SERIES 80, AMBASSADOR AND MATADOR

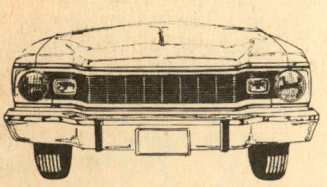

1972 Ambassador

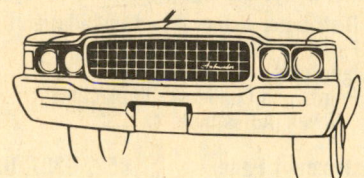

1973 Ambassador

1974 Ambassador

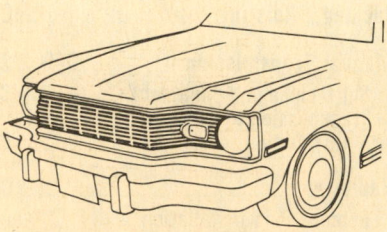

1975 Matador Sedan, Wagon

1976 Matador Sedan, Wagon

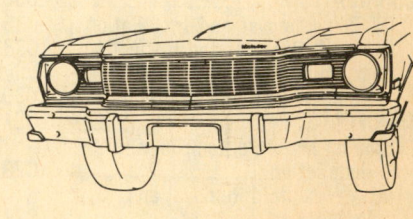

1977 Matador Sedan, Wagon

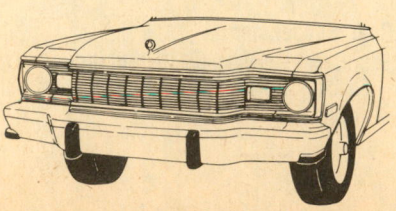

1978 Matador Coupe

SERIES 01 AND 40, GREMLIN, HORNET, CONCORD

1972 Hornet

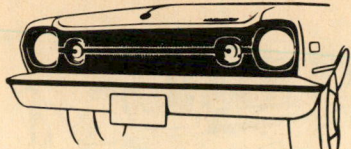

1973 Hornet

1974 Hornet

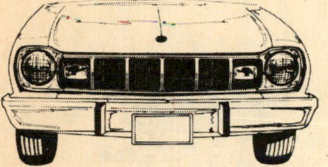

1975-76 Hornet

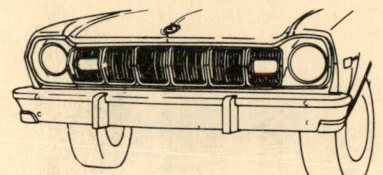

1977 Hornet

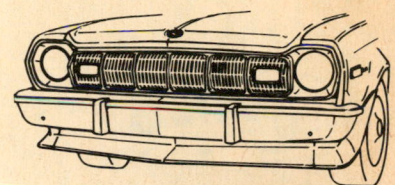

1977 Hornet AMX

1978 AMX

1978 Concord

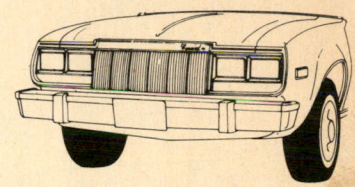

1979 Concord

1972 Gremlin

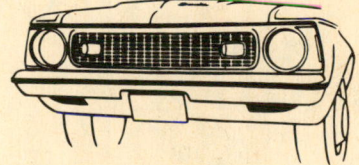

1973 Gremlin

1974 Gremlin

1975 Gremlin

1976 Gremlin

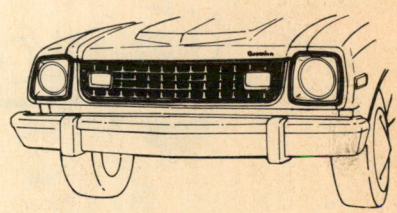

1977 Gremlin

1978 Gremlin

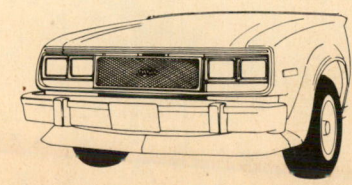

1979 AMX

1979 SPIRIT

YEAR IDENTIFICATION

SERIES 70, JAVELIN

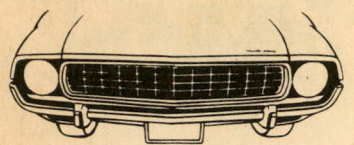

1972 Javelin SST

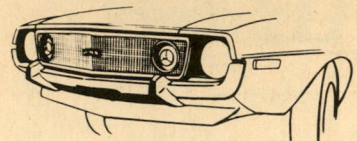

1973 Javelin

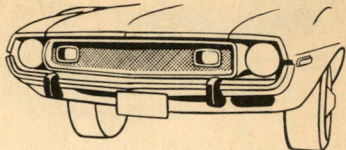

1974 Javelin

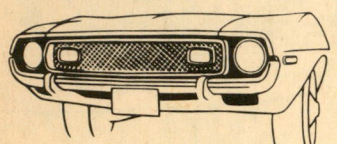

1972 Javelin AMX

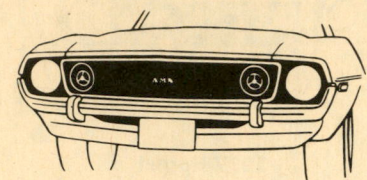

1973 Javelin AMX

1974 Javelin AMX

SERIES 60, PACER

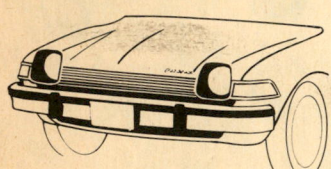

1975 Pacer

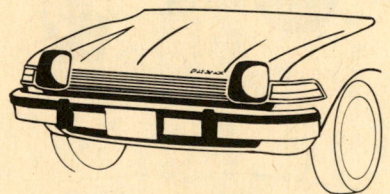

1976 Pacer

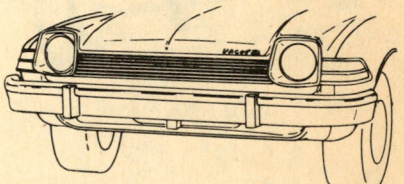

1977 Pacer

1978 Pacer

1979 Pacer

ENGINE CODE

The engine code is the 4th digit of the engine build code stamped on a machined surface of the cylinder block behind the dipstick on 4 cylinder engines, between No. 2 and No. 3 cylinders on 6 cylinder engines, and stamped on a tag attached to the right bank valve cover on V8 engines. All V8 engines also have their cubic inch displacement cast into block, on both banks, between the first and second core plugs. In addition, the engine code is the 7th digit of the Vehicle Identification Number (V.I.N.). The V.I.N. is stamped on a plate located at te left side of the instrument panel visible through the windshield.

Displacement	Carb. No. Bbls.	HP ■	'72	'73	'74	'75	'76	'77	'78	'79
4 Cylinder Models										
121	2	80						G	G	G
6 Cylinder Models										
232	1	90					E	E	E	E
232	1	100	E	E	E	E				
232	1	135								
258	1	95					A	A	A	A
258	1	110	A	A	A	A				
258	2	120					C	C	C	C
258	1	150								
8 Cylinder Models										
304	2	120					H	H	H	H
304	2	150	H	H	H	H				
304	2	210								
360	2	129						N	N	
360	2	140					N			
360	2	175	N	N	N	N				
360	4	180					P	P		
360	4	195,220#	P	P	P	P				
360	2	245								
360	4	290								
401	4	215					Z	Z		
401	4	225	Z	Z	Z	Z				
401	4	330								

\# With dual exhaust

■ Horsepower and torque are SAE net figures. They are measured at the rear of the transmission with all accessories installed and operating. Since the figures vary when a given engine is installed in different models, some are representative rather then exact.

GENERAL ENGINE SPECIFICATIONS

Year	Engine No. Cyl. Displacement Cu. In.	Carburetor Type	Horsepower @ rpm ■	Torque @ rpm (ft lbs) ■	Bore and Stroke (in.)	Compression Ratio	Oil Pressure @ 2000 rpm
'72	6-232	1 bbl	100 @ 3600	185 @ 1800	3.750 x 3.500	8.0:1	46
	6-258	1 bbl	110 @ 3500	195 @ 2000	3.750 x 3.900	8.0:1	46
	8-304	2 bbl	150 @ 4200	245 @ 2500	3.750 x 3.440	8.4:1	46
	8-360	2 bbl	175 @ 4000	285 @ 2400	4.080 x 3.440	8.5:1	46
	8-360	4 bbl	195 @ 4400	295 @ 2900	4.080 x 3.440	8.5:1	46
	8-401	4 bbl	255 @ 4600	345 @ 3300	4.165 x 3.680	8.5:1	46
'73	6-232	1 bbl	100 @ 3600	185 @ 1800	3.750 x 3.500	8.0:1	46
	6-258	1 bbl	110 @ 3500	195 @ 2000	3.750 x 3.900	8.0:1	46
	8-304	2 bbl	150 @ 4200	245 @ 2500	3.750 x 3.440	8.3:1	46
	8-360	2 bbl	175 @ 4000	285 @ 2400	4.080 x 3.440	8.3:1	46
	8-360	4 bbl	195 @ 4400	295 @ 2900	4.080 x 3.440	8.3:1	46
	8-360①	4 bbl	220 @ 4400	315 @ 3100	4.080 x 3.440	8.3:1	46
	8-401	4 bbl	255 @ 4600	345 @ 3300	4.165 x 3.680	8.5:1	46

GENERAL ENGINE SPECIFICATIONS (Cont'd)

Year	Engine No. Cyl. Displacement Cu. In.	Carburetor Type	Horsepower @ rpm ■	Torque @ rpm (ft lbs) ■	Bore and Stroke (in.)	Compression Ratio	Oil Pressure @ 2000 rpm
'74	6-232	1 bbl	100 @ 3600	185 @ 1800	3.750 x 3.500	8.0:1	46
	6-258	1 bbl	110 @ 3500	195 @ 2000	3.750 x 3.900	8.0:1	46
	8-304	2 bbl	150 @ 4200	245 @ 2500	3.750 x 3.440	8.4:1	46
	8-360	2 bbl	175 @ 4000	285 @ 2400	4.080 x 3.440	8.25:1	46
	8-360	4 bbl	195 @ 4400	295 @ 2900	4.080 x 3.440	8.25:1	46
	8-360①	4 bbl	220 @ 4400	315 @ 3100	4.080 x 3.440	8.25:1	46
	8-401	4 bbl	255 @ 4600	345 @ 3300	4.165 x 3.680	8.25:1	46
'75	6-232	1 bbl	100 @ 3600	185 @ 1800	3.750 x 3.500	8.0:1	46
	6-258	1 bbl	110 @ 3500	195 @ 2000	3.750 x 3.900	8.0:1	46
	8-304	2 bbl	150 @ 4200	245 @ 2500	3.750 x 3.440	8.4:1	46
	8-360	2 bbl	175 @ 4000	285 @ 2400	4.080 x 3.440	8.25:1	46
	8-360	4 bbl	195 @ 4400	295 @ 2900	4.080 x 3.440	8.25:1	46
	8-360①	4 bbl	220 @ 4400	315 @ 3100	4.080 x 3.440	8.25:1	46
	8-401②	4 bbl	255 @ 4600	345 @ 3300	4.165 x 3.680	8.25:1	46
'76	6-232	1 bbl	90 @ 3050	170 @ 2000	3.750 x 3.500	8.0:1	46
	6-258	1 bbl	95 @ 3050	180 @ 2100	3.750 x 3.900	8.0:1	46
	6-258	2 bbl	120 @ 3400	200 @ 2000	3.750 x 3.900	8.0:1	46
	8-304	2 bbl	120 @ 3200	220 @ 2200	3.750 x 3.440	8.4:1	46
	8-360	2 bbl	140 @ 3200	260 @ 1600	4.080 x 3.440	8.25:1	46
	8-360	4 bbl	180 @ 3600	280 @ 2800	4.080 x 3.440	8.25:1	46
	8-401②	4 bbl	215 @ 4200	320 @ 2800	4.165 x 3.680	8.25:1	46
'77	4-121	2 bbl	80 @ 5000	105 @ 2800	3.410 x 3.320	8.2:1	28.5③
	6-232	1 bbl	88 @ 3400	164 @ 1600	3.750 x 3.500	8.0:1	46
	6-258	1 bbl	98 @ 3200	193 @ 1600	3.750 x 3.900	8.0:1	46
	6-258	2 bbl	114 @ 3600	192 @ 2000	3.750 x 3.900	8.0:1	46
	8-304	2 bbl	121 @ 3450	219 @ 2000	3.750 x 3.440	8.4:1	46
	8-360	2 bbl	129 @ 3700	245 @ 1600	4.080 x 3.440	8.25:1	46
'78-'79	4-121	2 bbl	80 @ 5000	105 @ 2800	3.410 x 3.320	8.2:1	28.5③
	6-232	1 bbl	90 @ 3400	168 @ 1600	3.750 x 3.500	8.0:1	46
	6-258	1 bbl	100 @ 3400	200 @ 1600	3.750 x 3.900	8.0:1	46
	6-258	2 bbl	120 @ 3600	201 @ 1800	3.750 x 3.900	8.0:1	46
	8-304	2 bbl	130 @ 3200	238 @ 2000	3.750 x 3.440	8.4:1	46
	8-360	2 bbl	140 @ 3350	278 @ 2000	4.080 x 3.440	8.25:1	46

■ Beginning 1972, horsepower and torque are SAE net figures. They are measured at the rear of the transmission with all accessories installed and operating. Since the figures vary when a given engine is installed in different models, some are representative rather than exact.

① Dual exhaust
② Police only
③ At sending unit

Ambassador, Concord, Gremlin, Hornet, Matador, Pacer, Spirit

TUNE-UP SPECIFICATIONS

When analyzing compression test results, look for uniformity among cylinders rather than specific pressures.

Year	No. Cyl Displacement (cu in.)	hp	Orig. Type	Gap (in.)	Point Dwell (deg)	Point Gap (in.)	Man Trans	Auto Trans	Valves Intake Opens ■ (deg)	Fuel Pump Pressure (psi)	Idle Man Trans	Idle Auto Trans *
'72	6-232	100	N-12Y	.035	33	.016	5B(3B)	5B(3B)	12	4-5½	600(700)	550(600)
	6-258	110	N-12Y	.035	33	.016	5B(3B)	5B(3B)	12	4-5½	600(700)	550(600)
	8-304	150	N-12Y	.035	30	.016	5B	5B	14¾	4-5½	750	650(700)
	8-360	175	N-12Y	.035	30	.016	5B	5B	14¾	4-5½	750	700
	8-360	195	N-12Y	.035	30	.016	5B	5B	14¾	4-5½	750	700
	8-401	255	N-12Y	.035	30	.016	5B	5B	25½	4-5½	750	650(700)
'73	6-232	100	N-12Y	.035	33	.016	5B(3B)	5B(3B)	12	4-5½	700	600
	6-258	110	N-12Y	.035	33	.016	5B(3B)	5B(3B)	12	4-5½	700	600
	8-304	150	N-12Y	.035	30	.016	5B	5B	14¾	4-5½	750	700
	8-360	175	N-12Y	.035	30	.016	5B	5B	14¾	4-5½	750	700
	8-360	195	N-12Y	.035	30	.016	5B	5B	14¾	4-5½	750	700
	8-401	255	N-12Y	.035	30	.016	5B	5B	25½	4-5½	750	700
'74	6-232	100	N-12Y	.035	33	.016	5B(3B)	5B(3B)	12	4-5½	700	600
	6-258	110	N-12Y	.035	33	.016	5B(3B)	5B(3B)	12	4-5½	700	600
	8-304	150	N-12Y	.035	30	.016	5B	5B (2½ B)	14¾	5-6½	750	700
	8-360	175	N-12Y	.035	30	.016	5B	5B	14¾	5-6½	750	700
	8-360	195	N-12Y	.035	30	.016	5B	5B	14¾	5-6½	750	700
	8-401	255	N-12Y	.035	30	.016	5B	5B	25½	5-6½	750	700
'75	6-232	100	N-12Y	.035	electronic		5B	5B	12	4-5	600	550(700)
	6-258	110	N-12Y	.035	electronic		3B	3B	12	4-5	600	550(700)
	8-304	150	N-12Y	.035	electronic		5B	5B	14¾	5-6½	750	700
	8-360	175	N-12Y	.035	electronic		5B	5B	14¾	5-6½	750	700
	8-360	195	N-12Y	.035	electronic		5B	5B	14¾	5-6½	750	700
	8-401	255	N-12Y	.035	electronic		5B	5B	25½	5-6½	750	700
'76	6-232	90	N-12Y	.035	electronic		8B	8B	12	4-5	850	550(700)
	6-258	95	N-12Y	.035	electronic		6B	8B	12	4-5	850①	550(700)
	6-258	120	N-12Y	.035	electronic		6B	8B	12	4-5	850	550(700)
	8-304	120	N-12Y	.035	electronic		5B	10B(5B)	14¾	5-6½	750	700
	8-360	140	N-12Y	.035	electronic		—	10B(5B)	14¾	5-6½	—	700
	8-360	180	N-12Y	.035	electronic		—	10B(5B)	14¾	5-6½	—	700
	8-401	215	N-12Y	.035	electronic		—	10B(5B)	25½	5-6½	—	700
'77	4-121	80	N-8L	.035	47	.018	12B	12B(8B)	41¾	4-6	900	800
	6-232	88	N-12Y	.035	electronic		8B(10B)	10B	12	4-5	600(850)	550(700)
	6-258	98	N-12Y	.035	electronic		6B③	8B③	12	4-5	600	550(700)
	6-258	114	N-12Y	.035	electronic		6B	8B	12	4-5	600	550(700)
	8-304	121	N-12Y	.035	electronic		—	10B(5B)	14¾	5-6½	—	600(700)
	8-360	129	N-12Y	.035	electronic		—	10B(5B)	14¾	5-6½	—	600(700)
'78	4-121	2 bbl	N-8L	.035	47	.018	12B	12B(8B)	41¾	4-6	900	800
	6-232	1 bbl	N-13l	.035	electronic		8B	10B	12	4-5	600	550
	6-258	1 bbl	N-13L	.035	electronic		10B(6B)	10B(8D)	12	4-5	600(850)	550(700)
	6-258	2 bbl	N-13L	.035	electronic		6B	8B	14½	4-5	600	600

TUNE-UP SPECIFICATIONS (Cont'd)

When analyzing compression test results, look for uniformity among cylinders rather than specific pressures.

| | ENGINE | | SPARK PLUGS | | DISTRIBUTOR | | IGNITION TIMING (deg) ▲ | | VALVES | Fuel Pump | IDLE SPEED ● (rpm) ▲ | |
Year	No. Cyl Displacement (cu in.)	hp	Orig. Type	Gap (in.)	Point Dwell (deg)	Point Gap (in.)	Man Trans ●	Auto Trans	Intake Opens ■ (deg)	Pressure (psi)	Man Trans	Auto Trans *
	8-304	2 bbl	N-12Y	.035	electronic		—	10B(5B)	14¾	5-6½	—	600(700)
	8-360	2 bbl	N-12Y	.035	electronic		—	10B	14¾	5-6½	—	600(650)
'79	4-121	2 bbl	N-8L	.035	47	.018	12B	12B(8B)	41¾	4-6	900	800
	6-232	1 bbl	N-13L	.035	electronic		8B	10B	12	4-5	600	550
	6-258	1 bbl	N-13L	.035	electronic		—	8B	12	4-5	—	700
	6-258	2 bbl	N-13L	.035	electronic		4B	8B	12	4-5	700	600
	8-304	2 bbl	N-12Y	.035	electronic		5B	8B	14¾	5-6½	800	600

▲ See text for procedure
● Figure in parentheses indicates California engine
■ All figures Before Top Dead Center
* With transmission in Drive
B Before Top Dead Center
TDC Top Dead Center (zero degrees)

— Not applicable
① 600 rpm for Matador coupe and sedan
NOTE: The underhood specifications sticker often reflects tune-up specification changes made in production. Sticker figures must be used if they disagree with those in this chart.

MECHANICAL VALVE LIFTER CLEARANCE

Engine	Intake (Hot) In.	Exhaust (Hot) In.
4-121	.006-.009	.016-.019

Javelin — TUNE-UP SPECIFICATIONS

When analyzing compression test results, look for uniformity among cylinders rather than specific pressures.

| | ENGINE | | SPARK PLUGS | | DISTRIBUTOR | | IGNITION TIMING (deg) ▲ | | VALVES | Fuel Pump | IDLE SPEED (rpm) ▲ | |
Year	No. Cyl Displacement (cu in.)	hp	Orig. Type	Gap (in.)	Point Dwell (deg)	Point Gap (in.)	Man Trans ●	Auto Trans	Intake Opens ■ (deg)	Pressure (psi)	Man Trans ●	Auto Trans
'72	6-232	100	N-12Y	.035	31-34	.016	5B	5B	12½	4-5½	600(700)	550(600)
	6-258	110	N-12Y	.035	31-34	.016	—	3B	12½	4-5½	—	550(600)
	8-304	150	N-12Y	.035	29-31	.016	5B	5B	14¾	5-6½	750	650(700)
	8-360	175	N-12Y	.035	29-31	.016	—	5B	14¾	5-6½	—	700
	8-360	195	N-12Y	.035	29-31	.016	5B	5B	14¾	5-6½	750	700
	8-401	255	N-12Y	.035	29-31	.016	5B	5B	25½	5-6½	750	650(700)
'73	6-232	100	N-12Y	.035	31-34	.016	5B	5B	12½	4-5½	700	600
	6-258	110	N-12Y	.035	31-34	.016	—	3B	12½	4-5½	—	600
	8-304	150	N-12Y	.035	29-31	.016	5B	5B	14¾	5-6½	750	700
	8-360	175	N-12Y	.035	29-31	.016	—	5B	14¾	5-6½	—	700
	8-360	190	N-12Y	.035	29-31	.016	5B	5B	14¾	5-6½	750	700
	8-401	255	N-12Y	.035	29-31	.016	5B	5B	25½	5-6½	750	700
'74	6-232	100	N-12Y	.035	31-34	.016	5B	5B	12½	4-5½	600(700)	550(600)
	6-258	110	N-12Y	.035	31-34	.016	—	3B	12½	4-5½	—	550(600)
	8-304	150	N-12Y	.035	29-31	.016	5B	5B (2½ B)	14¾	5-6½	750	650(700)

Javelin   ## TUNE-UP SPECIFICATIONS

When analyzing compression test results. look for uniformity among cylinders rather than specific pressures.

	ENGINE		SPARK PLUGS		DISTRIBUTOR		IGNITION TIMING (deg) ▲		VALVES Intake Opens ■ (deg)	Fuel Pump Pressure (psi)	IDLE SPEED (rpm) ▲	
Year	No. Cyl Displacement (cu in.)	hp	Orig. Type	Gap (in.)	Point Dwell (deg)	Point Gap (in.)	Man Trans ●	Auto Trans			Man Trans ●	Auto Trans
	8-360	175	N-12Y	.035	29-31	.016	—	5B	14¾	5-6½	—	700
	8-360	190	N-12Y	.035	29-31	.016	5B	5B	14¾	5-6½	750	700
	8-401	255	N-12Y	.035	29-31	.016	5B	5B	25½	5-6½	750	650(700)

▲ See text for procedure
■ All figures Before Top Dead Center
● Figure in parentheses indicates California engine

B Before Top Dead Center
TDC Top Dead Center
— Not applicable

NOTE: The underhood specifications sticker often reflects tune-up specification changes made in production. Sticker figures must be used if they disagree with those in this chart.

FIRING ORDER

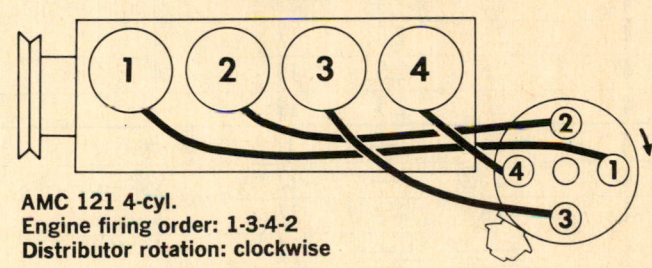

AMC 121 4-cyl.
Engine firing order: 1-3-4-2
Distributor rotation: clockwise

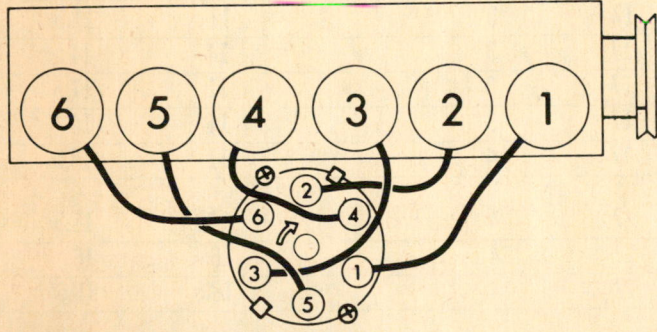

AMC 232, 258 6-cyl. Through 1977
Engine firing order: 1-5-3-6-2-4
Distributor rotation: clockwise

(Circles are position of latches on models through 1974; squares are position of latches on 1975 and later models.)

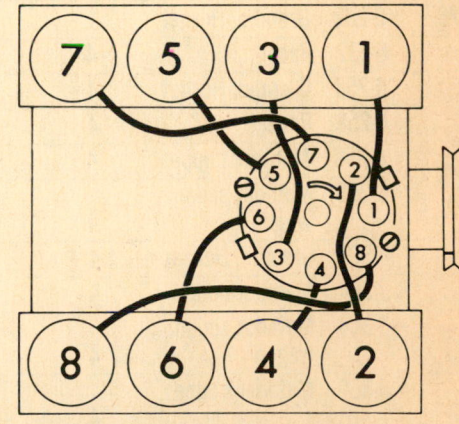

AMC 304, 360, 401 V8
Engine firing order: 1-8-4-3-6-5-7-2
Distributor rotation: clockwise

(Circles are position of latches on models through 1974; squares are the position of latches on 1975 and later models.)

AMC 232, 258 6-cyl. 1978 and later
Engine firing order 1-5-3-6-2-4
Distributor rotation: clockwise

CAPACITIES

Year	ENGINE No. Cyl. Displacement (cu in.)	MODEL	Engine Crankcase Add 1 Qt For New Filter	TRANSMISSION Pts To Refill After Draining			Drive Axle (pts)	Gasoline Tank (gals)	COOLING SYSTEM (qts)	
				Manual		Automatic			With Heater	With A/C
				3-Speed	4-Speed					
'72	6-232		4	1.5①	——	17	3③		10.5	10.5
	6-258		4	2.5	——	17	3③		10.5	10.5
	8-304		4	2.5	2.5	17	4		14	14
	8-360		4	2.5	2.5	19	4		13	13
	8-401		4	2.5	2.5	19	4		13	13
'73	6-232		4	2.5	——	17	3③		10.5	10.5
	6-258		4	2.5	——	17	3③		10.5	10.5
	8-304		4	2.5	2.5	17	4		14	14
	8-360		4	2.5	2.5	19	4		13	14
	8-401		4	2.5	2.5	19	4		13	14
'74	6-232		4	2.5	——	17	3③		11	11.5
	6-258		4	2.5	——	17	3③		11	11.5
	8-304		4	2.5	2.5	17	4		16④	16④
	8-360		4	2.5	2.5	19	4		15.5⑤	15.5⑤
	8-401		4	2.5	2.5	19	4		15.5⑤	15.5⑤
'75	6-232		4	3.5②	——	17	3③		11⑧	11.5⑥
	6-258		4	3.5②	——	17	3③		11⑧	11.5⑥
	8-304		4	3.5		17	4		16.5④	16④⑦
	8-360		4	——		19	4		15.5⑤	15.5⑤
	8-401		4	——		19	4		15.5⑤	15.5⑤
'76	6-232	Gremlin, Hornet	4	2.5②	——	17	3		11	11.5
	6-232	Pacer	4	3.5②	3.5	17	3		14	14
	6-258	Gremlin, Hornet	4	2.5②	——	17	3		11	11.5
	6-258	Pacer	4	3.5②	3.5	17	3		14	14
	6-258	Matador coupe	4	3.5	——	17	4		11	13.5
	6-258	Matador sedan, wagon	4	3.5	——	17	4		11	11.5
	8-304	Gremlin, Hornet	4	3.5	——	17	4		16	16
	8-304	Matador coupe	4	3.5	——	17	4		18.5	18.5
	8-304	Matador sedan, wagon	4	3.5	——	17	4		16.5	16.5⑨
	8-360, 401	Matador coupe	4	——		19	4		17.5	17.5
	8-360, 401	Matador sedan, wagon	4	——		19	4		15.5	15.5⑨
'77-'79	4-121	Gremlin	3.5⑩	——	2.4	14.2	3		6.5	——
	6-232	Gremlin	4	3.5⑪	3.5	17	3		11	14
	6-232•Hornet, Concord	4	3.5⑪	3.5	17	3		11	11.5⑬
	6-232	Pacer	4	3.5⑪	3.5	17	3		14	14
	6-258	Gremlin	4	3.5⑪	3.5	17	3		11	14
	6-258	Hornet, Concord	4	3.5⑪	3.5	17	3		11	11.5⑬
	6-258	Pacer	4	3.5⑪	3.5	17	3		14	14
	6-258	Matador coupe	4	——	——	17	4		13.5	13.5
	6-258	Matador sedan, wagon	4	——	——	17	4		11.5	11.5

CAPACITIES

Year	ENGINE No. Cyl. Displacement (cu in.)	MODEL	Engine Crankcase Add 1 Qt For New Filter	TRANSMISSION Pts To Refill After Draining Manual 3-Speed	4-Speed	Automatic	Drive Axle (pts)	Gasoline Tank (gals)	COOLING SYSTEM (qts) With Heater	With A/C
	8-304	Hornet, Concord, Pacer	4	—	—	17	4		16⑭	16⑭
	8-304	Matador coupe	4	—	—	17	4		18.5	18.5
	8-304	Matador sedan, wagon	4	—	—	17	4		16.5	16.5
	8-360	Matador coupe	4	—	—	19⑫	4		17.5	17.5
	8-360	Matador sedan, wagon	4	—	—	19⑫	4		15.5	15.5

① Fully synchronized transmission 2.25 pts
② 4 pts with overdrive
③ 8.875 ring gear—4 pts
④ Matador Coupe—18.5 qts, with coolant recovery system—20.5 qts; Hornet and Gremlin—16 qts
⑤ Matador Coupe—17.5 qts, with coolant recovery system—19.5 qts
⑥ 13.5 qts in Matador Coupe, 15.5 qts in Matador Coupe with coolant recovery system, 14.5 qts in Pacer

⑦ 16.5 qts in Matador Sedan and Wagon
⑧ 14.5 qts in Pacer
⑨ 2 qts more with coolant recovery system
⑩ Add 0.5 qt for new filter
⑪ 3 pts—1978-79
⑫ 16.4—1978-79
⑬ 14.0—1978-79
⑭ 18.0—1978-79
—— Not applicable

GASOLINE TANK CAPACITIES (gals.)

Model	'72	'73	'74	'75	'76	'77	'78	'79
Ambassador	19.5	19.5	24.9	—	—	—	—	—
Javelin	16	16	16	—	—	—	—	—
Gremlin 4 cyl.	—	—	—	—	—	15	15	15
Gremlin 6 cyl.	21	21	21	21	21	21	21	21
Hornet, Concord	16	16	16	22	22	22	22	22
Matador	19.5	19.5	24.9	24.5	24.5	24.5	25	25
Matador Wagon	20	20	21	21	21	21	21	21
Pacer	—	—	—	22	22	22	20	20

VALVE SPECIFICATIONS

Year	Engine No. Cyl. Displacement (cu in.)	Seat Angle (deg) ■	Face Angle (deg) ●	Outer Spring Test Pressure (lbs @ in.)	Spring Installed Height (in.)	STEM TO GUIDE Clearance (in.) Intake	Exhaust	STEM Diameter (in.) Intake	Exhaust
'72	6-232	45	44	195 @ 1.44	1 13/16	.0010-.0030	.0010-.0027	.3720	.3720
	6-258	45	44	195 @ 1.44	1 13/16	.0010-.0030	.0010-.0027	.3720	.3720
	8-304	45	44	218 @ 1.37	1 13/16	.0010-.0030	.0010-.0030	.3720	.3720
	8-360	45	44	218 @ 1.37	1 13/16	.0010-.0030	.0010-.0030	.3720	.3720
	8-401	45	44	218 @ 1.37	1 13/16	.0010-.0030	.0010-.0030	.3720	.3720
	8, All①	45	44	250 @ 1.33	1 13/16	.0010-.0030	.0010-.0030	.3720	.3720

VALVE SPECIFICATIONS

Year	Engine No. Cyl. Displacement (cu in.)	Seat Angle (deg) ■	Face Angle (deg) ●	Outer Spring Test Pressure (lbs @ in.)	Spring Installed Height (in.)	STEM TO GUIDE Clearance (in.) Intake	Exhaust	STEM Diameter (In.) Intake	Exhaust
'73	6-232	45	44	195 @ 1.44	1 13/16	.0010-.0030	.0010-.0027	.3720	.3720
	6-258	45	44	195 @ 1.44	1 13/16	.0010-.0030	.0010-.0027	.3720	.3720
	8-304	45	44	218 @ 1.37	1 13/16	.0010-.0030	.0010-.0030	.3720	.3720
	8-360	45	44	218 @ 1.37	1 13/16	.0010-.0030	.0010-.0030	.3720	.3720
	8-401	45	44	218 @ 1.37	1 13/16	.0010-.0030	.0010-.0030	.3720	.3720
'74	6-232	45	44	195 @ 1.44	1 13/16	.0010-.0030	.0010-.0027	.3720	.3720
	6-258	45	44	195 @ 1.44	1 13/16	.0010-.0030	.0010-.0027	.3720	.3720
	8-304	45	44	213 @ 1.37	1 13/16	.0010-.0030	.0010-.0030	.3720	.3720
	8-360	45	44	213 @ 1.37	1 13/16	.0010-.0030	.0010-.0030	.3720	.3720
	8-401	45	44	213 @ 1.37	1 13/16	.0010-.0030	.0010-.0030	.3720	.3720
'75	6-232	44.5	44	195 @ 1.44	1 13/16	.0010-.0030	.0010-.0027	.3720	.3720
	6-258	44.5	44	195 @ 1.44	1 13/16	.0010-.0030	.0010-.0027	.3720	.3720
	8-304	44.5	44	213 @ 1.38	1 13/16	.0010-.0030	.0010-.0030	.3720	.3720
	8-360	44.5	44	213 @ 1.38②	1 13/16	.0010-.0030	.0010-.0030	.3720	.3720
	8-401	44.5	44	223 @ 1.35②	1 13/16	.0010-.0030	.0010-.0030	.3720	.3720
'76	6-232, 258	44.5	44	195 @ 1.44	1 13/16	.0010-.0030	.0010-.0027	.3720	.3720'
	8-304, 360	44.5	44	213 @ 1.38②	1 13/16	.0010-.0030	.0010-.0030	.3720	.3720
	8-401	44.5	44	223 @ 1.35②	1 13/16	.0010-.0030	.0010-.0030	.3720	.3720
'77-'79	4-121	45⑤	45.20⑤	In.166 @ 1.30 Ex.160 @ 1.32⑥	1.936⑦	.0012-.0026	.0016-.0030	.3529	.3525
	6-232, 258	44.5	44	195 @ 1.41④	1 13/16	.0010-.0030	.0010-.0030	.3720	.3720
	8-304, 360	44.5	44	213 @ 1.38	1 13/16	.0010-.0030	.0010-.0030	.3720	.3720

● Exhaust valve face angles are shown
  All intake valve face angles are 29°, except 121 cu. in. engine
■ Exhaust valve seat angles are shown
  All intake valve seat angles are 30°, except 121 cu. in. engine
① With high-performance camshaft, dealer-installed 1972
② 1974-75 Police 360, 401:
   intake—270 @ 1.38;
   exhaust—270 @ 1.19,
   exhaust installed height—1⅝ in.

③ Not used
④ 204 @ 1.39 in. for two barrel engine
⑤ Intake and exhaust are the same
⑥ Inner spring test pressure—intake 39 @ 1.09; exhaust, 37 @ 1.11
⑦ Inner spring installed height—1.998 in.

CRANKSHAFT AND CONNECTING ROD SPECIFICATIONS
All measurements are given in inches

Year	Engine	CRANKSHAFT Main Brg. Journal Dia	Main Brg. Oil Clearance	Shaft End-Play	Thrust on No.	CONNECTING ROD Journal Diameter	Oil Clearance	Side Clearance
'77-'79	4-121	2.1581-2.1587	.001-.003	.004-.008	3	1.8880-1.8890	.001-.002	.002-.012
'72-'79	6-All	2.4986-2.5001	.001-.003	.002-.007	3	2.0934-2.0955	.001-.002	.005-.014
'72-'73	8-All	2.7474-2.7489①	.001-.002②	.003-.008	3	③	.001-.002	.009-.015
'74	8-All	2.7474-2.7489①	.001-.003	.003-.008	3	③	.001-.002	.009-.015
'75-'79	8-All	2.7474-2.7489①	.001-.003②	.003-.008	3	③	.001-.003	.006-.018

① No. 5—2.7464-2.7479
② Rear main—.002-.003
③ 401 through 1974—2.2471-2.2485 All 304, 360—
   2.0934-2.0955; 1975 and later 401—2.2464-2.2485

TORQUE SPECIFICATIONS
All readings in ft lbs

Year	Engine	Cylinder Head Bolts	Rod Bearing Bolts	Main Bearing Bolts	Crankshaft Bolt	Flywheel to Crankshaft Bolts	MANIFOLD Intake	MANIFOLD Exhaust
'77-'79	4-121	65 cold 80 hot	41	58, 47 rear	181	65	18	18
'72-'73	6-232, 258	80	26-30	75-85	48-64	95-120	18-28	18-28
'74-'76	6-232, 258	95-115	26-30	75-85	48-64	95-120	18-28	18-28
'77-'79	6-232, 258	95-115	30-35	75-85	70-90①	95-120	18-28	18-28
'72-'74	8-304, 360	100-120	26-30	90-105	48-64	95-120	37-47	20-30
'75	8-304, 360	100-120	26-30	90-105	70-90	95-120	37-47	20-30
'76-'79	8-304, 360	100-120	30-35	90-105	80-100②	95-120	37-47	20-30
'72-'74	8-401	100-120	35-40	90-105	48-64	95-120	37-47	20-30
'75-'76	8-401	100-120	35-40	90-105	70-90	95-120	37-47	20-30

① 48-64—1977
② 70-90—1976-77

RING GAP
All measurements are given in inches

Year	Engine	Top Compression	Bottom Compression
'72-'79	All engines	.010-.020	.010-.020

Year	Engine	Oil Control
'72-'79	6-232, 258, 8-304	.010-.025
'72-'79	8-360	.015-.045
'72-'76	8-401	.015-.055
'77-'79	4-121	.010-.016

RING SIDE CLEARANCE
All measurements are given in inches

Year	Engine	Top Compression	Bottom Compression
'72-'73	All engines	.0015-.0035	.0015-.0035
'74-'79	6-232, 258	.0015-.0030	.0015-.0030
'74-'79	8-304	.0015-.0035	.0015-.0030
'74-'79	8-360, 401	.0015-.0030	.0015-.0035
'77-'79	4-121	.0012-.0024	.0012-.0024

Year	Engine	Oil Control
'72-'79	6-232, 258, 8-304	.0011-.0080
'72-'79	8-360, 401	.0000-.0070
'77-'79	4-121	.0012-.0024

PISTON CLEARANCE

Year	Engine	Piston-to-Bore Clearance (in.)
'72-'79	6-232, 258	.0009-.0017
	V8-304, 401	.0010-.0018②
	V8-360	.0012-.0020①
'77	4-121	.0009-.0015
'78-'79	4-121	.0007-.0017

① 1974 and later police 360—.0016-.0024
② 1974 and later police 401—.0014-.0022

WHEEL ALIGNMENT SPECIFICATIONS

Year	Model	CASTER Range (deg)	CASTER Pref Setting (deg)	CAMBER Range (deg)	CAMBER Pref Setting (deg)	Toe-in (In.)	Steering Axis Inclin. (deg)	WHEEL PIVOT RATIO (deg) Inner Wheel	WHEEL PIVOT RATIO (deg) Outer Wheel
'72	All	½P to 1½P	1P	①	②	1/16 to 3/16	7¾	25	22
'73-'74	Hornet, Gremlin	½N to ½P	0	①	②	1/16 to 3/16	7¾	25	22
	Matador, Javelin, Ambassador	½P to 1½P	1P	①	②	1/16 to 3/16	7¾	25	22
'75-'77	Hornet, Gremlin	½N to ½P	0	①	②	1/16 to 3/16	7¾	25	22
	Matador, Pacer	½P to 1½P	1P	①	②	1/16 to 3/16	7¾	25	22
'78-'79	Concord, Gremlin, Matador	0-2P	1P	①	②	1/16 to 3/16	7¾	25	22
	Pacer	1P-3P	2P	①	②	1/16 to 3/16	7¾	25	22

① Left: 1/8P to 5/8P; Right: 0 to 1/2P
② Left 3/8P; Right: 1/8P
  N Negative   P Positive

CHARGING SYSTEM

Motorola alternators are used through 1975. Delco-Remy units are used starting 1975; Motorcraft alternators are also used starting 1976.

Information on alternator and regulator repair and troubleshooting can be found in the Unit Repair Section.

External Regulator Removal

Disconnect plug to the regulator. Remove the metal screws which hold the regulator to the sheet metal and lift off the regulator.

Alternator Removal and Installation

1. Disconnect battery cables.
2. Disconnect alternator wires or plug, then loosen adjusting bolt.
3. Remove V-belt, mounting bolts and alternator.
4. To install, reverse removal procedure.
5. There are several methods used for tightening the belt. Some alternator brackets have a hole through which you can insert a bar to pry out on the front alternator housing, others have a hole into which you can insert a 1/2 in. square socket drive to pull out on the alternator, and others have a square boss around the adjusting bolt which takes a 1 in. open end wrench. If there are none of these systems, use a bar to pry against the *front alternator housing*. The longest run of belt should deflect about 1/2 in. under moderate thumb pressure.

STARTING SYSTEM

American Motors cars are equipped with an integral positive engagement drive starter and a separate starter relay.

Starter repair procedures can be found in the Unit Repair Section.

Starter Removal and Installation

Disconnect the battery lead from the starter and the solenoid lead from the starter, if used. From underneath the car, remove the bolts which hold the starter to the bell housing, and remove the starter. Before installing the starter, make sure the mounting surfaces are free from burrs and foreign material. Install the starter to the housing, and tighten the bolts to 18 ft. lbs. on sixes and V8s; on 4s, tighten the larger bolt to 54 ft. lbs., the smaller bolt to 33 ft. lbs. Clean the terminal(s) and install the cable(s).

Disabling the Interlock System

Since the legal requirement for seat belt/starter interlock systems was dropped during the 1975 model year, those systems installed on cars built earlier may now be legally disconnected. However, the seat belt warning light is still required to operate.

1. Remove the pink wire and terminal from the two terminal connector at the emergency starter relay, located on the right inner fender panel, under the hood.
2. Cut off the pink wire close to the taped junction of the wire harness.
3. Remove the yellow wire and terminal from the three terminal connector at the starter relay.
4. Install the yellow wire into the two terminal connector at the location where the pink wire and terminal was removed.
5. From under the right side of the dash and along the right side of the glove box area, locate the interlock logic module and remove it from its bracket. Cut off the yellow with black tracer wire close to the taped junction of the wire harness and cut off the remaining end as close to the logic module as possible. Reinstall the logic module on its dash bracket.
6. The warning light should be off when the occupied seat belt is buckled and the car placed in gear with the ignition switch on.

NOTE: *Most models require the seating of both the driver and front seat passenger, prior to buckling of the belts or turning on of the ignition system, due to the programming of the logic module, for the seat belt warning light to go out. These series can be identified by a buff colored logic module. Other series are equipped with a green colored logic module which allows non-sequential operation and independent use of the seat belts.*

IGNITION SYSTEM

A conventional point-type ignition system is used on all models through 1974, and all 4 cylinder engines through 1977.

Starting 1975, all American Motors 6 and V8 cars are equipped with the Breakerless Inductive Discharge (BID) ignition system. The system consists of an electronic ignition control unit, a standard type ignition coil, a distributor that contains an electronic sensor and trigger wheel instead of a cam, breaker points and condenser, and the usual high tension wires and spark plugs. There are no contacting (and thus wearing) surfaces between the trigger wheel and the sensor. The dwell angle remains the same and never requires adjustment. The dwell angle is determined by the control unit and the angle between the trigger wheel spokes. In 1978 the system was modified to included a different ignition module and distributor, and was renamed Solid State Ignition (SSI). For more information and repair procedures, see the "Electronic Ignition systems" Unit Repair Section.

Distributor Removal

1. Remove the distributor cap, mark the position of the rotor relative to the distributor body and mark the body relative to the block. Remove the carburetor air cleaner if necessary, the distributor primary wire and the distributor vacuum lines.
2. Remove the hold-down bolt and take the distributor up out of the block.
   The rotor and body are marked so that they can be returned to the position from which they were removed. Do not turn the engine after the distributor has been taken off.

Distributor Installation

ENGINE NOT DISTURBED— TIMING RETAINED

Install the distributor in the reverse order of removal. Be sure that the rotor and distributor are installed with the marks, which were made during removal, in alignment. Adjust the timing as required.

ENGINE DISTURBED— TIMING LOST

If the rotor position was not noted during removal, or if the engine was cranked with the distributor out, install it as follows:
1. Remove the spark plug from the no. one cylinder and position a compression gauge or a thumb over the spark plug hole.
2. Slowly crank the engine, until compression pressure starts to build up.

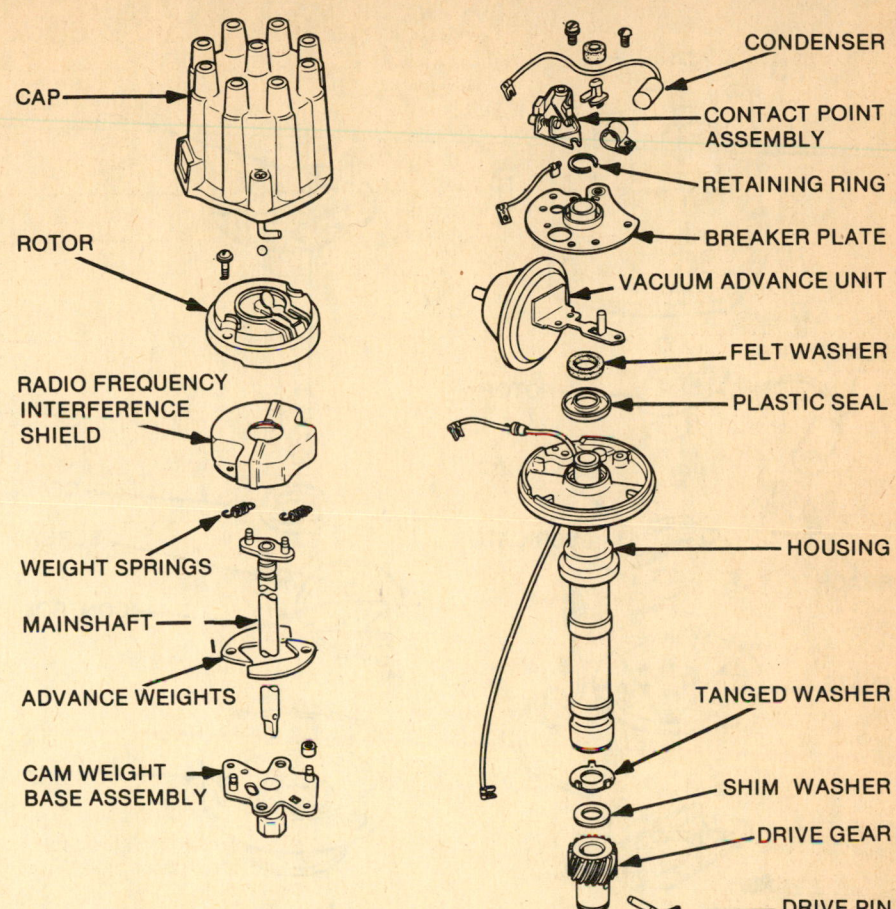

CAP
ROTOR
RADIO FREQUENCY INTERFERENCE SHIELD
WEIGHT SPRINGS
MAINSHAFT
ADVANCE WEIGHTS
CAM WEIGHT BASE ASSEMBLY

CONDENSER
CONTACT POINT ASSEMBLY
RETAINING RING
BREAKER PLATE
VACUUM ADVANCE UNIT
FELT WASHER
PLASTIC SEAL
HOUSING
TANGED WASHER
SHIM WASHER
DRIVE GEAR
DRIVE PIN

Distributor—all V8 through 1974

3. Continue cranking the engine so that the timing mark or pointer aligns with the TDC mark.
4. Install the distributor with its drive meshed, so that the rotor points to the no. one terminal on the distributor cap with engine at TDC.
5. Complete installation in the reverse order of removal and adjust the timing as required.

Breaker Points and Condenser Replacement, Dwell Angle Adjustment

The usual procedure is to replace the condenser each time the point set is replaced. Although this is not always necessary, it is easy to do at this time and the cost is negligible. Every time you adjust or replace the breaker points, the ignition timing must be checked and, if necessary, adjusted. No special equipment other than a feeler gauge is required for point replacement or adjustment, but a dwell meter is strongly advised.

1. Push down on the spring-loaded V8 distributor cap retaining screws and give them a half-turn to release. Unscrew the captive six-cylinder cap retaining screws. Use a small screwdriver to unclip the two latches on the four cylinder. Re-

move the cap. You might have to unclip or detach some or all of the plug wires to remove the cap.
2. Clean the cap inside and out with a clean rag. Check for cracks and carbon paths. A carbon path shows up as a dark line, usually from one of the cap sockets or inside terminals to a ground. Check the condition of the carbon button inside the center of the cap and the inside terminals. Replace the cap as necessary.
3. Pull the rotor up and off the shaft on fours and sixes. Remove the two screws and lift the round V8 rotor off. There is less danger of losing the screws if you just back them out all the way and lift them off with the rotor. Clean off the

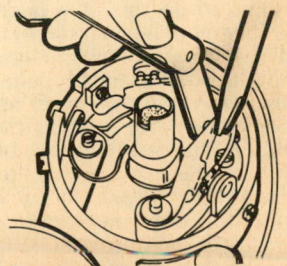

Point adjustment, 4 cylinder
(© American Motors Corp.)

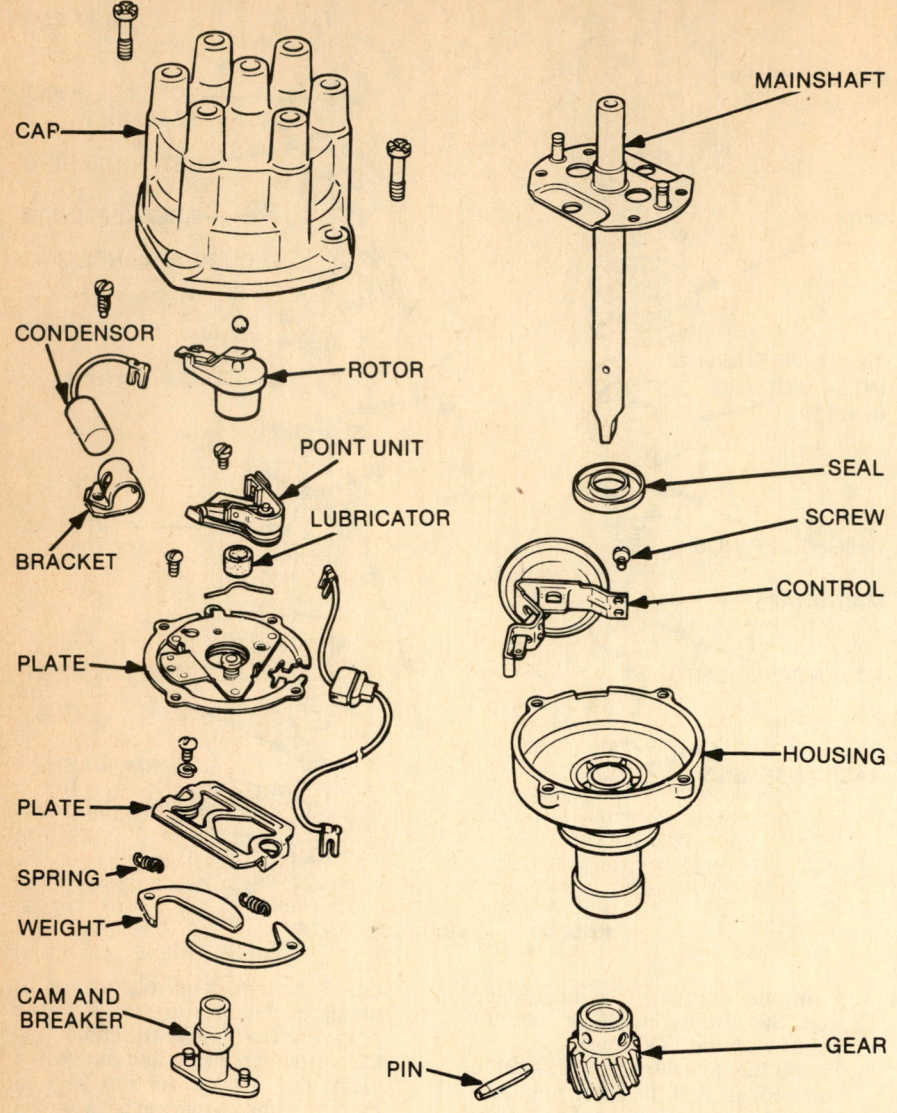

CAP

CONDENSOR

ROTOR

POINT UNIT

LUBRICATOR

BRACKET

PLATE

PLATE

SPRING

WEIGHT

CAM AND BREAKER

PIN

MAINSHAFT

SEAL

SCREW

CONTROL

HOUSING

GEAR

Distributor—6 cylinder through 1974

metal outer tip if it is burned or corroded. Don't file it. Replace the rotor as necessary or if one came with your tune-up kit.

4. The factory says that the points don't need to be replaced if metal transfer from one contact to the other doesn't exceed 0.020 in. However, experience shows that it is more economical and reliable in the long run to replace the point set while the distributor is open, than to have to do this at a later (and possibly more inconvenient) time.

5. Pull off the two wire terminals from the point assembly. One wire comes from the condenser and the other comes from within the distributor. The terminals are usually held in place by spring tension only. There might be a clamp screw securing the terminals on some older versions. There is now available a one-piece point/condenser assembly, except for the four cylinder. Loosen the point set

hold-down screw(s). Be very careful not to drop any of these little screws inside the distributor. If this happens, the distributor will probably have to be removed to get at the screw. If the hold-down screw is lost elsewhere, it must be replaced with one that is no longer than the original to avoid interference with the distributor workings. Remove the point set, even if it is to be reused.

6. If the points are to be reused, clean them with a few strokes of a special point file. This is done with the points removed to prevent tiny metal filings getting into the distributor.

7. Loosen the condenser hold-down screw and slide the condenser out of the clamp. This will save you a struggle with the clamp, condenser, and the tiny screw when you install the new one. If you have the type of clamp that is permanently fastened to the con-

denser, remove the screw and the condenser. On the four cylinder, remove the condenser and connector as an assembly from the side of the distributor. Don't lose the screw.

8. If possible replace the distributor cam lubricator at every tune-up. Most ignition point sets will have the cam lubricator wick as part of the kit, or a plastic tube of high melting point grease will be included. Use the grease sparingly on the distributor cam.

NOTE: *Don't oil or grease the lubricator. The foam is impregnated with a special lubricant.*

9. Install the new condenser. If you left the clamp in place, just slide the new condenser into the clamp.

10. Replace the point set and tighten the screws on a V8. Leave the screw slightly loose on sixes and fours. Replace the two wire terminals, making sure that the wires don't interfere with anything. Some V8 distributors have a ground wire that must go under one of the screws.

11. Check that the contacts meet squarely. If they don't, bend the tab supporting the fixed contact.

NOTE: *If you are installing preset points on a V8, go ahead to Step 16. If they are preset, it will say so on that package.*

12. Turn the engine until a high point on the cam that opens the points contacts the rubbing block on the point arm. You can turn the engine by hand if you can get a wrench on the crankshaft pulley nut, or you can grasp the fan belt and turn the engine with the spark plugs removed. Turn the crankshaft only in the direction of normal rotation.

─────── CAUTION ───────

If you try turning the engine by hand, be very careful not to get your fingers pinched in the pulleys.

On a stick-shift car, you can push it forward in High gear. Another alternative is to bump the starter switch or use a remote starter switch.

13. There is a screwdriver slot near the contacts. Insert a screwdriver and lever the points open or closed until they appear to be at about the gap specified in the "Tune-Up Specifications." On a V8, simply insert a 1/8 in. allen wrench into the adjustment screw and turn. The wrench sometimes comes with a tune-up kit.

14. Insert the correct size feeler gauge and adjust the gap until you can push the gauge in and out between the contacts with a slight drag, but without disturbing the point arm. Check by trying the gauges 0.001-0.002 larger and smaller than the setting size. The larger one should disturb the point arm, while

the smaller one should not drag at all. Tighten the point set holdown screw. Recheck the gap, because it often changes when the screw is tightened.

15. After all the point adjustments are complete, pull a white business card through (between) the contacts to remove any traces of oil. Oil will cause rapid contact burning.

NOTE: *You can adjust four and six-cylinder dwell at this point, if you wish. Refer to Step 18.*

16. Push the rotor firmly down into place. It will only go one way. Tighten the V8 rotor screws. If the rotor is not installed properly, it will probably break when the starter is operated.

17. Replace the distributor cap.

18. If a dwell meter is available, check the dwell. The dwell meter hookup is shown in the "Engine Troubleshooting" Section.

NOTE: *This hookup does not necessarily apply to electronic, capacitive discharge, or other special ignition systems. Some dwell meters won't work at all with such systems.*

Dwell can be checked with the engine running or cranking. Decrease dwell by increasing the point gap; increase by decreasing the gap. Dwell angle is simply the number of degrees of distributor shaft rotation during which the points stay closed. Theoretically, if the point gap is correct, the dwell should also be correct or nearly so. Adjustment with a dwell meter produces more exact consistent results since it is a dynamic adjustment. If dwell varies more than 3 degrees from idle speed to 1,750 engine rpm, the distributor is worn.

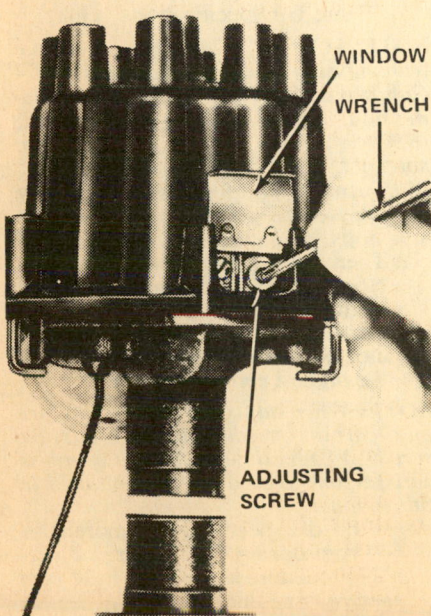

Point adjustment, V8
(© American Motors Corp.)

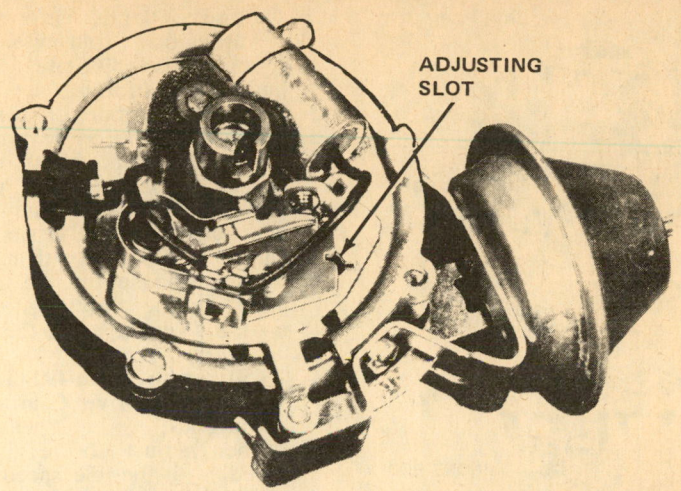

ADJUSTING SLOT

Point adjustment, 6 cylinder (© American Motors Corp.)

19. To adjust dwell on a four or a six, trial and error point adjustments are required. On a V8 simply open the metal window on the distributor and insert a 1/8 in. allen wrench. Turn until the meter shows the correct reading. Be sure to snap the window closed.

20. An approximate dwell adjustment can be made without a meter on a V8. Turn the adjusting screw clockwise until the engine begins to misfire, then turn it out 1/2 turn.

21. If the engine won't start, check:
    a. That all the spark plug wires are in place.
    b. That the rotor has been installed.
    c. That the two (or three) wires inside the distributor are connected.
    d. That the points open and close when the engine turns.
    e. That the gap is correct and the hold-down screw is tight.

22. After the first 200 miles or so on a new set of points, the point gap often closes up due to initial rubbing block wear. For best performance, recheck the dwell (or gap) at this time.

23. Since changing the gap affects the ignition point setting, the timing should be checked and adjusted as necessary after each point replacement or adjustment.

Ignition Timing Adjustment

A scale located on the timing chain cover and a notch milled into the vibration damper are used as references to set ignition timing.

NOTE: *Connect a tachometer to the BID or SSI ignition system in the conventional way; to the negative (distributor) side of the coil and to a ground. Some tachometers may not work with a BID or SSI ignition system and there is a possibility that some could be damaged. Check with the manufacturer of the tachometer to make sure it can be used.*

1. Disconnect the vacuum hose, at the distributor vacuum unit. Plug the vacuum line to prevent leakage.

2. Connect a timing light and a tachometer in accordance with the manufacturer's instructions. If the timing light has an advance control, be sure that it is in the "off" position.

3. Start the engine. Adjust the carburetor curb idle screw so that the engine idles at 500 rpm through 1977, and at the specified curb idle speed at operating temperature, 1978 and later. If there is a throttle stop solenoid, disconnect it electrically. Aim the timing light at the pointer marks.

4. Adjust the timing by loosening the distributor clamp nut and rotating the distributor. Set the timing to the proper specification.

NOTE: *On some models, a white paint mark is applied to the scale for the specified, initial timing setting. Do not mistake this mark for TDC.*

5. Check the timing again after tightening the distributor clamp.

6. Connect the vacuum hose and set the idle speed to normal specifications.

FUEL SYSTEM

Fuel Pump Removal and Installation

Disconnect both gas lines from the fuel pump, remove the two bolts which hold it to the block and lift off the pump.

Installation is the reverse of removal.

Fuel Filter Removal and Installation

These models use an inline fuel filter in the line from the carburetor to the fuel pump. Some V8 and all 1976 and later models also have a vapor return

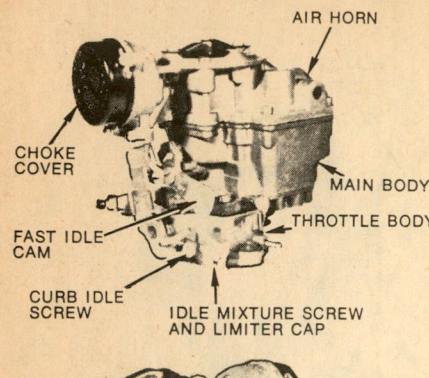

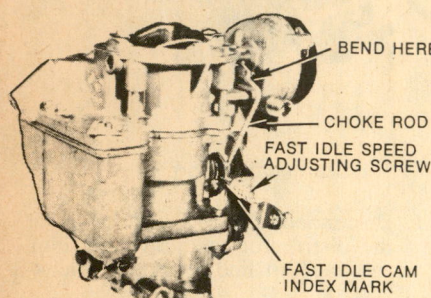

Carter YF carburetor adjustments
(© American Motors Corp)

line from the filter to the tank. To replace it:

1. Remove the air cleaner as necessary.
2. Put an absorbent rag under the filter to catch spillage.
3. Remove the hose clamps.
4. Remove the filter and short attaching hoses.
5. Assemble the new filter and hoses. If the filter has a return line, position the line at the top.

NOTE: *The original equipment type hose clamps can't be reused with much success. It is much better to replace them with screw type clamps. If there is an arrow on the new filter, it must point toward the carburetor. 1976 and later four barrel models also have a check valve with flow indicating arrows.*

6. Fit the filter in place, tighten the clamps, start the engine, and check for leaks. Discard the rag safely.

Carburetor Adjustments

1972

Adjust with the air cleaner installed. Do not allow the engine to idle for more than three minutes at a time. If the idle mixture adjustment is not completed at the end of three minutes, run the engine at 2000 rpm for one minute. Continue the adjustments at the specified rpm after that period.

1. Start the engine and warm to operating temperature. Connect a tachometer. On engines with air pumps, disconnect the air bypass hose at the valve.
2. Adjust the carburetor idle speed screw to obtain the following settings for six cylinder engines:
   Manual transmission—600 rpm/

49 States; 700 rpm/California.
   Automatic transmission—500 rpm (in Drive)/49 States; 600 rpm (in Drive)/California.

3. Adjust the carburetor idle speed screw to 750 rpm on V8s with manual transmission, or 600 rpm (in Drive)/49 States, 700 rpm (in Drive)/California for the 304 V8 with automatic transmission.
4. On 360 and 401 V8s with automatic transmission, set the idle speed by adjusting the throttle stop solenoid, if so equipped, to the following figures:
   650 rpm (in Drive)/49 States 401;
   700 rpm (in Drive)/California 401 and all 360s.
   Then adjust the engine idle speed, with the idle speed screw, to 500 rpm with the idle stop solenoid disconnected. Reconnect the solenoid after adjustment. If the engine does not have a solenoid, adjust the engine to the first set of figures with the idle speed screw.

----- CAUTION -----

When adjusting the idle speed on a car with an automatic transmission set in Drive, block the front wheels and set the parking brake firmly.

5. Starting from full rich stop(s) or two turns from seated on 4 bbl/manual V8, turn the mixture screw(s) equally clockwise until the engine speed drops off.
6. Turn the mixture screw(s) counterclockwise until the engine speed picks up to the former level. The highest idle speed obtainable within the range of the limiter caps (or between the rich drop-off points for the 4 bbl/manual V8) is the "lean best idle" setting. Both mixture screws should be turned equally unless the engine demands otherwise.
7. If the idle speed changes more than 30 rpm during the mixture adjustment, reset the idle speed screw and readjust the mixture.
8. On cars with air pumps, reconnect the air bypass valve hose.

NOTE: *If idle quality is poor within the range of the limiter caps, the caps may be removed and the idle speed set using the corrective procedure. Keep in mind that a combustion gas analyzer is necessary to meet the federal emission standards. All cars should have a 14:1 air/fuel ratio except 4 bbl/manual V8s, which should be set up at 13.5/1, with the air bypass hose disconnected.*

Idle Quality Corrective Procedure

1. Remove the idle limiter caps.
2. Adjust the idle speed screw to obtain 50 rpm less than specified for sixes, and V8 automatics. Manual V8s should be set to the specified idle.

3. Turn in the mixture screw(s) until they are gently seated, then back out one turn. Connect a tachometer.
4. Start the engine and turn the mixture screw(s) counterclockwise until the engine speed drops off slightly. On 2 and 4 bbl carburetors, turn both mixture screws equally unless the engine demands otherwise.
5. Turn the mixture screw(s) inward until the speed is regained, then continue inward until the speed begins to drop off again.
6. Turn the mixture screw(s) outward until the original speed is regained. This is the "lean best idle" setting.
7. Readjust the idle speed screw to obtain the proper idle speed. Disconnect the tachometer.
8. Install replacement idle limiter caps with ears against full rich stops.

1973-74

Adjust with air cleaner installed.
NOTE: *Do not allow the engine to idle more than three minutes at a time. If the idle/mixture adjustment is not completed by the end of three minutes, run the engine for one minute at 2,000 rpm. Return to specified rpm and continue the adjustment.*

1. Remove the idle limiter cap(s) by inserting a screw in its center. Turn the cap clockwise to remove it.
2. Discard the old cap(s).
3. Start the engine and allow it to reach normal operating temperature.
4. Install a tachometer of known accuracy in accordance with its manufacturer's instructions.
5. Adjust the idle speed to 30 rpm above the speed specified in the "Tune-Up Specifications" chart.

NOTE: *On 1973-74 V8, automatic transmission equipped cars and 1974 California sixes with automatic transmission, adjust the idle speed by turning the hex screw on the throttle stop solenoid.*

6. Turn the mixture screws until they are seated against their full-rich stops.
7. Then turn the mixture screws clockwise (leaner) until a drop in engine idle speed is noted.
8. Turn the mixture screws counterclockwise from this position until the highest rpm is obtained.

NOTE: *When adjusting the idle mixture on a carburetor which has two mixture screws, turn both screws equally unless satisfactory idle cannot be obtained in this manner.*

9. If the idle speed changes more than 30 rpm during the mixture adjusting procedure set the idle to 30 rpm above specification and repeat steps 6-8 again.
10. After completing steps 1-9 satisfactorily, turn the mixture screws clockwise until the engine idle

speed drops the amount specified below:

Engine/Transmission	RPM
6 cyl/manual	35
6 cyl/automatic	20
V8/All	40

11. Install new service idle limiter caps.

---------- CAUTION ----------

When adjusting the idle speed/mixture on a car with its automatic transmission set in Drive range, be sure that the parking brake is firmly on and that the front wheels are blocked.

1975-78

Six Cylinder and V8

Beginning with the 1977 models, special carburetors, incorporating an altitude compensating circuit to increase the air flow are used on cars that are sold for use at elevations above 4,000 feet. The single barrel YF-1 is manually adjusted for altitude while the two barrel 2150-2 has an automatic compensator system, controlled by an aneroid, which is sensitive to atmospheric pressures. At high altitudes, where the atmospheric pressure is lower, the aneroid expands and opens an altitude compensating valve, allowing extra air to enter the carburetor and lean out the fuel-air mixture.

NOTE: *The aneroid is factory calibrated and is not adjustable. With a change of altitude operation, ignition timing and carburetor adjustments must be reset on all models.*

NOTE: *This adjustment is performed with the air cleaner installed. Do not allow the engine to idle more than three minutes at a time. If the idle/mixture adjustment is not completed by the end of three minutes, run the engine for one minute at 2,000 rpm. Return to the specified rpm and continue the adjustment.*

1. Adjust the idle screw(s) to the full rich stop(s). Note the position of the screw head slot inside the limiter cap slots.
2. Carefully remove the idle limiter cap(s) by installing a sheet metal screw in the center of the cap and turning clockwise. Discard the old caps. Return the screws to their original positions.
3. Install a tachometer on the engine.
4. Start the engine and allow it to reach normal operating temperature.
5. Adjust the idle speed to 30 rpm above the specified idle speed. See the Tune-Up Specifications chart.

NOTE: *On most engines the idle speed is adjusted with the throttle stop solenoid. Use the following procedure for idle speed adjustment.*

   a. With the solenoid wire connected, turn the nut on the solenoid plunger in or out to obtain specified idle rpm.

   b. Tighten the solenoid lock nut, if so equipped.

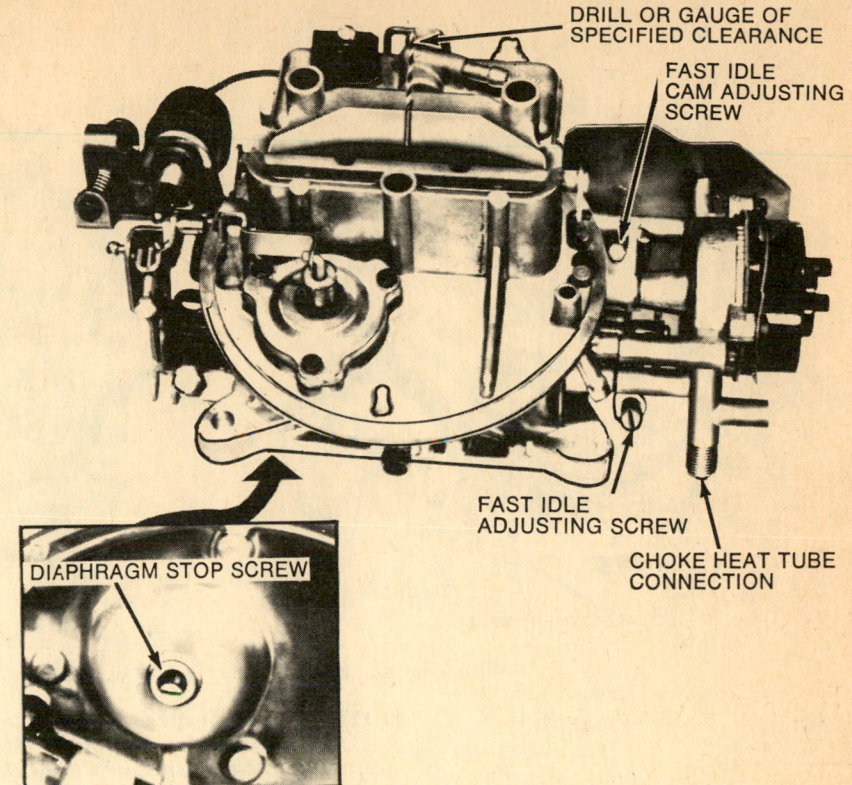

Autolite/Motorcraft 2100 carburetor adjustments (© American Motors Corp)

   c. Disconnect the solenoid wire and adjust curb idle speed screw to obtain 500 rpm.

   d. Connect the solenoid wire.

---------- CAUTION ----------

On the Carter BBD 2bbl., the curb idle and fast idle screws are side by side; it is easy to get the wrong one when setting idle speed on cars without a throttle stop solenoid. The screw for idle speed is the longer of the two.

6. Starting from the full rich stop position, as noted in step 1, turn the mixture screw(s) clockwise (leaner) until the engine looses speed.
7. Turn the mixture screw(s) counterclockwise until the highest rpm reading is obtained.

NOTE: *On engines with two mixture screws, turn both of the screws an equal number of turns unless the engine demands otherwise.*

8. If the idle speed has changed more than 30 rpm during the mixture adjustment, reset the idle to 30 rpm above the specified idle rpm as indicated in the "Tune-Up Specifications" chart.
9. Turn the mixture adjustment screw(s) clockwise until the rpm drops as follows:

1975-76 Six cylinder automatic	25 rpm
1975 Six cylinder manual	25 rpm
1976 Six cylinder manual	50 rpm
1975 Six cylinder manual with EGR and catalytic converter	35 rpm
1976 Six cylinder manual with EGR	50 rpm
1975-76 V8 automatic	20 rpm
1975 V8 manual	40 rpm
1976 V8 manual	100 rpm
1977-79 Six cylinder Manual	50 rpm
Matador–manual	25 rpm
automatic	25 rpm
1977-78 Six cylinder automatic Matador	175 rpm
1977-79 Six cylinder automatic, high altitude	25 rpm
1978-79 Six cylinder manual, high altitude	50 rpm
1978-79 Six cylinder two barrel automatic	25 rpm
1977-79 Six cylinder two barrel manual	50 rpm
1977-79 304-360 V8 automatic	20 rpm

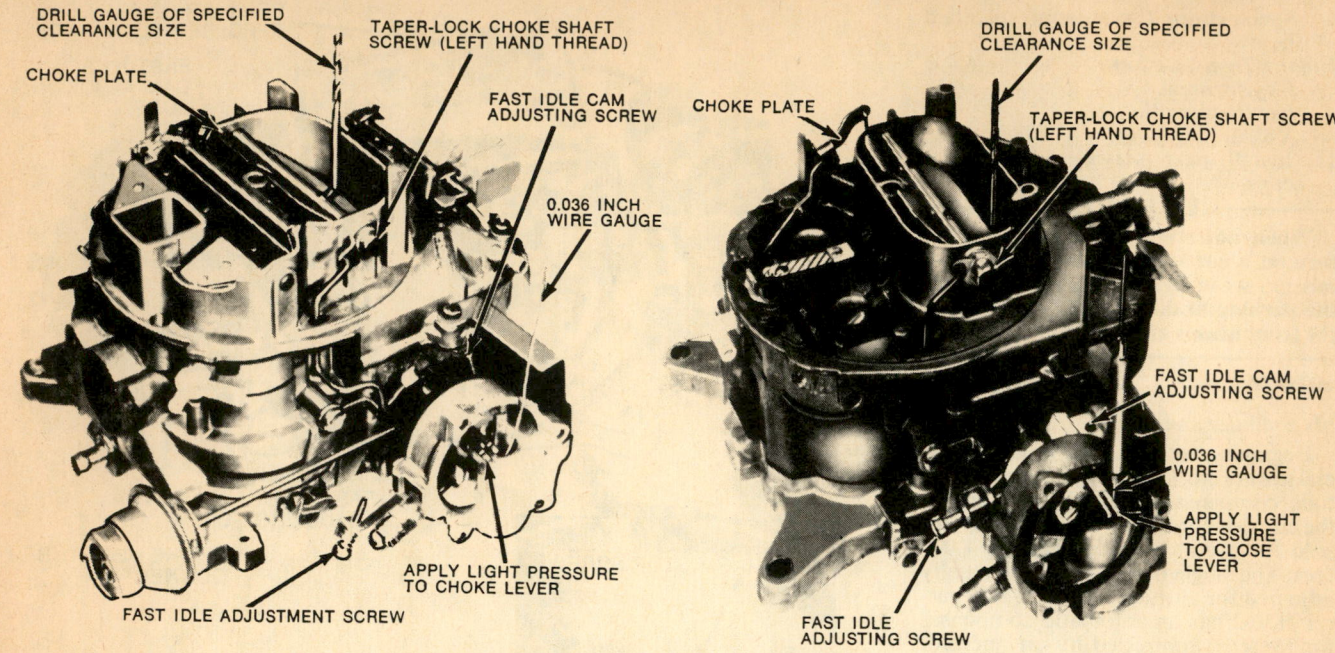

DRILL GAUGE OF SPECIFIED CLEARANCE SIZE

CHOKE PLATE

TAPER-LOCK CHOKE SHAFT SCREW (LEFT HAND THREAD)

FAST IDLE CAM ADJUSTING SCREW

0.036 INCH WIRE GAUGE

APPLY LIGHT PRESSURE TO CHOKE LEVER

FAST IDLE ADJUSTMENT SCREW

DRILL GAUGE OF SPECIFIED CLEARANCE SIZE

CHOKE PLATE

TAPER-LOCK CHOKE SHAFT SCREW (LEFT HAND THREAD)

FAST IDLE CAM ADJUSTING SCREW

0.036 INCH WIRE GAUGE

APPLY LIGHT PRESSURE TO CLOSE LEVER

FAST IDLE ADJUSTING SCREW

Autolite/Motorcraft 4300 carburetor (© American Motors Corp)

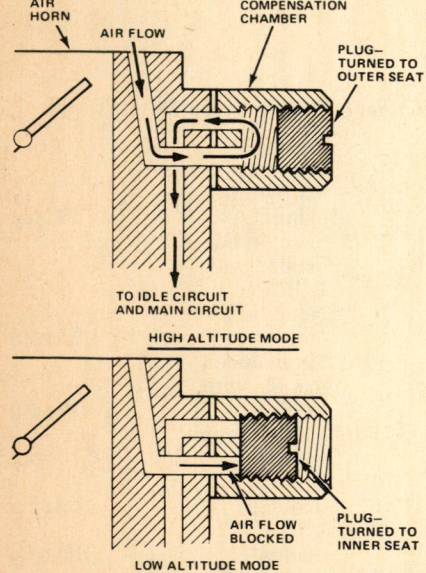

AIR HORN

AIR FLOW

COMPENSATION CHAMBER

PLUG—TURNED TO OUTER SEAT

TO IDLE CIRCUIT AND MAIN CIRCUIT

HIGH ALTITUDE MODE

AIR FLOW BLOCKED

PLUG—TURNED TO INNER SEAT

LOW ALTITUDE MODE

6 Cylinder altitude compensator plug operation and adjustment (© American Motors Corp.)

10. Install new blue service idle limiter cap(s) over the idle mixture screw(s) with the limiter cap tang(s) positioned against the full rich stop(s). Be careful not to disturb the idle mixture setting while installing the cap(s). Press the cap(s) firmly into place.

Four Cylinder

The four cylinder engine uses a staged, two barrel carburetor. The primary barrel is smaller than the secondary barrel, and mechanical linkage progressively opens the secondary barrel.

Idle speed and mixture setting procedures are as follows:

NOTE: *To compensate for temperature and fuel variations, while performing idle mixture adjustments, don't idle the engine over three minutes at a time. If settings are not completed within three minutes, operate the engine at 2,000 rpm for one minute. Repeat as necessary until the proper adjustments are attained.*

1. Note position of the screw head slot in the limiter cap.
2. Remove the limiter cap by installing a sheet metal screw in the center of the cap and turning the screw clockwise.
3. Reset the idle screw to its approximate original position.
4. Attach a tachometer. Start engine and warm to operating temperature.
5. A throttle stop solenoid is used to adjust curb idle. With the solenoid wire connected, turn the adjusting screw of the solenoid in or out to obtain the specified setting of 30 rpm above the specified rpm.
6. Disconnect the solenoid wire and adjust the solenoid off idle adjusting screw to obtain 500 rpm. Connect the solenoid wire.
7. Turn the mixture screw clockwise (lean) until a loss of rpm is indicated.
8. Turn the mixture screw counter-clockwise until the highest rpm reading is obtained at the best lean idle setting.
9. As a final adjustment, turn the mixture screw clockwise (leaner) until the specified drop in engine rpm is obtained.
10. Install a replacement limiter cap on the idle mixture screw, with the tab positioned inside the slot on the carburetor body, while being careful not to move the mixture screw.

Idle drop specifications are 120 rpm, except for high altitude manual transmission models (75 rpm).

Dashpot Adjustment

Some carburetors are equipped with a dashpot to prevent stalling. The dashpot adjustment procedure for these carburetors is as follows:

1. Be sure that the throttle valves are closed (curb idle position) and that the diaphragm stem is fully depressed.
2. Measure the clearance between the dashpot stem and the throttle lever with a feeler gauge. For the proper clearance specification see the chart below.
3. If the clearance is not correct, adjust it by loosening the locknut and rotating the dashpot until the proper clearance is obtained. Tighten the locknut.

Year	Carburetor		Clearance (Gauge size in.)
1972-74	YF (1-V)	All	0.095
	2100 (2-V)	2DM2	0.110
		2DA2, 3DM2, 4DM2	0.140
	4300 (4-V)	All	0.140
1975	YF (1-V)	All	0.075
	2100 (2-V)	All	0.093
1976-77	YF (1-V)	All	0.075
	2100 (2-V)	All	0.075
	BBD (2-V)	All	0.104

COOLING SYSTEM

American Motors cars are equipped with a conventional cooling system which utilizes a vertical flow radiator, a water pump, and a thermostat. The Pacer has a crossflow radiator. An internal by-pass port is used on the four and six-cylinder engine, which allows water to flow through the engine when the thermostat is closed. The V8 engine uses an external hose to perform the same function.

Information on the water temperature gauge can be found in the Unit Repair Section.

Radiator Removal

Raise the hood, drain the radiator, remove the upper and lower radiator hose. On models equipped with the optional coolant recovery system, disconnect its hose from the radiator. Remove the radiator shroud, if so equipped. Take out the bolts which hold the radiator to its cradle and, if the car is fitted with an automatic transmission, disconnect the fluid cooler lines and lift the core up and out. You may have to remove the fan.

Water Pump Removal and Installation

The water pump is a centrifugal unit having a non-adjustable packless seal. It is non-serviceable and must be replaced if defective—no maintenance is required.

4 CYLINDER

1. Drain the cooling system. Disconnect the negative (−) cable from the battery. Remove the fan shroud.
2. Rotate the crankshaft until the camshaft and crankshaft are at TDC for number one cylinder.
3. If equipped with power steering, loosen the pump and remove the belt. Loosen the air conditioner idler pulley and remove the belt, if so equipped.
4. Loosen the alternator and air pump.
5. Remove the fan, spacer, and pulley.
6. Remove the belt guard and air pump bracket.
7. Remove the camshaft and drive belt idler pulley.
8. Disconnect all the hoses from the pump except the hose from the thermostat.
9. Remove the water pump attaching bolts and pull the pump out of the hose from the thermostat.
10. Clean the gasket from the block, install a new gasket on the pump or block.
11. Insert the pump into the thermostat hose, install the pump attaching bolts and torque the small bolts to 7 ft. lbs. and the large bolts to 16 ft. lbs.
12. Reassemble in the reverse order, align the timing belt, apply tension to alternator, air pump, power steering (if equipped), belts.
13. Install coolant, operate engine for 3 to 5 minutes with the heater on to

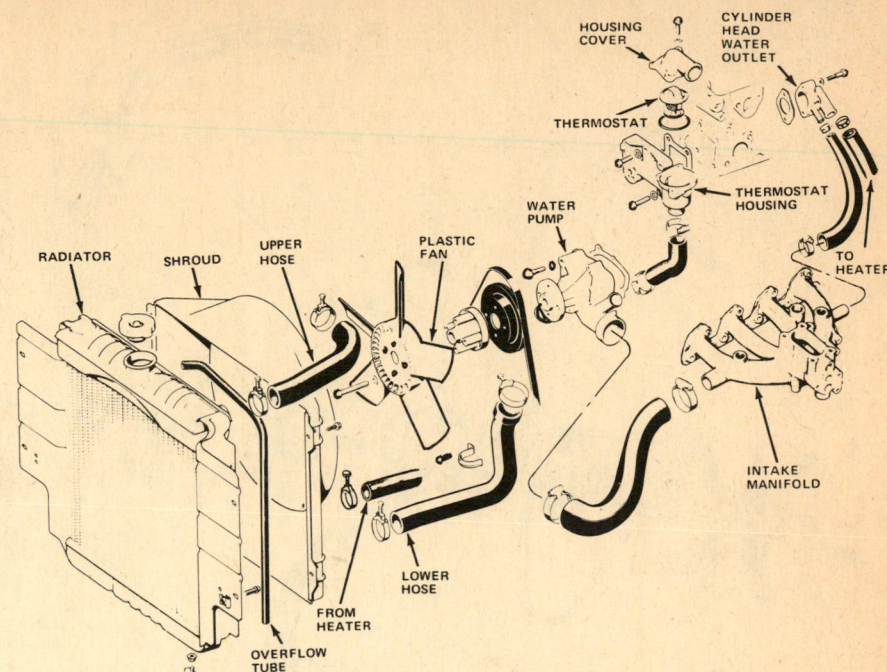

Water pump and hose routing, 4 cylinder (© American Motors Corp.)

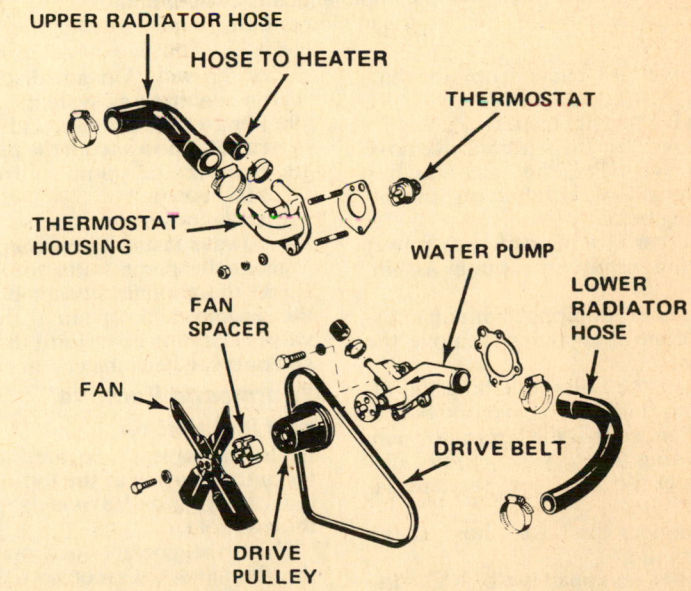

Cooling system components and coolant flow for 6 cylinder engines (© American Motors Corp)

check for leaks and correct fluid level.

6 CYLINDER

1. Drain the cooling system. Disconnect the negative (−) cable from the battery.
2. Unfasten the radiator and the heater hoses at the pump.
3. Loosen the adjustment bolts from the alternator and the power steering pump (if so equipped). Remove the V-belts.
4. Unfasten the fan ring securing bolts. Remove the fan and pump pulley assembly. Withdraw the fan ring (or shroud).

5. Remove the securing bolts from the water pump. Withdraw the pump along with its gasket.

Installation is the reverse order of removal. Always use a new pump gasket. Bleed the radiator by running the engine and opening the heater control valve. Run the engine long enough so that the thermostat opens. Check the coolant level.

The water pump securing bolts should be tightened to 10-15 ft. lbs.

V8

1. Drain the cooling system at the radiator. Remove the upper hose from the radiator. Disconnect the

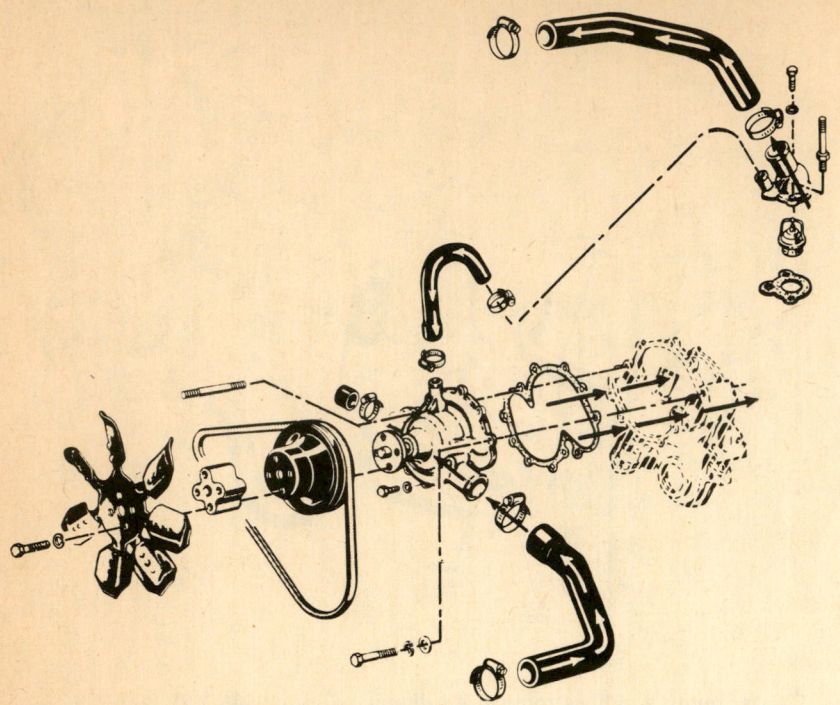

V8 Water pump components and coolant flow
(© American Motors Corp.)

negative (−) cable from the battery.

2. Remove the air cleaner.
3. Remove the fan shroud. Remove the drive belts, the fan, and hub assembly by withdrawing the attaching bolts.
4. If the car is equipped with power steering, remove the pump assembly.
5. If the car is equipped with an emission control air pump, remove the pump.
6. Loosen the bolts attaching the alternator bracket. Leave one bolt in position, so that the alternator may be swung to one side. Do not disconnect the wire from the alternator.
7. Disconnect the heater hose at the water pump.
8. On cars equipped with A/C, disconnect the compressor bracket and set it and the compressor out

of the way. Do not discharge the air conditioning system.
9. Remove the by-pass and the lower radiator hoses from the pump.
10. Remove the pump and clean the gasket areas.

Installation is the reverse of removal. Always install a new pump gasket. Tighten the pump bolts to 18 ft. lbs. Bleed the cooling system by starting the engine and opening the heater valve. Leave it open until the thermostat opens. Check the coolant level.

Thermostat Removal and Installation

The thermostat is located in the water outlet housing at the top of the cylinder head, or on V8 models in front of the manifold.

Drain the coolant to a point below the thermostat. Disconnect the upper radiator hose and remove the bolts which hold the water outlet neck to the engine. Remove the thermostat.

When installing the thermostat, be sure that the pellet or coil spring are facing the engine. Thermostats are marked on the outer flange with the proper installing direction. Replace the gasket.

The bleed hole on the thermostats used on six-cylinder engines must be installed up (at 12 o'clock), to prevent "burping" caused by air trapped in the block.

─────── CAUTION ───────

Tightening the housing bolts unevenly, or with the thermostat cocked in its recess, will cause the housing to crack.

Refill the cooling system and run the engine for a while with the heater on to bleed the system of air. Recheck the coolant level.

EMISSION CONTROLS

See the "Unit Repair Section" for testing and repair of the various emission control system components.

1972

The Evaporative Emission Control (EEC) system is used on all engines. It consists of a fuel expansion tank integral with the fuel tank, a closed vent system on the fuel tank, a fuel check valve to prevent the flow of liquid fuel through the vent system (all except Gremlin), and a special pressure and vacuum relief filler cap. The EEC routes fuel into the PCV system, where it is burned along with regular crankcase emissions. A charcoal canister is added to the EEC system on V8 models with automatic transmission, for fuel vapor storage.

The Air Guard air injection system is used on some engines. It consists of an air pump, air injection nozzles in the exhaust manifold, and detail changes in the carburetor and distributor. Its purpose is to ignite any unburned gases in the exhaust. More details can be found in the Unit Repair section.

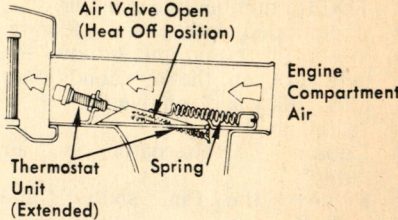

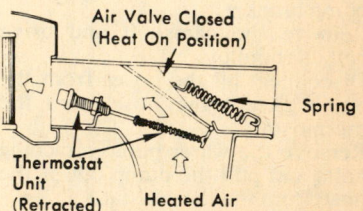

Thermostatically controlled air cleaner (TAC) —6 cylinder application
(© American Motors Corp)

Transmission Controlled Spark (TCS) is used on cars sold in California, and on 49 State 304 and 360 V8s with automatic transmission. Details can be found in the Unit Repair section.

A coolant temperature operated vacuum valve is used on cars equipped with V8 engines and automatic trans-

TIME SAVER

On V8 engines, water pumps have two different shaft lengths depending on application. Long-shaft pumps can be used in short-shaft applications if the flange on the pump shaft is pressed further down towards the pump (using an axle press) and the fan spacer drilled to receive the longer shaft.

missions. If the coolant temperature is above 160°F, intake manifold vacuum is blocked off and carburetor ported vacuum is sent through a hose to the distributor advance diaphragm, thus decreasing the amount of vacuum advance. On cars equipped with TCS, the distributor vacuum advance is controlled by the TCS system once 163°F is reached.

A thermostatically controlled air cleaner (TAC) is used on all engines in 1972. The TAC used on the V8 engines has a vacuum assist motor to operate the door in the air cleaner snorkle. The six cylinder TAC works by spring tension against a thermostatically controlled door.

1973

All six cylinder models are equipped with TCS.

New in 1973 is an Exhaust Gas Recirculation (EGR) system which is used on all V8s and six cylinder Matadors. This system directs a portion of the exhaust gases back into the intake manifold where they combine with the incoming mixture. This diluting of the mixture lowers peak combustion temperatures and reduces NOx. The EGR valve, which is controlled by carburetor vacuum, controls the amount of exhaust gas, if any, that is recycled into the engine. Two ambient temperature switches and one coolant temperature valve control the flow of vacuum to the valve. The low temperature ambient valve is mounted in the radiator support, near the grille, and opens at temperatures below 60° F to vent carburetor vacuum to the atmosphere. The high temperature ambient valve is mounted on the firewall and opens when ambient temperature rises above 115° F. When either of these valves is open the EGR valve will be closed, preventing exhaust gas from entering the engine. The coolant temperature valve is mounted in either the intake manifold or engine block and is closed to block vacuum when coolant temperature is below 115° F (160° on 304 V8 with manual transmission).

Also new for 1973 is an electrically-assisted automatic choke used on V8 models equipped with 4-bbl carburetors. Once under-hood temperatures reach 95°F (± 15°F), a bimetallic switch located in the choke cap closes, allowing a ceramic heating element to draw power from a special tap on the alternator. This causes the choke valve to open faster than normal, thus reducing CO emission during engine warm-up. After the engine is shut off, the bimetallic switch remains closed until under-hood temperature drops below 65°F. Thus, if the engine is turned off for only a short time or if the ambient temperature is above 65°F, the choke will function for only a limited period of time.

All Matador wagons and all V8s are equipped with an air pump. All engines

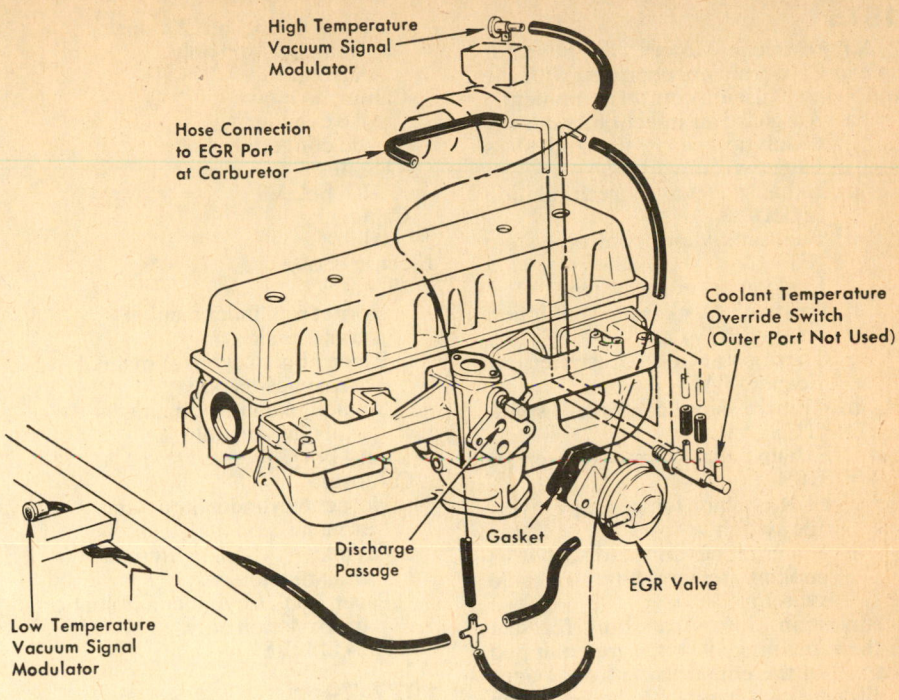

EGR valve installation and hose routing—6 cylinder
(© American Motors Corp)

have the charcoal canister added to the EEC system.

1973 1/2—74

Starting with vehicles made on or after 15 March 1973, the ambient temperature overrides were dropped from both the TCS and EGR systems.

Dropping these overrides on six-cylinder engines caused driveability problems, so a spark temperature override was added. This override provides normal vacuum advance below a coolant temperature of 160°F. Addition of the spark temperature override meant that the EGR coolant temperature override had to be dropped from the six-cylinder engines.

At the same time these changes were made, a new transmission controlled spark (TCS) was incorporated on all models equipped with automatic transmissions.

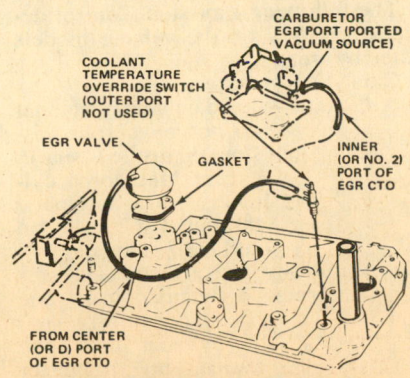

1974 V8 EGR system without backpressure sensor
(© American Motors Corp)

An adjustable TCS solenoid control switch, which is operated by transmission governor pressure, is mounted at the right rear of the block on sixes or at the rear of the right-hand valve cover on V8s. The switch is preset at the factory and should not normally require adjustment.

For 1974, most of the changes made in March are retained, except that the EGR coolant temperature override has been returned to the six-cylinder engines.

In addition, 1974 cars also have the following:
1. A back pressure sensing device to prevent EGR from occurring during idle, is used on all California six-cylinder engines when equipped with EGR valves, and V8s with automatic transmissions (except for the 401 cu in. V8).
2. Exhaust gas recirculation (EGR) has been extended to all six-cylinder engines, as well as V8s, except for the following:
   232 cu in. six—all Hornet sedans, Hornet hatchback, and Gremlin.
   258 cu in. six—Hornet 2-door sedan, Hornet hatchback, and Gremlin.
3. A new style diverter valve is used with air injection. The relief valve is now part of the diverter valve, rather than being mounted on the pump.
4. All engines for 1974 use a charcoal canister which is purged through the air cleaner snorkel. There is no purge valve on the canister.
5. The electrically assisted choke is retained on all 4-bbl V8 engines.

American Motors

1975

All American Motors cars built for sale in California are equipped with the following emission control equipment:

a. Air guard air injection system
b. Catalytic converter (all V8s have two converters)
c. Exhaust gas recirculation (EGR)
d. Fuel tank vapor control system (FTVC)
e. Fuel vapor return system
f. Positive crankcase ventilation system (PCV)
g. Thermostatically controlled air cleaner (TAC)
h. Transmission controlled spark (TCS)
i. Exhaust back-pressure sensor (BPS)
j. EGR coolant temperature override switch
k. Vacuum advance (distributor) coolant temperature override switch

American Motors cars built for sale in the remaining 49 states are equipped with all of the emission control devices California cars have with the following exceptions:

a. All six cylinder vehicles except manual transmission Matadors, do not have catalytic converters. All V8s and the 258 Matador Six with manual transmission have one catalytic converter; the 360 4 bbl V8 has two converters.
b. All Gremlin sixes and automatic transmission Hornet sixes and Pacers do not have the Air Guard air injection system.
c. All six cylinder vehicles except the Matador and Pacer automatic do not have the Fuel Vapor Return System.

See the "Emission Controls Unit Repair Section" for more information.

1976

No new emission control devices were introduced for 1976, but applications were changed as follows:

Air pump
  49 States
    Used on all V8 engines
    Pacer and Hornet 6 cylinder Manual Transmission only.
    Matador, all 6 cylinder
  California
    All models
Closed positive crankcase ventilation
Emission calibrated carburetor
Emission calibrated distributor
Single diaphragm vacuum advance
Exhaust gas recirculation
Vapor control, canister storage
Heated air cleaner
Transmission controlled spark
  49 States
    Not used
  California
    All models
Catalytic converter, single
  49 States

Matador 258 1 bbl. Manual Transmission only.
  All 2 bbl. V8
  California
    All 6 cylinder
Catalytic converter, dual
  49 States
    All 4 bbl. V8
  California
    All V8
Electric choke
  49 States
    Hornet 6 cylinder manual transmission only.
    Pacer 1 bbl. 6 cylinder manual transmission only.
    Matador 6 cylinder manual transmission only.
    All 4 bbl. V8
  California
    Hornet 6 cylinder automatic transmission only.
    Gremlin 6 cylinder automatic transmission only.
    Pacer 1 bbl. 6 cylinder automatic transmission only.
    All 4 bbl. V8

1977-79

Vehicles manufactured for sale at altitudes higher than 4,000 feet, must now be equipped with special emission control components. The emission control devices have been changed on some models and remain the same on others. All models have as standard equipment the following emission control components.

NOTE: *Refer to the Emission Control Systems section in the Unit Repair Section for further details on the emission control components.*

1. Air Guard system (air pump and components)
2. Closed positive crankcase ventilation system
3. Emission calibrated carburetor
4. Emission calibrated distributor
5. Single diaphragm vacuum advance unit
6. Vapor control, canister storage
7. Heated and thermostatically controlled air cleaner, (either vacuum or mechanically operated)
8. Exhaust gas recirculation valve

The following Emission Control devices are used on the vehicle models listed by area.

Catalytic Converter
  49 States—Used on all models that do not have transmission controlled spark, except Matador 6 cylinder automatic through 1977; used on all 1978-79 models
  Altitude—Used on all models
  California—4 cylinder uses one pellet converter
    6 cylinder uses one warm up converter and one pellet converter
    8 cylinder use two

warm up converters and two pellet converters
Transmission Controlled Spark
  49 States—Used on all models without catalytic converters, except Matador 6 cylinder automatic and 4 cylinder Gremlin models through 1977; not used 1978-79
  Altitude—Used on all automatic transmission models 1977 only
  California—Used on all models except 4 cylinder
Spark Coolant Temperature Override
  49 States—Used with 232 6 cylinder automatic and all other models except catalytic converter equipped manual transmission, and Matador 6 cylinder through 1977; used on all models 1978-79
  Altitude—Used on all models
  California—Used on all models
Carburetor Vent To Canister
  49 States—Used on all 4 and 6 cylinder models in 1977, and all 1978-79 models
  Altitude—Used on all models except 360 V8 Matador in 1977, and all 1978-79 models
  California—Used on all 4 and 6 cylinder in 1977, and all 1978-79 models
Electric Choke
  49 States—Used on 4 cylinder
  Altitude—Used on 4 cylinder and Matador 360 V8 and '78-'79 304 V8
  California—Used on all 4 cylinder and V8
Throttle Solenoid
  49 States—Used on 4 cylinder, 258 6 cylinder 2bbl automatic and all V8
  Altitude—Used on 4 cylinder and Matador 360 V8 and '78-'79 304 V8
  California—Used on all models

ENGINE

FOUR-CYLINDER

During the 1977 model year, a four cylinder, 2 litre (121 CID) engine was introduced for the Gremlin. The engine is of overhead camshaft design, belt driven from the crankshaft. The cylinder head is cast aluminum alloy and has removable camshaft bearing caps. Valve lash is controlled by manual adjustment of a tapered adjusting screw, located at the base of the tappet, under the camshaft. The intake and exhaust manifolds are on opposite sides of the cylinder head. The block is of cast iron and the crankshaft is set into five main bearings. Three grooved aluminum alloy pistons are used with full floating piston pins. The oil pump is located at the front of the block and is driven by the crankshaft.

SIX-CYLINDER

The base AMC engine is the 232 cubic inch six. Although American Motors has used this same engine since 1966, it is of relatively modern design. It has a seven main bearing crankshaft and overhead valves with hydraulic lifters. In engineer's parlance, this is an "oversquare" engine; the bore dimension exceeds that of the stroke. Beginning 1971, the 232 two-barrel was replaced by a very similar 258 cubic inch six, using a one barrel carburetor. A two-barrel 258 was introduced in 1976. The 258 is slightly "undersquare"; the stroke dimension exceeds the bore.

V8

All the AMC V8s are similar in design, having five main bearing crankshafts and overhead valves with hydraulic lifters.

The most common sizes are the 304 and 360. All of these V8 engines are "oversquare" or "short stroke" designs; their bore dimension exceeds that of the stroke. The base V8, the 304, has been offered only with a two-barrel carburetor. The 401 has been offered only with a four-barrel carburetor. The 360 has been available with a choice of two or four-barrel carburetion. Starting 1975, the 401 is available only to law enforcement agencies.

ENGINE REMOVAL AND INSTALLATION

4 CYLINDER

NOTE: *It is recommended by the manufacturer that the engine be removed from the car separately, and the transmission remain in the car.*

1. Mark the hinge locations and remove the hood.
2. Drain the coolant and remove the air cleaner and TAC hose.
3. Detach the negative cable at the alternator bracket and battery.
4. Remove the fuel and vacuum lines from the engine. Plug the fuel line.
5. Disconnect the necessary wiring, the throttle cable, and automatic transmission throttle valve linkage.
6. If your car has air conditioning, the system must be bled, the hoses disconnected, and the condenser moved.

———— CAUTION ————

Do not attempt to bleed the system unless you are familiar with air conditioning systems. Have it done by a qualified mechanic. Compressed refrigerant will freeze any surface it contacts, including your eyes. It also forms a poisonous gas in the presence of flame.

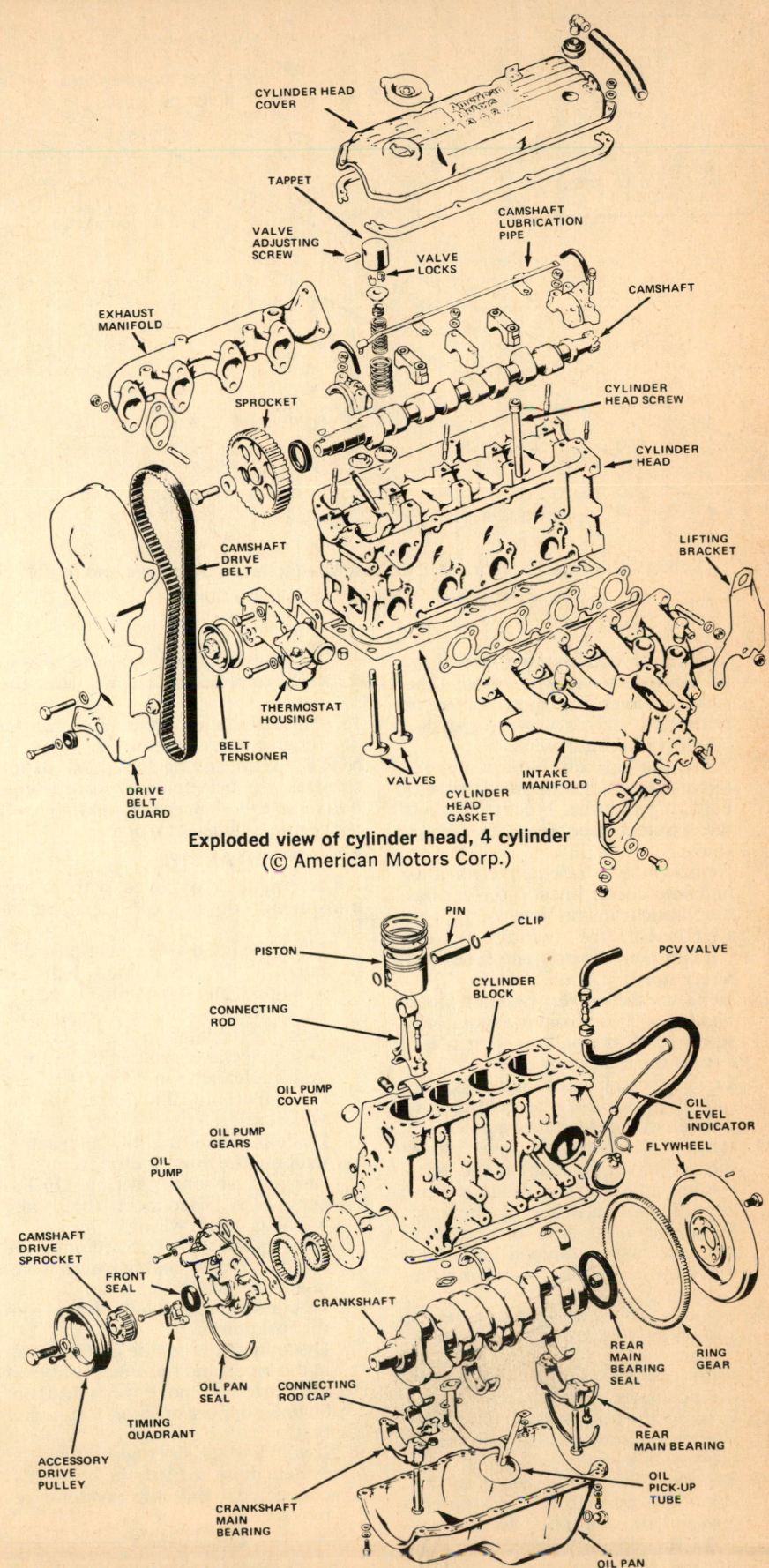

Exploded view of cylinder head, 4 cylinder
(© American Motors Corp.)

Exploded view of cylinder block, 4 cylinder (© American Motors Corp.)

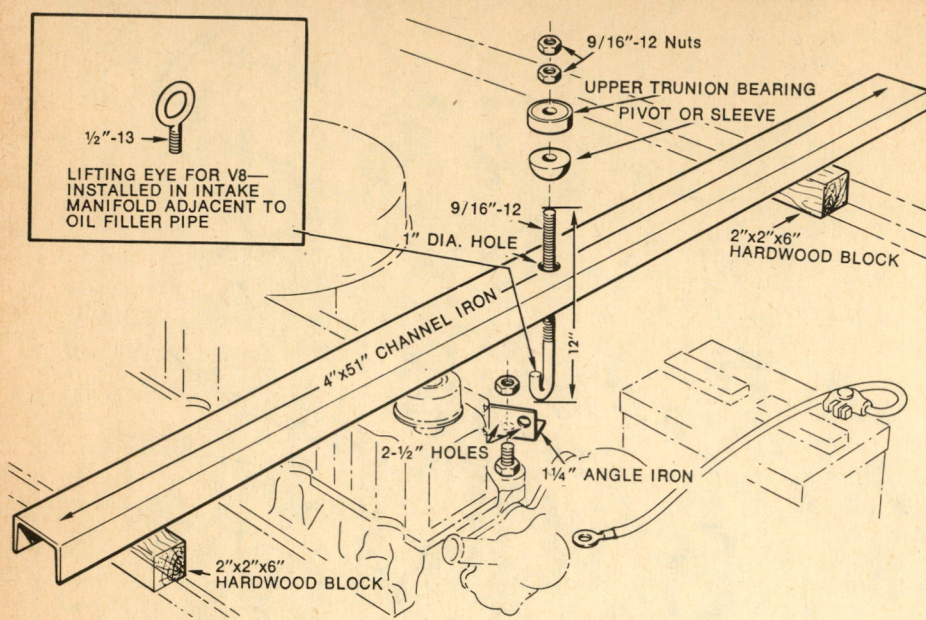

9/16"-12 Nuts

UPPER TRUNION BEARING

PIVOT OR SLEEVE

½"-13 →

LIFTING EYE FOR V8—
INSTALLED IN INTAKE
MANIFOLD ADJACENT TO
OIL FILLER PIPE

9/16"-12

1" DIA. HOLE

2"x2"x6" HARDWOOD BLOCK

4"x51" CHANNEL IRON

12"

2-½" HOLES

1¼" ANGLE IRON

2"x2"x6" HARDWOOD BLOCK

Lifting fixture can be fabricated as illustrated to facilitate oil pan and motor mount removal (© American Motors Corp)

With air conditioning, bleed off the compressor charge, remove the service valves, cap the compressor ports and service valves, and disconnect the clutch wire.

7. Raise the car, disconnect and remove the starter motor and exhaust pipe support bracket. Unbolt the exhaust pipe from the manifold.

8. Remove the torque convertor nuts and fluid cooler lines, if the car has automatic transmission.

9. Disconnect the wiring at the backup lamp switch and from the alternator.

10. Remove the lower radiator hose and heater hose from the radiator.

11. Remove all the bell housing bolts, except the top center bolt.

12. Lower the car and remove the top radiator hose and the cold air induction manifold at the radiator.

13. Remove the radiator screws, move the radiator one inch to the left, rotate, and lift the radiator and shroud assembly out of the car. With air conditioning, first remove the condenser attaching bolts and move the condenser away from the radiator.

14. Remove any other heater hoses and wiring that are still attached to the car.

15. With power steering, disconnect the hoses from the steering gear. Remove the transmission filler tube support screws with automatic transmission.

16. Remove the engine support cushion nuts on both sides of the engine and attach a lifting device.

17. With the engine partially raised, support the transmission and remove the center bolt from the

transmission bell housing. Carefully remove the engine from the car.

18. The installation procedure is in the reverse order of removal.

NOTE: *When mating the engine to the transmission bell housing, install three bolts for a more secure mounting until the engine is bolted into place.*

6 CYLINDER AND V8

The engine is removed without the transmission on all models except the Pacer.

1. Mark the hood hinge locations, disconnect the underhood light, if equipped, and remove the hood.

2. Drain the coolant and engine oil. Remove the filter on the Pacer.

3. Disconnect and remove the battery and air cleaner. On Pacers, first run the wipers to the center of the windshield.

4. Disconnect and tag the alternator, ignition coil, distributor, temperature and oil sender wiring. On Pacers, also disconnect the brake warning switch wiring.

5. If equipped with TCS, remove the switch bracket and vacuum solenoid wire harness.

6. Disconnect and plug the hose from the fuel pump.

7. Disconnect the engine ground strap at the block and the starter cable at the starter. Remove the right front engine support cushion-to-bracket bolt.

8. If your car has air conditioning, the system must be bled, the hoses disconnected, and the system removed.

CAUTION

Do not perform this operation if you are unfamiliar with A/C systems. Have

the system bled by a qualified mechanic. Compressed refrigerant will freeze any surface it contacts, including your eyes. It also forms a poisonous gas in the presence of flame.

Bleed the refrigerant from the system. Remove the service valves, cap the compressor ports and the service valves, and disconnect the clutch wire. On Pacers, also disconnect the receiver outlet at the coupling, and remove the receiver and condenser assembly.

9. Disconnect the return hose from the fuel filter, TAC hose from the manifold, carburetor vent hose, heater or A/C vacuum hose and /or power brake hose at intake manifold, and power brake vacuum check valve from booster, if equipped.

10. Disconnect the throttle cable and throttle valve rod, if equipped.

11. Disconnect the radiator and heater hoses from the engine, automatic transmission cooler lines from the radiator, radiator shroud, fan, and spacer, and remove the radiator.

12. Install a $5/16$ x $1/2$ in. bolt through the fan pulley into the water pump flange to maintain alignment (all but Pacer).

13. With power steering, disconnect the hoses, drain the reservoir, and cap the fittings.

14. On Pacers only, remove the carburetor and plug the fitting, remove the valve cover(s), and remove the vibration damper.

15. With automatic transmission, remove the filler tube.

16. Jack and support the front of the car. Remove the starter.

17. With automatic transmission on all except the Pacer, remove the converter cover, converter bolts (rotate the crankshaft for access), and the exhaust pipe/transmission linkage support.

With manual transmission on all but the Pacer, remove the clutch cover, bellcrank inner support bolts and springs, the bellcrank, outer bellcrank-to-strut retainer, and disconnect the back-up lamp wire harness at the firewall for access later.

On Pacers, disconnect the transmission and clutch linkage, speedometer cable at the transmission, remove the driveshaft (plug the transmission), and support the transmission with a jack. Remove the rear crossmember.

18. Attach the lifting device and support the engine. Remove the engine mount bolts.

19. Disconnect the exhaust pipe from the manifold.

20. On all but the Pacer, remove the upper converter or clutch housing bolts and loosen the lower bolts. Raise the car and move the jackstands to the jack pad area. Re-

move the A/C idler pulley and bracket, if equipped. Lift the engine off the front supports, support the transmission, remove the lower transmission cover attaching bolts, and lift the engine out of the car.

On Pacers, lift the engine slightly and remove the front support cushions. Remove the transmission support, raise the front of the car so that the bottom of the bumper is three feet from the floor, and partially remove the engine/transmission assembly until the rear of the cylinder head clears the cowl. Lower the car and remove the engine.

21. On installation with manual transmission, insert the transmission shaft into the clutch spline and align the clutch housing to the engine. Install and tighten the lower housing bolts. With automatic transmission, align the converter housing to the engine and loosely install the bottom housing bolts. Then install the next higher bolts and tighten all four bolts. With both transmissions, next remove the transmission support, lower the engine onto the mounts, and install the mounting bolts. The remainder of the installation is the reverse of removal.

On Pacers, raise the car with a jack as in Step 20. Lower the engine/transmission assembly into the compartment. Raise the transmission into position with a jack and install the rear crossmember. Install the front engine support cushions. The remainder of installation is the reverse of removal.

MANIFOLDS

Intake Manifold Removal and Installation

4 CYLINDER

1. Drain the cooling system.
2. Remove the EGR tube at the exhaust manifold and remove the air cleaner assembly.
3. Disconnect the fuel and vacuum lines and plug the main fuel line to avoid gasoline leakage.
4. Remove the accelerator cable and the air hose from the diverter valve.
5. Remove the fuel pump and the power brake cylinder vacuum hose. Loosen the air conditioner compressor mounting bracket, if so equipped. Do not discharge the system.
6. Remove the water inlet and outlet hoses from the manifold and the PCV hose at the block.
7. Remove the wires from the carburetor, accessories, and from the ignition coil.
8. Remove the manifold bracket lower screw, loosen and remove the manifold nuts, and remove the

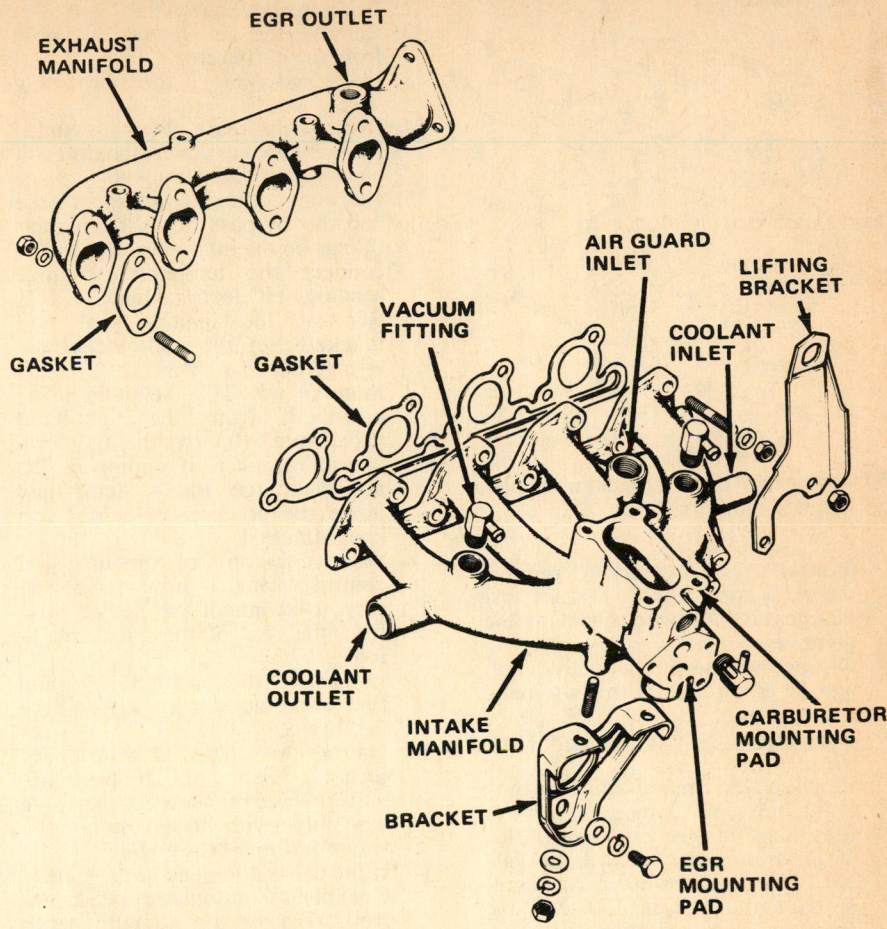

Intake and exhaust manifolds, 4 cylinder (© American Motors Corp.)

manifold and lift bracket from the engine.
9. Remove the gasket and clean the mating surfaces on the manifold and the cylinder head.
10. The installation of the intake manifold is in the reverse of the disassembly. When installing the manifold, don't tighten the manifold retaining nuts until the EGR tube is connected to the exhaust manifold. Then tighten the retaining nuts to 18 ft. lbs. torque and the bracket lower screw to 30 ft. lbs. When the installation is completed, operate the engine for 3 to 5 minutes and check for leaks.

6 CYLINDER

The intake manifold is mounted on the left-hand side of the engine and bolted to the cylinder head. A gasket is used between the intake manifold and the head, none is required for the exhaust manifold.

1. Remove the air cleaner. Disconnect the fuel line, vent hose, and solenoid wire, if equipped.
2. Disconnect the accelerator cable from the accelerator bellcrank.
3. Disconnect the PCV vacuum hose from the intake manifold and the TCS solenoid and bracket, if so equipped.

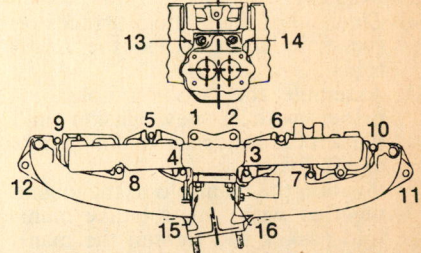

Intake manifold torque sequence —6 cylinder (© American Motors Corp)

4. Remove the spark CTO switch and EGR valve (or exhaust back-pressure sensor) vacuum lines from each of these components.
5. Disconnect the hoses from the air pump and the injection manifold check valve. Disconnect the vacuum line from the diverter valve and remove the diverter valve with hoses, if so equipped.
6. Remove the air pump and power steering bracket (if so equipped) and remove the air pump. Move the power steering pump aside, out of the way, without disconnecting the hoses.
7. Remove the air conditioning drive belt idler assembly from the cylinder head, if so equipped. On some

American Motors

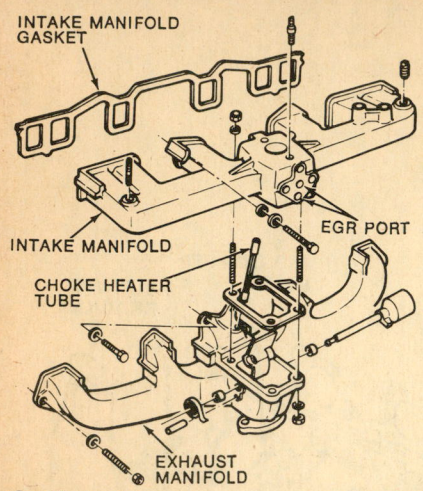

6 cylinder intake and exhaust manifold
(© American Motors Corp)

models it is necessary to remove the A/C compressor. Do not discharge the A/C system; just lay the compressor aside.

8. Disconnect the throttle valve linkage if equipped with automatic transmission.
9. Disconnect the exhaust pipe from the manifold.
10. Remove the manifold attaching bolts, nuts, and clamps and remove the intake and exhaust manifolds as an assembly. Discard the gasket. The two manifolds are separated at the heat riser. Discard the asbestos gasket if they are separated.

To install the intake and exhaust manifolds:

1. Clean all of the mating surfaces on the cylinder head and the manifolds.
2. Assemble the two manifolds together with a new gasket and tighten the heat riser retaining nuts to 5 ft. lbs.
3. Position the manifold to the engine together with a new intake manifold gasket and tighten the manifold attaching bolts and nuts in the proper sequence to the specified torque.
4. Install the remaining components in the reverse order of removal. Adjust the automatic transmission throttle linkage, if so equipped. Adjust the drive belt(s) tension.

V8

The cast iron manifold completely encloses and seals the tappet valley between the cylinder heads. The manifold contains water passages, a crankcase vent passage, exhaust crossover, induction, and in some cases EGR passages. A one-piece metal gasket seals the intake manifold to cylinder head joint and also serves as an oil splash baffle. The left-hand carburetor bores supply cylinders No. 1, 7, 4 and 6; the right-hand bores cylinders No. 3, 5, 2 and 8.

1. Drain the cooling system.
2. Remove the air cleaner assembly from the carburetor.
3. Mark and remove the spark plug wires.
4. Remove the spark plug wire guides from the rocker cover, ignition coil and by-pass valve brackets.
5. Disconnect the radiator upper hose and the by-pass hoses from their fittings on the intake manifold. Disconnect the temperature gauge sending unit electrical lead.
6. Remove the ignition coil and bracket. Set the coil/bracket assembly out of the way.
7. Remove the TCS solenoid if so equipped, from the right-hand valve cover. Remove the A/C compressor bracket, if equipped. Do not discharge the system, just move the compressor aside with lines attached.
8. Disconnect any of the emission control wiring or hoses as necessary. Disconnect the heater hose from the rear of the intake manifold.
9. Disconnect the throttle linkage and fuel and vacuum lines from the carburetor.
10. On the cars equipped with air injection, remove the by-pass (diverter) valve bracket. Set the valve assembly (with hoses) out of the way, forward of the engine.
11. If the car is equipped with "Cruise Command" (automatic speed control), remove the vacuum servo mounting bracket and set the servo assembly aside.
12. Remove the carburetor assembly from the manifold.
13. Remove the intake manifold assembly complete with gasket and end seals.

Always use a new gasket when installing the intake manifold. Use a good commercial sealer on both sides of the metal gasket and on the rubber end seals. Align the gasket at the rear first, then at the front.

The rest of the installation procedure is the reverse of removal. Torque the manifold bolts evenly to the specified torque, working from the center out.

Exhaust Manifold Removal and Installation

4 CYLINDER

1. Remove the TAC cold air induction manifold assembly and components.
2. Disconnect the EGR tube from the manifold.
3. Remove the exhaust pipe from the manifold.
4. Remove the manifold retaining nuts and washers.
5. Remove the manifold and gasket from the engine.
6. Clean the mating surfaces of the manifold and the head.

7. The installation of the manifold is the reverse of disassembly. Do not tighten the exhaust manifold nuts until the EGR tube is attached to the exhaust manifold, then torque the manifold nuts to 18 ft. lbs.

V8—EXCEPT GREMLIN AND HORNET w/AIR PUMP THROUGH 1976

NOTE: *The mating surfaces of both the exhaust manifold and the cylinder head are machined smooth, thus eliminating any need for a gasket between them.*

1. Disconnect the wires from the spark plugs after marking them for firing order.
2. On models equipped with air injection, disconnect the air delivery hoses from the injection manifold. Remove the injection manifold and nozzles from the exhaust manifold.
3. Disconnect the exhaust pipe from the exhaust manifold flange.
4. Remove the bolts and washers used to retain the manifold.
5. Remove the shields from the spark plugs. On 1977 and later Hornets and Concords only, before removing the right side manifold, remove the transmission filler tube bolt and tube. Use a new O-ring when installing the tube.
6. Remove the exhaust manifold from the cylinder head.
7. Clean the machined surfaces of the manifold and head. Installation is the reverse of removal.

GREMLIN AND HORNET V8 WITH AIR PUMP THROUGH 1976

The exhaust manifold on the left-side may be removed in the same manner as detailed for other V8 engines, however, the right-side manifold on Gremlins and Hornets equipped with air pumps, must be removed in the following order:

1. Raise the car and securely support it with jackstands.
2. Disconnect the exhaust pipe from the manifold flange.
3. Support the engine at the vibration damper, by placing a jack with a block of wood on its lifting pad underneath it.
4. Remove the bolts which secure the engine mounting bracket on the right-side.
5. Remove the air cleaner assembly, including the tube which runs to the manifold heat stove.
6. Disconnect the battery cables. Remove the spark plug leads after marking them for installation.
7. Disconnect the air supply hose from the air injection manifold.
8. Remove the air injection tubes from the exhaust manifold.
9. On cars with automatic transmissions, remove the dipstick and the screw which secures the transmission dipstick tube.
10. Working from the rear, unscrew

the exhaust manifold mounting bolts.

11. Raise the engine. Remove the exhaust manifold and the air injection manifold as an assembly.

Prior to installation, clean the joining surfaces of the manifold and cylinder head. Be careful not to nick or scratch either surface.

The rest of installation is the reverse of removal. Torque the manifold securing bolts to specification, starting from the rear and working forward.

6 CYLINDER

The exhaust manifold is removed along with the intake manifold; see previous instructions.

VALVE SYSTEM

4 CYLINDER

The valves are operated by an overhead cam, driven by a toothed rubber belt, connected to the crankshaft. The cam lobes contact "bucket" type tappets, which are set over the valve and valve springs, and force the valve and springs to move downward, moving the valve from its seat on the cylinder head. All the valves are fitted with outer and inner springs, to insure more positive valve action at all speeds. The exhaust valves have a rotator to prolong both valve and seat life. Both intake and exhaust valves are manually adjusted by a wedge type screw angled into the tappet, perpendicular to the valve stem. A flat area is milled onto the screw, which contacts the valve stem end. The threaded area locks to a threaded area within the tappet. Each turn changes the clearance .002 in. When tappet adjustment is done, the flat side of the adjusting screw must be toward the valve stem end at the completion of the adjustment. Refer to the Tune-Up Specifications Chart for hot valve clearances. Cold assembly clearances are 0.004-0.007, intake; and 0.014-0.017, exhaust.

4 Cylinder Valve Adjustment

NOTE: *Valve adjustment must be made with the engine at normal operating temperature.*

1. Remove the TAC hose, the cylinder head cover, the spark plug wires and distributor cap.
2. Rotate the crankshaft to bring the number one cylinder to TDC (the beginning of its firing stroke). The position of the distributor rotor will assist in determining this position.

NOTE: *There is a mark on the edge of the distributor housing at number one terminal position. Do not attempt to rotate the engine by turning the camshaft. Turn the crankshaft in the direction of normal rotation to avoid damage to the timing belt.*

3. With number one cylinder on TDC of its firing stroke, the clearance of the exhaust valves on cylinders

numbers one and three, and of the intake valves on cylinders number one and two, can be checked.

NOTE: *The front valve in each pair per cylinder is the intake valve. If the clearance requires adjustment, a special tool is required to move the adjusting screw.*

4. Adjust the screw by turning one complete turn until it clicks, and continue until the proper clearance is obtained.
5. After adjusting the clearance, use the special AMC gauge J-26860 to check the position of the screw in the tappet. If the gauge indicates the adjusting screw is turned too far into the tappet, the screw must be replaced. Five sizes of screws are available, identified by grooves on the end of the screws.

NOTE: *If the adjusting screws must be replaced, the tappets must be removed from the head. Note which tappets must be removed, then continue the adjustment procedure. When all eight adjustments are made, remove those tappets requiring screw replacement. Refer to camshaft removal and installation.*

6. Rotate the crankshaft 180 degrees. The distributor rotor should be 180 degrees opposite the mark on the distributor housing.
7. The clearance can now be checked on the exhaust valves for cylinders two and four, and the intake valve on cylinders three and four.
8. Reinstall the head cover, using a new gasket.

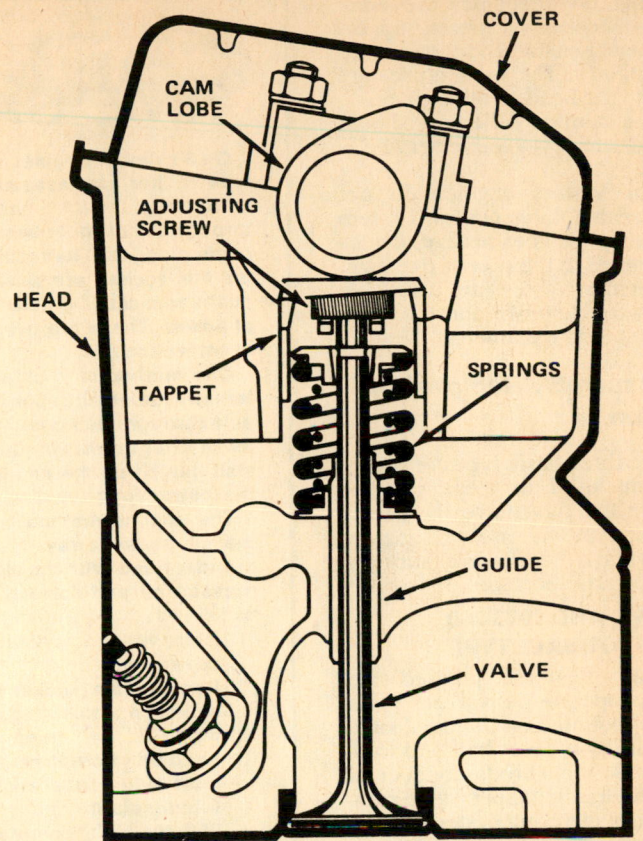

4 Cylinder valve train (© American Motors Corp.)

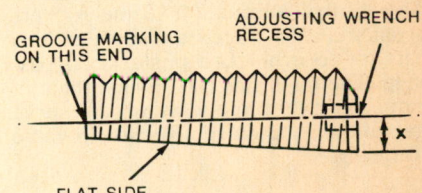

4 Cylinder valve tappet adjusting screw (© American Motors Corp.)

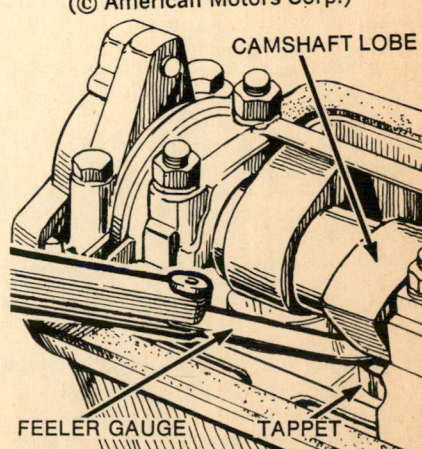

4 Cylinder valve clearance measurement

9. Reinstall the distributor cap and spark plug wiring. Reinstall the TAC flexible hose.

6 CYLINDER AND V8

American Motors cars use hydraulic

tappets; thus, no mechanical valve adjustment is necessary. Special tappets to permit higher sustained rpm are used in police engines. The valve guides are integral with the head on all engines.

The valve stem oil deflectors should be replaced whenever valve service is performed.

American Motors engines do not have replaceable valve guides. If stem to guide clearance is excessive, guides must be reamed to the proper oversize. Three oversize valves are available with stems 0.003, 0.015 and 0.030 in. larger than standard diameter.

Rocker Assembly Removal and Installation

There are three basic types of rocker arm systems used in these engines. Makes sure that you have the procedure for the type you are working on; there may have been some substitutions due to parts shortages.

1972 ALL V8, AND 1973 360, 401 V8—PIVOT BALL TYPE

Individually mounted, pressed steel rocker arms operate the valves. These rockers are mounted on threaded studs and are held by a pivot ball and locknut. The hollow pushrods conduct oil from each hydraulic tappet to the rockers. There is a metering system in each tappet consisting of a stepped lower pushrod cap surface and a flat plate. Any loss of lubrication to the rockers usually can be traced to failure of this part, or to a blocked pushrod oil passage. The pushrods rub against the cylinder head during operation and serve to maintain the correct rocker to valve stem angle.

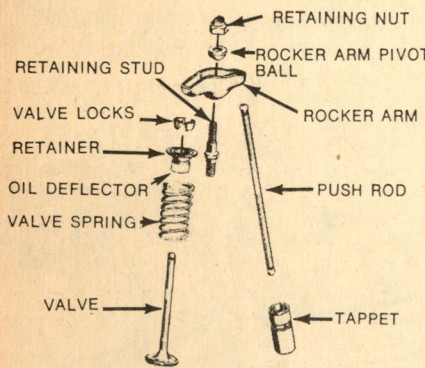

V8 rocker arm assembly—Pivot ball type
(© American Motors Corp)

1. Remove valve covers, after first removing any accessories and the air cleaner preheat tube.
2. Loosen and remove the retaining locknuts, ball pivots and rocker arms. It is a good idea to lay them out in order, along with their respective pushrods.
3. Installation is the reverse of removal.

On 6 cylinder engines with shaft type rocker arm assemblies, the lubricating oil passageway through the cylinder head can become clogged. The result is wear on the rocker arms, shaft, and push rods, causing noise and loss of power. These are two methods of correcting this.

One method is to obtain an externally routed oil supply kit, available through the manufacturer, or as an after market product. To install this kit on the engine, follow the instructions supplied.

The second method is to open the oil passageway through the cylinder head, with the aid of compressed air and solvent. Proceed as follows:

1. Remove the cylinder head cover.
2. Remove the rocker arm assembly and push rods.
3. Remove the third cylinder head bolt from the rear on the right side of the engine (distributor side).
4. With the aid of compressed air and/or solvent, open the oil passageway in the cylinder head bolt opening, and the passage to the number five rocker shaft support bolt hole.
5. Measure down from the top of the bolt threads ¼ inch and mark the bolt at this point. Measure up ¼ inch and mark the bolt shaft at this point.
6. Grind or machine off the threads in the marked ½ inch area of the bolt shaft. Go no deeper than the depth of the threads. You now have a bolt with a ½ in. indentation about ¹/₃₂ in. deep.
7. Replace the bolt in the cylinder head and torque to specifications.
8. Make the necessary repairs or replacement of parts to the rocker shaft assembly and install it and the push rods on the cylinder head and torque the retaining bolts to 18-26 ft lbs.
9. Temporarily attach the necessary lines and start the engine. Observe the oil supply at the rocker arm assembly. (Oil should drip from the shaft to the rocker arm area, and be flowing down the push rods.)
10. Stop the engine and install the cylinder head cover with a new gasket. The engine oil and filter should be changed to remove the loosened sludge.

NOTE: *When installing new threaded studs, make sure hex nut is fully seated and tightened to 65-70 ft. lbs. Retaining locknuts are tightened to 20-25 ft. lbs.*

1971-72 AND 1974 6 CYLINDER—SHAFT TYPE

The rocker arms on these engines are mounted on a common shaft. Oil pressure for rocker lubrication is supplied via No. 3 camshaft bearing from the main oil gallery to No. 5 rocker support.

1. Remove valve cover.
2. Unbolt cap bolts and remove rockers and shaft.
3. Installation is the reverse of removal. Torque mounting bolts to 18-26 ft. lbs.

NOTE: *Hold rockers in place using large rubber bands.*

1973 AND 1975-79 6 CYLINDER, 304 V8, AND ALL 1974-79 V8s —BRIDGED PIVOT TYPE

The intake and exhaust rocker arms for each cylinder pivot on a bridged pivot assembly bolted to the cylinder head. The pushrods are hollow to supply lubrication to the rocker arms. The pushrods act as guides to keep the rocker arms in alignment, so it is not abnormal for them to rub slightly on the cylinder head.

NOTE: *Be careful when ordering new valve train components, not to get parts for the wrong year. Some 1973 sixes*

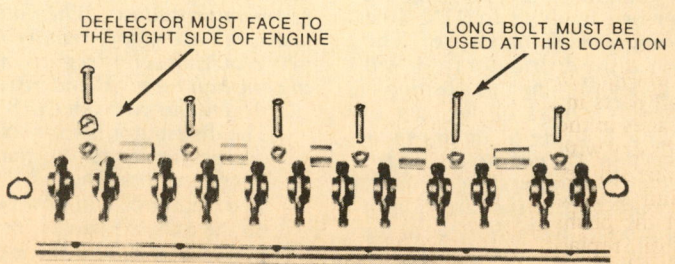

DEFLECTOR MUST FACE TO THE RIGHT SIDE OF ENGINE

LONG BOLT MUST BE USED AT THIS LOCATION

6 cylinder rocker shaft assembly
(© American Motors Corp)

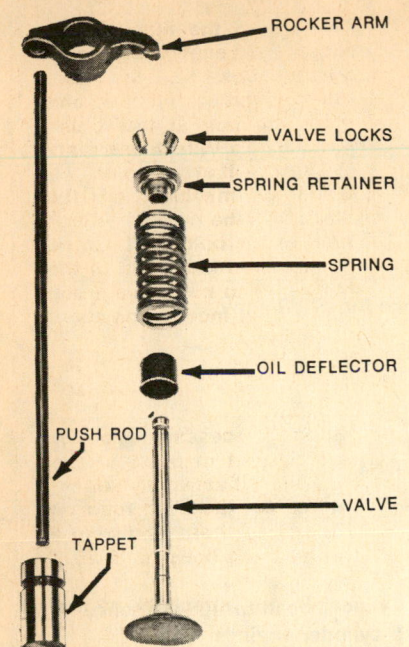

ROCKER ARM

VALVE LOCKS

SPRING RETAINER

SPRING

OIL DEFLECTOR

PUSH ROD

VALVE

TAPPET

Valve assembly sequence—shaft type
(© American Motors Corp)

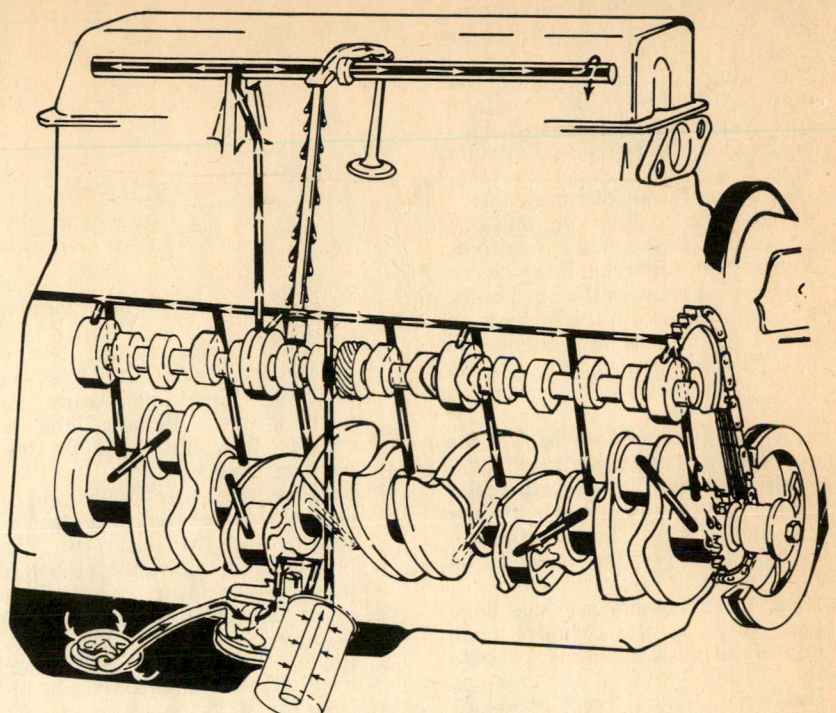

Oiling system, 6 cylinder with rocker arm shaft
(© American Motors Corp.)

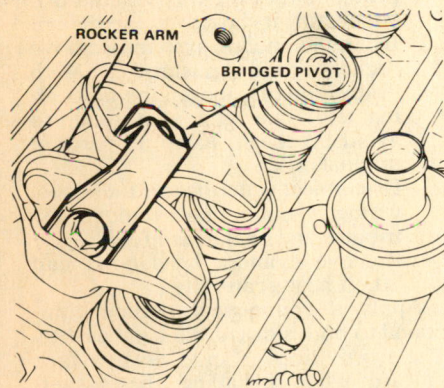

ROCKER ARM

BRIDGED PIVOT

Bridged pivot type rocker arms
(© American Motors Corp.)

may have come from the factory with the wrong tappets installed; check for this fault on any car which has noisy valves.

1. Remove any accessories which are in the way and remove the valve cover, complete with gasket.
2. Unscrew the rocker arm capscrews evenly to avoid breaking the bridge.
3. Remove the pivot assemblies, rocker arms, and pushrods.

NOTE: *Be sure to keep all parts in the same order in which they were removed*

4. Clean all parts in solvent. Blow all oil passages in the rocker arms and pushrods dry with compressed air.
   Replace any deeply pitted rocker arms and scuffed or worn pushrods. If the pushrod is worn from lack of oil, replace it, its valve lifter and rocker arm, as well.

Installation is performed in the following order:

1. Insert the pushrods in their bores,

be sure to center the bottom of each rod in the plunger cap of the hydraulic valve lifter.
2. Install the rocker arms, pivot assemblies and capscrews. Tighten the capscrews evenly to 21 ft. lbs.

NOTE: *Be sure that the pushrods, pivot assemblies, and capscrews are returned to exactly the same places from which they were removed.*

3. Install the valve cover and gasket; secure them with retaining screws and washers.
4. Install anything which was removed to gain access to the valve covers.

Cylinder Head Removal and Installation

CAUTION

Don't loosen the head bolts until the engine is thoroughly cool, to prevent warping.

If the head sticks, operate the starter to loosen it by compression or rap it upward with a soft hammer. Do not force anything between the head and the block.

NOTE: *Resurfacing (milling or grinding) the cylinder head will increase the compression ratio, and can affect the emission output, as well as the fuel octane requirement. For this reason the factory recommends replacing, rather than resurfacing cylinder heads.*

Cylinder head bolts should be retorqued after the first 500 miles or so unless a special AMC gasket is used.

The special gasket doesn't require retorquing.

CAUTION

Make sure to blow any coolant out of the cylinder head bolt holes before reassembly to prevent inaccurate torque readings.

4 CYLINDER

1. Drain the coolant from the system and disconnect the negative cable from the battery.
2. Remove the air cleaner assembly, vacuum hoses and flexible hoses from the cylinder head area.
3. Remove the radiator hoses, radiator bypass hose and the heater hoses.
4. Remove the accessory drive belts, camshaft drive belt cover, and the camshaft drive belt. Loosen the compressor mounting bracket if equipped with A/C.
5. Remove the fan belt, fan blades, spacer and pulley. Remove the air pump and also the alternator pivot bolt. Do not disconnect the wire harness from the alternator.
6. Remove the air pump front bracket, and the exhaust pipe from the manifold. Remove the air hose from the diverter valve and remove the EGR tube to bell housing screw.
7. Disconnect the remaining wires to the electrical units of the cylinder head, marking the wires for connection during assembly.
8. Remove the fuel line at the bottom

of the intake manifold, and remove the screw from the bottom of the manifold bracket.

9. Disconnect the power brake vacuum hose. Remove the remaining fuel vapor control hoses, PCV hoses, and the remaining vacuum lines.

10. Disconnect the accelerator cable.

11. Remove the coolant inlet and outlet hoses from the intake manifold.

12. Remove the cylinder head cover. Loosen and remove the head bolts. Loosen the bolts in the reverse order of the tightening sequence, in two passes. Remove the cylinder head, manifolds and carburetor as a unit.

13. Clean the machined surfaces of the cylinder head and the engine block. With a straight edge and feeler gauge, check the flatness of the mating surfaces. There should not be a distortion of over 0.002 in. on both surfaces.

14. After the necessary services have been done to the cylinder head and/or the block assembly, prepare the mating surfaces by cleaning thoroughly. Install a new head gasket, and place the head on the block with the aid of locating dowels. Torque the cylinder head bolts to 65 ft. lbs. following the cylinder head torque sequence illustration, and in three stages.

15. Complete cylinder head replacement by following the reverse procedure of disassembly. Temporarily install the head cover. Start the engine and allow it to warm up for five minutes.

16. When the engine has warmed up to operating temperature, stop the engine and remove the top engine cover.

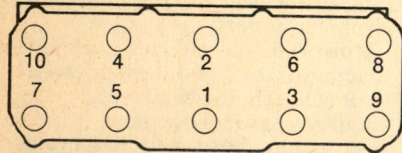

Head bolt torque sequence, 4 cylinder
(© American Motors Corp.)

17. Following the head torque sequence, loosen the first head bolt $1/8$ of a turn and retorque the bolt to 80 ft. lbs. Proceed to the second bolt and repeat the procedure for each head bolt until all the bolts have been retorqued to the new specification.

18. Replace the head cover and complete the assembly of the lines, tubes, wires, and air cleaner assembly.

19. Check the engine for leakage.

6 CYLINDER

NOTE: *On Pacers, run the wipers to the center of the windshield to ease valve cover removal.*

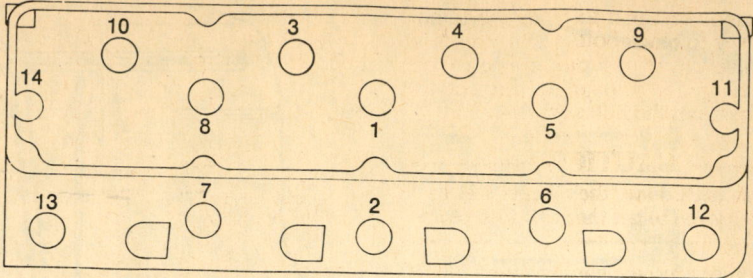

Cylinder head torque sequence for all V8 engines

1. Drain the cooling system. Disconnect throttle linkage, fuel lines, water hoses, spark plug wires and vacuum line. Remove the air cleaner, PCV hose, and the temperature sender.

2. Remove the valve cover and its gasket. Remove the rocker arm assembly and the pushrods. With bridged pivots, loosen each bolt alternately, one turn at a time, to avoid damage. Keep the pushrods in order.

3. Remove the intake and exhaust manifold assembly from the head.

4. Disconnect the spark plug wires and remove the plugs.

5. Disconnect the battery ground cable, the coil, and the coil bracket from the head. Disconnect the temperature sending unit wire.

6. If the vehicle is equipped with air conditioning, remove the drive the belt idler pulley bracket from the cylinder head. Loosen the alternator drive belt and remove the bolts from the compressor mounting bracket and set the compressor aside.

7. Remove the bolts and remove the cylinder head from the block.

8. Clean the gasket surfaces of both the head and the block. Remove the carbon deposits from the top of each piston and from the combustion chambers.

9. Check the head for straightness. If the head (or the block) is 0.008 in. out of true over its entire length, 0.001 in. in 1 in., or 0.002 in. in 6 in., the head requires resurfacing.

Installation of the cylinder head is performed in the following order:

1. Use a new head gasket and coat both of its sides with sealer. The word "top," on the gasket, faces upward.

2. Tighten the head bolts in three stages and proper sequence to the proper torque specification.

3. The rest of installation is the reverse of the removal. Refill the cooling system when completed.

V8

Maximum out of true is 0.006 in. for the entire length of head, 0.001 in every 1 in., or 0.002 in. in 6 in.

1. Remove oil filler tube, rocker covers, air pump, power steering pump, alternator support bracket,

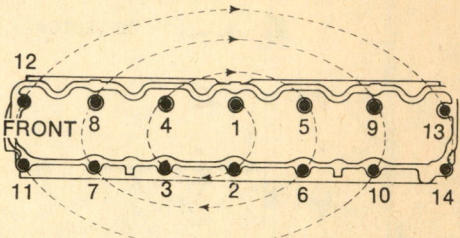

Cylinder head torque sequence for all 6 cylinder engines

exhaust manifolds and air conditioner. Move air conditioner compressor out of the way without disconnecting its hoses.

2. Drain the cooling system. Remove rockers and pushrods. With bridged pivots, loosen the bolts altenately, one turn at a time, to avoid breakage. Keep all parts in original order.

3. Disconnect water hoses, fuel lines, wiring, vacuum lines; remove distributor and intake manifold.

4. Remove cylinder head bolts and lift off heads carefully.

Apply a commercial sealing compound to both sides of the head gasket. The word "top" should always face upward when installing the gasket. Tighten the head bolts to specifications in three steps in the sequence illustrated. The rest of removal is the reverse of installation.

TIMING COVER, CHAIN, AND CAMSHAFT

Vibration Damper Removal

6 CYLINDER AND V8

Remove the radiator core, all drive belts, and the fan. Remove the nut from the center of the pulley. The best way to do this is to affix a heavy wrench and rap it with a substantial hammer. The nut must be unscrewed in the opposite direction of normal engine rotation. Using a puller, remove the pulley from the front of the crankshaft.

Timing Case Cover Removal and Installation

6 CYLINDER

1. Remove all V-belts, fan and pulley.
2. Remove vibration damper.

3. Remove oil pan to cover bolts and cover to block bolts.
4. Raise cover and pull oil pan front seal up far enough to extract the tabs from the holes in cover.

—————— CAUTION ——————

If this isn't done, the oil pan will have to be removed to get the seals into place.

5. Remove cover gasket from block; cut off seal tab flush with front face of block.

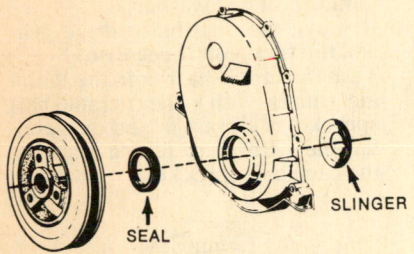

Timing chain cover assembly—6 cylinder
(© American Motors Corp.)

6. Clean all mating surfaces and remove oil seal.
7. Install a new front oil seal.
8. Install new neoprene front oil pan seal, cutting off protruding tabs to match original. Use sealer on the end tabs.
9. Position cover on block and install bolts. Tighten cover bolts to 4-6 ft. lbs.; four lower bolts to 10-12 ft. lbs. Use sealer on the gasket.
10. Install vibration damper, tightening the bolt to the specified torque.

NOTE: *Front oil seal can be installed with cover in place only if proper tool or duplicate is available.*

V8

The die-cast timing cover incorporates an oil seal at the vibration damper hub. This seal must be installed from the rear through 1976; therefore the cover must be removed from engine in every case to replace front seal. 1977 and later oil seals are installed from the front, and can be replaced without removing the cover using a special AMC tool.

1. Drain coolant and remove hoses from water pump.
2. Remove distributor, fuel pump, alternator drive belt, accessory drive belts, fan and hub assembly, alternator and bracket, and back idler pulley.
3. Remove the vibration damper bolts, then pull off the damper.
4. Remove air conditioner compressor and power steering pump, if so equipped, and swing them out of the way *without* disconnecting hoses.
5. Remove the two front oil pan bolts from beneath the car, then remove the cover bolts.

NOTE: *The timing case cover attaching*

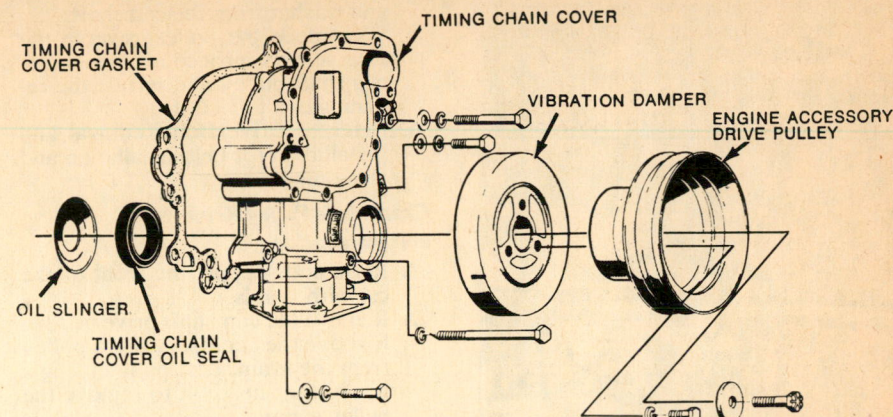

V8 timing chain cover assembly through 1976. 1977 and later are similar except for seal location (© American Motors Corp.)

bolts are of different lengths and must be replaced in their original locations.

6. Remove cover from block, then clean all parts and mating surfaces and remove oil seal.
7. Coat new seal lips with Petroleum jelly and seal surface with sealer, then drive the seal into the cover bore until it seats against the outer cover face. Use a proper size arbor for this job. 1972-76 seals are installed from the back of the cover; 1977 and later seals go on the front of the cover.
8. Remove lower dowel pin from cylinder block; this must be replaced when cover is in position but before bolts are installed.
9. Cut the oil pan gasket flush with the block on both sides of the oil pan.
10. Cut corresponding pieces of gasket from another oil pan gasket and cement them to cover. Install neoprene oil pan front seal into cover and align gasket tabs with pan seal.
11. Apply sealant to gaskets, then position cover. Install oil pan bolts and tighten evenly until cover lines up with upper dowel pin.
12. Install lower dowel pin, then cover to block bolts; tighten to 20-30 ft. lbs.
13. Install all removed pieces and adjust ignition timing.

Timing Chain and Sprocket Removal and Installation

4 CYLINDER

This engine uses a toothed rubber belt to drive the camshaft. Belt tension is controlled by an adjustable idler pulley. The distributor is at the rear of the cylinder head and is driven by a gear pressed on the rear of the camshaft.

—————— CAUTION ——————

Do not turn the engine backwards. Damage to the drive belt teeth could result. Turn the engine by the crankshaft bolt, not the camshaft.

Belt Removal and Installation.

1. Rotate the crankshaft in the normal direction of rotation, until the timing mark on the pulley is pointing to the zero position on the degree scale on the block. The timing mark on the rear of the camshaft pulley should be aligned with the pointer on the cylinder head cover.
2. Loosen the accessory pulley attaching bolts. Remove the belts and the cam drive belt shield.
3. Loosen the adjuster retaining screw to allow the belt to slacken and remove the belt from the pulleys.
4. To replace the belt, install the belt on the crankshaft pulley, and position it on the tensioner pulley. Slip the belt over the camshaft pulley using hand pressure only, while maintaining the pulleys at their respective timing marks.

NOTE: *Do not pry the belt with metal tools. The belt drive surface can be damaged and premature belt failure can result.*

5. Turn the offset adjusting nut on the tensioning pulley counterclockwise to increase the belt tension. The belt is properly tensioned when the drive side of the belt can be twisted 90 degrees with finger pressure.

NOTE: *When checking belt tension, apply tension on the crankshaft with a wrench, in a counterclockwise direction, to get all the slack on one side of the belt.*

6. With pressure on the tensioning pulley nut, tighten the retaining nut to 29 ft. lbs. torque. Recheck the belt tension.
7. Install the drive belt shield. Install the alternator belts and adjust their tension. Tighten the accessory pulley bolts to 15 ft. lbs.
8. Start the engine and adjust the ignition timing.

Camshaft Pulley Removal and Installation

1. Remove the drive belt.
2. Insert a bar or other suitable tool

Removing the 4 cylinder camshaft pulley (© American Motors Corp.)

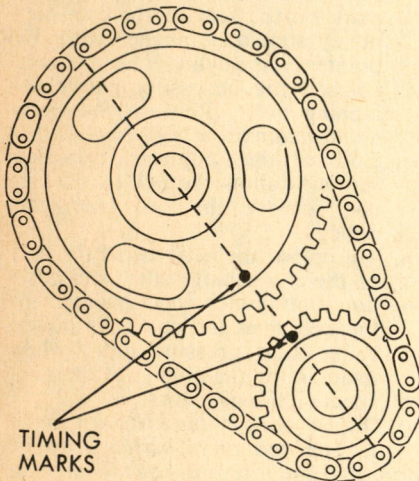

TIMING MARKS

Six-cylinder timing chain and sprockets

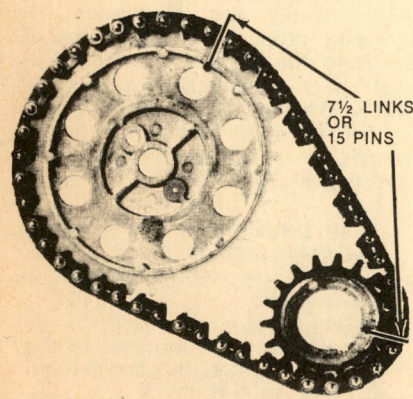

7½ LINKS OR 15 PINS

Correct timing chain installation— 6 cylinder
(© American Motors Corp.)

through the camshaft pulley to prevent it from turning.

3. Remove the pulley retaining bolt. Remove the pulley, woodruff key,

and washer from the camshaft.

4. To replace the pulley reverse the disassembly procedure. Hold the camshaft pulley and torque the retaining bolt to 58 ft lbs.

5. Refer to Drive Belt Removal and Installation for belt installation and tensioning.

Crankshaft Pulley Removal and Installation

1. Raise and support the front of the car with stands.
2. Remove the camshaft drive belt.
3. Remove the accessory drive pulley from the crankshaft pulley using a no. 40 torx head bit to remove the pulley screws.
4. The sprocket retaining bolt can be loosened and removed from the crankshaft. Hold the pulley from turning while the bolt is loosened.
5. Remove the pulley from the crankshaft.
6. Install in the pulley so that the indexing hole in the pulley engages with the pin on the crankshaft.
7. Hold the pulley from turning. Install the retaining bolt and torque to 181 ft. lbs.
8. Install the drive belt. See Belt Removal and Installation for tensioning.
9. Replace the belt guard. Replace the accessory drive pulley and torque the attaching bolts to 15 ft. lbs.
10. Complete the assembly in the reverse order of disassembly. Start the engine and reset the ignition timing.

6 CYLINDER

1. Remove the drive belt(s).
2. Remove the engine fan and hub assembly.
3. Remove the vibration damper pulley and remove the vibration damper.
4. Remove the timing case cover. Remove the seal from the timing case cover, because the seal should be replaced every time the cover is removed from the engine.
5. Remove the camshaft sprocket retaining bolt and washer.
6. Turn the crankshaft until the 0 timing mark on the crankshaft sprocket is closest to and on a centerline with the timing pointer of the camshaft sprocket.
7. Remove the crankshaft sprocket, camshaft sprocket and timing chain as an assembly. Disassemble the chain and sprockets.
To install the timing chain and sprockets:
8. Assemble the timing chain, crankshaft sprocket, and camshaft sprocket with the timing marks aligned.
9. Install the assembly to the crankshaft and camshaft.
10. Install the camshaft sprocket retaining bolt and washer and tighten the bolt to 50 ft. lbs.
11. To ensure the correct installation

of the timing chain, locate the timing mark of the camshaft sprocket at about the 1 o'clock position. This should place the timing mark on the crankshaft sprocket where the sprocket teeth mesh with the chain. There should be 15 timing chain pins between the timing marks of both sprockets.

V8

1. Remove the timing case cover and gasket.
2. Remove the crankshaft oil slinger.
3. Remove the camshaft sprocket retaining bolt and washer.
4. Remove the distributor drive gear and the fuel pump eccentric.
5. Turn the crankshaft until the 0 timing mark on the crankshaft sprocket is closest to and on a center line with the 0 timing mark on the camshaft sprocket.

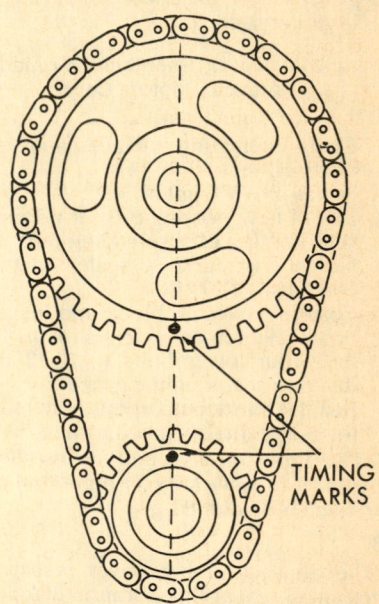

TIMING MARKS

V8 timing chain and sprockets

6. Remove the crankshaft sprocket, camshaft sprocket and the timing chain as an assembly.
To install the timing chain and sprockets:
7. Assemble the timing chain, and the two sprockets with the timing marks aligned vertically and install the assembly to the crankshaft and camshaft.
8. Install the fuel pump eccentric and the distributor drive gear. The fuel pump eccentric is installed with the word "REAR" toward the camshaft sprocket.
9. Install the camshaft sprocket, washer, and retaining bolt, tightening the bolt to 30 ft. lbs.
10. To ensure the timing chain is installed correctly, turn the crankshaft until the timing mark on the camshaft sprocket is placed horizontally at the 3 o'clock position. Starting with the timing chain pin

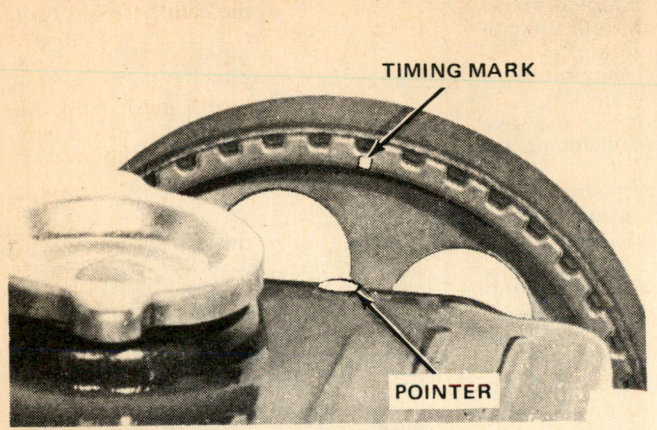

4 Cylinder camshaft sprocket timing mark
(© American Motors Corp.)

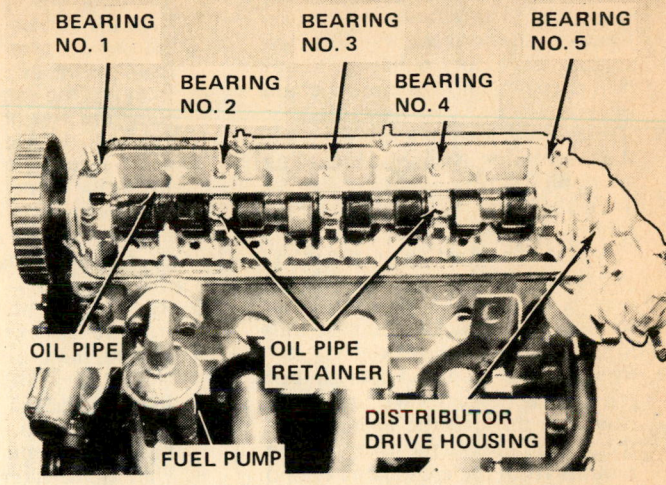

4 Cylinder camshaft and bearings (© American Motors Corp.)

directly opposite the camshaft sprocket timing mark, count the number of pins down to the timing mark on the crankshaft sprocket. There should be 20 pins between the two timing marks. The crankshaft timing mark must be between the 20th and 21st pin.

11. Install the crankshaft oil slinger.
12. Install the timing case cover together with a new gasket and seal.

Camshaft Removal and Installation

4 CYLINDER

1. Remove the air cleaner assembly, and the distributor cap with the wires attached.
2. Remove the accessory belts, and the belt guard. Loosen and remove the camshaft drive belt.
3. Remove the distributor and housing assembly from the rear of the cylinder head.
4. Remove the cylinder head cover, and the camshaft pulley from the camshaft.

NOTE: *Use a tool to prevent the sprocket from turning while removing the retaining bolt, and protect and head surface by wrapping a cloth around the end of the tool.*

5. Remove the bolts from number 5 camshaft bearing cap, (rear cap), and then remove the retaining nuts from caps 1, 3, and 5. Next remove the nuts on bearing caps number 2 and 4. Remove the oil pipe retainers from the bolts on bearing caps number 2 and 4.
6. Remove all the camshaft bearing caps from the cylinder head and keep them in their order of removal.
7. Remove the camshaft from the cylinder head.

NOTE: *The distributor drive gear should be removed from the camshaft with a puller. It can be replaced by driving the gear on the camshaft with the*

use of a block of wood and a hammer. Note the gear location before removal.

8. The tappets may be removed for service, by lifting them out of their bores in the cylinder head.
9. On installation, lubricate the camshaft lobes and bearing surfaces and install the shaft into the cylinder head. Install the camshaft bearing caps on their respective seats, and install the retaining nuts on cap numbers 1, 3, and 5.
10. Install the oil pipe on bearing cap studs number 2 and 4. Tighten the cap retaining nuts to a torque of 13 ft. lbs. Torque numbers 3 and 5 retaining nuts to 13 ft. lbs. Install the bolts in bearing cap number 5 and torque to 7 ft. lbs.
11. Install a replacement seal on the camshaft and tighten the number 1 bearing cap to 13 ft. lbs. torque.
12. Install the camshaft sprocket and torque the retaining bolt to 58 ft. lbs., while holding the sprocket to prevent its turning.
13. Temporarily install the cylinder head cover and position the camshaft pulley timing mark in line with the indicator on the cylinder head cover.
14. Install the distributor and housing on the rear of the cylinder head, setting the rotor to the number one cylinder position.
15. Install the distributor cap and wiring, attach the vacuum line, and connect the primary wire to the distributor.
16. Rotate the crankshaft to the TDC mark. Install the camshaft drive belt and adjust. Refer to Belt Removal and Installation for adjustment.
17. Reassemble the drive belt guard, replace the accessory belts and adjust.
18. Remove the cylinder head cover and adjust the tappet to camshaft clearance.
19. Install the cylinder head cover and complete the assembly. Start the

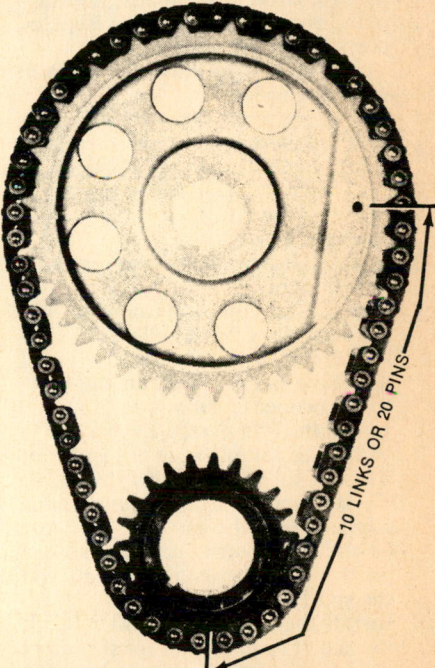

Correct timing chain installation—V8
(© American Motors Corp)

engine and adjust the ignition timing.

6 CYLINDER

1. Drain the cooling system and remove the radiator. Remove the hood (Pacers only).
2. If the car is equipped with air conditioning, remove the condenser and the receiver unit as a *charged assembly,* only.

NOTE: *Do not discharge the A/C system.*

3. Remove the valve cover and gasket.
4. Remove the rocker arm assembly and the cylinder head. Remove the tappets.

NOTE: *Pushrods and tappets should be kept in the proper order. They must be* *returned to their original places during assembly.*

5. Remove the drivebelt(s), fan assembly, accessory pulley(s), vibration damper, and the timing chain cover.
6. Remove the fuel pump. Take off the distributor assembly, including spark plug wires.
7. Turn the crankshaft until the "0" timing mark on the crankshaft sprocket is nearest to, on a centerline with, and aligns with the timing pointer on the camshaft sprocket.
8. Remove the sprockets and the timing chain as an assembly.
9. Remove the front bumper and/or grille as necessary. Withdraw the camshaft through the opening. On the Pacer, unbolt the front engine mounts from the crossmember and raise the engine.
10. Inspect the bearing journals, distributor drive, cam lobes, and tappets for wear or damage. Replace parts, as required.

Camshaft installation is performed in the following order:
1. Use a generous amount of an engine oil supplement on the camshaft. Install it in the block, using care not to damage any surfaces.
2. Install the timing chain and sprocket assembly.
3. Install the timing chain cover and a new oil seal.
4. Install the vibration damper and the accessory drive pulley(s).
5. Install the engine fan assembly and the drive belt(s). Tighten the belts to the proper tension.
6. Install the fuel pump.
7. With the number one piston at TDC of its compression stroke, fit the distributor so that the rotor is aligned with the no. one terminal on the cap (distributor fully seated on the block). Install the cap and the spark plug wires.
8. Install the tappets, cylinder head, its gasket, valve train (pushrods in the same order, as removed), valve cover and its gasket.

NOTE: *All valve train components must be lubricated with engine oil supplement. The supplement must remain in the engine for at least the first 100 miles. It does not require draining until the next regular oil change.*

9. Install the air conditioner receiver and condenser, without discharging any coolant (if so equipped).
10. Install the radiator and top up the cooling system.
11. Install the front bumper and/or grille. Bolt down the Pacer engine mounts and install the hood.

V8
1. Disconnect the battery cable.
2. Drain the radiator and both banks of the cylinder block. Remove the radiator, the hoses, and the thermostat housing. Remove the air conditioning condenser and receiver assembly as a charged unit,

if so equipped.
3. Remove the distributor, complete with spark plug wires and the coil from the intake manifold.
4. Remove the intake manifold as a complete assembly.
5. Take off the valve cover and take out the valve train, including the hydraulic tappets.

NOTE: *Keep the valve train components in proper order. They must be returned to their original place during assembly.*

6. Remove the power steering pump from its bracket, without disconnecting the hoses. Set it out of the way.
7. Remove the fan assembly and then the fuel pump. Disconnect heater hose at the water pump.
8. Unbolt the alternator bracket and set it out of the way, complete with the alternator. Do not disconnect the alternator wiring.
9. Remove the crankshaft pulley and the vibration damper.
10. With the timing marks in vertical alignment, remove the front cover, distributor/oil pump drive gear, fuel pump eccentric, sprockets, and the timing chain.
11. Remove the hood latch upper support bracket attachment screws. Move the bracket, as necessary, to permit removal of the camshaft. Remove the bumper and grille if necessary.
12. Use care during camshaft removal, so that the journal bearings are not damaged.
13. Inspect all parts for wear and damage. Replace them as required.

Installation of the cam is the reverse of removal. Install the timing chain and cover. Adjust the belt tension and fill up the cooling system.

NOTE: *Lubricate the camshaft tappets, and the valve train with an engine oil supplement. Add the remaining supplement to the crankcase, and leave it in*

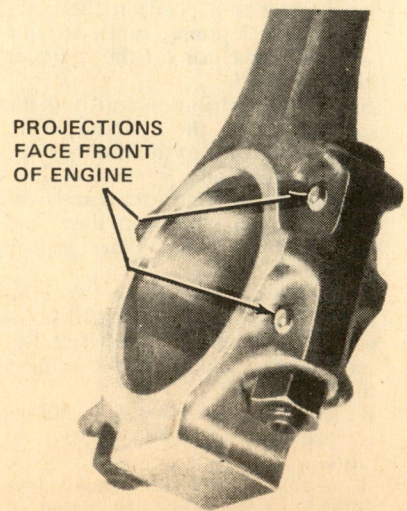

PROJECTIONS FACE FRONT OF ENGINE

Connecting rod installation, 4 cylinder
(© American Motors Corp.)

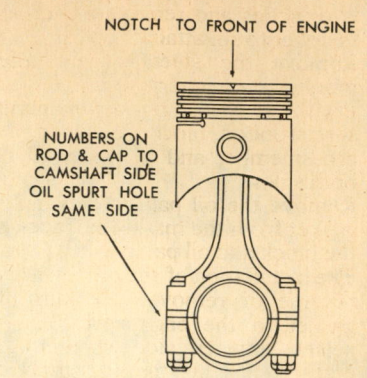

NOTCH TO FRONT OF ENGINE

NUMBERS ON ROD & CAP TO CAMSHAFT SIDE OIL SPURT HOLE SAME SIDE

Piston and rod assembly 6 cylinder engine

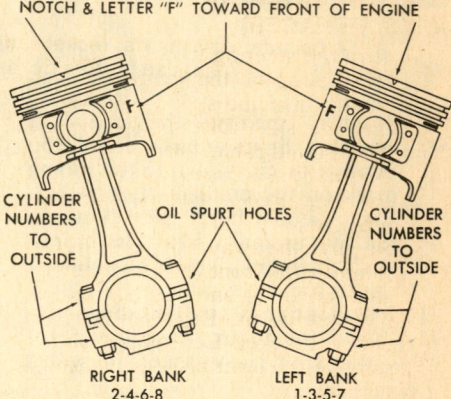

NOTCH & LETTER "F" TOWARD FRONT OF ENGINE

CYLINDER NUMBERS TO OUTSIDE — OIL SPURT HOLES — CYLINDER NUMBERS TO OUTSIDE

RIGHT BANK 2-4-6-8   LEFT BANK 1-3-5-7

Piston and rod assembly—V8 engines

the engine for at least the first 1000 miles. It does not require draining until the next regular oil change.

PISTON AND ROD ASSEMBLY

The piston and rod assemblies are installed from the top, and the dimple, notch, or dot, marked on the top of the piston, goes toward the front. On the four cylinder, the rod and piston assemblies must be marked on disassembly; the projections on the connecting rods must face towards the front of the engine. On the six cylinder, the connecting rod numbers must go toward the camshaft; on the V8, the numbers must go toward the outside of the engine.

ENGINE LUBRICATION
Oil Pan Removal and Installation
NOTE: *It is much easier to remove the engine in most cases.*

4 CYLINDER
1. Raise the car and support it with stands. Drain the oil.
2. Install an engine lifting device and support the weight of the engine, while removing the engine bracket to mount cushion nuts. Loosen the strut and bracket screws.
3. Raise the engine approximately

two inches and remove the cross-member to sill attaching parts.

4. Remove the steering gear idler bracket from the frame rail.

5. Pry the crossmember down and insert wooden blocks between the crossmember and the side sill on both sides.

6. Remove the oil pan and clean the gasket from the mating surfaces of the block and oil pan.

7. The installation of the oil pan is the reverse of removal. Cement the gasket to the engine block; use sealer between side gaskets and end seals; tighten the side pan bolts to 70 in. lbs. and the end bolts to 90 in. lbs.

6 CYLINDER AND V8 (EXCEPT PACER)

1. Turn the steering wheel to full left lock. Support the engine with a hoist. Raise and support the car at the side sills. Disconnect the engine ground cable.

2. Unbolt the idler arm at the side sill, and the engine cushions at the brackets.

3. Remove the sway bar, if equipped. Remove the front crossmember-to-side sill bolts and pull the cross-member down. Remove the right engine bracket. Loosen but do not remove the strut rods at the lower control arm.

4. Drain the engine oil.

5. Remove the starter.

6. Remove the oil pan bolts and pan. Remove the front and rear seals, and clean the gasket surfaces.

7. Install the new pan front seal to the timing cover, and apply sealer to end tabs. Cement new pan side gaskets to the block, and apply sealer to the ends of the gaskets.

8. Coat the inside surface of the new rear seal with soap, and apply sealer to end tabs. Install the seal in the rear main cap.

9. Coat front and rear seal contact surfaces with engine oil, and install the pan. The remainder of installation is the reverse of removal.

PACER

1. Drain the engine oil.

2. Install an engine lifting device and support the weight of the engine.

3. Disconnect the steering shaft flexible joint an hold it aside with a length of wire.

4. Raise and support the car.

5. Remove the front engine support through bolts.

6. Disconnect the front brake lines at the wheel cylinders.

7. Disconnect the upper ball joints from the spindles. Make sure the shock absorbers are attached securely.

8. Remove the upper control arm and move it aside.

9. Support the front crossmember with a jack.

10. Remove the nuts from the front

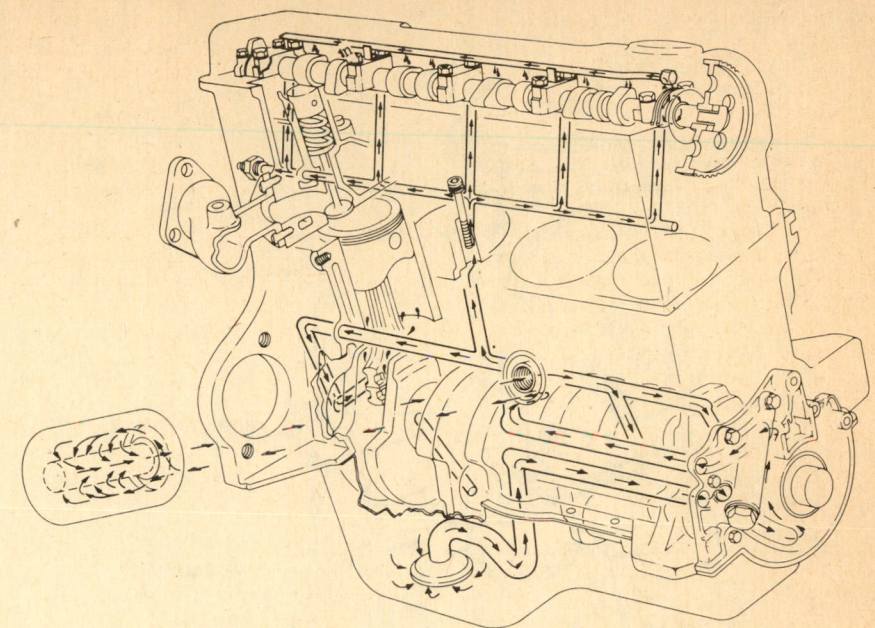

4 Cylinder lubrication system (© American Motors Corp.)

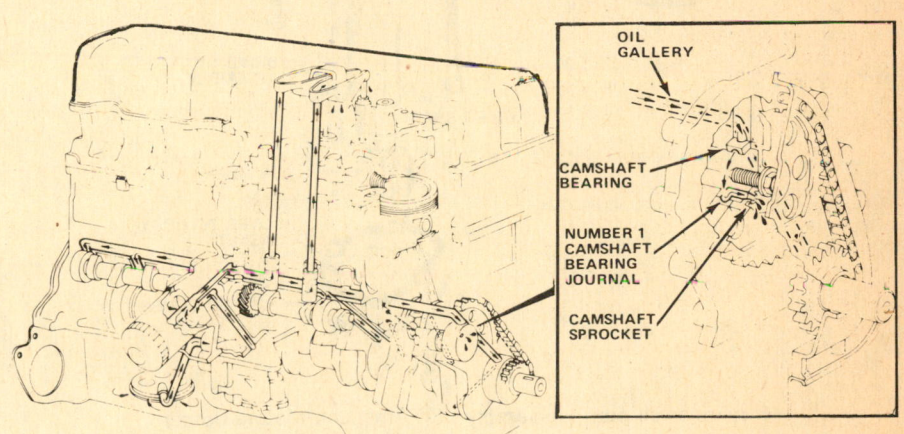

Six cylinder oiling system (© American Motors Corp.)

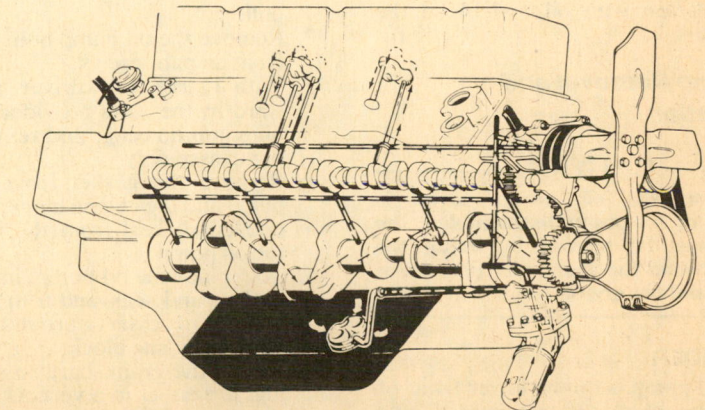

V8 oiling system (© American Motors Corp.)

crossmember rear mounts and swing the crossmember down and forward.

11. Follow Steps 5-9 of the preceding six cylinder and V8 procedure.

12. Install and assemble the remaining components in the reverse order of removal, tightening the 1/4 in. oil pan screws to 7 ft. lbs., the 5/16 in. oil pan screws to 11 ft. lbs., the crossmember attaching nuts to 50 ft. lbs., the upper control arm cross

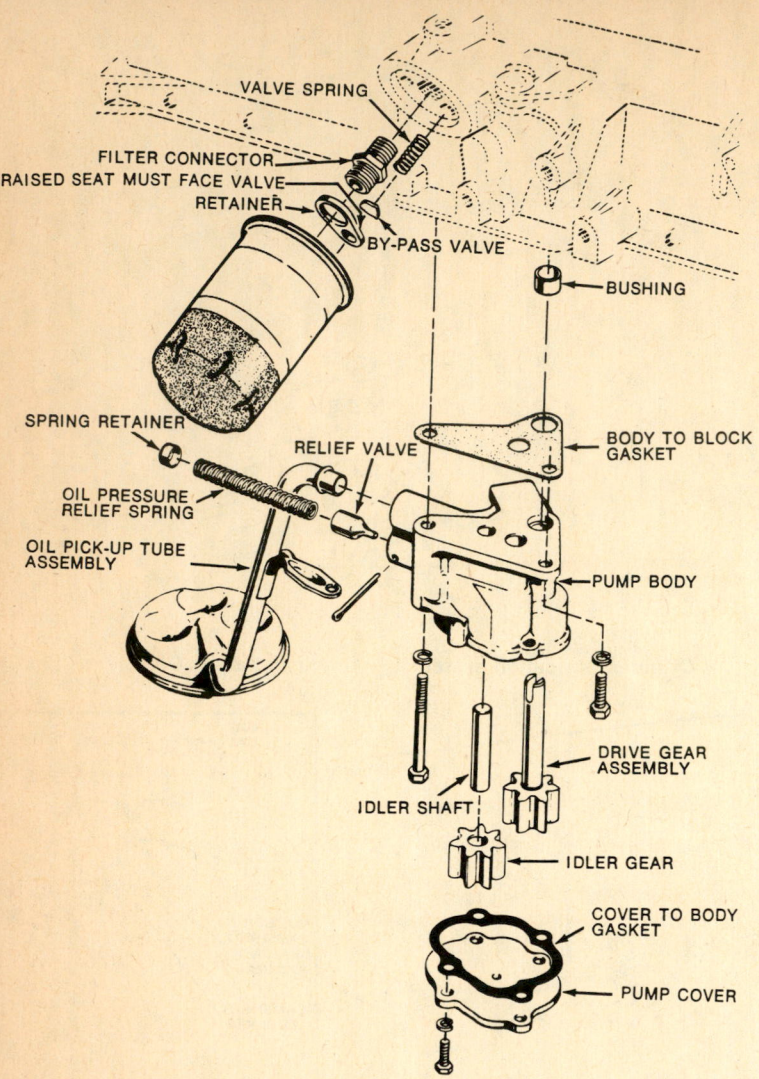

VALVE SPRING
FILTER CONNECTOR
RAISED SEAT MUST FACE VALVE
RETAINER
BY-PASS VALVE
BUSHING
SPRING RETAINER
RELIEF VALVE
OIL PRESSURE RELIEF SPRING
OIL PICK-UP TUBE ASSEMBLY
BODY TO BLOCK GASKET
PUMP BODY
DRIVE GEAR ASSEMBLY
IDLER SHAFT
IDLER GEAR
COVER TO BODY GASKET
PUMP COVER

6 cylinder oil pump assembly (© American Motors Corp.)

shaft bolt and nut to 60 ft. lbs., and the engine mount and steering shaft nuts to 25 ft. lbs. Fill the crankcase with oil and bleed the brakes.

Oil Pump Removal and Installation

> **CAUTION**
>
> Anytime the oil pump cover is removed or the pump disassembled, the pump must be primed by filling the spaces around the gears with petroleum jelly. Do not use grease.

4 CYLINDER

The oil pump is on the lower front of the engine block. It consists of two gears with meshing teeth, one with internal teeth and the other with external teeth. Oil pressure is controlled by a pressure relief valve and spring assembly. The inner gear is driven by the crankshaft at twice the speed of distributor driven oil pumps. To service the oil pump assembly, removal is necessary. Proceed as follows.

1. Remove the crankshaft timing belt pulley.
2. Remove the oil pump bolts and the front oil pan screws.
3. With a large screwdriver, pry outward in the slots provided on the oil pump housing, and remove the pump assembly.
4. Remove the gasket from the oil pump and the engine block, and the crankshaft seal from the front of the oil pump.
5. To replace the oil pump, install the gaskets and seals and trim the gaskets as necessary, around the oil pan and engine block.
6. Rotate the crankshaft so that the lugs are either in a vertical or horizontal position. Position the oil pump assembly over the crankshaft and align the oil pump gears to the crankshaft lugs.
7. Carefully tap the pump assembly into its seat as far as possible, while checking the alignment of the gears to the crankshaft lugs.

8. Install and tighten the oil pump bolts. Torque to 87 in. lbs. Install the front oil pan bolts and torque to 90 in. lbs.
9. Install the crankshaft seal in the front of the oil pump housing, with the use of a seal installer tool.
10. Replace the crankshaft timing pulley and install the drive belt. Refer to Belt Removal and Installation for adjusting belt tension. Assemble the belt guard and the accessory belts. Start the engine, check for oil pressure and oil leakage, and adjust the ignition timing.

> **CAUTION**
>
> It is important that the correct type oil filter, with a built-in bypass valve, be installed on the 4 cylinder engine.

6 CYLINDER

The oil pump is driven by the distributor drive shaft. Oil pump replacement does not, however, affect distributor timing because the drive gear remains in mesh with the camshaft gear.

1. Drain the oil and remove the oil pan.
2. Remove the oil pump attaching screws. Remove the pump and gasket from the engine block.

Installation is the reverse of removal. Prime the pump before installation; use a new cover gasket.

TIME SAVER

The original equipment-type oil filters for AMC engines have an anti-drainback diaphragm. This prevents the filter from emptying or partially emptying while the engine is stopped overnight. If a replacement filter without this feature is used, the result will be low or no oil pressure on startup. If this continues for any length of time, bearing damage will occur.

V8

The oil pump is located in, and as part of, the timing cover. The pump is driven by the distributor drive shaft. Oil pump replacement does not, however, affect distributor timing.

1. Remove the retaining bolts and separate the oil pump cover, complete with filter and gasket, from the timing cover.
2. The drive gear and shaft and the idler gear will slide out of the timing cover after removal of the pump cover.
3. Prime the pump before installation, and use a new gasket.

Rear Main Bearing Oil Seal Replacement

4 CYLINDER

The rear main bearing oil seal consists of a single piece of formed neoprene with a single lip. To replace the seal, proceed as follows.

1. Remove the transmission assembly. If manual transmission, remove the pressure plate and flywheel.
2. Remove the crankshaft seal from its seat in the block, while exercising care not to scratch the seal contacting area of the crankshaft.
3. Install the seal, after lubricating the lip with engine oil, into the recess of the block, until the seal bottoms. The seal should be about $1/32$ inch below the surface of the block.
4. Reinstall the flywheel and components. Reinstall the transmission assembly, adjust as necessary, start the engine and check for oil leakage.

6 CYLINDER AND V8

1. Remove oil pan, as previously described.
2. Scrape clean all gasket surfaces, then remove rear main cap.
3. Discard lower portion of seal; drive out upper portion, using a brass drift, until it can be grasped with pliers.
4. Clean main cap, then *loosen* all remaining main cap bolts.
5. Coat the lip of the new upper seal with SAE 40 engine oil.
6. Install upper seal portion with the lip facing the front.
7. Coat both sides of the lower seal end tabs with sealant.
8. Coat the back surface of new lower seal with soap, the lip with SAE 40 engine oil. Install lower seal firmly into main cap.
9. Coat both chamfered edges of rear main cap with sealant, install bearing inserts (if removed) and tighten all cap bolts to the specified torque.

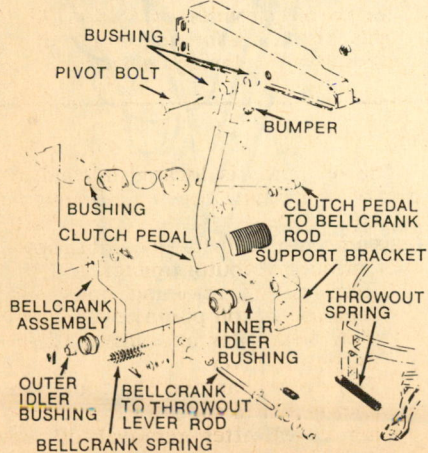

Typical clutch linkage
(© American Motors Corp.)

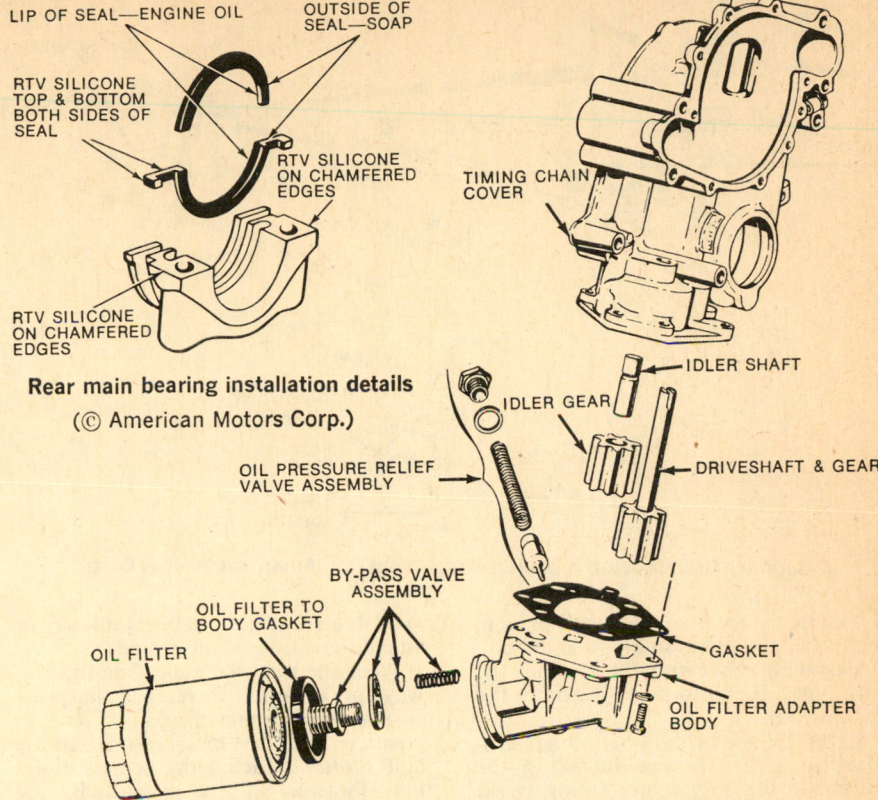

Rear main bearing installation details
(© American Motors Corp.)

V8 oil pump assembly (© American Motors Corp)

NOTE: *Do not apply sealer to the cylinder block mating surfaces of the cap.*
10. Install the pan.

CLUTCH

The clutch is a single-plate, dry-disc, coil spring type through 1976. A semi-centrifugal 11 inch diameter clutch assembly is used with 360 and larger V8s through 1974. A 10 inch direct spring pressure type is used with the 304 V8, while a $9^1/4$ inch indirect spring pressure type is used on sixes. 1977 and later models have a single dry-disc driven palte and a diaphragm-type clutch cover. Three speed transmission clutch covers have six mounting bolts, while 4-speeds have only three bolts. An $8^1/2$ inch clutch is used on the four cylinder models with a diaphragm type pressure plate.

Pedal travel decrease due to normal wear of the lining can be compensated for by adjusting the clutch pedal free-play.

Pedal Free Play Adjustment

SIX AND V8

Adjust the free play of the clutch pedal to $7/8$-$1^1/8$ inch. This is done by changing the length of the link between the throwout lever rod and the bellcrank assembly on 6 cylinder and V8.

4 CYLINDER

On the 4 cylinder, the clutch pedal free play is adjusted by varying the length of the control cable. The preferred free-play is $1^1/8$ inch.

1. To adjust the cable, loosen the cable locknut at the rear of the cable and pull the cable forward until the free play is eliminated from the throw out lever.
2. Rotate the adjuster nut toward the rear of the cable until the nut tabs contact the clutch housing.
3. Release the cable housing and turn the adjuster nut until the tabs engage the slots on the clutch housing.
4. Tighten the clutch cable locknut. Recheck clutch pedal free play.

Clutch Replacement

Remove the transmission and starter motor, then disconnect the clutch linkage at the release lever and remove the capscrews that hold the bellhousing (clutch housing) to the engine. It may be necessary to move the rear of the engine up or down to gain wrench clearance.

Any shims between the housing and engine must be replaced in exactly the same place to prevent misalignment.

Matchmark the clutch cover, pressure plate and flywheel before removal to ensure proper balance. Loosen each clutch cover capscrew a few turns at a time until spring tension is released, then remove the cover, pressure plate, and disc.

Check the pilot bushing in the end of the crankshaft for scoring or looseness.

American Motors

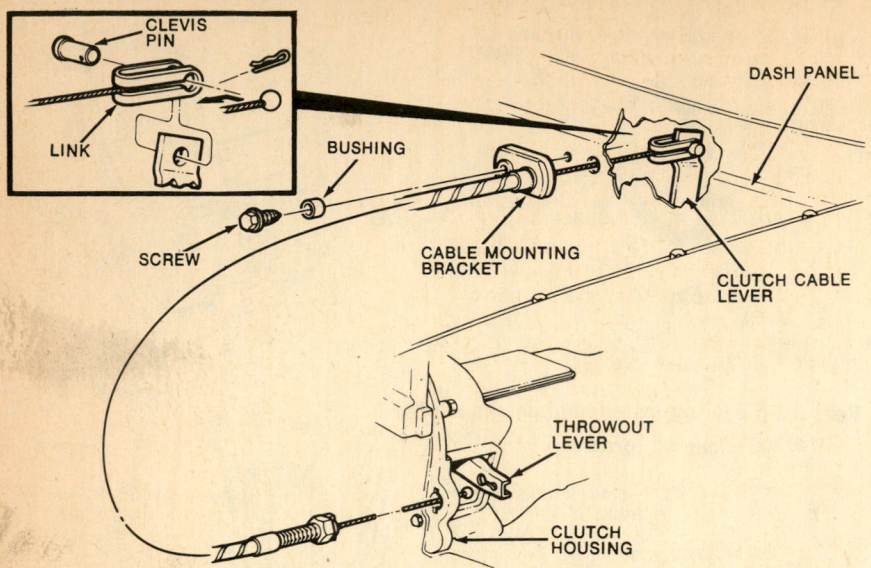

4 Cylinder Gremlin clutch cable arrangement (© American Motors Corp.)

If it is necessary to replace the bushing, use either an expanding-end slidehammer or a tap. Screwing the tap into the bore until it bottoms will force the bushing out.

Lubricate the bushing with high temperature grease before installing the clutch. If there is a lubricating wick, soak it in engine oil.

The 4 cylinder clutch uses a roller type pilot bearing. The removal and replacement procedures are the same with the exception that the bearing uses a grease seal at one end. During installation, the seal must be installed facing the crankshaft.

Inspect the flywheel surface for heat cracks, scoring, or blue heat marks. Check the flywheel capscrews for proper torque. It will be necessary to lock-up the flywheel ring gear with a block or flywheel holding clamp tool before tightening these capscrews.

The throwout (release) linkage consists of a forked, pivoted lever contacting the bearing at one end and the linkage pushrod on the other. A return spring keeps the lever in contact with the ball pivot.

The throwout bearing itself is pre-lubricated and cannot be repacked if dry. The slots in the inner groove of the throwout bearing sleeve should be filled with high temperature grease. Failure is evidenced by uneven clutch pedal pressure and a grinding, rattling noise when the pedal is depressed. Replace any noisy throwout bearings as soon as is practicable to prevent disintegration and possible transmission or clutch damage.

Slide the new clutch disc onto the transmission input shaft to check for binding. Remove any burrs from either the splines or hub using emery paper, then clean with a safe solvent. Place the clutch disc against the flywheel and secure it by inserting a dummy pilot shaft (such shafts, made of wood, are available from automobile jobbers) or an old transmission input shaft.

Place the new pressure plate (it is always good policy to replace the pressure plate when installing a new disc) in position, after first making sure that the clutch disc is facing the proper direction (flywheel side is so marked), and that matchmarks are aligned if old pressure plate is used.

Install all the capscrews fingertight. Tighten the screws a little at a time, working around the pressure plate to avoid distorting it, to 28 ft. lbs. on 6 cylinder engines and 38 ft. lbs. on V8s. Remove the pilot shaft.

The 4 cylinder model uses dowel pins on the flywheel to engage the locating holes on the pressure plate flange. Torque the attaching bolts to 23 ft. lbs.

Do not depress clutch pedal until transmission is installed or throwout bearing will fall out.

Install the clutch housing, throwout bearing and transmission. Hook up clutch linkage and check adjustment.

MANUAL TRANSMISSION

Most American Motors cars through 1974 use Warner manual transmissions. Starting 1975, they are used only in a few light duty applications, such as six-cylinder Gremlins without overdrive. The four-speed used through 1974 is the Warner T-10. A lightweight Warner SR4 four-speed was introduced in six cylinder models in late 1976. The four cylinder uses a Warner HR-1 four speed transmission. The SR4 transmission has a cast aluminum case and extension housing, while the HR-1 has a cast iron case and an aluminum extension housing. The SR4 and HR-1 have internal, non-adjustable shift linkage.

NOTE: *SR4 and HR-1 transmissions have metric fasteners in most threaded holes.*

An identification tag, containing Warner and American Motors part numbers, is located at the rear of the transmission. The Warner model number is also usually cast into the side of the case.

A few 1974, and most 1975 and later models, use the model 150T three-speed transmission. A nine-character identification code is stamped on the left front case flange, but does not give the model number.

The 150T can readily be identified by its nine-bolt top cover which is narrower in the front. Unlike the Warner transmissions, it does not have a drain plug; lubricant is drained by removing the lower extension housing bolt. Warner three-speeds have a rectangular top cover, usually with four or six bolts.

See the Manual Transmission Unit Repair Section for further applications and overhaul procedures.

Removal and Installation
NOTE: *Open the hood to avoid damage when the rear crossmember is removed. If the overdrive and transmission are to be separated, first engage then disengage the overdrive with the clutch pedal depressed and the engine running.*

1. Matchmark the driveshaft and rear axle yoke for correct installation. Split the rear universal joint and slide the driveshaft off the back of the transmission. Support the transmission with a jack.
2. Detach the column shift mechanism linkage to the transmission, and disconnect the clutch linkage and speedometer cable; disconnect the back-up light switch wiring, and TCS switch wiring, also.

On a floorshift, remove the shift lever. Remove the boot and unbolt the lever. Detach the column reverse lockup rod. On some Hurst units, the shift lever can be removed by inserting a 0.015-0.020

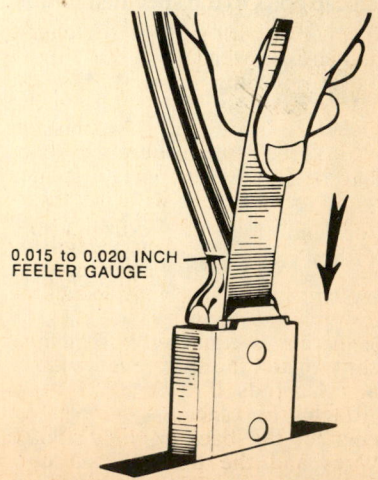

0.015 to 0.020 INCH FEELER GAUGE

Removing lever from Hurst shifter
(© American Motors Corp)

C40

in. feeler gauge along the driver's side of the lever, between the spring steel barb and the lower part of the lever. Pull the lever and gauge out together. Support the engine.

3. Disconnect the overdrive wiring. Remove the rear transmission support cushion bolts. Also remove the starter on four cylinder models.
4. On Pacers with overdrive, remove the cotter pin from the parking brake equalizer and disconnect the front cable from the equalizer. Remove the cable adjuster and hooks from the floorpan bracket and lower equalizer and rear brake cables to provide clearance. Also, remove the ground strap from the floorpan.

NOTE: *On V8 models with dual exhaust or dual catalytic converters, exhaust pipes must be disconnected from manifolds and lowered so to gain working clearance. On Javelin models having Hurst shifter, entire shifter should be removed so that transmission can slide back far enough for removal.*

5. Remove the transmission support crossmember except on Pacers; remove the crossmember with the transmission on those models. Remove the two lower studs which hold the transmission to the bell housing and replace these two studs with two long pilot studs on 150Ts and SR4s.
6. Remove the two top studs and slide the transmission assembly along the pilot studs and out of the car. On HR1s, support the engine and remove the clutch housing to engine bolts.

Installation is as follows:
1. Fill the slots in the inner groove of the throwout bearing with high temperature grease and soak the crankshaft pilot bushing wick in engine oil. Fit the throwout bearing and the sleeve assembly in the clutch fork. Center the bearing over the clutch lever. Shift 150Ts and SR4s into first gear.
2. Install two pilot studs in the clutch housing, instead of the lower clutch housing cap screws on 150Ts and SR4s.
3. Carefully slide the transmission into place. Be careful not to damage the clutch driven plate splines while mating them with the transmission input shaft.
4. Install the upper screws, which attach the case to the housing. Remove the pilot studs and install the lower cap screws.
5. If the car is equipped with a floor shift, install the shift lever retainer and shift rods, if removed.
6. Attach the speedometer cable, connect the back-up light switch wires and the transmission controlled spark (TCS) wire, if so equipped.
7. Raise the transmission. Attach the rear crossmember and support to the transmission. Fasten the crossmember to the side sills. Install the parking brake cables and ground strap on Pacer.
8. Attach the exhaust pipes to the exhaust manifolds, on V8 engines, if they were removed.
9. Install the front U-joint yoke on the transmission. Do the same for the rear U-joint at the differential. Be sure the alignment marks made earlier line up.
10. Connect the shift rods on the column shift transmissions and the reverse lockup rod on the floorshift transmission. Check the transmission oil level and add lubricant, as needed.
11. Remove the supports and lower the car.
12. Install the shift lever if the car has a floorshift transmission.
13. Adjust the shift linkage, if it was disturbed.

Shift Linkage Adjustment

COLUMN SHIFT

1. Disconnect the shift rods from the transmission shift levers. Insert a 3/16 in. drill through the column shift lever holes.
2. Shift into Reverse and lock the column with the ignition key. Position the transmission First/Reverse shift lever in Reverse.
3. Adjust the shift rod trunnion to a free pin fit in the transmission shift lever. Tighten the trunnion locknuts.
4. Unlock the column and move the gearshift to Neutral. Both of the transmission shift levers should be in the Neutral detent.
5. Repeat step three for the Second/Third shift rod trunnion.
6. Remove the drill from the column levers. Shift through all gears and check for a free crossover into Neutral.
7. Shift into Reverse and lock the column. The column should lock without any binding.

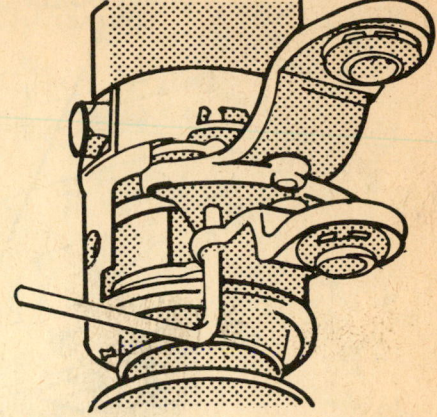

Aligning shift levers on column shift models

THREE-SPEED FLOORSHIFT

1. Place the transmission shift levers in their neutral positions.
2. Loosen the second-third lever adjuster.
3. Keeping the first-reverse shift rod and transmission lever in the neu-

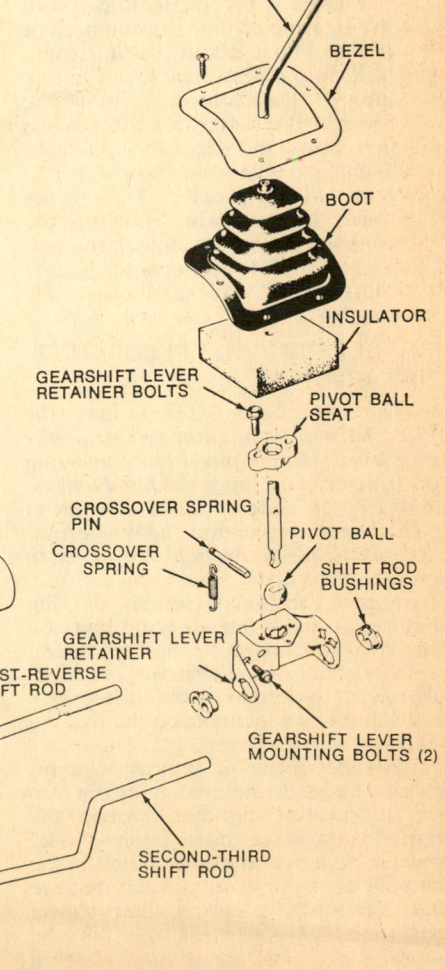

Three-speed floorshift linkage (© American Motors Corp.)

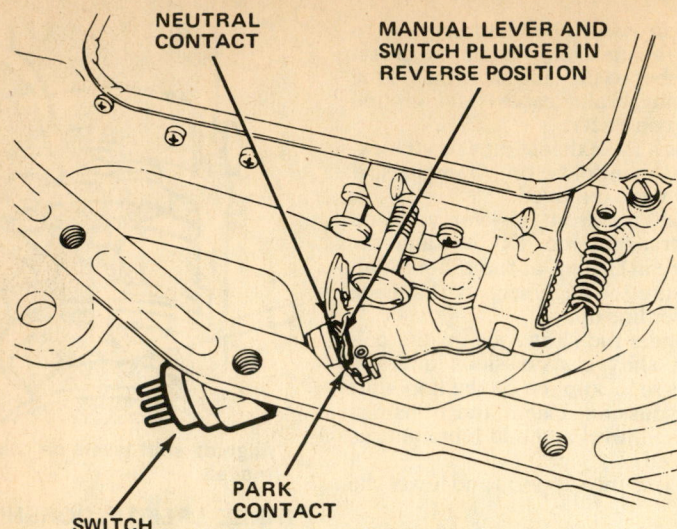

NEUTRAL CONTACT

MANUAL LEVER AND SWITCH PLUNGER IN REVERSE POSITION

SWITCH

PARK CONTACT

Torque-Command neutral start and backup light switch, pan removed - looking up
(© American Motors Corp.)

tral position, align the second-third rod so the shift notch is exactly aligned with the first-reverse shift notch. Tighten the adjuster.

4. Operate the linkage and check for full engagement of all gears and a smooth crossover from first to second.

5. If there is a reverse lockup rod to the steering column, loosen both of the locknuts about 1/2 in. each. Shift into reverse and lock the column. You may have to rotate the lever at the bottom of the column up into the locked position. Tighten the lower locknut until it contacts the trunnion. Tighten the upper locknut while holding the trunnion centered. Unlock the column and shift through the gears. Shift into reverse and check for binding.

FOUR-SPEED HURST FLOORSHIFT THROUGH 1974

NOTE: *It may be necessary to lower the rear of the transmission to install the shift lever aligning pin. Before lowering the transmission, open the hood and remove the air cleaner. Then disconnect the exhaust system and the rear crossmember. It would probably be easier to cut an access hole.*

Remove the boot assembly or plug and loosen the lower nuts and bolts on the two transmission forward speed shift levers. Loosen the two self-locking nuts at the center of the shift levers. Loosen the two locknuts on the reverse shift rod trunnion.

With the shifter in neutral position, insert a 1/4 in. diameter aligning pin into the shifter housing and through the center of the three shifter levers. Make sure that the pin enters the notch in the far side of the housing. Check that the transmission levers are in their neutral positions. Remove and reinsert the aligning pin. The pin should slide in freely. If it does not, the shifter is not

correctly aligned in the neutral position.

Tighten the lower bolts and nuts at the transmission forward speed shift levers. Tighten the self-locking nuts to 10 ft lbs. Make sure the transmission reverse lever is in the neutral position. Tighten the trunnion nuts, being careful not to bind the trunnion in the reverse lever, then remove the aligning pin.

Loosen the steering column reverse lock-up rod trunnion locknuts about 1/2 in. each. Shift into reverse and lock the column. It may be necessary to move the lower column lever upward until it is in the locked position. Tighten the lower trunnion locknut until it contacts .the trunnion. Tighten the upper locknut while holding the trunnion centered in the column lever. Unlock the column and check for proper shifting. The column should lock without binding.

AUTOMATIC TRANSMISSION

American Motors uses Chrysler Corporation Torque-flite automatic transmissions in all their cars. These transmissions are the same as the equivalent Chrysler units, the only differences being in case design required by the difference in American Motors' bell-housing configuration and driveshafts.

IDENTIFICATION

There are three models of Torque Command automatic transmissions; 904, 998, and 727. The 727 model is physically larger than the other two models, being designed for use with V8 engines and heavy duty applications. Physical identification of the 727 model transmission is assisted by the fact that the slope of the converter housing is

much more gradual than the other two.

The 904 and 998 models are similar in size and are designed for lighter duty applications. The 998 model has reinforcing ribs on the top of the rear servo boss on the case which distinguish it from the 904 model.

A seven-digit part number is stamped on the case on the left side above the pan mating surface. Following the part number is a coded, four-digit number which indicates the date of manufacture. The last group of numbers stamped on the case is the serial number.

TORQUE COMMAND TRANSMISSION IDENTIFICATION

Year	Transmission (Model)	Engine (cu. in.)
1972	904	232,258
	998	304
	727	360,401
1973-79	904	121,232[1],258
	998	304[1]
	727	360,401

① Model 727 optional on 258 six and all V8s except Pacer

Neutral Safety Switch Replacement and Adjustment

A combination back-up light/neutral safety switch is mounted on the left side of the transmission case. This switch cannot be adjusted; failure requires replacement.

To test the switch, proceed in the following manner:

1. Disconnect the wiring connector from the switch.
2. Use a 12V test lamp to check for continuity between the center pin of the switch and the transmission case. The lamp should only light in Park or Neutral.
3. If the lamp lights up in other positions, check the transmission linkage adjustments before replacing the switch.
4. To test the back-up light function of the switch repeat step two, by bridging the outside pins to test continuity. The light should only light in Reverse. No continuity should be present from either of the pins to the case.

To remove the switch, proceed as follows:

1. Place a container under the switch to catch transmission fluid. Unscrew the switch.
2. Select Park and then Neutral while checking to see that the operating fingers for the switch are centered in the case opening.
3. Screw a new switch and a *new* seal into the transmission. Tighten the switch to 24 ft. lbs.
4. Retest continuity. Replenish the transmission fluid, as required.

Shift Linkage Adjustment

1. Raise the car and loosen the shift rod trunnion jamnuts.
2. Remove the lockpin and separate the trunnion and shift rod at the bellcrank.
3. Place the shift lever in Park and lock the steering column.
4. Move the transmission shift lever into its Park detent, as far rearward as possible. Check for positive engagement by attempting to rotate the driveshaft.
5. Adjust the trunnion for a free pin fit and tighten the jamnuts. On column shift cars, eliminate lash by pulling down on the shift rod and pressing up on the outer bellcrank while making the adjustment.
6. Check for proper adjustment by attempting to start the engine in the Reverse and Drive positions of the shift lever. If the engine does not start in Park or Neutral, or starts in any of the other positions, the adjustment is incorrect or the neutral switch is defective.

Throttle Linkage Adjustment

This adjustment positions a valve which controls shift speed, shift firmness, and part-throttle downshift sensitivity. The linkage runs from the carburetor to the left side of the transmission.

1972-73

1. Make sure that the idle speed is correct.
2. Hook a spring in the hole on the transmission throttle lever.
3. Pull the spring forward and fasten it so that about 8-10 lbs. tension is exerted on the throttle lever.
4. Unfasten the retaining clip which holds the adjustable throttle rod link at its slotted end.
5. Take the tab washer out of the slot in the rod and loosen, but don't remove, the slip-joint retaining screw.
6. On sixes, lengthen the adjustable rod to remove all slack. On V8s, shorten the adjustable rod to remove all slack.
7. Tighten the retaining screw on the slip-joint.
8. On sixes place the rod slot over the bellcrank lever. On V8s, place it over the carburetor throttle lever.
9. Install the tab washer and the retaining clip, making sure that the tabs on the washer are inserted in the slot.
10. Remove the spring.

1974 AND LATER

1. Detach the throttle control rod spring and hook it so that the throttle control lever is held forward against its stop.
2. Block the choke open and set the carburetor throttle linkage off the fast idle cam.

NOTE: *On models with a throttle stop solenoid, energize the solenoid (turn the*

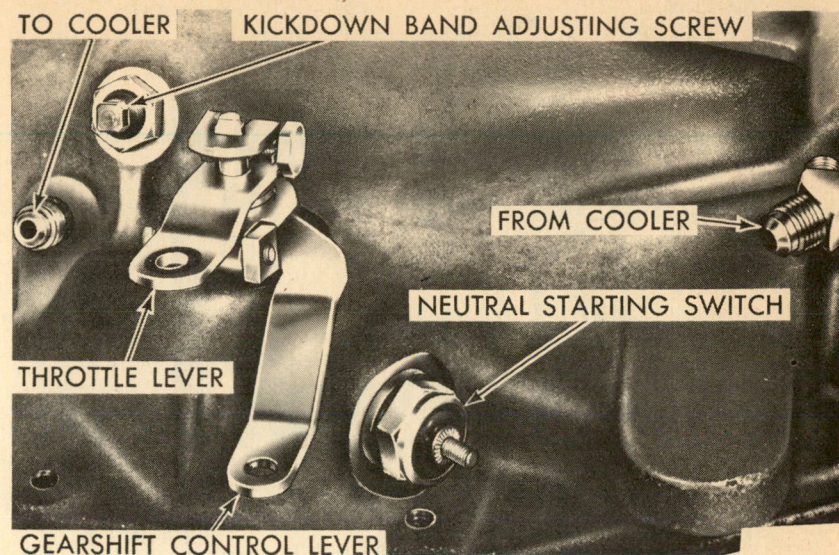

Torque-Command external adjustments (© Chrysler Corp)

ignition ON) and open the throttle halfway and then return the throttle to the idle position.

3. Loosen, but do not remove, the retaining bolt on the throttle control rod adjusting link.
4. On V8s, remove the spring clip and nylon washer; leave them in place on sixes.
5. On sixes, pull on the end of the link to remove all lash. On V8s, push on the end of the link to remove all lash.
6. Tighten the retaining bolt while performing Step 5.
7. Replace the throttle control rod spring in its original location. On V8s, install the nylon washer and spring clip on the retaining rod before replacing the spring.

Band Adjustments

KICKDOWN BAND—1972-73

The adjustment screw for the kickdown band is located on the left side of the transmission, above the throttle and shift linkage levers.

1. Loosen the locknut. Back off the screw five turns.
2. Using a torque wrench tighten the screw to 72 in. lbs.
3. Back off two turns on the adjustment screw on the 904 and 998 series transmission.
4. Back off two and one-half turns with the 360 cu. in. engines or two turns with the 401 cu. in. engine when used with the 727 series transmission.
5. Hold the adjusting screw and tighten the locknut to 29 ft. lbs.

KICKDOWN BAND—1974 AND LATER

The basic adjustment procedures are the same as for 1972-78 transmission. However, the adjustment screw on all 998 and all 727 transmissions should be backed off two and one-half turns in

Step 4 through 1977. On 1978 and later 904 and 998s, back the adjusting screw out 2 turns; back it out 2½ turns on the 727. On all transmissions, hold the adjusting screw and tighten the lock-nut to 35 ft. lbs., after completing the adjustment.

LOW AND REVERSE BAND, 904 1972-73; 998—THROUGH 1977; 727—1972 AND LATER

1. Remove the pan.
2. Loosen the locknut on the adjustment screw and back the screw off five turns.
3. Tighten the screw to 72 in. lbs.
4. Make the following adjustments:
   a. Series 904 transmission—back off three and one-quarter turns on the screw
   b. Series 998 transmission—back off four turns on the screw
   c. Series 727 transmission—back off two turns on the screw
5. Hold the adjusting screw while tightening the locknut to 35 ft. lbs.
6. Install the pan and a new gasket. Refill the transmission with DEXRON fluid.

LOW AND REVERSE BAND, 904—1974 AND LATER; 998—1978 AND LATER

1. Drain the fluid and remove the pan as detailed above.
2. Check the fluid for particles or burning.
3. Remove the locknut from the adjusting screw.
4. With a torque wrench and a ¼ in. socket, tighten the adjusting screw to 41 in. lbs.
5. Back the adjusting screw out 7 turns for 904s through 1977, and 7½ turns 1978 and later. Back the screw out four turns for 1978 and later model 998s.
6. While holding the adjusting screw,

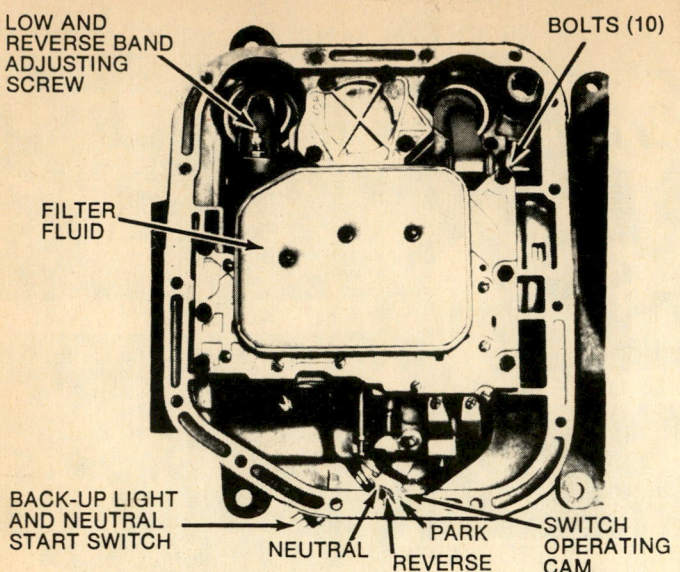

LOW AND REVERSE BAND ADJUSTING SCREW

BOLTS (10)

FILTER FLUID

BACK-UP LIGHT AND NEUTRAL START SWITCH

NEUTRAL

PARK REVERSE

SWITCH OPERATING CAM

Torque-Command adjustments with the pan removed
(© Chrysler Corp.)

install the locknut and tighten it to 35 ft. lbs.

7. Install the pan and a new gasket. Refill with DEXRON transmission fluid.

Pan Removal, Fluid and Filter Change

The manufacturer says that the transmission fluid doesn't ever have to be changed, unless the car is used for heavy work such as trailering. In this case, the fluid is to be changed every 25,000 miles. A band adjustment is also required at the same interval for these cars.

1. Drive the car until it is thoroughly warm.
2. Unbolt the pan. It holds six or more quarts so be ready.

NOTE: *If the fluid removed smells burnt, serious transmission troubles, probably due to overheating should be suspected.*

3. Unscrew and discard the filter.
4. Install a new filter. The proper torque is 28 in. lbs.
5. Clean out the pan, being extremely careful not to leave any lint from rags inside.
6. Replace the pan with a new gasket. Tighten the bolts to 11 ft. lbs. in a criss-cross pattern.
7. Pour six quarts of DEXRON or AMC automatic transmission fluid through the dipstick tube.
8. Start the engine in Neutral and let it idle for two minutes or more.
9. Hold your foot on the Brake and shift through D, 2, and R and back to N.
10. Add enough fluid to bring the level to the ADD ONE PINT mark.
11. Operate the car until the transmission is thoroughly warmed up, then check the level. It should be between the FULL and ADD ONE PINT mark.

12. If the level is at or below the ADD ONE PINT mark, add fluid through the dipstick tube to bring the level up to the FULL mark. One pint brings the level from ADD ONE PINT to FULL. Be very cautious not to overfill the transmission.

REAR AXLE

Two sizes of differential assemblies are used on the American Motor cars; 7⁹/₁₆ inch and 8⁷/₈ inch ring gear units. A Twin-Grip limited slip differential is available as an option on both units.

A letter code used to identify the axle ratio will be found on most differentials, stamped on the right axle tube housing boss, on the rear side, adjacent to the dowel hole. Some earlier cars have either a metal tag attached to one of the bolts of the differential housing cover or the code letter stamped on the right differential housing cover flange. It may be necessary to remove the cover from the differential to locate the letter. The codes and the axle ratios are listed in dealer parts books and shop manuals.

NOTE: *The 7⁹/₁₆ inch axle can be identified by the cover mounted filler plug, and the 8⁷/₈ inch axle by the front filler on the housing.*

Axle Shaft, Bearing and Seal Removal and Installation

1. The hub and drum are separate units and are removed after the wheel is removed. The hub and axle shaft are serrated together on the taper. An axle shaft key assures proper alignment during assembly.
2. Attach a puller to the rear hub and remove the hub. The use of a "Knock-out" puller should be dis-

couraged, since it may result in damage to the axle shaft or wheel bearings.

3. Disconnect the parking brake cable at the equalizer.
4. Disconnect the brake tube at the wheel cylinder and remove the brake support plate assembly, oil seal, and axle shims. Note that the axle shims are located on the left side only.
5. Using a screw type puller, remove the axle shaft and bearings from the axle housing.
6. Remove the axle shaft inner oil seal and install new seals at assembly.
7. The bearing is a press fit and should be removed with an arbor press.
8. The axle shaft bearings have no provision for lubrication after assembly. Before installing the bearings, they should be packed with a good quality wheel bearing lubricant.
9. Press the axle shaft bearings onto the axle shaft with the small diameter of the cone toward the outer (tapered) end of the shaft.
10. Soak the inner axle shaft seal in light lubricating oil. Coat the outer surface of the seal retainer with sealant.
11. Install the inner oil seal.
12. Install the axle shafts, indexing the splined end with the differential side gears.
13. Install the outer bearing cup.
14. Install the brake support plate. Sealant should be applied to the axle housing flange and brake support mounting plate.
15. Install the original shims, oil seal and brake support plate. Torque the nuts to 30-35 ft. lbs.

NOTE: *The oil seal and retainer go between the axle housing flange and the brake support plate on 9 in. brakes or 7⁹/₁₆ axle. On 10 in. brakes or 8⁷/₈ axle, they go on the outside of the brake support plate.*

16. To adjust the axle shaft end-play, strike the axle shafts with a lead mallet to seat the bearings. Install a dial indicator on the brake support plate and check the play while pushing and pulling the axle shaft. End-play should be 0.004-0.008 in., with 0.006 in. desirable. Add shims to the left side only to decrease the play and remove shims to increase the play.
17. Slide the hub onto the axle shafts aligning the serrations and the keyway on the hub with the axle shaft key.
18. Replace the hub and drum, install the wheel, lower the car onto the floor and tighten the axle shaft nut to 250 ft. lbs. If the cotter pin hole is not aligned with a castellation on the nut, tighten the nut to the next castellation.

NOTE: *A new hub must be installed*

whenever a new axle shaft is installed. Tighten the new hub onto the shaft until the hub is 1.17 in. from the end of the shaft on 7⁹/₁₆ in. differentials, and 1.30 in. on 8⁷/₈ in. models. Loosen the nut and torque to 250 ft. lbs. New hubs do not have serrations on the axle shaft mating surface. The serrations are cut when the hub is installed to the axle shaft.

19. Connect the parking brake cable at the equalizer.
20. Connect the brake tube at the wheel cylinder and bleed the brakes.

U-JOINTS

A one piece tubular drive shaft is used with a yoke at each end, to position the cross and roller type universal joints.

NOTE: *The drive shaft is a balanced unit; care must be used in handling. Do not bend or distort the tube or yokes, or vibration will result.*

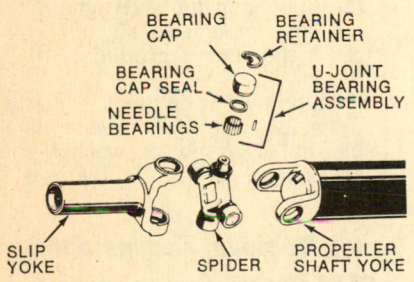

Front universal joint assembly
(© American Motors Corp)

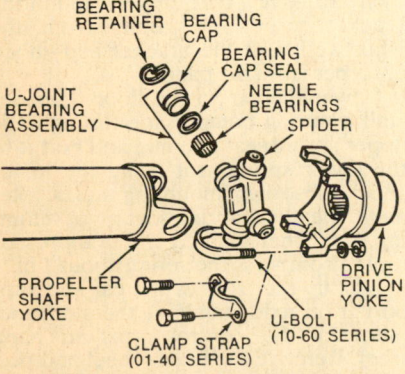

Rear universal joint assembly
(© American Motors Corp)

Removal and Installation

1. Matchmark and disassemble rear U-joint by removing nuts.
2. Drop rear of driveshaft and slide front yoke out of transmission.
3. To install, reverse removal procedure, tightening U joint nuts to 15 ft lbs.

Universal Joint Overhaul

1. Remove the lock rings from the inner side of two opposite bearings

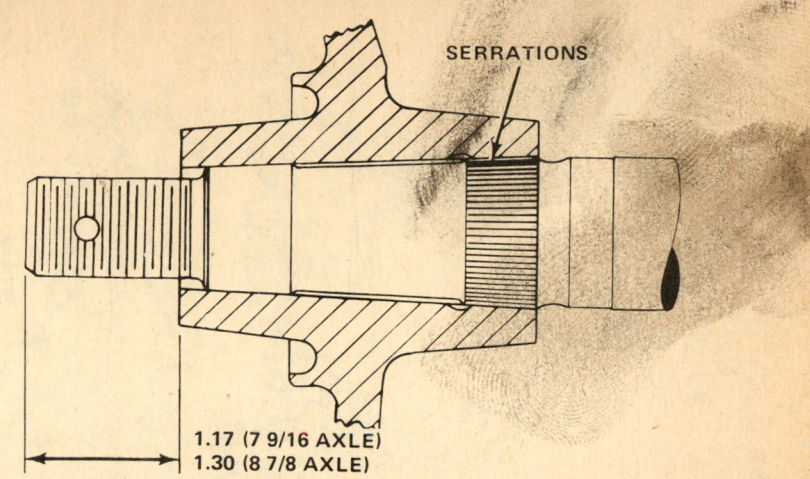

1.17 (7 9/16 AXLE)
1.30 (8 7/8 AXLE)

Measurements for installing a new rear axle hub (© American Motors Corp.)

and press on the outer side of one of the bearings, forcing the cross over. This will force the bearing on the opposite side out of its yoke.
2. Remove the bearing which was forced out of the yoke, then press the cross in the opposite direction to force the other bearing out.
3. Repeat this procedure on the third and fourth bearing.
4. When installing the new bearings in the universal joint yoke, press them into place.

JACKING, HOISTING

1. Jack car, at front, under lower support arms and, at rear, under rear axle housing.
2. To lift, contact car at rear lift pads marked lift just forward of rear wheels (at the rear spring hangers on Gremlin, Hornet, Concord, and Pacer). Front lift points are on underbody still just to the rear of strut rod-to-sill mounting bracket. On Pacer, the front lift points are located on the front wheelwell sill.

FRONT SUSPENSION

The front suspension on all models is an independent linked type with the coil springs located between seats in the wheelwell panels and seats in the upper control arms. Rubber insulators between the springs and seats reduce noise transmission to the body.

Direct acting, telescopic shock absorbers are located inside the coil springs and the control arms are attached to the body via rubber bushings.

The suspension system is a double ball joint design, both upper and lower control arms each having one joint.

On all models, strut rods serve to support the lower control arms. Stabilizer bars are used on some models.

The Pacer front suspension is different from all other AMC cars. The coil spring is mounted between the two control arms; seated at the bottom on the lower control arm and at the top in the suspension/engine mount crossmember. The crossmember is isolated from the rest of the body structure by rubber mounting points. The shock absorbers are mounted inside the coil spring. The steering knuckle is attached to the upper and lower control arms by upper and lower ball joints. A front stabilizer bar is optional.

NOTE: *The front end alignment must be checked after any disassembly procedure.*

Shock Absorber Replacement

NOTE: *When installing new shock absorbers, purge them of air by extending them in their normal position and compressing them while inverted. Do this several times. It is normal for there to be more resistance to extension than to compression.*

EXCEPT PACER

1. Remove the two lower shock absorber attaching nuts. Remove the washers and the grommets.
2. Remove the upper mounting bracket nuts and bolts.
3. Remove the bracket, complete with shock.
4. Remove the upper attaching nut and separate the shock from the mounting bracket.

Install the shock as follows:
1. Fit the grommets, washers, upper mounting bracket and nut on the shock, in the reverse order of removal. Tighten the nut to 30 ft. lbs. (through 1972) or to 8 ft. lbs. (1973 and later).
2. Fully extend the shock and install two grommets on the lower mounting studs.
3. Lower the shock through the hole in the wheel arch. Fit the lower at-

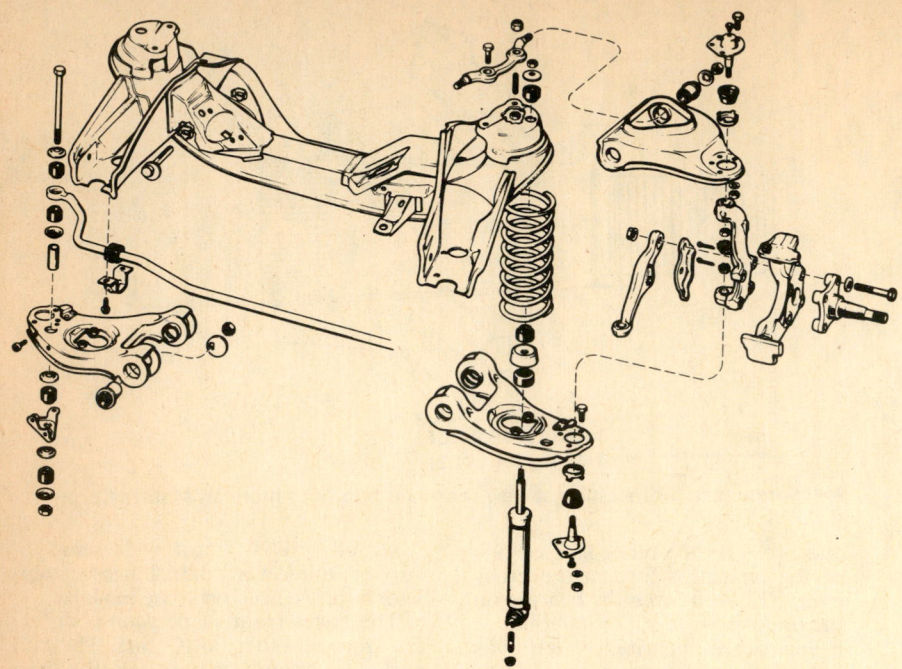

Exploded view of the Pacer front suspension

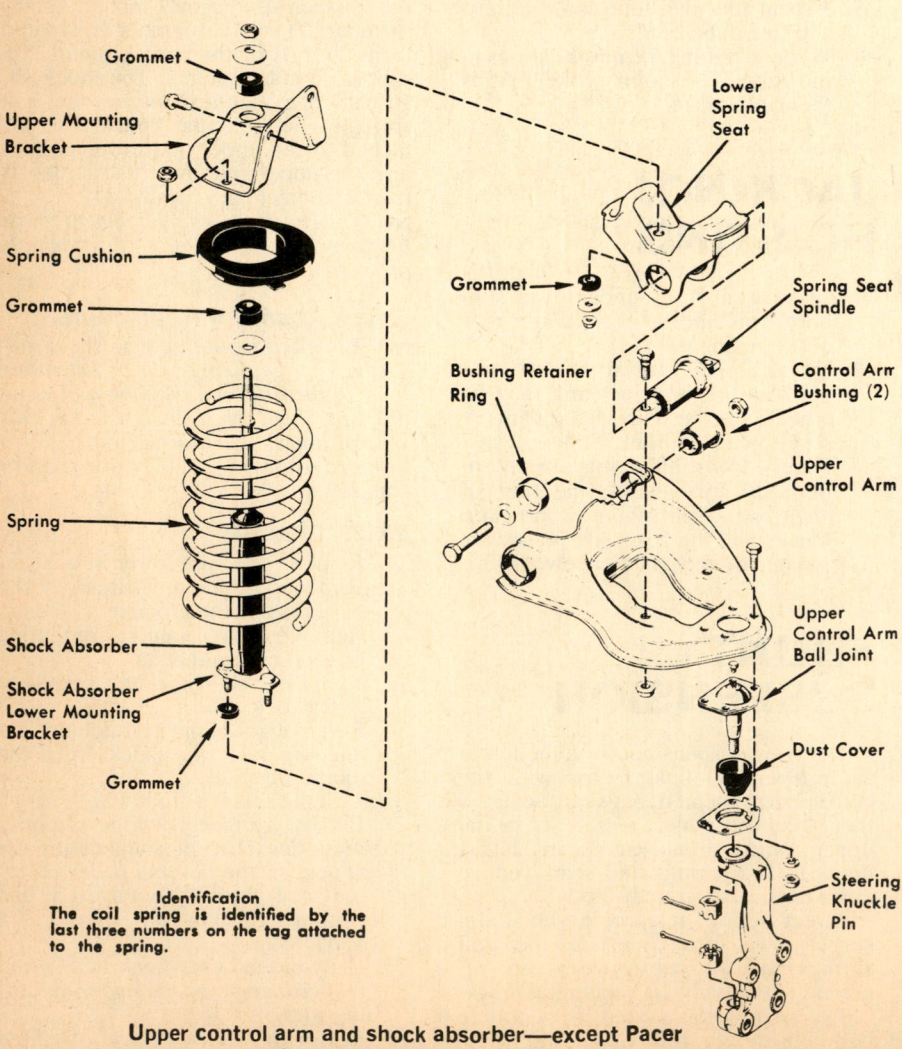

Grommet

Upper Mounting Bracket

Spring Cushion

Grommet

Spring

Shock Absorber

Shock Absorber Lower Mounting Bracket

Grommet

Lower Spring Seat

Grommet

Spring Seat Spindle

Bushing Retainer Ring

Control Arm Bushing (2)

Upper Control Arm

Upper Control Arm Ball Joint

Dust Cover

Steering Knuckle Pin

Identification
The coil spring is identified by the last three numbers on the tag attached to the spring.

Upper control arm and shock absorber—except Pacer
© American Motors Corp

tachment studs through the lower spring seat.

4. Install the grommets, washers, and nuts. Tighten the nuts to 8 ft. lbs. (through 1973) or 15 ft. lbs. (1974 and later).
5. Secure the upper mounting bracket with its attachment nuts and bolts. Tighten them to 20 ft. lbs.

PACER

1. Raise the front of the car and support it. Remove the wheels.
2. Remove the two lower shock absorber attaching bolts.
3. Remove the upper shock absorber attaching nut through the opening in the upper control arm.
4. Remove the shock absorber through the bottom of the lower control arm.

To install the front shock absorbers:

5. Install the rubber grommets and spacers to the shock absorber and install the shock up through the opening in the lower control arm. Place the rubber grommets and washers over the stud protruding through the mounting hole. Install the attaching nut and tighten the nut just enough to slightly compress the rubber grommets (8 ft. lbs.).
6. Position the lower shock mounting to the lower control arm and install the rubber grommets, washers and attaching nuts. Tighten the nuts to 20 ft. lbs.

Spring Removal and Installation
EXCEPT PACER

Jack up the car far enough to reach the two lower shock absorber nuts. Remove the nuts, washers and grommets, then remove the upper mounting bracket screws and bolts from the wheelwell. Lift the bracket and shock absorber from the panel.

Lower the car to the floor, then install a spring compressor through the upper spring seat opening and bolt it to the lower spring seat using the lower shock absorber mounting holes. Remove the lower spring seat pivot retaining nuts, then tighten the compressor tool to compress the spring about 1 in.

Jack up the front of the car and support it on axle stands at the subframe (allowing the control arms to hang free). Remove the front wheel and pull the lower spring seat out away from the car, then slowly release the spring tension and remove the coil spring and lower spring seat.

To install, place the spring compressor through the coil spring and tape the rubber spring cushion to the small-diameter end of the spring (upper). Place the lower spring seat against the spring with the end of the coil against the formed shoulder in the seat. The shoulder and coil end face inwards, toward the engine, when the spring is installed.

Place the spring up against the upper

seat, then align the lower spring seat pivot so that the retaining studs will enter the holes in the upper control arm. Compress the coil spring and install the spring, then install the wheel and tire and lower the car to the floor (to place weight on suspension). Install and tighten lower spring seat spindle retaining nuts and tighten them to 35 ft. lbs. Remove the spring compressor and install the shock absorber.

PACER

1. Disconnect the upper end of the shock absorber.
2. Raise the front end of the car and support it.
3. Disconnect the lower end of the shock absorber and remove it.
4. Disconnect the stabilizer bar at the lower control arm, if so equipped.
5. Remove the wheel, brake drum, or caliper and rotor. Do not allow the brake hose to support the weight of the caliper; use a length of wire to suspend the caliper from the frame.
6. Remove the two bolts that attach the steering arm to the steering knuckle and move the steering arm aside.
7. Use a spring compressor to compress the coil spring.
8. Remove the cotter pin and nut from the lower ball joint stud and disengage the stud from the steering knuckle with a puller.
9. Move the steering knuckle, steering spindle, and support plate, or anchor plate assembly, aside to provide working clearance. Do not allow the brake hose to support the weight of these components. Use wire to hang the components from the upper control arm.
10. Move the lower control arm aside and remove the spring.

    To install the front coil spring:

11. Position the upper end of the spring in the spring seat of the front crossmember. Align the cut-off end of the bottom coil with the formed shoulder in the spring seat. The top coil is flat and does not use an insulator. Use a floor jack or jack stand to support the spring until the spring compressor is installed. Install the spring compressor.
12. Assemble the remaining components of the front suspension in the reverse order of removal. Tighten the ball joint stud nut to 75 ft. lbs., the steering arm-to-knuckle attaching bolts to 80 ft. lbs. through 1976, 55 ft. lbs. 1977 and later, the shock absorber lower mounting nuts to 20 ft. lbs., and the stabilizer bar locknut to 8 ft. lbs.

Control Arm Removal and Installation

UPPER CONTROL ARM— EXCEPT PACER

Remove the shock absorber and

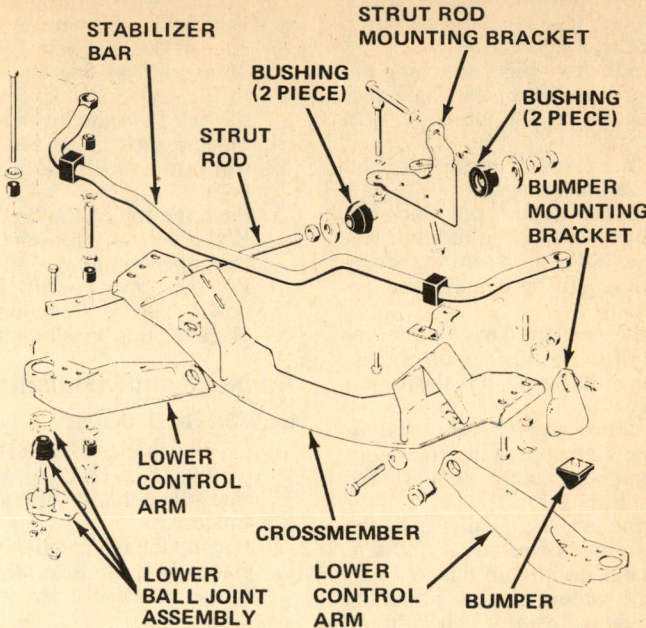

Lower control arm details—models except Pacer (© American Motors Corp.)

compress the coil spring approximately 2 in. using the procedure under Front Spring Removal and Installation.

Jack up the front of the car and support the body on jackstands placed under the subframes (allow the control arms to hang free). Remove the wheel and the upper ball joint cotter pin and retaining nut. Separate the ball joint stud from the steering knuckle using a ball joint removal tool. Remove the inner pivot bolts then remove the control arm.

To install, reverse the removal procedure. Do not tighten the pivot bolt nuts until the full weight of the car is on the wheels. The ball joint stud nut must be tightened to 40 ft. lbs. through 1976 and 75 ft. lbs. thereafter, the lower spring seat pivot retaining nuts to 35 ft. lbs., and the control arm inner pivot bolts to 45 ft. lbs. through 1976, 80 ft. lbs. 1977 and later.

UPPER CONTROL ARM—PACER

1. Raise and support the front of the vehicle.
2. Remove the wheel and tire.
3. Remove the cotter pin, locknut, and retaining nuts from the upper ball joint stud.
4. Loosen the stud from the steering knuckle with a ball joint removal tool.
5. Support the lower control arm with a floor jack.
6. Disengage the stud from the steering knuckle.
7. Remove the retaining nuts that attach the cross-shaft to the front crossmember and remove the upper control arm assembly.
8. Install the upper control arm in the reverse order of removal, tightening the cross-shaft retaining nuts to 80 ft. lbs., the upper ball joint stud

nut to 75 ft. lbs., and if new bushings were installed, tighten the nuts to 60 ft. lbs. after the car is lowered to the floor.

LOWER CONTROL ARM— EXCEPT PACER

The inner end of the lower control arm is attached to a removable crossmember. The outer end is attached to the steering knuckle pin and ball joint assembly.

To remove, jack up the car and support it on axle stands under the subframes. Remove the brake drum or caliper and rotor from the spindle, then disconnect the steering arm from the knuckle pin. Remove the lower ball joint stud cotter pin and nut. Separate the ball joint from the knuckle pin using a ball joint removal tool.

Disconnect the sway bar from the control arm, then unbolt the strut rod. Remove the inner pivot bolt and the control arm.

To install, reverse the removal procedure; do not tighten inner pivot bolt until car weight is on wheels. Tighten ball joint retaining nut to 40 ft. lbs. through 1976, 75 ft. lbs. thereafter, strut rod bolts to 75 ft. lbs., sway bar bolts to 8 ft. lbs., steering arm bolts to 65 ft. lbs., and control arm inner pivot bolt to 95 ft. lbs. through 1976, 110 ft. lbs. thereafter.

LOWER CONTROL ARM—PACER

1. Disconnect the upper end of the shock absorber, raise the front end of the car and disconnect the lower end of the shock absorber and remove the shock absorber.
2. Disconnect the stabilizer bar at the lower control arm, if so equipped.
3. Remove the wheel, brake drum, or caliper and rotor. Do not allow the

brake hose to support the weight of the caliper. Use wire to support it from the frame.

4. Remove the two bolts attaching the steering arm to the steering knuckle and move the steering arm aside.
5. Install a spring compressor and compress the spring.
6. Remove the cotter pin and nut from the lower ball joint stud. Remove the ball joint from the steering knuckle using a ball joint removal tool.
7. Move the steering knuckle assembly out of the way. Support the assembly with wire from the upper control arm.
8. Remove the two pivot bolts that attach the lower arm to the front crossmember and remove the lower control arm.
9. Install the lower control arm in the reverse order of removal, tightening the ball joint stud nut to 75 ft. lbs., the steering arm attaching bolts to 80 ft. lbs. through 1976, 55 ft. lbs. 1977 and later, the shock absorber lower attaching nuts to 20 ft. lbs., the stabilizer bar locknut to 8 ft. lbs., and lastly, after the car has been lowered to the ground with the wheel and tire installed, tighten the lower control arm pivot bolts to 95 ft. lbs. through 1976, and 110 ft. lbs. thereafter.

BALL JOINTS

Inspection

EXCEPT PACER

NOTE: *Be sure that the front wheel bearings are adjusted to specification before checking the upper ball joint.*

1. Jack up the front of the car and place jackstands under the frame side sills.

NOTE: *The control arms must hang free if an accurate reading is to be obtained.*

2. Check the lower ball joints by grasping the lower portion of the wheel and pulling it in and out.
3. If there is noticeable lateral free-play, the lower ball joint is worn and must be replaced.
4. To check the condition of the upper ball joint, place a dial indicator with its plunger against the tire scrub bead (just outside the whitewall).
5. Move the upper portion of the wheel and tire toward the car's center, while watching the dial indicator.
6. Move the wheel and tire back out while watching the indicator.
7. The upper ball joint should be replaced if its *total* movement is greater than 0.160 in.

PACER

1. Check that the front wheel bearings are adjusted properly.
2. Remove the lubrication plug from the lower ball joint. Insert a piece of stiff wire until it contacts the ball. Mark the wire even with the edge of the plug hole.
3. Measure from the end of the wire to the mark. If it exceeds $7/16$ in., the ball joint should be replaced.
4. Place a jack under the lower control arm and lift the wheel off the floor.
5. Push the top of the tire in and out. If there is any looseness, replace the upper ball joint.
6. Pry the upper control arm up and down. If there is any looseness, replace the upper ball joint.

Removal and Installation

LOWER BALL JOINT

1. On all vehicles except Pacer, place a 2 x 4 x 5 in. block of wood on the side sill so that it supports the control arm.
2. Jack up the front end of the car and place jackstands underneath the frame side sills to support the body.
3. Remove the wheel and the brake drum. On cars equipped with disc brakes, remove the caliper and rotor.
4. Disconnect the lower control arm strut rod, on models other than Pacer. Disconnect the stabilizer bar, if so equipped.
5. Separate the steering arm from the steering knuckle.
6. Remove the ball stud retaining nut, after removing its cotter pin.
7. Install a ball joint removal tool then loosen the ball stud in the knuckle pin. Leave the tool in place on the stud.
8. Place a jackstand under the lower control arm.
9. Chisel the heads off the rivets which secure the ball joint to the control arm. Use a punch to remove the rivets.
10. Remove the tool from the ball stud.
11. Remove the ball stud from the knuckle pin and remove the joint from the control arm.

Installation of a new lower ball joint is as follows:

1. Position the new ball joint so that its securing holes align with the rivet holes in the control arm.
2. Install the special $5/16$ in. bolts, used to secure the ball joint, loosely.

――――――― CAUTION ―――――――
Use only the hardened 5/16 in. bolts supplied with the ball joint replacement kit; standard bolts are not strong enough.
―――――――――――――――――――――

3. Install the steering strut and stop on the lower control arm. Tighten their bolts to 75 ft. lbs.
4. Tighten the $5/16$ in. ball joint securing bolts to 25 ft. lbs.
5. Fit the knuckle pin and retaining nut on the ball stud; tighten the nut to 40 ft. lbs. through 1976, 75 ft. lbs. thereafter, and 75 ft. lbs. on all Pacers. Install the cotter pin.
6. Complete the installation procedure in the reverse order of removal and then check front end alignment.

UPPER BALL JOINT

1. Perform Steps 1-3 of the "Lower Ball Joint Removal" procedure.

NOTE: *It is not necessary to remove the brake drum in Step 3.*

2. Next, perform Steps 6-9 of the "Lower Ball Joint Removal" procedure to the upper ball joint.
3. Separate the upper ball joint from the control arm.
4. Remove the ball joint puller from the knuckle pin.

Installation of a new upper ball joint is as follows:

1. Perform Steps 1-2 of the "Lower Ball Joint Installation" procedure.
2. Skip Step 3 and go on to Steps 4-5 of the "Lower Ball Joint Installation" procedure.
3. Complete the installation in the reverse order of removal and check front end alignment.

WHEEL BEARINGS

Inspection

Check to see that the inner cones of the bearings are free to "creep" on the spindle. Polish and lubricate the spindle to allow "creeping" movement and to keep rust from forming.

Adjustment

1. With the tire and wheel removed and the car supported by a suitable and safe means, remove the dust cover from the spindle.
2. Remove the cotter pin and nut retainer.
3. Rotate the wheel while tightening the spindle nut to 20-25 ft. lbs.
4. Loosen the spindle nut $1/3$ of a turn.
5. Rotate the wheel while tightening the spindle nut to 12 in. lbs. for models through 1973 and 6 in. lbs. for 1974 and later.
6. Fit the nut retainer over the spindle and align the slots in it with the cotter pin hole. Insert the cotter pin.
7. Install the dust cover.

Rear Suspension

All Pacers, Javelin, Hornet, and Gremlin models use a four or five-leaf semi-elliptic spring, and live axle rear suspension. Shock absorbers are mounted at their lower ends to studs and are bayonet or stud type at their upper ends. Upper shock nuts are accessible by removing cover plates or by removing trunk floormat on some models, or by removing underbody brackets bolted to the trunk pan on others, such as Pacer and Concord.

The rear suspension on Ambassador

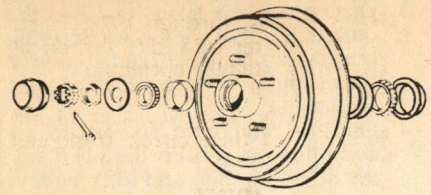

Front wheel bearing components
(© American Motors Corp)

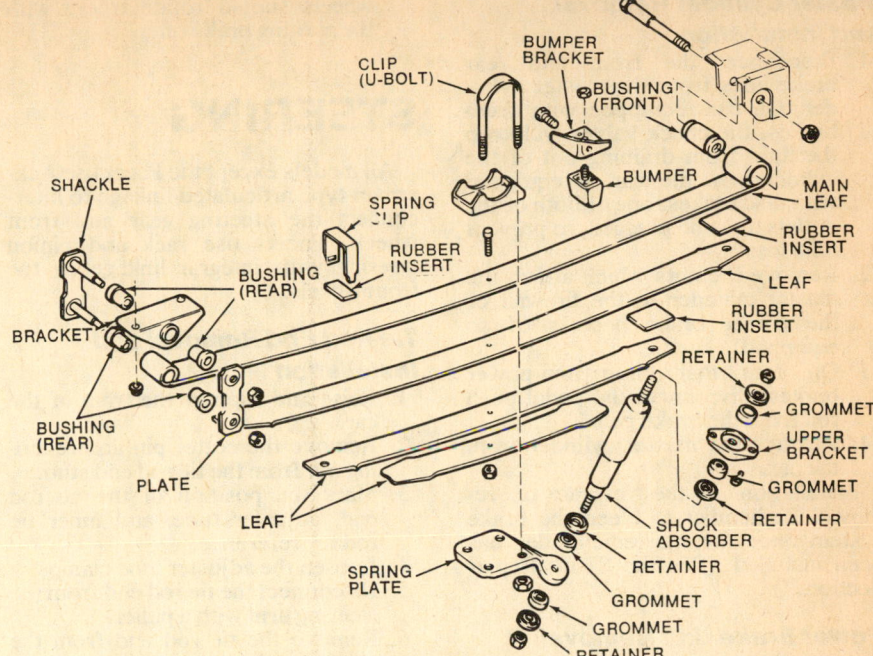

Typical leaf spring rear suspension (© American Motors Corp.)

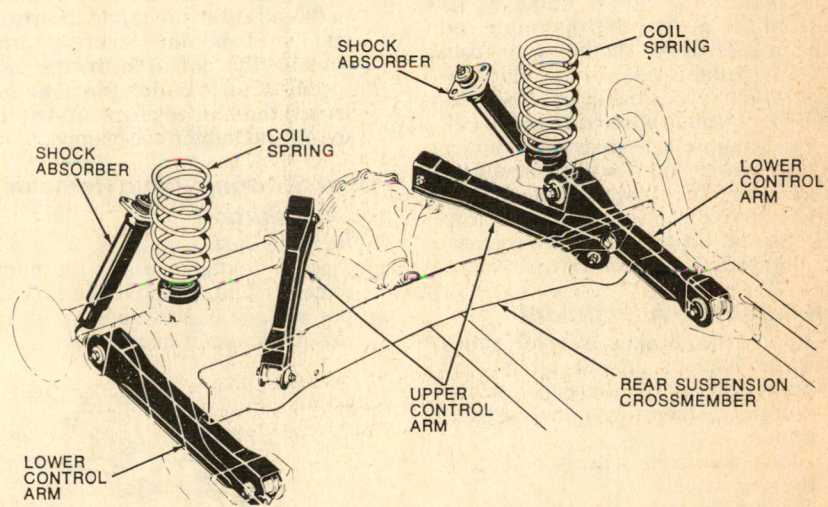

Typical coil spring rear suspension (© American Motors Corp.)

and Matador models is a four-trailing arm, coil spring type. The two lower control arms are attached to the differential housing and to a rear crossmember. Rubber bushings are used on the lower arms and on the crossmember ends of the upper arms. The lower ends of the upper arms are attached to the outer ends of the axle tubes and to the body side sills, while the two upper control arms are attached to pressed in bushings in ears on the differential case. Shock absorbers are accessible at their upper ends by removing cover plates in the body or by removing brackets from underneath the car.

Shock Absorber Replacement

NOTE: *When installing new shocks purge them of air by repeatedly extending them in their normal position and compressing them while inverted. It is normal for there to be more resistance to extension than to compression.*

1. Support the rear axle with jacks or a lift; this allows the weight of the car to compress the rear spring.
2. Remove the lower shock attachment.
3. Remove the access plate on the rear underbody panel and remove the upper securing nut. It may be necessary to hold the top of the shock while unfastening the nut.

NOTE: *Some models do not have an access plate. On these cars, remove the upper attachment plate complete as an assembly from under the car.*

4. Remove the shock from under the car.
5. Installation is the reverse of removal.

Spring Removal and Installation
PACER, JAVELIN, HORNET, CONCORD, AND GREMLIN

1. Raise the car. Support the rear axle with jacks or a lift to take the load off the rear springs.
2. Disconnect the rear shock from the lower mounting stud.
3. Disconnect the axle U-bolts.
4. Remove the nut from the bolt which attaches the eye of the spring to the front mount. Remove the bolt.
5. Remove the nuts from the rear shackle. Remove the shackle.
6. Installation is the reverse of removal.

AMBASSADOR AND MATADOR

1. Raise the rear of the car and support the rear axle with jacks or a lift to take the load off the rear springs.
2. Disconnect the shock from the axle tube. Lower the axle to the fullest extent of its travel (limited by the control arms). Detach the upper control arms at the axle on 1975 and later models.
3. Pull down the axle tube to completely release the spring.
4. Reverse the above to install the spring. Torque the control arm pivot bolts to 45-80 ft. lbs. with the weight of the car on the springs.

BRAKES

All American Motors cars are equipped with tandem master cylinders. This allows one set of brakes to operate, should the other set fail. A switch in the system, connected to a warning light on the instrument panel, indicates a difference in pressure between the front and rear brake lines, thus indicating the failure of one brake system. Repair procedures for both the master cylinder and the switch are found in the "Unit Repair Section".

All drum brakes have automatic brake adjusters. These automatically compensate for lining wear, by operating when the brakes are applied while the car is backing up. The automatic mechanism is attached to the star wheel adjuster, which it works through.

Information on brake adjustments, lining replacement, bleeding procedure, master and wheel cylinder overhaul can be found in the Unit Repair Section.

Master Cylinder Removal and Installation

1. Disconnect the front and rear brake lines from the master cylinder. On cars equipped with drum brakes, the check valves will keep the fluid from draining out of the cylinder. If the car is equipped with disc brakes, one or both of the outlets must be plugged, to prevent fluid loss.
2. Remove the nuts which attach the master cylinder to the firewall or the power brake booster (if so equipped).
3. On cars that have non-power brakes, disconnect the pedal push rod from the brake pedal.
4. Remove the master cylinder from the car.

Installation is the reverse of removal. Remember to bleed the brake system once the master cylinder has been installed. (See the "Unit Repair Section.")

Power Brake Unit Removal and Installation

Disconnect the power brake clevis pin from the power unit operating rod at the linkage under the hood, or from the brake pedal inside the car, depending on which type is being serviced. Remove the vacuum hose from the check valve. Separate the master cylinder from the power unit. Do not disconnect the hydraulic lines from the master cylinder. Remove the power unit mounting bolts and lift the unit from the car. Installation is the reverse of removal.

Parking Brake Adjustment

1. Apply the brakes several times while backing up to adjust the drum brakes. Set the pedal on the first notch from the released position.
2. Block the front wheels and raise the rear wheels.
3. Tighten the cable at the equalizer so that the wheels can just barely be turned forward.
4. Release the parking brake and check for rear brake drag. The wheels should rotate freely with the parking brake off.

STEERING

All models except the Pacer use Ackerman-type articulated linkage to interconnect the steering gear and front wheels. Pacers use rack and pinion steering with integral linkage to the front wheels.

Tie Rod End Removal and Installation

1. Raise and support the front of the car.
2. Remove the cotter pin and retaining nut from the tie rod end stud.
3. Mark the position of the tie rod end, adjuster tube, and inner tie rod for reference.
4. Loosen the adjuster tube clamps.
5. Disconnect the tie rod end from the steering arm with a puller.
6. Remove the tie rod end from the adjuster tube.
7. Install the replacement tie rod end in the adjuster tube, and insert the end stud in the steering arm. Tighten the nut to 35 ft. lbs. and install a new cotter pin. Do not loosen the nuts to align. Adjust the toe-in and tighten the clamps.

Power Steering Pump Removal and Installation

1. Remove the fan belt.
2. Place a container under the pump to catch fluid. Remove the fuel vapor storage canister and six-cylinder air cleaner if necessary.

3. Disconnect the hoses and cap the outlets, so that the power steering unit does not loose fluid. Remove the air pump belt on 1975 and later models.
4. On 1975 and later sixes with air conditioning, loosen the idler pulley adjusting bolt and idler pulley, air pump adjusting strap mounting bolt and remove the compressor drive belt from the idler pulley. Loosen the two nuts that attach the upper leg of the aluminum idler pulley mounting bracket to the cylinder head and remove the bolt that attaches the lower leg of the mounting bracket to the engine front cover.
5. On sixes through 1974 loosen the pump bracket pivot bolts. On V8s through 1974, remove the front pump mounting bracket. Remove the pump drive belt and the pump. On 1975 and later sixes, remove the nut from the air pump mounting stud, remove the power steering pump to engine front cover front adapter plate (do not unbolt the adapter plate from the pump), remove the long adjusting bolt that passes through the adapter plate, and remove the bolt hidden behind the flange in the rear adapter plate. Remove the pump, adapter plate and mounting bracket together.

On 1975 and later V8s, remove the two pump mounting stud nuts at the rear of the two-piece mounting bracket. Remove the pump, support strap bolts and the front half of the pump mounting bracket. Remove the nut from the stud holding the front half of the pump bracket. Remove the pump and the front half of the mounting bracket.

On four cylinder models, remove the adjuster locknuts and washers which retain the pump and pivot bracket to the mounting bracket. All of the pump mounting bolts are metric except for the $9/16$ in. adjuster locknuts. Move the pump and remove the belt. Remove the bolts which connect the front bracket to the rear bracket and engine block, and remove the pump complete with the pivot and front brackets.
6. After installation, fill the system with DEXRON or AMC power steering fluid. Bleed the system of air by raising the front of the car and turning the wheels from side to side without hitting the stops several times. Check the level frequently.

Steering Wheel Removal and Installation

1. Disconnect the battery and remove the horn button by one of the following methods:
   a. center button—lift upward.
   b. trim cover—remove the screws, which hold the cover on, from

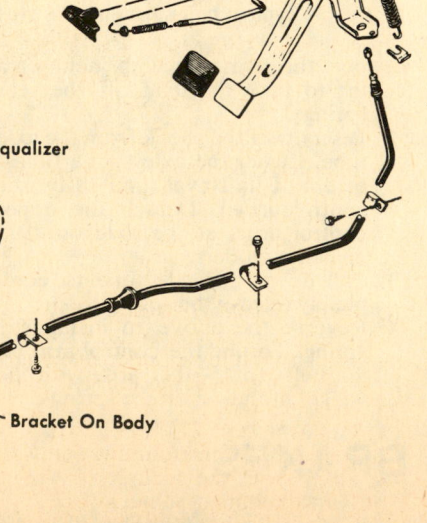

Typical foot pedal type parking brake linkage
(© American Motors Corp)

Cable Clevis

Left Rear Cable — *Equalizer*

Adjusting and Lock Nut

Right Rear Cable

Bracket On Body

the rear. On "rimblow" wheels, remove the center contact.

2. Remove the steering wheel center nut and washer. Before removing the wheel, note the position of the index marks on the wheel and the steering shaft. If none are present, paint an alignment mark on the shaft and wheel.
3. Remove the wheel with a puller.

Installation is the reverse of removal. Tighten the steering wheel nut to 20 ft. lbs.

NOTE: *Some shafts have metric threads. These can be identified by a groove in the shaft splines. Metric nuts are coded blue.*

─────── CAUTION ───────

Do not hammer on the end of the steering shaft; you could shear the plastic retainers which maintain the rigidity of the energy-absorbing steering column.

Turn Signal Switch Replacement

1. Disconnect the ground cable from the battery. Remove the steering wheel.
2. Loosen the anti-theft cover attaching screws and remove the cover from the column. Do not remove the screws from the cover; they are attached to it with plastic retainers.
3. To remove the lockplate, a special compressor is required. This tool is an inverted U-shape with a hole for the shaft. The shaft nut is used to force it down. Depress the lockplate and pry the snap-ring from the groove in the steering shaft. Remove the tool, snap-ring, plate, turn signal cam, upper bearing preload spring, and the thrust washer from the shaft.
4. Place the turn signal lever in the right turn position and remove it.
5. Depress the hazard warning switch button and remove it, by rotating it counterclockwise.
6. Disconnect the wire harness connector block at its mounting bracket, which is located on the right side of the lower column.

NOTE: *To aid in the removal and replacement of the directional switch harness, tape the harness connector to the wire harness to prevent snagging when removing the wiring harness assembly through the steering column. Prepare the new turn signal switch harness in the same manner for ease of installation.*

7. If the car (Gremlin, Hornet, Concord, only, after 1973) is equipped with a column-mounted automatic transmission selector, use a paper clip to depress the locktab that holds the shift quadrant light wire in the connector block (the grey wire at terminal "D").
8. Remove the switch attaching screws. Withdraw the switch and

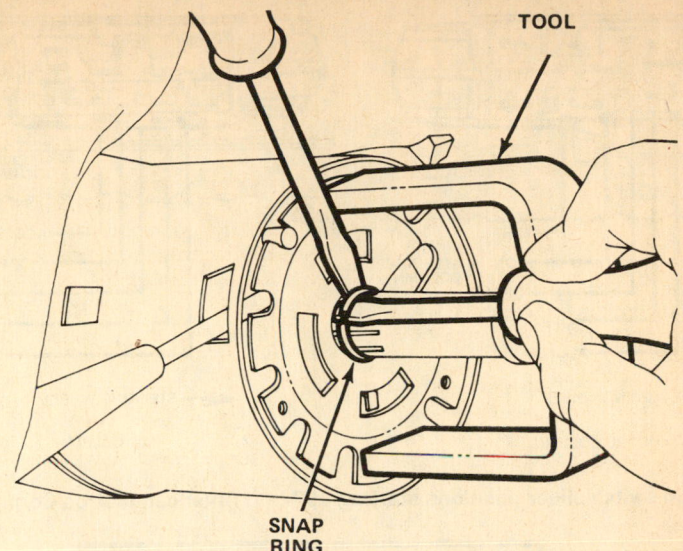

Using the special lockplate removal tool · (© American Motors Corp)

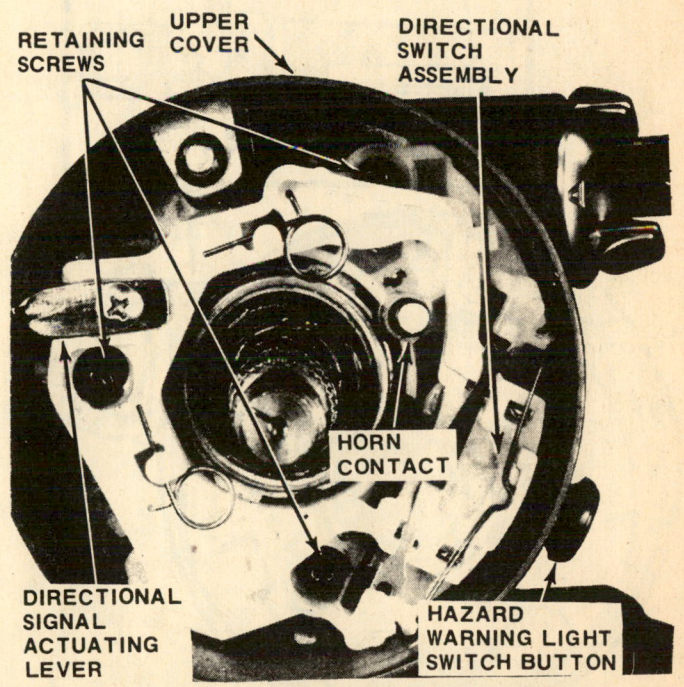

Turn signal switch (© American Motors Corp.)

wire harness from the column. You may have to remove the package tray, lower trim panel, and wire harness protector.

Install the new switch in the reverse order of removal.

Ignition Switch Replacement

The ignition switch on all models is mounted on the lower steering column tube and is connected to the lock cylinder via a lock rod.

1. Place the key in "OFF-LOCK."
2. Remove switch mounting screws.
3. Disconnect the lock rod, remove harness connector and switch.
4. To install on the standard column, move the switch slide as far as it will go to the left (toward the

wheel). On the tilt-column, push the slide to the extreme right.
5. Position the lock rod into the hole on the switch slide.
6. Install the switch on the steering column. Be sure that the slide stays in its detent.
7. On the tilt-column, do not tighten the mounting screws. Instead, push the switch down the column, away from the steering wheel. This will remove any slack from the lock rod.
8. Tighten the switch mounting screws.

Lock Cylinder Replacement

1. Remove the battery ground cable and the steering wheel. Loosen an-

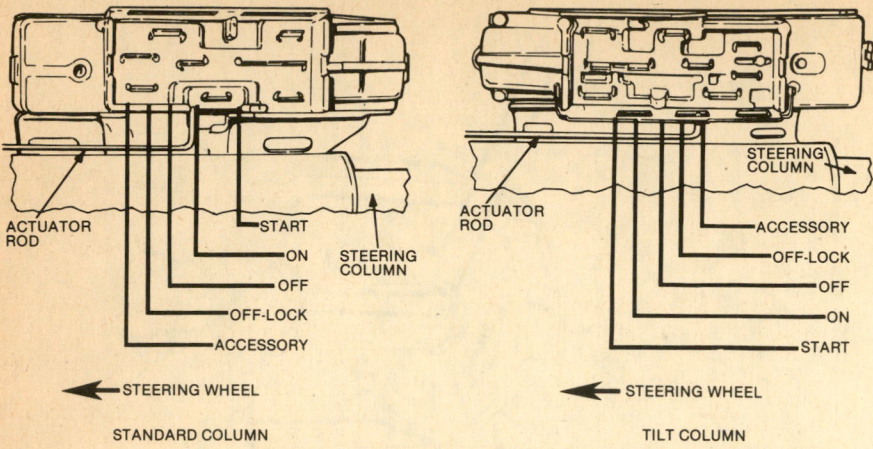

ACTUATOR ROD — START — ON — OFF — OFF-LOCK — ACCESSORY
STEERING COLUMN
← STEERING WHEEL
STANDARD COLUMN

ACTUATOR ROD — ACCESSORY — OFF-LOCK — OFF — ON — START
STEERING COLUMN
← STEERING WHEEL
TILT COLUMN

Ignition switch slider positions starting 1972 (© American Motros Corp.)

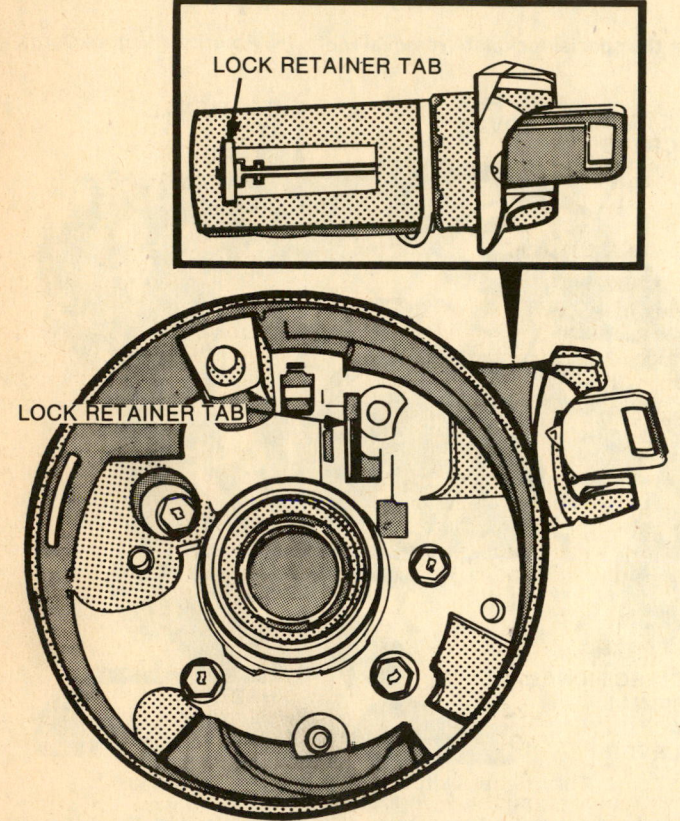

LOCK RETAINER TAB

LOCK RETAINER TAB

Lock cylinder removal   (© American Motors Corp)

ti-theft cover screws and remove cover from column.

2. Depress lock plate as far as possible, using a spacer and steering wheel nut.
3. Remove wire snap-ring from shaft groove, then remove compressor tool, snap-ring, lock plate, turn signal cam, upper bearing preload spring and thrust washer.
4. Place turn signal lever in "right turn" position and remove lever.
5. Depress hazard warning switch and remove button by turning counterclockwise.
6. Remove turn signal switch retain-

ing screws and pull switch and wires out of column, as far as wiring will allow.

7. Place key in "LOCK" position, then depress the lock cylinder retaining tab in the rectangular slot in the column housing and remove the cylinder.

To install the lock cylinder, proceed in the following manner:

1. Hold the lock cylinder sleeve and turn the lock cylinder clockwise (counterclockwise 1977 and later) until it contacts the stop.
2. Align the lock cylinder key with the keyway in the housing and slip

the cylinder into the housing.

3. Lightly depress the cylinder against the sector, while turning it counterclockwise, until the cylinder and sector are engaged.
4. Depress the cylinder until the retaining tab engages, and the lock cylinder is secured.
5. Install the turn signal switch. Be sure that the actuating lever pivot is properly seated and aligned in the top of the housing boss, before installing it with its screws.
6. Install the turn signal lever and check the operation of the switch.
7. Install the thrust washer, spring and turn signal cancelling cam on the steering shaft.
8. Align the lockplate and steering shaft splines, and position the lockplate so that the turn signal camshaft protrudes from the "dogleg" opening in the lockplate.
9. Use snap-ring pliers to install the snap-ring on the end of the steering shaft.
10. Secure the anti-theft cover with its screws.
11. Install the button on the hazard warning switch. Install the steering wheel, as detailed above.

INSTRUMENT PANEL

NOTE: *To remove the various units from the instrument panel it is necessary to remove the bezels, overlays, housings, and crash pads. Numerous fasteners are hidden. Caution must be exercised not to damage or break the panel trim.*

Current is supplied to the instruments and the instrument panel lights through a printed circuit which is attached to the rear of the instrument cluster. The disconnect plug is part of the panel wiring harness and connects to pins attached to the printed circuit. A keyway located on the printed circuit board insures that the plug is always mounted correctly.

— CAUTION —

Never pry under the plug to remove it, or damage to the printed circuit will result.

An instrument voltage regulator is wired in series with the gauges to supply a constant five volts to them. On the Hornet and Gremlin it is integral with the temperature gauge; on other models it is a separate unit. 1978 and later Concords and Gremlins have magnetic gauges, thus eliminating the constant voltage regulator.

Speedometer Cable Replacement

Two types of fasteners are used to attach the cable to the speedometer.

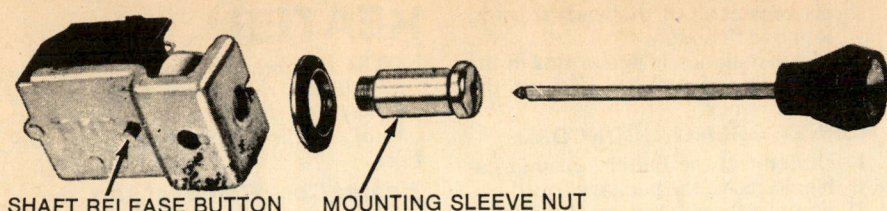

SHAFT RELEASE BUTTON   MOUNTING SLEEVE NUT

Light switch assembly (© American Motors Corp)

One type has a knurled round captive nut, which is screwed to the rear of the speedometer. The second type is a plastic finger, attached to the end of the cable. The finger lug locks to the rear of the speedometer housing. By depressing the plastic finger, the lug is raised, and the cable is released.

NOTE: *The negative battery cable should be detached before any repairs behind the instrument panel are attempted.*

Headlight Switch Replacement

EXCEPT JAVELIN

Light switches are similar in all models. Some variation occurs in the shape and position of the nut mounting the switch to dash.

1. Disconnect battery and remove the switch overlay cover attaching screws so the cover can be pulled forward.

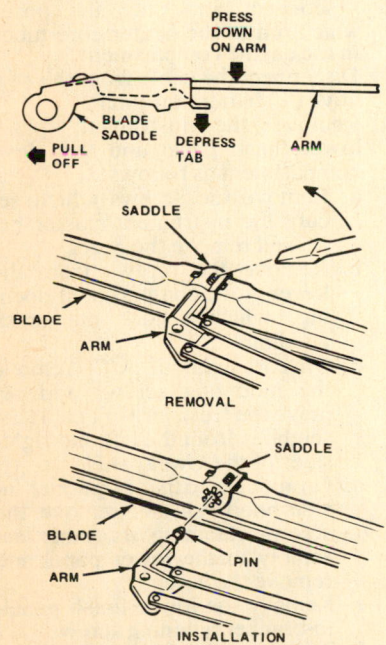

PRESS DOWN ON ARM

BLADE SADDLE   DEPRESS TAB   ARM

PULL OFF

SADDLE

BLADE

ARM

REMOVAL

SADDLE

BLADE

ARM   PIN

INSTALLATION

Wiper blade removal methods
(© American Motors Corp.)

2. With the switch in the on position, press the release button on the switch and remove the knob and shaft.
3. Remove screws, attaching switch or bracket to panel.
4. Reverse for installation, positioning switch so that the shaft is lined up properly before tightening the bracket screws.

JAVELIN

1. Remove the toggle switch knob by inserting a screwdriver in the groove on its left side. Pry upward, toward the knob, to release the spring clip that retains the knob.
2. Remove the screws that secure the lower cover to the steering column and withdraw the cover.
3. Disconnect the wire connectors and the retaining screws from the switch. Remove the switch.
4. Install the switch in the reverse order of removal.

WINDSHIELD WIPERS

Wiper Blade Removal and Replacement

Two types of wiper blade attaching methods are used. On the first type, the blade is attached to a straight or slightly curved arm, with the arm entering the wiper blade and locking into position. To release this type, depress the locking tab and remove the blade from the arm. The second type of blade is attached to a pin at a right angle to the arm. To release the pin, a tool is inserted into the wiper blade saddle to depress the spring clip and release the pin.

Motor Removal and Installation

JAVELIN, HORNET, GREMLIN THROUGH 1974; 1973-74 AMBASSADOR, MATADOR (EXCEPT 1974 COUPE)

The wiper motor is mounted on the engine side of the firewall and is easily accessible from under the hood.

1. Remove four screws that hold motor to firewall.
2. Remove vacuum wiper hose and control cable.
3. Unplug harness plug under dash, if equipped with electric wipers.
4. Disconnect motor link and remove motor.
5. To install, reverse removal procedure.

1975 AND LATER; GREMLIN, HORNET, CONCORD, MATADOR SEDAN AND WAGON

1. Remove the wiper arms and blades.
2. Remove the screws holding the

motor adapter plate to the dash panel.
3. Separate the wiper wiring harness connector at the motor.
4. Pull the motor and linkage out of the opening to expose the drive link-to-crank stud retaining clip. Raise up the lock tab of the clip with a screwdriver and slide the clip off the stud.
5. Install the windshield wiper motor in the reverse order of removal.

MATADOR AND AMBASSADOR THROUGH 1972

1. Remove wiper arms and blades and the cowl air intake cover.
2. Slide the link-to-motor retainer clip off the motor arm stud. Remove the link from the motor.
3. Disconnect control cable and vacuum hose or wiring harness from the motor.
4. Remove the motor and mounting plate-to-firewall screws, and the motor assembly.
5. Install by reversing removal procedure.

1974 AND LATER MATADOR COUPE

1. Remove the wiper arm/blade assemblies.
2. Open the hood and remove the cowl screen from the cowl opening.
3. Separate the linkage drive arm from the motor arm crankpin, by unfastening the retaining clip.
4. Disconnect the two multiconnectors from the motor.
5. Remove the wiper motor securing screws and withdraw the motor from the opening.

NOTE: *If the output arm hangs up on the firewall panel during motor removal, rotate the arm clockwise by hand, so that it clears the panel opening.*

Installation is performed in the reverse order of removal. Prior to installation, make sure that the output arm is in the "park" position. Tighten the motor securing screws to 90-120 in. lbs.

PACER

1. Remove the vacuum canister bracket and canister, if equipped.
2. Disconnect the linkage drive arm from the motor output arm crankpin by removing the retaining clip.
3. On vehicles equipped with air conditioning:
   a. Remove the two nuts on the left side of the heater housing.
   b. Remove the one nut on the right side of the heater housing.
   c. Remove the screw from the heater housing support.
4. On vehicles not equipped with air conditioning:
   a. Remove the two nuts and one screw on the left side of the heater housing.
   b. Remove the one nut on the right side of the heater housing.

c. Remove the screw from the heater housing support. Pull the heater housing forward.
5. Remove the wiper motor mounting plate attaching screws and remove the wiper motor assembly from the cowl.
6. Disconnect the two wire connectors from the wiper motor.
7. Remove the wiper motor attaching screws and remove the wiper motor.
8. Install the wiper motor in the reverse order of removal.

RADIO

The following precautions should be observed when working on a car radio:
1. Always observe the proper polarity of the power connections; i.e., positive (+) goes to the power source and negative (−) to ground (negative ground electrical system).
2. Never run the radio without a speaker; damage to the output transistors will result. If a replacement (or additional) speaker is used, be sure that it is the correct impedance (ohms) for the radio. The proper impedance is stamped on the case of American Motors radios.
3. If a new antenna or antenna cable is used, adjust the antenna trimmer for the best reception of a weak AM station around 1400kc; the trimmer is located behind or above the tuning knob or in the radio case near the antenna lead. On tape player radios, it is in the cartridge slot.

Removal and Installation

MATADOR AND AMBASSADOR THROUGH 1973
1. Disconnect the battery ground cable.
2. Disconnect the antenna, power, ground, and speaker wires from the radio.
3. Remove the radio bracket from the dash panel flange.
4. Remove the cluster overlay.
5. Remove the radio mounting screws and withdraw the radio.
Installation is the reverse of removal.

1974 AND LATER MATADOR AND AMBASSADOR
1. Disconnect the negative battery cable. Remove the knobs from the radio and unfasten the control shafts retaining nuts.
2. Remove the bezel securing screws, and remove the bezel.
3. Loosen, but do not remove, the upper radio securing screw.
4. Raise the rear of the radio to separate its bracket from the upper securing screw.
5. Pull the radio forward slightly, and

disconnect all of the leads from it. Remove the radio.
Radio installation is performed in the reverse order of removal. Adjust the antenna trimmer.

HORNET, GREMLIN, CONCORD
1. Disconnect the battery ground cable. Remove the package tray.
2. Remove the ash tray and bracket.
3. Pull off the radio knobs and remove shaft retaining nuts.
4. Remove the bezel retaining screws and remove the bezel. On 1978 and later models with A/C, remove the center housing of the instrument panel.
5. Disconnect the speaker, antenna, and power leads, and remove the radio.
Installation is the reverse of removal.

JAVELIN
1. Disconnect the battery ground lead.
2. Remove the upper crash pad retaining screws, which are located next to the windshield.
3. Open the passenger-side door and remove the two panel securing screws from the door pillar area.
4. Remove the five securing screws from the upper flange of the instrument cluster bezel.
5. Remove the molding attaching screws and the passenger assist handle.
6. Remove the map light to gain access to the crash pad mounting stud which is located behind it. Remove the nut from the stud.
7. Remove the entire crash pad assembly.
8. Remove the three speaker mounting plate screws. Remove the speaker.
9. Slide the radio rearward and lift it up, in order to disconnect the speaker and light bulb leads.
10. Disconnect the radio power lead at the fuse block. Tie a string to the power lead, to aid in pulling it back through to the fuse block during assembly.
11. Remove the radio, complete with power lead.
Installation is the reverse of removal. Be sure to install the upper radio attaching screws and the speaker bracket mounting bolts, as these are part of the ground system.

PACER
1. Disconnect the negative battery cable.
2. Remove the radio knobs, attaching nuts, cluster bezel, and overlay cover.
3. Loosen the radio-to-instrument panel attaching screw.
4. Lift the rear of the radio and pull forward slightly. Disconnect the electrical connections and the antenna and remove the radio.
5. Install in the reverse order of removal.

HEATER

NOTE: *It is recommended, unless you are trained in air conditioning servicing procedures, that you not disconnect any of the air conditioning refrigerant lines.*

Heater Core Removal and Installation

MATADOR AND AMBASSADOR THROUGH 1973
1. Disconnect hoses from core and plug hoses and tubes. It will not be necessary to drain entire cooling system. On A/C equipped cars disconnect vacuum hoses at damper vacuum motor.
2. Remove lower blower housing attaching nuts and washers in engine compartment.
3. Remove glove compartment door and glove compartment.
4. Remove remaining heater housing screws in passenger compartment, and remove core and housing as an assembly.
5. Slide core from housing.
6. Install in reverse order of above.

1974 MATADOR AND AMBASSADOR
1. Drain about two quarts of coolant from the cooling system.
2. Disconnect and plug the hoses which run to the heater core tubes in the engine compartment.
3. Disconnect the cable from the negative (−) battery terminal.
4. Remove the instrument panel lower finish panel and the glove compartment as follows:
   a. Remove the screws which secure the instrument cluster bezel and remove the bezel.
   b. Remove the screws from the lower glove compartment opening, which secure the crash padding.
   c. On cars without A/C, remove the mounting screws and remove the fresh air vent cable assemblies from the left and right sides of the lower panel.
   d. On models with an optional inside hood release, remove the screws retaining its cable assembly to the lower panel and remove the assembly.
   e. Remove the lower finish panel-to-bracket retaining screws.
   f. Pull the panel down, disconnect any electrical connections, and remove the panel.
   g. Working from underneath the instrument panel, remove the nuts securing the glove compartment door hinge, and remove the door and hinge as assembly.
   h. Remove the fuse panel retaining screws, disconnect the electrical leads (mark them for installation first), and lift out the fuse panel.

i. Remove the sheet metal screws which secure the glove compartment liner and remove the liner.
5. Disconnect the air blend door cable at the heater core housing.
6. On cars equipped with A/C, remove the hoses from the vacuum motors.
7. Remove the screws which secure the heater core housing. On models without A/C, unfasten the fresh air door cable.
8. Remove the housing and core as an assembly. Separate the core from the housing, as necessary.

Installation is the reverse of removal. Adjust the cable on the air blend door for proper operation. Refill the cooling system to capacity.

1975 AND LATER MATADOR

1. Disconnect the negative battery cable.
2. Drain about 2 quarts of coolant from the cooling system.
3. Disconnect the heater hoses from the heater core in the engine compartment and plug the core tubes.
4. On air conditioned cars, disconnect the blend-air damper cable at the heater core housing and remove the fuse panel. On non-A/C cars, disconnect the blend-air damper door and fresh air door cables.
5. Remove the lower instrument finish panel and remove the glove box door and liner.
6. Remove the right windshield pillar and corner finish mouldings for access to the upper right heater core housing mounting screws.
7. On air conditioned cars, remove the vacuum motor hoses.
8. Remove the remaining heater core housing attaching screws.
9. On air conditioned cars, remove the capscrew retaining the instrument panel to the right body pillar. Pull the right side of the instrument panel slightly rearward.
10. Remove the heater core housing and heater core. Remove the heater core from the housing.
11. Install the heater core and housing in the reverse order of removal.

JAVELIN

1. Drain 2 qts. of coolant from system.
2. Disconnect hoses from heater core tubes in engine compartment. Install corks in hoses and tubes.
3. Disconnect blower motor wires.
4. Remove housing attaching nuts at blower motor opening in dash.
5. Remove the instrument panel top cover, the right side mouldings, the assist handle, the lower right finish panel, and the right hand support brace for the instrument panel.
6. Disconnect air and defroster cables from damper levers.
7. Remove assembly.
8. Remove the core, defroster, and blower housing assembly from the car.

9. Remove the core from the housing assembly.

Installation is the reverse of removal.

GREMLIN, HORNET, CONCORD

1. Disconnect the negative battery cable and drain 2 qts. of coolant.
2. Disconnect heater hoses and plug hoses and core fittings.
3. Disconnect blower wires and remove motor and fan assembly.
4. On 1975 and later models, remove the housing attaching nut from the stud in the engine compartment.
5. Remove package shelf, if so equipped.
6. Disconnect wire at resistor, located below glove box.
7. Remove instrument panel center bezel, air outlet and duct, on A/C models.
8. Disconnect air and defroster cables from damper levers.
9. Remove right-side windshield pillar molding, the instrument panel upper sheet metal screws and the capscrew at the right door post.
10. Remove the right cowl trim panel and door sill plate on 1975 and later models.
11. Remove right kick panel and heater housing attaching screws.
12. Pull right side of instrument panel outward slightly and remove housing.
13. Remove core, defroster and blower housing.
14. Remove core from housing.

Installation is the reverse of removal.

PACER

1. Drain about two quarts of coolant from the radiator.
2. Disconnect the heater hoses from the heater core tubes and install plugs in the heater hoses and core tubes.
3. Remove the vacuum hoses from the heater core housing cover clip and move the lines aside. With A/C, disconnect the outside air door vacuum hose from the vacuum motor.
4. Remove the heater core housing cover screws.
5. Disconnect the overcenter spring from the cover and remove the cover.
6. Remove the heater core-to-housing attaching screws and remove the heater core.
7. Install the heater core in the reverse order of removal.

Heater Blower Removal and Installation

MATADOR AND AMBASSADOR THROUGH 1973

1. Remove water valve from blower housing. It is not necessary to disconnect hoses and control cable.
2. Remove nuts, washers and screws attaching blower housing to dash

panel in engine compartment.
3. Remove motor and fan, then separate fan from motor.
4. Install in reverse of above.

JAVELIN, HORNET, GREMLIN, CONCORD

1. Disconnect blower wires.
2. Remove retaining nut for cover and remove motor and fan assembly.
3. To install, reverse removal procedure.

1974 AND LATER MATADOR AND AMBASSADOR

1. Working from the engine compartment side of the firewall, disconnect the blower motor leads. Remove the motor cooling hose, if equipped.
2. Remove the screws which secure the blower motor mounting plate to the blower motor housing.
3. Remove the motor, mounting plate, and fan as an assembly.

Installation is the reverse of removal.

PACER WITHOUT A/C

1. Disconnect the negative battery cable.
2. Remove the right side windshield finish moulding.
3. Remove the instrument panel crash pad.
4. Remove the right scuff plate and cowl trim panel.
5. Remove the lower instrument panel-to-right A-pillar attaching screws.
6. Pull the instrument panel to the rear and replace the lower attaching screw in the right A-pillar. Allow the instrument panel to rest on the screw.
7. Remove the heater core housing attaching nuts and screw.
8. Remove the vacuum hoses from the heater core housing clip and set the lines aside.
9. Disconnect the blend-air door cable from the heater core housing.
10. Pull the heater core housing forward and set atop the upper control arm.
11. Remove the blower motor ground wire. Remove the blower motor housing attaching screw.
12. Disconnect the wires at the blower motor resistor.
13. Remove the blower motor housing brace.
14. Loosen the heater housing-to-dash panel attaching nuts.
15. Pull the blower housing to the rear and downward.
16. Disconnect the vacuum hoses from the vacuum motors.
17. Remove the blower housing.
18. Remove the blower housing cover.
19. Disconnect the white blower wire inside the housing.
20. Remove the blower motor mounting plate-to-housing screws and remove the blower motor assembly.

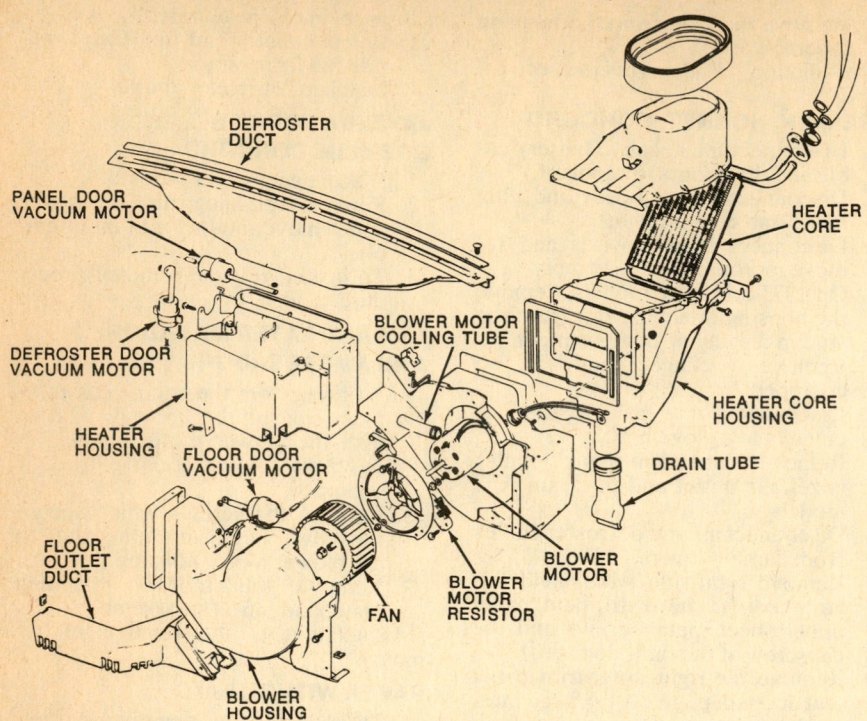

Pacer heater assembly (without air conditioning) (© American Motors Corp.)

21. Remove the blower fan from the motor shaft and remove the mounting plate from the motor housing.
22. Install the blower motor in the reverse order of removal.

PACER WITH A/C

1. Disconnect the negative battery cable.
2. Remove the right scuff plate and cowl trim panel.
3. Remove the radio overlay cover.
4. Remove the instrument panel crash pad.
5. Remove the instrument panel-to-right A-pillar attaching screws.
6. Remove the two upper instrument panel-to-lower instrument panel attaching screws above the glove box.
7. Disconnect the blend-air door cable from the heater core housing.
8. Remove the housing brace-to-floorpan screw.
9. Disconnect the wire at the blower motor resistor.
10. Disconnect the vacuum hoses from the vacuum motors.
11. Remove the heater core housing attaching nuts and screw.
12. Remove the vacuum hoses from the housing clip and set the lines aside.
13. Pull the heater core housing forward and set it atop the upper control arm.
14. Remove the floor outlet duct.
15. Disconnect the wires from the blower motor relay.
16. Remove the blower housing attaching screw located in the engine compartment on the firewall.
17. Loosen the evaporator housing-to-firewall panel attaching nuts.
18. Remove the blower housing to firewall attaching screw.
19. Pull the blower housing to the rear and downward.
20. Pull the right side of the instrument panel to the rear and remove the blower housing from under the panel.
21. Remove the floor door vacuum motor attaching screws and motor to gain access to the blower housing cover attaching screws.
22. Remove the blower housing cover attaching screws and remove the cover.
23. Remove the blower motor mounting plate and remove the blower motor assembly.
24. Remove the blower fan from the motor shaft and the mounting plate from the body of the motor.
25. Install the motor in the reverse order of removal.

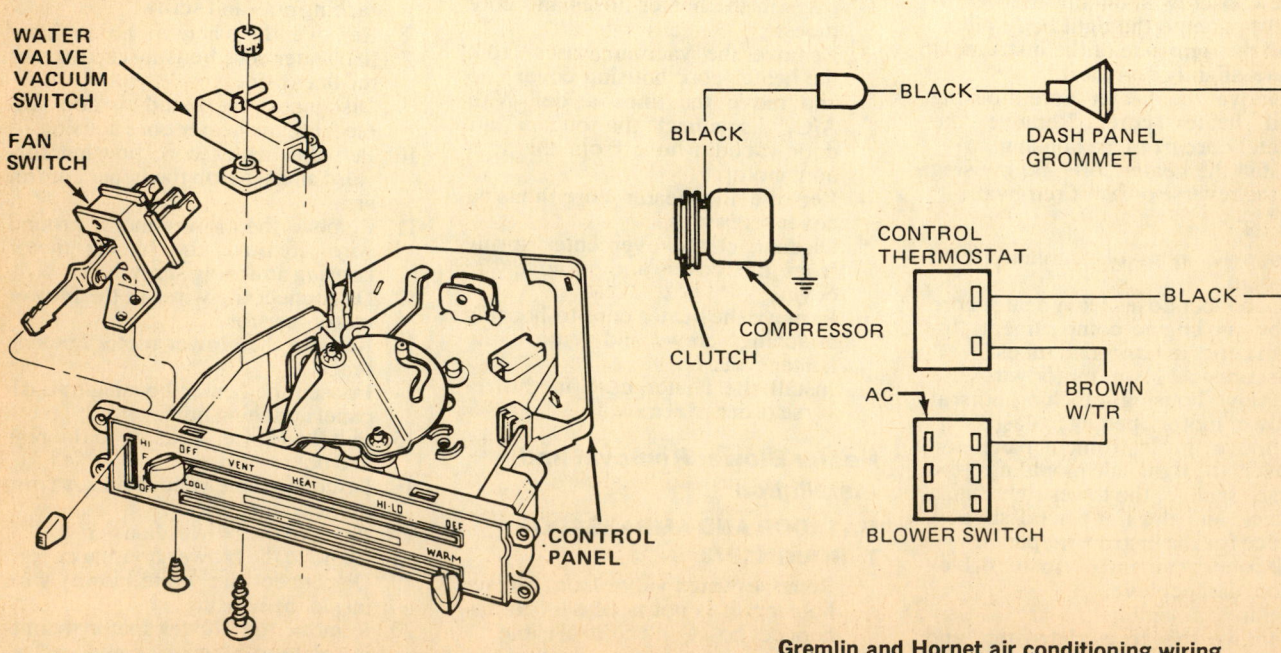

Pacer heater control panel (© American Motors Corp.)

Gremlin and Hornet air conditioning wiring
(© American Motors Corp.)

Astre · Firebird · Grand Am · GTO · Le Mans · Tempest · Ventura · Sunbird · Phoenix

Index

Astre • Firebird • Grand Am • GTO • Le Mans

YEAR IDENTIFICATION

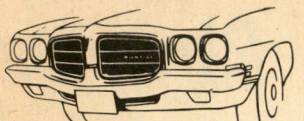
1972 Tempest

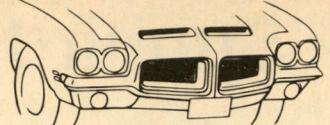
1972 GTO

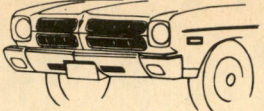
1971-72 Ventura II

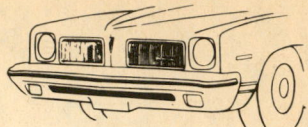
1973 LeMans

1973 Firebird

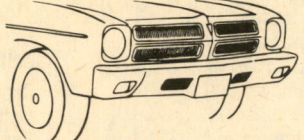
1973 Ventura II

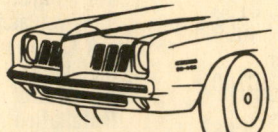
1973 Grand Am

1974 Firebird

1974 Ventura

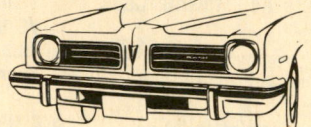
1974 LeMans

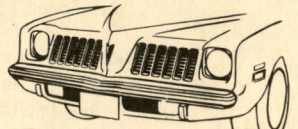
1974 Grand Am

1975-76 Astre

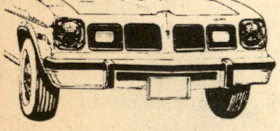
1975 Ventura

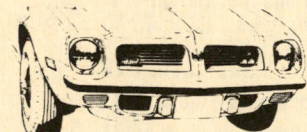
1975 Firebird

1975 Grand Am

1975 Grand LeMans

1976 Ventura

1976 Firebird

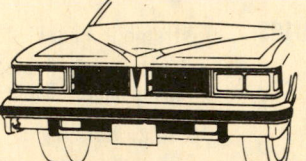
1976 LeMans

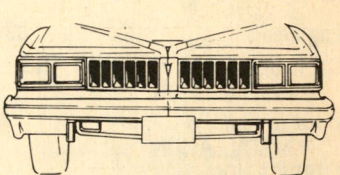
1977 LeMans

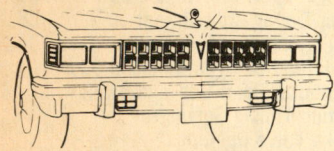
1977 Grand LeMans

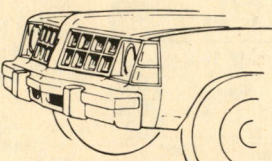
1977 Ventura

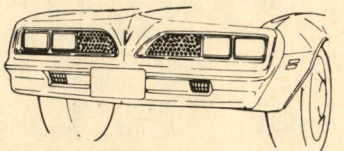
1977 Firebird

1977 Astre

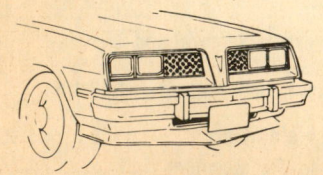
1977 Sunbird

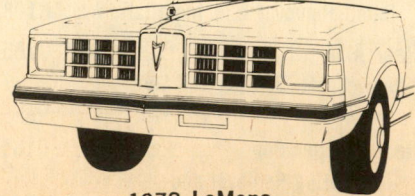
1978 LeMans

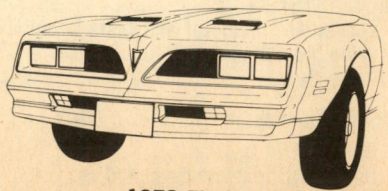
1978 Firebird

YEAR IDENTIFICATION

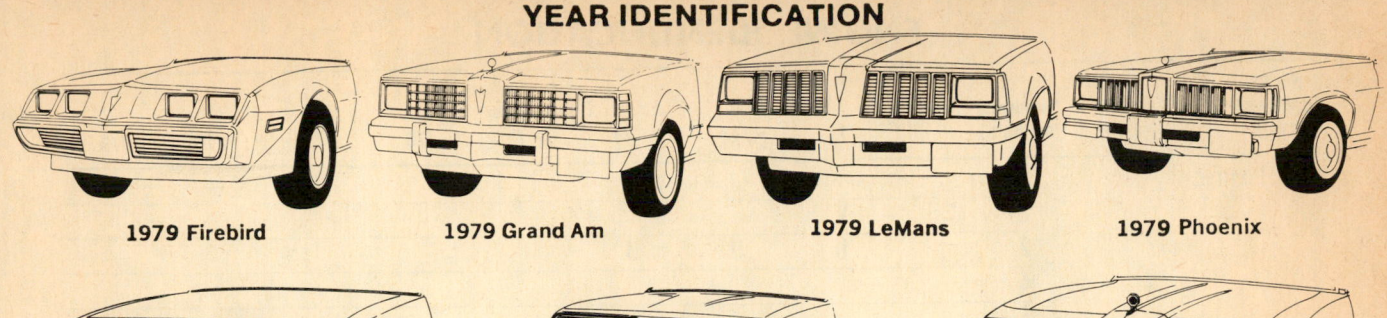

1979 Firebird   1979 Grand Am   1979 LeMans   1979 Phoenix

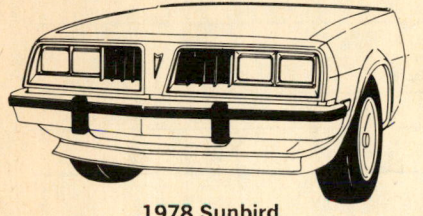

1978 Sunbird   1979 Sunbird   1978 Phoenix

ENGINE IDENTIFICATION

The engine code designation is the 5th digit of the vehicle identification number (V.I.N.). The V.I.N. is stamped on a plate located at the left side of the instrument panel visible through the windshield on all models.

No. Cyl. Displacement (cu. in.)	Carburetor (no. Bbls.)	'72	'73	'74	'75	'76	'77	'78	'79
4-140 Chev.	1				A	A			
	2				B	B	B		
4-151 Pontiac	2						V	V	V
6-231 Buick	2					C	C	A	A
6-250 Chev.	1	D	D	D	D	D			
8-260 Olds.	2				F	F			
8-301 Pontiac	2						Y	Y	Y
8-301 Pontiac	4							W	W
8-305 Chev.	2						U	U	G
8-305 Chev	4							H	H
8-307 Chev.	2	F	F						
8-350 Buick	2				H	H			
	4				J	J			
8-350 Chev.	4						L	L	L
8-350 Olds.	4						R		
8-350 Pontiac	2	N	N	N					
	2	M	M	M	M	M			
	4			A					
	4			B					
	4				E				
	4					P	P		
8-400 Pontiac	2								
	2	R	R	R	R				
	2	P	P	P					
	2					N			
	4								
	4	S	S	S	S				
	4	T	T	T					
	4					Z	Z	Z	Z
8-403 Olds.	4						K	K	K

ENGINE IDENTIFICATION

No. Cyl. Displacement (cu. in.)	Carburetor (no. Bbls.)	'72	'73	'74	'75	'76	'77	'78	'79
8-455 Pontiac	2								
	2	V							
	2	U	U	U					
	4								
	4								
	4	W	W	W	W	W			
	4	Y	Y	Y					
	4	X	X	X					

GENERAL ENGINE SPECIFICATIONS

Year	Engine No. Cyl. Displacement Cu. In.	Carburetor Type	Horsepower @ rpm ■	Torque @ rpm (ft lbs) ■	Bore x Stroke (In.)	Compression Ratio	Oil Pressure @ 2000 rpm
'72	6-250 Chev.	1 bbl	110 @ 3800	185 @ 1600	3.8750 x 3.530	8.5:1	40①
	8-307 Chev.	2 bbl	130 @ 4400	230 @ 2400	3.8750 x 3.250	8.5:1	40①
	8-350 Pont.	2 bbl	160 @ 4400	270 @ 2000	3.8762 x 3.750	8.2:1	35
	8-400 Pont.	2 bbl	175 @ 4000	310 @ 2400	4.1212 x 3.750	8.2:1	35
	8-400 Pont.	4 bbl	200 @ 4000	295 @ 2800	4.1212 x 3.750	8.2:1	35
	8-400 Pont.	4 bbl	250 @ 4400	325 @ 3200	4.1212 x 3.750	8.2:1	35
	8-455 Pont.	4 bbl	250 @ 3600	375 @ 2400	4.1522 x 4.210	8.2:1	35
	8-455 Pont.	4 bbl	300 @ 4000	415 @ 3200	4.1522 x 4.210	8.4:1	35
'73	6-250 Chev.	1 bbl	100 @ 3600	175 @ 1600	3.8750 x 3.530	8.2:1	50-65①
	8-350 SE Pont.	2 bbl	150 @ 4000	270 @ 2000	3.8762 x 3.750	7.6:1	55-60④
	8-350 DE Pont.	2 bbl	175 @ 4400	280 @ 2400	3.8782 x 3.750	7.6:1	55-60④
	8-400 SE Pont.	2 bbl	170 @ 3600	320 @ 2000	4.1212 x 3.750	8.0:1	55-60④
	8-400 DE Pont.	2 bbl	185 @ 4000	320 @ 2400	4.1212 x 3.750	8.0:1	55-60④
	8-400 DE Pont.	4 bbl	230 @ 4400	325 @ 3200	4.1212 x 3.750	8.0:1	55-60④
	8-455 DE Pont.	4 bbl	250 @ 4000	370 @ 2800	4.1522 x 4.210	8.0:1	55-60④
	8-455S.D. DE Pont.	4 bbl	310 @ 4000	390 @ 3600	4.1522 x 4.210	8.4:1	75-80④
'74	6-250 Chev.	1 bbl	100 @ 3600	175 @ 1600	3.8750 x 3.530	8.2:1	36-41①
	8-350 SE Pont.	2 bbl	155 @ 4000	275 @ 2400	3.8762 x 3.750	7.6:1	55-60④
	8-350 DE Pont.	2 bbl	170 @ 4400	290 @ 2400	3.8762 x 3.750	7.6:1	55-60④
	8-350 SE Pont.	4 bbl	170 @ 4000	280 @ 2000	3.8762 x 3.750	7.6:1	55-60④
	8-350 DE Pont.	4 bbl	200 @ 4000	295 @ 2800	3.8762 x 3.750	7.6:1	55-60④
	8-400 SE Pont.	2 bbl	175 @ 3600	315 @ 2000	4.1212 x 3.750	8.0:1	55-60④
	8-400 DE Pont.	2 bbl	190 @ 4000	330 @ 2400	4.1212 x 3.750	8.0:1	55-60④
	8-400 DE Pont.	4 bbl	225 @ 4000	330 @ 2800	4.1212 x 3.750	8.0:1	55-60④
	8-455 SE Pont.	4 bbl	215 @ 3600	355 @ 2400	4.1522 x 4.210	8.0:1	55-60④
	8-455 DE Pont.	4 bbl	250 @ 4000	380 @ 2800	4.1522 x 4.210	8.0:1	55-60④
	8-455S.D. DE Pont.	4 bbl	290 @ 4000	395 @ 3200	4.1522 x 4.210	8.4:1	75-80④
'75	4-140 OHC Chev.	1 bbl	78 @ 4200	120 @ 2000	3.501 x 3.625	8.0:1	40⑤
	4-140 OHC Chev.	2 bbl	87 @ 4400	122 @ 2800	3.501 x 3.625	8.0:1	40⑤
	6-250 Chev.	1 bbl	100 @ 3600	175 @ 1600	3.8750 x 3.530	8.5:1	36-41①
	8-260 Olds.	2 bbl	110 @ 3400	205 @ 1600	3.500 x 3.385	7.5:1	30-45③

GENERAL ENGINE SPECIFICATIONS

Year	Engine No. Cyl. Displacement Cu. In.	Carburetor Type	Horsepower @ rpm ■	Torque @ rpm (ft lbs) ■	Bore x Stroke (in.)	Compression Ratio	Oil Pressure @ 2000 rpm
'75	8-350 Pont.	2 bbl	155 @ 4000	275 @ 2400	3.8762 x 3.750	8.0:1	55-60④
	8-350 Pont.	4 bbl	170 @ 4000	280 @ 2000	3.8762 x 3.750	8.0:1	55-60④
	8-350 Ventura Buick	2 bbl	145 @ 3200	270 @ 2000	3.800 x 3.850	8.0:1	37⑥
	8-350 Ventura Buick	4 bbl	165 @ 3800	260 @ 2200	3.800 x 3.850	8.0:1	37⑥
	8-400 Pont.	2 bbl	175 @ 3600	315 @ 2000	4.1212 x 3.750	8.0:1	55-60④
	8-400 Pont.	4 bbl	210 @ 4000	315 @ 2800	4.1212 x 3.750	8.0:1	55-60④
	8-455 Pont.	4 bbl	215 @ 3600	355 @ 2400	4.1522 x 4.210	8.0:1	55-60④
'76	4-140 OHC Chev.	1 bbl	69 @ 4000	113 @ 2400	3.501 x 3.625	7.9:1	40⑤
	4-140 OHC Chev.	2 bbl	87 @ 4400	122 @ 2800	3.501 x 3.625	7.9:1	40⑤
	6-231 Buick	2 bbl	110 @ 4000	175 @ 2000	3.800 x 3.400	8.0:1	40⑤
	6-250 Chev.	1 bbl	100 @ 3600	175 @ 1600	3.875 x 3.530	8.3:1	36-41
	8-260 Olds	2 bbl	110 @ 3400	205 @ 1800	3.500 x 3.385	7.5:1	30-45④
	8-350 Ventura Buick	2 bbl	135 @ 3200	280 @ 1600	3.800 x 3.850	8.0:1	37⑥
	8-350 Ventura Buick	4 bbl	155 @ 3800	280 @ 1400	3.800 x 3.850	8.0:1	37⑥
	8-350 Pont.	2 bbl	155 @ 4000	280 @ 2000	3.876 x 3.750	7.6:1	55-60④
	8-350 Pont.	4 bbl	175 @ 4000	280 @ 2000	3.876 x 3.750	7.6:1	55-60④
	8-400 Pont.	2 bbl	170 @ 4000	305 @ 2000	4.121 x 3.750	7.6:1	55-60④
	8-400 Pont.	4 bbl	185 @ 3600	310 @ 1600	4.121 x 3.750	7.6:1	55-60④
	8-455 Pont.	4 bbl	200 @ 3500	330 @ 2000	4.152 x 4.210	7.6:1	55-60④
'77	4-140 OHC Chev.	2 bbl	87 @ 4400	122 @ 2800	3.501 x 3.625	7.9:1	40⑤
	4-151 Pont.	2 bbl	87 @ 4400	128 @ 2400	4.000 x 3.000	8.3:1	36-41
	6-231 Buick	2 bbl	105 @ 3200	185 @ 2000	3.800 x 3.400	8.0:1	40⑤
	8-301 Pont.	2 bbl	135 @ 4000	250 @ 1600	4.000 x 3.000	8.2:1	35-40⑥
	8-305 Chev.	2 bbl	145 @ 3800	245 @ 2400	3.736 x 3.480	8.5:1	32-40
	8-350 Olds.	4 bbl	170 @ 3800	275 @ 2000	4.057 x 3.385	8.0:1	32-40
	8-350 Chev.	4 bbl	170 @ 3800	270 @ 2400	4.000 x 3.480	8.5:1	30-45⑥
	8-350 Pont.	4 bbl	170 @ 4000	275 @ 1800	3.876 x 3.750	7.6:1	30-45⑥
	8-400 Pont.	4 bbl	180 @ 3600	325 @ 1600	4.121 x 3.750	7.6:1	35-40⑥
	8-403 Olds.	4 bbl	185 @ 3600	320 @ 2200	4.351 x 3.385	8.0:1	35-40⑥
'78	4-151 Pont.	2 bbl	87 @ 4400	128 @ 2400	4.000 x 3.000	8.3:1	36-41
	6-231 Buick	2 bbl	105 @ 3200	185 @ 2000	3.800 x 3.400	8.0:1	37④
	8-301 Pont.	2 bbl	135 @ 4000	250 @ 1600	4.000 x 3.000	8.2:1	35-40④
	8-301 Pont.	4 bbl	150 @ 4000	265 @ 1600	4.000 x 3.000	8.2:1	35-40④
	8-305 Chev.	2 bbl	145 @ 3800	245 @ 2400	3.736 x 3.480	8.4:1	32-40
	8-305 Chev.	4 bbl	155 @ 3800	260 @ 2400	3.736 x 3.480	8.4:1	32-40
	8-350 Chev.	4 bbl	170 @ 3800	270 @ 2400	4.000 x 3.480	8.2:1	30-45⑥
	8-400 Pont.	4 bbl	180 @ 3600	325 @ 1600	4.120 x 3.750	7.7:1	35-40④
	8-400 TA Pont.	4 bbl	188 @ 4000	340 @ 1700	4.120 x 3.750	8.1:1	35-40④
	8-403 Olds.	4 bbl	180 @ 3400	315 @ 2200	4.351 x 3.385	7.9:1	30-45③
'79	4-151 Pont.	2 bbl	85 @ 4400	123 @ 2800	4.000 x 3.000	8.3:1	36-41
	6-231 Buick	2 bbl	115 @ 3200	185 @ 2000	3.800 x 3.400	8.0:1	37
	8-301 Pont.	2 bbl	140 @ 3600	235 @ 2000	4.000 x 3.000	8.1:1	35-40
	8-301 Pont.	4 bbl	150 @ 4000	240 @ 2000	4.000 x 3.000	8.1:1	35-40

GENERAL ENGINE SPECIFICATIONS

Year	Engine No. Cyl. Displacement Cu. In.	Carburetor Type	Horsepower @ rpm ■	Torque @ rpm (ft lbs) ■	Bore x Stroke (in.)	Compression Ratio	Oil Pressure @ 2000 rpm
'79	8-305 Chev.	2 bbl	145 @ 4000	265 @ 2000	3.736 x 3.480	8.5:1	40
	8-305 Chev.	4 bbl	160 @ 4400	304 @ 2200	3.736 x 3.480	8.5:1	40
	8-400 Pont.	4 bbl	220 @ 4000	320 @ 2800	4.120 x 3.750	8.1:1	55-60
	8-403 Olds.	4 bbl	185 @ 3600	320 @ 2000	4.351 x 3.385	7.9:1	30-45

■ Beginning 1972 horsepower and torque are SAE net figures. They are measured at the rear of the transmission with all accessories installed and operating. Since the figures vary when a given engine is installed in different models, some are representative, rather than exact.

① Oil pressure at 2000 rpm
② For vehicles equipped with automatic transmissions, compression ratio is 10.0:1

③ Oil pressure at 1500 rpm
④ Oil Pressure above 2600 rpm
⑤ Pressure at 1000 rpm
⑥ Pressure at 2400 rpm
HO High Output
OHC Overhead Cam
SE Single Exhaust
DE Dual Exhaust

GTO through 1973, LeMans, Grand Am

TUNE-UP SPECIFICATIONS

When analyzing compression test results, look for uniformity among cylinders rather than specific pressures.

Year	ENGINE No. Cyl Displacement (cu in.)	hp	SPARK PLUGS Orig. Type	Gap (in.)	DISTRIBUTOR Point Dwell (deg)	Point Gap (in.)	IGNITION TIMING (deg) ▲ Man Trans •	Auto Trans	VALVES Intake Opens ■ (deg)	Fuel Pump Pressure (psi)	IDLE SPEED • (rpm) ▲ Man Trans	Auto Trans
'72	6-250 Chev.	110	R-45T	.035	32½	.019	4B	4B	16	4-5	700/450①	600/450①
	8-350 Pont.	160	R-46TS	.035	30	.016	8B	10B	26/30③	5-6½	800	625
	8-400 Pont.	175	R-46TS	.035	30	.016	—	10B	23/26③	5-6½	—	625
	8-400 Pont.	200	R-46TS	.035	30	.016	8B	10B	23	5-6½	1000/600①	700/500①
	8-455 Pont.	250	R-45TS	.035	30	.016	—	10B	23	5-6½	—	650/500①
	8-455 Pont.	300	R-45TS	.035	—	—	8B	10B	31	5-6½	1000/600①	700/500①
'73	6-250 Chev.	100	R-46T	.035	32½	.019	6B	6B	16	4-5	700/450①	600
	8-350 SE Pont.	150	R-46TS	.040	30	.016	10B	12B	26/30③	5-6½	900/600①	650
	8-350 DE Pont.	175	R-46TS	.040	30	.016	10B	12B	26/30③	5-6½	900/600①	650
	8-400 SE Pont.	170	R-46TS	.040	30	.016	10B	12B	26	5-6½	—	650
	8-400 DE Pont.	185	R-46TS	.040	30	.016	10B	12B	23/30③	5-6½	—	650
	8-400 DE Pont.	230	R-45TS	.040	30	.016	10B	12B	23/30③	5-6½	1000/600①	650
	8-455 DE Pont.	250	R-45TS	.040	30	.016	10B	12B	23	5-6½	—	650
	8-455 S.D. DE Pont.	310	R-44TS	.040	30	.016	10B	12B	42	5-6½	1000/600①	750/500①
'74	6-250 Chev.	all	R-46T	.035	32½	.019	6B	6B	16	4-5	850/450①	600/450①
	8-350 2 bbl Pont.	all	R-46TS	.040	30	.016	10B	12B(10B)	26	5-6½	900/600①	650(625)
	8-350 4 bbl Pont.	all	R-46TS	.040	30	.016	10B	12B(10B)	26	5-6½	1000/600	650(625)
	8-400 2 bbl Pont.	all	R-46TS	.040	30	.016	10B	12B(10B)	26	5-6½	—	650(625)
	8-400 4 bbl Pont.	all	R-45TS	.040	30	.016	10B	12B(10B)	23/30③	5-6½	1000/600①	650(625)
	8-455 Pont.	all	R-45TS	.040	30	.016	10B	12B(10B)	23	5-6½	—	650(625)
'75	6-250 Chev.	100	R-46TX	.060	Electronic		10B	10B	16	4-5	850	550(600)
	8-350 2 bbl Pont.	155	R-46TSX	.060	Electronic		—	16B	26	5-6½		600
	8-350 4 bbl Pont.	170	R-46TSX	.060	Electronic		—	16B(12)	26	5-6½	—	650(625)

TUNE-UP SPECIFICATIONS

GTO through 1973, LeMans, Grand Am

When analyzing compression test results, look for uniformity among cylinders rather than specific pressures.

Year	ENGINE No. Cyl Displacement (cu in.)	hp	SPARK PLUGS Orig. Type	Gap (in.)	DISTRIBUTOR Point Dwell (deg)	Point Gap (in.)	IGNITION TIMING (deg) ▲ Man Trans ●	Auto Trans	VALVES Intake Opens ■ (deg)	Fuel Pump Pressure (psi)	IDLE SPEED ● (rpm) ▲ Man Trans	Auto Trans
'75	8-400 2 bbl Pont.	175	R-46TSX	.060	Electronic		—	16B	26	5-6½	—	650
	8-400 4 bbl Pont.	210	R-45TSX	.060	Electronic		—	16B(12)	30	5-6½	—	650(600)
	8-455 4 bbl Pont.	215	R-45TSX	.060	Electronic		—	16B(10)	23	5-6½	—	650(675)
'76	6-250 Chev.	100	R-46TX	.035	Electronic		6B	10B	16	4½-5½	850	550④(600)
	8-260 Olds.	110	R-46SX	.080	Electronic		16B	18B⑤ (14B)	14	7-8½	750	550(600)
	8-350 Pont.	155	R46TSX	.060	Electronic		—	16B	22	7-8½	—	550
	8-350 Pont.	175	R45TSX	.060	Electronic		—	16B	26	7-8½	—	600
	8-400 Pont.	170	R46TSX	.060	Electronic		—	16B	26	7-8½	—	550
	8-400 Pont.	185	R46TSX	.060	Electronic		—	16B	30	7-8½	—	575
	8-455 Pont.	200	R45TSX	.060	Electronic		—	16B(12B)	23	7-8½	—	550(600)
'77	6-231 Buick	105	R-46TSX⑥	.060	Electronic		12B	12B	27	7-8½	800	600
	8-301 Pont.	135	R-46TSX	.060	Electronic		—	12B	17	4¼-5¾	—	550⑦
	8-350 Pont.	170	R-45TSX	.060	Electronic		—	16B	29	7-8½	—	575⑦
	8-350 Olds.	170	R-46SZ⑧	.080	Electronic		—	20B @ 1100	16	5½-6½	—	600⑨
	8-400 Pont.	180	R-45TSX	.060	Electronic		—	16B	29	7-8½	—	575⑦
	8-403 Olds.	180	R-46SZ	.080	Electronic		—	20B @ 1000	16	5½-6½	—	600⑨
'78	6-231 Buick	105	R-46TSX	.060	Electronic		15B	15B	27	7-8.5	800	670(600)
	8-301 Pont.	135	R-46TSX	.060	Electronic		—	12B	17	4.5-5.5	—	550
	8-301	150	R-45TSX	.060	Electronic		—	12B	17	4.5-5.5	—	550
	8-305 Chev.	145	R-45TS	.045	Electronic		—	⑩	29	4.5-5	—	⑪
	8-350 Chev.	170	R-45TS	.045	Electronic		—	8B	17	4-5	—	650
'79	6-231 Buick	115	R-46TSX	.060	Electronic		15B	15B	16	4.5-5.5	800	600
	8-301 Pont.	140	R-46TSX	.060	Electronic		—	12B	16	5.5-6.5	—	550
	8-301 Pont.	150	R-45TSX	.060	Electronic		12B	12B	16⑫	5.5-6.5	800	550
	8-305 Chev.	160	R-45TS,	.045	Electronic		—	4B	28	5.5-6.5	—	600
	8-350 Chev.	160	R-45TS	.045	Electronic		—	8B	28	5.5-6.5	—	600

SE Single Exhaust
DE Dual Exhaust
▲ See text for procedure
● Figure in parentheses indicates California engine
■ All figures are in degrees Before Top Dead Center. Where two figures appear, the first represents timing with manual transmission, the second with automatic transmission.
① Lower figure indicates idle speed with solenoid disconnected
③ Lower figure represents manual transmission models; higher figure indicates automatic transmission.
④ 575 w/air conditioning
⑤ Some early models may be 16B
⑥ High altitude and Calif.: R-45TSX
⑦ 650 w/AC on
⑧ High altitude: R-46SX

⑨ On AC equipped cars: 550 w/AC off; 640 w/AC on
⑩ Except California and High Altitude: 4B
   California: 6B
   High Altitude: 8B
⑪ Except California and High Altitude: 600
   California: 650
   High Altitude: 700
⑫ High performance: 27
B Before Top Dead Center
TDC Top Dead Center
— Not applicable

NOTE: The underhood specifications sticker often reflects tune-up specification changes made in production. Sticker figures must be used if they disagree with those in this chart.

Ventura, 1974 GTO, Astre, Sunbird, Phoenix

TUNE-UP SPECIFICATIONS

When analyzing compression test results, look for uniformity among cylinders rather than specific pressures.

Year	ENGINE		SPARK PLUGS		DISTRIBUTOR		IGNITION TIMING (deg) ▲		VALVES	Fuel Pump	IDLE SPEED • (rpm) ▲	
	No. Cyl Displacement (cu in.)	hp	Orig. Type	Gap (in.)	Point Dwell (deg)	Point Gap (in.)	Man Trans	Auto Trans	Intake Opens ■ (deg)	Pressure (psi)	Man Trans	Auto Trans
'72	6-250 Chev.	110	R-45T	.035	31-34	.019	4B	4B	16	4-5	700①/450	600①/450
	8-307 Chev.	130	R-45TS	.035	29-31	.019	4B	8B	28	5½-7½	900①/450	600①/450
	8-350 Pont.	160	R-46TS	.035	29-31	.019	10B	10B	16	5-6½	800	625
'73	6-250 Chev.	110	R-46T	.035	31-34	.019	6B	6B	16	4-5	700/450①	600
	8-350 SE Pont.	150	R-46TS	.040	29-31	.019	10B	12B	16	5-6½	900/600①	650
	8-350 DE Pont.	175	R-46TS	.040	29-31	.019	10B	12B	16	5-6½	900/600①	650
'74	6-250 Chev.	all	R-46T	.035	32½	.019	6B	6B	16	4-5	850/450①	600/450①
	8-350 2 bbl Pont.	all	R-46TS	.040	30	.019	10B	12B(10B)	26	5-6½	900/600①	650(625)
	8-350 4 bbl Pont.	all	R-46TS	.040	30	.019	10B	12B(10B)	26	5-6½	1000/600①	650(625)
'75	4-140 1 bbl Chev.	78	R-43TSX	.060	Electronic		8B	10B	22	3-4½	1000	750
	4-140 2 bbl Chev.	87	R-43TSX	.060⑥	Electronic		10B	12B	28	3-4½	1000	750
	6-250 Chev.	100	R-46TX	.060	Electronic		10B	10B	16	4-5	850	550(600)
	8-260 Olds.	110	R-46SX	.080	Electronic		16B	18B(16)	14	5-6½	—	600
	8-350 2 bbl Buick	145	R-45TSX	.060	Electronic		—	12B	19	5-6½	—	600
	8-350 4 bbl Buick	165	R-45TSX	.060	Electronic		—	12B	19	5-6½	—	650(625)
'76	4-140 Chev.	69	R-43TSX	.035	Electronic		8B	10B	22	3-4½	700	750
	4-140 Chev.	87	R-43TSX	.035	Electronic		8B	10B	28	3-4½	700	750
	V6-231 Buick	110	R-44SX	.060	Electronic		12B	12B	17	3-4½	800	600
	6-250 Chev.	100	R-46TX	.035	Electronic		6B	10B	10	4-5	850	550(600)
	8-260 Olds.	110	R-46SX	.080	Electronic		16B	18B⑤ (14B)	14	5-6½	750	550(600)
	8-350 Pont.	all	R-45TSX	.060	Electronic		—	12B	19	5-6½	—	600
'77	4-140 Chev.	87	R-43TS	.035	Electronic		10B	12B	34	3-4½	700	750
	4-151 Pont.	87	R-44TSX	.060	Electronic		14B	14B(12)	33	4-5½	1000	650
	6-231 Buick	105	R-46TSX②	.060	Electronic		12B	12B	17	3-4½③	800	600
	8-301 Pont.	135	R-46TSX	.060	Electronic		16B	12B	④	7-8.5	750⑦	550⑧
	8-305 Chev.	145	R-45TS	.045	Electronic		8B	8B(6)	28	7.5-9	800	600
	8-350 Chev.	170	R-45TS	.045	Electronic		8B	8B	28	7.5-9	800	600
	8-350 Olds.	170	R46SX	.080	Electronic		—	20B @ 1100⑨	16	5.5-6.5	—	600⑩
'78	4-151 Pont.	87	R-43TSX	.060	Electronic		14B	⑫	33	4-5.5	⑪	⑬
	6-231 Buick	105	R-46TSX	.060	Electronic		15B	15B	17	3-4.5	800	600
	8-305 Chev.	135	R-45TS	.045	Electronic		4B	6B⑭	29	4.5-5	700	⑮
	8-350 Chev.	170	R-45TS	.045	Electronic		—	8B	17	4-5	—	600
'79	4-151 Pont.	85	R-43TSX	.060	Electronic		12B(14B)	12B(14B)	33	5.0-6.5	1000	650
	6-231 Buick	115	R-46TSX	.060	Electronic		15B	15B	16	4.0-6.5	800	600
	8-305 Chev.	145	R-45TS	.045	Electronic		4B	4B	28	5.5-6.5	800	600
	8-350 Chev.	160	R-45TS	.045	Electronic		—	8B	28	5.5-6.5	—	600

SE Single Exhaust
DE Dual Exhaust
▲ See text for procedure
■ All figures Before Top Dead Center
  ① Lower figure indicates idle speed with solenoid disconnected
  ② High altitude and Calif.: R-45TSX
  ③ Ventura: 4¼-5¾
  ④ 31 manual, 27 automatic
  ⑤ Some Ventura's may be set at 16B
  ⑥ R-43TS at .035 if missing or hard starting.
  ⑦ 850 w/AC on
  ⑧ 650 w/AC on
  ⑨ At 1100 rpm
  ⑩ On air conditioned cars: 550 w/AC off
                       650 w/AC on
  ⑪ Sunbird with engine option code WH, WD: 1200 with air conditioning
                1000 without air conditioning

⑪ Sunbird with engine option code WB: 1000 with or without air conditioning
⑫ Sunbird except California: 12B
  Sunbird California: 14B
  Phoenix: 14B
⑬ Air conditioned models: 650
  Without air conditioning: 500
⑭ Sunbird high altitude: 8B
⑮ Sunbird and Phoenix with air conditioning, except Calif. and high alt.: 600
  Sunbird and Phoenix, high altitude: 700
  All others: 650
B Before Top Dead Center
• Figure in Parentheses for California
NOTE: The underhood specifications sticker often reflects tune-up specification changes made in production. Sticker figures must be used if they disagree with those in this chart.

Firebird   TUNE-UP SPECIFICATIONS

When analyzing compression test results, look for uniformity among cylinders rather than specific pressures.

Year	ENGINE No. Cyl Displacement (cu in.)	hp	SPARK PLUGS Orig. Type	Gap (in.)	DISTRIBUTOR Point Dwell (deg)	Point Gap (in.)	IGNITION TIMING (deg) ▲ Man Trans •	Auto Trans	VALVES Intake Opens ■ (deg)	Fuel Pump Pressure (psi)	IDLE SPEED • (rpm) ▲ Man Trans	Auto Trans
'72	6-250 Chev.	110	R-45T	.035	32½	.019	4B	4B	16	4-5	700①/450	600①/450
	8-350 Pont.	160	R-46TS	.035	30	.016	8B	10B	26/30④	5-6½	800	625
	8-400 Pont.	175	R-46TS	.035	30	.016	—	10B	23/26④	5-6½	—	625
	8-400 Pont.	250	R-45TS	.035	30	.016	8B	10B	23	5-6½	1000/600①	700/500①
	8-455 Pont.	300	R-45TS	.035	30	—	8B	10B	31	5-6½	1000/600①	700/500①
'73	6-250 Chev.	100	R-46T	.035	32½	.019	6B	6B	16	4-5	700/450	600/450
	8-350 SE Pont.	150	R-46TS	.040	30	.016	10B	12B	26/30④	5-6½	900/600①	1500/650
	8-350 DE Pont.	175	R-46TS	.040	30	.016	10B	12B	26/30④	5-6½	900/600①	650
	8-400 SE Pont.	170	R-46TS	.040	30	.016	10B	12B	26	5-6½	—	650
	8-400 DE Pont.	230	R-45TS	.040	30	.016	10B	12B	23/30④	5-6½	1000/600①	650
	8-455 DE Pont	250	R-45TS	.040	30	.016	10B	12B	23	5-6½	1000/600①	650
	8-455 S.D. DE Pont.	310	R-44TS	.040	30	.016	10B	12B	42	5-6½	1000/600①	750/500①
'74	6-250 Chev.	all	R-46T	.035	32½	.019	6B	6B	16	4-5	850/450①	600/450①
	8-350 2 bbl Pont.	all	R-46TS	.040	30	.016	10B	12B(10B)	26	5-6½	900/600①	650(625)
	8-350 4 bbl Pont.	all	R-46TS	.040	30	.016	10B	12B(10B)	26	5-6½	1000/600	650(625)
	8-400 2 bbl Pont.	all	R-46TS	.040	30	.016	10B	12B(10B)	26	5-6½	—	650(625)
	8-400 4 bbl Pont.	all	R-45TS	.040	30	.016	10B	12B(10B)	23/30④	5-6½	1000/600①	650(625)
	8-455 Pont.	all	R-45TS	.040	30	.016	10B	12B(10B)	23	5-6½	—	650(625)
	8-455 S.D. Pont.	290	R-45TS	.040	30	.016	10B	12B	38	5-6½	1000/600①	750/500①
'75	6-250 Chev.	100	R 46TX	.060	Electronic		10B	10B	16	4-5	850	550(600)
	8-350 2 bbl Pont.	155	R-46TSX	.060	Electronic		—	16B	26	5-6½	—	600

Firebird   TUNE-UP SPECIFICATIONS

When analyzing compression test results, look for uniformity among cylinders rather than specific pressures.

Year	ENGINE No. Cyl Displacement (cu in.)	hp	SPARK PLUGS Orig. Type	Gap (in.)	DISTRIBUTOR Point Dwell (deg)	Point Gap (in.)	IGNITION TIMING (deg) ▲ Man Trans ●	Auto Trans	VALVES Intake Opens ■ (deg)	Fuel Pump Pressure (psi)	IDLE SPEED ● (rpm) ▲ Man Trans	Auto Trans
'75	8-350 4 bbl Pont.	170	R-46TSX	.060	Electronic		12B	16B(12)	26	5-6½	775	650(625)
	8-400 4 bbl Pont.	210	R-45TSX	.060	Electronic		12B	16B(12)	30	5-6½	775	650(600)
	8-455 4 bbl Pont.	215	R-45TSX	.060	Electronic		16B	—	23	5-6½	675	
'76	6-250 Chev.	100	R46TX	.035	Electronic		6B	10B	16	4-5	850	550(600)
	8-350 Pont.	155	R-46TSX	.060	Electronic		—	16B	22	5-6½	—	550
	8-350 Pont.	175	R-45TSX	.060	Electronic		—	16B	26	5-6½	—	600
	8-400 Pont.	185	R-45TSX	.060	Electronic		12B	16B	30	5-6½	775	575
	8-455 Pont.	200	R-45TSX	.060	Electronic		12B	16B	23	5-6½	775	550(600)
'77	6-231 Buick	105	R-46TSX⑧	.060	Electronic		12B	12B	17	4½-5¾	800	600
	8-301 Pont.	135	R-46TSX	.060	Electronic		16B	12B	⑨	7-8½	800	550
	8-350 Pont.	170	R-45TSX	.060	Electronic		—	16B	29	7-8½	—	575
	8-350 Olds.	170	R-46SZ⑩	.080	Electronic		—	20B @ 1100	16	7-8½	—	575⑪
	8-400 Pont.	180	R-45TSX	.060	Electronic		18B	16B	⑫	7-8½	775	575⑪
	8-403 Olds.	185	R-46SZ⑩	.080	Electronic		—	20B @ 1200	16	5½-6½	—	600⑬
'78	6-231 Buick	105	R-46TSX	.060	Electronic		15B	15B	17	4.5-5.7	800	600
	8-305 Chev.	145	R-45TS	.045	Electronic		4B	4B(6B)	29	7-8.5	700	600(650)
	8-350 Chev.	170	R-45TS	.045	Electronic		6B	8B	17	4.5-5.7	700	500
	8-400 Pont.	180	R-45TSX	.060	Electronic		—	16B	29	7-8.5	—	650
	8-400 TA Pont.	188	R-45TSX	.060	Electronic		18B	18B	16	7-8.5	775	700
	8-403 Olds.	180	R-46SZ	.060	Electronic		—	20B	16	5.5-6.5	—	700(650)
'79	6-231 Buick	115	R-46TSX⑮	.06	Electronic		15B	15B	16	4.5-5.5	800	600
	8-301 Pont.	140	R-45TSX	.060	Electronic		—	12B	16	5.5-6.5	—	550
	8-301 Pont.	150	R-45TSX	.060	Electronic		12B	12B	16⑯	5.5-6.5	800	550
	8-305 Chev.	145	R-45TS	.045	Electronic		—	4B(6B)	28	5.5-6.5	—	600
	8-350 Chev.	160	R-45TS	.045	Electronic		—	8B	28	5.5-6.5	—	600
	8-400 Pont.	220	R-45TSX	.060	Electronic		18B	—	16	7.0-8.5	775	—
	8-403 Olds.	185	R-46SZ	.080	Electronic		—	20B @ 1100	16	5.5-6.5	—	550

SE Single Exhaust
DE Dual Exhaust
▲ See text for procedure
● Figure in parentheses indicates California engine
■ All figures are in degrees Before Top Dead Center. Where two figures appear, the first represents timing with manual transmission, the second with automatic transmission.
① Lower figure indicates idle speed with solenoid disconnected
④ Lower figure represents manual transmission models; higher figure indicates automatic transmission.
⑤ See engine compartment sticker
⑥ 31 with manual transmission
⑦ See underhood specifications sticker
⑧ High altitude and Calif.: R-45TSX
⑨ 31 manual, 27 automatic

⑩ High altitude: R-45SX
⑪ 650 rpm w/AC on
⑫ 21 manual, 29 automatic, 16 Trans Am
⑬ On Air Conditioned cars: 550 rpm w/AC off
                     650 rpm w/AC on
⑭ See the underhood specifications sticker
⑮ California: R45TSX
⑯ High performance: 27
B Before Top Dead Center
TDC Top Dead Center
— Not applicable
NOTE: The underhood specifications sticker often reflects tune-up specification changes made in production. Sticker figures must be used if they disagree with those in this chart.

NOTE: Most 1979 GM carburetors have idle mixture screws concealed by staked-in plugs. These are not meant to be removed, except at carburetor overhaul.

FIRING ORDER

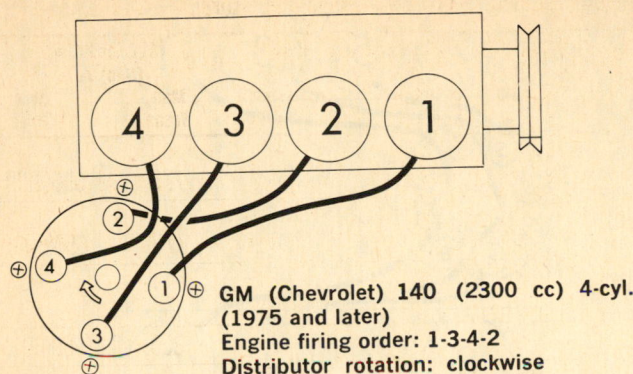

GM (Chevrolet) 140 (2300 cc) 4-cyl. (1975 and later)
Engine firing order: 1-3-4-2
Distributor rotation: clockwise

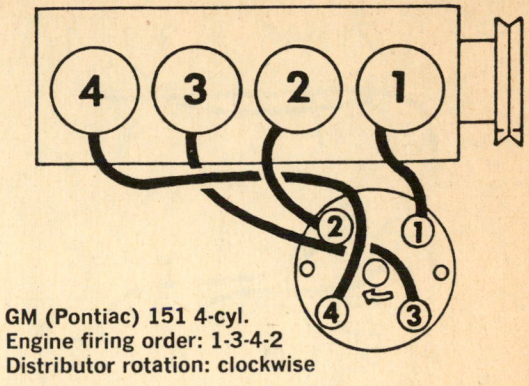

GM (Pontiac) 151 4-cyl.
Engine firing order: 1-3-4-2
Distributor rotation: clockwise

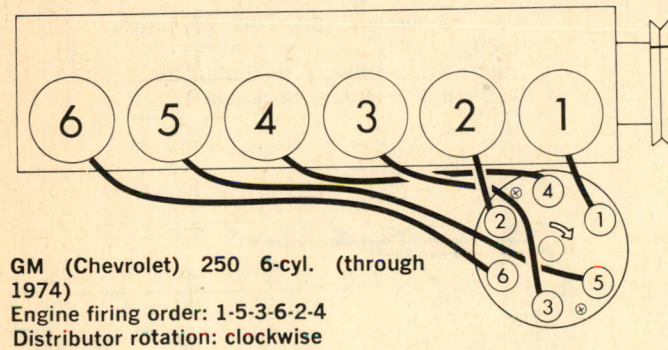

GM (Chevrolet) 250 6-cyl. (through 1974)
Engine firing order: 1-5-3-6-2-4
Distributor rotation: clockwise

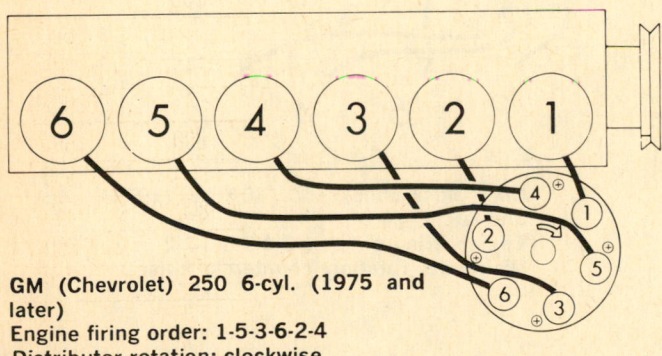

GM (Chevrolet) 250 6-cyl. (1975 and later)
Engine firing order: 1-5-3-6-2-4
Distributor rotation: clockwise

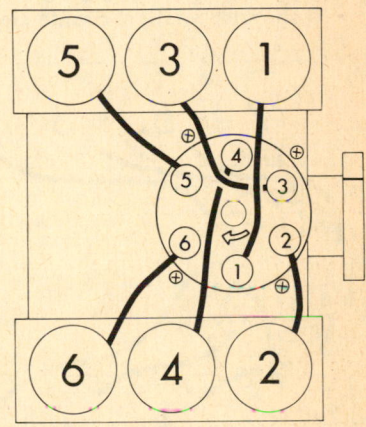

GM (Buick) 231 V6
Engine firing order: 1-6-5-4-3-2
Distributor rotation: clockwise

V6 harmonic balancers have two timing marks: one is 1/8 in. wide, and one is 1/16 in. wide. Use the 1/16 in. mark for timing with a hand held light. The 1/8 in. mark is used only with a magnetic timing pick-up probe.

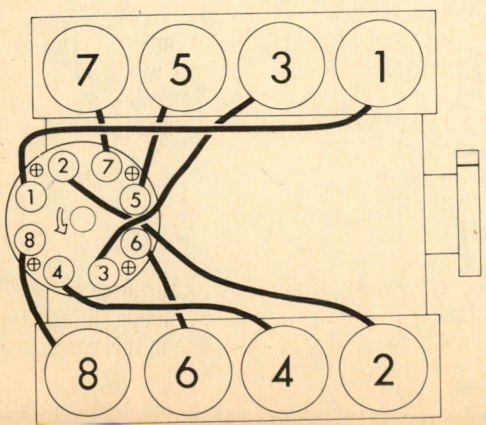

GM (Oldsmobile) 260 V8
Engine firing order: 1-8-4-3-6-5-7-2
Distributor rotation: counterclockwise

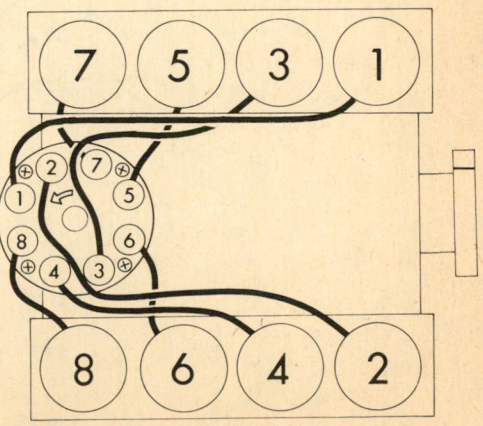

GM (Pontiac) 301, 350, 400, 455 V8 (1975 and later)
Engine firing order: 1-8-4-3-6-5-7-2
Distributor rotation: counterclockwise

FIRING ORDER

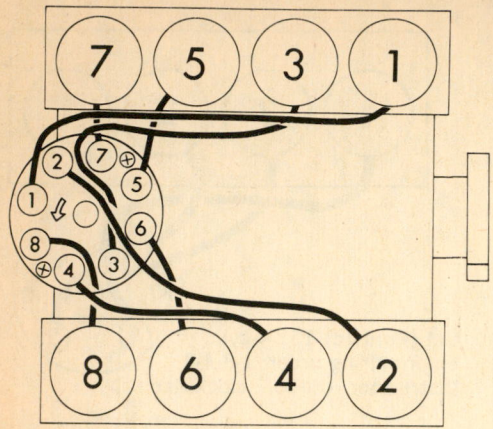

GM (Pontiac) 350, 400, 455 V8 (through 1974) exc. Ventura
Engine firing order: 1-8-4-3-6-5-7-2
Distributor rotation: counterclockwise

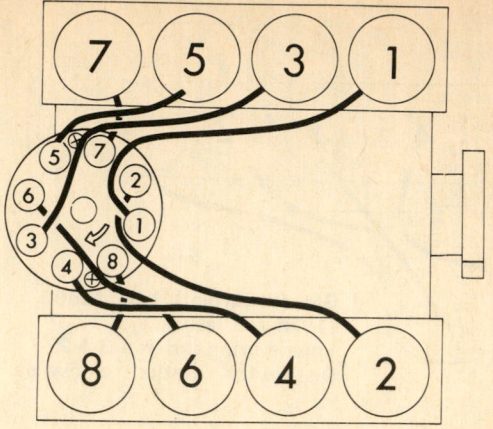

GM (Chevrolet) 307 V8 (Ventura through 1973)
Engine firing order: 1-8-4-3-6-5-7-2
Distributor rotation: clockwise

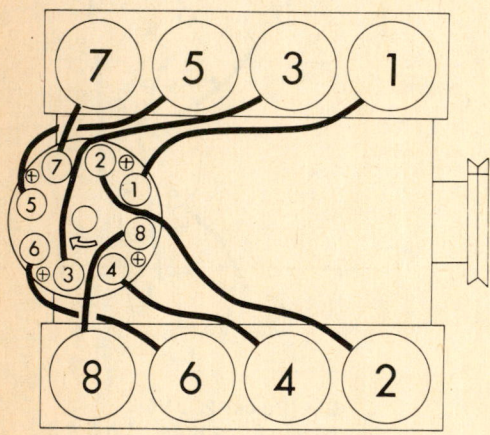

GM (Chevrolet) 305, 350 V8 (1975 and later)
Engine firing order: 1-8-4-3-6-5-7-2
Distributor rotation: clockwise

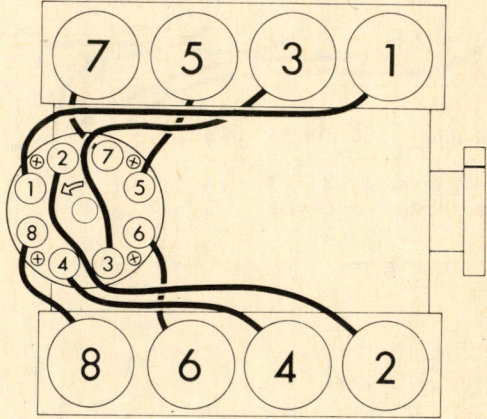

GM (Oldsmobile) 350, 403 V8 (1975 and later)
Engine firing order: 1-8-4-3-6-5-7-2
Distributor rotation: counterclockwise

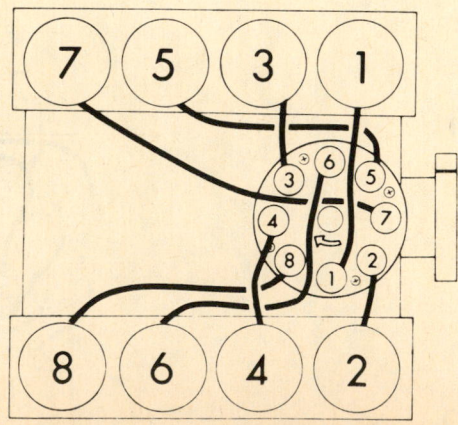

GM (Buick) 350 V8 (1975 and later)
Engine firing order: 1-8-4-3-6-5-7-2
Distributor rotation: clockwise

GTO
through 1973,
LeMans, Grand Am

CAPACITIES

Year	ENGINE No. Cyl. Displacement (Cu. In.)	Engine Crankcase Add 1 Qt For New Filter	TRANSMISSION Pts To Refill After Draining Manual 3-Speed	4/5 Speed	Automatic •	Drive Axle (pts)	Gasoline Tank (gals)	COOLING SYSTEM (qts) With Heater	With A/C			With Super-Cooling
'72	6-250 Chev.	4	3.5	—	6	3③	20①	13	12.4			—
	8-350 Pont.	5	3.5	2.5	6	3③	20①	20	20.5			—
	8-400 Pont.	5	2.8	2.5	7.5	3③	20①	18.6	20.8			—
	8-455 Pont.	5	—	2.5	7.5	3③	20①	17.9	19			—
'73	6-250 Chev.	4	3.5	—	7.5	4.25	21.8	13.3	—			—
	8-350 Pont.	5	3.5	2.5	7.5	4.25⑤	21.8⑥	22.0	23.1			—
	8-400 Pont.	5	2.8/3.5④	2.5	7.5	4.25⑤	21.8⑥⑦	22.0/23.0⑧	23.1/24.0⑧			—
	8-455 Pont.	5	—	2.5	7.5	4.25⑤	21.8⑦	21.1	22.2			—
'74	6-250 Chev.	4	3.5	—	7.5	4.25	21.8	13.3	—			—
	8-350 Pont.	5	2.8/3.5④	2.5	7.5	4.25⑤	21.8⑥	22.0	23.2			—
	8-400 Pont.	5	—	2.5	7.5	4.25⑤	21.8⑥⑦	22.0/23.0⑧	23.1/24.0⑧			—
	8-455 Pont.	5	—	—	7.5	4.25⑤	21.8⑦	21.2	21.3			—
'75-'76	6-250 Chev.	4	3.5	—	7.5	3	21.0	14.8	14.8			—
	8-260 Olds.	4	—	3.5	7.5	3	21.0	23.5	26			—
	8-350 Pont.	5	—	—	7.5⑩	3⑨	21.0⑥	21.8	21.8			—
	8-400 Pont.	5	—	—	7.5⑩	3⑨	21.0⑥⑦	23.8⑪	21.8⑪			—
	8-455 Pont.	5	—	—	7.5⑩	4.9	21.0⑦	21.6	21.6			—
'77	6-231 Buick	4	3.5	—	7.5	4.25	22	13.9	13.9			—
	8-301 Pont.	5	—	—	7.5	4.25	22					
	8-350 Pont.	5	—	—	7.5	4.25	22	21.0	21.0			
	8-350 Olds.	4	—	—	7.5	4.25	22	16.1	16.1			
	8-400 Pont.	5	—	—	7.5	4.25	22	19.4	19.4			—
	8-403 Olds	4	—	—	7.5	4.25	22	17.2	17.2			
'78	6-231 Buick	4	3.5	—	⑬	3.5	18.1⑭	14.3	14.2	14.2		
	8-301 Pont.	5	—	—	⑬	3.5	18.1⑭	20.3	20.2⑫	20.9		
	8-305 Chev.	4	—	—	6	3.5	18.1⑭	17.7	17.4	18.1		
	8-350 Chev.	4	—	—	7.5	3.5	18.1⑭	17.7	17.4	18.1		
'79	6-231 Buick	4	3.5	3.5	6	3.5	18.2	14.6	14.6			
	8-301 Pont.	5	—	3.5	6	3.5	18.2	23.0	23.0			—
	8-305 Chev.	4	—	—	6	3.5	18.2	17.0	17.0			
	8-350 Chev.	4	—	—	6	3.5	18.2	17.0	17.0			

• Specifications do not include torque converter
① Station wagons: 23 gals, less 1 gal for California cars
③ 5 pts with 8.875 in. ring gear
④ Lower figure for 3-speed Muncie transmission; higher figure for 3-speed Saginaw transmission
⑤ 5.5 pts with 8.875 in. ring gear (station wagon)
⑥ 22 gals station wagon
⑦ 25 gals Grand Am
⑧ Lower figure indicates 2 bbl engine; higher figure indicates 4 bbl engine

⑨ 4.9 on wagon, optional on sedans
⑩ on M-40; M-38, 8.0
⑪ 1976: 22 with A/C; 21.4 without
⑫ StaWgn: 20.9
⑬ TH 200: 6
 TH 350: 7.5
⑭ StaWgn: 18.2
—— Not applicable

Ventura, 1974 GTO, Astre, Sunbird, Phoenix   CAPACITIES

Year	Engine No. Cyl. Displacement (Cu. In.)	Engine Crankcase Add 1 Qt For New Filter	Transmission Pts To Refill After Draining — Manual 3-Speed	Manual 4/5 Speed	Automatic •	Drive Axle (pts)	Gasoline Tank (gals)	Cooling System (qts) With Heater	With A/C	With Super-Cooling
'72	6-250 Chev.	4	3	——	6	3.75	16	12	16	——
	8-307 Chev.	4	3	——	6①	3.75	16	15	16	——
	8-350 Pont.	5	——	——	5	3.75	16	19.4	20.3	——
'73	6-250 Chev.	4	3.5	——	6	4.25	21.5	12.1	——	——
	8-350 Pont.	5	3.5	2.5	5	4.25	21.5	12.1	12.1	——
'74	6-250 Chev.	4	3.5	——	6	4.25	20.5	12.1	——	——
	8-350 Pont.	5	3.5	2.5	7.5	4.25	20.5	19.2	19.3	——
'75-'76	4-140 OHC Chev.	3	2.4	2.4②	5.0	2.8	16③	7.0	7.5	——
	V6-231 Buick	3	2.4	2.4②	5.0	2.25	16③	7.0	7.5	——
	6-250 Chev.	4	3.5	——	5.0	3.75	20.5	13.5	13.5	——
	8-260 Olds.	4	3.5	——	5.0	3.75	20.5	18.5	19.5	——
	8-350 Buick and Pont.	4	——	——	5.0	3.75	20.5	18.5	19.5	——
'77	4-140 Chev.	3.5	——	3/3	8.0	2.8⑦	16③	7.0	8.0	——
	4-151 Pont.	3.0	——	3/3	6.0	2.8⑦	21④	10.7⑤	10.7⑤	——
	6-231 Buick	4.0	2.4	3/3	6.0	2.8⑦	21④	12.0⑥	12.0⑥	——
	8-301 Pont.	5.0	——	3	7.5	3.5	21	21.8	21.8	——
	8-305 Chev.	4.0	——	——	6.0	3.5	21	16.6	16.6	——
	8-350 Buick	4.0	——	——	7.5	3.5	21	16.0	16.0	——
	8-350 Chev.	4.0	——	——	7.5	3.5	21	16.6	16.6	——
'78	4-151 Pont.	3	——	3.5/3.5	6	3.5	⑭	⑧	⑨	⑩
	6-231 Buick	4	3.5	3.5/3.5	7.5	3.5	⑭	⑪	⑫	⑬
	8-305 Chev.	4	——	3.5	7.5	4.25	⑭	16.8	17.0	17.2
	8-350 Chev.	4	——	——	7.5	4.25	⑭	17.1	17.1	17.8
'79	4-151 Pont.	4	——	3.0	4.5	3.5	18.7⑰	10.7	10.7	——
	6-231 Buick⑮	4	——	3.0	6	3.5	18.7⑰	12.0	12.0	——
	6-231 Buick⑯	4	3.0	——	6	3.5	21.0	13.7	13.7	——
	8-305 Chev.⑮	4	——	3.0	6	3.5	18.7	15.5	15.5	——
	8-305 Chev.⑯	4	——	3.0	6	3.5	21.0	16.6	16.6	——
	8-350 Chev.	4	——	——	6	4.25	21.0	16.6	16.6	——

▲ 5-speed uses Dexron®
• Specifications do not include torque converter
① 5 pts with 3-speed transmission
② 3.5 with 5-speed
③ 18.5 with Sunbird
④ Astre 16; Sunbird 18.5
⑤ Ventura: 12.3
⑥ Ventura: 13.7
⑦ 3.5 with 7.5 in. ring gear axle
⑧ Sunbird MT: 10.9
    AT: 11.4
  Phoenix: 11.8
⑨ Sunbird MT: 10.9
    AT: 11.6
  Phoenix: 11.8
⑩ Sunbird MT: 10.9
    AT: 11.6

⑪ Sunbird: 12.7
  Phoenix: 14.0
⑫ Sunbird: 12.8
  Phoenix: 14.1
⑬ Sunbird Cpe: 13.0
  Sunbird StaWgn: 12.8
  Phoenix: 14.1
⑭ Ventura, Phoenix: 20.8
  Sunbird except Sta. Wgn: 18.5
  Sunbird Sta. Wgn., early production: 15.9
    Late production: 15.0
⑮ Sunbird
⑯ Phoenix
⑰ Sta. Wgn.: 15.2
—— Not applicable

Firebird | CAPACITIES

Year	ENGINE No. Cyl. Displacement (Cu. In.)	Engine Crankcase Add 1 Qt For New Filter	TRANSMISSION Pts To Refill After Draining Manual 3-Speed	4/5 Speed	Automatic ●	Drive Axle (pts)	Gasoline Tank (gals)	COOLING SYSTEM (qts) With Heater	With A/C	With Super-Cooling
'72	6-250 Chev.	4	3.5	—	6	4.25	17	12	12.4	—
	8-350 Pont.	5	3.5	2.5	6	4.25	17	20	20.5	—
	8-400 Pont.	5	2.8	2.5	7.5	4.25	17	18.6	18.7	—
	8-455 Pont.	5	—	2.5	7.5	4.25	17	17.9	19	—
'73	6-250 Chev.	4	3.5	—	7.5	4.25	18	12.5	—	—
	8-350 Pont.	5	3.5	2.5	7.5	4.25	18	22.4	22.7	—
	8-400 Pont.	5	—	2.5	7.5	4.25	18	22.4	22.7/23.5①	—
	8-455 Pont.	5	—	2.5	7.5	4.25	18	20.9	21.8	—
'74	6-250 Chev.	4	3.5	—	7.5	4.25	20.2	12.5	—	—
	8-350 Pont.	5	3.5	2.5	7.5	4.25	20.2	22.4	22.8	—
	8-400 Pont.	5	—	2.5	7.5	4.25	20.2	22.4	22.7/23.6①	—
	8-455 Pont.	5	—	2.5	7.5	4.25	20.2	20.9	21.9	—
'75-'76	6-250 Chev.	4	3.5	—	8.0	4.25	21.5	13.5	13.5	—
	8-350 Pont.	5	—	2.5	8.0	4.25	21.5	21.2	21.6	—
	8-400 Pont.	5	—	2.5	8.0	4.25	21.5	21.6	23.5	—
	8-455 Pont.	5	—	2.5	8.0	4.25	21.5	23.3	23.3	—
'77	6-231 Buick	4	3.5	—	7.5	4.25	21	15.8	15.8	—
	8-301 Pont.	5	—	3.0	7.5	4.25	21	20.9	20.9	—
	8-350 Pont.	5	—	—	7.5	4.25	21	20.0	20.0	—
	8-350 Olds.	4	—	—	7.5	4.25	21	15.4	15.4	—
	8-400 Pont.	5	—	3.0	7.5	4.25	21	18.4	18.4	—
	8-403 Olds.	4	—	—	7.5	4.25	21	20.4	20.4	—
'78	6-231 Buick	4	3.5	—	7.5	4.25	20.8	14.0	14.0	14.0
	8-305 Chev.	4	—	3.5	7.5	4.25	20.8	17.2	17.2	17.8
	8-350 Chev.	4	—	3.5	7.5	4.25	20.8	17.2	17.2	17.8
	8-400 Pont.	5	—	2.44	7.5	4.25	20.8	19.7	②	③
	8-403 Olds.	5	—	—	7.5	4.25	20.8	17.4	18.0	19.7
'79	6-231 Buick	4	3.5	—	6	4.25	21.0	15.8	15.8	—
	8-301 Pont.	5	—	3.5	6	4.25	21.0	23.0	23.0	—
	8-305 Chev.	4	—	—	6	4.25	21.0	17.5	17.5	—
	8-350 Chev.	4	—	—	7.5	4.25	21.0	17.5	17.5	—
	8-400 Pont.	5	—	3.5	7.5	4.25	21.0	18.4	18.4	—
	8-403 Olds.	4	—	—	7.5	4.25	21.0	20.4	20.4	—

● Specifications do not include torque converter
① Lower figure indicates 2 bbl model; higher figure indicates 4 bbl engine
② MT: 20.3 / AT: 22.1
③ MT: 22.0 / AT: 21.4
— Not applicable

GTO through 1973   VALVE SPECIFICATIONS
Lemans, Grand Am

Year	Engine No. Cyl. Displacement (cu in.)	Seat Angle (deg) ■	Face Angle (deg) ●	Outer Spring Test Pressure ▲ (lbs @ in.)	Spring Installed Height (in.)	STEM TO GUIDE Clearance (in.) Intake	Exhaust	STEM Diameter (in.) Intake	Exhaust
'72	6-250 Chev.	46③	45④	60 @ 1.66	1 21/32	.0010-.0027	.0010-.0027	.3414	.3414
	8-350 Pont.	45	44	61 @ 1.59	1 19/32	.0016-.0033	.0021-.0038	.3416	.3411
	8-400⑥ Pont.	30	29	60 @ 1.60	1 19/32	.0016-.0033	.0021-.0038	.3416	.3411
	8-400 2 bbl Pont.	45	44	61 @ 1.59	1 19/32	.0016-.0033	.0021-.0038	.3416	.3411
	8-400 4 bbl Pont.	30	29	65 @ 1.57	1 9/16	.0016-.0033	.0021-.0038	.3416	.3411
	8-455 Pont.	30	29	64 @ 1.57	1 9/16	.0016-.0033	.0021-.0038	.3416	.3416
	8-455 H.O. Pont.	30	29	66 @ 1.56	1 9/16	.0016-.0033	.0021-.0038	.3416	.3416
'73	6-250 Chev.	46③	45④	60 @ 1.66	1 21/32	.0010-.0027	.0010-.0027	.3414	.3414
	8-350 Pont.	45	44	61 @ 1.59	1 19/32	.0016-.0033	.0021-.0038	.3416	.3411
	8-400 4 bbl Pont.	30	29	60 @ 1.60	1 19/32	.0016-.0033	.0021-.0038	.3416	.3411
	8-400 2 bbl Pont.	45	44	61 @ 1.59	1 19/32	.0016-.0033	.0021-.0038	.3416	.3411
	8-400 4 bbl auto. Pont.	30	29	65 @ 1.57	1 9/16	.0016-.0033	.0021-.0038	.3416	.3411
	8-455 Pont.	30	29	64 @ 1.57	1 9/16	.0016-.0033	.0021-.0038	.3416	.3411
	8-455 S.D. Pont.	45	44	70 @ 1.82	1 9/16	.0016-.0033	.0021-.0038	.3416	.3416
'74	6-250 Chev.	46	45	60 @ 1.66	1 21/32	.0010-.0027	.0010-.0027	.3414	.3414
	8-350 Pont.	45	44	61 @ 1.59	1 19/32	.0016-.0033	.0021-.0038	.3416	.3411
	8-400 4 bbl Pont.	30	29	60 @ 1.60	1 19/32	.0016-.0033	.0021-.0038	.3416	.3411
	8-400 2 bbl Pont.	45	44	61 @ 1.59	1 19/32	.0016-.0033	.0021-.0038	.3416	.3411
	8-400 4 bbl auto. Pont.	30	29	65 @ 1.57	1 9/16	.0016-.0033	.0021-.0038	.3416	.3411
	8-455 Pont.		29	64 @ 1.57	1 9/16	.0016-.0033	.0021-.0038	.3416	.3411
'75-'76	6-250 Chev.	46	45	57 @ 1.66	1 21/32	.0010-.0027	.0010-.0027	.3414	.3414
	8-260 Olds.	46⑥	45⑦	70 @ 1.67	1 47/64	.0010-.0027	.0015-.0032	.3429	.3424
	8-350 Pont.	30	29	66 @ 1.56	1 19/32	.0016-.0033	.0021-.0038	3416	.3411
	8-400 2 bbl Pont.	30	29	70 @ 1.54	1 19/32	.0016-.0033	.0021-.0038	3416	.3411
	8-400 4 bbl Pont.	30	29	70 @ 1.54	1 9/16	.0016-.0033	.0021-.0038	3416	.3411
	8-455 Pont.	30	29	65 @ 1.57	1 9/16	.0016-.0033	.0021-.0038	3416	.3411
'77	6-231 Buick	45	45	64 @ 1.73	1 47/64	.0015-.0032	.0015-.0032	.3407	.3409
	8-301 Pont.	46	45	82 @ 1.66	1 21/32	.0010-.0027	.0010-.0027	.3422	.3422
	8-350 Pont.	30③	29④	68 @ 1.54	1 35/64	.0016-.0033	.0021-.0038	.3416	.3411
	8-350 Olds.	①	①	80 @ 1.67	1 21/32	.0010-.0027	.0015-.0032	34.29	.3424
	8-400 Pont.	30③	29④	68 @ 1.55	1 9/16	.0016-.0033	.0021-.0038	.3416	.3412
	8-403 Olds.	①	①	80 @ 1.67	1 21/32	.0010-.0027	.0015-.0032	.3429	.3424
'78-'79	6-231 Buick	45	45	182 @ 1.340	1.727	.0015-.0032	.0015-.0032	.3402-.3412	.3412-.3405
	8-301 Pont.	46	45	165 @ 1.290	1.660	.0010-.0027	.0010-.0027⑨	.3425	.3425
	8-305 Chev.	46	45	190 @ 1.160	⑧	.0010-.0037	.0010-.0047	.3414	.3414
	8-350 Chev.	46	45	190 @ 1.160	⑧	.0010-.0037	.0010-.0047	.3414	.3414

■ Intake valve seat angles are shown. All exhaust valve seat angles are 45° unless otherwise indicated.

● Intake valve face angles are shown. All exhaust valve face angles are 44° unless otherwise indicated.

① Intake seat 45°, intake face 44°; exhaust seat 31°, exhaust face 30°

② Not used

③ Exhaust valve seat angle 46°

④ Exhaust valve face angle 45°

⑤ All 400 cu in. engines with manual transmission

⑥ Exhaust valve seat: 31

⑦ Exhaust valve face: 30

— Not specified

⑧ Intake: 1 23/32
    Exhaust: 1 19/32

⑨ Clearance at bottom: .0020-.0037

▲INNER SPRING TEST PRESSURE
(lbs @ in.)

⑩ All 400 cu in. engines with manual transmission

Year	Engine No. Cyl Displacement (cu in.)	Test Pressure
'72	8-350	33 @ 1.55
	8-400⑩	56 @ 1.53
	8-400 2 bbl	33 @ 1.55
	8-400 4 bbl	36 @ 1.53
	8-455	37 @ 1.53
	8-455 HO	38 @ 1.52
'73	8-350	33 @ 1.55
	8-400 4 bbl	56 @ 1.53
	8-400 2 bbl	33 @ 1.55
	8-400 4 bbl auto.	36 @ 1.53
	8-455	37 @ 1.53
	8-455 S.D.	40 @ 1.75

Year	Engine No. Cyl Displacement (cu in.)	Test Pressure
'74	8-350	33 @ 1.55
	8-400 4 bbl	56 @ 1.53
	8-400 2 bbl	33 @ 1.55
	8-400 4 bbl auto.	36 @ 1.53
	8-455	37 @ 1.53
'75-'76	8-350	38 @ 1.52
	8-400 2 bbl	41 @ 1.50
	8-400 4 bbl	41 @ 1.50
	8-455	36 @ 1.53
'77	8-350 Pont.	39 @ 1.51
	8-400	40 @ 1.51

VALVE SPECIFICATIONS

Firebird, Ventura, 1974 GTO, Astre, Sunbird, Phoenix

Year	Engine No. Cyl. Displacement (cu in.)	Seat Angle (deg) ■	Face Angle (deg) ●	Outer Spring Test Pressure▲ (lbs @ in.)	Spring Installed Height (in.)	STEM TO GUIDE Clearance (in.) Intake	Exhaust	STEM Diameter (in.) Intake	Exhaust
'72	6-250 1 bbl Chev.	46③	45③	60 @ 1.66	1 21/32	.0010-.0027	.0010-.0027	.3414	.3414
	8-307 2 bbl Chev.	46③	45③	81 @ 1.70	1 45/64	.0010-.0027	.0010-.0027	.3414	.3414
	8-350④ 2 bbl Buick	46③	45③	60 @ 1.66	1 21/32	.0010-.0027	.0010-.0027	.3414	.3414
	8-350⑤ 2 bbl Pont.	45	44	61 @ 1.59	1 19/32	.0016-.0033	.0021-.0038	.3414	.3411
	8-400① Pont.	30	29	60 @ 1.60	1 19/32	.0016-.0033	.0021-.0038	.3416	.3411
	8-400 2 bbl Pont.	45	44	61 @ 1.59	1 19/32	.0016-.0033	.0021-.0038	.3416	.3411
	8-400 4 bbl Pont.	30	29	65 @ 1.57	1 9/16	.0016-.0033	.0021-.0038	.3416	.3411
	8-455 H.O. Pont.	30	29	66 @ 1.56	1 9/16	.0016-.0033	.0021-.0038	.3416	.3416
'73	6-250 1 bbl Chev.	46③	45③	60 @ 1.66	1 21/32	.0010-.0027	.0010-.0027	.3414	.3414
	8-350 2 bbl Pont.	45	44	61 @ 1.59	1 19/32	.0016-.0033	.0021-.0038	.3414	.3411
	8-400① Pont.	30	29	60 @ 1.60	1 19/32	.0016-.0033	.0021-.0038	.3416	.3411
	8-400 2 bbl Pont.	45	44	61 @ 1.59	1 19/32	.0016-.0033	.0021-.0038	.3416	.3411
	8-400 4 bbl Pont.	30	29	65 @ 1.57⑥	1 9/16	.0016-.0033	.0021-.0038	.3416	.3411
	8-455 Pont.	30	29	66 @ 1.56⑦	1 9/16	.0016-.0033	.0021-.0038	.3416	.3411⑦
'74	6-250 1 bbl Chev.	46③	45③	60 @ 1.66	1 21/32	.0010-.0027	.0010-.0027	.3414	.3414
	8-350 Pont.	45	44	61 @ 1.59	1 19/32	.0016-.0033	.0021-.0038	.3414	.3411
	8-400 2 bbl Pont.	45	44	61 @ 1.59	1 19/32	.0016-.0033	.0021-.0038	.3416	.3411
	8-400 4 bbl Pont.	30	29	65 @ 1.57⑧	1 9/16	.0016-.0033	.0021-.0038	.3416	.3411
	8-455 Pont.	30	29	66 @ 1.56	1 9/16	.0016-.0033	.0021-.0038	.3416	.3411
	8-455 SD Pont.	45	44	70 @ 1.82	1 9/16	.0016-.0033	.0021-.0038	.3416	.3416
'75-'76	4-140 Chev.	46③	45③	75 @ 1.75	1 3/4	.0010-.0027	.0017-.0027	.3414	.3414
	V6-231 Buick	45③	45③	64 @ 1.72	1 47/64	.0015-.0032	.0015-.0032	.3409	.3409
	6-250 Chev.	46③	45③	57 @ 1.66	1 21/32	.0010-.0027	.0010-.0027	.3414	.3414
	8-260 Olds.	46⑨	45⑩	80 @ 1.67	1 31/32	.0010-.0027	.0015-.0032	.3429	.3424
	8-350 Pont.	30	29	66 @ 1.56	1 19/32	.0016-.0033	.0021-.0038	.3416	.3411

Firebird, Ventura, 1974 GTO, Astre, Sunbird, Phoenix — VALVE SPECIFICATIONS

Year	Engine No. Cyl. Displacement (cu in.)	Seat Angle (deg) ■	Face Angle (deg) ●	Outer Spring Test Pressure▲ (lbs @ in.)	Spring Installed Height (in.)	STEM TO GUIDE Clearance (in.) Intake	Exhaust	STEM Diameter (In.) Intake	Exhaust
'75-'76	8-350 (Ventura) Buick	45③	45③	75 @ 1.73	1 23/32	.0015-.0035	.0015-.0032	.3725	.3727
	8-400 Pont.	30	29	70 @ 1.54	1 9/16	.0016-.0033	.0021-.0038	.3416	.3411
	8-455 Pont.	30	29	65 @ 1.27	1 9/16	.0016-.0033	.0021-.0038	.3416	.3411
'77	4-140 Chev.	46③	45③	75 @ 1.75	1 3/4	.0010-.0027	.0010-.0027	.3414	.3414
	4-151 Pont.	46③	45③	82 @ 1.66	1 21/32	.0010-.0027	.0010-.0027②	.3422	.3422
	6-231 Buick	45	45	64 @ 1.72	1 47/64	.0015-.0035	.0015-.0032	.3407	.3409
	8-301 Pont.	46	45	82 @ 1.66	1 21/32	.0010-.0027	.0010-.0027	.3422	.3422
	8-305 Chev.	46③	45③	80 @ 1.70	1 23/32⑪	.0010-.0027	.0010-.0027	.3414	.3414
	8-350 Chev.	46③	45③	80 @ 1.70	1 23/32⑪	.0010-.0027	.0010-.0027	.3414	.3414
	8-350 Olds.	⑫	⑫	80 @ 1.67	1 21/32	.0010-.0027	.0015-.0032	.3429	.3424
	8-350 Pont.	30	29	68 @ 1.54	1 19/32	.0016-.0033	.0021-.0038	.3416	.3412
	8-400 Pont.	30	29	68 @ 1.55	1 19/32	.0016-.0033	.0021-.0038	.3416	.3412
	8-403 Olds.	⑫	⑫	80 @ 1.67	1 21/32	.0010-.0027	.0015-.0032	.3429	.3424
'78-'79	4-151 Pont.	46	45	82 @ 1.66	1.69	.0010-.0027	.0010-.0027②	.3414	.3400
	6-231 Buick	45	45	182 @ 1.34	1.727	.0015-.0032	.0015-.0032	.3402-.3412	.3405-.3412
	8-305 Chev.	46	45	190 @ 1.16	⑭	.0010-.0037	.0010-.0047	.3414	.3414
	8-350 Chev.	46	45	190 @ 1.16	⑭	.0010-.0037	.0010-.0047	.3414	.3414
	8-400 Pont.	⑬	⑮	135 @ 1.18	1.54	.0016-.0033	.0021-.0038	.3425	.3425
	8-403 Olds.	⑫	⑫	190 @ 1.27	1.67	.0010-.0027	.0015-.0032	.3425-.3432	.3420-.3427

■ Intake valve seat angles are shown. All exhaust valve seat angles are 45° unless otherwise indicated.

● Intake valve face angles are shown. All exhaust valve face angles are 44° unless otherwise indicated.

① Manual transmission with 400 cu in. engine
② Figure given is at top of guide; .0020-.0037 at bottom
③ Exhaust valve seat and face angles are the same as intake valve seat and face angles
④ Ventura II only
⑤ Firebird only
⑥ 59 @ 1.50 with manual transmission
⑦ .3416 in. for 455 S.D. engine
⑧ 60 @ 1.60 with manual transmission
⑨ Exhaust—31
⑩ Exhaust—30
⑪ Exhaust: 1 19/32
⑫ Intake seat 45°, intake face 44°; exhaust seat 31°, exhaust face 30°
⑬ Intake: 30 Exhaust: 45
⑭ Intake: 1 23/32 Exhaust: 1 19/32
⑮ Intake: 29 Exhaust: 44
— Not specified

▲INNER SPRING TEST PRESSURE (lbs @ in.)

Year	Engine No. Cyl. Displacement (cu in.)	Test Pressure
'72	8-400	56 @ 1.53①
	8-400 2 bbl	33 @ 1.55
	8-400 4 bbl	36 @ 1.53
	8-455 H.O.	38 @ 1.52

'73	8-350	33 @ 1.55
	8-400	56 @ 1.53①
	8-400 2 bbl	33 @ 1.55
	8-400 4 bbl	36 @ 1.53
	8-455	36 @ 1.53②
'74	8-350④	33 @ 1.55
	8-400	56 @ 1.53①
	8-400 2 bbl	33 @ 1.55
	8-400 4 bbl	36 @ 1.53
	8-455	36 @ 1.53②

'75-'76	8-350 Pont.	38 @ 1.52
	8-400	41 @ 1.50
	8-455	36 @ 1.53
'77	8-350 Pont.	39 @ 1.51
	8-400	40 @ 1.51
'78-'79	8-400	97 @ 1.14

① 400 cu in. engine with manual transmission
② 40 @ 1.75 for 455 S.D.

PISTON CLEARANCE

Year	Engine No. Cyl. Displacement (cu. in.)	Piston-to-Bore Clearance (in.)
'72	6-250 Chev.	.0005-.0015
	8-350, 400, 455 Pont.	.0025-.0033
	8-307 Chev.	.0005-.0011
'73-'77	6-250 Chev.	.0005-.0015
	8-350, 400 Pont.	.0029-.0037
	8-455 Pont.	.0021-.0029①
	8-455 S.D. Pont.	.0060-.0068②
'75-'76	4-140 OHC Chev.	.0018-.0028③
	8-260 Olds.	.0010-.0020
	8-350 Ventura Buick	.0008-.0014
	V6-231 Buick	.0008-.0014
'77	4-140 Chev.	.0018-.0028③
	4-151 Pont.	.0025-.0033⑥
	6-231 Buick	.0008-.0020⑦
	8-301 Pont.	.0025-.0033⑥
	8-305 Chev.	.0017-.0042④

Year	Engine No. Cyl. Displacement (cu. in.)	Piston-to-Bore Clearance (in.)
	8-350 Chev.	.0007-.0017④
	8-350 Olds.	.0008-.0018⑤
	8-350 Pont.	.0025-.0033⑥
	8-400 Pont.	.0025-.0033⑥
	8-403 Pont.	.0008-.0018⑤
'78-'79	4-151 Pont.	.0025-.0033⑥
	6-231 Buick	.0008-.0020⑦
	8-301 Pont.	.0025-.0033⑥
	8-305 Chev.	.0007-.0027④
	8-350 Chev.	.0007-.0027④
	8-400 Pont.	.0025-.0033⑥
	8-403 Olds.	.0008-.0018⑤

① .0025-.0033 for 1973
② .0064-.0072 for 1974
③ 1.50″ from top of piston
④ 1.15″ from top of piston
⑤ .75″ below piston pin C/L
⑥ 1.11″ from top of piston
⑦ Top of skirt

RING GAP

All measurements are given in inches

Year	Engine No. Cyl. Displacement (cu. in.)	Top Compression	Bottom Compression
'72	8-307 Chev.	.010-.020	.010-.020
'72-'76	6-250 Chev.	.010-.020	.010-.020
'72-'76	8-455 Pont.	.010-.030	.010-.030
'72-'76	8-350, 400 Pont.	.010-.030	.010-.030
'75-'76	8-350 Buick	.010-.020	.010-.020
'75-'76	8-260 Olds.	.010-.023	.010-.023
'75-'77	4-140 Chev.	.015-.025	.009-.019
'77	8-350 Olds.	.010-.020	.010-.020
'77-'78	4-151 Pont.	.010-.020	.010-.020
'77-'79	8-305, 350 Chev.	.010-.020	.010-.025
'76-'77	6-231 Buick	.013-.023	.013-.023
'77-'78	8-301, 400 Pont.	.010-.020	.010-.020
'77-'79	8-403 Olds.	.010-.020	.010-.020
'79	4-151 Pont.	.015-.025	.009-.019
'79	8-301 Pont.	.014-.024	.014-.024
'79	8-400 Pont.	.009-.019	.005-.015

Year	Engine	Oil Control
'72	8-307 Chev.	.015-.055
'72-'76	6-250 Chev.	.015-.055
'72-'76	8-455 Pont.	.015-.055
'72-'76	8-350, 400 Pont.	.015-.055
'75-'76	8-350 Buick	.015-.035
'75-'76	8-260 Olds.	.015-.055
'75-'77	4-140 Chev.	.010-.030
'77	8-350 Olds.	.015-.055
'77-'78	4-151 Pont.	.010-.020
'77-'79	8-305, 350 Chev.	.010-.035
'76-'77	6-231 Buick	.015-.035
'77-'79	8-301, 400 Pont.	.015-.055
'77-'79	8-403 Olds.	.015-.055
'79	4-151 Pont.	.015-.055
'79	8-400 Pont.	.015-.035

RING SIDE CLEARANCE
All measurements are given in inches

Year	Engine No. Cyl. Displacement (cu. in.)	Top Compression	Bottom Compression
'72	8-307 Chev.	.0012-.0027	.0012-.0032
'72-'76	6-250 Chev.	.0012-.0027	.0012-.0032
'75-'77	4-140 Chev.	.0012-.0027	.0012-.0027
'72-'76	8-455 Pont.	.0015-.0050	.0015-.0050
'72-'76	8-350, 400 Pont.	.0015-.0050	.0015-.0050
'75-'76	8-350 Buick	.0030-.0050	.0030-.0050
'77	8-350 Olds.	.0020-.0040	.0020-.0040
'77-'79	8-350 Chev.	.0012-.0032	.0012-.0027
'75-'76	8-260 Olds.	.0020-.0040	.0020-.0040
'76-'79	6-231 Buick	.0030-.0050	.0030-.0050
'77-'79	8-301, 400 Pont.	.0015-.0035	.0015-.0035
'77-'79	8-305 Chev.	.0012-.0032	.0012-.0027
'77-'79	4-151 Pont.	.0025-.0033	.0025-.0033
'77-'79	8-403 Olds.	.0020-.0040	.0020-.0040

Year	Engine	Oil Control
'77-'79	4-151 Pont.	.0025-.0033
'72	8-307 Chev.	.0020-.0070
'72-'76	6-250 Chev.	.0010-.0050
'72-'76	8-455 Pont.	.0015-.0050
'72-'76	8-350, 400 Pont.	.0015-.0050
'75-'77	4-140 Chev.	.0000-.0050
'77	8-350 Olds.	.0006-.0096
'75-'76	8-350 Buick	.0035 max.
'77-'79	8-350 Chev.	.0000-.0050
'75-'76	8-260 Olds.	.0010-.0050
'76-'79	6-231 Buick	.0035 max.
'77-'79	8-305 Chev.	.0000-.0050
'77-'79	8-301, 400 Pont.	.0015-.0035
'77-'79	8-403 Olds.	.0006-.0096

CRANKSHAFT AND CONNECTING ROD SPECIFICATIONS
All measurements are given in inches

Year	Engine No. Cyl. Displacement (cu in.)	CRANKSHAFT Main Brg. Journal Dia	Main Brg. Oil Clearance	Shaft End-Play	Thrust on No.	CONNECTING ROD Journal Diameter	Oil Clearance	Side Clearance
'72-'74	6-250 Chev.	2.30	.0003-.0029	.002-.006	7	2.000	.0007-.0027	.009-.014⑦
	8-307 ('72) Chev.	②	③	.002-.006	5	2.099-2.100	.0013-.0035	.002-.006①
	8-350 Pont.	3.00	.0002-.0017	.003-.009	4	2.250	.0005-.0025	.012-.017①
	8-400 Pont.	3.00	.0002-.0017	.003-.009	4	2.250	.0005-.0025	.012-.017①
	8-455 Pont.	3.25	⑥⑧⑨	.003-.009	4	2.250	.0005-.0025⑩	.012-.017①
'75-'76	4-140 OHC Chev.	2.30	.0003-.0027⑫	.002-.007	4	2.000	.0007-.0038	.009-.014
	V6-231 Buick	2.50	.0004-.0015	.004-.008	2	2.000	.0002-.0023	.006-.014
	6-250 Chev.	2.30	.0003-.0029	.002-.006	7	2.000	.0007-.0027	.009-.014
	8-260 Olds.	2.50	.0005-.0021⑬	.004-.008	3	2.124	.0005-.0026	.006-.020
	8-350, 400 Pont.	3.00	.0002-.0017	.003-.009	4	2.250	.0005-.0025	.012-.017①
	8-350 Buick	3.00	.0004-.0015	.003-.009	3	2.000	.0005-.0026	.006-.020
	8-455 Pont.	3.25	.0005-.0021	.003-.009	4	2.250	.0005-.0025	.012-.017①
'77	4-140 Chev.	2.30	.0003-.0029	.002-.008	4	2.400	.0007-.0027	.009-.013
	4-151 Pont.	2.30	.0002-.0022	.0035-.0085	5	2.000	.0005-.0026	.006-.022
	6-231 Buick	2.50	.0004-.0015	.004-.008	2	2.000	.0005-.0026	.006-.026
	8-301 Pont.	3.00	.0002-.0020	.0035-.0085	4	2.250	.0005-.0026	.006-.022
	8-305 Chev.	⑪	⑭	.002-.007	5	2.100	.0013-.0035	.006-.016
	8-350 Chev.	⑪	⑭	.002-.007	5	2.100	.0013-.0035	.006-.016
	8-350 Olds.	⑮	⑯	.0035-.0135	5	2.120	.0004-.0033	.006-.020
	8-350 Pont.	3.00	.0002-.0017	.0035-.0085	4	2.250	.0005-.0026	.012-.017①
	8-400 Pont.	3.00	.0002-.0017	.0035-.0085	4	2.250	.0005-.0026	.012-.017①
	8-403 Olds.	⑮	⑯	.0035-.0135	5	2.120	.0004-.0033	.006-.020

CRANKSHAFT AND CONNECTING ROD SPECIFICATIONS

All measurements are given in inches

Year	Engine No. Cyl. Displacement (cu in.)	CRANKSHAFT Main Brg. Journal Dia	Main Brg. Oil Clearance	Shaft End-Play	Thrust on No.	Journal Diameter	CONNECTING ROD Oil Clearance	Side Clearance
'78-'79	4-151 Pont.	2.3000	.0002-.0022	.0035-.0085	5	2.000	.0005-.0026	.006-.022
	6-231 Buick	2.4995	.0003-.0017	.0030-.0090	2	2.2487-2.2495	.0005-.0026	.006-.027
	8-301 Pont.	3.0000	.0002-.0020	.0030-.0090	4	2.250	.0005-.0025	.006-.022
	8-305 Chev.	⑪	⑭	.0020-.0070	5	2.0990-2.1000	.0013-.0035	.006-.016
	8-350 Chev.	⑪	⑭	.0020-.0070	5	2.0990-2.1000	.0013-.0035	.006-.016
	8-400 Pont.	3.0000	.0002-.0020	.0030-.0090	4	2.250	.0005-.0025	.006-.022
	8-403 Olds.	⑮	⑯	.0035-.0135	5	2.1238-2.1248	.0005-.0026	.006-.020

① Total for 2 connecting rods
② No.'s 1, 2, 3, 4—2.4484-2.493
  No. 5—2.4479-2.4488
③ No. 1—.0008-.0020
  No.'s 2, 3, 4—.0011-.0023
⑥ No. 1 bearing cap w/small valve—.0003-.0019
  All others—.0005-.0021
⑦ .007-.016 in 1973
⑧ 1973-74—.0005-.0021 (455); .0010-.0026 (455 S.D.)
⑨ No. 1 on 1974 455—.0035-.0020
⑩ .0015-.0031 in 455 SD

⑪ No.'s 1, 2, 3, 4: 2.4502
  No. 5: 2.4508
⑫ .0003-.0020 for no. 1
⑬ .0005-.0031 for no. 5
⑭ No. 1: .0008-.0020
  No.'s 2, 3, 4: .0011-.0023
  No. 5: .0017-.0033
⑮ No. 1: 2.4988-2.4998
  No.'s 2, 3, 4, 5: 2.4985-2.4995
⑯ No.'s 1, 2, 3, 4: .0005-.0021
  No. 5: .0015-.0031

TORQUE SPECIFICATIONS

All readings in ft lbs

Year	Engine No. Cyl. Displacement (cu in.)	Cylinder Head Bolts	Rod Bearing Bolts	Main Bearing Bolts	Crankshaft Bolt	Flywheel to Crankshaft Bolts	MANIFOLD Intake	Exhaust
'72-'74	6-250 Chev.	95	35	65	Pressed on	60	25-30①	25
	8-350, 400, 455 Pont.	95	43②	90-110④	160	95	40	30
	8-307 (71-'72) Chev.	65	45	75	60	60	30	25
'75-'76	4-140 OHC Chev.	60	35	65	80	60	30	30
	V6-231 Buick	75	40	115	150	55	45	25
	6-250 Chev.	95	35	65	Pressed on	60	25-30①	25③
	8-260 Olds.	85	42	120	310	90	40	25
	8-350, 400, 455	95	43	100④	160	95	40	30
	8-350 Buick	80	40	115	140	60	45	28
'77	4-140 Chev.	60	35	65	80	60	30	30
	4-151 Pont.	95	30	65	160	55	40	40
	6-231 Buick	80	40	100	175 min.	60	45	25
	8-301 Pont.	85	30	70⑤	160	95	35	40
	8-305 Chev.	65	45	70	60	60	30	20
	8-350 Chev.	65	45	70	60	60	30	20
	8-350 Olds.	130	42	80⑥	310	60⑦	40	25
	8-350 Pont.	100	40	100⑥	160	95	35	40
	8-400 Pont.	100	40	100⑥	160	95	35	40
	8-403 Olds.	130	42	80⑥	310	60⑦	40	25

TORQUE SPECIFICATIONS
All readings in ft lbs

Year	Engine No. Cyl. Displacement (cu in.)	Cylinder Head Bolts	Rod Bearing Bolts	Main Bearing Bolts	Crankshaft Bolt	Flywheel to Crankshaft Bolts	MANIFOLD Intake	Exhaust
'78-'79	4-151 Pont.	95	30	65	160	55	40	40
	6-231 Buick	80	40	100	225	60	45	25
	8-301 Pont.	95	30	70⑤	160	95	35	40
	8-305 Chev.	65	45	70	60	60	30	20
	8-350 Chev.	65	45	70	60	60	30	20
	8-400 Pont.	95	40	100⑥	160	95	35	40
	8-403 Olds.	130	42	80⑥	220	60	40	25

① End bolts 15-20 ft. lbs.
② 63 ft lbs on 455 S.D. engine
③ With integral intake manifold cast into head—18-23 for four end bolts, 30-35 for all others

④ Rear cap—120
⑤ Rear main: 100
⑥ Rear main: 120
⑦ With Auto Trans: 90

WHEEL ALIGNMENT SPECIFICATIONS

Year	Model	CASTER Range (deg)	CASTER Pref Setting (deg)	CAMBER Range (deg)	CAMBER Pref Setting (deg)	Toe-in (in.)	Steering Axis Inclin. (deg)	WHEEL PIVOT RATIO (deg) Inner Wheel	Outer Wheel
'72	Tempest, LeMans	2N to 1N	1½N	½N to ½P	0	1/16 to 3/16	9	20	22
	Firebird	½N to ½P	0	½P to 1½P	1P	1/8 to 1/4	8.25 to 9.25	20	22
	Ventura II	0 to 1P	½P	1/4 to 3/4P	1/4P	1/8 to 1/4	N.A.	20	22
'73-'74	LeMans, Grand Am	③	④	①	②	0 to 1/8	10.35	20	22
	Firebird	½N to ½P	0	½P to 1½P	1P	1/8 to 1/4	10.35	20	22
	Ventura II	0 to 1P	½P	1/4N to 3/4P	1/4P	1/8 to 1/4	8.5 to 9.5	20	22
'74	LeMans, Grand Am	③	④	①	②	0 to 1/8	10.35	20	22
	Firebird	1N to 1P	0	3/4P to 1¾P	1P	1/16 to 5/16	10.35	20	22
	Ventura	½N to 1½P	½P	½N to 1P	1/4P	1/16 to 5/16	9	20	22
'75-'76	Astre/Sunbird	1¼N to 1/4N	3/4N	3/4N to 3/4P	1/4P	0 to 1/8	8.55	—	—
	Ventura	⑦	⑧	1/4P to 1¼P	3/4P	0 to 1/8	8.75	—	—
	Firebird	½N to ½P	0	½P to 1½P	1P	0 to 1/8	9.50	—	—
	LeMans, Grand Am	⑥	⑤	①	②	0 to 1/8	10.50	—	—
'77	Astre/Sunbird	1¼N to 1/4N	3/4N	1/4N to 3/4P	1/4P	0 to 1/8	8.55	—	—
	Ventura	⑨	⑨	⑩	⑩	0 to 1/8	10.00	—	—
	Firebird	1N to 1P	0	1/4P to 1¾N	1P	1/16 to 5/16	10.35	—	—
	LeMans	⑪	⑪	⑫	⑫	0 to 1/8	10.35	—	—
'78	Sunbird	1¼N to 1/4N	3/4N	1/4N to 3/4P	1/4P	0 to 1/8	8.55	—	—
	LeMans Man. Str.	1N to 3P	1P	1N to 2P	½P	1/8 to 3/16	10.50	—	—
	Pwr. Str.	1P to 5P	3P	1N to 2P	½P	1/8 to 3/16	10.50	—	—
	Firebird	1N to 3P	1P	½N to 2½P	1P	1/8 to 3/16	10.50	—	—
	Phoenix Man. Str.	3N to 1P	1N	3/5N to 2⅓P	4/5P	1/8 to 3/16	10.00	—	—
	Pwr. Str.	1N to 3P	1P	3/5N to 2⅓P	4/5P	1/8 to 3/16	10.00	—	—
'79	Sunbird	1¼N to 1/4N	3/4N	3/4N to 1/4P	1/4N	1/8 out to 0	8.55	—	—
	LeMans Man. Str.	½P to 1½P	1P	0 to 1P	½P	1/8 to 3/16	8.00	—	—
	Pwr. Str	2½P to 3½P	3P	0 to 1P	½P	1/8 to 3/16	8.00	—	—

WHEEL ALIGNMENT SPECIFICATIONS

Year	Model	CASTER		CAMBER		Toe-in (in.)	Steering Axis Inclin. (deg)	WHEEL PIVOT RATIO (deg)	
		Range (deg)	Pref Setting (deg)	Range (deg)	Pref Setting (deg)			Inner Wheel	Outer Wheel
'79	Firebird	½P to 1½P	1P	½P to 1½P	1P	0 to ⅛	10.35	—	—
	Phoenix Man. Str.	½N to 1½N	1N	½P to 1½P	1P	0 to ⅛	10.00	—	—
	Pwr. Str.	½P to 1½P	1P	½P to 1½P	1P	0 to ⅛	10.00	—	—

N Negative   P Positive

① LH: ½P to 1½P; RH: 0 to 1P
② LH: 1P; RH: ½P
③ Manual steering—1½N to ½N
   Power steering—½N to ½P
④ Manual steering—1N
   Power steering—0
⑤ Manual steering—1P
   Power steering—2P
⑥ Manual steering—½P to 1½P
   Power steering—1½P to 2½P
⑦ Manual steering—½N to 1½N
   Power steering—½P to 1½P
⑧ Manual steering—1N
   Power steering—1P
⑨ Manual steering—1¾N to ¼N; pref.: 1N
   Power steering—¾N to ¾P; pref.: 0
⑩ Manual steering—¼N to 1¾P; pref.: ¾P
   Power steering—0 to 1½P; pref.: ¾P
⑪ Manual steering—½P to 1½P; pref.: 1 P
   Power steering—1¼P to 2¼P; pref.: 1¾P
⑫ LH: ½P to 1½P; pref.: 1P
   RH: 0 to 1P; pref.: ½P
— Not specified

CHARGING SYSTEM

The charging system is the SI integral system. This system is composed of an alternator and integral regulator. Although several models of alternators are available, with different out-puts at different speeds, their basic operating principles are the same. The alternator features a solid state regulator mounted inside the alternator slip ring end frame. All regulator components are enclosed in a solid mold. The regulator voltage setting never needs adjustment and no means for adjustment is provided.

Alternator Removal and Installation

1. Disconnect the battery cables.
2. Remove the alternator wires or connector.
3. Loosen the adjusting and pivot bolts.
4. Remove the V-belt.
5. Remove the alternator adjusting and pivot bolts.
6. Remove the alternator.
7. To install, reverse the removal procedure.
   Adjust the belt tension so that the longest span of belt between the pulleys can be depressed about ½ in. in the middle by moderate thumb pressure.

--- CAUTION ---

Pull out on the alternator by hand to avoid damage to the housing and over-tightening, which could damage the bearings.

Tighten first the adjuster bolt, then the pivot bolt.

STARTING SYSTEM

The starter circuit consists of the battery, battery cables, starting motor, starter motor solenoid switch, ignition-starter switch and the neutral safety switch (automatic transmission) or clutch start switch (manual transmission).

The starting motor and solenoid assembly is mounted on the flywheel housing.

The solenoid switch closes the circuit between the battery and the starting motor. It also operates the shift lever that moves the drive pinion into mesh with the flywheel ring gear.

Troubleshooting procedures can be found in the Charging and Starting Systems section of the Unit Repair Section.

Starter Removal and Installation

ALL EXCEPT V6

1. Disconnect negative battery cable.
2. If necessary, jack-up and support the car.
3. Disconnect solenoid wires.
4. Disconnect starter brace, if any.
5. Remove starter-to-engine bolts and starter.

V6 WITH MANUAL TRANSMISSION

1. Disconnect the negative battery cable.
2. Raise the car and safely support it.
3. Remove the engine front cross-member to body bolts, then remove the right and left crossmember brace bolts.
4. Loosen all the brace bolts to let the crossmember braces hang down enough to allow removal of the crossmember.
5. Remove the crossmember and follow steps for all other engines.

V6 WITH AUTOMATIC TRANSMISSION

1. Raise the car and disconnect the negative battery cable.
2. Remove the exhaust crossover pipe and the flywheel cover.
3. Remove the two transmission mount to transmission bolts and place a jack under the extension housing of the transmission.
4. Remove the right transmission support bracket and pivot down.
5. Disconnect and plug the fluid cooler lines and lower the transmission enough to get at the two starter to engine block bolts.
6. Remove those two bolts, the terminals on the starter, and the starter.
7. Installation is the reverse of removal.

Disabling the Seat Belt/Starter System

Since the requirement for the interlock system was dropped during the 1975 model year, those systems installed on cars built earlier may now be legally disabled. The seat belt warning light is still required.

1. Disconnect the negative battery cable.
2. Locate the interlock harness connector under the left side of the in-

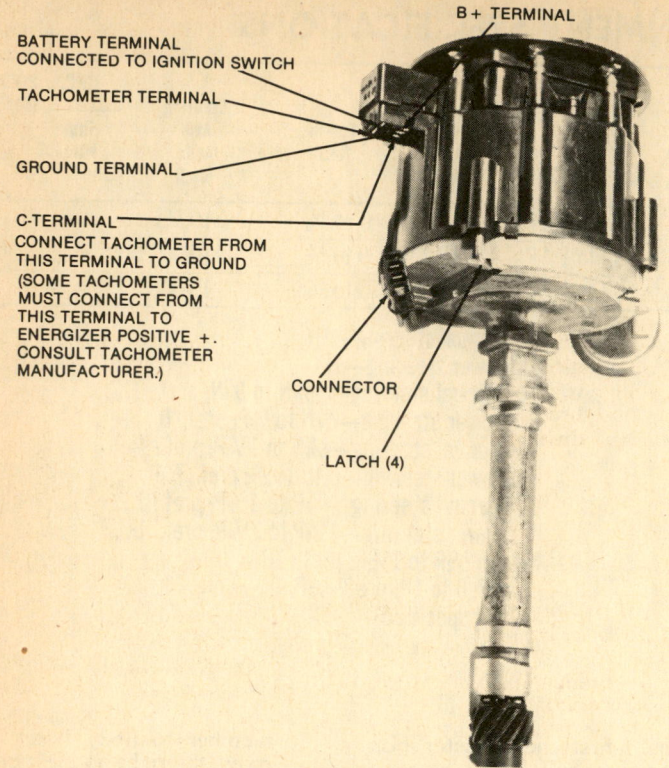

BATTERY TERMINAL
CONNECTED TO IGNITION SWITCH

TACHOMETER TERMINAL

GROUND TERMINAL

C-TERMINAL
CONNECT TACHOMETER FROM
THIS TERMINAL TO GROUND
(SOME TACHOMETERS
MUST CONNECT FROM
THIS TERMINAL TO
ENERGIZER POSITIVE +.
CONSULT TACHOMETER
MANUFACTURER.)

B+ TERMINAL

CONNECTOR

LATCH (4)

Tachometer hookup for V8 HEI system

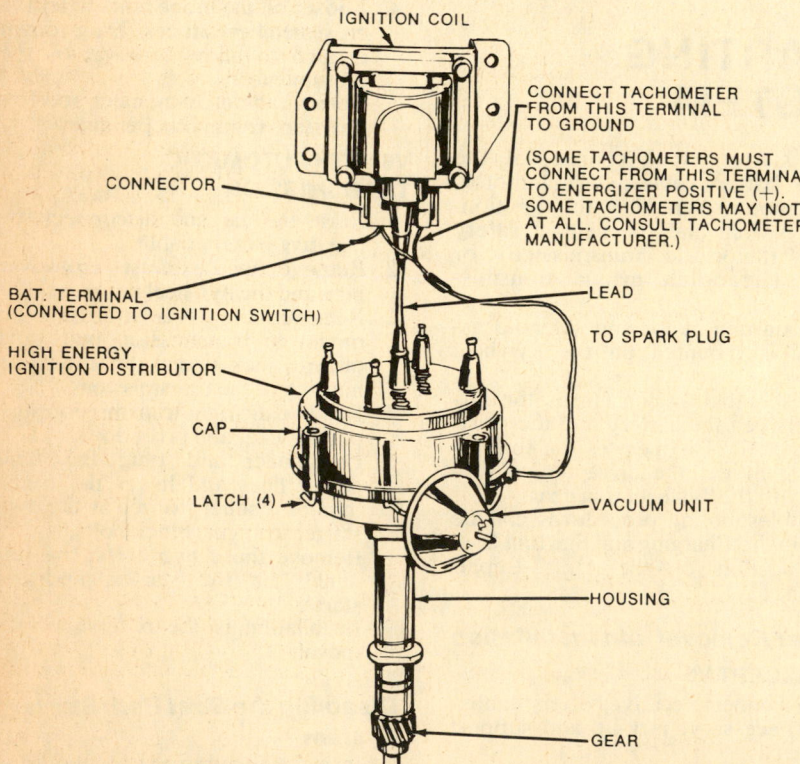

IGNITION COIL

CONNECT TACHOMETER
FROM THIS TERMINAL
TO GROUND

(SOME TACHOMETERS MUST
CONNECT FROM THIS TERMINAL
TO ENERGIZER POSITIVE (+).
SOME TACHOMETERS MAY NOT WORK
AT ALL. CONSULT TACHOMETER
MANUFACTURER.)

CONNECTOR

BAT. TERMINAL
(CONNECTED TO IGNITION SWITCH)

HIGH ENERGY
IGNITION DISTRIBUTOR

CAP

LATCH (4)

LEAD

TO SPARK PLUG

VACUUM UNIT

HOUSING

GEAR

Tachometer hookup for inline four and six HEI system

justment distributor used on six-cylinder engines, a 12 volt aluminum external point adjustment distributor used on eight-cylinder engines, and a 12 volt aluminum unitized transistor ignition distributor. During the 1974 model year, the unitized distributor was replaced by the similar HEI (High Energy Ignition) distributor used on other GM products. V8 and V6 HEI distributors have the coil mounted in the distributor cap. On the inline engines, the coil is mounted separately.

NOTE: *There is a tachometer connecting terminal next to the ignition switch connector on the V8 and V6 HEI or unitized distributor cap. On the inline engines, connect the tachometer to the terminal opposite the battery terminal on the remote-mounted coil. Most tachometers will work when connected to this terminal and to a ground. Some must connect from this terminal to the positive battery terminal. Some tachometers won't work at all with this system or may require a special hookup. Never ground the tachometer terminal; the system will be damaged.*

Distributor Removal

1. Disconnect the distributor primary wire (the thin wire) from the coil on breaker point systems. On inline systems, detach the wiring harness connector from the coil. On V6 and V8 HEI systems, disconnect the ignition switch battery feed wire from the distributor cap. Don't use a screwdriver or other tool to release the lock tab.
2. Remove the distributor cap. Unlatch the cap by using a screwdriver to disengage the spring-loaded latches. Sixes with breaker points have captive retaining screws.
3. Make reference marks on the block and the distributor housing that align with the tip of the rotor. Do not crank the engine after these marks have been made.
4. Disconnect the vacuum line at distributor.
5. Remove the distributor clamp screw and hold-down clamp.
6. Lift out the distributor. Notice the slight rotation of the rotor as the distributor is removed from the block.

Distributor Installation

Installation procedure is the reverse of the removal procedure. It should be noted, however, that while inserting a gear-driven distributor into the block, the rotor should be moved slightly to one side. This is necessary because of the helical cut of the distributor and camshaft gears. As the distributor seats in its bore, the rotor will turn slightly so the reference marks will once again be in line.

strument panel on or near the fuse block.
3. Cut and tape the ends of the green wire on the body side of the connector.
4. Remove the buzzer from the fuse block or connector.

IGNITION SYSTEM

Three types of distributors are used: a 12 volt aluminum internal point ad-

Distributor Installation If Engine Has Been Disturbed

ALL EXCEPT 4-140

1. With No. 1 piston coming up on compression stroke, continue cranking the engine until the pulley timing mark indexes with the zero (0) mark on the engine timing scale. There are devices available which will screw into the number one cylinder spark plug opening and indicate when TDC is reached.
2. Replace the distributor.
3. Install the distributor in the block so that the vacuum diaphragm faces the left side of the engine on V8 engines, and to the front of the engine on inline six-cylinder engines. The rotor should point toward the contact in the cap for N. 1 cylinder. Move the rotor slightly to the side because, as the distributor is pressed into its bore, it will turn a small amount.
4. Reverse the removal procedure to complete installation.

4-140

1. Remove No. 1 spark plug and place a finger over the plug hole. Remove the center coil wire and crank the engine until compression is felt in No. 1 cylinder. Rotate the engine until the timing pulley pointer is aligned with the 0° TDC mark.
2. Install the distributor with the vacuum advance unit pointing toward the front of the engine and the punchmarks on the drive gear (if any) in line with the No. 1 cap tower. The rotor must point to the No. 1 distributor cap tower.
3. Install the hold-down clamp. Tighten the clamp bolt.
4. Install the rotor, cap and vacuum line.
5. Connect the wiring connector to the coil.
6. Check and adjust the ignition timing.

Contact Point and Condenser Replacement and Adjustment

1. Remove the distributor cap and the rotor.
2. Remove the V8 radio frequency interference (R.F.I.) shield, if so equipped.
3. Remove the screws holding the points in place.
4. Remove the condenser lead and ignition primary lead from the points. Loosen the clamp and slide the condenser out. Remove the point set.
5. Install a new set of points and tighten the attaching screws.
6. Slide the new condenser into the clamp. Connect the condenser and primary leads to the points.
7. Apply a very small amount of high temperature grease to the distributor breaker cam.
8. On sixes, adjust the point gap after

turning the engine so that the fiber rubbing block of the point set is on the high point of the breaker cam. Set the dwell with the engine cranking. You don't have to adjust the gap on V8s at this point if you are installing present points.
9. Install the V8 R.F.I. shield. (The half covering the points should be installed first.) You don't need the shield if the unitized point and condenser set is being used on V8s.
10. Install the rotor and distributor cap.
11. Set the V8 dwell using a dwell meter with the engine running. Using a 1/8 in. allen wrench, rotate the adjusting screw through the cap window until the dwell meets specifications.

Ignition Timing

Timing marks are located on the front engine cover and harmonic balancer or pulley.

1. Disconnect and plug the distributor vacuum advance hose.
2. Make sure that the dwell is adjusted to specifications on models with breaker points.

NOTE: *it may be necessary to put a small amount of white paint or chalk on the timing marks to make them more visible.*

3. Connect a timing light to no. 1 spark plug.
4. Loosen the distributor hold-down clamp.
5. Start the engine and rotate the distributor until the correct mark on the cover lines up with the pulley or harmonic balancer mark. Tighten the distributor clamp, and recheck the timing.

FUEL SYSTEM

Information on the fuel gauge and carburetors will be found in the Unit Repair Section.

The fuel pump is of the single action diaphragm-type, equipped with a pulsation dampening chamber for stabilizing fuel flow.

A vapor diverter is incorporated into the fuel pumps used on air conditioned V8 and 4 bbl models. The fuel pump is not repairable and must be replaced as a unit if defective.

The Astre and Sunbird use an in-tank electric pump.

Fuel Pump Removal and Installation

ALL EXCEPT ASTRE AND SUNBIRD

1. Disconnect fuel inlet, outlet and vapor return lines at pump and plug pump inlet line.
2. Remove two pump mounting bolts and lockwashers; remove pump and gasket.
3. On Chevrolet 305, 307 & 350 V8

engines, if pushrod is to be removed: take out the two adapter bolts and lockwashers and remove adapter and gasket.
4. Install pump with new gasket coated with sealer. Coat mounting bolt threads with sealer and tighten bolts.

NOTE: *on Chevrolet 305, 307 & 350 V8 engines, mechanical fingers or heavy grease can be used to hold pump pushrod in place during installation. Coat pipe plug threads or adapter gasket with sealer if pushrod was removed.*

5. Connect inlet and outlet lines, start engine and check for leaks.

Chilton's TIME SAVER

When replacing a fuel pump on a Chevrolet 307 or 350 cu. in. engine, considerable time can be saved as follows:

1. **Before removing the old pump, remove the upper bolt from the engine's right front mounting boss. This bolt hole is in direct alignment with the fuel pump pushrod. The threaded bolt hole continues into the pump pushrod bore. The bolt acts as an oil plug.**
2. **Temporarily insert a longer bolt, (about 3/8—16 x 2 in.) into the hole. Screw the bolt into the bore until it bottoms against the pump pushrod. (Don't tighten the bolt with a wrench or the rod can be damaged.)**
3. **The mechanic is now free to remove and install the fuel pump without worrying about fuel pump pushrod misalignment.**

——— CAUTION ———

Don't forget to reinstall the original bolt.

ASTRE AND SUNBIRD

The electrical fuel pump is an integral part of the fuel tank unit assembly, which includes the fuel gauge metering unit. The fuel pump is energized by the ignition switch when the key is in the start position. After the engine starts, the pump receives current through the engine oil pressure safety switch as long as there is approximately 2 psi oil pressure.

1. Disconnect the battery ground cable and siphon the fuel from the tank.
2. Disconnect the gauge sending unit and pump wires at the rear harness connector.
3. Raise the car. Disconnect the fuel

line at the gauge unit pickup line.

4. Disconnect the tank vent line to the vapor separator, which is mounted in the tank.
5. Disconnect the gauge wire ground screw from the floorpan.
6. Remove the tank strap bolts and, very carefully, lower the tank.
7. Use a special wrench, or a suitable substitute, to unscrew the retaining cam ring. Do not strike any part of the tank with a metal tool, such as a hammer; there is a danger of explosion from sparks.
8. Remove the gauge sending-unit and fuel pump assembly.
9. Remove the flat wire conductor from the plastic clip on the fuel tube.
10. While squeezing the clamp, pull the pump straight back 1/2 in. for access to the terminals. Remove the two nuts, lockwashers, and wires from the pump.
11. Squeeze the clamp and pull the pump straight back to completely remove it from the sending unit.

——— CAUTION ———

Be careful not to bend the circular support bracket.

12. Slide the replacement pump through the circular support bracket until it rests against the rubber coupling. Be sure that the rubber isolator and saran strainer, supplied in the service package, are attached to the pump.
13. Attach the two pump terminals, using lockwashers and nuts. Be sure that the flat conductor is attached to the terminal farthest away from the float arm.
14. Squeeze the clamp and push the pump into the rubber coupling.
15. Replace the flat wire conductor in the plastic clip on the fuel tube.
16. Install the pump and gauge unit into the tank opening. Tighten the cam ring.
17. Install the fuel tank using a reverse of the removal procedure.

Fuel Filter Removal and Installation

1. Disconnect fuel line connection at inlet of carburetor.
2. Remove inlet fuel filter nut from carburetor using a box wrench.
3. Remove filter element and spring.
4. If a bronze element, blow through cone end—element should allow air to pass freely.
5. Install element spring and new element into carburetor. Bronze elements are installed with small section of cone facing outward.
6. Install new gasket on fitting nut and install nut.
7. Install fuel line and tighten securely. Start engine and check for leaks.

Idle Speed and Mixture Adjustments

1972

Adjust with air cleaner installed.

On some models, the idle stop solenoid is no longer used, having been replaced by the combination emission control valve. This valve is energized through the transmission to increase idle speed under conditions of high gear deceleration and to provide full vacuum spark advance during high gear operation. The valve is de-energized at curb idle and in the lower gears to provide a retarded spark under these conditions, the result of which is lower hydrocarbon emission. *The valve need not be adjusted unless the solenoid or throttle body is removed, or the carburetor overhauled.*

V8 Idle Speed

1. Disconnect carburetor "EVAP" hose from vapor storage canister.
2. Disconnect and plug carburetor-to-vacuum (distributor vacuum) solenoid hose at solenoid. Disconnect throttle solenoid wire on 4 bbl manual transmission engines.
3. Set dwell and timing (in that order) at specified idle speed.
4. Adjust carburetor speed screw to obtain specified idle speed, automatic in Drive, manual in Neutral.
5. On 4 bbl manual transmission models, reconnect throttle solenoid wire, manually extend solenoid screw and adjust to specified idle rpm.
6. Place automatic in Park, manual in Neutral and check fast idle speed with screw on top step of cam. Adjust fast idle screw to obtain 1,700 rpm.

NOTE: *2 bbl carburetors are not adjustable for fast idle.*

7. Reconnect distributor vacuum and vapor storage hoses.

Inline 6 Cyl. Idle Speed

1. Disconnect fuel tank "EVAP" hose from vapor storage canister.
2. Disconnect and plug distributor vacuum advance hose.
3. Set dwell and timing (in that order) at specified idle speed.
4. Adjust carburetor idle speed screw to obtain 550 rpm for manual, 500 rpm for automatic (in Drive). Do not adjust solenoid screw.
5. Place automatic in Park and manual in Neutral, then place fast idle tang on top step of fast idle cam and check fast idle speed. Adjust to obtain 2,400 rpm.

V8 and Inline 6 Cyl. Idle Mixture

If the carburetor has been overhauled, or the plastic locks removed from the mixture screws, the following procedure must be used to adjust idle speed and mixture. It must be emphasized that the manufacturer does not recommend this procedure as a substitute for the preceding methods, in that exhaust emission quality can be adversely affected unless the proper test equipment is available.

1. Turn in mixture screw/s until lightly seated, then back out 3 1/2 turns.
2. Start engine and adjust carburetor idle speed screw to obtain a speed 25 rpm above specified idle (automatic), 75 rpm higher for six and 2 bbl V8 (manual), or 100 rpm higher for 4 bbl V8 (manual).
3. Turn mixture screw/s in equally until specified idle speed is obtained. At this point, a CO meter should be employed to adjust mixture. A reading of 1.0% or less must be maintained.
4. Shut off engine and install new limiter caps.
5. Adjust fast idle speed, as described previously.

1973-74

Inline Six-Cylinder Idle Speed

1. Disconnect the fuel tank "EVAP" hose from the vapor canister in the engine compartment. Plug the line.
2. Disconnect and plug the distributor vacuum line.
3. Check that dwell and timing are correct.
4. Detach the idle stop solenoid wire (not the C.E.C. solenoid wire) and set the low idle speed to 450 rpm by using a 1/8 in. allen wrench inside the six-sided nut on the solenoid.

NOTE: *The engine must be at normal operating temperature.*

5. Reconnect the idle stop solenoid wire.
6. Set the normal idle speed to that specified in the Tune-Up Specifications chart. Adjust by turning the six-sided nut on the solenoid.

NOTE: *The automatic transmission must be in Drive. Block the wheels.*

7. On 1973 manual transmission models, pull the C.E.C. solenoid plunger out as far as it will go. The plunger should contact the throttle lever and produce an 850 rpm idle speed. Adjust by turning the plunger.
8. Set the automatic transmission in Park and the manual transmission in Neutral. Set the fast idle tang on the top step of the fast idle cam. The fast idle speed should be 2,400 rpm for 1973 and 1,800 rpm for 1974. Bend the tang to adjust.

V8 Idle Speed

1. Disconnect and plug the carburetor hose from the vapor canister.
2. Disconnect and plug the distributor and EGR valve vacuum hoses. Plug any open vacuum tubes on the carburetor.
3. Check the dwell and timing.
4. Disconnect the idle stop solenoid wire.
5. Adjust the carburetor idle speed screw to the low rpm specified in

the Tune-Up Specifications chart.

6. Reconnect the solenoid wire and adjust the solenoid plunger screw to obtain the specified idle speed.

NOTE: *You might have to work the throttle linkage by hand first, since the solenoid isn't always powerful enough to move it.*

7. On four-barrel carburetors, check the fast idle speed with the fast idle speed screw on the top step of the fast idle cam. Adjust the speed by turning the fast idle screw. Fast idle speed is 1,500 rpm for all engines except the 1974 455 S.D., which is 2,000 rpm.

NOTE: *The fast idle speed screw is NOT the same one used in Step 5. You can't make this adjustment on two-barrel carburetors.*

Idle Mixture

1. Set the parking brake and block the wheels.
2. Disconnect and plug the carburetor hose from the vapor canister in the engine compartment. Disconnect and plug the distributor vacuum hose.
3. If the idle mixture limiter caps are intact and a CO meter is available, attempt to obtain an idle setting of 0.2% CO by adjusting the mixture screws. If this doesn't work, remove the caps and proceed to the next step.

NOTE: *The engine must be at normal operating temperature.*

4. Remove the idle mixture limiter caps. If you have a CO meter, adjust the mixture screws equally to get a reading of 0.2% CO.
5. Run the screws in until they are lightly seated, then back them out six turns for 1973 and seven for 1974.

NOTE: *Sixes have only one screw.*

6. Turn the air conditioner off, place the automatic transmission in Drive (block the wheels), place the manual transmission in Neutral, leave the air cleaner off and plug the air cleaner manifold vacuum fitting. Adjust the idle speed screw or the idle stop solenoid to obtain the following temporary idle speed:

Engine	Year	Man.	Auto.
6-250	1973	800	700
8-350, 2 bbl	1973	1100	700
8-400, 2 bbl	1973	—	700
8-400, 455, 4 bbl	1973	1200	700
6-250	1974	950	650
6-250 Calif.	1974	950	630
8-350, 2 bbl	1974	1150	750
8-350, 2 bbl,	1974	—	720

Rochester 4 bbl

Engine	Year	Man.	Auto.
8-350, 4 bbl	1974	1200	730
8-350, 4 bbl, Calif.	1974	—	720
8-400, 2 bbl	1974	—	720
8-400, 2 bbl, Calif.	1974	—	690
8-400, 4 bbl	1974	1310	720
8-400, 4 bbl, Calif.	1974	—	685
8-455, 4 bbl	1974	—	680
8-455, 4 bbl, Calif.	1974	—	675
8-455, S.D.	1974	1420	825

7. Turn the mixture screws in equally to get the highest idle speed. Then set the speed back to that listed in Step 6.
8. Turn the mixture screws in equally until the engine speed drops to the normal idle speed given in the Tune-Up Specifications chart.
9. Install the air cleaner. If the idle speed changes, adjust the mixture screws slightly to compensate.

1975-76

Inline Six-Cylinder, OHC 4, V6, and V8

1. The adjustment must be made with the engine at normal operating temperature, with the air conditioner off, and the air cleaner removed. The air cleaner vacuum fitting in the manifold should be plugged. Automatic transmissions should be in Drive and manual transmissions in neutral.
2. Set the parking brake and block the wheels.
3. On all models, disconnect and plug the hose going to the carburetor from the vapor cannister. On 1975 350 V8 2 bbl except in the Ventura, detach and plug the distributor vacuum hose to block vacuum advance. On 1975 260 V8s with manual transmission, the distributor vacuum hose comes from the same carburetor port. Disconnect the EGR hose while leaving the distributor vacuum hoses connected. On 1976s, disconnect and plug the EGR hose to the carburetor at the EGR valve end. On the models indicated below, disconnect and plug the distributor vacuum hose; on all other models, leave it alone.

Firebird with 400/455 (except H.O.) and manual trans.
All Ventura with 350 V8
All Sunbird and Astre
All Calif. 250 inline sixes

On all 140 OHC fours with a 1 bbl carburetor and manual transmission, and all California 140 OHC fours with a 2 bbl and manual transmission, disconnect the idle stop solenoid.

4. Use pliers to break off the plastic

idle mixture screw limiter caps. Sixes have only one screw. Turn in the mixture screws until they seat lightly, then back them out five turns. Back out six turns on manual transmission Ventura 260 V8 and 455 H.O.

5. Adjust the idle speed screw or idle solenoid screw to get the "before lean drop idle" speed listed on the underhood specifications sticker. The tachometer hookup for the HEI ignition system is covered earlier under Ignition System.

6. Adjust the mixture screws equally (quarter-turn increments are recommended) to obtain the highest possible idle speed. Check the adjustment by shifting into Neutral, running the engine at 2,000 rpm for 5-10 seconds, returning to idle, shifting back into Drive, and letting the speed stabilize for 10 seconds.

7. Return the idle speed to that set in Step 5.

8. Repeat Steps 6 and 7, until no further speed increase is possible.

9. Turn in the mixture screws equally until the normal idle speed is reached.

10. Place the automatic transmission in Park and the manual in neutral. Check the tune-up sticker and adjust the fast idle with the fast idle speed screw. If there is no speed shown, you do not have to adjust the fast idle. For 4MC and 1MV carburetors, adjust with the fast idle speed screw on the high step of the cam; for the 5210-C carburetor, set the fast idle screw on the second step.

11. If there is an idle speed-up solenoid, place the transmission in Drive, disconnect the terminal connector at the air conditioner compressor clutch and adjust the solenoid to give 675 RPM; when finished reconnect the terminal connector.

12. If there is a dashpot, adjust it so that at idle, there is .040 in. clearance between the tip of the plunger (compressed) and the throttle lever.

13. Replace and connect the air cleaner. Use the mixture screws to make any slight idle speed correction necessary.

14. Replace the distributor and canister hoses.

1977 IDLE SPEED ADJUSTMENT

4-140, 4-151

1. Run the engine to normal operating temperature, choke open, A/C off, tachometer and timing light connected. Set the brake and block the wheels.

2. Disconnect and plug the PCV hose at the canister.

3. Disconnect and plug the vacuum hose at the distributor.

4. Start the engine and place the transmission in neutral with MT and Drive with AT.

5. Check, and adjust, if necessary, the timing.

6. Unplug and reconnect the vacuum advance hose.

7. Adjust the idle speed.

8. On cars with A/C, adjust the idle speed, then disconnect the lead at the wide open throttle A/C override switch located on the accelerator linkage bracket. Set the A/C to the on position and momentarily open the throttle to allow the solenoid plunger to extend. Adjust the solenoid to the specified rpm, reconnect the override and turn the A/C off.

9. Reconnect the PCV hose and remove the tachometer.

6-231, 8-305

1. Run the engine to normal operating temperature, choke open and A/C off. Connect a tach and timing light. Set the brake and block the wheels.

2. Disconnect and plug the canister and EGR hoses.

3. Start the engine and place the MT in neutral or the AT in Drive.

4. Disconnect the vacuum advance hose and set the timing.

5. Reconnect the advance hose and set the idle speed.

6. Connect the hoses and stop the engine.

8-301

1. Run the engine to normal operating temperature.

2. With the choke fully open, A/C off, parking brake set, wheels blocked and tachometer connected, place the transmission in neutral, MT, or Drive, AT. Set the timing.

3. Disconnect the A/C compressor clutch lead.

4. Disconnect and plug the vacuum advance line.

5. On cars with A/C, adjust the idle speed with the A/C on; this energizes the solenoid but not the compressor.

6. Open the throttle momentarily to extend the solenoid plunger. Adjust the solenoid screw to 650 rpm and reconnect the compressor lead.

7. Reconnect all hoses and stop the engine.

8-350, 400, 403

1. Run the engine to normal operating temperature.

2. With the choke fully open, A/C off, brake set, and wheels blocked, connect a tachometer and timing light.

3. Disconnect and plug the vacuum advance, canister, and EGR hoses. Disconnect the A/C compressor clutch lead wire.

4. Start the engine and place the transmission in neutral, MT, or Drive, AT. Adjust the timing.

5. Connect the vacuum advance line.

6. On cars with A/C, turn the system on. This will energize the solenoid. Open the throttle momentarily to extend the plunger.

7. Adjust the solenoid to the specified rpm.

8. Reconnect the compressor and turn the A/C off.

9. On cars with manual trans., adjust the idle speed screw to the specified rpm.

10. Connect all hoses and shut off engine.

1977 MIXTURE ADJUSTMENT

1. Run the engine to normal operating temperature, choke fully open, A/C off.

2. Set the brake and block the wheels.

3. Remove the air cleaner, but leave the vacuum hoses connected. If the car has level control, disconnect and plug the compressor vacuum hose.

4. Disconnect and plug the other hoses listed on the underhood sticker.

5. Connect tachometer to the engine.

6. With the advance hose plugged, check and if necessary, adjust the timing, with the MT in neutral and the AT in Drive. Connect the advance hose.

7. Carefully remove mixture the screw caps.

8. Lightly turn in the screws until they just seat, then back them out just enough so that the engine will run.

9. Back out each screw 1/8 of a turn at a time until maximum idle speed is obtained.

10. Set the idle speed to the higher of the two figures shown on the underhood sticker. Repeat step 9 to be sure you have maximum idle speed.

11. Turn in each screw 1/8 turn at a time until the lower of the two figures is reached.

12. Reset the idle to the specified rpm.

13. Reconnect the hoses and install the air cleaner.

1978-79 Idle Speed Adjustment

4-151 WITH 5210-C OR 6510-C CARBURETOR

1. Connect a tachometer to the engine according to the manufacturer's specifications.

2. Run the engine at normal operating temperature, turn the air conditioning off, disconnect and plug the vacuum line between the canister and the PCV valve at the canister, plug the distributor vacuum advance line at the distributor, make sure that the choke is fully opened, set the parking brake, block the wheels and place the transmission in Drive (AT) or neutral (MT).

3. Check, and if necessary, adjust the timing.

4. Unplug and reconnect the distributor vacuum advance hose.

5. Turn the idle screw to obtain the specified idle speed.

NOTE: *On cars with manual transmission and air conditioning, or cars with automatic transmission, set the idle as explained earlier, then disconnect the wide open throttle air conditioning override switch located on the accelerator linkage bracket. Turn the air conditioning on, momentarily open the throttle to allow the plunger to fully extend, and adjust the solenoid screw to the rpm specified on the underhood sticker. Reconnect the override switch and turn the A/C off.*

6. Unplug and reconnect the PCV-canister hose.

V6 WITH 2GE AND V8-305 WITH 2GC CARBURETOR

1. Connect a tachometer to the engine according to the manufacturer's instructions.

2. Run the engine at normal operating temperature. Turn the air conditioning off, make sure that the choke is fully open. Set the parking brake and block the wheels. Disconnect and plug the hoses from the vapor canister at the canister and the EGR valve at the valve.

3. Place the transmission in Park (AT) or neutral (MT).

4. Disconnect and plug the vacuum advance line.

5. Check and if necessary, adjust the timing.

6. Unplug and reconnect the vacuum advance line.

7. Turn the idle screw to the desired rpm.

8. Unplug and reconnect the hoses.

V8-301 WITH M2MC-210 CARBURETOR

1. Connect a tachometer to the engine according to the manufacturer's instructions. Run the engine at normal operating temperature. Disconnect the compressor clutch connector at the clutch. Set the parking brake and block the wheels. Make sure that the choke is fully opened and place the transmission in Drive (AT) or neutral (MT).

2. Disconnect and plug the vacuum advance line at the distributor.

3. Check and, if necessary, adjust the timing.

4. Unplug and reconnect the vacuum advance line.

5. Disconnect the purge hose from the canister.

6. On cars with air conditioning: Turn the idle screw to obtain the specified rpm. Turn the A/C switch on. Open the throttle momentarily to extend the idle solenoid plunger. Adjust the idle solenoid to the rpm specified on the underhood sticker. Turn the A/C off. On cars without air conditioning: Turn the idle

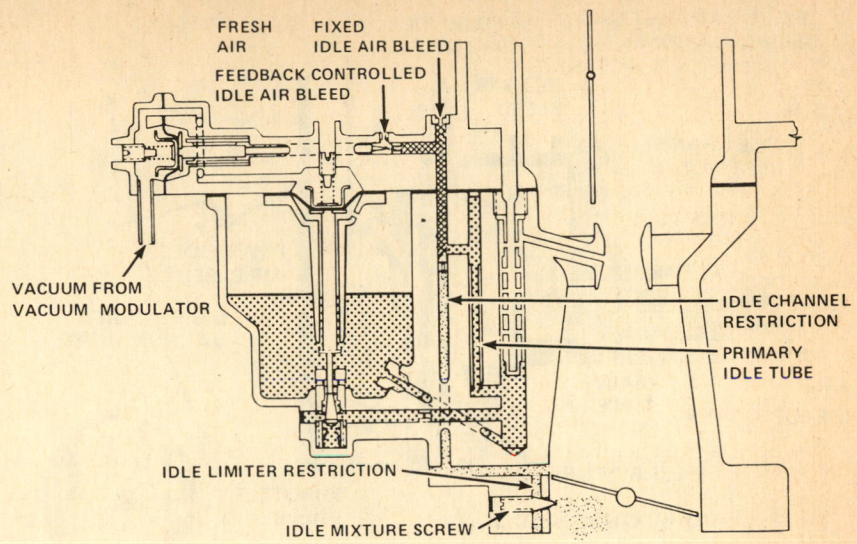

6510-C Idle System (© Pontiac Div., G.M. Corp.)

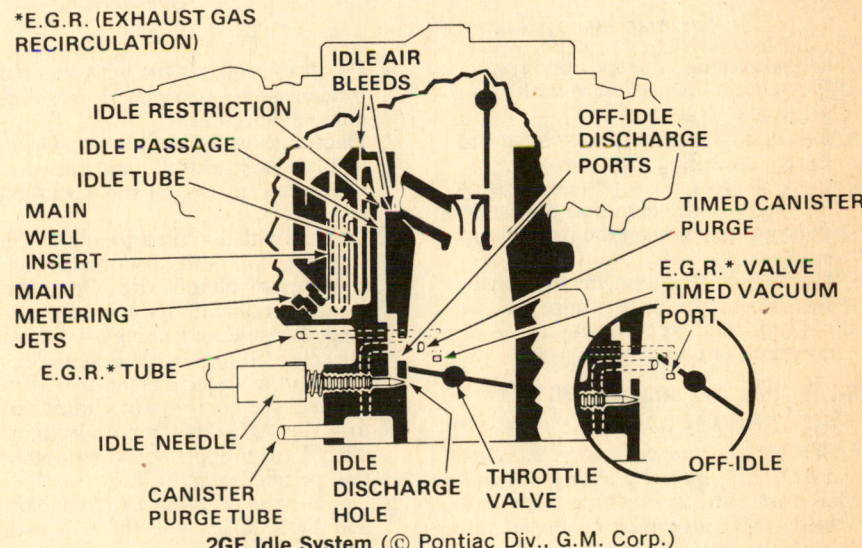

2GE Idle System (© Pontiac Div., G.M. Corp.)

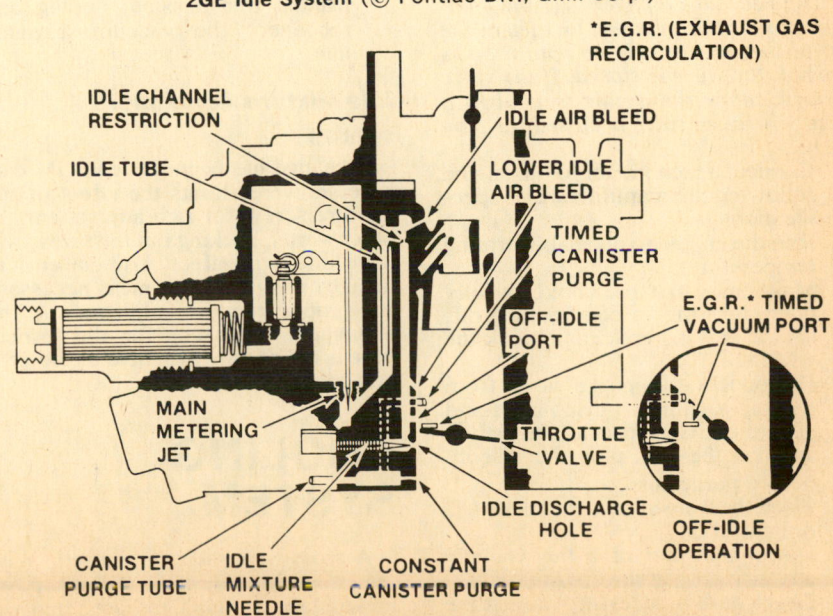

M2MC Idle System (© Pontiac Div., G.M. Corp.)

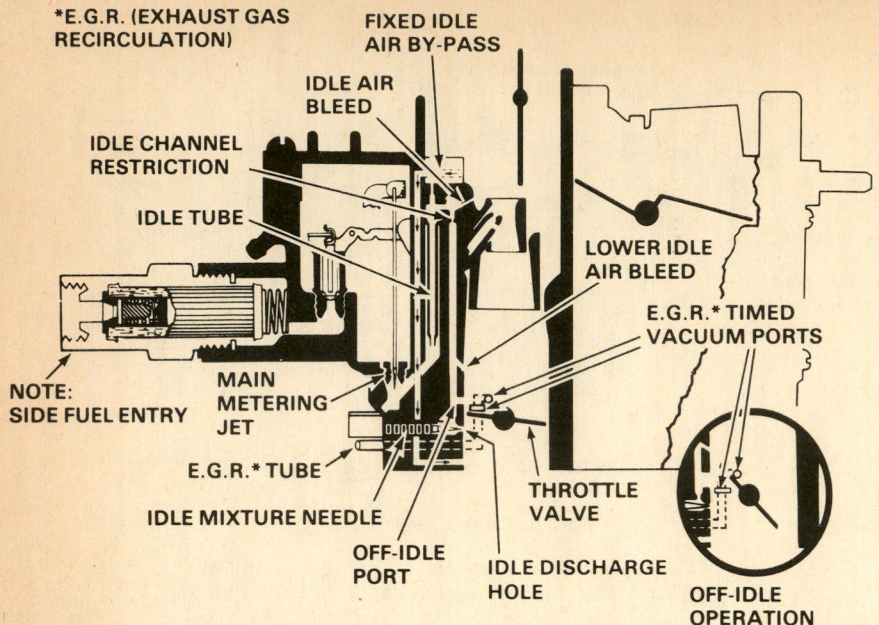

M4MC Idle System (© Pontiac Div., G.M. Corp.)

screw to obtain the specified rpm.

7. Place the transmission in Park (AT) or leave it in neutral (MT).
8. Disconnect the vacuum hose at the EGR valve. Plug the hose.
9. Place the fast idle screw on the second step of the cam and adjust to the rpm specified on the underhood sticker.
10. Unplug and reconnect the hose. Reconnect the purge hose at the canister and reconnect the A/C compressor clutch wire.

V8-301, 305, 350, 400, 403, WITH M4MC CARBURETOR

NOTE: *This carburetor, when used on the V8-301, is equipped with a hot idle compensator valve. For proper idle adjustment, this valve must be closed. To check this, place a finger over the compensator air inlet channel located at the top of the air horn. If no rpm drop is noticed, the valve is closed. If the valve is open, allow the engine to cool to a point where the valve is closed, or plug the hole.*

1. Connect a tachometer to the engine following the manufacturer's specifications.
2. Run the engine to normal operating temperature.
3. Make sure that the choke is fully open, turn the air conditioning off, set the parking brake and block the wheels.
4. Disconnect the purge hose from the vapor canister, disconnect and plug the EGR hose at the valve, and, on the 350, plug the disconnected purge hose.
5. Place the transmission in Park (AT) or neutral (MT).
6. Disconnect and plug the vacuum advance hose at the distributor.
7. Check and, if necessary, adjust the timing.

8. On all except the 400 with manual transmission, reconnect the vacuum advance line.
9. Place the transmission in Drive (AT) or neutral (MT) and turn the idle screw to obtain the specified rpm.
10. On cars with air conditioning: Turn the A/C on and disconnect the compressor clutch wire. Open the throttle momentarily to fully extend the solenoid plunger. Adjust the solenoid screw to the rpm specified on the underhood sticker. Reconnect the compressor clutch and turn the A/C off. On cars without A/C: Turn the idle screw to obtain the specified rpm.
11. Unplug and reconnect the canister and EGR hoses. On the 400 with manual transmission, unplug and reconnect the vacuum advance line.

Idle Mixture Adjustment

1978-79

A change has been made in GM carburetors which limits the effect of the mixture screw for rich adjustment. In other words, backing out the screw will have little or no effect. Artificial enrichment by means of propane is necessary for proper mixture adjustment. The equipment necessary for this procedure is not readily available to the general public.

COOLING SYSTEM

A cross-flow radiator is used. With the cross-flow design, coolant flows horizontally through the core and the tanks are located on each side.

Automatic transmission radiators have fluid coolers built into the right-hand tank, air-conditioned and high-performance models have greater cooling capacity than standard. The drain cock is located at the inside, lower left-hand corner of the radiator.

To refill and bleed the cooling system after repair, first fill the radiator with coolant mixture. Leave the cap off and run the engine with the heater on until the thermostat opens. Then fill the radiator as necessary, with the engine running. Replace the radiator cap. If there is a coolant reservoir, add coolant mixture until the level is between the two marks.

Radiator Removal and Installation

ALL EXCEPT 1975-77 ASTRE, SUNBIRD

1. Drain coolant.
2. Remove fan shield assembly on the six. Remove the fan.
3. Disconnect upper and lower hoses.
4. Disconnect and plug oil cooler lines, if equipped with automatic transmission.
5. Lift radiator and shroud straight up and out of car.
6. To install, reverse removal procedure, making sure lower cradles are properly located and automatic transmission is full.

1975-77 ASTRE, SUNBIRD

There are two radiators: a standard type and a larger heavy duty radiator equipped with a fan shroud.

1. Drain the radiator.
2. On models with the heavy duty radiator, remove the fan shroud.
3. Disconnect the intake and outlet hoses and the coolant recovery hose. Disconnect the coolant level indicator lead.
4. Remove the upper mounting panel or bracket.
5. Lift the radiator up and out of the lower brackets.
6. To install, reverse the removal procedure.

Water Pump Removal and Installation

EXCEPT 4-140, 4-151

This is a centrifugal-type water-pump. It is die cast, with sealed bearings and is pressed together. Therefore, it is serviced as a unit.

1. Disconnect the battery and drain the radiator.
2. Loosen the alternator and remove the fan belt.
3. Remove the power steering and air conditioning belts, if so equipped.
4. Remove the fan and water pump pulley.
5. Remove the V8 front alternator bracket.
6. Remove the heater hose and radiator hose at the pump.

7. Remove the water pump retaining bolts and the pump.
8. Install the pump by reversing the above steps. Make sure that all gasket surfaces are clean and smooth. Always use a gasket sealer on both sides of the gasket. Tighten the retaining bolts.

4-140

The water pump is located on the front of the engine block immediately above the crankshaft pulley. The pump bearings are permanently lubricated during manufacture and do not require periodic maintenance other than keeping the air vent (top of housing) and drain holes (bottom of housing) free of dirt and grease.

The pump components cannot be serviced separately and, in the event of pump failure, the complete assembly must be replaced as a unit, as follows:
1. Raise and support the hood.
2. Disconnect the battery negative cable.
3. Remove the fan and spacer.
4. Loosen, but do not remove, the two lower timing belt cover retaining screws. The holes in the cover are slotted so that the cover is easily removed.
5. Remove the two upper timing belt cover retaining screws and remove the cover.
6. Drain the coolant.
7. Loosen the water pump bolts to relieve the tension on the timing belt.
8. Remove the hoses from the water pump.
9. Remove the water pump bolts, pump and gasket.
10. Thoroughly clean the old gasket material from the pump and block.
11. To install, position the water pump on the block using a new gasket and loosely install the water pump bolts. Make sure theat the V grooves of the belt are aligned with the grooves in the water pump.

NOTE: *Use an anti-seize compound on the water pump bolt threads.*

12. A special tool is available to adjust the timing belt. It fits into the round hole in the square lug to the upper right (facing) of the water pump and bears against the pump housing midway between the bolt holes. If this tool is available, apply 15 ft. lbs. of torque against the water pump (and belt). If the tool is not available, apply a force to the pump in a similar manner. Tighten the pump bolts to 15 ft. lbs.
13. Install the radiator and heater hoses to the pump.
14. Install the timing belt cover, lowering the cover lower screw slots over the screws. Loosely tighten the screws against the cover.
15. Install the two upper timing cover screws, then tighten the upper and lower screws to 50 in. lbs.
16. Install the fan spacer and fan, tightening the bolts to 20 ft. lbs.
17. Fill the cooling system, connect

the battery negative cable, start the engine and check for leaks.

4-151
1. Drain the cooling system.
2. Remove all drive belts.
3. Remove the fan and pump pulley.
4. Unbolt and remove the pump from the engine.
5. Clean the gasket surfaces, coat the new gasket with non-hardening type sealer and position the gasket on the block.
6. Coat the threaded areas of the bolts with waterproof sealer and install the pump. Torque the bolts to 20 ft. lbs.
7. Install the pulley and fan.
8. Install the drive belts. The belts should be adjusted so that a 1/2" deflection is present when they are pushed on, mid-point along their longest straight run.

Thermostat Removal and Installation

EXCEPT 4-140
1. Drain coolant to below thermostat level.
2. Disconnect upper hose and remove water outlet assembly.
3. Replace by reversing the above steps. Clean the gasket surfaces and use a gasket sealer and a new gasket.
4. Refill and bleed cooling system.

4-140

The thermostat is located in a housing at the cylinder head water outlet adjacent to the intake manifold.
1. Drain the cooling system.
2. Disconnect the upper radiator hose at the engine.
3. Remove the alternator.
4. Unbolt the housing and remove the housing, gasket, and thermostat.
5. Replace the thermostat and housing, using a new gasket.
6. Install the alternator and adjust the drive belt.
7. Replace the radiator hose, fill the cooling system, start the engine, and check for leaks.

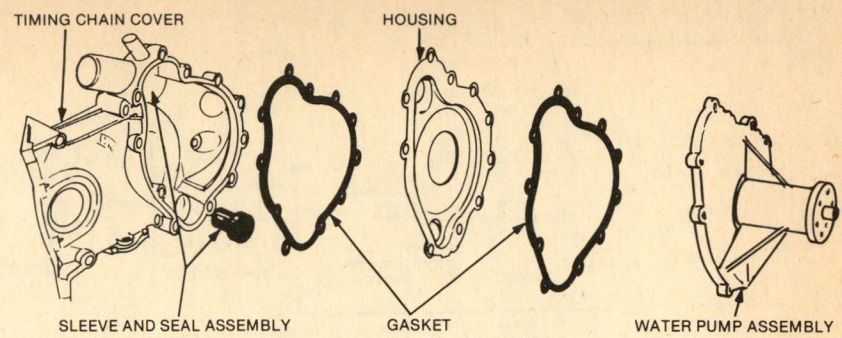

Pontiac V8 water pump assembly
(© Pontiac Div., G.M. Corp)

EMISSION CONTROLS

There are three types of emissions to be controlled: crankcase emissions, carburetor and gas tank gas vapor emissions, and exhaust emission. See the Unit Repair Section for troubleshooting and repair information.

1972

All six cylinder models with manual transmission, and all models with a 307 V8 use the C.E.C system. All six cylinder models with automatic transmission use the A.I.R. system. All V8s with four-speed transmission use the T.C.S. system. All V8s with a three-speed manual transmission or an automatic transmission use the Speed Control Spark System (S.C.S.)

The Speed Controlled Spark (S.C.S.), system uses a solenoid valve in the vacuum line running between the carburetor and the distributor. This valve is the same as the transmission-controlled spark valve. The difference in this system is that the valve is regulated by vehicle speed using a speed control spark switch. The S.C.S. solenoid valve is energized below 38 mph in any gear, under normal operating temperature, allowing no vacuum advance. Above 38 mph, in any gear, or any time engine temperature is higher or lower than normal operating temperature, the solenoid valve is de-energized allowing full vacuum advance to the distributor.

Normal S.C.S. engine operating temperatures range from 95° to 230°. An engine-temperature sensing switch is located in the head and de--energizes the solenoid until operating temperature is reached regardless of vehicle speed.

1973

The Controlled Combustion System (C.C.S.) is standard on all engines. The C.E.C./E.G.R. (Exhaust Gas Recirculation) system is used on all 6 cyl engines with manual transmission. The Air Injection Reactor (A.I.R.) is used

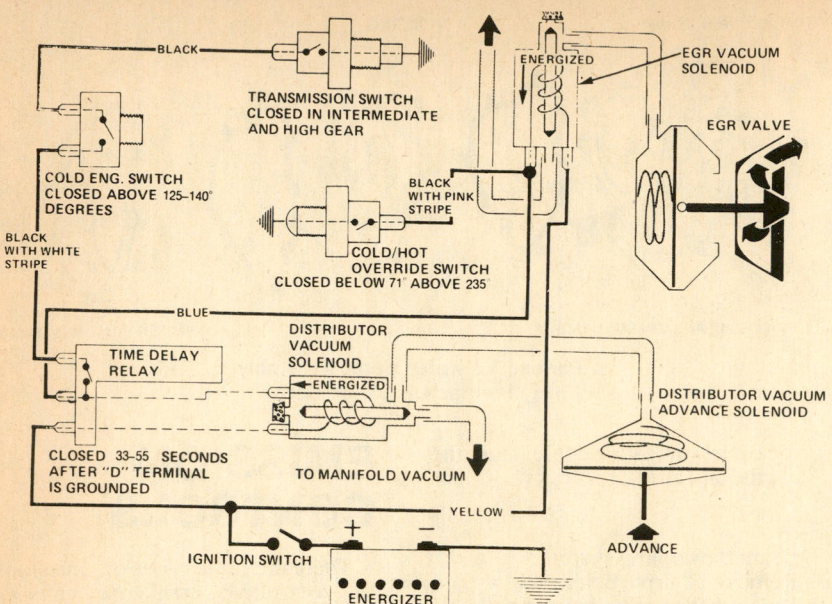

1973 combined TCS and EGR system (© Pontiac Div., G.M. Corp)

EXHAUST GAS RECIRCULATION (EGR)

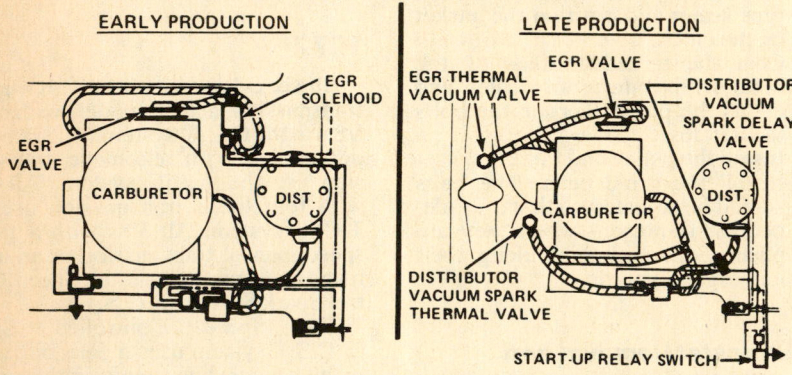

EGR system—1973 mid-year changes (© Pontiac Div, G.M. Corp)

on all 6 cyl, 350 with manual transmission, and 350/400 California engines. A combination of the Transmission Controlled Spark and Exhaust Gas Recirculation (E.G.R.) is on all V8 engines.

E.G.R. is a system used to reduce nitrous oxide (NOx) emissions. It functions by allowing a small amount of exhaust gas into the air fuel mixture in the intake manifold, under certain conditions. The EGR TCS system consists of a temperature switch which senses when the engine temperature is under 71° or over 230°, a second temperature switch sensing engine temperature between 140° and 230°, an EGR solenoid, a vacuum advance solenoid, a transmission switch, and a time delay relay. The under 71° and over 230° switch is mounted on the left cylinder head. The 140° to 230° switch is mounted in the right head. The time delay relay is mounted on the vacuum advance solenoid. The 71° to 230° switch grounds the circuit for the solenoids below 71° and above 230°. The 140° switch passes current to the transmission switch

when engine temperature is between 140° and 230°. The transmission switch then grounds the circuit for the solenoids in first gear only. Between 71° and 140° the temperature switches are both open and the solenoids are in the normal positions. The vacuum advance solenoid is normally closed, allowing no vacuum advance. The EGR solenoid is normally open, allowing exhaust gas recirculation. Below 71° there is a complete circuit and both solenoids are energized, allowing vacuum advance and cutting off EGR. From 71° to 140° there is an open circuit, the solenoids return to their normal positions, and vacuum advance is cut off and EGR is allowed. From 140° to 230°, in first gear, there is an open circuit and the solenoids are in their normal positions. The time delay relay maintains the open circuit for 33 to 55 seconds after the transmission shifts into second gear. However, after the time delay in second and third gear, the solenoids are energized to allow vacuum advance and cut off EGR. Over 235°

the solenoids are energized, vacuum advance occurs, and there is no EGR.

The C.E.C. system operates as previously, except that the time-delay relay now provides 20 seconds of vacuum advance before the solenoid is de-energized, and the engine temperature switch provides vacuum advance when engine coolant temperature is below 93°F.

1973 1/2

Mid-year A.I.R. cylinder heads can usually be identified by the absence of a drilled passage and by a metal sealing ball at the nos. 3 and 6 cylinder locations.

The new engines have a relocated vacuum source for the air cleaner. Vacuum is supplied through a tee in the hose feeding vacuum to the distributor vacuum spark thermal valve.

The mid-year EGR system operates on the same principle as the 1973 system, except for two major differences:
1. The EGR and TCS systems now work completely independently of each other.
2. A new EGR thermal vacuum valve is used to sense the temperature of the intake manifold coolant. Below 95°F, no EGR; above 95°F, EGR.

In the TCS system, full vacuum advance is provided below 62°F. When the temperature rises above 62°F, the distributor vacuum spark thermal valve closes and from this point on the distributor solenoid must be energized to get vacuum advance. The upper temperature limit for vacuum advance cut-in is now 240°F.

The Start-Up Relay Switch gives full advance in any gear for 20 seconds after all engine starts. After the 20 seconds has elapsed, the switch breaks ground and the distributor solenoid is de-energized, shutting off the vacuum advance.

1974

The A.I.R. system is carried over from 1973 and is used on all manual transmission and California six cylinder engines, 350 2 bbl manual transmission V8s, all 350 cu. in. California engines and 400 cu. in. 2 bbl California engines.

The EGR/TCS system is once again together, as in pre-1973 1/2 systems, and consists of a thermal vacuum valve, vacuum advance solenoid, EGR valve, hot coolant switch, cold feed switch and a time-delay relay for engine starting. The system is found on all V8s. In-line six-cylinder engines use the Chevrolet system without any changes.

On the EGR/TCS system, the distributor spark-EGR thermal vacuum valve senses the temperature of the air/fuel mixture inside the intake manifold. Below 62°F, EGR is off and full vacuum advance is provided. When the temperature rises above 62°F, EGR is on (operated by a port above the throttle blade, so that it only comes on above idle). From this point on the distributor vacuum advance solenoid must be energized by the other components and switches to provide vacuum advance.

When the cylinder head metal temperature goes above 125°, 140°, 155°F (depending on use), the cold feed switch closes. This sends the 12V current to the TCS switch. The TCS switch provides a ground only when the transmission shifts into high gear. There is no time delay after shifting into high gear.

Any time the coolant temperature goes over 240°F, the hot coolant switch provides a ground for the distributor solenoid. Since the hot coolant switch will ground whether the TCS switch does or not, vacuum advance will be supplied to the distributor in any gear when the coolant temperature reaches 240°F or above.

There is a distributor vacuum spark delay valve on some models, between the distributor solenoid and the distributor, acting as a restrictor on vacuum supplied to the distributor. This merely slows down the rate vacuum is initially supplied to the distributor. Full vacuum is eventually supplied.

The function of the start-up relay switch is identical to 1973 1/2.

1975

The Controlled Combustion System (C.C.S.) is continued on all non-California engines. It introduces preheated carburetor intake air during engine warmup.

The Air Injection Reactor (A.I.R.), or air pump system is continued in some applications.

E.G.R. (Exhaust Gas Recirculation) is used with the exhaust gas introduced into the intake mixture in the intake manifold and modulated by an exhaust backpressure modulating valve.

All models have high energy ignition (H.E.I.) to prevent any possible catalyst damage caused by ignition miss. Refer to the Electronic Ignition Unit Repair Section for details.

Catalytic converters are used on all models to control hydro-carbons and carbon monoxide. Refer to the Emission Control Unit Repair Section for details on this system.

All engines have outside air intakes. The cooler outside air improves driveability.

A heat valve on the exhaust manifold diverts exhaust gases through the intake manifold for a faster warmup.

Starting 1975, 350, 400, and 455 V8s, (except in the Ventura), are equipped with primary and secondary choke vacuum breaks. This dual choke break system ensures better driveability in both cold and hot weather. The system works as follows: When an engine is off or cold, the choke coil holds the choke valve in the carburetor closed. While

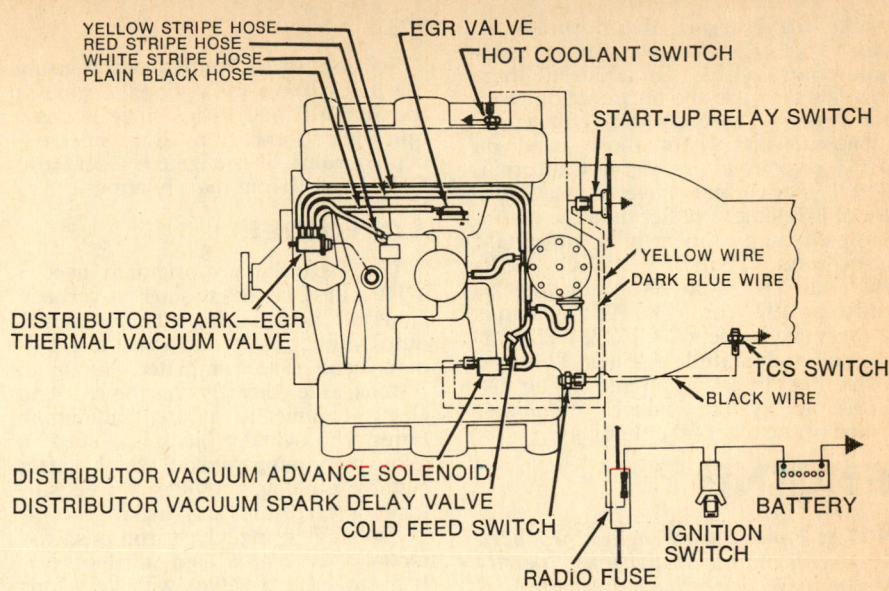

1974 Emissions Control System (© Pontiac Div., G.M. Corp)

cranking the engine, the choke allows the choke valve to be opened a little to ensure a rich starting mixture for easy starting. Once the engine is running, full manifold vacuum is applied to the primary vacuum break. The fast idle cam follower is pulled off the high step of the fast idle cam (coming to rest on the second step), and the choke valve is opened, allowing the car to be driven without stalling. When the engine is thoroughly warmed up, the choke is opened fully. In hot weather, the secondary choke vacuum break opens the choke valve a little further than normal.

The thermal vacuum valve in the air cleaner (which controls the secondary vacuum break) senses the temperature is above 62° and opens, allowing vacuum to flow to the secondary vacuum break, which opens the choke plate more than the primary vacuum break. This is accomplished after a slight time delay to allow the engine to stabilize at the leaner mixture. The leaning out of the mixture accomplished by the secondary vacuum break permits better driveability and reduced emissions.

1976

The 1976 Pontiac emission control systems are basically the same as those used in 1975. In a few cases the components have been changed, but the action of the system has remained the same. Examples of this are the EGR system and the vacuum advance circuit.

In the EGR system, the thermal vacuum valve has been replaced with a heat sensitive snap disc valve, attached to the intake manifold. This senses the engine radiant heat, and denies vacuum to operate the EGR valve when the engine is cold.

In the vacuum advance circuit, the spark retard delay valve has been re-

placed with a spark delay restrictor. The restrictor allows full manifold vacuum to the distributor except under full accereration or deceleration. In these cases, it delays vacuum for a few seconds.

Pontiac has added a distributor vacuum valve to the 260 V8, and testing procedures for this are the same as for other Pontiac distributor vacuum valves.

1977

For the most part, emission controls remain the same as 1976. This is true for the PCV, EGR, AIR and thermostatic air cleaner systems. The AIR system on California and high altitude V6 uses several new devices for regulating air injection: vacuum differential valve, air bypass valve, and differential and separator valve. On engines not equipped with AIR, a PAIR (Pulse Air Injection Reaction) system is used. This system uses a system of distribution pipes and check valves which rely on the pulses of the engine's exhaust system to siphon air into the exhaust port near the exhaust valve.

The Early Fuel Evaporation System (EFE) is used to provide a good source of heat during cold driveway. Two types are used. Some V8s use an orifice EFE system which consists of an orifice restriction in one leg of the exhaust crossover pipe. The other uses a valve which increases the exhaust gas flow under the intake manifold during cold temperatures. The valve is controlled by a TVS switch.

1978-79

The emission control systems for all 1978-79 engines include: catalytic converter, early fuel evaporation (EFE), exhaust gas recirculation (EGR), positive crankcase ventilation (PCV), choke calibration, thermostatic air cleaner (TAC), and evaporative emission control (EEC). In addition, some engines may use the air injection reactor system. The converter remains unchanged, except for those used on 4-151 engines intended for California. These converters have a platinum-rhodium element rather than the platinum-palladium element in all other GM converters. The EFE, EEC, EGR, PCV and TAC systems are the same as those on 1977 cars. The AIR system is a carryover except on V6-231 California and high altitude engines. This system differs in having an internal air distribution system which eliminates much of the external plumbing.

ENGINE

NOTE: *Pontiac uses engines produced by several other GM divisions. Identify the engine to be serviced, using the VIN code as explained at the beginning of this section, then determine the engine builder by using the Engine Identification Chart. When the engine has been identified, refer to the appropriate car section of this book. With the exception of engine removal and installation, service procedures for engines built by GM divisions other than Pontiac will not be covered in this section.*

INLINE SIX CYLINDER

This engine has a cast iron block and cylinder head, uses hydraulic valve lifters, and is a Chevrolet engine. Starting 1975, the intake manifold is integral with the cylinder head. This engine was last used in 1976.

V8

Pontiac has used several different V8s. Not all of them have been made by Pontiac Division. A run-down is as follows:

- 8-260—used in the 1975-76 Ventura; made by Oldsmobile.
- 8-301—new in 1977; made by Pontiac
- 8-305—used in 1977-78 in several car lines made by Chevrolet
- 8-307—used through 1973 in Ventura; made by Chevrolet
- 8-350—used in 1975-76 Ventura only; made by Buick
- 8-350—used in 1977-78 in several car lines made by Chevrolet
- 8-350—used in all 1977 cars except Astre/Sunbird; made by Oldsmobile
- 8-350—used in all cars through 1977 except Ventura through 1973 and Astre/Sunbird 1975-77; made by Pontiac
- 8-400—made by Pontiac
- 8-403—made by Oldsmobile
- 8-455—made by Pontiac

NOTE: *To determine which engine is in your car, check the code on the VIN label. Interpretation of this information is given at the front of this section.*

V6

Starting 1976, Pontiac began using the Buick V6 as the optional engine in the Sunbird line. It has since become optional or standard in all car lines except Firebird. This engine is a cast iron OHV V6 with four main bearings.

4 CYLINDER

The Astre/Sunbird originally used a 4-140 cid Chevrolet single overhead camshaft, design using a die cast aluminum cylinder block and a cast iron cylinder head. The iron-plated aluminum pistons ride directly on honed and electro-chemically treated aluminum bores. The cylinder block is cast of an alloy containing silicon which, after suitable etching, provides a bore surface for the pistons and rings.

Pontiac is using a cast iron push-rod model of its own design starting 1977. It has overhead valves with very long connecting rods. Using a short stroke (3 in.) and long connecting rods minimizes roughness.

ENGINE REMOVAL AND INSTALLATION

NOTE: *In most cases, engine work may be performed without disconnecting refrigerant lines on air conditioning systems. If, for any reason, the A/C system must be opened, the work is best performed by a professional. An A/C system is under high pressure. Refrigerant contact is harmful to the skin and can cause blindness. Failure to observe specific service procedures can permanently damage the system.*

4-151, INLINE SIX, V6, AND V8

1. Disconnect battery.
2. Drain cooling system.
3. Scribe alignment marks on hood and remove hood from hinges.
4. Disconnect the eingine wiring harness and ground straps, alternator wires, and the engine-temperature and oil-pressure sending-unit wires.
5. Remove air cleaner and fan shield or shroud.
6. Disconnect radiator and heater hoses.
7. Remove radiator.

NOTE: *On some models you can do the job by removing only the radiator or the fan, but it is generally easier to remove them both.*

8. Remove fan and fan pulley.

NOTE: *If equipped with power steering and/or air conditioning, disconnect and swing aside pump/compressor without disconnecting hoses.*

9. Disconnect accelerator linkage.
10. Disconnect all vacuum lines at the carburetor and disconnect the throttle cable.
11. Raise the front of the car and drain the engine oil.
12. Disconnect fuel lines at pump.
13. Disconnect exhaust pipes.
14. Disconnect the starter wires and

remove the starter on inline six-cylinder models.

15. If equipped with automatic transmission, remove converter cover and three converter retaining bolts, then slide converter to the rear. Make a mark on the flywheel and converter for later realignment.
16. If equipped with manual transmission, disconnect clutch linkage and remove clutch cross-shaft.

NOTE: *Remove starter and lower flywheel cover on V8s.*

17. Remove four lower bellhousing bolts (two per side). Remove the three right side bolts on the 260 V8.
18. Disconnect transmission filler tube support (automatic) and starter wire shield from cylinder heads.
19. Remove two front motor mount-to-frame bracket bolts.
20. Lower car to floor then, using a jack and a wood block, support the transmission. Support the engine with a hoist.
21. Remove two remaining bellhousing bolts. Remove the three left side bolts on the 260 V8.
22. Raise transmission slightly, using the jack and wood block, then, using a chain hoist, remove the engine.
23. To install, reverse removal procedure. Install the two upper bellhousing bolts first (with jack still under transmission).

NOTE: *Do not lower engine completely until jack and wood block are removed.*

4-140

1. Raise and secure the hood.
2. Disconnect the battery cables.
3. Drain the cooling system and disconnect the hoses at the radiator.
4. Disconnect the heater hoses at the water pump and at the heater inlet (bottom hose).
5. Disconnect the following emission hoses:
   a. PCV at the cam cover.
   b. The canister vacuum hose at the carburetor.
   c. PCV vacuum hose at the intake manifold.
   d. Bowl vent at the carburetor.
6. Remove the radiator, fan, fan spacer and air cleaner.
7. Disconnect the following electrical leads:
   a. Alternator.
   b. Ignition coil.
   c. Starter solenoid.
   d. Oil pressure sending unit.
   e. Temperature sending unit.
   f. Ground strap at the firewall.
8. Disconnect:
   a. Turbo Hydra-Matic detent cable.
   b. Fuel line at the rubber hose, rearward of the carburetor.
   c. Automatic transmission vacuum modulator and air conditioning vacuum line at the intake manifold.
   d. Throttle cable at the manifold bellcrank.

9. On cars with air conditioning, disconnect the compressor at the front support, rear support, rear lower bracket and remove the drive belt from the compressor.

NOTE: *Do not disconnect any air conditioning lines or fittings.*

10. Being careful not to crimp or bend the hoses, move the compressor slightly forward, allowing the front of the compressor to rest on the frame forward brace. Secure the rear of the compressor to the engine compartment so that it does not interfere with the engine removal.
11. If so equipped, disconnect the power steering pump and position it out of the way.
12. Raise the car on a hoist.
13. Disconnect the exhaust pipe at the exhaust manifold.
14. Remove the engine flywheel lower cover or the torque converter underpan.
15. On vehicles equipped with automatic transmission:
    a. Mark the converter-to-flywheel relationship for reassembly.
    b. Remove the converter to flywheel retaining bolts and install a converter safety strap, to keep the converter from falling out.
    c. Remove the converter housing to engine retaining bolts.
    d. Loosen the engine front mount retaining bolts at the frame attachment and lower the vehicle on the hoist.
    e. Install a floor jack under the transmission and an engine hoist to raise the engine slightly from its mounts.
    f. Remove the engine front mount retaining bolts.
    g. Remove the engine from the vehicle. Pull the engine forward enough to clear the transmission while slowly lifting the engine.
16. On vehicles with manual transmission:
    a. Remove the flywheel housing to engine retaining bolts.
    b. Proceed with Step 15, parts d, e, f, and g.
    To install engine:
17. Install two guide pins into the upper bolt holes in the engine block. Guide pins can be fabricated by cutting the heads off two bolts and sawing screwdriver slots into them.
18. Lower the engine into place, aligning the engine with the transmission.
19. Install the front mount bolts hand-tight.
20. Install the converter or clutch housing-to-engine bolts, replacing the guide pins. Remove the torque converter retaining strap, if one was used.
21. Torque the clutch housing-to-engine bolts to 25 ft. lbs. and the converter housing-to-engine bolts to 35 ft. lbs.
22. After checking to make sure that the front engine mounts are aligned and not making metal-to-metal contact, tighten them to 20 ft. lbs.
23. Align the previously made converter and flywheel marks, and torque the bolts to 35 ft. lbs.
24. Install the flywheel dust cover or torque converter underpan.
25. Connect the exhaust pipe at the manifold.
26. If so equipped, install the air conditioning compressor and power steering pump. Adjust the alternator belt.
27. Reconnect:
    a. the accelerator cable,
    b. the automatic transmission vacuum modulator line and the air conditioning vacuum line,
    c. the fuel line, and
    d. the Turbo Hydra-Matic detent cable.
28. Attach the following electrical connections:
    a. alternator
    b. coil
    c. starter solenoid
    d. oil pressure switch
    e. temperature switch
    f. engine ground strap
29. Replace the air cleaner and install these hoses:
    a. vent tube at the air cleaner base
    b. carburetor bowl vent
    c. PCV vacuum line
    d. vacuum canister hose
30. Install the radiator, radiator panel or shroud, spacer, and fan.
31. Connect the heater and radiator hoses. Fill the cooling system.
32. Connect the battery cables. Start the engine and check for leaks.

MANIFOLDS

Intake Manifold Removal and Installation

NOTE: *Pontiac doesn't recommend a specific manifold bolt torque sequence for V8 engines.*

V8

1. Remove the EGR valve on all engines except the 301. Drain the radiator and block.

NOTE: *You can drain most of the coolant through the radiator drain if you raise the rear of the car 15-18 in.*

2. Remove air cleaner and upper radiator hose.
3. Disconnect heater hose.
4. Disconnect temperature gauge wire, then remove two spark plug wire brackets from manifold.
5. Disconnect power brake vacuum and distributor vacuum lines.

NOTE: *Vacuum retard line is located at lower rear of vacuum unit on some exhaust emission distributors.*

6. Disconnect fuel line at carburetor.
7. Disconnect crankcase vent hose and accelerator linkage.

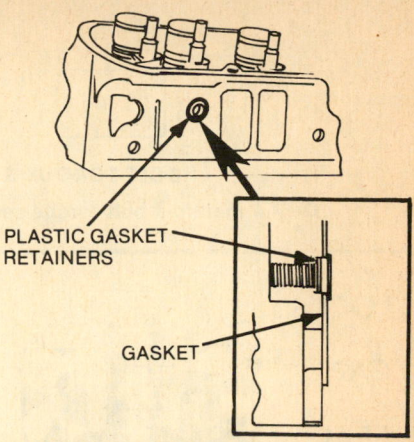

PLASTIC GASKET RETAINERS

GASKET

Pontiac V8 intake manifold gaskets can be held in place by using plastic retainers, available at Pontiac dealers

8. Remove bolts that secure accelerator linkage bracket, then remove intake manifold bolts and nuts. If the intake manifold will not clear the distributor, remove the distributor after noting the position of the rotor and the distributor housing.
9. Remove manifold and gasket.

—— CAUTION ——

Make sure the O-ring between the intake manifold and timing chain cover is in place, where used.

10. To install, reverse removal procedure, tightening timing chain cover to manifold bolts to 10-20 ft. lbs., manifold hold-down bolts and nuts evenly to the specified torque. Tighten all manifold bolts evenly.

4-151 Intake and Exhaust Manifold Removal

1. Remove the air cleaner and ducts.
2. Disconnect the fuel and vacuum lines.
3. Disconnect the electrical connectors.
4. Disconnect the carburetor linkage and remove the carburetor and heat shield.
5. Disconnect the exhaust pipe from the manifold.
6. Unbolt and remove the manifold assembly from the head.
7. Disconnect the EGR pipe and remove the four manifold attaching bolts.
8. Installation is the reverse of removal.
    When assembling the manifolds for installation, do the following:
    a. position the two manifolds together and loosely install the four bolts.
    b. place the manifolds on a straight, flat surface.
    c. Hold the manifolds securely while tightening the bolts. Failure to follow this procedure could result in stress cracking.

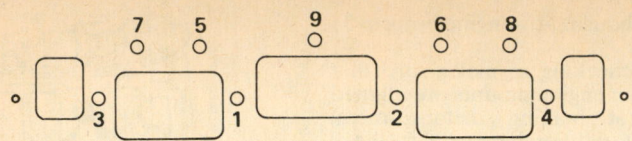

BOLT TORQUE 35 LB.FT.

OHV 4 manifold bolt torque sequence (© Pontiac Div., G.M. Corp.)

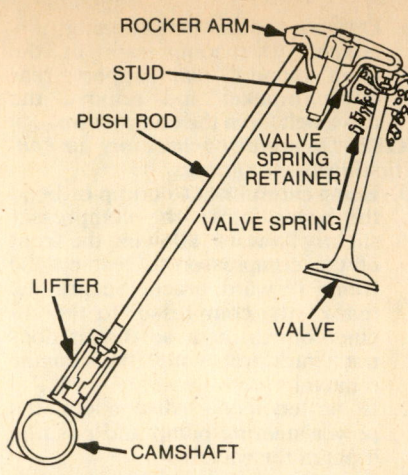

Pontiac V8 valve train assembly

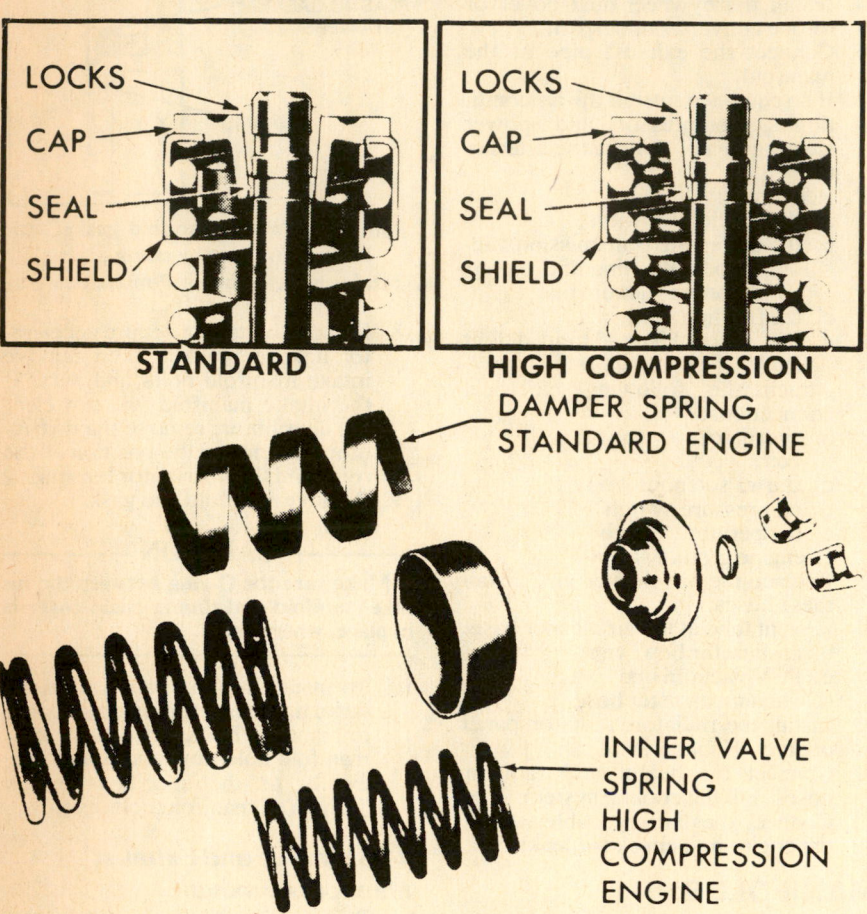

Typical Pontiac V8 valve spring assemblies

guides. Pontiac offers valves with over-size stems for worn guides (0.003 and 0.005 in. being available for most engines). To fit these, enlarge valve guide bores with valve guide reamers to an oversize that cleans up wear. If a large oversize is required, it is best to approach that size in stages. The correct valve stem to guide clearance is given in the Valve Specifications table at the beginning of this section.

As an alternate procedure, some local automotive machine shops fit replacement guides that use standard stem valves.

Rocker Arm Removal and Installation

4-151, AND V8

1. Remove the valve covers.
2. Remove the rocker arm nut and rocker arm ball.
3. Lift the rocker arm off the rocker arm stud. Always keep the rocker arm assemblies together and assemble them on the same stud.
4. Remove the pushrod from its bore. Make sure the rods are returned to their original bores, with the same end in the block.
5. Reverse the removal procedure to install the rocker arms. Tighten the rocker arm ball retaining nut to 20 ft. lbs.

Valve Adjustment

All engines are equipped with hydraulic lifters. No routine adjustment is necessary.

CYLINDER HEAD

Cylinder Head Removal and Installation

4-151

1. Drain the cooling system.
2. Disconnect the accelerator cable at the bellcrank, and the manifold vacuum and fuel lines at the carburetor.
3. Remove the intake and exhaust manifolds.

V8 Right Exhaust Manifold Removal and Installation

1. Disconnect the exhaust pipes from the manifolds.
2. Straighten the tabs on the manifold bolts, if used, and remove the manifold bolts, manifold, and gasket.
3. Clean the gasket surfaces.
4. Replace the exhaust manifold, using a new gasket; the holes in the end of the gasket are slotted.

NOTE: *The installation of the gasket may be simplified by first installing the manifold using only the front and rear bolts to retain the manifold. Allow clearance of about 1/8-3/16 in. between the cylinder head and the exhaust manifold. After inserting the gasket between the head and the manifold, the remaining bolts may be installed.*

5. Torque all bolts evenly to the specified torque.

6. Bend the tabs against the sides of the bolt heads.
7. Attach the exhaust pipe, using a new gasket.

V8 Left Exhaust Manifold Removal and Installation

1. Remove the alternator belt, alternator and mounting bracket as an assembly.
2. Disconnect the exhaust pipes from the manifolds.
3. Straighten the tabs, if used, on the manifold bolt locks and remove the bolts and manifold.
4. Clean the gasket surfaces.
5. Reverse the removal procedures for installation. The notes for the right-side apply here.

VALVE SYSTEM

Valve Guides

Pontiac engines have integral valve

4. Remove the alternator and power steering pump.
5. Disconnect all electrical connectors at the head.
6. Disconnect the radiator and heater hoses, and the battery ground strap.
7. Remove the spark plugs.
8. Remove the rocker arm cover, rocker arms, and push rods.
9. Unbolt and remove the cylinder head.
10. Clean the gasket surfaces thoroughly.
11. Install a new gasket over the dowels and position the cylinder head.
12. Coat the head bolt threads with sealer and install finger tight.
13. Tighten the bolts in sequence, in three equal steps to the specified torque.
14. Install all parts in the reverse of removal.

V8

1. Drain the cooling system.
2. Remove the intake manifold, pushrod cover and rocker cover.
3. Remove the rocker arms and pushrods.
4. Remove the battery ground and engine ground straps.
5. Remove the transmission dipstick tube from the head.
6. Remove the exhaust pipe from the manifold.
7. Remove the head bolts and lift off the head. On the left side, it will be necessary to raise the head slightly and move it forward to clear power steering and power brake equipment.
8. Right and left heads are identical. When installing new heads, the core plugs must be at the rear. On the 301 engine, coat all rocker stud lower threads and cylinder head bolts with sealer.
9. Clean all gasket surfaces thoroughly, and install the new gasket on the block. Position the head and install the head bolts finger tight, then tighten in three equal steps to the specified torque.
10. Install the remaining parts in the reverse order of removal.

TIMING CASE

Timing Gear or Chain Cover and Oil Seal Removal and Installation

V8

1. Drain radiator and cylinder block.
2. Losen alternator adjusting bolts.
3. Remove fan, fan pulley, and accessory drive belts.
4. Disconnect radiator hoses. Remove the water pump.
5. Remove fuel pump.

NOTE: *Fuel pump removal is not necessary if only the seal is being replaced.*

6. Remove harmonic balancer bolt and washer.
7. Remove harmonic balancer.

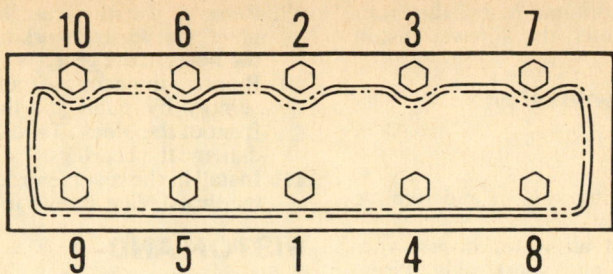

OHV 4 cylinder head bolt torque sequence (© Pontiac Div., G.M. Corp.)

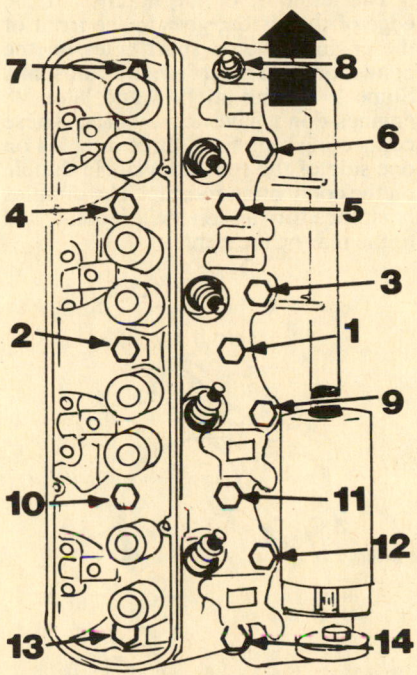

Cylinder head torque sequence Pontiac V8

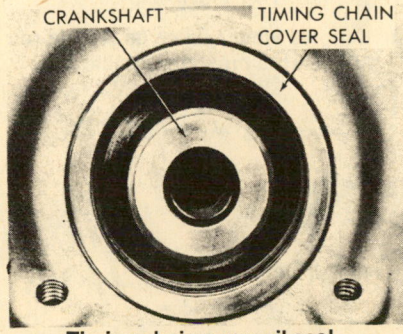

Timing chain cover oil seal (© Pontiac Div., G.M. Corp)

NOTE: *Do not pry on rubber-mounted balancers. Seal can be removed, using a screwdriver, at this point. Install a new seal with lip inward.*

8. Remove front four oil pan to timing cover bolts.
9. Remove timing cover bolts and nuts and cover to intake manifold bolt.
10. Pull cover forward and remove.
11. Remove O-ring from recess in intake manifold, then clean all gasket surfaces.
12. To replace seal, pry it out of the

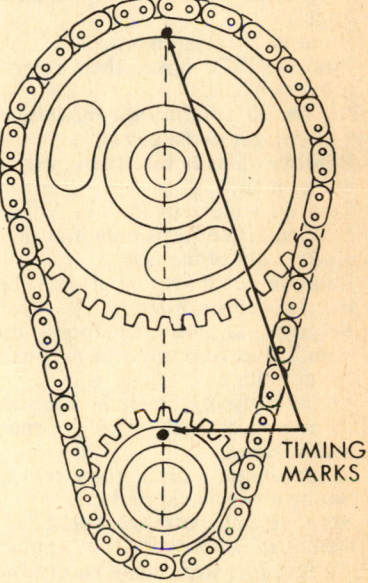

Pontiac V8 valve timing alignment marks (© Pontiac Div., G.M. Corp)

cover using a screwdriver. Install the new seal with lip inwards.

NOTE: *Seal can be replaced with cover installed.*

13. To install, reverse removal procedure, making sure all gaskets are replaced.

4-151

1. Remove the crankshaft hub.
2. Remove the oil pan-to-front cover screws.
3. Remove the front cover-to-block screws.
4. Pull the cover slightly forward, just enough to allow cutting of the oil pan front seal flush with the block on both sides.
5. Remove the front cover and attached portion of the pan seal.
6. Clean the gasket surfaces thoroughly.
7. Cut the tabs from the new oil pan front seal.
8. Install the seal on the front cover, pressing the tips into the holes provided.
9. Coat the new gasket with sealer and position it on the front cover.
10. Apply a 1/8 in. bead of silicone sealer to the joint formed at the oil pan and block.
11. Align the front cover seal with a

centering tool and install the front cover. Tighten the screws. Install the hub.

Camshaft Removal and Installation

V8

1. Drain cooling system and remove air cleaner.
2. Disconnect all water hoses, vacuum lines and spark plug wires. Remove the radiator.
3. Disconnect accelerator linkage, temperature gauge wire, and fuel lines.
4. Remove hood latch brace.
5. Remove PCV hose, then remove rocker covers.

NOTE: *On air-conditioned models, remove alternator and bracket.*

6. Remove distributor, then remove intake manifold.
7. Remove valley cover.
8. Loosen rocker arm nuts and pivot rockers out of the way.
9. Remove pushrods and lifters (keep them in proper order).
10. Remove harmonic balancer, fuel pump, and four oil pan to timing cover bolts.
11. Remove timing cover and gasket, then remove fuel pump eccentric and bushing.
12. Align timing marks, then remove timing chain and sprockets.
13. Remove camshaft thrust plate.
14. Remove camshaft by pulling straight forward, being careful not to damage cam bearings in the process.

NOTE: *It may be necessary to jack up the engine slightly to gain clearance, especially if motor mounts are worn.*

15. Install new camshaft, with lobes and journals coated with heavy (SAE 50-60) oil, into the engine, being careful not to damage cam bearings.

NOTE: *Most specialty cams come with a special "break-in" lubricant for the lobes and journals; if such lubricant is available, use it instead of heavy oil.*

16. Install camshaft thrust plate and tighten bolts to 20 ft. lbs.
17. To install, reverse Steps 1-12, tightening camshaft sprocket bolt to 40 ft. lbs., timing cover bolts and nuts to 30 ft. lbs., and oil pan bolts to 12 ft. lbs.

4-151

1. Drain the cooling system.
2. Remove the radiator.
3. Remove the fan and water pump pulley.
4. Remove the grille on Astre and Sunbird.
5. Remove the rocker cover, rocker arms, and pushrods.
6. Remove the distributor, spark plugs, and fuel pump.
7. Remove the pushrod cover and gasket. Remove the lifters.
8. Remove the crankshaft hub and timing gear cover.

9. Remove the two camshaft thrust plate screws by working through the holes in the gear.
10. Remove the camshaft and gear assembly by pulling it through the front of the block. Take care not to damage the bearings.
11. Install in the reverse order. Torque the thrust plate screws to 75 in. lbs.

PISTON AND CONNECTING ROD

The letter F, or the notches in the edge of the piston, goes to the front of the engine. The oil spurt holes on the connecting rod must face the camshaft. Some 1973, and all 1974 and later V8 engines don't have these holes. These connecting rods have three dimples on one side of the rod and a single dimple on the connecting rod cap. The dimples must face forward on the left bank, and to the rear on the right.

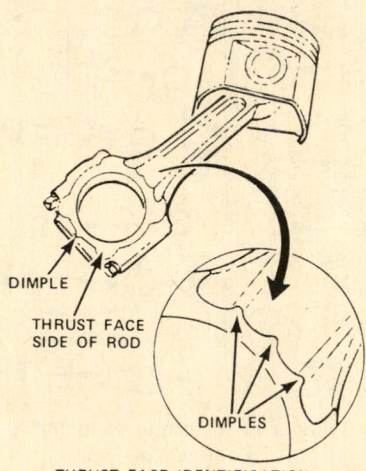

The dimples identify the connecting rod thrust faces on some Pontiac V8 engines (© Pontiac Div., G.M. Corp)

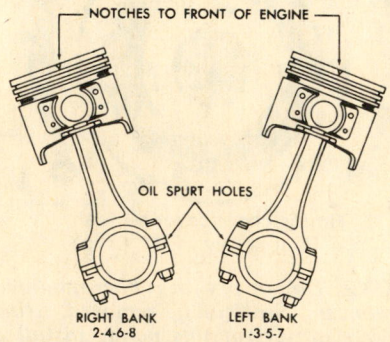

Pontiac V8 Piston and Rod Assembly (© Pontiac Div., G.M. Corp.)

LUBRICATION

Oil Pan Removal and Installation

V8

1. Disconnect battery cables.
2. Remove the fan and fan shroud.

Tilt the power steering pump out of the way. On some models, it may be necessary to dismount and set aside the A/C compressor. Do not disconnect the refrigerant lines.

3. Move all water hoses and wiring out of the way.
4. Raise car and drain engine oil. Disconnect idler arm from frame and pitman arm from shaft on 1972-77 Firebird.
5. Disconnect exhaust pipe/s at manifold.
6. On 1978 Firebird V8-400, rotate the crankshaft until # 1 piston is at bottom dead center.
7. Remove starter and bracket, then remove flywheel inspection cover.
8. Support engine with a wood-padded jack, located under the crankshaft damper. Special lifting tools are also available for this purpose.
9. Remove both frame-to-motor mount bolts.
10. Jack up engine for clearance, then remove oil pan bolts and pan.
11. To install, reverse the removal procedure. Silicone sealer is recommended at all gasket joints. Tighten pan bolts, and then tighten the rear bolts, through the reinforcement straps.

4-151

1. Disconnect the battery ground cable.
2. Remove the fan on Ventura.
3. Drain the oil.
4. On Astre and Sunbird, remove the rear section of the crossmember.
5. Disconnect the exhaust pipe at the manifold and loosen the hanger bracket.
6. Remove the starter.
7. Remove the flywheel housing inspection cover.
8. On Ventura, remove the hub bolt and install an engine support. Wrap chains around the frame and raise the engine enough to take the weight off the mounts. Remove the mounts. Remove the pan bolts and raise the engine enough to drop the pan.
9. On Astre/Sunbird, disconnect the steering linkage at the steering gear and idler arm support. Remove the pan.
10. Thoroughly clean the gasket surfaces and install the pan in the reverse order of removal. The bolts into the timing gear cover should be installed last.

Oil Pump Removal and Installation

ALL ENGINES

1. Remove engine oil pan. (See previous procedure.)
2. Remove pump attaching screws and carefully lower the pump.
3. Reinstall in reverse order. To ensure immediate oil pressure on start-up, the oil pump gear cavity

can be packed with petroleum jelly.

Rear Main Bearing Oil Seal Replacement

4-151

1. Remove the oil pan.
2. Remove the rear bearing cap.
3. Remove the oil seal from its groove by prying at the bottom with a small screwdriver.
4. Clean and oil the crankshaft surface.
5. Coat a new seal with clean engine oil and insert it in the bearing cap groove. Take care to keep oil off the rear edge, since it is treated with sealant. Gradually push the seal into place with a hammer handle.
6. The upper seal half may be removed by tapping it out of its groove with a hammer and blunt punch.
7. Push the new seal into place with the lip toward the front of the engine.
8. Install the bearing cap with the bolts loose.
9. Move the crankshaft first to the rear and then to the front with a rubber mallet. This will correctly position the thrust bearing.
10. Torque the cap bolts to 65 ft. lbs.
11. Install the oil pan.

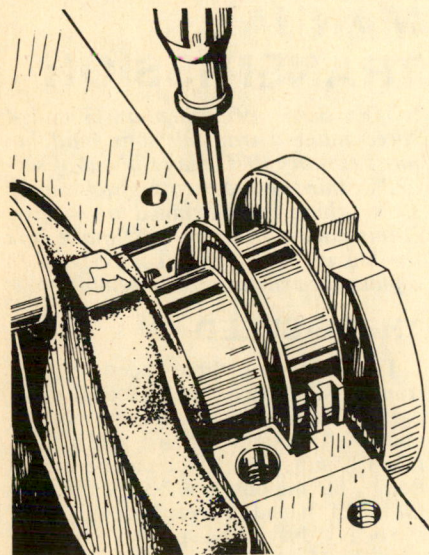

4-151 Upper Main Bearing Seal Removal
(© Pontiac Div., G.M. Corp.)

V8

1. Remove the oil pan and baffle.
2. Remove the rear main bearing cap.
3. Make a seal tool as illustrated.
4. Insert the tool against one end of the oil seal in the block and drive the seal gently into the groove until it bottoms. Repeat on the other end of the seal.
5. Form a new seal in the cap. Cut four ³/₈ in. long pieces from this seal.

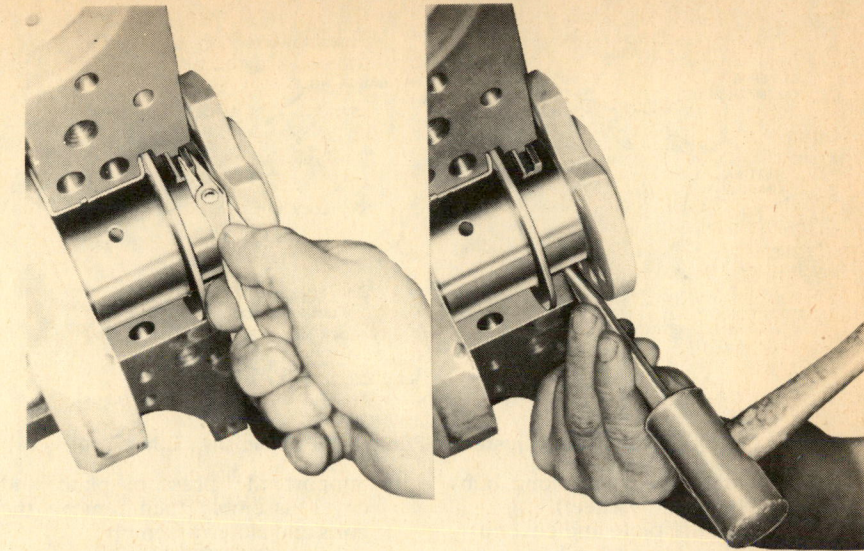

Rear main oil seal removal—upper half (© Pontiac Div., G.M. Corp)

6. Work two of the pieces into each of the gaps which have been made

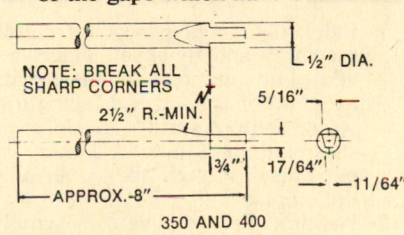

350 AND 400

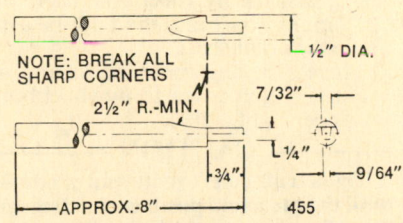

455

Pontiac V8 rear main bearing upper seal tool. The bottom tool is for the 455; the upper one is for the smaller engines.
(© Pontiac Div., G.M. Corp)

at the end of the seal in the block. Do not cut off any material to make them fit.

7. Form a new seal in the bearing cap.
8. Apply a ¹/₁₆ in. bead of silicone sealer from the center of the seal across to the external gasket groove.
9. Reassemble the cap and torque to specifications.

CLUTCH

A single-plate, dry-disc, diaphragm-spring clutch is used on all models. The clutch assembly consists of the driven plate, the pressure plate, and the release mechanism.

Two types of diaphragm type pressure plates are used—a bent finger type, in V8s of more than 350 cu. in. displacement, and a flat finger type, for all others. The diaphragm spring design is such that no overcenter spring is required.

A clutch safety switch prevents engine cranking unless the clutch is disengaged. The only periodic clutch service required, other than adjustment for normal wear, is the periodic lubrication of all linkage pivot points.

Clutch Replacement

EXCEPT ASTRE AND SUNBIRD

1. Raise car and support on jackstands. Disconnect the battery.
2. Support rear of engine.
3. Remove driveshaft.
4. Remove rear crossmember bolts from frame and transmission mounts, and remove crossmember.
5. Disconnect transmission shift linkage, speedometer cable and clutch return spring. Clutch fork pushrod will now hang free.
6. Remove clutch housing cover plate screws and let plate hang from starter gear housing.
7. Lower engine enough to gain access to clutch housing bolts at engine block, then remove all but uppermost bolt.
8. Hold transmission and clutch housing assembly against block over dowel pins while removing last bolt. Remove transmission and clutch housing as an assembly.
9. Matchmark pressure plate and flywheel with paint to make sure correct balance is maintained.
10. Loosen the cover plate attaching screws, a little at a time, until clutch diaphragm spring tension is released. Remove bolts and clutch assembly.
11. The pilot bearing is an oil-impregnated type bearing pressed into the crankshaft. Inspect and renew, if necessary.

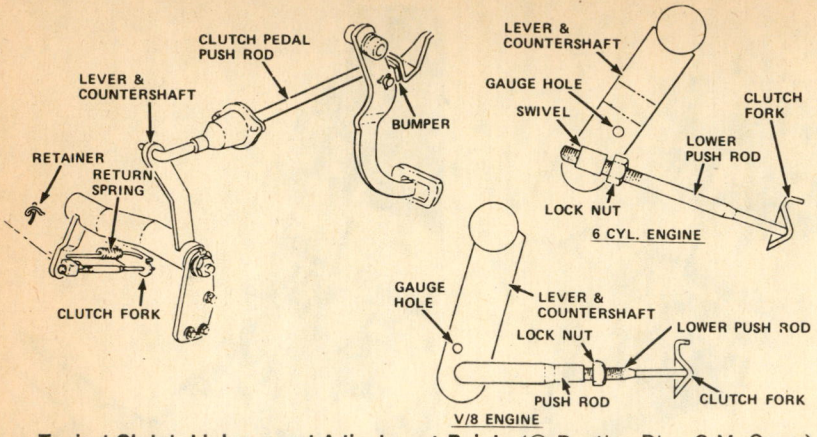

Typical Clutch Linkage and Adjustment Points (© Pontiac Div., G.M. Corp.)

12. Install clutch disc with long hub forward (toward flywheel).
13. Install pressure plate and cover assembly, then align clutch disc by inserting pilot tool, or old transmission mainshaft, into splines. Align mark on clutch cover with mark on flywheel, then align nearest bolt holes.
14. Install the bolts in the cover and tighten them alternately. Tighten them to 25 ft. lbs. (35 for Chevrolet engines).
15. Remove clutch pilot tool and check to see that it can be reinserted and moved freely.
16. Install clutch fork and dust boot into clutch housing. Lubricate throwout bearing with high melting point grease.
17. Complete the reassembly of clutch housing and transmission by reversing removal method. Tighten housing bolts to 40 ft. lbs. (30 for Ventura through 1973). Beginning 1974, tighten all models to 35 ft. lbs.
18. Adjust shifter and clutch release linkage.

ASTRE AND SUNBIRD

1. Raise vehicle on hoist.
2. Remove transmission.
3. Remove clutch fork cover then disconnect clutch return spring and control cable from clutch fork.
4. Remove input shaft oil seal from clutch release bearing sleeve.
5. Remove flywheel housing lower cover.
6. Remove flywheel housing from engine.
7. To remove the release bearing from clutch fork and sleeve, slide lever off ball stud against spring action. If necessary to replace ball stud, remove cap, locknut and stud from housing.
8. If assembly marks on clutch assembly and flywheel are not distinguishable, remark with paint or center-punch.
9. Loosen clutch cover to flywheel attaching bolts one turn at a time until spring pressure is released, to avoid bending clutch cover flange.

10. Support the pressure plate and cover assembly then remove the bolts and clutch assembly.

—————— CAUTION ——————
Do not disassemble the clutch cover, spring and pressure plate for repair. If defective replace complete assembly.

11. Index alignment marks on clutch assembly and flywheel. Place driven plate on pressure plate with long end of splined end facing forward, damper springs inside pressure plate, and insert a dummy input shaft through the cover and driven plate.
12. Position the complete assembly against the flywheel and insert the dummy shaft into the pilot bearing in the crankshaft.
13. Index the alignment marks and install clutch cover to flywheel bolts finger-tight.

—————— CAUTION ——————
Tighten all bolts evenly and gradually until tight to avoid possible clutch distortion. Torque bolts to 18 ft. lbs. and remove dummy shaft.

14. Lubricate the clutch fork ball socket and the fingers at the release bearing with high melting point grease.
15. Lubricate the recess on the inside of the throwout bearing collar and the fork groove with high melting point grease. Install fork in housing but not on stud.
16. Install bearing on sleeve, then position clutch fork over bearing in housing and slide fork onto ball stud.
17. Install flywheel housing and lower cover. Tighten bolts to 25 ft. lbs.
18. Install transmission.
19. Adjust clutch.
20. Lower and remove vehicle from hoist.

Clutch Adjustment

EXCEPT ASTRE AND SUNBIRD

1. Disconnect the clutch fork return spring.

2. Loosen the pushrod locknut.
3. Detach the swivel or pushrod from the countershaft lever.
4. Install the swivel or pushrod in the gauge hole on the countershaft lever.
5. Push on the countershaft lever so that the clutch pedal is up against the stop.
6. Hold the clutch fork to the rear so that the release bearing lightly contacts the release levers.
7. Adjust the pushrod length to remove all lash from the linkage.
8. Reinstall the swivel or pushrod in the original hole on the countershaft lever. Tighten the locknut.
9. Replace the spring. Pedal free travel should now be $3/4$-$1\frac{1}{4}$ in.

ASTRE AND SUNBIRD

Adjustment for normal clutch wear is accomplished by turning the clutch fork ball stud counterclockwise to give .90 ± .25 in. free play at clutch pedal.

1. Remove ball stud cap and loosen locknut on ball stud end located to the right of the transmission on the clutch housing.
2. Adjust ball stud to obtain .90 ± .25 in. free travel.
3. Tighten locknut being careful not to change adjustment and install ball stud cap.
4. Check operation of clutch.

MANUAL TRANSMISSION

NOTE: *Some 1975 Saginaw 3 and 4 speed manual transmissions built before February 1975, may slip out of second or third gear due to a synchronizer sleeve which was machined incorrectly. If this condition exists, first make sure the linkage is adjusted correctly, then replace the synchronizer assembly.*

THREE-SPEED

Two different three-speed manual transmissions have been used in these cars. All light and normal-duty models, and the Astre and Sunbird, use a Saginaw transmission, which can be identified by having only one bolt at the center top of the side cover. Through 1974, the heavy-duty three-speed is a Muncie unit. This is similar in appearance to the Saginaw, but has two bolts at the top of the cover.

Three-Speed Transmission Removal and Installation

1. Disconnect the battery and release the parking brake before raising the car.
2. Disconnect the speedometer cable.
3. Disconnect the transmission shifter levers from the transmission shifter shafts. Where used disconnect the electrical lead from the T.C.S. switch. On floorshift mod-

els, remove the two shifter assembly-to-shifter support bolts and remove the shifter from the transmission. If it is not necessary to remove the shifter from the car, it may be left hanging from its floor seal. Mark the differential flange and the driveshaft yoke to assure proper reassembly. Remove the driveshaft.

4. Support the rear of the engine and remove the transmission mount.
5. Remove the four crossmember bolts and slide the member rearward.
6. Remove the four transmission-to-bell housing bolts. It is a good idea to remove the upper bolts first and replace them with headless guide pins. This prevents any possible damage caused by the transmission hanging by its input shaft.
7. Slide the transmission rearward until it clears the clutch assembly and bell housing, then remove the transmission.
8. Reverse the removal procedure to install the transmission. Put the transmission in gear and turn the output shaft as necessary to start the splines into the clutch plate.

Three-Speed Linkage Adjustment—Column Shift

SAGINAW TRANSMISSION EXCEPT VENTURA, PHOENIX

1. Place gearshift lever in Reverse and lock ignition.
2. On the Firebird, loosen the swivel clamp nut at the rear transmission shift lever (First and Reverse) then loosen the nut at the idler lever.
3. Position the front transmission lever (Second and Third) in Neutral and the rear transmission shift lever (First and Reverse) in Reverse.
4. Tighten the First and Reverse swivel clamp bolt or nut, then unlock the steering column and shift into Neutral. On the Firebird, tighten both swivel clamp nuts, unlock the steering column, and check the complete shift pattern.
5. Unlock the column and align the lower gearshift levers (on column) in Neutral position, then insert a 0.185 in. diameter gauge pin through the hole in the lower control levers.
6. Tighten the swivel clamp bolt or nut, then remove the gauge pin and check the shift pattern.

VENTURA, PHOENIX

1. Set the shift lever in Reverse and lock the column. Loosen the swivel clamp nuts at both shifter levers.
2. Pull down slightly on 1st-Reverse rod to remove slack, then tighten swivel clamp nut at 1st-Reverse lever.
3. Unlock steering column and shift

into Neutral. Align column levers and insert a .185-.186 in. gauge pin through alignment holes.
4. Position 2nd-3rd transmission lever in Neutral, then tighten swivel clamp nut.
5. Remove gauge pin and check shift pattern and ignition lock. With lever in Reverse, key must move to LOCK freely. This should not be possible in any other gear.

Three-Speed Linkage Adjustment—Floor Shift

1. Place gearshift lever in Neutral.
2. Loosen swivel clamp on gearshift control rod.
3. Loosen trunnion locknuts on 1st-Reverse and 2nd-3rd transmission control rods.
4. Insert a 1/4 in. drill rod into shifter assembly.
5. If gearshift lever is not properly aligned with floor opening:
   a. *Console*—loosen two shifter to support bolts and align shifter. Tighten bolts.
   b. *Without console*—loosen two shifter to support bolts and center shifter in boot; tighten bolts.
6. Position both transmission shift levers in Neutral and tighten locknuts.
7. Remove gauge pin and check shift pattern.
8. Place gearshift lever in Reverse, then place steering column lower lever in Lock position and lock ignition.
9. Push up on gearshift control rod to take up lash in column lock mechanism, then tighten adjusting swivel clamp.

FOUR-SPEED

The Saginaw is used as the standard four-speed on all models. The four-speed Muncie is used in heavy duty applications through 1974. Both transmissions are fully synchronized in all forward gears. They can easily be identified by their shift linkage. On the Muncie, two shift rods go to levers on the side cover and one rod (reverse) goes to a lever on the case extension housing. On the Saginaw also known as the 76mm. transmission, all three shift rods go to levers on the side cover. Starting 1975, the heavy duty transmission, used only in the Firebird, with the 400 TA engine, is the Borg-Warner T-10, also known as the 82mm. transmission, which can be identified by a 9 bolt curved bottom side cover. It also has a reverse shift lever on the extension housing.

The GM 70 mm. 4-speed is offered on 1975-77 models using the 4 cylinder. The linkage is internal, with the shift lever attached to the extension housing; because of this, no linkage adjustments are necessary.

Four-Speed Transmission Removal and Installation

EXCEPT 1975-77 ASTRE AND SUNBIRD, AND ASTRE/SUNBIRD WITH 70mm. TRANSMISSION

The procedures for these four-speed transmissions are the same as for three-speed units.

1975-77 ASTRE AND SUNBIRD, FOUR-SPEED SAGINAW TRANSMISSION

1. Raise the car and drain the transmission.
2. Remove the driveshaft.
3. Disconnect the speedometer cable, TCS switch, and the backup light switch.
4. Detach the control rods and levers from the transmission, tie them together, and position them out of the way.
5. Remove the crossmember-to-transmission mounting bolts.
6. Support the engine and remove the crossmember-to-frame bolts. Remove the crossmember.
7. Remove the top transmission-to-clutch housing bolts and install guide pins in the holes.
8. Remove the lower bolts and pull the transmission back and out of the car.
9. On installation, guide the input shaft through the throwout bearing and into the pilot bearing.
10. Install the transmission retaining bolts and lockwashers. Tighten the bolts to 40 ft. lbs.
11. Position the crossmember on the frame and install the retaining bolts hand-tight.
12. Install the crossmember-to-transmission bolts and then tighten all bolts to 28 ft. lbs.
13. Remove the engine support.
14. Install the transmission control rods to the shifter. Adjust the linkage.
15. Connect the speedometer cable, TCS switch, and back-up light switch.
16. Install the driveshaft.
17. Fill the transmission to the level of the filler plug.
18. Lower the gear and check transmission operation.

ASTRE AND SUNBIRD, GM 70mm. 4-SPEED TRANSMISSION

1. Remove the shift lever by pulling down on the lever boot and loosening the locknut; then unscrew the upper part of the lever with the gearshift knob attached.
2. Raise the car on a hoist and drain the lubricant from the transmission.
3. Remove the driveshaft.
4. Disconnect the speedometer cable and TCS back-up light switch.
5. Disconnect the return spring and

clutch cable at the clutch release fork.

6. Remove the crossmember-to-transmission mount bolts.
7. Remove the exhaust manifold nuts and converter-to-tailpipe bolts and nuts. Remove the converter-to-transmission bracket bolts and remove the converter.
8. Remove the crossmember-to-frame bolts and the transmission damper if any.
9. Remove the crossmember.
10. Remove the clutch housing-to-engine retaining bolts, slide the transmission and clutch housing to the rear, and remove the transmission.
    To install:
11. Place the transmission in gear, position the transmission and clutch housing, and slide forward. Turn the output shaft to align the input shaft splines with the clutch hub.
12. Install the clutch housing retaining bolts and lockwashers. Torque the bolts to 25 ft. lbs.
13. Install the converter to transmission bracket and the transmission damper.
14. Position the crossmember to the frame and loosely install the retaining bolts. Install the crossmember-to-transmission mounting bolts. Torque the center nuts to 33 ft. lbs.; the end nuts to 21 ft. lbs. Torque the crossmember-to-frame bolts to 40 ft. lbs.
15. Install the exhaust pipe to the manifold and the converter bracket on the transmission. Torque the converter bracket rear support nuts to 150 in lbs.

Four-Speed Linkage Adjustment

EXCEPT ASTRE AND SUNBIRD

1. Place gearshift lever in Neutral and ignition switch in "off".
2. Loosen adjusting swivel clamp on gearshift control rod.
3. Loosen locknuts for all others.
4. Insert a 1/4 in. (1972-77), 3/16 in. (1978-79) drill rod into gauge pin hole in shifter.
5. If Muncie or Warner gearshift lever is not properly aligned with floor opening:
   a. *Console*—loosen two shifter to support bolts and align shifter. Tighten bolts.
   b. *Without console*—loosen two shifter to support bolts and center shifter in boot; tighten bolts.
6. Place transmission shift levers in Neutral and tighten locknuts.
7. Remove gauge pin and check shift pattern.
8. Place gearshift lever in Reverse, set steering column lower lever in Lock position and lock ignition.
9. Push up on gearshift control rod to take up lash in steering column lock mechanism, then tighten adjusting swivel clamp nut.

Astre and Sunbird Four-Speed Saginaw Linkage Adjustment

1. Turn the ignition switch to "Off" and place the shift lever in neutral.
2. Raise the car.
3. Loosen the lock nuts on the control rods. Position the transmission side cover levers in their neutral detents.
4. With the floor shift lever in neutral, align the shifter levers and insert a gauge pin into the levers and bracket.
5. Tighten the First/Second control rod lock nut against its swivel.
6. Tighten the Third/Fourth control rod lock nut against its swivel.
7. Tighten the Reverse control rod lock nut against its swivel.
8. Remove the gauge pin and check shifter operation.

5-SPEED

Starting 1976, a Borg-Warner 77mm. five speed is an option in Astre, Sunbird, LeMans, Phoenix and Ventura. In 1978, availability was limited to the Sunbird 4 and 6 cylinder, and the Phoenix 4 cylinder. Fifth gear in the transmission is an overdrive. The shift linkage is contained within the transmission and requires no adjustment.

Five Speed Transmission Removal and Installation

1. Remove the boot retainer and slide the boot upward on the shift lever.
2. Remove the foam insulator over the control assembly bolts.
3. Remove the four control lever bolts and remove the control lever.
4. Raise the car, mark the driveshaft to yoke position, and remove the driveshaft.
5. Remove the damper assembly, the torque converter bracket, and the torque arm bracket.
6. Disconnect the speedometer cable and the back-up light switch.
7. Remove the nut from the front of the torque arm, the catalytic converter bracket bolts, and the transmission damper, any. Remove the bolts holding the transmission rubber mount to the support then place a transmission jack under the transmission and remove the transmission support.
8. Remove the transmission-to-clutch housing bolts and slide the exhaust bracket forward. Install 1/2"-13 x 2" guidepins in place of the bolts to support the transmission. This will prevent clutch distortion. After this the transmission can be moved rearward and removed from the car.
9. Installation is the reverse of removal, but take note of the following: make sure the drive gear splines are clean and dry; use gui-

debolts in the bellhousing holes to aid in aligning the transmission to the engine; shift the lever through all the gears to make sure nothing is binding.

AUTOMATIC TRANSMISSION

Both two and three speed automatics have been used in Pontiac cars. The two speed (M35) was discontinued at the end of 1973. The Turbo Hydra-Matic 350 (M38) and 400 (M40) have been used for many years. The Turbo Hydra-Matic 250, also designated M38, was introduced in 1975; the Turbo Hydra-Matic 200 was introduced in 1976. To determine which unit is used in a particular vehicle, check the transmission ID plate on the transmission case. Visual identification is as follows: The 250 has an intermediate band adjustment on the side of the case, the others don't have any band adjustments. The Turbo Hydra-Matic 400 has an electric downshift switch, the others use a cable from the throttle linkage. The 400 is not available on 1978-79 cars. To distinguish a 200 from a 350, count the pan bolts: the 200 has 10; the 350 has 13.

NOTE: *Some 1975 M-38 transmissions may click or rattle in first gear because the intermediate steel clutch plates are flat instead of cone shaped. New clutch plates should be installed.*

Pan Removal, Fluid and Filter Change

The fluid should be drained with the transmission warm.

1. Support the Astre or Sunbird transmission at the vibration damper. Remove the crossmember.
2. Prepare a large pan to catch the transmission fluid.
3. Loosen all the pan screws, then pull one corner down to drain most of the fluid.
4. Remove the pan screws and empty out the pan. The pan can be cleaned out with solvent but it must be dried thoroughly before replacement. Be very careful not to leave any lint or threads from rags in the pan.
5. Remove the filter or strainer retaining bolt (two on Turbo Hydra-Matic 200, 250, and 350). A reusable strainer is used on two-speed transmissions and the Turbo Hydra-Matic 200 and 250. The strainer may be cleaned in solvent and air-dried thoroughly. Filters are to be replaced.
6. Assemble a new O-ring and filter to the intake pipe on the Turbo Hydra-Matic 400. Use a new gasket on all other models.
7. Install the new filter or cleaned strainer.
8. Install the pan with a new gasket.

Tighten the bolts evenly (12 ft. lbs.) in a criss-cross pattern.
9. Replace the Astre or Sunbird crossmember.
10. Add DEXRON or DEXRON II transmission fluid through the dipstick tube. Add 5 pts. for Turbo Hydra-Matic 250, 3 for the 200 and 350, and 7 for the 400.
11. Start the engine and let it idle. Do not race the engine. Shift through all the indicator positions, holding the brakes. Check the fluid level with the engine idling in Park. The level should be between the two dimples on the dipstick, about ¼ in. below the ADD mark. Add fluid as necessary.
12. Check the fluid level after the car has been driven enough to thoroughly warm up the transmission. The level should be at the FULL mark on the dipstick. If the transmission is overfilled, the excess must be drained off. Overfilling causes aerated fluid, resulting in transmission slippage and probable damage.

Band Adjustments

LOW BAND—TWO-SPEED (M-35)
This adjustment is required at fluid change intervals, or whenever slippage is evident.
1. Place the shifter lever in Neutral and raise the vehicle.
2. Remove the adjusting screw protecting cap.
3. Loosen the adjusting screw locknut ¼ turn.

—— CAUTION ——
Be sure to hold the adjusting screw locknut at 1/4 turn loose during the adjusting procedure.

4. Tighten the adjusting screw to 70 in. lbs. and then back off *exactly* four complete turns for a band with 6,000 miles or more of use, three turns for a band with less than 6,000 miles of use.
5. Tighten the locknut and install the protective cap.

TURBO HYDRA-MATIC 200, 350, 400
Band adjustments are made during overhaul and cannot be accomplished without disassembly of the transmission.

INTERMEDIATE BAND— TURBO HYDRA-MATIC 250
This adjustment is required at fluid change intervals, or whenever slippage is evident.
1. Position the shift lever in Neutral.
2. Loosen the locknut on the right side of the transmission and tighten the adjusting screw to 30 in. lbs.
3. Back the screw out three turns and then tighten the locknut.

Shift Linkage Adjustment through 1975

COLUMN SHIFT
1. Loosen screw (nut on Firebird) on adjusting swivel clamp.
2. Place gearshift lever in Park and lock ignition.
3. Place transmission shift lever in Park detent.
4. Push up on gearshift control rod until lash is taken up in steering column lock mechanism, then tighten screw or nut on swivel clamp.
5. Readjust the transmission neutral start switch if necessary.

TURBO HYDRA-MATIC FLOORSHIFT, EXCEPT TH-M 250 AND VENTURA TH-M 350 THROUGH 1974
1. Disconnect shift cable from transmission shift lever by removing nut from pin.
2. Adjust back drive linkage (as in Step 4, above).
3. Unlock ignition and rotate transmission shift lever counter-clockwise two detents.
4. Place console lever in Neutral and move against forward Neutral stop.
5. Assemble shift cable and pin to transmission shift lever so that no binding exists, then tighten nut.
6. Readjust the transmission neutral start switch if necessary.

TWO-SPEED FLOORSHIFT
1. Place console lever in Park and lock ignition.
2. Disconnect shift cable from transmission shift lever pin. Loosen the screw on the adjusting swivel at the shaft lever.
3. Rotate transmission shift lever clockwise to Park position and push up on control rod to take up slack.
4. Tighten swivel.
5. Unlock ignition and rotate range lever on transmission counter-clockwise two positions.
6. Place shift lever in Neutral and move forward against Neutral stop.
7. Assemble shift cable and pin to transmission lever (free fit) and tighten pin nut.
8. Readjust the transmission neutral start switch if necessary.

VENTURA TURBO HYDRA-MATIC 350 FLOORSHIFT THROUGH 1974
1. Loosen both swivel nuts on the shift control rod.
2. Place transmission lever in Drive position.
3. Set pawl rod into Drive notch.
4. Apply a forward load on actuating lever until pawl rod contacts detent.
5. Place a 0.094 in. spacer between front swivel nut and swivel. Run in

front nut until it hits spacer, then release load and tighten rear nut to 40 in. lbs.
6. Place transmission shift lever in Park position and lock ignition.
7. Loosen nut at the bottom of idler lever, then remove play by rotating shift lever downward. Tighten nut to 20 ft. lbs.

TURBO HYDRA-MATIC 250 FLOORSHIFT
1. Loosen the nut and swivel at the transmission lever.
2. Set the transmission lever in Neutral by moving it counter-clockwise to the L1 detent and then clockwise three detent positions to Neutral.
3. Position the shift lever in the Neutral notch of the detent plate.
4. Place the flat of the swivel into the slot of the control rod. Install the washer and cotter pin.
5. Tighten the locknut. Adjust the neutral safety switch, if necessary.

Shift Linkage Adjustment 1976 and Later

COLUMN SHIFT
1. Place the shift lever in the Neutral position, and then from underneath the car, loosen the screw on the shift linkage swivel clamp.
2. Put the transmission selector lever in the neutral detent.
3. Hold the swivel clamp flush against the shaft lever assembly and hand tighten the clamp screw against the gearshift control rod. While you are doing this make sure you do not force the control rod or the shaft lever assembly.
4. Tighten the clamp screw and check the shifting against the requirements listed below.

CONSOLE SHIFT EXCEPT 1978 LeMANS WITH TH-M 200
1. Place the console shift lever in the Park position, and then from underneath the car, loosen the pin from the selector lever.
2. Loosen the screw on the swivel clamp.
3. With the pin fitting freely in the selector lever, tighten the attaching nut.
4. Turn the ignition key to the Lock position, and then from underneath the car, pull the control rod down against the lock-stop to remove all the free play. Hold the swivel clamp flush against the shaft and lever assembly, and tighten the clamp screw against the control rod.
5. Check the shifting of the transmission against the requirements listed below.

Shift Linkage Requirements
1. Move the shift lever from Park to Low to make sure all the stops are available.

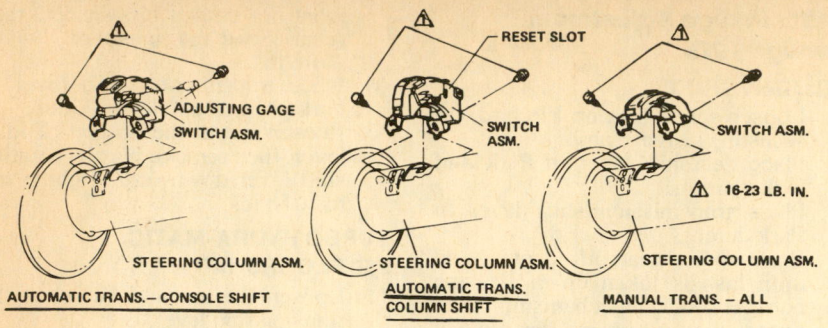

Neutral start switch (© Pontiac Div., G.M. Corp)

2. With the transmission in Drive there should be clearance between the shift lever and the gate; with the transmission in Reverse, there should also be clearance between the shift lever and gate.

3. Turn the ignition key to the On position and place the shift lever into Reverse; you should not be able to remove the key, but the steering will not be locked.

4. On column shift controls, with the key in Lock and the shift lever in Park, the key will be removeable, but the wheel will not turn and the shift lever will not move from Park.

5. On console shift cars, with the key in Lock and the shift lever in Park, the key will be removeable and the steering wheel will be locked.

1978-79 LeMANS WITH
TH-M 200 CONSOLE SHIFT

This adjustment is particularly sensitive. To assure proper operation of the ignition lock control and the selector lever, the following procedure must be performed in exact sequence.

1. Loosen the shift rod clamp screw. Loosen the pin nut in the transmission lever.

2. Place the console lever in Park and the ignition in Lock.

3. Rotate the transmission lever to the Park position.

4. Tighten the cable pin nut to 25 ft. lbs.

5. Rotate the transmission lever fully against the Park stop, then release the lever.

6. Pull the shift rod down against the lock stop to eliminate play and tighten the clamp screw.

7. With the brakes firmly applied, check to make sure that the starter will not work in any position but Neutral and Park.

Neutral Safety/Backup Light Switch Adjustment

Three types are used: a mechanical type inside the column on LeMans, a combination start/back-up light switch on top of the column used on Firebird, Ventura and Phoenix; and a combination switch located on the side of the floor mount mechanism on Astre/Sunbird.

ALL FLOORSHIFT, ALL
COLUMN SHIFT—EXCEPT
ASTRE AND SUNBIRD

NOTE: *This procedure applies to all switches with an adjusting pin hole in the back.*

1. Place the shift lever in Neutral. 1972 floorshift models must be in Park, except for Ventura, which must be in Drive.

2. Loosen the switch mounting screws.

3. Move the switch until you can insert a 0.092 (0.082 beginning 1975) in. diameter adjusting pin into the hole in the back of the switch about ³/₈ in.

4. Tighten the screws and remove the pin.

5. Step on the brake pedal and check that the engine will start only in Neutral or Park.

ASTRE AND SUNBIRD

1. Remove screws securing floor console.

2. Disconnect the electrical plugs on the back-up, seat belt warning, neutral start, and seat belt buzzer contacts of the neutral safety switch.

3. Place shift lever in Neutral.

4. Remove two screws securing shift indicator plate.

5. Remove two screws securing shift lever curved cover.

6. Remove two screws securing neutral start switch to lever assembly.

NOTE: *Screws are hidden beneath lever cover.*

7. Tilt switch assembly to right as you lift switch out of lever hole.

8. Make sure shift lever is in Neutral before installing switch assembly.

9. Assemble switch assembly to control lever bracket by inserting drive tang into hole in neutral start switch lever.

NOTE: *When installing the same neutral switch, align the contact support slot with the service adjustment hole in the switch and insert a ³/₃₂ in. drill to hold the switch in neutral. Remove the drill after the switch is fastened to the shift lever mounting bracket.*

10. Tighten two mounting screws securing switch assembly to lever bracket.

11. Install curved shift lever cover and secure with two screws.

12. Install shift indicator plate and attach with two screws.

13. Moving control lever out of Neutral will shear the new switch plastic locating pin.

14. Plug electrical connectors into switch assembly; apply parking brake and start vehicle—check for starting in Neutral and Park only. Also check for back-up lamps on in Reverse.

15. Turn off ignition and install console cover securing with four screws.

Downshift Cable Adjustment—
Turbo Hydra-Matic 200, 250, 350

LeMANS

1. With engine off and throttle butterflies closed (off fast idle), position retainer against insert on cable (from inside car).

2. To adjust, grasp accelerator pedal lever adjacent to downshift cable and pull carburetor cable to wide open throttle position. Check for full cable travel.

FIREBIRD

1. With engine off and throttle butterflies closed (off fast idle), position the retainer (under the hood) rearward against washer and insert (or Snap Lock up).

2. To adjust, push carburetor extension lever to wide open throttle position and push the Snap Lock down. Check for full cable travel.

VENTURA, PHOENIX

1. Disengage the Snap Lock on the detent cable.

2. Place carburetor lever at wide open position, against stop.

3. With detent cable through detent, push Snap Lock downward until its top is flush with the cable.

ASTRE AND SUNBIRD

1. Remove the air cleaner.

2. Insert a screwdriver on each side of the snap-lock on the bracket at the front of the transmission and pry up to release the lock.

3. Compress the lock tabs and disconnect the snap-lock assembly from the bracket.

4. Position the carburetor lever in the wide open throttle position.

5. Hold the carburetor lever in position and push the Snap Lock on the cable down until the top is flush with the cable.

NOTE: *The cable should not be lubricated.*

6. Install the air cleaner.

Throttle Valve (TV) Linkage
Adjustment—Two-Speed

INLINE 6 CYLINDER

1. Remove air cleaner.

2. Disconnect TV control rod swivel and clip from carburetor lever,

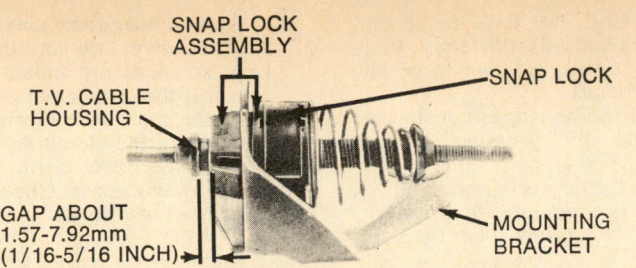

SNAP LOCK ASSEMBLY

SNAP LOCK

T.V. CABLE HOUSING

GAP ABOUT 1.57-7.92mm (1/16-5/16 INCH)

MOUNTING BRACKET

TH-M 200 Throttle Valve Cable Adjustment (© Pontiac Div., G.M. Corp.)

then disconnect TV return spring from bellhousing.

3. Push TV control rod rearward until transmission TV lever is against internal transmission stop.

4. Holding TV control rod in this position, hold carburetor lever in wide open throttle position and adjust TV control rod swivel so that pin freely enters hole in carburetor lever without binding.

5. Secure swivel, connect return spring and check linkage action for binding.

6. Install air cleaner.

V8

1. Remove air cleaner.

2. Disconnect accelerator linkage at carburetor.

3. Disconnect throttle and TV rod return springs.

4. Pull TV rod forward until transmission is through detent, hold in this position and open carburetor butterflies to wide open position.

5. The butterflies must reach wide open position at the same time that the ball stud contacts end of slot in upper TV rod ($\pm 1/32$ in.).

6. If necessary, adjust swivel end of upper TV rod.

7. Connect linkage and springs, then check linkage for binding.

8. Install air cleaner.

Turbo Hydra-Matic 200

1. Disengage the snap lock so that the cable slips freely through.

2. With the cable installed in the support and attached to the transmission and carburetor lever, move the carburetor lever to the wide open throttle position.

3. Push the snap lock flush and return the carburetor lever to the closed position.

U-JOINTS

A splined yoke and universal assembly and a rear universal joint are used to accommodate changes in length and orientation of the driveshaft as the car moves over bumps.

Driveshaft Removal and Installation

1. Mark the driveshaft rear yoke and the differential flange to assure correct alignment upon reassembly.

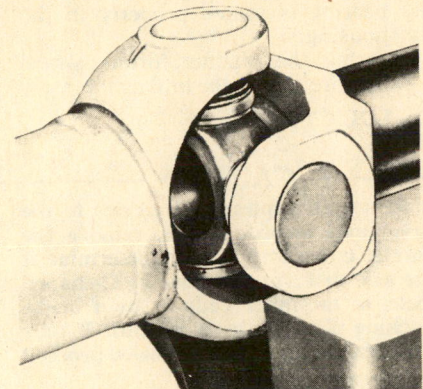

Supporting splined yoke
(© Pontiac Div., G.M. Corp)

2. Remove the U-bolts and nuts from the differential flange.

3. Remove the driveshaft assembly by first sliding the driveshaft sufficiently forward to disengage the differential flange, then slide the shaft downward and rearward to disengage the front splined yoke from the transmission output shaft.

4. Installation is the reverse of removal. Be sure to align the match mark made before disassembly.

U-Joint Removal and Installation—All Front and Rear U-Joints

1. Remove the driveshaft.

NOTE: *The universal may have snaprings that are used to retain the bearing cups in the yokes. These snap-rings may be located at the outside of each yoke or in a groove at the base or open end of each bearing cap. In both cases, there are four snap-rings for each universal joint and they must be removed before proceeding further.*

2. Support the splined yoke (front universal) or the journal (rear universal) in a manner that will allow the fixed yoke on the driveshaft to be moved. Support the opposite end so that the driveshaft will be in a horizontal position.

3. Using a piece of pipe, or a similar tool with a large enough diameter, apply force to the fixed yoke until the bearing is almost completely pushed out of the yoke and into the pipe. Remove the bearing completely by inserting a spacer be-

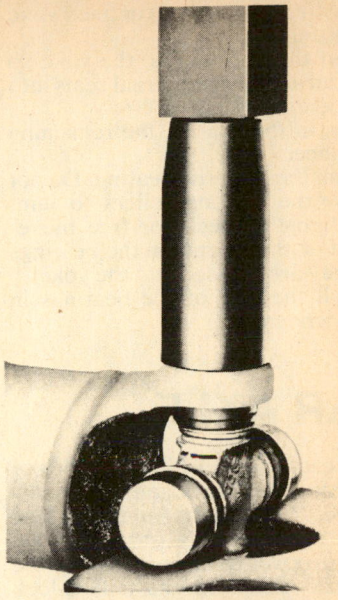

Bearing removal
(© Pontiac Div., G.M. Corp)

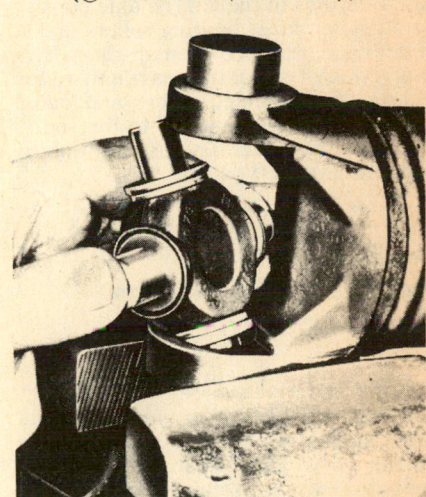

Installing journal
(© Pontiac Div., G.M. Corp)

tween the seal and the bearing cup and finish pressing the bearing out of its yoke, or by tapping around the circumference of the exposed portion of the bearing with a punch and small hammer.

NOTE: *The plastic which retains the bearing will be sheared when the bearing cup is pressed out. Be sure to remove the remains of the plastic retainer from the ears of the yoke. It is easier to remove the remains if a small pin or punch is first driven through the injection holes in the yoke. Failure to remove all of the plastic remains may prevent the bearing cups from being pressed into place and the bearing retainers from being properly seated.*

4. Remove the rest of the bearings following the same procedure.

On installation:

1. Install a bearing one-quarter of the way into one side of the splined

yoke (front universal) or fixed yoke (rear universal).

2. Insert the journal into the yoke so that an arm of the journal seats into the bearing.
3. Press in the bearing the remaining distance.
4. Install the opposite bearing. Do not allow the bearing rollers to jam. Continually check for free movement of the journal in the bearings as they are pressed into the yoke.
5. Install the rest of the bearings in the same manner.

REAR AXLE

These cars use two different types of drive anxle, the C-lock and the non C-lock type. Axle shafts in the C-lock type are retained by C-shaped locks, which fit grooves at the inner end of the shaft. Axle shafts in the non C-lock type are retained by the brake backing plate, which is bolted to the axle housing. Bearings in the C-type axle consist of an outer race, bearing rollers and a roller cage, retained by snap-rings. The non C-lock type axle uses a unit roller bearing (inner race, rollers and outer race), which is pressed onto the shaft, up to a shoulder. The Astre/Sunbird uses the C-lock type axle.

AXLE SHAFT, BEARING AND SEAL
Removal and Installation
NON C—LOCK TYPE

——————— CAUTION ———————

Before attempting any service to the drive axle or axle shafts, remove the axle carrier cover and visually determine if the axle shafts are retained by C-shaped locks at the inner end, or by the brake backing plate at the outer end. If the shafts are *not* retained by C-locks, proceed as follows.

Design allows for maximum axle shaft end-play of .025 in., which can be measured with a dial indicator. If end-play is found to be excessive, the bearing should be replaced. Shimming the bearing is not recommended as this ignores end-play of the bearing itself and could result in improper seating of the bearing.

1. Remove the wheel, tire and brake drum.
2. Remove the nuts holding the retainer plate to the backing plate. Disconnect the brake line.
3. Remove the retainer and install nuts, fingertight, to prevent the brake backing plate from being dislodged.
4. Pull out the axle shaft and bearing assembly, using a slide hammer.
5. Using a chisel, nick the bearing retainer in three or four places. The

retainer does not have to be cut, merely collapsed sufficiently, to allow the bearing retainer to be slid from the shaft.
6. Press off the bearing and install the new one by pressing it into position.
7. Press on the new retainer.

NOTE: *Do not attempt to press the bearing and the retainer on at the same time.*

8. Assemble the shaft and bearing in the housing, being sure that the bearing is seated properly in the housing.
9. Install the retainer, drum, wheel and tire. Bleed the brakes.

C—LOCK TYPE

——————— CAUTION ———————

Before attempting any service to the drive axle or axle shafts, remove the carrier cover and visually determine if the axle shafts are retained by C-shaped locks at the inner ends or by a brake backing plate at the outer end. If they are retained by C-shaped locks, proceed as follows.

1. Raise the vehicle and remove the wheels.
2. The differential cover has already been removed (see Caution note above). Remove the differential pinion shaft lockscrew and the differential pinion shaft.
3. Push the flanged end of the axle shaft toward the center of the vehicle and remove the C-lock from the end of the shaft.
4. Remove the axle shaft from the housing, being careful not to damage the oil seal.
5. Remove the oil seal by inserting the button end of the axle shaft behind the steel case of the oil seal. Pry the seal loose from the bore.
6. Seat the legs of the bearing puller behind the bearing. Seat a washer against the bearing and hold it in place with a nut. Use a slide hammer to pull the bearing.
7. Pack the cavity between the seal lips with wheel bearing lubricant and lubricate a new wheel bearing with the same.
8. Use a suitable driver and install the bearing until it bottoms against the tube. Install the oil seal.
9. Slide the axle shaft into place. Be sure that the splines on the shaft do not damage the oil seal. Make sure that the splines engage the differential side gear.
10. Install the axle shaft C-lock on the inner end of the axle shaft and push the shaft outward so that the C-lock seats in the differential side gear counterbore.
11. Position the differential pinion shaft through the case and pinions, aligning the hole for the case with the hole for the lockscrew.
12. Install the pinion shaft lockscrew.

13. Use a new gasket and install the carrier cover. Be sure that the gasket surfaces are clean before installing the gasket and cover.
14. Fill the axle with lubricant to the bottom of the filler hole.
15. Install the brake drum and wheels and lower the car. Check for leaks and road test the car.

JACKING, HOISTING

Jack car at front spring seats of lower control arms. Jack car at rear under axle housing, or under a frame member.

FRONT SUSPENSION

Shock Absorber Replacement
New shock absorbers must be purged of air before installation. This is done by repeatedly extending the shock in its normal mounted position, inverting, and compressing it.

EXCEPT ASTRE AND SUNBIRD
1. Remove the nut, retainer, and grommet which are attached to the upper end of the shock absorber and seat against the frame bracket.

NOTE: *It may be necessary to hold the shock absorber shaft to remove the nut. This may be done with a wrench on the end of the shaft.*

2. Raise the car to allow the shock to be dropped from the lower control arm.
3. Remove the two shock absorber lower attaching screws and lower the shock from the control arm.
4. Install the shock absorber by reversing the removal steps.
5. Make sure all grommets are in the correct position. Tighten the upper nut to 10 ft. lbs.

ASTRE AND SUNBIRD
1. Pry out the access plug in the engine compartment so that the upper mount is visible.
2. Raise the front of the car and safely support it.
3. Turn the wheels for clearance.
4. Hold the upper shock stud with a wrench. Loosen and remove the locknut.
5. Unbolt the lower end and pull the shock down and out.
6. Place the lower retainer and rubber grommet on the shock stud.
7. Put the shock in place and tighten the lower bolts. Torque to 20 ft. lbs.
8. Place the upper grommet, retainer, and nut on the shock stud.
9. Hold the stud with a wrench and

tighten the nut. Torque to 120 in. lbs.

Coil Spring Removal and Installation

EXCEPT ASTRE AND SUNBIRD

1. Jack up car and support on jack stands at frame side rails.
2. Remove shock absorber.
3. Disconnect stabilizer bar at lower control arm.
4. Support lower control arm with a hydraulic floor jack, then remove the two inner control arm to front crossmember pivot bolts.
5. Carefully lower the control arm, allowing the spring to relax.

——————— CAUTION ———————

Allow the spring to completely expand before attempting to remove it.

6. Reach in and remove spring.
7. To install, reverse the removal procedure. Tighten the lower control arm pivot bolts to 105 ft. lbs. or the nuts to 95 ft. lbs. with the weight of the car on the springs.

ASTRE AND SUNBIRD

1. Raise the front of the car and support it with jackstands placed under the front crossmember braces.
2. Remove the wheel, shock absorbers, and stabilizer bar.
3. Support the lower control arm outer end with a hydraulic floor jack and a block of wood.
4. Securely fasten the spring to the lower control arm with a heavy chain.
5. To detach the tie rod, remove the cotter pin and nut, and tap on the steering arm (not the tie-rod end) with a hammer. Hold another hammer behind the steering arm to take the force of the tapping. The tie rod should then fall free.
6. Remove the lower ball joint stud from the steering knuckle.
7. Very cautiously lower the jack until the spring is fully expanded.
8. Place the spring in its pads on the lower control arm and shock tower. Secure it with a chain as in step four.
9. Carefully raise the jack.
10. Place the lower ball joint stud in the steering knuckle. Torque the stud nut to 60 ft. lbs. If the cotter pin does not align, tighten it further ⅛ of a turn and insert a new cotter pin.
11. Install the tie-rod end to the steering arm. Torque the nut to 35 ft. lbs. If the cotter pin hole does not align, tighten further up to a maximum of 50 ft. lbs. Insert a new cotter pin.
12. Replace the shock absorber. Do not attach the top end of the shock at this point.
13. Install the stabilizer bar. Tighten the bracket bolts to 30 ft. lbs. and

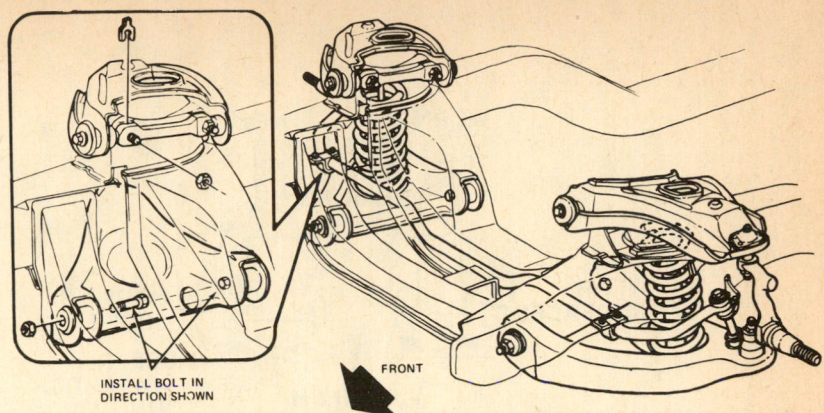

Front suspension—Ventura (© Pontiac Div., G.M. Corp)

the control arm bolts to 10 ft. lbs.
14. Replace the wheel and lower the car. Install the upper end of the shock absorber.

Upper Control Arm Removal and Installation

1. Support car weight at outer end of lower control arm.
2. Remove wheel and tire.
3. Remove cotter pin and loosen the nut on the upper control arm ball stud.
4. Remove the stud from the knuckle with a pry bar, while tapping with a hammer. The preferred method of doing this is to use a ball joint stud remover tool to push the stud out.
5. Remove two nuts that hold the upper control arm cross-shaft to front crossmember. Count number of shims at each bolt.
6. Install bolts through holes and install upper control arm to crossmember.
7. Secure two nuts and washers to the bolts holding the upper control arm shaft to front crossmember. Install same number of shims as removed at each bolt. Torque bolts to 50 ft. lbs. on all 1975 and later models and all Ventura. On 1972-74 Firebird, LeMans and Grand Am, tighten the bolts to 80 ft. lbs. Torque the bolts to 60 ft. lbs. on the Astre and Sunbird.
8. Lubricate ball joint with chassis lube.
9. Install ball joint stud through knuckle. Install nut, and torque to 40 ft. lbs. for all except Astre/Sunbird; 30 ft. lbs.—Astre and Sunbird. Insert cotter pin.

——————— CAUTION ———————

Care should be taken to insure that the steering knuckle hole, ball stud, and nut are free of dirt and grease before tightening the nut. Turn the nut only in the tightening direction to align the slot with the hole to insert the cotter pin. Do not back off the nut. Maximum torque to align the slot with the hole, except on Astre and Sunbird should not exceed 100 ft. lbs.

5. Install wheel and tire assembly.
6. Lower car to floor.
7. Be sure to recheck caster and camber.

Ball Joint Inspection

NOTE: *Before performing this inspection, make sure the wheel bearings are adjusted correctly and that the control arm bushings are in good condition.*

1. Jack the car up under the front lower control arm at the spring seat.
2. Raise the car until there is 1-2 in. of clearance under the wheel.
3. Insert a bar under the wheel and pry upward. If the wheel raises more than ⅛ in., the ball joints are worn. Determine whether the upper or lower ball joint is worn by visual inspection while prying on the weehl.

NOTE: *Due to the distribution of forces in the suspension, the lower ball joint is usually the defective joint.*

Alternate Ball Joint Inspection Method

UPPER

1. Disengage the ball stud from the steering knuckle, the weight of the car being supported by a jack under the spring seat on the side being checked.
2. Install the stud nut onto the stud and check the torque required to rotate the ball stud.
3. If the torque is less than ½ ft. lbs., the joint must be replaced.

LOWER

1. Place a jack under the lower control arm spring seat and jack up the car.
2. Remove the grease fitting from the lower ball joint.
3. Remove the hub and backing plate, or caliper assembly.
4. Separate the lower ball stud from the steering knuckle using a pry bar and hammer.

NOTE: *Make sure that the seal is not damaged.*

5. Place the probe of a dial indicator into the grease fitting hole until it

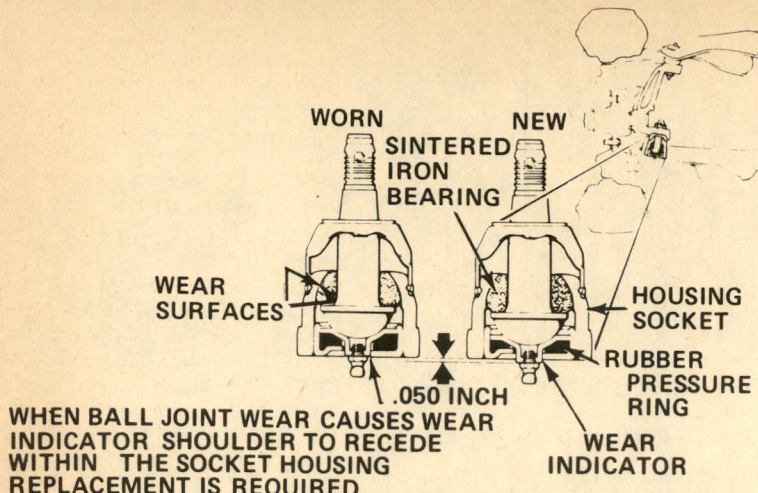

WORN NEW
SINTERED
IRON
BEARING

WEAR
SURFACES

HOUSING
SOCKET

RUBBER
PRESSURE
RING

.050 INCH

WEAR
INDICATOR

WHEN BALL JOINT WEAR CAUSES WEAR
INDICATOR SHOULDER TO RECEDE
WITHIN THE SOCKET HOUSING
REPLACEMENT IS REQUIRED

Lower ball joint wear indicator

(© Pontiac Div., G.M. Corp)

touches the base of the ball joint.
6. Preload and zero the indicator, then pull up and down on the threaded portion of the stud and measure the play.
7. If the play exceeds 0.050 in., the ball joint must be replaced.

Lower Ball Joint Wear Indicators—1974 Firebird and LeMans, All Models beginning 1975

These cars have a visual wear indicator on the lower ball joint. Wear is indicated by the position of the 1/2 in. nipple into which the grease fitting is screwed. On a new joint, the nipple should project .050 in. beyond the ball joint cover surface. If the nipple is flush or inside the cover surface, replace the ball joint.

Upper Ball Joint Removal and Installation

1. Perform Steps 1-4 of Upper Control Arm Removal. Prickpunch the center of the four rivets.
2. Drill through the heads of these rivets.
3. Chisel off rivet heads and tap out rivets with a punch.
4. Install new ball joint against top side of upper control arm. Secure joint to control arm with the four special alloy bolts and nuts furnished with the replacement part.
5. Torque these bolts and nuts to 9 ft. lbs.

Lower Control Arm and Ball Joint Removal and Installation

1. Remove coil spring and lower control arm inner bolts.
2. Separate lower ball joint from steering knuckle by prying, while hammering sharply on steering knuckle.
3. Press lower ball joint from lower control arm using suitable arbors and a large bench vise.

4. To install, reverse removal procedure, tightening lower ball joint stud nut to 70 ft. lbs. Tighten the nut to 60 ft. lbs. on the Astre and Sunbird.

NOTE: *If only ball joint is to be removed, remove brake caliper or hub and backing plate, with jack under lower arm. Begin with Step 2.*

Wheel Bearing Adjustment

1. Lift the wheel off the ground by jacking under the lower control arm.
2. Remove the dust cap from the hub.
3. Remove the cotter pin and discard it.
4. Snug up the spindle nut while spinning the wheel to seat the bearings (12 ft. lbs.). Then back off the nut 1/4-1/2 turn.
5. Retighten the nut by hand until it is finger-tight.
6. Loosen the nut until the nearest hole in the spindle lines up with a slot in the spindle nut and then insert a new cotter pin. When the bearing is properly adjusted, there will be 0.001-0.005 in. endplay.

NOTE: *Under no circumstances is the final bearing nut adjustment to be even finger-tight.*

7. Replace the dust cover and lower the car.

REAR SUSPENSION

Shock Absorber Replacement

New shock absorbers must be purged of air before installation. This is done by repeatedly extending the shock in its normal mounted position, inverting, and compressing it.

EXCEPT ASTRE AND SUNBIRD

1. Raise the car at the axle housing.
2. Remove the nut, retainer, and grommet, or nut, and lockwasher,

which attach the lower end of the shock absorber to its mounting.
3. Remove the two shock absorber upper attaching screws and the shock absorber.
4. Reverse the removal procedures to install. Tighten the lower nut to 65 ft. lbs. on LeMans and Grand Am, to 10 ft. lbs. on Firebird and to 55 (45 beginning 1975) ft. lbs. on Ventura and Phoenix.

ASTRE AND SUNBIRD

1. Raise the vehicle and support the rear axle.
2. Remove upper attaching bolts and lower through-bolt.
3. Remove the shock absorber.
4. Install retainer and rubber grommet onto the new shock.
5. Place shock absorber into installed position and install upper retaining bolts.
6. Install the through bolt and a rubber grommet on each side of the shock eye.
7. Lower the car.

Coil Spring Replacement

LeMANS, GRAND AM

1. Raise the rear of the car and support it solidly on the frame rails.
2. Remove the clip that attaches the brake hose to its bracket on the frame crossmember.
3. Support the rear axle with a jack.
4. Remove the nut and lockwasher from the shock absorber and disconnect the shock from the axle. It may be necessary to adjust the height of the jack to disconnect the shock. On models beginning 1973, disconnect the upper control arms from the axle housing.
5. Carefully lower the jack until the spring is free and remove the spring. Note the position of the spring and replace it with the lower coil pointing in the same direction.
6. Reverse the removal steps to install the spring.

ASTRE AND SUNBIRD

1. Raise vehicle and support the rear axle, with a hydraulic jack.
2. Disconnect both shock absorbers from lower brackets.
3. Lower axle and remove springs and spring insulators.

NOTE: *One or both springs may be removed at this point.*

— CAUTION —
When lowering axle do not stretch brake hose running from frame to axle.

4. Install insulators on top and bottom of springs and position on axle.
5. Raise axle and reconnect shock absorbers. Torque the bottom stud or bolt nuts to 42 in. lbs.
6. Lower the vehicle.

1976 AND LATER ASTRE AND SUNBIRD TRACK ROD REMOVAL AND INSTALLATION

1. Raise the car and support the rear axle.
2. Remove the mounting bolt at the body, and then remove the bolt at the axle bracket and remove the track rod.

1976 AND LATER ASTRE AND SUNBIRD TORQUE ROD REMOVAL AND INSTALLATION

1. Raise the car and support the rear axle.
2. Remove the mounting bracket from the transmission, then remove the through bolt.
3. Remove the mounting bolts from the transmission and remove the torque arm.

Leaf Spring Replacement

FIREBIRD, VENTURA, PHOENIX

1. Jack up the car at the rear axle. Then support the major portion of the weight of the car on the frame rails, leaving the jack in place under the axle. At this point the jack should be supporting the axle only; there should be no tension on the spring.
2. Disconnect the shock at the axle and move it out of the way.
3. Remove the spring and shock absorber anchor plate nuts and remove the anchor plate and lower spring cushion pad.
4. Raise the axle with the jack and remove the upper spring cushion pad.
5. Loosen the upper and lower spring shackle pin nuts.
6. Loosen the front spring eye bolt.
7. Remove the screws securing the spring front mounting bracket to the floor pan and carefully let the spring swing down.
8. Remove the lower shackle pin from the rear of the spring and remove the spring from the car.
9. Install the front spring mounting bracket on the front spring eye and loosely insert the bolt and nut. Do not tighten the spring eyebolt until the weight of the car is on the springs.
10. Place the spring into the shackles at the rear of the car and loosely install the lower shackle pin and nut. Do not tighten them.
11. Raise the front end of the spring and install the spring mounting bracket to the floor pan and torque the bolts to 30 ft. lbs. Make sure the tab on the spring mounting bracket is indexed in the slot in the floor pan and that the parking brake cables are on the top side of the spring.
12. Place the upper spring cushion pan on the spring and lower the axle onto spring.

Rear spring installation—Ventura with single leaf springs
(© Pontiac Div., G.M. Corp)

13. Install the lower spring cushion and shock absorber anchor plate and torque the anchor plate nuts to 40 ft lbs.
14. Install the shock absorber.
15. Put the weight of the car on the springs and torque the shackle pin nuts to 50 ft. lbs. Tighten front eyebolt to 80 ft. lbs.

BRAKES

Drum brakes are of the duo-servo, self-adjusting type.

A dual-type master cylinder is used. For detailed information on this cylinder, see Unit Repair Section.

Information on brake service can be found in the Unit Repair Section.

Parking Brake Adjustment

EXCEPT ASTRE AND SUNBIRD

The automatic self-adjusting feature incorporated in the rear brake mechanism normally maintains proper parking brake adjustment. For this reason, the rear brake adjustment must be checked before any adjustment of the parking brake cables is done. Check the parking brake mechanism and cables for free movement and lubricate all working surfaces before proceeding.

--- CAUTION ---

It is very important that the parking brake cables are not too tight. If the cables are too tight, they create a drag and position the secondary shoes so that the self-adjusters continue to operate in compensation for drag wear. The result is rapidly worn rear brake linings.

1. Jack up both rear wheels.
2. Push parking brake pedal 2 notches for 1975 and later Firebird, Ventura, and Phoenix, 3 notches for 1975 and later LeMans and Grand Am, 4-8 notches for all series 1972, 8 notches for all series 1973-74.
3. Loosen rear equalizer locknut and adjust forward nut until light rear

brake drag is felt as wheels are rotated by hand. On 1975 and later models, you should be able to turn the wheels backwards using two hands, but not forward.
4. Tighten locknut and release parking brake pedal; no drag should be felt.

ASTRE AND SUNBIRD

1. Raise and support the rear of the car.
2. Apply the parking brake one notch from the fully released position.
3. Loosen the adjusting locknut at the cable equalizer and tighten the adjusting nut until a slight drag is felt when the rear wheels are rotated.
4. Tighten the locknut securely.
5. The rear wheels should rotate freely when the parking brake is fully released.
6. Lower the vehicle.

Master Cylinder Removal and Installation

1. Disconnect hydraulic line/s at master cylinder; disconnect clevis at pedal (except on power brakes).
2. Remove the two retaining nuts and lockwashers that hold cylinder to the firewall or power booster.
3. Remove the master cylinder, gasket and rubber boot.
4. Position master cylinder on firewall; reconnect pushrod clevis to brake pedal.
5. Install nuts and lockwashers.
6. Install hydraulic line/s, then check brake pedal free play.
7. Bleed brakes, as described in Unit Repair Section.

Power Brake Booster Removal and Installation

1. Remove the vacuum hose from the front housing and discard the grommet. Remove the master cylinder and position away from the booster. It is not necessary to disconnect the lines from the master cylinder if it is not to be repaired.
2. Remove the clevis pin retainer from the brake pedal inside the car.
3. Remove the nuts from the vacuum cylinder studs under the dash and remove the vacuum power section.
4. Reverse the removal procedure to install the booster.

STEERING

The manual steering gear is the recirculating-ball nut type. The steering shaft, worm shaft, and worm nut are all in line. The steering shaft and worm shaft are separated by a flexible coupling. This coupling permits the gear to be removed independently of the steering shaft and steering column.

All models use a variable-ratio power steering gear. The gear is the recirculating-ball type, incorporating a worm-

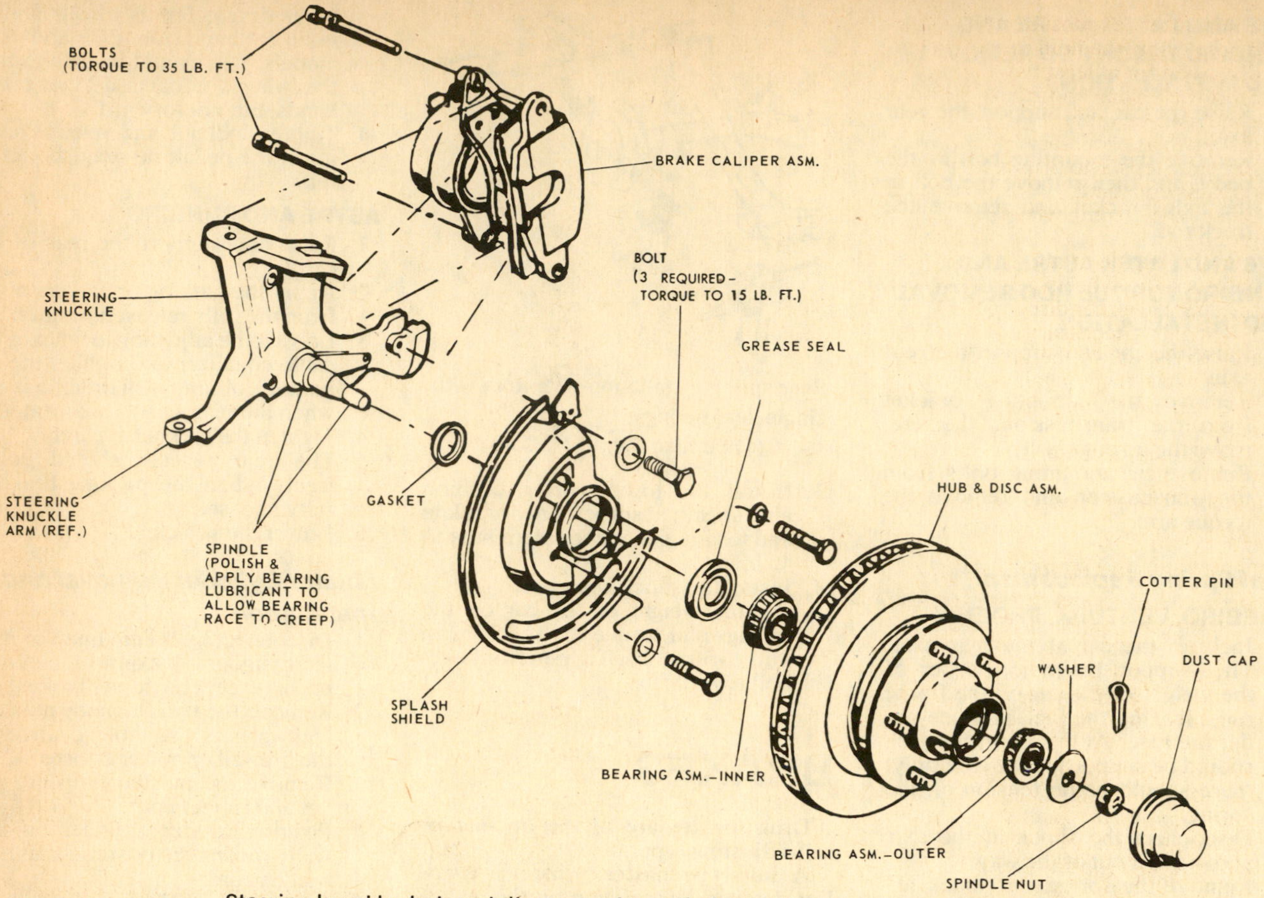

BOLTS
(TORQUE TO 35 LB. FT.)

BRAKE CALIPER ASM.

STEERING
KNUCKLE

BOLT
(3 REQUIRED -
TORQUE TO 15 LB. FT.)

GREASE SEAL

STEERING
KNUCKLE
ARM (REF.)

GASKET

SPINDLE
(POLISH &
APPLY BEARING
LUBRICANT TO
ALLOW BEARING
RACE TO CREEP)

HUB & DISC ASM.

COTTER PIN

WASHER

DUST CAP

SPLASH
SHIELD

BEARING ASM.–INNER

BEARING ASM.–OUTER

SPINDLE NUT

Steering knuckle, hub and disc assembly—Firebird, 1973 and later LeMans and Grand Am (© Pontiac Div., G.M. Corp)

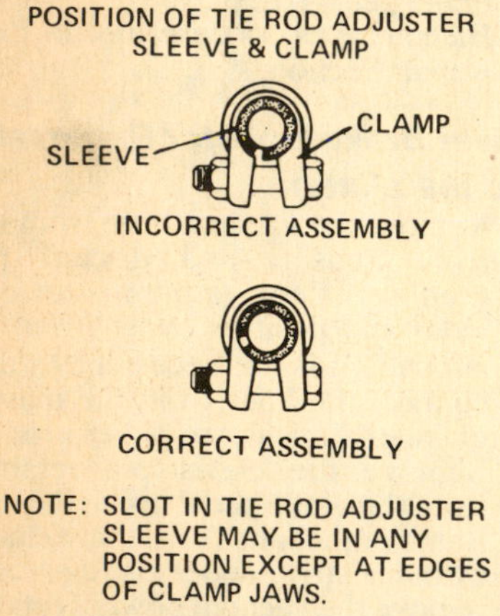

POSITION OF TIE ROD ADJUSTER
SLEEVE & CLAMP

SLEEVE — CLAMP

INCORRECT ASSEMBLY

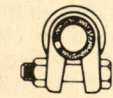

CORRECT ASSEMBLY

NOTE: SLOT IN TIE ROD ADJUSTER
SLEEVE MAY BE IN ANY
POSITION EXCEPT AT EDGES
OF CLAMP JAWS.

Tie rod clamp installation
(© Pontiac Div., G.M. Corp)

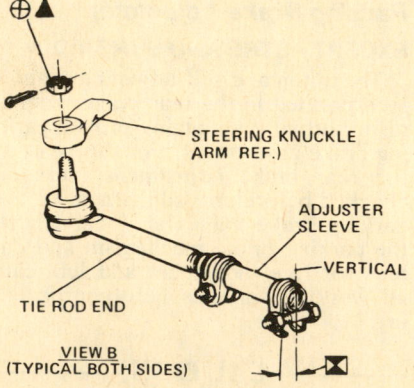

STEERING KNUCKLE
ARM REF.)

ADJUSTER
SLEEVE

VERTICAL

TIE ROD END

VIEW B
(TYPICAL BOTH SIDES)

Tie rod assembly—typical
(© Pontiac Div., G.M. Corp)

shaft and a rack-piston. A rotary valve is contained in the gear housing, eliminating the need for individually mounted valve and cylinder assemblies.

Hydraulic pressure for the power steering is provided by a constant displacement vane-type pump.

Tie Rod End Replacement

1. Loosen the tie rod adjuster sleeve clamp nuts.
2. Remove the tie rod stud nut cotter pin and nut.

3. Remove the tie rod stud from the steering arm or intermediate rod. This is a taper fit. Removal is accomplished by using a ball joint removal tool.
4. Unthread the tie rod from the adjuster sleeve. Outer tie rods have right-hand threads and inner tie rods have left-hand threads. Count the number of turns the tie rod must be rotated to remove it from the adjusting sleeve. This will allow a reasonably accurate realignment upon reassembly.

5. Reverse the removal procedures for installation. Clean all rust and dirt from the threads. Check the alignment and adjust if necessary.

Power Steering Pump Removal and Installation

1. Disconnect the hoses at the pump.
2. Remove the drive pulley attaching nut.
3. Loosen the bracket-to-pump mounting bolts and remove the drive belt.
4. Slide the pulley from the shaft with a gear puller. Do not hammer on the pulley.
5. Remove the bracket-to-pump mounting bolts and remove the pump.
6. Reverse the removal steps for installation. Bleed the pump of air by turning the pulley counter-clockwise until no bubbles appear in the reservoir.
7. Bleed the system.

Power Steering System Bleeding

The system must be bled of air whenever any parts of the pump circuit have been disconnected or replaced.

1. Fill the reservoir. Be careful not to overfill, because the level is normally checked at operating temper-

ature after expansion has taken place. Allow the fluid to remain undisturbed for at least two minutes.

2. Start the engine and run it for only about two seconds.
3. Fill again as necessary.
4. Repeat Steps 1 to 3 until the level remains constant.
5. Raise the front wheels off the ground.
6. Run the engine at about 1,500 rpm and turn the wheels gently against the stops in either direction.
7. Fill again as necessary.
8. Lower the car to the ground. Turn the wheels gently against the stops in either direction with the engine running.
9. Fill again as necessary.

Steering Wheel Removal and Installation

EXCEPT 1975-76 ASTRE/SUNBIRD

1. On deluxe models, remove the screws holding the trim cover to the wheel, or if equipped with a horn button, lift the button off.
2. Remove the snap-ring, if any, and steering wheel nut from the steering shaft.
3. Position the wheels in the straight-ahead position and make match marks on the steering shaft and steering wheel.
4. Using a puller, remove the steering wheel.

--- CAUTION ---

Don't pound on the steering wheel or the steering shaft. The collapsible column could be damaged enough to require replacement.

5. Disconnect the horn wire insulator by rotating the insulator counter-clockwise to the unlock position and then pull up.
6. Reverse the removal procedures for installation. Make sure the match marks are lined up when installing the wheel.

1975-76 ASTRE AND SUNBIRD

1. Disconnect the battery ground cable.
2. Remove the two screws from the back of the wheel, allowing the shroud (horn actuator bar) to be removed. Lift the Formula wheel horn button off.
3. Set the wheel straight ahead. Mark the relationship of the wheel to the shaft and remove the snap-ring and nut.
4. Remove the steering wheel with a puller, using the two threaded holes in the wheel. Disconnect the horn wire insulator by rotating the insulator counterclockwise to the unlock position and then pulling up.
5. Install the wheel, aligning the previously made marks. Make sure that the turn signal switch is in the

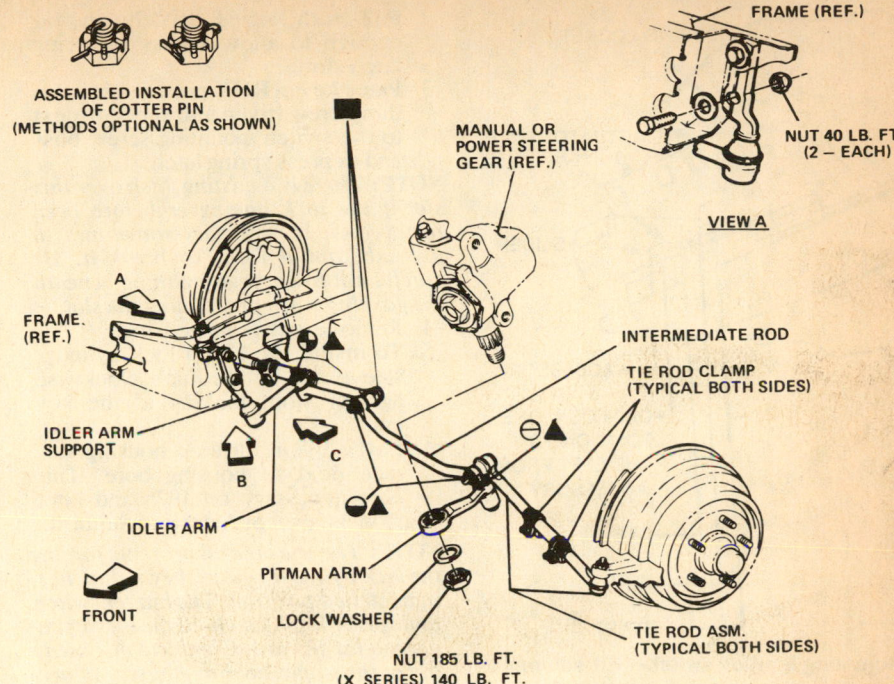

Steering linkage (© Pontiac Div., G.M. Corp)

neutral position. Torque the nut to 30 ft. lbs.
6. Make sure that the lower horn insulator, eyelet, and spring are in place.
7. Position the shroud, seating the pin on the right side of the wheel in the hole in the shroud. Replace the formula wheel horn button.
8. Replace the two screws in the rear of the wheel. Connect the battery cable.

Turn Signal Switch Replacement

1. Remove the steering wheel.
2. Remove the three cover screws and lift the cover off the shaft.
3. Depress the lockplate and remove the snap-ring. All 1976 and later steering columns have a redesigned lock plate which is removed by inserting a screwdriver in the cover slot and prying out. This is done in at least two of the slots to avoid breaking the plate. Remove the retaining ring and lockplate.
4. Slide the upper bearing spring and turn signal cam off the shaft. Remove the thrust washer.
5. Remove the turn signal lever screw and lever.
NOTE: *On LeMans with tilt steering wheel, the lever is held in place with a snap ring.*
6. Push the hazard warning switch in and remove the knob.
7. On models with a column mounted dimmer switch, remove the actuator arm screw and arm. On models with a tilt column, lift the tilt lever to remove the switch screws.
8. Pull the wiring connector out of the bracket and disconnect it. Wrap it

with tape to prevent snagging.
9. Pull the switch straight up and remove it from the housing.
10. Reverse the removal procedures for installation.

Ignition Switch Replacement

The ignition and steering wheel locking switch is located just below the gear selector lever on the steering column.
1. Disconnect battery.
2. Loosen toe pan screws.
3. Remove column to panel nuts, lower steering column, and disconnect switch wire connectors.

--- CAUTION ---

Be extremely careful with the steering column. Never let it hang unsupported.

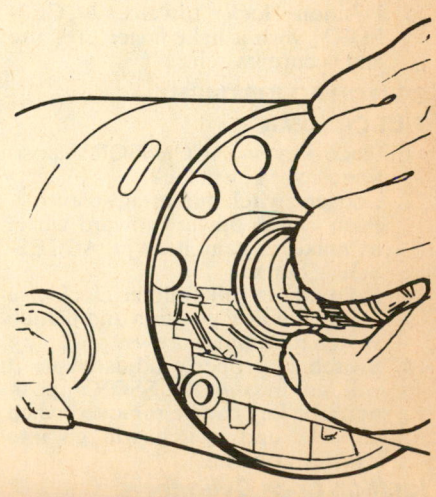

Depressing lock cylinder spring latch
(© Pontiac Div., G.M. Corp)

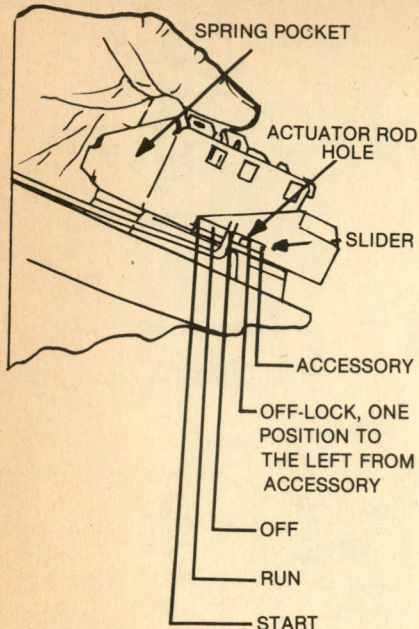

Adjusting ignition switch—tilt column
(© Pontiac Div., G.M. Corp)

4. Remove switch attaching screws and switch.
5. To install, move key lock to OFF-LOCK position.
6. Move actuator rod hole in switch to OFF-LOCK position.
7. Install switch, with rod in hole, then reverse removal procedure.

SWITCH ADJUSTMENT— STANDARD COLUMN
1. Place switch in OFF position.
2. Position switch on column, then move slider to extreme left (toward wheel).
3. Move slider back two positions to the right of ACCESSORY position.
4. Place key in any run position and shift transmission into any position but Park for automatics or Reverse for manual.
5. Position lock toward ACCESSORY with a light finger pressure and secure switch.

SWITCH ADJUSTMENT — TILT COLUMN
1. Place key in ACCESSORY position; leave key in lock.
2. Loosen switch mounting screws.
3. Push switch upward toward wheel to make certain it is in ACCESSORY detent.
4. Hold key in full counter clockwise ACCESSORY position and tighten switch mounting screws.
5. Switch is properly adjusted if: it will go into ACCESSORY position, the key can be removed when in lock, and switch will go into START position.

Ignition Lock Cylinder Replacement
1. Remove steering wheel.

2. Pull turn signal switch up far enough to allow access to spring latch slot.
3. Place key in RUN position, insert a thin screwdriver into the slot next to the switch mounting screw boss and depress spring latch.
NOTE: *There is a casting flash over this slot if the lock has never before been removed. It is necessary sometimes to use substantial force to break it. Be careful not to damage anything beneath the flashing when penetrating the slot.*
4. Remove lock from housing.
5. To install, first hold lock cylinder sleeve and rotate knob clockwise against stop, looking at the key end.
6. Lay a 1/16 in. drill on housing surface next to housing bore. This isn't necessary on 1975 and later models, except Astre and Sunbird.
NOTE: *The 1/16 in. drill prevents forcing the lock cylinder inward beyond its normal latched position. The buzzer switch and spring latch can hold the lock cylinder too far inward. Complete disassembly of the upper bearing housing is necessary to release an improperly installed lock cylinder.*
7. Insert cylinder into housing bore, aligning keyway, and push in to abutment.
8. Rotate knob counterclockwise, pushing in slightly, until cylinder mates with sector.
9. Push in until spring latch pops into groove, then remove drill.

INSTRUMENT PANEL

Light Switch Replacement
1. Disconnect battery.
2. Pull knob to on position.
3. Reach under instrument panel and depress the switch shaft retainer, then remove knob and shaft assembly.
NOTE: *Disconnect vacuum hose on vacuum-operated headlamp models.*
4. Remove retaining ferrule nut.
5. Remove switch from instrument panel.
6. Disconnect multi-plug connector from switch.
7. Install in reverse of above. (In checking lights before installation, switch must be grounded to test dome lights on some models).

Speedometer Cable Removal and Installation
1. Remove the lower A/C duct, if any, on LeMans.
2. Remove the lower instrument panel trim plates on all except Ventura and Phoenix.
3. Reach up behind the speedometer and find where the cable attaches to the speedometer head. Press the

retaining clip downward and slide the cable from the head.
4. Slide the old core from the casing. If the core is broken, raise the car and remove the cable retaining clip from the transmission. Pull out the remaining piece of the core.
5. Install in the reverse order of removal. Prior to installing, the core should be wiped clean and the casing flushed out with solvent. Before inserting the core into the case, coat the lower two-thirds of the core with a speedometer cable lubricant. Do not lubricate the upper third.

WINDSHIELD WIPERS

Motor Replacement
1. Remove hoses and wire terminals that are connected to wiper unit.
2. Remove clip or nut that secures wiper crank to wiper linkage arm.
NOTE: *This clip is under leaf screen on depressed-park (hidden wiper) motors, and accessible only after firewall bolts are removed on some standard motors. On some models, the wiper arm must be removed to facilitate motor removal.*
3. Remove screws that secure wiper motor assembly to firewall.
4. Position wiper assembly on firewall and secure.
5. Connect wire terminals and hoses.
6. Connect wiper crank with wiper linkage arm.

Blade Removal and Installation
Two types of blades are used, depending on the car model, the Anco and the Trico systems. Two types of blade attachment are used, the straight-in bayonet type and the side fit type. Each uses a simple catch and snap technique for attachment. Follow directions on the replacement blade package for installation.

RADIO

Removal and Installation
1972 LeMANS AND GTO ALL VENTURA AND PHOENIX
1. Disconnect battery.
2. Remove radio knobs, bezels and hex nuts.
3. Remove support bracket bolt. Remove the Ventura and Phoenix radio sidebrace screw.
4. Disconnect electrical and antenna leads; remove radio from under dash.
5. To install, reverse removal procedure.

FIREBIRD
1. Disconnect the battery ground cable.

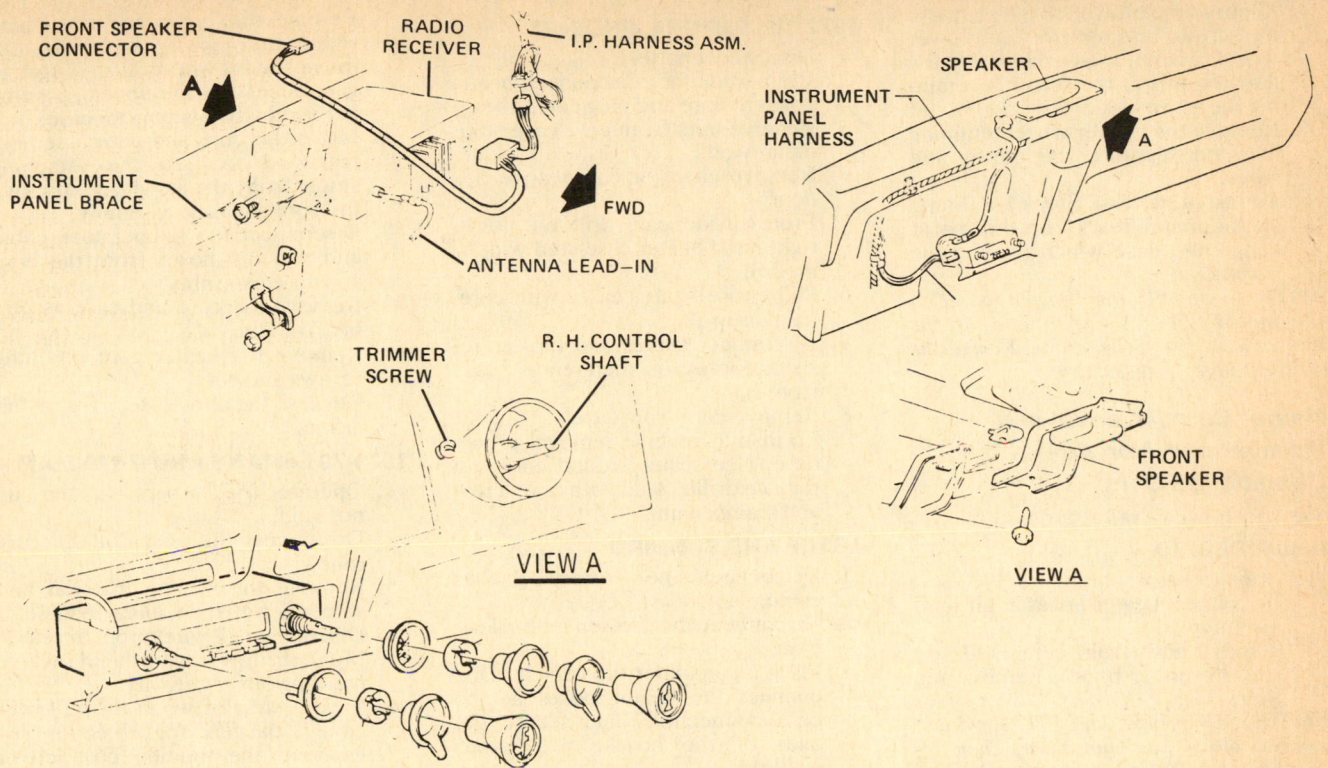

FRONT SPEAKER CONNECTOR • RADIO RECEIVER • I.P. HARNESS ASM. • INSTRUMENT PANEL BRACE • ANTENNA LEAD-IN • FWD • TRIMMER SCREW • R. H. CONTROL SHAFT • SPEAKER • INSTRUMENT PANEL HARNESS • A • FRONT SPEAKER • VIEW A • VIEW A

Ventura radio and front speaker installation (© G.M. Corp.)

2. Remove the glove box and lower right A/C duct.
3. Remove the knobs and trimplate.
4. Disconnect all wiring.
5. Remove the radio and bracket through the passenger side of the panel.
6. To install reverse the procedure.

1973-79 LeMANS

1. Disconnect the battery.
2. Remove the radio knobs and bezels.
3. Remove the upper and lower instrument panel trim plates.
4. Remove the two radio side (two front on 1974 and later) retaining screws.
5. Remove the radio from the panel opening, disconnecting the electrical connections and the antenna lead.
6. To install, reverse the removal procedure. If the radio is to be replaced, remove the bushing from the rear of the radio and install it on the replacement radio.

1973 AND LATER GRAND AM AND GRAND LeMANS

1. Disconnect the battery.
2. Remove the radio knobs and bezels and the retaining hex nut from the right-hand radio tuning shaft.
3. Remove the four retaining screws and the trim plate.
4. Remove the two side (one front on 1974 and later) retaining screws and the mounting bracket screw.
5. Remove the radio and the mounting bracket from the dash, discon-

necting the electrical connections and the antenna lead.
6. To install, reverse the removal procedure.

ASTRE AND SUNBIRD

1. Remove battery ground cable.
2. Remove knobs, controls, washers and nuts from radio bushings.
3. Disconnect antenna lead, power connector, and speaker connectors from rear of receiver.
4. Remove two screws securing radio mounting bracket to instrument panel lower reinforcement and lift out radio receiver.
5. To install, reverse the removal procedure.

HEATER

Heater Blower Removal and Installation—Non Air-Conditioned Cars

1972 LeMANS; FIREBIRD THROUGH 1976

1. Jack up front of car and remove right front wheel.
2. Cut access hole along stamped outline on right fender skirt, using an air chisel.
3. Disconnect blower power wire.
4. Remove blower.
5. To install, reverse removal procedure, covering access hole with a metal plate secured with sealer and sheet metal screws.

1973 AND LATER LeMANS & GRAND AM, 1977-79 FIREBIRD

1. Disconnect the blower motor feed wire and the ground wire.
2. Remove the blower motor retaining screws and remove the motor.
3. To replace, reverse the removal procedure.

VENTURA, PHOENIX

1. Disconnect the battery.
2. Detach the heater hoses from the clips on the right front fender skirt.
3. Raise the car and remove all fender skirt attaching bolts except those which attach the skirt to the radiator support.
4. Pull down on the skirt and block the skirt out to provide clearance for removal of the blower motor.
5. Disconnect the electrical wiring from the motor.
6. Remove the attaching screws and remove the blower motor. Pry the motor flange gently if the sealer acts as an adhesive.
7. Remove the blower impeller retaining nut and separate the motor from the impeller.
8. To replace, reverse the removal procedure.

ASTRE AND SUNBIRD

1. Disconnect the battery ground cable, and remove the coolant recovery tank.
2. Disconnect the blower motor lead wire. Disconnect the motor cooling tube on air-conditioned models.
3. Scribe the blower motor flange to case position.

4. Remove the blower to case attaching screws and remove the blower wheel and motor assembly. Pry the flange gently if the sealer is retaining the assembly.
5. Remove the blower wheel retaining nut and separate the motor and wheel.
6. To install, reverse Steps 1-5, lining up the match-marks on the motor flange and case which were made at removal.

NOTE: *Assemble the blower wheel to the motor with the open end of the blower away from the motor. Reseal the motor flange, if necessary.*

Heater Core Removal and Installation—Non Air-Conditioned Cars

1972-77 GTO, LeMANS, AND FIREBIRD

1. Drain radiator.
2. Disconnect heater hoses at air inlet assembly.
3. Remove nuts from core studs on firewall (under hood). Remove the glove box.

NOTE: *On Firebird, and 1977 LeMans, remove glove box and door, then remove heater outlet from case. Remove defroster duct screw on all models.*

4. From inside the car, pull the heater assembly from the firewall.
5. Disconnect control cables and wires, then remove heater assembly.
6. To remove core, unhook, retaining springs or strips.
7. To install, reverse removal procedure, making sure core is properly sealed during installation.

1978-79 LeMANS

1. Disconnect the hoses from the core tubes. Plug them to avoid coolant loss.
2. On the engine side of the firewall, remove the heater core cover from the case.
3. Remove the core bracket and ground screw.
4. Lift out the core.
5. Reverse the procedure for installation.

1978-79 FIREBIRD

1. Disconnect the battery ground.
2. Drain the radiator.
3. Disconnect the hoses from the core tubes.
4. Remove the heater box-to-core case screws and nuts from both sides of the firewall.
5. Remove the glove box and door.
6. Remove the heater and defroster outlet ducts.
7. Pull the heater case out and disconnect the cables.
8. Remove and discard sealing strips.
9. Lift out the core.
10. Installation is the reverse of removal. Transfer internal doors if replacing the case. Use new sealing material.

1972-79 VENTURA, PHOENIX

1. Disconnect battery.
2. Drain radiator, disconnect heater hoses at core and plug core tubes.
3. Remove nuts from core case studs on firewall.
4. Remove glove box and glove box door.
5. From inside car, drill out lower right hand heater case stud with 1/4 in. drill.
6. Pull entire heater case, with core, from firewall.
7. Disconnect cables and blower resistor connector, then remove case from car.
8. Remove core from case.
9. To install, reverse removal procedure. Use sealer around core and replace drilled stud with new screw and stamped nut.

ASTRE AND SUNBIRD

1. Disconnect the battery ground cable.
2. Disconnect the blower motor lead wire.
3. Place a pan under the vehicle. Disconnect the heater hoses at the core connections and secure the ends of the hoses in a raised position.
4. It may be necessary to remove the coil bracket to dash panel stud nut and move the coil out of the way.
5. Remove the blower intake to dash panel screws and nuts and remove the blower intake, blower motor and wheel as an assembly.
6. Remove the core retaining strap screws and remove the core from the vehicle.
7. To install, reverse Steps 1-6. Take great care when connecting hoses to core tubes. Undue inward or lateral pressure can easily cause stress cracks at the tube base. Use some sort of waterproof sealer on the core tubes to help the hoses slide into position.

NOTE: *Be sure that the blower intake sealer is intact, replace if necessary.*

Heater Blower Removal and Installation—Air-Conditioned Cars

This procedure is the same as for non air-conditioned cars.

Heater Core and Case Removal and Installation—Air-Conditioned Cars

GTO, LeMANS, AND GRAND AM THROUGH 1977

1. Drain the coolant.
2. Disconnect the water hoses at the heater core tubes to prevent spilling coolant during removal.
3. Remove the glove compartment.
4. Remove the cold air duct and heater outlet.
5. Remove the defroster duct attaching screw.

6. Remove the screws and nuts which retain the case to the dash. Remove the blower motor resistor to gain access to the upper retaining nut inside the evaporator case.
7. Move the core and case assembly rearward to free the attaching studs from the cowl and remove the core and case assembly.
8. Disconnect the temperature cable and vacuum hoses from the core and case assembly.
9. Remove the core and case assembly from the car.
10. Remove the heater core retaining screws and core.
11. Reverse the above steps for installation.

1978-79 LeMANS AND GRAND AM

1. Operate the wipers to the up position.
2. Disconnect the hoses at the core tubes.
3. Remove the sealing material and screens from the cooling module.
4. Disconnect all wires from the case.
5. Move the lower windshield reverse molding out of the way.
6. Tape a strip of wood to the lower edge of the glass for protection.
7. Remove the module core cover screws.
8. Cut the cover seal with a knife.
9. Pry the cover off from the side, not from the top.
10. Lift out the core.
11. Installation is the reverse of removal. Use all new sealer when installing.

FIREBIRD

1. Drain the coolant.
2. Remove the glove box and door.
3. Remove the cold air duct on the lower right-hand side.
4. Remove the left and center lower A/C ducts.
5. Raise the car and remove the rocker panel trim on the right side and remove the screws holding the forward trim brackets.
6. Remove the three lower fender bolts at rear of the fender.
7. Remove the four fender-to-skirt bolts at the rear of the wheel opening.
8. Remove the two fender skirt bolts near the blower motor area.
9. Pry the rear portion of the fender out at the bottom to gain access to the hose clamp on the water valve-to-core hose and disconnect the hose at the heater core.
10. Disconnect the water pump hose at the heater core.
11. Remove the two heater case retaining nuts under the hood at the dash.
12. Remove the two heater case retaining bolts inside the car.
13. Remove the console and tape player if equipped.
14. Disconnect the temperature cable at the heater case.
15. Remove the heater outlet duct.

16. Remove the lower defroster duct screw at the heater case.
17. Remove the right kick panel, and the heater core and case as an assembly.
18. Disconnect the vacuum hoses from the heater case and remove the core from the case.
19. Reverse the above steps for installation.

VENTURA, PHOENIX

1. Disconnect the battery and drain the coolant.
2. Disconnect the upper heater hose at the core pipe and remove the accessible heater core and case assembly attaching nuts.
3. Remove the right front fender skirt bolts and lower the skirt to gain access to the lower heater hose clamp. Loosen the clamp and disconnect the hose.
4. Remove the lower right-hand heater core and case assembly attaching nut.
5. Remove the glove compartment and door.
6. Remove the recirculation vacuum diaphragm at the right-hand kick panel.
7. Remove the heater outlet and cold air distributor duct.
8. Remove the heater case extension screws and separate the extension from the heater case on models through 1974.
9. Disconnect the heater cables and electrical connectors, and remove the case and core as an assembly.
10. Separate the core from the case.
11. Reverse the above steps for installation.

ASTRE

1. Disconnect the battery ground cable.
2. Disconnect the heater hoses at the core and plug them.
3. Remove the firewall selector stud nuts, the glove box, and door.
4. Disconnect the left-side flexible dash outlet hose from the center distributor duct.
5. Remove the right-side dash outlet and hose assembly.
6. Remove the steering column lower plastic retainer, insulation, and screws. Remove the column instru-

ment panel stud nuts and let the column rest on the seat.

7. Remove the instrument panel bezel, ash tray, and tray retainer.
8. Take out the air conditioning control panel screws.
9. Disconnect the radio and antenna leads.
10. Remove the instrument cluster to panel screws, cover the column to prevent scratches, and let the cluster rest on the column. Detach the speedometer cable.
11. Push the air conditioning controls forward and let them rest on the floor.
12. Remove the center distributor duct screws at the selector duct. Remove the duct to instrument panel upper retainer and remove the duct by sliding it to the left to clear the lower instrument panel to cluster tab, and then to the right.
13. Remove the defroster duct-to-selector duct screw. Remove the remaining selector duct-to-dash screws and pull the duct back far enough to allow the electrical and vacuum lines to be disconnected.
14. Disconnect the lines and the control cable and remove the selector duct assembly.
15. Pry off the temperature door bell-crank, being careful not to bend the arm or damage the selector case.
16. Remove the temperature door. Remove the backing plate and temperature door cable retainer screws.
17. Remove the heater core and backing plate as an assembly. Remove the core retaining straps and withdraw the core.
18. Reverse the removal procedure to install the core.

SUNBIRD

1. Have the air conditioning system purged of refrigerant.
2. Disconnect the negative battery cable.
3. Disconnect the inlet and outlet

lines and the oil bleed line from the VIR (receiver-dryer) assembly, on 1975-77 systems.
4. Remove the VIR to blower case strap screw, and remove the VIR unit on 1975-77 systems. Cap all the open connections immediately.
5. Remove the blower and case assembly.
6. Remove and plug the heater hoses at the core tubes and then hang them out of the way.
7. Remove the evaporator to firewall cover plate screws and remove the plate.
8. Remove (from inside the car), the floor outlet duct, the glove compartment assembly and the dash outlets on both sides. To remove the dash outlets, use a putty knife and pry them out.
9. Remove the eleven instrument panel pad screws and pry the pad off.
10. Remove the right side instrument panel to dash and kick pad screws, then loosen the left side instrument cluster to instrument panel screws.
11. Pull out on the right side of the instrument cluster to gain the necessary clearance to remove the right side instrument panel and lower duct.
12. Disconnect the vacuum hoses on the left side of the heater unit and tag them for later reinstallation.
13. Remove the modulator duct to heater unit screw, then pull the carpet and pad to the rear to make room for the heater unit removal.
14. Pull the heater unit toward you until the core tubes clear the firewall, then pull it to the right until there is enough clearance to disconnect the control cable.
15. After disconnecting the control cable, disconnect the wiring harness and remove the heater assembly.
16. Remove the screws and separate the heater case, then remove the core to case screws and remove the core.
17. Installation is the reverse of the above procedure, but before assembly, add 3 oz. of refrigerant oil to the evaporator core.
18. When installing the refrigerant lines, coat all the O-rings with refrigerant oil.

Barracuda · Challenger · Dart · Valiant · Volare · Aspen · LeBaron · Diplomat

Index

Volare • Aspen • Le Baron • Diplomat

YEAR IDENTIFICATION

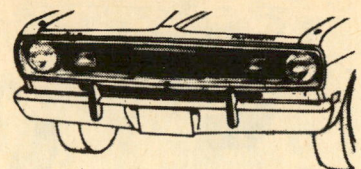

1972 Valiant and Duster

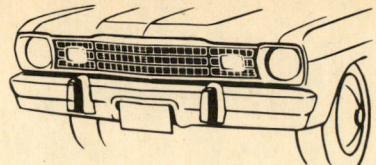

1973 Valiant and Duster

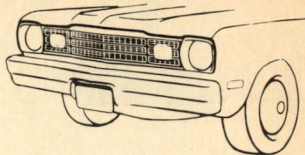

1974 Valiant and Duster

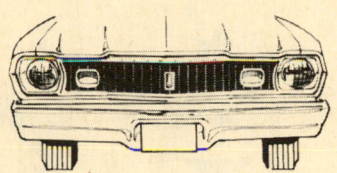

1975-76 Valiant

1972 Dart and Demon

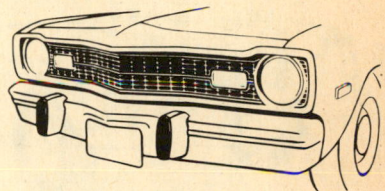

1973 Dart

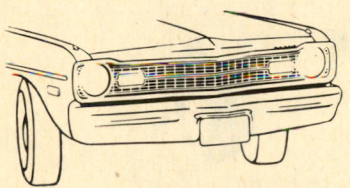

1974 Dart

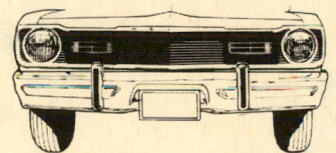

1975-76 Dart

1972 Cuda

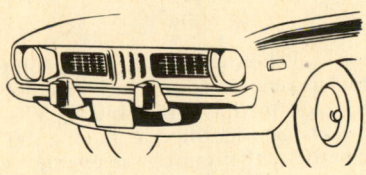

1973 Cuda

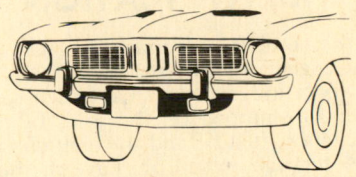

1974 Cuda

1972 Challenger

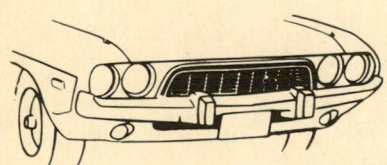

1973 Challenger

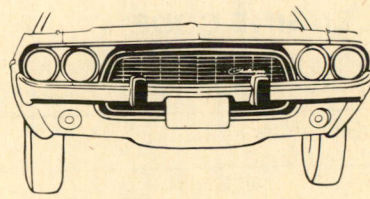

1974 Challenger

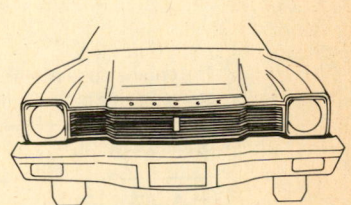

1976 Aspen

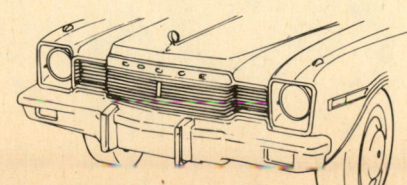

1977 Aspen SE

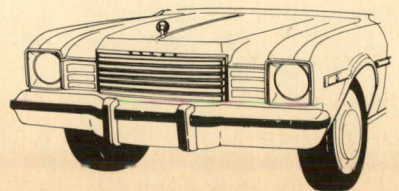

1978 Aspen

1979 Aspen

YEAR IDENTIFICATION

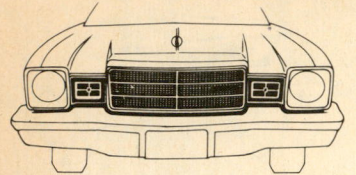

1976 Volare

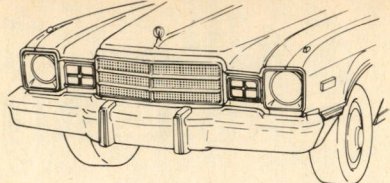

1977 Volare Premier

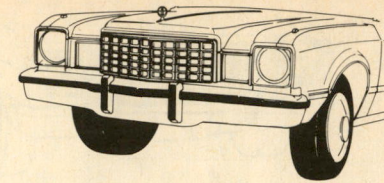

1978 Volare

1979 Volare

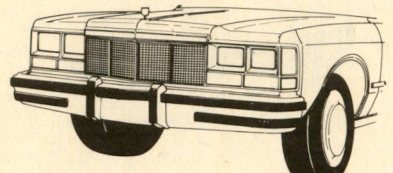

1978 Dodge Diplomat

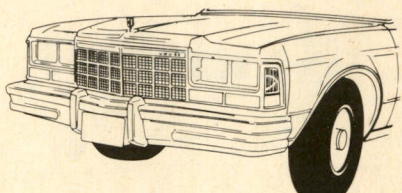

1979 Dodge Diplomat

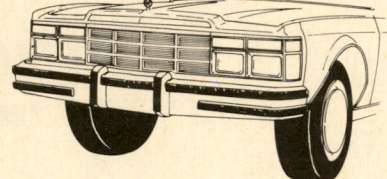

1978 Chrysler Le Baron

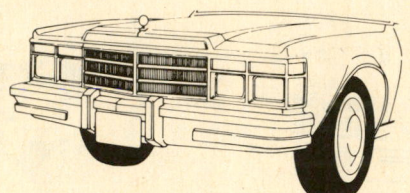

1979 Chrysler Le Baron

ENGINE IDENTIFICATION

The engine that the factory installed in the car can be identified by the fifth digit of the Vehicle Identification Number, as explained under Engine Code. The engine itself can be identified by the engine serial number. The cubic inch displacement is given by either the second, third, and fourth, or the third, fourth, and fifth digits of the engine serial number, depending on the year and engine.

Six cylinder engines have their serial number stamped on the joint face of the block, just behind the ignition coil. V8s through 360 cu. in. have the number on the front of the block, just below the left cylinder head. 383 and larger V8s have the number on the oil pan rail, below the starter opening, at the left rear corner of the block. 360 cu. in. and smaller (small block) V8s can quickly be identified as having the distributor at the rear of the engine, while 383 and larger versions have it at the front.

ENGINE CODE

The engine code designation is the 5th digit of the vehicle identification number (V.I.N.). The V.I.N. is stamped on a plate located at the left side of the instrument panel visible through the windshield.

Displacement	Bbl	'72	'73	'74	'75	'76	'77	'78	'79
6-Cylinder Models									
198	1	B	B	B	B				
225	1	C	C	C	C	C	C	C	C
225	2	D	D	D	D	D	D	D	D
8-Cylinder Models									
318	2	G	G	G	G	G	G	G	G
340 HP	4	H	H	H					
360	2					K	K	K	K
360 HP	4			L	L	L	L	L	L
360	4							J	J

HP High Performance

GENERAL ENGINE SPECIFICATIONS

Year	Engine No. Cyl. Displacement (Cu. In.)	Carburetor Type	Horsepower @ rpm ■	Torque @ rpm (ft lbs) ■	Bore x Stroke (in.)	Compression Ratio	Oil Pressure @ 2000 rpm
'72	6-198	1 bbl	100 @ 4400	160 @ 2400	3.406 x 3.640	8.4:1	55
	6-198 Calif.	1 bbl	94 @ 4400	158 @ 2400	3.406 x 3.640	8.4:1	55
	6-225	1 bbl	110 @ 4000	185 @ 2000	3.406 x 4.125	8.4:1	55
	6-225 Calif.	1 bbl	97 @ 4000	180 @ 2000	3.406 x 4.125	8.4:1	55
	8-318	2 bbl	150 @ 4000	260 @ 1600	3.910 x 3.310	8.6:1	55
	8-340 HP	4 bbl	240 @ 4800	290 @ 3600	4.040 x 3.310	8.5:1	55
'73	6-198	1 bbl	95 @ 4000	155 @ 1600	3.406 x 3.640	8.4:1	55
	6-225	1 bbl	105 @ 4000	185 @ 1600	3.406 x 4.125	8.4:1	55
	8-318	2 bbl	150 @ 3600	265 @ 2000	3.910 x 3.310	8.6:1	55
	8-340HP	4 bbl	240 @ 4800	295 @ 3600	4.040 x 3.310	8.5:1	55
'74	6-198	1 bbl	95 @ 4000	145 @ 2000	3.406 x 3.640	8.4:1	55
	6-225	1 bbl	105 @ 3600	180 @ 1600	3.406 x 4.125	8.4:1	55
	8-318	2 bbl	150 @ 4000	255 @ 2200	3.910 x 3.310	8.6:1	55
	8-360HP	4 bbl	245 @ 4800	320 @ 3600	4.000 x 3.580	8.4:1	55
'75	6-225	1 bbl	95 @ 3600	170 @ 1600	3.406 x 4.125	8.4:1	55
	6-225 Calif.	1 bbl	90 @ 3600	165 @ 1600	3.406 x 4.125	8.4:1	55
	8-318	2 bbl	145 @ 4000	255 @ 1600	3.910 x 3.310	8.5:1	55
	8-318 Calif.	2 bbl	140 @ 3600	255 @ 1600	3.910 x 3.310	8.5:1	55
	8-360 HP	4 bbl	230 @ 4400	300 @ 3600	4.000 x 3.580	8.4:1	55
	8-360 HP Calif.	4 bbl	190 @ 4000	270 @ 3200	4.000 x 3.580	8.4:1	55
'76	6-225	1 bbl	100 @ 3600	170 @ 1600	3.406 x 4.125	8.4:1	55
	6-225 Calif.	1 bbl	90 @ 3600	165 @ 1600	3.406 x 4.125	8.4:1	55
	8-318	2 bbl	150 @ 4000	255 @ 1600	3.910 x 3.310	8.5:1	55
	8-318 Calif.	2 bbl	140 @ 3600	250 @ 2000	3.910 x 3.310	8.5:1	55
	8-360	2 bbl	170 @ 4000	280 @ 2400	4.000 x 3.580	8.4:1	55
	8-360 HP	4 bbl	220 @ 4000	280 @ 3200	4.000 x 3.580	8.4:1	55
'77	6-225	1 bbl	100 @ 3600	170 @ 1600	3.406 x 4.125	8.4:1	55
	6-225 Calif.	1 bbl	90 @ 3600	170 @ 1600	3.406 x 4.125	8.4:1	55
	6-225	2 bbl	110 @ 3600	180 @ 2000	3.406 x 4.125	8.4:1	55
	8-318①	2 bbl	145 @ 4000	245 @ 1600	3.910 x 3.310	8.5:1	55
	8-318 Calif.	2 bbl	135 @ 3600	235 @ 1600	3.910 x 3.310	8.5:1	55
	8-360	2 bbl	155 @ 3600	275 @ 2000	4.000 x 3.580	8:4.1	55
'78	6-225	1 bbl	90 @ 3600	160 @ 1600	3.406 x 4.125	8.4:1	55
	6-225	2 bbl	110 @ 3600	180 @ 2000	3.406 x 4.125	8.4:1	55
	8-318	2 bbl	140 @ 4000	245 @ 1600	3.910 x 3.310	8.5:1	55
	8-318 Calif	4 bbl	155 @ 4000	245 @ 1600	3.910 x 3.310	8.5:1	55
	8-360	2 bbl	155 @ 3600	270 @ 2400	4.000 x 3.580	8.4:1	55
	8-360 HP	4 bbl	170 @ 4000	270 @ 1600	4.000 x 3.580	8.0:1	55
	8-360	4 bbl	160 @ 3600	265 @ 1600	4.000 x 3.580	8.4:1	55

Barracuda • Challenger • Dart • Valiant

GENERAL ENGINE SPECIFICATIONS

Year	Engine No. Cyl. Displacement (Cu. In.)	Carburetor Type	Horsepower @ rpm ■	Torque @ rpm (ft lbs) ■	Bore x Stroke (in.)	Compression Ratio	Oil Pressure @ 2000 rpm
'79	6-225	1 bbl	90 @ 3600	160 @ 1600	3.406 x 4.125	8.4:1	55
	6-225 ESC Calif	1 bbl	90 @ 3600	160 @ 1600	3.406 x 4.125	8.4:1	55
	6-225	2 bbl	110 @ 3600	180 @ 2000	3.406 x 4.125	8.4:1	55
	8-318 ESC	2 bbl	140 @ 4000	245 @ 1600	3.910 x 3.310	8.5:1	55
	8-318 ESC Calif	4 bbl	155 @ 4000	245 @ 1600	3.910 x 3.310	8.5:1	55
	8-360 ESC	2 bbl	155 @ 3600	270 @ 2400	4.000 x 3.580	8.4:1	55
	8-360 ESC Calif	4 bbl	160 @ 3600	265 @ 1600	4.000 x 3.580	8.4:1	55
	8-360 ESC HP	4 bbl	170 @ 4000	270 @ 1600	4.000 x 3.580	8.0:1	55

■ Horsepower and torque are SAE net figures. They are measured at the rear of the transmission with all accessories installed and operating. Since the figures vary when a given engine is installed in different models, some figures are representative rather than exact.

HP High Performance
① Also applies to lean burn 318 engines
ESC Electronic Spark Control

Valiant, Dart, Aspen, Volare, Diplomat, LeBaron
TUNE-UP SPECIFICATIONS

When analyzing compression test results, look for uniformity among cylinders rather than specific pressures.

Year	Engine No. Cyl Displacement (cu in.)	hp	Orig. Type	Gap (in.)	Point Dwell (deg)	Point Gap (in.)	Man Trans	Auto Trans	Valves Intake Opens ■ (deg)	Fuel Pump Pressure (psi)	Man Trans	Auto Trans
'72	6-198	100	N-14Y	.035	41-46	.020	2½B	2½B	16	2½-5	800(700)	800(700)
	6-225	110	N-14Y	.035	41-46	.020	TDC(2½B)	TDC(2½B)	16	2½-5	750(700)	750(700)
	8-318	150	N-13Y	.035	30-34	.017	TDC	TDC	10	5-7	750	750(700)
	8-340 HP	240	N-9Y	.035	30-34	.017	TDC(2½B)	2½B	22	5-7	900(850)	750
'73	6-198	95	N-14Y	.035	Electronic		2½B	2½B	16	4-5½	800	750
	6-225	105	N-14Y	.035	Electronic		TDC	TDC	16	4-5½	750	750
	8-318	150	N-13Y	.035	Electronic		2½B	TDC	10	6-7½	750	700
	8-360 HP	245	N-9Y	.035	Electronic		5B	2½B	22	6-7½	850	850
'74	6-198	95	N-14Y	.035	Electronic		2½B	2½B	16	3½-5	800	750
	6-225	105	N-14Y	.035	Electronic		TDC	TDC	16	5-7	800	750
	8-318	150	N-13Y	.035	Electronic		TDC	TDC	10	5-7	750	750
	8-360 HP	245	N-12Y	.035	Electronic		5B(2½B)	5B	22	5-7	850	850
'75	6-225	95	BL-13Y	.035	Electronic		TDC	TDC	16	3½-5	800	750
	8-318	145	N-13Y	.035	Electronic		2B	2B	10	5-7	750	750
	8-360 HP	230	N-12Y	.035	Electronic		—	2B	22	5-7	—	750
'76	6-225	100	RBL-13Y	.035	Electronic		6B(4B)	2B	16	3½-5	750(800)	750
	6-225①	100	RBL-13Y	.035	Electronic		12B	12B	16	3½-5	750(800)	750
	8-318	150	RN-12Y	.035	Electronic		2B	2B(TDC)	10	5-7	750	750
	8-318②	150	RN-12Y	.035	Electronic		—	2A	10	5-7	—	900
	8-360	170	RN-12Y	.035	Electronic		—	2B	18	5-7	—	850
	8-360 HP	230	RN-12Y	.035	Electronic		—	2B	22	5-7	—	850
'77	6-225	100	RBL-15Y	.035	Electronic		12B	12B(8B)	16	3½-5	700(750)	700(750)
	6-225	110	RBL-15Y	.035	Electronic		12B	12B	16	3½-5	700(750)	700(750)
	8-318	145	RN-12Y	.035	Electronic		8B	8B	10	5-7	700	700(850)
	8-360	155	RN-12Y	.035	Electronic		—	10B	18	5-7	—	700

Valiant, Dart, Aspen, Volare, Diplomat, LeBaron
TUNE-UP SPECIFICATIONS

When analyzing compression test results, look for uniformity among cylinders rather than specific pressures.

	ENGINE		SPARK PLUGS		DISTRIBUTOR		IGNITION TIMING (deg) ▲		VALVES Intake Opens ■ (deg)	Fuel Pump Pressure (psi)	IDLE SPEED (rpm) ▲	
Year	No. Cyl Displacement (cu in.)	hp	Orig. Type	Gap (in.)	Point Dwell (deg)	Point Gap (in.)	Man Trans •	Auto Trans			Man Trans •	Auto Trans
'78	6-225	1 bbl	RBL-16Y	.035	Electronic		12B(8B)	12B(8B)	16	3½-5	700(750)	700(750)
	6-225	2 bbl	RBL-16Y	.035	Electronic		12B(10B)	12B(10B)	16	3½-5	700(750)	700(750)
	8-318	2 bbl	RN-12Y	.035	Electronic		16B	16B	10	5¾-7¼	700(750)	700(750)
	8-318	4 bbl	RN-12Y	.035	Electronic		—	10B	10	5¾-7¼	700(750)	700(750)
	8-360	2 bbl	RN-12Y	.035	Electronic		—	20B	18	5¾-7¼	—	750
	8-360	4 bbl	RN-12Y	.035	Electronic		—	16B(6/8B)	18	5¾-7¼	—	750
'79	6-225	1 bbl	RBL-16Y	.035	Electronic		12B(15B)	12B(15B)	16	4-5½	700(750)	700(750)
	6-225	2 bbl	RBL-16Y	.035	Electronic		12B	12B	16	4-5½	700(750)	700(750)
	8-318	All	RN-12Y	.035	Electronic		—	16B	10	5¾-7¼	—	750
	8-360	All	RN-12Y	.035	Electronic		—	16B	18	5¾-7¼	—	750

Barracuda, Challenger   TUNE-UP SPECIFICATIONS

When analyzing compression test results, look for uniformity among cylinders rather than specific pressures.

	ENGINE		SPARK PLUGS		DISTRIBUTOR		IGNITION TIMING (deg) ▲		VALVES Intake Opens ■ (deg)	Fuel Pump Pressure (psi)	IDLE SPEED (rpm) ▲	
Year	No. Cyl Displacement (cu in.)	hp	Orig. Type	Gap (in.)	Point Dwell (deg)	Point Gap (in.)	Man Trans •	Auto Trans			Man Trans •	Auto Trans
'72	6-225	110	N-14Y	.035	44	.020	TDC(2½B)	TDC(2½B)	16	2½-5	750(700)	750(700)
	8-318	150	N-13Y	.035	32	.017	TDC	TDC	10	5-7	750	750(700)
	8-340 HP	240	N-9Y	.035	Electronic		TDC(2½B)	2½B	22	5-7	900(850)	750
'73	8-318	150	N-13Y	.035	Electronic		2½B	TDC	10	6-7½	750	700
	8-340 HP	240	N-9Y	.035	Electronic		5B	2½B	22	6-7½	850	850
'74	8-318	150	N-13Y	.035	Electronic		TDC	TDC	10	5-7	750	750
	8-360 HP	245	N-12Y	.035	Electronic		5B(2½B)	5B	22	5-7	850	850

MECHANICAL VALVE LIFTER CLEARANCE

Engine	Intake (Hot) In.	Exhaust (Hot) In.
All six cylinder	.010	.020

▲ See text for procedure
■ All figures Before Top Dead Center
• Figure in parentheses indicates California engine

① in Feather Duster/Dart Lite
② with air pump, no converter
A   After Top Dead Center
B   Before Top Dead Center
TDC   Top Dead Center
HP   High Performance

NOTE: The underhood specifications sticker often reflects tune-up specification changes made in production. Sticker figures must be used if they disagree with those in this chart.

TORQUE SPECIFICATIONS
All readings in ft lbs

Year	Engine No. Cyl Displacement (cu in.)	Cylinder Head Bolts	Rod Bearing Bolts	Main Bearing Bolts	Crankshaft Bolt	Flywheel to Crankshaft Bolts	MANIFOLD Intake	Exhaust
'72-'76	6-All	70	45	85	Press fit	55	10①	10
'77-'79	6-225	70	45	85	Press fit	55	10②	10

TORQUE SPECIFICATIONS
All readings in ft lbs

Year	Engine No. Cyl. Displacement (cu in.)	Cylinder Head Bolts	Rod Bearing Bolts	Main Bearing Bolts	Crankshaft Bolt	Flywheel to Crankshaft Bolts	MANIFOLD Intake	MANIFOLD Exhaust
'72-'73	8-318, 340	95	45	85	135	65	40	30
'74	8-318, 360	95	45	85	100	55	35	15/20③
'75-'76	8-318, 360	95	45	85	100	55	40	15/20③
'77-'79	8-318, 360	105④	45	85	100	55	45	15/20③

① Intake to exhaust manifold bolts—20 ft. lbs., studs—30 ft. lbs.
② Intake to exhaust manifold bolts—17 ft. lbs., studs—20 ft. lbs.
③ Nuts/screws
④ 95—1977

FIRING ORDER

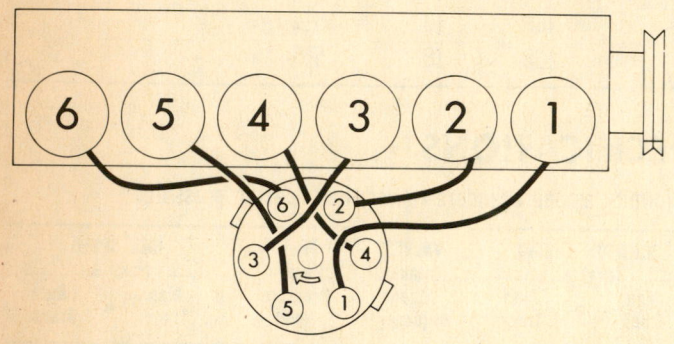

CHRYSLER CORP. 6-cyl.
Engine firing order: 1-5-3-6-2-4
Distributor rotation: clockwise

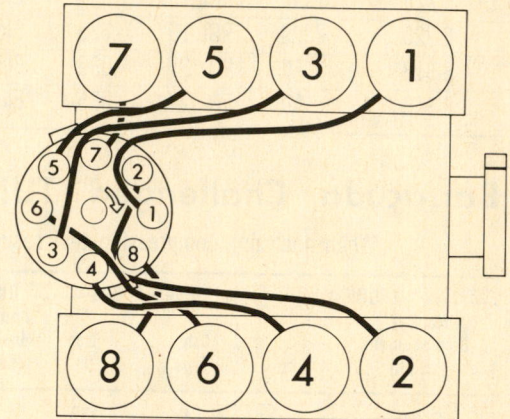

CHRYSLER CORP. 318, 340, 360 V8
Engine firing order: 1-8-4-3-6-5-7-2
Distributor rotation: clockwise

CAPACITIES

Year	ENGINE No. Cyl. Displacement (Cu. In.)	Engine Crankcase Add 1 Qt For New Filter	TRANSMISSION Pts To Refill After Draining Manual 3-Speed	4-Speed	Automatic	Drive Axle (pts)	Gasoline Tank (gals)	COOLING SYSTEM (qts) With Heater	With A/C
'72	6-198	4	6.5	——	17	2	16	13	14
	6-225	4	6.5①	——	17	2	16⑧	13	14
	8-318	4	4.75	——	17	4.5	16⑧	16	17
	8-340 HP	4	4.75	7②	16.3	4.5	16⑧	15	15
'73	6-198	4	6.5	——	17	2	16	13	13
	6-225	4	6.5	——	17	2	16	13	14
	8-318	4	4.75	——	17	4.5	16⑧	16	17.5
	8-340 HP	4	4.75	7②	16.3	4.5	16⑧	15.5⑨	15.5
'74	6-198	4	6.5	——	17	2	16⑦	13	——
	6-225	4	4.75	——	17	2	16⑦	13	14.0
	8-318	4	4.75	7.0②	17	4.5	16⑦	16	17.5
	8-360 HP	4	4.75	7.0②	16.5	4.5	16⑦	16	16.0
'75	6-225	4	3.5	7.0	17	2	16	13	14
	8-318	4	4.75	7.0	17	4.5	16	16	17.5
	8-360 HP	5	——	——	16.5	4.5	16	16	16

CAPACITIES

Year	Engine No. Cyl. Displacement (Cu. In.)	Engine Crankcase Add 1 Qt For New Filter	TRANSMISSION Pts To Refill After Draining Manual 3-Speed	4-Speed	Automatic	Drive Axle (pts)	Gasoline Tank (gals)	COOLING SYSTEM (qts) With Heater	With A/C
'76	6-225	4	3.5	7.0	17	2	16/18④	13	17.5
	8-318	4	4.75	7.0	17	4.5	16/18④	16	17.5
	8-360	4	—	—	17	4.5	18	16	16
	8-360 HP	5	—	—	16.5	4.5	16	16	16
'77-'78	6-225	4	4.75	7.0	17⑪	2.1⑥	18⑤⑩	12	14
	8-318	4	4.75	7.0	17⑪	2.1⑥	20⑩	16	17.5
	8-360	4	—	—	17⑪	4.5	20	16	17.5
'79	6-225	4	4.75	7.0	17⑪	2.0	18⑩⑫	11.5	12.5
	8-318	4	—	—	17⑪	2.0	19.5	15	16.5
	8-360	4	—	—	17⑪	4.5	19.5	15	15

① Barracuda, Challenger—4.75 pts
② Barracuda, Challenger—7.5 pts
③ Hi-performance—16 pts
④ Valiant, Dart/Aspen, Volare
⑤ 20 gal. on wagon
⑥ 4.4 pts for station wagon or High Altitude models.

⑦ Barracuda, Challenger—18 gals
⑧ Barracuda—16.5 gals, Challenger—18 gals
⑨ Barracuda, Challenger—15 qts
⑩ 19.5 gal. on Diplomat, LeBaron
⑪ 7.8 pts. if converter isn't drained
— Not applicable
⑫ 19.5 on wagon

VALVE SPECIFICATIONS

Year	Engine No. Cyl. Displacement (cu in.)	Seat Angle (deg)	Face Angle (deg)	Spring Test Pressure (lbs @ in.)	Spring Installed Height (in.)	STEM TO GUIDE Clearance (in.) Intake	Exhaust	STEM Diameter (in.) Intake	Exhaust
'72	6-198	45	①	144 @ 1.31	1 11/16	.0010-.0030	.0020-.0040	.3725	.3715
	6-225	45	①	144 @ 1.31	1 11/16	.0010-.0030	.0020-.0040	.3725	.3715
	8-318	45	①	177 @ 1.31	1 11/16	.0010-.0030	.0020-.0040	.3725	.3715
	8-340 HP	45	①	208 @ 1.31	1 11/16	.0015-.0035	.0025-.0045	.3720	.3710
'73	6-198	45	①	143 @ 1.31	1 21/32	.0010-.0030	.0020-.0040	.3725	.3715
	6-225	45	①	143 @ 1.31	1 21/32	.0010-.0030	.0020-.0040	.3725	.3715
	8-318	45	①	177 @ 1.31	1 21/32	.0010-.0030	.0020-.0040	.3725	.3715
	8-340 HP	45	①	208 @ 1.31	1 21/32	.0015-.0035	.0025-.0045	.3720	.3710
'74	6-198	45	①	143 @ 1.31	1 21/32	.0010-.0030	.0020-.0040	.3725	.3715
	6-225	45	①	143 @ 1.31	1 21/32	.0010-.0030	.0020-.0040	.3725	.3715
	8-318	45	①	177 @ 1.31	1 21/32	.0010-.0030	.0020-.0040	.3725	.3715
	8-360 HP	45	①	208 @ 1.31	1 21/32	.0010-.0030	.0025-.0045	.3725	.3715
'75	6-225	45	45	143 @ 1.31	1 21/32	.0010-.0030	.0020-.0040	.3725	.3715
	8-318	45	①	177 @ 1.31	1 21/32	.0010-.0030	.0020-.0040	.3725	.3715
	8-360 HP	45	①	208 @ 1.31	1 21/32	.0010-.0030	.0020-.0040	.3725	.3715
'76	6-225	45	45	143 @ 1.31	1 21/32	.0010-.0030	.0020-.0040	.3725	.3715
	8-318	45	①	177 @ 1.31	1 21/32	.0010-.0030	.0020-.0040	.3725	.3715
	8-360	45	①	182 @ 1.31	1 21/32	.0010-.0030	.0020-.0040	.3725	.3715
	8-360 HP	45	①	238 @ 1.22	1 11/16	.0020-.0040	.0030-.0050	.3720	.3710
'77-'79	6-225	45	①	143 @ 1.31	1 21/32	.0010-.0030	.0020-.0040	.3725	.3715
	8-318	45	①	177 @ 1.31	1 21/32	.0010-.0030	.0020-.0040	.3725	.3715
	8-360	45	①	177 @ 1.31	1 21/32	.0010-.0030	.0020-.0040	.3725	.3715
	8-360 HP	45	①	193 @ 1.25	1 21/32	.0015-.0035	.0025-.0045	.3720	.3710

① Intake 45°, Exhaust 43°
HP High Performance

CRANKSHAFT AND CONNECTING ROD SPECIFICATIONS

All measurements are given in inches

Year	Engine No. Cyl. Displacement (cu in.)	Crankshaft: Main Brg. Journal Dia	Crankshaft: Main Brg. Oil Clearance	Crankshaft: Shaft End-Play	Crankshaft: Thrust on No.	Connecting Rod: Journal Diameter	Connecting Rod: Oil Clearance	Connecting Rod: Side Clearance*
'72-'75	6-198, 225	2.7495-2.7505	.0005-.0020	.002-.007	3	2.1865-2.1875	.0005-.0020	.006-.012
'76	6-225	2.7495-2.7505	.0005-.0020	.002-.007	3	2.1865-2.1875	.0005-.0025	.006-.012
'77-'79	6-225	2.7495-2.7505	.0005-.0020	.002-.009	3	2.1865-2.1875	.0005-.0025	.006-.025
'72-'74	8-318, 340	2.4995-2.5005	.0005-.0015	.002-.007	3	2.1240-2.1250	.0005-.0020	.006-.014
'75-'76	8-318	2.4495-2.5005	.0005-.0020	.002-.007	3	2.1240-2.1250	.0005-.0025	.006-.014
'77-'79	8-318	2.4495-2.5005	.0005-.0020	.002-.009	3	2.1240-2.1250	.0005-.0025	.006-.014
'74	8-360	2.8095-2.8105	.0005-.0020	.002-.007	3	2.1240-2.1250	.0005-.0020	.006-.014
'75-'76	8-360	2.8095-2.8105	.0005-.0020	.002-.007	3	2.1240-2.1250	.0005-.0025	.006-.014
'77-'79	8-360	2.8095-2.8105	.0005-.0020	.002-.009	3	2.1240-2.1250	.0005-.0025	.006-.014

*Total for two rods

RING SIDE CLEARANCE

All measurements are given in inches

Year	Engine No. Cyl. Displacement (cu. in.)	Top Compression	Bottom Compression
'72-'79	All engines	.0015-.0030	.0015-.0030

Year	Engine No. Cyl. Displacement (cu. in.)	Oil Control
'72-'79	6-198, 225, 8-318, 340, 360	.0002-.0050

RING GAP

All measurements are given in inches

Year	Engine No. Cyl. Displacement (cu. in.)	Top Compression	Bottom Compression
'72	6-198, 225 8-318, 340	.010-.020	.010-.020
'73	All engines except 8-340	.010-.020	.010-.020
'73	8-340	.013-.023	.013-.023
'74-'79	6-198, 225 8-318, 360	.010-.020	.010-.020

Year	Engine No. Cyl. Displacement (cu. in.)	Oil Control
'72-'79	All	.015-.055

FRONT END HEIGHT

Year	Model	Front End Height (± ⅛ in.)
'72	All M.S.	②
	All P.S.	②
'73	All	③
'74	Dart, Valiant,	1⅞
	Barracuda, Challenger	1⅛
'75-'76	Valiant, Dart	10 15/16
'76-'79	Aspen, Volare Diplomat, LeBaron,	10¼

① Not used
② Dart, Valiant 4DR—2⅛
Dart, Valiant 2DR—1⅝
Barracuda, Challenger—1
③ Dart, Valiant 4DR—2⅛
Dart, Valiant 2DR—1⅞
Barracuda, Challenger—1⅛
M.S. Manual Steering
P.S. Power Steering

PISTON CLEARANCE

All measurements are given in inches

Year	Engine No. Cyl. Displacement (cu. in.)	Piston-to-Bore Clearance (in.)*
'72-'74	6-198	0.0005-0.0015
'77-'79	6-225	0.0005-0.0015
'72-'79	8-318	0.0005-0.0015
'73	8-340	0.0005-0.0015
'74-'79	8-360 2 bbl.	0.0005-0.0015
'74-'79	8-360 4 bbl.	0.0010-0.0020

* At top of skirt

WHEEL ALIGNMENT SPECIFICATIONS

Year	Model	CASTER Range (deg)	CASTER Pref Setting (deg)	CAMBER Range (deg)	CAMBER Pref Setting (deg)	Toe-in (In.)	Steering Axis Inclin. (deg.)	WHEEL PIVOT RATIO (deg) Inner Wheel	WHEEL PIVOT RATIO (deg) Outer Wheel
'72	Manual	1N to 0	½N	①	②	3/8 ± 5/32	7½	20	17.5
	Power	¼P to 1¼P	¾P	①	②	3/8 ± 5/32	7½	20	17.5
'73	Valiant, Dart, Barracuda, Challenger Manual	0 to 1N	½N	③	④	3/32 to 5/32	7½	20	17.5
	Power	¼P to 1¼P	¾P	③	④	3/32 to 5/32	7½	20	17.5
'74-'77	Valiant, Dart, Barracuda, Challenger Manual	1¾N to ½P	½N	⑦	⑧	1/16 to ¼	7½	20	18.5
	Power	½N to 1¾P	¾P	⑦	⑧	1/16 to ¼	7½	20	18.5
'76-'79	Aspen, Volare, Diplomat, LeBaron	1½P to 3¾P	2½P	⑦	④	1/16 to ¼	8	20	18

① Left wheel—½P ± ¼; Right wheel—¼P ± ¼
② Left wheel—½P; Right wheel—¼P
③ Left wheel—¼P to ¾P; Right wheel—0 to ½P
④ Left wheel—½P; Right wheel—¼P
⑤ Not used
⑥ Not used
⑦ Left wheel—0 to 1P; Right wheel—¼N to ¾P
⑧ Left wheel—½P; right wheel—¼P
N Negative   P Positive

CHARGING SYSTEM

NOTE: *See the Unit Repair Section for charging system troubleshooting.*

Alternator Removal and Installation

1. Disconnect battery ground cable.
2. Disconnect BAT and FLD leads from alternator. Disconnect the ground wire.
3. Remove alternator by removing two mounting bolts and belt tensioner bracket bolt.
4. To reinstall, reverse above. Tighten the belt so that it can be depressed about ½ in. by moderate thumb pressure in the center of the longest span between pulleys. Some alternator brackets have a square hole into which you can insert a ½ in. square socket drive to tension the belt.

NOTE: *Never attempt to polarize an alternator, or short the regulator.*

Regulator Removal and Installation

All models have a solid-state (silicon transistor) voltage regulator which is not adjustable. The regulator is in the engine compartment and clearly labeled.

1. Release the spring clips and pull off the regulator wiring plug.
2. Unbolt and remove the regulator.
3. Installation is the reverse of removal. Be sure that the spring clips engage the wiring plug and that the unit has a good ground.

STARTING SYSTEM

All models are equipped with either a reduction-gear starter, with a 3.5:1 or 2:1 reduction gear set, or a direct-drive starter. Both types have solenoids which are mounted on the starter assembly.

See the Unit Repair Section for starting system troubleshooting and repair.

Starter Removal and Installation

1. Disconnect the ground cable at the battery.
2. Remove the cable from the starter.
3. Disconnect the solenoid leads at their solenoid terminals.
4. Remove the starter securing nut and bolt and remove the starter from the engine flywheel housing. On some models with automatic transmissions, the oil cooler tube bracket will interfere with starter removal. In this case, remove the starter securing nut and bolt, slide the cooler tube bracket off the stud, and then remove the starter.
5. Installation is the reverse of the preceding. Be sure that the starter and flywheel housing mating surfaces are free of dirt and oil. Position the starter to flywheel housing seal. When tightening the bolt and nut, hold the starter away from the engine to ensure proper alignment.

Disabling the Seat Belt/Starter Interlock

All 1974 and some 1975 models have a seat belt/starter interlock system, which prevents starting the engine until

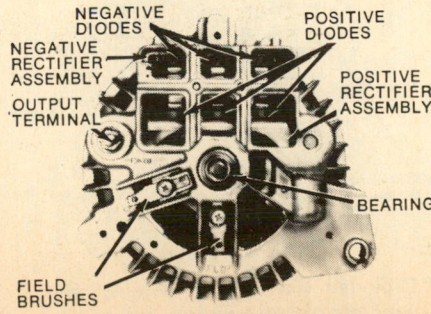

NEGATIVE DIODES
POSITIVE DIODES
NEGATIVE RECTIFIER ASSEMBLY
POSITIVE RECTIFIER ASSEMBLY
OUTPUT TERMINAL
BEARING
FIELD BRUSHES

Rear view of the alternator
(© Chrysler Corp)

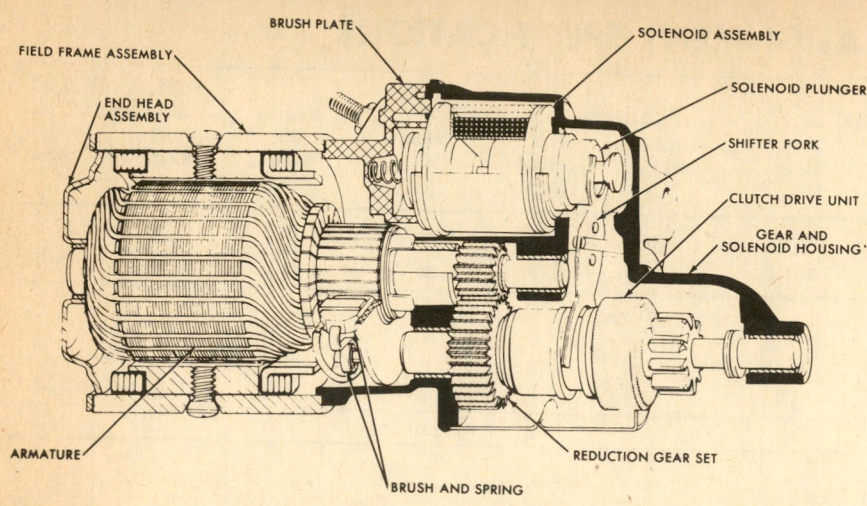

Starter motor details (© Chrysler Corp.)

front seat belts are fastened. Since the regulation requiring the interlock system was done away with during the 1975 model year, this device may now be legally disabled. All dealers have received a service bulletin on how to properly accomplish this modification for customers requesting it. It involves disconnecting the buzzer wire (you could easily do this yourself) and making some internal wiring changes to the printed circuit board in the interlock module (the bulletin recommends that this be done by a radio repair shop).

NOTE: *Although the interlock can be disabled by disconnecting the seat sensor wires at the connectors under the seat, this is not the recommended method, since it also disables the seat belt warning light. The warning light is still required.*

IGNITION SYSTEM

The ignition system used on early models is of the conventional breaker point type. A separate ballast resistor unit is wired in the primary circuit between the battery and the coil. This resistor controls the current flow in the primary circuit, according to engine speed, reducing the current flow at low engine speeds and increasing the current flow at higher engine speeds. The ballast resistor is bypassed during starter operation to allow full battery voltage to flow to the ignition primary circuit.

Some 1972 models are equipped with the Chrysler Electronic Ignition System. Beginning 1973, electronic ignition is standard on all models. For further details, refer to the section on electronic ignition systems in the Unit Repair Section. The Lean Burn system is covered in the Emission Control Systems Unit Repair Section.

NOTE: *Dwell/tachometer hookup with electronic ignition is the same as with conventional point-type systems. One tachometer lead connects to the negative primary coil terminal and the other to ground. Some meters will not work at all with this system.*

Distributor Removal

1. Disconnect the vacuum advance line at the distributor.
2. Disconnect the primary wire at the coil. On electronic ignition, disconnect the lead wire at the harness connector.
3. Unfasten the distributor cap retaining clips and lift off the cap.
4. Mark the distributor body and the engine block to indicate the position of the body in the block. Scribe a mark on the edge of the distributor housing to indicate the position of the rotor on the distributor. These marks can be used as guides when installing the distributor in a correctly timed engine.
5. Remove the distributor holdown clamp screw and clamp.
6. Carefully lift the distributor out of the block.

Distributor Installation

If the crankshaft has not been rotated while the distributor was removed from the engine, installation is the reverse of the removal procedure. (See step two or three of the procedure below.) Use the reference marks that were made before removal to correctly position the distributor in the block. Check the point gap and, before connecting the vacuum advance line, adjust the ignition timing.

If the crankshaft has been rotated or otherwise disturbed (as during engine rebuilding) after the distributor was removed, proceed as follows to install the distributor.

1. Bring the no. 1 piston to top dead center (TDC) by removing the no. 1 spark plug and inserting a finger

into the hole, while rotating the crankshaft. Compression pressure can be felt as the no. 1 piston approaches TDC. The TDC timing mark on the crankshaft vibration damper should now be opposite the indicator on the timing chain case. Make sure that you don't have no. 6 piston at TDC.

2. *For six-cylinder engines:* Note the position of the distributor cap (which should be connected to the engine by the spark plug cables). Hold the distributor so that the rotor will be in position *just ahead* of the distributor cap terminal for the no. 1 spark plug when the distributor is installed. Now lower the distributor into its engine block opening, engaging the distributor gear

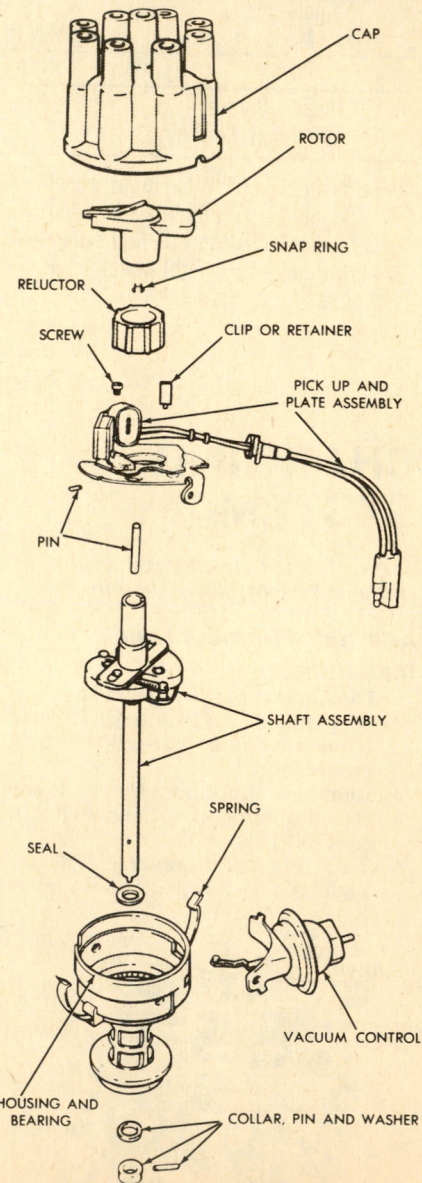

Exploded view of the V8 electronic ignition distributor. The six-cylinder distributor has a drive gear on the end of the shaft. (© Chrysler Corp.)

with the camshaft drive gear. Be sure that the rubber O-ring seal is in the groove in the distributor shank. When the distributor is properly seated, the rotor should be under the no. 1 distributor cap terminal with the contact points just opening. Proceed with step four.

3. *For eight-cylinder engines:* Clean the top of the engine block around the distributor opening to ensure a good seal between the distributor base and the block. Note the position of the distributor cap (which should be connected to the engine by the spark plug cables). Hold the distributor so that the rotor will be in position *directly under* the distributor cap terminal for the no. 1 spark plug when the distributor is installed. Now lower the distributor into its engine block opening,

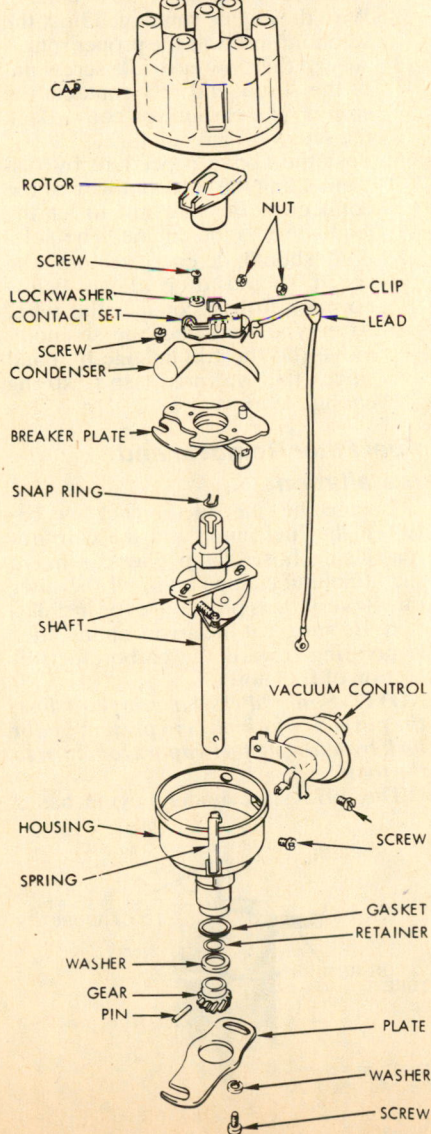

Distributor components—conventional ignition (© Chrysler Corp)

engaging the tongue of the distributor shaft with the slot in the distributor and oil pump drive gear. Proceed with step four.

4. Install the distributor hold-down clamp and tighten its retaining screw finger-tight.
5. Check the point gap and refit the distributor cap. Connect the primary wire to the coil or the lead wire to the harness.
6. Check and adjust the point dwell and the ignition timing.
7. Connect the vacuum advance line to the distributor.

Contact Point Replacement and Adjustment

1. Pull back the spring clips and lift off the distributor cap. Remove the rotor.
2. Loosen the terminal screw nut and remove the primary and condenser leads.
3. Remove the stationary contact lockscrew and remove the contact point set.
4. Remove the condenser and the retaining screw. Lift out the condenser.
5. Install the new condenser and tighten its retaining screw.
6. Install the point set but do not fully tighten its lockscrew.
7. Connect the condenser and primary leads.
8. If necessary, align the contacts by bending the stationary contact bracket only. *Never bend the movable contact arm to correct alignment.*
9. With the rubbing block of the movable contact arm resting on a peak of the cam lobe, adjust the point gap by inserting a screwdriver in the vee notch of the stationary contact base and using the screwdriver to move the stationary contact.
10. Tighten the lockscrew and recheck the gap setting. Reset if necessary.
11. Install the new rotor and refit the distributor cap.
12. Connect a dwell meter to the engine.
13. Start the engine and run it at idle speed. Note the dwell meter reading. If it is not within specifications, the point gap may be incorrect or the movable contact arm may be distorted. Readjust the contact points and recheck the dwell.

Ignition Timing

Ignition timing must be checked only when the engine is at normal running temperature and at its correct idle speed.
1. Disconnect and plug the vacuum line at the distributor (on all models).
2. Connect a stroboscopic timing light, start the engine, and adjust the idle speed to specification.

Check the underhood sticker for any further instructions.
3. Loosen the distributor hold-down screw so the housing can be rotated.
4. Check the ignition timing with the strobe light aimed at the crankshaft damper or pulley timing mark. If necessary, advance or retard the timing by rotating the distributor housing, until the correct timing is obtained.
5. Tighten the distributor hold-down screw and re-check the timing. Connect the vacuum line. Stop the engine and disconnect the timing light.

FUEL SYSTEM

CARBURETOR

Idle Speed and Mixture Adjustments (See Illustrations in Dodge Section)

NOTE: *These procedures all require the use of sophisticated testing equipment to ensure that the results are within legal limits. There is no way to avoid the need for this equipment; however, the procedures are given for those with access to the equipment.*

THROUGH 1974

Adjust with air cleaner installed.
1. Run engine at fast idle to stabilize engine temperature.
2. Make sure choke plate is fully released.
3. Attach a tachometer to the engine. Connect one tachometer lead to the negative coil primary lead and the other to a good ground.
4. Connect an exhaust analyzer to the engine and insert the probe as far into the tailpipe as possible. On vehicles with dual exhaust, insert the probe into the left tailpipe as this is the side without the heat riser valve.
5. Check ignition timing and adjust it as required.
6. If equipped with air conditioning, turn the air conditioner OFF. On models with six-cylinder engines, turn the headlights on high beam.
7. Place the transmission in the Neutral position. Make sure the hot idle compensator valve is fully seated in the closed position.
8. Turn the engine idle speed adjustment screw in or out to adjust idle speed to specification. If equipped with an electric solenoid, turn the solenoid adjusting screw in or out to obtain specified rpm. Then, adjust the curb idle speed screw until it just touches the stop on the carburetor body. Now, back the curb idle speed adjusting screw out one full turn.

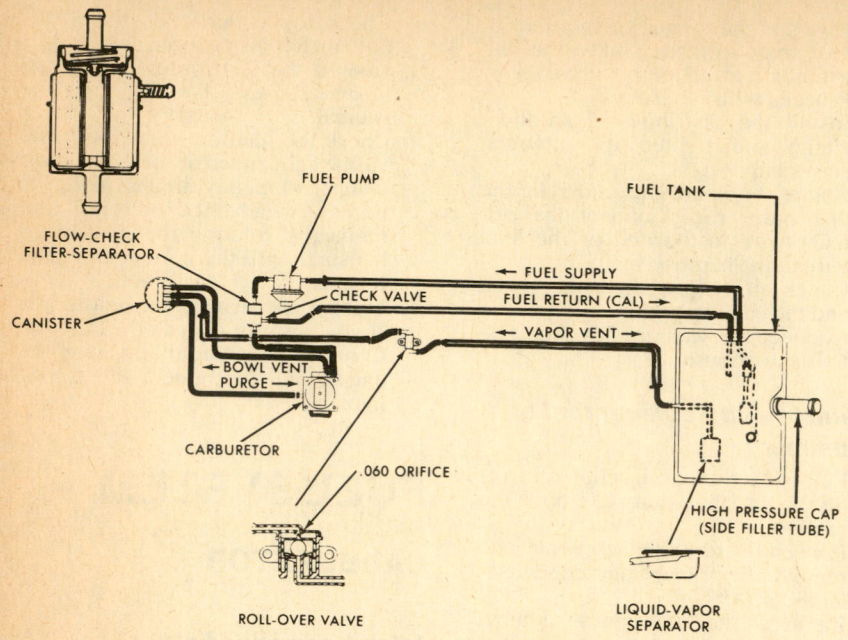

FLOW-CHECK FILTER-SEPARATOR

CANISTER

FUEL PUMP

FUEL TANK

← FUEL SUPPLY

CHECK VALVE

FUEL RETURN (CAL) →

← VAPOR VENT

BOWL VENT PURGE

CARBURETOR

.060 ORIFICE

HIGH PRESSURE CAP (SIDE FILLER TUBE)

ROLL-OVER VALVE

LIQUID-VAPOR SEPARATOR

Fuel system with roll-over protection introduced in 1976 (© Chrysler Corp.)

9. Turn each idle mixture adjustment screw $1/16$ turn richer (counterclockwise). Wait 30 seconds and observe the reading on the exhaust gas analyzer. Continue this procedure until the meter indicates a definite increase in the richness of the mixture.

NOTE: *This step is very important. A carburetor that is set too lean will cause the exhaust gas analyzer to give a false reading indicating a rich mixture. Because of this, the carburetor must first be known to have a rich mixture to verify the reading on the exhaust gas analyzer.*

10. After verifying the reading obtained on the meter, adjust the mixture screws to get an air/fuel ratio of 14.2:1. Turn the mixture screws clockwise (leaner) to raise the meter reading or counterclockwise (richer) to lower the meter reading.

1975 AND LATER

NOTE: *The factory recommended procedure for idle mixture and speed adjustment on 1977 and later 49 States models requires the addition of an artificial mixture enrichment substance (propane) to the air intake. This method requires special tools not generally available. The following procedure is specifically recommended by the factory for 1975-76 49 States and Canada models, and all 1975 and later California and high altitude models.*

1. The engine must have been off at least one hour.
2. Start the engine and run it in Neutral or Park on step 2 of the fast idle cam for about 5-10 minutes or until the thermostat opens and the engine warms up thoroughly. The top of the radiator should be hot.

3. Check the underhood sticker. Disconnect and plug the distributor vacuum line if it is required by the sticker for idle mixture setting. This is usually not required on 225 and 318 engines outside California. With Lean Burn, disconnect and plug the vacuum line to the transducer on the air cleaner.
4. Stop the engine. If there is an air pump, disconnect and plug the air tube on the engine.
5. If there is a catalytic converter, insert the probe of an emission analyzer into the exhaust system ahead of the converter. Use the left pipe on dual systems.
6. Start the engine and run it up to 2000 rpm for 10 seconds or more. Let it idle and wait at least 30 seconds but no more than 60 seconds, for the meters to stabilize. The transmission must be in Neutral or Park with the air conditioner and headlights off.
7. Adjust the idle speed and air/fuel mixture screws to get the percentage of carbon monoxide specified on the sticker and either the lowest hydrocarbon reading or the smoothest possible idle. Connect the air pump and correct the idle speed , if necessary.
8. Disconnect and plug the EGR vacuum line at the valve. On the 225 and 318 outside California, disconnect and plug the distributor vacuum hose. Adjust the fast idle speed with the screw on the second highest cam step.
9. If there is a problem with rough idle or low speed surge on 2 or 4-barrel carburetors, proceed as follows. Remove the plastic idle mixture limiter caps. Seat both idle speed screws gently, then back

them out $1^1/2$ or so turns. Start the engine and adjust the screws out equally (richer) $1/16$ turn at a time, checking the air/fuel ratio each time. Adjust to get both the specified air/fuel ratio and a smooth surgeless idle. Install new caps.

Idle Speed Solenoid Adjustment

This solenoid is energized whenever the ignition circuit is on. Its function is to allow the throttle plates to close farther when the ignition is switched off, thereby preventing running on. It must not be confused with the very similar catalyst protection system throttle position solenoid used on some 1975 models. This solenoid is energized only on deceleration. Further details on the catalyst protection system will be given in the Emission Control Systems Unit Repair Section, but it is not adjusted as part of tune-up.

1. Bring the engine to operating temperature and attach a tachometer.
2. With the engine running, adjust the solenoid screw to the proper rpm.
3. Adjust the slow curb idle screw until the screw end just contacts the stop on the carburetor body. Back the screw off one full turn.
4. Test the above procedure by disconnecting the solenoid wire at the connector. Be sure not to let the lead short to the engine. The solenoid should de-energize and idle speed should drop down below normal. Now reconnect the wire. After you reconnect the solenoid, move the throttle linkage by hand since the solenoid isn't strong enough to move it.

Fuel Filter Removal and Installation

Locate the filter in the fuel line between the fuel pump and the carburetor. Using hose-clamp pliers, remove the attaching clamps and pull the filter off. Reverse this procedure for installation. Be sure that the arrow on the filter is pointing toward the carburetor (direction of fuel flow).

NOTE: *Some filters have a third line, the purpose of which is to prevent vapor lock by allowing fuel vapors to return to the tank.*

The 1973 six-cylinder engine has a

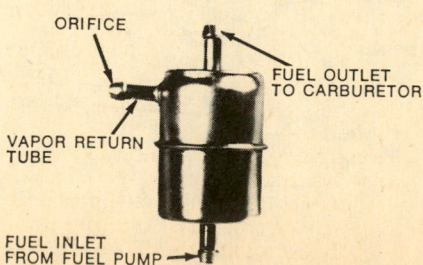

ORIFICE

FUEL OUTLET TO CARBURETOR

VAPOR RETURN TUBE

FUEL INLET FROM FUEL PUMP

The combination filter and vapor separator found on some models
(© Chrysler Corp.)

filter element screwed into the top of the fuel pump. This is not meant to be cleaned; it should be replaced.

Fuel Pump Removal and Installation

The fuel pumps used on the six-cylinder, 400 and 440 V8 engines are driven by a small cam eccentric cast into the main camshaft. On the 318, 340, and 360 V8 engines, the pump is driven by a pressed steel eccentric secured on the gear end of the camshaft. On the six-cylinder and 318, 340 and 360 V8 engines, the pump is driven directly by the pump rocker arm pressing on the cam eccentric. On the 400 and 440 big block V8s, there is a pushrod located between the pump rocker arm and the driving eccentric.

1. Wipe the pump exterior to remove all dirt and oil.
2. Taking note of positions, remove the pump fuel lines.
3. Remove the bolts securing the pump to the block and remove the pump.
4. Remove all gasket material from machined surfaces. Using a sealer of good quality, coat both sides of the pump gasket.
5. Install the pump to the block. If difficulty is encountered engaging the pump drive, rotate slightly.
6. Connect the fuel lines and tighten the pump bolts. Start the engine and check it for leaks.

COOLING SYSTEM

There are three levels of cooling: standard, air conditioning, and maximum cooling. Radiator size varies with the engine and cooling level. Other variable items are fan size, fan shrouds, thermostatically controlled fluid fan drives, and external automatic transmission fluid coolers. The maximum cooling system is usually used only in trailer-towing packages.

Radiator Removal and Installation

1. Drain the cooling system.
2. On cars with automatic transmissions, disconnect the fluid cooler lines at the radiator bottom tank. To avoid fluid loss or dirt contamination, plug the cooler lines.
3. Remove the upper and lower radiator hoses.
4. Remove the fan shroud securing screws and separate the shroud from the radiator. Move the shroud toward the engine as far as possible to obtain maximum clearance for removing the radiator.
5. Remove the radiator mounting screws.
6. Lift the radiator out of the engine compartment.

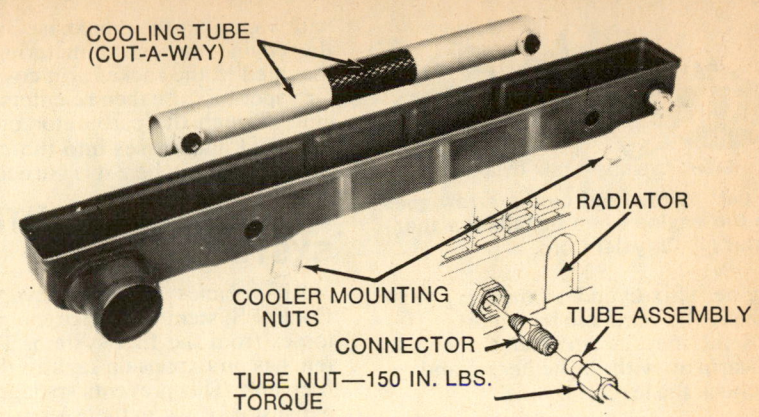

Internal details of the in-radiator transmission fluid cooler (© Chrysler Corp.)

— CAUTION —

Extreme care should be taken not to damage the radiator cooling fins or water tubes during removal.

7. Reverse the procedure to install the radiator. Fill the cooling system to 1 1/4 in. below the filler neck with the correct water and antifreeze mixture, without a coolant reserve tank. With a reserve tank, fill the radiator and fill the tank to the indicated level. Warm up the engine with the heater on and check the coolant level. On cars with automatic transmissions, check the fluid level after warm-up and add fluid as required.

Water Pump Removal and Installation

NOTE: *The water pump is serviced only as an assembly. When replacing the water pump, make sure to install the pump specified for the particular body, engine, and equipment. If the wrong pump is used, overheating may result.*

1. Drain the cooling system.
2. Remove the fan shroud securing screws and move the shroud out of the way.
3. It may be necessary to remove the radiator on some models to obtain the working clearance necessary to remove the water pump.
4. Loosen the alternator mounting bolts. Loosen the mounting bolts for the power steering pump, idler pulley, air conditioning compressor, and air pump (if so equipped). Remove all the accessory belts.
5. Remove the fan, spacer or fluid drive, and the pulley.

— CAUTION —

For fluid-coupled fan drives, do not position the drive unit with its shaft pointing downward. This will prevent the silicone fluid from leaking.

6. On some models, it may be necessary to remove the alternator or compressor mounting bracket bolts

from the water pump to swing the alternator or compressor out of the way.
7. Detach the hoses from the water pump. Remove the bolts which secure the water pump body to its engine block housing. Remove the water pump and discard the gasket.
8. Install the short bypass hose to the pump with the second clamp temporarily in the center of the hose. Install the water pump with a new gasket, using sealer, on its housing. Torque its securing bolts to 30 ft lbs.
9. Rotate the pump shaft by hand to be sure that it rotates freely. Refit the alternator or compressor mounting bracket to the pump if either was removed. Install the pulley, spacer or fluid drive, and the fan. Torque their retaining nuts to 15 ft lbs.
10. Refit all the accessory drive belts. Adjust them to get about 1/2 in. of play under moderate thumb pressure on the longest run of belt between pulleys.
11. Install the radiator if it was removed.
12. Install the fan shroud. Fill the cooling system to 1 1/4 in. below the filler neck with correct water and antifreeze mixture, without a coolant reserve tank. With a reserve tank, fill the radiator and fill the tank to the indicated level. Warm up the engine with the heater on and inspect the water pump for any leaks. Check the coolant level and add as required.

Thermostat Removal and Installation

All 1974 and later engines use a 195°F thermostat; earlier engines use a 185°F unit.

1. Drain the cooling system to below the level of the thermostat.
2. Remove the housing bolts and take out the thermostat and housing.
3. To install the thermostat, use a new gasket. On V8s, be sure that the pellet end is facing toward en-

EIGHT CYLINDER   SIX CYLINDER

The part pointed out by the arrow goes into the engine when installing a thermostat (© Chrysler Corp.)

gine. Six-cylinder models must have the vent hole facing up.
4. Refill the system. Let the engine warm up with the heater on and recheck the level.

EMISSION CONTROLS

POSITIVE CRANKCASE VENTILATION

All models are equipped with a positive crankcase ventilation (PCV) system which draws air into the engine through the air cleaner and circulates it through the engine. The air combines with vapors in the crankcase and exits the engine through a metering valve mounted in the rocker arm cover. The air vapor mixture then re-enters the engine through the carburetor or intake manifold and passes into the combustion chambers where it is burned.

EVAPORATIVE CONTROL SYSTEM

All vehicles have an Evaporation Control System to reduce evaporation losses from the fuel system. The system has an expansion tank in the main fuel tank. This prevents spillage due to expansion of warm fuel. A special filler cap with a two-way relief valve is used. An internal pressure differential, caused by thermal expansion, opens the valve, as does an external pressure differential caused by fuel usage. Fuel vapors from the carburetor and fuel tank are routed to the crankcase ventilation system. A separator is installed to prevent liquid fuel from entering the crankcase ventilation system.

Evaporation control systems used on 1972 and later vehicles also include a charcoal canister and an overflow limiting valve.

The limiting valve prevents the fuel tank from being overfilled by trapping fuel in the filler when the tank is full. When pressure in the tank becomes greater than the valve operating pressure, the valve opens and allows the gasoline vapors to flow into the charcoal canister.

The charcoal canister is mounted in the engine compartment. It absorbs vapors and retains them until clean air is drawn through a line from it that runs to the PCV valve. Absorption occurs while the car is parked and cleaning occurs when the car engine is running.

AIR INJECTION SYSTEM (AIR PUMP)

A belt-driven air pump, mounted on the front of the engine, is used to inject air into the exhaust ports. This causes oxidation of these gases and a considerable reduction in carbon monoxide and hydrocarbons. The system consists of the pump, a check valve to protect the hoses and pump from hot gases, and a diverter-pressure relief valve assembly. Later models add a vacuum and coolant temperature controlled air switching valve to the system. The switching valve allows air flow to the exhaust ports during warmup, then di-

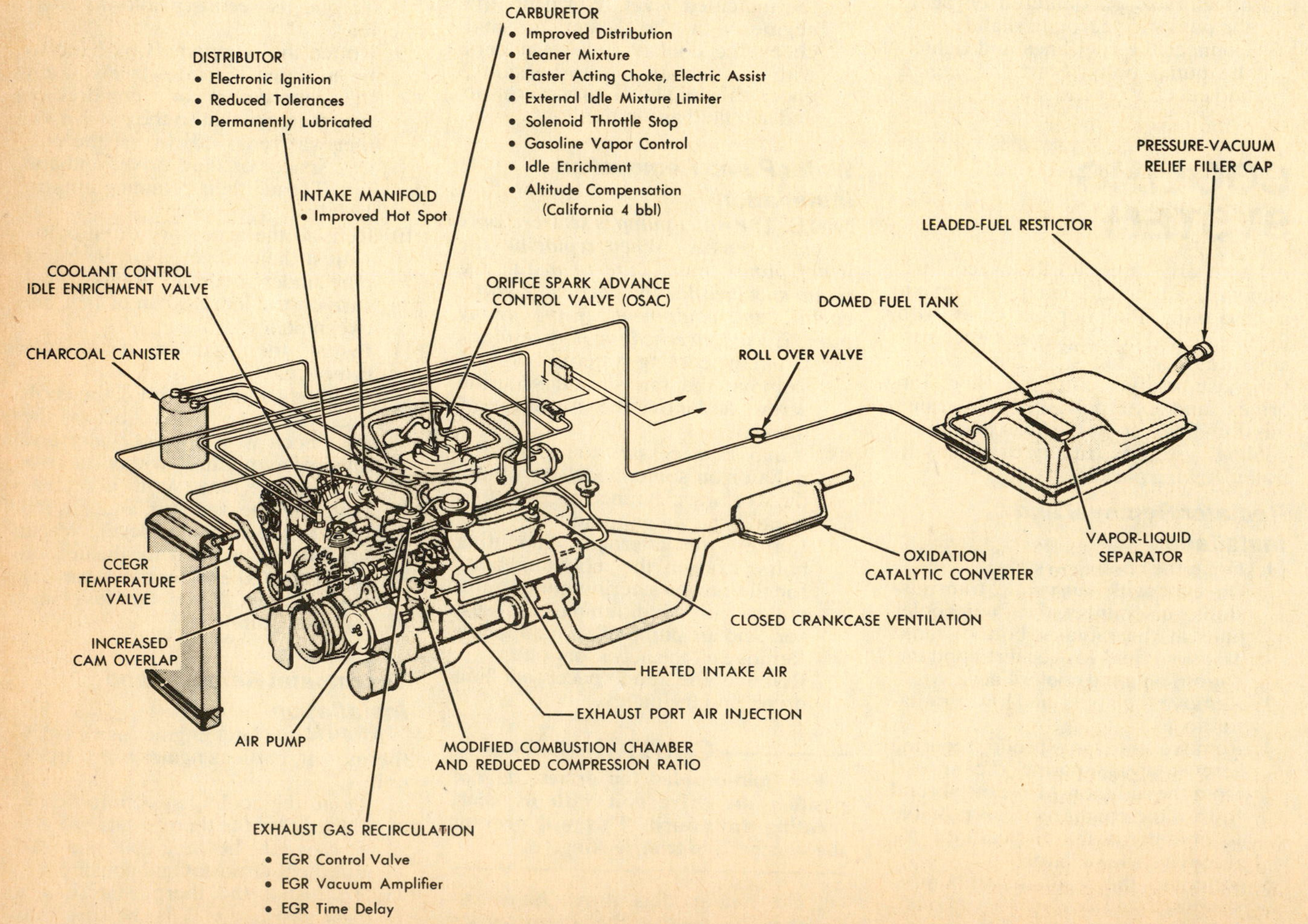

DISTRIBUTOR
• Electronic Ignition
• Reduced Tolerances
• Permanently Lubricated

CARBURETOR
• Improved Distribution
• Leaner Mixture
• Faster Acting Choke, Electric Assist
• External Idle Mixture Limiter
• Solenoid Throttle Stop
• Gasoline Vapor Control
• Idle Enrichment
• Altitude Compensation (California 4 bbl)

INTAKE MANIFOLD
• Improved Hot Spot

PRESSURE-VACUUM RELIEF FILLER CAP

LEADED-FUEL RESTRICTOR

COOLANT CONTROL IDLE ENRICHMENT VALVE

ORIFICE SPARK ADVANCE CONTROL VALVE (OSAC)

DOMED FUEL TANK

CHARCOAL CANISTER

ROLL OVER VALVE

CCEGR TEMPERATURE VALVE

VAPOR-LIQUID SEPARATOR

INCREASED CAM OVERLAP

OXIDATION CATALYTIC CONVERTER

CLOSED CRANKCASE VENTILATION

AIR PUMP

HEATED INTAKE AIR

EXHAUST PORT AIR INJECTION

MODIFIED COMBUSTION CHAMBER AND REDUCED COMPRESSION RATIO

EXHAUST GAS RECIRCULATION
• EGR Control Valve
• EGR Vacuum Amplifier
• EGR Time Delay

1975 Emission control systems (© Chrysler Corp)

verts it to the exhaust manifold or pipe, depending on the engine.

AIR ASPIRATOR SYSTEM

This system is a replacement for the air pump system. It utilizes a simple exhaust gas pulsation operated diaphragm valve to draw air from the air cleaner into the exhaust manifold.

EXHAUST GAS RECIRCULATION

In order to reduce the emission of oxides and nitrogen (NOx), exhaust gases are ducted from the intake manifold crossover passage to dilute (with inert, oxygen-free gas) the fuel/air mixture. These gases are introduced to the intake manifold floor by small jets on 1972 models. In 1973, all engines have floor jets. Floor jets were dropped from all 1974 and later engines. Most engines use an EGR control valve. This valve directs exhaust gas from the crossover passage into the intake manifold. By using either ported-vacuum (varies with throttle opening) or venturi-vacuum signals, the EGR valve is able to proportion the exhaust gas flow to the amount of vacuum present in the carburetor. Thermal switches on the engine and radiator prevent recirculation during engine warmup. All 1974 and later models have a delay timer relay and a solenoid valve to shut off vacuum to the system until the engine has run 30-40 seconds after startup. For 1979, the thermal switch in the system senses intake manifold fuel/air mixture, rather than coolant temperature.

ELECTRICALLY ASSISTED CHOKE

This system was introduced for 1973. There are two types, single and dual stage. Both use an electric assist heating element on the manifold mounted choke coil for faster choke release. The single stage unit applies heat to the choke coil only in summer temperatures, while the dual stage unit applies low heat during warmup and high heat after warmup.

NOx SYSTEM

Many 1972 vehicles sold in California have a NOx system to control the emission of oxides of nitrogen. Engines with this system all have a special camshaft and a 185°F thermostat.

The manual transmission NOx system uses a transmission switch, a thermal switch, and a solenoid vacuum valve. The transmission switch is screwed into the transmission housing and is closed, except in high gear. The thermal switch, mounted on the firewall, is open whenever the ambient temperature is above 70°F. With the transmission in any gear except high and the temperature above 70°, the solenoid vacuum valve is energized. This shuts off the distributor vacuum advance line preventing vacuum advance.

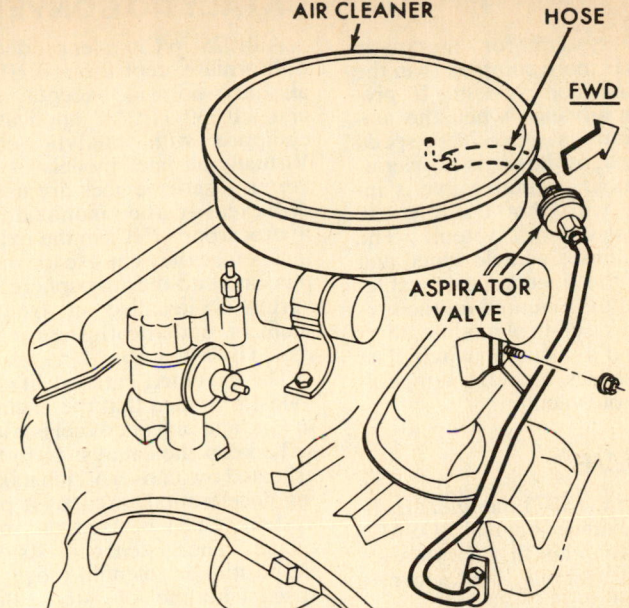

Typical air aspirator system (© Chrysler Corp.)

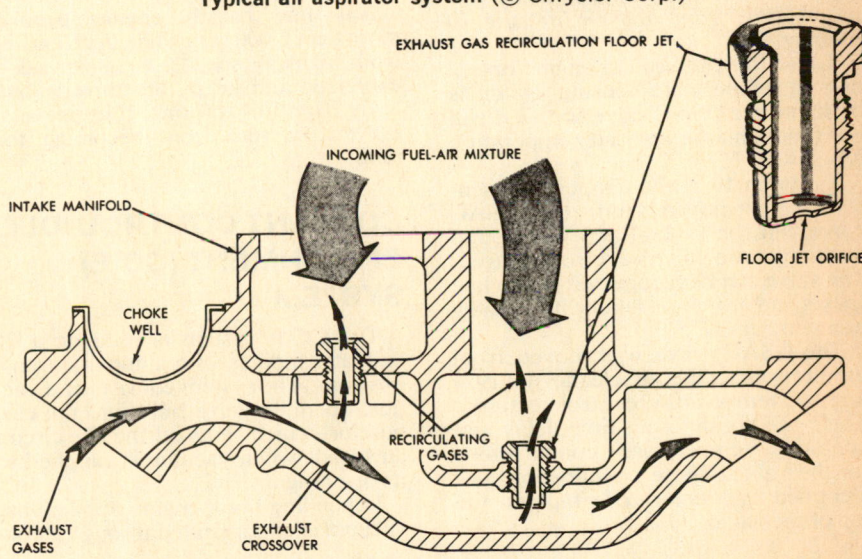

Exhaust Gas Recirculation—Floor Jet System (© Chrysler Corp)

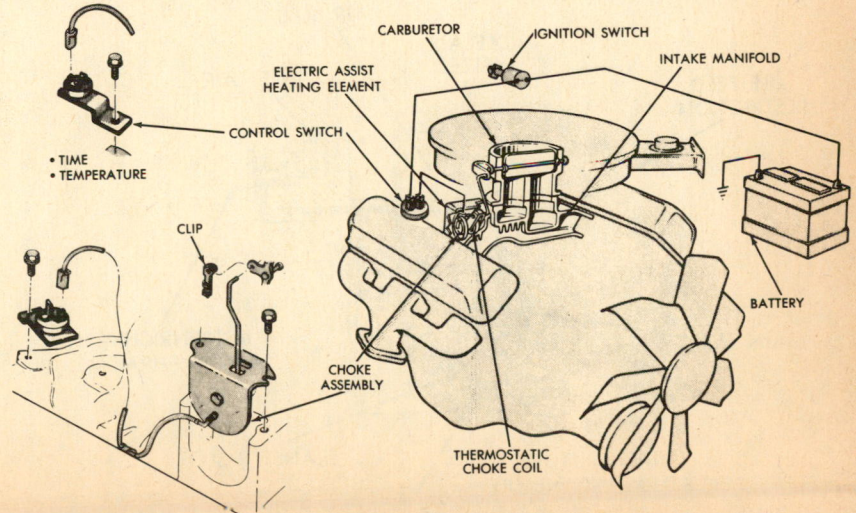

Electrically assisted choke system (© Chrysler Corp.)

Below 70°, the vacuum advance functions normally.

The NOx system for automatic transmissions is more complex than the manual transmission system. It prevents vacuum advance when the ambient temperature is above 70°F, speed is below 30 mph, or the car is accelerating. The solenoid vacuum valve is interchangeable with that used in the manual transmission system. The speed switch senses vehicle speed and is driven by the speedometer cable. The control unit is mounted on the firewall. It contains a control module, thermal switch, and a vacuum switch. The control unit senses ambient temperature and manifold vacuum.

OSAC VALVE

Starting with the 1973 models, an orifice spark advance control (OSAC) valve is used to delay distributor vacuum advance for about 15-27 seconds during acceleration.

NOTE: *The amount of time-delay varies slightly from one engine size to another.*

To aid in cold weather engine operation, a temperature sensing switch is built into the OSAC valve so that it will not function when the air temperature is below 68°F.

In March 1973, the temperature sensor was removed from the OSAC valve, but the general appearance and location of the valve were not changed. The valve can be recognized by a white gasket and a stick-on label with the new part number (3755499).

The OSAC valve was moved from the firewall to the air cleaner in 1974 and the temperature control restored. There are six different time delay and operating temperature combinations for the valve. These combinations are identified by a color code tape on the top of the valve.

CATALYTIC CONVERTER

All 1975-76 Chrysler products sold in California except the 360 HP V8, and all sold nationwide except some 318-2V and all 360 HP V8 applications, are equipped with catalytic converters. Virtually all later models use the converter. These devices are used to oxidize excess carbon monoxide (CO) and hydrocarbons (HC) in the exhaust system before they can escape out the tailpipe and into the atmosphere. The converter is installed in front of the mufflers, underneath the car, and protected by a heat shield.

The expected catalyst life is 50,000 miles, provided that the engine is kept in tune and unleaded fuel is used.

To keep the catalyst from being overheated by an overly rich mixture during deceleration, a catalyst protection system (CPS) is used on some 1975 models. The system consists of a throttle positioner solenoid (not to be confused with the idle stop solenoid), a control box, and an engine rpm sensor.

Any time that the engine speed is more than 2,000 rpm while decelerating from highway speeds, the solenoid is energized and keeps the throttle butterfly from fully closing, thus preventing the mixture from becoming too rich.

COOLANT CONTROL IDLE ENRICHMENT (CCIE) SYSTEM

The CCIE system is used on 1975 and later models with automatic transmissions. The system consists of a vacuum-operated valve built into the carburetor, which shuts off the idle circuit air bleeds when vacuum is supplied to its diaphragm.

Depending upon engine application, vacuum is either routed through a coolant controlled vacuum valve and an EGR vacuum control solenoid.

Vacuum is passed to the valve diaphragm below a predetermined temperature, and on models with an EGR control solenoid for only 35 seconds after the engine is started. The CCIE valve action closes off the air bleed passages, which richens the mixture, and allows a smoother cold idle.

LEAN BURN SYSTEM

Lean Burn is an electronic spark advance control system that permits operation at very lean air-fuel mixtures for improved emission control, economy, and driveability. It was introduced as standard equipment on the Diplomat and LeBaron. For 1979, the system is called Electronic Spark Control. For a description of the system, see the Dodge/Plymouth Section. For a more detailed description and troubleshooting, see the Emission Control Systems Unit Repair Section.

NOTE: *These cars use a "second-generation" improved, Lean Burn system. The new system has a single distributor pickup instead of the individual start and run pickups used in 1976 and 1977 versions.*

ENGINE

The standard equipment engine in most Chrysler Corporation compacts is the slant six. Although this engine has a long stroke, it presents a low profile because the entire block is canted 30 degrees to the right. An optional two barrel carburetor became available in 1977.

The 318, 340 and 360 cu. in. engines are Chrysler's "A" block series of V8s. All of the V8s utilize hydraulic tappets.

Chrysler's "B" block series consists of the 400 and 440 cu in. engines. Actually, these may be divided into two types: the 400 low-block engine and a 440 high-block. The difference is a larger, deeper block on the 440 to accommodate a longer stroke crank. In addition, main journal diameter, connecting rod length, pushrod length, and intake manifolds are different. Otherwise, these engines are similar and many parts will interchange.

SPECIAL ENGINE MARKINGS

Over and undersize engine components such as crankshaft and connecting rod journals, cylinder bores, tappets, and valve stems are identified by various marks. These marks may be located on top front engine pads, following the serial number, or on the crankshaft counterweights. In addition, some engines may have oversize valve stem markings stamped on cylinder head ends. For explanation of the

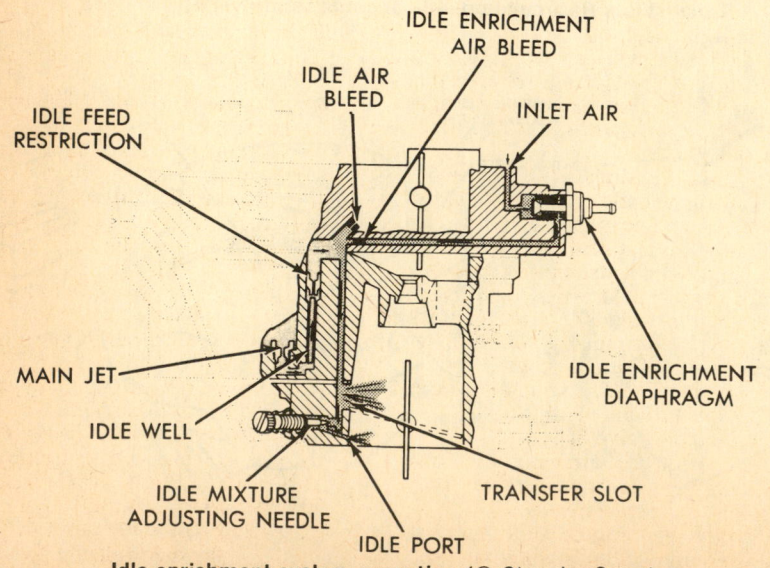

Idle enrichment system operation (© Chrysler Corp.)

meanings of the various markings, consult a dealer parts book.

ENGINE REMOVAL AND INSTALLATION

6 CYLINDER

1. Scribe the hood hinge outlines on the underside of the hood, then remove the hood.
2. Drain the cooling system, remove the battery and carburetor air cleaner.
3. Remove radiator and heater hoses, then the radiator. Remove PCV and evaporative control system.
4. Remove the outlet vent pipe from the cylinder head cover.
5. Disconnect fuel lines, linkage and wiring to the engine.
6. Disconnect exhaust pipe at exhaust manifold.
7. Raise car on hoist.
8. If equipped with automatic transmission, it must be drained. Remove the fluid cooler lines, filler tube and shift linkage.
9. Remove the clutch torque shaft, and rods.
10. Remove the speedometer cable and gear shift rods.
11. Disconnect driveshaft and tie out of the way.
12. Install an engine support fixture to the rear of the engine.
13. Remove the engine rear support crossmember.
14. Remove transmission mounting bolts from clutch housing.
15. Remove the transmission. With automatic transmission, the torque converter must be unbolted from the crankshaft flexplate first.
16. Lower the car.
17. Position engine lifting fixture onto the engine, and attach chain hoist to the fixture eyebolt.
18. Remove the engine support fixture.
19. Remove the engine front mounting bolts.

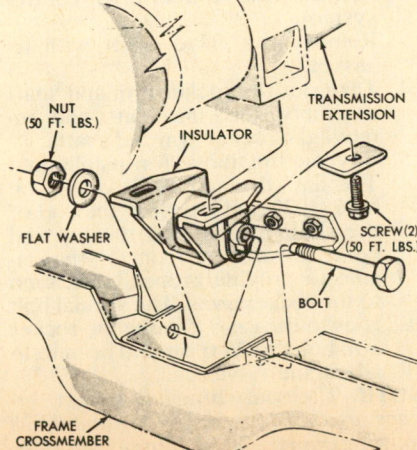

Typical rear engine mount
(© Chrysler Corp.)

Chilton's TIME SAVER

The procedure for engine removal requires first removing the transmission. The transmission can be left in the chassis, using the following procedure. If the vehicle is equipped with an automatic transmission, attach a remote starter switch to the engine, remove the inspection plate from the bellhousing, crank the engine to gain access to the torque converter-to-driveplate attaching nuts and remove the nuts. Remove the starter. If the vehicle is equipped with a manual transmission, disconnect the clutch torque shaft from the engine block and the clutch linkage from the adjustment rod. Remove the bolt that attaches the transmission filler tube to the engine (automatic transmission). Support the transmission and remove the bolts that attach the transmission to the engine or clutch bell housing. When removing the engine, place a block of wood on the lifting point of a floor jack and position the jack under the transmission. As the engine is removed from the vehicle, raise and lower the jack as required so the angle of the transmission duplicates as nearly as possible the angle of the engine. Use a clamp so that the torque converter doesn't fall out of the transmission.

When installing the engine into a vehicle with an automatic transmission, keep in mind that the crankshaft flange bolt circle, the inner and outer circle of holes in the driveplate, and the four tapped holes in the front face of the converter all have one hole offset. To insure proper engine-torque converter balance, the torque converter must be mounted to the driveplate in the same location it was originally installed.

When installing the engine into a vehicle with a manual transmission, it may be necessary to turn the crankshaft pulley, with the transmission in gear, to get the transmission input shaft spline to mesh with the inner hub on the clutch disc.

20. Lift the engine out of the engine compartment and lower it onto a substantial work stand.
21. To install the engine, reverse the procedure.

V8

1. Scribe the outline of the hood hinge brackets on the bottom of the hood and remove the hood.
2. Drain the cooling system and remove the radiator.
3. Remove the battery.
4. Remove the fuel line from the fuel pump and plug the line.
5. Remove all wires and hoses that attach to the engine.
6. If equipped with air conditioning and/or power steering, remove the unit from the engine and position it out of the way *without disconnecting the lines.*
7. Attach lifting sling to the engine.
8. Raise the vehicle on a hoist and install an engine support fixture to support the rear of the engine.
9. On automatic transmission models, drain the transmission and converter. On standard transmission models, disconnect the clutch torque shaft from the engine.
10. Disconnect the exhaust pipe/s from the exhaust manifold/s.
11. Remove the driveshaft.
12. Disconnect the transmission linkage and any wiring or cables that attach to the transmission.
13. Remove the engine rear support crossmember and remove the transmission.

14. Remove the bolts that attach the motor mounts to the chassis.
15. Lower the vehicle and attach a chain hoist or other lifting device to the engine.
16. Raise the engine and carefully remove it from the engine compartment.
17. Reverse the procedure to install the engine.

MANIFOLDS

6 Cylinder Combination Manifold Removal and Installation

1. Remove the air cleaner.
2. Disconnect the vacuum control tube at the carburetor.
3. Disconnect the fuel line at the carburetor.
4. Disconnect the crankcase ventilation tube at the carburetor.
5. Disconnect the automatic choke rod at the carburetor and remove the choke from the intake manifold.
6. Disconnect the throttle linkage at the carburetor.
7. Remove the carburetor from the intake manifold.
8. Disconnect the exhaust pipe at the exhaust manifold flange.
9. Remove the nuts and washers securing the manifold assembly to the cylinder head. Make note of the location of the different types of washers for installation.
10. Remove the manifold from the cylinder head.

11. Remove the three screws securing the intake manifold to the exhaust manifold.
12. Separate the intake and exhaust manifolds and discard the gasket.
13. Clean all gasket surfaces on the manifolds in solvent and blow them dry with compressed air.
14. Clean the manifold gasket surfaces on the cylinder head, wash them with solvent and blow them dry with compressed air.
15. Check the mating surfaces of the manifolds with a straightedge. Surfaces should be flat within .008″ per foot.
16. Inspect the manifolds for cracks or distortion.
17. Check the operation of the manifold heat control valve. If necessary to free up its operation, apply a manifold heat control valve solvent.
18. To install, first install a new gasket between the two manifolds.
19. Install the three long screws securing the two manifolds. *Do not tighten the screws yet.*
20. Position the manifold assembly on the cylinder head, using a new gasket with sealer on both sides.
21. Install the triangular washers and nuts on the upper studs and on the four lower studs opposite numbers 2 and 5 cylinders. The eight triangular washers should be positioned squarely on the machined surfaces of both intake and exhaust manifold retaining pads. These washers must be installed with the *cup side* against the manifold. Install the nuts and washers only when the engine is cold.
22. Install the steel conical washers with the cup (concave) side to the manifold, one on the center upper stud and two on the center lower studs. Install the brass washers at each end, with the flat side to the manifold. Install the nuts with the flat side away from the washers. Snug up the nuts.
23. Tighten the intake to exhaust manifold screws to the specified torque, starting with the inner stud. Tighten the manifold to head screws and nuts to the specified torque.
24. Attach the exhaust pipe to manifold flange, using a new gasket and tighten the nuts to 35 ft lbs.
25. Install the carburetor and connect the automatic choke rod and throttle linkage. Assemble the crankcase ventilation hose, vacuum control tube, and fuel line to the carburetor. Install the carburetor air cleaner, and connect the closed breather cap hose to the air cleaner inlet tube.

V8 Intake Manifold Removal and Installation

1. Drain the cooling system. Disconnect the negative battery cable.
2. Remove the air cleaner and disconnect the fuel line from the carburetor.
3. Disconnect all vacuum lines and throttle linkage that attach to the carburetor or intake manifold.
4. Disconnect the spark plug wires from the plugs and remove the distributor cap and wires as an assembly.
5. Disconnect the wires from the coil and the temperature sending unit.
6. Disconnect the heater hose and bypass hose from the intake manifold.
7. Remove the intake manifold attaching bolts and remove the manifold, carburetor and coil from the engine as an assembly.
8. Clean all gasket mounting surfaces and firmly cement new gaskets to the engine.

NOTE: *Do not use sealer on the composition side gaskets used on 1973 and later 340 and 360 engines.*

9. Reverse the procedure to install. Torque the bolts to specification in three passes, in the sequence shown.

V8 Exhaust Manifold Removal and Installation

Disconnect the exhaust manifold at the pipe flange. Access to these bolts is underneath the vehicle. If so equipped, disconnect the Air Injection nozzles and carburetor heated air stove. Disconnect any components of the EGR system which are in the way. Remove the exhaust manifold by removing the securing bolts and washers. To reach these bolts, it may be necessary to jack the engine slightly off its front mounts. When the exhaust manifold is removed, sometimes the securing studs will come out with the nuts. If this occurs, studs must be replaced with the aid of sealing compound on the coarse thread ends. If this is not done, water leaks may develop at the studs. To install the exhaust manifold, reverse the removal procedure. On the center branch of the 318, 340, and 360 manifold, no conical washers are used.

VALVE SYSTEM

All valves used in Chrysler engines are arranged in line in the cylinder head; they ride in guides that are integrally cast with the head. Service valves with oversize stems are available; therefore, valve guides may be reamed if required.

Rocker Shaft Removal and Installation

SIX CYLINDER

1. Remove the closed ventilation system.
2. Remove the evaporative control system.
3. Remove the valve cover with its gasket.
4. Take out the rocker arm and shaft assembly securing bolts and remove the rocker arm and shaft.
5. Reverse the above for installation. The flat (through 1973) or the oil hole (1972 and later) on the end of the shaft must be on the top and point toward the front of the engine to provide proper lubrication to the rocker arms. The special bolt goes to the rear. Torque the rocker arm bolts to 25 ft lbs and be sure to adjust the valves.

NOTE: *The cold valve adjustment settings are 0.012 in. for intake, and 0.028 in. for exhaust. These settings are to be used only for reassembly; adjust the valves to the normal hot setting as soon as the engine has been warmed up.*

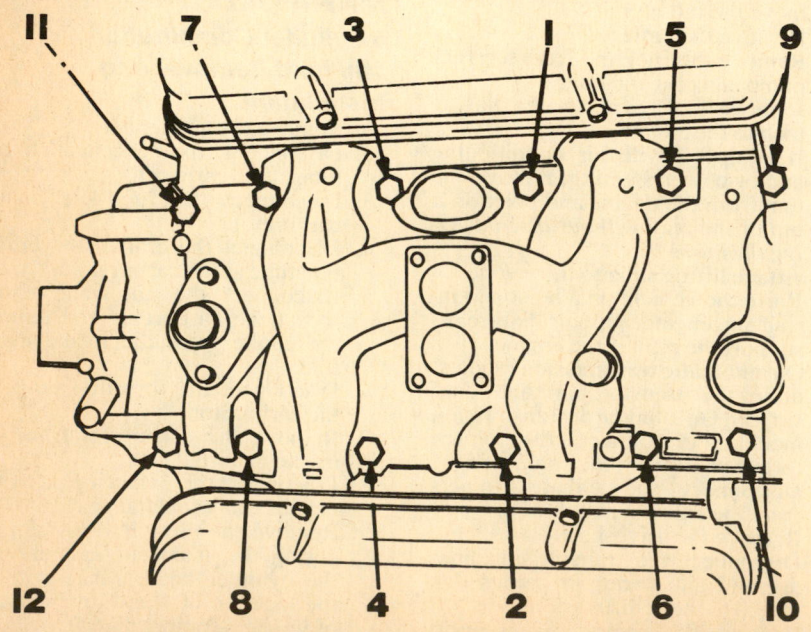

Intake manifold tightening sequence for V8 engines. 400 and 440 V8s do not have bolts 9, 10, 11, and 12 (© Chrysler Corp)

V8

The stamped steel rocker arms are arranged on one rocker arm shaft per cylinder head. To remove the rocker arms and shaft:

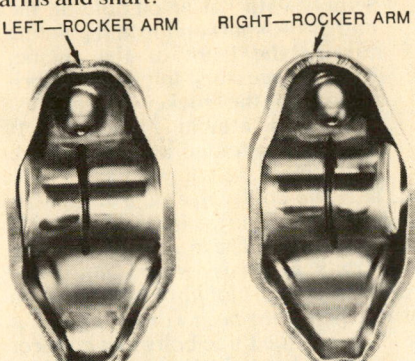

Left and right rocker arm identification for 318, 340, 360 V8s (© Chrysler Corp)

1. Disconnect the spark plug wires.
2. Disconnect the closed ventilation and evaporative control system.
3. Remove the valve covers with their gaskets.
4. Remove the rocker shaft bolts and retainers, and lift off the rocker arm assembly.

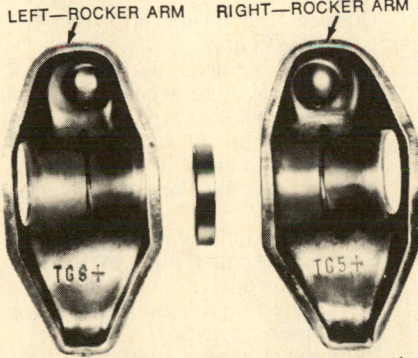

Left and right rocker arm identification for 400 and 440 V8s (© Chrysler Corp)

5. Reverse the above procedure to install. The notch on the end of both rocker shafts on the 318, 340, and 360 should point to the engine centerline and toward the front of the engine on the left cylinder head, or toward the rear on the right cylinder head. On the 400 and 440, the rocker arm lubrication holes must point down and toward the valves. Torque the rocker shaft bolts to 17 ft lbs on the 318, 340, and 360, and 25 ft lbs on the 400 and 440.

Valve Adjustment

This adjustment is required only on the six cylinder engines. The sixes use solid lifters and adjustable rocker arms. All V8s use hydraulic lifters and non-adjustable rocker arms; the lifters take up lash automatically and no adjustment is possible. After engine reassembly, these lifters adjust themselves shortly after oil pressure builds up.

NOTE: *Some 1978 two barrel six cylin-*

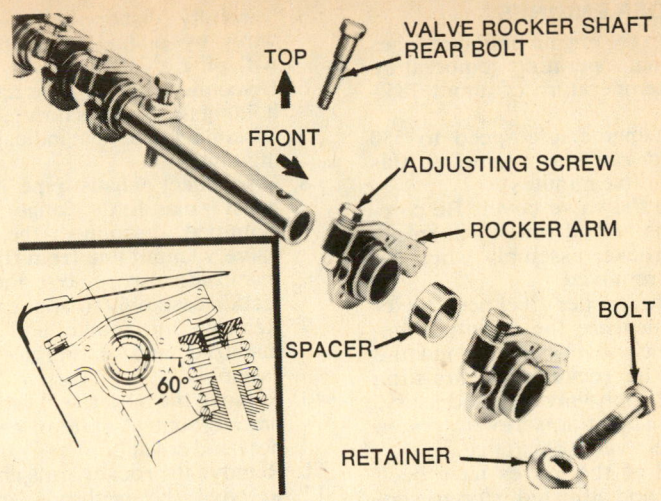

Six-cylinder rocker shaft details (© Chrysler Corp.)

der engines were assembled with hydraulic lifters. These are identified by a sticker on the rocker arm cover. The sales code is Y39, and the engines were all assembled at the Newark plant, plant code F, seventh digit of the Vehicle Identification Number. The emission sticker also does not list a valve lash setting.

Valve lash should be adjusted whenever there is excessive noise from the valve mechanism.

CAUTION

Do not set the valve lash closer than specified in an attempt to quiet the valve mechanism. This will cause burned valves.

Chilton's TIME SAVER

The factory recommends adjusting the valves on six cylinder engines with the engine running, but the amateur mechanic will have better luck with the following procedure:

1. The engine must be at normal operating temperature. Mark the crankshaft pulley into three equal 120° segments, starting at the timing mark.
2. Remove the valve (rocker) cover and the distributor cap.
3. Set the engine at TDC on the No. 1 cylinder by aligning the mark on the crankshaft pulley with the 0° mark on the timing cover pointer. The distributor rotor should point at the position of the No. 1 spark plug wire in the distributor cap. Both rocker arms on No. 1 cylinder should be free to move slightly. If all this isn't the case, you have No. 6 cylinder at TDC and will have to turn the engine 360° in the normal direction of rotation.
4. The cylinders are numbered from front to rear. The intake and exhaust valves are in the following sequence, starting at the front: E-I, E-I, E-I, I-E, I-E, I-E. Note that intake and exhaust valves have different settings.
5. The lash is measured between the rocker arm and the end of the valve.
6. To check the lash, insert the correct size feeler gauge between the rocker arm and the valve. Press down lightly on the other end of the rocker arm. If the gauge cannot be inserted, loosen the self-locking adjustment nut on top of the rocker arm. Tighten the nut until the gauge can just be inserted and withdrawn without buckling.
7. After both valves for the No. 1 cylinder are adjusted, turn the engine so that the pulley turns 120° in the normal direction of rotation (clockwise). The distributor rotor will turn 60°, since it turns at half engine speed.
8. Check that the rocker arms are free and adjust the valves for the next cylinder in the firing order, No. 5. The firing order is 1-5-3-6-2-4.
9. Turn the engine 120° to adjust each of the remaining cylinders in the firing order. When you are done the engine will have made two complete revolutions (720°) and the rotor one complete revolution (360°).
10. Replace the rocker cover with a new gasket. Replace the distributor cap. Start the engine and check for leaks.

SIX CYLINDER ENGINES

1. Warm up the engine until it reaches its normal operating temperature (water temperature of about 185°-F).
2. Set the engine idle speed to 550 rpm and run the engine at this speed for five minutes.
3. Remove the valve cover. Be careful of the hot oil which will splash off the rocker assembly when the cover is removed.
4. Using the proper thickness feeler gauge, measure the clearance between the valve stem tip and the end of the rocker arm adjusting screw at each valve. If necessary, turn the adjusting screw to obtain the correct valve clearance.
5. After all of the valves have been checked and adjusted, stop the engine and replace the valve cover, using a new gasket between the cover and cylinder head. If much oil was lost during the valve adjustment procedure, check the oil level in the crankcase.

CYLINDER HEAD

─── CAUTION ───

Don't loosen the head bolts until the engine is thoroughly cool, to prevent warping the head. If the head sticks to the block, operate the starter to loosen it by compression or rap it upward with a soft hammer. Do not force anything between the head and the block. Cylinder head bolts should be retorqued after the first 500 miles, unless a special gasket is used.

6 Cylinder Removal

1. Drain the cooling system.
2. Remove carburetor air cleaner and fuel lines.
3. Disconnect accelerator linkage.
4. Remove all of the vacuum lines from the carburetor.
5. Carefully disconnect spark plug wires by pulling straight, in line with plug.
6. Disconnect heater hose and clamp holding the by-pass hose.
7. Disconnect the heat indicator sending-unit wire.
8. Disconnect exhaust pipe at the exhaust manifold flange. If so equipped, disconnect the diverter valve vacuum line from the intake manifold; also remove the air injection assembly (if applicable).
9. Remove the intake and exhaust manifold and carburetor as an assembly.
10. Remove the outlet vent tube, evaporative control system, and cylinder head cover.
11. Remove the rocker arms and shaft.
12. Remove the pushrods and keep them in order.
13. Remove the head bolts and lift off the cylinder head.
14. Place cylinder head on bench and remove the spark plugs and tubes (through 1974).

6 Cylinder Installation

1. Clean carbon from the combustion area. Clean all gasket surfaces of both head and cylinder block. Install spark plugs. (No gaskets are used.)
2. If there is any cause to suspect leakage, check all surfaces with a straightedge. If out of flatness exceeds 0.00075 times the span length in any direction, replace head or machine head gasket surface. For example, on a 12 in. span the maximum allowable out of flat is 12 x 0.00075 or 0.009 in.
3. Apply a reliable sealer to the new gasket and install the gasket and cylinder head.
4. Install the 14 cylinder head bolts. Starting at the top center, tighten all cylinder head bolts to specification in three steps.

5. Inspect all push rods for bends or wear. Replace if necessary.
6. Insert the pushrods, small ends down into the tappets.
7. Install rocker arms and shaft assembly with flat or oil hole on the end of the shaft on top and pointing toward the front of the engine. This is necessary to provide lubrication to the rocker assemblies. Torque the attaching bolts to 25 ft lbs. Make a temporary, cold, valve adjustment.

NOTE: *The cold valve adjustment settings are 0.012 in. for intake, and 0.028 in. for exhaust. These settings are to be used only for reassembly; adjust the valves to the normal hot setting as soon as the engine has been warmed up.*

8. Loosen the three bolts that connect the intake and exhaust manifolds. (This is necessary to obtain proper alignment.)
9. Position intake and exhaust manifold and carburetor assembly onto the cylinder head. Put the cup side of the conical washers against the manifolds, install the attaching nuts and torque to specifications.
10. Retighten the three intake-to-exhaust manifold bolts to specifications. Be sure to torque the inner bolt first.
11. Connect the heater hose and by-pass hose clamp.
12. Connect the heat indicator sending-unit wire, the accelerator linkage and the spark plug wires. If applicable, install vacuum control tube at the carburetor, the air injection assembly, and the diverter valve.
13. Install carburetor vacuum line(s).
14. Connect exhaust pipe to the exhaust manifold.
15. Install the fuel line and carburetor air cleaner.
16. Refill the cooling system.
17. Start the engine and let run until operating temperatures have been reached.
18. Adjust valve tappet clearance. The adjusting screw in the pushrod end of the rocker arm should have a minimum of 3 ft lbs (36 in lbs) tension as it is turned. If less, replace the adjusting screw and the rocker arm.
19. Place the new cylinder head cover gasket in position and install cylinder head cover.
20. Install outlet vent tube, and evaporative control system (if applicable).

V8 Removal and Installation

1. Drain cooling system and disconnect battery.
2. Remove alternator, air cleaner and fuel line.
3. Disconnect accelerator linkage.
4. Remove vacuum hose(s) from the carburetor.
5. Remove distributor cap and wires. If removing heads in vehicle, re-

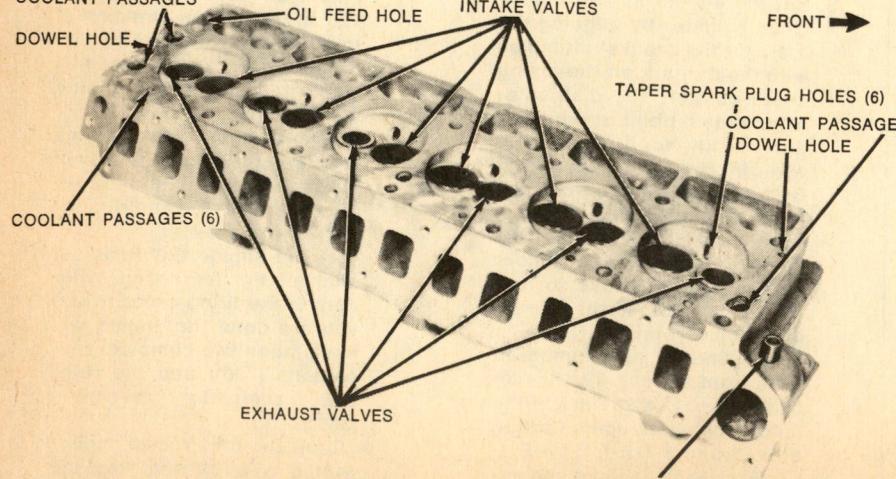

Cylinder head, showing valve sequence—six cylinder engines (© Chrysler Corp)

move plugs to prevent breaking them.

6. Disconnect coil wires, temperature sending wire, heater hoses, and by-pass hose.
7. Remove closed ventilation system (PCV), evaporative control system if so equipped, and valve covers.
8. Remove intake manifold, ignition coil, and carburetor as an assembly. Remove the tappet chamber cover, if used.
9. Remove exhaust manifolds.
10. Remove rocker arm and shaft assemblies. Remove pushrods and identify to ensure installation in original location.
11. Remove the head bolts from each cylinder head and lift off heads.

TIME SAVER

If only one head is to be removed, it is possible to leave the intake manifold on the engine while removing the head:

1. Remove the head bolts from the intake manifold on the side from which the head is to be removed.
2. Loosen, but do not remove, the bolts on the opposite side of the manifold 1½-2 turns.
3. Perform steps 9-11 of the V8 head removal procedure.
4. Slip the head out from under the intake manifold.
5. Perform steps 12-14 of the V8 head removal procedure.

TIME SAVER

Frequently valves become bent or warped or their seats become blocked with carbon or other material. Left unattended, this can cause burnt valves, damaged cylinder heads and other expensive troubles. To detect leaking valves early, perform this test whenever the cylinder head is removed.

1. After removing head, replace sparkplugs. Removing sparkplugs before removing heads eliminates breakage.
2. Place head on bench with valves, springs, retainers and keys installed and combustion chambers up.
3. Pour enough safe solvent in each combustion chamber to completely cover both valves. Watch combustion chambers for two minutes for any leakage.

12. Clean all surfaces.
13. Inspect all surfaces with straight edge if there is any reason to suspect leakage. If out of flatness exceeds 0.00075 times span length in any direction, replace head or machine mating surface. For example, if span length is 12 in., maximum out of flatness is 12 x 0.00075 or 0.009 in.
14. Reverse procedure to install. Be sure to use sealer and torque the cylinder head to specifications in three stages.

NOTE: *318 cylinder heads were changed during the 1976 model year; 360 heads were changed during the 1977 model year. A new type gasket must be used with the new heads.*

Cylinder Head Bolt Tightening Sequences

NOTE: *Torque to specifications in three steps.*

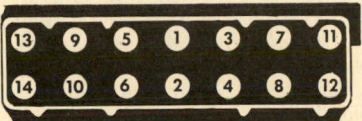

6 cylinder

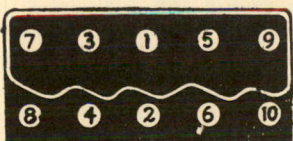

360 cu. in. and smaller V8

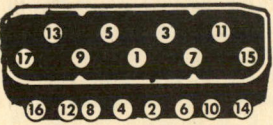

400 and 440 V8

TIMING COVER, CHAIN, AND CAMSHAFT

Timing Chain and Cover Replacement

NOTE: *It is normal to find particles of neoprene between the seal retainer and the crankshaft oil slinger after the seal has been in service on sixes through 1973 and V8s through 1974.*

SIX-CYLINDER

1. Drain the cooling system and disconnect the battery.
2. Remove the radiator and fan.
3. With a puller, remove the vibration damper.
4. Loosen the oil pan bolts to allow clearance and remove the timing case cover and gasket.

5. Slide the crankshaft oil slinger off the front of the crankshaft.
6. Remove the camshaft sprocket bolt.
7. Remove the timing chain with the camshaft sprocket.
8. On installation: Turn the crankshaft to line up the timing mark on the crankshaft sprocket with the centerline of the camshaft (without the chain).
9. Install the camshaft sprocket and chain. Align the timing marks.

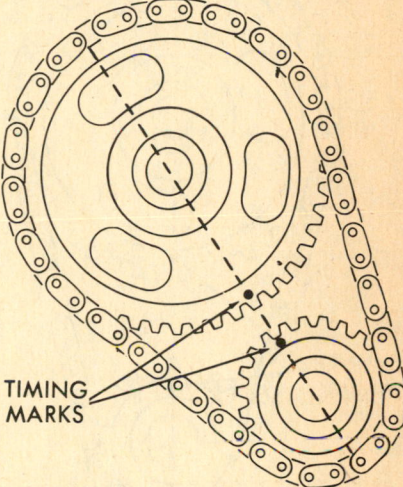

Alignment of timing marks—6 cylinder

10. Torque the camshaft sprocket bolt to 35 ft lbs.
11. Replace the oil slinger. Apply a ⅛ in. bead of sealer to the junction of the rubber and cork oil pan seals.
12. Reinstall the timing case cover with a new gasket and torque the bolts to 17 ft lbs. Retighten the engine oil pan to 17 ft lbs.
13. Press the vibration damper back on.
14. Replace the radiator and hoses.
15. Refill the cooling system.

V8

1. Disconnect the battery and drain the cooling system. Remove the water pump. Remove the power steering pump attaching bolts and move the pump aside. If so equipped. Move the air conditioning compressor aside, if equipped.
2. Remove the vibration damper pulley. Unbolt and remove the vibration damper with a puller. On 318, 340, and 360 engines, remove the fuel lines and fuel pump, then loosen the oil pan bolts and remove the front bolt on each side.
3. Remove the timing gear cover and the crankshaft oil slinger.
4. On 318, 340, and 360 engines, remove the camshaft sprocket lockbolt, securing cup washer, and fuel pump eccentric. Remove the timing chain with both sprockets. On 400, 426, and 440 engines, remove the camshaft sprocket lockbolt and remove the timing chain with the

camshaft and crankshaft sprockets.

5. To begin the installation procedure, place the camshaft and crankshaft sprockets on a flat surface with the timing indicators on an imaginary centerline through both sprocket bores. Place the timing chain around both sprockets. Be sure that the timing marks are in alignment.

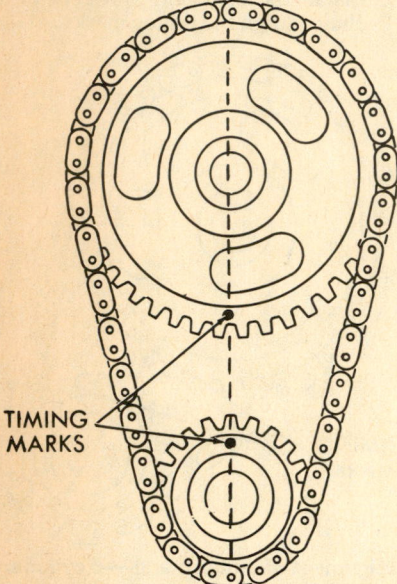

TIMING MARKS

Alignment of timing marks—V8

CAUTION

When installing the timing chain, have an assistant support the camshaft with a screwdriver to prevent it from contacting the plug in the rear of the engine block. Remove the distributor and the oil pump/distributor drive gear. Position the screwdriver against the rear side of the cam gear and be careful not to damage the cam lobes.

6. Turn the crankshaft and camshaft to align them with the keyway location in the crankshaft sprocket and the keyway or dowel hole in the camshaft sprocket.
7. Lift the sprockets and timing chain while keeping the sprockets tight against the chain in the correct position. Slide both sprockets evenly onto their respective shafts.
8. Use a straightedge to measure the alignment of the sprocket timing marks. They must be perfectly aligned.
9. On 318, 340, and 360 engines, install the fuel pump eccentric, cup washer, and camshaft sprocket lockbolt, and torque to 35 ft lbs. If camshaft end play exceeds 0.010 in., install a new thrust plate. It should be 0.002-0.006 in. with the new plate.

On 400 and 440 V8s, install the washer and camshaft sprocket lockbolt and then torque the lockbolt to 35 ft. lbs. through 1972, 50

ft. lbs. 1973 and later. Check to make sure that the rear face of the camshaft sprocket is flush with the camshaft end.

Timing Cover Seal Replacement
NOTE: *A seal remover and installer tool is required to prevent seal damage.*
1. Using a seal puller, separate the seal from the retainer.
2. Pull the seal from the case.
3. To install the seal place it face down in the case with the seal lips downward.
4. Seat the seal tightly against the cover face. There should be a maximum clearance of .0014 in. between the seal and the cover. Be careful not to overcompress the seal.

Camshaft Removal and Installation
NOTE: *Whenever a new camshaft and/or new tappets are installed, the manufacturer recommends that one qt of their crankcase conditioner, or equivalent, be added to the engine oil to aid break-in. This oil mixture should be left in the engine for a minimum of 500 miles.*
The manufacturer recommends that the engine be removed from the vehicle before removing the camshaft. However, in some cases it may be possible to remove the camshaft from the engine with the engine still in the car by removing the radiator and grille and sliding the camshaft out through the front of the vehicle.

6 CYLINDER
1. Remove the cylinder head, timing gear cover, camshaft sprocket, and timing chain.
2. Remove the valve tappets, keeping them in order to ensure installation in their original location.
3. Remove the crankshaft sprocket.
4. Remove the distributor and the oil pump.
5. Remove the fuel pump.
6. Fit a long bolt into the front of the camshaft to facilitate camshaft removal.
7. Remove the camshaft, being careful not to damage the cam bearings with the cam lobes.
8. Lubricate the camshaft lobes and bearing journals with camshaft lu-

bricant. Insert the camshaft into the engine block.
9. Install the fuel pump and oil pump.
10. Install the distributor. (Refer to the ''Distributor Installation'' procedure.)
11. Inspect the crowns of all the tappet faces with a straightedge. Replace any tappets that have dished or worn surfaces. Install the tappets.
12. Replace the timing chain and timing gear cover.

V8
1. Remove the valve covers, intake manifold, timing gear cover, camshaft and crankshaft sprocket, and the timing chain.
2. Remove the pushrods and valve tappets, keeping them in order to ensure installation in their original location.
3. Remove the distributor and lift out the oil pump and distributor driveshaft.
4. Remove the camshaft thrust plate (318, 340, 360). Note the location of the oil tab.
5. Fit a long bolt into the front of the camshaft and remove the camshaft, being careful not to damage the cam bearings with the cam lobes.
6. Lubricate the camshaft lobes and bearing journals with camshaft lubricant. Insert the camshaft into the engine block within 2 in. of its final position in the block.
7. Have an assistant support the camshaft with a screwdriver to prevent the camshaft from contacting the plug in the rear of the engine block. Remove the distributor and the oil pump/distributor drive gear. Position the screwdriver against the rear side of the cam gear and be careful not to damage the cam lobes.
8. Replace the camshaft thrust plate. Make sure the tang is in the lower right hole in the plate. The top edge of the chain oil tab must be flat against the plate. If camshaft end play exceeds 0.010 in., install a new thrust plate. Play should be 0.002-0.006 in. with the new plate.
9. Install the oil pump and the distributor driveshaft. Install the distributor. (Refer to the ''Distributor Installation'' procedure.)
10. Inspect the crown of all the tappet

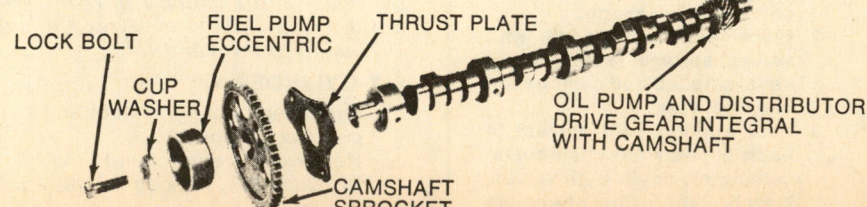

LOCK BOLT
CUP WASHER
FUEL PUMP ECCENTRIC
THRUST PLATE
CAMSHAFT SPROCKET
OIL PUMP AND DISTRIBUTOR DRIVE GEAR INTEGRAL WITH CAMSHAFT

Camshaft and sprocket assembly—V8 through 360 cu. in.
(© Chrysler Corp)

faces with a straightedge. Replace any tappets that have dished or worn surfaces. Install the tappets.

11. Install the timing chain, cover, and cylinder heads.

PISTONS AND CONNECTING RODS

For all models the notch on the top of each piston must face the front of the engine.

To position the connecting rod correctly, the oil squirt hole should point to the right-side on all six-cylinder engines except those with cast iron crankshafts; the hole should face forward on those engines. On all V8 engines the larger chamfer of the lower connecting rod bore must face toward the crankpin journal fillet (toward the front on the left bank and toward the rear on the right bank).

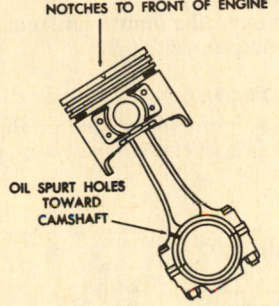

Piston and connecting rod assembly — six cyl. through 1977

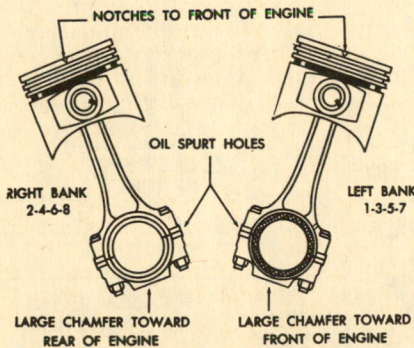

V8 piston and connecting rod assembly

ENGINE LUBRICATION

Oil Pan Removal and Installation

SLANT SIX——DART, VALIANT, ASPEN, VOLARE, DIPLOMAT, LEBARON

1. Disconnect the battery and drain the radiator. Disconnect the upper and lower radiator hoses, and remove the oil dipstick.
2. Remove the radiator shroud attaching screws and position it rearward on the engine.
3. Jack up the vehicle and drain the

oil. Remove the engine-to-transmission bracket, the exhaust pipe, and the torque converter inspection shield with automatic transmission.

4. Remove the steering center link from the steering and idler arms.
5. Position a jack stand at the right front corner of the engine oil pan. Be sure not to support the engine at the crankshaft pulley or vibration damper.
6. Remove the front engine mount bolts. Raise the engine about 1½-2 in.
7. Remove the oil pan bolts, rotate the engine crankshaft to clear the counterweights, and remove the oil pan.
8. Using a new pan gasket set, apply sealer to the four junctions of the gaskets, install the oil pan and torque it to 200 in lbs. Make sure the pickup screen contacts the bottom of the pan.
9. Lower the engine into its original position and install the front engine mount bolts. Torque to specifications.
10. Connect the steering and idler arms to the center link. Torque to specification; be sure to install the cotter pins. Install the torque converter cover, exhaust pipe, and support bracket.
11. If removed, install the radiator hoses and replace the fan shroud.
12. Fill the cooling system, install the dipstick, replace the oil, and check for leaks. Connect the battery and start the vehicle. Run for five minutes with the heater on, then check again for leaks.

SLANT SIX—BARRACUDA AND CHALLENGER

1. Disconnect the battery and remove the oil dipstick. Jack up the vehicle and drain the oil.

2. Remove the steering center link with the idler arm attached.
3. Disconnect the exhaust pipe from its manifold and secure it out of the way.
4. Remove the oil pan attaching bolts. Rotate the engine crankshaft in order to clear the counterweights. Remove the oil pan.
5. To install the oil pan, reverse the removal procedure. Torque the pan bolts to 200 in. lbs.

318, 340, AND 360 V8—ALL MODELS

1. Disconnect the battery and remove the dipstick.
2. Jack up the vehicle and drain the oil. If so equipped, remove the torque converter-to-engine left housing strut.
3. Disconnect the steering center link from the steering and idler arms.
4. Disconnect the exhaust pipes from the manifolds and secure them out of the way. On Aspens, Volares, Diplomats, LeBarons, and Chryslers, remove the starter, and the torque converter inspection plate if equipped with automatic transmission.
5. Visually check to see if there is sufficient clearance to reach all of the oil pan bolts. If there is not, it will be necessary to raise the engine about 1½-2 in. Do this by loosening the motor mounts and jacking or hoisting the engine until the bolts become accessible. Be sure to raise the engine only the minimum amount necessary to reach these bolts. Remove the distributor cap for clearance. Remove the oil pan bolts, rotate the engine crankshaft to clear the counterweights, and remove the pan with a twisting motion. On 1976 and later models, unbolt the transmission mount and raise the transmission

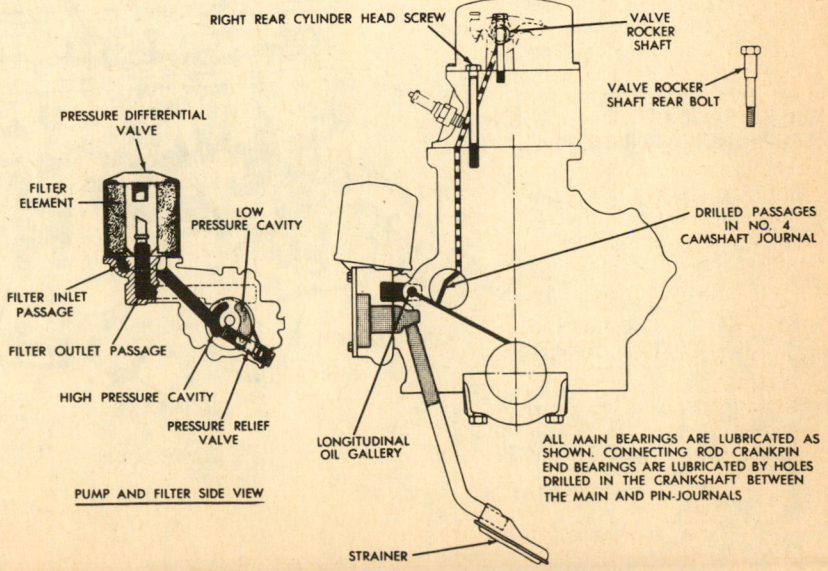

Six-cylinder lubrication system (© Chrysler Corp.)

till the pan clears. On 1975 and later 360 HP engines, raise first the transmission to clear the rear of the pan, then the front of the engine to remove the pan.

6. When installing the oil pan, be sure that the oil strainer will be parallel with and will contact the pan bottom. Use a new gasket and apply sealer to the junctions of the cork and rubber gaskets. The side gaskets should overlap the rear seal. On 360s, be sure the notches in the side gaskets are at the rear. Torque the pan bolts to 200 in. lbs.

7. If it was necessary to jack the engine from its mounts, return it to its proper position at this time. Tighten the engine mount bolts.

8. Install the engine-to-converter housing strut (if so equipped).

9. From this point, reverse the removal procedure.

400 AND 440 V8

1. Disconnect the battery and remove the dipstick.

2. Jack up the vehicle and remove the center steering link from the steering and idler arms.

3. Disconnect the exhaust pipes from the manifolds and secure them out of the way.

4. If there is not sufficient clearance for the oil pan to clear the exhaust pipe, remove the clamp attaching the exhaust pipe to the extension and remove the exhaust pipe.

5. Drain the oil.

6. Remove the dust shield from the torque converter.

7. Extract the oil pan bolts. On some models, it may be necessary to jack the engine off its mounts (1½-2 in.) to reach the oil pan bolts. Do this by loosening the motor mounts and jacking or hoisting the engine. Raise the engine only the minimum amount required to reach the bolts. When removing the oil pan, be sure to rotate the crankshaft to clear the counterweights. Remove the pan with a twisting motion.

8. When installing the oil pan, be sure to use a new gasket. Torque the pan bolts to 200 in. lbs.

9. If it was necessary to jack the engine, lower it now and torque the engine mounts to specifications. To proceed, reverse the order of removal. After completion, be sure to start the vehicle and idle for at least five minutes. Check for leaks.

Oil Pump Removal and Installation

NOTE: *Prime the oil pump before installation by filling it with engine oil.*

SIX CYLINDER

1. Drain radiator, disconnect upper and lower hoses, and remove fan shroud.

2. Raise vehicle on hoist, support front of engine with jack stand placed under right front corner of oil pan, and remove engine mount bolts. Do not support engine at crankshaft pulley or vibration damper.

3. Raise engine approximately 1½-2 in.

4. Remove oil filter, oil pump attaching bolts, and pump assembly.

318, 340, AND 360 V8

1. Remove oil pan.

2. Remove oil pump from rear main bearing cap.

400 AND 440 V8

1. The oil pump is located on the bottom side of the engine block at the filter.

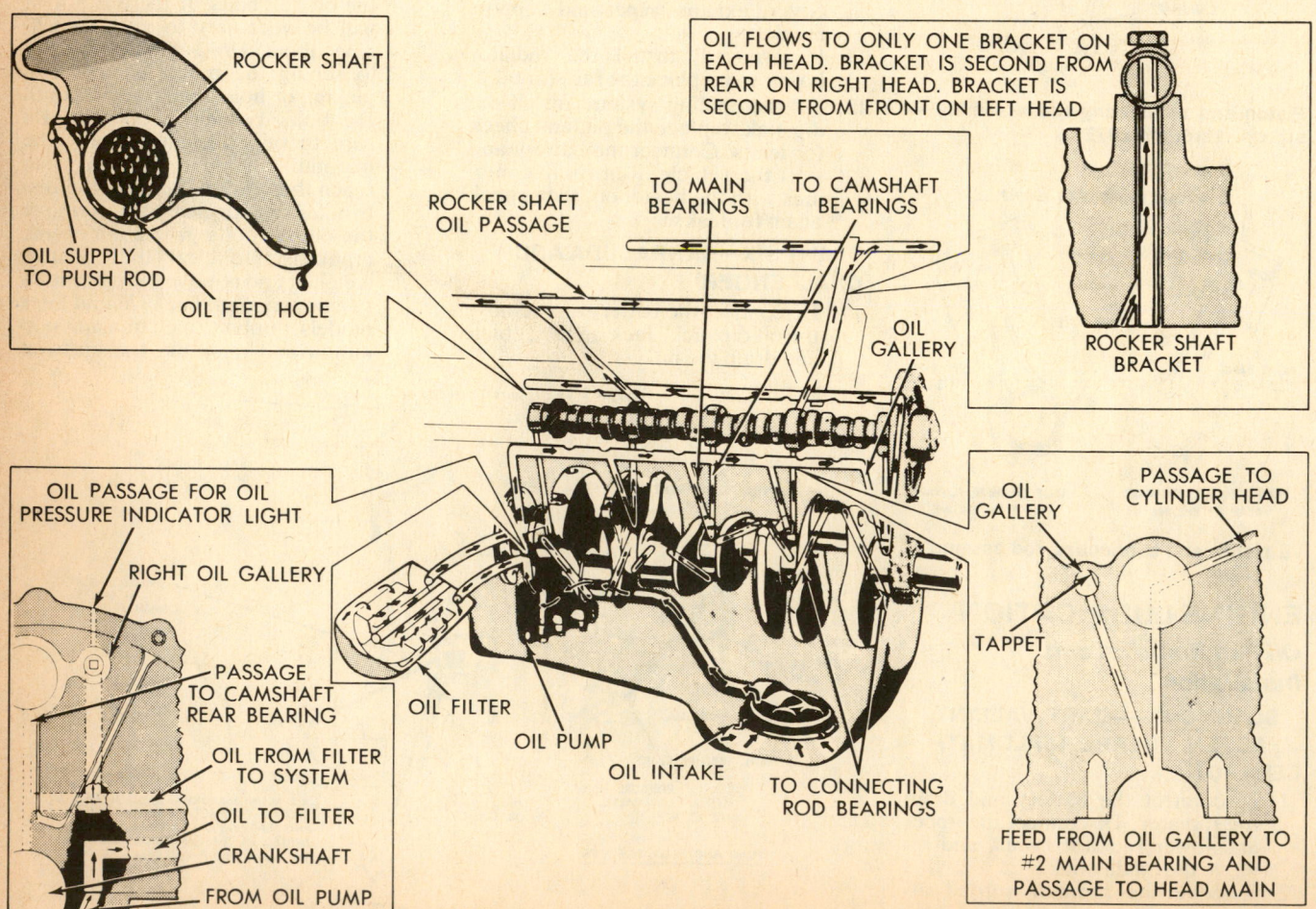

V8 (through 360 cu. in.) Lubrication system (© Chrysler Corp.)

2. Removal consists of taking out the attaching bolts and removing the pump and filter as an assembly.
3. To install the pump, reverse the removal procedure.

Rear Main Bearing Oil Seal Replacement

Service replacement seals are of split rubber type composition. This type of seal makes it possible to replace the upper half of the rear main oil seal without removing the engine from the car, or the crankshaft from the engine. When installing rubber seals, they must be replaced as a set and cannot be combined with the rope type rear main seal. The following procedure is for removing the rope type seal and replacing it with the rubber type seal.

1. Remove the oil pan.
2. Remove the rear seal retainer and the rear main bearing cap.
3. Remove the lower rope seal by prying from the side with a small screwdriver.
4. To remove the upper rope seal, drive up on either exposed end of the seal with a 6 in. piece of $3/16$ in. brazing rod. When the opposite end of the seal starts to protrude from the block, have an assistant grasp it with pliers and gently pull it from the block while the opposite end is being driven. There are also screw type extractor tools available.
5. Wipe crankshaft clean and lightly oil crankshaft and new seal before installing seal.
6. If necessary, loosen all main bearing caps slightly to lower the crankshaft which will ease installation.

CAUTION

Do not allow the crankshaft to drop enough to permit the main bearings to become displaced on the crankshaft.

---

7. Hold the seal tightly against the crankshaft with the thumb (with paint stripe to the rear) and install the seal in the block groove. Rotate the crankshaft if necessary while installing the seal in the groove. *Make sure the sharp edges on the block groove do not cut or nick the rear of the seal.*
8. Install lower half of seal (with paint stripe to the rear) into the lower seal retainer. On 318s only, insert the cap seals into the slots in the bearing cap; the one with the yellow paint goes on the right side. Be sure the narrow edge is facing up. Pull outward on the small end of the seal until its edge lines up with the shoulder. On 360s only, apply a dot of sealer to the main bearing cap surface adjacent to the seal. Do not use sealer on any other engine. On all engines, lightly oil the seal lips before installation.
9. Install rear main bearing cap.

10. Tighten all main bearing caps to specification.

NOTE: *Make sure all main bearings are located in their proper position before tightening the main bearing caps.*

CLUTCH

All models utilize a single, dry plate clutch operated by a pedal suspended under the dash. All models are equipped with a return spring; some models have centrifugal rollers assembled between the pressure plate and cover.

NOTE: *It is normal for the centrifugal rollers to rattle before the cover is installed.*

Removal

1. Remove the transmission.
2. Remove the clutch housing pan.
3. Disconnect the fork return spring from the clutch housing and release fork.
4. Remove the spring washer fastening the fork rod to the torque shaft lever pin. Remove the pin from the rod and release fork.
5. On models with the A-903 or A-250 three-speed transmission, remove the clip and plain washer securing the interlock rod to the torque shaft lever and remove the washers and rod from the torque shaft.
6. Remove the sleeve assembly and clutch release bearing from the clutch release fork.

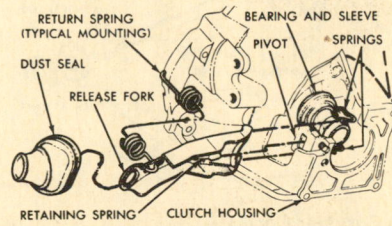

Clutch release fork, bearing and sleeve (© Chrysler Corp)

7. Punch-mark the clutch cover and flywheel so they may be installed in the same relative positions.
8. Loosen the clutch cover attaching screws one or two turns at a time, in rotation, to avoid bending the cover.
9. Remove the clutch assembly. Be careful not to contaminate the clutch with grease or oil.

Installation

1. Lightly lubricate the drive pinion bushing in the end of the crankshaft. Use about $1/2$ teaspoonful of long-life chassis grease. Lubricant should be inserted in the cavity in front of the bushing.
2. Thoroughly clean the surfaces of the flywheel and pressure plate with fine sandpaper. All oil or grease must be removed at this time.
3. Position the clutch disc, pressure plate, and cover in the mounting position. Springs on disc damper must be facing away from the flywheel. Do not touch the disc facing at any time. Insert a clutch disc aligning arbor or suitable substitute (such as a spare transmission input shaft) through the disc hub and into the bushing.
4. Align the punch marks that were made at removal. Install the clutch cover bolts but do not tighten them.
5. Tighten all bolts a few turns at a time in an alternate sequence. Torque $5/16$ in. bolts to 17 ft lbs and $3/8$ in. bolts to 30 ft lbs. Remove the alignment tool.

NOTE: *11 in. clutches don't use lockwashers on the bolts.*

6. Pack the release bearing sleeve cavity with high temperature grease. Apply the same lubricant to the release fork pads on the sleeve.
7. Insert the release bearing and sleeve assembly into the clutch housing as far forward as possible. Lightly lubricate the fork fingers and retaining spring.
8. Insert the fork fingers under the

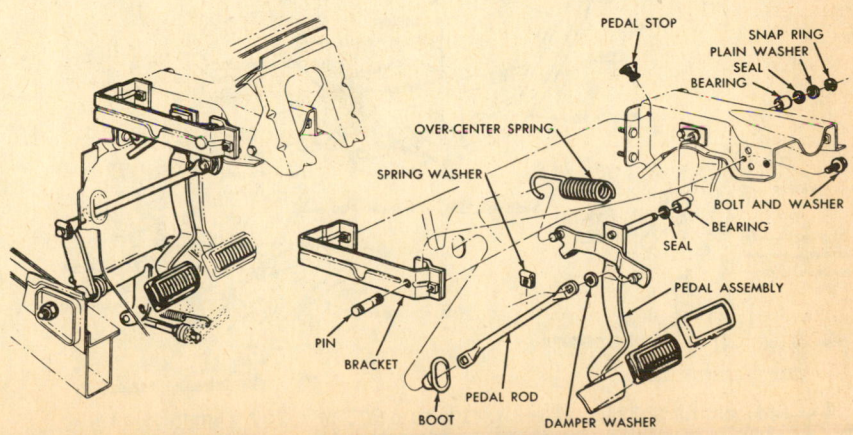

Typical clutch pedal and linkage (© Chrysler Corp)

clutch sleeve retaining springs. Retaining springs on the sleeve must have lateral freedom.

9. Make sure that the groove in the seal is properly seated in the seal opening flange in the clutch housing. Replace the pedal rod on the torque shaft lever pin and secure it with a spring washer.

10. Insert the threaded end of the fork rod assembly in the opening provided in the end of the release fork rod. Replace the eye end of the fork rod on the torque shaft lever pin and lock it with a spring washer.

11. If applicable, install the fork return spring between the release fork and the clutch housing.

12. With the A-903 or A-250 transmission install the spring and plain washer with interlock rod in the torque shaft lever and lock it in position with a washer and clip.

13. When installing the transmission, be sure not to allow grease to get on the splines or pilot end of the transmission drive pinion.

14. Install the transmission and adjust the clutch pedal free-play.

Linkage Free-Play Adjustment

1. If the vehicle is equipped with a gearshift interlock rod (A-903 or A-250 transmission), disconnect it by loosening the rod swivel clamp screw.

2. Adjust the fork rod by rotating the self-locking nut to provide $5/32$ in. free-play at the fork end. This adjustment will result in the proper 1 in. free-play at the clutch pedal.

3. Adjust the A-903 or A-250 gearshift interlock.

Gearshift Interlock Adjustment, Six Cylinder with A-903 or A-250 Transmission

This type of transmission has an external interlock to prevent the clutch from being engaged if two transmission gears are engaged at once.

1. Disconnect the interlock pawl from the clutch rod swivel on the side of the transmission.

2. Adjust the clutch pedal free-play.

3. With the first-reverse lever on the transmission in the neutral (middle detent) position, the interlock pawl should enter the slot in the first-reverse lever.

4. Loosen the swivel clamp bolt and move the swivel on the rod to enter the pawl. Install the washers with a clip. Hold the interlock pawl forward and torque the swivel clamp bolt to 100-125 in. lbs. The clutch pedal must be in the fully returned position during this adjustment.

NOTE: *Under no circumstances should the clutch rod be pulled rearward to engage the pawl swivel.*

5. Shift the clutch through all gear positions at least three times. Clutch action should be normal.

6. Disengage the clutch and shift halfway to first or reverse gear. The clutch pedal should be held down by the interlock to within 1-2 in. of the floor.

MANUAL TRANSMISSION

Manual transmission applications are as follows: a top cover three-speed A-903 with synchromesh on second and third gears only used on 6-cylinder models through 1972; a top cover three-speed A-250 with synchromesh on second and third gears only used on 1973-74 6-cylinder models; a side cover fully synchronized three-speed A-230 used on V8 and 6-cylinder models; a top cover fully synchronized three-speed A-390 used on 1975-76 6-cylinder models; a side cover fully synchronized four-speed A-833 transmission. The A-833 transmission was offered with V8s only through 1975, and with both sixes and V8s with an overdrive fourth gear beginning 1976.

All manual transmissions have a serial number stamped on a pad on the right side of the case. The third, fourth, and fifth digits are the transmission model number.

NOTE: *The A-390 transmission is drained by removing the lower extension housing to case bolt.*

Removal and Installation

1. Raise and support the car safely.

2. Remove the shift rods and the clutch interlock rod (A-903 and A-250 only) from the transmission levers.

3. After marking both parts for reassembly, detach the driveshaft and the rear universal joint.

— CAUTION —

Don't nick or scratch the ground surface on the sliding spline yoke.

4. Disconnect the speedometer cable, transmission controlled spark

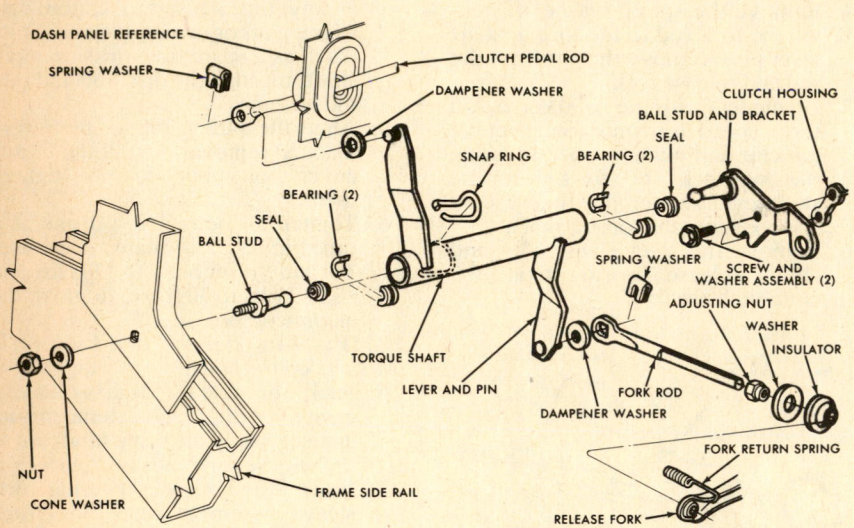

Typical clutch linkage (© Chrysler Corp.)

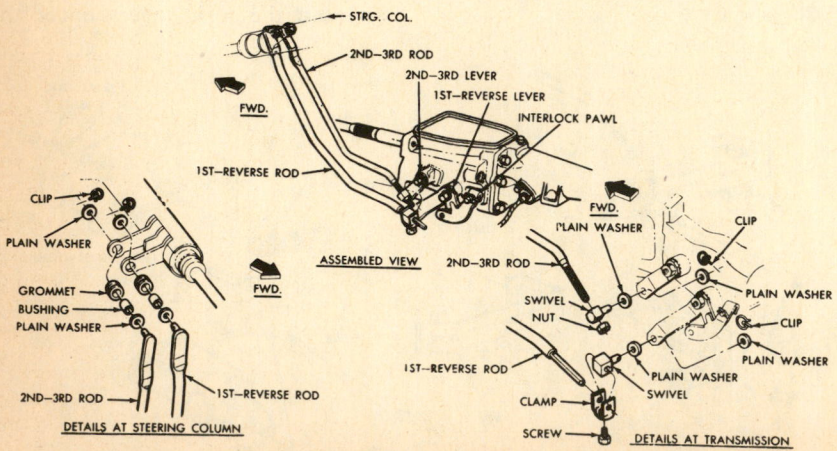

3-speed column shift linkage—sixes with A-903 or A-250 transmission with clutch/gearshift interlock
(© Chrysler Corp)

switch, and back-up light switch. Remove the console, if necessary, and unbolt the shifter from the extension housing on floor-shift models. The shift lever unbolts from the shifter, except on 1976 and later Overdrive—4 models. On these, insert a 0.014 in. feeler gauge alongside the driver's side of the lever and pull the lever out.

5. Unfasten the transmission extension housing from the center crossmember and jack up the engine and transmission about 1 in.

6. Remove the center crossmember.

7. On some models it may be necessary to disconnect or loosen the exhaust system and position it to one side to gain clearance in order to remove the transmission.

8. Support the transmission on a jack. Remove the bolts which secure the transmission to the clutch housing.

9. Slide the transmission toward the rear until the input shaft clears the clutch disc. Lower the transmission and remove it from the car.

10. Installation is the reverse of removal. Lubricate the input shaft pilot bearing in the flywheel and the bearing retainer pilot (for the clutch release sleeve). Do not lubricate the clutch splines or the clutch release levers.

11. Position the transmission so that the drive pinion is centered in the clutch housing bore. Push the transmission forward until the pinion shaft enters the clutch disc. Place the transmission in gear. Twist the output shaft until the splines are in alignment. Push the transmission forward until it is seated against the clutch housing.

——— CAUTION ———

The transmission must not hang after the pinion is inside the clutch.

12. Replace the transmission housing bolts. Torque them to 50 ft lbs. With a drift, align the crossmember bolt holes and install the bolts. Torque them to 40-50 ft lbs. Remove the engine support fixture. Tighten the engine mount-to-crossmember bolt. Install and perform the gearshift linkage adjustment. Connect the driveshaft and universal joints. Connect the exhaust system and fill the transmission with lubricant.

Linkage Adjustment
COLUMN SHIFT THROUGH 1974

1. Loosen both shift rod swivels at the ends of the two long rods from the column. Be sure that the transmission shift levers are in the neutral (middle) positions.

2. Move the column shift lever into reverse to line up the locating slots in the bottom of the steering column shift housing and the bearing

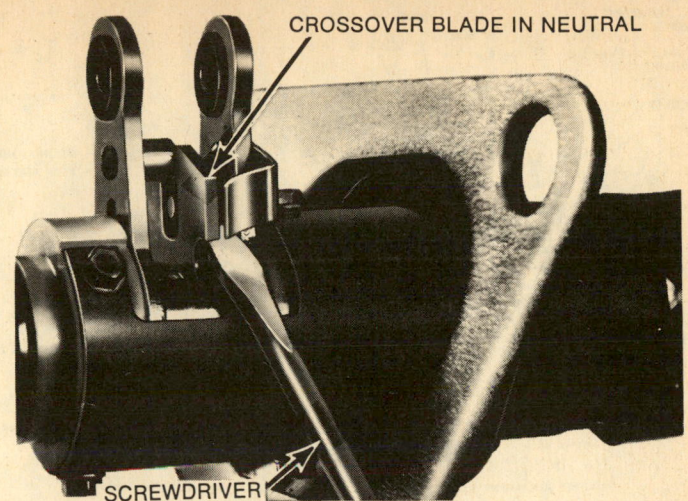

CROSSOVER BLADE IN NEUTRAL

SCREWDRIVER

Holding cross-over blades in neutral (© Chrysler Corp)

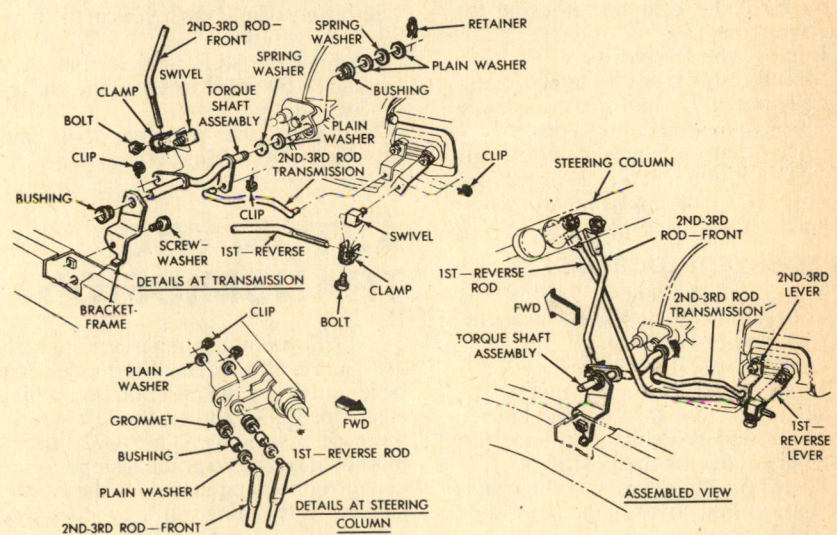

Typical three-speed column shift linkage (© Chrysler Corp)

housing. Place a tool in the slot to hold the lever in place.

3. Place a screwdriver between the crossover blade (between the two column levers) and the second-third lever (the top one) at the steering column so that both lever pins are engaged by the cross-over blade.

4. Set the first-reverse lever (the back one) on the transmission to the reverse position (rotate it clockwise).

5. Adjust the first-reverse rod swivel by sliding the swivel along the rod. Tighten the swivel bolt.

6. Remove the gearshift housing locating tool and shift the column lever into the neutral position.

7. Adjust the second-third rod swivel by sliding the swivel along the rod. Tighten the swivel bolt.

8. Remove the screwdriver from the crossover blade at the steering column, and shift through all gears to check adjustment and cross-over (through neutral) smoothness.

9. Check that the ignition switch will lock with the shift lever in reverse only, without applying pressure to the shift lever.

1975 AND LATER COLUMN SHIFT

1. Loosen both shift rod swivels at the ends of the two long rods from the column.

2. Make sure the transmission levers are in the neutral or middle positions.

3. Move the column shift lever into neutral to line up the locating slots in the bottom of the steering column shift housing and the bearing housing. Install a tool into the slot to hold the lever in place.

4. Place a screwdriver between the crossover blade (between the two column levers) and the second-third (the upper one) lever so that both lever pins are engaged by the crossover blade.

5. Tighten both swivel bolts.

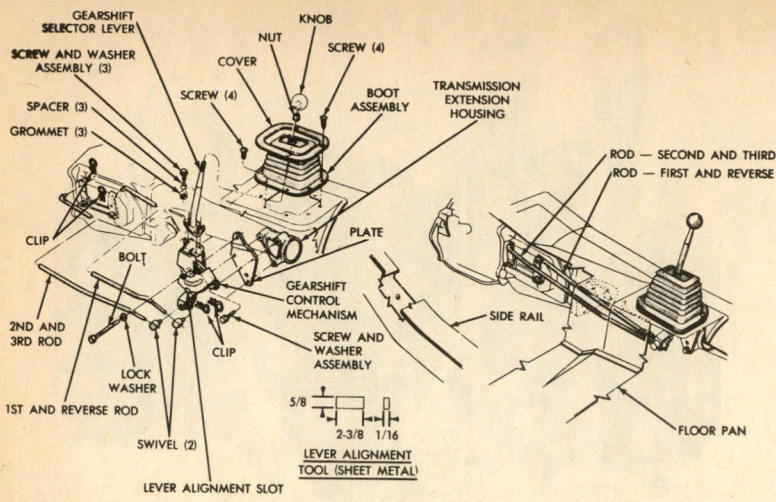

Three-speed floor shift linkage—Barracuda and Challenger; Valiant and Dart similar (© Chrysler Corp)

6. Remove the gearshift housing locating tool.
7. Remove the screwdriver.
8. Shift through all gears to check the adjustment and cross-over (through neutral) smoothness.
9. Check that the ignition switch will lock with the shift lever in reverse only, without applying any pressure to the shift lever.

THREE-SPEED FLOORSHIFT

1. Make an alignment tool out of $1/16$ in. thick metal. It should be $5/8$ in. wide and $2^3/8$ in. long.
2. Detach the shift rod swivels.
3. From under the car, insert the alignment tool through the shifter levers and the shifter to hold the levers in the neutral positions.
4. Place both shift levers on the transmission side cover in the neutral or middle position.
5. Adjust the swivels so that they can be installed freely in the shifter lever holes.
6. Remove the alignment tool and check the shifting action.

FOUR-SPEED FLOORSHIFT

1. Remove all the shift rods from the transmission shift levers.
2. Place all the transmission shift levers in their neutral positions.
3. From under the car, insert a $1/4$ in. rod or drill bit about $2^1/4$ in. long through the shifter levers and the

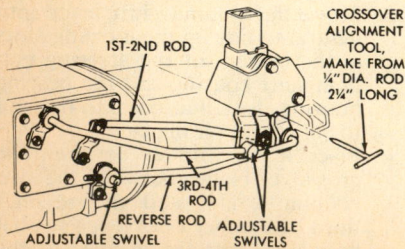

Four-speed shift linkage adjustment (© Chrysler Corp)

shifter to hold the levers in the neutral positions.
4. Adjust the shift rods so that they can be installed freely in the shifter lever holes.
5. Remove the aligning tool and check the shifting action.

AUTOMATIC TRANSMISSION

Two different transmission models are used in all models. The model may be identified by the part number, which is stamped on a pad on the left side of the case pan flange. The A-727 transmission has a more gradual slope to the converter housing than does the A-904. Generally speaking, all 6 cylinder and 318 V8 engines for normal use are equipped with a model A-904 Torqueflite, while all larger V8s use the model A-727. Starting 1976, most V8s use an A-904 LA transmission, which includes slight internal modifications in the number of clutch plates and discs for added strength. However, all adjustments are the same as for the A-904. Fleet, police, and taxi service 6 cylinder and 318 V8 engines use the A-727 also.

Neutral Safety/Backup Light Switch Replacement

The neutral safety switch is mounted in the transmission case. When the gearshift lever is placed in either the Park or Neutral position, a cam, which is attached to the transmission lever inside the transmission, contacts the neutral safety switch and provides a ground to complete the starter solenoid circuit.

The back-up lamp switch is incorporated into the neutral safety switch. The center terminal is for the neutral safety switch and the two outer terminals are for the back-up lamps.

There is no adjustment for the switch. If a malfunction occurs, first check to make sure that the transmission gearshift linkage is properly adjusted. If the malfunction continues, the switch must be removed and replaced.

To remove the switch, disconnect the electrical leads and unscrew the switch from the transmission. Use a drain pan to catch the transmission fluid that drains out of the mounting hole. Install a new seal and refill the transmission to the proper level.

Shift Linkage Adjustment

1. Under the car, loosen the adjustable rod swivel lock bolt.
2. Put the floorshift or column shift lever into Park.
3. Move the transmission shift lever all the way to the rear.
4. Tighten the swivel lock bolt without putting any pressure on the linkage.

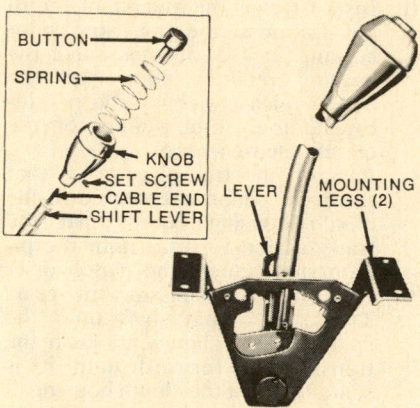

Automatic console shift unit disassembled (© Chrysler Corp)

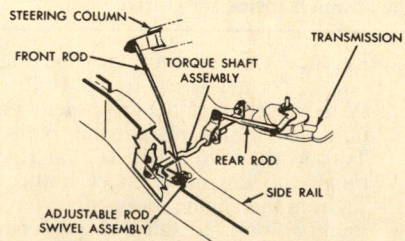

Column shift linkage—Barracuda and Challenger (© Chrysler Corp)

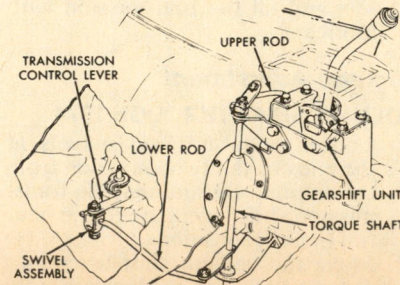

Typical automatic console shift linkage (© Chrysler Corp)

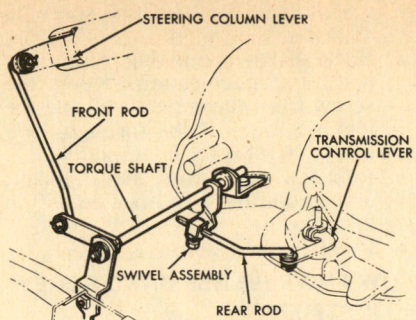

Typical automatic column shift linkage
(© Chrysler Corp)

5. The shift effort must be free and the detents should feel crisp. All gate stops must be positive. It should be possible to start the engine in Park and Neutral only.

Throttle Rod Adjustment

1972-73 Six Cylinder

1. Disconnect the choke or block the choke fully open. Open the throttle to release the fast idle cam, then allow the throttle to close to curb idle.
2. Have an assistant hold the transmission lever fully forward against its stop. It must remain firmly against the stop throughout the adjustment.
3. Loosen the lock bolt on the slotted link at the carburetor. Pull the link fully forward to remove all slack.
4. Tighten the lock bolt to 100 in. lbs.
5. Have your assistant release the throttle lever. Check for free linkage movement by pushing the slotted link fully rearward, then allowing it to return slowly. It should return to the full forward position.
6. Reconnect or unblock the choke.

1974-79 All

1. Follow Steps 1 and 2 of the 1972-73 6 cyl. procedure.
2. Adjustment is made at the adjustable swivel on the transmission throttle lever. Loosen the swivel lock bolt and make sure the swivel is able to slide freely on the throttle rod. With the throttle lever fully forward, tighten the swivel bolt to 100 in. lbs.
3. Follow Steps 5 and 6 of the 6 cyl. procedure

1972-73 V8 WITH 3 PIECE THROTTLE ROD

1. Follow Steps 1 and 2 of the 6 cyl. procedure.
2. Insert a 3/16 in. diameter rod (1) into the holes in the upper bell-crank and lever (2). Thread the ball socket (3) up or down to align it with the ball end when a slight downward push is applied to the intermediate rod (4). Make sure the throttle lever is fully forward.
3. Slip the socket over the ball end

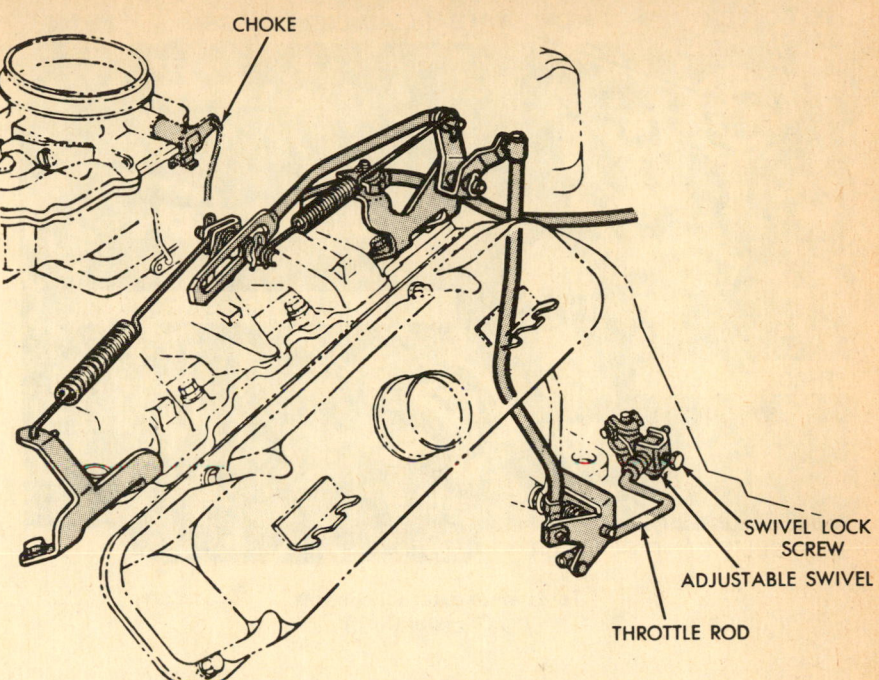

1974 and later V8 throttle rod adjustment — 6 cyl. similar (© Chrysler Corp)

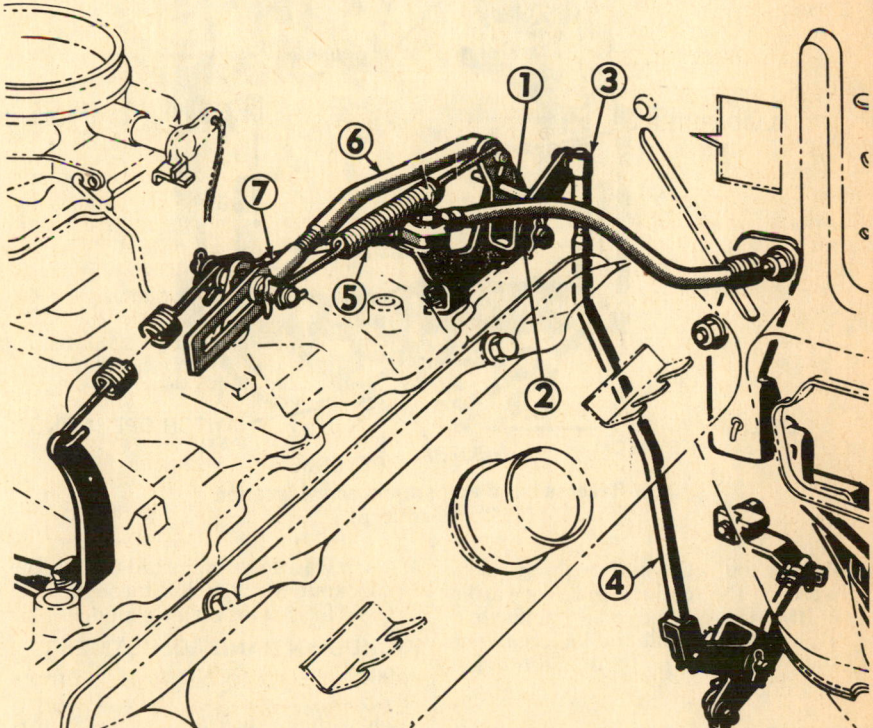

1972-73 three piece throttle rod adjustment (© Chrysler Corp)

and remove the rod.
4. Disconnect the return spring (5), clip and washer. Adjust the carburetor rod (6) length, while pushing it slightly rearward to remove backlash, by turning the threaded adjustment (7), so that the rear end of the slot contacts the carburetor throttle lever pin. When the slotted link is in its normal position it should exert no force on the pin.

5. Reassemble the clip, washer, and spring. Follow Steps 5 and 6 of the 6 cyl. procedure.

1972-73 V8 WITH 1 PIECE THROTTLE ROD

1. Follow Steps 1 and 2 of the 6 cyl. procedure.
2. Loosen the transmission throttle rod lock bolt at the rear of the carburetor linkage.

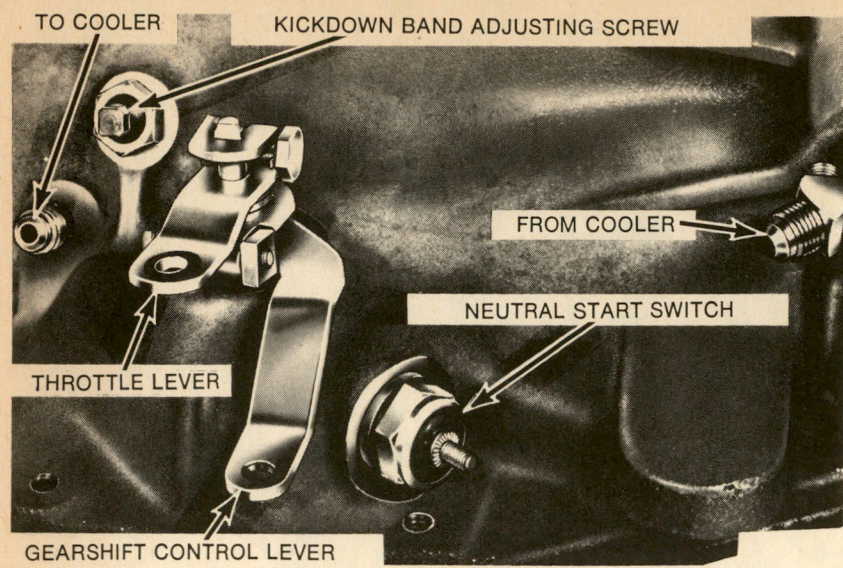

Torqueflite external controls
(© Chrysler Corp)

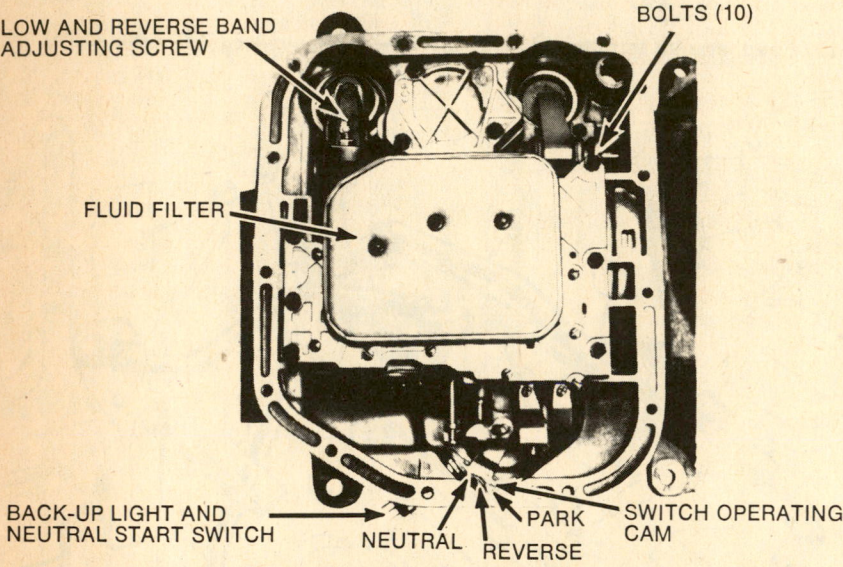

Low-Reverse band adjustment screw location
(© Chrysler Corp)

gine, torque the adjusting screw to 41 in lbs.

4. Back off the adjusting screw exactly to specification. Keep the screw from turning and torque the locknut to 35 ft lbs through 1973 and to 30 ft lbs for later models.

5. Reinstall pan, using new gasket, and torque the pan bolts to 150 in lbs.

6. Refill transmission.

LOW AND REVERSE BAND SCREW ADJUSTMENT

A-904	
Six (through 1973)	3½ turns
Six (1974 and later)	7 turns
318, 360 V8	4 turns
A-727	2 turns

Pan Removal and Installation, Fluid and Filter Change

1. Drive the car until it is thoroughly warm.

2. Unbolt the pan. Be ready with a large container.

NOTE: *If the fluid removed smells burnt, serious transmission troubles, probably due to overheating should be suspected.*

3. Remove the access plate in front of the torque converter. With the aid of a socket wrench on the vibration damper bolt, rotate the engine clockwise to bring the converter drain to the bottom. Position the container under the converter, remove the drain plug, and allow the fluid to drain.

Replace the converter drain plug and torque it to 110 in lbs for a $^7/_{16}$ in. head plug and 90 in lbs for a $^5/_{16}$ in. plug.

Install the access plate.

NOTE: *Starting January 1977, the torque converter no longer has a drain plug.*

4. Unscrew and discard the filter.

5. Install a new filter. The proper torque is 35 in lbs.

6. Clean out the pan, being extremely careful not to leave any lint from rags inside.

7. Replace the pan with a new gasket. Tighten the bolts to 150 in lbs in a crisscross pattern.

8. Pour six quarts (four qts. if the converter wasn't drained) of DEXRON® automatic transmission fluid through the dipstick tube.

9. Start the engine in Neutral and let it idle for two minutes or more.

10. Hold your foot on the Brake and shift through D, 2, 1, and R and back to N.

11. Add enough fluid to bring the level to the ADD ONE PINT mark.

12. Operate the car until the transmission is thoroughly warmed up, then check the level. Engage the parking brake and place the selector lever in the Neutral position. After the engine has idled for about two minutes, move the selector lever slowly through all the gear posi-

3. Adjust the rod while pushing forward on the retainer and rearward on the rod to remove all backlash. Tighten the throttle rod lock bolt.

4. Follow Steps 5 and 6 of the 6 cyl. procedure.

Band Adjustments

KICKDOWN BAND

The kickdown band adjusting screw is located on the left-hand side of the transmission case near the throttle lever shaft.

1. Loosen the locknut and back off about five turns. Be sure the adjusting screw is free in the case.

2. Torque the adjusting screw to 72 in lbs.

3. Back off the adjusting screw exactly to specification. Keep the

screw from turning, and tighten the locknut to 29 ft lbs through 1973 and to 35 ft lbs on later models.

KICKDOWN BAND ADJUSTMENT

A-904	2 turns
A-727	2½ turns
440 w/dual exhaust	2 turns

LOW AND REVERSE BAND

Access to the low and reverse band requires pan removal.

1. Raise the car, drain transmission and remove the transmission pan.

2. Loosen the band adjusting screw locknut and back it off about five turns. Be sure the adjusting screw turns freely in the lever.

3. Tighten the adjusting screw to 72 in lbs. On 1974 and later A-904 transmissions with a six-cylinder en-

tions, pausing momentarily in each and ending with the lever in the Neutral position. When the fluid is hot, the fluid level should be at the FULL mark, or slightly below. Add fluid as necessary.

U-JOINTS

The driveshaft is a one-piece tubular shaft with two universal joints, one at each end. The front joint yoke serves as a slip yoke on the transmission output shaft. The rear universal joint is the type that must be disassembled to be removed. See the Chrysler Section for an illustration of these parts.

DRIVESHAFT AND U-JOINTS

Removal and Installation

You can avoid loss of lubricant from the rear of the transmission by raising the rear of the car before removing the driveshaft.

1. Match mark the driveshaft, U-joint and pinion flange before disassembly. These marks must be realigned during reassembly to maintain the balance of the driveline. Failure to align them may result in excessive vibration.
2. Remove both of the clamps from the differential pinion yoke and slide the driveshaft forward slightly to disengage the U-joint from the pinion yoke. Tape the two loose U-joint bearings together to prevent them from falling off.

──────── CAUTION ────────

Do not disturb the bearing assembly retaining strap. Never allow the driveshaft to hang from either of the U-joints. Always support the unattached end of the shaft to prevent damage to the joints.

3. Lower the rear end of the driveshaft and gently slide the front yoke/driveshaft assembly rearward disengaging the assembly from the transmission output shaft. Be careful not to damage the splines or the surface which the output shaft seal rides on.
4. Check the transmission output shaft seal for signs of leakage.
5. Installation is the reverse of removal. Be sure to align the match marks. The torque for the clamp bolts is 14 ft lbs.

U-Joint Overhaul

1. Remove the driveshaft.
2. To remove the bearings from the yoke, first remove the bearing retainer snap rings located at the base or open end of each bearing cap.
3. Pressing on one of the bearings, drive the bearing in toward the cen-

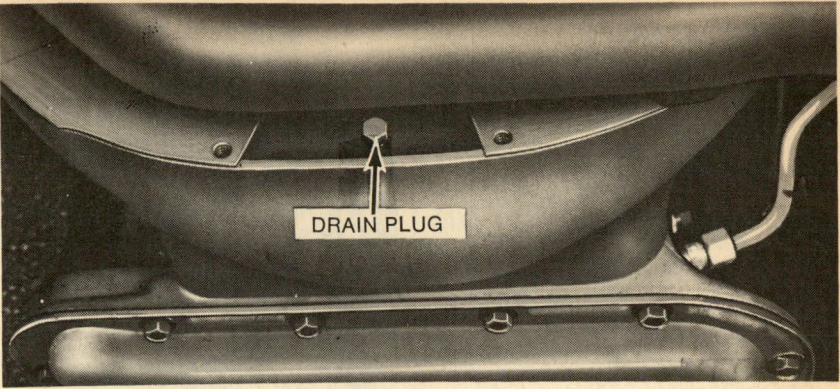

Converter drain plug
(© Chrysler Corp)

ter of the joint. This will force the cross to push the opposite bearing out of the universal joint. This step may be performed using a hammer and drift or a vise and sockets or pieces of pipe. However installation of bearings must be done using the vise or a press.
4. After the bearing has been pushed all the way out of the yoke, pull up the cross slightly and pack some washers under it. Then press on the end of the cross from which the bearing was just removed to force the first bearing out of the yoke. Repeat steps 3 and 4 to remove the remaining two bearings.
5. If a grease fitting is supplied with the new U-joint assembly, install it. If no fitting is supplied, make sure that the joint is amply greased. Pack grease in the recesses in the end of the cross.
6. To reassemble start both bearing cups into the yoke at the same time and hold the cross carefully in the fingers in its installed position. Be careful not to knock any rollers out of position.
7. Squeeze both bearings in a vise or press, moving the bearings into place. Continually check for free movement of the cross in the bearings as they are pressed into the yoke. If there is a sudden increase in the force needed to press the bearings into place, or the cross starts to bind, the bearings are cocked in the yoke. They must be removed and restarted in the yoke. Failure to do so will greatly reduce the life of the bearing. Repeat steps 6 and 7 to reinstall the remaining two bearings. Install the snap rings, or in the case of the rear U-joint, tape the bushings to the cross until they are assembled into the clamps.

REAR AXLE

Three different rear axle assemblies have been used. A 7¼ in. (ring gear diameter) unitized carrier axle is used

with all six cylinder applications and on some late production 318 V8 models. An 8¼ in. unitized carrier axle is installed in most mid 1972 and later models with 318, 340, or 360 V8s. An 8¾ in. removable differential carrier axle is used on models through 1974 with 318 or 340 engines.

These axles can be visually identified as follows:

The 7¼ in. axle has a 9 bolt rear cover with a filler plug. The 8¼ in. has a 10 bolt rear cover without a filler plug; starting 1977 there is a filler plug in the cover. The 8¾ in. has a welded rear cover.

All axles, except the 7¼ in. unit through 1973, have a ratio identification tag under one of the cover or carrier bolts. The 7¼ in. axle through 1973 has an axle ratio code marking on the front of the pad at the bottom of the housing.

AXLE SHAFT, BEARING, AND SEAL

Removal and Installation

Because the axle shafts are slightly different from one rear axle assembly to another, individual service procedures are required for each axle shaft assembly. Two very important points to remember when servicing any rear axle assembly are:

1. Always elevate *both* rear wheels when performing any rear axle service, or when using the engine or other means to rotate the axle.
2. On those cars that are equipped with a Sure-Grip differential, you must never rotate one axle shaft without rotating the other. If it is necessary to rotate one of the axle shafts, *both* shafts must be in position and both must be rotated. Otherwise, alignment of the axle shafts will be very difficult.
NOTE: *This procedure also covers axle shaft end-play adjustment, on those axles on which it is possible.*

7¼ IN. AXLE

NOTE: *Whenever this axle assembly is serviced, both the brake support plate gaskets and the inner axle shaft oil seal must be renewed. There is no provision for adjusting axle shaft end-play.*

1. Support the rear of the car and remove the rear wheels.
2. Detach the clips which secure the brake drum to the axle shaft studs and remove the brake drum.
3. Disconnect the brake lines at the wheel cylinders and block off the lines.
4. Through the access hole in the axle shaft flange, remove the axle shaft retaining nuts.
5. Attach a puller or slide hammer to the axle shaft flange and remove the axle shaft.
6. Remove the brake assembly from the axle housing.
7. Remove the axle shaft oil seal from the axle housing.

CAUTION

Never use a torch or other heat source as an aid in removing any axle shaft components as this will result in serious damage to the axle assembly.

8. Place the axle shaft housing retaining collar in a vise. With a chisel, cut deeply into the retaining collar at 90° intervals. This will loosen it enough so it can be removed. The bearing can be pressed off.
9. To assemble and install the axle shaft, replace the retainer plate, bearing, and bearing retainer collar on the axle shaft, using a press.
10. Insert new axle shaft oil seals in the axle housing and lightly grease the outside diameter of the bearing.
11. Replace the foam gasket on the studs of the axle housing and install the brake support plate assembly on the axle housing studs. Refit the outer gasket.
12. Very carefully slide the axle shaft assembly through the oil seal and engage the splines of the differential slide gear. Using a non-metallic hammer, lightly tap the end of the axle shaft to position the axle shaft bearing in the recess of the axle housing. Install the retainer plate over the axle housing studs and torque the securing nuts to 35 ft lbs.
13. Reconnect the brake lines to the wheel cylinders and bleed the hydraulic system.
14. Install the brake drum and retaining clips.
15. Refit the rear wheels and lower the car.

8¼ AND 9¼ IN. AXLES

NOTE: *There is no provision for adjusting axle shaft endplay on this axle.*
1. Raise the vehicle and remove the wheels.
2. Clean all dirt from the housing cover and remove the cover to drain the lubricant.
3. Remove the brake drum.
4. Rotate the differential case until the differential pinion shaft lock-

Removal of differential pinion shaft lock screw on the 8¼ in. rear axle (© Chrysler Corp.)

screw can be removed. Remove the lockscrew and pinion shaft.
5. Push the axle shaft toward the center of the vehicle and remove the C-lock from the groove on the axle shaft.
6. Pull the axle shaft from the housing, being careful not to damage the bearing which remains in the housing.
7. Inspect the axle shaft bearings and replace any doubtful parts. Whenever the axle shaft is replaced, the bearings should also be replaced.
8. Remove the axle shaft seal from the bore in the housing, using the button end of the axle shaft.
9. Remove the axle shaft bearing from the housing with a slide hammer. Do not reuse the bearing or the seal.
10. Check the bearing shoulder in the axle housing for imperfections. These should be corrected with a file or polish.
11. Clean the axle shaft bearing cavity.
12. Install the axle shaft bearing in the cavity. Be sure that the bearing is not cocked and that it is seated firmly against the shoulder.
13. Install the axle shaft bearing seal. It should be seated beyond the end of the flange face.
14. Insert the axle shaft, making sure that the splines do not damage the seal. Be sure that the splines are properly engaged with the differential side gear splines.
15. Install the C-locks in the grooves on the axle shafts. Pull the shafts outward so that the C-locks seat in the counterbore of the differential side gears.
16. Install the differential pinion shaft through the case and pinions. Install the lockscrew and secure it in position.
17. Clean the housing and gasket surfaces. Install the cover and a new gasket.

NOTE: *Replacement gaskets may not be available for differential covers. In*

this case, the use of a gel type nonsticking sealant is recommended.

Be sure that the rear axle ratio identification tag is replaced under one of the cover bolts. Refill the axle with lubricant. The proper lubricant level is ⅛-¼ in. below the filler plug hole on axles with the filler plug in the axle housing, and at the filler plug hole to ½ in. below on axles with the filler plug in the cover (1977 and later). MOPAR Hypoid lubricant and Friction Modifier additive must be used in Sure-Grip limited slip units.
18. Install the brake drum and wheel.
19. Lower the vehicle.

8¾ AND 9¾ IN. AXLES

NOTE: *Whenever this axle assembly is serviced, both the brake support plate gaskets and the inner axle shaft oil seal must be renewed.*
1. Jack up the rear of the car and remove the rear wheels.
2. Detach the clips which secure the brake drum to the axle shaft studs, and remove the brake drum.
3. Through the access hole in the axle shaft flange, remove the axle shaft retaining nuts. The right-side axle shaft has a threaded adjuster in the retainer plate and a lock under one of its studs which should be removed at this time.
4. Remove the parking brake strut.
5. Attach a puller to the axle shaft. Remove the shaft.
6. Remove the brake assembly from the axle housing.
7. Remove the axle shaft oil seal from the axle housing.

CAUTION

It is advisable to position some sort of a protective sleeve over the axle shaft seal surface next to the bearing collar to protect the seal surface. Never use a torch or other heat source as an aid in removing any axle shaft components as this will result in serious damage to the axle assembly.

8. Wipe the axle housing seal bore clean. Install a new axle shaft oil seal.

NOTE: *All 8¾ in. axle shaft bearings are factory packed with a special lubricant. If the roller bearing must be repacked, the factory lubricant must be washed out; it is not compatible with the other lubricants.*
9. Place the axle shaft housing retaining collar in a vise. With a chisel, cut deeply into the retaining collar at 90° intervals. Remove the bearing with a puller.
10. Remove the bearing roller retainer flange by cutting off the lower edge with a chisel.
11. Grind or file a section off the flange of the inner bearing cone and remove the bearing rollers.
12. Pull the bearing roller retainer down as far as possible and cut it off with side cutters.

13. Remove the roller bearing cup with its protective sleeves.

14. To prevent damage to the seal journal when the bearing cone is removed, protect the journal with a single wrap of shim stock that is 0.002 in. thick and is held in place by a rubber band.

15. Using a puller, remove the bearing cone. Remove the seal in the bearing retainer plate and replace it with a new seal.

16. To assemble the axle, first install the retainer plate and seal assembly on the axle shaft.

17. Grease the wheel bearings and install them.

18. Install a new axle shaft bearing cup, cone and collar on the shaft. Check the axle shaft seal journal for imperfections and if necessary, polish with no. 600 crocus cloth.

19. Thoroughly clean the axle housing flange face and brake support. Install a new rubber/asbestos gasket onto the axle housing studs. Next, install the brake support plate assembly on the left side of the axle housing.

20. Lightly grease the outside edge of the bearing cup. Install the bearing cup in the bearing bore.

21. Replace the foam gasket on the studs of the left-side axle housing and very carefully slide the axle shaft assembly through the oil seal and engage the splines of the differential side gear.

22. Using a non-metallic hammer, lightly tap the end of the axle shaft to position the axle shaft bearing in the recess of the axle housing. Install the retainer plate over the axle housing studs and, starting with the bottom securing nut, torque the nuts to 30-35 ft lbs.

23. Repeat step 19 for the right-side axle housing.

24. At the right side of the axle housing, back off the threaded adjuster until the inner face of the adjuster is flush with the inner face of the retainer plate. Very carefully slide the axle shaft assembly through the oil seal and engage the splines of the differential side gear. Repeat step 22.

25. Mount a dial indicator on the left brake support. Turn the adjuster clockwise until both wheel bearings are seated and there is zero end-play in the axle shafts. Back off the adjuster about four notches to establish an end-play of 0.008-0.018 in. on 8¾ in. axles and 0.008-0.012 for the 9¾.

26. Lightly tap the end of the left shaft with a non-metallic hammer. This will seat the right wheel bearing cup against the adjuster. Turn the axle shaft several times so that a true end-play reading is obtained.

27. Remove one retainer plate nut and install the adjuster lock. If the lock tab does not mate with the notch in

the adjuster, turn the adjuster slightly until it does. Refit the nut and torque it to 30-35 ft lbs.

28. Recheck the axle shaft end-play. If it is not correct, repeat the adjustment. When the adjustment is complete, remove the dial indicator.

29. Install the parking brake strut. Refit the brake drum and retaining clips.

30. Install the rear wheels and lower the car.

JACKING, HOISTING

Jack car at front control arms and at rear under axle housing.

To lift at frame use adapters, so that contact will be made at points shown. Lifting pads must extend beyond sides of supporting structure.

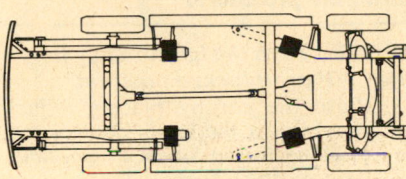

Positioning lift adapter
(© Chrysler Corp)

FRONT SUSPENSION

All Chrysler vehicles in this section utilize a torsion bar type front suspension. Aspen, Volare, Diplomat, and LeBaron have transverse torsion bars; all others have longitudinal (parallel to the frame) bars. Compression type lower ball joints are located in the steering knuckles. When servicing the front suspension, it should be kept in mind that rubber bushings must not be lubricated. Any front suspension part that contains rubber should be tightened with full vehicle weight on the suspension.

See the Front End Alignment Unit Repair Section for front end height adjustment and alignment.

Shock Absorber Removal and Replacement

1. Remove the washer and nut from shock absorber upper end. Be sure to note the positions of all small parts.

2. Jack the vehicle until the wheels clear the floor. Remove the shock absorber lower attaching bolt or nut. Allow the control arm to lower itself.

3. Fully compress the shock absorber

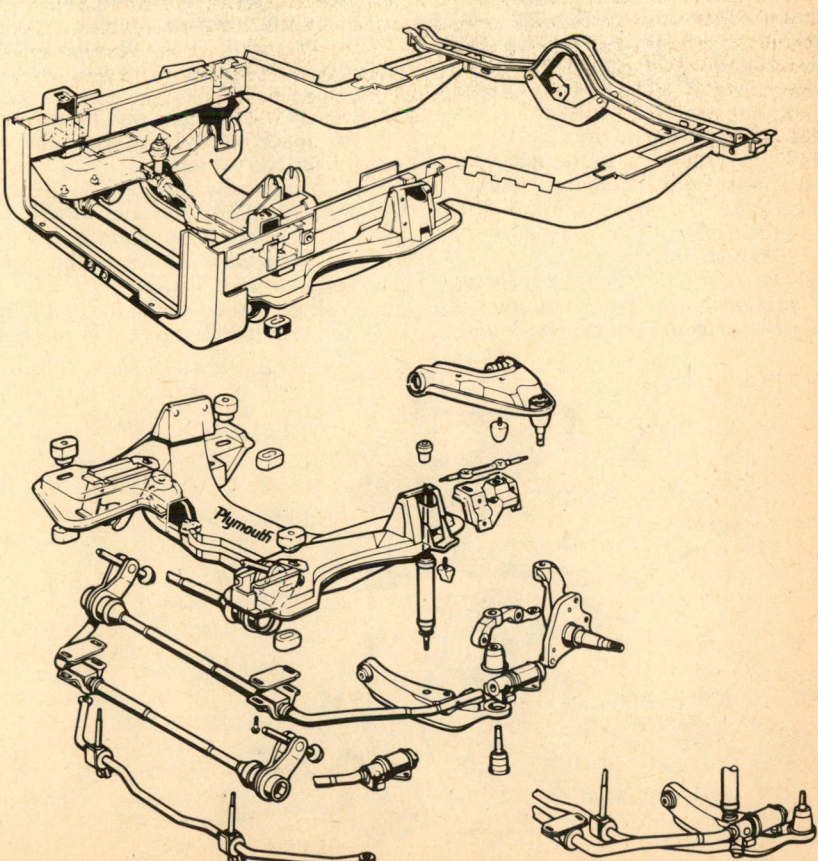

Aspen, Volare, Diplomat, LeBaron isolated front suspension with transverse torsion bars
(© Chrysler Corp.)

by pushing upward. Pull the shock firmly and remove it from the vehicle.

4. Purge the new shock of air by repeatedly extending it in its normal position and compressing it while inverted. It is normal for there to be more resistance to extension than to compression. Fully compress the new shock absorber. Insert the mount through the upper bushing and install the retainer and nut. Torque the nut to 25 ft lbs. Be sure that all the retainers are installed with the concave side in contact with rubber.

5. Position and align the lower mount of shock absorber. Install the bolt (from the rear) or nut and fingertighten it. Lower the vehicle and torque the nut to 50 ft lbs. (35 on Aspen/Volare/Diplomat/LeBaron) with the full weight of the vehicle on the wheels.

BALL JOINTS
Inspection
NOTE *Before performing the inspection, make sure the wheel bearings are adjusted correctly and that the control arm bushings are in good condition.*

1. Place a jack under the lower control arm as close to the wheel as possible.
2. Raise the car until there is 1-2 in. of clearance under the wheel.
3. Insert a bar under the wheel and pry upward. If the wheel raises noticeably the ball joints are worn. Determine if the upper or lower ball joint is worn by visual inspection while prying on the wheel.
4. You can make a more accurate measurement by clamping a dial indicator to the lower control arm and measuring the lower ball joint stud movement.

NOTE *Due to the distribution of forces in the suspension the lower ball joint is usually the defective joint. The manu-facturer's limit for lower ball joint play, measured at the joint, is 0.020 in. for Aspen and Volare and 0.070 in. for all others through 1976. Starting 1977, it is 0.030 in. for all models. This limit may not agree with your state's inspection regulations.*

5. Lower the jack enough to let the tire lightly contact the floor. Tighten the wheel bearing nut enough to remove all play. Have an assistant try to move the top of the tire in and out while you observe the upper ball joint. If there is any noticeable side play, replace the upper ball joint.
6. Correct the wheel bearing adjustment.

Removal and Installation
UPPER BALL JOINT

— CAUTION —
The torsion bar remains under tension during this procedure.

NOTE: *Turn the ignition key to the OFF or unlocked position.*

1. Raise the car by placing a jack stand under the lower control arm as close to the wheel as possible. Remove the wheel.
2. Remove the nut that attaches the upper ball joint to the steering knuckle. Loosen the ball joint stud from the steering knuckle. Press the ball joint stud out with a ball joint removal tool. Never strike the ball joint stud.
3. Unscrew the upper ball joint from the upper control arm and remove it from the vehicle.
4. Position a new ball joint on the upper control arm and screw the joint into the arm. Be careful not to cross thread the joint in the arm. Torque it to 125 ft lbs.
5. Position a new seal on the ball joint stud and install the seal in the ball joint making sure the seal is fully seated on the ball joint housing.
6. Position the ball joint stud in the steering knuckle and install the retaining nut. Torque the nut to 100 ft lbs. Install a new cotter pin.
7. Lubricate the ball joint. Adjust the wheel alignment.

LOWER BALL JOINT—VALIANT, DART, BARRACUDA, CHALLENGER
The lower ball joint and the steering arm are an integral unit. Because of this, they cannot be replaced separately.

1. Take the upper control arm rebound bumper off.
2. Raise the car. Be sure that the suspension is under no load (full rebound).

— CAUTION —
If jacks are used, there must be a support placed between the K-member and the jack.

3. Back-off (counterclockwise) the torsion bar adjuster to remove the load on the torsion bar.
4. Remove the wheel, tire, and the drum or disc brake.
5. Unfasten the two lower bolts from the brake support which secure the ball joint/steering arm assembly to the steering knuckle.
6. Remove the end of the tie rod from the steering arm with a puller or removal tool.
7. Use a ball joint stud puller to remove the ball joint stud from the lower control arm. The ball joint/steering arm assembly may now be removed.
8. Position a new seal over the new ball joint, being certain that the lip of the seal is fully seated in the housing.
9. Attach the ball joint/steering arm assembly to the steering knuckle and tighten the attachment bolts to 110 ft lbs through 1972 and to 160 ft lbs starting 1973.
10. Fit the ball joint stud into the opening in the lower control arm. Tighten the stud retaining nut to 100 ft lbs for 1976, or 85 ft lbs (through 1975). Install the cotter pin. Lubricate the ball joint.
11. Check the tie rod seal for signs of damage and replace it if necessary. Attach the tie rod end to the steering knuckle arm. Torque its securing nut to 40 ft lbs. Install the cotter pin.
12. Load the torsion bar by rotating its adjusting nut clockwise.
13. Install the wheel and brake assembly. Adjust the front wheel bearing.
14. Lower the car. Install the upper control arm rebound bumper and tighten its securing nut.
15. Adjust the front end height and wheel alignment.

Typical Valiant, Dart, Barracuda, Challenger upper control arm and steering knuckle (© Chrysler Corp.)

LOWER BALL JOINT—ASPEN, VOLARE, DIPLOMAT, LEBARON

NOTE: *Turn the ignition key to the OFF or unlocked position.*

1. Remove the lower control arm rebound bumper.
2. Raise the vehicle so that the front suspension drops to the downward limit of its travel. Position jackstands beneath the front frame for extra support.
3. Remove the wheel and tire assembly.
4. Remove the brake caliper from its mounts and tie it up out of the way so that there is no strain on the flexible brake hose.
5. Remove the hub and rotor assembly, splash shield, and lower shock absorber mounting nut and bolt.
6. Unload the torsion bar by rotating the adjusting bolt counterclockwise.
7. Remove the lower ball joint stud cotter pin and nut. Use a ball joint removal tool to press the ball joint out. Never strike the ball joint stud.
8. Press the ball joint out of the lower control arm.
9. Press the new ball joint into the lower control arm.
10. Place a new seal over the ball joint. Press the retainer portion of the seal down over the ball joint housing until it locks into position.
11. Insert the ball joint stud through the opening in the knuckle arm and install the stud retaining nut. Tighten to 100 ft lbs. Install the cotter pin and lubricate the ball joint.
12. Load the torsion bar by rotating the adjusting bolt clockwise.
13. Install the shock absorber nut and bolt, the splash shield, hub and rotor assembly, and brake caliper. Install the wheel and tire assembly.
14. Adjust the front wheel bearings. Remove the jackstands and lower the car. Install the rebound bumper. Adjust the front suspension height and alignment.

Upper Control Arm Removal and Installation

1. Follow Steps 1-2 of the Upper Ball Joint Removal and Installation Procedure.
2. On Valiant, Dart, Barracuda, and Challenger, remove the nuts, lockwashers, cams, and cam bolts holding the upper control arm to the support bracket. On installation, tighten the adjusting bolts to 70 ft lbs.
3. On Aspen, Volare, Diplomat, and LeBaron remove the rubber splash shield and remove the pivot shaft nuts. It will be easier to reset the alignment if you mark the original pivot bar location. Remove the control arm and pivot shaft assem-

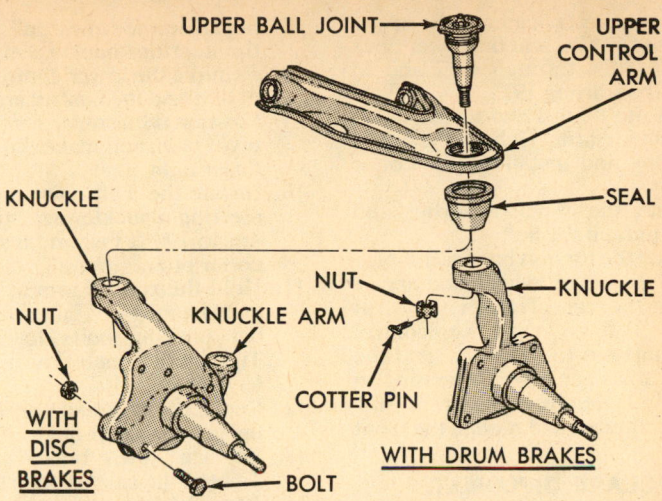

Steering knuckle and upper control arm details—Aspen, Volare
(© Chrysler Corp.)

bly. On installation, tighten the pivot shaft nuts to 150 ft lbs.
4. Follow Steps 3-7 of the Upper Ball Joint Removal and Installation procedure.

Lower Control Arm Removal and Installation

VALIANT, DART, BARRACUDA, CHALLENGER

1. Raise the car and support it under the frame. Let the suspension hang down. Remove the wheel, tire and brake drum or disc. Remove the rebound bumper.
2. Remove the shock absorber at the bottom attachment and swing it up out of the way. Remove the torsion bar from its mounting at the lower control arm after releasing its tension.
3. Remove the tie rod end from the steering knuckle arm. Be careful not to damage the seal.
4. Remove the sway bar link from the lower control arm. Remove the steering knuckle arm-to-brake support bolts and remove the steering knuckle arm, as in Lower Ball Joint Removal.

5. At the forward end of the crossmember, remove the strut spring pin, nut, and bushings, taking note of their positions. Remove the nut and washer from the lower control arm shaft.
6. Using a soft hammer, tap the end of the lower control arm shaft and remove it from the crossmember.
7. Remove the lower control arm, strut and shaft as an assembly.
8. On installation, position the front strut bushing half and sleeve into the crossmember and install the control arm, strut, and shaft assembly. Replace the shaft bushing outer retainer and finger tighten the nut.
9. Replace the lower control arm shaft washer and finger tighten the nut.
10. Replace the lower ball joint stud into the lower control arm and tighten it to 85 ft lbs through 1975, and to 100 ft lbs for 1976. Install a new cotter pin.
11. Install the brake support to steering knuckle and replace the two upper bolts and finger tighten them.
12. Install the steering knuckle on the steering knuckle arm and insert the

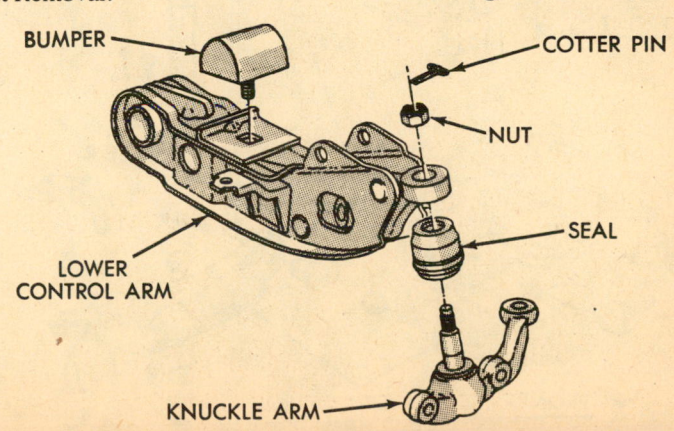

Typical Valiant, Dart, Barracuda, Challenger lower control arm (© Chrysler Corp.)

two lower bolts. Tighten the upper bolts to 55 ft lbs and the lower ones to 110 ft lbs through 1972 and to 160 ft lbs starting 1973.

13. Install the tie rod end to the steering knuckle arm. Tighten the nut to 40 ft lbs and install a new cotter pin.
14. Connect the shock absorber and finger tighten the bolt.
15. Replace the torsion bar assembly.
16. Install the brake, wheel, and tire.
17. Lower the car. Tighten the strut nut to 70 ft lbs, the lower control arm shaft nut to 145 ft lbs, and the shock absorber lower mounting to 50 ft lbs. Readjust the front suspension height and realign the front end.

ASPEN, VOLARE, DIPLOMAT, LEBARON

1. Raise the car and remove the wheel.
2. Remove the brake caliper and wire it up.
3. Remove the lower shock absorber attachment.
4. Remove the hub, rotor and splash shield.
5. Unload both torsion bars by turning the adjusting bolts counterclockwise.

CAUTION

Unload both bars even if you are removing only one control arm.

6. Raise the lower control arm until there is 2⅞ in. clearance between the crossmember ledge at the jounce bumper and the torsion bar bushing on the lower control arm. Unbolt the torsion bar bushing from the control arm.

7. Separate the lower ball joint from the steering knuckle arm.
8. Remove the lower control arm pivot bolt and the control arm.
9. Position the control arm, install the pivot bolt, and make the flange nut finger tight.
10. Install the ball joint stud in the steering knuckle arm, tighten the nut to 100 ft lbs, and install a new cotter pin.
11. Hold the control arm at the height used in Step 6. Tighten the torsion bar bushing bolts to 50 ft lbs. Tighten the control arm pivot bolt to 75 ft. lbs.
12. Replace the shock absorber and tighten the lower nut to 35 ft. lbs.
13. Replace the brake assembly. Tighten the caliper bolts to 15 lbs.
14. Turn the adjusting screws clockwise to load the torsion bars.
15. Lower the car and adjust suspension height and wheel alignment.

Torsion Bar Removal and Installation

The torsion bars are not interchangeable from right to left. Longitudinal bars are marked with an R or an L, according to their location.

VALIANT, DART, BARRACUDA, CHALLENGER

1. Remove the upper control arm rebound bumper before raising the car.
2. Lift the car high enough to free the front suspension of all load.
3. Release load from torsion bar by backing off anchor adjusting nuts counterclockwise.
4. Remove the lock ring from the rear of torsion bar rear anchor. Remove the automatic transmission torque

shaft on 1974-76 models, if necessary.
5. Remove the torsion bar from its mounts. A special tool is available for this job, it clamps to the bar and provides a striking surface for driving the bar out.

CAUTION

The torsion bar may be under some load so be careful when removing it. Never use heat to ease removal of the bar as this will destroy the temper of the bar.

6. It may be necessary to move the rear balloon seal out of the way to ease removal. Slide the torsion bar out through the rear mounting. Be careful not to damage the balloon seal.
7. Inspect the torsion bar and lightly dress any sharp edges. Coat the dressed area with a rust preventive. Clean and lightly lubricate the bar.
8. Start replacement by sliding the bar into the rear anchor. Slide the balloon seal over the bar with the cupped end toward the rear of the bar. Coat both hex ends of the bar with waterproof grease.
9. Insert the torsion bar through the hex opening of the lower control arm. Replace the lockring in the rear anchor.
10. Fully pack the ring opening in the rear anchor with waterproof grease.
11. Install the balloon seal on the rear anchor so the seal lip engages the anchor grove.
12. Rotate the adjusting bolt clockwise to load the torsion bar. Lower the vehicle and adjust the front suspension height. Replace the upper control arm rebound bumper.

ASPEN, VOLARE, DIPLOMAT, LEBARON

1. Raise the car so that the front suspension hangs down.
2. Release the load on both torsion bars by turning the anchor adjusting bolts counterclockwise.
3. Remove the adjusting bolt on the bar to be removed.
4. Raise the lower control arms until there is 2⅞ in. clearance between the crossmember ledge at the jounce bumper and the torsion bar bushing on the lower control arm.
5. Unbolt the sway bar from the control arm.
6. Unbolt the torsion bar pivot bushing from the crossmember. Remove the bar and anchor assembly from the crossmember.
7. Check the seals on the bar for damage. If corrosion is evident, replace the bar assembly. Touch up any paint nicks or scratches. Check the adjusting bolt and swivel for corrosion or damage. Replace them if necessary.

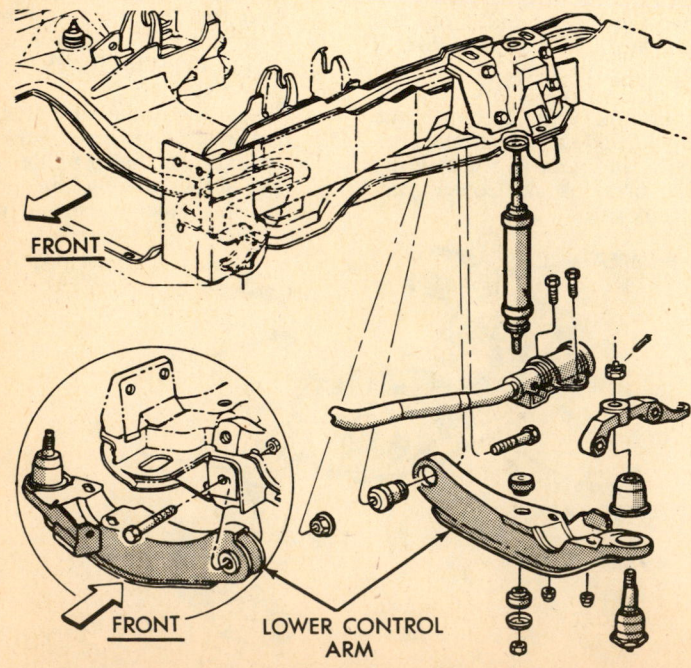

Aspen, Volare lower control arm details (© Chrysler Corp.)

8. Slide the balloon seal over the end of the bar with the cupped end toward the hex.
9. Coat the hex end of the bar with high-temperature waterproof grease.
10. Install the hex end of the bar into the anchor bracket. The ears of the bracket should be nearly straight up.
11. Install the bar anchor bracket assembly into the crossmember anchor retainer. Install the adjusting bolt and bearing. Attach the pivot bushing to the crossmember, finger tight.
12. Support the lower control arms at the height specified in Step 4 and install the torsion bar bushing to lower control arm bolts. Tighten them to 50 ft lbs for 1976, and to 70 ft lbs for 1977 and later.
13. Check that the anchor bracket is fully seated in the crossmember. Tighten the pivot bushing bolts to 75 ft lbs for 1976, and to 85 ft lbs for 1977 and later.
14. Put the balloon seal over the anchor bracket.
15. Install a new sway bar end bolt and tighten to 50 ft lbs.
16. Load the bars by turning the adjusting bolts clockwise. Lower the car and adjust the front end height.

Wheel Bearing Adjustment

1972

1. Raise the front of the car and remove the hub caps and grease caps from the front wheels. Remove the cotter pin from the spindle and remove the adjusting nut lock.
2. The wheel must be rotated while the bearing adjusting nut is tightened. The adjusting nut should be tightened to 90 in lbs.
3. Place the lock over the nut so that one pair of slots aligns with the cotter pin hole.
4. Back the nut and lock assembly off one slot. Install the cotter pin. This adjustment should yield 0.001-0.003 in. end-play.
5. Clean the grease cap. Coat, but do not fill, the cap with grease. Install it on the hub.
6. Lower the car and road-test it.

1973 AND LATER

1. Jack up or hoist the car, so that the front wheels are off the floor.
2. Remove the hub caps, grease cup, cotter pin and nut lock.
3. Back off on the adjusting nut.
4. Check for free wheel rotation.
5. While rotating the wheel, tighten the wheel bearing adjustment nut to 240-300 in. lbs.
6. Release the torque. Retighten the nut so that it is finger tight.
7. Position the nut lock so that one pair of slots is in line with the cotter pin hole and install the cotter pin. This adjustment should give 0.001-0.003 in. end play.

8. Install the rest of the items removed. Repeat the procedure for the other wheel and lower the car.

REAR SUSPENSION

All models utilize rear springs of the semi-elliptical leaf type. They are engineered to operate with little or no camber under conditions of small or no load. Heavy-duty springs are offered as an option on most models. They serve to increase the stability of the vehicle under conditions of heavy load. All vehicles with leaf springs are constructed with zinc interleaves between the normal leaves. They have the purpose of reducing spring corrosion and lengthening spring life.

Shock Absorber Removal and Installation

1. Jack the vehicle under the axle assembly in such a manner as to relieve load from the shock absorbers.
2. Remove the nut attaching the shock to the spring mounting plate.
3. At the upper mount, remove the shock attaching bolt or nut and the shock. On Barracuda and Challenger, access is through a rubber plug in the trunk.
4. Purge the new shock of air by repeatedly extending it in its normal position and compressing it while inverted. It is normal for there to be more resistance to extension than to compression. To install the shock, position it so the upper bolt or nut may be replaced. Hand-tighten only.
5. Align the shock with the spring mounting plate and install the bolt or nut. Hand-tighten only.
6. Lower the vehicle and tighten the shock absorber mounting bolts. Torques are 50 ft lbs at the bottom,

except for Aspen, Volare, Diplomat, and LeBaron stud nuts, which are 35 ft lbs. Top bolt torques are 70 ft lbs, except on Valiant and Dart stud nuts, which are 50 ft lbs.

Spring Removal and Installation

1. Jack up the vehicle and remove the wheels. Position jack stands under the axle in such a manner so as to relieve weight from the rear springs.
2. Disconnect the rear shock absorbers at the bottom. Lower the axle assembly to allow the rear springs to hang free. Disconnect the rear sway bar links, if so equipped.
3. Remove the U-bolt nuts and remove the bolts and spring plates. Remove the nuts securing the front spring hanger to the body mounting bracket.
4. Remove the rear spring hanger bolts and allow the spring to drop enough to allow the front spring hanger bolts to be removed. On the Barracuda and Challenger, loosen and remove the rear shackle nuts and plate and remove the shackle.
5. Remove the front pivot bolt from the front spring hanger.
6. Remove the shackle nuts and shackle from the rear of the spring.
7. To begin installation, assemble the shackle and bushings in the rear of the spring and hanger. Start the shackle bolt nut. Do not lubricate rubber bushings to ease installation. Do not tighten the bolt nut.
8. Install the front spring hanger to the front spring eye and insert the pivot bolt and nut. Do not tighten them.
9. Install the rear spring hanger-to-body bracket and torque the bolts to 30 ft lbs.
10. With the aid of a helper, raise the spring and insert the bolts in the spring hanger mounting bracket holes. Install the nuts and torque them to 30 ft lbs.
11. Position the axle assembly so it is

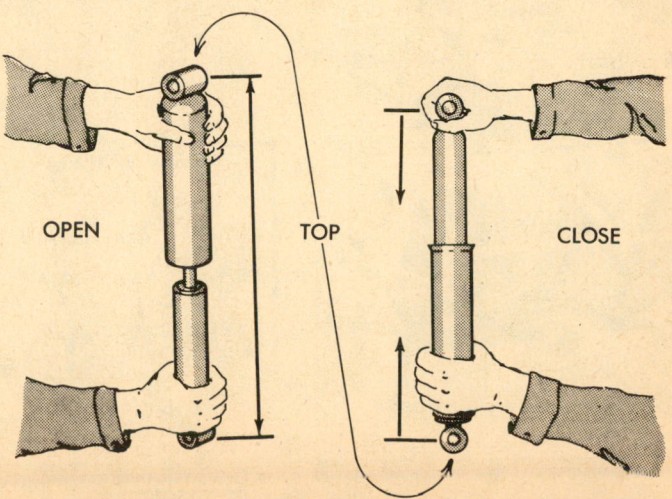

OPEN   TOP   CLOSE

Purging new shock absorbers of air (© Chrysler Corp.)

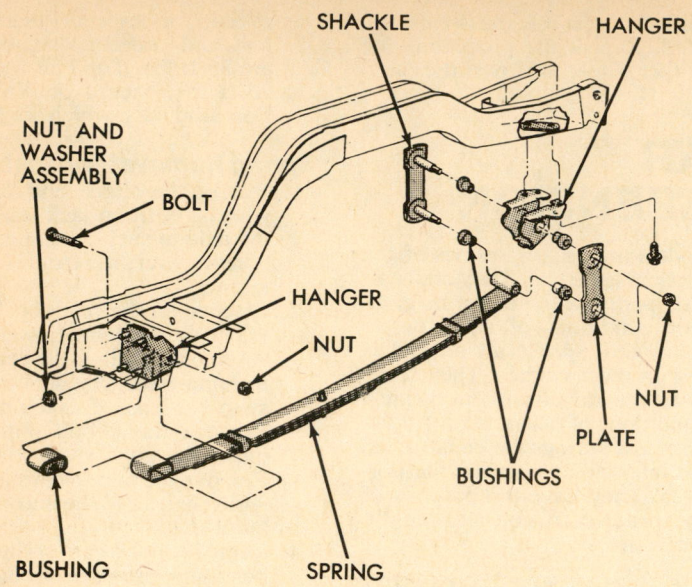

Rear spring details for Aspen, Volare, Diplomat, and LeBaron (© Chrysler Corp.)

correctly aligned with the spring center bolt.

12. Position the center bolt over the lower spring plate. Insert the U-bolt and nut. Tighten the U-bolts to 45 ft lbs (40 ft lbs with 2½ in. diameter axle tube). Connect the rear shock absorbers.

13. Lower the vehicle. Torque the pivot bolts to 125 ft lbs (85 on Dart and Valiant through 1972). Tighten the shackle nuts to 30 ft lbs on Valiant and Dart, 40 ft lbs on all others.

BRAKES

A dual (tandem) master cylinder is used. In operation, this type master cylinder provides braking even if one section of the system should develop a leak. Power assist is offered as an option.

With the exception of heavy-duty fleet units, brakes are self-adjusting.

Beginning 1973, front disc brakes are standard on all models with the exception of six-cylinder Valiants and Darts.
NOTE: *Disc brake squeal in 1973 and later models can be minimized by installing pads with riveted linings in place of the original equipment bonded linings.*

Master Cylinder Removal and Installation

1. Disconnect the brake lines from the master cylinder. Plug the brake line outlets to prevent fluid loss.
2. Remove the nuts that attach the master cylinder to the cowl panel or brake booster.

3. On models with non-power brakes, disconnect the pushrod from the brake pedal. On 1977 and later non-power brake models, disconnect the stop light switch bracket and pull the brake pedal back hard enough to separate the push rod from the master cylinder piston. This will destroy the pushrod grommet; it must be replaced. Lubricate the new one with a drop of water on installation.
4. Slide the master cylinder straight out and off the cowl panel or brake booster.
5. Reverse above procedure to install and bleed brake system.

Power Brake Booster Removal and Installation

1. Remove the nuts that attach the master cylinder to the brake booster and position the master cylinder out of the way without disconnecting the lines. Use care not to kink the brake lines.
2. Disconnect the vacuum hose from the brake booster.
3. Working under the dash, remove the nut and bolt that attaches the brake booster pushrod to the brake pedal. On 1978 and later models, use a small screwdriver to expand the retainer clip and remove the clip from the brake pedal pin. Discard the clip. Unbolt and remove the lower pivot bolt and nut.
4. Remove the brake booster attaching nuts and washers.
5. Remove booster assembly from the vehicle.
6. Reverse above procedure to install. Use a new retainer clip on models so equipped.

Parking Brake Adjustment

1. Apply the brakes several times while backing up to adjust the rear

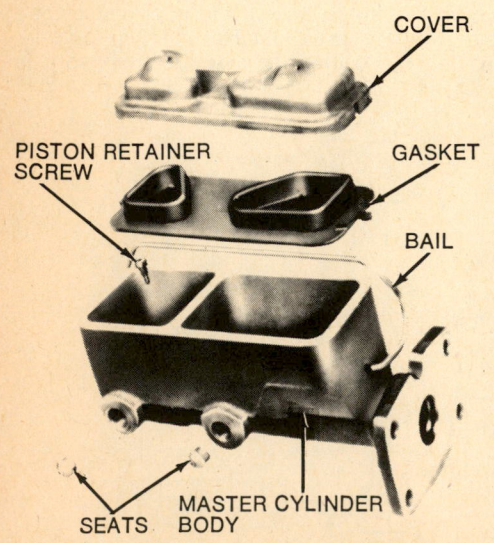

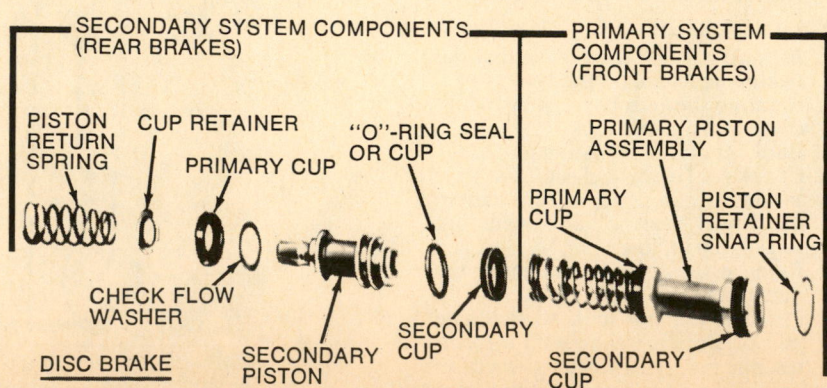

Dual type master cylinder (disc brakes) (© Chrysler Corp.)

drum brakes. Release the parking brake lever and clean and lubricate the parking brake cable adjusting nut and threads. Loosen the cable adjusting nut.

2. Tighten the cable adjusting nut until a slight drag is felt in the rear wheels when the rear wheels are rotated. Loosen the cable adjusting nut until the rear wheels can be rotated freely. Back off the cable adjusting nut two additional turns.

3. Apply and release the parking brake several times and check to verify that the rear wheels rotate freely, without any brake drag.

STEERING

A worm and recirculating ball type steering gear is used with the manual steering system.

Power steering is an option on all models. Hydraulic power is provided by a belt-driven pump. Some power steering pumps were equipped from the factory with fluid coolers. These were used on vehicles with high-performance engines and/or special axle ratios.

Tie-Rod End Removal and Installation

1. Loosen the tie rod adjuster sleeve clamp nuts.
2. Remove the tie rod end stud nut and cotter pin.
3. If the outer tie rod end is being removed, remove the stud from the steering knuckle. If the inner tie rod end is being removed, remove the stud from the center link. The studs on all the tie rod ends fit in a tapered hole. They can be removed with a ball joint stud removal tool.
4. Unscrew the tie rod end from the threaded sleeve. The threads may be left or right-hand threads. Count the number of turns required to remove it.
5. To install, reverse the above. Turn the tie rod end in as many turns as was needed to remove it. This will give approximately correct toe-in.
6. Tighten the stud nuts to 40 ft lbs and install new cotter pins.
7. Set the toe-in.

Power Steering Pump Removal and Installation

1. Back off the pump mounting and locking bolts, and remove the pump drive belt.
2. Disconnect all hoses at the pump.
3. Remove the pump bolts and pump with the bracket.
4. To install the pump, place the pump in position and install the mounting bolts.
5. Install the pump drive belt and adjust. There should be no more than ½ in. of play, under moderate

thumb pressure, on the longest run of belt. Some pump brackets have a ½ in. square hole for use in tensioning the belt. Torque the mounting bolts to 30 ft lbs.
6. Connect the pressure and return hoses. Replace the pressure hose O-ring, if there is one.
7. Fill the pump with power steering fluid.
8. Start the engine and rotate the steering wheel from stop to stop several times. This will bleed the system. Check the pump fluid level and fill as required.
9. Be certain the hoses are away from the exhaust manifolds and are not kinked or twisted.

Steering Wheel Removal and Installation

---------- CAUTION ----------

All models are equipped with collapsible steering columns. A sharp blow or excessive pressure on the column will cause it to collapse. Do not hammer on the steering wheel.

1. Disconnect the ground cable from the battery.
2. Remove the padded center assembly. This center assembly is often held on only by spring clips. There are usually holes in the back of the wheel so the pad can be pushed off. However, on some deluxe interiors it is held on by screws behind the arms of the wheel.
3. On the tilt and telescoping steering column remove the locking lever knob by releasing the clip on its underside. Remove the locking lever screws and the lever.
4. Remove the large center nut. Mark the steering wheel and steering shaft so that the wheel may be replaced in its original position. In most cases, the wheel can only go on one way.

5. Using a puller, pull the steering wheel from the steering shaft.
6. Reverse the procedure to install the wheel. When placing the wheel on the shaft, make sure the tires are straight ahead and the match marks are aligned. Tighten the nut to 28 ft lbs on models through 1972, and 60 ft lbs on 1973 and later models.

Chilton's TIME SAVER

A steering wheel puller can be made by drilling two holes in a piece of steel the same distance apart as the two threaded holes in the steering wheel. Sometimes an old spring shackle will have the right dimensions. Drill another hole in the center. Place a center bolt with the head against the steering shaft and a nut against the bottom of the homemade puller bar. Thread the two outer bolts into the holes in the wheel. Unscrew the nut on the center bolt to draw the wheel off the shaft.

Turn Signal/Hazard Warning Switch Removal and Installation

1972-75

1. Disconnect the negative battery ground cable.
2. Disconnect the wiring connectors at the base of the steering column.
3. Remove the steering wheel.
4. Remove the turn signal lever. The lever is held by a nut.

NOTE: On models with cruise control, do not remove the turn signal lever, allow it to hang by the wire.

5. Remove the screws which attach the turn signal switch upper bear-

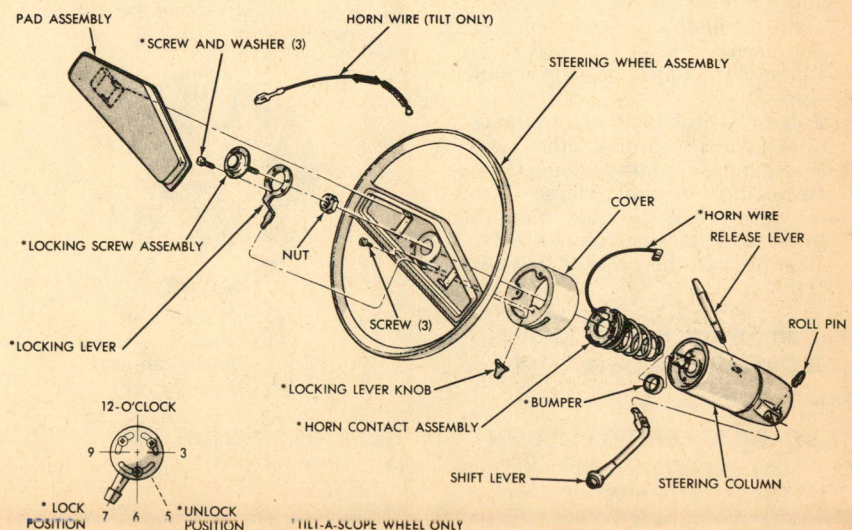

Typical steering wheel details (© Chrysler Corp.)

ing retainer and remove the retainer.

6. If the column has a cover, remove it.
7. Unfasten the wire which holds the horn wire on its mounting stud.
8. Remove the nuts which attach the mounting bracket to the steering column.
9. Separate the wiring harness trough from the column by unfastening its screws. Remove the tape from the harness and unfasten the harness multiconnector.
10. Pull the switch out of the column, while carefully guiding its wires through the column.
11. Work the connector through the column opening and completely remove the switch from the column.
   Installation is the reverse of removal.

1976 AND LATER

1. Disconnect the battery ground cable.
2. Remove the steering wheel.
3. Remove the steering column cover.
4. With tilting steering wheel, remove the shift position indicator, unbolt the steering column from the lower instrument panel reinforcement and the mounting bracket from the column, and remove the column wiring trough.

— CAUTION —

Support the steering column to prevent damage.

5. With standard column, unsnap the wiring trough from the column.
6. Position the automatic transmission column shift lever fully clockwise. Set the tilting steering wheel at its midpoint.
7. Disconnect the harness wire connector.
8. Remove the turn signal lever screw and the lever. If the car has speed control, just let the lever hang; don't remove it.
9. Remove the upper bearing retainer screws.
10. Pull the switch gently from the column while guiding the wires through the column opening.
11. Installation is the reverse of removal. Tighten the mounting bracket to steering column bolts to 10 ft lbs and the bracket bolts to 9 ft lbs.

Ignition Switch and/or Ignition Lock Cylinder Removal and Installation

STANDARD STEERING COLUMN

1. Disconnect the negative battery cable. Remove the steering wheel.
2. Remove the screw that attaches the turn signal lever to the steering column.

3. Remove the three screws that attach the upper bearing retainer to the turn signal switch.
4. Pull the turn signal switch as far upward as possible.
5. Using snap-ring pliers, remove the upper bearing housing snap-ring from the steering shaft.
6. Remove the screw that attaches the ignition key light assembly to the upper bearing housing.
7. Using care not to damage any components, pry the upper bearing housing off the steering shaft by lifting upward on alternate sides of the bearing housing with screwdrivers.
8. Lift upward as far as possible on the steering shaft lockplate and place a screwdriver or other object under it to hold it in the raised position. If this operation does not provide adequate working room under the lockplate, it will be necessary to press out the pin that attaches the lockplate to the steering shaft and remove the lockplate from the steering shaft. If the ignition switch is being replaced, the lockplate must be removed.
9. Using an offset screwdriver, remove the two screws that attach the lock lever guide plate to the steering column.
10. With the ignition lock cylinder in the "lock" position and the ignition key removed, insert a stiff wire into the lock cylinder release hole in the steering column. Push in on the wire to release the spring-loaded lock retainer and pull the lock cylinder out of the steering column.
11. If the ignition switch is being replaced, remove the two screws that attach the ignition key buzzer switch to the steering column and the three screws that attach the ignition switch to the steering column. Lift the ignition switch out of the housing.
12. Reverse the above procedure for installation.

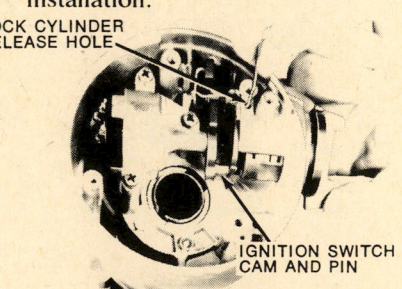

LOCK CYLINDER RELEASE HOLE

IGNITION SWITCH CAM AND PIN

Lock cylinder removal
(© Chrysler Corp)

TILT STEERING COLUMN

1. Disconnect the negative battery cable.
2. Remove the steering wheel.
3. Remove the three attaching screws and the shaft lock cover.

4. Remove the screws that attach the tilt control lever and the turn signal lever to the steering column and remove the levers.
5. Push the hazard warning knob in and unscrew the knob from the turn signal switch. Remove the ignition key lamp assembly.
6. Using a suitable tool, depress the lockplate to gain access to the lockplate retaining snap-ring. Remove the snap-ring from the steering shaft.
7. Remove the lockplate, cancelling cam, and spring.
8. Remove the three turn signal switch attaching screws, place the shift lever in the low position, and pull the switch and wires as far upward as possible.
9. With the ignition lock cylinder in the "lock" position through 1975, or "accessory" position 1976 and later, insert a small screwdriver into the lock release slot in the housing cover.
10. Press down with the screwdriver to release the spring latch at bottom of the slot and pull the lock cylinder from the housing.

The following steps are for ignition switch replacement only.
11. Remove the three screws that attach the upper steering column housing to the steering column and remove the housing.
12. Install the column tilt control lever and move the column to the full "up" position.
13. Insert a screwdriver into the slot in the spring retainer and press the retainer in approximately 3/16 in. Turn the retainer approximately 1/8 turn to the left until the ears align with the grooves in the housing. Remove the spring retainer, spring, and guide.
14. Push the steering shaft inward to enable removal of the inner race and seat. Remove the race and seat.
15. Make sure the ignition switch is in the "lock" position through 1975, or "accessory" position 1976 and later, then remove the wire connector from the ignition switch and remove the screws that attach the ignition switch to the outside of the steering column.
16. Lift the ignition switch from the column and twist it to disengage the switch actuating rod from the rack. Remove the switch.
17. To install the ignition lock cylinder, insert the cylinder into the housing with the cylinder in the lock position and the key removed.
18. Move the cylinder into the housing until it contacts the switch actuator. Move the switch actuator rod up and down to align the parts. When the parts are aligned the cylinder will move inward and lock into place.

The following steps are for ignition switch installation only.

19. With the ignition switch in the "lock" position through 1975, or "accessory" position thereafter, insert the actuating rod into the steering column.
20. Twist the switch and rod assembly as required to engage the actuating rod with the rack. Make sure the ignition lock cylinder is in the correct position.
21. Install the ignition switch mounting screws but do not tighten them.
22. Move the ignition switch downward away from the steering wheel and tighten the switch mounting screws. Make sure the ignition switch has not moved out of the lock detent.
23. Attach the switch wiring connector.

INSTRUMENT PANEL

Headlight Switch Removal and Installation

VALIANT AND DART

1. On models through 1973, remove the fuse box attaching screw and position the fuse box out of the way.
2. Press the release button on the body of the headlight switch and pull the control knob and shaft from the switch.
3. Disconnect the multiple connector from the rear of the headlight switch.
4. Remove the bezel nut that attaches the headlight switch to the dash and remove the switch.
5. Reverse above procedure to install.

BARRACUDA AND CHALLENGER

1. Disconnect the negative battery cable.
2. Remove the six lamp panel mounting screws and carefully slide the lamp panel out of the dash and lay it on top of the instrument panel. It is not necessary to disconnect the wiring harness.
3. Remove the four switch bezel mounting screws. Carefully slide the switch bezel out and to the right, overlapping the center instrument cluster, then lower it until it is free of the instrument panel and disconnect the wiring harness.
4. Remove the two headlight switch mounting screws and remvoe the switch from the bezel assembly.
5. Install in reverse order.

ASPEN, VOLARE, DIPLOMAT, LEBARON

1. Remove the instrument cluster bezel by removing the four screws

along the lower edge, placing the automatic transmission selector in 1, and pulling out to detach the top edge clips.
2. Remove the switch module assembly mounting screws, pull the assembly out, and let it hang.
3. Depress the switch stem, release the button on the switch, and pull out the knob and stem.
4. Insert a Phillips screwdriver through the stem opening in the switch bezel and remove the switch mounting nut.
5. Disconnect the switch wiring connector. Remove the switch.
6. Reverse the procedure for installation, making sure the stem locks into place.

Speedometer Cable Replacement

A bent or kinked inner speedometer drive cable is often the cause of a jerky or noisy speedometer. To replace a bent cable, detach the outer cable from the back of the speedometer and pull out the inner cable. Insert the new cable, make sure it engages with the speedometer head, and connect it to the back of the speedometer. If the cable is broken, you will have to detach the transmission end of the cable to remove the broken piece.

WINDSHIELD WIPERS

Motor Removal
VALIANT AND DART

1. Disconnect battery.
2. Disconnect wiper motor wiring harness.
3. Remove three wiper motor mounting nuts. On vehicles without air conditioning it is easier to remove crank arm nut and crank arm from under instrument panel first and omit steps 4 and 5.
4. Work motor off mounting studs far enough to gain access to crank arm mounting nuts.
5. Using an open end wrench, remove the motor crank arm nut while

holding the motor crank arm with a second wrench. Carefully pry arm off shaft.
6. Remove wiper motor.

——— CAUTION ———

Do not force or pry motor from mounting studs as drive link can be easily distorted.

BARRACUDA AND CHALLENGER

1. Disconnect battery.
2. Carefully remove wiper arm and blade assemblies.
3. Remove left cowl screen.
4. Remove drive crank arm retaining nut and drive crank. Disconnect wiring to motor.
5. Remove three wiper motor mounting nuts and remove motor.

ASPEN, VOLARE, DIPLOMAT, LEBARON

1. Disconnect the battery ground cable.
2. Remove the wiper arms.
3. Remove the cowl screen.
4. Hold the motor crank with a wrench while removing the crank arm nut. Detach the motor wiring.
5. Remove the three mounting nuts and the motor.

Blade Replacement

When wiper blades wear out, you can either replace the entire wiper blade assembly or just the rubber inserts. The wiper arms can also be replaced if necessary.

1. Park concealed wipers on the windshield by turning off the ignition key while they are running. Push the release lever on top of the wiper arm and remove the blade assembly. Just push the blade back onto the arm to replace.
2. Non-concealed wipers usually have a release lever under the arm. Push the lever, wiggle the blade, and pull it off. Just push the blade back onto the arm to replace.
3. To replace the blade inserts, push the release button on the end bridge to release it from the center bridge. Sometimes there is an end clip on replacement inserts; if so, remove it. Slide the old insert out

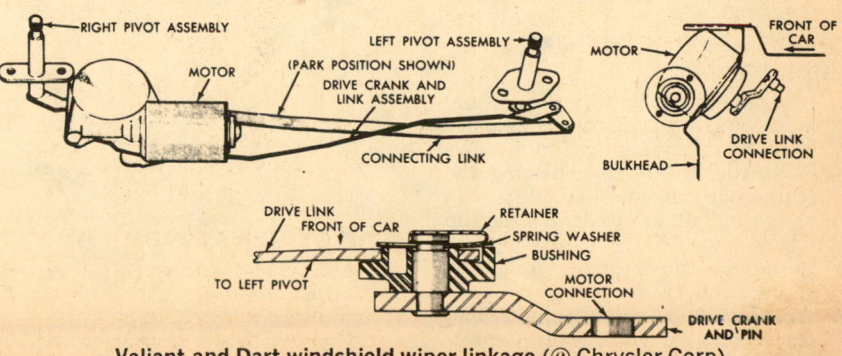

Valiant and Dart windshield wiper linkage (© Chrysler Corp)

of the claws of the two bridges. Slide the new insert into place, install the end clip, if any, and reassemble the blade.

RADIO

The following should be observed when working on a car radio:

1. Always observe the proper polarity of the connections; i.e., positive (+) goes to the power source and negative (−) to ground (negative ground electrical system).
2. Never operate the radio without a speaker; damage to the output transistors will result. If a replacement speaker is used, be sure that it is the correct impedance (ohms) for the radio.
3. If a new antenna or antenna cable is used, adjust the antenna trimmer for the best reception of a weak AM station around 1400 kc; the trimmer screw is located either behind the tuning knob or on the radio case.
4. For best FM reception, the best antenna height is 31-33 in.; for best AM reception, the antenna should be at its full length.

Removal

VALIANT, DART, BARRACUDA, AND CHALLENGER

1. Disconnect battery.
2. From under panel, disconnect speaker, antenna, and wiring leads at radio.
3. Pull off the knobs and remove the shaft nuts.
4. Remove two radio mounting nuts from panel and remove radio to lower support bracket mounting screw. Hold radio in position and remove radio bracket.
5. Move radio toward the front of the car, down, and out from under instrument panel.

NOTE: *If the car is equipped with air conditioning, it will be necessary to remove the two air outlet assembly-to-instrument panel mounting nuts from the underside of the panel and drop the assembly down and remove it from under the instrument panel. It will also be necessary to remove the ash tray and ash tray housing.*

VOLARE, ASPEN, DIPLOMAT, LEBARON

1. Disconnect the battery ground cable. Remove the instrument cluster bezel by removing the four screws along the lower edge, placing the automatic transmission selector in 1, and pulling out to detach the top edge clips.
2. Remove the radio mounting screws.
3. Pull the radio from the panel and disconnect the wiring and antenna.
4. Remove the radio.

HEATER

Heater Assembly Removal— Non Air-Conditioned Cars

Heater assembly removal is required in order to service the blower motor or heater core on cars without A/C.

VALIANT AND DART

1. Drain radiator and disconnect battery.
2. Disconnect heater hoses from heater and remove heater hoses to dash retainer plate. Disconnect heater motor wires.
3. Remove heater motor seal retainer plate from dash panel.
4. Disconnect heater-defroster and temperature control cables from heater assembly.
5. Remove the heater motor resistor wire from the resistor at the top of the unit. Remove the three mounting nuts.
6. Remove defroster tubes from heater assembly.
7. Disconnect heater housing support rod from fresh air duct.
8. Remove heater assembly.

BARRACUDA AND CHALLENGER

1. Disconnect battery.
2. Drain coolant.
3. Disconnect heater hoses from core tubes at dash panel. Plug core tubes to prevent spilling coolant on interior of car.
4. Remove three mounting nuts from studs around blower motor and remove flange and air seal.
5. Unplug antenna from radio and place wire to one side.
6. Remove screw from housing to plenum support rod on right side of housing above fresh air opening.
7. Disconnect three air door cables.
8. Disconnect wires from blower motor resistor.
9. Tip unit down and out from under instrument panel.

ASPEN, VOLARE, DIPLOMAT, LEBARON

CAUTION

This is a major disassembly operation.

1. Disconnect the battery ground cable and drain the coolant.
2. Disconnect the heater hoses at the firewall. Plug the core tubes to prevent spillage.
3. Slide the front seat all the way back.
4. Remove the core tube firewall seals and retainer.
5. Remove the instrument cluster bezel by removing the four screws along the lower edge, placing the automatic transmission selector in 1, and pulling out to detach the upper edge clips.
6. Remove the instrument panel upper cover by removing the mounting screws at the top inner surface of the glove box, at the brow above the instrument cluster, at the left end cap mounting, at the right side of the pad brow, and in the defroster outlets.
7. Remove the steering column cover (the instrument panel piece under the column).
8. Remove the right intermediate side cowl trim panel. Remove the lower instrument panel (the part with the glove box). Remove the instrument panel center to lower reinforcement.
9. Remove the right vent control cable, the temperature, and heating mode door control cables from the unit.
10. Disconnect the blower motor resistor block wiring.
11. Remove the mounting nuts on the engine side of the firewall.
12. Remove the heater support-to-plenum bracket.
13. Remove the heater unit.

Heater Blower Motor Removal— Non Air-Conditioned Cars

VALIANT AND DART

1. Remove the heater assembly.
2. Remove the seal from around the heater blower motor mounting studs.
3. Remove the spring clips that retain the spacers and the blower motor to the heater housing on models through 1972. On later models, re-

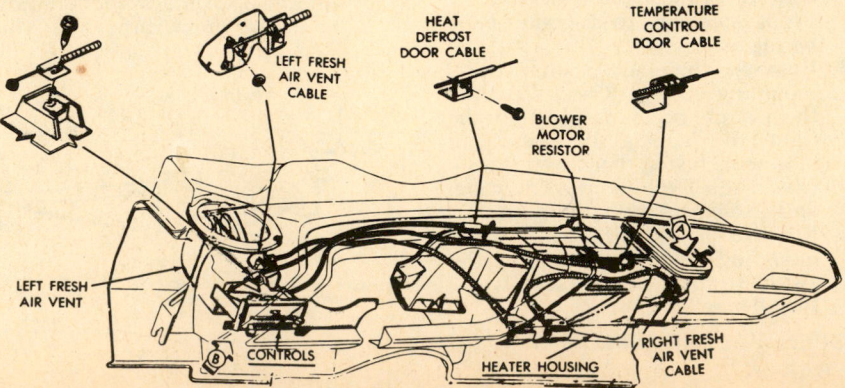

Barracuda and Challenger heater assembly
(© Chrysler Corp)

move the backplate from the housing and the fan from the motor.
4. Remove the blower motor from the heater housing.

BARRACUDA AND CHALLENGER

1. Remove heater assembly from car.
2. Disconnect blower motor lead from resistor block and ground wire from mounting plate.
3. Remove six sheet metal screws and six retaining clips holding blower motor assembly from housing.
4. Remove blower wheel from motor shaft.
5. Remove two retaining nuts and separate motor from mounting plate.

ASPEN, VOLARE, DIPLOMAT, LEBARON

1. Remove the heater assembly from the car.
2. Remove the retainer clips and separate the housing halves.
3. Remove the screw attaching the seal retainer and seal around the core tubes. Remove the core tube support clamp.
4. Slide the core out.
5. Remove the blower vent tube and the blower mounting nuts. Remove the blower motor.

Heater Core Removal—Non Air-Conditioned Cars

VALIANT AND DART

1. Remove the heater assembly and the heater blower motor as outlined above. Remove the motor resistor assembly.
2. Remove the fresh air door seal from either the inner or outer heating housing half only.
3. Remove the clips that retain the heater housing halves together.
4. Separate the heater housing halves.
5. Remove the screw that attaches the seal retainer and seal around the heater core tubes.
6. Remove the heater core tube support clamp.
7. Remove the screws that attach the heater core to the heater housing and remove the heater core.
8. Reverse above procedure to install.

BARRACUDA AND CHALLENGER

1. Remove the heater assembly.
2. Remove the nine spring clips and four screws that hold the front cover to the heater housing.
3. Cut the sponge rubber plenum-to-heater housing air seal in two places where the front cover separates the cover from the housing.
4. Remove the core tube retaining screw from behind the housing, between the core tubes.
5. Remove the two sponge rubber gaskets from the heater core tubes

and remove the core from the heater housing.

ASPEN, VOLARE. DIPLOMAT, LEBARON

This procedure is the same as for Heater Blower Motor Removal.

Heater Blower Motor Removal— Air-Conditioned Cars

VALIANT, DART, BARRACUDA, AND CHALLENGER

The blower motor can be removed from the engine compartment.
1. Detach the motor wiring. Remove the air tube, if any.
2. Remove the nuts holding the mounting plate.
3. Remove the mounting plate and blower motor.

ASPEN, VOLARE, DIPLOMAT, LEBARON

The blower motor is removed from inside the car.
1. Disconnect the motor wiring.
2. Remove the motor mounting nuts from the bottom of the recirculation housing.
3. Separate the lower blower motor housing from the upper housing.
4. Remove the mounting plate screws and remove the mounting plate and blower motor.

Heater Core Removal— Air-Conditioned Cars

DART AND VALIANT THROUGH 1973

1. The core and cover are serviced as an assembly. They are located just forward of the instrument panel.
2. Disconnect the battery and remove the air cleaner. Remove glove box, the air outlet assembly, and the right defroster tube.

3. Drain the cooling system and remove the heater hoses at the core.
4. Disconnect the vacuum hoses from the fresh air recirculating actuator, the electrical wires from the resistor block, the temperature control cable, the evaporator temperature control switch control cable, and the ground wire from the heater core.
5. Extract the screws holding the heater to the evaporator assemblies. Disconnect the heater housing support rod from its position at the fresh air duct.
6. Take out the entire heater assembly.
7. Remove the fresh air recirculating door actuator.
8. Remove the operating link between the recirculating door and the bellcrank.
9. Remove the fresh air intake seal from either the front or rear heater housing halves only.
10. Remove the clips holding the heater housing halves together. Pull the halves apart. Take out the screws which secure the heater core to the housing and remove the core.
11. To begin installation, place a small amount of sealer into the heater housing flange. Replace the heater core in the housing and install the attaching screws.
12. Place weatherseal on the inner lip of the heater core flange. Squeeze a small amount of sealer onto the heater housing cover.
13. Install the two housing halves together and install their retaining clips. Wipe off any excess sealer.
14. Install the link between the recirculating door and the bellcrank. It may require some adjustment; the fresh air door should be fully open when the recirculating door is closed. Replace the fresh air door recirculating actuator.

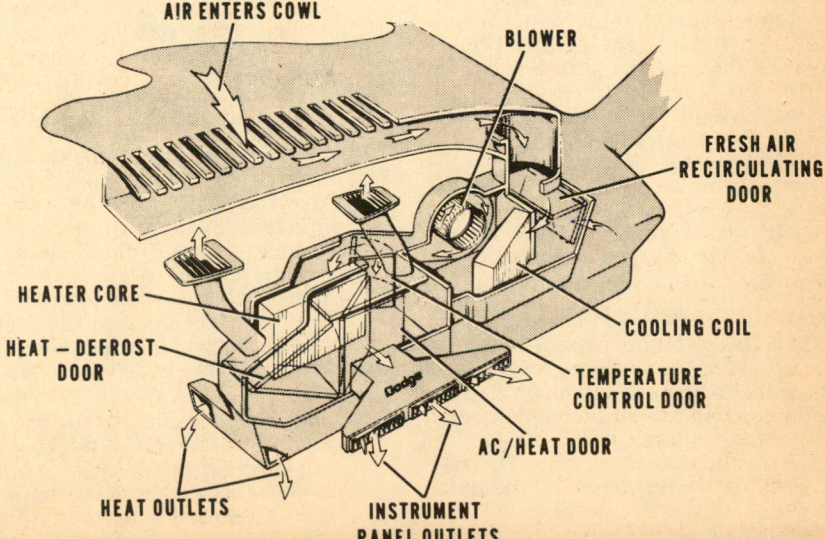

Dart and Valiant heater and air conditioner assembly through 1973
(© Chrysler Corp)

15. Place the heater assembly in the vehicle. Replace the temperature control cable on the outer operating arm; position it so that it is in the full heat position with the end of the cable housing 1/4 in. beyond the edge of the retainer clip.
16. Replace the evaporator temperature control switch cable on the inner operating arm. In the full heat position, the end of the cable housing should be 1/4 in. beyond the edge of the cable clip.
17. Install the heater assembly on the dash panel. Replace the heater support rod to the fresh air duct and install the evaporator assembly screw.
18. Replace the electrical connections to the resistor block. Install the vacuum hoses to the fresh air recirculating actuator. Be certain the red stripe is facing the rod side. Install the heater core ground wire.
19. Install the defroster tube, the glove box, and the air outlet assembly.
20. Replace the heater hoses, fill the cooling system, connect the battery and replace the air cleaner.
21. Start engine and bring to operating temperature. Test operation of the heater.

1974-76 VALIANT AND DART

1. Disconnect the battery.
2. Drain the cooling system and disconnect the heater hose from the unit.
3. Remove the core tube seal nut, bracket and seal.
4. Remove the air conditioning duct.
5. Remove the ash tray and housing.
6. Remove the radio.
7. Remove the heat-defrost vacuum actuator pot and let it hang by its rod.
8. To remove the heat distribution duct, remove the three screws on the front cover, two on each end and work the housing out of the lip and remove it to the left-side.
9. Remove the left defroster duct. Remove the right defroster duct from the unit and let it hang from the top.
10. Remove the rear distribution housing. You may reach through the radio opening for some of the screws; three on top, three on the bottom, and one at the left end.
11. With the distribution housing off, the heater core will be loose. Separate it from the seal and lift it out.

BARRACUDA AND CHALLENGER

NOTE: *This procedure requires evacuation of the air conditioner refrigerant. Use proper safety precautions.*
1. Remove the air cleaner and disconnect the battery.
2. Drain the cooling system. Disconnect the heater hoses at the dash panel. Plug the core tubes to prevent spillage.
3. Discharge refrigerant from the system.

4. Disconnect the refrigerant lines at the dash panel (use two wrenches for this procedure). Leave the expansion valve attached to the line. Plug all refrigerant openings.
5. Disconnect the blower motor electrical connections. Remove the motor cooling tube and remove the blower motor.
6. Remove the glove box assembly.
7. Remove the appearance shield from the lower edge of the instrument panel.
8. Remove the left spot cooler duct and the air distribution housing.
9. Disconnect all wires from the blower motor resistor, and the antenna wires from the radio bottom.
10. Remove the radio.
11. Disconnect the vacuum harness from the control switch rear.
12. Remove the water valve cable from the bracket on the housing left end.
13. In the engine compartment, remove the nuts from the housing mounting studs.
14. Remove the rubber drain tube.
15. Take the support bracket from the plenum-to-housing panel.
16. Remove the unit from beneath the instrument panel.
17. With the unit removed from the vehicle, remove the plenum air seal.
18. Remove the vacuum hose from the fresh air door actuator and bypass door actuator. Remove the air seal from the evaporator core tubes and heater.
19. Remove the 18 screws securing the front and rear covers, extract one screw from between the evaporator core tubes. Pull the housings apart.
20. Extract the three screws from the evaporator core access plate and remove the plate. With access now clear to the 2 evaporator core mounting screws, remove them. In addition, remove the four screws securing the evaporator core to the front cover and remove the core.
21. Carefully lift the left housing half seal from the rear cover. Do not remove the entire seal; the lower portion acts as a water seal.
22. Remove the two core retaining screws from the mounting plate. From the back of the rear cover, remove one screw from between the core tubes. Lift the heater core from the housing.
23. To begin assembly and installation, place the heat door in the "up" position. Place the heater core into the rear cover. Install its retaining screws.
24. Apply rubber cement to the bottom of the raised portion of the housing seal; carefully replace it in its original position over the heater core.
25. Insert the evaporator core into the front cover and replace its four securing screws.
26. Place the front and rear covers to-

gether. Make sure the cover seal is seated properly. Replace the 18 securing screws (and the screw between the evaporator core tubes at the back of the rear cover).
27. Replace the air seal over the heater and evaporator core tubes.
28. Connect all vacuum hoses to their respective actuators. Connect the hose with the red tracer to the actuator rod side.
29. Install the evaporator core access cover plate to the housing front and replace its three sheet metal screws.
30. Apply rubber cement to the plenum air seal and install it in position.
31. Position the housing up under the instrument panel. Connect the housing-to-plenum support bracket.
32. In the engine compartment, install four retaining nuts on the housing mounting studs; torque them to 24 in lbs.
33. Install the vacuum harness to the rear of the control switch. Install the water valve control cable in its retaining bracket.
34. Install the radio.
35. Install all blower motor resistor wiring. Plug the antenna lead into the radio bottom.
36. Replace the center outlet air distribution housing. Replace the left spot cooler duct.
37. Replace the appearance shield at the instrument panel bottom.
38. Replace the glove box.
39. Replace the blower motor and connect its wiring. Install the blower motor cooling tube and replace the evaporator drain tube.
40. Connect the refrigerant lines to the evaporator core tubes. Freely lubricate the fittings and O-rings with refrigerant oil. Use two wrenches to avoid twisting the tubes.
41. Connect the heater hoses to the core tubes. Fill the cooling system.
42. Sweep the system. Evacuate the system. Charge the system and check for leaks.

ASPEN, VOLARE, DIPLOMAT, LEBARON

--- CAUTION ---
This procedure requires evacuation of the air conditioner refrigerant. Do not attempt this yourself unless you are familiar with air conditioning service. This is also a major disassembly operation.

1. Discharge the air conditioning system.
2. Disconnect the battery ground cable, drain the coolant, remove the air cleaner, and disconnect the heater hoses. Plug the core tubes to prevent spillage.
3. Remove the H-type expansion valve.

4. Slide the front seat all the way back.
5. Remove the instrument cluster bezel assembly by removing the four screws along the lower edge, placing the automatic transmission selector in 1, and pulling out to detach the upper edge clips.
6. Remove the instrument panel upper cover by removing the mounting screws at the top inner surface of the glove box, at the brow above the instrument cluster, at the left end cap mounting, at the right side of the pad brow, and in the defroster outlets.
7. Remove the steering column cover (the instrument panel piece under the column).
8. Remove the right intermediate side cowl trim panel. Remove the lower instrument panel. Remove the lower instrument panel (the part with the glove box). Remove the instrument panel center to lower reinforcement.
9. Remove the floor console, if any.
10. Remove the right center air distribution duct. Detach the locking tab on the defroster duct.
11. Disconnect the temperature control cable from the housing. Disconnect the blower motor resistor block wiring.
12. Detach the vacuum lines from the

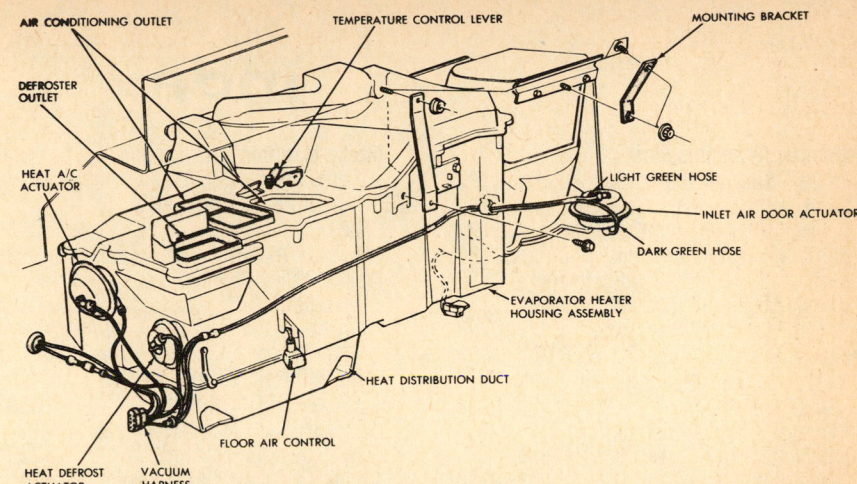

Aspen, Volare, Diplomat, LeBaron heater/air-conditioner unit (© Chrysler Corp.)

water valve and tee in the engine compartment. Detach the wiring from the evaporator housing. Remove the vacuum lines from the inlet air housing and disconnect the vacuum harness coupling.
13. Remove the drain tube in the engine compartment. Remove the mounting nuts from the fire-wall.
14. Remove the hanger strap from the rear of the evaporator and plenum

stud.
15. Roll the unit back so that the pipes clear and remove it.
16. Remove the blend air door lever from the shaft. Remove the screws and lift off the top cover. Lift the heater core out.
17. Reverse the procedure for installation. Sweep, leak test, and charge the air conditioning system. Refill the cooling system.

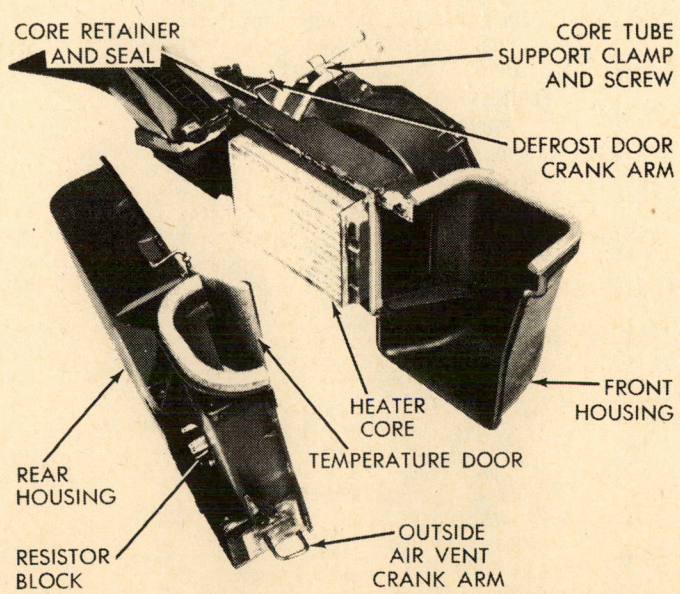

Heater core removal—Aspen, Volare, Diplomat, LeBaron (© Chrysler Corp.)

Bobcat · Mustang II · Pinto

Index

YEAR IDENTIFICATION

1976 Bobcat

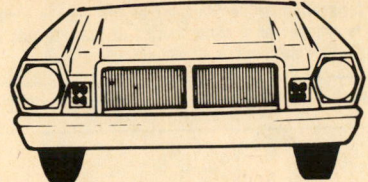

1977 Bobcat

1978 Bobcat

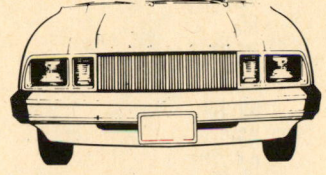
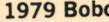

1979 Bobcat

1974 Mustang II

1975-76 Mustang II

1977 Mustang II

1978 Mustang II

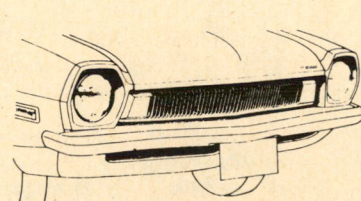

1972 Pinto

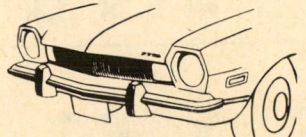

1973 Pinto

1974 Pinto

1975 Pinto

1976 Pinto

1977 Pinto

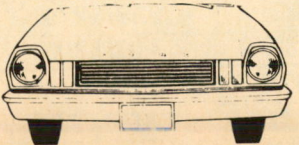

1978 Pinto

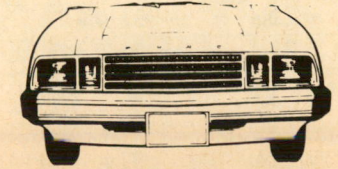

1979 Pinto

ENGINE CODE

The engine code designation is the 5th digit of the vehicle identification number (V.I.N.). The V.I.N. is stamped on a plate located at the left side of the instrument panel visible through the windshield on all models.

Disp	Bbl	Hp ■	'72	'73	'74	'75	'76	'77	'78	'79
4-Cylinder Models										
98 (1600cc)	1	54	W	W						
98 (1600cc)	1	75								
122 (2000cc)	2	80			X					
122 (2000cc)	2	85, 86	X	X						
122 (2000cc)	2	100								
140 (2300cc)	2	82, 88				Y			Y	Y
140 (2300cc)	2	83					Y			
140 (2300cc)	2	92						Y	Y	
6-Cylinder Models										
171 (2800cc)	2	105			Z					
171 (2800cc)	2	97				Z				
171 (2800cc)	2	103, 100, 99, 90					Z	Z	Z	Z
8-Cylinder Models										
302 (4950cc)	2	129				F				
302 (4950cc)	2	134					F	F	F	

■ Horsepower and torque are SAE net figures. They are measured at the rear of the transmission with all accessories installed and operating. Since the figures vary when a given engine is installed in different models, some are representative rather than exact.

GENERAL ENGINE SPECIFICATIONS

Year	Engine No. Cyl. Displacement (Cu. In., cc.)	Carburetor Type	Horsepower @ rpm ■	Torque @ rpm (ft lbs) ■	Bore x Stroke (in.)	Compression Ratio	Oil Pressure @ 2000 rpm
'72	4-97.6 (1600 cc)	1 bbl	54 @ 4600	80 @ 2400	3.188 x 3.056	8.0:1	38
	4-122 (2000 cc)	2 bbl	86 @ 5400	103 @ 3200	3.575 x 3.029	8.2:1	50①
'73	4-97.6 (1600 cc)	1 bbl	54 @ 4600	80 @ 2400	3.188 x 3.056	8.0:1	38
	4-122 (2000 cc)	2 bbl	86 @ 5400	103 @ 3200	3.575 x 3.029	8.2:1	50①
'74	4-122 (2000 cc)	2 bbl	80 @ 5400	98 @ 3000	3.575 x 3.029	8.2:1	50①
	4-140 (2300 cc)	2 bbl	88 @ 5000②	116 @ 2600	3.781 x 3.126	8.4:1	50
	6-170.8 (2800 cc)	2 bbl	105 @ 4600	140 @ 3200	3.660 x 2.700	8.2:1	40-55①
'75	4-140 (2300 cc)	2 bbl	83 @ 4800	109 @ 2800	3.781 x 3.126	8.4:1	50
	6-170.8 (2800 cc)	2 bbl	97 @ 4400	138 @ 3200	3.660 x 2.700	8.2:1	40-55①
	8-302 (4950 cc)	2 bbl	129 @ 4000	213 @ 1800	4.000 x 3.000	8.0:1	50-70
'76-'77	4-140 (2300 cc)	2 bbl	92 @ 5000	121 @ 3000	3.781 x 3.126	9.0:1	40-60
	6-170.8 (2800 cc)	2 bbl	103 @ 4300	149 @ 2800	3.660 x 2.700	8.7:1	40-60
	6-170.8 (2800 cc) Calif.	2 bbl	99 @ 4400	144 @ 2200	3.660 x 2.700	8.7:1	40-60

GENERAL ENGINE SPECIFICATIONS

Year	Engine No. Cyl. Displacement (Cu. In., cc.)	Carburetor Type	Horsepower @ rpm ■	Torque @ rpm ■ (ft lbs)	Bore x Stroke (in.)	Compression Ratio	Oil Pressure @ 2000 rpm
	6-170.8 (2800 cc) Mustang II, Auto.	2 bbl	100 @ 4600	143 @ 2600	3.660 x 2.700	8.7:1	40-60
	6-170.8 (2800 cc) Mustang II, Auto., Calif.	2 bbl	100 @ 4400	143 @ 2600	3.660 x 2.700	8.7:1	40-60
	8-302 (4950 cc)	2 bbl	134 @ 3600	247 @ 1800	4.000 x 3.000	8.0:1	40-60
'78-'79	4-140 (2300 cc)	2 bbl	88 @ 4800	118 @ 2800	3.781 x 3.126	9.0:1	50
	6-170.8 (2600 cc)	2 bbl	90 @ 4200	143 @ 2200	3.660 x 2.700	8.7:1	40-55①
	8-302 (4950 cc)	2 bbl	139 @ 3600	250 @ 1600	4.000 x 3.000	8.4:1	40-60
	8-302 (4950 cc) Calif	2 bbl	133 @ 3600	243 @ 1600	4.000 x 3.000	8.1:1	40-60

■ Horsepower and torque are SAE net figures. They are measured at the rear of the transmission with all accessories installed and operating. Since the figures vary when a given engine is installed in different models, some are representative rather than exact.
① Oil pressure at 1500 rpm.
② 88 hp in Mustang II; 82 hp in Pinto

TUNE-UP SPECIFICATIONS

When analyzing compression test results, look for uniformity among cylinders rather than specific pressures.

	ENGINE	SPARK PLUGS		DISTRIBUTOR		IGNITION TIMING (deg) ▲		VALVES Intake Opens	Fuel Pump Pressure (psi)	IDLE SPEED (rpm) ▲	
Year	No. Cyl. Displacement cu in. (cc)	Orig. Type ●	Gap (in	Point Dwell (deg)	Point Gap (in.)	Man Trans ●	Auto Trans	■ (deg)		Man Trans	Auto Trans
'72	4-97.6 (1600)	AGR-22	.030	40	.025	12B	—	17	3½-5½	800/500③	—
	4-122 (2000)	BRF-42	.034	40	.025	6B-10B	6B-10B	24	3½-5½	750/500③	650/500③
'73	4-97.6 (1600)	AGR-32	.034	40	.025	12B	—	17	3½-5½	800/500③	—
	4-122 (2000)	BRF-42	.034	40	.025	6B-10B	6B-10B	24	3½-5½	750/500③	650/500③
'74	4-122 (2000)	BRF-42	.034	39	.025	6B(3B)	6B(3B)	24	3½-4½	750	750
	4-140 (2300)	AGRF-52	.034	38	.027	6B	6B	22	3½-4½	750④	650④
	6-170.8 (2800)	AGR-42	.034	38	.025	12B	12B	20	3½-4½	750	650
'75	4-140 (2300)	AGRF-52	.034	Electronic		6B	6B(10B)	22	3½-5½	550	550
	6-170.8 (2800)	AGR-42	.034	Electronic		10B(8B)	12B(6B)	20	3½-5½	850	700
	8-302	ARF-42	.044	Electronic		—	6B	20	5-7	—	650
'76	4-140 (2300)	AGRF-52	.034	Electronic		6B	20B	22	5-7	750	650
	6-170.8 (2800)	AGR-42	.034	Electronic		10B(8B)	12B(6B)	20	3½-6	850	700
	8-302 (4950)	ARF-42	.044	Electronic		12B	6B(8B)	16	6-8	800	700
'77	4-140 (2300)	AWRF-42	.034	Electronic		6B	20B	22	5½-6½	850	750⑤
	6-170 (2800)	AWSF-42	.034	Electronic		10B	12B(6B)	20	3½-5¾	850	750⑥
	8-302 (4950)	ARF-52	.054	Electronic		12B	4B(12B)	16	5½-6½	850	700
'78	4-140 (2300)	AWRF-42	.034	Electronic		6B	20B	22	5½-6½	850	800(750)
	6-170 (2800)	AWSF-42	.034	Electronic		10B	12B(6B)	20	3½-5¾	700	650⑧(600)
	8-302 (4950)	ARF-52 (ARF-52-6)	.050 (.060)	Electronic		6B	4B(12B)⑦	16	5½-6½	900	700

TUNE-UP SPECIFICATIONS

When analyzing compression test results, look for uniformity among cylinders rather than specific pressures.

ENGINE		SPARK PLUGS		DISTRIBUTOR		IGNITION TIMING (deg) ▲		VALVES Intake Opens ■ (deg)	Fuel Pump Pressure (psi)	IDLE SPEED (rpm) ▲	
Year	No. Cyl. Displacement cu in. (cc)	Orig. Type ●	Gap (in.)	Point Dwell (deg)	Point Gap (in.)	Man Trans ●	Auto Trans			Man Trans	Auto Trans
'79	All					See Underhood Specifications Sticker					

NOTE: The underhood specifications sticker often reflects tune-up specification changes made in production. Sticker figures must be used if they disagree with those in this chart.

B Before Top Dead Center
— Not applicable
① and ② Not used
③ First figure is for idle speed with solenoid energized and automatic transmission in Drive, while the second figure is for idle speed with solenoid disconnected and automatic transmission in Neutral. Cars without a solenoid use higher figure.

▲ See text for procedure
■ All figures Before Top Dead Center
● Figure in parentheses is for California
④ 850 man, 750 auto in Pinto
⑤ Pinto/Bobcat wagon with 3.18 rear, except calif.—800
⑥ Without A/C, with 3.00 or 3.18 rear; except Calif.—700
⑦ 16B for high altitude
⑧ 700 with A/C on

FIRING ORDER

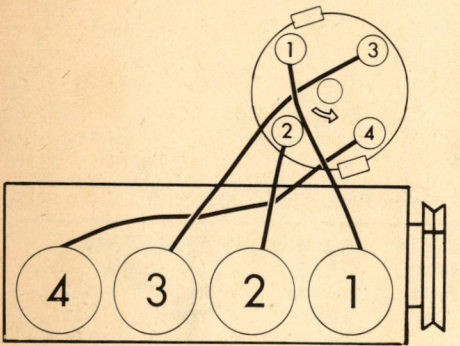

FORD MOTOR CO. 1600 cc 4-cyl.
Engine firing order: 1-2-4-3
Distributor rotation: counterclockwise

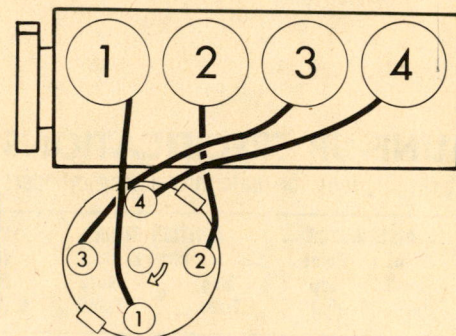

FORD MOTOR CO. 2000 cc 4-cyl.
Engine firing order: 1-3-4-2
Distributor rotation: clockwise

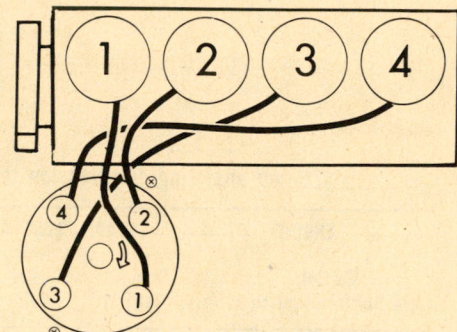

FORD MOTOR CO. 2300 cc 4-cyl.
Engine firing order: 1-3-4-2
Distributor rotation: clockwise

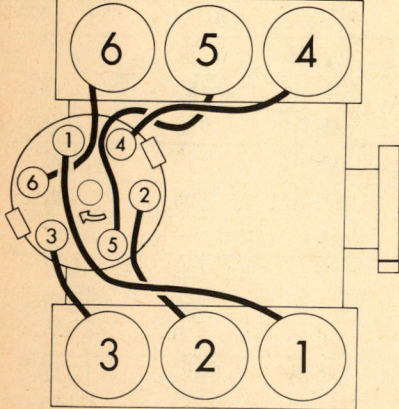

FORD MOTOR CO. 2800 cc V6 (1974)
Engine firing order: 1-4-2-5-3-6
Distributor rotation: clockwise

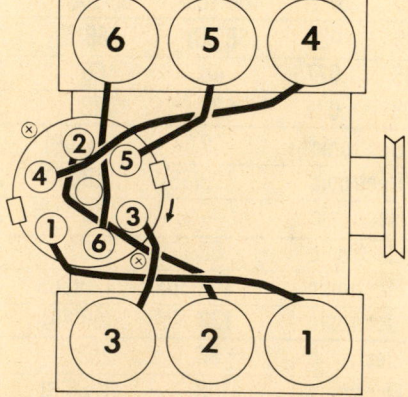

FORD MOTOR CO. 2800 cc V6 (1975 and later)
Engine firing order: 1-4-2-5-3-6
Distributor rotation: clockwise

(Circles are position of latches on 1975-76 models; squares are position of latches on 1977 and later models.)

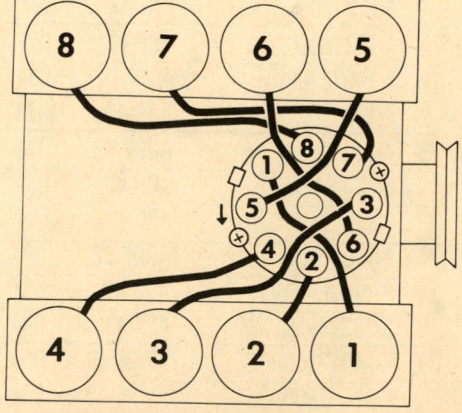

FORD MOTOR CO. 302 V8
Engine firing order: 1-5-4-2-6-3-7-8
Distributor rotation: clockwise

(Squares are position of latches through 1976; circles are position of latches on 1977-78 models).

VALVE SPECIFICATIONS

Year	Engine No. Cyl. Displacement (cu in.)	Seat Angle (deg)	Face Angle (deg)	Spring Test Pressure (lbs @ in.)	Spring Installed Height (in.)	STEM TO GUIDE Clearance (in.) Intake	STEM TO GUIDE Clearance (in.) Exhaust	STEM Diameter (in.) Intake	STEM Diameter (in.) Exhaust
'72	4-97.6 (1600 cc)	45	45	50 @ 1.26	1 $\frac{17}{64}$	.0008-.0027	.0017-.0036	.3102	.3093
	4-122 (2000 cc)	45	46	69 @ 1.42	1 $\frac{13}{32}$	.0008-.0025	.0018-.0035	.3163	.3153
'73	4-97.6 (1600 cc)	45	44	47 @ 1.263	1 $\frac{17}{64}$	.0008-.0027	.0017-.0036	.3102	.3093
	4-122 (2000 cc)	45	44	69 @ 1.418	1 $\frac{13}{32}$	.0008-.0025	.0018-.0035	.3163	.3153
'74	4-122 (2000 cc)	45	46	69 @ 1.418	1 $\frac{47}{64}$	.0008-.0025	.0018-.0035	.3163	.3153
	4-140 (2300 cc)	45	46	75 @ 1.560	1 $\frac{53}{64}$	.0010-.0027	.0015-.0022	.3419	.3415
	6-170.8 (2800 cc)	45	44	64 @ 1.585	1 $\frac{29}{32}$	.0008-.0025	.0018-.0035	.3162	.3153
'75-'79	4-140 (2300 cc)	45	46①	75 @ 1.56	1 $\frac{9}{16}$	.0006-.0023②	.0015-.0032	.3424③	.3415
	4-170.8 (2800 cc)	45	46①	64 @ 1.59	1 $\frac{19}{32}$	.0008-.0025	.0018-.0035	.3162	.3153
	8-302 (4950 cc)	45	46①	80 @ 1.69④	1 $\frac{39}{64}$⑤	.0010-.0027	.0015-.0032	.3420	.3415

① 1977-79: 44
② 1977-79: .0010-.0027
③ 1977-79: .3419

④ 80 @ 1.60—1975-76 exhaust
⑤ 1977-78: 1 $\frac{11}{16}$ intake, 1 $\frac{5}{8}$ exhaust

TORQUE SPECIFICATIONS
All readings in ft lbs

Year	Engine No. Cyl. Displacement (cu in.)	Cylinder Head Bolts	Rod Bearing Bolts	Main Bearing Bolts	Crankshaft Pulley Bolt	Flywheel to Crankshaft Bolts	MANIFOLD Intake	MANIFOLD Exhaust
'72-'79	4-97.6 (1600 cc)	65-70	30-35	65-70	24-28	50-55	12-15	15-18
	4-122 (2000 cc)	65-80	29-34	65-75	39-43	47-51	12-15	12-15①
	4-140 (2300 cc)	80-90	30-36	80-90	80-114② ④	54-64	14-21	16-23
	6-170.8 (2800 cc)	65-80	21-25	65-75	92-103②	47-51	15-18	14-18③
	8-302 (4950 cc)	65-72	19-24	60-70	70-90②	75-85	23-25	18-24

① 15-18 in 1974
② Crankshaft damper bolt

③ 16-23 1975-76; 20-30 in 1977-79
④ 1977-79: 100-120

CAPACITIES

Year	ENGINE No. Cyl. Displacement (Cu. In.)	Engine Crankcase Add 1 Qt For ■ New Filter	TRANSMISSION Pts To Refill After Draining 4-Speed Manual	TRANSMISSION Automatic (Total capacity)	Drive Axle (pts)	Gasoline Tank (gals)	COOLING SYSTEM (qts) With Heater	COOLING SYSTEM (qts) With A/C
'72	4-97.6 (1600 cc)	3	2.5	—	2.2	11①	7.75	—
	4-122 (2000 cc)	4	2.5	16	2.2	11①	8.50	8.50
'73	4-97.6 (1600 cc)	3	2.8	—	2.2	11①	7.80	—
	4-122 (2000 cc)	4	2.8	16	2.2	11①	8.50	8.50
'74	4-122 (2000 cc)	4	2.8	16	3	13①	8.50	8.50
	4-140 (2300 cc)	4	4④	16	3	13①	8.80③	9.20③
	6-170.8 (2800 cc)	4.5	4	16	3	13	12.5	12.8

Bobcat • Mustang II • Pinto

CAPACITIES

Year	ENGINE No. Cyl. Displacement (Cu. In.)	Engine Crankcase Add 1 Qt For ■ New Filter	TRANSMISSION Pts To Refill After Draining 4-Speed Manual	Automatic (Total capacity)	Drive Axle (pts)	Gasoline Tank (gals)	COOLING SYSTEM (qts) With Heater	With A/C
'75	4-140 (2300 cc)	4	3.5④	16	3⑧	13⑤⑥	8.7	9.0
	6-170.8 (2800 cc)	4.5	3.5④	15⑦	4	13⑤⑥	12.5	13.2
	8-302	4	—	15	4	13⑥	16.3	16.3
'76-'79	4-140 (2300 cc) Pinto, Bobcat	4	2.8	16/14②	2.2/4.0⑨	13⑤⑭	8.7	9.0
	4-140 (2300 cc) Mustang II	4	3.5	16	3/4.0⑨	13⑥	8.5	9.1
	6-170.8 (2800 cc) Pinto, Bobcat	4.5	3.5	16/14②	2.2/4.0⑨	13⑤⑭	12.5⑩	13.2⑪
	6-170.8 (2800 cc) Mustang II	4.5	3.5	14	3/4.0⑨	13⑥	12.3⑫	13.2⑬
	8-302 (4950 cc)	4	3.5	14	4.0	13⑥	16.3⑮	16.3⑮

■ ½ quart for 1600, 2800
— Not applicable
① Wagon—12 gals
② C3/C4
③ 8.5 qt in Pinto
④ 2.8 pt in Pinto
⑤ 14 gals on station wagon
⑥ 16.5 gals with auxiliary tank in Mustang II
⑦ 14 pt in Pinto

⑧ 2.3 pt in Pinto
⑨ 6.75/8.00 in. axle
⑩ 1977-79:8.5
⑪ 1977-79:9.2
⑫ 1977-78 M.T.: 8.3
     A.T.: 8.8
⑬ 1977-78: 9.0
⑭ Bobcat Sedan, Calif.: 11.7
⑮ 1978:14.6

CRANKSHAFT AND CONNECTING ROD SPECIFICATIONS

All measurements are given in inches

Year	Engine No. Cyl. Displacement (cu in.)	CRANKSHAFT Main Brg. Journal Dia	Main Brg. Oil Clearance	Shaft End-Play	Thrust on No.	CONNECTING ROD Journal Diameter	Oil Clearance	Side Clearance
'72-'73	4-97.6 (1600 cc)	2.1253-2.1261	.0005-.0016	.003-.011	3	1.9368-1.9376	.0004-.0024	.004-.010
	4-122 (2000 cc)	2.2432-2.2440	.0006-.0016	.003-.011	3	2.0464-2.0472	.0006-.0026	.004-.010
'74	4-122 (2000 cc)	2.2432-2.2440	.0006-.0016	.003-.011	3	2.0464-2.0472	.0006-.0015	.004-.011
	4-140 (2300 cc)	2.3982-2.3990	.0008-.0015	.004-.012	3	2.0465-2.0472	.0006-.0027	.0008-.0026
	6-170.8 (2800 cc)	2.2433-2.2441	.0006-.0019	.003-.011	3	2.0464-2.0472	.0006-.0022	.004-.011
'75	4-140 (2300 cc)	2.3982-2.3990	.0008-.0015	.004-.008	3	2.0464-2.0472	.0008-.0015	.0035-.0105
	6-170.8 (2800 cc)	2.2433-2.2441	.0005-.0016	.004-.008	3	2.1252-2.1260	.0005-.0015	.004-.011
	8-302 (4950 cc)	2.2482-2.2490	.0005-.0015①	.004-.008	3	2.1228-2.1236	.0008-.0015	.010-.020
'76-'79	4-140 (2300 cc)	2.3982-2.3990	.0008-.0015	.004-.008	3	2.0464-2.0472	.0008-.0015	.0035-.0105
	6-170.8 (2800 cc)	2.2433-2.2441	.0008-.0015	.004-.008	3	2.1252-2.1260	.0006-.0015	.004-.011
	8-302 (4950 cc)	2.2482-2.2490	.0005-.0015①	.004-.008	3	2.1228-2.1236	.0008-.0015	.010-.020

① .0001-.0015 on No. 1

RING GAP
All measurements are given in inches

Year	Engine	Top Compression	Bottom Compression
'72-'73	4-97.6 (1600 cc)	.009-.014	.009-.014
'72	4-122 (2000 cc)	.019-.021	.019-.021
'73-'74	4-122 (2000 cc)	.015-.023	.015-.023
'74	4-140 (2300 cc)	.010-.020	.010-.020
'74	6-170.8 (2800 cc)	.015-.023	.015-.023
'75-'79	4-140 (2300 cc)	.010-.020	.010-.020
'75-'79	6-170 (2800 cc)	.015-.023	.015-.023
'75-'78	8-302 (4950 cc)	.010-.020	.010-.020

Year	Engine	Oil Control
'72-'73	1600 cc	.009-.014
'72-'74	2000 cc	.016-.055
'74	2300 cc	.015-.055
'74	2800 cc	.015-.055
'75-'79	2300 cc	.015-.055
'75-'79	2800 cc	.015-.055
'75-'78	8-302	.015-.055

RING SIDE CLEARANCE
All measurements are given in inches

Year	Engine	Top Compression	Bottom Compression
'72-'73	4-97.6 (1600 cc)	.0016-.0036	.0016-.0036
'72-'74	4-122 (2000 cc)	.0019-.0038	.0019-.0038
'74-'79	4-140 (2300 cc)	.0020-.0040	.0020-.0040
'74-'79	6-170.8 (2800 cc)	.0020-.0033	.0020-.0033
'75-'78	8-302 (4950 cc)	.002-.004	.002-.004

Year	Engine	Oil Control
'72-'73	1600 cc	.0018-.0038
'72-'74	2000 cc	Snug
'74-'79	2300 cc	Snug
'74-'79	2800 cc	Snug
'75-'78	8-302	Snug

PISTON CLEARANCE

Year	Engine	Piston-to-Bore Clearance (in.)
'72-'73	4-1600 cc	.0016-.0022* .0019-.0025**
'72-'74	4-2000 cc	.0010-.0020
'74-'79	4-2300 cc	.0014-.0022
'74-'79	6-2800 cc	.0011-.0019
'75-'78	8-302	.0018-.0026

* No. 1, 2, and 3   ** No. 4

WHEEL ALIGNMENT SPECIFICATIONS

Year	Model	Caster Range (deg)	Caster Pref Setting (deg)	Camber Range (deg)	Camber Pref Setting (deg)	Toe-in (in.)	Steering Axis Inclin.	Wheel Pivot Ratio Inner Wheel (deg)	Outer Wheel
'72	All models	½N to 3½P	1½P	¼N to 1¾P	¾P	1/16 to 7/16	8.968	20	18.94
'73	All models	1N to 3P	1P	¼N to 1¾P	¾P	0 to ¼	8.968	20	18.94
'74-'76	Pinto, Bobcat	½P to 2P	1¼P	0 to 1½P	¾P	⅛ to ⅜	10.018	20	18.84
'74-'76	Sta. Wag.	¾P to 2¼P	1½P	0 to 1½P	¾P	⅛ to ⅜	10.018	20	18.84
'74-'76	Mustang II	⅛P to 1⅝P	⅞P	¼N to 1¼P	½P	0 to ¼	9.763	20	18.84
'77-'79	Pinto, Bobcat	¼P to 1¾P	1P	¼N to 1¼P	½P	0 to ¼	10.018	20	18.84
'77-'79	Sta. Wag.	½N to 1P	¼P	¼N to 1¼P	½P	0 to ¼	10.018	20	18.84
'77-'78	Mustang II	⅛P to 1⅝P	⅞P	¼N to 1¼P	½P	0 to ¼	9.763	20	18.84

N Negative   P Positive

NOTE: *The Mustang II, 1974-1978, is in this section. Mustang models are in the Comet car section.*

CHARGING SYSTEM

The charging system consists of an alternator, regulator, battery, charge indicator and fusible link. The alternator produces power in the form of alternating current. The regulator automatically adjusts the alternator field current to maintain the alternator output within prescribed limits to maintain battery charge. The alternator is self-current limiting.

Testing and adjustment of the alternator and regulator are covered in the "Unit Repair Section."

Alternator Removal

1. Disconnect the battery negative cable.
2. Disconnect the electrical leads.
3. Loosen the mounting bolts and tilt the alternator in toward the engine.
4. Remove the fanbelt, then remove the mounting bolts and the alternator.

Alternator Installation

1. Position the alternator and loosely install the mounting bolts.
2. Install fanbelt, pry on the front of the alternator so as to place tension on the belt (1/4 in. deflection at belt midpoint), then tighten mounting bolts.
3. Connect alternator wires and the battery cable.

Regulator Replacement

1. Disconnect the battery ground cable.
2. Remove the wiring harness from the regulator.
3. Remove the regulator retaining screws and remove the regulator.
4. Position the regulator on the car and install the retaining screws.
5. Attach the wiring to the regulator and connect the ground cable.

STARTING SYSTEM

The engine is equipped with a positive engagement starter. Internal starter repair procedures can be found in the Unit Repair Section.

Starter Removal and Installation

THROUGH 1973

1. Remove the ground cable from the battery.
2. Raise the car on a hoist and disconnect the starter cable. On the 1600, remove the right steering gear housing clamp and grommet from the crossmember, and loosen the left clamp bolts.
3. Remove the 3 starter retaining bolts. Remove the starter. On the 2000, you may have to turn the steering gear bellows clamp.
4. Position the starter motor to the engine.
5. Install the 3 retaining bolts and connect the starter cable. Tighten the steering clamps and bolts.
6. Lower the car and install the battery ground cable.

1974 AND LATER

1. Disconnect the battery ground cable.
2. Raise the car on a hoist and remove the four bolts retaining the crossmember under the bellhousing.
3. Remove the flex coupling clamping screw at the attachment point to the steering gear.
4. Remove the 3 nuts and bolts which attach the steering gear to the crossmember.
5. Disengage the steering gear from the flex coupling and pull the steering gear down to provide access to the starter motor.
6. Disconnect the starter cable from the starter motor.
7. Remove the starter motor attaching bolts and remove the starter.
8. Install the starter motor in the reverse order of removal.

Disabling the Interlock System

New automobiles are no longer required to have the seat belt/starter interlock system. The system may legally be disabled on cars that do have it, but the following procedure must be used.

1. Locate the override switch and terminal connector attached to it.
2. Remove the no. 32 (red with a light blue stripe) wire(s) and no. 33 (white with pink dots) wire(s) and splice them together.

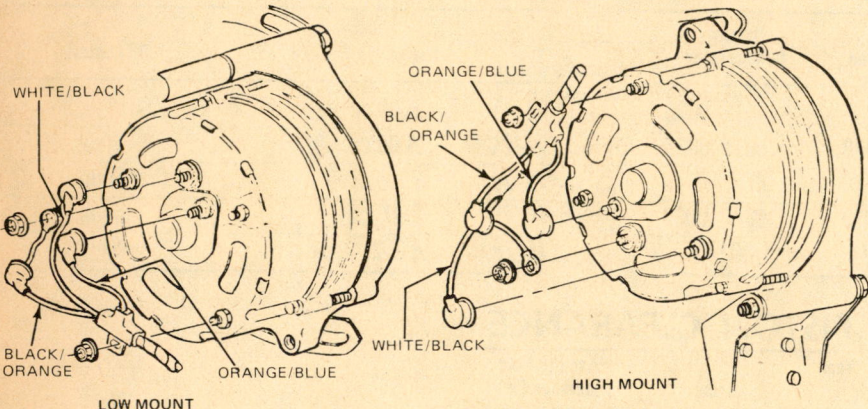

Typical connector details for the rear terminal alternator (© Ford Motor Co.)

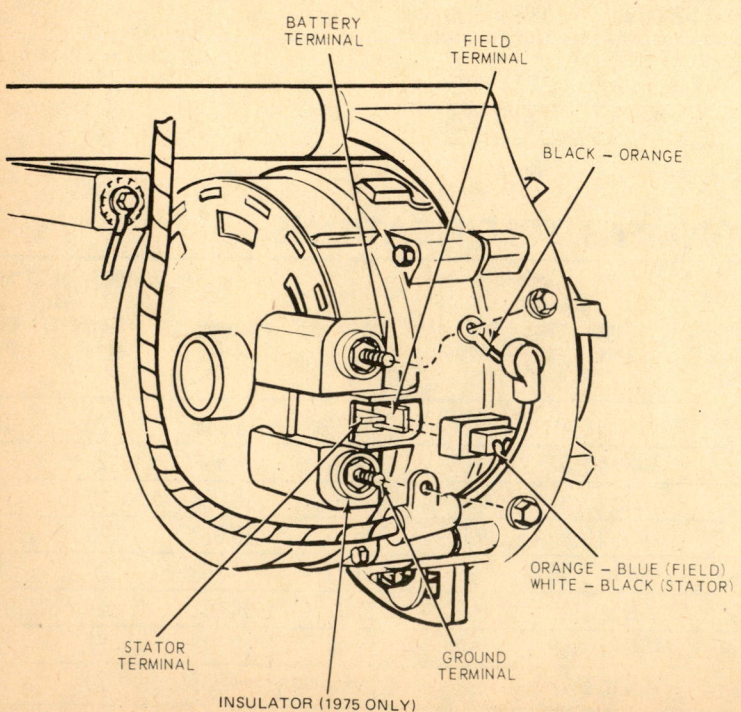

Typical connector details for the side terminal alternator (© Ford Motor Co.)

3. To remove the buzzer, remove the terminal connector from the buzzer, and tape it to the wiring harness to prevent rattling; then remove the buzzer unit.
4. To remove the warning light, remove the bulb from its socket, and replace the empty socket.

IGNITION SYSTEM

All distributors are the dual advance type; that is, they have both centrifugal and vacuum advance. Some models are equipped with a vacuum retard mechanism which retards ignition timing during deceleration and idling.

Beginning 1975, all Ford engines have electronic ignition which does not use replaceable contacts. This system, while retaining most of the features of the conventional system, uses a unique armature and magnetic pickup coil assembly inside the distributor and a solid state amplifier module.

NOTE: *The ignition wires used with electronic ignition can be easily damaged. Ford recommends the use of a special plier-like tool when installing or removing the wires. See the Electronic Ignition Unit Repair Section for details.*

Tachometer Hookup for Solid State Ignition

The new solid state ignition coil connector allows a tachometer test lead with an alligator clip type tip to be connected to the distributor electronic control terminal without removing the connector.

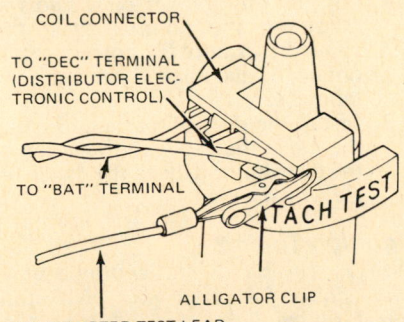

COIL CONNECTOR
TO "DEC" TERMINAL (DISTRIBUTOR ELECTRONIC CONTROL)
TO "BAT" TERMINAL
TACH TEST
ALLIGATOR CLIP
TACHOMETER TEST LEAD

Electronic ignition test tachometer hookup (© Ford Motor Co.)

Connect the clip to the Tach Test cavity. If the coil connector must be removed pull it out straight until it disconnects.

Distributor Removal and Installation

1. Remove the air cleaner on V6 and V8 engines. On the 4 cylinder engines equipped with an air pump, remove the one mounting bolt and the drive belt, then swing the pump to one side to gain access to the distributor. It may be necessary to

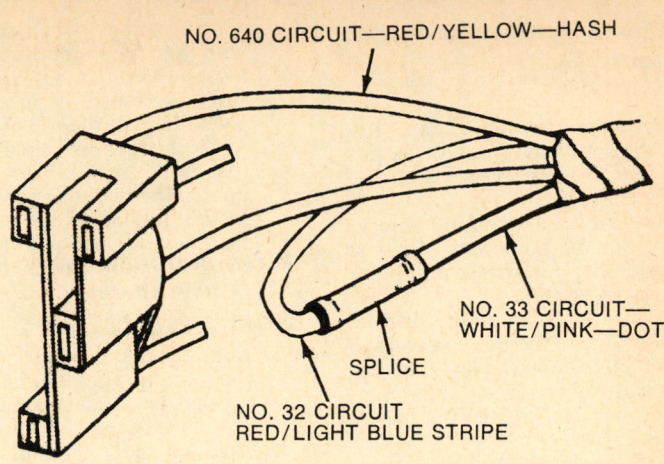

NO. 640 CIRCUIT—RED/YELLOW—HASH
NO. 33 CIRCUIT— WHITE/PINK—DOT
SPLICE
NO. 32 CIRCUIT RED/LIGHT BLUE STRIPE

Seatbelt interlock override switch terminal connector and wires (© Ford Motor Co.)

disconnect the air pump system air filter and lines. Unsnap the two clips or loosen the two screws and remove the distributor cap.
2. Note their positioning, and then disconnect the vacuum lines from the distributor. Disconnect the electronic ignition wiring harness.
3. Matchmark the distributor housing and the engine block, then scribe another mark on the housing to indicate the rotor position.
4. Remove the bolt that holds the distributor, then carefully pull out the unit.

NOTE: *The hex shaft which drives the oil pump may stick in the distributor shaft and be withdrawn from the pump. When installing the distributor coat one end of the hex shaft with heavy grease and insert that end into the hex hole in the distributor shaft.*

On the V8, make sure the oil pump intermediate shaft is fully engaged with the distributor. You may have to turn the engine with the starter to get full engagement.

Installation is as follows:
1. Align matchmarks, if engine has not been disturbed, and install distributor.

NOTE: *Keep in mind that the helical gear will tend to rotate the distributor as it is pushed down.*

2. If engine has been disturbed, turn crankshaft until No. 1 piston is at TDC on compression stroke and crankshaft damper timing marks are aligned. Place the cap on the distributor and scribe the location of No. one spark plug tower. Install the distributor so that the rotor points toward No. one. Install the hold-down bolt.
3. Tighten the hold-down bolt and connect the primary and high-tension wires. Adjust contact breaker points, if any, and ignition timing. Connect the vacuum line(s).

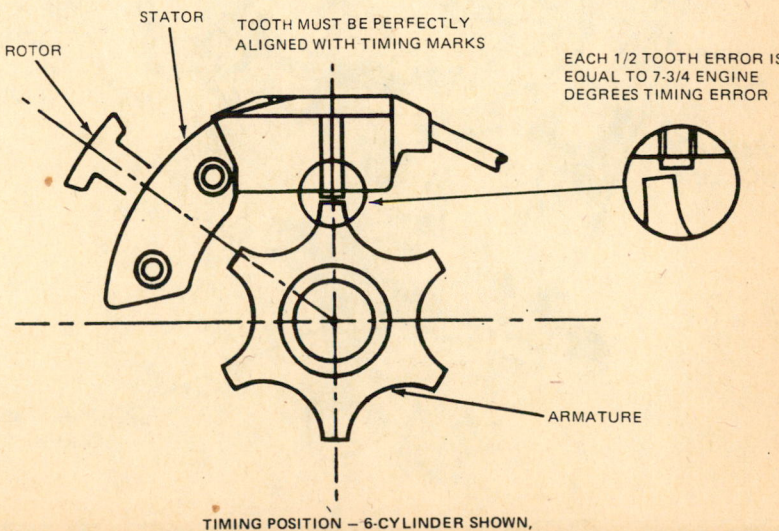

ROTOR
STATOR
TOOTH MUST BE PERFECTLY ALIGNED WITH TIMING MARKS
EACH 1/2 TOOTH ERROR IS EQUAL TO 7-3/4 ENGINE DEGREES TIMING ERROR
ARMATURE
TIMING POSITION – 6-CYLINDER SHOWN, 8-CYLINDER SIMILAR

Distributor firing position with electronic ignition (© Ford Motor Co.)

Contact Point Replacement and Adjustment

1600 CC

1. Remove the distributor cap. Remove the screw that retains the primary and condenser wires to the point set.
2. Remove the two retaining screws and lift out the point set. It is best to replace the condenser and point set at the same time.
3. Lubricate the cam with silicone cam lube. Place the point set on the breaker plate, making sure the tab on the bottom engages the indentation in the plate. Tighten the retaining screw.
4. Install the primary and condenser wires to the point set, making sure that the connectors are parallel to each other and to the ground when tightened.
5. Turn the engine to bring the point set rubbing block onto one of the cam's high points. Insert a feeler gauge, thickness equal to the point gap specified in the ''Tune-Up Specifications'' chart, between the contacts.
6. Adjust the gap if the feeler gauge does not fit between the contacts with just a slight drag. Partially loosen the retaining screws and insert a screwdriver in the breaker plate notch at the top of the points. Twist the screwdriver until the correct gap is obtained, and then tighten the retaining screws.
7. Install the distributor cap, aligning the tab in the cap with the notch in the distributor. Check the dwell angle with a meter.

2000 CC, 2300 CC, AND 2800 CC V6

1. Remove the distributor cap. Pull the breaker point wire from the condenser connector near the outside edge of the distributor body.
2. Remove the retaining screws and lift out the point set.
3. To replace the condenser: remove the attaching screw, grasp the condenser and wire, and work the rubber grommet out of the distributor body. Disconnect the ignition wire connector from the coil and disconnect the coil wire from the condenser.

   The condenser is mounted inside the distributor on the 2300 cc engine. Remove it by disconnecting the condenser lead, removing the retaining screw, and lifting the condenser from the distributor.
4. To install the condenser: place the condenser and wire assembly on the side of the distributor and work the grommet into the distributor body. Install the retaining screw and position the end of the wire attached to the condenser on the ''dist'' coil post. Install the ignition wire on the coil post over the condenser wire.

   Install the condenser on the 2300 cc engine by placing the condenser in position in the distributor, installing the hold-down screw and connecting the condenser lead to the points terminal.
5. Position the point set on the breaker plate and tighten the retaining screw. Connect the breaker point wire to the condenser. Lubricate the cam with silicone cam lube.
6. Turn the engine to bring the point set rubbing block onto one of the cam's high points. Insert a feeler gauge, the thickness of which is equal to the point gap specified in the ''Tune-Up Specifications'' chart, between the contacts.

CAUTION

When rotating the engine manually, never turn the overhead camshaft engine pulley counterclockwise or the camshaft drive belt may slip and alter the timing.

---

7. Adjust the gap if the feeler gauge does not fit between the contacts with just a slight drag. Slightly loosen the retaining screw and insert a screwdriver between the boss on the breaker plate and the notch on the points. Twist the screwdriver until the correct gap is obtained, and then tighten the retaining screw.
8. Install the distributor cap, aligning the tab in the cap with the notch in the distributor. Check the dwell angle with a meter.

Ignition Timing

NOTE: *The Electronic Ignition System may cause false-triggering of a standard timing light. An inductive type light should be used.*

1. Locate the timing marks and pointer on the lower engine pulley and front cover. Clean the marks and pointer, and then scribe the mark and pointer with chalk. (See ''Tune-Up Specifications'' chart for the correct timing.)
2. Hook up a timing light to number one spark plug according to the manufacturer's instructions. Disconnect the one or two vacuum lines and plug the open end(s).
3. Attach a tachometer and adjust the engine idle speed to 600 rpm or the timing speed specified on the underhood specifications sticker. (See ''Idle Speed Adjustment''.)

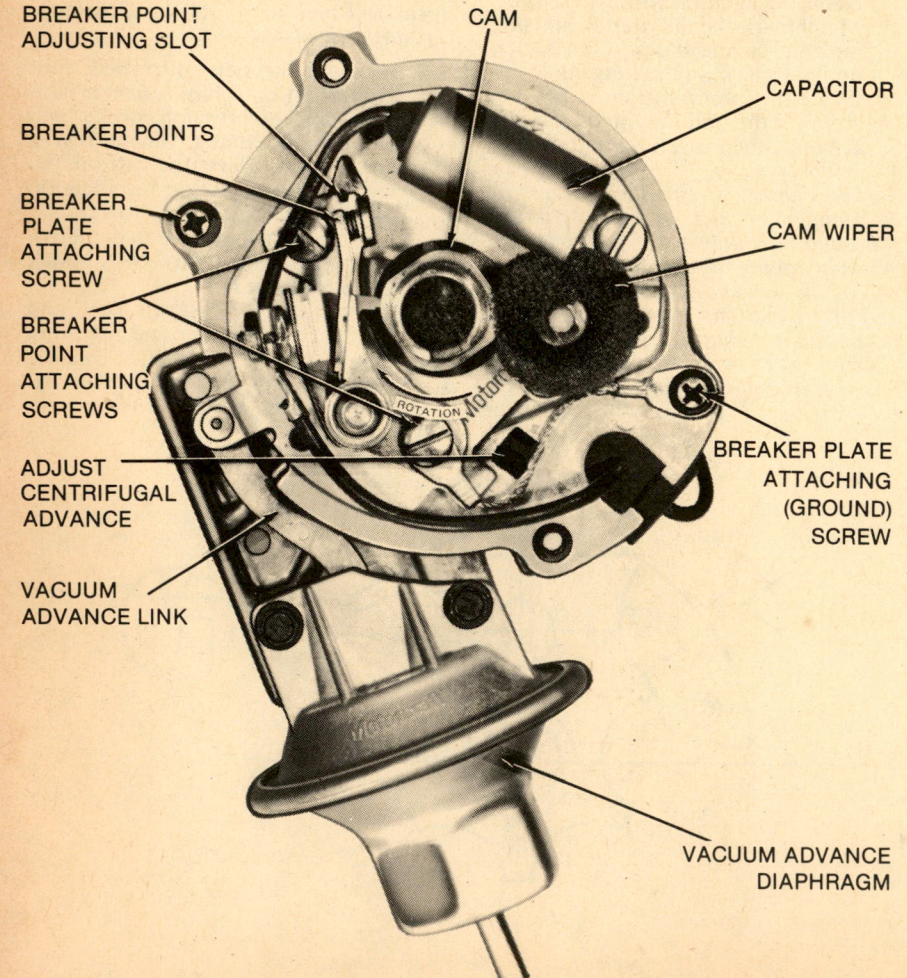

BREAKER POINT ADJUSTING SLOT

BREAKER POINTS

BREAKER PLATE ATTACHING SCREW

BREAKER POINT ATTACHING SCREWS

ADJUST CENTRIFUGAL ADVANCE

VACUUM ADVANCE LINK

CAM

CAPACITOR

CAM WIPER

BREAKER PLATE ATTACHING (GROUND) SCREW

VACUUM ADVANCE DIAPHRAGM

View of the inside of the 2300 cc point-type distributor (© Ford Motor Co)

4. Aim the timing light at the pulley marks. If the marks do not align, loosen the distributor hold-down screw or bolt and slowly rotate the distributor until the marks align. Tighten the hold-down screw or bolt.

NOTE: *A variance of plus or minus two degrees from the specified timing is acceptable.*

5. Recheck the timing, and then adjust the engine to normal idle speed.

FUEL SYSTEM

CARBURETOR

The carburetor used on the 1600 cc engine is an Autolite 1250 single-barrel downdraft unit.

All other four-cylinder engines are equipped with an Autolite model 5200 carburetor, except in California. The 5200 model is a two stage, two venturi carburetor. The primary stage venturi bore is of smaller diameter than the secondary stage venturi bore. The secondary stage is actuated by mechanical linkage when the primary throttle plates reach an opening of approximately 45°. 1978 and later Pintos and Bobcats sold in California with the 2.3 liter engine use a model 6500 feedback carburetor, which is a model 5200 modified with an externally variable fuel metering system to more precisely control engine emissions.

V6 and V8 engines use the Motorcraft 2150 two-barrel carburetor. This

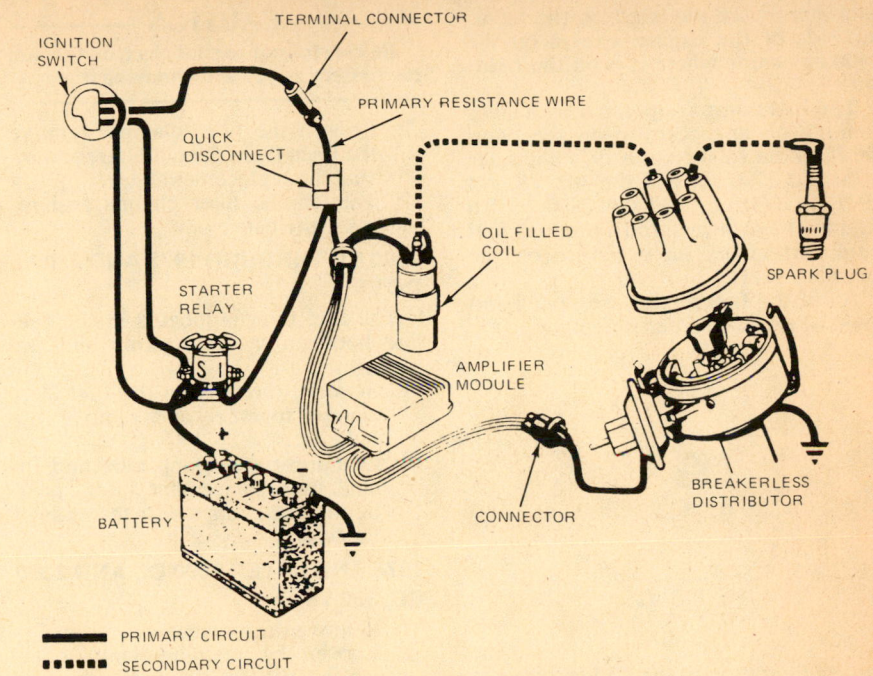

Typical electronic ignition system schematic (© Ford Motor Co.)

is a non-progressive two-barrel; both barrels operate simultaneously.

1977-78 California 302 V8s, and 1978 and later California 2.6 V6s have the Motorcraft 2700VV. This unit is equipped with a variable venturi, capable of varying the venturi area according to engine speed and load. It uses a dual element venturi valve which moves in and out of the air flowing through the two carburetor throats, controlled by vacuum and throttle position.

FUEL PUMP

All of the engines use a diaphragm-type mechanical fuel pump. All of the

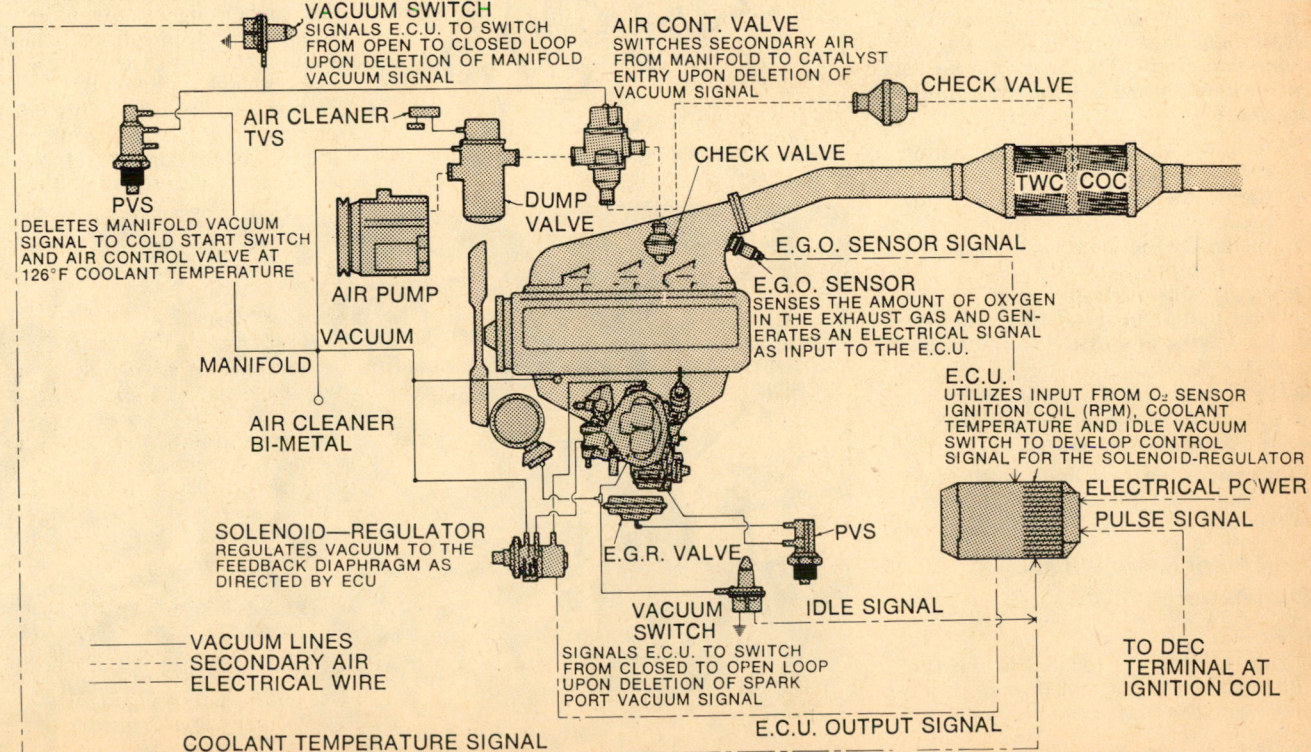

Electronically controlled feedback carburetor with three-way catalyst first used on 1978 2300 California engines (© Ford Motor Co.)

fuel pumps are mounted on the front, left-side of the engine, except on the 1600 cc engine where it is on the right-side.

The fuel pump is operated by a lever running on an eccentric on the camshaft on the 1600 cc, the 1974 and later 2000 and 2300 V8, and the 302 V8. All 1971-73 2000 cc, and the 2800 cc V6 engines have a pushrod operated fuel pump driven by an eccentric on the auxiliary shaft.

All of the fuel pumps are sealed and must be replaced when defective.

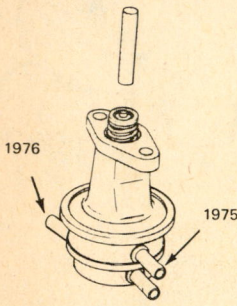

The configuration of the V6 fuel pump is changed, starting 1976
(© Ford Motor Co.)

Removal and Installation

1. Disconnect the fuel lines from the fuel pump and plug the inlet line from the gas tank to prevent gas leakage.
2. Remove the fuel pump retaining screws and remove the pump.

NOTE: *Before removing the pump, rotate the engine so that the low point of the cam lobe is against the pump arm. This can be determined by loosening the pump mounting bolts, then rotating the engine until tension is removed from the pump arm.*

3. Remove the fuel pump actuating rod, is so equipped.
4. Clean all gasket mounting surfaces.
5. Install the fuel pump actuating rod, if so equipped.
6. Apply oil-resistant sealer to the fuel pump, position the pump on the engine and install the retaining screws.

NOTE: *Make sure the fuel pump rocker arm or rod is riding on the camshaft or intermediate shaft eccentric.*

7. Connect the fuel lines to the fuel pump, start the engine and check for leaks.

Fuel Filter Removal and Installation

1600 CC

The fuel filter is located in the fuel line beneath the battery; therefore, it is necessary to remove the battery to replace the filter.

1. Disconnect the battery cables. Remove the hold-down retaining nut and remove the battery.

---

2. Loosen the filter clamps, remove the lines from the old filter, and install the replacement filter.
3. Tighten the filter clamps and replace the battery.

2000 CC THROUGH 1973 AND 2800 CC V6

The fuel filter is located in the fuel line between the fuel pump and the carburetor.

1. Squeeze the tabs on the fuel filter clamps together and remove the old filter.
2. Compress the clamp tabs and install the replacement filter, positioning the clamps near the ends of the filter.

1974 AND LATER 2000 CC AND 2300 CC, 302 V8

1. Remove the air cleaner.
2. Loosen the retaining clamp securing the fuel inlet hose to the fuel filter.
3. Unscrew the fuel filter from the carburetor. Disconnect the fuel filter from the hose. Model 2700 VV carburetor fuel filters are behind the fuel inlet fitting. After removing the hose, unscrew the fitting

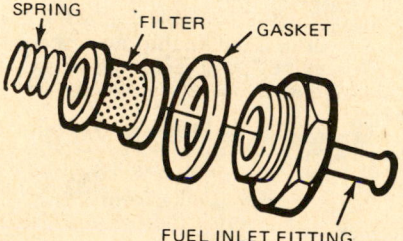

Model 2700 VV fuel filter (© Ford Motor Co.)

---

and be ready to catch the filter; it is located by a spring. Install the new filter over the spring in the carburetor body, then replace the inlet fitting.

4. Install the fuel filter in the reverse order of removal.

Idle Speed and Mixture Adjustment

NOTE: *The factory recommended procedure for adjusting the idle mixture on 1975 and later models requires the addition of an artificial mixture enrichment substance (propane) to the air intake. This method requires special tools not generally available to the public. The procedures that follow are specifically recommended by the factory only for models through 1974.*

1600 CC

1. Check the idle speed with the air cleaner removed and the headlights on high beam. If it is necessary to make an adjustment, turn the nut on the bottom of the carburetor solenoid to correct the speed.
2. When the idle speed is correct, disconnect the solenoid at the quick-disconnect.
3. Idle speed should equal the lower figure in the "Tune-Up Specifications" chart. Turn the carburetor idle screw if an adjustment is necessary.
4. Reconnect the solenoid. Open the throttle slightly and check to see that the solenoid plunger extends. Idle speed should be increased to the higher figure given in the "Tune-Up Specifications" chart.
5. Adjust the idle mixture screw until a smooth idle is obtained.
6. Turn the engine off and install the air cleaner. Recheck the idle speed and, if it is not correct, remove the air cleaner and readjust the idle

1600 cc idle speed and mixture adjustment screws

speed. Repeat this operation until the idle speed is correct.

2000 CC, 2300 CC WITHOUT AIR CONDITIONING, AND ALL V6

1. Start the engine and check the idle speed. Make this check on automatic-equipped cars with the selector in Drive and the wheels blocked.
2. Turn the carburetor curb idle screw in or out as necessary to correct the idle speed to the figure in the "Tune-Up Specifications" chart.
3. Adjust the carburetor idle mixture adjusting screw to obtain the smoothest idle.
4. Turn off the engine and install the air cleaner. Restart the engine and check the idle speed. If the idle speed has changed, remove the air cleaner and readjust the idle speed. Repeat this operation until the idle speed is correct.

2000 CC, 2300 CC WITH AIR CONDITIONING

1. Turn the air conditioner on and, if equipped with automatic transmission, block the wheels and place the selector in Drive.
2. Check the idle speed and, if it isn't equal to the higher figure given in the "Tune-Up Specifications" chart, turn the adjusting nut on the bottom of the carburetor solenoid to correct it.

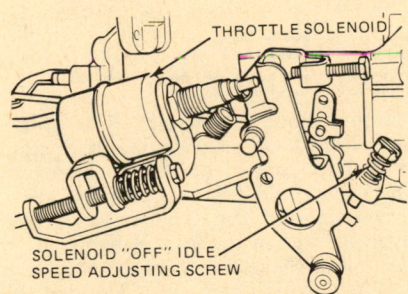

THROTTLE SOLENOID

SOLENOID "OFF" IDLE SPEED ADJUSTING SCREW

Model 2150 carburetor idle speed adjustment   (© Ford Motor Co.)

3. Disconnect the solenoid at the quick-disconnect. Turn the air conditioner off and, on automatic-equipped cars, put the selector in neutral.
4. Check the idle speed. If it does not conform with the lower figure in the "Tune-Up Specifications" chart, adjust the carburetor curb idle screw to correct it.
5. Reconnect the solenoid. Open the throttle slightly and check to see that the solenoid plunger extends. The idle speed should be increased to the higher figure listed in the "Tune-Up Specifications" chart.
6. Turn the carburetor idle mixture screw until the smoothest idle is obtained.
7. Turn the engine off and install the air cleaner. Restart the engine and

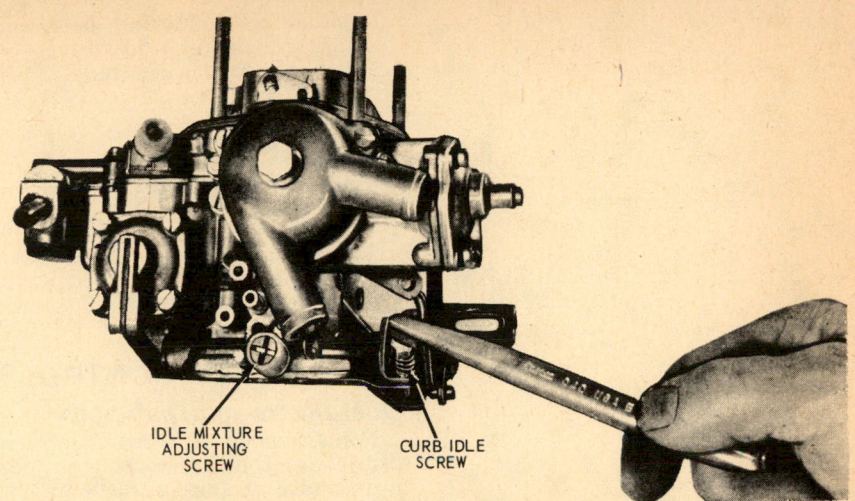

IDLE MIXTURE ADJUSTING SCREW

CURB IDLE SCREW

Autolite 5200 carburetor idle adjustments
(© Ford Motor Co)

check the idle speed (A/C on, automatic transmission in Drive). If an adjustment is necessary, turn the engine off and remove the air cleaner. Start the engine and adjust the idle speed. Repeat this operation as many times as necessary.

COOLING SYSTEM

Coolant is circulated from the bottom of the radiator up through the water pump and into the cylinder block and cylinder head to the thermostat. If the engine is at operating temperature (or hotter), the coolant is returned to the radiator top tank, from where it flows down through the radiator tubes to be cooled by air. If the engine is cold, the coolant flows through a by-pass hose to allow the coolant in the block and head to warm up quickly.

NOTE: *Early 1975 models require that air be bled from the cooling system to prevent overheating at low speeds. Fill the engine block through the upper radiator hose; to bleed the system, detach the heater core return hose momentarily with the engine running. Do not attempt this with the engine at normal operating temperature; serious burns could result.*

Overheating at high speeds on the early 1975 V8 Mustang II may be caused by incorrect radiator air deflectors. The top deflector should be removed and the lower one replaced with the updated part.

Radiator Removal and Installation

1. Remove the radiator cap and drain the coolant.
2. Disconnect the charcoal canister line from the clip on the radiator.
3. Disconnect the radiator hoses from the radiator.
4. Disconnect the transmission fluid

cooler lines from the bottom of the radiator, if so equipped.
5. Place a block of wood under the radiator for support and remove the mounting bolts. Position the fan shroud, if so equipped, rearward over the fan. Remove the radiator.
6. Reverse the removal procedure to install the radiator. Refill the cooling system.

Water Pump Removal and Installation

1. Drain the cooling system.
2. Disconnect the lower radiator hose and heater hose from the water pump.
3. Loosen the alternator retaining and adjusting bolt, and remove the drive belt.
4. Remove the fan shroud, fan and water pump pulley. On 2000 and 2300 cc engines, remove the camshaft drive belt cover first. It is not necessary to remove the cam belt or inner cover
5. Remove the water pump retaining bolts and remove the pump from the engine.
6. Clean all mating surfaces and install the pump with a new gasket coated with sealer. If a new pump is being installed, transfer the heater hose fitting from the old pump.
7. Reverse the removal steps to install the pump. Refill the cooling system.

Thermostat Removal and Installation

1. Drain the cooling system.
2. Remove the thermostat housing attaching bolts.

NOTE: *On the 2800 cc V6, the thermostat is located on the bottom of the water pump housing. The thermostat housing connects to the radiator lower hose, instead of the upper hose.*

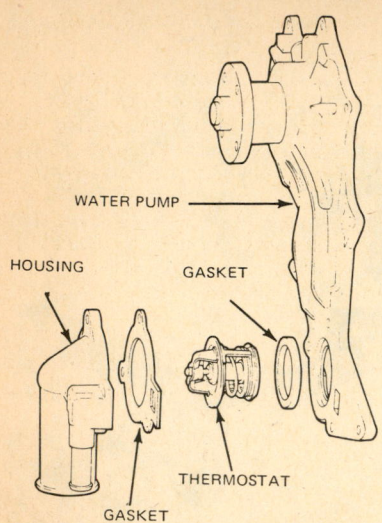

V6 engine thermostat installation
(© Ford Motor Co.)

V8 engine thermostat installation
(© Ford Motor Co.)

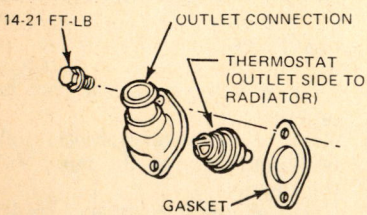

2300 cc engine thermostat installation
(© Ford Motor Co.)

3. On 1600 cc, 2300 cc, and 302 V8 engines, lift the thermostat housing from the engine and remove the thermostat and gasket.
4. On 2000cc engines, remove the retaining clip, thermostat, thermostat seal, and gasket from the housing.
5. Clean the gasket mating surfaces and the thermostat housing.
6. Install the thermostat, gasket, seal, and retaining clip (2000 cc only) in the thermostat housing. On the 2300 cc and V8 engines, twist the thermostat to lock it into place in the housing. Coat the gasket with sealer.

7. Install the attaching bolts and tighten them to 12-15 ft lbs.
8. Refill the cooling system.

EMISSION CONTROLS

Testing and diagnosis of emission control equipment is included in the "Emission Control Systems" section of the "Unit Repair Section."

DISTRIBUTOR CONTROLS

Dual-Diaphragm Distributor

Certain models use a dual-diaphragm distributor. This distributor has a normal set of centrifugal advance weights and vacuum diaphragm advance, with the addition of another diaphragm controlled by manifold vacuum. This second diaphragm acts to retard the spark at deceleration and idle, when manifold vacuum is greatest. While this decreases the power of the engine at these times, there is an increase in the braking effect of the engine and hydrocarbon emissions are reduced.

Coolant Temperature Control Valve

Certain models use a coolant temperature control valve which screws into the water jacket. Vacuum lines connect it to the carburetor, outer distributor vacuum chamber (advance), and the intake manifold. This valve helps prevent overheating by connecting intake manifold vacuum to the distributor and allowing vacuum advance during idling when the coolant temperature reaches a certain point.

Cold Start Spark Advance System

On some 1975 and later engines, a cold start spark advance system is added to the distributor control system. Intake manifold vacuum is routed to the distributor when the coolant temperature is below 125°F or above 235°F. Thus full advance is provided when the engine is cold or overheated at idle.

Spark Delay Valve

Some models utilize a spark delay in the vacuum line to the vacuum advance chamber of the distributor. This valve cuts off vacuum advance during certain heavy throttle applications for a period of seconds.

Electronic Spark Control

This system, used in 1972 only, blocks carburetor vacuum to the distributor vacuum advance mechanism under certain speed and temperature conditions. It consists of a temperature sensor, a speed sensor, an amplifier, and a distributor modulator vacuum valve. This system prevents ignition advance by blocking carburetor vacuum from the distributor advance mechanism until the car reaches 35 mph when the ambient temperature is over 65°F.

The temperature sensor monitors outside air temperature and relays this information to the amplifier. The amplifier controls the distributor modulator vacuum valve, which is connected into the carburetor-to-distributor vacuum line and is normally open. When the temperature is over 65°F, the sensor sends a signal to the amplifier which relays the signal to the distributor vacuum modulator. The modulator closes, cutting off ignition advance, until vehicle speed reaches 35 mph as signaled by the speed sensor in the speedometer cable. When the ambient temperature is below 49° the system does not function.

EXHAUST GAS RECIRCULATION

Some models, starting 1974, utilize an Exhaust Gas Recirculation System (EGR) to control oxides of nitrogen. On V6 and V8 engines, exhaust gases travel through the exhaust gas crossover passage in the intake manifold. A portion of these gases are diverted into a spacer which is mounted under the carburetor. The EGR control valve, which is attached to the rear of the spacer, consists of a vacuum diaphragm with an attached plunger which normally blocks off exhaust gases from entering the intake manifold. On 4 cylin-

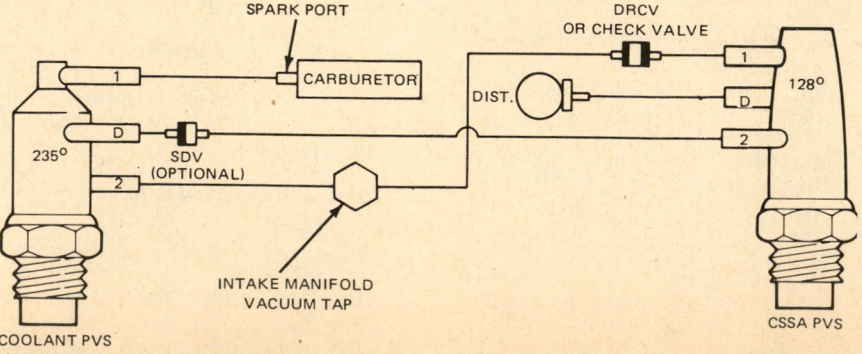

CSSA system, PVS means ported vacuum switch (© Ford Motor Co.)

der engines, an external tube carries exhaust manifold gases to the carburetor spacer. The EGR valve is controlled by a vacuum line from the carburetor.

The vacuum diaphragm opens the EGR valve permitting exhaust gases to flow through the carburetor spacer and enter the intake manifold where they combine with the fuel mixture and enter the combustion chambers. The exhaust gases are relatively oxygen-free, and tend to dilute the combustion charge. This lowers peak combustion temperature thereby reducing oxides of nitrogen.

THERMACTOR

From 1974 on, some models are equipped with an air injection system. The thermactor system consists of an air pump, check valves, anti-backfire valve, and air distribution and injection tubes. The belt driven air pump injects air into the exhaust manifold near the cylinder head. The air combines with the gases leaving the cylinders and burns off some of the harmful exhaust gases.

CATALYTIC CONVERTER

Starting 1975, some Pintos, Bobcats, and Mustang IIs and all California cars, are equipped with catalytic converter units. All 1976 and later models have them. While the unit does not require servicing until replacement, there are some precautions that must be observed.

1. Use unleaded fuel; the use of leaded fuel in a converter equipped car will invalidate the warranty.
2. Running out of gas may cause damage to the catalyst.
3. Proper engine maintenance is important. Misfires and other malfunctions can cause overheating and converter damage.
4. Do not run the engine for more than 30 seconds with a plug wire off or shorted.
5. Do not run an overly rich mixture for a long period of time.
6. Check ignition performance with an oscilloscope rather than by pulling a plug wire off.

FUEL SYSTEM CONTROLS

Carburetors

Carburetors are calibrated for leaner mixtures to decrease unburned hydrocarbon emissions. Idle mixture adjusting screws are equipped with limiter caps to prevent their being adjusted for excessively rich air-fuel mixtures at idle. The 1600 cc engine and 2000 cc engines equipped with air conditioning have a throttle positioning solenoid, which raises the idle speed when energized and retracts from the throttle lever when de-energized to prevent dieseling.

FEEDBACK CARBURETOR

1978 and later Pintos and Bobcats sold in California with the 2300 engine have a feedback carburetor electronic engine control system. The system works in conjunction with the Thermactor and catalytic converter systems to continually monitor and modify the fuel/air mixture for optimum performance and minimal exhaust emissions. Full details can be found in the Unit Repair Section.

Heat Riser Valve

Starting 1975, some engines use a vacuum operated heat riser valve. The valve preheats the fuel-air mixture by directing exhaust gases through passages in the intake manifold. The heat riser operates only during engine warmup.

Deceleration Valve

This valve is a vacuum-actuated valve which is attached to the intake manifold and connected to the carburetor with an air-fuel line. High vacuum during deceleration opens the valve and draws a metered air-fuel mixture through the hose from the carburetor. This enters the intake manifold and then the combustion chamber, where it is burned. This extra mixture slows the engine's deceleration rate and reduces the usually high exhaust emissions during slow-down.

Heated Intake Air Cleaner

The air cleaner is equipped with a thermostatically controlled door in the air cleaner snorkel. When the underhood temperature is under about 90°F, the door is closed, blocking off cooler underhood air from the air cleaner and allowing heated air from a shroud over the exhaust manifold to enter. When the temperature is over about 130°F, the door opens allowing the cooler underhood air to enter the air cleaner.

Evaporative Emission Control System

All models are equipped with a fuel vapor control system. The system has three major components—the fuel tank, the vapor separator, and the vapor absorbing charcoal canister. The fuel tank is equipped with a pressure-vacuum relief filler cap and has the vapor separator mounted on the top.

Fuel vapors are stored in the vapor canister to be drawn into the engine to be consumed.

CRANKCASE EMISSION CONTROLS

Crankcase emission control equipment consists of an oil separator (mounted on the side of the four-cylinder engine block), a positive crankcase ventilation (PCV) valve (mounted on the top of the oil separator on four-cylinders, in the intake manifold on 1974 V6s, and in the rocker cover on 1975 and later V6 and V8), a closed oil filler cap, and connecting hoses.

ENGINE

The standard engine used in the Pinto through 1973 is a 1600 cc, four-cylinder, inline overhead valve unit having a cross-flow cylinder head. The cylinder bores are machined in the cast-iron block and cooled by full-length water jackets.

The crankshaft is made of cast iron and runs in five main bearings. Endplay is controlled by thrust washers on each side of the center main bearing.

The camshaft is driven in a conventional manner, at one-half engine speed, by a single-row roller chain. A helical gear on the cam drives the distributor and oil pump, while an eccentric operates the fuel pump.

The cast-iron cylinder head has integral valve guides; although guide replacement is possible and sleeves are

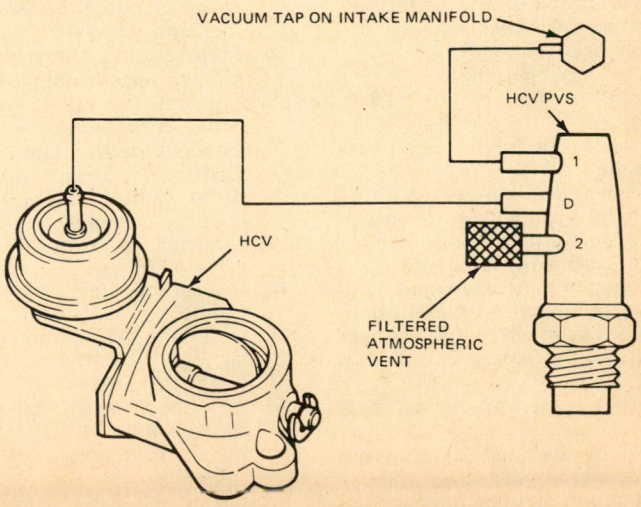

VACUUM TAP ON INTAKE MANIFOLD

HCV PVS

HCV

FILTERED ATMOSPHERIC VENT

Vacuum operated heat riser valve system (© Ford Motor Co.)

available. Intake valves are aluminum coated, and cannot be refaced.

The 2000 and 2300 cc, overhead camshaft, four-cylinder engine is of cast-iron construction. The crankshaft is supported by five main bearings and the camshaft by three bearings. The camshaft is belt driven by the crankshaft. Belt tension is adjusted by a spring loaded idler pulley.

The pistons are made from an aluminum alloy and forged steel connecting rods are used.

The 2800 cc engine is a V6 overhead valve design. The cylinder heads and engine block are made of cast-iron. Four main bearings support the crankshaft. The distributor and the oil pump are driven by an eccentric at the front of the camshaft. The connecting rods are forged steel with replaceable copper-lead alloy insert bearings. The intake manifold is made from aluminum and has individual passages to the openings in the cylinder heads. The V6 has a full pressure lubrication system fed by a rotor type oil pump mounted at the rear of the crankcase.

Starting 1975, the Mustang II was offered with an optional 302 cubic inch V8. This is the same engine as used in other Ford cars, an overhead valve design with wedge shaped combustion chambers.

CAUTION

Metric and standard thread bolts are used in the four and six cylinder engines and transmissions. Only metric tools should be used to remove metric bolts.

If any repair operation requires the removal of a component of the air conditioning system (on vehicles so equipped), do not disconnect the refrigerant lines. If it is impossible to move the component out of the way with the lines attached, have the system evacuated. Air conditioning systems contain pressurized Freon, which is very dangerous to the untrained.

Engine Removal—1600 cc

1. Remove hood, after scribing matchmarks around hinges.
2. Disconnect battery cables.
3. Drain the cooling system.

NOTE: *Drain engine block as well as radiator.*

4. Disconnect radiator hoses and remove radiator.
5. Remove air cleaner assembly.
6. Disconnect heater hoses from water pump and intake manifold.
7. Disconnect throttle linkage.
8. Disconnect oil pressure and temperature sender wires, then disconnect alternator wires. Disconnect the carburetor solenoid and coil battery wires.

NOTE: *It is a good idea to tag these wires.*

9. Disconnect exhaust pipe from manifold and remove hot air tubes.
10. Disconnect fuel inlet line at fuel pump.

NOTE: *Plug the line so that gas does not siphon from tank.*

11. Disconnect coil wires, then remove spark plug wires and distributor cap.
12. Jack up the front of the car and support on axle stands.
13. Disconnect starter wires, remove starter and oil pan shield.
14. Remove clutch cover. Drain the oil.
15. Lower the car to the floor.
16. Remove clutch housing-to-engine bolts, then install lifting brackets and chain hoist.
17. Disconnect the front motor mounts, while supporting engine with chain hoist.
18. Place an axle stand or wooden block under the transmission.
19. Raise the engine slightly, while pulling forward to separate the transmission input shaft from the clutch; lift engine out of car.

Engine Installation—1600 cc

1. Position the engine assembly in the engine compartment and start the input shaft into the clutch disc. It may be necessary to adjust the position of the transmission if the input shaft doesn't enter the clutch disc properly. If the engine won't move after the shaft enters the clutch, turn the crankshaft pulley slowly with the transmission in gear until the splines on the input shaft align with those on the clutch disc.
2. Slide the engine rearward, making sure the flywheel upper cover plate engages the dowels on the clutch housing. Align the front motor mounts and the exhaust manifold with the exhaust pipe.
3. Install the front motor mount nuts and tighten them to 20-30 ft lbs.
4. Install and tighten the upper clutch housing-to-engine attaching bolts. Make sure that the engine ground strap is secured by the upper left bolt.
5. Install the distributor cap and wires. Connect the fuel line to the fuel pump.
6. Connect the oil pressure and water temperature sending unit wires. Connect the carburetor solenoid and distributor battery wires.
7. Connect the alternator wires.
8. Connect the exhaust pipe to the exhaust manifold and install the heat duct on the manifold.
9. Connect the throttle linkage to the carburetor.
10. Connect the heater hoses to the engine.
11. Install the radiator and connect the hoses.
12. Install the air cleaner.
13. Jack the front of the car up and support it with stands.
14. Install the starter and connect the cable.
15. Install the lower clutch housing cover.

16. Install the oil pan drain plug and the cooling system drain plug in the block. Close the radiator petcock.
17. Remove the jack stands and lower the car.
18. Fill the engine with oil and the cooling system with coolant.
19. Connect the negative battery cable.
20. Start the engine and allow it to idle. Check for leaks and perform any necessary adjustments.
21. Install the hood.

Engine Removal—2000 cc

1. Drain the engine of coolant and oil. Remove the hood.
2. Remove the air cleaner and the exhaust manifold shroud.
3. Disconnect the battery ground cable.
4. Remove the upper and lower hoses from the radiator.
5. Remove the radiator and fan.
6. Disconnect the heater hose from the water pump and carburetor choke fitting.
7. Disconnect the wires from the alternator and starter. It is good practice to tag these wires to prevent confusion during installation.
8. Disconnect the carburetor accelerator cable. If the vehicle is equipped with air conditioning, remove the compressor from the mounting bracket and lay it aside.

NOTE: *Leave the refrigerant lines attached.*

9. Disconnect the flexible fuel line from the fuel tank line and plug the fuel tank line.
10. Disconnect the coil primary wire and the water temperature and oil temperature sending units.
11. Jack up the vehicle and remove the starter.
12. Remove the flywheel (or converter housing) upper mounting bolts.

NOTE: *Two 10 mm X ³/₈ in. studs are used to attach the upper housing to the engine. If the studs are removed, make sure they are reinstalled with the metric threads in the engine block.*

13. Disconnect the exhaust pipe at the exhaust manifold. Unbolt the engine right and left mount at the underbody bracket. Remove the flywheel (or converter housing) cover.
14. On vehicles equipped with manual transmissions, remove the flywheel housing lower mounting bolts. On automatic transmission vehicles, disconnect the converter from the flywheel and remove the converter housing lower mounting bolts. It is necessary to turn the crankshaft pulley to gain access to the four converter – to – flywheel attaching nuts.
15. Lower the vehicle and support the transmission or converter housing with a hydraulic jack.
16. Attach the engine lifting apparatus

and carefully pull the engine from the engine compartment.

17. On automatic transmission-equipped vehicles, match-mark the flywheel and the torque converter so they can be rejoined correctly.

Engine Installation—2000 cc

1. Place a new gasket over the exhaust pipe.
2. Carefully, lower the engine into the engine compartment. Be sure that the exhaust manifold studs are aligned with the holes in the exhaust pipe flange. On a vehicle with automatic transmission, start the converter pilot shaft into the crankshaft. On manual transmission cars, start the transmission input shaft into the clutch disc. It may be necessary to adjust the position of the transmission with relation to the engine if the input shaft fails to enter the clutch disc. If the engine hangs up after the shaft enters, turn the crankshaft slowly with the transmission in gear, until the input shaft splines mesh with the clutch disc splines.
3. Remove the lifting apparatus and install the flywheel (or converter housing) upper mounting bolts.
4. Remove the jack from the transmission and jack up vehicle.
5. Install the flywheel (or converter housing) lower mounting bolts. On an automatic transmission car, attach the converter to the flywheel and torque to 23-28 ft lbs.
6. Install the flywheel (or converter housing) dust cover.
7. Install the engine left and right mounting brackets to the underbody.
8. Unplug the fuel tank line and connect it to the flexible line. Tighten the exhaust pipe and exhaust manifold.
9. Lower the vehicle and connect the water and oil temperature sending units, coil primary wire and accelerator cable.
10. Install and connect the starter. Connect the alternator wires, and heater hose to the water pump and carburetor choke fitting.
11. Install the fan pulley, fan and drive belt. On vehicles equipped with air conditioning, install the compressor on the mounting bracket and adjust the belt tension. Drive belt should sag approximately 1/2 in. under thumb pressure at the middle of the longest side.
12. Install the radiator and connect the upper and lower hoses. Fill and bleed the cooling system. Fill the engine with proper amount and grade of engine oil.
13. Connect the battery ground cable and operate the engine at fast idle, checking all gaskets and hoses for leaks.
14. On automatic transmission vehi-

cles, adjust the transmission control linkage.

15. Install the air cleaner and connect the crankcase ventilation hose.
16. Install the hood.

Engine Removal—2300 cc

1. Raise the hood and fasten it up.
2. Drain the coolant from the radiator and the oil from the crankcase.
3. Remove the air cleaner and the exhaust manifold shroud.
4. Disconnect the ground cable from the battery.
5. Remove the radiator upper and lower hoses.
6. Remove the radiator and fan.
7. Disconnect the heater hose from the water pump and carburetor choke fitting.
8. Disconnect the alternator wires from the alternator, starter cable from the starter, and the accelerator cable from the carburetor. With air conditioning, remove the compressor from the mounting bracket, and position it out of the way, leaving the refrigerant lines attached. Label the wires.
9. Disconnect the flexible fuel line at the fuel pump line and plug the fuel line.
10. Disconnect the coil primary wire at the coil. Disconnect the oil pressure and the water temperature sending unit wires at the sending units.
11. Remove the starter.
12. Raise the vehicle. Remove the flywheel or converter housing upper attaching bolts.
13. Disconnect the headpipe at the exhaust manifold. Disconnect the engine right and left mounts at the underbody bracket. Remove the flywheel or converter housing cover.

   With automatic transmission, disconnect the converter from the flywheel. Remove the converter housing lower attaching bolts.

   With manual tranmission, remove the flywheel housing lower attaching bolts.
14. Lower the vehicle. Support the transmission and the flywheel or converter housing with a jack.
15. Attach the engine lifting device to the existing lifting brackets.
16. Carefully lift the engine out of the engine compartment.

Engine Installation—2300 cc

1. Carefully lower the engine into the engine compartment.
2. Make sure that the studs on the exhaust manifold are aligned with the holes in the head pipe.

   With automatic transmission, start the converter pilot into the crankshaft.

   With manual transmission, start the transmission input shaft into the clutch disc. It may be necessary to adjust the position of the

transmission in relation to the engine if the input shaft will not enter the clutch disc. If the engine hangs up after the shaft enters, turn the crankshaft slowly clockwise, with the transmission in gear, until the shaft splines mesh with the clutch disc splines.

3. Install the flywheel or converter housing upper attaching bolts. Remove the engine lifting sling hooks.
4. Remove the jack from the transmission. Raise the vehicle.
5. Install the flywheel or converter housing lower attaching bolts.

   With automatic transmission, attach the converter to the flywheel. Torque the bolts to 27-49 ft. lbs. for the C3, 20-30 ft. lbs. for the C4.
6. Install the flywheel or converter housing dust cover.
7. Install the engine left and right mount to the underbody bracket.
8. Remove the plug from the flexible fuel line and connect the flexible fuel line to the fuel pump line. Install the exhaust manifold to headpipe nuts.
9. Lower the vehicle. Connect the oil pressure and engine temperature sending unit wires. Connect the coil primary wire. Connect the accelerator cable.
10. Install the starter motor. Connect the starter cable. Connect the alternator wires. Connect the heater hose at the water pump and carburetor for the choke fitting.
11. Install the pulley, fan, and drive belt. Adjust the drive belt tension. With air conditioning, install the compressor on the mounting bracket and adjust the belt tension. Install the radiator. Connect the radiator upper and lower hoses. Fill and bleed the cooling system. Fill the crankcase with the proper type and quantity of motor oil.
12. Connect the battery ground cable.
13. Operate the engine at fast idle and check all gaskets and hose connections for leaks.

   With an automatic transmission, adjust the transmission control linkage, as necessary.
14. Install the air cleaner and connect the PCV hose.

Engine Removal—2800 cc V6

1. Remove any interfering air pump system components. Disconnect the battery, drain the cooling system and remove the hood.
2. Remove the air cleaner and intake duct assembly.
3. Disconnect the upper and lower hoses at the radiator.
4. Remove the fan shroud attaching bolts and position the shroud over the fan. Remove the radiator and shroud.
5. Remove the alternator and bracket. Position the alternator out of the way. Disconnect the alterna-

tor ground wire from the cylinder block.

6. Disconnect the heater hoses at the block and water pump.
7. Remove the ground, oil pressure, and temperature sender wires from the cylinder block.
8. Disconnect the fuel line at the fuel pump. Plug the fuel tank line.
9. Disconnect the accelerator cable or linkage at the carburetor and intake manifold. Disconnect the automatic transmission downshift linkage.
10. Disconnect the engine wire loom at the ignition coil. Disconnect the brake booster vacuum line.
11. Raise the vehicle on a hoist.
12. Disconnect the headpipes at the exhaust manifolds.
13. Disconnect the starter cable and remove the starter.
14. Remove the engine front support through-bolts.
15. With automatic transmission, remove the converter inspection cover and disconnect the flywheel from the converter.
    Remove the downshift rod.
    Remove the converter housing-to-engine block bolts and the adapter plate-to-converter housing bolt.
    With manual transmission, remove the clutch linkage and remove the bellhousing-to-engine block bolts.
16. Lower the vehicle.
17. Attach an engine lifting device to the lifting brackets at the exhaust manifolds.
18. Position a jack under the transmission.
19. Raise the engine slightly and carefully pull it from the transmission. Carefully lift the engine out of the engine compartment so that the rear cover plate is not bent or parts damaged.

Engine Installation—2800 cc V6

1. Lower the engine carefully into the engine compartment. Make sure that the exhaust manifolds are properly aligned with the headpipes.
2. With manual transmission, start the transmission input shaft into the clutch disc. It may be necessary to adjust the position of the transmission in relation to the engine if the input shaft will not enter the clutch disc. If the engine hangs up after the shaft enters, turn the crankshaft slowly, with the transmission in gear, until the shaft splines mesh with the clutch disc splines.
    With automatic transmission, start the converter pilot into the crankshaft.
3. Install the bellhousing or converter housing upper bolts, making sure that the dowels in the cylinder block engage the flywheel housing.

Remove the jack from under the transmission.

4. Remove the lifting device from the engine.
5. With automatic transmission, position the downshift rod on the transmission and engine.
6. Raise the vehicle on a hoist.
7. With automatic transmission, position the transmission linkage bracket and install the remaining converter housing bolts. Install the adapter plate-to-converter housing bolts. Install the converter-to-flywheel nuts and install the inspection cover. Connect the downshift rod on the transmission.
    On manual transmission cars, install the lower bellhousing bolts and connect the clutch linkage to the engine block.
8. Install the starter and connect the cable.
9. Connect the muffler inlet pipes at the exhaust manifolds.
10. Install the engine front support through-bolts.
11. Lower the vehicle.
12. Install the ground wire. Install the engine wire loom and connect it to the ignition coil, then connect the water temperature sending unit and oil pressure sending unit. Connect the brake booster vacuum line.
13. Install the accelerator linkage and connect the automatic transmission downshift rod. Connect the vacuum lines. Connect the fuel tank line at the fuel pump.
14. Connect the ground wire at the cylinder block. Install the heater hoses at the water pump and cylinder block.
15. Install the alternator and bracket. Connect the alternator ground wire to the cylinder block. Install the drive belt and adjust the belt tension.
16. Position the fan shroud over the fan. Install the radiator and connect the upper and lower radiator hoses. Install the fan shroud attaching bolts.
17. Fill and bleed the cooling system. Fill the crankcase with oil. Adjust the automatic transmission downshift linkage. Connect the battery.
18. Operate the engine at fast idle until it reaches normal operating temperature and check all gaskets and hose connections for leaks. Adjust the ignition timing and idle speed.
19. Install the air cleaner and intake duct. Install and adjust the hood.

Engine Removal and Installation—V8

1. Remove or disconnect any interfering air pump system components.
2. Drain the coolant. Remove the hood. Disconnect the battery and alternator ground cables.
3. Remove the air cleaner assembly.
4. Detach the upper radiator hose

from the engine and the lower hose from the pump.

5. Detach the automatic transmission cooler lines from the radiator. Unbolt the fan shroud and remove the shroud, radiator fan pulley and spacer.
6. Unbolt the alternator and set it aside.
7. Disconnect and plug the fuel line. Detach any gauge wires from the engine.
8. Disconnect the accelerator rod at the carburetor. With automatic transmission, disconnect the throttle valve vacuum line and shift linkage. Remove the filler tube bracket from the engine.
9. Set the air conditioner assembly aside without disconnecting any lines. See the Caution at the beginning of this section.
10. Unbolt and set the power steering pump aside without disconnecting the lines.
11. Detach the power brake vacuum line.
12. Detach the heater hoses at the water pump and intake manifold.
13. Remove the upper flywheel or converter housing to engine bolts.
14. Detach the ignition system wiring harness at the coil. Detach the engine ground strap.
15. Raise and support the car safely. Remove the starter.
16. Unbolt the headpipes from the engine manifolds. Detach the engine mount insulators from the frame brackets.
17. With manual transmission, unbolt the clutch linkage from the frame and the engine. Remove the rest of the flywheel housing bolts.
18. With automatic transmission, remove the converter housing cover. Unbolt the flywheel from the converter. Remove the rest of the converter housing bolts. Arrange a strap or clamp to keep the converter in the housing.
19. Lower the car to the floor and support the transmission. Attach the hoist to the engine and raise it slightly, carefully pulling it from the transmission.
20. Installation is the same as that shown previously for the V6 engine. Flywheel housing to engine bolt torque is 28-32 ft lbs. Converter housing to engine and flywheel to converter bolt torques are 28-38 ft lbs.

ENGINE MANIFOLDS

Intake Manifold Removal

1600 CC

1. Drain the cooling system.
2. Remove the air cleaner and disconnect the throttle shaft at the carburetor throttle lever.
3. Disconnect the fuel line and vacuum line from the carburetor. Dis-

connect the carburetor solenoid wire at the quick-disconnect.

4. Remove the choke thermostatic spring and water housing.
5. Disconnect the water outlet hose and crankcase ventilation hose from the intake manifold.
6. Disconnect the decel valve-to-carburetor hose at the carburetor.
7. Remove the intake manifold attaching bolts and remove the manifold.
8. Remove all gasket material.
9. If the intake manifold is to be replaced, transfer all necessary components to the new manifold. Loosen the union fitting on the manifold and remove the decel valve from the intake manifold. Remove the decel valve adaptor from the manifold by inserting a large allen wrench into the adaptor and turning the adaptor out of the manifold.

2000 AND 2300 CC

1. Remove the air cleaner assembly.
2. Disconnect the fuel line from the carburetor.
3. Disconnect the vacuum lines from the distributor at the intake manifold.
4. Disconnect the crankcase ventilation hose at the intake manifold.
5. On engines with a heated manifold, drain the cooling system. Disconnect the heater hoses from the intake manifold and the choke cover.
6. Remove the intake manifold attaching bolts and remove the manifold, carburetor, and decel valve from the studs, as an assembly.

Intake Manifold Installation

1600 CC

1. Clean the cylinder head and intake manifold mating surfaces thoroughly.
2. Carefully coat the mating surfaces with sealer and position a new gasket on the studs. Install the manifold and torque the nuts alternately and evenly.
3. Further installation is the reverse of removal.

2000 AND 2300 CC

1. Clean all dirt and gasket material from the surfaces on the cylinder head and intake manifold.
2. Position a new gasket and the manifold on the studs. Torque the bolts and nuts to the specified torque in two stages.
3. Connect the crankcase ventilation hose to the manifold. Connect the heater hoses to the choke cover and manifold, if equipped.
4. Connect the distributor vacuum lines to the manifold.
5. Connect the fuel line to the carburetor.
6. Install the air cleaner assembly. Fill the cooling system, if drained, and check for leaks.

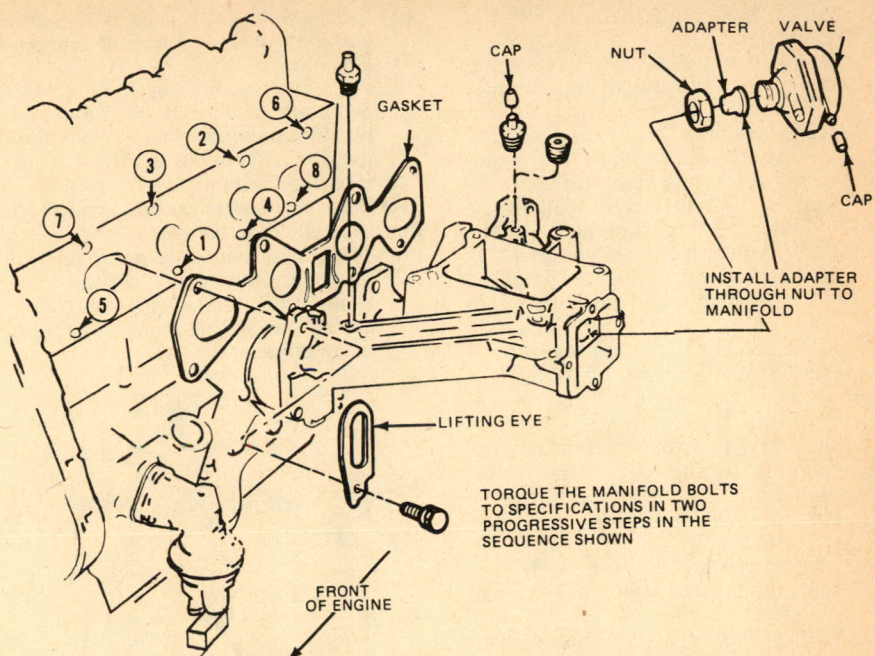

Intake manifold tightening sequence—2300 cc engine (© Ford Motor Co.)

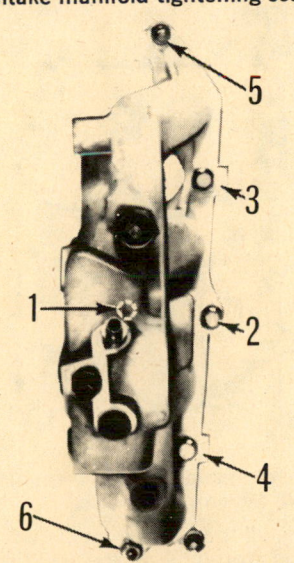

Intake manifold tightening sequence—2000 cc engine (© Ford Motor Co.)

Intake Manifold Removal and Installation

2800 CC V6

1. Remove the air cleaner assembly and disconnect the battery.
2. Disconnect the throttle cables.
3. Drain the cooling system. Disconnect and remove the hose from the water outlet to the radiator and the hoses and line from the water outlet to the water pump.
4. Remove the distributor cap and spark plug wires as an assembly. Disconnect the distributor wire and the vacuum line.
5. Mark the position of the distributor and remove it.
6. Remove the fuel line and filter between the fuel pump and the carburetor and then remove the rocker arm covers.
7. Remove the intake manifold bolts and nuts. Tap the manifold lightly with a plastic hammer to break the

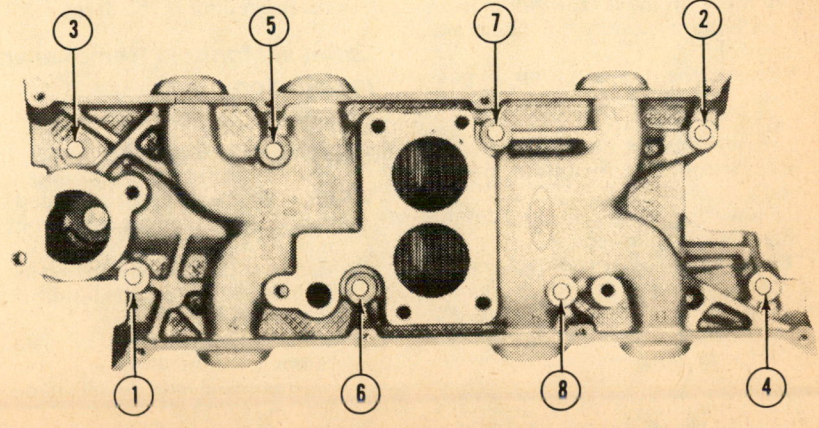

V6 intake manifold bolt torque sequence (© Ford Motor Co.)

gasket seal, and then lift off the manifold.
8. Remove all the gasket material and dirt from the manifold and cylinder heads.
9. Apply sealing compound to the joining surfaces. Place the manifold gasket in place. (Make sure that the tap on the right bank of the cylinder head gasket fits into the cutout of the manifold gasket.)
10. Install the intake manifold. Tighten the attaching bolts until they are hand tight, and then tighten them, in sequence, to the proper torque.

NOTE: *Tightening bolt no. 7 with a torque wrench will require an attachment called a "crow's foot."*

11. Install the distributor so the rotor is pointing to the mark made previously.
12. Connect the distributor wire and vacuum line.
13. Install the carburetor, fuel line, fuel filter, and the rocker arm covers.
14. Install the distributor cap and wires.
15. Install and adjust the carburetor linkage. Install the coolant hoses and refill the cooling system.
16. Install the air cleaner assembly and air cleaner tube to the carburetor. Connect the battery.
17. Adjust the ignition timing.

302 V8

1. Drain the cooling system, remove the air cleaner assembly and disconnect the crankcase ventilation hose and choke heated air inlet hose.
2. Disconnect the throttle linkage from the carburetor; remove the automatic transmission and brake booster lines from the intake manifold.
3. Remove the air pump; remove the spark plug wires and distributor cap assembly with wires attached.
4. Remove the EGR vacuum amplifier, gas inlet line and automatic choke heat tube.
5. Remove the distributor and thermostat upper hose and sending unit assembly; remove the hose from the choke assembly to the intake manifold.
6. Remove the water pump bypass hose, and crankcase vent hose at the rocker arm cover.
7. Remove the air conditioner compressor-to-intake manifold brackets.
8. Remove the carburetor and intake manifold as an assembly.

NOTE: *It may be necessary to pry the manifold away from the cylinder heads. Use caution to avoid damaging the sealing surfaces. Discard the intake manifold attaching bolt sealing washers.*

9. If the manifold is to be disassembled, mark all vacuum hoses before disconnecting them.

10. For installation, clean the mating surfaces of the manifold and engine block.
11. Put new gaskets on the cylinder head and new seals on the engine block, checking to make sure they interlock. Apply sealer to the outside of each seal.

NOTE: *Most sealers set up quickly so it is important that the rest of the operation be done as quickly as possible.*

12. Lower the manifold to the block. When it is in place, run your finger around the seals to make sure they are in place.

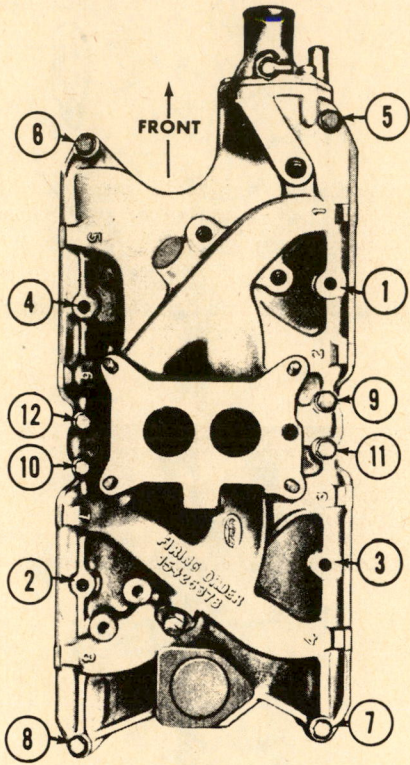

Intake manifold tightening sequence— 302 V8 (© Ford Motor Co.)

13. Install the attaching nuts and bolts and torque to specifications in sequence.
14. Replace the distributor.
15. To complete the operation, reverse the procedure in the Steps 1-7.

Exhaust Manifold Removal and Installation

1600 CC

1. Remove the air cleaner.
2. Place a block of wood under the front of the exhaust pipe and disconnect the exhaust pipe from the manifold.
3. Remove the exhaust manifold attaching nuts and bolts, and remove the manifold.
4. If a new manifold is to be installed, remove the heat shroud from the old manifold and install it on the new manifold.
5. Clean the exhaust manifold and cylinder head mating surfaces.

6. Install a new gasket over the center studs on the cylinder head.
7. Position the exhaust manifold near the cylinder head and install the end exhaust manifold gaskets between the manifold and the head.
8. Install the attaching nuts and bolts and tighten them to the proper torque.
9. Connect the exhaust pipe to the manifold, remove the wood support, and install the air cleaner.

2000 AND 2300 CC

1. Remove the air cleaner. Remove the heat shroud from the exhaust manifold. Disconnect the hose from the Thermactor check valve, if equipped. On 1978 and later California 2300s, disconnect the oxygen sensor wiring.
2. Place a block of wood under the exhaust pipe, and then disconnect it from the manifold.

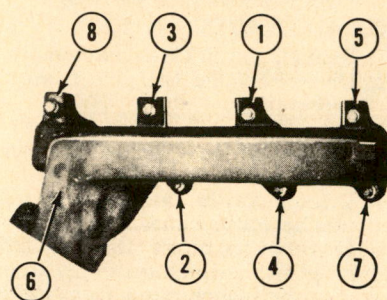

Exhaust manifold tightening sequence— 2000 cc engine   (© Ford Motor Co.)

3. Remove the attaching nuts and remove the manifold from the head. Clean the mating surfaces.
4. Install a light coat of graphite grease on the exhaust manifold mating surface and position the manifold on the cylinder head.
5. Install the attaching nuts and tighten them to the proper torque.
6. Connect the exhaust pipe to the manifold and remove the wood support from under the pipe.
7. Install the air cleaner, and check valve hose and oxygen sensor wiring if present.

2800 CC

1. Remove the air cleaner.
2. Remove the four attaching nuts from the exhaust manifold shroud (right side only).
3. Disconnect the attaching nuts from the muffler inlet pipe. Remove air pump hoses and components as necessary. Disconnect the choke heat tube at the carburetor, if present.
4. Remove the exhaust manifold attaching nuts and remove the manifold.
5. These manifolds do not use gaskets. When installing the manifold, smear a light coat of graphite grease on the mating surfaces.
6. Position the manifold on the studs and install the bolts handtight then

torque them evenly to the proper torque.

7. Install a new inlet pipe gasket and the attaching nuts.
8. Position the exhaust manifold shroud on the manifold and install the attaching nuts (right side).
9. Install the air cleaner. Install any air pump components removed and the choke heat tube.

302 V8

1. On the right exhaust manifold, remove the air cleaner, automatic choke heat tube and air cleaner heat ducts.
2. Disconnect the exhaust manifold(s) from the muffler inlet pipe(s). Label and remove the spark plug wires, plugs, and heat shields.
3. Remove the manifold attaching bolts and remove the manifold(s).
4. Reverse the procedure to reinstall, using new inlet pipe gaskets.

VALVE SYSTEM

1600 CC

The valves are mounted vertically in the cylinder head, the intake valve heads being larger than the exhaust valve heads. The exhaust valves are stellite-coated for better heat and wear resistance, while the intake valves are coated with diffused aluminum for the same reason. *The factory does not recommend grinding the intake valves or lapping the intake valve seats, because the grinding operation removes the coating and shortens the life of the valve.* Exhaust valves, on the other hand, may be ground if necessary.

Valve stems are phosphate-coated for better wear resistance. Valve guides are cast integral with the head, although sleeves are available if guides become worn. In addition, valves are available with 0.003 and 0.015 in. oversize stem diameters.

The valve keepers do not grip the stem, allowing the valves to rotate freely during operation.

Valve Adjustment

1600 CC

Valves are set with the engine at normal operating temperature and turned off.

1. Remove the air cleaner. Disconnect the carburetor solenoid wire at the connector near the rear of the valve cover.
2. Remove the throttle cable retaining screw, pry the end of the throttle cable off the carburetor stud, and position the cable out of the way.
3. Remove the valve cover. Identify the spark plug wires and disconnect them.
4. Turn the engine to depress the proper valves by turning the crankshaft pulley.

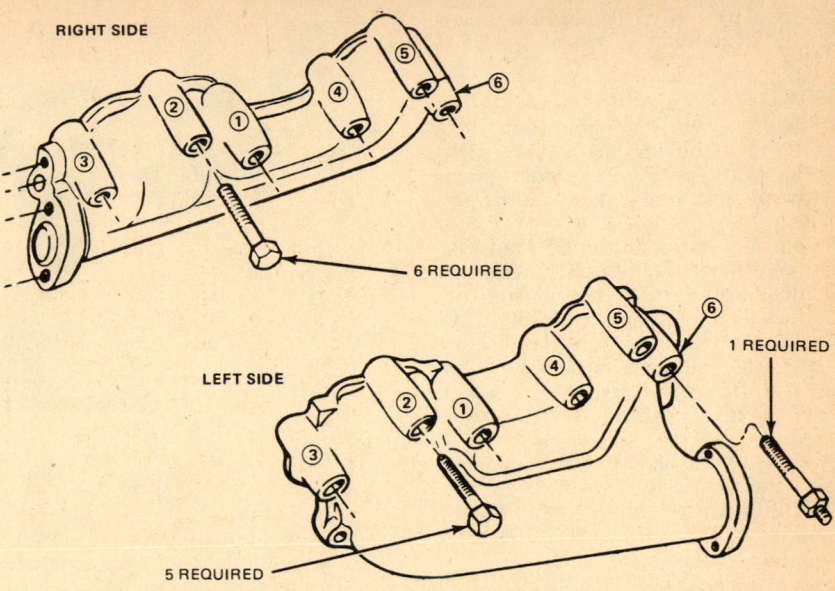

V6 exhaust manifold torque sequence (© Ford Motor Co.)

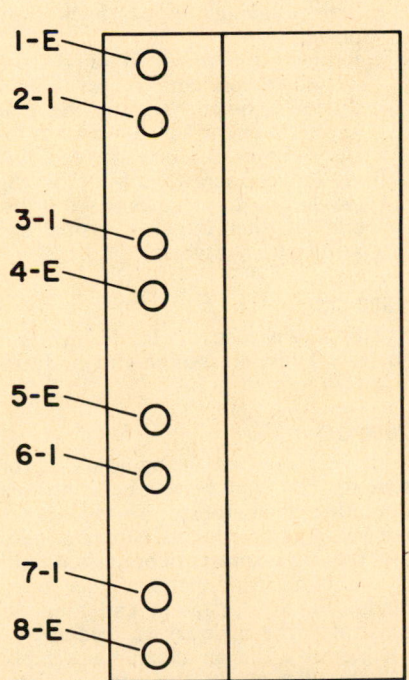

1600 cc engine valve identification

Valve Clearance Adjustment

1600 cc Engine—Set Hot		
Valve Depressed	Valves to Adjust to .010	.017
No. 1	No. 3	No. 8
No. 2	No. 7	No. 5
No. 3	No. 6	No. 1
No. 5	No. 2	No. 4

5. Insert a feeler gauge of the specified thickness between the tip of the rocker arm and the top of the valve. If an adjustment is necessary, turn the adjusting screw in or out as necessary.
6. Install the removed or disconnected components in a reverse or-

Chilton's TIME SAVER

The following is a method for replacing valve springs, oil seals or spring retainers without removing the cylinder head.

1. Obtain an air hose spark plug hole adaptor.
2. Remove the valve rocker cover.
3. Remove the rocker arm from the valve to be worked on.
4. Remove the spark plug from the cylinder to be worked on.
5. Turn the crankshaft to bring the piston of this cylinder down, away from possible contact with the valve head. Sharply tap the valve retainer to loosen the valve lock.
6. Then turn the crankshaft to bring the piston in this cylinder to the Exact Top of its Compression Stroke.
7. Screw in the spark plug hole adaptor.
8. Hook up an air hose to the chuck and turn on the pressure.
9. With a strong and constant supply of air holding the valve closed, compress the valve spring and remove the lock and retainer.
10. Make the necessary replacements and reassemble.

NOTE: *It is important that the operation be performed exactly as stated, in this order. The piston in the cylinder must be on exact top-center to prevent air pressure from turning the crankshaft.*

der of removal. Tighten the valve cover retaining screws to 2.5-3.5 ft lbs.

2000 CC

Valves are set with engine cold.

1. Remove the air cleaner. Identify the spark plug wires and remove them, positioning them out of the way.
2. On non-air-conditioned models, move the heater hose attached to the carburetor choke housing off the valve cover and out of the way. On air-conditioned models, disconnect the carburetor choke heater hose from the heater hot water valve and position it out of the way.
3. Remove the valve cover retaining screw (note the position of the screws with rubber coated washers) and remove the valve cover.

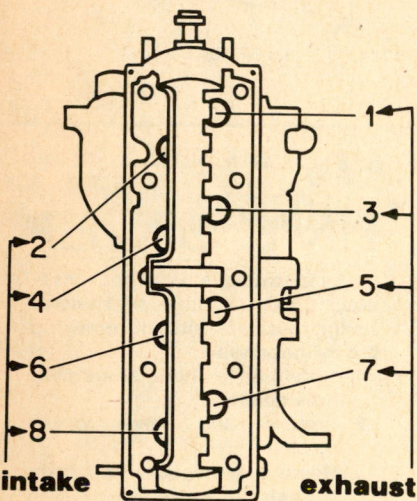

2000 cc engine valve identification

4. Turn the crankshaft pulley to depress the valves specified in the chart.

─── CAUTION ───

Never turn the pulley in a counterclockwise direction, as the camshaft drive belt may slip and alter the timing.

5. Check clearance according to the following chart:

Valve Clearance Adjustment

2000 cc Engine—Set Cold

Valve Depressed	Valves to .008	Adjust to .010
No. 1	No. 6	No. 7
No. 2	No. 8	No. 3
No. 3	No. 2	No. 5
No. 6	No. 4	No. 1

Clearance is checked between the rocker arm and the cam. Use a screwdriver to snap the retaining spring off the rocker arm until it hangs loose. Use a feeler gauge of the specified thickness to check the clearance.

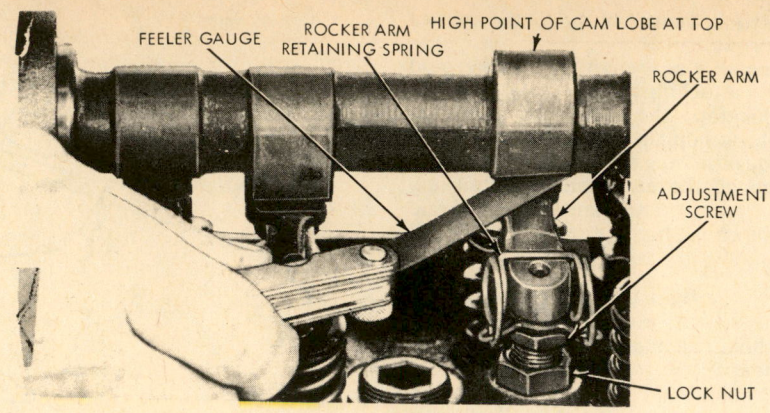

Checking valve clearance—2000 cc
(© Ford Motor Co)

6. If an adjustment is necessary, loosen the locknut and turn the adjusting screw in or out as necessary. When the adjustment is correct, tighten the locknut and snap the retaining spring back into place.
7. Replace the removed or disconnected components in a reverse order of removal. Tighten the rear valve cover cap screws to 4-6 ft lbs from the back forward, the two vertical cap screws to 1-2 ft lbs, the two lateral cap screws to 4-6 ft lbs, and retighten the two vertical cap screws to 4-6 ft lbs.

2300 CC

This engine uses hydraulic lash adjusters. Thus, no routine valve adjustment is required.

2800 CC

If the valves are being adjusted for tune-up, the engine must be at normal operating temperature. If the valves are being adjusted after engine assembly, the engine must not be started until a preliminary adjustment has been made. Final adjustment can then be made after the engine is warmed up.

1. Remove the air cleaner assembly and disconnect the negative battery cable.
2. Remove the Thermactor air bypass valve and its mounting bracket.
3. Remove the two engine lifting eyes; remove the alternator drive belt, loosen the alternator mounting bolts and swing the alternator outward toward the fender.
4. Remove the plug wires and remove the rocker covers.

NOTE: *Some 1975 engines were assembled so that the distributor diaphragm housing interferes with rocker cover removal. This can be corrected by removing the distributor and resetting it one tooth clockwise.*

5. When removing the rocker covers, remove or reposition any wires or the rocker covers.
6. Torque the rocker arm support bolts to 46 ft lbs.

7. Reconnect the battery cable, place hoses which block the removal of the rocker covers.
   the transmission in Neutral (manual) or Park (automatic), and apply the parking brake.
8. Place a finger on the adjusting screw of the intake valve rocker arm for cylinder No. 5. Cylinder numbering is shown under Firing Order at the start of the section. Valve arrangement, from front to rear, on the left bank is I-E-E-I-E-I; on the right it is I-E-I-E-E-I. You will be able to feel the rocker arm begin to move.
9. Use a remote starter switch or manual means to turn the engine until you can just feel the valve begin to open. Now the engine is in position to adjust the intake and exhaust valves on the No. 1 cylinder.
10. Adjust the No. 1 cylinder intake valve so that a 0.014 in. feeler gauge has a slight drag while a 0.015 in. feeler gauge is a tight fit. To decrease lash, turn the adjusting screw clockwise; to increase lash, turn the adjusting screw counterclockwise. There are no locknuts to tighten; the adjusting screws are self-locking.

─── CAUTION ───

Do not use a step-type, "go-no go" feeler gauge. When checking lash, insert the feeler gauge and move it parallel with the crankshaft. Do not move it in and out perpendicular with the crankshaft: this will give an erroneous feel which will result in overtightened valves.

11. Adjust the exhaust valve the same way so that an 0.018 in. feeler gauge has a slight drag, while a 0.019 in. gauge is a tight fit.
12. The rest of the valves are adjusted in the same way, in their firing order (1-4-2-5-3-6), by positioning the engine according to the following chart:

V6 Valve Clearance Adjustment

Intake valve just opening in cylinder No.:	Adjust both valves in this cylinder: (Intake —0.014 in.; Exhaust—0.018 in.)
5	1
3	4
6	2
1	5
4	3
2	6

13. Remove all the old gasket material from the cylinder heads and rocker cover gasket surfaces, and disconnect the negative cable from the battery.
14. Remove the spark plug wires and reinstall the rocker arm covers.
15. Reinstall any hoses and wires which were removed.
16. Reinstall the spark plug wires, the alternator drive belt, and the Thermactor air by-pass valve and its mounting bracket.
17. Reconnect the battery cable, replace the air cleaner assembly, start the engine, and check for leaks.

302 V8

This rocker arm nut tightening procedure is needed only if the valve train has been disturbed, as in cylinder head removal and replacement. It is not a normal tune-up procedure.
1. Crank the engine until No. 1 cylinder is at TDC of the compression stroke and the timing pointer is aligned with the 0 mark on the crankshaft damper.
2. Tighten the following rocker arms: no. 1, 7, and 8 intake; no. 1, 5, and 4 Exhaust. Tighten the nut until it contacts the shoulder of the rocker and then torque to 18-20 ft lbs.
3. Rotate the crankshaft 180° clockwise and tighten the following valves: no. 5 and 4 intake; no. 2 and 6 exhaust.
4. Rotate the crankshaft 270° clockwise and tighten the following valves: no. 2, 3, and 6 intake; no. 7, 3, and 8 exhaust.

Rocker Arm or Shaft Replacement

1600 CC

1. Remove the valve cover as described under "Valve Adjustment." Disconnect the spark plug wires and move them out of the way.
2. Loosen each rocker shaft attaching bolt one turn at a time until all the bolts are loose.
3. Remove the rocker shaft.
4. To install, position the rocker shaft on the head and align the pushrods with the rocker arm adjusting screws.
5. Starting from the front of the en-

gine and working back, tighten each bolt one turn at a time until the shaft is mounted on the head. Finally, tighten each bolt to 25-30 ft lbs.
6. Adjust the valves as previously described. Install the valve cover and spark plug wires.

2000 CC

1. Remove the valve cover as described under "Valve Adjustment."
2. Rotate the crankshaft in a clockwise direction until the cam lobe for the rocker arm that is to be removed is pointing straight up.
3. Remove the retaining spring from the rocker arm.
4. Depress the valve spring that corresponds to the rocker arm that is to be removed just enough to remove the rocker arm.
5. To install, position the rocker arm on the valve and adjusting screw and install the rocker arm retaining spring.
6. Adjust the valve clearance as previously described.
7. Install the valve cover, air cleaner, and any other components that were removed or disconnected in a reverse order of removal.

2300 CC

1. Remove the valve cover and associated parts as required.
2. Rotate the camshaft so that the base circle of the cam is against the cam follower you intend to remove.
3. Remove the retaining spring from the cam follower, if so equipped.
4. Using a valve spring compressor tool for a 2300 cc engine, collapse the lash adjuster and/or depress the valve spring, as necessary, and slide the cam follower over the lash adjuster and out from under the camshaft.
5. Install the cam follower in the reverse order of removal. Make sure that the lash adjuster is collapsed and released before rotating the cam shaft.

2800 CC

1. Remove any emission control equipment as necessary to remove the rocker cover(s), remove the spark plug wires, remove the throttle linkage to the carburetor as necessary, and remove the valve rocker cover(s).
2. Remove the rocker arm shaft stand retaining bolts; loosen them each 2 turns at a time in sequence. Lift the rocker arm and shaft assembly and the oil baffle.
3. Before installing the rocker shaft assemblies, back off the adjusting screws on the rockers a few turns. Install the rocker shafts in the reverse order of removal; tighten the rocker shaft stand retaining bolts 2 turns at a time in sequence until

they are tightened to 46 ft lbs. Adjust the valve clearance as previously described.

302 V8

The 302 V8 is equipped with individual stud-mounted rocker arms. Use the following procedure to remove the rocker arms:
1. On the right cylinder head, disconnect the choke heat chamber air hose.
2. Remove the air cleaner and inlet duct assembly, the choke heat tube, PCV valve and hose, and the EGR hoses. Remove the Thermactor by-pass valve and air supply hoses.
3. Label and disconnect the spark plug wires at the plugs. Remove the plug wires from the harness.
4. Remove the valve cover attaching bolts and remove the covers.
5. Remove the valve rocker arm stud nut, fulcrum seat, and then the rocker arm.
6. Reverse the above procedure to install. Tighten each stud nut to 17-23 ft lbs after the nut contacts the shoulder. Install and tighten the nuts in the sequence given under Valve Adjustment.

CYLINDER HEAD

NOTE: *To prevent distortion or warping of the cylinder head, allow the engine to cool completely before removing the head bolts.*

If the head sticks, operate the starter to loosen it by compression or rap it upward with a soft hammer. Do not force anything between the head and the block. Coat all valve train components with a pre-lube before assembly.

Removal—1600 cc

1. Remove the air cleaner, then disconnect the fuel line at the pump and the carburetor.
2. Drain the cooling system.
3. Disconnect spark plug wires, then disconnect heater and vacuum hoses from the intake manifold and choke housing.
4. Disconnect temperature sender wire, then disconnect exhaust pipe at manifold flange.
4. Disconnect throttle linkage and distributor vacuum line at carburetor. Disconnect the carburetor solenoid wire.
6. Remove thermostat housing and thermostat.
7. Remove rocker arm cover and gasket, then remove the rocker shaft bolts, evenly, and the rocker shaft assembly.
8. Remove pushrods and place them aside in proper order for correct installation.
9. Remove cylinder head bolts, head, and gasket.

Installation—1600 cc

1. Place a new head gasket on the block.
2. Position the cylinder head and install the bolts. Tighten evenly in sequence to proper torque in two stages.

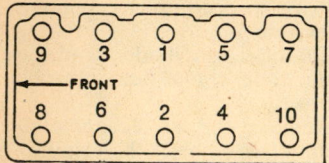

1600 cc cylinder head bolt tightening sequence (© Ford Motor Co.)

NOTE: *Manifolds may be installed prior to placing head on block.*

3. Install pushrods in correct order, then place rocker arms and shaft assembly on head and locate pushrods in rocker arm screws. Tighten rocker arm bolts to 25-30 ft lbs.
4. Adjust valve clearance, then install rocker arm cover and gasket.
5. Continue installation by reversing Steps 1-6 of removal procedure.

Removal—2000 cc and 2300 cc

1. Drain the cooling system.
2. Remove the air cleaner and the valve rocker cover.
3. Remove the intake and exhaust manifolds. The intake manifold, decel valve and carburetor can be removed as an assembly.
4. Remove the camshaft drive belt cover.
5. Loosen the drive belt tensioner and remove the drive belt.
6. Remove the water outlet from the cylinder head.
7. Remove the cylinder head bolts evenly, and remove the cylinder head.

NOTE: *A special 12-point allen wrench is necessary to remove the head bolts on the 2000 cc engine.*

Installation—2000 cc and 2300 cc

1. Position a new cylinder head gasket on the block. On the 2300, rotate the camshaft so that the locating pin is at the five o'clock position, to avoid valve damage.
2. Position the cylinder head and camshaft assembly on the block. Install the bolts finger tight, then torque to specifications in two stages.

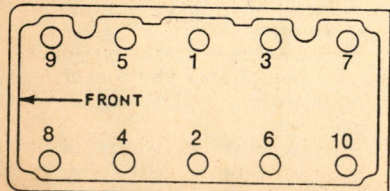

Cylinder head bolt tightening sequence 2000 cc and 2300 cc (© Ford Motor Co.)

NOTE: *If difficulty in positioning the head on the block is encountered, guide pins may be fabricated by cutting the heads off two extra cylinder head bolts.*

3. Set the crankshaft at TDC and be sure that the camshaft drive gear and distributor are positioned correctly as explained under Timing Belt Replacement.
4. Install the camshaft drive belt and release the tensioner. Rotate the crankshaft two full turns clockwise (facing the engine) to remove all slack from the belt. The timing marks should again be aligned. Tighten the tensioner lockbolt and pivot bolt.
5. Install the camshaft drive belt cover.
6. Apply sealer to the water outlet and new gasket, and install.
7. Install the intake and exhaust manifolds.
8. Adjust the valve clearance.
9. Install a new valve cover gasket and install the valve cover.
10. Install the air cleaner and crankcase ventilation hose.
11. Refill the cooling system.

Removal and Installation— 2800 cc

1. Remove the air cleaner assembly and disconnect the battery and accelerator linkage. Drain the cooling system.
2. Remove the distributor cap with the spark plug wires attached. Remove the distributor vacuum line and distributor. Remove the hose from the water pump to the water outlet which is on the carburetor.
3. Remove the valve covers, fuel line and filter, carburetor, and the intake manifold.
4. Remove the rocker arm shaft and oil baffles. Remove the pushrods, keeping them in the proper sequence for installation.
5. Remove the exhaust manifold, referring to the appropriate procedures.
6. Remove the cylinder head retaining bolts and remove the cylinder heads and gaskets.
7. Remove all gasket material and carbon from the engine block and cylinder heads.
8. Place the head gaskets on the engine block.

NOTE: *The left and right gaskets are not interchangeable.*

9. Install guide studs in the engine block. Install the cylinder head as-

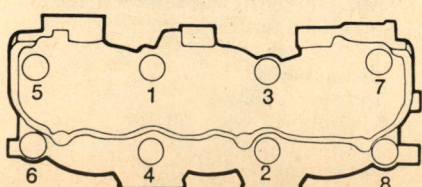

V6 cylinder head bolt torque sequence (© Ford Motor Co.)

semblies on the engine block one at a time. Tighten the cylinder head bolts in sequence, and in steps, to the specified torque.
10. Install the intake and exhaust manifolds.
11. Install the pushrods (ends lubricated) in the proper sequence. Install the oil baffles and the rocker arm shaft assemblies. Install the distributor. Adjust the valve clearances.
12. Install the valve covers with new gaskets.
13. Install the carburetor and the distributor cap with the spark plug wires. Set the ignition timing.
14. Connect the accelerator linkage, fuel line, with fuel filter installed, and distributor vacuum line to the carburetor. Fill the cooling system.

302 V8

1. Drain the cooling system.
2. Remove the intake manifold and the carburetor as an assembly, following the procedures under "Intake Manifold Removal."
3. Disconnect the spark plug wires, marking them as to placement. Position them out of the way of the cylinder head. Remove the spark plugs.
4. Disconnect the exhaust pipes at the manifolds.
5. Remove the rocker arm covers.
6. On cars with air conditioning, remove the mounting bolts and the drive belt, and position the compressor out of the way of the left cylinder head. Remove the compressor upper mounting bracket from the cylinder head.

—————— CAUTION ——————

If the compressor refrigerant lines do not have enough slack to permit repositioning of the compressor without first disconnecting the refrigerant lines, the air conditioning system will have to be evacuated by a trained air conditioning serviceman. Under no circumstances should an untrained person attempt to disconnect the air conditioning refrigerant lines.

7. In order to remove the left cylinder head, on cars equipped with power steering, it may be necessary to remove the steering pump and bracket, remove the drive belt, and wire or tie the pump out of the way, but in such a way as to prevent the loss of its fluid.
8. In order to remove the right head it may be necessary to remove the alternator mounting bracket bolt and spacer, the ignition coil, and the air cleaner inlet duct from the right cylinder head.
9. In order to remove the left cylinder head on a car equipped with a Thermactor air pump system, disconnect the hose from the air manifold on the left cylinder head.

10. If the right cylinder head is to be removed on a car equipped with a Thermactor system, remove the Thermactor air pump and its mounting bracket. Disconnect the hose from the air manifold on the right cylinder head.

11. Loosen the rocker arm stud nuts enough to rotate the rocker arms to the side, in order to facilitate the removal of the pushrods. Remove the pushrods in sequence, so that they may be installed in their original positions. Remove the exhaust valve stem caps.

12. Remove the cylinder head attaching bolts, noting their positions. Lift the cylinder head off the block. Remove and discard the old cylinder head gasket.

Installation is as follows:

1. Position the new cylinder head gasket over the dowels on the block. Position new gaskets on the muffler inlet pipes at the exhaust manifold flange.

2. Position the cylinder head to the block, and install the head bolts, each in its original position. On engines on which the exhaust manifold has been removed from the head to facilitate removal, it is necessary to properly guide the exhaust manifold studs into the muffler inlet pipe flange when installing the head.

3. Step-torque the cylinder head retaining bolts first to 50 ft lbs then to 60 ft lbs, and finally to the torque specification listed in the "Torque Specifications" chart. Tighten the exhaust manifold-to cylinder head attaching bolts to specifications.

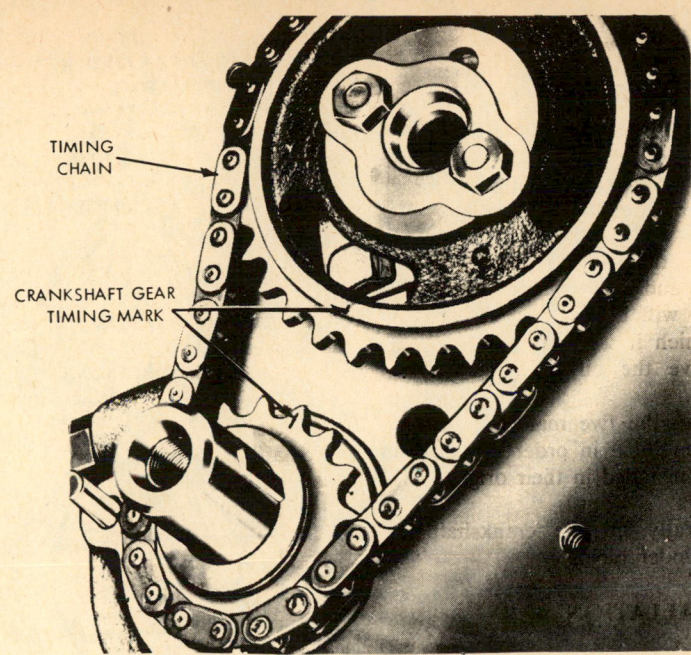

Valve timing mark alignment—1600 cc
(© Ford Motor Co)

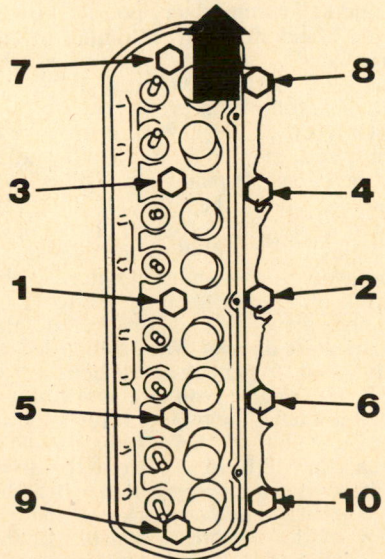

Cylinder head bolt tightening sequence 302 V8

4. Tighten the nuts on the exhaust manifold studs at the muffler inlet flanges to 18 ft lbs.

5. Clean and inspect the pushrods one at a time. Clean the oil passage within each pushrod with solvent and blow the passage out with compressed air. Check the ends of the pushrods for nicks, grooves, roughness, or excessive wear. Visually inspect the pushrods for straightness, and replace any bent ones. Do not attempt to straighten pushrods.

6. Install the pushrods in their original positions. Apply Lubriplate® or a similar product to the valve stem tips and to the pushrod guides in the cylinder head. Install the exhaust valve stem caps.

7. Apply Lubriplate® or a similar product to the fulcrum seats and sockets. Turn the rocker arms to their proper position and tighten the stud nuts enough to hold the rocker arms in position. Make sure that the lower ends of the pushrods have remained properly seated in the valve lifters. Tighten the stud nuts to 17-23 ft lbs in the order given under Valve Adjustment.

8. Install the valve covers.

9. Install the intake manifold and carburetor, following the procedure under "Intake Manifold Installation."

10. Replace all other items removed.

TIMING COVER, CHAIN, AND CAMSHAFT—1600 cc

Timing Cover and Chain Replacement

1. Drain coolant.
2. Disconnect radiator hoses at the engine, then remove radiator.
3. Remove fanbelt, fan, and water pump pulley.
4. Remove the water pump.
5. Remove the crankshaft pulley, using a puller only.
6. Remove the front cover.

NOTE: *Cover is secured by four oil pan bolts as well.*

Perform steps 7 through 13 to remove and install the timing chain.

7. With the transmission in Neutral, have an assistant tap the starter to align the cam and crankshaft sprockets.
8. Remove the timing chain tensioner.
9. Remove the timing chain sprocket attaching bolts.
10. Slide the timing chain and the camshaft sprocket off the engine as an assembly.

NOTE: *The timing chain tensioner pad is designed so that two grooves are gradually worn into it. Do not alter the grooves. Replace the chain and tensioner as a unit.*

11. Install the replacement timing chain on the camshaft and crankshaft sprockets and align the timing marks.
12. Position the sprockets and timing chain on the engine. Be sure that the timing marks on the sprockets are aligned.
13. Install the camshaft sprocket attaching bolts.
14. Coat the front cover gasket with sealer and position it and the cover on the engine.
15. Using a large socket wrench or other tool to center the cover on the engine, install the cover attaching bolts.
16. Tighten the bolts to 5-7 ft lbs and remove the centering tool.
17. Install the four front oil pan bolts and tighten them to 7-9 ft lbs.
18. Install the lower engine pulley and

the water pump. Adjust the engine drive belts.

19. Install the radiator and fill the cooling system.

Camshaft and Valve Lifter Replacement

The 1600 cc engine utilizes mushroom lifters, i.e., the bottom diameter is larger than the top diameter. For this reason, it is necessary to remove the engine, remove most of its external components, and invert it to remove the camshaft and/or lifters.

1. Remove the engine from the car and mount it securely on a stand.
2. Remove the fuel and oil pumps.
3. Remove the distributor.
4. Remove the valve cover, rocker shaft, and pushrods.
5. Remove the front cover and timing chain.
6. Place a pan under the engine and invert it on the stand.
7. Remove the oil pan.
8. Remove the camshaft thrust plate and remove the camshaft.
9. Remove the lifters.
10. Install the camshaft and/or lifters using a reverse of the removal procedure. Be sure to utilize the specific instructions on installing the timing chain and distributor. Adjust the valve clearance as previously described.

CAMSHAFT, AUXILIARY SHAFT AND TIMING BELT —2000 CC and 2300 CC

Should the camshaft drive belt jump timing by a tooth or two, the engine

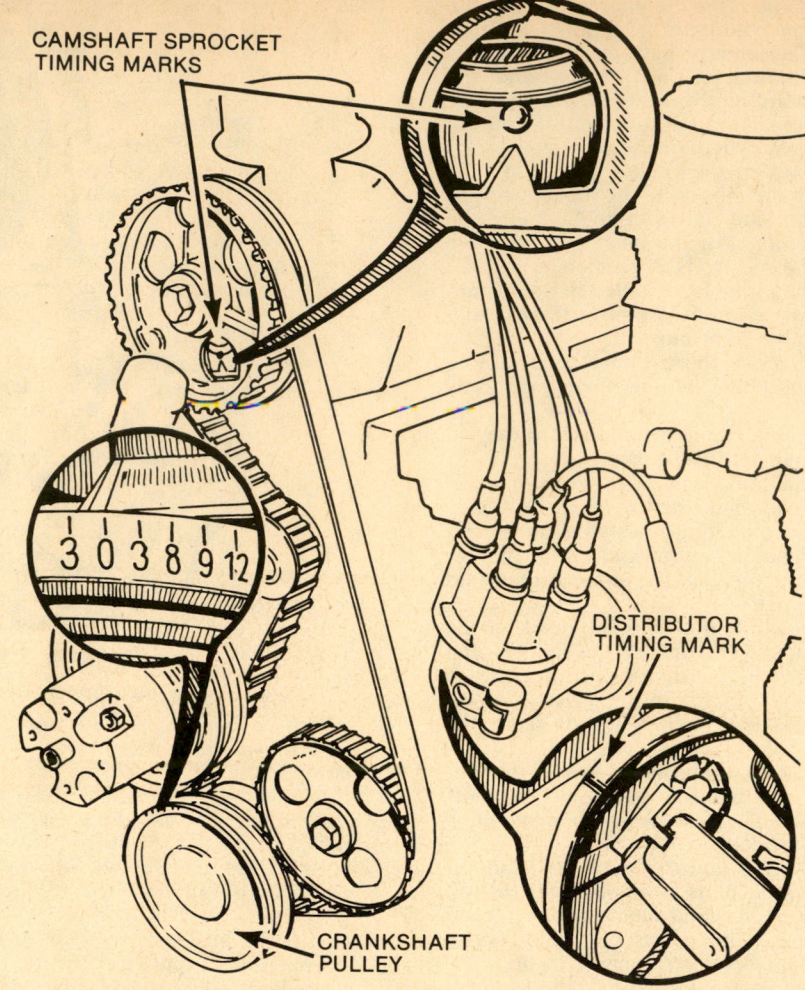

Crankshaft, camshaft, and distributor timing marks—2000 cc engine

could still run; but very poorly. To visually check for correct timing of the crankshaft, auxiliary shaft, and the camshaft on the 2000 cc and 2300 cc engines, follow this procedure:

On 2000 cc engines, turn the crankshaft until the two round locating holes in the camshaft pulley are visible from the rear side of the pulley, looking forward from the left-side of the car. When these two holes are parallel to the ground, the timing pointer on the crankshaft pulley should point to TDC. If the drive belt is dislocated, the crankshaft damper will be retarded or advanced 19° per cog on the belt.

If the engine you are working on does not have the two locating holes on the rear side of the camshaft pulley, then you will have to remove the drive belt cover and observe that when the crankshaft timing marks are aligned to TDC of the compression stroke of the No. 1 cylinder, the distributor rotor is pointing to the index mark on the upper lip of the distributor housing which coincides with No. 1 spark plug tower, and the pointer on the camshaft pulley is aligned with the index mark on the cylinder head.

On 2300 cc engines, there is an access plug provided in the cam drive belt

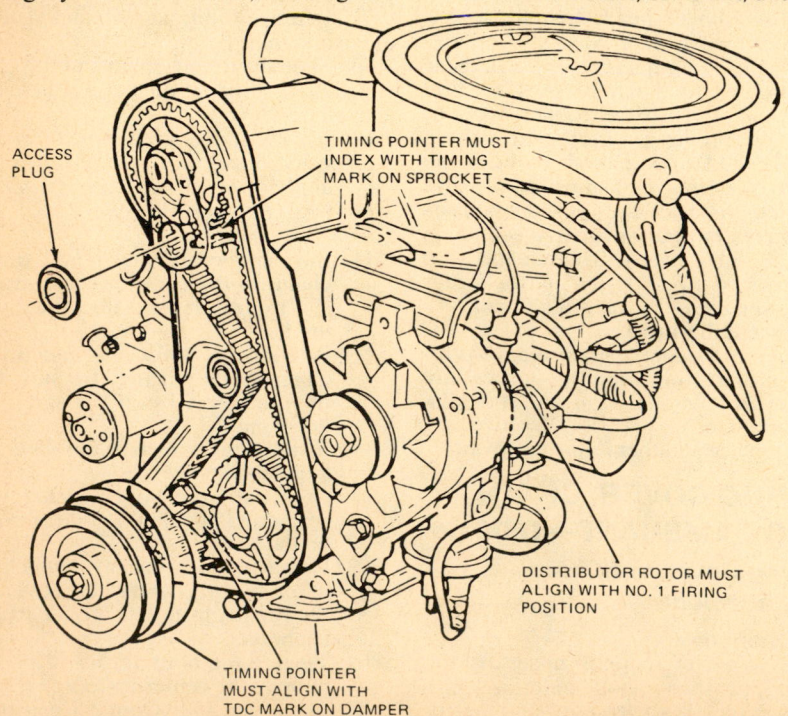

Crankshaft, camshaft, and distributor timing marks—2300 cc engine
(© Ford Motor Co.)

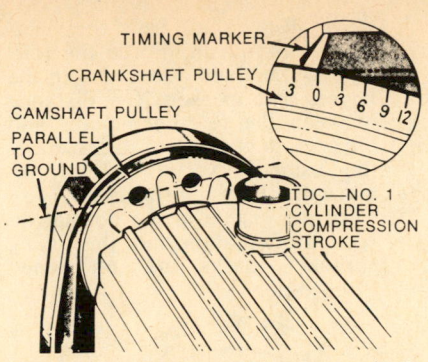

Checking 2000 cc overhead camshaft timing (© Ford Motor Co)

cover so that the camshaft timing can be checked without removing the drive belt cover. Remove the access plug, turn the crankshaft until the timing mark on the crankshaft damper indicates TDC, and observe that the timing mark on the camshaft drive sprocket is aligned with the pointer on the inner belt cover. Also, the rotor of the distributor must align with the No. 1 cylinder firing position.

NOTE: *Never turn the crankshaft of any of the overhead cam engines in the opposite direction of normal rotation. Backward rotation of the crankshaft may cause the timing belt to slip and alter the timing.*

CAUTION

After any procedure requiring removal of the rocker arms on the 2300, each lash adjuster must be fully collapsed after assembly, then released. This must be done before the camshaft is turned.

Timing Belt Replacement

1. Set the engine to TDC as described for checking valve timing. The crankshaft and camshaft timing marks should align with their respective pointers and the distributor rotor should point to the No. 1 plug tower.
2. Loosen the adjustment bolts on the alternator and accessories and remove the drive belts. To provide clearance for removing the camshaft belt, remove the fan and pulley.
3. Remove the belt outer cover.
4. Remove the distributor cap from the distributor and position it out of the way.
5. Loosen the belt tensioner adjustment and pivot bolts. Lever the tensioner away from the belt and retighten the adjustment bolt to hold it away.
6. Remove the crankshaft bolt and pulley. Remove the belt guide behind the pulley.
7. Remove the camshaft drive belt.
8. Install the new belt over the crankshaft pulley first, then counterclockwise over the auxiliary shaft sprocket and the camshaft sprocket. Adjust the belt fore and aft so that it is centered on the sprockets.
9. Loosen the tensioner adjustment bolt, allowing it to spring back against the belt.
10. Rotate the crankshaft two complete turns in the normal rotation direction to remove any belt slack. Turn the crankshaft until the timing check marks are lined up. If the timing has slipped, remove the belt and repeat the procedure.
11. Tighten the tensioner adjustment bolt to 14-21 ft lbs, and the pivot bolt to 28-40 ft lbs.
12. Replace the belt guide and crankshaft pulley, distributor cap, belt outer cover, fan and pulley, drive belts and accessories. Adjust the accessory drive belt tension. Start the engine and check the ignition timing.

Camshaft Replacement

1. Remove the cylinder head as previously described.
2. Remove the rocker arms.
3. Remove the camshaft drive gear attaching bolt and washer, and remove the gear and belt guide plate.
4. Remove the camshaft thrust plate from the rear of the head. Carefully slide the camshaft out of the rear of the cylinder head on the 2000 cc engine.

   On the 2300 cc engine, the camshaft is removed through the front of the cylinder head after removing the front cam bearing seal. Use a new seal during asembly.
5. Reverse the removal procedure to install the camshaft and cylinder head.

NOTE: *Coat the camshaft with oil before sliding it into the cylinder head. Apply a coat of sealer or teflon tape to the cam drive gear bolt before installation.*

CAUTION

After any procedure requiring removal of the rocker arms on the 2300, each lash adjuster must be fully collapsed after assembly, then released. This must be done before the camshaft is turned.

Auxiliary Shaft Replacement

1. Remove the camshaft drive belt cover.
2. Remove the drive belt. Remove the auxiliary shaft sprocket. A puller may be necessary to remove the sprocket.
3. Remove the distributor and fuel pump.
4. Remove the auxiliary shaft cover and thrust plate.
5. Withdraw the auxiliary shaft from the block.

NOTE: *The distributor drive gear and the fuel pump eccentric on the auxiliary shaft must not be allowed to touch the auxiliary shaft bearings during removal and installation. Completely coat the*

shaft with oil before sliding it into place.

6. Slide the auxiliary shaft into the housing and insert the thrust plate to hold the shaft.
7. Install a new gasket and auxiliary shaft cover.

NOTE: *The auxiliary shaft cover and cylinder front cover share a gasket. Cut off the old gasket around the cylinder cover and use half of the new gasket on the auxiliary shaft cover.*

8. Fit a new gasket into the fuel pump and install the pump.
9. Insert the distributor and install the auxiliary shaft sprocket.
10. Align the timing marks and install the drive belt.
11. Install the drive belt cover.
12. Check the ignition timing.

TIMING CASE, GEARS, AND CAMSHAFT—V6

Front Cover Removal and Installation

1. Remove the oil pan as described in the following section.
2. Remove the radiator and any other necessary parts such as the water pump, to allow clearance.
3. Remove the alternator and drive belts. Remove the water pump and water lines.
4. Remove the fan.
5. Remove the crankshaft pulley with a puller.
6. Remove the front cover retaining bolts and remove the front cover. If the front cover plate gasket needs replacement, remove the two screws and the plate to replace the gasket. If necessary, remove the guide sleeves from the cylinder block.
7. To install, reverse the procedures, cleaning all surfaces of gasket material and installing new gaskets and sealing compound.

NOTE: *If the guide sleeves were removed, install them with new seal rings but do not use sealing compound.*

Front Oil Seal Removal and Installation

1. Remove the timing cover.
2. Drive out the old seal with a punch and make sure that the inside rim is clean.
3. Coat a new seal with grease and place it into position on the case.
4. Drive the seal in until fully seated; check to make sure that the spring is properly positioned in the seal.
5. Reinstall the timing cover.

Camshaft Removal and Installation

1. Drain the cooling system.
2. Remove the radiator, fan, spacer, pulley, and drive belts.
3. Remove the distributor cap with the spark plug wires attached. Re-

move the distributor vacuum line, distributor, alternator, rocker arm covers, fuel line and filter, carburetor, and intake manifold.

4. Remove the rocker arm and shaft assemblies. Lift out the pushrods and mark them so they can be replaced in the same location.
5. Remove the oil pan. (See the following sections.)
6. Remove the timing chain cover and water pump as an assembly.
7. Remove the camshaft gear retaining bolt and slide the gear off the camshaft. Remove the camshaft thrust plate.
8. Remove the valve lifters from the engine block with a magnet. Lifters should be identified to permit installation in the same location.
9. Carefully pull the camshaft from the engine block, avoiding damage to the camshaft bearings. Remove the key and spacer ring.
10. Coat the camshaft with a cam lubricant or heavy engine oil.
11. Install the camshaft, carefully avoiding damage to the bearings.

NOTE: *When installing the camshaft, do not push it hard into the engine. There is an oil plug at the rear of the engine block called the "bore plug." If the camshaft is forced into the engine, it could push this plug out, resulting in oil leaking on the clutch and pressure plate.*

12. Install the spacer ring with the chamfered side toward the engine. Insert the camshaft key. Install the thrust plate. Camshaft end-play should be 0.001-0.004 in. The spacer ring and thrust plate are available in two sizes for adjustment.
13. Install the camshaft timing gear and align the timing marks. Install the retaining washer and bolt.

V6 timing gear alignment
(© Ford Motor Co)

14. Install the valve lifters.
15. Install the timing cover.
16. Install the belt drive pulley and secure it with the washer and retaining bolt.
17. Install the oil pan.

18. Install the pushrods in the same locations from which they were removed. Install the intake manifold.
19. Install the oil baffles and rocker arm shaft assemblies. Adjust the valves.
20. Install the carburetor, fuel line and filter, alternator, distributor cap, and wires.
21. Fill the cooling system.
22. Install the rocker arm covers but not permanently. Run the engine, check for leaks, and set the ignition timing.
23. Set the valves at their hot setting. Install the valve covers with sealer.

TIMING COVER, CHAIN, AND CAMSHAFT—V8

Timing Cover and Chain
Removal and Installation

1. Drain the cooling system and the crankcase. Disconnect the negative battery cable.
2. Remove the fan shroud retaining bolts and position the shroud to the rear. Remove the bolts attaching the spacer to the water pump and remove the fan and spacer (or fan drive clutch) from the water pump shaft. Remove the fan shroud.
3. Remove the air conditioner drive belt and idler pulley bracket. Remove the alternator and alternator drive belt. Remove the power steering pump and drive belt. Remove the Thermactor air pump and drive belt.
4. Remove the water pump pulley.
5. Disconnect the radiator hose, heater hose, and the water pump by-pass hose from the water pump.
6. Remove the crankshaft pulley from the crankshaft vibration damper. After removing the damper retaining screw and washer, install a universal gear puller on the damper and pull it off.
7. Disconnect the fuel pump outlet line at the fuel pump. Remove the fuel pump retaining bolts and position the pump to one side with the flexible fuel line still attached.
8. Remove the engine dip-stick.
9. Remove the bolts attaching the oil pan to the front cover. Using a thin-bladed knife, cut the oil pan gasket flush with the cylinder block face prior to separating the cover from the cylinder block. Then remove the front cover and water pump as an assembly.
10. Discard the old front cover gasket, and remove the crankshaft front oil slinger.
11. Check the timing chain deflection. Gently rotate the crankshaft in a counter-clockwise direction until all slack is removed from the left-side of the timing chain. Scribe a mark on the engine block parallel to the present position of the left-side of the chain. Turn the crankshaft in a clockwise direction to re-

move all the slack from the right-side of the chain. Force the left-side of the chain outward with the fingers and measure the distance between the reference point and the present position of the chain. If the distance exceeds 1/2 in., replace the chain and sprockets.
12. Turn the engine in the normal direction of rotation until the timing sprocket marks are positioned "dot-to-dot."

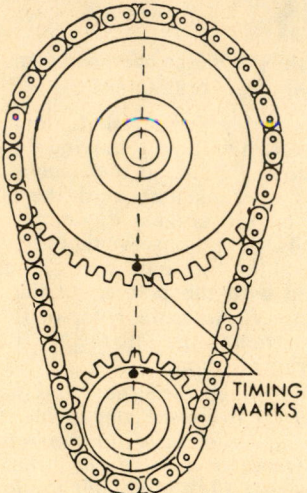

Aligning the camshaft timing marks—302 V8 (© Ford Motor Co.)

13. Remove the camshaft sprocket capscrew, washers and the fuel pump eccentric. Slide both sprockets and the timing chain forward, and remove them as an assembly.

To install:

1. Position the sprockets and timing chain on the camshaft and crankshaft simultaneously, aligning the marks.
2. Install the fuel pump eccentric, washers and camshaft sprocket capscrew. Tighten the capscrew to 30-35 ft lbs. Install the front oil slinger, if equipped.
3. Clean the front cover, oil pan and cylinder block mating surfaces to remove all old gasket material.
4. Replace the cover oil seal.
5. Lubricate the timing chain with engine oil.
6. Coat the gasket surface of the oil pan with oil-resistant sealer. Cut and position the required sections of a new gasket on the oil pan and apply oil-resistant sealer at the corners. Install the oil pan seal. Coat the gasket surfaces of the block and front cover with oil-resistant sealer, and position the new gasket on the block.
7. Place the front cover on the block, taking care to avoid seal damage or gasket mislocation.
8. Install the front cover. To align the holes in the block with those in the cover, it may be necessary to insert two phillips head screwdrivers in two of the bolt holes and force the

cover downward, compressing the new pan gasket. Then, with the attaching bolts coated with oil resistant sealer for ease of installation, install the bolts, tightening them diagonally, in rotation, to a final torque of 12-15 ft lbs.

9. Apply white grease to the rubbing surface of the vibration damper inner hub to prevent damage to the seal. Apply a light coating of grease to the front of the crankshaft for damper installation. Then, align the vibration damper keyway. Install the vibration damper on the crankshaft and install the capscrew and washer. Tighten the screw to 70-90 ft lbs. Install the crankshaft pulley.

10. Using a new gasket, install the fuel pump to the block. Connect the fuel outlet line.

11. Install the dipstick.

12. Connect the radiator hose, heater hose, and the water pump by-pass hose at the water pump.

13. Install the Thermactor air pump and drive belt. Install the power steering pump and drive belt. Install the alternator and drive belt. Install the air conditioner idler pulley and drive belt.

14. Position the fan shroud over the water pump pulley. Install the fan and spacer (or fan clutch drive). Install the fan shroud retaining bolts.

15. Adjust all drive belts.

16. Fill the crankcase and cooling system. Connect the battery cable. Bleed the cooling system.

17. Start the engine and operate it at a fast idle. Check for coolant and oil leaks.

18. Adjust the ignition timing.

Front Oil Seal Removal and Installation

This procedure is identical to that shown for the V6.

Camshaft Removal and Installation

1. Drain the cooling system. Disconnect the radiator hoses and the automatic transmission cooler lines. Remove the fan shroud retaining bolts. Remove the radiator. If equipped with air conditioning, remove the bolts securing the air conditioning condenser and position the condenser to one side.

--- CAUTION ---

Do not disconnect the refrigerant lines.

2. Remove the intake manifold as outlined under ''Intake Manifold Removal and Installation.''

3. Remove the front cover timing chain and sprockets as outlined under ''Timing Cover and Chain Removal and Installation.''

4. Remove the crankcase ventilation valve and hoses and the EGR cooler, if equipped. Remove the rocker arm covers. Loosen the rocker arm stud nuts and rotate the rocker arms to one side (away from the pushrods).

5. Lift out the pushrods, keeping them in order so that they may be installed in their original positions. Using a magnet, remove the valve lifters, also keeping them in order. If the lifters become stuck in their bores, use a claw-type tool to remove them.

6. Remove the camshaft thrust plate and remove the camshaft by carefully pulling it to the front of the engine. Take care not to damage the camshaft lobes or the cam bearing journals while removing the camshaft from the engine.

7. Prior to installing the camshaft, coat the cam lobes with a camshaft lubricant, and the bearing journals and all valve parts with heavy engine oil.

8. Reverse the above procedure to install, taking care to tighten the rocker arm nuts in the order specified under valve adjustment before starting the engine. Permissible camshaft end-play is 0.001-0.007 in., adjusted by replacement of the thrust plate.

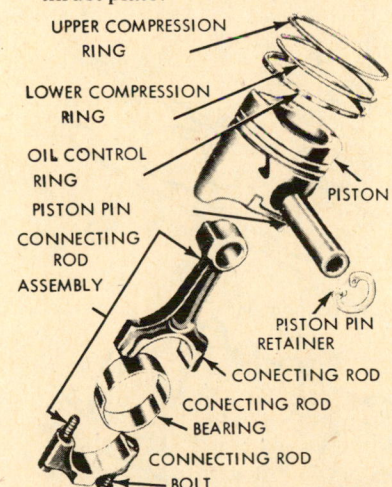

Connecting rod and piston assembly for the 1600 cc engine (© Ford Motor Co)

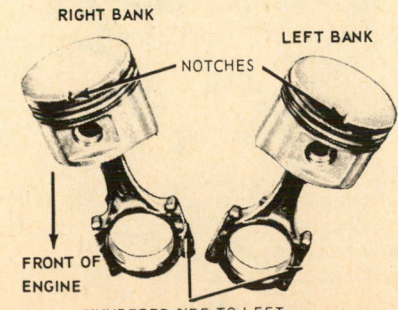

Piston and rod positioning for installation 2800 cc V6 (© Ford Motor Co)

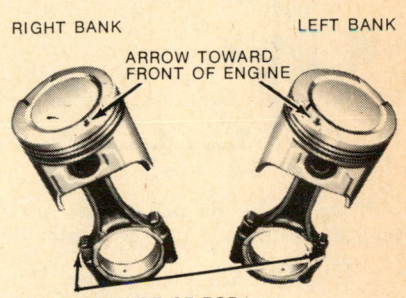

Piston and rod positioning for installation in 2000 cc and 2300 cc engines (© Ford Motor Co)

Piston and connecting rod positioning for installation—302 V8 (© Ford Motor Co.)

ENGINE LUBRICATION

NOTE: *The Brazilian-built 2300 cc engine has an oil restrictor pin in the oil gallery behind the pressure sender. This pin restricts oil pressure to the tappets during cold and full throttle operation. If the pin is removed, the valves will not seat properly. The Brazilian engine has a 900 through 922 series number on the white engine timing belt cover tag.*

Oil Pan Removal and Installation

1600, 2000, AND 2300 CC

1. Drain the crankcase.

2. Remove the oil dipstick.

3. On 1600 cc engines, disconnect the negative battery cable, remove the starter motor retaining bolts and remove the starter from the engine.

4. Disconnect the steering shaft connection from the rack and pinion.

5. Disconnect the rack and pinion from the crossmember and move it forward to provide clearance.

6. Remove the flywheel housing inspection cover.

7. Remove the oil pan attaching bolts and remove the pan.

8. Clean the gasket mounting surface of the block and the pan.

9. Coat the block surface and the oil pan gasket with oil resistant sealer and position the gasket on the block. The 2000 has a two piece gasket.

10. Coat the oil pan front oil seal and the front cover with oil resistant sealer and position the seal on the

front cover, making sure the ends of the seal contact the oil pan gasket.

11. Coat the rear oil pan seal with oil resistant sealer and install it in the rear main bearing cap.

12. Position the pan on the block and tighten the bolts to specification.

Tighten all bolts to 7-9 ft lbs, except 8 mm bolts on the 2300. Tighten these to 11-13 ft lbs.

13. Reverse steps 1-6 to complete installation.

2800 CC V6

1. Remove the dipstick. Remove the bolts attaching the fan shroud to

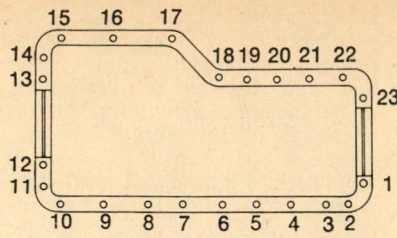

2000 cc engine oil pan torque sequence (© Ford Motor Co.)

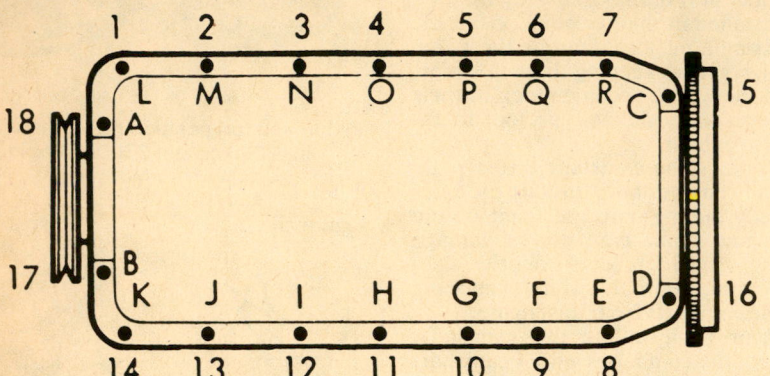

1600 cc engine oil pan torque sequence—use the alphabetical pattern first, then the numerical (© Ford Motor Co.)

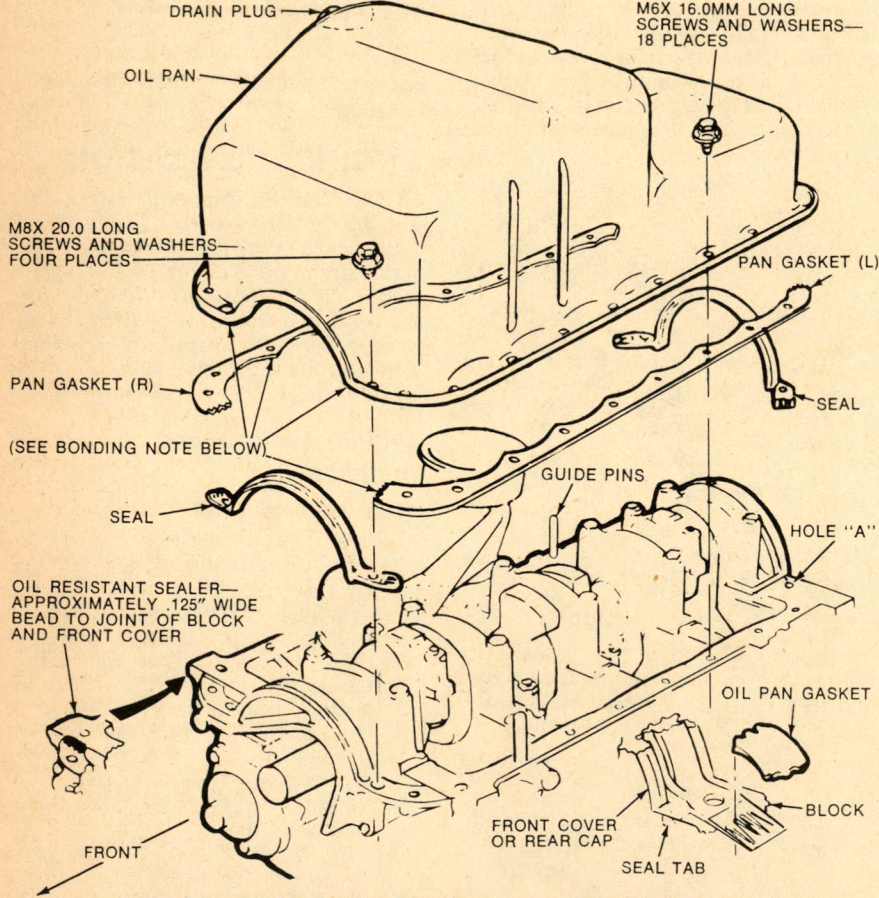

1. APPLY GASKET ADHESIVE EVENLY TO OIL PAN FLANGE AND TO PAN SIDE GASKETS. ALLOW ADHESIVE TO DRY PAST WET STAGE, THEN INSTALL GASKETS TO OIL PAN.
2. APPLY SEALER TO JOINT OF BLOCK AND FRONT COVER. INSTALL SEALS TO FRONT COVER AND REAR BEARING CAP AND PRESS SEAL TABS FIRMLY INTO BLOCK. BE SURE TO INSTALL THE REAR SEAL BEFORE THE REAR MAIN BEARING CAP SEALER HAS CURED.
3. POSITION 2 GUIDE PINS AND INSTALL THE OIL PAN. SECURE THE PAN WITH THE FOUR M8 BOLTS SHOWN ABOVE.
4. REMOVE THE GUIDE PINS AND INSTALL AND TORQUE THE EIGHTEEN M6 BOLTS, BEGINNING AT HOLE "A" AND WORKING CLOCKWISE AROUND THE PAN.

2300 cc engine oil pan torque sequence (© Ford Motor Co,)

the radiator. Position the shroud over the fan. Disconnect the battery ground cable at the battery. Loosen the alternator bracket and adjusting bolts. Drain the coolant and remove the radiator hoses and automatic transmission cooler lines.

2. Raise the vehicle on a hoist. Disconnect the steering gear and set it out of the way. Disconnect the sway bar ends.

3. Drain the crankcase.

4. Remove the splash shield. Remove the starter.

5. Remove the engine front support nuts.

6. Raise the engine and place wood blocks between the engine front supports and the chassis brackets. Remove the clutch or converter housing cover.

7. Remove the oil pan attaching bolts and remove the oil pan.

8. Clean the gasket surfaces of the block and the oil pan. The oil pan has a two-piece gasket.

9. Coat the block surface and the oil pan gasket with sealer. Position the oil pan gaskets on the cylinder block.

10. Position the oil pan front seal on the cylinder front cover. Be sure that the tabs on the seal are over the oil pan gasket.

11. Place the end seals in position flush with the cylinder block oil pan rail, if previously removed. Position the oil pan rear seal on the rear main bearing cap. Be sure that the tabs on the seal are over the oil pan gasket.

12. Position the oil pan centered on the cylinder block. Install two bolts at both ends (front and rear) of the oil pan, then install the remaining bolts and tighten them to 5-7 ft lbs, starting with the bolt at the left front corner on the leading edge of the oil pan and working clockwise around the circumference of the pan.

13. Replace the converter housing or clutch cover.

14. Raise the engine and remove the wood blocks from between the engine supports and chassis brackets. Lower the engine and install the engine support nuts.

15. Replace the starter and splash shield, steering gear, and swaybar.

16. Lower the vehicle.

17. Install the alternator.
18. Connect the battery ground wire.
19. Install the fan shroud.
20. Install the dipstick. Fill the crankcase with oil. Start engine and check for leaks.

302 V8

1. Disconnect the battery ground cable.
2. Unbolt the fan shroud and place it over the fan.
3. Raise the car safely.
4. Drain the oil.
5. Remove the four bolts and the crossmember.
6. Remove the steering shaft flex joint attaching screw. Unbolt the steering gear from the crossmember.
7. Unbolt the sway bar from the chassis and move it down.
8. Disconnect the battery cable at the starter and remove the starter.
9. Remove the pan bolts and the pan.
10. On installation, clean the gasket surfaces. Cement the pan gasket and seals to the block. Install the pan.
11. Replace all the other items removed. Torque the steering gear to crossmember bolts to 80-100 ft lbs and the coupling bolt to 20-30 ft lbs.

Oil Pump Removal and Installation

CAUTION

When installing the oil pump, prime it by filling the inlet or outlet port with engine oil and rotating the pump by hand. This must be done to prevent engine damage.

1600 CC

The oil pump and filter assembly is bolted to the left side of the block and can be serviced with the engine installed in the car.

Two types of oil pump have been installed during production—an eccentric bi-rotor type and a sliding vane type. These pumps are readily identified by their end covers—the eccentric bi-rotor type has four recesses cast into its cover while the sliding vane type has a flat cover. These two pumps are interchangeable, although their internal parts are not.

1. Lift the hood and place a drain pan under the oil pump.
2. Remove the three bolts which hold the pump and filter assembly.

NOTE: *Tighten these bolts to 13-15 ft lbs when installing pump.*

3. Remove filter from pump.
4. To install, reverse removal procedure.

2000 AND 2300 CC

The oil pump, of bi-rotor design, is mounted to the bottom of the cylinder block, inside the oil pan. To remove the

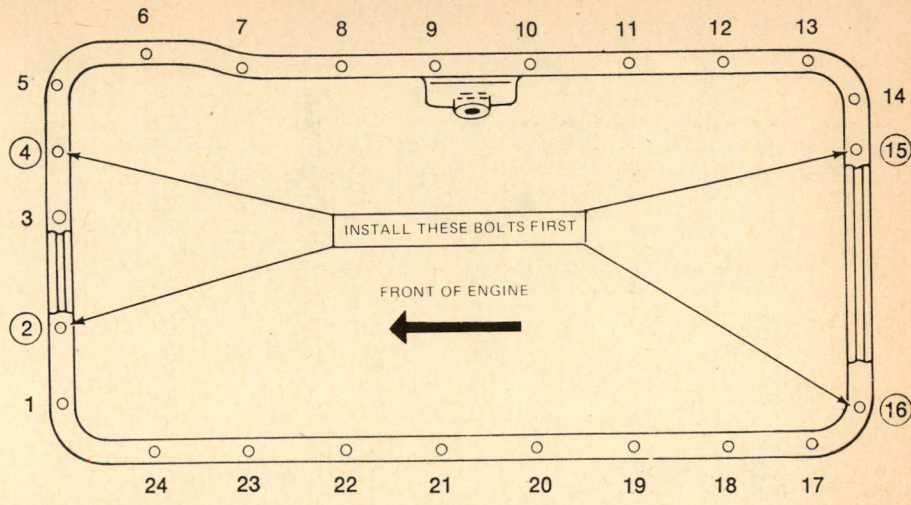

V6 oil pan bolt torque sequence (© Ford Motor Co.)

pump, remove the oil pan and remove the two bolts that mount the oil pump to the block.

NOTE: *Under no circumstances should the three-bolt cover oil pump on a 2300 cc engine be disassembled. If the pump is found to be defective, it should be replaced as a unit. Four-bolt cover pumps (introduced in 1976) may be disassembled.*

V6

1. Remove the oil pan and unbolt the oil pickup screen from the main bearing cap.
2. Remove the pump bolts.
3. Remove the pump and pump drive shaft.
4. On installation, prime the pump. Insert the driveshaft into the engine block with the pointed end inward. The pointed end is closest to the pressed-on flange.
5. Install the pump with a new gasket and tighten the screws; install the inlet tube and screen assembly with a new gasket.
6. Replace the oil pan, start the engine, and check for leaks.

302 V8

1. Remove the oil pan. Remove the pump inlet tube and screen assembly.
2. Unbolt and remove the pump, gasket, and driveshaft.
3. On installation, prime the pump. Insert the driveshaft in the distributor socket. The stop on the shaft should touch the roof of the crankcase. Remove the shaft and position the stop if necessary.
4. Insert the driveshaft into the pump. Install the pump and shaft as an assembly. If the pump won't go into place, the driveshaft is probably not correctly aligned with the distributor shaft.
5. Tighten the pump bolts and replace the inlet and screen assembly. Replace the pan.

Crankshaft Rear Main Oil Seal Replacement

1600 cc

1. Remove the transmission and unbolt the right and left engine mounts from the cylinder block.
2. Raise and support the engine above the engine mounts.
3. Remove the pressure plate bolts in sequence, a few turns at a time, and remove the pressure plate and clutch disc.
4. Remove the flywheel.
5. Remove the oil pan and gaskets.
6. Remove the rear oil seal carrier.
7. Remove the seal from the carrier and install a new one.
8. Locate a new gasket on the rear oil seal carrier. Fit the carrier to the block rear face. Tighten the bolts evenly to 12-15 ft lbs.
9. Position new gaskets on the block flange. Position the cork packing strips with the chamfered ends into the grooves. Install the oil pan.
10. Assemble the clutch, transmission, and motor mounts in the reverse order of removal.

2000 CC AND 2800 CC V6

1. Remove the transmission. Remove the clutch pressure plate and clutch disc, if so equipped.
2. Remove the flywheel, flywheel housing and rear plate.

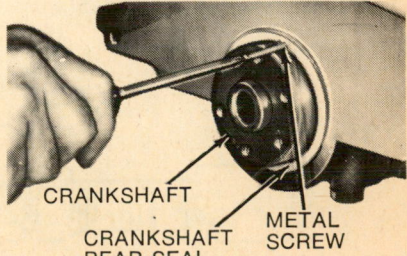

Removing the crankshaft rear main oil seal—2000 cc and 2800 cc V6
(© Ford Motor Co)

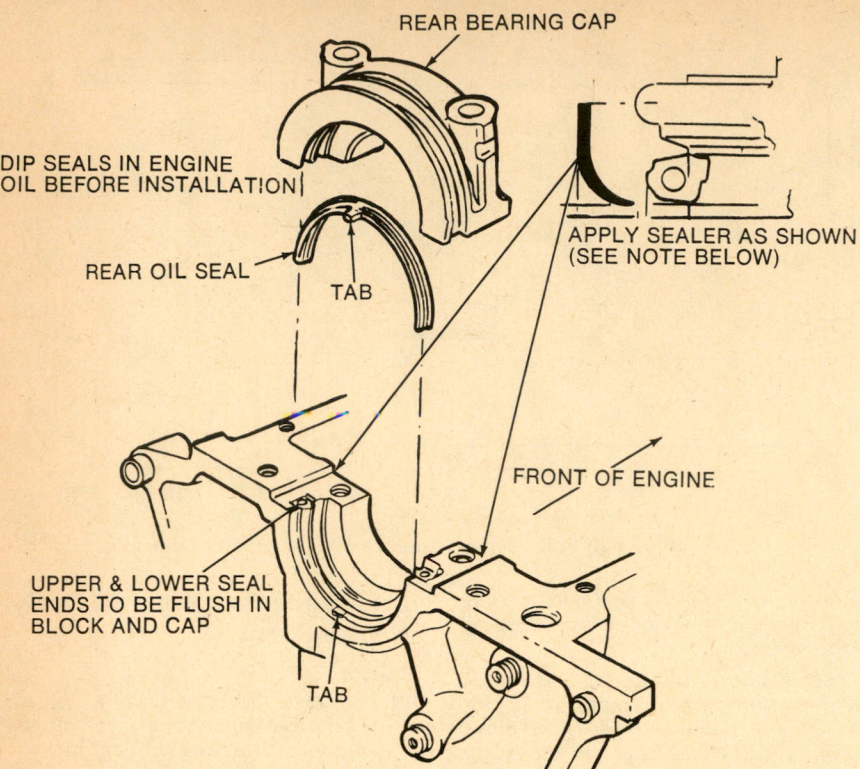

DIP SEALS IN ENGINE OIL BEFORE INSTALLATION

REAR BEARING CAP

REAR OIL SEAL

TAB

APPLY SEALER AS SHOWN (SEE NOTE BELOW)

FRONT OF ENGINE

UPPER & LOWER SEAL ENDS TO BE FLUSH IN BLOCK AND CAP

TAB

NOTE: CLEAN THE AREA WHERE SEALER IS TO BE APPLIED BEFORE INSTALLING THE SEALS. AFTER THE SEALS ARE IN PLACE, APPLY A 1/16 INCH BEAD OF SEALER AS SHOWN. *SEALER MUST NOT TOUCH SEALS*

Replacement of the crankshaft rear main oil seal—2300 cc engine (© Ford Motor Co)

3. Punch two holes in the crankshaft rear oil seal on opposite sides of the crankshaft just above the bearing cap-to-cylinder block split line. Install a sheet metal screw in each of the holes and pry the crankshaft rear main oil seal from the block.

NOTE: *Use extreme caution not to scratch the crankshaft oil seal surface.* Clean the oil seal recess in the cylinder block and main bearing cap.

4. Coat the seal and all of the seal mounting surfaces with oil and install the seal in the recess, driving it in place with an oil seal installation tool or a large socket.

5. Install the clutch and/or transmission in the reverse order of removal.

2300 CC AND 302 V8

1. Remove the oil pan and oil pump, if required.

2. Loosen all the main bearing cap bolts, thereby lowering the crankshaft slightly but not more than 1/32 in.

3. Remove the rear main bearing cap, and remove the oil seal from the bearing cap and the cylinder block. Install a small sheet metal screw in one end of the cylinder block half of the seal, and pull on the screw to remove the seal.

4. Clean the seal grooves in the cap and block with a brush and solvent. Dry the area thoroughly. No solvent should come in contact with the seal.

5. Dip the seal halves in clean engine oil.

6. Carefully install the upper seal (block half) into its groove with the undercut side of the seal toward the front of the engine, by rotating it on the seal journal of the crank-

shaft unil about 3/8 in. protrudes below the parting surface. Be sure that no rubber has been shaved off. Wipe all oil from the mating surface of the bearing cap and cylinder block.

7. Tighten the bearing cap bolts to specifications.

8. Install the lower seal in the rear main bearing cap with the undercut side of the seal toward the front of the engine. Allow the seal to protrude about 3/8 in. above the parting surface to mate with the upper seal when the cap is installed.

NOTE: *Install the seals so that the locating tab faces the rear of the engine. (2300 cc only).*

9. Apply a *small* amount of sealer to the mating surface of the bearing cap. No sealer compound should come in contact with the rubber seals when the bearing cap is installed and tightened.

10. Install the oil pump (if removed) and oil pan. Fill the crankcase with oil, and operate the engine, checking for leaks.

CLUTCH

A single plate, dry disc type clutch is used. Actuation is by means of adjustable, mechanical linkage.

Adjustment
PINTO THROUGH 1974

1. Working under the car, loosen the clutch adjusting nut, the front locknut and the rear locknut (if so equipped).

2. Pull the clutch cable toward the front of the car until all free play is removed from the clutch release lever.

3. Holding the cable in this position, place a 1/4 in. spacer against the engine side of the flywheel housing and tighten the adjusting nut fingertight against the spacer.

4. Hold the adjusting nut so that it maintains its position and tighten the front locknut against the adjusting nut.

5. Remove the spacer and tighten the rear locknut (if so equipped) against the transmission side of the flywheel housing.

1975 AND LATER PINTO AND BOBCAT

1. Loosen the cable locknut on the transmission side of the flywheel housing.

2. Pull the cable toward the front of the car until the tabs on the adjuster nut are clear of the housing. Rotate the nut toward the front of the car about 1/4 in.

3. Release the cable. Then pull the cable forward again until there is no release lever free movement. Rotate the adjusting nut toward the

LOCKNUT

RELEASE LEVER

CABLE

1/4 INCH

Pinto clutch linkage adjustment through 1974 (© Ford Motor Co.)

housing until the tabs touch the housing, then drop the tabs into the nearest groove.

4. Tighten the locknut.

MUSTANG II

1. Remove the cable retaining clip at the firewall.
2. Remove the screw holding the cable attaching bracket on the fender apron.
3. Pull the cable toward the front of the vehicle until the adjusting nut can be turned. Rotate the nut away from the adjustment sleeve about 1/4 in.
4. Release the cable, and then pull the cable again until free movement of the release lever is eliminated.
5. Rotate the adjusting nut toward the adjustment sleeve until contact is made, then index it into the next notch.
6. Reinstall the cable retaining clip and cable attaching bracket, and the screw on the fender apron.

Clutch, Clutch Housing, And Manual Transmission

REMOVAL, PINTO AND BOBCAT

1. Place the gearshift lever in the neutral position. Raise the car and remove the back-up light switch from the transmission extension housing.
2. Loosen the shift lever locknut. Remove the knob and the locknut from the shift lever. Remove the four rubber boot attaching screws and remove the boot.
3. Compress the corrugated rubber spring, then remove the retaining snap-ring and slide the spring upward on the lever.
4. Bend the shift lever locktabs up, then thread the plastic dome nut from the extension housing.
5. Lift the shift lever from the extension housing.
6. Working from under the hood, remove the upper flywheel housing-to-engine attaching bolts.
7. Raise the vehicle and match-mark the driveshaft and the rear axle pinion flange.
8. Disconnect and remove the driveshaft. Place rags in the extension housing to prevent loss of lubricant.
9. Remove the clutch release lever dust cover.
10. Disconnect the clutch cable from the clutch release lever.
11. Remove the starter motor attaching bolts and position the motor out of the way.
12. Remove the speedometer cable-to-transmission attaching screw and remove the cable and gear from the transmission. Plug the opening in the transmission to prevent lubricant spillage.
13. Support the rear of the engine with a jack and remove the crossmember-to-body attaching bolts.

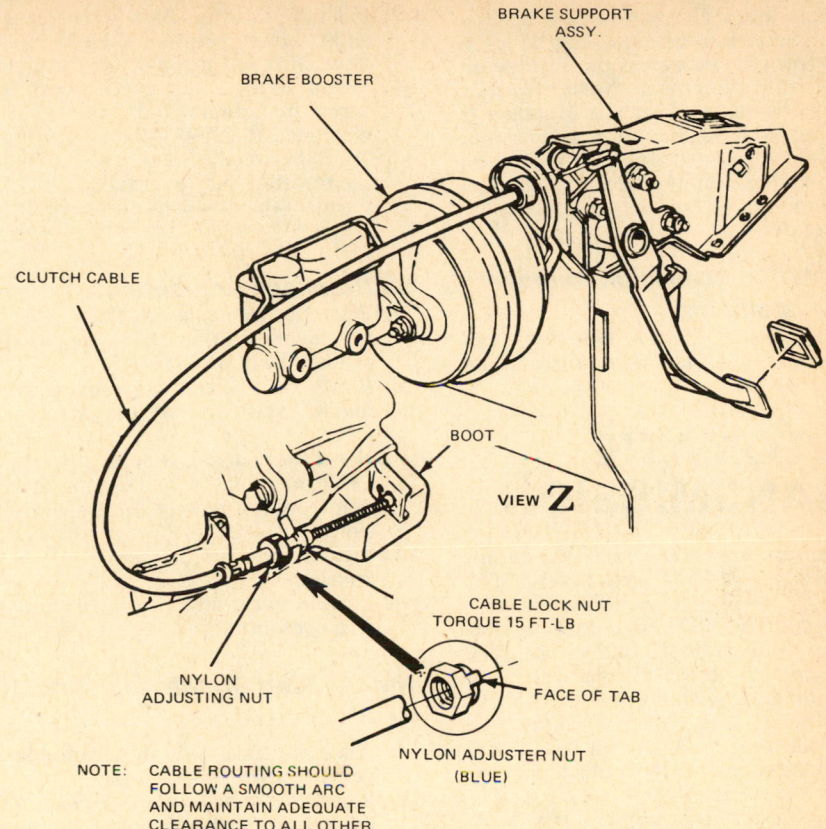

1975 and later Pinto and Bobcat clutch linkage (© Ford Motor Co.)

NOTE: CABLE ROUTING SHOULD FOLLOW A SMOOTH ARC AND MAINTAIN ADEQUATE CLEARANCE TO ALL OTHER COMPONENTS

14. Remove the bolts that attach the crossmember to the transmission extension housing and remove the crossmember from the car.
15. Lower the engine to gain working room, and remove the remaining flywheel housing-to-engine attaching bolts.
16. Slide the transmission rearward and remove it from the car.
17. If the clutch is to be removed loosen the six pressure plate attaching bolts evenly to release spring pressure gradually. If the same pressure plate and cover are to be reused, mark the position of the pressure plate and flywheel so they can be returned to their original location.
18. Remove the pressure plate attaching bolts and remove the pressure plate and clutch from the car.

REMOVAL, MUSTANG II

1. Place the shift lever in neutral. Remove the carpet and boot. Remove the three metric lever base bolts and remove the shift lever.
2. Raise the car safely. Remove the driveshaft, after matchmarking its location, and plug the end of the transmission.
3. Disconnect the seat belt sensing switch, if any, and the backup light wires.
4. Remove the attaching screw and pull out the speedometer cable. Plug the hole.

5. The remainder of the procedure is the same as for Pinto and Bobcat, starting with Step 13. The major difference is that the transmission is removed separately, leaving the clutch housing in place.

INSTALLATION PINTO, BOBCAT, MUSTANG II

1. Position the clutch and pressure plate on the flywheel and install the attaching bolts loosely.

NOTE: *The three dowel pins on the flywheel must be aligned with the pressure plate.*

2. Align the clutch assembly, using a pilot shaft or other tool, and alternately tighten the bolts.
3. Position the transmission and flywheel assembly on the studs on the cylinder block and install the retaining bolts.
4. Reverse removal procedure to install remaining equipment. The shift lever must be installed before the back-up light switch.

MANUAL TRANSMISSION

A four-speed manual transmission is standard equipment on all models. Some 1600 cc Pintos have an English built transmission. The majority of 1600 cc Pintos and all other Pintos and

Bobcats use a German built transmission. These transmissions can be identified from the transmission ID code on the identification tag at the left front of the extension housing. The Mustang II uses an American built transmission. No linkage adjustment is possible on any of these units. See the Manual Transmissions Unit Repair section for further details.

Manual Transmission Removal and Installation

See *Clutch, Clutch Housing, and Transmission Removal and Installation* in this car section.

AUTOMATIC TRANSMISSION

The 1600 cc, 2000 cc and 302 cu. in. engines use the C4 exclusively. The 2300 cc engine uses only the C3 through 1976. 1977 and later models may use either the C3 or C4. The 2800 cc engine may have either a C3 or C4, depending on availability at the time of manufacture. The transmission code letter for the C3 is V and for the C4, W. It may be found on the Vehicle Certification Label.

NOTE: *Perform the adjustments in the order listed below.*

Downshift Linkage Adjustment

1. Disconnect the downshift lever return spring on models through 1972.

2. Hold the throttle shaft lever in the wide open position. Hold the downshift rod against the through detent stop. Adjust the downshift screw to obtain 0.050-0.070 in. clearance (0.010-0.080 in. starting 1973) between the screw tip and the throttle shaft lever tab.
3. Connect the downshift lever return spring.

Shift Linkage Adjustment

1. Place the transmission floor selector lever in the Drive position against the rear stop.
2. Raise the vehicle and loosen the linkage shift rod at the selector lever.
3. Move the transmission lever to the Drive position (second detent position from the rear of the transmission).
4. Tighten the adjustment on the linkage.
5. Lower the car and check transmission operation.

Neutral Start Switch Adjustment
C4

1. Place the transmission selector lever in the Neutral position.
2. Raise the vehicle on a hoist and loosen the two bolts that attach the neutral switch to the transmission.
3. Rotate the switch until a gauge pin (shank end of a no. 43 drill bit) can be inserted through the gauge pin holes in the switch. The gauge pin must be inserted a full $31/64$ in. into

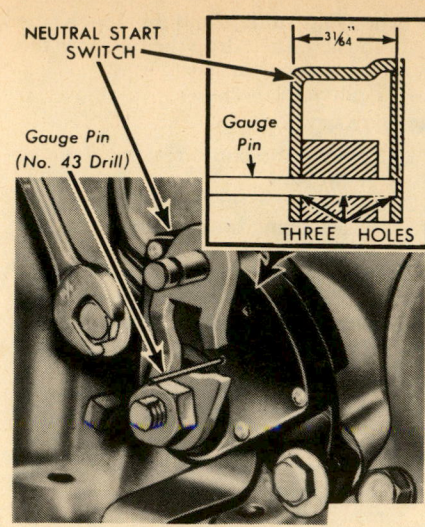

C4 Neutral start switch adjustment (© Ford Motor Co)

the switch, through all three holes in the switch.
4. Tighten the switch retaining bolts and remove the pin.

Neutral Start Switch Replacement
C4

1. Raise the car, with the transmission in neutral, and disconnect the downshift linkage.
2. Remove the neutral switch attaching bolts and remove the switch and disconnect the wires.

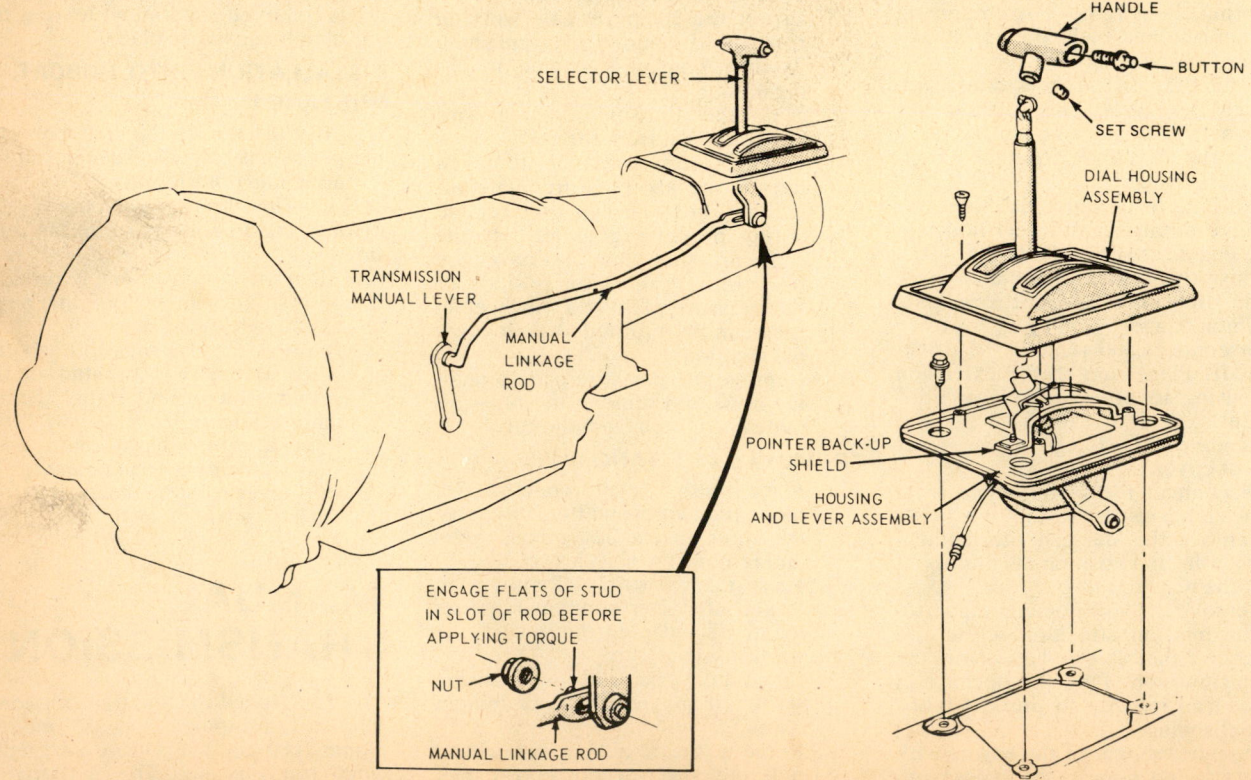

Automatic transmission shift linkage (© Ford Motor Co.)

3. Install the replacement switch and adjust it as described above.
4. Install the downshift outer lever.
5. Connect the downshift linkage rod to the downshift lever.

C3
1. Unplug the connector from the switch and unscrew the switch from the transmission case.
2. Replace the switch with a new O-ring.
3. Carefully check that the back-up lights work only in Reverse and that the engine will start only in Neutral and Park. No adjustment is required.

Band Adjustments

— CAUTION —

The torque figures and numbers of turns given in these procedures must be exactly correct to prevent transmission damage.

NOTE: *The only band adjustment required on the C3 transmission is on the front band.*

INTERMEDIATE (FRONT) BAND
1. Wipe clean the area around the adjusting screw on the side of the transmission, near the left-front corner of the transmission.
2. Remove the adjusting screw locknut and discard it.
3. Install a new locknut on the adjusting screw but do not tighten it.
4. Tighten the adjusting screw to *exactly 10 ft lbs.*

MUSTANG, PINTO & BOBCAT
TOOL # 71P—77370A OR
Tool # T70P—713200A

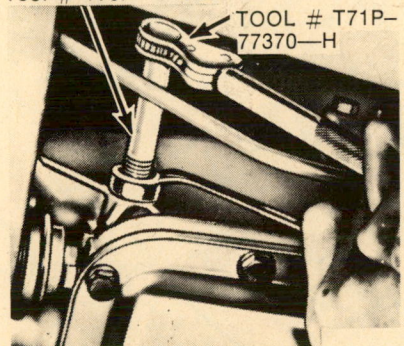

Intermediate band adjustment
(© Ford Motor Co)

5. Back off the adjusting screw *exactly 1³/₄ turns; 1¹/₂ turns on the C3.*
6. Hold the adjusting screw so that it *does not turn* and tighten the adjusting screw locknut to 35-45 ft lbs.

LOW-REVERSE BAND
1. Wipe clean the area around the adjusting screw on the side of the transmission, near the right-rear corner.

C4 Low-reverse band adjustment
(© Ford Motor Co)

2. Remove the adjusting screw locknut and discard it.
3. Install a new locknut on the adjusting screw but do not tighten it.
4. Tighten the adjusting screw to *exactly 10 ft lbs.*
5. Back off the adjusting screw *exactly 3 full turns.*
6. Hold the adjusting screw so that it *does not turn* and tighten the adjusting screw to 35-45 ft lbs.

Pan Replacement, Fluid and Filter Change
1. Raise the car up on a lift.
2. Some C4 models require that the transmission fluid filler tube be disconnected to drain the pan; all others can be drained by loosening the pan bolts and letting the fluid drain out when the pan is lowered.
3. After the fluid has drained out, remove the rest of the attaching bolts, the pan and the gasket.
4. Remove the bolts holding the filter in place, remove the filter, clean, and replace it. The filter may be reused after cleaning in a non-detergent solution, such as new transmission fluid.

— CAUTION —

The C4 filter holds the throttle pressure limit valve and spring in place in the control valve body. These parts will drop out when the filter is removed. When replacing, put the valve in first, then place the gasket and filter in place over the parts.

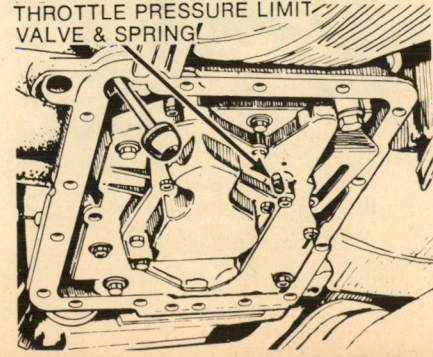

C4 filter, throttle pressure limit valve, and spring

5. Replace the filter and gasket and attach the mounting bolts. Clean the edge of the transmission pan before installing the new gasket; bolt the pan to the transmission, and reattach the fluid filler tube if applicable.
6. Refill the transmission with Type F fluid, and check for leaks around the pan.

— CAUTION —

Add a little less than the amount of drained fluid at first, run the engine, shift through all positions, and check the level. It should be between ADD and FULL. The level should be at FULL after the transmission is fully warmed up. Be very cautious not to overfill.

U-JOINTS

The drive shaft incorporates two universal joints and a slip yoke. The splines in the yoke and on the transmission output shaft permit the drive shaft to move forward and rearward as the axle moves up and down. All drive shafts are balanced. If the driveshaft is serviced, all mating parts should be marked prior to disassembly. If the vehicle is undercoated, the driveshaft and U-joints should be covered to prevent application of undercoating material.

Driveshaft Removal and Installation
1. Raise the vehicle.
2. Mark the position of the rear driveshaft yoke in relation to the pinion flange so the driveshaft can be returned to its original location.
3. Disconnect the rear U-Joint from the pinion flange and remove the loose bearing caps. Pull the driveshaft rearward until it clears the transmission extension housing. Plug the extension housing. Remove the driveshaft from the car.
4. To install, insert the driveshaft front yoke into the transmission extension housing, mating the output shaft splines with the driveshaft splines. Align the rear driveshaft flange with the differential companion flange according to the marks made during disassembly. Torque the bolts to 8-15 ft. lbs.

Universal Joint Overhaul
1. Remove the driveshaft.
2. Remove the snap rings which retain the bearings in the yokes.
3. Select two sockets. One must be small enough to pass through the bearing yoke hole, and the other must be large enough to receive the trunnion bearing. Using a press or a vise, press on the smaller socket until the bearing cap is pressed out on the other side. If it does not come all the way out, grasp it with

a pair of pliers and work it from the yoke.

4. Repeat the procedure for the other bearing caps.
5. To install, start a new bearing cap into the yoke. Position the trunnion into the yoke and press the cap far enough below the surface of the yoke to install the snap ring, using the smaller socket.
6. Position the opposite cap into place, and install the snap ring. It may be necessary to grind the facing surface of the snap ring to permit easier entry.
7. Repeat the procedure for the other bearings. After all the trunnions and bearings are in place, check the joints for free movement. Install the driveshaft.

REAR AXLE

Two basic types of axles are used: the integral carrier type and removeable carrier type. The removeable carrier type can also be equipped with "Traction-lok" limited slip unit.

The I.D. tag for the integral carrier is attached by one of the rear cover bolts. The tag for the removeable carrier is attached by one of the carrier-to-housing bolts. It is important to use the axle model designation when ordering any parts.

AXLE SHAFT, BEARING AND SEAL REMOVAL AND INSTALLATION

NOTE: *Bearings must be pressed on and off the shaft with an arbor press.*

1. Remove the wheel, tire, and the brake drum.
2. Working through the axle shaft flange access hole, remove the nuts holding the axle retainer plate to the backing plate.
3. Remove the retainer and install the nuts fingertight to prevent the backing plate from being dislodged.
4. Using a slide hammer, remove the axle shaft and bearing assembly. If the end play is excessive, replace the bearing.
5. Using a chisel, nick the bearing retainer in three or four places.
6. Press off the old bearing and install the new one by pressing it into position.
7. Press on the new retainer.

NOTE: *Do not try to press on the bearing and retainer at the same time.*

8. With a slide hammer, remove the seal from the axle housing; when

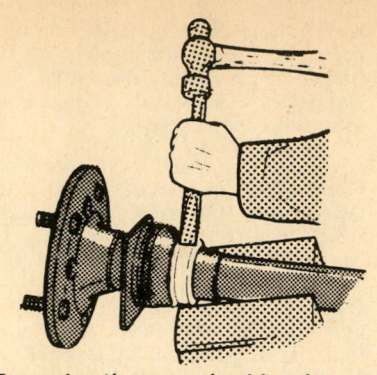

Removing the rear wheel bearing retainer ring (© Ford Motor Co.)

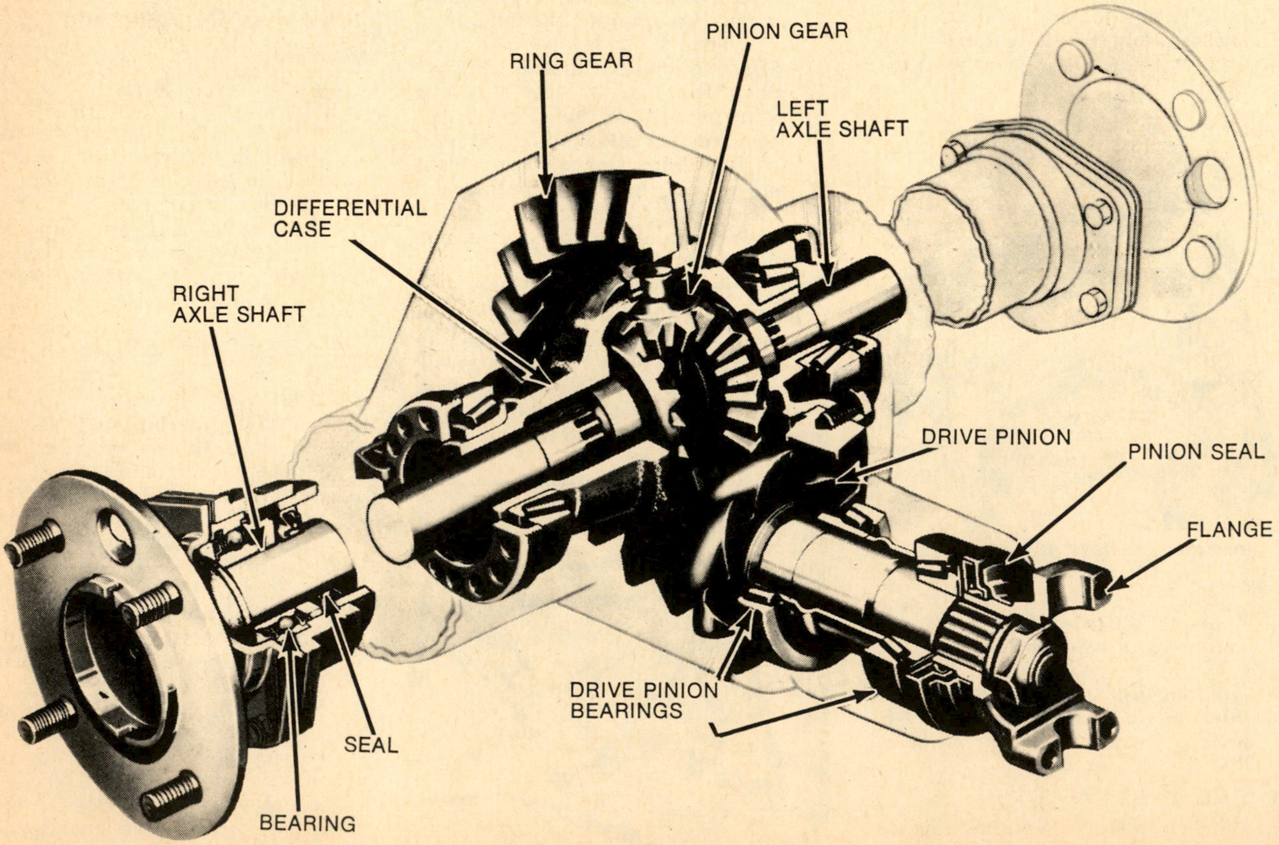

removed, clean the seal recess in the axle housing.

9. Place a new seal in position and drive it into place with a seal installation tool. The right and left seals are not interchangeable, so make sure that the seal is on the proper axle.
10. Assemble the shaft and bearing in the housing and make sure that the bearing is seated properly. Be careful not to contact the seal with the rough forging of the shaft up to the seal journal or the splines, as this will result in early seal failure.
11. Install the retainer, the drum, the wheel, and the tire.

RING GEAR

PINION GEAR

LEFT AXLE SHAFT

DIFFERENTIAL CASE

RIGHT AXLE SHAFT

DRIVE PINION

PINION SEAL

FLANGE

DRIVE PINION BEARINGS

SEAL

BEARING

Cutaway view of rear axle (© Ford Motor Co.)

JACKING, HOISTING

Lift and jacking points are shown in the figure. A floor jack may also be used under the center of the number two crossmember or under the differential housing.

FRONT SUSPENSION

Each front wheel rotates on a spindle. The spindles are attached to an upper and lower arm. The upper arm pivots on a bushing and shaft assembly which is bolted to the number 2 crossmember. The lower arm pivots on a bolt in the number two crossmember. A coil spring seats between the upper and lower arm. The shock absorber is

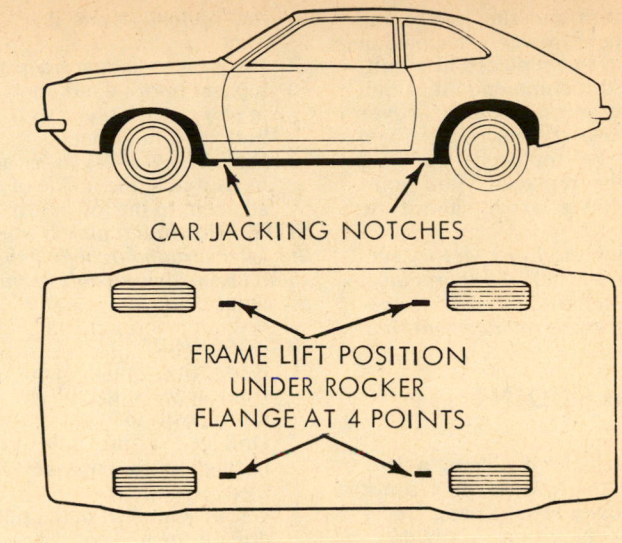

CAR JACKING NOTCHES

FRAME LIFT POSITION
UNDER ROCKER
FLANGE AT 4 POINTS

Lifting and jacking points
(© Ford Motor Co)

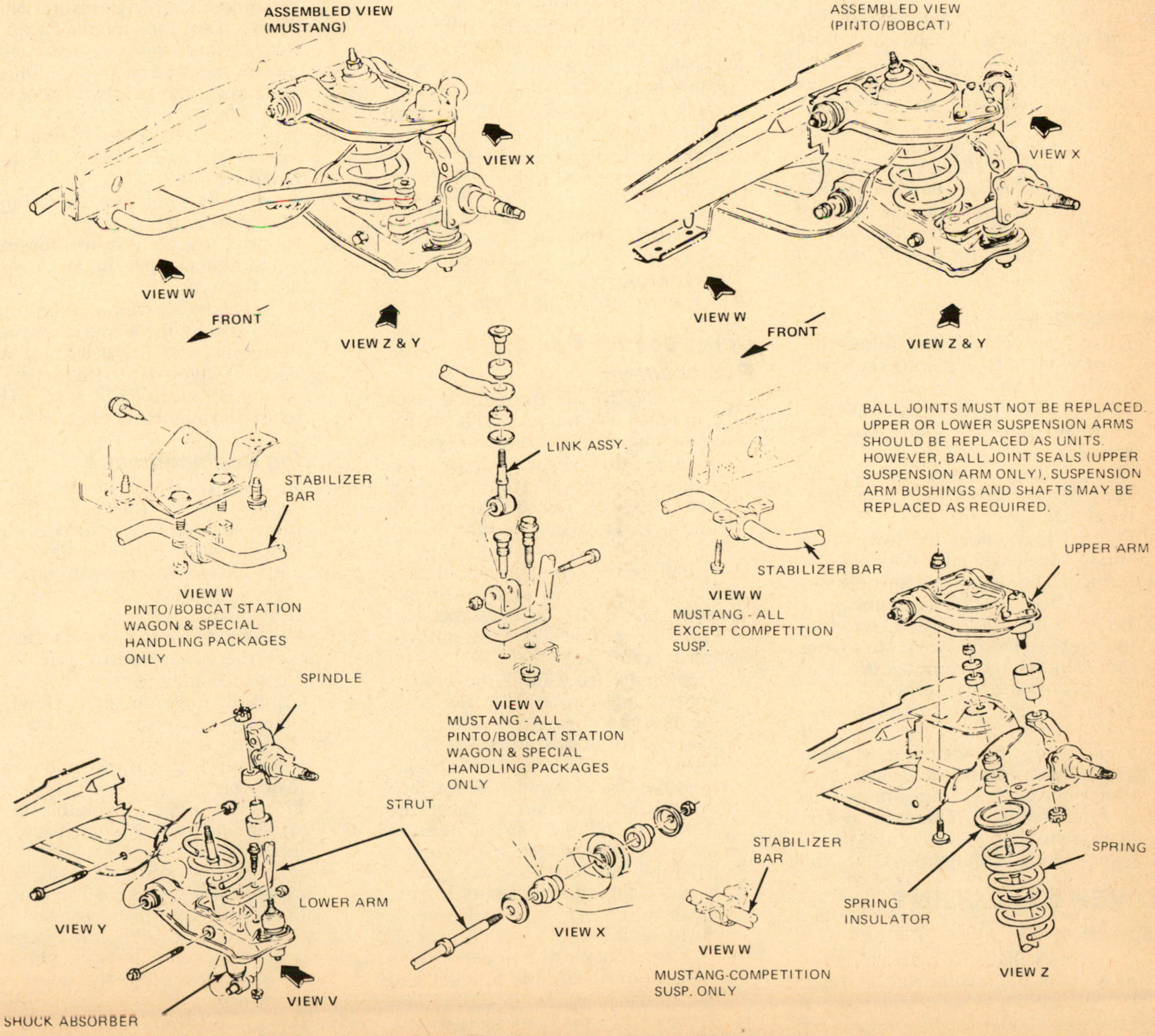

ASSEMBLED VIEW
(MUSTANG)

VIEW X

VIEW W

FRONT

VIEW Z & Y

ASSEMBLED VIEW
(PINTO/BOBCAT)

VIEW X

VIEW W

FRONT

VIEW Z & Y

STABILIZER
BAR

LINK ASSY.

STABILIZER BAR

BALL JOINTS MUST NOT BE REPLACED.
UPPER OR LOWER SUSPENSION ARMS
SHOULD BE REPLACED AS UNITS.
HOWEVER, BALL JOINT SEALS (UPPER
SUSPENSION ARM ONLY), SUSPENSION
ARM BUSHINGS AND SHAFTS MAY BE
REPLACED AS REQUIRED.

UPPER ARM

VIEW W
PINTO/BOBCAT STATION
WAGON & SPECIAL
HANDLING PACKAGES
ONLY

VIEW W
MUSTANG - ALL
EXCEPT COMPETITION
SUSP.

SPINDLE

VIEW V
MUSTANG - ALL
PINTO/BOBCAT STATION
WAGON & SPECIAL
HANDLING PACKAGES
ONLY

STRUT

STABILIZER
BAR

SPRING

SPRING
INSULATOR

LOWER ARM

VIEW Y

VIEW V

VIEW X

VIEW W
MUSTANG-COMPETITION
SUSP. ONLY

VIEW Z

SHOCK ABSORBER

Front suspension details (© Ford Motor Co.)

bolted to the arm and the top of the spring housing. Lower suspension arms must always be replaced as a unit. Since 1973 Ford recommends that ball joints and other sub-assemblies never be installed in a used arm. Upper arm bushings may be replaced, but ball joints cannot be replaced. Ball joint seals on the lower arms cannot be replaced.

NOTE: *Although the Ford factory recommends against ball joint replacement, several suspension parts manufacturers do market replacement ball joints.*

UPPER BALL JOINT

Inspection

1. Raise the vehicle by placing a floor jack under the lower arm. Do not allow the lower arm to hang freely with the vehicle on a hoist or bumper jack.
2. Have an assistant grasp the bottom of the tire and move the wheel in and out.
3. As the wheel is being moved, observe the upper control arm where the spindle attaches to it. Any movement between the upper part of the spindle and the upper ball joint indicates a bad ball joint which must be replaced.

NOTE: *During this check the lower ball joint will be unloaded and may move; this is normal and not an indication of a bad ball joint. Also, do not mistake a loose wheel bearing for a defective ball joint.*

Replacement

1. Raise the vehicle and allow the front wheels to fall into their full down position.
2. Drill a $1/8$ in. hole completely through each ball joint attaching rivet.
3. Using a large chisel, cut off the head of each rivet and drive them from the upper arm.
4. Place a jack under the lower arm and lower the vehicle about 6 in.
5. Remove the cotter pin and attaching nut from the ball joint stud.
6. Using a ball joint stud removal tool, loosen the ball joint stud from the spindle and remove the ball joint from the upper arm.
7. Clean all metal burrs from the upper arm and install the new ball joint, using the service part nuts and bolts to attach the ball joint to the upper arm. Do not attempt to re-rivet the ball joint once it has been removed.
8. Check front end alignment.

LOWER BALL JOINT

Inspection

1. Raise the vehicle by placing a floor jack under the lower arm; or, raise the vehicle on a hoist and place a jack stand under the lower arm and lower the vehicle onto it to remove

the preload from the lower ball joint.
2. Have an assistant grasp the wheel top and bottom and apply alternate in and out pressure to the top and bottom of the wheel.
3. Radial play of $1/4$ in. is acceptable measured at the inside of the wheel adjacent to the lower arm.

NOTE: *This radial play is multiplied at the outer circumference of the tire and should be measured only at the inside of the wheel.*

Replacement

1. Raise the vehicle and allow the front wheels to fall to their full down position.
2. Drill a $1/8$ in. hole completely through each ball joint attaching rivet.
3. Use a $3/8$ in. drill in the pilot hole to drill off the head of the rivet.
4. Drive the rivets from the lower arm.
5. Place a jack under the lower arm and lower the vehicle about 6 in.
6. Remove the lower ball joint stud cotter pin and attaching nut.
7. Using a ball joint stud removal tool, loosen the ball joint from the spindle and remove the ball joint from the lower arm.
8. Clean all metal burrs from the lower arm and install the new ball joint, using the service part nuts and bolts to attach the ball joint to the lower arm. Do not attempt to re-rivet the ball joint once it has been removed.
9. Check front end alignment.

Upper Control Arm
Replacement

1. Raise the front of the car and place safety stands on each side of the frame just behind the lower arm.
2. Remove the wheel and tire. Remove the cotter pin from the upper ball joint stud. Loosen the stud nut one or two turns, but don't remove it.
3. Install a ball joint removal tool beween the upper and lower ball joint studs. Be careful the tool ends are not against the nuts or lower cotter pin.
4. Tighten the tool until the stud is under compression. Tap the spindle near the upper stud with a soft hammer to loosen the stud. Don't loosen the stud with only the tool.
5. Remove the tool and place a jack under the lower arm. Raise the jack and relieve spring tension from the arm. Remove the upper ball joint stud nut.
6. Remove the attaching nuts for the upper arm inner shaft and remove the upper arm.
7. To install, place the upper arm in position on the frame bracket and install the nuts to 95-120 ft lbs. Connect the upper ball joint stud to the spindle and install the nut.

Torque the nut to 75 ft lbs, then tighten as necessary to line up the cotter pin holes. Do not loosen it, once tightened. Install the wheel and tire and adjust the front end alignment.

Lower Arm Control
Replacement

1. Raise the car and support it with stands placed under the frame.
2. Remove the wheel and tire.
3. Disconnect the sway bar from the lower arm, if equipped.
4. Disconnect the shock absorber and remove it.
5. Remove the cotter pin from the lower ball joint stud nut.
6. Remove the two bolts and nuts holding the strut to the lower arm.
7. Loosen the lower ball joint stud nut two turns. Do not remove this nut.
8. Install a spreader tool between the upper and lower ball joint studs.
9. Expand the tool until the tool exerts considerable pressure on the studs. Tap the spindle near the lower stud with a hammer to loosen the stud in the spindle. Do not loosen the stud with tool pressure only.
10. Position a floor jack under the lower arm and remove the lower ball joint nut.
11. Lower the floor jack and remove the spring and insulator.
12. Remove the A arm-to-crossmember attaching parts, and remove the arm from the car.
13. Reverse the above procedure to install. Torque the arm to crossmember bolts to 95-120 ft lbs, the strut bolts to 40-60 ft lbs, and the ball joint stud nut to 75-90 ft lbs. Have front-end alignment checked.

Spring Replacement

1. Jack up the front of the car and support it with jackstands.
2. Remove the shock absorber.
3. Disconnect the strut bar and sway bar from the lower control arm.
4. Place a floor jack under the lower control arm.
5. Remove the nut and bolt that attach the lower control arm to the front crossmember.
6. Carefully lower the jack, slowly, to relieve the spring pressure from the lower arm.
7. Remove the spring and upper insulator.
8. Place the upper insulator on the spring and secure it in place with tape.
9. Position the spring on the lower control arm. Make sure that the bottom of the spring properly engages the seat on the lower control arm. The end of the spring must be $1/2$ in. or less from the depression in the arm.
10. Raise the lower control arm with the floor jack and guide the lower

control arm and the top of the spring into place. Install the lower control arm attaching bolt and nut. Tighten the lower control arm attaching bolt to 75-110 ft lbs after the car is resting on its wheels.

11. Install the shock absorber after removing the jack. Connect the sway bar, if equipped, and tighten the bolt to 10-18 ft. lbs.

12. Remove the jack stands and lower the car.

Shock Absorber Replacement

1. Remove the nut, washer, and bushing from the upper end of the shock. If the shaft of the shock absorber turns while you are attempting to remove the nut, hold the shaft in place with an adjustable wrench while removing the nut.
2. Raise the front end of the car and install jackstands.
3. Disconnect the bottom of the shock absorber from the lower control arm. It may be necessary to raise the lower arm to remove the bottom bolt.
4. Remove the shock absorber from under the car.
5. Purge the new shock of air by repeatedly extending it in its normal position and compressing it while inverted. Position the replacement shock absorber on the lower control arm and install the attaching bolts.
6. Remove the jackstands and lower the car.

7. Connect the top of the shock absorber to the upper spring pad.

Wheel Bearing Adjustment

1. Jack the front of the car up and support it with jackstands.
2. Remove the dust cap and spindle nut cotter pin. Slide the nut lock off. Discard the pin.
3. With disc brakes, loosen the adjusting nut three turns and rock the wheel in and out to push the brake pads away from the disc. Tighten the adjusting nut on all models to 17-25 ft lbs while turning the wheel. Back the nut off one-half turn.
4. Tighten the nut to 10-15 in lbs.
5. Install the nut lock on the adjusting nut so that two of the slots align with the hole in the spindle.
6. Install a new cotter pin and bend back its ends.
7. Install the dust cap and lower the car.

REAR SUSPENSION

Two spring pads, integral with the axle housing rest on two leaf springs. The axle housing is fastened to the center of each spring assembly by U-bolts, retainers and nuts. Each spring assembly is attached to the underbody side rail by hanger and shackle assemblies.

Shock Absorber Replacement

1. Disconnect the lower end of the shock absorber from the spring plate.
2. Remove the three bolts retaining the shock absorber mounting bracket at the upper end of the shock. Station wagons have two stud nuts holding the top of the shock to the body.
3. Compress and remove the shock from the car.
4. Purge the new shock of air by repeatedly extending it in its normal position and compressing it while inverted. Transfer the mounting bracket to the new shock except on the station wagon.
5. Position the shock absorber on the car and install the attaching parts.

Spring Replacement

1. Disconnect the lower end of the shock absorber from the spring plate and position the shock out of the way.
2. Raise the vehicle on a hoist and place supports under the axle and the underbody.
3. Remove the spring plate attaching nuts from the U-bolts. Remove the spring plate.
4. Disconnect and remove the rear shackle from the spring.
5. Remove the front hanger bolt and nut from the eye of the spring. Remove the spring from the car.
6. Reverse above procedure to install.

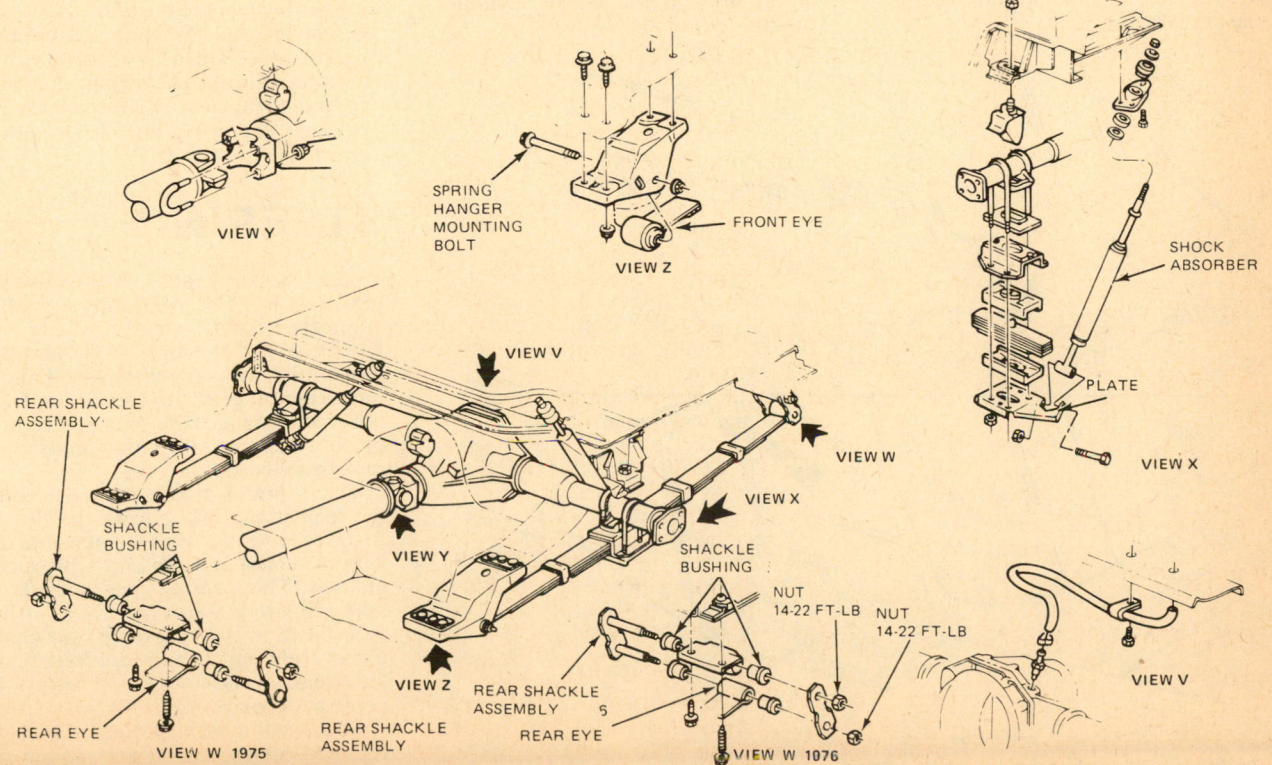

Mustang II rear suspension (© Ford Motor Co)

BRAKES

The drum brake system incorporates single anchor, internal expanding and self adjusting brake assemblies. The brake hydraulic system employs a dual reservoir master cylinder, a control valve and a single cylinder, dual piston wheel cylinder mounted on each backing plate. Front disc brakes are available as an option on early Pintos, and standard on later models.

The parking brake is operated through a floor-mounted lever located between the front seats. Pulling the lever transmits force through a cable linkage to operate the rear drum brakes. A self-adjusting feature operates when there is excessive clearance between the brake shoes and drums.

Replacement, overhaul, and bleeding procedures are included in the "Unit Repair Section."

Master Cylinder Removal and Installation

STANDARD BRAKES

1. Working under the dash, disconnect the stop light switch wires from the stop light switch and remove the switch and master cylinder pushrod from the brake pedal. Use care not to damage the stop light switch during removal.
2. Raise the hood and remove the brake lines from the master cylinder.
3. Remove the capscrews and lockwashers that attach the master cylinder to the firewall and remove the master cylinder.

4. Reverse above procedure to install, but, leave the brake lines loose on the master cylinder.
5. Fill the master cylinder with Extra Heavy Duty Brake Fluid.
6. Bleed the master cylinder by slowly depressing the foot pedal.
7. Refill master cylinder and bleed the front, then the rear, brakes.

POWER BRAKES

1. Disconnect the brake lines from the master cylinder.
2. Remove the nuts holding the master cylinder to the booster.
3. Remove the master cylinder.
4. Reverse the procedure for installation. Bleed the system.

Vacuum Brake Booster Removal and Installation

1. From inside the car, remove the stoplight switch connector from the switch; remove the pin retainer and washer from the pedal pin and slide the stoplight switch far enough to clear the pin and remove the switch. Slide the booster push rod, bushing and washer off the brake pin.
2. On four and six cylinder models, remove: air cleaner, accelerator cable (at carburetor), accelerator cable bracket, choke water inlet hose (at thermostat), and vacuum hose from EGR valve.
3. Disconnect the manifold vacuum hose from the booster.
4. Remove the primary and secondary brake lines from the outlet ports on the master cylinder. Cap the lines and the master cylinder ports.

5. Remove the master cylinder retaining nuts and remove the master cylinder.
6. From inside the car, remove the booster to firewall retaining nuts. From the engine side, pull the booster until the pushrod clears the firewall, rotate the booster ninety degrees, and pull up until it comes clear.
7. To install, put the booster in position with the check valve on the upper right side. Replace the booster pushrod pin; secure the booster to the firewall and tighten the bolts.
8. Place the stoplight switch on the booster push rod with the slot toward the pedal and the hole just clearing the pin. Be careful not to damage the switch. Install the retaining washer and pin and connect the wiring connector.
9. Reconnect the manifold vacuum hose to the booster unit.
10. Reattach the master cylinder assembly, reconnect the items removed in Step 2 and bleed the brakes.

Parking Brake Adjustment

1. Fully release the parking brake.
2. Place the transmission in Neutral and raise the rear axle until the rear wheels clear the floor. The weight of the car must be on the springs.
3. Pry the handle cover up inside the car. The rear of the cover is held by two screws on 1975 and later models. Tighten the adjusting nut until the rear brakes drag when the rear wheels are turned.
4. Loosen the adjusting nut until the rear wheels can be turned without the rear brakes dragging.
5. Lower the rear of the vehicle and check the operation of the parking brake.

STEERING

The steering gear is of the rack and pinion type. The gear input shaft is connected to the steering shaft by a flexible cable through 1973, and a u-joint and flexible coupling, 1974 and later. A pinion gear, machined on the input shaft, engages the rack and rotation of the input shaft pinion causes the rack to move laterally.

The tie-rod is attached at each end of the rack joint. This allows the tie-rods to move with the front suspension. The gear is sealed at each end with rubber bellows. The steering gear is filled with approximately 5-8 oz. of SAE-90 E.P. type oil at initial assembly and checking or refilling is not required unless fluid leakage is evident or repairs become necessary.

Couplings attaching the tie-rods are retained on the rack, are pinned and cannot be disassembled in service through 1973; 1974 and later models are

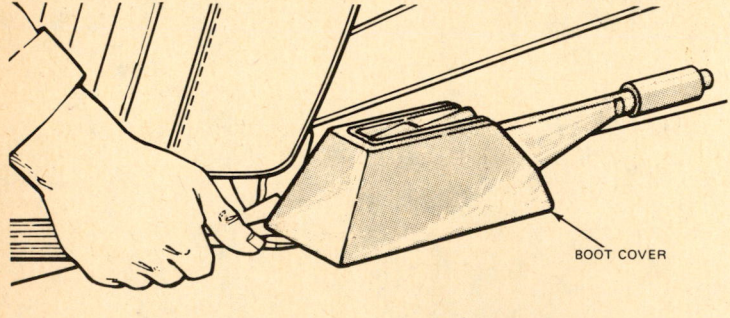

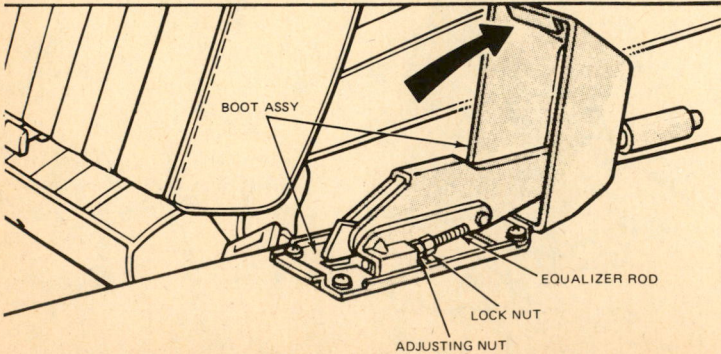

BOOT COVER

BOOT ASSY

EQUALIZER ROD

LOCK NUT

ADJUSTING NUT

Parking brake adjustment; starting 1975 the rear of the boot cover has two hold-down screws. (© Ford Motor Co)

replaceable. Replacement of inner tie-rods, rack, housing, or upper pinion bearing requires installation of a new steering gear assembly through 1973 only.

Integral power rack and pinion steering is a hydraulic-mechanical unit, which uses an integral piston and rack design. Internal valving directs the flow of fluid from the pump and controls the pressure, as required. The unit contains a rotary hydraulic fluid control valve integrated to the input shaft of the steering gear and a boost cylinder integrated with the rack. See the Power Steering Unit Repair Section for details.

——— CAUTION ———

When the front wheels of the vehicle are suspended completely off the ground, do not turn the wheels quickly or forcefully from lock to lock. This could cause a build-up of hydraulic pressure within the steering gear which could damage or blow out the bellows.

Power Steering Pump Removal and Installation

1. Disconnect the fluid return hose at the reservoir, and drain the fluid from the pump.
2. Disconnect the pressure hose from the pump.
3. Remove the bolts or nuts from the pump attaching it to the mounting bracket. Disconnect the belt from the pulley and remove the pump.
4. Install the pump in the reverse order of removal.

NOTE: *On 1978 and later units, do not overtighten the pressure hose to pump fitting. The torque limit is 10-15 ft. lbs. Use a flare (tube) nut wrench to avoid damage. This fitting is designed to swivel; movement does not indicate an undertightened nut.*

5. Fill the reservoir with fluid.
6. Turn the steering wheel from stop-to-stop several times. Do not hold the steering wheel in the far left or right position.
7. Recheck the fluid level and add fluid as necessary.
8. Start the engine and allow it to run for several minutes.
9. Stop the engine and recheck the fluid level in the reservoir; add fluid, as necessary.

Steering Wheel Removal and Installation

1. Disconnect the battery ground cable.
2. On models with a small horn button, remove the horn button by pushing down and turning it counterclockwise.
3. On deluxe steering wheels, remove the pad by removing the two screws from behind the steering wheel. Disconnect the horn wires from the pad.

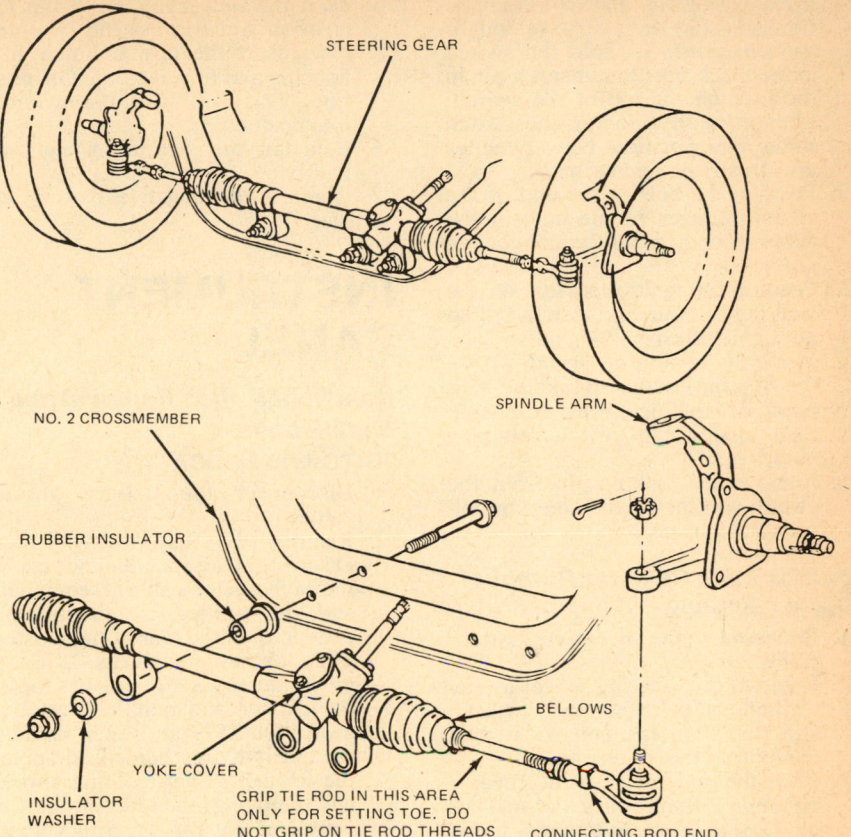

1974 and later rack and pinion steering linkage (© Ford Motor Co.)

4. Remove the steering wheel attaching nut and, using a puller, remove the steering wheel.
5. Align the mark on the hub with the mark on the shaft and install the wheel on the shaft.
6. Install the attaching nut and tighten it to 30-40 ft lbs.
7. Install the horn button or pad.

Turn Signal and Flasher Switch Removal and Installation

1. Remove the steering wheel as previously outlined.
2. Remove the turn signal lever by unscrewing it from the steering column.
3. Remove the lower steering column shroud.
4. Disconnect the steering column wiring connectors from the steering column by lifting up on the tabs and removing the connectors from the brackets.
5. Remove the three screws that attach the head of the switch to the top of the steering column.
6. Pull the switch and wire assembly up and out of the steering column. A thin wire attached to the connector will make it easy to pull it down through the column on installation.
7. With speed control, transfer the ground brush to the new switch. To install the switch, position it and the wires in the steering column

and work the wires down the steering column.
8. Secure the wires and connectors to the base of the steering column.
9. Connect the wire connector at the base of the column.
10. Install the switch head attaching screws.
11. Install the turn signal lever and steering wheel.

IGNITION SWITCH

Removal

1. To gain access to the switch, remove the steering column shroud and disconnect and lower the steering column from the brake support bracket.
2. Disconnect the negative battery cable.
3. Disconnect the switch wiring at the multiple connector.
4. Remove the two nuts that retain the ignition switch to the steering column.
5. Remove the pin that connects the switch plunger to the actuating rod and remove the switch.

Installation

1. When installing the ignition switch, both the switch and the ignition lock must be in the LOCK position. The parts can be held in place by turning the ignition lock cylinder to the LOCK position with the

transmission in Park (automatic transmission) or reverse (standard transmission). To hold the switch in the Lock position, insert a pin in the hole on the top of the switch, after manually moving the switch to the lock position. New switches are already pinned in Lock.

2. Position the hole in the end of the switch plunger to the hole in the actuator and install the connecting pin.
3. Position the ignition switch on the steering column, and install, but do not tighten the retaining nuts.
4. Move the switch up and down on the steering column to find the mid-point of the actuating rod lash, then tighten the switch retaining nuts.
5. Remove the locking pin from the switch and install the steering column and shroud.

Ignition Lock Cylinder Removal and Installation

1. Disconnect the negative battery cable.
2. Remove the steering wheel as described under "Steering." Insert a stiff wire into the hole located in the lock cylinder housing.
3. Place the gearshift lever in Reverse on standard shift cars and in Park on cars with an automatic transmission, and turn the ignition key to the Run position.
4. Depress the wire and remove the lock cylinder and wire.

5. Turn the new cylinder to the On position and depress the retaining pin. Insert the new cylinder into housing and turn it to the Off position. This will lock the cylinder into position.
6. Reinstall the steering wheel and pad.
7. Connect the negative battery cable.

INSTRUMENT PANEL

Headlight Switch Removal and Installation

PINTO AND BOBCAT

1. Disconnect the battery ground cable.
2. Remove the instrument cluster. Disconnect the speedometer cable, the tachometer cable if equipped, and the printed circuit multiple connector at the rear of the cluster. Then, on models through 1976, remove the two screws at the top of the cluster and pull it down and away. On 1977 and later models, remove the two screws attaching the lower steering column shroud and remove it; then loosen the forward and rearward steering column attaching nuts 1/2 inch. Remove the four screws at the top and the bottom of the cluster and pull it down and away.

3. Pull the headlamp switch On and depress the release button. Remove the headlight switch control knob, shaft and retaining nut.
4. Disconnect the multiple connector from the switch and remove the switch from instrument cluster opening.
5. Reverse above procedure to install.

MUSTANG II

1. Disconnect the battery ground cable.
2. Through the hole in the underside of the instrument panel, press the release button with a screwdriver, and remove the knob and shaft assembly.
3. Remove the bezel nut, lower the switch and disconnect the multiple connector.
4. Remove the switch.
5. Install the headlight switch in the reverse order of removal.

Speedometer Cable Removal and Installation

1. Reach behind the speedometer head and press the flat surface of the quick connect lever of the cable away from the head.
2. Lower the cable end and pull the core from the casing.
3. If the core is broken, raise and support the vehicle and remove the bolt retaining the cable mounting clip to the transmission.

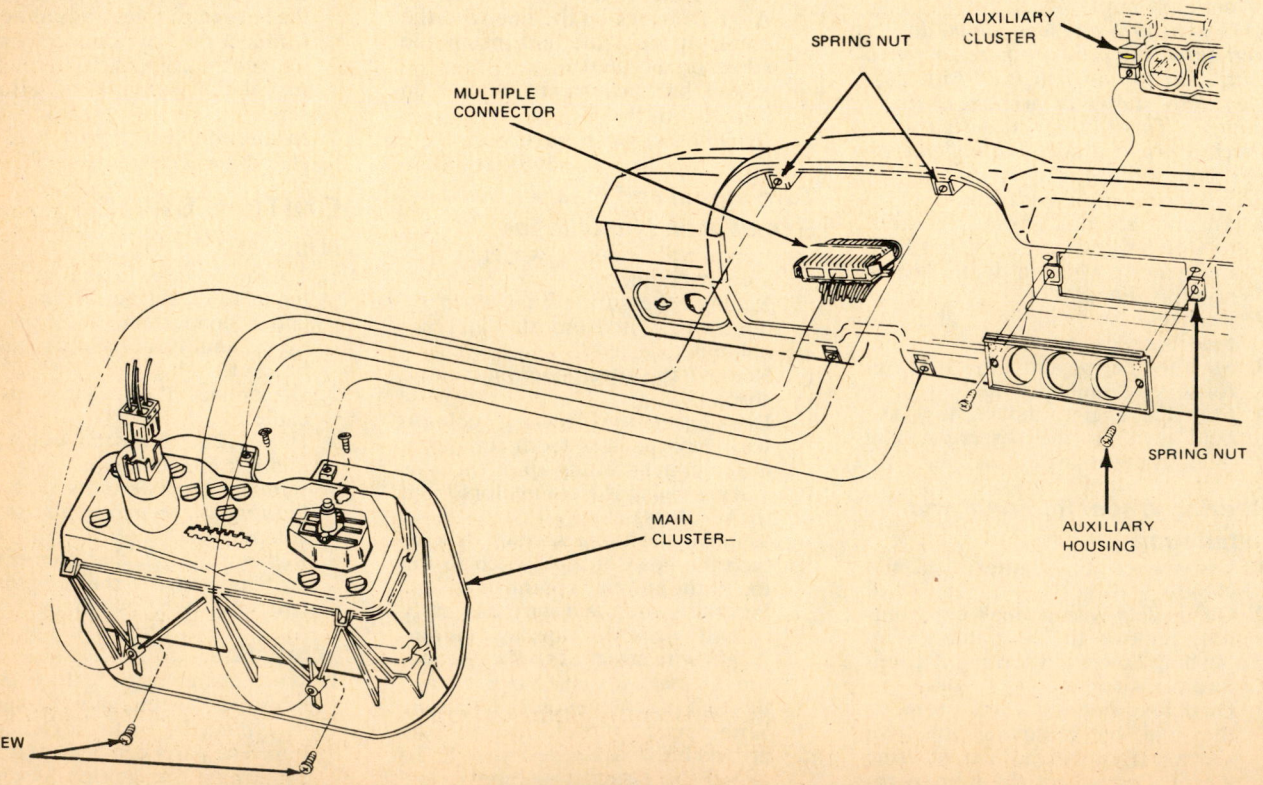

Instrument cluster mounting details, 1978 shown (© Ford Motor Co.)

4. Remove the shaft and driven gear from the transmission.
5. Remove the retainer and remove the driven gear and shaft from the cable.
6. Installation is the reverse of the above.

NOTE: *Ford sells new cores in kits. The exact length of the old core must be determined and a new core cut. DO NOT cut from the square end of the core. Remove any burrs or frayed edges. The core should be seated and crimped in the tip. When installing the cable to the head, apply a 3/16" ball of silicone grease in the drive hole of the head.*

WINDSHIELD WIPERS

Motor Removal and Installation

1. Loosen the two nuts and disconnect the wiper pivot shaft and link assembly from the motor drive arm ball. A link retaining clip is used on the Mustang II.
2. Remove the three motor attaching screws and lower the motor away from the left side of the instrument panel.
3. Disconnect the wiper motor wires and remove the motor.
4. To install, position the motor and install the wires. Operate the motor to ensure it is in Park position.
5. Position the motor and install the retaining screws.
6. Position the wiper pivot shaft and link assembly to the motor drive arm ball and tighten the two nuts. On the Mustang II, install the retaining clip.

Wiper Blade Replacement

Wiper blades used are from either Trico or Anco companies. With a bayonet type blade, the blade saddle slides over the end of the arm and is engaged by a locking stud. With a side saddle pin type, a pin on the arm enters the side of the blade saddle and engages a loaded spring (Trico) or a loaded clip (Anco) in the saddle.

RADIO

For best FM reception, adjust the antenna to 31 in. height. Fading or weak AM reception may be adjusted by adjusting the trimmer control. The trimmer control will be located either on the right rear or the front side of the radio. See the owner's manual for position if you are in doubt. To adjust the trimmer:

1. Extend the antenna to its maximum height.
2. Tune the radio to a weak station around 1600 KC. Adjust the volume so that the sound is barely audible.

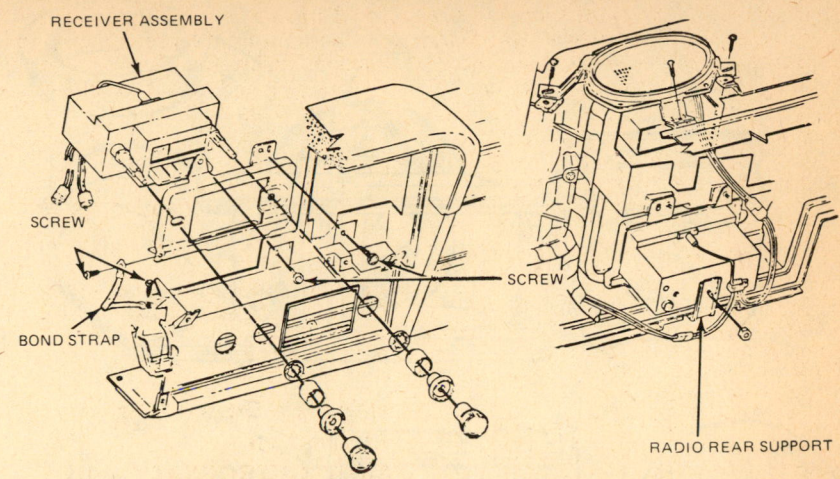

Radio installation Mustang II (© Ford Motor Co.)

3. Adjust the trimmer to obtain maximum volume.

Removal and Installation

1. Disconnect the negative battery cable from the battery.
2. Remove the control knobs, discs, control shaft nuts and washers on Mustang II. Remove the panel trim brace cover on Pinto or Bobcat.
3. On the Mustang II, pull the ash tray out to expose the lower mounting bolt. Remove the bolt.
4. Remove the radio rear support attaching nut or bolt.
5. On Pinto or Bobcat, remove the four screws attaching the bezel to the instrument panel opening.
6. Remove the radio from the instrument panel; out through the front on Pinto or Bobcat, or down from behind the instrument panel on Mustang II.
7. Disconnect the electrical lead, antenna lead, and speaker leads from the radio and remove the radio from the vehicle.
8. Install the radio in the reverse order of removal.

HEATER

NOTE: *Improved heater performance is available, through the installation of revised components, for 1974-78 Bobcats, Pintos, and Mustangs equipped with the 2300 engine. The parts include a new water outlet connection, hose tee, thermostat, and the necessary hoses and clamps, to revise the coolant circulation pattern. In the revised system, coolant first flows to the core, then to the intake manifold, rather than vice versa. The parts are available from your dealer. Details are given in Technical Service Bulletin 155, dated April 1978.*

Heater Assembly Removal and Installation, Non-Air Conditioned Cars

1. Drain the cooling system and dis-

connect the negative battery cable.
2. Disconnect the blower motor ground wire (black) at the engine side of the firewall.
3. Disconnect the heater hoses at the engine block.
4. Remove the four nuts that attach the heater assembly to the firewall, from the engine side.
5. Working inside the car, remove the glove box.
6. Disconnect the control cables from the heater. Disconnect the motor lead. Remove the radio.
7. Remove the snap-rivet that attaches the forward side of the defroster air duct to the heater assembly. Move the air duct back into the defroster nozzle and disengage it from the tabs on the heater box. Tilt the forward edge of the duct up and forward to disengage it from the nozzle, and remove it from the left side of the heater assembly.
8. Remove the heater assembly to instrument panel support bracket mounting screw and remove the heater assembly. At the same time, pull the heater hoses through the firewall. Then, disconnect the hoses from the heater core in the case.
9. Install in the reverse order of removal.

Blower Motor Removal and Installation, Non-Air Conditioned Cars

1. Remove the heater assembly.
2. Disconnect the blower motor lead wire from the resistor.
3. Remove the four blower motor mounting plate attaching nuts and remove the motor and wheel.
4. Install in the reverse order.

Heater Core Removal and Installation, Non-Air Conditioned Cars

1. Remove the heater assembly.

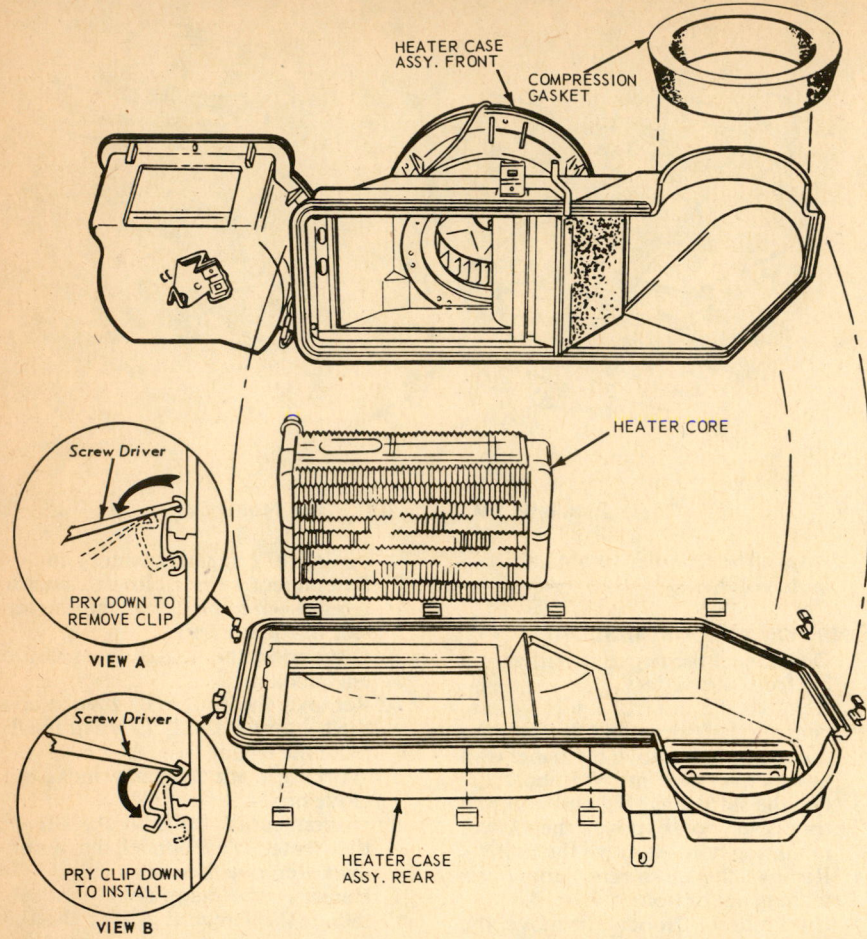

HEATER CASE ASSY. FRONT

COMPRESSION GASKET

Screw Driver

PRY DOWN TO REMOVE CLIP

VIEW A

HEATER CORE

Screw Driver

PRY CLIP DOWN TO INSTALL

VIEW B

HEATER CASE ASSY. REAR

Heater core removal—non-air conditioned models
(© Ford Motor Co)

2. Remove the compression gasket from the cowl air inlet and remove the eleven clips from the case. Separate the case and remove the heater core.

3. Install in the reverse order.

Heater Assembly Removal and Installation, Air Conditioned Cars

1972 PINTO

NOTE: *This procedure requires evacuation of the air conditioning refrigerant. Failure to exercise proper safety precautions could cause personal injury.*

1. Disconnect the negative battery cable and drain the cooling system.
2. Evacuate the air conditioning system.
3. Disconnect the heater hose from the heater housing.
4. Remove the expansion valve from the evaporator core and tape the openings on the core closed.
5. Disconnect the green and brown vacuum hoses from the hot water valve and remove the two screws that attach the hot water valve and vacuum motor to the firewall.
6. Remove the three heater housing attaching nuts from the engine side of the firewall.

7. Remove the glove box door and the glove box. On models equipped with a console, remove the console.
8. Remove the radio and the kick panel from under the right side of the instrument panel.
9. Remove the three bolts that attach the right pillar brace to the lower edge of the instrument panel.
10. Disconnect the temperature control cable from the heater housing, and the purple and green vacuum hoses from the water valve vacuum switch on the heater housing.
11. Disconnect the white hose from the vacuum motor and the electrical leads from the blower motor resistor.
12. Disconnect the blower motor ground wire from the cowl and the red and yellow vacuum hoses from the vacuum motor above the heater blower motor.
13. Remove the cover plate from the bottom of the defroster duct that runs out of the blower motor.
14. Remove the two screws that attach the air distribution duct to the blower motor and remove the duct.
15. Reach through the opening left by the removal of the air distribution duct and remove the nut and lock

plate that attaches the blower housing to the heater housing.
16. Turn the blower housing counterclockwise to disconnect it from the heater housing. Position the blower housing out of the way on the transmission tunnel.
17. Remove the drain hose from the heater housing and remove the screw that attaches the right side of the heater housing to the cowl support.
18. Remove the heater housing from under the instrument panel.
19. Reverse the above procedure to install the heater housing. After installation, charge the refrigerant system.

1973 PINTO

NOTE: *This procedure requires evacuation of the air conditioning refrigerant. Failure to exercise proper safety precautions could cause personal injury.*

1. Disconnect the negative battery cable and drain the cooling system.
2. Evacuate the air conditioning system.
3. Disconnect the heater hoses from the heater core tubes.
4. Disconnect the expansion valve from the evaporator core tubes and plug the openings in the core tubes.
5. Remove the three nuts that attach the heater assembly to the firewall.
6. Remove the glove box and disconnect the right and left air ducts from the heater housing.
7. Disconnect the blue vacuum hose from the A/C-defroster distribution housing. Open the access door in the bottom of the housing and remove the two screws that attach the housing to the instrument panel defroster ducts. Remove the housing from the top of the blower motor housing.
8. Disconnect the red and the yellow vacuum hoses from the A/C-heat door vacuum motor (upper left side of housing).
9. Disconnect the white vacuum hose from outside recirculation door vacuum motor (upper right side of housing).
10. Disconnect the multiple vacuum connector from the rear of the A/C-heater control on the instrument panel.
11. Disconnect the control cable from the temperature control door crank arm.
12. Disconnect the purple and the green vacuum hoses from the water valve switch. The water valve switch is located on the heater housing just above the temperature door crank arm.
13. Remove the bracket that attaches the heater housing to the underside of the instrument panel.
14. Move the heater assembly rearward until it clears its mounting studs, then detach the vacuum

hoses that are taped or clipped to the top of the housing.

15. Tag and disconnect the wiring that attaches to the heater housing.
16. Remove the heater housing from the car.
17. Reverse the above procedure to install the heater housing. Charge the refrigerant system.

1974 MUSTANG II, 1974 AND LATER PINTO AND BOBCAT

NOTE: *This procedure requires evacuation of the air conditioning refrigerant. Failure to exercise proper safety precautions could cause personal injury.*

1. Drain the engine coolant, discharge the air conditioning system and disconnect the battery.
2. Remove the A/C refrigerant lines and the front half of the refrigerant manifold through 1976 only.
3. Remove the manifold mounting stud to provide clearance when removing the evaporator case assembly through 1976 only.
4. On 1977 and later models, remove the two hex screws attaching the evaporator manifold plate to the expansion valve body, then separate the expansion valve body and the STV housing manifold from the evaporator manifold plate. Use new O-rings between the valve body and manifold plate on reassembly.
5. Disconnect the two heater hoses from the core tubes in the engine compartment.
6. Remove the A/C condensate drain hose in the engine compartment.
7. Remove the glove box.
8. Disconnect the vacuum hoses from the evaporator case.
9. Disconnect the temperature control cable from the blend door crank arm.
10. Remove the heat distribution duct. On the Mustang II, remove the mode door vacuum motor which is retained to the evaporator case assembly by two nuts and a spring nut.
11. On the Pinto or Bobcat, to remove the A/C defrost plenum:
    a. Cut and remove the two staples which retain the fold down door in the closed position on the plenum.
    b. Bend the fold down door away from the locating tabs on each side of the plenum to allow removal of the adaptor duct.
    c. Remove the adapter duct.
    On the Mustang II, remove the lower section of the A/C defrost plenum which is retained by 3 screws and two retaining tabs.
12. Remove the blower motor and wheel from the blower scroll.
13. Install one 1/4-20 hex-washer head screw to the mounting tab on the inlet duct to upper cowl bracket to hold the duct in place. Leave this

screw in place when installing the case assembly.

14. Remove the three inlet duct-to-evaporator case attaching screws through the blower scroll opening.
15. Remove the one upper case-to-inlet duct attaching screw located under the outside-recirculating motor mounting bracket.
16. Remove the two evaporator-to-upper cowl bracket attaching screws.
17. Remove the four evaporator-to-dash panel attaching nuts in the engine compartment.
18. Rotate the evaporator assembly down and away from the dash panel and out from under the instrument panel.
19. Install the heater/evaporator case in the reverse order of removal. During installation, position the fold down door of the defrost plenum between the locating tabs on each side of the plenum and tape it in position with two pieces of black tape 1 in. wide by 4 in. long.

1975 AND LATER MUSTANG II

NOTE: *This procedure requires evacuation of the air conditioning system. This should not be attempted by untrained persons; personal injury may result. This is also a major disassembly operation.*

1. Remove the battery, drain the coolant, and discharge the air conditioner.
2. Remove the instrument panel pad, the radio speaker, both A-pillar moldings, both side kick panel assemblies, and the lower steering column cover.
3. Remove the steering column to cowl panel brace.
4. Remove the accelerator pedal. Disconnect the heater control cables.
5. Remove the bottom bolt holding the center brace to the instrument panel.
6. Disconnect the radio antenna lead. Detach the five connectors at the left cowl panel. Unplug the dimmer switch. Disconnect the blower motor resistor.
7. Disconnect the temperature control cable. Remove the two upper cowl bracket screws.
8. Detach the main wiring harness in the engine compartment. Push the harness into the passenger compartment. Do the same with the last three connectors.
9. Disconnect the turn signal switch. Remove the four steering column nuts, unplug the ignition switch, unplug the stoplight switch, and remove the column center support bracket.
10. Remove the four retaining bolts and the instrument panel.
11. Detach the heater hoses from the core tubes. Disconnect the two lines at the evaporator manifold assembly. Remove the manifold

from the bracket. Remove the outer manifold.

12. Remove the nuts and remove the assembly from the firewall.
13. Installation is carried out in the reverse order of removal. Fill the cooling system and charge the air conditioner.

Blower Motor Removal and Installation, Air Conditioned Cars

1972

1. Disconnect the negative battery cable. If equipped with a console, remove the console from the car.
2. Remove the radio.
3. Remove the fuse panel attaching screw, disconnect the multiple connector from the fuse panel and remove the fuse panel from the fuse panel support bracket which is attached to the brake pedal support bracket.
4. Remove the fuse panel support bracket from the brake pedal support bracket and position it out of the way.
5. Remove the instrument panel-to-cowl brace and position the fuse panel on the lower edge of the instrument panel.
6. Disconnect the lead wires from the blower motor resistor and the blower motor ground wire from the cowl.
7. Remove the red and yellow vacuum hoses from the vacuum motor over the blower motor.
8. Remove the cover plate from the bottom of the defroster outlet duct of the blower motor.
9. Remove the two screws that attach the air distribution duct to the blower motor housing.
10. Reach through the opening left by the removal of the air distribution duct and remove the nut and lock plate that attaches the blower motor housing to the heater housing.
11. Turn the blower motor counterclockwise to disconnect it from the heater housing and position the blower motor on the transmission tunnel.
12. Remove the steering column-to-instrument panel brace. It may be necessary to move the blower housing slightly rearward to gain access to the upper brace attaching bolt.
13. Cut the blower housing-to-heater housing gasket at the break in the two blower housing pieces.
14. Disconnect the A/C-heat door rod from the A/C-heat door.
15. Remove the seven clips and separate the two halves of the blower housing.
16. Remove the left half of the blower housing with the blower motor attached.
17. Remove the three blower motor

mounting nuts and remove the blower motor and wheel.

18. Reverse the above procedure to install the blower motor.

1973

1. Disconnect the negative battery cable.
2. Remove the two screws that attach the hot air distribution duct to the bottom of the blower housing and remove the duct.
3. Open the access door in the bottom of the A/C-defroster distribution housing and remove the two screws that attach the distribution housing to the instrument panel defroster ducts.
4. Working through the opening left by removal of the bottom heat distribution duct, remove the nut and lock plate that attaches the blower housing to the heater housing.
5. Turn the blower motor housing clockwise to disengage the two locking tabs on the blower housing from the pin on the heater housing.
6. Remove the blower housing from the car.
7. Cut the blower outlet gasket at the blower housing seams.
8. Remove the clips that secure the two halves of the blower housing, and separate the housing.

9. Remove the three blower motor attaching nuts and the motor.

1974 AND LATER

The blower motor and wheel is integrally located within the scroll portion of the evaporator assembly on the right-side of the evaporator case. To remove the blower motor and wheel, remove the glove box and remove the four screws retaining the blower motor and wheel in the blower scroll. It may be necessary to remove the instrument panel to right side cowl bolt, to allow the panel to be pulled rearward for clearance. Install the blower motor and wheel in the reverse order of removal.

Heater Core Removal and Installation, Air Conditioned Cars

1972-73

1. Remove the heater housing and remove the rubber seal from the housing.
2. Remove the eleven clips that hold the two halves of the heater housing together and separate the housing.
3. Remove the A/C thermostatic de-icing switch from the top of the housing.
4. Remove four screws and remove the evaporator core from the upper housing.
5. Remove four screws and the temperature blend door upper frame.
6. Remove the spring clip and crank arm and remove the temperatur-blend door from the housing.
7. Remove for screws and the temperature blend door lower frame.
8. Remove the heater core and gasket from the lower housing.

1974 AND LATER

1. Remove the evaporator case assembly from the vehicle.
2. Remove the upper-to-lower case attaching screws. Remove the blower motor and wheel.
3. Remove the rubber seal from the heater core tubes.
4. Remove the upper half of the evaporator case.
5. Move the rubber seal on the evaporator core forward to clear the case mounting stud and pull the core out of the lower case.
6. Install in the reverse order of removal. Be sure to install new rope sealer around the flange of the lower case before installing the upper half of the case. Install new O-rings on the manifold plate. Dip the new O-rings in refrigerant oil before installing them.

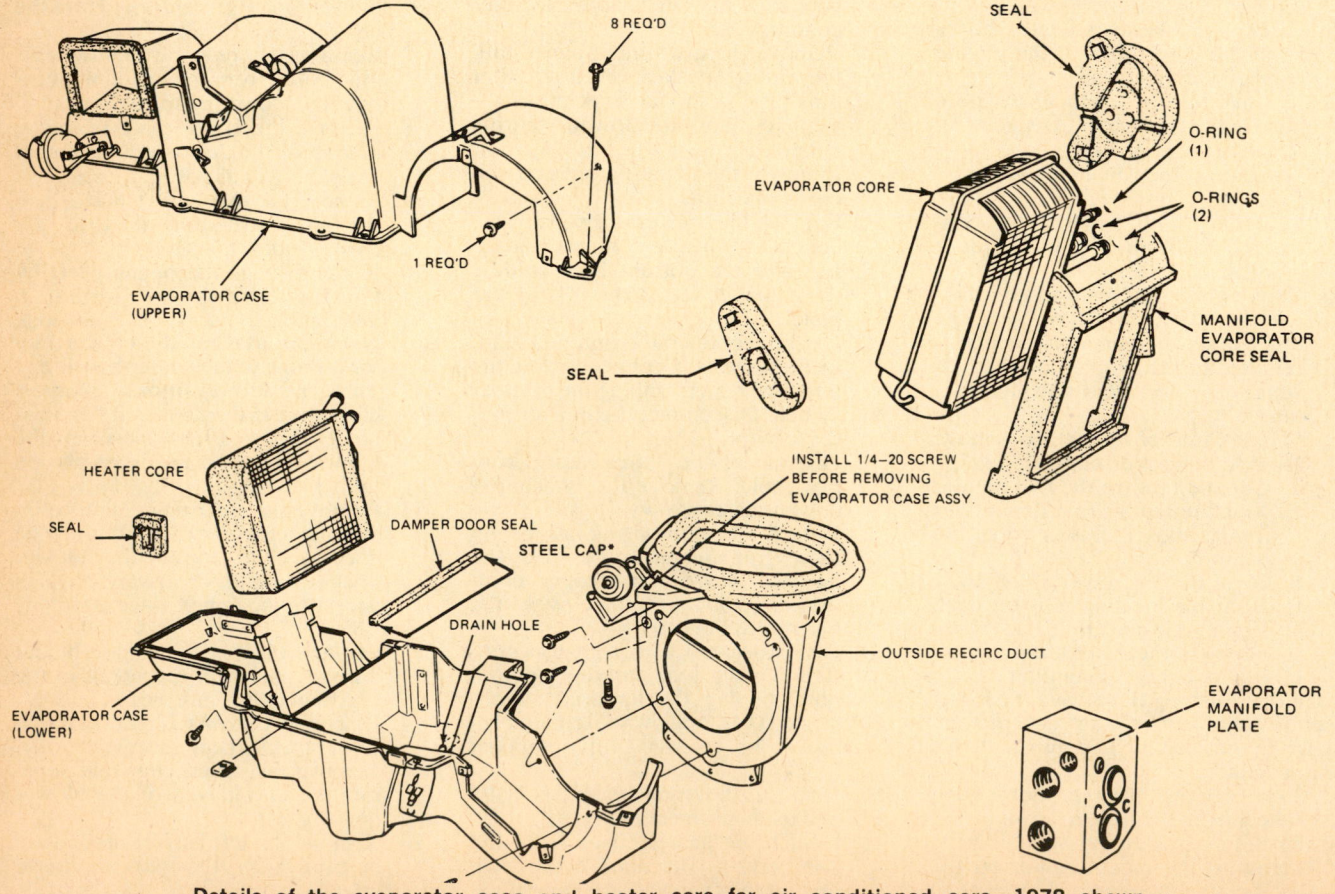

Details of the evaporator case and heater core for air conditioned cars, 1978 shown
(© Ford Motor Co.)

Index

Buick

YEAR IDENTIFICATION

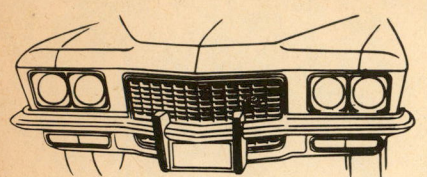

1972 Riviera

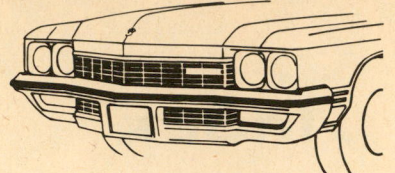

1972 Electra

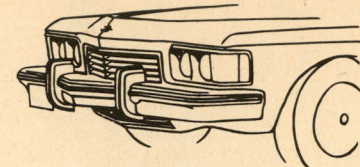

1973 Riviera

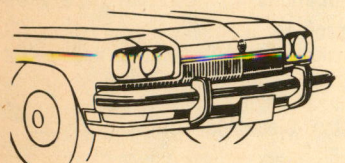

1973 Buick

1974 Riviera

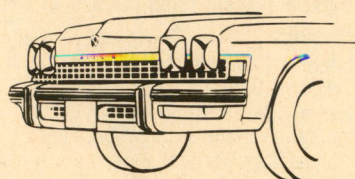

1974 Electra

1974 Le Sabre

1975 Riviera

1975 Electra

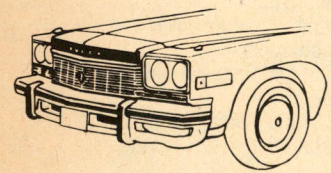

1975 LeSabre

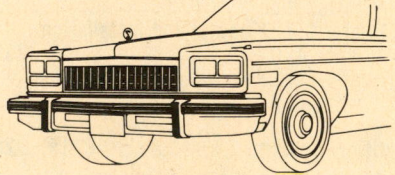

1976 Electra

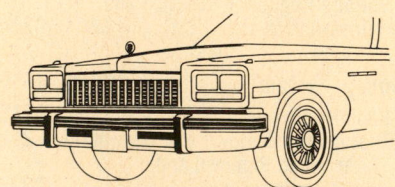

1976 Electra Limited

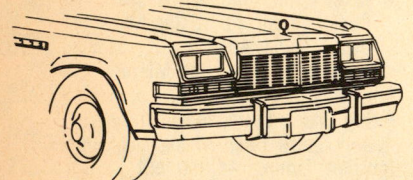

1977 LeSabre

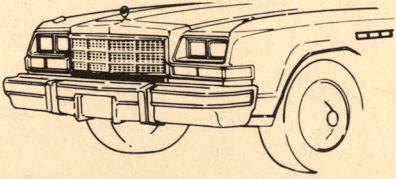

1977 Electra

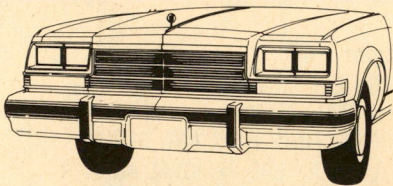

1978 Le Sabre

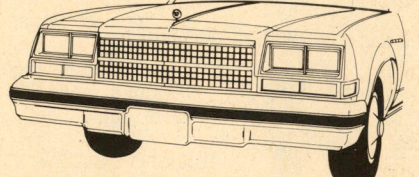

1978 Electra

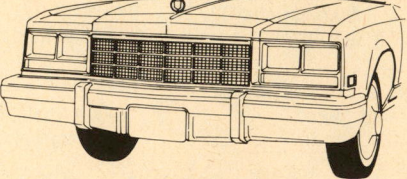

1979 Electra

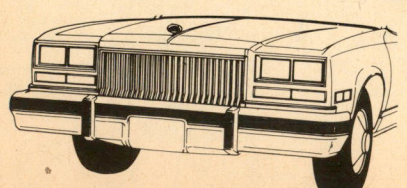

1978 Riviera

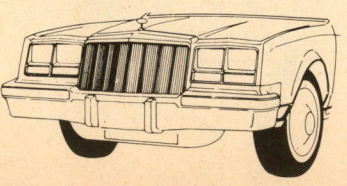

1979 Riviera

ENGINE IDENTIFICATION CODE

The vehicle identification number plate is on the top left side of the instrument panel, visible through the windshield. The engine code is the fifth digit of the VIN number.

Disp		Bbl	Hp	'72	'73	'74	'75	'76	'77	'78	'79
V6											
231	Buick	2	Turbo.							G	
231	Buick	4	Turbo.							3	3
231	Buick	2	105						C	A	A
V8											
301	Pont.	2	135						Y	Y	Y
305	Chev.	2	145							U	
350	Buick	2	150	H	H	H					
					G#						
350	Buick	4	155-165				J	J	J	X	X
350	Olds.	4	170						R	R	R
350	Buick	4	175	J	J	J					
350	Buick	4	190	K	K#						
350	Buick	4	260	B							
350	Chev.	4	170							L	
403	Olds.	4	185						K	K	K
455	Buick	2	145			P					
455	Buick	2	190		R#						
455	Buick	4	205					T	Y		
455	Buick	4	210			T					
455	Buick	4	225	T							
455	Buick	4	230			U#					
455	Buick	4	245			V#					
455	Buick	4	250	U	U#						
455	Buick	4	255		T	W#					
455	Buick	4	260	V	V#						
455	Buick	4	270	W	W#						

\# Dual exhaust

■ Horsepower and torque are SAE net figures. They are measured at the rear of the transmission with all accessories installed and operating. Since the figures vary when a given engine is installed in different models, some are representative rather than exact.

GENERAL ENGINE SPECIFICATIONS

Year	Engine No. Cyl. Displacement (cu. in.)	Carburetor Type	Horsepower @ rpm ■	Torque @ rpm (ft lbs) ■	Bore x Stroke (in.)	Compression Ratio	Oil Pressure @ 2000 rpm (psi)
'72	8-350	2 bbl	155 @ 3800	270 @ 2400	3.800 x 3.850	8.5:1	37
	8-350 Calif.	2 bbl	150 @ 3800	265 @ 2400	3.800 x 3.850	8.5:1	37
	8-350	4 bbl	180 @ 3800	275 @ 2400	3.800 x 3.850	8.5:1	37
	8-350 Calif.	4 bbl	175 @ 3800	270 @ 2400	3.800 x 3.850	8.5:1	37
	8-455	4 bbl	225 @ 4000	360 @ 2600	4.3125 x 3.900	8.5:1	40
	8-455 DE	4 bbl	250 @ 4000	375 @ 2800	4.3125 x 3.900	8.5:1	40
	8-455	4 bbl	260 @ 4400	380 @ 2800	4.3125 x 3.900	8.5:1	40
'73	8-350	2 bbl	150 @ 3800	265 @ 2400	3.800 x 3.850	8.5:1	37
	8-350	4 bbl	175 @ 3800	270 @ 2400	3.800 x 3.850	8.5:1	37
	8-455	4 bbl	225 @ 4000	360 @ 2600	4.3125 x 3.900	8.5:1	37
	8-455 DE	4 bbl	250 @ 4000	375 @ 2800	4.3125 x 3.900	8.5:1	37
	8-455	4 bbl	260 @ 4400	380 @ 2800	4.3125 x 3.900	8.5:1	37
'74	8-350 SE	2 bbl	150 @ 3600	270 @ 2000	3.800 x 3.850	8.5:1	37
	8-350 DE	2 bbl	165 @ 3800	285 @ 2000	3.800 x 3.850	8.5:1	37
	8-350 SE	4 bbl	175 @ 3800	260 @ 2000	3.800 x 3.850	8.5:1	37
	8-350 DE	4 bbl	195 @ 4000	280 @ 2000	3.800 x 3.850	8.5:1	37

GENERAL ENGINE SPECIFICATIONS

Year	Engine No. Cyl. Displacement (cu. in.)	Carburetor Type	Horsepower @ rpm ■	Torque @ rpm (ft lbs) ■	Bore x Stroke (in.)	Compression Ratio	Oil Pressure @ 2000 rpm (psi)
	8-455 SE	2 bbl	175 @ 3400	355 @ 2000	4.3125 x 3.900	8.5:1	37
	8-455 DE	2 bbl	190 @ 3600	370 @ 2000	4.3125 x 3.900	8.5:1	37
	8-455 SE	4 bbl	210 @ 3600	335 @ 2200	4.3125 x 3.900	8.5:1	37
	8-455 DE	4 bbl	230 @ 3800	355 @ 2200	4.3125 x 3.900	8.5:1	37
	8-455 DE Stage I	4 bbl	245 @ 4000	360 @ 2400	4.3125 x 3.900	8.5:1	37
'75	8-350	4 bbl	165 @ 3800	260 @ 2200	3.800 x 3.850	8.0:1	37
	8-350 Calif.	4 bbl	160 @ 3800	260 @ 2200	3.800 x 3.850	8.0:1	37
	8-455	4 bbl	205 @ 3800	345 @ 2000	4.3125 x 3.900	7.9:1	40
'76	6-231	2 bbl	105 @ 3400	185 @ 2000	3.800 x 3.400	8.0:1	37
	8-350	4 bbl	155 @ 3400	280 @ 1800	3.800 x 3.850	8.0:1	34
	8-455	4 bbl	205 @ 3800	345 @ 2000	4.3125 x 3.900	7.9:1	40
'77	6-231 Buick	2 bbl	105 @ 3200	185 @ 2000	3.800 x 3.400	8.0:1	37
	8-301 Pont.	2 bbl	135 @ 4000	250 @ 1600	4.000 x 3.000	8.2:1	34
	8-350 Buick	4 bbl	155 @ 3400	275 @ 1800	4.057 x 3.385	8.0:1	35
	8-350 Olds.	4 bbl	170 @ 3800	275 @ 2100	4.057 x 3.385	8.0:1	35
	8-403 Olds.	4 bbl	185 @ 3600	315 @ 2400	4.351 x 3.385	7.9:1	34
'78	6-231 Buick	2 bbl	105 @ 3400	185 @ 2000	3.800 x 3.400	8.0:1	37
	6-231 Buick	2 bbl Turbo	150 @ 3800	245 @ 2400	3.800 x 3.400	8.0:1	37
	6-231 Buick	4 bbl Turbo	165 @ 4000	265 @ 2800	3.800 x 3.400	8.0:1	37
	8-301 Pont.	2 bbl	140 @ 3600	235 @ 2000	4.000 x 3.000	8.2:1	34
	8-305 Chev.	2 bbl	145 @ 3800	245 @ 2400	3.736 x 3.480	8.5:1	35
	8-350 Buick	4 bbl	155 @ 3400	280 @ 1800	3.800 x 3.850	8.0:1	35
	8-350 Chev.	4 bbl	170 @ 3800	275 @ 2000	4.000 x 3.480	8.5:1	35
	8-350 Olds.	4 bbl	170 @ 3600	265 @ 2000	4.057 x 3.385	8.0:1	35
	8-403 Olds.	4 bbl	185 @ 3600	320 @ 2000	4.351 x 3.385	8.0:1	35
'79	6-231 Buick	2 bbl	115 @ 3800	190 @ 2000	3.800 x 3.400	8.0:1	37
	6-231 Buick Turbo	4 bbl	165 @ 4000	265 @ 2800	3.800 x 3.400	8.0:1	37
	8-301 Pont.	2 bbl	140 @ 3600	235 @ 2000	4.000 x 3.000	8.2:1	34
	8-350 Buick	4 bbl	155 @ 3400	280 @ 1800	3.800 x 3.850	8.0:1	35
	8-350 Olds	4 bbl	170 @ 3800	275 @ 2000	4.057 x 3.385	8.0:1	35
	8-403 Olds	4 bbl	185 @ 3600	320 @ 2000	4.351 x 3.385	8.0:1	35

■ Beginning 1972, horsepower and torque are SAE net figures. They are measured at the rear of the transmission with all accessories installed and operating. Since the figures vary when a given engine is installed in different models, some are representative rather than exact.

SE Single Exhaust   DE Dual Exhaust

NOTE: Most 1979 GM carburetors have idle mixture screws concealed by staked-in plugs. These are not meant to be removed, except at carburetor overhaul.

TUNE-UP SPECIFICATIONS

Year	Engine No. Cyl Displacement (cu in.)	hp	SPARK PLUGS Orig. Type	Gap (in.)	DISTRIBUTOR Point Dwell (deg)	Point Gap (in.)	IGNITION TIMING (deg) ▲ ● Man Trans	Auto Trans	VALVES Intake Opens ■ (deg) ●	Fuel Pump Pressure (psi)	IDLE SPEED (rpm) ▲ ● Man Trans	Auto Trans
'72	8-350	155	R-45TS	.040	30	.016	—	4B	24	4¼-5¾	—	650② /500
	8-350	180	R-45TS	.040	30	.016	—	4B	24	4¼-5¾	—	650② /500
	8-455	225	R-45TS	.040	30	.016	—	4B	12(14)	4¼-5¾	—	650② /500

TUNE-UP SPECIFICATIONS

	ENGINE No. Cyl Displacement		SPARK PLUGS		DISTRIBUTOR		IGNITION TIMING (deg) ▲ ●		VALVES Intake Opens	Fuel Pump Pressure	IDLE SPEED (rpm) ▲ ●	
Year	(cu in.)	hp	Orig. Type	Gap (in.)	Point Dwell (deg)	Point Gap (in.)	Man Trans	Auto Trans	■ (deg) ●	(psi)	Man Trans	Auto Trans
	8-455	250	R-45TS	.040	30	.016	—	4B	12(14)	4¼-5¾	—	650②/500
	8-455	260	R-45TS	.040	30	.016	—	4B	12(14)	4¼-5¾	—	650②/500
'73	8-350	150	R-45TS	.040	30	.016	—	4B	24	4¼-5¾	—	600/500②
	8-350	175	R-45TS	.040	30	.016	—	4B	24	4¼-5¾	—	600/500②
	8-455	225	R-45TS	.040	30	.016	—	4B	14	4¼-5¾	—	650/500②
	8-455	250	R-45TS	.040	30	.016	—	4B	14	4¼-5¾	—	650/500②
	8-455	260	R-45TS	.040	30	.016	—	4B	14	4¼-5¾	—	650/500②
'74	8-350	All⑤	R-45TS	.040	30	.016	—	4B	19(25)	4¼-5¾	—	650/500②
	8-455	All⑤	R-45TS	.040	30	.016	—	4B	10	4¼-5¾	—	650/500②
'75	8-350	165	R-45TSX	.060	Electronic		—	12B	19	4¼-5¾	—	600
	8-455	205	R-45TSX	.060	Electronic		—	12B	10	4¼-5¾	—	600
'76	6-231	105	R-44SX	.060	Electronic		—	12B	17	4¼-5¾	—	600
	8-350	155	R-45TSX	.060	Electronic		—	12B	13.5	5-6½	—	600
	8-455	205	R-45TSX	.060	Electronic		—	12B	10	7½-9	—	600
'77	6-231 Buick	105	R-46TS	.060	Electronic		—	12B	17	4¼-5¾	—	600
	8-301 Pont.	135	R-46TS	.045	Electronic		—	12B	27	7-8½	—	650
	8-350 Buick	155	R-46TSX	.060	Electronic		—	12B	13.5	7½-9	—	600
	8-350 Olds.	170	R-46SZ	.060	Electronic			20B @ 1100	16	5½-6½	—	650(550)⑥
	8-403 Olds	180	R-46SZ	.060	Electronic		—	24B(20B) @1100③	16	6-7½	—	650(550)⑥
'78	6-231 Buick	105	R-46TSX	.060	Electronic		—	15B	17	4.5-5.5	—	600
	6-231 Buick Turbo		R-44TSX	.060	Electronic		—	15B	17	4.5-5.5	—	650
	8-301 Pont.	140	R-46TSX	.060	Electronic		—	12B	27	7-8.5	—	550
	8-305 Chev.	145	R-45TS	.045	Electronic		—	①	28	4-5	—	500④
	8-350 Buick	155	R-46TSX	.060	Electronic		—	15B	16	7.5-9	—	550
	8-350 Chev.	170	R-45TS	.045	Electronic		—	8B	28	4-5	—	600(500)
	8-350 Olds.	170	R-46SZ	.060	Electronic		—	20B@ 1100	16	5.5-6.5	—	600(550)
	8-403 Olds.	185	R-46SZ	.060	Electronic		—	20B@ 1100	16	5.5-6.5	—	550⑦
'79	6-231 Buick	115	R-46TSX	.060	Electronic		—	15B	16	4.25-5.75	—	600
	6-231 Buick Turbo		R-44TSX	.060	Electronic		—	15B	16	4.25-5.75	—	650
	8-301 Pont.	140	R-46TSX	.060	Electronic		—	12B	27	7-8.5	—	550
	8-350 Buick	155	R-46TSX	.060	Electronic		—	15B	13.5	6-7.5	—	550
	8-350 Olds	170	R-46SZ	.080	Electronic		—	20B@ 1100	16	6-7.5	—	550
	8-403 Olds	185	R-46SZ	.080	Electronic		—	20B@ 1100	16	6-7.5	—	550

▲ See text for procedure
■ All figures Before Top Dead Center
● Figure in Parentheses indicates California engine
① Except Calif. and High Altitude: 4B
   Calif.: 6B
   High Altitude: 8B
② Lower figure indicates idle speed with solenoid disconnected
③ 20B for high altitude
④ High Altitude: 600

⑤ See underhood specifications sticker on engines with H.E.I. electronic ignition system.
   B Before Top Dead Center
⑥ 650(600) for high altitude
⑦ High Altitude: 600
TDC Top Dead Center
— Not applicable

NOTE: The underhood specifications sticker often reflects tune-up specification changes made in production. Sticker figures must be used if they disagree with those in this chart.

Buick

FIRING ORDER

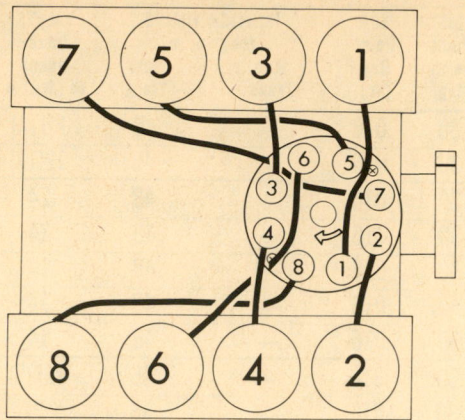

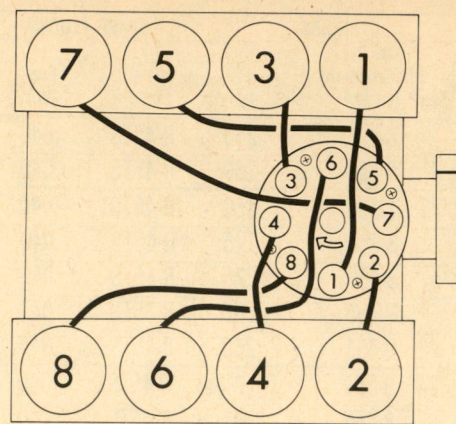

GM (Buick) 196, 231 V6
Engine firing order: 1-6-5-4-3-2
Distributor rotation: clockwise

V6 harmonic balancers have two timing marks: one is 1/8 in. wide, and one is 1/16 in. wide. Use the 1/16 in. mark for timing with a hand held light. The 1/8 in. mark is used only with a magnetic timing pick-up probe.

GM (Buick) 350, 455 V8 (through 1974)
Engine firing order: 1-8-4-3-6-5-7-2
Distributor rotation: clockwise

GM (Buick) 350, 455 V8 (1975 and later)
Engine firing order: 1-8-4-3-6-5-7-2
Distributor rotation: clockwise

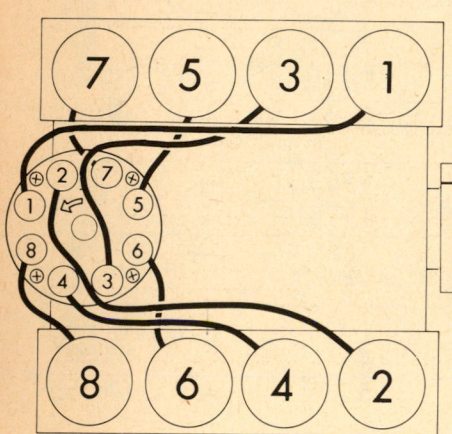

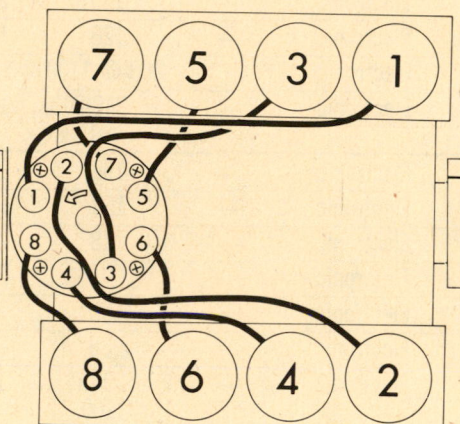

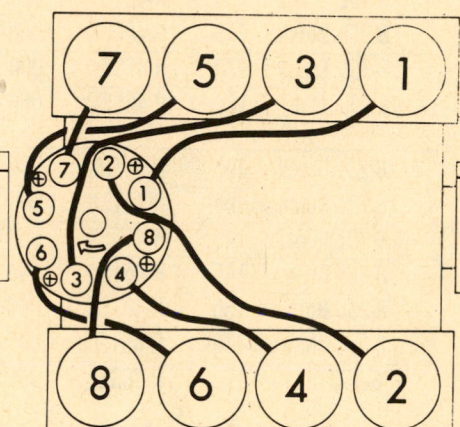

GM (Oldsmobile) 350, 403 V8 (1975 and later)
Engine firing order: 1-8-4-3-6-5-7-2
Distributor rotation: counterclockwise

GM (Pontiac) 301 V8
Engine firing order: 1-8-4-3-6-5-7-2
Distributor rotation: counterclockwise

GM (Chevrolet) 305, 350 V8
Firing Order: 1-8-4-3-6-5-7-2
Distributor rotation: clockwise

TORQUE SPECIFICATIONS

All readings in ft lbs

Year	Engine Displacement (cu in.)	Cylinder Head Bolts	Rod Bearing Bolts	Main Bearing Bolts	Crankshaft Pulley or Balancer Bolt	Flywheel to Crankshaft Bolts	MANIFOLD Intake	Exhaust
'72	350	75	35	95	120	60	55	18
	430, 455	100	35	110	200	60	55②	18
'73	350	80	35③	115	140	60	55	18
	455	100	45	115	200	60	65	18
'74-'75	350	80	40	115	140	60	45	28
	455	100	45	115	200	60	45	28
'76	231, 350	80	40	115	175	60	45	25
	455	100	45	115	225	60	45	25

TORQUE SPECIFICATIONS

All readings in ft lbs

Year	Engine Displacement (cu in.)	Cylinder Head Bolts	Rod Bearing Bolts	Main Bearing Bolts	Crankshaft Pulley or Balancer Bolt	Flywheel to Crankshaft Bolts	MANIFOLD Intake	Exhaust
'77	231 Buick	85	42	80④	310	60	40	25
	301 Pont.	90	35	60①	160	95	40	35
	8-350 Buick	80	40	115	175	60	45	25
	350, 403 Olds.	130	42	80④	200-310	60	40	25
'78-'79	6-231 Buick	80	40	100	225	60	45	25
	8-301 Pont.	90	35	60①	160	95	40	35
	8-305 Chev.	65	45	70	60	60	30	20
	8-350 Buick	80	40	100	225	60	45	25
	8-350 Chev.	65	45	70	60	60	30	20
	8-350 Olds.	130	42	80④	300	60	40	25
	8-403 Olds.	130	42	80④	300	60	40	25

① Rear main—100 ft. lbs.
② 1970-72 455 cu in.—65 ft. lbs.
③ 40 with cap screws
④ Rear main—120 ft. lbs.

VALVE SPECIFICATIONS

Year	Engine No. Cyl. Displacement (cu in.)	Seat Angle (deg)	Face Angle (deg)	Spring Test Pressure (lbs @ in.)	Spring Installed Height (in.)	STEM TO GUIDE Clearance (in.) Intake	Exhaust	STEM Diameter (in.) Intake	Exhaust
'72	8-350	45	45	180 @ 1.34	1 23/32	.0015-.0035	.0015-.0032	.3725	.3727
	8-455	45	45	177 @ 1.45	1 29/32	.0015-.0035	.0015-.0032	.3725	.3727
'73	8-350	45	45	180 @ 1.34	1 23/32	.0015-.0035	.0015-.0032	.3725	.3730
	8-455	45	45	177 @ 1.45	1 29/32	.0015-.0035	.0015-.0032	.3725	.3730
'74	8-350	45	45	180 @ 1.34	1 23/32	.0015-.0035	.0015-.0032	.3725	.3730
	8-455	45	45	177 @ 1.45	1 29/32	.0015-.0035	.0015-.0032	.3725	.3730
'75-'76	6-231	45	45	164 @ 1.34	1 47/64	.0015-.0035	.0015-.0032	.3407	.3409
	8-350	45	45	180 @ 1.34①	1 47/64	.0015-.0035	.0015-.0032	.3725	.3727
	8-455	45	45	177 @ 1.45	1 57/64	.0015-.0035	.0015-.0032	.3725	.3727
'77	6-231 Buick	45	45	164 @ 1.34	1 47/64	.0015-.0035	.0015-.0035	.340	.340
	8-301 Pont.	46	45	170 @ 1.26	1 47/64	.0017-.0020	.0015-.0020	.340	.340
	8-350 Olds.	45②	44②	180 @ 1.34	1 47/64	.0010-.0027	.0015-.0032	.3425	.3420
	8-350 Buick	45	45	180 @ 1.34	1 47/64	.0015-.0032	.0015-.0032	.3730	.3727
	8-403 Olds.	45②	44②	180 @ 1.27	1 47/64	.0010-.0027	.0015-.0032	.3425	.3420
'78-'79	6-231 Buick	45	45	168 @ 1.327	1 47/64	.0015-.0032	.0015-.0032	.3405-.3412	.3405-.3412
	8-301 Pont.	46	45	170 @ 1.260	1 46/64	.0017-.0020	.0017-.0020	.3400-.3405	.3400-.3405
	8-305 Chev.	46	45	200 @ 1.160	④	.0010-.0037	.0010-.0037	.3410-.3417	.3410-.3417
	8-350 Buick	45	45	③	1 47/64	.0015-.0035	.0015-.0032	.3720-.3730	.3723-.3730
	8-350 Chev.	46	45	200 @ 1.160	④	.0010-.0037	.0010-.0037	.3410-.3417	.3410-.3417
	8-350 Olds.	45②	44②	187 @ 1.270	1 2/3	.0010-.0027	.0015-.0032	.3425-.3432	.3420-.3427
	8-403 Olds.	45②	44②	187 @ 1.270	1 2/3	.0010-.0027	.0015-.0032	.3425-.3432	.3420-.3427

① Exhaust—175 @ 1.34
② Exhaust valve seat angle—31, exhaust valve face angle—30
③ intake: 180 @ 1.340
   exhaust: 177 @ 1.450
④ intake: 1 23/32
   exhaust: 1 19/32

Buick

CAPACITIES

Year	ENGINE No. Cyl. Displacement (cu. in.)	Engine Crankcase Add 1 Qt For New Filter	TRANSMISSION Pts To Refill After Draining Manual 3-Speed	4-Speed	Automatic •	Drive Axle (pts)	Gasoline Tank (gals)	COOLING SYSTEM (qts) With Heater	With A/C	Heavy Duty
'72	8-350	4	—	—	6	4.25	25	19	19.3	—
	8-455	4	—	—	7	5.5	25②	18.7	19	—
	Riviera	4	—	—	7	5.5	24	18.7	19	—
'73	8-350	4	—	—	6	4.25	26	18.9	19.3	—
	8-455	4	—	—	7	5.4	26③	18.7	19	20.4
'74	8-350	4	—	—	6	4.25	26	18.9	19.3	—
	8-455	4	—	—	7	5.4	26③	18.7	19	20.4
'75	8-350	4	—	—	6	4.25	26	16.9	17.2	—
	8-455	4	—	—	7	5.4	26③	19.6	21.4	—
'76	6-231	4	—	—	6	4.25	26	16.9	17.2	—
	8-350	4	—	—	6	4.25	26	16.9	17.2	—
	8-455	4	—	—	7	5.4	26③	19.7	20	—
'77	6-231 Buick	4	—	—	6	4.25	18.5	12.7	12.7	—
	8-301 Pont.	5.5	—	—	6	4.25	21	18.3	19.1	—
	8-350 Buick, Olds.	4	—	—	6	4.25	21	14.6	15.4	—
	8-403 Olds.	4	—	—	7	4.25	21①	15.7	16.6	—
'78	6-231 Buick	4	—	—	⑤	⑥	21.0	12.9	12.9	12.9
	8-301 Pont.	5	—	—	7.5	⑥	21.0③	20.9	20.9	21.6
	8-305 Chev.	4	—	—	7.5	⑥	21.0③	16.6	16.7	16.7
	8-350 Buick	5	—	—	⑧	⑥	25.3③	14.1	14.1	14.9
	8-350 Chev.	4	—	—	7.5	⑥	21.0③	16.6	16.7	18.0
	8-350 Olds.	4	—	—	7.5	⑥	21.0③⑦	14.6	14.5	15.4
	8-403 Olds.	4	—	—	7.5	⑥	25.3③	15.7	16.6	16.6
'79	6-231 Buick	4	—	—	⑤	⑥	25.3⑨	13.3	13.34	13.34
	8-301 Pont.	5	—	—	⑤	⑥	25.3⑨	20.9	20.9	21.6
	8-350 Buick	4	—	—	⑤	⑥	25.3⑨	14.6	14.5	15.0
	8-350 Olds	4	—	—	⑤	⑥	25.3⑨	14.6	14.5	15.0
	8-403 Olds	4	—	—	⑤	⑥	25.3⑨	15.7	16.6	16.6

• Specifications do not include torque converter
① Riviera and Electra—24.5, Estate wagon—22
② Estate wagon—23 gals
③ Estate wagon—22 gals
⑤ TH-M 200: 6 TH-M 350: 7.5
⑥ 7.5 inch ring gear: 3.5
   8.5 inch ring gear: 4.25
   8.75 inch ring gear: 5.4
⑧ TH-M 200: 6 TH-M 350, 400: 7.5
⑦ Electra: 25.3
⑨ Estate Wagon: 22.5 Riviera: 20
— Not applicable

CRANKSHAFT AND CONNECTING ROD SPECIFICATIONS

All measurements are given in in.

Year	Engine Displacement (cu in.)	CRANKSHAFT Main Brg. Journal Dia	Main Brg. Oil Clearance	Shaft End-Play	Thrust on No.	CONNECTING ROD Journal Diameter	Oil Clearance	Side Clearance*
'72	350	2.9995	.0004-.0015	.003-.009	3	2.0000	.0002-.0023	.006-.014
	455	3.2500	.0007-.0018	.003-.009	3	2.2495	.0002-.0023	.005-.012
'73	350	2.9995	.0004-.0015	.003-.009	3	2.0000	.0002-.0023	.006-.020
	455	3.2500	.0007-.0018	.003-.009	3	2.2495	.0002-.0023	.005-.012
'74	350	3.0000	.0004-.0015	.003-.009	3	2.0000	.0002-.0023	.006-.020
	455	3.2500	.0007-.0018	.003-.009	3	2.2495	.0002-.0023	.005-.012

CRANKSHAFT AND CONNECTING ROD SPECIFICATIONS

All measurements are given in in.

Year	Engine Displacement (cu in.)	CRANKSHAFT				CONNECTING ROD		
		Main Brg. Journal Dia	Main Brg. Oil Clearance	Shaft End-Play	Thrust on No.	Journal Diameter	Oil Clearance	Side Clearance*
'75-'76	231	2.4995	.0004-.0015	.004-.008	2	1.9995	.0002-.0023	.006-.014
	350	2.9995	.0004-.0015	.002-.006	3	1.9995	.0005-.0026	.006-.026
	455	3.2500	.0007-.0018	.003-.009	3	2.2491	.0005-.0026	.005-.025
'77	231 Buick	2.4995	.0004-.0015	.004-.008	2	2.000	.0005-.0026	.006-.027
	301 Pont.	3.0000	.0004-.0020	.003-.009	4	2.000	.0005-.0025	.006-.027
	8-350 Buick	2.9995	.0004-.0015	.002-.006	3	1.9995	.0005-.0026	.006-.026
	350 Olds.	2.4990	.0005-.0021①	.004-.014	3	2.1243	.0004-.0015	.006-.027
	403 Olds.	2.4990	.0005-.0021①	.004-.014	3	2.1243	.0005-.0026	.006-.020
'78-'79	6-231 Buick	2.4995	.0003-.0017	.004-.008	2	2.2487-2.2495	.0005-.0026	.006-.027
	8-301 Pont.	3.0000	.0004-.0020	.006-.022	4	2.2500	.0005-.0025	.006-.022
	8-305 Chev.	③	.0010-.0035④	.002-.006	3	2.0990-2.1000	.0010-.0035	.008-.014
	8-350 Buick	3.0000	.0004-.0015	.003-.009	3	1.9910-2.0000	.0005-.0026	.006-.027
	8-350 Chev.	③	.0010-.0035④	.002-.006	3	2.0990-2.1000	.0010-.0035	.008-.014
	8-350 Olds.	2.4985-2.4995②	.0005-.0021①	.0035-.0135	3	2.1238-2.1248	.0004-.0033	.006-.020
	8-403 Olds.	2.4985-2.4995②	.0005-.0021①	.0035-.0135	3	2.1238-2.1248	.0004-.0033	.006-.020

* Total for two rods
① Number five main bearing clearance—.0015-.0031
② #1: 2.4988-2.4998

③ #1: 2.4484-2.4493
  #2,3,4: 2.4481-2.4490
  #5: 2.4479-2.4488
④ #1: .0020 maximum

RING GAP

All measurements are given in inches

Year	Engine No. Cyl Displacement (cu in.)	Top Compression	Bottom Compression	Oil Control
'72	8-350	.013-.023	.013-.023	.015-.035
	8-455	.013-.023	.013-.023	.015-.055
'73-'74	8-350	.010-.020	.010-.020	.015-.035
	8-455	.013-.023	.013-.023	.015-.055
'75-'76	6-231, 8-350	.013-.023	.013-.023	.015-.035
	8-455	.013-.023	.013-.023	.015-.035
'77	6-231 Buick	.010	.010	.015
	8-301 Pont.	.010-.020	.010-.020	.035
	8-350 Buick	.013-.023	.013-.023	.015-.055
	8-350 Olds.	.010-.023	.010-.023	.015-.055
	8-403 Olds.	.010-.023	.010-.023	.015-.055
'78-'79	6-231 Buick	.010-.020	.010-.020	.015-.035
	8-301 Pont.	.010-.020	.010-.020	.035
	8-305 Chev.	.010-.030	.010-.035	.015-.065
	8-350 Buick	.010-.020	.010-.020	.015-.035
	8-350 Chev.	.010-.030	.010-.035	.015-.065
	8-350 Olds.	.010-.023	.010-.023	.015-.055
	8-403 Olds.	.010-.023	.010-.023	.015-.055

PISTON CLEARANCE

Year	Engine No. Cyl. Displacement (cu. in.)	Piston to Bore Clearance (in.)
'74	8-350	.0008-.0020
	8-455	.0010-.0016
'75-'76	6-231, 8-350	.0008-.0014
	8-455	.0010-.0016
'77	6-231 Buick	.0008-.0020
	8-301 Pont.	.0025-.0033
	8-350 Buick	.0008-.0014
	8-350 Olds.	.0010-.0020
	8-403 Olds.	.0010-.0020
'78-'79	6-231 Buick	.0013-.0035
	8-301 Pont.	.0025-.0033
	8-305 Chev.	.0027 max.
	8-350 Buick	.0013-.0035
	8-350 Chev.	.0027 max.
	8-350 Olds.	.0010-.0020
	8-403 Olds.	.0010-.0020

RING SIDE CLEARANCE
All measurements are given in inches

Year	Engine	Top Compression	Bottom Compression	Oil Control
'72	All	.003-.005	.003-.005	.0035-.0095
'73-'76	All	.003-.005	.003-.005	.0035 Maximum
'77	8-301 Pont.	.0015-.0035	.0015-.0035	.0015-.0035
	6-231, 8-350 Buick	.003-.005	.003-.005	.0035 Maximum
	8-350, 403 Olds.	.002-.004	.002-.004	.0015-.0035
'78-'79	6-231 Buick	.0030-.0050	.0030-.0050	.0035
	8-301 Pont.	.0015-.0035	.0015-.0035	.0015-.0035
	8-305 Chev.	.0012-.0042	.0012-.0042	.0020-.0080
	8-350 Buick	.0030-.0050	.0030-.0050	.0035
	8-350 Chev.	.0012-.0042	.0012-.0042	.0020-.0080
	8-350 Olds.	.0020-.0040	.0020-.0040	.0015-.0035
	8-403 Olds.	.0020-.0040	.0020-.0040	.0015-.0035

WHEEL ALIGNMENT SPECIFICATIONS

Year	Model	CASTER Range (deg)	CASTER Pref Setting (deg)	CAMBER Range (deg)	CAMBER Pref Setting (deg)	Toe-in (in.)	Steering Axis Inclin. (deg)	WHEEL PIVOT RATIO (deg) Inner Wheel	WHEEL PIVOT RATIO (deg) Outer Wheel
'72	All	½P to 1½P	1P	0 to 1P	½P	⅛ to ¼	10.5	20	18½
'73	All	½P to 1½P	1P	¼N to ¾P	¼P	⅛ to ¼	10.5	20	18½
'74	All	½P to 1½P	1P	½P to 1½P LH 0 to 1P RH	1P LH ½P RH	0 to ⅛	10.5	20	18½
'75-'76	All	1P to 2P	1½P	½P to 1½P LH 0-1P RH	1P LH ½ RH	0 to ⅛	10.5	20	18½
'77	All	2P to 4P	3P	0 to1 ½P	¾P	1/16 to 3/16	10.5	20	18½
'78-'79	All	2½P to 3½P	3P	⅓P to 1⅓P	⅘P	1/16 to 3/16 ①	——	——	——

N Negative   P Positive   RH Right-hand side
LH Left-hand side   ① '79 Riviera: 0 to 1/16

CHARGING SYSTEM

Voltage Regulator Removal and Installation

All Buicks are equipped with a Delcotron 10 SI alternator with internal voltage regulator. The regulator requires no adjustment and is not serviceable without overhauling the alternator.

Alternator Removal and Installation

Remove the bolt holding the tension bar to the alternator. On some models, it may be necessary to loosen and rotate the fan shroud to get at the pivot bolt. Push the alternator in toward the engine to release the drive belt. Remove the alternator mounting bolt to release the alternator from the engine.

When reinstalling, adjust the alternator drive belt to allow ½ in. play on the longest run between pulleys.

NOTE: *On A/C models, remove the compressor brace.*

STARTING SYSTEM

See the Charging and Starting Systems Unit Repair Section for troubleshooting.

Starter Removal and Installation

1. Disconnect the battery negative cable.
2. Jack up the car and remove the four flywheel inspection cover screws.
3. Disconnect the wires from the solenoid.
4. Remove the starter bolts.
5. Remove the starter.

NOTE: *On some models, it may be necessary to move the exhaust pipe to gain clearance.*

6. Reverse the steps to install.

Disabling the Seat Belt/Starter Interlock System

It is legal to disconnect the seat belt interlock, but not the seat belt warning light. Disconnect the system as follows:

1. Disconnect the negative battery cable.
2. Locate the interlock wiring harness

under the left side of the instrument panel on or near the fuse block. The connector has orange, yellow and green wires.

3. Cut and tape the ends of the green wire on the body side of the harness.

4. Disconnect the seat belt warning buzzer from the installed position under the left side of the instrument panel by removing the buzzer from the fuse block or connector and removing the two yellow wires with black tracers from the multiple connector into which the buzzer is plugged. Tape the terminal and reinstall the buzzer.

5. Connect the battery ground cable.

IGNITION SYSTEM

The ignition system used on models through 1974 is the conventional contact point type.

In 1974, a solid state, high energy ignition (HEI) system was offered as an option. Beginning 1975, the HEI system became standard equipment. There are no points or condenser to replace, nor any cam or rubbing block to wear out.

HEI System Tachometer Hookup

There is a convenient tachometer terminal at the top of the distributor cap on the HEI systems. The terminal is marked "TACH." Connect the positive tachometer lead to the distributor terminal and the negative tachometer lead to a ground. Some tachometers must connect from the distributor terminal to the positive terminal of the battery. Follow the tachometer manufacturer's instructions.

The procedure for checking the ignition timing on this system is the same as for the conventional ignition systems.

— CAUTION —

Never ground the HEI tachometer terminal.

Distributor Removal

Disconnect the distributor primary wire from the coil and the hose from the vacuum unit. On the HEI system, first disconnect the battery ground cable, then disconnect the terminal connectors from the distributor and remove the vacuum advance hose. Remove distributor cap by inserting a screwdriver into upper slotted end of cap latches, pressing down and turning 90° counterclockwise.

Make a mark on the distributor body in line with the rotor. Match-mark position of vacuum unit to the engine.

Remove clamp to release distributor and remove from crankcase.

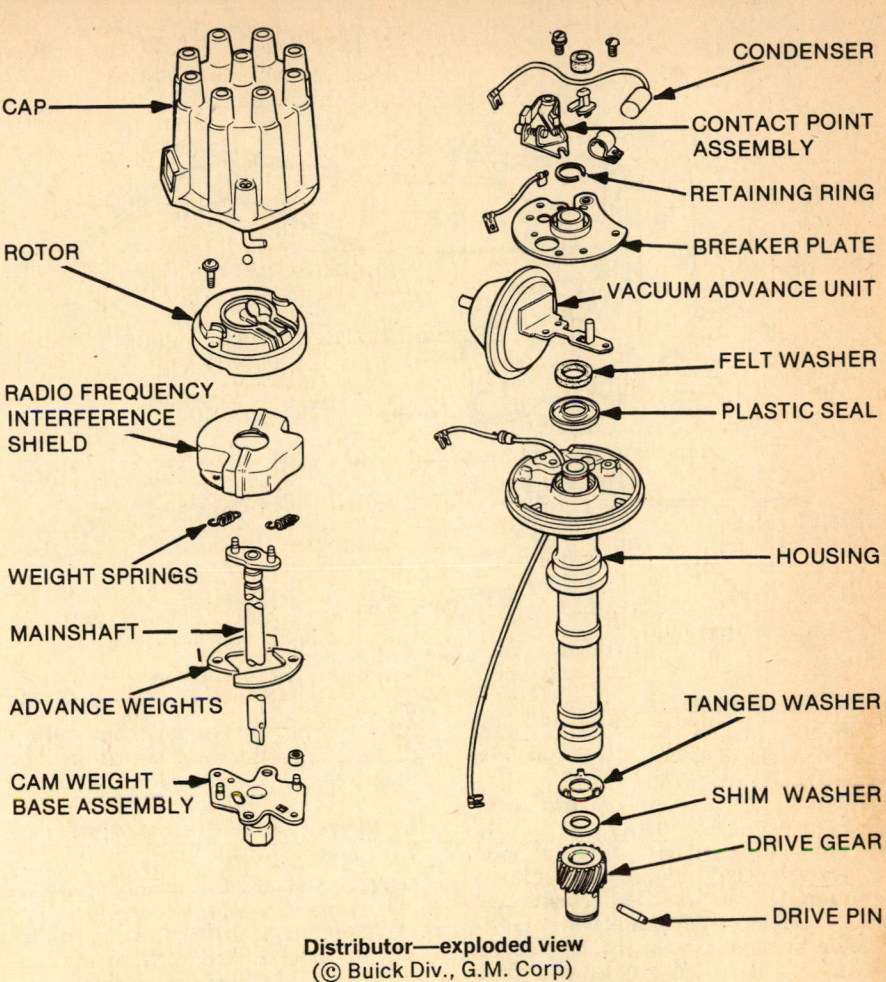

CAP
ROTOR
RADIO FREQUENCY INTERFERENCE SHIELD
WEIGHT SPRINGS
MAINSHAFT
ADVANCE WEIGHTS
CAM WEIGHT BASE ASSEMBLY

CONDENSER
CONTACT POINT ASSEMBLY
RETAINING RING
BREAKER PLATE
VACUUM ADVANCE UNIT
FELT WASHER
PLASTIC SEAL
HOUSING
TANGED WASHER
SHIM WASHER
DRIVE GEAR
DRIVE PIN

Distributor—exploded view
(© Buick Div., G.M. Corp)

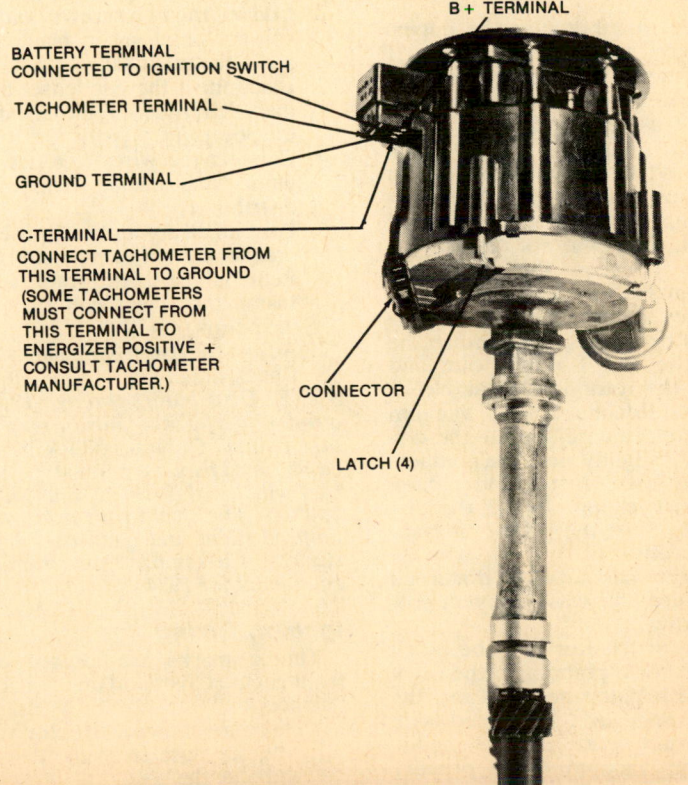

B + TERMINAL
BATTERY TERMINAL CONNECTED TO IGNITION SWITCH
TACHOMETER TERMINAL
GROUND TERMINAL
C-TERMINAL
CONNECT TACHOMETER FROM THIS TERMINAL TO GROUND (SOME TACHOMETERS MUST CONNECT FROM THIS TERMINAL TO ENERGIZER POSITIVE + CONSULT TACHOMETER MANUFACTURER.)
CONNECTOR
LATCH (4)

Tachometer connection for the HEI system

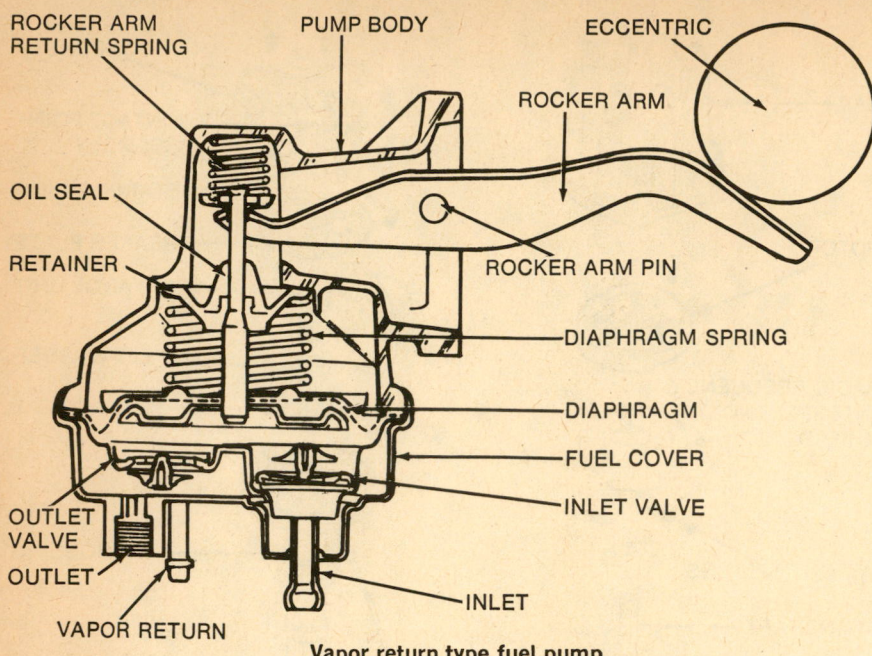

ROCKER ARM
RETURN SPRING

PUMP BODY

ECCENTRIC

ROCKER ARM

OIL SEAL

RETAINER

ROCKER ARM PIN

DIAPHRAGM SPRING

DIAPHRAGM

FUEL COVER

INLET VALVE

OUTLET
VALVE

OUTLET

VAPOR RETURN

INLET

Vapor return type fuel pump

Distributor Installation

If the engine was inadvertently turned while distributor was out, proceed as follows:

Remove the right rocker arm cover. Using a wrench on the crankshaft pulley bolt, turn the engine over until both valves for No. 1 cylinder are closed. The timing mark on the harmonic balancer behind the crankshaft pulley should be aligned with the zero degree mark. No. 1 cylinder is now at firing point.

Install the distributor in the engine with the rotor in position to fire No. 1 cylinder. The vacuum unit should align with the match-mark made when the distributor was removed. Press down lightly on the distributor if it does not seat correctly. Use the starter to turn the engine until the tang on the distributor shaft slips into the slot in the oil pump shaft. This will not disturb the relationship between the distributor and the camshaft because the drive gear engages before the tang. However, it will be necessary to return the engine to the No. 1 firing point and check that the rotor is also at No. 1 firing point. Reconnect the vacuum tube and primary wire. Rotate the distributor body slightly until the contacts just start to open. Install and tighten the distributor clamp. Install the distributor cap. Start the engine and adjust point dwell.

If the engine has not been disturbed since the distributor was removed, proceed as follows:

Insert the distributor into the block so that the rotor is pointing to the mark made on distributor housing and the vacuum advance unit is aligned with the match-mark made on the engine. Connect the vacuum tube, primary wire, and install the distributor cap. Install the distributor clamp. Check that

the spark plug wires are correctly routed. Start the engine and adjust point dwell and then adjust ignition timing.

Contact Point Replacement and Adjustment

NOTE: *The condenser should be replaced when the points are replaced.*

1. Remove the distributor cap and rotor. If equipped with an interference shield, remove the shield.
2. Loosen the two screws holding the contact point set in place and remove the point set.
3. Disconnect the condenser and primary leads from their terminals on the points.
4. Connect the wires to a new set of points and install them into the distributor.
5. Put a small amount of grease on the breaker cam or turn the lubricator.
6. Reinstall the shield, rotor, and cap. Install the shield half that covers the points first.
7. Adjust the dwell to specification.
8. Check the timing.

NOTE: *Distributors through 1973 have a radio interference shield over the contact points. Only snap-lock point sets can be used because screw-type connectors will hit this shield and short the ignition. The shield isn't necessary if a unitized point and condenser set is installed. The unitized set is standard equipment for 1974.*

Ignition Timing

Timing marks are located on the front engine cover and on the harmonic balancer.

1. Disconnect the distributor vacuum advance hose from the distributor and plug the hose.
2. Make sure the dwell is correct.

NOTE: *It may be necessary to put a*

small amount of white paint or chalk on the timing marks to make them more visible.

3. Connect a timing light to No. 1 cylinder.
4. Loosen the distributor clamp.
5. Start the engine and rotate the distributor until the correct marks line up. Tighten the distributor clamp and recheck the timing.
6. Reconnect the vacuum hose.

FUEL SYSTEM

These models use a single action fuel pump mounted on the lower side of the engine front cover, on Buick built engines, and on the lower left side of the block on engines built by other GM divisions.

The fuel pump is not rebuildable.

All air-conditioner equipped cars have a special fuel pump with a metering outlet for a vapor return system. Hot fuel and fuel vapor is returned to the fuel tank. The fuel pump is continuously cooled by circulating fuel from the tank, thus greating reducing the possibility of vapor lock.

Fuel Pump Removal and Installation

1. Disconnect the fuel inlet, outlet, and vapor return hoses.
2. Remove the two bolts holding the pump to the engine.
3. Remove the old fuel pump.
To install:
1. Install a new pump and gasket.
2. Install the two bolts.
3. Reconnect the hoses to the pump. Do not force the threaded fittings, use very light pressure until it is obvious that the threads are started properly.
4. Start the engine and check for leaks.

Fuel Filter Replacement

The filter is located in the carburetor inlet behind the large hex nut. This is a small pleated paper or sintered bronze filter.

1. Remove the fuel inlet line from the carburetor.
2. Remove the large nut from the carburetor body.
3. Remove the old filter.
4. Install a new filter with the spring inserted before the filter.
5. Install the large hex nut and fuel line.
6. Start the engine and check for leaks.

Idle Speed and Mixture Adjustments

1972-73

1. Connect a tachometer to the engine.
2. Start the engine and run it until it is warmed up.

3. Remove and plug the vacuum hose to the distributor.
4. Place transmission in Drive.
5. Open the throttle sufficiently to allow the solenoid to extend and contact the throttle lever pad in the idle position.
6. Adjust the solenoid set screw to obtain the specified rpm. This is the higher figure in the specification chart.
7. Disconnect the solenoid wire to disengage solenoid.
8. Adjust the carburetor idle screw to obtain specified idle speed, which is the lower figure in the specification chart.
9. Reconnect the solenoid wire.
10. Adjust the idle mixture needles, one at a time, to obtain the highest tachometer reading. After the highest reading is reached, readjust the solenoid plunger to obtain 50 rpm over the specified idle speed. Turn each mixture needle in to reduce the idle speed 25 rpm for each needle. This reduces the idle speed to the recommended rpm.
11. Adjust the fast idle speed on all four-barrel carburetors. Fast idle must be adjusted after slow idle speed and mixture have been adjusted. Make the adjustment on the low step of the fast idle cam in Drive to 700 RPM.
12. Connect the distributor vacuum hose.
13. Install the ''red'' service idle needle limiter caps on the mixture screws.

1974-76

NOTE: *Idle speed and mixture must be set with the engine at normal operating temperature, the air conditioner off, the air cleaner on, and the transmission in drive. If a CO meter is available, set the idle mixture to that specified on the underhood specifications sticker.*

1. Set the parking brake and block the wheels.
2. Disconnect the evaporative emission hose at the air cleaner. Disconnect and plug the distributor vacuum line at the distributor. Disconnect and plug the EGR vacuum line at the EGR valve.
3. Adjust the idle speed to that specified in the ''Tune-Up Specifications'' chart. On 1974-75 models, first adjust the idle speed screw with the solenoid disconnected to get the lower speed, then adjust the solenoid screw with the solenoid connected to get the higher speed. On 1976 models, adjust the idle speed with the idle speed screw.
4. Cut the tabs off the mixture screw caps, then equally richen (turn out) the mixture screws until the maximum idle speed is achieved.
5. Using the solenoid screw or idle speed screw, adjust, if necessary, the idle speed to 70 rpm above the specified speed for 455 engines,

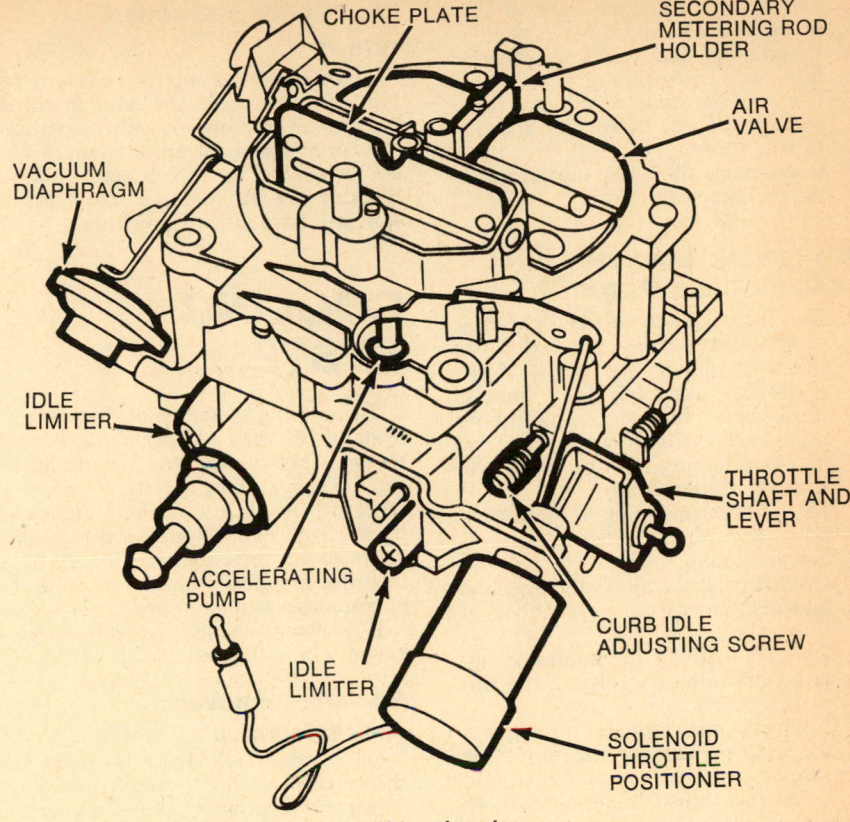

4 bbl carburetor

and 60 rpm above for the 350 (1974). On 1975-76 vehicles, adjust the idle speed to 80 rpm above specification.
6. Turn in (lean) the mixture screws equally to the specified idle speed.
7. Reconnect all the hoses removed in Step 2.

1977

1. Set the parking brake and block the drive wheels. Bring the engine to normal operating temperature.
2. Loosen and relocate the air cleaner to gain access to the carburetor adjusting screws, if necessary, but keep the vacuum hoses connected.
3. Disconnect and plug other vacuum lines as directed on the underhood Emission Control Information label.
4. Disconnect and plug the vacuum advance hose. Adjust the ignition timing, if necessary, and reconnect the vacuum advance hose.
5. Remove the caps from the idle mixture screws and turn each screw inward to lightly seat and then back them out equally so that the engine will just run.
6. Place the transmission in drive, back each screw out, 1/8 turn at a time, until a maximum idle speed is obtained.
7. Adjust the idle speed screw to 25 RPM higher than the idle speed specifications.
8. Turn the idle mixture screws in-

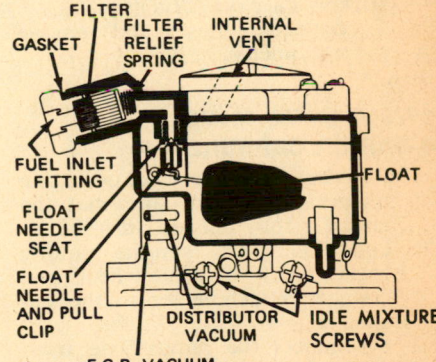

2 bbl carburetor
(© Buick Div., G.M. Corp)

ward until the idle speed reaches the specified idle speed.
9. Reset the idle speed to specification.
10. Recheck the idle speed and mixture, connect all the vacuum hoses, and reinstall the air cleaner.

1978-79 2GC, 2GE
2-BARREL CARBURETOR

1. Run the engine to normal operating temperature, turn the air conditioning Off, make sure that the choke is fully opened, set the parking brake, block the drive wheels and connect a tachometer to the engine according to the manufacturer's instructions.
2. Disconnect and plug the hoses at

the vapor canister and EGR valve.
3. Place the transmission in Park.
4. Disconnect the vacuum advance hose and set the timing.
5. Connect the vacuum advance hose and set the idle by turning the adjusting screw.
6. Reconnect all hoses and remove the tachometer.

1978-79 M2MC-210, M2ME-210 2-BARREL CARBURETOR

1. Run the engine to normal operating temperature, make certain that the choke is fully opened, set the parking brake, block the drive wheels, disconnect the air conditioning compressor clutch wire, turn the air conditioning Off and place the transmission in Drive.
2. Disconnect and plug the vacuum advance hose at the distributor.
3. Set the timing.
4. Connect the vacuum advance line and disconnect the purge hose at the canister.
5. On cars without air conditioning, adjust the idle by turning the adjusting screw.
    On cars with air conditioning, set the idle by turning the adjusting screw. Turn the A/C control to On. Open the throttle momentarily to extend the solenoid idle speed by turning the solenoid to achieve the rpm specified on the underhood sticker. Turn the A/C Off.
6. Reconnect all hoses and remove the tachometer.

1978-79 M4MC, M4ME 4-BARREL CARBURETOR

1. Run the engine to normal operating temperature, make sure that the choke is fully opened, turn the air conditioning Off, set the parking brake, block the drive wheels and connect a tachometer to the engine.
2. Disconnect the purge hose from the vapor canister. Disconnect and plug the EGR vacuum hose at the valve. On 350 cid. engines, plug the purge hose.
3. Place the transmission in Park.
4. Disconnect and plug the vacuum advance line at the distributor.
5. Check and adjust the timing.
6. Connect the vacuum advance line.
7. Place the transmission in Drive, and adjust the idle speed by turning the adjusting screw. On air conditioned cars, disconnect the compressor clutch wire and turn the A/C control On. Open the throttle momentarily to extend the solenoid plunger and adjust the solenoid speed by turning the solenoid until the rpm specified on the underhood sticker is achieved. Turn the A/C Off.
8. Connect all hoses and remove the tachometer from the engine.

Idle Mixture Adjustment
1978-79

Changes in the mixture system for 1978-79 have made the adjustment of the fuel-air mixture impossible without the use of a propane enrichment device not available to the general public. Backing-out the mixture screw, of itself, will have little or no effect.

COOLING SYSTEM

The cooling system is of the conventional type, with a larger capacity systems for heavy duty and air conditioning. The cooling system uses a reservoir to collect coolant displaced by the heat expansion. As the system cools down, the coolant is drawn back into the radiator by vacuum, and the coolant level is maintained.

If coolant is needed, add it to the reservoir, not to the radiator.

Radiator Removal and Installation

On models equipped with a fan shroud, remove the shroud from the radiator and position it rearward over the fan.

Remove the capscrews that hold the fan blades to the fan hub and take off the blades, spacer and pump pulley. Drain the cooling system and remove the top and bottom radiator hoses and the two automatic transmission cooler lines from the radiator. Remove the bolts that hold the radiator core to the cradle and lift the core straight up. Reverse the above steps to install.

Water Pump Removal and Installation

It is possible to remove and replace the water pump on all Buicks without disturbing the radiator core. This is accomplished by removing the fan belt, fan blades, and pulley, disconnecting the hoses and removing the water pump attaching bolts. Reverse the removal procedure to install. Use a new gasket and make sure all gasket surfaces are clean.

Thermostat Removal and Installation

The thermostat is contained in the water outlet elbow mounted on the front of the intake manifold.

To replace the thermostat, disconnect the upper radiator hose, remove the water outlet attaching bolts, lift off the outlet and take out the thermostat.

--- CAUTION ---
When installing a thermostat, always place the end of the thermostat with the spring inside of engine.

EMISSION CONTROLS

There are three types of emissions to be controlled: crankcase emissions, carburetor and gas tank fuel vapor emissions, and exhaust emissions. See the "Unit Repair Section" for troubleshooting and repair information.

1972

In 1972, all engines are equipped with positive crankcase ventilation, transmission controlled vacuum spark advance (TCS) and the controlled combustion system (CCS). The air injection reactor system is standard on all engines except the non-California 350 cu in. with automatic transmission. All California cars have Exhaust Gas Recirculation (EGR).

The EGR system is used to reduce oxides of nitrogen emissions. To lower the formation of nitrogen oxides, it is necessary to reduce combustion temperatures. This is done by introducing exhaust gases into the intake manifold to be burned.

An EGR valve is mounted on the right rear of the intake manifold and is used to regulate the amount of exhaust gases and the time the exhaust gases enter the intake manifold. As the engine speeds up, carburetor vacuum is applied to the valve which opens a port connecting the intake manifold to the exhaust gas passage that is cast in the intake manifold. This allows exhaust gases to pass into the intake manifold. The EGR system is not in operation during engine idle.

1973

All engines are equipped with Positive Crankcase Ventilation, Controlled Combustion, Air Injection Reactor System, Exhaust Gas Recirculation, Transmission Controlled Vacuum Spark Advance System and Evaporative Emission Control. With the exception of a low temperature cut-out valve that was added to the EGR system, the emission control systems remain unchanged from previous years.

The EGR system is the same one that was used on 1972 California cars with a new temperature valve. This black and white plastic valve is located in the vacuum line to the EGR valve and it senses ambient temperature above the the engine intake manifold. At temperatures below 55°F, the temperature valve closes to prevent carburetor vacuum from opening the EGR valve. When the temperature above the manifold rises above 60°F, the valve opens and allows carburetor vacuum to control the operation of the EGR valve. Whenever installing a new valve, always make sure the side of the valve marked EGR faces toward the EGR valve.

1974

The 1974 Buick emission control system is unchanged from 1973, except for a change in the EGR temperature sensor. Instead of ambient temperature, it measures coolant temperature. Although the system design remains unchanged, there has been an extensive refinement and recalibration of components to insure greater efficiency.

1975-76

All 1975-76 models are equipped with a catalytic converter. Details on this system will be found in the Emission Control Systems Unit Repair Section. A fast warm-up system is used to heat incoming fuel by directing exhaust gas flow through the intake manifold crossover passage below the carburetor when engine temperatures are low. A choke modulator is used to keep the choke on longer in cold weather by restricting the flow of exhaust gas warmed air to the choke. In warm weather, the modulator allows normal choke operation. High Energy Ignition became standard equipment in 1975. For 1976, the emission control systems are the same as 1975, but air cleaner cold air ducts on some engines have been dropped.

1977-79

The emission control system remains virtually unchanged from previous year, except for minor modifications and specifications changes. Specifications vary for vehicles sold over 4,000 feet elevation, vehicles sold in California, and for vehicles sold in the remaining 49 states. The back pressure type exhaust gas recirculation valve has been modified to incorporate a small heat deflector plate at the top of the exhaust pressure sensing tube. This prevents hot exhaust gases from flowing directly onto the diaphragm and prolongs the life of the EGR valve.

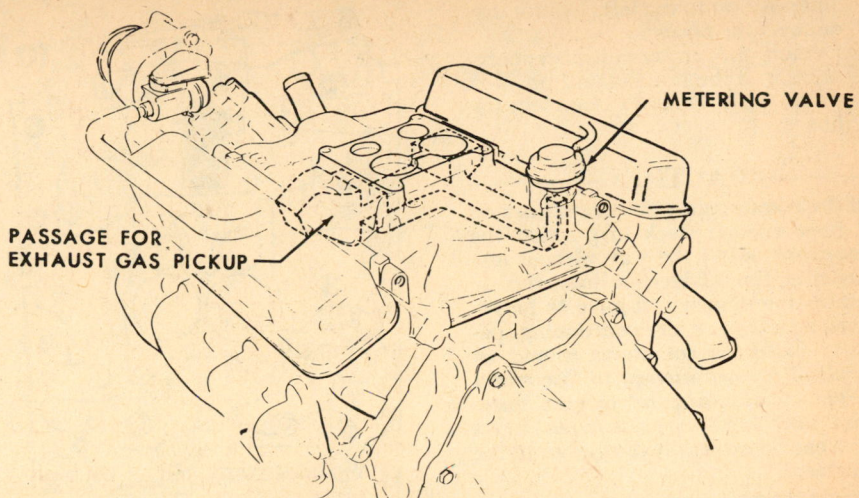

Exhaust Gas Recirculation system
(© Buick Div., G.M. Corp)

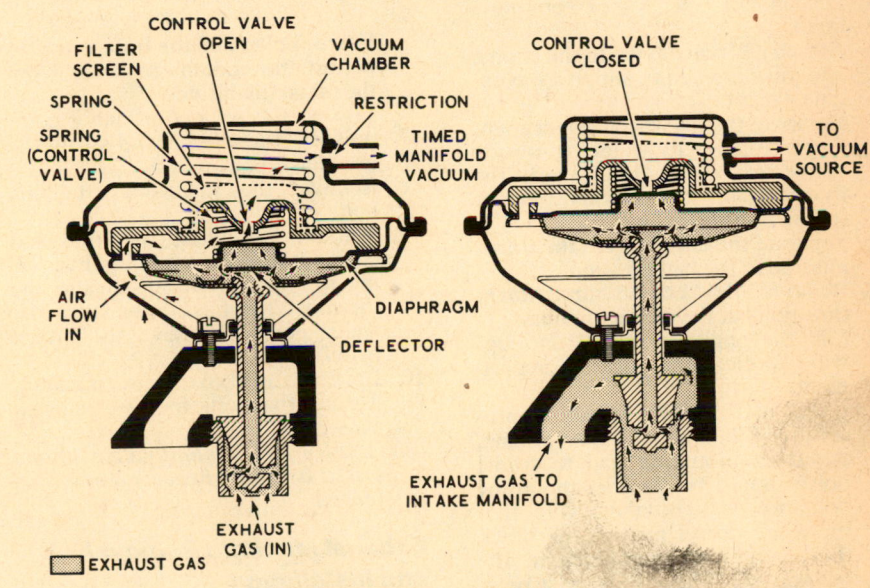

Back pressure type EGR valve
(© Buick Div., G.M. Corp)

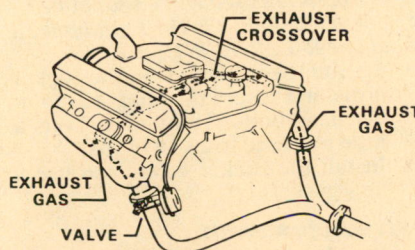

Beginning 1975 Fast warm-up system
(© Buick Div., G.M. Corp)

ENGINE

Beginning 1977, Oldsmobile 350 and 403 V8, and Pontiac 301 V8 engines were installed in various Buick models. In 1978 the Chevrolet 305 and 350 V8s were added. The 305 is used only in LeSabre and the 350 is used only in LeSabre models for sale in locations above 4,000 ft. altitude. To identify the engine, locate the engine code in the Vehicle Identification Number and refer to the Engine Identification Code Chart at the front of this section. Refer to the appropriate car section for major engine repairs.

NOTE: Engine service procedures in this section are for Buick V8s only. The V6 is covered in the Buick Apollo Section; Pontiac V8s are covered in the Pontiac and Astre Sections; Oldsmobile V8s are covered in the Oldsmobile Section; Chevrolet V8s are covered in the Chevrolet Section.

ENGINE REMOVAL AND INSTALLATION

1. Drain the cooling system.
2. Scribe the hinge outline on the underside of the hood. Remove the hood attaching bolts and remove the hood.
3. Disconnect the battery cables.
4. Remove the radiator and heater hoses and remove the air cleaner.
5. Disconnect the transmission oil cooler lines. Remove the fan shroud, fan belts, and pulleys.
6. Remove the attaching bolts and lift out the radiator.
7. Disconnect the exhaust pipe or pipes at the exhaust manifold/s.
8. Disconnect the vacuum line to the power brake unit.
9. Disconnect the accelerator to carburetor linkage.
10. Disconnect all the engine component wiring that would interfere with the engine removal, such as alternator wires, gauge sending unit wires, primary ignition wires, engine-to-body ground strap, etc.
11. Disconnect the gas line at the fuel pump.
12. Detach the power steering pump

and position to the left. Do not disconnect the hoses.
13. Detach the air conditioner compressor at the bracket and position to the right. Do not disconnect the hoses.

CAUTION

If the compressor refrigerant lines do not have enough slack to position the compressor out of the way without disconnecting the refrigerant lines, the air conditioning system will have to be removed by a trained air conditioning specialist. Under no conditions should an untrained person attempt to disconnect the air conditioning refrigerant lines. These lines contain pressurized freon which can be extremely dangerous to the untrained.

---

14. Disconnect the transmission control linkage.
15. Disconnect the vapor emission lines.
16. Attach a lifting device to the engine and raise enough to support the engine weight.
17. Remove the flywheel cover pan. Remove the flywheel to-torque converter bolts. Match-mark the flywheel and torque converter for reassembly.
18. Separate the engine from the transmission at the bell housing.
19. Remove the engine attachment thru-bolts at the engine mounts.
20. Lift the engine forward and upward to clear the engine compartment.
21. Install by reversing the above procedure. When installing an engine, the front mounting pad to frame bolts should be the last mounting bolts to be tightened. Note that there are dowel pins in the block that have matching holes in the bellhousing. These pins must be in almost perfect alignment before the engine will go together with the transmission.

MANIFOLDS

Intake Manifold Removal and Installation

1. Drain the cooling system and disconnect the battery.
2. Remove the carburetor air cleaner. Disconnect all the tubes and hoses from the carburetor. Disconnect and remove the coil.
3. Disconnect the temperature indicator wire from sending unit.
4. Disconnect the accelerator and transmission linkage at the carburetor. Disconnect the throttle return spring.
5. Slide the front thermostat bypass hose clamp back on the hose. Disconnect the upper radiator hose at the outlet.
6. Disconnect the heater hose at the temperature control valve inlet.

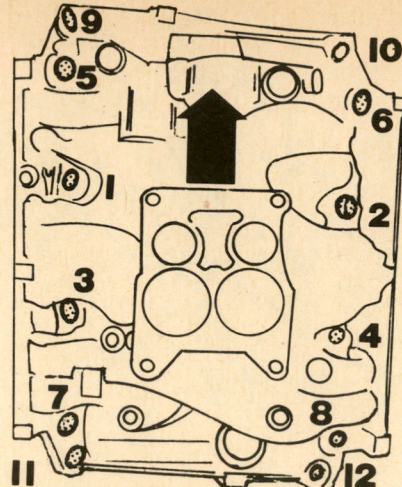

Intake manifold tightening sequence—Buick 350 and 455 V8
(© Buick Div., G.M. Corp)

Force the end of the hose down to permit the coolant to drain from the intake manifold.
7. Loosen the air conditioning compressor bracket bolt and swing the bracket out of the way.
8. Remove the manifold attaching bolts.
9. Remove the intake manifold and carburetor as an assembly by sliding it rearward to disengage the thermostat bypass hose from the water pump. Remove the intake manifold gasket.
10. Reverse the above steps to install. Torque the bolts in the sequence shown.
NOTE: *New intake manifold gasket and seals must be used whenever a manifold is removed.*

Exhaust Manifold Removal and Installation

1. Jack up the car and support on jack stands.
2. Disconnect the exhaust pipe from the manifolds on both sides of the engine and lower. If equipped with dual exhaust, disconnect and lower only on the side being worked on.
NOTE: *On the right side, it may be necessary to remove the air conditioning compressor, the power steering pump, or alternator. On 1972 left-side exhaust manifolds, on models other than Le-Sabre, the pitman arm must be removed and the steering linkage pushed out of the way.*
3. Remove the exhaust manifold-to-cylinder head bolts.
4. Remove the manifold from beneath the car.
5. Reverse the above steps to install.

VALVE SYSTEM

Rocker Arm Removal and Installation

1. Remove the rocker arm cover.
2. Remove the rocker arm shaft as-

sembly bolts and then the assembly.
3. Remove the nylon arm retainers by prying them out with pliers or breaking them with a chisel.
4. Remove the rocker arms. Remove any retainer pieces from the inside of the shaft.
   On installation:
1. Install the rocker arms on the shaft and lubricate them with oil.
2. Center each arm on the 1/4 in. hole in the shaft. Install new nylon rocker arm retainers in the holes using a drift 1/2 in. in diameter.

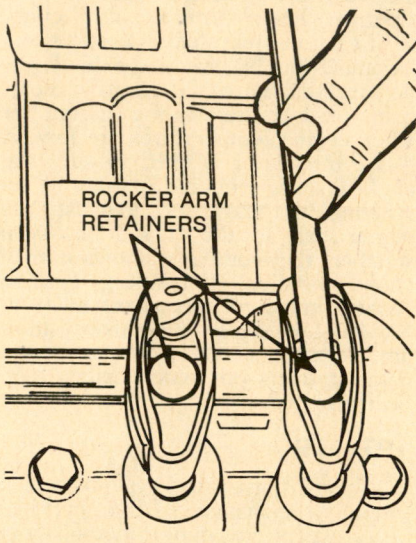

Removing nylon rocker arm retainers —350 and 455 Buick V8
(© Buick Div., G.M. Corp)

NOTE: *On 1972 engines, each pair of rocker arms must be installed so that the external rib on each arm points away from the rocker arm shaft bolt that is located between each pair of rocker arms. On 1973 and later engines, replacement rocker arms are marked R and L. From the front of the engine on the left bank, the sequence should be L-R, L-R, L-R, L-R. On the right bank, it should be R-L, R-L, R-L, R-L.*
3. Locate the push rods in the rocker arms and insert the shaft-to-cylinder head bolts. Tighten the bolts a little at a time to 25-30 ft. lbs.
4. Install the rocker cover and use a new gasket.

Valve Adjustment

After the shaft assembly-to-cylinder head bolts are torqued to specification, the valves are automatically adjusted.

Valve Guide Replacement

Valve guides are cast into the cylinder heads of all engines. The valve guides must be reamed and fitted with valves with oversize stems to be repaired.
NOTE: *Some of the engines use progressively wound valve springs. The coils are closer together at one end than at the other. The close wound end must*

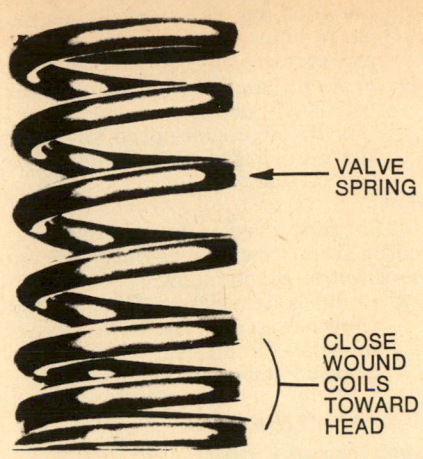

Progressively wound valve spring
(© Buick Div., G.M. Corp)

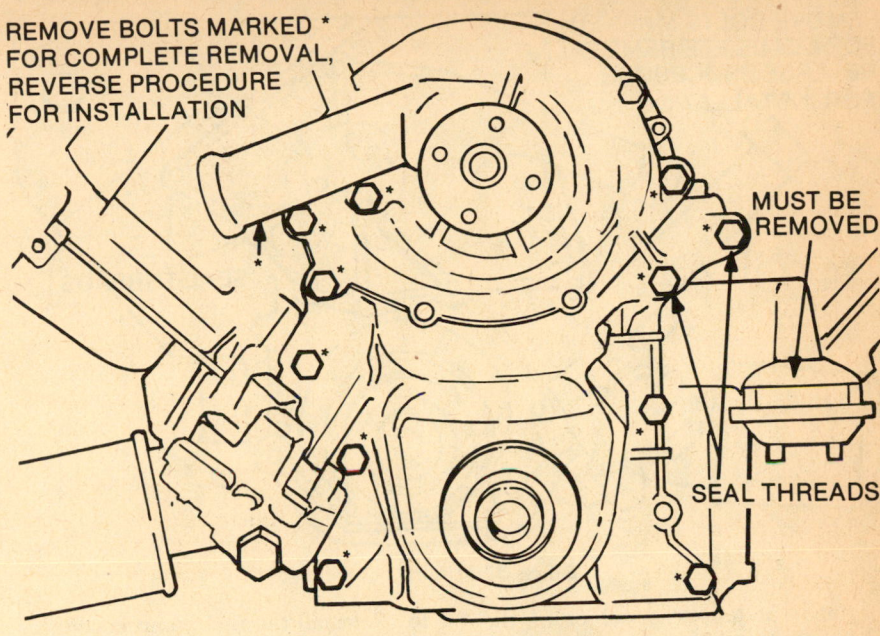

Buick 455 timing cover bolts

go against the cylinder head. 0.010 in. oversize lifters are sometimes installed at the factory. These are identified by an O on the lifter bore and two grooves on the lifter body.

CYLINDER HEAD

Cylinder Head Removal and Installation

1. Disconnect the battery.
2. Drain the coolant.
3. Remove the air cleaner.
4. Remove the air conditioning from the engine, but do not disconnect any lines.
5. Remove the intake manifold.
6. When removing the right cylinder head, loosen the alternator belt and remove the alternator; if equipped with an air conditioning compressor, remove the compressor from the mounting bracket and position it out of the way with the hoses connected, then remove the alternator with the mounting bracket; finally, disconnect the metal temperature indicator wire (1973 and later models only).

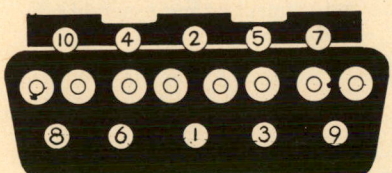

Cylinder head torque sequence
for 350, 455 Buick V8

7. When removing the left cylinder head, remove the dipstick and the power steering pump without disconnecting any hoses.
8. Disconnect the plug wires.
9. Disconnect the exhaust manifold from the head being removed.
10. Remove the rocker arm cover and rocker shaft assembly. Lift out the push rods. Disconnect the AIR hoses from the cylinder head.
11. Remove the cylinder head bolts.
12. Remove the cylinder head and gasket.
13. Reverse the above steps to install. Torque the head bolts to specifications in three steps.

TIMING CASE COVER, TIMING CHAIN AND CAMSHAFT

Timing Chain and Front Oil Seal Replacement

350

1. Drain the cooling system and remove the radiator, shroud, fan, pulleys, and belts.
2. Remove the crankshaft pulley, fuel pump and distributor.
3. Remove the Delcotron and the power steering pump, if necessary.
4. Loosen and slide rearward the front clamp on the thermostat bypass hose. Remove the harmonic balancer.
5. Remove the bolts attaching the timing chain cover to the cylinder block and the oil pan to timing chain cover bolts. Remove the timing chain cover assembly and gasket. Clean the cover thoroughly, being careful not to damage the gasket surface.
6. Turn the crankshaft so that the timing marks on the sprockets are adjacent to each other on a line with the shaft centers.
7. Remove the crankshaft oil slinger.
8. Remove the bolt, special washer, distributor drive gear, and fuel pump eccentric from the camshaft.
9. Alternately pry the camshaft and the crankshaft sprockets forward until the camshaft sprocket and

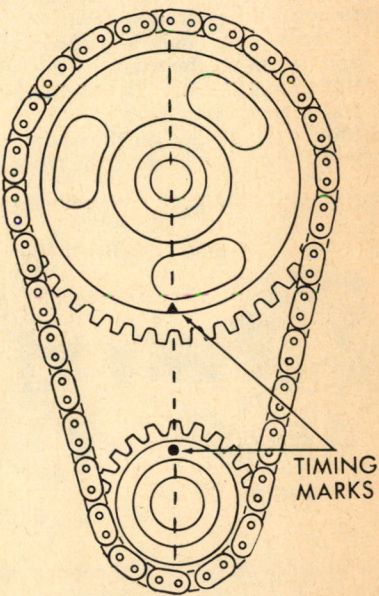

Timing chain and sprocket marks

chain are free. Then remove the crankshaft sprocket.

If the oil seal appears worn or has been leaking, replace it as follows:

10. Use a punch to drive out the old seal and retainer. Drive from front to rear of the timing chain cover.
11. Coil new packing around the opening so that the ends are at the top. Drive in the retainer. Stake the retainer in at least three places. Size the packing by rotating a hammer handle, etc. around the packing until the balancer hub fits through the packing.

If engine has been disturbed since chain and sprockets were removed:

12. Turn the crankshaft until No. 1 pis-

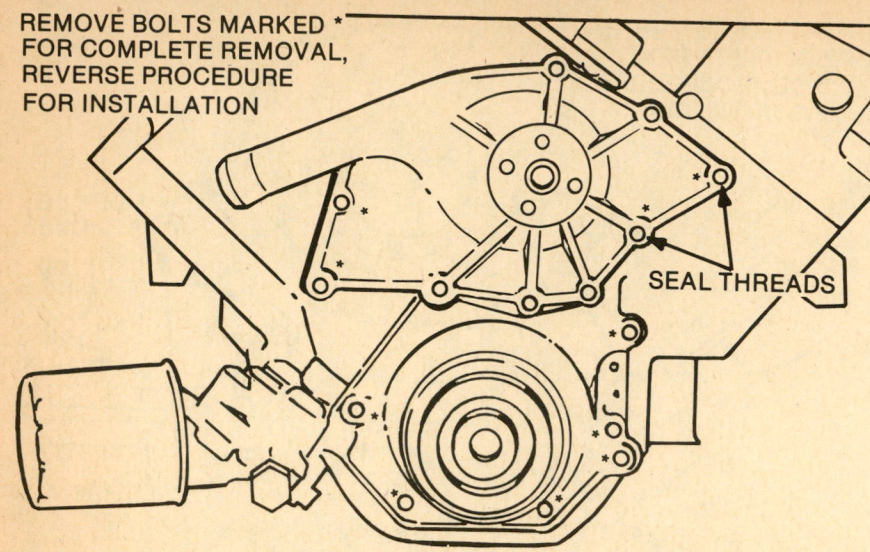

REMOVE BOLTS MARKED *
FOR COMPLETE REMOVAL,
REVERSE PROCEDURE
FOR INSTALLATION

SEAL THREADS

Buick 350 timing cover bolts

ton is at top dead center of the compression stroke.

13. Mount the sprocket temporarily and turn the camshaft so that the timing mark is straight down.

14. Assemble the chain and sprockets and mount on the shafts with their timing marks closest to each other and aligned vertically.

15. Mount the slinger on the sprocket with the concave side to the front.

16. Reinstall the fuel pump eccentric, distributor drive gear, special washer, and bolt on the camshaft. Reinstall the Woodruff key with the oil groove forward.

17. Remove the oil pump cover and pack the space around the oil pump gears full of petroleum jelly, leaving no air spaces. Reinstall the oil pump cover with a new gasket. This step is very important. If it is

not done the oil pump will not begin to pump oil as soon as the engine is started.

18. Reinstall the timing chain cover with a new gasket.

Keep the engine speed low for a short time after installation of a new oil seal.

455

This procedure is identical to that outlined for 350 cu. in. engines with the substitution of the following steps:

8. Remove the oil pan. Remove the camshaft sprocket bolts.

16. Reinstall the oil pan. Reinstall the camshaft sprocket bolts.

Camshaft Removal and Installation

1. Remove the intake manifold, distributor, radiator, air conditioning condenser and grille.

2. Remove the rocker arm covers.

3. Remove the rocker arm and shaft assemblies, push rods, and valve lifters.

4. Remove the timing chain cover, timing chain, and camshaft sprocket.

5. Slide the camshaft forward, through the grille opening, and out from the bearing bores. Carefully avoid marring the bearing surfaces.

6. Reverse the above steps to install.

CONNECTING RODS AND PISTONS

When the rod assemblies are re-

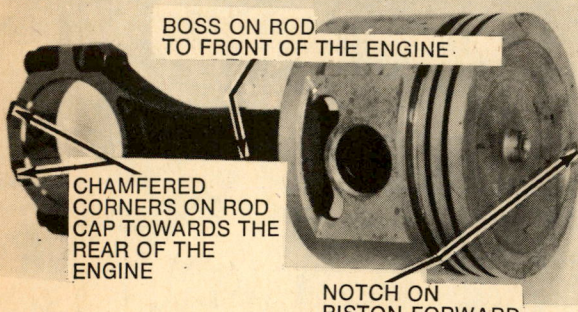

RIGHT NO. 2-4-6-8

BOSS ON ROD TO FRONT OF THE ENGINE

CHAMFERED CORNERS ON ROD CAP TOWARDS THE REAR OF THE ENGINE

NOTCH ON PISTON FORWARD

350 Buick V8 piston and connecting rod assembly —right bank
(© Buick Div., G.M. Corp)

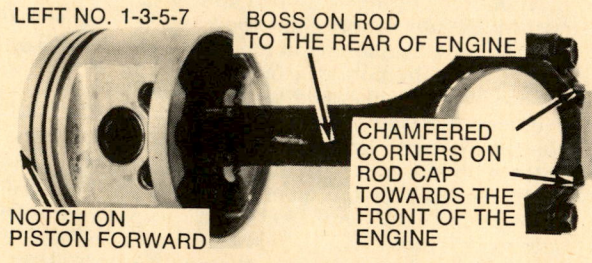

LEFT NO. 1-3-5-7

BOSS ON ROD TO THE REAR OF ENGINE

CHAMFERED CORNERS ON ROD CAP TOWARDS THE FRONT OF THE ENGINE

NOTCH ON PISTON FORWARD

350 Buick V8 piston and connecting rod assembly —left bank
(© Buick Div., G.M. Corp)

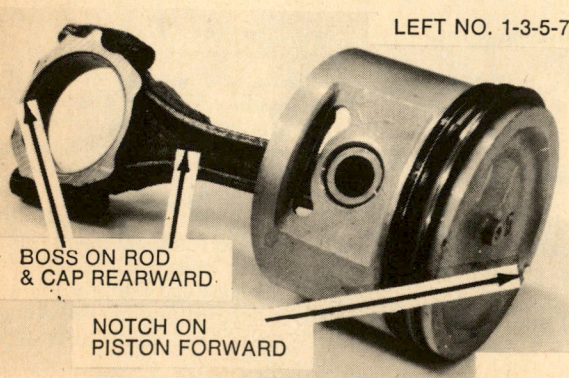

LEFT NO. 1-3-5-7

BOSS ON ROD & CAP REARWARD

NOTCH ON PISTON FORWARD

455 Buick V8 piston and connecting rod assembly—left bank
(© Buick Div., G.M. Corp)

RIGHT NO. 2-4-6-8

BOSS ON ROD & CAP FORWARD

NOTCH ON PISTON FORWARD

455 Buick V8 piston and connecting rod assembly—right bank
(© Buick Div., G.M. Corp)

placed in the engine, the connecting rod bearing oil spurt hole must point up toward the camshaft.

ENGINE LUBRICATION

Oil Pan Removal and Installation

1. Disconnect the battery.
2. Remove the fan shroud-to-radiator tie bar screws.
3. Remove the air cleaner and disconnect the throttle linkage.
4. Raise the car and support it on jackstands.
5. Drain the oil.
6. Remove the lower flywheel housing, remove the shift linkage attaching bolt and swing it out of the way, and disconnect the exhaust crossover pipe at the engine.
8. On 1972 models, disconnect the idler arm at the frame and push the steering linkage forward to the crossmember.
9. Remove the front engine mounting bolts.
10. Raise the engine by placing a jack under the crankshaft pulley mounting.

CAUTION

On air conditioned cars, place a support under the right-side of the transmission before raising the engine. If you don't do this, the engine and transmission will cock to the right due to the weight of the air conditioning equipment.

11. Remove the oil pan bolts and remove the pan. It may be necessary to rotate the crankshaft to get enough clearance to remove the pan. Remove the rear main seal on the 455.
12. Reverse the above steps to install. Use gasket sealer and new gaskets. Tighten the bolts evenly to 14 ft. lbs.

Oil Pump Removal

The oil pump is located in the timing chain cover on the right-hand side. It is connected by a drilled passage in the crankcase to an oil screen housing and pipe assembly. The screen is submerged in the oil supply in the oil pan.

The pump can be disassembled as follows:

1. Remove the oil filter.
2. Unbolt the pump cover assembly from the timing chain cover.
3. Remove the cover assembly and slide out the pump gears.
4. Remove the oil pressure relief valve cap, spring, and valve. Do not remove the oil filter by-pass valve and spring.
5. Check that the relief valve spring isn't worn on its side or collapsed. Check that the relief valve is no more than an easy slip fit in its bore in the cover. If there is any perceptible side-play, replace the valve. If

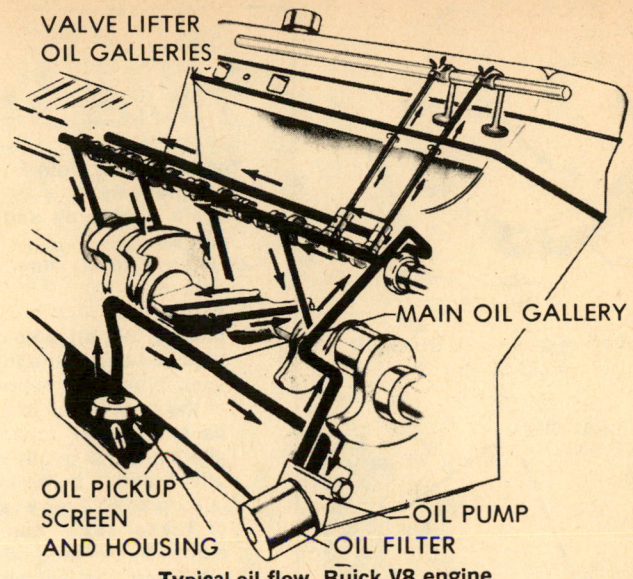

Typical oil flow, Buick V8 engine
(© Buick Div., G.M. Corp)

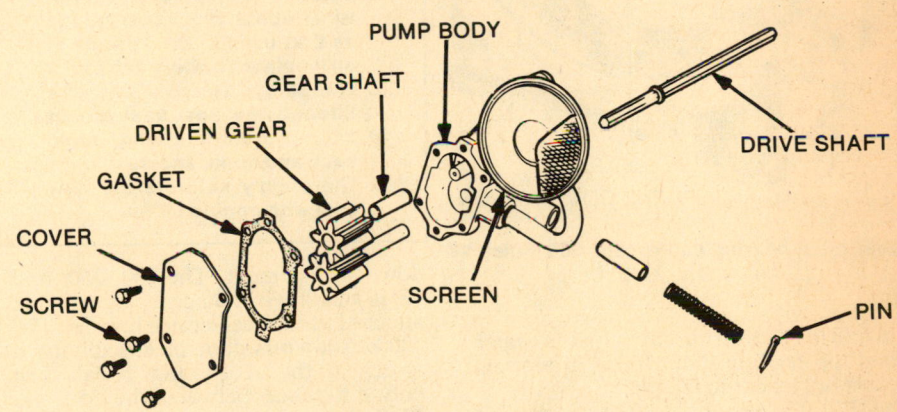

Typical oil pump assembly
(© Buick Div., G.M. Corp)

there is still side-play, replace the cover.
6. Check the filter by-pass valve for good condition.

To assemble the pump:

7. Lubricate and install the pressure relief valve and spring in the cover bore. Install the gasket and cap, torquing the cap to 35 ft. lbs.
8. Install the gears and check that gear-to-cover end clearance is between 0.002-0.006 in. If the clearance is less, check the timing cover gear pocket for wear.
9. Remove the gears and pack the gear pocket full of petroleum jelly. Don't use grease.

CAUTION

Unless the pump is primed this way, it won't produce any oil pressure when the engine is started.

10. Install the gears. Install a new gasket and the cover. Torque the bolts evenly to 10 ft. lbs. Replace the filter.

Rear Main Bearing Oil Seal Replacement

Buick uses an oil slinger and groove, a braided fabric seal and two neoprene strips to seal the rear main bearing. The braided fabric seal can be installed in the crankcase half (upper) only when crankshaft is removed. However, the seal can be replaced in the lower half whenever the lower half (cap) has been removed. To renew the seals in the cap proceed as follows:

Remove the oil pan. Remove the old seals and clean the cap. Place the new braided seal in the groove with both ends projecting above the parting surface of the cap. Force the seal into the groove by rubbing down with a hammer handle or other smooth tool until the seal is seated in the groove and the ends project above the parting face of the cap, not more than $1/16$ in. Using a razor blade, cut off the ends flush with the parting surface.

On 350 cu. in. engines only, just before installing the bearing cap, lightly lubricate the neoprene side seals and

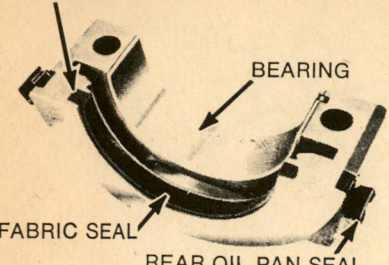

CUT ENDS OF FABRIC SEAL SQUARE & FLUSH

BEARING

FABRIC SEAL

REAR OIL PAN SEAL

Rear main bearing cap—455 Buick V8
(© Buick Div., G.M. Corp)

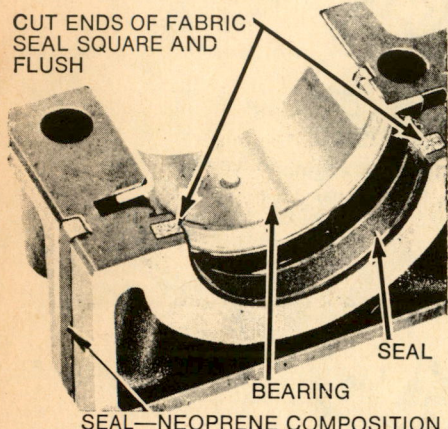

CUT ENDS OF FABRIC SEAL SQUARE AND FLUSH

SEAL

BEARING

SEAL—NEOPRENE COMPOSITION

Rear main bearing cap-except 455 Buick V8
(© Buick Div., G.M. Corp)

install in the bearing cap with the upper ends protruding about $1/16$ in. The seals must not be cut to length.

NOTE: *The neoprene side seals may fit loosely in the side grooves of the rear main bearing cap when first installed, and may even leak for a short time. However, the seals swell considerably when they come in contact with oil and heat and will soon seal properly if installed correctly.*

After installing the cap, force the seals up into the cap with a blunt instrument to insure a seal at the line between the cap and the case.

NOTE: *The 455 cu. in. engines use a rear bearing cap which does not have the neoprene side seals. These engines are sealed at this point by a rear oil pan seal.*

— CAUTION —

The engine must be operated at slow speed when first started after installation of new braided seals.

AUTOMATIC TRANSMISSION

Turbo Hydra-Matic 200, 350, 375B, and 400 transmissions are used on Buicks. The most notable distinguishing feature among them is the kick-

Chilton's TIME SAVER

Top Half, Rear Main Bearing Oil Seal Replacement
1. Drain engine oil and remove oil pan.
2. Remove rear main bearing cap.
3. With a 6 in. length of 3/16 in. brazing rod, drive up on either exposed end of the top half oil seal. When the opposite end of the seal starts to protrude, have a helper grasp it with pliers and pull gently while the driven end is being tapped. It is surprising how easily most of these seals can be removed by this method.

To replace the woven fabric-type seal:
1. Obtain a 12 in. piece of copper wire (about the same gauge as that used in the strands of an insulated battery cable).
2. Thread one strand of this wire through the new seal, about 1/2 in. from the end, bend back and make secure.
3. Thoroughly saturate the new seal with engine oil.

4. Push the copper wire up through the oil seal groove until it comes down on the opposite side of the bearing.
5. Pull, (with pliers), on the protruding copper wire while the crankshaft is being turned and the new seal is slowly fed into place.

— CAUTION —

This snaking operation slightly reduces the diameter of the new seal and care will have to be used to keep the seal from slipping too far through the top half of the bearing.

6. When an equal amount of seal is extending from each side, cut off the copper wire close to the seal and tamp both ends of the seal up into the groove (this will tend to expand the seal again).

NOTE: Don't worry about the copper wire left in the groove, it is too soft to cause damage.

7. Replace in the usual way and replace the oil pan.

down arrangement. The 200, 350, and 375B kickdown linkage is by a cable attached to the accelerator linkage. The 400 kickdown is done electrically by a switch at the accelerator pedal. The only difference between the 350 and 375B transmissions is that the 375B has more direct clutch plates, to increase torque capacity. There is no way to differentiate between the two externally. The 200 transmission was first used in 1977. It is an all-metric transmission and sometimes has the word METRIC stamped in the pan. It can be distinguished from the 350 by the number of pan bolts; the 200 has 10 bolts, while the 350 has 13 bolts. The designation 375B was last used in 1976.

Neutral Start Switch Adjustment

This safety switch prevents starting except in Neutral or Park positions. The switch combines function with the back-up light switch and is actuated by the transmission linkage. The switch is on the steering column under the instrument panel. To check switch adjustment:
1. Turn on the ignition switch.
2. Place the shift control lever in Reverse, and make sure the back-up lights are on.
3. Set the parking brake. Hold the foot brake. Place shift control in Neutral and make sure the engine will start. Repeat in Park, Drive, and Reverse. The engine must start only in Neutral or Park.

4. To adjust the switch, place the shift lever in the Neutral position and insert a $3/32$ in. (No. 41) drill bit through the hole marked N. Move the switch until the bit goes in about $3/8$ in. Tighten the mounting screws.
5. Check the adjustment as in Step 3.

Shift Linkage Adjustment

COLUMN SHIFT
1. Loosen the adjusting clamp bolt.
2. Place the selector lever in Neutral.
3. Place the transmission lever, at the transmission, in the neutral position.
4. Tighten the adjusting clamp bolt.
5. Start the engine. Check for proper shifting into all ranges.

FLOORSHIFT

These units are operated by a cable linkage. Adjust as follows:
1. Pull the clip from the cable housing at the side of the transmission.
2. Set the shift lever in the Park detent.
3. Set the transmission lever in the Park, or most forward, position.
4. Replace the clip to hold the cable housing in position.
5. Loosen the reverse rod clamp screw or nut.
6. Push the reverse rod (from linkage to steering column) up and hold lightly against the stop.
7. Tighten the screw in the clamp at the end of the reverse rod.

8. Start the engine. Check for proper shifting into all ranges.

Kickdown Detent Cable Adjustment, Turbo Hydra-Matic 200, 350, 375B

Throttle Valve Adjustment 1978-79 Turbo Hydra-Matic 200

1. Release the snap-lock on the cable connected to the carburetor linkage.
2. Hold the carburetor linkage in the wide open throttle position and close the snap-lock.

Detent Switch Adjustment, Turbo Hydra-Matic 400

The initial adjustment on installation is made by pushing the switch lever all the way toward the firewall. The final adjustment is made automatically the first time the accelerator pedal is fully depressed.

Pan Replacement, Fluid and Filter Change

TURBO HYDRA-MATIC 200, 350, and 375B

1. Raise the car and support it with jack stands.
2. Place a container under one of the pan corners and loosen the pan attaching screws. Pull the corner down to drain some of the fluid.
3. After the fluid has drained, remove the pan, clean and dry it thoroughly. Be very careful not to leave any lint from cleaning rags in the pan.
4. Remove the filter assembly and gasket by removing the two retaining screws.
5. Install a new filter-to-valve body gasket on the filter and install the filter. Tighten the retaining screws.
6. Install the pan with a new gasket.

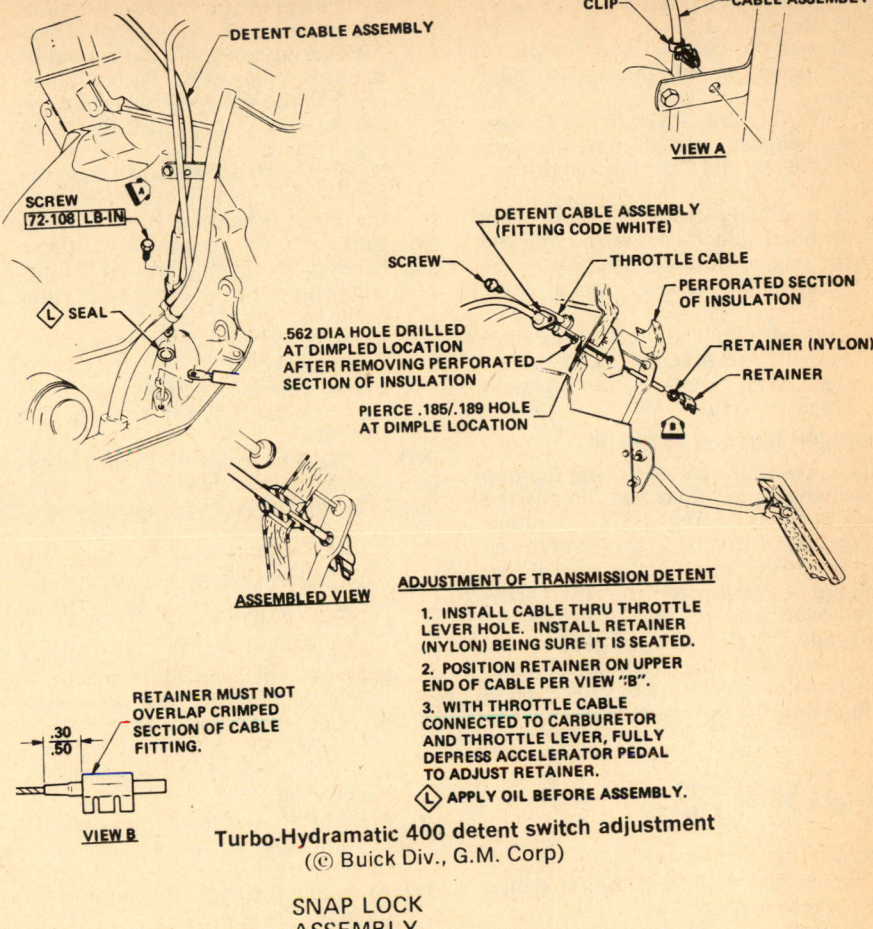

Turbo-Hydramatic 400 detent switch adjustment
(© Buick Div., G.M. Corp)

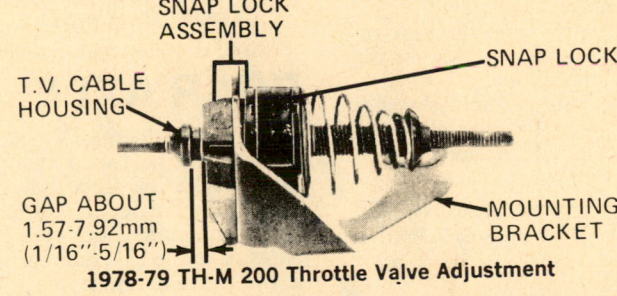

1978-79 TH-M 200 Throttle Valve Adjustment

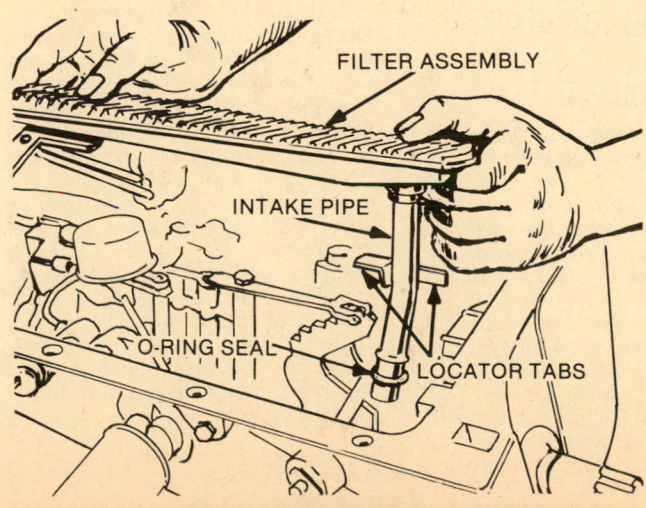

Removing/installing the filter and O-ring seal on a 400 automatic transmission
(© Buick Div., G.M. Corp)

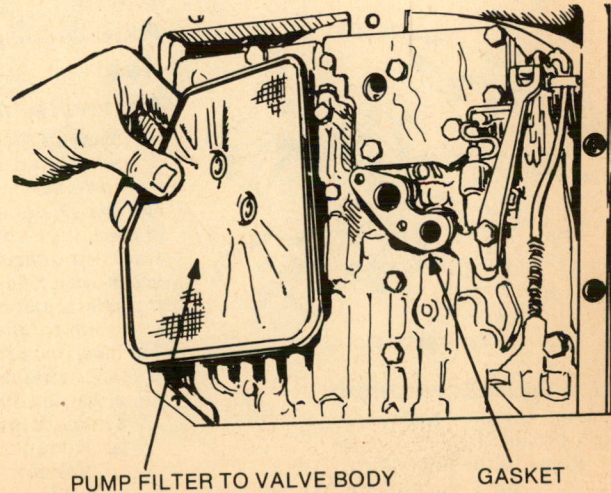

Removing/installing the filter and gasket on a 350 or 375B automatic transmission
(© Buick Div., G.M. Corp)

Tighten the retaining screws to 13 ft. lbs.

7. Lower the car and add 3 pints of transmission fluid through the filler neck.
8. With the shift lever in Park, start the engine, but do not race it. Move the shift lever through each range.
9. Immediately check the fluid level with the selector lever in Park and the engine running. Make sure the vehicle is resting on a level surface.
10. Add additional fluid as necessary to bring the level to 1/4 in. below the ''ADD'' mark on the dipstick. Do not overfill.

TURBO HYDRA-MATIC 400

The procedure for removing the pan and changing the fluid and filter is the same as for the 350 and 375. The filter of the 400 is attached by one bolt and has an O-ring seal on the end of the intake pipe. Make sure that the O-ring is removed from its seat if it does not come out with the filter and intake pipe. Install a new O-ring. Tighten the filter retaining bolt to 12 ft. lbs. Add 5 pints of fluid through the filler tube.

U-JOINTS

Driveshaft Removal

1. Mark the shaft and pinion flange for reassembly.
2. Remove U-bolts from the rear pinion flange. Use tape to secure the bearings on the spider.
3. Remove the shaft assembly by sliding it rearward to disengage the splines on the transmission shaft.

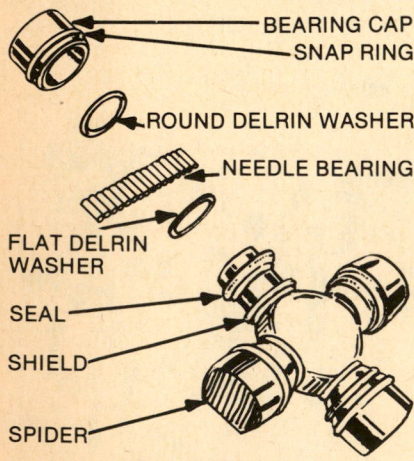

BEARING CAP
SNAP RING
ROUND DELRIN WASHER
NEEDLE BEARING
FLAT DELRIN WASHER
SEAL
SHIELD
SPIDER

Typical U-joint

Driveshaft Disassembly

Nylon-injected composite universal joints are used.
1. Remove the driveshaft.
2. By using a piece of pipe or similar tool, slightly larger than 1 1/8 in. to encircle the bearing shell, apply force on the yoke until downward

movement of the yoke and stationary position of the journal, force the bearing assembly almost out of the top of the yoke. (The force applied on the yoke will shear the nylon retainers which lock the bearings in place).
3. Rotate the shaft 180° and repeat the preceding step to partially remove the opposite bearing.
4. Complete the removal of these bearings by tapping around the circumference of the exposed portion of the bearing.
5. Remove the journal from the driveshaft rear yoke.
6. Remove the bearings and the journal from the splined yoke in the same way.

NOTE: *New bearings and journal assembly kits must be used upon reassembly. The kit includes snap-rings and Delrin washers.*

7. Install by inserting one bearing one-quarter way in one side of the splined yoke, using a brass hammer.
8. Insert the journal into the splined yoke (with dust shields installed).
9. Install the opposite bearing, ensuring that the bearing rollers do not jam on the journal. Check for free rotary movement of the journal in the bearing.
10. Press both bearings into place (just far enough to install the snap rings).
11. Assemble the opposite end universal in the same way.

REAR AXLE

The manufacturer's identification number will be found stamped on the right or left axle tube adjacent to the differential carrier, on all axles except those with an 8 1/2 inch ring gear. These axles have the I.D. number stamped on a tag located under one of the rear cover attaching bolts.

Axle Shaft, Bearing and Seal

Removal and Installation

1. Jack up the vehicle and remove the wheel and brake drum on the side to be serviced.

NOTE: *There are two types of axles installed in Buicks; one with the axle shafts attached to the differential side gears with C-clips and the other with the axle shafts held in by retainer plates attached to the brake backing plate. The only way to be sure of which type you are working on is to remove the differential cover and look for the C-clips.*

2. On models with the C-clips:
   a. Remove the bolts and differential carrier cover and allow the lubricant to drain out.
   b. Remove the pinion shaft lock bolt and pinion shaft from the differential.

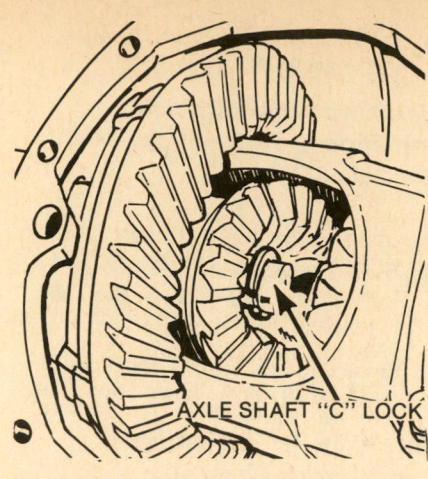

AXLE SHAFT "C" LOCK

Axle shaft C-clips inside the differential

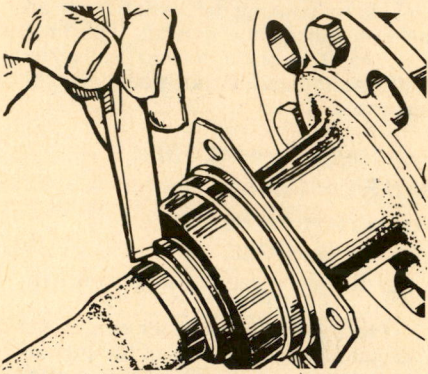

Breaking the bearing retainer with a chisel

   c. Push the axle shafts inward to permit the removal of the C-clips and remove the axle shafts.
3. On models with retainer plates:
   a. Remove the nuts holding the retainer plates to the brake backing plates.
   b. Pull the retainers clear of the bolts and reinstall two opposite nuts finger tight to hold the brake backing plate in position.
   c. Pull the axle shaft out using an axle puller (slide hammer).
4. On axles with C-clips, the bearing and seal are removed and installed from the axle housing with special bearing and seal tools.
5. On axles with the retainer plates, the axle bearing retainer ring must be cracked with a chisel, and the bearing pressed off and on with an arbor press. Press on a new retainer ring.
6. Install the axle shafts in the reverse order of removal. Apply a small amount of lubricant to the splines of the axle shaft to facilitate installation. If the differential is a limited slip type, use a limited slip differential type lubricant.

JACKING HOISTING

To raise the front of the car, jack at

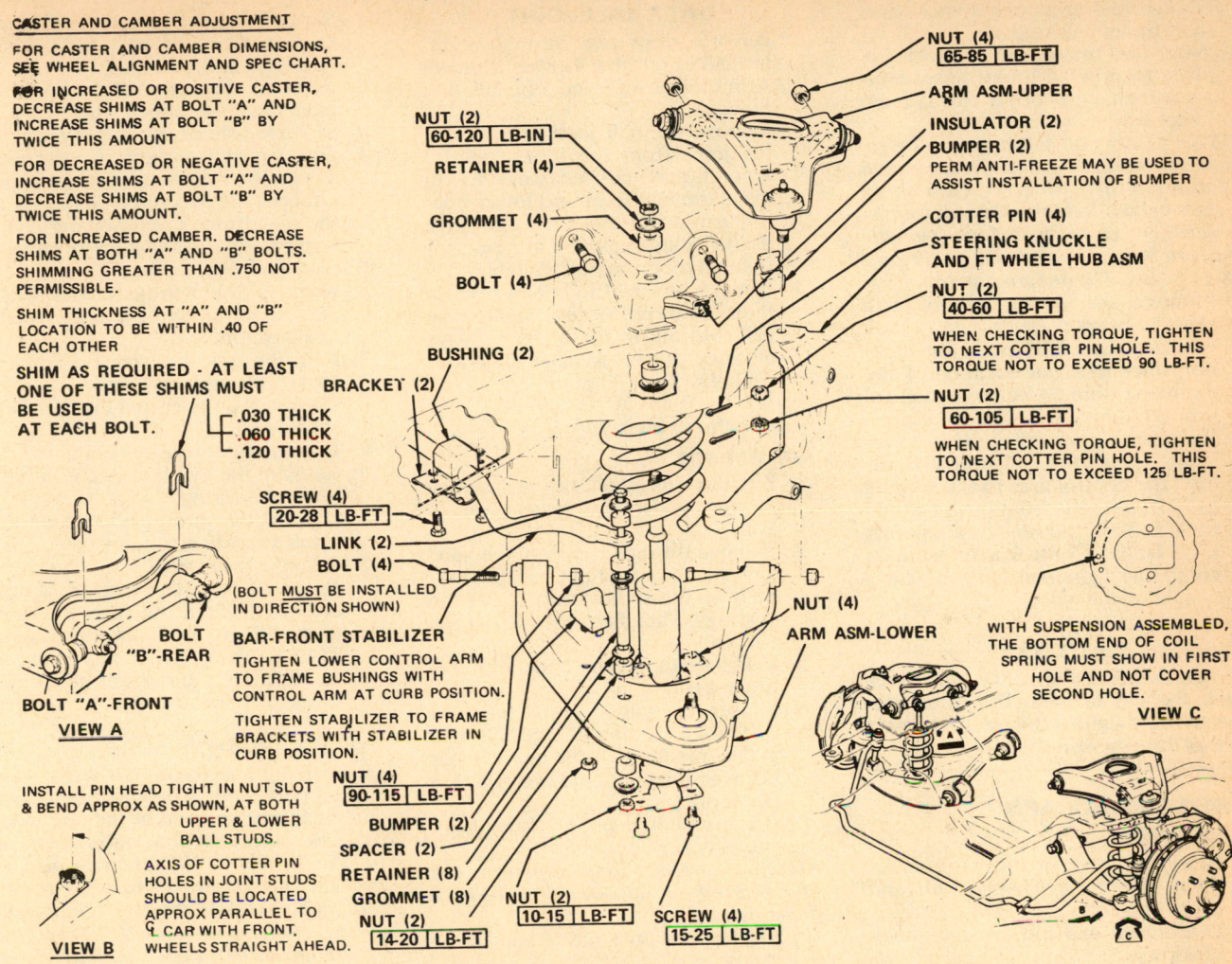

CASTER AND CAMBER ADJUSTMENT

FOR CASTER AND CAMBER DIMENSIONS, SEE WHEEL ALIGNMENT AND SPEC CHART.

FOR INCREASED OR POSITIVE CASTER, DECREASE SHIMS AT BOLT "A" AND INCREASE SHIMS AT BOLT "B" BY TWICE THIS AMOUNT

FOR DECREASED OR NEGATIVE CASTER, INCREASE SHIMS AT BOLT "A" AND DECREASE SHIMS AT BOLT "B" BY TWICE THIS AMOUNT.

FOR INCREASED CAMBER, DECREASE SHIMS AT BOTH "A" AND "B" BOLTS. SHIMMING GREATER THAN .750 NOT PERMISSIBLE.

SHIM THICKNESS AT "A" AND "B" LOCATION TO BE WITHIN .40 OF EACH OTHER

SHIM AS REQUIRED - AT LEAST ONE OF THESE SHIMS MUST BE USED AT EACH BOLT.
- .030 THICK
- .060 THICK
- .120 THICK

NUT (2) | 60-120 LB-IN
RETAINER (4)
GROMMET (4)
BOLT (4)
BUSHING (2)
BRACKET (2)
SCREW (4) | 20-28 LB-FT
LINK (2)
BOLT (4)
(BOLT MUST BE INSTALLED IN DIRECTION SHOWN)

BOLT "B"-REAR
BOLT "A"-FRONT
VIEW A

BAR-FRONT STABILIZER
TIGHTEN LOWER CONTROL ARM TO FRAME BUSHINGS WITH CONTROL ARM AT CURB POSITION.
TIGHTEN STABILIZER TO FRAME BRACKETS WITH STABILIZER IN CURB POSITION.

NUT (4) | 90-115 LB-FT
BUMPER (2)
SPACER (2)
RETAINER (8)
GROMMET (8)
NUT (2) | 14-20 LB-FT
NUT (2) | 10-15 LB-FT
SCREW (4) | 15-25 LB-FT

INSTALL PIN HEAD TIGHT IN NUT SLOT & BEND APPROX AS SHOWN, AT BOTH UPPER & LOWER BALL STUDS.
AXIS OF COTTER PIN HOLES IN JOINT STUDS SHOULD BE LOCATED APPROX PARALLEL TO ₵ CAR WITH FRONT WHEELS STRAIGHT AHEAD.
VIEW B

NUT (4) | 65-85 LB-FT
ARM ASM-UPPER
INSULATOR (2)
BUMPER (2)
PERM ANTI-FREEZE MAY BE USED TO ASSIST INSTALLATION OF BUMPER
COTTER PIN (4)
STEERING KNUCKLE AND FT WHEEL HUB ASM
NUT (2) | 40-60 LB-FT
WHEN CHECKING TORQUE, TIGHTEN TO NEXT COTTER PIN HOLE. THIS TORQUE NOT TO EXCEED 90 LB-FT.
NUT (2) | 60-105 LB-FT
WHEN CHECKING TORQUE, TIGHTEN TO NEXT COTTER PIN HOLE. THIS TORQUE NOT TO EXCEED 125 LB-FT.

NUT (4)
ARM ASM-LOWER

WITH SUSPENSION ASSEMBLED, THE BOTTOM END OF COIL SPRING MUST SHOW IN FIRST HOLE AND NOT COVER SECOND HOLE.
VIEW C

Typical front suspension (© Buick Div., G.M. Corp)

the front spring seat of the lower control arm, or at the center of the front crossmember.

To raise the car at the rear, place the jack under the axle housing, being careful not to damage the inspection cover.

To lift the car at the frame, use the side rails in front of the body floor pan and at the rear side rail at the lower rear control arm front pivot.

FRONT SUSPENSION

Shock Absorber Replacement

1. Remove the upper shock absorber attaching nut, grommet retainer, and grommet.
2. Remove the lower retaining screws. Lower the shock through the hole in the lower control arm.
3. Reverse the above steps to install. Tighten the upper nut to 11 ft. lbs.; the lower bolts to 27 ft. lbs.

NOTE: *To purge the shock absorber of air, repeatedly extend it in its normal*

position and compress it while inverted.

BALL JOINTS

Inspection

1972

NOTE: *Before performing this inspection, make sure that the wheel bearings are adjusted correctly and that the control arm bushings are in good condition. Due to the distribution of forces in the suspension, the lower ball joint is usually the defective joint.*

1. Jack the car up under the front lower control arm at the spring seat.
2. Raise the car until there is 1-2 in. of clearance under the wheel.
3. Insert a bar under the wheel and pry upward. If the wheel raises more than 1/8 in., the ball joints are worn. Determine whether the upper or lower ball joint is worn by visual inspection while prying on the wheel.

1973 AND LATER

The lower ball joints contain a visual wear indicator. The lower ball joint grease plug screws into the wear indi-

cator which protrudes from the bottom of the ball joint housing. As long as the wear indicator extends out of the ball joint housing, the ball joint is not worn. If the tip of the wear indicator is parallel with, or recessed into the ball joint housing, the ball joint is defective.

Control Arms and/or Ball Joint, Spring—Removal and Installation

UPPER CONTROL ARM

1. Raise the car with a jack under the frame. Remove the wheel and tire.
2. Remove the cotter pin from the upper ball joint stud.
3. Loosen, but do not remove the nut.

——— **CAUTION** ———

If the nut is removed, the full force of the coil spring could be released.

Rap the knuckle sharply in the area of the tapered stud to free the stud from the knuckle.

4. With another jack, support the car weight under the outer edge of the lower control arm. Raise jack

enough to free upper control arm from upper ball stud.

5. Wire the brake and knuckle in place to prevent brake hose damage, then, lift upper arm from knuckle.

NOTE: *If only ball joints are to be replaced, stop at this point. Center punch and drill out the four rivets, then chisel off their heads. Remove old ball joint—the new joint comes with four specially hardened bolts, which must be torqued to 8-11 ft. lbs. The nut goes on top.*

6. Remove the upper control arm shaft-to-bracket nuts and lock washers. Carefully note the number, thickness, and location of the adjusting shims. Remove control arm assembly.

7. Reverse the preceding steps to install. Tighten the ball stud to 61 ft. lbs.; the control arm-to-frame nuts to 75 ft. lbs.; the front bushing nuts to 90 ft. lbs.; the rear bushing nuts to 55 ft. lbs. Control arm fasteners should be tightened with the car's weight on the wheels.

--- **CAUTION** ---

When installing the cotter pin, never loosen the nut to align the cotter pin holes. Always tighten the nut to the next slot that lines up with the hole.

LOWER CONTROL ARM, OR SPRING

1. Raise the front of the car and remove the tires, wheels, hub and drum or rotor.
2. Disconnect and remove the shock absorber.
3. Remove the front stabilizer rod link from the lower control arm.
4. Disconnect the brake reaction rod from the lower control arm.
5. As a safety precautuion to gain maximum leverage, place a jack about 1/2 in. below the lower ball joint stud. Now, remove the ball stud cotter pin and loosen the nut about 1/8 in. Do not remove the nut.
6. Rap the steering knuckle in the area of the stud to separate the stud from the knuckle.
7. After the stud has broken loose from the knuckle, raise the jack against the control arm. Remove the nut and separate the steering knuckle from the tapered stud.
8. Carefully lower the jack under the control arm and release the spring. With the jack entirely lowered, it may be necessary to pry the spring off its seat on the lower control arm with a pry bar.
9. After the spring is removed, the lower control arm may be removed by removing the lock nut attaching the control arm to the frame.
10. Install by reversing removal procedure. Tighten the ball stud nut to 85 ft. lbs.; the control arm to frame nuts to 95 ft. lbs. front and 125 ft. lbs. rear.

LOWER BALL JOINT

1. Perform steps two through eight, inclusive, in the Lower Control Arm Removal and Installation procedure.
2. Remove the ball joint by pressing the joint from the lower control arm. It may be necessary to remove the ball joint and lower control arm as an assembly and have the ball joint removed in a press if suitable tools are not available.
3. Install a new ball joint and reverse the removal procedure. Tighten the ball stud nut to 85 ft. lbs. Always advance the nut to align the cotter pin hole.

Front Wheel Bearing Adjustment

1. Lift the wheel off the ground by jacking under the lower control arm.
2. Remove the dust cap from the hub.
3. Remove the cotter pin and discard.
4. Snug up the spindle nut to seat the bearings. Then back off the nut 1/4-1/2 turn.
5. Retighten the nut by hand until it is finger-tight.
6. Loosen the nut 1/12 of a turn (no more than 1/6) and line up the hole in the spindle with the nearest slot in the spindle nut, and insert a new cotter pin.
   There should be 0.001-0.005 in. end-play.

NOTE: *Under no circumstances is the final bearing nut adjustment to be even finger-tight.*

7. Replace the dust cover and lower the car.

REAR SUSPENSION

Shock Absorber Replacement

1. Raise the car at the axle housing.
2. Remove the nut, retainer, and grommet or nut, and lockwasher, as equipped, which attach the lower end of the shock absorber to its mounting.
3. Remove the two shock absorber upper attaching screws and remove the shock absorber.
4. Reverse the removal procedures to install. On models through 1977 the upper attaching nut should be tightened to 10-15 ft. lbs. On 1978 and later models the upper nuts should be torqued to 12 ft. lbs.; the lower nut to 65 ft. lbs.

NOTE: *To purge the new shock absorber of air, repeatedly extend it in its normal position and compress it while inverted.*

Leaf Spring Replacement

1. Jack up the car at the axle housing. Make sure you don't crush the exhaust pipe.

2. Support the car at both frame side rails in front of and behind the springs, using axle stands.
3. Remove the nut and lockwasher from the lower shock stud.
4. Move the shock out of the way.
5. Disconnect the right side exhaust system by removing the screw that attaches the exhaust pipe hanger to the rear frame crossmember. Support the exhaust system to prevent damage from bending.
6. Remove the spring anchor plate nuts, then remove the anchor plate and cushion.
7. Jack the axle housing up and remove the upper cushion.
8. Loosen the upper and lower spring shackle nuts.
9. Loosen the spring eye bolt.
10. Remove the eye bolt and carefully lower the spring.
11. Support the spring and remove the lower shackle pin.
12. Remove the spring.
13. To install, reverse the removal procedure. Tighten the front eye bolt to 80-100 ft. lbs., shackle nuts to 75-95 ft. lbs., anchor plate nuts to 35-50 ft. lbs., and lower shock nut to 55-75 ft. lbs.

Coil Spring Replacement

1. Jack up the back of the car and support both sides with stands, on the frame, in front of the rear axle. Disconnect the shock absorbers.

NOTE: *It may be necessary to disconnect the rear brake line in order to obtain sufficient axle drop to remove the spring. If this is done, first depress and secure the brake pedal at least 1 in. from the relaxed position to prevent the master cylinder from draining when the rear brake line is disconnected.*

2. Place a jack under the lower control arms and remove the bolts which hold the upper control arms to the rear axle housing.

NOTE: *The spring can often be removed without disconnecting the lower control arm.*

3. Slowly, and very carefully, let the trailing arms come down until the tension is released from the rear coil springs. Then, take off the coil spring. Note the direction the end of the last coil is pointing. Reinstall the spring in the same position.
4. When starting a new coil spring, make certain that the bottom of the coil is properly inserted into the socket in the frame and into the form plate on the trailing arm.
5. Jack the trailing arms into place and reinstall, but do not tighten the bolts yet.
6. Lower the car to rest on its wheels.
7. Tighten the bolts to 65-85 ft. lbs.

BRAKES

A dual master cylinder is used on all models. Information on the system and brake adjustments, lining replacement, bleeding procedure, master and wheel cylinder overhaul can be found in the Unit Repair Section.

Master Cylinder Removal and Installation

1. Disconnect the brake pipes from the master cylinder and tape the ends of the pipes to prevent entrance of dirt.
2. Disconnect the brake pedal from the master cylinder at the pushrod.

NOTE: *Step 2 is not necessary with power brakes.*

3. Remove the master cylinder-to-firewall or booster retaining bolts. Remove the master cylinder.
4. Reverse the steps to install. Bleed the brakes and check for leaks after installation.

Power Brake Unit Removal and Installation

1. Unbolt the master cylinder from the power unit. Being careful not to kink or bend the brake lines, pull the master cylinder away from the power unit without disconnecting the brake lines.
2. Disconnect and plug the vacuum hose.
3. Disconnect the power brake pushrod from the brake pedal.
4. Unbolt the power brake unit from the firewall.
5. Remove the unit.
6. Mount the unit to the firewall.
7. Install the master cylinder to the power unit and torque the nuts to 25 ft. lbs.
8. Connect the vacuum hose.
9. Connect the power brake pushrod to the brake pedal.

Parking Brake Adjustment

Adjustment of the parking brake is necessary whenever the rear brake cables have been disconnected or the parking brake pedal can be depressed more than sixteen rachet clicks under foot pressure. The car should first be raised on a lift.

1. Make sure that the service brakes are properly adjusted.
2. Depress the parking brake pedal three rachet clicks (2 on 1978 and later models; 6 on 1974-75 station wagons).
3. Loosen the jam nut on the equalizer adjusting nut. On cars through 1977 tighten the adjusting nut until the rear wheels can just be turned rearward by hand but not forward. On 1978 and later cars, tighten the nut until the left rear wheel can be turned backward with two hands, but not forward.
4. Release the rachet one click; the rear wheels should rotate rearward freely and forward with a slight drag.
5. Release the rachet fully; the rear wheels should turn freely in either direction.

NOTE: *Be sure that the parking brake*

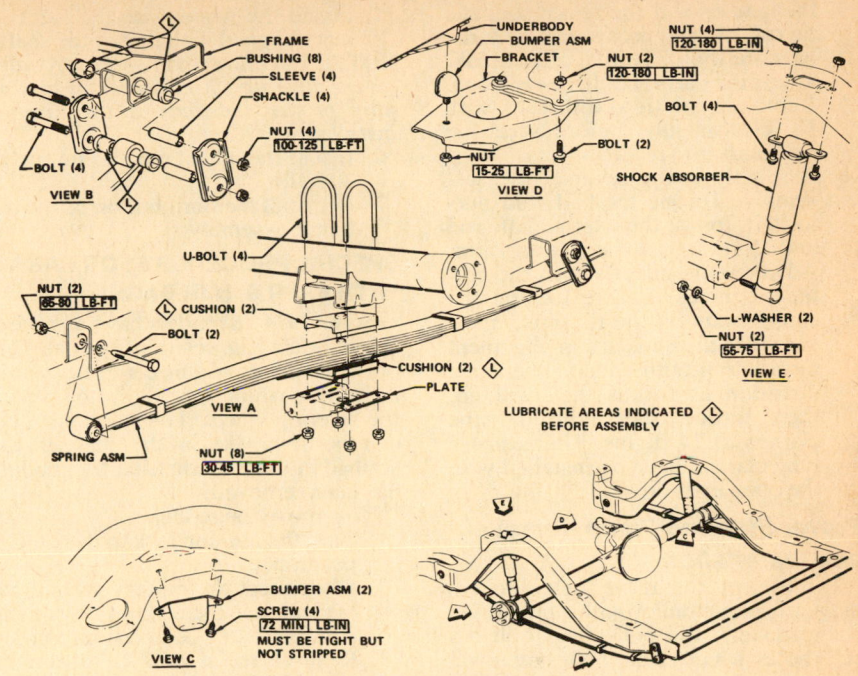

Rear suspension details—Estate Wagon with leaf springs
(© Buick Div., G.M. Corp)

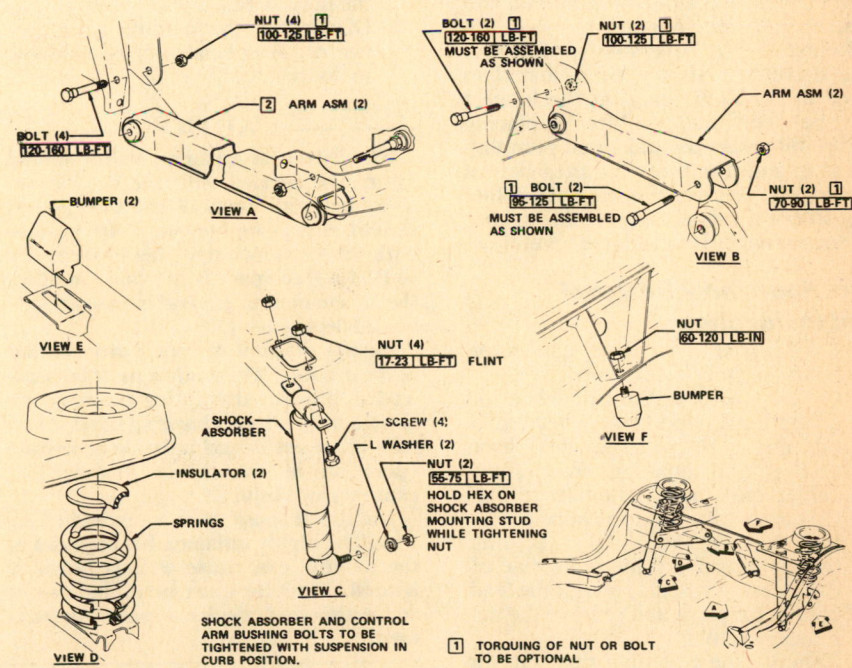

Rear suspension details—typical with coil springs (© Buick Div., G.M. Corp)

does not drag. An overtightened, dragging parking brake on a car with automatic brake adjusters will result in an extremely short life for rear brake linings.

STEERING

Tie Rod End Removal and Installation

NOTE: *If either tie rod end is replaced, front end toe-in will have to be reset.*

1. Raise the car and support it on jackstands.
2. Remove the cotter pins from the castellated nuts and remove the nuts from the ball studs.
3. Remove the outer ball stud with a ball joint remover, then remove the inner ball stud in the same manner.
4. Remove the clamp bolts and unscrew the tie rod end from the adjuster tube. NOTE: Before removal count the number of threads on the tie rod for proper positioning of

the new end. If the removal of the tie rod end requires a turning force of more than 7 ft. lbs. after breakaway, the parts should be replaced.

5. Lubricate the tie rod threads with EP chassis lube before screwing new ends into place.

6. Assembly is the reverse of disassembly. Torque the ball stud nuts to 40 ft. lbs. at the intermediate rod and 35 ft. lbs. at the steering arm. Advance the nuts to align the cotter pin holes. Before locking the clamp bolts on the tie rods, make sure that the ends are in alignment by rotating both ends in the same direction as far as they will go, then torque the adjuster tube clamps to 14 ft. lbs. The adjuster tube clamps must be installed with the open ends down.

Power Steering Pump Removal and Installation

Disconnect the drive belt and remove the pump pulley with a puller. On some models, the pulley has bolt access holes which make pulley removal unnecessary. Disconnect the hoses from the pump and unbolt the pump from the bracket. Use caps or tape to cover the hose connectors, unions, and hose ends to keep out dirt.

Reinstall by reversing procedure. The drive belt should be adjusted to have about 1/2 in. play on the longest run between pulleys. After replacing pump, fill reservoir and bleed pump by idling engine for three minutes before moving the steering wheel. Then rotate the steering wheel slowly throughout its entire range. Recheck the level.

Steering Wheel Removal and Installation

1. Unplug the horn wire connector from the steering column.

2. On cars with a standard wheel or an optional wood-rim wheel, pull off the cap, remove the three screws and bushing spacer, receiver cup, and Belleville spring. On cars with a bar-type horn actuator, remove the screws securing the actuator from the underside of the steering wheel, pull out the lead connector plug, and remove the actuator assembly.

3. Remove the retaining ring. On tilt wheel models, remove the flange and lever retaining bolts and remove the flange and lever. Loosen the steering wheel nut several turns but do not remove it.

4. Apply a steering wheel puller and pull the wheel up to the nut. Now remove the puller, nut and steering wheel.

——— CAUTION ———
Don't pound on the steering wheel in either direction or the collapsible steering column will collapse, requiring replacement.

5. Install the wheel with the location mark aligned with that of the shaft.

NOTE: *Location marks are provided on the steering wheel and shaft to simplify proper indexing at the time of installation.*

6. Install the wheel nut and torque to 30 ft. lbs.

7. Reinstall the horn button or the actuator assembly.

SPECIAL PROCEDURE FOR CARS WITH A.C.R.S. (AIR BAGS)

Some 1974-76 models have an air cushion, or air bag, restraint system. One of the elements of this complex system is an air cushion module in the top of the steering wheel. The steering wheel can be removed in the manner described in this section after the module has been removed.

To remove the module:

1. Turn the ignition lock to the LOCK position.

2. Disconnect the battery ground cable and tape the end to prevent any possibility of a complete circuit.

3. Remove the 4 module-to-steering wheel screws. A special tool is available to do this.

4. Lift up the module and disconnect the horn wire.

5. Disconnect the module wire connector. A special tool is available to do this, too.

——— CAUTION ———
The driver air cushion module should always be carried with the vinyl cover away from all parts of one's body and should always be laid on a flat surface with the vinyl side up. This is necessary so that a free space is provided to allow the air cushion to expand in case of accidental deployment.

Do not attempt to repair any portion of the module. The module must be serviced as a unit. Attempting repairs such as soldering wires, changing covers, etc. may cause accidental inflation or impair operation of the driver module and cause serious injury.

Do not dispose of a module in any way. The highly inflammable material in the module can cause serious burns if ignited. Modules must be exchanged at an authorized dealer's parts department.

To install the module:

6. Hold the module with the emblem in the lower right corner.

7. Loop the air cushion harness clockwise from the 11 O'clock position to the 6 O'clock position.

8. Install the module connector by pushing it onto the column circuit firmly. Check that it is fully seated.

9. Install the horn wire.

10. Position the module, making sure that the wiring is still in place, and install the 4 screws. Torque them to 40 in. lbs.

11. Reconnect the battery ground cable.

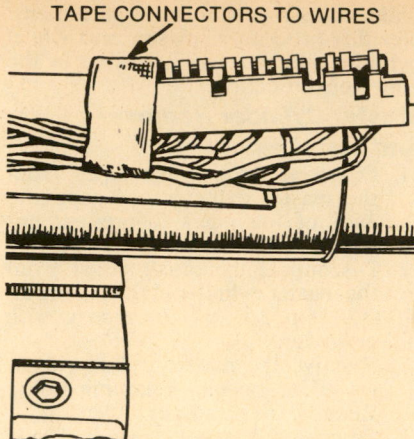

TAPE CONNECTORS TO WIRES

Tape the connector to the wires so that it will slip easily up the steering column

12. Turn the ignition lock to any position other than LOCK and check that the restraint indicator light operates correctly.

Turn Signal Switch Replacement

NOTE: *The steering wheel must always be supported. Use extreme care not to bend the steering column.*

1. Remove the steering wheel.

2. Remove the three cover screws and remove the cover. On 1976 and later models, insert a screwdriver in the slot and pry up on the cover plate to remove it.

3. Depress the lockplate and remove the snap-ring. Remove the lockplate. On tilt and telescoping models remove the cancelling cam at this time.

4. Remove the spring and horn contact signal cancelling cam. Remove the thrust washer from the upper steering shaft.

5. Remove the turn signal lever, depress and remove the hazard warning knob, and tilt column lever, if equipped. On models with column mounted dimmer switch, it may be necessary to remove the dimmer switch to gain access to the turn signal switch.

6. Tape the wiring harness connector to the wires so it will slip easily up the steering column.

7. Remove the three turn signal switch mounting screws. Pull the connector out from the bracket on the column. On 1978 and later models, remove the lower instrument panel trimplate and the toe pan.

8. Pull the switch straight up with the wire protector and wire harness.

9. Reverse the above steps to install.

1974-76 AND LATER WITH A.C.R.S. (AIR BAGS)

Follow the procedure for removing the steering wheel and air cushion module which appears previously under

"Steering Wheel Removal and Installation, Special Procedure for Cars with A.C.R.S."

1. Remove the 3 screws from the retainer and cover. Carefully lift the cover and retainer from the column.
2. Carefully insert a screwdriver blade into the locking tab at the side and lift the slip ring from the column.
3. Now proceed with Steps 3-8 of the Turn Signal Switch Replacement procedure.
4. To replace the slip ring, align the slip ring locating tab with the slot in the bowl and push the slip ring into position. Make sure that all 3 locking tabs are securely positioned.
5. Install the cover and retainer, aligning the cover over the locating tab. Torque the screws to 15 in. lbs.

Ignition Lock Cylinder and/or Switch Replacement

The ignition switch occupies a position on the steering column, just above the gear selector lever. This lock prevents shifting the transmission and locks the steering. The ignition lock cylinder cannot be removed until the steering column is partially disassembled to gain access to the internal lock cylinder retainer. The steering wheel, lock plate, and turn signal switch assembly must be removed first.

STANDARD COLUMN

1. Remove the steering wheel using a puller.
2. Remove the three cover screws and the cover; remove the retainers.
3. Depress the lock plate, then remove the wire snap-ring and lock plate.
4. Slide the upper bearing preload spring and cancelling cam off the shaft.
5. Slide the thrust washer off the shaft, then remove the turn signal lever screw and lever.
6. Push in the four-way flasher switch; remove the knob.
7. Remove the three turn signal switch mounting screws, pull the connector out of its bracket on the column and tape the upper part of the connector and wires together.
8. Pull the turn signal switch out of the column jacket.
9. Insert a small screwdriver into the slot next to the turn signal switch mounting screw boss (right-hand slot), depress the spring latch and remove the key lock.
10. Pull the buzzer switch straight out, depressing the switch clip with pliers. If the ignition switch is to be removed, disconnect the steering column mounting bracket from the lower edge of the instrument panel and lower the steering column. Support the column so that it does not flex.
11. Place the ignition switch in the accessory position by pulling up on the connecting rod until there is a definite stop or detent felt.
12. Remove the two attaching screws and the ignition switch.
13. Assembly is the reverse of the above. However, note the following steps before proceeding with the reassembly.
14. To install the steering lock, hold the lock cylinder sleeve and rotate the knob clockwise against the stop. Insert the cylinder into the cover bore with the key on the cylinder sleeve aligned with the keyway in the housing. Then push the cylinder in until it bottoms. Maintaining a light inward pressure, rotate the knob counterclockwise until the drive section of the cylinder mates with the drive shaft. Push in until the snap ring pops into the groove and the lock cylinder is secured in the cover. Check for free rotation.
15. When installing the ignition switch, be sure the lock cylinder is in the lock position. Put the shift bowl or shroud in the Park position. Then insert the actuator rod into the switch and assemble the switch to the column.

TILT COLUMN

1. Remove the column mounting bracket from the column.
NOTE: *Be careful not to damage the "breakaway" capsules.*
2. Remove the steering wheel using a puller.
3. Remove the turn signal wire protector (lower column).
4. Remove the three column cover screws and cover.
5. Remove the tilt release lever and turn signal switch lever. Push the four-way flasher knob in and remove the knob, and remove the upper shift lever.
6. Depress the lock plate and remove the snap-ring; remove the lock plate.
7. Remove the cancelling cam and spring.
8. Remove the three turn signal switch screws, tape the wires to the wire connector at the upper end and place the shift bowl in Low. Pull the switch straight up and out.
9. Insert a small screwdriver into the slot next to the turn signal switch mounting screw boss (right-hand slot), depress the spring latch and remove the key lock.
10. If the ignition switch is to be replaced, remove the buzzer switch straight out, depressing the switch clip with pliers.
11. Remove the three housing cover screws and the cover.
12. Install the tilt release lever and place the column in full up position.
13. Place a screwdriver in the slot of

the tilt spring retainer, press in about $3/16$ in. and turn counterclockwise. Remove the spring and guide.
NOTE: *The spring is very strong—be careful.*
14. Place the column in the neutral position, push in on the upper steering shaft, remove the inner race seat and race.
15. Remove the upper flange pinch bolt, place the ignition switch in the accessory position, remove the two switch mounting screws and the switch.
NOTE: *The neutral start switch can be removed at this time, if necessary.*
16. Assembly is the reverse of the above. However, note the following steps before proceeding with the reassembly.
17. To install the steering lock, hold the lock cylinder sleeve and rotate the knob clockwise against the stop. Insert the cylinder into the cover bore with the key on the cylinder sleeve aligned with the keyway in the housing. Then push the cylinder in until it bottoms. Maintaining a light inward pressure, rotate the knob counterclockwise until the drive section of the cylinder mates with the drive shaft. Push in until the snap ring pops into the groove and the lock cylinder is secured in the cover. Check for free rotation.
18. When installing the ignition switch, be sure the lock cylinder is in the lock position. Put the shift bowl or shroud in the park position. Make sure the ignition switch is in the lock position. Then insert the actuator rod into the switch and assemble the switch to the column.

INSTRUMENT PANEL

Speedometer Cable Replacement

The speedometer cable is attached to the rear of the speedometer by a knurled nut or a spring clip on the cable casing. To remove the casing from the speedometer, unscrew the knurled nut or release the clip and pull the cable rearward and down. The cable can be serviced or replaced, as needed, by pulling the cable from the casing. If the core is broken, raise the car and support it on jackstands. Disconnect the cable from the transmission, remove the snap ring and gear, and pull the core from the cable.
NOTE: *On models equipped with air bags, do not attempt to perform any service on the instrument panel components, until you turn the ignition switch to the lock position, disconnect the negative battery cable and tape the end of the cable to avoid any accidental grounding.*

Buick

Light Switch Replacement
1. Disconnect the battery negative cable.
2. For 1975-76, remove the left side trim panel by moving the steering column rubber ring up and prying the trim panel off; then remove the three screws and lift the switch out of the instrument panel. Disconnect the terminal connector.
3. Pull the switch knob to the last notch and depress the spring loaded latch button on top of the switch, while pulling the knob and rod out of the switch.
4. Remove the escutcheon and the retaining nut. Remove the switch from the cluster.

NOTE: *Remove the left trim plate on 1973 and later models.*
5. Disconnect the multiple connector.
6. Install in the reverse of above.

WINDSHIELD WIPERS

Wiper Blade Replacement
The windshield wiper blades are attached to a pin on the side of the wiper arms. To disengage the blade from the pin, insert a tool into the slot on the top of the wiper blade, near the pin. Depress the spring and remove the blade from the arm.

Motor Removal and Installation
1. Raise the hood and remove the cowl screen.
2. Loosen the transmission drive link-to-crankarm attaching nuts through the cowl screen opening.
3. Remove the transmission drive link(s) from the motor crank arm.
4. Disconnect the wiring and washer hoses.
5. Remove the motor attaching screws.
6. Remove the motor while guiding the crank arm through the hole.
7. Install the wiper motor in the reverse order of removal. The motor must be in the Park position when assembling the crank arm to the transmission drive link(s).

RADIO

Always disconnect the battery ground cable before working on any part of the instrument panel.
NOTE: *The radio antenna trimmer screw is located above the station selector shaft. The knob most be removed to gain access to the trimmer screw. To trim the AM radio, extend the antenna fully, tune to a weak station around 1400 on the dial. Turn the volume up and adjust the trim screw until maximum volume is achieved.*

Removal and Installation
THROUGH 1976
1. Remove the knobs and escutcheons from the radio. If equipped with Trip-Set and/or Speed-Alert, remove the cone-shaped knobs.
2. Remove the face plate by pulling outward. Disconnect the terminal connector before completely removing the face plate, if equipped with Trip-Set/Speed-Alert.
3. Remove the two hex nuts from the control shafts.
4. Remove the ash tray and frame.
5. Disconnect the two connectors behind the dash and unplug the antenna.
6. Unscrew the support bracket nuts and remove the radio to the rear and downward.
7. Install by reversing the removal procedure.

1977 AND LATER
1. Disconnect the battery ground cable.
2. Remove the ashtray and bracket.
3. Pull off the radio knobs and trim washers.
4. Remove the lower left air duct.
5. Remove the two retaining nuts from the control shafts.
6. Unplug the power lead, speaker wire, and antenna lead.
7. Remove the rear radio mounting nut.
8. Reverse the procedure for installation.

1974-76 WITH A.C.R.S. (AIR BAGS)
1. Turn the ignition lock to the LOCK position.
2. Disconnect the battery ground cable and tape its end thoroughly to prevent any possibility of a short circuit.
3. Remove both lower instrument panel cover trim plates after prying them out.
4. Disconnect the parking brake release cable and remove the lower left instrument panel cover assembly by removing the 8 retaining screws.
5. Remove:
   a. 2 horizontal screws below the instrument panel
   b. 4 vertical screws on the upper horizontal instrument panel surface.
   c. 2 screws from the outside of the glove box door hinge.
   d. 1 screw from the right-side of the instrument panel cover.
6. Disconnect the radio, speakers, convector (remote unit) connectors, and antenna lead cable from the radio.
7. Release the 4 clips behind the instrument panel by grasping the tongue of the far right-side clip, squeezing, and pulling forward.
8. Remove the radio knobs and escutcheons from the shafts.
9. Carefully pull the trim plate off the instrument panel housing.
10. Remove the retaining nuts from the shafts.
11. Unscrew and remove the power antenna relay.
12. Loosen the nut on the left radio support. Remove the right support nut.
13. Lower the radio from beneath the instrument panel.
14. If the car has a radio/tape unit, remove the two convector (remote unit) mounting screws and remove the convector from the right-side of the instrument panel housing support.
15. Reverse all these steps on installation.

HEATER

NOTE: *Vacuum hose routing clips, electrical wires and relays, weather seals, and other items, may be attached to the heater housing, and will have to be relocated during removal and replacement of the heater core and/or the blower motor.*

Blower Motor Removal and Installation
ALL CARS WITH OR WITHOUT A/C 1972-77
1. Support the hood and loosen the hood hinge from the extension and plate assembly.
2. Remove the extension and plate assembly.
NOTE: *Steps 1 and 2 are only necessary on the 1974-76 Riveria.*
3. Disconnect the blower motor wire.
4. Remove the blower motor attaching screws and the motor.

ALL CARS WITH OR WITHOUT A/C 1978-79
1. Disconnect the blower motor wires.
2. On A/C equipped cars, disconnect the cooling tube from the case.
3. Remove the motor attaching screws and lift the motor from the case.
4. Installation is the reverse of removal. Replace any damaged sealer.

Heater Core Removal and Installation w/o A/C
THROUGH 1976
1. Drain the radiator and disconnect the heater inlet and outlet hoses at the dash.
2. Disconnect the control wires from the defroster door and vacuum hose diverter door actuator diaphragm and control cable from the temperature door lever.
3. Remove the 4 nuts securing the heater assembly to the firewall.
4. Remove the screw securing the defroster outlet tab to the heater assembly.

5. Remove the heater from the car.
6. Reverse the above steps to install.

1977 AND LATER

1. Drain the radiator.
2. Disconnect the heater core inlet and outlet hoses at the firewall.
3. Detach the electrical connections.
4. Remove the screws holding the front case to the heater module assembly.
5. Remove the front case, then the heater core.
6. On installation, reseal the case.

Heater Core Removal and Installation with A/C

THROUGH 1976

NOTE: *This procedure does not apply to those models with the A.C.R.S. (air bag) system. For those models with air bags, it is advisable to take the car to a dealer for proper servicing.*

1. Drain the radiator and disconnect the hoses from the core.
2. Disconnect the wires from the defroster door, diverter door and temperature door.
3. Remove the four nuts securing the core assembly to the dash.
4. Remove the screw securing the defroster outlet tab to the heater assembly.
5. Remove the core assembly.
6. Reverse the above steps to install.

1977 AND LATER

1. Disconnect the battery ground cable.

2. Drain the coolant. Disconnect the heater hoses at the firewall.
3. Disconnect the electrical connections. Remove the diagnostic connector.
4. Remove the thermostatic switch from the heater/air conditioning module cover.
5. Remove the weather seal on top of the module cover.
6. Remove the cowl screen and windshield washer nozzle.
7. Remove the screws and take off the module cover.
8. Remove the core retaining clip, twist the heater core, and pull it up and out.
9. On installation, reseal the module cover.

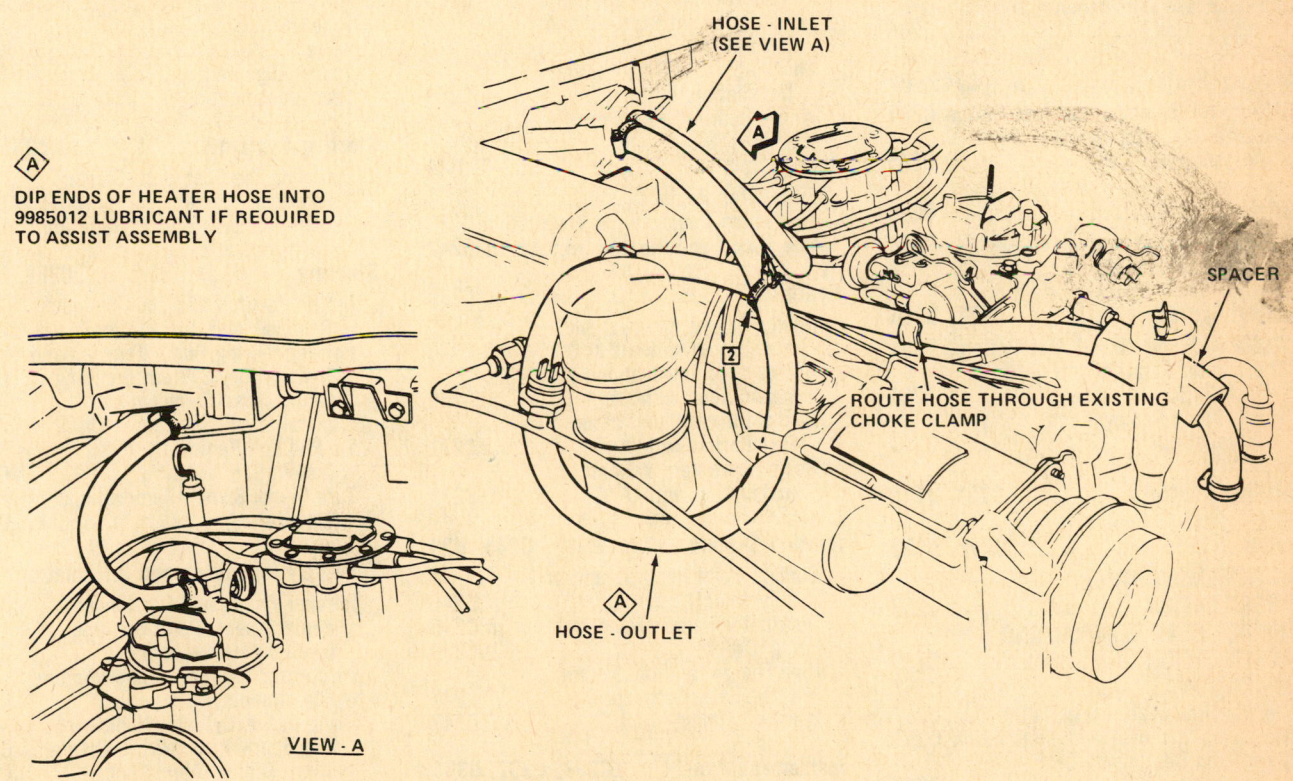

Ⓐ
DIP ENDS OF HEATER HOSE INTO 9985012 LUBRICANT IF REQUIRED TO ASSIST ASSEMBLY

HOSE - INLET
(SEE VIEW A)

Ⓐ

SPACER

ROUTE HOSE THROUGH EXISTING CHOKE CLAMP

HOSE - OUTLET
Ⓐ

VIEW - A

Heater hose installation, vehicles without A/C (© Buick Div., G.M. Corp.)

Buick Apollo · Century · Gran Sport · Regal · Skyhawk · Skylark

Index

YEAR IDENTIFICATION

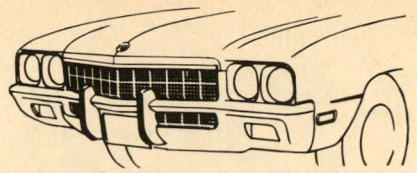

1972 Skylark

1972 Buick Gran Sport

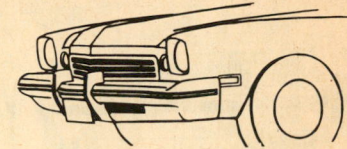

1973 Buick Century

1973 Buick Regal

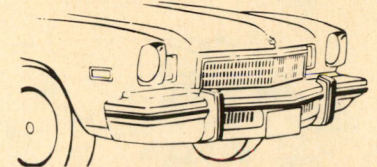

1974 Buick Regal

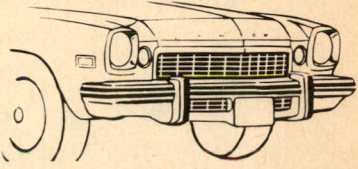

1974 Buick Century

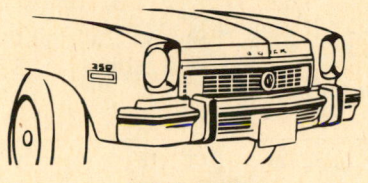

1974 Apollo

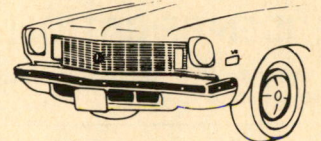

1975 Century

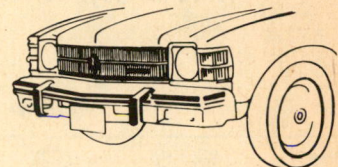

1975 Skylark, Apollo

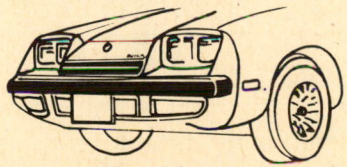

1975 Skyhawk

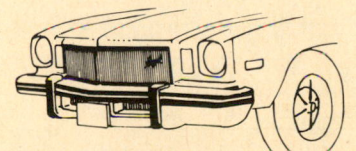

1975 Regal

1976 Century

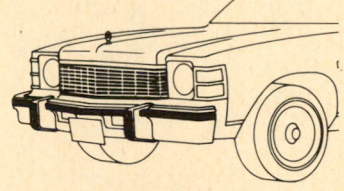

1976 Skylark, Apollo

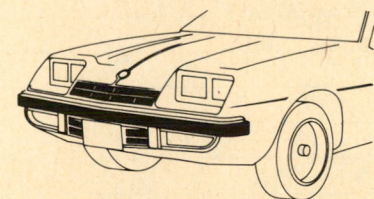

1976 Skyhawk

1976 Century Special

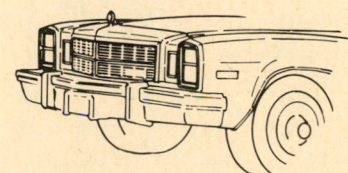

1977 Century

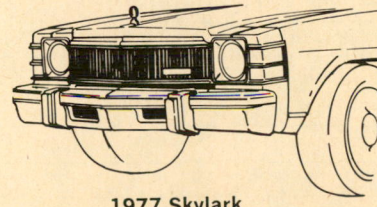

1977 Skylark

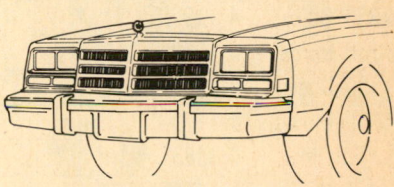

1977 Century Special

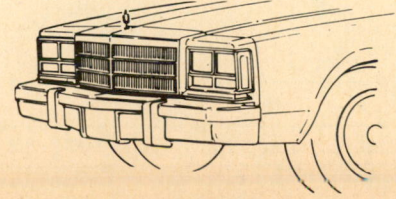

1977 Regal

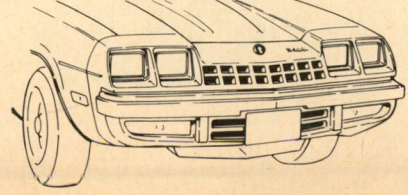

1977 Skyhawk

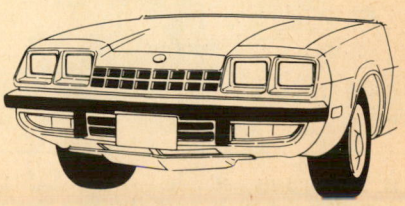

1978 Skyhawk

YEAR IDENTIFICATION

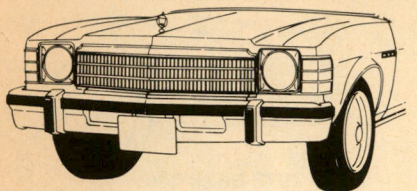

1978 Skylark

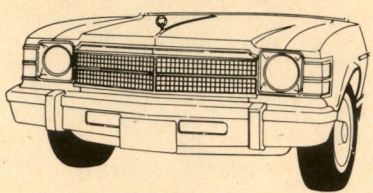

1978 Buick Century

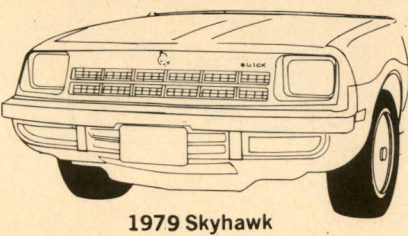

1978 Buick Regal

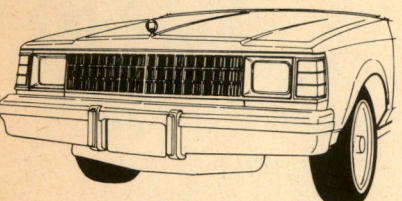

1979 Century

1979 Skylark

1979 Skyhawk

ENGINE IDENTIFICATION CODES

* Skyhawk California only
DE: dual exhaust

The VIN engine code is the fifth digit of the VIN number found on a plate on the upper left side of the instrument panel pad, visible through the windshield.

Disp.	Bbl	Hp	'72	'73	'74	'75	'76	'77	'78	'79
6-196 Buick	2	90							C	C
6-231 Buick	2	105				C	C	C	A	A
6-231 Buick	2	150							G	
6-231 Buick	2	100*							2	
6-231 Buick	4	165							3	3
6-250 Chev.	1	100			D	D				
8-260 Olds.	2	110				F	F			
8-301 Pont.	2	135						Y		Y
8-301 Pont.	4	160								W
8-305 Chev.	2	145						U	U	U
8-305 Chev.	4	155							H	H
8-350 Buick	2	135	H	H	H		H	H		
8-350 Buick	2	150DE		G						
8-350 Buick	4	155				J	J	J		
8-350 Buick	4	165DE			G					
8-350 Buick	4	175	J	J	J					
8-350 Buick	4	190DE	K	K	K					
8-350 Buick	4	260	B							
8-350 Chev.	4	170						L	L	L
8-350 Olds.	4	170						R		
8-403 Olds.	4	185						K		
8-455 Buick	2	190DE			R					
8-455 Buick	4	225	T	T						
8-455 Buick	4	230DE			U					
8-455 Buick	4	255DE			W					
8-455 Buick	4	260DE	V	V						
8-455 Buick	4	270DE	W	W						

■ Horsepower and torque are SAE net figures. They are measured at the rear of the transmission with all accessories installed and operating. Since the figures vary when a given engine is installed in different models, some are representative rather than exact.

GENERAL ENGINE SPECIFICATIONS

Year	Engine Displacement (Cu. In.)	Carburetor Type	Horsepower @ rpm ■	Torque @ rpm (ft lbs) ■	Bore x Stroke (in.)	Compression Ratio	Oil Pressure @ 2400 rpm
'72	8-350	2 bbl	155 @ 3800	270 @ 2400	3.800 x 3.850	8.5:1	37②
	8-350	4 bbl	180 @ 3800	275 @ 2400	3.800 x 3.850	8.5:1	37②
	8-350 DE	4 bbl	195 @ 4000	290 @ 2800	3.800 x 3.850	8.5:1	37②
	8-455	4 bbl	225 @ 4000	360 @ 2600	4.3125 x 3.900	8.5:1	40
	8-455 Stage 1	4 bbl	270 @ 4400	390 @ 3000	4.3125 x 3.900	8.5:1	40
'73	8-350	2 bbl	150 @ 3800	265 @ 2400	3.800 x 3.850	8.5:1	37
	8-350	4 bbl	175 @ 3800	270 @ 2400	3.800 x 3.850	8.5:1	37
	8-350	4 bbl	190 @ 4000	285 @ 2800	3.800 x 3.850	8.5:1	37
	8-455	4 bbl	225 @ 4000	360 @ 2600	4.3125 x 3.900	8.5:1	37
	8-455	4 bbl	270 @ 4400	390 @ 3000	4.3125 x 3.900	8.5:1	37
'74	6-250	1 bbl	100 @ 3600	175 @ 1600	3.875 x 3.530	8.3:1	40④
	8-350	2 bbl	150 @ 3600	270 @ 2000	3.800 x 3.850	8.5:1	37
	8-350	4 bbl	175 @ 3800	260 @ 2000	3.800 x 3.850	8.5:1	37
	8-455 DE	2 bbl	190 @ 3600	370 @ 2000	4.3125 x 3.900	8.5:1	40
	8-455 DE	4 bbl	230 @ 3300	355 @ 2200	4.3125 x 3.900	8.5:1	40
	8-455 DE③	4 bbl	255 @ 4400	370 @ 2800	4.3125 x 3.900	8.5:1	40
'75	6-231	2 bbl	110 @ 4000	175 @ 2000	3.800 x 3.400	8.0:1	37
	6-250	1 bbl	105 @ 3800	185 @ 1200	3.875 x 3.530	8.25:1	36-41④
	8-260	2 bbl	110 @ 3400	210 @ 1600	3.550 x 3.385	8.5:1	30-45
	8-350	2 bbl	145 @ 3200	270 @ 2000	3.800 x 3.850	8.1:1	37
	8-350	4 bbl	165 @ 3800	260 @ 2200	3.800 x 3.850	8.0:1	37
'76	6-231	2 bbl	105 @ 3400	185 @ 2000	3.800 x 3.400	8.0:1	37
	8-260	2 bbl	110 @ 3400	210 @ 1600	3.550 x 3.385	8.5:1	30-45④
	8-350	2 bbl	140 @ 3400	280 @ 1600	3.800 x 3.850	8.0:1	37
	8-350	4 bbl	155 @ 3400	280 @ 1800	3.800 x 3.850	8.0:1	37
'77	6-231 Buick	2 bbl	105 @ 3200	185 @ 2000	3.800 x 3.400	8.0:1	37
	8-301 Pont.	2 bbl	135 @ 4000	250 @ 1600	4.000 x 3.000	8.2:1	34
	8-305 Chev.	2 bbl	140 @ 3800	245 @ 2000	3.736 x 3.480	8.5:1	40
	8-350 Buick	2 bbl	140 @ 3200	280 @ 1400	4.057 x 3.385	8.0:1	35
	8-350 Buick	4 bbl	155 @ 3400	275 @ 1800	4.057 x 3.385	8.0:1	35
	8-350 Olds.	4 bbl	170 @ 3800	275 @ 2400	4.057 x 3.385	8.0:1	30-40
	8-350 Chev.	4 bbl	170 @ 3800	270 @ 2400	4.000 x 3.480	8.5:1	40
	8-403 Olds.	4 bbl	185 @ 3600	315 @ 2400	4.351 x 3.385	7.9:1	34
'78	6-196 Buick	2 bbl	90 @ 3600	165 @ 2000	3.500 x 3.400	8.0:1	37
	6-231 Buick	2 bbl	105 @ 3400	185 @ 2000	3.800 x 3.400	8.0:1	37
	6-231 Buick Turbo	2 bbl	150 @ 3800	245 @ 2400	3.800 x 3.400	8.0:1	37
	6-231 Buick Turbo	4 bbl	165 @ 4000	285 @ 2800	3.800 x 3.400	8.0:1	37
	8-305 Chev.	2 bbl	145 @ 3800	245 @ 2400	3.736 x 3.480	8.5:1	34
	8-305 Chev.	4 bbl	160 @ 4000	285 @ 2400	3.736 x 3.480	8.5:1	34
	8-350 Chev.	4 bbl	160 @ 3800	260 @ 2400	4.000 x 3.480	8.5:1	34
'79	6-196 Buick	2 bbl	105 @ 3800	160 @ 2000	3.500 x 3.400	8.0:1	37
	6-231 Buick	2 bbl	115 @ 3800	190 @ 2000	3.800 x 3.400	8.0:1	37
	6-231 Buick Turbo	4 bbl	165 @ 4000	285 @ 2800	3.800 x 3.400	8.0:1	37
	8-301 Pont.	2 bbl	140 @ 3600	235 @ 2000	4.000 x 3.000	8.2:1	34
	8-301 Pont.	4 bbl	150 @ 3800	255 @ 2400	4.000 x 3.000	8.2:1	34
	8-305 Chev.	2 bbl	140 @ 3800	270 @ 2400	3.736 x 3.480	8.5:1	40

GENERAL ENGINE SPECIFICATIONS

Year	Engine Displacement (Cu. In.)	Carburetor Type	Horsepower @ rpm ■	Torque @ rpm (ft lbs) ■	Bore x Stroke (in.)	Compression Ratio	Oil Pressure @ 2400 rpm
	8-305 Chev.	4 bbl	160 @ 4000	235 @ 2400	3.736 x 3.480	8.5:1	40
	8-350 Chev.	4 bbl	170 @ 3800	260 @ 2400	4.000 x 3.480	8.5:1	40

■ Horsepower and torque are SAE net figures. They are measured at the rear of the transmission with all accessories installed and operating. Since the figures vary when a given engine is installed in different models, some are representative rather than exact.

① Not used
② Oil pressure at 2600 rpm
③ Stage I Gran Sport
④ Oil pressure at 2000 rpm
DE Dual exhaust

TUNE-UP SPECIFICATIONS

When analyzing compression test results, look for uniformity among cylinders rather than specific pressures.

	ENGINE		SPARK PLUGS		DISTRIBUTOR		IGNITION TIMING (deg) ▲		VALVES	Fuel Pump	IDLE SPEED (rpm) ▲	
Year	No. Cyl Displacement (cu in.)	hp	Orig. Type	Gap (in.)	Point Dwell (deg)	Point Gap (in.)	Man Trans ●	Auto Trans	Intake Opens ■ (deg) ●	Pressure (psi)	Man Trans ● *	Auto Trans
'72	8-350	155	R-45TS	.040	30	.016	4B	4B	24	4¼-5¾	800/600	650/500
	8-350	180	R-45TS	.040	30	.016	4B	4B	24	4¼-5¾	800/600	650/500
	8-350	195	R-45TS	.040	30	.016	4B	4B	24	4¼-5¾	800/600	650/500
	8-455	225	R-45TS	.040	30	.016	4B	4B	24(14)	4¼-5¾	900/600	650/500
	8-455 Stage 1	360	R-45TS	.040	30	.016	8B	10B	24(14)	4¼-5¾	900/600	650/500
'73	8-350	150	R-45TS	.040	30	.016	4B	4B	24	4¼-5¾	800/600	650/500
	8-350	175	R-45TS	.040	30	.016	4B	4B	24	4¼-5¾	800/600	650/500
	8-350	190	R-45TS	.040	30	.016	4B	4B	24	4¼-5¾	800/600	650/500
	8-455	225	R-45TS	.040	30	.016	4B	4B	24	4¼-5¾	900/600	650/500
	8-455 Stage 1	270	R-45TS	.040	30	.016	8B	10B	24	4¼-5¾	900/600	650/500
'74	6-250	All	R-46T	.035	31-34	.019	8B	6B	16	4-5	950/450	600/450
	8-350	All	R-45TS	.040	30	.016	—	4B	19(25)	4¼-5¾	—	650/500
	8-455	All	R-45TS	.040	30	.016	—	4B	10	4¼-5¾	—	650/500
	8-455 Stage 1	255	R-45TS	.040	30	.016	—	10B	10	4¼-5¾	—	650/500
'75	6-231	175	R-44SX	.060	Electronic		12B	12B	17	3-4½④	800/600	700
	6-250	100	R-46TX	.060	Electronic		10B	10B	14	4-5	850	550
	8-260	110	R-465X	.060	Electronic		—	18B(14B)	22	4¼-5¾	—	650
	8-350	All	R-45TSX	.060	Electronic		12B	12B	19	4¼-5¾	—	600
'76	6-231	105	R-44SX	.060③	Electronic		12B	12B	17	3-4½④	800/600	600
	8-260	110	R-46SX	.080	Electronic		18B(14B) @ 1100	18B(14B) @ 1100	22	4½-5¾	—	650/550 (650/600)
	8-350	All	R-45TSX	.060	Electronic		12B	12B	13½	5-6½	—	600
'77	6-231 Buick	105	R46TSX	.060③	Electronic		12B	12B	17	4¼-5¾	800/500	600
	8-301 Pont.	135	R46TS	.060	Electronic		16B	12B	27	7-8½	875/750	650/550
	8-305 Chev.	145	R45TS	.045	Electronic		8B	8B	28	7½-9	700	650/500
	8-350 Chev.	155	R45TS	.045	Electronic		8B	8B(6B)①	28	7½-9	700	650/500
	8-350 Buick	155	R46TS	.045⑤	Electronic		12B	12B	13	7½-9	600	600
	8-350 Olds.	170	R46SZ	.060	Electronic		—	20B @ 1100	16	5½-6½	—	650/550
	8-403 Olds.	180	R46SZ	.060	Electronic		—	24B(20B) @ 1100②	16	6-7½	—	650/550
'78	6-196 Buick	90	R46TSX	.060	Electronic		15B	15B	18	4.5-5.5	600	600
	6-231 Buick	105	R46TSX	.060	Electronic		15B	15B	17	4.5-5.5	600	600

TUNE-UP SPECIFICATIONS

When analyzing compression test results, look for uniformity among cylinders rather than specific pressures.

Year	No. Cyl Displacement (cu in.)	hp	SPARK PLUGS Orig. Type	Gap (in.)	DISTRIBUTOR Point Dwell (deg)	Point Gap (in.)	IGNITION TIMING (deg) ▲ Man Trans ●	Auto Trans	VALVES Intake Opens ■ (deg) ●	Fuel Pump Pressure (psi)	IDLE SPEED (rpm) ▲ Man Trans ● *	Auto Trans
	6-231 Buick Turbo		R44TSX	.060	Electronic		—	15B	17	4.5-5.5	—	650
	8-305 Chev.	145	R45TS	.045	Electronic		—	⑥	28	7.5-9	—	500⑦
	8-305 Chev.	160	R45TS	.045	Electronic		—	4B	28	7.5-9	—	650
	8-350 Chev.	160	R45TS	.045	Electronic		—	8B	28	7.5-9	—	500(600)
'79	6-196 Buick	105	R46TSX	.060	Electronic		15B	15B	16	4.25-5.75	800	600
	6-231 Buick	115	R46TSX	.060	Electronic		15B	15B	16	4.25-5.75	800	600
	6-231 Buick Turbo		R44TSX	.060	Electronic		—	15B	16	4.25-5.75	—	600
	8-301 Pont.	140	R46TSX	.060	Electronic		—	12B	27	7-8.5	—	550
	8-301 Pont.	160	R45TSX	.060	Electronic		—	12B	27	7-8.5	—	550
	8-305 Chev.	140	R45TS	.045	Electronic		—	⑥	28	7.5-9	—	500⑦
	8-305 Chev.	160	R45TS	.045	Electronic		—	4B	28	7.5-9	—	650
	8-350 Chev.	160	R45TS	.045	Electronic		—	8B	28	7.5-9	—	500(600)

NOTE: The underhood specifications sticker often reflects tune-up specification changes made in production. Sticker figures must be used if they disagree with those in this chart.

▲ See text for procedure
● Figure in parentheses indicates California engine
■ All figures Before Top Dead Center
* Lower figure indicates idle speed with solenoid disconnected
① 6B for high altitude
② 20B for high altitude

③ .040 with R46TS
④ 4¼-5¾ on mechanical pumps
⑤ .060 with R46TSX
⑥ 49 states: 4B
   Calif.: 6B
   High Altitude: 8B
⑦ High Altitude: 600
B Before Top Dead Center
TDC Top Dead Center

NOTE: Most 1979 GM carburetors have idle mixture screws concealed by staked-in plugs. These are not meant to be removed, except at carburetor overhaul.

FIRING ORDER

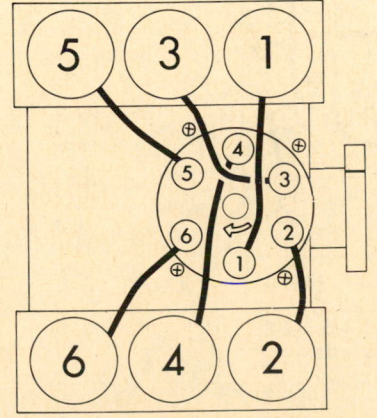

GM (Buick) 231 V6
Engine firing order: 1-6-5-4-3-2
Distributor rotation: clockwise

V6 harmonic balancers have two timing marks: one is 1/8 in. wide, and one is 1/16 in. wide. Use the 1/16 in. mark for timing with a hand held light. The 1/8 in. mark is used only with a magnetic timing pick-up probe.

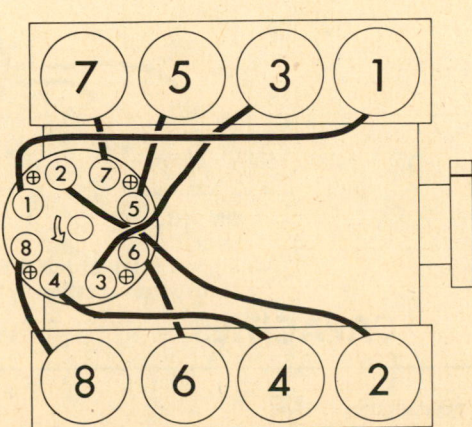

GM (Oldsmobile) 260 V8
Engine firing order: 1-8-4-3-6-5-7-2
Distributor rotation: counterclockwise

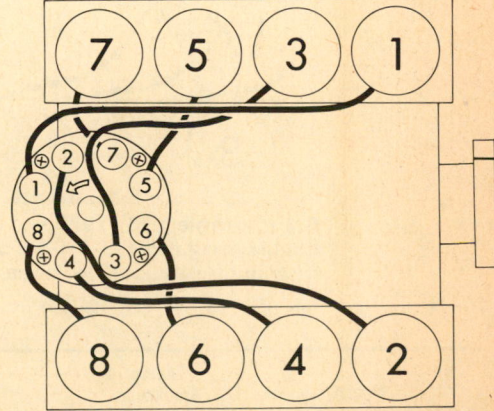

GM (Pontiac) 301, 350, 400, 455 V8
(1975 and later)
Engine firing order: 1-8-4-3-6-5-7-2
Distributor rotation: counterclockwise

FIRING ORDER

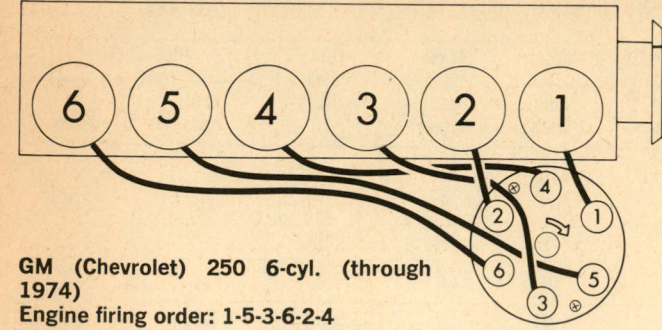

GM (Chevrolet) 250 6-cyl. (through 1974)
Engine firing order: 1-5-3-6-2-4
Distributor rotation: clockwise

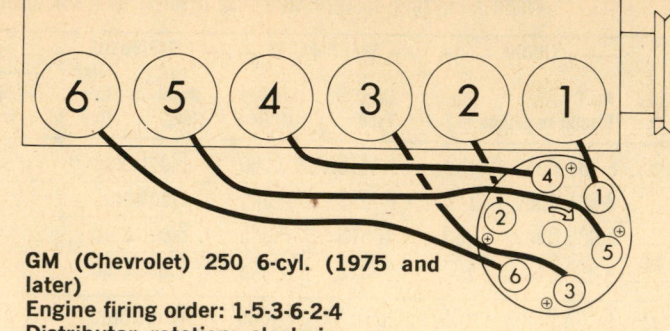

GM (Chevrolet) 250 6-cyl. (1975 and later)
Engine firing order: 1-5-3-6-2-4
Distributor rotation: clockwise

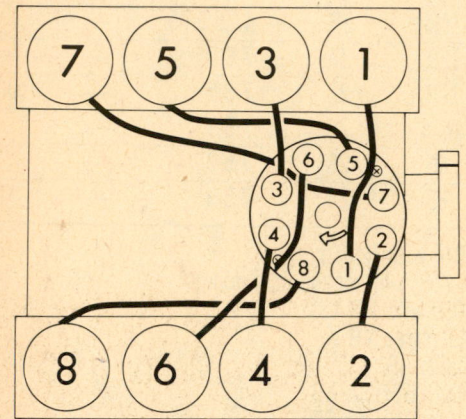

GM (Buick) 350, 455 V8 (through 1974)
Engine firing order: 1-8-4-3-6-5-7-2
Distributor rotation: clockwise

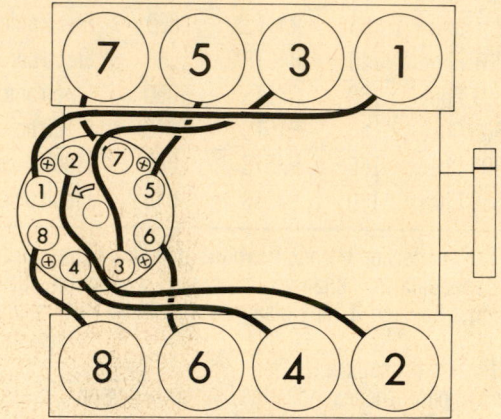

GM (Oldsmobile) 350, 403 V8
Engine firing order: 1-8-4-3-6-5-7-2
Distributor rotation: counterclockwise

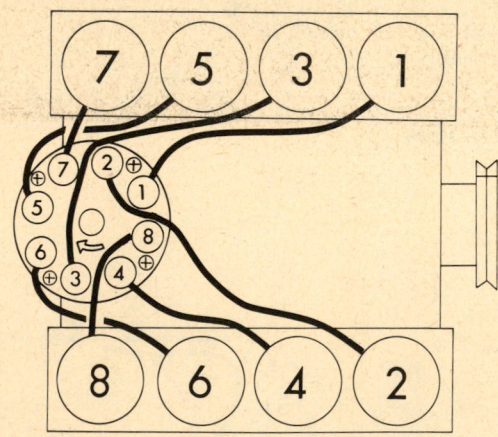

GM (Chevrolet) V8 (1975 and later)
Engine firing order: 1-8-4-3-6-5-7-2
Distributor rotation: clockwise

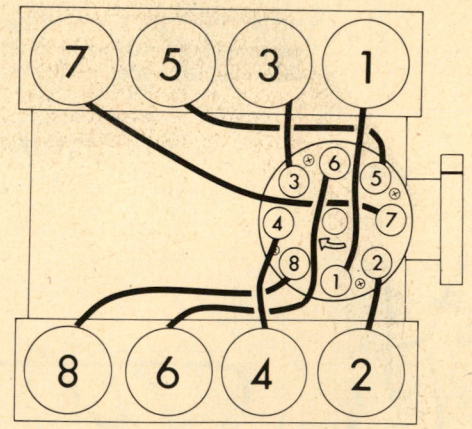

GM (Buick) 350, 455 V8 (1975 and later)
Engine firing order: 1-8-4-3-6-5-7-2
Distributor rotation: clockwise

CAPACITIES

Year	ENGINE No. Cyl. Displacement (cu. in.)	Engine Crankcase Add 1 Qt For New Filter	TRANSMISSION Pts To Refill After Draining			Drive Axle (pts)	Gasoline Tank (gals)	COOLING SYSTEM (qts)		
			Manual		Automatic •			With Heater	With A/C	With Heavy Duty
			3-Speed	4/5-Speed						
'72	8-350	4	3.4	—	6	4.25	20①	16.5	16.9	—
	8-350 Gran Sport	4	3.4	3	6	4.25	20	16.2	16.6	
	8-455	4		3	7	5.5	20	19.2	19.7	—

CAPACITIES

Year	ENGINE No. Cyl. Displacement (cu. in.)	Engine Crankcase Add 1 Qt For New Filter	TRANSMISSION Pts To Refill After Draining Manual 3-Speed	Manual 4/5-Speed	Automatic •	Drive Axle (pts)	Gasoline Tank (gals)	COOLING SYSTEM (qts) With Heater	With A/C	With Heavy Duty
'73	8-350	4	3.4	——	6	4.25	22	16.5	16.9	——
	8-350	4	3.4	3.4	6	4.25	22	16.5	16.9	——
	8-455	4	——	3.4	6	4.25	22	16.2	16.6	——
'74	6-250	4	3.5	——	6	4.25	21	14.0	②	——
	8-350 Apollo	4	——	——	6	4.25	21	18.9	19.3	——
	8-350	4	——	——	6	4.25	22	16.5	16.9	——
	8-455	4	——	——	6	4.25	22	16.2	16.6	——
'75-'76	6-231 Skyhawk	4	——	3.5③	6	2.8	18.5	13.35	14.19	——
	6-231 Skylark	4	3.5	——	6	4.25	21	16.6	16.7	——
	6-231 Other	4	3.5	——	6	4.25	22	15.5	15.4	——
	6-250	4	3.5	——	6	4.25	21	16.92	17.0	——
	8-260	4	——	——	6	4.25	21	22.4	22.9	——
	8-350, Apollo/Skylark	4	——	——	6	4.25	21	18.9	19.3	——
	8-350, Other	4	——	——	6	4.25	22	17.9	18.5	——
'77	6-231 Skyhawk	4	——	3.1/3.5	6	2.8	18.5	12.0	12.0	——
	6-231 Skylark	4	3.1	——	6	2.8	21	12.7	12.8	——
	6-231 Other	4	3.1	——	6	4.25	22	12.9	12.7	——
	8-301 Pont.	5.5	——	——	6	4.25	22	18.6	19.2	——
	8-305 Chev.	4	——	——	6	4.25	22	14.9	16.4	——
	8-350 Buick	4	——	——	6	4.25	22	14.9	16.4	——
	8-350 Olds.	4	——	——	6	4.25	22	15.0	15.6	——
	8-350 Chev.	4	——	——	6	4.25	22	14.8	16.9	——
	8-403 Olds.	4	——	——	6	4.25	22	16.4	18.5	——
'78	6-196 Buick	4	3.5	——	3.0	4.25	18.1	13.1	13.2	13.1
	6-231 Buick④	4	3.5	3.5	⑤	4.25	18.1	13.1	13.2	13.1
	6-231 Buick⑥	4	3.5	——	3.0	4.25	20.8	13.6	13.7	13.5
	6-231 Buick⑦	4	——	3.5③	3.0	3.75	18.5	⑧	⑧	⑧
	8-305 Chev.④	4	——	——	⑤	4.25	18.1	19.2	18.9	19.6
	8-305 Chev.⑥	4	——	——	⑤	4.25	20.8	15.9	16.3	16.9
	8-350 Chev.④	4	——	——	3.0	4.25	18.1	19.2	18.9	19.6
	8-350 Chev.⑥	4	——	——	3.0	4.25	20.8	16.1	16.9	16.9
'79	6-196 Buick	4	3.12	——	⑤	3.5	18.1	13.3	13.34	13.34
	6-231 Buick⑦	4	——	3.5③	⑤	⑨	18.5	12.32	12.29	12.19
	6-231 Buick⑥	4	3.12	——	6.0	⑨	21.0	13.74	13.8	——
	6-231 Buick④	4	——	3.5③	⑤	⑨	18.1	13.3	13.34	13.34
	8-301 Pont.	5	——	——	⑤	⑨	18.1	20.2	20.1	20.8
	8-305 Chev.⑥	4	——	——	⑤	⑨	21.0	15.9	16.3	16.9
	8-305 Chev.④	4	——	——	⑤	⑨	18.1	19.2	18.9	19.6
	8-350 Chev.④	4	——	——	⑤	⑨	18.1	19.2	18.9	19.6
	8-350 Chev.⑥	4	——	——	⑤	⑨	21.0	16.1	16.9	16.9

• Specifications do not include torque converter
① Sportwagon—23 gals
② Optional—16 qts
③ 5-speed uses Dexron® II ATF
④ Century and Regal
⑤ TH-M 200: 6 TH-M 350: 3
⑥ Skylark
⑦ Skyhawk
⑧ Manual trans., without A/C: 11.8
   Manual trans., 49 states, with A/C: 12.4
   Manual trans., 49 states, with A/C and Heavy Duty: 12.4

Buick Apollo • Century • Gran Sport

Manual trans., Calif., with A/C: 12.2
Manual trans., Calif. and High Altitude, with A/C and Heavy
Duty: 12.9
Auto. trans., without A/C: 11.7
Auto. trans., 49 states, with A/C: 11.7
Auto. trans., 49 states, with 2.93:1 rear axle, with A/C and
Heavy Duty: 12.3

Auto. trans., Calif. and High Altitude, with A/C: 12.1
Auto. trans., Calif. and High Altitude, with A/C and Heavy
Duty: 12.8
⑨ 7 inch ring gear: 3.5
7.5 inch ring gear: 3.75
8.5 inch ring gear: 4.25

CRANKSHAFT AND CONNECTING ROD SPECIFICATIONS

All measurements are given in inches

Year	Engine No. Cyl. Displacement (cu in.)	CRANKSHAFT Main Brg. Journal Dia	Main Brg. Oil Clearance	Shaft End-Play	Thrust on No.	CONNECTING ROD Journal Diameter	Oil Clearance	Side Clearance
'72-'74	6-250	2.3004	.0003-.0029	.002-.006	7	2.0000	.0007-.0027	.009-.014
	8-350	2.9995②	.0004-.0015	.002-.006①	3	2.0000	.0002-.0023	.006-.020
	8-455	3.2500	.0007-.0018	.003-.009	3	2.2500	.0002-.0023	.005-.019
'75-'76	6-231	2.4995	.0004-.0015	.004-.008	2	2.0000	.0002-.0023	.006-.014
	6-250	2.2999	.0003-.0029	.002-.006	7	2.0000	.0007-.0027	.007-.016
	8-260	2.4995	.0005-.0021	.004-.008	3	2.1240	.0005-.0026	.006-.020
	8-350	2.9995	.0004-.0015	.002-.006	3	2.0000	.0005-.0026	.006-.026
'77	6-231 Buick	2.4995	.0004-.0015	.004-.008	2	2.000	.0005-.0026	.006-.027
	8-301 Pont.	3.0000	.0004-.0020	.003-.009	4	2.000	.0005-.0025	.006-.027
	8-305 Chev.	2.4480	.0035 max.④	.002-.006	5	2.200	.0035 max.④	.008-0.14
	8-350 Buick	3.0000	.0004-.0015	.003-.009	3	2.000	.0005-.0026	.006-.027
	8-350 Olds.	2.4995	.0005-.0021③	.003-.013	3	2.125	.0004-.0015	.006-.027
	8-350 Chev.	2.4480	.0035 max.④	.002-.006	5	2.200	.0035 max.④	.008-.014
	8-403 Olds.	2.4995	.0005-.0021③	.003-.013	3	2.125	.0005-.0026	.006-.020
'78-'79	6-196, 231 Buick	2.4995	.0003-.0017	.004-.008	2	2.2487-2.2495	.0005-.0026	.006-.027
	8-301 Pont.	3.0000	.0004-.0020	.003-.009	4	2.000	.0005-.0025	.006-.027
	8-305, 350 Chev.	⑤	.0035 max.④	.002-.006	.0035 max.	.008-.014	5	2.0990-2.1000

① 1972-74 V8—350; .003-.009 in.
② 3.0000 for 1974
③ No. 5—.0015-.0031
④ No. 1—.002 max.

⑤ #1: 2.4484-2.4493
#2,3,4: 2.4481-2.4490
#5: 2.4479-2.4488

VALVE SPECIFICATIONS

Year	Engine No. Cyl. Displacement (cu in.)	Seat Angle (deg)	Face Angle (deg)	Spring Test Pressure (lbs @ in.)	Spring Installed Height (in.)	STEM TO GUIDE Clearance (in.) Intake	Exhaust	STEM Diameter (in.) Intake	Exhaust
'72	8-350	45	45	180 @ 1.34	1 23/32	.0015-.0035	.0015-.0032	.3725	.3727
	8-455	45	45	198 @ 1.45	1 29/32	.0015-.0035	.0015-.0032	.3725	.3727
'73	8-350	45	45	180 @ 1.34	1 23/32	.0015-.0035	.0015-.0032	.3720	.3730
	8-455	45	45	198 @ 1.45	1 29/32	.0015-.0035	.0015-.0032	.3725	.3727
'74	6-250	46	45	186 @ 1.27	1 21/32	.0010-.0027	.0010-.0027	.3413	.3413
	8-350	45	45	180 @ 1.34	1 29/32	00015-.0035	.0015-.0032	.3725	.3727
	8-455	45	45	178 @ 1.45	1 29/32	.0015-.0035	.0015-.0032	.3725	.3727
'75-'76	6-231	45	45	164 @ 1.34②	1 47/64	.0015-.0035	.0015-.0032	.3407	.3407
	6-250	46	45	186 @ 1.27	1 21/32	.0010-.0027	.0010-.0020	.3413	.3413
	8-260	45④	46④	187 @ 1.27	1 43/64	.0010-.0027	.0015-.0032	.3428	.3424
	8-350	45	45	180 @ 1.34③	1 47/64	.0015-.0035	.0015-.0032	.3725	.3727

VALVE SPECIFICATIONS

Year	Engine No. Cyl. Displacement (cu in.)	Seat Angle (deg)	Face Angle (deg)	Spring Test Pressure (lbs @ in.)	Spring Installed Height (in.)	STEM TO GUIDE Clearance (in.) Intake	Exhaust	STEM Diameter (in.) Intake	Exhaust
'77	6-231 Buick	45	45	164 @ 1.34	1 47/64	.0015-.0035	.0015-.0032	.3400	.3400
	8-301 Pont.	46	45	170 @ 1.26	1 47/64	.0017-.0020	.0017-.0020	.3400	.3400
	8-305 Chev.	46	45	206 @ 1.25	1 23/32 ⑤	.0010-.0037	.0010-.0037	.3410	.3410
	8-350 Buick	45	45	180 @ 1.34	1 47/64	.0015-.0032	.0015-.0032	.3730	.3730
	8-350 Olds.	45④	44④	180 @ 1.34	1 47/64	.0010-.0027	.0015-.0032	.3425	.3420
	8-350 Chev.	46	45	206 @ 1.25	1 23/32 ⑤	.0010-.0037	.0010-.0037	.3410	.3410
	8-403 Olds.	45④	44④	180 @ 1.34	1 47/64	.0010-.0027	.0015-.0032	.3425	.3420
'78-'79	6-196 Buick	45	45	168 @ 1.327	1 47/64	.0015-.0032	.0015-.0032	.3405-.3412	.3405-.3412
	6-231 Buick	45	45	168 @ 1.327	1 47/64	.0015-.0032	.0015-.0032	.3405-.3412	.3405-.3412
	8-301 Pont.	46	45	170 @ 1.26	1 47/64	.0017-.0020	.0017-.0020	.3400	.3400
	8-305 Chev.	46	45	200 @ 1.160	1 23/32 ⑤	.0010-.0037	.0010-.0037	.3410	.3410
	8-350 Chev.	46	45	200 @ 1.160	1 23/32 ⑤	.0010-.0037	.0010-.0037	.3410	.3410

① Not used ② Exhaust—182 @ 1.34 ③ Exhaust—175 @ 1.34 ④ Exhaust—31 seat, 30 face ⑤ Exhaust—1 19/32

TORQUE SPECIFICATIONS
All readings in ft lbs

Year	Engine No. Cyl. Displacement (cu in.)	Cylinder Head Bolts	Rod Bearing Bolts	Main Bearing Bolts	Crankshaft Bolt	Flywheel to Crankshaft Bolts	MANIFOLD Intake	Exhaust
'72-'76	6-250	95	35	60-70	60	55-65	35	②
	6-231	75	40	115	150 min.	55⑤	45	25
	8-260	85	42	120	200 min.	60	40	25
	8-350	80	35④	115	140 min.	60	45	28
	8-455	100	45	115	200 min.	60	45	28
'77	6-231 Buick	85	42	80③	310	60	40	25
	8-301 Pont.	90	35	60①	160	95	40	35
	8-305 Chev.	65	45	70	60	60	30	20
	8-350 Buick	80	40	115	175	60	45	25
	8-350 Olds.	130	42	80③	310	60	40	25
	8-350 Chev.	65	45	70	60	60	30	20
	8-403 Olds.	130	42	80	310	60	40	25
'78-'79	6-196, 231 Buick	80	40	100	225	60	45	25
	8-301 Pont.	90	35	60①	160	95	40	35
	8-305, 350 Chev.	65	45	70	60	60	30	20

① 100—rear main
② Center Bolts 25-30; End Bolts 15-20
③ 120—rear main
④ 40 with capscrews
⑤ 60—1976 and later

PISTON CLEARANCE

Year	Engine No. Cyl. Displacement (cu. in.)	Piston to Bore Clearance (in.)
'74-'75	6-250 Chev.	.0005-.0015
'75-'79	6-231 Buick	.0008-.0020
'75-'76	8-260 Olds.	.0010-.0020
'77-'79	8-301 Pont.	.0025-.0033
'72-'77	8-350 Buick	.0008-.0020

Year	Engine No. Cyl. Displacement (cu. in.)	Piston to Bore Clearance (in.)
'77-'79	8-305, 350 Chev.	.0027 Max.
'77	8-350, 403 Olds.	.0010-.0020
'72-'74	8-455 Buick	.0010-.0016
'78-'79	6-196 Buick	.0008-.0020

RING SIDE CLEARANCE

All measurements are given in inches

Year	Engine No. Cyl. Displacement (cu. in.)	Top Compression	Bottom Compression	Oil Control
'74-'75	6-250 Chev.	.0012-.0027	.0012-.0032	.0000-.0050
'75-'79	6-231 Buick	.0030-.0050	.0030-.0050	.0035 Max.
'75-'76	8-260 Olds.	.0020-.0040	.0020-.0040	.0010-.0035
'77-'79	8-301 Pont.	.0015-.0035	.0015-.0035	.0015-.0035
'72	8-350 Buick	.0030-.0050	.0030-.0050	.0035-.0095
'73-'77	8-350 Buick	.0030-.0050	.0030-.0050	.0035 Max.
'77-'79	8-305, 350 Chev.	.0012-.0042	.0012-.0042	.0020-.0080
'77	8-350 Olds.	.0020-.0040	.0020-.0040	.0010-.0050
'77	8-403 Olds.	.0020-.0040	.0020-.0040	.0150-.0550
'72	8-455 Buick	.0030-.0050	.0030-.0050	.0035-.0095
'73-'74	8-455 Buick	.0030-.0050	.0030-.0050	.0035 Max.
'78-'79	6-196 Buick	.0030-.0050	.0030-.0050	.0035 Max.

RING GAP

All measurements are given in inches

Year	Engine No. Cyl. Displacement (cu. in.)	Top Compression	Bottom Compression	Oil Control
'74-'75	6-250 Chev.	.010-.020	.010-.020	.015-.055
'75-'79	6-231 Buick	.010-.020	.010-.020	.015-.035
'75-'76	8-260 Olds.	.010-.023	.010-.023	.015-.055
'77-'79	8-301 Pont.	.010-.020	.010-.020	.035 max.
'72	8-350 Buick	.013-.023	.013-.023	.015-.035
'73	8-350 Buick	.010-.020	.010-.020	.015-.035
'77-'79	8-305, 350 Chev.	.010-.030	.010-.035	.015-.065
'77	8-350, 403 Olds.	.010-.023	.010-.023	.015-.055
'72	8-455 Buick	.013-.023	.013-.023	.015-.055
'73-'74	8-455 Buick	.013-.023	.013-.023	.015-.035
'78-'79	6-196 Buick	.010-.020	.010-.020	.015-.035

WHEEL ALIGNMENT SPECIFICATIONS

Year	Model	CASTER Range (deg)	CASTER Pref Setting (deg)	CAMBER Range (deg)	CAMBER Pref Setting (deg)	Toe-in (in.)	Steering Axis Inclin. (deg)	WHEEL PIVOT RATIO (deg) Inner Wheel	WHEEL PIVOT RATIO (deg) Outer Wheel
'72	All	1N to 0	½N	0 to 1P	½P	⅛ to ¼	8	20	18½
'73	All	0 to 1P	½P	0 to 1P ①	½P	1/16 to ⅛	8	20	②
'74	Apollo	½N to 1½P	½P	½N to 1P	¾P	1/16 to 5/16	9	20	②
	Century, Regal, Luxus	1N to 1P	0	¼N to 1¼P RH ¼P to 1¾P LH	½P RH 1P LH	0 to 3/16	8	20	②
'75-'77	Skyhawk	1¼N to ¼N	¾N	½N to ¾P	¼P	0 to ⅛	8.55	20	②
	Apollo/Skylark, manual steer.	½N to 1½N	1N	¼P to 1¼P	¾P	0 to ⅛	10	20	②
	Apollo/Skylark, power steer.	½P to 1½P	1P	¼P to 1¼P	¾P	0 to ⅛	10	20	②
	Century, Regal	1½P to 2½P ③	2P	0 to 1P ½P to 1½P LH	½P RH 1P LH	0 to ⅛	8	20	②
'78-'79	Century, Regal manual steer.	½P to 1½P	1P	0 to 1P	½P	1/16 to 3/16	—	—	—
	Century, Regal power steer.	2½P to 3½P	3P	0 to 1P	½P	1/16 to 3/16	—	—	—
	Skylark manual steer.	½N to 1½N	1N	⅓P to 1⅓P	⅘P	0 to ⅛	—	—	—
	Skylark power steer.	½P to 1½P	1P	⅓P to 1⅓P	⅘P	0 to ⅛	—	—	—
	Skyhawk	¼N to 1¼N	¾N	¼N to ¾P	¼P	0 to ⅛	—	—	—

① Right wheel given, left wheel is 0 to 2P, preferred 1P
   N Negative   P Positive
② Manual steering and station wagon: RH—19³/₁₆, LH—18¹³/₁₆;
   Power steering, except station wagon: RH—19, LH—18¹¹/₁₆
③ 1977 Caster with radial tires, 1½P to 2½P—2P preferred;
   Caster with bias tires, ½P to 1½ P—1P preferred

RH Right hand side
LH Left hand side
—Not specified

CHARGING SYSTEM

The Delco ST alternator system is standard on all models.

Charging system troubleshooting can be found in the Unit Repair Section.

Alternator Removal and Installation

Remove the bolt holding the tension bar to the unit. Release the drive belt. Unfasten the mounting bolt to release the Delcotron from the engine. When reinstalling, adjust the drive belt to allow 1/2 in. play on the longest run between pulleys.

NOTE: *On some models, it may be necessary to loosen and rotate the fan shroud. On all A/C models, remove the compressor bracket.*

Voltage Regulator Removal and Installation

The voltage regulator is in the alternator, and requires no adjustment. The alternator must be disassembled to remove the regulator.

STARTING SYSTEM

Starter Removal and Installation

INLINE SIX

1. Disconnect the battery and solenoid wires.
2. Remove the flywheel inspection cover.
3. On 1974 models, disconnect the starter support bracket.
4. Remove the attaching bolts and lift out the starter.

V6

Disconnect the negative battery cable from the battery. Note the locations of the wiring connections and disconnect the electrical leads from the starter. Remove the capscrew which secures the starter motor to the angle bracket on the side of the engine. Remove the two capscrews which secure the drive end of the starter motor to the cylinder block and remove the starter. Install the starter in the reverse order of removal.

V8

1. Disconnect the battery.
2. Jack up the car.
3. Remove the four screws (3/8 in.) that hold the flywheel inspection cover.
4. Disconnect the wires from the solenoid.
5. Remove one bolt from the starter bracket to the engine block, then remove the two rear starter bolts using a 9/16 in. socket.

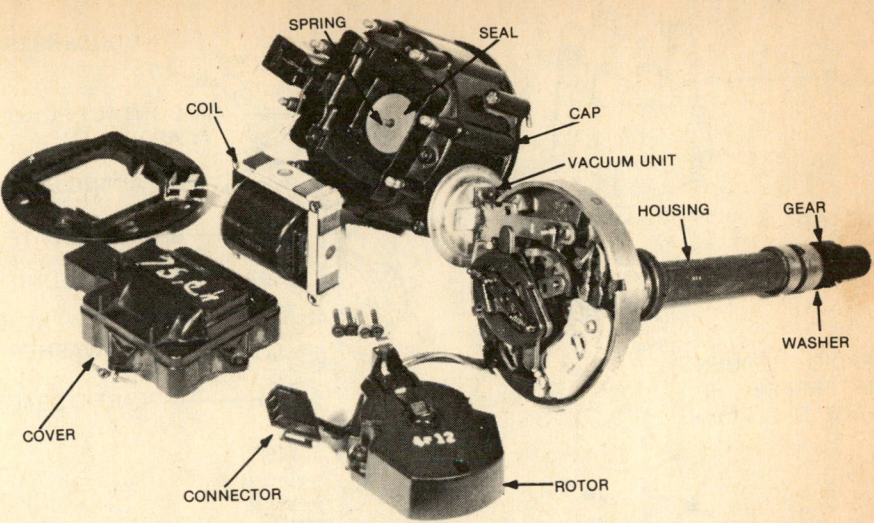

Exploded view of V8 or V6 HEI distributor

NOTE: *The bracket bolt is hidden and must be removed using a short 1/2 in. open-end wrench. This bolt must be started by hand when installing. The bracket was used only in 1972.*

6. Remove the starter motor.

SKYHAWK, AUTOMATIC TRANSMISSION

1. Disconnect the battery and raise the car.
2. Remove the exhaust crossover pipe and flywheel cover.
3. Remove the two transmission mount to transmision bolts and support the transmission extension housing.
4. Remove the right transmission support bolt and loosen the left bolt enough to let the transmission support pivot down.
5. Lower the transmission and disconnect the fluid cooler lines at the transmission.
6. Remove the starter mounting bolts; remove the starter wires, and lower the starter from the engine.
7. Installation is the reverse of removal.

Disabling the Seat Belt/Starter Interlock System

The seat belt interlock and warning buzzer are no longer mandatory. These may now be disabled, but the seat belt warning light must remain in operation.

1. Disconnect the battery, and locate the interlock terminal connector. This is a connector with orange, yellow and green wires, located under the left side of the instrument panel, near the fuse box.
2. Cut and tape the green wire on the body harness side of the connector.
3. Remove the warning buzzer from the fuse block or terminal connector on all Skyhawk, Skylark, and Apollo models.
4. On all other models, remove and tape the terminal with two yellow wires with black stripes. This terminal is located near the fuse block.

IGNITION SYSTEM

A conventional breaker point ignition system was used on all Buick engines through 1974. During 1974, a solid-state, High Energy Ignition system was offered as an option on the V8. This system was standard equipment, beginning 1975. There are no contact points or condensor to replace, nor any cam or rubbing block to wear out, thus eliminating distributor maintenance.

Distributor Removal

1. Remove the distrisbutor cap, primary wire and vacuum line at the distributor. On inline sixes with HEI, remove No. 1 and 2 spark plug wires and the coil connectors. Unplug the V6 and V8 distributor cap HEI connectors.
2. Scribe a mark on the distributor body, locating the position of the rotor and scribe another mark on the engine block, showing the position of the body in the block.
3. Remove the hold-down clamp and lift the distributor out of the block.

Distributor Installation

For firing order and cylinder numbering, see the specifications.

1. If the engine has been disturbed, rotate the crankshaft to bring the piston of No. 1 cylinder to the top of its compression stroke. If the engine has not been disturbed, insert the distributor into the engine, making sure the tip of the rotor is aligned with the marks that were

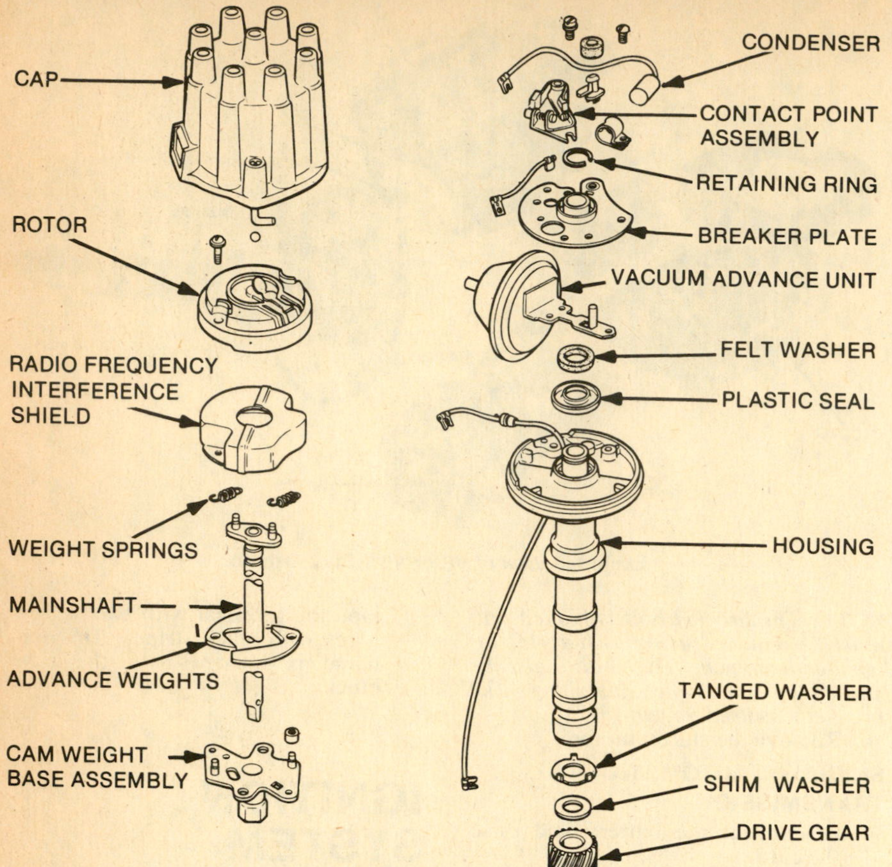

CAP

ROTOR

RADIO FREQUENCY
INTERFERENCE
SHIELD

WEIGHT SPRINGS

MAINSHAFT

ADVANCE WEIGHTS

CAM WEIGHT
BASE ASSEMBLY

Point type V8 distributor assembly
(© Buick Div., G.M. Corp.)

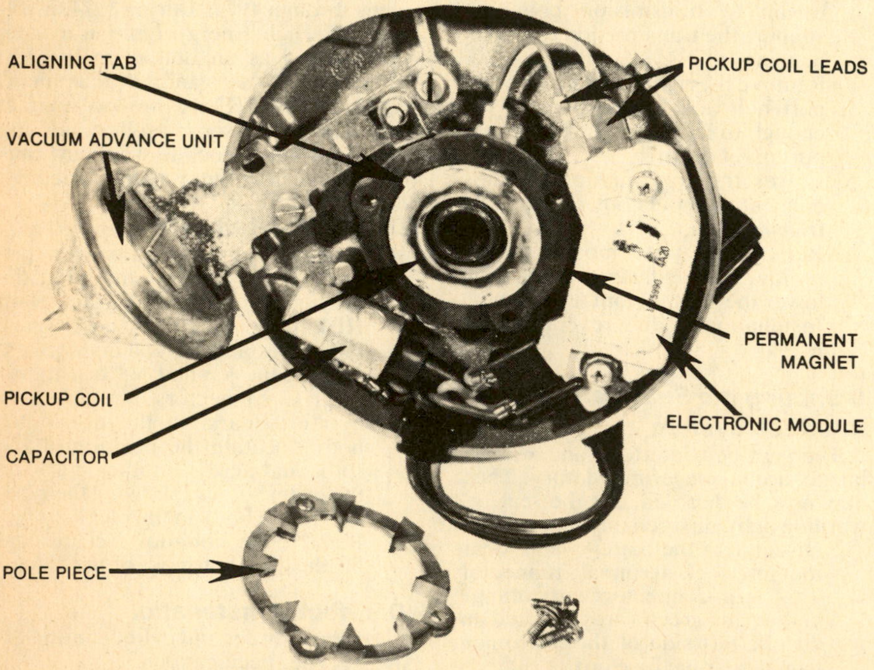

CONDENSER

CONTACT POINT
ASSEMBLY

RETAINING RING

BREAKER PLATE

VACUUM ADVANCE UNIT

FELT WASHER

PLASTIC SEAL

HOUSING

TANGED WASHER

SHIM WASHER

DRIVE GEAR

DRIVE PIN

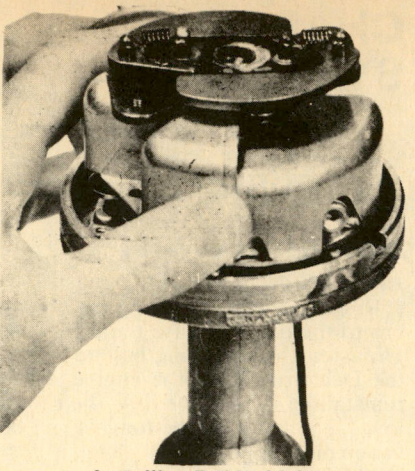

Installing R.F.I. shield
(© Buick Div., G.M. Corp)

ALIGNING TAB

VACUUM ADVANCE UNIT

PICKUP COIL LEADS

PERMANENT
MAGNET

PICKUP COIL

CAPACITOR

ELECTRONIC MODULE

POLE PIECE

Internal Components of the HEI distributor
(© Buick Div., G.M. Corp)

wise until the breaker points are just starting to open. Tighten the retaining screw.
5. Connect the primary wire and the vacuum line to the distributor, then install distributor cap.
6. Start the engine and check the timing with a timing light.

Contact Point Replacement and Adjustment

INLINE SIX THROUGH 1974

1. Loosen the captive distributor cap retaining screws and remove the cap.
2. Pull off the rotor.
3. Disconnect the primary and condenser leads from the point set.
4. Remove the retaining screw and the point set.
4. Remove the retaining screw and the point set.
5. Remove the condenser and clamp.
6. Rotate the sponge cam lubricator or apply a trace of distributor lubricant to the cam.
7. Insert the new point set and the attaching screw.
8. Install the new condenser and clamp.
9. Connect the leads to the point set.
10. Turn the engine so that the points are open to their maximum.
11. Adjust the gap with a feeler gauge. Use the screwdriver slot to lever the points open or closed.
12. Check the dwell with the engine either cranking or running. Set the dwell by adjusting the point gap.
13. Check the timing.

V8 THROUGH 1974

NOTE: *The condenser should be replaced when the points are replaced.*

1. Remove the distributor cap and rotor. If there is an interference shield, remove the shield.
2. Disconnect the condenser and primary leads from their terminal on the points.
3. Loosen the two screws holding the

scribed on the distributor housing and the engine block.
2. Position the distributor in the block with the rotor at No. 1 firing position. Make sure the oil pump inter-

mediate drive shaft is properly seated in the oil pump.
3. Install the distributor lock but do not tighten.
4. Rotate the distributor body clock-

contact point set in place and re-move the point set.

4. Connect the wires to a new set of points and install them into the distributor.

NOTE: *Distributors through 1973 have a radio interference shield over the contact points. Only snap-lock point sets can be used because screw-type connectors will hit this shield and short the ignition. The shield isn't needed if the later type unitized point/condenser set is installed.*

5. Put a small amount of grease on the breaker cam or rotate the lubricator.
6. Reinstall the shield, rotor, and cap. Install the shield half that covers the points first. The shield isn't necessary if a unitized point and condenser set is installed. The unitized set is standard equipment beginning 1974. It can be installed in all General Motors V8 distributors.
7. Adjust the dwell to specifications using a 1/8 in. allen wrench through the cap window.
8. Check the timing.

Ignition Timing

Timing marks are located on the front engine cover and on the harmonic balancer.

1. Disconnect the distributor vacuum advance hose from the distributor and plug the hose.
2. Make sure the dwell is adjusted and the timing marks are clean and readable.

NOTE: *It may be necessary to put a small amount of white paint or chalk on the timing marks to make them more visible.*

3. Connect a timing light to No. 1 cylinder.
4. Loosen the distributor clamp.
5. Start the engine and rotate the distributor until the correct marks line up. Tighten the distributor clamp and recheck the timing.
6. Reconnect the vacuum hose.

High Energy Ignition System Tachometer Hookup

Some 1974, and all 1975 and later Buicks are equipped with the High Energy Ignition System which uses a different tachometer hookup than was used in previous years.

1. On the V6 and V8 engines, connect the tachometer to the TACH terminal on the distributor and to a suitable ground.

NOTE: *Some tachometers must connect to the TACH terminal on the distributors and to the positive terminal on the battery. If there is any doubt, check the tachometer manufacturer's instructions.*

2. On the inline engines, connect the tachometer to the TACH terminal on the coil, opposite the BAT terminal, and to a ground.

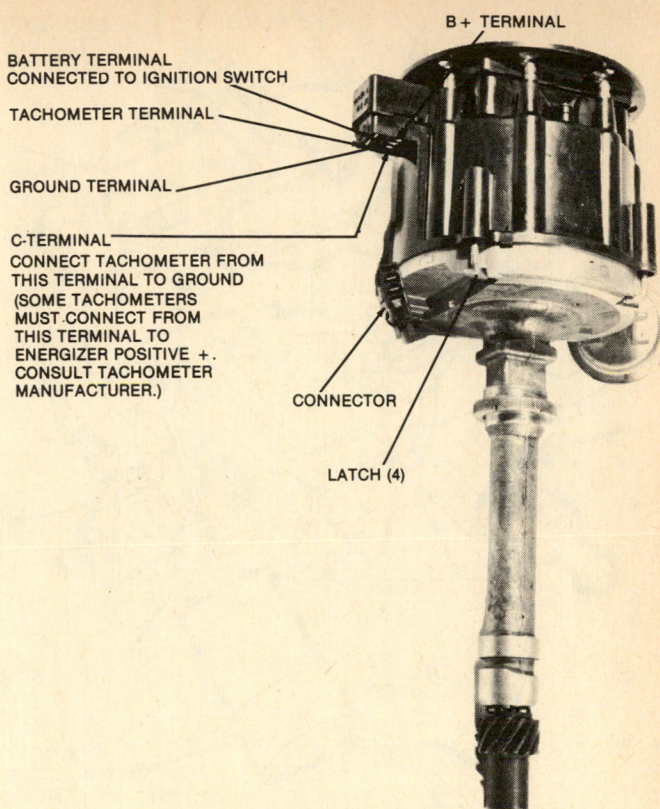

BATTERY TERMINAL
CONNECTED TO IGNITION SWITCH

TACHOMETER TERMINAL

GROUND TERMINAL

C-TERMINAL
CONNECT TACHOMETER FROM THIS TERMINAL TO GROUND (SOME TACHOMETERS MUST CONNECT FROM THIS TERMINAL TO ENERGIZE POSITIVE +. CONSULT TACHOMETER MANUFACTURER.)

B + TERMINAL

CONNECTOR

LATCH (4)

V8 HEI system distributor tachometer hookup
(© Buick Div., G.M. Corp)

FUEL SYSTEM

Information on the fuel gauge, carburetor, and carburetor specifications will be found in the Unit Repair section.

Idle Speed and Mixture Adjustment

1972-73

NOTE: *Check to see that the compressor for the Automatic Level Control, if equipped, is not running. The compressor has a regulating valve to turn off vacuum at idle speed. If the compressor is running, this valve is faulty and must be adjusted or replaced before a good idle can be obtained.*

1. Connect a tachometer to the engine.
2. Start the engine and run it until it is warmed up.
3. Remove and plug the vacuum hose to the distributor.
4. Place manual transmissions in Neutral and automatic transmissions in Drive.
5. Open the throttle sufficiently to allow the solenoid to extend and contact the throttle lever pad in the idle position.
6. Adjust the solenoid plunger to obtain the specified rpm. This is the higher figure in the specification chart.

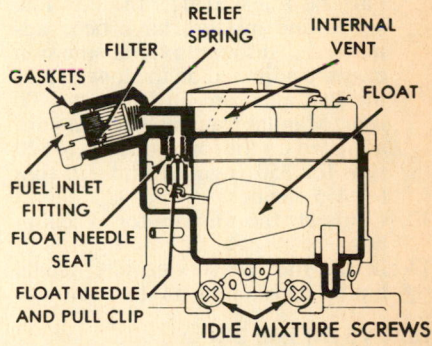

RELIEF SPRING

FILTER

INTERNAL VENT

GASKETS

FLOAT

FUEL INLET FITTING

FLOAT NEEDLE SEAT

FLOAT NEEDLE AND PULL CLIP

IDLE MIXTURE SCREWS

2 bbl carburetor
(© Buick Div., G.M. Corp)

7. Disconnect the solenoid wire to disengage solenoid.
8. Adjust the carburetor idle screw to obtain specified idle speed, this is the lower figure in the specification chart.
9. Reconnect the solenoid wire.
10. Adjust the idle mixture needles, one at a time, to obtain the highest tachometer reading. After the highest reading is reached, readjust the solenoid plunger to obtain 50 rpm over the specified idle speed. Turn each mixture needle in to reduce the idle speed 25 rpm for each needle. This reduced the idle speed to the recommended rpm.
11. Adjust the fast idle speed on all four-barrel carburetors. Fast idle

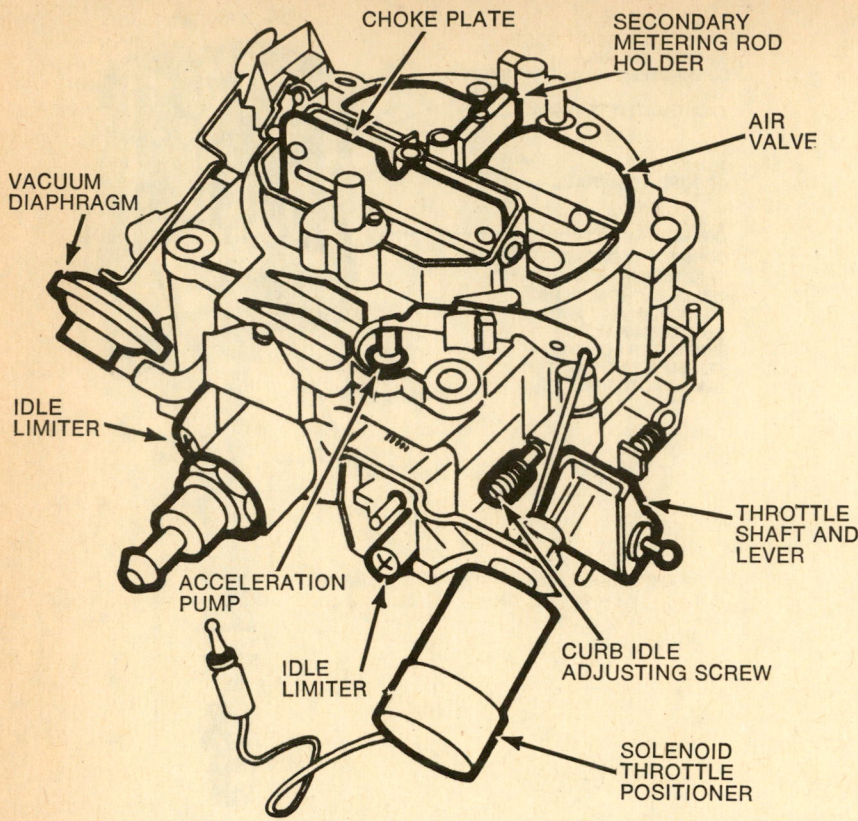

4 bbl carburetor

(Diagram labels:) CHOKE PLATE, SECONDARY METERING ROD HOLDER, AIR VALVE, VACUUM DIAPHRAGM, IDLE LIMITER, ACCELERATION PUMP, IDLE LIMITER, THROTTLE SHAFT AND LEVER, CURB IDLE ADJUSTING SCREW, SOLENOID THROTTLE POSITIONER

must be adjusted after the slow idle speed and mixture have been adjusted. Automatic transmission cars are adjusted on the low step of the fast idle cam, in Drive, to 700 rpm. Manual transmission cars are adjusted on the low cam step to 820 rpm for 350 engines, and 920 rpm for 455 engines.

12. Connect the distributor vacuum hose.

13. Install the red service idle needle limiter caps on the mixture screws.

1974-75 INLINE SIX

NOTE: *Idle speed and mixture must be set with the engine at normal operating temperature, the air conditioner off, the air cleaner on, and the automatic transmission in Drive.*

1. Set the parking brake and block the wheels.

2. Disconnect the fuel tank vent hose at the vapor canister. Disconnect and plug the distributor vacuum line at the distributor.

3. Adjust the idle speed to the higher figure specified in the "Tune-Up Specifications" chart. Adjust the solenoid screw with the solenoid connected.

4. Cut the tab off the idle mixture screw cap.

5. Using the solenoid screw, set the idle speed to the higher speed specified on the underhood sticker. This is usually 30-350 rpm above normal idle speed.

6. Adjust the mixture screw (usually out) until the maximum engine idle speed is reached.

7. Lean the mixture by turning the mixture screw in until the engine slows to the idle speed you started with in Step 3. Adjust the idle speed to the lower figure from the "Tune-Up Specifications" chart with the solenoid disconnected.

8. Reconnect all the hoses removed in Step 2.

1974-76 V6 AND V8 (EXCEPT 260)

NOTE: *Idle speed and mixture must be set with the engine at normal operating temperature, the air conditioner off, the air cleaner on, and the transmission in Drive.*

1. Set the parking brake and block the wheels.

2. Disconnect the evaporative emission hose at the air cleaner. Disconnect and plug the distributor vacuum line at the distributor. Disconnect and plug the EGR vacuum line at the EGR valve on all 1974 models, and all 1975-76 V6s.

3. Adjust the idle speed to that specified in the "Tune-Up Specifications" chart. First adjust the idle speed screw with the solenoid disconnected to get the lower speed, then adjust the solenoid screw with the solenoid connected to get the higher speed on models so equipped. If there is no solenoid,

adjust the idle speed with the idle speed screw.

4. Cut the tabs off the mixture screw caps then turn them out to obtain the maximum idle speed.

5. Using the solenoid screw (if equipped), or the idle speed screw, adjust the idle speed to the higher speed specified on the underhood sticker, which is usually 60-100 rpm above the normal idle speed.

6. Turn in the mixture screws equally until the engine returns to the normal idle speed. On the V6, reset the idle speed with the solenoid de-energized, if necessary.

7. Reconnect all the hoses removed in Step 2.

260 V8

1. Follow the first two steps under the 1974-76 V6 and V8 procedure, but plug the EGR line at the carburetor.

2. Remove the caps on the mixture screws and then lightly seat each screw.

3. Back out each screw *exactly* five turns.

4. Adjust the idle speed screw to obtain 610 rpm for non-California models or 700 rpm for California models.

5. Turn in the mixture screws 1/2 turn at a time until the idle speed is 550 rpm for non-California models or 600 rpm for California models.

6. If the car is equipped with air conditioning, it may have an idle speed-up solenoid on the carburetor which must be adjusted when adjusting the idle speed.

Turn on the air conditioning and disconnect the terminal connector at the compressor clutch. With the solenoid energized, adjust the screw to obtain 650 rpm with the transmission in Drive. When completed, reconnect the connector at the compressor clutch.

1977

NOTE: *Engines produced by several GM divisions are used in Buicks. The vehicle emission control information sticker in the engine compartment should be checked for the individual engine specifications.*

1. With the engine at normal operating temperature, set the parking brake and block the wheels.

2. Remove the air cleaner, if necessary, to gain access to the idle air screws, but leave the vacuum lines connected.

3. Disconnect and plug the other vacuum lines as indicated by the emission control sticker.

4. Connect a tachometer and timing light to the engine, and if necessary, adjust the ignition timing to specifications. Disconnect the vacuum advance line, if directed by the instructions on the emission control sticker.

5. Carefully remove the idle mixture

screw limiter caps. Lightly seat the screws by turning them into the carburetor base, and then back the screws out equally until the engine will run without stalling.

6. If the car has automatic transmission, place the selector lever in Drive.
7. Back out the idle mixture screws, 1/8 of a turn at a time, until the maximum idle speed is obtained.
8. Adjust the engine idle speed to 50 rpm over the specified low rpm setting. Repeat step 7, if necessary.

NOTE: *Two idle speed adjustments are normally required. One is the normal rpm setting, controlled by the adjustment of the electric solenoid screw, and the second adjustment, or low setting, is controlled by a screw on the carburetor throttle shaft lever. If the car has air conditioning, the solenoid may be used as an idle speed up control. To determine the type used, turn the air conditioning on, if the engine idle speed increases, the solenoid is used as a speed-up device. The idle speed setting is then adjusted by the screw on the throttle shaft lever.*

9. Turn each screw in, 1/8 of a turn at a time, until the idle speed reaches the specified idle rpm.
10. Reset the idle speed.
11. Connect all the vacuum lines and install the air cleaner. Recheck the idle speed and correct as necessary.

1978-79 2GC, 2GE CARBURETOR

1. Run the engine to normal operating temperature. Make sure that the choke is fully opened, set the parking brake, block the drive wheels, turn the air conditioning Off and connect a tachometer to the engine according to the manufacturer's instructions.
2. Disconnect and plug the vacuum hoses at the vapor canister and EGR valve.
3. Place the transmission in Park (AT) or Neutral (MT).
4. Disconnect and plug the vacuum advance hose at the distributor. Set the timing.
5. Reconnect the vacuum advance hose and turn the idle speed screw to obtain the specified rpm.
6. Connect all hoses and remove the tachometer.

1978-79 M2MC-210 CARBURETOR

1. Run the engine to normal operating temperature.
2. Make sure that the choke is fully opened, set the parking brake, block the wheels, connect a tachometer to the engine according to the manufacturer's instructions, disconnect the compressor clutch wire, turn the A/C Off, place the transmission in Drive, and disconnect and plug the vacuum advance hose at the distributor.
3. Set the timing, if necessary.

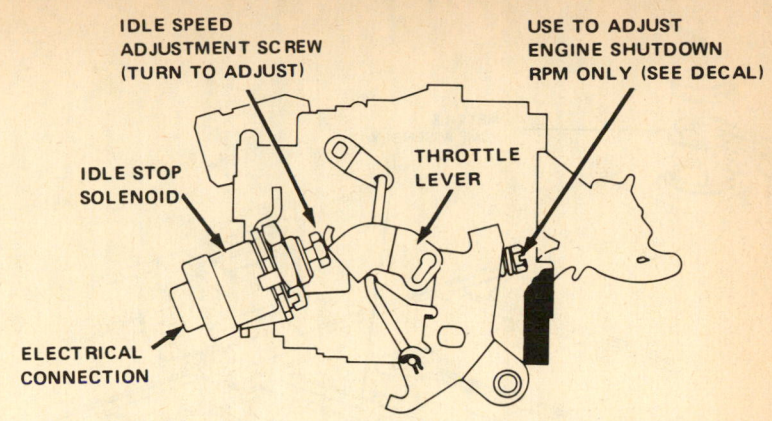

IDLE SPEED ADJUSTMENT SCREW (TURN TO ADJUST)

USE TO ADJUST ENGINE SHUTDOWN RPM ONLY (SEE DECAL)

IDLE STOP SOLENOID

THROTTLE LEVER

ELECTRICAL CONNECTION

(MODELS NOT EQUIPPED WITH A/C)

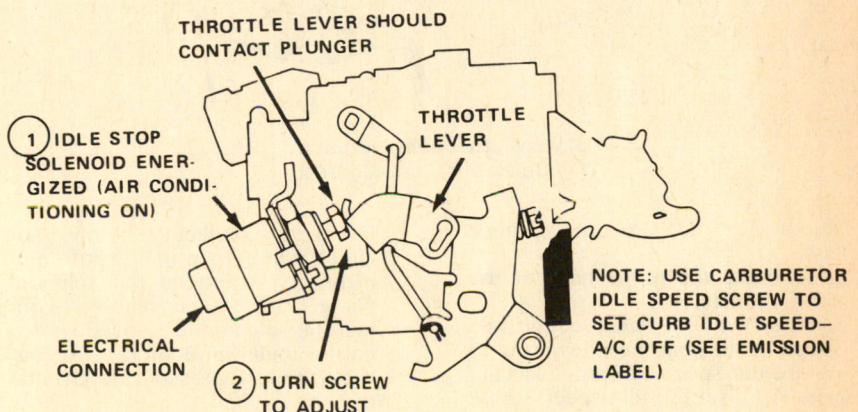

THROTTLE LEVER SHOULD CONTACT PLUNGER

THROTTLE LEVER

① IDLE STOP SOLENOID ENERGIZED (AIR CONDITIONING ON)

ELECTRICAL CONNECTION

② TURN SCREW TO ADJUST

NOTE: USE CARBURETOR IDLE SPEED SCREW TO SET CURB IDLE SPEED—A/C OFF (SEE EMISSION LABEL)

(MODELS EQUIPPED WITH A/C)

Typical 2 bbl idle speed adjustment locations
(© Buick Div., G.M. Corp)

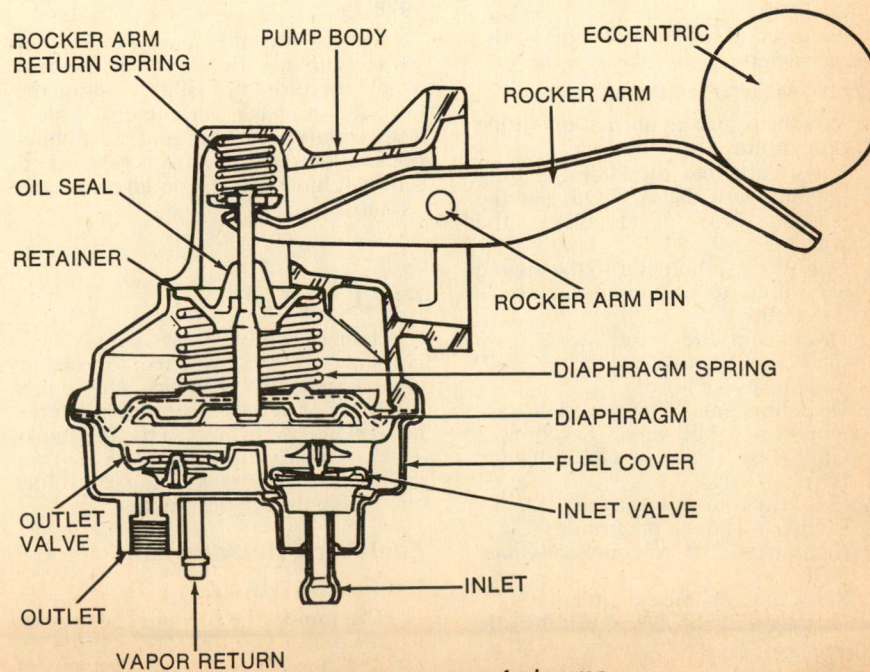

ROCKER ARM RETURN SPRING

PUMP BODY

ECCENTRIC

ROCKER ARM

OIL SEAL

RETAINER

ROCKER ARM PIN

DIAPHRAGM SPRING

DIAPHRAGM

FUEL COVER

INLET VALVE

OUTLET VALVE

OUTLET

INLET

VAPOR RETURN

Vapor return type fuel pump

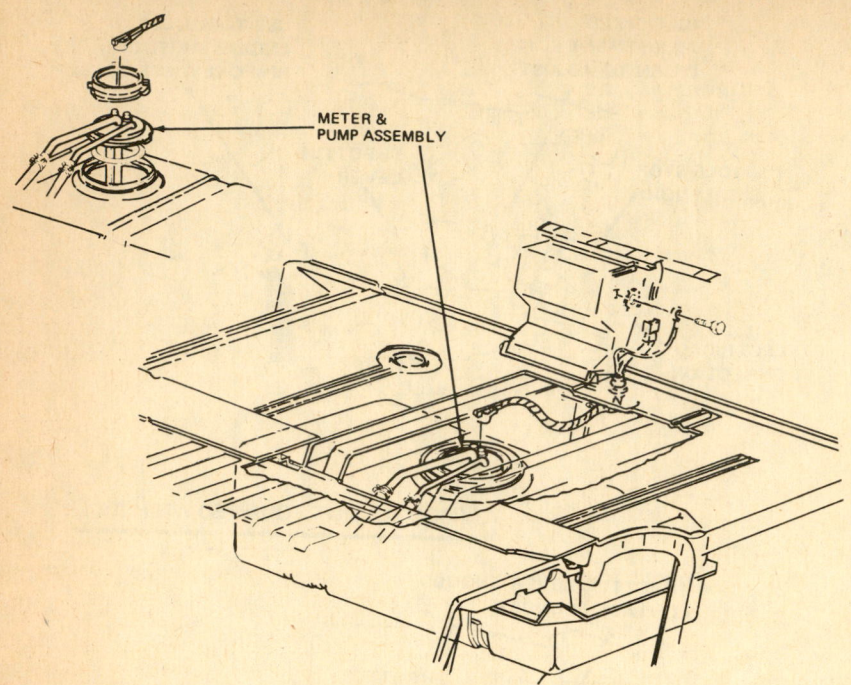

Skyhawk fuel pump location
(© Buick Div., G.M. Corp)

2. Remove the two 1/2 inch (in.) bolts.
3. Remove the fuel pump.
4. Install a new gasket.
5. Install a new pump and bolts.
6. Tighten the bolts alternately and evenly.
7. Reconnect the hoses, start the engine, and check for leaks.

SKYHAWK

The fuel pump used in the Skyhawk is an electric pump, mounted in the gas tank.

1. Disconnect the fuel pump wires at the rear wiring harness connector.
2. Raise the car on a hoist and drain the gas tank.
3. Disconnect the gas line hose at the tank, and the vent hose.
4. Remove the gas gauge ground wire from the bottom of the tank.
5. Remove the tank retaining straps, and lower the tank carefully.
6. A special spanner wrench is needed to unscrew the pump retaining ring.
7. Installation is the reverse of removal.

Fuel Filter Replacement

1. Disconnect the fuel line connection at the inlet of the carburetor.
2. Remove the inlet fuel filter nut from the carburetor with a box wrench.
3. Remove the filter element and spring.
4. If it is a bronze element, blow through the cone end—the element should allow air to pass freely.
5. Install the element spring and a new element into the carburetor. Bronze elements are installed with the small section of the cone facing outward.
6. Install a new gasket on the fitting nut and install the nut.
7. Install the fuel line and tighten it securely. Start the engine and check for leaks.

4. Reconnect the vacuum advance hose.
5. Disconnect the purge hose at the vapor canister.
6. On cars without A/C: set the idle speed by turning the idle screw to obtain the specified rpm. On cars with A/C: set the idle speed screw to the specified rpm. Turn the A/C on. Open the throttle momentarily to extend the solenoid plunger, then adjust the solenoid to obtain the solenoid idle speed shown on the underhood sticker. Turn the A/C Off.
7. Connect all hoses, and remove the tachometer.

1978-79 M4MC CARBURETOR

1. Run the engine to normal operating temperature.
2. Make sure that the choke is fully opened, turn the A/C Off, set the parking brake and block the wheels.
3. Connect a tachometer to the engine according to the manufacturer's instructions.
4. Disconnect the purge hose from the vapor canister. On the 350, plug the purge hose.
5. Disconnect and plug the EGR vacuum hose at the valve. Disconnect and plug the vacuum advance hose.
6. Place the transmission in Park.
7. Check and adjust the timing.
8. Reconnect the vacuum advance hose.
9. Place the transmission in Drive.
10. On cars without A/C: Turn the idle speed screw to obtain the specified rpm.
    On cars with A/C: Turn the A/C

ON and disconnect the compressor clutch wire. Open the throttle momentarily to extend the solenoid plunger. Adjust the solenoid to obtain the solenoid idle speed shown on the underhood sticker. Reconnect the compressor clutch and turn the A/C Off.
11. Reconnect all hoses and remove the tachometer.

Idle Mixture Adjustment

1978-79

Changes in the carburetors for 1978-79 cars have made the adjustment of idle mixture impossible without the use of a propane enrichment system not available to the general public. Backing out the mixture screw, of itself, will have little or no effect on the mixture.

FUEL PUMP

All air conditioned cars with V8 engines and all cars with the 455 engine have a special fuel pump. This pump has a vapor return line which returns hot fuel and fuel vapor to the fuel tank. The possibility of vapor lock is thus greatly reduced by keeping cool fuel circulating though the pump.

Fuel Pump Replacement

EXCEPT SKYHAWK

1. Disconnect the fuel inlet hose from the pump. Disconnect the vapor return hose, if equipped. Disconnect the inlet hose.

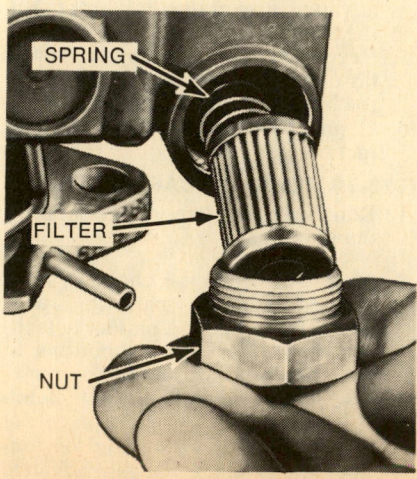

Fuel filter
(© Buick Div., G.M. Corp)

COOLING SYSTEM

Thermostat Replacement

To replace the thermostat, remove the two bolts holding the water neck in place. Remove the water neck and the thermostat will lift out. Use a new gasket when installing a new thermostat.

--- CAUTION ---

Be sure the thermostat is not reversed in its installed position. The spring should extend toward the rear or down.

Water Pump Removal and Installation

INLINE SIX

1. Drain the radiator.
2. Disconnect the heater hose and the lower radiator hose from the pump.
3. Loosen the alternator bolt and remove the belt.
4. Remove the fan blades and pulley.
5. Unbolt the power steering pump from the water pump. Unbolt the water pump from the engine.
6. Remove the pump. Be careful to pull it straight out, to avoid impeller damage.
7. On installation, use a new, sealer coated gasket.
8. Reverse the procedure for installation.

V6 AND V8

1. Drain the cooling system; on all 1975 and later models, the fan shroud must be removed. On the Skyhawk, the fan shroud and fan must be removed together.
2. Loosen the belt or belts, then remove the fan blades and pulley or pulleys from the hub on the water pump shaft. Remove the belt or belts.
3. Disconnect the hose from the water pump inlet and the heater hose from the nipple. Remove the bolts, then remove the pump and gasket from the timing case cover.

To install the pump:

1. Install the pump assembly with a new gasket. Bolts and lock washers must be torqued evenly.
2. Connect the radiator hose to the pump inlet and the heater hose to the nipple. Fill the cooling system and check all points of possible coolant leaks.
3. Install the fan pulley or pulleys and the fan blade. Install the belt or belts and adjust for correct tension.

Radiator Removal and Installation

The radiator mounting is a four-point system using rubber inserts on U shaped brackets for the lower mounting. The radiator upper mounting points are part of the upper radiator panel. The radiator is removed by removing the upper radiator panel, disconnecting the hoses and automatic transmission lines if equipped, and lifting the radiator out of the car. On models equipped with a fan shroud, remove the shroud from the radiator and position it rearward over the fan. Installation is the reverse of removal.

EMISSION CONTROLS

There are three types of emissions to be controlled: crankcase emissions, carburetor and gas tank gas vapor emissions, and exhaust emissions. See the ''Unit Repair Section'' for troubleshooting and repair information.

1972

In 1972, all engines are equipped with Positive Crankcase Ventilation, Transmission Controlled Vacuum Spark Advance, and the Controlled Combustion System. The Air Injection Reactor System is standard on all engines except non-California 350 cu in. engines with automatic transmissions. All California cars and all cars with manual transmissions have Exhaust Gas Recirculation (EGR).

The EGR System is used to reduce oxides of nitrogen emissions. To lower the formation of nitrogen oxides, it is necessary to reduce combustion temperatures. This is done by introducing exhaust gases into the intake manifold to be burned.

An EGR valve is mounted on the right rear of the intake manifold and is used to regulate the amount of exhaust gases and the time the exhaust gases enter the intake manifold. As the engine speeds up, carburetor vacuum is applied to the valve which opens a port connecting the intake manifold to the exhaust gas passage that is cast in the intake manifold. This allows exhaust gases to pass into the intake manifold. The EGR system is not in operation during engine idle.

1973

All engines are equipped with Positive Crankcase Ventilation, Controlled Combustion, Air Injection Reactor System, Exhaust Gas Recirculation, Transmission Controlled Vacuum Spark Advance System, and Evaporative Emission Control. With the exception of a low temperature cut-out valve that added to the EGR system, the emission control systems remain unchanged from previous years.

The EGR system is the same one that was used on 1972 California cars with a new temperature valve. This black and white plastic valve is located in the vacuum line to the EGR valve and it senses ambient temperature above the engine intake manifold. At temperatures below 0°F, the temperature valve closes to prevent carburetor vacuum from opening the EGR valve. When the temperature above the manifold rises above 60°F, the valve opens and allows carburetor vacuum to control the operation of the EGR valve.

1974

The 1974 Buick emission control system is unchanged from 1973, except for a required change in the EGR temperature sensor. The EGR temperature sensor now records coolant temperature rather than ambient (engine compartment) temperature. Although the system design remains unchanged, there has been an extensive refinement and recalibration of components to insure greater efficiency.

1975

The 1975 Buick emission control system has three additions to the 1974 system, while dropping the Transmission Controlled Spark system. The additions are: a catalytic converter, a choke air modulator, and an early fuel evaporation system (EFE).

The catalytic converter is a device used to reduce hydrocarbons and carbon monoxide in the exhaust system. See the Unit Repair Section for more details.

The choke air modulator, located in the bottom of the air cleaner, provides heated air to the choke thermostatic coil housing to improve drivability and performance.

The EFE valve promotes quick heating of the incoming fuel to the carburetor by directing the flow of exhaust gas through the intake manifold crossover passage underneath the carburetor.

1976

The 1976 emission control system is a carryover from 1975. The only changes are the addition of a spark advance vacuum modulator to the distributor advance circuit on the 260 V8 to more closely match timing to engine demand, and the dropping of the cold air intake snorkel to the air cleaner.

1977-79

The emission controls remain basically the same as in the previous years, other than for re-introduction of the Air Injection Reactor System (AIR) on some Buick engines. This system injects air into the exhaust ports of only four cylinders; it uses a belt driven air pump, tubing, valves, and a special head assembly. The distributor and the carburetor are specially calibrated.

Additional vacuum and spark control monitors are used on turbocharged engines.

ENGINE

NOTE: Engines manufactured by other GM divisions are used in some Buicks. Refer to the Engine Identification Codes Chart at the beginning of this section for identification.

Buick engines used are the 196, 231 V6, 350 V8, and 455 V8. These have a front mounted distributor and valve rocker shafts. For repair procedures on Buick V8s, see the Buick section of this manual. Engine coverage in this section is only for the V6.

In 1978 Buick introduced a turbocharged version of the 6-231.

Oldsmobile engines used are the 260, 350, and 403 V8s. Complete repair information is given in the Oldsmobile Section.

Repair information on the Pontiac 301 V8 is given in the Astre and Pontiac sections.

Chevrolet engines used are the 250 inline six, and the 305 and 350 V8s. Complete repair information is given in the Camaro and Chevrolet Sections.

TURBOCHARGER PRECAUTIONS

There are certain steps to be taken when performing maintenance on a turbocharged engine.

  a. When changing the oil and filter, or performing any other operation which results in oil loss or drainage, before restarting the engine, disconnect the pink wire from the distributor, crank the engine several times for short intervals, until the oil light goes out.
  b. Any time a main bearing, connecting rod bearing or camshaft bearing is in need of replacement, the oil and filter should be changed as part of the procedure. If the change is the result of sudden damage to the bearing, the turbocharger should be flushed with clean engine oil to reduce the chance of contamination.
  c. Any time the center housing or part of the turbocharger which includes the center housing, is replaced, the oil and filter should be changed as part of the procedure.

ENGINE REMOVAL AND INSTALLATION

1. Scribe marks at the hood hinges and the hinge brackets. Remove the hood.
2. Disconnect the battery and drain the coolant.
3. Remove the air cleaner.
4. On cars with air conditioning (A/C), disconnect the compressor ground wire from the bracket. Remove the electrical connector from the compressor. Remove the compressor and position the compressor out of the way. Do not disconnect any hoses.

――――――― CAUTION ―――――――

If the compressor refrigerant lines do not have enough slack to position the compressor out of the way without disconnecting the refrigerant lines, the air conditioning system will have to be discharged by a trained air conditioning specialist. Under no conditions should an untrained person attempt to disconnect the air conditioning refrigerant lines. These lines contain pressurized freon, which can be extremely dangerous.

5. Remove the fan blade, pulley, and belts.
6. Disconnect the radiator and heater hoses. Remove the radiator and shroud assembly.
7. Remove the power steering pump and move it out of the way. Do not disconnect any hoses.
8. Remove the fuel pump hoses and plug them.
9. Disconnect the vapor emission lines, from the carburetor, the vacuum supply hose from the carburetor to the vacuum manifold, and the power brake vacuum hoses, if equipped.
10. Disconnect the throttle linkage at the carburetor.
11. Disconnect the oil and coolant switch.
12. Disconnect the engine-to-body ground strap.
13. Raise the car and disconnect the starter wires.
14. Disconnect the pipe from the exhaust manifold and support the exhaust system.
15. Remove the flywheel and converter cover.
16. On cars with automatic transmission, remove the fly-wheel-to-converter attaching bolts. Match-mark the converter to the flywheel. On standard transmission models, disconnect the clutch linkage.
17. Remove the transmission-to-engine attaching bolts.

NOTE: *On inline sixes, leave the engine and transmission bolted together. They are removed as a unit. Unbolt the transmission rear mount from the crossmember and remove the driveshaft before removing the engine.*

18. Support the transmission.
19. Remove the thru-bolts from the motor mounts.
20. Lower the car, making sure the transmission is adequately supported.
21. Disengage the engine from the transmission and remove the engine from the car.
22. Install the engine in the reverse order of removal. Note that there are dowel pins in the block that have matching holes in the bellhousing. These dowel pins must be in almost perfect alignment before the engine will go together with the transmission.

TURBOCHARGER ASSEMBLY

Component Parts

NOTE: *In the course of servicing the engine, component parts of the turbocharger assembly, including the unit itself, piping, hoses and lines, and electrical connections, may have to be removed or disconnected. If removal and installation of turbocharger components becomes necessary, refer to the proper service procedure below.*

――――――― CAUTION ―――――――

If the turbocharger unit has to be removed, first clean around the unit thoroughly with a non-caustic solution. Secondly, when removing the turbocharger, take great care to avoid bending, nicking or in ANY WAY damaging the compressor or turbine blades. Any damage to the blades will result in imbalance, failure of the center housing bearing, damage to the unit and possible personal injury or damage to other engine parts.

ESC Detonation Sensor Removal and Installation

1. Squeeze, the side of the connector and carefully pull it straight up.
2. Using a deep socket, unscrew the sensor.
3. To install, reverse the removal procedure. Torque the sensor to 14 ft. lb. Do not over-torque the sensor or apply a side load when installing.

Wastegate Actuator Assembly Removal and Installation

1. Disconnect the two hoses from the actuator.
2. Remove the wastegate linkage-to-actuator rod clip.
3. Remove the two bolts attaching the actuator to the compressor housing.
4. Installation is the reverse of removal.

Center Housing Removal and Installation

1. Disconnect the exhaust outlet pipe from the elbow assembly.
2. Raise and support the car.
3. Disconnect the exhaust outlet pipe from the catalytic converter.
4. Lower the car.
5. Disconnect the exhaust inlet pipe from the turbine housing.
6. Disconnect the exhaust inlet pipe from the right exhaust manifold.
7. Remove the two turbine housing-to-intake manifold bolts.
8. Disconnect the oil feed pipe from

the center housing rotating assembly.

9. Remove the oil drain hose from the oil drain pipe.
10. Remove the wastegate linkage-to-actuator rod clip.
11. Remove the six bolts and three clamps attaching the center housing to the compressor housing.
12. Installation is the reverse of removal.

Turbocharger Unit and Actuator Assembly Removal and Installation

1. Disconnect the exhaust inlet and outlet pipes from the turbocharger.
2. Disconnect the oil feed pipe from the center housing.
3. Remove the nut attaching the air intake elbow to the carburetor and remove the elbow and flex tube from the carburetor.
4. Disconnect the accelerator, cruise and detent linkages from the carburetor. Disconnect the plenum linkage bracket.
5. Remove the two bolts attaching the plenum to the side bracket.
6. Disconnect the fuel line and all vacuum lines from the carburetor.
7. Drain the cooling system.
8. Disconnect the coolant lines from the front and rear of the plenum.
9. Disconnect the power brake vacuum line from the plenum.
10. Remove the two bolts attaching the turbine housing to the intake manifold bracket.
11. Remove the two bolts attaching the EGR valve manifold to the plenum. Loosen the two bolts attaching the EGR valve to the intake manifold.
12. Remove the AIR bypass hose from the check valve.
13. Remove the three bolts attaching the compressor housing to the intake manifold.
14. Remove the turbocharger, actuator, carburetor and plenum from the engine.
15. Remove the six bolts attaching the carburetor and plenum to the turbocharger and actuator.
16. Remove the oil drain from the center housing.

To install:
1. Install the oil drain on the center housing. Torque to 15 ft. lb.
2. Install the six turbocharger/actuator-to-carburetor/plenum bolts.
3. Place the assembly on the engine and connect all vacuum hoses.
4. Install the three bolts attaching the compressor housing to the intake manifold. Torque to 35 ft. lb.
5. Install the AIR bypass hose.
6. Loosely install the two bolts attaching the EGR valve manifold to the plenum. Tighten the two bolts attaching the EGR valve to 15 ft. lb. Tighten the EGR manifold-to-plenum bolts to 14 ft. lb.

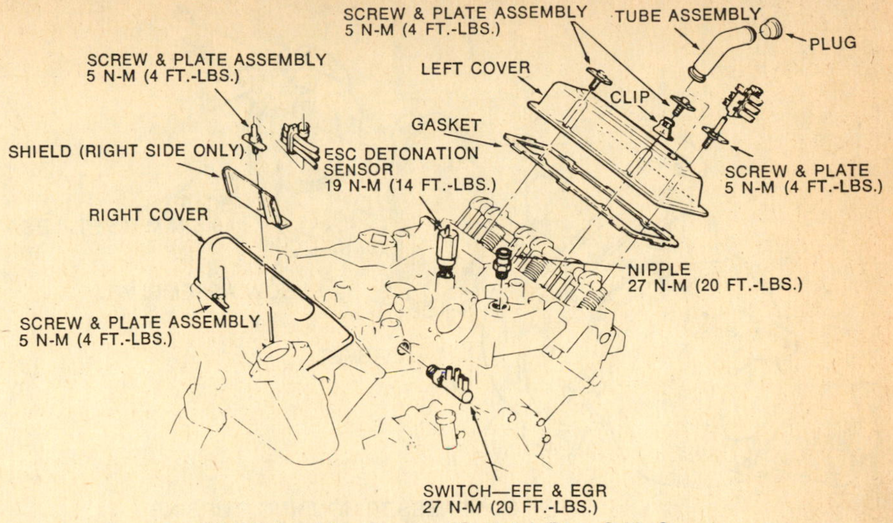

SCREW & PLATE ASSEMBLY 5 N-M (4 FT.-LBS.)
SCREW & PLATE ASSEMBLY 5 N-M (4 FT.-LBS.)
TUBE ASSEMBLY
PLUG
LEFT COVER
CLIP
GASKET
SHIELD (RIGHT SIDE ONLY)
ESC DETONATION SENSOR 19 N-M (14 FT.-LBS.)
SCREW & PLATE 5 N-M (4 FT.-LBS.)
RIGHT COVER
NIPPLE 27 N-M (20 FT.-LBS.)
SCREW & PLATE ASSEMBLY 5 N-M (4 FT.-LBS.)
SWITCH—EFE & EGR 27 N-M (20 FT.-LBS.)

ECS Detonation Sensor (© Buick Div., G.M. Corp.)

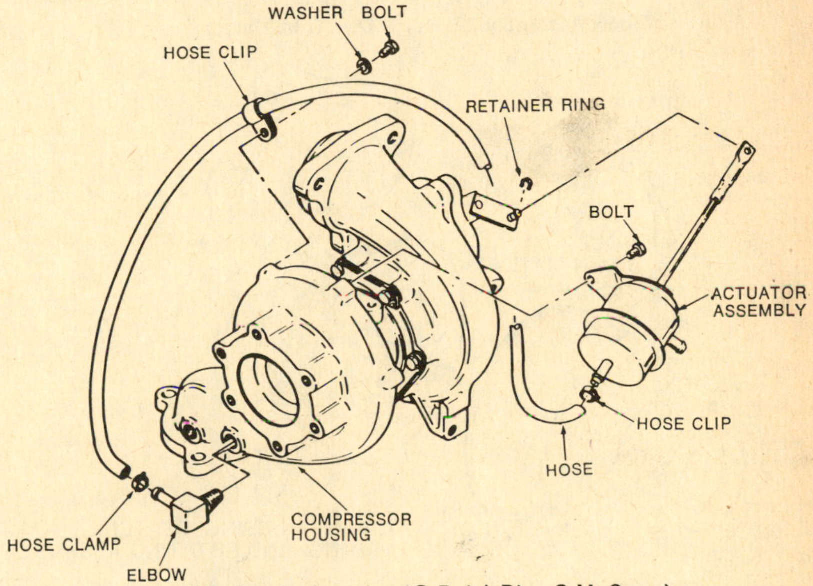

WASHER BOLT
HOSE CLIP
RETAINER RING
BOLT
ACTUATOR ASSEMBLY
HOSE CLIP
HOSE
COMPRESSOR HOUSING
HOSE CLAMP
ELBOW

Wastegate Actuator (© Buick Div., G.M. Corp.)

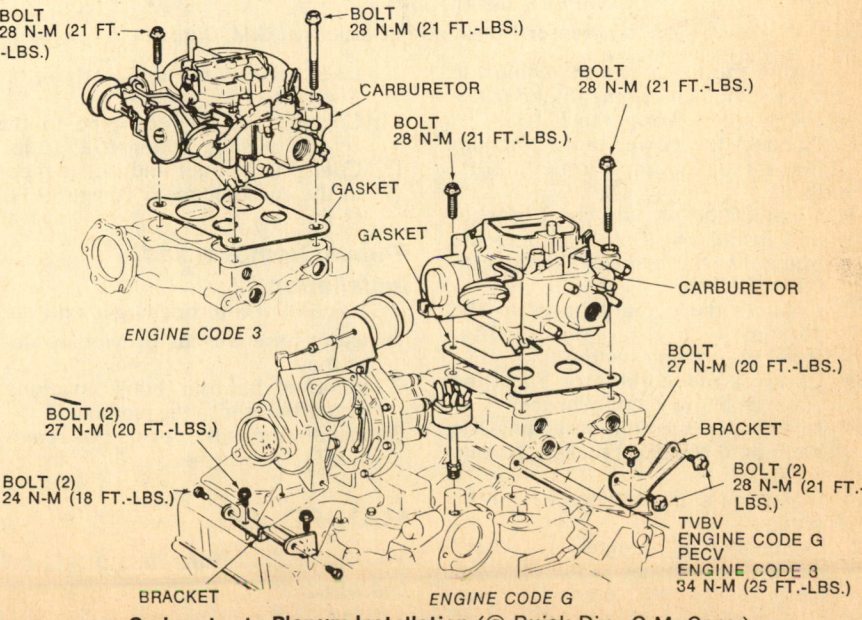

BOLT 28 N-M (21 FT.-LBS.)
BOLT 28 N-M (21 FT.-LBS.)
CARBURETOR
BOLT 28 N-M (21 FT.-LBS.)
BOLT 28 N-M (21 FT.-LBS.)
GASKET
GASKET
CARBURETOR
ENGINE CODE 3
CARBURETOR
BOLT 27 N-M (20 FT.-LBS.)
BOLT (2) 27 N-M (20 FT.-LBS.)
BRACKET
BOLT (2) 24 N-M (18 FT.-LBS.)
BOLT (2) 28 N-M (21 FT.-LBS.)
TVBV ENGINE CODE G
PECV ENGINE CODE 3 34 N-M (25 FT.-LBS.)
BRACKET
ENGINE CODE G

Carburetor to Plenum Installation (© Buick Div., G.M. Corp.)

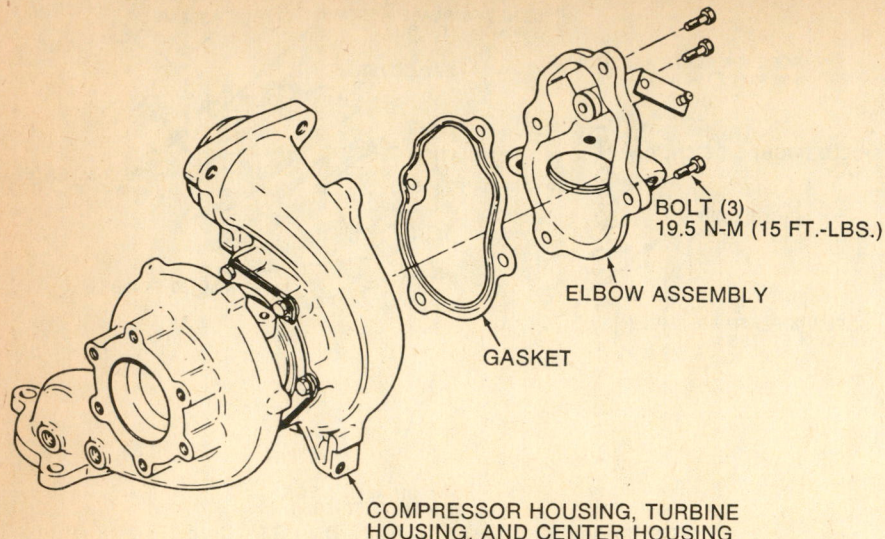

BOLT (3)
19.5 N-M (15 FT.-LBS.)

ELBOW ASSEMBLY

GASKET

COMPRESSOR HOUSING, TURBINE
HOUSING, AND CENTER HOUSING
ROTATING ASSEMBLY

Elbow Assembly (© Buick Div., G.M. Corp.)

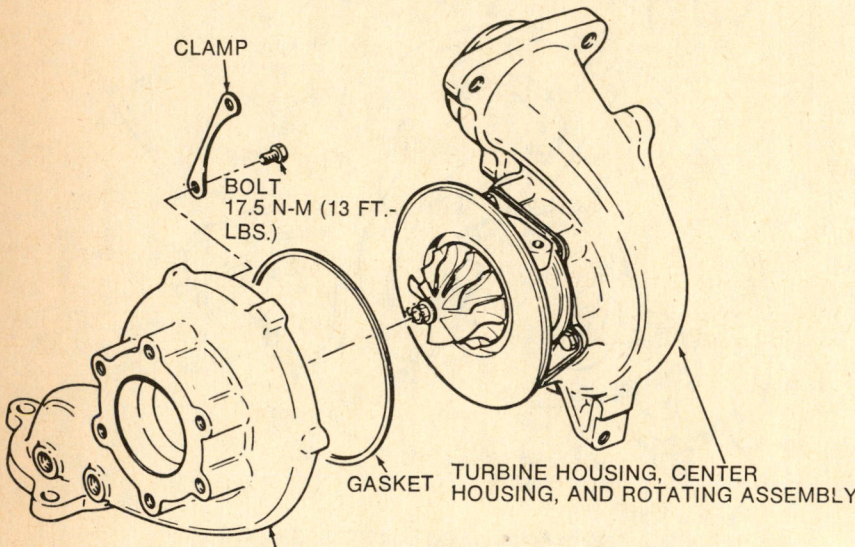

CLAMP

BOLT
17.5 N-M (13 FT.-
LBS.)

GASKET

TURBINE HOUSING, CENTER
HOUSING, AND ROTATING ASSEMBLY

COMPRESSOR HOUSING

Compressor Housing (© Buick Div., G.M. Corp.)

7. Install the two bolts attaching the turbine housing to the intake manifold bracket. Torque to 20 ft. lb.
8. Connect the power brake vacuum line at the plenum. Torque to 21 ft. lb.
9. Connect the plenum front bracket and install one bolt attaching the bracket to the manifold. Torque to 25 ft. lb.
10. Connect the coolant hoses to the plenum.
11. Refill the cooling system.
12. Connect the carburetor fuel line and remaining vacuum hoses.
13. Install the two bolts attaching the plenum to the side bracket. Torque to 20 ft. lb.
14. Connect the linkage bracket to the plenum.
15. Connect the accelerator, detent and cruise linkages to the carburetor.
16. Install the nut attaching the air in-

take elbow to the carburetor. Torque to 15 ft. lb.
17. Connect the oil feed pipe to the center housing. Torque to 15 ft. lb.
18. Connect the inlet and outlet pipes to the turbocharger. Torque to 14 ft. lb.

Plenum Removal and Installation

1. Remove the turbocharger and actuator assembly as previously described.
2. Remove the four bolts attaching the carburetor to the plenum.
3. Installation is the reverse of removal. Torque the bolts to 20 ft. lb.

MANIFOLDS

V6 Intake Manifold Removal and Installation

The manifold incorporates an ex-

haust heat passage to warm the carburetor throttle body. Engine coolant flows out of the engine through the water passages in the manifold and through the thermostat and water outlet elbow located at the front of the manifold.

1. Drain the cooling system and disconnect the battery.
2. Remove the air cleaner and disconnect all lines, wires and hoses from the carburetor.
3. Disconnect the temperature indicator wire from the sending unit. Loosen the air conditioning compressor bracket bolt and alternator bracket and swing the bracket out of the way.
4. Disconnect the accelerator and transmission linkage at the carburetor. Disconnect the throttle return spring.
5. Slide the front thermostat by-pass hose clamp back on the hose. Disconnect the upper radiator hose at the outlet.

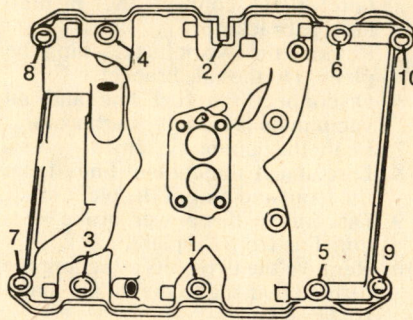

V6 intake manifold torque sequence

6. Disconnect the heater hose at the temperature control valve inlet. Force the end of the hose down to permit the coolant to drain from the intake manifold.
7. Remove the vacuum hoses from the distributor thermal vacuum switch, the EFE valve pipe and the vacuum tank hose.
8. Remove the manifold-to-heat attaching bolts. Remove the distributor cap rotor to get at the left manifold torx head bolt which requires a special wrench for removal. After removing this bolt, remove the plug wires.
9. Remove the intake manifold and carburetor as an assembly by sliding it rearward to disengage the thermostat by-pass hose from the water pump. Remove the intake manifold gasket. Reverse the above steps to install, torquing the bolts in the sequence illustrated.

V6 Exhaust Manifold Removal and Installation

1. Jack up car and support on axle stands.
2. Disconnect the exhaust crossover pipe from the manifolds on both

sides of the engine and lower it. Disconnect the choke pipe if you are working on the right side, the EFE line if you are working on the left side. On the Apollo or Skylark; to remove the left manifold, you must remove the engine left mounting bracket through bolt, loosen the right one and jack the engine up enough to provide the clearance to remove the manifold.

3. If equipped with manual transmission, remove the equalizer shaft.

NOTE: *On the right side, it may be necessary to remove the A/C, power steering, or alternator.*

4. Remove the exhaust manifold-to-cylinder head bolts.
5. Remove the manifold from beneath the car.
6. Reverse the above to install. Always use the bolt locks.

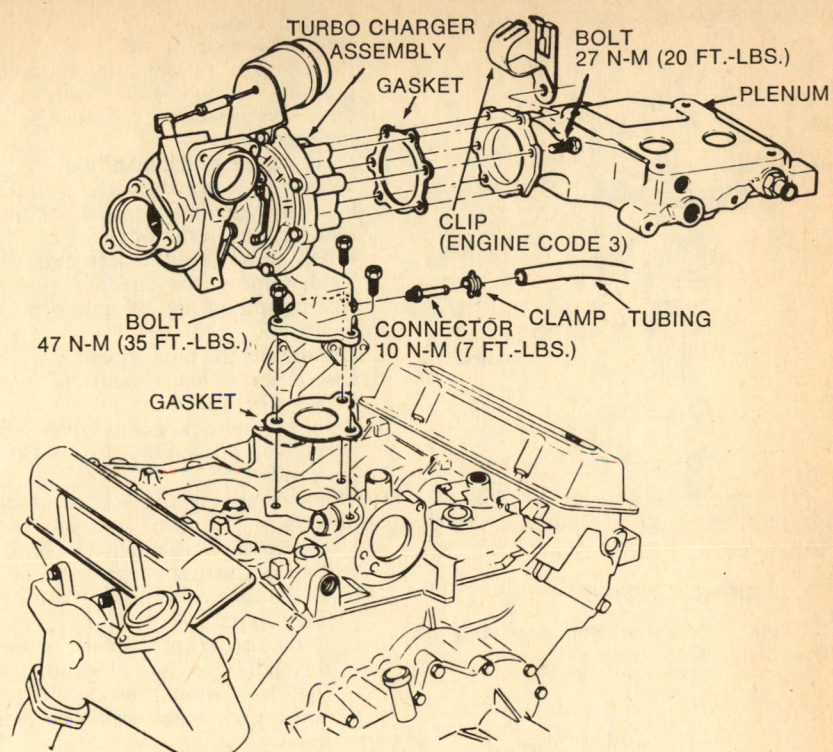

Turbocharger and Plenum Assembly (© Buick Div., G.M. Corp.)

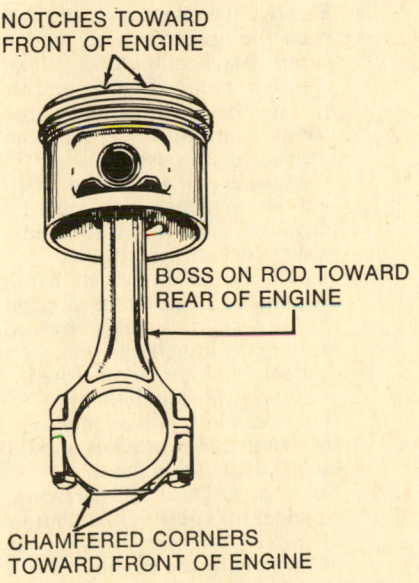

NOTCHES TOWARD FRONT OF ENGINE

BOSS ON ROD TOWARD REAR OF ENGINE

CHAMFERED CORNERS TOWARD FRONT OF ENGINE

LEFT NO. 1-3-5

Left Bank Piston and Rod Assembly (© Buick Div., G.M. Corp.)

VALVE SYSTEM

All V6 engines of Buick design use rocker arm shafts, while the engines from other GM Divisions, use separate rocker arms mounted on studs. All lifters are the hydraulic type.

NOTE: *Some of the engines use progressively wound valve springs. The coils are closer together at one end than the other. The close wound end must go against the cylinder head.*

Valve Adjustment

The V6 valves cannot be adjusted. If there is excessive clearance in the valve train, look for worn push rods, rocker arms, valve springs or collapsed or stuck lifters. For procedures on the Chevrolet engines see the Camaro section.

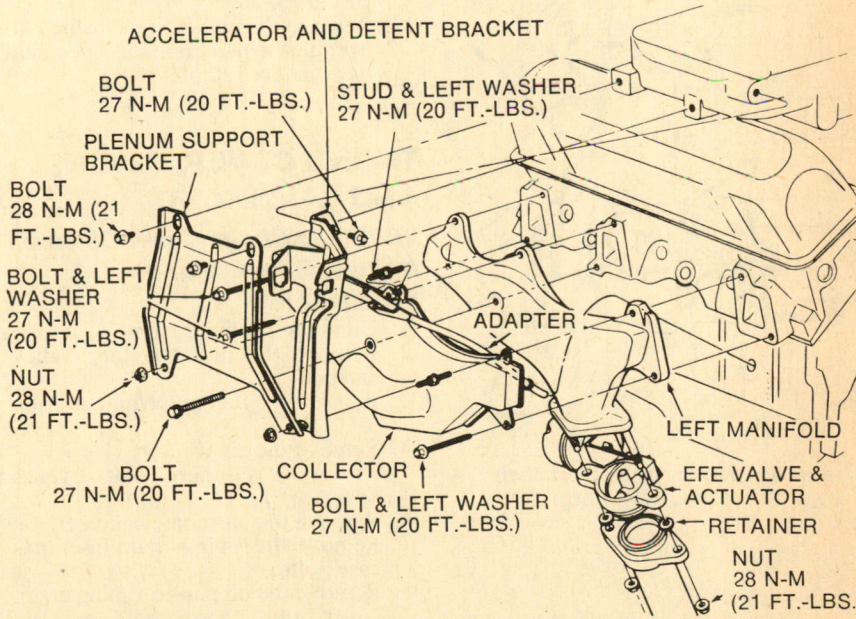

Left Exhaust Manifold and Attachments (© Buick Div., G.M. Corp.)

V6 Rocker Arm Removal and Installation

1. Remove the rocker arm cover.
2. Remove the rocker arm shaft assembly bolts and the assembly.
3. Remove the nylon arm retainers by breaking them below their head with a chisel.
4. Remove the rocker arms.
5. Install the rocker arms on the shaft and lubricate them with oil.
6. Center each arm on the 1/4 in. hole in the shaft. Install new nylon rocker arm retainers in the holes using a 1/2 in. drift.
7. Locate the push rods in the rocker arms and insert the shaft-to-cylinder head bolts. Tighten the bolts a little at a time until they are tightened to 30 ft. lbs.
8. Install the rocker cover and use a new gasket.

V6 Cylinder Head Removal and Installation

1. Disconnect the battery.

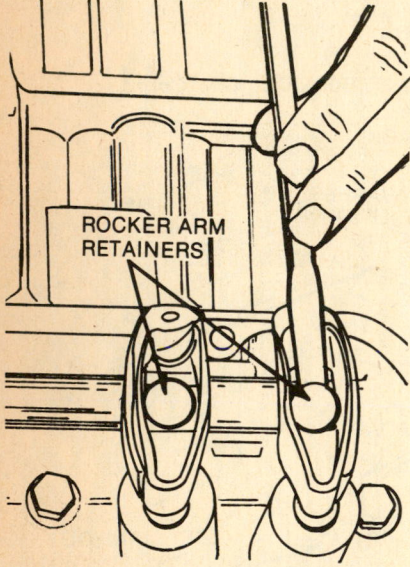

NOTCHES TOWARD FRONT OF ENGINE

BOSS ON ROD TOWARD FRONT OF ENGINE

CHAMFERED CORNERS TOWARD REAR OF ENGINE

RIGHT NO. 2-4-6

Right Bank Piston and Rod Assembly
(© Buick Div., G.M. Corp.)

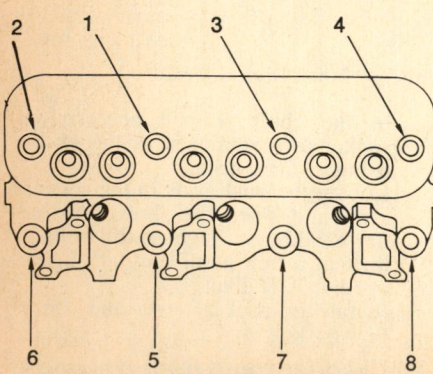

ROCKER ARM RETAINERS

Removing nylon rocker arm retainer
(© Buick Div., G.M. Corp)

V6 cylinder head bolt torque sequence
(© Buick Div., G.M. Corp)

2. Drain the coolant.
3. Remove the air cleaner.
4. Remove the air conditioning compressor, *but do not disconnect any lines.* Disconnect the AIR hose at the check valve.
5. Remove the intake manifold.
6. When removing the right cylinder head, loosen the alternator belt and remove the alternator.
7. When removing the left cylinder head, remove the dipstick, power steering pump and air pump if so equipped.
8. Disconnect the plug wires.
9. Disconnect exhaust manifold from the head being removed.
10. Remove the rocker arm cover and rocker shaft assembly. Lift out the push rods.
11. When removing the left head on Skylark:
    a. Disconnect the power brake hose at the rear of the head.
    b. Disconnect the exhaust crossover pipes.
    c. Remove the left engine mount through-bolt, and loosen the right front mount through-bolt.
    d. Raise the engine with a jack or hoist.
12. Remove the cylinder head bolts.
13. Remove the cylinder head and gasket.
14. Reverse the above steps to install. Torque the head bolts to specifications in three steps.

TIMING COVER, CHAIN, AND CAMSHAFT

V6 Timing Chain, Cover Oil Seal, & Cover Removal and Installation

1. Drain the cooling system.
2. Remove the radiator, fan, pulley and belt.
3. Remove the fuel pump and alternator.
4. Remove the distributor.
5. Remove the thermostat bypass hose.
6. Remove the harmonic balancer.
7. Remove the timing chain-to-crankcase bolts.
8. Remove the oil pan-to-timing chain cover bolts, thoroughly clean the cover and crankcase surface, and pry the seal out without disturbing the cover.
9. Align the timing marks on the sprocket.
10. Remove the bolt, washer, distributor drive gear and fuel pump eccentric from the camshaft. Remove the crankshaft oil slinger.

To install:

1. Make sure, with sprockets temporarily installed, that No. 1 piston is at top dead center and the camshaft sprocket O-mark is straight down and on the centerline of both shafts.

2. Remove the camshaft sprocket and assemble the timing chain on both sprockets. Then slide the sprockets-and-chain assembly on the shafts with the O-marks in their closest together position and on a centerline with the sprocket hubs.
3. Assemble the slinger on the crankshaft with I.D. against the sprocket, (concave side toward the front of engine).
4. Slide the fuel pump eccentric on the camshaft and the Woodruff key with the oil groove forward.
5. Install the distributor drive gear.
6. Install the drive gear and eccentric bolt and retaining washer. Torque to 40-55 ft. lbs.
7. Reinstall the timing case cover. Install a new seal by lightly tapping it in place. The lip of the seal faces inward. Pay particular attention to the following points.
    A. Remove the oil pump cover and pack the space around the oil pump gears completely full of petroleum jelly. There must be no air space left inside the pump. Reinstall the pump cover using a new gasket.
    B. The gasket surface of the block and timing chain cover must be clean and smooth. Use a new gasket correctly positioned.
    C. Install the chain cover being certain the dowel pins engage the dowel pin holes before starting the attaching bolts.
    D. Lube the bolt threads before installation and install them.
    E. If the car has power steering, the front pump bracket should be installed at this time.
    F. Lube the O.D. of the harmonic balancer hub before installation to prevent damage to the seal when starting the engine.

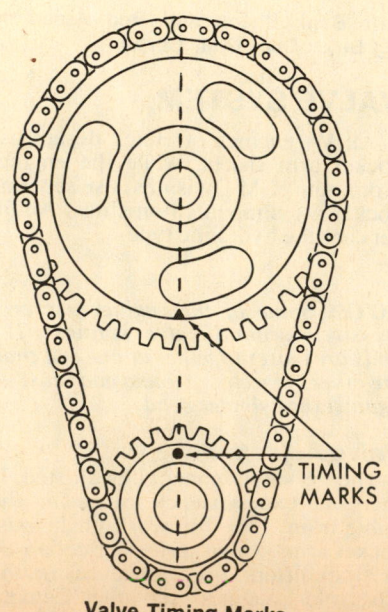

TIMING MARKS

Valve Timing Marks

V6 Camshaft Removal and Installation

1. Drain the cooling system.
2. Remove the radiator, fan, and water pump pulley.
3. Remove the grille.
4. Remove the valve cover, rocker shaft assemblies, and push rods. Keep these parts in order. They must be reassembled in the same order.
5. Remove the distributor and fuel pump.
6. Remove the harmonic balancer, water pump timing chain cover assembly, timing chain, and sprocket.
7. Remove the intake manifold.
8. Remove the hydraulic lifters and keep them in order.

NOTE: *0.010 in. oversize lifters are sometimes installed. These are identified by an O on the lifter bore and two grooves on the lifter body.*

9. Slide the camshaft forward out of the bearing bores. Do this very carefully to avoid marring the bearing surfaces.
10. Reverse the above steps to install. Clean all gasket surfaces and use new gaskets. Make sure the camshaft timing marks are aligned. Lubricate the camshaft lobes and bearings with heavy oil.

PISTON ASSEMBLY

On the V6, starting at the front, the cylinders in the right bank are numbered 2-4-6 and in the left bank are numbered 1-3-5.

All compression rings are marked with a dimple, a letter "T", a letter "O", or the word "TOP" to identify the side of the ring which must face toward the top of the piston.

When the piston and connecting rod assembly is properly installed, the oil spurt hole in the connecting rod will face the camshaft. The rib on the edge of the bearing cap will be on the same side as the conical boss on the connecting rod web. These marks on the rib and the boss will be toward the other connecting rod on the same crankpin. The notch on the piston will face the front of the engine.

LUBRICATION

Oil Pump Removal and Installation

On the inline 6, the oil pump is located in the oil pan and mounted to the front section of the cylinder block where it is connected to an oil screen housing and pipe assembly. On the V6 and V8, the oil pump is located in the left side of the timing chain cover, where it is connected by a drilled passage in the cylinder crankcase to an oil screen housing and standpipe assembly.

INLINE SIX

1. Drain the oil and remove the oil pan.
2. Remove the two flange mounting bolts and the pickup pipe bolt and remove the pump and screen as an assembly.
3. To install, reverse the above procedure, being sure to tighten the mounting bolts to 9 ft lbs.

NOTE: *The oil pump should slide easily into place. If not, remove it and relocate the slot.*

BUICK V6 AND V8

The pump can be disassembled as follows:

1. Remove the oil filter.
2. Unbolt the pump cover assembly from the timing chain cover.
3. Remove the cover assembly and slide out the pump gears.
4. Remove the oil pressure relief valve cap, spring, and valve. Do not remove the oil filter by-pass valve and spring.
5. Check that the relief valve spring isn't worn on its side or collapsed. Check that the relief valve is no more than an easy slip fit in its bore in the cover. If there is any perceptible sideplay, replace the valve. If there is still side-play, replace the cover.
6. Check the filter by-pass valve for good condition.
   To assemble the pump:
7. Lubricate and install the pressure relief valve and spring in the cover bore. Install the gasket and cap, torquing the cap to 35 ft. lbs.
8. Install the gears and check that gear-to-cover end clearance is between 0.002-0.006 in. If the clearance is less, check the timing cover gear pocket for wear.
9. Remove the gears and pack the gear pocket full of petroleum jelly. Don't use grease.

CAUTION

Unless the pump is primed this way, it won't produce any oil pressure when the engine is started.

---

10. Install the gears. Install a new gasket and the cover. Torque the bolts evenly to 10 ft. lbs. Replace the filter.

OLDSMOBILE V8

1. Remove the oil pan.
2. Remove the oil pump to rear main bearing cap mounting bolts.
3. Remove the pump and drive shaft extension.
4. Installation is the reverse of removal.

Oil Pan Removal and Installation

BUICK V6 AND V8 ENGINES

1. Disconnect the battery ground cable.
2. Remove the fan shroud-to-radiator screws.
3. Remove the air cleaner and disconnect the throttle linkage.
4. Raise the front end and support it on jackstands.
5. Drain the oil.
6. Disconnect the exhaust crossover pipe at the engine. The clutch equalizer bracket will have to be unbolted from the frame on some earlier models.
7. Remove the lower flywheel housing cover.
8. Remove the shift linkage bolt and swing it out of the way.
9. Remove the front engine mount bolts.
10. Raise the front of the engine, either by placing a block of wood and a jack under the crankshaft pulley mounting or lifting it with a hoist.

CAUTION

On air conditioned cars, place a support under the right-side of the transmission before raising the engine. If you don't do this, the engine and transmission will flip to the right due to the weight of the air conditioning equipment.

---

11. On 1974 and later Apollo and Skylark, disconnect the idler arm at the frame and swing the assembly down.
12. Unbolt and remove the pan. It may be necessary to turn the crankshaft so that it doesn't interfere with the front of the pan.
13. Reverse the procedure for installation.

OLDSMOBILE V8

1. Remove the distributor cap and place the rotor at TDC for No. 1 cylinder by turning the crankshaft pulley.
2. Disconnect the battery cable; remove the dipstick.
3. Put the car on a lift and drain the oil.
4. Remove the flywheel cover and starter assembly.
5. Disconnect the exhaust and exhaust crossover pipes.
6. Jack up the engine to disconnect the engine mounts then raise the front of the engine as far as possible.
7. Remove the oil pan mounting bolts and remove the pan.
8. Install the front and rear seals, the pan gasket, and replace the pan.
9. Reverse the removal steps to install.

INLINE SIX

1. Disconnect the battery, remove the air cleaner and disconnect the throttle linkage.
2. Remove the fan shroud-to-radiator screws.
3. Jack up the car and support on axle stands under the lower A-frames.
4. Drain the engine oil.

5. If equipped with automatic transmission:
   a. Remove the flywheel housing inspection cover.
   b. Remove the shift linkage bolt and swing the linkage out of the way.
   c. Disconnect the exhaust pipe at the manifold.
6. Remove the front motor mount bolts.
7. Jack up the engine as far as it will go, with a padded jack under the crank pulley mounting.
8. Remove the front motor mounts completely to gain clearance. Remove the left mount and frame bracket, on 1974 and later Apollo and Skylark.
9. On 1974 and later Apollo and Skylark, disconnect the steering rod at the idler lever, then move the linkage to one side.
10. On 1974 and later Apollo and Skylark, unbolt and move the brake line away from the front crossmember.
11. Turn the crankshaft until the timing mark on the damper is at the bottom.
12. Unbolt the pan. On 1974 and later Apollo and Skylark, lower it slightly and roll it into the area from which you removed the left engine mount, tilt the front of the pan up and pull it down and out to the rear.
13. Reverse the procedure on installation. Tighten the bolts to 7-10 ft. lbs., except for those that go into the front cover. These must be installed last and tightened to 5 ft. lbs.

Rear Main Bearing Oil Seal Replacement

INLINE SIX

1. The rear main bearing oil seal can be replaced without removing the crankshaft. Remove the oil pan and rear main bearing cap.
2. Remove the seal from the bearing cap and clean the groove.
3. Remove the upper seal half by tapping the seal out with a brass punch until it can be grasped with pliers.
4. To replace the bearing cap seal, lubricate the groove in the cap and lightly press the seal in place. Do not cut the end of the seal. Do not get any oil on the parting line surface.
5. To replace the upper seal, lubricate the new seal with oil. Gradually push the seal in the groove in the block, while turning the crankshaft, until the seal is rolled into place.
6. Install the rear main bearing cap and torque it to specifications. Be sure the cross seal tabs are in place and properly seated. Make sure there is no oil on the parting line between the bearing cap and the

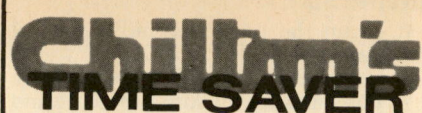

Chilton's TIME SAVER

Top Half, Rear Main Bearing Oil Seal Replacement

Although the factory recommends removing the crankshaft to replace the top half of the oil seal, the following procedure can be used without removing the crankshaft.

1. Remove the oil pan and rear main bearing cap.
2. Loosen the rest of the crankshaft main bearings and allow the crankshaft to drop about 1/16 in.
3. Remove the old upper half of the oil seal.
4. Wrap some soft copper wire around the end of the new seal and leave about 12 in. on the end. Generously lubricate the new seal with oil.
5. Slip the free end of the copper wire into the oil seal groove and around the crankshaft. Pull the wire until the seal protrudes an equal amount on each side. Rotate the crankshaft as the seal is pulled into place.
6. Remove the wire. Push any excess seal that may be protruding back into the groove.
7. Before tightening the crankshaft bearing caps, visually check the bearings to make sure they are in place. Torque the bearing cap bolts to specifications. Make sure there is no oil on the parting surfaces.
8. Replace the oil pan. Run the engine slowly for the first few minutes of operation.

block. Run the engine slowly for the first few minutes.

BUICK V6 AND V8

1. Braided fabric seals are used. The upper seal half cannot be replaced without removing the crankshaft, unless you use the Time Saver in this section.
2. Remove the oil pan and rear main bearing cap.
3. Remove the old seal from the bearing cap and place a new seal in the groove with both ends projecting above the parting surface of the cap.
4. Force the seal into the groove by rubbing down with a hammer handle or smooth tool, until the seal projects above the groove not more than 1/16 in. Cut the ends off flush with the surface of the cap. Use a razor blade.
5. Use the same procedure to install a new upper seal half after removing the engine from the car and the crankshaft from the engine.

CLUTCH

The only service adjustment necessary on the clutch is to maintain the correct pedal free-play.

Removal and Installation

1. Remove the pedal return spring from the clutch fork. On the Skyhawk, remove the clutch fork cover, then disconnect the clutch return spring and control cable from the clutch fork. Remove the transmission.
2. Remove the flywheel housing.
3. Remove the throw-out bearing from the clutch fork.
4. Disconnect the clutch fork from the ball stud.
5. Mark the clutch cover and the flywheel to assure proper balance on reassembly.
6. Loosen the clutch cover to flywheel bolts one turn at a time until the spring pressure is released.
7. Support the pressure plate and cover assembly while removing the last bolts, then remove the cover assembly and the driven plate.
8. Install the clutch by reversing the removal procedure. Use a clutch aligning pilot or a spare transmission input shaft through the hub of the driven plate and into the pilot bushing. Be sure to align the clutch cover-to-flywheel index marks.

Linkage Adjustment

THROUGH 1974

Check the pedal lash (free-play) by pushing down on the pedal by hand. Lash should be approximately 3/4 in. measured at the pedal pad.

1. Make sure the pedal is at full release position, contacting the rubber bumper stop. Remove the return spring.
2. Adjust the clutch release rod underneath the car to give zero lash at the clutch pedal.
3. Back off the release rod adjustment 2-3 turns to give 3/4 in. lash at the pedal pad. (Equals 1/16-1/8 in. at the pushrod.)
4. Tighten the locknut on the clutch release rod.

1975-77 EXCEPT SKYHAWK

1. Disconnect the return spring at the clutch operating fork.
2. Use the linkage to push the clutch pedal up against its rubber bumper stop.

3. Push the end of the clutch operating fork to the rear until the release bearing can just be felt to contact the pressure plate fingers.
4. Detach the front end of the operating rod from the clutch pivot shaft arm and place it in the gauge hole on the arm.
5. Loosen the locknut and lengthen the rod just enough to take all the play out of the linkage. Tighten the locknut.
6. Replace the operating rod in its original location.
7. Replace the return spring and check the free play at the pedal pad. It should be 3/4-1 in.

SKYHAWK
1. Make sure that the pedal is at full release position, contacting the rubber bumper stop. Remove the return spring.
2. Push the clutch fork forward until the throwout bearing just touches the clutch spring (about 1 3/4 in.).
3. Tighten the screw pin on the cable to obtain about 1/4 in. fork free play; this will produce 3/4-1 in. free play at the clutch pedal.
4. Attach the return spring.

1978-79 SKYLARK
1. Turn the clutch lever and shaft assembly until the pedal is firmly against the stop.
2. Push the outer end of the clutch fork to the rear until the throw-out bearing lightly touches the spring fingers.
3. Place the lower pushrod in the fork and gauge hole, and increase the length until all play is gone from the linkage.
4. Place the swivel or rod in the hole furthest from the centerline of the lever and shaft assembly and install the retainer.
5. Tighten the locknut and spacer against the swivel.
6. Install the clutch fork retainer spring. This procedure should produce 1 2/3 to 2 1/3 in. of travel when measured at the pedal pad centerline.

1978-79 CENTURY, REGAL
1. Remove the return spring.
2. Turn the clutch lever and shaft assembly until the pedal is firmly against the stop.
3. Push the outer end of the clutch fork to the rear until the throwout bearing touches the spring fingers.
4. Install the lower pushrod in the fork and the swivel in the gauge hole. Turn the rod clockwise as viewed from the front to remove all play from the linkage.
5. Remove the swivel from the gauge hole and install it in the hole furtherest from the centerline of the lever and shaft assembly. Install the washers and retainer.
6. Tighten the locknut against the swivel, being careful not to change the rod length.

7. Install the clutch retainer spring. The above procedure should produce 2/3 to 1 1/3 in. of free play when measured at the pedal pad center.

MANUAL TRANSMISSION

A fully-synchronized Saginaw three-speed transmission has been available in these cars. It can be identified by the single bolt at the top of the side cover. The production code and transmission serial number are on the right side of the transmission case.

The Muncie 4-speed is the only 4-speed transmission used in cars made before 1975.

Since 1978 the only 4 speed used has been the Saginaw unit. The production code and transmission serial number are stamped on the right side of the transmission case.

Starting 1976, the Skyhawk was available with the Borg-Warner 5-speed transmission. The linkage on this model is internal and does not require any adjustment.

For repair procedures, see the Unit Repair Section.

Removal and Installation
EXCEPT 5-SPEED
1. Mark the universal joint and transmission shaft companion flange for proper indexing at the time of installation. Remove the two U-bolts and disconnect the driveshaft at the rear joint. Slide the driveshaft rearward as far as possible and remove it.
2. Disconnect the shift linkage from the transmission.
3. Disconnect the speedometer cable at the transmission.
4. Loosen all exhaust pipe joints to permit the transmission and the

rear of the engine to be lowered if necessary.
5. Remove the two bolts holding the transmission mounting pad to the transmission support. Leave the mounting pad bolted to the transmission.
6. With a padded jack under the engine, raise the unit until the transmission mounting pad just clears the transmission support.
7. Remove the four bolts holding the transmission support to the body members. Remove the support, then lower the jack to allow the transmission to clear the underbody.
8. Remove the two top transmission-to-flywheel housing bolts and install guide pins.
NOTE: *If guide pins are not used, damage to the clutch driven plate can result.*
9. Remove the other transmission attaching bolts. Slide the transmission back until the drive gear shaft disengages the clutch disc and clears the flywheel housing. Lower the transmission.
10. On installation, install the guide pins in the upper and lower right-side bolt holes for alignment. If the guide pins aren't used, the clutch plate might be damaged.

5-SPEED
1. Remove the boot retainer and slide the boot upward on the shift lever.
2. Remove the foam insulator over the control assembly bolts.
3. Remove the four control lever bolts and remove the control lever.
4. Raise the car and remove the driveshaft.
5. Remove the damper assembly, the torque converter bracket, and the torque arm bracket.
6. Disconnect the speedometer cable and the back-up light switch.
7. Place a transmission jack under the transmission and remove the transmission support.

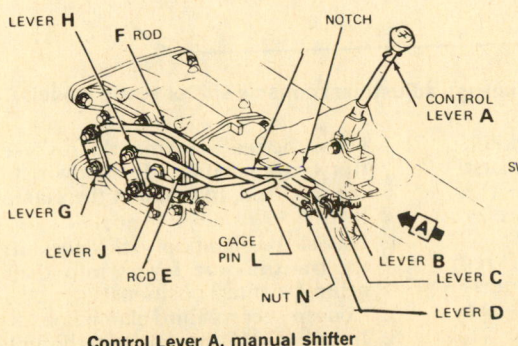

Control Lever A. manual shifter
Lever B. Reverse control lever
Lever C. 1ST-2ND control lever
Lever D. 3RD-4TH control lever

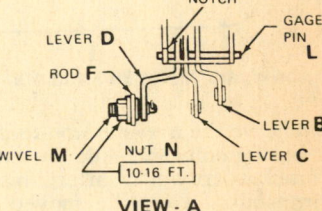

VIEW - A
Rod E. 1ST-2ND connecting rod
Rod F. 3RD-4TH connecting rod
Rod I. Reverse connecting rod
Lever G. 3RD-4TH transmission lever
Lever H. 1ST-2ND transmission lever
Lever J. Reverse transmission lever

Skyhawk 4 speed transmission linkage
(© Buick Div., G.M. Corp)

Buick Apollo • Century • Gran Sport

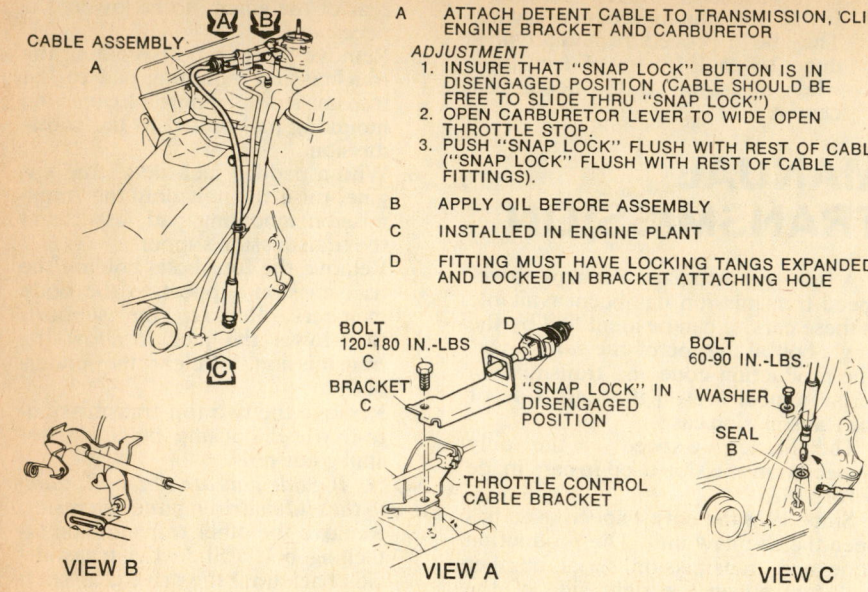

A ATTACH DETENT CABLE TO TRANSMISSION, CLIP, ENGINE BRACKET AND CARBURETOR

ADJUSTMENT
1. INSURE THAT "SNAP LOCK" BUTTON IS IN DISENGAGED POSITION (CABLE SHOULD BE FREE TO SLIDE THRU "SNAP LOCK")
2. OPEN CARBURETOR LEVER TO WIDE OPEN THROTTLE STOP.
3. PUSH "SNAP LOCK" FLUSH WITH REST OF CABLE ("SNAP LOCK" FLUSH WITH REST OF CABLE FITTINGS).

B APPLY OIL BEFORE ASSEMBLY
C INSTALLED IN ENGINE PLANT
D FITTING MUST HAVE LOCKING TANGS EXPANDED AND LOCKED IN BRACKET ATTACHING HOLE

Turbo Hydra-Matic 200, 350, 375B detent cable adjustment
(© Buick Div., G.M. Corp)

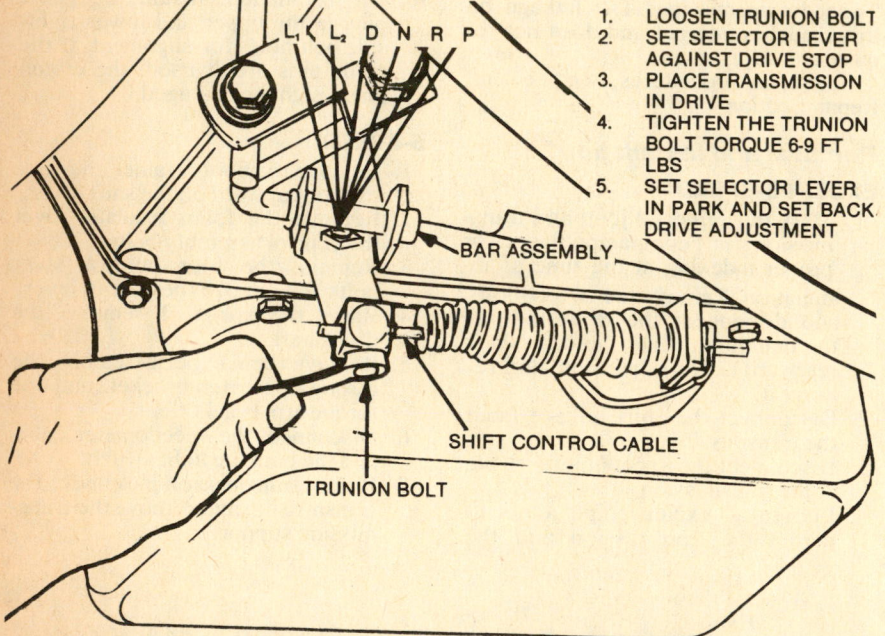

1. LOOSEN TRUNION BOLT
2. SET SELECTOR LEVER AGAINST DRIVE STOP
3. PLACE TRANSMISSION IN DRIVE
4. TIGHTEN THE TRUNION BOLT TORQUE 6-9 FT LBS
5. SET SELECTOR LEVER IN PARK AND SET BACK DRIVE ADJUSTMENT

Turbo Hydra-Matic 350 and 400 linkage adjustment console shifter (early models)

8. Remove the transmission-to-clutch housing bolts and slide the exhaust bracket forward; after this the transmission can be moved rearward and removed from the car.
9. Installation is the reverse of removal. Make sure that the transmission input shaft splines are clean and dry.

Linkage Adjustment

COLUMN SHIFT
1. Place the column shift lever in Reverse. Turn the ignition lock to the LOCK position.
2. Loosen first-reverse clamp bolt.
3. Place the transmission first-reverse lever (the rear one) into the reverse (forward) position. Pull down on the shift rod and tighten the clamp bolt.
4. Unlock the ignition lock and shift the transmission levers into their neutral (center) positions.
5. Loosen second-third clamp bolt.
6. Install a 3/16 in. dia. rod through the second-third lever, selector plate, first-reverse lever, and alignment plate at the bottom of the column.
7. Tighten second-third clamp bolt.
8. With the shift lever in Reverse, the key must move freely to the LOCK position. You should not be able to

get into the LOCK position in any gear position other than Reverse.

THREE-SPEED FLOORSHIFT
1. Place the transmission levers into neutral.
2. Loosen the shift rod adjusting clamp bolts.
3. Place a 5/16 in. dia. rod in the notch in the rear portion of the shift bracket assembly.
4. Move both shift levers back against the rod.
5. Tighten the shift rod adjusting bolts.

FOUR-SPEED FLOORSHIFT, EXCEPT SKYHAWK
1. Place the transmission levers in neutral positions.
2. Place a 5/16 in. dia. rod in the rear lower portion of the shift bracket assembly.
3. Adjust all three shift levers back against the rod.
4. Tighten the adjusting clamp bolts.

FOUR-SPEED FLOORSHIFT, SKYHAWK
1. Loosen the rod retaining nuts at the base of the shift lever; set the third and fourth, first and second, and reverse gear levers into neutral. This can be done by moving the levers counterclockwise one detent and then clockwise one detent.
2. Move the shift lever into neutral and then align the holes of the reverse, first and second, and third and fourth gear levers with the notch on the shifter assembly. When they are aligned, insert a pin to hold them in place.
3. Attach the third and fourth gear rod to the third and fourth gear lever.
4. Attach the third and fourth gear rod and retaining nut loosely to the swivel on the third and fourth gear lever. When installed, tighten the retaining nut.
5. Repeat steps 3 and 4 for the first and second, and for the reverse gear adjustment.
6. When the adjustments have been completed, remove the pin.

HURST LINKAGE
1. Shift the transmission into Reverse.
2. Push the back drive (steering lock) rod up into the reverse detent in the steering column (if applicable).
3. Tighten the clamp screw.
4. Place all the transmission and control levers in Neutral.
5. Insert a 1/4 in. drill rod through the adjustment hole in the shifter and make sure all the shift rods fit into their respective levers without tension. Adjust the length of rods as necessary, then tighten the swivel nuts.

AUTOMATIC TRANSMISSION

All of the Buick models covered in this section, use the 350 and 375B Turbo Hydra-Matic transmissions, with the 200 series added during the 1976 model year.

The identification number on the 350, and 375B, transmissions is on the left side of the transmission. The identification number for the 200 transmission is on the right side of the transmission. It can sometimes be identified by the word METRIC stamped on the pan. The 200 can readily be identified visually; it has ten pan bolts, while the 350 or 375B has thirteen.

Detent Cable Adjustment

Refer to the accompanying illustration for this procedure.

Throttle Valve Adjustment

1978-79 TURBO HYDRA-MATIC 200

1. Disengage the snap lock so that the cable slides freely.
2. With the cable in the support and attached to the carburetor lever, move the lever to the wide open throttle position.
3. Push the snap lock flush and return the throttle lever to the closed position.

Shift Linkage Adjustment

COLUMN SHIFT

1. Place selector lever in Neutral.
2. Loosen adjusting clamp bolt.
3. Place lever at transmission in Neutral position.
4. Tighten clamp bolt.

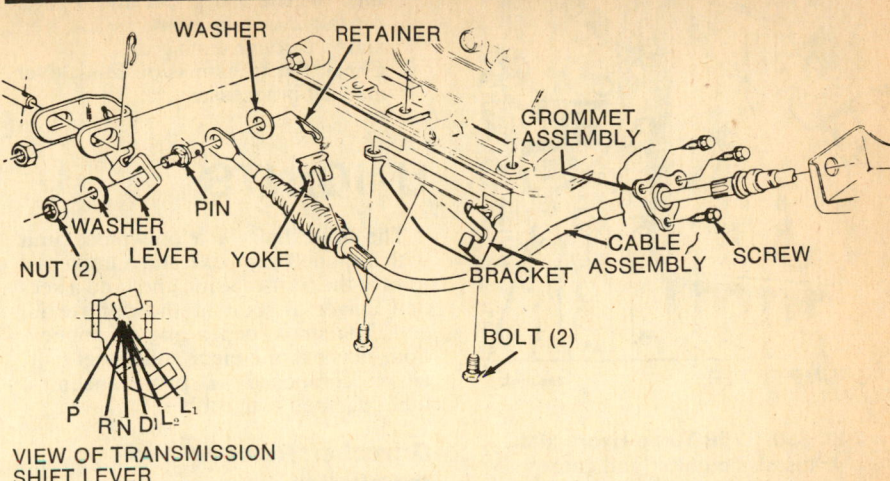

VIEW OF TRANSMISSION SHIFT LEVER

Typical floorshift cable control (© Buick Div., G.M. Corp)

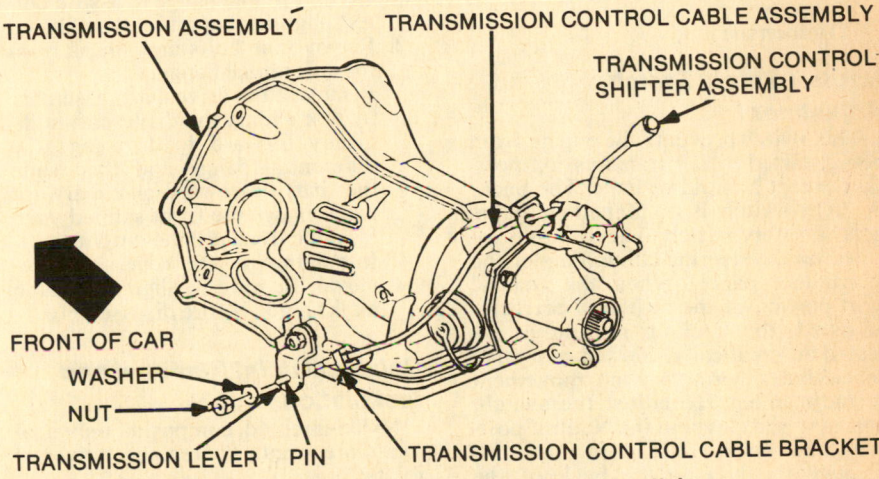

FRONT OF CAR

1976 and later Skyhawk automatic transmission linkage

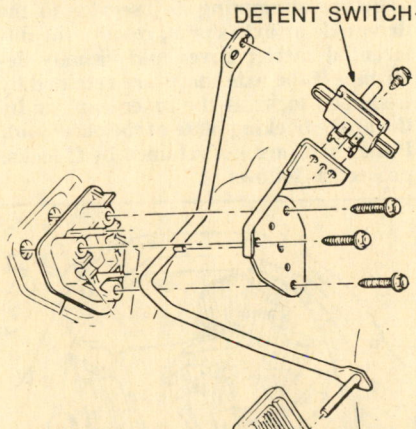

Detent switch, Turbo Hydra-Matic 400
(© Buick Div., G.M. Corp)

FLOORSHIFT EXCEPT SKYHAWK

There are two procedures that can be used, depending on the shape of the transmission end of the shifter cable. On early models, the cable ends in a straight rod with a clamp (trunnion) bolt. On later models, the cable ends in a flattened eye with a fixed bolt through it.

1. Loosen the trunnion bolt at the transmission end of the cable on early models. On later models, pull the clip from the cable housing at the side of the transmission.
2. Set the console shift lever against the Drive stop on early models. On later models, set it in the Park detent.
3. Set the transmission shift lever in the Drive position on early models and on the Apollo and Skylark. This is the third position from the back. On later models, set it in the Park, or most forward, position.
4. On early models, tighten the trunnion bolt against the cable end. On later models, replace the clip to hold the cable housing in position.
5. Place the console shift lever in the Park position.
6. Set the console shift lever in Park. Loosen the clamp at the bottom of the back drive rod (the one that goes to the steering column). Push the back drive rod up against the

stop and tighten the clamp screw.

1975 SKYHAWK FLOORSHIFT

1. Loosen the nut and swivel at the transmission lever.
2. Place the transmission lever in Neutral by moving it counterclockwise to the L1 detent and then clockwise three detent positions to Neutral.
3. Position the shift lever in the Neutral notch of the detent plate.
4. Place the flat of the swivel into the slot of the control rod. Install the washer and cotter pin.
5. Tighten the locknut and adjust the neutral safety switch if necessary.

1976 AND LATER SKYHAWK FLOORSHIFT

1. Loosen the nut on the transmission lever, with the control cable on the pin and connected to the shifter assembly and the cable bracket.
2. Place the shifter in Neutral, and the transmission lever in Neutral. You can find neutral on the transmission lever by moving it to the

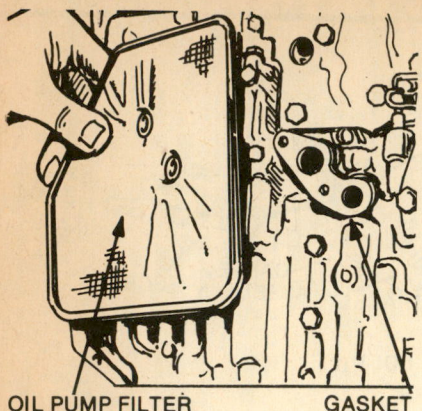

OIL PUMP FILTER
TO VALVE BODY   GASKET

**200, 350, 375B Turbo Hydra-Matic
transmission filter and gasket**

L1 detent, and then forward four stops.
3. Tighten the nut.

Neutral Safety Switch Adjustment

This switch prevents the engine from being started in any transmission position except Neutral or Park. The back-up light switch is combined with the neutral safety switch. The switch is located on the steering column under the instrument panel. When the neutral start portion of the switch is correctly adjusted, the back-up portion is adjusted automatically. Slotted mounting screw holes permit switch movement for adjustment. To adjust the switch, place the shift lever in the Neutral position and insert a 3/32 in. drill bit through the hole in the back of the switch. Move the switch until the bit goes in about 3/8 in. Tighten the mounting screws and check the adjustment.

--- CAUTION ---

When checking to see if engine will start in transmission positions other than Neutral or Park, always hold the service brake firmly.

Pan Removal and Installation, Fluid and Filter Change

1. Raise the car on a lift, remove the pan bolts and washers. Loosen the bolts gradually so that the fluid can drain out of one corner of the pan without spilling.
2. Remove the old gasket and clean the pan.
3. Remove the two screws holding the filter in place and remove it, remove the filter to valve body gasket.
4. Install the new filter to valve body gasket on the filter and install the assembly. Replace the pan, torquing the bolts to 13 ft. lbs. for the 350, 375B and 10 ft. lb. for the 200.
5. Lower the car and add three pints of Dexron automatic transmission

fluid for the 350, 375B and 6 pints for the 200; then start the car and shift it through each gear.
6. Check the transmission fluid level and add if necessary.

U-JOINTS

The driveshaft is a one piece unit with a splined slip yoke and a universal joint at the transmission end, and a second universal joint at the differential end. The shaft, depending on application, can be a one-piece solid steel unit, or be composed of two concentric tubes damped with rubber.

Driveshaft Removal and Installation

1. Mark the driveshaft rear yoke and the differential flange to assure correct alignment upon reassembly.
2. Remove the bolts and straps from the differential flange.
3. Remove the driveshaft assembly by first sliding the driveshaft sufficiently forward to disengage the differential flange and then slide the shaft downward and rearward to disengage the front splined yoke from the transmission output shaft.
4. Installation is the reverse of removal. Be sure to align the match marks made before disassembly.

Universal Joint Removal and Installation

Nylon-injected composite universal joints are used. To replace universal joints:
1. Remove the driveshaft.
2. By using a piece of pipe or similar tool, slightly larger than 1 1/8 in. to encircle the bearing shell, apply force on the yoke until downward movement of the yoke and stationary position of journal force the bearing assembly almost out of the top of the yoke (the force applied on the yoke will shear nylon retainers which lock bearings in place).
3. Rotate the shaft 180° and repeat preceding step to partially remove the opposite bearing.
4. Complete the removal of these bearings by tapping around the circumference of the exposed portion of bearing.
5. Remove the journal from the driveshaft rear yoke.
6. Remove the bearings and the journal from the splined yoke in the same way.
NOTE: *New bearings and journal assembly kits must be used upon reassembly. The kit includes snap-rings and Delrin washers.*
7. Install by inserting one bearing one-quarter way in one side of the splined yoke, using a brass hammer.

8. Insert the journal into the splined yoke (with the dust shields installed).
9. Install the opposite bearing, ensuring that the bearing rollers do not jam on the journal. Check the free rotary movement of the journal in the bearing.
10. Press both bearings into place (just far enough to install snap-rings).
11. Assemble the opposite end universal in the same way.

REAR AXLE

Axle, Shaft, Bearing, and Seal Removal and Installation

These cars use two different types of drive axle, the C-lock and the non C-lock type. Axle shafts in the C-lock type are retained by C-shaped locks, which fit grooves at the inner end of the shaft. Axle shafts in the non C-lock type are retained by the brake backing plate, which is bolted to the axle housing. Bearings in the C-lock type axle consist of an outer race, bearing rollers and a roller cage, retained by snaprings. The non C-lock type axle uses a unit roller bearing (inner race, rollers and outer race), which is pressed onto the shaft up to a shoulder. It is imperative to determine the axle type before attempting any service.

The axle identification number is stamped on the rear of the axle tube next to the differential carrier on all models except those with an 8 1/2 in. ring gear. These models have the I.D. on a tag under one of the differential rear cover bolts.

NON C-LOCK TYPE

--- CAUTION ---

Before attempting any service to the drive axle or axle shafts, remove the differential carrier cover and visually determine if the axle shafts are retained by C-shaped locks at the inner end, or by the brake backing plate at the outer end. If the shafts are *not* retained by C-locks, proceed as follows.

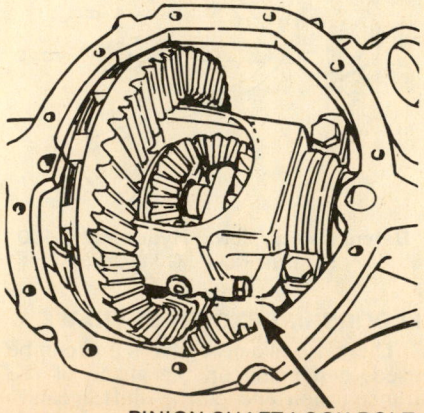

PINION SHAFT LOCK BOLT

**Removing pinion shaft lock bolt
from differential!**

Design allows for maximum axle shaft end-play of 0.022 in., which can be measured with a dial indicator. If end-play is found to be excessive, the bearing should be replaced. Shimming the bearing is not recommended as this ignores end-play of the bearing itself and could result in improper seating of the bearing.

1. Remove the wheel, tire and brake drum.
2. Remove the nuts holding the retainer plate to the backing plate. Disconnect the brake line.
3. Remove the retainer and install nuts, fingertight, to prevent the brake backing plate from being dislodged.
4. Pull out the axle shaft and bearing assembly, using a slide hammer.
5. Using a chisel, nick the bearing retainer in three or four places. The retainer does not have to be cut, merely collapsed sufficiently, to allow the bearing retainer to be slid from the shaft.
6. Press off the bearing and install the new one by pressing it into position.
7. Press on the new retainer.

NOTE: *Do not attempt to press the bearing and the retainer on at the same time.*

8. Assemble the shaft and bearing in the housing, being sure that the bearing is seated properly in the housing.
9. Install the retainer, drum, wheel and tire. Bleed the brakes.

C-LOCK TYPE

CAUTION

Before attempting any service to the drive axle or axle shafts, remove the carrier cover and visually determine if the axle shaft(s) are retained by C-shaped locks at the inner ends or by a brake backing plate at the outer end. If they *are* retained by C-shaped locks, proceed as follows.

---

1. Raise the vehicle and remove the wheels.
2. The differential cover has already been removed (see Caution note above). Remove the differential pinion shaft lockscrew and the differential pinion shaft.
3. Push the flanged end of the axle shaft toward the center of the vehicle and remove the C-lock from the end of the shaft.
4. Remove the axle shaft from the housing, being careful not to damage the oil seal.
5. Remove the oil seal by inserting the button end of the axle shaft behind the steel case of the oil seal. Pry the seal loose from the bore.
6. Seat the legs of the bearing puller behind the bearing. Seat a washer against the bearing and hold it in place with a nut. Use a slide hammer to pull the bearing.
7. Pack the cavity between the seal

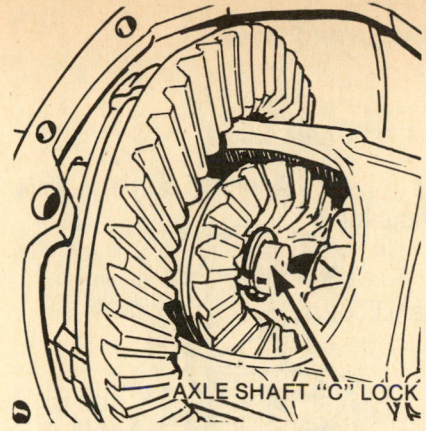

Removing the axle shaft C lock

lips with wheel bearing lubricant and lubricate a new wheel bearing with same.
8. Use a suitable driver and install the bearing until it bottoms against a tube. Install the oil seal.
9. Slide the axle shaft into place. Be sure that the splines on the shaft do not damage the oil seal. Make sure that the splines engage the differential side gear.
10. Install the axle shaft C-lock on the inner end of the axle shaft and push the shaft outward so that the C-lock seats in the differential side gear counterbore.
11. Position the differential pinion shaft through the case and pinions,

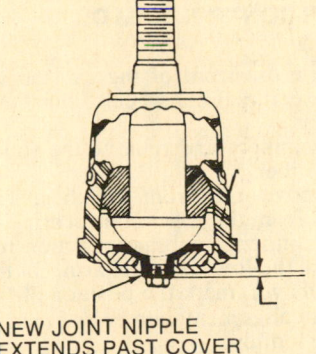

NEW JOINT NIPPLE EXTENDS PAST COVER

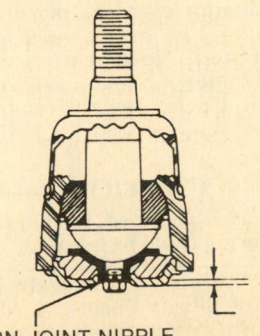

WORN JOINT NIPPLE IS FLUSH OR BELOW COVER

The wear indicating lower ball joint is used beginning 1973 on all models except Apollo, and beginning 1975 on Apollo

(© Buick Div., G.M. Corp)

aligning the hole in the case with the hole for the lockscrew.
12. Install the pinion shaft lockscrew.
13. Use a new gasket and install the carrier cover. Be sure that the gasket surfaces are clean before installing the gasket and cover.
14. Fill the axle with lubricant to the bottom of the filler hole.
15. Install the brake drum and wheels and lower the car. Check for leaks and road test the car.

JACKING, HOISTING

Jack the car at the front spring seat of the lower control arm or center of the cross member.

Jack the car at the rear at the axle housing.

To lift at the frame, use the side rails in front of the body floor pan and at the rear side rail at the lower control arm front pivot.

FRONT SUSPENSION

Ball Joint Inspection

ALL MODELS THROUGH 1972 AND 1973-74 APOLLO

NOTE: *Before performing this inspection, make sure the wheel bearings are adjusted correctly and that the A arm bushings are in good condition.*

1. Jack up the car under the front lower control arm at the spring seat.
2. Raise the car until there is 1-2 in. of clearance under the wheel.
3. Insert a bar under the wheel and pry upward. If the wheel raises more than 1/8 in. the ball joints are worn. Determine if the upper or lower ball joint is worn by visual inspection while prying on the wheel.
4. You can also measure the total length of the ball joint, with calipers, from the tip of the grease fitting to the end of the stud. Compare measurements taken with the wheel hanging free, and raised as in Step 3. If the difference exceeds 1/16 in., the joint is worn.

NOTE: *Due to the distribution of force in the suspension, the lower ball joint is usually the defective joint.*

1973 AND LATER

Beginning 1973, on all cars except the 1973-74 Apollo, lower ball joints have a visual wear indicator. The lower ball joint grease plug screws into the wear indicator which protrudes from the bottom of the ball joint housing. As long as the wear indicator extends out of the ball joint housing, the ball joint is not

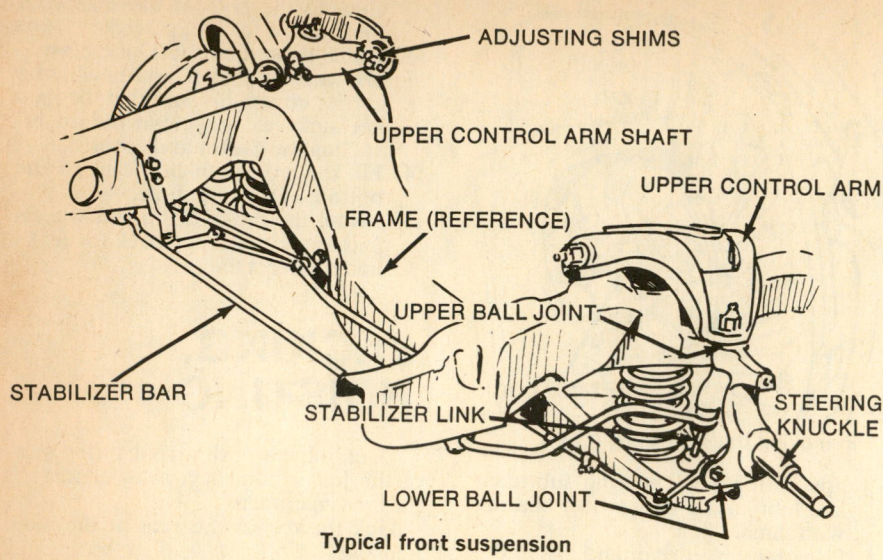

ADJUSTING SHIMS

UPPER CONTROL ARM SHAFT

FRAME (REFERENCE)

UPPER CONTROL ARM

UPPER BALL JOINT

STABILIZER BAR

STABILIZER LINK

STEERING KNUCKLE

LOWER BALL JOINT

Typical front suspension

worn. If the tip of the wear indicator is parallel with, or recessed into the ball joint housing, the ball joint is defective.

Control Arm, and/or Ball Joint, Spring—Removal and Installation

UPPER CONTROL ARM AND/OR BALL JOINT

1. Raise the car and place a jack under the frame. Remove the wheel and tire.
2. Remove the cotter pin from the upper ball joint stud.
3. Loosen, but do not remove, the nut.

——— CAUTION ———

If the nut is removed, the full force of the coil spring could be released.

Use a ball joint removal tool to free the stud from the knuckle.

4. With another jack, support the car weight under the outer edge of the lower control arm. Raise the jack enough to free the upper control arm from the upper ball stud.
5. Wire the brake and knuckle in place to prevent brake hose damage, then lift the upper arm from the knuckle.

NOTE: *If only the ball joints are to be replaced, stop at this point. Center punch and drill out the four rivets, then chisel off their heads. Remove the old ball joint. The new joint comes with four specially hardened bolts which must be torqued to 8 ft. lbs. The nut goes on top.*

6. Remove the upper control arm shaft-to-bracket nuts and lock washers. Carefully note the number, thickness, and location of the adjusting shims. Remove the control arm assembly.
7. Reverse the above steps to install. Observe the following torque fig-

ures: Upper control arm-to-frame nuts, 60 ft. lb. for Skyhawk; 75 ft. lb. for Skylark; 46 ft. lb. for all others. Ball joint stud nut 30 ft. lb. for Skyhawk; 60 ft. lb. for all others. Upper control arm bushing nuts, 55 rear, 90 front.

——— CAUTION ———

When installing the cotter pin, never loosen the nut to align the cotter pin holes. Always tighten the nut to the next slot that lines up with the hole.

LOWER CONTROL ARM OR SPRING

1. Raise the front of the car and remove the tires, wheels, hub, and rotor.
2. Disconnect and remove the shock absorber.
3. Remove the front stabilizer rod link from the lower control arm.
4. Disconnect the brake reaction rod from the lower control arm. On the Skyhawk, mark the position of the front alignment cam bolts to aid in reassembly.
5. As a safety precaution and to gain maximum leverage, place a jack about 1/2 in. below the lower ball joint stud. Now, remove the ball stud cotter pin and loosen the nut about 1/8 in. Do not remove the nut.

——— CAUTION ———

If the nut is removed, the full force of the coil spring could be released.

6. Rap the steering knuckle in the area of the stud or use a ball joint removal tool to separate the stud from the knuckle.
7. After the stud has broken loose from the knuckle, raise the jack against the control arm. Remove the nut and separate the steering knuckle from the tapered stud.

8. Carefully lower the jack under the control arm and release the spring. With the jack entirely lowered, it may be necessary to pry the spring off its seat on the lower control arm with a pry bar.
9. After the spring is removed, the lower control arm may be removed by removing the lock nut which attaches the control arm to the frame.
10. Install by reversing the removal procedure. Observe the following toque specifications: Lower control arm-to-frame nuts, Skyhawk 125 ft. lb., Skylark 95 ft. lb., all others 61 ft. lb.; ball joint stud nut, Skyhawk 60 ft. lb., Skylark 85 ft. lb., all others 80 ft. lb.

Lower Ball Joint Removal and Installation

1. Perform Steps 1-7, inclusive, as in the Lower Control Arm procedure. In Step 1, the rotor does not have to be removed.
2. Remove the ball joint by pressing the joint from the lower control arm. It may be necessary to remove the ball joint and lower control arm as an assembly and have the ball joint removed in a press if suitable tools are not available.
3. Install a new ball joint and reverse the removal procedure.

Wheel Bearing Adjustment

1. Lift the wheel off the ground by jacking under the lower control arm.
2. Remove the dust cap from the hub.
3. Remove the cotter pin and discard it.
4. Snug up the spindle nut to seat the bearings while turning the wheel. Then back off the nut 1/4-1/2 turn.
5. Retighten the nut by hand until it is finger-tight.
6. Loosen the nut until the nearest hole in the spindle lines up with a slot in the spindle nut, and insert a new cotter pin.

NOTE: *Under no circumstances is the final bearing nut adjustment to be even finger-tight.*

7. Feel the looseness in the hub assembly. There will be 0.001-0.005 in. end-play.
8. Replace the dust cover and lower the car.

Shock Absorber Removal and Installation

NOTE: *Purge new shocks of air by repeatedly extending them in their normal position and compressing them while inverted.*

1. Remove the upper shock absorber attaching nut, grommet retainer, and grommet.
2. Remove the lower retaining screws. Lower the shock through the hole in the lower control arm.
3. Reverse the above steps to install.

Tighten the upper nut to 8 ft. lb.; the lower bolts to 20 ft. lb.

REAR SUSPENSION

Shock Absorber Removal and Installation

NOTE: *Purge new shocks of air by repeatedly extending them in their normal position and compressing them while inverted.*

1. Raise the car at the axle housing.
2. Remove the nut, retainer, and grommet, or nut and lockwasher, as equipped, which attachs the lower end of the shock absorber to its mounting.
3. Remove the two shock absorber upper attaching screws and remove the shock absorber.
4. Reverse the removal procedures to install. Tighten the upper bolts to 18-20 ft. lb., the lower nut to 45 ft. lb. for the Skyhawk; 65 ft. lb.; for all others.

Leaf Spring Replacement

1. Raise the rear of the car on stands.
2. Support the rear axle to take its weight off the springs.
3. Disconnect the bottom of the shock absorber.
4. Loosen the front spring eye bolt.
5. Unbolt the spring front bracket from the underbody.
6. Lower the axle slightly and remove the front bracket from the spring.
7. Pry the parking brake cable out of its retainer bracket on the axle spring mounting plate.
8. Unbolt the spring from the axle.
9. Remove the spring plate and cushion from the bottom of the spring. There should also be a cushion between the axle and the spring.
10. Remove the upper bolt from the rear spring shackle. Lower the spring and remove the bottom bolt.
11. On installation, attach the front bracket to the spring eye. The head of the bolt should be toward the center of the car.
12. Assemble the shackle loosely to the rear spring eye.
13. Raise the rear end of spring and install the upper shackle bolt loosely, making sure that the parking brake cable goes under the spring.
14. Raise the front end of the spring and loosely attach the front bracket to the underbody. Make sure that the bracket tab goes into its slot.
15. Make sure that the upper and lower spring cushions are aligned properly. The upper one has locating ribs and the lower one, a locating dowel.

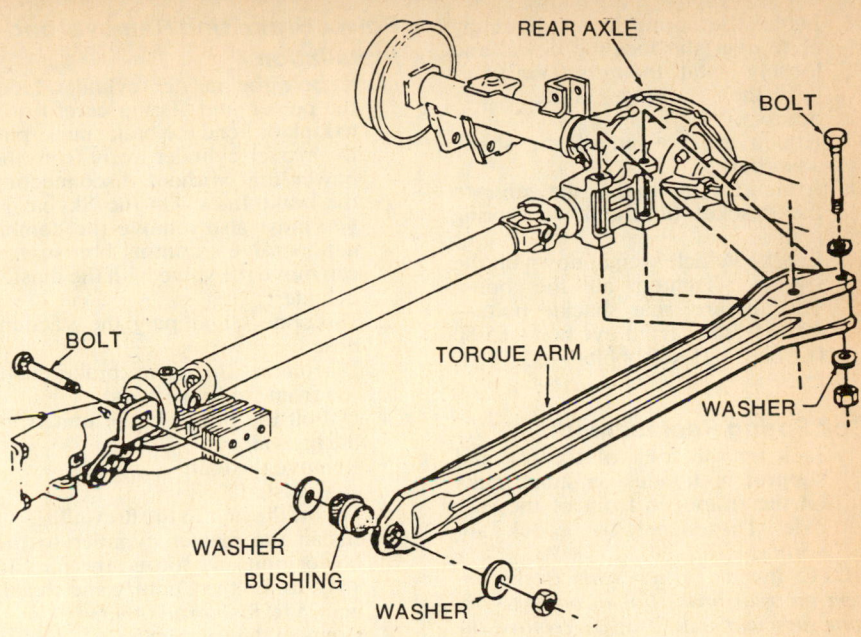

1976 and later Skyhawk rear suspension
(© Buick Div., G.M. Corp)

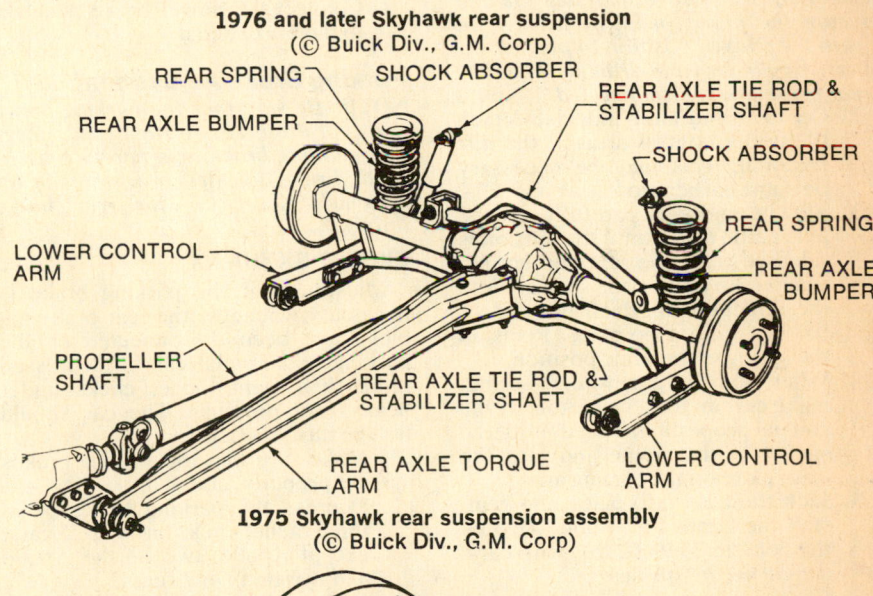

1975 Skyhawk rear suspension assembly
(© Buick Div., G.M. Corp)

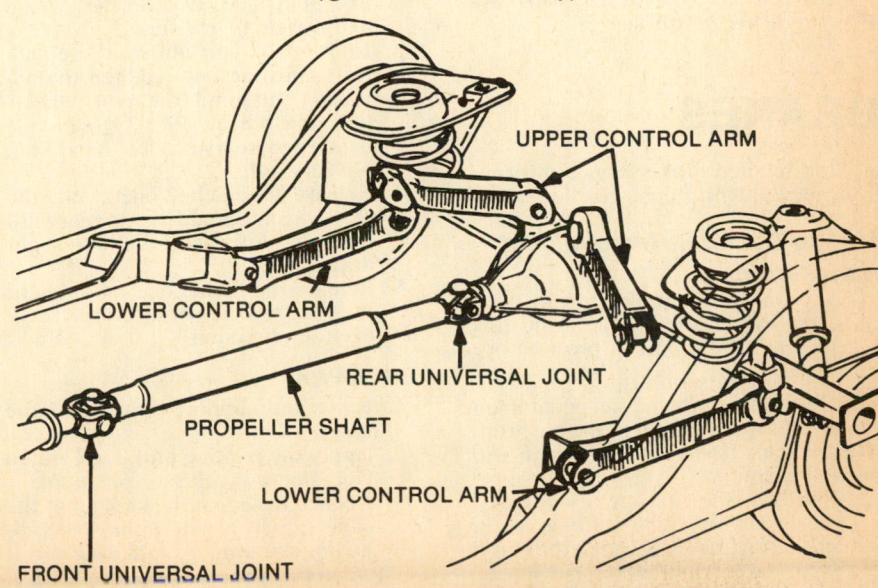

Rear suspension, except Apollo/Skylark and Skyhawk

16. Install the spring lower mounting plate over the locating dowel and loosely install the nuts. Don't forget the parking brake cable bracket.
17. Attach the bottom of the shock absorber.
18. Attach the parking brake cable to the bracket on the lower spring plate.
19. Let the vehicle weight down on the springs. Tighten all the bolts. Torques are: rear shackle bolts—40-60 ft. lbs., front eye bolt—65-80 ft. lbs., and axle bolts —35-50 ft. lbs.

Coil Spring Replacement

1. Jack up the back of the car and support both sides on stand jacks on the frame, in front of the rear axle. Disconnect the shock absorber.

NOTE: *It may be necessary to disconnect the rear brake line in order to obtain sufficient axle drop to remove the spring. If this is done, first depress and secure the brake pedal at least 1 in. from the relaxed position to prevent the master cylinder from draining when the rear brake line is disconnected.*

2. On 1973 and later models, detach the upper control arms at the differential. This may be necessary on some earlier models also.
3. Slowly, and very carefully, let the axle come down until the tension is released from the rear coil spring. Then, take off the coil spring. Note the direction in which the end of the last coil is pointing. Reinstall the spring in the same position.
4. When starting a new coil spring, make certain that the bottom of the coil is properly inserted into the socket in the frame and into the form plate on the trailing arm.
5. Jack the axle into place and reinstall the control arm bolt. Tighten the bolts to 75-95 ft. lbs. with car's weight on the springs.

BRAKES

For detailed brake service information, see the Unit Repair Section.

Master Cylinder Removal and Installation

1. Disconnect the brake pipe or pipes from the master cylinder and tape the end of the pipe or pipes to prevent entrance of dirt.
2. Disconnect the brake pedal from the master cylinder at the pushrod.

NOTE: *This step isn't required with power brakes.*

3. Remove the master cylinder-to-dash retaining bolts. Remove the master cylinder. Reverse the above steps to install. Bleed the master cylinder after it is reinstalled.

Power Brake Unit Removal and Installation

1. Unbolt the master cylinder from the power unit. Being careful not to kink or bend the brake lines, pull the master cylinder away from the power unit without disconnecting the brake lines. On the Skyhawk, you must also remove the combination valve mounting bolt so you can move the valve with the master cylinder.
2. Disconnect and plug the vacuum hose.
3. Disconnect the power brake pushrod from the brake pedal.
4. Unbolt the power brake unit from the firewall.
5. Remove the unit.
   To install:
6. Mount the unit to the firewall.
7. Install the master cylinder to the power unit and torque the nuts to 15 ft. lb. on the Century and Regal, and 25 ft. lbs. on all others.
8. Connect the vacuum hose.
9. Connect the power brake pushrod to the brake pedal.

Parking Brake Adjustment

NOTE: *Be sure that the parking brake does not drag. An overtightened, dragging parking brake on a car with automatic brake adjusters will result in an extremely short life for rear brake linings.*

EXCEPT SKYHAWK

Adjustment of the parking brake is necessary whenever the rear brake cables have been disconnected or the parking brake pedal can be depressed more than eight rachet clicks under heavy foot pressure. The car should first be raised on a lift.

1. Make sure that the service brakes are properly adjusted.
2. Depress the parking brake pedal three rachet clicks on 1972-75 cars, except Apollo, two on the Apollo and two on 1976-79 cars.
3. Loosen the jam nut on the equalizer adjusting nut. Tighten the adjusting nut until the rear wheels (lift rear wheel, 1978-79) can just be turned rearward by hand, but not forward.
4. Release the rachet one click; the rear wheels should rotate rearward freely and forward with a slight drag.
5. Release the rachet one more click; the rear wheels should turn freely in either direction.

SKYHAWK

1. Raise and support the rear of the car.
2. Apply the parking brake one notch from the fully released position.
3. Loosen the adjusting locknut at the cable equalizer and tighten the adjusting nut until a slight drag is felt when the rear wheels are rotated.
4. Tighten the locknut securely.

5. The rear wheels should rotate freely when the parking brake is fully released.
6. Lower the vehicle.

STEERING

Refer to the Unit Repair Section for adjustments and repairs to steering gear, both manual and power assisted.

Power Steering Pump Removal and Installation

1. Remove the hoses at the pump and tape the openings shut to prevent contamination. Position the disconnected lines in a raised position to prevent leakage.
2. Remove the pump belt.
3. Loosen the retaining bolts and any braces, and remove the pump.
4. Install the pump on the engine with the retaining bolts hand-tight.
5. Connect and tighten the hose fittings.
6. Refill the pump with fluid and bleed by turning the pulley counterclockwise (viewed from the front). Stop the bleeding when air bubbles no longer appear.
7. Install the pump belt on the pulley and adjust the tension.

Power Steering System Bleeding

The system must be bled of air whenever any parts of the pump circuit have been disconnected or replaced.

1. Fill the reservoir. Be careful not to overfill, because the level is normally checked at operating temperature after expansion has taken place. Allow the fluid to remain undisturbed for at least two minutes.
2. Start the engine and run it for only about two seconds.
3. Fill again as necessary.
4. Repeat Steps 1 to 3 until the level remains constant.
5. Raise the front wheels off the ground.
6. Run the engine at about 1,500 rpm and turn the wheels gently against the stops in either direction.
7. Fill again as necessary.
8. Lower the car to the ground. Turn the wheels gently against the stops in either direction with the engine running.
9. Fill again as necessary.

Steering Wheel Removal and Installation

EXCEPT TILT AND TELESCOPE COLUMN

1. Unplug the horn wire connector from the steering column.
2. On cars with a standard wheel or optional wood-rim wheel, pull off the cap, remove the three screws and the contact, insulator, and

spring. On cars with the bar-type horn actuator, remove the screws securing the actuator from the underside of the steering wheel, pull out the lead connector plug, and remove the actuator assembly.

3. Loosen the steering wheel nut.
4. Apply the steering wheel puller and pull the wheel up to the nut. Now remove the puller, nut and steering wheel.

— CAUTION —

Don't pound on the steering wheel in either direction or the collapsible steering column will collapse, requiring replacement.

On installation:

NOTE: *Location marks are provided on the steering wheel and shaft to simplify proper indexing at the time of installation.*

1. Install wheel with the location mark aligned with that of the shaft.
2. Install the wheel nut and torque to 30 ft lbs.
3. Reinstall horn button or actuator assembly.

TILT AND TELESCOPE COLUMN

1. Disconnect the battery ground.
2. Remove the three attaching screws and lift the pad from the column.
3. Disconnect the horn wire by pushing in the connector and turning it counterclockwise.
4. Push the locking lever counterclockwise until full release is obtained.
5. Mark the lock plate-to-locking lever position and remove the plate and lever.
6. Remove the steering wheel retaining nut and remove the wheel with a puller.
7. Install a 5/16 in. x 18 set screw into the upper shaft at the fully extended position and lock it.
8. Install the steering wheel, observing the aligning mark on the hub and the slash mark on the end of the shaft. Make certain that the unattached end of the horn upper contact assembly is seated flush against the top of the horn contact carrier button.
9. Install the nut on the upper steering shaft and torque to 30 ft. lb.
10. Remove the set screw installed in step 7.
11. Install the plate assembly finger tight.
12. Position the locking lever in the vertical position and move it counterlockwise until the holes in the plate align with the holes in the lever. Install the attaching screws.
13. Align the pad assembly with the holes in the steering wheel and install the retaining screws.
14. Connect the battery.
15. Make certain that the locking lever securely locks the wheel travel and that the wheel travel is free in the unlocked position.

Tie-Rod End Removal and Installation

1. Loosen the tie-rod adjuster sleeve clamp nuts.
2. Remove the tie-rod stud nut cotter pin and nut.
3. Remove the tie-rod stud from the steering arm or intermediate rod. This is a taper fit. Removal is accomplished using a ball joint removal tool or by hitting the steering arm sharply with a hammer, while using a heavy hammer as a backup. If the joint is to be reused, the removal tool must be used.

NOTE: *If a turning force of more than 7 ft. lb. is needed for end removal, after breakaway, the nuts and bolts should be replaced.*

4. Unthread the tie rod from the adjuster sleeve. Outer tie rods have right-hand threads and inner tie rods have left-hand threads. Count the number of turns the tie rod must be rotated to remove it from the adjusting sleeve. This will allow a reasonably accurate realignment upon reassembly.
5. Reverse the removal procedures to install. Clean rust and dirt from the threads. Observe the following torque specifications: steering arm-to-tie rod end nut, 35 ft. lb.; tie rod clamp nuts, 11-14 ft. lb.; tie rod-to-intermediate nut, 40 ft. lb. Check the alignment and adjust if necessary.

Turn Signal Switch Removal and Installation

EXCEPT TILT AND TELESCOPE COLUMN

NOTE: *The steering wheel must always be supported. Use extreme care not to bend the steering column.*

1. Remove the steering wheel.
2. Remove the three cover screws and the cover. All 1976 and later steering columns have a redesigned lock plate which is removed by inserting a screwdriver in the cover slot and prying out. This is done in at least two of the slots to avoid breaking the plate.
3. Depress the lock plate and remove the snap-ring. Remove the lock plate.
4. Remove the spring and horn contact signal cancelling cam. Remove the thrust washer.
5. Remove the turn signal lever, depress the hazard warning knob, and remove the knob and tilt column lever—if equipped.
6. Remove the three turn signal switch mounting screws. Pull the connector out of the bracket on the column.
7. Pull the switch straight up with the wire protector and wire harness.
8. Reverse the above steps to install.

TILT AND TELESCOPE COLUMN

1. Disconnect the battery ground.

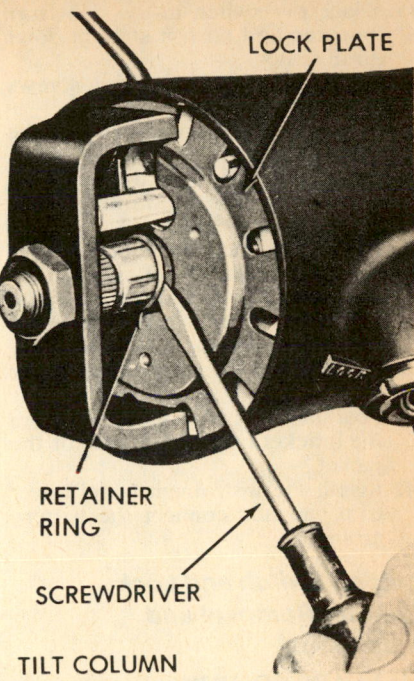

LOCK PLATE

RETAINER RING

SCREWDRIVER

TILT COLUMN

Removing lock plate
(© Buick Div., G.M. Corp)

2. Remove the steering wheel and lock plate as previously described.
3. Remove the upper bearing preload spring.
4. Position the turn signal lever in the right turn position and remove the lever and screw.
5. With column mounted dimmer switches, remove the actuator arm and screw, then remove the turn signal arm by pulling it straight out.
6. Push in on the warning hazard knob, then remove the retaining screw and knob.
7. Position the column in the center position and remove the three turn signal switch attaching screws.
8. Remove the instrument panel lower trim pad and disconnect the turn signal harness connector. Lift the connector from the mounting bracket on the right side of the jacket.
9. Remove the toe pan bolts.
10. Remove the four bolts attaching the bracket assembly to the jacket.
11. Remove the shift indicator retaining clip.
12. Support the column and remove the bracket assembly. Remove the wire protector from the turn signal wiring. Pull the turn signal switch and wiring from the column.
13. Prior to installation, coat all moving parts with lithium based grease.
14. Insert switch wiring into the column.

— CAUTION —

Angling or cocking of the switch can cause damage to the buzzer terminal or tangs.

15. Place the switch in the right turn position and push it straight down until seated.
16. Install the switch attaching screws and torque them to 25 in. lb.
17. Position the turn signal in the center.
18. Connect the wiring to the harness.
19. Install the hazard warning knob and turn signal lever.
20. Install the lock plate and carrier and the steering wheel.
21. Install the wiring protector and bracket. Torque the bracket bolts to 18 ft. lb. and the nuts to 24 ft. lb.
22. Install the shift indicator needle or clip.
23. Position the harness connector in the bracket on the right side of the jacket.
24. Install the instrument panel lower trim pad and connect the battery ground.

Ignition Switch and Lock Cylinder Removal and Installation

STANDARD COLUMN

1. Remove the steering wheel using a proper puller.
2. Remove the three cover screws and cover; remove the retainers. All 1976 and later steering columns have a redesigned lock plate which is removed by inserting a screwdriver in the cover slot and prying out. This is done in at least two of the slots to avoid breaking the plate.
3. Depress the lock plate, then remove the wire snap-ring and lock plate.
4. Slide the upper bearing preload spring and cancelling cam off the shaft. Remove the steering column-to-instrument panel attaching bolts (2), and carefully lower the column.
5. Slide the thrust washer off the shaft, then remove the turn signal lever screw and lever.
6. Push in the four-way flasher switch; remove the knob.
7. Remove the three turn signal switch mounting screws, pull the connector out of its bracket on the column and tape the upper part of the connector and wires together.
8. Pull the turn signal switch out of the column jacket.
9. Insert a small screwdriver into the slot next to the turn signal switch mounting screw boss (right-hand slot), depress the spring latch and remove the key lock.
10. Pull the buzzer switch straight out, depressing the switch clip with pliers.
11. Place the ignition switch in the accessory position by pulling up on the connecting rod until there is a definite stop or detent felt.
12. Remove the two attaching screws and the ignition switch.

13. Assembly is the reverse of the above. However, note the following steps before proceeding with the reassembly.
14. To install the steering lock, hold the lock cylinder sleeve and rotate the knob clockwise against the stop. Insert the cylinder into the cover bore with the key on the cylinder sleeve aligned with the keyway in the housing. Then push the cylinder in until it bottoms. Maintaining a light inward pressure, rotate the knob counterclockwise until the drive section of the cylinder mates with the drive shaft. Push in until the snap-ring pops into the groove and the lock cylinder is secured in the cover. Check for free rotation.
15. When installing the ignition switch, be sure the lock cylinder is in the LOCK position. Put the shift bowl or shroud in the PARK position. Make sure the ignition switch is in the LOCK position. Then insert the actuator rod into the switch and assemble the switch to the column.
16. The neutral start switch is adjusted with the shift is adjusted with the shift lever in the Drive position.

TILT COLUMN

1. Remove column mounting bracket from column.
NOTE: *Be careful not to damage the "breakaway" capsules.*
2. Remove the steering wheel using a proper puller.
3. Remove the turn signal wire protector (lower column).
4. Remove the three column cover screws and cover. All 1976 and later steering columns have a redesigned lock plate which is removed by inserting a screwdriver in the cover slot and prying out. This is done in at least two of the slots to avoid breaking the plate.
5. Remove the tilt release lever, turn the signal switch lever, push the four-way flasher knob in and remove the knob, and remove the upper shift lever.
6. Depress the lock plate and remove the snap-ring; remove the lock plate.
7. Remove the cancelling cam and spring.
8. Remove the three turn signal switch screws, tape the wires to the wire connector at the upper end and place the shift bowl in Low. Pull the switch straight up and out.
9. Insert a small screwdriver into the slot next to the turn signal switch mounting screw boss (right-hand slot) depress the spring latch and remove the key lock.
10. Remove the buzzer switch straight out, depressing the switch clip with pliers.
11. Remove the three housing cover screws and cover.
12. Install the tilt release lever and

place column in full UP position.
13. Place a screwdriver in the slot of the tilt spring retainer, press in about 3/16 in. and turn counterclockwise. Remove the spring and guide.
NOTE: *The spring is very strong—be careful.*
14. Place the column in neutral position, push in on the upper steering shaft, remove the inner race seat and race.
15. Remove the upper flange pinch bolt, place the ignition switch in the accessory position, remove the two switch mounting screws and switch.
NOTE: *The neutral start switch can be removed at this time, if necessary.*
16. Assembly is the reverse of the above. However, note the following steps before proceeding with the reassembly.
17. To install the steering lock, hold the lock cylinder sleeve and rotate the knob clockwise against the stop. Insert the cylinder into the cover bore with the key on the cylinder sleeve aligned with the keyway in the housing. Then push the cylinder in until it bottoms. Maintaining a light inward pressure, rotate the knob counterclockwise until the drive section of the cylinder mates with the drive shaft. Push in until the snap-ring pops into the groove and the lock cylinder is secured in the cover. Check for free rotation.
18. When installing the ignition switch, be sure the lock cylinder is in the LOCK position. Put the shift bowl or shroud in the PARK position. Make sure the ignition switch is in the LOCK position. Then insert the actuator rod into the switch and assemble the switch to the column.
19. The neutral start switch is adjusted with the shift lever in the Drive position.

INSTRUMENT PANEL

Light Switch Replacement
1. Disconnect the battery.
2. Disconnect the multiple connector from the switch.
3. Pull the switch knob to the last notch and depress the spring loaded latch button on top of the switch while pulling the knob and rod out of the switch.
NOTE: *On A/C cars, remove the left duct.*
4. Remove the escutcheon and the switch.
5. Install in the reverse of the above.

Speedometer Cable Replacement
1. Reach up underneath the instru-

ment panel and disconnect the cable housing from the cluster housing. On some models you might first have to remove the left air conditioning duct.
2. Carefully pull the cable housing down and pull out the cable.
3. Hold the cable vertically and turn it slowly between your fingers. If it is kinked, you will notice it flopping around. Replace any kinked cable.
4. Install the new cable in the cable housing after lubricating it.
5. If the cable core is broken, raise and support the car. Disconnect the cable from the transmission, remove the gear and pull the core from the cable.

WINDSHIELD WIPERS

Wiper Motor Removal and Installation

NON-HIDDEN WIPERS
1. Disconnect the battery.
2. Remove the cowl screen. Beginning 1974, this is necessary only on Apollo.
3. Loosen the two nuts on the adjustable motor drive link at the crank arm and slip the drive link off.
4. Remove the electrical connectors from the washer motor and pump.
5. Disconnect the washer pump hoses.
6. Remove the three bolts securing the motor to the cowl and carefully lift the motor away from the cowl.
7. Reverse the above steps for installation.

HIDDEN WIPERS
1. Disconnect the battery.
2. Remove the hoses from the washer nozzles.
3. Remove the rubber weatherstrip and cowl screen.
4. Loosen the two nuts on the adjustable motor drive link at the crank arm and slip the drive link off.
5. Disconnect the washer hoses and electrical connectors.
6. Remove the three wiper motor-to-cowl retaining screws and the motor.
7. Reverse the above steps to install.

Wiper Blade Removal and Installation
Any one of three methods of blade attachment may be used on these models. If there is a small tab on top of the blade, depress it and slide off the blade. If there is a small spring visible in the top of the blade, insert a screwdriver in the opening, press down and slide the blade off. If there is a clip on the underside of the arm, press down on the clip and slide the blade off.

RADIO

The antenna trim must be adjusted on AM radios, when major repair has been done to the unit or the antenna changed. The trimmer screw is located behind the right side knob. Raise the antenna to its full height. Tune to a weak station around 1400 and turn the volume up. Turn the trimmer screw until the maximum volume is achieved.

Removal and Installation

— **CAUTION** —

Don't turn on the radio without the speaker connected. Failure will result.

1972
NOTE: *If equipped with stereo tape, remove the tape player before starting Step 2.*
1. Disconnect the battery ground lead.
2. Remove the radio knobs, escutcheons, and hex nuts.
3. Remove the two screws from the radio filler plate and remove the plate.
4. Remove the ashtray assembly.
5. Remove the center air conditioning duct, if so equipped.
6. Remove the radio bracket.
7. Remove the two instrument panel attaching nuts at the radio face.
8. Disconnect the wiring and remove the radio downward.
9. Install in the reverse order of removal.

1973 AND LATER, EXCEPT SKYHAWK
NOTE: *Use Steps 1, 2, 5, and 6 on the Apollo and Skylark.*
1. Disconnect the battery ground cable.
2. Remove the radio knobs and trim rings.
3. Remove the two screws and remove the center air conditioning duct assembly control. Disconnect the left air conditioning hose. Remove the glove box, if necessary.
4. Disconnect the antenna, power, and speaker leads.
5. Loosen the support nut or screw at the side of the radio.
6. Remove the radio shaft nuts and slide the radio back and down.
7. Reverse the procedure on installation, adjusting the trimmer screw before replacing the right knob.

1975 SKYHAWK
1. Disconnect the battery; remove the clock knob and trim panel.
2. Remove the instrument panel cover, glove compartment, and four attaching nuts from above the glove compartment door.
3. Lower the steering column by removing the nuts holding the column to the upper bracket guide.

— **CAUTION** —

Be extremely careful not to let the column drop or hang unsupported.

4. Disconnect the speedometer cable from the speedometer; remove the instrument cluster assembly.
5. Remove all the knobs and escutcheons from the radio; remove the radio support bracket retaining screw from the lower dash.
6. Disconnect the electrical connections and antenna lead wire, remove the radio.
7. Installation is the reverse of removal.

1976 AND LATER SKYHAWK
1. Disconnect the battery negative cable and pull off the radio control knobs and bezels.
2. With a deep well socket, remove the control shaft nuts and washers.
3. Remove the antenna wire, and remove the two screws holding the radio to the instrument panel.
4. Lower the radio with the mounts attached and remove the lead wires.
5. Remove the radio mounts and put them on the new radio, then install the radio reversing Steps 1 through 4.

HEATER

Heater Core Removal and Installation without A/C

1972
1. Remove the right front inner fender panel.
2. Drain the radiator.
3. Disconnect the control cables from the defroster door and the outside air inlet door. Disconnect the temperature control cable from the temperature door.
4. Remove the nuts from the heater assembly studs.
5. Disconnect the inlet and the outlet hoses.
6. Remove the connector from the blower motor resistor.
7. Remove the screws securing the defroster outlet assembly to the top of the heater assembly.
8. Work the heater assembly rearward until the studs clear the firewall. Remove the heater assembly.
9. Install in the reverse of the above.

1973-77, EXCEPT APOLLO/ SKYLARK
1. Drain the radiator and disconnect the heater inlet and outlet hoses at the dash. On the Skyhawk, remove the blower inlet to firewall screws, remove the blower inlet, motor and wheel as an assembly.
2. Disconnect the control wires from the defroster door and vacuum hose diverter door actuator diaphragm and control cable from the

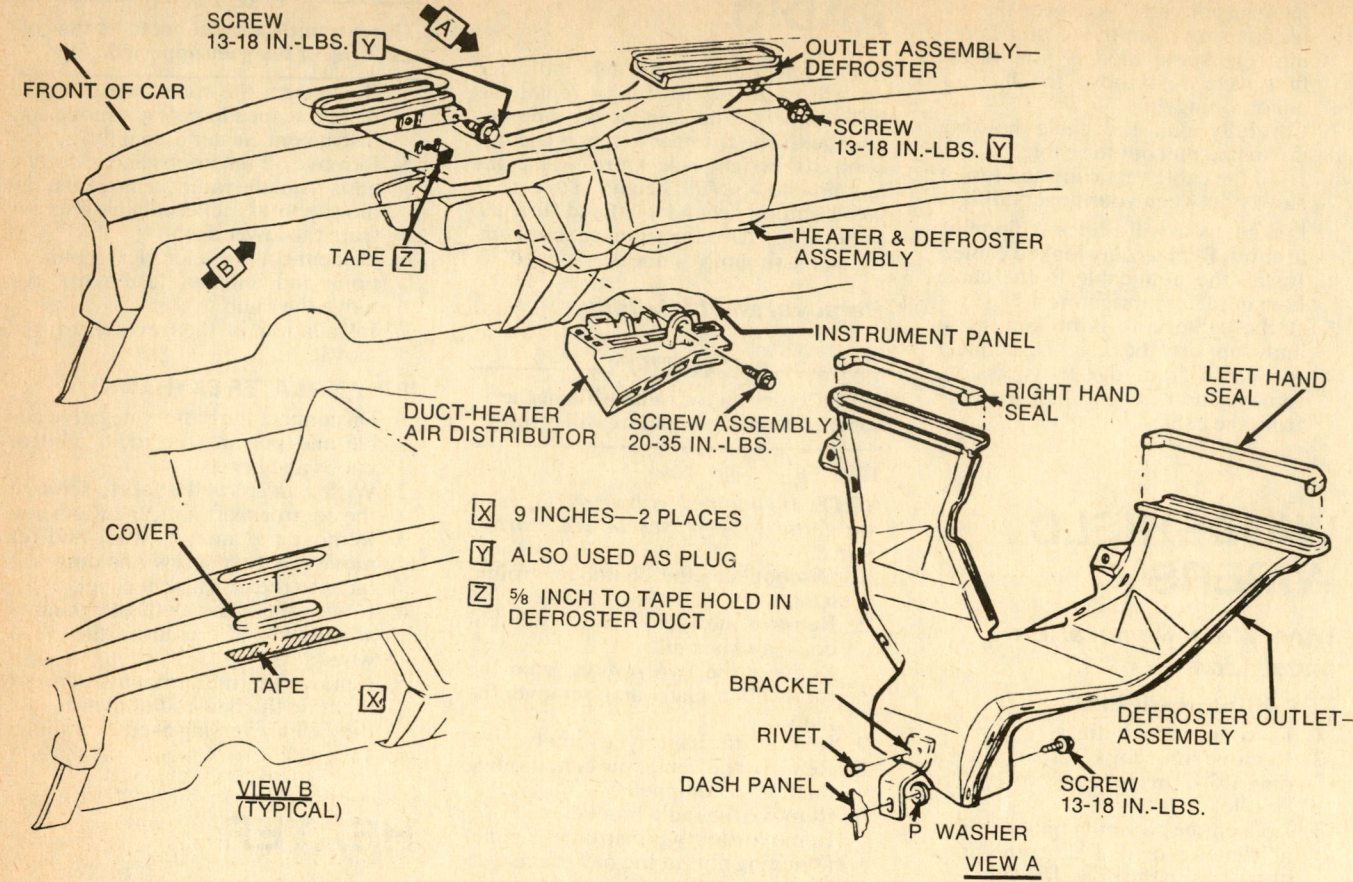

SCREW 13-18 IN.-LBS. [Y]

FRONT OF CAR

OUTLET ASSEMBLY— DEFROSTER

SCREW 13-18 IN.-LBS. [Y]

HEATER & DEFROSTER ASSEMBLY

TAPE [Z]

INSTRUMENT PANEL

DUCT-HEATER AIR DISTRIBUTOR

SCREW ASSEMBLY 20-35 IN.-LBS.

RIGHT HAND SEAL

LEFT HAND SEAL

COVER

[X] 9 INCHES—2 PLACES

[Y] ALSO USED AS PLUG

[Z] ⅝ INCH TO TAPE HOLD IN DEFROSTER DUCT

TAPE [X]

BRACKET

RIVET

DASH PANEL

P WASHER

DEFROSTER OUTLET— ASSEMBLY

SCREW 13-18 IN.-LBS.

VIEW B (TYPICAL)

VIEW A

Heater-defroster outlets and defroster opening cover, Skylark (© Buick Motor Div.)

temperature door lever, except on the Skyhawk.
3. Remove the four nuts securing the heater assembly to the dash. On the Skyhawk, remove the core retaining strap screws and remove the core.
4. Remove the screw securing the defroster outlet tab to the heater assembly, except on the Skyhawk.
5. Remove the heater from the car.
6. Reverse the above steps to install.

1973-75 APOLLO, 1973-79 SKYLARK

1. Disconnect the battery ground cable.
2. Drain the radiator.
3. Disconnect the heater hoses and plug the tubes to prevent spillage, when you remove the assembly from inside the car.
4. Remove the retaining nuts from the studs on the engine side of the firewall.
5. Remove the glove compartment and door.
6. Drill out the lower right heater case stud from inside the car.
7. Pull the core and case assembly from below the instrument panel.
8. Detach the cables and wiring from the case and remove the case from the car.

9. Remove the core from the case.
10. Reverse the procedure on installation, replacing the drilled out stud with a new screw and stamped nut.

1978-79 SKYHAWK

1. Disconnect the battery ground.
2. Disconnect the blower wire.
3. Disconnect the heater hoses at the core tubes. Position the hose up to prevent coolant loss.
4. Remove the blower inlet-to-firewall screws and remove the inlet, motor and wheel assembly.
5. Remove the core straps and lift out the core.
6. Installation is the reverse of the above. Replace all insulation when installing.

1978-79 CENTURY, REGAL

1. Disconnect the heater hoses at the core tubes.
2. Place the hoses in an up position to prevent excess coolant loss.
3. Disconnect all electrical connectors at the module case.
4. Remove the front case from the module.
5. Lift out the core.
6. Reverse the above for installation. Replace any damaged sealer.

Heater Blower Removal and Installation without A/C

1972

1. Remove the right front inner fender panel.
2. Remove the nuts and screws securing the blower and air inlet assembly to the cowl.
3. Disconnect the blower motor wire and remove the assembly.
4. Install in the reverse of the above/

1973-77, EXCEPT APOLLO/ SKYLARK, SKYHAWK

1. Disconnect the blower motor wire.
2. Remove the blower motor attaching screws and the motor.

1973-77 APOLLO/SKYLARK

1. Disconnect the battery ground cable.
2. Raise the car. Remove all the fender skirt bolts except those holding the skirt to the radiator support.
3. Pull out and down on the fender skirt. Put a wood block between the skirt and fender to allow clearance for removing the motor.
4. Disconnect the motor wiring.
5. Remove the screws and the motor.
6. Reverse the procedure on installation.

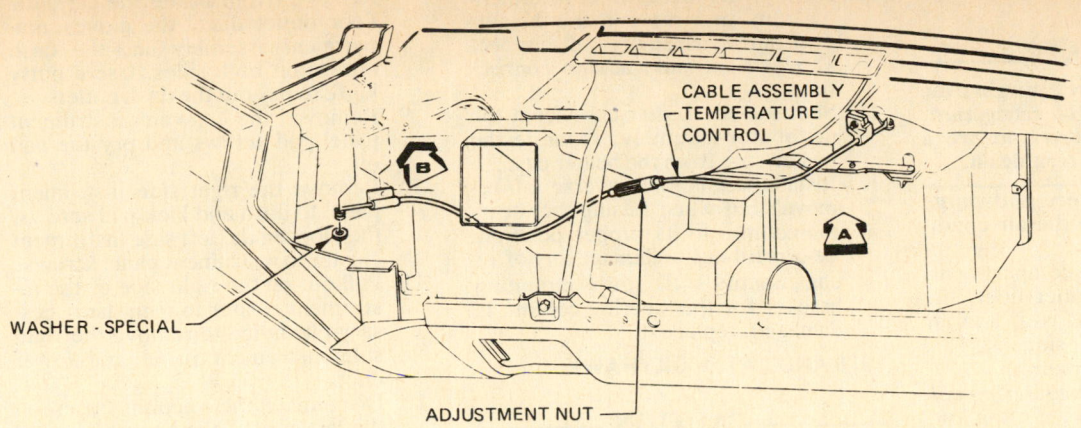

WASHER - SPECIAL

CABLE ASSEMBLY
TEMPERATURE
CONTROL

ADJUSTMENT NUT

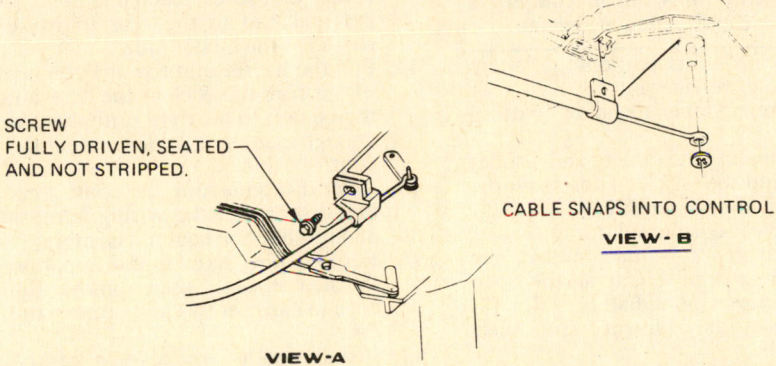

SCREW
FULLY DRIVEN, SEATED
AND NOT STRIPPED.

CABLE SNAPS INTO CONTROL

VIEW-B

VIEW-A

CONTROL WIRE ASSEMBLE & ADJUSTMENT

1 — SUB-ASSEMBLE CONTROL WIRE TO
AIR CONDITIONING HEATER CONTROL
ASSEMBLY.

A.   SECURE TEMPERATURE WIRE TO
TEMPERATURE CONTROL VALVE (RED)

B.   ADJUST CONTROL CABLE SO THAT
1/16" TO 1/8" SPRINGBACK IS
OBTAINED IN THE HOT POSITION.

CONTROLS MUST BE 100% INSPECTED FOR
CORRECT OPERATION & FREE MOVEMENT.

Typical manual A/C control cable adjustment
(© Buick Div., G.M. Corp)

SKYHAWK

See Heater Core Removal and Installation without A/C.

Blower Motor Removal and Installation with A/C

1972

1. Support the hood and remove the extension and plate assembly from the hood hinge.
2. Disconnect the motor wiring.
3. Remove the screws securing the motor to the firewall and remove the motor.
4. Reverse the above steps to install.

1973 AND LATER

1. Follow the same procedures as described in Blower Removal and Installation without A/C.

Heater Core Removal and Installation with A/C

1972

1. Drain the radiator and disconnect the heater inlet and outlet hoses from the dash.
2. Disconnect the control wires from the defroster door and vacuum hose diverter door actuator dia-

phragm and control cable from the temperature door lever.
3. Remove the four nuts securing the heater assembly to the firewall.
4. Remove the screw securing the defroster outlet to the heater assembly.
5. Move the heater assembly rearward until the studs clear the firewall and then remove the heater assembly.
6. Reverse the above steps to install.

1973 AND LATER, EXCEPT APOLLO/SKYLARK, SKYHAWK

1. Drain the radiator and disconnect the heater hoses.
2. Disconnect the temperature control cable and the vacuum hoses.
3. Remove the resistor assembly. Reach through the opening and remove the attaching nut. Remove the attaching nut directly over the transmission and the two attaching nuts to the upper and lower inboard evaporator case half.
4. From inside the car, remove the screw in the lower right corner on the passenger side.
5. Remove the lower attaching outlets. Work the assembly to the rear until the studs clear. Remove the heater assembly.
6. On installation, adjust the control

cable to get about 1/8 in. springback in the hot position.

APOLLO/SKYLARK

1. Disconnect the battery ground cable.
2. Drain the coolant.
3. Disconnect the upper heater hose and remove all the heater case assembly nuts you can reach.
4. Remove the right front fender skirt bolts and lower the skirt to remove the lower heater hose clamp. Remove the lower right case nut while you're in there.
5. Plug the heater core tubes to prevent spillage inside the car.
6. Remove the glove compartment and door.
7. Remove the diaphragm at the right kick panel.
8. Remove the heater outlet at the bottom of the heater case.
9. Remove the cold air duct from the heater case.
10. Remove the heater case extension screws and separate the extension from the case.
11. Disconnect the heater cables and wiring.
12. Remove the core and case assembly.
13. Reverse the whole procedure on installation.

1975 SKYHAWK

—————— CAUTION ——————

This procedure requires purging the air conditioning system of refrigerant. Do not attempt this unless you are a qualified air conditioning technician.

1. Disconnect the battery and purge the refrigerant from the air conditioning system.
2. Remove the glove compartment, the right side air outlet duct, the instrument bezel and pad, and air outlet duct on the left side.
3. Lower the steering column.

NOTE: *Make sure that the steering column is adequately supported when lowered to avoid major damage.*

4. Remove the instrument panel assembly and heater-air conditioner control assembly from the instrument panel.
5. Remove the radio and the defroster duct.
6. Remove the large center distributor duct, and the heater hoses at the core pipes.
7. Clean the VIR (receiver vessel) of any dirt which may have accumulated on it. Disconnect the compressor inlet line, oil bleed line and condenser outlet line; cap all these lines.
8. Loosen the evaporator inlet and outlet lines; remove the accumulator mounting clamp and slide the accumulator off the evaporator, outlet line first.
9. Remove and discard all the old O-ring gaskets and plug all open lines to prevent contamination.
10. Remove the heater to cowl attaching nuts and remove the heater-distributor assembly, disconnect all electrical and vacuum connections.
11. Separate the heater case from the distributor assembly; separate the heater core from the heater case.
12. Installation is the reverse of removal, but when raising the steering column to its proper position, be careful not to damage any of its components. If the mounting bracket for the steering column is damaged, replace it.

1976 AND LATER SKYHAWK

—————— CAUTION ——————

This procedure requires purging the air conditioning system of refrigerant. Do not attempt this unless you are a qualified air conditioning technician.

1. Have the air conditioning system purged of refrigerant.
2. Disconnect the negative battery cable.
3. Disconnect the inlet and outlet lines and the oil bleed line from the accumulator assembly.
4. Remove the accumulator to blower case strap screw, and remove the accumulator unit. Cap all the open connections immediately.
5. Remove the blower and case assembly.
6. Remove and plug the heater hoses at the core tubes and then hang them out of the way.
7. Remove the evaporator to firewall cover plate screws and remove the plate.
8. Remove (from inside the car), the floor outlet duct, the glove compartment assembly and the dash outlets on both sides. Use a putty knife to pry out the dash outlets.
9. Remove the eleven instrument panel pad screws and pry the pad off.
10. Remove the right side instrument panel to dash and kick pad screws, then loosen the left side instrument cluster to instrument panel screws.
11. Pull out on the right side of the instrument cluster to gain the necessary clearance to remove the right side instrument panel and lower duct.
12. Disconnect the vacuum hoses on the left side of the heater unit and tag them for later reinstallation.
13. Remove the modulator duct to heater unit screw, then pull the carpet and pad to the rear to make room for the heater unit.
14. Pull the heater unit toward you until the core tubes clear the firewall, then pull it to the right until there is enough clearance to disconnect the control cable.
15. After disconnecting the control cable, disconnect the wiring harness and remove the heater assembly.
16. Remove the screws and separate the heater case, then remove the core to case screws and remove the core.
17. Installation is the reverse of the above procedure, but before assembly, add 3 oz. of refrigerant oil to the evaporator core.
18. When installing the refrigerant lines, coat all the O-rings with refrigerant oil.

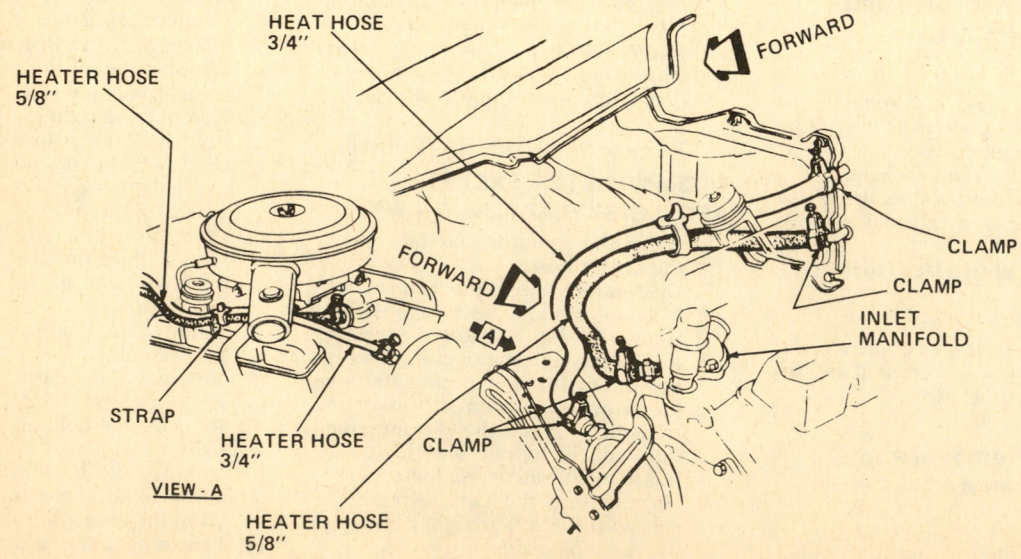

Heater hose installation, vehicles with A/C (© Buick Div., G.M. Corp.)

Index

Cadillac & Seville

YEAR IDENTIFICATION

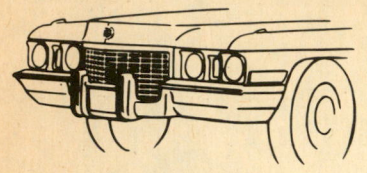

1972 Cadillac

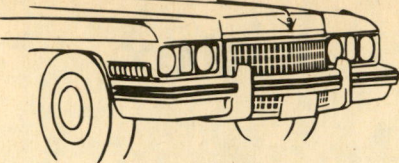

1973 Cadillac

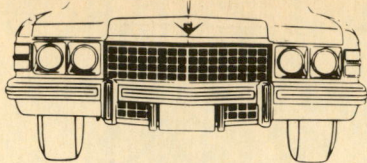

1974 Cadillac

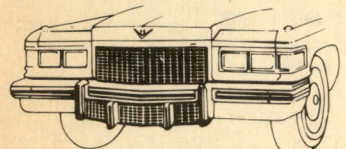

1975-76 Cadillac

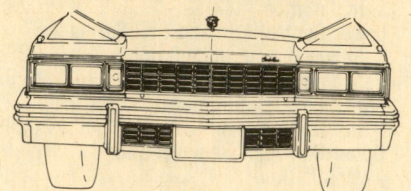

1977 Cadillac

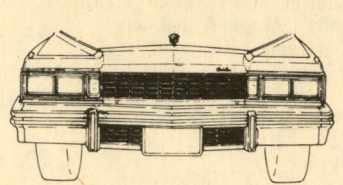

1978 Cadillac

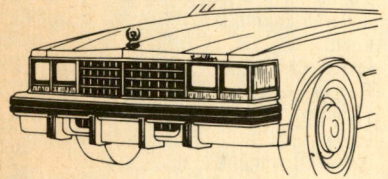

1976 Seville

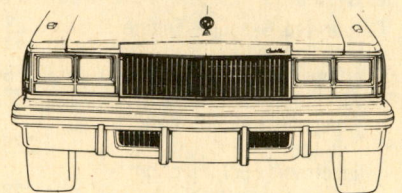

1977 Seville

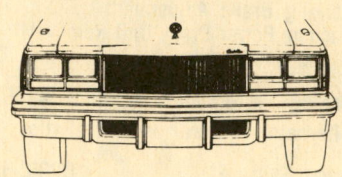

1978 Seville

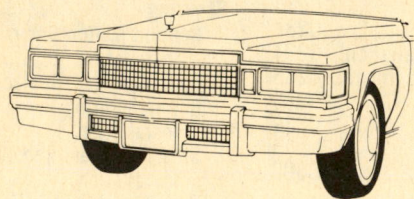

1979 Cadillac

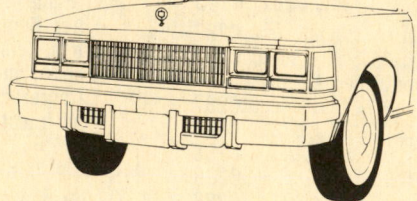

1979 Seville

ENGINE IDENTIFICATION

The vehicle identification number plate is on the top left side of the instrument panel, visible through the windshield. The engine code is the fifth digit of the Vehicle Identification Number.

No. Cyls.	Cu. in. Displ.	Type	1972	1973	1974	1975	1976	1977	1978	1979
8	472	All	R	R	R					
8	500	All	S	S	S	S	S			
8	350	EFI(Olds.)					R	R	B	B
8	350	Diesel(Olds.)							N	N
8	425	4 bbl.							S	S
8	425	EFI						T	T	T

EFI—Electronic fuel injection

C274

GENERAL ENGINE SPECIFICATIONS

Year	Engine Displacement Cu. In.	Carburetor Type	Horsepower @ rpm ■	Torque @ rpm (ft lbs) ■	Bore x Stroke (in.)	Compression Ratio	Oil Pressure @ 2000 rpm
'72	8-472	4 bbl	220 @ 4000	365 @ 2400	4.300 x 4.060	8.5:1	35
'73	8-472	4 bbl	220 @ 4000	365 @ 2400	4.300 x 4.060	8.5:1	35
'74	8-472	4 bbl	220 @ 4000	365 @ 2400	4.300 x 4.060	8.25:1	35
'75	8-500	4 bbl	235 @ 3800	386 @ 2400	4.300 x 4.304	8.5:1	35
'76	8-500	4 bbl	190 @ 3600	360 @ 2000	4.300 x 4.304	8.5:1	35
	8-500	EFI	215 @ 3600	400 @ 2000	4.300 x 4.304	8.5:1	35
	8-350	EFI	180 @ 4400	275 @ 2000	4.057 x 3.385	8.0:1	35
'77	8-425	4 bbl	180 @ 3600	260 @ 2000	4.082 x 4.060	8.5:1	35
	8-425	EFI	215 @ 3600	260 @ 2000	4.082 x 4.060	8.5:1	35
	8-350	EFI	180 @ 4400	275 @ 2000	4.057 x 3.385	8.0:1	35
'78	8-425	4 bbl	180 @ 3600	260 @ 2000	4.082 x 4.060	8.5:1	35
	8-425	EFI	215 @ 3600	260 @ 2000	4.082 x 4.060	8.5:1	35
	8-350	EFI	180 @ 4400	275 @ 2000	4.057 x 3.385	8.0:1	35
	8-350	Diesel	120 @ 3600	220 @ 1800	4.057 x 3.385	22.0:1	40
'79	8-350	EFI	170 @ 4200	270 @ 2000	4.057 x 3.385	8.0:1	35
	8-350	Diesel	120 @ 3600	220 @ 1600	4.057 x 3.385	22.5:1	40
	8-425	4 bbl	180 @ 4000	320 @ 2000	4.082 x 4.060	8.2:1	35
	8-425	EFI	185 @ 3800	320 @ 2400	4.082 x 4.060	8.2:1	35

■ Beginning 1972 Horsepower and torque are SAE net figures. They are measured at the rear of the transmission with all accessories installed and operating. Since the figures vary when a given engine is installed in different models, some are representative rather than exact.
EFI Electronic fuel injection

NOTE: Most 1979 GM carburetors have idle mixture screws concealed by staked-in plugs. These are not meant to be removed, except at carburetor overhaul.

TUNE-UP SPECIFICATIONS

When analyzing compression test results, look for uniformity among cylinders rather than specific pressures.

ENGINE Year No. Cyl Displacement (cu in.)		hp	SPARK PLUGS Orig. Type	Gap (in.)	DISTRIBUTOR Point Dwell (deg)	Point Gap (in.)	IGNITION TIMING (deg) ▲ Man Trans ●	Auto Trans	VALVES Intake Opens ■ (deg)	Fuel Pump Pressure (psi)	IDLE SPEED (rpm) ▲ Man Trans	Auto Trans
'72	8-472	220	R-46-N	.035	30	.016	—	8B	34	5¼-6½	—	600② /400
'73	8-472	220	R-46-N	.035	30	.016	—	8B	34	5¼-5¾	—	600② /400
'74*	8-472	220	R-45-NS	.035	30	.016	—	10B	21	5¼-6½	—	600② /400
'75	8-500	235	R-45NSX	.060	Electronic		—	6B	34	5¼-6¼	—	600② /400
	8-500 EFI	235	R-45NSX	.060	Electronic		—	12B	34	5¼-6¼	—	600② /400
'76	8-500	190	R-45NSX	.060	Electronic		—	6B	21	5¼-6½	—	600
	8-500 EFI	215	R-45NSX	.060	Electronic		—	12B	21	39 min.	—	600
	8-350 EFI	180	R-46SX	.080	Electronic		—	10B(6B)	22	39 min.	—	600
'77	8-425	All	R-45NSX	.060	Electronic		18B @ 1400		21	5¼-6½	—	675
	8-350	All	R-47SX	.060	Electronic		—	10B(8B)	22	5¼-6½	—	650
'78	8-425	All	R-45NSX	.060	Electronic		18B @ 1400		21	5¼-6½	—	650
	8-350	EFI	R-47SX	.060	Electronic		—	10B(8B)	22	5¼-6½	—	600
	8-350	Diesel	—	—	—		—	5B②	16	—	—	575

TUNE-UP SPECIFICATIONS

When analyzing compression test results, look for uniformity among cylinders rather than specific pressures.

Year	ENGINE No. Cyl. Displacement (cu in.)	hp	SPARK PLUGS Orig. Type	Gap (in.)	DISTRIBUTOR Point Dwell (deg)	Point Gap (in.)	IGNITION TIMING (deg) ▲ Man Trans ●	Auto Trans	VALVES Intake Opens ■ (deg)	Fuel Pump Pressure (psi)	IDLE SPEED (rpm) ▲ Man Trans	Auto Trans
'79	8-350	EFI	R-45SX	.060	Electronic		—	10B	22	5.5-6.5	—	600
	8-350	Diesel	—		—		—	5B③	16	—	—	575
	8-425	All	R-45NSX	.060	Electronic		—	23B④	11	5.5-6.5	—	600

▲ See text for procedure
■ All figures Before Top Dead Center
① Not used
② Lower figure indicates idle speed with solenoid disconnected
③ Static fuel injection timing, injector opening pressure is 1800 psi.
④ EFI: 18B

B Before Top Dead Center
EFI Electronic fuel injection
— Not applicable
● California figures in parentheses
* No point gap or dwell with electronic ignition
NOTE: The underhood specifications sticker often reflects tune-up specification changes made in production. Sticker figures must be used if they disagree with those in this chart.

FIRING ORDER

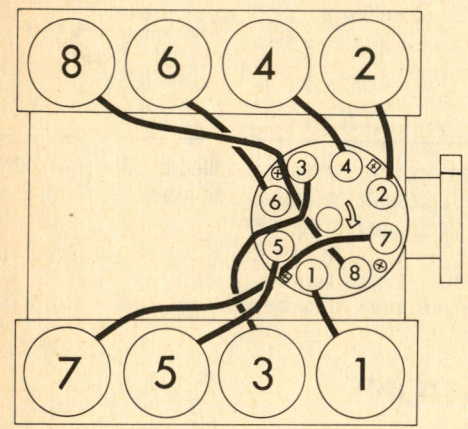

GM (Cadillac) 425, 472, 500 V8
Engine firing order: 1-5-6-3-4-2-7-8
Distributor rotation: clockwise

(Circles only are position of latches with point-type ignition: circles and squares are position of latches with electronic ignition).

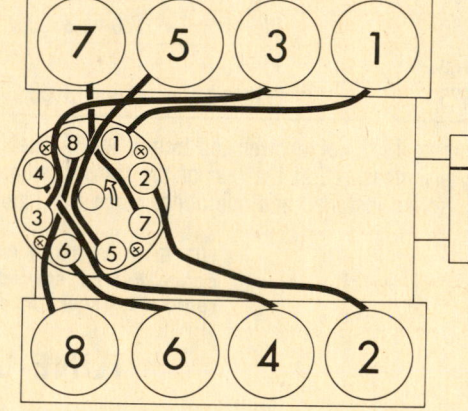

GM (Oldsmobile) 350 V8 w/EFI (1976 and later)
Engine firing order: 1-8-4-3-6-5-7-2
Distributor rotation: counterclockwise

VALVE SPECIFICATIONS

Year	Engine No. Cyl. Displacement (cu in.)	Seat Angle (deg)	Face Angle (deg)	Spring Test Pressure (lbs @ in.)	Spring Installed Height (in.)	STEM TO GUIDE Clearance (in.) Intake	Exhaust	STEM Diameter (in.) Intake	Exhaust
'72	8-472	45	44	168 @ 1.50	1 15/16	.0010-.0027	.0012-.0027	.3420	.3418
'73	8-472	45	44	168 @ 1.50	1 15/16	.0010-.0027	.0012-.0027	.3420	.3418
'74	8-472	45	44	165 @ 1.50	1 15/16	.0010-.0027	.0016-.0027	.3420	.3418
'75-'76	8-500	45	44	168 @ 1.50	1 15/16	.0010-.0027	.0010-.0027	.3418	.3416
'76-'79	8-350	①	②	187 @ 1.27	1 43/64	.0010-.0027	.0015-.0032	.3429	.3424
'77-'78	8-425	45	44	160 @ 1.50	1 15/16	.0010-.0027	.0010-.0027	.3416	.3416
'78-'79	8-350 Diesel	①	②	151 @ 1.30	1 43/64	.0010-.0027	.0015-.0032	.3429	.3424
'79	8-425	45	44	162 @ 1.489	1 15/16	.0010-.0027	.0012-.0029	.3416	.3435

① Intake 45°; exhaust 31°
② Intake 44°; exhaust 30°

CAPACITIES

Year	ENGINE No. Cyl. Displacement (Cu. In.)	Engine Crankcase Add 1 Qt For New Filter	TRANSMISSION Pts To Refill After Draining Manual 3-Speed	4-Speed	Automatic ●	Drive Axle (pts)	Gasoline Tank (gals)	COOLING SYSTEM (qts) With Heater	With A/C
'72	All	4	—	—	8	5	27.5	21.3	21.8②③
'73	All	4	—	—	8	5	27.5	21.3	21.8②③
'74	All	4	—	—	8	5	27.5	21.3	23.8④
'75-'76	8-500	4	—	—	8	5	27.5	21.3	23.0②
'76-'77	8-350	4	—	—	8	5	21	18.9①	18.9①
'77	8-425	4	—	—	8	5	24.5	20.8	20.8
'78	8-350	4	—	—	8	4.3	21	18.9	18.9
'78	8-350 Diesel	7	—	—	6	4.3	21	18.9	18.9
'78	8-425	4	—	—	8	4.3	24	19.8	19.8
'79	8-350	4	—	—	9	4.3	19.6	17.2	17.2
'79	8-350 Diesel	7.5	—	—	9	4.3	19.6	17.2	17.2
'79	8-425	4	—	—	9	4.25	25.0	20.8	20.8

- ● Specifications do not include torque converter
- ① 17.2—1977 and later
- ② Fleetwood—25.8 qts
- ③ Trailer package—2 qts additional
- ④ Fleetwood—26.8 qts

TORQUE SPECIFICATIONS

All readings in ft lbs

Year	Engine Displacement (cu in.)	Cylinder Head Bolts	Rod Bearing Bolts	Main Bearing Bolts	Crankshaft Bolt	Flywheel to Crankshaft Bolts	MANIFOLD Intake	Exhaust
'72-'76	472, 500	115	40	90	Press fit	75	30	35
'76-'79	350	85③	42	80②	310	60	40	25
'77-'79	425	95	40	90	Press fit	75	30	①
'78-'79	350 Diesel	130	42	120	200-310	60	40	25

- ① Long bolt—35, Short bolt—12
- ② 120 ft lbs. on No. 5
- ③ 130—1977 and later

CRANKSHAFT AND CONNECTING ROD SPECIFICATIONS

All measurements are given in inches

Year	Engine Displacement (cu in.)	CRANKSHAFT Main Brg. Journal Dia	Main Brg. Oil Clearance	Shaft End-Play	Thrust on No.	CONNECTING ROD Journal Diameter	Oil Clearance	Side Clearance
'72-'73	472	3.250	.0003-.0026	.002-.012	3	2.5000	.0005-.0035	.008-.016
'74	472	3.250	.0013-.0026	.002-.012	3	2.5000	.0005-.0028	.011-.021
'75-'76	500	3.250	.0010-.0026	.002-.012	3	2.5000	.0005-.0028	.008-.020
'76-'79	350	2.4985-2.4995①	.0005-.0021②	.004-.014	3	2.1238-2.1248	.0004-.0033	.006-.020
'77-'79	425	3.250	.0010-.0026	.002-.012	3	2.5000	.0005-.0028	.008-.020
'78-'79	350 Diesel	2.9993-3.0003	.0005-.0021②	.004-.014	3	2.1238-2.1248	.0005-.0026	.006-.020

- ① No. 1—2.4988-2.4988 in.
- ② No 5—.0015-.0031 in.

RING GAP

All measurements are given in inches

Year	Engine	Top Compression	Bottom Compression
'72-'76	472, 500	.013-.025	.013-.025
'76-'79	350	.010-.023	.010-.023
'77-'79	425	.013-.023	.013-.023
'78-'79	350 Diesel	.015-.025	.015-.025

Year	Engine	Oil Control
'72-'79	All	.015-.055

RING SIDE CLEARANCE

All measurements are given in inches

Year	Engine	Top Compression	Bottom Compression
'72-'74	472	.0017-.0040	.0017-.0040
'75-'76	500	.0017-.0040	.0017-.0040
'76-'79	350	.0020-.0040	.0020-.0040
'77-'79	425	.0017-.0040	.0017-.0040
'78-'79	350 Diesel	.005-.007	.0018-.0038

Year	Engine	Oil Control
'72-'76	472, 500	None (side sealing)
'76-'79	350	.0006-.0096
'77-'79	425	None (side sealing)
'78-'79	350 Diesel	None

PISTON CLEARANCE

Year	Engine	Piston to Bore Clearance (in.)
'72-'74	472	.0006-.0010
'75-'76	500	.0006-.0010
'76-'78	350	.0010-.0020
'77-'79	425	.0006-.0014
'78-'79	350 Diesel	.0005-.0006
'79	350	.0008-.0018

WHEEL ALIGNMENT SPECIFICATIONS

Year	Model	CASTER Range (deg)	CASTER Pref Setting (deg)	CAMBER Range (deg)	CAMBER Pref Setting (deg)	Toe-in (in.)	Steering Axis Inclin. (deg)	WHEEL PIVOT RATIO (deg) Inner Wheel	WHEEL PIVOT RATIO (deg) Outer Wheel
'72-'73	All Series	1½N to ½N	1N	①	①	⅛ to ¼	6	20	18
'74-'76	Cadillac	②	②	①	①	1/16 to 3/16	6	20	18
'76	Seville	1½P to 2½P	2P	③	③	0 to ⅛	——	——	——
'77-'78	Cadillac	2½P to 3½P	3P	⅛P to ⅞P	½P	1/16N to 1/16P	5	——	——
'77-'78	Seville	1½P to 2½P	2P	⅜N to ⅜P	0	0 to ⅛	5	——	——
'79	Seville	0 to 1P	½P	0 to ⅘P	⅖P	0 to 1/16	10.35	——	——
'79	Cadillac	0 to 2P	1P	0 to 1⅓P	⅘P	0 to ⅛	10.59	——	——

① Left ⅜P to ⅜N; zero preferred
   Right ⅛P to ⅝N; ¼N preferred

② All except Fleetwood—½N to ½P; zero preferred
   Fleetwood 75 models—1½N to ½N; 1N preferred

③ Left—⅛P to ⅞P; ½P preferred
   Right—⅛N to ⅝P; ¼P preferred

N Negative   P Positive

CHARGING SYSTEM

Diesel engine models use a single, standard, alternator to supply two parallel-connected 12 volt batteries. The two batteries are needed to handle the load of eight glow plugs and a larger starter. There are no special switches or relays in the starting system.

See Charging and Starting Systems in the Unit Repair Section for charging system test procedures.

Alternator Removal and Installation

1972

Disconnect the battery. Disconnect the wire leads at the alternator. Remove alternator adjusting strap drive belt. Remove alternator.
NOTE: *The heavy duty alternator. used on the commercial chassis, is slid backward off its lower mounting bolts, after first loosening the belt tensioner and removing the fan belt and upper bolt.*

1973 AND LATER

1. Disconnect the negative battery cable.
2. Disconnect the electrical leads from the alternator.
3. Remove the screw from the alternator adjusting link.
4. Remove the screw from the rear of the alternator, retaining the shims for reinstallation.
5. Loosen the alternator pivot bolt and remove the drive belt.
6. Remove the air pump pulley for access to the pump bolt behind the pulley.
7. Loosen the two screws securing the front bracket to the engine.
8. Remove the alternator, spacer and lower through bolt by twisting the alternator toward the fender for clearance.
9. Install the alternator in the reverse order of removal.

STARTING SYSTEM

Cadillac V8 starter motors are located on the right hand side of the engine; on the 350 V8, both gasoline and diesel, it is on the left side.

Information on starter motors and systems can be found in the Unit Repair Section.

The diesel engine starter is of conventional design, but somewhat larger and with a greater power output to turn the engine at least 100 rpm for starting. An electric glow plug in each combustion chamber is used to heat the chamber prior to starting. When the key is turned to the RUN position, before starting, they go on. They automatically turn off after startup.

Starter Removal and Installation

1. Disconnect the battery cable and raise the car.
2. Disconnect the battery lead and the two wires from the solenoid.
3. Remove the bolt that holds the support bracket to the starter.
4. Remove the two starter-to-engine bolts.
5. Remove the motor by pulling it forward and down, or toward the front wheel and over the steering linkage.
6. To install, reverse the removal procedure.

Disabling the Seat Belt/Starter Interlock and Buzzer

It is now legal to disconnect the seat belt interlock and buzzer system, but not the seat belt warning light.

1. Disconnect the negative battery cable.
2. Locate the interlock harness connector under the left side of the instrument panel on or near the fuse block with orange, yellow and green wires.
3. Cut and tape the green wire on the body harness side of the interlock connector.
4. Disconnect the seat belt warning buzzer from its position under the left side of the instrument panel by removing the lower steering column cover. Remove the connector and seat belt buzzer from the left body bracket and disconnect the buzzer from the harness and reinstall the connector to the bracket. Install the lower steering column cover.

IGNITION SYSTEM

The High Energy Ignition system was optional in 1974 and became standard equipment in 1975. The HEI system consists of an ignition coil, electronic module and a magnetic pick-up assembly all within the distributor.

A terminal in the top of the distributor cap is provided for the connection of a tachometer. The terminal is marked TACH.

More detail and HEI service procedures are given in the Electronic Ignition unit repair section

Starting 1978, an electronic spark selection system was introduced on the 350 V8. The system continuously and automatically controls ignition system spark advance (or retard) to improve fuel economy, reduce emissions, and aid hot starting. Details on the system

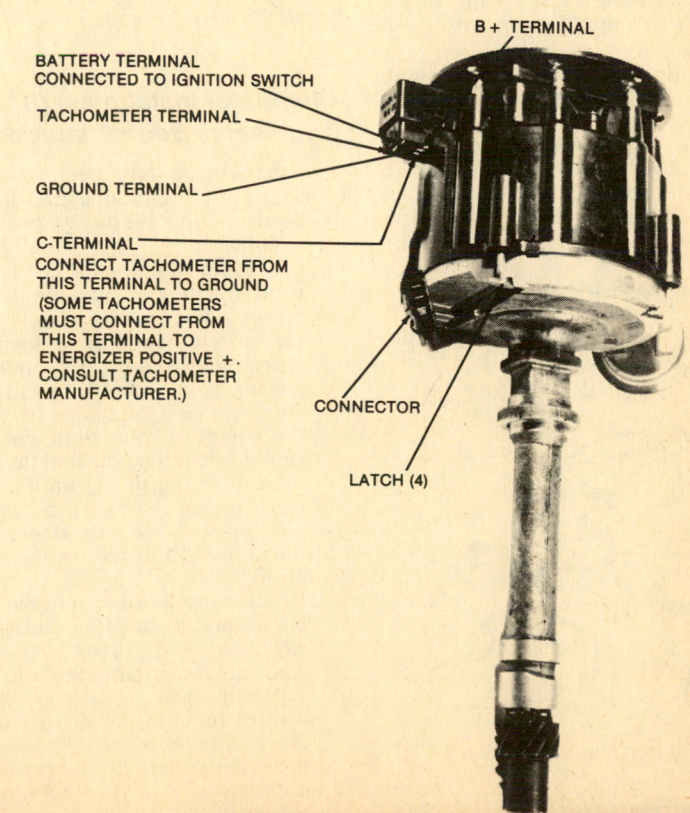

BATTERY TERMINAL CONNECTED TO IGNITION SWITCH

TACHOMETER TERMINAL

GROUND TERMINAL

C-TERMINAL
CONNECT TACHOMETER FROM THIS TERMINAL TO GROUND (SOME TACHOMETERS MUST CONNECT FROM THIS TERMINAL TO ENERGIZER POSITIVE +. CONSULT TACHOMETER MANUFACTURER.)

B + TERMINAL

CONNECTOR

LATCH (4)

Tachometer connection on HEI system

are in the Emission Control Systems unit repair section.

Unlike the gasoline engine, which is a spark-ignition design, the diesel engine is a compression-ignition type. When air is highly compressed, high temperatures are produced. At the moment of peak compression a small quanity of fuel is sprayed, under high pressure, into the combustion chambers. The temperature of compression ignites the tiny fuel droplets. A temperature of about 1750°F is required for ignition. Glow plugs are required, as an aid to cold starting.

Distributor Point Replacement Through 1974

1. Remove the distributor cap by depressing and turning the retaining screws.
2. Remove the two screws securing the rotor and remove it.
3. Remove the condenser and primary leads from the nylon insulated connection.
4. Loosen the two screws holding the base of the contact assembly in place and remove the points.
5. Inspect the weight assembly, replace or lubricate as required.
6. Place the new points under the two screws and tighten the screws.
7. Connect the condenser and primary leads at the nylon insulated connection.

NOTE: *Be sure the leads do not interfere with the cap, weight base, or advance.*

8. Install the rotor. The square and round lugs must be properly aligned.
9. With a 1/8 in. Allen wrench inserted, turn until the points close while the rubbing block is on the high point of the lobe. Then turn the screw counterclockwise one-half turn.
10. Replace the distributor cap.
11. With the engine warmed up and off fast idle, set the points to get the proper dwell angle.

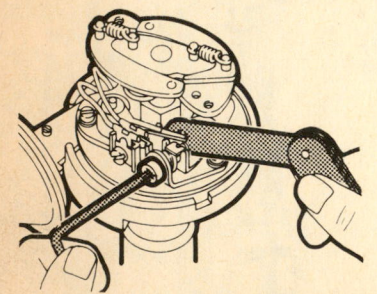

Distributor point adjustment

Distributor Removal

Unplug (HEI) and remove the distributor cap. On EFI cars, disconnect the speed sensor connector at the distributor trigger. Disconnect the vacuum line. Disconnect the primary lead at the distributor.

Turn the engine to top dead center for No. 1 cylinder so that the rotor points to the No. 1 cylinder tower in the distributor cap and the pointer on the timing case cover points to the O-mark on the crankshaft pulley.

Using a scribe mark, index the vacuum advance unit to the cylinder block, and the tip of the rotor to the distributor housing so that the distributor body will be correctly replaced at reassembly. Remove the clamp bolt and distributor.

Distributor Installation

Install the distributor so that the vacuum advance unit aligns with the match-mark made at removal. Turn the rotor slightly left of center so that as the gear engages the camshaft it will revolve into the proper position, pointing to the No. 1 contact in the cap.

Install the hold-down clamp. Connect the primary lead and install the cap. Rotate the lubricator. Plug the distributor vacuum line to the carburetor. Insert an adapter pin alongside the No. 1 wire in the distributor cap and connect a timing light. Clean the crankshaft pulley markings and the pointer. Set the timing to specifications. Tighten the clamp bolt. Remove the plug and adapter pin and reconnect the vacuum line to the advance unit.

Distributor Installation (If Engine Has Been Disturbed)

If the engine has been disturbed (cranked) after removing the distributor, perform the following procedure for installation:

1. Crank the engine until no. 1 piston is at the top of its compression stroke. The compression stroke can be determined by removing the spark plug from no. 1 cylinder and placing your thumb over the hole while an assistant slowly cranks the engine. Crank until compression is felt at the hole and then continue cranking slowly until the timing mark on the crankshaft pulley lines up with the zero degrees (0°) timing mark located on the timing chain cover.
2. Position the distributor in the block but do not, at this time, allow it to engage with its drive gear at the base of the mounting hole. Observe the position of the vacuum control unit on the distributor. If the distributor is located correctly, the vacuum unit will be positioned normally so that the vacuum hose can easily connect to it.
3. Rotate the distributor shaft so that the rotor points to the front of the engine, turn the rotor counterclockwise about 1/8 turn toward the left (driver's side), and push the distributor down to engage the camshaft. It may be necessary to turn the rotor a small amount in either direction in order to achieve this engagement. If installed correctly, the rotor should point toward the No. 1 spark plug terminal in the distributor cap.
4. Press firmly downward on the distributor housing. This will ensure that the distributor shaft engages the oil pump shaft, thereby allowing the distributor to fully contact the engine block.
5. Install the hold-down clamp and tighten the bolt until it is snug.
6. Turn the distributor slightly until the points just open and then tighten down on the bolt.
7. Install the distributor cap, making sure that the rotor points to No. 1 terminal in the cap.
8. Attach all wires and the vacuum advance hose.
9. Start the engine. If it fails to start, or runs roughly, the distributor may be 180° out of time. Lift up on the distributor, turn the rotor one-half revolution, and install the distributor. Repeat steps 1-9 if the engine continues to run poorly.
10. Check the timing and change it as necessary.

Ignition Timing

1. Loosen the distributor hold-down bolt so that the distributor can be turned without it being too loose.
2. Remove the hose from the vacuum advance unit and plug the free end. The end must be plugged as a manifold leak will affect the timing.
3. Remove the vacuum hose from the parking brake and plug the end.
4. Connect the timing light. With HEI, connect it at the No. 1 distributor terminal. Make certain that the timing marks are visible.
5. Connect a tachometer to the engine and, after securing the parking brake and blocking the wheels, start the engine and place the selector lever in Drive.
6. Adjust the idle speed to the specified rpm, then place the transmission in Park or Neutral.
7. Point the timing light at the pulley and observe the notch in the pulley in relation to the notches on the front cover. Check the specification chart for the correct timing setting.
8. If the setting is not correct, rotate the distributor until the correct timing is obtained then tighten the distributor clamp nut and recheck the timing.
9. Untape and reconnect the vacuum hoses on the parking brake and the vacuum advance.

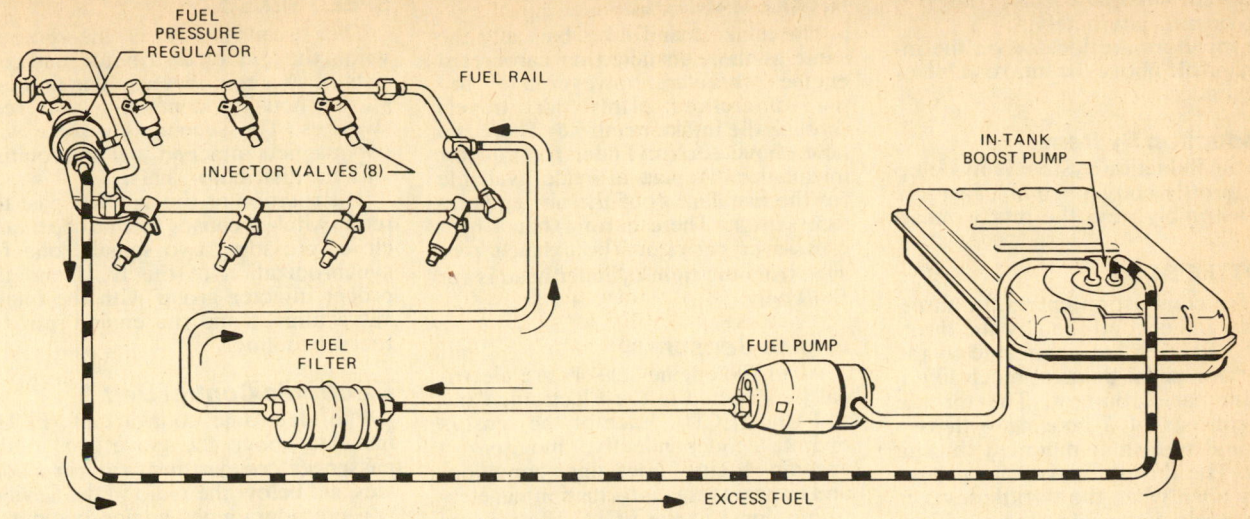

Fuel delivery system—EFI
(© Cadillac Div., G.M. Corp.)

FUEL SYSTEM

CARBURETED GASOLINE ENGINES

The standard Cadillac fuel system (except Seville) includes the fuel pump, fuel filter, lines, carburetor and intake manifold.

DIESEL ENGINE

The diesel engine is produced by General Motor's Oldsmobile division. Details on the diesel fuel system will therefore be found in the Oldsmobile car section.

FUEL INJECTED GASOLINE ENGINES

Electronic Fuel Injection (EFI) is standard on Seville and optional on 1976 and later full size models.

EFI provides a means of precisely controlling the air/fuel mixture for combustion by monitoring selected engine operating conditions and electronically metering the fuel requirements to meet those conditions.

The EFI system consists of four basic subsystems; the fuel delivery system, air induction system, the network of sensors, and the electronic control unit (ECU).

Fuel Delivery System

The fuel delivery subsystem is made up of an in-tank fuel pump and a chassis mounted fuel pump, fuel filter, a fuel pressure regulator, fuel rails, an injector for each cylinder, and supply and return lines.

FUEL PUMPS

The electric fuel pumps are connected in parallel to the ECU and are activated by the ECU when the ignition is turned on and the engine is cranking

In-tank fuel pump—EFI
(© Cadillac Div., G.M. Corp.)

or operating. If the engine stalls or if the starter is not engaged, the fuel pumps will stop in about one second. The fuel is pumped from the fuel tank, through the supply line and filter, through the pressure regulator, fuel rails and to the injectors, with excess fuel being returned to the fuel tank.

The in-tank boost pump is located in the fuel tank and is an integral part of the fuel gauge tank unit. This pump supplies fuel to the chassis mounted fuel pump and helps prevent vapor lock on the suction side of the system.

The chassis mounted fuel pump is a constant-displacement, roller-vane pump with a check valve to prevent fuel from flowing back into the tank. This pump has a flow rate of 33 gallons per hour and maintains a minimum pressure of 39 psi. An internal relief valve opens at 55-95 psi to protect the system from excessive pressure. The

pump is mounted under the vehicle, forward of the left rear wheel on all vehicles except the Eldorado, where it is mounted in front of the right rear wheel.

FUEL FILTER

The fuel filter is located on a bracket on the lower left front of the engine. The filter consists of a casing with an internal throwaway type paper filter element.

FUEL PRESSURE REGULATOR

The fuel pressure regulator, located on the fuel rail at the front of the engine, maintains a constant 39 psi pressure across the fuel injectors. The regulator contains an air chamber and fuel chamber separated by a spring-loaded diaphragm. The air chamber is connected by a hose to the throttle body assembly. The pressure in the air chamber of the regulator is identical to the pressure in the intake manifold. The changing manifold pressure and the spring control the action of the diaphragm valve, opening or closing an orifice in the fuel chamber of the regulator. At this point excess fuel is routed out of the regulator and back to the fuel tank.

FUEL INJECTOR

The fuel injector is a solenoid operated pintle valve that meters fuel to each cylinder. The injectors are controlled by an electronic pulse signal from the ECU. When energized, the valve opens for precisely the proper amount of time to spray the exact amount of fuel droplets required by the engine. When the injector is deenergized, it prevents any further fuel flow to the engine.

The eight injectors are divided into two groups of four each. Cylinders 1, 2, 7, and 8 form group 1 and the remaining injectors form group 2. All four injectors in each group are opened and closed simultaneously; the two groups operate alternately.

The injectors are located on the intake manifold above the intake valve of each cylinder.

Air Induction System

The air induction system is made up of the throttle body assembly, fast idle valve assembly, and the intake manifold.

THROTTLE BODY

Air for combustion enters the throttle body and is controlled by the throttle valves which are connected to the accelerator pedal linkage, much like a conventional carburetor. The throttle body consists of a housing with two bores and two shaft mounted throttle valves. The throttle valves are pre-set slightly open when the throttle lever is resting against the idle stop position. *The adjustment is not to be tampered with.* An adjustable set screw on the front of the throttle body adjusts an idle by-pass air passage incorporated within the throttle body and allows a regulated amount of air to by-pass the throttle valves, adjusting warm engine idle speed.

A large port on top of the throttle body contains the fast idle valve.

Starting 1978 on Seville, a solenoid operated idle air compensator is added to provide more air to the engine when the air conditioner clutch is engaged at idle.

FAST IDLE VALVE

The fast idle valve, installed on the top of the throttle body, consists of a plastic body that houses an electric heater, a spring and plunger, and a temperature sensitive unit.

The fast idle valve is connected electrically to the fuel pump circuit through the ECU. When the engine is started cold, the open valve allows extra air to bypass the throttle valves. The heater warms the thermal element which expands and forces the spring and plunger toward the air orifice, restricting the flow of extra air and gradually reducing the engine speed to the normal idle rpm. The fast idle valve has no effect after the thermal element reaches about 140°F. The rate at which the valve closes is a function of time and temperature. The warmer the air, the faster the valve closes. At 68°F the valve will close in about 90 seconds and at −20°F the valve will require about 5 minutes to close.

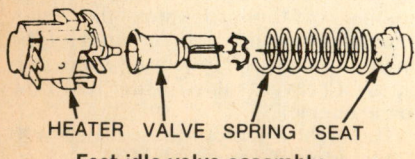

HEATER VALVE SPRING SEAT
**Fast idle valve assembly—
exploded view—EFI**
(© Cadillac Div., G.M. Corp.)

INTAKE MANIFOLD

The intake manifold is basically the same as those installed on carbureted engines. There are, however, a few minor differences: Only air travels through the intake manifold. There is a hole above each cylinder for injector installation. A port is made available for the installation of the air temperature sensor. There is no exhaust heat cross-over passage. The exhaust passage from the right cylinder head is for EGR only.

Engine Sensors

All of the engine sensors are electrically connected to the Electronic Control Unit (ECU). Each of the sensors operates independently, monitors a specific engine operating condition, and transmits this information via electronic signal to the ECU. The sensors continuously send information signals to the ECU while the ignition switch is in the On or Start position.

MANIFOLD ABSOLUTE PRESSURE SENSOR

The manifold absolute pressure (MAP) sensor monitors pressure changes within the intake manifold which are the direct result of engine load, speed, and barometric pressure. As pressure in the intake manifold increases, additional fuel is required. The MAP sensor sends this information to the ECU so that the length of time the injectors are energized is increased or decreased accordingly.

The sensor is mounted within the electronic control unit. A manifold pressure line is routed with the engine harness and is connected to the front of the throttle body at one end to the MAP sensor at the other end.

THROTTLE POSITION SWITCH

The throttle position switch is mounted to the throttle body, connected to the throttle valve shaft, and monitors the opening or closing of the throttle valves. The switch senses the shaft movement and position and transmits electrical signals to the ECU. The ECU processes these signals to determine the fuel requirement for the engine.

TEMPERATURE SENSORS

The two air and coolant temperature sensors vary electrical current resistance as a function of temperature. Low temperatures provide low resistance and vice versa. Voltage changes across each sensor are monitored by the ECU.

The air temperature sensor is located on the rear of the intake manifold and is connected to the engine harness. The coolant temperature sensor is located on the heater hose fitting at the rear of the right cylinder head.

The sensors are identical and completely interchangeable.

SPEED SENSOR

The speed sensor is incorporated within the ignition distributor, and consists of two components. The first is a plastic housing containing two reed switches. The second is a rotor with two magnets attached to it and rotating with the distributor shaft.

The rotation of the magnets past the reed switches causes them to open and close, providing two signals: one for synchronization of the ECU and the proper injector group with the intake valve timing; and the engine rpm for fuel scheduling.

Electronic Control Unit

The electronic control unit (ECU), installed above the glove box in the passenger compartment on big Cadillacs and below the radio in the Seville, is a preprogrammed analog computer. The ECU is electrically connected to the vehicle's power supply, all of the EFI system electrical components, plus the EGR activation solenoid by a harness routed through the firewall.

When the ECU is energized by the ignition switch being turned to the On or Crank position, it continuously receives information from all of the engine sensors, and activates the fuel pumps, fast idle valve, fuel injectors, and the EGR solenoid.

The commands for proper air/fuel ratios for various driving and atmospheric conditions are designed into the ECU. As the electronic signals are received from the sensors, the ECU analyzes the signals and computes the exact fuel requirement for the engine. The ECU then causes the fuel injectors to open for a specific amount of time. The duration of time the injectors are open varies as the engine operating conditions change.

The electronic control units are calibrated differently depending on where the car is sold (California or 49 states) and in which vehicle the unit is installed. Each ECU is labeled for its intended use. The proper unit must be used for each application.

ELECTRONIC FUEL INJECTION TROUBLESHOOTING

NOTE: *Because a special electronic tester is necessary to diagnose problems in the ECU, this section will deal with troubleshooting only mechanical and basic electrical problems of the EFI system. If the ECU is diagnosed as being the possible cause of a problem, the car should be taken to a Cadillac dealer where the special electronic tester and trained personnel are available.*

Before disconnecting any part of the fuel delivery system on EFI equipped vehicles, the pressure within the fuel lines must be bled off. On early model cars without a pressure fitting in the rear fuel rail, cover the fitting to be removed with a shop towel while loosening. Dispose of the gasoline soaked cloth safely.

On models with the Schrader pressure relief valve in the rear fuel rail, arrange a shop towel or suitable container at the valve so the fuel will be contained. Remove the protective cap, depress the valve, and bleed the pressure out of the system. Dispose of the fuel or fuel soaked cloth safely. Replace the protective cap on the valve and proceed with the service.

PROBLEM: Engine cranks but will not start.
POSSIBLE CAUSE:
NOTE: *The following possible causes assume that the rest of the vehicle electrical system is functioning properly.*
1. Blown 10 amp in-line fuel pump fuse (located under the instrument panel near the ECU wiring harness connectors). To check, listen for the whine of the chassis-mounted fuel pump when the ignition key is turned to the On position. The fuel pump should only operate for one second before shutting off. Do not turn the ignition key to the Start position.
2. Poor connection of the green wire at the fuel pump wiring harness near the ECU harness below the instrument panel. Check the operation of the fuel pump in the same manner as in POSSIBLE CAUSE 1 above.
3. Malfunction in the chassis-mounted pump.
4. Open circuit in the purple wire between the starter solenoid and the ECU.
5. Open circuit in the green wire between the alternator BAT terminal and the ECU.
6. Poor connection at the engine coolant sensor or an open circuit in the wiring or the sensor, with the engine cold only. To check, connect an ohmmeter to the temperature sensor connector terminals. If the resistance in the sensor is greater than 1600 ohms, replace the sensor.
7. Poor connection of the ECU wiring harness.
8. Poor connection at the speed sensor on the distributor.
9. The speed sensor trigger is stuck closed.
10. The wide-open-throttle section of the throttle position switch is shorted. To check, disconnect the switch; the engine should start.
11. A restriction in the fuel delivery system.

PROBLEM: Hard starting
POSSIBLE CAUSE:
1. Open circuit in the engine coolant temperature sensor. This should occur only when the engine is cold or partially warm. The engine

should start satisfactorily when hot.
2. The wide-open-throttle section of the throttle position switch is shorted. To check, disconnect the switch; the engine should start.
3. The fuel pressure regulator is malfunctioning.
4. The chassis-mounted fuel pump is malfunctioning.

PROBLEM: Poor fuel economy
POSSIBLE CAUSE:
1. The manifold absolute air pressure sensor is disconnected or leaking.
2. The vacuum hose at the fuel pressure regulator or throttle body is disconnected.
3. The air temperature or coolant temperature sensors are malfunctioning. Check the coolant temperature sensor as outlined under Engine cranks but will not start, number 6. Check the air temperature sensor by connecting an ohmmeter to the sensor connector terminals; if the sensor resistance is less than 700 ohms, replace the sensor.

PROBLEM: Engine stalls after being started
POSSIBLE CAUSE:
1. A poor connection or open circuits in the black and yellow ignition signal wire between the fuse block and the ECU.
2. A poor connection or open circuit in the wiring or body of the engine coolant temperature sensor; cold or warm engine only. Check as outlined under Engine cranks but will not start, number 6.
3. On 1978 and later Seville, a malfunctioning idle air compensator solenoid will cause stalling at idle.

PROBLEM: Rough idle
POSSIBLE CAUSE:
1. Disconnected, leaking, or pinched manifold absolute air pressure sensor vacuum hose.
2. Poor connection or an open circuit in the air temperature sensor or wiring; cold engine only. See Poor fuel economy, number 3.
3. Poor connection or short in the sensor or wiring of the engine coolant temperature sensor. See Engine cranks but will not start, number 6.
4. Poor connection at the injectors.

PROBLEM: Fast idle condition is prolonged
POSSIBLE CAUSE:
1. Throttle position switch needs adjusting.
2. Poor connection at the fast idle valve or an open circuit in the heating element.
3. A vacuum leak in or around the throttle body.

PROBLEM: Hesitation of the engine under acceleration
POSSIBLE CAUSE:
1. Leaking, restricted, or disconnected manifold absolute air pressure sensor vacuum hose.
2. Throttle position switch needs adjusting or is malfunctioning.
3. Poor connection of the ECU wiring harness at the ECU.
4. Poor connection at the EGR valve solenoid or solenoid stuck open; cold engine only.
5. Intermittent malfunction of the speed sensor trigger at the distributor.

PROBLEM: High speed performance is poor
POSSIBLE CAUSE:
1. The wide-open-throttle section of the throttle position switch needs adjusting or the switch is malfunctioning.
2. The fuel filter is blocked or restricted.
3. The chassis-mounted fuel pump is malfunctioning.
4. Intermittent malfunction of the speed sensor trigger.
5. An open circuit in the purple wire between the starter solenoid and the ECU.

FUEL PUMP AND FILTER

The fuel pump on carbureted engines is mounted on the left-hand side of the engine. The pump is operated by an eccentric on the camshaft. The fuel filter is mounted inside the fuel pump on models through 1974. Beginning 1975, the fuel filter is mounted in the carburetor behind the fuel inlet nut. Beginning 1976, a check valve is included in the fuel filter. On air conditioned cars, the fuel filter has a passage and a connecting line to the fuel tank to return fuel

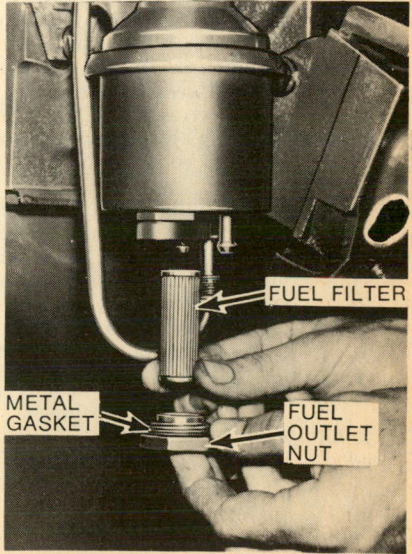

Fuel filter—models through 1974
(© Cadillac Div., G.M. Corp.)

vapors to the tank under high temperature conditions.

Vehicles with EFI have two electric fuel pumps; one is mounted in the fuel tank and is integral with the fuel level sending unit and the other, a chassis-mounted pump, is located in front of the rear axle either on the right or left side. A fuel filter is mounted on a bracket at the lower left front of the engine. On Seville models the fuel filter is mounted on the left side of the frame near the fuel pump.

Fuel Pump Removal and Installation

CARBURETED ENGINES

NOTE: *On air conditioned cars, be sure to disconnect the flexible line connecting the fuel filter to the vapor return line from the tank.*

1. If equipped with A.I.R. system, it may be necessary to remove air pump and bracket for clearance.
2. Remove center coil wire. Jack up front of car and support on axle stands so that pump can be removed from underneath.
3. Loosen one bolt and one stud nut.
4. Turn engine so that tension on mounting bolts is relieved.
5. Disconnect pump inlet line and pump outlet line. Plug inlet line. Disconnect the vapor return line.
6. Remove two mounting bolts and pump.
7. To install, reverse removal procedure. Make sure pump arm is properly positioned on cam eccentric; tighten bolts to 15 ft lbs.

FUEL INJECTED ENGINES

Chassis-Mounted Pump

1. Relieve the pressure in the fuel lines and remove the fuel inlet and outlet hoses from nipples on the pump.
2. Peel back the rubber boot and remove the two nuts, one from each electrical terminal. Remove the electrical leads.

NOTE: *These nuts have metric threads.*

3. Remove the two screws and flat washers holding the fuel pump to the bracket and remove the pump assembly.
4. Install the fuel pump in the reverse order of removal. Connect the green wire to the positive terminal on the pump and the black wire to the negative terminal. Check to make sure the fuel pump is resting evenly on its two mounts and not grounding against the bracket or frame.

In-Tank Pump

1. Disconnect the battery, open the fuel tank filler door and disconnect the tan sending unit feed wire.
2. Siphon the fuel from the fuel tank. If the rear of the car is raised one foot higher than the front, more fuel can be taken out.

3. Raise the rear of the car and remove the screw securing the ground wire to the cross member.
4. Disconnect the fuel line, evaporative emission lines and the fuel return lines at the front of the tank.
5. Support the tank with a jack and wooden block and remove one screw on each side securing the fuel tank support straps to the body at the front of the tank.
6. Lower the jack and tank enough so that the fuel pump electrical lead can be disconnected. Disconnect the wire.
7. Remove the fuel tank from the car.
8. Remove the locknuts securing the fuel gauge tank unit and fuel pump feed wires to the tank unit.
9. Turn the cam locking ring counterclockwise with a soft non-ferrous punch and hammer. When the lock ring is disengaged, remove it and lift the gauge/pump unit from the tank.
10. Install in the reverse order of removal. Tighten the fuel tank retaining strap screws to 25 ft lbs.

Filter Removal and Installation

CARBURETED ENGINES

Through 1974

1. Jack up car and support on stands.
2. Clamp or plug rubber section of inlet hose.
3. Disconnect fuel pump outlet line at fuel pump.
4. Remove fuel outlet nut and remove filter.

NOTE: *Use two wrenches to prevent loosening of nut welded to pump cover.*

5. Install in reverse of above.

1975 and Later

1. Disconnect the fuel line at the carburetor inlet.

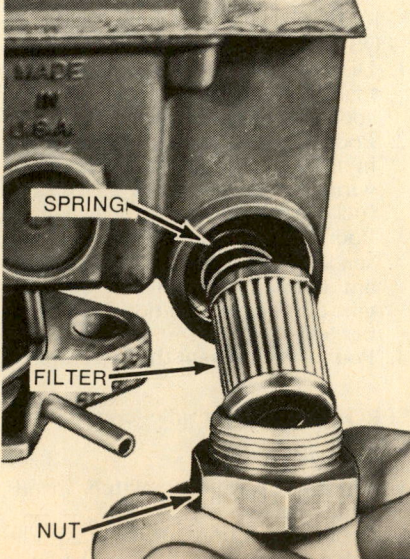

Fuel filter—1975 and later models
(© Cadillac Div., G.M. Corp.)

2. Remove the fuel inlet nut from the carburetor using a box wrench.
3. Remove the fuel filter element and spring.
4. Install the filter spring and new fuel filter element into the carburetor.
5. Install a new gasket on the fuel inlet nut and install the nut.
6. Connect the fuel line to the fuel inlet nut and tighten securely. Start the engine and check for leaks.

FUEL INJECTED ENGINES

NOTE: *The fuel filter element can be replaced by unscrewing the bottom cover and removing it.*

1. Bleed the pressure from the fuel delivery system and remove the fuel inlet and outlet hoses from the fuel filter.
2. Remove the two screws retaining the fuel filter to the bracket and remove the filter from the engine or frame.
3. Remove the inlet and outlet fittings from the filter assembly if they are needed for the new filter.
4. Install the fittings to the new filter, using a sealer on the threads.
5. Attach the filter to the bracket and tighten the retaining screws to 12 ft lbs.
6. Connect the inlet and outlet line, using new clamps.

NOTE: *It may require considerable cranking before the engine starts due to the drained fuel lines.*

Throttle Body Assembly Removal and Installation, Fuel Injected Engines

1. Remove the air cleaner.
2. Disconnect the two throttle return springs from the throttle lever.
3. Remove the cruise control chain retainer and chain, if so equipped.
4. Remove the clip and disconnect the throttle cable from the throttle lever.
5. Remove the left rear throttle body mounting screw and remove the one screw holding the throttle bracket to the intake manifold.
6. Remove the downshift switch from the throttle lever and position bracket. Move the switch and linkage aside.
7. Disconnect the throttle position and fast idle valve electrical connectors. Slide the fast idle valve wiring out of the notch in the throttle body.
8. Disconnect the vacuum lines from the throttle body.
9. Remove the remaining throttle body retaining screws and remove the throttle body.
10. Remove all gasket material from the intake manifold and the throttle body.
11. Install the throttle body in the reverse order of removal. Install the throttle return springs between the throttle lever and pressure regulator bracket with the open end of

the spring on the outside of the throttle lever.

Throttle Position Switch Removal and Installation, Fuel Injected Engines

1. Remove the throttle body from the engine.
2. Remove the two mounting screws and remove the switch from the throttle body.
3. Install the switch on the right side of the throttle body so that the tab on the switch engages the flat on the throttle shaft.
4. Install the two mounting screws and tighten the screws so that the switch will move but is still firmly attached.
5. Adjust the throttle position switch as outlined under Adjustments.
6. Reinstall the throttle body.

Fast Idle Valve Removal and Installation, Fuel Injected Engines

1. Remove the air cleaner and disconnect the fast idle valve heater electrical connection.
2. Remove the air cleaner mounting stud.
3. Push down and twist the fast idle valve heater counterclockwise 90° to remove it.
4. Remove the fast idle valve, spring and seat from the throttle body.
5. Install the fast idle valve seat, spring and valve in the throttle body.
6. Position the heater on top of the fast idle valve and push it down to compress the spring. Be careful to avoid damaging the micro-switch contact arm on the bottom of the heater housing.
7. Align the tabs on the fast idle valve heater with the cut-out portion of the throttle body and compress the spring further.
8. Rotate the heater clockwise 90° to secure it in position.
9. Connect the electrical lead and install the air cleaner stud and air cleaner.

Fuel Injector Removal and Installation, Fuel injected Engines

1. Remove the front and rear fuel rails.
2. Remove the electrical conduit from the injector brackets.
3. Remove the two screws holding each injector bracket to the intake manifold and remove the brackets and grommets.
4. Disconnect the electrical lead from all of the injectors on the fuel rail being removed.
5. Remove the fuel rail and injectors from the engine as an assembly. Some injectors may stick to the intake manifold and others will come

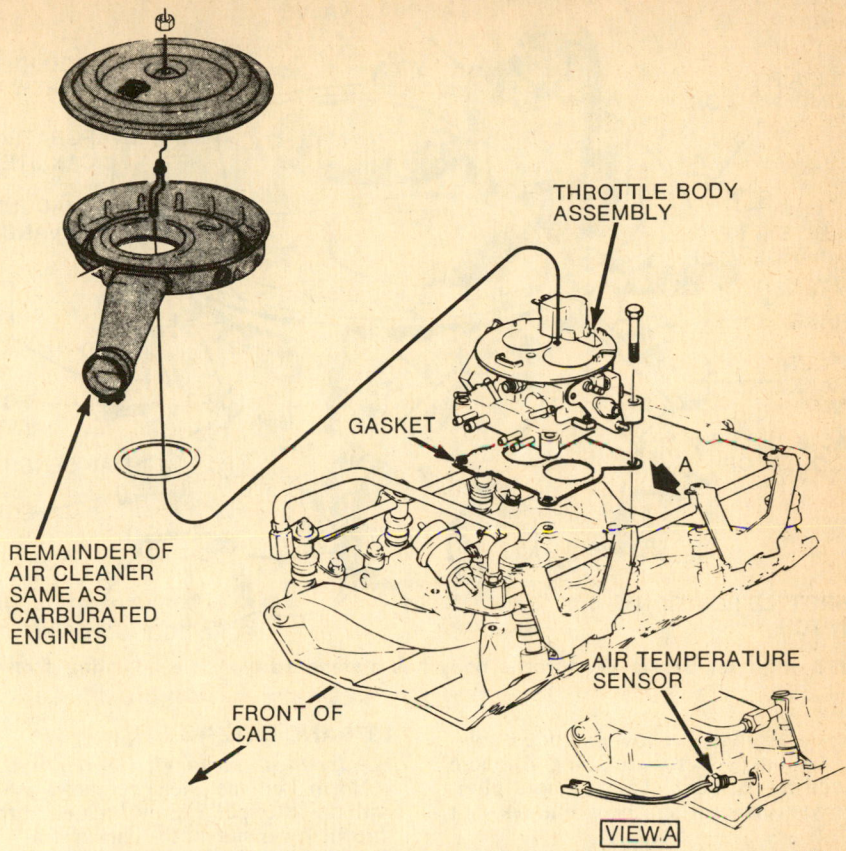

Mounting of the throttle body assembly and air temperature sensor—EFI
(© Cadillac Div., G.M. Corp.)

off with the fuel rail. Remove the injectors from the fuel rail and manifold as required.
6. Remove and discard all of the used O-rings used to seal the injectors at the fuel rail and intake manifold.
7. Before installing the new O-ring seals, lubricate them with a suitable lubricant and install the O-rings on the fuel rail end of each injector.
8. Install the injectors into the fuel rail with the electrical connector facing inward.
9. Install new O-rings into each injector port in the intake manifold.
10. Install the fuel rail/injector assembly to the intake manifold. Make certain that each injector is properly positioned in the manifold O-ring.
11. Install the rubber grommets, flanges down, on the fuel rail and install the injector brackets in position.
12. Install and tighten the bracket retaining screws to 5 ft. lbs.
13. Route and secure the electrical harness along the bracket. Connect all eight injectors as follows: the two front and two rear cylinders' injectors are connected to the red/black wires; the four center cylinders' injectors are connected to the black/white wires.
14. Install the front and rear fuel rails.

15. Turn the ignition On and Off a few times to build up fuel pressure in the system and check for leaks.
16. Start the engine and check for leaks. It may require considerable cranking to start the engine due to the drained condition of the fuel lines.

Fuel Pressure Regulator Removal and Installation, Fuel Injected Engines

1. Remove the vacuum hose from the top of the pressure regulator.
2. Bleed off the pressure in the fuel delivery system and disconnect the flexible fuel hose between the fuel rail and the regulator. Disconnect the fuel return line.
3. Remove the one nut securing the pressure regulator to the bracket. This nut has metric threads.
4. Remove the regulator.
5. Install the regulator in the reverse order of removal.

Carbureted Engine Idle Speed and Mixture Adjustments
THROUGH 1974

Adjust with the air cleaner removed.
Idle speed is adjusted at an anti-dieseling solenoid. The throttle must be opened slightly to allow the plunger to move out all the way, then it must be

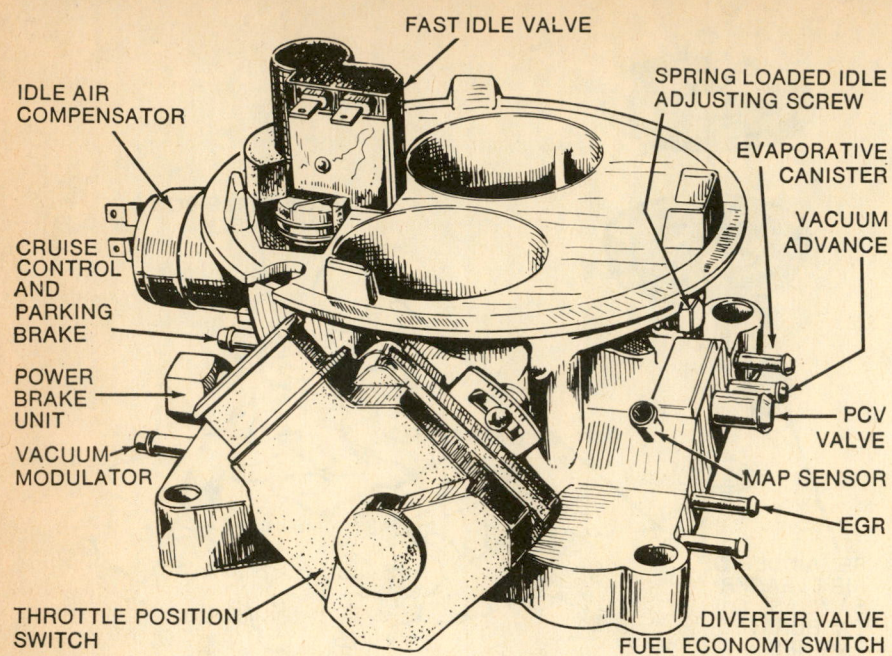

1978 and later Seville EFI throttle body has a standard type idle adjusting screw.

Labels on diagram: IDLE AIR COMPENSATOR, FAST IDLE VALVE, SPRING LOADED IDLE ADJUSTING SCREW, EVAPORATIVE CANISTER, VACUUM ADVANCE, CRUISE CONTROL AND PARKING BRAKE, POWER BRAKE UNIT, VACUUM MODULATOR, PCV VALVE, MAP SENSOR, EGR, THROTTLE POSITION SWITCH, DIVERTER VALVE FUEL ECONOMY SWITCH

closed against the now-extended solenoid plunger before making the idle speed adjustment. The solenoid plunger will retract when the ignition is shut off.

1. Disconnect and plug the distributor vacuum advance hose and parking brake vacuum hose (at the release cylinder). If equipped with self-leveling, remove and plug the air leveling compressor hose at the air cleaner. Remove the air cleaner but keep the vacuum hoses connected.
2. Connect a tachometer and set the parking brake with transmission in Neutral.
3. Turn in the mixture screws until they seat gently, then turn the screws out approximately 6 turns through 1973 or 4 turns for 1974.
4. Start the engine and allow it to warm up. Make sure the choke is off.
5. Place the car in Drive with A/C off.

NOTE: *Press down on the hot idle compensator pin while making adjustments to Fleetwood 75 and Commercial models only.*

6. Set idle speed to 620 rpm through 1973 or 640 rpm for 1974 by adjusting the anti-dieseling solenoid.
7. Turn each mixture screw clockwise 1/4 turn at a time alternately until an idle speed of 600 rpm is obtained.
8. Install the limiter caps, then disconnect the wire that energizes the solenoid. The plunger should retract to allow a slower idle speed of 350-400 rpm.
9. Shut off the engine, disconnect the tach, connect the vacuum lines and solenoid wire and install the air cleaner.

1975 AND LATER

Adjust with the air cleaner removed.
Normal engine idle speed is adjusted with the idle speed screw located at the throttle lever side of the carburetor.

1. Disconnect and plug the distributor vacuum advance hose and parking brake vacuum hose (at the release cylinder). Disconnect the air leveling compressor hose at the air cleaner and plug it. Remove the air cleaner, but keep the vacuum hoses connected.
2. Connect a tachometer to the engine, set the parking brake, and block the wheels. Place the transmission in Neutral.
3. Turn in the mixture screws until they seat gently, then turn them out 5 turns.
4. Start and warm the engine to normal operating temperature. Be sure that the choke is off and that the throttle lever stop tang is contacting the carburetor idle speed screw (slow idle position).
5. Place the transmission in Drive with A/C off.
6. Set the idle speed to the higher of the two figures on the underhood sticker by adjusting the idle speed screw located at the throttle lever side of the carburetor.

NOTE: *Do not depress the brake pedal on cars equipped with the Hydro-boost brake system as engine speed will be decreased.*

7. Alternately turn each mixture screw inward 1/4 turn at a time until 600 rpm for 1975-76 or 675 rpm for 1977 and later is reached.
8. Install replacement mixture screw limiter caps and recheck idle speed.

9. Stop the engine, remove the tachometer, connect all vacuum lines, and install the air cleaner.

Fuel Injected Engine Idle Speed Adjustment

1. Adjust the ignition timing to the correct specifications.
2. Disconnect and plug the distributor vacuum line, the parking brake release cylinder vacuum line, and the air leveling compressor hose at the air cleaner.
3. Connect a tachometer to the engine, start it, allow the engine to reach normal operating temperature.
4. Place the transmission selector in Drive, and turn the air conditioning Off.
5. Loosen the lock nut on the idle by-pass adjusting screw on the front of the throttle body. Starting 1978 on Seville, a conventional spring-loaded adjusting screw is used.
6. Adjust the idle by-pass adjusting screw to obtain an idle speed of 600 rpm for 1976 or 650 rpm for 1977 and later. An Allen wrench is required through 1977 and on full-size models.
7. Tighten the lock nut on the adjusting screw, stop the engine, remove the tachometer, and install the air cleaner and vacuum hoses.

Fuel Injected Engine Throttle Position Switch Adjustment

1. Loosen the two throttle position switch mounting screws.
2. While holding the throttle valves in the idle position, turn the throttle position switch counterclockwise carefully until the end-stop is reached.
3. Tighten the mounting screws.
4. Check and make sure that the throttle valves close to the throttle stop. Readjust, if necessary.

COOLING SYSTEM

Cadillac uses a cooling system designed to remain sealed at all times. A coolant reservoir allows fresh coolant to be added. There is no need to open the radiator cap.

Information on the water temperature light or gauge can be found in the Unit Repair Section.

Radiator Removal and Installation

1. Disconnect the battery ground cable.
2. Drain the cooling system.
3. Disconnect the air conditioning compressor, if so equipped, and position it out of the way without disconnecting the hoses.

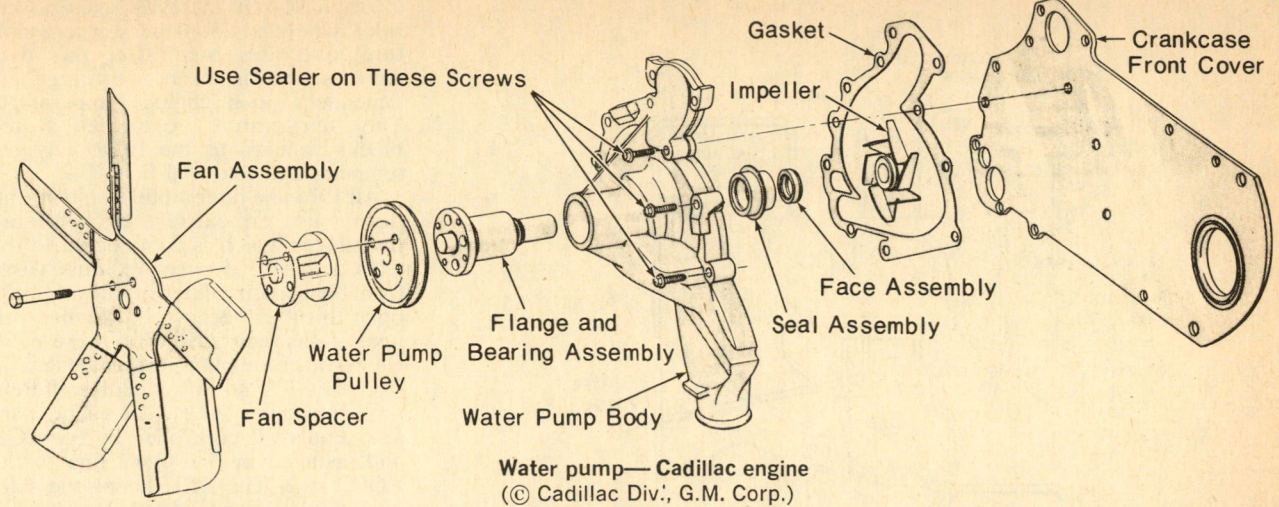

Water pump— Cadillac engine
(© Cadillac Div., G.M. Corp.)

4. Remove the clamp that holds the A/C high pressure vapor line to the cradle.
5. Loosen the hose clamps and disconnect the upper and lower radiator hoses.
6. Disconnect the two transmission cooler lines and plug them.

NOTE: *Disconnect the heater return hose, if so equipped.*

7. Remove the two top radiator cradle clamps or straps and the fan shroud. Disconnect the reservoir hose from the filler neck.
8. Remove the vacuum hoses, if so equipped. Mark them for proper installation.
9. Pull the radiator straight up and out of the car.
10. Reverse thew procedure for installation.

Water Pump Removal and Installation

1. Disconnect the negative battery cable.
2. Drain the radiator and remove the fan shroud. In some cases, the rivets holding the two fan pieces together will have to be drilled out.
3. Remove the fan assembly. The screws cannot be removed entirely due to lack of clearance between fan and radiator. Slide the loosened assembly near the power steering pump to remove the bolts and spacer.
4. Loosen the alternator mounting screws and remove the belt.
5. Loosen the power steering pump mounting screws and remove the belts.
6. On applicable models, remove the air pump and belt.
7. Remove the water pump pulley, disconnect the water inlet hose and remove fuel line.
8. Loosen the four screws holding the crankshaft pulley to the hub halfway and move the pulley out, on Cadillac engines.
9. Unbolt and remove the pump.

10. On installation, use a new gasket. Use sealer on the bolts, on Cadillac engines. The rest of the job is the reverse of removal.

Thermostat Removal and Installation

1. Drain the cooling system until the coolant level is below the level of the thermostat.
2. Remove the upper radiator hose at the thermostat housing.
3. Remove the thermostat housing.
4. Pull the thermostat from the engine block.
5. Position the thermostat in the block with the valve up.
6. Install a new gasket coated with sealer onto the engine block.
7. Position and secure the thermostat housing; tighten the screws.
8. Connect the radiator hose and refill the system to the proper level.

EMISSION CONTROLS

POSITIVE CRANKCASE VENTILATION (PCV) SYSTEM

A simple valve, operated by intake manifold vacuum, is used to meter the flow of air and vapors through the crankcase. Air is drawn in through the breather assembly, located between the rocker cover and the carburetor air cleaner (closed system). When the car is decelerating or the engine is idling, high manifold vacuum opens the valve; this allows full flow of the crankcase vapor into the intake manifold. During acceleration or at a constant speed, the intake manifold vacuum drops, the valve spring forces the valve closed and restricts the flow of vapors into the intake manifold from the crankcase. If

a backfire occurs the valve closes, preventing the vapor in the crankcase from being ignited.

AIR INJECTION

The Air Injection Reactor (AIR) system consists of an engine-driven air pump which forces air into the exhaust port of each cylinder to promote further oxidation and reduce the concentration of hydrocarbons.

THERMOSTATICALLY CONTROLLED AIR CLEANER

The Thermac air cleaner regulates the air temperature at the air cleaner inlet so that it maintains a constant temperature of 105°F. A damper in the air cleaner, when the engine is cold (85°F or below) allows the intake air to be heated by the exhaust manifold before it enters the carburetor. As the engine reaches operating temperature, the damper opens and allows a mixture of outside cool air and heated air to mix to obtain the 105°F intake air.

The Thermac air cleaner is not used on fuel injected engines.

EVAPORATIVE LOSS CONTROL (ELC)

Evaporative Loss Control (ELC), is known as evaporative control system (E.C.S.). The concept of this system is, the venting of the fuel tank through a canister containing charcoal. Both liquid fuel and fuel vapors from the tank are fed into the liquid vapor separator which is located ahead of or in the fuel tank. The vapors are collected in the charcoal canister which is mounted on the front of the radiator. The vapors are drawn from the canister by a vacuum line which is connected to the air cleaner. The liquid fuel which is ducted to the separator is returned to the fuel tank.

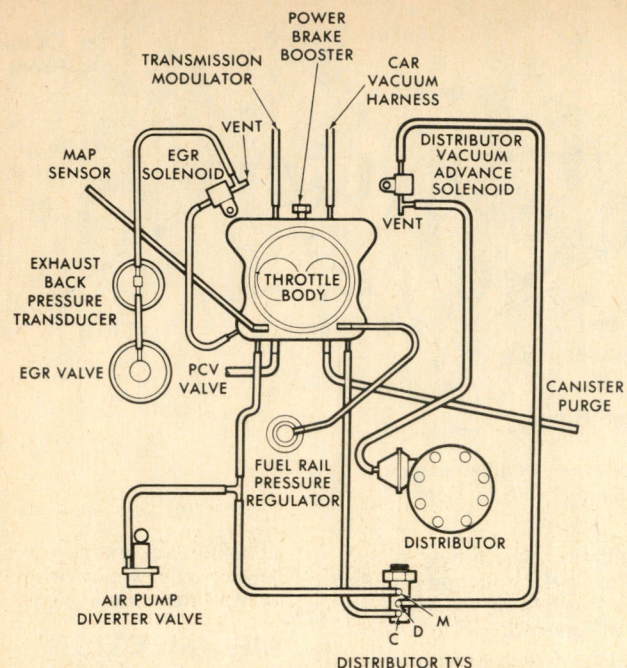

1978 425 California EFI engine vacuum diagram
(© Cadillac Div., G.M. Corp.)

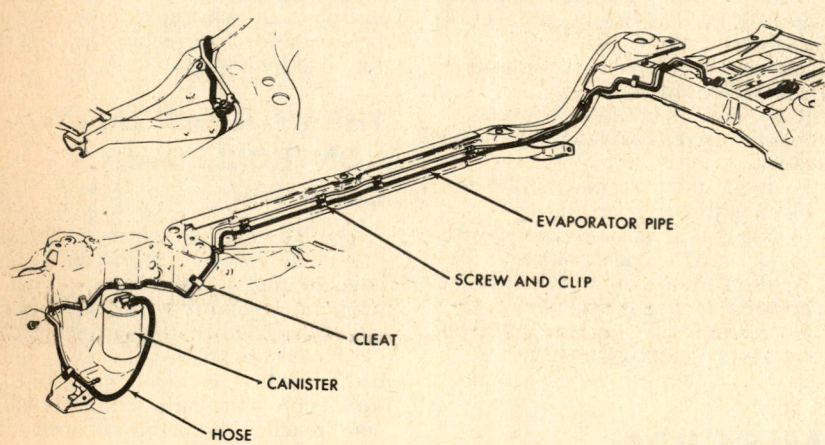

Evaporative control system (© Cadillac Div., G.M. Corp)

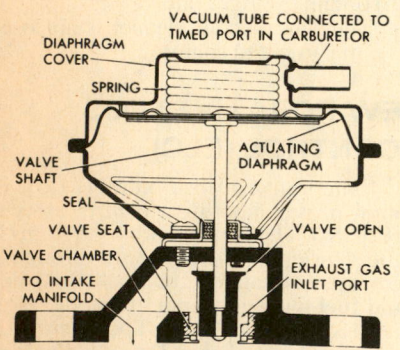

E.G.R. valve in the open position
(© Cadillac Div., G.M. Corp)

EXHAUST GAS RECIRCULATION (EGR)

The Exhaust Gas Recirculation System (EGR), used from 1973 on, is a control system used to reduce oxides of nitrogen released into the air. The basic function of the system is to reduce the temperature in the combustion chambers. This will lessen nitrogen oxidation and reduce pollution. It is accomplished by recirculating a small amount of engine exhaust through ports in the intake manifold and into the carburetor for reburning.

This channeling of exhaust is governed by the EGR valve which is mounted at the rear of the intake manifold. As the engine speed increases, vacuum is applied to the vacuum diaphragm in the valve and this opens the exhaust port allowing exhaust gases to enter. As vacuum decreases at idle speed and wide open throttle, the valve closes and the gases are cut off.

Temperature overrides are used to prevent exhaust gas recirculation from occurring when the engine is cold.

Prior to March 15, 1973, these overrides depended upon ambient temperature; overrides used after this date were enclosed in shrouds, making them dependent upon engine temperature. The temperature override switch blocks vacuum to the EGR valve at temperatures below 60°F.

All 1974 and later models sold in California use an exhaust backpressure transducer which is connnected to the EGR valve to prevent exhaust gases from being recirculated at idle and wide open throttle, because the higher volume of gas recirculated on these models would cause poor performance.

The EGR system is slightly different on EFI engines. The EGR vacuum solenoid valve is controlled by the ECU and installed in the signal line to the EGR valve. The ECU keeps the solenoid valve closed when coolant temperatures are below about 130°F, blocking the signal to the EGR valve. This is to improve cold starting and engine warm up. When the coolant temperature goes above 130°F, vacuum is directed to the EGR valve and exhaust pressure transducer. A thermal delay valve is not used.

CATALYTIC CONVERTER

Catalytic converters are used on 1975 and later Cadillac and Seville models. The converter is located in the exhaust pipe, under the floor on the passenger's side.

For more information on how the converter works, as well as service procedures for it, see the Emission Controls Unit Repair Section.

EARLY FUEL EVAPORATION (EFE)

Early Fuel Evaporation (EFE) is used on 1975 and later Cadillacs (except fuel injected models). The system consists of a valve installed on the right-hand exhaust manifold which is controlled by a thermostatic vacuum switch (TVS), located in the upper left front of the cylinder block.

Below approximately 150°F (120°F for 1977 and later) engine coolant temperature, the TVS routes intake manifold vacuum to the EFE valve. The vacuum closes the EFE valve, forcing exhaust gases through the exhaust crossover passage in the intake manifold to heat the intake manifold for better fuel vaporization. At approximately 150°F (120°F for 1977 and later) coolant temperature, the TVS blocks manifold vacuum to the EFE valve. This causes the EFE valve to open, ending heating of the intake manifold.

MODEL USAGE

The 1972 cars use the PCV, AIR, ELC, and a Speed Control Spark (SCS) which controls the spark advance to the distributor at low speeds. The switch is mounted to the transmission and connected to the speedometer gear. The switch is closed up to 33 mph, allowing no vacuum advance to the distributor during speeds from 0 to 33 mph. When the vehicle reaches 33 mph, the contacts in the switch separate, allowing the vacuum port to be uncovered. Once the port is uncovered the vacuum causes the distributor to advance.

1973-74 models use EGR, PCV, AIR, and ELC.

1975 models use PCV, AIR (Calif. cars and Commercial Chassis), EGR, EFE, ECS, and catalytic converters.

1976-79 Cadillac models use PCV, AIR (Calif. cars and fuel injected models), EGR, EFE (except fuel injected models), ECS, and catalytic converters.

All 1976-79 Seville models use PCV, AIR, EGR, ECS, and catalytic converters.

ENGINE

NOTE: *The diesel engine is produced by General Motor's Oldsmobile division. Diesel engine service procedures will therefore be found in the Oldsmobile car section.*

ENGINE REMOVAL AND INSTALLATION

FULL SIZE CADILLAC

1. Disconnect negative battery cable.
2. Remove hood, after scribing hood hinge outline for proper alignment.
3. Remove air cleaner and heat shroud.
4. Drain cooling system. Unfasten the fender struts from the radiator shroud.
5. Remove radiator hose bracket, radiator cover and fan.
6. Remove upper radiator hose.
7. Disconnect throttle and Cruise Control linkage at carburetor.
8. Remove Cruise Control power unit on cars so equipped.
9. Disconnect power steering pump bracket and swing pump out of way with hoses still connected. Position power steering fluid cooler out of the way.
10. Remove A/C compressor bracket bolts and swing compressor out of way with hoses still connected.
11. Disconnect temperature sender wire, idle speed-up wire (if so equipped), ignition primary wire, downshift switch wire, S.C.S. solenoid (if so equipped) and anti-dieseling solenoid wires, electronic ignition connector, block temperature sender lead, and all ground straps. On fuel injected engines, disconnect the EFI manifold harness and move it out of the way.

12. Bend back clips and position wiring harness out of the way.
13. Disconnect all vacuum hoses, and purge hose from E.L.C. canister. Disconnect the automatic level control line, on models so equipped.
14. Disconnect alternator, heater switch and oil pressure sender wires.
15. Remove wiring harness from clips.
16. Remove water hose from fitting at rear of right-hand cylinder head.
17. Loosen and remove alternator and A.I.R. pumps and remove belts.
18. Disconnect tie struts and swing out of the way.
19. Remove upper two transmission-to-engine bolts. Remove two screws that secure right air deflector to lower radiator cradle.
20. Jack up car and support on axle stands.
21. Relieve fuel pressure on EFI cars. See the note under EFI Troubleshooting.
22. Remove starter motor, then disconnect exhaust pipes from manifolds.
23. Remove front engine mount bolts, then disconnect and plug vapor return line at fuel pump (A/C cars only) and fuel inlet line. Remove oil filter, after draining engine oil.
24. Disconnect lower radiator hose and remove flywheel housing cover.
25. Remove the three screws that secure flex plate to converter. Engine must be rotated for acess.
26. Remove four transmission-to-engine bolts.
27. Lower the car to the ground.
28. Connect a lifting bracket to the engine.
29. Support transmission with a wood-padded floor jack.
30. Raise engine slightly and pull forward to disengage from transmission, then pull engine up and out.
31. Reverse the above procedure to install the engine.

SEVILLE

1. Disconnect the negative battery cable. On the diesel, remove the rear battery and the engine vacuum pump.
2. Drain the cooling system.
3. Remove the hood. Scribe marks on the hinges and their mounting points for installation.
4. Remove the air cleaner assembly.
5. Remove the struts from both right and left wheelhousings.
6. Remove the radiator cover.
7. Disconnect the power brake hose at the point where it joins the steel tube to the rear of the left cylinder head.
8. Disconnect the left and right side sections of the wiring harness and position them out of the way.
9. Disconnect the heater hose from the rear of the intake manifold.

10. Disconnect the upper and lower radiator hoses from the engine and remove the fan assembly from the water pump.
11. Remove the distributor cap and spark plug wires.
12. Disconnect the two ground wires from the compressor bracket and position the harness out of the way.
13. Disconnect the accelerator linkage and vapor canister hose from the throttle body.
14. Relieve fuel pressure on EFI cars. See the note under EFI Troubleshooting.
15. Disconnect the fuel inlet line from the fuel rail and plug the line.
16. Remove the power steering hoses at the steering gear and plug the hoses and gear. Secure hoses to engine.
17. Disconnect the fuel return line from the pressure regulator outlet fitting.
18. Remove the air conditioner compressor from the engine without disconnecting the refrigerant lines and move it out of the way.
19. Raise the car on a hoist.
20. Disconnect the exhaust pipe and exhaust crossover pipe from the exhaust manifolds.
21. Remove the torque converter cover.
22. Remove the starter motor.
23. Remove the screw and clip securing the transmission oil cooler lines to the engine oil pan.
24. Remove the three screws securing the flexplate to the converter.
25. Remove the through-bolt from each engine mount.
26. Remove the screws holding the engine and transmission together.
27. Lower the car.
28. Remove the screws securing the heater water valve to the evaporator and move the valve out of the way.
29. Support the transmission with a jack and a block of wood placed between the jack and the transmission case.
30. Install a suitable lifting device on the engine and raise the engine off the motor mounts. Reposition the transmission support.
31. Raise the engine carefully, pull it forward and lift it from the car.
32. Install the engine in the reverse order of removal.

MANIFOLDS

Exhaust Manifold Removal and Installation

1. In order to remove the left exhaust manifold, remove the air cleaner assembly, then remove the air cleaner bracket and heat stove from the manifold, by unfastening the manifold nuts from the studs on the Nos. 2 and 8 cylinders.
2. Unfasten the nuts which secure the

downpipes to either manifold. Remove the two studs retaining the EFE valve to the right-side manifold and remove the EFE valve.

3. Remove the bolts which secure the manifold to the cylinder heads.

NOTE: *It may not be possible to remove the fifth bolt from the front of the cylinder head completely on Cadillac engines. Back the bolt all the way out and remove it with the manifolds.*

4. Lift the manifold out of the engine compartment.
5. Installation is the reverse of removal. Lubricate the cylinder head installation surface with moly grease. Install the fifth screw from the front prior to installing the manifold. Tighten the bolts to specifications. On the right-side manifold, position the EFE valve on the manifold with the actuator toward the engine block. Tighten the two stud bolts.

Intake Manifold Removal and Installation
CARBURETED ENGINES

1. Remove the negative battery cable, air cleaner, heat tube, and crankcase vent.
2. Disconnect the throttle linkage and the Cruise Control.
3. Remove the coil leads and the connector from the SCS solenoid.
4. Disconnect the downshift switch and the temperature sender. On some models it is necessary to remove the anti-dieseling solenoid and the SCS solenoid.
5. Disconnect all vacuum lines. Remove the carburetor fuel line.
6. On cars with air conditioning, it is necessary to partially remove the compressor.
7. Remove the manifold hold-down bolts and lift the manifold from the engine.
8. To install the intake manifold, reverse the procedure. The intake manifold bolts are torqued using a diagonal torque pattern beginning from the center of the manifold and working toward the ends.

FUEL INJECTED ENGINES

1. Disconnect the negative battery cable and remove the air cleaner and crankcase filter.
2. Disconnect the throttle cable and cruise control linkage at the throttle body. Remove the cable from the bracket and move it aside.
3. Disconnect the coolant temperature switch wire, the HEI wire, speed sensor wire, downshift switch wire, and the injector wiring harness from the fuel rail brackets and move the harness out of the way.
4. Disconnect the two vacuum hoses from the throttle body to the thermal vacuum switch (TVS).
5. Disconnect the vacuum hoses and

power brake pipe from the rear of the throttle body.
6. Bleed the pressure from the fuel delivery system, as explained in the note under EFI Troubleshooting, and disconnect the fuel line from the fuel rail.
7. Disconnect the EGR solenoid wires, air temperature sensor wire and the MAP sensor vacuum hose.
8. Remove the PCV valve from the rocker cover and move it out of the way.
9. Remove the spark plug wires and the distributor cap.
10. Remove the front fuel rail.
11. Remove the air conditioner compressor from the engine. Do not disconnect the refrigerant lines.
12. Remove the fuel return line hose from the fuel pressure regulator.
13. On the 1978 and later Seville aluminum manifold, remove the oil pressure switch and oil fill tube. Remove the intake manifold retaining screws and remove the manifold. Do not pry or lift the manifold by the fuel rails or their mounting brackets.
14. Clean all gasket material from the mating surfaces of the manifold, cylinder heads and block.
15. Place new rubber intake manifold seals over the rails at the front and rear of the cylinder block. The tabs on the gasket should be positioned in the holes in the rails and the beveled ends of the gasket tucked into the slot at the mating of the head and rail.
16. Apply gasket sealer to the sheet metal gasket-shield on the engine. The holes in the gasket should engage the dowel pins on the cylinder heads. Be careful not to use too much sealer near the injector tips.
17. Carefully position the manifold on the top of the engine. Install and tighten the intake manifold retaining screws to the specified torque.
18. Assemble and install the remaining components in the reverse order of removal. Make sure to replace the two large washers on the aluminum manifold.

VALVE SYSTEM

All Cadillac engines use hydraulic lifters. Valve systems with hydraulic lifters operate with zero clearance in the valve train. The rocker arms are non-adjustable. The lifter itself will compensate if there is slack in the system but if there is excessive play, the entire system should be examined.

If the valve guides are found to be worn past allowable limits, they will have to be rebored and valves with oversize stems installed. Three oversize valves of different stem diameters are available for each engine.

Sometimes a valve guide bore is made oversize at the factory. Oversize valve guide bores from the factory are marked on the inboard side of the cyl-

inder heads on a machined surface just above the intake manifold surface on the 350 V8 in the Seville and on the cylinder head gasket surface in line with the oversize valve in the full-size Cadillacs.

NOTE: *Some 350 V8 Seville engines have both standard and .010 in. oversize valve lifters. The oversize lifters have O etched on the side of the lifter and the same marking on the lifter housing boss on the cylinder block.*

Rocker Arm Removal and Installation

The rocker arms are mounted in pairs (four pairs to each cylinder head). They are of the modified pedestal-mounted type.

Rocker arms may be removed in pairs and do not require cylinder-head removal.

Torque rocker arm mounting screws to 60 ft. lbs. through 1973; 70 ft. lbs. on 1974 and later Cadillac models; or 25 ft. lbs. on 1976 and later Seville models.

Cylinder Head Removal and Installation

Care must be used when replacing Cadillac engine cylinder-head bolts. They are different lengths.
1. Remove intake manifold.
2. Drain engine coolant.
3. Disconnect ground strap at rear of cylinder heads from cowl. Disconnect wiring connector for high engine temperature warning system from sending unit at rear of left cylinder head.
4. Remove alternator, if working on the right cylinder head, or partially remove the steering pump if working on the left head. Remove the heater hose from the rear of the right cylinder head.
5. Disconnect A.I.R. injection pump tubes from cylinder heads.
6. Remove clamps holding the wire harness to the cylinder heads and tie harness back out of the way.
7. Remove screws holding exhaust manifolds to cylinder heads.
8. Remove screws holding the rocker arm cover to the heads.
9. Remove the rocker cover.
10. Remove screws holding each rocker arm support to cylinder head, then remove rocker arm assemblies. Store these assemblies so that they may be reinstalled in their correct locations.
11. Remove pushrods and store them with their respective rocker arm assemblies.
12. Install two 7/16 x 6 in. screws to be used as lifting handles in two of the rocker arm support screw holes.
13. Remove ten cylinder-head bolts.
14. Lift cylinder head off the block.
15. Remove all gasket material from the cylinder head and block mating surfaces.
16. Install by reversing removal procedures.

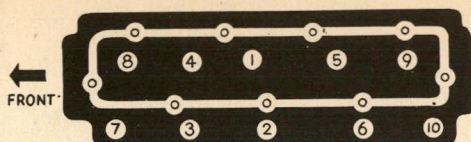

Cylinder head bolt tightening sequence
—Cadillac engine

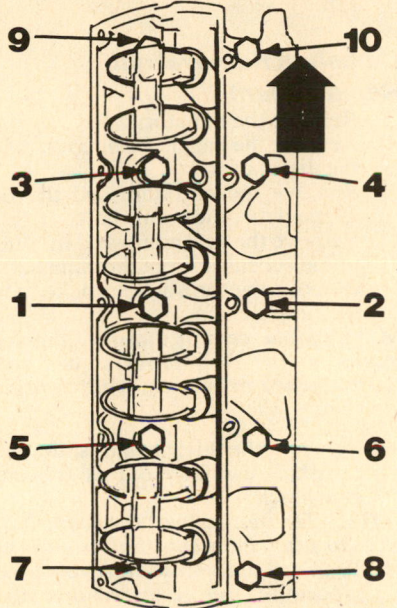

Cylinder head bolt tightening sequence
—Seville 350 V8

17. When torquing the head bolts, use the three-step method. Torque the bolts to 1/3 of the total torque listed in the sequence shown. Once this is done, repeat the same procedure, this time torquing all the bolts to 2/3 of the total listed torque. Finally torque the bolts to the recommended torque.

TIMING CASE COVER—CHAIN, AND CAMSHAFT

Timing Chain Cover, Chain, and Sprocket Removal

1. Disconnect negative battery cable and drain cooling system.
2. Detach upper radiator hose retainer from cradle and position hose out of the way.
3. Remove fan, generator belt and power steering belts.
4. Remove four capscrews that secure crank pulley to harmonic balancer, then remove both pulley and balancer.
5. Remove plug from end of crankshaft, and install balancer puller pilot in one bore in the end of the crankshaft and remove balancer hub from the end of the crankshaft.
6. Drain engine oil and remove oil pan.

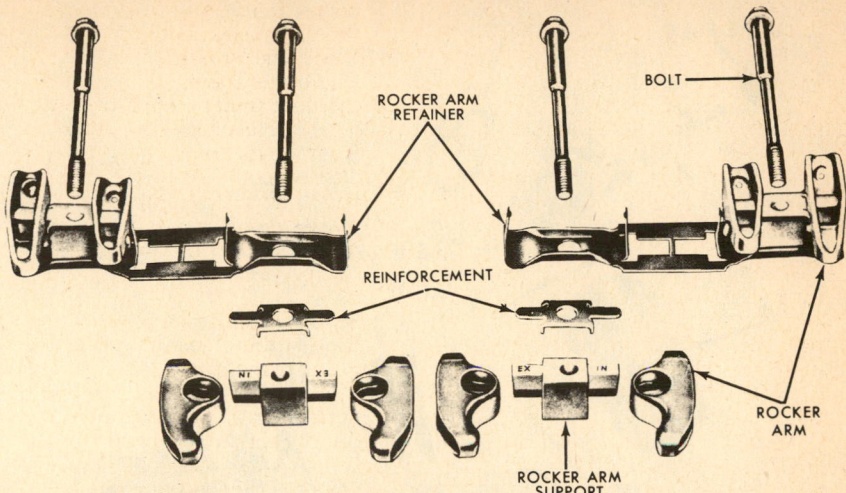

Cadillac engine rocker arm assembly (ⓒ Cadillac Div., G.M. Corp)

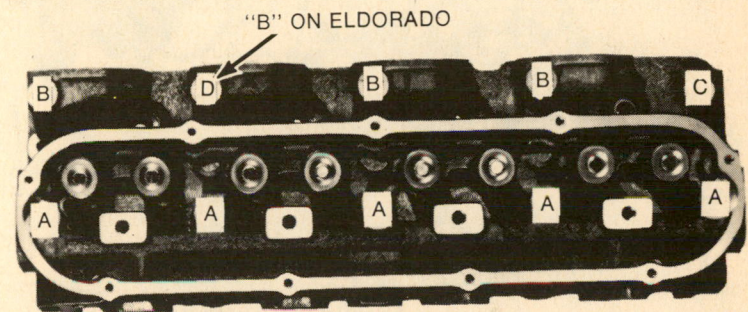

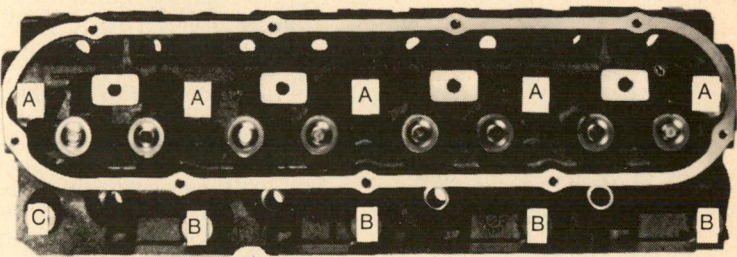

Cylinder head bolt location and length— Cadillac engine

BOLT LOCATION	LENGTH
A—BOLT	4.36"
B—BOLT	4.77"
C—BOLT	3.02"
D—BOLT/STUD	3.02"

(ⓒ Cadillac Div., G.M. Corp.)

7. Disconnect lower radiator hose from water pump, then remove the ten screws that hold front cover to engine. Remove cover with water pump attached.
8. Remove distributor and fuel pump.
9. Remove oil slinger and fuel pump eccentric.
10. Remove two capscrews that secure camshaft sprocket.
11. Remove camshaft sprocket along with timing chain.
12. To install, reverse removal procedure. Mount the timing chain over the camshaft and the crankshaft sprocket and start the camshaft sprocket over the shaft, being certain the aligning dowel is in a position where it will enter the hole in the camshaft freely. Make certain

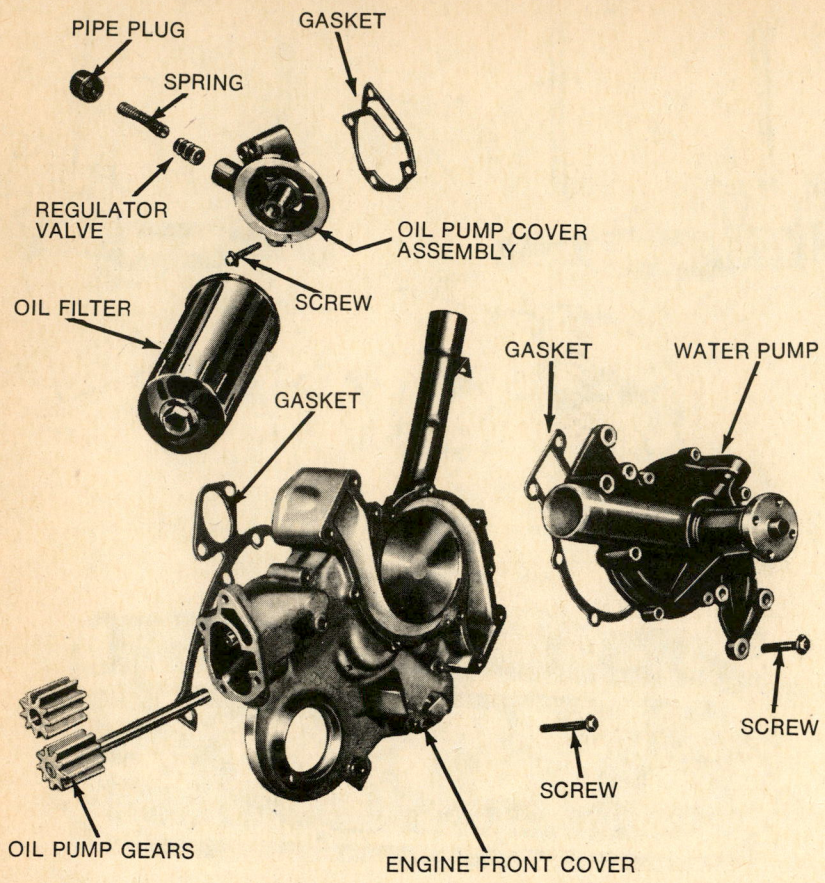

Engine front cover disassembled—Cadillac engine
(© Cadillac Div., G.M. Corp)

Labels: PIPE PLUG, GASKET, SPRING, REGULATOR VALVE, OIL PUMP COVER ASSEMBLY, OIL FILTER, SCREW, GASKET, GASKET, WATER PUMP, SCREW, SCREW, OIL PUMP GEARS, ENGINE FRONT COVER

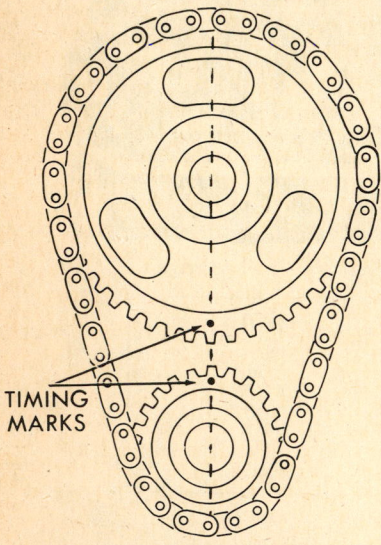

Labels: TIMING MARKS

Timing mark alignment

that the timing marks on the sprockets are in line between shaft centers.

Camshaft sprockets sometimes install a little stiffly. However, a comparatively easy way to install a tight-fitting sprocket is to draw it on carefully with two bolts somewhat longer then the regular

mounting bolts. By drawing alternately against each bolt, and tapping gently with a plastic hammer, even a very tight camshaft gear sprocket can be installed.

13. When the camshaft is secured, turn the engine two full revolutions until the timing marks again assume the original position. Check to make certain that the punch marks, which are stamped into the front face of the sprockets, are in line between the shaft centers.

Timing Cover Oil Seal Removal and Installation

All models are equipped with a molded-type front cover crankshaft oil seal. The seal may be replaced without removing the engine front cover.

1. Disconnect the battery and remove carburetor air cleaner.
2. Remove power steering pump drive belt.
3. Remove generator drive belt.
4. On air conditioned cars, and cars equipped with the A.I.R. system, remove the pump drive belts.
5. Raise and support the front of the car on stands. Remove the fan.
6. Remove pulley and harmonic balancer, as outlined in Timing Chain and Sprocket Removal.

7. With a thin blade screwdriver, pry out front cover oil seal.
8. Lubricate new dual-lip oil seal with wheel bearing grease. Position seal on end of crankshaft with garter spring side toward engine.
9. Using a seal installer drive the front seal into the front cover until it bottoms.
10. Assemble and install the remaining parts in reverse order of disassembly.

Camshaft Removal and Replacement

1. Remove the radiator.
2. Remove the engine front cover and the distributor.
3. Remove the oil pump and the oil slinger from the crankshaft.
4. Remove the fuel pump and the fuel pump eccentric from the camshaft.
5. Remove the camshaft sprocket and the timing chain.

NOTE: *Make certain that the aligning marks on the two sprockets are correctly aligned before removing the timing chain.*

6. Remove the lifters and slide the camshaft carefully out of the engine block.

NOTE: *Do not allow the camshaft lobes to scratch the camshaft bearings.*

7. To install the camshaft, reverse the procedure. Before installation, the camshaft should be lubricated with a thin coat of rear axle lubricant and then carefully inserted to avoid bearing damage.
8. The camshaft sprocket screws should be torqued to 18 ft lbs while the fuel pump eccentric screw is tightened to 35 ft lbs.

PISTON AND ROD INSTALLATION

The numbers on the connecting rods face away from the camshaft; that is, the numbers on the left bank (even) face to the left; the numbers on the right bank (odd) face to the right. As a double check, the word *rear*, (or R), stamped on the piston, faces the rear of the engine on both banks and an arrow on the piston top points to the front of the engine.

On the 350 Seville V8, the piston is placed in the cylinder with the notch in the top of the piston and the F on the side of the piston facing toward the front of the engine. The oil spurt hole in the connecting rod faces toward the camshaft.

LUBRICATION

Oil Pump Removal and Installation

425, 472, 500 V8

1. Jack up car and remove oil filter.
2. Remove five capscrews that secure oil pump to engine.

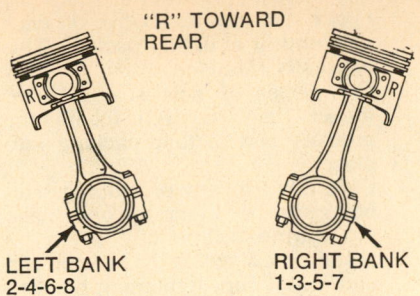

"R" TOWARD REAR

LEFT BANK
2-4-6-8

RIGHT BANK
1-3-5-7

**Piston to connecting rod relationship
—Cadillac engine**

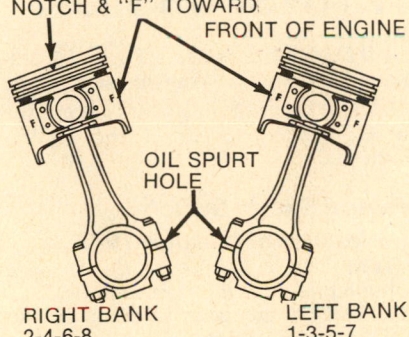

NOTCH & "F" TOWARD FRONT OF ENGINE

OIL SPURT HOLE

RIGHT BANK
2-4-6-8

LEFT BANK
1-3-5-7

**Piston and connecting rod positioning
—Seville 350 V8**

NOTE: *Remove screw nearest pressure regulator last.*

3. Slide drive shaft, drive gear and driven gear out of housing.
4. Remove plug from housing cover, using 5/16 in. wrench. Remove pressure regulator valve and spring.
5. Check free length of regulator spring—it should be 2.57-2.69 in.
6. Inspect gears and housing for burrs or scoring.
7. Check pump clearance limits.
8. On installation, pack the pump with petroleum jelly. Use a new gasket, engage the pump driveshaft with the distributor drive, and install screw nearest pressure regulator first. Install remaining screws and tighten all five screws to 15 ft. lbs. Install oil filter, add one quart oil to engine, run engine and check for leaks.

350 V8

1. Remove the oil pan.
2. Remove the oil pump-to-rear main bearing cap attaching bolts and remove the oil pump and drive shaft extension.
3. Remove the drive shaft extension. Do not attempt to remove the washers from the shaft. The shaft extension and washers must be replaced as an assembly if the washers are not 1-11/32 in. from the end of the shaft.
4. Remove the cotter pin, spring and the pressure regulator valve. Place your thumb over the pressure regulator bore before removing the cotter pin to contain the spring.

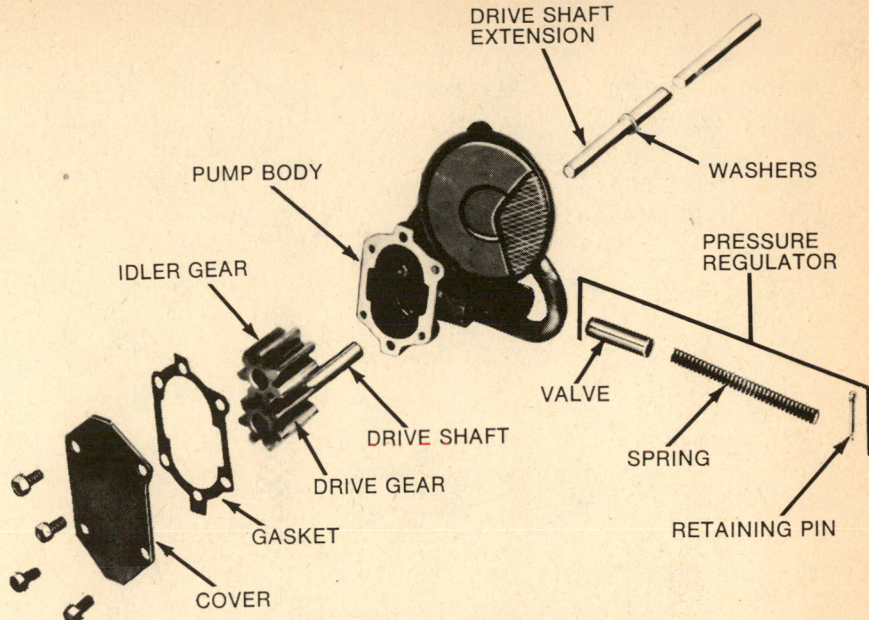

Exploded view of Seville 350 V8 oil pump
(© Cadillac Div., G.M. Corp.)

(labels: DRIVE SHAFT EXTENSION, WASHERS, PRESSURE REGULATOR, PUMP BODY, IDLER GEAR, VALVE, SPRING, DRIVE SHAFT, RETAINING PIN, DRIVE GEAR, GASKET, COVER)

5. Remove the oil pump cover attaching screws and remove the cover and gasket.
6. Remove the idler gear and drive gear from the pump body.
7. Check the gears for scoring and any other damage. Install new gears, if necessary.
8. Assemble and install the oil pump in reverse order of removal. The end of the drive shaft extension nearest the washers is inserted into the drive shaft.

Oil Pan Removal and Installation

425, 472, 500 V8

1. Drain engine oil and disconnect positive battery cable.
2. Disconnect exhaust crossover pipe at exhaust manifold.
3. Disconnect exhaust support bracket at transmission extension housing, and position exhaust system to one side.
4. Remove starter motor.
5. Remove two idler arm support mounting screws from frame side member, and lower support.
6. Disconnect pitman arm at drag link, and lower steering linkage.
7. Remove transmission lower cover.
8. Remove engine oil pan.
9. When reinstalling, reverse above procedure and torque oil pan screws and nuts to 10 ft. lbs. The transmission cover screws should be torqued to 20 ft. lbs.

350 V8

1. Remove the wheelhousing struts from the fenders.
2. Remove the radiator cover.
3. Raise the car.
4. Remove the through-bolt from each motor mount.

5. Remove the exhaust crossover pipe.
6. Remove the starter motor.
7. Remove the torque converter cover.
8. Drain the crankcase and remove the oil pan attaching screws.
9. Raise the engine as far as necessary with a jack placed under the crankshaft pulley and remove the oil pan.
10. Clean all of the gasket material from the oil pan and engine block mating surfaces and install the oil pan in the reverse order of removal, using a new gasket kit and sealer. The rubber front and rear seals cover the tabs on the oil pan gaskets at the front cover. Torque the oil pan screws to 10 ft. lbs.

Rear Main Seal Removal and Installation

425, 472, 500 V8

1. Remove the oil pan, after removing spark plug wires and plugs.
2. Remove the rear main bearing cap and loosen the bolts holding the other four bearings about three turns each. Remove the old rear main bearing seals.
3. Clean the groove in the cap and in the block. Lubricate seals with engine oil.
4. Make an installation tool.

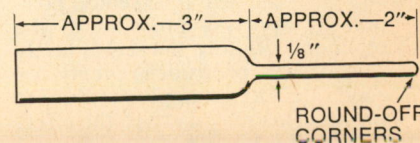

←APPROX.—3"→ ←APPROX.—2"→
↓1/8"
ROUND-OFF CORNERS

Rear main bearing oil seal installation tool

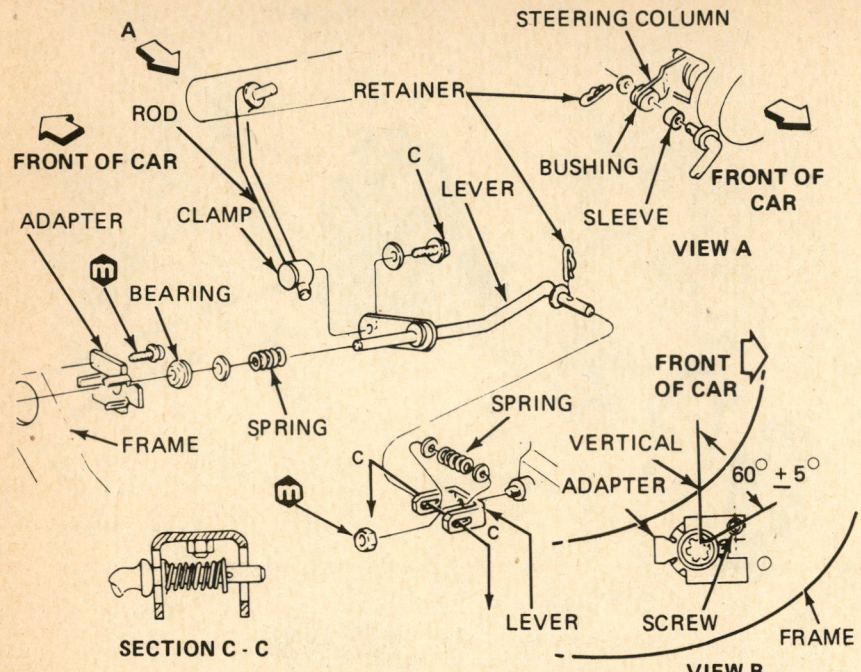

Typical Seville shift linkage—adjustment is made at screw C (© Cadillac Div., G.M. Corp.)

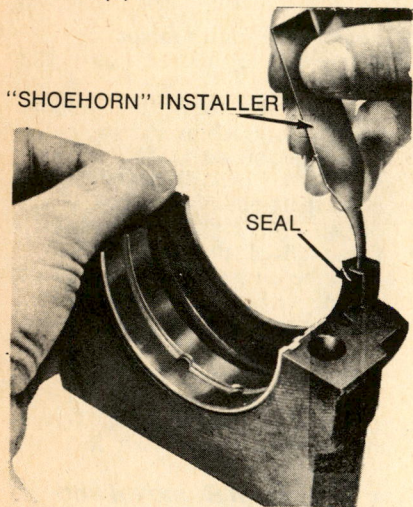

Installing rear main bearing oil seal
(© Cadillac Div., G.M. Corp)

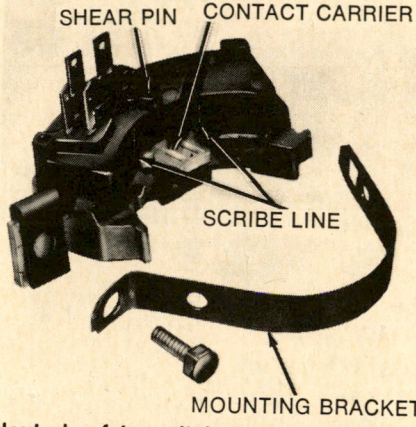

Neutral safety switch used through 1973
(© Cadillac Div., G.M. Corp.)

5. Start the upper half into the groove in the block with the lip facing forward and rotate it into position, using the tool as a guide. Press firmly on both ends to be sure it is protruding uniformly on each side.

6. Install the lower half of the seal into the bearing cap with the lip facing forward and one end of the seal over the ridge and flush with the split line. Hold one finger over this end to prevent it from slipping, and push the seal into seated position by applying pressure to the other end. Be sure the seal is firmly seated and protrudes evenly on each side. Do not apply pressure to the lip. This may damage the effectiveness of the seal.

7. Apply rubber cement to the mating surfaces of the block and cap being careful not to get any cement on the bearing, the crankshaft or the seal. The cement coating should be about .010 in. thick.

8. Install the bearing cap, tightening the bolts with the fingers only.

9. Move the crankshaft forward and rearward by pounding on the counterweight with a plastic hammer to assure alignment of the rear main bearing thrust surfaces.

10. Tighten the bearing bolts to 90-100 ft. lbs. Be sure to tighten the bolts of the other four bearings also.

11. Reinstall the oil pan.

350 V8

The crankshaft need not be removed to replace the rear main bearing upper oil seal.

1. Drain the crankcase and remove the oil pan and rear main bearing cap.

2. Using a blunt-ended tool, drive the upper seal into its groove on each side until it is tightly packed. This is usually 1/4-3/4 in.

3. Cut pieces of new seal 1/16 in. longer than required to fill the grooves and install, packing into place.

4. Carefully trim any protruding seal, being sure not to scratch or damage the bearing surface.

5. Install a new seal in the bearing cap and install cap, tightening bolts to 120 ft. lbs. Install the oil pan.

AUTOMATIC TRANSMISSION

All Cadillac cars use a Turbo Hydramatic automatic transmission. The model 400 is used on all cars except the diesel, which uses the Turbo Hydramatic 200.

Neutral Safety Switch Replacement through 1973

NOTE: *The switch is on the steering column under the instrument panel.*

1. Position the gear selector in the Neutral position.

2. Release the clamp and remove the switch without moving the contact carrier. The position of the carrier should be marked.

3. Remove the vacuum hoses after they have been marked and disconnect the wires from the switch.

4. Installation is accomplished by reversing the above procedure.

To adjust the switch:

1. Check that the gear lever is correctly adjusted and that the neutral safety switch is properly positioned by this check.

2. Set the handbrake. Put the lever on the steering column in drive. Hold the ignition key on and slowly move the lever toward Neutral or Park until the starter cranks and the engine runs.

3. Without moving the lever farther, press the accelerator to determine whether the transmission is really in Neutral or Park.

4. If all is correct, the engine will have started when the lever got to the neutral position and the transmission will not be in gear. Also, back-up lights will go on with transmission in Reverse.

NOTE: *A vacuum leak that can be corrected by moving the shift lever is an indication that the switch only needs adjustment and is not defective.*

5. Adjust the neutral safety switch by turning it and its mounting bracket until the above conditions are met.

Neutral Safety Switch—1974 and later

On all models 1974 and later, the neutral safety switch works mechanically, rather than electrically. When the transmission selector is any position other than Park or Neutral, the key cannot be turned to Start.

Shift Linkage Adjustment

1. Loosen the nut on the steering column manual lever on full-size Cadillacs and the adjustment screw on the relay lever on Seville.
2. From under the car, pull relay rod up, positioning transmission shift valve in Park, then push rod down to the Neutral third step.
3. Position selector lever in Neutral.
4. Tighten nut on steering column manual lever on full-size Cadillacs and the adjustment screw on the relay lever on Seville.
5. Check that positions selected on selector lever correspond with appropriate detents on transmission.

Kickdown Adjustment, Turbo Hydra-Matic 400

1. Remove the air cleaner.
2. Make certain that the idle speed is set correctly and that the carburetor is operating on the low-speed circuit.
3. Loosen the switch mounting screws and insert a 0.094 in. wire gauge into the hole in the lower wire terminal.
4. With the gauge in place, adjust the position of the switch so that the lever just touches the carburetor adaptor plate arm. The switch should make contact above 60° of throttle opening.
5. After adjusting, tighten the mounting screws and remove the gauge.
6. Reinstall the air cleaner.

Throttle Valve Adjustment, Turbo Hydra-Matic 200

The throttle valve cable controls line pressure, shift points, shift feel, part throttle and full throttle downshifts.

1. Remove the engine air cleaner.
2. Push up on the bottom of the snap-lock at the cable bracket. Make sure that the cable is free to slide through the snap-lock.
3. Move the carburetor lever to the wide open throttle position and hold it there.
4. Push the snap-lock flush and let the carburetor lever return to the closed position.
5. If the preceding adjustment does not correct late shifting or no part throttle downshift, a transmission fluid pressure test should be made.

Pan Removal and Installation, Fluid and Filter Change

1. Raise the vehicle and loosen one corner of the transmission pan and allow the fluid to drain into a container.
2. Remove the remaining pan attaching screws and remove the pan and gasket. Discard the gasket.
3. Clean the pan with solvent and dry it thoroughly.

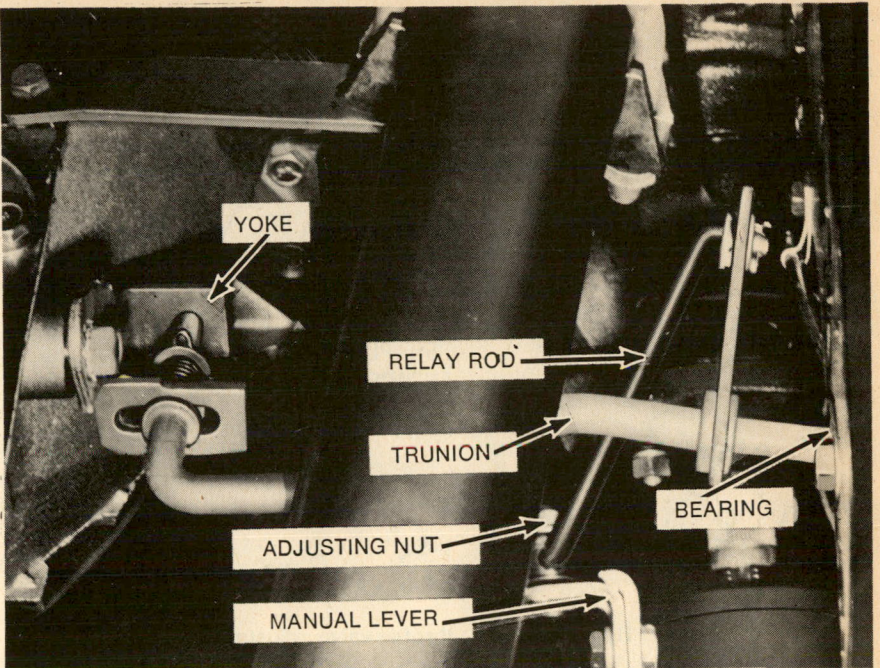

1972 Shift linkage adjustment (© Cadillac Div., G.M. Corp.)

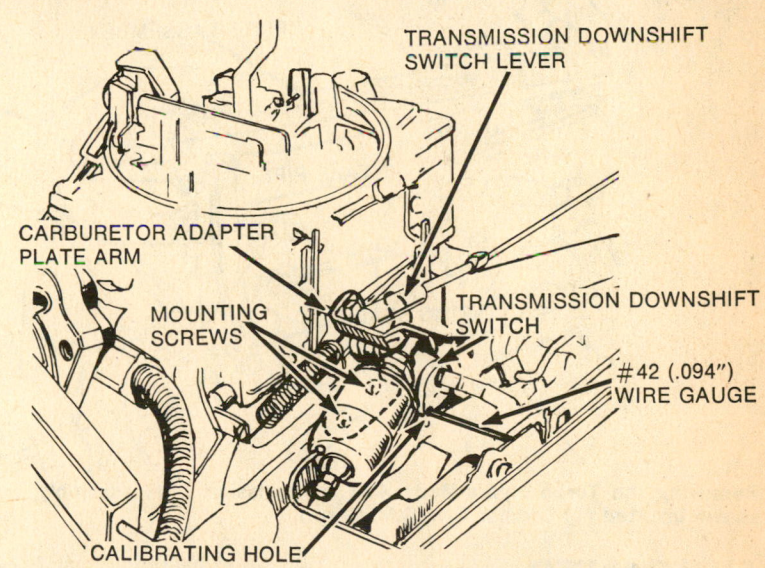

Turbo Hydra-Matic 400 downshift switch adjustment

4. Remove the filter retaining bolt on the 400.
5. On the 400, remove the intake pipe and filter assembly. Remove the intake pipe O-ring and discard the filter and O-ring. Install the new intake pipe O-ring on the pipe and install the intake pipe into the new filter assembly. Install the intake pipe and filter assembly into the case bore. Install the filter retaining bolt.
6. On the 200 transmission, remove the screen bolts, screen, and gasket. Clean the screen and replace with a new gasket. Tighten the bolts to 6-10 ft. lbs.
7. Install a new gasket on the pan and

8. install the pan, tightening the retaining screws to 12 ft lbs.
8. Lower the car and add 4 quarts of Dexron automatic transmission fluid through the filler tube. If the filter was not replaced, only add 2 quarts. Add 3 quarts for the 200 transmission.
9. Start the engine and allow it to run at normal idle speed for 1-1/2 minutes with the gear selector in Park.
10. Check the fluid level. With the fluid below normal operating temperature the level should be 1/4 in. below the ADD mark on the dip stick for the 400, and between the two dimples on the 200. Add fluid as necessary.

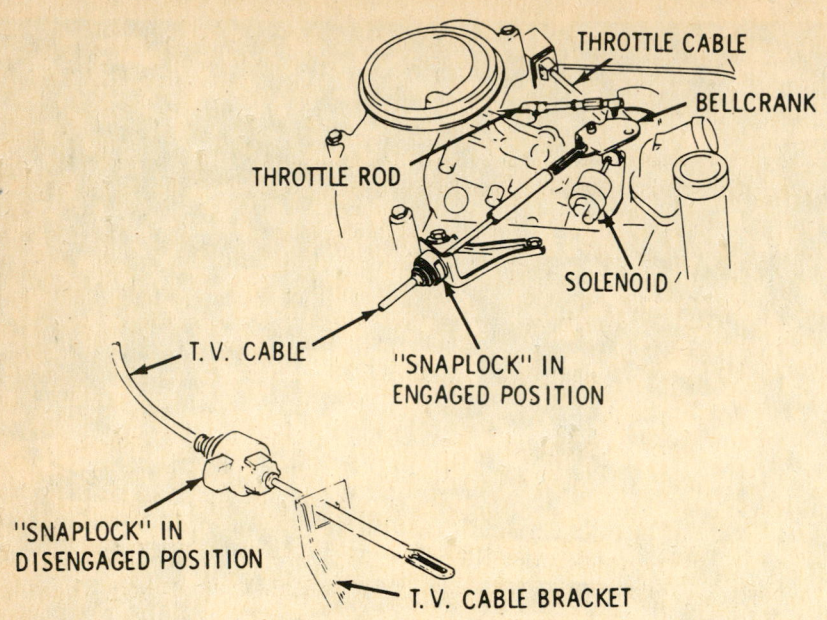

Turbo Hydra-Matic 200 throttle valve adjustment
(© Cadillac Div., G.M. Corp.)

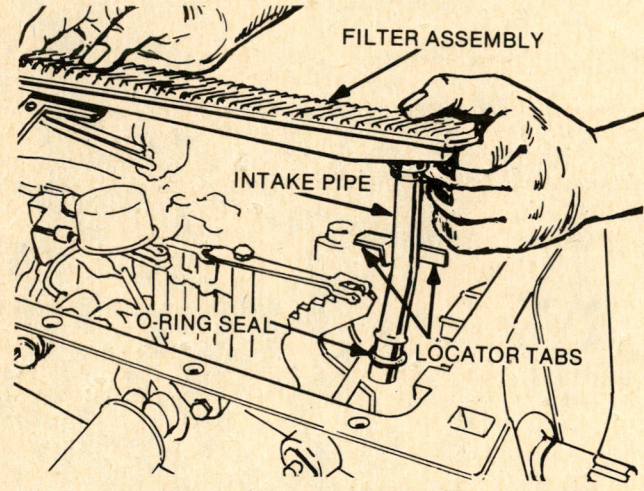

Removing the Turbo Hydra-Matic 400 transmission filter assembly, transmission shown inverted (© Cadillac Div., G.M. Corp.)

U-JOINTS

Universal joints and driveshafts can be divided into two groups: single-piece shaft models (full-size Cadillac and Seville models except Fleetwood 75 sedan and limousine and Commercial Chassis), and two-piece shaft models (Fleetwood 75 sedan and limousine and Commercial Chassis models only).

Single-Piece Shaft Removal and Installation

FULL SIZE CADILLAC

1. Place transmission in Neutral and jack up car; support on axle stands.
2. Remove the two accessible rear U-joint flange capscrews.
3. Rotate driveshaft and remove other two capscrews, after sup-porting rear of shaft on a chain. Never let the full weight of the driveshaft be supported only by the front constant velocity joint.
4. Push shaft forward to clear pinion flange, then pull rearward to disengage slip yoke from transmission. Plug transmission to prevent oil leak.
5. Lubricate slip yoke inside diameter with gear lube, outside of splines with A.T.F.
6. To install, reverse removal procedure, tightening rear U-joint fasteners to 70 ft. lbs. Place transmission in Park to hold shaft while tightening capscrews.

SEVILLE

1. Raise the vehicle with the transmission in Park and the front of the car slightly lower than the rear, if possible.

2. Mark the position of the ball support yoke in relation to the axle pinion flange.
3. Remove the ball support yoke attaching screws. Support the drive shaft as the last screw is being removed.
4. Remove the drive shaft by pushing it forward into the rear of the transmission until the ball support yoke clears the differential pinion flange, and then pulling it rearward out of the transmission. Fluid could leak out of the rear of the transmission if the front isn't lowered enough. Plug the opening with a clean lint free cloth, if necessary.
5. Install the drive shaft in the reverse order of removal. Tighten the ball support yoke attaching screws to 70 ft. lbs.

Two-Piece Shaft Removal and Installation

1. Follow Steps 1-6 of *Single-Piece Shaft Removal and Installation*, with the addition of the following step:
2. Remove center bearing support after matchmarking it and crossmember. When installing, tighten the bolts to 16 ft lbs.

U-Joint Overhaul

1. Remove the drive shaft.
2. Remove the lockrings from the bearings. If the original universal joints are being replaced, the nylon ring will shear off when the bearing is removed.
3. Match-mark the yoke and the shaft so that the shaft parts can be reassembled easily.
4. Position the yoke or bearing trunnion on vise jaws. Using a bearing remover, or a similar tool, and a hammer tap the remover until the bearing is driven out of the yoke about 1/2 in.
5. Place the tool in the vise and then drive the yoke away from the tool until the bearing is removed.
6. Use Steps 4 and 5 for all other bearings.

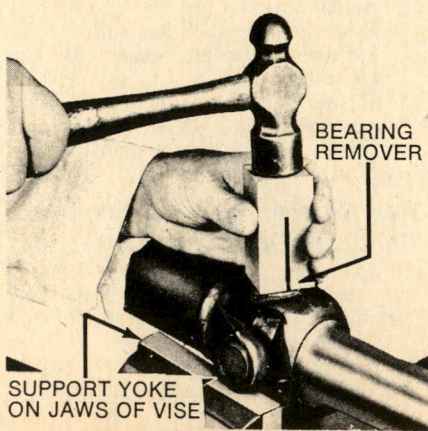

Using the bearing removal tool
(© Cadillac Div., G.M. Corp)

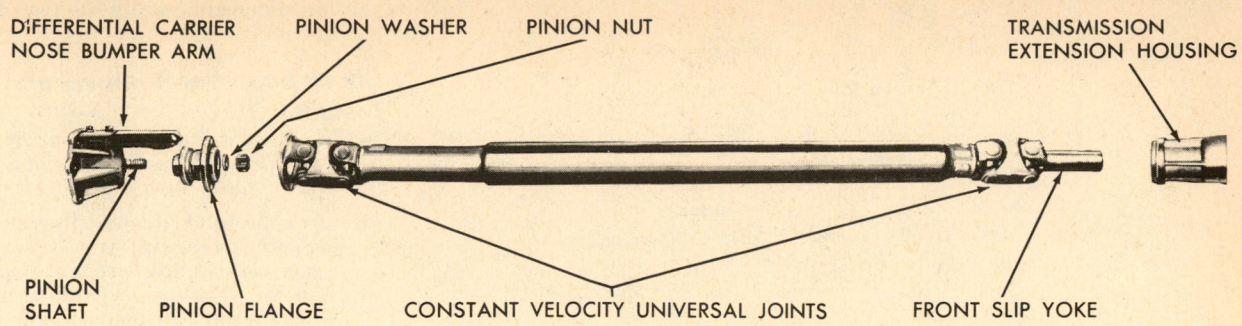

DIFFERENTIAL CARRIER NOSE BUMPER ARM — PINION WASHER — PINION NUT — TRANSMISSION EXTENSION HOUSING

PINION SHAFT — PINION FLANGE — CONSTANT VELOCITY UNIVERSAL JOINTS — FRONT SLIP YOKE

Single-piece driveshaft (© Cadillac Div., G.M. Corp)

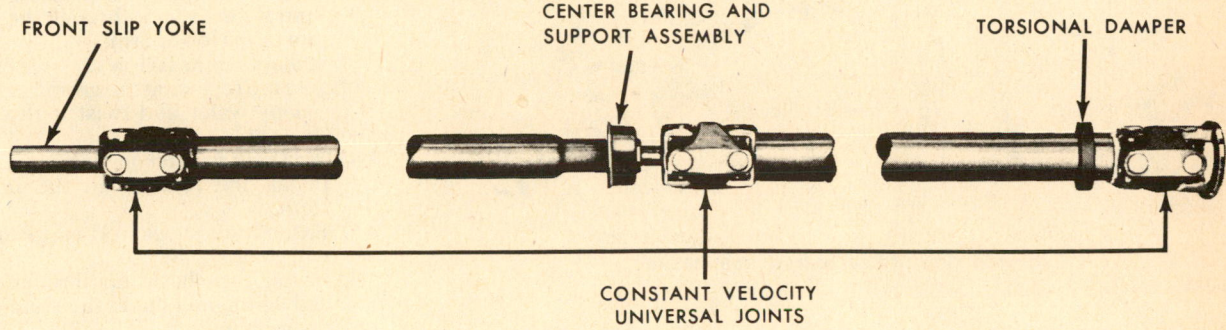

FRONT SLIP YOKE — CENTER BEARING AND SUPPORT ASSEMBLY — TORSIONAL DAMPER

CONSTANT VELOCITY UNIVERSAL JOINTS

Two-piece driveshaft with C.V. joints (© Cadillac Div., G.M. Corp)

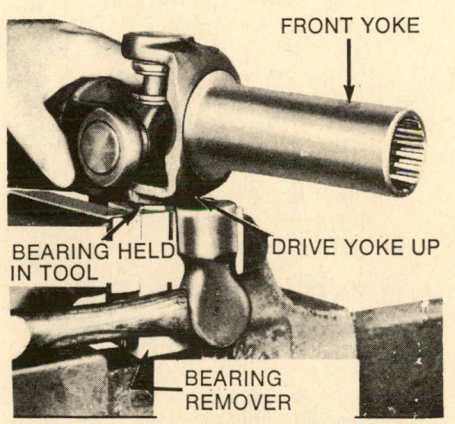

FRONT YOKE

BEARING HELD IN TOOL — DRIVE YOKE UP

BEARING REMOVER

Removing the universal joint bearing
(© Cadillac Div., G.M. Corp)

7. To install the bearings lubricate the cross arm ends with universal joint grease and install the joint cross into position.
8. Start the bearings into the driveshaft yoke and press them into position using a vise.

NOTE: *If the bearings are not positioned with normal vise pressure, there is a possibility that one of the needle bearings has fallen out of place.*

9. Use the same installation procedure for the other bearings.
10. Install the lock rings.

REAR AXLE

Axle Shaft, Bearing, and Seal Removal and Installation

FULL SIZE CADILLAC

1. Raise the rear of the car and sup-

port it. Remove the wheel and brake drum.
2. Remove the four nuts that secure the retainer and backing plate to the axle housing.
3. Remove the axle shaft with a slide hammer.

NOTE: *When the axle shaft is removed the outer bearing race may remain in the axle housing. This does not indicate bearing failure. If the bearing is to be replaced, make sure the old outer bearing race is removed from the axle housing.*

4. Using a chisel and hammer, split the bearing retainer next to the bearing. Be careful not to damage the bearing of the axle shaft. Remove and discard the retainer.
5. Stand the axle shaft upright on the flanged end and use two screwdrivers to pry the oil seal away from the bearing.
6. Remove axle bearing from the axle shaft with a press.
7. Make sure that the axle shaft and bearing are clean and install the bearing seal onto the axle shaft. The oil seal is properly installed when it can't be pushed on any further.
8. Apply a light coat of wheel bearing grease to the bearing.
9. If a tapered roller bearing is used, position the bearing on the axle shaft with the narrow ring of the bearing facing the flanged end of the axle shaft. If a straight roller bearing is installed, the loose ring at one end of the inner race must be installed toward the flange.

10. Press the bearing onto the axle shaft until the bearing bottoms against the shoulder on the shaft.
11. Press the retainer on the axle shaft until the retainer bottoms against the bearing.
12. If the axle bearing has been replaced because of bearing failure, inspect the axle housing and differential carrier for metal chips and clean thoroughly.
13. Apply a thin film of wheel bearing grease to the wheelbearing bore in the axle housing. Also, lubricate the oil seal and the outer race of the bearing with wheel bearing grease.
14. Install a new gasket on the brake backing plate.
15. Install the axle shaft onto the axle housing, using extreme care to align the oil seal cover with the axle housing mounting bolts. Rotate the axle shaft so the axle shaft splines engage the differential side gear splines.
16. Install the four nuts on the axle housing flange bolts to hold the gasket, brake backing plate, and oil seal cover in place. Tighten the nuts to 50 ft. lbs. Install the brake drum and one nut to push it on. Remove the nut to install the wheel. Lower the car.

SEVILLE

1. Raise the car on a hoist and remove the wheel and brake drum.
2. Clean any dirt from the differential cover and loosen the cover attaching screw, allowing the lubricant to drain out into a suitable container.

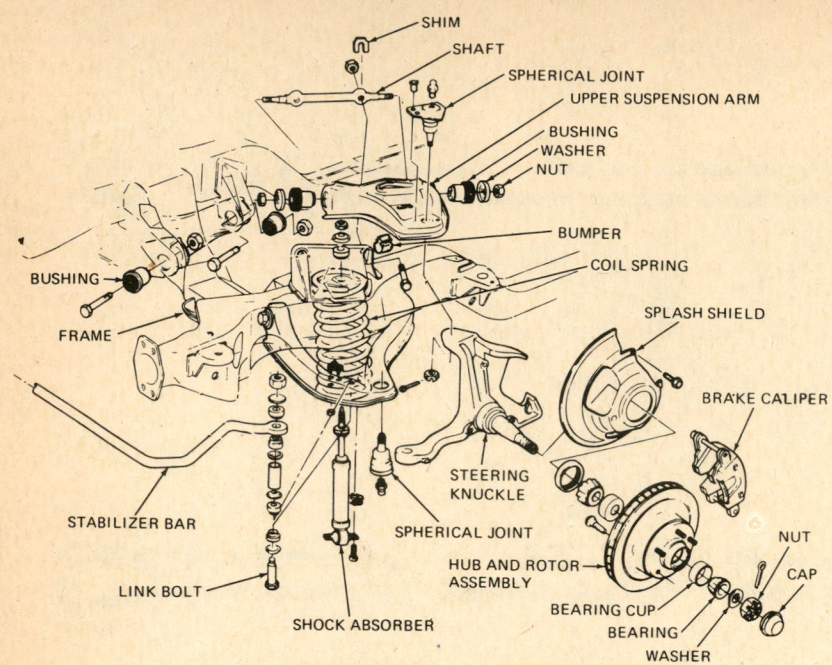

SHIM
SHAFT
SPHERICAL JOINT
UPPER SUSPENSION ARM
BUSHING
WASHER
NUT
BUMPER
COIL SPRING
SPLASH SHIELD
BRAKE CALIPER
BUSHING
FRAME
STEERING KNUCKLE
SPHERICAL JOINT
STABILIZER BAR
HUB AND ROTOR ASSEMBLY
NUT
CAP
LINK BOLT
BEARING CUP
BEARING
WASHER
SHOCK ABSORBER

Exploded view of Seville front suspension
(© Cadillac Div., G.M. Corp.)

3. Remove the pinion shaft lockscrew and remove the pinion shaft.
4. Push in on the flanged end of the axle shaft and remove the C-lock from the splined end of the axle shaft.
5. Remove the axle shaft from the housing, being cautious not to damage the oil seal.
6. Use a screwdriver to pry the oil seal out of the bore. Use an axle shaft bearing puller on a slide hammer to remove the axle bearing from the bearing bore.
7. Install the new bearing in the bearing bore until it is 0.550 in. from the end of the axle tube. Use a block of wood and a hammer to tap the bearing in place. Install the axle shaft bearing seal until it is flush with the end of the axle tube.
8. Slide the axle shaft into the housing until the splines on the end of the shaft engage the splines of the differential side gear. Handle the shaft gently when trying to engage the splines.
9. Install the axle shaft C-lock on the splined end of the axle shaft in the differential. Push the shaft outward so that the shaft lock seats in the counterbore of the differential side gear.
10. Install the pinion cross shaft through the differential case and pinion gears. Align the lock screw hole and install the lock screw, tightening it to 25 ft. lbs.
11. Clean the differential housing and cover mating surfaces and install the cover with a new gasket.
12. Fill the differential with lubricant, install the brake drum and wheel, and lower the car.

JACKING, HOISTING

FULL SIZE CADILLAC

When jacking under front suspension arms, make sure lift is made from the flattened portion on the flange of the lower arms.

When lifting on frame area, make sure of solid contact at the corners of the perimeter of the frame with the lift points close to the bend at front and rear of the frame.

SEVILLE

To raise the car on a twin-post suspension hoist, place the lift adapters under the lower control arms at the front and under the axle tube near the spring mounting pads at the rear.

When using a frame hoist, place the lift adapters under the front subframe members just in front of the rear cross member and under the rear sub-frame members opposite the front rear spring shackles.

FRONT SUSPENSION

All rear-drive Cadillacs and Sevilles use the same front suspension system. The system is a coil spring suspension which consists of two upper and two lower control arm assemblies, shock absorbers, a stabilizer bar, and two steering knuckles, and a pair of coil springs.

For further information on front sus-

pension alignment consult the Unit Repair Section.

Shock Absorber Removal and Installation

NOTE: *Purge a new shock of air by repeatedly extending it in its normal position and compressing it while inverted.*

1. Open the hood. Remove the retaining nut from the frame spring tower. Use a box wrench to prevent the shock stem from turning while the nut is being unfastened.
2. Take off the bolt, nut, and lockwasher which secure the lower end of the shock to the suspension arm.
3. Remove the shock through the bottom of the lower arm.
   Installation is as follows:
   If you are replacing the grommet, dip it in soapy water and twist it through the frame hole.
NOTE: *Don't use silicone lubricant.*
4. Install the retainer in the upper stem.
5. Extend the shock rod as far as it will go.
6. Install the shock up through the coil spring and guide the stem into the grommet.
7. Position the lower end of the shock on the lower control arm. Install the bolt, lockwasher, and nut. Tighten the bolt to 55 ft. lbs. (19 ft. lbs. on Seville).
8. Tighten the retaining nut on the upper stem to 15 ft. lbs., while holding the stem with a box wrench to keep it from turning. On Seville, tighten the nut to the end of the threads (about 1-1/8 in. of stud is above the nut).

Lower Control Arm and Coil Spring Removal and Installation

1. Disconnect front shock at its upper mount.
2. Raise car and support under front frame side rails.
3. Remove wheel and tire assembly.
4. Disconnect stabilizer link from lower arm or spring to be removed.
5. Disconnect tie-strut at lower arm.
6. Remove bolt holding shock to lower arm, and remove shock from car.
7. Remove nut from pivot bolt in lower arm at frame mount.
8. Position jack under outboard end of lower suspension arm so that jack is supporting the arm.
9. Remove locknut from lower ball joint stud. Install standard nut on joint stud and run nut to within two threads of knuckle.
10. Strike knuckle with a hammer in area of ball joint stud to loosen the joint. Raising the opposite rear corner of the car will help compress the spring and assist in removing the joint stud from the knuckle.
11. Use jack to lift spring load from nut and remove nut from joint stud. Wrap a chain around the

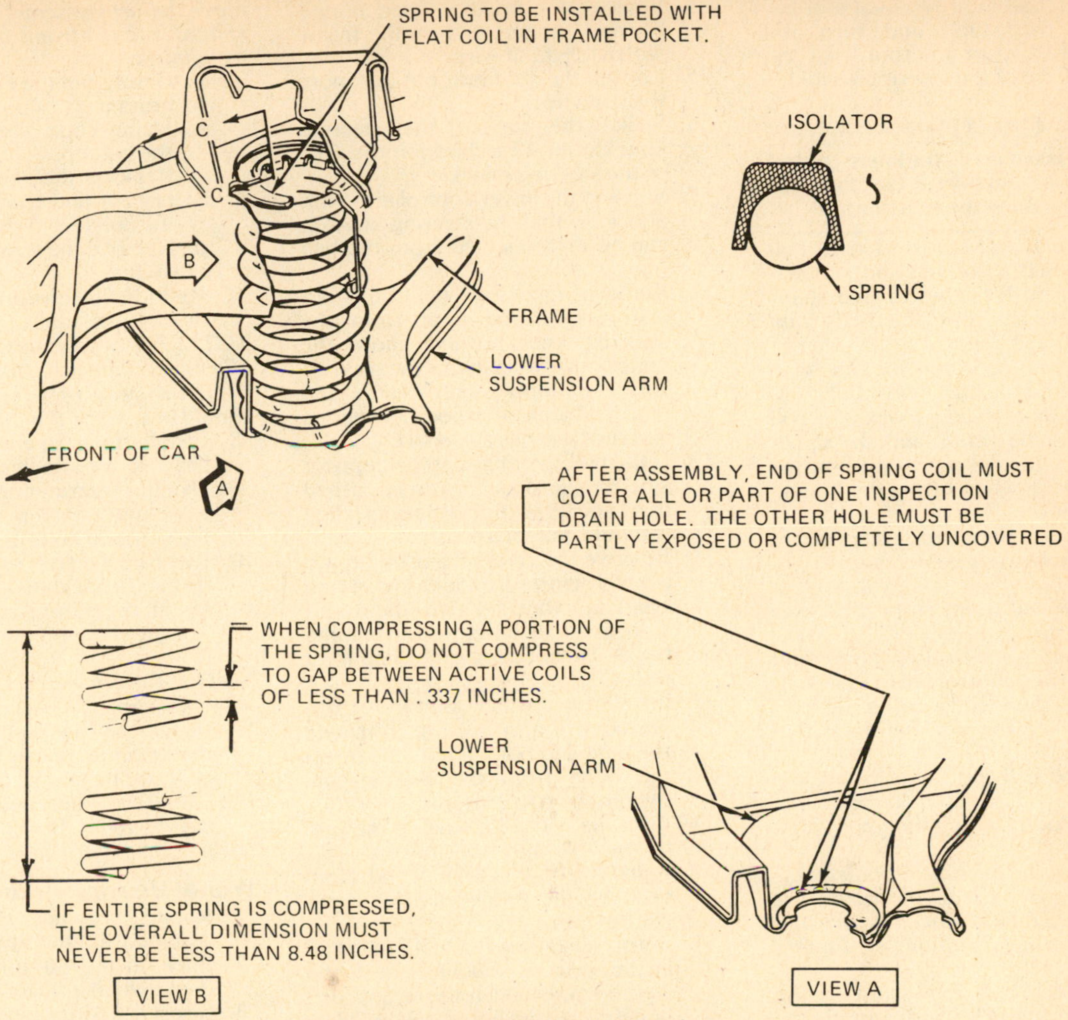

SPRING TO BE INSTALLED WITH
FLAT COIL IN FRAME POCKET.

C

C

B

FRAME

LOWER
SUSPENSION ARM

FRONT OF CAR

A

ISOLATOR

SPRING

AFTER ASSEMBLY, END OF SPRING COIL MUST
COVER ALL OR PART OF ONE INSPECTION
DRAIN HOLE. THE OTHER HOLE MUST BE
PARTLY EXPOSED OR COMPLETELY UNCOVERED

WHEN COMPRESSING A PORTION OF
THE SPRING, DO NOT COMPRESS
TO GAP BETWEEN ACTIVE COILS
OF LESS THAN .337 INCHES.

LOWER
SUSPENSION ARM

IF ENTIRE SPRING IS COMPRESSED,
THE OVERALL DIMENSION MUST
NEVER BE LESS THAN 8.48 INCHES.

VIEW B

VIEW A

Installation of Seville front coil spring
(© Cadillac Div., G.M. Corp.)

spring and through the lower control arm as a safety measure.
12. Slowly lower jack and remove spring.
13. Remove pivot bolt from lower arm at frame mount and remove the arm.
14. Install by reversing the removal procedure.

Ball Joint Inspection

NOTE: *Before performing this inspection, make sure the wheel bearings are adjusted correctly and that the control arm bushings are in good condition.*

1. Jack the car up under the front lower control arm at the spring seat.
2. Raise the car until there is 1-2 in. of clearance under the wheel.
3. Insert a bar under the wheel and pry upward. If the wheel raises more than 1/8 in. the ball joints are worn. Determine if the upper or lower ball joint is worn by visual inspection while prying on the wheel.

NOTE: *Due to the distribution of forces in the suspension, the lower ball joint is usually the defective joint. Also, 1973 and later Cadillacs and Sevilles are equipped with wear indicators on the lower ball joint. As long as the wear indicator neck extends below the ball stud seat, replacement is unnecessary.*

Lower Ball Joint Removal and Installation

FULL SIZE CADILLAC

1. Follow Steps 1-12 of *Lower Control Arm and Coil Spring Removal and Installation.*
2. Remove band and seal from ball joint.
3. If ball joint vertical movement exceeds 1/16 in. (.062 in.), press old ball joint out of lower control arm, using press tool.
4. Press new joint into arm until it bottoms on flange, using standard nut and flat washer to pull joint into position
5. Reverse Steps 1-12 of *Lower Control Arm and Coil Spring Removal*

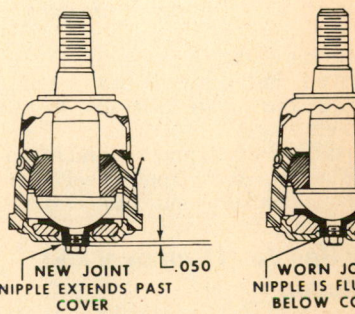

NEW JOINT
NIPPLE EXTENDS PAST
COVER

.050

WORN JOINT
NIPPLE IS FLUSH OR
BELOW COVER

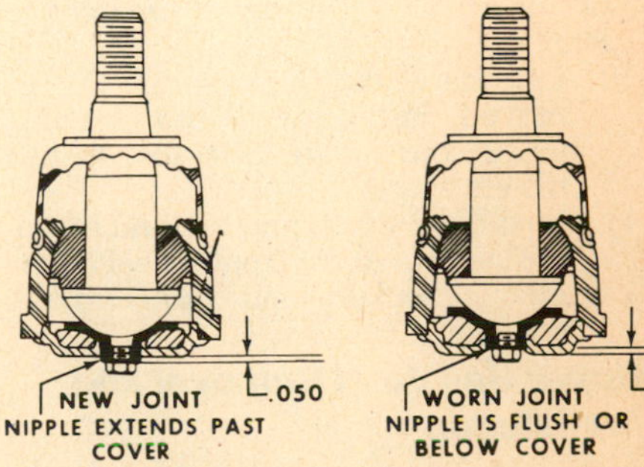

**Lower ball joint wear indicator—
1973 and later**
(© Cadillac Div., G.M. Corp.)

and Installation, tightening stud nut to 85 ft. lbs.

SEVILLE

1. Raise the car and remove the wheel and tire.
2. Remove the lower ball joint stud cotter pin. Loosen (not more than one turn), but do not remove, the stud nut.

3. Install a ball joint removal tool between the studs and turn the threaded end of the tool until the stud is free of the steering knuckle.

——— CAUTION ———

If a hoist is not used, the lower control arm must be supported so that the spring cannot force the arm down.

4. Remove the lower stud nut. Pull out on bottom of tire and simultaneously push tire up to free steering knuckle from the ball joint stud.
5. Lift up on upper control arm (with steering knuckle and hub attached), and place a block of wood between the frame and the upper arm. Be careful not to pull on the brake hose when lifting the knuckle and hub.

NOTE: *Remove the tie-rod end from the steering knuckle only if necessary.*

6. Use a ball joint removal tool to push the ball joint from the lower control arm.
7. To install, place the lower ball joint in the lower control arm and seat it. Position the bleed vent in the rubber boot of the new ball joint facing inward.
8. Turn the ball joint stud cotter pin hole fore and aft. Remove the wood block holding the upper control arm.

NOTE: *Examine the tapered hole in the steering knuckle. Clean the area. The knuckle MUST be replaced if any out-of-roundness, deformation, or damage is found.*

9. Attach the ball joint stud to the steering knuckle and install the stud nut. Torque the nut to 80 ft. lbs. and install a new cotter pin.

NOTE: *125 ft. lbs. or 1/6 turn maximum is allowed to align the cotter pin slot. Do not back off the nut to install the cotter pin.*

10. Lubricate the ball joint. If removed, install the tie-rod end and torque the nut to 35 ft. lbs. Install the cotter pin.
11. Install the wheel and tire and lower the car. Have the front wheel alignment checked and adjusted as necessary.

Upper Ball Joint Removal and Installation

FULL SIZE CADILLAC

The upper ball joints are pressed into the upper control arms and are tack-welded to the arms at two places. Do not attempt to remove the upper ball joints as any rewelding could damage the joint seals or weaken the control arms. The upper control arms and ball joints are replaced as an assembly.

SEVILLE

1. Raise the car on a hoist.
2. Remove the wheel and tire.
3. Remove the upper ball joint stud cotter pin.

---

4. Remove the brake caliper assembly and support it from the frame with a length of wire.
5. Loosen the stud nut, but not more than one turn.
6. Strike the top of the steering knuckle until the ball joint is free of the steering knuckle.
7. Support the lower control arm with a jack so that the steering knuckle can be disconnected from the ball joint.
8. Remove upper ball joint stud nut and remove the joint from the steering knuckle and allow the knuckle to swing out of the way.
9. Lift the upper control arm and place a block of wood between it and the frame as a support.
10. If the ball joint has any perceptible side-to-side shake or can be turned in its socket with your fingers, then it should be replaced.
11. Remove the rivets from the upper control arm with either a chisel or a grinding wheel. Drive them out with a punch after removing the heads. Do not damage the ball joint seat.
12. Install the new ball joint in the upper control arm and attach it with the nuts and bolts provided. Insert the bolts from the bottom and tighten them to 25 ft. lbs.
13. Turn the ball joint stud so the cotter pin hole runs front-to-rear.
14. Remove the block of wood from between the frame and the upper control arm.
15. Before installing the ball joint stud in the steering knuckle, check the tapered hole and remove any dirt or debris. If the hole is distorted or damaged, the steering knuckle must be replaced.
16. Install the ball joint stud in the hole in the top of the steering knuckle. Install the castellated nut and tighten it to 60 ft. lbs. Tighten the nut to a maximum of 100 ft. lbs. to install the cotter pin. Do not back the nut off in order to install the cotter pin.
17. Install the brake caliper assembly.
18. Grease the ball joint.
19. Install the wheel and tire and lower the car.

Upper Control Arm Removal and Installation

1. Raise and support the car.
2. Place a jack stand under the lower control arm.
3. Remove the wheel.
4. Remove the upper ball joint stud from the steering knuckle.
5. Remove the two nuts securing the upper arm shaft to the frame bracket and remove the arm.
6. Note the number and position of shims for reassembly.

NOTE: *In some cases, on Seville, it is necessary to remove the upper arm attaching bolts to allow clearance to re-*

---

move the arm assembly. The bolts are splined into the frame and are removed as follows:

 a. Gently tap the bolt down with a brass drift.
 b. Using a box wrench, gently pry the bolt up.
 c. Remove the nut, and, using a pry bar and block of wood, pry the bolts from the frame.
 d. Remove the arm from the car.

To install:

7. Position the new upper arm attaching bolts in frame.

NOTE: *For Seville only, install the pre-alignment shim with the thick area toward the rear of the car. The plate should be against the shaft.*

8. Install the suspension arm cross shaft on the attaching bolts.
9. Using a freerunning nut instead of a locknut, tighten both nuts until the serrated bolts are reseated.
10. Remove the free running nuts and install the locknuts.
11. Install the shims as removed.
12. Torque the mounting nuts to 75 ft. lb.

NOTE: *Tighten the nut on the thinner shim pack first.*

13. Install the ball joint stud through the knuckle and tighten the nut to 60 ft. lb. Install the cotter pin.
14. Install the wheel and torque the lug nuts to 100 ft. lb.

Wheel Bearing Adjustment

1. Rotate the wheel and tighten the adjusting nut to 15 ft. lbs.
2. Back off the nut until it is free and then tighten it finger tight.
3. Insert the cotter pin. If the pin cannot be installed in this position, back off the nut until the holes align. Make certain that the pin fits tight. If it can be moved with your fingers, it should be replaced.

REAR SUSPENSION

FULL SIZE CADILLAC

A four-link rear suspension system, consisting of upper and lower control arms, coil springs and shock absorbers is used. The coil springs are placed on brackets on the rear axle housing at their lower ends, the upper ends being seated in the frame crossmember. Cars can be equipped with Automatic Level Control.

COMMERCIAL CHASSIS AND SEVILLE

The Commercial Chassis and Seville use semi-elliptic leaf springs. Automatic Level Control is standard on Seville models and optional on Commercial Chassis.

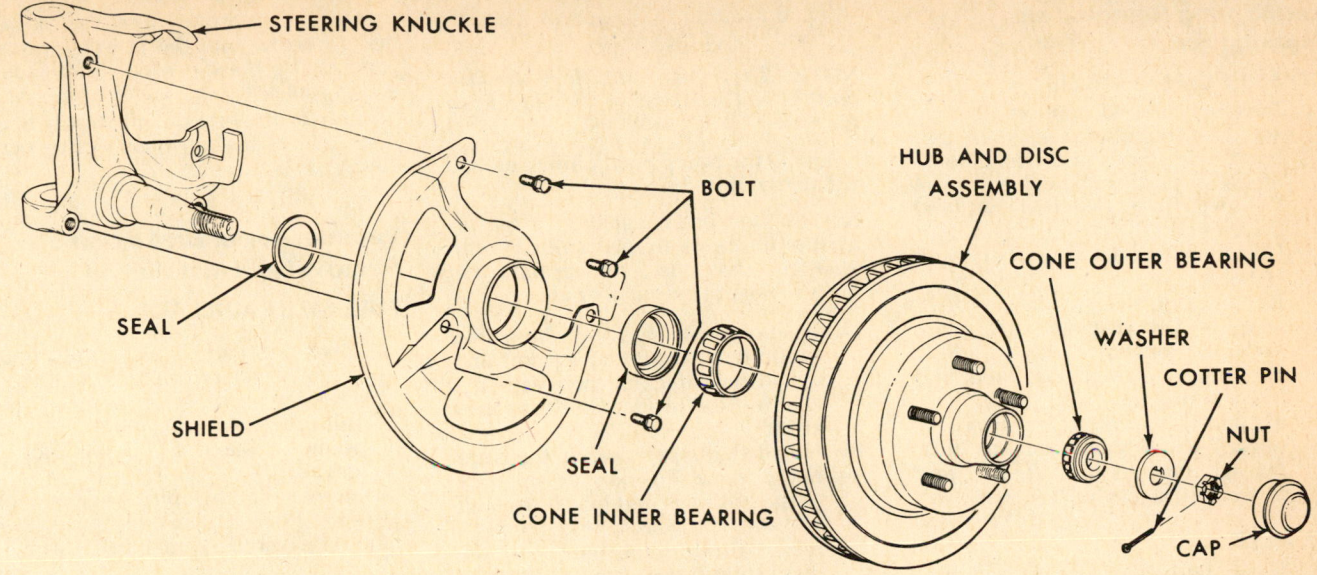

Front disc brake hub assembly (© Cadillac Div., G.M. Corp)

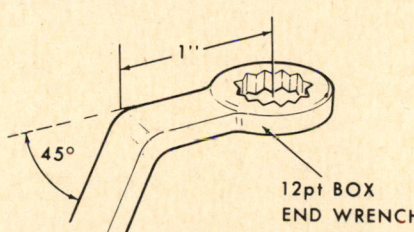

Rear shock absorber wrench
(© Cadillac Div., G.M. Corp)

Shock Absorber Removal and Installation

NOTE: *Purge a new shock of air by repeatedly extending it in its normal position and compressing it while inverted.*

FULL SIZE CADILLAC

1. Raise the rear of the vehicle and support both the frame and the axle with separate jacks.
2. If the vehicle is equipped with Automatic Level Control, remove the air lines at the shocks.

— CAUTION —

The shocks act as rebound stops for the rear suspension and under no circumstances should the rear end be raised excessively high while disconnecting the shocks, unless both the rear axle and the frame are supported.

3. Remove the upper retaining bolts and nuts. To do this, bend a 1/2 in. box end wrench to form a 45° angle at a point one inch from the center of the box diameter. This is used to hold the upper mounting nut.
4. Remove the lower retaining nut while holding the stem by the grommet to keep the stem from turning. Pull the shock off.
5. Installation is the reverse of removal.

SEVILLE

1. Raise the car and support both the frame and rear axle.
2. Remove the air lines at the shock absorbers.

— CAUTION —

The shocks act as rebound stops for the rear suspension and under no circumstances should the rear end be raised excessively high while disconnecting the shocks, unless both the rear axle and the frame are supported.

3. Remove the shock absorber upper and lower retaining bolts and remove the shock absorber.

NOTE: *The left-hand shock absorber has two air line connections; the right has only one.*

4. To install, position the crossbar of the upper mount to the underbody so that the shock angles toward the lower mount. The line connections are to the front on the left-side; to the rear on the right-side.
5. Install and tighten the upper retaining bolts to 12 ft. lbs.
6. Place the shock absorber lower mount into the mounting bracket. Install and tighten the retaining bolt and nut to 45 ft. lbs.
7. Install the air line fittings at the shocks. (The line with the black and white stripe goes to the lower port on the left-hand shock). Tighten the fittings to 35 in. lbs.
8. Inflate the reservoir through the service valve to 140 psi.
9. Disconnect the overtravel lever at the underbody bracket and push the arm up to inflate the shock absorbers. Do not put the car weight on the shocks until they are inflated as they may be damaged.

10. Return the overtravel lever to the normal position and reconnect it to the axle bracket.
11. Lower the car and check system for proper operation.

Coil Spring Removal and Installation

1. Raise and support the car.
2. Place a jack under the differential housing.
3. Remove the wheels.
4. If the car has automatic level control, disconnect the link at the overtravel lever and position it in its center location.
5. Remove the shock absorber lower retaining nuts and washers.

— CAUTION —

The shock absorbers act as stops for the suspension. Make certain that both the axle and the frame are supported before continuing.

6. Position container to catch brake fluid, then disconnect brake hose from steel line at frame.
7. Remove brake hose and clip from frame.
8. Disconnect rear U-joint and support driveshaft on a chain.
9. Remove nuts and bolts that secure both upper control arms to axle brackets.
10. Lower rear axle assembly slowly until springs are free.

— CAUTION —

Do not allow the differential to wind up as it is lowered as the spring may fly out.

11. To install, reverse removal procedure. Tighten upper and lower control arm bolts to 75 ft. lbs.

Cadillac & Seville

Leaf Spring Removal and Installation

COMMERCIAL CHASSIS

1. Jack up car and support on axle stands at frame side rails.
2. Place axle stands under axle housing, after jacking up housing.
3. Remove front eye bolt nut and drive out bolt.
4. Disconnect shock absorber from U-bolt plate.
5. Remove rear shackle nuts.
6. Remove U-bolt plate nuts, plate and insulators.
7. Disconnect rear shackle links and lower spring.
8. To install, reverse removal procedure. Tighten shackle nuts to 70 ft. lbs., U-bolt nuts to 45 ft. lbs., and lower shock nuts to 50 ft. lbs.

SEVILLE

1. Raise the rear of the car and support it so the axle can be raised or lowered. Raise the axle so that all tension is relieved from the spring.
2. Disconnect the rear automatic leveling valve overtravel lever from its link and hold the lever in the exhaust position (down) to deflate the shock absorbers.
3. Disconnect the lower half of the shock absorbers and move them out of the way.
4. Loosen the parking brake adjustment at the equalizer and remove the parking brake cable clip from the front retaining bracket on the spring. Remove the cable clamps from the under side of the springs.
5. Loosen the spring front eye bushing-to-retaining bracket bolt.
6. Remove the bolts retaining the front spring bracket to the underbody.
7. Lower the axle enough to permit access to the front eye bolt and remove the bracket from the spring.

NOTE: *The front eye bushing can be replaced at this time.*

8. Remove the U-bolt and T-bolt nuts retaining the lower spring plate to the axle and stabilizer bar brackets.
9. Remove the upper and lower spring pads and spring plate.
10. Support the spring with a jack stand and remove the two nuts from the rear shackle.
11. Separate the shackle and remove the spring from the vehicle.
12. If the spring is being replaced, remove the spring damper for installation on the new spring by removing the clamp bolt and bending the bottom half of the clamp down about 2 in. Slide the clamp rearward over the damper and remove the damper from the spring.
13. Position the spring damper on the new spring and position it 1/8 in. from the front spring eye. Slide the clamp forward over the damper

and position the clamp at the second leaf of the spring.

NOTE: *The clamp must face upward and the nut must be on the outside of the spring.*

Install the clamp bolt pointing up and tighten to 20 ft. lbs.

NOTE: *Do not tighten any of the attaching hardware to specifications until step 25. Allow the retaining nuts and bolts to remain only finger tight.*

14. Position the front eye of the spring to the front mounting bracket and install the attaching bolt with the head on the inside. Bolt torque is 105 ft. lbs.
15. Install the upper shackle bushings in the frame. Position the shackles to the bushings and install the bolt and nut. Torque is 50 ft. lbs.
16. Install the bushing halves in the rear spring eye and install the spring to the shackle. Lower shackle bolt and nut torque is 50 ft. lbs.
17. Raise the front end of the spring and position the bracket to the underbody. Make sure the tab on the bracket is aligned in the slot in the underbody.
18. Install the screws retaining the front spring bracket to the underbody. Torque is 30 ft. lbs.
19. Position the spring upper cushion between the spring and the axle bracket so the cushion ribs align with the bracket locating ribs.
20. Position the lower mounting plate over the locating dowel on the lower spring pad and install the retaining nuts. Torque is 45 ft. lbs.
21. Position the stabilizer brackets to the lower spring plate. Retaining bolts and nut torque is 30 ft. lbs.
22. Connect the lower shock absorber mount to the lower spring bracket. Torque is 45 ft. lbs.
23. Install the parking brake cable under the leaf spring and secure it at the front of the spring with the wire clip and clamp. Adjust the parking brake cable.
24. Connect the rear leveling alve overtravel lever to its link.
25. Tighten all of the attaching hardware to the specified torques.
26. Lower the vehicle.

BRAKES

For information relating to brake shoe replacement and adjustment, wheel cylinder and caliper overhaul, and brake bleeding refer to the brake Unit Repair Section.

Beginning 1976, Hydro-boost is installed on Fleetwood 75 limousine models and the Commercial Chassis. Hydro-boost is a hydraulically-assisted power brake booster. The power steering pump provides the hydraulic fluid

pressure to operate both the power brake booster and the power steering gear. Hydro-boost is used with the diesel, as well.

Refer to the brake Unit Repair Section for Hydro-boost service procedures.

Vacuum Power Brake Unit Removal and Installation

FULL SIZE CADILLAC

1. Disconnect and cap hydraulic lines from master cylinder.
2. Disconnect vacuum line from vacuum check valve on unit.
3. Remove steering column lower cover.
4. Remove cotter pin, washer and spring spacer that secure power unit pushrod to brake pedal arm.
5. Remove the four nuts that secure power unit to firewall, then remove power unit.
6. To install, reverse removal procedure. Bleed the hydraulic system.

SEVILLE

1. Remove any vacuum from the booster by depressing the brake pedal several times.
2. Disconnect the two front and one rear brake outlet lines and electrical connector from the combination valve. Plug the lines and outlets to prevent entry of dirt.
3. Remove the two attaching nuts securing the master cylinder to the booster, and discard the nuts. Remove the master cylinder and combination valve assembly from the car.
4. Disconnect the booster vacuum hose from the check valve.
5. From under the instrument panel, remove the clip and washer from the brake pedal push rod pin. Do not remove the push rod from the brake pedal assembly yet.
6. Remove the two screws retaining the twilight sentinel amplifier, if so equipped, to the brake pedal bracket. Lower the amplifier and discard the connectors.
7. Remove the four booster-to-cowl retaining nuts and discard the nuts. Slide the studs through the cowl. Move the booster toward the engine and keep the mounting surface parallel to the cowl. Slide the push rod from the brake pedal pin and remove the booster from the car.
8. Install the booster in the reverse order of removal, using new attaching nuts. Tighten the booster-to-cowl nuts to 15 ft lbs, and the master cylinder-to-booster nuts to 20 ft lbs.
9. Bleed the brake hydraulic system. Start the engine and check the brake vacuum system for leaks and operation.

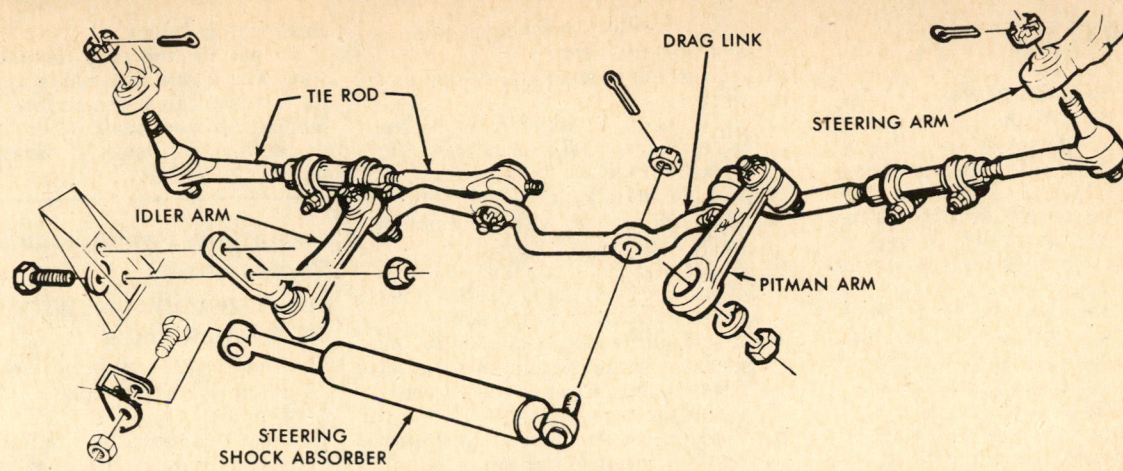

Cadillac Steering linkage (© Cadillac Div., G.M. Corp)

Hydro-Boost Power Brake Unit Removal and Installation

—— CAUTION ——
Power steering fluid and brake fluid are incompatible. If brake seals contact steering fluid or steering seals contact brake fluid, the seals will be ruined.

1. With the engine off, pump the brake pedal four or five times to empty the accumulator of pressurized fluid.
2. Remove the two master cylinder-to-booster attaching nuts and move the master cylinder away from the booster with the brake lines attached.
3. Remove and plug the three hydraulic lines from the booster. Remove the washer and retainer that secures the booster pedal rod to the brake pedal arm.
4. Remove the four nuts holding the booster to the firewall.

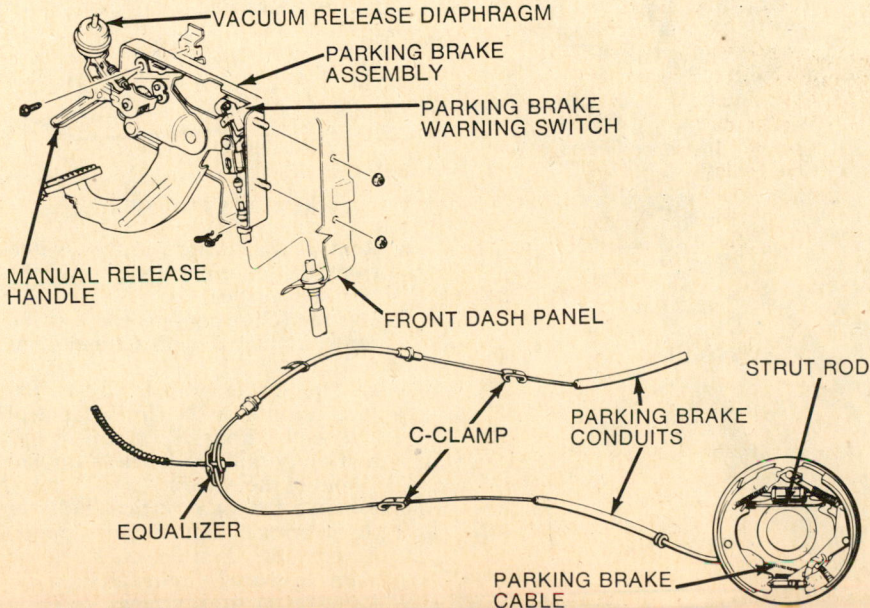

Parking brake system details for full-size models (© Cadillac Div., G.M. Corp.)

NOTE: *To avoid booster damage, do not pry the pedal rod off the pedal arm.*

5. Loosen the booster from the firewall and move the booster pedal rod inboard until it disconnects from the brake pedal arm. Remove the spring washer from the brake pedal arm and remove the booster.
6. To install, reverse the removal procedure. Tighten the booster mounting nuts to 15 ft. lbs. and the master cylinder to booster mounting nuts to 20 ft. lbs. Bleed the Hydro-boost system as explained in the Brakes Unit Repair Section.

Parking Brake Adjustment
REAR DRUM BRAKES
NOTE: *Make certain that the rear brakes are properly adjusted before adjusting the parking brake.*

1. Make a check of the parking brake linkage for the free movement of all the cables. Lubricate, if necessary.

2. Depress the parking brake pedal as follows: 1-3/4 in.—1972; 1 in.—1973-75; 1-1/2 in.—1976 and later.
3. Raise the rear wheels off the ground.
4. While holding the cable stud to keep it from turning, tighten the equalizer nut until a light drag is felt on either wheel when they are spun in the forward direction.
5. When the parking brake is released there should be no brake shoe drag.

REAR DISC BRAKES
1. Lubricate the parking brake cables at the underbody rub points, and at the equalizer hooks on Seville.
2. Make sure the parking brake pedal is in the fully released position.
3. Raise the rear wheels.
4. Hold the brake cable stud from turning and tighten the equalizer nut until the cable slack is removed.
5. Make sure the caliper levers are against the stops on the caliper housing after tightening the equalizer nut.
6. If the levers are off the stops, loosen the cable until the levers return to stops.
7. Operate the parking brake several times to check the adjustment.
8. Lower the car.
NOTE: *The levers must be on the caliper stops after adjustment. Back off the adjuster if necessary.*

Master Cylinder Removal and Installation
NOTE: *It is possible to remove the master cylinder unit without removing the power booster from the vehicle.*

1. Disconnect and plug the front and rear brake lines at the master cylinder.
2. Remove the two securing nuts which hold the master cylinder to the power booster.
3. Remove the master cylinder.
4. To install, reverse the removal procedure. Bleed the hydraulic system.

STEERING

Steering Wheel Removal

NOTE: *For 1974-76 models equipped with air bags, perform the special procedure following, prior to removing steering wheel.*

1. Remove the screws on the underside of the steering wheel spokes near the center and remove the pad assembly.
2. Remove the horn contact wire from the plastic tower by pushing in on the wire and turning it counterclockwise.
3. Remove the nut holding the steering wheel to the steering shaft.
4. On tilt wheels, remove locking lever and flange and screw assembly.
5. Note the match-marking of the shaft and wheel and use a puller to remove the steering wheel.
6. On installation, tighten the steering shaft nut to 30 ft. lbs.

SPECIAL PROCEDURE FOR CARS WITH A.C.R.S. (AIR BAGS)

Some 1974-76 models have an air cushion, or air bag, restraint system. One of the elements of this complex system is an air cushion module in the top of the steering wheel. The steering wheel can be removed in the manner described in this section after the module has been removed.

To remove the module:

1. Turn the ignition lock to the LOCK position.
2. Disconnect the battery ground cable and tape the end to prevent any possibility of a complete circuit.
3. Remove the 4 module-to-steering wheel screws. A special tool is available to do this.
4. Lift up the module and disconnect the horn wire.
5. Disconnect the module wire connector. A special tool is available to do this, too.

To install the module:

6. Hold the module with the emblem in the lower right corner.
7. Loop the air cushion harness clockwise from the 11 o'clock position to the 6 o'clock position.
8. Install the module connector by pushing it onto the column circuit firmly. Check that it is fully seated.
9. Install the horn wire.
10. Position the module, making sure that the wiring is still in place, and install the 4 screws. Torque them to 40 in lbs.
11. Reconnect the battery ground cable.
12. Turn the ignition lock to any position other than LOCK and check that the restraint indicator light operates correctly.

--- CAUTION ---

The driver air cushion module should always be carried with the vinyl cover away from all parts of one's body and should always be laid on a flat surface with the vinyl side up. This is necessary so that a free space is provided to allow the air cushion to expand in case of accidental deployment.

Do not attempt to repair any portion of the module. The module must be serviced as a unit. Attempting repairs such as soldering wires, changing covers, etc. may cause accidental inflation or impair operation of the driver module and cause serious injury.

Do not dispose of a module in any way. The highly flammable material in the module can cause serious burns if ignited. Modules must be exchanged at an authorized dealer's parts department.

Turn Signal Switch Removal and Replacement

FULL SIZE CADILLAC WITHOUT A.C.R.S. (AIR BAGS)

1. Remove the steering wheel.
2. Remove the lockplate cover assembly.
3. After compressing the lockplate spring, remove the snap-ring from the groove in the shaft.

--- CAUTION ---

When the snap-ring is removed do not allow the shaft to slide out the bottom of the column.

4. Remove the lockplate and slide the turn signal cam and the upper bearing preload spring off the upper steering shaft. Remove horn contact carrier.
5. Remove the thrust washer from the shaft.

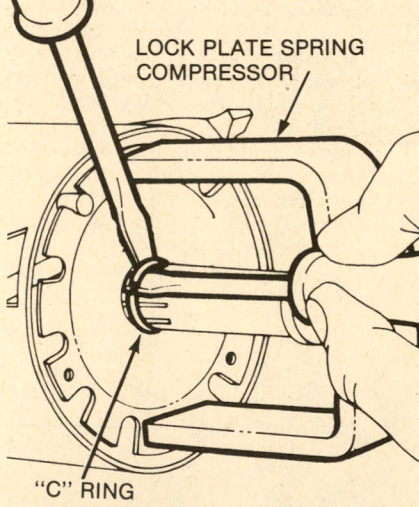

LOCK PLATE SPRING COMPRESSOR

"C" RING

Removing the C-ring

6. Remove the hazard warning switch from the column along with the turn signal lever.
7. Use the following procedure if the car is equipped with Cruise Control.
   a. Attach a length of wire to the connector on the Cruise Control switch harness.
   b. Gently pull the harness up and out of the column.
8. Remove the two vertical bolts at the steering column upper support. Remove the shim packs. Keep the shims in order for reinstallation.
9. Remove the four screws securing the column upper mounting bracket to the column and remove

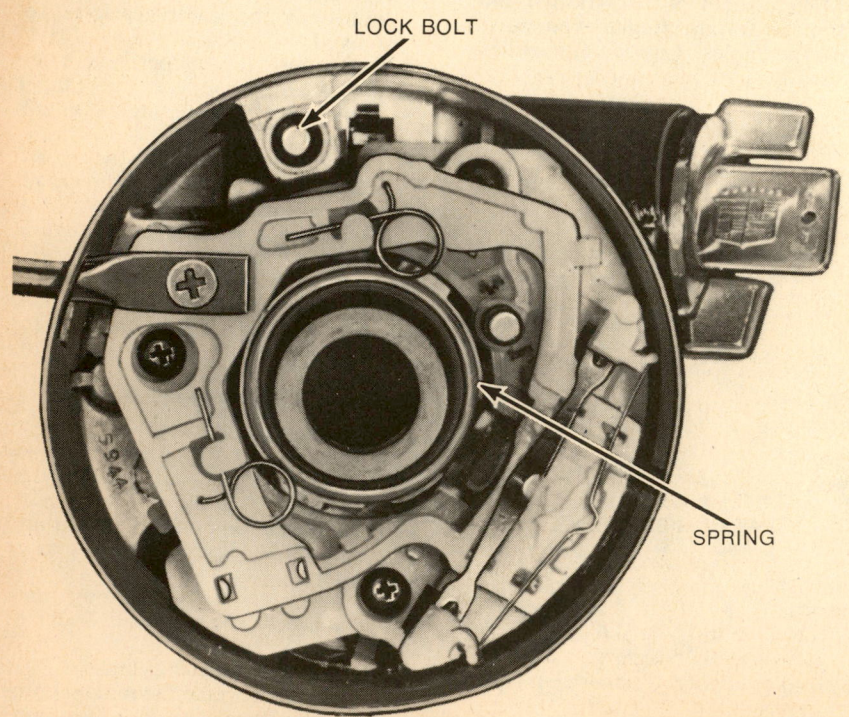

LOCK BOLT

SPRING

Turn signal switch (© Cadillac Div., G.M. Corp.)

the bracket.
10. Remove the turn signal switch mounting screws.
11. Slide the switch connector out of the bracket on the steering column.
12. If the switch is known to be bad, cut the wires and discard the switch. Tape the connector of the new switch to the old wires, and pull the new harness down through the steering column while removing the old wires.
13. If the original switch is to be reused, wrap tape around the wire and connector and pull the harness up through the column. It may be helpful to attach a length of wire or string to the harness connector before pulling it up through the column to facilitate installation.
14. After freeing the switch wiring protector from its mounting, pull the turn signal switch straight up and remove the switch, switch harness, and the connector from the column.
15. To reassemble reverse the removal procedure.

1974-76 FULL SIZE CADILLAC WITH A.C.R.S. (AIR BAGS)

Follow the procedure for removing the steering wheel and air cushion module which appears previously under Steering Wheel Removal, Special Procedure for Cars with A.C.R.S.
1. Remove the 3 screws from the retainer and cover. Carefully lift the cover and retainer from the column.
2. Carefully insert a screwdriver blade into the locking tab at the side and lift the slip-ring from the column.
3. Now proceed with Steps 3-10 of the Turn Signal Switch Removal and Replacement procedure.
4. To replace the slip-ring, align the slip-ring locating tab with the slot in the bowl and push the slip-ring into position. Make sure that all 3 locking tabs are securely positioned.
5. Install the cover and retainer, aligning the cover over the locating tab. Torque the screws to 15 in lbs.

SEVILLE
1. Disconnect the battery and remove the steering wheel.
2. Remove the rubber sleeve bumper from the steering shaft.
3. Remove the plastic retainer with a screwdriver, disengaging the tabs on the retainer from the C-ring.
4. Compress the upper steering shaft preload spring with a compressor and remove the C-ring.
5. Remove the spring compressor and remove the upper steering shaft lock plate, horn contact carrier and the preload spring.

6. Remove the steering column lower cover.
7. Unscrew and remove the turn signal lever. If equipped with cruise control:
   a. Disconnect the cruise control wire from the harness near the bottom of the steering column.
   b. Slide the protector off the cruise control wire and wind the wire around the turn signal lever until the lever is disconnected. Do not remove the wire from the column.
8. Remove the two nuts and shim packs from the upper column support. Keep the shims together as a unit for reinstallation.
9. Remove the bracket from the steering column.
10. Disconnect the turn signal wiring harness from the car harness and remove the wires from the plastic protector.
11. Remove the turn signal switch retaining screws and pull the switch up out of the steering column.
12. If the switch is to be replaced, cut the wires from the switch and tape the new switch connector to the old wires. Carefully pull the new harness down through the column as the old wires are removed.
13. If the old switch is to be reused, tape the connector to the wires and carefully pull the harness up out of the column.
14. Feed the wiring harness down through the steering column to replace the old switch.
15. Secure the switch in the steering column.
16. Install the upper shaft preload spring.
17. Install the lock plate and carrier assembly. Make sure that the flat on the lower end of the steering shaft is pointing up and that the small plastic tab on the carrier is up or nearest the top of the column. The flat surface of the lock plate must be installed facing down against the turn signal switch.
18. Install the spring compressor, compress the preload spring and lock plate and install the C-ring with the wide side toward the keyway.
19. Remove the spring compressor and install the plastic retainer on the C-ring.
20. Install the rubber sleeve bumper over the steering shaft and install the steering wheel.
21. Install the turn signal lever. If the vehicle is equipped with cruise control:
   a. Turn the turn signal lever clockwise exactly 6 turns to wind the harness tightly around the lever.
   b. Position the lever to the switch and screw it in, unwinding the harness as the lever is installed.

22. Remove the tape from the end of the harness and connect the switch and cruise control, if so equipped, to the car harness.
23. Cover both harnesses with the plastic protector and position it to the column. The turn signal connector slides on the tabs of the column.
24. Position the steering column upper bracket over the turn signal switch harness plastic protector.
25. Install the mounting bracket nuts and shims in their original positions.
26. Install the steering column lower cover.

Steering Linkage Removal and Replacement
1. Remove the steering shock damper, if any, from the frame bracket. Remove cotter pins and nuts from outer tie-rod pivots.
2. Remove outer tie rod pivots from steering knuckles using tie-rod end puller.
3. Remove idler arm screws and lockwashers from side member.
4. Remove pitman arm cotter pin, nut and washer at steering linkage.
5. Remove steering linkage from pitman arm.
6. Remove intermediate rod with tie-rods and idler arm attached.
7. Remove cotter pins and nuts from idler arm pivot and inner tie-rod pivots.
8. Remove tie-rod.
9. Remove idler arm from intermediate rod.
10. Remove dust seals from pitman arm and idler arm pivot studs.
11. Remove outer tie-rod pivots by loosening nuts on outer clamp bolts and unscrewing the pivot from adjuster tubes.
12. To install, reverse removal procedure. Tighten the idler arm nuts to 45 ft. lbs. and install the cotter pin. Do not tighten above 55 ft. lbs.

Power Steering Pump Removal and Installation
1. On Seville, remove the alternator and bracket.
2. Disconnect the pump lines and seal them to prevent fluid loss.
3. Remove the pump mounting from the engine block. Remove the drive belt.
4. By releasing the bottom pivot screw the pump can be removed with the mounting bracket attached.
5. The installation procedure is the reverse of removal. Remember to adjust the pump belt tension and bleed the hydraulic system.

NOTE: *To adjust the power steering pump belt, loosen the pump to mounting bracket screws, and move the pump upward until the belt is tight. Tighten the mounting bracket screws. Run the engine faster than idle speed, and turn the steering wheel full right or left. If the belt squeals, it is too loose and should be tightened more.*

Ignition Switch Replacement

1. Disconnect battery.
2. Position lock cylinder in lock position.
3. Remove steering column lower cover.
4. Loosen two nuts on upper steering column, allowing column to drop.

———— **CAUTION** ————

Do not remove the nuts, as the column may bend under its own weight.

5. Disconnect ignition switch connector at switch.
6. Remove two screws securing ignition switch to steering column. Remove switch.
7. To install, first assemble ignition switch on actuator rod and adjust to lock position, as follows:
   a. Standard Column—Hold switch actuating rod stationary with one hand while moving switch toward bottom of column until switch reaches end of travel (Acc. position). Back off one detent, then, with key also in lock position, tighten two switch mounting screws to 35 in. lbs.
   b. Tilt column—Hold switch actuating rod stationary with one hand while moving switch toward upper end of column until switch reaches end of travel (Acc. position). Back off one detent, then, with key also in lock position, tighten two switch mounting screws to 35 in. lbs.
8. Connect wires, tighten two steering column nuts, install lower cover and reconnect battery.

Lock Cylinder Replacement

NOTE: *On 1974-76 models, equipped with air bags (A.C.R.S.), perform the special procedure for removing the air bag module from the steering wheel, prior to removing the lock cylinder.*

STANDARD STEERING COLUMN

1. Remove the steering wheel.
2. Remove the lockplate cover assembly.
3. After compressing the lockplate spring, remove the snap-ring from the groove in the shaft.

———— **CAUTION** ————

When the snap-ring is removed do not allow the shaft to slide out the bottom of the column.

4. Remove the lockplate and slide the turn signal cam and the upper bearing preload spring off the upper steering shaft.
5. Remove the thrust washer from the shaft.
6. Remove the hazard warning switch from the column along with the turn signal lever.
7. Use the following procedure if the car is equipped with Cruise Control.
   a. Attach a piece of stiff wire to the connector on the Cruise Control switch harness.
   b. Gently pull the harness up and out of the column.
8. Remove the turn signal switch mounting screws.
9. Slide the switch connector out of the bracket on the steering column.
10. After freeing the switch wiring protector from its mounting, pull the turn signal switch straight up and remove the switch, switch harness and the connector from the column.
11. Turn the ignition switch to on or run and then insert a small screwdriver into the slot next to the switch mounting screw boss. Push the lock cylinder tab and remove the lock cylinder.

TILT COLUMN

1. Remove the steering wheel.
2. Remove the rubber sleeve bumper from the steering shaft.
3. Using a small screwdriver, remove the plastic retainer.
4. Using a spring compressor, compress the upper steering shaft spring and remove the C-ring. Release the steering shaft lockplate, the horn contact carrier, and the upper steering shaft preload spring.
5. Remove the four screws which hold the upper mounting bracket and then remove the bracket.
6. Slide the harness connector out of the bracket on the steering column. Tape the upper part of the harness and connector.
7. Disconnect the hazard button and position the shift bowl in Park. Remove the turn signal lever from the column.
8. Use the following procedure for cars with Cruise Control.
   a. Remove the harness protector from the harness.
   b. Attach a piece of piano wire to the switch harness connector.
   c. Before removing the turn signal lever, loop a piece of piano wire and insert it into the turn signal lever opening. Using the wire, pull the Cruise Control harness out through the opening.
   d. Pull the rest of the harness up through and out of the column.
   e. Remove the guide wire from the connector and secure the wire to the column.

f. Remove the turn signal lever.
9. Pull the turn signal switch up until the end connector is within the shift bowl. Remove the hazard flasher lever. Allow the switch to hang.
10. Place the ignition key in the run position.
11. Depress the center of the lock cylinder retaining tab with a screwdriver and then remove the lock cylinder.
12. To install reverse the procedure.

INSTRUMENT PANEL

Headlight Switch Removal and Installation

FULL SIZE CADILLAC THROUGH 1976

1. Disconnect the negative battery cable and remove the lower cover of the steering column.
2. Release the wiring harness retainer which runs below the headlight switch.
3. Depress the knob release button which is located on the top of the headlight switch. While the button is depressed, remove the rod and knob.
4. Remove the two mounting screws and the ground wire which is located at the bottom of the switch housing.
5. Pull the headlight switch assembly down and rearward, disconnect the wiring harness connectors, and the two bulbs, and then remove the assembly.
6. Unfasten the hex-head sleeve which holds the headlight switch to the housing case, then remove the switch from the case.
7. On units with Guide-Matic or Twilight Sentinel, use the following additional procedure.
   a. Remove the two screws securing the backplate and the lens to the bezel. Then remove the backplate and the lens.
   b. Remove the control ring and the washer on units equipped with one of the systems only. On cars with both systems, a dual control with an inner and outer shaft is used.
   c. Remove the hex nut securing the control switch and then remove the switch from the backplate.
8. To reassemble reverse the removal procedure.

1977 AND LATER FULL SIZE CADILLAC

1. Disconnect the battery ground.
2. Remove the left instrument panel insert.
3. Remove the three screws securing

the switch to the instrument panel.

4. On cars equipped with Cruise Control and Twilight Sentinel, remove the two screws securing the Cruise Control switch to the instrument panel.
5. Slide the cruise control switch forward to remove the light switch.
6. Disconnect the wires and Guide-Matic, if equipped.
7. Installation is the reverse of removal.

1976 SEVILLE

1. Disconnect the negative battery cable.
2. Remove the lower steering column cover and instrument cluster bezel.
3. Remove the trim screw from the left side of the lower panel.
4. Remove the 2 screws securing the left lower instrument panel to the top cover.
5. Loosen the screw securing the lower panel to the reinforcement.
6. Pull the left lower instrument panel out to gain access to the connectors. Disconnect the climate control electrical and vacuum connectors, cruise control and headlight connectors, illumination bulbs and sockets, and ground wires.
7. Pull the knob on the headlight switch On and depress the spring loaded button on the bottom of the switch. Remove the headlight switch knob and rod.
8. Remove the headlight switch case-to-instrument panel insert screws and separate the headlight switch assembly from the left lower instrument panel assembly.
9. Remove the sleeve that secures the switch to the case.
10. Without Guide-Matic and/or Twilight Sentinel, remove the sleeve that secures the escutcheon, washer and lens to the backplate.
   If the vehicle is equipped with Guide-Matic and/or Twilight Sentinel, remove the Guide-Matic knob, wave washer and Twilight Sentinel lever by carefully pulling straight out. The lens may be removed without any further disassembly. Remove the spanner nut to remove the potentiometer(s) from the backplate.
11. Install the headlight switch in the reverse order.

1977 AND LATER SEVILLE

1. Remove the left lower instrument panel assembly.
2. Pull the switch to the ON position.
3. Depress the spring-loaded button on the bottom of the switch and remove the knob and rod assembly.
4. Remove the four headlamp switch case-to-panel screws and separate the switch assembly from the panel.
5. Remove the sleeve which secures the switch to the case.

6. On cars without Guide-Matic or Twilight Sentinel, remove the sleeve which secures the escutcheon, lens and backplate.
7. On cars with those options, remove the Guide-Matic knob, wave washer and Twilight Sentinel lever by pulling straight out.
8. Installation is the reverse of removal.

Speedometer Cable Removal and Installation

FULL SIZE CADILLAC THROUGH 1976

1. Disconnect the battery ground.
2. Reach up behind the speedometer cluster and depress the retaining tab while pulling back on the cable.
3. Pull the core from the cable. If the core is broken, raise the car and remove the cable end from the transmission.
4. Installation is the reverse of removal.

1977 AND LATER FULL SIZE CADILLAC

1. Remove the left instrument panel insert.
2. Disconnect the battery ground.
3. Place the shift lever in Park and remove the screw securing the shift indicator cable to the column.
4. Remove the two upper screws securing the cluster assembly to the panel horizontal support.
5. Remove the two lower inside screws securing the cluster to the horizontal support.
6. Remove the screw located directly above the steering column securing the cluster to the speedometer mounting plate.
7. Pull the cluster outward to disengage the cable.
8. Disconnect the cable housing from the locking spring on the mounting plate and pull it through the firewall.
9. Pull the core from the cable. If the core is broken, raise and support the car and disconnect the cable from the transmission.
10. Installation is the reverse of removal.

SEVILLE

1. Disconnect the battery ground.
2. Remove the lower steering column cover.
3. Remove the 4 screws securing the cluster bezel to the instrument panel and cluster.
4. Press the bezel downward slightly, rotate the top outward and remove the bezel.
5. Place the shift lever in Park and remove the screw holding the indicator cable to the column.
6. Remove the two upper cluster screws and the two lower inboard screws.

7. Pull the cluster outward to disengage the cable.
8. Disconnect the cable housing from the locking spring and pull it through the firewall.
9. Remove the core from the cable. If the core is broken, raise the car and remove the cable from the transmission.
10. Installation is the reverse of removal.

WINDSHIELD WIPERS

Wiper and Washer Motor Removal and Installation

1. Disconnect the negative battery cable.
2. Remove the cowl screen.
3. Reach through the opening and disengage the transmission drive link from the wiper crank arm by loosening two nuts.
4. Disconnect the wiring and washer hoses.
5. Remove the three screws that secure the wiper/washer unit to firewall.
6. Remove the entire assembly.
7. To install, reverse the removal procedure, making sure the wiper crank arm is in the Park position.

Wiper Blade Replacement

Two methods are used to retain the blades to the arms. One method uses a press type tab. When the tab is depressed, the blade assembly can be slid off the arm. The other method uses a spring retainer. A screwdriver must be inserted on top of the spring and the spring pushed downward. The blade assembly can then be slid off the pin.

RADIO

Removal and Installation

THROUGH 1973

1. Remove the steering column lower cover.
2. Remove the defroster hose behind the radio.
3. Remove the radio knobs, washers and rings by pulling straight out.
4. Remove the nuts securing the control shafts to the panel.
5. Disconnect any wiring from the radio.
6. Remove the support bolts and remove the radio.
7. Installation is the reverse of removal.

1974-76 FULL SIZE CADILLAC WITHOUT AIR BAGS (A.C.R.S.)

1. Remove the 4 screws each which secure the lower steering column

Cadillac & Seville

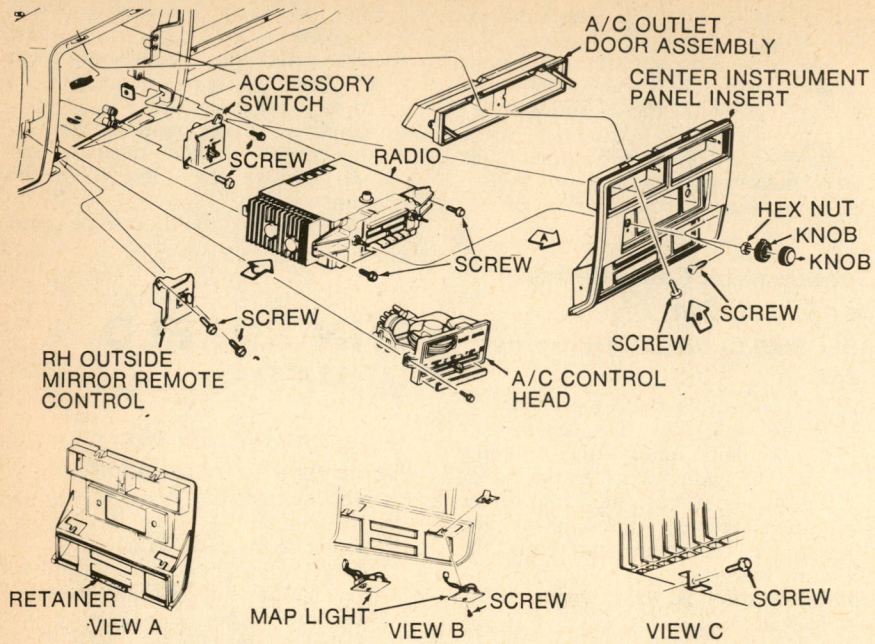

ACCESSORY SWITCH

A/C OUTLET DOOR ASSEMBLY

CENTER INSTRUMENT PANEL INSERT

SCREW

RADIO

HEX NUT

KNOB

KNOB

SCREW

SCREW

SCREW

SCREW

RH OUTSIDE MIRROR REMOTE CONTROL

A/C CONTROL HEAD

RETAINER

VIEW A

MAP LIGHT

SCREW

VIEW B

SCREW

VIEW C

1977 and later full-size car radio details (© Cadillac Div., G.M. Corp.)

cover to its reinforcement and the instrument panel support.
2. Take the lower cover off.
3. Unfasten the screws which secure the lower ash tray bracket, and then remove the two screws from the left-hand ash tray bracket.
4. Unfasten the right-hand ash tray securing screw. Remove the ash tray assembly from the dash panel.
5. Remove the knobs, washers, outer rings, and shaft retaining nuts.
6. Remove the radio-to-dash panel lower support brace nut from the back of the radio.
7. Loosen, but don't remove, the screw which secures the brace to the support, and turn the brace clockwise.
8. Slide the radio back from the instrument panel. Detach the speaker connector, power connector, and antenna lead from it.
9. Turn the dial side of the radio (front) so that it is facing down, and lower the left-side of the receiver. Withdraw it through the ash tray opening.
10. Installation is the reverse of removal.

1974-76 FULL SIZE CADILLAC WITH AIR BAGS (A.C.R.S.)

1. Turn the ignition switch to Lock.
2. Remove the negative (—) battery cable and tape its terminal end.

------ **CAUTION** ------

If the battery cable is not disconnected and taped, there is a chance that the air bag could accidentally deploy.

3. Remove the 3 screws which retain the glovebox in the dash, but don't remove the two striker screws.
4. Remove the glovebox partition

screws, and set the glovebox aside, without disconnecting the wiring.
5. Remove the tape storage compartment retaining screws and remove the compartment.
6. Remove the ash tray assembly retaining screws, pull the assembly out partway, unfasten the electrical leads, and remove the assembly.
7. Remove the knee restraint left trim screw.
8. Remove the screws, and loosen, but don't remove, the fifth screw (under the steering column) from the bottom of the knee restraint.
9. Remove the 4 knee restraint securing screws working from the tape storage compartment and ash tray openings.
10. Perform Steps 5-7 of the radio removal procedure for 1974 and later Cadillacs without air bags.
11. Through the knee restraint opening, disconnect the antenna lead, depress the locktabs and push the electrical connections upward to disengage them.
12. Clear the instrument panel support by turning the radio to the left. Slide the radio away from you, lower the front of the radio (dial), and withdraw it, front first, through the knee restraint opening.
13. Installation is the reverse of removal.

1977 AND LATER EXCEPT SEVILLE

1. Remove the radio knobs and anti-rattle springs.
2. Remove the two hex nuts securing the bezel to the radio.
3. Remove the two center air conditioning outlet grilles. Remove the one screw in each outlet.

4. Remove the maplights and remove the center panel insert.
5. Unbolt and remove the radio from the panel.
6. Disconnect wiring.
7. Installation is the reverse of removal.

SEVILLE

1. Disconnect the battery ground.
2. Loosen the right forward screw which secures the fuel injection electronic control unit cover to the unit.
3. Remove the remaining three screws from the cover.
4. Remove the three screws which secure the unit to the panel supports.
5. Remove the screw securing the climate control outlet extension to the heater case.
6. Disconnect the antenna.
7. Remove the radio support rod.
8. Remove the control knobs, anti-rattle springs, control rings and both hex nuts.

NOTE: *The control knobs on radios with 8-track are retained with 5/64 in. allen screws.*

9. Remove the radio. Installation is the reverse of removal.

HEATER

Heater Blower Removal, Non-Air Conditioned Cars through 1975

1. Disconnect negative battery cable.
2. Disconnect electrical connector.
3. Remove five blower-to-case screws and blower motor.

Heater Blower Removal, Air Conditioned Cars

1. Disconnect the negative battery cable.
2. Remove the rubber cooling hose from the nipple and blower motor.
3. Disconnect the electrical connector.
4. Remove the screws that secure the motor to the case, then twist the motor 180° and pull out.

Heater Core Removal, Non-Air Conditioned Cars through 1975

1. Drain cooling system.
2. Remove heater hoses from core nipples. Plug the nipples.
3. Remove instrument panel top cover.
4. Remove screws and position center ventilator duct and sleeve out of the way.
5. Remove vacuum hoses from diverter door and defroster door vacuum actuators.
6. Unfasten the bowden cable from temperature door and case and move out of way.
7. Take out the screws, securing heater case to cowl.

8. Work heater case from position under instrument panel.
9. Remove the screws and clips securing the core to heater case, and lift out core.
10. To install, reverse removal procedure.

Heater Core Removal, Air Conditioned Cars

FULL SIZE CADILLAC THROUGH 1976

NOTE: *On 1974-76 models equipped with air bags (A.C.R.S.), the passenger air bag restraint assembly must be removed first. This procedure is best left to a dealer shop.*

1. Drain cooling system.
2. Remove hoses from heater core nipples. Plug the nipples.
3. Remove instrument panel top cover.
4. Remove right and left A/C outlet hoses and center outlet connector.
5. Remove screws securing A/C distributor to heater case and lift off distributor.
6. Remove defroster nozzle.
7. Remove glove box.
8. Disconnect vacuum hoses at recirculator door, water valve, control head supply hose, and programmer (if equipped).
9. Disconnect aspirator hose from in-car sensor.
10. Take off instrument panel braces.
11. On engine side of cowl remove the nuts securing heater case to cowl.
12. Work the heater case out from under dash.
13. Remove rubber seals from around core nipples.
14. Remove the screw and clip from beneath the seal.
15. Take out screws and clip from opposite end of core and remove core.
16. Reverse the procedure for installation.

1977 AND LATER FULL SIZE CADILLAC

1. Disconnect wiring from the blower, resistors, and thermostatic cycling switch.
2. Remove the right windshield washer nozzle.
3. Remove the right air inlet screen from the plenum.
4. Remove the two screws securing the thermostatic cycling switch to the module and carefully reposition the switch off the module cover.
5. Remove the 16 fasteners securing the module cover and remove the cover.
6. Remove the hoses from the core nipples.
7. Remove one screw and retainer holding the core to the frame at the top.
8. Place the temperature door in the max. hot position and reach through the temperature housing and push the lower forward corner of the heater core away from the housing. This causes the core to snap out of the lower clamp. The core may not be removed in a vertical direction.
9. Installation is the reverse of removal.

SEVILLE

NOTE: *In order to remove the heater core, the air conditioning system must be discharged and the evaporator case assembly removed from the car. If you are not knowledgeable about or properly equipped to service automotive air conditioning systems, do not attempt to discharge the system.*

1. Discharge the air conditioning system.
2. Drain the cooling system and remove the right side wheelhousing strut.
3. Support the front of the hood and tape a pad to the right rear corner of the hood. Remove the right hood hinge.
4. Remove the electrical connections from the components mounted on the evaporator assembly and move the wiring harness out of the way.
5. Remove the heater hose at the heater core side of the hot water valve. Remove the two screws securing the valve to the evaporator case and move the valve out of the way.
6. Jack up the front of the car and support it with jackstands. Remove the right front wheel.
7. Remove the five screws securing the wheelhousing to the fender at the wheel opening.
8. Remove the two screws attaching the wheelhousing at the front.
9. Remove the three plastic retainers securing the wheel housing seal at the rear of the wheelwell, front of the wheelwell, and at the fender, forward of the wheel opening.
10. Remove the two screws behind the wheelwell securing the wheelhousing to the cowl brace.
11. Remove the battery and battery tray.
12. Remove the three screws and retainer securing the wheelhousing to the radiator support under the horns.
13. Remove the wheelhousing damper upper mounting bolt and move the damper out of the way.
14. Remove the wheelhousing from the car. Some prying and bending may be necessary.
15. Remove the heater hoses from the heater core nipples.
16. Disconnect and plug the refrigeration lines at the receiver.
17. Remove the screws and nuts retaining the evaporator case and remove the case from the vehicle.
18. Separate the case and remove the heater core.
19. Install in the reverse order. Use new O-rings at the connection of the refrigeration lines to the receiver. Fill the cooling system and evacuate and recharge the air conditioning system.

Cadillac Eldorado

Index

YEAR IDENTIFICATION

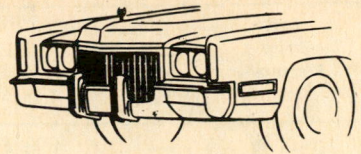

1972

1973

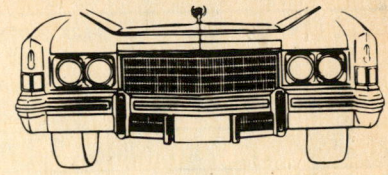

1974

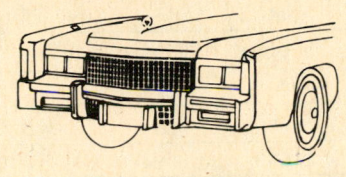

1975-76

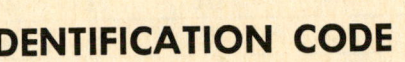
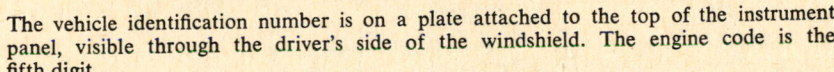

1977

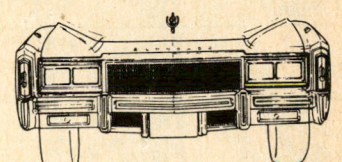

1978

ENGINE IDENTIFICATION CODE

The vehicle identification number is on a plate attached to the top of the instrument panel, visible through the driver's side of the windshield. The engine code is the fifth digit.

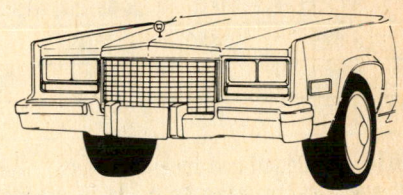

1979

No. Cyl.	Cu. in. Disp.	Type	1972	1973	1974	1975	1976	1977	1978	1979
8	500	4 bbl.	S	S	S	S	S			
8	500	EFI				S	S			
8	425	4 bbl.						S	S	S
8	425	EFI						T		
8	350	EFI								B
8	350	Diesel								N

GENERAL ENGINE SPECIFICATIONS

Year	Engine No. Cyl Displacement (cu in.)	Carburetor Type	Horsepower @ rpm ■	Torque @ rpm (ft lbs) ■	Bore Stroke (in.)	Compression Ratio	Oil Pressure @2000 rpm
'72	8-500	4 bbl	235 @ 3800	385 @ 2400	4.300 x 4.304	8.5:1	35
'73	8-500	4 bbl	235 @ 3800	385 @ 2400	4.300 x 4.304	8.5:1	35
'74	8-500	4 bbl	210 @ 3600	380 @ 2000	4.300 x 4.304	8.25:1	35
'75	8-500	4 bbl	210 @ 3600	380 @ 2000	4.300 x 4.304	8.25:1	35
	8-500	EFI	210 @ 3600	380 @ 2000	4.300 x 4.304	8.25:1	35
'76	8-500	4 bbl	190 @ 3600	360 @ 2000	4.300 x 4.304	8.5:1	35
	8-500	EFI	215 @ 3600	400 @ 2000	4.300 x 4.304	8.5:1	35
'77-'78	8-425	4 bbl	180 @ 3600	260 @ 2000	4.082 x 4.060	8.2:1	35
	8-425	EFI	215 @ 3600	260 @ 2000	4.082 x 4.060	8.2:1	35
'79	8-350	EFI	170 @ 4200	270 @ 2000	4.057 x 3.385	8.0:1	35
	8-350	Diesel	120 @ 3600	220 @ 1600	4.057 x 3.385	22.5:1	40

■ Horsepower and torque are SAE net figures. They are measured at the rear of the transmission with all accessories installed and operating. Since the figures may vary when a given engine is installed in different models, some are representative rather than exact.
EFI—Electronic Fuel Injection

Cadillac Eldorado

TUNE-UP SPECIFICATIONS

When analyzing compression test results, look for uniformity among cylinders rather than specific pressures.

Year	ENGINE No. Cyl Displacement (cu in.)	hp	SPARK PLUGS Orig. Type	Gap (in.)	DISTRIBUTOR Point Dwell (deg)	Point Gap (in.)	IGNITION TIMING (deg) ▲ Man Trans	Auto Trans	VALVES Intake Opens ■ (deg)	Fuel Pump Pressure (psi)	IDLE SPEED (rpm) ▲ Man Trans *	Auto Trans
'72	8-500	235	R-46-N	.035	30	.016	—	8B	34	5¼-6½	—	600/400
'73	8-500	235	R-46-N	.035	30	.016	—	8B	34	5¼-6½	—	600/400
'74	8-500	210	R-45NS	.035	30	.016	—	10B	21	5¼-6½	—	600/400
	8-500 H.E.I.	210	R-45NS	.035	Electronic		—	10B	21	5¼-6½	—	600/400
'75	8-500	210	R-45NSX	.060	Electronic		—	6B	21	5¼-6½	—	600
	8-500 EFI	210	R-45NSX	.060	Electronic		—	6B	21	39 min.	—	600
'76	8-500	190	R-45NSX	.060	Electronic		—	6B	21	5¼-6½	—	600
	8-500 EFI	215	R-45NSX	.060	Electronic		—	12B	21	39 min.	—	600
'77	8-425	180	R-45NSX	.060	Electronic		—	18B@2000	21	5¼-6½	—	675
	8-425 EFI	215	R-45NSX	.060	Electronic		—	18B@2000	21	39 min.	—	650
'78	8-425	180	R-45NSX	.060	Electronic		—	18B@2000	21	5¼-6½	—	675
'79	8-350	EFI	R-47SX	.060	Electronic		—	10B	22	5.5-6.5①	—	600
'79	8-350	Diesel	—	—	—	—		5B③	16	5.5-6.5②	—	575

NOTE: The underhood specifications sticker often reflects tune-up specification changes made in production. Sticker figures must be used if they disagree with those in this chart.

▲ See text for procedure
■ All figures Before Top Dead Center
* Lower figure indicates idle speed with solenoid disconnected
B Before Top Dead Center

— Not applicable
H.E.I.—High Energy Ignition
EFI—Electronic Fuel Injection
① Injection pressure: 39 psi
② Injection pressure: 1800 psi
③ Static

FIRING ORDER

NOTE: Most 1979 GM carburetors have idle mixture screws concealed by staked-in plugs. These are not meant to be removed, except at carburetor overhaul.

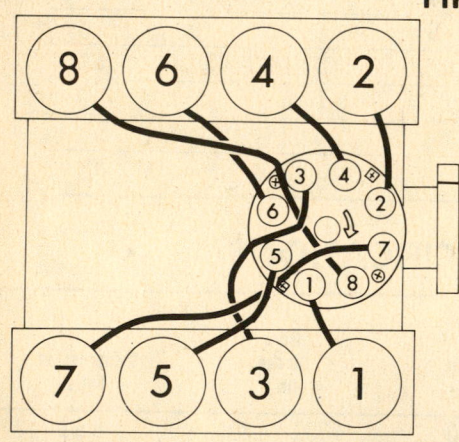

GM (Cadillac) 425, 500 V8
Engine firing order: 1-5-6-3-4-2-7-8
Distributor rotation: clockwise

(Circles only are position of latches with point-type ignition; circles and squares are position of latches with electronic ignition).

VALVE SPECIFICATIONS

Year	Engine No. Cyl. Displacement (cu in.)	Seat Angle (deg)	Face Angle (deg)	Spring Test Pressure (lbs @ in.)	Spring Installed Height (in.)	STEM TO GUIDE Clearance (in.) Intake	Exhaust	STEM Diameter (in.) Intake	Exhaust
'72	8-500	45	44	168 @ 1.50	1 15/16	.0010-.0027	.0012-.0027	.3418	.3416
'73	8-500	45	44	168 @ 1.50	1 15/16	.0010-.0027	.0012-.0027	.3418	.3416
'74	8-500	45	44	168 @ 1.50	1 15/16	.0010-.0027	.0012-.0029	.3418	.3416
'75-'78	8-425 500	45	44	160 @ 1.50	1 15/16	.0010-.0027	.0010-.0027	.3416	.3416
'79	8-350 EFI	①	②	187 @ 1.27	1 43/64	.0010-.0027	.0015-.0032	.3429	.3424
'79	8-350 Diesel	①	②	151 @ 1.30	1 43/64	.0010-.0027	.0015-.0032	.3429	.3424

① Intake 45; exhaust 31
② Intake 44; exhaust 30

CAPACITIES

Year	ENGINE No. Cyl. Displacement (cu. in.)	Engine Crankcase Add 1 Qt For New Filter	TRANSMISSION Pts To Refill After Draining Manual 3-Speed	4-Speed	Automatic ●	Drive Axle (pts)	Gasoline Tank (gals)	COOLING SYSTEM (qts) With Heater	With A/C
'72	8-500	5	—	—	11.9	4.0	27.5	21.3	21.8①
'73	8-500	5	—	—	11.9	4.0	27.5	21.3	21.8①
'74	8-500	5	—	—	11.9	4.0	27.5	21.3	21.8①
'75	8-500	5	—	—	10.0	4.0	27.5	25.8	25.8
'76	8-500	5	—	—	11.5	4.0	27.5	23.0	23.0
'77	8-425	5	—	—	10.0	4.0	27.5	25.8	25.8
'78	8-425	5	—	—	10.0	4.0	27.5	24.3	24.3
'79	8-350 EFI	4	—	—	10.0	3.17	19.6	17.2	17.2
'79	8-350 Diesel	7.5	—	—	10.0	3.17	19.6	17.2	17.2

● Specifications do not include torque converter   ① Trailer package—2 qts additional   — Not applicable

TORQUE SPECIFICATIONS

All readings in ft lbs

Year	Engine Displacement (cu in.)	Cylinder Head Bolts	Rod Bearing Bolts	Main Bearing Bolts	Crankshaft Bolt	Flywheel Bolts	MANIFOLD Intake	Exhaust
'72-'76	500	115	40	90	Press fit	75	30	35①
'77-'78	425	95	40	90	Press fit	75	30	35①
'79	350 EFI	130	42	80②	310	60	40	25
'79	350 Diesel	130	42	120	310	60	40	25

① 12 for short bolt
② 120 on No. 5

CRANKSHAFT AND CONNECTING ROD SPECIFICATIONS

All measurements are given in inches

Year	Engine Displacement (cu in.)	CRANKSHAFT Main Brg. Journal Dia	Main Brg. Oil Clearance	Shaft End-Play	Thrust on No.	CONNECTING ROD Journal Diameter	Oil Clearance	Side Clearance①
'72-'73	500	3.250	.0003-.0026	.002-.012	3	2.500	.0005-.0035	.008-.016
'74	500	3.250	.0003-.0026	.002-.012	3	2.500	.0005-.0028	.011-.021
'75-'78	425, 500	3.250	.0001-.0026	.002-.012	3	2.500	.0005-.0028	.008-.020
'79	350 EFI	2.4990	.0005-.0021②	.004-.014	3	2.1240	.0004-.0033	.006-.020
'79	350 Diesel	2.9998	.0005-.0021②	.004-.014	3	2.1240	.0005-.0026	.006-.020

① Total 2 Rods

RING SIDE CLEARANCE

All measurements are given in inches

Year	Engine	Top Compression	Bottom Compression	Year	Engine	Oil Control
'72-'78	8-425, 500	.0017-.0040	.0017-.0040	'72-'78	8-425, 500	None (side sealing)
'79	8-350 EFI	.0020-.0040	.0020-.0040	'79	8-350 EFI	.0006-.0096
'79	8-350 Diesel	.0050-.0070	.0018-.0038	'79	8-350 Diesel	None (side sealing)

RING GAP

All measurements are given in inches

Year	Engine No. Cyl. Displacement (cu in.)	Top Compression	Bottom Compression
'72-'76	8-500	.013-.025	.013-.025
'77-'78	8-425	.013-.023	.013-.023
'79	8-350 EFI	.010-.023	.010-.023
'79	8-350 Diesel	.015-.025	.015-.025

Year	Engine	Oil Control
'72-'79	All	.015-.055

WHEEL ALIGNMENT SPECIFICATIONS

Year	CASTER Range (deg)	Pref Setting (deg)	CAMBER Range (deg)	Pref Setting (deg)	Toe-in (in.)	Steering Axis Inclin.	WHEEL PIVOT RATIO (deg) Inner Wheel	Outer Wheel
'72-'73	½N to 1½N	1N	⅜N to ⅜P	0	¹⁄₁₆N to ¹⁄₁₆P	11	20	18⅙
'74-'76	½N to ½P	0	LH—⅜N to ⅜P RH—⅝N to ⅛P	¼N	¹⁄₁₆N to ¹⁄₁₆P	11	20	18⅙
'77-'78	½N to ½P	0	⅖N to ⅖P	0	¹⁄₁₆N to ¹⁄₁₆P	11	—	—
'79	0 to 1P	½P	0 to 1P	½P	0 to ¹⁄₁₆	11	—	—

N Negative   P Positive   RH—Right-hand
LH—Left-hand   — Not specified

CHARGING SYSTEM

Alternator Removal and Installation

EXCEPT 80 AMP ALTERNATOR

1. Disconnect negative battery cable.
2. Disconnect air pump hose at check valve and remove heater hose clip from adjusting link (if so equipped).
3. Remove cap, if installed, from + terminal.
4. Disconnect wires from + terminal.
5. Unplug multiple connector.
6. Disconnect black wire from ground terminal (if used).
7. Remove link adjusting screw and raise link, then loosen lower alternator mounting screw and remove V-belt.
8. Remove lower mounting screw, spacer and washer.

NOTE: *It may be necessary to twist the alternator toward the fender to do this.*

9. Remove the alternator.
10. To install, reverse the removal procedure. Tighten the mounting screw to 17-20 ft. lbs.

80 AMP H.D. ALTERNATOR

1. Disconnect the negative battery cable.
2. Disconnect all wiring connections from the alternator.
3. Loosen the belt tension adjusting bolts and remove the belt.
4. Remove the 2 nuts and lockwash-

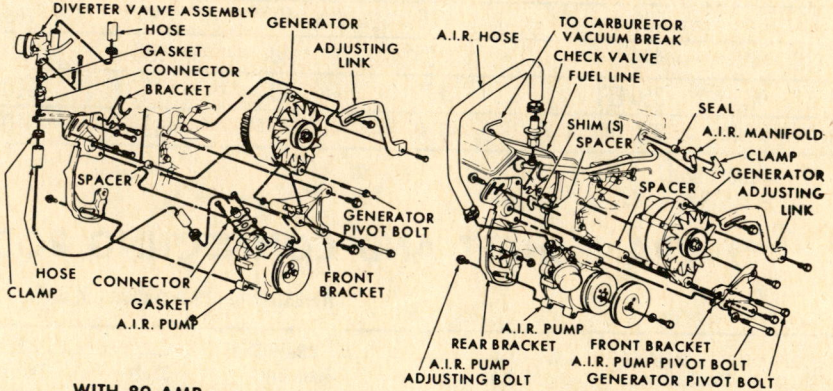

Alternator mounting positions (© Cadillac Div., G.M. Corp)

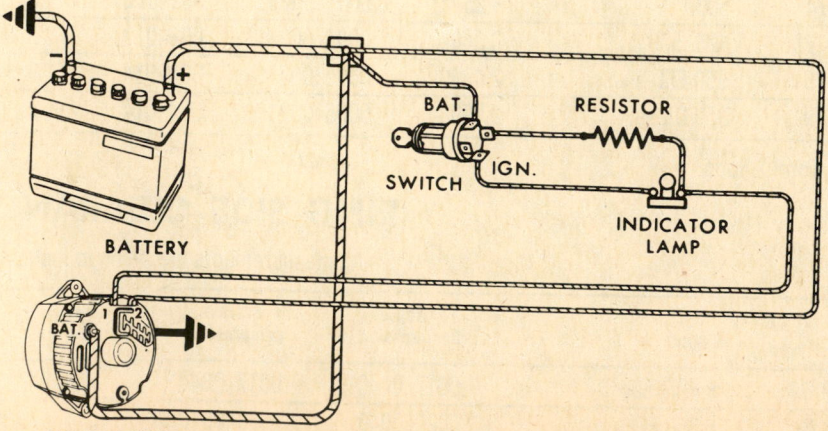

Charging system diagram (© Cadillac Div., G.M. Corp)

ers from the lower mounting bolts, leaving the bolts in place.
5. Remove the upper mounting bolt and remove the alternator by sliding it rearward off the lower mounting bolts.
6. Installation is the reverse of removal. Adjust the belt tension.

STARTING SYSTEM

For detailed testing and repair procedures consult the Unit Repair Section.

Starter Removal and Installation
1. Disconnect the negative battery cable.
2. Disconnect the starter harness at the right rear of the engine.
3. Raise the front of the car.
4. Remove the spring clip securing wire which is attached to the solenoid housing.
5. Remove the support bracket which holds the starter to the crankcase.
6. Remove the two screws which attach the starter to the crankcase.
7. Remove the starter from the car by first pulling it forward and then toward the right front wheel and then up over the steering linkage.
8. To install the unit, position it properly onto the engine crankcase and then tighten the attaching screws to 46 ft. lbs.
9. Install the support bracket. Tighten the screws to 12 ft. lbs. and the nut to 6 ft. lbs.
10. Install the spring clip and lower the car. Connect the starter harness and the negative battery cable.

Disabling the Seat Belt/Starter Interlock and Buzzer
The seat belt/starter interlock was used only on early production 1975s.
It is now legal to disable the seat belt/starter interlock, but *not* the warning light. To do this, proceed as follows:
1. Disconnect the negative (—) battery cable.
2. Locate the interlock harness connector, which is on or near the fuse block. The connector has orange, yellow, and green leads running to it.
3. Cut and tape the green lead on the body harness side of the interlock connector.
4. Remove the steering column lower cover.
5. Remove the buzzer connector from its mounting bracket and separate the buzzer from it. Install the connector back on the bracket.
6. Replace the steering column lower cover.
7. Connect the negative battery cable.

8. Check system operation by starting the car with the seat belt unfastened.

IGNITION SYSTEM

In 1974, GM High Energy Ignition (HEI) was offered as an option; it became standard equipment in 1975.
HEI is a breakerless system which has the coil and the control module integral with the distributor. For further description as well as repair procedures, see Electronic Ignition in the Unit Repair Section.

Contact Point Replacement and Adjustment through 1974
1. Remove distributor cap by depressing and turning the retaining screws.
2. Remove the two rotor screws.
3. Remove condenser and primary leads from nylon insulated connection.
4. Loosen two screws holding base of contact assembly in place and remove points.
5. Inspect weight assembly, replace or lubricate as required.

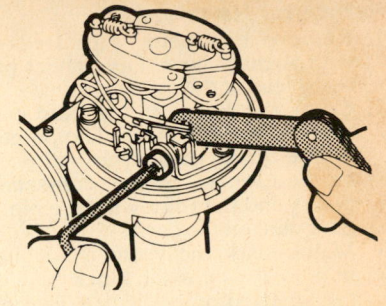

Adjusting distributor points

6. Place new points under the two screws and tighten screws.
7. Connect the condenser and primary leads at the nylon insulated connection.

NOTE: *Be sure the leads do not interfere with the cap, weight base, or advance.*

8. Install rotor. Square and round lugs must be properly aligned.
9. With 1/8 in. Allen wrench, turn until points close while rubbing block is on high point of lobe. Then turn screw counterclockwise one-half turn.
10. Replace distributor cap.
11. With engine warmed up and at idle, set points to proper dwell angle.

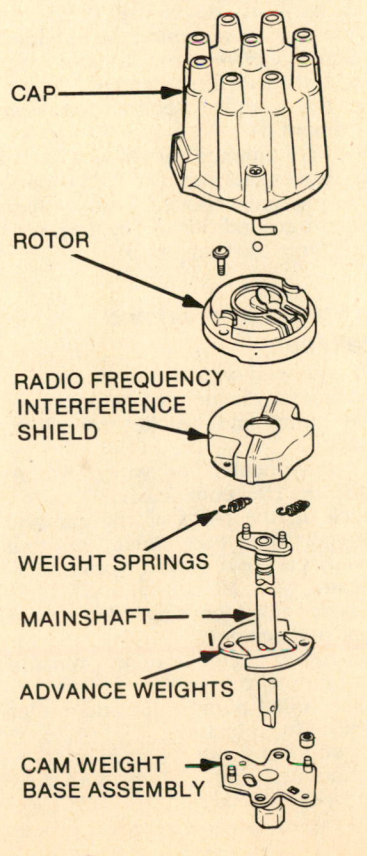

CAP
ROTOR
RADIO FREQUENCY INTERFERENCE SHIELD
WEIGHT SPRINGS
MAINSHAFT
ADVANCE WEIGHTS
CAM WEIGHT BASE ASSEMBLY

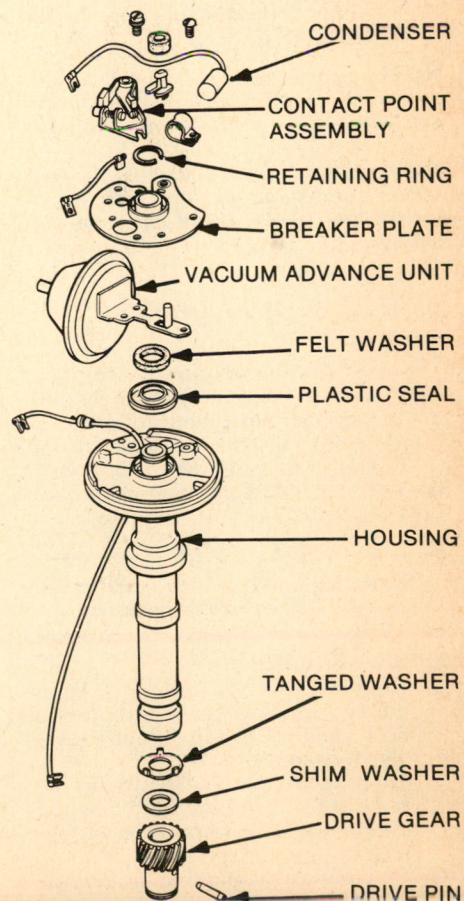

CONDENSER
CONTACT POINT ASSEMBLY
RETAINING RING
BREAKER PLATE
VACUUM ADVANCE UNIT
FELT WASHER
PLASTIC SEAL
HOUSING
TANGED WASHER
SHIM WASHER
DRIVE GEAR
DRIVE PIN

Conventional distributor

Distributor Removal

1. Remove distributor cap. Disconnect vacuum hose. Disconnect primary lead at the coil.
2. Crank the engine to top dead center for No. 1 cylinder. The pointer on the timing case cover will point to the O-mark on the crankshaft pulley and the rotor will face No. 1 plug wire on the cap.
3. Match-mark the vacuum advance unit to the cylinder block so that the distributor body will be correctly replaced at reassembly.
4. Remove hold-down clamp and lift the distributor straight up.

Distributor Installation

1. Install rubber seal-ring below distributor housing mounting flange.
2. Install the distributor so that the vacuum advance unit aligns with the match-mark made at removal. Turn the rotor slightly left of center so that as the gear engages the camshaft it will revolve into the proper position, pointing to No. 1 contact in the cap.
3. Install the distributor hold-down and connect the distributor lead to the coil.
4. Check the condition of the contact points and the breaker gap.
5. Install the cap and set the timing. (See Ignition Timing.)
6. Reconnect the vacuum hose to the vacuum advance unit.

NOTE: *If the engine has been cranked, remove No. 1 spark plug. Crank the engine until No. 1 piston is in firing position with the pointer and the O-mark on the crankshaft pulley aligned. Lower the distributor into position with the rotor pointing to No. 1 contact on the distributor cap.*

Tachometer Hookup to HEI Ignition

In the distributor cap, there is a TACH terminal. Connect the tachometer to this terminal and to ground. Some tachometers must connect from the TACH terminal to the battery positive (+) terminal; follow the manufacturer's instructions.

—— CAUTION ——

Grounding the TACH terminal could damage the HEI electronic module.

Ignition Timing

1. Loosen the distributor clamp enough to allow the distributor to be turned by hand without excessive looseness.
2. Disconnect the vacuum advance hose at the distributor and tape the end of the hose to prevent any air leaks.
3. Disconnect the parking brake vacuum hose at the diaphragm and tape the end.

4. Connect a timing light to the engine.
5. Connect a tachometer to the engine.

NOTE: *Make sure that the timing mark on the pulley and the aligning plate on the front cover are clean.*

6. Disconnect the automatic level control hose on cars so equipped.
7. Allow the engine to reach operating temperature.
8. Set the idle speed with the selector lever in Drive.
9. Set the timing to specifications with transmission in Park or Neutral. At the correct setting tighten the hold-down bolt of the distributor and recheck the timing.
10. Connect the 3 vacuum hoses and remove both the timing light and the tachometer from the engine.

FUEL SYSTEM

MECHANICAL FUEL PUMP

The fuel pump is mounted on the left-front of the engine and is driven by an eccentric on the camshaft. The fuel filter is an integral part of the fuel pump on models through 1974. A strainer is also located behind the fuel inlet nut on the carburetor. Beginning 1975, the fuel filter is located behind the fuel inlet nut. Starting 1976, a check valve is included in the fuel filter element.

See the Cadillac section for filter replacement.

All air conditioned cars have a line to return excess fuel vapor to the gasoline tank to prevent vapor lock under high temperature conditions. The line runs directly from the fuel pump.

Fuel Pump Removal and Installation

1. If equipped with the air pump system, it may be necessary to remove air pump and bracket for clearance.
2. Remove center coil wire. Disconnect the HEI connector.
3. Jack up the front of the car and support on axle stands so that pump can be removed from underneath.
4. Loosen two mounting bolts, or one bolt and one nut.
5. Turn over engine to relieve tension on pump arm.
6. Disconnect pump inlet and outlet lines. Plug inlet line.
7. Disconnect vapor return line.
8. Remove mounting bolts and fuel pump.
9. To install, reverse removal procedure.

Fuel Filter Replacement

See the Cadillac section.

ELECTRIC FUEL PUMP

Models equipped with electronic fuel injection (EFI) have two electric fuel pumps. For fuel pump service on cars so equipped, see the Cadillac section.

CARBURETOR

Idle Speed and Mixture Adjustments

1972-74

Adjust with air cleaner removed.

Idle speed is adjusted at an anti-dieseling solenoid. The throttle must be opened slightly to allow the plunger to move out all the way, then it must be closed against the now-extended solenoid plunger before making the idle speed adjustment. The solenoid plunger will retract when the ignition is shut off.

1. Disconnect and plug distributor vacuum advance hose and parking brake vacuum hose (at the release cylinder).
2. Connect a tachometer and set the parking brake with transmission in Neutral.
3. Remove the air cleaner and turn in mixture screws until they seat gently, then turn the screws out approximately 6 turns (4 turns, 1974).
4. Start engine and allow it to warm up.
5. Place car in Drive with A/C off.
6. Set idle speed to 620 rpm (640 rpm, 1974) by adjusting anti-dieseling solenoid. Tighten jam nut.
7. Alternately, turn each mixture screw clockwise 1/4 turn at a time until idle speed reaches 600 rpm.
8. Disconnect wire that energizes solenoid. The plunger should retract to allow a slower idle speed of 350-400 rpm.
9. Shut off engine, disconnect tach, connect vacuum lines and solenoid wire and install air cleaner.

1975-76

1. Disconnect the hose from the parking brake vacuum release cylinder. Plug the hose.
2. Apply the parking brake. Block the wheels. Remove and plug the air leveling compressor hose at the air cleaner.
3. Connect a tachometer. Allow the engine to reach normal operating temperature. The choke should fully open and the cam follower should be off the fast idle cam completely.

—— CAUTION ——

Do not allow the engine to idle or fast idle for excessive periods of time; catalyst damage could result.

4. Place the transmission in Drive and shut off the air conditioner.
5. Adjust the idle speed screw to obtain 600 rpm (unless the mixture is to be adjusted).

NOTE: *Do not depress the brake pedal when adjusting idle speed on 1976 and later models. These cars are equipped with the Hydro-boost power brake system; brake application will decrease engine speed.*

6. Remove the air cleaner but leave its vacuum hoses connected.
7. Remove the limiter caps and screw both mixture screws out 5 turns from fully seated.
8. Set the idle speed to 650 rpm on 49-state cars on 620 rpm on California cars with the idle speed screw.
8. Use a hex-driver with an extension to turn in each mixture screw 1/4-turn at a time until the normal idle speed of 600 rpm is obtained.
9. Shut off the engine. Install service replacement limiter caps on the idle mixture screws and install the air cleaner.
10. Remove the tachometer. Connect all the vacuum hoses.

1977-79

1. Set the parking brake, block the wheels and disconnect and plug the vacuum line at the parking brake.
2. Remove the air cleaner, but keep the vacuum lines connected.
3. On cars with automatic level control, disconnect and plug the compressor vacuum lines.
4. Disconnect and plug all other hoses listed on the underhood specifications sticker.
5. Run the engine to normal operating temperature, with the A/C off.
6. Connect an accurate tachometer.
7. Disconnect and plug the vacuum advance hose and check and set the timing.
8. Reconnect the vacuum advance line.
9. Remove the idle mixture screw caps.
10. Lightly seat the screws, then back them out equally about 2 turns each, so that the engine will just run.
11. Block the wheels. Place the transmission in Drive.
12. Back out each screw 1/8 turn at a time until maximum idle speed is reached. Then set the idle speed to 670 rpm (630 in Calif.).
13. Turn each screw in 1/8 turn at a time until speed reaches 600 rpm.
14. Adjust the idle speed screw to the specified idle speed.
15. Reconnect all equipment.

ELECTRONIC FUEL INJECTION (EFI)

Starting 1975, electronic fuel injection (EFI) was offered as an option on all Cadillacs, including Eldorado. It was not offered on 1978 models.

For a description of the EFI system, as well as adjustment and service procedures, see the Cadillac section.

COOLING SYSTEM

Eldorados use a sealed cooling system which maintains 15 lbs. maximum pressure. The radiator is constructed with two vertical tanks that connect to the enclosed cross-flow tubing. The coolant enters the upper left-hand inlet tank and circulates through the cross-flow tubes and enters the right return tank. A coolant reservoir is attached to the radiator filler neck by a hose. The reservoir allows for coolant expansion and indicates the need for additional coolant. Coolant should be added to the reservoir, not the radiator.

Further information on the cooling system may be found in the Cadillac section under the same year model. Also, system capacities can be found in the Capacities chart.

Radiator Removal and Installation

1. Remove the 6 screws securing the radiator cover and one screw securing the hose bracket. Remove the cover. Remove the negative battery cable.
2. Open the drain plug on the radiator and drain the coolant. Remove the radiator cap so that the liquid drains faster.
3. Remove the hose clamps and remove the upper hose.
4. Remove the heater return hose which is located at the right radiator tank.
5. Disconnect the two transmission cooler lines from the bottom of the radiator. Plug the ends of the lines to prevent loss of fluid.
6. Remove the reservoir hose from the filler neck and the two straps from the top of the radiator.
7. Remove the radiator, being careful not to damage the radiator or the fan. Pull the unit straight up.
8. Installation is the reverse of removal.

Water Pump and Thermostat Removal and Installation

See the Cadillac section.

EMISSION CONTROLS

The Cadillac Eldorado uses the same emission control systems as the rest of the Cadillac line.

For a description of these controls see Emission Controls in the Cadillac car section.

For emission control tests and adjustments, see Emission Control Systems in the Unit Repair Section.

ENGINE

On the Eldorado, special mounting brackets welded to the frame provide the front attaching points and a special crossmember is used for the rear mount.

ENGINE REMOVAL AND INSTALLATION

CAUTION

If it is necessary to reposition the air conditioner compressor or the lines, do not disconnect the lines.

1. Follow Steps 1-16 of procedure in Cadillac Section.
2. Disconnect left exhaust pipe at manifold flange.
3. Remove screw that holds transmission cooler lines to motor mount.
4. Remove the nut that secures the dipstick tube to manifold. Remove the upper screw holding the steering gear flex coupling shroud to the frame.
5. Jack up car and remove the steering gear flex coupling shroud.
6. Remove starter motor.
7. Disconnect right exhaust pipe at manifold flange.
8. Remove transmission inspection cover.
9. Disconnect and plug vapor return line and fuel inlet at fuel pump.
10. Remove lower radiator hose at water pump.
11. Remove three screws that secure flywheel to converter.
12. Remove four screws that secure engine to transmission.
13. Remove front motor mount bolts and bolt that secures final drive to mount.
14. Remove right drive axle spindle nut and cotter pin.
15. Remove the drive axle-to-output shaft screws and lockwashers.

NOTE: *Discard the screws and washers. Have an assistant hold the brake pedal to prevent the shaft from turning.*

16. Remove shaft support-to-engine bolts, and one support-to-brace screw.
17. Rotate inboard end of drive axle rearward toward starter motor.
18. Pull output shaft straight out, then lower and remove from underside of car. Proceed with engine removal procedure.
19. Lower car, install lifting bracket and chain hoist and place a wood-padded jack under the transmission pan.
20. Raise engine and pull forward to disengage transmission. Lift engine out of car.
21. To install, reverse removal procedure.

MANIFOLDS

Intake Manifold Removal and Installation

WITH CARBURETOR

1. Remove the negative battery cable.
2. Remove the air cleaner, heat tube, crankcase breather, carburetor linkage, and the Cruise Control linkage.
3. Remove the coil wires or HEI connector and disconnect the SCS solenoid.
4. Remove the primary coil wire (if so equipped) and then remove the distributor cap.
5. Disconnect the single connector near the ignition coil and the green wire to the temperature sender.
6. Remove the two orange wires from the downshift switch and disconnect the anti-dieseling solenoid.
7. Remove the ignition coil (if so equipped) anti-dieseling solenoid, and the SCS solenoid.
8. Remove the power brake vacuum hose and the vacuum modulator hose which is located at the rear of the carburetor.
9. On air-conditioned cars, disconnect the compressor clutch electrical connection. Remove the vacuum hose for the air conditioner and the TVS hose from the rear of the manifold.
10. Remove the fuel line from the carburetor and remove the distributor vacuum advance hose at the carburetor.
11. Disconnect the PCV valve from the right valve cover and the automatic level control (ALC) vacuum hose. Remove the 12 manifold retaining bolts.
12. Remove the manifold. Also remove the inner manifold shield and gasket and the front and rear gaskets.
13. To reassemble reverse the procedure.

WITH ELECTRONIC FUEL INJECTION (EFI)

For intake manifold removal and installation on models with electronic fuel injection, see the Cadillac section.

Exhaust Manifold Removal and Installation

1. If the work is to be done on the left-side manifold, remove the carburetor air cleaner and the heat duct. Remove the nuts from No. 2 and No. 6 cylinders and the heat shroud from around the manifold.
2. Remove the dipstick tube.
3. Release the eight securing screws, disconnect the manifold from the exhaust pipe, and remove the manifold. The 5th screw from the front may not be removable due to frame interference. Back it out and remove it with the manifold.

4. Use the same procedure for removing the right-side manifold except remove the two studs retaining the EFE vacuum operated heat riser valve (if equipped) to the manifold and remove the valve. EFI cars have a spacer in place of the valve.
5. Reassembly is the reverse of the procedure. Lubricate the cylinder head mounting surface with a thin coat of graphite. Right manifold with EFE valve: Install the EFE valve on the manifold with the actuator toward engine block. Tighten stud bolts to 35 ft. lbs.

VALVE SYSTEM

See the Cadillac section.

Cylinder Head Removal and Installation

NOTE: *Care must be used when replacing cylinder-head bolts. They are of different lengths.*

1. Remove intake manifold.
2. Drain engine coolant.
3. Disconnect ground strap at rear of cylinder heads from cowl. Disconnect wiring connector for high engine temperature warning system from sending unit at rear of left cylinder head.
4. Remove alternator and heater hose, if working on the right cylinder head, or partially remove the steering pump if working on the left head.
5. Disconnect AIR injection pump tubes from cylinder heads.
6. Remove clamps holding the wire harness to the cylinder heads and tie harness back out of the way.
7. Remove screws holding exhaust manifolds to cylinder heads.
8. Remove screws holding the rocker arm cover to the heads.
9. Remove the cover.
10. Remove the screws holding each rocker arm support to cylinder head, then remove rocker arm assemblies. Store these assemblies so that they may be reinstalled in their correct locations.
11. Remove pushrods and store them with their respective rocker arm assemblies.
12. Install two 7/16 x 6 in. screws to be used as lifting handles in two of the rocker arm support screw holes.
13. Remove the cylinder-head bolts.
14. Lift cylinder head off the block.
15. Remove all gasket material from the cylinder head and block mating surface.
16. The bottom rear bolt must be installed prior to the positioning of the head.

When torquing the head bolts, use the three-step method. Torque the bolts to 1/3 of the total torque listed in sequence. Once this is done, repeat the same procedure, this time torquing all the bolts to 2/3 of the total listed

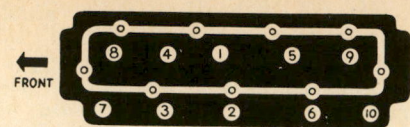

Cylinder head bolt tightening sequence. See Cadillac section for bolt location and length.

torque. Finally torque the bolts to the recommended torque.

ROD AND PISTON ASSEMBLIES

The numbers on the connecting rods face away from the camshaft; that is, the numbers on the left bank face to the left; the numbers on the right bank face to the right. As a double check, the word *rear,* (or R), stamped on the piston, faces the rear of the engine on both banks and an arrow or notch on the piston top points to the front of the engine.

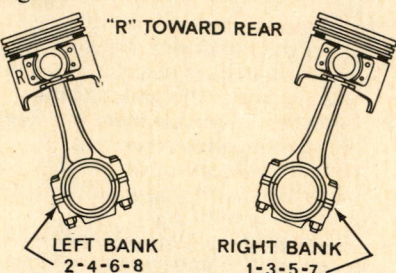

"R" TOWARD REAR

LEFT BANK 2-4-6-8   RIGHT BANK 1-3-5-7

Piston-to-connecting rod relationship

TIMING COVER, CHAIN AND CAMSHAFT

Timing Cover, Chain and Sprockets Removal and Installation

THROUGH 1974

The engine must be removed from the car before the front cover can be removed. The procedure is otherwise identical to that for the same year Cadillac as found in the Cadillac Section.

1975 AND LATER

The front cover may be removed with the engine in the car. This procedure eliminates the necessity of removing the oil pan.

1. Disconnect the negative battery cable.
2. Drain the crankcase and the radiator.
3. Loosen the radiator inlet (top) hose clamp and remove the one screw retaining the hose to the radiator cover. Place the hose out of the way.
4. Remove the fan assembly and the alternator and power steering pump drive belts.
5. Remove the four capscrews retaining the crankshaft pulley and the plug from the end of the crankshaft.
6. Use suitable puller tools to remove

the crankshaft hub. It may be necessary to hold one piston within its compression stroke with compressed air to avoid turning the crankshaft. Remove a spark plug and use the proper adapter to apply air pressure to the cylinder.

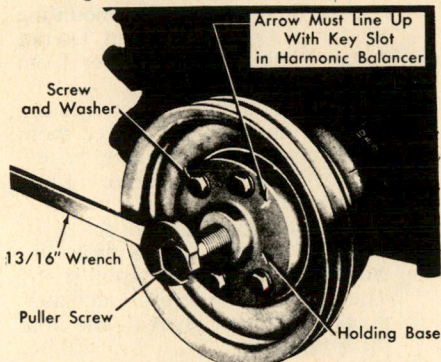

Balancer assembly removal
(© Cadillac Div., G.M. Corp.)

7. Loosen the starter enough to gain access to the oil pan screws. Loosen the oil pan nuts and screws and lower the front of the oil pan.
8. Loosen the hose clamp at the water pump inlet and remove the lower radiator hose from the water pump.
9. Remove the 10 screws retaining the front cover to the block. Remove the cover with the water pump attached and discard the gasket.
10. Inspect the oil pan front seal to make sure that it was not damaged on removal. Replace the seal if damaged. If the seal is satisfactory, remove any oil and coat the sealing surface with gasket cement.
11. Place a new front cover gasket over the locating dowels on the block. Hold the gasket in place with a small amount of gasket cement.
12. Position the front cover over the end of the crankshaft and down over the oil pan lip. Align the holes in the cover with the dowels on the block. Tighten the retaining screws.
13. Lubricate the bore of the hub and seal with E.P. lubricant to prevent seizure to crankshaft. Position the hub on the crankshaft aligning the slot in the hub with the key on the crankshaft.
14. Press the hub onto the crankshaft with the proper tools. Again use of compressed air may be necessary to avoid turning the crankshaft. Install the crankshaft pulley onto the hub. Tighten the four capscrews to 15 ft. lbs.
15. If used, exhaust air pressure from the cylinder, remove the adapter, and install the spark plug.
16. Install the fan assembly on the water pump and install the power steering pump and alternator drive belts. Adjust drive belt tension.

17. Connect the upper radiator hose at the radiator inlet and secure with the hose clamp. Secure the hose to the radiator cover with one screw.
18. Tighten the oil pan nuts and screws to 10 ft. lbs; tighten the starter motor mounting bolts to 45 ft. lbs.
19. Connect the lower radiator hose to the water pump inlet and secure with hose clamp. Refill the cooling system and add engine oil. Connect the negative battery cable. Start the engine and check for coolant and oil leaks.

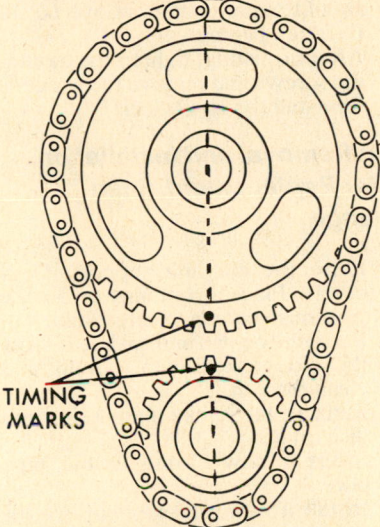

Timing sprocket location marks

Camshaft Removal and Installation

See Cadillac section.

LUBRICATION

Oil Pan Removal and Installation

1. Remove engine as previously described in Engine Removal and Installation.
2. Drain engine oil.
3. Remove the transmission lower cover.
4. Remove two brackets-to-block bolts on each side of engine front mounting support.
5. Remove nuts and cap screws that hold oil pan to cylinder block and engine front cover, then remove the oil pan.
6. Remove side gaskets and rubber front and rear seals from oil pan. Discard the gaskets and seals.
7. Install by reversing the removal procedure. Torque to 10 ft lbs.

Oil Pump Removal and Installation

1. Raise and support the car.
2. Remove the oil filter.
3. Unbolt and remove the pump. The bolt nearest the pressure regulator should be removed last.

4. Remove the pump driveshaft.
5. Installation is the reverse of removal. Fill the pump with oil. Torque the bolts to 15 ft. lbs.

Rear Main Bearing Oil Seal Replacement

1. Remove the oil pan, after removing spark plug wires and plugs.
2. Remove the rear main bearing cap and loosen the bolts holding the other four bearings about three turns each. Remove the old rear main bearing seals.
3. Clean the groove in the cap and in the block. Lubricate seals with engine oil.
4. Make an installation tool.
5. Start the upper half into the groove in the block with the lip facing forward and rotate it into position, using the tool as a guide. Press firmly on both ends to be sure it is protruding uniformly on each side.
6. Install the lower half of the seal into the bearing cap with the lip facing forward and one end of the seal over the ridge and flush with the split line. Hold one finger over this end to prevent it from slipping, and push the seal into seated position by applying pressure to the other end. Be sure the seal is firmly seated and protrudes evenly on each side. Do not apply pressure to the lip. This may damage the effectiveness of the seal.
7. Apply rubber cement to the mating surfaces of the block and cap being careful not to get any cement on the bearing, the crankshaft or the seal. The cement coating should be about .010 in. thick.
8. Install the bearing cap, tightening the bolts with the fingers only.
9. Tighten the bearing bolts to specifications. Be sure to tighten the bolts of the other four bearings also.
10. Reinstall the oil pan.

AUTOMATIC TRANSMISSION

The Turbo Hydra-Matic 425 transmission used on the Eldorado is an automatic transmission used for front wheel drive applications. It consists primarily of a three-element hydraulic torque converter, dual sprocket and link assembly, compound planetary gear set, three multiple-disc clutches, a sprag clutch, a roller clutch, two band assemblies, and a hydraulic control system.

Neutral Safety Switch Replacement and Adjustment through 1973

NOTE: *The switch is on the steering column under the instrument panel.*

Cadillac Eldorado

1. Position the gear selector in the Neutral position.
2. Release the clamp and remove the switch without moving the contact carrier. The position of the carrier should be marked.
3. Remove the vacuum hoses after they have been marked and disconnect the two wires from the switch.
4. Installation is the reversal of removal.
5. To adjust, check that the gear lever is correctly adjusted and that the neutral safety switch is properly positioned by this check.
6. Set the handbrake. Put the lever on the steering column in Drive. Hold the ignition key on and slowly move the lever toward Neutral or Park until the starter cranks and the engine runs.
7. Without moving the lever farther, press the accelerator to determine whether the transmission is really in Neutral or Park.
8. If all is correct, the engine will start with the lever in Park. The transmission will not be in gear. Also, back-up lights will go on with transmission in Reverse.

NOTE: *A vacuum leak that can be corrected by moving the shift lever is an indication that the switch only needs adjustment and is not defective.*

9. Adjust the neutral safety switch by turning it and its mounting bracket until the above conditions are met.

Neutral Safety Switch—1974 and Later

On all models from 1974, the neutral safety switch works mechanically rather than electrically. When the transmission selector is in any position other than Park or Neutral, the key cannot be turned to Start.

This mechanical system is contained within the steering column.

Shift Linkage Adjustment

1. Place the transmission shift valve into the Park position and then move the relay rod to the Neutral step which is the third one down.
2. Loosen the adjusting screw on the relay lever and place the selector lever in the Neutral detent position.
3. Tighten the relay rod adjusting screw with the shift lever held against the neutral stop.
4. Check the adjustment by:
   a. Moving the selector level to the Neutral detent making sure that the lever fits securely into the notch on the steering column.
   b. Move the lever to Drive. Make sure that the lever is secure in this gear. Move the lever to Reverse and check for gear security.

NOTE: *When the linkage is adjusted, check the operation of the Neutral Safety Switch, parking brake release and the back-up lights.*

Kickdown Adjustment

1. Remove the air cleaner.
2. Make certain that the idle speed is set correctly and that the carburetor is operating on the low-speed circuit.
3. Loosen the switch mounting screws and insert a 0.094 in. wire gauge into the hole in the lower wire terminal.
4. With the gauge in place, adjust the position of the switch so that the lever just touches the carburetor adapter plate stud. The switch should make contact above 60° of throttle opening.
5. After adjusting, tighten the mounting screws and remove the gauge.
6. Reinstall the air cleaner.

Pan Removal and Installation, Filter Replacement, Fluid Change

1. Raise the car and support it securely. Place a container under the transmission pan to catch fluid.
2. Remove the pan and gasket. Throw the old gasket away. Drain and clean the pan.
3. Remove the intake pipe O-ring and discard it.
4. Insert a new O-ring in the pipe bore.
5. Install a new intake pipe/filter assembly in the pipe bore.
   Installation is as follows:
1. Place a new gasket on the pan and install the pan. Tighten the attaching screws to 12 ft. lbs.
2. Lower the car.
3. Add 4 qts of DEXRON® II transmission fluid through the filler tube.
4. Start the engine and run it at 800 rpm for 1-1/2 minutes with the gear selector in Park (P).
5. Return the engine speed to idle. Check the level and add fluid as necessary. The level should be between *ADD* and *FULL*.

DRIVE AXLES

Drive axles are a complete flexible assembly and consist of an axle shaft and an inner tri-pot joint and outer constant velocity joint. The inner tri-pot joint has complete flexibility, plus inward and outward movement. The outer constant velocity joint has complete flexibility at the angle of operation.

The constant velocity joints are to be replaced as a unit and are only disassembled for repacking and replacement of seals.

Right Drive Axle Removal

1. Remove the negative battery cable and the wheel disc.
2. If the drive axle is to be removed, release the cotter pin and loosen but do not remove the spindle nut.
3. Raise the car at the lower control arms.
4. Loosen but do not remove the right front shock absorber lower mounting nut. Then pry the shock absorber along the lower mounting stud until it reaches the nut. Do not remove the shock absorber from the lower mount.
5. To keep the torsion bar connectors from being damaged, cover them with a short length of rubber hose.
6. Remove the screws securing the drive axle to the output shaft.
7. Position the inside end of the drive axle toward the starter motor to gain access to the output shaft. Then remove the screw which supports the output shaft to the final drive housing.
8. Remove the two screws which support the right output shaft support to the engine.
9. Remove the output shaft, support and strut as an assembly in the following manner.
   a. Slide the output shaft outward to disengage the splines.
   b. Move the inside end of the assembly forward and downward until it is clear of the car.
10. If the drive axle is to be removed, use the following procedure.
    a. Using a hammer and a wooden block tap the end of the drive axle to unseat the axle at the hub.

NOTE: *The spindle nut should be loosened but not removed.*

    b. Rotate the axle inward and toward the front of the car positioning the axle over the front crossmember and out from under the car.

——— CAUTION ———

Care must be exercised so that constant velocity joints do not turn to full extremes, and that seals are not damaged against shock absorber or stabilizer bar.

Right Drive Axle Installation

1. Carefully place right-hand drive axle assembly into lower control arm and enter outer race splines into knuckle.
2. Lubricate final drive output shaft seal, with wheel bearing grease.
3. Install right-hand output shaft into final drive and attach the support bolts to engine and brace. Torque the bolts to 50 ft. lbs.
4. Install brace.
5. Move right-hand drive axle assembly toward front of car and align with right-hand output shaft. Install attaching bolts and torque to 65 ft. lbs.
6. Install washer and nut on drive axle.
7. Remove floor stands and lower hoist.

8. Tighten wheel lugs to 105 ft. lbs.—1972; 130 ft. lbs.—1973 and later; and drive axle nut to 110 ft. lbs., (1972-73 to 150 ft. lbs.). Install cotter pin.

NOTE: *Align the hole by tightening the nut.*

Left Drive Axle Removal and Installation

1. Hoist car under lower control arms.
2. Remove wheel and tire.
3. Remove drive axle cotter pin, nut and washer.
4. Install a piece of rubber hose over lower control arm torsion bar connector.
5. Remove six drive axle-to-output shaft screws and washers.
6. Loosen upper shock mounting bolt.
7. Remove upper control arm ball joint cotter pin and nut.
8. Using hammer and brass drift, drive on knuckle until upper ball joint stud is free.
9. Remove brake hose bracket.
10. Tip upper part of knuckle and support outward so that brake hose is not damaged.
11. Carefully guide drive axle assembly outward. Remove left output shaft retaining bolt by installing two screws in the shaft flange to prevent shaft rotation. Pull the shaft straight out toward side of car.

NOTE: *Care must be exercised so that constant velocity joints do not turn to full extremes and that seals are not damaged against shock absorber or stabilizer bar.*

12. To install, reverse removal procedure. Tighten output shaft retaining bolt to 50 ft. lbs., output shaft-to-axle screws to 65 ft. lbs., upper ball joint stud nut to 60 ft. lbs., upper shock absorber bolt to 75 ft. lbs. Tighten wheel lug nuts to 105 ft. lbs.—1972; 130 ft. lbs.—1973 and later. Tighten drive axle nut to 110 ft. lbs. (150 ft. lbs.—1972-73).

JACKING, HOISTING

When jacking the front of the vehicle, make certain that the jack is placed so that it contacts the lower suspension arm just inside the stabilizer bar. If the vehicle is lifted from the rear, place the jack as far into the middle of the frame as possible so that the Automatic Level Control and the fuel and brake lines are not damaged.

Ideally, the best lift is one which contacts both the front and rear suspension at the same time.

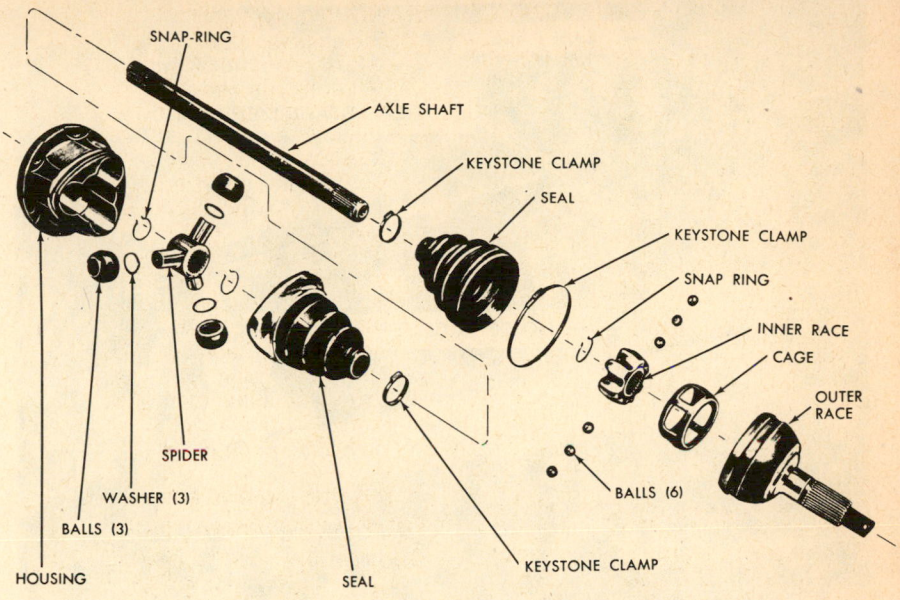

Drive axle—exploded view
(© Cadillac Div., G.M. Corp)

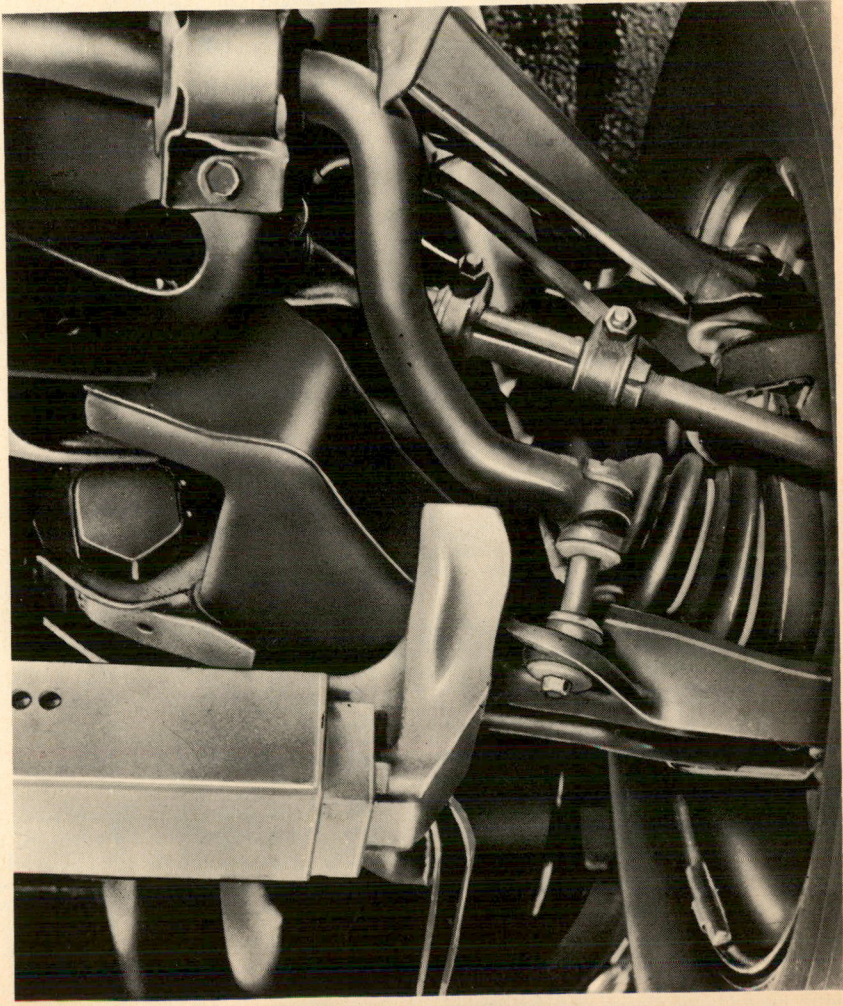

Front jacking position
(© Cadillac Div., G.M. Corp)

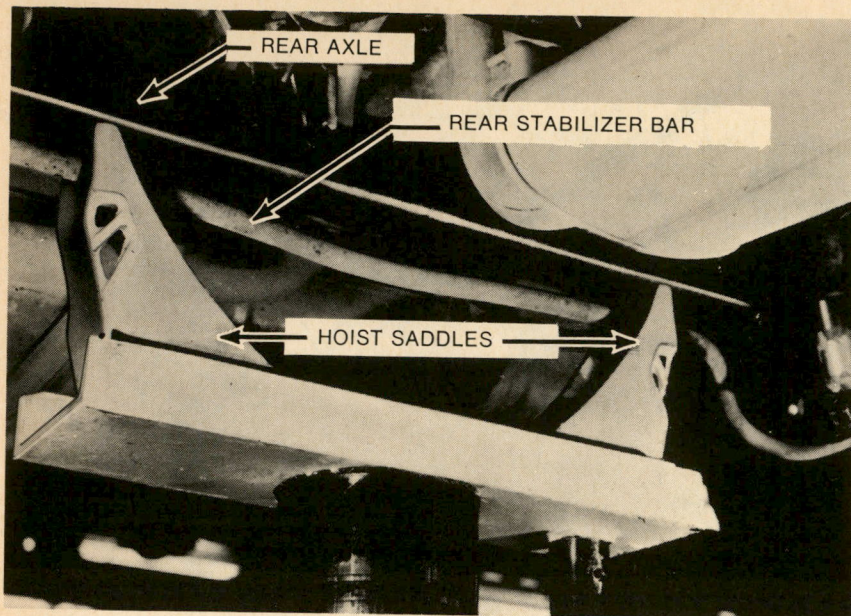

REAR AXLE

REAR STABILIZER BAR

HOIST SADDLES

Rear jacking position
(© Cadillac Div., G.M. Corp.)

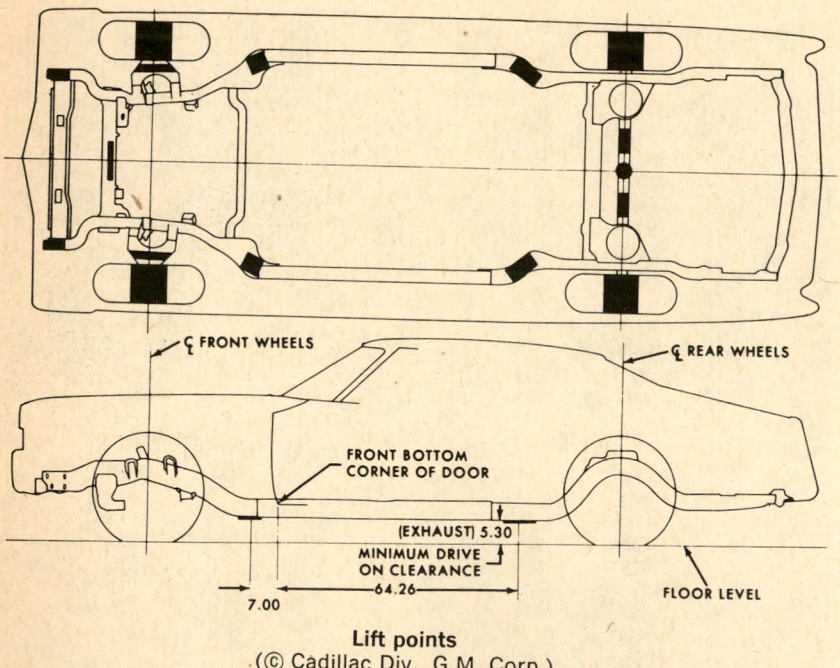

Ç FRONT WHEELS

Ç REAR WHEELS

FRONT BOTTOM
CORNER OF DOOR

(EXHAUST) 5.30

MINIMUM DRIVE
ON CLEARANCE

7.00

64.26

FLOOR LEVEL

Lift points
(© Cadillac Div., G.M. Corp.)

⸺ CAUTION ⸺

The rear lower control arm should never be used as a lift point for the vehicle.

When working on the vehicle in the raised position, it is recommended that two jackstands be placed under the front frame crossmember. Also, the vehicle should never be supported at the very ends of the frame with anything other than the jack provided with the car.

DIFFERENTIAL

A bevel gear-type differential is used. Overhauling the differential assembly is not recommended. Cadillac recommends that the unit be serviced by replacement only.

Removal

1. Disconnect the negative battery cable.
2. Unbolt the transmission filler tube bracket and remove the filler tube.

3. Remove screws A, B and the nut H.
4. Disconnect the transmission cooler lines from the final drive support bracket and slide the clip out of the way.
5. Remove the locknut, washer and long through-bolt holding the final drive support brace to the engine mount bracket.
6. Remove the right-hand output shaft.

⸺ CAUTION ⸺

The shock absorbers act as rebound stops. Before performing the following Step, be sure that the right-hand shock absorber lower sleeve cannot be dislodged from the stud.

7. Place jackstands under the front frame side rails and lower the hoist that was used when removing the right-hand output shaft.
8. Remove the final drive cover and allow the lubricant to drain into a drain pan.
9. Remove the 6 screws holding the left-hand drive axle to the output shaft. Compress the drive axle inner C.V. joint and hold it in this position to remove the final drive unit with the left-hand output shaft installed.
10. Remove the bolt, washer, and nut holding the left tie strut to the frame crossmember. Loosen the bolt holding the strut to the side rail and rotate the strut outboard until the strut is clear of the final drive area.
11. Remove the large through-bolt nut and washers, securing the final drive support bracket to the final drive.
12. Remove the final drive support bracket.
13. Remove the final drive cover and gasket(s).
14. Remove the final drive with a transmission lift and adapter. The adapter should have a rotating feature to ease removal and installation.
15. Place a drain pan under the transmission and remove screws C, D, E, F and nut G.
16. Disengage the final drive splines from the transmission and let the unit drain.
17. Remove the final drive unit from under the car by sliding the unit toward the front of the car and permitting the ring gear to rotate over the steering linkage. Lower the housing from the car.
18. Remove and discard the final drive-to-transmission gasket.

Installation

1. Positioning new gasket on transmission, install final drive unit, permitting ring gear to rotate up over steering linkage.
2. Align final drive splines with splines in transmission.

3. Align bolt studs G and H on transmission with holes in final drive.
4. Install bolts C, D, E and F and nut G finger tight.
5. Install support bracket on final drive unit.
6. Install other support brackets.
7. Install bolt in fluid cooler lines, clamp and tighten to 8 ft. lbs.
8. Tighten bolts C, D, E and F and nut G to 25 ft. lbs.
9. Reposition left drive axle and install screws to 65 ft. lbs.
10. Install right output shaft and axle.
11. Position final drive cover to final drive and install screws to 30 ft. lbs.—through 1973; 13 ft. lbs.—1974 and later.
12. Fill final drive unit. Tighten lower shock nut to 75 lbs.
13. Install wheels and tires, tightening nuts finger tight.
14. Lower car and tighten wheel nuts to 105 ft. lbs.—through 1972; 130 ft. lbs.—1973 and later.
15. Install bolts A and B and nut H, tightening to 25 ft. lbs.
16. Install new O-ring on transmission filler tube, remove plug in filler tube hole and install filler tube.
17. Position the transmission cooler line clips and secure the support bracket with the screw.
18. Connect battery.
19. Check engine oil and transmission fluid. Start engine and add fluid as needed.
20. After running check the seals for leaks.

FRONT SUSPENSION

The front suspension consists of control arms, stabilizer bar, shock absorbers and a right and left torsion bar. Torsion bars are used in place of conventional coil springs. The front end of the torsion bar is attached to the lower control arm. The rear of the torsion bar is mounted into an adjustable arm at the torsion bar crossmember. The ride height of the car is controlled by this adjustment. See the Front End Alignment Unit Repair Section for ride height adjustment and alignment.

Wheel Hub and Upper Ball Joint Removal and Installation

1. Remove hub cap, loosen wheel nuts, remove drive axle cotter pin and loosen drive axle nut.
2. Jack up car and place axle stands under lower control arms.
3. Remove axle nut and wheel and tire assembly.
4. Remove brake hose and caliper.
NOTE: *Match-mark disc and hub, then remove the disc.*
5. Remove upper ball joint cotter pin and loosen stud nut.

6. Strike steering knuckle near upper joint to separate it from taper.
7. Cover the lower control arm torsion bar connector with a short piece of rubber hose to avoid damaging the inboard tri-pot joint seal when the hub and knuckle are removed.
8. Remove tie-rod end cotter pin and nut.
9. Separate tie-rod end from steering knuckle using a tie-rod splitter.
10. Remove lower ball joint cotter pin and stud nut.
11. Disconnect lower ball joint.
12. Remove hub, backing plate and steering knuckle as an assembly.
13. To install, reverse removal procedure. Tighten upper ball joint stud to 60 ft. lbs.; tighten lower ball joint stud to 80 ft. lbs. Tighten tie-rod end nut to 40 ft. lbs. Tighten drive axle nut to 110 ft. lbs. (150 ft. lbs.—1972-73). Tighten wheel lug nuts to 105 ft. lbs.—1972; 130 ft. lbs.—1973 and later models.

Torsion Bar Removal and Installation

1. Jack up car and support so that front suspension hangs at full rebound.
2. Remove adjusting bolt from both torsion bar locknuts.
3. Install torsion bar remover and installer tool on torsion bar crossmember.
4. Tighten center bolt of tool until adjusting arm is raised high enough to permit removal of locknut. Remove locknut.

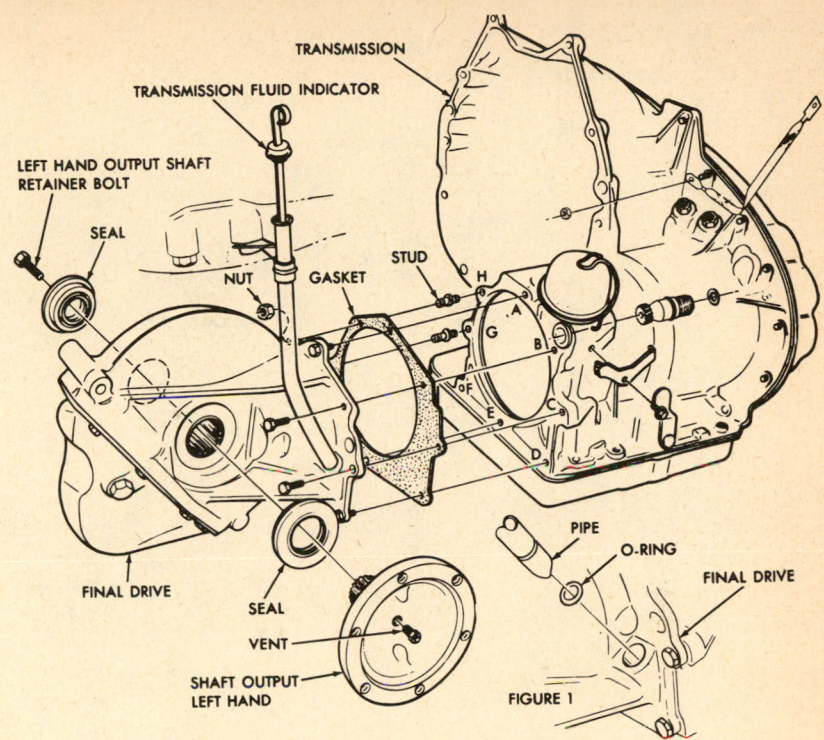

Final drive-to-transmission assembly
(© Cadillac Div., G.M. Corp.)

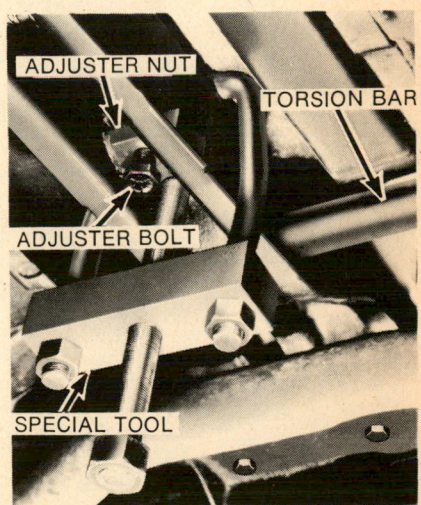

Torsion bar remover and installer
(© Cadillac Div., G.M. Corp.)

5. Repeat Steps 3 and 4 on other side of crossmember.
6. Remove parking brake cable guide at right side of underbody.
7. Remove torsion bar crossmember bolts and retainers from both sides. On 1974-76 models with air bags (ACRS), remove the lock pins and retainers from either end of the crossmember.
8. Move crossmember toward side opposite the torsion bar being removed. One side of crossmember should clear frame at this point.
9. Lower the free end on the crossmember and drive it rearward until torsion bar is free. It may be neces-

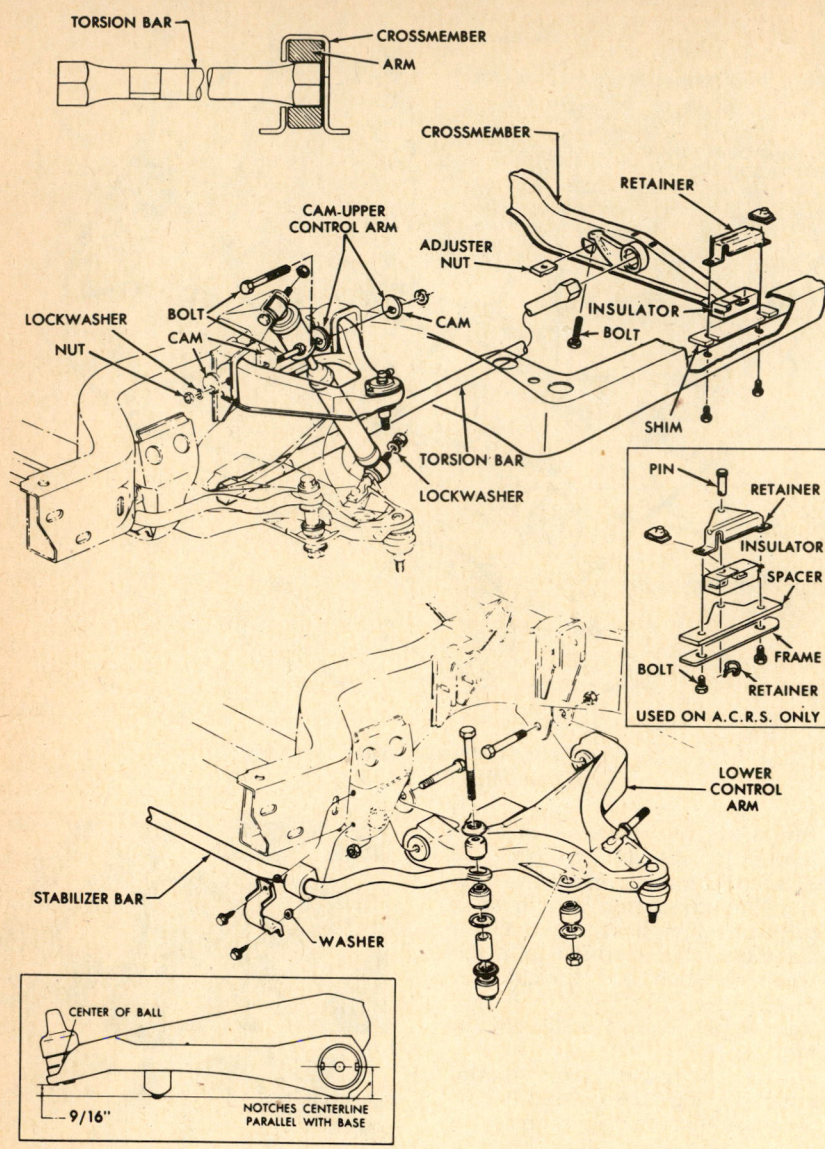

CASTER AND CAMBER CAMS

Front suspension disassembled—1975 shown. Right inset shows crossmember lockpins and retainers used on cars equipped with air bags (ACRS).
(© Cadillac Div., G.M. Corp.)

Caster and camber cam locations

5. Using hammer and a drift, drive on spindle until upper ball joint stud is disengaged.
6. Remove upper control arm cam assemblies and remove control arm from car.
7. To replace guide upper control arm over shock absorber and install bushing ends into frame horns.
8. Install cam assemblies.

NOTE: *Both cams are mounted with the bolt holes downward.*

9. Install ball joint stud into knuckle. Install caliper.
10. Install brake hose clip on ball joint stud.
11. Install ball joint nut. Torque 60 ft. lbs. and insert cotter pin, crimp.

NOTE: *The cotter pin must be crimped toward the upper control arm to prevent interference with the outer C. V. joint seal.*

12. Install upper shock attaching bolt and nut. Torque to 75 ft. lbs.
13. Install wheel.
14. Lower hoist.
15. Check camber, caster and toe-in, and adjust if necessary.

Lower Control Arm Removal and Installation

1. Remove wheel disc and loosen wheel mounting nuts.
2. Remove hub cotter pin. Loosen nut.
3. Raise car and remove wheel and tire.
4. Remove torsion bar, as described previously.
5. Remove hub nut and washer, and brake line clips attached to frame.

sary to loosen parking brake adjuster nut to gain slack in cable.

NOTE: *Although both torsion bars can be removed at this point, it has been found much easier to do only one side at a time.*

10. Remove torsion bar from lower control arm.

NOTE: *Nicks or scratches in the torsion bar can cause its failure.*

11. Lubricate 3 in. of each end of torsion bar. Bars are marked L or R for left and right sides—do not interchange.
12. Slide torsion bar into lower control arm as far as it will go after installing the torsion bar seal.
13. Position adjusting arm in crossmember. Holding arm in place, slide torsion bar rearward until it is seated in adjusting arm. The torsion bars are stamped L for left

and R for right. The stamped end is installed in the lower control arm.

14. Position crossmember to frame and reverse Steps 1-7 of Removal procedure.

Upper Control Arm Removal and Installation

NOTE: *The upper control arm can be serviced as an assembly, although bushings and upper ball joint kits are available.*

1. Hoist car and remove wheel. Support the car on jackstands as close to the ball joints as possible.
2. Remove upper shock absorber attaching bolt.
3. Remove cotter pin and nut on upper ball joint.
4. Disconnect brake hose clamp from ball joint stud. Remove caliper.

6. Remove cotter pin, nut and brake line clip from upper ball joint and remove joint from steering knuckle with a hammer and drift.
7. Disconnect shock absorber and remove.
8. Disconnect tie-rod end at steering knuckle with tie-rod end puller.
9. Disconnect stabilizer bar and nut and link bolt.
10. Disconnect lower ball joint with ball joint puller and adapter.
11. Disengage hub, knuckle and disc as an assembly and secure to upper control arm with wire.
12. Remove lower control arm to frame nuts and bolts and disengage arm from frame mounts.
13. Install hub, disc and knuckle assembly on drive axle.
14. Install lower control arms into mounts at chassis.

NOTE: *Do not tighten the nuts now.*

15. Install lower control arm ball joint into steering knuckle. Tighten nut to 80 ft. lbs. Install the cotter pin.
16. Tighten lower control arm bolts to 80 ft. lbs.
17. Install shock absorber and tighten nut to 75 ft. lbs.
18. Install upper control arm ball joint into steering knuckle and install brake line clip. Tighten nut to 60 ft. lbs. Install cotter pin.
19. Install brake line clip to chassis.
20. Install tie-rod end in steering knuckle, tightening nut to 40 ft. lbs.
21. Install stabilizer bar.
22. Install hub to drive axle washer and nut.
23. Install torsion bar.
24. Install wheel and tire.
25. Lower car.
26. Tighten hub-to-drive axle nut to 110 ft. lbs. (150 ft. lbs. for 1972-73), and install the cotter pin. Tighten the wheel lug nuts to 105 ft. lbs.—1972; 130 ft. lbs.—1973 and later.
27. Install wheel disc.

Ball Joint Checks

VERTICAL CHECK

1. Raise the car and position floor stands under the left and right lower control arm, as near as possible to each lower ball joint. Car must be stable and should not rock on floor stands.
2. Position dial indicator to register vertical movement at wheel hub.
3. Place a pry bar between the lower control arm and the outer race, and pry down on the bar. Very little pressure is necessary. Often the weight of the bar is sufficient. Care must be used so that the drive axle seal is not damaged. The vertical reading must not exceed 0.125 in.

HORIZONTAL CHECK

1. Place car on floor stands as outlined in Step 1 in the Vertical Check.

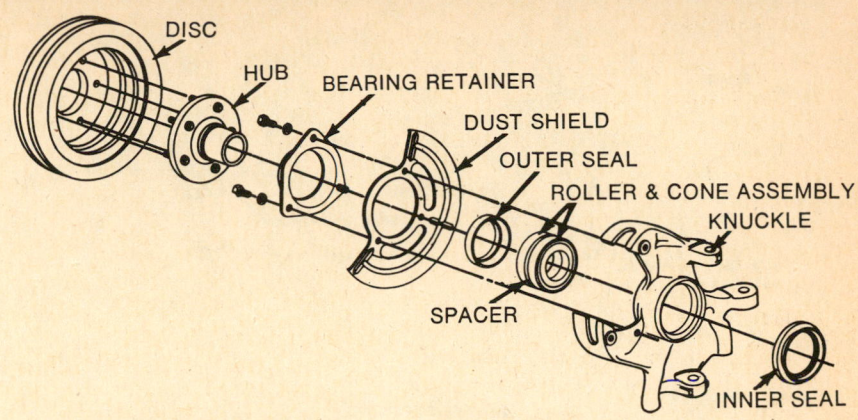

Front hub, bearing, and retainer (© Cadillac Div., G.M. Corp)

2. Position dial indicator at the rim of the wheel, to indicate side play.
3. Grasp wheel, top and bottom, and push in on the bottom of the tire while pulling out at the top. Read gauge, then reverse the push-pull procedure. Horizontal deflection on the gauge should not exceed 0.125 in. at the wheel rim.

Lower Ball Joint Removal and Installation

1. Remove the lower control arm.
2. Using chisel, cut the three rivet heads off.
3. By using a 7/32 in. drill bit, drill side rivets 3/16 in. deep.
4. Using hammer and punch, drive center rivet of joint, until joint is out of the control arm.
5. Install service ball joint into control arm and torque bolts and nut.
6. Reverse lower control arm removal.

Lower Ball Joint Seal Removal and Installation

The lower ball joint seal can be installed with the lower control arm either in or out of the car.

1. Remove steering knuckle.
2. Using hammer and chisel, tap lightly on the seal retainer.
3. Work the retainer off the joint with a small screwdriver.
4. Wipe grease from ball joint and stud.
5. Position new seal over ball joint stud.
6. Lubricate jaws of camber adjusting wrench and carefully slide jaw between seal and retainer.
7. Tap lightly with hammer on center bolt of the wrench until retainer is fully seated.
8. Install knuckle.
9. Lubricate the ball joint fitting until grease is apparent in seal.

Shock Absorber Replacement

The front shock absorbers should be removed with the car on a platform type hoist, so that the vehicle weight is supported on the front suspension. If a platform hoist is available, ignore Steps

1-3. If no platform hoist is available, support the car as indicated in Steps 1-3.

1. Remove wheel disc and loosen wheel mounting nuts.
2. Raise car, place on stands, and remove wheel and tire.
3. Place a hydraulic jack under lower control arm and raise so that load is taken off shock absorber.
4. Disconnect shock absorber at upper and lower mount.
5. Compress shock absorber, working lower mount free from mount bolt.
6. Remove shock absorber.

NOTE: *Purge new shocks of air by repeatedly extending them in the normal postion and compressing them while inverted.*

7. Install by reversing procedure, tightening shock absorber nuts to 75 ft. lbs. and wheel mounting nuts to 105 ft. lbs. (130 ft. lbs. for 1973 and later).

Front Wheel Bearing Adjustment

1. Raise the front of the car and remove the wheel covers from the wheels and the dust covers, nut locks and cotter pins from the spindles.
2. Tighten the adjusting nut to 15 ft. lbs.
3. Once the correct torque is obtained, back the nut off until it is just loose (1 flat).
4. Tighten the nut finger tight only.
5. Install cotter pin.

NOTE: *If the cotter pin cannot be installed, back the adjusting nut off to the next hole.*

REAR SUSPENSION

This system is a four-link, coil spring suspension having no components interchangeable with other Cadillac models.

The rear axle is a straight, hollow tube design. The spindles are pressed

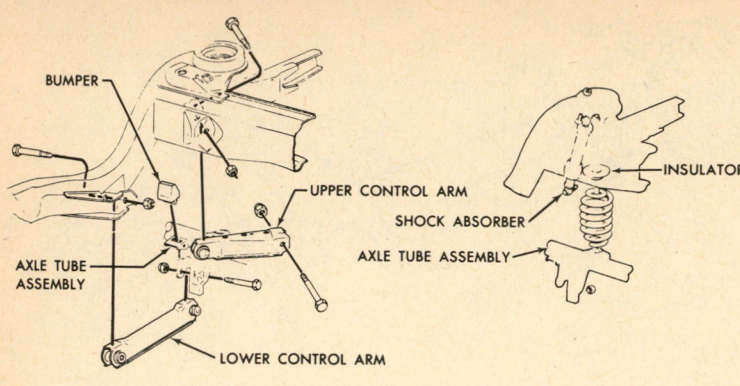

Rear suspension
(© Cadillac Div., G.M. Corp.)

and bolted to the axle flanges and tapered roller bearings are used. The Track Master system, optional on 1972 models, uses a hollow spindle through which the drive cables for the speed sensors run.

Upper Control Arm Removal and Installation

1. Jack up car and support rear on axle stands under frame side members.
2. Disconnect Automatic Level Control system over-travel link at right upper control arm axle bracket, then position lever in center position.
3. Disconnect lower shock bolt and position shock out of the way.
4. Jack up under rear axle to unload upper control arm.

5. Remove bolt and nut that secures upper arm to axle bracket.
6. Remove bolt and nut that secures upper arm to crossmember; remove arm.

NOTE: *Bushings can be replaced at this point.*

7. Install upper arm to brackets and install bolts and nuts. Do not tighten nuts at this time.
8. Install lower shock bolt and shock.
9. Jack up on rear axle and remove axle stands under frame side members.
10. With weight of car on axle only, tighten upper arm-to-crossmember nuts to 100 ft. lbs. (145 ft. lbs. 1973 and later) and lower axle bracket nuts to 75 ft. lbs. (110 ft. lbs. 1973 and later).
11. Install A.L.C. overtravel lever,

lower car and inflate system to 140 psi.

NOTE: *Control arm pivot bolts must be tightened at standing height or ride will be affected.*

12. Inspect brake lines for damage.

Lower Control Arm Removal and Installation

1. Jack up car.
2. Remove bolts and nuts that secure lower arm to axle and frame.
3. Remove lower control arm.
4. Install lower arm and tighten bolts to 100 ft. lbs. (145 ft. lbs. 1973 and later).

Coil Spring Removal and Installation

1. Remove both upper control arms from their axle mountings.
2. Disconnect both rear shocks at lower ends.
3. Disconnect brake hose and cap brake line.
4. Lower axle carefully, using a floor jack, until springs can be removed.

--- CAUTION ---

If the axle is lowered beyond full rebound, the springs can jump from their seats with considerable force. For this reason lower only far enough to allow the springs to be lightly compressed by hand and removed.

5. Inspect rubber insulators for damage.
6. Insert springs and jack up axle until springs are compressed.
7. Reconnect shocks and upper control arms.
8. Connect brake hose and bleed rear brake circuit.

Shock Absorber Removal and Installation

1. Raise and support the car.
2. If the car is equipped with ALC, disconnect the air lines at the shock absorbers.
3. Remove the upper and lower mounting nuts and bolts.
4. Remove the shock absorber from its mounts.
5. Installation is the reverse of removal. Torque the upper nuts to 20 ft. lbs. and the lower nuts to 60 ft. lbs.

NOTE: *Purge new shocks of air by repeatedly extending them in the normal postion and compressing while inverted.*

Rear Wheel Bearing Adjustment

Regularly scheduled wheel bearing repacking is not required. When major brake service is required, it is recommended that the rear wheel bearings be cleaned and repacked with a high melting point grade 2 lithium grease.

1972

1. Adjustment should be made

Location of the automatic level control components (© Cadillac Div., G.M. Corp)

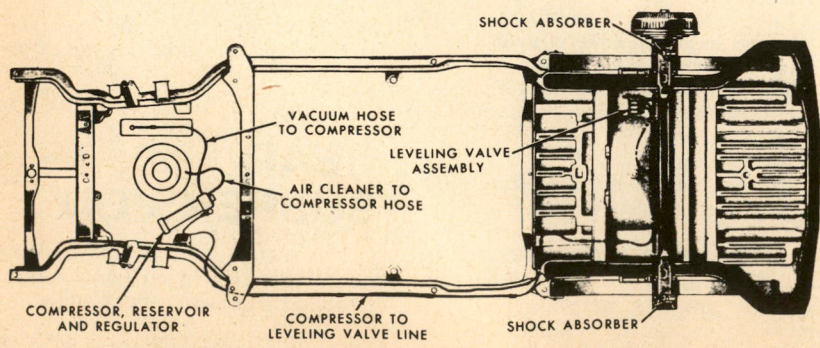

Automatic leveling system (© Cadillac Div., G.M. Corp)

while revolving the wheel at least 3 times the speed of nut rotation through at least 3 revolutions.

2. Check to be sure that the hub is completely seated on the spindle.
3. While rotating the wheel assembly, tighten the spindle nut to 15 ft. lbs.
4. Back the spindle nut off until it is free.
5. Tighten the nut finger-tight and insert the cotter pin.
6. If the cotter pin cannot be inserted in either of the 2 holes, back the nut off until it can be inserted.
7. Peen the end of the pin securely.
8. If equipped with Track Master, insert the pin into the end of the sensor assembly using pliers, and install insulators on each end of the pin. The pin should protrude equally from each end of the sensor.
9. Install the dust cap, or if equipped with Track Master, install the drive cap.

1973 AND LATER

1. Adjustment should be made while rotating the wheel at least 3 times the speed of the nut rotation through at least 3 revolutions.
2. While rotating the hub, tighten the spindle nut to 25-30 ft. lbs.
3. Back the nut off 1/2 turn and tighten it to 24 in. lbs. Install the cotter pin.
4. If the cotter pin cannot be installed, back the nut off until it can be installed.
5. The final adjustment should be 24 in. lbs nut torque to 0.004 in. bearing play.
6. Peen the end of the cotter pin and install the dust cap.

BRAKES

Single-piston, sliding caliper Delco-Moraine disc brakes are standard equipment on the front wheels of all Eldorado models. The master cylinders used with these brakes are the same as for the same year Cadillac, even though the Eldorado uses tandem power booster units.

A foot-operated, vacuum-released parking brake working on the rear drums via mechanical linkage is used through 1975. This is virtually identical to the parking brake used on other Cadillac models.

Beginning 1976, hydraulically-assisted four-wheel disc brakes are standard. 11 in. diameter single-piston disc brakes with integral parking brake and automatic adjusters are used on the rear. Front and rear brake calipers and pads are not interchangeable.

The hydraulic power booster is called Hydro-boost. The booster uses power steering pump fluid pressure to multiply brake pedal force applied to the master cylinder. The booster unit is

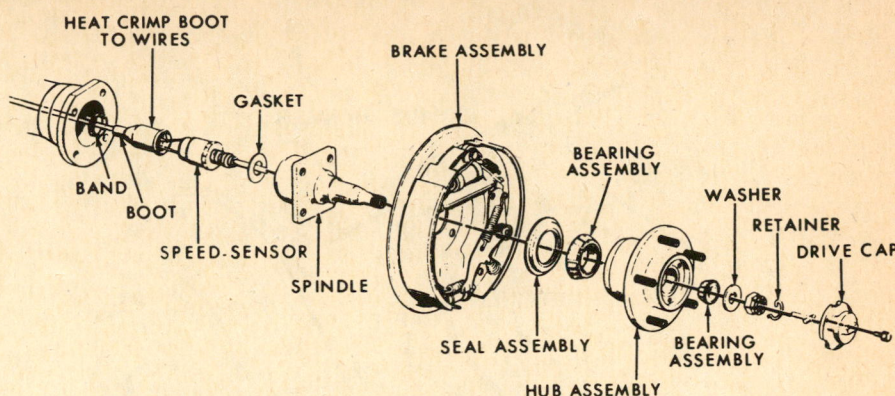

Rear axle disassembled— with Track Master (© Cadillac Div., G.M. Corp.)

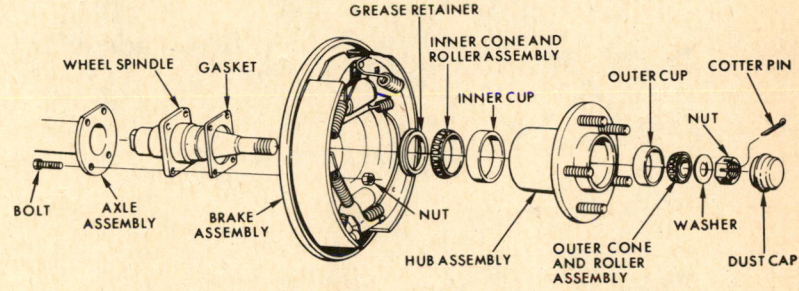

Rear axle disassembled (© Cadillac Div., G.M. Corp.)

mounted on the firewall in the same location as previous vacuum boosters. A larger capacity power steering pump reservoir is used in addition to a fluid cooler and filter. A reserve accumulator system stores pressurized fluid to provide a minimum of three power-assisted brake applications should pump pressure be stopped. Non-assisted braking is available when the reserve system is exhausted.

For brake service, see the Unit Repair Section of this manual.

Master Cylinder Removal and Installation

See the Cadillac section.

Power Brake Vacuum Booster Removal and Installation

1. Disconnect hydraulic lines from master cylinder.
2. Disconnect vacuum line from vacuum check valve on unit.
3. Remove steering column lower cover.
4. Remove cotter pin, washer and spring spacer that secure power unit pushrod to brake pedal arm.
5. Remove the four nuts that secure power unit to firewall, then remove power unit.
6. To install, reverse removal procedure.

Hydro-Boost Removal and Installation

1. With engine off, pump brake pedal four or five times to empty accumulator of pressurized fluid.

CAUTION

Power steering fluid and brake fluid are incompatible. If brake seals contact steering fluid or steering seals contact brake fluid, the seals will be damaged.

---

2. Remove the two master cylinder-to-booster attaching nuts and move the master cylinder away from the booster with brake lines attached.
3. Remove and plug the three hydraulic lines from the booster. Remove the washer and retainer that secures the booster pedal rod to the brake pedal arm.
4. Remove the four nuts which attach the booster to the firewall.

NOTE: *To avoid damaging the booster, never pry the pedal rod off the pedal arm.*

5. Loosen the booster from the firewall and move the booster pedal rod inboard until it disconnects from the brake pedal arm. Remove the spring washer from the brake pedal arm and remove the booster.
6. To install, reverse the removal procedure. Tighten the booster mounting nuts to 15 ft. lbs. and the master cylinder-to-booster mounting nuts to 20 ft. lbs. Bleed the Hydroboost system as explained in the Brakes Unit Repair Section.

Parking Brake Adjustment
THROUGH 1975

See the Cadillac section.

1976 AND LATER

1. Lubricate the parking brake cables at the equalizer hooks and un-

Cadillac Eldorado

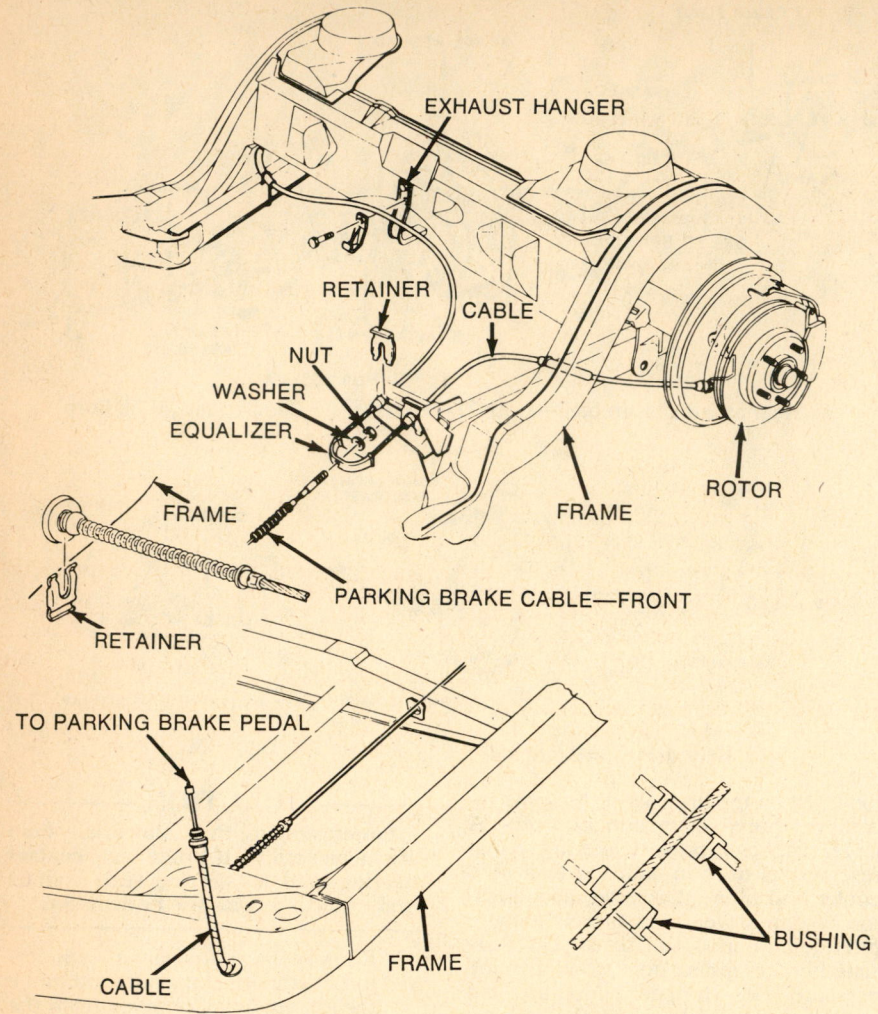

Parking brake cables—1976 and later
(© Cadillac Div., G.M. Corp.)

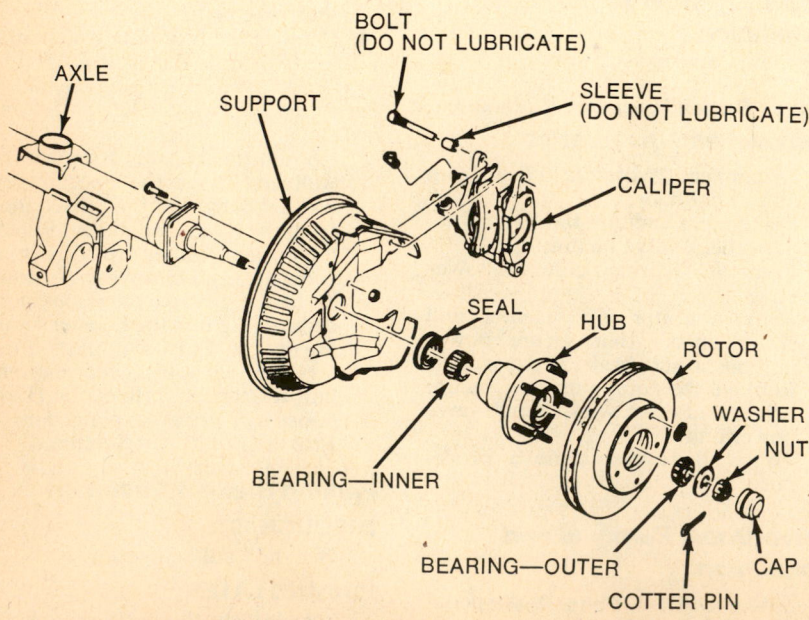

Rear disc brake details   (© Cadillac Div., G.M. Corp.)

derbody rub points. Check for free movement of all cables.
2. With the parking brake in the fully released position, jack the rear of the car to raise the rear wheels off the floor.
3. Hold the brake cable stud from turning and tighten the equalizer nut until slack is removed.
4. Make sure that the caliper levers are against their stops on the caliper housings. If the levers are off their stops, loosen the cable until the levers return to their stops.
5. Operate the parking brake pedal several times to check the adjustment. After adjustment, the parking brake pedal should travel 4-5$\frac{1}{2}$ in. with an approximate force of 125 lbs. on the pedal.
6. Lower the car.

NOTE: *The caliper levers must be on their stops after adjustment.*

STEERING

The steering linkage on the Eldorado is composed of a pitman arm, idler arm, a pair of tie rod assemblies, a drag link, and a shock absorber. The pitman arm connects the left side of the drag link to the steering gear while the idler arm connects the right side of the drag link to the frame. The small shock absorber connects the drag link to the frame and serves to dampen the vibrations in the linkage. The tie rods connect the drag link with the steering knuckles.

Steering Linkage Removal and Installation
1. Remove the front wheels.
2. Remove the steering damper from the frame.
3. Remove all the cotter pins and nuts from the pitman arm and the idler arm pivots on the drag link.
4. Using a puller, remove both the idler and pitman arm pivots from the drag link.

NOTE: *It may be necessary to loosen the steering gear from the frame to remove the drag link from the pitman arm.*

5. The cotter pins and nuts from the outer tie rod pivots should be removed at the steering knuckles. Then separate the tie rod pivots from the steering knuckles.
6. The linkage can be removed from the frame.
7. If the idler arm is to be removed, loosen the locknut and bolt which fastens it to the frame.
8. Installation is accomplished by reversing the removal procedure. The torque on the damper should be 40 ft. lbs. while the tie rod torque is 60 ft. lbs.

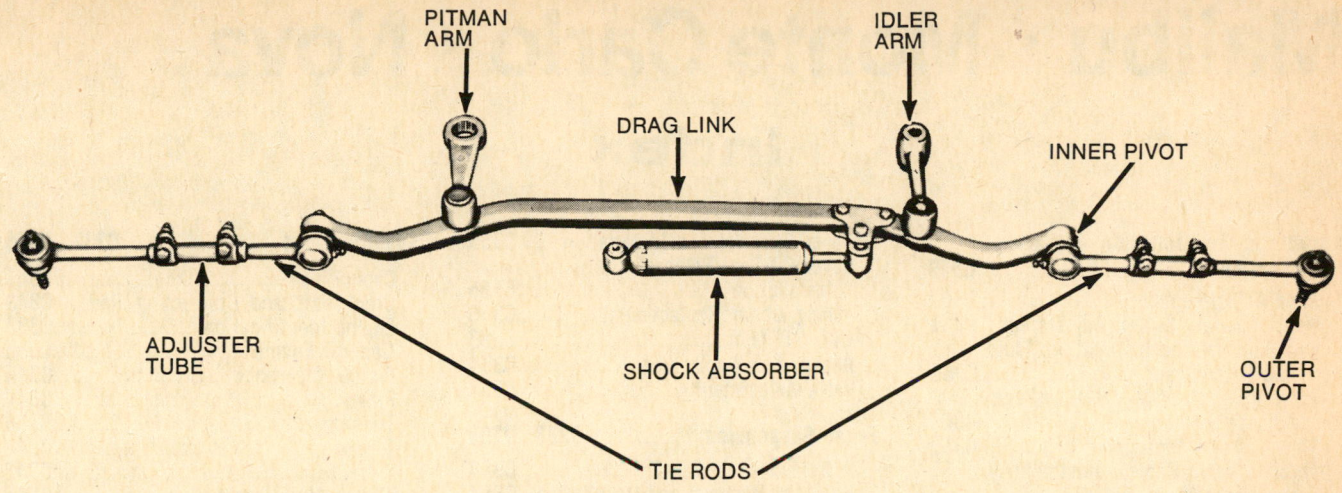

Steering linkage
(© Cadillac Div., G.M. Corp.)

Power Steering Pump, Steering Wheel, Turn Signal Switch, Ignition Switch, and Lock Cylinder Removal and Installation

See the Cadillac Section.

INSTRUMENT PANEL

Headlight Switch Removal and Installation

1. Disconnect negative battery cable. Remove steering column lower cover.
2. Disconnect wiring harness retainer below headlight switch assembly.
3. Depress spring loaded release button on top of headlight switch and remove switch, knob and rod assembly (switch "on").
4. Remove screw with ground wire at bottom of switch housing.
5. Pull assembly down and rearward, disconnect wiring harness connectors, two bulbs and remove assembly.
6. Install in reverse of above.

Speedometer Cable Removal and Installation

See the Cadillac Section

WINDSHIELD WIPERS

See the Cadillac Section

RADIO

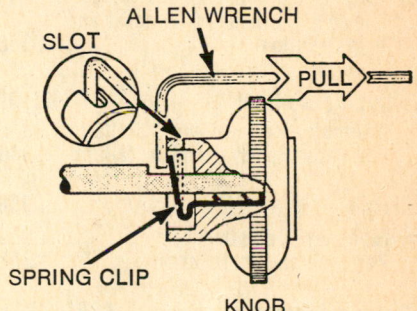

Radio knob removal
(© Cadillac Div., G.M. Corp.)

HEATER

See the Cadillac Section.

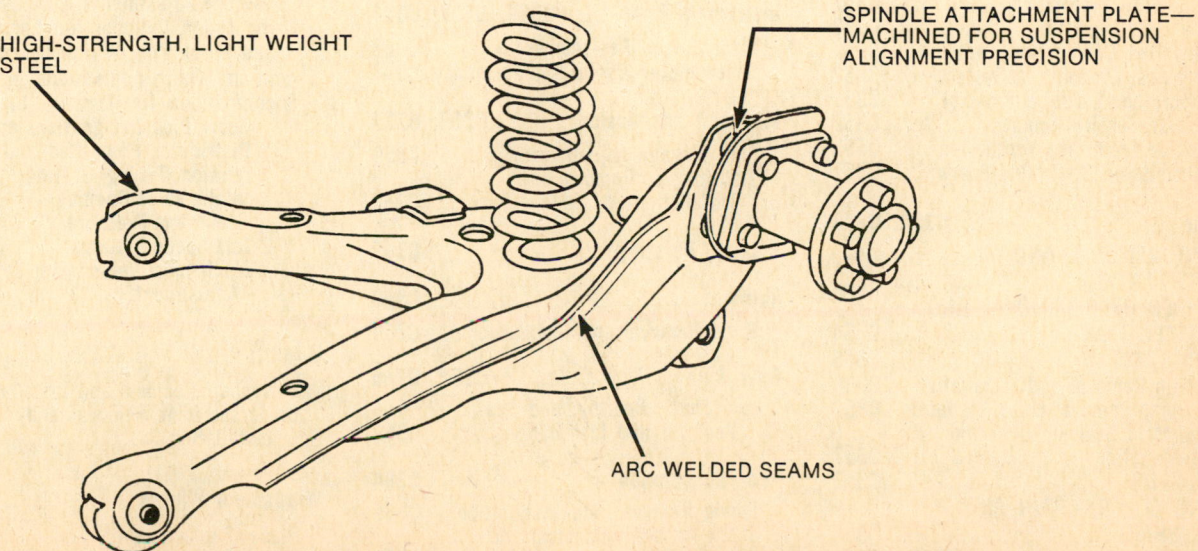

1979 Eldorado independent rear suspension. Toe-in is adjusted at the inner pivot of the control arm. The rear (and front) wheel bearings require no service or adjustment, and are replaced as a unit. This system is also used on the 1979 Toronado and Riviera.

Camaro · Chevelle · Malibu · Monte Carlo · Nova

Index

Camaro • Chevelle • Malibu • Monte Carlo • Nova

YEAR IDENTIFICATION

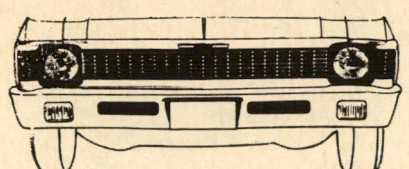

1972 Nova

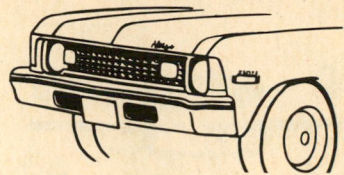

1973 Nova

1974 Nova

1975 Nova LN

1975 Nova LN

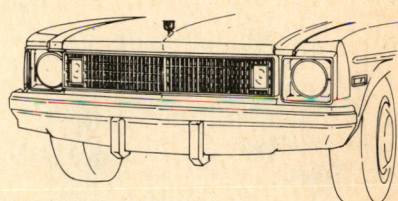

1977 Nova

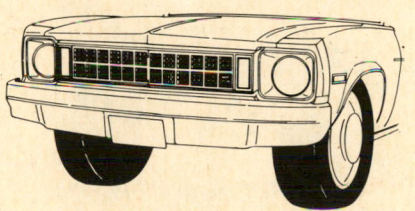

1978 Nova

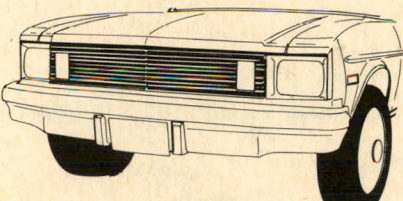

1979 Nova

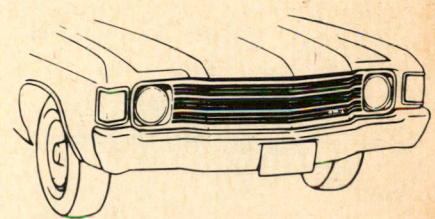

1972 Chevelle

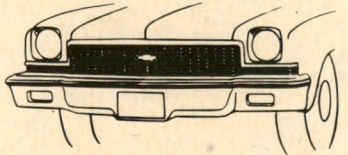

1973 Chevelle

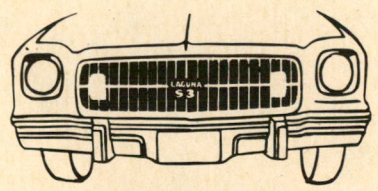

1974 Chevelle Laguna

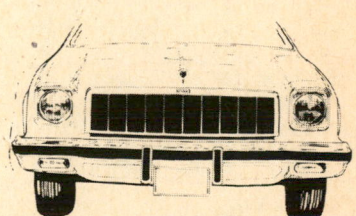

1975 Malibu Classic

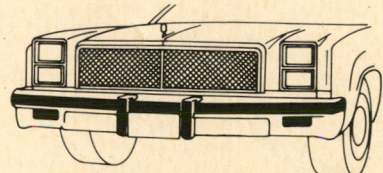

1976 Malibu Classic

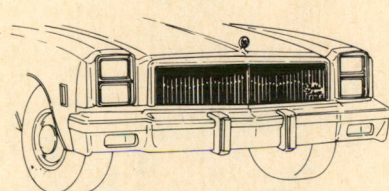

1977 Malibu Classic

1978 Malibu Classic

1979 Malibu Classic

1972 Camaro

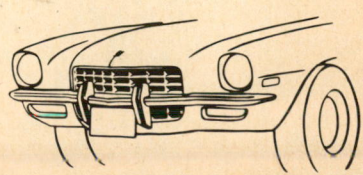

1973 Camaro

Camaro • Chevelle • Malibu • Monte Carlo • Nova

YEAR IDENTIFICATION

1974 Camaro

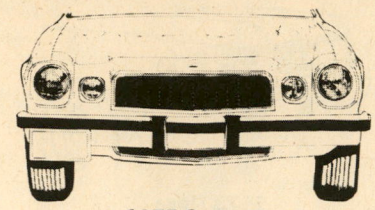

1975 Camaro

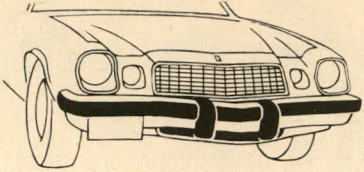

1976-77 Camaro

1978 Camaro

1979 Camaro

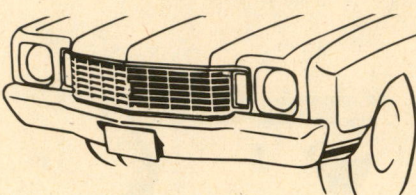

1972 Monte Carlo

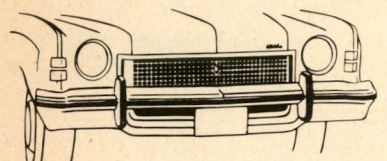

1973 Monte Carlo

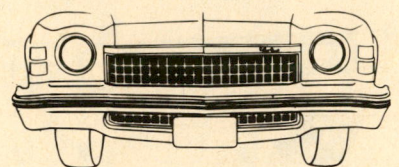

1974 Monte Carlo

1975 Monte Carlo

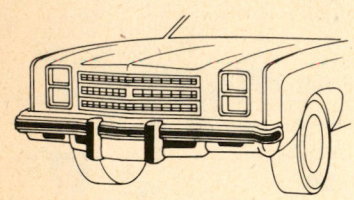

1976 Monte Carlo

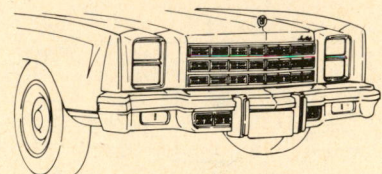

1977 Monte Carlo

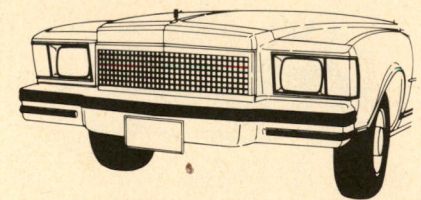

1978 Monte Carlo

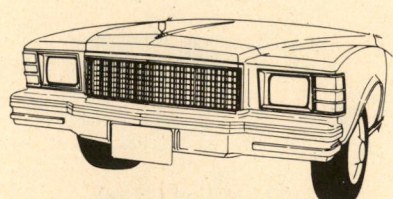

1979 Monte Carlo

ENGINE IDENTIFICATION

Engine identification can be determined in one of two ways. Some 1972-73 cars with V8 engines have a 3 letter engine identification code stamped on a pad on the front side of the block. All other cars have the engine identification code stamped as the fifth digit of the Vehicle Identification Code on a plate on the upper left corner of the instrument panel pad, visible through the windshield.

Camaro

No. Cyls.	Cu. In. Displ.	Type	YEAR AND CODE							
			1972	1973	1974	1975	1976	1977	1978	1979
6	250	All	D	D	D	D	D	D	D	D
8	305	2bbl					Q	U	U	U
8	307	All	F	F						
8	350	MT 2bbl	CKA	CKA						
8	350	MT 4bbl		CLJ CKB						
8	350	Z28 MT	CKS							
8	350	MT 2bbl w/EEC	CMH	CKY						
8	350	MT 4bbl w/EEC	CDG	CLL CKH						
8	350	TH350 2bbl	CTL	CKW						
8	350	TH350 4bbl	CKD	CLK						
8	350	TH400	CKD	CLK						
8	350	AT Z28	CKT	CLK						
8	350	AT 2bbl w/EEC	CMB	CKX						
8	350	AT 4bbl w/EEC	CDD	CKD						
8	350	2bbl			H	H				
8	350	4bbl			T	T	L	L	L	L
8	400	MT	CLA							
8	400	MT w/AIR	CTA							
8	400	AT	CLB							
8	400	AT w/AIR	CTB							

MT: Manual Transmission
AT: Automatic Transmission
PG: Power Glide
TH: Turbo Hydra-Matic
AIR: Air Injection Reactor
EEC: Exhaust Emission Control
DE: Dual exhaust

Chevelle, Monte Carlo, Malibu

No. Cyls.	Cu. In. Displ.	Type	YEAR AND CODE							
			1972	1973	1974	1975	1976	1977	1978	1979
6	200	All							M	M
6	231	All							A	A
6	250	All	D	D	D	D	D	D		
8	267	2bbl								
8	305	2bbl					Q	U	U	
8	305	4bbl								H
8	307	All	F	F						
8	350	MT 2bbl	CKA	CKA						
8	350	MT 4bbl	CKK	CKB						
8	350	MT 2bbl w/EEC	CDA	CKC						

Camaro • Chevelle • Malibu • Monte Carlo • Nova

Chevelle, Monte Carlo, Malibu

No. Cyls.	Cu. In. Displ.	Type	1972	1973	1974	1975	1976	1977	1978	1979
						YEAR AND CODE					
8	350	MT 4bbl w/EEC	CDG	CKH						
8	350	PG	CKB							
8	350	PG w/EEC	CDB							
8	350	TH350 2bbl	CTL	CKL						
8	350	TH350 4bbl	CKD	CKJ						
8	350	TH350 2bbl w/EEC	CMD	CKK						
8	350	TH350 4bbl w/EEC	CDD	CKD						
8	350	Police	CSH							
8	350	Police/EEC	CAR							
8	350	2bbl			H	H	V			
8	350	4bbl			J	J	L	L	L	L
8	350	4bbl DE			T	T				
8	400	MT	CLA CLS							
8	400	MT w/AIR	CTA							
8	400	MT w/HD 3sp.	CTH							
8	400	AT 2bbl	CLB							
8	400	AT 4bbl			R	U	U			
8	400	AT 2bbl w/AIR	CTA							
8	400	AT 4bbl w/AIR	CTB							
8	454	MT 365hp	CPA	CWA						
8	454	AT	CPD	CWB	Y	Y				
8	454	AT w/AIR	CRW							
8	454	AT w/EEC		CWD	Z					
8	454	MT w/AIR	CRX	CWC						

Nova

No. Cyls.	Cu. In. Displ.	Type	1972	1973	1974	1975	1976	1977	1978	1979
						YEAR AND CODE					
6	250	All	D	D	D	D	D	D	D	D
8	262	All				G	G			
8	305	2bbl					Q	U	U	U
8	307	All	F	F						
8	350	MT 2bbl	CKA	CKA						
8	350	MT 4bbl	CKK	CKB						
8	350	MT 2bbl w/EEC	CDA	CKC						
8	350	MT 4bbl w/EEC	CDG	CKH						
8	350	MT 4bbl w/AIR	CRL							
8	350	AT 2bbl	CTL	CKU						
8	350	AT 4bbl	CKD	CKW						
8	350	AT 2bbl w/EEC	CMD	CKK						

Nova

No. Cyls.	Cu. In. Displ.	Type	1972	1973	YEAR AND CODE						
					1974	1975	1976	1977	1978	1979	
8	350	AT 4bbl w/EEC	CDD	CKD							
8	350	AT 4bbl w/AIR	CRL								
8	350	2bbl			H	L					
8	350	4bbl			J	J	L	L	L	L	

GENERAL ENGINE SPECIFICATIONS

Year	Engine No. Cyl. Displacement (cu in.)	Carburetor Type	Horsepower @ rpm ∎	Torque @ rpm (ft lbs) ∎	Bore x Stroke (in.)	Compression Ratio	Oil Pressure @ 2000 rpm
'72	6-250	1 bbl	110 @ 3800	185 @ 1600	3.875 x 3.530	8.5:1	40
	8-307	2 bbl	130 @ 4000	230 @ 2400	3.875 x 3.250	8.5:1	40
	8-350	2 bbl	165 @ 4000	280 @ 2400	4.000 x 3.480	8.5:1	40
	8-350	4 bbl	200 @ 4400	300 @ 2800	4.000 x 3.480	8.5:1	40
	8-350	4 bbl	255 @ 5600	280 @ 4000	4.000 x 3.480	9.0:1	40
	8-402	4 bbl	240 @ 4400	345 @ 3200	4.126 x 3.760	8.5:1	40
	8-454	4 bbl	220 @ 4000	390 @ 3200	3.875 x 3.530	8.25:1	40
'73	6-250	1 bbl	100 @ 3800	175 @ 1600	4.251 x 4.000	8.5:1	40
	8-307	2 bbl	115 @ 4000	205 @ 2000	3.875 x 3.250	8.5:1	40
	8-350	2 bbl	145 @ 4000	255 @ 2400	4.000 x 3.480	8.5:1	40
	8-350	4 bbl	175 @ 4400	270 @ 2400	4.000 x 3.480	8.5:1	40
	8-350	4 bbl	245 @ 5200	280 @ 4000	4.000 x 3.480	9.0:1	40
	8-454	4 bbl	245 @ 4000	375 @ 2800	4.251 x 4.000	8.5:1	40
'74	6-250	1 bbl	100 @ 3600	175 @ 1800	3.875 x 3.530	8.25:1	40
	8-350	2 bbl	145 @ 3600	250 @ 2200	4.000 x 3.480	8.5:1	40
	8-350	4 bbl	160 @ 3800	245 @ 2400	4.000 x 3.480	8.5:1	40
	8-350	4 bbl	185 @ 4000	270 @ 2600	4.000 x 3.480	8.5:1	40
	8-350	4 bbl	245 @ 5200	280 @ 4000	4.000 x 3.480	9.0:1	40
	8-400	2 bbl	150 @ 3200	295 @ 2600	4.126 x 3.750	8.5:1	40
	8-400	4 bbl	180 @ 3800	290 @ 2400	4.126 x 3.750	8.5:1	40
	8-454	4 bbl	235 @ 4000	360 @ 2800	4.251 x 4.000	8.25:1	44
'75	6-250	1 bbl	105 @ 3800	185 @ 1200	3.875 x 3.530	8.25:1	40
	8-262	2 bbl	110 @ 3600	200 @ 2000	3.671 x 3.10	8.5:1	40
	8-350	2 bbl	145 @ 3800	250 @ 2200	4.000 x 3.480	8.5:1	40
	8-350	4 bbl	155 @ 3800	245 @ 2400①	4.000 x 3.480	8.5:1	40
	8-400	4 bbl	175 @ 3600	305 @ 2000	4.126 x 4.000	8.5:1	40
	8-454	4 bbl	215 @ 4000	350 @ 2400	4.251 x 4.000	8.15:1	44
'76-'77	6-250	1 bbl	105 @ 3800	185 @ 1200	3.875 x 3.530	8.25:1	40
	8-305	2 bbl	140 @ 3800	245 @ 2000	3.736 x 3.480	8.5:1	40
	8-350	2 bbl	145 @ 3800	250 @ 2200	4.000 x 3.480	8.5:1	40
	8-350	4 bbl	165 @ 3800	260 @ 2400	4.000 x 3.480	8.5:1	40
	8-400	4 bbl	175 @ 3600	305 @ 2000	4.126 x 4.000	8.5:1	40
'78-'79	6-200 Chev.	2 bbl	95 @ 3800	160 @ 2000	3.500 x 3.480	8.2:1	40
	6-231 Buick	2 bbl	105 @ 3400	185 @ 2000	3.800 x 3.400	8.0:1	37
	6-250 Chev.	1 bbl	110 @ 3800	190 @ 1600	3.875 x 3.530	8.1:1	40

GENERAL ENGINE SPECIFICATIONS

Year	Engine No. Cyl. Displacement (cu in.)	Carburetor Type	Horsepower @ rpm ■	Torque @ rpm (ft lbs) ■	Bore x Stroke (in.)	Compression Ratio	Oil Pressure @ 2000 rpm
'78-'79	8-305	4 bbl	155 @ 3800	260 @ 2800	3.736 x 3.480	8.4:1	45
	8-305 Chev.	2 bbl	145 @ 3800	245 @ 2400	3.736 x 3.480	8.5:1	40
	8-267	2 bbl	N.A.	N.A.	3.500 x 3.480	8.2:1	45
	8-350 Chev.	4 bbl	170 @ 3800	270 @ 2400	4.000 x 3.480	8.5:1	40
	8-350 Chev.	Z-28	185 @ 4000	280 @ 2400	4.000 x 3.480	8.5:1	40

■ Horsepower and torque are SAE net figures. They are measured at the rear of the transmission with all accessories installed and operating. Since the figures vary when a given engine is installed in different models, some are representative rather than exact.
① 250 @ 2400 in wagon
N.A.: Not Available

Camaro　　TUNE-UP SPECIFICATIONS

When analyzing compression test results, look for uniformity among cylinders rather than specific pressures.

Year	ENGINE No. Cyl. Displacement (cu in.)	hp	SPARK PLUGS Orig. Type	Gap (in.)	DISTRIBUTOR Point Dwell (deg)	Point Gap (in.)	IGNITION TIMING (deg) ▲ ● Man Trans	Auto Trans	VALVES Intake Opens ■ (deg) ●	Fuel Pump Pressure (psi)	IDLE SPEED (rpm) ▲ * Trans Man ●	Trans Auto
'72	6-250	110	R-46T	.035	31-34	.019	4B	4B	16	3½-4½	700	600
	8-307	130	R-44T	.035	29-31	.019	4B	8B	28	5-6½	900	600
	8-350	165	R-44T	.035	29-31	.019	6B	6B	28(44)	7-8½	900	600
	8-350	200	R-44T	.035	29-31	.019	4B	8B	28(44)	7-8½	800	600
	8-350	255	R-44T	.035	29-31	.019	8B	12B	43	7-8½	900	700
	8-402	240	R-44TS	.035	28-30	.019	8B	8B	28	7-8½	800	600
'73	6-250	100	R-46T	.035	31-34	.019	6B	6B	16	3½-4½	700/450	600/450
	8-307	115	R-44T	.035	29-31	.019	4B	8B	28	5-6½	900/450	600/450
	8-350	145	R-44T	.035	29-31	.019	8B	8B	28	7½-8½	900/450	600/450
	8-350	175	R-44T	.035	29-31	.019	8B	12B	28	7½-8½	900/450	600/450
	8-350	245	R-44T	.035	29-31	.019	8B	12B	52	7½-8½	900/450	700/450
'74	6-250	100	R-46T	.035	31-34	.019	6B	6B	16	4-5	800/450	600/450
	8-350	145	R-44T	.035	29-31	.019	4B	8B	28	7½-9	900/450	600/450
	8-350	160	R-44T	.035	29-31	.019	4B	8B	44	7½-9	900/450	600/450
	8-350	185	R-44T	.035	29-31	.019	4B	8B	28	7½-9	900/450	600/450
	8-350	245	R-44T	.035	29-31	.019	8B	8B	52	7½-9	900/450	700/450
'75	6-250	105	R-46TX	.060	Electronic		10B	10B	16	4-5	800/425	550/425① (600/425)
	8-350	145	R-44TX	.060	Electronic		6B	6B	28	7½-9	800	600
	8-350	155	R-44TX	.060	Electronic		6B	8B(6B)	28	7½-9	800	600
'76	6-250	105	R-46TS	.035	Electronic		6B	6B	16	4-5	850	550②(600)
	8-305	140	R-45TS	.045	Electronic		6B	8B(TDC)	28	7½-9	800	600
	8-350	165	R-45TS	.045	Electronic		8B(6B)	8B(6B)	28	7½-9	800	600
'77	6-250	All	R-46TS	.035	Electronic		6B	8B(6B)③	16	4-5	④	550(600)
	8-305	All	R-45TS	.045	Electronic		8B	8B(6B)	28	7½-9	600	500
	8-350	All	R-45TS	.045	Electronic		8B	8B	28	7½-9	700	500

Camaro

TUNE-UP SPECIFICATIONS

When analyzing compression test results, look for uniformity among cylinders rather than specific pressures.

Year	ENGINE No. Cyl. Displacement (cu in.)	hp	SPARK PLUGS Orig. Type	Gap (in.)	DISTRIBUTOR Point Dwell (deg)	Point Gap (in.)	IGNITION TIMING (deg) ▲ ● Man Trans	Auto Trans	VALVES Intake Opens ■ (deg) ●	Fuel Pump Pressure (psi)	IDLE SPEED (rpm) ▲ * Trans Man	● Trans Auto
'78	6-250 Chev.	All	R-46TS	.035	Electronic		6B	②	16	4-5	800/425	550(600)/425(400)
	8-305 Chev.	All	R-45TS	.045	Electronic		4B	4B	28	7.5-9	600	500
	8-350 Chev.	All	R-45TS	.045	Electronic		6B	⑤	28	7.5-9	700	500
'79	6-250 Chev.	All	R-46TS	.035	Electronic		8B	10B(6B)	16	4.5-6.0	800	550
	8-305 Chev.	All	R-45TS	.045	Electronic		4B	4B	28	7.5-9.0	600	500
	8-350 Chev.	All	R-45TS	.045	Electronic		6B	6B(8B)	28	7.5-9.0	700	500

▲ See text for procedure.
● Figure in parentheses indicates California engine
■ All figures Before Top Dead Center
 * When two idle speed figures are separated by a slash, the lower figure is with the idle speed solenoid disconnected.
① Without intake manifold integral with head—600/450
② Non A/C; Non Calif: 10B
  with A/C, except Calif: 8B
  Calif.: 6B
③ 6B for Calif. engines exc. engine code CCC which is 8B
  10B for high altitude engines
④ 750 w/o AC
  800 w/AC
⑤ AT, except Calif. and High Altitude: 6B
  Calif: 8B
  High Alt. w/o A/C: 6B
  High Alt. with A/C: 8B
  A After Top Dead Center
  B Before Top Dead Center
TDC Top Dead Center
 — Not applicable

MECHANICAL VALVE LIFTER CLEARANCE

Year	Engine		Intake (Hot) In.	Exhaust (Hot) In.
1972	V8-350	255 hp	.024	.030

NOTE: The underhood specifications sticker often reflects tune-up specification changes made in production. Sticker figures must be used if they disagree with those in this chart.

Chevelle, Monte Carlo, Malibu

TUNE-UP SPECIFICATIONS

When analyzing compression test results, look for uniformity among cylinders rather than specific pressures.

Year	ENGINE No. Cyl. Displacement (cu in.)	hp	SPARK PLUGS Orig. Type	Gap (in.)	DISTRIBUTOR Point Dwell (deg)	Point Gap (in.)	IGNITION TIMING (deg) ▲ ● Man Trans	Auto Trans	VALVES Intake Opens ■ (deg) ●	Fuel Pump Pressure (psi)	IDLE SPEED (rpm) ▲ * Trans Man	● Trans Auto
'72	6-250	110	R-46TS	.035	31-34	.019	4B	4B	16	3½-4½	700	600
	8-307	130	R-44T	.035	29-31	.019	4B	8B	28	5-6½	900	600
	8-350	165	R-44T	.035	29-31	.019	6B	6B	28	7-8½	900	600
	8-350	175	R-44T	.035	29-31	.019	4B	8B	28	7-8½	800	600
	8-402	240	R-44T	.035	29-31	.019	8B	8B	30	7-8½	750	600
	8-454	270	R-44T	.035	29-31	.019	8B	8B	56	7-8½	750	600
'73	6-250	100	R-46T	.035	31-34	.019	6B	6B	16	3½-4½	700/450	600/450
	8-307	115	R-44T	.035	29-31	.019	4B	8B	28	5-6½	900/450	600/450
	8-350	145	R-44T	.035	29-31	.019	8B	8B	28	7-8½	900/450	600/450
	8-350	175	R-44T	.035	29-31	.019	8B	12B	28	7-8½	900/450	600/450
	8-454	245	R-44T	.035	29-31	.019	10B	10B	55	7-8½	900/450	600/450

Chevelle, Monte Carlo, Malibu   TUNE-UP SPECIFICATIONS

When analyzing compression test results, look for uniformity among cylinders rather than specific pressures.

Year	ENGINE No. Cyl. Displacement (cu in.)	hp	SPARK PLUGS Orig. Type	Gap (in.)	DISTRIBUTOR Point Dwell (deg)	Point Gap (in.)	IGNITION TIMING (deg) ▲ ● Man Trans	Auto Trans	VALVES Intake Opens ■ (deg) ●	Fuel Pump Pressure (psi)	IDLE SPEED (rpm) ▲ * Trans Man	● Trans Auto
'74	6-250	100	R-46T	.035	31-34	.019	6B	6B	16	4-5	800/450	600/450
	8-350	145	R-44T	.035	29-31	.019	4B	8B	28	7½-9	900/450	600/450
	8-350	160	R-44T	.035	29-31	.019	4B	8B	44	7½-9	900/450	600/450
	8-400	150	R-44T	.035	29-31	.019	—	8B	28	7½-9	—	600/450
	8-400	180	R-44T	.035	29-31	.019	—	8B	44	7½-9	—	600/450
	8-454	235	R-44T	.035	29-31	.019	10B	10B	55	7½-9	800/450	600/450
'75	6-250	105	R-46TX	.060	Electronic		10B	10B	16	4-5	850/425	550/425 (600/425)
	8-350	145	R-44TX	.060	Electronic		6B	6B	28	7½-9	—	600
	8-350	155	R-44TX	.060	Electronic		—	6B	28	7½-9	800	600
	8-400	175	R-44TX	.060	Electronic		—	8B	28	7½-9	—	600
	8-454	215	R-44TX	.060	Electronic		—	16B	55	7½-9	—	600/500
'76	6-250	105	R-46TS	.035	Electronic		6B	6B	16	3½-4½	850	550(600)
	8-305	140	R-45TS	.045	Electronic		—	8B(TDC)	28	7-8½	—	600
	8-350	145	R-45TS	.045	Electronic		—	6B	28	7-8½	—	600
	8-350	165	R-45TS	.045	Electronic		—	8B(6B)	28	7-8½	—	600
	8-400	175	R-45TS	.045	Electronic		—	8B	28	7-8½	—	600
'77	6-250	All	R-46TS	.035	Electronic		6B	8B(6B)①	16	4-5	②	550(600)
	8-305	All	R-45TS	.045	Electronic		8B	8B(6B)	28	7½-9	600	500
	8-350	All	R-45TS	.045	Electronic		8B	8B	28	7½-9	700	500
'78	6-200 Chev.	95	R-45TS	.045	Electronic		8B	8B	28	7.5-9	700	600
	6-231 Buick	105	R-46TSX	.060	Electronic		15B	15B	17	6-7	600	500
	8-305 Chev.	145	R-45TS	.045	Electronic		4B	③	28	7.5-9	600	500④
	8-350 Chev.	170	R-45TS	.045	Electronic		—	8B	28	7.5-9	—	500
'79	6-200 Chev.	All	R-45TS	.045	Electronic		8B	14B	34	4.5-6.0	700	600
	6-231 Buick	All	R-46TSX	.060	Electronic		15B	15B	16	4.25-5.75	600	500
	8-267 Chev.	All	R-45TS	.045	Electronic		4B	10B	28	7.5-9.0	600	500
	8-305 Chev.	All	R-43TS	.045	Electronic		4B	4B	28	7.5-9.0	600	500
	8-350 Chev.	All	R-43TS	.045	Electronic		—	8B	28	7.5-9.0	—	500

NOTE: The underhood specifications sticker often reflects tune-up specification changes made in production. Sticker figures must be used if they disagree with those in this chart.

▲ See text for procedure
● Figure in parentheses indicates California engine
■ All gures Before Top Dead Center
* When two idle speed figures are separated by a slash, the lower figure is with the idle speed solenoid disconnected
① 6B for Calif. engines except engine code CCC which is 8B
  10 B for high altitude engines

② 750 w/o AC
  800 w/AC
③ 49 states: 4B
  Calif.: 6B
  High Altitude: 8B
④ High Altitude: 600
A After Top Dead Center
B Before Top Dead Center
TDC Top Dead Center
— Not applicable

NOTE: Most 1979 GM carburetors have idle mixture screws concealed by staked-in plugs. These are not meant to be removed, except at carburetor overhaul.

Nova   TUNE-UP SPECIFICATIONS

When analyzing compression test results, look for uniformity among cylinders rather than specific pressures.

Year	ENGINE No. Cyl. Displacement (cu in.)	hp	SPARK PLUGS Orig. Type	Gap (in.)	DISTRIBUTOR Point Dwell (deg)	Point Gap (in.)	IGNITION TIMING (deg) ▲ • Man Trans	Auto Trans	VALVES Intake Opens ■ (deg) •	Fuel Pump Pressure (psi)	IDLE SPEED (rpm) ▲ * Trans Man	• Trans Auto
'72	6-250	110	R-46T	.035	31-34	.019	4B	4B	16	4-5	700	600
	8-307	130	R-44T	.035	29-31	.019	4B	8B	28	5½-7½	900	600
	8-350	165	R-44T	.035	29-31	.019	6B	6B	28(44)	7½-9	900	600
	8-350	200	R-44T	.035	29-31	.019	4B	8B	28(44)	7½-9	800	600
'73	6-250	100	R-46T	.035	31-34	.019	6B	6B	16	3½-4½	700/450	600/450
	8-307	115	R-44T	.035	29-31	.019	4B	8B	28	5-6½	900/450	600/450
	8-350	145	R-44T	.035	29-31	.019	8B	8B	28	7-8½	900/450	600/450
	8-350	175	R-44T	.035	29-31	.019	8B	12B	28	7-8½	900/450	600/450
'74	6-250	100	R-46T	.035	31-34	.019	6B	6B	16	4-5	800/450	600/450
	8-350	145	R-44T	.035	29-31	.019	4B	8B	28	7½-9	900/450	600/450
	8-350	160	R-44T	.035	29-31	.019	4B	8B	44	7½-9	900/450	600/450
	8-350	185	R-44T	.035	29-31	.019	4B	8B	28	7½-9	900/450	600/450
'75	6-250	105	R46TX	.060	Electronic		10B	10B	16	4-5	800/425	550/425③ (600/425)
	8-262	110	R-44TX	.060	Electronic		8B	8B	26	7½-9	800	600
	8-350	145	R-44TX	.060	Electronic		6B	6B	28	7½-9	800	600
	8-350	155	R-44TX	.060	Electronic		6B	8B(6B)	28	7½-9	800	600
'76	6-250	105	R-46TS	.035	Electronic		6B	6B	16	3½-4½	850	550(600)
	6-250①	105	R-46TS	.035	Electronic		6B	8B	16	3½-4½	850	600
	8-305	140	R-45TS	.045	Electronic		6B	8B(TDC)	28	7-8½	800	600
	8-350	165	R-45TS	.045	Electronic		8B(6B)	8B(6B)	28	7-8½	800	600
'77	6-250	All	R-46TS	.035	Electronic		6B	8B(6B)④	16	4-5	⑤	550(600)
	8-305	All	R-45TS	.045	Electronic		8B	8B(6B)	28	7½-9	600	500
	8-350	All	R-45TS	.045	Electronic		8B	8B	28	7½-9	700	500
'78	6-250 Chev.	All	R-46TS	.035	Electronic		6B	②	16	4-5	800/425	500(600)/ 425(400)
	8-305 Chev.	All	R-45TS	.045	Electronic		4B	4B(6B)	28	7.5-9	600	500
	8-350 Chev.	All	R-45TS	.045	Electronic		——	8B	28	7.5-9		500
'79	6-250 Chev.	All	R-46TS	.035	Electronic		8B	10B(6B)	16	4.5-6.0	800	500
	8-305 Chev.	All	R-45TS	.045	Electronic		4B	4B	28	7.5-9.0	600	500
	8-350 Chev.	All	R-45TS	.045	Electronic		—	8B	28	7.5-9.0		500

NOTE: The underhood specifications sticker often reflects tune-up specification changes made in production. Sticker figures must be used if they disagree with those in this chart.

▲ See text for procedure
• Figure in parentheses indicates California engine
■ All figures before top dead center
* When two idle speed figures are separated by a slash, the lower figure is with the idle speed solenoid disconnected.
① not used
② 49 states without A/C: 10B
   49 states with A/C: 8B
   Calif.: 6B

③ Without intake manifold integral with head—600/450
④ 6B for Calif. engines except engine code CCC which is 8B
   10B for high altitude engines
⑤ 750 w/o AC; 800 w/AC
A After Top Dead Center
B Before Top Dead Center
TDC Top Dead Center
— Not applicable

FIRING ORDER

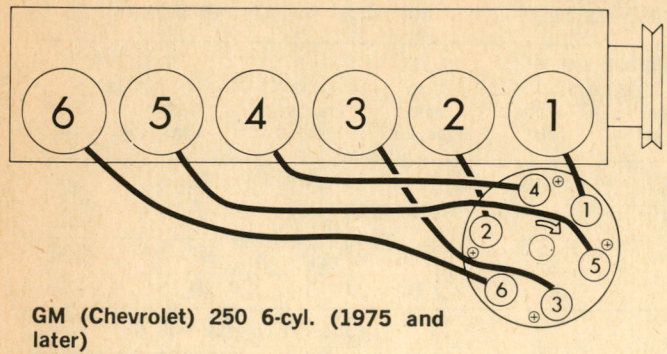

GM (Chevrolet) 250 6-cyl. (1975 and later)
Engine firing order: 1-5-3-6-2-4
Distributor rotation: clockwise

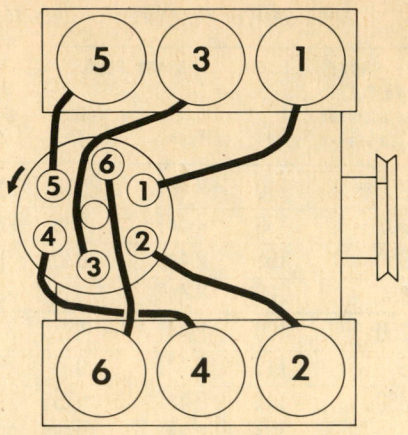

GM (Chevrolet) 200 V6
Engine firing order: 1-6-5-4-3-2
Distributor rotation: counterclockwise

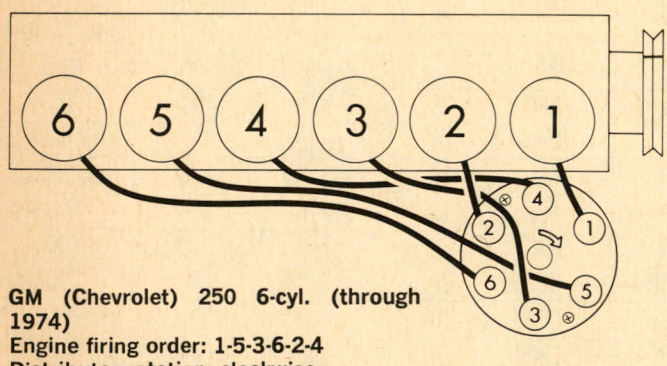

GM (Chevrolet) 250 6-cyl. (through 1974)
Engine firing order: 1-5-3-6-2-4
Distributor rotation: clockwise

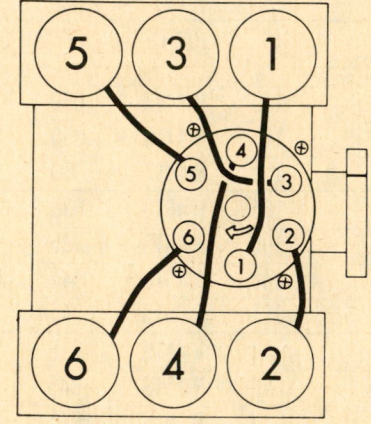

GM (Buick) 231 V6
Engine Firing Order: 1-6-5-4-3-2
Distributor rotation: clockwise

V6 harmonic balancers have two timing marks: one is 1/8 in. wide, and one is 1/16 in. wide. Use the 1/16 in. mark for timing with a hand held light. The 1/8 in. mark is used only with a magnetic timing pick-up probe.

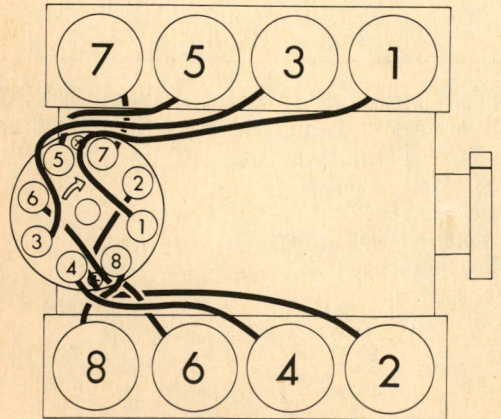

GM (Chevrolet) V8 (through 1974) Exc. 1973-74 Corvette
Engine firing order: 1-8-4-3-6-5-7-2
Distributor rotation: clockwise

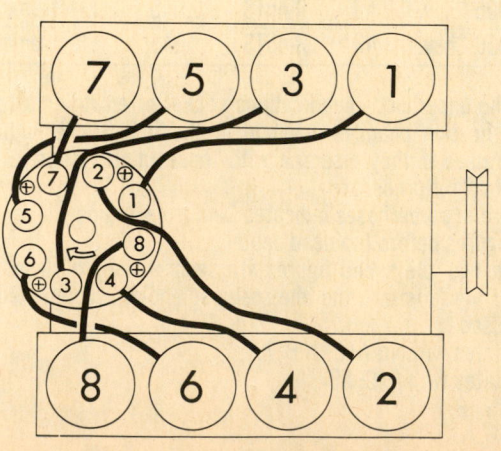

GM (Chevrolet) V8 (1975 and later)
Engine firing order: 1-8-4-3-6-5-7-2
Distributor rotation: clockwise

CAPACITIES

Year	Engine No. Cyl. Displacement (Cu. In.)	Engine Crankcase Add 1 Qt For New Filter	TRANSMISSION Pts To Refill After Draining			Drive Axle (pts)	Gasoline Tank (gals) (See Accompanying Chart)	COOLING SYSTEM (qts)	
			Manual 3-Speed	4-Speed	Automatic ●			With Heater	With A/C
'72	6-250	4	3	—	6⑤	4.25		12	—
	8-307	4	3	—	6⑤	4.25		15	16
	8-350	4	3	3	6.5③⑤	4.25		16	16
	8-402	4	—	3	8	4.25④		24	24
	8-454	4	—	3	8	4.25④		23	24
'73	6-250	4	3	—	6⑤	4.25		12.5	—
	8-307	4	3	—	5	4.25		16⑥	17⑦
	8-350	4	3	3	5③	4.25		16⑥	17⑦
	8-454	4	—	3	8	4.25④		23	24
'74	6-250	4	3	—	8	4.25		12.5	—
	8-350	4	3	3	8	4.25		16⑥	17⑦
	8-400	4	—	—	8	4.25④		16	17
	8-454	4	—	3	9	4.9		23	24
'75	6-250	4	3	—	8	4.25		14⑨	15⑧
	8-262	4	3	—	8	4.25		17	18
	8-350	4	3	3	8	4.25		17	18⑩
	8-400	4	—	—	8	4.25④		17⑪	18
	8-454	4	—	3	9	4.9		23	23
'76-'77	6-250	4	3	—	8	4.25		15⑫	17⑨
	8-262, 305	4	3	3	8	4.25		17	18
	8-350	4	—	3	8	4.25		17	18
	8-400	4	—	—	8	4.25		17	18
'78	6-200 Chev.	4	3	—	6	3.5		16.8	16.8
	6-231 Buick	4	3	3	6	3.5		14.79	14.79
	6-250 Chev.	4	3	—	6	⑬		14.6	14.6
	8-305 Chev.	4	—	3	6	⑬		①	①
	8-350 Chev.	4	—	3	6	⑬		②	②
'79	6-200 Chev.	4	3.0	—	8.0	3.25		N.A.	N.A.
	6-231 Buick	4	3.0	—	8.0	3.25		N.A.	N.A.
	6-250 Chev.	4	3.0	—	8.0	13		N.A.	N.A.
	8-267 Chev.	4	—	3.4	8.0	3.25		N.A.	N.A.
	8-305 Chev.	4	—	3.4	8.0	13		N.A.	N.A.
	8-350 Chev.	4	3.0	3.4	8.0	13		N.A.	N.A.

● Specifications do not include torque converter
① Malibu, Monte Carlo 19.2
  Camaro: 17.2
  Nova: 16.0
② Malibu: 19.2
  Camaro: 17.3
  Nova: 16.1
③ 8 pts with Z-28 350
④ 4.9 pts in Monte Carlo or Chevelle with 8⅞ in. ring gear
⑤ 5 pts with Turbo Hydramatic 350
⑥ 15.5 Nova

⑦ 16.5 Nova
⑧ 16 Chevelle
⑨ 15 Nova, 1977 and later Chevelle and Camaro
⑩ 17 Nova
⑪ 18 Monte Carlo
⑫ 14 Nova, 1977 and later Chevelle and Camaro
⑬ with 7.5 inch ring gear: 3.5
  with 8.5 inch ring gear: 4.25
— Not applicable
N.A. Information not Available

Camaro • Chevelle • Malibu • Monte Carlo • Nova

VALVE SPECIFICATIONS

Year	Engine No. Cyl. Displacement (cu in.)	Seat Angle (deg)	Face Angle (deg)	Spring Test Pressure (lbs @ In.)	Spring Installed Height (in.)	STEM TO GUIDE Clearance (in.) Intake	Exhaust	STEM Diameter (in.) Intake	Exhaust
'72	6-250	46	45	60 @ 1.66	1 21/32	.0010-.0037	.0015-.0052	.3414	.3414
	8-307	46	45	80 @ 1.70	1 23/32	.0010-.0037	.0012-.0049	.3414	.3414
	8-350	46	45	80 @ 1.70	1 23/32	.0010-.0037	.0012-.0049	.3414	.3414
	8-402	46	45	75 @ 1.88②	1 7/8	.0010-.0037	.0012-.0047	.3719	.3717
	8-454	46	45	75 @ 1.88②	1 7/8	.0010-.0037	.0012-.0047	.3719	.3717
'73	6-250	46	45	60 @ 1.66	1 21/32	.0010-.0027	.0015-.0032	.3414	.3414
	8-307	46	45	80 @ 1.61③	1 5/8	.0010-.0027	.0012-.0029	.3414	.3414
	8-350	46	45	80 @ 1.70③	1 23/32④	.0010-.0027	.0012-.0027	.3414	.3414
	8-454	46	45	80 @ 1.88	1 7/8	.0010-.0027	.0012-.0027	.3719	.3417
'74	6-250	46	45	60 @ 1.66	1 21/32	.0010-.0027	.0010-.0027	.3414	.3414
	8-350	46	45	80 @ 1.70③	1 23/32④	.0010-.0027	.0010-.0027	.3414	.3414
	8-400	46	45	80 @ 1.70③	1 23/32④	.0010-.0027	.0010-.0027	.3414	.3414
	8-454	46	45	80 @ 1.88	1 7/8	.0010-.0027	.0010-.0027	.3719	.3719
'75-'77	6-250	46	45	60 @ 1.66⑥	1 21/32	.0010-.0027	.0010-.0027⑤	.3414	.3414
	8-262	46	45	80 @ 1.70③	1 23/32④	.0010-.0027	.0010-.0027	.3414	.3414
	8-305	46	45	80 @ 1.70③	1 23/32①	.0010-.0027	.0010-.0027	.3414	.3414
	8-350	46	45	80 @ 1.70③	1 23/32④ ①	.0010-.0027	.0010-.0027	.3414	.3414
	8-400	46	45	80 @ 1.70③	1 23/32④ ①	.0010-.0027	.0010-.0027	.3414	.3414
	8-454	46	45	90 @ 1.80	1 51/64	.0010-.0027	.0010-.0027	.3719	.3719
'78-'79	6-200 Chev.	46	45	200 @ 1.25	1 23/32①	.0010-.0027	.0010-.0027	.3414	.3414
	6-231 Buick	45	45	168 @ 1.33	1 47/64	.0015-.0032	.0015-.0032	.3407	.3409
	6-250 Chev.	46	45	175 @ 1.26	1 21/32	.0010-.0027	.0015-.0032	.3414	.3414
	8-267 Chev.	46	45	180 @ 1.25⑦	1.70	.0010-.0027	.0010-.0027	.3414	.3414
	8-305 Chev.	46	45	200 @ 1.25	1 23/32①	.0010-.0027	.0010-.0027	.3414	.3414
	8-350 Chev.	46	45	200 @ 1.25	1 23/32①	.0010-.0027	.0010-.0027	.3414	.3414

① exhaust valve—1 19/32
② Inner spring—30 @ 1.78
③ 80 @ 1.61 for exhaust
④ 1 39/64 for exhaust
⑤ 1976—.0015-.0032
⑥ 1976 and later—82 @ 1.66
⑦ Exhaust:

TORQUE SPECIFICATIONS

All readings in ft lbs

Year	Engine No. Cyl. Displacement (cu in.)	Cylinder Head Bolts	Rod Bearing Bolts	Main Bearing Bolts	Crankshaft Bolt	Flywheel to Crankshaft Bolts	MANIFOLD Intake	Exhaust
'72-'78	6-250	95	35	65	60	60	35⑦	30⑥⑨
'72-'77	8-262, 305, 307, 350, 400	70⑩	45	75②⑪	60⑤	60	30	④
'72	8-402	80	50	110	85⑤	65	30	30
'72-'75	8-454	80	50③	110	85⑤	65	30	20
'78-'79	200, 8-267, 8-305, 350	65	45	70	60	60	30	20
'78-'79	6-231	80	40	100	175	60	45	25

① not used
② Engines with 4-bolt mains—Outer bolts 65
③ 7/16 Rod bolts—70
④ Center bolts—30, end bolts 20
⑤ Where applicable
⑥ Exhaust-to-intake
⑦ Manifold-to-head
⑧ 65 starting 1975
⑨ With intake manifold integral with head—30 center, 20 on four end bolts
⑩ 65 starting 1976
⑪ 70 starting 1976

CRANKSHAFT AND CONNECTING ROD SPECIFICATIONS

All measurements are given in inches

Year	Engine No. Cyl. Displacement (cu in.)	Main Brg. Journal Dia	CRANKSHAFT Main Brg. Oil Clearance	Shaft End-Play	Thrust on No.	Diameter Journal	CONNECTING ROD Clearance Oil	Clearance Side
'72	6-250	2.2983-2.2993	.0003-.0029	.002-.006	7	1.999-2.000	.0007-.0027	.009-.014
	8-307, 350	2.4484-2.4493⑩	.0008-.0020⑪	.002-.006	5	2.099-2.100	.0013-.0035	.008-.014
	8-350 (Z28)	2.4484-2.4493⑩	.0013-.0025④	.002-.006	5	2.099-2.100	.0013-.0035	.008-.014
	8-402	2.7487-2.7496⑤	.0007-.0019⑥	.006-.010	5	2.199-2.200	.0009-.0025	.013-.023
	8-454	2.7485-2.7494②	.0013-.0025⑦	.006-.010	5	2.199-2.200	.0009-.0025	.015-.021
'73	6-250	2.3004	.0003-.0029	.002-.006	7	1.999-2.000	.0007-.0027	.009-.014
	8-307, 350	2.4502⑫	.0008-.0020⑪	.002-.007	5	2.099-2.100	.0013-.0035	.008-.014
	8-454	2.7492⑬	.0007-.0019⑭	.006-.010	5	2.199-2.200	.0009-.0025	.015-.023
'74-'77	6-250	2.2988	.0003-.0029	.002-.006	7	1.9928-2.000	.0007-.0027	.007-.016
	8-262	2.4489⑮	④	.002-.006	5	2.099-2.100	.0012-.0035	.008-.014
	8-305	2.4489⑮	④	.002-.006	5	2.099-2.100	.0013-.0035	.008-.014
	8-350	2.4489⑮	④	.002-.006	5	2.099-2.100	.0035-.0035	.008-.014
	8-400	2.6489⑯	.0008-.0002⑰	.002-.006	5	2.099-2.100	.0035-.0035	.008-.014
	8-454	2.7490	.0013-.0025⑱	.006-.010	5	2.199-2.200	.0009-.0025	.015-.021
'78-'79	6-200 Chev.	2.4489⑮	.0011-.0023⑲	.002-.006	5	2.0988-2.0998	.0013-.0035	.008-.014
	6-231 Buick	2.4995	.0004-.0015	.004-.008	2	2.2487-2.2495	.0005-.0026	.006-.027
	6-250 Chev.	2.2988	.0010-.0024⑳	.002-.006	7	1.9980-2.0000	.0010-.0026	.006-.017
	8-267 Chev.	2.4489⑮	.0020-.0035㉑	.002-.007	5	2.0978-2.0988	.0013-.0035	.006-.016
	8-305 Chev.	2.4489⑮	.0011-.0023⑲	.002-.006	5	2.0988-2.0998	.0013-.0035	.008-.014
	8-350 Chev.	2.4489⑮	.0011-.0023⑲	.002-.006	5	2.0988-2.0998	.0013-.0035	.008-.014

① Not Used
② No. 1—2.7484-2.7493
　　Nos. 2-4—2.7481-2.7490
　　No. 5—2.7478-2.7488
③ Not used
④ w/Man. trans.—No. 5—.0023-.0033
　　w/Auto. trans.—No. 1—.0019-.0031
　　　　　　Nos. 2-4—.0013-.0025
　　　　　　No. 5—.0023-.0033
⑤ Nos. 3-4—2.7481-2.7490
　　No. 5—2.7473-2.7483
⑥ Nos. 2-4—.0013-.0025
　　No. 5—.0019-.0035
⑦ No. 5—.0024-.0040
⑧ No. 5—2.6479-2.6488
⑨ Not Used
⑩ Nos. 2-4—2.4481-2.4490

No. 5—2.4479-2.4488
⑪ Nos. 2-4—.0011-.0023
　　No. 5—.0017-.0033
⑫ No. 5—2.4508
⑬ Nos. 2-4—2.7504
　　No. 5—2.7499
⑭ Nos. 2-4—.0013-.0028
　　No. 5—.0019-.0035
⑮ No. 2-4: 2.4486
　　No. 5: 2.4485
⑯ No. 5: 2.6485
⑰ No. 2-4: .001-.0023
　　No. 5: .0017-.0033
⑱ No. 5: .0024-.0070
⑲ #1: .0008-.0020
⑳ #7: .0016-.0035
㉑ #4: .0005-.0015

GAS TANK CAPACITIES (Gals)

Year	Nova	Chevelle, Monte Carlo	Camaro
'72	16	19①	18
'73	21	22	18
'74	21	22	21

Year	Nova	Chevelle, Monte Carlo	Camaro
'75-'77	21	22	21
'78	21	②	21
'79	21	③	21

① 18 gals in station wagon
② Malibu, exc. Sta. Wgn.: 18.08
　　Malibu Sta. Wgn.: 18.18
　　Monte Carlo: 17.5
③ Sedan & Coupe: 18.1
　　S.W.: 18.2

RING SIDE CLEARANCE

All measurements are given in inches

Year	Engine	Top Compression	Bottom Compression
'72-'79	6-250	.0012-.0027	.0012-.0032
'72-'73	8-307, 400	③	③
'72-'77	8-262, 305, 350	.0012-.0032①	.0012-.0027②
'72-'75	8-402, 454	.0017-.0032	.0017-.0032
'78-'79	6-200	.0012-.0032	.0012-.0032
'78-'79	8-305, 350	.0012-.0032	.0012-.0032
'78-'79	6-231	.0030-.0050	.0030-.0050

Year	Engine	Oil Control
'72-'79	6-250	.0000-.0050
'72-'77	8-262, 305, 307, 350, 400	.0000-.0050④⑤
'72-'75	8-402, 454	.0005-.0065
'78-'79	6-200, 8-305, 350	.002-.007
'78-'79	6-231	.0035 Max.

① .0012-.0027 on 1975 2 bbl. 350

② 145, 155, 165, 245, 250 hp 350 cu in. engine .0012-.0032

③ 330 hp 400 cu in. engine
  Top .0017-.0032
  2nd .0017-.0032

④ .002-.007 for '72-'74 350 2 bbl and 1974-77 350 4 bbl, except 1974 Z28

⑤ 1977 and later: .0020-.0070

RING GAP

All measurements are given in inches

Year	Engine	Top Compression	Bottom Compression
'72-'77	6-250, 8-307, 400, 454	.010-.020	.010-.020
'72	8-350①	.010-.020	.013-.025
'73-'75	8-350	.010-.020	.013-.025
'75-'76	8-262	.010-.020	.013-.025
'76-'77	8-305	.010-.020	.010-.025
'76	8-350 2 bbl	.010-.020	.010-.020
'76-'77	8-350 4 bbl	.010-.020	.013-.025
'78	6-200 8-305, 350	.010-.020	.010-.025
'78-'79	6-231	.010-.020	.010-.020
'79	8-267	.010-.020	.010-.025
'79	6-200	.010-.020	.010-.020
'79	8-305, 350	.010-.020	.013-.025

① 255, 330 hp Top .010-.020
  2nd .013-.023

Year	Engine	Oil Control
'72-'78	All Chev. Engines	.015-.055
'78-'79	6-231 Buick	.015-.035
'79	6-200	.010-.030
'79	6-250, 8-350	.015-.055
'79	8-267, 305	.010-.035

PISTON CLEARANCE

Year	Engine	Horsepower	Piston to Bore Clearance (in.)
'72-'76	6-250	All	.0010
'77-'79	6-250	All	.0015
'72-'73	8-307	All	.0008
'72-'76	8-400	All	.0017
'72	8-402	All	.0022
'72	8-350	165, 175, 200	.0010
'72	8-350	255	.0039
'72	8-454	All	.0029
'73-'76	8-454	All	.0023
'73	8-350	145, 175	.0010
'73	8-350	245, 250	.0039
'75-'76	8-262, 350	2bbl	.0008
'74-'76	8-350	4bbl	.0010
'75-'76	8-350	Dual Exh.	.0039
'77-'79	8-305, 350	All	.0012
'78-'79	6-231	105	.0008-.0020
'78-'79	6-200	95	.0012
'79	8-267	All	.0012

WHEEL ALIGNMENT SPECIFICATIONS

Year	Model	CASTER Range (deg)	Pref Setting (deg)	CAMBER Range (deg)	Pref Setting (deg)	Toe-in (in.)	Steering Axis (deg) Inclination	WHEEL PIVOT RATIO (deg) Inner Wheel	Outer Wheel
'72	Nova	0 to 1P	1/2P	1/4N to 3/4P	1/4P	1/8 to 1/4	8³/4 to 9¹/4	—	—
	Chevelle	1¹/2N to 1/2N	1N	1/4P to 1¹/4P	1P	1/8 to 1/4	7³/4 to 8¹/4	—	—
	Monte Carlo	1/2N to 1/2P	0	1/4P to 1¹/4P	3/4P	1/8 to 1/4	7³/4 to 8¹/4	—	—
	Camaro	1/2N to 1/2P	0	1/2P to 1¹/2P	3/4P	1/8 to 1/4	9 to 10	—	—
	Camaro Z28	1¹/2N to 1/2N	1N	1/4P to 1¹/4P	3/4P	1/8 to 1/4	9¹/4 to 10¹/4	—	—
'73	Nova	1/2N to 1¹/2P	1/2P	1/2N to 1P	3/4P	1/16 to 5/16	9	— .	—
	Chevelle	1³/4N to 3/4N	1¹/4N	1/2P to 1¹/2P	1P②	1/8 to 1/4	9¹/2	—	—
	Monte Carlo	4¹/4P to 5¹/4P	4³/4P	1/2P to 1¹/2P	1P②	0 to 1/8	9¹/2	—	—
	Camaro	1N to 1P	0	1/4P to 1³/4P	1P	1/16 to 5/16	10¹/2	—	—
	Camaro Z28	2N to 0	1N	1¹/2N to 0	3/4N	1/16 to 5/16	10¹/2	—	—
'74	Nova	0 to 1P	1/2P	1/4P to 3/4P	1/4P	1/8 to 1/4	8³/4	—	—
	Chevelle Man. Steer.	1¹/2 to 1/2N	1N	1/2P to 1¹/2P	1P	0 to 1/8	10¹/2	—	—
	Chevelle Pow. Steer.	1/2N to 1/2P	0	1/2P to 1¹/2P	1P	0 to 1/8	10¹/2	—	—
	Monte Carlo	4¹/2 to 5¹/2P	5	1/2P to 1¹/2P	1P	0 to 1/8	10¹/2	—	—
	Camaro	1/2N to 1/2P	0	1/2P to 1¹/2P	1P	1/8 to 1/4	9¹/2	—	—
	Camaro Z28	1¹/2N to 1/2N	1N	1/4P to 1¹/4P	3/4P	1/8 to 1/4	9³/4	—	—
'75-'76	Nova Man. Steer.	1¹/2N to 1/2N	1N	1/4P to 1¹/4P	3/4P	0 to 1/8	10	—	—
	Nova Pow. Steer.	1/2P to 1¹/2P	1P	1/4P to 1¹/4P	3/4P	0 to 1/8	10	—	—
	Chevelle	1¹/2P to 2¹/2P	2P	0 to 1P②	1/2P	0 to 1/8	9¹⁹/32	—	—
	Monte Carlo	4¹/2P to 5¹/2P	5P	0 to 1P②	1/2P	0 to 1/8	9¹⁹/32	—	—
	Camaro	1/2N to 1/2P⑤	C⑥	1/2P to 1¹/2P	1P	0 to 1/8	10¹¹/32	—	—
'77	Nova Man. Steer.	1/2N to 1¹/2N	1N	1/3P to 1¹/3P	4/5P	0 to 1/8	10	—	—
	Nova Pow. Steer.	1/2P to 1¹/2P	1P	1/3P to 1¹/3P	4/5P	0 to 1/8	10	—	—
	Chevelle	③	③	④	④	0 to 1/8	9¹⁹/32	—	—
	Monte Carlo	4¹/2P to 5¹/2P	5P	④	④	0 to 1/8	9¹⁹/32	—	—
	Camaro	1/2P to 1¹/2N	1P	1/2P to 1¹/2P	1P	0 to 1/8	10¹¹/32	—	—
'78	Nova Man. Steer.	1/2N to 1¹/2N	1N	1/3P to 1¹/3P	4/5P	1/16 to 3/16	—	—	—
	Nova Pow. Steer.	1/2P to 1¹/2P	1P	1/3P to 1¹/3P	4/5P	1/16 to 3/16	—	—	—
	Camaro	1/2P to 1¹/2P	1P	1/2P to 1¹/2P	1P	1/16 to 3/16	—	—	—
	Malibu/Monte Carlo	1/2P to 1¹/2P	1P	2¹/2P to 3¹/2P	3P	1/16 to 3/16	—	—	—
'79	Nova Man. Steer.	2N to 0	1N	1/3P to 1¹/3P	4/5P	.10-.20⑦	10	—	—
	Nova Pwr. Steer.	0 to 2P	1P	1/3P to 1¹/3P	4/5P	.10-.20⑦	10	—	—
	Camaro	1/2P to 1¹/2P	1P	1/2P to 1¹/2P	1P	.05-.15⑦	10.35	—	—
	Malibu, Monte Carlo	1/2P to 1¹/2P	1P	2¹/2P to 3¹/2P	3P	1/16 to 3/16	7.86	—	—

N Negative   P Positive

① not used
② Left wheel given, right wheel is 1/2P ± 1/2
③ With power steering and radial tires: 1¹/2P to 2¹/2P; pref.: 2P
   With power steering and belted tires: 1/2P to 1¹/2P; pref.: 1P
   With manual steering: 1/2P to 1¹/2P; pref.: 1P

④ Left side: 1/2P to 1¹/2P; pref.: 1P
   Right side: 0 to 1P; pref.: 1/2P
⑤ '76—1/2P to 1¹/2P
⑥ '76—1P
⑦ degrees
— Not specified

CHARGING SYSTEM

Alternator and regulator trouble-shooting are covered in the Charging and Starting Systems Unit Repair Section.

Alternator Removal and Installation

1. Disconnect battery ground cable to prevent diode damage.
2. Disconnect the alternator wiring.
3. Remove brace bolt. If power steering equipped, loosen pump brace and mount nuts. Detach drive belt(s).
4. Support the alternator and remove mount bolt(s). Remove unit from vehicle.

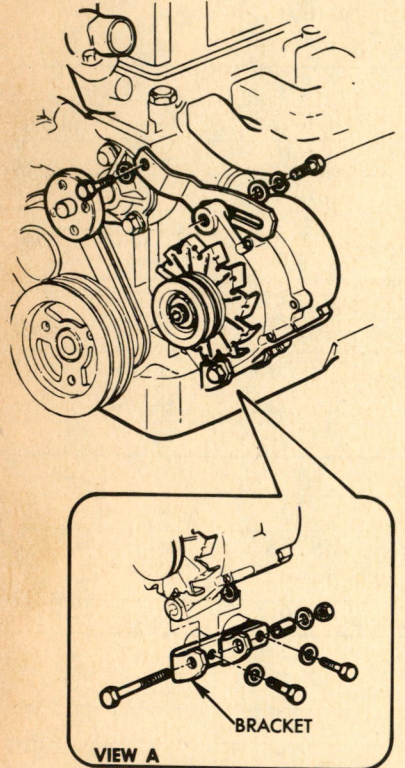

VIEW A
BRACKET

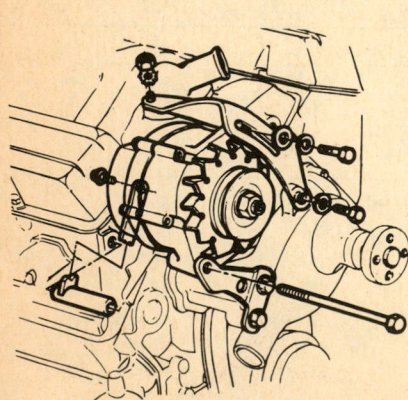

Delcotron installation
(© Chevrolet Div., G.M. Corp)

5. Reverse procedure to install. Adjust drive belt to have 1/4-1/2 in. play on longest run of belt.

1972 External Regulator

1. Disconnect the ground cable at the battery.
2. Disconnect the wiring harness from the regulator.
3. Remove the mounting screws and remove the regulator.
4. Make sure that the regulator base gasket is in place before installation.
5. Clean the attaching area for proper grounding.
6. Install the regulator. Do not over-tighten the mounting screws, as this will cancel the cushioning effect of the rubber grommets.

Integral Voltage Regulator

An alternator with an integral voltage regulator has been optional and became standard equipment in 1973. There are no adjustments possible with this unit; testing procedures will be found in the Charging And Starting Systems Unit Repair Section.

STARTING SYSTEM

Starter motor troubleshooting and repairs are covered in the Charging and Starting Systems Unit Repair Section.

Starter Removal and Installation

1. Disconnect battery ground cable.
2. Raise and support vehicle.
3. Disconnect all wires at solenoid terminals. Note color coding of wires for reinstallation.
4. Remove starter front bracket and two mount bolts. On engines with solenoid heat shield, remove front bracket upper bolt and detach bracket from starter motor.
5. Remove front bracket bolt or nut.

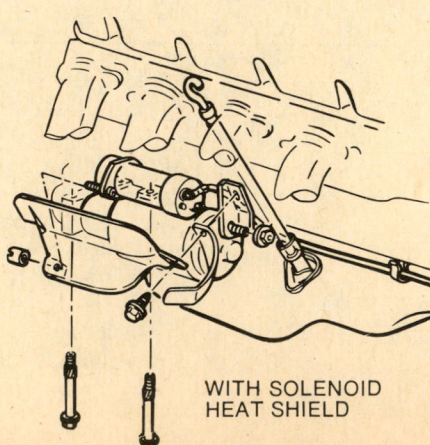

WITH SOLENOID HEAT SHIELD

Starter motor installation
(© Chevrolet Div., G.M. Corp)

Rotate bracket clear. Lower starter front end first. Remove starter.
6. Reverse procedure to install. Torque mount bolts to 25-35 ft lbs.

Disabling the Seat Belt/Starter Interlock System

Since the requirement for the interlock system was dropped during the 1975 model year, those systems installed on cars built earlier may now be legally disabled. The seat belt warning light is still required.

1. Disconnect the negative battery cable.
2. Locate the interlock harness connector under the left side of the instrument panel on or near the fuse block. It has orange, yellow, and green leads.
3. Cut and tape the ends of the green wire on the body side of the connector.
4. Remove the buzzer from the fuse block or connector.

IGNITION SYSTEM

All models are equipped with the HEI distributor and ignition system starting 1975. This system uses no points and is, therefore, relatively maintenance free. See the Electronic Ignition section for unit description.

When using an auxiliary starter switch the primary distributor lead on point-type systems must be disconnected from the negative post of the ignition coil and the ignition switch must be on. On HEI systems, the distributor BATT lead must be disconnected. Failure to do this may cause damage to the grounding circuit in the ignition switch.

HEI System Tachometer Hookup

There is a terminal marked TACH on the side of the V6 and V8 HEI distributor. Connect one tachometer lead to this terminal and the other to ground. On some tachometers, the leads must be connected to the TACH terminal and to the battery positive terminal. The hookup is the same for the inline six-cylinder HEI system, except that the TACH terminal is opposite the BAT terminal on the connector plug on the remote-mounted coil.

--- CAUTION ---

Never ground the TACH terminal; serious system damage will result. If there is any doubt as to the correct tachometer hookup, check with the tachometer manufacturer.

Distributor Removal and Installation

The drive gear is attached to the distributor shaft. If it becomes necessary to remove the distributor, carefully mark the position of the rotor in relation to the engine block and the distributor housing so that, if the engine is not turned after the distributor is taken out, the rotor can be returned to the position from which it was removed without difficulty.

To remove the distributor, take off the V8 carburetor air cleaner, disconnect the coil primary wire and the vacuum line, remove the distributor cap, take out the distributor body. Mark the position of the body relative to the block, and then work the distributor up out of the block.

When installing the distributor, turn the rotor about 1/8 turn counterclockwise past the alignment mark before pushing the distributor into place. The marks should align when the distributor seats. Check the timing.

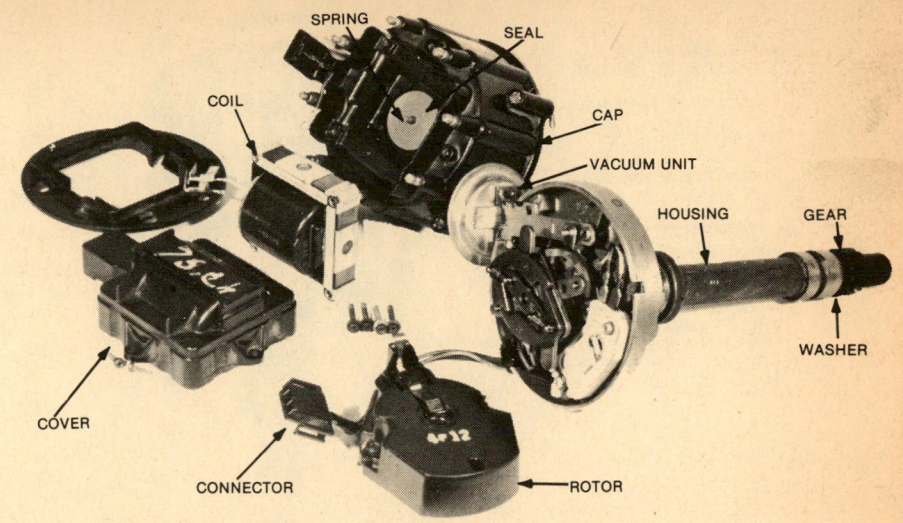

V8 HEI distributor

Distributor Installation (Engine Disturbed)

1. Turn the crankshaft until the No. 1 cylinder is at the top of its compression stroke. Remove the No. 1 spark plug to feel the compression.
2. Align the timing mark on the vibration damper with the TDC indicator or 0 mark on the timing scale.
3. With distributor body oriented in its normal position, hold the rotor pointing toward the No. 1 plug wire location, then turn the rotor approximately 1/8 turn counterclockwise and push the distributor down until it engages the camshaft, rotating the shaft slightly if necessary.

NOTE: *On Mark IV (big block) V8 engines there is a punch mark on the distributor drive gear which indicates the rotor position. Thus, the distributor may be installed with the cap in place. Align the punch mark 2° clockwise from the No. 1 cap terminal, then rotate the distributor body 1/8 turn counterclockwise and push the distributor down into the block.*

4. Press down on the distributor and crank the engine to make sure the oil pump shaft is engaged.
5. Return the crankshaft to No. 1 cylinder compression stroke with the timing marks aligned.
6. Turn the distributor body counterclockwise until the points are just beginning to open, then tighten the distributor clamp bolt.
7. Install the distributor cap, checking that the rotor points to the No. 1 terminal. Make sure that the spark plug wires are in their supports and are securely connected.
8. Connect distributor vacuum line and primary wire.
9. Start engine and set the timing.

Breaker Point Adjustment

NOTE: *Distributors through 1973 are equipped with a radio static-shield which must be removed for access to the points. If a unitized point and con-*

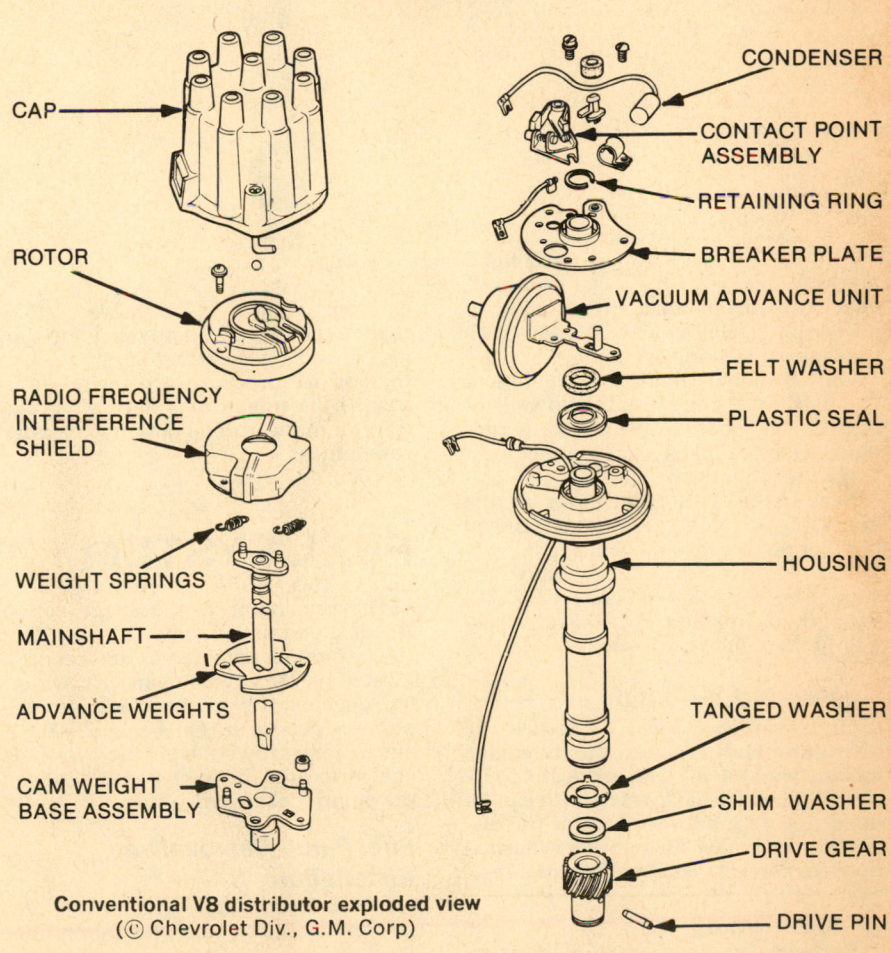

Conventional V8 distributor exploded view
(© Chevrolet Div., G.M. Corp)

denser set is used, the shield isn't needed.

Breaker point gap (dwell) adjustment is accomplished for six cylinder engines by loosening the point assembly attaching screw and adjusting the points with a screwdriver until the correct gap clearance is obtained (use a feeler gauge). Tighten the point assembly attaching screw and install the distributor cap. Use a dwell meter to

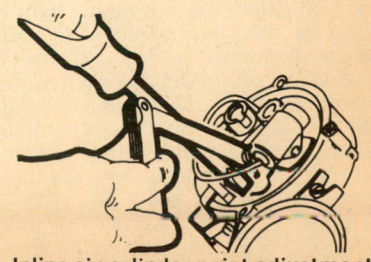

Inline six-cylinder point adjustment

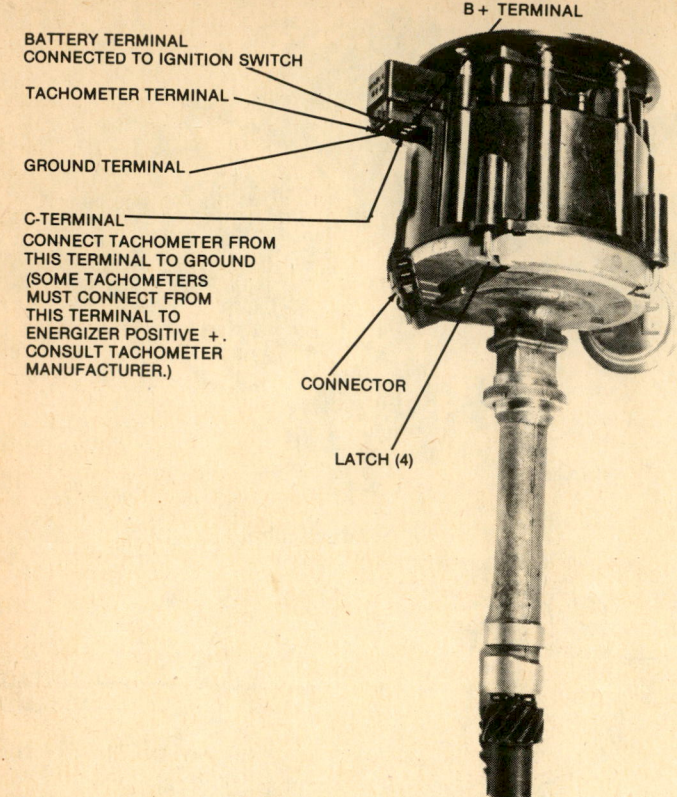

BATTERY TERMINAL
CONNECTED TO IGNITION SWITCH

TACHOMETER TERMINAL

GROUND TERMINAL

C-TERMINAL
CONNECT TACHOMETER FROM
THIS TERMINAL TO GROUND
(SOME TACHOMETERS
MUST CONNECT FROM
THIS TERMINAL TO
ENERGIZER POSITIVE +.
CONSULT TACHOMETER
MANUFACTURER.)

B+ TERMINAL

CONNECTOR

LATCH (4)

HEI tachometer hookup

check the dwell angle, readjusting if necessary. Dwell can be checked with the engine cranking or running.

On V8 models there is a window in the distributor cap so that the dwell angle may be set while the engine is running. Use an allen (hex) wrench to make the adjustment.

See Tune-Up Specifications at the beginning of this section for correct breaker point gap and dwell angle.

The distributor cam lubricator should be rotated 180°, switched end-for-end, or replaced periodically. Do not oil these lubricator wicks.

—— CAUTION ——

On Chevrolet V6 and V8 models the distributor body is involved in the engine lubricating system. The lubricating circuit to the right-bank valve train can be interrupted by misalignment of the distributor body. See Firing Order illustrations for correct distributor positioning.

Ignition Timing

Remove the spark plug wire from No. 1 plug and attach a timing light between the wire and the plug. With HEI, use an adapter at the No. 1 distributor terminal. No. 6 may be used if it is more convenient. Disconnect the distributor spark advance hose and plug the vacuum opening. Start the engine and run it at idle speed. Aim the timing light at the degree scale just over the harmonic balancer. Adjust the timing by loosening the securing clamp and rotating the distributor until the desired

ignition advance is achieved, then tighten the clamp. To advance the timing, rotate the distributor opposite to the normal direction of rotor rotation. Retard the timing by rotating the distributor in the normal direction of rotor rotation.

FUEL SYSTEM

The fuel pump is the single action AC diaphragm type.

The pump is actuated by an eccentric located on the engine camshaft. On inline engines, the eccentric actuates the pump rocker arm. On V6 and V8 engines, a pushrod between the camshaft eccentric and the fuel pump actuates the pump rocker arm.

Fuel Pump Removal and Installation

1. Disconnect fuel inlet and outlet lines at pump and plug pump inlet line.
2. Remove two pump mounting bolts and lockwashers; remove pump and gasket.
3. On all small block engines, if rocker arm pushrod is to be removed: take out the two adapter bolts and lockwashers and remove adapter and gasket.
4. On big block V8 engines, if rocker arm pushrod is to be removed: take out pipe plug.
5. Install pump with new gasket

coated with sealer. Coat mounting bolt threads with sealer and tighten bolts.

NOTE: *On Chevrolet V6 and V8 engines, mechanical fingers or heavy grease can be used to hold pump pushrod in place during installation. Coat pipe plug threads or adapter gasket with sealer if pushrod was removed.*

6. Connect inlet and outlet lines, start engine and check for leaks.

Chilton's TIME SAVER

When replacing a fuel pump on small block V8 and V6-200 engines, considerable time can be saved as follows:

1. Before removing the old pump, remove the upper bolt from the engine's right front mounting boss on the front of the block. This bolt hole is in direct alignment with the fuel pump pushrod. The threaded bolt hole continues into the pump pushrod bore. The bolt acts as an oil plug.
2. Temporarily insert a longer bolt, (about 3/8—16 x 2 in.) into the hole. Screw the bolt into the bore until it bottoms against the pump pushrod. (Don't tighten the bolt with a wrench or the rod can be damaged.)
3. The mechanic is now free to remove and install the fuel pump without worrying about fuel pump pushrod misalignment.

—— CAUTION ——

Don't forget to reinstall the original bolts.

Fuel Filter Removal and Installation

All 1976 and later fuel filters use a check valve to prevent fuel spillage in an accident. When you replace the filter, make sure the new one has a check valve.

1. Disconnect fuel line connection at inlet of carburetor.
2. Remove inlet fuel filter nut from carburetor using a box wrench.
3. Remove filter element and spring.
4. If a bronze element, blow through cone end—element should allow air to pass freely.
5. Install element spring and new element into carburetor. Bronze elements are installed with small section of cone facing outward.
6. Install new gasket on fitting nut and install nut.
7. Install fuel line and tighten securely. Start engine and check for leaks.

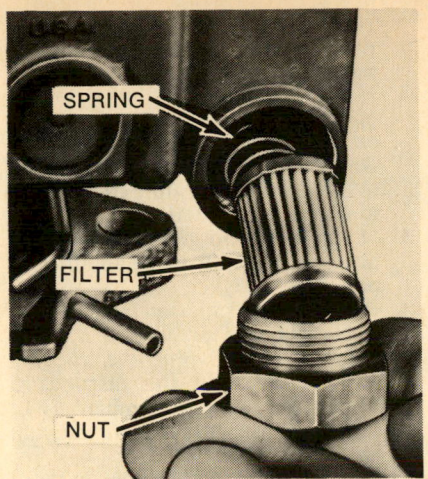

Paper fuel filter
(© Chevrolet Div., G.M. Corp)

Idle Speed and Mixture Adjustments

1972

Disconnect the fuel tank line from the vapor canister. Disconnect the distributor vacuum hose and plug the opening. All carburetors are equipped with idle mixture limiter caps. Do not try to adjust the mixture or remove the caps. Adjust the idle speed with the engine running at its normal temperature, choke open, and parking brake set. Turn the air conditioner off, if so equipped. Chock the wheels on automatic transmission cars. Manual transmissions should be in Neutral, and automatic transmissions in Drive.

250 cu. in. 6 cylinder

Adjust the idle stop solenoid (not the C.E.C. solenoid, which is the larger of the two carburetor-mounted solenoids) for a speed of 700 rpm (M.T.) or 600 rpm (A.T.).

307, 350 and 400 cu. in. V8s (two-barrel carburetor)

Adjust the idle stop solenoid screw for 900 rpm (M.T.) or 600 rpm (A.T.). Set the carburetor fast idle cam screw for 1850 rpm on 307 engines and 2200 rpm on 350 and 400 engines.

350 cu. in. V8 (Quadrajet four-barrel carburetor)

Adjust the idle stop solenoid screw to obtain 800 rpm (M.T.) or 600 rpm (A.T.). Position the fast idle follower on the second step of the fast idle cam and set the fast idle to 1350 rpm (M.T.) or 1500 rpm (A.T.).

350 cu. in. V8 (Holley four-barrel carburetor)

Adjust the idle stop solenoid screw for 900 rpm.

402 and 454 cu. in. V8s (Quadrajet four-barrel carburetor)

Adjust the idle stop solenoid screw for 800 rpm (M.T.) or 600 rpm (A.T.). Position the fast idle follower on the second step of the fast idle cam and set the fast idle at 1350 rpm (M.T.) or 1500 rpm (A.T.).

1973

All models are equipped with idle limiter caps and idle solenoids. Disconnect the fuel tank line from the evaporative canister. The engine must be running at operating temperature, choke off, parking brake on, and rear wheels blocked. Disconnect the distributor vacuum hose and plug it. After adjustment, reconnect the vacuum and evaporative hoses.

250 cu. in. 6 cylinder

Adjust the idle stop solenoid for 700 rpm on manual transmission models or 600 rpm on automatics. On manual models, make no attempt to adjust the CEC solenoid (the larger of the two carburetor solenoids) or a decrease in engine braking could result.

Two-barrel 307, 350, and 400 cu. in. V8s

1. With air conditioning switched off, if so equipped, adjust the idle stop solenoid screw for a speed of 900 rpm on manual models; 600 rpm on automatics.
2. De-energize the idle stop solenoid and adjust the idle speed screw (screw resting on lower step of the cam) for 450 rpm on 307, 400 rpm on 350 and 400 engines with automatic transmission, or 500 rpm on 350 engines with a manual transmission.

Four-barrel 350 and 454 cu. in. V8s

1. Adjust the idle stop solenoid screw for 900 rpm on manual transmission models; 600 rpm on automatics.
2. Connect the distributor vacuum hose and position the fast idle cam follower on the top step of the fast idle cam (turn air conditioning off if so equipped) and adjust the fast idle to 1300 rpm on manual transmission 350 engines; 1600 on manual 454 engines and all automatics (in Park).

Z28

1. Adjust the idle stop solenoid screw (air conditioning off if so equipped) for a speed of 900 rpm on manual transmission; 700 rpm on automatic (in Drive).
2. Connect the distributor vacuum hose and position the fast idle cam follower on the top step of the cam (turn air conditioning off if so equipped) and adjust the fast idle to 1300 rpm on manual models; 1600 rpm on automatics.

1974

The same preconditions as 1973 apply.

250 cu. in. 6 cylinder

Adjust the idle stop solenoid hex nut for 850 rpm on manual transmission; 600 rpm on automatics (in Drive).

Two-barrel 350 and 400 cu. in. V8s

1. Turn the air conditioning off, if so equipped. Adjust the idle stop solenoid screw for 900 rpm on manual transmission models; 600 rpm on automatics (in Drive).
2. De-energize the solenoid and adjust the carburetor idle cam screw (on low step of cam) for 400 rpm on automatic models (in Drive); 500 rpm on 350 engines with manual transmission.

Four-barrel 350 and 400 cu. in. V8s

1. Turn the air conditioning off, if so equipped. Adjust the idle stop solenoid screw for 900 rpm on manual transmission models; 600 rpm on automatics (in Drive).
2. Connect the distributor vacuum hose. Position the fast idle cam follower on the top step of the fast idle cam and adjust the fast idle speed to 1300 rpm on manual transmission models; 1600 on automatics (in Park).

Z28

1. Turn the air conditioning off, if so equipped. Adjust the idle stop solenoid for 900 rpm on manual transmission models; 700 rpm on automatics (in Drive).
2. Connect the distributor vacuum hose. Position the fast idle cam follower on the top step of the cam and adjust the fast idle to 1300 rpm on manual transmission cars; 1500 rpm on automatics (in Park).

454 cu. in. V8

1. Shut off the air conditioning, if so equipped. Adjust the idle stop solenoid screw for 800 rpm on manual transmission models; 600 rpm on automatics (in Drive).
2. Connect the distributor vacuum hose and position the fast idle cam follower on the top step of the cam and adjust the fast idle to 1600 rpm on manual transmission cams; 1500 rpm on automatics (in Park).

1975-76

The engine must be at normal operating temperature with the air cleaner on, the choke open, the air conditioner off, and the timing correctly set.
1. Set the brake and block the wheels.
2. Set the automatic transmission in Drive and the manual in neutral. Disconnect the fuel tank hose from the vapor canister in the engine compartment.
3. Use needle nose pliers to break off the mixture screw cap or caps.

1 bbl

Adjust the idle speed by turning the solenoid in or out to obtain the higher of the two speeds listed on the sticker. Disconnect the electrical connector from the solenoid and turn the 1/8 in. allen screw in the end of the solenoid body to lower the idle speed to the second figure on the sticker.

2 bbl

Adjust the idle speed with the idle speed screw to obtain the higher idle speed shown on the sticker.

4 bbl

Disconnect the electrical connector at the idle solenoid, and adjust the idle speed to the lower of the two figures given on the sticker. Reconnect the electrical connector, open the throttle to extend the solenoid plunger, then turn the solenoid plunger screw to obtain the higher of the two idle speed figures. For 1976, the idle solenoid has been dropped; the idle is adjusted with an idle speed screw.

On all but the 2 bbl, turn out the mixture screws until the highest possible idle speed is reached. If the idle speed becomes excessive (more than that set in Step 4), reset the idle speed to that set in Step 4. On the 2 bbl, turn out the mixture screws to obtain the highest idle and then, turn in the mixture screws to obtain the lower of the two figures listed on the sticker.

Turn in the mixture screws equally until the normal idle speed is reached.

Replace the vapor canister hose.

1977 Idle Speed

Run the engine to normal operating temperature, A/C off, vacuum advance line disconnected and plugged, FUEL TANK line at canister disconnected. Place the manual transmission in neutral; automatic transmission in Drive. Connect a tachometer to the engine.

1 bbl

1. Turn the bolt head of the solenoid to set speed with solenoid energized to: MT-750 wo/AC; 800 w/ AC; AT-550 wo/AC, 600 w/AC.
2. Disconnect the solenoid lead and turn the hex bolt (inside the bolt head) to achieve 425 rpm.

2 bbl without solenoid

1. Place the idle speed screw on the low step of the fast idle cam.
2. Turn the idle speed screw to achieve 600 rpm-MT; 500 rpm-AT.

2 bbl with solenoid

1. Turn the idle speed screw to achieve 600 rpm-MT; 500 rpm-AT.
2. Disconnect the A/C compressor clutch lead and energize the solenoid by turning the A/C on.
3. Open the throttle slightly to allow the solenoid plunger to extend.
4. Turn the solenoid screw to achieve 700 rpm-MT; 650 rpm-AT.
5. Reconnect the A/C lead.

4 bbl without solenoid

Turn the idle speed screw to achieve the following rpm according to the carburetor part number (found on a tag under a carburetor bolt): 17057203, 17057210, 17057510-700 rpm; 17057202-500 rpm; 17057582, 17057584-600 rpm; 17057211-800 rpm.

4 bbl with solenoid

Adjustments are made according to the carburetor number (found on a tag under a carburetor bolt).

1. Turn the idle speed screw to set the curb idle to: 17057204, 17057504-500 rpm; 17057228, 17057528-700 rpm; 17057584-600 rpm.
2. Disconnect the A/C compressor lead and turn the system on.
3. Open the throttle slightly to allow solenoid plunger to extend fully.
4. Turn the solenoid screw to adjust to: 17057204, 17057504-650 rpm; 17057228, 17057528-800 rpm; 17057584-650 rpm.

1977 IDLE MIXTURE

1. Set the idle speed.
2. Check the ignition timing and adjust if necessary.
3. Carefully remove the cap(s) from the mixture screw(s).
4. Lightly seat the screw(s).
5. Back out each screw 1/8 turn at a time until maximum idle speed is attained. Then set the idle speed screw to: MT-950 rpm; AT-575 rpm; AT, Calif.-640 rpm; AT, High Altitude-650 rpm for 6 cylinder engines. For 2 bbl V8s: MT-650; AT-550. For 4 bbl V8s: MT-800; AT-550; MT, Calif.-900; AT, Calif.-750; AT, High Altitude-650.
6. Repeat step 5 to make sure you have the highest possible idle speed.
7. Turn the screws in 1/8 turn at a time until the idle speed reaches: MT-750 rpm; AT-550 rpm; AT, Calif.-640 rpm; AT, High Altitude-600 rpm for 6 cylinder models. For 2bbl V8s: MT-600; AT-500 rpm. For 4 bbl V8s: MT-700; AT-500; MT, Calif.-800; AT, Calif.-700; AT, High Altitude-600 rpm.
8. Reset the idle speed.
9. Reconnect and reinstall all parts.

1978-79 IDLE SPEED ADJUSTMENT

6-250

1. Run the engine to normal operating temperature.
2. Make sure that the choke is fully opened.
3. Turn the A/C Off and disconnect the vacuum line at the vapor canister. Plug the line.
4. Set the parking brake, block the drive wheels and place the transmission in Drive (AT) or Neutral (MT). Connect a tachometer to the engine according to the manufacturer's instructions.
5. Turn the solenoid assembly to achieve the solenoid-on speed.
6. Disconnect the solenoid wire and turn the 1/8 inch hex screw in the solenoid end, to achieve the solenoid-off speed.
7. Remove the tachometer, connect the canister vacuum line and shut off the engine.

6-200, 6-231, 8-305

1. Run the engine to normal operating temperature.
2. Make sure that the choke is fully opened, turn the A/C Off, set the parking brake, block the drive wheels and connect a tachometer to the engine according to the manufacturer's instructions.
3. Disconnect and plug the vacuum hoses at the EGR valve and the vapor canister.
4. Place the transmission in Park (AT) or Neutral (MT).
5. Disconnect and plug the vacuum advance hose at the distributor. Check and adjust the timing.
6. Connect the distributor vacuum line.
7. Manual transmission cars without A/C: place the idle speed screw on the low step of the fast idle cam and turn the screw to achieve the specified idle speed.

Cars with A/C: set the idle speed screw to the specified rpm. Disconnect the compressor clutch wire and turn the A/C On. Open the throttle momentarily to extend the solenoid plunger. Turn the solenoid screw to obtain the specified rpm.

Automatic transmission cars without A/C: momentarily open the throttle to extend the solenoid plunger. Turn the solenoid screw to obtain the specified rpm. Disconnect the solenoid wire and turn the idle speed screw to obtain the slow engine idle speed.

8-350

1. Run the engine to normal operating temperature.
2. Set the parking brake and block the drive wheels.
3. Connect a tachometer to the engine according to the manufacturer's instructions.
4. Disconnect and plug the purge hose at the vapor canister. Disconnect and plug the EGR vacuum hose at the EGR valve.
5. Turn the A/C Off.
6. Place the transmission in Park (AT) or Neutral (MT).
7. Disconnect and plug the vacuum advance line at the distributor. Check and adjust the timing.
8. Connect the vacuum advance line. Place the automatic transmission in Drive.
9. Manual transmission cars without A/C: adjust the idle stop screw to obtain the specified rpm. Cars with A/C: Disconnect the compressor clutch wire and turn the A/C On. Open the throttle momentarily to extend the solenoid plunger. Turn the idle speed screw to obtain the specified rpm, then turn the solenoid screw to obtain the solenoid rpm listed on the Underhood Sticker.

10. Connect all hoses and remove the tachometer.

1978-79 Idle Mixture Adjustment

Changes in the carburetors have made the adjustment of the idle mixture impossible without a propane enrichment system not available to the general public. Backing out the mixture screw will have little or no effect on the mixture.

COOLING SYSTEM

A standard pressure cooling system is used on all models. The radiator cap is designed to maintain a cooling system pressure of about 13 or 15 psi above atmospheric. The water pump requires no attention except to make certain the air vent at the top of the housing and the drain holes in the bottom do not become clogged.

Radiator Removal and Installation

1. Drain radiator.
2. Disconnect hoses and oil cooler lines.
3. Remove radiator upper panel and shroud (if so equipped).
4. Remove radiator attaching bolts and lift radiator out of car.
5. Slide radiator into position.
6. Install attaching bolts, shroud, and upper panel.
7. Install hoses and close drain.
8. Fill cooling system, run engine with radiator cap off until operating temperature has been reached. Again fill cooling system and check for leaks.

Water Pump Removal and Installation

1. Drain the radiator and loosen the fan pulley bolts.
2. Disconnect the heater hose, lower radiator hose and, if applicable, the bypass hose at the water pump.
3. On V6 and V8 engines, remove the alternator upper brace. Loosen the swivel bolt and remove the fan belt.
4. On Mark IV (big block) engines, disconnect the power steering and air conditioning belts and swivel the power steering pump to one side.
5. Remove the fan blade and pulley.
NOTE: *Thermostatic fan clutches must be kept in an "in-car" position. When removed from the car the assembly should be supported so that the clutch disc remains in a vertical plane to prevent silicone fluid leakage.*
6. Remove the water pump attaching bolts and, if applicable, the power steering-to-pump bolts and remove the pump and gasket.

NOTE: *On inline six-cylinder engines, pull the pump straight out of the block first to avoid damage to the impeller.*

7. Install the pump assembly using a new gasket. Coat the gasket on both sides with sealer. Tighten the 5/16 in. bolts to 15 ft lbs (inline six-cylinder) and the 3/8 in. bolts (V6 and V8) to 30 ft lbs.
8. Install the pulley and fan.
9. On big block engines, install the power steering and air conditioning bolts.
10. Connect the hoses and fill the cooling system.
11. On V6 and V8 engines, install the alternator upper brace and fan belt. Install the power steering pump bolt.
12. Adjust the belts, then start the engine and check for leaks.

Thermostat Removal and Installation

The thermostat is located inside a housing on the front of the cylinder head on inline six-cylinder engines and inside the front of the intake manifold casting V6 and V8 engines. It is not necessary to remove the radiator hose from the thermostat housing when removing the thermostat.

1. Remove the two retaining bolts from the thermostat housing and lift up the housing with the hose attached. Remove the thermostat.
2. Insert the new thermostat, spring end down, and install the housing with a new gasket. Tighten the housing retaining bolts to 30 ft lbs.

EMISSION CONTROLS

NOTE: *See the Unit Repair Section for emission control system troubleshooting.*

POSITIVE CRANKCASE VENTILATION

In this system, crankcase vapors are drawn into the intake manifold and burned as part of engine combustion. The system draws clean air from the carburetor air cleaner. The ventilation flow is regulated by the PCV valve.

AIR INJECTION REACTOR

The AIR system injects air into the exhaust system, near enough to the exhaust valves to continue the burning of the normally unburned segment of the exhaust gases. To do this it employs an air injection pump and a system of hoses, valves, tubes, etc., necessary to carry the compressed air from the pump to the exhaust manifolds. Carburetors and distributors for AIR engines have specific modifications to adapt them to the air injection system; those components should not be inter-

changed with those intended for use on engines that do not have the system.

A diverter valve is used to prevent backfiring. The valve senses sudden increases in manifold vacuum and ceases the injection of air during fuel-rich periods. During coasting, this valve diverts the entire air flow through the pump muffler and during high engine speeds, expels it through a relief valve. Check valves in the system prevent exhaust gases from entering the pump.

CONTROLLED COMBUSTION SYSTEM

C.C.S. increases combustion efficiency through leaner carburetor adjustments and revised distributor calibration. Thermostatically controlled air intakes are also used on most models. A higher temperature thermostat is used on C.C.S. cars.

EVAPORATIVE EMISSION CONTROL

This system reduces the amount of escaping gasoline vapors. Float bowl emissions are controlled by internal carburetor modifications. Redesigned bowl vents, reduced bowl capacity, heat shields, and improved intake manifold-to-carburetor insulation serve to reduce vapor loss into the atmosphere. The venting of fuel tank vapors into the air has been stopped. Fuel vapors are now directed through lines to a canister containing an activated charcoal filter. Unburned vapors are trapped here until the engine is started. When the engine is running, the canister is purged by air drawn in by manifold vacuum. The air and fuel vapors are then directed into the engine to be burned. Most 1973 and later models have integral vapor separators within the fuel tank.

TRANSMISSION CONTROLLED SPARK

This system controls exhaust emissions by eliminating vacuum advance in the lower forward gears.

The system consists of a transmission switch, solenoid vacuum switch, time delay relay and thermostatic water temperature switch. The vacuum solenoid, called a Combination Emissions Control or CEC solenoid serves two functions. One function is to control distributor vacuum; the added function is to act as a deceleration throttle stop in high gear. This cuts down on emissions when the vehicle is coming to a stop in high gear. The CEC solenoid is controlled by a temperature switch, a transmission switch, and a 20 second time delay relay. This system also contains a reversing relay, which energizes the solenoid when the transmission switch, temperature switch or time delay completes the CEC circuit to ground. The system is normally closed blocking vacuum advance and when energized, opens to allow vacuum advance. The temperature switch completes the CEC circuit to ground when engine temperature is below 82°. Some Camaros also have a high temperature terminal on the switch to complete the CEC circuit when coolant temperature reaches 232°. The time delay relay allows vacuum advance (and raised idle speed) for 20 seconds after the ignition key is turned to the "on" position. Models with an automatic transmission and air conditioning also have a solid state timing device which engages the air conditioning compressor for three seconds after the ignition key is turned to the "off" position to prevent the engine from running-on.

In the energized position, an idle stop solenoid maintains engine speed at a predetermined fast idle. When the solenoid is de-energized by turning off the ignition, the solenoid allows the throttle plates to close beyond the normal idle position; thus cutting off the air supply and preventing engine run-on. The 6 cylinder is the only 1972 engine with a C.E.C. valve. The time delay relay delays full vacuum 20 seconds after the transmission is shifted into high gear. V8 engines use a vacuum advance solenoid. This relay is normally closed to block vacuum and opens when energized to allow vacuum advance. The solenoid controls distributor vacuum advance and performs no throttle positioning function. The idle stop solenoid used operates in the same manner as the one on 6 cylinder engines. All air-conditioned cars have an additional anti-diesel (run-on) solenoid which engages the compressor clutch for three seconds after the ignition is switched off. The 1973 TCS system differs from the 1972 system in three ways. The 32 second upshift delay has been replaced by a 20 second starting relay. This relay closes to complete the TCS circuit and open the TCS solenoid, allowing vacuum advance, for 20 seconds after the key is turned to the "on" position. The

operating temperature of the temperature overide switch has been raised to 93°, and the switch that was used to engage the A/C compressor when the key was turned "off" has been eliminated. All models are equipped with an electric throttle control solenoid to prevent run-on. The 1973 TCS system is used on all models equipped with a 307 engine, all V8 models equipped with a manual transmission, and all full-size station wagons equipped with a 165 hp 350 or a 170 hp 400.

The 1974 TCS system is used only on manual transmission models. System components remain unchanged from 1973. The vacuum advance solenoid is located on the coil bracket.

For diagnosis procedures, see the Unit Repair Section.

EARLY FUEL EVAPORATION SYSTEM

1975 and later models are equipped with this system to reduce engine warm-up time, improve driveability, and reduce emissions. On start-up, a vacuum motor acts to close a heat valve in the exhaust manifold which causes exhaust gases to enter the intake manifold heat riser passages. Incoming fuel mixture is then heated and more complete fuel evaporation is provided during warm-up.

CATALYTIC CONVERTER

All 1975 and later models are equipped with a catalytic converter. The converter is located midway in the exhaust system. Stainless steel exhaust pipes are used ahead of the converter. The converter is stainless steel with an aluminized steel cover and a ceramic felt blanket to insulate the converter from the floorpan. The catalyst pellet bed inside the converter consists of noble metals which cause a reaction that

converts hydrocarbons and carbon monoxide into water and carbon dioxide. See the "Unit Repair" section for a complete description.

EXHAUST GAS RECIRCULATION

All 1973 and later engines are equipped with exhaust gas recirculation (EGR). This system consists of a metering valve, a vacuum line to the carburetor, and cast-in exhaust gas passages in the intake manifold. The EGR valve is controlled by carburetor vacuum, and accordingly opens and closes to admit exhaust gases into the fuel/air mixture. The exhaust gases lower the combustion temperature, and reduce the amount of oxides of nitrogen (NOx) produced. The valve is closed at idle and wide open throttle, but is open between the two extreme throttle positions.

Some California engines are equipped with a dual diaphragm EGR valve. This valve further limits the exhaust gas opening (compared to the single diaphragm EGR valve) during high intake manifold vacuum periods, such as high-speed cruising, and provides more exhaust gas recirculation during acceleration when manifold vacuum is low. In addition to the hose running to the thermal vacuum switch, a second hose is connected directly to the intake manifold.

ENGINE

The 250 six cylinder engines are of the inline type, with seven main bearings. V8 engines are of two basic types. All engines of each type are generally similar in design and have some interchangeability of parts. The first type is the small block V8 series. This includes the 262, 305, 307, 350, and 400 cu. in. engines. The second type is the big block, or Mark IV, V8 series. This includes engines of 402 and 454 cu. in. displacement.

The big block 402 was last offered in 1972; the 454 was dropped after 1975. The small block 400 was offered starting 1974. The V6-200 is a cut down small block V8, sharing common parts with the V8.

NOTE: The V6-231 is built by Buick and is not covered in this section. For 231 V-6 service procedures see the Apollo section.

NOTE: *Interchangeability of parts is rather limited between the 400 and the smaller small block V8s.*

ENGINE REMOVAL AND INSTALLATION

NOTE: *Unless otherwise stated, the following operations cover all engines.*

DIAPHRAGM COVER
SPRING
VALVE SHAFT
SEAL
VALVE SEAT
VALVE CHAMBER
TO INTAKE MANIFOLD
VACUUM TUBE CONNECTED TO PORT IN CARBURETOR
ACTUATING DIAPHRAGM
VALVE OPEN
EXHAUST GAS INLET PORT

Cutaway view of an EGR valve
(© Chevrolet Div., G.M. Corp)

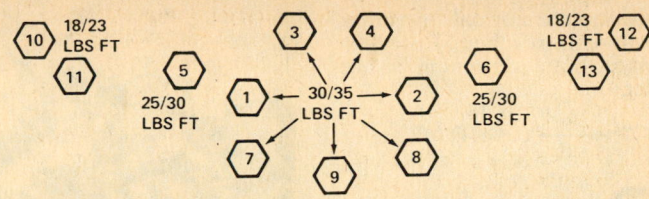

Exhaust manifold torque sequence—inline six cylinder with integral intake manifold (© Chevrolet Div., G.M. Corp.)

CAUTION

Do not discharge the compressor or disconnect the A/C lines. Damage to the A/C system or personal injury could result.

1. Raise car and place on jackstands.
2. Drain cooling system, transmission, and crankcase.
3. Scribe alignment marks on underside of hood and around hood hinges, and remove hood from hinges.
4. Disconnect coolant and heater hoses at engine attachment.
5. Disconnect battery cables at battery.
6. Remove radiator and shroud assembly. Remove fan and pulley.
7. Remove air cleaner.
8. Disconnect coil, starter and alternator wires, engine-to-body ground strap, oil pressure and engine temperature sender wires, C.E.C. wire, and any other wires.
9. Disconnect gas line at fuel pump.
10. Disconnect accelerator control linkage at firewall.
11. Disconnect power brake vacuum line.
12. Disconnect exhaust pipe from manifold. Disconnect the crossover pipe on V8 models, if so equipped.
13. Disconnect clutch shaft bracket at frame and disconnect clutch linkage. On automatic transmission models, remove transmission oil filler tube and plug the opening.
14. Attach engine lifting apparatus. Attach to hoist and secure the engine.
15. Remove driveshaft.
16. Remove and set aside power steering pump and air conditioning compressor. Do not disconnect hoses.
17. Remove engine rear mounting bolts.
18. Disconnect speedometer cable, transmission control rod linkage lower ends, T.C.S. switch, and transmission oil cooler lines.
19. Loosen front engine mounting bolts.
20. Raise engine slightly and remove bolts.
21. Remove transmission crossmember and free the transmission rear mounting.
22. Remove engine and transmission as a unit from the car.
    On installation:
1. Bolt engine lifting equipment to engine and lower engine and transmission into chassis as a unit. Guide engine to align front engine mounts with mounts on frame.
2. Install one rear transmission crossmember side bolt, swing crossmember up under transmission mount and install bolt in opposite side rail.
3. Align and install rear mount bolts.
4. Install engine front mount bolts and remove lifting equipment from engine.

5. Install and connect all items in reverse order of engine removal procedure.

MANIFOLDS

Refer to the Chevrolet and Corvette section for intake and exhaust manifold removal and installation procedures for all engines. Use the following procedures for exhaust manifold removal and installation on inline sixes with the intake manifold integral with the cylinder head.

Exhaust Manifold Removal and Installation, 1975 and Later Six Cylinder Engine with Integral Intake Manifold

1. Remove the air cleaner.
2. Remove the power steering and air pump brackets.
3. Remove the EFE valve bracket.
4. Disconnect the throttle linkage and return spring.
5. Unbolt the exhaust pipe from the flange.
6. Unbolt and remove the manifold.
7. Reverse the procedure for installation. Tighten the four end bolts to specifications last.

VALVE SYSTEM

Chevrolet uses a hydraulic tappet system with adjustable rocker mounting nuts to obtain zero lash.

A few 1972 high-performance V8s use mechanical tappets (valve lifters) which require periodic adjustment.

Mechanical Valve Lifter Adjustment

1. Set engine in No. 1 firing position.
2. Adjust the clearance between the valve stems and the rocker arms using a feeler gauge. Adjust the rocker arm mounting nut. Check the Tune-Up Specifications table for the proper clearance. Adjust the following Valves in No. 1 firing position: Intake No. 2, 7, Exhaust No. 4, 8.
3. Turn crankshaft one-half revolution (180°) clockwise. Adjust the following valves: Intake No. 1, 8, Exhaust No. 3, 6.
4. Turn crankshaft one-half revolution clockwise to No. 6 firing position. Adjust the following valves in No. 6 firing position: Intake No. 3, 4, Exhaust No. 5, 7.
5. Turn crankshaft one-half revolution clockwise. Adjust the follow-

ing valves: Intake No. 5, 6, Exhaust No. 1, 2.

VALVE ARRANGEMENT

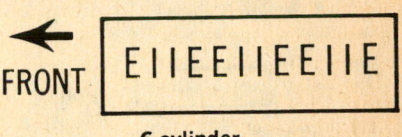

6 cylinder

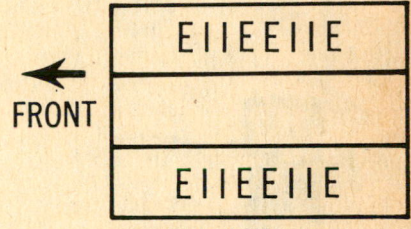

Small block V8s

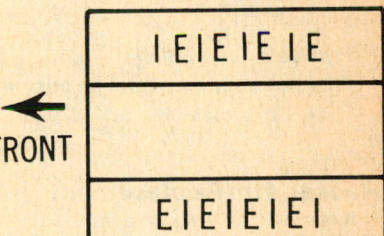

Big block V8s

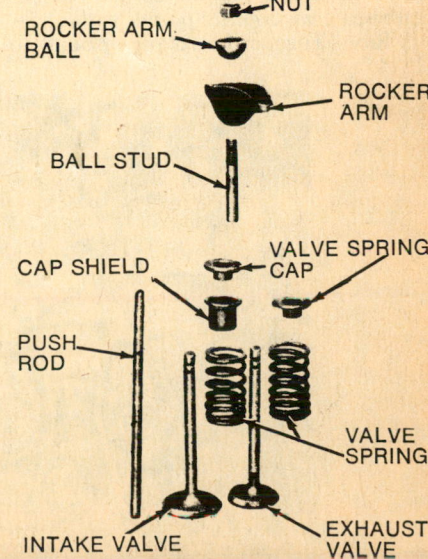

V8 valve assembly
(© Chevrolet Div., G.M. Corp)

6. Run engine until normal operating temperature is reached. Reset all clearances, hot and running, using oil deflectors.

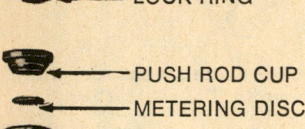

— LOCK RING

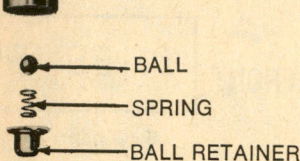

— PUSH ROD CUP
— METERING DISC
— PLUNGER

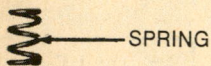

— BALL
— SPRING
— BALL RETAINER

— SPRING

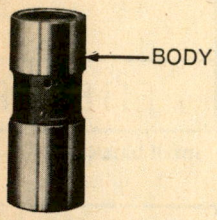

— BODY

Hydraulic lifter plunger and body are fitted pairs and must not be mismated
(© Chevrolet Div., G.M. Corp)

Rocker Arm Replacement

Remove the rocker arm cover. Remove the rocker arms in mated pairs. Install the rocker arms for each cylinder only when the lifters are off the cam lobes and the valves are closed. Lubricate all contact points with chassis lube. Torque the retaining bolts to 25 ft.lb.

Adjusting valve clearance—6 cyl hydraulic lifters
(© Chevrolet Div., G.M. Corp)

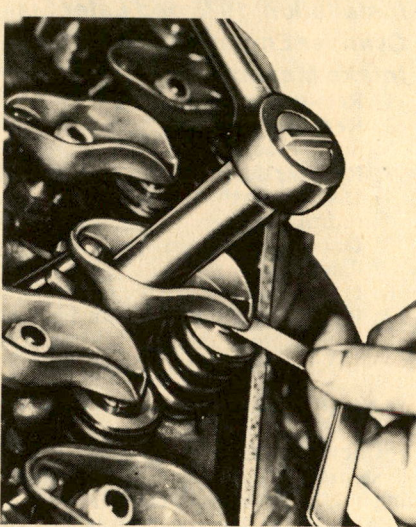

Adjusting valve clearance—V8 w/mechanical lifters
(© Chevrolet Div., G.M. Corp)

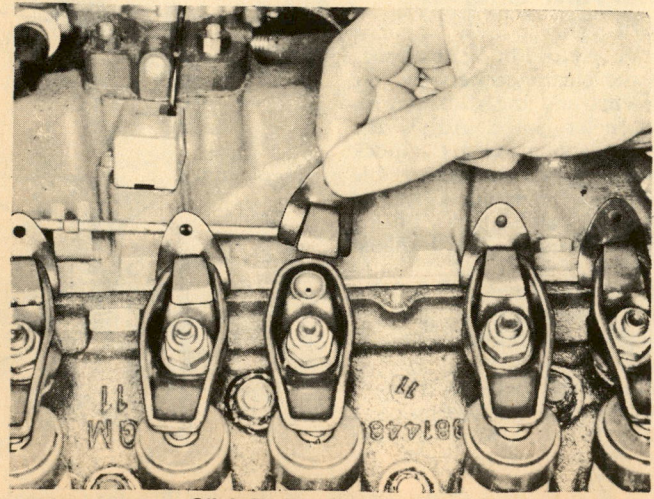

Oil deflector clips installed
(© Chevrolet Div., G.M. Corp)

Cylinder Head Removal and Installation

—————— CAUTION ——————
Do not discharge the compressor or disconnect the A/C lines. Personal injury could result.

INLINE 6 CYLINDER

1. Drain cooling system and remove air cleaner. Disconnect P.C.V. hose.
2. Disconnect accelerator pedal rod at bell crank on manifold, and fuel and vacuum lines at carburetor.
3. Disconnect exhaust pipe at manifold flange, then remove manifold bolts and clamps and remove manifolds and carburetor as an assembly.
4. Remove fuel and vacuum line retaining clip from water outlet. Then disconnect wire harness from heat sending unit and coil, leaving harness clear of clips on rocker arm cover.
5. Disconnect radiator hose at water outlet housing and battery ground strap at cylinder head.
6. Disconnect wires and remove spark plugs. On the 6 cylinder engine disconnect coil to distributor primary wire lead at coil and remove the coil.
7. Remove rocker arm cover. Back off rocker arm nuts, pivot rocker arms to clear push rods and remove push rods.

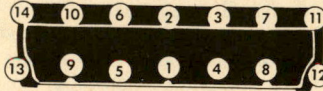

6 cylinder engine cylinder head torque sequence

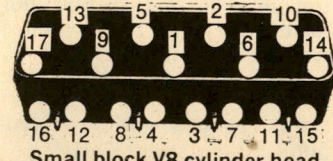

Small block V8 cylinder head torque sequence

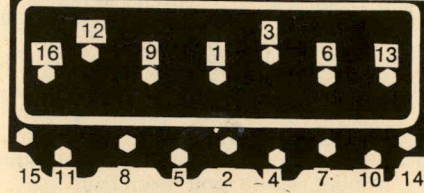

Big block V8 cylinder head torque sequence

8. Remove cylinder-head bolts, cylinder head and gasket.
9. Place a new cylinder-head gasket over dowel pins in cylinder block.
10. Guide and lower cylinder head into place over dowels and gasket.

11. Oil cylinder-head bolts, install and run them down snug.
12. Tighten the cylinder-head bolts a little at a time with a torque wrench in the correct sequence. Final torque should be as specified.
13. Install valve pushrods down through the cylinder-head openings and seat them in their lifter sockets.
14. Install rocker arms, balls and nuts and tighten rocker arm nuts until all pushrod play is taken up.
15. Install thermostat, thermostat housing and water outlet using new gaskets. Then connect radiator hose.
16. Install heat sending switch and torque to 15-20 ft lbs.
17. Clean spark plugs or install new ones.
18. Torque 5/8 in. plugs to 15 ft lbs. Tapered seat plugs are used on all engines.
19. Install coil (on six cylinder engine) then connect heat sending unit and coil primary wires, and connect battery ground cable at the cylinder head.
20. Clean surfaces and install new gasket over manifold studs. Install manifold. Install bolts and clamps and torque as specified.
21. Connect throttle linkage.
22. Connect P.C.V., fuel and vacuum lines and secure lines in clip at water outlet.
23. Fill cooling system and check for leaks.
24. Adjust valve lash.
25. Install rocker arm cover and position wiring harness in clips.
26. Clean and install air cleaner.

V6 and V8

1. Drain coolant. Remove air cleaner.
2. Disconnect:
   a. battery
   b. radiator and heater hose from manifold
   c. throttle linkage
   d. fuel line
   e. coil wires
   f. temperature sending unit
   g. power brake hose, distributor vacuum hose, and crankcase vent hoses.
3. Remove:
   a. distributor, marking position
   b. alternator upper bracket
   c. coil and bracket
   d. manifold attaching bolts
   e. intake manifold and carburetor.
4. Remove:
   a. rocker arm covers
   b. rocker arm nuts, balls, rocker arms, and pushrods. These items must be replaced in their original locations.
5. Remove cylinder head bolts, cylinder head, and gasket.
6. Reverse procedure to install. Tighten head bolts evenly to the specified torque. On engines having steel gasket, use sealer on both sides. No sealer should be used on steel-asbestos gaskets. Adjust the valve lash.

TIMING COVER, CHAIN, AND CAMSHAFT

All inline 6 cylinder engines have gear driven camshafts, while all V6 and V8 camshafts are driven by a timing chain. Inline 6 cylinder timing gear replacement requires camshaft removal.

Cover Removal and Installation

1. Drain and remove radiator.
2. Remove harmonic balancer, using a puller.
3. Drain the engine oil and remove the oil pan on all 1972 engines and on small block V8s through 1974. Remove the V6 and V8 water pump. If the oil pan isn't to be removed, cut the pan seal off flush with the block.
4. Remove timing gear cover attaching screws, and cover and gasket.
5. Reverse procedure to install. Use silicone sealer at the oil pan to cylinder block joint.

Chilton's TIME SAVER

When replacing the crankshaft damper, it has been found that lightly polishing the inside diameter with crocus cloth will greatly ease replacement. This procedure will also assist in any future removals, as it is sometimes difficult to pull a damper even with a puller. Be sure that the polishing is not overdone, or the damper will wobble on the crankshaft.

CAUTION

The engines use a harmonic balancer. Breakage may occur if the balancer is hammered back onto the crankshaft. A press or special installation tool is necessary.

Oil Seal Removal and Installation

1. After removing gear cover, pry oil seal out of front of cover with large screwdriver.
2. Install new lip seal with lip (open side of seal) inside and drive or press seal carefully into place.

V6 and V8 Timing Chain Replacement

V6 and V8 models are equipped with a timing chain. To replace the chain, remove the radiator, water pump harmonic balancer, and the crankcase front cover. This will allow access to the timing chain. Crank the engine until the marks punched on both sprockets are closest to one another and in line between the shaft centers. Take out the three bolts that hold the camshaft sprocket to the camshaft. This sprocket is a light press fit on the camshaft and will come off readily. It is located by a dowel. The chain comes off with the camshaft sprocket. A gear puller will be required to remove the crankshaft sprocket.

Without disturbing the position of the engine, mount the new crank sprocket on the shaft, then mount the chain over the camshaft sprocket. Arrange the camshaft sprocket in such a way that the timing marks will line up between the shaft centers and the camshaft locating dowel will enter the dowel hole in the cam sprocket.

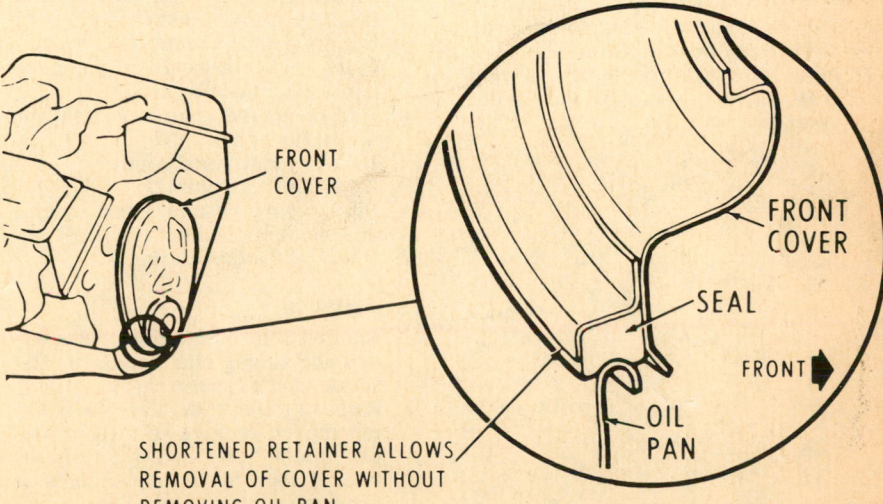

FRONT COVER

FRONT COVER

SEAL

FRONT

OIL PAN

SHORTENED RETAINER ALLOWS REMOVAL OF COVER WITHOUT REMOVING OIL PAN

On 1975 and later small block V8s, it is no longer necessary to remove or lower the oil pan to remove the timing cover. The seal retainer is shortened enough to clear the pan

(© Chevrolet Div., G.M. Corp)

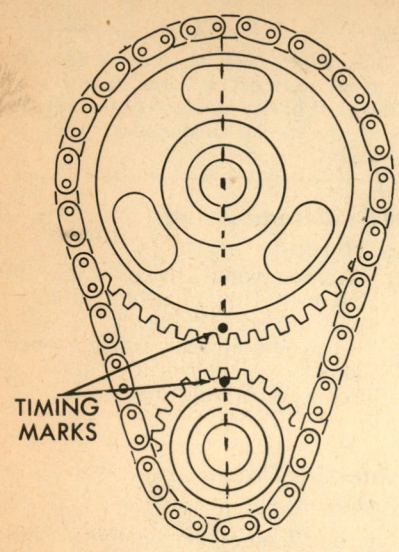

TIMING MARKS

V8 engine timing marks

Place the cam sprocket, with its chain mounted over it, in position on the front of the camshaft and pull up with the three bolts that hold it to the camshaft.

After the sprockets are in place, turn the engine two full revolutions to make certain that the timing marks are in correct alignment between the shaft centers.

Camshaft Removal and Installation

NOTE: *Cam lobes must be lubricated with engine assembly lubricant or heavy oil before installation. All cam journals are the same diameter, so be careful that the cam bearings are not dislodged during installation.*

INLINE 6 CYLINDER

The manufacturer recommends that the engine be removed from the car to remove the camshaft. However, in most cases the following procedure can be used. You may also have to raise the front of the engine for clearance.

1. In addition to removing the timing gear cover, remove the grille assembly.

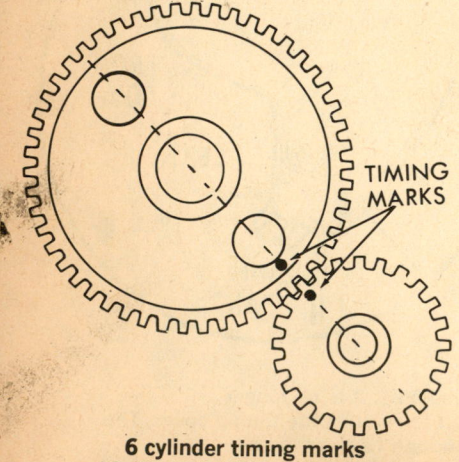

TIMING MARKS

6 cylinder timing marks
(© Chevrolet Div., G.M. Corp)

2. Remove valve cover and gasket, loosen all the valve rocker arm nuts and pivot the arms clear of the pushrods.
3. Remove distributor and fuel pump.
4. Remove coil, side cover and gasket. Remove pushrods and valve lifters.
5. Remove the two camshaft thrust plate retaining screws by working through holes in the camshaft gear.
6. Remove camshaft and gear assembly by pulling it out through the front of the block.

NOTE: *If renewing either camshaft or camshaft gear, the gear must be pressed off the camshaft. The replacement parts must be assembled in the same manner (under pressure). In placing the gear on the camshaft, press the gear onto the shaft until it bottoms against the gear spacer ring. The end clearance of the thrust plate should be .001 to .005 in.*

7. Install camshaft assembly in the engine.
8. Turn crankshaft and camshaft to align and bring the timing marks together. Push the camshaft into this aligned position. Install camshaft thrust plate-to-block screws and torque them to 6-7 1/2 ft lbs.
9. Runnout on either crankshaft or camshaft gear should not exceed .003 in.
10. Backlash between the two gears should be between .004 and .006 in.
11. Install timing gear cover and gasket.
12. Install oil pan and gaskets.
13. Install harmonic balancer.
14. Line up keyway in balancer with key on crankshaft and drive balancer onto shaft until it bottoms against crankshaft gear.
15. Install valve lifters and pushrods. Install side cover with new gasket. Attach coil wires; install fuel pump.
16. Install distributor and set timing as described under distributor at the beginning of the section.
17. Pivot rocker arms over pushrods and adjust the valves.
18. Add oil to the engine. Install and adjust fan belt.
19. Install radiator or shroud.
20. Install grille assembly.
21. Fill cooling system, start engine and check for leaks.
22. Check and adjust timing.

V6 and V8

1. Remove intake manifold, valve lifters and timing chain cover as described in this section.
2. Remove grille, except on Nova. On this model, remove both front motor mount bolts and right motor mount, then lower engine until it rests on frame.
3. On Nova, remove the two center bolts and the one lower bolt that secure the hood latch support. This will give adequate clearance for the cam.

4. Remove fuel pump and pump pushrod.
5. Remove camshaft sprocket bolts, sprocket and timing chain. A light blow to the lower edge of a tight sprocket should free it (use a plastic mallet).
6. Install two 5/16—18 x 4 in. bolts in cam bolt holes and pull cam from block.
7. To install, reverse removal procedure aligning the sprocket timing marks.

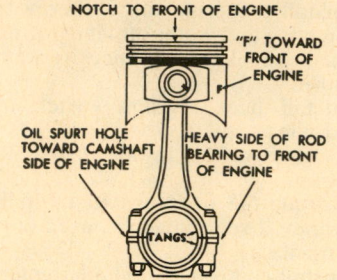

NOTCH TO FRONT OF ENGINE

"F" TOWARD FRONT OF ENGINE

OIL SPURT HOLE TOWARD CAMSHAFT SIDE OF ENGINE

HEAVY SIDE OF ROD BEARING TO FRONT OF ENGINE

TANGS

Piston and rod assembly—6 cylinder
(© Chevrolet Div., G.M. Corp)

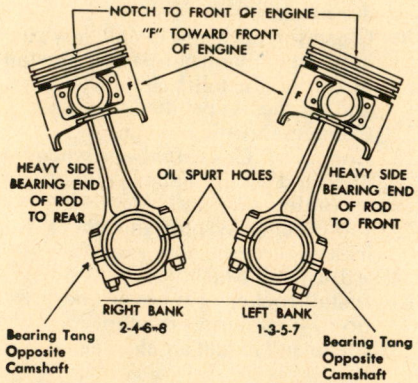

NOTCH TO FRONT OF ENGINE

"F" TOWARD FRONT OF ENGINE

HEAVY SIDE BEARING END OF ROD TO REAR

OIL SPURT HOLES

HEAVY SIDE BEARING END OF ROD TO FRONT

RIGHT BANK 2-4-6-8

LEFT BANK 1-3-5-7

Bearing Tang Opposite Camshaft

Bearing Tang Opposite Camshaft

Piston-to-rod relationship small block V8

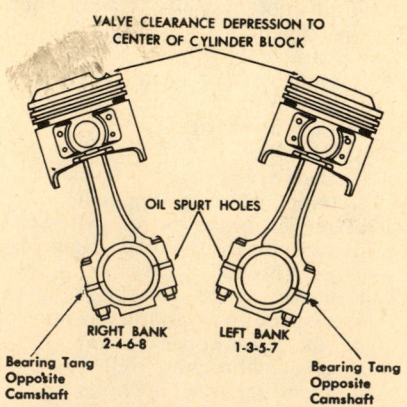

VALVE CLEARANCE DEPRESSION TO CENTER OF CYLINDER BLOCK

OIL SPURT HOLES

RIGHT BANK 2-4-6-8

LEFT BANK 1-3-5-7

Bearing Tang Opposite Camshaft

Bearing Tang Opposite Camshaft

Piston-to-rod relationship— Mk IV (big block) V8

LUBRICATION

Oil Pan Removal and Installation

NOVA, CAMARO—INLINE 6 CYLINDER

1. Disconnect battery ground cable.
2. Remove front engine mount bolts.

Remove upper radiator panel or side mount bolts.

3. Drain coolant. Remove radiator hoses.
4. Remove fan.
5. Drain engine oil.
6. On all models through 1974, and 1975 and later models with manual transmission, disconnect and remove the starter.
7. Disconnect oil cooler lines and remove converter or flywheel housing underpan.
8. On Nova through 1974 and 1972 Camaro disconnect steering rod at idler lever. Swing linkage to one side for pan clearance.
9. Rotate crankshaft until timing mark on torsional damper is at 6:00 o'clock position.
10. On Camaro, raise engine enough to insert 2 x 4 in. blocks under engine mounts.
11. Unbolt oil pan. On some models it may be necessary to remove the oil pump and intake pipe for clearance. On Nova, remove the left engine mount and frame bracket. Lower the pan slightly and roll it into the area where the mount was. Then tilt the front of the pan up and pull it down and to the rear. Lower pan.

1972 CHEVELLE—6 CYLINDER

1. Disconnect battery ground cable.
2. Remove radiator upper mounting panel. Place a piece of heavy cardboard between fan and radiator.
3. Remove starter. Disconnect fuel line.
4. Drain engine oil; disconnect brake line from front crossmember.
5. Remove converter housing underpan and splash shield.
6. Rotate crankshaft until timing mark on torsional damper is at 6:00 o'clock position.
7. Remove front engine mount through bolts.
8. Raise engine approximately three inches, remove engine mounts, and lower oil pan.

V8 EXCEPT 402, 454

See the next procedure for 1972 Chevelle and Monte Carlo with big block V8.

1. Disconnect battery ground cable.
2. Remove distributor cap.
3. Remove radiator upper mounting panel.
4. Remove fan. On big block (Mark IV) engine models, place a piece of heavy cardboard betwen the radiator and fan.
5. Drain engine oil.
6. Disconnect exhaust or crossover pipes.
7. Remove converter housing underpan and splash shield.
8. On 1972 Camaro disconnect steering idler lever at the frame. Swing linkage down.
9. Rotate crankshaft until timing

Installing blocks for oil pan removal—V8
(© Chevrolet Div., G.M. Corp)

mark on torsional damper is at 6:00 o'clock position.
10. Remove starter.
11. On 1973-74 big block Chevelles with a 4-speed, remove the transmission mount to crossmember nut and raise the rear of the transmission.
12. Remove front engine mount through bolts.
13. Raise engine and insert blocks under engine mounts. Bock thickness should be 2 in. for Nova and Camaro, and 3 in. for Chevelle.
14. Remove oil pan.

ALL V6

1. Drain the oil.
2. Remove the oil dipstick and tube.
3. Raise and support the car.
4. Remove the exhaust crossover pipe.
5. On cars with automatic transmission, remove the converter housing under pan.
6. Remove the oil pan and discard the gaskets and seals.
7. Thoroughly clean the gasket surfaces and install the pan in reverse of removal. Always use new gaskets and seals.

1972 CHEVELLE AND MONTE CARLO—402, 454 V8

1. Disconnect battery ground cable.
2. Remove:
   a. air cleaner
   b. dipstick
   c. distributor cap
   d. radiator shroud and upper mounting panel.
3. Disconnect engine ground straps.
4. Disconnect accelerator control cable.
5. Drain oil.
6. Remove driveshaft and plug rear of transmission.
7. Remove starter.
8. Disconnect transmission linkage at transmission or remove floorshift lever.
9. Disconnect speedometer cable and back-up switch connector.
10. On manual transmission vehicles disconnect clutch chaft at frame.

On automatic transmission vehicles, disconnect cooler lines, detent cable, rod or switch wire, and modulator pipe.
11. Remove crossmember bolts. Jack up engine. Move crossmember rearward.
12. Remove crossover or disconnect dual exhaust pipes.
13. Remove:
   a. flywheel housing cover
   b. transmission
   c. flywheel housing and throwout bearing (manual transmission)
   d. front engine mount through bolts.
14. Raise rear of engine approximately 4 inches. Support engine by hoist.
15. Raise front of engine approximately 4 inches and insert 2 in. blocks under front engine mounts.
16. Rotate crankshaft until timing mark on torsional damper is at 6:00 o'clock position.
17. Unbolt and remove oil pan.

Oil Pump Removal and Installation

1. Remove oil pan.
2. Remove pump and pickup tube and screen assembly on inline engine and pump to rear main bearing cap bolt on V6 and V8. Remove the pump and extension shaft on the V6 and V8.
3. To install, reverse removal procedure.

Rear Main Seal Removal and Installation

The rear main bearing seal may be replaced without removing the crankshaft. Seals should only be replaced as a pair. The seal lips should face the front of the engine when properly installed.

1. Remove the oil pan, and pump as previously outlined, and remove the rear main bearing cap.
2. Pry the lower seal out of the bearing cap with a screwdriver, being careful not to gouge the cap surface.

3. Remove the upper seal by lightly tapping on one end with a brass pin punch until the other end can be grasped and pulled out with pliers.
4. Clean the bearing cap, cylinder block, and crankshaft mating surfaces with solvent. Inspect all these surfaces for gouges, nicks, and burrs.
5. Apply light engine oil on the seal lips and bead, but keep the seal ends clean.

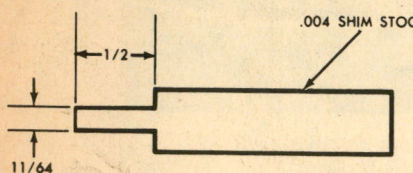

Rear main bearing seal installation tool
(© Chevrolet Div., G.M. Corp)

6. Insert the tip of the installation tool between the crankshaft and the seal seat of the cylinder block. Place the seal between the tip of the tool and the crankshaft, so that the bead contacts the tip of the tool.
7. Be sure that the seal lip is facing the front of the engine, and work the seal around the crankshaft using the installation tool to protect the seal from the corner of the cylinder block.

NOTE: *Do not remove the tool until the opposite end of the seal is flush with the cylinder block surface.*

8. Remove the installation tool, being careful not to pull the seal out at the same time.
9. Using the same procedure, install the lower seal into the bearing cap. Use your finger and thumb to lever the seal into the cap.
10. Apply sealer to the cylinder block only where the cap mates to the surface. Do not apply sealer to the seal ends.

11. Install the rear cap and torque the bolts to specifications. Install the oil pan and pump as previously described.

CLUTCH

The only service adjustment necessary on the clutch is to maintain the correct pedal free play. Clutch pedal free play, or throwout bearing lash, decreases with driven disc wear.

Removal and Installation

1. Support engine and remove transmission.
2. Disconnect clutch fork push rod and spring.
3. Remove flywheel housing.
4. Slide clutch fork from ball stud and remove fork from dust boot. Ball stud is threaded into clutch housing and may be replaced, if necessary.
5. Install an alignment tool (dummy shaft) to support the clutch assembly during removal. Mark flywheel and clutch cover for reinstallation, if they do not already have X marks.
6. Loosen clutch to flywheel attaching bolts evenly, one turn at a time, until spring pressure is released. Remove bolts and clutch assembly.
   On installation:
1. Clean pressure plate and flywheel face.
2. Support clutch disc and pressure plate with alignment tool. The driven disc is installed with the damper springs on the transmission side. The grease slinger is always on the transmission side.
3. Turn clutch assembly until mark on cover lines up with mark on flywheel, then install bolts. Tighten down evenly and gradually to avoid distortion.
4. Remove alignment tool.

5. Lubricate ball socket and fork fingers at release bearing end with high melting point grease. Lubricate recess on inside of throwout bearing and throwout fork groove with a light coat of graphite or other high melting point grease.
6. Install clutch fork and dust boot into housing. Install throwout bearing to throwout fork. Install flywheel housing. Install transmission.
7. Connect fork push rod and spring. Lubricate spring and pushrod ends.
8. Adjust shift linkage and clutch pedal free play.

Free Play Adjustment

This adjustment must be made under the vehicle on the clutch operating linkage. Free play is measured at the clutch pedal.

1. Disconnect the return spring at the clutch operating fork.
2. Use the linkage to push the clutch pedal up against its rubber bumper stop. On the 1973 Chevelle, more clearance can be obtained by loosening the rubber bumper bracket and moving the bracket. On 1978-79 models, rotate the clutch lever until the pedal is firmly against the bumper.
3. Push the end of the clutch operating fork to the rear until the release bearing can just be felt to contact the pressure plate fingers.

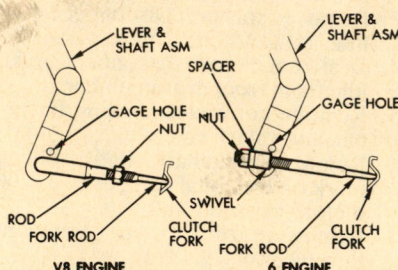

Clutch pedal free-play adjustment
(© Chevrolet Div., G.M. Corp)

4. Detach the front end of the operating rod from the clutch pivot shaft arm and place it in the gauge hole on the arm.
5. Loosen the locknut and lengthen the rod just enough to take all the play out of the linkage. Tighten the locknut.
6. Replace the operating rod in its original location.
7. Replace the return spring and check the free play at the pedal pad. It should be about 1 in. or more.

New Clutch Linkage Adjustment

1978-79 New Novas or Nova with new replacement clutches
1. Rotate the clutch lever and shaft assembly until the clutch pedal is firmly against the stop on the firewall.

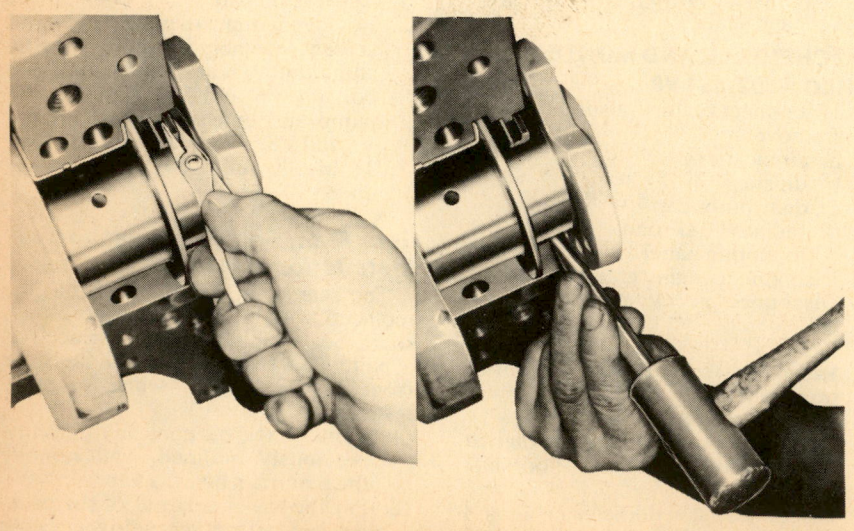

Rear main seal installation
(© Chevrolet Div., G.M. Corp)

2. Push the outer end of the clutch fork rearward until the throw-out bearing lightly touches the pressure plate springs.
3. Place the lower push rod in the fork and gauge hole, and increase the length until all-lash is removed.
4. Install the swivel or rod in the hole furthest from the centerline of the lever and shaft assembly and install the retainer.
5. Shorten the lower push rod by .16 inch, by turning the rod an additional 2½ turns, if necessary to remove clutch interference.
6. Tighten the locknut and spacer against the swivel or rod.
7. Install the clutch fork retainer spring.
8. A maximum of 1.6-2.3 inches when measured at the center of the pedal pad, is necessary to prevent the release fingers from contacting the clutch disc hub.

MANUAL TRANSMISSION

The normal-duty three-speed transmission is the Saginaw unit, while the heavy-duty three-speed used through 1974 is the Muncie. The Saginaw has one bolt at the center top of the side cover, while the Muncie has two.

The normal-duty four-speed is the Saginaw, while the heavy-duty unit used through 1974 is the Muncie. During 1974, the Muncie four-speed was phased out and the Warner T-10 heavy-duty four-speed introduced in the Camaro only. On the Saginaw, all three shift linkage rods go to the levers on the side cover. On the Muncie, two shift rods go to levers on the side cover and one rod (reverse) goes to a lever on the case extension housing. The Warner T-10 linkage is similar to that on the Muncie, but the transmission has a 9 bolt curved bottom side cover.

Transmission Removal and Installation

1. On floorshift models, remove the shift knob, and the spring and T-handle on four-speeds. Remove the boot.
2. Raise the car.
3. Disconnect the speedometer cable and TCS switch wiring at the transmission.
4. Remove the driveshaft.
5. On 1972 models remove the crossmember to shifter brace.
6. Support the rear of the engine and remove the crossmember. On 1972 models the crossmember may be slid rearward.
7. Detach the shift rods from the transmission levers.
8. On floorshift models, remove the shifter from the transmission.
9. Remove the upper transmission to clutch housing bolts and replace them with headless guide pins. Remove the lower bolts.
10. Slide the transmission back along the guide pins until the input shaft clears the clutch. Remove the transmission.
11. Reverse the procedure for installation. If the input shaft won't engage the clutch splines, put the transmission in gear and turn the output shaft slightly. Torque the transmission to clutch housing bolts to 55 ft lbs for 1972 models, and to 75 ft lbs beginning 1973. Torque for the Warner T-10 is 52 ft. lb.

Shift Linkage Adjustment

COLUMN SHIFT

1. With transmission in Reverse, place ignition switch in Lock.
2. Loosen shift rod lock nuts.
3. Set transmission first-reverse lever in reverse position. Pull down on first-reverse control rod until column lever is in reverse detent position. Tighten first-reverse lock nut.
4. Unlock the switch and shift the column and transmission levers to neutral position. Insert a 3/16 in. dia. rod into alignment holes in levers.
5. Tighten second-third locknut.
6. Remove alignment rod. Shift column lever to reverse. Turn key to Lock. Ignition switch must move freely to Lock position and it must not be possible to turn key to Lock when in any transmission position other than reverse. If this interlock binds, leave switch in Lock position and readjust first-reverse rod.
7. Check shifting.

FLOORSHIFT

1. Turn ignition switch to Off.
2. Loosen locknuts on shift rods and reverse rod.
3. Set transmission levers in neutral positions.
4. Set floorshift lever in neutral. Install locating gauge, 1/8 in. thick, 41/64 in. wide, 3 in. long, into control lever bracket assembly alignment slot. Some later models may take a locating pin.
5. Adjust length of shift rods. Tighten locknuts.
6. Remove locating gauge. Shift into reverse and lock the switch.
7. Pull down slightly on back drive (to column) rod to remove any slack and tighten locknut. Ignition switch must move freely to Lock position and it must not be possible to turn key to Lock when in any transmission position other than reverse. If this interlock binds, leave the switch in Lock position and readjust back drive rod.
8. Check shifting operation.

AUTOMATIC TRANSMISSION

There are two basic automatic transmissions. The first is the two speed Powerglide. A variation on the Powerglide is the Torque Drive transmission. The Torque Drive unit is a Powerglide with the automatic shifting provisions removed. Torque Drive is shifted manually, but has no clutch. Powerglide was dropped in mid-1973. The second type is the three speed Turbo Hydra-Matic. It is available in several load capacities, the Turbo Hydra-Matic 200, 250, 350, 375, and 400.

The Turbo Hydra-Matic 250 is used only in 1974-76 six-cylinder models. Only the 200 and the 350 are used in 1978-79 models. The 250 may be identified by the intermediate band adjusting screw on the right side of the case. The intermediate band replaces the intermediate clutch on the larger capacity models. The 200 is externally similar to the 350 but differs in having 10 pan bolts. The 350 has 13. The 200, 250, and 350 have a cable operated downshift linkage running from the accelerator linkage to the right side of the transmission, while the 375 and 400 have a downshift solenoid activated by a switch on the accelerator linkage. There is no external difference between the 375 and 400; they differ internally in numbers of clutch plates and other items related to torque capacity.

—— CAUTION ——

Any inaccuracies in shift linkage adjustments may result in premature failure of the transmission due to operation without the controls in full detent. Such operation results in reduced fluid pressure and in turn, partial engagement of the affected clutches. Partial engagement of the clutches, with sufficient pressure to permit apparently normal vehicle operation will result in failure of the clutches and/or other internal parts after only a few miles of operation.

Powerglide Shift Linkage Adjustment

COLUMN SHIFT

1. Loosen adjustment clamp at cross-shaft. Set transmission lever in drive by rotating lever counterclockwise to low detent, then clockwise one detent to drive.
2. Set selector lever in Drive. Remove any free play by holding cross-shaft upward and pulling shift rod downward.
3. Tighten the clamp and check the adjustment.
4. Place shift lever in Park and ignition switch in Lock. Loosen back drive rod clamp nut. Remove column lash and tighten clamp nut.
5. With selector lever in Park, the ig-

nition key should move freely to Lock position. Lock position should be obtainable only when transmission is in Park.

CAMARO, CHEVELLE, MALIBU, MONTE CARLO FLOORSHIFT

These models use a cable operated linkage.
1. Place shift lever in Drive position.
2. Disconnect cable from transmission lever. Place transmission lever in drive by rotating lever counterclockwise to low detent, then clockwise one detent to drive.
3. Measure distance from rearward face of attachment bracket to center of cable attachment pin. Adjust this dimension to 5.5 in. by loosening and moving cable end stud nut.
4. Place shift lever in Park and ignition switch in Lock position.
5. Loosen and adjust column (back drive) rod.
6. With selector lever in Park position, the ignition key should move freely to Lock position. Lock position should not be obtainable in any transmission position other than Park.

1972-77 Turbo Hydra-Matic 250, 350, 375, 400 Shift Linkage Adjustment

COLUMN SHIFT
1. Loosen the swivel at the lower end of the rod that comes from the column.
2. On 1973 and later models, set the transmission lever in the Neutral detent by turning the lever counterclockwise to the L1 detent, then clockwise three positions. On 1972 models set the lever in the Drive detent by turning the Lever counterclockwise to the L1 detent, then clockwise two positions.
3. Put the column lever in Neutral for 1973 and later models, and in Drive for 1972 models. The important thing here is not where the indicator points but that the lever be in the correct position.
4. Tighten the swivel.
5. Check that the key cannot be removed and that the wheel is not locked with the key in RUN. Check that the key can be removed in LOCK with the lever in Park, and that the steering wheel is locked.

1978-79 Turbo Hydra-Matic 350 Column Shift Linkage Adjustment
1. The shift tube must be free in the mast jacket.
2. Lift the selector lever towards the steering wheel. Allow the selector lever to be positioned in Drive by the detent. Do not use the indicator pointer as a reference.

3. Release the lever. The lever should be stopped from engaging low unless the lever is lifted.
4. Lift the lever towards the steering wheel and allow it to be positioned in Neutral by the detent.
5. Release the lever, it should now be stopped from engaging reverse unless lifted.
6. If adjustment is required, remove the screw and washer from the swivel.
7. Place the transmission lever in neutral by moving the lever counterclockwise to the L1 detent, then clockwise three detent positions to neutral.
8. Position the selector lever in Neutral as determined by the mechanical stop in the steering column.
9. Assemble the swivel, spring washer and screw and tighten the screw to 20 ft. lb. No lateral force should be exerted on the rod.
10. If necessary, adjust the indicator pointer to agree with the detent positions.
11. If necessary, readjust the neutral start switch.
12. Check the linkage operation.

NOVA FLOORSHIFT THROUGH 1974

This is a rod operated linkage. It is adjusted in Neutral. The Turbo Hydra-Matic Drive position is obtained by turning the transmission lever counterclockwise to the L1 detent, then clockwise two positions. The Neutral position is obtained by turning the level clockwise three positions from the L1 detent.

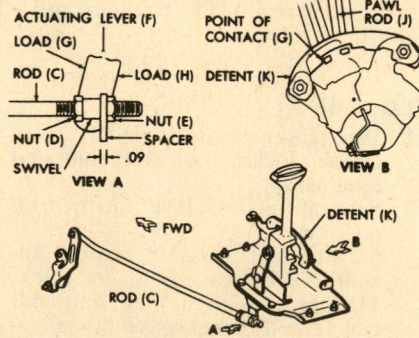

Automatic transmission rod operated floorshift linkage, Nova
(© Chevrolet Div., G.M. Corp)

1972 CAMARO, CHEVELLE, MONTE CARLO FLOORSHIFT

This is a cable operated linkage, very similar to the cable linkage used on the Camaro, Chevelle, and Monte Carlo Powerglide floorshift. The adjustment procedure is the same, except that the Turbo Hydra-Matic Drive position is obtained by turning the transmission lever counterclockwise to the L1 detent, then clockwise two positions.

CAMARO, CHEVELLE, MONTE CARLO, MALIBU FLOORSHIFT 1973 AND LATER; NOVA FLOORSHIFT 1975 AND LATER

This is a cable operated linkage.
1. Loosen the swivel at the lower end of the rod that comes from the steering column.

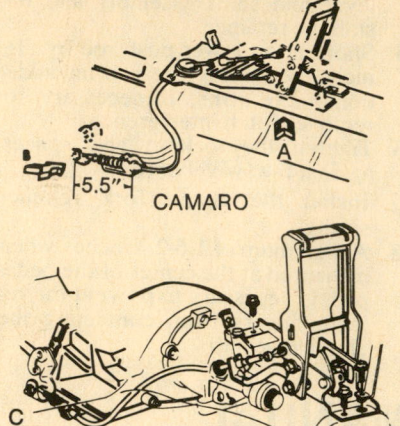

Automatic transmission cable operated floorshift linkage, Camaro and Chevelle
(© Chevrolet Div., G.M. Corp)

2. Loosen the pin at the transmission end of the cable.
3. Set the floorshift lever in the Drive detent.
4. Set the transmission lever in the Drive detent by moving it counterclockwise to the L1 detent, then clockwise three detent positions.
5. Tighten the nut on the pin at the transmission end of the cable.
6. Put the floorshift lever in Park and the ignition switch in LOCK.
7. Pull down lightly on the rod from the column and tighten its clamp nut to 20 ft. lb.

Turbo Hydra-Matic 200 Shift Linkage Adjustment
1. Place shifter assembly in the Neutral position.
2. Place the lever on the transmission in the Neutral position.
NOTE: *Neutral may be obtained by moving the lever on the transmission clockwise to the maximum detent position then counterclockwise two detent positions.*
3. Insert the pin and lock in the lever fork and adjust the column rod until the hole in the rod lines up with the pin in the shifter assembly and install the rod on the pin.

Powerglide Throttle Valve Linkage Adjustment

INLINE ENGINES THROUGH 1973
1. Fully depress the accelerator pedal.

2. Bellcrank must be at wide open throttle position.
3. On models through 1971, the dash lever at the firewall must be 1/64-1/16 in. off the lever stop.
4. Transmission lever must be against transmission internal stop.
5. Adjust linkage to simultaneously obtain conditions in Steps 1-4.

1972 V8 ENGINES
1. Remove air cleaner.
2. Disconnect accelerator linkage at carburetor.
3. Disconnect both return springs.
4. Pull throttle valve upper rod forward until transmission is through detent.
5. Open carburetor to wide open throttle position. Adjust swivel on end of upper throttle valve rod so carburetor reaches wide open throttle position at the same time that the ball stud contacts the end of the slot in the upper throttle valve rod. A tolerance of 1/32 in. is allowable.

Turbo Hydra-Matic 200 Throttle Valve Cable Adjustment
1. Disengage the snap lock so the cable is free.
2. With the cable installed in the support and attached to the transmission end carburetor lever, move the lever to the wide open throttle position.
3. Push the snap lock flush and close the throttle.

Turbo Hydra-Matic 200, 250, and 350 Detent Cable Adjustment
The Turbo Hydra-Matic 200, 250, and 350 have a detent, or downshift, cable between the carburetor linkage and the transmission.

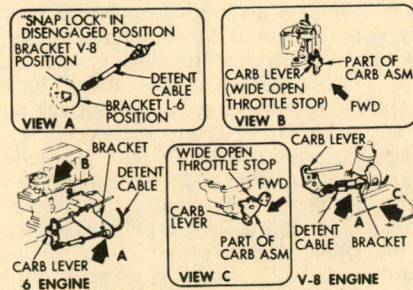

Turbo Hydra-Matic 350 detent cable adjustment
(© Chevrolet Div., G.M. Corp)

ALL NOVA AND CAMARO; 1972 CHEVELLE AND MONTE CARLO
1. Remove air cleaner.
2. Loosen detent cable screw or disengage snap lock.
3. Place carburetor lever in wide open throttle position. Make sure lever is against stop. On vehicles with Quadrajet carburetors, disengage the secondary lock out before placing lever in wide open throttle position.

NOTE: *Detent cable must be pulled through detent position.*
4. Engage snap lock or tighten detent screw.

1973 AND LATER CHEVELLE, MALIBU AND MONTE CARLO
On these models, the cable adjusts itself the first time the accelerator pedal is floorboarded.

Turbo Hydra-Matic 375 and 400 Detent Switch Adjustment
The Turbo Hydra-Matic 375 and 400 transmission has an electrical detent, or downshift, switch operated by the throttle linkage.

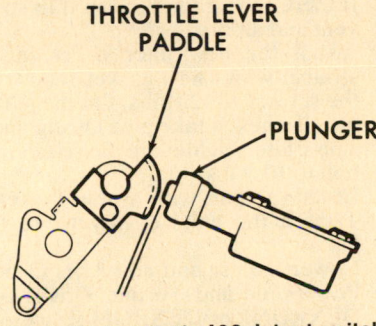

Turbo Hydra-Matic 400 detent switch adjustment—Nova and Camaro
(© Chevrolet Div., G.M. Corp)

1972 NOVA AND CAMARO
1. Loosen the switch mounting bolts. Place the carburetor lever in the wide open throttle position.
2. Make sure the choke is off.
3. Depress the switch plunger all the way.
4. Adjust switch mounting to obtain distance between depressed switch plunger and throttle lever paddle of .22-.24 in.
5. Tighten the switch mounting bolts.

1972 CHEVELLE AND MONTE CARLO
1. Pull detent switch driver rearward until hole in switch body aligns with hold in driver. Insert a .092 in. dia. pin through the aligned holes to hold the driver in position.
2. Loosen mounting bolt.
3. Depress accelerator to wide open throttle position. Move switch forward until driver contacts accelerator lever.
4. Tighten mounting bolt. remove pin.

1973 AND LATER
After installation, the switch adjusts itself the first time the accelerator is floorboarded.

Neutral Safety Swtich Adjustment
The neutral safety switch prevents the engine from being started in any transmission position except Neutral or Park. On all column shift and floorshift models from late 1972, the switch is located on the upper side of the steering column under the instrument panel. On early 1972 models with floorshift, the switch is located inside the shift console.
1. Remove console for access on early floorshift models.
2. Disconnect wiring connectors.
3. Remove switch.

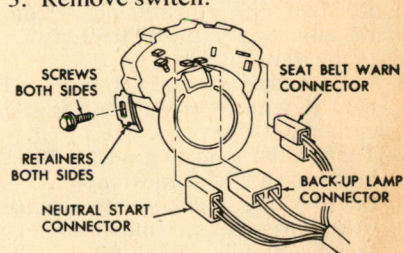

1973 combination neutral start switch connections
(© Chevrolet Div., G.M. Corp)

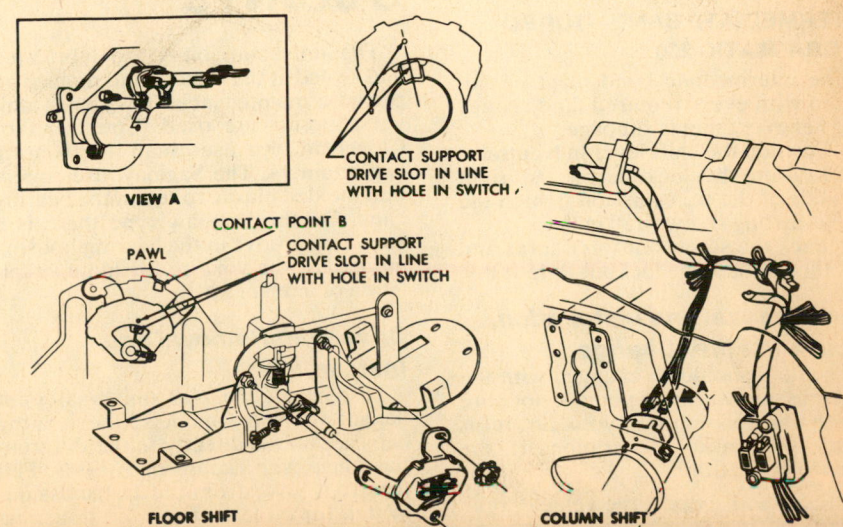

Typical neutral safety switch installation (© Chevrolet Div., G.M. Corp)

4. Position the shift lever in Neutral on column shift models from late 1972. Put it in Drive on earlier column shift models, and in Park on floorshift models with the column mounted switch. On column shift models, locate lever tang against transmission selector plate.

5. Align slot in contact support with hole in switch. Insert 3/32 in. dia. pin to hold support in place. Switch is now aligned.

NOTE: *1973 and later neutral safety switches have a shear-pin installed to aid in proper new switch alignment so that insertion of a pin is unnecessary. Moving the shift lever shears the pin.*

6. Place contact support drive slot over drive tang. Install screws.
7. Remove pin. Connect wiring. Replace console.
8. Set parking brake and footbrake. Check to see that engine will start only in Drive or Neutral.

Band Adjustments

There are no band adjustments possible or required for the Turbo Hydra-Matic 200, 350, 375, or 400.

LOW BAND—POWERGLIDE AND TORQUE DRIVE

The low band must be adjusted at the first required fluid change or whenever there is slippage.

1. Position the shift lever in Neutral.
2. Remove the protective cap from the adjusting screw on the left side of the transmission.
3. Loosen the locknut 1/4 turn and hold it with a wrench during the entire adjusting procedure.
4. Tighten the adjusting nut to 70 in lbs, using a 7/32 allen wrench.
5. Back off the adjusting nut exactly three turns for a band used less than 6,000 miles. Back off exactly four turns for a band used 6,000 miles or more.
6. Torque the locknut to 15 ft lbs and replace the cap.

INTERMEDIATE BAND—TURBO HYDRA-MATIC 250

The intermediate band must be adjusted with every required fluid change or whenever there is slippage.

1. Position the shift lever in Neutral.
2. Loosen the locknut on the right side of the transmission tighten the adjusting screw to 30 in lbs.
3. Back the screw out three turns and then tighten the locknut to 15 ft lbs.

Pan Removal and Installation, Fluid and Filter Change

The fluid should be changed with the transmission warm. If you are not sure which transmission is in your car, refer to the pan gasket illustrations in the Chevrolet Section.

1. Raise and support the vehicle, preferably in a level attitude.
2. On Nova with Turbo Hydra-Matic

200, 250 or 350, support the transmission and remove the support crossmember.

3. Place a large pan under the transmission pan. Remove all the front and side pan bolts. Loosen the rear bolts about four turns.
4. Pry the pan loose and let it drain.
5. Remove the pan and gasket. Clean the pan thoroughly with solvent and air dry it. Be very careful not to get any lint from rags in the pan.
6. Remove the strainer to valve body screws, the strainer, and the gasket. Most 200 and 350 transmissions will have a throw-away filter instead of a strainer. On the 400 transmission, remove the filter retaining bolt, filter, and intake pipe O-ring.
7. If there is a strainer, clean it in solvent and air dry.
8. Install the new filter or cleaned strainer with a new gasket. Tighten the screws to 12 ft lbs. On the 400, install a new intake pipe O-ring and a new filter, tightening the retaining bolt to 10 ft lbs.
9. Install the pan with a new gasket. Tighten the bolts evenly to 12 ft lbs.
10. Lower the car and add 5 pts (3 on Powerglide and Torque Drive) of DEXRON® or DEXRON II® automatic transmission fluid through the dipstick tube.
11. Start the engine in Park and let it idle. Do not race the engine. Shift into each shift lever position, shift back into Park, and check the fluid level on the dipstick. The level should be 1/4 in. below. ADD. Be very careful not to overfill. Recheck the level after the car has been driven long enough to thoroughly warm up the transmission. Add fluid as necessary. The level should then be at FULL.

U JOINTS

The universal joints are lubricated and sealed at the factory and require no periodic maintenance. Two basic universal joints are used. The Dana or Cleveland type uses snap-ring bearing cap retainers. The Saginaw uses injection molded plastic to retain the bearing caps. On the Saginaw type there is a snap-ring groove in the bearing housing inboard of the yoke to facilitate installation of a repair kit.

Driveshaft Removal and Installation

Disconnect the rear universal joint flange. On some models, the bearing caps are bolted directly to the differential flange with clamps or U-bolts. Pull the front yoke from the transmission. Watch for oil leaks from the transmission output housing. Install in the reverse order of removal.

Universal Joint Removal and Installation

SNAP-RING TYPE

1. Remove the driveshaft.
2. Remove the snap-rings from the trunnion yoke.
3. Using a vise and suitably sized sockets, press on the trunnion until the bearing cap is almost out. Grasp the cap in the vise and work it out of the yoke. Repeat the above procedure for the rest of the bearing caps.
4. Pack the rollers in grease and fill the grease reservoir.
5. To install, position the trunnion in the yoke and partially install one bearing cap. Start the trunnion in the bearing cap and partially install the other cap. Align the trunnion with the caps and press into place.
6. If necessary, repeat Step 5 above for the other yoke.
7. Install the snap-rings.
8. Install the driveshaft in the vehicle.

PLASTIC RETAINER TYPE

Remove and install the bearing caps and trunnion as described for the snap-ring type universal joints. On an original universal joint, however, the bearing caps will be secured in the yokes with injected plastic. The plastic will shear when the bearing caps are pressed. Service snap-rings are installed in the groove on the inside (of yoke) of the installed caps.

REAR AXLE

Axle Shaft, Bearing and Seal Removal and Installation

These cars use two different types of drive axle, the C-lock and the non C-lock type. Axle shafts in the C-lock type are retained by C-shaped locks, which fit grooves at the inner end of the shaft. Axle shafts in the non C-lock type are retained by the brake backing plate, which is bolted to the axle housing. Bearings in the C-lock type axle consist of an outer race, bearing rollers and a roller cage, retained by snap-rings. The non C-lock type axle uses a unit roller bearing (inner race, rollers and outer race), which is pressed onto the shaft, up to a shoulder. It is imperative to determine the axle type before attempting any service.

NON C-LOCK TYPE

--- **CAUTION** ---

Before attempting any service to the drive axle or axle shafts, remove the axle carrier cover and visually determine if the axle shafts are retained by C-shaped locks at the inner end or by the brake backing plate at the outer end. If the shafts are *not* retained by C-locks, proceed as follows.

Design allows for maximum axle shaft end-play of 0.022 in., which can be measured with a dial indicator. If end-play is found to be excessive, the bearing should be replaced. Shimming the bearing is not recommended as this ignores end-play of the bearing itself and could result in improper seating of the bearing.

1. Remove the wheel, tire and brake drum.
2. Remove the nuts holding the retainer plate to the backing plate. Disconnect the brake line.
3. Remove the retainer and install nuts, fingertight, to prevent the brake backing plate from being dislodged.
4. Pull out the axle shaft and bearing assembly, using a slide hammer.
5. Using a chisel, nick the bearing retainer in three or four places. The retainer does not have to be cut, merely collapsed sufficiently, to allow the bearing retainer to be slid from the shaft.
6. Press off the bearing and install the new one by pressing it into position.
7. Press on the new retainer.

NOTE: *Do not attempt to press the bearing and the retainer on at the same time.*

8. Assemble the shaft and bearing in the housing, being sure that the bearing is seated properly in the housing.
9. Install the retainer, drum, wheel and tire. Bleed the brakes.

C-LOCK TYPE

—————— CAUTION ——————

Before attempting any service to the drive axle or axle shafts, remove the carrier cover and visually determine if the axle shaft(s) are retained by C-shaped locks at the inner ends or by a brake backing plate at the outer end. If they *are* retained by C-shaped locks, proceed as follows.

1. Raise the vehicle and remove the wheels.
2. The differential cover has already been removed (see Caution). Remove the differential pinion shaft lock-screw and the differential pinion shaft.
3. Push the flanged end of the axle shaft toward the center of the vehicle and remove the "C" lock from the end of the shaft.
4. Remove the axle shaft from the housing, being careful not to damage the oil seal.
5. Remove the oil seal by inserting the button end of the axle shaft behind the steel case of the oil seal. Pry the seal loose from the bore.
6. Seat the legs of the bearing puller behind the bearing. Seat a washer against the bearing and hold it in place with a nut. Use a slide hammer to pull the bearing.

7. Pack the cavity between the seal lips with wheel bearing lubricant and lubricate a new wheel bearing with same.
8. Use a suitable driver and install the bearing until it bottoms against the tube. Install the oil seal.
9. Slide the axle shaft into place. Be sure that the splines on the shaft do not damage the oil seal. Make sure that the splines engage the differential side gear.
10. Install the C-lock on the inner end of the axle shaft and push the shaft outward so that the C-lock seats in the differential side gear counterbore.
11. Position the differential pinion shaft through the case and pinions, aligning the hole in the case with the hole for the lock-screw.
12. Use a new gasket and install the carrier cover. Be sure that the gasket surfaces are clean before installing the gasket and cover.
13. Fill the axle with lubricant to the bottom of the filler hole.
14. Install the brake drum and wheels and lower the car. Check for leaks and road test the car.

JACKING, HOISTING

1. Jack car at front spring seat of lower control arm. Jack car at rear axle housing except when equipped with rear stabilizer bar. On these models, jack at frame rails.
2. To lift at frame, use side rails in front of body floor pan and at rear corner at squared off corner of box ahead of rear wheel.

FRONT SUSPENSION

Coil Spring Removal and Installation

1. Remove the shock absorber. Disconnect the stabilizer bar.
2. Support the car at the frame so the control arms hang free.
3. Support the inner end of the control arm with a floor jack. (dealers have a device that cradles the inner bushings).
4. Raise the jack enough to take the tension off the lower control arm pivot bolts.
5. Chain the spring to the lower control arm, for safety's sake.
6. Remove first the rear, then the front pivot bolt.
7. Cautiously lower the jack until all spring tension is released.

8. Note the way in which the spring is installed to the control arm and remove it.
9. On installation, position the spring to the control arm and raise it into place.
10. Install the pivot bolts and torque the nuts to 100 ft lbs for all 1974 and later models except for 1974 Nova. Torque the 1974 Nova and all models through 1973 to 85 ft lbs.
11. Replace the shock absorber and stabilizer bar.

Shock Absorber Removal and Installation

1. Remove the upper stem nut while holding the stem to keep it from turning.
2. Remove the two bolts holding the shock absorber to the lower control arm, and pull the shock through the arm.
3. Extend the new shock absorber and insert it up through the lower control arm. Make sure that the upper stem goes through the hole in the upper control arm frame bracket.

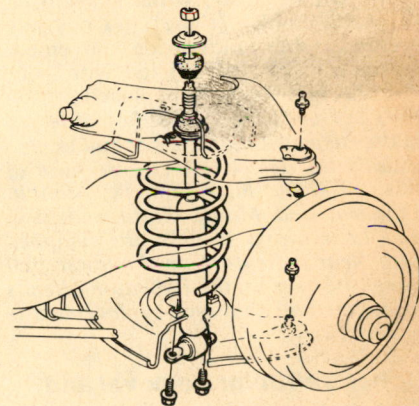

Chevelle and Camaro shock absorber installation
(© Chevrolet Div., G.M. Corp)

NOTE: *Purge new shocks of air by repeatedly compressing them while inverted and extending them in their normal installed position.*

4. Install the grommet, retainer cup, and nut to the shock absorber upper stem.
5. Hold the shock absorber stem and tighten the upper nut to 8 ft lbs.
6. Install the lower control arm retaining bolts and tighten to 20 ft lbs.

Front Wheel Bearing Adjustment

1. Jack the car up and support it at the lower arm.
2. Remove the hub dust cover and spindle cotter pin. Loosen the nut.
3. While spinning the wheel, snug the nut down to seat the bearings. Do not exert over 12 ft lbs of force on the nut.

4. Back the nut off 1/4-1/2 a turn or until it is just loose. Line up the cotter pin hole in the spindle with the hole in the nut.

5. Insert a new cotter pin. Endplay should be between 0.001 and 0.005 in. If play exceeds this tolerance, the wheel bearings should be replaced.

BALL JOINTS

Inspection

NOTE: *Before performing this inspection, make sure the wheel bearings are adjusted correctly and that the control arm bushings are in good condition.*

1. Jack the car up under the front lower control arm at the spring seat.
2. Raise the car until there is 1-2 in. of clearance under the wheel.
3. Insert a bar under the wheel and pry upward. If the wheel raises more than 1/8 in., the ball joints are worn. Determine if the upper or lower ball joint is worn by visual inspection while prying on the wheel.
4. The upper ball joint can be further inspected after partial suspension disassembly. If the stud has any detectable side-to-side movement or if it can be twisted with your fingers it should be replaced.

NOTE: *Due to the distribution of forces in the suspension, the lower ball joint is usually the defective joint. Because of this, 1974 and later Chevelle, Malibu, Camaro, and Monte Carlo and 1975 and later Nova models are equipped with wear indicators on the lower ball joint. As long as the indicator extends below the ball stud seat, replacement is unnecessary.*

Upper Ball Joint Removal and Installation

1. Raise the car on a hoist.

2. Remove the tire and wheel assembly.
3. Support the lower control arm with a jack.
4. Remove the upper ball stud nut.
5. Remove the ball stud from the knuckle.
6. Chisel or grind off the ball joint mounting rivets.
7. Drill out the ball stud attaching holes to accept the service ball joint attaching bolts.
8. Install the ball joint with the nuts and bolts supplied with the new joint, nuts on top.
9. Install the lube fitting in the new joint.
10. Mate the upper control arm to the steering knuckle and install the bal stud through the knuckle boss.
11. Tighten the ball stud nut to 55 ft lbs plus whatever is necessary to align the cotter pin holes. Install the cotter pin.

NOTE: *Do not back off on the nut to align the cotter pin.*

12. Install the wheel and lower the vehicle.

Lower Ball Joint Removal and Installation

1. Raise the vehicle on a hoist and remove the wheel.
2. Support the lower control arm with a jack.
3. Loosen the lower ball stud nut. Break the ball stud loose. Remove the ball stud nut.
4. Remove the ball stud from the steering knuckle.
5. The ball joint is pressed in and must be pressed out.
6. Install the new ball joint, using the bolts supplied with the service ball joint. The thick-headed bolt is installed on the forward side of control arm. Press in the ball joint.
7. Install the ball stud in the steering knuckle boss. This may be done by

raising the lower control arm with the jack.
8. Install the nut on the ball stud, tightening to 50 ft lbs on all models through 1973 and 1974 Nova; 60 ft lbs on 1974 Chevelle, Monte Carlo, and Camaro, and 83 ft lbs on all 1975 and later models.
9. Install the lube fitting.

Lower Control Arm Removal and Installation

1. Remove the spring as described earlier.
2. Remove the ball stud from the steering knuckle.
3. Remove the control arm.
4. To install, reverse the above procedure.

Upper Control Arm Removal and Installation

1. Raise the vehicle on a hoist.
2. Support the outer end of the lower control arm with a jack.
3. Remove the wheel.
4. Separate the upper ball joint from the steering knuckle as described above under Upper Ball Joint Removal and Installation.
5. Remove the control arm shaft to frame nuts.

NOTE: *Tape the shims together and identify them so that they can be installed in the positions from which they were removed.*

6. Remove the bolts which attach the control arm shaft to the frame and remove the control arm. Note the positions of the bolts.
7. Install in the reverse order of removal. Make sure the shaft to frame bolts are installed in the same position they were in before removal and that the shims are in their original positions. Tighten the shaft to frame bolts to 55 ft lbs on Nova through 1974 and 1972 Chevelle and Monte Carlo; 75 ft lbs on all 1975 and later models; 80 ft lbs on Camaro through 1973; and 90 ft lbs on 1973-74 Chevelle and Monte Carlo, and 1974 Camaro. The control arm shaft nuts are torqued to 40 ft lbs on Chevelle and Monte Carlo through 1973 and Nova through 1974; 65 ft lbs on Camaro through 1974 and 1974 Chevelle and Monte Carlo; and 75 ft lbs on all 1975 and later models.

1974 and later Chevelle, Monte Carlo, and Camaro and 1975 and later Nova models are equipped with wear indicators on the lower ball joint
(©Chevrolet Div., G.M. Corp)

REAR SUSPENSION

The Chevelle, Malibu, and Monte Carlo have a coil spring rear suspension located by two lower control arms and two diagonally mounted upper control arms. Fore and aft axle movement is prevented by the lower control arms. Lateral movement is prevented by the upper control arms and the axle-to-frame tie-rod.

The Camaro and Nova have a leaf spring rear suspension.

All models use staggered shock absorbers to prevent axle hop on hard acceleration. The right shock absorber is mounted forward of the axle and the left shock absorber is mounted behind the axle.

Shock Absorber Removal and Installation

1. Jack the car to a convenient working height.
2. If the car is equipped with superlift shock absorbers, disconnect the air line.
3. On Chevelle, Malibu, and Monte Carlo: remove the two retaining bolts from the upper mounting bracket. Hold the hex on the bottom stud and disconnect the lower mounting. Remove the shock absorber.
4. On Camaro: with the rear axle supported, remove the lower shock absorber nut, retainer, and grommet. Remove the upper bolts, and remove the shock.
5. On Nova: remove the lower shock absorber eye bolt. Remove the upper bolts, and remove the shock absorber.

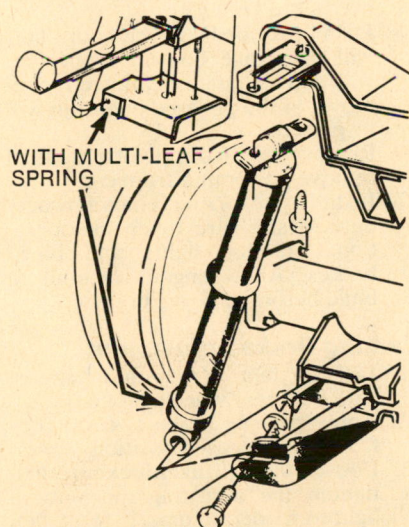

WITH MULTI-LEAF SPRING

Nova rear shock absorber mounting
(© Chevrolet Div., G.M. Corp)

NOTE: *Purge new shocks of air by repeatedly compressing them while inverted and extending them in their normal installed position.*

6. Install the shock absorbers in a reverse of the removal procedure. Torque the upper fasteners: 12 ft lbs on Chevelle and Monte Carlo and 18 ft lbs on Nova and Camaro. Torque the bottom fasteners: 65 ft lbs on Chevelle, Malibu, and Monte Carlo, 45 ft lbs on Nova (60 ft lbs with performance suspension) and 8 ft lbs on Camaro.

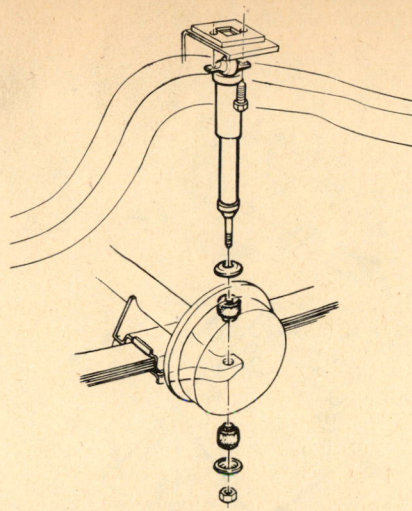

Camaro rear shock absorber mounting
(© Chevrolet Div., G.M. Corp)

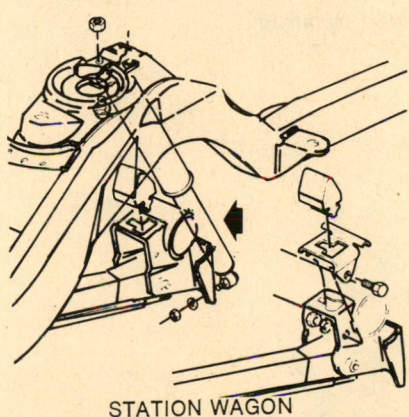

STATION WAGON

Chevelle rear shock absorber mounting
(© Chevrolet Div., G.M. Corp)

Spring Removal and Installation
CHEVELLE, MALIBU, AND MONTE CARLO

If the springs have been in use for any length of time, it will probably be necessary to replace both to maintain an even ride height.

1. Raise the car by frame so that the rear axle can be independently raised and lowered.
2. Support the rear axle with a floor jack.
3. Disconnect the shock absorber from the axle. You don't have to disconnect both shocks unless you are removing both springs.
4. On 1973 and later models, disconnect the brake line at the axle housing junction block. Disconnect the upper control arm at the axle. You don't have to disconnect both unless you are removing both springs.
NOTE: *This step makes the job easier on earlier models too.*
5. Lower the axle to the limits of its travel, being careful of the brake lines.
6. Pry the lower end of the spring over the axle bracket vertical retai-

ner. Remove the spring and insulator. Reverse the procedure for installation. Torque the upper control arm to axle mount to 80 ft lbs.

NOVA AND CAMARO

1. Raise the car by the frame so that the rear axle can be independently raised and lowered.
2. Support the rear axle with a floor jack.
3. Disconnect the shock absorber lower mount.
4. Loosen the retaining bolt through the front spring eye. Unbolt the front bracket from the body.
5. Lower the axle enough to remove the bracket and retaining bolt from the front spring eye.
6. Pry the parking brake cable from the spring mounting plate retainer.
7. Remove the U-bolt nuts, the spring plate, and the upper and lower spring pads.
8. Remove the lower rear shackle bolt. Remove the spring.
9. On installation, install the front bracket to the spring eye, install the rear shackle, bolt the front bracket in place, install the U-bolts, and replace the shock absorber. Tighten the bolts with the weight of the car on the springs. Torque the front bracket mounting bolts to 25-30 ft lbs, the front eye bolt to 75 ft lbs, the U-bolts to 40 ft lbs, and the rear shackle bolts to 50 ft lbs.

BRAKES

Brake lining replacement and adjustment wheel and master cylinder overhaul and brake bleeding procedures can be found in the Unit Repair Section.

Master Cylinder Removal and Installation

1. Disconnect hydraulic lines at master cylinder.
2. Remove the retaining nuts and lockwashers that hold cylinder to firewall. Disconnect pushrod at brake pedal.
3. Remove the master cylinder, gasket and rubber boot.
4. Position master cylinder on firewall, making sure pushrod goes through the rubber boot into the piston. Reconnect pushrod clevis to brake pedal.
5. Install nuts and lockwashers.
6. Install hydraulic lines then check brake pedal free play.
7. Bleed brakes, as described in Unit Repair Section.
NOTE: *Cars having disc brakes do not have a check valve in the front outlet port of the master cylinder. If one is installed, front discs will quickly wear out due to residual hydraulic pressure holding pads against rotor.*

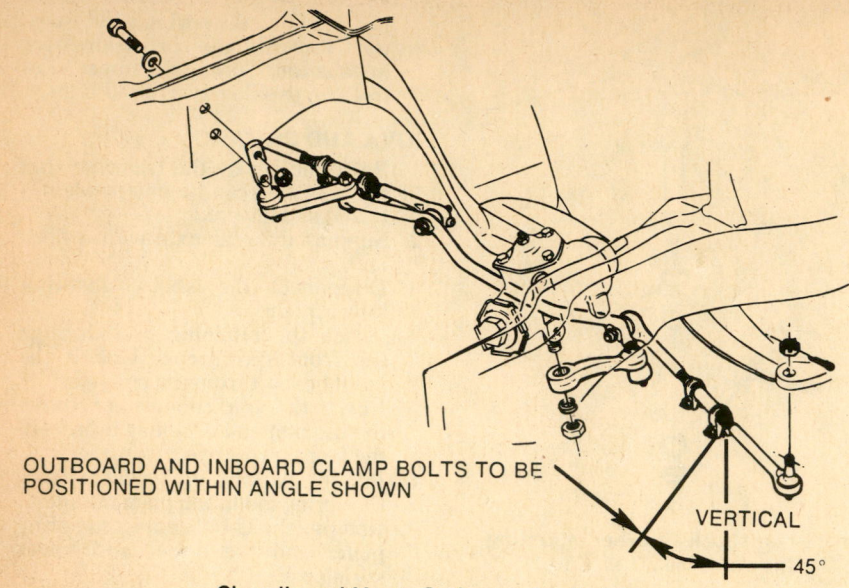

OUTBOARD AND INBOARD CLAMP BOLTS TO BE
POSITIONED WITHIN ANGLE SHOWN

Chevelle and Monte Carlo steering linkage
(© Chevrolet Div., G.M. Corp)

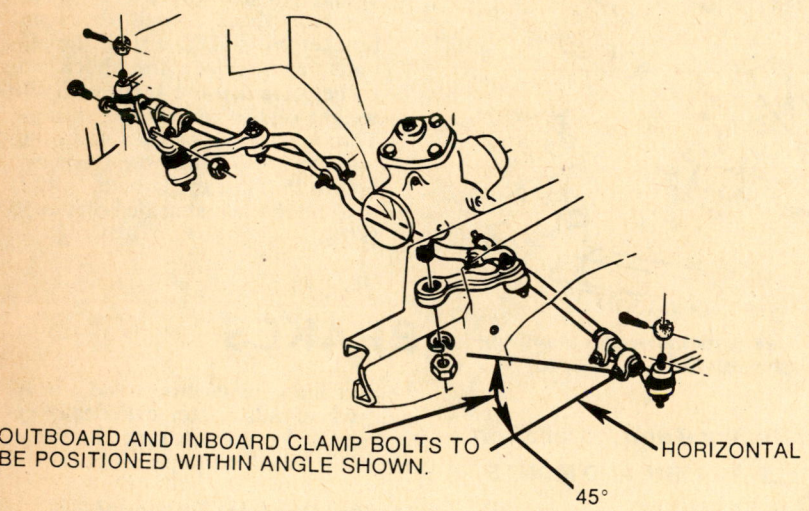

OUTBOARD AND INBOARD CLAMP BOLTS TO
BE POSITIONED WITHIN ANGLE SHOWN.

Camaro steering linkage
(© Chevrolet Div., G.M. Corp)

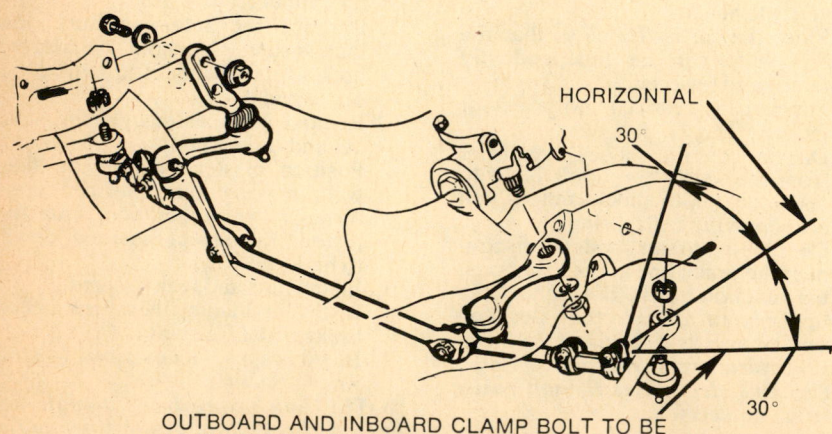

OUTBOARD AND INBOARD CLAMP BOLT TO BE
POSITIONED WITHIN ANGLE SHOWN.

Nova steering linkage
(© Chevrolet Div., G.M. Corp)

Power Brake Booster Removal and Installation

EXCEPT CHEVELLE AND MONTE CARLO THROUGH 1975

1. Disconnect vacuum hose from vacuum check valve.
2. Disconnect hydraulic lines at master cylinder.
3. Disconnect pushrod at brake pedal assembly.

NOTE: *Some Nova-Camaro brake boosters may also be held on with a sealant. This can be easily removed with tar remover.*

4. Remove nuts and lockwashers that secure booster to firewall and remove booster from engine compartment.
5. Install by reversing removal procedure. Make sure to check operation of stop lights and bleed brakes. Allow engine vacuum to build before applying brakes.

CHEVELLE AND MONTE CARLO THROUGH 1975

1. Remove master cylinder from vacuum booster.
2. Remove vacuum line from vacuum check valve.
3. Remove brake line clip from booster.
4. From inside vehicle, remove nuts and lockwashers that secure booster to firewall.
5. Push brake pedal to the floor. This will disengage booster from firewall and adequate clearance for removal of the pushrod pivot pin will be gained.
6. Remove clip from pivot pin, then remove power unit from car.
7. Install by reversing removal procedure. Make sure to check operations of stop lights and bleed brakes. Allow engine vacuum to build before applying brakes.

Parking Brake Adjustment

1. Jack up rear of car and support with both rear wheels off floor.
2. Apply parking brake two notches from fully released position.
3. Loosen the equalizer locknut, then tighten the adjusting nut until a light to moderate drag is felt when the rear wheels are rotated.
4. Tighten the locknut.
5. Fully release parking brake and rotate rear wheels—no drag should be felt.

STEERING

Tie-Rod Removal and Installation

1. Remove the cotter pins and nuts from the tie-rod end studs.
2. Tap on the steering arm near the tie-rod end (use another hammer as backing) and pull down on the tie-rod if necessary, to free it.

3. Remove the inner stud in the same manner as the outer.

4. Loosen the clamp bolts and un-screw the ends if they are being replaced.

5. Lubricate the tie-rod end threads with chassis grease if they were re-moved. Installed each end assem-bly an equal distance from the sleeve.

6. Ensure that the tip-rod end stud threads and nut are clean. Install new seals and install the studs into the steering arms and relay rod.

7. Install the stud nuts. Tighten to 35 ft lbs. If necessary, you can tighten the nuts to as much 50 ft lbs to in-stall the cotter pins.

8. Adjust the toe-in.

NOTE: *Before tightening the sleeve clamps, ensure that the clamps are po-sitioned so that adjusting sleeve slot is covered by the clamp.*

Power Steering Pump Removal and Installation

All models use integral power steer-ing. A pump delivers hydraulic pres-sure through two hoses to the steering gear itself.

Detailed service coverage is in the Unit Repair Section.

1. Remove the hoses at the pump and tape the openings shut to prevent contamination. Position the dis-connected lines in a raised position to prevent leakage.

2. Remove the pump belt.

3. Loosen the retaining bolts and any braces, and remove the pump.

4. Install the pump on the engine with the retaining bolts handtight.

5. Connect and tighten the hose fittings.

6. Refill the pump with fluid and bleed by turning the pulley counterclock-wise (viewed from the front). Stop the bleeding when air bubbles no longer appear.

7. Install the pump belt on the pulley and adjust the tension. Bleed the system.

Bleeding Power Steering System

1. Fill the fluid reservoir.

2. Let the fluid stand undisturbed for two minutes, then crank the engine for about two seconds. Refill reser-voir if necessary.

3. Repeat Steps 1 and 2 above until the fluid level remains constant af-ter cranking the engine.

4. Raise the front of the car until the wheels are off the ground, then start the engine. Increase the en-gine speed to about 1,500 rpm.

5. Turn the wheels lightly against the stops to the left and right, checking the fluid level and refilling if necessary.

Steering Wheel Removal and Installation

--- CAUTION ---

Disconnect the battery ground cable before removing the steering wheel. When installing a steering wheel, always make sure that the turn signal lever is in the neutral position.

PADDED RIM WHEEL

1. Pry out the center cap and retainer. Remove the shaft snap-ring on 1975 and later models.

NOTE: *On the tilt-telescope wheel, re-move the three upper contact retaining screws, the contact and shim if used. Then remove the center star screw and lever.*

2. Remove the steering wheel nut and washer.

3. Remove the three receiving cup screws and remove the cup belle-ville spring, bushing, and pivot ring.

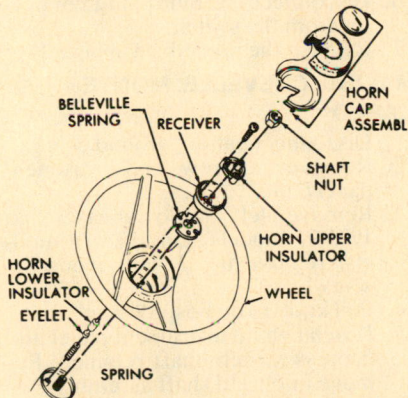

Cushioned rim steering wheel assembly
(© Chevrolet Div., G.M. Corp)

4. Mark the wheel-to-shaft relation-ship, and then remove the wheel with a puller.

5. Install the wheel on the shaft, aligning the previously made marks. Tighten the nut to 30 ft lbs.

6. Install the belleville spring (dished side up), pivot ring, bushing, and receiving cup. Install the center cap and reconnect the battery.

STANDARD WHEEL

1. Remove the trim retaining screws from behind the wheel.

2. Lift the trim off and pull the horn wires from the turn signal cancel-ling cam.

NOTE: *On the tilt-telescope wheel, re-move the three upper contact retaining screws, the contact and shim if used. Then remove the center star screw and lever.*

3. Remove the shaft snap-ring on 1975 and later models. Remove the steering wheel nut.

4. Mark the wheel-to-shaft relation-ship, and then remove the wheel with a puller.

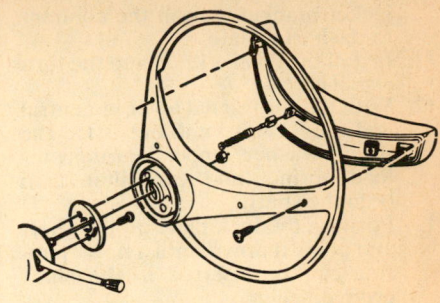

Standard steering wheel
(© Chevrolet Div., G.M. Corp)

5. Install the wheel on the shaft align-ing the previously made marks. Tighten the nut to 30 ft lbs.

6. Insert the horn wires into the can-celling cam.

7. Install the center trim and recon-nect the battery cable.

Turn Signal Switch Removal and Installation

1. Remove the steering wheel as pre-viously outlined. Remove the trim cover.

2. Loosen the cover screws (on 1976 and later models, pry the cover off with a screwdriver), and lift the cover off the shaft.

3. Position the U-shaped lockplate compressing tool on the end of the steering shaft and compress the lock plate by turning the shaft nut clockwise. Pry the wire snap-ring out of the shaft groove.

4. Remove the tool and lift the lock-plate off the shaft.

5. Slip the cancelling cam, upper bearing preload spring, and thrust washer off the shaft.

6. Remove the turn signal lever. Push the flasher knob in and unscrew it.

7. Pull the switch connector out of the mast jacket and tape the upper part to facilitate switch removal. Attach a long piece of wire to the turn signal switch connector. When installing the turn signal switch, feed this wire through the column first, and then use this wire to pull the switch connector into position. On tilt wheels, place the turn signal and shifter housing in low position and remove the har-ness cover.

8. Remove the three switch mounting screws. Remove the switch by pulling it straight up while guiding the wiring harness cover through the column.

9. Install the replacement switch by working the connector and cover down through the housing and un-der the bracket. On tilt models, the connector is worked down through the housing, under the bracket, and then the cover is installed on the harness.

10. Install the switch mounting screws and the connector on the mast

jacket bracket. Install the column-to-dash trim plate.

11. Install the flasher knob and the turn signal lever.

12. With the turn signal lever in neutral and the flasher knob out, slide the thrust washer, upper bearing pre-load spring, and cancelling cam onto the shaft.

13. Position the lock plate on the shaft and press it down until a new snap-ring can be inserted in the shaft groove.

14. Install the cover and the steering wheel.

Ignition Switch Replacement

All models have the ignition lock cylinder located on the upper right side of the steering column. The ignition switch is inside the channel section of the brake pedal support. The switch is inaccessible unless the steering column is lowered.

1. Lower steering column. The column must be carefully supported to prevent damage.

2. Remove lock cylinder.

NOTE: *Pull actuating rod for switch up until a definite stop is felt, then push it down one detent to Lock position.*

3. Remove two switch screws and switch assembly.

4. When replacing switch, make sure switch and lock are in Lock position. Do not use switch screws longer than the originals, or the compressibility feature of the column may be lost.

Ignition Lock Cylinder Replacement

1. Remove steering wheel and directional signal switch as previously outlined.

2. Place lock cylinder in Run position.

—— CAUTION ——

Do not remove the ignition key buzzer.

3. Insert a small screwdriver into the turn signal housing slot. Keeping the screwdriver to the right side of the slot, break the housing flash loose and depress the spring latch at the lower end of the lock cylinder. Remove the lock cylinder.

NOTE: *Considerable force may be necessary to break this casting flash, but be careful to damage any other parts.*

4. To install, hold the lock cylinder sleeve and rotate the knob clockwise against the stop. Insert the cylinder into the housing, aligning the key and keyway. Hold a .070 in. drill between the lock bezel and housing. Rotate the cylinder counterclockwise, maintaining a light pressure until the drive section of the cylinder mates with the sector. Push in until the snap ring pops into the grooves. Remove drill. Check cylinder operation.

—— CAUTION ——

The drill prevents forcing the lock cylinder inward beyond its normal position. The buzzer switch and spring latch can hold the lock cylinder in too far. Complete disassembly of the upper bearing housing is necessary to release an improperly installed lock cylinder.

INSTRUMENT PANEL

Light Switch Replacement

NOVA

1. Disconnect battery.
2. Pull knob out to on position.
3. Reach under instrument panel and depress the switch shaft retainer, and remove knob and shaft assembly.
4. Remove the retaining ferrule nut.
5. Remove switch from instrument panel.
6. Disconnect the multi-plug connector from the switch.
7. Reverse the procedure to install.

MALIBU, CHEVELLE, MONTE CARLO

1. Disconnect battery ground cable.
2. Remove six screws and instrument panel pad.
3. Remove left radio speaker on 1972-77 models. On 1978-79 models, remove the 3 with mounting screws.
4. Pull knob to on position.
5. Reach behind instrument panel and depress switch shaft retainer. Remove knob and shaft assembly.
6. Remove ferrule nut and switch assembly from instrument panel.
7. Reverse procedure to install.

CAMARO

1. Disconnect battery negative cable.
2. Remove steering column lower cover (six screws).
3. Reach up under cluster on the left side and depress light switch shaft retainer, while pulling gently on shaft.
4. Remove nut that secures switch to cluster carrier.
5. Remove four cluster carrier screws in front and two from rear, then tilt right side of cluster out. Cigarette lighter grounding ring may have to be freed.
6. Unplug harness connector from switch.
7. Remove switch.
8. To install, reverse removal procedure. Make sure all ground connections are refastened.

Speedometer Cable Replacement

CAMARO

1. Disconnect the battery ground cable.

2. Reach up behind the speedometer and depress the retaining tab while pushing in, then out on the cable end.

3. Remove the firewall panel sealing plug to allow movement of the cable.

4. Pull the core from the casing. If the core is broken, it will be necessary to raise the car and disconnect the cable from the transmission.

5. Lubricate the core with cable lubricant and insert it into the casing. Connect the case to the speedometer and install the dash sealing plug.

NOVA

Remove the radio, then follow the procedure under Camaro.

1972 CHEVELLE AND MONTE CARLO

1. Remove the lower steering column cover and driver's air conditioning lap cooler.

2. Follow the procedure under Camaro.

1973 AND LATER MALIBU, CHEVELLE AND MONTE CARLO

1. Disconnect the battery ground cable.

2. Remove the radio knobs and clock stem.

3. Remove the instrument bezel retaining screws.

4. Disconnect the tailgate release or defogger switch.

5. Remove the instrument cluster bezel.

6. Remove the speedometer head.

7. Disconnect the cable from the head by depressing the clip.

8. Pull the core from the casing. If the core is broken, raise the vehicle and remove the lower cable end from the transmission.

9. Lubricate the core with cable lubricant and install it in the casing.

WINDSHIELD WIPERS

Motor Removal and Installation

1. Make sure wiper motor is in park position.

2. Disconnect washer hoses and electrical connectors.

3. Remove the plenum chamber grille or access cover. Disconnect the drive link from the motor crank arm.

4. Remove the retaining screws or nuts and remove motor.

5. Reverse procedure to install, checking sealing gaskets at motor.

Wiper Blade Replacement

Two methods are used to retain the wiper blades to the arms. One is the press tab type release; the tab is pressed and the blade may be pulled from the arm. The other is the coil spring retainer; a screwdriver must be inserted on top of the spring and the spring pushed downward. The blade may then be pulled off.

RADIO

Removal and Installation 1972

1. Disconnect battery ground cable.
2. Remove ash tray and ash tray housing as necessary.
3. Remove knobs, controls, washers, trim plate, and nuts from radio.
4. Remove hoses from center air conditioning duct as necessary.
5. Disconnect all wiring leads.
6. Remove screw from radio rear mounting bracket and lower radio.
7. To install, reverse above procedure.

1973-77 LATER CHEVELLE AND MONTE CARLO

1. Disconnect the battery ground cable.
2. Remove the left air conditioner lap cooler duct.
3. Pull off the knobs and bezels.
4. Remove the control shaft nuts and washers. You will probably need a deep well socket.
5. Remove the support bracket stud nut. Disconnect the antenna, speaker, and power wires.
6. Move the radio back until the shafts clear the instrument panel. Lower it from behind the panel.
7. Reverse the procedure for installation. Make sure to hook up the speaker leads before turning the radio on; operating without a speaker will damage the transistors.

1978-79 MALIBU AND MONTE CARLO

1. Disconnect the battery ground.
2. Pull the control knobs from the shaft.
3. Remove the trim plate.
4. Remove the wiring and antenna.
5. Remove the receiver stud nut at the right side bracket.
6. Remove the control knob nuts.
7. Remove the instrument panel bracket.
8. Remove the radio through the panel opening.
9. Installation is the reverse of removal.

1973 AND LATER NOVA AND CAMARO

1. Disconnect the battery ground cable.
2. Pull off the knobs and bezels.
3. Remove the control shaft nuts and washers. A deep well socket will be needed on the Camaro.
4. Remove the mounting bracket screws or nuts.
5. Move the radio back until the shafts clear the instrument panel.

Lower it and disconnect the antenna, speaker, and power wires.
6. Remove the radio. Reverse the procedure for installation. Make sure to hook up the speaker leads before turning the radio on; operating without a speaker will damage the transistors.

HEATER

Heater Blower Removal and Installation with or without Air Conditioning

1978-79 MALIBU AND MONTE CARLO WITHOUT AIR CONDITIONING

1. Disconnect battery ground cable.
2. Disconnect hoses and wiring from right side inner fender panel.
3. Remove all right side inner fender panel attaching bolts except those attaching panel to radiator support. On 1974 and later Nova, remove the eight rear fender skirt screws instead.
4. Pull out, then down, on panel. Place a block between panel and fender.
5. Remove blower to case attaching screws. Remove the air-cooling hose from the motor on air-conditioned cars. Remove blower assembly. On 1974 and later Nova, separate the blower wheel and motor first.
6. Remove blower wheel retaining nut and separate the motor and wheel.
7. Reverse procedure to install. Open end of blower should be away from motor.

1973 AND LATER MALIBU, CHEVELLE AND MONTE CARLO

1. Disconnect the battery ground cable.
2. Disconnect the motor lead wire. On cars with A/C, disconnect the cooling tube.
3. Remove the blower to case screws and the blower.
4. Remove the retaining nut to separate the motor and wheel.
5. Reverse the procedure for installation. The open end of the blower wheel should be away from the motor.

1978-79 CAMARO

1. Disconnect the battery ground.
2. Disconnect the electrical connectors at the motor.
3. Remove the heater front module screws and nuts.

4. Lift off the front module and motor.
5. Installation is the reverse of removal. Replace all sealer.

Heater Core Removal and Installation

ALL MODELS WITHOUT AIR CONDITIONING EXCEPT 1978-79 MALIBU AND MONTE CARLO

1. Disconnect battery ground cable.
2. Drain radiator.
3. Disconnect heater hoses. Plug core inlet and outlet.

NOTE: *The larger hose goes to the water pump.*

4. Remove nuts from air distributor duct studs on firewall.
5. On Nova, remove glove compartment and door assembly.
6. From under Nova dash, drill out lower right hand distributor duct stud with a 1/4 in. drill.
7. On Camaro: remove glove box and radio, then defroster duct to distributor duct screw.
8. Pull distributor duct from firewall mounting. Remove resistor wires.
9. Remove core assembly from distributor duct.
10. Reverse procedure to install.

1978-79 MALIBU AND MONTE CARLO WITHOUT AIR CONDITIONING

1. Remove the heater hoses from the core tubes.
2. Disconnect the wiring from the module case.
3. Unbolt and remove the module front cover.
4. Lift out the core.
5. Installation is the reverse of removal. Replace all sealer.

1972 CHEVELLE AND MONTE CARLO WITH AIR CONDITIONING

1. Drain the cooling system and disconnect the battery ground cable. It is not necessary to purge the A/C refrigerant.
2. Remove the heater hoses at the firewall and plug the openings.
3. Remove the case stud nuts from the firewall.
4. Remove the right kick pad cover and the recirculating air valve.
5. Remove the center duct from the distributor, and remove the floor distributor duct.
6. From inside the passenger compartment, drill the lower right distributor duct stud out.
7. Remove the remaining air distributor-to-firewall screws, electrical connectors, and control cables.
8. Scribe the temperature door camming plate-to-distributor duct relationship and remove the plate.
9. Remove the heater core housing and core.

10. Reverse the removal procedure to install the core. Replace the drilled-out stud with a screw and speed nut.

1973 AND LATER CHEVELLE AND MONTE CARLO WITH AIR CONDITIONING

1. Disconnect the battery ground cable and drain the radiator. Don't purge the air conditioning system.
2. Detach the heater hoses and plug the core tubes.
3. Remove the nuts from the firewall distributor case studs inside the car.
4. Remove the resistor assembly, reach through the opening, and remove the last distributor stud nut.
5. Remove the screws holding the right lap cooler duct to the instrument panel. Remove the duct.
6. Remove the center duct.
7. Remove the glove box strap screw, strap, and glove box.
8. Remove the floor outlet.
9. Remove the defroster to distributor duct screw at the lower right of the duct.
10. Pull the distributor assembly back far enough that the studs and core tubes clear. Lower it and detach the electrical and vacuum connections.
11. Disconnect the temperature door cable.
12. Remove the distributor assembly.
13. Remove the screws holding the core clamps to the distributor assembly and remove the core.
14. Reverse the procedure for installation.

1978-79 MALIBU AND MONTE CARLO WITH AIR CONDITIONING

1. Drain the cooling system.
2. Disconnect the hoses at the core tubes.
3. Remove the retaining bracket and ground strap.
4. Remove the module rubber seal.
5. Remove the module screen.
6. Remove the right windshield wiper arm.
7. Remove the diagonal connector, high blower relay and thermostatic switch.
8. Disconnect all wiring from the module.
9. Remove the module top cover.
10. Lift out the core.
11. Installation is the reverse of removal. Replace all sealing material.

NOVA WITH AIR CONDITIONING

1. Disconnect the battery ground cable and drain the cooling system. It is not necessary to purge the refrigerant from the A/C system.
2. Disconnect the heater hose from the upper pipe at the firewall.
3. Remove the nuts from the heater studs in the firewall.
4. Remove the right front inner fender panel screws and lower the panel onto the tire.
5. Remove the remaining stud nut and the lower heater hose.
6. Remove the glove compartment.
7. Remove the right kick pad recirculating air valve.
8. Detach the center duct from the selector duct.
9. Remove the floor duct and separate the two selector halves.

10. Remove the selector duct from the firewall.
11. Disconnect the control cables and electrical wires.
12. Scribe the temperature door camming plate-to-selector duct relationship and remove the plate.
13. Place the selector duct on the floor and remove the heater core housing and core.
14. Reverse the removal steps to install the core.

CAMARO WITH AIR CONDITIONING

1. Disconnect the battery ground cable and drain the cooling system. It is not necessary to purge the refrigerant from the cooling system. On 1974 and later models, remove the 8 to 10 rearmost inner fender skirt screws and block the skirt out with a 4 in. wood block for access.
2. Disconnect the heater hoses at the firewall and plug the openings.
3. Remove the nuts from the heater studs protruding through the firewall.
4. Remove the glove compartment and radio.
5. Remove the defroster duct-to-distributor duct screw and pull the defroster duct rearward.
6. Pull the distributor duct from its dash mounting. Disconnect the control cables and electrical wires when there is sufficient clearance.
7. Remove the distributor duct and core from the car.
8. Remove the retainers and remove the heater core.
9. Reverse the removal procedure to install the heater core.

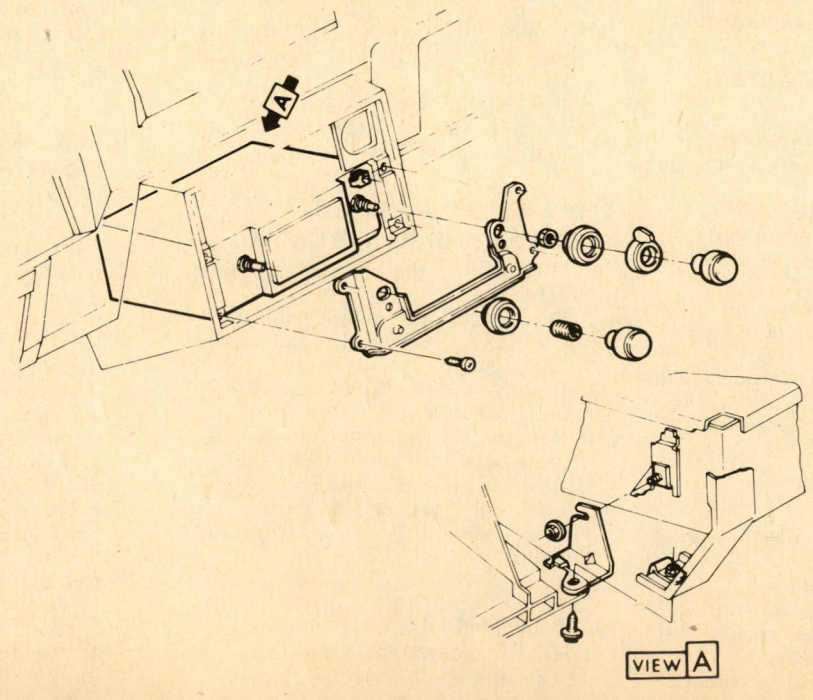

VIEW A

Radio mounting details, 1978 and later Malibu and Monte Carlo (© Chevrolet Div., G.M. Corp.)

Index

Chevrolet & Corvette

YEAR IDENTIFICATION

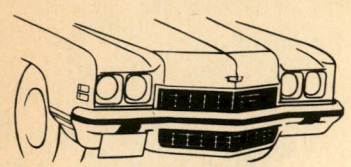

1972 Caprice

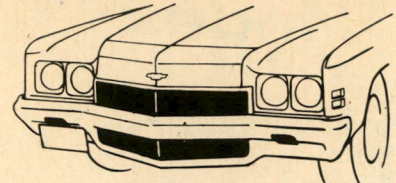

1972 Impala

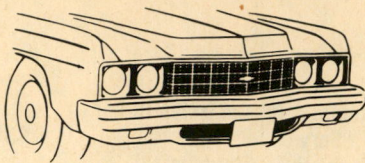

1973 Impala

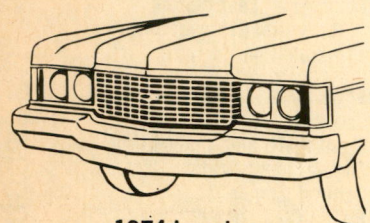

1974 Impala

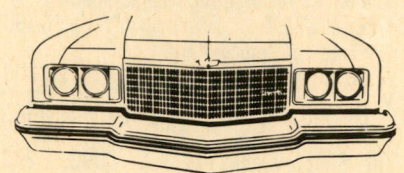

1974 Caprice

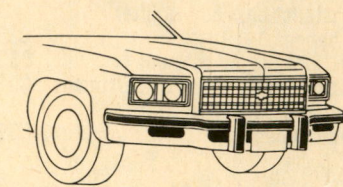

1975 Caprice

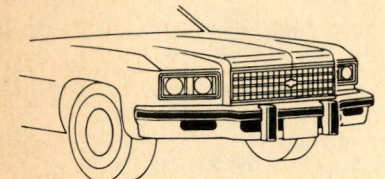

1976 Impala

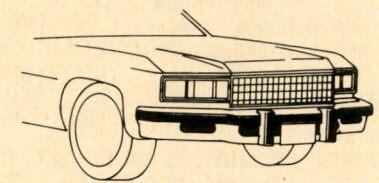

1976 Caprice

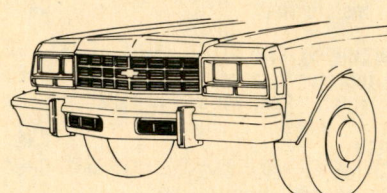

1977 Impala

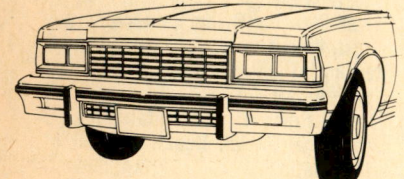

1978 Impala

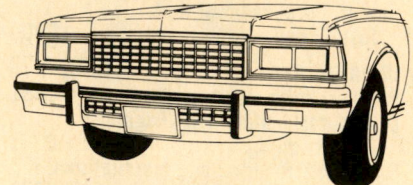

1978 Caprice

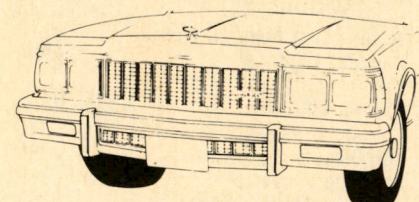

1979 Caprice

1972 Corvette

1973 Corvette

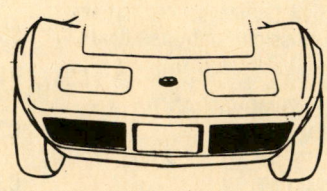

1974 Corvette

1975 Corvette

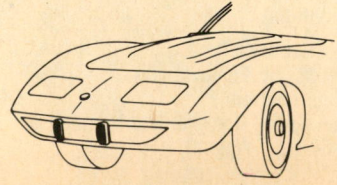

1976 Corvette

1977 Corvette

YEAR IDENTIFICATION

1978 Corvette

1979 Corvette

ENGINE IDENTIFICATION

The engine code is the fifth digit of the Vehicle Identification Number stamped on the VIN plate on the upper left corner of the instrument panel pad, visible through the windshield.

Chevrolet

No. Cyls.	Cu. in. Displ.	Type	1972	1973	1974	1975	1976	1977	1978	1979
6	250	All	D	D	D	D	D	D	D	D
8	305	All						U	U	U
8	350	2 bbl	J	H	H	H	H			
8	350	4 bbl	K	K	L	L	L	L	L	L
8	400	2 bbl	R	R	R					
8	400	4 bbl				U	U	U		
8	454	4 bbl	W	Y	Y	Y	S			
8	454	4 bbl DE		Z	Z					

(Header: YEAR AND CODE)

DE: Dual Exhaust

Corvette

No. Cyls.	Cu. in. Displ.	Type	1972	1973	1974	1975	1976	1977	1978	1979
8	350	200 hp	L	J	J	J	L	L	L	L
8	350	HP	L	P	P	T	X	X	4	4
8	454	All	W	Z	Z					

(Header: YEAR AND CODE)

hp: horsepower
HP: High Performance

GENERAL ENGINE SPECIFICATIONS

Year	Engine No. Cyl. Displacement Cu. In.	Carburetor Type	Horsepower @ rpm ■	Torque @ rpm (ft lbs) ■	Bore X Stroke (in.)	Compression Ratio	Oil Pressure @ 2000 rpm
'72	6-250	1 bbl	110 @ 3800	185 @ 1600	3.875 x 3.530	8.5:1	40
	8-350	2 bbl	165 @ 4000	280 @ 2400	4.000 x 3.480	8.5:1	40
	8-350	4 bbl	200 @ 4400	300 @ 2800	4.000 x 3.480	8.5:1	40
	8-350	4 bbl	255 @ 5600	280 @ 4000	4.000 x 3.480	9.0:1	40
	8-400	2 bbl	170 @ 3400	325 @ 2000	4.126 x 3.750	8.5:1	40
	8-402	4 bbl	210 @ 4400	320 @ 2400	4.126 x 3.760	8.5:1	40
	8-454	4 bbl	270 @ 4000	390 @ 3200	4.251 x 4.000	8.5:1	40

GENERAL ENGINE SPECIFICATIONS

Year	Engine No. Cyl. Displacement Cu. In.	Carburetor Type	Horsepower @ rpm ■	Torque @ rpm (ft lbs) ■	Bore X Stroke (in.)	Compression Ratio	Oil Pressure @ 2000 rpm
'73	6-250	1 bbl	100 @ 3600	175 @ 1600	3.875 x 3.530	8.25:1	40
	8-350	2 bbl	145 @ 4000	255 @ 2400	4.000 x 3.480	8.5:1	40
	8-350	4 bbl	175 @ 4000	260 @ 2800	4.000 x 3.480	8.5:1	40
	8-350	4 bbl	190 @ 4400	270 @ 2800	4.000 x 3.480	8.5:1	40
	8-350	4 bbl	250 @ 5200	285 @ 4000	4.000 x 3.480	9.0:1	40
	8-400	2 bbl	150 @ 3200	295 @ 2000	4.126 x 3.750	8.5:1	40
	8-454	4 bbl	245 @ 4000①	375 @ 2800②	4.251 x 4.000	8.25:1	40
	8-454	4 bbl	275 @ 4400	395 @ 2800	4.251 x 4.000	8.25:1	40
'74	8-350	2 bbl	145 @ 3600	250 @ 2200	4.000 x 3.480	8.5:1	40
	8-350	4 bbl	160 @ 3800	245 @ 2400	4.000 x 3.480	8.5:1	40
	8-350	4 bbl	195 @ 4400	275 @ 2800	4.000 x 3.480	8.5:1	40
	8-350	4 bbl	250 @ 5200	285 @ 4000	4.000 x 3.480	9.0:1	40
	8-400	2 bbl	150 @ 3200	295 @ 2000	4.126 x 3.750	8.5:1	40
	8-400	4 bbl	180 @ 3800	290 @ 2400	4.126 x 3.750	8.5:1	40
	8-454	4 bbl	235 @ 4000	360 @ 2800	4.251 x 4.000	8.25:1	40
	8-454	4 bbl	270 @ 4400	380 @ 2800	4.251 x 4.000	8.25:1	40
'75	8-350	2 bbl	145 @ 3800	250 @ 2200	4.000 x 3.480	8.5:1	40
	8-350	4 bbl	155 @ 3800	250 @ 2400	4.000 x 3.480	8.5:1	40
	8-350	4 bbl	165 @ 3800	255 @ 2400	4.000 x 3.480	8.5:1	40
	8-350	4 bbl	205 @ 4800	255 @ 3600	4.000 x 3.480	9.0:1	40
	8-400	4 bbl	175 @ 3600	305 @ 2000	4.126 x 3.750	8.5:1	40
	8-454	4 bbl	215 @ 4000	350 @ 2400	4.251 x 4.000	8.15:1	40
	6-250	1 bbl	105 @ 3800	185 @ 1200	3.875 x 3.530	8.25:1	40
	8-305	2 bbl	140 @ 3800	245 @ 2000	3.736 x 3.480	8.5:1	40
'76	8-350	2 bbl	145 @ 3800	250 @ 2200	4.000 x 3.480	8.5:1	40
	8-350	4 bbl	165 @ 3800	260 @ 2400	4.000 x 3.480	8.5:1	40
	8-350	4 bbl	180 @ 4000	270 @ 2400	4.000 x 3.480	8.5:1	40
	8-350	4 bbl	210 @ 5200	255 @ 3600	4.000 x 3.480	9.0:1	40
	8-400	4 bbl	175 @ 3600	305 @ 2000	4.126 x 3.750	8.5:1	40
	8-454	4 bbl	225 @ 3800	360 @ 2400	4.251 x 4.000	8.25:1	46
'77	6-250	1 bbl	110 @ 3800	195 @ 1600	3.875 x 3.530	8.3:1	40
	8-305	2 bbl	145 @ 3800	245 @ 2400	3.736 x 3.480	8.5:1	40
	8-350	4 bbl	170 @ 3800	270 @ 2400	4.000 x 3.480	8.5:1	40
	8-350	4 bbl	180 @ 4000	270 @ 2400	4.000 x 3.480	8.5:1	40
	8-350	4 bbl	210 @ 5200	255 @ 3600	4.000 x 3.480	9.0:1	40
'78-'79	6-250	1 bbl	110 @ 3800	190 @ 1600	3.875 x 3.530	8.1:1	40
	8-305	2 bbl	145 @ 3800	245 @ 2400	3.736 x 3.480	8.4:1	40
	8-350	4 bbl	170 @ 3800	270 @ 2400	4.000 x 3.480	8.4:1	40
	8-350	4 bbl	185 @ 4000	280 @ 2400	4.000 x 3.480	8.4:1	40
	8-350	4 bbl	220 @ 5200	260 @ 3600	4.000 x 3.480	8.9:1	40

■ Horsepower and torque are SAE net figures. They are measured at the rear of the transmission with all accessories installed and operating. Since the figures vary when a given engine is installed in different models, some are representative rather than exact.

① 215 in wagon
② 345 in wagon

Chevrolet   TUNE-UP SPECIFICATIONS

When analyzing compression test results, look for uniformity among cylinders rather than specific pressures.

Year	No. Cyl Displacement	hp (cu in.)	Orig. Type	Gap (in.)	Point Dwell (deg)	Point Gap (in.)	Man Trans	● Auto Trans	Valves Intake Opens ■ (deg) ●	Fuel Pump Pressure (psi)	Man Trans	Auto Trans
'72	6-250	110	R46T	.035	31-34	.019	4B	4B	16	4-5	700	600
	8-350	165	R44T	.035	29-31	.019	6B	6B	28(44)	7½-9	900	600
	8-400	170	R44T	.035	29-31	.019	2B	6B	28(44)	7½-9	900	600
	8-402	210	R44T	.035	29-31	.019	8B	8B	30(44)	7½-9	750	600
	8-454	270	R44T	.035	29-31	.019	8B	8B	56	7½-9	750	600
'73	6-250	100	R46T	.035	31-34	.019	6B	—	16	3½-4½	700/450②	—
	8-350	145	R44T	.035	29-31	.019	—	8B	28	7½-9	—	600/450②
	8-350	175	R44T	.035	29-31	.019	—	12B	28	7½-9	—	600/450②
	8-400	140	R44T	.035	29-31	.019	—	8B	28	7½-9	—	600/450②
	8-454	245	R44T	.035	29-31	.019	—	10B	55	7½-9	—	600/450②
'74	8-350	145	R44T	.035	29-31	.019	—	8B	28(44)	7½-9	—	600
	8-350	160	R44T	.035	29-31	.019	—	12B(8B)	28(44)	7½-9	—	600
	8-400	150	R44T	.035	29-31	.019	—	8B	28(44)	7½-9	—	600
	8-400	180	R44T	.035	29-31	.019	—	8B	28(44)	7½-9	—	600
	8-454	235	R44T	.035	29-31	.019	—	10B	55	7½-9	—	600
'75	8-350	145	R-44TX	.060	Electronic		—	6B	28	7½-9	—	600
	8-350	155	R-44TX	.060	Electronic		—	6B	28	7½-9	—	600
	8-400	175	R-44TX	.060	Electronic		—	8B	28	7½-9	—	600
	8-454	215	R-44TX	.060	Electronic		—	16B	55	7½-9	—	650
'76	8-350	145	R-45TS	.045	Electronic		—	6B	28	7½-9	—	600
	8-350	165	R-45TS	.045	Electronic		—	8B (6B)	28	7½-9	—	600
	8-400	175	R-45TS	.045	Electronic		—	8B	28	7½-9	—	600
	8-454	225	R-45TS	.045	Electronic		—	12B	55	7½-9	—	550
'77	6-250	All	R-46TS	.035	Electronic		—	8B(6B)③	16	4-5	—	550/600④
	8-305	All	R-45TS	.045	Electronic		—	8B(6B)	28	7½-9	—	500
	8-350	All	R-45TS	.045	Electronic		—	8B	28	7½-9	—	500/600④
'78	6-250	110	R-46TS	.035	Electronic		—	①	16	4-5	—	550(600)
	8-305	145	R-45TS	.045	Electronic		—	4B(6B)	28	7-9	—	500
	8-350	170	R-45TS	.045	Electronic		—	6B(8B)	28	7-9	—	500
'79	6-250	110	R-46TS	.035	Electronic		—	10B(6B)	16	4.5-6.0	⑥	⑥
	8-305	145	R-45TS	.045	Electronic		—	4B	28	7.5-9.0	⑥	⑥
	8-350	170	R-45TS	.045	Electronic		—	6B(8B)	28	7.5-9.0	⑥	⑥

▲ See text for procedure
● Figure in parentheses indicates California engine
■ All figures Before Top Dead Center
① Non-California, non-air conditioning: 10B
   Non-California, with air conditioning: 8B
   California: 6B
② Lower figure with Idle Solenoid disconnected

③ High altitude—10B
④ High figure with A/C
⑤ See underhood specifications sticker
⑥ See Underhood Sticker
B Before Top Dead Center
TDC Top Dead Center
— Not applicable

NOTE: Most 1979 GM carburetors have idle mixture screws concealed by staked-in plugs. These are not meant to be removed, except at carburetor overhaul.

Corvette   TUNE-UP SPECIFICATIONS

When analyzing compression test results, look for uniformity among cylinders rather than specific pressures.

| | ENGINE | | SPARK PLUGS | | DISTRIBUTOR | | IGNITION TIMING (deg) ▲ | | VALVES | Fuel Pump | IDLE SPEED ● (rpm) ▲ | |
Year	No. Cyl Displacement (cu in.)	hp	Orig. Type	Gap (in.)	Point Dwell (deg)	Point Gap (in.)	Man Trans ●	Auto Trans	Intake Opens ■ (deg)	Pressure (psi)	Man Trans	Auto Trans
'72	8-350	200	R44T	.035	29-31	.019	8B	8B	28(44)	7½-9	800	600
	8-350	255	R44T	.035	29-31	.019	4B	8B	42½	7½-9	900	700
	8-454	270	R44T	.035	29-31	.019	8B	8B	56	7½-9	800	600
'73	8-350	190	R44T	.035	29-31	.019	12B	12B	28	7½-9	900/450①	600/450
	8-350	250	R44T	.035	29-31	.019	8B	8B	52	7½-9	900/450①	700/450
	8-454	275	R44T	.035	29-31	.019	10B	10B	55	7½-9	900/450①	600/450
'74	8-350	195	R44T	.035	29-31	.019	8B(4B)	8B	28(44)	7½-9	900	600
	8-350	250	R44T	.035	29-31	.019	8B	8B	52	7½-9	900	700
	8-454	270	R44T	.035	29-31	.019	10B	10B	55	7½-9	800	600
'75	8-350	165	R-44TX	.060	Electronic		6B	6B	28	7½-9	800	600
	8-350	205	R-44TX	.060	Electronic		12B	12B	52	7½-9	900	700
'76	8-350	180	R-45TS	.045	Electronic		8B	8B(6B)	28	7½-9	800	600
	8-350	210	R-45TS	.045	Electronic		12B	12B	52	7½-9	1000	700
'77	8-350	180	R-45TS	.045	Electronic		8B	8B	28	7½-9	700	500/600②
	8-350	210	R-45TS	.045	Electronic		12B	12B	52	7½-9	800	500/600②
'78	8-350	185	R-45TS	.045	Electronic		6B	6B(8B)	28	7-9	700	500③
	8-350	220	R-45TS	.045	Electronic		12B	12B	52	7-9	900	700
'79	8-350	185	R-45TS	.045	Electronic		6B	④	28	7.5-9.0	⑤	⑤
	8-350	220	R-45TS	.045	Electronic		12B	12B	52	7.5-9.0	⑤	⑤

▲ See text for procedure
● Figure in parentheses iindicates California engine
■ All figures Before Top Dead Center
① Lower figure with Idle Solenoid disconnected
② Higher figure with A/C
③ High Altitude: 600
④ Except Calif. and High Altitude: 6B
　Calif. and High Altitude: 8B
⑤ See Underhood Sticker
B Before Top Dead Center
— Not applicable

MECHANICAL VALVE LIFTER CLEARANCE

Year	Engine		Intake (Hot) In.	Exhaust (Hot) In.
1972	V8-350	255 hp	.024	.030

FIRING ORDER

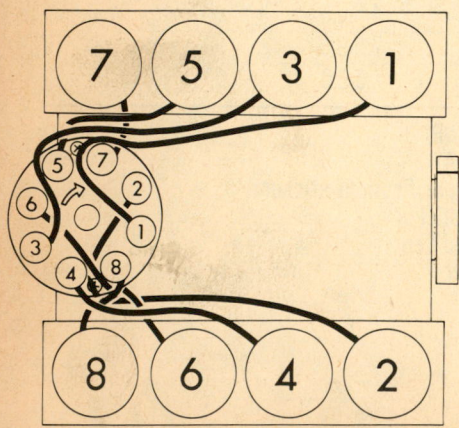

GM (Chevrolet) V8, (through 1974)
Engine firing order: 1-8-4-3-6-5-7-2
Distributor rotation: clockwise

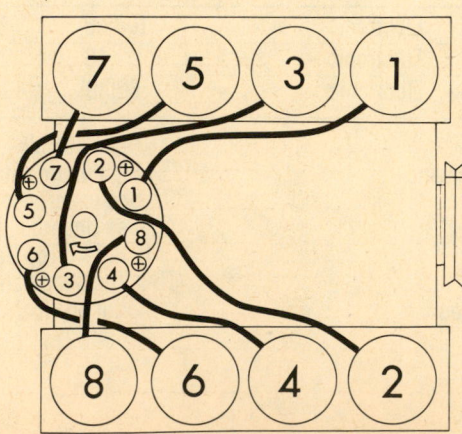

GM (Chevrolet) V8 (1975 and later)
Engine firing order: 1-8-4-3-6-5-7-2
Distributor rotation: clockwise

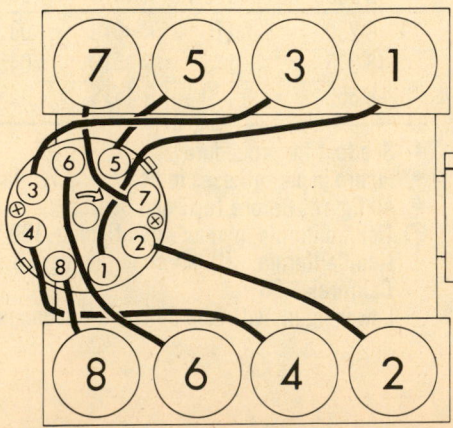

GM (Chevrolet) Corvette 350, 454 V8 (1973-74)
Engine firing order: 1-8-4-3-6-5-7-2
Distributor rotation: clockwise

FIRING ORDER

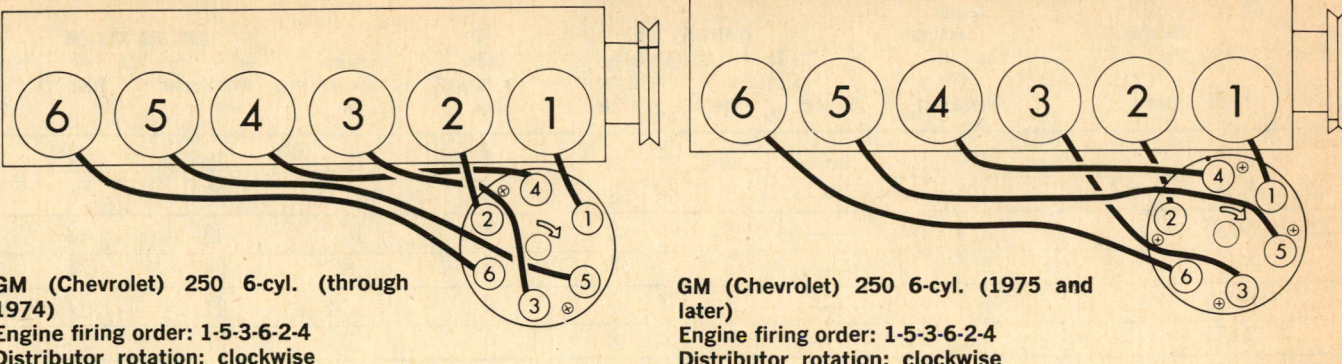

GM (Chevrolet) 250 6-cyl. (through 1974)
Engine firing order: 1-5-3-6-2-4
Distributor rotation: clockwise

GM (Chevrolet) 250 6-cyl. (1975 and later)
Engine firing order: 1-5-3-6-2-4
Distributor rotation: clockwise

Chevrolet

CAPACITIES

Year	ENGINE No. Cyl. Displacement (cu. in.)	Engine Crankcase Add 1 Qt For New Filter	TRANSMISSION Pts to Refill After Draining Automatic ●		Drive Axle (pts) ▲	Gasoline Tank (gals) ■	COOLING SYSTEM (qts)		
							With Heater	With A/C	With Heavy Duty
'72	6-250	4	3	—	6	4.25	23	12	—
	8-350	4	—	—	5	4.25	23	16	17
	8-400	4	—	—	5	4.25	23	16	17
	8-402	4	—	—	8	4.25	23	23	24
	8-454	4	—	—	8	4.25	23	22	23
'73	6-250	4	3	—	5	4.25	26	12	12
	8-350	4	—	—	5	4.25	26	16	17
	8-400	4	—	—	5	4.25	26	16.5	17.5
	8-454	4	—	—	8	4.25	26	23	24
'74	8-350	4	—	—	8	4.25	26	16	16
	8-400	4	—	—	8①	4.25	26	16	16
	8-454	4	—	—	9	4.25	26	22	23
'75	8-350	4	—	—	8	4.25	26	16	16
	8-400	4	—	—	9	4.25	26	16	16
	8-454	4	—	—	9	4.25	26	22	23
	6-250	4	3	—	5	4.25	26	12	12
	8-305	4	—	—	8	4.25	26	18	20
'76	8-350	4	—	—	8	4.25	26	18	20
	8-400	4	—	—	9	4.25	26	18	20
	8-454	4	—	—	9	4.25	26	23	25
'77	6-250	4	—	—	8	3.25	21	14.6	15.2
	8-305	4	—	—	8	3.25	21	17.2	17.8
	8-350	4	—	—	8	3.25	21	17.2	17.8
'78	6-250	4	—	—	6	3.25	21	14.2	14.2
	8-305	4	—	—	6	3.25	21	16.6	16.6
	8-350	4	—	—	6	3.25	21	16.6	16.6
'79	6-250	4	—	—	7	4.0	21	14.2	14.2
	8-305	4	—	—	8	4.0②	21	16.6	16.6
	8-350	4	—	—	8	4.0②	21	16.6	16.6

● Specifications do not include torque converter
■ Station wagons: 22 gals
▲ With 8.875 diameter ring gear: through 1976: 4.9 pts, '77 and later 8.5 and 8.75: 4.0 pts

① 9 with 400 4 bbl
② with 7.5 inch ring gear: 3.25
— Not applicable

Corvette   CAPACITIES

Year	ENGINE No. Cyl. (Cu. In.) Displacement	Engine Crankcase Add 1 Qt For New Filter	TRANSMISSION Pts To Refill After Draining Manual 3-Speed	4-Speed	Automatic ●	Drive Axle (pts) ▲	Gasoline Tank (gals) ■	COOLING SYSTEM (qts) With Heater	With A/C
'72	8-350	4	—	3	8	4	18	15②	18
	8-454	5	—	3	8	4	18	22	24
'73	8-350	4	—	3	8	4	18	18	18
	8-454	5	—	3	8	4	18	24	24
'74	8-350	4	—	3	8	4	18	17	17
	8-454	5	—	3	8	4	18	22	23
'75	8-350	4	—	3	8	4	18	17	17
'76	8-350	4	—	3	8	4	18	18	18
'77	8-350	4	—	3	8	4	17	21	21
'78	8-350	4	—	3	8	4	24	21.6	21.6
'79	8-350	4	—	3.4③	8	3.75	24	21.6	21.6

● Specifications do not include torque converter   ③ Optional close-ratio 4 sp.: 2.75   ② 18 qts with 330 hp

① Not used   — Not applicable

VALVE SPECIFICATIONS

Year	Engine No. Cyl. Displacement (cu in.)	Seat Angle (deg)	Face Angle (deg)	Spring Test Pressure (lbs @ in.)	Spring Installed Height (in.)	STEM TO GUIDE Clearance (in.) Intake	Exhaust	STEM Diameter (in.) Intake	Exhaust
'72	6-250	46	45	60 @ 1.66	1 21/32	.0010-.0037	.0010-.0047	.3414	.3414
	8-350	46	45	80 @ 1.70	1 23/32	.0010-.0037	.0010-.0047	.3414	.3414
	8-400	46	45	80 @ 1.70	1 23/32	.0010-.0037	.0010-.0047	.3414	.3414
	8-402	46	45	90 @ 1.88	1 7/8	.0010-.0037	.0010-.0047	.3719	.3717
	8-454	46	45	75 @ 1.88①	1 7/8	.0010-.0037	.0010-.0047	.3719	.3717
'73	6-250	46	45	60 @ 1.66	1 21/32	.0010-.0027	.0010-.0027	.3414	.3414
	8-350	46	45	80 @ 1.70②	1 23/32	.0010-.0027	.0010-.0027	.3414	.3414
	8-400	46	45	80 @ 1.70②	1 23/32	.0010-.0027	.0010-.0027	.3414	.3414
	8-454	46	45	80 @ 1.88	1 7/8	.0010-.0027	.0010-.0027	.3719	.3717
'74	8-350	46	45	80 @ 1.70②	1 23/32	.0010-.0027	.0010-.0027	.3414	.3414
	8-400	46	45	80 @ 1.70②	1 23/32	.0010-.0027	.0010-.0027	.3414	.3414
	8-454	46	45	80 @ 1.88	1 7/8	.0010-.0027	.0010-.0027	.3719	.3717
	6-250	46	45	60 @ 1.66	1 21/32	.0010-.0027	.0015-.0032	.3414	.3414
	8-305	46	45	80 @ 1.70	1 23/32	.0010-.0027	.0010-.0027	.3414	.3414
'75-'76	8-350	46	45	80 @ 1.70②	1 23/32	.0010-.0027	.0010-.0027	.3414	.3414
	8-400	46	45	80 @ 1.70②	1 23/32	.0010-.0027	.0010-.0027	.3414	.3414
	8-454	46	45	80 @ 1.88	1 7/8	.0010-.0027	.0010-.0027	.3719	.3717
'77	6-250	46	45	82 @ 1.66	1 21/32	.0010-.0027	.0010-.0027	.3414	.3414
	8-305	46	45	82 @ 1.70②	1 23/32	.0010-.0027	.0010-.0027	.3414	.3414
	8-350	46	45	82 @ 1.70②	1 23/32	.0010-.0027	.0010-.0027	.3414	.3414
'78	6-250	46	45	175 @ 1.26	1 21/32	.0010-.0027	.0015-.0032	.3414	.3414
	8-305	46	45	200 @ 1.25	1 23/32	.0010-.0027	.0010-.0027	.3414	.3414
	8-350	46	45	200 @ 1.25③	1 23/32④	.0010-.0027	.0010-.0027	.3414	.3414
'79	6-250	46	45	175 @ 1.26	1 21/32	.0010-.0027	.0010-.0027	.3414	.3414
	8-305	46	45	180 @ 1.25⑤	1 23/32⑥	.0010-.0027	.0010-.0027	.3414	.3414
	8-350⑦	46	45	180 @ 1.25⑤	1 23/32⑥	.0010-.0027	.0010-.0027	.3414	.3414

VALVE SPECIFICATIONS

Year	Engine No. Cyl. Displacement (cu in.)	Seat Angle (deg)	Face Angle (deg)	Spring Test Pressure (lbs @ in.)	Spring Installed Height (in.)	STEM TO GUIDE Clearance (in.) Intake	Exhaust	STEM Diameter (in.) Intake	Exhaust
'79	8-350⑧	46	45	184 @ 1.25	1 ²³/₃₂⑥	.0010-.0027	.0010-.0027	.3414	.3414
	8-350⑩	46	45	200 @ 1.25⑪	1 ²³/₃₂	.0010-.0027	.0010-.0027	.3414	.3414

① Inner spring 30 @ 1.78
② Intake, 80 @ 1.61 for exhaust spring
③ Corvette exhaust valve: 200 @ 1.16
④ Corvette exhaust valve: 1 ¹⁹/₃₂
⑤ Exhaust: 190 1.16
⑥ Exhaust: 1 ¹⁹/₃₂
⑦ Chevrolet
⑧ Corvette base engine Not Used
⑩ Corvette optional engine
⑪ Exhaust: 203 1.25

RING GAP

All measurements are given in inches

Year	Engine No. Cyl.	Top Compression	Bottom Compression
'72-'79	6-250	.010-.020	.010-.020
'77-'78	8-305	.010-.020	.010-.025
'72-'76	8-400, 402, 454	.010-.020	.010-.020
'72-'79	8-350	.010-.020①	.013-.025②①
'79	8-305	.010-.020	.013-.025

Year	Engine No. Cyl.	Oil Control
'72-'79	All exc. '79 8-305	.015-.055
'79	8-305	.015-.035

① 250, 300 hp 350 cu in. Top .013-.023
2nd .013-.025
② 210, 250, 255 hp 350 cu in. .013-.023

CRANKSHAFT AND CONNECTING ROD SPECIFICATIONS

All measurements are given in inches

Year	Engine No. Cyl. Displacement (cu in.)	CRANKSHAFT Main Brg. Journal Dia	Main Brg. Oil Clearance	Shaft End-Play	Thrust on No.	CONNECTING ROD Journal Diameter	Oil Clearance	Side Clearance
'72	6-250	2.2983-2.2993	.0003-.0029	.002-.006	7	1.9990-2.0000	.0007-.0027	.009-.014
	8-350	2.4484-2.4493⑫	.0008-.0020⑨	.002-.006	5	2.0990-2.1000	.0013-.0035	.008-.014
	8-350 (255 H.P.)	2.4484-2.4493⑫	.0013-.0025⑬	.002-.006	5	2.0990-2.1000	.0013-.0035	.008-.014
	8-400 (170 H.P.)	2.6484-2.6493⑭	.0008-.0020⑨	.002-.006	5	2.0990-2.1000	.0013-.0035	.008-.014
	8-402 (210 H.P.)	2.7487-2.7496⑮	.0007-.0019⑯	.006-.010	5	2.1990-2.2000	.0009-.0025	.013-.023
	8-454 (270 H.P.)	2.7485-2.7494⑰	.0013-.0025⑩	.006-.010	5	2.1990-2.2000	.0009-.0025	.015-.021
'73-'77	6-250 All	2.2983-2.2993	.0003-.0029	.002-.006	7	1.9990-2.000	.0007-.0027	.009-.014
	8-305, 350, 145, 175 HP	2.4484-2.4493⑱	.0008-.0020⑨	.002-.006	5	2.0990-2.1000	.0013-.0035	.008-.014
	8-350 245, 250 HP auto. trans	2.4484-2.4493⑱	.0019-.0031	.002-.006	5	2.0990-2.1000	.0013-.0035	.008-.014
	8-350 245, 250 HP Manual Trans	2.4484-2.4493⑱	.0013-.0025	.002-.006	5	2.0990-2.1000	.0013-.0035	.008-.014
	8-400	2.6484-2.6493⑲	.0008-.0020⑨	.002-.006	5	2.0990-2.1000	.0013-.0035	.008-.014
	8-454	2.7485-2.7494⑰	.0013-.0025⑩	.006-.010	5	2.1990-2.2000	.0009-.0025	.015-.021
'78-'79	6-250	2.2979-2.2994	.0010-.0024⑧	.002-.006	7	1.9980-2.0000	.0010-.0026	.006-.017
	8-305, 350	2.4484-2.4493⑦	.0008-.0020⑨	.002-.006	5	2.0988-2.0998	.0013-.0035	.008-.014

①-⑥ Not used
⑦ No. 2, 3, 4: 2.4481-2.4490
No. 5: 2.4479-2.4488
⑧ No. 7: .0016-.0035
⑨ No.'s 2, 3, 4—.011-.0023; No. 5—.0017-.0033
⑩ No. 5—.0024-.0040
⑪ Not used
⑫ No.'s 2, 3, 4—2.4481-2.4490; No. 5—2.4479-2.4488

⑬ No. 5—.0023-.0033; with auto. trans. No. 1—.0019-.0031
⑭ No. 5—2.6479-2.6488
⑮ No.'s 3, 4—2.7481-2.7490; No. 5—2.7473-2.7483
⑯ No.'s 2, 3, 4—.0013-.0025; No. 5—.0019-.0035
⑰ No.'s 2, 3, 4—2.7481-2.7490; No. 5—2.7478-2.7488
⑱ No. 5—2.4508
⑲ No. 5—2.6509

RING SIDE CLEARANCE

All measurements are given in inches

Year	Engine No. Cyl.	Top Compression	Bottom Compression
'72-'79	6-250	.0012-.0027	.0012-.0032
'72-'76	8-350 2 bbl	.0012-.0032	.0012-.0032
'72-'77	8-305, 8-350 4 bbl	.0012-.0032	.0012-.0027
'72-'76	8-400	.0012-.0027①	.0012-.0032①
'72-'76	8-402, 454	.0017-.0032	.0017-.0032
'78-'79	8-305, 350	.0012-.0032	.0012-.0032

Year	Engine No. Cyl.	Oil Control
'72-'79	6-250, 400	.000-.005②
'72-'76	8-350 2 bbl	.002-.007
'72-'79	8-305, 350 4 bbl	.000-.005
'72-'76	8-402, 454	.0005-.0065

① 330 hp 400 cu in. Top .0017-.0032
② 330 hp 400 cu in. .0005-.0065
2nd .0012-.0032

TORQUE SPECIFICATIONS

All readings in ft lbs

Year	Engine No. Cyl. Displacement (cu in.)	Cylinder Head Bolts	Rod Bearing Bolts	Main Bearing Bolts	Crankshaft Bolt	Flywheel to Crankshaft Bolts	MANIFOLD Intake	MANIFOLD Exhaust
'72-'73	6-250	95	35	65	——	60	30⑧	25⑦
'77-'79	6-250	95	35	65	——	60	—	③
'72-'79	8-305, 350, 400	70⑥	45	75②	60	60	30	⑤
'72	8-402 (Big Block)	80	50	105	85	65	30	30
'72-'75	8-454	80	50④	110	85	65	30	30

① Not used
② Engines with 4-bolt mains—Outer bolts 65; 70 starting 1976
③ 30 center, 20 on four end bolts
④ 7/16 Rod bolts—70
⑤ Center bolts—30, end bolts 20
⑥ 65 starting 1976
⑦ Exhaust-to-intake
⑧ Manifold-to-head

WHEEL ALIGNMENT SPECIFICATIONS

Year	Model	CASTER Range (deg)	CASTER Pref Setting (deg)	CAMBER Range (deg)	CAMBER Pref Setting (deg)	Toe-in (In.)	Steering Axis Inclin. (deg)	WHEEL PIVOT RATIO (deg) Inner Wheel	WHEEL PIVOT RATIO (deg) Outer Wheel
'72	Corvette⑦	½P to 1½P①	1P	¼P to 1¼P	¾P	3/16 to 5/16	6½ to 7½	—	—
'72	Chevrolet	½P to 1½P	1P	0 to 1P	½P	3/16 to 5/16	9½ to 10½	—	—
'73	Chevrolet	0 to 2P	1P	¼P to 1¾P⑤	1P	1/16N to 3/16P	10½	—	—
	Corvette⑦	0 to 2P③	1P	0 to 1½P④	¾P	1/8 to 3/8④	6⅞	—	—
'74	Chevrolet	½-1½P	1P	½-1½P⑤	1P⑥	1/16 to 3/16	9½	—	—
	Corvette⑦	½P-1½P①	1P	¼P-1¼P④	¾P	3/32 to 5/32④	7¾	—	—
'75-'76	Chevrolet	½P-2½P⑧	1½P	½-1½P⑤	1P⑥	1/16 to 3/16	9⁷/₆₄	—	—
	Corvette⑦⑨	½P-1½P①	1P	¼P-1¼P	¾P	1/32 to 3/32	7¾	—	—
'77-'78	Chevrolet	2½P to 3½P	3P	1/3P to 1 1/3P	4/5P	1/16 to 3/16	9⁷/₆₄	—	—
	Corvette⑨	2P to 2½P	2¼P	¼P to 1¼P	¾P	3/16 to 5/16	7¾	—	—
'79	Chevrolet	2½P to 3½P	3P	1/3P to 1 1/3P	4/5P	.10-.20⑩	9.785	—	—
	Corvette	2P to 2½P	2¼P	¼P to 1P	¾P	.19-.31⑩	7.680	—	—

① W/power steering—1¾P to 2¾P
② Not used
③ W/power steering—1¼P to 3¼P, 2¼ preferred
④ Rear wheel alignment: camber ⅞N ± ¼. toe-in 2/32 ± 1/32
⑤ Left wheel given, right wheel is ¼N to 1¼P, preferred ½P
⑥ Left wheel given, right wheel is ½P
⑦ Rear wheel alignment through 1975: Camber—¹¹/₁₆N ± ¼; Toe-in—0 ± ¹/₃₂
⑧ ½P-1½P W/bias belted tires
⑨ 1976 and later Rear Wheel Alignment: Camber, ⅞N ± ¼; Toe-In, ¹/₃₂-³/₃₂
⑩ degrees

N Negative   P Positive
— Not specified

PISTON CLEARANCE

Year	Engine	Horsepower	Piston to Bore Clearance (in.)
'72-'76	6-250	all	.0010
'77-'79	6-250	all	.0015
'72-'76	8-400	all	.0017
'72	8-350	165, 175, 200	.0010
'72	8-350	255	.0039
'72	8-454	all	.0029
'73-'76	8-454	all	.0023
'73	8-350	145, 175	.0010
'73	8-350	245, 250	.0039
'74	8-350	all	.0010
'75-'76	8-350	2 bbl	.0008
'75-'76	8-350	4 bbl	.0010
'75-'76	8-350	Dual Exh.	.0039
'77-'78	8-305, 350	all exc. L82	.0012
'78-'79	8-350	L82	.0051
'79	8-305, 350	all exc. L82	.0025*

* measured 1.56 inches from top of piston

CHARGING SYSTEM

Test details can be found in the Charging and Starting Systems Unit Repair Section.

Alternator Removal and Installation

1. Disconnect the battery cables from the battery terminals.
2. Disconnect and identify the wire leads from the alternator.
3. Remove the alternator brace bolt, then remove belt(s).
4. Remove the alternator pivot attaching bolt and remove alternator from vehicle.
5. To install, reverse the above procedure and adjust belt tension.

1972 Regulator Removal and Installation

NOTE: *An integral alternator/regulator is used starting 1973. Separate removal or adjustment of the regulator is not possible with this unit. This unit is described in the Unit Repair Section.*

1. Disconnect the ground cable at the battery.
2. Disconnect the wiring harness from the regulator.
3. Remove the mounting screws and remove the regulator.
4. Make sure that the regulator base

gasket is in place before installation.
5. Clean the attaching area for proper grounding.
6. Install the regulator. Do not overtighten the mounting screws, as this will cancel the cushioning effect of the rubber grommets.

STARTING SYSTEM

More information on starters can be found in the Unit Repair Section under Charging and Starting Systems.

Starter Removal and Installation

1. Disconnect the battery and the wires from the solenoid.

NOTE: *1975 and later models do not have a solenoid-to-ignition coil wire, thus eliminating the R terminal on the solenoid.*

2. Remove the starter mounting bolt and lock washers. On V8s, a stud nut and lock washer are at the front of the starter.
3. Pull starter forward and out of car.
4. To install, reverse the above procedure.

Disabling the Seat Belt/Starter Interlock System

Since the requirement for the interlock system was dropped during the 1975 model year, these systems may now be legally disabled. The seat belt warning light is still required.

1. Disconnect the battery ground cable.
2. Locate the interlock harness connector under the left side of the instrument panel on or near the fuse block. It has orange, yellow, and green leads.
3. Cut and tape the ends of the green wire on the body side of the connector.
4. Remove the buzzer from the fuse block or connector.

IGNITION SYSTEM

Two types of ignition systems have been available: a conventional breaker type, and a High Energy Ignition (HEI) system.

A resistance wire connects the ignition switch and the coil on the breaker type system. The magnetic pulse system utilizes two; one between the negative coil terminal and ground, the other provides a voltage drop for the engine run circuit. The HEI system doesn't use a resistance wire.

The HEI system was used starting 1974 on 454 cu. in. Chevrolets. All 1975

and later models are equipped with HEI. Description and troubleshooting for both the magnetic pulse and HEI systems are found in the Electronic Ignition Unit Repair Section.

Distributor Removal

6 CYLINDER

The distributor assembly is mounted on the right side of the block and is driven directly from the camshaft.

To remove the distributor, first detach the vacuum lines from the vacuum advance unit and lift off the distributor cap. Detach the coil wire or the HEI connector.

The distributor body is fastened to the block by a single cap screw. Scribe marks so that the distributor body and rotor can be installed in their original locations. Do not turn engine while the distributor is removed. Remove the retaining screw and lift the distributor out of the block.

V8

The distributor is located between the two banks of cylinders at the back of the block.

The drive gear is attached to the distributor shaft; therefore, if it becomes necessary to remove the distributor, carefully mark the position of the rotor. Then, if the engine is not turned after the distributor is taken out, it can be intalled in the same position from which it was removed.

To remove the distributor, disconnect the carburetor air cleaner, disconnect the coil primary wire or HEI connector and the vacuum line, remove the distributor cap, take out the single hold-down bolt located under the distributor body, mark the position of the body relative to the block and then work the distributor up out of the block.

Distributor Installation (Engine Disturbed)

1. Turn the crankshaft until the No. 1 cylinder is at the top of its compression stroke. Remove the No. 1 spark plug to feel the compression.
2. Align the timing mark on the vibration damper with the indicator.
3. With distributor body oriented in its normal position, hold the rotor pointing toward the front of the engine, then turn the rotor approximately 1/8 turn counterclockwise down until it engages the camshaft, rotating the shaft slightly if necessary.

NOTE: *On Mark IV (big block V8) engines there is a punch mark on the distributor drive gear which indicates the rotor position. Thus, the distributor may be installed with the cap in place. Align the punch mark 2° clockwise from the No. 1 cap terminal, then rotate the distributor body 1/8 turn counterclockwise and push the distributor down into the block.*

4. Press down on the distributor and crank the engine to make sure the oil pump shaft is engaged.
5. Return the crankshaft to No. 1 cylinder compression stroke with the timing marks aligned.
6. Turn the distrubtor body counterclockwise until the points are just beginning to open, then tighten the distributor clamp bolt.
7. Install the distributor cap, checking that the rotor points to the No. 1 terminal. Make sure that the spark plug wires are in their supports and are securely connected.
8. Connect distributor vacuum line and primary wire.
9. Start engine and set the timing.

CAUTION

When using an auxiliary starter switch for bumping the engine into position for timing, the primary distributor lead must be disconnected from the negative post of the ignition coil and the switch must be in the on position. Failure to do this may cause damage to the grounding circuit in the ignition switch.

Breaker Point Adjustment

NOTE: *Some distributors are equipped with a radio static shield, which must be removed for access to the points.*

Breaker point gap (dwell) adjustment is accomplished for 6-cylinder engines by loosening the point assembly attaching screw and adjusting it with a screwdriver until correct gap clearance is obtained (use a feeler gauge). Tighten the point assembly attaching screws and install the distributor cap. Use a dwell meter, if available, to check the dwell angle, readjusting if necessary.

On V8 models there is a window in the distributor cap so that the dwell angle may be set while the engine is running. Use a 1/8 in. Allen (hex) wrench to make the adjustment.

See Tune-Up Specifications at the beginning of this section for correct breaker point gap and dwell angle.

CAUTION

On V8 models the distributor body is involved in the engine lubricating system. The lubricating circuit to the right-bank valve train can be interrupted by mis-alignment of the distributor body. See Firing Order illustrations for correct distributor positioning.

HEI System Tachometer Hookup

Connect one dwell/tach lead to the TACH terminal on the side of the V8 distributor and the other to ground. Some tachometers must be connected to the TACH terminal and the battery positive terminal. The hookup is the same for inline engine systems, except that the TACH terminal is opposite the BAT terminal on the remote-mounted coil. Not all tachometers will operate correctly with the HEI system. Check

with the manufacturer if there is any doubt.

CAUTION

The TACH terminal should never be connected to ground.

When hooking up a remote starter switch, disconnect the BATT terminal.

Ignition Timing

Remove the spark plug wire from no. one plug and attach a timing light between the wire and the plug. Disconnect the distributor spark advance hose and plug the vacuum opening. Start the engine and run it at idle speed. Aim the timing light at the degree scale just over

ADJUST DWELL ANGLE SETTING OR POINT OPENING

6 cylinder point adjustment
(© Chevrolet Div., G M. Corp)

the harmonic balancer. Adjust the timing by loosening the securing clamp and rotating the distributor until the desired ignition advance is achieved, then tighten the clamp. To advance the timing, rotate the distributor opposite to the normal direction of rotor rotation. Retard the timing by rotating the distributor in the normal direction of rotor rotation. When timing an engine equipped with HEI, use an adapter at the No. 1 distributor or plug terminal. You can also use No. 6 wire, if it is more convenient.

FUEL SYSTEM

Data on capacity of the gas tank can be found in the Capacities table. Data on correct engine idle speed and fuel pump pressure can be found in the Tune-up Specifications table.

Information covering operation and troubles of the fuel gauge is in the Unit Repair Section.

Fuel Pump Removal and Installation

To remove the fuel pump, disconnect the input line and the output line to the carburetor. The fuel pump then can be unbolted from the side of the block

and lifted off. On V8 models, the pump is actuated by a pushrod in the block.

CAUTION

A fuel pump may fail to function at the time of replacement as a result of error in positioning or damage to the fuel pump pushrod of the V8 engine. This pushrod can slip out of place during the process of pump replacement and result in no pump action from the newly replaced unit. Before tightening the fuel pump to the engine, have someone spin the engine with the starter while feeling the fuel pump body for movement. If the pump and pushrod are in correct position, movement will be felt in the pump as the pushrod pressure is applied and released from the pump arm.

Fuel Filter Removal and Installation

Fuel filters are integral with the car-

Chilton's TIME SAVER

When replacing a fuel pump on a small block V8 engine, considerable time can be saved as follows:
1. Before removing the old pump, remove the upper bolt from the engine's right front mounting boss. This bolt hole is in direct alignment with the fuel pump pushrod. The threaded bolt hole continues into the pump pushrod bore. The bolt acts as an oil plug.
2. Temporarily insert a longer bolt, (about 3/8—16 x 2 in.) into the hole. Screw the bolt into the bore until it bottoms against the pump pushrod. (Don't tighten the bolt with a wrench or the rod can be damaged.)
3. The mechanic is now free to remove and install the fuel pump without worrying about fuel pump pushrod misalignment.

CAUTION: Don't forget to reinstall the original bolt.

The design of big block V8 engines prevents the use of the bolt method of simplifying fuel pump pushrod positioning while installing a fuel pump. However, to hold the pump pushrod in position while installing the fuel pump, the following works satisfactorily;
1. Clean oil from pushrod.
2. Pack a small quantity of non-fibrous grease in the area around the fuel pump pushrod to hold it in suspension long enough to position the fuel pump.
3. Install and check pump action, then torque attaching bolts.

buretor body. The filter element can be replaced as follows:
1. Disconnect the fuel line.
2. Remove the fuel filter nut from the carburetor.

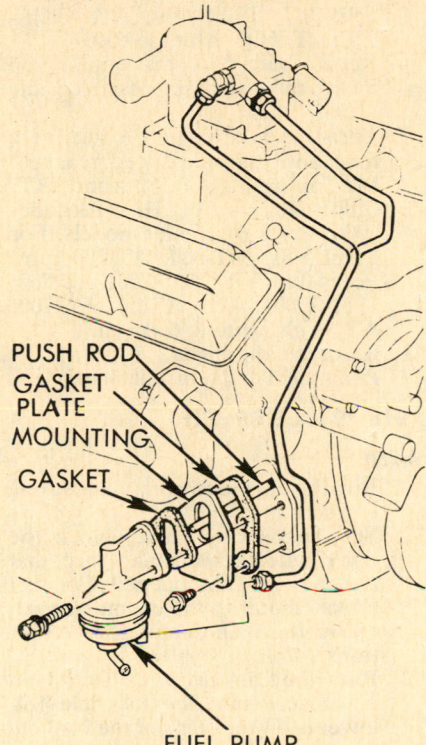

Typical small block V8 fuel pump
(© Chevrolet Div., G.M. Corp)

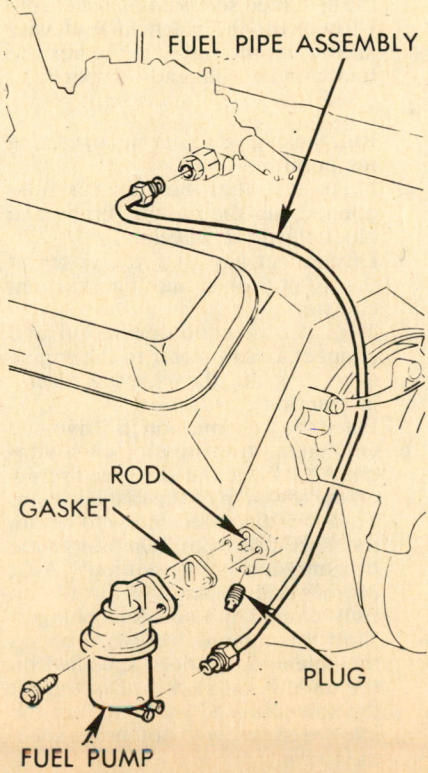

Typical big block V8 fuel pump

3. Remove the filter element and spring. Blow through the filter end. If the air does not flow freely, replace the element. Do not attempt to clean the filter element.
4. Install the spring, then the element. Bronze filters in Holley carburetors must have the small section of the cone facing out.
5. Install the inlet fitting using a new gasket.
6. Install the fuel line.

Carburetor Adjustments

When adjusting a carburetor with two idle mixture screws, adjust them alternately and evenly, unless otherwise stated.

In the following adjustment procedures the term "lean roll" means turning the mixture adjusting screws in (clockwise) from optimum setting to obtain an obvious drop in engine speed (usually 20 rpm).

1972

NOTE: *All carburetors are equipped with idle limiter caps and idle mixture is preset at the factory and should not require adjustment.*
1. On Chevrolet models, disconnect the fuel tank line from the vapor storage canister. On Corvettes, remove the fuel filler cap but do not remove the vapor line.
2. Detach the distributor vacuum hose and plug the hose.
3. Set the parking brake and turn the air conditioner (if so equipped) off. On cars equipped with an automatic transmission, chock the wheels.
4. Allow the engine to reach normal operating temperature. Be sure that the choke is open.
5. If the car has an automatic transmission, set the selector in Drive. If the car has a manual transmission keep the transmission in Neutral.
6. Adjust the anti-dieseling solenoid to the *higher* of the two rpm figures given in the specifications.

— CAUTION —
Do not turn the solenoid more than one complete turn unless the electrical lead is disconnected (solenoid de-energized).

7. Disconnect the solenoid lead and set the idle speed to the *lower* of the two figures given in the specifications. Use an allen wrench in the end of the solenoid for this adjustment, on six cylinder engines. On V8s use the normal idle speed adjusting screw.
NOTE: *If no lower figure is given, adjust the idle to 450 rpm.*
8. Reconnect all of the wires and hoses which were disconnected in order to perform these adjustments.

1973

All models are equipped with idle limiter caps and idle solenoids. Disconnect the fuel tank line from the evaporative canister. The engine must be running at operating temperature, choke off, parking brake on, and rear wheels blocked. Disconnect the distributor vacuum hose and plug it. After adjustment, reconnect the vacuum and evaporative hoses.

250 cu. in. Six Cylinder
Adjust the idle stop solenoid for 700 rpm on manual transmission models or 600 rpm on automatics. On manual models, make no attempt to adjust the CEC solenoid (the larger of the two carburetor solenoids) or a decrease in engine braking could result.

Two barrel 350 and 400 cu. in. V8
1. With air conditioning switched off, adjust the idle stop solenoid screw for a speed of 900 rpm on manual models; 600 rpm on automatics.
2. De-energize the idle stop solenoid and adjust the idle speed screw (screw resting on lower step of the cam) for 400 rpm on 350 and 400 engines with automatic transmission, or 500 rpm on 350 engines with manual transmission.

Four barrel 350 and 454 cu. in. V8
1. Adjust the idle stop solenoid screw for 900 rpm on manual, 600 rpm on automatic.
2. Connect the distributor vacuum hose and position the fast idle cam follower on the top step of the fast idle cam (turn air conditioning off) and adjust the fast idle to 1300 rpm on manual transmission 350 engines; 1600 on manual 454 engines and all automatics (in Park).

Optional Corvette 350 cu. in. (L82) V8
1. Adjust the idle stop solenoid screw (air conditioning off) for a speed of 900 rpm on manual transmission; 700 rpm on automatic (in Drive).
2. Connect the distributor vacuum hose and position the fast idle cam follower on the top step of the cam (turn air conditioning off) and adjust the fast idle to 1300 rpm on manual; 1600 on automatic.

1974

The same preconditions as for 1973 apply.

Two barrel 350 and 400 cu. in. V8
1. Turn the air conditioning off. Adjust the idle stop solenoid screw for 900 rpm on manual; 600 rpm on automatic (in Drive).
2. De-energize the solenoid and adjust the carburetor idle cam screw (on low step of cam) for 400 rpm on automatic models (in Drive); 500 rpm on 350 engines with manual transmission.

Four barrel 350 and 400 cu. in. V8
1. Turn the air conditioning off. Ad-

just the idle stop solenoid screw for 900 rpm on manual transmission models; 600 rpm on automatic (in Drive).

2. Connect the distributor vacuum hose. Position the fast idle cam follower on the top step of the fast idle cam and adjust the fast idle speed to 1300 rpm on manual; 1600 on automatic (in Park).

Optional Corvette 350 cu. in. (L82) V8

1. Turn the air conditioning off. Adjust the idle stop solenoid for 900 rpm on manual; 700 rpm on automatic (in Drive).
2. Connect the distributor vacuum hose. Position the fast idle cam follower on the top step of the cam and adjust the fast idle to 1300 rpm on manual; 1600 rpm on automatic (in Park).

454 cu. in. V8

1. Shut off the air conditioning. Adjust the idle stop solenoid screw for 800 rpm on manual; 600 rpm on automatic (in Drive).
2. Connect the distributor vacuum hose and position the fast idle cam follower on the top step of the cam and adjust the fast idle to 1600 rpm on manual; 1500 rpm on automatic (in Park).

1975-76

The engine must be at normal operating temperature with the air cleaner on, the choke open, the air conditioner off, and the timing correctly set.

1. Set the brake and block the wheels.
2. Set the automatic transmission in Drive and the manual in neutral. Disconnect the fuel tank hose from the vapor canister in the engine compartment.
3. Use needle nose pliers to break off the mixture screw cap or caps.

2 bbl

4. Adjust the idle speed with the idle speed screw to obtain the higher idle speed shown on the sticker.

4 bbl

Disconnect the electrical connector at the idle solenoid, and adjust the idle speed to the lower of the two figures given on the sticker. Reconnect the electrical connector, open the throttle to extend the solenoid plunger, then turn the solenoid plunger screw to obtain the higher of the two idle speed figures. For 1976, the idle solenoid has been dropped; the idle is adjusted with an idle speed screw.

5. On the 4 bbl, turn out the mixture screws until the highest possible idle speed is reached. If the idle speed becomes excessive (more than that set in Step 4), reset the idle speed to that set in Step 4. On the 2 bbl., turn out the mixture screws to obtain the highest idle and then, turn in the mixture screws to obtain the lower of the two figures listed on the sticker.

6. Turn in the mixture screws equally until the normal idle speed is reached.
7. Replace the vapor canister hose.

1977 IDLE SPEED

Run the engine to normal operating temperature, A/C off, vacuum advance line disconnected and plugged, FUEL TANK line at canister disconnected. Place the manual transmission in neutral; automatic transmission in Drive. Connect tachometer to the engine.

1 bbl

1. Turn the bolt head of the solenoid to set speed with solenoid energized to: MT-750 wo/AC; 800 w/AC; AT-550 wo/AC; 600 w/AC.
2. Disconnect the solenoid lead and turn the hex bolt (inside the bolt head) to achieve 425 rpm.

2 bbl without solenoid

1. Place the idle speed screw on the low step of the fast idle cam.
2. Turn the idle speed screw to achieve 600 rpm-MT; 500 rpm-AT.

2 bbl with solenoid

1. Turn the idle speed screw to achieve 600 rpm-MT; 500 rpm-AT.
2. Disconnect the compressor clutch lead and energize the solenoid by turning the A/C on.
3. Open the throttle slightly to allow the solenoid plunger to extend.
4. Turn the solenoid screw to achieve 700 rpm-MT; 650 rpm-AT.
5. Reconnect the A/C lead.

4 bbl without solenoid

Turn the idle speed screw to achieve the following rpm according to the carburetor part number (found on a tag under a carburetor bolt): 17057203, 17057210, 17057510-700 rpm; 17057202-500 rpm; 17057582, 17057584-600 rpm; 17057211-800.

4 bbl with solenoid

Adjustments are made according to the carburetor number (found on a tag under a carburetor bolt).

1. Turn the idle speed screw to set the curb idle to: 17057204, 17057504-500 rpm; 17057228, 17057528-700 rpm; 17057584-600 rpm.
2. Disconnect the A/C compressor lead and turn the system on.
3. Open the throttle slightly to allow solenoid plunger to extend fully.
4. Turn the solenoid screw to adjust to: 17057204, 17057504-650 rpm; 17057228, 17057528-800 rpm; 17057584-650 rpm.

1977 IDLE MIXTURE

1. Set the idle speed.
2. Check the ignition timing and adjust if necessary.
3. Carefully remove the cap(s) from the mixture screw(s).
4. Lightly seat the screw(s).
5. Back out each screw 1/8 turn at a time until maximum idle speed is

attained. Then set the idle speed screw to: MT-950 rpm; AT-575 rpm; AT, Calif.-640 rpm; AT, High Altitude-650 rpm for 6 cylinder engines. For 2 bbl V8s; MT-650; AT-550. For 4 bbl V8s: MT-800; AT-550; MT, Calif.-900; AT, Calif.-750; AT, High Altitude-650.

6. Repeat step 5 to make sure you have the highest possible idle speed.
7. Turn the screws in 1/8 turn at a time until the idle speed reaches: MT-750 rpm; AT-550 rpm; AT, Calif.-640 rpm; AT, High Altitude-600 rpm for 6 cylinder models. For 2 bbl V8s: MT-600; AT-500 rpm. For 4 bbl V8s: MT-700; AT-500; MT, Calif.-800; AT, Calif.-700; AT, High Altitude-600 rpm.
8. Reset the idle speed.
9. Reconnect and reinstall all parts.

1978-79 IDLE SPEED

6-250

1. Run the engine to normal operating temperature.
2. Set the parking brake, block the drive wheels and make sure that the choke is fully opened. Connect a tachometer to the engine according to the manufacturer's instructions.
3. Place the transmission in Drive and make sure that the fast idle follower is off the steps of the fast idle cam.
4. Momentarily open the throttle to extend the solenoid plunger. Turn the A/C Off.
5. Turn the solenoid hex nut to obtain the specified solenoid-on speed.
6. Disconnect the solenoid lead wire and adjust the screw in the hex nut to obtain the solenoid-off speed.

8-305

1. Run the engine to normal operating temperature.
2. Make sure that the choke is fully opened, set the parking brake and block the drive wheels.
3. Disconnect and plug the hoses at the EGR valve and the vacuum canister.
4. Turn the air conditioning Off and connect a tachometer to the engine according to the manufacturer's instructions.
5. Place the transmission in Drive.
6. On manual transmission cars without A/C: Place the idle speed screw on the low step of the fast idle cam. Turn the idle speed screw to obtain the specified rpm. On automatic transmission cars without A/C: Momentarily open the throttle to fully extend the solenoid plunger. Turn the solenoid screw to obtain the solenoid-on speed specified on the underhood sticker. Disconnect the solenoid lead wire and turn the idle speed screw to obtain the specified rpm. On cars with air conditioning: Turn the idle speed screw

to obtain the specified rpm. Momentarily open the throttle to extend the solenoid plunger. Disconnect the compressor clutch wire and turn the A/C ON. Turn the solenoid screw to obtain the rpm specified on the underhood sticker.

7. Reconnect all hoses and connect the compressor clutch lead.

8-350

1. Run the engine to normal operating temperature.
2. Make sure that the choke is fully opened, set the parking brake, block the drive wheels, turn the air conditioning Off and connect a tachometer to the engine according to manufacturer's instructions.
3. Disconnect and plug the purge hose at the vapor canister and the vacuum hose at the EGR valve.
4. Place the manual transmission in Neutral and the automatic transmission in Drive.
5. On cars without an idle solenoid, turn the idle speed screw to obtain the specified rpm. On cars with an idle solenoid, turn the idle screw to obtain the rpm specified on the underhood sticker. Disconnect the compressor clutch lead and turn the A/C On. Momentarily open the throttle to extend the solenoid plunger. Turn the solenoid screw to obtain the specified rpm.

1978-79 IDLE MIXTURE

Changes in the idle systems of these models make it impossible to adjust the mixture without the aid of a propane enrichment system, not available to the general public. Backing out the mixture screw, of itself, will have little or no effect.

COOLING SYSTEM

Cooling system capacities can be found in the capacities table at the beginning of this section. Information on the water temperature gauge can be found in the Unit Repair Section.

Radiator Removal and Installation

CHEVROLET

1. Drain the cooling system.
2. Disconnect the radiator upper and lower hoses and, if applicable, transmission coolant lines. Remove the coolant recovery system line, if so equipped.
3. Remove the radiator upper panel if so equipped.
4. If there is a radiator shroud in front of the radiator, the radiator and shroud are removed as an assembly.
5. If there is a fan shroud, remove the

shroud attaching screws let the shroud hang on the fan.
6. Remove the radiator attaching bolts and remove the radiator.
7. Installation is the reverse of the removal procedure.

CORVETTE THROUGH 1974

1. Drain the radiator.
2. Raise the hood and insert a bolt in the hole of the hood support. Remove the hood.
3. Remove the radiator inlet and outlet hoses and, if applicable, the transmission coolant hoses.
4. If applicable, remove the supply tank hose at the radiator connection.
5. Remove the shroud to radiator support bracket screws (the L88 engine does not have a fan shroud).
6. Remove the shroud to radiator baffle bracket screws and let the shroud rest on the fan.
7. Remove the radiator upper support bracket screws and carefully lift the radiator from the car.
8. Install in the reverse order of removal.

1975 AND LATER CORVETTE

1. Drain the radiator and disconnect the battery ground cable. Disconnect cooler lines on automatic transmission models.
2. Remove the hood. This is a two man job.
3. Remove the radiator support brackets attached to the fan shroud.
4. Remove the two front hood hinge bolts.
5. From inside the wheel well, remove the six radiator side support bolts.
6. Remove the two bottom radiator support bolts and the center brace.
7. Pull the radiator support forward and use a clamp to retain it to the right hood hinge.
8. Disconnect the two radiator hoses and the overflow hose.
9. Carefully lift the radiator out of the car.
10. If replacing the radiator, remove the shrouds and mount them on the new unit.
11. Installation is the reverse of removal.

Water Pump Removal and Installation

1. Drain the radiator and loosen the fan pulley bolts.
2. Disconnect the heater hose, lower radiator hose and, if applicable, the bypass hose at the water pump.
3. On V8 engines, remove the Delcotron upper brace. Loosen the swivel bolt and remove the fan belt.
4. On big block engines, disconnect the power steering and air conditioning belts and swivel the power steering pump to one side.

5. Remove the fan blade and pulley. Replace a bent or damaged fan.

NOTE: *Thermostatic fan clutches must be kept in an "in-car" position. When removed from the car the assembly should be supported so that the clutch disc remains in a vertical plane to prevent silicone fluid leakage.*

6. Remove the water pump attaching bolts and, if applicable, the power steering-to-pump bolts and remove the pump and gasket.

NOTE: *On six cylinder engines, pull the pump straight out of the block first to avoid damage to the impeller.*

7. Install the pump assembly using a new gasket. Coat the gasket on both sides with sealer. Tighten the 5/16 in. bolts to 15 ft lbs (six cylinder) and the 3/8 in. bolts (V8) to 30 ft lbs.
8. Install the pulley and fan.
9. On big block engines, install the power steering and air conditioning bolts.
10. Connect the hoses and fill the cooling system.
11. On V8 engines, install the Delcotron upper brace and fan belt. Install the power steering pump bolt.
12. Adjust the belts, then start the engine and check for leaks.

Thermostat Removal and Installation

The thermostat is located inside a housing on the front of the cylinder head on six cylinder engines and between the intake manifold and the cylinder head (forward) on V8 engines. It is not necessary to remove the radiator hose from the thermostat housing.

1. Remove the two retaining bolts from the thermostat housing and lift up the housing with the hose attached. Remove the thermostat.
2. Insert the new thermostat, spring end down, and install the housing with a new gasket.

EMISSION CONTROLS

POSITIVE CRANKCASE VENTILATION

In this system, crankcase vapors are drawn into the intake manifold and burned as part of the engine combustion. The "closed positive" system draws clean air from the carburetor air cleaner. The ventilation flow is regulated by a PCV valve located in the valve cover.

AIR INJECTION REACTOR

The A.I.R. system injects compressed air into the exhaust system, close enough to the exhaust valves to continue the burning of the normally

Chevrolet & Corvette

unburned segment of the exhaust gases. To do this it employs an air injection pump and a system of hoses, valves, tubes, etc., necessary to carry the compressed air from the pump to the exhaust manifolds. Carburetors and distributors for A.I.R. engines have specific modifications to adapt them to the air injection system; these components should not be interchanged with those intended for use on engines that do not have the system.

A diverter valve is used to prevent backfiring. The valve senses sudden increases in manifold vacuum and ceases the injection of air during fuel-rich periods. During coasting, this valve diverts the entire air flow through the muffler and during high engines speeds, expels it through a relief valve. Check valves in the system prevent exhaust gases from entering the pump.

On models with catalytic converters, it is not necessary to inject the air close to the exhaust valves. For this reason, not all models are equipped with manifolds on the exhaust manifolds for air injection as in previous years. Instead, one large pipe is used to inject air into the exhaust pipe ahead of the converter. Some models use part of the old system, but utilize only two or three of the injection nozzles on the exhaust manifold.

CONTROLLED COMBUSTION SYSTEM

This system increases combustion efficiency by means of leaner carburetor mixtures and revised distributor calibration. On most installations, thermostatically controlled air cleaner intakes draw warm air from an exhaust manifold shroud. This allows leaner carburetor settings and improves engine warm-up. A higher temperature thermostat is employed on C.C.S. cars.

EVAPORATIVE EMISSION CONTROL

This system reduces the amount of

escaping gasoline vapors. Float bowl emissions are controlled by internal carburetor modifications. Redesigned bowl vents, reduced bowl capacity, heat shields, and improved intake manifold-to-carburetor insulation serve to reduce vapor loss into the atmosphere. The venting of fuel tank vapors into the air has been stopped. Fuel vapors are now directed from lines to a canister containing an activated charcoal filter. Unburned vapors are trapped here until the engine is started. When the engine is running, the canister is purged by air drawn in by manifold vacuum. The air and fuel vapors are then directed into the engine to be burned. This system is designed to reduce fuel vapor emission. The canister filter should be replaced periodically.

The filter is located in the bottom of the canister. Pull out the old filter and work the new filter into place. It may be necessary, on earlier models, to remove the bottom of the canister for access.

ANTI-DIESELING SOLENOID

Some models may have an idle speed solenoid on the carburetor. All 1972-74 models have idle solenoids. Due to the leaner carburetor settings required for emission control, the engine may have a tendency to "diesel" or "run-on" after the ignition is turned off. The carburetor solenoid, energized when the ignition is on, maintains the normal idle speed. When the ignition is turned off, the solenoid is de-energized and permits the throttle valves to fully close, thus preventing run-on. For adjustment of carburetors with idle solenoids see Carburetor Adjustments.

TRANSMISSION CONTROLLED SPARK

The 1972-73 6 cyl. system uses an idle stop solenoid which has been added to the system. In the energized position, the solenoid maintains engine

speed at a predetermined fast idle. When de-energized the solenoid allows the throttle plates to close beyond the normal idle position; thus cutting off the air supply and preventing engine run-on. The 6-250 is the only 1972-74 engine with a CEC valve. The 1972 time delay relay delays full vacuum 20 seconds after the transmission is shifted into high gear. On 1973-74 models, the delay relay is replaced by a time relay which energizes the CEC valve for 20 seconds after the key is turned to the On position. This relay is not used on 1973 V8 engines with small blocks. V8 engines use a vacuum advance solenoid similar to that used in 1970. This relay is normally closed to block vacuum and opens when energized to allow vacuum advance. The solenoid controls distributor vacuum advance and performs no throttle positioning function. The idle stop solenoid used operates in the same manner as the one on 6-250 engines. All air-conditioned cars have an additional anti-diesel (run-on) solenoid which engages the compressor clutch for three seconds after the ignition is switched off. The 1973-74 Chevrolet TCS system differs from the 1972 system in three ways. The 23 second upshift delay has been replaced by a 20 second starting relay. This relay closes to complete the TCS circuit and open the TCS solenoid, allowing vacuum advance, for 20 seconds after the key is turned to the "on" position. The operating temperature of the temperature override switch has been raised to 93°, and the switch that was used to engage the A/C compressor when the key was turned "off" has been eliminated. All models are equipped with an electric throttle control solenoid to prevent run-on. The 1973 TCS system is used on all full-size station wagons equipped with a 165 hp 350 or a 170 hp 400. The 1974 TCS system is used only on manual transmission models. System components remain unchanged from 1973. The vacuum advance solenoid is located on the coil bracket.

1973-74 Corvette models are equipped with a Thermo-Override system instead of the normal TCS system. This system consists of a three-position temperature switch, which is mounted in the right cylinder head and a two-position vacuum advance solenoid. Three vacuum lines are connected to the solenoid, a ported vacuum line from the carburetor, a vacuum line from the intake manifold, and a vacuum line that runs to the distributor vacuum advance unit. When the engine temperature is between 93°F and 232°F, the temperature switch contacts are open and the vacuum solenoid is de-energized. This causes carburetor-ported vacuum to control the operation of the distributor vacuum advance unit. When the engine temperature is below 93°F or above 232°F, the temperature switch contacts are closed and the vac-

1973-74 Corvette Thermo-Override System (© Chevrolet Div., G.M. Corp)

C386

uum solenoid is energized. This moves the plunger in the solenoid to block the ported vacuum opening and connect manifold vacuum to the distributor. When the engine reaches normal temperature, the temperature switch contacts open and ported vacuum is restored to the distributor.

For diagnosis procedures, see the Unit Repair Section. TCS is not used on 1975 and later models.

EXHAUST GAS RECIRCULATION

All 1973 and later engines are equipped with exhaust gas recirculation (EGR). This system consists of a metering valve, a vacuum line to the carburetor, and cast-in exhaust gas passages in the intake manifold. The EGR valve is controlled by carburetor vacuum, and accordingly opens and closes to admit exhaust gases into the fuel/air mixture. The exhaust gases lower the combustion temperature, and reduce the amount of oxides of nitrogen (NOx) produced. The valve is closed at idle, deceleration, and wide open throttle, but is open between the two extreme throttle positions.

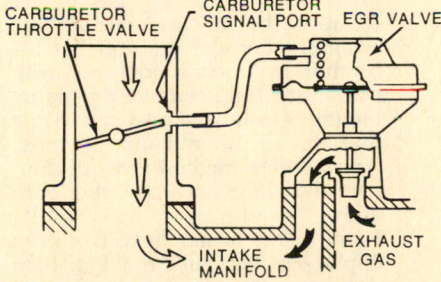

EGR system schematic
(© Chevrolet Div., G.M. Corp)

As the car accelerates, the carburetor throttle plate uncovers the vacuum port for the EGR valve. At 3-5 in. Hg, the EGR valve opens and then some of the exhaust gases are allowed to flow into the air/fuel mixture to lower the combustion temperature. At full-throttle the valve closes again.

400 cu. in. California engines are equipped with a dual diaphragm EGR valve. This valve further limits the exhaust gas opening (compared to the single diaphragm EGR valve) during high intake manifold vacuum periods, such as high-speed cruising, and provides more exhaust gas recirculation during acceleration when manifold vacuum is low. In addition to the hose running to the thermal vacuum switch, a second hose is connected directly to the intake manifold.

EARLY FUEL EVAPORATION SYSTEM

1975 and later models are equipped with this system to reduce engine warm-up time, improve driveability,

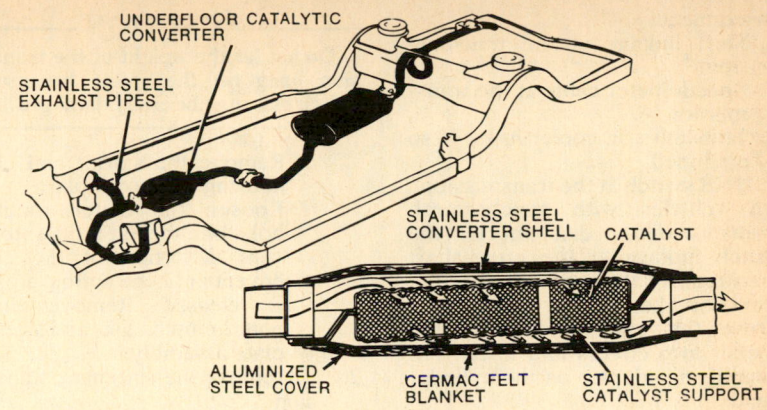

Catalytic converter
(© Chevrolet Div., G.M. Corp)

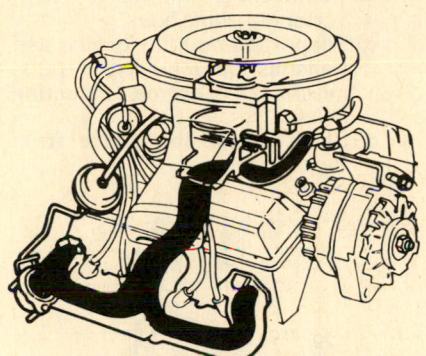

Early fuel evaporation system
(© Chevrolet Div., G.M. Corp)

and reduce emissions. On start-up, a vacuum motor acts to close a heat valve in the exhaust manifold which causes exhaust gases to enter the intake manifold heat riser passages. Incoming fuel mixture is then heated and more complete fuel evaporation is provided during warm-up.

CATALYTIC CONVERTER

All 1975 and later models are equipped with a catalytic converter. The converter is located midway in the exhaust system. Stainless steel exhaust pipes are used ahead of the converter. The converter is stainless steel with an aluminized steel cover and a ceramic felt blanket to insulate the converter from the floorpan. The catalyst pellet bed inside the converter consists of noble metals which cause a reaction that converts hydrocarbons and carbon monoxide into water and carbon dioxide.

ENGINE

Engine application and specification tables may be found at the beginning of this section.

The following service procedures apply to all engines, except where differences are specified. The 402 and 454 V8 (big blocks) are essentially the same engine. Similarly, the 305, 350, and 400

small block series engines utilize much the same design.

NOTE: *There is limited parts interchangeability between the 400 and the other small block V8s.*

The big block 402 was last offered in 1972. The 454 was last offered in passenger cars in 1976. The small block 400 was offered in 1974 in both two and four-barrel form. The 400 was last offered in passenger cars in 1976.

ENGINE REMOVAL AND INSTALLATION

CHEVROLET

1. Remove the hood. Scribe lines around the hinges so that the hood can be installed in its original location.
2. Remove the air cleaner.
3. Disconnect the battery cables at the battery.
4. Remove the radiator and shroud.
5. Remove the fan blade and pulley.
6. Disconnect wires at:
   a. C.E.C. solenoid.
   b. Coil.
   c. Temperature switch.
   d. Delcotron.
   e. Starter solenoid.
   f. Oil pressure sending unit.
7. Disconnect:
   a. Accelerator linkage at the pedal.
   b. Oil pressure gauge line, if so equipped.
   c. Exhaust pipes at the manifold flanges.
   d. Engine cooler lines, if so equipped.
   e. Vacuum line to the power brake unit, if so equipped.
   f. Fuel line (from tank) at the fuel pump.
8. Remove the power steering pump, leaving the hoses attached to the pump.
9. Raise the car on a hoist.
10. Drain the cooling system and the crankcase.
11. Remove the driveshaft.

NOTE: *If a plug for the driveshaft opening in the transmission is not available, drain the transmission.*

12. Disconnect:
    a. Shift linkage at the transmission.
    b. Speedometer cable at the transmission.
    c. Transmission cooler lines, if so equipped.
    d. TCS switch at the transmission.
13. On vehicles with synchromesh transmissions, disconnect the clutch linkage at the cross-shaft then remove the cross-shaft at the frame bracket.
14. Lower the vehicle and remove the rocker arm covers and install engine lifting adapter on the cylinder heads.
15. Raise the engine enough to take the weight off the front mounts, then remove the front mount through bolts.
16. Remove the rear mount to crossmember bolts.
17. Raise the engine enough to take the weight off the rear mount, then remove the crossmember.

NOTE: *It is necessary to remove the mount from the transmission before the crossmember can be removed.*

18. Remove the engine/transmission assembly as a unit.
19. To remove the clutch and transmission from the engine:
    a. Remove the clutch housing cover plate screws.
    b. Remove the clutch housing to engine attaching bolts, then, remove the transmission and clutch housing as a unit.

— **CAUTION** —
Do not let the weight of the transmission hang on the spline because the clutch disc may be easily damaged.

    c. Remove the starter and clutch housing rear cover plate.
    d. Loosen the clutch mounting bolts one turn at a time (to prevent distortion of the clutch cover) until the spring pressure is released. Remove all the bolts, clutch disc and pressure plate assembly.
20. To remove the automatic transmission:
    a. Remove the starter and the converter housing underpan.
    b. Remove the flywheel to converter attaching bolts.
    c. Supporting both the engine and transmission, remove the transmission to engine mounting bolts.
    d. Slowly guide the engine from the transmission.

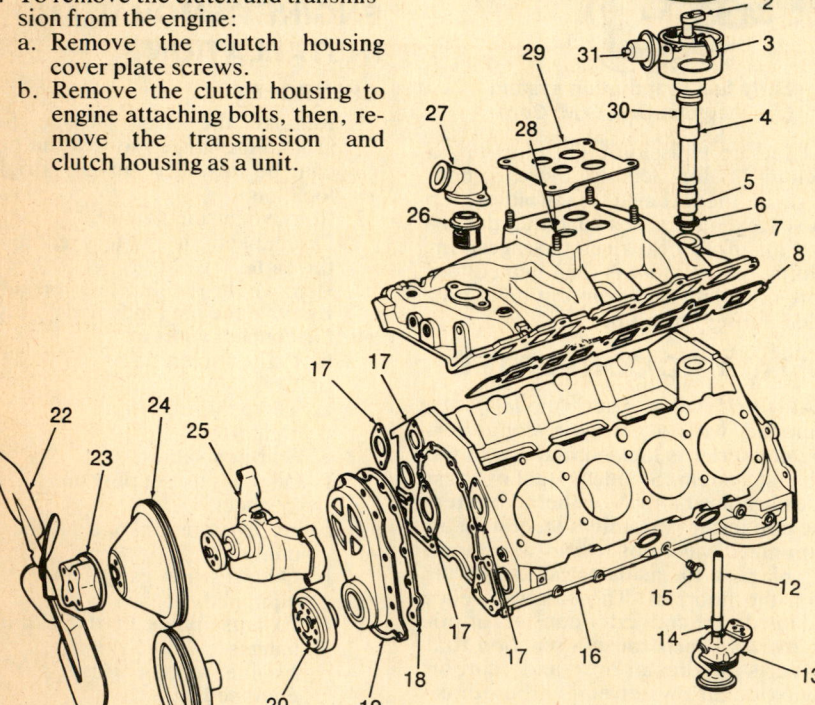

Mark IV (big block) exploded view (© Chevrolet Div., G.M. Corp)

1 Cap nipple	14 Sleeve	24 Pulley
2 Rotor	15 Drain plug	25 Water pump
3 Spring clip	16 Cylinder block	26 Thermostat
4 Distributor	17 Gasket	27 Water neck
5 Distributor gear	18 Gasket	28 Carburetor stud
6 Gasket	19 Timing cover	29 Gasket
7 Intake manifold	20 Damper	30 Shaft
8 Gasket	21 Pulley	31 Vacuum unit
12 Oil pump shaft	22 Fan	32 Distributor cap
13 Oil pump	23 Spacer	

CORVETTE

This procedure is basically the same for all engines regardless of size and model year. Certain pieces of optional equipment require minor specific changes but the overall operation remains the same.

1. The engine may be removed separately from the transmission, through the top of the engine compartment. Begin by draining the cooling system and the engine crankcase.
2. Disconnect the battery cables from the battery terminals and remove the air cleaner and ignition shields. Cover the carburetor.
3. Disconnect wiring at the alternator, temperature sending unit, oil pressure switch, primary coil lead, and CEC solenoid when applicable. Also disconnect the engine ground wires and the accelerator rod at the bellcrank.
4. Disconnect the power brake hose at the manifold end when applicable. Disconnect the tachometer drive cable at the distributor and the throttle valve if so equipped. Scribe the hood hinge locations on the support brackets and remove the hood.
5. Remove the radiator shroud and radiator, then the fan and fan assembly. If the car is equipped with power steering, remove the pump mounting bolts and push the pump into the vacant radiator opening. An alternate method is to disconnect the pump lines and plug both ends.
6. Remove the heater hose from the clip at the alternator bracket, then disconnect the hose from the engine connections and move back for extra clearance. Remove the rocker arm covers and place the vehicle on jack stands.
7. Remove the center head bolt on each head, and install the lift tool to the engine. Unhook the distributor cap and move it forward. Cover the distributor with a clean cloth.
8. Disconnect the exhaust pipes at the manifold flanges. On cars equipped with big block V8 engines, the front stud on each manifold must be removed before the exhaust pipes can be removed.
9. Disconnect the wire leads at the starter solenoid. Remove the gas tank line at the fuel pump and plug the line to prevent fuel siphoning.
10. Block the clutch pedal in the return position and remove the clutch cross-shaft. Remove the oil filter and oil cooler lines if so equipped. Remove the starting motor. If the Corvette is equipped with a manual transmission, remove the flywheel cover plate. If equipped with an automatic transmission, remove the converter underpan.
11. Remove the front engine mount thru-bolts. Support the transmis-

sion with a floor jack and remove the transmission-to-engine bolts. If the car has an automatic transmission, remove the converter-to-flywheel bolts and install a converter holding bracket to the transmission.

12. Move the engine forward and upward as needed to clear the engine compartment.
13. Replacement is the reversal of this procedure.

MANIFOLDS

Combination Manifold on 6 Cylinder Engines

Most Chevrolet six cylinder engines are equipped with a combination intake and exhaust manifold. See the Camaro section for details on the six with integral head and intake manifold. The exhaust manifold is equipped with a heat riser valve which, when the engine is cold, deflects the hot exhaust gases against the intake manifold to assist in rapid warm up.

To remove the manifold assembly, disconnect the exhaust pipe flange and remove all connections to the carburetor. Take off the vacuum lines at the manifold and at the carburetor.

Remove the carburetor, and the manifold may be unbolted from the side of the cylinder head. If necessary to remove either exhaust or intake manifolds they may be separated by removing one bolt and two nuts at center of assembly.

Before reinstalling the manifold, thoroughly clean all mating surfaces.

Intake Manifold Removal and Installation—V8

NOTE: *Some engines will require the use of RTV silicone sealant during installation of the manifold.*

1. Remove the air cleaner.
2. Drain the radiator.
3. Disconnect:
   a. Battery cables at the battery.
   b. Upper radiator and heater hoses at the manifold.
   c. Crankcase ventilation hoses as required.
   d. Fuel line at the carburetor.
   e. Accelerator linkage at the pedal lever.
   f. Vacuum hose at the distributor.
   g. Power brake hose at the carburetor base or manifold, if applicable.
   h. Ignition coil and temperature sending switch wires.
4. Remove the distributor cap and scribe the rotor position relative to distributor body.
5. Remove the distributor.
6. If applicable, remove the Delcotron upper bracket.
7. Remove the manifold to head attaching bolts, then remove the manifold and carburetor as an assembly.
8. If the manifold is to be replaced,

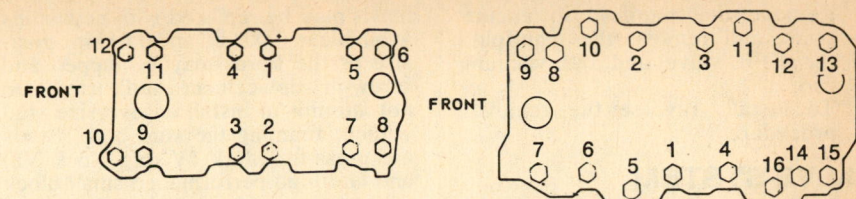

Intake manifold tightening sequence (left—small block V8; right—Mk. IV (big block) V8) (© Chevrolet Div., G.M. Corp)

transfer the carburetor (and mounting studs), water outlet and thermostat (use a new gasket), heater hose adapter and, if applicable, the choke coil and EGR valve with its vacuum line.

9. Before installing the manifold, thoroughly clean the gasket and seal surfaces of the cylinder heads and manifold.
10. Install the manifold end seals, folding the tabs if applicable, and the manifold/head gaskets, using a sealing compound around the water passages. Make sure the gaskets are firmly cemented in place before installing the manifold.

NOTE: *On those engines not having front and rear manifold seals, place a 3/16 inch bead of RTV silicone sealant on the front and rear ridges of the cylinder case. Extend the bead 1/2 inch up each cylinder head to seal and retain the manifold side gaskets.*

11. When installing the manifold, care should be taken not to dislocate the end seals. It is helpful to use a pilot in the distributor opening. Tighten the manifold bolts in the sequence illustrated.
12. Install the ignition coil.
13. Install the distributor with the rotor in its original location as indicated by the scribe line. If the engine has been disturbed, refer to Distributor Removal and Installation.
14. If applicable, install the Delcotron upper bracket and adjust the belt tension.
15. Connect all components disconnected in Step 3 above.
16. Fill the cooling system, start the engine, check for leaks and adjust the ignition timing and carburetor idle speed and mixture.

Exhaust Manifold Removal and Installation—V8

THROUGH 1973

1. If equipped with A.I.R., remove the air injector manifold assembly. The 1/4 in. pipe threads in the manifold are straight threads. Do not use a 1/4 in. tapered pipe tap.
2. Disconnect the battery.
3. If applicable, remove the air cleaner pre-heater shroud.
4. Remove the exhaust pipe flange nuts, then hang the pipe with wire.
5. Remove the manifold mounting bolts (end bolts first), then remove the manifold.

6. To install, clean the mating surfaces, then install the manifold with the center bolts first. Install the end bolts, then tighten all bolts.
7. To complete installation, reverse Steps 1 through 3.

1974 AND LATER LEFT SIDE

1. Disconnect the battery ground cable and raise the car. Disconnect the exhaust pipe at the manifold.
2. Remove the front manifold to exhaust pipe flange stud, and then remove the rear spark plug shield; lower the car.
3. On all models except the Corvette, remove the air conditioning compressor and set it aside. Do not disconnect any air conditioning lines.
4. Disconnect the spark plug wires and their holder, the temperature sending unit lead and the dipstick.
5. Remove the attaching bolts and remove the manifold.
6. To install, reverse the removal procedure.

1974 AND LATER RIGHT SIDE

1. Disconnect the ground cable, and remove the fan shroud upper bolts and loosen the fan shroud. Remove the air cleaner intake pipe. On the Corvette, remove and set aside the air conditioning compressor and then remove the compressor lower mounting bracket. Do not disconnect any air conditioning lines. On models to 1974, if equipped with an air pump, remove the air injector manifold assembly.
2. Raise the car and disconnect the exhaust pipe at the manifold.
3. Remove the right side engine mounting bracket through bolt, and loosen the left side mounting bracket through bolt. Jack up the right side of the engine, reinstall the right side through bolt, and lower the engine until the through bolt is resting on the mounting bracket.
4. Remove the rear spark plug shield bolt. On the Corvette only, disconnect the AIR tube from the exhaust pipe and move it aside; also remove the rear spark plug shield and the three rear manifold attaching bolts.
5. Lower the vehicle and remove the spark plug wires, air cleaner heat stove pipe, and the air cleaner intake pipe. Remove the rear spark plug shield.

6. Remove the manifold to engine bolts, and remove the manifold, the EFE valve and the vacuum can.

7. To install, reverse the removal procedure.

VALVE SYSTEM

Valve guides are integral with the cylinder head. Valve guide bores may be reamed to accommodate oversize valve stems or the guides may be knurled (if wear permits) to allow the retention of standard size valves.

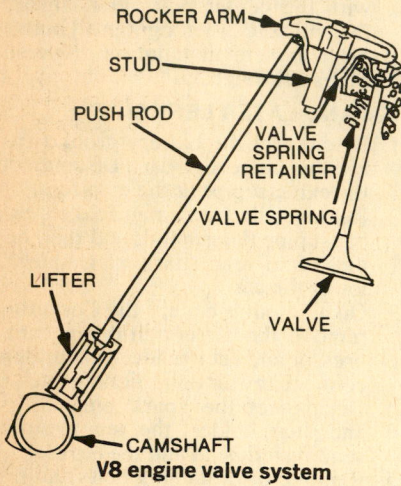

V8 engine valve system

Rocker Arm Removal and Installation

NOTE: *Some engines are assembled using RTV silicone sealant in place of rocker arm cover gasket. If the engine was assembled using RTV, never use a gasket when reassembling. Conversely, if the engine was assembled using a rocker arm cover gasket, never replace it with RTV.*

When using RTV, an 1/8 inch bead is sufficient. Always run the bead on the inside of the bolt holes.

Rocker arms are removed by removing the adjusting nut. Be sure to adjust valve lash after replacing rocker arms.

NOTE: *When replacing an exhaust rocker, move an old intake rocker to the exhaust rocker arm stud and install the new rocker arm on the intake stud.*

Rocker arm studs that have damaged threads or are loose in the cylinder heads may be replaced with new studs available in 0.003 in. and 0.013 in. oversize or the bores may be tapped and screw-in replacement studs used. Do not attempt to install an oversize stud without reaming the stud bore. Studs are press-fit. Mark IV (big block V8) and late high performance small-block engines use screw-in studs and pushrod guide plates.

NOTE: *If engine is equipped with the A.I.R. exhaust emission control system, the interfering components of the system must be removed. Disconnect the lines at the air injection nozzles in the exhaust manifolds.*

Valve Clearance Adjustment

HYDRAULIC LIFTERS

On six-cylinder engines, crank the engine until the distributor rotor points to the No. 1 firing position and the breaker points are just opening. The following valves may be adjusted:

No. 1	exhaust	intake
No. 2		intake
No. 3	exhaust	
No. 4		intake
No. 5	exhaust	

To adjust the rest of the valves, crank the engine until the distributor rotor points to the No. 6 firing position and the breaker points are just opening. The following valves may be adjusted:

No. 2	exhaust	
No. 3		intake
No. 4	exhaust	
No. 5		intake
No. 6	exhaust	intake

On V8 engines, crank the engine until the No. 1 piston is at TDC of its compression stroke (the compression can be felt by placing a finger over the spark plug hole or by feeling the valves

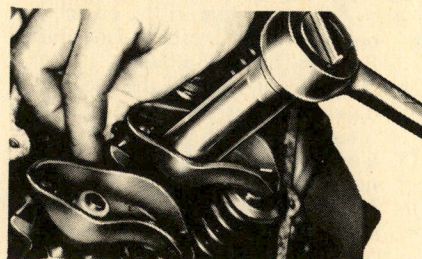

V8 valve adjustment
(© Chevrolet Div., G.M. Corp)

as the timing mark passes "0"—if the valves don't move, the No. 1 piston is at the top of its compression stroke). With the crankshaft in this position the following valves may be adjusted:

Exhaust—1, 3, 4, 8
Intake—1, 2, 5, 7

Rotate the crankshaft one full revolution until the timing pointer is again aligned with the "0". With the crankshaft thus in No. 6 cylinder firing position, the following valves may be adjusted:

Exhaust—2, 5, 6, 7
Intake—3, 4, 6, 8

Adjustment is made by backing off the rocker arm adjusting nut until there is play in the pushrod. Tighten the nut to remove the pushrod clearance (this can be felt by rotating the pushrod with the fingers while tightening the adjusting nut). When the pushrod cannot be freely turned, tighten the nut one additional turn to place the hydraulic lifter in the center of its travel. No further adjustment is required.

MECHANICAL LIFTERS

Position the crankshaft for No. 1, then No. 6 cylinder firing positions as described for adjusting hydraulic lifters above. In the case of mechanical lifters, however, use a feeler gauge between the rocker arm and the valve stem to obtain the correct clearance. The final valve lash setting is made with the engine running at normal operating temperature. Specified valve lash (hot) can be found in the Tune-Up Specifications at the beginning of this section.

Cylinder Head Removal and Installation

6-250

To remove the cylinder head, detach the air cleaner and all rods, lines and vacuum tubes at the carburetor and manifold.

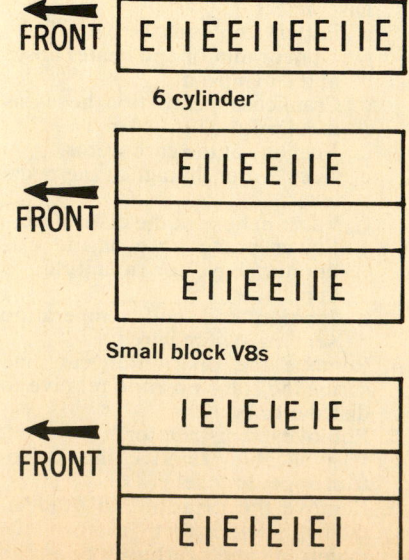

FRONT EIIEEIIEEIIE

6 cylinder

FRONT EIIEEIIE
EIIEEIIE

Small block V8s

FRONT IEIEIEIE
EIEIEIEI

Big block V8s

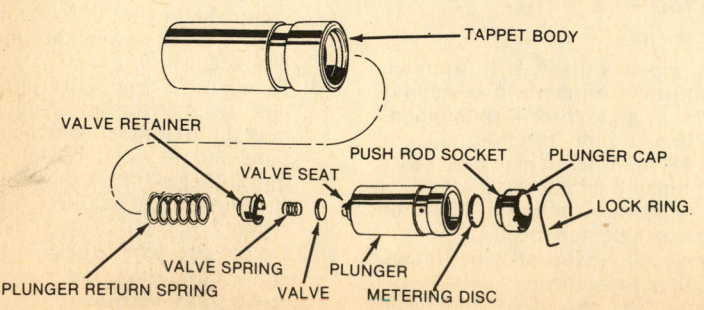

Typical hydraulic lifter exploded

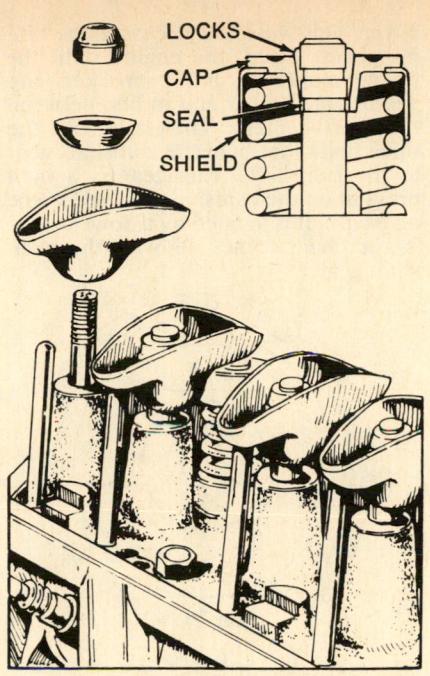

6-cylinder head and rocker arm assembly, 250 cu. in. engine

NOTE: *If the engine is equipped with an exhaust emission control system, the injector connections must be disconnected at the cylinder head. Disconnect any interfering components and tie back out of the way.*

When installing, do not use sealer on the composition steel asbestos gasket. Coat the threads of the head bolts with sealing compound before installation. Tighten the head bolts in sequence a little at a time until each is tightened to the specified torque. Install all components which were removed. Adjust the valve mechanism as described later.

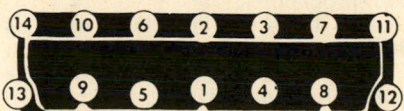

6 cylinder

--- CAUTION ---

The 1/4 in. pipe threads at the cylinder head air injection nozzles are a straight pipe thread. Do not use a 1/4 in. tapered pipe tap. Hoses used in this air injection system are of special material. Do not substitute.

1. Unbolt the manifold from the cylinder head, but not from the exhaust pipe flange. The manifold is simply pulled away from the head.
2. Remove the engine side plate covers and the gas lines at the fuel pump. Unbolt and lift off the rocker cover, disconnect the oil line leads to the rockers.
3. The rocker arms are supported separately and may be left intact until the head is removed.

4. Unbolt and lift off the cylinder head.

V8

1. Remove the intake manifold as described above. Remove the alternator lower mounting bolt, and lay the unit aside.
2. Remove the exhaust manifolds as described above. If the vehicle has A/C, dismount the compressor and position it out of the way. Do not disconnect the refrigerant lines.

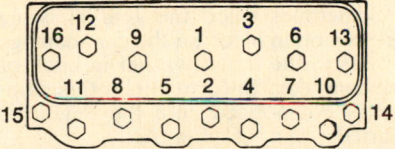

Big block V8s

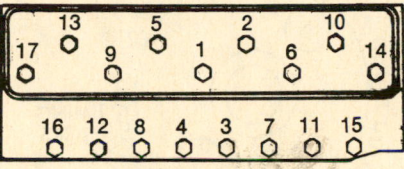

Small block V8s

3. Back off the rocker arm nuts and pivot the rocker arms out of the way so that the pushrods can be removed. Identify the pushrods so that they can be reinstalled in their original locations.
4. Remove the cylinder head bolts and cylinder heads.
5. Install using new gaskets. The head gasket is installed with the bead up.

NOTE: *Coat a steel gasket, thinly and evenly, on both sides with sealer. If a steel asbestos gasket is used, do not apply sealer. Clean the bolt threads, apply sealing compound and install the bolts finger tight.*

6. Tighten the head bolts a little at a time in the sequence illustrated to the specified torque.
7. Install the exhaust and intake manifolds as described previously.
8. Adjust the valves.

TIMING CASE

Crankshaft Pulley Replacement

NOTE: *To prevent vibration damper damage, it is important that a puller be used to draw the pulley on the crankshaft.*

6-250

1. Remove the radiator core and the fan belt. Remove accessory drive pulley and belt, if so equipped.
2. Use a screw-type puller to remove the balancer-pulley assembly.

V8

1. Drain radiator and disconnect the hoses. Take off the fan belt, and the fan pulley assembly. Remove the battery.
2. Remove the fan shroud. Remove the radiator core. Unbolt the pulley

portion of the balancer-pulley assembly.

3. Install screw-type puller and remove the balancer portion from the crankshaft.

Timing Case Cover and Front Oil Seal Replacement

NOTE: *The timing case cover oil seal may be replaced without removing the case cover on all Corvettes and Chevrolets.*

After gaining access to the oil seal, pry the old seal out of the cover with a screwdriver. Then, lubricate the new seal and drive it into place with a seal installer.

6-250, 8-402, 454

1. Remove the radiator, fan belts and, using a puller, remove the crankshaft pulley. On V8 engines, remove the water pump.
2. Remove the timing case-to-engine attaching bolts and remove the two oil pan-to-timing case bolts.
3. Slide the front cover forward until a knife can be positioned behind the cover, then cut the ends of the oil pan front seal off flush with the cylinder block on the two ends of the front cover.

Cutting oil pan front seal
(© Chevrolet Div., G.M. Corp)

CUT THIS PORTION
FROM NEW SEAL

Fitting new oil pan front seal
(© Chevrolet Div., G.M. Corp)

4. Remove the front cover and clean all gasket mounting surfaces on the front cover, the block and the exposed portion of the oil pan.
5. Temporarily position a new oil pan front seal on the front of the oil pan and trim off the edges of the new seal so that it will fit flush with the engine block.
6. Remove the new front seal, coat it with sealer and install it on the front cover. Apply a bead of silicone rubber sealer to the place on the front of the oil pan where the cut off portion of the old seal will mate with the new oil pan front seal.
7. Install a centering tool in the crankshaft snout hole in the front cover and install the front cover on the engine.
8. Install the front cover bolts finger tight, remove the centering tool and tighten the cover bolts. Install the pulley, fan belts and radiator.

305, 350 AND 400 V8

1. Remove the crankshaft pulley. Remove the oil pan on engines through 1974. Remove the water pump. Remove the screws holding the timing case cover to the block and remove the cover and gaskets.
2. Use a large screwdriver to pry the old seal out of the front face of the cover.
3. Install the new seal so that open end is toward the inside of the cover.
4. Check that the timing chain oil slinger is in place against the crankshaft sprocket.
5. Install the cover carefully onto the locating dowels.
6. Tighten the attaching screws to 6-8 ft lbs.

Timing Chain Replacement

6-250

Chevrolet timing gears are arranged so that (unless deliberately disturbed) the valve timing will remain as set at the factory. Unless the gears are badly worn or seriously damaged, the valve timing will remain constant within reasonable limits.

If it becomes necessary to replace the timing gears due to wear or damage, remove the radiator, disconnect the front motor mounts and jack up the front of the engine. Remove the fan belt, fan pulley, oil pan and timing case cover.

NOTE: *The manufacturer recommends*

that the camshaft be removed from the car in order to remove and replace the gear in an arbor press.

Sometimes when the gear is being pressed on in place on the car, damage results to the thrust washer in back of the cam gear. Unfortunately, this damage is not noticed until the engine is started.

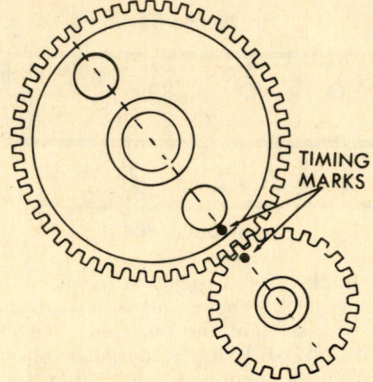

TIMING MARKS

Timing mark alignment, 6 cylinder

To replace the gear by removing the camshaft, remove the rocker arm assemblies and the distributor, take out all of the pushrods and all of the lifters. The camshaft may then be pulled out toward the front of the engine. It will be necessary to retime the ignition.

Runout of the timing gear should not exceed .004 in. Backlash between the two gears should not be less than .004 in. nor more than .006 in. End clearance of the thrust plate should be .001 to .005 in.

CAUTION

The use of a dial indicator will reduce the possibility of driving the gear too far onto the camshaft. This would alter the desired camshaft thrust clearance of .001 to .005 in. Use care when approaching the final position of the gear on the shaft, because it is impossible to increase the thrust clearance without pulling the new gear. In the absence of a dial indicator, this end thrust can be measured with a feeler gauge. In this case, the thrust clearance is to be measured between the camshaft gear hub and the thrust plate. A feeler gauge strip, inserted in either of the two large gear holes, will reach this point.

V8

To replace the chain, remove the radiator core, water pump, the harmonic balancer and the crankcase front

cover. This will allow access to the timing chain. Crank the engine until the timing marks on both sprockets are nearest each other and in line between the shaft centers. Then take out the three bolts that hold the camshaft gear to the camshaft. This gear is a light press fit on the camshaft and will come off easily. It is located by a dowel. The chain comes off with the camshaft gear.

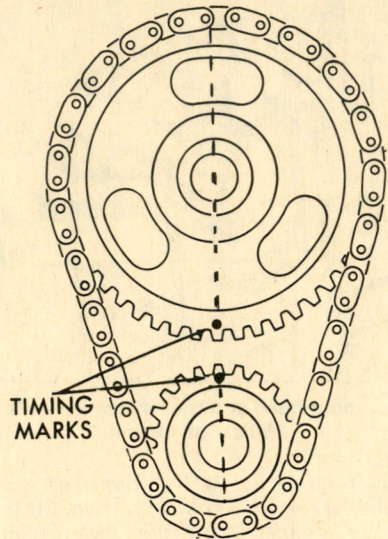

TIMING MARKS

Timing mark alignment, V8

A gear puller will be required to remove the crankshaft gear.

Without disturbing the position of the engine, mount the new crankshaft gear on the shaft, and mount the chain over the camshaft gear. Arrange the camshaft gear in such a way that the timing marks will line up between the shaft centers and the camshaft locating dowel will enter the dowel hole in the cam sprocket.

Place the cam sprocket, with its chain mounted over it, in position on the front of the car and pull up with the three bolts that hold it to the camshaft.

After the gears are in place, turn the engine two full revolutions to make certain that the timing marks are in correct alignment between the shaft centers.

End-play of the V8 camshaft is zero.

Camshaft Replacement

6-250

Due to the length of the six cylinder camshaft, a large amount of working room will be required in front of the engine to remove the camshaft. There are two ways to go about this task: either remove the engine assembly from the car, or remove the radiator, grille and supports that are mounted directly in front of the engine, disconnect the motor mounts and raise the front of the engine as required to gain enough clearance to remove the cam from the engine. In either case the following equipment will have to be removed from the engine:

1. Remove the valve cover. Loosen each rocker arm mounting stud enough to turn it sideways and remove the pushrods. Keep the pushrods in their proper order.
2. Remove the fuel pump.
3. Remove the inspection plates from the side of the engine and remove the valve lifters. Keep the lifters in order when they are removed.
5. Remove the timing case cover.
6. Turn the crankshaft until the timing marks on the camshaft and crankshaft gears are aligned.
7. Remove the distributor cap and mark the position of the distributor rotor relative to the distributor body and the position of the distributor body relative to the engine block. Remove the distributor.
8. Remove the camshaft from the engine.

V8
1. Drain the cooling system and remove the radiator. On Corvettes, remove the hood. On some 1978-79 models it may be necessary to remove the grill.
2. Remove the water pump and the timing case cover.
3. Turn the crankshaft until the timing marks on the camshaft and crankshaft sprockets are aligned.
4. Remove the valve covers and loosen each rocker arm nut enough to turn the rocker to the side and remove the pushrods. Keep the pushrods in order when they are removed from the engine.
5. Remove the distributor cap and mark the position of the rotor relative to the distributor body and the position of the distributor body relative to the engine. Remove the distributor.
6. Remove the intake manifold, then remove the valve lifters from the engine. Keep the lifters in order when they are removed from the engine.
7. Remove the fuel pump.
8. Remove the timing chain and sprockets from the engine.
9. Install two 5/16 inch-18 x 4 inch bolts in the holes in the front of the cam and carefully slide it out of the engine.

NOTE: *On some engine and model combinations it will be necessary to disconnect the motor mounts and jack up the front of the engine or remove the grille from the car in order to gain adequate clearance in front of the engine to get the camshaft out of the engine.*

PISTONS AND CONNECTING RODS

NOTE: *Complete engine rebuilding procedures are contained in the Engine Rebuilding Section.*

6-250

Where split skirt-type pistons are being installed, the split in the skirt of the piston should be placed opposite the clamp screw of the wrist-pin. This is also opposite the number on the bottom of the connecting rod.

Where solid skirt slipper-type pistons are being replaced, it is unimportant which way the piston is mounted onto the connecting rod. However, if the old pistons are being reinstalled, the piston should be carefully marked before it is detached from the connecting rod in order that it may be replaced on the same side from which it was removed.

When assembling the rods to the pistons and installing the pistons in their respective bores, be sure that the flange, or heavy side of the rod at the bearing end, is toward the front of the

NOTCH TO FRONT OF ENGINE

HEAVY SIDE OF ROD BEARING TO FRONT OF ENGINE

OIL SPURT HOLE TOWARD CAMSHAFT SIDE OF ENGINE

TANGS

Correct relation of piston to rod, 6-cylinder 250 cu. in. engine

VALVE CLEARANCE DEPRESSION TO CENTER OF CYLINDER BLOCK

OIL SPURT HOLES

RIGHT BANK 2-4-6-8   LEFT BANK 1-3-5-7

BEARING TANG OPPOSITE CAMSHAFT

Piston-to-rod relationship—Mk. IV (big block) V8

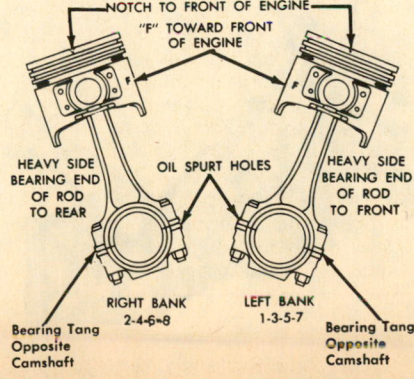

NOTCH TO FRONT OF ENGINE
"F" TOWARD FRONT OF ENGINE

HEAVY SIDE BEARING END OF ROD TO REAR   OIL SPURT HOLES   HEAVY SIDE BEARING END OF ROD TO FRONT

RIGHT BANK 2-4-6-8   LEFT BANK 1-3-5-7

Bearing Tang Opposite Camshaft   Bearing Tang Opposite Camshaft

Piston-to-rod relationship—small block V8

piston (cast depression in top of piston head). The oil hole in the connecting rod goes toward the camshaft side of the engine.

V8

Pistons are marked with a cast depression at the top of the piston and also the letter F on the piston strut. This depression and F always go toward the front.

For the left bank, pistons Nos. 1, 3, 5, and 7, the heavy flange at the bottom of the connecting rod goes on the side of the piston having the depression and F mark. For the right bank, cylinders Nos. 2, 4, 6, and 8, the heavy flange on the connecting rod goes to the side opposite the stamped letter F and the cast depression in the top of the piston.

Place the piston and rod assemblies into the cylinder so that the depression cast into the top of the piston (and the letter F stamped on the boss of the piston) face front. Double check that the pistons are in the correct bank by noting that on the left bank, pistons Nos. 1, 3, 5 and 7, the heavy flange on the connecting rod will also face forward, but on the right bank, cylinders Nos. 2, 4, 6 and 8, the heavy flange on the connecting rod will face toward the rear.

LUBRICATION

Oil Pan Removal

6-250

The oil pan can be removed, either after removing the engine, or as follows:

1. Drain radiator and oil pan.
2. Disconnect gas tank line at fuel pump and upper and lower radiator hoses.
3. Remove clutch housing-to-engine block bolt above dowel on right side.
4. Raise vehicle on hoist or place on jack stands.
5. Rotate engine to align distributor rotor between No. 3 and No. 5 plug wire. (This locates No. 6 crank throw part way up.)
6. Remove starter and flywheel front cover plate (or converter housing shield).
7. Remove front mount through bolts.
8. Jack up front of engine. Raise as far as possible always using care by checking various dash and body tunnel clearances.
9. Remove front engine mount frame bracket on right side and remove oil filter where necessary.
10. Remove oil pan screws and lower pan to frame.
11. Remove oil pump to gain clearance, then remove oil pan by sliding and rotating front to right and then to rear, and down at an angle. (On certain earlier models, these procedures may vary).
12. Install in reverse of above.

V8 CHEVROLET CARS

1. Disconnect battery negative cable.
2. Remove distributor cap from distributor to prevent breakage against firewall.
3. Drain cooling system. Remove radiator hoses, and remove oil dipstick and tube, where necessary.
4. Remove fan blade assembly. On cars with A/C, remove the vacuum reservoir.
5. Raise car, and drain engine oil.
6. Remove bolts from engine front mounts. Disconnect and remove starter.
7. On cars with automatic transmissions, remove converter housing underpan.
8. Disconnect the exhaust Y pipe from the manifolds.
9. Rotate crankshaft until timing mark on the damper is at six o'clock position.
10. Using a block of wood and a suitable jack, raise engine enough to insert 2 x 4 in. wood blocks under engine mounts then lower engine onto blocks.
11. Remove engine oil pan.
12. Install by reversing removal procedures. Torque the pan bolts to 7 1/2 ft. lb. Torque the engine mount bolts to 50 ft. lb.

NOTE: *The 402, and 454 cu. in. engines use three 1/4 in. attaching bolts at crankcase front cover; one at each corner, and one at the lower center.*

CORVETTE

1. Disconnect battery, and remove dipstick and tube.
2. Raise car and support on stands. Drain engine oil.
3. Remove starter and flywheel splashshield.
4. Disconnect steering idler arm and lower steering linkage.

5. Remove oil pan and discard gaskets and seals.
6. On high performance engines, the oil baffle must be removed before additional operations can be performed.

NOTE: *On the 454 cu. in. engine, the oil pan has three 1/4 in. attaching bolts at crankcase front cover; one at each front corner, and one at lower center.*

7. Install by reversing removal procedure.

Oil Pump Replacement

The oil pump is located in the oil pan, and it is driven by a tang from the distributor shaft.

On six-cylinder engines, the pump is flange-mounted to the under side of the crankcase with two cap screws.

On V8 models, the oil pump is bolted to the rear, main bearing cap. Oil is fed from the pump up through the rear, main bearing cap.

Rear Main Bearing Oil Seal Removal and Installation

1. Remove rear main bearing cap and pry old seal from groove. Insert new seal with lubricant only on the lip. Do not get oil on the glue-treated parting line surfaces. Lip faces front of engine.
2. Using a hammer and small punch, revolve the upper half of the seal until it protrudes far enough to remove with pliers.
3. Oil the seal except at the glue-treated ends and, using a hammer handle, roll the seal into place in the block.
4. These seals are made to size and require no trimming. Install the lower half over the crankshaft and in place onto the block.

CLUTCH

Clutches are of the diaphragm spring type. The throwout bearing is a ball bearing with no provision for lubrication. The throwout fork pivots on a ball stud which is mounted in the rear face of the bellhousing.

Clutch Removal and Installation

1. Support the engine and remove the transmission as described in Manual Transmission.
2. Disconnect the clutch fork pushrod and spring.
3. Remove the flywheel housing.
4. Slide the clutch fork from the ball stud and remove the fork from the dust boot. The ball stud is threaded into the clutch housing and is easily replaced, if necessary.
5. Install a clutch pilot tool.

NOTE: *Look for the assembly markings "X" on the flywheel and the clutch cover (pressure plate assembly). If there are none, scribe marks to identify the position of the clutch cover relative to the flywheel.*

6. Loosen the clutch cover bolts evenly until the spring pressure is relieved, then remove the bolts and clutch assembly.
7. Before installing, clean the pressure plate and the flywheel face.
8. Position the disc and pressure plate assembly on the flywheel and install a pilot tool.

NOTE: *The disc on six cylinder engines is installed with the springs facing the flywheel. On V8 engines, the grease slinger must face the transmission.*

9. Install the pressure plate assembly bolts. Make sure the mark on the cover is aligned with the mark on the flywheel. Tighten the bolts alternately and evenly to 35 ft lbs.
10. Remove the pilot tool.
11. Remove the release fork and lubricate the ball socket and the fork fingers at the throwout bearing with graphite or Moly Grease. Reinstall the release fork.
12. Lubricate the inside recess and the fork groove of the throwout bearing with a light coat of graphite or Moly Grease.
13. Install the clutch release fork and dust boot in the clutch housing and the throwout bearing on the fork, then install the flywheel housing. Tighten flywheel housing bolts to 30 ft lbs.
14. Connect the fork pushrod and spring.
15. Adjust the shift linkage.
16. Adjust the clutch pedal free play.

Clutch Adjustment

CORVETTE THROUGH 1974

1. Disconnect the spring between the clutch push rod and cross shaft lever.
2. While holding the clutch pedal against the stop, loosen the two

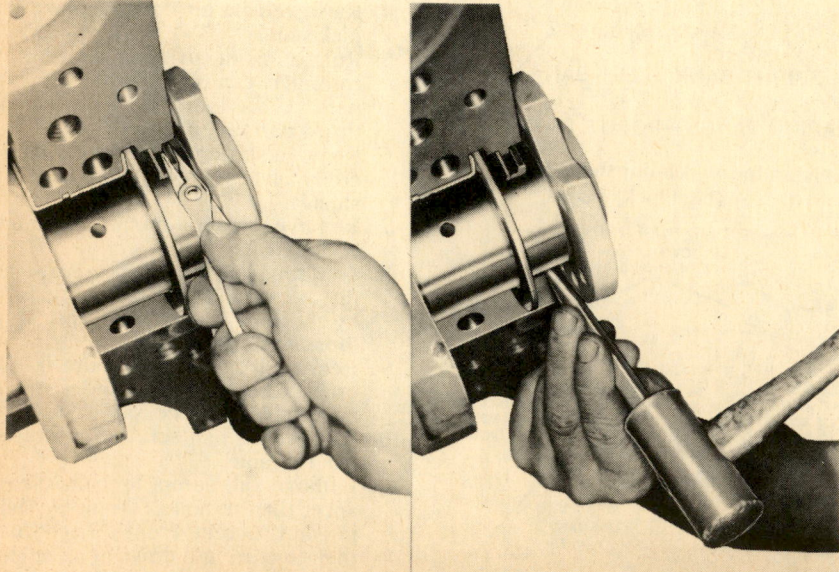

Rear main seal removal
(© Chevrolet Div., G.M. Corp)

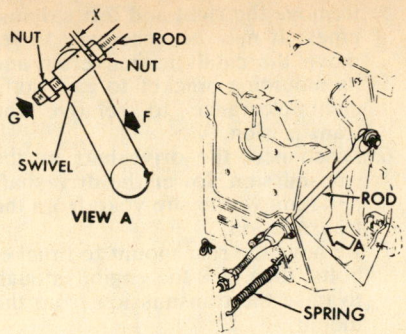

Corvette clutch linkage through 1974
(© Chevrolet Div., G.M. Corp)

locknuts enough to allow the adjusting rod to move against the clutch fork until the throwout bearing light touches the pressure plate springs.

3. Turn the upper nut against the swivel and then back it off 4 1/2 turns. Tighten the bottom locknut to lock the swivel against the top nut.
4. Reinstall the return spring. Pedal free travel, the distance the pedal can be moved before the throwout bearing contacts the pressure plate spring, should be:
1972 1 1/4-1 3/4 in.
1973 1 1/4-1 1/2 in.
1974 1-1 1/2 in.

CHEVROLET THROUGH 1973

1. Disconnect the return spring at the clutch fork.
2. Push the clutch lever and shaft assembly until the clutch pedal is tight against the rubber stop under the dash.
3. Push the outer end of the clutch fork backward until the throwout bearing just touches the pressure plate.
4. Install the pushrod into the upper hole on the lever and increase its length until all play is removed.
5. Remove the rod from the upper hole and reinsert it into the lower hole.

6. Tighten the locknut, being careful not to change the length of the push rod.
7. Install the return spring.
8. Check the pedal free travel. It should be 1 1/4-1 3/4 in.

1975 AND LATER CORVETTE

1. Disconnect the return spring between the floor and the cross shaft.
2. Push the clutch lever and shaft assembly until the clutch pedal is tightly against the rubber stop under the dash.
3. Loosen the two locknuts on the shaft.
4. Push the shaft until the throwout bearing just touches the pressure plate spring.
5. Tighten the top locknut towards the swivel until the distance between it and the swivel is 0.4 in.
6. Tighten the bottom locknut against the swivel.
7. Check pedal free travel. It should be 1-1 1/2 in.

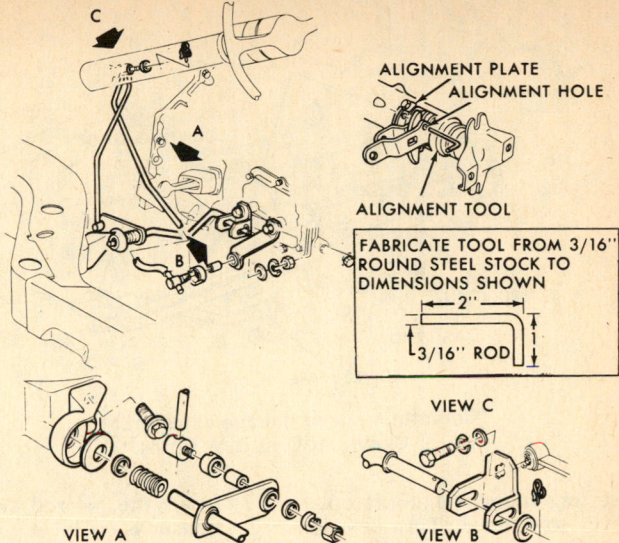

3-speed column shift linkage adjustment through 1973
(© Chevrolet Div., G.M. Corp)

MANUAL TRANSMISSION

Transmission refill capacities are in the Capacities table of this section.

Manual transmissions used in these models are the Muncie 3-speed, Saginaw 3-speed, Saginaw 4-speed, Muncie 4-speed, and Warner 4-speed. The Warner was installed in Corvettes beginning in mid-year 1974. The base unit in Corvette is the Saginaw, with the Warner available on the L82 engine option. Identification is determined by side cover design and linkage. The 3-speed Muncie side cover has two bolts on the side cover top edge and the Saginaw 3-speed one. The Saginaw 4-speed linkage arms are all mounted through the side cover. The Muncie and Warner 4-speeds have the reverse fork mounted in the tailshaft. These two may be differentiated by the shape of the side cover; the Warner has a nine bolt curved bottom and the Muncie a seven bolt straight bottom.

Repair of manual transmissions is covered in the Unit Repair Section.

Shift Linkage Adjustment

THREE-SPEED COLUMN SHIFT THROUGH 1973

1. With transmission in Reverse, place ignition switch in Lock.
2. Loosen shift rod lock nuts.
3. Set transmission first-reverse lever in reverse position. Pull down on first-reverse control rod until column lever is in reverse detent position. Tighten first-reverse lock nut.
4. Shift column and transmission levers to neutral position. Insert a 3/16 in. dia. rod into alignment holes in levers and alignment plate.
5. Tighten second-third locknut.

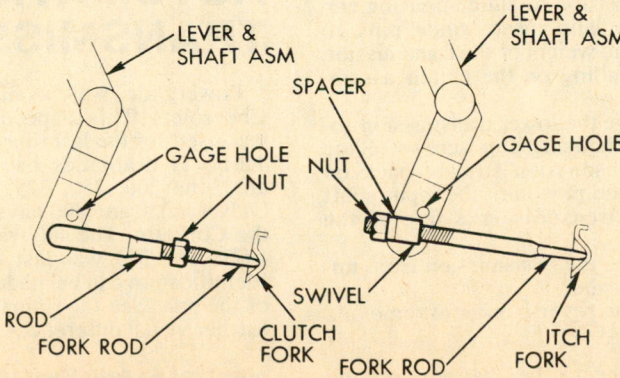

Chevrolet clutch linkage through 1973
(© Chevrolet Div., G.M. Corp)

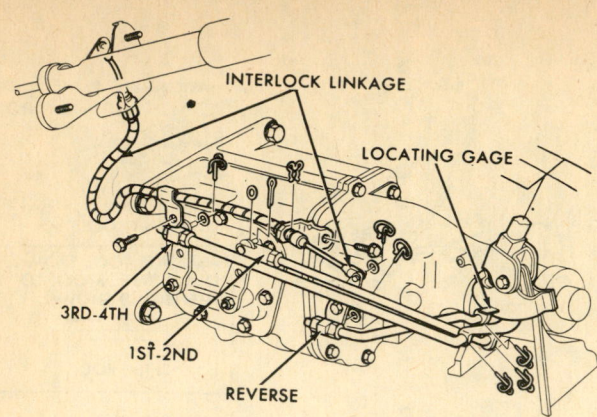

INTERLOCK LINKAGE

LOCATING GAGE

3RD-4TH

1ST-2ND

REVERSE

Corvette 4-speed linkage adjustment
(© Chevrolet Div., G.M. Corp)

6. Remove alignment rod. Shift column lever to reverse. Turn key to Lock. Ignition switch must move freely to Lock position and it must not be possible to turn key to Lock when in any transmission position other than reverse. If this interlock binds, leave switch in Lock position and readjust first-reverse rod.
7. Check shifting.

1972-77 CORVETTE FOUR-SPEED— WARNER OR SAGINAW

1. Place the ignition switch in "lock."
2. Loosen locknuts at swivels on shift rods and reverse control rod.
3. Set transmission shift levers in neutral positions.
4. Shift lever into neutral. Insert locating gauge, 1/8 thick x 41/64 wide x 3 in. long, into control lever bracket assembly.
5. Hold each lever against the gauge and adjust in turn. Tighten shift rod locknuts and remove gauge.
6. Loosen the interlock bracket assembly bolts at the bottom of the steering column. Make sure that the bracket is not stuck to the dash and then tighten the bracket again.
7. Move the ignition key through "off" and "lock" positions. If there is any binding, readjust the interlock linkage.

1978-79 CORVETTE—WARNER OR SAGINAW

1. Place the ignition switch in Lock.
2. Loosen the swivels on the shift rods.
3. Place the transmission shift levers in Neutral. Neutral may be found by moving the levers all the way forward (counterclockwise), then back one detent.
4. Place the shift lever in Neutral.
5. Align the notches in the shift control levers with the notch in the lever and bracket assembly. Install a locating gauge, 1/8 inch thick by 41/64 inch wide by 3 inches long into the control lever bracket assembly.
6. Attach the 3-4 shift rod to the shift control lever with a cotter pin.

7. Insert the 3-4 rod swivel into the transmission lever and attach the washer and cotter pin.
8. Push the 3-4 lever rearward to take up the slack and tighten the rear adjusting nut against the swivel.
9. Repeat this procedure for the 1-2 and reverse levers.
NOTE: *After the adjustments have been made, the centerlines of the levers must be aligned to prevent rubbing.*

Transmission Removal
CHEVROLET

1. Raise the car on a hoist and drain the transmission. Disconnect the speedometer cable and the control levers. Disconnect the driveshaft. Remove two bolts attaching the center bearing to the frame. Remove nuts and U-bolts retaining the rear universal joint bearing to the differential pinion drive flange. Move the driveshaft rearward to the left and under the rear axle housing to withdraw the front universal joint from the transmission output shaft. Remove the transmission rear mounting pad bolts and unbolt the support member from the frame.
2. On all models, remove the two top transmission-to-clutch housing cap screws, and insert guide pins to keep the weight of the transmission from falling on the clutch assembly.
3. Remove the lower transmission-to-clutch housing cap screws. Slide the transmission straight back on the guide pins until the input shaft of the transmission is free of the clutch.
4. Remove the transmission from under the car.
5. Install in reverse order of removal.

CORVETTE

1. Disconnect the battery ground cable.
2. Remove the shifter ball and "T" handle.
3. Remove the console trim plate.
4. Raise the vehicle on a hoist.

5. Remove the right and left exhaust pipes. It may be necessary to remove the catalytic converter and its mounting bracket to gain sufficient clearance to remove the transmission.
6. Disconnect the driveshaft at the transmission, lower the driveshaft and remove the slip yoke from the transmission.
7. Remove the rear mount to bracket bolts, then jack the engine enough to raise the transmission from the mount.
8. Remove the transmission linkage mounting bracket to frame bolts.
9. Disconnect the shift levers at the transmission.
10. Remove the bolts attaching gearshift assembly to mounting bracket and remove the mounting bracket. Remove the shifter mechanism with the rods and levers attached.
11. Disconnect the speedometer cable and the TCS switch wiring.
12. Remove the transmission mount bracket.
13. Remove the transmission to clutch housing retaining bolts and the lower left extension bolt.
14. Pull the transmission rearward until it is clear of the clutch housing, then rotate it clockwise while pulling to the rear. Carefully lower the rear of the engine until the tachometer drive cable at the distributor (used through 1974) just clears the firewall.

— CAUTION —

The tachometer cable is easily damaged if it hits the firewall. Slide the transmission rearward until it clears the clutch, then tilt the front of it down and lower it from the rear.

15. Installation is the reverse of removal. Adjust the shift linkage. Torque the transmission-to-clutch housing bolts to 52 ft. lb. Torque the crossmember bolts to 25 ft. lb.

AUTOMATIC TRANSMISSION

Powerglide was available only in Chevrolets. This 2-speed transmission was used for the last time in 1972. Four Turbo HydraMatics have been available, the 200, 350, 375, and the 400. Only the 350 and 400 have been used in the Corvette. The 400 was last used in 1977. The 375 was last used in 1976. Identification can be made by the shape of the pan. See the Camaro section for further visual differences.

Neutral Safety Switch Adjustment
1972 COLUMN SHIFT

1. Disconnect the wiring at the switch.

Powerglide pan

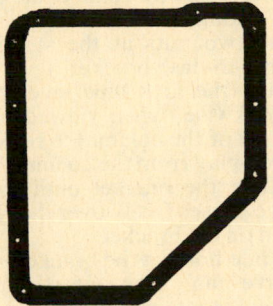

Turbo Hydra-Matic 200 pan

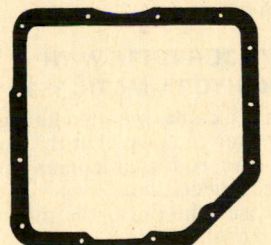

Turbo Hydra-Matic 350 pan

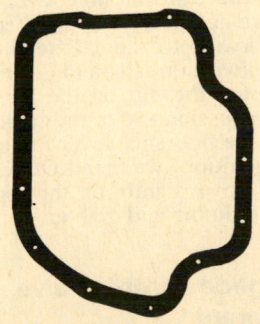

Turbo Hydra-Matic 375 and 400 pan

2. Remove the retaining screws and remove the switch from the steering column.
3. Put the shift level in neutral when installing the switch.
4. Align the slot in the contact support with the hole in the switch and insert a 3/32 in. pin to hold the support in position. The switch is now in the Drive position.
5. Put the contact support drive slot over the shifter tube drive tang and tighten the screws. Remove the clamp and the pin.
6. Connect the wiring and check the switch for proper operation.

1972 FLOORSHIFT
1. Disconnect the shift control lever arm from the control rod.

2. Remove the shift knob.
3. Remove the trim plate.
4. Remove the control assembly retaining screws and lift the assembly away from the seal.
5. Remove the neutral switch from the control assembly.
   To install:
6. On early 1972 models put the shifter into Drive, Park on later Chevrolets (with neutral switch on column), or Neutral on later Corvettes.
7. Align the hole in the contact support with the hole in the switch and insert a 3/32 in. pin to hold the support in place.
8. Place the contact support drive slot over the drive tang and tighten the switch mounting screws. Remove the pin.
9. Install the control assembly mounting screws. Connect the switch wiring and check the switch operation.
10. Install the trim plate and shift knob.
11. Connect the shift lever arm to the transmission control rod.

1973 AND LATER
Use the procedure outlined previously except that during installation, the shift lever is positioned in Neutral on column shift or Drive on floor shift models. It is only necessary to use 3/32 in. pin for alignment on a used switch.

Shift Linkage Adjustment
1972 COLUMN SHIFT
1. Make sure that the shift lever works freely in the mast jacket.
2. Check for proper linkage adjustment:
   a. Pull the selector lever back and

allow the lever to be positioned in Drive by the transmission detent.

NOTE: *Do not use the indicator pointer as a reference. The indicator pointer will be adjusted after the linkage.*

   b. Release the lever. The lever should not go into Low range unless it is lifted.
   c. Lift the shift lever and allow the lever to be positioned in Neutral by the transmission detent.
   d. Release the lever. The lever should not go into Reverse unless it is lifted.
   e. If the selector lever can move beyond the Neutral and Drive detents without being lifted, then the mechanical stops in the steering column are not coordinated with the transmission detents and adjustment is required.
3. To adjust, place the selector lever in Drive as determined by the transmission detent.
4. Loosen the adjustment clamp or swivel at the cross-shaft and position the selector lever in Drive.
5. With the selector lever in Drive and the transmission lever in Drive detent position, tighten the clamp or swivel bolt.
6. Repeat Step 2 above to check for proper adjustment.
7. If necessary, readjust the selector pointer to agree with the transmission detents.
8. Readjust the neutral safety switch if necessary.
9. When properly adjusted:
   a. From Reverse to Drive position travel, the transmission detent must be noted and related to the indicated position on the dial.
   b. In Drive and Reverse positions,

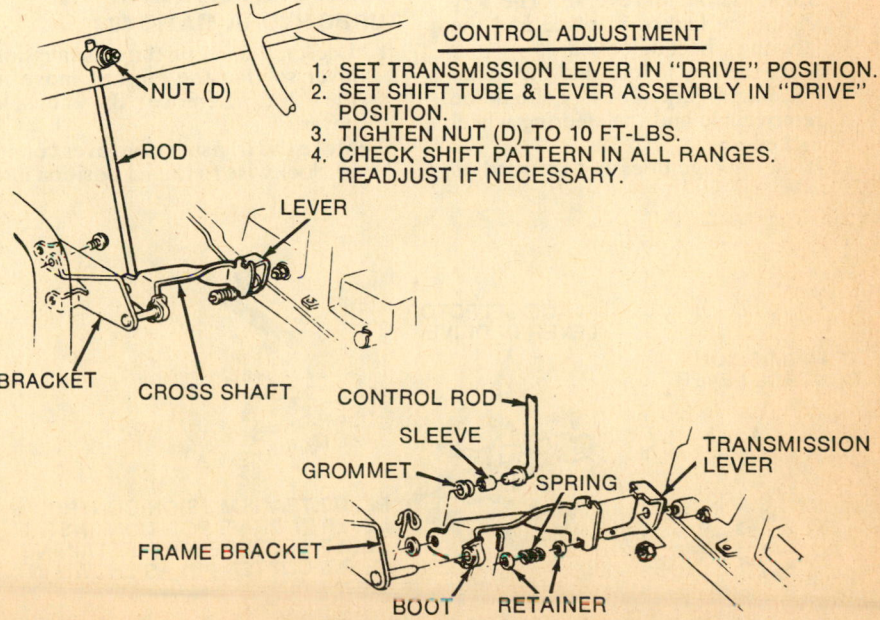

CONTROL ADJUSTMENT
1. SET TRANSMISSION LEVER IN "DRIVE" POSITION.
2. SET SHIFT TUBE & LEVER ASSEMBLY IN "DRIVE" POSITION.
3. TIGHTEN NUT (D) TO 10 FT-LBS.
4. CHECK SHIFT PATTERN IN ALL RANGES. READJUST IF NECESSARY.

Turbo Hydra-Matic column linkage adjustment (© Chevrolet Div., G.M. Corp) the selector lever must drop back into position freely when lifted.

1973 AND LATER COLUMN SHIFT

1. Follow steps 1 and 2 of the preceding procedure.
2. Remove the retaining screw and spring washer from the linkage swivel.
3. Set the lever on the transmission in neutral by moving it counterclockwise to the L1 detent and then clockwise three detent positions to neutral.
4. Place the transmission selector lever in Neutral as determined by the stop in the steering column. Don't use the indicator pointer for reference. The pointer will be adjusted last.
5. Assemble the swivel, spring washer, and screw to the lever and tighten to 20 ft lbs.
6. Readjust the indicator needle, if necessary, to match the transmission detent positions. Readjust the neutral switch.
7. Make sure that the key cannot be removed with the key in the run position and the transmission in reverse. When the key is in the Lock position and shift lever in Park, be sure that the key can be removed, the steering is locked, and that the transmission remains in Park when the steering column is locked.

TURBO HYDRA-MATIC 350 CONSOLE SHIFT EXCEPT CORVETTE

1. Move the transmission control lever into each gear position and make sure that the transmission lever is in each detent position
2. Turn the key to Run and place the transmission in reverse. The key should be locked in place and the steering wheel unlocked.
3. Place the key in lock and the transmission in Park. The key should be removeable and the steering wheel locked.
4. If the linkage does not respond as

described, proceed with the following steps for adjustment.
5. Loosen the screw from the swivel so that the rod is free.
6. Place the control lever in Drive and loosen the nut so that the pin moves in the slot of the transmission lever.
7. Position the transmission lever in Drive by moving the lever counterclockwise to the L1 detent and then clockwise three detent positions.
8. Tighten the nut to 20 ft. lb.
9. Position the transmission lever in Park and turn the key to Lock.
10. Pull down on the vertical rod so that it rests lightly against its stop and tighten the screw to 20 ft. lb.

TURBO HYDRA-MATIC 200

1. Place the shifter in the NEUTRAL position of the detent plate.
2. Place the cross lever in the NEUTRAL position.

NOTE: *Neutral may be obtained by moving the cross lever clockwise to the maximum detent position then counterclockwise two detent positions.*

3. Insert the pin and lock in the cross lever fork and adjust the column rod until the hole in the rod lines up with the pin in the shifter assembly and install the rod on the pin.

1972 CORVETTE

1. Disconnect the pushrod at the transmission lever.
2. With the transmission lever in Drive detent and the selector lever in Drive, rotate the pushrod until the hole lines up with the lever pin.
3. Install the pushrod on the pin and install the retainer clip.
4. Check operation of the linkage in all positions.

1973-77 CORVETTE WITH TURBO HYDRA-MATIC 400

1. Loosen the nut on the transmission lever so that the pin can move in the slot. Remove the console cover.
2. Move the transmission lever counter-clockwise to the L1 position and

then clockwise five detents to Park.
3. Place the shift lever in Park and insert a 0.40 in. spacer in front of the pawl.
4. Tighten the nut on the transmission lever to 20 ft lbs.
5. Turn the ignition switch to Lock with the shift lever in Park.
6. Remove the cotter pin and washer from the backdrive cable at the column lever. Disconnect the cable.
7. Working under the dash, remove the two nuts at the steering column-to-dash bracket.
8. Turn the lock tube lever counterclockwise (when viewed from the front of the column) to remove any free-play from the column.
9. Move the bracket until the cable eye passes freely over the retaining pin on the bracket.
10. While holding the bracket in place, have an assistant tighten the bracket retaining nuts.
11. Install the cotter pin and washer to retain the cable to the lever retaining pin.

1976-79 CORVETTE WITH TURBO HYDRA-MATIC 350

This is a cable operated linkage.
1. Loosen the swivel at the lower end of the rod that comes from the steering column.
2. Loosen the pin at the transmission end of the cable.
3. Set the floorshift lever in the Drive detent.
4. Set the transmission lever in the Drive detent by moving it counterclockwise to the L1 detent, then clockwise three detent positions.
5. Tighten the nut on the pin at the transmission end of the cable.
6. Put the floorshift lever in Park and the ignition switch in LOCK.
7. Pull down lightly on the rod from the column and tighten its clamp nut.

Powerglide Throttle Valve Adjustment

6-CYLINDER THROUGH 1973

Adjustment is made with the throttle pedal completely depressed and the bellcrank in wide open position.
Adjust the length of the linkage to obtain a 1/64 in. to 1/16 in. clearance between the lever on the firewall and its stop when the transmission lever is against its stop.

1972 V8

1. Remove the air cleaner and disconnect:
   a. Accelerator linkage at the carburetor.
   b. Accelerator return spring.
   c. Throttle valve rod return spring.
2. Pull the throttle valve upper rod forward until the transmission is through detent and place the carburetor in wide open position. The

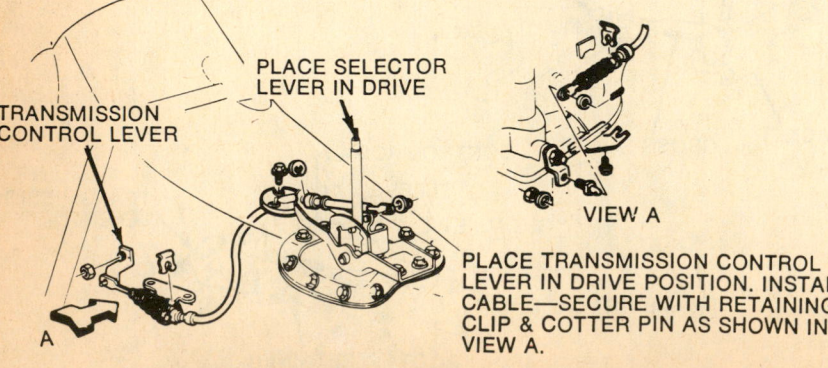

TRANSMISSION CONTROL LEVER

PLACE SELECTOR LEVER IN DRIVE

VIEW A

PLACE TRANSMISSION CONTROL LEVER IN DRIVE POSITION. INSTALL CABLE—SECURE WITH RETAINING CLIP & COTTER PIN AS SHOWN IN VIEW A.

Corvette Turbo Hydra-Matic linkage adjustment
(© Chevrolet Div., G.M. Corp)

carburetor must reach wide open position at the same time that the ball stud contacts the end of the slot in the upper throttle valve rod.

3. Adjust the swivel on the end of the upper throttle valve rod to obtain the setting described in Step 2 above. Allowable tolerance is approximately 1/32 in.
4. Connect and adjust the carburetor linkage.

Detent Cable Adjustment and Throttle Valve Cable Adjustment

1972 CHEVROLET TURBO HYDRA-MATIC 350, 1976 AND LATER CORVETTE, 1978-79 TURBO HYDRA-MATIC 200

1. Disengage the snap lock on the detent cable.
2. Place the carburetor in wide open position (lever against the stop). On Quadrajet carburetors, disengage the secondary locknut before placing the lever in wide open position.

Throttle Valve Cable Adjustment-Turbo Hydra-Matic 200 (© Chevrolet Motor Division, G.M. Corp.)

NOTE: *Detent cable must be through detent.*

3. Holding the carburetor in wide open position, push the snap lock on the detent cable downward until the top is flush with the cable.

1973-79 TURBO HYDRA-MATIC 350, 1976-77 TURBO HYDRA-MATIC 200

The cable adjusts itself the first time the accelerator pedal is depressed to the floor.

Detent Switch Adjustment

1972 CORVETTE TURBO HYDRA-MATIC 400

The detent switch is located on the carburetor.
1. Pull the detent switch driver rearward until the hole in the switch body aligns with the hole in the driver.
2. Insert a 0.092 in. pin through the aligned holes to a depth of 0.10 in. to hold the driver in position.
3. Loosen the switch mounting bolt.
4. With the throttle held in wide open position, move the switch forward until the driver contacts the accelerator lever.

5. Tighten the mounting bolt and remove the pin.

1972 CHEVROLET TURBO-HYDRA-MATIC 400 (CHEVROLET)

The detent switch is located on the carburetor.
1. Loosen the switch mounting bolt.
2. Holding the throttle in wide open position (choke fully open), depress the detent switch plunger until it bottoms in the switch. Move the switch toward the throttle lever paddle until there is a clearance of 0.23 ± 0.01 in. between the face of the lever paddle and the depressed detent switch plunger.
3. Tighten the switch mounting bolts.

1973-77 TURBO HYDRA-MATIC 375 AND 400 (CHEVROLET AND CORVETTE)

The switch is located over the accelerator pedal. After installing a new switch, adjustment is made by pressing the plunger in. This presets the switch and it will self-adjust the first time the pedal is fully depressed.

Band Adjustment, Pan Removal and Installation, Fluid and Filter Change

Follow the procedures given in the Camaro section.

U-JOINTS

For driveshaft and U-joint procedures, see the Camaro section.

REAR AXLE

For Chevrolet axle shaft, bearing, and seal service, refer to the Camaro section.

Corvette Differential Removal and Installation

Corvette is equipped with an independent rear suspension. The differential is solidly attached to the car frame, the rear wheels being driven through tubular rear axles, each fitted with two universal joints. A transverse, multiple leaf rear spring provides rear suspension. Brake torque and driving forces are transmitted through radius arms to the frame. The spring supports vertical loads, while lateral forces, on turns etc., are taken by the axles and control rods to the fixed differential and to the frame.
1. Raise the vehicle on a hoist.
2. Disconnect the spring and link bolts.
3. Disconnect the axle shafts at the carrier by removing the U-bolts on the universal joint trunnions.
4. Disconnect the carrier front support bracket at the frame crossmember.

5. Disconnect the driveshaft at the companion flange.
6. Scribe marks indicating the cam and bolt relative location on the strut rod bracket and loosen the cam bolts.
7. Remove the four bolts which secure the bracket to the carrier lower surface and drop the bracket. Remove the camber cam bolts and swing the strut rods up and out of the way.
8. Remove the eight carrier to cover bolts, loosening the bolts gradually to permit the lubricant to drain out.
9. Pull the carrier partially out of the cover, drop the nose to clear the crossmember, then gradually work the carrier down and out.
10. To install, clean the carrier cover and grease the gasket surface.
11. Using a new gasket and two 1/2 in.-13 x 1-1/4 in. studs as aligning studs, raise the carrier into position. Cut the head off of a 9/16 in.-18 x 1-1/4 in. bolt and slot the unthreaded end. Install this bolt into the carrier underside to aid in installing the strut rod bracket.
12. Install the carrier to cover bolts, tightening securely.
13. Install the driveshaft to the companion flange, tightening the clamp bolts securely.
14. Install the rubber cushion on the bracket and position to the frame crossmember. Install the nut, tightening to 50 ft lbs.
15. Install the axle trunnions to the yokes with the U-bolts.
16. Assemble the strut rods to the bracket and raise the bracket into position under the carrier. Install the four bolts, tightening to 35 ft lbs.
17. Move the camber cams to the marked locations and tighten the cam nuts.
18. Connect the spring end link bolts.
19. Fill the housing with lubricant to the level of the filler hole.

JACKING, HOISTING

When jacking the car, place the jack at the spring seat of the lower control arm in the front and at the axle housing in the rear. A bumper jack may be used on Chevrolet models, but not Corvettes.

To hoist the car, position the hoist arms at the frame side rails immediately in front of the rear wheels and immediately behind the front wheels.

FRONT SUSPENSION

Both Chevrolet and Corvette utilize conventional short-long arm suspension, with coil springs and tube shocks. A stabilizer bar is used between the lower arms to reduce roll.

Shock Absorber Removal and Installation

1. Remove the upper stem nut while holding the stem to keep it from turning.
2. Remove the two bolts holding the shock absorber to the lower control arm and pull the shock through the arm.
3. Purge the new shock of air by repeatedly extending it in its normal position and compressing it while inverted. Extend the shock absorber and insert it up through the lower control arm. Make sure that the upper stem goes through the hole in the upper control arm frame bracket.

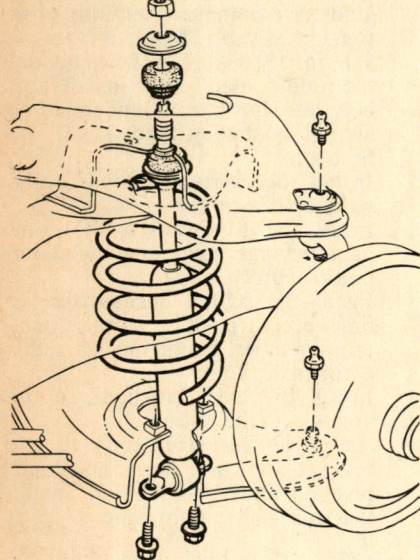

Installing shock absorbers—typical
(© Chevrolet Div., G.M. Corp)

4. Install the grommet, retainer cup, and nut to the shock absorber upper stem.
5. Hold the shock absorber stem and tighten the upper nut to 8 ft lbs.
6. Install the lower control arm retaining bolts and tighten to 20 ft lbs (Chevrolet) or 13 ft lbs (Corvette).

Spring Removal and Installation

1. Raise car on hoist and remove nut, retainer and grommet from top of shock absorber. Support car so that control arms swing free.
2. Disconnect stabilizer bar from lower control arm and remove shock absorber.
3. Bolt a spring remover tool to a suitable jack and place it under the lower control arm bushings so that the bushings seat in the grooves of the tool.

NOTE: *This tool is a cradle which, when fastened to a hydraulic jack, allows the lowering of the control arm*

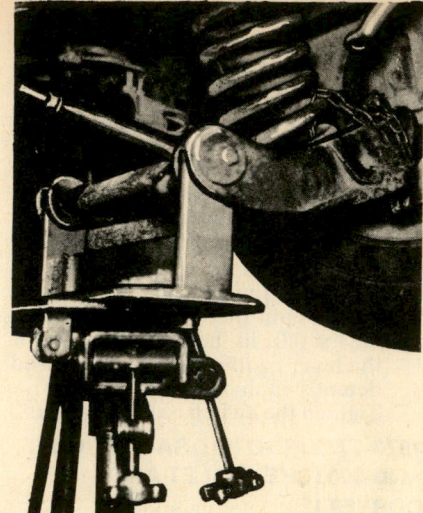

Corvette front spring removal
(© Chevrolet Div., G.M. Corp)

and slow decompression of the spring. A similar tool can be fabricated in the shop. Always safety-chain the spring and control arm when using this method.

4. Remove cross shaft rear retaining nut and the two front retaining bolts.
5. Slowly release jack, swing control arm forward, then remove spring.
6. Install by reversing procedure above. Torque the retaining nut to 92 ft. lb. Torque the retaining bolts to 75 ft. lb.

NOTE: *Chevrolet recommends this cradle spring removal tool for all models. Other methods may be used, depending on the availability of tools.*

Ball Joint Inspection

NOTE: *Before performing this inspection, make sure the wheel bearings are adjusted correctly and that the control arm bushings are in good condition.*

1. Jack the car up under the front lower control arm at the spring seat.
2. Raise the car until there is 1-2 in. of clearance under the wheel.
3. Insert a bar under the wheel and pry upward. If the wheel raises more than 1/8 in. the ball joints are worn. Determine if the upper or lower ball joint is worn by visual inspection while prying on the wheel.

NOTE: *Due to the distribution of forces in the suspension, the lower ball joint is usually the defective joint. Also, 1973 and later Chevrolets are equipped with wear indicators on the lower ball joint. As long as the wear indicator neck extends below the ball stud seat, replacement is unnecessary.*

Upper Ball Joint Removal and Installation

1. Raise the car on a hoist.

2. Remove the tire and wheel assembly.
3. Support the lower control arm with a jack.
4. Loosen the upper ball stud nut.
5. Install a ball joint remover tool and unseat the upper joint from the steering knuckle. Remove the upper stud nut and install a block of wood under the upper control arm.
6. Chisel or grind off the ball joint mounting rivets.
7. Drill out the ball stud attaching holes to accept the service ball joint attaching bolts.
8. Install the ball joint with the nuts and bolts supplied with the new joint.
9. Install the lube fitting in the new joint.
10. Mate the upper control arm to the steering knuckle and install the ball stud through the knuckle boss.
11. Tighten the ball stud nut to 50 ft lbs plus whatever is necessary to align the cotter pin holes. Install the cotter pin. Never back-off the nut to align the cotter pin holes.
12. Install the wheel and lower the vehicle.

Lower Ball Joint Removal and Installation

NOTE: *On Corvette, the lower ball joint removal and installation is the same as that described for the upper ball joint above. For all others:*

1. Support the lower control arm with a jack.
2. Loosen the lower ball stud nut. Break the ball stud loose. Remove the ball stud nut.
3. Remove the ball stud from the steering knuckle.
4. The ball joint is pressed in and must be pressed out.
5. Press in the ball joint.
6. Install the ball stud in the steering knuckle boss. This may be done by raising the lower control arm with the jack.
7. Install the nut on the ball stud, tightening to 80-90 ft lbs. Advance the nut as necessary to align the ball stud nut. Never back-off the nut.
8. Install the lube fitting.

Lower Control Arm Removal and Installation

1. Remove the spring as described above.
2. Remove the ball stud from the steering knuckle as described above.
3. Remove the control arm pivot bolts and remove the control arm. On some Corvettes, the pivot bolt is secured to the frame with two bolts.
4. To install, reverse the above procedure.

Upper Control Arm
Removal and Installation
1. Raise the vehicle on a hoist.
2. Support the outer end of the lower control arm, with a jack.
3. Remove the wheel.
4. Separate the upper ball joint from the steering knuckle as described above under Upper Ball Joint Removal and Installation.
5. Remove the control arm shaft to frame nuts.

NOTE: *Tape the shims together and identify them so that they can be installed in the positions from which they were removed.*

6. Remove the bolts which attach the control arm shaft to the frame and remove the control arm. Note the positions of the bolts.
7. Install in the reverse order of removal. Make sure the shaft to frame bolts are installed in the same position they were in before removal and that the shims are in their original positions. Tighten the shaft to frame bolts to 85 ft lbs on the Chevrolet and to 55 ft lbs on the Corvette. The control arm shaft nuts are torqued to 60 ft lbs.

Front Wheel Bearing
Adjustment
1. Jack the car up and support it at the lower arm.
2. Remove the hub dust cover and spindle cotter pin.
3. While spinning the wheel, snug the nut down to seat the bearings. Do not exert over 12 ft lbs of force on the nut.
4. Back the nut off 1/4-1/2 a turn. Tighten the nut *finger-tight* (if the roller bearings are preloaded with the wheel off the ground, the inner edges of the bearings will be forced against the bearing cage), then *loosen* the nut as required to line up the cotter pin hole in the spindle with the hole in the nut.
5. Insert the cotter pin. End-play should be between 0.001 and 0.008 in. If play exceeds this tolerance, the wheel bearings should be replaced.

REAR SUSPENSION

The Chevrolet uses a coil sprung axle located by two trailing arms on each side, except the station wagon through 1976 which has semi-elliptical leaf springs. The Corvette uses a three-link, independent suspension with a transverse spring.

Shock Absorber Removal and Installation
NOTE: *Purge new shocks of air by repeatedly extending them in their normal position and compressing them while inverted.*

CHEVROLET
1. Jack the car to a convenient working height.
2. If the car is equipped with superlift shock absorbers, disconnect the air line.
3. Remove the two retaining bolts from the upper mounting bracket.
4. Hold the hex on the bottom stud and disconnect the lower mounting. Remove the shock absorber.
5. Install the top two bolts hand-tight.
6. Install the lower stud into the axle bracket and install the lock-washer and nut hand-tight.
7. Torque the upper bolts to 12 ft lbs.
8. While holding the hex stud, torque the nut to 65 ft lbs.
9. Attach the air line, if so equipped, and lower the car.

CORVETTE
1. Jack the car to a convenient working height.
2. Remove the upper bolt and nut.
3. Remove the lower mounting nut and washers.
4. Pivot the top of the shock absorber out of the frame bracket and pull the bottom off the strut shaft.
5. Slide the upper shock absorber eye into the frame bracket and install the bolt, lockwasher, and nut.
6. Install the rubber grommets on the lower shock eye and place the shock over the strut shaft. Install the washers and nut.

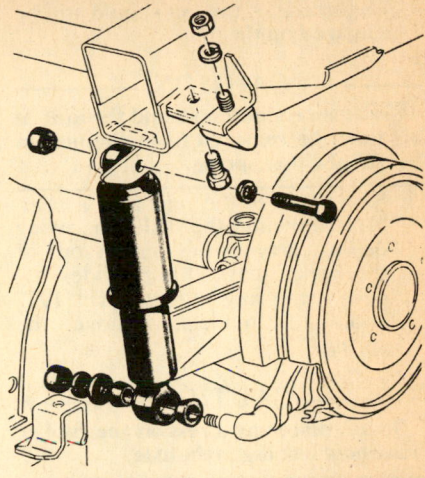
Shock absorber installation, Corvette
(© Chevrolet Div., G.M. Corp)

7. Torque the upper bolt to 50 ft lbs and the lower nut to 35 ft lbs. Lower the car.

Coil Spring Removal and Installation (Chevrolet)
1. Raise rear of vehicle and place jack stands under frame. Support weight of vehicle at rear axle housing separately from the frame position.
2. Remove both rear wheels.
3. With car supported as in Step 1, and springs compressed by weight of vehicle:
   a. Disconnect both rear shocks from anchor pin lower connection.
   b. Loosen the upper control arm(s) rear pivot bolt (do not remove the nut).
   c. Loosen both left and right lower control arm rear attachment (do not disconnect from axle brackets).
   d. Remove rear suspension tie rod from stud on axle tube.
4. On models through 1976, slightly loosen the nut on the bolt that retains the spring and seat to control arm at lower seat of both rear springs. When bolt has been backed off the maximum distance,

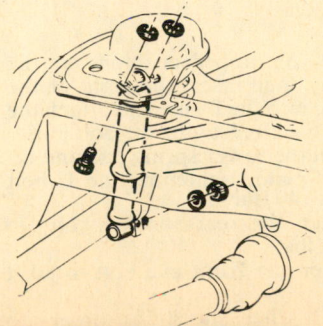
EXCEPT WAGONS
Chevrolet rear shock absorber mounting
(© Chevrolet Div., G.M. Corp)

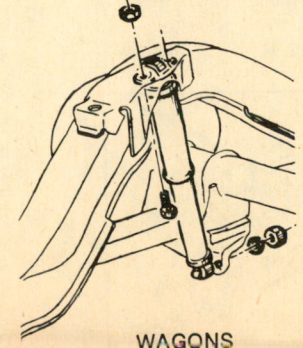
WAGONS

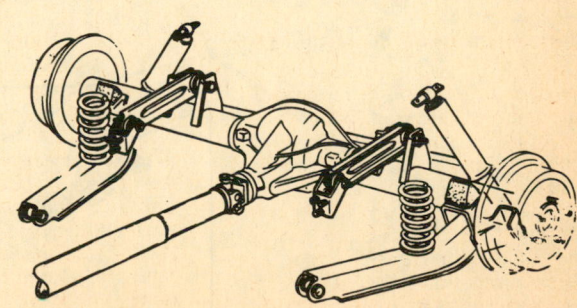
Chevrolet rear suspension except station wagon through 1976
(© Chevrolet Div., G.M. Corp)

all threads of the nut should still be engaged on the bolt.

---------------- **CAUTION** ----------------

Under no condition should the nut, at this time, be removed from the bolt in the seat of either spring.

5. Slowly lower the rear axle assembly, allowing the axle to swing down, carrying the springs out of the upper seat. This provides access for spring removal. On 1977 and later models, remove the springs.

---------------- **CAUTION** ----------------

Do not place any stress on the rubber brake hose leading to the axle.

6. On models through 1976, remove the lower seat attaching parts from each spring, then remove springs from vehicle.
7. Position springs in upper seat and axle on 1977 and later models. On models through 1976, install lower seat parts on control arm. Install nut of spring retaining bolt finger-tight.

NOTE: *Omit the lockwasher under the special high carbon bolt, so that sufficient threads will be available to start the nut. Lockwashers will be installed later.*

8. On models through 1976, alternately raise the axle slightly and re-tighten the nut on each spring lower seat bolt. Continue in until the weight is fully supported on the jack or lift. With spring now completely compressed to approximate curb position, completely position the springs in the lower seats by torquing the nut on the lower seat bolt.
9. On 1978 and later models, raise the axle and align the control arm bolt holes. Reconnect shock absorbers, torque the upper control arm bolts

to 80 ft. lb. and the lower control arm bolts to 125 ft. lb.
10. On models through 1976, while still jacked under axle, remove the nut from the lower seat bolt of one rear spring and install lockwasher and replace nut and tighten. Similarly install lockwasher at other spring.
11. Install rear wheels and lower car to floor.

Transverse Leaf Spring Removal and Installation (Corvette)

1. Raise car and support it by the frame, slightly forward of torque control pivot points. Remove wheel assemblies.
2. Place floor jack under spring near link bolt, and raise spring until nearly flat.
3. Tie the end of the spring to the suspension crossmember to hold this flat attitude, with a 1/4 in. or 5/16 in. chain and grab hook wrapped around the spring and crossmember. To prevent chain slipping, use a C-clamp on the spring adjacent to the chain.
4. Remove link bolt and rubber bushings.
5. Support and raise spring end, as before, and remove chain.
6. Carefully lower jack to completely relax spring.

7. Repeat foregoing procedure on the other side of car.
8. Remove four bolts and washers attaching the spring at the center.
9. Remove the spring by sliding it over the exhaust pipes and out one side of the car.
10. Install by reversing removal procedure. Always use new link bolts and cushions. Torque anchor plate nuts to 40 ft. lb. Install the nut on the link bolt just far enough to expose the cotter pin hole, then insert the pin.

Leaf Spring Removal and Installation (Chevrolet Station Wagon through 1976)

1. Raise the vehicle on a hoist and place an adjustable jack under the axle.
2. Raise the axle until all tension is relieved from the spring.
3. Disconnect the shock absorber from the spring retainer plate.
4. Remove the upper shackle retaining bolt, then the front spring eye bolt.
5. Remove the spring/axle U-bolts, lower plate, spring pads, and spring.
6. Remove the shackle from the spring.
7. Before installing the spring, install the shackle on the rearward end.

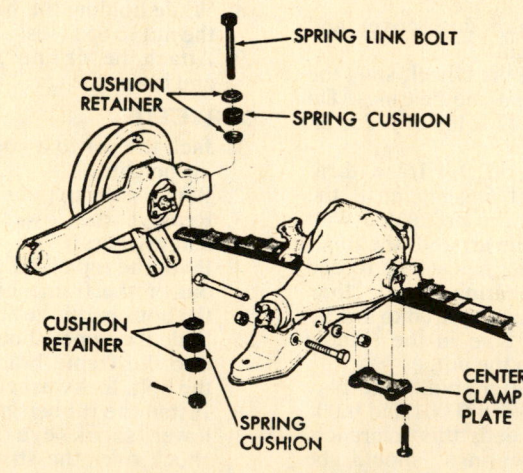

CUSHION RETAINER — SPRING LINK BOLT — SPRING CUSHION — CUSHION RETAINER — SPRING CUSHION — CENTER CLAMP PLATE

Spring mounting, Corvette
(© Chevrolet Div., G.M. Corp)

8. Place the upper cushion on the spring, then insert the front of the spring into the frame and attach the rear shackle, leaving the bolt loose.
9. Install the lower spring pad and retainer plate, tightening the U-bolt nuts to 40 ft lbs.
10. Tighten the rear shackle bolts to 115 ft lbs.
11. Tighten the front eye bolt to 80 ft lbs.
12. Attach the shock absorber to spring retainer plate, tightening to 65 ft lbs.
13. Remove the jack and lower the vehicle.

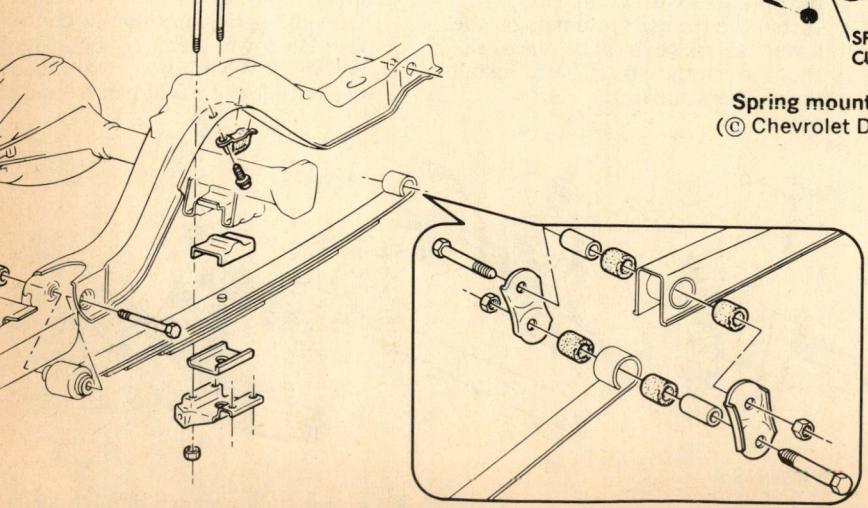

Station wagon rear suspension through 1976 (© Chevrolet Div., G.M. Corp)

Strut Rod and Bracket Removal and Installation (Corvette)

1. Raise car on a hoist.
2. Disconnect shock absorber lower eye from strut rod shaft.
3. Remove strut rod shaft cotter pin and nut. Withdraw shaft by pulling toward the front of the car.
4. Mark related position of camber adjustment, so that adjustment is maintained upon reassembly.
5. Loosen camber bolt and nut. Remove four bolts holding strut rod bracket to carrier and lower the bracket.
6. Remove cam bolt and cam bolt assembly. Pull strut down out of bracket and remove bushing caps.
7. Inspect strut rod bushings for wear and replace where necessary. Replace strut rod if it is bent or damaged in any way.
8. Install by reversing removal procedure. Torque the strut rod-to-spindle support to 75 ft. lb. plus as needed to align cotter pin hole. Torque the bracket-to-carrier to 35 ft. lb.
9. Check rear wheel camber and adjust to specifications.

Torque Control Arm Removal and Installation (Corvette)

1. Disconnect spring on the side from which the torque arm is to be removed. Follow procedure for Spring Removal and Installation.

NOTE: *If so equipped, disconnect stabilizer rod from torque arm.*

2. Remove shock absorber lower eye from strut rod shaft.
3. Disconnect and remove strut rod shaft and swing strut rod down.
4. Remove four bolts holding the axle driveshaft to spindle flange and disconnect drive shaft.
5. Disconnect brake line at wheel cylinder inlet or caliper and from torque arm. Disconnect parking brake cable.
6. Remove torque arm pivot bolt and toe-in shims, then pull torque arm out of frame. Tape shims together

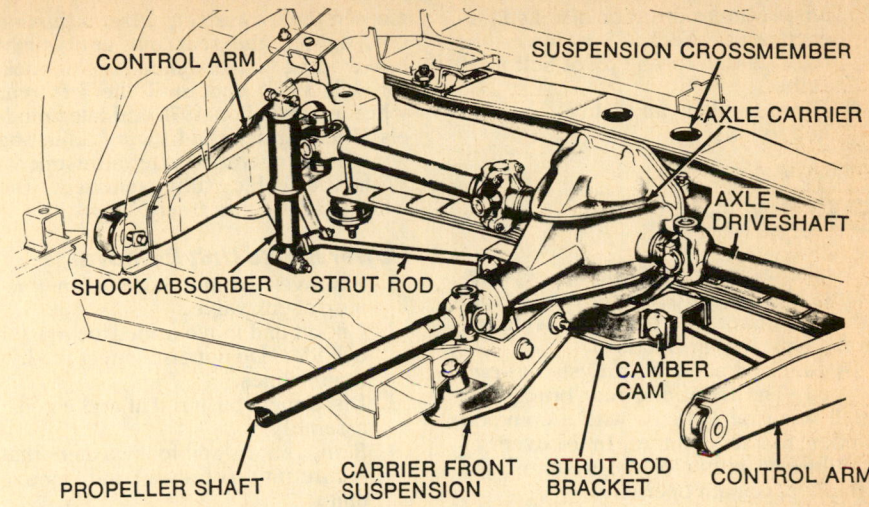

Corvette rear suspension
(© Chevrolet Div., G.M. Corp)

to assure relationship for reassembly.
7. To install, place torque arm in frame opening.
8. Position toe-in shims in original location on both sides of torque arm. Install pivot bolt and lightly tighten at this time.
9. Raise axle driveshaft into position and install to drive flange. Torque bolts to 75 ft lbs

10. Raise strut into position and insert strut rod shaft so that flat lines up with flat in spindle support fork. Install nut and torque to 80 ft lbs.
11. Install shock absorber lower eye and tighten nut to 35 ft lbs.
12. Connect spring end as outlined under Leaf Spring Removal and Installation.

NOTE: *If car is so equipped, connect stabilizer shaft.*

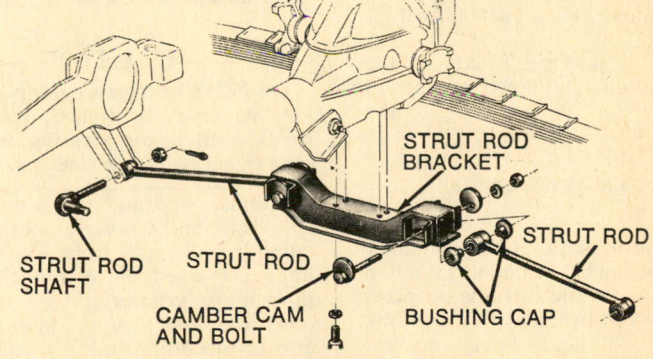

Strut rods, Corvette
(© Chevrolet Div., G.M. Corp)

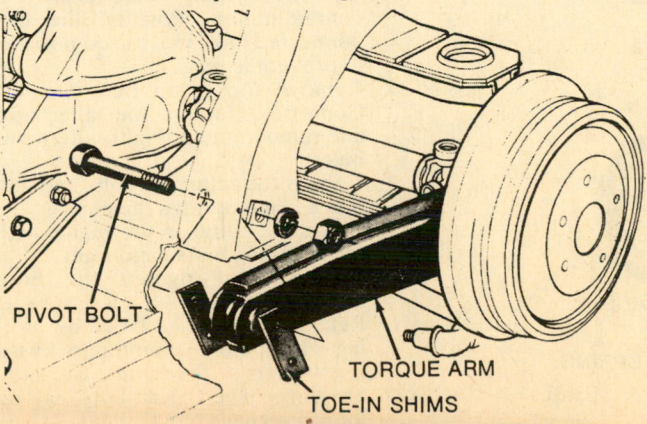

Torque control arm, Corvette
(© Chevrolet Div., G.M. Corp)

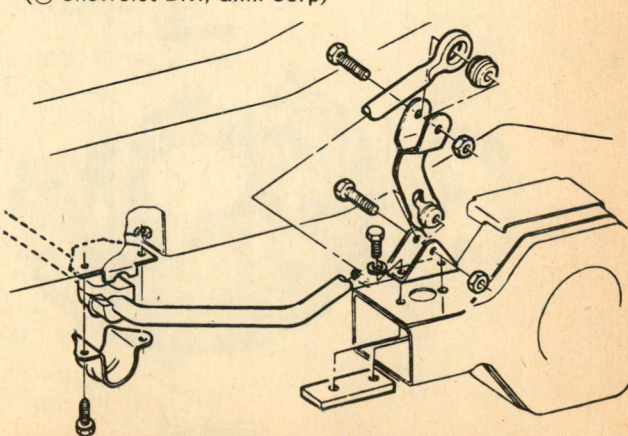

Stabilizer shaft installation, Corvette
(© Chevrolet Div., G.M. Corp)

13. Install brake drum or disc and caliper, and wheel. Then lower the car. Tighten torque pivot bolt to 50 ft lbs.
14. Bleed brakes and check camber and toe-in.

BRAKES

Brake adjustments, lining replacement, bleeding procedure, master and wheel cylinder overhaul can be found in the Unit Repair Section.

A dual hydraulic brake system is employed. The front and rear brakes are each separate systems with a common tandem master cylinder. In the event of a failure in either of the systems, the other will remain operable.

Parking Brake Adjustment

CORVETTE

1. Jack the rear wheels off the ground and remove the wheels. Loosen the brake cables at the equalizer nuts, until the parking brake levers move freely to the Off position with slack in the cables.
2. Rotate the disc until the adjusting screw can be seen through the hole in the disc.
3. Insert a screwdriver and adjust with an up-and-down motion.
4. Tighten the adjuster until the disc cannot move, then back off 6 to 8 notches.
5. Apply the parking brake to the fourth notch. Tighten the cables at the equalizer to give a light drag with the wheel mounted.
6. Release the parking brake and check for a no drag condition.

CHEVROLET

Adjustment is made at the equalizer while the parking brake pedal is applied two notches from the full release position on models through 1977, and one notch on 1978 and later models.

Loosen the forward equalizer adjusting nut, tighten the rear nut until slight brake drag is obtained on models through 1977, and until the left rear wheel is locked on 1978 and later models. Then tighten the forward adjusting nut. Check operation after adjustment. With the cable fully released, the wheels should turn freely.

Power Brake Unit Removal

1. Remove vacuum hose from vacuum check valve.
2. Unbolt and move aside, the master cylinder. Do not disconnect the hydraulic lines.
3. Disconnect push rod at brake pedal assembly.
4. Remove nuts and lockwashers that secure unit to firewall and remove unit.
5. Installation is the reverse of removal. Torque the mounting nuts to 24 ft. lb.

Master Cylinder Removal

1. Disconnect the brake pipes at the master cylinder.
2. Remove the two mounting nuts and lift off the cylinder.
3. Installation is the reverse of removal. Torque the nuts to 24 ft. lb. and bleed the system.

STEERING

——— CAUTION ———

On 1973 Chevrolets equipped with the air bag restraint system, refer to the Buick section for steering wheel and turn signal switch service.

Manual steering gear on both the Chevrolet and Corvette is of the recirculating ball type. Relay-type steering linkage is used on all models, with a pitman arm connected to one end of a relay rod and a frame-mounted idler arm at the other end. Two tie-rod assemblies connect the relay rod to the steering arms. The tie-rod ends are threaded into sleeves to provide adjustment.

Chevrolet power steering is the integral-gear type. The only external hydraulic lines on this sytem are the pressure and return hoses to the pump. The Corvette uses a linkage assist system. A valve attached to the linkage modulates pressure according to power requirements. A power cylinder supplies the actual assist.

Tie-Rod Removal and Installation

1. Remove the cotter pins and nuts from the tie-rod end studs.
2. Tap on the steering arm near the tie-rod end (use another hammer as backing) and pull down on the tie rod, if necessary, to free it.
3. Remove the inner stud in the same manner as the outer.
4. Loosen the clamp bolts and unscrew the ends if they are being replaced.
5. Lubricate the tie-rod end threads with chassis grease if they were removed. Install each end assembly an equal distance from the sleeve.
6. Ensure that the tie-rod end stud threads and nut are clean. Install new seals and install the studs into the steering arms and relay rod.
7. Install the stud nuts. Tighten the outer end nut to 35 ft lbs plus as needed to align the cotter pin hole, and the inner nut to 60 ft lbs on models through 1976, 35 ft. lb. on 1977 and later models (35 ft lbs on Corvette).
8. Adjust the toe-in as described in the Front End Alignment section.

NOTE: *Before tightening the sleeve clamps, ensure that the clamps are positioned so that the adjusting sleeve slot is covered by the clamp.*

Power Steering Pump Removal and Installation

1. Remove the hoses at the pump and tape the openings shut to prevent contamination. Position the disconnected lines in a raised position to prevent leakage.
2. Remove the pump belt. On 454 Corvettes, loosen the alternator and remove the pump-to-alternator belt.
3. Loosen the retaining bolts and any braces, and remove the pump.
4. Install the pump on the engine with the retaining bolts hand-tight.
5. Connect and tighten the hose fittings.
6. Refill the pump and bleed by turning the pulley counterclockwise (viewed from the front). Stop the bleeding when air bubbles no longer appear.
7. Install the pump belt on the pulley and adjust the tension. Bleed the system.

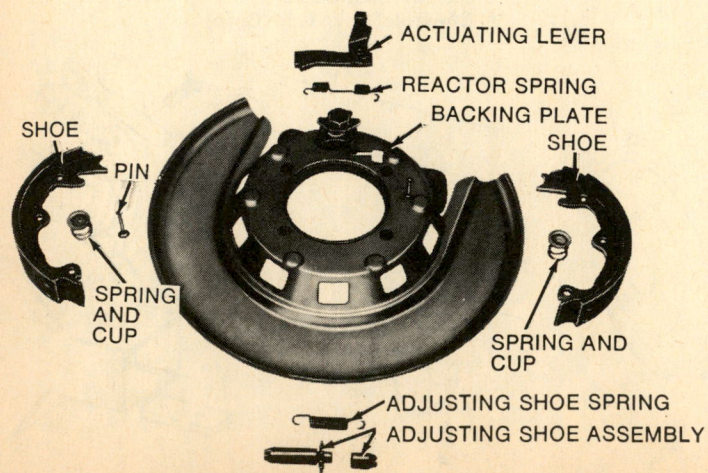

Corvette parking brake components
(© Chevrolet Div., G.M. Corp)

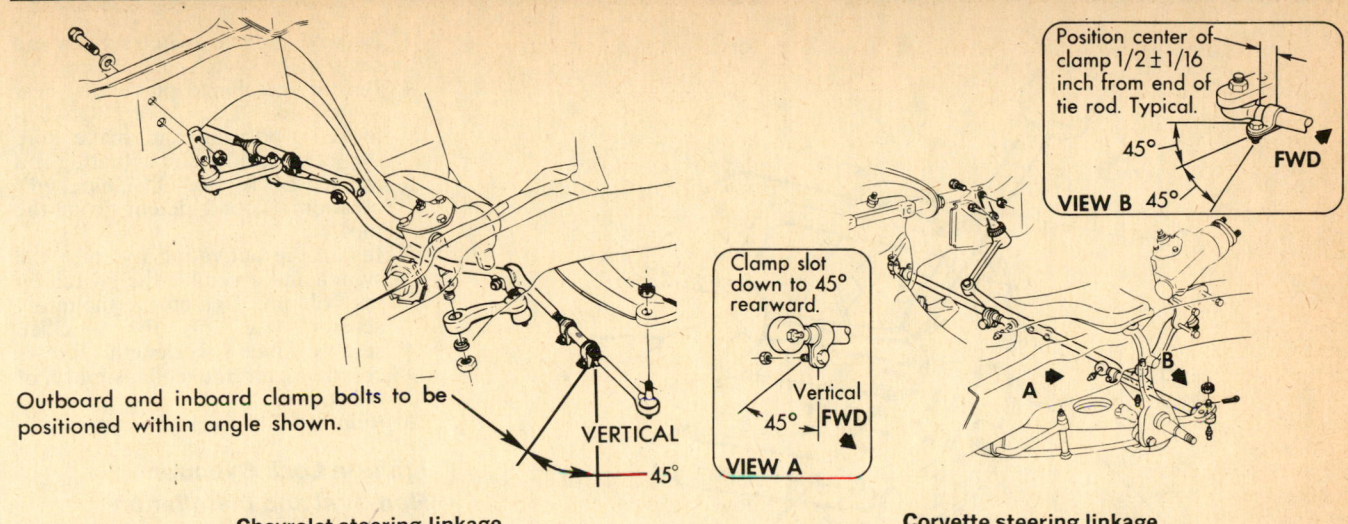

Outboard and inboard clamp bolts to be positioned within angle shown.

VERTICAL

45°

Clamp slot down to 45° rearward.

Vertical
45° FWD

VIEW A

Position center of clamp 1/2 ± 1/16 inch from end of tie rod. Typical.

45° FWD

VIEW B 45°

A B

Chevrolet steering linkage
(© Chevrolet Div., G.M. Corp)

Corvette steering linkage
(© Chevrolet Div., G.M. Corp)

Bleeding the Power Steering System

1. Fill the fluid reservoir.
2. Let the fluid stand undisturbed for two minutes, then crank the engine for about two seconds. Refill reservoir if necessary.
3. Repeat Steps 1 and 2 above until the fluid level remains constant after cranking the engine.
4. Raise the front of the car until the wheels are off the ground, then start the engine. Increase the engine speed to about 1,500 rpm.
5. Turn the wheels to the left and right, checking the fluid level and refilling if necessary.

Steering Wheel Removal and Installation

— CAUTION —

Disconnect the battery ground cable before removing the steering wheel. When installing a steering wheel, always make sure that the turn signal lever is in the neutral position.

1975 and later models have a snap ring on the steering column which must be removed for steering wheel service.
1. Remove the four trim retaining screws from behind the wheel.
2. Lift the trim off and pull the horn wires from the turn signal cancelling cam.
3. Remove the steering wheel nut.
4. Mark the wheel-to-shaft relationship, and then remove the wheel with a puller.
5. Install the wheel on the shaft, aligning the previously made marks. Tighten the nut to 30 ft lbs.
6. Insert the horn wires into the canceling cam.
7. Install the center trim and reconnect the battery cable.

NOTE: *The 1973 Chevrolet cushioned rim wheel, and the Corvette wheel do not require pulling for removal. Pry off the center cap and horn contact assembly. On the tilt/telescope Corvette wheel, remove the shim, center lock-screw, lock lever or knob, and the spacer. The wheel is held to the hub by phillips screws. Reverse the disassembly procedure to install the wheel.*

Turn Signal Switch Removal and Installation
EXCEPT TILT-TELESCOPE

1. Remove the steering wheel as previously outlined.
2. Loosen the three cover screws and lift the cover off the shaft. On 1976 and later models, use a screwdriver blade to pry the cover from the lock plate.
3. Position the special lockplate compressing tool or a substitute on the end of the steering shaft and compress the lockplate. Pry the wire snap-ring out of the shaft groove.
4. Remove the tool and lift the lockplate off the shaft.
5. Slip the cancelling cam, upper bearing pre-load spring, and thrust washer off the shaft.
6. Remove the turn signal lever. Push the flasher knob in and unscrew it.
7. Pull the switch connector out of the mast jacket and tape the upper part to facilitate switch removal. On tilt wheels, place the turn signal and shifter housing in low position and remove the harness cover.

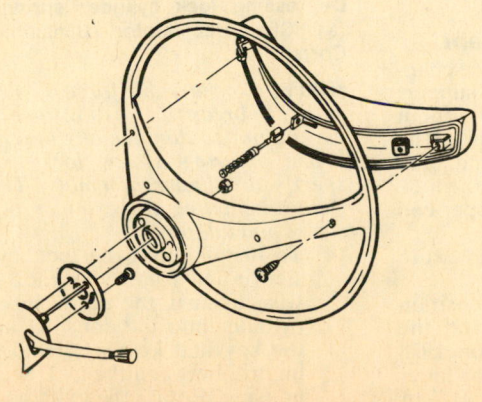

Chevrolet standard steering wheel
(© Chevrolet Div., G.M. Corp)

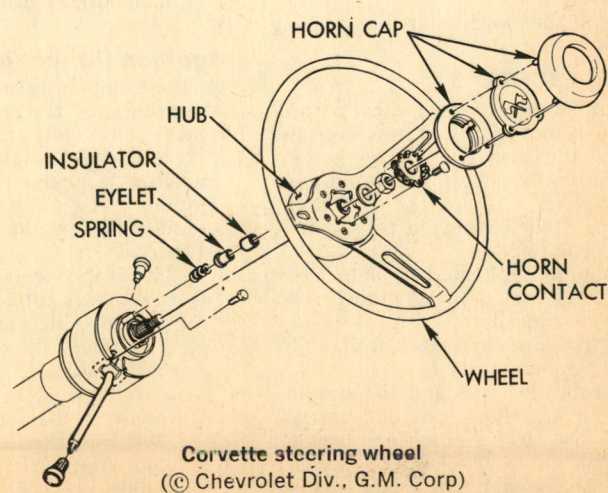

HORN CAP

HUB

INSULATOR

EYELET

SPRING

HORN CONTACT

WHEEL

Corvette steering wheel
(© Chevrolet Div., G.M. Corp)

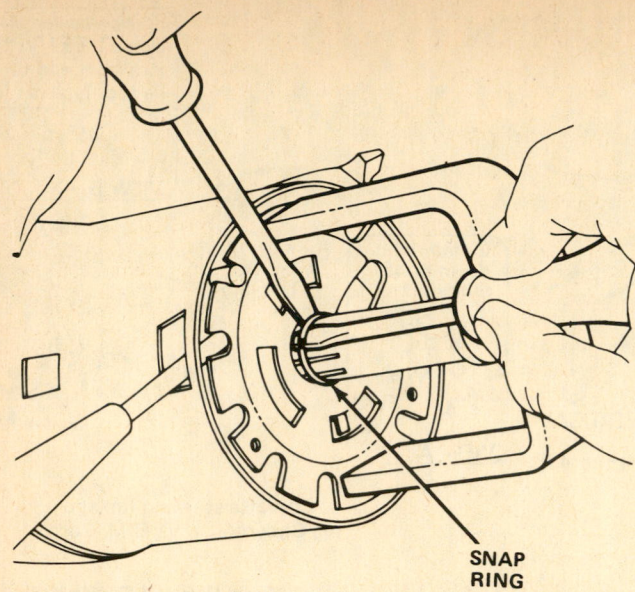

SNAP RING

Compressing steering wheel lockplate and removing snap-ring

8. Remove the three switch mounting screws. Remove the switch by pulling it straight up while guiding the wiring harness cover through the column.
9. Install the replacement switch by working the connector and cover down through the housing and under the bracket. On tilt models, the connector is worked down through the housing, under the bracket, and then the cover is installed on the harness.
10. Install the switch mounting screws and the connector on the mast jacket bracket. Install the column trim plate.
11. Install the flasher knob and the turn signal lever.
12. With the turn signal lever in neutral and the flasher knob out, slide the thrust washer, upper bearing pre-load spring, and cancelling cam onto the shaft.
13. Position the lockplate on the shaft and press it down until a new snap-ring can be inserted in the shaft groove.
14. Install the cover and the steering wheel.

TILT-TELESCOPE
1. Remove the steering wheel as previously outlined and press off the hub with a puller.
2. Remove the steering column/dash trim cover.
3. Remove the C-ring plastic-retainer, if so equipped.
4. Install the special lockplate compressing tool or a substitute over the steering shaft.
5. Compress the lockplate until the C-ring can be removed.
6. Remove the tool and lift out the lock plate, horn contact carrier, and the upper bearing preload spring.
7. Pull the switch connector out of

the mast jacket and tape the upper part to facilitate switch removal.
8. Remove the turn signal lever. Push the flasher in and unscrew it.
9. Position the turn signal and shifter housing in low position. Remove the switch by pulling it straight up while guiding the wiring harness out of the housing.
10. Install the replacement switch by working the harness connector down through the housing and under the mounting bracket.
11. Install the harness cover and clip the connector to the mast jacket.
12. Install the switch mounting screws, signal lever, and the flasher knob.
13. With the turn signal lever in neutral and the flasher knob out, install the upper bearing pre-load spring and lockplate onto the shaft.
14. Position the tool as in step four and compress the plate far enough to allow the C-ring to be installed.
15. Remove the tool. Install the plastic C-ring retainer.
16. Install the column/dash trim cover. Install the steering wheel.

Ignition Switch Replacement
The switch is located inside the channel section of the brake pedal support and is completely inaccessible without first lowering the steering column. The switch is actuated by a rod and rack assembly. A gear on the end of the lock cylinder engages the toothed upper end of the rod.
1. Lower the steering column; be sure to properly support it.
2. Put the switch in "Lock" position on models through 1977 and the "Off-Unlocked" position on 1978 and later models. With the cylinder removed, the rod is in "Lock" or "Off-Unlocked" position when it is in the next to the uppermost detent.

3. Remove the two switch screws and remove the switch assembly.
4. Before installing, place the new switch in "Lock" or "Off-Unlocked" position and make sure the lock cylinder and actuating rod are in "Lock" or "Off-Unlocked" position (second detent from the top).
5. Install the activating rod into the switch and assemble the switch on the column. Tighten the mounting screws. Use only the specified screws since overlength screws could impair the collapsibility of the column.
6. Reinstall the steering column.

Ignition Lock Cylinder
Removal and Installation
THROUGH 1977
1. Remove the steering wheel and directional signal switch.
2. Place the lock cylinder in Run position.

--- **CAUTION** ---

Do not remove the ignition key buzzer.

3. Insert a small screwdriver into the turn signal housing slot. Keeping the screwdriver to the right side of the slot, break the housing flash loose and depress the spring latch at the lower end of the lock cylinder. Remove the lock cylinder.

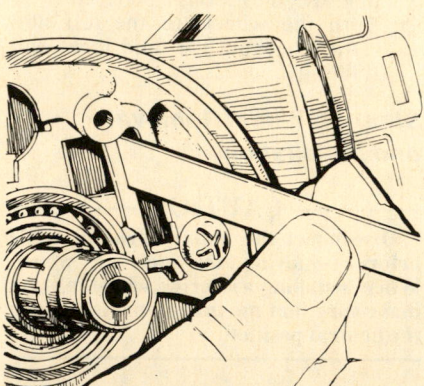

Depressing lock cylinder spring latch (© Chevrolet Motor Division, G.M. Corp.)

NOTE: *Considerable force may be necessary to break this casting flash, but be careful not to damage any other parts. When ordering a new lock cylinder, specify a cylinder assembly. This will save assembling the cylinder, washer, sleeve and adaptor.*

4. To install, hold the lock cylinder sleeve and rotate the knob clockwise against the stop. Insert the cylinder into the housing, aligning the key and keyway. Hold a .070 in. drill between the lock bezel and housing. Rotate the cylinder counterclockwise, maintaining a light pressure until the drive section of the cylinder mates with the sector.

Push in until the snap-ring pops into the grooves. Remove drill. Check cylinder operation.

——— CAUTION ———

The drill prevents forcing the lock cylinder inward beyond its normal position. The buzzer switch and spring latch can hold the lock cylinder in too far. Complete disassembly of the upper bearing housing is necessary to release an improperly installed lock cylinder.

1978-79

1. Remove the steering wheel as previously described.
2. Remove the turn signal as previously described.
3. On all models except Corvette, do not remove the buzzer switch or lock damage will result.
4. Place the cylinder in the Lock position. Insert a small screwdriver or similar tool into the turn signal housing slot. Keep the tool to the right of the slot, break the housing slot loose and at the same time, depress the spring latch at the lower end of the cylinder. With the latch depressed, the lock cylinder can be removed from the housing.
5. Hold the lock cylinder sleeve and rotate the knob clockwise against the stop. Insert the cylinder into the housing bore with the key on the cylinder sleeve aligned with the keyway in the housing. Push the cylinder into the abutment of the sector and cylinder.
6. Rotate the cylinder counterclockwise, maintaining a light pressure until the drive section of the cylinder mates with the sector.
7. Push in until the snap ring pops into the grooves and the lock cylinder is secured in the housing. Check for free rotation.
8. Install the turn signal and steering wheel.

Mid-1978 through 1979 Corvette

1. Place the lock in the Run position.
2. Remove the lock plate, turn signal switch and buzzer switch.
3. Remove the screw and lock cylinder.

——— CAUTION ———

If the screw is dropped on removal, it could fall into the column, requiring complete disassembly to retrieve the screw.

4. Rotate the cylinder clockwise to align the cylinder key with the keyway in the housing.
5. Push the lock all the way in.
6. Install the screw. Tighten the screw to 14 in.lb. for adjustable columns and 25 in.lb. for standard columns.

INSTRUMENT PANEL

Headlight Switch Replacement

CHEVROLET

1. Disconnect battery.
2. Pull knob out to On position.
3. Reach under instrument panel and depress the switch shaft retainer. Remove knob and shaft assembly. On 1978 and later models, remove the windshield wiper switch.
4. Remove the retaining ferrule nut.
5. Remove switch from instrument panel.
6. Disconnect the multi-plug connector from the switch.
7. Replace in reverse of above. (In checking lights before installation, switch must be grounded to test dome light.)

CORVETTE THROUGH 1977

1. Disconnect the battery.
2. Remove mast jacket trim covers.
3. Unclip and remove the left forward console side trim panel.
4. Lower the steering column.
5. Remove the screws and washers which secure the left instrument panel to the door opening, the top of the dash and the left side of the center instrument cluster.
6. Pull the cluster assembly down and tilt it forward.
7. Depress the switch shaft retainer and remove the knob and shaft assembly.
8. Remove the switch retaining bezel.
9. Disconnect the vacuum lines, identifying them for correct reconnection.
10. Pry the connector from the switch.
11. Install in the reverse order of removal.

1978-79 CORVETTE

1. Disconnect the battery ground.
2. Remove the left air distribution duct.
3. Remove the instrument cluster attaching screws and pull the cluster rearward.

4. Disconnect the speedometer cable, electrical connectors and remove the cluster.
5. Remove the instrument panel to left door pillar attaching screws and pull the left side of the instrument panel slightly rearward for access.
6. Depress the shaft retainer, pull the knob and shaft assembly out and remove the switch bezel.
7. Disconnect the vacuum hoses from the switch, tagging them for installation.
8. Pry the connector from the switch and remove the switch from the panel
9. Installation is the reverse of removal.

Speedometer Cable Removal and Installation

CHEVROLET THROUGH 1975

1. Disconnect the battery ground.
2. Remove the cigarette lighter knob and one screw located above the knob.
3. Pull out on the headlight switch shaft, then remove one screw hidden above the shaft.
4. Remove the two screws at the bottom corners of the shroud and lift off the shroud.
5. Remove the clock stem knob.
6. Remove the three screws at the top of the lens retaining strip and lift off the strip, being careful not to scratch the lens.
7. Remove the four lower filter housing illumination bulb sockets by gently giving them 1/4 turn.
8. Lift up on the bottom of the filter housing containing the lens and rotate the housing up and rearward, toward the seat.
9. Remove the two attaching screws and lift out the speedometer.
10. Pull the core from the casing. If the core is broken, raise the car and disconnect the cable from the transmission.
11. Lubricate the new cable with speedometer cable lubricant and insert it into the casing.

Chevrolet speedometer cable removal

Chevrolet & Corvette

12. Install all parts in reverse order of removal.

1976 AND LATER CHEVROLET
1. Disconnect the battery ground.
2. Remove the four attaching screws and lower the steering column bottom cover.
3. Disconnect the shift lever indicator from the steering column.
4. Unbolt the column from the instrument panel.
5. Remove the six screws and three plastic snap retainers and lift off the lens.
6. Remove the two screws from the upper surface of the grey sheet metal trim plate.
7. Remove the nuts from two studs in the lower corner of the cluster.
8. Reach behind the cluster, depress the cable retaining clip and remove the speedometer cable.
9. Pull the core from the casing. If the core is broken, raise the car and disconnect the cable from the transmission.
10. Lubricate the new cable core with speedometer cable lubricant and install it in the casing.
11. Assemble all parts in reverse order of removal.

CORVETTE
Reach behind the speedometer and depress the retaining clip. Pull the cable from the casing. If the cable is broken, raise the car and disconnect the cable at the transmission. Lubricate only the bottom 3/4 of the cable core with speedometer cable lubricant. Reconnect all parts.

WINDSHIELD WIPERS

Motor Removal and Installation
1. With wiper motor in park position and hood open, disconnect the washer hoses and all wiring from the motor assembly.
2. Remove the plenum chamber grill on Corvettes or the access cover on Chevrolet models.
3. Loosen the nuts which retain the drive link to the crank arm ball stud on Chevrolet models. Remove the nut which retains the crank arm to the motor assembly on Corvette models.
4. On Corvettes, remove the ignition shield, if used, and distributor cap. Remove and identify the left bank spark plug leads.
5. Remove the motor mounting screws or nuts and remove the motor.
6. To install, reverse the above procedure.

Wiper Blade Replacement
Two methods are used to retain the

blades to the arms. One uses a press-release tab. By depressing the tab, the blade can be slid off the arm. The other method uses a coil spring retainer. A screwdriver must be inserted on top of the spring and the spring pushed downward. The blade can then be slid off.

RADIO

Removal and Installation
1972 CHEVROLET
1. Disconnect battery.
2. Remove ash tray, retainer attaching screws and retainer.
3. Remove heater control panel retaining screws and push panel assembly from console.
NOTE: *If interference between control panel and radio is met, loosen radio retaining nuts.*
4. Remove radio control knobs, bezels and retaining nuts.
5. Disconnect radio wiring harness, and antenna lead-in.
6. Remove radio rear brace attaching screw, and remove radio from the car.
7. Remove speaker retaining bolt and remove speaker.
8. To install, reverse removal procedure.

1973-76 CHEVROLET
1. Disconnect the negative battery cable.
2. On cars with A/C, remove the lap cooler duct.
3. Turn the radio control knobs until the slots in the bottom of the knobs are visible. Depress the metal retainers with a screwdriver and remove the knobs and bezels.
4. Remove the control shaft nuts and washers.
5. Remove the right side bracket-to-instrument panel bolt and the stud nut on the left side of the radio.
6. Pull the radio forward and disconnect the wiring from the radio and remove the radio from the car.

1977 AND LATER CHEVROLET
1. Disconnect the battery ground cable.
2. Pull the knobs off.
3. Take off the three screws and the trim plate.
4. Remove the two screws and the bottom nut holding the radio to the instrument panel.
5. Detach the wiring and the antenna.
6. Remove the radio and the mounting bracket.
7. Reverse the procedure for installation.

CORVETTE THROUGH 1977
1. Disconnect the negative battery cable and remove the right instrument panel pad.
2. Disconnect the radio speaker connectors.

3. Remove the wiper switch trim plate screws and tip the plate forward to gain access to the switch connector. Remove the switch connector and trim plate from the dash.
4. Unclip and remove the right and left forward console trim pads. Remove the forwardmost screw on the left and right sides of the console.
5. Working with a flexible drive socket between the console and the metal horseshoe brace, remove the nuts from the studs on the lower edge of the console cluster.
6. Remove the remaining console attaching screws and disconnect the radio electrical connectors, antenna wire and radio brace from the rear of the console. Remove the radio knobs and nuts.
7. Pull the top of the console rearward and separate the radio from the console and remove it from the right side opening.
NOTE: *The center instrument cluster trim panel is designed to collapse under impact. Do not deflect the panel to gain access to the radio. Also, the remotely located radio heat sink should be removed with the radio when servicing is required.*

1978-79 CORVETTE
1. Disconnect the battery ground.
2. Pull off the radio control knobs.
3. Remove the instrument cluster.
4. Remove the screw holding the radio bracket reinforcement to the floorpan.
5. Pull the radio outward and disconnect the wiring from the back.
6. Installation is the reverse of removal. If a new radio is being installed, save the mounting bracket from the rear of the old one.

HEATER

Blower Removal and Installation
CHEVROLET THROUGH 1976, WITH OR WITHOUT A/C
1. Disconnect battery.
2. Unclip hoses from fender skirt.
3. Disconnect electrical feed from motor. Disconnect the motor air-cooling hose on air-conditioned cars.
4. Turn vehicle front wheels to extreme right.
5. Remove right front fender skirt bolts and allow skirt to drop, resting it on top of tire. It may be wedged away from fender lower flange with block of wood to provide better access to bolts.
6. Remove screws attaching motor mounting plate to air inlet housing.
7. Remove screws attaching motor to mounting plate.

C408

8. Remove clip attaching cage to shaft and remove blower motor.
9. Install in reverse of above.

1977 AND LATER CHEVROLET, WITH OR WITHOUT A/C

1. Disconnect the battery ground.
2. Disconnect the blower lead wire.
3. Remove the attaching screws and gently pry the blower from the case. The sealer may act as an adhesive.
4. To install, reverse the procedure. Replace the sealer if it was damaged.

CORVETTE THROUGH 1976, NON-AIR CONDITIONED

1. Remove the radiator supply tank from its retaining straps. Move it out of the way. Disconnect the battery.
2. Remove blower motor electrical connectors.
3. Scribe a reference mark on the blower motor mounting plate and the blower motor.
4. Remove the five screws that mount the blower mounting plate to the blower inlet assembly.
5. Withdraw the blower assembly from the inlet assembly.
6. Install in reverse of removal procedure.

CORVETTE THROUGH 1976, WITH AIR CONDITIONING

1. Remove the battery ground cable.
2. Disconnect the air cooling tube and electrical wire from the blower motor.

3. Remove the first three sill molding screws and pry the molding out to allow access to the right splash shield bolts.
4. Remove the splash shield.
5. Remove the motor retaining screws and drop the motor out through the splash shield opening. Pry on the mounting flange gently, if necessary to break the motor loose.
6. Reverse the removal steps to install the motor.

ALL 1977 AND LATER CORVETTE

1. Disconnect the battery ground.
2. Remove the radiator supply tank screws and move the tank out of the way.
3. Disconnect the blower motor lead wires.
4. Remove the attaching screws and gently pry the motor out of the case. The sealer may act as an adhesive.
5. To install, reverse the procedure.

Core Removal and Installation

ALL THROUGH 1976 EXCEPT AIR CONDITIONED CARS

1. Drain radiator.
2. Remove heater hoses at connections beside air inlet assembly.
3. Remove cable and electrical connectors from heater and defroster assembly.
4. On engine side of dash, remove screws and nuts holding air inlet to dash panel.
5. Inside vehicle, pull entire assembly

from firewall and remove assembly from vehicle.
6. Remove core assembly retaining springs and remove core.
7. Install in reverse of above.

1972-76 CHEVROLET WITH AIR CONDITIONING

1. Drain the cooling system. It is not necessary to evacuate the A.C. refrigerant.
2. Disconnect the battery ground cable and compressor clutch connector.
3. Disconnect the vacuum line from the vacuum check valve and push the grommet through the firewall into the passenger compartment.
4. Disconnect the heater hoses at the firewall.
5. Remove the three screws and nuts retaining the heater and selector duct. The inner fender must be pried out from the firewall to gain access to one screw.
6. Remove the lap cooler assembly.
7. Remove the glove compartment.
8. Remove the floor outlet duct and panel pad.
9. Disconnect the distributor duct hoses and connector.
10. Remove the duct from the selector.
11. Loosen the defroster duct and move it to provide access to the selector and core assembly.
12. Disconnect the temperature door cable.
13. Separate the inline vacuum connector and the outside air diaphragm line.

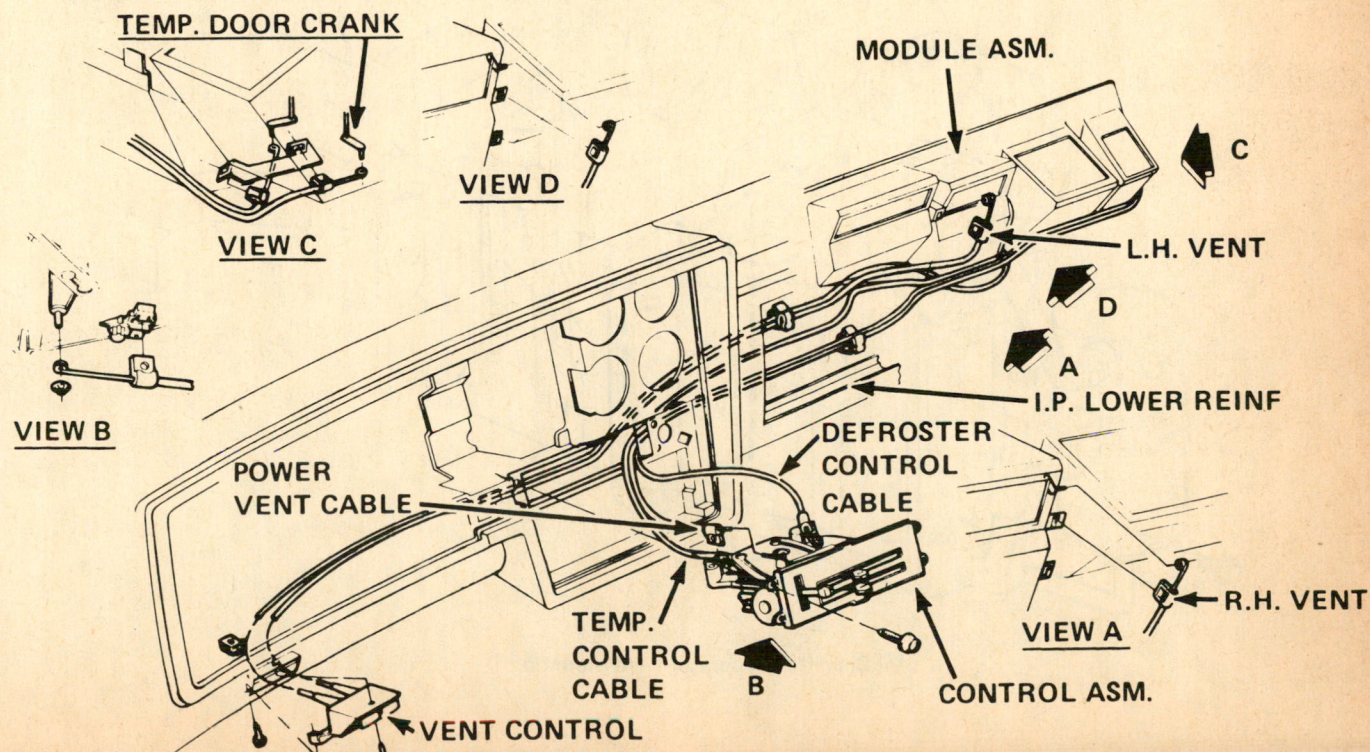

Chevrolet heater control cable adjustments

14. Lift the heater and air selector duct out as an assembly.
15. Remove the retaining screws and remove the heater core from the selector.

ALL 1977 CHEVROLET, WITH OR WITHOUT A/C
1978-79 CHEVROLET WITHOUT A/C

1. Disconnect the battery ground.
2. Drain the radiator.
3. Disconnect the heater hoses at the core and plug the core tubes.
4. Remove the screws from the perimeter of the core cover on the engine side of the firewall.
5. Pull the core cover from the firewall mounting.
6. Pull the core assembly from the module.
7. To install, reverse the procedure.

1978-79 CHEVROLET WITH A/C

1. Drain the cooling system.
2. Disconnect the hoses at the core tubes.
3. Remove the module retaining bracket and ground strap.
4. Remove the module rubber seal.
5. Remove the module screen.
6. Remove the right windshield wiper arm.
7. Remove the diagnostic connector, high blower relay and thermal switch mounting screws.

8. Remove all electrical connectors from the module top.
9. Remove the module top cover.
10. Lift out the core.
11. Installation is the reverse of removal. Replace all sealer.

CORVETTE THROUGH 1976 WITH AIR CONDITIONING

1. Disconnect the battery ground cable.
2. Drain the cooling system. It is not necessary to evacuate the A/C refrigerant.
3. Disconnect the heater hoses at the firewall and plug the pipes.
4. Remove the nuts from the distributor studs protruding through the firewall.
5. Remove the right side dash pad and center dash cluster (described under ''instruments'').
6. Disconnect the right outlet from the center duct.
7. Remove the center duct from the selector duct.
8. Remove the selector duct and pull it to the right and to the rear.
9. Remove the cables and wiring connectors from the selector and remove it from the car.
10. Remove the temperature door cam plate from the selector duct.
11. Remove the heater core and housing from the selector.
12. Reverse the removal procedure to install.

ALL 1977 CORVETTE, WITH OR WITHOUT A/C

1. Remove the right instrument panel pad.
2. Remove the right side firewall braces.
3. Remove the center dash console duct and floor outlet duct.
4. Remove the radio and center dash console.
5. Pull the distributor assembly from the center firewall mounting.
6. Disconnect the cables and wires and remove the distributor duct assembly from the car.
7. Remove the core from the distributor assembly.
8. To install, reverse the procedure.

1978-79 CORVETTE

1. Disconnect the battery ground.
2. Drain the cooling system.
3. Disconnect the hoses from the core tubes.
4. Remove the nuts from the heater distributor on the engine side of the firewall.
5. Disconnect the cables from the distributor.
6. Remove the distributor from the firewall.
7. Remove the core from the distributor.
8. Installation is the reverse of removal. Replace any damaged sealer.

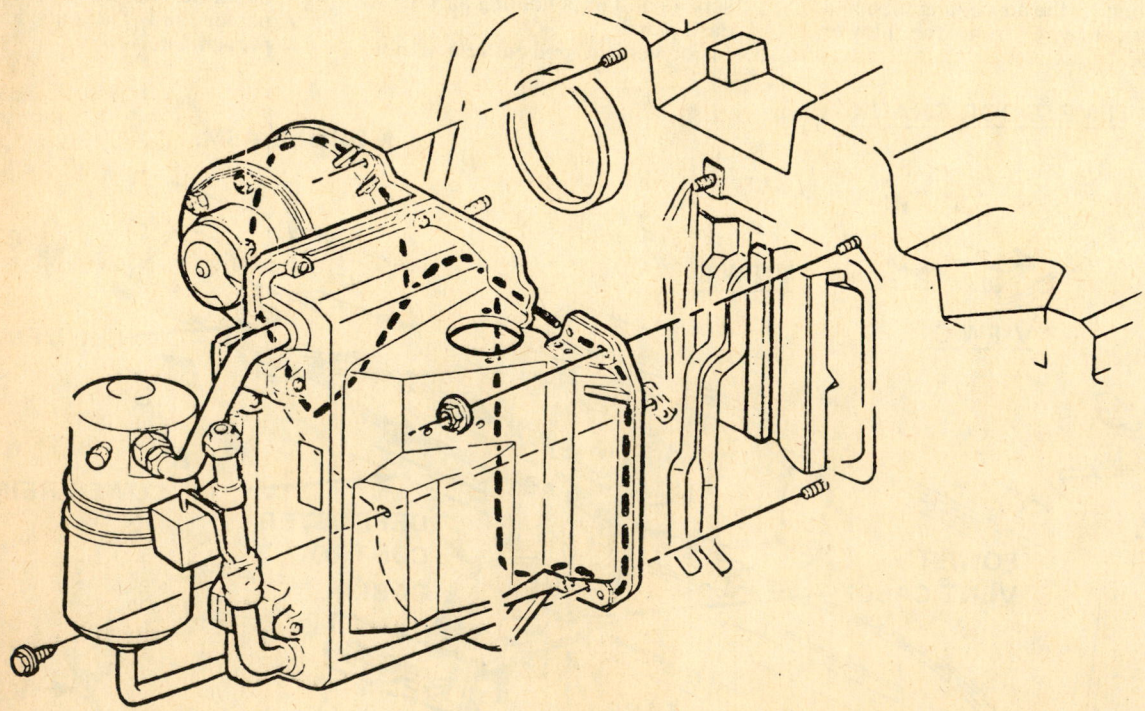

Corvette evaporator case mounting

Chevette

Index

YEAR IDENTIFICATION

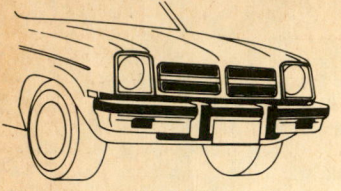

1976-77

1978

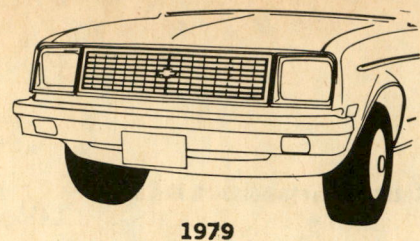

1979

ENGINE IDENTIFICATION

The vehicle identification number (VIN) is on a tag on the top left of the instrument panel, visible through the windshield. The engine identification code is the fifth digit of the Vehicle Identification Number.

No. Cyls.	Cu. in.(cc) Displacement	1976	1977	1978	1979
4	85 (1400)	A	A		
4	97.6(1600)	B	B	E	E
4	97.6(1600) HO			J	J

GENERAL ENGINE SPECIFICATIONS

Year	Engine No. Cyl. Displacement liters (cu in.)	Carburetor Type	Horsepower @ rpm ■	Torque @ rpm (ft lbs) ■	Bore x Stroke (in.)	Compression Ratio	Oil Pressure @ 2000 rpm
'76-'77	4-1.4 (85)	1 bbl	52 @ 5300	67 @ 3400	3.228 x 2.606	8.5:1	39-46
	4-1.6 (97.6)	1 bbl	60 @ 5300	77 @ 3200	3.228 x 2.980	8.5:1	39-46
'78-'79	4-1.6 (97.6)	1 bbl	63 @ 4800	82 @ 3200	3.228 x 2.980	8.6:1	34-42
	4-1.6 (97.6)	1 bbl HO	68 @ 5000	84 @ 3200	3.228 x 2.980	8.6:1	34-42

■ Horsepower and torque are SAE net figures. They are measured at the rear of the transmission with all accessories installed and operating. Since the figures vary when a given engine is installed in different models, some are representative rather than exact.

TUNE-UP SPECIFICATIONS

When analyzing compression test results, look for uniformity among cylinders rather than specific pressures.

Year	ENGINE No. Cyl. Displacement (liters)		SPARK PLUGS Orig. Type	Gap (in.)	DISTRIBUTOR Point Dwell (deg)	Point Gap (in.)	IGNITION TIMING (deg) ▲ Man Trans	Auto Trans	VALVES Intake Opens ■ (deg)	Fuel Pump Pressure (psi)	IDLE SPEED (rpm) ▲ Man Trans ●	Auto Trans.
'76	4-1.4		R43TS	.035	Electronic		10B	10B	32	5-6.5	800(1000)	800(850)
	4-1.6		R43TS	.035	Electronic		8B	10B	32	5-6.5	800(1000)	800(850)
'77	4-1.4		R43TS	.035	Electronic		12B	12B	32	5-6.5	800(1000)	800(850)
	4-1.6		R43TS	.035	Electronic		8B	8B	32	5-6.5	800(1000)	800(850)
'78	4-1.6	base	R-43TS	.035	Electronic		8B	8B	28	5-6.5	800	800
	4-1.6	HO	R-43TS	.035	Electronic		8B	8B	31	5-6.5	800	800

TUNE-UP SPECIFICATIONS

When analyzing test results, look for uniformity among cylinders rather than specific pressures.

	ENGINE No. Cyl. Displacement (liters)		SPARK PLUGS		DISTRIBUTOR		IGNITION TIMING (deg) ▲		VALVES Intake Opens	Fuel Pump Pressure	IDLE SPEED (rpm) ▲	
Year			Orig. Type	Gap (in.)	Point Dwell (deg)	Point Gap (in.)	Man Trans	Auto Trans	■ (deg)	(psi)	Man Trans •	Auto Trans.
'79	4-1.6	base	R-42TS	.035	Electronic		①	①	28	5-6.5	①	①
	4-1.6	HO	R-42TS	.035	Electronic		①	①	31	5-6.5	①	①

▲ See text for procedure
• Figure in parentheses indicates California engine
■ All figures Before Top Dead Center
B Before Top Dead Center
HO High Output

① See Underhood Specifications Sticker
NOTE: The underhood specifications sticker often reflects tune-up specification changes made in production. Sticker figures must be used if they disagree with those in this chart.

NOTE: Most 1979 GM carburetors have idle mixture screws concealed by staked-in plugs. These are not meant to be removed, except at carburetor overhaul.

FIRING ORDER

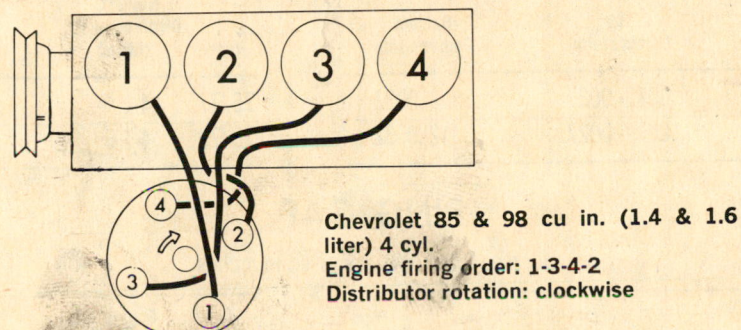

Chevrolet 85 & 98 cu in. (1.4 & 1.6 liter) 4 cyl.
Engine firing order: 1-3-4-2
Distributor rotation: clockwise

CAPACITIES

Year	ENGINE No. Cyl. Displacement (liters)	Engine Crankcase Add ½ Qt For New Filter	TRANSMISSION Pts To Refill After Draining Manual 4-Speed	Automatic •	Drive Axle (pts)	Gasoline Tank (gals)	COOLING SYSTEM (qts) With Heater	With A/C
'76	4-1.4	4	3	7	2.8	13	8.5	8.5
	4-1.6	4	3	7	2.8	13	9.0	9.0
'77	4-1.4	4	3	7	1.8	13	8.5	8.5
	4-1.6	4	3	7	1.8	13	9.0	9.0
'78-'79	4-1.6	4	3.4	5.7	1.8	12.5	9.0	9.0

• Specifications do not include torque converter

VALVE SPECIFICATIONS

Year	Engine No. Cyl. Displacement (liters)	Seat Angle (deg)	Face Angle (deg)	Spring Test Pressure (lbs @ in.)	Spring Installed Height (in.)	STEM TO GUIDE Clearance (in.) Intake	Exhaust	STEM Diameter (in.) Intake	Exhaust
'76-'77	4-1.4	46	45	68 @ 1.26	1.26	.0018-.0021①	.0026-.0029②	.3141	.3133
'76-'79	4-1.6	46	45	68 @ 1.26	1.26	.0018-.0021①	.0026-.0029②	.3141	.3133

① 1977 and later: .0006-.0017
② 1977 and later—.0014-.0025

CRANKSHAFT AND CONNECTING ROD SPECIFICATIONS

All measurements are given in inches

Year	Engine No. Cyl. Displacement (liters)	Main Brg. Journal Dia	CRANKSHAFT Main Brg. Oil Clearance	Shaft End-Play	Thrust on No.	Journal Diameter	CONNECTING ROD Oil Clearance	Side Clearance
'76	4-1.4	2.0075-2.0085	.0009-.0025	.004-.008	4	1.809-1.810	.0014-.0030	.004-.012
	4-1.6	2.0075-2.0085	.0009-.0025	.004-.008	4	1.809-1.810	.0014-.0030	.004-.012
'77	4-1.4	2.0078-2.0088	.0006-.0026①	.004-.008	4	1.809-1.810	.0014-.0031	.004-.012
'77-'79	4-1.6	2.0078-2.0088	.0006-.0026①	.004-.008	4	1.809-1.810	.0014-.0031	.004-.012

① no. 5: .00094-.0026

RING SIDE CLEARANCE

All measurements are given in inches

Year	Engine No. Cyl. Displacement (liters)	Top Compression	Bottom Compression
'76-'77	4-1.4	.0012-.0027	.0012-.0032
'76-'79	4-1.6	.0012-.0027	.0012-.0032

Year	Engine No. Cyl. Displacement (liters)	Oil Control
'76-'77	4-1.4	.0000-.0050
'76-'79	4-1.6	.0000-.0050

RING GAP

All measurements are given in inches

Year	Engine No. Cyl. Displacement (liters)	Top Compression	Bottom Compression
'76-'77	4-1.4	.009-.019	.008-.018
'76-'79	4-1.6	.009-.019	.008-.018

Year	Engine No. Cyl. Displacement (liters)	Oil Control
'76-'77	4-1.4	.015-.055
'76-'79	4-1.6	.015-.055

PISTON CLEARANCE

Year	Engine No. Cyl. Displacement (liters)	Piston① to Bore Clearance (in.)
'76-'77	4-1.4	.0008-.0016
'76-'79	4-1.6	.0008-.0016

① Measured 1½ in. from top of piston

TORQUE SPECIFICATIONS

All readings in ft lbs

Year	Engine No. Cyl. Displacement (liters)	Cylinder Head Bolts	Rod Bearing Bolts	Main Bearing Bolts	Crankshaft Bolt	Flywheel to Crankshaft Bolts	MANIFOLD Intake	Exhaust
'76-'79	4-1.4, 1.6	70-80	34-40	40-52	65-85	40-52	13-18	①

① Center bolts—13-18; end bolts—19-25

WHEEL ALIGNMENT SPECIFICATIONS

Year	Model	CASTER Range (deg)	CASTER Pref Setting (deg)	CAMBER Range (deg)	CAMBER Pref Setting (deg)	Toe-in (in.)	Steering Axis Inclination (deg)	WHEEL PIVOT RATIO (deg) Inner Wheel	WHEEL PIVOT RATIO (deg) Outer Wheel
'76	All	4P to 5P	4½P	¼N to ¾P	¼P	1/16	7½	—	—
'77-'78	All	3½P to 5½P	4½P	⅕N to ⅗P	⅕P	1/32 to 3/32	7½	—	—
'79	All	2½P to 6½P	4½P	½N to 1P	⅕P	1/32 to 3/32	7½	—	—

N Negative
P Positive
— not specified

CHARGING SYSTEM

A Delcotron 10-SI series alternator is used. This unit contains a solid state, integrated circuit voltage regulator. The alternator is nonadjustable and requires no periodic maintenance. Refer to the Unit Repair Section for applicable testing and overhaul procedures.

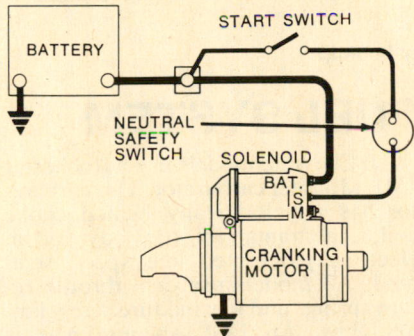

Typical starting system (© Chevrolet Div., G.M. Corp.)

Alternator Removal and Installation

1. Disconnect the negative battery cable.
2. Disconnect the alternator wiring.
3. Remove the brace bolt and the drive belt.
4. Support the alternator, remove the mounting bolt, and remove the alternator.
5. Installation is the reverse of removal. Adjust drive belt deflection to 1/2 in. under moderate thumb pressure.

STARTING SYSTEM

Engine cranking is accomplished by a solenoid-actuated starter motor powered by the vehicle battery. The motor is a Delco-Remy unit similar to other Chevrolet starters. No periodic lubrica-

tion of the motor or solenoid is necessary. Testing procedures can be found in the Unit Repair Section.

Starter Removal and Installation
CARS WITHOUT POWER BRAKES

1. Disconnect the negative battery cable and remove the air cleaner.
2. Disconnect and remove the oil pressure sending unit.
NOTE: *The oil pressure sending unit has a harness lock. To disconnect the electrical connector, lift the tab on the collar of the lock and remove the lock assembly.*
3. Disconnect the starter solenoid.
4. Remove the brace screw from the bottom of the starter housing.
5. Remove the two starter-to-flywheel housing mounting screws.
6. Hold the starter with both hands and tip it past the engine mount bracket, then upward between the intake manifold and wheelarch.
7. Installation is the reverse of removal.

CARS WITH POWER BRAKES (WITHOUT AIR CONDITIONING)

1. Disconnect the battery negative cable and remove the air cleaner.
2. Remove the distributor cap.
3. Remove the fuel line from the carburetor.
4. Disconnect the electrical connector from the ignition coil. Remove the three coil bracket retaining screws and remove the coil with bracket.
5. Disconnect the vacuum hose at the distributor.
6. Disconnect and remove the oil pressure sending unit. See the preceding Note concerning the oil pressure sender harness lock.
7. Disconnect the wires from the starter solenoid.
8. Remove the brace screw from the bottom of the starter housing.
9. Remove the two starter-to-flywheel housing mounting screws.
10. Hold the starter with both hands and remove it by sliding it toward the front of the car.
11. Installation is the reverse of removal.

CARS WITH POWER BRAKES AND AIR CONDITIONING

1. Disconnect the negative battery cable and remove the air cleaner.
2. Remove the upper starter-to-flywheel housing mounting screw.
3. Remove the two steering column lever cover screws.
4. Remove the mast jacket lower bracket screw.
5. Remove the upper steering column mounting bracket.
6. Disconnect the four electrical connectors from the steering column.
7. Raise the car on a hoist.
8. Disconnect the steering flexible coupling (rag joint) and push it aside.
9. Disconnect the wires from the starter solenoid.
10. Remove the brace screw from the bottom of the starter housing.
11. Remove the lower starter-to-flywheel housing mounting screw.
12. To gain clearance, raise the engine 1/2 in. with a jack placed under the left-side of the engine.
13. Remove the starter by lowering it through the opening at the bottom of the engine.
14. Installation is the reverse of removal.

IGNITION SYSTEM

All Chevette models are equipped with High Energy Ignition (HEI). This is a pulse triggered, transistor-controlled, inductive discharge ignition system that uses no breaker points. The HEI distributor contains a pick-up assembly and an electronic module which perform the function of breaker points. Centrifugal and vacuum advance mechanisms are basically the same as those in breaker point distributors. The capacitor in the distributor only serves to reduce radio noise. The ignition coil is mounted externally, on the left side of the engine, beneath the intake manifold, and is not visible on A/C equipped cars. The coil has a plastic cover.

Distributor mounting is at the front of the engine on the left-side.

HEI System Tachometer Hookup

Connect a tachometer to the negative terminal on the coil and to a ground. However, some tachometers must connect to the negative terminal and the battery positive terminal. Some old tachometers, without a relay, won't work at all with HEI. Check the tachometer manufacturer's instructions.

Distributor Replacement

1. If the vehicle is air conditioned: Disconnect the electrical lead at the air conditioning compressor. Remove the compressor mounting thru bolt and two adjusting bolts. Remove two bolts and remove the compressor upper mounting bracket. Raise the vehicle on a hoist. Remove the two bolts securing the compressor lower mounting bracket and pull the bracket outward for clearance. Lower the vehicle.
2. Remove the air cleaner.
3. Remove the distributor cap and place it aside.
4. Remove the ignition coil cover by prying on the flat on the front edge of the cover.
5. Remove the ignition coil mounting bracket bolts.
6. Disconnect the electrical connector with red and brown wires that goes from the ignition coil to the distributor.
7. Remove the fuel pump, gasket, and push rod, noting the direction in which push rod was installed.

NOTE: *It is important that the push rod be installed in exactly the same direction as removed.*

8. Scribe a mark on the engine in line with the distributor rotor. Note the approximate position of the distributor housing in relation to the engine.
9. Remove the distributor hold-down bolt and clamp.
10. Remove the distributor.
11. Install the distributor, making sure it is fully seated. Replace the distributor and fuel pump gaskets as required.

Ignition Timing

NOTE: *Use an adapter to make timing light connections at the distributor No. 1 terminal.*

1. Bring the engine to normal operating temperature. Stop the engine and connect a tachometer. Disconnect and plug the PCV hose at the vapor canister and the vacuum hose at the distributor vacuum advance unit. Start the engine and check curb idle speed. Adjust as necessary.
2. Stop the engine, clean the timing marks and mark them with chalk. Connect a timing light.
3. Start the engine and aim the timing light at the timing marks. If the marks align, stop the engine, reconnect the PCV and vacuum hoses, and remove the timing light.
4. If adjustment is necessary, loosen the distributor clamp and rotate the distributor to align the marks. Tighten the clamp and recheck the timing.

NOTE: *Air conditioned models require removal of the compressor, bracket, and belt to reach the distributor clamp.*

5. Reset the curb idle speed if necessary, stop the engine, and remove the tachometer and timing light. Reconnect the PCV and vacuum hoses.

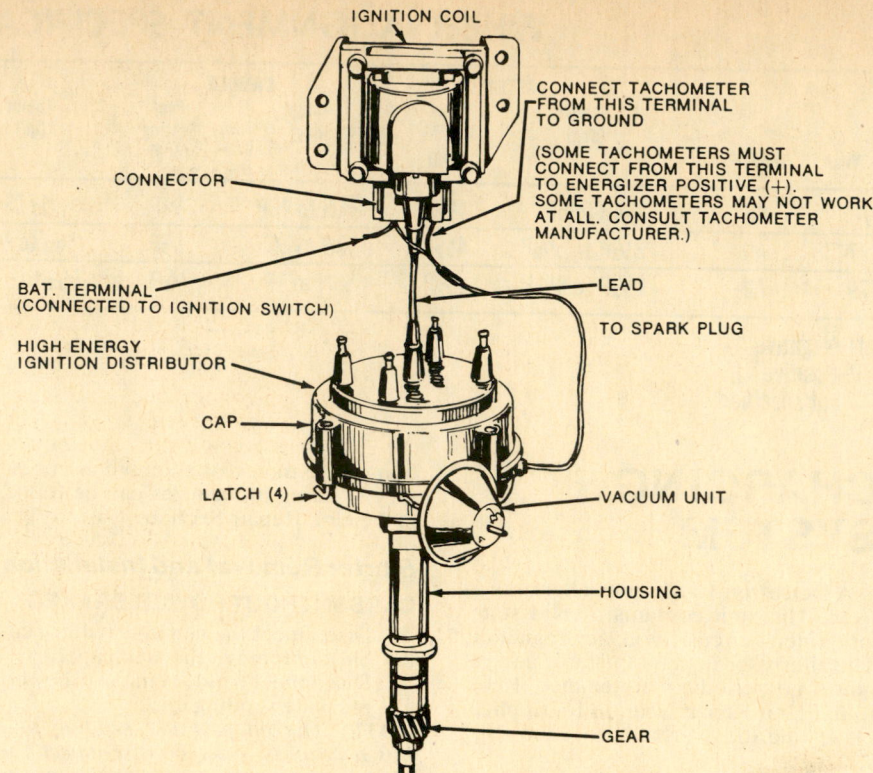

IGNITION COIL

CONNECT TACHOMETER FROM THIS TERMINAL TO GROUND

(SOME TACHOMETERS MUST CONNECT FROM THIS TERMINAL TO ENERGIZER POSITIVE (+). SOME TACHOMETERS MAY NOT WORK AT ALL. CONSULT TACHOMETER MANUFACTURER.)

CONNECTOR

BAT. TERMINAL (CONNECTED TO IGNITION SWITCH)

HIGH ENERGY IGNITION DISTRIBUTOR

CAP

LATCH (4)

LEAD

TO SPARK PLUG

VACUUM UNIT

HOUSING

GEAR

HEI tachometer hookup

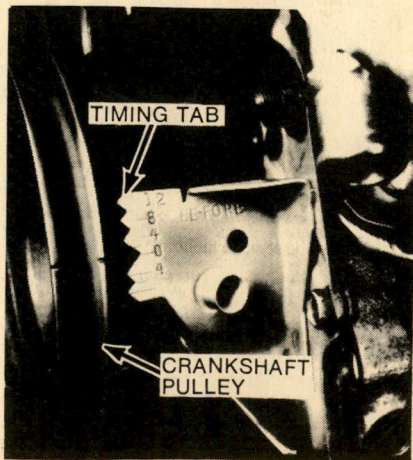

TIMING TAB

CRANKSHAFT PULLEY

Ignition timing marks
(© Chevrolet Div., G.M. Corp)

FUEL SYSTEM

All Chevette models use a Rochester 1ME Monojet carburetor. The carburetor has an electrically heated choke coil, an aluminum throttle body, and an electrically-operated idle speed solenoid. All models use dual throttle return springs and idle mixture screw limiter caps. An EGR vacuum port is located in the throttle body.

Fuel is filtered by an internal paper element located in the fuel bowl behind the fuel inlet nut. Also in the fuel inlet is a check valve to prevent fuel spillage in the event of a roll over accident.

The fuel pump is located on the left side of the engine under the intake manifold.

Fuel Pump Removal and Installation

NOTE: *Air conditioned cars require the removal of the rear compressor bracket to gain working room.*

1. Working from under the car, remove the ignition coil.
2. Disconnect the fuel inlet and outlet lines at the pump and plug the inlet line.
3. Remove the two pump mounting bolts and lockwashers and remove the fuel pump and gasket.
4. Install the fuel pump with a new gasket coated with sealer. Tighten the two mounting bolts.
5. Connect the fuel inlet and outlet lines at the pump. Install the ignition coil.

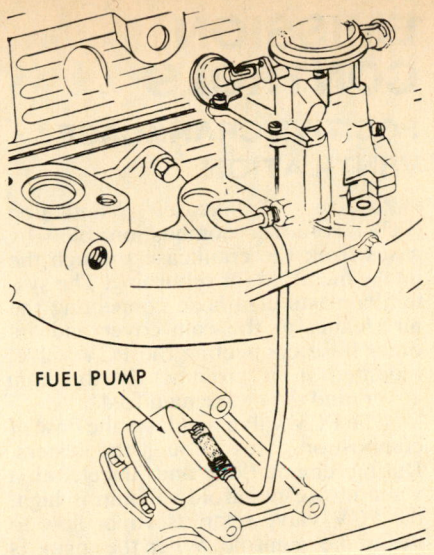

FUEL PUMP

Chevette fuel pump location (© Chevrolet Div., G.M. Corp.)

6. Start the engine and check for leaks.

Fuel Filter Removal and Installation

1. Disconnect the fuel line fitting at the carburetor fuel inlet nut.
2. Remove the fuel inlet nut from the carburetor.
3. Remove the fuel filter element and spring from the carburetor.
4. Install the spring and the fuel filter element into the carburetor.
5. With a new gasket on the fuel inlet nut, install the nut into the carburetor and tighten it securely.
6. Install the fuel line fitting into the fuel inlet nut and tighten securely.

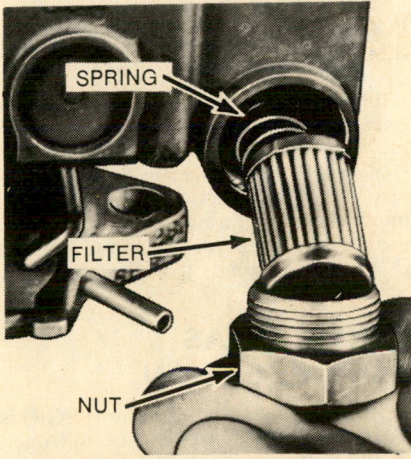

SPRING

FILTER

NUT

Fuel filter and check valve assembly (© Chevrolet Div., G.M. Corp.)

Idle Speed Adjustment

Two idle speeds are controlled by a solenoid on models without both automatic transmission and air conditioning. One is normal curb idle speed (solenoid energized). The second is low idle speed (solenoid de-energized) which prevents dieseling when the ignition is turned off. On cars with both automatic transmission and air conditioning the solenoid is energized when air conditioning is on to maintain curb idle speed.

WITHOUT BOTH A/C AND AUTOMATIC TRANSMISSION

1. The engine must be warmed up, the air cleaner on, the air conditioner off, the choke open, the parking brake on, manual transmission in neutral, automatic in Drive, the rear wheels blocked, the PCV hose disconnected and plugged at the canister, and the distributor vacuum advance hose disconnected and plugged at the distributor. Connet a tachometer.
2. Open the throttle momentarily to let the solenoid plunger extend. Turn the solenoid body nut to get the curb idle speed specified on the underhood specifications sticker or in the tune-up specifications chart.
3. Disconnect the solenoid wire. Use a 1/8 in. Allen wrench to turn the screw in the end of the solenoid to the specified low idle, or solenoid off, speed.
4. Reconnect the solenoid wire. Stop the engine and replace the hoses.

WITH BOTH A/C AND AUTOMATIC TRANSMISSION

1. The engine must be warmed up, the air cleaner on, the air conditioner on with the compressor lead disconnected, the choke open, the parking brake on, automatic transmission in Drive, the rear wheels blocked, the PCV hose disconnected and plugged at the canister, and the distributor vacuum advance hose disconnected and plugged at the distributor. Connect a tachometer. Open the throttle momentarily to let the solenoid plunger extend.
2. Turn the solenoid body nut to get an idle speed of 950 rpm.
3. Reconnect the compressor lead, and turn the air conditioner off.
4. Adjust the curb idle speed by turning the 1/8 in. Allen screw in the end of the solenoid.
5. Stop the engine and replace the hoses.

Idle Mixture Adjustment

THROUGH 1977

Carburetor idle mixture is present at the factory and a plastic limiter cap is mounted on the idle mixture screw. The cap limits the mixture screw to approximately one turn leaner (clockwise) without breaking the cap. Idle mixture should be adjusted at major carburetor overhaul.

1. With engine at normal operating temperature, air cleaner on, choke open, and air conditioning off, attach a tachometer to the engine. Apply parking brake, block the rear wheels, and disconnect and plug the PCV hose at vapor canister and vacuum advance hose at the distributor.
2. Start the engine and check ignition timing. Adjust timing as necessary. Replace vacuum advance hose.
3. Place automatic transmission in Drive or manual transmission in Neutral.
NOTE: *If the mixture screw is removed from the carburetor, gently seat it, then back it out 3 turns. Continue with Step 4.*
4. Remove the air cleaner and cut the tab off the limiter cap, but do not remove the cap from the screw. Replace the air cleaner. Obtain the maximum idle speed by turning the mixture screw clockwise (leaner) or counterclockwise (richer).
5. Turn the idle speed solenoid in or out to obtain the higher idle speed stated on the underhood tune-up specifications sticker.
6. While turning the idle mixture screw clockwise (leaner), watch the tachometer to obtain the lower idle speed stated on the underhood specifications sticker.
7. Stop engine, remove the tachometer, and replace the PCV and vacuum advance hoses.

1978 and later

Turning the mixture screw on these carburetors will have no appreciable effect. The factory-recommended idle mixture adjustment procedure requires special apparatus to artificially enrich the mixture with propane gas. This equipment is not available to, or practical for, the general public.

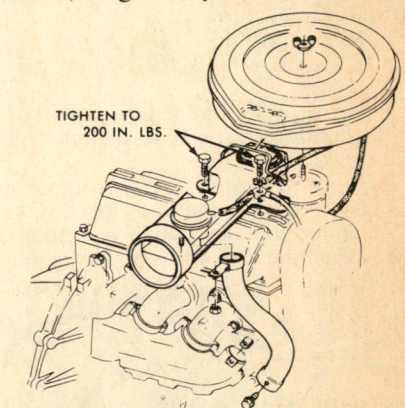

TIGHTEN TO 200 IN. LBS.

Air cleaner details (© Chevrolet Div., G.M. Corp.)

COOLING SYSTEM

A standard pressurized cooling system is used. A permanently-lubricated impeller-type water pump forces coolant through engine and cylinder head water jackets and into a cross-flow radiator. Some models use a heavy-duty radiator with a fan shroud. The pressure-type radiator cap pressurizes the cooling system to 15 psi. A 190°F thermostat in the coolant outlet passage is used to control coolant flow. A translucent plastic coolant recovery reservoir is used to provide for coolant expansion. Coolant level is checked by observing the amount present in the reservoir with the engine at normal operating temperature. Add coolant to the reservoir, not the radiator. A 50/50 mixture of ethylene glycol antifreeze and water yielding freeze protection to —20°F should be used as coolant.

Radiator Removal and Installation

1. Drain the radiator.
2. Disconnect the upper and lower radiator hoses and the coolant recovery reservoir hose.
3. Remove the radiator baffle or shroud. Remove the baffle by removing the four baffle-to-radiator support screws. Remove the shroud by removing the two upper screws and the two middle screws. Remove the upper radiator shroud. The lower shroud is removed from its mounting clips.
4. Disconnect and plug the transmission cooler lines if necessary.
5. Remove the radiator upper mounting panel or brackets and lift the radiator out of the lower brackets.
6. To install, reverse the removal procedure. Fill the system and run the engine with the heater on until the thermostat opens. Recheck the level.

Water Pump Removal and Installation

1. Disconnect the battery negative cable and remove the engine drive belt(s).
2. Remove the engine fan, spacer (air conditioned models), and the pulley.
3. Remove the timing belt front cover by removing the two upper bolts, center bolt, and two lower nuts.
4. Drain the coolant from the engine.

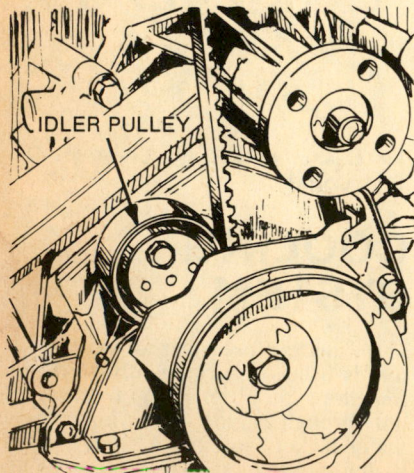

Timing belt idler pulley

5. Remove the lower radiator hose and the heater hose at the water pump.
6. Turn the crankshaft pulley so that the mark on the pulley is aligned with the 0 mark on the timing scale and that a 1/8 in. drill bit can be inserted through the timing belt upper rear cover and camshaft sprocket.
7. Remove the idler pulley and pull the timing belt off the sprocket. Don't disturb crankshaft position.
8. Remove the water pump retaining bolts and remove the pump and gasket from the engine.
9. Clean all the old gasket material from the cylinder case.
10. With a new gasket in place on the water pump, position the water pump in place on the cylinder case and install the water pump retaining bolts.
11. Install the timing belt onto the cam sprocket.
12. Apply sealer to the idler pulley attaching bolt and install the bolt and the idler pulley. Turn the idler pulley counterclockwise on its mounting bolt to remove the slack in the timing belt.
13. Use a tension gauge to adjust timing belt tension. Check belt tension midway between the tensioner and the cam sprocket on the idler pulley side. Correct belt tension is 55 lbs. Torque the idler pulley mounting bolt to 13-18 ft. lbs.
14. Remove the 1/8 in. drill bit from the upper rear timing belt cover and cam sprocket.
15. Install the lower radiator hose and the heater hose to the water pump.
16. Install the timing belt front cover.
17. Install the water pump pulley, spacer (if equipped), and engine fan.
18. Install the engine drive belt(s).
19. Refill the cooling system.
20. Connect the battery negative cable.
21. Start the engine and check for leaks. Run the engine with the heater on until the thermostat opens, the recheck the coolant level.

Thermostat Removal and Installation

1. Drain the radiator and remove the upper radiator hose at the water outlet.
2. Remove the thermostat housing bolts and remove the housing, gasket, and thermostat.
3. Install the thermostat. Use a new gasket on the thermostat housing and install the thermostat housing bolts.
4. Install the upper radiator hose at the water outlet.
5. Fill the cooling system. Run the engine with the heater on until the thermostat opens, then recheck the coolant level.

EMISSION CONTROLS

POSITIVE CRANKCASE VENTILATION

Positive Crankcase Ventilation (PCV) reroutes combustion blow-by gases from the crankcase through the intake manifold for reburning. The system consists of a hose connecting the air cleaner to the cam cover and another hose connecting the PCV valve, mounted in a grommet in the cam cover, and the intake manifold.

The PCV valve regulates the flow of combustion gases through the system. During engine idle and deceleration when intake manifold vacuum is high, the PCV valve restricts vapor flow to the intake manifold. When the engine is accelerated or is at constant speed, intake manifold vacuum is low and the PCV valve allows crankcase gases to flow into the intake manifold. Should the engine backfire, the plunger inside the valve is forced against its seat preventing the backfire from traveling through the PCV valve and into the engine crankcase.

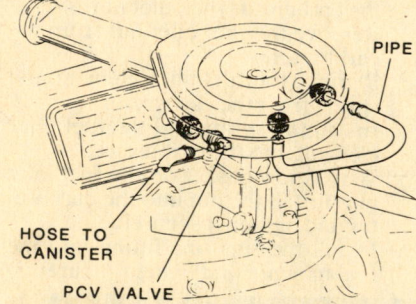

PCV system details (© Chevrolet Div., G.M. Corp.)

The PCV valve is checked for proper operation simply by removing it from the grommet in the cam cover and shaking. If the plunger in the valve rattles, the valve is good. At the specified intervals, install a new PCV valve and use compressed air to blow out the PCV valve hose to eliminate any restriction.

EXHAUST GAS RECIRCULATION

Exhaust Gas Recirculation (EGR) is used to reduce oxides of nitrogen (NOx) exhaust emissions. NOx formation occurs at very high combustion temperatures so that the EGR system reduces combustion temperature slightly by introducing small amounts of inert exhaust gas into the intake manifold. The result is reduced formation of NOx.

An EGR valve is mounted on the intake manifold. It contains a vacuum diaphragm and is operated by intake manifold vacuum to control the flow of

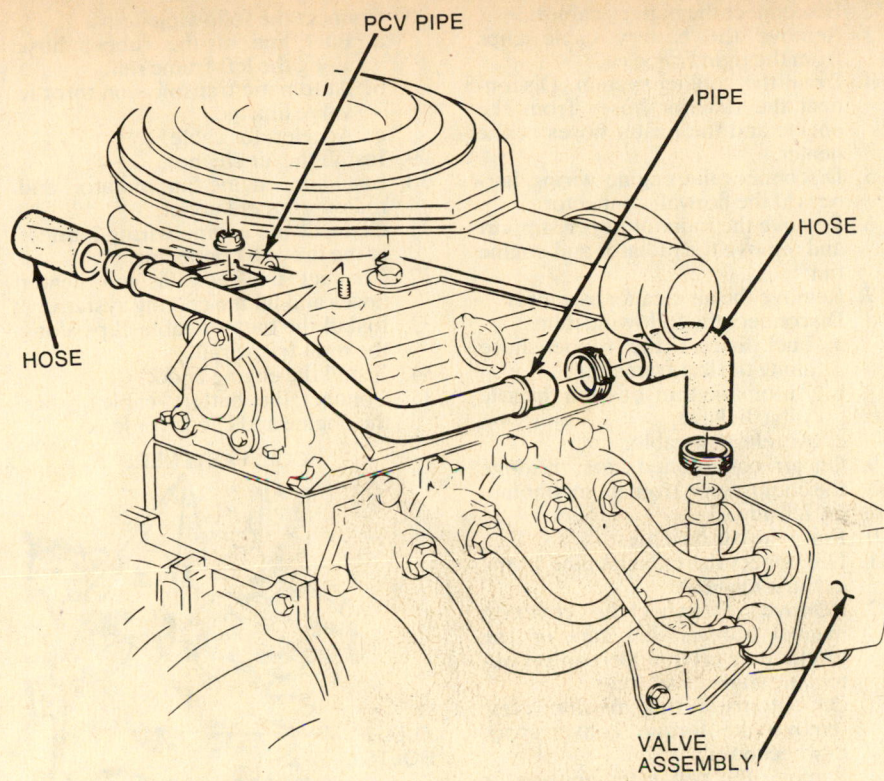

Pulse air system (© Chevrolet Div., G.M. Corp)

high rpm operation, the valve will remain closed.

EVAPORATIVE EMISSION CONTROL

The Evaporative Control System (ECS) limits gasoline vapor escape into the atmosphere. A domed fuel tank and pressure-vacuum filler cap is used with a plastic, charcoal-filled storage canister.

Fuel vapors travel from the fuel tank vent pipe (located above fuel level in the dome of the fuel tank), by way of steel tubing and fuel-resistant rubber hose to the plastic vapor storage canister in the engine compartment. Fuel vapors are routed into the PCV system for burning when carburetor vacuum operates a valve in the canister. As fuel is pumped from the tank, a relief valve in the tank cap opens to allow air to enter the fuel tank.

CONTROLLED COMBUSTION SYSTEM

The Controlled Combustion System (CCS) increases combustion efficiency by way of leaner carburetor mixtures and revised distributor calibration. Also, a thermostatically - controlled damper in the air cleaner snorkel maintains warm air intake to the carburetor to optimize fuel vaporization.

An air intake duct routes air from the radiator support to the air cleaner snorkel, then to the 50,000 mile, one-piece air cleaner. Air temperature is automatically controlled by a thermostatic damper inside the air cleaner snorkel. The damper selects warm air from the exhaust manifold heat stove when air temperature is below 50°F. When air temperature is above 110°F, the damper selects outside air from the air intake duct.

When replacing the 50,000 mile air cleaner, remove the air cleaner from the air intake snorkel and the carbure-

exhaust gases. A vacuum signal supply port is located in the throttle body of the carburetor above the throttle plate. Vacuum is supplied to the EGR valve (causing recirculation), at part-throttle conditions. EGR does not occur at idle or at wide open throttle. A 0.030 in. orifice in the EGR valve vacuum tube further regulates vacuum.

Some models also use a thermal vacuum switch (TVS), mounted in the water outlet housing to block vacuum to the EGR valve until engine coolant temperature is approximately 100°F.

AIR INJECTION REACTOR

The Air Injection Reactor (AIR) system reduces carbon monoxide and unburned hydrocarbon emissions by injecting air into the exhaust system after the exhaust valves. The AIR system is used on some California cars only. The system consists of an air pump, air injection tubes (one for each cylinder), a vacuum differential valve, an air by-pass valve, a differential vacuum delay and separator valve, a check valve, and the required hoses to connect the components.

The air pump (with an integral filter), compresses and injects the air through the air manifolds into the exhaust system to the rear of the exhaust valves. The additional air brings about further combustion of hydrocarbons and carbon monoxide in the exhaust manifold. The vacuum differential valve stops air injection to prevent backfiring during engine deceleration by activating the air by-pass valve. The vacuum differen-

tial valve is triggered by sharp increases in manifold vacuum. On engine deceleration total air pump output is vented to the atmosphere through a muffler in the air by-pass valve. Also in the air by-pass valve is a pressure relief valve which vents excess air from the air pump at high engine speeds. The by-pass valve also vents air through its muffler at times of low intake manifold vacuum (engine acceleration). This low manifold vacuum venting is controlled by the differential vacuum delay and separator valve which blocks this venting for very short periods of 20 seconds or less, to prevent possible overheating of the catalytic converter. The check valve prevents exhaust gases from entering the air pump.

PULSE AIR SYSTEM (PAIR)

Some 1977 and later Chevettes are equipped with the PAIR system. This is a greatly simplified air injection system, replacing AIR. It consists of a pulse air valve which has four check valves, one for each exhaust port. The firing of the engine creates a pulsating flow of gases which have positive or negative pressure, depending on whether the exhaust valve is seated or not. If the pressure is positive, the check valve is forced closed and no exhaust gas will flow past the valve and into the fresh air supply line. If there is negative pressure, the check valve will open and fresh air will be drawn in and mixed with the exhaust gases. During

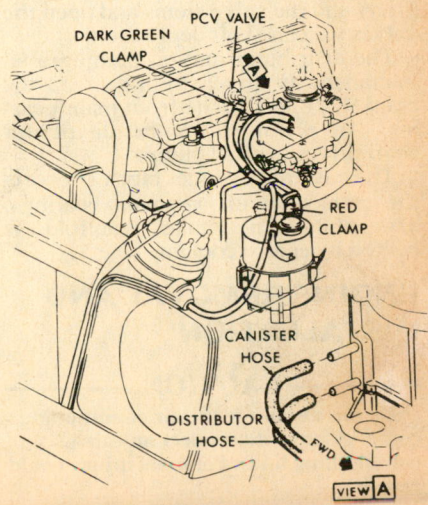

ECS canister and lines
(© Chevrolet Div., G.M. Corp)

tor and throw it away. Check the carburetor air horn gasket and replace it if damaged or cracked, and install a new air cleaner.

CATALYTIC CONVERTER

All models are equipped with an underfloor catalytic converter. The converter contains pellets coated with the catalyst material containing platinum and palladium. The converter reduces hydrocarbon and carbon monoxide emissions by transforming them into carbon dioxide and water through a chemical reaction which takes place at high temperature.

Unleaded fuel only must be used with converter equipped cars because lead in leaded fuel is not consumed in the combustion process and will enter the converter and coat the pellets, eventually rendering the catalytic converter useless for emission control. There is also the possibility of the converter clogging, causing excessive exhaust back pressure and poor performance. To ensure the use of unleaded fuel only, all models have a small diameter fuel inlet filler which will accept only the smaller unleaded fuel nozzle.

See Emission Control Systems in the Unit Repair Section for additional information on emission controls.

ENGINE

All Chevette models are powered by a 1.4 or 1.6 liter inline four-cylinder overhead camshaft engine of 85 or 98 cu. in. respectively. A high output (HO) version of the 1.6 engine was added in 1978.

The belt-driven camshaft is supported on five bearing surfaces in an aluminum carrier on top of the cast iron cylinder head. The crossflow cylinder head has induction-hardened exhaust valve seats for greater durability. Rocker arms bridge hydraulic valve lifters and the valve stems and open the valves via camshaft depression.

The distributor and oil pump are simultaneously driven by a gear on the crankshaft next to the front main bearing. An eccentric on the distributor shaft drives the fuel pump.

The cast iron cylinder block supports the crankshaft in five main bearings. The aluminum intake manifold is heated by engine coolant.

ENGINE REMOVAL AND INSTALLATION

--- CAUTION ---
Do not discharge the air conditioning compressor or disconnect any air conditioning lines. Personal injury could result.

1. Remove the engine hood from the car.

2. Disconnect the battery cables.
3. Remove the battery cable clips from the right frame rail.
4. Drain the cooling system. Disconnect the radiator hoses from the engine and the heater hoses at the heater.
5. Disconnect the engine wiring harness at the firewall connector.
6. Remove the radiator upper support and remove the radiator and engine fan.
7. Remove the air cleaner assembly.
8. Disconnect the following items:
   a. Fuel line at the rubber hose along the left frame rail.
   b. Automatic transmission throttle valve linkage.
   c. Accelerator cable.
9. On air conditioned cars, remove the compressor from its mount and lay it aside.
10. Raise the car on a hoist.
11. Disconnect the exhaust pipe at the exhaust manifold.
12. Remove the flywheel dust cover on manual transmission cars or the torque converter underpan on automatic transmission cars.
13. On automatic transmission cars, remove the torque converter-to-flywheel bolts.
14. Remove the converter housing or flywheel housing-to-engine retaining bolts and lower the car.
15. Position a floor jack or other suitable support under the transmission.
16. Remove the safety straps from the front engine mounts and remove the mount nuts.
17. Install the engine lifting apparatus.
18. Remove the engine by pulling forward to clear the transmission while lifting slowly. Check to make sure that all necessary disconnections have been made and that proper clearance exists with surrounding components. Remove the lifting apparatus.

To install the engine:
19. Install the engine lifting apparatus and install guide pins in the engine block.
20. Install the engine in the car by aligning the engine with the transmission housing.
21. Install the front engine mount nuts and safety straps.
22. Raise the car on a hoist.
23. Install the engine-to-transmission housing bolts. Torque them to 25 ft. lbs.
24. On automatic transmission cars, install the torque converter to the flywheel. Torque the bolts to 35 ft. lbs.
25. Install the flywheel dust cover or torque converter underpan as applicable.
26. Install the exhaust pipe to the exhaust manifold and lower the car.
27. Install the air conditioning compressor if necessary, and adjust drive belt tension.

28. Connect the following items:
   a. Fuel line at the rubber hose along the left frame rail.
   b. Automatic transmission throttle valve linkage.
   c. Accelerator cable.
29. Install the air cleaner.
30. Install the engine fan, radiator, and radiator upper support.
31. Connect the engine wiring harness at the firewall connector.
32. Connect the radiator and heater hoses and fill the cooling system.
33. Install the battery cable clips along the right frame rail.
34. Install the engine hood.
35. Connect the battery cables, start the engine and check for leaks.

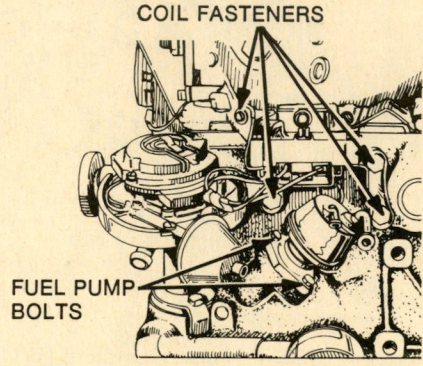

Fuel pump and coil bolt locations

MANIFOLDS

Intake Manifold Removal and Installation

1. Disconnect the battery ground.
2. Drain the cooling system.
3. Remove the air cleaner.
4. Disconnect the upper radiator and heater hoses.
5. Remove the EGR valve.
6. Disconnect all electrical wiring, vacuum hoses and the accelerator linkage from the carburetor.
7. Disconnect the fuel line from the carburetor.
8. If the car is equipped with A/C:
   a. Remove the upper radiator support.
   b. Remove the alternator and compressor drive belts and the compressor adjusting bolts.
   c. Remove the fan and pulley.
   d. Remove the timing belt cover.
   e. Move the compressor out of the way without disconnecting the refrigerant lines.
   f. Raise the car and remove the lower compressor brackets.
   g. Lower the car and remove the upper compressor brackets.
9. Remove the coil.
10. Remove the manifold.
11. If installing a new manifold, transfer all good parts. Installation is the reverse of removal. Torque all bracket bolts to 30 ft. lbs., and intake manifold bolts to the specified torque.

Exhaust Manifold Removal and Installation

1. Disconnect the battery ground.
2. Raise the vehicle and support it on stands.
3. Disconnect the exhaust pipe from the flange.
4. Lower the vehicle.
5. Remove the carburetor heat tube.
6. Remove the pulse air tubing, if any.
7. Remove the manifold.
8. Installation is the reverse of removal. Tighten the bolts to the specified torque.

VALVE SYSTEM

Valve operation is accomplished by rocker arms bridging hydraulic lash adjusters and the valve stems being depressed by the camshaft.

Adjustment of the hydraulic valve lash adjusters is not possible.

Cleanliness should be exercised when handling the valve lash adjusters. Before installation of lash adjusters, check the lash adjuster oil hole in the cylinder head to make sure that it is free of foreign matter and fill the lash adjusters with oil.

Rocker Arm Removal and Installation

NOTE: *A special valve spring compressor is necessary for this procedure. Also prelubricate new rocker arms and contacting parts with engine assembly lubricant.*

1. Remove the camshaft cover.
2. Using the special valve spring compressor, compress the valve springs and remove the rocker arms. Keep the rocker arms and guides in order so that they can be installed in their original locations.
3. To install the rocker arms, compress the valve springs and install the rocker arm guides.
4. Position the rocker arms in the guides and on the valve lash adjusters.
5. Install the camshaft cover.

Valve Guides

Valve with oversize stems are available. To install, remove the cylinder head and remove the camshaft from the head. The valve guides must be reamed to fit the oversize valves.

Cylinder Head Removal and Installation

1. Remove the timing belt.
2. Drain the cooling system and disconnect the upper radiator hose and heater hose at the intake manifold.
3. Remove the air cleaner and snorkel (silencer) assembly.
4. Remove the accelerator cable support bracket.
5. Disconnect the spark plug wires.
6. Disconnect the wires from the idle solenoid, choke, temperature sender, and alternator.
7. Raise the car on a hoist and disconnect the exhaust pipe from the exhaust manifold.
8. Lower the car.
9. Remove the dipstick tube bracket-to-manifold attaching bolt.
10. Disconnect the fuel line at the carburetor.
11. Take off the coil cover. Remove the coil bracket bolts and lay the coil aside.
12. Remove the camshaft cover.
13. Remove the camshaft cover-to-camshaft housing attaching studs.
14. Remove the rocker arms, rocker arm guides, and valve lash adjusters. Keep the parts in order so that they can be installed in their original locations.
15. Remove the camshaft carrier bolts and remove the camshaft carrier. A sharp wedge may be necessary to separate the camshaft carrier from the cylinder head. Be very cautious not to damage the mating surfaces.
16. Remove the manifold and cylinder head assembly.

To install the cylinder head:

17. Install a new cylinder head gasket with the words This Side Up facing up over dowel pins in the block. Make sure that the gasket is absolutely clean.
18. Install the manifold and cylinder head assembly.
19. Apply a light, thin continuous bead of sealant to the joining surfaces of the cylinder head and the camshaft carrier and install the camshaft carrier. Clean any excess sealer from the cylinder head. Apply sealing compound to the camshaft carrier/cylinder head bolts and install the bolts finger-tight. Tighten the bolts a little at a time and in the proper sequence until the final specified torque figure is reached.

```
         7    3    2    6   10
F       ┌─────────────────────┐
R       │  O    O    O    O    O │
O       │                       │
N       │  O    O    O .  O    O │
T       └─────────────────────┘
         8    4    1    5    9
```

1.4 and 1.6 liter cylinder head torque sequence (© Chevrolet Div., G.M. Corp)

20. Install the camshaft cover-to-camshaft housing attaching studs.
21. Install the valve lash adjusters and rocker arm guides. Prelube the rocker arms with engine assembly lubricant and install the rocker arms.
22. Using new gaskets, install the camshaft covers.
23. Install the coil bracket mounting bolt.
24. Connect the fuel line to the carburetor.
25. Install the dipstick tube bracket-to-manifold attaching bolt.
26. Raise the car on a hoist and attach the exhaust pipe to the exhaust manifold.
27. Lower the car.
28. Connect the wires to the idle solenoid, choke, temperature sender, and alternator.
29. Connect the spark plug wires.
30. Apply Teflon tape or its equivalent to the threads of the accelerator cable support bracket attaching bolts and install the bracket.
31. Install the air cleaner and snorkel (silencer) assembly.
32. Connect the upper radiator hose and heater hose to the intake manifold.
33. Fill the cooling system.
34. Install the timing belt.

TIMING COVER, BELT, AND CAMSHAFT

Timing Belt Cover Removal and Installation

UPPER FRONT COVER

1. Disconnect the negative battery cable. Remove the radiator upper mounting panel or fan shroud.
2. Remove engine accessory drive belts.
3. Remove the engine fan.
4. Remove the cover retaining screws and nuts and remove the cover.

To install the cover:

5. Align the screw slots on the upper and lower parts of the cover.
6. Install the cover retaining screws and nuts.
7. Install the engine fan.
8. Install the engine accessory drive belts.
9. Connect the negative battery cable.

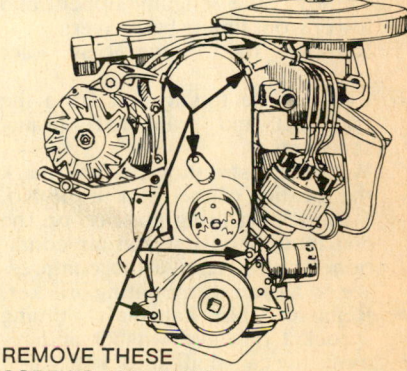

REMOVE THESE
SCREWS AND NUTS

Timing belt fasteners

LOWER FRONT COVER

1. Disconnect the negative battery cable.
2. Remove the crankshaft pulley.
3. Remove the upper front timing belt cover.
4. Remove the one cover-to-block retaining nut.
5. To install the cover, align the cover with the studs on the engine block.

6. Install the lower front cover retaining nut.
7. Install the upper front timing belt cover.
8. Install the crankshaft pulley. Torque the retaining bolt to the specified torque.

UPPER REAR COVER

1. Disconnect the negative battery cable.
2. Remove the upper and lower front cover, the timing belt, and the camshaft timing sprocket.
3. Remove the three screws retaining the camshaft sprocket cover to the camshaft carrier.
4. Inspect the condition of the cam seal.
5. Position and align a new gasket over the end of the camshaft and against the camshaft carrier.
6. Install the three camshaft sprocket cover retaining screws.
7. Install the camshaft sprocket, timing belt, and the upper and lower front covers.
8. Connect the negative battery cable.

Timing Belt and Sprockets Removal and Installation

——— CAUTION ———

Do not discharge the air conditioning compressor or disconnect the air conditioning lines. Personal injury could result.

1. Disconnect the negative battery cable.
2. Remove the alternator and air conditioning compressor (if equipped) drive belts.
3. Remove the engine fan and pulley.
4. Remove the engine upper and lower front timing belt covers.
5. Remove the timing belt idler pulley.
6. Remove the timing belt from the camshaft and crankshaft timing sprockets.
7. With the distributor cap off, mark the location of the rotor in the No. 1 spark plug firing position on the distributor housing. On air conditioned cars, remove the compressor and lower its mounting bracket.
8. Remove the camshaft timing sprocket bolt and washer and remove the camshaft sprocket.
9. Remove the crankshaft sprocket.
  To install:
10. Place the crankshaft sprocket on the crankshaft making sure that the locating dowels face outward.
11. Install the crankshaft sprocket.
12. Align the camshaft sprocket dowel with the hole in the end of the camshaft and install the sprocket on the camshaft.
13. Apply thread locking compound to the camshaft sprocket retaining bolt and washer and torque to 65-85 ft. lbs.

14. Position the timing belt over the crankshaft sprocket.
15. Install the crankshaft pulley.
16. Align the crankshaft pulley timing mark with the 0 mark on the timing scale and the distributor rotor with the scribed mark on the distributor housing.

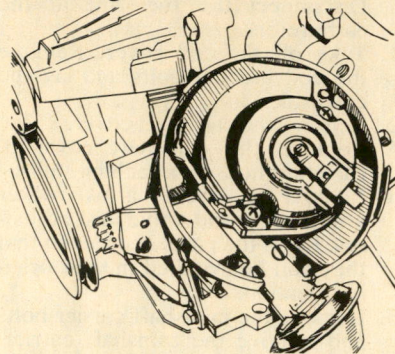

Correct distributor rotor alignment for timing belt installation

17. Align the hole in the camshaft sprocket with the hole in the upper rear timing belt cover. Insert a 1/8 in. drill bit to hold the sprocket in alignment.

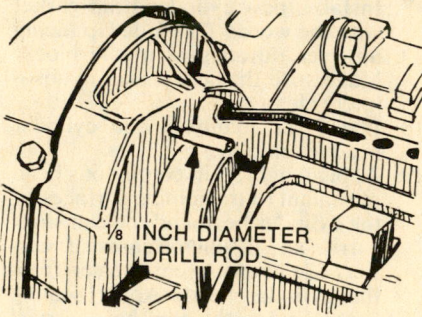

1/8 INCH DIAMETER DRILL ROD

Correct camshaft sprocket alignment for timing belt installation

18. Install the timing belt on the camshaft and crankshaft sprockets.
19. To adjust timing belt tension see the adjustment procedure.
20. Install the distributor cap. On air conditioned cars, install the lower compressor bracket and the compressor.
21. Install the upper and lower front timing belt covers.
22. Install the engine fan and pulley.
23. Install the alternator and, if necessary, the air conditioning compressor drive belts.
24. Connect the negative battery cable.

Timing Belt Adjustment

1. Remove the fan, fan belt, water pump pulley and upper cam belt cover.
2. Rotate the crankshaft clockwise a minimum of one revolution. Stop with No. 1 piston at TDC. **DO NOT TURN THE ENGINE BACKWARD!**
3. Install a belt tension gauge on the same side as the idler pulley, mid-

way between the cam sprocket and the idler pulley. Be sure that the center finger of the gauge extension fits in a notch between the teeth on the belt. Correct belt tension is 40-60 lbs. for 1976, 50-80 lbs. for 1977 and later.
4. If the tension is incorrect, loosen the idler pulley attaching bolt and, using a 1/4 in. Allen wrench, rotate the pulley counterclockwise on its attaching bolt until the proper tension is obtained. Torque the bolt to 15 ft. lbs.
5. Replace all parts.

Camshaft Removal and Installation.

NOTE: *A special valve spring compressor is necessary for this procedure. If replacing the camshaft or rocker arms, prelube new parts with engine assembly lubricant.*

1. Disconnect the negative battery cable.
2. Remove engine accessory drive belts.
3. Remove the engine fan and pulley.
4. Remove the upper and lower front timing belt covers.
5. Loosen the idler pulley and remove the timing belt from the camshaft sprocket.
6. Remove the camshaft sprocket attaching bolt and washer and remove the camshaft sprocket.
7. Remove the camshaft cover. Using the special valve spring compressor, remove the rocker arms and guides. Keep the rocker arms and guides in order so that they can be installed in their original locations.
8. Remove any components necessary to gain working clearance.

NOTE: *The heater assembly will probably have to be removed from the firewall.*

9. Remove the camshaft carrier rear cover.
10. Remove the camshaft thrust plate bolts. Slide the camshaft slightly to the rear and remove the thrust plate.
11. Remove the engine mount nuts and wire retainers.
12. Using a floor jack, raise the front of the engine.
13. Remove the camshaft from the camshaft carrier. Heavy pressure will be needed to pull the camshaft and seal forward.
  To install:
14. Install the camshaft into the camshaft carrier.
15. Lower the engine.
16. Install the engine mount nuts and attach the retaining wires.
17. Slide the camshaft to the rear and install the thrust plate. Slide the camshaft forward and install the carrier rear cover.
18. Position and align a new gasket over the end of the camshaft, against the camshaft carrier.

19. Install any components which were removed to gain working clearance.
20. Install the valve rocker arms and guides in their original locations using the special valve spring compressor.
Install the camshaft covers.
21. Align the dowel in the camshaft sprocket with the hole in the end of the camshaft and install the sprocket.
22. Apply thread locking compound to the sprocket retaining bolt threads and install the bolt and washer. Torque the sprocket retaining bolt to 65-85 ft. lbs.
23. Turn the crankshaft clockwise to bring the No. 1 cylinder to top dead center. Make sure that the distributor rotor is in position to fire the No. 1 spark plug. Aligh the hole in the camshaft sprocket with the hole in the upper rear timing belt cover and install the timing belt on the camshaft sprocket.
24. Adjust timing belt tension as described previously.
25. Install the upper and lower front timing belt covers.
26. Install the engine fan and pulley.
27. Install the engine accessory drive belts.
28. Connect the negative battery cable.

PISTONS AND CONNECTING RODS

Install piston and connecting rod assemblies into their original cylinders. Install the piston and rod assemblies with the notch on the piston crown facing to the front of the engine. The numbers on the connecting rods and bearing caps must be on the same side when installing pistons and connecting rods.

LUBRICATION

Oil Pan Removal and Installation

NOTE: *This procedure requires removal of the heater assembly. On cars with air conditioning, discharge of the A/C system is required. Unless you are trained in air conditioning system maintenance, it is recommended that this not be attempted.*
1. On cars without A/C:
   a. disconnect the battery ground.
   b. drain the cooling system.
   c. Disconnect the heater hoses at the core connections and plug the tubes.
   d. remove the screws from the heater core cover perimeter and remove the core cover.
   e. remove the core from the case.
2. On cars with air conditioning:
   a. discharge the system.
   b. disconnect the battery ground.
   c. remove the core case-to-distributor assembly screws and roll the assembly forward and away from the case.

d. remove the accumulator and brackets.
e. remove the insulation and clamp from the sensing element of the thermostatic switch.
f. bend the sensing capillary tube forward, away from the case.
g. remove the temperature door cable and door arm access cover. Position the door so as not to interfere with removal of the upper case cover.
h. remove the blower motor.
i. remove the sealer around the exposed portion of the outlet tube located at the upper case surface.
j. remove the upper evaporator case cover attaching screws and remove the upper case.
k. remove the core.
3. Remove the motor mount nuts and wire restraints.
4. Remove the upper radiator support and fan shroud.
5. Disconnect the fuel line from the canister.
6. Drain the oil.
7. Remove the flywheel splash shield.
8. On cars with manual transmission, remove the rack and pinion-to-front crossmember attaching bolts.
9. Loosen the rear converter-to-exhaust pipe clamp.
10. Raise the engine with a jack and lifting adapter under the ears at the front of the block.
11. Remove the oil pan bolts.
12. On cars with manual transmission:
    a. lower the oil pan about 1 in.
    b. rotate the front of the pan right and the rear left.
    c. tilt the pan 45° and remove it.
13. Installation is the reverse of removal. On cars with A/C, evacuate, charge, and leak test the system. Sealant should be applied to the area where the pan gasket meets the crankcase cover and the rear main cap meets the block.

NOTE: *Early production oil pans, through about January, 1977, have a raised center sealing bead around the pan rail; these may be used either with a gasket or with RTV (room temperature vulcanizing) sealant. Later pans do not have the sealing bead; these should be used only with RTV sealant.*

Oil Pump Removal and Installation
1. Remove the ignition coil attaching bolts and lay the coil aside.
2. Raise the car and remove the fuel pump, pushrod, and gasket.
3. Lower the car and remove the distributor. On air conditioned cars, remove the compressor mounting bolts and lay it aside. Do not disconnect any refrigerant lines.
4. Raise the car and remove the oil pan.
5. Remove the oil pump pipe and screen assembly clamp and remove the bolts attaching the pipe and

screen assembly.
6. Remove the pipe and screen assembly from the oil pump.
7. Remove the pick-up tube seal from the oil pump.
8. Remove the oil pump attaching bolts and remove the oil pump.
To install:
9. Install the oil pump. Torque the oil pump bolts to 45-60 in lbs.
NOTE: *Make certain that the pilot on the oil pump engages the case.*
10. Install the pick-up tube seal in the oil pump.
11. Install the pick-up pipe and screen assembly in the oil pump and install the pick-up pipe and screen clamp. Torque the clamp bolt to 70-95 in. lbs. Torque the pick-up tube and screen mounting bolt to 19-25 ft. lbs.
12. Install the oil pan.
13. Lower the car and install the distributor.
14. Raise the car and install the fuel pump with gasket and pushrod.
15. Lower the car and install the ignition coil.

Rear Main Oil Seal Replacement
1. Remove the engine from the car and place it in a stand.
2. Remove the oil pan.
3. Remove the rear main bearing cap.
4. Clean the bearing cap and case.
5. Check the crankshaft seal for excessive wear, etc.
6. Install a new crankshaft seal. Make sure that it is properly seated against the rear main bearing seal bulkhead.
7. Apply RTV sealer or its equivalent to the bearing cap horizontal split line.
8. With the sealer still wet, install the rear main bearing cap. Tighten the cap bolts to the specified torque.
9. Apply RTV sealer or its equivalent in the vertical grooves of the rear main bearing cap.
10. Remove any excess sealer and install the oil pan. Torque the oil pan bolts to 45-60 in. lbs.
11. Install the engine in the car.

CLUTCH

Chevette manual transmission models use a cable-operated diaphragm spring-type clutch. The clutch cable is attached to the clutch pedal at its upper end and is threaded at its lower end where it attaches to the clutch fork. The clutch release fork pivots on a ball stud located opposite the clutch cable attaching point. The pressure plate, clutch disc, and throwout bearing are of conventional design.

When the clutch pedal is depressed, the clutch release fork pivots on the ball stud and pushes the throwout bearing forward. The throwout bearing presses against the inner ends of the pressure plate diaphragm spring fingers to release pressure on the clutch disc, disengaging the clutch. The return spring preloads the clutch release mechanism to remove any looseness. Clutch pedal free-play will increase with release mechanism wear and will decrease with clutch disc wear.

Clutch Disc Removal and Installation

1. Raise the car on a hoist.
2. Remove the transmission.
3. Remove the throwout bearing from the clutch fork by sliding the fork off the ball stud against spring tension. If the ball stud is to be replaced, remove the locknut and stud from the bellhousing.
4. If the balance marks on the pressure plate and the flywheel are not easily seen, remark them with paint or a centerpunch.
5. Alternately loosen the pressure plate-to-flywheel attaching bolts one turn at a time until spring tension is released.
6. Support the pressure plate and cover assembly, then remove the bolts and the clutch assembly.

CAUTION

Do not disassemble the clutch cover and pressure plate for repair. If defective, replace the assembly.

---

7. Align the balance marks on the clutch assembly and the flywheel. Place the clutch disc on the pressure plate with the long end of the splined hub facing forward and the damper springs inside the pressure plate. Insert a dummy shaft through the cover and clutch disc.
8. Position the assembly against the flywheel and insert the dummy shaft into the pilot bearing in the crankshaft.
9. Align the balance marks and install the pressure plate-to-flywheel bolts finger-tight.

CAUTION

Tighten all bolts evenly and gradually until tight to avoid possible clutch distortion. Torque the bolts to 18 ft. lbs. and remove the dummy shaft.

---

10. Pack the groove on the inside of the throwout bearing with graphite grease. Also coat the fork groove and ball stud depression with the lubricant.
11. Install the throwout bearing and release fork assembly in the bellhousing with the fork spring hooked under the ball stud and the fork spring fingers inside the bearing groove.
12. Position the transmission and clutch housing and install the clutch housing attaching bolts and lockwashers. Torque the bolts to 25 ft. lbs.
13. Complete the transmission installation.

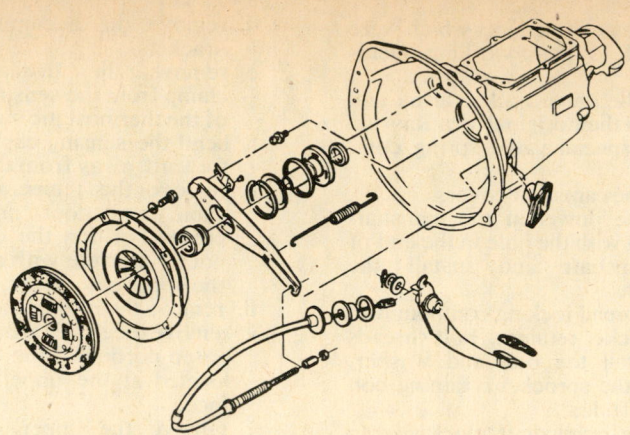

Clutch assembly (© Chevrolet Div., G.M. Corp)

CAUTION

Check the position of the engine in the front mounts and realign as necessary.

NOTE: *A special gauge (J-23644 or J-28449) is necessary to adjust ball stud position if it has been removed.*

14. Adjust clutch pedal free-play.
15. Lower the car and check operation of the clutch and transmission.

Clutch Pedal Free-Play Adjustment

1976-77

Adjustment for normal wear is made by turning the release fork ball stud counterclockwise to give 0.812 ± 0.25 in. (20.6 ± 6 mm) lash at the clutch pedal.

1. Loosen the locknut on the ball stud

end located to the right of the transmission on the clutch housing.
2. Adjust the ball stud to obtain the correct free-play.
3. Tighten the locknut to 25 ft. lbs., being careful not to change the adjustment.
4. Check for proper clutch operation.

1978-79

Adjustment is made at the firewall end of the outer clutch cable. Pedal free-play should be 0.83 ± 0.25 in. at the pedal.

1. Pull the adjusting ring clip from the cable at the firewall.
2. To increase free-play, move the cable into the firewall, one notch at a time, and replace the clip.
3. To decrease free-play, pull the cable out, one notch at a time, and replace the clip.

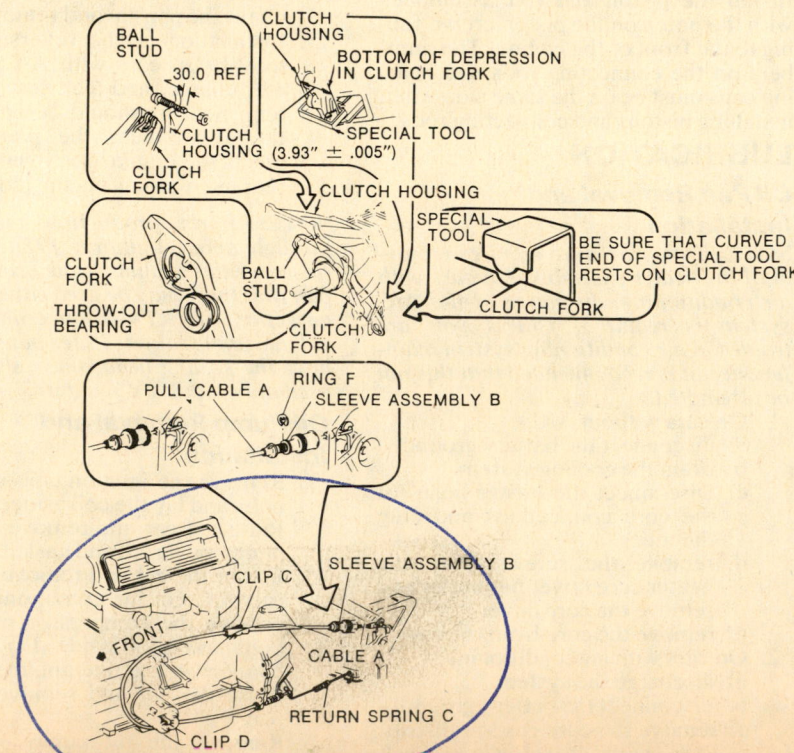

1978-79 clutch cable and ball stud adjustment details (© Chevrolet Div., G.M. Corp.)

4. If, after the adjustment, the pedal won't return tight against the bumper, the ball stud will have to be adjusted. Use either the special gauge mentioned in the clutch replacement procedure, or the method for 1976-77 free-play adjustment.

MANUAL TRANSMISSION

Chevettes use a 70mm Muncie four-speed fully synchronized transmission. Gear shifting is accomplished by an internal shifter shaft. No adjustment of the shift mechanism is possible.

Transmission Removal and Installation

1. Remove the shift lever.
2. Raise the car on a hoist and drain the lubricant from the transmission.
3. Remove the driveshaft.
4. Disconnect the speedometer cable and back-up light switch.
5. Disconnect the return spring and clutch cable at the clutch release fork.
6. Remove the crossmember-to-transmission mount bolts.
7. Remove the exhaust manifold nuts and converter-to-tailpipe bolts and nuts. Remove the converter-to-transmission bracket bolts and remove the converter.
8. Remove the crossmember-to-frame bolts and remove the crossmember.
9. Remove the dust cover.
10. Remove the clutch housing-to-engine retaining bolts, slide the transmission and clutch housing to the rear, and remove the transmission.

To install:

11. Place the transmission in gear, position the transmission and clutch housing, and slide forward. Turn the output shaft to align the input shaft splines with the clutch hub.
12. Install the clutch housing retaining bolts and lockwashers. Torque the bolts to 25 ft. lbs.
13. Install the dust cover.
14. Position the crossmember to the frame and loosely install the retaining bolts. Install the crossmember-to-transmission mounting bolts. Torque the center nuts to 33 ft. lbs.; the end nuts to 21 ft. lbs. Torque the crossmember-to-frame bolts to 40 ft. lbs.
15. Install the exhaust pipe to the manifold and the converter bracket on the transmission.
16. Connect the clutch cable. Adjust clutch pedal free-play.
17. Connect the speedometer cable and back-up light switch.
18. Install the driveshaft.
19. Fill the transmission to the correct level with SAE 80W or SAE 80W-90 GL-5 gear lubricant. Lower the car.
20. Install the shift lever and check operation of the transmission.

Shift Lever Removal and Installation

1. Remove the floor console and/or boot retainer.
2. Raise the shift lever boot to gain access to the locknut on the lever. Loosen the locknut and unscrew the upper portion of the shift lever with the knob attached.
3. Remove the foam insulator to gain access to the control assembly bolts.
4. Remove the three bolts on the extension and remove the control assembly.
5. Use caution when removing the clip on the control housing as the internal components are under spring pressure.

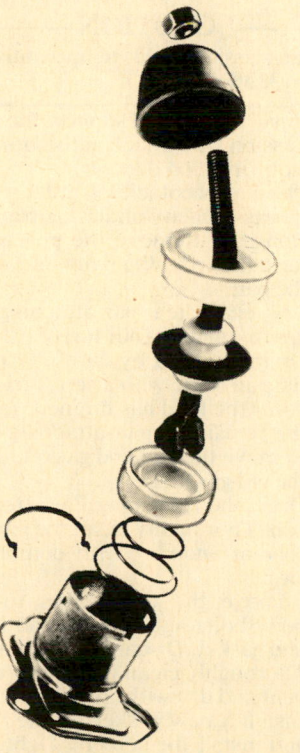

Shift lever components
(© Chevrolet Div., G.M. Corp)

6. Remove the locknut, boot retainer, and seat from the threaded end of the shift lever.
7. Remove the spring and guide from the forked end of the shift lever.
8. To assemble the shift lever, install the spring and guide on the forked end of the lever.
9. Install the seat, boot retainer, and the locknut over the threaded end of the lever.
10. Assemble the components in the control housing and install the clip on the control housing.
11. Install the control assembly on the extension making sure that the fork at the lower end of the lever engages the shifter shaft lever arm pin. Tighten the shift lever retaining bolts.
12. Install the foam insulator, boot, retainer, and/or floor console.
13. Slide the boot below the threaded portion of the shift lever and install the upper shift lever. Tighten the locknut.

AUTOMATIC TRANSMISSION

Chevettes use the Turbo Hydra-Matic 200 transmission for 1976-77. 1978 and later models use the Turbo Hydra-Matic 180.

Neutral Safety Switch Replacement and Adjustment

1. Remove the floor console cover.
2. Disconnect the electrical connectors on the back-up, seat belt warning, and neutral starter contacts on the switch.
3. Place the shift lever in Neutral.
4. Remove the two switch attaching screws and remove the switch.
5. Make sure that the shift lever is in the Neutral position before installing the switch assembly.
6. Place the neutral start switch assembly in position on the shift lever making sure that the pin on the lever is in the slot of the switch.

NOTE: *When replacing the original switch, align the contact support slot with the service adjustment hole in the switch and insert a 3/32 in. drill bit to hold the switch in Neutral. Remove the drill bit after the switch is fastened to the shift lever mounting bracket.*

7. Install the two switch attaching screws.

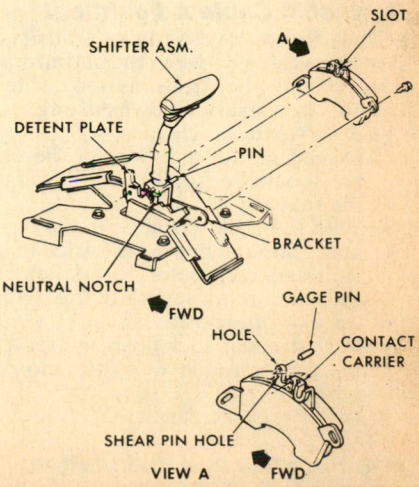

Neutral safety switch adjustment, Turbo Hydra-Matic (© Chevrolet Div., G.M. Corp.)

8. Move the shift lever out of Neutral to shear the plastic pin.
9. Connect the electrical connectors to the switch contacts. Apply the parking brake and start the engine. Check to make sure that the engine starts only in Park or Neutral. Make sure that the back-up lights work only in Reverse. Check that the seat belt warning system operates.
10. Stop the engine and install the floor console cover.

Shift Linkage Adjustment

1. Place the shift lever in the Neutral position of the detent plate.
2. Disconnect the rod from the lower end of the shift lever. Place the transmission lever in the Neutral position. Do this by moving the lever clockwise to the maximum detent (Park), then counterclockwise two (2) detent positions to Neutral.
3. Adjust the rod until the hole in the rod aligns with the pin on the lower end of the shift lever. Install the rod on the pin and secure it by adding the washer and spring clip.

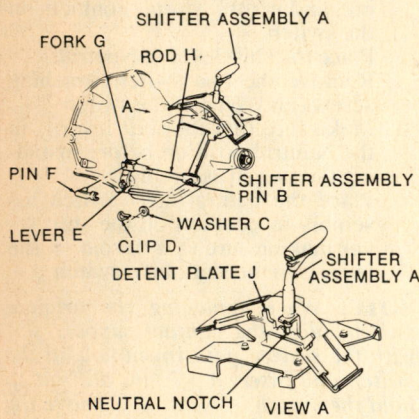

Shift linkage adjustment, Turbo Hydra-Matic (© Chevrolet Div., G.M. Corp.)

Downshift Cable Adjustment

The Turbo Hydra-Matic transmission has a cable between the carburetor linkage and the transmission which controls transmission downshifting.

1. Remove the air cleaner.
2. Disengage the snap lock. (The cable should be free to slide through the snap lock).
3. With the cable installed in the support and attached to the transmission and carburetor levers, move the carburetor lever to the wide open throttle position.
4. Push the snap lock flush and return the carburetor lever to the closed position.
5. Install the air cleaner.

Pan Removal and Installation, Fluid and Filter Change

Transmission fluid should be drained while at normal operating temperature.

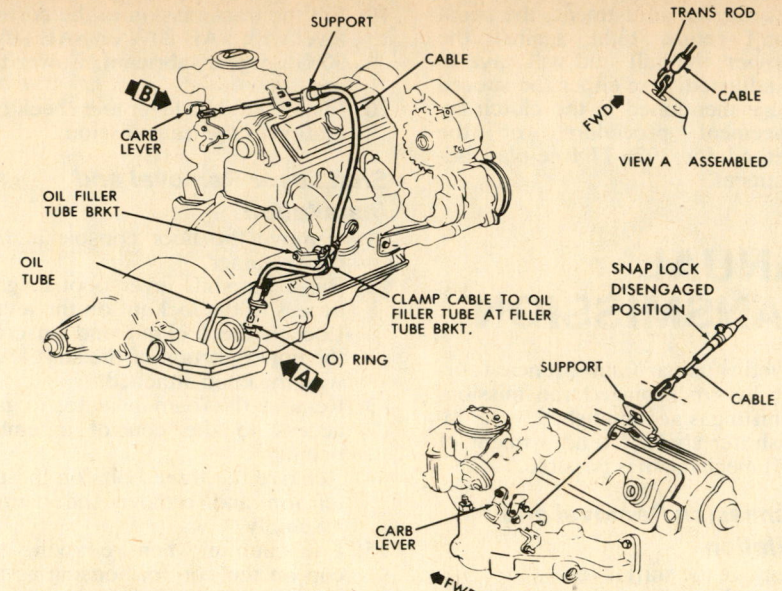

Downshift cable adjustment, Turbo Hydra-Matic (© Chevrolet Div., G.M. Corp.)

——— CAUTION ———
Transmission fluid temperature can exceed 350°F.

1. Raise the car and support the transmission with a jack at the transmission vibration damper.
2. Place a receptacle of at least three quarts capacity under the transmission pan. Remove the pan attaching bolts from the front and side of the pan.
3. Loosen the rear pan attaching bolts approximately four turns.
4. Drain the fluid by carefully prying the pan loose with a screwdriver.
5. After the fluid has drained, remove the remaining pan attaching bolts. Remove the pan and gasket. Throw the old gasket away.
6. Drain the remaining fluid from the pan. Thoroughly clean the pan with solvent and dry with compressed air.
7. Remove the two screen-to-valve body bolts and remove the screen and gasket. Discard the gasket.
8. Thoroughly clean the screen in solvent and dry with compressed air.
9. Install a new gasket on the screen and install the screen. Tighten the screen attaching bolts.
10. Install the pan using a new gasket. Tighten the pan bolts and washers to 10 ft. lbs.
11. Lower the car and add approximately six pints of DEXRON® or DEXRON® II automatic transmission fluid through the filler tube.
12. With the transmission in Park, apply the parking brake, start the engine and let it idle (not fast idle). Do not race the engine.
13. Move the gear selector lever slowly through all positions, return the lever to Park, and check the transmission fluid level.
14. Add fluid as necessary to raise the level between the dimples on the dipstick. Be careful not to overfill the transmission.

U-JOINTS

A one-piece driveshaft is mounted to the companion flange with a conventional universal joint at the rear. The driveshaft is connected to the transmission output shaft with a splined slip yoke. The slip yoke contains a thrust spring which seats against the end of the transmission output shaft. The thrust spring must be installed for proper operation.

The universal joints are of the long-life design and do not require periodic inspection or lubrication. When the joints are disassembled, repack the bearings and lubricate the reservoirs at the end of the trunnions with chassis grease and replace the dust seals.

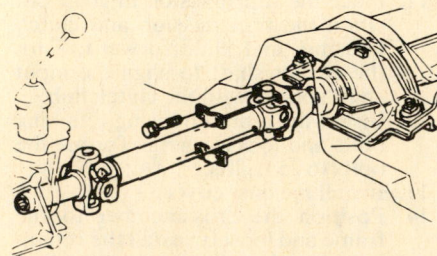

Chevette driveshaft assembly (© Chevrolet Div., G.M. Corp)

Driveshaft Removal and Installation

1. Raise the car on a hoist. Scribe matchmarks on the driveshaft and the companion flange and disconnect the rear universal joint by removing the trunnion bearing straps.
2. Move the driveshaft to the rear under the axle to remove the slip

yoke from the transmission. Watch for leakage from the transmission output shaft housing.

3. Install the driveshaft in the reverse order of removal. Tighten the trunnion strap bolts to 16 ft. lbs.

Universal Joint Overhaul

1. Remove the driveshaft.
2. For reassembly purposes, scribe a line on the transmission end of the driveshaft and on the slip yoke. Remove the snap-rings from the trunnion yoke.
3. Support the trunnion yoke with a piece of 1-1/4 in. ID pipe on an arbor press or bench vise. Use a suitable socket to press on the trunnion until the bearing cup is almost out. Grasp the cup in the vise and work the cup out of the yoke. Press the trunnion in the opposite direction to remove the other cup.
4. Clean and inspect the dust seals, bearing rollers, and trunnions. Lubricate the bearings. Make sure that the lubricant reservoir at the end of each trunnion is completely filled with lubricant. A squeeze bottle is recommended to fill the reservoirs from the bottom to prevent air pockets.
5. When installing a U-joint rebuilding kit, place the dust seals on the trunnions with the cavities of the seals toward the end of the trunnions. Use caution when pressing the seals onto the trunnions to prevent seal distortion and to assure proper seal seating.

NOTE: *Install the transmission yoke on the front of the driveshaft as marked in Step 2. If this is not done, driveline vibration may result.*

6. To assemble, position the trunnion into the yoke. Partially install one bearing cup into the yoke and start the trunnion into the bearing cup. Partially install the other cup, align the trunnion into the cup, and press the cups into the yoke.
7. Install the snap-rings.
8. Install the driveshaft.

REAR AXLE

Axle Shaft, Bearing, and Seal Removal and Installation

1. Raise the car on a hoist. Remove the wheel and tire assembly and the brake drum.
2. Clean the area around the differential carrier cover.
3. Remove the differential carrier cover to drain the rear axle lubricant.
4. Use a metric Allen wrench to unscrew the differential pinion shaft lockscrew and remove the differential pinion shaft. It may be necessary to shorten the Allen wrench to do this.

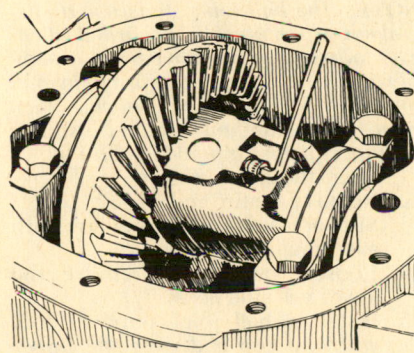

Removing the differential pinion shaft lockscrew

5. Push the flanged end of the axle shaft toward the center of the car and remove the C-lock from the inner end of the shaft.
6. Remove the axle shaft from the housing making sure not to damage the oil seal.
7. If replacing the seal only, remove the oil seal by using the inner end of the axle shaft. Insert the end of the shaft behind the steel case of the oil seal and carefully pry the seal out of the bore.
8. To remove bearings, insert a bearing and seal remover into the bore so that the tool head grasps behind the bearing. Slide the washer against the seal or bearing and turn the nut against the washer. Attach a slide hammer and remove the bearing.

NOTE: *If you don't have a special bearing installer tool, measure and note the bearing location.*

9. Lubricant a new bearing with hypoid lubricant and install it into the housing with a bearing installer tool. Make sure that the tool contacts the end of the axle tube to make sure that the bearing is at the proper depth.
10. Lubricate the cavity between the seal lips with a high melting point wheel bearing grease. Place a new oil seal on the seal installation tool and position the seal in the axle housing bore. Tap the seal into the bore flush with the end of the housing.
11. To install the axle shaft, slide the axle shaft into place making sure that the splines on the end of the shaft do not damage the oil seal and that they engage the splines of the differential side gear. Install the C-lock on the inner end of the axle shaft and push the shaft outward so that the shaft lock seats in the counterbore of the differential side gear.
12. Position the differential pinion

BEARING RETAINER

BEARING CUP

ROUND PLASTIC WASHER

ROLLER BEARINGS

SEAL

FLAT PLASTIC WASHER

CROSS

U-joint repair components

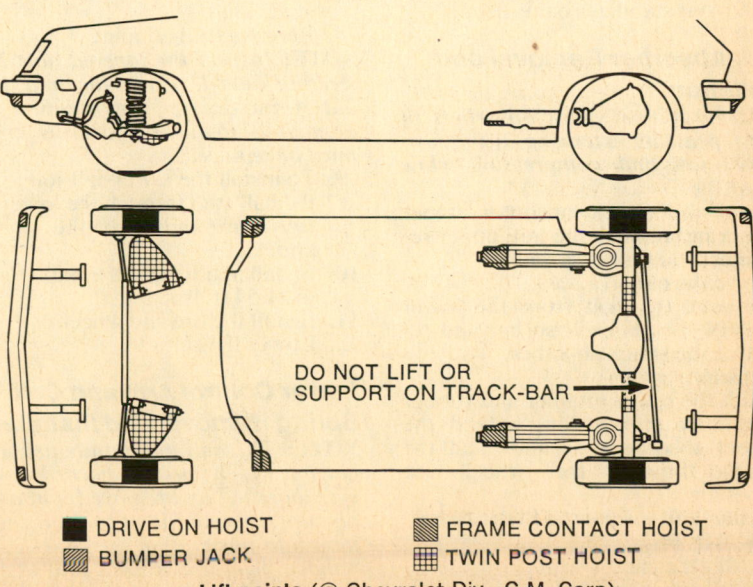

DO NOT LIFT OR SUPPORT ON TRACK-BAR

■ DRIVE ON HOIST   ▨ FRAME CONTACT HOIST
▨ BUMPER JACK   ▦ TWIN POST HOIST

Lift points (© Chevrolet Div., G.M. Corp)

shaft through the case and pinions, aligning the hole in the shaft with the lockscrew hole. Install the lockscrew.

13. Clean the gasket mounting surfaces on the differential carrier and the carrier cover. Install the carrier cover using a new gasket and tighten the cover bolts in a crosswise pattern to 22 ft. lbs.

14. Fill the rear axle with lubricant to the bottom of the filler hole.

15. Install the brake drum and the wheel and tire assembly.

16. Lower the car.

JACKING, HOISTING

The illustration shows the recommended areas for jacking and hoisting. When using a twin post hoist, be sure that it is positioned properly on the rear axle to avoid damaging the rear stabilizer. Never lift the car by the rear lower control arms.

—————— CAUTION ——————
When jacking or lifting on the side rails be certain that the lift pads do not contact the catalytic converter.

FRONT SUSPENSION

The Chevette front suspension is of conventional long and short control arm design with coil springs. The control arms attach with bolts and bushings at the inner pivot points and to the steering knuckle/front wheel spindle assembly at the outer pivot points. Lower ball joints are the wear indicator type. A front stabilizer bar is used.

Shock Absorber Removal and Installation

NOTE: *Purge new shock absorbers of air by repeatedly extending in the normal position and compressing while inverted.*

1. Hold the shock absorber upper stem and remove the nut, upper retainer, and rubber grommet
2. Raise the car on a hoist.
3. Remove the bolt from the lower end of the shock absorber and remove the shock absorber.
  To install:
4. With the lower retainer and rubber grommet in position, extend the shock absorber stem and install the stem through the wheelhouse opening.
5. Install and torque the lower bolt to 35-50 ft. lbs.
6. Lower the car.
7. Install the upper rubber grommet,

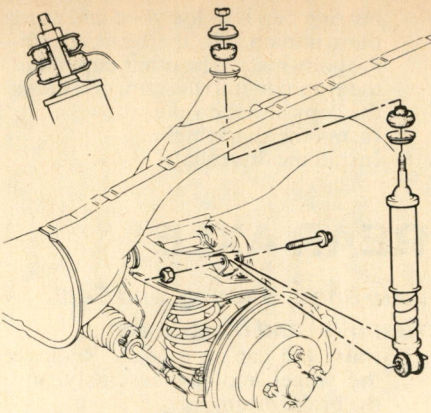

Front shock absorber mounting
(© Chevrolet Div., G.M. Corp)

retainer, and nut to the shock absorber stem.

8. Hold the shock absorber upper stem and torque the nut to 60-120 in. lbs.

Lower Ball Joint Removal and Installation

NOTE: *The ball joint studs use a special nut which must be discarded whenever loosened and removed. On assembly, use a standard nut to draw the ball joint into position on the knuckle, then remove the standard nut and install a new special nut for final installation.*

1. Raise the car on a hoist.
2. Remove the tire and wheel.
3. Support the lower control arm with a hydraulic floor jack.
4. Loosen, but do not remove the lower ball stud nut.
5. Install a ball joint removal tool with the cup end over the upper ball stud nut.
6. Turn the threaded end of the ball joint removal tool until the ball stud is free of the steering knuckle.
7. Remove the ball joint removal tool and remove the nut from the ball stud.
8. Remove the ball joint.

NOTE: *Inspect the tapered hole in the steering knuckle. Clean the area. If any out-of-roundness, deformation, or damage is found, the steering knuckle must be replaced.*

9. To install the lower ball joint, mate the ball stud through the lower control arm and into the steering knuckle.
10. Install and torque the ball stud nut to 41-54 ft. lbs.
11. Install the tire and wheel.
12. Lower the car.

Lower Control Arm and Coil Spring Removal and Installation

NOTE: *The ball joint studs use a special nut which must be discarded whenever loosened and removed. On assembly, use a standard nut to draw the ball joint into position on the knuckle, then remove the standard nut and install a new special nut for final installation.*

1. Raise the car on a frame contact hoist.
2. Remove the wheel and tire.
3. Disconnect the stabilizer bar from the lower control arm and disconnect the tie-rod from the steering knuckle.
4. Support the lower control arm with a jack.
5. Remove the nut from the lower ball joint, then use a ball joint removal tool to press out the lower ball joint.
6. Swing the knuckle and hub aside and attach them securely with wire.
7. Loosen the lower control arm pivot bolts.
8. As a safety precaution, install a chain through the coil spring.
9. Slowly lower the jack.
10. When the spring is extended as far as possible, use a pry bar to carefully lift the spring over the lower control arm seat. Remove the spring.
11. Remove the pivot bolts and remove the lower control arm.
  To install:
12. Install the lower control arm and pivot bolts to the underbody brackets. Torque the lower control arm pivot bolts to 49 ft. lbs.
13. Position the spring correctly and install it in the upper pocket. Use tape to hold the insulator onto the spring.

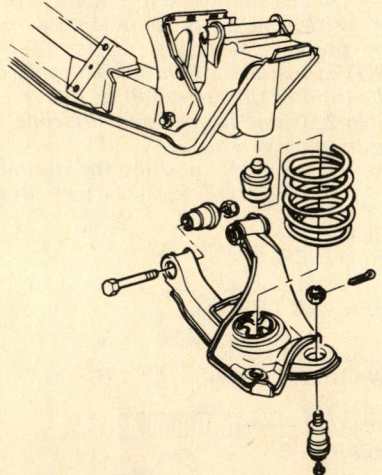

Correct position for front spring installation (© Chevrolet Div., G.M. Corp)

14. Install the lower end of the spring onto the lower control arm. An assistant may be necessary to compress the spring far enough to slide it over the raised area of the lower control arm seat.
15. Use a jack to raise the lower control arm and compress the coil spring.
16. Install the ball joint through the lower control arm and into the steering knuckle. Install the nut on the ball stud nut and torque to 41-54 ft. lbs.
17. Connect the stabilizer bar to the

lower control arm. Connect the tie-rod to the steering knuckle. Install the wheel and tire.

18. Lower the car.

Upper Ball Joint Removal and Installation

NOTE: *The ball joint studs use a special nut which must be discarded whenever loosened and removed. On assembly, use a standard nut to draw the ball joint into position on the knuckle, then remove the standard nut and install a new special nut for final installation.*

1. Raise the car on a hoist.
2. Remove the tire and wheel.
3. Support the lower control arm with a floor jack.
4. Loosen, but do not remove the upper ball stud nut.
5. Install a ball joint removal tool with the cup end over the lower ball stud nut.
6. Turn the threaded end of the ball joint removal tool until the upper ball stud is free of the steering knuckle.
7. Remove the ball joint removal tool and remove the nut from the ball stud.
8. Remove the two nuts and bolts attaching the ball joint to the upper control arm and remove the ball joint.

NOTE: *Inspect the tapered hole in the steering knuckle. Clean the area. If any out-of-roundness, deformation, or damage is found, the steering knuckle must be replaced.*

9. To install the upper ball joint, install the nuts and bolts attaching the ball joint to the upper control arm. Torque the nuts to 29 ft. lbs. Then mate the upper control arm ball stud to the steering knuckle.
10. Install and torque the ball stud nut to 29-36 ft. lbs.
11. Install the tire and wheel.
12. Lower the car.

Upper Control Arm Removal and Installation

NOTE: *The ball joint studs use a special nut which must be discarded whenever loosened and removed. On assembly, use a standard nut to draw the ball joint into position on the knuckle, then remove the standard nut and install a new special nut for final installation.*

1. Raise the car on a hoist.
2. Remove the tire and wheel.
3. Support the lower control arm with a floor jack.
4. Remove the upper ball joint from the steering knuckle as previously described.
5. Remove the upper control arm pivot bolts and remove the upper control arm.
6. To install the upper control arm, install the upper control arm with its pivot bolts.

NOTE: *The inner pivot bolt must be in-*

stalled with the bolt head toward the front.

7. Install the pivot bolt nut.
8. Position the upper control arm in a horizontal plane and torque the nut to 43-50 ft. lbs.
9. Install the ball joint to the upper control arm and to the steering knuckle as previously described. Torque the ball joint-to-upper control arm attaching bolts to 29 ft. lbs. Torque the ball stud nut to 29-36 ft. lbs.
10. Install the tire and wheel.
11. Lower the car.

Front Wheel Bearing Adjustment

1. Raise the car and support at the front lower control arm.
2. Remove the hub cap or wheel cover from the wheel. Remove the dust cap from the hub.
3. Remove the cotter pin from the spindle and spindle nut.
4. Spin the wheel forward by hand and tighten the spindle nut to 12 ft. lbs. This will fully seat the bearings.
5. Back off the nut to a just loose position.
6. Hand-tighten the spindle nut. Loosen the spindle nut until either hole in the spindle aligns with a slot in the nut, but not more than 1/2 flat.
7. Install a new cotter pin, bend the ends of the pin against the nut, and cut off any extra length to avoid interference with the dust cap.
8. Proper bearing adjustment should give 0.001-0.005 in. of end-play.
9. Install the dust cap on the hub and the hub cap or wheel cover on the wheel.
10. Lower the car.
11. Adjust the opposite front wheel bearings.

REAR SUSPENSION

Chevettes use a solid rear axle and coil springs. The axle is attached to the body by two tubular lower control arms, a straight track rod, two shock absorbers, and a bracket at the front end of the rear axle extension.

The lower control arms maintain fore and aft relationship of the axle to the chassis. The coil springs are located between brackets on the axle tube and spring seats in the frame. They are held in place by the weight of the car and, during rebound, by the shock absorbers which limit axle movement. The shock absorbers are angle-mounted on brackets behind the axle housing and the rear spring seats in the frame. A rear stabilizer bar is used.

When using a hoist contacting the rear axle, be sure that the stabilizer

links and the track rod are not damaged.

Shock Absorber Removal and Installation

NOTE: *Purge new shock absorbers of air by repeatedly extending in the normal position and compressing while inverted.*

1. Raise the car on a hoist.
2. Support the rear axle.
3. Remove the shock absorber upper attaching nut and lower attaching bolt and nut, and remove the shock absorber.

To install:

4. Install the retainer and the rubber grommet onto the shock absorber.
5. Place the shock absorber into its installed position and install and tighten the upper retaining nut to 7 ft. lbs.
6. Install the lower shock absorber nut and bolt and torque to 33 ft. lbs.
7. Remove the rear axle supports and lower the car.

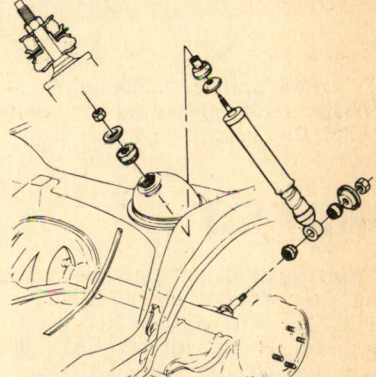

Rear shock absorber mounting
(© Chevrolet Div., G.M. Corp)

Rear Spring Removal and Installation

1. Raise the car on a hoist.
2. Support the rear axle with a floor jack.
3. Disconnect both shock absorbers from their lower brackets.
4. Disconnect the rear axle extension center support bracket from the underbody. Use caution when disconnecting the extension and safely support it when disconnected.
5. Lower the rear axle and remove the springs and spring insulators. One or both springs can be removed now.

--- CAUTION ---

Do not stretch the rear brake hose when lowering the rear axle.

6. To install, place the insulators on top and on the bottom of the springs and position the springs between their upper and lower seats.
7. Raise the rear axle. Connect the rear axle extension center support

bracket to the underbody. Torque the bolts to 37 ft. lbs.

8. Connect the shock absorbers to their lower brackets. Torque the nuts to 33 ft. lbs.
9. Remove the jack from the axle.
10. Lower the car.

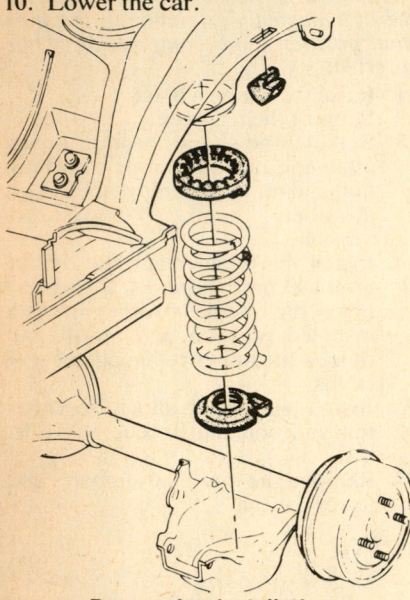

Rear spring installation—position both insulators as shown
(© Chevrolet Div., G.M. Corp)

BRAKES

Front disc brakes are standard equipment. Power brakes are available as an option. The 9.68 in. diameter disc is a one-piece casting with the hub. Single-piston sliding calipers are used.

The rear brakes are of conventional leading-trailing shoe design. Brake drum diameter is 7.87 in. Automatic adjusters are used in the rear brakes to provide adjustment when needed whenever the brakes are applied, forward or reverse.

The master cylinder is a two-piece design: a cast housing containing the primary and secondary pistons and a stamped steel reservoir. The reservoir is attached to the cast housing with two retainers and sealed with two O-rings. The reservoir is not divided, however a dual braking system is used. The front (secondary) piston operates the rear brakes, while the rear (primary) piston operates the front brakes.

The front and rear brake lines are routed through a distributor and switch assembly located on the left-hand engine compartment side panel. The switch is a pressure differential type which lights the brake warning light on the instrument panel if either the front or rear hydraulic system fails. It automatically resets after repair. The switch is nonadjustable and nonserviceable; it must be replaced if defective.

Master Cylinder Removal and Installation

1. Disconnect the master cylinder pushrod from the brake pedal.
2. Remove the pushrod boot.
3. Remove the air cleaner.
4. Thoroughly clean all dirt from the master cylinder and the brake lines. Disconnect the brake lines from the master cylinder and plug them to prevent the entry of dirt.
5. Remove the master cylinder securing nuts and remove the master cylinder.
6. Install the master cylinder with its spacer. Tighten the securing nuts.

7. Connect the brake lines to their ports.
8. Place the pushrod boot over the end of the pushrod. Secure the pushrod to the brake pedal with the pin and clip.
9. Fill the master cylinder and bleed the entire hydraulic system. After bleeding, fill the master cylinder to within 1/4 in. from the top of the reservoir. Check for leaks.
10. Install the air cleaner.
11. Check brake operation before moving the car.

Parking Brake Adjustment

1. Raise the car on a hoist.
2. Apply the parking brake one notch from the fully released position.
3. Tighten the parking brake cable equalizer adjusting nut under the car until a light drag is felt when the rear wheels are rotated forward.
4. Fully release the parking brake and rotate the rear wheels. There should be no drag.
5. Lower the car.

Power Brake Booster Removal and Installation

1. Remove the air cleaner.
2. Disconnect the vacuum hose from the check valve.
3. Remove the master cylinder brace.
4. Remove the master cylinder-to-power cylinder nut, and pull forward on the master cylinder until it clears the power cylinder mounting studs. Move the master cylinder aside and support it, being careful of the brake lines.
5. Remove the nuts securing the power cylinder to the firewall.
6. Remove the pushrod-to-pedal retainer and slip the pushrod off the pedal pin. Remove the power cylinder.
7. Installation is the reverse of removal.

STEERING

All Chevette models use manual rack and pinion steering which encloses the steering gear and linkage in one unit. Power steering is not available.

Rotary motion of the steering wheel is converted into linear motion to turn the wheels by the meshing of the helical pinion with the teeth of the rack. The pinion and a major portion of the rack are encased in a die cast aluminum housing. Inner tie-rod assemblies are threaded and staked to the rack. The inner tie-rods contain a belleville spring-loaded ball joint which permits both rocking and rotating tie-rod movement. The outer tie-rods thread onto the inners and are held in position by jam nuts. Two convoluted boots are secured by clamps to the housing and in-

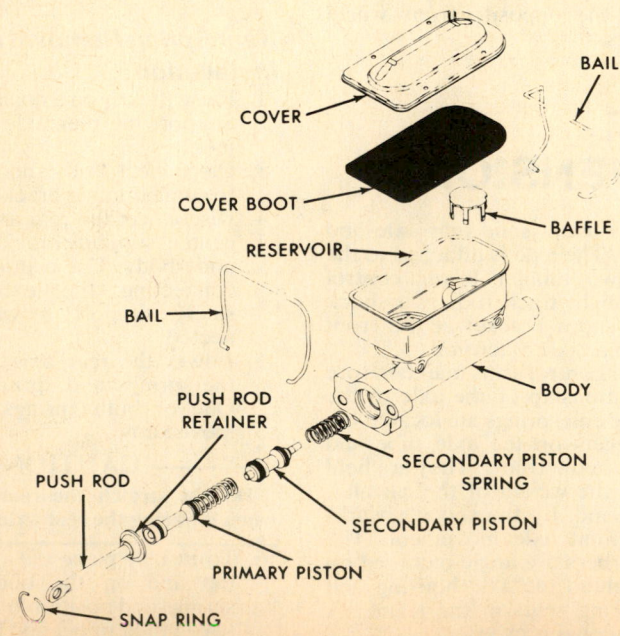

Dual piston master cylinder with common reservoir
(© Chevrolet Div., G.M. Corp)

ner tie-rods to prevent the entrance of dirt. The rack and pinion assembly is secured to the front suspension crossmember with two clamps and bushings.

The energy-absorbing steering column has a switch which operates the turn signals (up and down movement), the headlight dimmer switch (front and back movement), the windshield wipers (rotation), and the windshield washers (by pushing the lever into the column).

Steering Wheel Removal and Installation

1. Disconnect the negative battery cable.
2. Remove the two steering wheel shroud screws at the underside of the steering wheel and remove the shroud.
3. Remove the wheel nut retainer and the wheel nut.

CAUTION

Do not overexpand the retainer.

---

4. Using a steering wheel puller, thread the puller anchor screws into the threaded holes in the steering wheel. With the center bolt of the puller butting against the steering shaft, turn the center bolt to remove the steering wheel.
5. To install, place the turn signal lever in the neutral position and install the steering wheel. Torque the steering wheel nut to 30 ft. lbs. and install the nut retainer. Use caution not to overexpand the nut retainer.
6. Connect the negative battery cable.

Turn Signal Switch Removal and Installation

1. Remove the steering wheel as previously described.
2. Position a screwdriver blade into one of the three cover slots. Pry up and out (at least two slots) to free the cover.

3. Press down on the lockplate, but do not relieve the full load of the spring because the ring will rotate and make removal difficult. Pry the round wire snap-ring out of the shaft groove and discard it. Lift the lockplate off the end of the shaft.
4. Slide the turn signal cancelling cam, upper bearing preload spring, and thrust washer off the end of the shaft.
5. Remove the multi-function lever by rotating it clockwise to its stop (off position), then pull the lever straight out to disengage it.
6. Push the hazard warning knob in and unscrew the knob.
7. Remove the two screws, pivot arm, and spacer.
8. Wrap the upper part of the connector with tape to prevent snagging the wires during switch removal.
9. Remove the three switch mounting screws and pull the switch straight up, guiding the wiring harness through the column housing.

CAUTION

On installation it is extremely important that only the specified screws, bolts, and nuts be used. The use of overlength screws could prevent the steering column from compressing under impact.

---

10. Position the switch into the housing.
11. Install the three switch mounting screws. Replace the spacer and pivot arm. Be sure that the spacer protrudes through the hole in the arm and that the arm finger encloses the turn signal switch frame.
12. Install the hazard warning knob.
13. Make sure that the turn signal switch is in the neutral position and that the hazard warning knob is out. Slide the thrust washer, upper bearing preload spring, and the cancelling cam into the upper end of the shaft.
14. Place the lockplate and a new snap-

ring onto the end of the shaft. Compress the lockplate as far as possible. Slide the new snap-ring into the shaft groove.

CAUTION

On assembly, always use a new snap-ring

---

15. Install the multi-function lever, guiding the wire harness through the column housing. Align the lever pin with the switch slot. Push on the end of the lever until it is seated securely.
16. Install the steering wheel as previously described.

Lock Cylinder Removal and Installation

The lock cylinder is located on the right-side of the steering column and should be removed only in the Run position. Removal in any other position will damage the key buzzer switch. The lock cylinder cannot be disassembled; if replacement is required, a new cylinder coded to the old key must be installed.

1. Remove the steering wheel and turn signal switch as previously described.
2. Do not remove the buzzer switch or damage to the lock cylinder will result.
3. Insert a small screwdriver or similar tool into the turn signal housing slot to the upper right of the steering shaft. Keep the tool to the right-side of the slot and depress the retainer at the bottom to release the lock cylinder. Remove the lock cylinder.
4. To install the lock cylinder, hold the cylinder sleeve in the left hand and rotate knob (key in) clockwise to stop. (This retracts the actuator). Insert the cylinder into the housing bore with the key on the cylinder sleeve aligned with the keyway in the housing. Push the

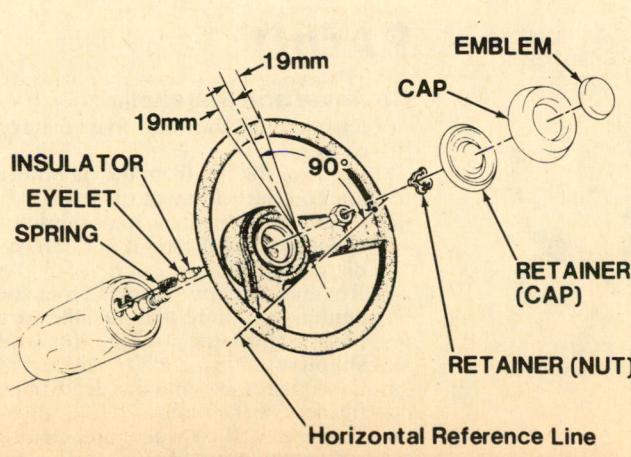

Chevette steering wheel assembly
(© Chevrolet Div., G.M. Corp)

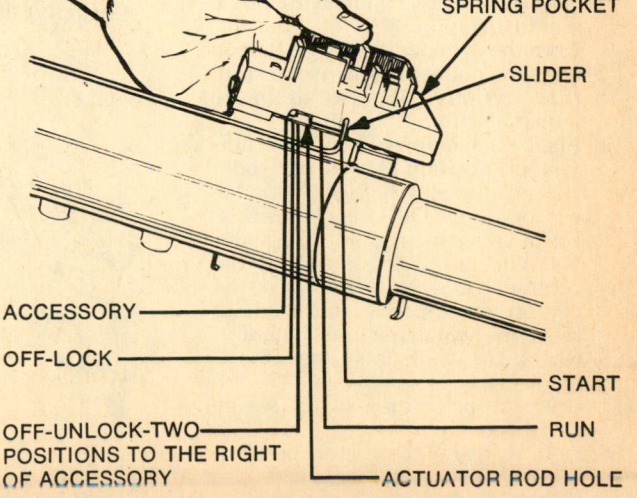

Positioning the ignition switch for installation

cylinder in until it bottoms. Rotate the knob counterclockwise while maintaining a light pressure inward until the drive section of the cylinder mates with the sector. Push the cylinder in fully until the retainer pops into the housing groove.

5. Install the turn signal switch and the steering wheel as previously described.

Ignition Switch and Dimmer Switch Removal and Installation

The ignition switch is mounted on top of the mast jacket near the front of the instrument panel. The switch is located inside the channel section of the brake pedal support and is completely inaccessible without first lowering the steering column.

1. Disconnect the negative battery cable.
2. Remove the steering wheel as previously described.
3. Move the driver's seat as far back as possible.
4. Remove the floor pan bracket screw.
5. Remove the two column bracket-to-instrument panel nuts and lower the column far enough to disconnect the ignition switch wiring harness.

--- CAUTION ---

Be sure that the steering column is properly supported before proceeding.

6. The switch should be in the Lock position before removal. If the lock cylinder has already been removed, the actuating rod to the switch should be pulled up until there is a definite stop, then moved down one detent to the Lock position.
7. Remove the two mounting screws and remove the ignition and dimmer switch.
8. Refer to the lock cylinder installation procedure previously described in Lock Cylinder Removal and Installation.
9. Turn the cylinder clockwise to stop and then counterclockwise to stop, then counterclockwise again to stop (Off-Unlock position).
10. Place the ignition switch in the Off-Unlock position. Move the slider two positions to the right from Accessory to the Off-Unlock position.
11. Fit the actuator rod into the slider hole and install the switch on the column. Be sure to use only the correct screws. Be careful not to move the switch out of its detent.
12. Check the dimmer switch adjustment.
13. Connect the ignition switch wiring harness.
14. Loosely install the column bracket-to-instrument panel nuts.
15. Install the floor pan bracket screw and tighten it to 20 ft. lbs.

16. Tighten the column bracket-to-instrument panel nuts to 20 ft. lbs.
17. Install the steering wheel as previously outlined.
18. Connect the battery negative cable.

INSTRUMENT PANEL

The standard instrument cluster contains a speedometer and fuel gauge with warning lights for oil pressure, coolant temperature, alternator, brakes, and seat belts. The optional cluster adds a tachometer, but retains all warning lights.

Instrument Cluster and Speedometer Cable Replacement

The instrument cluster must be removed to replace light bulbs, gauges, and printed circuit.

1. Disconnect the negative battery cable.
2. Remove the clock stem knob.
3. Remove the four screws and remove the instrument cluster bezel and lens.
4. Remove the two nuts securing the instrument cluster to the instrument panel and pull the cluster slightly forward.
5. Disconnect the electrical connector and speedometer cable from the cluster and remove it.
6. Installation is the reverse of removal.

Headlight Switch Removal and Installation

1. Disconnect the negative battery cable.
2. Pull the headlight switch control knob to the On position.
3. Reach up under the instrument panel and depress the switch shaft retainer button while pulling on the switch control shaft knob.

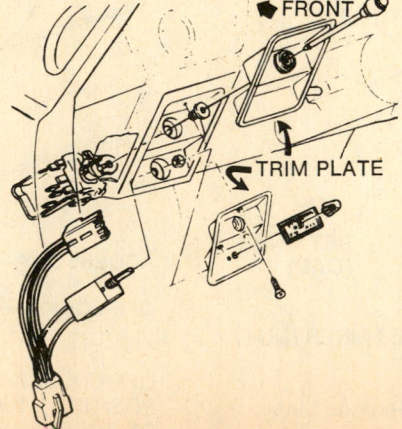

Headlight switch mounting
(© Chevrolet Div., G.M. Corp)

4. Remove the three screws and remove the headlight switch trim plate.
5. Use a large-bladed screwdriver to remove the light switch ferrule nut from the front of the instrument panel.
6. Disconnect the multi-contact connector from the bottom of the headlight switch. (A small screwdriver will aid removal).
7. Installation is the reverse of removal.

WINDSHIELD WIPERS

Motor Removal and Installation

1. Working inside the car, reach up under the instrument panel above the steering column and loosen, but do not remove, the transmission drive link-to-motor crank arm attaching nuts.
2. Disconnect the transmission drive link from the motor crank arm.
3. Raise the hood and disconnect the motor wiring.
4. Remove the three motor attaching bolts.
5. Remove the motor while guiding the crank arm through the hole.
6. To install, align the sealing gasket to the base of the motor and reverse the rest of the removal procedure.

NOTE: *If the wiper motor-to-firewall sealing gasket is damaged during removal, it should be replaced with a new gasket to prevent possible water leaks.*

Wiper Blade Replacement

To remove the blade from the arm, depress the spring type blade clip away from the underside of the arm and slide the arm out of the blade clip. To install the blade, slide the tip end of the arm into the blade clip until the pin on the tip end engages the hole in the clip.

RADIO

Removal and Installation

1. Disconnect the negative battery cable.
2. Remove the nut from the mounting stud on the bottom of the radio.
3. Remove all control knobs and/or spacers from the right and left radio control shafts.
4. Remove the four screws from the center trim plate and pull the trim plate and the radio forward slightly.
5. Disconnect the antenna lead from the rear of the radio.
6. Disconnect the speaker and electrical connectors from the radio harness.
7. Disconnect the electrical connec-

tors from the rear window defogger and cigarette lighter.

8. Use a deep well socket to remove the retaining nuts from both control shafts and remove the radio.
9. To install, reverse the removal procedure.

HEATER

Blower Motor Removal and Installation

1. Disconnect the negative battery cable.
2. Disconnect the electrical lead from the blower motor.
3. Scribe a mark to reference the blower motor flange-to-case position.
4. Remove the blower motor-to-case attaching screws and remove the blower motor and wheel as an assembly. Pry the flange gently if the sealer acts as an adhesive.
5. Remove the blower wheel retaining nut and separate the motor and wheel.
6. Reverse Steps 1-5 to install. Be sure to align the scribe marks made during removal.

NOTE: *Assemble the blower wheel to the motor with the open end of the wheel away from the motor. If necessary, replace the sealer at the motor flange.*

Heater Core Removal and Installation

1. Disconnect the negative battery cable.

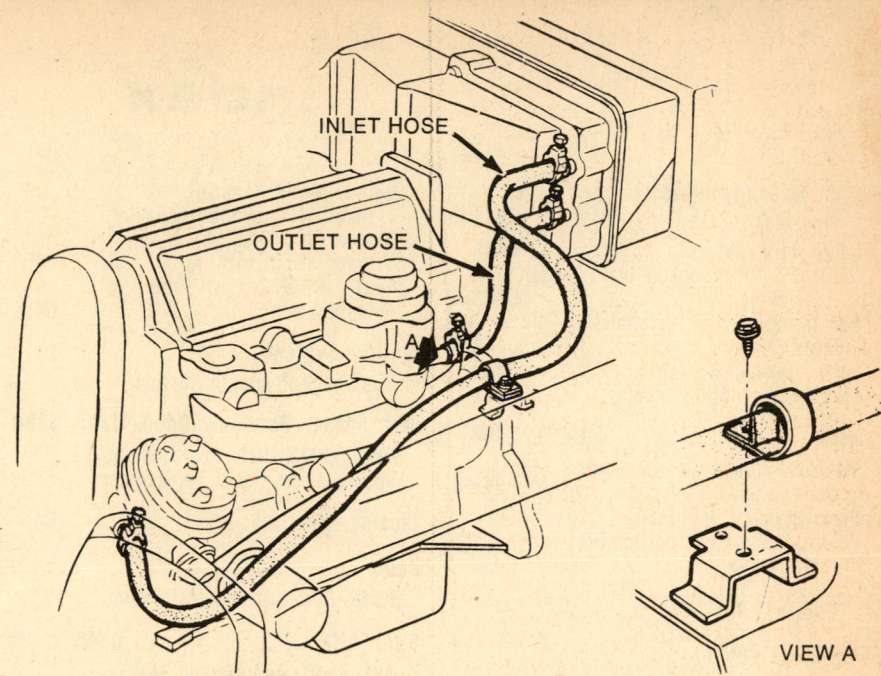

Heater hose details (© Chevrolet Div., G.M. Corp.)

2. Drain the radiator.
3. Disconnect the heater hoses at the heater core tube connections. Use care when removing the hoses as the core tube attachment seams can be easily damaged if too much force is used on them. When the hoses are removed, install plugs in the core tubes to avoid spilling coolant when removing the core.

NOTE: *The larger diameter hose goes to the water pump; the smaller diameter hose goes to the thermostat housing.*

4. Remove the screws around the perimeter of the heater core cover on the engine side of the firewall.
5. Pull the heater core cover from its mounting in the firewall.
6. Remove the core from the distributor assembly.
7. Reverse the removal procedure to install. Be sure that the core-to-case sealer is intact before replacing the core; use new sealer if necessary. When installation is complete, check for coolant leaks.

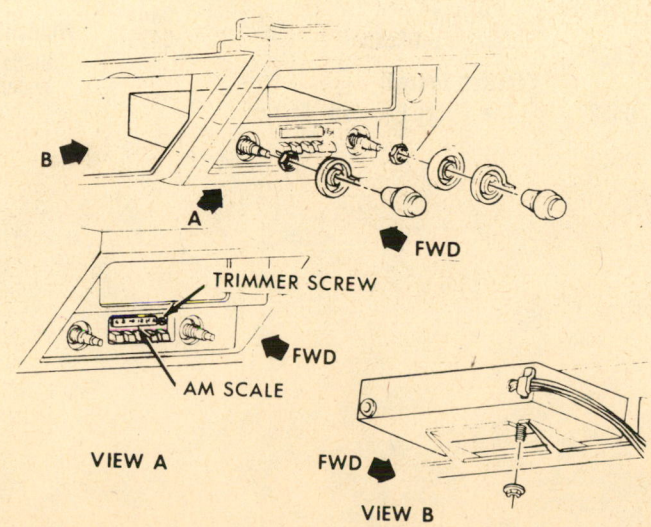

Radio installation details (© Chevrolet Div., G.M. Corp.)

Chrysler · Cordoba · Imperial

Index

YEAR IDENTIFICATION

Chrysler

1972 Newport

1972 New Yorker

1973 Newport

1973 New Yorker

1974 New Yorker

1975 Newport

1975 Cordoba

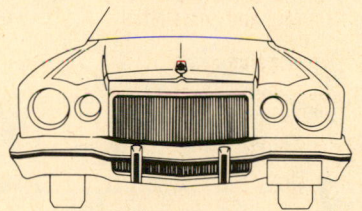

1976 Cordoba

1975 New Yorker Brougham

1976 Newport

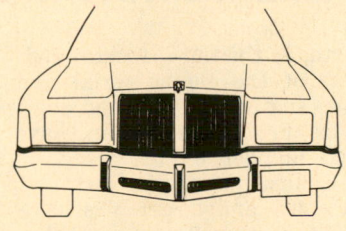

1976 New Yorker Brougham

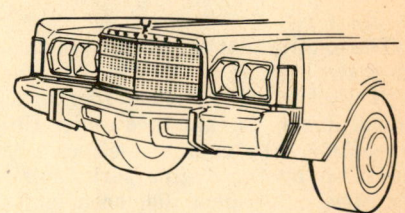

1977 Newport

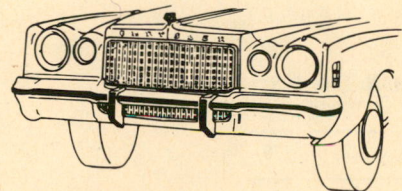

1977 Cordoba

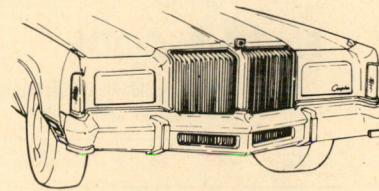

1977 New Yorker Brougham

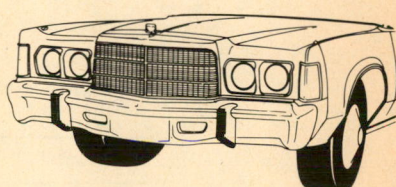

1978 Newport

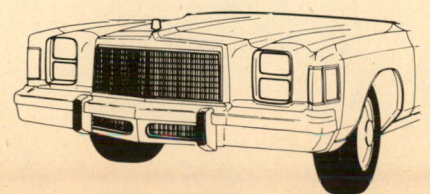

1978 Cordoba

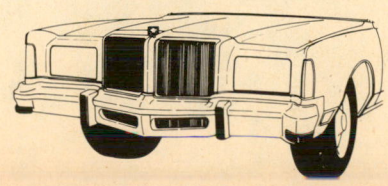

1978 New Yorker

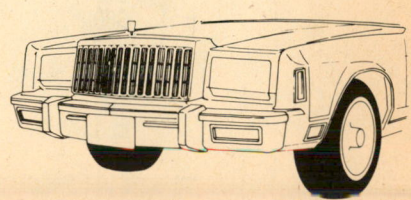

1979 New Yorker

YEAR IDENTIFICATION

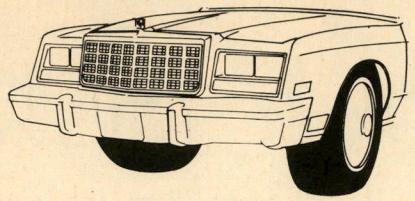

1979 Newport

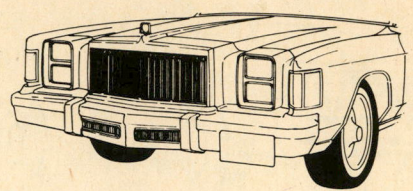

1979 Cordoba

Chrysler Imperial

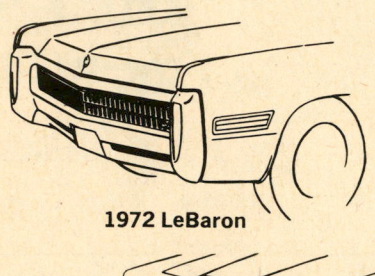

1972 LeBaron

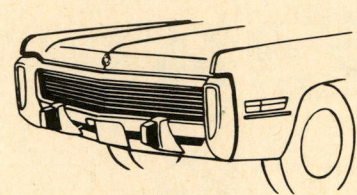

1973 LeBaron

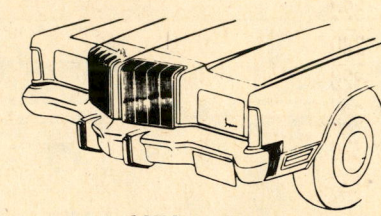

1974 Le Baron

1975 Imperial LeBaron

ENGINE IDENTIFICATION

The engine that the factory installed in the car can be identified by the fifth digit of the Vehicle Identification Number, as explained under Engine Code. The engine itself can be identified by the engine serial number. The cubic inch displacement is given by either the second, third, and fourth, or the third, fourth, and fifth digits of the engine serial number, depending on the year and engine.

V8s through 360 cu. in. have the serial number on the front of the block, just below the left cylinder head. 400 and larger V8s have the number on the oil pan rail, below the starter opening, at the left rear corner of the block; in front of the distributor; or along the left front tappet rail. 360 cu. in. and smaller (small block) V8s can quickly be identified as having the distributor at the rear of the engine, while 400 and larger versions have it at the front.

ENGINE CODE

The engine code designation is the 5th digit of the vehicle identification number (V.I.N.). The V.I.N. is stamped on a plate located at the left side of the instrument panel visible through the windshield.

Displacement	Bbl	'72	'73	'74	'75	'76	'77	'78	'79
318	2				G	G	G	G	G
318	4							H	H
360	2	K			K	K	K	K	K
360	4				J	J	J	J	J
360	4							L	L
400	2	M	M	M	M	M	M		
400	4			N	N	N	N	N	
400 HP	4				P	P	P		
440	4	T	T	T	T	T	T	T	
440 HP	4				U	U	U		

HP High Performance

GENERAL ENGINE SPECIFICATIONS

Year	Engine No. Cyl. Displacement (Cu. In.)	Carburetor Type	Horsepower @ rpm ■	Torque @ rpm (ft lbs) ■	Bore X Stroke (in.)	Compression Ratio	Oil Pressure @ 2000 rpm
'72	8-360	2 bbl	175 @ 4000	285 @ 2400	4.000 x 3.580	8.8:1	45-65
	8-400	2 bbl	190 @ 4400	310 @ 2400	4.342 x 3.375	8.2:1	45-65
	8-440	4 bbl	225 @ 4400	345 @ 3200	4.320 x 3.750	8.2:1	45-65
'73	8-400	2 bbl	185 @ 3600	310 @ 2400	4.340 x 3.380	8.2:1	45-65
	8-440	4 bbl	215 @ 3600	345 @ 2000	4.320 x 3.750	8.2:1	45-65
	8-440 Calif.	4 bbl	208 @ 3600	340 @ 2000	4.320 x 3.750	8.2:1	45-65
'74	8-360	4 bbl	200 @ 4000	290 @ 3200	4.000 x 3.580	8.4:1	45-65
	8-400	2 bbl	185 @ 4000	315 @ 2400	4.340 x 3.380	8.2:1	45-65
	8-400	4 bbl	205 @ 4400	310 @ 2400	4.340 x 3.380	8.2:1	45-65
	8-440	4 bbl	230 @ 4000	350 @ 3200	4.320 x 3.750	8.2:1	45-65
	8-440 Calif.	4 bbl	220 @ 4000	345 @ 3200	4.320 x 3.750	8.2:1	45-65
'75	8-318	2 bbl	150 @ 4000	255 @ 1600	3.910 x 3.310	8.5:1	45-65
	8-318 Calif.	2 bbl	135 @ 3600	245 @ 1600	3.910 x 3.310	8.5:1	45-65
	8-360	2 bbl	180 @ 4000	290 @ 2400	4.000 x 3.580	8.4:1	45-65
	8-360	4 bbl	190 @ 4000	270 @ 3200	4.000 x 3.580	8.4:1	45-65
	8-400	2 bbl	175 @ 4000	300 @ 2400	4.340 x 3.380	8.2:1	50-75
	8-400 Cordoba	2 bbl	165 @ 4000	295 @ 3200	4.340 x 3.380	8.2:1	50-75
	8-400	4 bbl	195 @ 4000	285 @ 3200	4.340 x 3.380	8.2:1	50-75
	8-400 Cordoba	4 bbl	190 @ 4000	290 @ 3200	4.340 x 3.380	8.2:1	50-75
	8-400 Cordoba Calif.	4 bbl	185 @ 4000	285 @ 3200	4.340 x 3.380	8.2:1	50-75
	8-400 HP	4 bbl	235 @ 4200	320 @ 3200	4.340 x 3.380	8.2:1	50-75
	8-440	4 bbl	215 @ 4000	330 @ 3200	4.320 x 3.750	8.2:1	50-75
	8-440 Calif.	4 bbl	210 @ 4000	320 @ 3200	4.320 x 3.750	8.2:1	50-75
	8-440 HP	4 bbl	260 @ 4400	355 @ 3200	4.320 x 3.750	8.2:1	50-75
	8-440 HP Calif.	4 bbl	250 @ 4000	350 @ 3200	4.320 x 3.750	8.2:1	50-75
'76	8-318	2 bbl	150 @ 4000	255 @ 1600	3.910 x 3.310	8.5:1	45-65
	8-318 Calif.	2 bbl	140 @ 3600	250 @ 2000	3.910 x 3.310	8.5:1	45-65
	8-360	2 bbl	170 @ 4000	280 @ 2400	4.000 x 3.580	8.4:1	45-65
	8-360 Calif.	4 bbl	175 @ 4000	270 @ 1600	4.000 x 3.580	8.4:1	45-65
	8-400	2 bbl	175 @ 4000	300 @ 2400	4.340 x 3.380	8.2:1	50-75
	8-400	4 bbl	210 @ 4400	305 @ 3200	4.340 x 3.380	8.2:1	50-75
	8-400 Calif.	4 bbl	185 @ 3600	285 @ 3200	4.340 x 3.380	8.2:1	50-75
	8-400 HP	4 bbl	240 @ 4400	325 @ 3200	4.340 x 3.380	8.2:1	50-75
	8-440	4 bbl	205 @ 3600	320 @ 2000	4.320 x 3.750	8.2:1	50-75
	8-440 Calif.	4 bbl	200 @ 3600	310 @ 2400	4.320 x 3.750	8.2:1	50-75
'77	8-318	2 bbl	145 @ 4000	245 @ 1600	3.910 x 3.310	8.6:1	35-65
	8-318 Calif.	2 bbl	135 @ 3600	235 @ 1600	3.910 x 3.310	8.6:1	35-65
	8-360	2 bbl	155 @ 3600	275 @ 2000	4.000 x 3.580	8.4:1	30-80
	8-360 Calif.②	4 bbl	170 @ 4000	270 @ 1600	4.000 x 3.580	8.4:1	30-80
	8-400①	4 bbl	190 @ 3600	305 @ 3200	4.340 x 3.380	8.2:1	30-80
	8-440①	4 bbl	195 @ 3600	320 @ 2000	4.320 x 3.750	8.2:1	30-80
	8-440 Calif.①②	4 bbl	185 @ 3600	310 @ 2400	4.320 x 3.750	8.2:1	30-80
'78	8-318①	2 bbl	140 @ 4000	245 @ 1600	3.910 x 3.310	8.5:1	35-65
	8-318 Calif.①	4 bbl	155 @ 4000	245 @ 1600	3.910 x 3.310	8.5:1	35-65
	8-360①	2 bbl	155 @ 3600	270 @ 2400	4.000 x 3.580	8.4:1	30-80

GENERAL ENGINE SPECIFICATIONS

Year	Engine No. Cyl. Displacement (Cu. In.)	Carburetor Type	Horsepower @ rpm ■	Torque @ rpm (ft lbs) ■	Bore X Stroke (in.)	Compression Ratio	Oil Pressure @ 2000 rpm
	8-360②	4 bbl	170 @ 4000	270 @ 2400	4.000 x 3.580	8.4:1	30-80
	8-360 Calif.	4 bbl	170 @ 3600	265 @ 1600	4.000 x 3.580	8.4:1	30-80
	8-360 Calif. HD	4 bbl	160 @ 3600	265 @ 1600	4.000 x 3.580	8.0:1	30-80
	8-400①	4 bbl	190 @ 3600	305 @ 3200	4.340 x 3.380	8.2:1	30-80
	8-440①	4 bbl	195 @ 3600	320 @ 2000	4.320 x 3.750	8.2:1	30-80
	8-440 Calif. ①②	4 bbl	185 @ 3600	310 @ 2400	4.320 x 3.750	8.2:1	30-80
'79	6-225	2 bbl	110 @ 3600	180 @ 2000	3.406 x 4.125	8.4:1	35-65
	8-318 ESC	2 bbl	140 @ 4000	245 @ 1600	3.910 x 3.310	8.5:1	35-65
	8-318 ESC	2 bbl	140 @ 4000	245 @ 1600	3.910 x 3.310	8.5:1	35-65
	8-318 ESC Calif	4 bbl	155 @ 4000	245 @ 1600	3.910 x 3.310	8.5:1	35-65
	8-360 ESC	2 bbl	155 @ 3600	270 @ 2400	4.000 x 3.580	8.4:1	30-80
	8-360 ESC Calif	4 bbl	160 @ 3600	265 @ 1600	4.000 x 3.580	8.4:1	30-80
	8-360	EFM	160 @ 3600	265 @ 1600	4.000 x 3.580	8.4:1	30-80
	8-360 ESC HP	4 bbl	170 @ 4000	270 @ 1600	4.000 x 3.580	8.0:1	30-80

HP High Performance
① Lean burn
② High altitude
ESC Electronic Spark Control
EFM Electronic Fuel Metering

HD Heavy Duty

■ Horsepower and torque are SAE net figures. They are measured at the rear of the transmission with all accessories installed and operating. Since the figures vary when a given engine is installed in different models, some are representative rather than exact.

TUNE-UP SPECIFICATIONS

When analyzing compression test results, look for uniformity among cylinders rather than specific pressures.

Year	ENGINE No. Cyl Displacement (cu in.)	hp	SPARK PLUGS Orig. Type	Gap (in.)	DISTRIBUTOR Point Dwell (deg)	Point Gap (in.)	IGNITION TIMING (deg) ▲ ● Man Trans	Auto Trans	VALVES Intake Opens ■ (deg)	Fuel Pump Pressure (psi) ●	IDLE SPEED (rpm) ▲ ● Man Trans	Auto Trans
'72	8-360	175	N-13Y	.035	28½-32½	.017	—	TDC	16	5-7	—	700
	8-400	255	J-13Y	.035	28½-32½	.018	—	①5B(2½B)	18	3½-5	—	700
	8-440	280	J-11Y	.035	28½-32½	.018	—	10B(5B)	18	3½-5	—	900
'73	8-400	185	J-13Y	.035	Electronic		—	10B	18	3½-5	—	700
	8-440	215	J-11Y	.035	Electronic		—	10B	18	3½-5	—	700
'74	8-360	200	N-12Y	.035	Electronic		—	5B	22	5-7	—	750
	8-400	185	J-13Y	.035	Electronic		—	10B(5B)	18	3½-5	—	750
	8-400	205	J-11Y	.035	Electronic		—	10B(2½B)	21	3½-5	—	900
	8-440	230	J-11Y	.035	Electronic		—	10B	21	3½-5	—	750
'75	8-318	150, 135	N-13Y	.035	Electronic		—	2B	10	5-7	—	750
	8-360	180	N-12Y	.035	Electronic		—	6B	18	5-7	—	750
	8-360	190	N-12Y	.035	Electronic		—	6B	18	5-7	—	750
	8-400	2 bbl	J-13Y	.035	Electronic		—	10B	18	6-7½	—	750
	8-400	4 bbl	J-13Y	.035	Electronic		—	8B	18	3½-5(6-7½)	—	750
	8-440	4 bbl	RY-87P	.040	Electronic		—	8B	18	4-5½	—	750

TUNE-UP SPECIFICATIONS

When analyzing compression test results, look for uniformity among cylinders rather than specific pressures.

Year	ENGINE No. Cyl Displacement (cu in.)	hp	SPARK PLUGS Orig. Type	Gap (in.)	DISTRIBUTOR Point Dwell (deg)	Point Gap (in.)	IGNITION TIMING (deg) ▲ ● Man Trans	Auto Trans	VALVES Intake Opens ■ (deg)	Fuel Pump Pressure (psi) ●	IDLE SPEED (rpm) ▲ ● Man Trans	Auto Trans
'76	8-318	150, 140	RN-12Y	.035	Electronic		—	2B(TDC)	10	5-7	—	750
	8-360	170, 175	RN-12Y	.035	Electronic		—	6B	18	5-7	—	700(750)
	8-400	175	RJ-13Y	.035	Electronic		—	10B	18	5-7	—	700
	8-400	210, 185	RJ-13Y	.035	Electronic		—	6B(8B)	18	5-7	—	850(750)
	8-400 HP	240	RJ-86P	.035	Electronic		—	6B	18	5-7	—	850
	8-440	205, 200	RJ-13Y	.035	Electronic		—	8B	18	5-7	—	750
'77	8-318	145(135)	RN-12Y	.035	Electronic		—	8B(TDC)	10	5¾-7¼	—	700(850)
	8-360	155(170)	RN-12Y	.035	Electronic		—	10B(6B)	18	5¾-7¼	—	700(750)
	8-400②	190	RJ-13Y	.035	Electronic		—	10B	20	5¾-7¼	—	750
	8-440②	195(185)	RJ-13Y	.035	Electronic		—	12B(8B)	20	5¾-7¼	—	750
'78	8-318②	2 bbl	RN-12Y	.035	Electronic		—	16B	10	5¾-7¼	—	750
	8-318②	4 bbl	RN-12Y	.035	Electronic		—	10B	10	5¾-7¼	—	750
	8-360②	2 bbl	RN-12Y	.035	Electronic		—	20B	18	5¾-7¼	—	750
	8-360	4 bbl	RN-12Y	.035	Electronic		—	③	18	5¾-7¼	—	750
	8-400②	4 bbl	OJ-13Y	.035	Electronic		—	20B	18	5¾-7¼	—	750
	8-440②	4 bbl	OJ-13Y	.035	Electronic		—	12B(8B)	18	5¾-7¼	—	750
'79	6-225	2 bbl	RBL-16Y	.035	Electronic		—	12B	16	4-5½	—	750
	8-318	All	RN-12Y	.035	Electronic		—	16B	10	5¾-7¼	—	750
	8-360	All	RN-12Y	.035	Electronic		—	16B	18	5¾-7¼	—	750

▲ See text for procedure
● Figure in parentheses for California and high altitude
■ All figures Before Top Dead Center
① Non-California cars built after Feb. 2, 7½B
② Lean burn
③ 6B—High Altitude
   8B—Calif. and HD

A After Top Dead Center
B Before Top Dead Center
TDC Top Dead Center
— Not applicable
NOTE: The underhood specifications sticker often reflects tune-up specification changes made in production. Sticker figures must be used if they disagree with those in this chart.

FIRING ORDER

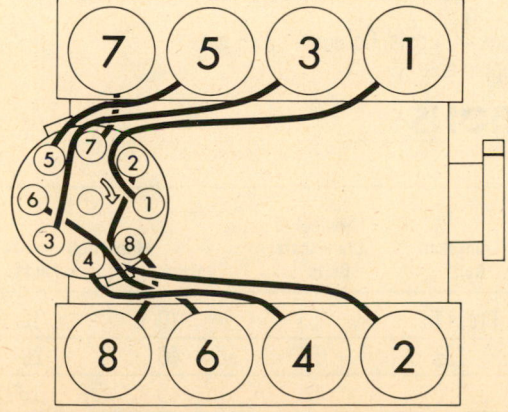

CHRYSLER CORP. 318, 360 V8
Engine firing order: 1-8-4-3-6-5-7-2
Distributor rotation: clockwise

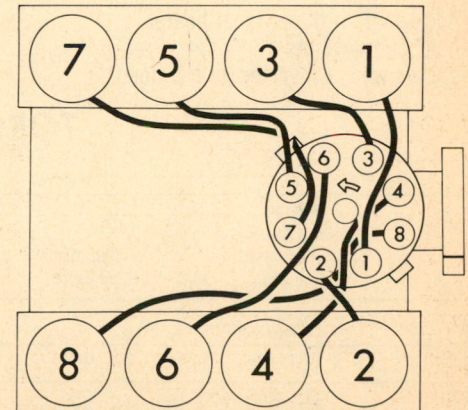

CHRYSLER CORP. 400 and 440 V8
Engine firing order: 1-8-4-3-6-5-7-2
Distributor rotation: counterclockwise

CAPACITIES

Year	Engine No. Cyl. Displacement (Cu. In.)	Engine Crankcase Add 1 Qt For New Filter	TRANSMISSION Pts To Refill After Draining Manual 3-Speed	4-Speed	Automatic	Drive Axle (pts)	Gasoline Tank (gals)	COOLING SYSTEM (qts) With Heater ▲	With A/C
'72	8-360	4	—	—	16.3	4.4	23	15.5	16.5
	8-400	4	—	—	19.0	4.4	23	14.5	15.5
	8-440	4	—	—	19.0	4.4	23	17.5	17.5
	Town & Country	4	—	—	19.0	4.4	23	16	17
	Imperial	4	—	—	19.0	4.4	23	17.5	17.5
'73	8-400	4	—	—	19.0	4.5	23	16	16
	8-440	4	—	—	19.0	4.5	23	15.5	15.5
	Imperial	4	—	—	19.0	4.5	23	18	18
'74	8-360	4	—	—	16.1	4.5	26.5④	16	16
	8-400	4	—	—	18.9	4.5	26.5④	16.5	16.5
	8-440	4	—	—	18.9	4.5	26.5④	16	16
	Imperial	4	—	—	16.5	4.5	26.5	17	17
'75	8-318	4	—	—	16.5	4.5	25.5	16.5	18
	8-360	4	—	—	16.5	4.5	26.5④	16.0	16.0
	8-400	4	—	—	16.5	4.5	26.5④	16.5	16.5
	8-400 HP	4	—	—	16.5	4.5	20.5	16.5	16.5
	8-440	4	—	—	16.5	4.5	26.5④	16.0	16.0
	Imperial	4	—	—	16.5	4.5	26.5	17.0	17.0
'76	8-318	4	—	—	17	4.5	25.5	16.5	18
	8-360	4	—	—	19	4.5	26.5④	16	16
	8-400	4	—	—	19	4.5	26.5④	16.5	16.5
	8-400 HP	5	—	—	19	4.5	20.5	16.5	16.5
	8-440	4	—	—	19	4.5	26.5	16	16
'77-'78	8-318	4	—	—	17②	4.5	26.5④	16.5	18.0
	8-360	4	—	—	17②	4.5	26.5④	16.0	16.0
	8-400	4	—	—	16.5②	4.5	26.5④	16.5	17.0
	8-440	4	—	—	16.5②	4.5	26.5④	16.0	16.5
'79	6-225	4	—	—	17②	4.5	21	11.5	14.5
	8-318	4	—	—	17②	4.5	21	15.0	17.5
	8-360	4	—	—	17②	4.5	21	16.0	16.0

▲ Add 1.5 qts with rear seat heater
① 4 bbl carb—16 pts
② 7.8 pts when converter isn't drained.

③ 2 bbl only
④ Wagons—24 gals, Cordoba—25.5 gals
— Not applicable

TORQUE SPECIFICATIONS
All readings in ft lbs

Year	Engine No. Cyl. Displacement (cu in.)	Cylinder Head Bolts	Rod Bearing Bolts	Main Bearing Bolts	Crankshaft Bolt	Flywheel to Crankshaft Bolts	MANIFOLD Intake	Exhaust
'79	6-225	70	45	85	Press fit	55	10③	10
'72	8-360	95	45	85	135	55	40	20
'74-'79	8-318, 360	95②	45	85	100	55	45	20/15①
'72-'78	8-400, 440	70	45	85	135	55	45	30

① Screw/nut
② 105—1978-79

③ Intake to exhaust manifold bolts—17 ft. lbs., studs—20 ft. lbs.

VALVE SPECIFICATIONS

ENGINE No. Cyl. Displacement (cu. in.)		Seat Angle (deg)	Face Angle (deg)	Spring Test Pressure (lbs @ in.)	Spring Installed Height (in.)	STEM TO GUIDE Clearance (in.)		STEM Diameter (in.)	
						Intake	Exhaust	Intake	Exhaust
'72	8-360	45	④	177 @ 1.31	1 ¹¹⁄₁₆	.0010-.0030	.0020-.0040	.3725	.3715
	8-400	45	45	200 @ 1.44	1 ⁷⁄₈	.0010-.0030	.0020-.0040	.3725	.3715
	8-440	45	45	200 @ 1.44	1 ⁷⁄₈	.0010-.0030	.0020-.0040	.3725	.3715
'73	8-400	45	45	200 @ 1.42	1 ⁵⁵⁄₆₄	.0015-.0032	⑤	.3722	⑥
	8-440	45	45	200 @ 1.42	1 ⁵⁵⁄₆₄	.0015-.0032	⑤	.3722	⑥
'74	8-360	45	④	208 @ 1.31	1 ⁴³⁄₆₄	.0010-.0030	.0020-.0040	.3725	.3720
	8-400	45	45	200 @ 1.43	1 ⁵⁵⁄₆₄	.0010-.0027	⑤	.3727	⑥
	8-440	45	45	234 @ 1.40	1 ⁵⁵⁄₆₄	.0015-.0032	⑥	.3722	⑥
'75	8-318	45	④	177 @ 1.31	1 ²¹⁄₃₂	.0010-.0030	.0020-.0040	.3725	.3715
	8-360	45	④	177 @ 1.31	1 ²¹⁄₃₂	.0010-.0030	.0020-.0040	.3725	.3715
	8-400	45	45	200 @ 1.43	1 ⁵⁵⁄₆₄	.0010-.0027	⑤	.3726	⑥
	8-400 HP	45	45	246 @ 1.36	1 ⁵⁵⁄₆₄	.0015-.0032	③	.3722	②
	8-440	45	45	200 @ 1.43	1 ⁵⁵⁄₆₄	.0010-.0027	⑤	.3726	⑥
'76	8-318	45	④	177 @ 1.31	1 ²¹⁄₃₂	.0010-.0030	.0020-.0040	.3725	.3715
	8-360	45	④	177 @ 1.31	1 ²¹⁄₃₂	.0010-.0030	.0020-.0040	.3725	.3715
	8-400	45	45	200 @ 1.43	1 ⁵⁵⁄₆₄	.0011-.0028	⑤	.3726	⑥
	8-400 HP	45	45	246 @ 1.36	1 ⁵⁵⁄₆₄	.0016-.0033	③	.3722	②
	8-440	45	45	200 @ 1.43	1 ⁵⁵⁄₆₄	.0011-.0028	⑤	.3726	⑥
'77-'79	6-225	45	④	143 @ 1.31	1 ²¹⁄₃₂	.0010-.0030	.0020-.0040	.3725	.3715
	8-318	45	④	177 @ 1.31	1 ⁵⁄₈	.0010-.0030	.0020-.0040	.3725	.3715
	8-360 2 bbl	45	④	177 @ 1.31	1 ⁵⁄₈	.0010-.0030	.0020-.0040	.3725	.3715
	8-360 HD	45	④	193 @ 1.25	1 ⁵⁄₈	.0015-.0035	.0025-.0045	.3720	.3710
	8-400	45	45	200 @ 1.44	1 ⁵³⁄₆₄	.0011-.0028	⑤	.3726	②
	8-440	45	45	200 @ 1.44	1 ⁵³⁄₆₄	.0011-.0028	⑤	.3726	②

① not used
② Hot end—.3712, cold end—.3722
③ Hot end—.0026-.0043, cold end—.0016-.0033
④ Intake valve face angle 45°
   Exhaust valve face angle 43°

⑤ Hot end—.0020-.0037, cold end—.0010-.0027
⑥ Hot end—.3716, cold end—.3726
HP High Performance
HD Heavy Duty

PISTON CLEARANCE

Year	Engine	Piston to bore clearance (in.)*
'72-'79	318, 360 2 bbl	.0005-.0015
	6-225	.0005-.0015
	360 4 bbl HD	.0010-.0020
	400, 440	.0003-.0013

* at top of skirt

RING GAP

All measurements are given in inches

Year	Engine No. Cyl. Displacement (cu. in.)	Top Compression	Bottom Compression	Year	Engine No. Cyl. Displacement (cu. in.)	Oil Control
'72-'79	8-360, 318	.010-.020	.010-.020	'72-'79	All	.015-.055
'72-'79	8-400, 440	.013-.023	.013-.023			

RING GAP
All measurements are given in inches

Year	Engine No. Cyl. Displacement (cu. in.)	Top Compression	Bottom Compression
'79	6-225	.010-.020	.010-.020
'72-'79	8-360, 318	.010-.020	.010-.020
'72-'78	8-400, 440	.013-.023	.013-.023

Year	Engine No. Cyl. Displacement (cu. in.)	Oil Control
'72-'79	All	.015-.055

CRANKSHAFT AND CONNECTING ROD SPECIFICATIONS
All measurements are given in inches

Year	Engine No. Cyl. Displacement (cu in.)	CRANKSHAFT Main Brg. Journal Dia	Main Brg. Oil Clearance	Shaft End-Play	Thrust on No.	CONNECTING ROD Journal Diameter	Oil Clearance	Side Clearance*
'79	6-225	2.7495-2.7505	.0005-.0020	.002-.009	3	2.187-2.188	.0005-.0025	.006-.025
'74-'79	8-318	2.4995-2.5005	.0005-.0020	.002-.007①	3	2.124-2.125	.0005-.0025	.006-.014
'72-'79	8-360	2.8095-2.8105	.0005-.0020	.002-.007①	3	2.124-2.125	.0005-.0025	.006-.014
'72-'74	8-400 2 bbl	2.6245-2.6255	.0005-.0020	.002-.007	3	2.374-2.375	.0005-.0020	.009-.017
'75-'77	8-400 2 bbl	2.6245-2.6255	.0005-.0020	.002-.007	3	2.375-2.376	.0005-.0025	.009-.017
'74	8-400 4 bbl	2.6245-2.6255	.0005-.0020	.002-.007	3	2.374-2.375	.0010-.0025	.009-.017
'75-'78	8-400 4 bbl	2.6245-2.6255	.0005-.0020	.002-.007①	3	2.375-2.376	.0010-.0030②	.009-.017
'72-'78	8-440	2.7495-2.7505	.0005-.0020	.002-.007①	3	2.375-2.376	.0005-.0030②	.009-.017

* Total for two rods
① 1977 and later—.002-.009
② 1977 and later—.0005-.0025

WHEEL ALIGNMENT SPECIFICATIONS

Year	Model	CASTER Range (deg)	Pref Setting (deg)	CAMBER Range (deg)	Pref Setting (deg)	Toe-in (in.)	Steering Axis Inclin. (deg.)	WHEEL PIVOT RATIO (deg) Inner Wheel	Outer Wheel
'72	Manual Steering Chry.	0 to 1P	½N	④	⑤	3/32 to 5/32	7½	20	18.8
	Power Steering Chry.	¼P to 1¼P	¾P	④	⑤	3/32 to 5/32	7½	20	18.8
	Imperial	¼P to 1¼P	¾P	④	⑤	3/32 to 5/32	9	20	17.9
'73	Chrysler	1/16N to 1 5/16P	5/8P	⑦	⑤	1/8 ± 3/32	7½	20	18.8
	Imperial	1/16N to 1 5/16P	5/8P	⑦	⑤	1/8 ± 3/32	9	20	17.9
'74	Chrysler, Imperial	½N to 1¾P	¾P	⑧	⑤	1/16 to ¼	9	20	18.3
'75	Cordoba	½N to 1¾P	¾P	⑦	⑤	1/16 to ¼	8	20	18.0
	Chrysler, Imperial	½N to 1¾P	¾P	⑦	⑤	1/16 to ¼	9	20	18.3
'76	Cordoba	½N to 1¾P	¾P	⑧	½P⑥	1/16 to ¼	8	20	18
	Chrysler	½N to 1¾P	¾P	⑧	½P⑥	1/16 to ¼	9	20	18.3
'77-'79	Cordoba	½N to 2P	¾P	⑧	½P⑥	1/16 to ¼		20	18
'78	Chrysler	½N to 2P	¾P	⑧	½P⑥	1/16 to ¼	9	20	18.3
'79	Chrysler	½N to 2P	¾P	⑧	½P⑥	1/16 to ¼	8	20	18.3

①②③ not used
④ Left side—½P ± ¼; Right side—¼P ± ¼
⑤ Left side—½P; Right side—¼P
⑥ ¼P on right side
⑦ Left side—⅛P to ⅞P
   Right side—⅛N to ⅝P
⑧ Left side—0 to 1P
   Right side—¼N to ¾P
N Negative   P Positive

FRONT END HEIGHT

Year	Model	Front End Height (± ⅛ in.)		Year	Model	Front End Height (± ⅛ in.)
'72-'73	Chrysler	1⅛		'75-'79	Chrysler	10⅛
	Imperial	1¾			Imperial	10⅛
'74	Chrysler	1			Cordoba	10¾
	Imperial	1				

Service procedures for the Charging System, Starting System, Ignition System, Fuel System, Cooling System, Emission Controls, Engine, Clutch, and Manual Transmission on Chrysler, Cordoba, and Imperial cars can be found in the Dodge-Plymouth section.

The Chrysler LeBaron is covered in the Barracuda car section.

AUTOMATIC TRANSMISSION

The model may be identified by the part number, which is stamped on a pad on the left side of the case fluid pan flange. All models use the A-727 transmission, except for Cordobas with the 318 engine, which use the smaller A-904. 1977 and later 360 Cordobas also use the A-904. The A-727 transmission can be visually identified as having a more gradual slope to the converter housing than the A-904; the 727 pan has a bulge at the right front corner while the 904 pan is nearly square.

Neutral Safety/Backup Light Switch Replacement, Shift Linkage Adjustment, Throttle Rod Adjustment, Pan Removal and Installation, Fluid Change

These procedures are covered for all Chrysler Corporation cars in the Barracuda car section.

Band Adjustments

KICK-DOWN BAND

The kick-down band adjusting screw is located on the left-hand side of the transmission case near the throttle lever shaft.

1. Loosen the locknut and back it off about five turns. Be sure that the adjusting screw is free in the case.
2. Using an inch pounds torque wrench, torque the adjusting screw to 72 in. lbs.
3. Back off the adjusting screw the exact number of turns specified below. Keep the screw from turning and tighten the locknut.

A-727 2 1/2 turns
A-904 2 turns

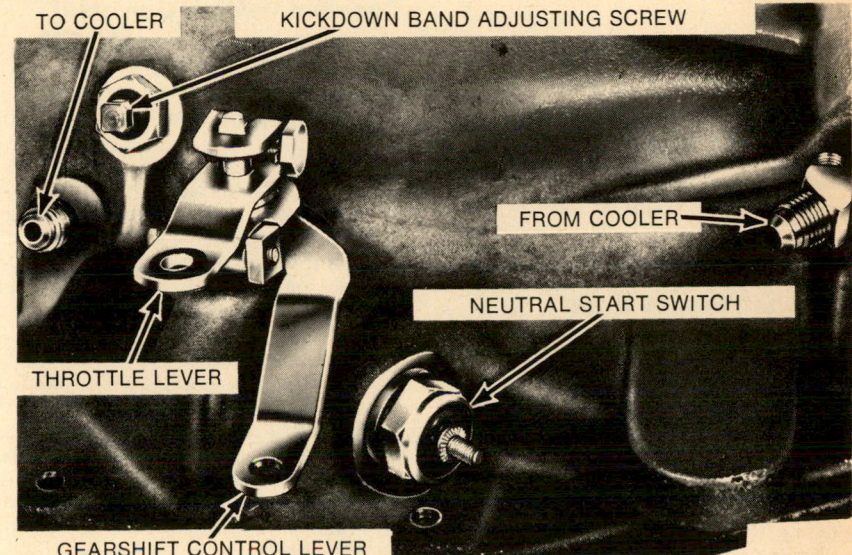

TorqueFlite transmission external controls, showing the location of the kick-down band adjustment
(© Chrysler Corp)

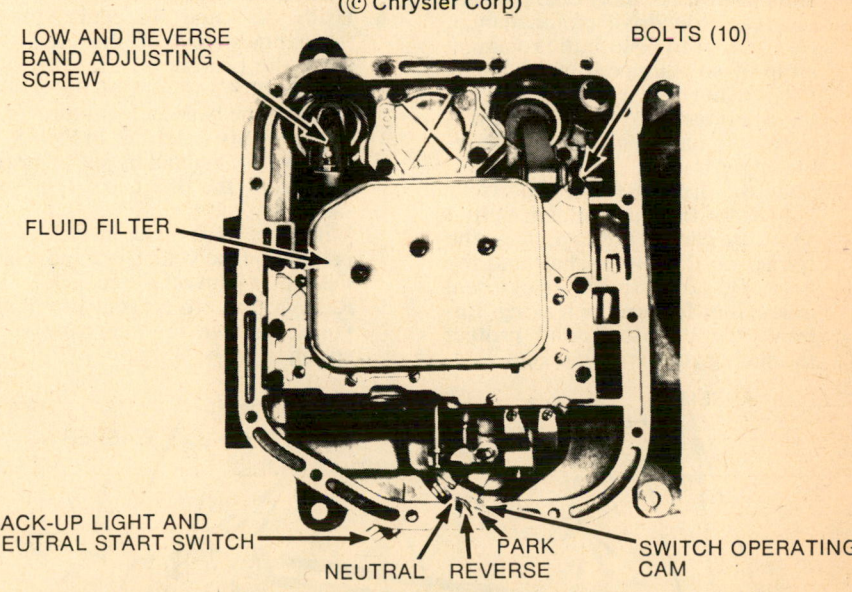

TorqueFlite transmission bottom view with the pan removed. Note the low and reverse band adjusting screw location
(© Chrysler Corp)

LOW AND REVERSE BAND

The pan must be removed from the transmission to gain access to the low and reverse band adjusting screw.

1. Drain the transmission and remove the pan.
2. Loosen the band adjusting screw locknut and back it off about five turns. Be sure that the adjusting screw turns freely in the lever.
3. Using an inch pounds torque wrench, tighten the adjusting screw to 72 in. lbs.

4. Back off the adjusting screw the exact number of turns specified below. Keep the screw from turning and tighten the locknut.
   A-727   2 turns
   A-904   4 turns
5. Using a new gasket, install the pan and tighten the attaching bolts to 150 in. lbs.
6. Fill the transmission.

U-JOINTS

All models use one-piece driveshafts with two U-joints. All full size Chrysler, Cordoba, and 1974-75 Imperial models have two cross-and-roller U-joints with a slip spline at the front U-joint. There are two constant-velocity U-joints on Imperials through 1973.

Driveshaft Removal and Installation

You can avoid loss of lubricant from the rear of the transmission by raising the rear of the car before removing the driveshaft.

1. Scribe alignment marks on the driveshaft, rear U-joint, and the drive pinion flange. This is necessary to ensure proper drive train balance upon installation of the various parts.
2. Remove both of the U-joint roller and bushing assembly clamps from the rear axle drive pinion flange. Be sure not to disturb the retaining strap (if so equipped) which holds the bushing assemblies on the U-joint cross. Do not allow the driveshaft to hang loose while removing either U-joint.
3. Slide the driveshaft with the front yoke from the transmission output shaft. Be careful not to damage the splines on the output shaft and the yoke. Do not disturb the yoke seal unless it is damaged or leaking. Remove the driveshaft and protect the sliding yoke from damage.

4. To install the driveshaft, clean the sliding yoke and inspect its machined surface. File off burrs if necessary. Carefully engage the yoke splines with the splines on the end of the transmission output shaft.
5. At the rear, align the scribe marks and install the U-joint cross and roller bushings into the drive pinion flange. Fit the bushing clamps and securing screws.

Constant Velocity Universal Joint—Imperial through 1973

Remove the driveshaft and, before disassembling any parts, mark the joints for proper indexing at the time of assembly.

1. Remove the four screws and lockwashers. Remove the spline yoke.
2. Remove the two loose bearings from the centering socket yoke.
3. Remove the snap-rings holding the bearing assemblies in the center socket yoke shaft, and the center yoke bores.
4. Press the bearing assemblies from the yokes by using a 3/4 in. socket as a remover and a pipe or socket with an inside diameter of not less than 1 1/16 in. as a receiver on the opposite bearing. With the aid of a press or vise, press one of the rear yoke bearings about 3/8 in. out of the yoke.
5. Clamp the exposed bearing in the vise and drive the yoke from the bearing with a brass drift.
6. Using the same procedure, press the exposed end of the cross to force the bearing on the opposite end about 3/8 in. out of the yoke. Remove the bearing from the yoke as previously described in Step 5.
7. Remove the remaining set of bearings from the shaft yoke in the same way.
8. With the shaft held in the vise, press in on the yoke shaft and work the center joint off the cross.
9. Remove the cross from the shaft yoke. Remove the centering stud spring from the shaft.

10. Remove the four roller bearing assemblies to separate the yoke shaft from the center yoke, as previously described.
    If it is necessary to remove the centering ball and socket assembly, proceed as follows:
11. Carefully pry the centering ball seal assembly from the yoke shaft.
12. Remove the seal from the centering stud seal retainer and the bearing rollers from the centering ball.
13. Fill the cavity behind the centering ball and inside the ball with lithium base grease.
14. Insert a rod, slightly smaller than the inside diameter of the centering ball, into the ball, then strike it sharply with a hammer. The force applied should force the ball and retainer from the yoke.
15. On assembly, position the centering assembly in the yoke with the large diameter hole up, and press it firmly into its seat.
16. Apply grease on the inside surface of the centering ball. Install the 34 rollers. Install the centering stud seal in the ball.
17. Install the centering ball seal assembly on the yoke and press firmly into place.
18. Coat the inside surfaces of the bearing races with the same grease, and install the 32 rollers. Also, pack the reservoirs in the ends of the cross with the same grease.
19. Place the cross in the shaft yoke. Insert one bearing assembly in the bearing bore of the shaft yoke. With the bar stock or socket used as a remover when disassembling, press the bearing into the bore. At the same time, guide the cross into the bearing. Press the bearing into the yoke far enough to install the snap-ring. Install the snap-ring. Reverse the position of the yoke and install the opposite bearing and snap-ring in the same manner.
20. Place the center yoke on the cross installed in the shaft yoke. Install the two bearings and snap-rings in the yoke, as previously described.
21. Install the cross and two bearings in the shaft yoke, in the same manner as previously described. Install the snap-rings.
22. Install the centering stud spring on the centering stud, (large end first). Apply grease to the stud.
23. Position the cross in the center universal joint of the propeller shaft while guiding the centering ball on the centering stud, applying pressure at the same time. Work the center yoke over the cross. Don't damage the cross seals.
24. Install the two bearing assemblies in the rear bores of the center yoke as previously described. Install the snap-rings.
25. Coat the splines of the center socket yoke with grease.
26. Install the slip spline yoke on the

Constant Velocity U-joints and drive shaft—Imperial through 1973
(© Chrysler Corp)

constant velocity joints with screws and lockwashers. Torque to specifications.

Cross and Roller Bearing U-Joints/Chrysler, Cordoba, and 1974-75 Imperial

1. To disassemble the joint, remove the four bolts that hold the two bearing assemblies to the companion flange and knock the bearings off the flange.
2. To remove the bearings from the yoke, first remove the bearing retainer lock washers or C-washers, then pressing on one of the bearings, drive the bearing in toward the center of the joint. This will force the cross to push the opposite bearing out of the universal joint yoke. After it has been pushed all the way out of the yoke, pull up the cross slightly and pack some washers under it. Then press on the end of the cross from which the bearing was just removed to force the first bearing out of the yoke.
3. Perhaps the easiest way to reassemble is to start both bearing retainers into the yoke at the same time, hold the cross carefully in the fingers and squeeze both bearings in a vise or heavy C-clamp. Driving the bearings into place usually cocks the rollers, greatly reducing the life of the bearings.
4. Install the locking devices.

REAR AXLE

Three different rear axle assemblies are being used on Chrysler, Imperial and Cordoba models. A removable carrier axle with an 8 3/4 in. ring gear diameter differential was installed on all models through 1972. Beginning 1973, two integral carrier axles are used; an 8 1/4 and a 9 1/4 in. unit. Both the 8 1/4 and 9 1/4 in. axles use C-clips to retain the axle shafts.

These axles can be visually identified as follows:

The 8 1/4 in. axle has a 10 bolt rear cover, the 8 3/4 in. axle has a welded nonremovable rear cover, and the 9 1/4 in. axle has a 12 bolt rear cover.

All axles have a ratio identification tag under one of the cover or carrier bolts.

Axle Shaft, Bearing and Seal Removal and Installation

See the Dodge/Plymouth section for these procedures. They are arranged by differential ring gear diameter size.

JACKING, HOISTING

Jack the car at the front under the lower control arm and at the rear under the axle housing.

To lift at the frame, use adapters so that contact will be made at the points

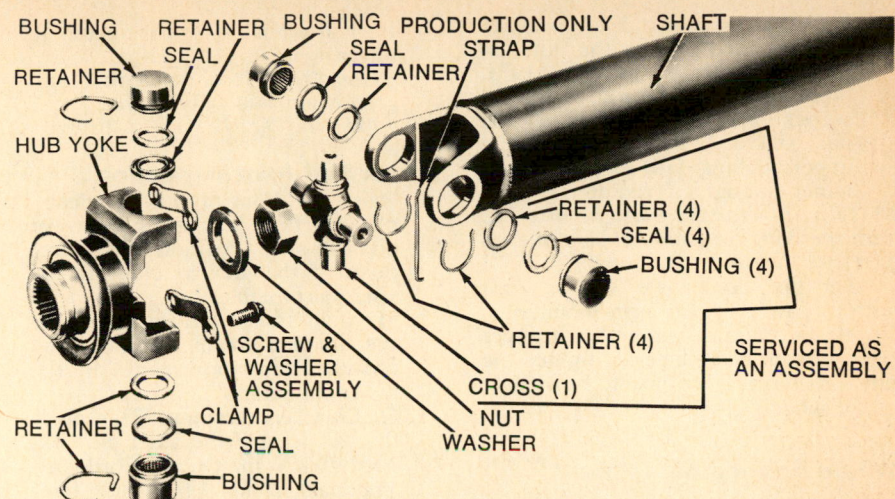

Rear cross and roller U-joint—All Chrysler, Cordoba, and 1974-75 Imperial

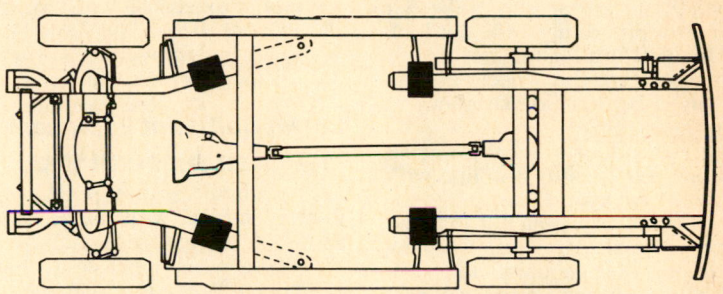

Positioning lift adapter (© Chrysler Corp)

shown. The lifting pad must extend beyond the sides of the supporting structure.

FRONT SUSPENSION

See the Unit Repair Section for front end height adjustment and alignment.

NOTE: The downsized 1979 Chryslers use the Chrysler Corporation intermediate-size front suspension system. The suspension service procedures and torques for the Cordoba should be used for this model.

Shock Absorber Removal and Installation

1. Remove the nut and retainer from the shock absorber top.
2. Jack up the front of the vehicle. It is sometimes necessary to remove the tire and wheel assembly and perform the removal operation from beneath the fender.
3. Remove the shock absorber lower attaching bolt or stud nut. Remove the bolt from the shock absorber eye.
4. Push upward on the shock absorber and fully compress it; pull the shock downward and out of its upper mounting bushings and remove from the vehicle. On Imperial models through 1973, the dust shield is removed with the shock absorber. It may be necessary to remove the upper control arm

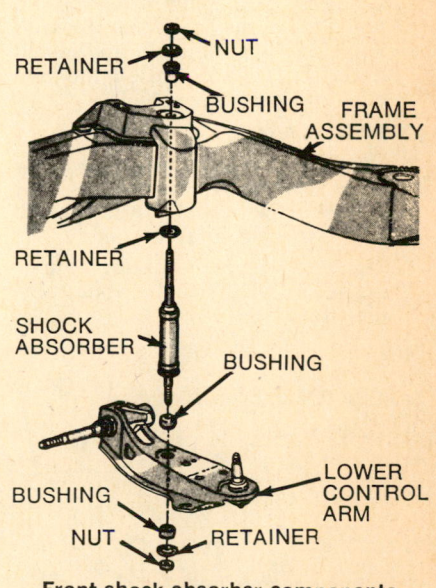

Front shock absorber components —1974 and later Chrysler and Imperial (© Chrysler Corp)

bumper, on some models, to obtain enough clearance to remove the shock absorber assembly.
5. Purge the new shock of air by repeatedly extending it in its normal position and compressing it while inverted. To begin the installation procedure fully compress the shock. Insert the rod through the

upper bushing, install the retainer and nut, and tighten the nut. On Imperial models through 1973, place the retainer on the shock absorber upper rod; then install the dust shield. Install the rod to the upper bushing with its nut and retainer and tighten the nut.

NOTE: *All retainers must be installed with the concave (sunken) side in contact with the rubber.*

Align the shock lower eye or shaft with its lower control arm mountings. Install its retaining nut and bolt finger tight. Lower the vehicle and tighten the nut with the full weight of the vehicle on the wheels.

Wheel Bearing Adjustment

1972

1. Jack the vehicle and remove the hub cap and grease cup. Take out the cotter pin, remove the nut lock and loosen the adjusting nut.
2. While rotating the wheel, tighten the wheel bearing adjusting nut to 90 in lbs.
3. Align the nut lock on the nut so that one pair of slots is in line with the cotter pin hole.
4. Back off the adjusting nut lock assembly one slot and install a new cotter pin. This should yield an adjustment between zero (no preload) and 0.003 in. end-play.
5. Clean the grease cup. Coat, but do not fill, the inside of the cup with wheel bearing lubricant and install it on the vehicle. Install the hub caps and lower the vehicle.

1973 AND LATER

1. Raise the front of the car to allow the wheels to spin freely.
2. Remove the wheel cover, grease cup, cotterpin, and lock nut.
3. Tighten the wheel bearing adjusting nut to 240-300 in lbs while spinning the wheel.

4. Back the nut off and retighten to finger tight.
5. Reinstall the lock nut, cotter pin, grease cup, and wheel cover.
6. Lower the car.

Lower Ball Joint Inspection

1. Raise the front of the vehicle by placing a floor jack under the lower control arm. Position the lifting point of the jack as close to the wheel as possible.
2. Have an assistant raise and lower the tire and wheel assembly and observe any movement at the lower ball joint.
3. On Chryslers through 1973, replace the ball joint if the axial play exceeds 0.070 in. On all Cordobas, Imperials, and 1974 and later Chryslers, the lower ball joints are preloaded and, if any free-play exists in excess of 0.020 in. through 1976, or .030 in. 1977 and later, the lower ball joint control arm assembly must be removed for service.

Lower Ball Joint Replacement

CHRYSLER THROUGH 1973

The compression-type lower ball joint is integral with the steering arm and is not serviced separately.

1. Remove the upper control arm rebound bumper. Raise the vehicle on a hoist so the front suspension will drop to the downward limit of its travel.
2. Place a jack stand under the lower control arm, near the ball joint.
3. Lower the vehicle onto the jack stand. Off-load the torsion bars by rotating the adjusting bolts counterclockwise.
4. Remove the tire, wheel, and brake drum from the vehicle as an assembly. If equipped with disc brakes, remove the tire and wheel. Remove the brake pads, and remove the caliper from the steering

knuckle and position it out of the way with the brake line attached. Remove the rotor from the spindle.
5. Remove the two lower bolts that attach the steering arm-ball joint assembly to the brake assembly mounting plate.
6. Using a suitable tool, disconnect the tie rod end from the steering arm, taking care not to damage the seal.
7. Remove the ball joint stud retaining nut and cotter pin.
8. Using a suitable tool, separate and remove the ball joint from the lower control arm.
9. On installation, position the ball joint-steering arm assembly on the steering knuckle and install the two retaining bolts.
10. Insert the ball joint stud in the lower control arm and install the retaining nut and cotter pin.
11. Position the tie rod end in the steering knuckle and install the retaining nut and cotter pin.
12. Place a load on the torsion bar by turning the adjusting bolt in a clockwise direction.

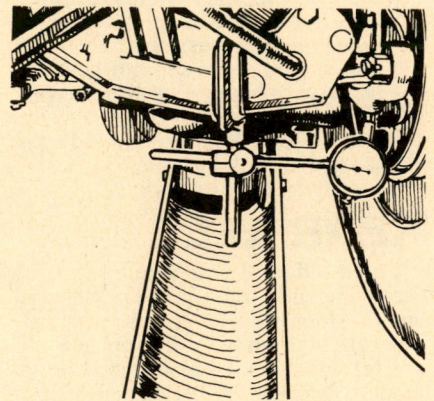

Measuring lower ball joint play; see text for specifications
(© Chrysler Corp)

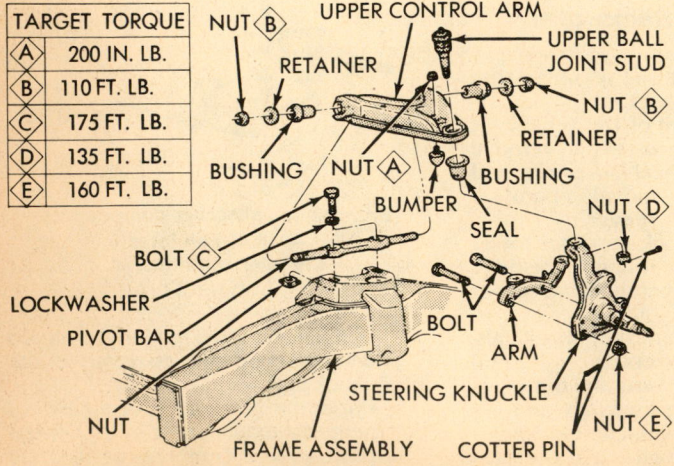

TARGET TORQUE	
Ⓐ	200 IN. LB.
Ⓑ	110 FT. LB.
Ⓒ	175 FT. LB.
Ⓓ	135 FT. LB.
Ⓔ	160 FT. LB.

Upper control arm assembly exploded view— 1974 and later Chrysler and Imperial
(© Chrysler Corp.)

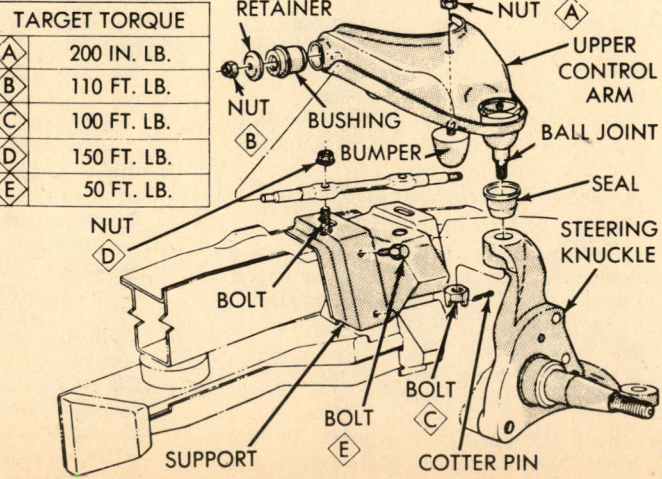

TARGET TORQUE	
Ⓐ	200 IN. LB.
Ⓑ	110 FT. LB.
Ⓒ	100 FT. LB.
Ⓓ	150 FT. LB.
Ⓔ	50 FT. LB.

Cordoba upper control arm assembly
(© Chrysler Corp.)

13. Install the tire, wheel and brake drum assembly. If equipped with disc brakes, install the rotor, caliper, brake pads and tire and wheel assembly.
14. Lower the vehicle and install the upper control arm rebound bumper if so equipped.
15. Check and adjust the front suspension height as required.

IMPERIAL THROUGH 1973

Lower ball joints on Imperial models are serviced only as ball joint-control arm assemblies.

1. Raise the vehicle on a hoist so the front suspension drops to the downward limit of its travel.
2. Remove the wheel and tire as an assembly.
3. Remove the load from *both* torsion bars by turning the adjusting bolts in a counterclockwise direction.
4. Disconnect the shock absorber from the lower control arm and position the shock out of the way. Disconnect the strut bar from the lower control arm.
5. Disconnect the brake hose from the caliper.
6. Remove the lower ball joint retaining nut and cotter pin.
7. Using a suitable tool, separate the ball joint stud from the steering knuckle.
8. Remove the nut and washer that attaches the lower control arm pivot shaft to the frame.
9. Using a brass drift and hammer, tap the end of the pivot shaft to loosen it (the shaft is a tapered fit in the front crossmember).
10. Remove the lower control arm and shaft from the vehicle as an assembly.
11. Position the control arm assembly in a press with the hex opening for the torsion bar in the up position and place a support under the outer edge of the control arm.
12. Insert a brass drift in the hex opening and press the shaft out of the control arm. The bushing inner arm will remain on the shaft.
13. Remove the torsion bar adjusting bolt and swivel from the control arm.
14. On installation, position a new bushing on the pivot shaft (flange end of the bushing first) and seat the bushing on the shoulder of the pivot shaft.
15. Press the shaft and bushing assembly into the new control arm.
16. Install the torsion bar adjusting bolt and swivel on the new control arm.
17. Position a new seal on the ball joint and install the seal. To ease installation of the seal, the ball joint stud should be perpendicular to the body of the ball joint.
18. Position the control arm assembly on the crossmember in approximate operating position and install

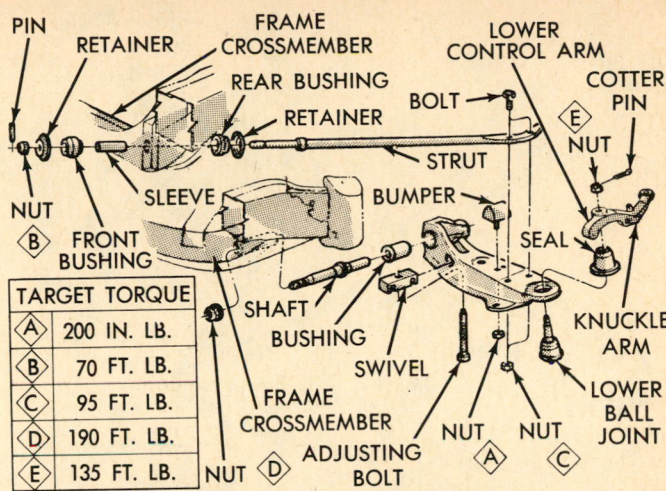

Lower control arm assembly exploded view—
1974 and later Chrysler and Imperial
(© Chrysler Corp)

TARGET TORQUE	
A	200 IN. LB.
B	70 FT. LB.
C	95 FT. LB.
D	190 FT. LB.
E	135 FT. LB.

the nut and washer. *Do not tighten the nut until the full weight of the vehicle is on the wheels.*
19. Insert the lower ball joint stud in the steering knuckle and install the retaining nut and cotter pin.
20. Install the strut bar rear bushing and retainer on the strut bar and insert the strut bar through the crossmember.
21. Install the front strut bar bushing and retainer on the strut bar and install the retaining nut finger tight only.
22. Position the rear of the strut bar over the lower control arm and install the bumper and plate.
23. Connect the shock absorber to the lower control arm and install the retaining nut finger tight. Place a load on each torsion bar by turning the adjusting bolt clockwise.
24. Connect the brake line to the disc brake caliper and bleed the brakes.
25. Install the tire and wheel assembly.
26. Lower the vehicle to the floor. Tighten the strut bar, shock absorber and lower control arm attaching nuts.
27. Check and adjust the front end height and alignment.

1974 AND LATER CHRYSLER, CORDOBA, AND IMPERIAL

Lower ball joints on these models may be serviced separately. The ball joints are a press-fit.

1. Place the ignition switch in the off or unlocked position.
2. Remove the rebound bumper.
3. Raise the vehicle on a hoist so that the front suspension drops to the downward limit of its travel. Position jackstands beneath the front frame for extra support.
4. Remove the wheel and tire assembly.
5. Remove the caliper from its mounts and tie it up out of the way

so that there is no strain on the flexible brake hose.
6. Remove the hub and rotor assembly, splash shield, lower shock absorber mounting nut, retainer and insulator.
7. Off-load the torsion bars by rotating the adjusting bolts counterclockwise.
8. Remove the upper and lower ball joint stud cotter pins and nuts. Using a ball joint press tool, slide the tool over the upper stud until the tool rests on the steering knuckle.
9. Then, turn the threaded portion of the tool so that it locks snugly against the lower stud. Tighten the tool enough to load the lower ball joint stud, and then strike the steering knuckle arm with a hammer to loosen the stud. Under no circumstances should you attempt to force the stud from the knuckle using the tool alone.

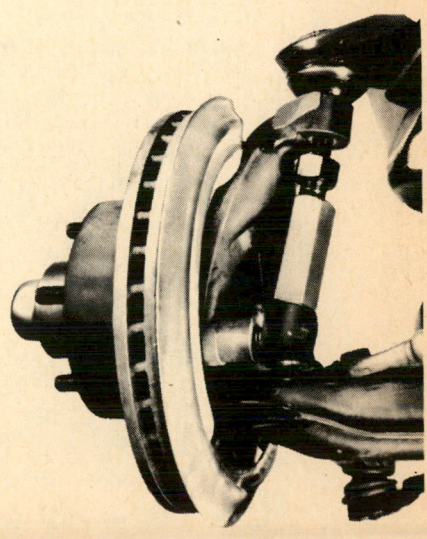

Removing the ball joint stud with a stud remover tool (© Chrysler Corp)

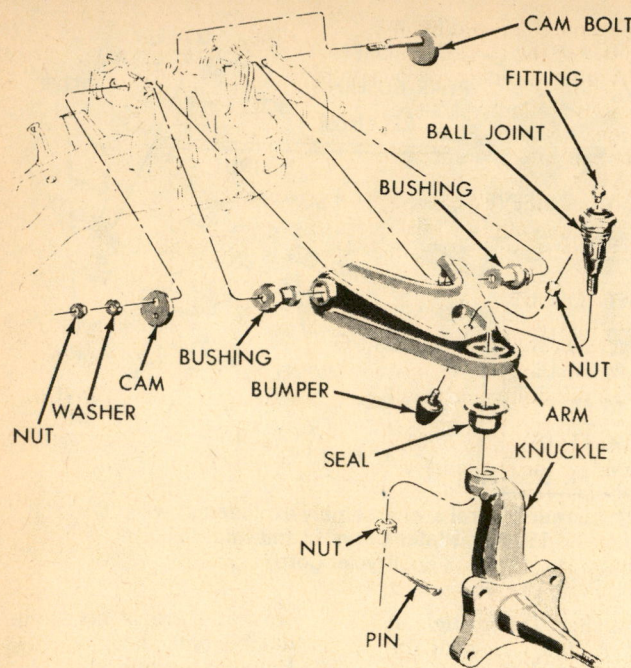

Chrysler upper control arm—through 1973
(© Chrysler Corp)

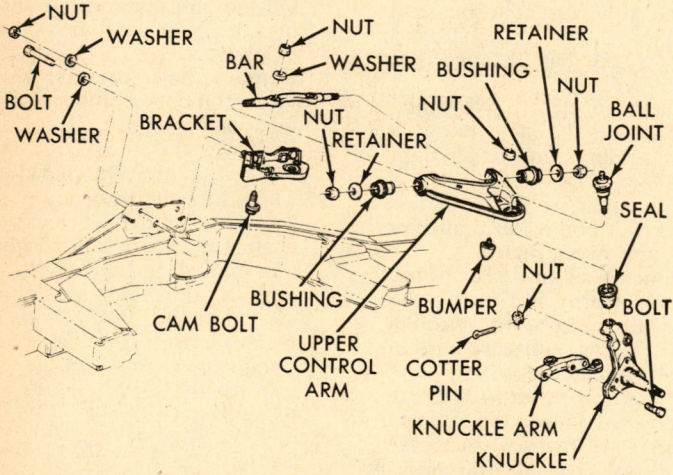

Imperial upper control arm—through 1973
(© Chrysler Corp)

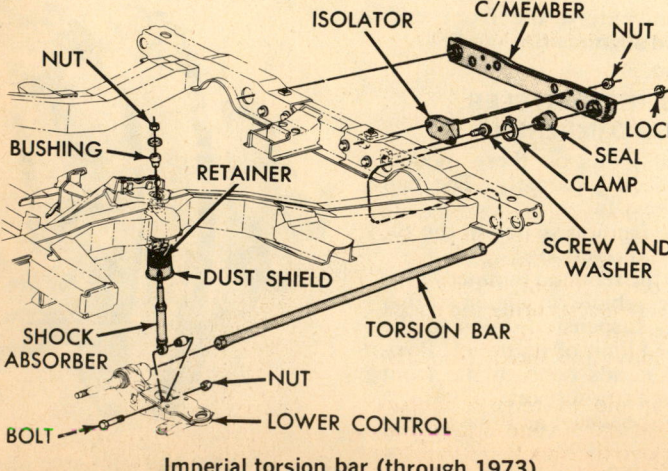

Imperial torsion bar (through 1973)
(© Chrysler Corp)

Front shock absorber and lower control arm assembly—Cordoba
(© Chrysler Corp)

10. Using a press, press the ball joint out of the lower control arm.
11. On installation, press the new ball joint into the lower control arm.
12. Place a new seal over the ball joint (as necessary). Press the retainer portion of the seal down over the ball joint housing until it locks into position.
13. Insert the ball joint stud through the opening in the knuckle arm and install the stud retaining nut. Tighten the stud nut to 100 ft. lbs. for Chrysler through 1973 and Cordoba, and to 135 ft. lbs. for 1974 and later Chrysler and all Imperial. Install the cotter pins and lubricate the ball joint.
14. Load the torsion bar by rotating the adjusting bolt clockwise.
15. Install the shock absorber retaining nut, retainer and insulator, the splash shield, hub and rotor assembly, and brake caliper. Install the wheel and tire assembly.
16. Adjust the front wheel bearings.
17. Remove the jackstands and lower the car. Install the rebound bumper. Adjust the front suspension height.

Upper Ball Joint Replacement
1. Place the ignition in the off or unlocked position. Raise the vehicle by placing a floor jack under the lower control arm. Place the lifting point of the jack as close as possible to the wheel.
2. Remove the wheel, tire and drum as an assembly. On models with disc brakes, remove the tire and wheel, remove the disc brake pads, remove the disc brake caliper from the steering knuckle and position the caliper out of the way with the brake line attached. Remove the brake rotor from the steering knuckle.

3. Remove the nut that attaches the upper ball joint to the steering knuckle and, using a ball joint stud removal tool, loosen the ball joint stud from the steering knuckle.

4. Unscrew the upper ball joint from the upper control arm and remove it from the vehicle.

5. Position a new ball joint on the upper control arm, screw the ball joint into the control arm until it bottoms and tighten the ball joint to a minimum of 125 ft. lbs. for Cordoba, 150 ft. lbs. for Imperial and Chrysler models.

NOTE: *When installing a ball joint, make certain the ball joint threads engage those of the upper control arm squarely if the original control arm is being used.*

6. Position a new seal on the ball joint stud and install the seal in the ball joint making sure the seal is fully seated on the ball joint housing.

7. Position the ball joint stud in the steering knuckle and install the retaining nut. Tighten the stud nut to 100 ft. lbs. for Chrysler through 1973 and Cordoba, and to 135 ft. lbs. for 1974 and later Chrysler and all Imperial.

8. Lubricate ball joint and, if replacement ball joint is equipped with knock-off type grease fitting, break off that portion of the fitting over which the lubrication gun was installed.

9. If equipped with disc brakes, install the rotor, caliper and brake pads. Install the tire and wheel.

10. Lower the vehicle and adjust the wheel alignment.

Torsion Bar Removal and Installation

The torsion bars are not interchangeable from right to left. They are marked with an R or an L.

1. Raise the vehicle so the front suspension drops to the limit of its downward travel.

2. Remove the upper control arm rebound bumper if so equipped.

3. On all models except Imperials through 1973, remove the tension from the torsion bar to be replaced by turning the anchor adjusting bolt in a counterclockwise direction. On Imperials through 1973, release the load on both torsion bars by turning each anchor adjusting bolt in a counterclockwise direction. This is necessary because the rubber insulator rear crossmember would be under load and could possibly cause severe damage or personal injury.

4. Slide rear anchor balloon seal off the rear anchor and remove the lockring from the anchor. On Imperial models remove the balloon seal clamp. Remove the automatic transmission torque shaft on 1974 and later models, if necessary.

5. On all models, remove the torsion bar from the vehicle by sliding it rearward and out of the torsion bar rear anchor. A special tool is available for this job; it clamps to the bar and provides a striking surface for driving the bar out. Do not apply heat to the bar or the anchors.

6. On installation, position the torsion bar in the chassis and apply a coating of chassis lubricant to both ends.

7. Install the lockring in the anchor, making sure it is seated in the groove. If the torsion bar and control arm hex openings are not aligned, loosen the control arm pivot shaft nut and rotate the pivot shaft. Do not retighten the nut until weight is placed on the suspension.

8. Pack the annular opening in the rear anchor, completely full of chassis lubricant and position the lip of the balloon seal in the groove of the anchor. On Imperial models, install the balloon seal clamp.

9. On all Chrysler, Cordoba, and 1974-75 Imperial models, turn the adjusting bolt clockwise to load the torsion bar. On Imperial models through 1973, turn both adjusting bolts to load both torsion bars.

10. Lower the vehicle to the floor and adjust front end height as required. If the pivot shaft nut was loosened, tighten it to 145 ft. lbs. for cordobas, 190 ft. lbs. for Chryslers and Imperials.

REAR SUSPENSION

All models use a leaf-spring rear suspension and double-acting shock absorbers. The springs are of the semi-elliptical type, with zinc interleaves between the normal leaves to increase spring life and reduce corrosion. On most models, rubber insulators are used where the springs attach to the body to reduce road noise and vibration.

Shock Absorber Removal and Installation

NOTE: *Purge new shocks of air by repeatedly extending them in the normal position and compressing them while inverted.*

1. Jack the vehicle under the rear axle. Position the jackstands in such a manner that the shock absorbers are under no load.

2. At the bottom mount, remove the nut and retainer securing the shock to the spring seat isolator retainer plate; remove the shock from the stud.

3. At the top mount, remove the retaining bolt and nut and washer and then remove the shock. To replace the shock absorber, reverse the removal procedure. Remember that

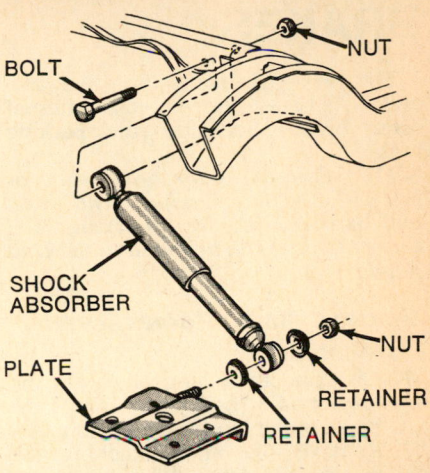

Rear shock absorber components—1974 and later Chrysler and Imperial
(© Chrysler Corp)

the shock absorber mounting bolts must not be fully tightened until the full vehicle weight is resting on the wheels.

Spring Removal and Installation

1. Raise the vehicle on a hoist.

2. Place jack stands under the differential and lower the vehicle until the weight is removed from the rear springs.

3. Disconnect the rear shock absorber. If so equipped, remove the sway bar.

4. Loosen and remove the U-bolt nuts and U-bolts. Remove the spring plate.

5. Loosen and remove the nuts holding the front spring hanger to the front body mounting bracket.

--- CAUTION ---

1974 and later full-size models have preloaded rear springs. A special spring stretcher (tool no. C-4211) must be installed before releasing either end of the spring. Do not try to remove the spring without the stretcher; its sudden release could cause serious injury.

6. Remove the rear spring hanger bolts and let the spring drop far enough to pull the front spring hanger bolts out of the body mounting bracket.

7. Remove the front pivot bolt from the front spring hanger.

8. Loosen and remove rear shackle nuts and remove the rear shackle from the spring.

9. Remove rear spring from the vehicle.

10. Reverse above procedure to install. When installing the front and rear pivot nuts and bolts, do not tighten the bolts until the vehicle has been lowered to the floor and weight is on the wheels.

BRAKES

The 1974-75 Imperial uses rear disc brakes. The system employs internal drum brake shoes for the parking brake.

NOTE: *Procedures for brake shoe or pad replacement and adjustment, wheel and master cylinder overhaul, and brake bleeding can be found in the Unit Repair Section.*

Master Cylinder Removal and Installation

1. Disconnect the fluid lines. On the disc brake cylinders, plug the brake outlets to prevent leakage.
2. Remove the nuts attaching the master cylinder to the firewall or to the power brake unit.

NOTE: *It is not necessary to disconnect the pedal push rod as it is possible to separate the master cylinder from the rod by pulling them apart after the master cylinder attaching nuts have been removed.*

3. Disconnect the pedal push rod (non-power brakes) from the brake pedal.
4. Remove the master cylinder from the vehicle.
5. Reverse the procedure to install.
6. Bleed the brake system.

Power Brake Booster Removal and Installation

1. Remove the nuts attaching the master cylinder to the brake booster and position the master cylinder out of the way. If the brake lines do not have enough slack to allow the master cylinder to be moved without kinking the brake lines, it will be necessary to disconnect the brake lines.
2. Disconnect the vacuum hose from the brake booster.
3. Working under the dash, remove the attaching nut and bolt from the brake booster pushrod and disconnect the pushrod from the brake pedal. On 1978 and later Cordobas, use a small screwdriver to expand and remove the retainer clip from the brake pedal pin. Discard the clip; use a new one on reassembly. Remove the lower pivot bolt and nut.
4. Remove the nuts and washers that attach the brake booster to the firewall.
5. Remove the booster from under the hood.
6. Reverse the above procedure to install.
7. If the brake lines were disconnected, bleed the brake system.

Parking Brake Adjustment

NOTE: *On 1974-75 Imperials, the internal drum parking brake is first adjusted by inserting an adjusting spoon through an opening in the intermediate adapter (from the inboard side) and turning the starwheel until the parking brake shoes seat against the drum/disc surface. Then, back off the starwheel exactly 12 clicks so that the disc turns freely. Finally, adjust the cable as described below.*

1. Apply the brakes several times while backing up to adjust the rear drum brakes. Raise and support the vehicle. Release the parking brake lever. Loosen the cable adjusting nut.
2. Tighten the cable adjusting nut until a slight drag is felt while rotating the wheel.
3. Loosen the cable adjusting nut until both rear wheels can be rotated freely. Back off the cable adjusting nut two full turns.
4. Apply the parking brake several times. Check to see that the rear wheels rotate freely without dragging.

STEERING

A worm and recirculating ball type steering gear is used with the manual steering system. Constant-Control power steering is an option on all models. Hydraulic power is provided by a belt-driven pump. Some power steering pumps were equipped from the factory with fluid coolers. These were used on vehicles with air conditioning, high-performance engines, and/or vehicles equipped with special axle ratios.

Power Steering Pump Removal and Installation

1. Before beginning the removal procedure, carefully take note of the exact hose routing. The hoses must be installed in the exact same position as before the removal.
2. Back off the pump mounting and locking bolts and remove the pump drive belt.
3. Disconnect all hoses at the pump.
4. Remove the pump bolts and remove the pump with its bracket.
5. To install the pump, place it in position and install the mounting bolts.
6. Install the pump drive belt and adjust. There should be no more than 1/2 in. of play, under moderate thumb pressure, on the longest run of belt. Some pump brackets have a 1/2 in. square hole for use in tensioning the belt. Torque the pump mounting bolts 30 ft. lbs.
7. Connect the pressure and return hoses. Install a new pressure-hose O-ring if there is one.
8. Fill the pump with power steering fluid.
9. Start the engine and rotate the steering wheel from stop to stop several times. This will bleed the system. Check the pump fluid level and fill as required.

10. Be certain the hoses are away from the exhaust manifolds and are not kinked or twisted.

Steering Wheel Removal and Installation

— CAUTION —

Be careful when removing the steering wheel from vehicles that are equipped with a collapsible steering column. A sharp blow or excessive pressure on the column could cause it to collapse.

1. Disconnect the battery.
2. Remove the padded center assembly. This center assembly is often held on only by spring clips. There are usually holes in the back of the wheel so the pad can be pushed off. On some deluxe interiors, and with the rim blow horn, it is held on by screws behind the arms of the wheel. On the tilt and telescoping steering column, remove the locking lever knob by releasing the clip on its underside. Remove the locking lever screws and the lever.
3. Remove the large center nut. Remove the steering wheel from the column with a puller.
4. Reverse the procedure to install.

Turn Signal/Hazard Warning Switch, Ignition Switch and/or Ignition Lock Cylinder Removal and Installation

These procedures are covered for all Chrysler Corporation cars in the Barracuda car section.

INSTRUMENT PANEL

Speedometer Cable Replacement

The speedometer cable end has a sleeve with a spring clip, which locks to the speedometer housing. The sleeve also functions as a noise damper between the cable and the speedometer. To release the cable, depress the end of the spring clip arm and pull the cable from the speedometer housing. The core can then be pulled from the cable housing for replacement or servicing.

Headlight Switch Replacement

THROUGH 1973

1. Disconnect the battery. If equipped with air conditioning, remove the left air conditioning duct.
2. Remove the headlight switch shaft and knob by pulling the switch to the On position, reaching under the dash, and depressing the button on the bottom of the headlight switch case. Pull the knob and shaft from the switch.

3. Remove the sentinel and automatic dimmer control knobs if equipped with automatic headlight dimmer.
4. Remove the headlight switch attaching nut.
5. Remove the headlight switch from under the dash and disconnect the wires.
6. Reverse above procedure to install.

1974-78 CHRYSLER AND IMPERIAL

1. Disconnect the battery ground cable. Remove the instrument cluster bezel.
2. Pull the air conditioner outlet housing seal loose at the top to get at the lower switch bracket mounting screws. Remove the screws.
3. Pull the assembly out from the carrier housing and disconnect all the wires.
4. Pull the light switch to the on position and depress the release button on the side of the switch. Pull the knob and stem from the switch.
5. Remove the sentinel and dimmer control knobs, if any.
6. Remove the illumination lamp assembly mounting screw and the lamp.
7. Remove the mounting clips and the headlight switch lens.
8. Remove the switch to mounting plate nut and remove the switch.
9. Reverse the procedure for installation.

1979 CHRYSLER NEWPORT, NEW YORKER

1. Disconnect the battery ground cable.
2. Remove the knob and shaft assembly by pushing the release button on the switch from underneath the instrument panel.
3. Snap out the switch trim bezel using the knob and shaft assembly as a tool.
4. Remove the spanner nut.
5. Disconnect the wires and remove the switch.
6. Reverse the procedure for installation.

CORDOBA

1. Disconnect the battery ground cable. Remove the instrument cluster upper bezel.
2. Remove the escutcheon mounting screw.
3. Remove the screws holding the switch mounting plate to the cluster housing.
4. Detach the wires.
5. Depress the switch stem release button and pull the knob and stem from the switch.
6. Remove the escutcheon and switch mounting nut. Remove the switch.
7. Reverse the procedure for installation.

WINDSHIELD WIPERS

Wiper Blade Replacement

The wiper blades are attached to the arms by one of two methods. One is a spring loaded lever in the blade bridge, which locks to a tapered lug on the side of the arm. To release the blade, depress the release lever and pull the blade from the lug. The second type has the arm inserted into a pivot bridge on the blade and locked into place by a flat spring in the bridge, engaging a lug on the arm. To release the blade, depress the flat spring end and pull the blade from the arm.

Motor Removal and Installation

1. Disconnect the negative battery cable.
2. Lift the latch on each wiper arm and remove the arms and blades as an assembly.
3. Remove the cowl screen.
4. Remove the drive crank retaining nut and drive crank. To prevent damage to the gears, hold the crank arm with a wrench when removing the crank nut from the motor. Disconnect the motor wiring.
5. Disconnect the lead wires from the wiper motor.
6. Remove the three wiper motor mounting bolts and remove the motor from the vehicle.
7. Reverse above procedure to install. When installing the wiper arms and blades, make sure the wiper motor is in the Park position.

RADIO

NOTE: *When installing the radio, adjust the antenna trimmer for peak volume. The antenna trimmer screw is usually near the antenna socket on the radio. Sometimes it is behind the tuning knob.*

Removal and Installation

THROUGH 1973

1. Disconnect the battery ground cable.
2. Remove the left ash tray.
3. Unscrew the stereo tape reset knob, if so equipped.
4. Disconnect the radio wiring.
5. Move the defroster vacuum actuator to facilitate the radio removal.
6. Remove the two radio mounting screws through the access openings in the lower instrument panel. On search-tune and AM radios, remove the knobs, bezels, and nuts.
7. Remove the radio support bracket (if so equipped) mounting screw from lower reinforcement. Support the radio.
8. Remove the radio support bracket or mounting screws through the access openings in the lower instrument panel. Remove the radio from under the instrument panel.
9. Reverse the procedure to install.

1974-78 CHRYSLER AND IMPERIAL

1. Disconnect the battery ground cable.
2. Remove the instrument cluster bezel.
3. On monaural radios, remove the lamp assembly from the front of the radio.
4. Remove the radio to panel screws.
5. Remove the instrument panel upper cover. Work through the access hole in the top of the instrument panel to disconnect the antenna and speaker leads. Remove the bracket mounting nut.
6. Remove the radio and detach the electrical lead.
7. Reverse the procedure for installation.

1979 CHRYSLER NEWPORT, NEW YORKER

1. Remove the center bezel.
2. Remove the radio to panel mounting screws.
3. Pull the radio out through the front face of the panel. Detach the antenna lead, ground strap, power wire, and speaker leads.
4. Reverse the procedure for installation.

CORDOBA

1. Disconnect the battery ground cable.
2. Remove the instrument cluster lower bezel.
3. Disconnect the antenna, speaker, and electrical leads.
4. Remove the nut holding the radio to the support bracket. The nut is at the back of the radio and on the side of tape player/radios.
5. Remove the screws holding the radio to the cluster housing from the front.
6. Remove the radio.
7. Reverse the procedure for installation.

HEATER

NON-AIR CONDITIONED CARS

Blower Motor Removal and Installation

CHRYSLER AND IMPERIAL

THROUGH 1978

The blower motor is mounted to the housing under the right front fender between the inner fender shield and the fender. The inner fender shield must be removed to service the blower motor.

1979 CHRYSLER NEWPORT, NEW YORKER

1. Disconnect the battery ground cable.

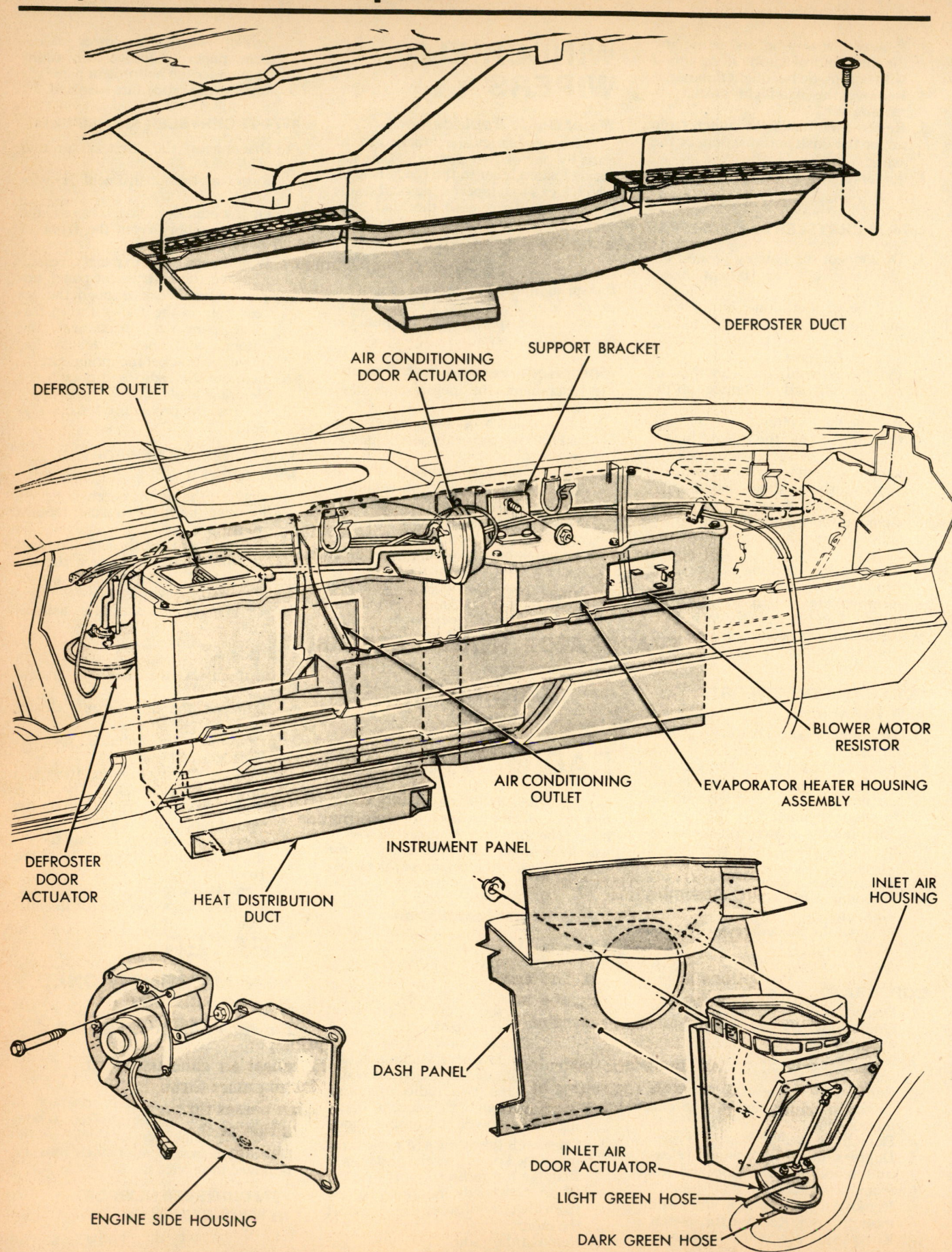

DEFROSTER DUCT

AIR CONDITIONING
DOOR ACTUATOR

SUPPORT BRACKET

DEFROSTER OUTLET

BLOWER MOTOR
RESISTOR

AIR CONDITIONING
OUTLET

EVAPORATOR HEATER HOUSING
ASSEMBLY

DEFROSTER
DOOR
ACTUATOR

INSTRUMENT PANEL

HEAT DISTRIBUTION
DUCT

INLET AIR
HOUSING

DASH PANEL

INLET AIR
DOOR ACTUATOR

LIGHT GREEN HOSE

DARK GREEN HOSE

ENGINE SIDE HOUSING

1974-78 Chrysler heater and air conditioner details (© Chrysler Corp.)

2. Remove the glovebox.
3. Disconnect the blower motor wires.
4. Remove the heater assembly to plenum brace.
5. Remove the screws holding the blower motor to the heater housing. Remove the blower motor.
6. Reverse the procedure for installation.

CORDOBA

1. Disconnect the battery ground cable.
2. Remove the entire heater assembly from the car, as outlined under Heater Core Removal and Installation, Non-Air Conditioned Models.
3. Disconnect the blower motor lead from the resistor block, and the ground wire from the mounting plate.
4. Remove the 6 sheet metal screws and clips retaining the blower mount to the housing. Separate the mount and blower from the housing.
5. Remove the blower wheel from the motor shaft.
6. Remove the two retaining nuts and separate the motor from its mount.
7. Reverse the procedure to install.

Heater Core Removal and Installation

THROUGH 1973

1. Disconnect the battery ground cable. Drain the coolant.
2. Disconnect the heater hoses and plug the fittings.
3. Slide the front seat back. Unplug the antenna from the radio.
4. Remove the vacuum hoses from the trunk lock, if so equipped.
5. Disconnect the blower motor resistor block.
6. Remove the vacuum hoses from the defroster actuator and heater shut off door actuator.
7. Swing the support bracket up out of the way.
8. Remove the four retaining nuts from the studs on the engine side housing.
9. Remove the locating bolt from the bottom center of the passenger side housing.
10. Roll or tip the housing out from under the instrument panel.
11. Remove the temperature control cable retaining clip and the cable from the heat shut off door crank.
12. From inside the housing, remove the two retaining nuts from the right side of the heater core and the four screws from the outside of the housing.
13. Remove the core tube locating metal screw from the top of the housing.
14. Carefully pull the heater core out of the housing.
15. Reverse the procedure to install.

1974-78 CHRYSLER AND IMPERIAL

1. Disconnect the battery ground cable and drain the coolant.
2. Detach the heater hoses at the firewall and plug the core tubes.
3. Slide the front seat back. Remove the instrument panel lower cover.
4. Unplug the antenna from the radio. Disconnect the upper level ventilation actuator vacuum line.
5. Remove the screw holding the upper level vent ducts to the heater housing and the screw holding the bracket to the instrument panel. Swing back the duct.
6. Disconnect the blower motor resistor connectors at the lower right end of the housing.
7. Detach the mode cable from the mode door crank on the front of the housing.
8. Remove the bottom retaining nut and swing the support bracket out of the way.
9. On the engine side, remove the five nuts.
10. Tip the housing out from under the instrument panel.
11. Detach the temperature control cable at the top.
12. Remove the core tube locating screw between the tubes. Remove the six nuts holding the front and rear housings together. Remove the four core retaining screws and separate the housings. Slide the core out.
13. Reverse the procedure for installation.

1979 CHRYSLER NEWPORT, NEW YORKER

1. Disconnect the battery ground cable. Drain the coolant.
2. Disconnect the heater hoses and plug the core tubes.
3. Remove the four nuts holding the heater assembly to the firewall.
4. Slide the front seat all the way back. Remove the console, if any.
5. Remove the heater controls and disconnect the vacuum harness from the harness extension.
6. Remove the ash tray and housing, and the glove box.
7. Disconnect the right lap cooler tube from the lap cooler and remove the trim bezel. Remove the right cowl trim pad.
8. Disconnect the blower motor wires.
9. Detach the temperature control cable from the heater housing.
10. Remove the heater distribution housing.
11. Hold the assembly up and remove the mounting brace to the plenum.
12. Pull the assembly back and rotate it to the right and out from under the instrument panel. Remove the top cover for access to the heater core.
13. Reverse the procedure for installation.

CORDOBA

1. Disconnect the battery ground cable and drain the coolant.
2. Disconnect the heater hoses at the firewall and plug the core tubes. Remove the blower motor vent tube.
3. Remove the three mounting nuts around the blower motor and the one near the center.
4. Remove the lower instrument panel bezel, glove box, and glove box door.
5. Unplug the antenna from the radio.
6. Remove the screw from the housing to plenum support rod on the right side above the outside air opening.
7. Detach the two air door cables and the blower motor resistor wires.
8. Tip the unit out from under the instrument panel.
9. Remove the front cover screws. Cut the plenum to housing air seal in two places where the front cover separates the cover from the housing.
10. Remove the core tube retaining screw between the tubes. Remove the heater core.
11. Reverse the procedure for installation. Seal the plenum air seal with rubber cement.

AIR CONDITIONED CARS

Blower Motor Removal and Installation

CHRYSLER AND IMPERIAL THROUGH 1978

1. The blower motor is mounted on the engine side housing, under the right front fender, between the inner fender shield and the fender. To service the motor, it is necessary to remove the inner fender panel by extracting its securing bolts. If the vehicle is equipped with a power antenna, it is necessary to disconnect it before the inner fender panel is removed.
2. For all models, disconnect the battery and feed wires and remove the air tube (if so equipped). Remove its mounting bolts and remove the blower assembly.
3. Installation is the reverse of removal.

1979 CHRYSLER NEWPORT, NEW YORKER

This procedure is the same as for non-air conditioned cars.

CORDOBA

1. Disconnect the feed wire at its connector. Remove the air tube.
2. Remove the three nuts retaining the blower mount to the firewall (from the engine side.)
3. Lift out the blower motor and fan assembly.
4. Reverse the procedure to install.

Heater Core Removal and Installation

THROUGH 1973

1. The heater core is located in the front cover of the passenger side housing. The air conditioning system need not be discharged to remove the heater core.
2. Disconnect the battery and drain the cooling system. Remove the air cleaner and disconnect the heater hoses. Plug the heater core tubes to prevent fluid loss.
3. Remove the left spot cooler duct and the steering column cover. On 1972 models, remove the linkage shield.
4. Disconnect the two actuator rods at the linkage on the left side of the housing. Remove the two cover retaining screws.
5. Remove the heat distribution duct securing screws, the duct, and the now-exposed screws in the bottom lip of the front cover.
6. Remove the glove box and the center spot cooler duct; also the right spot cooler duct and the air distribution housing.
7. Working in the glovebox opening, remove the top and right side retaining screws from the housing. On vehicles with Auto-Temp, remove the aspirator tube from its clip before performing the above.
8. Disconnect all electrical leads at the resistor block. Remove the vacuum hoses from the recirculating housing actuator. On cars with Auto-Temp, remove the wires from the plastic strips and metal clip; remove the amplifier, master, and compressor switches.
9. Remove the nut from the housing end of the support bracket. Swing the bracket upward and out of the way, and carefully roll the heater core and front cover out from beneath the instrument panel. Remove the core from the housing by cutting the adhesive away, grasping it at the top, and pulling it from the housing.
10. To begin the installation procedure, remove the condensate seal from the heater core flange and cement a new seal in position. Install the heater core in the rear housing and secure with a screw at either end. Install the core and rear housing to the front housing. Hold the rear housing in position and swing the support bracket down and over the stud on the rear housing face; install its retaining nut.
11. Working through the glove box opening, install the housing top retaining screws and the screws at the right side of the rear housing.
12. Working beneath the instrument panel, replace all the screws securing the housings together. Install the two screws on the left side of the rear housing.
13. Install the heat distribution duct to the bottom of the housing.
14. Connect the actuator rods.
15. Connect all of the vacuum hoses to the actuators; install all electrical connections to the resistor block. On cars with Auto-Temp, secure the wires with the plastic straps and metal clip. Install the aspirator tube in the clip.
16. Working through the glove box opening, replace the air distribution housing, the center spot cooler duct, and the right spot cooler duct.
17. Install the steering column cover and the left spot cooler duct. Replace the glove box assembly. On Auto-Temp equipped vehicles, install the amplifier, master, and compressor switches.
18. From this point, reverse the removal procedure.

1974-78 CHRYSLER AND IMPERIAL

NOTE: *This procedure requires evacuation of the refrigerant in the air conditioning system. Therefore, it should not be attempted by persons not having the special tools and training required to perform the job safely.*

1. Purge the system of refrigerant.
2. Disconnect the battery ground cable. Drain the coolant.
3. Remove the air cleaner and disconnect the heater hoses. Plug the core tubes.
4. Remove the 5/16″ bolt in the center of the plumbing sealing plate.
5. Pull the refrigerant line assembly toward the front of the car.
6. Remove the two 1/4-20 Allen screws and remove the H valve.
7. Slide the front seat back, out of the way. Remove the lap cooler and lower instrument panel cover.
8. Remove the A/C distribution duct.
9. Unplug the antenna lead from the radio.
10. Disconnect the wires and vacuum lines from unit.
11. Remove the drain tube. With automatic temperature control (ATC), remove the electrical connections and vacuum connector from the servo. Disconnect the amplifier wires. Disconnect the wires and vacuum hoses from the master and compressor switches. Disconnect the aspirator tube.
12. Remove the temperature control cable from the clip on the unit.
13. Remove the retaining nut from the support bracket.
14. Remove the six retaining nuts from the studs in the engine compartment.
15. Remove the housing from under the instrument panel, and place it on a work table.
16. Remove the mode door and the blend air door levers from the shaft. Remove the screws and lift off the top cover.
17. Remove the 4 retaining screws and the 3 screws for the core tube seal. Lift out the core.
18. Reverse the procedure to install.

1979 CHRYSLER NEWPORT, NEW YORKER

NOTE: *This procedure requires evacuation of the refrigerant in the air conditioning system. Therefore, it should not be attempted by persons not having the special tools and training required to perform the job safely.*

1. Discharge the air conditioning system completely.
2. Disconnect the battery ground cable. Drain the coolant.
3. Disconnect the heater hoses and plug the core tubes.
4. Remove the air conditioning system H-valve. Cap all openings.
5. Remove the condensate drain tube.
6. Disconnect the vacuum lines in the engine compartment and push the rubber grommet and vacuum lines through the firewall.
7. Remove the four nuts holding the heater assembly to the firewall.
8. Slide the front seat all the way back. Remove the console, if any.
9. Remove the heater/air conditioning controls and disconnect the vacuum harness from the harness extension.
10. Remove the ash tray and housing, and the glove box.
11. Disconnect the right lap cooler tube from the lap cooler and remove the trim bezel. Remove the right cowl trim pad.
12. Disconnect the blower motor wires.
13. Detach the temperature control or bimetal sensor cable from the evaporator/heater housing.
14. Remove the heater distribution housing.
15. Remove the center distribution duct.
16. Remove the mode door actuator or vacuum servo from the lower left corner of the housing.
17. Remove the automatic temperature control system in-car air hose from the compensator.
18. Hold the assembly up and remove the mounting brace to the plenum.
19. Pull the assembly back and rotate it to the right and out from under the instrument panel. Remove the top cover for access to the heater core.
20. Reverse the procedure for installation.

CORDOBA

See the Heater Core Removal procedure (for air-conditioned cars) for Satellite, Coronet, Charger, 1975-78 Fury, 1977-78 Monaco in the Dodge-Plymouth car section.

—Capri • Comet • Cougar • Elite Fairmont • Granada • LTD II Maverick • Monarch • Montego Mustang • 1977-79 Thunderbird Torino • Versailles • Zephyr

Index

YEAR IDENTIFICATION

1979 Capri

1972 Comet GT

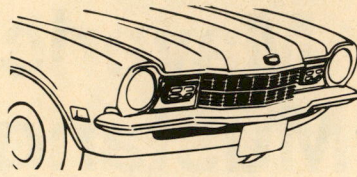

1972 Comet

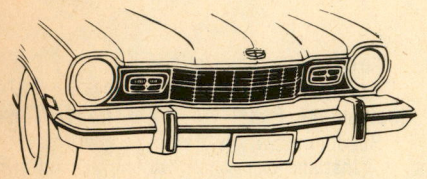

1973 Comet

1974 Comet

1975 Comet

1976 Comet

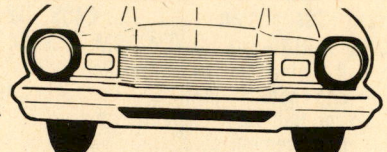

1977 Comet

1972 Cougar XR-7

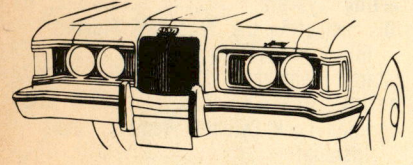

1973 Cougar

1974-75 Cougar

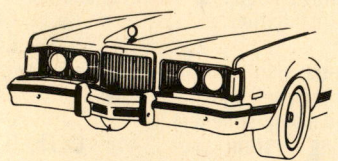

1976 Cougar

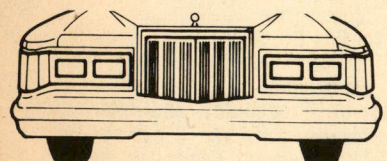

1977 Cougar

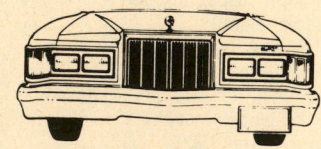

1978 Cougar

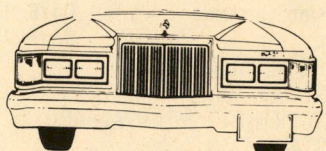

1979 Cougar

1972 Mustang

1973 Mustang

1979 Mustang

Monarch • Montego • Mustang • 1977-79 Thunderbird
Torino • Versailles • Zephyr

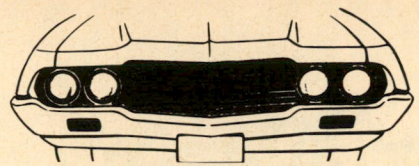

1972 Torino

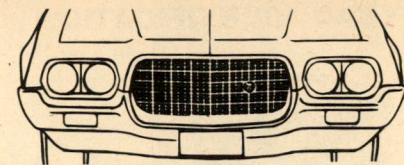

1972 Gran Torino

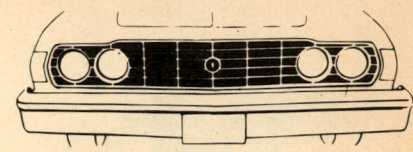

1973 Torino

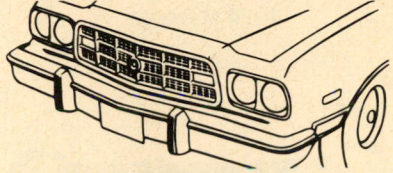

1973 Gran Torino

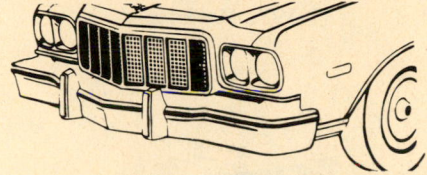

1974 Gran Torino

1975 Gran Torino Brougham

1976 Gran Torino Brougham

1974-75 Ford Elite

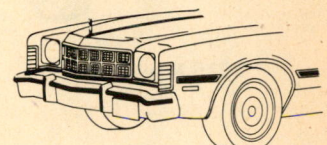

1976 Ford Elite

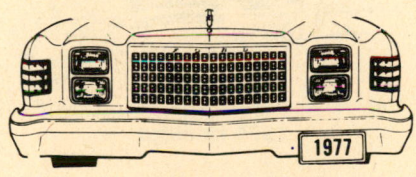

1977 LTD II

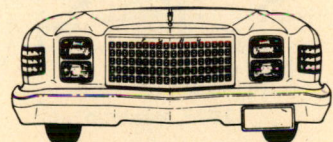

1978 LTD II

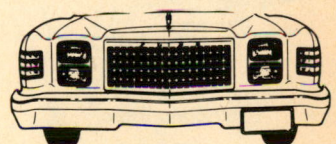

1979 LTD II

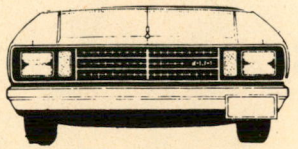

1978 Fairmont

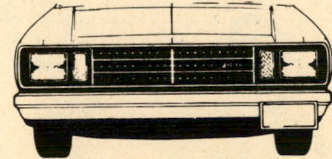

1979 Fairmont

1978 Versailles

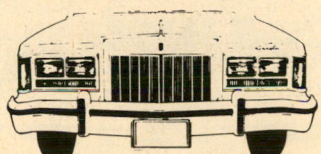

1979 Versailles

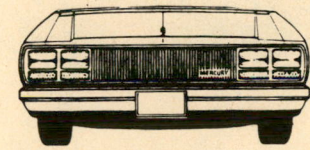

1978 Zephyr

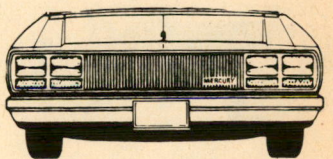

1979 Zephyr

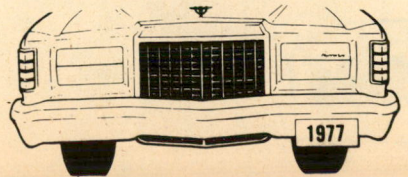

1977 Thunderbird

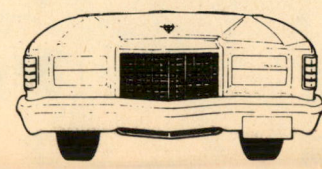

1978 Thunderbird

1979 Thunderbird

C457

YEAR IDENTIFICATION

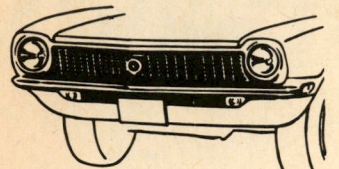

1972 Maverick

1973 Maverick

1974 Maverick

1975 Maverick

1976 Maverick

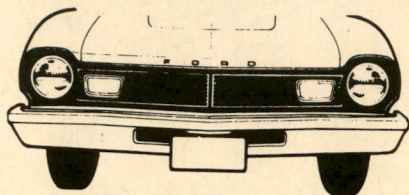

1977 Maverick

1972 Montego

1973 Montego

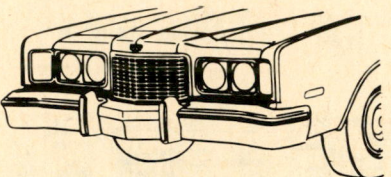

1974 Montego

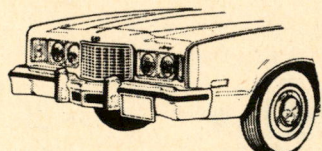

1975 Montego

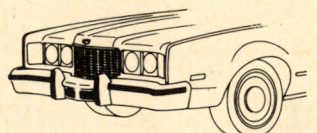

1976 Montego

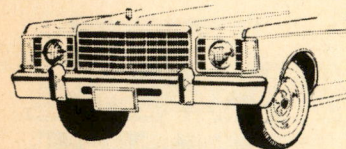

1975 Granada

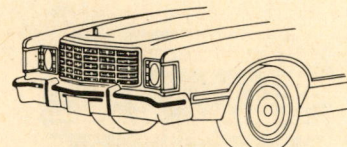

1976 Granada

1977 Granada

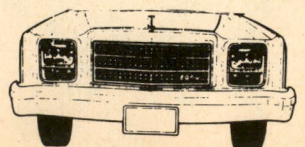

1978 Granada

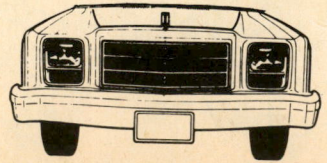

1979 Granada

Monarch • Montego • Mustang • 1977-79 Thunderbird
Torino • Versailles • Zephyr

1975 Monarch

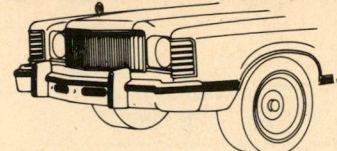

1976 Monarch

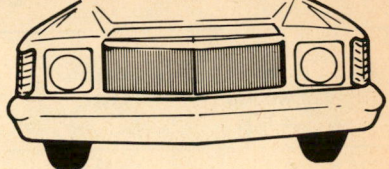

1977 Monarch

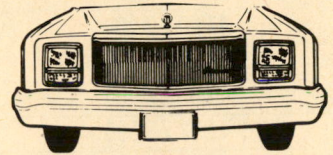

1978 Monarch

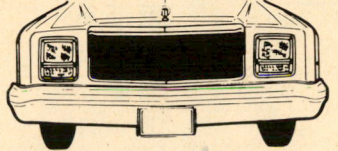

1979 Monarch

ENGINE IDENTIFICATION CODE

The engine code designation is the 5th digit of the vehicle identification number (V.I.N.). The V.I.N. is stamped on a plate located at the left side of the instrument panel, visible through the windshield.

Disp	Bbl	'72	'73	'74	'75	'76	'77	'78	'79
4-Cylinder Models									
140 (2300cc)	2							Y	Y
6-Cylinder Models									
170 (2800cc)	1	U							
170 (2800cc) V6	2								Z
200 (3300cc)	1	T	T	T	T	T	T	T	T
250 (4100cc)	1	L	L	L	L	L	L	L	L
8-Cylinder Models									
302 (4950cc)	2	F	F	F	F	F	F	F	F
351W (5750cc)①	2	H	H	H	H	H	H	H	H
351C (5750cc)①	2	H	H	H					
351M (5750cc)①	2				H	H	Q	Q	Q
351CJ (5750cc)	4	Q	Q						
351HO (5750cc)	4	R							
400 (6550cc)	2	S	S	S	S	S	S		
429 (7200cc)	4	N	N						
460 (7540cc)	4			A	A	A			
460PI (7540cc)	4				C	C			

① Windsor and Cleveland versions of the 351 2 bbl engine were used interchangeably through 1974. Starting 1975, Windsor and Modified Cleveland engines were used. A quick visual means of identification is the location of the thermostat housing/water outlet; Windsor engines have it mounted to the front face of the intake manifold, Cleveland and Modified Cleveland engines have it on top of the engine block.

- C Cleveland
- CJ Cobra Jet
- HO High Output
- M Modified Cleveland
- PI Police Interceptor
- W Windsor

Transmission Codes
The transmission code is found on the vehicle certification label, on the driver's door.

1. Three speed
5. Four speed (RUG—through 1973 only)
7. Four speed Overdrive (RUG)
7. Four speed (ET—1978 Fairmont/Zephyr only)
- S. JATCO Automatic
- U. C6 Automatic
- V. C3 Automatic
- W. C4 Automatic
- X. FMX Automatic
- Z. C6 Police Automatic

GENERAL ENGINE SPECIFICATIONS

Year	Engine No. Cyl. Displacement (Cu. In.)	Carburetor Type	Horsepower @ rpm ■	Torque @ rpm (ft lbs) ■	Bore X Stroke (in.)	Compression Ratio	Oil Pressure @ 2000 rpm
'72	6-170	1 bbl	82 @ 4400	129 @ 1800	3.500 x 2.940	8.3:1	35-60
	6-200	1 bbl	91 @ 4000	154 @ 2200	3.680 x 3.130	8.3:1	35-60
	6-250	1 bbl	99 @ 3600	184 @ 1600	3.680 x 3.910	8.0:1	35-60
	8-302	2 bbl	141 @ 4000	242 @ 2000	4.000 x 3.000	8.5:1	35-60
	8-351 C or W	2 bbl	164 @ 4000	276 @ 2000	4.000 x 3.500	8.6:1	35-85
	8-351 CJ	4 bbl	248 @ 5400	290 @ 3800	4.000 x 3.500	8.6:1	35-85
	8-351 HO	4 bbl	266 @ 5400	301 @ 3600	4.000 x 3.500	8.6:1	35-85
	8-400	2 bbl	168 @ 4200	297 @ 2200	4.000 x 4.000	8.4:1	35-85
	8-429	4 bbl	205 @ 4400	322 @ 2600	4.362 x 3.590	8.5:1	35-75

GENERAL ENGINE SPECIFICATIONS

Year	Engine No. Cyl. Displacement (Cu. In.)	Carburetor Type	Horsepower @ rpm ■	Torque @ rpm (ft lbs) ■	Bore X Stroke (in.)	Compression Ratio	Oil Pressure @ 2000 rpm
'73	6-200	1 bbl	91 @ 4000	154 @ 2200	3.680 x 3.130	8.3:1	35-60
	6-250	1 bbl	99 @ 3600	184 @ 1600	3.680 x 3.910	8.0:1	35-60
	8-302	2 bbl	141 @ 4000	242 @ 2000	4.000 x 3.000	8.5:1	35-60
	8-351	2 bbl	164 @ 4000	276 @ 2000	4.000 x 3.500	8.6:1	35-85
	8-351	4 bbl	248 @ 5400	290 @ 3800	4.000 x 3.500	8.0:1	35-85
	8-400	2 bbl	168 @ 4200	297 @ 2200	4.000 x 4.000	8.0:1	35-85
	8-429	4 bbl	205 @ 4400	322 @ 2600	4.362 x 3.590	8.5:1	35-75
	8-460 PI	4 bbl	269 @ 4600	388 @ 280C	4.362 x 3.850	8.8:1	35-75
'74	6-200	1 bbl	84 @ 3800	150 @ 1800	3.680 x 3.130	8.3:1	35-55
	6-250	1 bbl	91 @ 3200	190 @ 1600	3.680 x 3.910	8.0:1	35-55
	8-302	2 bbl	140 @ 3800	230 @ 2600	4.000 x 3.000	8.0:1	35-55
	8-351 W	2 bbl	162 @ 4000	275 @ 2200	4.000 x 3.500	8.0:1	50-70
	8-351 C	2 bbl	163 @ 4200	278 @ 2000	4.000 x 3.500	8.0:1	50-70
	8-351	4 bbl	255 @ 5600	290 @ 3400	4.000 x 3.500	7.9:1	50-70
	8-400	2 bbl	170 @ 3400	330 @ 2000	4.000 x 4.000	8.0:1	50-70
	8-460	4 bbl	195 @ 3800	355 @ 2600	4.362 x 3.850	8.0:1	35-75
	8-460	4 bbl	220 @ 4000	355 @ 2600	4.362 x 3.850	8.0:1	35-75
	8-460 PI	4 bbl	260 @ 4400	380 @ 2700	4.362 x 3.850	8.8:1	50-75
'75	6-200 MT	1 bbl	75 @ 3200	145 @ 2000	3.680 x 3.130	8.3:1	30-50
	6-200 AT	1 bbl	74 @ 3400	132 @ 2400	3.680 x 3.130	8.3:1	30-50
	6-250 MT	1 bbl	85 @ 2900	180 @ 2000	3.680 x 3.910	8.0:1	40-60
	6-250 AT	1 bbl	72 @ 2900	180 @ 1400	3.680 x 3.910	8.0:1	40-60
	6-250 MT Cal.	1 bbl	79 @ 2800	177 @ 1600	3.680 x 3.910	8.0:1	40-60
	6-250 AT Cal.	1 bbl	70 @ 2800	175 @ 1400	3.680 x 3.910	8.0:1	40-60
	8-302 Granada, Monarch	2 bbl	129 @ 3800	220 @ 1800	4.000 x 3.000	8.0:1	40-60
	8-302 Maverick, Comet	2 bbl	122 @ 3800	208 @ 1800	4.000 x 3.000	8.0:1	40-60
	8-302 Cal.	2 bbl	115 @ 3600	203 @ 1800	4.000 x 3.000	8.0:1	40-60
	8-351 W Compact	2 bbl	143 @ 3600	255 @ 2200	4.000 x 3.500	8.2:1	40-65
	8-351-W Inter- mediate	2 bbl	154 @ 3800	268 @ 2200	4.000 x 3.500	8.2:1	40-65
	8-351 W Cal.	2 bbl	153 @ 3400	270 @ 2400	4.000 x 3.500	8.2:1	40-65
	8-351 M 49	2 bbl	148 @ 3800	243 @ 2400	4.000 x 3.500	8.0:1	50-75
	8-351 M Cal.	2 bbl	150 @ 3800	244 @ 2800	4.000 x 3.500	8.0:1	50-75
	8-400 49	2 bbl	158 @ 3800	276 @ 2000	4.000 x 4.000	8.0:1	50-75
	8-400 Cal.	2 bbl	144 @ 3600	255 @ 2200	4.000 x 4.000	8.0:1	50-75
	8-460 49	4 bbl	216 @ 4000	366 @ 2600	4.362 x 3.850	8.0:1	40-65
	8-460 Cal.	4 bbl	217 @ 4000	365 @ 2600	4.362 x 3.850	8.0:1	40-65
	8-460 PI	4 bbl	226 @ 4000	374 @ 2600	4.362 x 3.850	8.0:1	40-65
'76	6-200 MT	1 bbl	81 @ 3400	151 @ 1700	3.682 x 3.126	8.3:1	30-50
	6-200 AT	1 bbl	78 @ 3300	152 @ 1600	3.682 x 3.126	8.3:1	30-50
	6-250 MT①	1 bbl	90 @ 3000	190 @ 2000	3.682 x 3.910	8.0:1	40-60
	6-250 MT②	1 bbl	87 @ 3000	187 @ 1900	3.682 x 3.910	8.0:1	40-60
	6-250 AT①	1 bbl	81 @ 3000	192 @ 2000	3.682 x 3.910	8.0:1	40-60
	6-250 AT②	1 bbl	78 @ 3000	187 @ 1900	3.682 x 3.910	8.0:1	40-60

Monarch • Montego • Mustang • 1977-79 Thunderbird
Torino • Versailles • Zephyr

GENERAL ENGINE SPECIFICATIONS

Year	Engine No. Cyl. Displacement (Cu. In.)	Carburetor Type	Horsepower @ rpm ■	Torque @ rpm (ft lbs) ■	Bore X Stroke (in.)	Compression Ratio	Oil Pressure @ 2000 rpm
	6-250 MT Cal.	1 bbl	74 @ 3000	181 @ 1900	3.682 x 3.910	8.0:1	40-60
	6-250 AT Cal.①	1 bbl	78 @ 3000	183 @ 1400	3.682 x 3.910	8.0:1	40-60
	6-250 AT Cal.②	1 bbl	76 @ 3000	179 @ 1300	3.682 x 3.910	8.0:1	40-60
	8-302 MT①	2 bbl	138 @ 3600	245 @ 2000	4.000 x 3.000	8.0:1	40-60
	8-302 MT②	2 bbl	134 @ 3600	242 @ 2000	4.000 x 3.000	8.0:1	40-60
	8-302 AT①	2 bbl	137 @ 3600	246 @ 1800	4.000 x 3.000	8.0:1	40-60
	8-302 AT②	2 bbl	133 @ 3600	243 @ 1800	4.000 x 3.000	8.0:1	40-60
	8-302 AT Cal.①	2 bbl	137 @ 3600	247 @ 1800	4.000 x 3.000	8.0:1	40-60
	8-302 AT Cal.②	2 bbl	130 @ 3600	238 @ 1600	4.000 x 3.000	8.0:1	40-60
	8-351 AT②	2 bbl	143 @ 3200	285 @ 1600	4.000 x 3.500	8.0:1	45-65
	8-351 W	2 bbl	154 @ 3400	286 @ 1800	4.000 x 3.500	8.0:1	45-65
	8-351 M	2 bbl	152 @ 3800	274 @ 1600	4.000 x 3.500	8.0:1	45-65
	8-351 AT Cal.②	2 bbl	140 @ 3400	276 @ 1600	4.000 x 3.500	8.0:1	45-65
	8-400	2 bbl	180 @ 3800	336 @ 1800	4.000 x 4.000	8.0:1	35-65
	8-460	4 bbl	202 @ 3800	352 @ 1600	4.362 x 3.850	8.0:1	35-65
	8-460 PI	4 bbl	226 @ 3800	371 @ 1600	4.362 x 3.850	8.0:1	35-65
'77	6-200 MT	1V	96 @ 4400	151 @ 2000	3.682 x 3.126	8.5:1	40
	6-200 AT	1V	97 @ 4400	153 @ 2000	3.682 x 3.126	8.5:1	40
	6-250 MT	1V	98 @ 3400	182 @ 1800	3.682 x 3.910	8.1:1	50
	6-250 AT	1V	98 @ 3600	190 @ 1400	3.682 x 3.910	8.1:1	50
	6-250 AT Cal.	1V	86 @ 3000	185 @ 1800	3.682 x 3.910	8.1:1	50
	8-302 MT	2V	122 @ 3200	237 @ 1600	4.000 x 3.000	8.4:1	50
	8-302 AT	2V	134 @ 3600	245 @ 1600	4.000 x 3.000	8.4:1	50
	8-302 AT Cal.	2V	122 @ 3400	222 @ 1400	4.000 x 3.000	8.1:1	50
	8-351W AT②	2V	135 @ 3200	275 @ 1600	4.000 x 3.500	8.3:1	55
	8-351W	2V	149 @ 3200	291 @ 1600	4.000 x 3.500	8.3:1	55
	8-351M	2V	161 @ 3600	285 @ 1800	4.000 x 3.500	8.3:1	55
	8-400	2V	173 @ 3800	326 @ 1600	4.000 x 4.000	8.0:1	55
	8-400 Cal.	2V	168 @ 3800	323 @ 1600	4.000 x 4.000	8.0:1	55
'78-'79	4-121	2 bbl	88 @ 4800	118 @ 2800	3.781 x 3.126	9.0:1	50
	4-121 T	2 bbl	147 @ 6000	143 @ 2800	3.781 x 3.126	9.0:1	50
	V6-170	2 bbl	90 @ 4200	143 @ 2200	3.660 x 2.700	8.7:1	40-55③
	6-200	1 bbl	85 @ 3600	154 @ 1600	3.682 x 3.126	8.5:1	30-50
	6-250	1 bbl	97 @ 3200	210 @ 1400	3.682 x 3.910	8.5:1	40-60
	8-302	2 bbl	134 @ 3400	250 @ 1600	4.000 x 3.000	8.4:1	40-60
	8-302 Cal	2VV	133 @ 3600	243 @ 1600	4.000 x 3.000	8.1:1	40-60
	8-351 M	2 bbl	152 @ 3600	278 @ 1800	4.000 x 3.500	8.0:1	50-75
	8-351 W	2 bbl	144 @ 3200	277 @ 1600	4.000 x 3.500	8.3:1	40-60
	8-400	2 bbl	166 @ 3800	319 @ 1800	4.000 x 4.000	8.0:1	50-75

■ Beginning 1972 horsepower and torque are SAE net figures. They are measured at the rear of the transmission with all accessories installed and operating. Since the figures vary when a given engine is installed in different models, some are representative rather than exact.

W Windsor
C Cleveland
M Modified Cleveland
PI Police Interceptor
VV Variable Venturi
T Turbocharged

MT Manual Transmission
AT Automatic Transmission
49 49 states only
Cal California only
① Maverick/Comet
② Granada/Monarch, Versailles
③ @ 1500 rpm

C461

Capri • Comet • Cougar • Elite • Fairmont • Granada LTD II • Maverick

TUNE-UP SPECIFICATIONS

Torino, Montego, Mustang through 1973 Cougar, Elite, LTD II, 1977 and later Thunderbird

When analyzing compression test results, look for uniformity among cylinders rather than specific pressures.

Year	ENGINE No. Cyl Displacement (cu in.)	hp	SPARK PLUGS Orig. Type	Gap (in.)	DISTRIBUTOR Point Dwell* (deg)	Point Gap (in.)	IGNITION TIMING (deg)▲ Man Trans	Auto Trans	VALVES Intake Opens ■(deg)	Fuel Pump Pressure (psi)	IDLE SPEED (rpm)▲ Man Trans	Auto Trans
'72	6-250	95	BRF-82	.034	37	.027	6B	6B	10(16)	4½-6½	750/500	600/500
	8-302	140	BRF-42	.034	28	.017	6B	6B	16	5½-6½	800/500	575 600/500
	8-351C	165	ARF-42	.034	28	.017	6B	6B	12	5½-6½		575/500 (625/500)
	8-351W	165	BRF-42	.034	28	.017	—	6B	12	5½-6½	—	575 600/500
	8-351CJ	266	ARF-42	.034	28	.017/.020	16B	16B④	14	5½-6½		700/500④ (800/500)
	8-351HO	N.A.	ARF-42	.034	28	.020	10B	—	17½	5½-6½	1000/500	—
	8-400	168	ARF-42	.034	28	.017	—	6B	17	4½-5½	—	625/500
	8-429	205	ARF-42	.034	28	.017	—	10B	8	5½-6½	—	600/500
'73	6-250	95	BRF-82	.034	37	.027/.025	6B	6B	16	4½-6½	750/500	600/500
	8-302	140	BRF-42	.034	28	.017	6B	6B	16	5½-6½	800/500	575 600/500
	8-351C	165	ARF-42	.034	28	.017	—	6B	12	5½-6½	—	625/500
	8-351W	165	BRF-42	.034	28	.017	—	6B	12	5½-6½	—	575 600/500
	8-351CJ	266	ARF-42	.034	28⑤	.017③	16B	16B④	14	5½-6½	1000/500	800/500④
	8-400	168	ARF-42	.034	28	.017	—	6B	17	5½-6½	—	625/500
	8-429	205	ARF-42	.034	28	.017	—	10B	8	5½-6½	—	600/500
	8-460PI	269	ARF-42	.035	28	.017	—	10B	18	5½-7½	—	600
'74	6-250	91	BRF-82	.034①	37⑩	.027	6B	6B	26	5½-6½	800/500	625/500
	8-302	140	BRF-42	.034①	28⑩	.017	10B	6B	16⑦	5½-6½	800/500	625/500
	8-351W	162	BRF-42	.034①	28⑩	.017	—	6B	15	5½-6½	—	600/500
	8-351C	163	ARF-42	.034①	28⑩	.017	—	14B	11.5	5½-6½	—	600/500
	8-351CJ	255	ARF-42	.034①	28⑩	.017	—	20B⑥	14	5½-6½	—	800/500
	8-400	170	ARF-42	.044	Electronic		—	12B⑥	17	5½-6½	—	625/500
	8-460	195, 220, 260	ARF-42	.054	Electronic		—	14B	8	5½-6½	—	650/500
'75	8-351W	153, 154	ARF-42	.044	Electronic		—	6B	15	5½-6½	—	600/500
	8-351M	148, 150	ARF-42	.044	Electronic		—	6B	19½	5½-6½	—	700/500
	8-400	144, 158	ARF-42	.044	Electronic		—	6B	17	5½-6½	—	625/500
	8-460	216, 217	ARF-52	.044	Electronic		—	14B	8	5½-6½	—	650/500
	8-460PI	226	ARF-52	.044	Electronic		—	14B	18	5½-7	—	700/500
'76	8-351W	All	ARF-42/52⑧	.054	Electronic		—	⑧	15	5½-6½	—	650
	8-351M	All	ARF-42/52⑧	.044	Electronic		—	⑧	19½	5½-6½	—	650 (650/675⑧)
	8-400	All	ARF-42/52⑧	.044	Electronic		—	⑧	17	5½-6½	—	650(625)
	8-460	All	ARF-52	.044	Electronic		—	8/14B⑧⑨	8	5½-6½	—	650
	8-460PI	226	ARF-52	.044	Electronic		—	14B⑨	18	5½-7	—	650

C462

TUNE-UP SPECIFICATIONS

Torino, Montego, Mustang through 1973 Cougar, Elite, LTD II, 1977 and later Thunderbird

When analyzing compression test results, look for uniformity among cylinders rather than specific pressures.

Year	ENGINE No. Cyl Displacement (cu in.)	hp	SPARK PLUGS Orig. Type	● Gap (in.)	DISTRIBUTOR Point Dwell* (deg)	Point Gap (in.)	IGNITION TIMING (deg)▲ Man Trans	● Auto Trans	VALVES Intake Opens ■(deg)	Fuel Pump Pressure (psi)	IDLE SPEED (rpm)▲ Man Trans	● Auto Trans
'77	8-302	All	ARF-52 (ARF-52-6)	.050(.060)	Electronic		—	8B	16	5½-6½	—	650
	8-351W	All	ARF-52 (ARF-52-6)	.050(.060)	Electronic		—	4B	23	4-6	—	650
	8-351M	All	ARF-52 (ARF-52-6)	.050(.060)	Electronic		—	8B(9B)	19½	6½-7½	—	650
	8-400	All	ARF-52 (ARF-52-6)	.050(.060)	Electronic		—	8B	17	7-8	—	650
'78	8-302	All	ARF-52 (ARF-52-6)	.050(.060)	Electronic		—	14B	16	5½-6½	—	650
	8-351W	All	ARF-52 (ARF-52-6)	.050(.060)	Electronic		—	14B	23	4-6	—	650
	8-351M	All	ARF-52 (ARF-52-6)	.050(.060)	Electronic		—	14B(16B)	19½	6½-7½	—	650
	8-400	All	ARF-52 (ARF-52-6)	.050(.060)	Electronic		—	13B(16B)	17	6½-7½	—	650
'79		All	See Underhood Specifications Sticker									

NOTE: The underhood specifications sticker often reflects tune-up specification changes made in production. Sticker figures must be used if they disagree with those in this chart.

* Where two dwell or point gap figures are separated by a slash, the first figure is for engines equipped with dual diaphragm distributors and the second figure is for engines equipped with single diaphragm distributors

▲ See text for procedure

● In all cases where two idle speed figures are separated by a slash, the first is for idle speed with solenoid energized and automatic transmission in Drive, while the second is idle speed with solenoid disconnected and automatic transmission in Neutral. Figures in parentheses are for California.

■ All figures are in degrees Before Top Dead Center

① .044 with electronic ignition
② Not used

③ Figure is .020 for manual transmission with dual point distributor
④ On Cougars with automatic transmission, set ignition timing to 6B and set idle speed to 650 rpm
⑤ Figure is 32°-35° on manual transmission model with dual point distributor with both point sets combined
⑥ At 500 rpm
⑦ 20° BTC for 302 automatic
⑧ Depends on emission equipment; check underhood specifications sticker
⑨ In Drive
⑩ Electronic ignition used on all engines assembled after May, 1974
B Before Top Dead Center
C Cleveland
M Modified Cleveland
CJ Cobra Jet
HO High Output
W Windsor
— Not applicable

MECHANICAL VALVE LIFTER CLEARANCE

Year	Engine	Intake (Hot) In.	Exhaust (Hot) In.
1972	351 HO	.025	.025
1979	170 V6	.014 (cold)	.016 (cold)

Lincoln Versailles   TUNE-UP SPECIFICATIONS

When analyzing compression test results, look for uniformity among cylinders rather than specific pressures.

Year	ENGINE No. Cyl Displacement (cu in.)	hp	SPARK PLUGS Orig. Type	Gap (in.)	DISTRIBUTOR Point Dwell* (deg)	Point Gap (in.)	IGNITION TIMING (deg)▲ Man Trans	Auto Trans	VALVES Intake Opens ■(deg)	Fuel Pump Pressure (psi)	IDLE SPEED (rpm)▲ Man Trans	Auto Trans
'77	8-302	All	ARF-52-6	.060	Electronic		—	12B	16	5-6	—	700
	8-351W	All	ARF-52	.050	Electronic		—	4B	23	5-6	—	625
'78	8-302	All	ARF-52	.050	Electronic		Variable	EEC	16	5½-6½	—	650
'79	8-302	All	See Underhood Specifications Sticker									

Maverick, Granada, Comet, Monarch, Fairmont, Zephyr, 1979 Mustang and Capri   TUNE-UP SPECIFICATIONS

When analyzing compression test results, look for uniformity among cylinders rather than specific pressures.

Year	ENGINE No. Cyl Displacement (cu in.)	hp	SPARK PLUGS Orig. Type	Gap (in.)	DISTRIBUTOR Point Dwell* (deg)	Point Gap (in.)	IGNITION TIMING (deg)▲ Man Trans	Auto Trans	VALVES Intake Opens ■(deg)	Fuel Pump Pressure (psi)	IDLE SPEED (rpm)▲ Man Trans	Auto Trans
'72	6-170	82	BRF-82	.034	37	.027/	6B	—	9	4-6	750	—
	6-200	91	BRF-82	.034	37	.027	6B	6B	9	4-6	800/500	600/500
	6-250	98	BRF-82	.034	37	.027	6B	6B	10	4-6	750/500	600/500
	8-302	143	BRF-42	.034	28	.017	6B	6B	16	4-6	800/500	600/500
'73	6-200	91	BRF-82	.034	37	.027/ .025	6B	6B	9	4-6	800/500	600/500
	6-250	98	BRF-82	.034	37	.027/ .025	—	6B	10	4-6	—	600/500
	8-302	143	BRF-42	.034	28	.017	6B	6B	16	4-6	800/500	600/500
'74	6-200	84	BRF-82	.034⑥	37⑤	.024/ .030	6B	6B	28	4½-5½	750/500	550/500
	6-250	91	BRF-82	.034⑥	37⑤	.024/ .030	6B	6B	26	4½-5½	750/500	600/500
	8-302	140	BRF-42	.034⑥	27⑤	.014/ .020	6B	6B	②	5½-6½	800/500	650/500①
'75	6-200	All	BRF-82	.044	Electronic		6B	6B	20	4½-5½	750/500	600/500
	6-250	All	BRF-82	.044	Electronic		6B	6B	26	4½-5½	850/500	600/500
	8-302	All	ARF-42	.044	Electronic		6B	6B	20	5½-6½	900/500	650/500
	8-302	115	ARF-42	.044	Electronic		6B	8B	20	5½-6½	900/500	650/500
	8-351 W	143	ARF-42	.044	Electronic		—	4B	15	5½-6½	—	700/500
	8-351 W④	153	ARF-42	.044	Electronic		—	6B	15	5½-6½	—	650/500
'76	6-200	All	BRF-82	.044	Electronic		③	③	20	4½-5½	800	650
	6-250	All	BRF-82	.044	Electronic		③	③	26	4½-5½	850	600
	8-302	All	ARF-42/52③	.044	Electronic		③	③	20	5½-6½	750	650(700)
	8-351W	All	ARF-52	.044	Electronic		—	8(10B) @ 625(650)	15	5½-6½	—	625(650)
'77	6-200	All	BRF-82	.050	Electronic		6B	6B	20	5½-6½	800	650
	6-250	All	BRF-82	.050	Electronic		4B	68(8B)	18	5½-6½	850	600
	8-302	All	ARF-52 (ARF-52-6)	.050 (.060)	Electronic		6B	4B(12B)	16	5½-6½	750	650(700)
	8-351W	All	ARF-52 (ARF-52-6)	.050 (.060)	Electronic		—	4B	23	5½-6½	—	625

Maverick, Granada, Comet, Monarch, Fairmont, Zephyr, 1979 Mustang and Capri

TUNE-UP SPECIFICATIONS

When analyzing compression test results, look for uniformity among cylinders rather than specific pressures.

ENGINE			SPARK PLUGS			DISTRIBUTOR		IGNITION TIMING (deg)▲		VALVES	Fuel Pump	IDLE SPEED (rpm)▲	
Year	No. Cyl Displacement (cu in.)	hp	Orig. Type	•	Gap (in.)	Point Dwell* (deg)	Point Gap (in.)	Man Trans	• Auto Trans	Intake Opens ■ (deg)	Pressure (psi)	Man Trans	• Auto Trans
'78	4-140	All	AWRF-42		.034	Electronic		6B	20B	22	5½-6½	850	800
	6-200	All	BRF-82		.050 (.060)	Electronic		10B	10B(6B)	20	5½-6½	800	650
	6-250	All	BRF-82		.050	Electronic		4B	14B(6B)	18	5½-6½	800	600
	8-302	All	ARF-52 (ARF-52-6)		.050 (.060)	Electronic		10B	6B(12B⑦)	16	5½-6½	500	650
'79		All				See Underhood Specifications Sticker							

* Where two dwell or point gap figures are separated by a slash, the first figure is for engines equipped with dual diaphragm distributors and the second figure is for engines equipped with single diaphragm distributors

▲ See text for procedure

■ All figures Before Top Dead Center

• Where two idle speed figures are separated by a slash, the first figure is for idle speed with solenoid energized and automatic transmission in Drive, while the second is for idle speed with solenoid disconnected and automatic transmission in Neutral. Figures in parentheses are for California

B Before Top Dead Center

— Not applicable

① 600/500 with air conditioning

② 16° B—manual transmission
20° B—automatic transmission

③ Depends on emission equipment; check underhood specifications sticker

④ Granada/Monarch

⑤ Electronic ignition used on all engines assembled after May, 1974

⑥ .044 in. with electronic ignition

⑦ 14B for high altitude

NOTE: The underhood specifications sticker often reflects tune-up specification changes made in production. Sticker figures must be used if they disagree with those in this chart.

FIRING ORDER

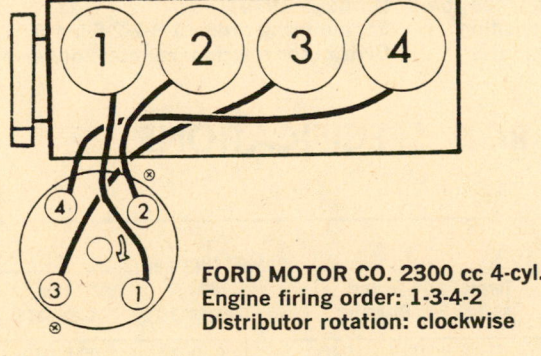

FORD MOTOR CO. 2300 cc 4-cyl.
Engine firing order: 1-3-4-2
Distributor rotation: clockwise

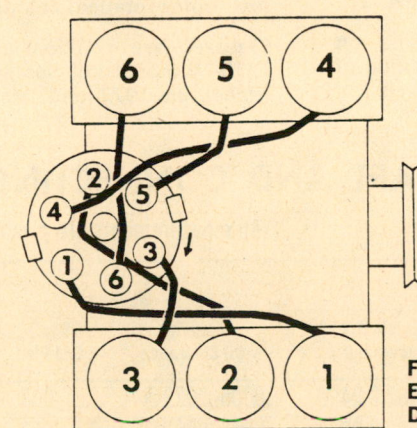

FORD MOTOR CO, 2800cc V6
Engine firing order: 1-4-2-5-3-6
Distributor rotation: Clockwise

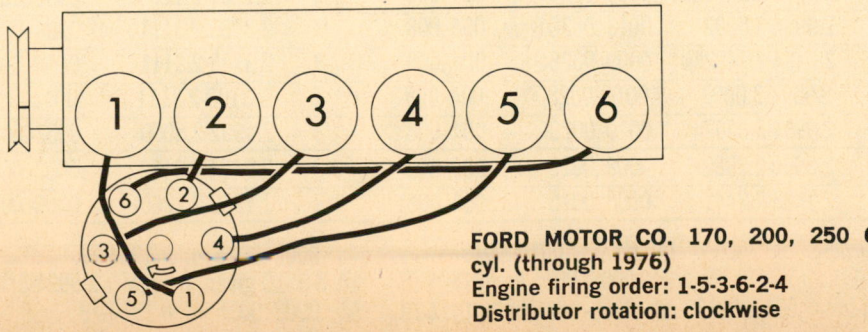

FORD MOTOR CO. 170, 200, 250 6-cyl. (through 1976)
Engine firing order: 1-5-3-6-2-4
Distributor rotation: clockwise

Capri • Comet • Cougar • Elite • Fairmont • Granada
LTD II • Maverick

FIRING ORDER

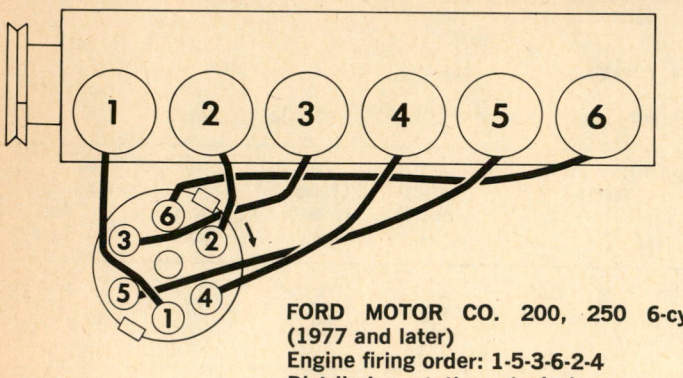

FORD MOTOR CO. 200, 250 6-cyl.
(1977 and later)
Engine firing order: 1-5-3-6-2-4
Distributor rotation: clockwise

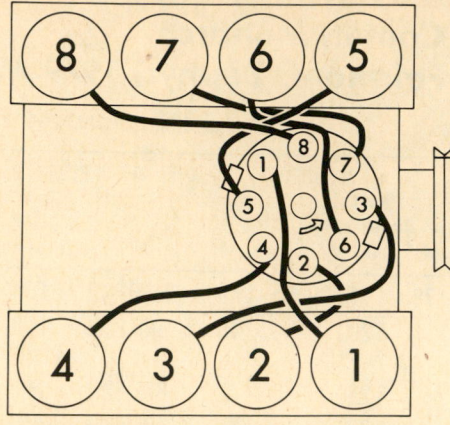

FORD MOTOR CO. 302, 429, 460 V8
(through 1974)
Engine firing order: 1-5-4-2-6-3-7-8
Distributor rotation: counterclockwise

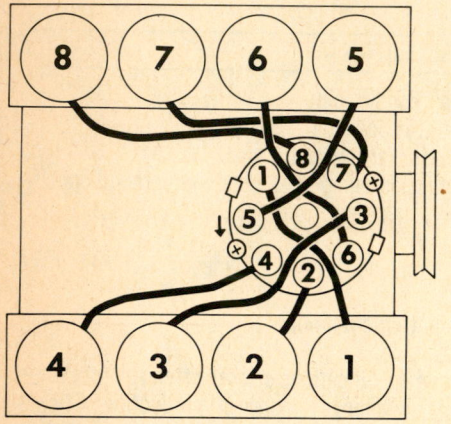

FORD MOTOR CO. 302, 460 V8 (1975 and later)
Engine firing order: 1-5-4-2-6-3-7-8
Distributor rotation: counterclockwise

(Squares are position of latches on 1975-76 models; circles are position of latches on 1977 and later models.)

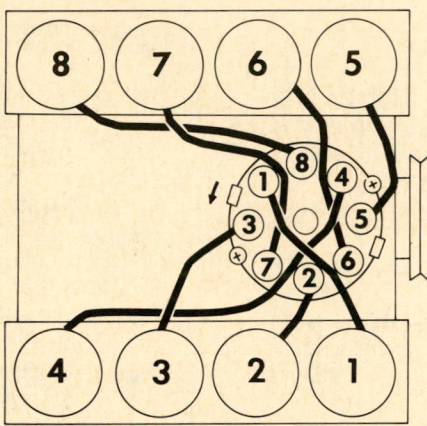

FORD MOTOR CO. 351, 400 V8 (1975 and later)
Engine firing order: 1-3-7-2-6-5-4-8
Distributor rotation: counterclockwise

(Squares are position of latches on 1975-76 models; circles are position of latches on 1977 and later models.)

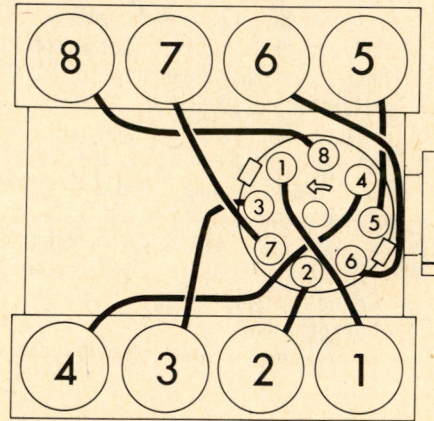

FORD MOTOR CO. 351, 400 V8
(through 1974)
Engine firing order: 1-3-7-2-6-5-4-8
Distributor rotation: counterclockwise

CRANKSHAFT AND CONNECTING ROD SPECIFICATIONS

All measurements are given in inches

Year	Engine No. Cyl. Displacement (cu in.)	Main Brg. Journal Dia	CRANKSHAFT Main Brg. Oil Clearance	Shaft End-Play	Thrust on No.	Journal Diameter	CONNECTING ROD Oil Clearance	Side Clearance
'72-'79	6-200	2.2482-2.2490	.0005-.0022⑬	.004-.008	5	2.1232-2.1240	.0008-.0015	.004-.011
	6-250	2.3982-2.3990	.0005-.0022⑬	.004-.008	5	2.1232-2.1240	.0008-.0015	.004-.011
	8-302	2.2482-2.2490	.0005-.0024⑤⑪	.004-.008	3	2.1228-2.1236	.0008-.0026⑥	.010-.020
	8-351W	2.9994-3.0002	.0013-.0030⑩⑤	.004-.008	3	2.3103-2.3111	.0008-.0026⑥	.010-.020
	8-351C or M	2.7484-2.7492⑫	.0009-.0026⑦⑨	.004-.008	3	2.3103-2.3111	.0008-.0026⑦⑨	.010-.020
	8-400	2.9994-3.0002	.0011-.0028⑨	.004-.008	3	2.3103-2.3111	.0011-.0026⑨	.010-.020
'72-'76	8-460	2.9994-3.0002	.0010-.0020⑧	.004-.008	3	2.4992-2.5000	.0008-.0028	.010-.020
'78-'79	4-140	2.3990-2.3982	.0008-.0015	.004-.008	3	2.0464-2.0472	.0008-.0015	.0035-.0105
'79	V6-170	2.2433-2.2441	.0008-.0015	.004-.008	3	2.1252-2.1260	.0006-.0015	.004-.011

⑤ .0001-.0015 No. 1 bearing only

⑥ .0008-.0015 in. in 1977-79

⑦ 351 HO and 351 C or M 4-bbl—.0011-.0015

⑧ No. 1—.0010-.0015

⑨ .0008-.0015 in. in 1974-79

⑩ .0008-.0015 in. in 1974-79

⑪ .0005-.0015 in. in 1974-79

⑫ 8-351C given; 8-351M—2.9994-3.0002

⑬ .0008-.0015 in. in 1977-79

Monarch • Montego • Mustang • 1977-79 Thunderbird
Torino • Versailles • Zephyr
CAPACITIES

Year	ENGINE No. Cyl. Displacement (Cu. In.)	Engine Crankcase Add 1 Qt For New Filter	TRANSMISSION Pts To Refill After Draining Manual 3-Speed	4-Speed	Automatic (Total Capacity)	Drive Axle (pts)	Gasoline Tank (gals)	COOLING SYSTEM (qts) With Heater	With A/C
'72	MAVERICK, COMET								
	6-170, 200	3.5	3.5	—	16	4	15	9	9
	6-250	3.5	3.5	—	18	4	15	9.5	10.5
	8-302	4	3.5	—	18	4	15	13.5	14.5
	TORINO, MONTEGO								
	6-250	3.5	3.5	—	18	4	22.5⑩	11.5	11.5
	8-302	4	3.5	—	18	4	22.5⑩	15	15
	8-351	4	—	4	20.5⑪	4	22.5⑩	15.5	16
	8-400	4	—	—	26	4	22.5⑩	17.5	17.5
	8-429	4	—	—	26	5	22.5	19	19
	MUSTANG								
	6-250	3.5	3.5	—	18	4	19.5	11	11
	8-302	4	3.5	—	18	4	19.5	15	15.5
	MUSTANG, COUGAR								
	8-351	4	3.5	4	22⑫	5	19.5	16	16
'73	MAVERICK, COMET								
	6-200	3.5	3.5	—	16	4	15	9	9
	6-250	3.5	3.5	—	18	4	15	9.5	10.5
	8-302	4	3.5	—	18	4	15	13.5	14.5
	TORINO, MONTEGO								
	6-250	3.5	3.5	—	18	4	22.5⑩	11.5	11.5
	8-302	4	3.5	—	18	4	22.5⑩	15	15
	8-351	4	—	4	20.5⑪	4	22.5⑩	15.5	16
	8-400	4	—	—	26	4	22.5⑩	17.5	17.5
	8-429	4	—	—	26	5	22.5⑩	19	19
	8-460	6	—	—	26	5	22.5⑩	19.5	19.5
	MUSTANG								
	6-250	3.5	3.5	—	18	4	19.5	11	11
	8-302	4	3.5	—	18	4	19.5	15	15.5
	MUSTANG, COUGAR								
	8-351	4	—	4	22⑫	5	19.5	16	16
'74	MAVERICK, COMET								
	6-200	4	3.5	—	16	4	15	9.0	9.0
	6-250	4	3.5	—	18	4	15	9.7	9.7
	8-302	4	3.5	—	18	4	15	13.4	14.2
	TORINO, MONTEGO								
	6-250	4	—	—	⑬	4	26.5⑰	11.5	—
	8-302	4	3.5	—	⑬	4	26.5⑰	15.7	15.7
	TORINO, MONTEGO, COUGAR, ELITE								
	8-351	4	—	—	⑭	4⑯	26.5⑰	⑱	⑲
	8-400	4	—	—	25⑮	5	26.5⑰	17.7	18.3
	8-460	6	—	—	25⑮	5	26.5⑰	18.9	19.5
'75-'77	MAVERICK, COMET								
	6-200	4	3.5	—	16	4.5①	19.5㉓	9.0	9.0
	6-250	4	3.5	—	18	4.5①	19.5㉓	9.7	9.7
	8-302	4	3.5	—	20㉗	4.5①	19.5㉓	13.4	14.2

C467

Capri • Comet • Cougar • Elite • Fairmont • Granada
LTD II • Maverick

CAPACITIES

Year	ENGINE No. Cyl. Displacement (Cu. In.)	Engine Crankcase Add 1 Qt For New Filter	TRANSMISSION Pts To Refill After Draining — Manual 3-Speed	4-Speed	Automatic (Total Capacity)	Drive Axle (pts)	Gasoline Tank (gals)	COOLING SYSTEM (qts) With Heater	With A/C
'75-'76 TORINO, MONTEGO									
	8-351	4	—	—	⑳	4②	26.5⑰	15.9㉑	16.2㉑
	8-400	4	—	—	⑳	5	26.5⑰	17.1	17.5
	8-460	4	—	—	⑳	5	26.5⑰	19.2③	19.2③
'75-'76 COUGAR, ELITE									
	8-351	4	—	—	㉒	5	26.5	16.3④	16.8⑤
	8-400	4	—	—	㉒	5	26.5	17.7④	18.3⑤
	8-460	4	—	—	㉒	5	26.5	18.9⑥	20.5⑥
'77-'79 COUGAR									
	8-302	4	—	—	㉒	5	21㉔	14.3㉕	14.6
	8-351W	4	—	—	㉒	5	21㉔	15.9	16.3
	8-351M	4	—	—	㉒	5	21㉔	17.1 ㉖	17.5 ㉖
	8-400	4	—	—	㉒	5	21㉔	17.1 ㉖	17.5 ㉖
'77-'79 VERSAILLES									
	8-302	4	—	—	20.5	5	19.2	14.6	14.6
	8-351W	4	—	—	20.5	5	19.2	15.7	15.7
'75-'79 GRANADA, MONARCH									
	6-200	4	3.5	4⑨	—	4⑦	19.2⑧	9.9	9.9
	6-250	4	3.5	4⑨	17.0㉙	4⑦	19.2⑧	10.5	10.7
	8-302	4	3.5	4⑨	17.0㉘	4⑦	19.2⑧	14.6	14.6
	8-351	4	—	—	20.0	4⑦	19.2⑧	15.7	16.7
'77-'79 LTD II, THUNDERBIRD									
	8-302	4	—	—	20	5	21㉔	13.5	14.1
	8-351W	4	—	—	22	5	21㉔	15.5	16.0
	8-351W	4	—	—	22	5	21㉔	17.1 ㉖	17.5 ㉖
	8-400	4	—	—	25	5	21㉔	17.1 ㉖	17.5 ㉖
'78-'79 FAIRMONT, ZEPHYR, MUSTANG, CAPRI									
	4-140	4	—	2.8⑨	16	3.5 ㉛	16	8.6	10.3
	V6-170	4	—	3.5	14.5	3.5 ㉛	16	8.6	9.0
	6-200	4	3.5	—	㉚	3.5	16	9.0	9.0
	8-302	4	—	4.5	20.5	3.5	16	13.9	14.0

① 4 pts in 1975
② 5 pts in 1976
③ 19.7 qts in 1976
④ 17.1 qts in 1976
⑤ 17.5 qts in 1976
⑥ 19.2 qts in 1976
⑦ 8 in.—4.5 pts
   8.7 in.—4.0 pts
   9.0 in.—5.0 pts
⑧ 1 gal less on certain 1976 models; 18 gals 1978-79
⑨ 4-Speed overdrive—4.5 pts.
⑩ Less 2 gals—station wagon, Ranchero
⑪ 26 pts for 351 CJ
⑫ Less 1 pt with 4 bbl
⑬ C4—18 or 20 pts; FMX—22 pts

⑭ 351 2V with C-4—20 pts; 351-2V with FMX—22pts; 351 2V with C-6—25 pts; 351-4V (C6)—21 pts
⑮ Cougar—21 pts
⑯ Cougar—5 pts
⑰ Station wagon—21.2 gallons
⑱ 351 W 2V—16.4 qts
   351 C 2V—15.9 qts
   351 C 4V—15.9 qts
⑲ 351 W 2V—16.8 qts
   351 C 2V—16.5 qts
   351 C 4V—16.9 qts
⑳ C4—20 pts; C6—25 pts; FMX—22 pts
㉑ 17.1 qts with heater, 17.5 qts with AC on 351 C 2 bbl

㉒ C4—21 pts; C6—24.5 pts; FMX—22 pts
㉓ 16 in 1975
㉔ 1977—26 gals; 1977 station wagon—21.3 gals; 1979 optional tank: 27.5 gals.
㉕ 13.5—1977
㉖ 16.5—1978-79
㉗ 18 in 1975
㉘ 20 in 1977-79
㉙ 16.5 with C4
㉚ C3—16pts; C4—14.5 pts
㉛ Mustang and Capri—3.0 pts

— Not applicable

C468

VALVE SPECIFICATIONS

Year	Engine No. Cyl. Displacement (cu in.)	Seat Angle (deg)	Face Angle (deg)	Spring Test Pressure (lbs @ in.)	Spring Installed Height (in.)	STEM TO GUIDE Clearance (in.) Intake	Exhaust	STEM Diameter (in.) Intake	Exhaust
'72	6-170, 200	45	44	150 @ 1.22	1 19/32	.0008-.0025	.0010-.0027	.3104	.3102
	6-250	45	44	150 @ 1.22	1 19/32	.0008-.0025	.0010-.0027	.3104	.3102
	8-302	45	44	200 @ 1.23	1 11/16	.0010-.0027	.0015-.0032	.3420	.3415
	8-351W	45	44	200 @ 1.34	1 25/32	.0010-.0027	.0015-.0032	.3420	.3415
	8-351⑥	45	44	210 @ 1.42	1 13/16	.0010-.0027	.0015-.0032	.3420	.3415
	8-351⑦	45	44	285 @ 1.23	1 13/16	.0010-.0027	.0015-.0032	.3420	.3415
	8-351④	45	44	315 @ 1.23	1 13/16	.0010-.0027	.0015-.0032	.3420	.3415
	8-400	45	44	226 @ 1.39	1 13/16	.0010-.0027	.0015-.0032	.3420	.3415
	8-429	45	45	229 @ 1.33	1 13/16	.0010-.0027	.0010-.0027	.3420	.3420
'73-	6-200	45	44	150 @ 1.22	1 19/32	.0008-.0025	.0010-.0027	.3104	.3102
'78	6-250	45	44	150 @ 1.22	1 19/32	.0008-.0025	.0010-.0027	.3104	.3102
	8-302	45	44	①	③	.0010-.0027	.0015-.0032	.3420	.3415
	8-351W	45	44	②	⑤	.0010-.0027	.0015-.0032	.3420	.3415
	8-351⑥	45	44	228 @ 1.39	1 13/16	.0010-.0027	.0015-.0032	.3420	.3415
'73-'76	8-351⑦	45	44	285 @ 1.32	1 13/16	.0010-.0027	.0015-.0032	.3420	.3415
'73-'78	8-400	45	44	226 @ 1.39	1 13/16	.0010-.0027	.0015-.0032	.3420	.3415
'73-'76	8-460	45	44	253 @ 1.33	1 13/16	.0010-.0027	.0010-.0027	.3420	.3420
'78-'79	4-140	45	44	180-198 @ 1.16	1 9/16	.0010-.0027	.0015-.0032	.3420	.3415
'79	V6-170	45	44	138-149 @ 1.22	1 19/32	.0008-.0025	.0018-.0035	.3163	.3152

① Intake: 200 @ 1.31
Exhaust: 200 @ 1.20
② Intake: 200 @ 1.34
Exhaust: 200 @ 1.20
③ Intake: 1 11/16
Exhaust: 1 5/8
④ Boss
⑤ Intake: 1 25/32
Exhaust: 1 5/8
⑥ Cleveland or modified Cleveland 2 bbl
⑦ Cleveland or modified Cleveland 4 bbl

TORQUE SPECIFICATIONS

All readings in ft lbs

Year	Engine No. Cyl. Displacement (cu in.)	Cylinder Head Bolts*	Rod Bearing Bolts	Main Bearing Bolts	Crankshaft Pulley or Damper Bolt	Flywheel to Crankshaft Bolts	MANIFOLD Intake	Exhaust
'72-'73	6-170, 200, 250	70-75	19-24②	60-70	85-100	75-85	—	13-18
	8-302	65-72	19-24	60-70	70-90	75-85	23-25	12-16
	8-351	95-100①	40-45⑥	95-105⑦	70-90	75-85	23-25 (5/16) 28-32 (3/8) 6-9 (1/4)	12-22
	8-400	95-105⑨	40-45	⑩	70-90	75-85	21-25 (5/16) 27-33 (3/8) 6-9 (1/4)	12-16
	8-429, 460	130-140	40-45	95-105⑤	70-90	75-85	25-30	28-33
	8-429 Boss	90-95	85-90	70-80	70-90	75-85	25-30	28-33
'74-'79	6-200	70-75	19-24	60-70	85-100	75-85	—	13-18⑪
	6-250	70-75	21-26	60-70	85-100	75-85	—	13-18⑪

TORQUE SPECIFICATIONS

All readings in ft lbs

Year	Engine No. Cyl. Displacement (cu in.)	Cylinder Head Bolts*	Rod Bearing Bolts	Main Bearing Bolts	Crankshaft Pulley or Damper Bolt	Flywheel to Crankshaft Bolts	MANIFOLD Intake	MANIFOLD Exhaust
'74-'79	8-302	65-72	19-24	60-70	70-90	75-85	19-27	18-24
	8-351W	105-112	40-45	95-105	70-90	75-85	19-27	18-24
	8-351C, 351M	95-105⑧	40-45	⑨	70-90	75-85	⑩	18-24
	8-400	95-105⑧	40-45	⑨	70-90	75-85	⑩	18-24
'74-'76	8-460	130-140	40-45	95-105	70-90	75-85	22-32	28-33
'78-'79	4-140	80-90	30-36	80-90	100-120	54-64	③	16-23
'79	V6-170	65-80	21-25	65-75	92-103	47-51	④	20-30

① 351 HO three steps—40, 80, 120 ft. lbs.
② 250—21-26
③ Two steps: 5-7, then 14-21
④ Four steps: 3-6, 6-11, 11-15, 15-18; retorque to 15-18 with engine hot
⑤ 7/16 in. bolts—70-80
⑥ 351 HO—43-48 ft. lbs.
⑦ 3/8 in. bolts—34-45 ft. lbs.
⑧ Three steps—55, 75, then maximum figure
⑨ 1/2 in—13 bolts, 95-105, 3/8 in—16 bolts, 35-45
⑩ 5/16 in. bolt, 21-25; 3/8 in. bolt, 22-32; 1/4 in. bolt, 6-9
⑪ 1977 and later: 18-24
* Tighten cylinder head bolts in three steps

RING GAP

All measurements are given in inches

Year	Engine	Top Compression	Bottom Compression
'72-'73	All	.010-.020	.010-.020
'74-'79	Inline 6 Cyl.	.008-.016	.008-.016
	8 Cyl. and 4 Cyl.	.010-.020	.010-.020
'79	V6	.015-.023	.015-.023

Year	Engine	Oil Control
'72-'79	6-170, 200, 250; 4-140	.015-.055
'72-'79	8-302, 351	.015-.055①
'72-'76	8-400	.015-.069
'77-'78	8-400	.015-.055
'72-'76	8-429, 460	.015-.055

① .015-.069 in Cleveland built engine through 1973

RING SIDE CLEARANCE

All measurements are given in inches

Year	Engine	Top Compression	Bottom Compression
'72-'79	All except V6	.002-.004	.002-.004
'79	V6	.002-.0033	.002-.0033

Year	Engine	Oil Control
'72-'79	All	Snug

PISTON CLEARANCE

Year	Engine	Piston-to-Bore Clearance (in.) Minimum	Piston-to-Bore Clearance (in.) Maximum
'72-'79	302, 351W	0.0018	0.0026
'72-'79	170, 200, 250	0.0013	0.0021
'72-'79	351C, 351M, 400, 429, 460	0.0014	0.0022
'72	351HO (CJ)	0.0034	0.0042
'78-'79	4-140	0.0014	0.0022
79	V6-170	0.0011	0.0019

WHEEL ALIGNMENT SPECIFICATIONS

Year	Model	CASTER Range (deg)	CASTER Pref Setting (deg)	CAMBER Range (deg)	CAMBER Pref Setting (deg)	Toe-in (in.)	Steering Axis Inclin. (deg)	WHEEL PIVOT RATIO (deg) Inner Wheel	WHEEL PIVOT RATIO (deg) Outer Wheel
'72	Torino, Montego	1¼N to 2¾P	¾P	¼N to 1¾P	¾P	¹⁄₁₆ to ⁷⁄₁₆	7⅔	20	17¾
	Mustang, Cougar	2N to 2P	0	½N to 1½P	½P	¹⁄₁₆ to ⅜	6¾	20	17¾
	Maverick, Comet	2½N to 1½P	½N	¾N to 1¼P	¼P	¹⁄₁₆ to ⅜	6¾	20	18½④
'73	Torino, Montego	¾N to 2¼P	¾P	¼N to 1¾P	¾P	³⁄₁₆ to ⁹⁄₁₆	7⅔	20	17.73
	Mustang, Cougar	2N to 2P	0	½N to 1½P	½P	¹⁄₁₆ to ⅜	6¾	20	17.72
	Maverick, Comet	2½N to 1½P	½N	¾N to 1¼P	¼P	¹⁄₁₆ to ⅜	6¾	20	18.44④
'74	Torino, Montego, Cougar, Elite	½P to 3½P	2P	⑥	⑦	0 to ⅜	9	20	18.11
	Maverick, Comet	2½N to 1½P	½N	¾N to 1¼P	¼P	¹⁄₁₆ to ⅜	6¾	20	18.39④
'75-'79	Torino, Montego, Cougar, Elite, LTD II, 1977-79 Thunderbird	3¼P to 4¾P	4P	⑨	⑩	0 to ¼	9⑪	20	18.06
	Maverick, Comet, Monarch, Granada, Versailles	1¼N to ¼P	½N	½N to 1P	¼P	0 to ¼	6¾	20	⑧
'78-'79	Fairmont, Zephyr, Mustang, Capri	⑫	⅞P	⑫	⅜P	³⁄₁₆-⁷⁄₁₆	—	20	19.74

①② Not used
③ Manual steering—17°19′; power steering—17°49′
④ 18.16° for power steering.
⑤ Not used
⑥ Left—⅜N to 1⅝P
Right—⅞N to 1⅛P
⑦ Left—⅝P
Right—⅛P

⑧ Maverick/Comet w/PS—18.13; w/o PS—18.36
Granada/Monarch, Versailles w/PS—18.20; w/o PS—18.43
⑨ Left—¼N to 1¼P
Right—½N to 1P
⑩ Left—½P
Right—¼P
⑪ Thunderbird—9½
⑫ Caster and camber is preset and nonadjustable
N Negative   P Positive

NOTE: 1972-73 and 1979 Mustang is covered in this section. Refer to the Bobcat, Mustang II, Pinto car section for coverage of 1974-78 Mustang II. Beginning 1977, Thunderbird and Lincoln Versailles are covered in this section. See the Ford, Mercury, Thunderbird car section for coverage of Thunderbird through 1976.

CHARGING SYSTEM

Charging system troubleshooting procedures can be found in the Unit Repair Section under Charging and Starting Systems.

Alternator Removal and Installation

1. Disconnect the battery ground cable.
2. Loosen the alternator mounting bolts and remove the adjustment arm to alternator attaching bolt. On 1979 Mustangs and Capris with the 302 V8, lever the belt tensioner away from the belt, then slip the serpentine belt off the alternator pulley.

On 302 V8s with serpentine belt, raise the tensioner with a short bar.

3. Remove the electrical connectors from the alternator and remove the alternator. On some models it is necessary to remove the alternator mounting bolts and the alternator wiring ground bolt from engine to gain access to the electrical connectors.
4. Install the alternator to the bracket and connect the electrical connectors. Adjust the drive belt tension

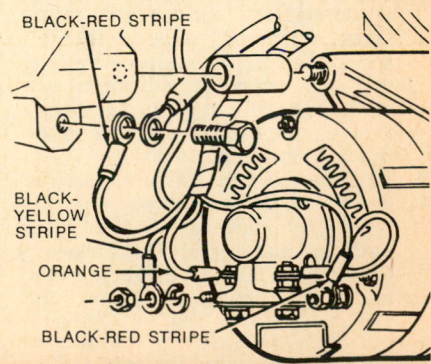

BLACK-RED STRIPE
BLACK-YELLOW STRIPE
ORANGE
BLACK-RED STRIPE

Typical alternator mounting
(© Ford Motor Co)

so that there is approximately 1/4-1/2 in. of deflection on the longest span of belt between pulleys. Use a soft piece of wood to pry against the alternator housing, if necessary. On 1979 Mustangs and Capris with the 302 V8, install the alternator to the bracket, attach the electrical connectors, slide the serpentine belt over the alternator pulley, and release the automatic tensioner.

Voltage Regulator Removal and Installation

1. Disconnect the negative battery cable.
2. Remove the regulator mounting screws.
3. Remove the cable quick-disconnect from the old regulator and attach to the new regulator.
4. Place the mounting bracket for the radio suppression capacitor over the hole for the lower regulator's mounting screw and install the screws.
5. Connect the negative battery cable.
6. Test the system for proper voltage regulation.

STARTING SYSTEM

Starting system troubleshooting procedures can be found in the Charging and Starting Systems Unit Repair Section.

All engines except 429 or 460 V8 have a positive engagement starter with a self-contained engagement mechanism. The 429 and 460 V8 models use a solenoid activated starter with an outboard solenoid. There is no difference in procedures for removing or installing these two types of starters.

Starter Removal and Installation

Due to interference of the exhaust inlet pipe on some models, the steering idler arm must be lowered to provide clearance for starter removal.

1. Disconnect the starter cable at the starter terminal, remove the flywheel housing to starter retaining screws. Remove the starter assembly and the rubber dust ring.
2. Position the rubber dust ring on the flywheel housing.
3. Position the starter assembly to the flywheel housing, and begin on the starter retaining screws. On a car with an automatic transmission, the transmission dipstick tube bracket is mounted under the starter side mounting bolt. Snug all bolts, then tighten to 15 ft lbs, tightening the middle bolt first.

NOTE: *Intermittent starter operation on solenoid starter motor equipped 429*

and 460 V8s may be due to the loosening of screws and terminals on the solenoid switch assembly. To remedy this, apply a small amount of bolt locking compound.

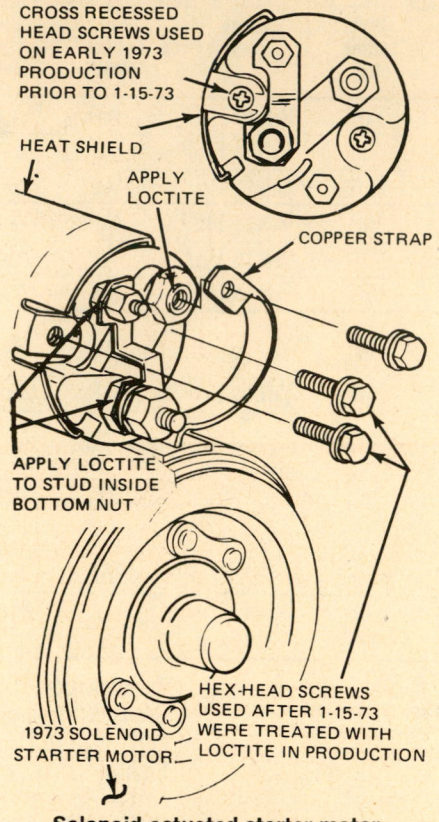

CROSS RECESSED HEAD SCREWS USED ON EARLY 1973 PRODUCTION PRIOR TO 1-15-73

HEAT SHIELD

APPLY LOCTITE

COPPER STRAP

APPLY LOCTITE TO STUD INSIDE BOTTOM NUT

HEX-HEAD SCREWS USED AFTER 1-15-73 WERE TREATED WITH LOCTITE IN PRODUCTION

1973 SOLENOID STARTER MOTOR

Solenoid-actuated starter motor
(© Ford Motor Co)

Disconnecting the Seat Belt/Starter Interlock

It is now legal to disconnect the seat belt/starter interlock system. However the warning light portion of the system must be left operational.

1. Apply the parking brake and remove the ignition key.
2. Open the hood and locate the system emergency override switch and connector. Remove the connector.
3. Cut the white wire(s) with the pink dots (# 33 circuit) and the red wire(s) with the light blue stripe (# 32 circuit).
4. Splice the two (four) wires together and tape the splice. Use a butt connector if available.

NOTE: *Do not cut and splice the other connector wires. If the red/yellow hash wire is spliced to any of the other wires the car will start in gear.*

5. Install the connector back on the override switch. Close the hood.
6. Apply the parking brakes, buckle the seat belt, and turn the key to the ON position. If the starter cranks in ON or any gear selected, the wrong wires have been cut and spliced. Repeat steps 3-6.
7. Unbuckle the belt and try to start the car. If the car doesn't start, re-

peat steps 3-6. If the car starts, everything is OK.

9. To stop the warning buzzer from operating, remove it from its connector and throw it away. Tape the connector to the wiring harness so that it can't rattle.

IGNITION SYSTEM

Beginning 1974, Ford uses a solid state or breakerless ignition system on all California engines and on all 400 and 460 cu in. V8s. All engines assembled after May, 1974 have the system.

Starting 1975, breakerless ignition is standard on all Ford engines. This system eliminates the contact breaker points, replacing them with a permanent magnet low voltage generator.

Beginning 1977, an improved breakerless ignition system called DuraSpark is standard. Two versions of the Dura-Spark system are used: one for California cars and one for all other engines. Both utilize higher spark voltages of up to 42,000 volts to allow wider spark plug gaps necessary to fire leaner air/fuel mixtures.

NOTE: *On 1975 and later models there is a terminal on the coil provided for connecting a tachometer. The terminal is labeled Tach Test and has a small arrowhead pointing to the proper terminal.*

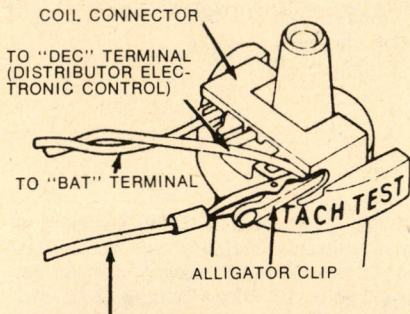

COIL CONNECTOR

TO "DEC" TERMINAL (DISTRIBUTOR ELECTRONIC CONTROL)

TO "BAT" TERMINAL

TACH TEST

ALLIGATOR CLIP

TACHOMETER TEST LEAD

Attaching dwell/tachometer lead to coil connector—1975 and later with breakerless ignition (© Ford Motor Co)

Distributor Removal

1. Remove the distributor cap. Disconnect the primary wire at the coil and the vacuum control line at the distributor.
2. Scribe a mark on the distributor body, showing position of the rotor. Then, scribe another mark on the distributor body and engine block, showing the position of the body in the block. These marks can be used to advantage when reassembling the distributor in an undisturbed engine.
3. Remove the screw, lockwasher and hold-down clamp. Pull the distributor out of the block. Do not rotate crankshaft while distributor

is out of block because it will then be necessary to retime ignition.

Distributor Installation

1. If the engine was not cranked while the distributor was removed, install the distributor in the engine, aligning the tip of the rotor with the marks that were made on the distributor body and the engine. Proceed to Step 3. If the engine was cranked while the distributor was removed, rotate the crankshaft to bring No. 1 piston to T.D.C. of its compression stroke.
2. Position the distributor in the block with the rotor at No. 1 firing position. Be sure that the oil pump intermediate driveshaft is properly seated in the oil pump.
3. Install, but do not tighten, the distributor retaining clamp and screw.
4. Rotate the distributor body clockwise until the breaker points start to open on point-type models.
5. Tighten the retaining clamp screw.
6. Install distributor cap.
7. Connect distributor primary wire.
8. Start engine and run long enough to obtain engine operating temperature.
9. Idle engine to 500 rpm. Then, with a timing light, check the timing marks at the front pulley and make necessary corrections.
10. Connect the vacuum control line to the distributor and check advance characteristics with the timing light when the engine is accelerated.

Contact Point Replacement and Adjustment—through 1974

1. Unsnap the distributor cap retaining clips and position the cap clear of the breaker plate. Remove the rotor by pulling it straight up.
2. Remove the metal point shield, if so equipped.
3. Disconnect the primary lead and condenser wires from the contact point assembly. On dual-point distributors, remove the jumper strap also.
4. Remove the contact point and condenser retaining screws. Lift the contact point assembly and condenser from the distributor.
5. Lightly lubricate the distributor cam with heat-resistant lubricant.
6. Place the new contact point assembly and condenser in the distributor. Install, but do not tighten, the retaining screws.
7. On all V8 engines, except those equipped with a centrifugal advance distributor, place the ground wire under the contact point assembly screw farthest from the contacts. This ground wire is positioned under the condenser retaining screw on all six cylinder engines.
8. Turn the engine until the rubbing block on the point assembly is resting on the high point of the distrib-

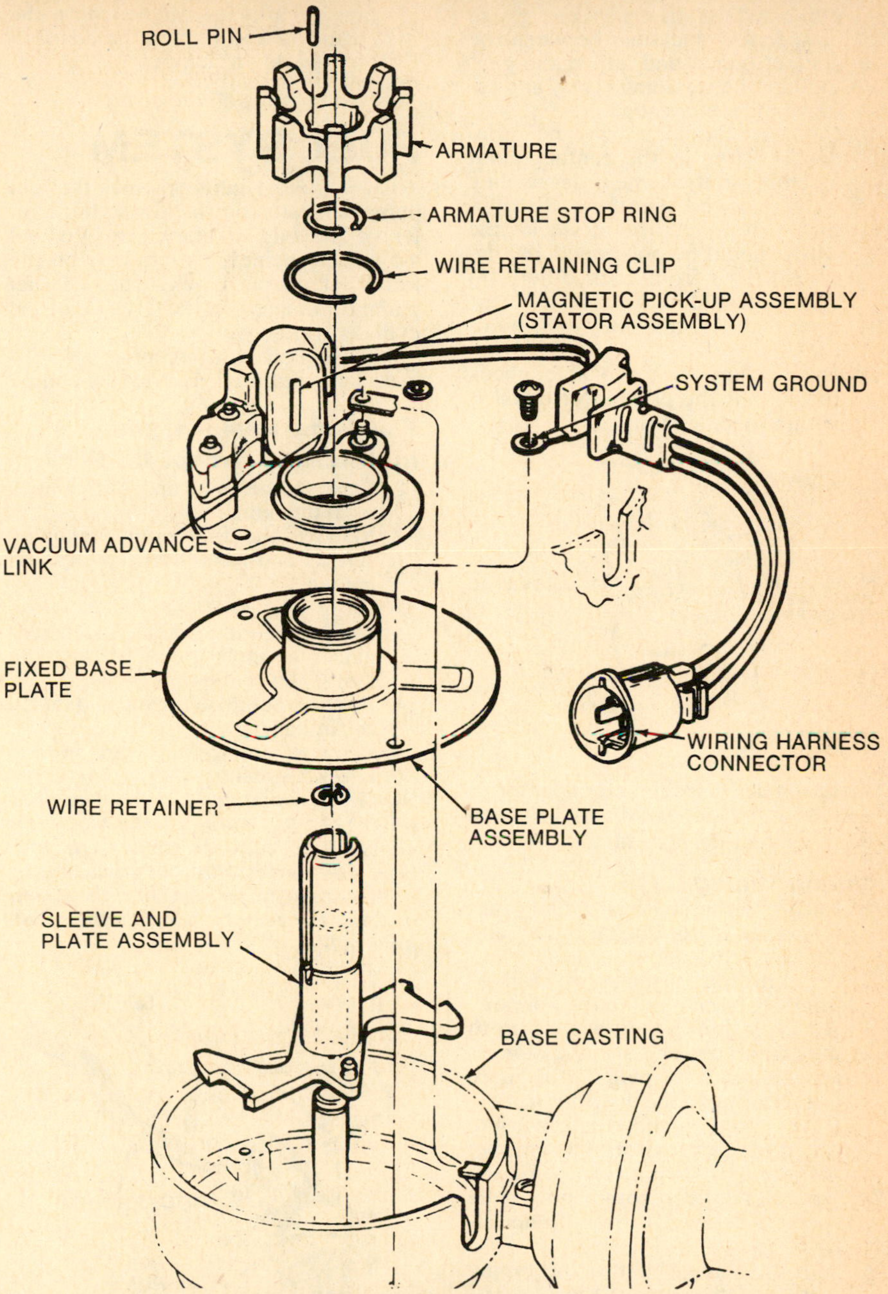

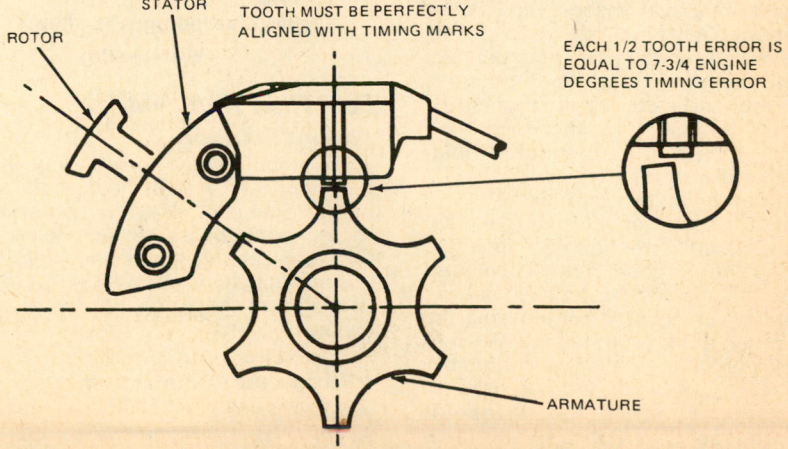

ROLL PIN

ARMATURE

ARMATURE STOP RING

WIRE RETAINING CLIP

MAGNETIC PICK-UP ASSEMBLY (STATOR ASSEMBLY)

SYSTEM GROUND

VACUUM ADVANCE LINK

WIRING HARNESS CONNECTOR

FIXED BASE PLATE

BASE PLATE ASSEMBLY

WIRE RETAINER

SLEEVE AND PLATE ASSEMBLY

BASE CASTING

Breakerless V8 distributor diassembled (© Ford Motor Co)

STATOR

ROTOR

TOOTH MUST BE PERFECTLY ALIGNED WITH TIMING MARKS

EACH 1/2 TOOTH ERROR IS EQUAL TO 7-3/4 ENGINE DEGREES TIMING ERROR

ARMATURE

Breakerless ignition distributor static timing position (© Ford Motor Co)

utor cam lobe. Insert a feeler gauge of specified thickness between the contact points and adjust the gap. Tighten the retaining screw and remove the feeler gauge.

9. Connect the primary and condenser wires to the contact point assembly in the same order as they were removed. On those distributors with a metal point shield, the wires should be positioned 180 degrees (180°) from each other. Install the shield.

10. Install the rotor and distributor cap.

11. If a dwell meter is available, check to see that the distributor dwell is within specifications.

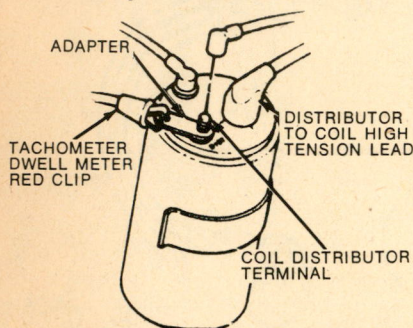

Installing dwell/tachometer adaptor on coil-1974 and earlier with conventional ignition (© Ford Motor Co)

Ignition Timing

1. Locate the timing marks and pointer on the lower engine pulley and engine's front cover.
2. Clean the marks and apply chalk or bright-colored paint to the pointer.
3. Attach a timing light according to the manufacturer's specifications.
4. Disconnect and plug all vacuum lines leading to the distributor.
5. If the recommended engine idle speed is in excess of 500 rpm, set the idle at 500 rpm for setting the timing. If the recommended idle speed is below 500 rpm, do not alter it.
6. Aim the timing light at the timing mark and pointer on the front of the engine. If the marks align when the timing light flashes, remove the timing light, set the idle to its proper specification, and connect the vacuum lines at the distributor. If the marks do not align when the light flashes, turn the engine off and loosen the distributor hold-down clamp slightly.
7. Start the engine again, and observe the alignment of the timing marks. To advance the timing, turn the distributor counterclockwise, on six cylinder engines, or clockwise, for V8 engines. When altering the timing, it is wise to tap the distributor lightly with a wooden hammer handle to move it in the desired direction. Grasping the distributor with your hand may result in a painful electric shock. When the

timing marks are aligned, turn the engine off and tighten the distributor hold-down clamp.

FUEL SYSTEM

On 6-cylinder inline engines the fuel pump is located on the lower, left center of the engine block. On V6 and 4-cylinder engines, the pump is on the left front of the block. The V8 fuel pump is mounted on the left side of the cylinder front cover.

1975-76 Police Interceptor 460 V8s use a tank-mounted electric fuel pump.

Fuel Pump Removal and Installation—except 460 PI V8

1. Remove the inlet and outlet lines from the pump.
2. Remove the fuel pump retaining screws and remove the pump and gasket.
3. Clean all gasket material from the pump mounting surface on the engine, and apply a coat of oil-resistant sealer to the new gasket.
4. Position pump on engine and install retaining screws.
5. Reinstall lines, start engine and check for leaks.

NOTE: *If resistance is felt while positioning the fuel pump on the block, the camshaft eccentric is in the high position. To ease installation, connect a remote engine starter switch to the engine and tap the remote switch until resistance fades.*

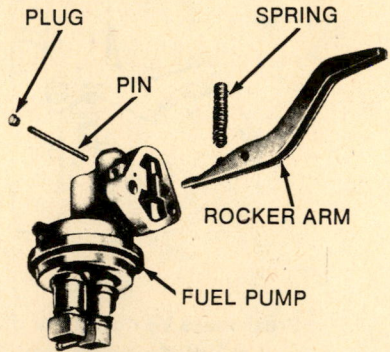

Typical fuel pump—V8 shown

(© Ford Motor Co)

Fuel Filter Removal and Installation

All models use a throw-away inline fuel filter which is located at the carburetor fuel inlet. The filter is removed by removing the air cleaner, loosening the hose clamp on the inlet line, and unscrewing the filter. When installing, use a new hose clamp to prevent leakage.

Idle Speed and Mixture Adjustments

NOTE: *Adjust with air cleaner installed.*

IDLE SPEED ADJUSTMENT

This is the procedure for adjusting all carburetors; any exceptions are listed below.

NOTE: *If the following adjustment fails to produce a satisfactory idle, the following items should be checked: vacuum leaks, ignition wiring continuity, spark plug condition, dwell angle, breaker point condition, ignition timing, carburetor float level, PCV valve condition, valve clearance, cylinder compression, and, failing all else, check for an overly lean air fuel mixture with a CO meter.*

1. Run engine at fast idle to equalize operating temperature.
2. Make sure the choke plate is fully released.
3. Turn headlights on high beam. On models equipped with an automatic transmission, apply the parking brake and put the transmission selector lever in Drive.
4. If engine is equipped with hot idle compensator valve, make sure it is fully seated in the closed position.
5. Attach tachometer of known accuracy to the engine.
6. On cars equipped with air conditioning, the idle speed is set with the air conditioner turned OFF.
7. On models equipped with a temperature sensing valve in the distributor vacuum line, remove and plug the vacuum hoses from the intake manifold to the valve, at the valve located in the intake manifold. Also plug the intake manifold hose fitting on the valve.
8. Make sure the dashpot is working freely and not binding.
9. If it is not possible to adjust the idle speed with the air cleaner installed, the engine idle speed must be rechecked after installing the air cleaner. On cars with vacuum controlled heat ducts in the air cleaner, the vacuum line must be plugged if the carburetor is to be adjusted with the air cleaner removed.
10. On carburetors which do not have an electric throttle solenoid, turn the idle speed adjusting screw inward or outward to obtain the specified idle speed. On models which are equipped with a throttle solenoid, turn the throttle solenoid adjustment screw inward or outward to obtain the higher of the two idle speeds listed in the Tune-up Specifications table.
11. If equipped with a throttle solenoid, disconnect the lead wire from the solenoid and turn the curb idle adjusting screw on the carburetor to obtain the lower of the two idle speeds listed in the Tune-up Specifications table. On models equipped with an automatic transmission, place the transmission selector lever in Park or neutral before adjusting the lower idle speed.

NOTE: *With the electric solenoid disengaged, the carburetor adjusting screw*

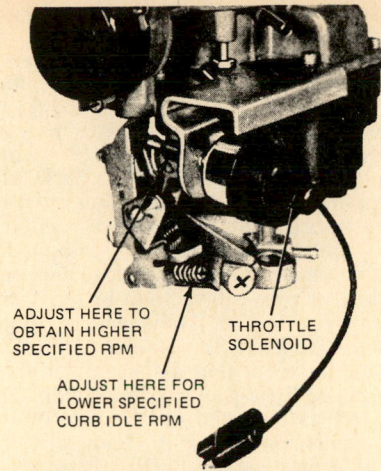

Carburetor adjustments—solenoid equipped Carter YF 1 bbl; Carter YFA similar (© Ford Motor Co)

ADJUST HERE TO OBTAIN HIGHER SPECIFIED RPM

ADJUST HERE FOR LOWER SPECIFIED CURB IDLE RPM

THROTTLE SOLENOID

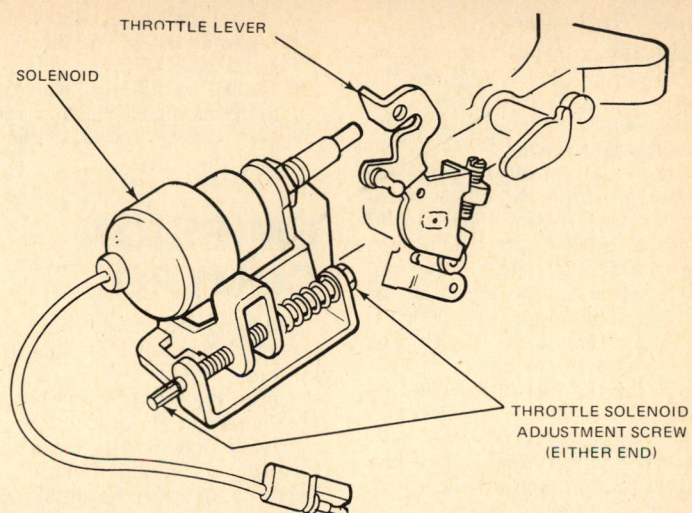

THROTTLE LEVER

SOLENOID

THROTTLE SOLENOID ADJUSTMENT SCREW (EITHER END)

1972-74 throttle solenoid adjustment—Motorcraft 2100-D and 4300 shown (© Ford Motor Co)

must make contact with the throttle shaft to prevent the throttle plates from jamming in the throttle bore when the engine is shut off.

FUEL MIXTURE ADJUSTMENT

NOTE: *The factory recommended procedure for adjusting the idle mixture on 1975 and later models requires the addition of an artificial mixture enrichment substance (propane) to the air intake. This method requires special tools not generally available to the public. The following procedure is specifically recommended by the factory only for models through 1974.*

Adjust by turning the idle mixture adjusting screw(s) inward to obtain the smoothest idle possible within the range of the idle limiters. Limiter caps should not be removed, unless a CO meter is available to bring the emissions within the legal limits.

COOLING SYSTEM

In the 4-cylinder and inline 6-cylinder engines, coolant flows from the cylinder head, past the thermostat (if it is open) and into the radiator upper tank. In the V6, coolant enters the block through the lower inlet, through the thermostat if open, and exits into the radiator through the intake manifold outlet. In the V8 engine, coolant from each cylinder head flows through water passages in the intake manifold, then past the thermostat (if it is open) and into the radiator upper tank.

A single water pump assembly is used. The pump has a sealed bearing integral with the water pump shaft. The bearing requires no lubrication. There is a bleed hole in the water pump housing. This is not a lubrication hole.

Some models are equipped with a coolant recovery or constant full system. These systems have a non-vented radiator cap that forces coolant expansion into an expansion reservoir. When adding coolant to these systems, add coolant to the reservoir only, not the radiator.

Radiator Removal and Installation

1. Drain cooling system.
2. Disconnect upper and lower hoses at the radiator.
3. On automatic transmission-equipped cars, disconnect oil cooler lines at radiator.
4. On vehicles equipped with a fan shroud, remove the shroud retaining screws and position the shroud out of the way.
5. Remove radiator attaching bolts and lift out the radiator.
6. If a new radiator is to be installed, transfer the petcock from the old radiator to the new one. On cars equipped with automatic transmissions, transfer the fluid cooler line fittings from the old radiator to the new one.
7. Position the radiator and install, but do not tighten, the radiator support bolts. On cars equipped with automatic transmissions, connect the fluid cooler lines. Then tighten the radiator support bolts.
8. On vehicles equipped with a fan shroud, reinstall the shroud.
9. Connect the radiator hoses. Close the radiator petcock. Then fill and bleed the cooling system.
10. Start the engine and bring to operating temperature. Check for leaks.
11. On cars equipped with automatic transmissions, check the cooler lines for leaks and interference. Check transmission fluid level.

Water Pump Removal and Installation

1. Drain cooling system.
2. On 351C, 351M, and 400 V8, disconnect the negative battery cable.
3. On cars with power steering, remove the drive belt.
4. If the vehicle is equipped with air conditioning, remove the idler pulley bracket and air conditioner drive belt.
5. On engines with Thermactor, remove the belt.
6. Disconnect the lower radiator hose and heater hose from the water pump.
7. On cars equipped with a fan shroud, remove the retaining screws and position the shroud rearward.
8. Remove the fan and spacer from the engine, and if the car is equipped with a fan shroud, remove the fan and shroud from the engine as an assembly.
9. Loosen alternator mounting bolts, remove the alternator belt and remove the alternator adjusting arm bracket from the water pump.
10. Loosen bypass hose at water pump.
11. Remove water pump retaining screws and remove pump from engine. On V6s, the two bolts through the thermostat housing must also be removed; they retain the lower portion of the pump housing.
12. Clean any gasket material from the pump mounting surface, and on 429 V8 remove the water pump backing plate and replace the gasket.

NOTE: *The 250 6-cylinder engine originally uses a one-piece gasket for the cylinder front cover and water pump. Trim away the old gasket at the edge of the cylinder cover and replace with service gasket. Replace the thermostat housing gasket on V6s.*

13. Remove the heater hose fitting from the old pump and install it on the new pump.
14. Coat both sides of the new gasket with a water-resistant sealer, then re-install pump reversing the procedure.

Thermostat Removal and Installation

1. Open the drain cock and drain the radiator so the coolant level is below the coolant outlet elbow which houses the thermostat.
2. Remove the outlet elbow retaining bolts and position the elbow sufficiently clear of the intake manifold or cylinder head to provide access to the thermostat. The V6 thermostat is located on the lower water pump housing, under the lower radiator hose inlet. See the Bobcat section for an illustration
3. Remove the thermostat by rotating it in a counterclockwise direction and lifting it from the housing.
4. Clean the mating surfaces of the outlet elbow and the engine to remove all old gasket material and sealer. Coat the new gasket with water-resistant sealer and install it on the engine. Install the thermostat in the outlet elbow. The thermostat must be rotated clockwise to lock it in position. On V6s, the thermostat must be installed into the pump housing first, then the O-ring, and finally the gasket and inlet elbow.
5. Install the outlet elbow and retaining bolts on the engine. Torque the bolts to 12-15 ft lbs.
6. Refill the radiator. Run the engine at operating temperature and check for leaks. Recheck the coolant level.

EMISSION CONTROLS

All Ford cars covered in this text use positive crankcase ventilation (PCV) systems. The PCV system routes a harmful mixture of blow-by gases and condensation vapors, which were formerly dispelled into the atmosphere, through a modulating valve (PCV valve) and into the intake manifold where they combine with the carburetor air fuel mixture and are burned in the combustion chamber. For system checks and adjustments, see Emission Control Systems in the Unit Repair Section.

1972

In 1972, an Electronic Spark Control (ESC) system is used. It consists of an amplifier and distributor modulator valve, a speed sensor located in the speedometer cable, and a thermal switch located in the right door pillar. The speed sensor generates a small current which increases in direct proportion to speed. The thermal switch opens at temperatures above 58°F. The amplifier judges the signals sent to it by the speed and temperature switches and tells the distributor modulator valve when to open and close and thus allow or prevent vacuum to reach the distributor. The Transmission Regulated Spark (TRS) is similar to the ESC system except that the speed sensor is replaced by a transmission switch. The switch is mounted on the side of the transmission and is hydraulically actuated on cars equipped with an automatic transmission and manually actuated on models equipped with a manual transmission. When the ambient temperature is above 55°, the transmission switch is closed whenever the transmission is in any gear other than high gear (manual transmission), or high gear or reverse (automatic transmission). When the transmission switch closes, it signals the distributor modulator valve to close and thus prevents carburetor vacuum from reaching the distributor. As in past systems, neither of these systems is functional below 55-58°, and both are bypassed by the PVS if the engine should overheat.

On most 1972 and later models, a spark delay valve was inserted into the vacuum advance line to the distributor. The valve closes under hard acceleration, blocking carburetor vacuum to the distributor for a predetermined period of seconds. The valves are color coded for identification purposes.

1973

1973 and later models utilize an Exhaust Gas Recirculation System (EGR) to control oxides of nitrogen. On V8 engines, exhaust gases travel through the exhaust gas crossover passage in the intake manifold. A portion of these gases is diverted into a spacer which is mounted under the carburetor. The EGR control valve, which is attached to the rear of the spacer, consists of a vacuum diaphragm with an attached plunger which normally blocks off exhaust gases from entering the intake manifold. On 6 cylinder engines, an external tube carries exhaust manifold gases to the carburetor spacer. On all models except those equipped with a 250 six cylinder and manual transmission, the EGR valve is controlled by a vacuum line from the carburetor which passes through a ported vacuum switch. The EGR ported vacuum switch provides vacuum to the EGR valve at coolant temperature above 125°F. The vacuum diaphragm then opens the EGR valve permitting exhaust gases to flow through the carburetor spacer and enter the intake manifold where they combine with the

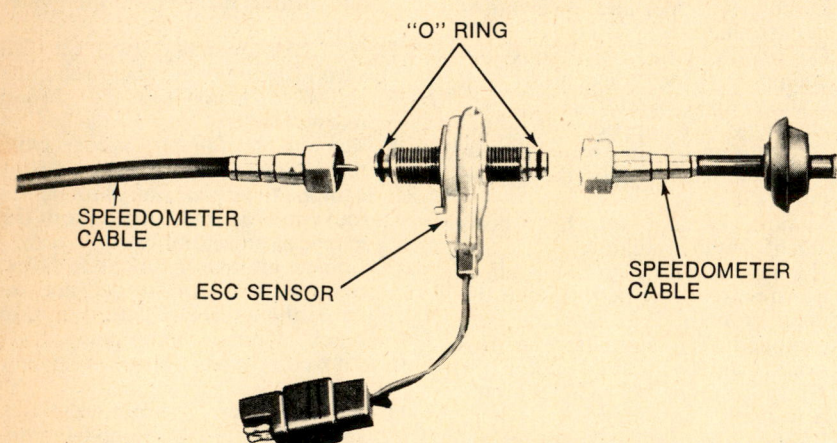

Speed sensor location (© Ford Motor Co)

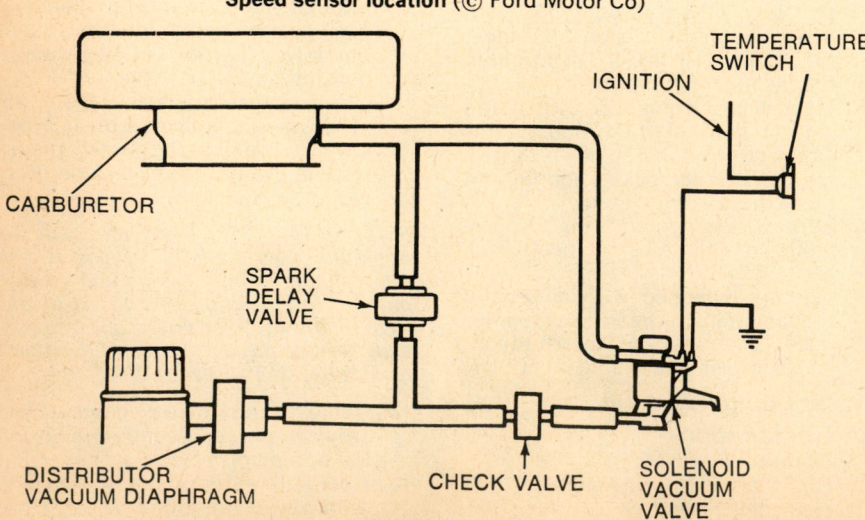

Delay vacuum by-pass system—DVB (© Ford Motor Co)

fuel mixture and enter the combustion chambers. The exhaust gases are relatively oxygen-free, and tend to dilute the combustion charge. This lowers peak combustion temperature thereby reducing oxides of nitrogen.

1973-74 Torinos and Montegos equipped with a 250 six-cylinder engine and manual transmission have a combined spark control and EGR system called TRS+1. The spark control portion of this system is identical to the TRS system described under 1972. Operation of the EGR control valve is governed by vacuum from either the distributor vacuum port on the carburetor or the EGR vacuum port. When the TRS system is not in operation, EGR valve vacuum comes from the EGR port on the carburetor. The vacuum passes through a coolant temperature vacuum valve and a three-way solenoid valve. The coolant valve blocks vacuum from the EGR valve until the engine coolant temperature has reached 60°F. The vacuum lines from both the EGR and distributor vacuum ports on the carburetor connect to the three-way solenoid valve. The third line is an outlet line to the EGR valve. When the TRS system is not in operation, the three-way solenoid valve is deenergized. When the TRS system is in operation, the solenoid is energized, blocking the EGR port on the three-way solenoid, and opening the distributor port to the EGR valve. When the transmission is shifted into high gear, the TRS and three-way solenoids are de-energized. This restores normal vacuum to the distributor and the EGR valve.

All models equipped with a 250 six-cylinder engine and automatic transmission and built prior to March 15, 1973, use another system to control distributor spark advance. The system, known as the Temperature Activated Vacuum (TAV) system, contains a three-way solenoid valve, an ambient temperature switch, and a vacuum bleed line to the air cleaner. The operation of the three-way solenoid valve is identical to the valve described for 250 manual transmission engines. The only difference is that the output line of the three-way valve is connected to the distributor. When the ambient temperature is above 60°, the contacts in the temperature sensor close and complete the circuit to the three-way solenoid. This energizes the solenoid and connects the EGR vacuum port on the carburetor to the distributor vacuum advance. When the ambient temperature is below 49°, the solenoid is de-energized and the distributor vacuum advance operates in the normal manner.

1973 Torino and Montego station wagons equipped with a 302 or 351W V8 and manual transmission and all 1973 models that are equipped with a 351C, 400, or 429 V8 built prior to March 15, 1973, use a Delay Vacuum By-Pass (DVB) spark control system. This system provides two paths by which carburetor vacuum can reach the distributor vacuum advance. The system consists of a spark delay valve, a check valve, a solenoid vacuum valve, and an ambient temperature switch. When the ambient temperature is below 49°F. the temperature switch contacts and the vacuum solenoid are open (de-energized). Under these conditions, vacuum will flow from the carburetor, through the open solenoid, and to the distributor. Since the spark delay valve resists the flow of carburetor vacuum, the vacuum will always flow through the vacuum solenoid when it is open, since this is the path of least resistance. When the ambient temperature rises above 60°F. the contacts in the temperature switch (which is located in the door post) close. This passes ignition switch current to the solenoid, energizing the solenoid. This blocks one of the vacuum paths. All distributor vacuum must now flow through the spark delay valve. When carburetor vacuum rises above a certain level on acceleration, a rubber valve in the spark delay valve blocks vacuum from passing through the valve for 5-30 seconds. After this delay, normal vacuum is supplied to the distributor. When the vacuum solenoid is closed (temperature above 60°), the vacuum line from the solenoid to the distributor is vented to atmosphere. To prevent the vacuum that is passing through the spark delay valve from escaping through the solenoid into the atmosphere, a one-way check valve is installed in the vacuum line from the solenoid to the distributor.

All 1973 and later models use an electric choke heating element. When ambient temperature is above 63°, and the ignition switch is turned on, a heating element in the choke housing raises the temperature of the choke bimetallic spring, thus preventing the choke from engaging.

1974

1974 models sold in California and all 1975 models are equipped with a Thermactor (air injection) system to reduce hydrocarbons and carbon monoxide. This system is used in addition to the previously mentioned EGR system.

A Cold Temperature Actuated Vacuum (CTAV) System is installed on some 1973 models manufactured after March 15, 1973 and many 1974 models to control distributor spark advance. It is basically a refinement of the DVB or TAV spark control systems with the temperature switch relocated in the air cleaner and a latching relay added to maintain a strong vacuum signal at the distributor, whether it be EGR port or spark port carburetor vacuum, and to keep the system from intermittently switching vacuum signals when the intake air is between 49 and 60°F. When the temperature switch closes at 60°F, the latching relay (normally off) is energized and stays on until the ignition switch is turned off. The latching relay then overrides the temperature switch and forces the solenoid valve to keep the spark port vacuum system closed and open the EGR port vacuum system. This prevents full vacuum advance, once the engine is warmed-up, thereby lowering emissions.

The EGR/CSC system is used on most 1974 and later models. It regulates both distributor spark advance and EGR valve operaton, according to coolant temperature, by sequentially switching vacuum sources. The major components are:

a. 95°F EGR-PVS valve,
b. spark delay valve (SDV), and
c. a vacuum check valve.

When coolant temperature is below 85°F, the EGR-PVS valve admits carburetor EGR port vacuum (at about 2500 rpm) directly to the distributor advance diaphragm through a one-way check valve. At the same time, the EGR-PVS valve shuts off carburetor EGR vacuum to the EGR valve and transmission diaphragm.

When coolant temperature is above 95°F, the EGR-PVS valve is actuated and admits carburetor EGR vacuum to the EGR valve and transmission instead of the distributor. At temperatures between 82° and 95°F, the EGR-PVS valve may be open, closed, or in midposition.

1975-76

Catalytic converters are installed in all 1975 and later cars sold in California, and on most 1975 models sold in the 49 states with the following exceptions; 250 six-cylinder and 302 V8 Mavericks and Comets, 250 six-cylinder 2-door Granadas and Monarchs. Torino, Elite, Montego and Cougar models sold in California use dual converters.

All 1976 models use a catalytic converter system.

The catalyst units convert emissions of hydrocarbons and carbon monoxide into harmless carbon dioxide and water, and in some cases, small amounts of possibly harmful sulfur dioxide (rotten egg odor) or (when mixed with water) sulphuric acid. The reaction takes place inside the converters at great heat (1300-1500°F) using platinum and palladium metals as the catalyst. The units are installed in the exhaust system, upstream from the mufflers. They are designed, if the engine is kept in proper tune and *only* unleaded fuel is used, to last 50,000 miles before replacement.

On models using the 460 V8 engine, a Cold Start Spark Advance (CSSA) System is used to improve cold engine operation. When the coolant temperature is below 125°F, carburetor ported vacuum is routed to the distributor through a spark delay valve and coolant temperature operated vacuum valve (PVS).

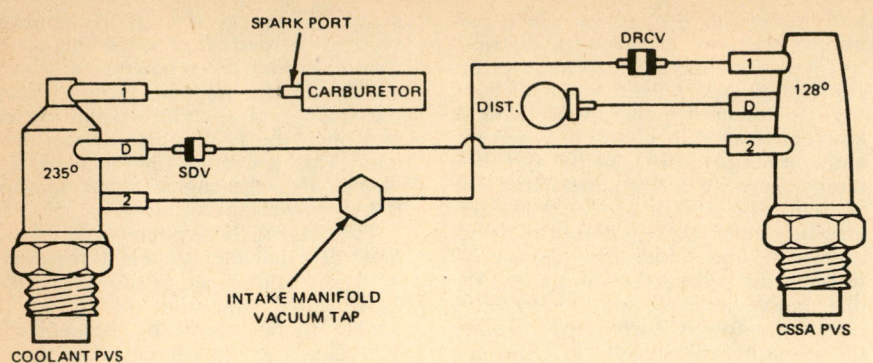

CSSA System schematic
(© Ford Motor Co)

Another aid to cold engine operation is a cold weather modulator, which is added to the heated air intake system. When the ambient temperature is below 55°F and the engine is cold, the cold weather modulator prevents the door in the air cleaner snorkel from opening to the fresh air position under hard acceleration. Above 55°F, the door works the same as in other years; i.e., opening under hard acceleration or when the engine has reached normal operating temperatures.

All 1975 engines have a spacer entry EGR valve mounted on a spacer beneath the carburetor. This replaces the floor entry system used on some 1974 engines.

Positive crankcase ventilation (PCV) and evaporative emission control systems are carryovers from previous years.

To further aid cold start driveability during engine warmup, most 1975 engines use a Vacuum Operated Heat

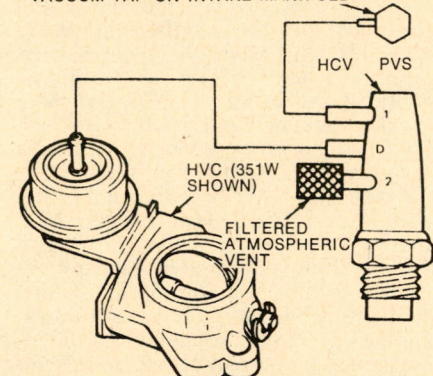

VOHV System schematic (© Ford Motor Co)

Valve (VOHV) located between the exhaust manifold and the exhaust inlet (header) pipe.

When the engine is first started, the valve is closed, blocking exhaust gases from exiting from one bank of cylinders. These gases are then diverted back through the intake manifold crossover passage under the carburetor and choke. The VOHV is controlled by a ported vacuum switch which uses manifold vacuum to keep the vacuum motor on the valve closed until the coolant reaches a predetermined warm-up value. When the engine is warmed up, the PVS shuts off vacuum to the VOHV, and a strong return spring opens the VOHV butterfly.

The complexity of the emission control equipment on all Ford vehicles has been substantially reduced in 1976 due to the more extensive use of catalytic converters. All 1976 model passenger cars have catalytic converters. The average number of emission control components has been reduced from 25 to 11 on most cars.

In addition, a new exhaust gas recirculation signal vacuum control system is used on all 1976 V8 engines. The new system uses an exhaust back-pressure transducer to regulate the EGR valve spark port vacuum signal which modulates the flow of EGR. This more accurately matches the amount of EGR to the engine load; improving engine driveability and fuel economy.

1977-79

1977-79 models carry over the emis-

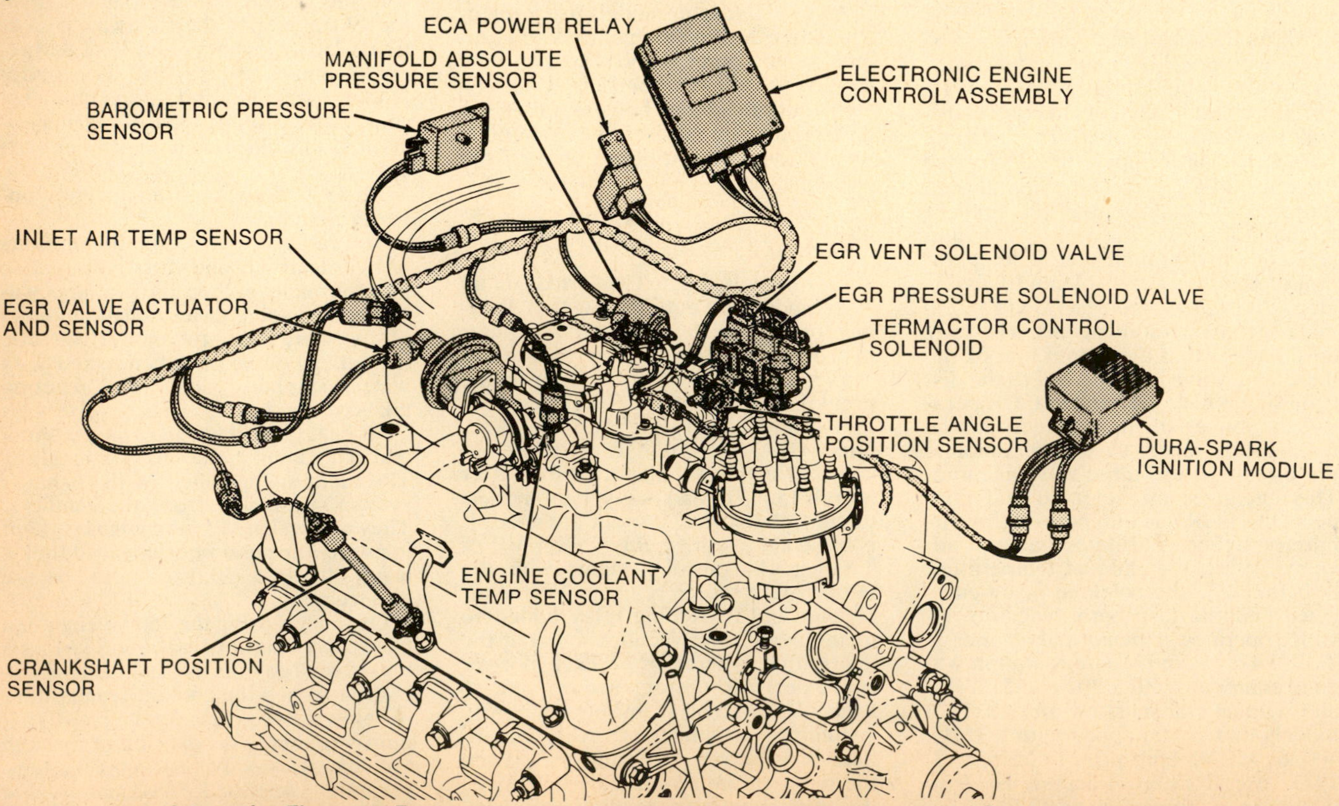

Interactive Electronic Engine Control System, introduced on 1978 Versailles (© Ford Motor Co)

sion controls used in 1976: air injection, PCV, EGR, evaporative controls, and catalytic converters. However some revisions have been made.

Physically larger catalytic converters are used. Improved breakerless electronic ignition called Dura-Spark which generates up to 42,000 volts is standard on all engines. Engine modifications include larger intake valves and revised combustion chambers for the 200 and 250 cu in. six-cylinder engines. The 302 and 351W V8 engines have modified combustion chambers and pistons. Cylinder heads also have larger coolant passages for improved spark plug and exhaust valve cooling. There are reduced size passages in the intake manifolds to increase velocity of the air/fuel mixture which aids combustion and improves performance at low rpm.

Also new is a variable venturi two-barrel carburetor (the Motorcraft 2700 VV), for use on the California 302 V8 and 2800 V6 engines. It is also used on all 1978 and later Versailles in conjunction with the EEC system. This carburetor changes the size of the venturis as a function of speed and load. Tapered metering rods, attached to the venturi valves, slide in the main jets to control fuel flow. Venturi valve position is controlled by a spring (closed), and by control vacuum operating through a rubber diaphragm (open). The venturi valves are not directly linked to the throttle shaft. Throttle plate opening results in a stronger control vacuum signal which causes the venturi valves to open, increasing venturi size. The control vacuum and opposing spring select the precise air/fuel ratio for all speed and load conditions except wide open throttle.

Electronic Engine Control (EEC) was introduced on the Versailles in 1978. This is an integrated electronic system designed to continuously monitor engine and ambient conditions, and continuously compute and alter timing, EGR flow rate, and Thermactor air flow accordingly. More details on the EEC system, and all emission controls, can be found in the Emission Controls Unit Repair Section.

ENGINE

There were three six-cylinder engines available in compact and intermediate size Ford products in 1972: the 170, the 200 and the 250 cu. in. engines. The 170 engine was dropped from production in 1973. These engines are all of the same family, and the only great difference among them is their bore and stroke. One distinguishing characteristic that makes these engines easily identifiable is the fact that the intake manifold is cast as an integral part of the cylinder head.

Optional V8 engines have a great amount of similarity. The 302 V8 is a compact engine with stud-mounted

rockers and wedge-shaped combustion chambers. The 351 Windsor engine has the wedge-shaped combustion chambers and stud-mounted rockers of the small block engine in an intermediate sized block. The 351 Cleveland has the same bore and stroke as the Windsor engine, and there most of the resemblance ends. It has different main bearing size, larger valves, and semi-hemispherical combustion chambers. It is used concurrently with the Windsor engine and is found in many of the same models. See the Engine Identification Code Chart to identify the 351 engines. A longer stroke, 400 cu. in. version of the 351 Cleveland V8 was introduced in 1972. Starting 1975, all 351C engines are designated 351M, for modified Cleveland. A high-performance version of the 351 Cleveland engine is designated as the 351 HO (High Output) engine, available on 1972 models. Some models used the big block 429 V8 which is the same as was used in full sized Mercury and Ford cars. The standard 429-4V V8 was available through 1973. Beginning 1974, a similar 460 4V V8 is used in some heavy-duty applications. The 460 4V V8 was dropped from the mid-size line in 1976. The 400 V8 was dropped in 1979.

A four cylinder engine was introduced in 1978 for the Fairmont and Zephyr. This is the same all metric 2300cc engine originally designed for the Pinto. It is a modern, belt driven overhead cam design with a crossflow head, hemispherical combustion chambers, and hydraulic lash adjusters eliminating routine valve clearance adjustments. The engine is offered in a turbocharged version in the Mustang and Capri.

The 2800cc V6 installed in 1979 Mustangs and Capris is the same Ford of Germany engine installed in the Pinto, Bobcat, and Mustang II. It is a lightweight, thin wall cast iron engine, with cylinder banks displaced 60°.

NOTE: *Most fasteners used in the four cylinder and V6 engines are metric. Use only metric tools to remove and install them. Do not replace metric fasteners with standard inch fasteners.*

Service procedures for the four and V6 are found in the Bobcat/Pinto section, except for engine removal and installation, and oil pan removal, which are found in this section under the appropriate headings.

ENGINE REMOVAL AND INSTALLATION

1. Scribe the hood hinge outline on the under-hood, disconnect the hood and remove.
2. Drain the entire cooling system and crankcase.
3. Remove the air cleaner, disconnect the battery at the cylinder head. On automatic transmission equipped cars, disconnect oil cooler lines at the radiator.

4. Remove upper and lower radiator hoses and remove radiator. If equipped with air conditioning, unbolt compressor and position compressor out of way with refrigerant lines intact. Unbolt and lay refrigerant condenser forward without disconnecting refrigerant lines.

NOTE: *If there is not enough slack in the refrigerant lines to position the compressor out of the way, the refrigerant in the system must be evacuated (using proper safety precautions) before the lines can be disconnected from the compressor.*

5. Remove fan, fan belt and upper pulley.
6. Disconnect the heater hoses from the engine. On four cylinder engines, disconnect the heater hose from the water pump and choke fittings.
7. Disconnect the alternator wires at the alternator, the starter cable at the starter, the accelerator rod at the carburetor.
8. Disconnect fuel tank line at the fuel pump and plug the line.
9. Disconnect the coil primary wire at the coil. Disconnect wires at the oil pressure and water temperature sending units.
10. Remove the starter and dust seal.
11. With manual transmission, remove the clutch retracting spring. Disconnect the clutch equalizer shaft and arm bracket at the underbody rail and remove the arm bracket and equalizer shaft.
12. Raise the car. Remove the flywheel or converter housing upper retaining bolts.
13. Disconnect the exhaust pipe or pipes at the exhaust manifold. Disconnect the right and left motor mount at the underbody bracket. Remove the flywheel or converter housing cover.
14. On manual shift, remove the flywheel housing lower retaining bolts.
15. On automatic transmission, disconnect throttle valve vacuum line at the intake manifold (2 lines on 1973 models) and disconnect the converter from the flywheel. Remove the converter housing lower retaining bolts. On power steering, disconnect power steering pump from cylinder head. Remove the drive belt and wire steering pump out of the way. Do not disconnect the hoses.
16. Lower the car. Support the transmission and flywheel or converter housing with a jack.
17. Attach an engine lifting hook. Lift the engine up and out of the compartment and onto an adequate workstand.

On installation:
1. Place a new gasket over the studs of the exhaust manifold/s.
2. Attach engine sling and lifting device. Lift engine from workstand.

3. Lower the engine into the engine compartment. Be sure the exhaust manifold/s is in proper alignment with the muffler inlet pipe/s, and the dowels in the block engage the holes in the flywheel housing.

On a car with automatic transmission, start the converter pilot into the crankshaft.

On manual transmission, start the transmission main drive gear into the clutch disc. If the engine hangs up after the shaft enters, rotate the crankshaft slowly (with transmission in gear) until the shaft and clutch disc splines mesh. Rotate 4-cyl. engines clockwise only, when viewed from the front.

4. Install the flywheel or converter housing upper bolts.
5. Install engine support insulator to bracket retaining nuts. Disconnect engine lifting sling and remove lifting brackets.
6. Raise front of car. Connect exhaust line/s and tighten attachments.
7. Position dust seal and install starter.
8. On manual transmission, install remaining flywheel housing-to-engine bolts. Connect clutch release rod. Position the clutch equalizer bar and bracket, and install retaining bolts. Install clutch pedal retracting spring.
9. On automatic transmission, remove the retainer holding the converter in the housing. Attach the converter to the flywheel. Install the converter housing inspection cover and the remaining converter housing retaining bolts.
10. Remove the support from the transmission and lower the car.
11. Connect engine ground strap and coil primary wire.
12. Connect water temperature gauge wire and the heater hose at coolant outlet housing. Connect accelerator rod at the bellcrank.
13. On automatic transmission, connect the transmission filler tube bracket. Connect the throttle valve vacuum line.
14. On power steering, install the drive belt and power steering pump bracket. Install the bracket retaining bolts. Adjust drive belt to proper tension.
15. Remove plug from the fuel tank line. Connect the flexible fuel line and the oil pressure sending unit wire.
16. Install the pulley, belt, spacer, and fan. Adjust belt tension.
17. Tighten alternator adjusting bolts. Connect generator wires and the battery ground cable.
18. Install radiator. Connect radiator hoses. On air conditioned cars, install compressor and refrigerant radiator.
19. On automatic transmission, connect fluid cooler lines.
20. Install oil filter. Connect heater hose at water pump and carburetor choke (4 cyl.).
21. Bring crankcase to level with correct grade of oil. Run engine at fast idle and check for leaks. Install air cleaner and make final engine adjustments.
22. Install and adjust hood.
23. Road-test car.

Intake Manifold Removal and Installation

6 CYLINDER

Sixes have intake manifolds that are integral with the cylinder head and cannot be removed.

V8

1. On the 302, 351W, 429, and 460 V8s, drain the cooling system, disconnect the upper radiator hose from the thermostat housing, and the bypass hose from the manifold.
2. On all engines, remove the air cleaner and intake duct.
3. Disconnect the high tension lead and wires from the coil. Disconnect the engine wiring loom and position out of the way.
4. Disconnect the spark plug wires at the plugs by twisting and pulling on the molded plug cap only. Remove the distributor cap and wires as an assembly. Disconnect the vacuum hose(s) from the distributor.
5. Mark the position of the rotor in relation to the manifold, remove the distributor hold down bolt, and remove the distributor.
6. Remove the Thermactor by-pass valve and air supply hoses, if equipped.
7. Remove all vacuum lines from the manifold. Also remove the temperature sending unit wire on 302, 351W, 429, and 460 V8s.
8. Disconnect the fuel line and vacuum hoses at the carburetor. Disconnect the accelerator linkage and downshift linkage, if so equipped, and position out of the way.
9. Disconnect the crankcase vent hose at the rocker cover.
10. On 351 C, 351 M, 351 HO, and 400 V8s, remove the heater hoses from the retaining strap, and position out of the way. If the car is air conditioned, remove the compressor mounting brackets from the manifold and position the compressor out of the way. Do not disconnect any A/C hoses.
11. Remove the intake manifold and carburetor as an assembly. Be careful not to damage any gasket sealing surfaces.
12. Clean the mating surfaces of the manifold, block, and heads. Apply a 1/8 in. bead of silicone seal to the four engine block-to-cylinder head mating surfaces. Do not apply any sealer to the waffle section of the end seals on 351 C, M, HO, and 400 V8s.

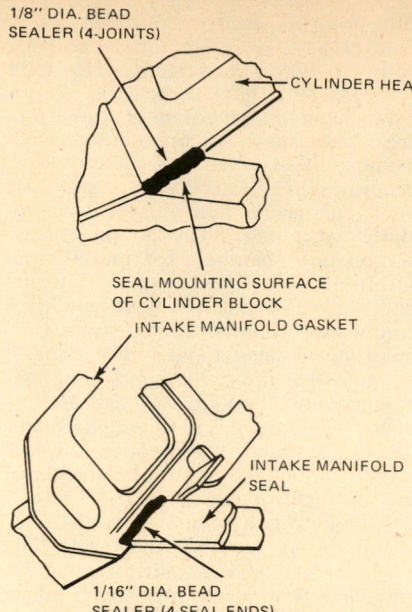

Intake manifold sealer application (© Ford Motor Co.)

13. Position the new end seals into place on the block, pressing the locating tabs into place. Position new manifold gaskets into place on the heads, and apply a 1/8 in. bead of silicone seal to the four end seal-to-manifold gasket joints. Do not allow the sealer to fall into the engine valley.
14. Carefully lower the manifold into place. After it is positioned, run

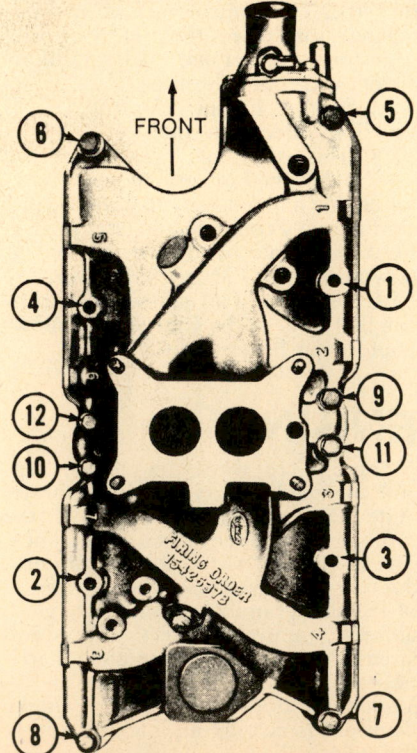

Intake manifold torque sequence—302 V8, 1976 and later 351 W (© Ford Motor Co.)

your finger around the seal area to be sure the seals are properly positioned. If they are not, remove the manifold and reposition the seals.

15. Torque the manifold to specification in three stages, according to the pattern given. The rest of installation is the reverse of removal. After installation, run the engine to operating temperature and retorque the manifold bolts.

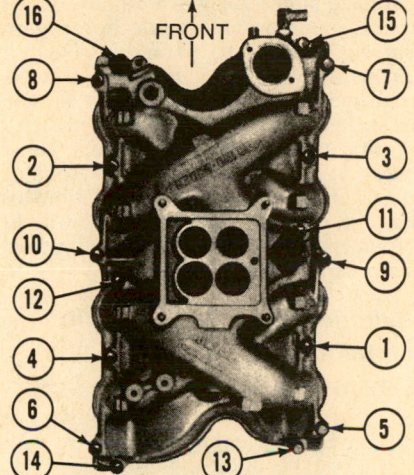

Intake manifold torque sequence—429, 460 V8 (© Ford Motor Co)

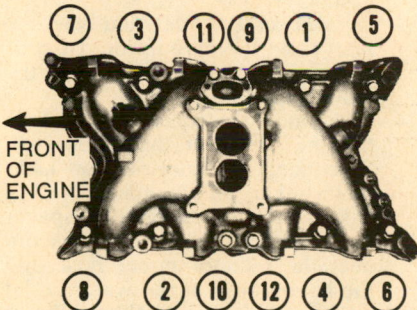

Intake manifold torque sequence—351C, 351M, 400 V8 (© Ford Motor Co)

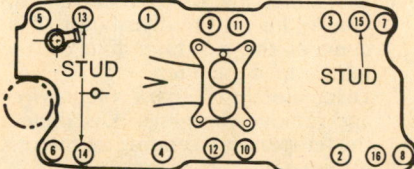

Intake manifold torque sequence—351 W V8 through 1975 (© Ford Motor Co.)

Exhaust Manifold Removal and Installation

6 CYLINDER

1. Remove the air cleaner and heat duct body.
2. Disconnect the muffler inlet pipe and remove the choke hot air tube from the manifold.
3. Bend the exhaust manifold attaching bolt lock tabs back, remove the bolts and the manifold.

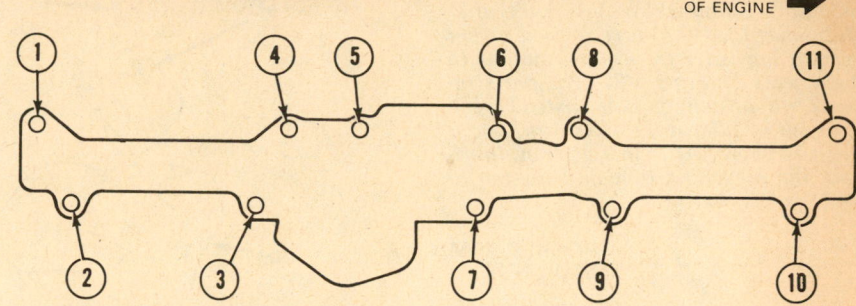

INSTALL 3/8-16 STUD & WASHER ASSEMBLY — HOLES NUMBERED 4 & 5
3/8-16 X 2.62 BOLT — HOLES 3-6-7-8
3/8-16 X 1.12 BOLT — HOLES 1-2-9-10-11

Six cylinder exhaust manifold torque sequence—1975 and later (© Ford Motor Co.)

4. Clean all manifold mating surfaces and place a new gasket on the muffler inlet pipe.
5. Reinstall manifold by reversing the procedure. Torque attaching bolts in sequence from the centermost bolt outward through 1974. For 1975 and later models, use the sequence shown. After installation, warm the engine to operating temperature and re-torque to specifications.

V8

1. On right exhaust manifold, remove the air cleaner, automatic choke heat tube and air cleaner heat ducts.
2. Disconnect the exhaust manifold(s) from the muffler inlet pipe(s).
3. Remove the spark plug wires, spark plugs, and heat shields.
4. Remove the manifold attaching bolts and remove the manifold(s).
5. Reverse the procedure to reinstall, using new inlet pipe gaskets. Torque the manifold bolts in sequence from the center to the ends.

NOTE: *To remove the left side exhaust manifold from a car equipped with a 351C, 351M, or 400 engine, it is necessary to remove the oil filter and the transmission selector cross shaft or clutch linkage and equalizer shaft bracket, depending on transmission type.*

VALVE SYSTEM

V8 engines use hydraulic tappets. The pushrods in the V8s also transfer oil under pressure to the friction areas of the rocker arms.

Rocker Arm Assembly Removal and Installation

6 CYLINDER

1. Remove the air cleaner and PCV line, and the accelerator control cable bracket.
2. Remove the rocker arm cover and gasket.
3. Remove the rocker shaft bolts, two turns at a time each, working from the ends toward the center.
4. Lift off the rocker shaft assembly.

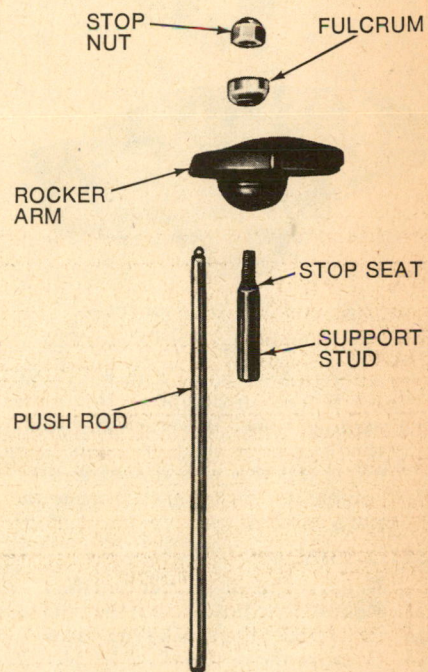

Positive Stop Rocker Arm Stud and Nut (© Ford Motor Co)

Keep the pushrods in order, if removed.

5. Installation is the reverse of removal. Torque the rocker shaft bolts, two turns at a time, working from the center toward the ends, to 30-35 ft lb.

302, 351W

1. Right side:
   a. disconnect the automatic choke heat chamber air inlet hose.
   b. remove the air cleaner and duct.
   c. remove the automatic choke heat tube (302).
   d. remove the PCV fresh air tube from the rocker cover, and disconnect the EGR vacuum amplifier hoses.
2. Remove the Thermactor by-pass valve and air supply hoses.
3. Disconnect the spark plug wires.
4. On the left side:
   a. remove the wiring harness from the clips.
   b. remove the rocker arm cover.

5. Remove the rocker arm stud nut, fulcrum seat and rocker arm.

NOTE: *302 and 351W V8s built after December 12, 1977, have revised rocker arms using valve train parts similar to those used on other V8s. The parts include an attaching bolt instead of a stud nut, a fulcrum, rocker arm, and a fulcrum guide. After installation, lubricate the attaching bolt and tighten to 18-25 ft. lbs.*

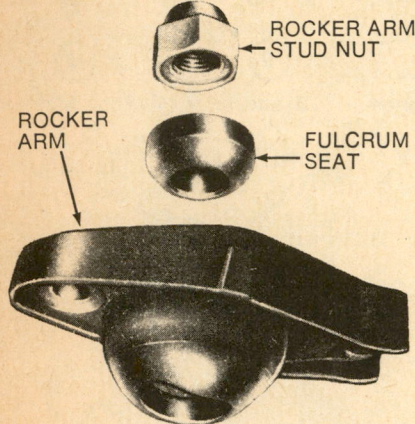

302, and 351 Windsor rocker arm assembly (© Ford Motor Co)

6. Lubricate all parts with heavy SE oil before installation. When installing, rotate the crankshaft until the lifter is on the base of the cam circle (all the way down) and assemble the rocker arm. Torque the nut to 17-23 ft lb.

351C, 351M, 400

1. Remove the air cleaner and duct.
2. Remove the hoses from the cover.
3. Disconnect the spark plug wires.
4. Remove the cover(s).
5. Remove the rocker arm bolt, oil deflector, fulcrum seat and arm.
6. Before installation, lubricate all parts with heavy SE engine oil. When installing, position no. 1 piston on TDC of the compression stroke and assemble the rocker arms on the following valves:

    no. 1 intake and exhaust
    no. 4 intake
    no. 3 exhaust
    no. 8 intake
    no. 7 exhaust

    Turn the crankshaft 180° clockwise and assemble the rocker arms for:

    no. 3 intake
    no. 2 exhaust
    no. 7 intake
    no. 6 exhaust

    Turn the crankshaft 270° clockwise and assemble the rocker arms for:

    no. 2 intake
    no. 4 exhaust
    no. 5 intake and exhaust
    no. 6 intake
    no. 8 exhaust

    Torque the bolts to 18-25 ft lb. Be sure the fulcrum seat base is seated before tightening the bolts.
7. Assemble the remaining parts.

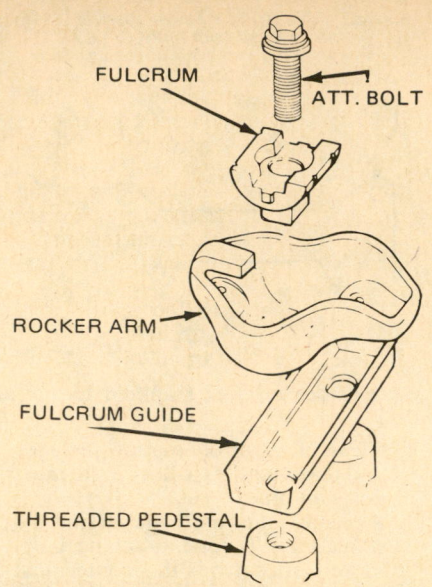

Rocker arm design on 1978 and later 302 and 351W V8s (© Ford Motor Co)

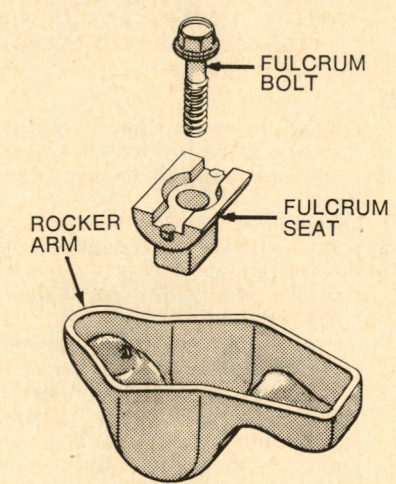

351 Cleveland V8 rocker arm assembly; 351M, 400 V8 similar (with oil deflector) (© Ford Motor Co)

429, 460

The procedure is the same as that for the 351C, 351M, and 400. With the engine in the first position install rocker arms:

    no. 1 intake and exhaust
    no. 7 intake and 5 exhaust
    no. 8 intake and 4 exhaust

With the engine in the second position install rocker arms:

    no. 4 intake and 2 exhaust
    no. 5 intake and 6 exhaust

With the engine in the third position install rocker arms:

    no. 2 intake and 3 exhaust
    no. 3 intake and 7 exhaust
    no. 6 intake and 8 exhaust

V8 Mechanical Valve Lifter Adjustment

1972 351 HO ONLY

1. Run engine to bring to operating temperature.

2. Remove rocker covers.
3. Insert a feeler gauge of specified thickness between the rocker arm and valve, and with engine running, adjust rocker arm to obtain desired clearance.
4. Reinstall rocker cover.

Valve Guides

Ford Motor Company engines use integral valve guides offer valves with oversize stems for worn guides. To fit these, enlarge valve guide bores with valve guide reamers to an oversize that cleans up wear. If a large oversize is required it is best to approach that size in stages to maintain the concentricity of the guide bore. The correct valve guide to stem clearance is at front of this section. As an alternative, some local automotive machine shops will fit replacement guides that use standard stem valves.

Cylinder Head Removal and Installation

6 CYLINDER

1. Drain cooling system, remove the air cleaner and disconnect the battery cable at the cylinder head.
2. Disconnect exhaust pipe at the manifold end, spring the exhaust pipe down and remove the flange gasket.
3. Disconnect the fuel and vacuum lines from the carburetor. Disconnect the intake manifold line at the intake manifold.
4. Disconnect the accelerator and retracting spring at the carburetor. Disconnect the transmission kickdown linkage, if equipped.
5. Disconnect the carburetor spacer outlet line at the spacer. Disconnect the radiator upper hose and the heater hose at the water outlet elbow. Disconnect the radiator lower hose and the heater hose at the water pump.
6. Disconnect the distributor vacuum control line at the distributor. Disconnect the gas filter line on the inlet side of the filter.
7. Disconnect the spark plug wires and remove the plugs. Disconnect the temperature sending unit wire.
8. Remove the rocker arm cover.
9. Loosen the rocker arm shaft attaching bolts and remove the rocker arm and shaft assembly. Remove the valve pushrods, in order, and keep them that way.
10. Remove one cylinder-head bolt from each end of the head (at opposite corners) and install cylinder head guide studs. Remove the remaining cylinder head bolts and lift off the cylinder head.

    To help in removal and installation of cylinder head, two 6 in. x 7/16—14 bolts with heads cut off and the head end slightly tapered and slotted for installation and removal, with a screwdriver, will reduce the possibility of damage during head replacement. These guide studs make a handy tool during head removal and gasket and head replacement.

11. Clean the cylinder head and block surfaces. Be sure of flatness and no surface damage.

12. Apply cylinder head gasket sealer to both sides of the new gasket and slide the gasket down over the two guide studs in the cylinder block.

NOTE: *Apply gasket sealer only to steel shim head gaskets. Steel/asbestos composite head gaskets are to be installed without any sealer.*

13. Carefully lower the cylinder head over the guide studs. Place the exhaust pipe flange on the manifold studs (new gasket).

14. Coat the threads of the end bolts for the right side of the cylinder head with a small amount of water-resistant sealer. Install, but do not tighten, two head bolts at opposite ends to hold the head gasket in place. Remove the guide studs and install the remaining bolts.

15. Cylinder head torquing should proceed in three steps and in prescribed order. Tighten to 55 ft lbs, then give them a second tightening to 65 ft lbs. The final step is to 75 ft lbs, at which they should remain undisturbed.

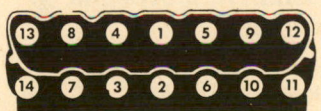

Cylinder head bolt tightening sequence —170, 200, 250 cu. in. 6 cyl. through 1977

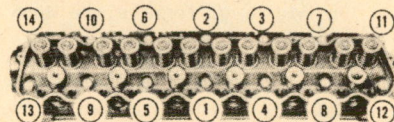

Cylinder head bolt tightening sequence— 200, 250 6 cyl., 1978 and later
(© Ford Motor Co.)

16. Lubricate both ends of the pushrods and install them in their original locations.

17. Apply lubricant to the rocker arm pads and the valve stem tips and position the rocker arm shaft assembly on the head. Be sure the oil holes in the shaft are in a down position.

18. Tighten all the rocker shaft retaining bolts to 30-35 ft lbs and do a preliminary valve adjustment (make sure there are no tight valve adjustments).

19. Hook up the exhaust pipe.

20. Reconnect the heater and radiator hoses.

21. Reposition the distributor vacuum line, the carburetor gas line and the intake manifold vacuum line on the engine. Hook them up to their respective connections and reconnect the battery cable to the cylinder head.

22. Connect the accelerator rod and retracting spring. Connect the choke control cable and adjust the choke. Connect the transmission kickdown linkage.

23. Reconnect the vacuum line at the distributor. Connect the fuel inlet line at the fuel filter and the intake manifold vacuum line at the vacuum pump.

24. Lightly lubricate the spark plug threads and install them. Connect spark plug wires and be sure the wires are all the way down in their sockets. Connect the temperature sending unit wire.

25. Fill the cooling system. Run the engine to stabilize all engine part temperatures.

26. Adjust engine idle speed and idle fuel-air adjustment.

27. Coat one side of a new rocker cover gasket with oil-resistant sealer. Lay the treated side of the gasket on the cover and install the cover. Be sure the gasket seals evenly all around the cylinder head.

V8

1. Remove the valve covers and disconnect the negative battery cable.

2. Remove the intake manifold and carburetor assembly.

3. On cars equipped with air conditioning, remove the compressor from the engine and position it to one side, *without disconnecting the refrigerant lines.*

4. If removing the left cylinder head, on cars equipped with power steering, remove the pump, bracket, and drive belt and position to one side *without disconnecting the lines.* On cars with Thermactor emission control system, disconnect the hose from the air manifold on the left cylinder head.

5. If removing the right cylinder head, remove the alternator mounting bracket bolt and spacer, ignition coil, and air cleaner inlet duct. On cars equipped with Thermactor emission control, remove the air pump and bracket. Disconnect the hose from the right cylinder head.

6. Disconnect the exhaust manifold/s from the exhaust pipe/s.

7. Loosen the rocker arm stud nuts so that the arms can rotate to the side to clear the pushrods. Remove the pushrods. Keep them in order.

8. Remove the cylinder head bolts and lift off the cylinder head. On some 351 engines, it may be necessary to remove the exhaust manifold to gain access to the lower cylinder head bolts.

9. Reverse the procedure for installation taking care to follow the specified torque sequence. Perform a preliminary valve adjustment before starting the engine.

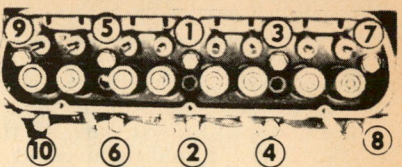

Cylinder head bolt tightening sequence —302, 351W, 351C, 400 V8 shown
(© Ford Motor Co)

Chilton's TIME SAVER

Frequently valves become bent or warped or their seats become blocked with carbon or other material. Left unattended, this can cause burnt valves, damaged cylinder heads and other expensive troubles. To detect leaking valves early, perform this test whenever the cylinder head is removed.

1. After removing head, replace spark plugs. Removing spark plugs before removing heads eliminates breakage.

2. Place head on bench with valves, springs, retainers and keys installed and combustion chambers up.

3. Pour enough gasoline in each combustion chamber to completely cover both valves. Watch combustion chambers for two minutes for any leakage.

TIMING COVER, CHAIN, AND CAMSHAFT

Cover and Chain Removal and Installation

6 CYLINDER

1. Drain the cooling system and crankcase.

2. Disconnect the upper radiator hose from the intake manifold and the lower hose from the water pump. On cars with automatic transmission, disconnect the cooler lines from the radiator.

3. Remove the radiator, fan and pulley, and engine drive belts. On models with air conditioning, remove the condenser retaining bolts and position the condenser forward. *Do not disconnect the refrigerant lines.*

4. On 170 and 200 cu. in. engines remove the cylinder front cover retaining bolts and front oil pan bolts and gently pry the cover away from the block. On 250 engines, it is necessary to remove the oil pan before removing the front cover.

5. Remove the crankshaft pulley bolt and use a puller to remove the vibration damper.

6. With a socket wrench of the proper size on the crankshaft pulley bolt,

gently rotate the crankshaft in a clockwise direction until all slack is removed from the left side of the timing chain. Scribe a mark on the engine block parallel to the present position of the left side of the chain. Next, turn the crankshaft in a counterclockwise direction to remove all the slack from the right side of the chain. Force the left side of the chain outward with the fingers and measure the distance between the reference point and the present position of the chain. If the distance exceeds 1/2 inch, replace the chain and sprockets.

7. Crank the engine until the timing marks are aligned as shown in the illustration. Remove the bolt, slide sprocket and chain forward and remove as an assembly.

8. Position the sprockets and chain on the engine, making sure that the timing marks are aligned, dot to dot.

9. Reinstall the front cover, applying oil resistant sealer to the new gasket.

NOTE: *On 170 and 200 engines, trim away the exposed portion of the old oil pan gasket flush with front of the engine block. Cut and position the required portion of a new gasket to the oil pan, applying sealer to both sides of it.*

10. On 250 engines, reinstall the oil pan.

11. Install the fan, pulley and belts. Adjust belt tension.

12. Install the radiator, connect the radiator hoses and transmission cooling lines. If equipped with air conditioning, install the condenser.

13. Fill the crankcase and cooling system. Start the engine and check for leaks.

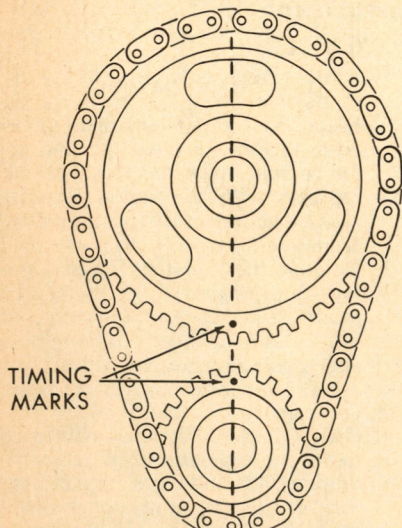

TIMING MARKS

Timing mark alignment

V8

1. Drain cooling system, remove air cleaner and disconnect the battery.

2. Disconnect radiator hoses and remove the radiator.

3. Disconnect heater hose at water pump. Slide water pump by-pass hose clamp toward the pump.

4. Loosen alternator mounting bolts at the alternator. Remove the alternator support bolt at the water pump. Remove Thermactor pump on all engines so equipped. If equipped with power steering or air conditioning, unbolt the component, remove the belt, and lay the pump aside with the lines attached.

5. Remove the fan, spacer, pulley, and drive belt.

6. Remove pulley from crankshaft pulley adapter. Remove cap screw and washer from front end of crankshaft. Remove crankshaft pulley adapter with a puller.

7. Disconnect fuel pump outlet line at the pump. Remove fuel pump retaining bolts and lay the pump to the side.

8. Remove the front cover attaching bolts. On the 351C, 351M, and 400 engines, it is necessary to remove the oil pan before the front cover can be removed.

9. Remove the crankshaft oil slinger if so equipped.

10. Check timing chain deflection, using the procedure outlined in Step 6 of the six cylinder cover and chain removal.

11. Crank engine until sprocket timing marks are aligned as shown in valve timing illustration.

12. Remove crankshaft sprocket cap screw, washers, and fuel pump eccentric. Slide both sprockets and chain forward and off as an assembly.

13. Position sprockets and chain on the camshaft and crankshaft with both timing marks dot to dot on a centerline. Install fuel pump eccentric, washers and sprocket attaching bolt. Torque the sprocket attaching bolt to 30-35 ft lbs.

14. Install crankshaft front oil slinger.

15. Clean front cover and mating surfaces of old gasket material. Install a new oil seal in the cover. Use a seal driver tool, if available. Oil the lips of the seal to prevent damage.

16. Coat a new cover gasket with sealer and position it on the block.

NOTE: *On all except 351C, 351M, and 400 engines, trim away the exposed portion of the oil pan gasket flush with the cylinder block. Cut and position the required portion of a new gasket to the oil pan, applying sealer to both sides of it. On 351C, 351M, and 400 engines, after installing the cylinder front cover, install the oil pan using a new gasket.*

17. Install front cover, using a crankshaft-to-cover alignment tool. Coat the threads of the attaching bolts with sealer. Torque attaching bolts to 12-15 ft lbs.

18. Install fuel pump, connect fuel pump outlet tube.

19. Install crankshaft pulley adapter and torque attaching bolt. Install crankshaft pulley.

20. Install water pump pulley, drive belt, spacer and fan.

21. Install alternator support bolt at the water pump. Tighten alternator mounting bolts. Adjust drive belt tension. Install Thermactor pump if so equipped.

22. Install radiator and connect all coolant and heater hoses. Connect battery cables.

23. Refill cooling system.

24. Start engine and operate at fast idle.

25. Check for leaks, install air cleaner. Adjust ignition timing and make all final adjustments.

Cover Seal Removal and Installation

It is recommended to replace the cover seal any time the front cover is removed.

1. With the cover removed from the car, drive the old seal from the rear of cover with a pinpunch. Clean out the recess in the cover.

2. Coat the new seal with grease and drive it into the cover until it is fully seated. Check the seal after installation to be sure the spring is properly positioned in the seal.

Camshaft Removal and Installation

6 CYLINDER

1. Remove the cylinder head.

2. Remove the cylinder front cover, timing chain and sprockets as outlined in the preceding section.

3. Disconnect and remove the grille. On Mustang, remove the gravel deflector.

4. Using a magnet, remove the valve lifters and keep them in order so that they can be installed in their original positions.

5. Remove the camshaft thrust plate and remove the camshaft by pulling it from the front of the engine. Use care not to damage the camshaft lobes or journals while removing the cam from the engine.

6. Before installing the camshaft, coat the lobes with engine assembly lubricant and the journals and all valve parts with heavy oil. Clean the oil passage at the rear of the cylinder block with compressed air.

7. Reverse the procedure to install, following recommended torque settings and tightening sequences.

V8

1. Remove the intake manifold as outlined previously.

2. Remove the cylinder front cover, timing chain and sprockets as directed previously.

3. Remove the grille, and, on models with air conditioning, remove the condenser retaining bolts and posi-

tion it out of the way. *Do not disconnect refrigerant lines.* On the Versailles, the hood latch assembly, ambient temperature switch wiring, and the support bracket must be removed.

4. Remove the rocker arm covers.
5. Remove the pushrods and lifters and keep them in order so that they can be installed in their original positions.
6. Remove the camshaft thrust plate and washer if so equipped. Remove the camshaft from the front of the engine. Use care not to damage camshaft lobes or journals while removing the cam from the engine.
7. Before installing the camshaft, coat the lobes with engine assembly lubricant and the journals and valve parts with heavy oil.
8. Reverse the procedure to install.

NOTE: *Perform a preliminary valve adjustment before starting the engine.*

PISTON AND CONNECTING ROD

Six cylinder engines should have their piston and rod assemblies installed with the notch on the piston crown toward the front and the oil squirt hole in the rod toward the right side. V8 pistons are assembled with the notch or arrow on the piston crown toward the front and the numbered side of the rod toward the outside.

ENGINE LUBRICATION

All engines are equipped with full-flow-type oil filters to condition the oil before it reaches the main bearings. The filter is equipped with an internal bypass relief valve.

Oil Pan Removal and Installation

NOTE: *On certain engine-chassis combinations, interference will be encountered between the oil pan and oil pump while attempting to remove the oil pan. If this occurs, lower the oil pan and reach inside it and remove the two bolts retaining the oil pump and pickup tube to the engine block. Lower the pump and pickup tube assembly into the pan and remove it with the pan. To ensure proper gasket sealing, the oil pan retaining bolts should be tightened from the center outward.*

MAVERICK AND COMET 170 AND 200 6 CYLINDER

1. Drain the crankcase. Remove the dipstick and the flywheel inspection plate.
2. Remove the retaining bolts and oil pan. Reverse the procedure to install, taking care to place the tabs of the front and rear oil seals over the pan gasket.

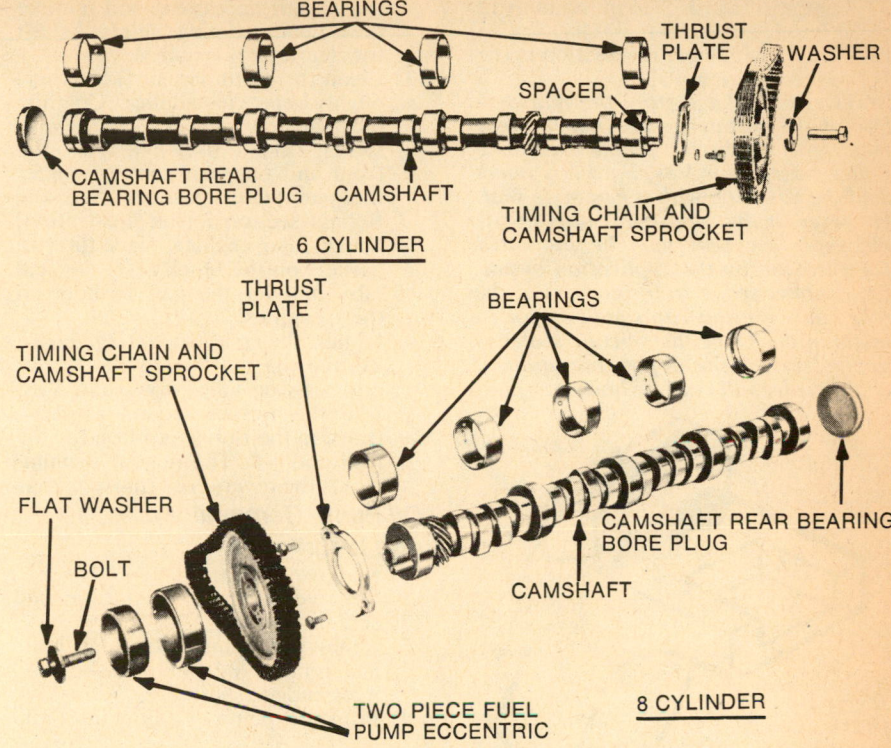

Camshaft and related parts (© Ford Motor Co)

TORINO, MONTEGO, MAVERICK, MONARCH, GRANADA AND COMET 250 6 CYLINDER, MUSTANG 6 CYLINDER THROUGH 1973

1. Drain the crankcase and cooling system. Remove the dipstick and the flywheel inspection plate.
2. Remove the radiator. On cars with automatic transmissions, the cooler lines must be disconnected and plugged.
3. Raise the vehicle. Remove the stabilizer bar.
4. Remove the engine support thru-bolts and nuts. Loosen the two rear insulator-to-crossmember bolts, if equipped.
5. Raise the engine with a jack and place two 2 in. wooden blocks between the engine supports and the chassis brackets. Also raise the transmission slightly on Granadas and Monarchs.
6. Remove the retaining bolts and the starter motor.
7. Remove the retaining bolts and oil pan.
8. Clean the gasket mounting surfaces. Coat the block and the pan gaskets with sealer and place the pan gaskets on the block. Install the front seal on the timing cover and the rear seal on the main bearing cap. The seal tabs go over the gasket ends. Install the pan and tighten the bolts from the center outward to 7-9 ft. lbs. The rest of installation is the reverse of removal.

V8

1. Remove the dipstick.

2. Remove the fan shroud retaining bolts, on models so equipped, and position the shroud over the fan.
3. Raise the vehicle and drain the crankcase.
4. On vehicles with 351C, 351M, 400, and 429 engines, disconnect the negative battery cable and remove the starter.
5. Disconnect the stabilizer bar links and remove the stabilizer bar.
6. Remove the engine front support thru-bolts. On Granadas and Monarchs with power steering, remove the bolt holding the lines to the rear of the lower arm.
7. Install a wooden block on a jack and position the jack beneath the leading edge of the pan.
8. Raise the engine and place 1-1 1/2 in. wood blocks between the engine supports and the chassis. Remove the jack from beneath the engine.
9. Remove the oil pan retaining bolts and lower the pan to the crossmember.
10. If the car is equipped with an automatic transmission, position the cooler lines out of the way.
11. Turn the crankshaft as required to obtain clearance to remove the pan. On the Versailles, the rear throw must be horizontal to clear the pan flange.
12. Clean the gasket mounting surfaces. Coat the block and the pan gaskets with sealer and place the gaskets on the block. Install the front and rear seals with their tabs over the gasket ends. Install the pan, and tighten the bolts from the

center outward: 5/16 in. bolts to 12 ft lbs, 1/4 in. bolts to 8 ft lbs.

13. The remainder of installation is the reverse of removal.

NOTE: *Oil leakage from the rear section of the oil pan gasket (not the rear main seal) has been a problem on some Police Interceptor V8s. Ford has remedied the situation with a new style seal. However, if the neoprene seal is of the old type, the seal may be prevented from leaking by the application of silicone rubber sealer to the corners of the rear main bearing cap saddle, prior to installation. Once the silicone sealer is applied, install the oil pan immediately, as the sealer will begin to harden.*

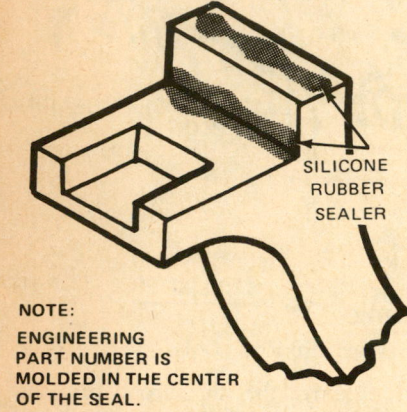

Old style oil pan gasket seal—460 PI (© Ford Motor Co.)

FAIRMONT, ZEPHYR, 1979 MUSTANG, 1979 CAPRI—ALL ENGINES

1. Remove the oil dipstick. Disconnect the two cooler lines at the radiator, if equipped.
2. On the four cyl. and inline six cyl., remove the two radiator top support bolts.
3. On the V6 only, drain the cooling system and disconnect the upper and lower radiator hoses at the radiator.
4. Remove the fan shroud bolts and position the shroud over the fan.
5. Raise the car and drain the oil.
6. Remove the sway bar attaching bolts and allow it to hang down. Remove the K brace.
7. Remove the steering gear to crossmember attaching bolts and allow the steering gear to rest on the frame away from the pan.
8. Disconnect the battery lead and remove the starter except on V8s.
9. Remove the engine mount bolts.
10. Raise the engine and place a 1 1/4 in. spacer between the mount and chassis on each side. Use a 2 x 4 in. wood block on each side with the V8.
11. On the four and inline six only, place a jack under the transmission and raise it slightly.
12. Remove the oil pan bolts and lower the pan to the crossmember. Move the transmission cooler lines out of

the way, if necessary, and remove the oil pan, rotating the crankshaft for clearance if required.

13. Clean the mounting surfaces thoroughly before installation. Coat the block and pan gasket surfaces with sealer. On the four cyl. only, the front and rear seal tabs go under the pan (side) gaskets. See the Bobcat section for an illustration. On all other engines, place the pan gaskets on the block first; the seal tabs go over the pan gaskets on these engines.
14. Install the pan mounting bolts. Torque the bolts from the center outwards on inline sixes and V8s. Use the torque sequences illustrated in the Bobcat section for the four and V6. The rest of installation is the reverse of removal.

Oil Pump Removal and Installation

1. Remove oil pan.
2. Remove oil pump inlet tube and screen assembly.
3. Remove oil pump attaching bolts and remove oil pump gasket and intermediate shaft.
4. Prime oil pump by filling inlet and

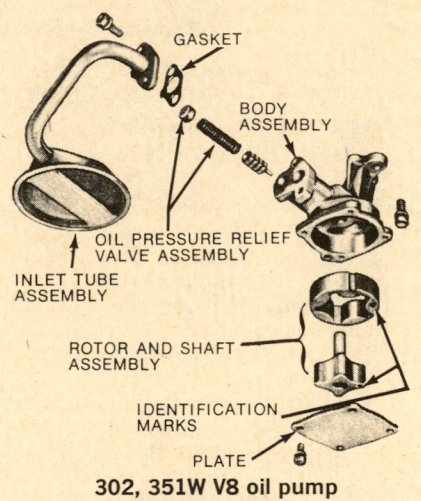

302, 351W V8 oil pump (© Ford Motor Co)

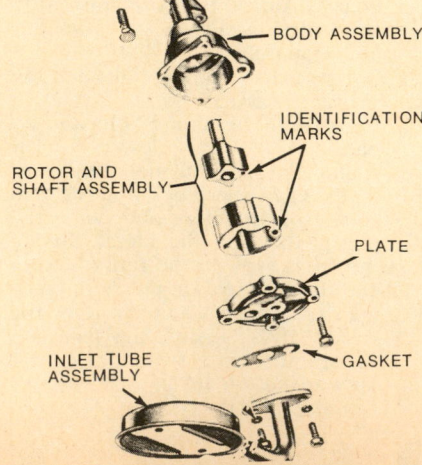

6 cyl oil pump (© Ford Motor Co)

outlet port with engine oil and rotating shaft of pump to distribute it.

5. Position intermediate drive shaft into distributor socket.
6. Position new gasket on pump body and insert intermediate drive shaft into pump body.
7. Install pump and intermediate shaft as an assembly.

NOTE: *Do not force pump if it does not seat readily. The drive shaft may be misaligned with the distributor shaft. To align rotate intermediate drive shaft into a new position.*

8. Install and torque oil pump attaching screws to 12-15 ft lbs on six cylinder, 20-25 ft lbs on V8s.
9. Install oil pan.

Rear Main Oil Seal Removal and Installation

NOTE: *The rear oil seal installed in these engines is a rubber type seal.*

1. Remove the oil pan, and; if required, the oil pump.
2. Loosen all main bearing caps allowing the crankshaft to lower slightly.

NOTE: *The crankshaft should not be allowed to drop more than 1/32 in.*

3. Remove the rear main bearing cap and remove the seal from the cap and block. Remove the old seal retaining pin from the cap, if

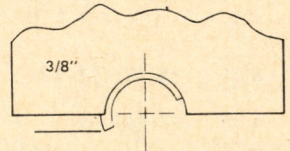

SEAL HALVES TO PROTRUDE BEYOND PARTING FACES THIS DISTANCE TO ALLOW FOR CAP TO BLOCK ALIGNMENT

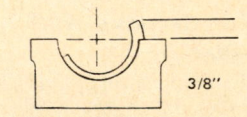

REAR FACE OF REAR MAIN BEARING CAP AND CYLINDER BLOCK

INSTALL SEAL WITH LIP TOWARDS FRONT OF ENGINE

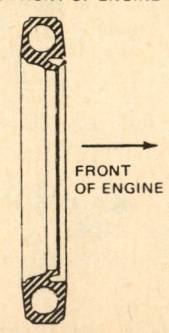

VIEW LOOKING AT PARTING FACE OF SPLIT, LIP-TYPE CRANKSHAFT SEAL

Rear main seal installation (© Ford Motor Co.)

equipped. It is not used with the replacement seal.

4. Carefully clean the seal grooves in the cap and block with solvent.
5. Soak the new seal halves in clean engine oil.
6. Install the upper half of the seal in the block with the undercut side of the seal toward the front of the engine. Slide the seal around the crankshaft journal until 3/8 in. protrudes beyond the base of the block.
7. Tighten all the main bearing caps (except the rear main bearing) to specifications.
8. Install he lower seal into the rear cap, with the undercut side facing the front of the engine. Allow 3/8 in. of the seal to protrude above the surface, at the opposite end from the block seal.
9. Squeeze a 1/16 in. bead of silicone seal onto the areas shown.
10. Install the rear cap and torque to specifications.
11. Install the oil pump and pan. Fill the crankcase with oil, start the engine, and check for leaks.

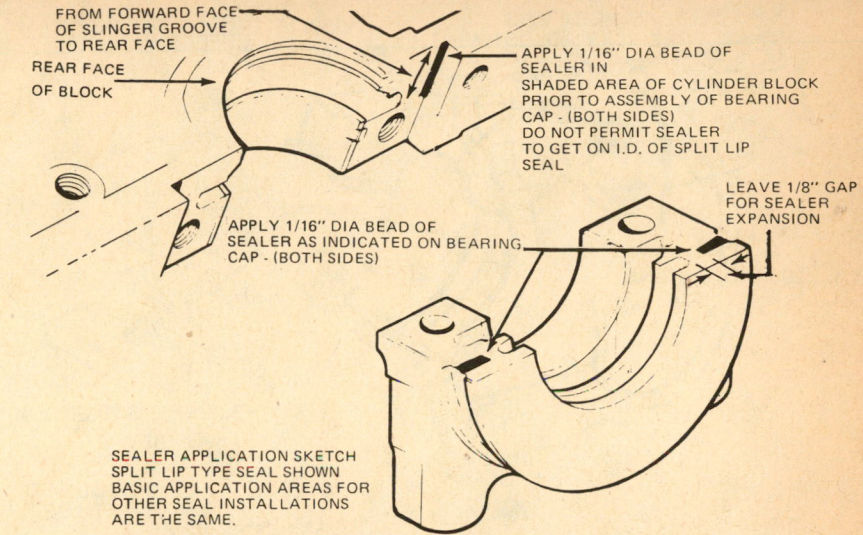

Rear main bearing cap sealer application (© Ford Motor Co.)

CLUTCH

The clutch is a single dry disc type and is mechanically engaged. Centrifugal weights are used to increase pressure plate grip at high rpm.

Pedal Adjustment

ALL EXCEPT FAIRMONT, ZEPHYR, 1979 MUSTANG AND CAPRI

1. Disconnect clutch return spring from release lever.
2. Loosen release lever rod locknut and adjusting nut. On 1977 and later models, remove the release lever rod locking pin and loosen the adjusting nut.
3. Move clutch release lever rearward until release bearing lightly contacts clutch pressure plate release fingers.
4. Adjust rod length until rod seats in release lever pocket.
5. Insert specified feeler gauge between adjusting nut and swivel sleeve. Tighten adjusting nut against gauge.
6. Tighten locknut against adjusting nut, taking care not to disturb adjustment. On 1977 and later models, rotate the rod to align the flat with the pin hole in the adjusting nut and install the pin. Remove feeler gauge.
7. Install clutch return spring.
8. Check free travel at pedal. Readjust if necessary to obtain specified travel. Moving adjusting nut away from swivel sleeve increases travel. Moving adjusting nut toward swivel sleeve decreases travel.

9. As final check, measure pedal free travel with transmission in neutral and engine running at 3,000 rpm. If pedal travel is not minimum of 1/2 in., readjust free travel.

If a problem is encountered with clutch adjustment rods bending, check the clutch equalizer shaft. A bent or distorted equalizer shaft will allow the clutch pedal to travel too far, which will bend the adjustment rod.

Clutch Pedal Adjustment

Year and Engine	Clearance* (in.)	Free Travel (in.)
1972-74 Torino, Montego, Cougar and 1972-73 Mustang	0.194	7/8–1-1/8
1972 and later Comet, Maverick, Monarch and Granada	0.136	7/8–1-1/8

* Between adjusting nut and swivel sleeve

FAIRMONT, ZEPHYR, 1979 MUSTANG, 1979 CAPRI

Four Cylinder Engine

1. Working under the car, remove the release lever spring and the dust boot.

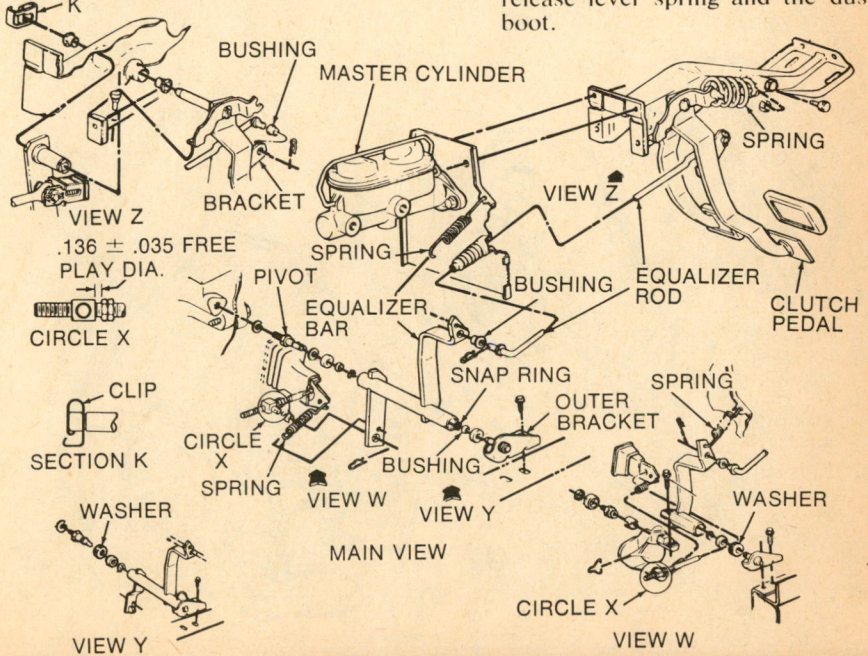

Clutch pedal and linkage adjustment—Maverick and Comet through 1974
(© Ford Motor Co)

Capri • Comet • Cougar • Elite • Fairmont • Granada
LTD II • Maverick

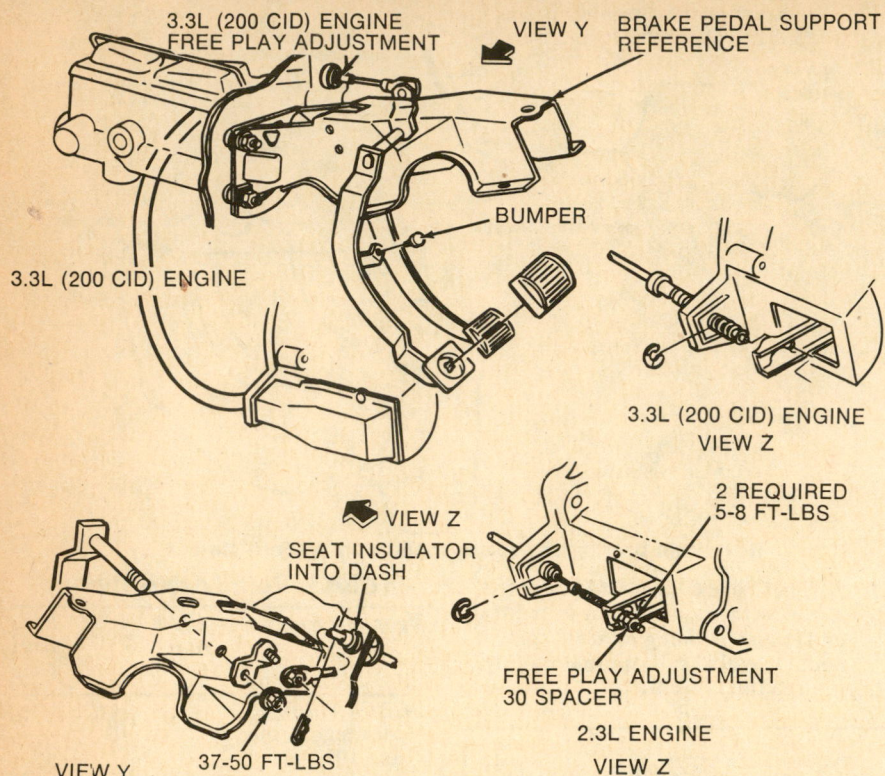

3.3L (200 CID) ENGINE
FREE PLAY ADJUSTMENT

VIEW Y

BRAKE PEDAL SUPPORT
REFERENCE

BUMPER

3.3L (200 CID) ENGINE

3.3L (200 CID) ENGINE
VIEW Z

VIEW Z

SEAT INSULATOR
INTO DASH

2 REQUIRED
5-8 FT-LBS

VIEW Y

37-50 FT-LBS

FREE PLAY ADJUSTMENT
30 SPACER

2.3L ENGINE
VIEW Z

Fairmont, Zephyr, 1979 Mustang, Capri clutch pedal and linkage adjustment
(© Ford Motor Co.)

2. Loosen the cable locknut and adjusting nut at the release lever.
3. Move the lever forward until free movement is eliminated. Hold forward during adjustment.
4. Insert a 0.30 in. spacer against the release lever cable spacer. Tighten the adjusting nut against the spacer finger tight.

5. Tighten the locknut against the adjusting nut. Remove the spacer. Apply and release the clutch five times. Check for about 1 1/2 ins. of free play. Install the dust boot and return spring.

Six Cylinder Engines
1. Pull the clutch cable forward until

PILOT BEARING   CLUTCH DISC

RELEASE BEARING

FLYWHEEL HOUSING

RELEASE
LEVER

PIVOT
BALL STUD

BOOT

INPUT SHAFT

Exploded view of clutch and related parts (© Ford Motor Co)

the adjusting nut can be rotated. Unscrew the adjusting nut approximately 0.30 in. from the rubber insulator. The nylon nut will not rotate until it is free of the insulator. It may be necessary to remove the clutch pedal bumper to provide enough slack. Replace the rubber bumper before continuing.
2. Release the cable. Pull the cable slightly forward again to remove slack. Free movement of the lever should be eliminated.
3. Tighten the adjusting nut until it contacts the insulator, then index the tabs into the next notch. Apply and release the clutch five times and check the free play. It should measure approximately 1 1/2 inches.

Clutch and/or Manual Transmission Removal and Installation

1. Disconnect and remove starter and dust ring, if the clutch is to be removed. On floorshift models, remove the boot retainer and shifter lever.
2. On 1978 and later Fairmonts and Zephyrs, and 1979 Mustangs and Capris with the four speed transmission: working under the hood, remove the upper clutch housing-to-engine bolts.
3. Raise the car.
4. Matchmark the driveshaft and axle flange for reassembly. Disconnect the driveshaft at the rear universal joint and remove the driveshaft. Plug the extension housing.
5. Disconnect the speedometer cable at the transmission extension. On cars with transmission regulated spark, disconnect the lead wire at the connector. Disconnect the seat belt sensor wires. Remove the clutch lever boot and cable on Fairmonts, Zephyrs, Mustangs, and Capris so equipped.
6. Disconnect the gear shift rods from the transmission shift levers. If car is equipped with four speed, remove bolts that secure shift control bracket to extension housing. Support the engine with a jack.
7. Remove the bolt holding the extension housing to the rear support, and remove the muffler inlet pipe bracket to housing bolt.
8. Remove the two rear support bracket insulator nuts from the underside of the crossmember. Remove crossmember.
9. Place a jack (equipped with a protective piece of wood) under the rear of the engine oil pan. Raise or lower the engine slightly as necessary to provide access to the bolts.
10. Remove transmission-to-flywheel housing bolts.

NOTE: *On 429 and 460 cu in. engines the upper left-hand transmission attaching bolt is a seal bolt. Carefully* *note its position so that it may be reinstalled in its original position.*

11. Slide the transmission back and out of the car. It may be necessary to slide the catalytic converter bracket forward to provide clearance on some models.
12. To remove the clutch, remove release lever retracting spring. Disconnect pedal at the equalizer bar, or the clutch cable from the housing, as applicable.
13. Remove bolts that secure engine rear plate to front lower part of bellhousing.
14. Remove bolts that attach bell housing to cylinder block and remove housing and release lever as a unit.
15. Loosen six pressure plate cover attaching bolts evenly to release spring pressure. Mark cover and flywheel to facilitate reassembly in same position.
16. Remove six attaching bolts while holding pressure plate cover. Remove pressure plate and clutch disc.

CAUTION

Do not depress the clutch pedal while the transmission is removed.

---

17. To install the clutch, first wash flywheel surface with alcohol.
18. Attach the clutch disc and pressure plate assembly to the flywheel with the bolts finger tight.
19. Align the clutch disc with the pilot bushing. Torque cover bolts to 12-20 ft lbs.
20. Lightly lubricate the release lever fulcrum ends. Install the release lever in the flywheel housing and install the dust shield.
21. Apply very little lubricant on the release bearing retainer journal. Fill the groove in the release bearing hub with grease. Clean all excess grease from the inside bore of the hub to prevent clutch disc contamination. Attach the release bearing and hub on the release lever.
22. Make sure the flywheel housing and engine block are clean. Any missing or damaged mounting dowels must be replaced. Install the flywheel housing and torque the attaching bolts to 38-61 ft. lbs. on all V8s and 250 sixes, 38-55 ft. lbs. on 200 sixes, and 28-38 ft. lbs. on fours and V6s. Install the dust cover and torque the bolts to 17-20 ft lbs.
23. Connect the release rod or cable and the retracting spring. Connect the pedal-to-equalizer-rod at the equalizer bar.
24. Install starter and dust ring.
25. After moving the transmission back just far enough for the pilot shaft to clear the clutch housing, move it upward and into position on the flywheel housing. It may be necessary to put the transmission

in gear and rotate the output shaft to align the input shaft and clutch splines.

26. Move the transmission foward and into place against the flywheel housing, and install the transmission attaching bolts finger-tight.
27. Tighten the transmission bolts to 37-42 ft lbs on all cars.
28. Install the crossmember and torque the mounting bolts to 20-30 ft. lbs. Slowly lower the engine onto the crossmember.
29. Torque the rear mount to 30-50 ft. lbs. except: Cougars through 1974 and Mustangs through 1973 to 25-35 ft. lbs.
30. Connect gear shift rods and the speedometer cable. On transmission regulated spark equipped cars, connect the lead wire at the connector.
31. Remove the plug from the extension housing and install the driveshaft, aligning the marks made previously.
32. Refill transmission to proper level. On floorshift models, install the boot retainer and shift lever.

MANUAL TRANSMISSION

There are four manual transmissions used: (1) a heavy-duty, top cover, fully synchromesh three-speed used on all three-speed applications, (2) a heavy-duty, top cover, fully synchromesh, Ford-built four-speed used on V8 engines through 1974, (3) beginning 1977, a fully synchromesh four-speed overdrive transmission available on Granada and Monarch, (4) a fully synchronized Model 78ET four-speed first available on Fairmonts and Zephyrs with the 2300 four cylinder. The 78ET has an internal shift rail; linkage adjustments are neither possible nor necessary.

Linkage Adjustment
COLUMN SHIFT

With the transmission in neutral, the shift lever should be in a horizontal plane and parallel to the instrument

panel line. Corrective adjustments should be made at the gear shift rods.

1. Place lever in neutral.
2. Loosen two gear shift rod adjustment nuts.
3. Insert 3/16 in. diameter alignment pin through first and reverse gear shift lever and second and third gear shift lever. Align levers to insert pin.
4. Tighten gear shift rod adjustment nuts, and remove pin.
5. Check gear lever for smooth crossover.

THREE-SPEED FLOOR AND CONSOLE SHIFT

1. Loosen three shift linkage adjustment nuts.
2. Install a 1/4 in. diameter alignment pin through control bracket and levers.
3. Tighten three shift linkage adjustment nuts and remove alignment pin.
4. Check gear lever for smooth crossover.

FOUR-SPEED

NOTE: *This procedure is for four speed transmissions through 1974, and 1977-78 Granada and Monarch four speed overdrive transmssions. 1978 and later Fairmont and Zephyr, and all 1979 four speeds have internal shift rails with no provision for adjustment.*

1. Place shifter lever in neutral position, then raise car on a hoist.
2. Insert a 1/4 in. rod into the alignment holes of the shift levers.
3. If the holes are not in exact alignment, check for bent connecting rods or loose lever locknuts at the rod ends. Make replacements or repairs, then adjust as follows.
4. Loosen the three rod-to-lever retaining lock nuts and move the levers until the 1/4 in. gauge rod will enter the alignment holes. Be sure that the transmission shift levers are in neutral and the reverse shifter lever is in the neutral detent.
5. Install the shift rods and tighten the locknuts.
6. Remove the 1/4 in. gauge rod.
7. Operate the shift levers to assure correct shifting.
8. Lower the car and road test.

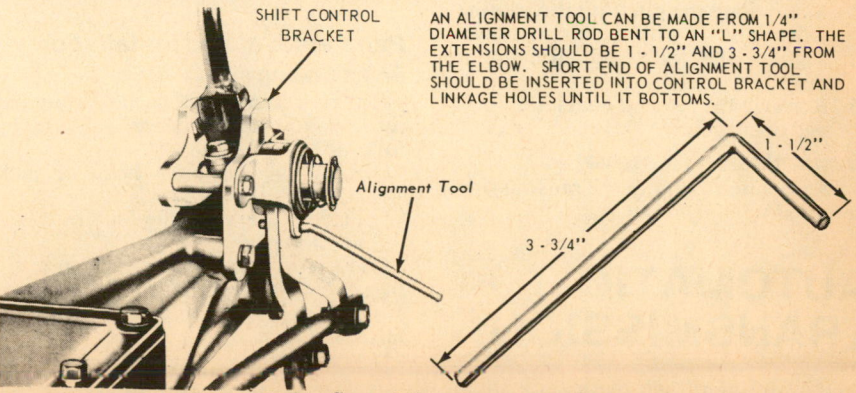

SHIFT CONTROL BRACKET

Alignment Tool

AN ALIGNMENT TOOL CAN BE MADE FROM 1/4" DIAMETER DRILL ROD BENT TO AN "L" SHAPE. THE EXTENSIONS SHOULD BE 1 - 1/2" AND 3 - 3/4" FROM THE ELBOW. SHORT END OF ALIGNMENT TOOL SHOULD BE INSERTED INTO CONTROL BRACKET AND LINKAGE HOLES UNTIL IT BOTTOMS.

1 - 1/2"

3 - 3/4"

Manual transmission floor shift adjustment (© Ford Motor Co)

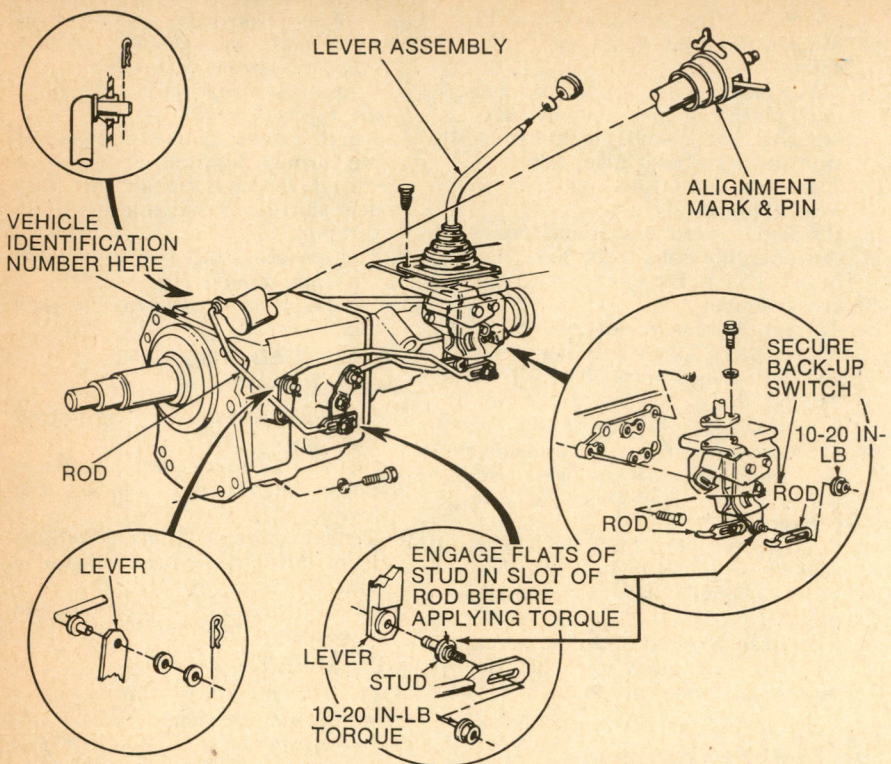

VEHICLE IDENTIFICATION NUMBER HERE

LEVER ASSEMBLY

ALIGNMENT MARK & PIN

ROD

LEVER

SECURE BACK-UP SWITCH

10-20 IN-LB

ROD

ROD

ENGAGE FLATS OF STUD IN SLOT OF ROD BEFORE APPLYING TORQUE

LEVER

STUD

10-20 IN-LB TORQUE

Three-speed floor shift linkage and lock rod (© Ford Motor Co)

Transmission Lock Rod Adjustment

Models through 1976 with floor or console mounted shifters and manual transmissions incorporate a transmission lock rod which prevents the shifter from being moved from the reverse position when the ignition lock is in the OFF position. The lock rod connects the shift tube in the steering column to the transmission reverse lever. The lock rod cannot be properly adjusted until the manual linkage adjustment is correct.

1. With the transmission selector lever in the neutral position, loosen the lock rod adjustment nut on the transmission reverse lever.
2. Insert a .180 in. diameter rod (No. 15 drill bit) in the gauge pin hole located at the 6 o'clock position on the steering column socket casting, directly below the ignition lock.
3. Manipulate the pin until the casting will not move with the pin inserted.
4. Tighten the lock rod adjustment nut.
5. Remove the pin and check the linkage operation.

Transmission Removal

See Clutch and/or Transmission Removal.

AUTOMATIC TRANSMISSION

Five different automatic transmissions are used in Ford compact and in-

termediate cars: a C3, a C4, a C6, an FMX, and beginning March 1977, a Jatco unit. The Jatco is used in the Granada/Monarch with column shift, except in California. The C3 is a light duty unit used with four cylinder and some six cylinder engines. The C4 is a light duty transmission used on six cylinder and small block V8 engines. The FMX is an intermediate duty transmission used on medium duty V8s. The C6 is a heavy duty transmission used on high-performance and large displacement V8 engines. The Jatco is a light duty unit used only with the 250 engine. The Jatco is easily identified by the word Japan on the left side of the case.

The transmission identification code can be found on the vehicle certification label affixed to the left front door lock panel or door pillar. Interpret the code by the Transmission Identification Codes chart at the beginning of this section.

Pan Removal and Installation, Fluid Change

The procedure for a partial drain and refill of the transmission fluid is as follows:

1. Raise the car on a hoist or jack stands.
2. Place a drain pan under the transmission pan.

NOTE: *On some models of the C4 transmission, the fluid is drained by disconnecting the filler tube from the transmission fluid pan.*

3. Loosen the pan attaching bolts to allow the fluid to drain.
4. When the fluid has stopped drain-

ing to level of the pan flange, remove the pan bolts starting at the rear and along both sides of the pan, allowing the pan to drop and drain gradually.

5. When all the transmission fluid has drained, remove the pan and the fluid filter and clean them.

NOTE: *On C4 models only, the filter and gasket retain the throttle pressure limit valve within the lower control valve body. Be careful not to lose this valve when removing the filter. The valve is installed large end first into the valve body; the spring fits over the valve shaft.*

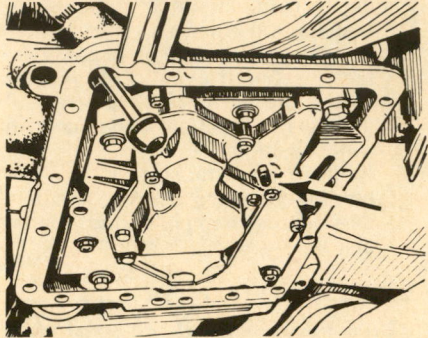

C4 Throttle pressure limit valve and filter

6. After completing the transmission repairs or adjustments, install the fluid filter screen, a new pan gasket, and the pan on the transmission. Tighten the pan attaching bolts on C3, C4 and C6 transmissions to 12-16 ft lbs. On FMX transmissions, tighten the pan attaching bolts to 10-13 ft lbs. Tighten to 4-6 ft lb. on the Jatco.

--- CAUTION ---

With the exception of the 1977 and later C6 and JATCO, all Ford automatic transmissions use Type F fluid. The 1977 and later C6 and JATCO use a new fluid, Ford Type CJ.

7. Install three quarts of transmission fluid through the filler tube. If the filler tube was removed to drain the transmission, install the filler tube using a new 0-ring.
8. Start and run the engine for a few minutes at low idle speed and then at the fast idle speed (about 1,200 rpm) until the normal operating temperature is reached. Do not race the engine.
9. Move the selector lever through all gear positions and place it at the Park position. Check the fluid level, and add fluid until the level is between the add and full marks on the dipstick. Do not overfill.

C3

Throttle and Downshift Linkage, Shift Linkage Adjustment

See the C4 section.

Band Adjustment

Only the front band requires adjustment.

1. Remove the downshift rod from the transmission lever.
2. Clean any dirt from the area, and remove and discard the locknut from the band adjusting screw.
3. Install a new locknut. Tighten the adjusting screw to exactly 10 ft. lbs. This figure is not approximate; it must be exact.
4. Back off the adjusting screw exactly one and a half turns.
5. Hold the adjusting screw so that it cannot turn and tighten the locknut to 35-45 ft. lbs. Reinstall the downshift rod.

C4

Throttle Linkage Adjustment

INITIAL ADJUSTMENT

1. Apply parking brake and place selector lever at N. Block the wheels.
2. Run engine at normal idle speed. If engine is cold, run engine at fast idle speed (about 1200 rpm) until it reaches normal operating temperature. When engine is warm, slow it down to normal idle speed.
3. Connect tachometer to engine.
4. Adjust engine idle speed to specified rpm with transmission selector lever at D.
5. The carburetor throttle lever must be against hot idle speed adjusting screw at specified idle speed in D.

FINAL ADJUSTMENT

1. With engine stopped, disconnect throttle and downshift return springs.
2. Hold carburetor throttle lever in wide open position against stop.
3. Hold transmission in full downshift position against internal stop.
4. Turn adjustment screw on carburetor downshift lever to within 0.050-0.070 in. on 1972 models, and 0.010-0.080 on 1973 and later models, of contacting pickup surface of carburetor throttle lever.
5. Release transmission and carburetor to normal free positions.
6. Install throttle and downshift return springs.

Shift Linkage Adjustment

COLUMN SHIFT

1. With engine stopped, loosen clamp at shift lever at point A so that shift rod is free to slide in clamp. On vehicles equipped with a shift cable, remove the nut at point A and at manual lever stud.
2. Place transmission shift lever into D position.
3. Shift manual lever at transmission into D. D is the second detent from the rear.
4. Tighten clamp on shift rod. On vehicles equipped with a shift cable, position the cable end on the transmission manual lever stud, aligning the flats. Start the adjusting nut.
5. Check pointer alignment and transmission operation for all selector lever positions.

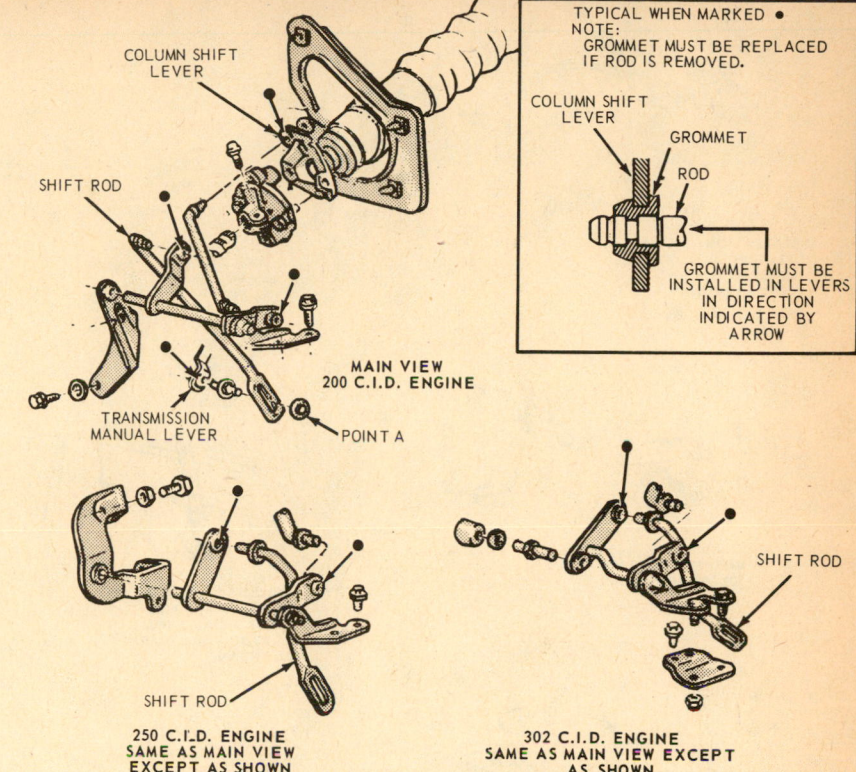

MAIN VIEW 200 C.I.D. ENGINE

250 C.I.D. ENGINE SAME AS MAIN VIEW EXCEPT AS SHOWN

302 C.I.D. ENGINE SAME AS MAIN VIEW EXCEPT AS SHOWN

Column shift—Maverick and Comet
(© Ford Motor Co)

FLOOR OR CONSOLE SHIFT

1. Place transmission shift lever in D.
2. Raise vehicle and loosen manual lever shift rod retaining nut. Move transmission lever to D position. D is second from rear.
3. With transmission shift lever and transmission manual lever in position, tighten nut.
4. Check transmission operation for all selector lever detent positions.

NOTE: *Some models (Maverick, Comet, 1972-73 Mustang and Cougar) with a floor or console mounted selector lever have a transmission lockout rod to prevent the transmission selector from being moved out of the park position when the ignition lock is in the OFF position. The lock rod connects the shift tube in the steering column to the transmission manual lever. The lock rod cannot be properly adjusted until the manual linkage adjustment is correct.*

Lock Rod Adjustment

1. With the transmission selector lever in the Drive position, loosen the lock rod adjustment nut on the transmission lever.
2. Insert a .180 in. diameter rod (No. 15 drill bit) in the gauge pin hole in the steering column socket casting, it is located at the 6 o'clock position directly below the ignition lock.
3. Manipulate the pin so that the casting will not move when the pin is fully inserted.

4. Tighten the lock rod adjustment nut.
5. Remove the pin and check the linkage operation.

Band Adjustment

INTERMEDIATE BAND

1. Clean all the dirt from the adjusting screw and remove and discard the locknut.
2. Install a new locknut on the adjusting screw. Using a torque wrench, tighten the adjusting screw to exactly 10 ft. lbs.
3. Back off the adjusting screw exactly 1-3/4 turns.
4. Hold the adjusting screw steady and tighten the locknut.

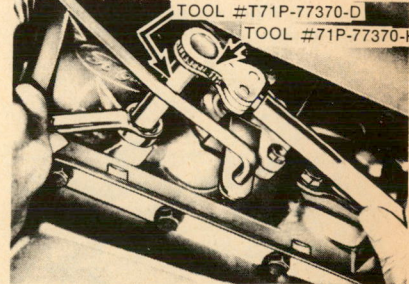

TOOL #T71P-77370-D
TOOL #71P-77370-H

C4 Intermediate band adjustment
(© Ford Motor Co)

LOW-REVERSE BAND

1. Clean all dirt from around the band adjusting screw, and remove and discard the locknut.

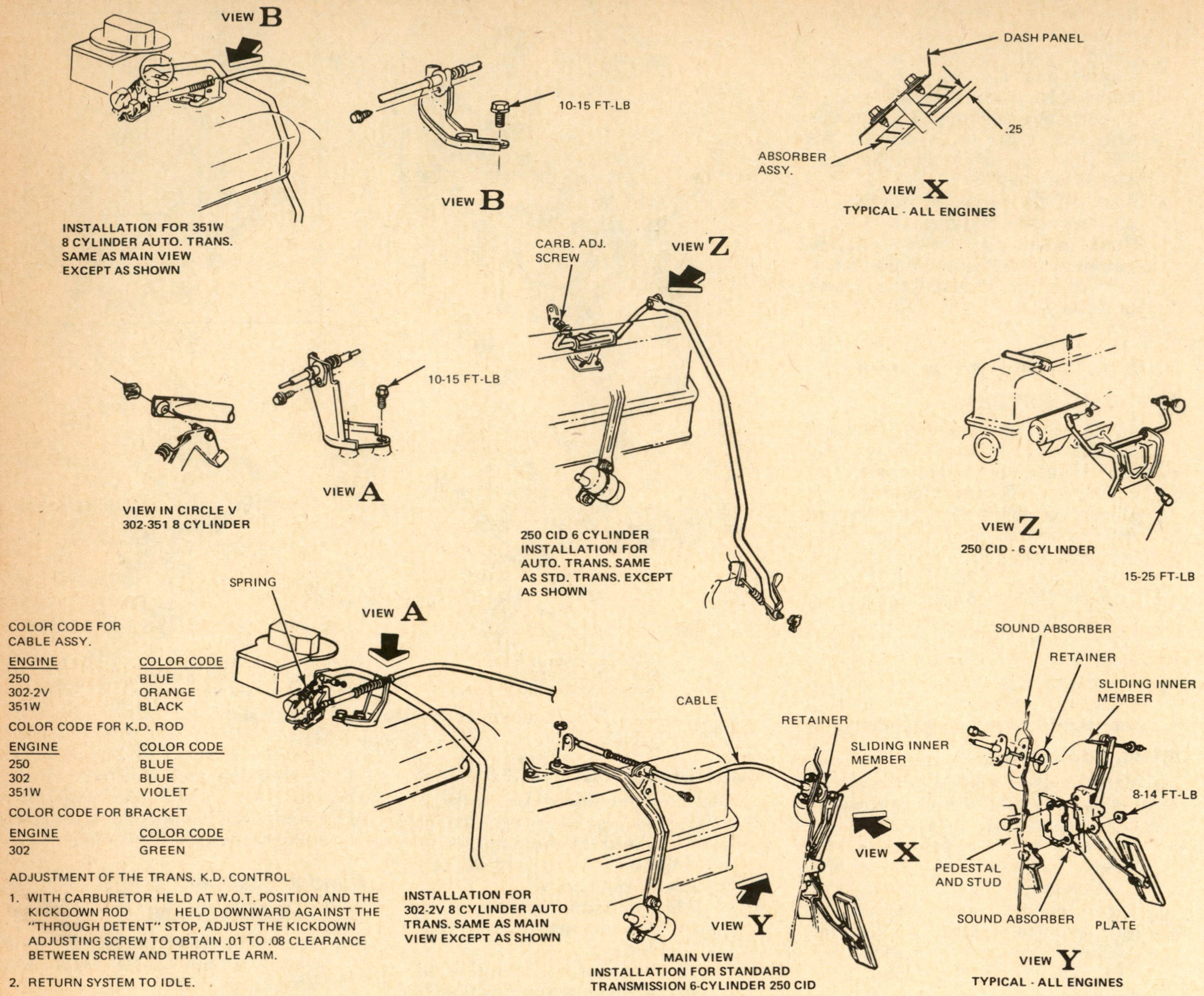

VIEW **B**

DASH PANEL

.25

ABSORBER ASSY.

VIEW **X**
TYPICAL - ALL ENGINES

VIEW **B**

10-15 FT-LB

INSTALLATION FOR 351W
8 CYLINDER AUTO. TRANS.
SAME AS MAIN VIEW
EXCEPT AS SHOWN

CARB. ADJ. SCREW

VIEW **Z**

10-15 FT-LB

VIEW **A**

VIEW IN CIRCLE V
302-351 8 CYLINDER

250 CID 6 CYLINDER
INSTALLATION FOR
AUTO. TRANS. SAME
AS STD. TRANS. EXCEPT
AS SHOWN

VIEW **Z**
250 CID - 6 CYLINDER

15-25 FT-LB

SPRING

VIEW **A**

SOUND ABSORBER

RETAINER

SLIDING INNER MEMBER

COLOR CODE FOR
CABLE ASSY.

ENGINE	COLOR CODE
250	BLUE
302-2V	ORANGE
351W	BLACK

COLOR CODE FOR K.D. ROD

ENGINE	COLOR CODE
250	BLUE
302	BLUE
351W	VIOLET

COLOR CODE FOR BRACKET

ENGINE	COLOR CODE
302	GREEN

CABLE

RETAINER

SLIDING INNER MEMBER

8-14 FT-LB

PEDESTAL AND STUD

SOUND ABSORBER

PLATE

VIEW **X**

ADJUSTMENT OF THE TRANS. K.D. CONTROL

1. WITH CARBURETOR HELD AT W.O.T. POSITION AND THE KICKDOWN ROD HELD DOWNWARD AGAINST THE "THROUGH DETENT" STOP, ADJUST THE KICKDOWN ADJUSTING SCREW TO OBTAIN .01 TO .08 CLEARANCE BETWEEN SCREW AND THROTTLE ARM.

2. RETURN SYSTEM TO IDLE.

INSTALLATION FOR
302-2V 8 CYLINDER AUTO
TRANS. SAME AS MAIN
VIEW EXCEPT AS SHOWN

VIEW **Y**

MAIN VIEW
INSTALLATION FOR STANDARD
TRANSMISSION 6-CYLINDER 250 CID

VIEW **Y**
TYPICAL - ALL ENGINES

Throttle and downshift linkage—Granada and Monarch (© Ford Motor Co)

2. Install a new locknut on the adjusting screw. Using a torque wrench, tighten the adjusting screw to exactly 10 ft lbs.
3. Back off the adjusting screw exactly 3 full turns.
4. Hold the adjusting screw steady and tighten the locknut.

TOOL #T70P-713200-B

TOOL #T71P-77370-H

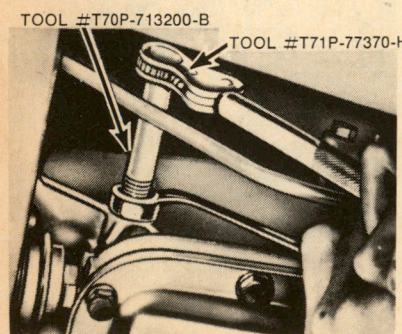

C4 Low-Reverse band adjustment
(© Ford Motor Co)

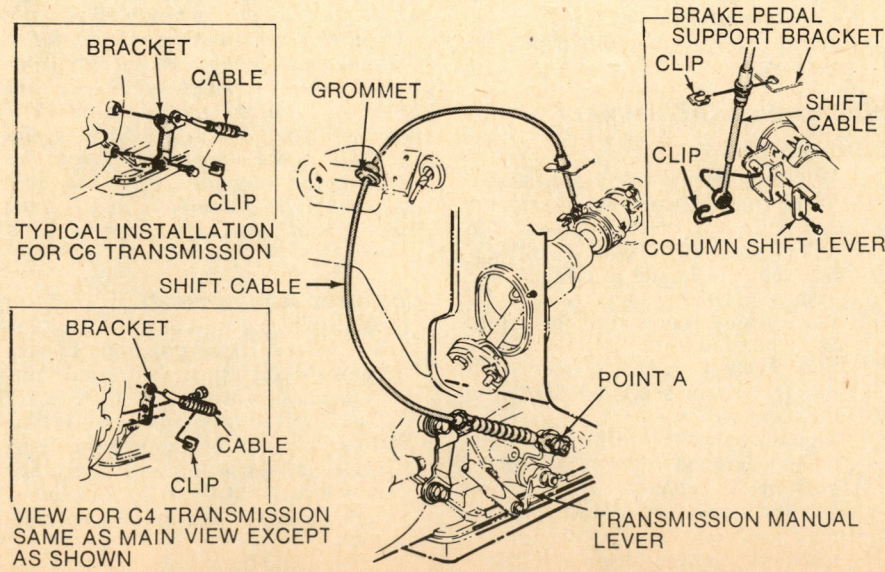

BRACKET

CABLE

CLIP

TYPICAL INSTALLATION
FOR C6 TRANSMISSION

GROMMET

SHIFT CABLE

BRACKET

CABLE

CLIP

VIEW FOR C4 TRANSMISSION
SAME AS MAIN VIEW EXCEPT
AS SHOWN

BRAKE PEDAL
SUPPORT BRACKET

CLIP

SHIFT CABLE

CLIP

COLUMN SHIFT LEVER

POINT A

TRANSMISSION MANUAL
LEVER

**Automatic transmission column shift linkage—Torino, Montego, Elite,
LTD II, 1977 and later Thunderbird, 1972 and later Cougar**

C6

Throttle and Downshift Linkage, Shift Linkage, Transmission Lock Rod Adjustment

See the C4 section.

Intermediate Band Adjustment

1. Raise the car on a hoist or place it on jackstands.
2. Clean the threads of the intermediate band adjusting screw.
3. Remove and discard the adjustment screw lock nut. Loosely install a new locknut.
4. Tighten the adjusting screw to 10 ft. lbs. and back the screw off *exactly 1-1/2 turns*. Tighten the adjusting screw locknut.

FMX

The throttle and downshift linkage adjustments are the same as with the C4 transmission.

Band Adjustments

See the Ford car section.

JATCO

Intermediate Band Adjustment

1. Raise and support the vehicle.
2. Remove the servo cover.
3. Loosen the intermediate band adjusting screw locknut and tighten the adjusting screw to 10 ft. lbs.
4. Back off the adjusting screw exactly two turns, hold it stationary and tighten the locknut to 22-29 ft. lbs.
5. Replace the cover using a new gasket.

Shift Linkage Adjustment

See the C4 section.

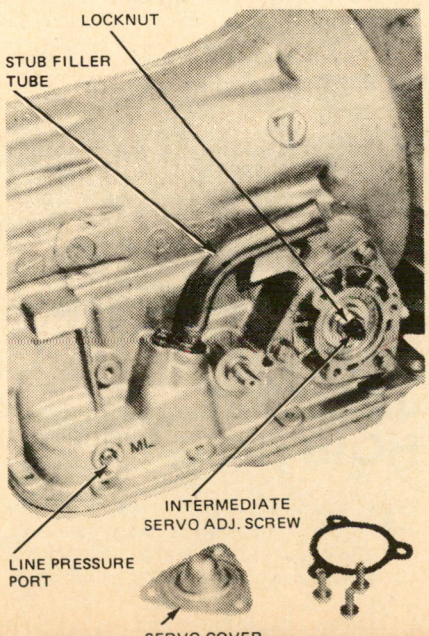

JATCO intermediate band adjustment location (© Ford Motor Co.)

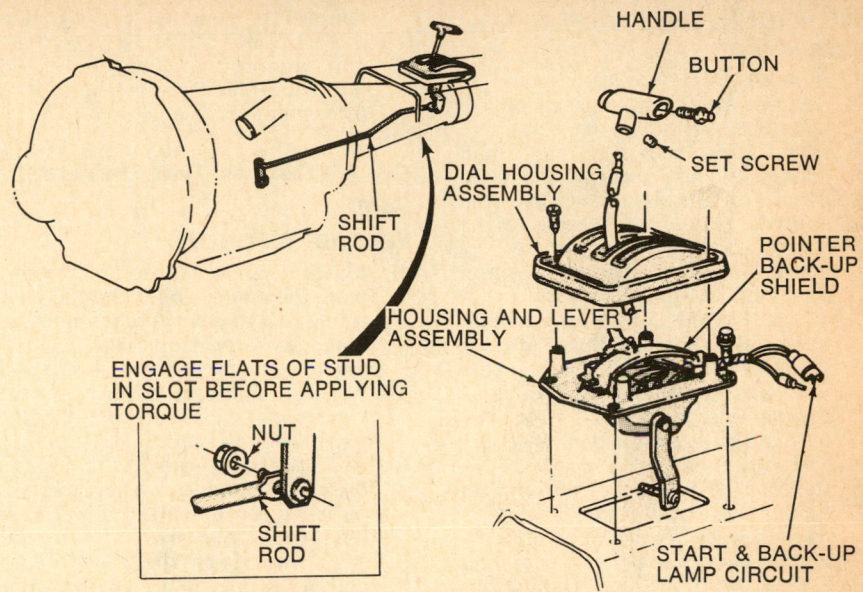

Automatic transmission floorshift linkage—Torino, Montego, Elite, LTD II, 1977 and later Thunderbird, 1972 and later Cougar (© Ford Motor Co)

U-JOINTS

Universal joints are retained at the rear by U-bolts on all models except the Fairmont, Zephyr, 1979 Mustang, Capri, and Versailles, which are retained in a coupling flange which is bolted to the pinion (differential) flange. The Versailles uses a double Cardan-type universal joint at the rear. Service for the front U-joint on the Versailles is the same as for other models.

Driveshaft Removal and Installation

1. Matchmark the rear driveshaft yoke and the companion flange so that the parts may be reassembled in the same way to maintain balance.
2. Remove the U-bolts and straps at the rear of the driveshaft, and tape the loose bearing caps to the spider. On Fairmonts, Zephyrs, 1979 Mustangs, Capris, and Versailles, remove the coupling flange nuts and bolts.
3. Allow the rear of the driveshaft to drop down slightly. Pull the driveshaft and slip yoke out of the transmission extension housing.
4. Plug the transmssion to prevent fluid leakage.
5. To install, lubricate the yoke splines and install the yoke into the transmission extension housing, aligning the splines. Be careful not to bottom the slip yoke hard against the transmission seal.
6. Rotate the pinion flange as necessary to align the matchmarks made earlier. Install the U-bolts and tighten to 8-15 ft. lbs. On the Versailles, tighten the coupling-to-pinion flange bolts to 70-90 ft. lbs.

The Fairmont and Zephyr use special wax dipped coupling-to-pinion flange bolts which may not be reused. They must be replaced with special new bolts, torqued to 60-70 ft. lbs.

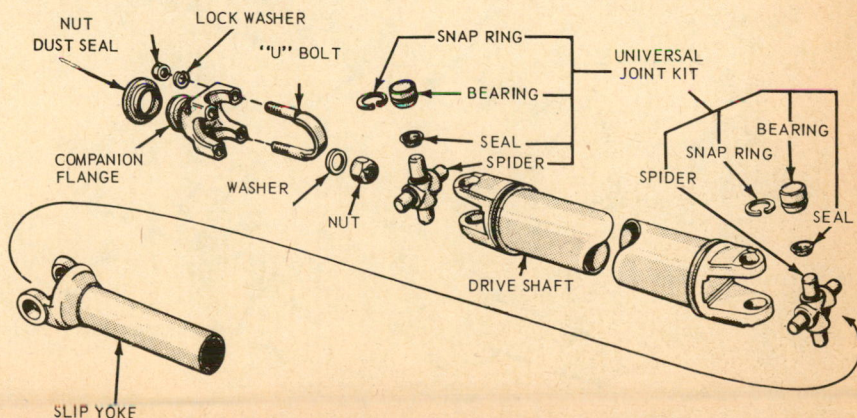

Driveshaft and universal joint assembly (© Ford Motor Co)

Universal Joint Removal and Installation

1. Remove the driveshaft.
2. Remove the snap rings which retain the bearings.
3. Select two sockets, one small enough to pass through the yoke holes for the bearing caps, the other large enough to receive the bearing cap.
4. Using a vice or a press, position the small and large sockets on either side of the U-joint. Press in on the smaller socket so that it presses the opposite bearing cap out of the yoke and into the larger socket. If the cap does not come all the way out, grasp it with a pair of pliers and work it out.
5. Reverse the position of the sockets so that the smaller socket presses on the spider. Press the other bearing cap out of the yoke.
6. Repeat the procedure on the other bearings.
7. To install, grease the bearing caps and needles thoroughly if they are not pregreased. Start a new bearing cap into one side of the yoke. Position the spider in the yoke.
8. Select two sockets small enough to pass through the yoke holes. Put the sockets against the spider and the cap, and press the bearing cap 1/4 in. below the surface of the yoke.
9. Install a new snap ring.
10. Start a new bearing into the opposite side. Place a socket on it and press in until the opposite bearing contacts the snap ring.
11. Install a new snap ring. It may be necessary to grind the facing surface of the snap ring to permit easier installation.
12. Install the other bearings in the same manner.
13. Check the joint for free movement. If binding exists, smack the yoke ears with a brass or plastic faced hammer to seat the bearing needles. Do not strike the bearings, and support the shaft firmly. Do not install the driveshaft until free movement exists at all joints.

Double Cardan-Type Universal Joint

VERSAILLES ONLY

1. Matchmark the position of the spiders, the center yoke, and the centering socket yoke in relation to the companion flange. The spiders must be reassembled with the bosses in the same position to provide proper clearance and to maintain proper driveline balance.
2. Remove the driveshaft.
3. Using either the socket method outlined for universal joints earlier, or a U-joint press, remove the snap rings from the center yoke and press one of the bearings out until it protrudes 3/8 in. out of the yoke.
4. Remove the driveshaft from the vise and tighten the bearing cap in the vise. Tap on the yoke with a hammer to free the bearing. Do not under any circumstances tap on the driveshaft tube.
5. Remove the other bearings in a similar manner.
6. Insert a screwdriver into the centering ball socket located in the companion flange and pry out the rubber seal. Remove the retainer, three piece ball seat, washer, and spring from the socket.
7. Inspect the centering socket assembly for worn or damaged parts and replace as required.
8. Install the spring, washer, three piece ball seat, and retainer into the socket.
9. Install the ball socket seal.
10. Position the spider in the driveshaft yoke. Be sure the spider bosses are in the same position as originally installed. Press the bearing cups into place and install the internal snap rings.
11. Position the center yoke over the spider ends and press in the bearing cups. Install the snap rings.
12. Install the spider in the companion flange yoke. The spider bosses must be as originally installed. Install the bearing cups and snap rings.
13. Position the center yoke over the spider ends and press in the cups. Install the snap rings.
14. Install the driveshaft, aligning the matchmarks made during removal.

REAR AXLE

Both integral and removable carrier type axles are used. Traction-Lok (limited slip) axles are available only as removable carrier types.

The axle type and ratio are stamped on a plate attached to a rear housing cover bolt. Axle types also indicate whether the axle shafts are retained by C-locks; on these axles, the bearing is removed with a slide hammer. On other axles, the bearing is housed in a retainer ring which must be split for removal. WER and WGX axles have C-locks. All other axles have bearing retainer rings. If the second letter of the axle code is F, it is a Traction-Lok axle (WFA, WFB, etc.). Always use the axle codes and ratio when ordering parts.

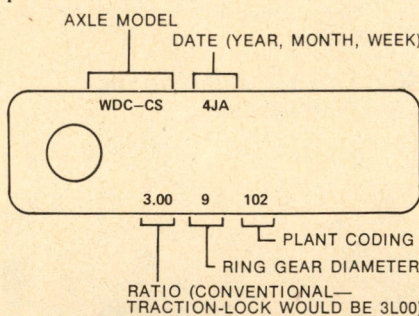

Axle code tag (© Ford Motor Co.)

Axle Shaft, Bearing, and Seal Removal and Installation

These procedures are covered in the Ford section.

JACKING, HOISTING

Jack car at front under spring seat of lower control arm. Jack car at rear axle housing close to differential case.

On twin post lifts, the front adapters must be carefully placed and large enough to cover the entire spring seat area. On models with leaf spring rear suspension, rear adapters or forks must be placed under axle not more than 1

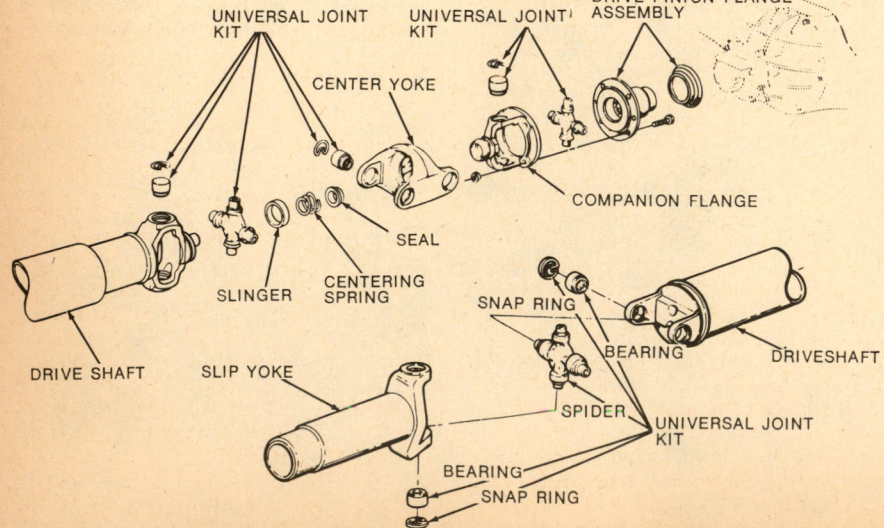

Versailles driveshaft and universal joint assembly (© Ford Motor Co.)

in. outboard from welds near the differential housing. Do not allow the lifts to contact the steering linkage.

On 1972 and later Torinos and Montegos, 1974 and later Cougars and Elites, 1977 and later LTD IIs and Thunderbirds, and all Fairmonts, Zephyrs, 1979 Mustangs and Capris, *do not* position the fork lifts outboard of the rear suspension lower arms. Place the forklifts under the axle housing inboard of the suspension arm brackets.

On frame contact lifts, on all except 1972 Torino and Montego and 1974 and later Cougar and Elite, and 1977 and later LTD II and Thunderbird, place the adapters as shown. Be sure that the pads cover at least 12 sq. in. in area.

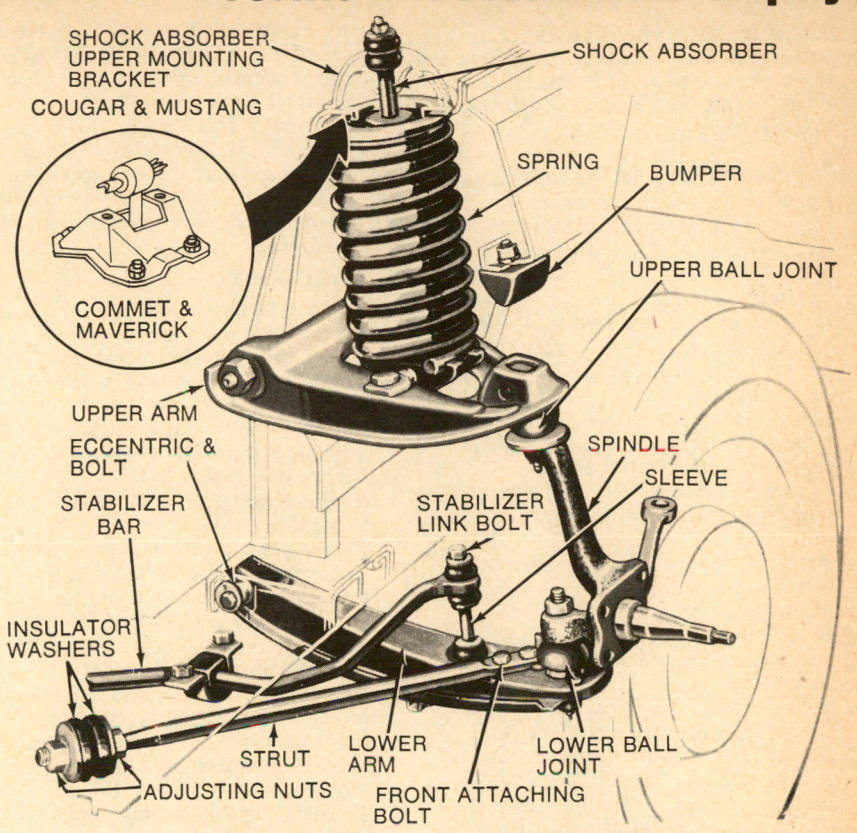

Front suspension—spring on upper arm (© Ford Motor Co)

Rear hoist contact area—cars with unitized construction (© Ford Motor Co)

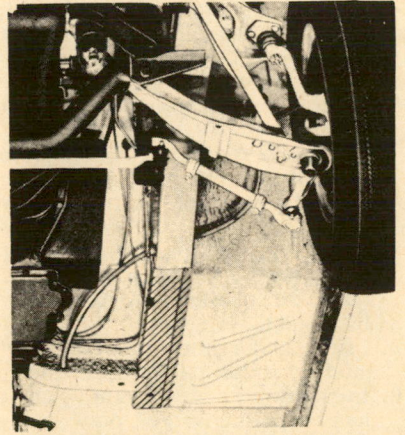

Front hoist contact area—cars with unitized construction (© Ford Motor Co)

FRONT SUSPENSION

On all compact and intermediate Ford Products, except the Torino and Montego, 1974 and later Cougar and Elite, 1977 and later LTD II and Thunderbird, and Fairmonts, Zephyrs, 1979 Mustangs and Capris, the front coil springs are mounted on top of the upper control arm to a tower in the sheet metal of the body. This type of mounting provides good stability. The lower arm and stabilizing strut substitute for the conventional control arm and serve to guide the lower part of the spindle through its cycle of up-and-down movement. The rod-type stabilizing strut is mounted between two rubber buffer pads at the front end to cushion fore and aft thrust of suspension. The effective length of this rod is variable and must be considered in maintenance.

On 1972 and later Torinos and Montegos and 1974 and later Cougars and Elites, and 1977 and later LTD IIs and Thunderbirds, the front coil springs are mounted between the upper and lower control arm. This type of mounting, used on standard-sized Fords for many years, aids cornering ability by lowering the roll center.

Fairmonts, Zephyrs, 1979 Mustangs, and Capris employ a modified MacPherson strut single arm design utilizing shock struts and coil springs mounted between the lower arm and a spring pocket in the number two crossmember. The suspension is designed with a zero scrub radius providing good steering stability. Advantages of the design include a reduction in weight, minimal intrusion into the engine compartment, and elimination of the need for a spring compressor when replacing the strut.

Front end alignment procedures are given in the Unit Repair Section.

COIL SPRING ON UPPER ARM
Shock Absorber Removal and Installation

NOTE: *Purge a new shock of air by repeatedly extending it in its normal position and compressing it while inverted.*

1. Raise the hood and remove the three shock absorber-to-spring tower attaching bolts.
2. Raise the front of the vehicle and place jackstands under the lower control arms.
3. Remove the shock absorber lower attaching nuts, washers, and insulators.
4. Lift the shock absorber and upper bracket from the spring tower and remove the bracket from the shock absorber. Remove the insulators from the lower attaching studs.
5. Install the upper mounting bracket on the shock absorber. Torque to 22-30 ft. lbs. on Mustangs and Cougars through 1973, and 10-16 ft. lbs. on all other cars. Install the insulators on the lower attaching studs.
6. Place the shock absorber and upper bracket assembly in the spring tower, making sure that the shock absorber lower studs are in the pivot plate holes.
7. Install the two washers and attaching nuts on the lower studs of the shock absorbers. Torque to 8-12 ft. lbs.

Capri • Comet • Cougar • Elite • Fairmont • Granada
LTD II • Maverick

8. Install the three shock absorber upper mounting bracket attaching nuts. Torque to 32-48 ft. lbs.
9. Remove the jackstands and lower the vehicle.

Spring Removal and Installation
1. Remove the shock absorber.
2. Remove wheel cover on hub cap.
3. Remove grease cap, cotter pin, nut lock, adjusting nut, and outer bearing.
4. Pull wheel, tire and hub and drum off spindle as an assembly. Remove the disc brake assembly, if so equipped.
5. Install spring compressor.
6. Compress spring until all tension is removed from control arms.
7. Remove two upper control arm attaching nuts and swing control arm outboard.
8. Release spring compressor and remove.
9. Remove spring.
10. To install, place upper spring insulator on spring and secure in place with tape.
11. Position spring in spring tower and compress with spring compressor.
12. Swing upper control arm inboard and install attaching nuts. Torque the nuts to 85-100 ft. lbs. through 1977, and 110-130 ft. lbs. thereafter.
13. Release spring pressure and guide spring into upper arm spring seat. The end of the spring must be not more than 1/2 in. from tab on spring seat.
14. Remove spring compressor and position wheel, tire, and hub and drum on spindle. Install disc brake assembly, if so equipped.
15. Install bearing, washer and adjusting nut.
16. On disc brake cars, loosen adjusting nut three turns, and rock wheel hub and rotor assembly in and out to push disc brake pads away from rotor.
17. While rotating wheel, hub and drum assembly, adjust the wheel bearings.
18. Install the shock absorber.

Lower Ball Joint
On all intermediate size Ford cars which have the coil springs mounted on the upper control arm, the lower ball joint is an integral part of the lower control arm. If the lower ball joint is defective the entire lower control arm must be replaced.

INSPECTION
1. Raise the vehicle on a hoist or floor jack so that the front wheel falls to the full down position.
2. Have an assistant grasp the bottom of the tire and move the wheel in and out.
3. As the wheel is being moved, observe the lower control arm where the spindle attaches to it.

4. Any movement between the lower part of the spindle and the lower control arm indicates a worn ball joint which must be replaced.

NOTE: *During this check, the upper ball joint will be unloaded and may move; this is normal and not an indication of a bad ball joint. Also, do not mistake a loose wheel bearing for a worn ball joint.*

REPLACEMENT
1. Position a support between the upper arm and side rail.
2. Raise the vehicle, position jack stands and remove the wheel and tire.
3. Remove the stabilizer bar to link attaching nut and disconnect the bar from the link.
4. Remove the link bolt from the lower arm.
5. Remove the strut bar to lower control arm attaching nuts and bolts.
6. Remove the lower ball joint cotter pin and back off the nut. Using a ball joint removal tool, loosen the ball joint stud in the spindle.
7. Remove the nut from the lower ball joint stud and lower the arm.
8. Remove the lower arm to underbody cam attaching parts and remove the arm.
9. To install, position the lower arm in the underbody and install the ball joint and cam attaching parts loosely.
10. Raise the lower arm, install the ball joint stud into place and loosely install the stud nut.
11. Install the stabilizer and strut and tighten the stabilizer nuts to 6-12 ft. lbs. Tighten the strut-to-arm nuts to 60-80 ft. lbs. through 1977, and 90-115 ft. lbs. thereafter.
12. Tighten the ball joint stud to 60 ft. lbs. through 1977, or 75 ft. lbs. 1978 and later, then continue to tighten until the cotter pin holes align. Install a new cotter pin. Tighten the lower arm bolts to 85-100 ft. lbs.
13. Lower the car and remove the upper arm support.
14. Front end alignment must be rechecked.

Upper Ball Joint
INSPECTION
1. Raise the vehicle on a hoist or floor jack so that the front wheels hang in full down position.
2. Have an assistant grasp the wheel top and bottom and apply alternate in and out pressure to the top and bottom of the wheel.
3. Radial play of 1/4 in. is acceptable measured at the inside of the wheel adjacent to the upper arm on all models except the Granada, Monarch, and Versailles; on those models only, any detectable play indicates worn ball joints.

NOTE: *This radial play measurement is multiplied at the outer circumference of*

the tire and should not be measured here. Measure only at the inside of the wheel.

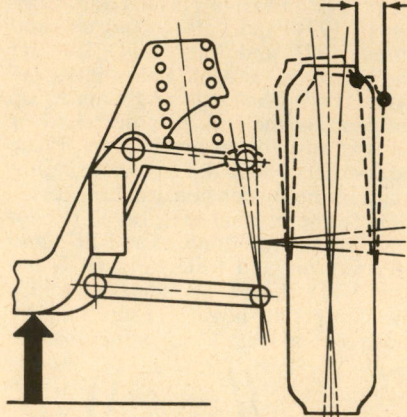

Measuring upper ball joint radial play
—spring on upper arm
(© Ford Motor Co)

REPLACEMENT
NOTE: *The factory procedure for ball joint replacement is to install a new upper control arm. The factory does not recommend installation of a new ball joint. However, ball joint replacements are available from auto parts dealers, and may be installed using the following procedure.*
1. Position a support between the upper arm and frame rail.
2. Raise the vehicle and remove the tire and wheel.
3. Remove the upper ball joint cotter pin and loosen the nut.
4. Using a ball joint removal tool, loosen the ball joint in the spindle.
5. Remove the three ball joint retaining rivets using a large chisel.
6. Remove the nut from the ball joint stud and remove the ball joint.
7. Clean and remove all burrs from the ball joint mounting area of the control arm before installing new ball joint.
8. Install the ball joint in the upper arm using the service part nuts and bolts. Do not attempt to rivet a new ball joint to the arm.
9. Install and tighten the ball joint stud nut and install the cotter pin.
10. Lubricate the new joint with a hand type grease gun only; using an air pressure gun may loosen the ball joint seal.
11. Install wheel, lower vehicle and remove upper arm support.
12. Check front end alignment.

Upper Control Arm Replacement
NOTE: *The upper arm shaft and bushings may not be replaced separate from the upper arm.*
1. Remove the shock absorber and upper mounting bracket from the car as an assembly. Install a wood block as a support between the upper arm and the body.

2. Raise the vehicle and remove the wheel and tire as an assembly.
3. Install spring compressor tool.
4. Place a safety stand under the lower arm.
5. Remove the cotter pin from the upper ball joint stud and loosen the nut.
6. Using a ball joint removal tool, loosen the ball joint in the spindle, then remove the nut and lift the stud from the spindle.
7. Remove the upper arm attaching nuts from the engine compartment and remove the upper arm.
8. To install the arm, position it on the mounting bracket and install the attaching nuts on the inner shaft attaching bolts. Torque to 85-100 ft. lbs. through 1977, or 110-130 ft. lbs. thereafter.

NOTE: *The original equipment (through 1977) keystone-type lockwashers must be used with the inner shaft attaching nuts and bolts.*

9. Install the upper ball joint stud in the spindle and tighten the nut according to the procedure in Step 12 of the lower ball joint procedure. Install a new cotter pin.
10. Remove spring compressor and position spring on upper arm. Install wheel and check front end alignment.

Chilton's TIME SAVER

When upper control arm bushings become low on lubrication, they become very noisy. This can often be corrected by lubrication; it is not necessary to replace the bushings. On early models that do not contain grease plugs it is necessary to drill and tap the bushing to accept a grease fitting. On later models with grease plugs it is difficult to remove the plug and grease the bushing with conventional tools. Ford Motor Co. has available an upper A-arm lubrication kit which greatly eases the performance of this operation.

T70P-3068-D

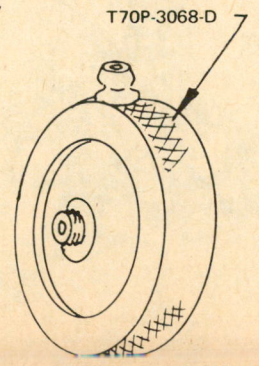

Upper control arm lubricating tool
© Ford Motor Co

COIL SPRING ON LOWER ARM

Shock Absorber Removal and Replacement

NOTE: *Purge a new shock of air by repeatedly extending it in its normal position and compressing it while inverted.*

1. Remove the nut, washer, and bushing from the upper end of the shock absorber.
2. Raise the vehicle and install jackstands under the frame rails.
3. Remove the two bolts securing the shock absorber to the lower control arm and remove the shock absorber.
4. Install a new bushing and washer on the top of the shock absorber and position the unit inside the front spring. Install the two lower attaching bolts and torque them to 8–15 ft lbs:
5. Remove the jackstands and lower the vehicle.
6. Place a new bushing and washer on the shock absorber top stud and install a new attaching nut. Torque to 22–30 ft lbs.

Coil Spring and Lower Control Arm Removal and Installation

1. Raise car and support it with stands placed in back of lower arms.
2. If equipped with drum type brakes, remove the wheel and brake drum as an assembly. Remove the brake backing plate attaching bolts and remove the backing plate from the spindle. Wire the assembly back out of the way.
3. If equipped with disc brakes, remove the wheel from the hub. Remove the bolts and washers that hold the caliper and brake hose bracket to the spindle. Remove the caliper from the rotor and wire it back out of the way. Then, remove the hub and rotor from the spindle.
4. Disconnect lower end of the shock absorber and push it up to the retracted position.
5. Disconnect stabilizer bar link from the lower arm.
6. Remove cotter pins from the upper and lower ball joint stud nuts.
7. Remove two bolts and nuts holding the strut to the lower arm. Remove the jounce bumper, if equipped.
8. Loosen the lower ball joint stud nut two turns. Do not remove this nut.
9. Install a spreader tool between the upper and lower ball joint studs.
10. Expand the tool until the tool exerts considerable pressure on the studs. Tap the spindle near the lower stud with a hammer to loosen the stud. Do not loosen the stud with tool pressure only.
11. Position floor jack under the lower arm and remove the lower ball joint stud nut.

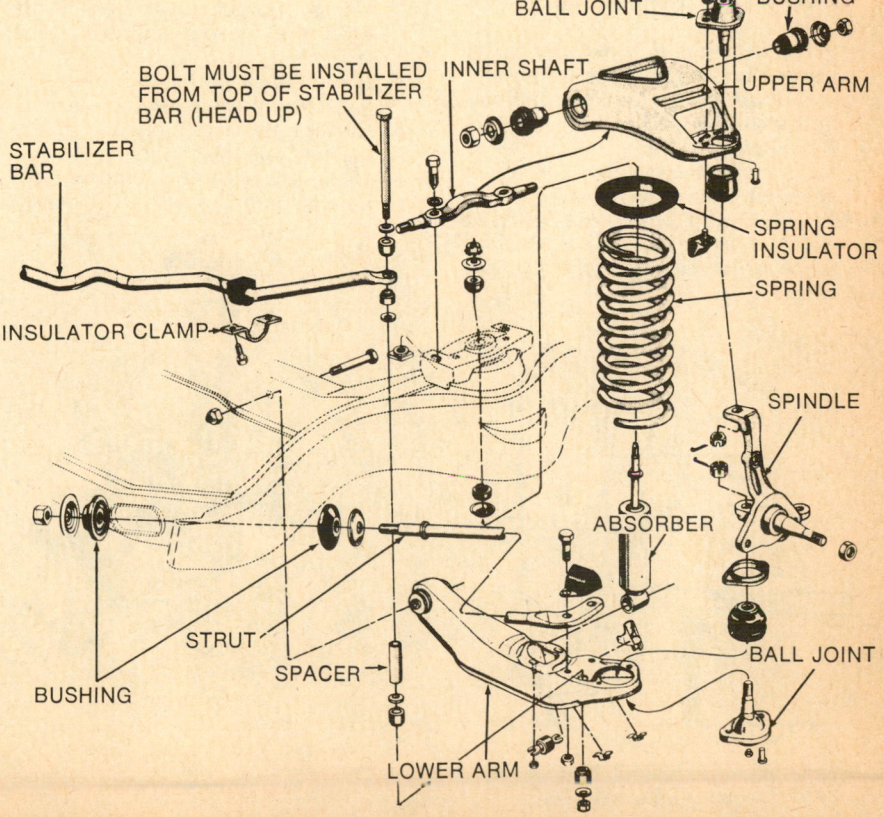

Front suspension—spring on lower arm © Ford Motor Co

12. Lower floor jack and remove the spring and insulator.
13. Remove the A-arm to crossmember attaching parts, and remove the arm from the car.
14. To install, loosely attach the lower arm to the crossmember using a new pivot bolt and nut. Do not tighten.
15. Position the spring and insulator within the control arms; the lower end of the spring must be no more than 1/2 in. from the end of the lower arm depression. Raise the arm with the floor jack, aligning the ball joint stud with the spindle.
16. Install the stud nut and torque to 75 ft. lbs., then continue to tighten until the holes align. Install new cotter pins in the upper and lower studs.
17. Reattach the shock absorber (8-15 ft. lbs.) and the jounce bumper. Using new bolts and nuts, install the stabilizer bar and torque to 6-12 ft. lbs. Reinstall the wheel and brake parts, and lower the car. Torque the lower arm pivot bolt to 95-110 ft. lbs. Check the alignment.

Lower Ball Joint
INSPECTION
1. Raise the vehicle by placing a floor jack under the lower arm; or, raise the vehicle on a hoist and place a jack stand under the lower arm and lower the vehicle onto it to remove the preload from the lower ball joint.
2. Have an assistant grasp the wheel top and bottom and apply alternate in and out pressure to the top and bottom of the wheel.
3. Radial play of 1/4 in. is acceptable measured at the inside of the wheel adjacent to the lower arm.

NOTE: *This radial play is multiplied at the outer circumference of the tire and should be measured only at the inside of the wheel.*

Upper Ball Joint
INSPECTION
1. Raise the vehicle by placing a floor jack under the lower arm. Do not allow the lower arm to hang freely with the vehicle on a hoist or bumper jack.
2. Have an assistant grasp the bottom of the tire and move the wheel in and out.
3. As the wheel is being moved, observe the upper control arm where the spindle attaches to it. Any movement between the upper part of the spindle and the upper ball joint indicates a bad ball joint which must be replaced.

NOTE: *During this check the lower ball joint will be unloaded and may move; this is normal and not an indication of a bad ball joint. Also, do not mistake a loose wheel bearing for a defective ball joint.*

REPLACEMENT
NOTE: *Ford Motor Company recommends replacement of the control arm and ball joint as an assembly. However, aftermarket replacement parts are available, which can be installed using the following procedure. This procedure may be used on both upper and lower ball joints.*

1. Raise the vehicle on a hoist and allow the front wheels to fall to their full down position.
2. Drill a 1/8 in. hole completely through each ball joint attaching rivet.
3. Using a large chisel, cut off the head of each rivet and drive them from the arm.
4. Place a jack under the lower arm and lower the vehicle about 6 in.
5. Remove the cotter pin and attaching nut from the ball joint stud.
6. Using a ball joint removal tool, loosen the ball joint stud from the spindle and remove the ball joint from the arm.
7. Clean all metal burrs from the arm and install the new ball joint, using the service part nuts and bolts to attach the ball joint. Do not attempt to rerivet the ball joint once it has been removed.
8. Check front end alignment.

Upper Control Arm
Replacement
1. Raise the front of the car and support the frame with stands.
2. Remove the tire and wheel. With drum brakes, remove the brake drum.
3. Remove the upper ball joint stud nut cotter pin. Loosen the stud nut but do not remove it.
4. Install a ball joint stud removal tool. Tighten the tool, then tap the spindle near the upper stud to loosen the stud in the spindle. Do not loosen the stud with tool pressure only.
5. Remove the tool. Raise the lower arm with a jack to relieve pressure on the upper stud nut. Remove the nut.
6. Remove the upper arm shaft attaching bolts and the arm.
7. To install, attach the upper arm bolts to a snug fit but do not tighten yet.
8. Install the ball joint stud into the spindle and install the stud nut. Tighten the stud nut to 75 ft. lbs., then continue to tighten until the cotter pin holes align. Install new cotter pin.
9. Install the wheel and tire (and drum with drum brakes) and adjust the front wheel bearing. Lower the car and adjust the front end alignment, then tighten the upper arm attaching bolts to 120-140 ft. lbs.

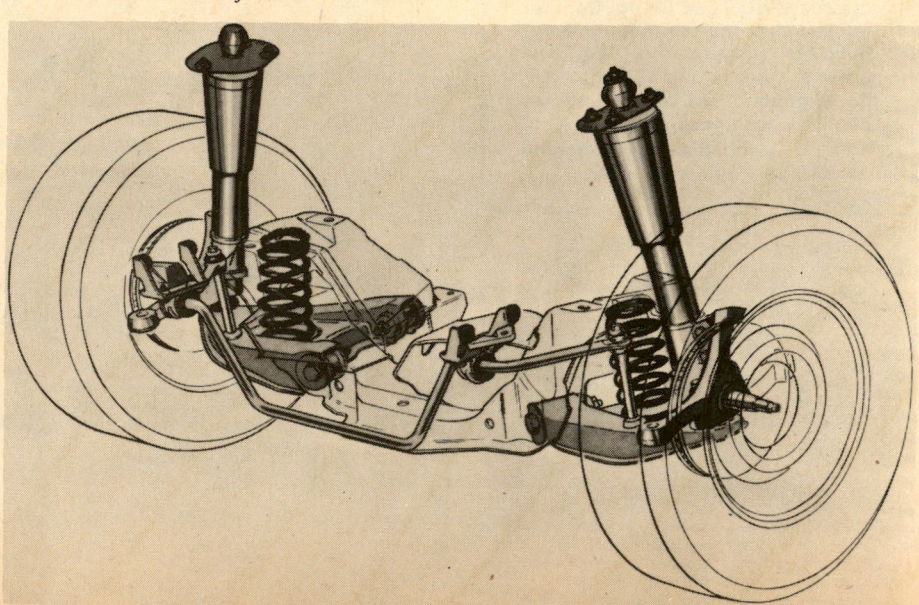

MAXIMUM TOLERANCE

Measuring lower ball joint radial play —spring on lower arm
(© Ford Motor Co)

Fairmont and Zephyr Front Suspension (© Ford Motor Co.)

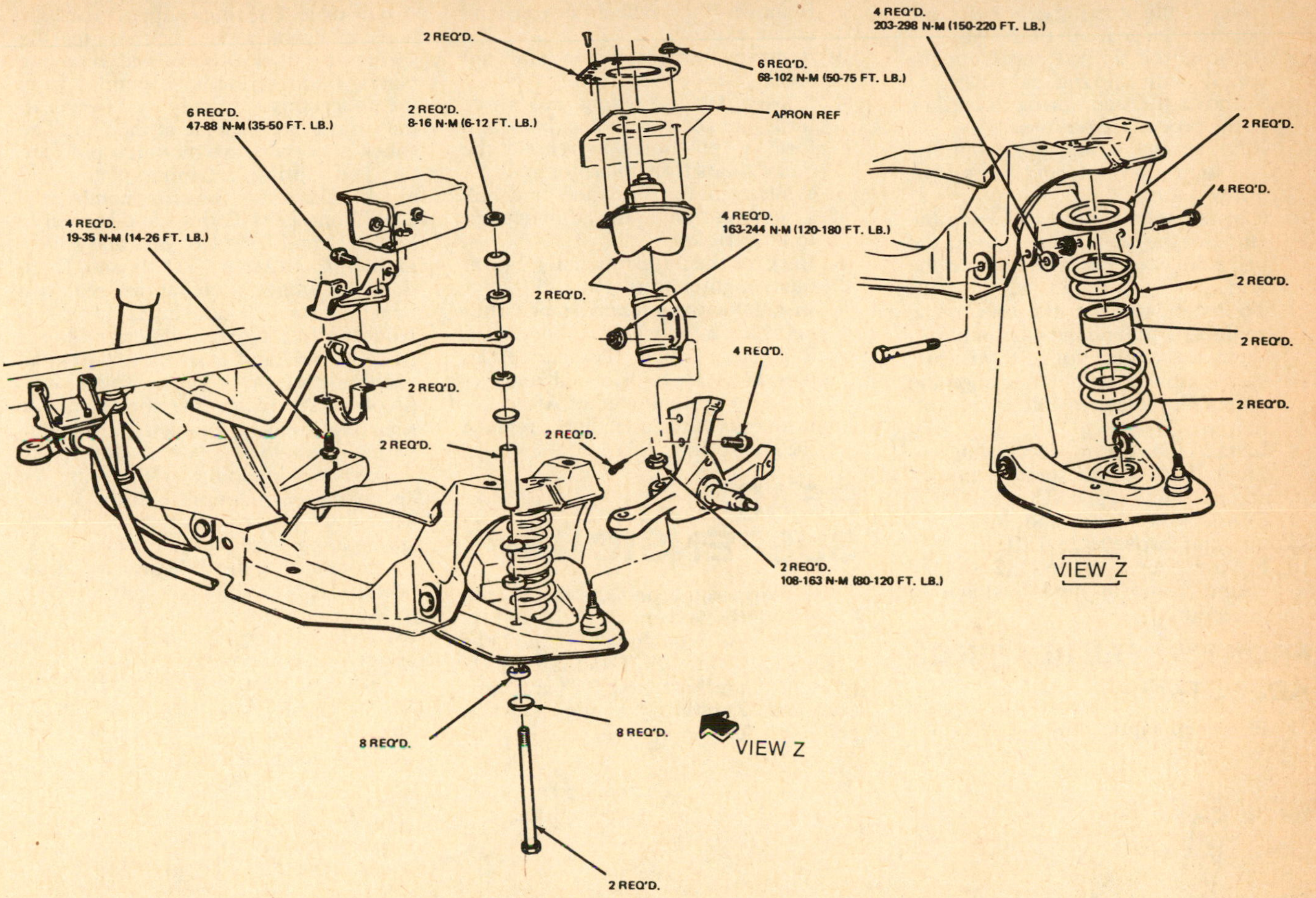

2 REQ'D.

6 REQ'D.
68-102 N·M (50-75 FT. LB.)

4 REQ'D.
203-298 N·M (150-220 FT. LB.)

APRON REF

6 REQ'D.
47-88 N·M (35-50 FT. LB.)

2 REQ'D.
8-16 N·M (6-12 FT. LB.)

2 REQ'D.

4 REQ'D.
19-35 N·M (14-26 FT. LB.)

4 REQ'D.
163-244 N·M (120-180 FT. LB.)

2 REQ'D.

4 REQ'D.

2 REQ'D.

2 REQ'D.

2 REQ'D.

2 REQ'D.

2 REQ'D.

2 REQ'D.

2 REQ'D.

4 REQ'D.

2 REQ'D.

2 REQ'D.
108-163 N·M (80-120 FT. LB.)

VIEW Z

8 REQ'D.

8 REQ'D.

VIEW Z

2 REQ'D.

Fairmont/Zephyr single arm suspension; 1979 Mustang and Capri similar (© Ford Motor Co.)

SINGLE ARM FRONT SUSPENSION

Shock Strut Removal and Installation

1. Raise the front of the car and place stands under the jacking pads just aft of the lower arms.
2. Remove the wheel and tire. Raise the lower arm with a floor jack to compress the spring.
3. Remove the two lower shock strut nuts and bolts. Leave the strut in position.
4. Remove the three upper strut mounting nuts from within the engine compartment.
5. Compress the strut to clear the upper mount and remove the strut.
6. To install, place the lower end into the spindle, then extend the upper portion until the bolts are positioned. Install the upper nuts and torque to 60-75 ft. lbs.
7. Install the two lower retaining bolts and tighten to 150-180 ft. lbs.
8. Lower the jack and install the wheel and tire.

Ball Joint
INSPECTION

Only one ball joint is used on each side, located in the lower arm. It is pro-

vided with a grease fitting, which projects beyond the ball joint cover. When the checking surface (the round boss into which the grease fitting is threaded) is flush with the cover, the ball joint is due for replacement.

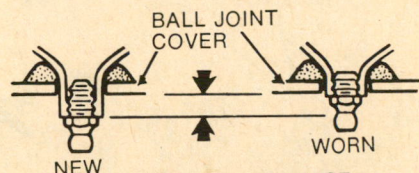

BALL JOINT COVER

NEW   WORN

CHECKING SURFACE

Ball joint wear indicator (© Ford Motor Co.)

REPLACEMENT

The ball joint and lower arm must be replaced as an assembly. Follow the instructions for arm replacement.

Coil Spring Removal and Installation

1. Raise and support the car with stands placed under the pads just behind the lower arms.
2. Remove the wheel and tire. Disconnect the stabilizer bar from the arm.
3. Remove the brake rotor dust shield.
4. Support the arm with a jack placed under both bushings.

5. Remove the steering gear bolts and move the gear out of the way.
6. Remove the two lower arm to crossmember bolts and nuts. Slowly lower the jack to relieve spring tension, and remove the spring.
7. To install, secure the upper spring insulation to the spring with tape. Install the spring damper within the spring, and the rubber hose over the last coil.
8. Place the spring in the upper pocket. Position the lower end between the two holes in the arm.
9. Raise the arm with the floor jack. Install the two bolts and nuts, and tighten to a snug fit.
10. Install the steering gear bolts; torque to 80-100 ft. lbs.
11. Install the rotor shield. Install the stabilizer bar link, and tighten to 9-12 ft. lbs.
12. Install the wheel and tire, remove the stands, and lower the car. With the weight of the car on the suspension, tighten the arm nuts to 200-220 ft. lbs.

Lower Arm Removal and Installation

1. Perform Steps 1-3 of the spring removal and installation procedure.

2. Remove the steering gear bolts and position the gear out of the way.
3. Remove the tie rod end from the spindle with a tie rod end puller.
4. Remove the coil spring according to the procedure outlined.
5. Remove the cotter pin from the ball joint stud nut, and loosen the nut two turns.
6. Rap the spindle boss to loosen the stud in the spindle. Remove the ball joint stud nut and remove the arm.
7. To install, position the arm to the spindle, installing the stud in place. Tighten the stud nut to 80 ft. lbs., then continue to tighten to align the cotter pin holes. Install a new cotter pin.
8. Install the spring according to Steps 7-10 of the spring removal and installation procedure.
9. Connect the tie rod end, install the nut, and torque to 35-47 ft. lbs.
10. Follow Steps 11 and 12 of the spring removal and installation procedure.

FRONT WHEEL BEARING ADJUSTMENT

1. Raise and support the vehicle.

2. Remove the wheel cover and grease cap.
3. Remove the cotter pin and nut lock.
4. Loosen the adjusting nut three turns and rock the wheel back and forth a few times to release the brake shoes from the rotor.
5. While rotating the wheel and hub assembly, tighten the adjusting nut to 17-25 ft. lbs.
6. Back off the adjusting nut 1/2 turn, then retighten to 10-15 in. lbs.
7. Install the locknut and a new cotter pin. Check the wheel rotation. If it is noisy or rough, the bearings either need to be cleaned and repacked, or readjusted. After adjustments are complete, replace the grease cap.

REAR SUSPENSION

All intermediate and compact-sized Ford products, except the 1972 and later Torino and Montego, 1974 and later Cougar and Elite, 1977 and later LTD II and Thunderbird, and 1978 and later Fairmont, Zephyr, Mustang, and Capri, use a leaf-spring rear suspension.

A pair of leaf springs support the axle housing, which is secured to the springs by two U-bolts and retaining plates. Each spring is suspended from the underbody side rails by a hanger at the front and a shackle at the rear. The shock absorbers are mounted between the leaf spring retaining plates and brackets bolted to the crossmember.

1972 and later Torinos and Montegos and 1974 and later Cougars and Elites, and 1977 and later LTD IIs and Thunderbirds, utilize a coil spring rear suspension. The axle housing is suspended from the frame by an upper and lower trailing arm, and a shock absorber at each side of the vehicle. These arms pivot in the frame members and the rear axle housing brackets. Each coil spring is mounted between a lower seat which is welded to the axle housing and an upper seat integral with the frame. The shock absorbers are bolted to the spring upper seats at the top and brackets mounted on the axle housing at the bottom. A rear stabilizer bar, attached to the frame side rail brackets and the two axle housing brackets, is available as optional equipment.

1978 and later Fairmonts, Zephyrs, Mustangs, and Capris have a four bar link coil spring suspension. The lower

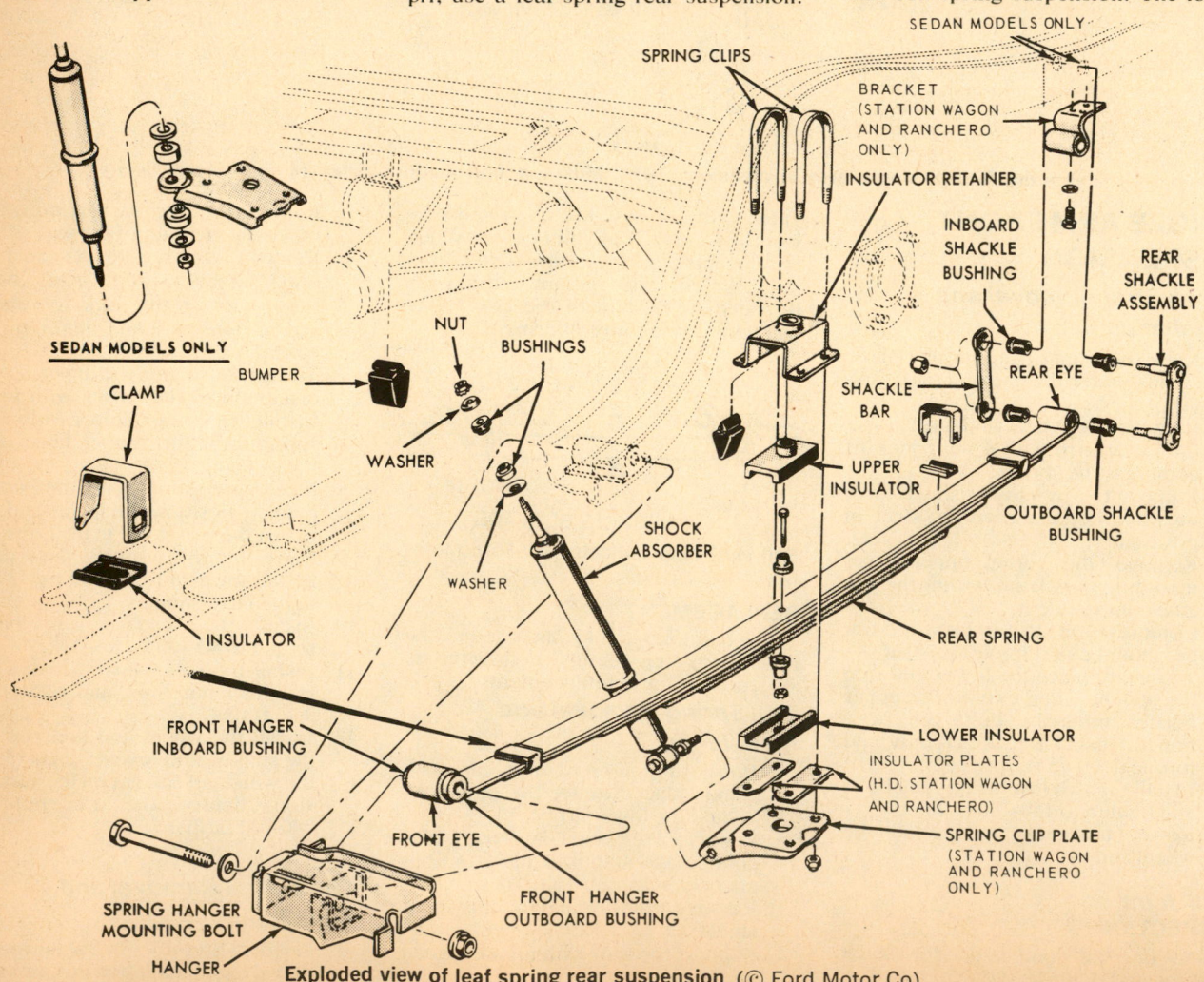

Exploded view of leaf spring rear suspension (© Ford Motor Co)

links are parallel to the frame, and serve to locate the lower end of the coil springs. The upper links are angled 45° toward the differential housing. Shock absorbers are mounted vertically at the outside of the frame rails. The rear stabilizer bar, optional on some models, mounts to the two lower links.

LEAF SPRING SUSPENSION

Spring Removal and Installation

1. Raise the vehicle and place supports beneath the underbody and axle.
2. Disconnect the lower end of the shock absorber from the spring clip plate and position it out of the way. Remove the supports from under the axle.
3. Remove the spring plate nuts from the U-bolt and remove the spring plate. With a jack, raise the rear axle just enough to remove the weight of the housing from the spring.
4. Remove the two rear shackle attaching nuts, the shackle bar, and the two inner bushings.
5. Remove the rear shackle assembly and the two outer bushings.
6. Remove the nut from the spring mounting bolt and tap the bolt out of the bushing at the front hanger. Lift out the spring assembly.

NOTE: *All used attaching components (nuts, bolts, etc.) must be discarded and replaced with new ones prior to assembly. Bushings may be lubricated with soap and water to ease bolt installation; do not use grease or oil.*

7. Position the leaf spring under the axle housing and insert the shackle assembly into the rear hanger bracket and the rear eye of the spring.
8. Install the shackle inner bushings, the shackle plate, and the locknuts. Hand-tighten the locknuts.
9. Position the spring eye in the front hanger, slip the washer on the front hanger bolt, and, from the inboard side, insert the bolt through the hanger and eye. Install the locknut on the hanger bolt finger-tight.
10. Lower the rear axle housing so that it rests on the spring. Place the spring plate on the U-bolt and tighten the nuts.
11. Attach the lower end of the shock absorber to the spring plate using a new nut.
12. Place jackstands under the rear axle. Lower the vehicle until the spring is in the approximate curb load position, and tighten the front hanger locknut.
13. Tighten the rear shackle locknuts.
14. Remove the jackstands and lower the vehicle.

Shock Absorber Removal and Installation

NOTE: *Purge a new shock of air by re-*

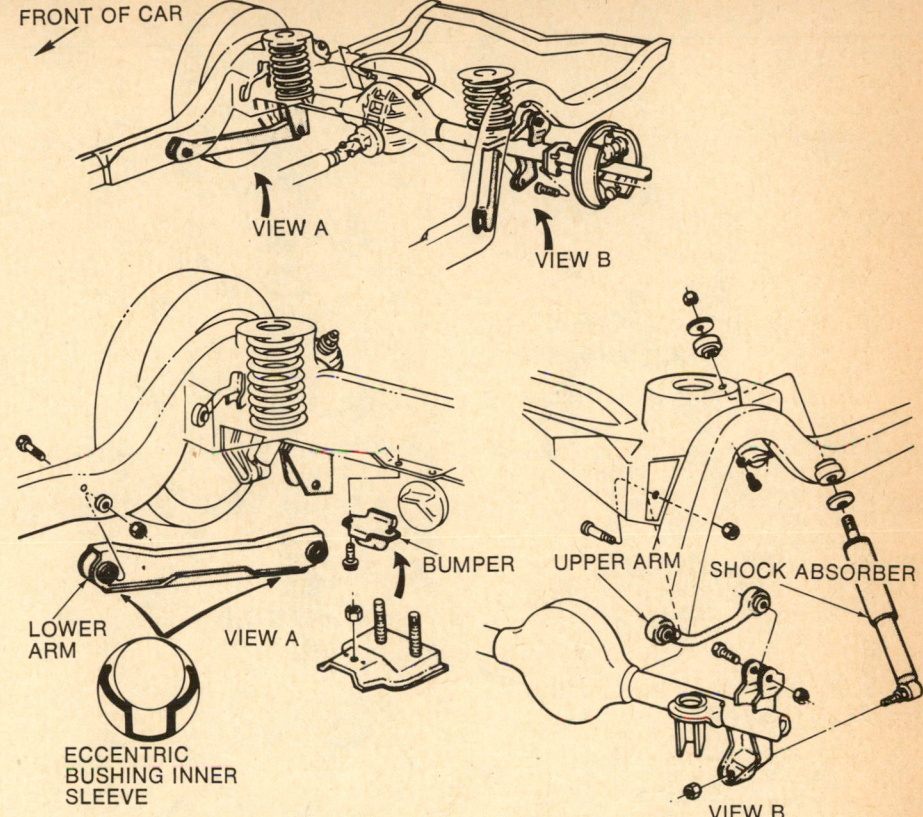

Coil spring rear suspension (© Ford Motor Co)

peatedly extending it in its normal position and compressing it while inverted.

MUSTANG AND COUGAR THROUGH 1973

1. Disconnect the shock absorber at the spring plate.
2. Remove the shock absorber access cover from the trunk. Remove the rear seat from convertibles to reach the access cover.
3. Remove the shock absorber upper retaining nut.
4. Compress and remove the shock absorber. Remove all bushings and washers from the unit.
5. Place new inner bushings and washers on the shock absorber studs.
6. Connect the upper stud to the mounting. Install a new outer bushing, washer, and nut on the stud. Install the access cover.
7. Connect the lower stud to the spring plate. Install a new outer bushing, washer, and nut on the stud. Be sure that the spring plate is free of burrs.

MAVERICK, COMET, GRANADA, MONARCH, VERSAILLES

1. Remove the lower end of the shock absorber from the spring plate.
2. Remove the nut retaining the upper end of the shock absorber to the mounting bracket underneath the car.

3. Compress and remove the shock absorber. Discard the nuts.
4. Transfer the washers and bushings to the new shock absorber. Insert the upper stud through the mounting bracket, and install a new attaching nut finger-tight.
5. Compress and install the shock absorber to the spring plate. Install the washers, bushings, and attaching nuts.
6. Tighten the upper and lower attaching nuts.

COIL SPRING SUSPENSION

Spring Removal and Installation

ALL EXCEPT FAIRMONT, ZEPHYR, 1979 MUSTANG AND CAPRI

1. Place a jack under the rear axle housing. Raise the vehicle and place jackstands under the frame side rails.
2. Disconnect the lower studs of the shock absorbers from the mounting brackets on the axle housing.
3. Lower the axle housing until the springs are fully released.
4. Remove the springs and insulators from the vehicle.
5. Place the insulators in each upper seat and position the springs between the upper and lower seats.
6. With the springs in position, raise the axle housing until the lower studs of the rear shock absorbers

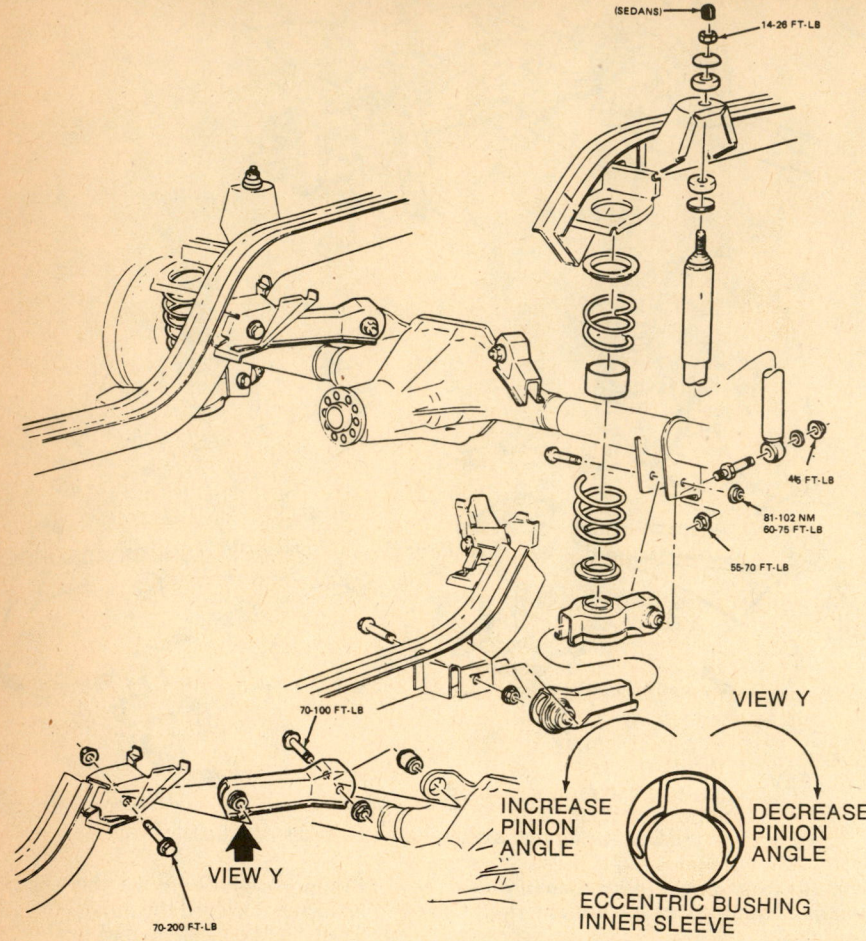

(SEDANS) 14-26 FT-LB

45 FT-LB

81-102 NM
60-75 FT-LB

55-70 FT-LB

70-100 FT-LB

70-200 FT-LB

VIEW Y

VIEW Y

INCREASE PINION ANGLE

DECREASE PINION ANGLE

ECCENTRIC BUSHING INNER SLEEVE

Four-bar link coil spring suspension (© Ford Motor Co.)

reach the mounting brackets on the axle housing. Connect the lower studs and install the attaching nuts.
7. Remove the jackstands and lower the vehicle.

FAIRMONT, ZEPHYR, 1979 MUSTANG, CAPRI

NOTE: *If one spring must be replaced, the other should be replaced also. If the car has a stabilizer bar, the bar must be removed first.*

1. Raise and support the car at the rear crossmember, while supporting the axle with a jack.
2. Lower the axle until the shocks are fully extended.

3. Place a jack under the lower arm pivot bolt. Remove the pivot bolt and nut. Carefully and slowly lower the arm until the spring load is relieved.
4. Remove the spring and insulators.
5. To install, tape the insulator in place in the frame, and place the lower insulator in place on the arm. Install the internal damper in the spring.
6. Position the spring in place and slowly raise the jack under the lower arm. Install the pivot bolt and nut, with the nut facing outwards. Do not tighten the nut.
7. Raise the axle to curb height, and

tighten the lower pivot bolt to 70-100 ft. lbs.
8. Install the stabilizer bar, if removed. The proper torque is 30-40 ft. lbs. Remove the crossmember stands and lower the car.

Shock Absorber Removal and Installation

NOTE: *Purge a new shock of air by repeatedly extending it in its normal position and compressing it while inverted.*

ALL EXCEPT FAIRMONT, ZEPHYR, 1979 MUSTANG AND CAPRI

1. Raise the vehicle and install jackstands.
2. Remove the shock absorber outer attaching nut, washer and insulator from the stud at the top side of the spring upper seat. Compress the shock sufficiently to clear the spring seat hole, and remove the inner insulator and washer from the upper attaching stud.
3. Remove the locknut and disconnect the shock absorber lower stud at the mounting bracket on the axle housing. Remove the shock absorber.
4. Position a new inner washer and insulator on the upper attaching stud. Place the upper stud in the hole in the upper spring seat. While maintaining the shock in this position, install a new outer insulator, washer, and nut on the stud from the top side of the spring upper seat.
5. Extend the shock absorber. Locate the lower stud in the mounting bracket hole on the axle housing and install the locknut.

FAIRMONT, ZEPHYR, 1979 MUSTANG, CAPRI

1. Remove the upper attaching nut, washer, and insulator. Access is through the trunk on sedans or side panel trim covers on station wagons. Sedan studs have rubber caps.
2. Raise the car. Compress the shock to clear the upper tower. Remove the lower nut and washer; remove the shock.
3. Purge the shock of air and compress. Place the lower mounting eye over the lower stud and install the washer and a new locking nut. Do not tighten the nut yet.
4. Place the insulator and washer on the upper stud. Extend the shock, installing the stud through the upper mounting hole.
5. Torque the lower mounting nut to 40-55 ft.lbs.
6. Lower the car. Install the outer insulator and washer on the upper stud, and install a new nut. Tighten to 14-26 ft. lbs. Install the trim panel on station wagons or the rubber cap on sedans.

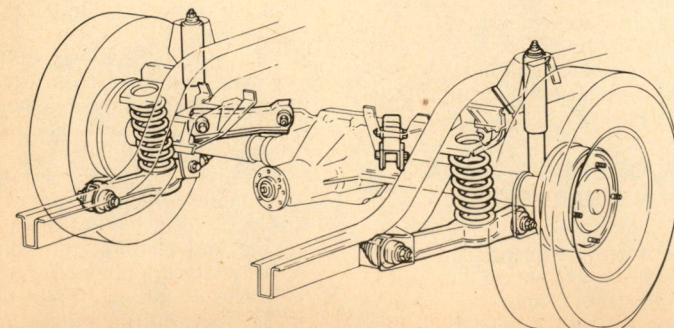

1979 Mustang and Capri rear suspension (© Ford Motor Co.)

BRAKES

An independent parking brake operates the rear wheel brake shoes or pads through a mechanical cable linkage. Front disc brakes have been available on front wheels of most models. Rear disc brakes are standard on Versailles and available on Granada and Monarch when equipped with the hydraulically assisted Hydro-Boost System. Complete Service Procedures are in the Unit Repair Section.

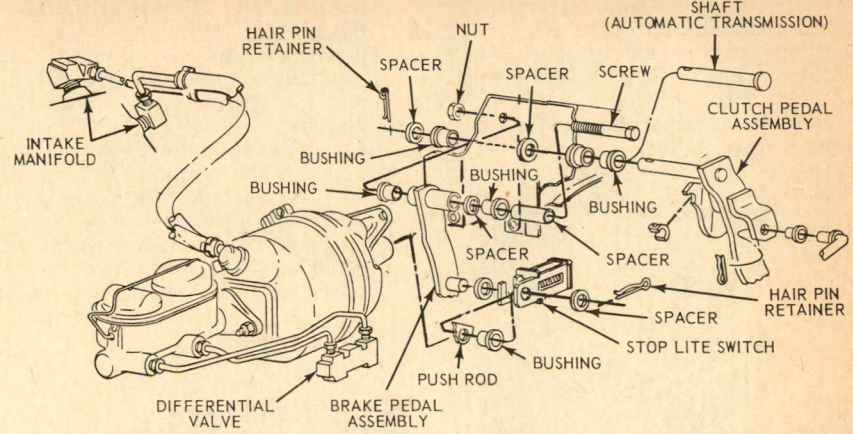

Typical vacuum brake booster installation (© Ford Motor Co.)

Master Cylinder Removal and Installation

A tandem-type (dual) master cylinder is used on all models. This design divides the brake hydraulic system into two independent and hydraulically separated halves. In the event of a single hydraulic failure, 50% braking efficiency is maintained.

STANDARD BRAKES

1. Working under the dash, disconnect the master cylinder pushrod from the brake pedal. The pushrod cannot be removed from the master cylinder.
2. Disconnect the stoplight switch wires and remove the switch from the brake pedal, using care not to damage the switch.
3. Disconnect the brake lines from the master cylinder.
4. Remove the attaching screws from the firewall and remove the master cylinder from the car.
5. Reinstall in reverse order, leaving the brake line fittings loose at the master cylinder.
6. Fill the master cylinder, and with the brake lines loose, slowly bleed the air from the master cylinder using the foot pedal.

POWER BRAKES

1. Disconnect the brake lines from the master cylinder.
2. Remove the two nuts and lockwashers that attach the master cylinder to the brake booster.
3. Remove the master cylinder from the booster.
4. Reverse the procedure to reinstall.
5. Fill master cylinder and bleed entire brake system.
6. Refill master cylinder.

Power Brake Vacuum Unit Removal and Installation

1. Working inside the car below the instrument panel, disconnect booster valve operating rod from the brake pedal assembly.

   To do this, disconnect the stop light switch wires at the connector. Remove the hairpin retainer and nylon washer from the pedal pin. Slide the switch off just enough for the outer arm to clear the pin. Re-

move the switch. Slide the booster push rod, bushing and inner nylon washer off the pedal pin.
2. Remove the air cleaner for working clearance if necessary. On four cylinder models, disconnect the accelerator cable at the carburetor. Remove the securing screw from the accelerator shaft bracket and remove the cable from the bracket. Remove the two screws attaching the bracket to the manifold; rotate the bracket toward the engine.
3. Disconnect the brake lines at the master cylinder outlet fittings.
4. Disconnect manifold vacuum hose from the booster unit. On cars equipped with speed control, remove the left cowl screen in the engine compartment. Remove three nuts retaining the speed control servo to the firewall and move the servo out of the way.
5. Remove the four bracket-to-firewall attaching bolts.
6. Remove the booster and bracket assembly from the firewall, sliding the valve operating rod out from the engine side.
7. Installation is the reverse of removal. Bleed the brakes after installation is complete.

Hydro-Boost Power Unit Removal and Installation

See the Lincoln section.

Parking Brake Adjustment

NOTE: *If a new cable is installed, pre-stretch it by applying and releasing five times before making any adjustments.*

REAR DRUM BRAKES

In most cases, a rear brake shoe adjustment will provide satisfactory parking brake action. However, if parking brake cables are excessively loose after releasing the handbrake, proceed as follows:

1. On handle-actuated systems pull up the handle to the third notch. On pedal-actuated systems, depress the parking brake pedal one notch from its normal released position.
2. Loosen locknut on equalizer rod under the car. Then loosen the nut in front of the equalizer, several turns.
3. Turn the locknut forward against the equalizer until the cables are tight enough so that the rear wheels cannot be turned by hand. Then,

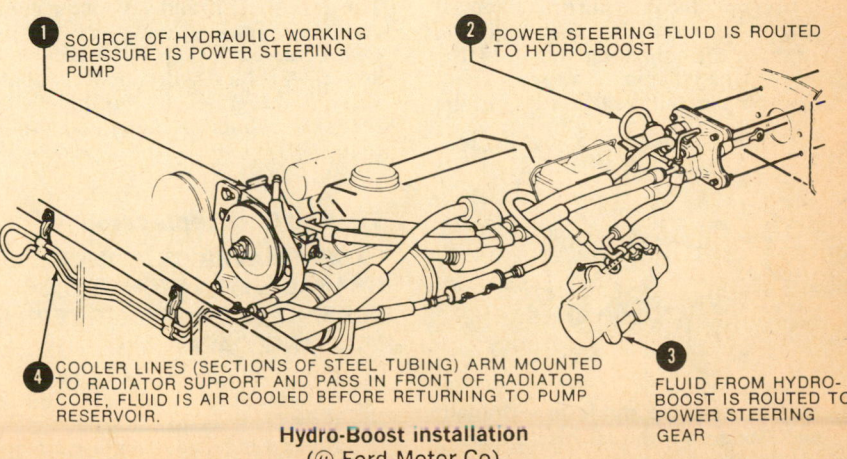

Hydro-Boost installation
(© Ford Motor Co)

back off the adjustment until the rear wheels turn freely.

4. When cables are properly adjusted, tighten both nuts against the equalizer.

5. Release the brake and feel for freeness of rear wheels.

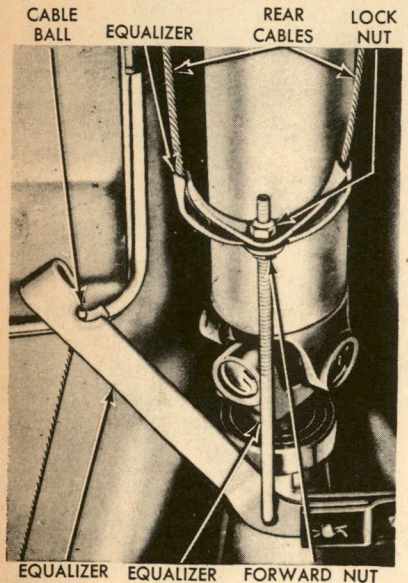

Parking brake linkage (© Ford Motor Co)

DISC BRAKES

1. Fully release the parking brake.
2. Place the transmission in Neutral. If it is necessary to raise the car to reach the adjusting nut and observe the parking brake levers, use an axle hoist or a floor jack positioned beneath the differential. This is necessary so that the rear axle remains at the curb attitude, not stretching the parking brake cables.

—— CAUTION ——

If you are raising the rear of the car only, block the front wheels.

3. Locate the adjusting nut beneath the car on the driver's side. While observing the parking brake actuating levers on the rear calipers, tighten the adjusting nut until the levers just begin to move. Then, loosen the nut sufficiently for the

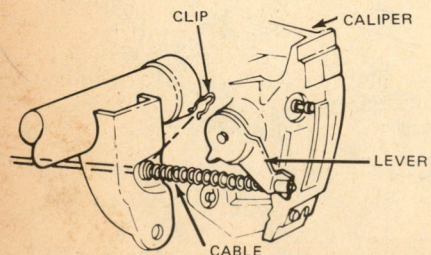

Parking brake cable and lever—Granada and Monarch with rear disc brakes
(© Ford Motor Co)

levers to fully return to the stop position. The levers are in the stop position when a 1/4 in. pin can be inserted past the side of the lever into the holes in the cast iron housing.

4. Check the operation of the parking brake. Make sure the actuating levers return to the stop position by attempting to pull them rearward. If the lever moves rearward, the cable adjustment is too tight, which will cause a dragging rear brake and consequent brake overheating and fade.

STEERING

The manual steering gear is of the worm and recirculating ball type except on Fairmont, Zephyr, 1979 Mustang and Capri which have rack and pinion steering.

Power steering is available as an option. On all compact and intermediate Ford products, except the Mustang through 1973, 1972 and later Torino and Montego, the 1974 and later Cougar and Elite, the 1977 and later LTD II and Thunderbird, and the Fairmont, Zephyr, 1979 Mustang and Capri, the power steering system is the Bendix non-integral type. The Bendix system utilizes the manual worm and recirculating ball steering gear. Hydraulic assist is provided externally to the steering linkage via a power steering pump, power cylinder, and control valve. The Mustangs and Cougars use the Saginaw integral system, while the 1972 and later Torinos and Montegos and 1974 and later Cougars and Elites, and 1977 and later LTD IIs and Thunderbirds use the Ford integral system. On both types, hydraulic assist is directly applied to the steering gear, eliminating all hoses and hardware which were previously mounted under the chassis on the Bendix system.

Fairmonts, Zephyrs, 1979 Mustangs and Capris use an integral rack and pinion variable ratio rack and pinion gear, manufactured by either Ford or TRW. The gear housing and valve housing are combined into a one-piece casting. Quick connect fittings allow the lines to swivel. A rotary hydraulic fluid control valve is integrated to the input shaft; the boost cylinder is integrated with the rack.

Tie Rod End Replacement

EXCEPT MAVERICK, COMET, GRANADA, MONARCH, VERSAILLES, FAIRMONT, ZEPHYR, MUSTANG, CAPRI

1. Raise and support the front end.
2. Remove the cotter pin and nut from the rod end ball stud.
3. Loosen the sleeve and clamp bolts and remove the rod end from the

spindle arm center link using a ball joint separator.

4. Remove the rod end from the sleeve, counting the exact number of turns required.
5. Install the new end using the exact number of turns it took to remove the old one.
6. Install all parts. Torque the stud to 40-43 ft lbs, and the clamp to 20-22 ft lbs.
7. Check the toe-in.

MAVERICK, COMET, GRANADA, MONARCH, VERSAILLES

1. Raise and support the front end.
2. Remove and discard the cotter pin and nut from the rod end ball stud.
3. Disconnect the rod end from the spindle arm or center link.
4. Loosen the rod sleeve clamp bolts and turn the rod to remove. Count the exact number if turns required.
5. Install a new rod end using the exact number of turns it took to remove the old one.
6. Install all parts in reverse of removal. Torque stud to 40-43 ft lbs and clamp to 20-22 ft lbs.
7. Check the toe-in.

FAIRMONT, ZEPHYR, 1979 MUSTANG, CAPRI

1. Remove the cotter pin and nut at the spindle. Separate the tie rod end stud from the spindle with a puller.
2. Matchmark the position of the locknut with paint on the tie rod. Unscrew the locknut. Unscrew the tie rod end, counting the number of turns required to remove.
3. Install the new end the same number of turns. Attach the tie rod end stud to the spindle. Install the nut and torque to 35 ft. lbs., then continue to tighten until the cotter pin holes align. Install a new cotter pin. Check the toe and adjust if necessary, then torque the tie rod end locknut to 35 ft. lbs.

Power Steering Pump Removal and Installation

1. Drain the fluid from the pump reservoir by disconnecting the fluid return hose at the pump. Then, disconnect the pressure hose from the pump.
2. Remove the mounting bolts from the front of the pump. On eight cylinder engines through 1977, there is a nut on the rear of the pump that must be removed. After removal, move the pump inward to loosen the belt tension and remove the belt from the pulley. Then, remove the pump from the car.
3. To reinstall the pump, position on mounting bracket and loosely install the mounting bolts and nuts. Put the drive belt over the pulley and move the pump outward

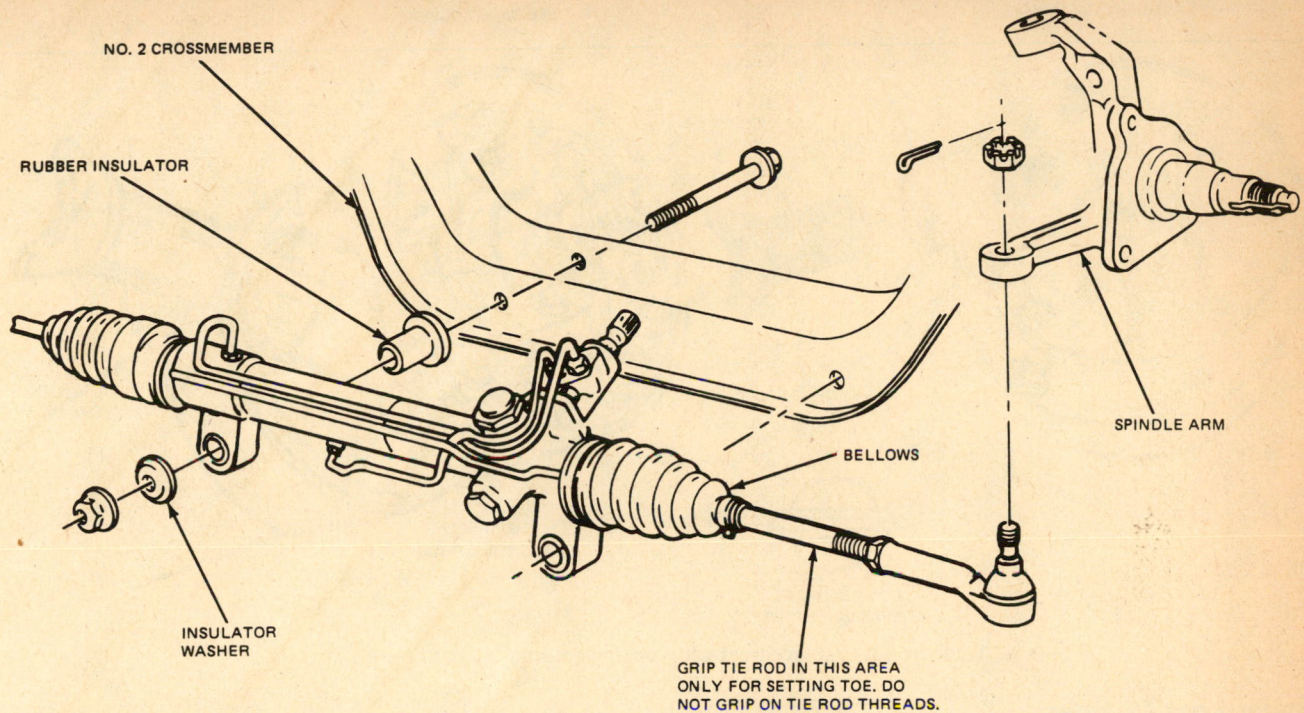

NO. 2 CROSSMEMBER

RUBBER INSULATOR

SPINDLE ARM

BELLOWS

INSULATOR WASHER

GRIP TIE ROD IN THIS AREA ONLY FOR SETTING TOE. DO NOT GRIP ON TIE ROD THREADS.

Fairmont, Zephyr, 1979 Mustang and Capri power steering gear and tie rod end installation (© Ford Motor Co.)

against the belt until the proper belt tension is obtained. Do not pry against the pump body. Measure the belt tension with a belt tension gauge for the proper adjustment. Only in cases where a belt tension gauge is not available should the belt deflection method be used.

4. Tighten the mounting bolts and nuts.

Steering Wheel Removal and Installation

1. Open the hood and disconnect the negative cable from the battery.
2. On models with safety crash pads, remove the crash pad attaching screws from the underside of the steering wheel spoke and remove the pad. On all models equipped with a horn button, remove the horn button or ring by pressing down evenly and turning it counterclockwise approximately 20° and then lifting it from the steering wheel. On Fairmonts, Zephyrs, 1979 Mustangs and Capris, pull straight out on the hub cover. Disconnect the horn wires from the crash pad on models so equipped.
3. Remove and discard the nut from the end of the shaft. Install a steering wheel puller on the end of the shaft and remove the wheel.

—————— CAUTION ——————
The use of a knock-off type steering wheel puller or the use of a hammer on the steering shaft will damage the collapsible column.

4. Lubricate the upper surface of the steering shaft upper bushing with white grease. Transfer all serviceable parts to the new steering wheel.
5. Position the steering wheel on the shaft so that the alignment marks line up. Install a locknut and torque it to 20-30 ft lbs. Connect the horn wires.
6. Install the horn button or ring by turning it clockwise or install the crash pad.

Turn Signal Switch Removal and Installation

ALL EXCEPT FAIRMONT, ZEPHYR, 1979 MUSTANG AND CAPRI

1. Open the hood and disconnect the negative battery cable.
2. Remove the steering wheel.
3. Unscrew the turn signal handle from the side of the column. Remove the emergency flasher retainer and knob, if so equipped.
4. Remove the wire assembly cover and disconnect the wire connector plugs. Record the location and color code of each wire and tape the wires together. Make sure that the horn wires are disconnected. Remove the plastic cover from the wiring harness. Attach a piece of heavy cord to the switch wires to pull them through the column during installation.
5. Remove the retaining clips and attaching screws from the turn signal switch and pull the switch and wire assembly from the top of the column.

6. Tape the ends of the new switch wires together and transfer the pull cord to these wires.
7. Pull the wires down through the column with the cord and attach the new switch to the column hub.
8. Connect the wiring plugs to their mating plugs at the lower end of the column and install the plastic cover at the harness.
9. Install all retaining clips and wire assembly covers that were removed and install the turn signal handle. Install the emergency flasher retainer and knob, if so equipped.
10. Install the steering wheel and retaining nut.
11. Connect the negative battery cable.

FAIRMONT, ZEPHYR, 1979 MUSTANG AND CAPRI

1. Remove the four screws retaining the steering column shroud.
2. Remove the turn signal lever by pulling and twisting straight out
3. Peel back the foam shield. Disconnect the two electrical connectors.
4. Remove the two attaching screws and disengage the switch from the housing.
5. To install, position the switch to the housing and install the screws. Stick the foam to the switch.
6. Install the lever by aligning the key and pushing the lever fully home.
7. Install the two electrical connectors, test the switch, and install the shroud.

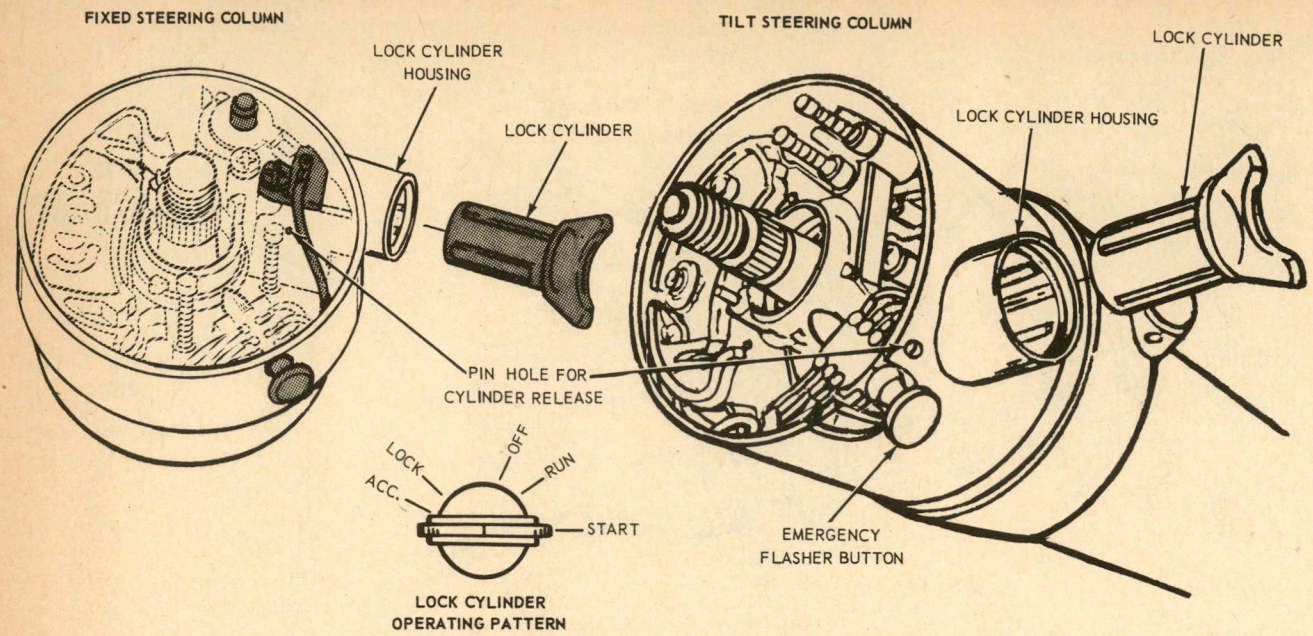

FIXED STEERING COLUMN

TILT STEERING COLUMN

LOCK CYLINDER HOUSING

LOCK CYLINDER

LOCK CYLINDER

LOCK CYLINDER HOUSING

PIN HOLE FOR CYLINDER RELEASE

LOCK
OFF
RUN
ACC.
START

EMERGENCY FLASHER BUTTON

LOCK CYLINDER OPERATING PATTERN

Lock cylinder replacement with locking column (© Ford Motor Co)

Ignition Lock Cylinder Replacement

1. Disconnect the negative battery cable.
2. On cars with a fixed steering column, remove the steering wheel trim pad and the steering wheel. Insert a stiff wire into the hold located in the lock cylinder housing. On cars with a tilt steering wheel, this hole is located on the outside of the steering column near the emergency flasher button and it is not necessary to remove the steering wheel. On Fairmonts, Zephyrs, 1979 Mustangs and Capris, remove the four column shroud screws. The hole in the casting is angled down toward the seat. Insert a 1/8 in. diameter wire.
3. Place the gear shift lever in Reverse on standard shift cars and in Park on cars with automatic transmission, and turn the ignition key to the ON or RUN position.
4. Depress wire and remove lock cylinder and wire.
5. Insert new cylinder into housing and turn to the OFF position. This will lock the cylinder into position.
6. Reinstall steering wheel and pad.
7. Connect negative battery cable.

Ignition Switch Replacement

1. Disconnect the negative battery cable.
2. Remove shrouding from the steering column. Detach and lower the steering column from the brake support bracket on all models except the Fairmont, Zephyr, 1979 Mustang and Capri.
3. Disconnect the switch wiring at the multiple plug.

4. Remove the two nuts that retain the switch to steering column. On Fairmont, Zephyr, 1979 Mustang and Capri, the break-off head bolts that attach the switch to the lock cylinder housing must be drilled out with a 1/8 in. drill. Remove the bolts with an Easy-Out extractor. Disengage the ignition switch from the pin.
5. On models with a steering column-mounted gearshift lever, disconnect the ignition switch plunger from the ignition switch actuator rod and remove the ignition switch. On models with a floor mounted gearshift lever, remove the pin that connects the switch plunger to the switch actuator and remove the switch.
6. To re-install the switch, place both locking mechanism at top of column and switch itself in lock position for correct adjustment. To hold column in lock position, place automatic shift lever in PARK or manual shift lever in reverse, and turn to LOCK and remove the key. New switches are held in lock by plastic shipping pins. To pin existing switches, pull the switch plunger out as far as it will go and push back in to first detent. Insert 3/32 in. diameter wire into locking hole in the top of the switch.
7. Connect the switch plunger to the switch actuator rod.
8. Position the switch on the column and install the attaching nuts. Be sure the proper break-off head bolts are used on the Fairmont, Zephyr, 1979 Mustang and Capri. Do not tighten them.
9. Move the switch up and down to locate the mid-position of rod lash, and then tighten the nuts. On Fair-

monts, Zephyrs, 1979 Mustangs and Capris, tighten the bolts until the heads break off.
10. Remove the locking pin or wire. Connect the electrical connector. Reconnect the battery cable and check for proper switch operation.
11. Attach the steering column to the brake support bracket and install the shrouding.

INSTRUMENT PANEL

Headlight Switch Replacement

1. Disconnect the negative battery cable.
2. Remove the headlight switch control knob and shaft after depressing the release button on the rear of the switch. Some models require special procedures to gain access to the release button. They are:
   a. On Mavericks, Comets, Fairmonts, Zephyrs, 1979 Mustangs and Capris, equipped with air conditioning, disconnect the left A/C duct from the duct-to-register connector, loosen the two nuts that retain the left register to the utility shelf and remove the connector from the register.
   b. On 1972-73 Mustangs and Cougars, insert a screwdriver through the hole in the bottom of the instrument panel beneath the headlight switch and depress the headlight switch release button with the screwdriver.
3. After pulling the switch shaft and knob from the switch, remove the bezel nut that attaches the switch to the instrument panel.

4. Lower the switch and disconnect the lead wires from the switch.
5. On models equipped with headlight doors, disconnect the vacuum hoses from the headlight switch.
6. Reverse the procedure to install the new switch. When installing the new switch, insert the control knob and shaft into the switch until a distinct click is heard, signifying that the shaft is locked in place.

Headlight switch (© Ford Motor Co)

Speedometer Cable Replacement

1. Reach up behind the speedometer and depress the flat, quick-disconnect tab, while pulling back on the cable.
2. If the inner cable is broken, raise and support the car and remove the cable-to-transmission clamp and pull the cable from the transmission.
3. Pull the core from the cable.
4. Installation is the reverse of removal. Lubricate the core.with speedometer cable lubricant prior to installation.

WINDSHIELD WIPERS

Motor Removal and Installation

1972 AND LATER TORINO AND MONTEGO, 1977 AND LATER LTD II (NON-HIDDEN WIPERS), MUSTANG AND COUGAR THROUGH 1973

1. Disconnect battery and wiper motor connector.
2. Remove cowl top left vent screen by removing four retaining drive pins.
3. Remove wiper link retaining clip from wiper motor arm.
4. Remove three wiper motor retaining bolts, and remove wiper motor and mounting bracket.
5. To install motor, place wiper motor and mounting bracket against firewall and install three retaining bolts.
6. Position wiper link on motor drive arm, and install connecting clip. Be sure to force clip locking flange into locked position.
7. Install cowl top vent screen and secure with four drive pins.

8. Check motor operation and connect wiring plugs.

MAVERICK, COMET, MONARCH, GRANADA, VERSAILLES THROUGH 1977

1. Remove instrument cluster.
2. If air conditioned, remove center connector and duct assembly. Remove mounting bracket screw behind center duct, disconnect assembly from plenum chamber and left duct, and pull center connector and duct assembly out through cluster opening.
3. Working through cluster opening, disconnect two pivot shaft links from motor drive arm by removing retaining clip.
4. Disconnect wiring plug at motor, remove three retaining bolts, and remove motor through cluster opening.
5. To install motor, bolt motor to mounting plate with three retaining bolts.
6. Connect right pivot shaft link to motor and then connect left pivot shaft link. Lock clip.
7. On air conditioned vehicles, insert end of center connector and duct assembly near mounting bracket into left duct and opposite end into plenum chamber.
8. Secure assembly with mounting bracket screw.
9. Install instrument cluster, and check operation of wiper motor.

1978 AND LATER GRANADA, MONARCH, VERSAILLES

1. Disconnect the battery ground cable.
2. Remove the instrument panel pad, retained by eight screws.
3. Remove the speaker mounting bracket, disconnect and remove the speaker.
4. Remove the interlock module from the bracket and disconnect the multiple connector.
5. Remove the motor bracket bolts and the drive arm clip. Remove the motor.
6. Install in reverse order.

1972-73 TORINO AND MONTEGO (HIDDEN WIPERS)

1. Disconnect the negative battery cable.
2. Remove the wiper arms from the pivot shafts.
3. Disconnect the linkage drive arm from the motor output arm crankpin by removing the retaining clip.
4. From the engine side of the dash, disconnect the two wire connectors from the motor.
5. Remove the three retaining bolts and the motor from the firewall.
6. If the output arm catches on the firewall during removal, hand-turn

the arm clockwise so it will clear the opening in the firewall.
7. Reverse the procedure for installation, making sure that the output arm is in the park position prior to installation.

1974 AND LATER TORINO, ELITE, MONTEGO, COUGAR, LTD II, 1977 AND LATER THUNDERBIRD (HIDDEN WIPERS)

1. Disconnect the battery ground cable.
2. Remove the wiper arm and blade assemblies from the pivot shafts.
3. Remove the left cowl screen for access through the cowl opening. Disconnect the linkage drive arm from the motor output arm crankpin by removing the retaining clip. From the engine side of the firewall, disconnect the two push-on wire connectors from the motor.
4. Remove the three bolts which retain the motor to the firewall and remove the motor. If the output arm catches on the firewall during removal, hand turn the arm clockwise, so that it will clear the opening in the firewall.
5. Before installing the motor, be sure that the output arm is in the Park position.

FAIRMONT, ZEPHYR, 1979 MUSTANG, CAPRI

1. Disconnect the ground cable.
2. Remove the left hand wiper arm from the pivot shaft and lay it on the top grille.
3. Remove the cowl top grille screws.
4. Reach under the left front corner of the grille to disconnect the linkage drive arm from the motor crank by removing the retaining clip.
5. Disconnect the electrical connector. Remove the motor mounting bolts and remove the motor.
6. Install in reverse order.

Wiper Blade Replacement

These cars use two types of blade attachment, the bayonet type and the side pin type. The bayonet type has two kinds of latches. One latch made by Trico uses a tab which is pressed down to release the blade; the other type, made by Anco, uses a button, which is pressed inward to release the blade. The side pin type, made by Trico, has a opening into which a screwdriver must be inserted to depress the tab.

RADIO

For best FM reception, adjust the antenna, if adjustable, to 31 in. height. Fading or weak AM reception may be adjusted by adjusting the trimmer control. The trimmer control is located either on the right rear or front side of the radio. See the owner's manual for position if you are in doubt. To adjust the trimmer:

1. Extend the antenna to maximum height.
2. Tune the radio to a weak station around 1600 KC. Adjust the volume so that the sound is barely audible.
3. Adjust the trimmer to obtain maximum volume.

Removal and Replacement

TORINO, MONTEGO, ELITE, LTD II, 1974 AND LATER COUGAR, 1977 AND LATER THUNDERBIRD

1. Disconnect battery.
2. Pull radio control knobs off shafts.
3. Remove radio support to instrument panel attaching screw.
4. Remove two bezel nuts from radio control shafts.
5. Lower radio and disconnect antenna, speaker, and power leads. Remove radio.
6. To install, connect antenna, speaker and power leads to radio.
7. Position radio in instrument panel and install two bezel nuts.
8. Install radio support bracket to instrument panel attaching screw.
9. Connect battery.

MUSTANG AND COUGAR THROUGH 1973

1. Disconnect the negative battery cable.
2. Disconnect the radio antenna wire from the radio.

3. Pull off the radio control knobs and remove the two radio bezel nuts from the radio.
4. Remove the four radio bezel attaching screws.
5. Pull the radio away from the instrument panel and disconnect the lead wires from the radio as they become accessible.
6. To install the radio, position it on the instrument panel and connect the lead wires to it.
7. To complete installation, reverse the removal procedure. When positioning the radio in the instrument panel, make sure the radio support bracket on the rear of the radio engages the tab on the instrument panel.

MAVERICK AND COMET

1. Disconnect the battery, and remove the seatbelt interlock module, if any, beneath the radio.
2. Remove radio rear support nut and lock washer.
3. Remove four radio to instrument panel retaining screws.
4. Pull radio from instrument panel and disconnect antenna, speaker, and power leads.
5. Remove radio.
6. Remove knob and disc assemblies from radio shafts.
7. Remove two bezel retaining nuts and remove bezel.
8. To install radio, position bezel on radio and install two bezel retaining nuts.
9. Install disc and knob assemblies on radio shafts.

10. Connect antenna, speaker, and power connectors.
11. Position radio so that rear support mounting bolt enters hole in rear support mounting bracket.
12. Install four radio to instrument panel retaining screws.
13. Install radio rear support nut and lock washer.
14. Place speaker and power wire harnesses in clip on bezel.
15. Connect battery and check operation of radio.

GRANADA, MONARCH, VERSAILLES

1. Disconnect the negative battery cable.
2. Remove the headlight switch from the instrument panel. Remove the heater, air conditioner, windshield wiper/washer knobs, and radio knobs and discs.
3. Remove the six screws which attach the applique to the instrument panel and remove the applique. Disconnect the antenna lead-in cable from the radio.
4. Remove the four screws which attach the radio bezel to the instrument panel. Slide the radio and bezel out of the lower rear support bracket and instrument panel opening toward the interior far enough to disconnect the electrical connections, and remove the radio.
5. Remove the nut attaching the rear support bracket to the radio and remove the bracket. Remove the

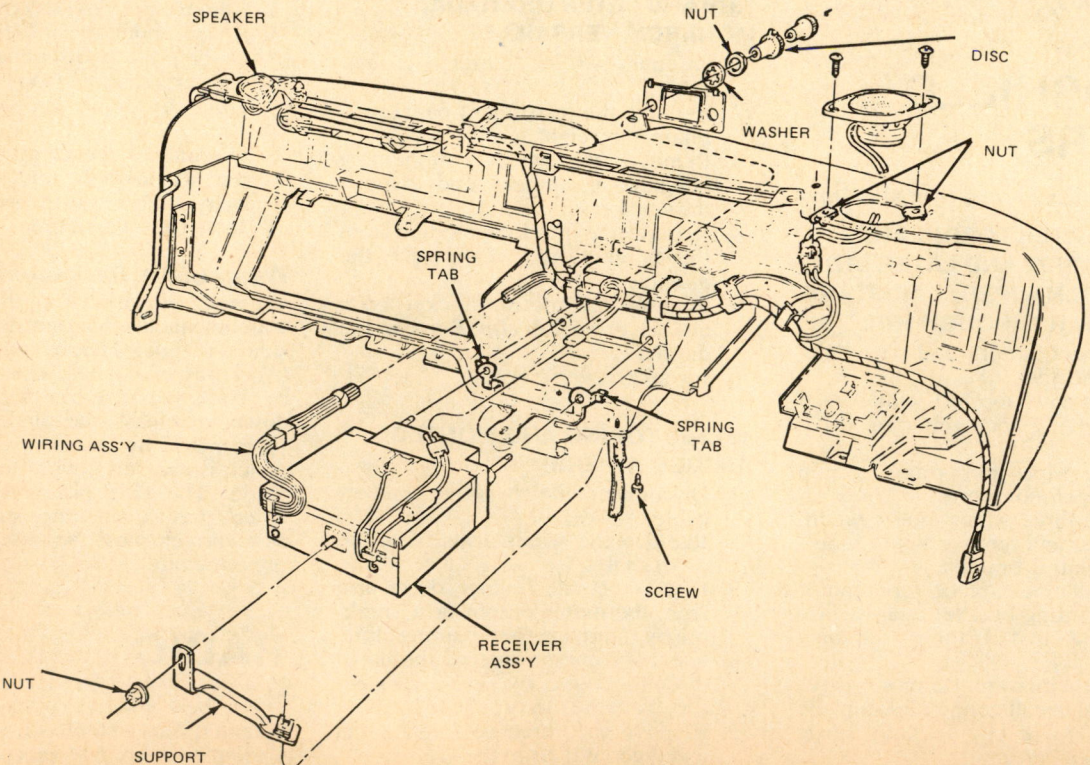

Fairmont and Zephyr radio installation (© Ford Motor Co.)

nuts and washer from the radio control shafts and remove the bezel.

6. To install, install the rear support bracket on the radio. Install the bezel, washers and nuts on the radio shafts.
7. Insert the radio with rear support bracket and bezel through the instrument panel opening far enough to connect the electrical leads and antenna lead-in cable. Install the radio upper rear support bracket into the lower rear support bracket.
8. Center the radio and bezel in the opening and install the four bezel attaching screws.
9. Install the instrument panel applique with its six attaching screws. Install all knobs removed from the instrument panel and radio. Install the headlight switch.
10. Connect the negative battery cable.

FAIRMONT, ZEPHYR, 1979 MUSTANG AND CAPRI

1. Disconnect the negative battery cable. Remove the seat belt interlock module underneath the radio.
2. Disconnect the electrical, speaker, and antenna leads from the radio.
3. Remove the knobs, discs, and control shaft nuts and washers from the radio shafts.
4. Remove the rear support nut from the radio.
5. Remove the radio from the rear support, and drop the radio down and out from behind the instrument panel.
6. To install, slide the radio up into position from underneath the instrument panel. Slip the support over the rear bolt and install the nut finger tight. Install the front washers and nuts on the control shafts, tighten, then tighten the rear support nut. Connect the leads, install the knobs, connect the battery cable. Install the seatbelt module.

HEATER

NOTE: *Heater and air conditioner case removal and installation procedures are included only where necessary to replace the heater core.*

VEHICLES WITHOUT AIR CONDITIONING

Heater Case Removal and Installation

COUGAR AND MUSTANG THROUGH 1973

1. Disconnect battery and drain coolant.

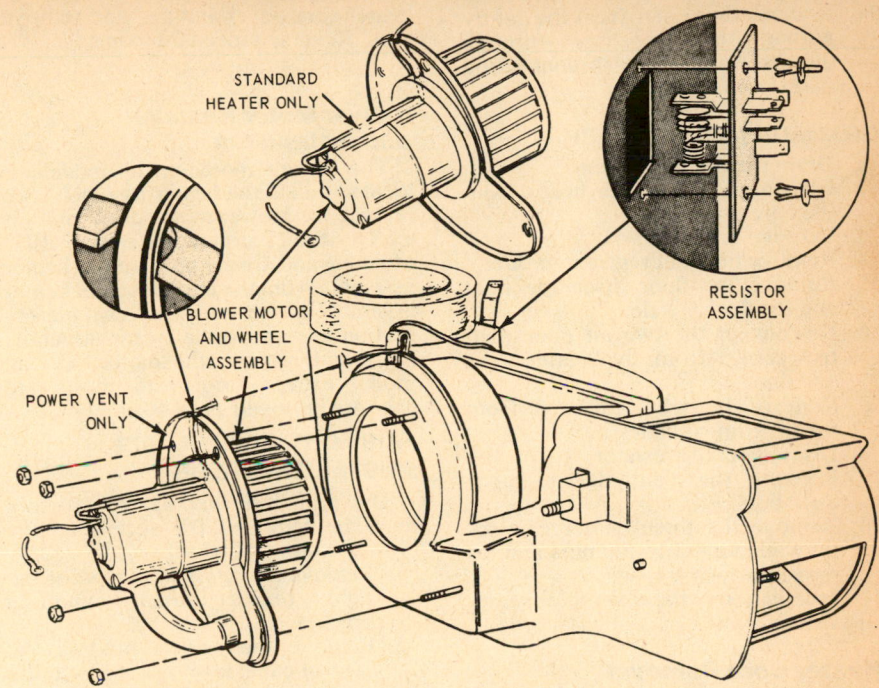

Heater blower and motor installation—Mustang and Cougar through 1973, Maverick, Comet (© Ford Motor Co)

2. Remove instrument panel pad.
3. Remove glove compartment liner and door.
4. Remove air distribution duct from heater.
5. Disconnect control cables from heater assembly.
6. Disconnect wires from blower motor resistor.
7. Remove right courtesy light located on underside of instrument panel, if so equipped.
8. Remove heater support to dash panel retaining screw.
9. Disconnect vacuum hoses and remove power air vent duct, if so equipped.
10. Remove blower motor ground wire grounding screw.
11. Disconnect heater hoses from heater at firewall.
12. Working in engine compartment, remove five heater assembly retaining nuts.
13. Remove instrument panel to cowl attaching screws.
14. Remove instrument panel right side brace.
15. Pull heater assembly and right side of instrument panel rearward, and remove heater assembly. Reverse procedure to install.

TORINO, MONTEGO, ELITE, LTD II, 1974 AND LATER COUGAR, 1977 AND LATER THUNDERBIRD

1. Drain coolant.
2. Disconnect both heater hoses at firewall.
3. Remove nuts retaining heater assembly to firewall.

4. Disconnect temperature and defroster cables at heater.
5. Disconnect wires from resistor, and disconnect blower motor wires and clip retaining heater assembly to defroster nozzle.
6. Remove glove box.
7. Remove bolt and nut connecting the right air duct control to instrument panel. Remove nuts retaining right air duct and remove duct assembly.
8. Remove heater assembly to bench.

MAVERICK, COMET

1. Drain the cooling system and disconnect the negative battery cable.
2. Disconnect the blower ground wire (black) from the fender apron.
3. Disconnect the heater hoses from the engine block.
4. Remove the five heater assembly to firewall attaching bolts from the firewall.
5. Working inside the car, on models through 1976, remove the ignition switch and plate from the package tray and remove the tray from the dash. On 1977 models, remove the glove compartment.
6. Remove the right kick panel and remove the package tray bracket.
7. Disconnect the heater control cables from the heater.
8. Disconnect the defroster air duct from the top of the heater.
9. Disconnect the heater blower motor lead wires from the resistor at the bottom of the heater.
10. Remove the one screw from the bracket that mounts the heater to the dash.

11. Remove the heater from the car by pulling the heater hoses through the firewall, then disconnecting them from the heater.

GRANADA AND MONARCH

1. Drain the cooling system.
2. Disconnect the heater hoses from the core tubes.
3. Remove the glove box.
4. Remove the right register air duct.
5. Remove the floor discharge duct and the floor nozzle.
6. Disconnect the two air door control cables from the heater case and doors.
7. Remove the right vent cable from the instrument panel.
8. Disconnect the resistor.
9. Remove the vent duct-to-upper cowl bolt.
10. Remove the three heater case-to-firewall mounting stud nuts and remove the heater case.
11. Installation is the reverse of removal.

Heater Core Removal and Installation

MAVERICK AND COMET

1. Remove heater assembly.
2. Remove air inlet seal from heater assembly.
3. Remove eleven clips from heater assembly flange and separate heater assembly housing.
4. Remove heater core from heater assembly housing. Reverse procedure to install.

FAIRMONT, ZEPHYR, 1979 MUSTANG AND CAPRI

It is not necessary to remove the heater case for access to the heater core.

1. Drain enough coolant from the radiator to drain the heater core.
2. Loosen the heater hose clamps on the engine side of the firewall and disconnect the heater hoses. Cap the heater core tubes.
3. Remove the glove box liner.
4. Remove the instrument panel-to-cowl brace retaining screws and remove the brace.
5. Move the temperature lever to warm.
6. Remove the heater core cover screws. Remove the cover through the glove box.
7. Loosen the heater case mounting nuts on the engine side of the firewall.
8. Push the heater core tubes and seal toward the interior of the car to loosen the core.
9. Remove the heater core through the glove box opening.

ALL OTHER MODELS

The heater core is located in the heater case in a diagonal position. It is serviced through an opening in the back plate. With the heater assembly removed from the vehicle, remove heater core cover and pad and remove core. Reverse procedure to install.

Blower Motor Removal and Installation

The blower motor on all models is located inside the heater assembly. To replace the blower motor on all models except the Fairmont, Zephyr, 1979 Mustang and Capri, remove the heater assembly from the car. Once the heater assembly is removed, it is a simple operation to remove the motor attaching bolts and remove the motor. On all models except as noted, the motor and cage are removed as an assembly.

FAIRMONT, ZEPHYR, 1979 MUSTANG AND CAPRI

The right side ventilator assembly must be removed for access to the blower motor and wheel.

1. Remove the retaining screw for the right register duct mounting bracket.
2. Remove the screws holding the control cable lever assembly to the instrument panel.
3. Remove the glove box liner.
4. Remove the plastic rivets securing the grille to the floor outlet, and remove the grille.
5. Remove the right register duct and register assembly:
   a. Remove the register duct bracket retaining screw on the lower edge of the instrument panel, and disengage the duct from the opening and remove through the glove box opening.
   b. Insert a thin blade under the retaining tab and pry the tab toward the louvers until the retaining tab pivot clears the hole in the register opening. Pull the register assembly end out from the housing only enough to prevent the pivot from going back into the pivot hole. Pry the other retaining tab loose and remove the register assembly from the opening.
6. Remove the retaining screws securing the ventilator assembly to the blower housing. The upper right screw can be reached with a long extension through the register opening; the upper left screw can be reached through the glove box opening. The other two screws are on the bottom of the assembly.
7. Slide the assembly to the right, then down and out from under the instrument panel.
8. Remove the motor lead wire connector from the register and push it back through the hole in the case. Remove the right side cowl trim panel for access, and remove the ground terminal lug retaining screw.
9. Remove the hub clamp spring from the motor shaft and remove the blower wheel.
10. Remove the blower motor bolts from the housing and remove the motor.

VEHICLES WITH INTEGRAL HEATER-AIR CONDITIONING

NOTE: *Removal of the heater-air conditioner housing requires evacuation of the air conditioner refrigerant. This operation requires special tools and training. Failure to follow proper safety precautions may cause personal injury.*

Heater-Air Conditioner Removal and Installation

MAVERICK, COMET

NOTE: *To facilitate installation, tag vacuum lines and electrical wires, as to their proper location, before disassembling unit. To remove the core, it is necessary to remove the entire evaporator assembly.*

1. Disconnect the battery and remove the air cleaner.
2. Drain the cooling system.
3. Connect a manifold gauge set to the compressor, and discharge the system.
4. Remove the expansion valve and disconnect the heater hoses from the heater core. Tape over openings to avoid entry of dirt.
5. Remove the three A/C assembly-to-firewall mounting stud nuts. Remove the utility shelf and bracket from the lower edge of the instrument panel, and remove the right cowl trim panel and radio. Remove the glove compartment.
6. Disconnect the right and left A/C register air ducts from the plenum chamber.
7. Remove the floor distribution duct from the blower housing.
8. Remove the center register from the instrument panel. Then pull the plenum chamber part way through the register opening to disengage it from the blower housing. Disconnect the hose from the door motor on the plenum chamber.
9. Disconnect the vacuum hoses from the door motors.
10. Disconnect the vacuum harness multiple connector from the control assembly.
11. Disconnect the temperature control cable from the evaporator housing, and disconnect the vacuum hoses from the adjacent water valve vacuum switch.
    On 1977 models, remove the blower motor at this point.
12. Remove the screw which retains the evaporator housing to the cowl upper support and move A/C assembly rearward and away from the firewall.
13. Remove any remaining hoses and disconnect wires from the blower

resistor, the de-icing switch and the blower motor ground wire.

14. Remove the evaporator and blower housing assembly from the vehicle.
15. Install assembly into the vehicle by reversing the removal procedures, being careful to correctly connect the vacuum hoses. When making connections to the water valve vacuum switch, connect the purple hose to the nipple closest to the switch plunger and attach the green hose to the water valve motor.
16. After installation, adjust the temperature control cable and, if necessary, the water valve vacuum switch.
17. Evacuate, leak test and charge the system.

MUSTANG AND COUGAR THROUGH 1973

NOTE: *To remove the core, it is necessary to remove the entire evaporator assembly.*

1. Remove the carburetor air cleaner.
2. Disconnect the battery.
3. Drain the cooling system.
4. Purge the system of refrigerant.
5. Disconnect the evaporator tubes from the expansion valve, disconnect the heater hoses.
6. Remove the housing-to-firewall mounting stud nuts.
7. Remove the glove box and map light from the lower edge, right side of instrument panel.
8. Disconnect the vacuum hoses at the motor.
9. Disconnect the two hoses from the water valve vacuum switch, and disengage the hoses from the clip at the top of the housing.
10. Disconnect the wires from the thermostatic (de-icing) switch.
11. Disconnect the cable from the door crank arm.
12. Remove the motor from the housing to allow clearance at the lower edge of the instrument panel, and remove the motor bracket.
13. Remove the motor to allow clearance at the right side of the housing during removal.
14. Remove the housing-to-cowl bracket.
15. Pull the drain hose from the hole in the floor pan.
16. Remove the two blower housing-to-cowl attaching screws, lower the blower housing slightly. Pull the housing away from the firewall, move it to the right to separate it from the blower housing and remove it from the vehicle.
17. To install, reverse the removal procedure. Evacuate, leak test, and charge the refrigerant system.

Heater Core Removal and Installation
TORINO AND MONTEGO
1. Remove the heater-air conditioner assembly.

2. Separate the heater housing from the plenum.
3. Slip the heater core out of the plenum.
4. Transfer the old heater core seal to the new core.
5. Slip the new core with seal into the plenum.
6. Install the heater housing to the plenum. Connect the wires at the resistor block, and install the seal and retainer at the evaporator tubes.
7. Install the heater-air conditioner assembly.

MUSTANG AND COUGAR THROUGH 1973, MAVERICK AND COMET
1. Remove the heater-air conditioner assembly.
2. Remove the flange clips and upper half of the housing assembly.
3. Remove the water valve vacuum switch from the lower half of the housing.
4. Remove the screw, retaining clip and temperature blend door shaft, the four screws and door upper frame, the door, and the four screws and door lower frame from the lower half of the housing.
5. Lift the heater core from the lower housing.
6. Transfer the pads from the old core to the new core.
7. Reverse the procedure to install. Leak-test, evacuate and charge the refrigeration system.

1972-76 TORINO, MONTEGO, AND ELITE; 1974-6 COUGAR
1. Drain the cooling system and disconnect the heater hoses at the core.
2. Remove the glove box.
3. Remove the two snap clips and the heater air outlet register from the plenum.
4. Remove the temperature control cable assembly mounting screw, and disconnect the end of the cable from the blend door crank arm.
5. Remove the blue and red vacuum hoses from the high-low door vacuum motor; the yellow hose from the panel-defrost door motor, and the brown hose from the inline tee connector.
6. Disconnect the wires at the resistor block.
7. Remove the ten screws and the rear half of the plenum.
8. Remove the mounting nut from the heater core tube support bracket.
9. Reverse the procedure to install, taking care to apply body sealer around the case flanges to insure a positive seal.

1977 AND LATER LTD II, THUNDERBIRD, COUGAR
1. Drain the engine coolant and disconnect the hoses from the core.

2. Remove the heater core cover plate, under the hood.
3. Press down on the core and tilt it toward the front of the vehicle to release it from the seal.
4. Pull the core up and out.
5. To install, press downward on the core and tilt it toward the rear to engage the notch on the seal with the flange on the housing. Replace any deformed sealer. Install all other parts.

GRANADA, MONARCH, VERSAILLES
NOTE: *The refrigerant system components and charge do not have to be disturbed when removing and installing the heater core.*

1. Drain the coolant and disconnect the battery.
2. Disconnect 2 heater hose clamps at the firewall in the engine compartment. Plug the core tubes to prevent coolant leakage during removal.
3. Remove the heat distribution duct from the instrument panel.
4. Remove the seat belt interlock module and bracket.
5. Remove the glovebox liner.
6. Loosen the right door sill scuff plate, right A pillar trim cover, and remove the right cowl side trim panel.
7. Loosen instrument panel-to-right cowl side bolt and remove the instrument panel brace bolt at the lower rail, below the glove box.
8. On 1975-76 models and Versailles with ATC, remove the instrument panel crash pad.
9. On 1975-76 models and Versailles with ATC, remove the radio speaker or panel cowl brace.
10. Remove the 4 nozzle-to-cowl bracket mounting screws.
11. Lift the defroster nozzle upward through the crash pad opening.
12. Disconnect the vacuum hoses from the A/C-Defrost and Heat/Defrost door motors. Remove the screw from the clip holding the vacuum harness to the plenum.
13. Remove 2 Heat/Defrost door mounting nuts and swing the motor rearward on the door crankarm.
14. Remove 2 screws attaching the plenum to the left mounting bracket. Then remove the screws and clips securing the plenum to the evaporator case.
15. Swing the bottom of the plenum away from the evaporator case to disengage the S-clip on the forward flange of the plenum. Raise the plenum to clear the tabs on the top of the evaporator case.
16. Move the plenum to the left as far as possible (about 4 inches), pulling rearward on the instrument panel to gain clearance. Take care when pulling back on the instrument panel to avoid cracking the plastic panel.

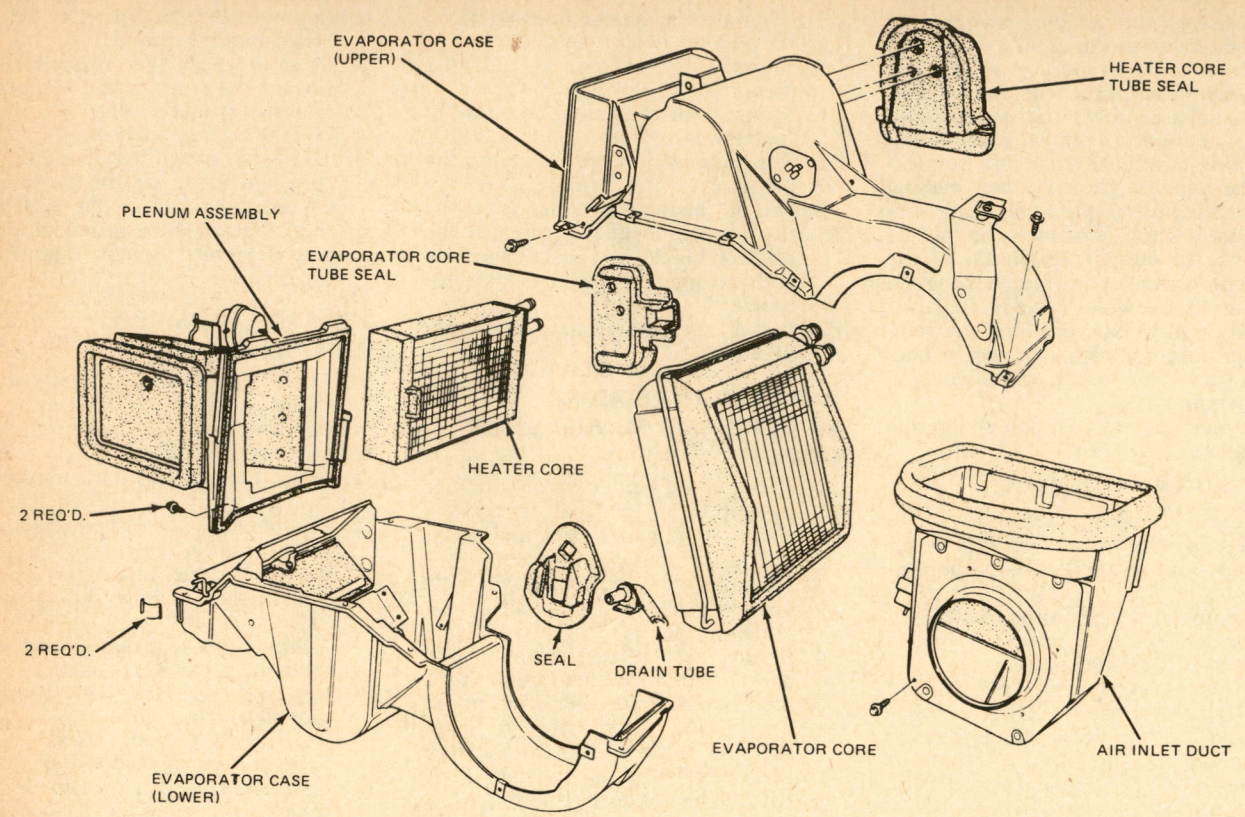

EVAPORATOR CASE (UPPER)

HEATER CORE TUBE SEAL

PLENUM ASSEMBLY

EVAPORATOR CORE TUBE SEAL

HEATER CORE

2 REQ'D.

2 REQ'D.

SEAL

DRAIN TUBE

EVAPORATOR CORE

AIR INLET DUCT

EVAPORATOR CASE (LOWER)

Granada and Monarch evaporator case assembly (© Ford Motor Co.)

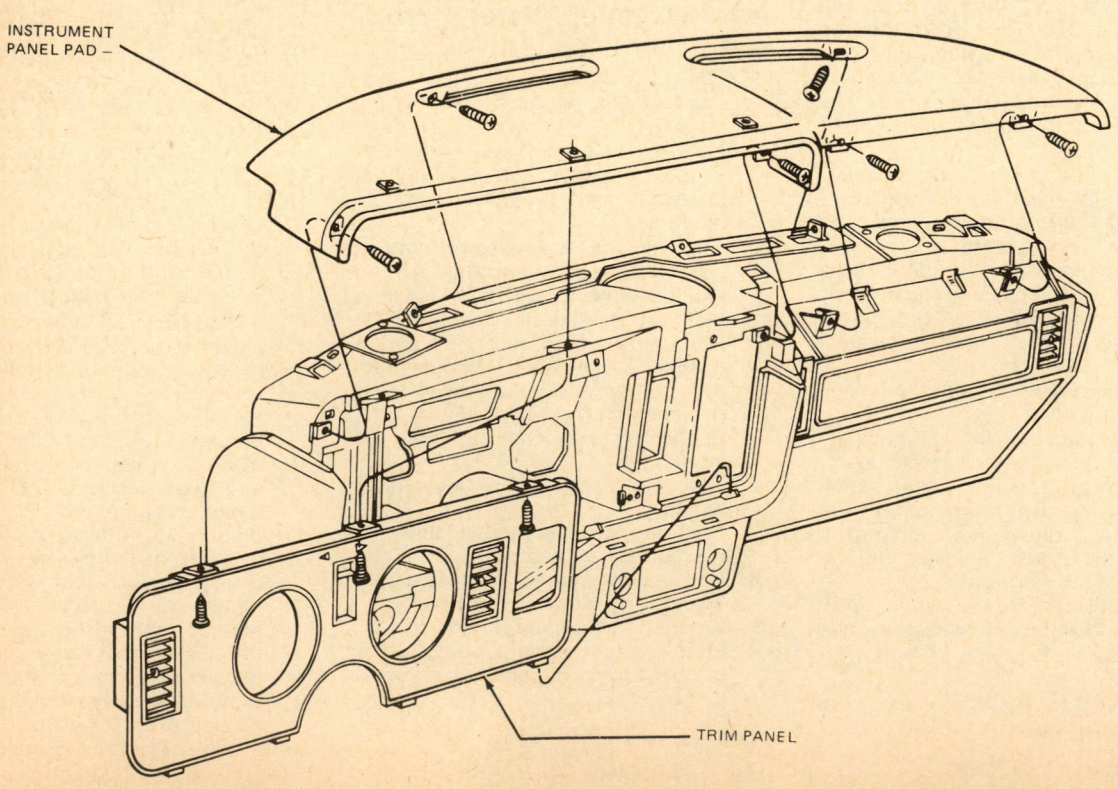

INSTRUMENT PANEL PAD

TRIM PANEL

Fairmont and Zephyr instrument panel pad and trim panel removal (© Ford Motor Co.)

NOTE: *There is very little clearance between the plenum and the wiper motor assembly.*

17. Pull the heater core to the left using the tab molded into the rear heater core seal. As the rear surface of the heater core clears the evaporator case, pull the core rearward and downward to clear the instrument panel.
18. Reverse the procedure to install.

NOTE: *Before installing the core, make sure that the heater core tube to firewall seal is in place between the evaporator case and the firewall.*

FAIRMONT, ZEPHYR, 1979 MUSTANG AND CAPRI

The instrument panel must be removed for access to the heater core.

1. Disconnect the battery ground cable.
2. Remove the instrument panel pad:
   a. Remove the screws attaching the instrument cluster trim panel to the pad.
   b. Remove the screw attaching the pad to the panel at each defroster opening.
   c. Remove the screws attaching the edge of the pad to the panel.
3. Remove the steering column opening cover.
4. Remove the nuts and bracket retaining the steering column to the instrument panel and lay the column against the seat.
5. Remove the instrument panel to brake pedal support screw at the column opening.
6. Remove the screws attaching the lower brace to the panel below the radio, and below the glove box.
7. Disconnect the temperature cable from the door and case bracket.
8. Unplug the 7-port vacuum hose connectors at the evaporator case.
9. Disconnect the resistor wire connector and the blower feed wire.
10. Remove the screws attaching the top of the panel to the cowl. Support the panel while doing this.
11. Remove one screw at each end attaching the panel to the cowl side panels.
12. Move the panel rearward and disconnect the speedometer cable and any wires preventing the panel from lying flat on the seat.
13. Drain the coolant and disconnect the heater hoses from the heater core. Plug the core tubes.
14. Remove the nuts retaining the evaporator case to the firewall in the engine compartment.
15. Remove the case support bracket screws and air inlet duct support bracket.
16. Remove the nut retaining the bracket to the dash panel at the left side of the evaporator case, and the nut retaining the bracket below the case to the dash panel.
17. Pull the case assembly away from

the panel to get to the screws retaining the heater core cover to the case.
18. Remove the cover screws and the cover.
19. Lift the heater core and seals from the evaporator case.

Blower Motor Removal and Installation

TORINO, MONTEGO, ELITE THROUGH 1976; 1974 AND LATER COUGAR; 1977 AND LATER LTD II AND THUNDERBIRD

1. Disconnect the battery and take out the glove box.
2. Remove the recirculating air duct. On 1975 and later models, remove the instrument panel pad and side cowl trim.
3. Remove the screws which attach the blower lower housing to the firewall and bracket.
4. Disconnect the vacuum line from the actuator and move it out of the way.
5. Disconnect the plug from the resistor block and lift out the resistor block.
6. Remove all blower housing flange screws, separate blower housing halves, and unscrew and remove blower assembly.
7. Remove the blower wheel.
8. Install the blower wheel on the motor.
9. Install the motor and shell and ground wire in the case.
10. Install blower assembly into lower housing, and reassemble housing.
11. Connect the wires.
12. Fasten the resistor block to the plenum.
13. Install the recirculating air duct.
14. Install the screws which attach the blower lower housing to the firewall and bracket.
15. Install the glove box and connect the battery. Install the pad and trim.

MAVERICK AND COMET THROUGH 1973

1. Disconnect the battery and remove the radio assembly.
2. Remove the utility shelf, and air ducts from the plenum chamber.
3. Remove the air duct from the bottom of the blower housing.
4. Remove the blower housing mounting stud nut and lock plate.
5. Rotate the blower housing from the evaporator housing.
6. Disconnect the vacuum hoses, resistor and ground wires, and remove the housing.
7. Separate the left and right halves.
8. Set the motor in place.
9. Install the motor attaching nuts.
10. Set the blower fan on the motor shaft.

11. Install the blower motor and fan assembly.
12. Set the blower housing in place.
13. Install the blower housing attaching nuts, washers, and screws.
14. Install the water valve.
15. Reverse steps 1-3 to complete assembly.

1974 AND LATER MAVERICK AND COMET

1. Disconnect the battery and remove the radio, and lower instrument panel extension.
2. Remove the floor air distribution duct retaining bolts, and on 1974-75 models disconnect the right and left A/C register air duct assemblies from the plenum chamber.
3. Remove the floor air distribution duct from the bottom of the blower housing.
4. Remove the blower housing mounting stud nut and lockplate.
5. Rotate the blower housing to unlock the slotted tabs on the blower housing from their lock pins on the evaporator housing. There are two tabs and pins. Disconnect the red and yellow hoses at the vacuum motor on the blower housing. Disconnect the resistor and ground wires, and remove the blower housing.
6. Cut the gaskets around the A/C outlets at the break line.
7. Remove the seven clips, and separate the left and right halves of the blower housing.
8. Remove the three blower motor mounting plate retaining nuts, and remove the motor and wheel assembly from the housing.
9. Assemble and install in the reverse order of removal, making sure that the A/C-Heat door is positioned properly before clipping the right and left housing halves together. Connect the battery.

MUSTANG AND COUGAR THROUGH 1973

1. Disconnect the battery. Remove the blower housing mounting bracket stud nut (engine side of the firewall).
2. Remove the two blower housing-to-instrument panel support mounting screws.
3. Disconnect the blower motor ground wire (black) from the resistor.
4. Disconnect the blower motor lead wire (orange-black) from the resistor.
5. Rotate the blower housing to a diagonal position. Remove the blower motor mounting screws, and remove the blower motor and wheel as an assembly.
6. Position the assembly and secure the mounting screws.
7. Connect the blower motor lead and ground wires.

NOTE: NO COOLING TUBE RE-
QUIRED ON UNITS
EQUIPPED WITH STEEL
SHELL BLOWER MOTORS.

RESISTOR ASSEMBLY

BLOWER MOTOR AND
WHEEL ASSEMBLY

ADAPTOR

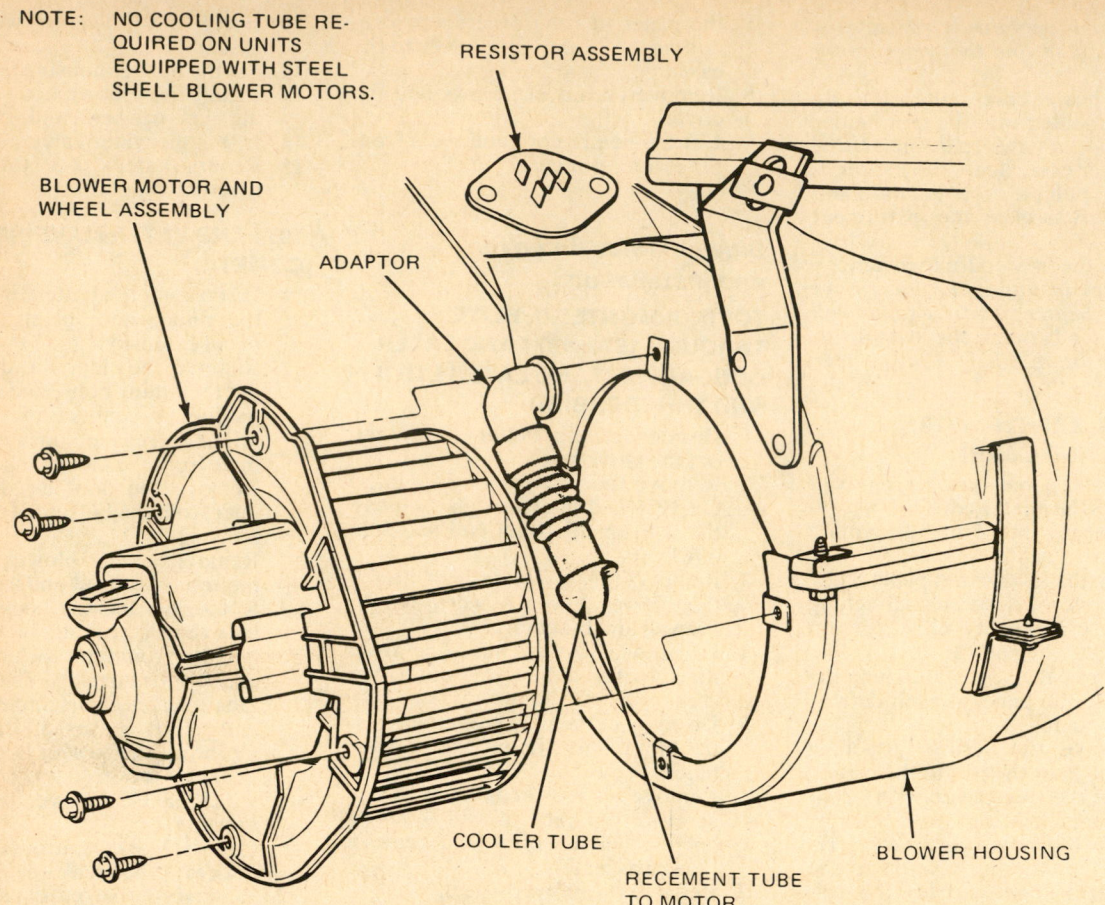

COOLER TUBE

RECEMENT TUBE
TO MOTOR

BLOWER HOUSING

Blower motor removal—Granada and Monarch with heater/air conditioner system
(© Ford Motor Co)

8. Position the blower motor on the blower housing and install the mounting bracket.
9. Install the battery.

GRANADA, MONARCH, VERSAILLES

1. Disconnect the negative battery cable.
2. Loosen the passenger side door sill scuff plate and the right A pillar trim cover. Remove the right cowl side trim panel.
3. Remove the bolt retaining the lower side of the instrument panel to the cowl. Remove the right cowl side brace bolt.
4. Disconnect the wiring harness connectors at the blower motor.
5. If so equipped, remove the cooling tube from the blower motor.

6. Remove the 4 screws retaining the blower motor and wheel assembly to the scroll. To remove the motor, pull rearward on the lower edge of the instrument panel to provide clearance. Do not remove the mounting plate from the blower motor.
7. Installation is the reverse of removal. If necessary, cement the cooling tube to the blower motor.

FAIRMONT, ZEPHYR, 1979 MUSTANG, CAPRI

The air inlet duct and blower housing assembly must be removed for access to the blower motor.

1. Remove the glove box liner and disconnect the hose from the vacuum motor.
2. Remove the instrument panel

lower right side to cowl attaching bolt.
3. Remove the screw attaching the brace to the top of the air inlet duct.
4. Disconnect the motor wire.
5. Remove the housing lower support bracket to case nut.
6. Remove the side cowl trim panel and remove the ground wire screw.
7. Remove the attaching screw at the top of the air inlet duct.
8. Remove the air inlet duct and housing assembly down and away from the evaporator case.
9. Remove the four blower motor mounting plate screws and remove the blower motor and wheel as an assembly from the housing. Do not remove the mounting plate from the motor.

Index

Dodge & Plymouth

YEAR IDENTIFICATION

1972 Polara

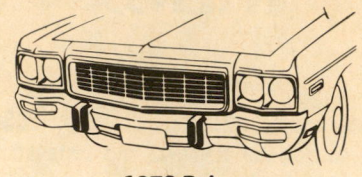

1973 Polara

1972 Charger

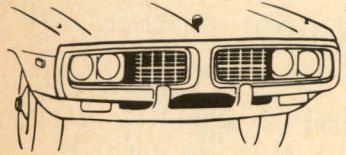

1973 Charger

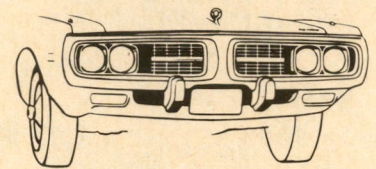

1974 Charger

1975 Charger S.E.

1976 Charger S.E.

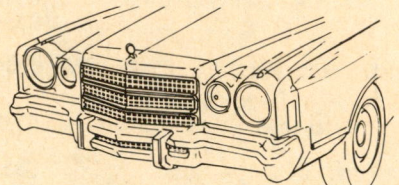

1977 Charger SE

1978 Charger

1972 Coronet

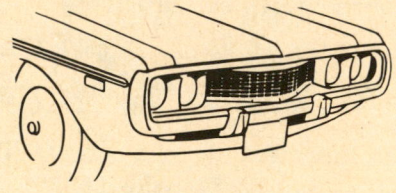

1973 Coronet

1974 Coronet

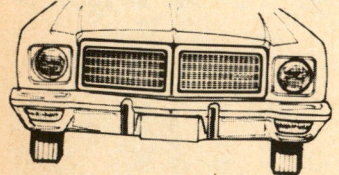

1975-76 Coronet

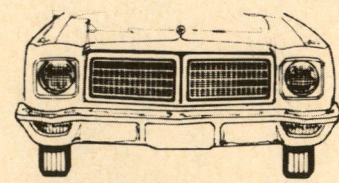

1975-76 Coronet Brougham

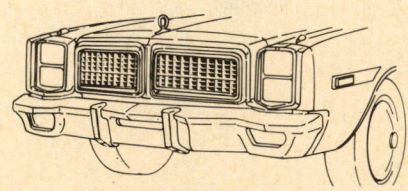

1977 Monaco

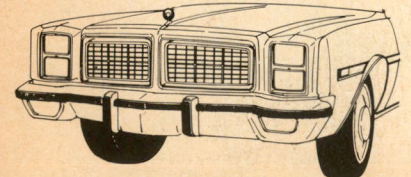

1978 Royal Monaco

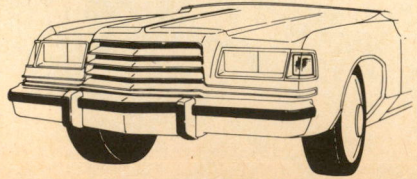

1978 Magnum XE

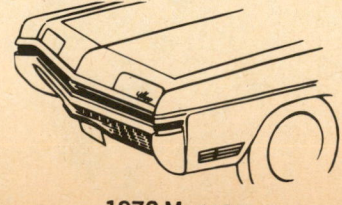

1972 Monaco

Dodge & Plymouth

YEAR IDENTIFICATION

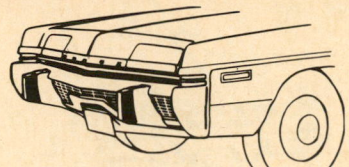
1973 Monaco

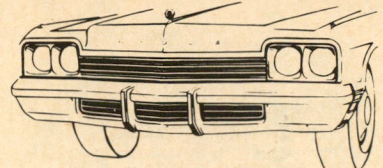
1974 Monaco

1975 Monaco

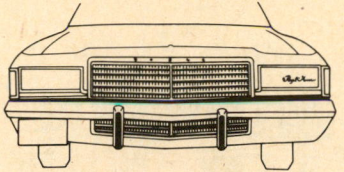
1976 Monaco

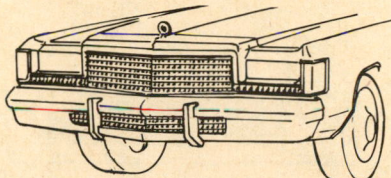
1977 Royal Monaco

1972 Fury

1973 Fury

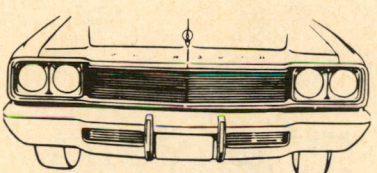
1974 Fury

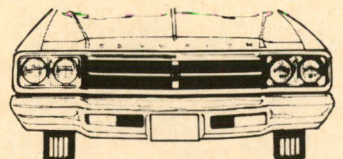
1975 Gran Fury

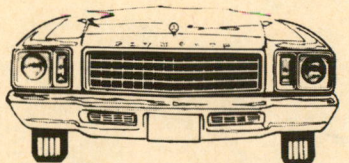
1975 Gran Fury Brougham

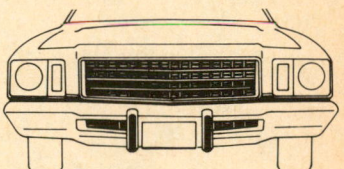
1976 Gran Fury

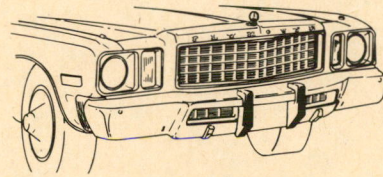
1977 Gran Fury

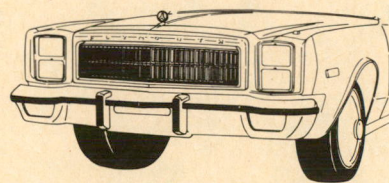
1978 Plymouth Gran Fury

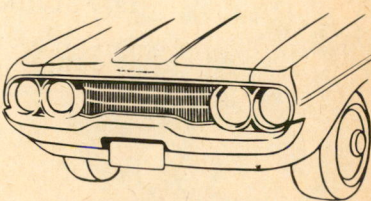
1972 Satellite

1972 Sebring

1972 Road Runner

1973 Satellite

C517

Dodge & Plymouth

YEAR IDENTIFICATION

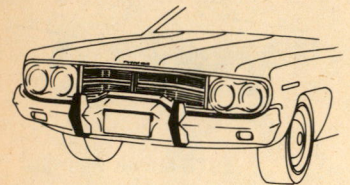

1974 Satellite

1974 Sebring

1974 Road Runner

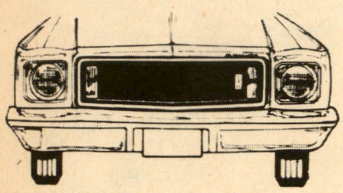

1975 Road Runner

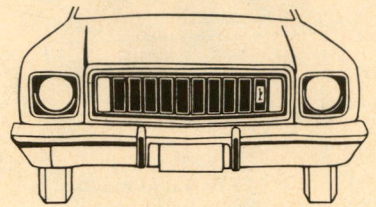

1976 Road Runner

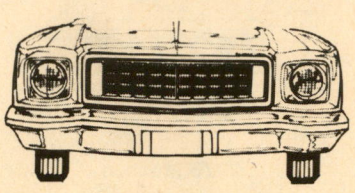

1975-76 Fury

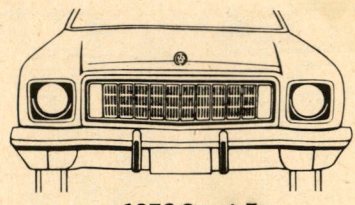

1976 Sport Fury

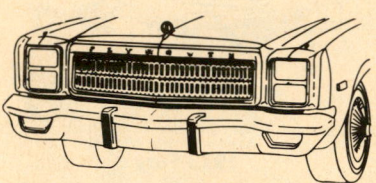

1977 Fury

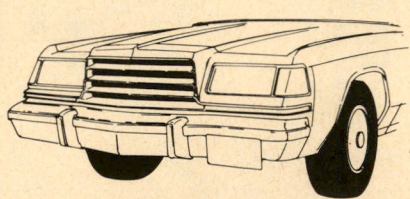

1979 MAGNUM XE

1979 ST. REGIS

ENGINE CODE

The engine code designation is the 5th digit of the vehicle identification number (V.I.N.). The V.I.N. is stamped on a plate located at the left side of the instrument panel visible through the windshield.

Disp	Bbl	'72	'73	'74	'75	'76	'77	'78	'79
6 Cylinder Models									
225	1	C	C	C	C	C	C	C	C
225	2						D	D	D
8 Cylinder Models									
318	2	G	G	G	G	G	G	G	G
318 HP	2			G					
318	4							H	H
340 HP	4	H	H						
360	2	K	K	K	K	K	K	K	K
360	4			J	J	J	J	J	J
360 HP	4			L				L	L
400	2	M	M	M	M	M	M		
400	4			N	N	N	N	N	
400 HP	4	P	P	P	P	P	P		
440	4	T	T	T	T	T	T		
440 HP	4	U	U	U	U	U	U	U	

HP High Performance

Engine Identification

The engine that the factory installed in the car can be identified by the fifth digit of the Vehicle Identification Number, as explained under Engine Code. The engine itself can be identified by the engine serial number. The cubic inch displacement is given by the second, third, and fourth, or the third, fourth, and fifth digits of the engine serial number, depending on the year and engine.

Six cylinder engines have their serial number stamped on the joint face of the block, just behind the ignition coil. V8s through 360 cu. in. have the number on the front of the block, just below the left cylinder head. 400 and larger V8s have the number either on the oil pan rail, below the starter opening, at the left rear corner of the block; ahead of the base of the distributor; or on the left bank front tappet rail. 360 cu. in. and smaller (small block) V8s can quickly be identified as having the distributor at the rear of the engine, while 400 and larger versions have it at the front.

GENERAL ENGINE SPECIFICATIONS

Year	Engine No. Cyl. Displacement Cu. In.	Carburetor Type	Horsepower @ rpm ■	Torque @ rpm (ft lbs) ■	Bore x Stroke (in.)	Compression Ratio	Oil Pressure @ 2000 rpm
'72	6-225	1 bbl	110 @ 4000	185 @ 2000	3.400 x 4.125	8.40:1	55
	6-225 Calif.	1 bbl	97 @ 4000	180 @ 2000	3.400 x 4.125	8.40:1	55
	8-318	2 bbl	150 @ 4000	260 @ 1600	3.910 x 3.310	8.60:1	55
	8-340 HP	4 bbl	240 @ 4800	290 @ 3600	4.040 x 3.310	8.50:1	55
	8-360	2 bbl	175 @ 4000	285 @ 2400	4.000 x 3.580	8.80:1	55
	8-400	2 bbl	190 @ 4400	310 @ 2400	4.340 x 3.380	8.20:1	55
	8-400 Calif.	2 bbl	181 @ 4400	305 @ 2400	4.340 x 3.380	8.20:1	55
	8-400 HP	4 bbl	255 @ 4800	340 @ 3200	4.340 x 3.380	8.20:1	55
	8-400 Calif.	4 bbl	246 @ 4800	335 @ 3200	4.340 x 3.380	8.20:1	55
	8-400 HP	4 bbl	265 @ 4800	345 @ 3200	4.340 x 3.380	8.20:1	55
	8-440	4 bbl	225 @ 4400	345 @ 3200	4.320 x 3.750	8.20:1	55
	8-440 Calif.	4 bbl	216 @ 4400	340 @ 3200	4.320 x 3.750	8.20:1	55

GENERAL ENGINE SPECIFICATIONS

Year	Engine No. Cyl. Displacement Cu. In.	Carburetor Type	Horsepower @ rpm ■	Torque @ rpm (ft lbs) ■	Bore x Stroke (in.)	Compression Ratio	Oil Pressure @ 2000 rpm
	8-440	4 bbl	280 @ 4800	375 @ 3200	4.320 x 3.750	8.20:1	55
	8-440 HP	4 bbl	290 @ 4800	380 @ 3200	4.320 x 3.750	8.20:1	55
'73	6-225	1 bbl	105 @ 4000	185 @ 1600	3.400 x 4.125	8.4:1	55
	8-318	2 bbl	150 @ 3600	265 @ 2000	3.910 x 3.310	8.6:1	55
	8-340 HP	4 bbl	240 @ 4800	295 @ 3600	4.040 x 3.310	8.5:1	55
	8-360	2 bbl	170 @ 4000	285 @ 2400	4.000 x 3.580	8.4:1	55
	8-400	2 bbl	185 @ 3600	310 @ 2400	4.340 x 3.380	8.2:1	55
	8-400 HP	4 bbl	260 @ 4800	335 @ 3600	4.340 x 3.380	8.2:1	55
	8-440	4 bbl	220 @ 3600	350 @ 2400	4.320 x 3.750	8.2:1	55
	8-440 HP	4 bbl	275 @ 4800	380 @ 3200	4.320 x 3.750	8.2:1	55
'74	6-225	1 bbl	105 @ 3600	180 @ 1600	3.400 x 4.125	8.4:1	55
	8-318	2 bbl	150 @ 4000	255 @ 2200	3.910 x 3.310	8.6:1	55
	8-318 HP	2 bbl	170 @ 4000	265 @ 2600	3.910 x 3.310	8.6:1	55
	8-360	2 bbl	180 @ 4000	290 @ 2400	4.000 x 3.580	8.4:1	55
	8-360	4 bbl	200 @ 4000	290 @ 3200	4.000 x 3.580	8.4:1	55
	8-360 HP	4 bbl	245 @ 4800	320 @ 3600	4.000 x 3.580	8.4:1	55
	8-400	2 bbl	185 @ 4000	315 @ 2400	4.340 x 3.380	8.2:1	55
	8-400	4 bbl	205 @ 4400	310 @ 2400	4.340 x 3.380	8.2:1	55
	8-400 HP	4 bbl	250 @ 4800	330 @ 3400	4.340 x 3.380	8.2:1	55
	8-440	4 bbl	230 @ 3600	350 @ 3200	4.320 x 3.750	8.2:1	55
	8-440 Calif.	4 bbl	220 @ 3600	345 @ 3200	4.320 x 3.750	8.2:1	55
	8-440 HP	4 bbl	275 @ 4400	375 @ 3200	4.320 x 3.750	8.2:1	55
'75	6-225	1 bbl	95 @ 3600	170 @ 1600	3.400 x 4.125	8.4:1	55
	6-225 Calif.	1 bbl	90 @ 3600	165 @ 1600	3.400 x 4.125	8.4:1	55
	8-318	2 bbl	150 @ 4000	255 @ 1600	3.910 x 3.310	8.5:1	55
	8-318①	2 bbl	150 @ 4000	260 @ 1600	3.910 x 3.310	8.5:1	55
	8-318 Calif.	2 bbl	135 @ 3600	245 @ 1600	3.910 x 3.310	8.5:1	55
	8-318 Calif.①	2 bbl	145 @ 3600	250 @ 1600	3.910 x 3.310	8.5:1	55
	8-360	2 bbl	180 @ 4000	290 @ 2400	4.000 x 3.580	8.4:1	55
	8-360	4 bbl	190 @ 4000	270 @ 3200	4.000 x 3.580	8.4:1	55
	8-400	2 bbl	165 @ 4000	295 @ 3200	4.340 x 3.380	8.2:1	55
	8-400①	2 bbl	175 @ 4000	300 @ 3200	4.340 x 3.380	8.2:1	55
	8-400②	2 bbl	165 @ 4000	295 @ 3200	4.340 x 3.380	8.2:1	55
	8-400	4 bbl	190 @ 4000	290 @ 3200	4.340 x 3.380	8.2:1	55
	8-400①	4 bbl	195 @ 4000	285 @ 3200	4.340 x 3.380	8.2:1	55
	8-400 Calif.	4 bbl	185 @ 4000	285 @ 3200	4.340 x 3.380	8.2:1	55
	8-400 HP	4 bbl	235 @ 4200	320 @ 3200	4.340 x 3.380	8.2:1	55
	8-400 HP①	4 bbl	240 @ 4200	325 @ 3200	4.340 x 3.380	8.2:1	55
	8-440	4 bbl	215 @ 4000	330 @ 3200	4.320 x 3.750	8.2:1	55
	8-440 Calif.	4 bbl	210 @ 4000	320 @ 3200	4.320 x 3.750	8.2:1	55
	8-440 HP	4 bbl	260 @ 4000	355 @ 3200	4.320 x 3.750	8.2:1	55
	8-440 Calif.	4 bbl	250 @ 4000	350 @ 3200	4.320 x 3.750	8.2:1	55
'76	6-225	1 bbl	100 @ 3600	170 @ 1600	3.400 x 4.125	8.4:1	55
	8-318	2 bbl	150 @ 4000	255 @ 1600	3.910 x 3.310	8.5:1	55
	8-318 Calif.	2 bbl	140 @ 3600	250 @ 2000	3.910 x 3.310	8.5:1	55
	8-360	2 bbl	170 @ 4000	280 @ 2400	4.000 x 3.580	8.4:1	55

GENERAL ENGINE SPECIFICATIONS

Year	Engine No. Cyl. Displacement Cu. In.	Carburetor Type	Horsepower @ rpm ■	Torque @ rpm (ft lbs) ■	Bore x Stroke (in.)	Compression Ratio	Oil Pressure @ 2000 rpm
	8-360	4 bbl	175 @ 4000	270 @ 1600	4.000 x 3.580	8.4:1	55
	8-400	2 bbl	175 @ 4000	300 @ 2400	4.340 x 3.380	8.2:1	55
	8-400	4 bbl	240 @ 4400	325 @ 3200	4.340 x 3.380	8.2:1	55
	8-400 Calif.	4 bbl	185 @ 3600	285 @ 3200	4.340 x 3.380	8.2:1	55
	8-400 Lean Burn	4 bbl	210 @ 4400	305 @ 3200	4.340 x 3.380	8.2:1	55
	8-400 HP	4 bbl	240 @ 4400	325 @ 3200	4.340 x 3.380	8.2:1	55
	8-440	4 bbl	205 @ 3600	320 @ 2000	4.320 x 3.750	8.2:1	55
	8-440 Police	4 bbl	255 @ 4400	355 @ 3200	4.320 x 3.750	8.2:1	55
	8-440 Police Calif.	4 bbl	250 @ 4000	350 @ 3200	4.320 x 3.750	8.2:1	55
	8-440 Calif.	4 bbl	200 @ 3600	310 @ 2400	4.320 x 3.750	8.2:1	55
'77	6-225	1 bbl	100 @ 3600	170 @ 1600	3.400 x 4.125	8.4:1	30-70
	6-225 Calif.	1 bbl	90 @ 3600	170 @ 1600	3.400 x 4.125	8.4:1	30-70
	6-225	2 bbl	110 @ 3600	180 @ 2000	3.400 x 4.125	8.4:1	30-70
	8-318	2 bbl	145 @ 4000	245 @ 1600	3.910 x 3.310	8.6:1	35-65
	8-318 Calif.	2 bbl	135 @ 3600	235 @ 1600	3.910 x 3.310	8.6:1	35-65
	8-360	2 bbl	155 @ 3600	275 @ 2000	4.000 x 3.580	8.4:1	30-80
	8-360 Calif.⑤	4 bbl	170 @ 4000	270 @ 1600	4.000 x 3.580	8.4:1	30-80
	8-400④	4 bbl	190 @ 3600	305 @ 3200	4.340 x 3.380	8.2:1	30-80
	8-440④	4 bbl	195 @ 3600	320 @ 2000	4.320 x 3.750	8.2:1	30-80
	8-440 Calif.④⑤	4 bbl	185 @ 3600	310 @ 2400	4.320 x 3.750	8.2:1	30-80
'78	6-225	1 bbl	100 @ 3600	170 @ 1600	3.400 x 4.125	8.4:1	30-70
	6-225	2 bbl	110 @ 3600	180 @ 2000	3.400 x 4.125	8.4:1	30-70
	8-318④	2 bbl	140 @ 4000	245 @ 1600	3.910 x 3.310	8.5:1	35-65
	8-318 Calif.④	4 bbl	155 @ 4000	245 @ 1600	3.910 x 3.310	8.5:1	35-65
	8-360④	2 bbl	155 @ 3600	270 @ 2400	4.000 x 3.580	8.4:1	30-80
	8-360⑤	4 bbl	170 @ 4000	270 @ 2400	4.000 x 3.580	8.4:1	30-80
	8-360 Calif.	4 bbl	170 @ 3600	265 @ 1600	4.000 x 3.580	8.4:1	30-80
	8-360 Calif. HP	4 bbl	160 @ 3600	265 @ 1600	4.000 x 3.580	8.0:1	30-80
	8-400④	4 bbl	190 @ 3600	305 @ 3200	4.340 x 3.380	8.2:1	30-80
	8-440④⑥	4 bbl	225 @ 4400	360 @ 3200	4.320 x 3.750	7.8:1	30-80
	8-440 Calif.④⑥	4 bbl	240 @ 4000	330 @ 3200	4.320 x 3.750	7.8:1	30-80
'79	6-225	2 bbl	110 @ 3600	180 @ 2000	3.400 x 4.125	8.4:1	30-70
	8-318 ESC	2 bbl	140 @ 4000	245 @ 1600	3.910 x 3.310	8.5:1	35-65
	8-318 ESC Calif	4 bbl	155 @ 4000	245 @ 1600	3.910 x 3.310	8.5:1	35-65
	8-360 ESC	2 bbl	155 @ 3600	270 @ 2400	4.000 x 3.580	8.4:1	30-80
	8-360 Calif	4 bbl	160 @ 3600	265 @ 1600	4.000 x 3.580	8.4:1	30-80
	8-360 ESC HP	4 bbl	170 @ 4000	270 @ 1600	4.000 x 3.580	8.0:1	30-80

■ Horsepower and torque are SAE net figures. They are measured at the rear of the transmission with all accessories installed and operating. Since the figures vary when a given engine is installed in different models, some are representative rather than exact.

① Gran Fury, Monaco
② Charger SE
④ Lean burn
⑤ High altitude
⑥ Police only
HP High Performance
ESC Electronic Spark Control

TUNE-UP SPECIFICATIONS

Satellite, Coronet,
Charger, 1975-78
Fury, 1977-78 Monaco, Magnum XE, ST. Regis
(intermediate size)

When analyzing compression test results, look for uniformity among cylinders rather than specific pressures.

Year	ENGINE No. Cyl Displacement (cu in.)	hp●	SPARK PLUGS Orig. Type	Gap (in.)	DISTRIBUTOR Point Dwell (deg)	Point Gap (in.)	IGNITION TIMING (deg) ▲ Man Trans ●	Auto Trans	VALVES Intake Opens ■ (deg)	Fuel Pump Pressure (psi)	IDLE SPEED (rpm) ▲ Man Trans ●	Auto Trans
'72	6-225	110	N-14Y	.035	44	.020	TDC	TDC	16	3½-5	750(700)	750(700)
	8-318	150	N-13Y	.035	32	.017	TDC	TDC	10	5-7	750	750(700)
	8-340 HP	240	N-9Y	.035	Electronic		2½B	2½B	22	5-7	900(850)	750
	8-400	190	J-13Y	.035	30	.018	—	5B①	18	3½-5	—	700
	8-400 HP	255, 265	J-11Y	.035	Electronic		TDC(2½B)	10B(5B)	21	3½-5	900(800)	750
	8-440 HP	290	J-11Y	.035	Electronic		2½B	10B(5B)	21	3½-5	900(800)	900
'73	6-225	105	N-14Y	.035	Electronic		TDC	TDC	16	4-5½	750	750
	8-318	150	N-13Y	.035	Electronic		2½B	TDC	10	6-7½	750	700
	8-340 HP	240	N-9Y	.035	Electronic		5B	2½B	22	6-7½	850	850
	8-400	175	J-13Y	.035	Electronic		—	10B	18	4-5½	—	700
	8-400 HP	260	J-11Y	.035	Electronic		2½B	10B	21	4-5½	900	850
	8-440 HP	275	J-11Y	.035	Electronic		—	10B	21	4-5½	—	800
'74	6-225	105	N-14Y	.035	Electronic		TDC	TDC	16	3½-5	800	750
	8-318	150	N-13Y	.035	Electronic		TDC	TDC	10	5-7½	750	750
	8-318 HP	170	N-13Y	.035	Electronic		TDC	TDC	22	5-7½	750	750
	8-360	180	N-12Y	.035	Electronic		—	5B	16	5-7½	—	750
	8-360	200	N-12Y	.035	Electronic		—	5B	16	6-7½	—	750
	8-360 HP	245	N-12Y	.035	Electronic		5B(2½B)	5B	22	6-7½	850	850
	8-400	205	J-13Y	.035	Electronic		—	5B	18	4-5½	—	900
	8-400 HP	250	J-11Y	.035	Electronic		5B	5B(2½B)	21	4-5½	900	900
	8-440	275	J-11Y	.035	Electronic		—	10B(5B)	21	7-8.2	—	800
'75	6-225	95	BL-13Y	.035	Electronic		TDC	TDC	16	3½-5	—	750
	8-318	150	N-13Y	.035	Electronic		2B	2B	10	5-7	—	750
	8-360	All	N-12Y	.035	Electronic		—	6B	18	5-7	—	750
	8-400	All	J-13Y	.035	Electronic		—	8B	18	4-5½	—	750
'76	6-225	100	RN-12Y	.035	Electronic		6B(4B)	2B	16	3½-5	750(800)	750
	8-318	150, 140	RBL-13Y	.035	Electronic		2B	2B(TDC)	10	5-7	750	750
	8-360	170	RN-12Y	.035	Electronic		—	2B	18	5-7	—	850
	8-400	175	RJ-13Y	.035	Electronic		—	10B	18	5-7	—	700
	8-400	4 bbl	RJ-13Y	.035	Electronic		—	8B	18	5-7	—	750
	8-400 HP	240	RJ-86P	.035	Electronic		—	6B	18	5-7	—	850
'77	6-225	110(100)	RBL-15Y	.035	Electronic		12B(8B)	12B(8B)	16	3½-5	700(750)	700(750)
	8-318	145(135)	RN-12Y	.035	Electronic		8B(TDC)	8B(TDC)	10	5¾-7¼	700(850)	700(850)
	8-360	155(170)	RN-12Y	.035	Electronic		—	10B(6B)	18	5¾-7¼	—	700(750)
	8-400②	190	RJ-13Y	.035	Electronic		—	10B	20	5¾-7¼	—	750
'78	6-225	1 bbl	RBL16Y	.035	Electronic		—	12B	16	3½-5	—	700(750)
	6-225	2 bbl	RBL16Y	.035	Electronic		12B	12B	16	3½-5	750	750
	8-318②	2 bbl	RN12Y	.035	Electronic		—	16B	10	5-7	—	750
	8-318②	4 bbl	RN12Y	.035	Electronic		—	10B	10	5-7	—	750
	8-360②	2 bbl	RN12Y	.035	Electronic		—	20B	18	5-7	—	750

TUNE-UP SPECIFICATIONS

Satellite, Coronet,
Charger, 1975-78
Fury, 1977-78 Monaco, Magnum XE, ST. Regis
(intermediate size)

When analyzing compression test results, look for uniformity among cylinders rather than specific pressures.

| ENGINE | | | SPARK PLUGS | | DISTRIBUTOR | | IGNITION TIMING (deg) ▲ | | VALVES | Fuel | IDLE SPEED (rpm) ▲ | |
No. Cyl Displacement Year (cu in.)	hp●	Orig. Type	Gap (in.)	Point Dwell (deg)	Point Gap (in.)	Man Trans ●	Auto Trans	Intake Opens ■ (deg)	Pump Pressure (psi)	Man Trans ●	Auto Trans
8-360	4 bbl	RN-12Y	.035	Electronic		—	③	18	5-7	—	750
8-400②	4 bbl	OJ-13Y	.035	Electronic		—	20B	18	5-7	—	750
8-440②	4 bbl	OJ-11Y	.035	Electronic		—	16B(8B)	18	6-7½	—	750
'79 6-225	2 bbl	RBL-16Y	.035	Electronic		—	12B	16	4-5½	—	750
8-318	All	RN-12Y	.035	Electronic		—	16B	10	5¾-7¼	—	750
8-360	All	RN-12Y	.035	Electronic		—	16B	18	5¾-7¼	—	750

▲ See text for procedure
● Figure in parentheses for California and high altitude
■ All figures Before Top Dead Center
① For non-California vehicles built after February 2, 1972—7½B
② Lean burn
③ 6B—High Altitude
   8B—Calif. and HD
  A After Top Dead Center
  B Before Top Dead Center

TDC Top Dead Center
— Not applicable
HP—High performance
NOTE: The underhood specifications sticker often reflects tune-up specification changes made in production. Sticker figures must be used if they disagree with those in this chart.

MECHANICAL VALVE LIFTER CLEARANCE

Engine	Intake In.	Exhaust In.
All 6 cylinder	.010 (Hot)	.020 (Hot)

TUNE-UP SPECIFICATIONS

Polara, Monaco through 1976, 1977
Royal Monaco,
Fury through 1974, 1975-1977
Gran Fury (full size)

When analyzing compression test results, look for uniformity among cylinders rather than specific pressures.

| ENGINE | | | SPARK PLUGS | | DISTRIBUTOR | | IGNITION TIMING (deg) ▲ | | VALVES | Fuel | IDLE SPEED (rpm) ▲ | |
No. Cyl Displacement Year (cu in.)	hp●	Orig. Type	Gap (in.)	Point Dwell (deg)	Point Gap (in.)	Man Trans ●	Auto Trans	Intake Opens ■ (deg)	Pump Pressure (psi)	Man Trans ●	Auto Trans
'72 8-318	150	J-11Y	.035	28-32	.018	—	TDC	10	5-7	—	750(700)
8-360	175	N-13Y	.035	30-34	.017	—	TDC	16	5-7	—	750
8-400	190	J-13Y	.035	28-32	.018	—	5B②	18	3½-5	—	700
8-440	225	J-11Y	.035	28-32	.018	—	10B	18	3½-5	—	750(700)

Dodge & Plymouth

TUNE-UP SPECIFICATIONS

Polara, Monaco through 1976, 1977
Royal Monaco,
Fury through 1974, 1975-1977
Gran Fury (full size)

When analyzing compression test results, look for uniformity among cylinders rather than specific pressures.

ENGINE			SPARK PLUGS		DISTRIBUTOR		IGNITION TIMING (deg) ▲		VALVES	Fuel	IDLE SPEED (rpm) ▲	
Year	No. Cyl Displacement (cu in.)	hp●	Orig. Type	Gap (in.)	Point Dwell (deg)	Point Gap (in.)	Man Trans ●	Auto Trans	Intake Opens ■ (deg)	Pump Pressure (psi)	Man Trans ●	Auto Trans
'73	8-318	150	N-13Y	.035	Electronic		—	TDC	10	6-7½	—	700
	8-360	170	N-13Y	.035	Electronic		—	TDC	16	6-7½	—	750
	8-400	185	J-13Y	.035	Electronic		—	10B	18	4-5½	—	700
	8-440	220	J-11Y	.035	Electronic		—	10B	18	4-5½	—	700
'74	8-360	180	N-12Y	.035	Electronic		—	5B	16	5-7½	—	750
	8-400	185	J-13Y	.035	Electronic		—	5B	18	4-5½	—	750
	8-400	205	J-13Y	.035	Electronic		—	5B	18	4-5½	—	900 (750)
	8-440	275	J-11Y	.035	Electronic		—	10B	18	7-8.2	—	750
'75	8-318	150	N-13Y	.035	Electronic		—	2B	10	5-7	—	750
	8-360	All	N-12Y	.035	Electronic		—	6B	18	5-7	—	750
	8-400	175	J-13Y	.035	Electronic		—	10B	18	4-5½	—	750
	8-400	190	J-13Y	.035	Electronic		—	8B	18	4-5½	—	750
	8-440	215	RY-87P	.040	Electronic		—	8B	18	4-5½	—	750
'76	8-318	150	RN-12Y	.035	Electronic		—	2B	10	5-7	—	750
	8-360	170	RN-12Y	.035	Electronic		—	2B	18	5-7	—	850
	8-360	175	RN-12Y	.035	Electronic		—	6B	18	5-7	—	750
	8-400	175	RJ-13Y	.035	Electronic		—	10B	18	5-7	—	700
	8-400	4 bbl	RJ-13Y	.035	Electronic		—	8B	18	5-7	—	750
	8-440	200, 205	RJ-13Y	.035	Electronic		—	8B	18	5-7	—	750
'77	8-318	145(135)	RN-12Y	.035	Electronic		8B(TDC)	8B(TDC)	10	5¾-7¼	700(850)	700(850)
	8-360	155(170)	RN-12Y	.035	Electronic		—	10B(6B)	18	5¾-7¼	—	700(750)
	8-400①	190	RJ-13Y	.035	Electronic		—	10B	20	5¾-7¼	—	750
	8-440①	195(185)	RJ-13Y	.035	Electronic		—	12B(8B)	20	5¾-7¼	—	750

▲ See text for procedure
■ Before Top Dead Center
● Figure in parentheses for California and high altitude
① Lean burn
② Non-California cars built after Feb. 2, 7½B
NOTE: The underhood specifications sticker often reflects tune-up specification changes made in production. Sticker figures must be used if they disagree with those in this chart.

A After Top Dead Center
B Before Top Dead Center
TDC Top Dead Center
HP High Performance

MECHANICAL VALVE LIFTER CLEARANCE

Engine	Intake (Hot) In.	Exhaust (Hot) In.
All six cylinder	.010	.020

FIRING ORDER

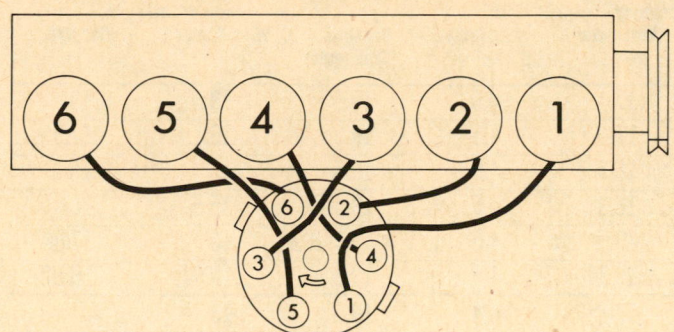

CHRYSLER CORP. 6-cyl.
Engine firing order: 1-5-3-6-2-4
Distributor rotation: clockwise

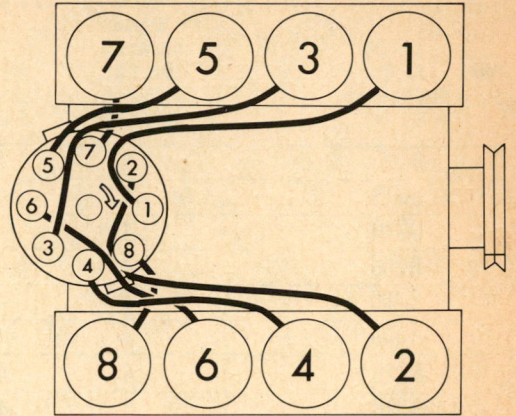

CHRYSLER CORP. 318, 340, 360 V8
Engine firing order: 1-8-4-3-6-5-7-2
Distributor rotation: clockwise

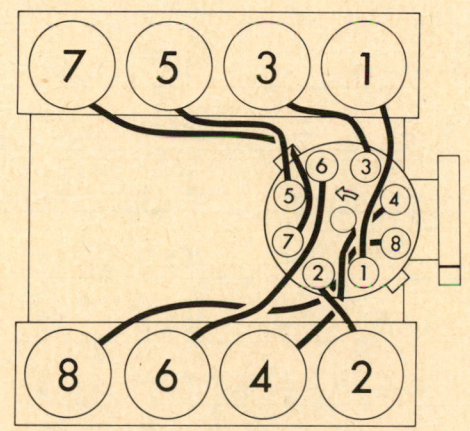

CHRYSLER CORP. 383, 400, 440 V8
Engine firing order: 1-8-4-3-6-5-7-2
Distributor rotation: counterclockwise

CAPACITIES

Year	ENGINE No. Cyl. Displacement (Cu. In.)	Engine Crankcase Add 1 Qt For New Filter	TRANSMISSION Pts To Refill After Draining			Drive Axle (pts)	Gasoline Tank (gals)	COOLING SYSTEM (qts)	
			Manual		Automatic			With Heater	With A/C
			3-Speed	4-Speed					
'72	6-225	4	6.5	—	17	4.5	21	13	14
	8-318	4	4.75	—	17	4.5	21⑪	16	17.5
	8-340	4	—	7.5	16.3	4.5	21	15	15.5
	8-360	4	—	—	16.3	4.5	23	16	16
	8-400 2 bbl	4	—	—	19	4.5	21⑪	14.5	15
	8-440	4	4.75	7.5	16.3	4.5	21⑪	14.5	14.5

Dodge & Plymouth

CAPACITIES

Year	ENGINE No. Cyl. Displacement (Cu. In.)	Engine Crankcase Add 1 Qt For New Filter	TRANSMISSION — Pts To Refill After Draining — Manual 3-Speed	4-Speed	Automatic	Drive Axle (pts)	Gasoline Tank (gals)	COOLING SYSTEM (qts) With Heater	With A/C
'73	6-225	4	4.75	——	17	4.5	19.5	13	13
	8-318	4	4.75	7.5	17	4.5	19.5[11][18]	16	17.5
	8-340	4	——	7.5	16.3	4.5	19.5	15	15.5
	8-360	4	——	——	16.3	4.5	19.5[11]	15.5	16
	8-400	4	——	7.5	19[16]	4.5	19.5[11][18]	16	17[19]
	8-440	4	——	——	16.3[17]	4.5	19.5[11]	16.5[20]	16.5[20]
'74	6-225	4	4.75	——	17	4.4	19.5	13	——
	8-318	4	4.75	7.5	17	4.4	19.5[18]	16	18
	8-360 Satellite, Charger, Coronet	4	——	7.5	16.5	4.4	19.5[18]	16.5	16.5
	8-360 Fury, Polara, Monaco	4	——	——	16.5	4.4[12]	25.0[8]	16	16
	8-400 Satellite, Charger, Coronet	4	——	——	19	4.4[12]	19.5[18]	16.5	16.5
	8-400 HP Satellite, Charger, Coronet	4	——	7.5	16.5	4.4[12]	19.5[18]	16.5	17.5
	8-400 Fury, Polara, Monaco	4	——	——	19	4.4[12]	25.0[8]	16.5	16.5
	8-440 HP Satellite, Charger, Coronet	4	——	——	16.5	4.4	19.5	16	16
	8-440 Fury, Polara, Monaco	4	——	——	19	4.5	25.0[8]	16	16
'75	6-225 Charger, Coronet, Fury	4	4.75	——	16.5	4.5	25.5	13.0	——
	8-318 Charger, Coronet, Fury	4	4.75	——	16.5	4.5	25.5[18]	16.5	18.0
	8-318 Gran Fury, Monaco	4	——	——	16.5	4.5	26.5	17.5	17.5
	8-360 Charger, Coronet, Fury	4	——	——	16.5	4.5	25.5[18]	16.0	16.0
	8-360 Gran Fury, Monaco	4	——	——	16.5	4.5	26.5[8]	16.0	16.0
	8-400 Charger, Coronet, Fury	4	——	——	16.5	4.5	25.5[18][21]	16.5	16.5
	8-400 Gran Fury, Monaco	4	——	——	16.5	4.5	26.5[8]	16.5	16.5
	8-440 Gran Fury, Monaco	4	——	——	16.5	4.5	26.5[8]	16.0	16.0
'76	6-225 Charger, Coronet, Fury	4	4.75	——	17	4.5	20.5	13.0	14.5
	8-318 Charger, Coronet, Fury	4	4.75	——	17	4.5	25.5[14]	16.5	18.0
	8-318 Gran Fury, Monaco	4	——	——	19	4.5	26.5	17.5	17.5
	8-360 Charger, Coronet, Fury	4	——	——	17[5]	4.5	25.5[14]	16.0	16.0
	8-360 Gran Fury, Monaco	4	——	——	19	4.5	26.5	16.0	16.0
	8-400 Charger, Coronet, Fury	4	——	——	19	4.5	25.5[14]	16.5	16.5

CAPACITIES

Year	ENGINE No. Cyl. Displacement (Cu. In.)	Engine Crankcase Add 1 Qt For New Filter	TRANSMISSION — Pts To Refill After Draining			Drive Axle (pts)	Gasoline Tank (gals)	COOLING SYSTEM (qts)	
			Manual 3-Speed	4-Speed	Automatic			With Heater	With A/C
	8-400 HP Charger	5	—	—	19	4.5	20.5	16.5	16.5
	8-400 Gran Fury, Monaco	4	—	—	19	4.5	26.5⑧	16.5	16.5
	8-440 Gran Fury, Monaco	4	—	—	19	4.5	26.5⑧	16.0	16.0
'77	6-225 Fury, Monaco	4	4.75	—	17	4.5	20.5	13	14.5
	8-318 Fury, Monaco, Charger	4	4.75	—	16.5	4.5	25.5④	16.5	18
	8-318 Gran Fury, Royal Monaco, Charger	4	—	—	16.5	4.5	25.5④	17.5	17.5
	8-360 Fury, Gran Fury, Charger, Monaco, Royal Monaco	4	—	—	16.5	4.5	25.5④	16	16
	8-400 Fury, Gran Fury, Charger, Monaco, Royal Monaco	4	—	—	16.5	4.5	25.5④	16.5	16.5
	8-440 Gran Fury, Royal Monaco	4	—	—	16.5	4.5	26.5	16	16
'78	6-225	4	4.75	—	17⑥	4.4	20.5①	13	14.5
	8-318	4	—	—	17⑥	4.4	25.5④②	16	17.5
	8-360	4	—	—	17⑥	4.4	25.5④②	15.5	15.5
	8-400	4	—	—	16.5⑥	4.4③	25.5④②	16	16.5
	8-440	4	—	—	16.5⑥	4.5	25.5	16.5	16.5
'79	6-225	4	—	—	17⑥	4.5	21	11.5	14.5
	8-318	4	—	—	17⑥	4.5	21	15.0	17.5
	8-360	4	—	—	17⑥	4.5	21	16.0	16.0

① 25.5 with optional tank
② Dual exhaust—20.5
③ Station wagons—4.5
④ Station wagons—20.5 gals
⑤ Charger SE—19
⑥ 7.8 pts if converter isn't drained
⑦ Not used
⑧ Station wagons—24 gals
⑨ Not used
⑩ Not used
⑪ Fury, Polara, Monaco—23 gals
⑫ Station wagons—4.5 pts
⑬ Not used
⑭ Station wagons—20.5 leaded, 20 unleaded
⑮ Not used
⑯ Charger, Coronet, Satellite with 4 bbl—16.3 pts
⑰ Fury, Polara, Monaco—19 pts
⑱ Station wagons—21 gals
⑲ Fury, Polara, Monaco—16 qts
⑳ Fury, Polara, Monaco—15.5 qts
㉑ 400 4 bbl w/dual exhaust—20.5 gals.
—— Not applicable

Dodge & Plymouth

TORQUE SPECIFICATIONS

All readings in ft lbs

Year	Engine Displacement (cu in.)	Cylinder Head Bolts	Rod Bearing Bolts	Main Bearing Bolts	Crankshaft Bolt	Flywheel to Crankshaft Bolts	MANIFOLD Intake	MANIFOLD Exhaust
'72-'79	6-225	70	45	85	Press fit	55	10①	10
'72-'76	8-318, 340, 360	95	45	85	100	55	40	15/20②
'77-'79	8-318, 360	105③	45	85	100	55	45	15/20②
'72-'78	8-400, 440	70	45	85	135	55	45	30

① Intake to exhaust manifold bolts—20 ft. lbs., studs—30 ft. lbs. through 1976, Intake to exhaust manifold bolts—17 ft. lbs., studs—20 ft. lbs. 1977 and later
② Nuts/screws
③ 95—1977

VALVE SPECIFICATIONS

Year	Engine No. Cyl. Displacement (cu in.)	Seat Angle (deg)	Face Angle (deg)	Spring Test Pressure (lbs @ in.)	Spring Installed Height (in.)	STEM TO GUIDE Clearance (in.) Intake	STEM TO GUIDE Clearance (in.) Exhaust	STEM Diameter (in.) Intake	STEM Diameter (in.) Exhaust
'72	6-225	45	45①	144 @ 1.31	1 11/16	.0010-.0030	.0020-.0040	.3725	.3715
	8-318	45	45①	177 @ 1.31	1 11/16	.0010-.0030	.0020-.0040	.3725	.3715
	8-340	45	45①	208 @ 1.31	1 11/16	.0015-.0035	.0025-.0045	.3720	.3710
	8-360	45	45①	177 @ 1.31	1 11/16	.0010-.0030	.0020-.0040	.3725	.3715
	8-400 2 bbl	45	45	200 @ 1.44	1 7/8	.0010-.0030	.0020-.0040	.3727	.3717
	8-400 4 bbl	45	45	246 @ 1.72	1 7/8	.0015-.0032	.0025-.0042	.3722	.3712
	8-440	45	45	200 @ 1.44	1 7/8	.0010-.0030	.0020-.0040	.3727	.3717
	8-440 HP	45	45	246 @ 1.72	1 7/8	.0015-.0032	.0025-.0042	.3722	.3712
'73	6-225	45	45②	160 @ 1.24	1 21/32	.0010-.0030	.0020-.0040	.3725	.3715
	8-318	45	45②	189 @ 1.28	1 21/32	.0010-.0030	.0020-.0040	.3725	.3715
	8-340	45	45②	238 @ 1.22	1 21/32	.0015-.0035	.0025-.0045	.3720	.3710
	8-360	45	45②	195 @ 1.24	1 21/32	.0010-.0030	.0020-.0040	.3725	.3715
	8-400 2 bbl	45	45	200 @ 1.42	1 55/64	.0010-.0027	⑦	.3727	⑨
	8-400 4 bbl	45	45	234 @ 1.40	1 55/64	.0015-.0032	⑧	.3722	⑩
	8-440	45	45	200 @ 1.42	1 55/64	.0010-.0027	⑦	.3727	⑨
	8-440 HP	45	45	234 @ 1.40	1 55/64	.0015-.0032	⑧	.3722	⑩
'74	6-225	45	45①	143 @ 1.31	1 21/32	.0010-.0030	.0020-.0040	.3725	.3715
	8-318	45	45①	177 @ 1.31	1 21/32	.0010-.0030	.0020-.0040	.3725	.3715
	8-360	45	45①	208 @ 1.31⑪	1 21/32	.0010-.0030	.0025-.0040	.3725	.3715
	8-400, 440 std.	45	45	200 @ 1.43	1 55/64	.0010-.0027	⑦	.3727	⑨
	8-400 HP	45	45	246 @ 1.36	1 55/64	.0015-.0032	⑧	3722	⑩
	8-440 HP	45	45	246 @ 1.36	1 55/64	.0015-.0032	⑧	.3722	⑩
'75	6-225	45	45	143 @ 1.31	1 21/32	.0010-.0030	.0020-.0040	.3725	.3715
	8-318	45	45①	177 @ 1.31	1 21/32	.0010-.0030	.0020-.0040	.3725	.3715
	8-360	45	45①	208 @ 1.31⑪	1 21/32	.0010-.0030	.0020-.0040	.3725	.3715
	8-400, 440 std.	45	45	200 @ 1.44	1 55/64	.0011-.0028	⑦	.3727	⑨
	8-400, 440 HP	45	45	246 @ 1.36	1 55/64	.0016-.0033	⑧	.3722	⑩
'76-	6-225	45	45	143 @ 1.31	1 21/32	.0010-.0030	.0020-.0040	.3725	.3715
	8-318	45	45①	177 @ 1.31⑪	1 21/32	.0010-.0030	.0020-.0040	.3725	.3715
	8-360	45	45①	182 @ 1.31⑪	1 21/32	.0010-.0030	.0020-.0040	.3725	.3715
	8-400, 440 std.	45	45	200 @ 1.44	1 55/64	.0011-.0028	⑦	.3725	⑨

VALVE SPECIFICATIONS

Year	Engine No. Cyl. Displacement (cu in.)	Seat Angle (deg)	Face Angle (deg)	Spring Test Pressure (lbs @ in.)	Spring Installed Height (in.)	STEM TO GUIDE Clearance (in.) Intake	Exhaust	STEM Diameter (in.) Intake	Exhaust
	8-400 HP	45	45	246 @ 1.36	1 55/64	.0016-.0033	⑧	.3722	⑩
'77-	6-225	45	45①	143 @ 1.31	1 21/32	.0010-.0030	.0020-.0040	3720-.3730	.3710-.3720
'79	8-318, 360	45	45①	177 @ 1.31	1 21/32	.0010-.0030	.0020-.0040	3720-.3730	.3710-.3720
	8-360 HP	45	45①	193 @ 1.25	1 21/32	.0015-.0035	.0025-.0045	3715-.3725	.3705-.3715
	8-400	45	45	200 @ 1.44	1 53/64	.0011-.0028	⑦	3723-.3730	⑩
	8-440	45	45	200 @ 1.44	1 53/64	.0011-.0028	⑦	3723-.3730	⑩

① Exhaust 43°
② Exhaust 47°
③ to ⑥ Not used
⑦ Hot end—.0021 .0038, cold end—.0011-.0028
⑧ Hot end—.0026 .0043, cold end—.0016-.0033

⑨ Hot end—.3716, cold end—.3726
⑩ Hot end—.3711, cold end—.3721
⑪ 177 @ 1.31 on 2 bbl engine
HP High Performance

CRANKSHAFT AND CONNECTING ROD SPECIFICATIONS

All measurements are given in inches

Year	Engine Displacement (cu in.)	CRANKSHAFT Main Brg. Journal Dia	Main Brg. Oil Clearance	Shaft End-Play	Thrust on No.	CONNECTING ROD Journal Diameter	Oil Clearance	Side* Clearance
'72-'79	6-225	2.7495-2.7505	.0005-.0020	.002-.007①	3	2.1865-2.1875	.0005-.0020	.006-.012②
'72-'79	8-318, 340	2.4495-2.5005	.0005-.0015③	.002-.007①	3	2.124-2.125	.0005-.0020	.006-.014
'72-'79	8-360	2.8095-2.8105	.0005-.0020	.002-.007①	3	2.124-2.125	.0005-.0020	.006-.014
'72-'74	8-400	2.6245-2.6255	.0005-.0020	.002-.007	3	2.3740-2.3750	.0005-.0020	.009-.017
'75-'78	8-400	2.6245-2.6255	.0005-.0020	.002-.007①	3	2.3750-2.3760	.0005-.0030④	.009-.017
'72-'74	8-440	2.7495-2.7505	.0005-.0020	.002-.007	3	2.3740-2.3750	.0010-.0025	.009-.017
'75-'78	8-440	2.7495-2.7505	.0005-.0020	.002-.007①	3	2.3750-2.3760	.0005-.0030④	.009-.017

* Total for two rods
① .002-.009 for 1977 and later
② .006-.025—1977 and later
③ .0005—.0020—1975 and later
④ .0005-.0025—1977 and later

RING SIDE CLEARANCE

All measurements are given in inches

Year	Engine No. Cyl. Displacement (cu. in.)	Top Compression	Bottom Compression	Year	Engine No. Cyl. Displacement (cu. in.)	Oil Control
'72-'79	All	.0015-.0030	.0015-.0030	'72-'79	6-225, 8-318, 340, 360	.0002-.005
				'72-'77	8-400, 440	.0000-.005
				'78	8-400, 440	.0002-.005

RING GAP

All measurements are given in inches

Year	Engine No. Cyl. Displacement (cu. in.)	Top Compression	Bottom Compression
'72	6-225	.010-.020	.010-.020
'72	8-318, 340, 360, 400, 440	.013-.023	.013-.023
'73-'79	6-225, 8-318, 360	.010-.020	.010-.020
'73-'78	8-340, 400, 440	.013-.023	.013-.023

Year	Engine	Oil Control
'72-'79	All	.015-.055

PISTON CLEARANCE

Year	Engine No. Cyl. Displacement (cu. in.)	Piston to Bore Clearance (in.)*
'72-'79	6-225, 8-318, 340, 360	.0005-.0015
'72-'78	8-400, 440	.0003-.0013

* At top of skirt

WHEEL ALIGNMENT SPECIFICATIONS

Year	Model	CASTER Range (deg)	CASTER Pref Setting (deg)	CAMBER Range (deg)	CAMBER Pref Setting (deg)	Toe-in (in.)	Steering Axis Inclin. (deg)	WHEEL PIVOT RATIO (deg) Inner Wheel	WHEEL PIVOT RATIO (deg) Outer Wheel
'72	M.S.—Coronet, Charger, Satellite	1/2N ± 1/2	1/2N	①	①	3/32 to 5/32	7 1/2	20	17.8
	P.S.—Coronet, Charger, Satellite	3/4P ± 1/2	3/4P	①	①	3/32 to 5/32	7 1/2	20	17.8
	M.S.—Fury, Monaco, Polara	1/2N ± 1/2	1/2N	①	①	3/32 to 5/32	7 1/2	20	18.8
	P.S.—Fury, Monaco, Polara	1/4 to 1 1/4P⑤	3/4P⑤	①	①	3/32 to 5/32	7 1/2	20	18.8
'73	M.S.—Coronet, Charger, Satellite	1 5/16N to 1/16P	5/8N	⑥	⑥	1/8 ± 3/32	7 1/2	20	17.8
	P.S.—Coronet Charger, Satellite	1/16N to 1 5/16P	5/8P	⑥	⑥	1/8 ± 3/32	7 1/2	20	17.8
	P.S.—Fury, Monaco, Polara	1/16N to 1 5/16P	5/8P	⑥	⑥	1/8 ± 3/32	7 1/2	20	18.8
'74	M.S.—Coronet, Charger, Satellite	1 3/4N to 1/2P	5/8N	⑦	⑦	1/16 to 1/4	8	20	18.0
	P.S.—Coronet, Charger, Satellite	1/2N to 1 3/4P	5/8P	⑦	⑦	1/16 to 1/4	8	20	18.0
	P.S.—Fury, Monaco, Polara	1/2N to 1 3/4P	5/8P	⑦	⑦	1/16 to 1/4	9	20	18.3

WHEEL ALIGNMENT SPECIFICATIONS

Year	Model	CASTER Range (deg)	CASTER Pref Setting (deg)	CAMBER Range (deg)	CAMBER Pref Setting (deg)	Toe-in (in.)	Steering Axis Inclin. (deg)	WHEEL PIVOT RATIO (deg) Inner Wheel	WHEEL PIVOT RATIO (deg) Outer Wheel
'75	M.S.—Coronet, Charger, Fury	1 5/16 N to 1/16 P	1/2 N	⑥	⑥	3/32 to 9/32	8	20	18.0
	P.S.—Coronet, Charger, Fury	1/16 N to 1 5/16 P	3/4 P	⑥	⑥	3/32 to 9/32	8	20	18.0
	P.S.—Gran Fury, Monaco	1/16 N to 1 5/16 P	3/4 P	⑥	⑥	3/32 to 9/32	9	20	18.3
'76	M.S.—Coronet, Charger, Fury	1 3/4 N to 1/2 P	1/2 N	⑦	⑦	1/16 to 1/4	8	20	18.0
	P.S.—Coronet, Charger, Fury	1/2 N to 1 3/4 P	3/4 P	⑦	⑦	1/16 to 1/4	8	20	18.0
	P.S.—Gran Fury, Monaco	1/2 N to 1 3/4 P	3/4 P	⑦	⑦	1/16 to 1/4	9	20	18.3
'77-'78	M.S.—Monaco, Fury, Charger, Magnum	1 3/4 N to 3/4 P	1/2 N	⑦	⑦	1/16 to 1/4	8	20	18.0
	P.S.—Monaco, Fury, Charger, Magnum	1/2 N to 2 P	3/4 P	⑦	⑦	1/16 to 1/4	8	20	18.0
	P.S.—Gran Fury, Royal Monaco	1/2 N to 2 P	3/4 P	⑦	⑦	1/16 to 1/4	9	20	18.3
'79	St. Regis, Magnum XE	1/2 N to 2 P	3/4 P	⑦	⑦	1/16 to 1/4	8	20	18.0

M.S. Manual steering
P.S. Power steering
P Positive
N Negative

① Left—1/4 P to 3/4 P; 1/2 P preferred
   Right 0 to 1/2 P; 1/4 P preferred
② to ⑤ not used

⑥ Left—1/8 P to 7/8 P; 1/2 P preferred
   Right—1/8 N to 5/8 P; 1/4 P preferred
⑦ Left—0 to 1P; 1/2 P preferred
   Right—1/4 N to 3/4 P; 1/4 P preferred

FRONT END HEIGHT (± 1/8 in.)

Year	Model	Front End Height	Year	Model	Front End Height
'72-'74	Coronet, Charger, Satellite	1 7/8 ②	'75-'76	Coronet, Satellite, Charger, Fury	10 3/4
	Fury, Monaco, Polara	1 3/8 ① ③		Wagon	11 1/4
				Gran Fury Monaco	10 1/8
			'77-'79	Monaco, Fury, Charger, Magnum	10 3/4
				Wagon	11 1/4
				Gran Fury, Royal Monaco	10 1/8

① Monaco, Polara—1 1/8
② '72-'73—1 5/8
③ 1974—1 in.

NOTE: Service procedures for the Charging System, Starting System, Ignition System, Cooling System, Fuel System, Emission Control Systems, Engine, Clutch and Manual Transmission apply to Chrysler, Cordoba, and Imperial models, as well.

CHARGING SYSTEM

Before undertaking any electrical system service, the battery must be disconnected. Never attempt to polarize or short any component of the system.

Charging System troubleshooting can be found in the Unit Repair Section.

Alternator Removal and Installation

To remove the alternator:
1. Disconnect the battery.
2. Disconnect the Bat. and Fld. leads from the alternator.
3. Remove the alternator by removing two mounting bolts and the belt tensioner bracket bolt.
4. To reinstall: reverse the above. Tighten the belt so that it can be depressed about 1/2 in. by moderate thumb pressure in the center of the longest span between pulleys. Some alternator brackets have a square hole into which you can insert a 1/2 in. square socket drive to tension the belt.

NOTE: *Never attempt to polarize an alternator, nor short the regulator.*

Regulator Removal and Installation

All models have a solid-state (silicon transistor) voltage regulator which is not adjustable. The regulator is in the engine compartment and clearly labeled.
1. Release the spring clips and pull off the regulator wiring plug.
2. Unbolt and remove the regulator.
3. Installation is the reverse of removal. Be sure that the spring clips engage the wiring plug and that the unit has a good ground.

STARTING SYSTEM

All models are equipped with one of two types of starter: a direct-drive type or a 3.5:1 or 2.0:1 reduction gear type. The reduction gear type of starter may be identified by the battery terminal on the starter being installed at an angle; the direct-drive type starter battery terminal is parallel to the starter case. Both types of starters have solenoids which are mounted directly on the starter assembly.

Starter Removal and Installation
1. Disconnect the ground cable at the battery.
2. Remove the cable from the starter.
3. Disconnect the solenoid leads at their solenoid terminals.
4. Remove the starter securing bolts and remove the starter from the engine flywheel housing. On some models with automatic transmissions, the fluid cooler tube bracket will interfere with starter removal. In this case, remove the starter securing bolts, slide the cooler tube bracket off the stud and then remove the starter.
5. Installation is the reverse of the above. Be sure that the starter and flywheel housing mating surfaces are free of dirt and oil. When tightening the bolt and nut, hold the starter away from the engine to ensure proper alignment.

Disabling the Seat Belt/Starter Interlock System

Since the regulation requiring the interlock system was done away with during the 1975 model year, this device may now be legally disabled. All dealers have received a service bulletin on how to properly accomplish this modification for customers requesting it. It involves disconnecting the buzzer wire and making internal wiring changes to the printed circuit board in the interlock module. It is recommended that this work be done by the dealer, a radio shop, or a person skilled in circuit board repairs.

NOTE: *Although the interlock can be disabled by disconnecting the seat sensor wires at the connectors under the seat, this is not the proper method, since it also disables the seat belt warning light, which is still required by law.*

IGNITION SYSTEM

Chrysler used conventional ignition systems on most 1972 models.

An electronic ignition system is standard on all 1973 and later Chrysler Corporation vehicles. This type of ignition system has no contact points; consequently, there is no dwell adjustment. The only regular ignition system maintenance required is inspection of the wiring and spark plug replacement (check timing on occasion only). To determine whether a car is equipped with electronic ignition, check for a double primary lead from the distributor, a dual ballast resistor located on the firewall, and a control unit located either on the left wheel housing or the firewall. Further details and troubleshooting on electronic ignition are in the Unit Repair Section.

NOTE: *Test tachometer hookup with electronic ignition is the same as with conventional point-type systems. One tachometer lead connects to the negative primary coil terminal and the other to ground. Check the instructions for the operation of the tachometer being used, as some meters will not register correctly with this system.*

1972-74 400 OR 440 4-V V8 IGNITION ADVANCE SOLENOID

This solenoid, located on the distributor side, is connected to the starter relay so that it operates only during engine cranking to improve starting.

When the engine fires, this solenoid ceases to operate. If the solenoid is not operating, it will affect starting, but not drivability. A possible sign of non-operation is popping through the carburetor during engine cranking.

To check operation, idle engine and connect a jumper wire from the battery to the solenoid lead. If the solenoid is operating properly, the engine speed will increase noticeably.

--- CAUTION ---

Disconnect the jumper wire as soon as possible after checking solenoid operation.

Distributor Removal
1. Take off the cap and wire assembly.
2. Disconnect the primary coil wire and vacuum tube. With electronic ignition, disconnect the lead wire at the harness connector.
3. Mark the relative positions of the distributor and rotor on the engine block.
4. Loosen the distributor mounting and lift out the distributor.

NOTE: *To simplify reinstallation, do not disturb the engine while the distributor is out.*

5. Reinstall by reversing the above procedure, aligning the distributor rotor and the mark on the block when installing the distributor.

Distributor Replacement (When Engine has been Disturbed)
SLANT 6 ENGINE
1. Rotate the engine until No. 1 piston is up on the compression stroke at top dead center. This is determined by the compression pressure and the 0 mark on the crankshaft pulley hub being aligned with the timing pointer, as the engine is rotated.
2. Rotate the rotor to a position just ahead of the No. 1 distributor cap terminal.
3. Lower the distributor into the opening, engaging the distributor gear with the drive gear on the camshaft. With the distributor

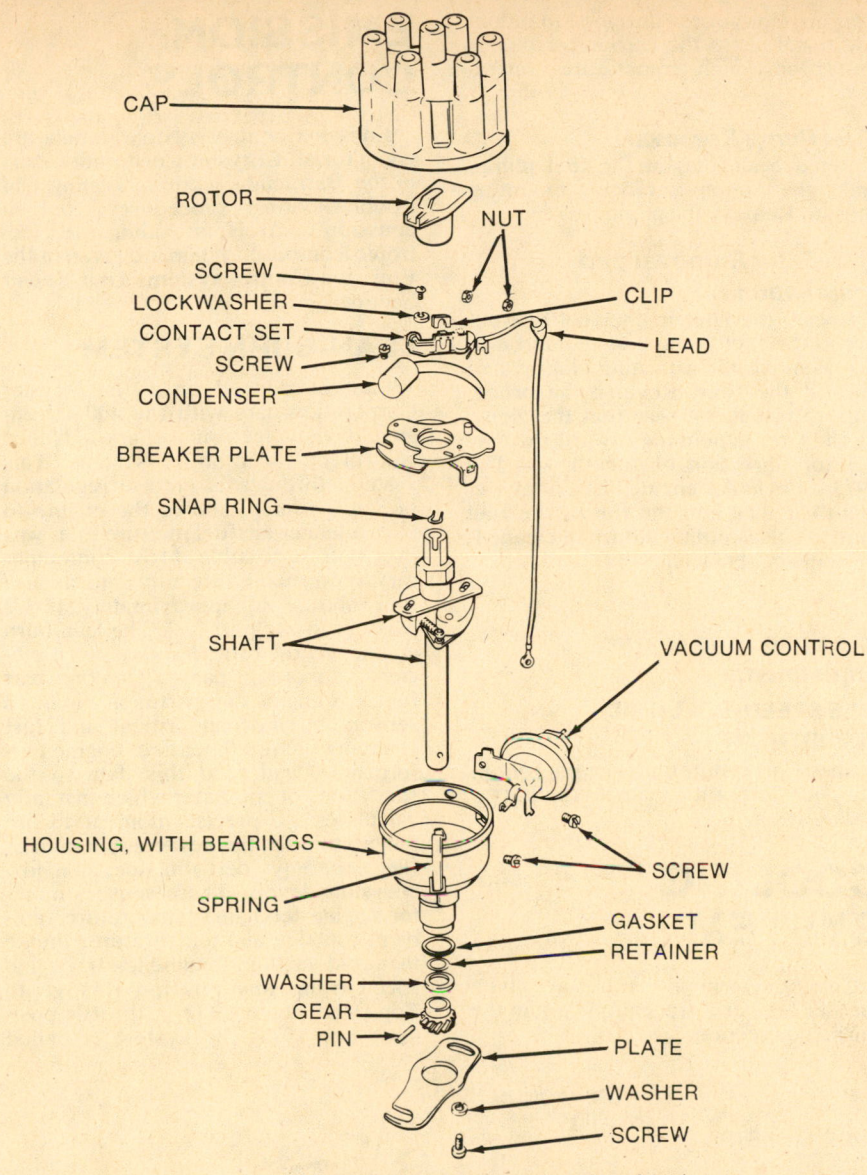

6 cylinder distributor (conventional ignition)
(© Chrysler Corp)

Labels on left diagram: CAP, ROTOR, NUT, SCREW, LOCKWASHER, CLIP, CONTACT SET, LEAD, SCREW, CONDENSER, BREAKER PLATE, SNAP RING, SHAFT, VACUUM CONTROL, HOUSING, WITH BEARINGS, SPRING, SCREW, GASKET, RETAINER, WASHER, GEAR, PIN, PLATE, WASHER, SCREW

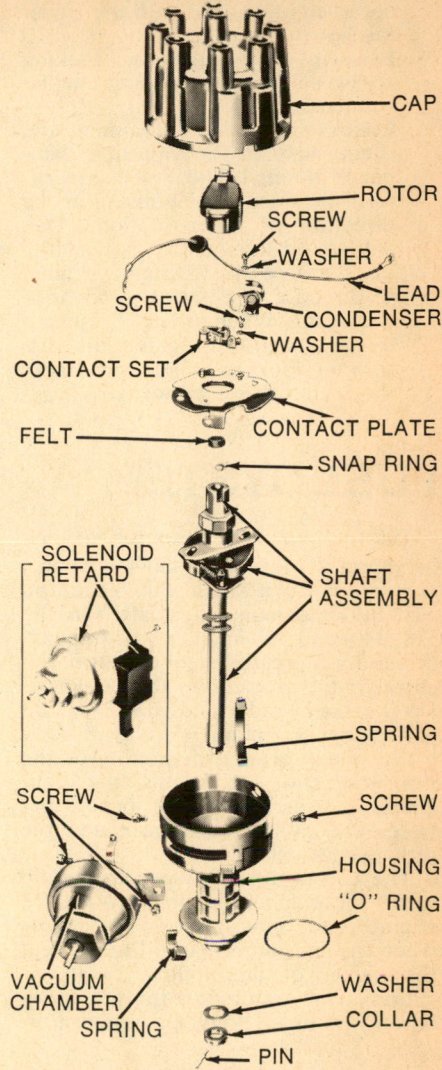

V8 distributor (conventional ignition)
(© Chrysler Corp)

Labels on right diagram: CAP, ROTOR, SCREW, WASHER, LEAD, SCREW, CONDENSER, WASHER, CONTACT SET, CONTACT PLATE, FELT, SNAP RING, SOLENOID RETARD, SHAFT ASSEMBLY, SPRING, SCREW, SCREW, HOUSING, "O" RING, VACUUM CHAMBER, SPRING, WASHER, COLLAR, PIN

fully seated on the engine, the rotor should be under the cap No. 1 tower with the distributor contact points just opening.

4. Install the cap, tighten the hold-down arm screw and check the timing with a timing light.

V8 ENGINE

Rotate the crankshaft until No. 1 cylinder is at top dead center. The pointer on the chain case cover should be over the 0 mark on the crankshaft pulley. The slot in the intermediate shaft which carries the gear that drives the oil pump and the distributor, should be parallel (or nearly so) with the crankshaft.

Hold the distributor over the mounting pad on the cylinder block so that the distributor body flange coincides with the mounting pad and the rotor points to the No. 1 cylinder firing position.

Install the distributor while holding the rotor in position, allowing it to move only enough to engage the slot in the drive gear.

Breaker Points and Condenser Replacement

1. Remove the distributor cap. Do not pull the wires from the cap. Pull the rotor from the shaft.
2. Carefully note the position of all leads and remove the securing nut. Loosen the point plate lock-screw and remove the points and condenser from the vehicle.
3. With a clean, lint-free rag, wipe any of the old cam grease from the distributor cam. Apply fresh cam lubricant sparingly.
4. Insert a new point set with the contact heel resting on the highest point of the cam lobe. Set the point

gap to specifications with a feeler gauge. The setting is correct when the feeler gauge is removed with a light drag. Install the condenser and secure the leads. Lock the point securing screws.

5. Replace the distributor cap and rotor. Check the dwell with a dwell meter. Adjust the point gap as necessary.
6. Road-test the vehicle.

Ignition Timing

NOTE: *Before timing the engine, check information on ignition retard/advance solenoids.*

The ignition timing test indicates correct timing of the engine only at idle and with the engine hot. Check timing as follows:

1. Disconnect the vacuum hose at the distributor and plug the line.
2. Connect a timing light to No. 1 spark plug and to the battery terminals.
3. Start the engine and set it to the

specified idle speed with the transmission in Neutral.

4. Loosen the distributor locking screw so that the housing can be rotated.

5. Check the timing by aiming the timing light at the vibration damper. If timing is ahead of the mark, turn the distributor housing in the direction of rotor-rotation. This will retard timing. If it is past the mark, rotate the distributor against its direction of rotation to advance the timing. When timing is adjusted to specifications, tighten the distributor lockscrew and reconnect the vacuum hose to the distributor.

FUEL SYSTEM

The fuel pumps used on the six-cylinder and all big blocks (400-440 cu. in.) are driven by a small cam eccentric cast into the main camshaft. On the 318, 340, and 360 engines, the pump is driven by a pressed steel eccentric secured on the gear end of the camshaft. On the six-cylinder and 318, 340, and 360 engines, the pump is driven directly by the pump rocker arm pressing on the cam eccentric. On the big block engines, there is a push rod located between the pump rocker arm and the driving eccentric.

The carburetor idle speed solenoid raises the engine idle speed to reduce engine emissions, but de-energizes when the ignition is shut off to prevent the engine from dieseling.

Some carburetors incorporate an internally mounted hot idle compensator.

This compensator is designed to induct additional air to the carburetor during low-speed, high-temperature operation.

Fuel Pump Removal

Remove all lines at the fuel pump, and the pump-to-block mounting screws. Remove the pump.

Fuel Filter Removal and Installation

Locate the filter in the fuel line between the fuel pump and the carburetor. Remove the attaching clamps and pull off the filter. Reverse the procedure to install. Be sure that the arrow on the filter is pointing toward the carburetor (direction of fuel flow). The 1973 six-cylinder engine has a filter element screwed into the top of the fuel pump. This is not meant to be cleaned; it should be replaced.

Idle Speed and Mixture Adjustments

IDLE SPEED, SOLENOID ADJUSTMENT

These procedures are given for all Chrysler Corporation cars in the Barracuda section.

COOLING SYSTEM

Cooling system procedures are given for all Chrysler Corporation cars in the Barracuda section.

EMISSION CONTROLS

Emission control system details are given for all Chrysler Corporation cars in the Barracuda section. Testing and troubleshooting procedures for all emission controls, including the electronic lean-burn system are given in the Emission Control systems Unit Repair Section.

LEAN-BURN SYSTEM

First introduced on 1976 Chrysler Corporation cars with the 400-4V engine is the electronic spark advance control or "lean-burn" system. This system, through its precise regulation of spark timing, allows the engine to burn a leaner air/fuel mixture than was ever before possible. Most contemporary powerplants are tuned to an air/fuel mixture of approximately 14-1/2 parts air to one part fuel. The lean-burn engine, on the other hand, is most efficient at about 18 parts air to one part fuel. Six engine compartment-mounted sensors monitor all critical and fast changing factors that affect engine performance, and feed this data to the spark control computer which instantly calculates the precise moment to fire the mixture for the best combination of fuel economy, performance, and low emissions levels. These sensors monitor engine (coolant) temperature, ambient (outside air) temperature, intake manifold vacuum (engine load), engine speed (rpm) and position relative to Top Dead Center (TDC), throttle position. For 1979, the system is called

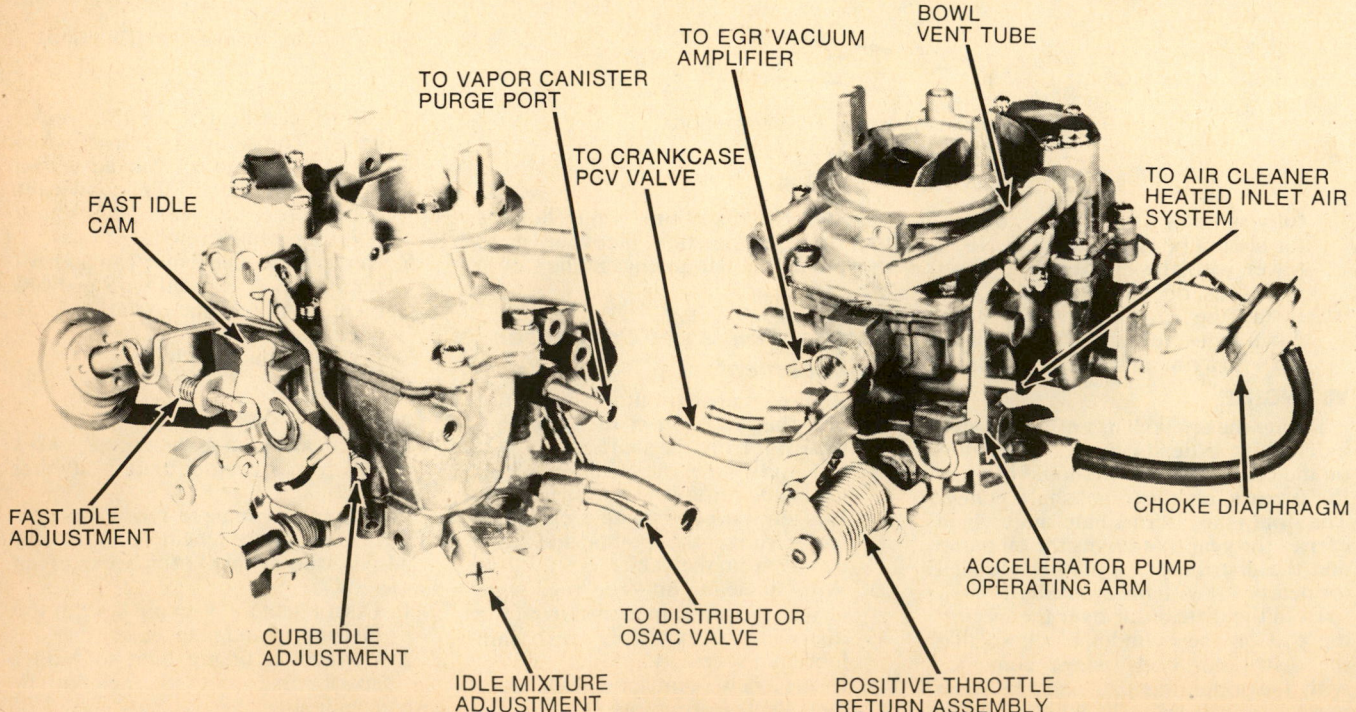

Holley 1945 carburetor adjustments (© Chrysler Corp)

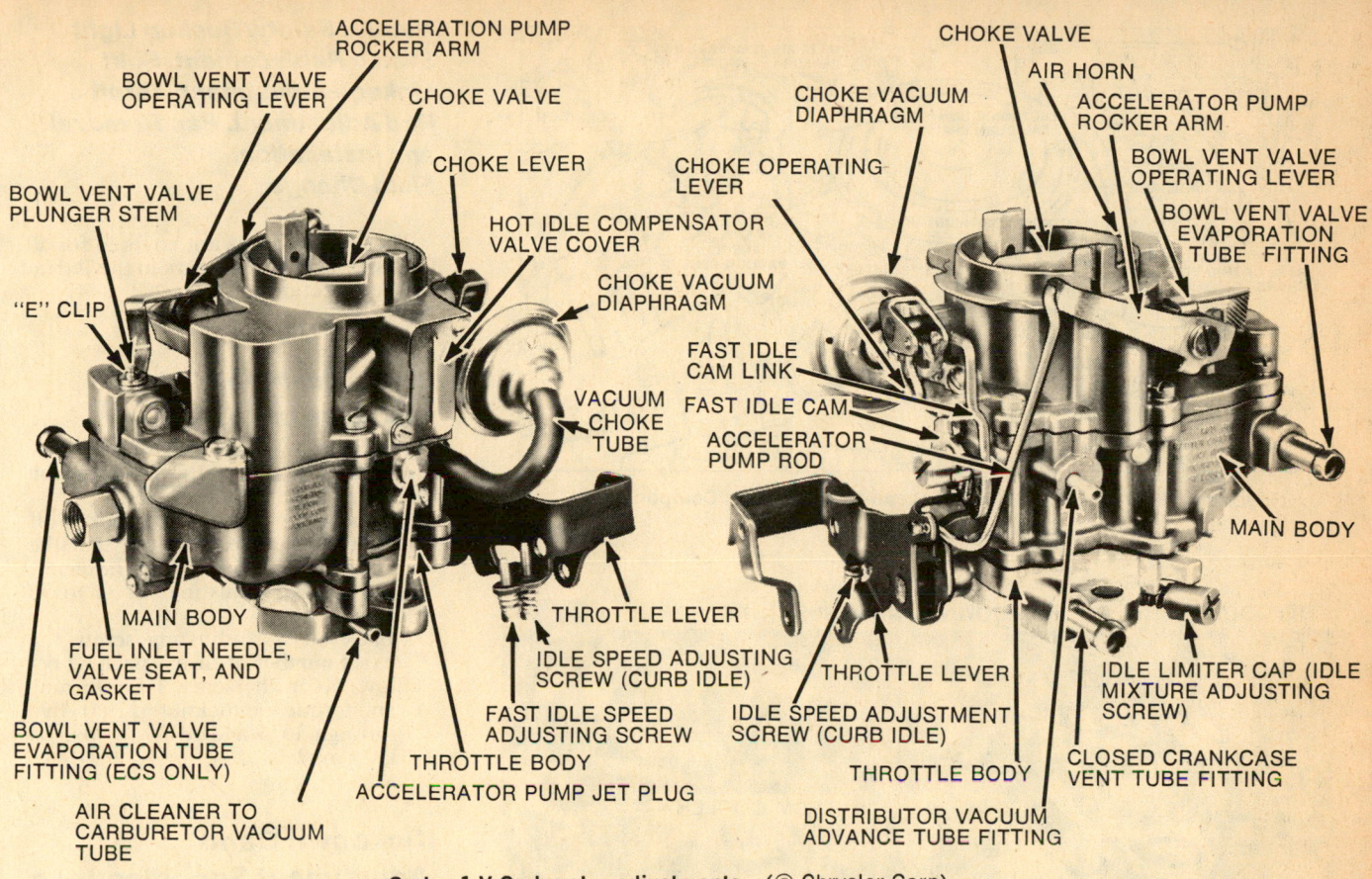

BOWL VENT VALVE OPERATING LEVER

ACCELERATION PUMP ROCKER ARM

CHOKE VALVE

CHOKE LEVER

BOWL VENT VALVE PLUNGER STEM

HOT IDLE COMPENSATOR VALVE COVER

"E" CLIP

CHOKE VACUUM DIAPHRAGM

VACUUM CHOKE TUBE

MAIN BODY

FUEL INLET NEEDLE, VALVE SEAT, AND GASKET

THROTTLE LEVER

IDLE SPEED ADJUSTING SCREW (CURB IDLE)

BOWL VENT VALVE EVAPORATION TUBE FITTING (ECS ONLY)

FAST IDLE SPEED ADJUSTING SCREW

AIR CLEANER TO CARBURETOR VACUUM TUBE

THROTTLE BODY

ACCELERATOR PUMP JET PLUG

CHOKE VACUUM DIAPHRAGM

CHOKE VALVE

AIR HORN

ACCELERATOR PUMP ROCKER ARM

CHOKE OPERATING LEVER

BOWL VENT VALVE OPERATING LEVER

BOWL VENT VALVE EVAPORATION TUBE FITTING

FAST IDLE CAM LINK

FAST IDLE CAM

ACCELERATOR PUMP ROD

MAIN BODY

THROTTLE LEVER

IDLE SPEED ADJUSTMENT SCREW (CURB IDLE)

IDLE LIMITER CAP (IDLE MIXTURE ADJUSTING SCREW)

THROTTLE BODY

CLOSED CRANKCASE VENT TUBE FITTING

DISTRIBUTOR VACUUM ADVANCE TUBE FITTING

Carter 1-V Carburetor adjustments   (© Chrysler Corp)

THROTTLE POSITION SOLENOID

CURB IDLE ADJUSTMENT SCREW

SECONDARY AIR VALVE

ALTITUDE COMPENSATOR (CALIFORNIA MODELS)

IDLE ENRICHMENT VALVE ASSEMBLY

CHOKE DIAPHRAGM

TO AIR PUMP DIVIRTER VALVE (ON SOME MODELS)

TO PCV VALVE

TO DISTRIBUTOR OSAC VALVE

TO AIR CLEANER HEATED INLET AIR SYSTEM

TO VAPOR CANISTER PURGE PORT

IDLE MIXTURE SCREWS WITH LIMITER CAPS (2)

FAST IDLE CAM

FAST IDLE ADJUSTMENT SCREW

Carter Thermo-Quad® Carburetor Adjustments   (© Chrysler Corp.)

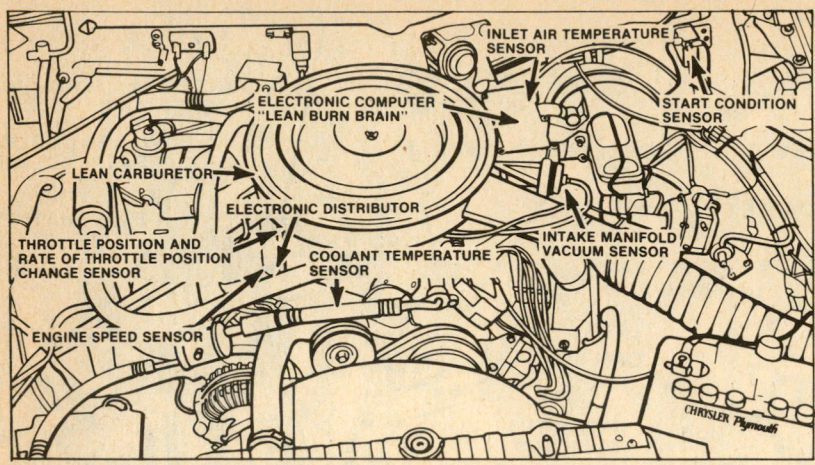

Electronic Spark Advance Control (Lean-Burn) System Components
(© Chrysler Corp.)

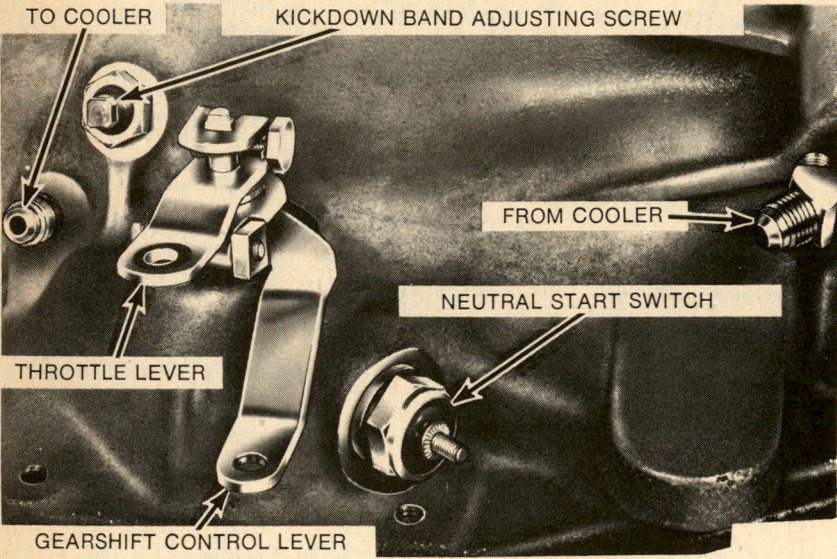

Torqueflite external adjustments and controls
(© Chrysler Corp)

Electronic Spark Control. Full details on this system are given in the Emission Control Systems Unit Repair Section.

ENGINE

NOTE: Engine service procedures for all Chrysler Corporation engines are given in the Barracuda car section.

CLUTCH

MANUAL TRANSMISSION

Clutch and manual transmission service procedures for all Chrysler Corporation cars are covered in the Barracuda car section.

AUTOMATIC TRANSMISSION

The model may be identified by the part number, which is stamped on a pad on the left side of the case pan flange. Visual identification is aided by the fact that the A-727 transmission has a more gradual slope to the converter housing than does the A-904, the 727 also has a bulge at the right front corner of the pan.

As a general rule, the A-904 Torqueflite is used on all 6 cylinder and light duty (318) V8 applications. The A-727 Torqueflite is used on all medium and heavy duty V8 applications. Starting 1976, normal duty 360 V8s in the Fury and Coronet use the A-904.

Neutral Safety/Backup Light Switch Replacement, Shift Linkage Adjustment, Throttle Rod Adjustment, Pan Removal and Installation, Fluid Change

These procedures are covered for all Chrysler Corporation cars in the Barracuda car section.

Band Adjustments
KICKDOWN BAND

The kickdown band adjusting screw is on the left side of the transmission case near the throttle lever shaft.
1. Loosen the locknut and back it off about five turns. Be sure that the adjusting screw is free in the case.
2. Torque the adjusting screw to 72 in. lbs.
3. Back off the adjusting screw the exact number of turns specified below. Keep the screw from turning and torque the locknut to 29 ft. lbs. through 1973 and to 35 ft. lbs. on later models.

Kickdown Band Adjustment Specifications

A—904	2 turns
A—727	
440 dual exhaust	2 turns
All others	2-1/2 turns

LOW AND REVERSE BAND

The pan must be removed from the transmission to gain access to the First and Reverse band adjusting screw.
1. Drain the transmission and remove the pan.
2. Loosen the band adjusting screw locknut and back it off about five turns. Be sure that the adjusting screw turns freely in the lever.
3. Torque the adjusting screw to 72 in. lbs. (1974 and later A-904 six cylinder applications—41 in. lbs).
4. Back off the adjusting screw the exact number of turns specified below. Keep the screw from turning and torque the locknut to 35 ft. lbs. through 1973 and to 30 ft. lbs. for later models.
5. Using a new gasket, refit the pan and torque the pan bolts to 150 in. lbs. Refill the transmission to the proper fluid level.

Low and Reverse Band Adjustment Specifications

A—904	
6 Cyl. (through 1973)	3-1/4 turns
6 Cyl. (1974 and later)	7 turns
318, 360 V8	4 turns
A—727	2 turns

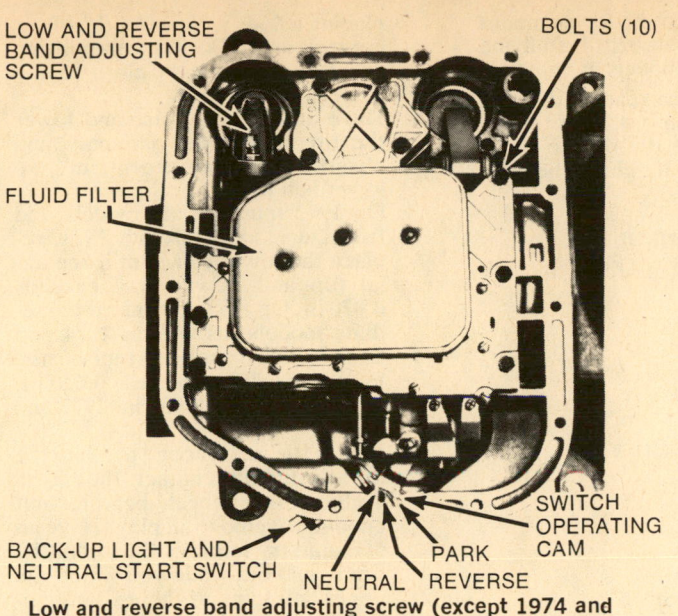

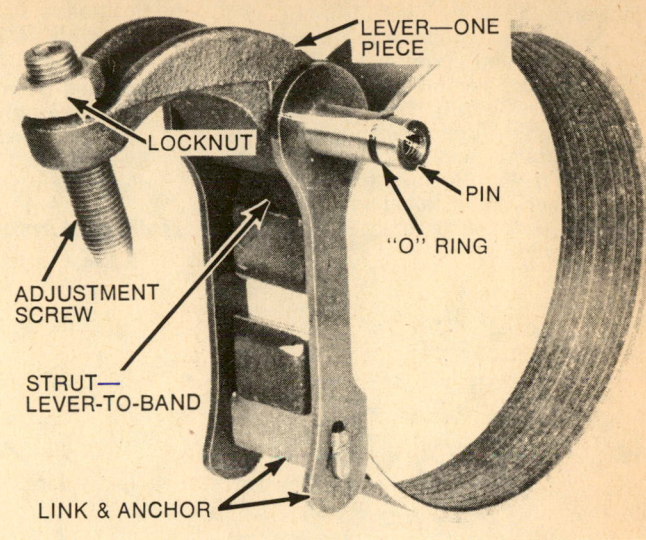

Low and reverse band adjusting screw (except 1974 and later A-904 six cylinder applications) (© Chrysler Corp)

1974 and later A-904 six-cylinder low-reverse band adjustment (© Chrysler Corp)

U-JOINTS

Driveshaft Removal and Installation, U-Joint Overhaul

These procedures are given in the Barracuda car section.

REAR AXLE

Several rear axle assemblies have been used on intermediate and full-sized Dodge and Plymouth models. An 8-1/4 in. unitized carrier axle is installed in many models equipped with the heavy-duty six cylinder or small block (318, 340, 360) V8 engines, an 8-3/4 in. removable carrier axle is used through 1974 with the heavy-duty six cylinder, and all small block V8s. Starting 1974, a 9-1/4 in. unitized carrier axle is installed in models equipped with the 400 or 440 V8. A 9-3/4 in. unitized carrier axle is used on 1972 intermediates equipped with the high-performance 440 V8s.

These axles can be visually identified as follows: The 8-1/4 in. axle has a 10 bolt rear cover. The 8-3/4 in. axle has a welded rear cover. The 9-1/4 in. axle has a 12 bolt rear cover. The 9-3/4 in. axle has a 10 bolt rear cover.

All axles have a ratio identification tag under one of the cover or carrier bolts.

Axle Shaft, Bearing, and Seal Removal and Installation

These procedures are given for all Chrysler Corporation axles in the Barracuda car section. Use the 8-1/4 in. axle procedure for the 9-1/4 in. axle.

JACKING, HOISTING

Jack the car at the front lower con-

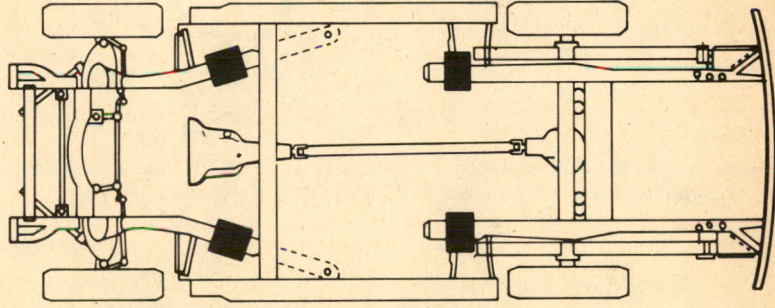

Positioning lift adapter

trol arm and at the rear under the axle housing.

To lift at the frame, use adapters so that contact will be made at the points shown. Lifting pads must extend beyond the sides of the supporting structure.

FRONT SUSPENSION

NOTE: The downsized Dodge St. Regis uses the intermediate-size Dodge front suspension system. The suspension service procedures and torques for intermediate-size models should be used for this model.

All Chrysler Corporation passenger vehicles utilize a torsion-bar front suspension. Compression-type lower ball joints are located in the steering arms on 1972 intermediates and full size cars through 1973. 1973 Satellite, Charger and Coronet models use screw-in type lower ball joints. All 1974 and later models utilize serviceable lower ball joints which are *pressed* into the lower control arms. When servicing the front suspension, it should be kept in mind that rubber bushings must not be lubricated at any time. Any front suspen-

sion component that contains rubber should be tightened with the suspension at the proper height and with full vehicle weight on the wheels. See the Unit Repair Section for front end height adjustment and alignment.

Shock Absorber Removal and Installation

1. Remove the washer and nut from the upper end of the shock absorber. Be sure to note the positions of all small parts.
2. Jack the vehicle until the wheels are off the floor. Remove the shock absorber lower attaching bolt.
3. Fully compress the shock absorber by pulling upward. Pull the shock firmly and remove it from the vehicle.
4. Check the shock absorber bushings, if they are worn or scored, replace them. Remove and install the bushings with a press or a drift and hammer. To ease installation, lubricate with water.

— CAUTION —
Do not use oil to ease installation.

5. Purge the new shock of air by repeatedly extending it in its normal position and compressing it while inverted. To install the shock, compress it fully. Insert the mount through the upper bushing, replace the retainer and nut, and torque it to 25 ft. lbs. Be sure that all of the retainers are installed with the concave side in contact with the rubber.

6. Position and align the lower mount of the shock absorber. Install the bolt (on some models it must be installed from the rear) with a nut and finger-tighten it. Lower the vehicle and torque the bolt to 50 ft. lbs. with the full weight of the vehicle on the wheels.

Ball Joint Inspection

1. Raise the front of the vehicle by

placing a floor jack under the lower control arm. Position the lifting point of the jack as close to the wheel as possible.

2. Have an assistant raise and lower the tire and wheel assembly and observe any movement at the lower ball joint.

3. On 1972 intermediate models and full size models through 1973, replace the lower ball joint if the axial (up and down) play exceeds 0.070 in. On 1973 and later intermediate models, as well as 1974 and later full size models, replace the joint if axial play exceeds 0.020 in. through 1976, or 0.030 in. 1977 and later.

4. Lower the jack enough to allow the tire to lightly contact the floor. Tighten the wheel bearing nut enough to remove all play. Have an assistant try to move the top of the tire in and out while you watch the upper ball joint. If there is any noticeable side play, replace the upper ball joint.

5. Correct the wheel bearing adjustment.

Lower Ball Joint Removal and Installation

1972 INTERMEDIATES, FULL SIZE THROUGH 1973

The lower ball joint is integral with the steering arm and is not serviced separately.

1. Raise the vehicle on a hoist so the front suspension will drop to the downward limit of its travel.

2. Place a jack stand under the lower control arm.

3. Lower the vehicle onto the jack stand.

4. Remove the tire, wheel, and brake drum from the vehicle as an assembly. If equipped with disc brakes, remove the tire and wheel, remove the brake pads, and remove the caliper from the steering knuckle and position it out of the way with the brake line attached. Remove the rotor from the spindle.

5. Remove the two lower and upper bolts that attach the steering arm-ball joint assembly to the brake assembly mounting plate and move the backing plate out of the way.

6. Using a suitable tool, disconnect the tie-rod end from the steering arm.

7. Remove the ball joint stud retaining nut and cotter pin.

8. Using a suitable tool, separate and remove the ball joint from the lower control arm.

On installation:

1. Position ball joint-steering arm assembly on the steering knuckle and install the two retaining bolts.

2. Insert the ball joint stud in the lower control arm and install the retaining nut and cotter pin.

3. Position the tie-rod end in the

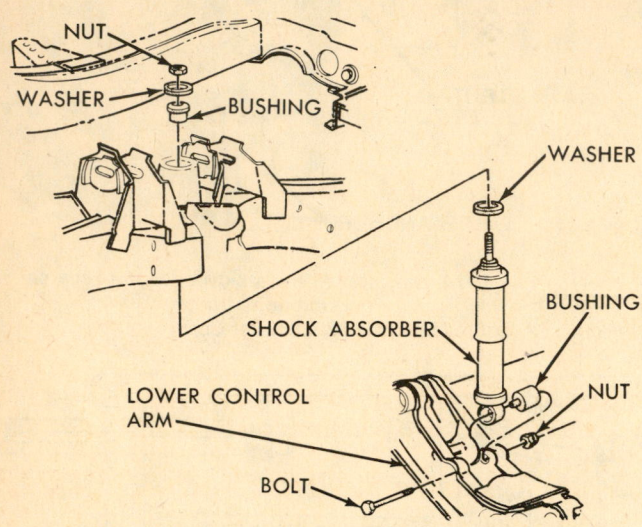

Front shock absorber replacement—Fury through 1973, Polara, Monaco; Satellite, Coronet, Charger 1973 and later; 1975 and later Fury
(© Chrysler Corp)

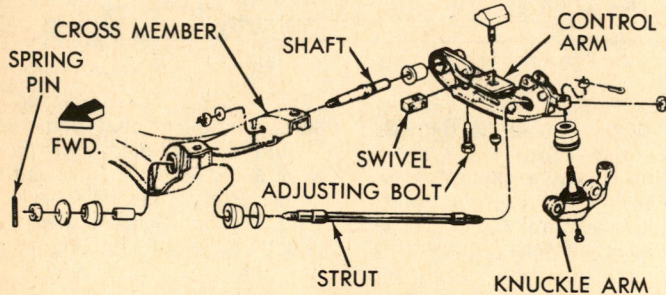

Lower control arm—Belvedere, Satellite, Coronet and Charger through 1972
(© Chrysler Corp)

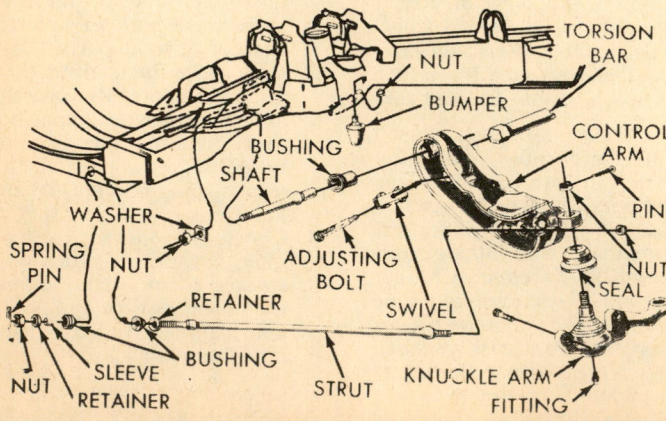

Lower control arm—Fury, Polara and Monaco through 1973
(© Chrysler Corp)

steering knuckle and install the retaining nut and cotter pin.

4. Place a load on the torsion bar by turning the adjusting bolt in a clockwise direction.

NOTE: *Loading the torsion bar is only necessary if it was removed.*

5. Install the tire, wheel and brake drum assembly. If equipped with disc brakes, install the rotor, caliper, brake pads and tire and wheel assembly.

6. Lower vehicle and install upper control arm rebound bumper if it was removed.

7. Check and adjust front suspension height and alignment.

ALL 1974 AND LATER MODELS AND 1973 INTERMEDIATES

Lower ball joints on these models may be serviced separately.

1. Place the ignition switch in the "Off" or "Unlocked" position.

2. Remove the rebound bumper.

3. Raise the vehicle on a hoist so that the front suspension drops to the downward limit of its travel. Position jackstands beneath the front frame for extra support.

4. Remove the wheel and tire assembly.

5. Remove the caliper from its mounts and tie it up out of the way so that there is no strain on the flexible brake hose.

6. Remove the hub and rotor assembly, splash shield, lower shock absorber mounting nut, retainer and insulator.

7. Off-load the torsion bars by rotating the adjusting bolts counterclockwise.

8. Remove the upper and lower ball joint stud cotter pins and nuts. Using a ball joint press tool, slide the tool over the upper stud until the tool rests on the steering knuckle.

9. Turn the threaded portion of the

Removing ball joint stud—1973 and later intermediates and 1974 and later full size models (© Chrysler Corp)

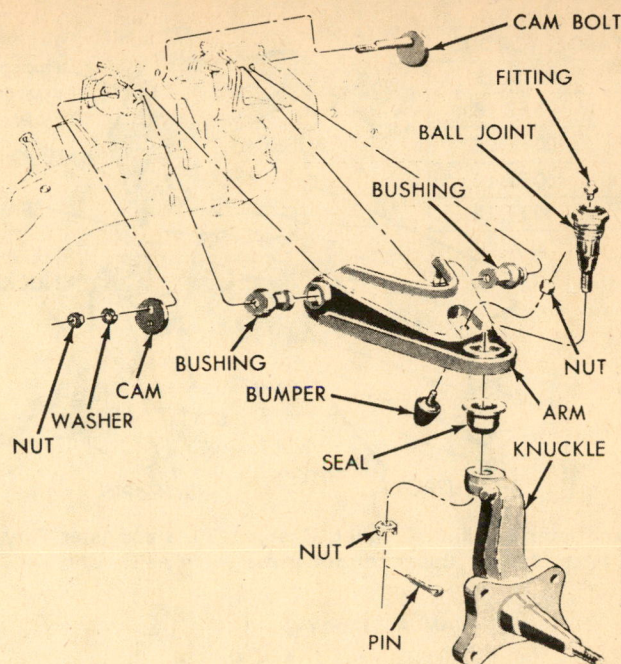

Upper control arm—Fury, Polara, and Monaco through 1973 (© Chrysler Corp)

bumper. Adjust the front suspension height and alignment.

tool so that it locks snugly against the lower stud. Tighten the tool enough to load the lower ball joint stud, and then strike the steering knuckle arm with a hammer to loosen the stud. Under no circumstances should you attempt to force the stud from the knuckle using the tool alone.

10. On all 1974 and later models, use a press to press the ball joint out of the lower control arm. On 1973 intermediates, unscrew the ball joint from the lower control arm.

On installation:

1. On all 1974 and later models, use a press to press the new ball joint into the lower control arm. On 1973 intermediates, screw in the ball joint and tighten to 125 ft. lbs.

2. Place a new seal over the ball joint (as necessary). Press the retainer portion of the seal down over the ball joint housing until it locks into position.

3. Insert the ball joint stud through the opening in the knuckle arm and install the stud retaining nuts. Tighten to 100 ft. lbs. on intermediates and 135 ft. lbs. on full-size. Install the cotter pins and lubricate the ball joint.

4. Load the torsion bar by rotating the adjusting bolt clockwise.

5. Install the shock absorber retaining nut, retainer and insulator, splash shield, hub and rotor assembly, and brake caliper. Install the wheel and tire assembly.

6. Adjust the front wheel bearings.

7. Remove the jackstands and lower the car. Install the rebound

Upper Ball Joint Replacement

1. Turn the ignition key to the "Off" or "Unlocked" position. Raise the vehicle by placing a floor jack under the lower control arm. Place the lifting point of the jack as close as possible to the wheel.

2. Remove the wheel, tire and drum as an assembly. On models with disc brakes, remove the tire and wheel, remove the disc brake pads, remove the disc brake caliper from the steering knuckle and position the caliper out of the way with the brake line attached. Remove the brake rotor from the steering knuckle.

3. Remove the nut that attaches the upper ball joint to the steering knuckle and, using a ball joint stud removal tool, loosen the ball joint stud from the steering knuckle.

4. Unscrew the upper ball joint from the upper control arm and remove it from the vehicle.

5. Position the new ball joint on the upper control arm, screw the ball joint into the control arm until it bottoms on the control arm and tighten the ball joint to a minimum of 125 ft. lbs.

NOTE: *When installing a ball joint, make certain the ball joint threads engage those of the upper control arm squarely if the original control arm is being used.*

6. Position a new seal on the ball joint stud and install the seal in the ball joint making sure the seal is fully seated on the ball joint housing.

7. Position the ball joint stud in the steering knuckle and install the retaining nut. Tighten the nut to 100

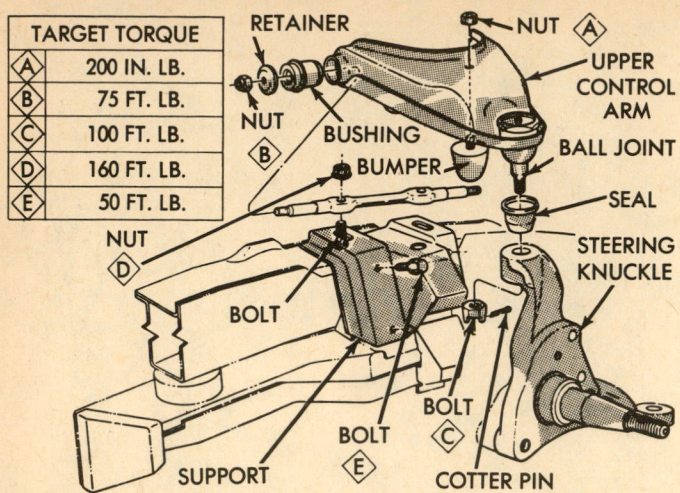

TARGET TORQUE	
Ⓐ	200 IN. LB.
Ⓑ	75 FT. LB.
Ⓒ	100 FT. LB.
Ⓓ	160 FT. LB.
Ⓔ	50 FT. LB.

1973 and later Satellite, Coronet, Charger, 1975 and later Fury, 1977 and later Monaco upper control arm assemblies (© Chrysler Corp)

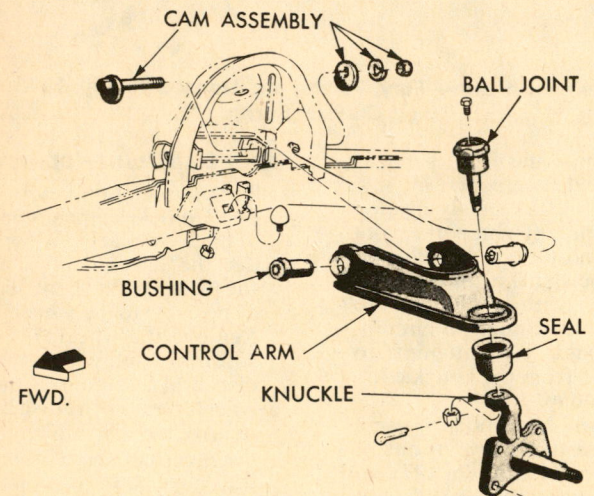

Upper control arm Belvedere, Satellite, Coronet and Charger through 1972 (© Chrysler Corp)

ft. lbs. on intermediates and 135 ft. lbs. on full size.

8. Lubricate the ball joint.
9. If equipped with disc brakes, install the rotor, caliper and brake pads. Install the tire and wheel.
10. Lower the vehicle and adjust the front suspension height and alignment.

Torsion Bar Removal and Installation

NOTE: *Torsion bars are not interchangable side-for-side. Do not mix them.*

1. Remove the upper control arm rebound bumper (if so equipped).
2. If the vehicle is jacked on a hoist, be sure that it is lifted in such a manner that the front suspension is under no load. If the vehicle is to be lifted with a floor jack, at the crossmember, first place a support between the jack and the cross-

member. The front suspension must be under no load.
3. Remove all loads from the torsion bars by rotating the anchor adjusting bolts counterclockwise.
4. At the torsion bar rear anchor, remove the lockring. Remove the automatic transmission torque shaft on 1974 and later models, if necessary.
5. Remove the torsion bar from its mounts. A special tool is available for this job; it clamps to the bar and provides a striking surface for driving the bar out.

CAUTION

The torsion bar may be under some load so be careful when removing it. Heat must never be used to ease bar removal.
---

6. It may be necessary to move the rear balloon seal out of the way to ease removal of the torsion bar.

Slide the torsion bar out through the rear of the anchor. Be careful not to damage the balloon seal.

7. Inspect the torsion bar and lightly dress all sharp edges. Coat the area of repair with a rust preventive. Clean the bar and lubricate it lightly to ease installation.
8. To begin replacement, slide the torsion bar into the rear anchor. Slide the balloon seal over the bar with the cupped end toward the rear of the bar.
9. Lightly grease the hex ends of the bar. Insert the torsion bar through the hex opening of the lower control arm. If the torsion bar hex opening does not align with the lower control arm opening, loosen the control arm pivot shaft nut and rotate the pivot shaft. Do not retighten the pivot shaft nut until the car is lowered to the floor. Replace the lockring in the rear anchor.
10. Fully pack the ring opening in the rear anchor with grease.
11. Install the balloon seal on the rear anchor so the seal lip engages with the anchor groove.
12. Rotate the adjusting bolt clockwise to load the torsion bar. Lower the vehicle and adjust the front suspension height. If the pivot shaft nut was loosened, tighten it to 145 ft. lbs. Replace the upper control arm rebound bumper.

Lower Control Arm and Steering Knuckle Removal and Installation

1972 INTERMEDIATES, FULL SIZE THROUGH 1973

1. Raise the car and support it under the frame; let the suspension hang down. Remove the wheel/tire and drum (or disc) as an assembly.
2. Remove the shock absorber at the bottom attachment and swing it up out of the way. Remove the torsion bar from its attachment at the lower control arm after releasing its tension.
3. Using a puller, remove the tie rod end from the steering knuckle arm. Be careful not to damage the seal during this operation. At this point, it is a good idea to match-mark the wheel alignment cam to act as an aid in assembly.
4. Remove the sway bar link from the lower control arm (or strut attaching straps). Remove the knuckle arm-to-brake support bolts and remove the knuckle arm. Position the brake support assembly to one side.
5. With a puller, remove the ball joint stud from the lower control arm. Be sure not to damage the seal during this operation.
6. At the forward end of the crossmember, remove the strut spring, pin, nut, and retainer, taking note of their relative positions. Remove

the nut and washer from the lower control arm shaft.

7. Using a non-metallic object, tap the end of the lower control arm shaft to aid in the shaft removal from the crossmember. Take off the lower control arm, strut, and shaft as an assembly.

8. To begin the installation (on some models), insert a new strut bushing into the crossmember with a twisting motion. Use water as a lubricant to aid installation—grease or oil must not be used. Position the strut bushing inner retainer on the strut and install the control arm, strut, and shaft assembly. Replace the shaft bushing retainer and finger-tighten the nut.

9. Replace the lower control arm shaft washer and finger-tighten the nut.

10. Replace the lower ball joint stud into the lower control arm and torque it to 85 ft. lbs. on intermediates and 100 ft. lbs. on full size. Install the cotter pin.

11. Install the brake support to the steering knuckle and replace the two upper bolts with nuts. Finger-tighten them only.

12. Install the steering knuckle on the steering knuckle arm and insert the two lower bolts with nuts. Torque the upper bolts to 55 ft. lbs. and the lower bolts to 120 ft. lbs. Inspect the tie rod end seal and replace it if necessary. Install the tie rod end to the steering knuckle arm and torque it to 40 ft. lbs. At this point, install the cotter pin.

13. Connect the shock absorber and finger-tighten it.

14. Replace the torsion bar assembly.

15. Install the wheel/tire/brake assembly.

16. Lower the vehicle. Adjust the front suspension height. Torque the strut nut at the crossmember to 52 ft. lbs. and insert the strut pin. Torque the lower control arm shaft nut to 145 ft. lbs. on intermediates and 185 ft. lbs. on full size and complete the installation of the shock absorber.

17. Align the front end.

1973 AND LATER INTERMEDIATES, 1974 AND LATER FULL SIZE

1. Remove the rebound bumper from the lower control arm.

2. Raise and support the car so that the front suspension hangs down.

3. Remove the wheel and brake caliper. Don't let the caliper hang by the brake line.

4. Remove the hub and brake disc, splash shield, and the lower shock absorber mount.

5. Remove the two strut bar attaching bolts.

6. Remove the automatic transmission gearshift torque shaft on intermediates, if it interferes.

7. Measure and record the torsion bar

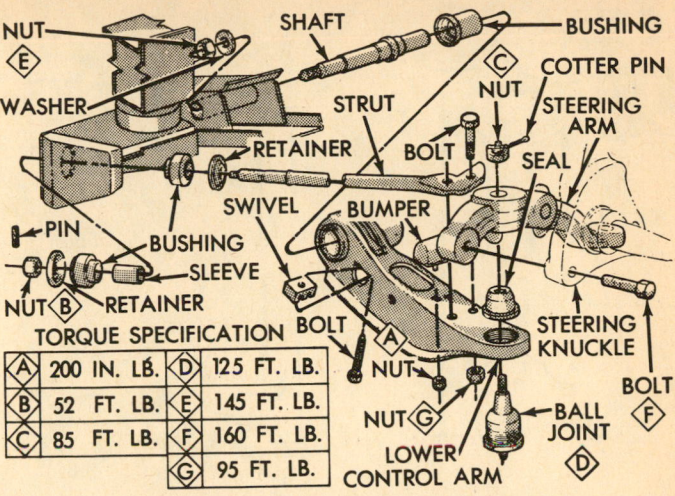

1973 and later Satellite, Coronet, Charger, 1975 and later Fury lower control arm assembly
(© Chrysler Corp)

TORQUE SPECIFICATION			
A	200 IN. LB.	D	125 FT. LB.
B	52 FT. LB.	E	145 FT. LB.
C	85 FT. LB.	F	160 FT. LB.
		G	95 FT. LB.

anchor bolt depth into the lower control arm and release the bar tension.

8. Remove the torsion bar as described earlier.

9. Use a ball joint removal tool to separate the lower ball joint stud from the steering knuckle.

10. Remove the lower control arm shaft nut from the control arm shaft and push the shaft out from the frame crossmember. Tap the threaded end of the shaft with a soft hammer to loosen it.

11. Remove the lower control arm and shaft as an assembly.

12. On installation, position the control arm and shaft in the crossmember. Install the shaft nut finger tight.

13. Install the lower ball joint stud into the steering knuckle and tighten the nut to 100 ft. lbs. on intermediates and 135 ft. lbs. on full size. Install a new cotter pin.

14. Install the torsion bar. Tighten the adjusting bolt to its original position.

15. Replace the gearshift torque shaft.

16. Replace the strut bar on the control arm and tighten the bolts to 95 ft. lbs.

17. Attach the brake splash shield and replace the lower shock absorber mount, but don't tighten it yet.

18. Attach the hub and rotor. Adjust the bearing. Install the caliper.

19. Replace the wheel. Lower the car to the floor and tighten the lower shock mount. Adjust the suspension height and wheel alignment. Tighten the control arm pivot shaft nut to 145 ft. lbs. on intermediates and 190 ft. lbs. on full size.

Wheel Bearing Adjustment

1. The wheel must be rotated while the bearing adjusting nut is tightened. 1972 models should be ad-

justed to 90 in lbs, and 1973 and later models to 240-300 in lbs.

2. Place the lock over the nut so that one pair of slots align with the cotter pin hole.

3. On 1972 models, back the nut and lock assembly off one slot. On 1973 and later models, loosen the nut and tighten it finger tight. Install the cotter pin. This adjustment should yield zero to .003 in. endplay.

4. Clean the grease cap. Coat, but do not fill, the cap with grease. Install it on the hub.

5. Lower the car and road test.

REAR SUSPENSION

Shock Absorber Removal and Installation

1. Jack up the vehicle under the axle assembly in such a manner as to relieve the load from the shock absorbers.

2. Remove the nut attaching the shock to the spring mounting plate stud.

3. At the upper mount, remove shock attaching bolt and the shock.

4. Purge the new shock of air by repeatedly extending it in its normal position and compressing it while inverted. To install the shock, position it so that the upper bolt may be inserted. Hand-tighten the bolt.

5. Align the shock with the spring mounting plate stud and install the bolt and nut. Hand-tighten only.

6. Lower the vehicle to the ground. Torque the lower nut to 50 ft. lbs. through 1976, 35 ft. lbs. 1977 and later, and the upper nut to 70 ft. lbs.

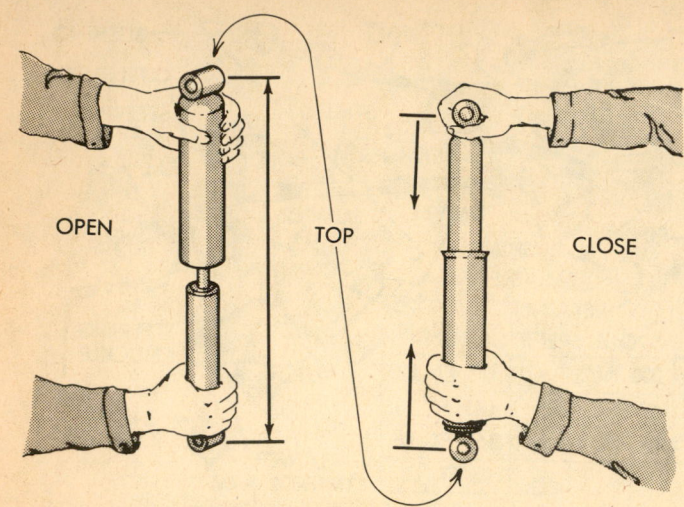

Purging air from shock absorbers (© Chrysler Corp)

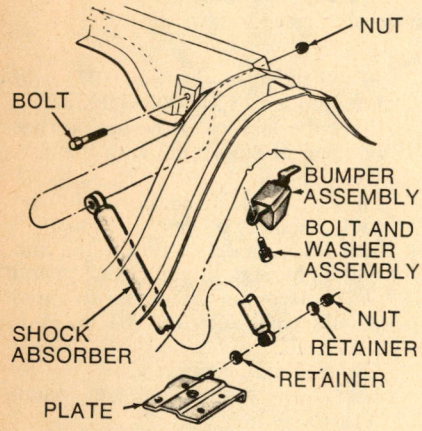

Rear shock absorber installation—
Satellite, Coronet, Charger, 1975
and later Fury, 1977 and later
Monaco (© Chrysler Corp)

Spring Removal and Installation

1. Jack up the vehicle and remove the wheels. Position jack stands under the axle to relieve the weight on the rear springs.
2. Disconnect the rear shock absorbers at the bottom attaching bolts. Lower the axle assembly to allow the rear springs to hang free. Disconnect the sway bar links, if equipped.
3. Remove the U-bolt nuts and withdraw the bolts and spring plates. Remove the nuts securing the front spring hanger to the body mounting bracket.

--- CAUTION ---

1974-77 full-size models have preloaded rear springs. A special spring stretcher (tool no. C-4211) must be installed before releasing either end of the spring. Do not try to remove the spring without the stretcher; its sudden release could cause serious injury.

4. Remove the rear spring hanger bolts and allow the spring to drop

enough to allow the front spring hanger bolts to be removed.
5. Remove the front pivot bolt from the front spring hanger.
6. Remove the shackle nuts and remove the shackle from the rear spring.
7. To begin installation, assemble the shackle and bushings in the rear of the spring and hanger. Start the shackle bolt nuts. Do not lubricate the rubber bushings to ease installation. Do not tighten the bolt nut.
8. Install the front spring hanger to the front spring eye and insert the pivot bolt and nut. Do not tighten them.
9. Install the rear spring hanger to the body bracket and torque the bolts to 30 ft. lbs.
10. With the aid of a helper, raise the spring and insert the bolts in the spring hanger mounting bracket holes. Install the nuts and torque them to 30 ft. lbs.
11. Position the axle assembly so it is correctly aligned with the spring center bolt.
12. Position the center bolt over the lower spring plate. Insert the U-bolt and nut. Torque the bolt to 45 ft. lbs. and connect the shock absorbers. Connect the sway bar, if equipped.
13. Lower the vehicle. Torque the pivot bolts to 125 ft. lbs. Torque the shackle nuts to 40 ft. lbs.
14. After this operation, drive the vehicle, check the front suspension height, and make adjustments as necessary.

BRAKES

Information on brake adjustments, lining replacement, disc brakes, bleeding procedure, master and wheel cylinder overhaul can be found in the Unit Repair Section.

Master Cylinder, Power Brake Booster Removal and Installation, Parking Brake Adjustment

These procedures are covered for all Chrysler Corporation cars in the Barracuda car section.

STEERING

A worm and recirculating ball-type steering gear is used with the manual steering system.

Constant-Control power steering is an option or standard on all models. Hydraulic power is provided by a belt-driven pump.

Some power steering pumps were equipped by the factory with oil coolers. These were used on vehicles with high-performance engines and/or special axle ratios. Steering service procedures for all Chrysler Corporation cars are given in the Barracuda car section.

INSTRUMENT PANEL

To service the instrument cluster, the cluster bezel must be removed. On some models, it will be necessary to remove the instrument panel upper cover and the sub-bezel to gain access to the speedometer cable and the electrical wire connectors that must be disconnected before the cluster can be removed. Care should be exercised not to force the finish panels when removing or installing, or breakage can occur. The speedometer cable is attached to the speedometer housing by a tensioned arm, which locks into a groove on the speedometer housing. To release the cable, depress the tensioned arm to disengage it from the groove, and pull the cable away from the speedometer housing.

Headlight Switch Replacement

1972-74 CORONET, CHARGER, SATELLITE; 1972-73 FURY, POLARA, MONACO

1. Disconnect the negative battery cable.
2. On cars equipped with air conditioning, disconnect the air duct from the spot cooler on the instrument panel.
3. Reach up under the instrument panel and depress the headlight switch control knob release button on the headlight switch.
4. While depressing the release button, pull the headlight switch control knob and shaft from the front of the instrument panel.
5. Disconnect the electrical leads from the rear of the switch.
6. Using a spanner wrench, remove the spanner nut that attaches the front of the headlight switch to the

front of the instrument panel.
7. Remove the headlight switch from the rear of the instrument panel.
8. Reverse the above procedure to install the new switch.

1975 AND LATER CORONET, CHARGER, FURY, MAGNUM, 1977-78 MONACO

1. Disconnect the battery ground cable. Remove the instrument cluster upper bezel by removing the screws and pulling out at the top.
2. Remove the escutcheon mounting screw.
3. Remove the screws holding the switch mounting plate to the cluster housing.
4. Pull the switch assembly from the cluster housing and disconnect the wires.
5. Depress the switch stem release button and pull the knob and stem from the switch.
6. Remove the switch mounting nut and remove the switch from the plate.
7. Reverse the procedure for installation.

1974 AND LATER GRAN FURY, 1974-76 MONACO, 1977 ROYAL MONACO

1. Disconnect the battery ground cable. Remove the instrument cluster bezel by placing the automatic transmission lever in 1 position, removing the ashtray and lighter, removing the screws under the lower bezel edge, pulling the top out, and disengaging the locking tabs.
2. Remove the wiper/washer switch mounting screws.
3. Pull the switch and mounting plate out and disconnect the wires.
4. Pull the switch to the on position and depress the release button on the side of the switch. Pull the knob and stem out.
5. Remove the escutcheon plate screw and remove the escutcheon. Remove the mounting plate nut and the switch.
6. Reverse the procedure for installation.

1979 DODGE ST. REGIS

This procedure is the same as for 1979 Chrysler Newport and New Yorker, given in the Chrysler car section.

WINDSHIELD WIPERS

The wiper blades are attached to the arms by one of two methods. One is a spring loaded lever in the blade bridge, which locks to a tapered lug on the side of the arm. To release the blade, depress the release lever and pull the blade from the lug. The second type has the arm inserted into a pivot bridge on the blade and locked into place by a flat spring in the bridge, engaging a lug

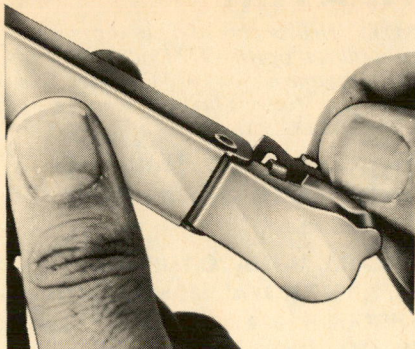

Movement of locking latch to release wiper arm from pivot
(© Chrysler Corp)

on the arm. To release the blade, depress the flat spring end and pull the blade from the arm.

Motor Removal and Installation

ALL THROUGH 1975 WITH NON-CONCEALED WIPERS

1. Disconnect the negative battery cable.
2. Disconnect the wiper motor wiring at the multiple connector.
3. On models without air conditioning, working under the dash, remove the nut that attaches the drive link to the wiper motor and disconnect the drive link from the motor. Remove the nuts that attach the wiper motor to the studs in the cowl panel and remove the motor from the vehicle.
4. Remove the wiper motor mounting nuts. Work the motor off the mounting studs far enough to gain access to the nut that attaches the drive link to the wiper motor. Do not force or pry the wiper motor off the mounting studs as this could damage the wiper drive link. Using a 1/2 in. open end wrench, remove the motor crank arm nut. Remove the arm from the wiper motor and remove the motor from the vehicle.

THROUGH 1975 WITH CONCEALED WIPERS, ALL 1976 AND LATER

1. Disconnect the negative battery cable.
2. Lift the latch on each wiper arm and remove the arms and blades as an assembly.
3. Remove the cowl screen.
4. Remove the drive crank retaining nut and drive crank. Hold the crank with a wrench when removing the crank arm nut to avoid gear breakage.
5. Disconnect the lead wires from the wiper motor.
6. Remove the three wiper motor mounting bolts and remove the motor from the vehicle.
7. Reverse the procedure to install. When installing the wiper arms and

blades, make sure the wiper motor is in the Park position.

RADIO

Removal and Installation

NOTE: *When installing the radio, adjust the antenna trimmer for peak radio volume. The antenna trimmer screw is near the antenna socket on the radio housing.*

FURY, POLARA, AND MONACO THROUGH 1973

1. Disconnect the battery.
2. Remove the nine lamp panel mounting screws, lower the lamp panel assembly slightly, disconnect the lamp harness from the main harness, and remove the lamp panel from the instrument panel.
3. Remove the steering column cover.
4. Remove the radio trim bezel mounting screws and bezel.
5. Remove the center lower air conditioner duct, if so equipped.
6. Disconnect the electrical leads and the antenna lead at the radio.
7. Remove the radio support mounting bracket.
8. Remove the two radio mounting bolts.
9. Move the radio down through the bottom of the instrument panel carefully to avoid damage to the vacuum hoses and electrical leads. Reverse the procedure to install.

1974 AND LATER GRAN FURY, 1974-76 MONACO, 1977 ROYAL MONACO

1. Disconnect the battery ground cable. Remove the instrument cluster bezel by placing the automatic transmission lever in 1 position, removing the ashtray and lighter, removing the screws under the lower bezel edge, pulling the top out, and disengaging the locking tabs.
2. Remove the sub bezel by removing the nylon attaching pins with pliers.
3. Remove the lamp assembly from the front of the monaural radio.
4. Remove the radio to panel screws.
5. Remove the instrument panel upper cover, first pulling the rear edge up.
6. Disconnect the antenna and speaker wires. Remove the radio bracket mounting nut.
7. Pull the radio out and disconnect the wire.
8. Reverse the procedure for installation.

SATELLITE, CORONET, CHARGER THROUGH 1973

1. Disconnect the negative battery cable.
2. Remove the radio control knobs

and retaining nuts. Remove the rear radio support brackets.

3. Disconnect the lead wires from the radio and remove the radio from the vehicle.

1974 SATELLITE, CORONET, CHARGER

1. Disconnect the battery ground cable.
2. Remove the ashtray.
3. Remove the right radio mounting screw from the right cluster leg. You can reach the screw through the lower left corner of the ashtray housing.
4. Loosen the support bracket nut on the right side of the radio.
5. Pull the knobs off. Remove the mounting nuts from the panel.
6. Detach the antenna, speaker, and power wires.
7. Remove the radio. Reverse the procedure for installation.

1975 AND LATER CORONET, CHARGER, FURY, MAGNUM, 1977-78 MONACO

1. Disconnect the battery ground cable.
2. Remove the instrument cluster lower bezel by removing the right remote control mirror mounting nut, removing the mounting screws, and pulling it off.
3. Disconnect the power, speaker, and antenna leads.
4. Remove the nut holding the radio to the support bracket at the rear. On tape player/radios, it is at the side.
5. Remove the radio mounting screws from the front of the panel.
6. Remove the radio from the front of the panel. Reverse the procedure for installation.

1979 DODGE ST. REGIS

This procedure is the same as for 1979 Chrysler Newport and New Yorker, given in the Chrysler car section.

HEATER

NOTE: *Heater core and blower removal procedures for the 1979 Dodge St. Regis are the same as for 1979 Chrysler Newport and New Yorker, given in the Chrysler car section.*

Heater Assembly Removal and Installation—Non Air-Conditioned Cars

POLARA, MONACO THROUGH 1976, 1977 ROYAL MONACO, FURY THROUGH 1974, 1975 AND LATER GRAN FURY

NOTE: *This is the removal procedure for the heater housing that attaches to the passenger compartment side of the firewall. Do not remove the part of the housing that attaches to the engine side of the firewall.*

1. Disconnect the battery and drain the radiator.
2. Disconnect the heater hoses at the firewall. Plug the hose fittings on the heater to prevent spilling coolant.
3. Slide the front seat back to allow room. Remove the instrument panel lower cover.
4. Disconnect the radio antenna and the upper level ventilator actuator vacuum line. Remove the screw holding the vent ducts to the heater housing, detach the bracket, and swing the ducts back.
5. Disconnect the electrical conductors from the blower motor resistor block on the face of the housing.
6. Remove the vacuum hoses from the trunk lock switch if so equipped.
7. Remove the control cables from the defroster door crank and the heat shut off door crank.
8. Remove the bottom retaining nut from the support bracket and swing the bracket up and out of way.

9. In the engine compartment, remove the retaining nuts from the studs.
10. Remove the locating bolt from the bottom center of the passenger side housing.
11. Roll or tip the housing out from under the instrument panel.
12. Remove the temperature control cable.

SATELLITE, CORONET, CHARGER; 1975 AND LATER FURY, 1977 AND LATER MONACO, MAGNUM

1. Disconnect the negative battery cable.
2. Drain the cooling system.
3. Disconnect the heater hoses from the heater core tubes at the firewall. Plug the core tubes to prevent spilling coolant on the interior of the car. Remove the blower motor vent tube.
4. Remove the three mounting nuts from the studs around the blower motor, the one nut from the heater housing near the center. On 1975 and later models, remove the lower instrument panel bezel, glove box, and glove box door.
5. Disconnect the antenna lead wire from the radio and position it out of the way.
6. Remove the screw that attaches the housing to the support rod for the plenum. It is located on the right-side of the housing above the outside air opening.
7. Disconnect the air door cables.
8. Disconnect the wires from the blower motor resistor.
9. Tip the heater assembly down and out.

Blower Motor Removal and Installation—Non Air-Conditioned Cars

SATELLITE, CORONET, CHARGER; 1975 AND LATER FURY, 1977 AND LATER MONACO, MAGNUM

1. Remove the heater assembly.
2. Disconnect the wiring from the blower motor to heater assembly.
3. Remove the motor cooler tube.
4. Remove the heater back plate assembly from the heater.
5. Remove the fan from the motor shaft.
6. Remove the blower motor from the back plate.

POLARA, MONACO THROUGH 1976, 1977 ROYAL MONACO, FURY THROUGH 1974, 1975 AND LATER GRAN FURY

The blower motor is mounted to the engine side housing under the right front fender, between the inner fender shield and the fender. The inner fender shield must be removed to service the blower motor.

1. Raise the hood and remove all brackets and clips that attach to the

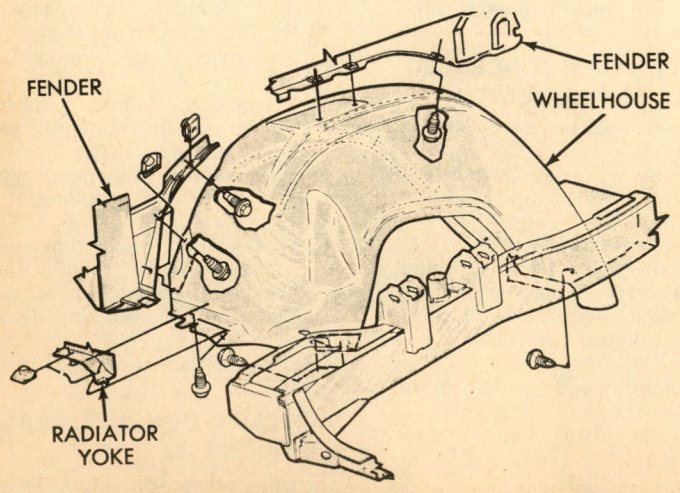

Inner fender shield attaching points—Fury, Polara, and Monaco through 1973 (© Chrysler Corp)

inner fender shield under the hood.
2. Raise the car on a hoist and remove the right front tire and wheel assembly.
3. From under the fender, remove the bolts that attach the inner fender shield to the fender.
4. Remove the fender shield from the vehicle.
5. Disconnect the blower motor wiring at the multiple connector.
6. Remove the nuts that attach the blower motor to the heater housing and remove the blower motor.

Heater Core Removal and Installation—Non Air-Conditioned Cars

POLARA, MONACO THROUGH 1976, 1977 ROYAL MONACO, FURY THROUGH 1974, 1975 AND LATER GRAN FURY

1. Remove the heater assembly.
2. Separate the housing.
3. Remove the heater core attaching screws.
4. Remove the heater core locating screw.
5. Carefully pull the heater core from the heater housing.

SATELLITE, CORONET, CHARGER; 1975 AND LATER FURY, 1977 AND LATER MONACO, MAGNUM

1. Remove the heater assembly.
2. Remove the screws that attach the front cover to the heater housing.
3. Cut the sponge rubber plenum-to-housing air seal in two places, where the front cover separates the cover from the housing.
4. Remove the one core tube retaining screw from behind the heater housing, between the heater core tubes.
5. Remove the sponge rubber gaskets from the heater core tubes. Remove the heater core from the heater housing.

Heater Core Removal and Installation—Air-conditioned Cars

SATELLITE, CORONET, CHARGER THROUGH 1974

NOTE: *This procedure requires evacuation of the refrigerant system which requires special tools and training.*

1. Remove the air cleaner and disconnect the battery.
2. Drain the cooling system. Disconnect the heater hoses at the dash panel. Plug the core tubes to prevent spillage.
3. Discharge refrigerant from the system.
4. Disconnect the refrigerant lines at the firewall (use two wrenches for this procedure). Leave the expansion valve attached to the line. Plug all refrigerant openings.
5. Disconnect the blower motor

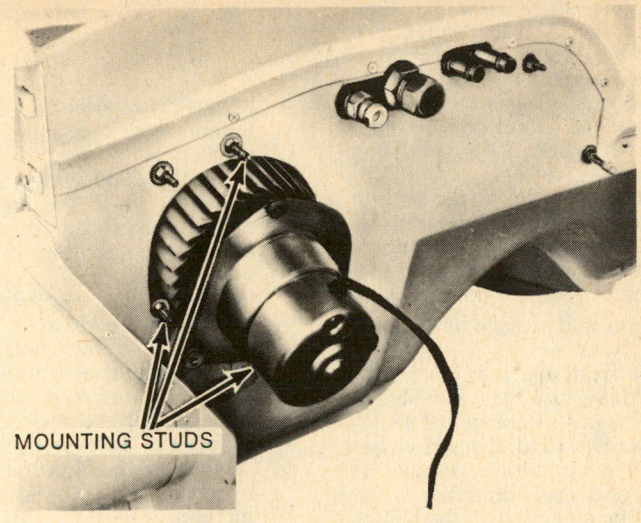

Blower motor removal—mid size cars (© Chrysler Corp)

electrical connections. Remove the motor cooling tube and the blower motor.
6. Remove the glove box assembly.
7. Remove the left spot cooler duct and the air distribution housing.
8. Disconnect all wires from the blower motor resistor, and the antenna wire from the radio bottom.
9. Remove the radio.
10. Disconnect the vacuum harness from the control switch rear.
11. Remove the water valve cable from the bracket on the housing left end.
12. In the engine compartment, remove the nuts from the housing mounting studs.
13. Remove the rubber drain tube.
14. Remove the support bracket from the plenum-to-housing panel.
15. Remove the unit from beneath the instrument panel.
16. With the unit removed from the vehicle, remove the plenum air seal.

17. Remove the vacuum hose from the fresh air door actuator and bypass door actuator. Remove the air seal from the evaporator core tubes and heater.
18. Remove the 18 screws securing the front and rear covers; extract one screw from between the evaporator core tubes. Pull the housings apart.
19. Extract the three screws from the evaporator core access plate; remove the plate. With access now clear to the two evaporator core mounting screws, remove them. In addition, remove the four screws securing the evaporator core to the front cover; remove the core.
20. Carefully lift the left housing half seal from the rear cover. Do not remove the entire seal; the lower portion acts as a water seal.
21. Remove the two core retaining screws from the mounting plate. From the back of the rear cover,

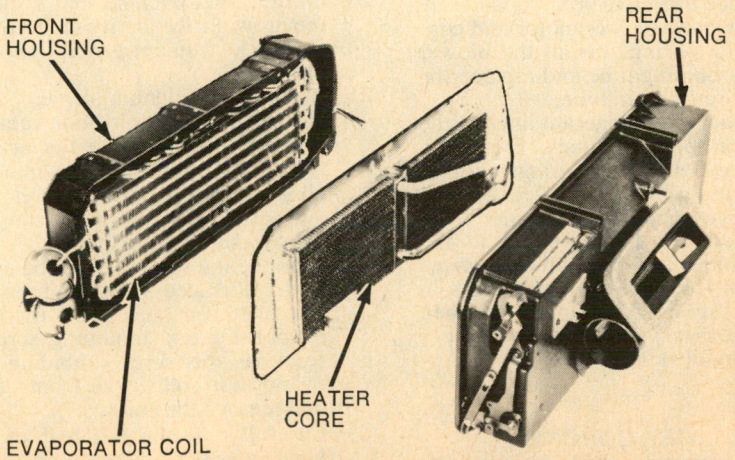

Heater and evaporator core—1972-73 Polara, Monaco and Fury
(© Chrysler Corp)

remove one screw from between the core tubes. Lift the heater core from the housing.

22. To begin assembly and installation, place the heat door in the up position. Place the heater core into the rear cover. Install its retaining screws.

23. Apply rubber cement to the bottom of the raised portion of the housing seal; carefully replace it in its original position over the heater core.

24. Insert the evaporator core into the front cover and replace its four securing screws.

25. Place the front and rear covers together. Make sure the cover seal is seated properly. Replace the 18 securing screws (and the screw between the evaporator core tubes at the back of the rear cover).

26. Replace the air seal over the heater and evaporator core tubes.

27. Connect all vacuum hoses to their respective actuators. Connect the hose with the red tracer to the actuator rod side.

28. Install the evaporator core access cover plate to the housing front and replace its three sheet metal screws.

29. Apply rubber cement to the plenum air seal and install it in position.

30. Position the housing up under the instrument panel. Connect the housing-to-plenum support bracket.

31. In the engine compartment, install four retaining nuts on the housing mounting studs.

32. Install the vacuum harness to the control switch rear. Install the water valve control cable in its retaining bracket.

33. Install the radio.

34. Install all blower motor resistor wiring. Plug the antenna lead into the radio bottom.

35. Replace the center outlet air distribution housing. Replace the left spot cooler duct.

36. Replace the glove box.

37. Replace the blower motor and connect its wiring. Install the blower motor cooling tube and replace the evaporator drain tube.

38. Connect the refrigerant lines to the evaporator core tubes. Freely lubricate fittings and O-rings with refrigerant oil. Use two wrenches to avoid twisting the tubes.

39. Connect the heater hoses to the core tubes. Fill the cooling system.

40. Check for and repair any leaks in the system. Evacuate, and then charge the system with the proper amount of refrigerant.

1975 AND LATER CORONET, CHARGER, FURY, 1977 AND LATER MONACO, MAGNUM

NOTE: *This procedure requires evacuation of the air conditioning system which requires special tools and training.*

1. Remove the carburetor air cleaner.
2. Disconnect the battery ground cable.
3. Drain the coolant. Disconnect the heater hoses at the firewall. Plug the core tubes.
4. Discharge the air conditioning system.
5. Disconnect the refrigerant line assembly at the H-valve. Cover the plumbing sealing plate. Remove the expansion valve attached to the evaporator and cover the evaporator sealing plate and both sealing surfaces of the expansion valve.
6. Disconnect the blower motor wires and remove the blower motor cooling tube.
7. Remove the glove box, the ashtray, and housing.
8. Remove the appearance shield and right lap cooler duct from the lower edge of the instrument panel.
9. Remove the right front passenger side cowl panel.
10. Remove the air distribution duct.
11. Remove the air conditioner mode door vacuum actuator from its mounting bracket and shift the actuator forward 90 degrees.
12. Remove the wiring from the seat belt interlock control unit and leave it hanging from the glove box opening.
13. Disconnect the blower motor resistor wires and the radio antenna wire.
14. Remove the radio.
15. Disconnect the vacuum housing from the extension to the control.
16. Remove the nuts from the housing mounting studs in the engine compartment.
17. Remove the rubber drain tube.
18. Adjust the front seat all the way back.
19. Remove the support bracket from the rear unit to the plenum.
20. Pull the unit back so that it clears the firewall. Rotate it out from under the instrument panel, right end first.
21. Remove the plenum air seal. Disconnect the inlet air door vacuum actuator hose. Remove the air seal from the heater and evaporator core tubes. Remove the clamps and screws holding the housing together and separate them.
22. Remove the screws from the evaporator coil access plate and remove the plate for access to the two evaporator coil mounting screws. Remove the screws holding the evaporator coil to the front cover and remove the coil.
23. Carefully lift the left half of the housing seal from the rear cover; do not remove the entire seal.
24. Remove the two core retaining screws from the mounting plates and the one between the core tubes. Lift the core out of the housing.
25. Reverse the procedure for installation.

1972-73 POLARA, MONACO, FURY

To remove only the heater core, it is not necessary to discharge the air conditioning system. The heater core is positioned in the rear housing of the passenger-side unit.

1. Disconnect the battery and drain the cooling system. Remove the air cleaner and disconnect the heater hoses. Plug the heater core tubes to prevent coolant loss when the core is removed.
2. Remove the steering column cover and remove the left spot cooler duct.
3. On the left side of the housing, remove the linkage shield and disconnect the actuator rods. Remove the screws from the housing left side.
4. Remove the screws holding the heat distribution duct and remove it. With duct removed, the screws in the bottom lip of the rear housing will become visible. Remove them.
5. Remove the glove box. In addition, remove the right spot cooler duct, the air distribution housing, and the center outlet duct.
6. Working in the glove box opening, remove the top retaining screws and the right-side housing screws. If the vehicle is Auto-Temp equipped, remove the aspirator tube from the clip first and then remove the amplifier and master compressor switches. Now remove the right-side housing screws.
7. Disconnect all electrical connections at the resistor block. On Auto-Temp equipped vehicles, remove the wires from the two plastic straps and the metal clip.
8. Remove the nut from the housing end of the support bracket. Swing the bracket upward and out of the way. Carefully roll the housing out from under the instrument panel. The heater core may be removed by pulling it out from the top. Cut the adhesive along the bottom and sides with a knife to ease removal.
9. To begin installation, scrape all the remaining sealer from the heater core flange and fit a new seal. Position the heater core in the rear housing and secure it with a screw at either end. Place the front housing in position; hold the rear housing in place and swing the support bracket down. Secure it in position with its retaining nut.
10. Working in the glove box opening, install the top two housing screws and the screws at the right side of the rear housing.

11. From beneath the instrument panel, install the screws along the housing bottom and the screws at the left side of the rear housing. It is not necessary to reinstall the linkage shield.
12. Replace the heat distribution duct to the housing bottom.
13. Connect the actuator rods.
14. Working in the glove box opening, connect the resistor block wires. Tighten the support bracket nuts. On Auto-Temp equipped vehicles, fasten the wires with the plastic straps and metal clip. Install the aspirator tube in the clip.
15. Replace the center outlet duct, the air distribution housing, and the right spot cooler duct.
16. Install the steering column cover, the left spot cooler duct, and the glove box assembly. On Auto-Temp equipped vehicles, install the amplifier and the master and compressor switches.
17. From this point, reverse the removal procedure. Be sure to fill the cooling system with the proper amount and type of antifreeze.

POLARA, 1974 FURY, 1975 AND LATER GRAN FURY, 1974-76 MONACO, 1977 ROYAL MONACO

NOTE: *This procedure requires evacuation of the refrigerant in the air conditioning system. Therefore, it should not be attempted by persons not having the special tools and training required to perform the job safely.*

1. Purge the system of refrigerant.
2. Disconnect the battery ground cable.

3. Remove the air cleaner and disconnect the heater hoses. Plug the core tubes.
4. Remove the 5/16″ bolt in the center of the plumbing sealing plate.
5. Pull the refrigerant line assembly toward the front of the car.
6. Remove the two 1/4-20 Allen screws and remove the "H" valve.
7. Slide the front seat back, out of the way. Remove the lap cooler and lower instrument panel cover.
8. Remove the A/C distribution duct.
9. Unplug the antenna lead from the radio.
10. Disconnect wires and vacuum lines from unit.
11. Remove the drain tube. With automatic temperature control (ATC), remove the electrical connections and vacuum connector from the servo. Disconnect the amplifier wires. Disconnect the wires and vacuum hoses from the master and compressor switches. Disconnect the aspirator tube.
12. Remove the temperature control cable from the clip on the unit.
13. Remove the retaining nut from the support bracket.
14. Remove the six retaining nuts from the studs in the engine compartment.
15. Remove the housing from under the instrument panel, and place it on a work table.
16. Remove the mode door and the blend air door levers from the shaft. Remove the screws and lift off the top cover.
17. Remove the 4 retaining screws and the 3 screws for the core tube seal. Lift out the core.
18. Reverse the procedure to install.

Blower Motor Removal and Installation—Air-Conditioned Cars

CORONET, CHARGER, SATELLITE, 1975 AND LATER FURY, 1977 AND LATER MONACO, MAGNUM

1. Working inside the engine compartment, disconnect the feed wire and ground wire. Remove the air tube (if so equipped).
2. Remove the mounting screws located on the outer surface of the mounting plate.
3. Remove the mounting plate, blower motor, and fan as an assembly.
4. To install the motor, if the motor was removed from its mounting plate, be sure mounting grommets are installed at the attaching bolts. In addition, be sure the blower wheel is free and does not rub.
5. Install the blower motor assembly to the evaporator casing with the air tube opening toward the bottom. Install its retaining screws.
6. Install the air tube, ground, and feed wires.
7. Check blower motor operation.

POLARA, FURY THROUGH 1974, 1975 AND LATER GRAN FURY, MONACO THROUGH 1976, 1977 ROYAL MONACO

The blower motor is located under the right front fender between the inner fender shield and the fender. Remove the inner fender shield to provide access to the blower motor. Service consists of removing its electrical leads and attaching screws. The blower motor is not repaired; replace if defective.

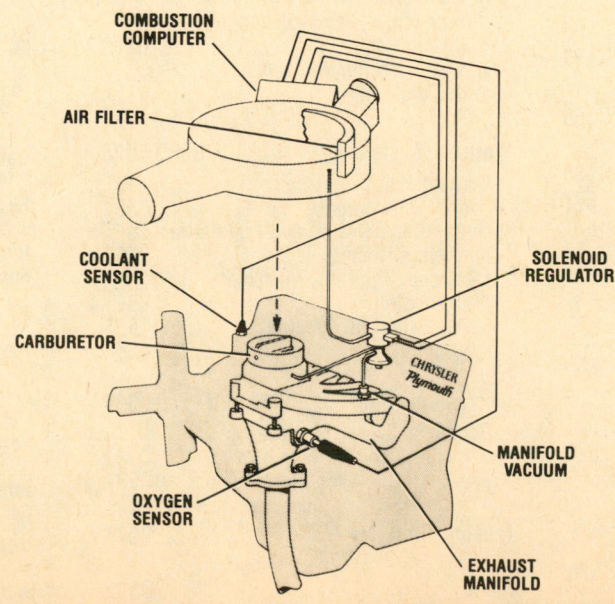

Electronic feedback carburetor control system used on 1979 automatic sixes in California (© Chrysler Corp.)

Ford · Mercury · Thunderbird

Index

YEAR IDENTIFICATION

FORD

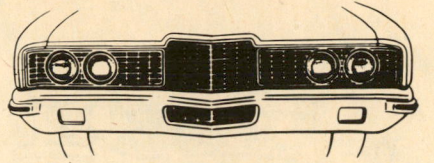

1972 Galaxie

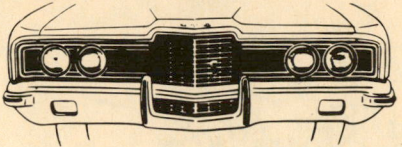

1972 LTD

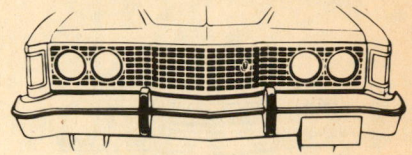

1973 Galaxie

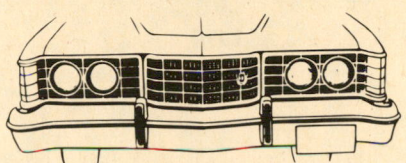

1973 LTD

1974 LTD

1975 Ford LTD Landau

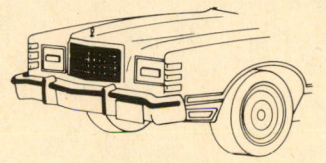

1976 LTD

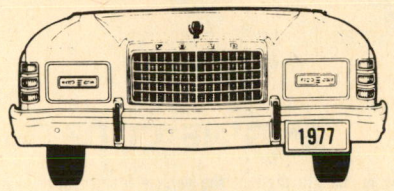

1977 LTD

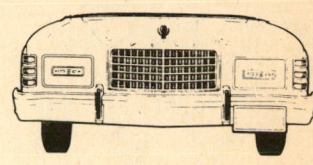

1978 LTD

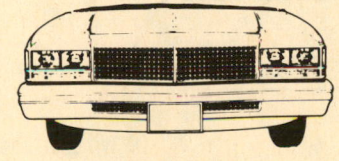
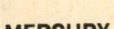

1979 LTD

MERCURY

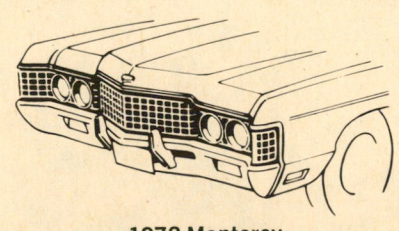

1972 Monterey

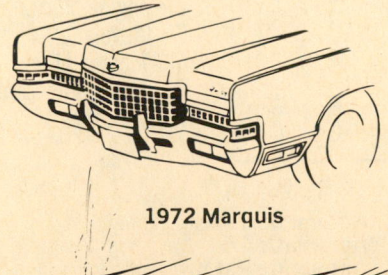

1972 Marquis

1973 Marquis

1974 Monterey

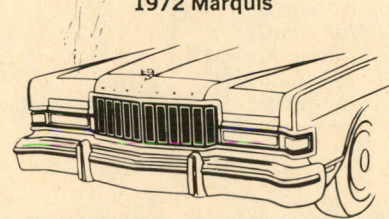

1974 Marquis

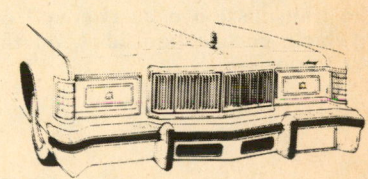

1975 Marquis

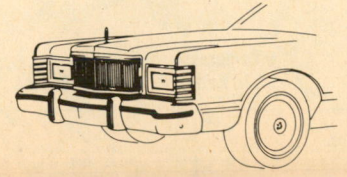

1976 Mercury

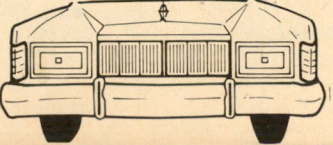

1977 Marquis

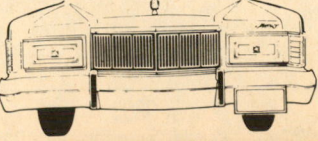

1978 Marquis

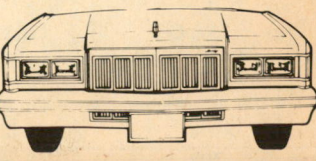

1979 Marquis

Ford • Mercury • Thunderbird

YEAR IDENTIFICATION

THUNDERBIRD

1972

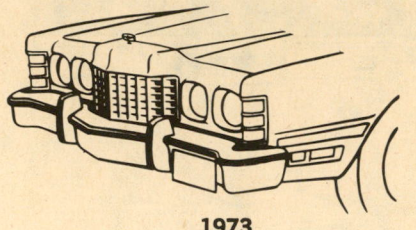

1973

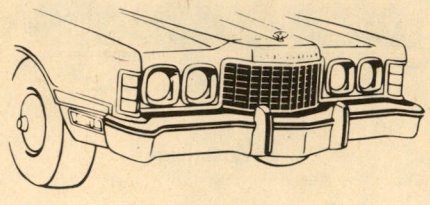

1974

1975

1976

ENGINE CODE

The engine code is the 5th digit of the vehicle identification number (V.I.N.). The V.I.N. is stamped on a plate on the top left side of the instrument panel, visible through the windshield.

Disp (Cu in.)	Carb no. bbls	'72	'73	'74	'75	'76	'77	'78	'79
6 Cylinder Models									
240	1	V							
8 Cylinder Models									
302	2	F						F	F
351W①	2	H	H	H					
351C①	2	H	H	H				H	H
351M①	2				H	H	Q	Q	
400	2	S	S	S	S	S	S	S	
429	4	N	N						
429 PI	4	P							
460	4	A	A	A	A	A	A	A	
460 PI	4		C	C	C	C	C	C	

① Windsor and Cleveland versions of the 351 2 bbl engine were used interchangeably through 1974. Starting 1975, only Modified Cleveland engines were used. A quick visual means of identification is the location of the thermostat housing/water outlet; Windsor engines have it mounted to the front face of the intake manifold, Cleveland and Modified Cleveland engines have it on top of the engine block.
C   Cleveland
M   Modified Cleveland
PI   Police Interceptor
W   Windsor

TRANSMISSION CODE

The transmission code is found on the vehicle certification label, on the driver's door.

W. Automatic C4
U. Automatic C6
X. Automatic FMX
Y. Automatic CW
Z. Automatic C6   Special—Police trailer towing

The CW transmission is a Warner unit used on 1973-74 400 V8 Ford and Mercury sedans with a 2.75:1 rear axle ratio only.

GENERAL ENGINE SPECIFICATIONS

Year	Engine No. Cyl. Displacement (Cu. In.)	Carburetor Type	Horsepower @ rpm ■	Torque @ rpm (ft lbs) ■	Bore X Stroke (in.)	Compression Ratio	Oil Pressure @ 2000 rpm
'72	6-240	1 bbl	103 @ 3800	170 @ 2200	4.000 x 3.180	8.5:1	35-60
	8-302	2 bbl	140 @ 4000	239 @ 2000	4.000 x 3.000	8.5:1	35-60
	8-351 W	2 bbl	153 @ 3800	266 @ 2000	4.000 x 3.500	8.3:1	35-60

GENERAL ENGINE SPECIFICATIONS

Year	Engine No. Cyl. Displacement (Cu. In.)	Carburetor Type	Horsepower @ rpm ■	Torque @ rpm (ft lbs) ■	Bore X Stroke (in.)	Compression Ratio	Oil Pressure @ 2000 rpm
	8-351 C	2 bbl	163 @ 3800	277 @ 2000	4.000 x 3.500	8.6:1	35-60
	8-400	2 bbl	172 @ 4000	298 @ 2200	4.000 x 4.000	8.4:1	50-70
	8-429	4 bbl	208 @ 4400	322 @ 2800	4.362 x 3.590	8.5:1	35-75
	8-429	4 bbl	212 @ 4400	327 @ 2600	4.362 x 3.590	8.5:1	35-75
	8-460	4 bbl	200 @ 4400	326 @ 2800	4.362 x 3.850	8.5:1	35-75
	8-460	4 bbl	212 @ 4400	342 @ 2800	4.362 x 3.850	8.5:1	35-75
'73	8-351 W	2 bbl	153 @ 3800	266 @ 2000	4.000 x 3.500	8.3:1	35-60
	8-351 C	2 bbl	163 @ 3800	277 @ 2000	4.000 x 3.500	8.6:1	35-60
	8-400	2 bbl	172 @ 4000	298 @ 2200	4.000 x 4.000	8.4:1	50-70
	8-429	4 bbl	208 @ 4400	322 @ 2800	4.362 x 3.590	8.5:1	35-75
	8-429	4 bbl	212 @ 4400	327 @ 2600	4.362 x 3.590	8.5:1	35-75
	8-460	4 bbl	200 @ 4400	326 @ 2800	4.362 x 3.850	8.5:1	35-75
	8-460	4 bbl	212 @ 4400	342 @ 2800	4.362 x 3.850	8.5:1	35-75
'74	8-351 W	2 bbl	162 @ 4000	275 @ 2200	4.000 x 3.500	8.2:1	45-65
	8-351 C	2 bbl	163 @ 4200	278 @ 2000	4.000 x 3.500	8.0:1	45-75
	8-400	2 bbl	170 @ 3400	330 @ 2000	4.000 x 4.000	8.0:1	45-75
	8-460	4 bbl	195 @ 3800	335 @ 2600	4.362 x 3.850	8.0:1	35-65
	8-460 PI	4 bbl	275 @ 4400	395 @ 2800	4.362 x 3.850	8.8:1	35-65
'75-'76	8-351 M	2 bbl	148 @ 3800	243 @ 2400	4.000 x 3.500	8.0:1	45-75
	8-351 M Calif.	2 bbl	150 @ 3800	244 @ 2800	4.000 x 3.500	8.0:1	45-75
	8-400	2 bbl	158 @ 3800	276 @ 2000	4.000 x 4.000	8.0:1	45-75
	8-400 Calif.	2 bbl	144 @ 3600	255 @ 2200	4.000 x 4.000	8.0:1	45-75
	8-460	4 bbl	218 @ 4000	369 @ 2000	4.362 x 3.850	8.0:1	35-65
	8-460 Calif.	4 bbl	218 @ 4000	367 @ 2600	4.362 x 3.850	8.0:1	35-65
	8-460 T-Bird①	4 bbl	224 @ 4000	370 @ 2600	4.362 x 3.850	8.0:1	35-65
	8-460 T-Bird②	4 bbl	194 @ 3800	347 @ 2600	4.362 x 3.850	8.0:1	35-65
	8-460 T-Bird Calif.	4 bbl	223 @ 4000	366 @ 2600	4.362 x 3.850	8.0:1	35-65
	8-460 PI	4 bbl	226 @ 4000	374 @ 2600	4.362 x 3.850	8.0:1	35-65
'77	8-351 M	2 bbl	161 @ 3600	285 @ 1800	4.000 x 3.500	8.0:1	45-75
	8-400	2 bbl	173 @ 3800	326 @ 1600	4.000 x 4.000	8.0:1	45-75
	8-400 Calif.	4 bbl	168 @ 3800	323 @ 1600	4.000 x 4.000	8.0:1	45-75
	8-460	4 bbl①	197 @ 4000	353 @ 2000	4.362 x 3.850	8.0:1	35-65
	8-460 PI	4 bbl①	202 @ 3800	352 @ 1600	4.362 x 3.850	8.0:1	35-65
'78	8-302	2 bbl	134 @ 3400	248 @ 1600	4.000 x 3.000	8.4:1	40-60
	8-351 W	2 bbl	144 @ 3200	277 @ 1600	4.000 x 3.500	8.3:1	40-60
	8-351 M	2 bbl	145 @ 3400	273 @ 1800	4.000 x 3.500	8.0:1	50-75
	8-400	2 bbl	160 @ 3800	314 @ 1800	4.000 x 4.000	8.0:1	50-75
	8-460	4 bbl	202 @ 4000	348 @ 2000	4.362 x 3.850	8.0:1	35-65
	8-460 PI	4 bbl①	202 @ 3800	352 @ 1600	4.362 x 3.850	8.0:1	35-65
'79	8-302	VV	134 @ 3400	248 @ 1600	4.000 x 3.000	8.4:1	40-60
	8-351 W	2 bbl	144 @ 3200	277 @ 1600	4.000 x 3.500	8.3:1	40-60
	8-351 W Calif.	VV	139 @ 3200	270 @ 1600	4.000 x 3.500	8.3:1	40-60

■ Horsepower and torque are SAE net figures. They are measured at the rear of the transmission with all accessories installed and operating. Since the figures vary when a given engine is installed in different models, some are representative rather than exact.

W Windsor Design
C Cleveland Design
M Modified Cleveland Design
PI Police Interceptor
VV Variable Venturi

① Dual exhaust
② Single exhaust

FORD

TUNE-UP SPECIFICATIONS

Year	Engine No. Cyl. Displacement (cu. In.)	hp	Spark Plugs Orig. Type	Gap (in.)	Distributor Point Dwell (deg)	Point Gap (in.)	Ignition Timing (deg) ▲ Man Trans •	Auto Trans	Valves Intake Opens ■ (deg)	Fuel Pump Pressure (psi)	Idle Speed (rpm) ▲ Man Trans *	Auto Trans •
'72	6-240	103	BRF-42	.034	35-39	.027	—	6B	18	4-6	—	500
	8-302	140	BRF-42	.034	26-30	.017	—	6B	16	5-7	—	575 600/500
	8-351W	153	BRF-42	.034	26-30	.017	—	6B	11	5-7	—	575 600/500
	8-351C	163	ARF-42	.034	26-30	.017	—	6B	12	5-7	—	600/500
	8-400	172	ARF-42	.034	26-30	.017	—	6B	17	5-7	—	625/500
	8-429	208	BRF-42	.034	26-30	.017	—	10B	8	5-7	—	600/500
	8-429PI	N.A.	ARF-42	.034	26-30	.017	—	10B	32	4½-6½	—	650/500
'73	8-351W	153	BRF-42	.034	26-30	.017	—	6B	11	5-7	—	575 600/500
	8-351C	163	ARF-42	.034	26-30	.017	—	6B	12	5-7	—	600/500
	8-400	172	ARF-42	.034	26-30	.017	—	6B	17	5-7	—	625/500
	8-429	208	BRF-42	.034	26-30	.017	—	10B	8	5-7	—	600/500
	8-460PI	267, 274	ARF-42	.034	26-30	.017	—	10B	32	4½-6½	—	650/500
'74	8-351W	162	BRF-42	.034②	26-30③	.014-.020③	—	6B	15	4-6	—	600/500
	8-351C	163	ARF-42	.044	26-30③	.014-.020③	—	14B	19½	5½-6½	—	700/500
	8-400	170	ARF-42	.044 (.054)	Electronic		—	12B	17	5½-6½	—	625/500
	8-460	195	ARF-52	.054 (.044)	Electronic		—	14B	8	5½-6½	—	650(675) 500
	8-460PI	275	ARF-52	.054	Electronic		—	10B	18	Electric	—	700/500
'75	8-351M	148, 150	ARF-42	.044	Electronic		—	8B	19½	5½-6½	—	700
	8-400	144, 158	ARF-42	.044	Electronic		—	6B④	17	5½-6½	—	625
	8-460	218	ARF-52	.044	Electronic		—	14B	8	6.2-7.2	—	650
	8-460PI	226	ARF-52	.044	Electronic		—	14B	18	6.2-7.2	—	650
'76	8-351M	2 bbl	ARF-52	.044	Electronic		—	8B	19½	5½-6½	—	650
	8-351M	4 bbl	ARF-42	.044	Electronic		—	8B	19½	5½-6½	—	650
	8-400	2 bbl	ARF-52	.044	Electronic		—	10B	17	5½-6½	—	650
	8-400	4 bbl	ARF-42	.044	Electronic		—	10B	17	5½-6½	—	650
	8-460	All	ARF-52	.044	Electronic		—	8B(14B)	8	5-7	—	650
	8-460	PI	ARF-52	.044	Electronic		—	14B	18	6-7	—	650
'77	8-351M	All	ARF-52	.050	Electronic		—	8B	19½	6½-7½	—	650
	8-400	All	ARF-52	.050	Electronic		—	8B	17	6½-7½	—	650(625)
	8-460	All	ARF-52-6	.060	Electronic		—	16B	8	7-8	—	650
	8-460	PI	ARF-52-6	.060	Electronic		—	16B	8	7-8	—	650
'78	8-302	All	ARF-52 (ARF-52-6)	.050 (.060)	Electronic		—	14B	16	5½-6½	—	650
	8-351W	All	ARF-52 (ARF-52-6)	.050 (.060)	Electronic		—	4B	23	4-6	—	650
	8-351M	All	ARF-52 (ARF-52-6)	.050 (.060)	Electronic		—	12B(16B)	19½	6½-7½	—	650
	8-400	All	ARF-52 (ARF-52-6)	.050 (.060)	Electronic		—	13B(16B)	17	6½-7½	—	650
	8-460	All	ARF-52 (ARF-52-6)	.050 (.060)	Electronic		—	10B	8	7¼-8¼	—	580

FORD

TUNE-UP SPECIFICATIONS

Year	ENGINE No. Cyl. Displacement (cu. In.)	hp	SPARK PLUGS Orig. Type	• Gap (in.)	DISTRIBUTOR Point Dwell (deg)	Point Gap (in.)	IGNITION TIMING (deg) ▲ Man Trans •	Auto Trans	VALVES Intake Opens ■ (deg)	Fuel Pump Pressure (psi)	IDLE SPEED (rpm) ▲ Man Trans *	• Auto Trans
	8-460	PI	ARF-52-6	.060	Electronic		—	16B	18	7¼-8¼	—	580
'79	8-302	All	ARF-52	.050	Electronic		—	14B	16	5½-6½	—	650
	8-351 W	All	ARF-52	.050	Electronic		—	4B (EECII)①	23	4-6	—	650

NOTE: The underhood specifications sticker often reflects tune-up specification changes made in production. Sticker figures must be used if they disagree with those in this chart.

▲ See text for procedure
● Figure in parentheses indicates California engine
■ All figures Before Top Dead Center
* In all cases where two idle speed figures are separated by a slash, the first is for idle speed with solenoid energized and the automatic transmission in Drive, while the second is for idle speed with solenoid disconnected and automatic transsion in Neutral.
① California engines have variable EEC II timing; see text for description.

② .044 on California models and all cars using Solid State Ignition
③ Solid State Ignition used on all engines nationwide on cars assembled after May, 1974.
④ 8B with 3.25:1 rear axle, Code 9 or R on Certification label, except in California
B Before Top Dead Center
C Cleveland
M Modified Cleveland
PI Police Interceptor
TDC Top Dead Center
W Windsor
— Not applicable

Mercury

TUNE-UP SPECIFICATIONS

When analyzing compression test results, look for uniformity among cylinders rather than specific pressures.

Year	ENGINE No. Cyl. Displacement (cu. In.)	hp	SPARK PLUGS Orig. Type	• Gap (in.)	DISTRIBUTOR Point Dwell (deg)	Point Gap (in.)	IGNITION TIMING (deg) ▲ Man Trans •	Auto Trans	VALVES Intake Opens ■ (deg)	Fuel Pump Pressure (psi)	IDLE SPEED (rpm) ▲ Man Trans *	• Auto Trans
'72	8-351C	163	ARF-42	.034	28	.017	—	6B	12	5½-6½	—	575/500 (625/500)
	8-400	172	ARF-42	.034	28	.017	—	8B(6B)	17	5½-6½	—	625/500
	8-429	208	BRF-42	.034	28	.017	—	10B	8	5½-6½	—	650/500
	8-429PI	N.A.	ARF-42	.034	28	.020	—	10B	32	5½-6½	—	650/500
	8-460	200	BRF-42	.034	28	.017	—	10B(6B)②	8	5½-6½	—	625/500
'73	8-351C	163	ARF-42	.034	28	.017	—	6B	12	5½-6½	—	650/500
	8-400	172	ARF-42	.034	28	.017	—	6B	17	5½-6½	—	650/500
	8-429	208	BRF-42	.034	28	.017	—	10B	8	5½-6½	—	650/500
	8-429PI	N.A.	ARF-42	.034	28	.020	—	10B	32	5½-6½	—	650/500
	8-460	200	BRF-42	.034	28	.017	—	6B	8	5½-6½	—	(625/500)
'74	8-351C	163	ARF-42	.044	28③	.017③	—	14B	19½	5½-6½	—	600/500
	8-400	170	ARF-42	.044 (.054)	Electronic		—	12B	17	5½-6½	—	625/500
	8-460	195	ARF-52	.054	Electronic		—	10B	8	5½-6½	—	625/500
'75	8-400	144, 158	ARF-42	.044	Electronic		—	12B	17	5.5-6.5	—	625
	8-460	218	ARF-52	.044	Electronic		—	14B	8	6.2-7.2	—	650
	8-460PI	226	ARF-52	.044	Electronic		—	14B	18	6.2-7.2	—	650
'76	8-400	2 bbl	ARF-52	.044	Electronic		—	10B	17	5½-6½	—	650
	8-400	4 bbl	ARF-42	.044	Electronic		—	10B	17	5½-6½	—	650
	8-460	All	ARF-52	.044	Electronic		—	8B(14B)	8	5-7	—	650
	8-460	PI	ARF-52	.044	Electronic		—	14B	18	6-7	—	650
'77	8-400	All	ARF-52	.050	Electronic		—	8B	17	6½-7½	—	650(625)
	8-460	All	ARF-52-6	.060	Electronic		—	16B	8	7-8	—	650
	8-460	PI	ARF-52-6	.060	Electronic		—	16B	8	7-8	—	650

Mercury   TUNE-UP SPECIFICATIONS

When analyzing compression test results, look for uniformity among cylinders rather than specific pressures.

Year	ENGINE No. Cyl. Displacement (cu. In.)	hp	SPARK PLUGS Orig. Type	Gap • (in.)	DISTRIBUTOR Point Dwell (deg)	Point Gap (in.)	IGNITION TIMING (deg) ▲ Man Trans •	Auto Trans	VALVES Intake Opens ■ (deg)	Fuel Pump Pressure (psi)	IDLE SPEED (rpm) ▲ Man Trans *	Auto Trans •
'78	8-351M	All	ARF-52 (ARF-52-6)	.050 (.060)	Electronic		—	12B	19½	6½-7½	—	650(625)
	8-400	All	ARF-52 (ARF-52-6)	.050 (.060)	Electronic		—	13B(16B)	17	6½-7½	—	650(625)
	8-460	All	ARF-52 (ARF-52-6)	.050 (.060)	Electronic		—	16B	8	7¼-8¼	—	580
	8-460 PI	All	ARF-52 (ARF-52-6)	.050 (.060)	Electronic		—	16B	18	7¼-8¼	—	580
'79	8-302	All	ARF-52	.050	Electronic		—	14B	16	5½-6½	—	650
	8-351W	All	ARF-52	.050	Electronic		—	EEC II①	23	4-6	—	650

NOTE: The underhood specifications sticker often reflects tune-up specification changes made in production. Sticker figures must be used if they disagree with those in this chart.
▲ See text for procedure
• Figure in parentheses indicates California engine
■ All figures Before Top Dead Center
* In all cases where two figures are separated by a slash, the first figure is for idle speed with solenoid energized and automatic transmission in Drive, while the second is for idle speed with solenoid disconnected and automatic transmission in Neutral.

① All 351W engines have variable EEC II timing; see text for description.
② For all vehicles with 3.00 axles, Code 6 or 0 on certification label, figure is 6B
③ Solid State Ignition used on all engines nationwide on cars assembled after May 1974.
  B Before Top Dead Center
  C Cleveland
  PI Police Interceptor
  W Windsor
— Not applicable

Thunderbird   TUNE-UP SPECIFICATIONS

When analyzing compression test results, look for uniformity among cylinders rather than specific pressures.

Year	ENGINE No. Cyl Displacement (cu in.)	hp	SPARK PLUGS Orig. Type	Gap (in.)	DISTRIBUTOR Point Dwell (deg)	Point Gap (in.)	IGNITION TIMING (deg) ▲ Man Trans •	Auto Trans	VALVES Intake Opens ■ (deg)	Fuel Pump Pressure (psi)	IDLE SPEED (rpm) ▲ Man Trans *	Auto Trans
'72	8-429	208, 212	BRF-42	.034	26-30	.020	—	10B	8	5½-6½	—	650/500
	8-460	200, 212	BRF-42	.034	26-30	.020	—	10B(6B)	8	5½-6½	—	650/500
'73	8-429	208, 212	BRF-42	.034	26-30	.020	—	10B	8	5½-6½	—	650/500
	8-460	200, 212	BRF-42	.034	26-30	.020	—	6B	8	5½-6½	—	650/500
'74	8-460	195	ARF-52	.044	Electronic		—	14B	8	5½-6½		675/500
'75	8-460	All	ARF-52	.044	Electronic		—	14B	8	6½-7½	—	650
'76	8-460	All	ARF-52	.044	Electronic		—	8B(14B)	8	6-7	—	650
'77 and Later							See Capri Car Section					

NOTE: The underhood specifications sticker often reflects tune-up specification changes made in production. Sticker figures must be used if they disagree with those in this chart.
▲ See text for procedure
• Figure in parentheses indicates California engine
■ All figures Before Top Dead Center
— Not applicable

* First figure is for idle speed with solenoid energized and automatic transmission in Drive, while the second figure is for idle speed with solenoid disconnected and automatic transmission in Neutral

B Before Top Dead Center

FIRING ORDER

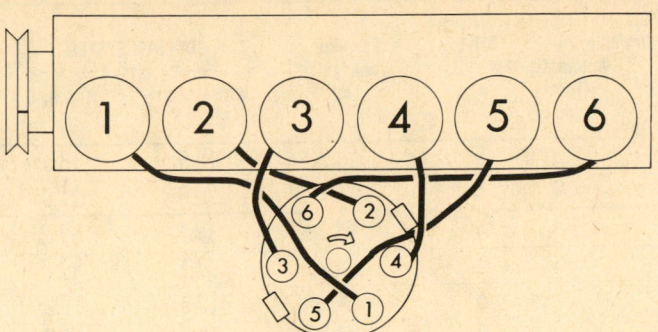

FORD MOTOR CO. 240 6-cyl.
Engine firing order: 1-5-3-6-2-4
Distributor rotation: clockwise

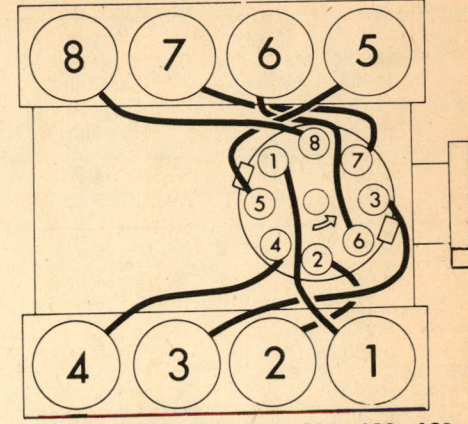

FORD MOTOR CO. 302, 390, 429, 460 V8 (through 1974)
Engine firing order: 1-5-4-2-6-3-7-8
Distributor rotation: counterclockwise

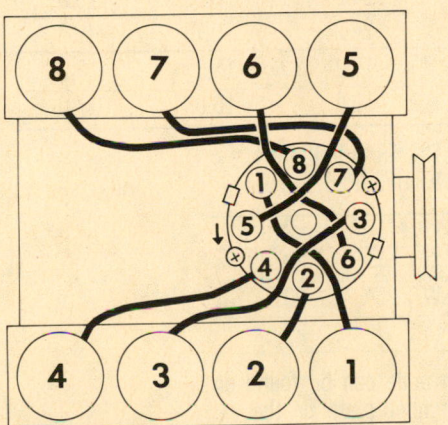

FORD MOTOR CO. 302, 460 V8 (1975 and later)
Engine firing order: 1-5-4-2-6-3-7-8
Distributor rotation: counterclockwise

(Squares are position of latches on 1975-76 models; circles are position of latches on 1977 and later models.)

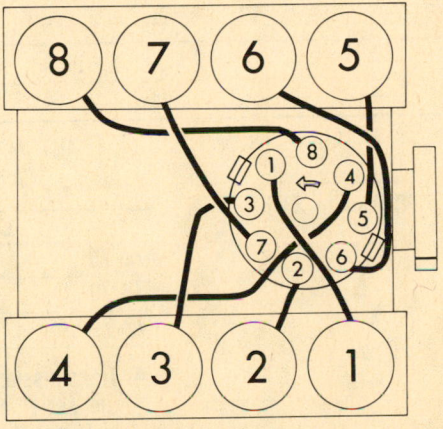

FORD MOTOR CO. 351, 400 V8 (through 1974)
Engine firing order: 1-3-7-2-6-5-4-8
Distributor rotation: counterclockwise

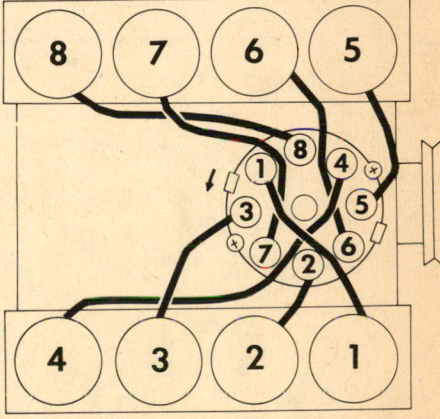

FORD MOTOR CO. 351, 400 V8 (1975 and later)
Engine firing order: 1-3-7-2-6-5-4-8
Distributor rotation: counterclockwise

(Squares are position of latches on 1975-76 models; circles are position of latches on 1977 and later models.)

Ford

CAPACITIES

Year	ENGINE No. Cyl. Displacement (Cu. In.)	Engine Crankcase Add 1 Qt For New Filter	Manual 3-Speed	Manual 4-Speed	Automatic (Total capacity)	Drive Axle (pts)	Gasoline Tank (gals) ■	COOLING SYSTEM (qts) With Heater	With A/C
'72-'73	6-240	4	—	—	⑥	4	22	14.2	14.2
	8-302	4	—	—	⑥	4.5	22	15.2	15.2
	8-351	4	—	—	⑥	4.5	22	16.3	16.3
	8-400	4	—	—	⑥	5	22	17.7	18.3
	8-429	4	—	—	⑥	5	22	18.8	19.5
'74	8-351	4	—	—	⑥	4.5	22	16.3	①
	8-400	4	—	—	⑥	5	22	18.0	18.0
	8-460	4	—	—	⑥	5	22	19.4	19.4
'75-'76	8-351 M	4	—	—	⑥	4.5④	24.2③	17.1	17.6
	8-400	4	—	—	⑥	4.5④	24.2③	17.1	17.6

Ford
CAPACITIES

Year	ENGINE No. Cyl. Displacement (Cu. In.)	Engine Crankcase Add 1 Qt For New Filter	TRANSMISSION Pts To Refill After Draining Manual 3-Speed	4-Speed	Automatic (Total capacity)	Drive Axle (pts)	Gasoline Tank (gals) ■	COOLING SYSTEM (qts) With Heater	With A/C
	8-460	4	—	—	⑥	5	24.2③	18.5	18.5
	8-460 PI	6②	—	—	⑥	5	24.2③	20.0	20.0
'77	8-351 M	4	—	—	⑥	4⑤	24.2③	17.1	17.2
	8-400	4	—	—	⑥	4⑤	24.2③	17.1	17.5
	8-460	4	—	—	⑥	5	24.2③	19.2	19.2
	8-460 PI	6②	—	—	⑥	5	24.2③	19.7	19.7
'78	8-302	4	—	—	⑥	4⑤	24.2	15.1	15.1
	8-351W	4	—	—	⑥	4⑤	24.2	16.2	16.2
	8-351M	4	—	—	⑥	4⑤	24.2	16.9	16.9⑦
	8-400	4	—	—	⑥	4⑤	24.2	16.9	16.9⑦
	8-460	4	—	—	⑥	5	24.2	18.6	19.0
	8-460PI	6②	—	—	⑥	5	24.2	19.7	19.7
'79	8-302	4	—	—	⑥	4	19.0	15.0	16.0
	8-351W	4	—	—	⑥	4	19.0	16.0	17.0

① 351W—17.1 qts.; 351C—16.3 qts
② 7.5 w/oil cooler
③ With auxiliary fuel tank: sedan—32.3 gals; wagon—29.0 gals.
④ 5 with locker or 3.25:1 ratio
⑤ 5 with locker or 3.0:1 ratio
⑦ Trailer Towing: 17.4
■ Station wagons:
   '79—20 gals
   through '78—21 gals
M Modified Cleveland
PI Police interceptor
—— Not applicable

⑥AUTOMATIC TRANSMISSION CAPACITIES (Pts)

Year	Code▲	Capacities
'72-'79	X, Y, #	22
'72-'79	W	20.5
'72-'79	U, Z	25

▲ Transmission code can be found on the serial number plate or the vehicle certification label.

Mercury
CAPACITIES

Year	ENGINE No. Cyl. Displacement (Cu. In.)	Engine Crankcase Add 1 Qt For New Filter	TRANSMISSION Pts To Refill After Draining Manual 3-Speed	4-Speed	Automatic (Total capacity)	Drive Axle (pts)	Gasoline Tank (gals) ■	COOLING SYSTEM (qts) With Heater	With A/C
'72	8-351	4	—	—	22	4	22	15.8	16.3
	8-400	4	—	—	25.5	5	22	17.7	18.3
	8-429	4	—	—	25.5	5	22	18.8	19.5
'73-'74	8-351	4	—	—	22	4	22	15.8	16.3
	8-400	4	—	—	25.5	5	22	17.7	18.3
	8-429	4	—	—	25.5	5	22	18.8	19.5
	8-460	4	—	—	26	5	22	19.5	19.5
'75-'76	8-400	4	—	—	22	4④	24.2②	17.1	17.6
	8-460	4	—	—	25③	4④	24.2②	18.5	18.5
	8-460 PI	6①	—	—	25	4④	24.2②	20.0	20.0
'77	8-400	4	—	—	25	4④	24.2②	17.1	17.5
	8-460	4	—	—	25	5	24.2②	19.2	19.2
	8-460 PI	6①	—	—	25	5	24.2②	19.7	19.7

Mercury   CAPACITIES

Year	ENGINE No. Cyl. Displacement (Cu. In.)	Engine Crankcase Add 1 Qt For New Filter	TRANSMISSION Manual 3-Speed	4-Speed	Automatic (Total capacity)	Drive Axle (pts)	Gasoline Tank (gals) ■	COOLING SYSTEM (qts) With Heater	With A/C
'78	8-351	4	—	—	25③	4④	24.2	16.9	16.9⑦
	8-400	4	—	—	25③	4④	24.2	16.9	16.9⑦
	8-460	4	—	—	25③	5	24.2	18.6	19.0
	8-460 PI	6①	—	—	25	5	24.2	19.7	19.7
'79	8-302	4	—	—	24③⑤	3.75⑥	19.0	15.0	16.0
	8-351W	4	—	—	24③⑤	3.75⑥	19.0	16.0	17.0

■ Station Wagons:
  '79—20 gals.
  through '78—21 gals.
  with 400 engine—19 gals.

① 7.5 with oil cooler
② With auxiliary fuel tank: sedan—32.3 gals; wagon—29.0 gals.

③ 22 for FMX
④ 5 for removeable differential carrier axle
⑤ 20 for C4
⑥ 4.25 pts with 8½ in. axle
⑦ Trailer Towing—17.4
— Not applicable
PI Police interceptor

Thunderbird   CAPACITIES

Year	ENGINE No. Cyl. Displacement (Cu. In.)	Engine Crankcase Add 1 Qt For New Filter	TRANSMISSION Manual 3-Speed	4-Speed	Automatic (Total capacity)	Drive Axle (pts)	Gasoline Tank (gals) ■	COOLING SYSTEM (qts) With Heater	With A/C
'72-'74	8-429	4	—	—	26	5	22.5	18.8	18.8
	8-460	4	—	—	26	5	22.5	20	20
'75	8-460	4	—	—	25	5	26.5	19.3②	19.3②
'76	8-460	4	—	—	25	5	26.5	—	19.8
'77 and later				See Capri Car Section					

① Not used   ② 19.8 with Class III towing package   — Not applicable

VALVE SPECIFICATIONS

Year	Engine No. Cyl. Displacement (cu in.)	Seat Angle (deg)	Face Angle (deg)	Spring Test Pressure (lbs @ in.)	Spring Installed Height (in.)	STEM TO GUIDE Clearance (in.) Intake	Exhaust	STEM Diameter (in.) Intake	Exhaust
'72	6-240	45	44	197 @ 1.30	1 11/16	.0010-.0027	.0010-.0027	.3420	.3420
	8-302	45	44	200 @ 1.31	1 11/16	.0010-.0027	.0015-.0032	.3420	.3415
	8-351W	45	44	200 @ 1.34	1 25/32	.0010-.0027	.0015-.0032	.3420	.3415
	8-351C	45	44	210 @ 1.42	1 13/16	.0010-.0027	.0015-.0032	.3420	.3415
	8-400	45	44	226 @ 1.39	1 13/16	.0010-.0027	.0015-.0032	.3420	.3415
	8-429	45	45	229 @ 1.33	1 13/16	.0010-.0027	.0010-.0027	.3420	.3420
	8-460	45	45	229 @ 1.33	1 13/16	.0010-.0027	.0010-.0027	.3420	.3420
'73-'74	8-351W	45	44	200 @ 1.34	1 25/32	.0010-.0027	.0015-.0032	.3420	.3415
	8-351C	45	44	210 @ 1.42②	1 13/16	.0010-.0027	.0015-.0032	.3420	.3415
	8-400	45	44	226 @ 1.39	1 13/16	.0010-.0027	.0015-.0032	.3420	.3415
	8-429	45	45	229 @ 1.33	1 13/16	.0010-.0027	.0010-.0027	.3420	.3420
	8-460	45	45	229 @ 1.33	1 13/16	.0010-.0027	.0010-.0027	.3420	.3420
'75	8-351M	44½-45	45½-45¾	226 @ 1.39	1 13/16	.0010-.0027	.0015-.0032	.3420	.3415
'76	8-400	44½-45	45½-45¾	226 @ 1.39	1 13/16	.0010-.0027	.0015-.0032	.3420	.3415

VALVE SPECIFICATIONS

Year	Engine No. Cyl. Displacement (cu in.)	Seat Angle (deg)	Face Angle (deg)	Spring Test Pressure (lbs @ in.)	Spring Installed Height (in.)	STEM TO GUIDE Clearance (in.) Intake	STEM TO GUIDE Clearance (in.) Exhaust	STEM Diameter (in.) Intake	STEM Diameter (in.) Exhaust
	8-460	44½-45	45½-45¾	253 @ 1.33	1 13/16	.0010-.0027	.0010-.0027	.3420	.3420
	8-460 PI	44½-45	45½-45¾	315 @ 1.32	1 13/16	.0010-.0027	.0010-.0027	.3420	.3420
'77-	8-302	45	44	①	1 11/16 ⑥	.0010-.0027	.0015-.0032	.3420	.3415
'79	8-351W	45	44	⑤	1 13/16 ⑥	.0010-.0027	.0015-.0032	.3420	.3415
	8-351 M	44½-45	45½-45¾	226 @ 1.39	1 13/16	.0010-.0027	.0015-.0032	.3420	.3415
	8-400	44½-45	45½-45¾	226 @ 1.39	1 13/16	.0010-.0027	.0015-.0032	.3420	.3415
	8-460	44½-45	45½-45¾	③	1 13/16	.0010-.0027	.0010-.0027	.3420	.3420
	8-460 PI	44½-45	45½-45¾	④	1 13/16	.0010-.0027	.0010-.0027	.3420	.3420

① Intake: 200 @ 1.31, Exhaust: 200 @ 1.20
② 1974 models—226 @ 1.39
③ Intake: 240 @ 1.33, Exhaust: 253 @ 1.33
④ Intake: 315 @ 1.32, Exhaust: 315 @ 1.33
⑤ Intake: 200 @ 1.34, Exhaust: 200 @ 1.20
⑥ Exhaust: 1 5/8

PI Police interceptor
W Windsor engine
C Cleveland engine
M Modified Cleveland engine

RING GAP
All measurements are given in inches

Year	Engine	Top Compression	Bottom Compression
'72-'79	All	.010-.020	.010-.020

Year	Engine	Oil Control
'72	6-240	.015-.055
'72	8-302	.015-.055
'72-'74	8-351C, 351W	.015-.069
'72-'74	8-351C	.015-.055
'72-'74	8-400	.015-.069
'75-'78	8-351M, 400	.015-.055
'72-'78	8-429, 460	.015-.055
'79	8-302, 351W	.015-.055

PISTON CLEARANCE

Year	Engine	Piston-to-Bore Clearance (in.)
'72	240 Six	.0014-.0022
'72-'79	8-302, 351W	.0018-.0026
'72-'78	8-351C, 351M, 400, 429, 460	.0014-.0022

RING SIDE CLEARANCE
All measurements are given in inches

Year	Engine	Top Compression	Bottom Compression
'72-'79	All	.002-.004	.002-.004

Year	Engine	Oil Control
'72-'79	All	Snug

CRANKSHAFT AND CONNECTING ROD SPECIFICATIONS
All measurements are given in inches

Year	Engine No. Cyl. Displacement (cu in.)	CRANKSHAFT Main Brg. Journal Dia	CRANKSHAFT Main Brg. Oil Clearance	Shaft End-Play	Thrust on No.	CONNECTING ROD Journal Diameter	CONNECTING ROD Oil Clearance	Side Clearance
'72	6-240	2.3982-2.3990	.0005-.0022	.004-.008	5	2.1228-2.1236	.0008-.0026	.006-.013
	8-302	2.2482-2.2490	.0005-.0024①	.004-.008	3	2.1228-2.1236	.0008-.0026	.010-.020
	8-351W	2.9994-3.0002	.0008-.0026	.004-.008	3	2.3103-2.3111	.0008-.0026	.010-.020
	8-351C	2.7484-2.7492	.0011-.0028	.004-.010	3	2.3103-2.3111	.0011-.0026	.010-.020
	8-400	2.9994-3.0002	.0011-.0028	.004-.010	3	2.3103-2.3111	.0011-.0026	.010-.020
	8-429	2.9994-3.0002	.0010-.0020②	.004-.008	3	2.4992-2.5000	.0008-.0028	.010-.020
	8-460	2.9994-3.0002	.0010-.0020②	.004-.008	3	2.4992-2.5000	.0008-.0026	.010-.020

CRANKSHAFT AND CONNECTING ROD SPECIFICATIONS

All measurements are given in inches

Year	Engine No. Cyl. Displacement (cu in.)	CRANKSHAFT Main Brg. Journal Dia	Main Brg. Oil Clearance	Shaft End-Play	Thrust on No.	CONNECTING ROD Journal Diameter	Oil Clearance	Side Clearance
'73-'74	8-351W	2.9994-3.0002	.0008-.0026	.004-.008	3	2.3103-2.3111	.0008-.0026	.010-.020
	8-351C	2.7484-2.7492	.0011-.0028	.004-.010	3	2.3103-2.3111	.0008-.0015④⑤	.010-.020
	8-400	2.9994-3.0002	.0011-.0028	.004-.010	3	2.3103-2.3111	.0011-.0026	.010-.020
	8-429	2.9994-3.0002	.0010-.0020②	.004-.008	3	2.4992-2.5000	.0008-.0028	.010-.020
	8-460	2.9994-3.0002	.0010-.0020②	.004-.008	3	2.4992-2.5000	.0008-.0026	.010-.020
'75-'76	8-351M	2.7484-2.7492	.0009-.0026④	.004-.008	3	2.3103-2.3111	.0008-.0015④	.010-.020
	8-400	2.9994-3.0002	.0011-.0028	.004-.008	3	2.3103-2.3111	.0011-.0026	.010-.020
	8-460	2.9994-3.0002	.0012-.0028③	.004-.008	3	2.4992-2.5000	.0008-.0028	.010-.020
'77-'79	8-302	2.2482-2.2490	.0005-.0015⑥	.004-.008	3	2.1228-2.1236	.0008-.0015	.010-.020
	8-351W	2.9994-3.0002	.0008-.0015	.004-.008	3	2.3103-2.3111	.0008-.0015	.010-.020
	8-351M, 400	2.9994-3.0002	.0008-.0015	.004-.008	3	2.3103-2.3111	.0008-.0015	.010-.020
	8-460	2.9994-3.0002	.0008-.0015	.004-.008	3	2.4992-2.5000	.0008-.0015	.010-.020

① #1—.0001-.0018
② #1—.010-.015
③ #1 bearing—.0010-.0015
④ 4 bbl: .0011-.0015
⑤ 1973: .0008-.0026
⑥ #1 bearing—.0001-.0015

TORQUE SPECIFICATIONS

All readings in ft lbs

Year	Engine No. Cyl. Displacement (cu in.)	Cylinder Head Bolts	Rod Bearing Bolts	Main Bearing Bolts	Crankshaft Bolt	Flywheel to Crankshaft Bolts	MANIFOLD Intake	Exhaust
'72	6-240	70-75	40-45	60-70	130-150	75-85	23-28	23-28
	8-302	65-72	19-24	60-70	70-90	75-85	23-25	12-16
	8-351W	105-112	40-45	95-105	100-130	75-85	23-25	18-24
	8-351C, 400	95-105	40-45⑥	⑦	70-90	75-85	⑧	12-16
	8-429, 460	130-140	40-45	95-105	70-90	75-85	25-30	28-33
'73-'79	8-302	65-72	19-24	60-70	70-90	75-85	23-25	18-24
	8-351W	105-112	40-45	95-105	70-90	75-85	23-25	18-24
	8-351C, 351M, 400	95-105	40-45	⑦	70-90	75-85	⑩	18-24⑨
	8-460	130-140	40-45	95-105	70-90	75-85	22-32	28-33

①②③ Not used
④ 351C engine—12-16
⑤⑥ Not used
⑦ 1/2 x 13 in. bolt—95-105
3/8 x 16 in. bolt—35-45
⑧ 5/16 in. bolt—21-25
3/8 in. bolt—27-23
1/4 in. bolt—6-9
⑨ 1973-74 351—12-22
1973-74 400—12-16
⑩ 5/16 bolt: 21-25
3/8 bolt: 22-32
1/4 bolt: 6-9

WHEEL ALIGNMENT SPECIFICATIONS

Year	Model	CASTER Range (deg)	Pref Setting (deg)	CAMBER Range (deg)	Pref Setting (deg)	Toe-in (in.)	Steering Axis Inclin. (deg)	WHEEL PIVOT RATIO (deg) Inner Wheel	Outer Wheel
'72	Ford, Mercury	1N to 3P	1P	1/2N to 1 1/2P	1/2P	1/16 to 7/16	7 3/4	20	19 4/25
	T-Bird	1N to 3P	1P	1/4N to 1 3/4P	3/4P	1/16 to 7/16	7 3/4	20	17 37/50
'73	Ford, Mercury	0 to 4P	2P	1N to 1P	0	1/16 to 7/16	7 3/4	20	18 3/4
	T-Bird	1/2N to 3 1/2P	1 1/2P	1/4N to 1 3/4P	3/4P	1/16 to 7/16	7 3/4	20	17 3/4

WHEEL ALIGNMENT SPECIFICATIONS

Year	Model	CASTER Range (deg)	CASTER Pref Setting (deg)	CAMBER Range (deg)	CAMBER Pref Setting (deg)	Toe-in (in.)	Steering Axis Inclin. (deg)	WHEEL PIVOT RATIO (deg) Inner Wheel	WHEEL PIVOT RATIO (deg) Outer Wheel
'74	Ford	0 to 4P	2P	①	②	3/16	9½	20	18¾
	Mercury	0 to 4P	2P	③	②	3/16	9½	20	18¾
	T-Bird	½P to 3½P	2P	¼N to 1¾P	¾P	3/16	9	20	18
'75-'76	Ford, Mercury	0 to 4P	2P	③	②	3/16	9⁷/₁₆	20	18¾
	T-Bird	2½P to 5½P	4P	④	⑤	3/16	9	20	18
'77 and later T-Bird				See Capri Car Section					
'77-'78	Ford, Mercury	1¼P to 2¾P	2P	⑥	⑦	1/16 to 5/16	9.44	20	18.69⑧
'79	Ford, Mercury	2¼P to 3¾P	3P	¼N to 1¼P	½P	1/16 to 5/16	11.20	20	18

① Left wheel—0 to 1P
Right wheel—¼N to ¾P

② Left wheel—½P
Right wheel—¼P

③ Left wheel—½N to 1½P
Right wheel—¾N to 1¼P

④ Left wheel—0 to 2P
Right wheel—½N to 1½P

⑤ Left wheel—1P
Right wheel—½P

⑥ Left ¼N to 1¼P
Right ½N to 1P

⑦ Left ½P
Right ¼P

⑧ 18.72—1978

N Negative
P Positive

— Not specified

NOTE: The Thunderbird through 1976 is in this section. Thunderbird, starting 1977, is in the Capri, Comet car section.

CHARGING SYSTEM

More information on starters can be found in the Unit Repair Section under Charging and Starting Systems.

Alternator Removal and Installation

1. Disconnect the negative battery cable.
2. Loosen the alternator mounting bolts, remove the alternator to adjusting arm bolt and remove the belt.
3. Remove the alternator mounting bolt and spacer, position the alternator so that the wire connectors can be disconnected and remove the alternator.
4. Reverse the above procedure to reinstall, applying pressure only to the front of the alternator housing when tightening the drive belt. The bolt should deflect 1/4 to 1/2 in. between the longest span of pulleys when properly tensioned.

Regulator Removal and Installation

1. Disconnect the negative battery cable. The regulator is located behind the battery on some models and it is necessary to remove the battery to remove the regulator.
2. Remove the regulator mounting screws, unlock the wire connectors, and remove the regulator.

NOTE: *1979 models have electronic voltage regulators. Always disconnect the connector plug from the regulator before removing the mounting screws on these models.*

3. Reverse the procedure to reinstall. On electromechanical regulators, the radio suppression condenser mounts under one screw.

STARTING SYSTEM

All models, except 429 and 460 V8, use positive engagement starters. These medium-duty starters have a self-contained engagement mechanism. The 429 and 460 V8 are equipped with heavy-duty, solenoid-actuated starters, to which an outboard solenoid is mounted. There is no difference in procedures for removing or installing these two types of starters.

Starting system troubleshooting may be found in the Unit Repair Section under Charging and Starting Systems.

Starter Removal and Installation

1. Disconnect the negative battery cable.
2. Disconnect the starter cable from the starter.
3. Remove the starter mounting bolts. On Thunderbird, remove the 2 front brace attaching bolts.
4. Manipulate the starter so that it can be lowered through the steering linkage. On some engine/chassis combinations this can be done by turning the steering wheel all the way to the right; on others it will be necessary to remove the idler arm bracket attaching bolts and lower the assembly away from the engine.
5. Reverse the procedure to reinstall.

Disabling the Seat Belt/Starter Interlock

It is now legal to disable the seat belt/starter interlock system. However the warning light portion of the system must be left operational.

1. Apply the parking brake and remove the ignition key.
2. Open the hood and locate the system emergency override switch and connector. It is always under the hood and sometimes on the left fender apron. Remove the connector.
3. Cut the white wire(s) with the pink dots (# 33 circuit) and the red wire(s) with the light blue stripe (# 32 circuit).
4. Splice the two (or four) wires together and tape the splice. Use a butt connector if available.

NOTE: *Do not cut and splice the other connector wires. If the red/yellow hash wire is spliced to any of the other wires the car will not start in gear.*

5. Install the connector back on the override switch. Close the hood.
6. Apply the parking brakes, buckle the seat belt, and turn the key to the ON position. If the starter cranks in ON or any gear selected, the wrong wires have been cut and spliced. Repeat steps 3-6.
7. Unbuckle the belt and try to start the car. If the car doesn't start, repeat steps 3-6. If the car starts, everything is O.K.
8. To stop the warning buzzer from operating, remove it from the connector. Tape the connector to the wiring harness so that it can't rattle.

IGNITION SYSTEM

Beginning 1974, Ford utilized a solid state or breakerless ignition system on all 351 cubic inch and larger engines in the state of California, and on all 400 and 460 cubic inch V8 engines nationwide. All engines assembled after May, 1974, use this maintenance-saving ignition system. This system is unique in that it eliminates the contact breaker points, replacing them with a permanent magnet, low voltage generator.

Complete service information for the Ford Solid State Ignition System can be found in the Electronic Ignition Unit Repair Section.

Tachometer Connection—
Electronic Ignition

Install a tachometer alligator clip into the Tach Test cavity. If the coil connector must be removed, grasp the wires and pull horizontally until it disconnects from the terminals.

An alligator type clip from the tachometer test lead can also be connected to the DEC (Distributor Electronic Control) without removing the connector.

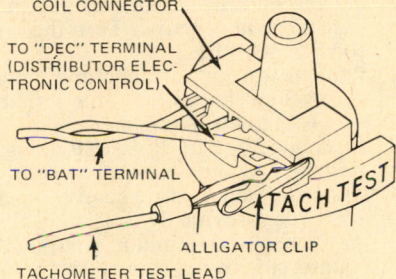

Electronic ignition tach connection
(© Ford Motor Co.)

Distributor Removal and
Installation

Remove the distributor cap and mark the position of tip of the rotor in relation to the body of the distributor and the engine block. Disconnect the ignition primary wires, the vacuum line(s) then take out the holdown bolt that holds the distributor down in the block and lift it up out of the block.

Do not disturb the engine after the distributor has been removed. If the engine is cranked with the distributor removed, the engine will have to be retimed.

Ignition Retiming—Point Type
Distributor

If the timing relationship has been disturbed, proceed to retime the ignition as follows: bring No. 1 cylinder up into the firing position. This can be checked by removing the spark plug, placing your thumb in the spark plug hole, then cranking the engine until the compression blows by your thumb. Now, slowly bring the crankshaft around until the TDC mark on the crankshaft pulley lines up with the pointer. This is the approximate firing position for No. 1 cylinder.

Scribe a mark on the engine that corresponds with the position of the No. 1 spark plug wire in the distributor cap. Remove the distributor and reinstall it so that the tip of the rotor aligns with the mark on the engine.

Viewed from above, rotation of dis-

tributor for six cylinder engine is clockwise; for eight cylinder, counterclockwise.

Ignition Retiming—Solid State
Distributor

1. Rotate the engine until No. 1 piston is on TDC of the compression stroke.
2. Align the correct initial timing mark with the pointer.
3. Position the distributor in the block with one of the armature segments aligned with the stator tooth and the rotor at No. 1 firing position.
4. Be sure that the oil pump intermediate shaft properly engages the distributor shaft. Install, but do not tighten, the distributor clamp bolt.
5. Rotate the distributor to advance the timing to a point where the armature tooth is properly aligned. Tighten the clamp.
6. Connect the distributor wiring and check the timing with a timing light.

Contact Point Replacement and
Adjustment

1. Unsnap the distributor cap retaining clips and position the cap clear of the breaker plate. Remove the rotor by pulling it straight up.
2. Remove the metal point shield, if so equipped.
3. Disconnect the primary lead and condenser wires from the contact point assembly. On dual-point distributors, remove the jumper strap also.
4. Remove the contact point and condenser retaining screws. Lift the contact point assembly and condenser from the distributor.
5. Lightly lubricate the distributor cam with heat-resistant lubricant.
6. Place the new contact point assembly and condenser in the distributor. Install, but do not tighten, the retaining screws.
7. On all V8 engines, place the ground wire under the contact point assembly screw farthest from the

contacts. On all six-cylinder engines, this ground wire is positioned under the condenser retaining screw.
8. Turn the engine until the rubbing block on the point assembly is resting on the high point of the distributor cam lobe. Insert a feeler gauge of specified thickness between the contact points and adjust the gap. Tighten the retaining screw and remove the feeler gauge.
9. Connect the primary and condenser wires to the contact point assembly in the same order in which they were removed. On distributors equipped with a metal point shield, the wires should be positioned 180° from each other, then install the shield.
10. Install the rotor and distributor cap.
11. If a dwell meter is available, check to see that the distributor dwell is within specifications.

Ignition Timing

1. Locate the timing marks and pointer on the lower engine pulley and engine front cover.
2. Clean the marks and apply chalk or bright-colored paint to the pointer.
3. Attach a timing light according to the manufacturer's specifications.
4. Disconnect and plug all vacuum lines leading to the distributor.
5. If the recommended engine idle speed is in excess of 500 rpm, set the idle 500 rpm for setting the timing. If the recommended idle speed is below 500 rpm, do not alter it.
6. Aim the timing light at the timing mark and pointer on the front of the engine. If the marks align when the timing light flashes, remove the timing light, set the idle to its proper specification, and connect the vacuum lines at the distributor. If the marks do not align when the light flashes, loosen the distributor hold-down clamp slightly.
7. Start the engine again, and observe

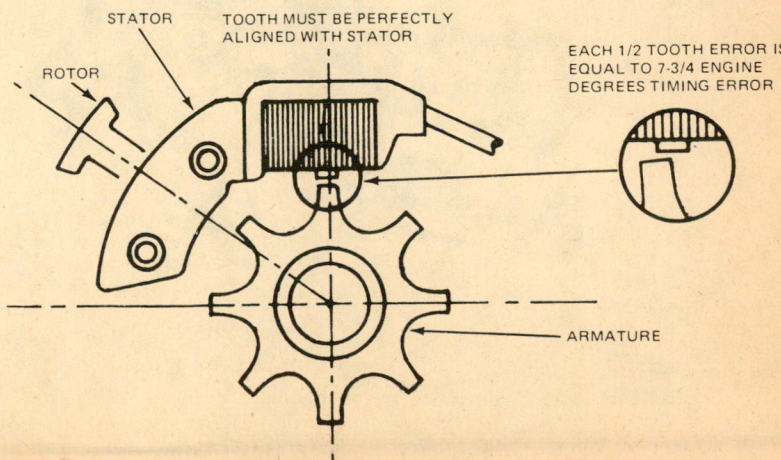

Static timing position—electronic ignition (© Ford Motor Co.)

the alignment of the timing marks. To advance the timing, turn the distributor counterclockwise on six-cylinder engines and clockwise on V8 engines. When the timing marks are aligned, turn the engine off and tighten the distributor hold-down clamp. Start the engine and re-check the timing.

FUEL SYSTEM

Fuel Pump Replacement

A single-action, permanently sealed fuel pump is used on all models. On 6-cylinder engines, the fuel pump is located on the lower left center of the engine block. The V8 fuel pump is mounted on the left side of the cylinder front cover.

NOTE: *Before removing the pump, rotate the engine so that the low point of the cam lobe is against the pump arm. This can be determined by rotating the engine with the fuel pump mounting bolts loosened; when tension is removed from the arm, proceed.*

1. Remove the inlet and outlet lines from the pump.
2. Remove the fuel pump retaining screws and remove the pump and gasket.
3. Clean all gasket material from the pump mounting surface on the engine, and apply a coat of oil-resistant sealer to the new gasket.
4. Position pump on engine and install retaining screws.
5. Reinstall lines, start engine and check for leaks.

NOTE: *If resistance is felt while positioning the fuel pump on the block, the camshaft eccentric is in the high position. To ease installation, connect a remote engine starter switch to the engine and tap the remote switch until resistance fades.*

Fuel Filter Replacement

All models use a non-serviceable in-line fuel filter which is located at the carburetor fuel inlet.
1. Remove the air cleaner.
2. Loosen the hose clamp or crimp type clamp at the fuel inlet hose connection.
3. Unscrew the filter from the carburetor.
4. Disconnect the filter from the hose and discard the hose clamp.
5. Reverse the above procedure to install, using a new hose clamp. After installation, start the engine and check for fuel leakage.

Idle Speed Adjustment

THROUGH 1974

Adjust with air cleaner installed.
1. Run engine at fast idle to equalize operating temperature.
2. Make sure the choke plate is fully released.
3. Turn headlights on high beam.
4. If engine is equipped with hot idle compensator valve, make sure it is fully seated in the closed position.
5. Attach tachometer of known accuracy to the engine.
6. The idle speed is set off with the air conditioner turned OFF.
7. On models equipped with a temperature sensing valve in the distributor vacuum line, remove and plug the vacuum hoses from the distributor to the valve and from the intake manifold to the valve, at the valve located in the intake manifold.
8. Make sure the dashpot is working freely and not binding.
9. If it is not possible to adjust the idle speed with the air cleaner installed, the engine idle speed must be rechecked after installing the air cleaner. On cars with vacuum controlled heat ducts in the air cleaner,

the vacuum line must be plugged if the carburetor is to be adjusted with the air cleaner removed.
10. On models with an electric solenoid, the higher idle speed is adjusted by turning the adjusting screw in the solenoid mounting bracket. On all models with a solenoid, the lower idle speed is obtained by putting the transmission in Park or Neutral, disconnecting the solenoid and adjusting the carburetor idle screw in the normal manner.

NOTE: *With the electric solenoid disengaged, the carburetor adjusting screw must make contact with the throttle shaft to prevent the throttle plates from jamming in the throttle bore when the engine is shut off.*

1975-78 351M AND 400 V8

1. Set the parking brake and put the transmission in Drive. Turn the air conditioner OFF.
2. Remove the air cleaner and plug the vacuum hoses from the intake manifold to the air cleaner.
3. Disconnect the EGR valve by plugging the vacuum hose at the valve.
4. If the idle fuel mixture screws have not been previously set, be sure they are at maximum rich (full counterclockwise) against the limiter stops. Otherwise, do not disturb the mixture screws.
5. Start the engine and warm it thoroughly.
6. Set the ignition timing.
7. Adjust the idle speed to specifications with the TSP (throttle solenoid positioner) energized. Use the TSP screw in the solenoid mounting bracket. After adjustment, place the transmission in Neutral and increase the rpm slightly to clear up any loading condition. Return the engine to idle and check the speed in Drive.
8. Reconnect the EGR valve and install the air cleaner.

1975-78 460 V8

1. Warm the engine to operating temperature.
2. Check the timing with the advance line disconnected and plugged. Connect the hose after checking.
3. Set the idle rpm to specification in Drive with the solenoid positioner engaged.
4. Run the engine briefly at fast idle in Neutral and check the idle speed again in Drive.
5. Readjust the idle speed if necessary.

1978 AND LATER 302 AND 351W V8 EXCEPT WITH EEC II

1. The air cleaner must be installed. If engine speed fluctuates, use the average engine speed. Do not depress the brake pedal on models with hydro-boost brakes. On cars with automatic parking brake release, disconnect and plug the vacuum hose

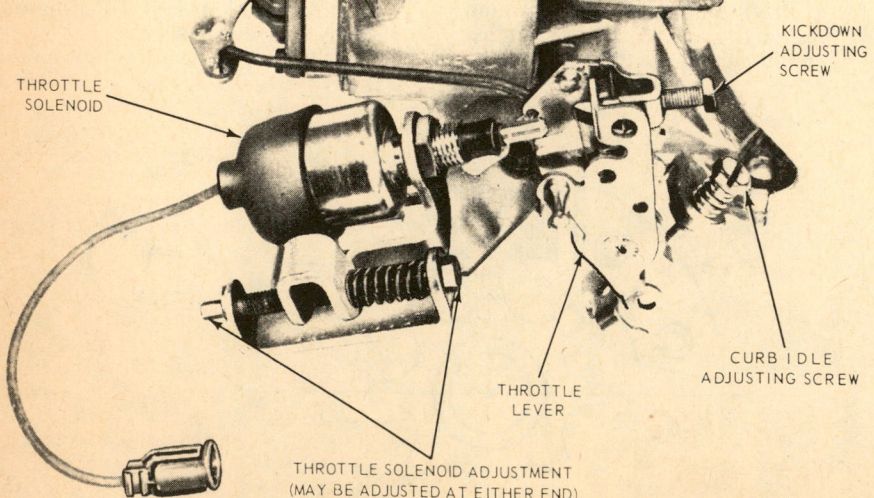

THROTTLE SOLENOID

KICKDOWN ADJUSTING SCREW

CURB IDLE ADJUSTING SCREW

THROTTLE LEVER

THROTTLE SOLENOID ADJUSTMENT (MAY BE ADJUSTED AT EITHER END)

Throttle solenoid adjusting locations—Motorcraft 2100 shown; Motorcraft 4300 similar.
(© Ford Motor Co)

at the parking brake pedal. Set the parking brake, turn off all accessories, warm the engine to operating temperature, and shut off.

2. Disconnect the fuel evaporation purge valve hose by tracing the hose from the charcoal cannister to the first fitting. Disconnect and plug the hose; also cap the fitting. Connect a tachometer. A special tachometer is needed on California engines with Dura-Spark I ignitions.

3. On all models except those with the Model 2700 VV (variable venturi) carburetor: Remove the spark delay valve (if equipped) and route the hose directly to the distributor advance fitting.

   On engines with the VV carburetor: disconnect and plug the distributor vacuum advance hose.

4. Trace the EGR hose to the carburetor. If an EGR/PVS valve is located in the hose, disconnect and plug the hose at the EGR valve.

5. Start the engine (choke fully open, transmission in Park). Place the fast idle lever on the specified step of the cam (see the emission control sticker on the engine for specification). Adjust if not within 100 rpm of specifications. Run the engine to 2500 rpm for 15 seconds and recheck the adjustment.

6. On engines with the VV carburetor only, turn off the engine and disconnect and plug the hose from the throttle modulator. Attach a spare length of vacuum hose from an engine vacuum source to the modulator. Start the engine, open the throttle until the modulator plunger is fully extended. Release the throttle. Check the auxiliary fast idle rpm (engine sticker). Adjustment is made by loosening the modulator locknut and turning the modulator. Reconnect the hose after adjustment.

7. After fast idle rpm is set, reconnect the vacuum lines (and spark delay valve, if equipped) removed earlier.

8. Before each idle speed check following, run the engine at 2500 rpm for 15 seconds (transmission in Neutral), then allow the engine to return to curb idle.

9. The air conditioning must be off, engine warm, choke fully open, parking brake set, and transmission in gear specified on the engine sticker (usually in Drive). If engine rpm in each case is not within 50 rpm of specifications, adjustment is required.

10. If no solenoid is present: turn the throttle stop adjusting screw until specified rpm (engine sticker) is obtained. If equipped with a dashpot, shut off the engine, collapse the dashpot plunger, and measure the clearance between the plunger and the throttle lever pad. Adjust to specifications (sticker) if necessary.

11. On non-air conditioned cars with an anti-diesel TSP (throttle solenoid positioner): adjust the TSP by rotating the long screw (part of the mounting bracket) until the specified curb idle rpm (engine sticker) is obtained. Then, collapse the TSP plunger by forcing the throttle lever pad against the plunger. Adjust the throttle stop screw until the specified TSP-OFF rpm (sticker) is obtained.

12. On air conditioned cars with an A/C TSP:
    a. Turn the A/C on;
    b. open the throttle to allow the TSP plunger to extend, then release the throttle;
    c. disconnect the A/C compressor clutch wire at the compressor;
    d. check A/C-ON rpm and adjust, if necessary, by turning the long screw on the TSP bracket until the specified A/C-ON rpm is obtained. Then turn the A/C off, connect the compressor clutch wire, and adjust the throttle stop screw until the specified A/C-OFF rpm is obtained.

Fuel Mixture Adjustment

THROUGH 1974

On models with idle mixture limiters, adjust to obtain the highest rpm possible. Limiter caps should not be removed.

1975 AND LATER

Fuel mixture adjustment requires an artificial enrichment substance (propane). This should not be attempted unless you have the special equipment.

Dashpot Adjustment

1. With the engine idle speed and the mixture properly adjusted and with the engine at operating temperature, loosen the dashpot locknut.

2. Hold the throttle in the closed position and depress the dashpot plunger. Measure the clearance between the plunger and cam. Adjust the dashpot adjusting nut to give the proper clearance. For years not listed, see the engine emission control sticker.

3. Tighten the locknut and check the setting of the accelerator pump.

Dashpot Adjustment

Model	Clearance (in.)
1972 302, 351, 400, 429 2V	1/8
1972 240 1V	7/64

COOLING SYSTEM

Both the 6 cylinder and V8 engines employ cooling systems that are basically similar.

In the 6 cylinder engine, coolant flows from the cylinder head, past the thermostat (if it is open) and into the radiator upper tank. In the V8 engine, coolant from each cylinder head flows through water passages in the intake manifold, then past the thermostat (if it is open) and into the radiator upper tank.

A single water pump assembly is used. The pump has a sealed bearing integral with the water pump shaft. The bearing requires no lubrication. There is a bleed hole in the water pump housing. This is not a lubrication hole.

Radiator Removal and Installation

1. Drain the cooling system.
2. Remove the upper and lower radiator hoses from the radiator.
3. On models with a fan shroud, remove the shroud attaching screws and move the shroud rearward to gain clearance.
4. Disconnect and plug the automatic transmission cooler lines at the bottom of the radiator.
5. Remove the radiator attaching screws and remove the radiator from the car.
6. Reverse the above procedure to install.
7. Fill the cooling system, run the engine at fast idle and check for leaks. Check the transmission fluid level and add, if necessary.

Water Pump Removal and Installation

1. Drain the cooling system. Disconnect the negative battery cable.
2. On cars with power steering, remove the drive belt; remove the power steering mounting retaining screws and remove the pump and bracket as an assembly and position it out of the way.
3. If vehicle is equipped with air conditioning, remove the idler pulley and drive belt from the engine.
4. Disconnect the lower radiator hose, heater hose and bypass hose from the water pump.
5. On cars with a fan shroud, remove the shroud retaining screws and position the shroud rearward over the fan.
6. Remove the fan attaching screws and remove the fan, fan spacer and shroud from the engine compartment.
7. Loosen the alternator mounting bolts and remove the belt.
8. Remove the air pump pulley and pivot bolt. Remove the air pump adjusting bracket. Swing the upper bracket aside. Detach the air conditioner compressor and lay it aside.
9. Remove any accessory mounting brackets from the water pump.
10. Disconnect the heater and lower radiator hoses from the water pump.

11. Remove the water pump mounting bolts and remove the pump from the engine.

12. Clean all gasket surfaces, and on 429 and 460 V8, remove the water pump backing plate and replace the gasket.

NOTE: *The 240 6-cylinder engine originally had a one-piece gasket for the cylinder front cover and the water pump. Trim away the old gasket at the edge of the cylinder cover and replace with service gasket.*

13. Remove the water pump fitting from the old pump and install it in the new pump.

14. Coat both sides of the new gasket with water resistant sealer, then install pump by reversing above procedure.

Thermostat Replacement

1. Drain the radiator so that the coolant level is below the thermostat housing.

2. Remove the outlet elbow retaining bolts and position the elbow clear of the intake manifold or cylinder head sufficiently to provide access to the thermostat.

3. Remove the thermostat and old gasket. The thermostat must be rotated counterclockwise for removal on all engines through 1974, and all 302 and 351W V8s.

4. Clean the mating surfaces of the outlet elbow and the engine to remove all old gasket material and sealer. Coat the new gasket with water-resistant sealer. Install the thermostat in the block on 1975 and later 351W and 400 V8s (or in the intake manifold on 460 V8s), then install the gasket. On all other engines, position the gasket on the engine, and install the thermostat in the coolant elbow. The thermostat must be rotated clockwise to lock it in position on all engines through 1974, and all 302 and 351W V8s.

5. Install the outlet elbow and retaining bolts on the engine. Torque the bolts to 12-15 ft lbs.

6. Refill the radiator. Run the engine at operating temperature and check for leaks. Recheck the coolant level.

EMISSION CONTROL SYSTEMS

All cars use positive crankcase ventilation (PCV) systems. The PCV system routes a harmful mixture of blow-by gases and condensation vapors, which were formerly dispelled into the atmosphere, through a modulating valve (PCV valve) and into the intake manifold where they combine with the carburetor air/fuel mixture and are burned in the combustion chamber. The system is closed to the atmosphere, deriving its fresh air from the air cleaner.

1972

The Electronic Spark Control (ESC) system is two pieces, an amplifier and a distributor modulator valve. The amplifier judges the signals sent to it by the speed and temperature switches and causes the distributor modulator valve to open and close and thus allow or prevent vacuum to reach the distributor. The Transmission Regulated Spark (TRS) is similar to the ESC system except that the speed sensor is replaced by a transmission switch. The switch is mounted on the side of the transmission and is hydraulically actuated. When the ambient temperature is above 55°F, the transmission switch is closed whenever the transmission is in any gear other than high gear or reverse (automatic transmission).

When the transmission switch closes, it signals the distributor modulator valve to close and thus prevent carburetor vacuum from reaching the distributor. Neither of these systems is functional below 55-58°F, and both are bypassed by the PVS if the engine should overheat.

On some 1972 models, a spark delay valve has been inserted into the vacuum advance line to the distributor. The valve closes under hard acceleration, blocking carburetor vacuum to the distributor for a predetermined period of a few seconds. The valves are color coded for identification purposes.

1973-74

1973-74 models use an Exhaust Gas Recirculation System (EGR) to control oxides of nitrogen. On V8 engines, exhaust gases travel through the exhaust gas crossover passage in the intake manifold. A portion of these gases is diverted into a spacer which is mounted under the carburetor. The EGR control valve, which is attached to the rear of the spacer, consists of a vacuum diaphragm with an attached plunger which normally blocks off exhaust gases from entering the intake manifold. The EGR valve is controlled

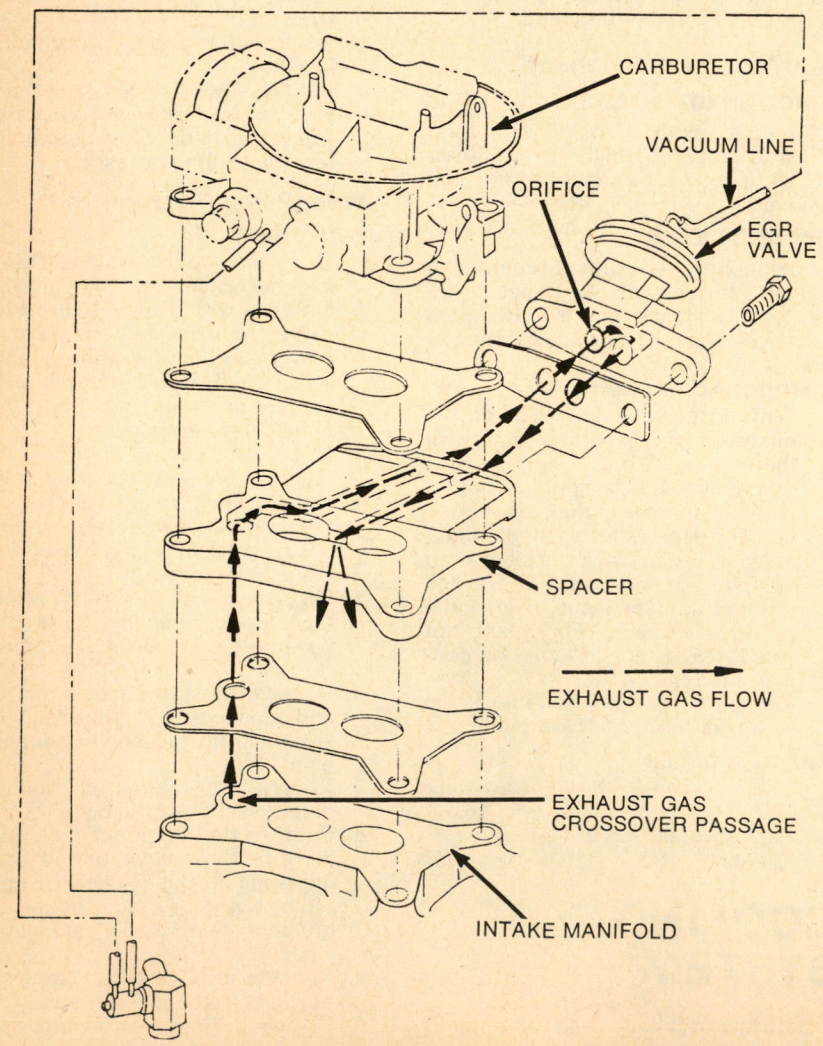

CARBURETOR

VACUUM LINE

ORIFICE

EGR VALVE

SPACER

EXHAUST GAS FLOW

EXHAUST GAS CROSSOVER PASSAGE

INTAKE MANIFOLD

Exhaust Gas Recirculation (EGR) System (© Ford Motor Co)

by a vacuum line from the carburetor which passes through a ported vacuum switch. The EGR ported vacuum switch provides vacuum to the EGR valve at coolant temperatures above 125°F. The vacuum diaphragm then opens the EGR valve permitting exhaust gases to flow through the carburetor spacer and enter the intake manifold where they combine with the fuel mixture and enter the combustion chambers. The exhaust gases are relatively oxygen-free and tend to dilute the combustion charge. This lowers peak combustion temperature thereby reducing oxides of nitrogen.

All models with a 351C, 400, 429, or 460 V8 use the new Delay Vacuum By-Pass (DVB) spark control system. This system provides two paths by which carburetor vacuum can reach the distributor vacuum advance. The system consists of a spark delay valve, a check valve, a solenoid vacuum valve, and an ambient temperature switch. When the ambient temperature is below 49°F, the temperature switch contacts are open and the vacuum solenoid is open (de-energized). Under these conditions, vacuum will flow from the carburetor, through the open solenoid, and to the distributor. Since the spark delay valve resists the flow of carburetor vacuum, the vacuum will always flow through the vacuum solenoid when it is open, since this is the path of least resistance. When the ambient temperature rises above 60°F, the contacts in the temperature switch (which is located in the door post) close. This passes ignition switch current to the solenoid, energizing the solenoid. This blocks one of the two vacuum paths. All distributor vacuum must now flow through the spark delay valve. When carburetor vacuum rises above a certain level on acceleration, a rubber valve in the spark delay valve blocks vacuum from passing through the valve for from 5 to 30 seconds.

After this time delay has elapsed, normal vacuum is supplied to the distributor. When the vacuum solenoid is closed, (temperature above 60°), the vacuum line from the solenoid to the distributor is vented to atmosphere. To prevent the vacuum that is passing through the spark delay valve from escaping through the solenoid into the atmosphere, a one-way check valve is installed in the vacuum line from the solenoid to the distributor.

In order to meet 1974 California emission control standards, all 1974 Ford cars sold in that state will be equipped with a Thermactor (air injection) system to control hydrocarbons and carbon monoxide. The EGR and IMCO systems are retained, as in 1973, to control oxides of nitrogen.

1975

All full size Ford Motor Co. cars are equipped with catalytic converters. California models are equipped with two converters, while models sold in the 49 states have only one unit.

Catalytic converters convert noxious emissions of hydrocarbons (HC) and carbon monoxide (CO) into harmless carbon dioxide and water. The units are installed in the exhaust system ahead of the mufflers and are designed, if the engine is properly tuned, to last 50,000 miles before replacement.

In addition to the converters, most 1975 Ford, Mercury and Thunderbird cars are equipped with the Thermactor air pump (air injection system) previously mentioned. The air injection system, which afterburns the uncombusted fuel mixture in the exhaust ports, is needed with the converters to prevent an overly rich mixture from reaching the converter, and to help supply oxygen to aid in converter reaction.

Other emission control equipment for 1975 includes a carryover of the Positive Crankcase Ventilation (PCV) System, the Fuel Evaporative Control System, and exhaust gas recirculation.

Emission control related improvements for 1975 include standard Solid State (breakerless) Ignition, induction hardened exhaust valve seats, exhaust manifold redesign, vacuum operated heat riser valves, and improved carburetors with more precise fuel metering control and a mechanical high-speed bleed system.

All cars equipped with the 460 V8 engine use a Cold Start Spark Advance (CSSA) System in 1975 to aid in cold start driveability. Basically, the system will allow full vacuum advance to the distributor until the coolant temperature reaches 125°F.

1976

For 1976, the complexity of emission control equipment has been reduced on Ford products. The average number of emission control components has been

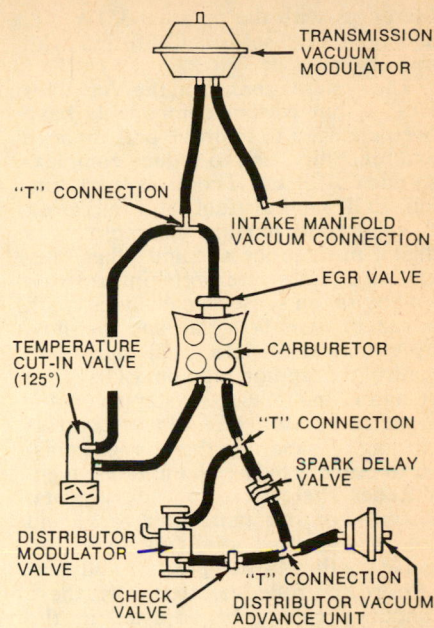

Typical vacuum hose schematic with EGR
(© Ford Motor Co)

reduced from 25 to 11 on most cars. All 1976 models have catalytic converters. In addition, a new proportional exhaust gas recirculation system has been introduced. Exhaust backpressure regulates the EGR valve spark port vacuum signal to modulate the recirculation of gases, matching EGR flow to engine load.

1977-78

See the Capri, Comet car section for details on these emission control systems.

1979

Most emission controls are carryover from 1978. One exception, however, is the EEC II (Electronic Engine Control) system. It is installed on all

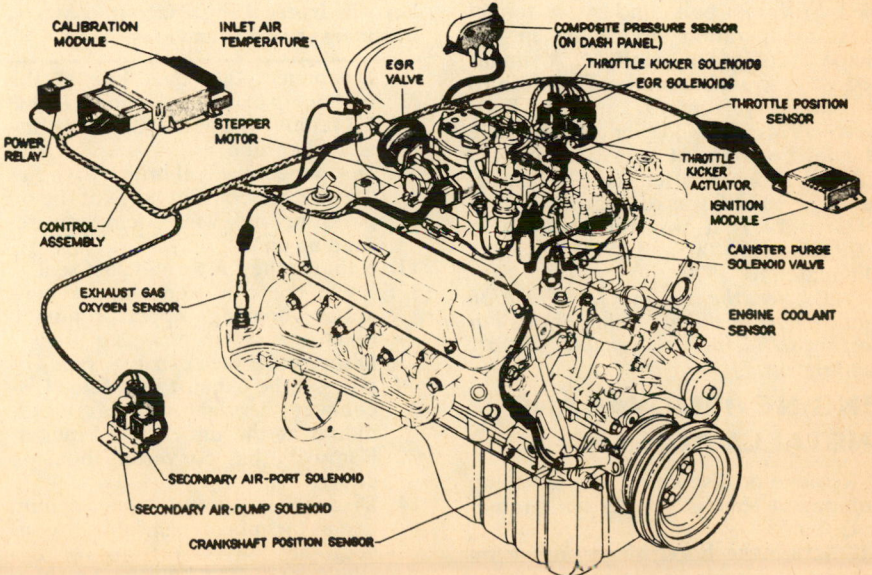

351W V8 EEC II components (© Ford Motor Co)

Mercurys with the optional 351W V8, and on LTDs sold in California with that engine.

The system is based on the Versailles EEC I, but certain components have been changed to improve performance and reliability, and to reduce complexity and cost. EEC II controls spark timing, EGR, and air/fuel ratio (mixture). A solid state module incorporating a digital microprocessor and other integrated circuits interprets information sent by seven sensors, calculates spark advance, EGR flow rate and fuel-flow trim, and sends electrical signals to control the ignition module, EGR valve actuator, and an electric stepper motor in the carburetor. EEC II also controls purging of vapors in the storage canister to prevent over-rich mixtures, high-altitude fuel mixture adjustments, Thermactor (air pump) air flow, and cold engine (fast idle) functions. Because the throttle idle position and mixture are controlled electronically, these functions cannot be adjusted in the conventional manner.

ENGINE

The only 6 cylinder engine available on full sized Fords is the 240 cu. in. version in 1972. The intake manifolding on this six is mounted conventionally on the right-hand side and is detachable, unlike the intake manifolding on Ford sixes in smaller cars. The 302, 351W, 351C, 351M and 400 V8 engines are the most popular engines in full sized Fords. The 302 is notably compact, about 20 in. across. The larger displacement 351W is wider and bulkier although nearly identical in layout and conformation. The 351M, a modified 351C, was introduced in 1975.

The 429 engine was the first of a new series of big block Ford engines. It has been available in two-barrel and four-barrel versions. The engine is identifiable by its great bulk, and by the tunnel port configuration noticeable in the shape of its intake manifold. A similar 460 V8 is available on the Thunderbird and Mercury from 1972 and the Ford from 1974. The 351 engine became standard equipment in 1973. The 429 V8 was dropped after the 1973 model run. The 302 V8 was discontinued from 1973 to 1977; it was reintroduced in 1978. The 460, 400, and 351M V8s were eliminated for 1979.

NOTE: *See the Engine Identification Code Chart at the beginning of this car section to identify the engine you are working on.*

ENGINE REMOVAL AND INSTALLATION

Remove or disconnect any air pump equipment that interferes with removal.

1. Scribe the hood hinge outline on the underside of the hood, disconnect the hood and remove.
2. Drain the entire cooling system and oil from engine oil pan.
3. Remove the air cleaner, disconnect the battery ground cable. Disconnect the transmission fluid cooler lines at the radiator.
4. Remove the upper and lower radiator hoses from the engine and, if the engine has a fan shroud, disconnect the shroud from the radiator and position it rearward. Remove the radiator from the car.
5. Remove the fan attaching screws and remove the fan, fan spacer and shroud from the engine as an assembly. Loosen and remove all drive belts. Remove the water pump pulley.
6. Disconnect the heater hoses from the engine. If the vehicle has power steering, remove the pump from the engine and position it out of the way.
7. Remove the alternator mounting bolts and ground wire from the block and remove the alternator. Disconnect the carburetor kickdown linkage and speed control wire from the engine.
8. On models with power brakes, remove the vacuum line from the engine. On cars with air conditioning, remove the compressor mounting bracket from the engine and position the compressor out of the way without disconnecting the refrigerant lines.

NOTE: *If the compressor lines do not have enough slack to move the compressor out of the way without disconnecting the refrigerant lines, the air conditioning system must be evacuated, using the required tools, before the refrigerant lines can be disconnected.*

--------- CAUTION ---------
Do not disconnect any refrigerant lines unless you have experience with air conditioning systems. Escaping refrigerant will freeze any surface it contacts, including your skin and eyes.

9. Disconnect fuel tank line at the fuel pump and plug the line. On 460 V8 remove the automatic transmission filler tube.
10. Disconnect the coil primary wire at the coil. Disconnect wires at the oil pressure and water temperature-sending units.
11. Remove the starter and dust seal.
12. Raise the car. Remove the converter housing upper retaining bolts.
13. Disconnect the exhaust pipe or pipes at the exhaust manifold. Disconnect the right and left motor mount at the underbody bracket. Remove the converter housing cover.
14. Disconnect throttle valve vacuum line at the intake manifold, disconnect the converter from the flywheel rotating the flywheel as necessary for access. Remove the

converter housing lower retaining bolts.
15. Lower the car. Support the transmission and converter housing with a jack.
16. Attach an engine lifting hook. Lift the engine up and out of the compartment and onto an adequate work stand.

On installation:
1. Place a new gasket over the studs of the exhaust manifold/s.
2. Attach engine sling and lifting device. Then lift engine from work stand.
3. Lower the engine into the engine compartment. Be sure the exhaust manifold/s properly line up with the muffler inlet pipe/s and the dowels in the block engage the holes in the converter housing.

Start the converter pilot into the crankshaft.
4. Install the converter housing upper bolts.
5. Install the engine support insulator to the bracket retaining nuts. Disconnect the engine lifting sling and remove the lifting brackets.
6. Raise the front of car. Connect the exhaust line/s and tighten the attachments.
7. Position the dust seal and install the starter.
8. Attach the converter to the flywheel. Install the converter housing inspection cover. Install the remaining converter housing retaining bolts.
9. Remove the support from the transmission and lower the car.
10. Connect the engine ground strap and coil primary wire.
11. Connect the water temperature gauge wire and the heater hose at the coolant outlet housing. Connect the accelerator rod at the bellcrank.
12. Connect the transmission filler tube bracket. Connect the throttle valve vacuum line.
13. With power steering, install the drive belt and power steering pump bracket. Install the bracket retaining bolts. Adjust the drive belt to proper tension.
14. Remove the plug from the fuel tank line. Connect the flexible fuel line and the oil pressure sending unit wire.
15. Install the pulley, belt spacer, and fan. Adjust the belt tension.
16. Install the alternator and the negative battery cable.
17. With power brakes, connect vacuum line at intake manifold. With air conditioning, install compressor on mounting bracket.
18. Install the radiator. Connect the radiator hoses.
19. Connect the transmission fluid cooler lines.
20. Connect the heater hose at the water pump, after bleeding the system.

21. Bring the crankcase to level with the correct grade of oil. Run the engine at fast idle and check for leaks. Install the air cleaner and make final engine adjustments.
22. Install and adjust hood.

MANIFOLDS

Intake and Exhaust Manifold Removal—6 Cylinder

1. Remove the air cleaner. Remove the carburetor linkage and kickdown linkage from the engine.
2. Disconnect the fuel line from the carburetor and all vacuum lines from the manifolds.
3. Remove the negative battery cable, then remove the alternator mounting bolts and move the alternator from the engine with the wires attached.
4. Disconnect the muffler inlet pipe from the engine.
5. Remove the manifold attaching parts from the engine, and remove the two manifolds as an assembly.
6. To separate the manifolds, remove the carburetor and then remove the nuts that secure the manifolds together.
7. Clean all gasket surfaces. If the manifolds were separated, coat the mating surfaces lightly with graphite grease, then assemble them with the nuts hand tight. Install the carburetor with a new gasket.
8. Install a new intake gasket and exhaust pipe gasket. Coat the mating surfaces on the engine lightly with graphite grease, install the manifold assembly, and torque the attaching nuts in three stages to 23-28 ft. lbs. in the sequence shown.
9. If the manifolds were separated, tighten the nuts after the manifolds are attached to the engine. The remainder of installation is the reverse of removal.

Intake Manifold Removal—V8

Intake manifold removal and installation procedures for all V8s are covered in the Capri section.

Exhaust Manifold Removal—V8

Exhaust manifold removal and installation procedures for all V8s are covered in the Capri section.

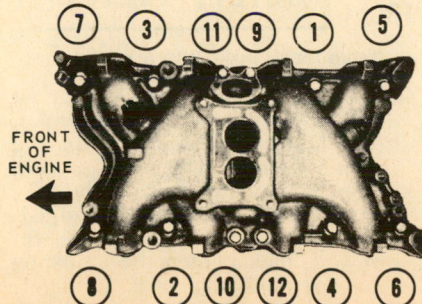

Intake manifold torque sequence—351C, 351M, 400 V8 (© Ford Motor Co)

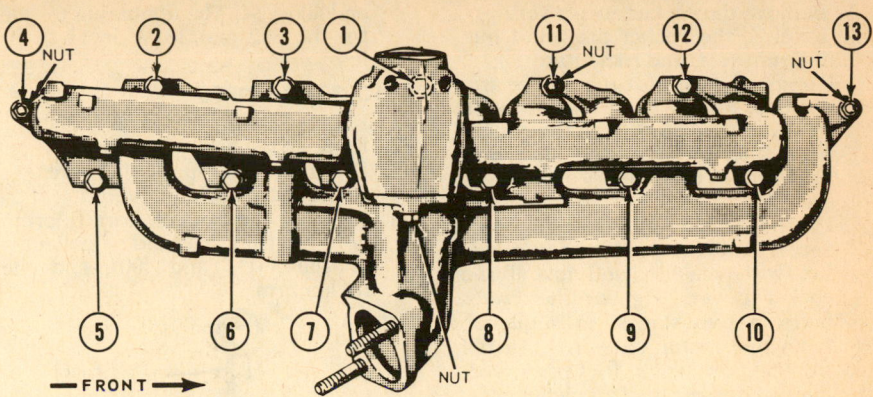

Intake and exhaust manifold torque sequence—240 six cyl. (© Ford Motor Co)

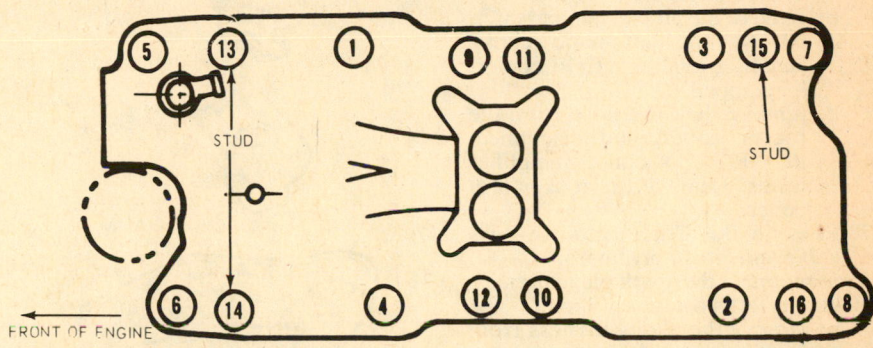

Intake manifold torque sequence—351W V8 through 1975 (© Ford Motor Co)

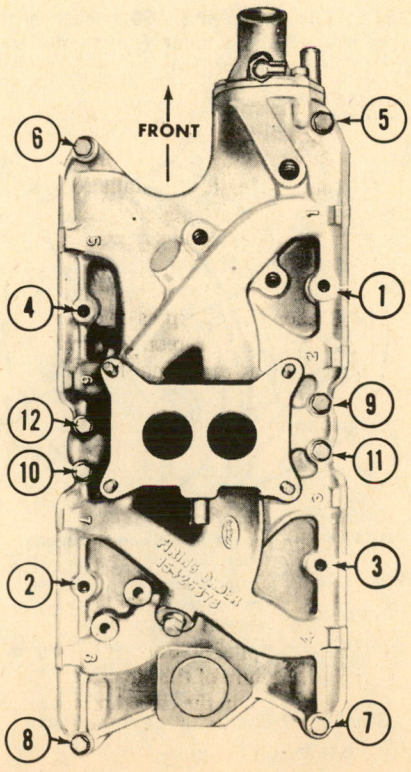

Intake manifold torque sequence—302 V8 and 1976 and later 351W V8 (© Ford Motor Co)

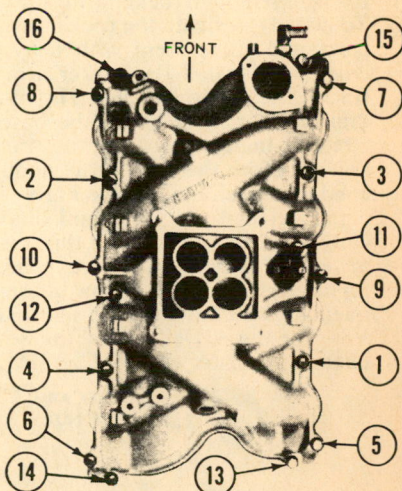

Intake manifold torque sequence—429 and 460 V8 (© Ford Motor Co)

VALVE SYSTEM

Rocker Arm Removal and Installation

6 CYLINDER

1. Disconnect the PCV hoses from the rocker arm cover. Remove the air cleaner assembly. Disconnect any vacuum hoses and fuel lines crossing the rocker cover. Disconnect the carburetor linkage.

2. Remove the rocker arm cover.
3. Remove the rocker arm stud nut, fulcrum seat, and rocker arm.
4. To install, first coat the rocker arm surfaces and valve stem with heavy engine oil. Install the rocker arm, fulcrum seat, and stud nut. Perform a preliminary valve adjustment.
5. Clean the gasket mounting surfaces, coat a new rocker cover gasket with sealant, and install the rocker cover. Tighten the cover bolts in two stages, in sequence from the center outwards. Install the vacuum hoses, fuel lines, carburetor linkage, and air cleaner.

302, 351W V8

1. On the right side:
   a. disconnect the automatic choke heat chamber air inlet hose.
   b. remove the air cleaner and duct.
   c. remove the automatic choke heat tube (302) and EGR cooler, if equipped.
   d. remove the PCV hose from the rocker cover, and disconnect the EGR vacuum amplifier hoses. Remove the rocker arm cover.
2. Remove the Thermactor by-pass valve and air supply hoses.
3. Disconnect the spark plug wires.
4. On the left side:
   a. remove the wiring harness from the clips.
   b. remove the rocker arm cover.
5. Remove the rocker arm stud nut, fulcrum seat, and rocker arm.
6. To install, lubricate the rocker arm parts and valve stem with heavy engine oil. Install the rocker arm, fulcrum seat, and stud nut. The hydraulic lifter must be on the base circle of the cam lobe (all the way down) before the stud nut is tightened. If an individual rocker arm is being reinstalled, the crankshaft can be rotated until this is achieved. If all rockers are being replaced, for the 302, follow the sequence given for the 429 and 460 V8s; for the 351W, follow the sequence given for the 351C, 351M,

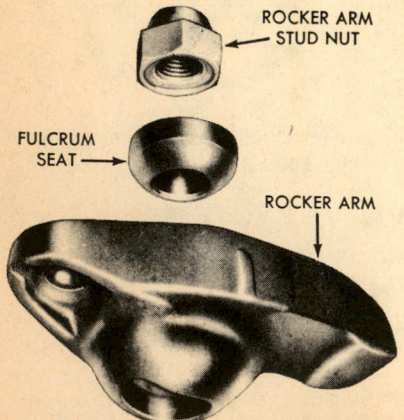

302 and 351W rocker arm assembly
(© Ford Motor Co)

and 400 V8s. The tightening torque for the 302 and 351W is 17-23 ft. lbs.

351C, 351M, 400 V8

1. Remove the air cleaner and duct.
2. Remove the hoses from the cover.
3. Disconnect the spark plug wires.
4. Remove the rocker cover(s).
5. Remove the rocker arm fulcrum bolt, fulcrum seat (and oil deflector on the 351M and 400), and the rocker arm.

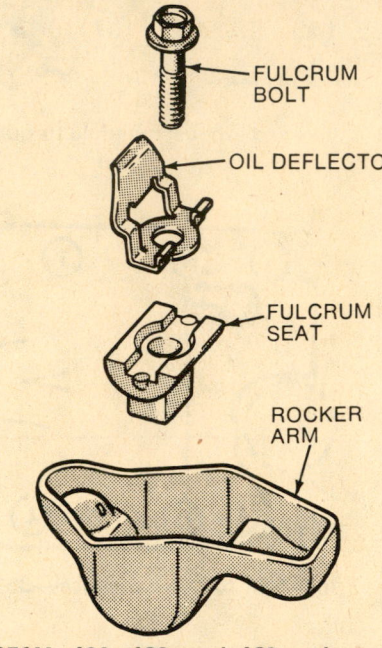

351M, 400, 429, and 460 rocker arm assembly; 351C similar (no oil deflector) (© Ford Motor Co)

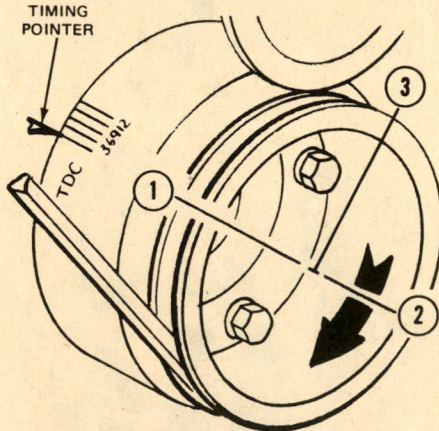

POSITION 1 — No. 1 at TDC at end of compression stroke.
POSITION 2 — Rotate the crankshaft 180 degrees (one half revolution) clockwise from POSITION 1.
POSITION 3 — Rotate the crankshaft 270 degrees (three quarter revolution) clockwise from POSITION 2.

Crankshaft positions for rocker arm installation (© Ford Motor Co)

6. When installing, the lifter must be on the base circle of the cam lobe. If all rockers are being replaced,

position no. 1 piston on TDC of the compression stroke, and assemble the rocker arms on the following valves:
no. 1 intake and exhaust
no. 4 intake and no. 3 exhaust
no. 8 intake and no. 7 exhaust
   Turn the crankshaft 180° clockwise and assemble the rocker arms for:
no. 3 intake and no. 2 exhaust
no. 7 intake and no. 6 exhaust
   Rotate the crankshaft 270° clockwise and assemble the rocker arms for:
no. 2 intake and no. 4 exhaust
no. 5 intake and exhaust
no. 6 intake and no. 8 exhaust
   Torque the fulcrum bolts to 18-25 ft. lbs.
7. Assemble the remaining parts.

429, 460 V8

The procedure is the same as that for the 351C, 351M, and 400 V8s, but the tightening sequence is different. With the engine in the first position, tighten the fulcrum bolts on the following valves:
no. 1 intake and exhaust
no. 7 intake and no. 5 exhaust
no. 8 intake and no. 4 exhaust
   With the engine in the second position, tighten the fulcrum bolts for:
no. 4 intake and no. 2 exhaust
no. 5 intake and no. 6 exhaust
   With the engine in the third position:
no. 2 intake and no. 3 exhaust
no. 3 intake and no. 7 exhaust
no. 6 intake and no. 8 exhaust
   Tightening torque for the 429 and 460 V8 fulcrum bolts is 18-25 ft. lbs.

Preliminary Valve Adjustment

6 CYLINDER

1. Crank the engine until the TDC mark on the crankshaft damper is aligned with timing pointer on the cylinder front cover.
2. Scribe a mark on the damper at this point.
3. Scribe two more marks on the damper, each equally spaced from the first mark.

Valve locations—240 6 cylinder

4. With the number one cylinder on TDC of the compression stroke, (the first mark aligned with the pointer) back off the rocker arm adjusting nut until there is end-play in the pushrod. Tighten the adjusting nut until all clearance is removed, then tighten the adjusting nut one additional turn. To determine when all clearance is removed from the rocker arm, turn the pushrod with the fingers. When

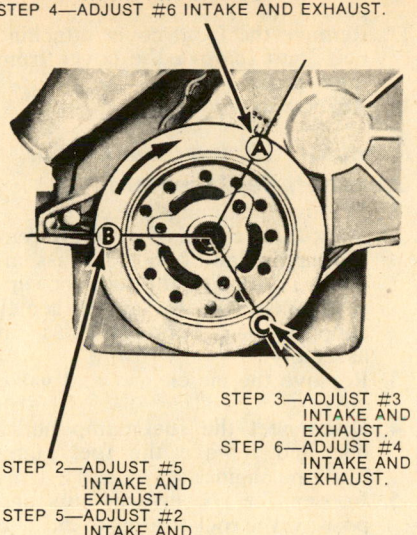

STEP 1—SET #1 PISTON ON T.D.C. AT END OF COMPRESSION STROKE—ADJUST #1 INTAKE AND EXHAUST.
STEP 4—ADJUST #6 INTAKE AND EXHAUST.

STEP 3—ADJUST #3 INTAKE AND EXHAUST.
STEP 6—ADJUST #4 INTAKE AND EXHAUST.
STEP 2—ADJUST #5 INTAKE AND EXHAUST.
STEP 5—ADJUST #2 INTAKE AND EXHAUST.

Position of crankshaft for valve adjustment 6 cylinder (© Ford Motor Co)

the pushrod can no longer be turned, all clearance has been removed.

5. Repeat this procedure for each valve, turning the crankshaft 1/3 turn to the next mark each time and following the engine firing order of 1-5-3-6-2-4.

V8

All V8 engines use hydraulic lifters with no provision for preliminary adjustment, except for the installation procedure. When a rocker arm is installed, the lifter must be on the base circle of the cam lobe (all the way down) before the rocker nut or bolt is tightened. The rocker must be tightened until the nut contacts the stud shoulder on the 302 and 351W V8s, then torqued to specification. On all other V8s, torque the fulcrum bolt to specification.

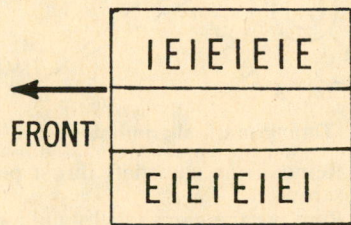

Valve locations—302, 351W, 351C, 351M, 400, 429 and 460 V8

Valve Guides

Valve guides on all the engines are an integral part of the cylinder head casting. If valve guides become worn, they can be reamed oversize or bronze replacement bushings can be installed. Oversize valves are available with stem diameters .003, .015, and .030 in. larger than standard. If the guides are to be reamed more than .003 in. oversize, they must be reamed in steps.

Cylinder Head Removal and Installation

6 CYLINDER

1. Drain the coolant and remove the air cleaner. Disconnect the battery cable at the cylinder head.
2. Disconnect the exhaust pipe at the manifold.
3. Disconnect the accelerator retracting spring, choke control cable and accelerator rod at the carburetor.
4. Disconnect the fuel line and the distributor control vacuum line at the carburetor.
5. Disconnect the coolant tubes from the carburetor spacer. Disconnect the coolant and heater hoses.
6. Disconnect the distributor control vacuum line at the distributor and the fuel inlet line at the filter. Remove the lines as an assembly.
7. Disconnect the PVC hose.
8. Disconnect the spark plug wires at the plugs and the small wire from the temperature-sending unit. With a Thermactor exhaust emission control system, disconnect the air pump hose at the air manifold assembly. Unscrew the tube nuts and remove the air manifold. Disconnect the anti-backfire valve air and vacuum lines at the intake manifold. With power brakes, disconnect the brake vacuum line at the intake manifold.
9. Remove the rocker arm cover.
10. Loosen the rocker arm stud nut so that the rocker arm can be rotated to one side. Remove the valve pushrods and keep them in sequence.

11. Remove the remaining cylinder head bolts, then remove the cylinder head.
On installation:
1. Clean the head and block surfaces.
2. Apply sealer to both sides of the head gasket. Position the gasket over guide studs or dowel pins.
NOTE: *Apply gasket sealer only to steel shim head gaskets. Steel/asbestos composite head gaskets are to be installed without any sealer.*
3. Install a new gasket on the exhaust pipe flange.
4. Lift the cylinder head over the guide studs and slide it carefully into place while guiding the exhaust manifold studs into the exhaust pipe flange.
5. Coat the cylinder-head attaching bolts with water-resistant sealer and install (but do not tighten), the head bolts.
6. Torque the head, in proper sequence, and in three progressive steps to specifications.

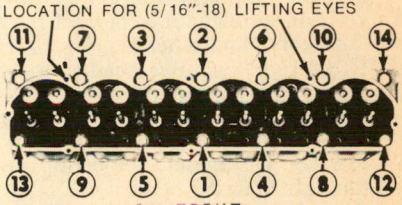

LOCATION FOR (5/16"-18) LIFTING EYES

Cylinder head torque sequence—240 six cyl. (© Ford Motor Co)

7. Lubricate both ends of the pushrods and insert them in their original bores and sockets.
8. Lubricate the valve stem tips and the rocker arm pads.
9. Position the rocker arms and tighten the stud nuts enough to hold the pushrods in position. Adjust the valves.
10. Install the exhaust pipe-to-manifold nuts and lockwashers. Torque to 17-22 ft lbs.
11. Connect the radiator and the heater hoses. Connect the coolant tubes at the carburetor spacer.
12. Connect the distributor vacuum line and the carburetor fuel line. Connect the battery cable to the cylinder head.
13. With a Thermactor exhaust emission control system, install the air manifold assembly on the cylinder head. Connect the air pump outlet hose to the air manifold. Connect the anti-backfire valve, air and vacuum lines to the intake manifold.
14. Connect the accelerator rod pullback spring. Connect the choke control cable and the accelerator rod at the carburetor.
15. Connect the distributor control vacuum line at the distributor. Connect the carburetor fuel line at the fuel filter.
16. Connect the temperature-sending unit wire at the sending unit. Connect the spark plug wires.

17. Fill the cooling system.
18. Run the engine to stabilize the engine temperature. Check for coolant and oil leaks.
19. Adjust the engine idle mixture and speed.

V8

1. Remove the intake manifold and carburetor as an assembly.
2. Remove the rocker arm covers.
3. With air conditioning, remove the compressor. Do not disconnect any air conditioning lines.
4. If the left cylinder head is involved on a car with power steering, remove the steering pump and bracket and remove the drive belt. Tie the assembly out of the way.
5. If the left cylinder head is involved on a car with a Thermactor exhaust emission control system, disconnect the hose from the air manifold on the left cylinder head.
6. If the right head is involved, remove the alternator mounting bracket bolt and spacer, ignition coil and air cleaner inlet duct from the right cylinder head.
7. If the right cylinder head is to be removed on an engine with a Thermactor exhaust emission control system, remove the air pump and bracket. Disconnect the hose from the right cylinder head.
8. Disconnect the exhaust manifold/s at the exhaust pipe/s.
9. Loosen the rocker arm stud nuts so that the arms can rotate to the side to clear the pushrods. Remove the pushrods. Keep the pushrods in order. On 351 engines, remove the exhaust manifold to get access to the lower cylinder head bolts.
10. Remove the cylinder-head bolts and lift off the cylinder head.
11. To install, clean the block and head gasket mounting surfaces. Install a new head gasket on the block, install the head, and install the head bolts. Torque the head bolts to specification in three progressive steps in the sequence shown.
12. Install the exhaust manifolds, if removed.
13. Clean the pushrods and check for straightness. Lubricate both ends and install in their original positions. Lubricate the valve stem tips, install the exhaust valve stem caps (if equipped) and install the rocker arms. Follow the procedure given earlier. Install the remaining components in the reverse order of removal.

TIMING CASE

6 Cylinder Timing Gear Cover Removal and Installation

1. Drain the cooling system and the crankcase.
2. Remove the radiator from the car.
3. Loosen and remove all engine drive belts.
4. With power steering, disconnect the pump mounting bracket from the cylinder front cover and position the pump and bracket out of the way.
5. With air conditioning, remove the condenser mounting bolts and position the condenser out of the way. *Do not disconnect the refrigerant lines.*
6. Disconnect and remove the fan and fan spacer.
7. Remove any accessory drive pulleys from the crankshaft damper. Remove the capscrew and washer from the crankshaft end; then, using a puller, remove the crankshaft damper.
8. Remove the alternator adjusting arm bolt and position the arm out of the way.
9. Remove the starter cable and attaching bolts, and remove the starter.
10. Remove the engine front support insulator to intermediate support bracket nuts on both supports. Remove the engine rear support insulator to crossmember bolt and insulator to transmission extension housing bolts. Raise the transmission and remove the support insulator. Lower the transmission to the crossmember.
11. Raise the engine and place 2 in. thick blocks of wood between both supports and brackets.
12. Remove the oil pan bolts, and lower the oil pan. Reach inside the oil pan and remove the two oil pump to block bolts, and lower the pump and screen into the pan.

Turn the crankshaft as required to gain clearance and remove the oil pan.
13. Remove the front cover attaching bolts and remove the cover from the engine.
14. Reverse the procedure to install.

6 Cylinder Timing Gear and/or Camshaft Replacement

1. Remove the timing case cover.
2. Mark the location of the grille center support and hood lock assembly in relation to the radiator support. Remove the grille, center support, and hood lock as an assembly.
3. Remove the air cleaner and valve cover.
4. Disconnect the fuel pump outlet line and remove the fuel pump from the engine.
5. Loosen the rocker arm nuts and position the rocker arms to the side so the pushrods can be removed. Keep the pushrods in order so that they can be returned to their original location in the engine.
6. Remove the pushrod cover from the side of the engine, and, using a magnet, remove the lifters from their bores. Keep the lifters in order so they can be returned to their original location in the engine.
7. Rotate the engine until the timing marks are aligned on the timing gears.

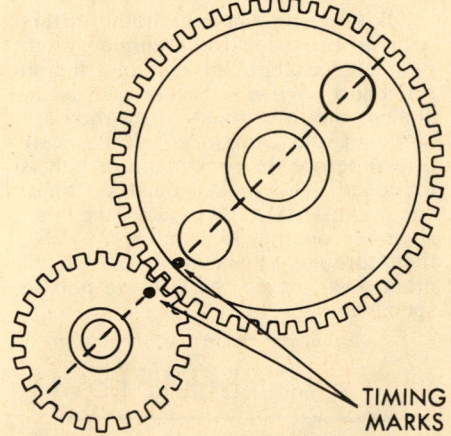

TIMING MARKS

Timing mark alignment—6 cyl.

8. Remove the camshaft thrust plate screws.
9. Remove the camshaft by pulling it out the front of the engine. Use care not to damage the camshaft lobes or journals while removing the cam from the engine.
10. Place the camshaft/gear assembly in a press and press the cam from the gear.
11. Position a new gear on the camshaft and press into position.
12. Using a puller, remove the crankshaft timing gear.
13. Press the new gear onto the crankshaft.
14. Before installing the camshaft in

Cylinder head torque sequence—all V8 (© Ford Motor Co)

the engine, coat the lobes with engine assembly lubricant and the journals and all valve train components with heavy oil.

15. Reverse the procedure to install, following recommended torque settings and performing preliminary valve adjustment before starting engine.

V8 Cover and Chain Removal and Installation

1. Drain the cooling system and crankcase.
2. Disconnect the negative battery cable.
3. With a fan shroud, disconnect it from the radiator and position it rearward.
4. Remove the radiator. Remove the fuel pump.
5. Remove the fan attaching bolts, remove the fan, fan spacer and shroud from the engine.
6. Loosen and remove all engine drive belts.
7. Remove the power steering pump mounting bracket and position the pump and bracket out of the way.
8. With air conditioning, remove the compressor and condenser and position them out of the way. *Do not disconnect the refrigerant lines.*
9. Disconnect the alternator adjusting arm from the engine and position it out of the way.
10. With Thermactor, remove the air pump from the engine.
11. Disconnect the heater hose and bypass hose from the water pump.
12. Remove any accessory drive pulleys from the crankshaft damper and remove the crankshaft front bolt and washer.
13. Using a puller, remove the crankshaft damper from the engine.
14. Remove the front cover attaching bolts and the front oil pan bolts.
15. Remove the front cover and water pump from the engine.
16. Remove the crankshaft front oil slinger.
17. To check timing chain free play, rotate the crankshaft clockwise until all slack is removed from the left side of the chain. Scribe a mark on the engine parallel to the present position of the chain. Next, rotate the crankshaft counterclockwise to remove all the slack from the right side of the chain. Force the left side of the chain outward with the fingers and measure the distance between the present position of the chain and the reference mark on the engine. If the distance exceeds 1/2 in., replace the chain and sprockets.
18. To replace the chain and sprockets, crank the engine until the timing marks are aligned.
19. Remove the camshaft sprocket attaching bolt and remove the chain and sprockets from the engine by

sliding them forward as an assembly.
20. Position the chain and sprockets on the engine, making sure that the timing marks on the sprockets are aligned.

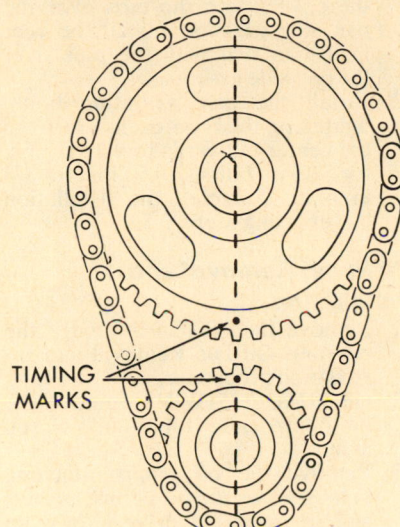

Timing mark alignment—V8

21. Clean all gasket surfaces. Trim away the exposed portion of the oil pan gasket flush with the front of the block.
22. Cut and position the required portion of a new gasket to the oil pan, applying sealer to both sides.
23. Reinstall the front cover, applying oil resistant sealer to the new gasket.
24. Install the components that were removed from the engine by reversing the removal procedure.

Timing Case Oil Seal Replacement

To replace the oil seal, it is necessary to take off the timing case cover and drive the seal out with a pin punch. Clean out the recess in the cover and install a new seal using a seal driving tool.

Coat the new seal with grease to reduce friction when installing and starting the engine.

V8 Camshaft Replacement

1. Remove the intake manifold.
2. Remove the cylinder front cover, timing chain and sprockets as outlined previously.
3. Remove the rocker arm covers.
4. On engines with individual rocker arms, loosen the rocker arm fulcrum bolts or nuts and rotate the rocker arms to the side.
5. Remove the pushrods and lifters and keep them in order so that they can be installed in their original location.
6. Remove the camshaft thrust plate and washer if so equipped. Remove the camshaft from the front of the engine. On certain engine/

chassis combinations it may be necessary to remove the grille to gain adequate clearance to remove the camshaft. Use care not to damage the camshaft lobes or journals while removing the cam from the engine.
7. Before installing the camshaft in the engine, coat the lobes with engine assembly lubricant and the journals and all valve train components with heavy oil.
8. Reverse the procedure to install.

PISTON AND ROD ALIGNMENT

When installing the assembled piston and rod, positioning is as follows:

240 cu. in.—bearing tang side of rod toward the left; notch on top of piston toward the front.

V8—numbered side of rod outboard; notch or arrow on top of piston toward the front.

ENGINE LUBRICATION

Oil Pan Removal

6 CYLINDER

1. Drain the crankcase and the cooling system.
2. Remove the radiator.
3. Disconnect the flexible fuel line at the fuel pump.
4. Disconnect the transmission kickdown rod at the bellcrank assembly.
5. Raise the car on a hoist.
6. Disconnect the starter cable at the starter. Remove the retaining bolts and remove the starter.
7. Remove the nuts on both engine front support insulator-to-support brackets.
8. Remove the bolt and insulators at the transmission extension housing.
9. Raise the transmission, remove the support insulator, lower the transmission to crossmember.
10. Raise the engine with a transmission jack and place a 3-in. thick wood block between both the front support insulators and the intermediate support brackets.
11. Remove the oil pan retaining bolts and the oil pump mounting bolts. With the oil pump in the pan, rotate the crankshaft as needed to remove the pan.
12. Clean all gasket surfaces. Remove the rear main bearing cap oil seal, and the front cover seal. Clean the grooves.
13. Apply sealer in the cavities between the bearing cap and the block. Install a new seal in the cap. Apply a bead of sealer to the ends of the seal. Install new side gaskets on the pan with sealer. Install a new front cover seal onto the pan.
14. Prime the oil pump and position in the pan. Place the pan under the engine, install the pump with a new

gasket, and install the oil pan. Torque the oil pan bolts in sequence from the center out, to 10-12 ft. lbs. Reverse Steps 1-10 to complete installation.

V8

1. Remove the shroud from the radiator and position it rearward over the fan. Disconnect the battery negative cable. On 429 V8s, remove the bolt attaching the vacuum line retaining clip to the upper right side of the converter housing.
2. Raise and support the car. Drain the oil. Position the transmission cooler lines out of the way, if necessary. Remove the sway bar attaching bolts and move the sway bar forward on the struts.
3. Remove nuts and lockwashers from the engine front support insulator-to-intermediate support bracket.
4. Install a block of wood on a jack and position a jack under the leading edge of the pan.
5. Raise the engine approximately 1-1/4 in. and insert a 1-in. block between the insulators and crossmember. Remove the floor jack. On 351C, 351M, 400, 429, and 460 V8s, remove the starter. On 1972-77 429 and 460 V8s, remove the oil filter.
6. Remove the oil pan attaching screws and lower the pan to the frame crossmember.
7. Turn the crankshaft to obtain clearance between the crankshaft counterweight and the rear of the pan.
8. Remove the oil pump attaching bolts.
9. Position the tube and the screen out of the way and remove the pan.

10. To install, clean the gasket mounting surfaces thoroughly. Coat the surfaces on the block and pan with sealer. Position the pan side gaskets on the engine block.
11. Install the front cover oil seal on the cover, with the tabs over the pan side gaskets. Install the rear main cap seal with the tabs over the pan side gaskets.
12. Install the pan mounting bolts, tightening them on each side from the center outwards to 9-11 ft. lbs. for 5/16 in. bolts, 7-9 ft. lbs. for 1/4 in. bolts. Complete the installation by reversing Steps 1-5.

Oil Pump Removal and Installation

1. Remove the oil pan as under the previous Oil Pan Removal and Installation procedure.
2. On 302 and 351W V8, remove the oil pump inlet tube and screen assembly.
3. Remove the oil pump attaching bolts. Lower the oil pump, gasket, and intermediate driveshaft from the crankcase. If not already removed, remove and clean the inlet tube and screen assembly.
4. To install, prime the oil pump by filling either the inlet or outlet port with engine oil. Rotate the pump shaft to distribute the oil within the pump body.
5. Position the intermediate driveshaft into the distributor socket. With the shaft firmly seated in the socket, the stop on the shaft should contact the roof of the crankcase. Remove the shaft and position the stop as necessary.
6. Insert the intermediate driveshaft into the oil pump. Using a new gas-

ket, install the pump and shaft as an assembly. Do not attempt to force the pump into position if it will not seat readily. If necessary, rotate the intermediate driveshaft hex into a new position so that it will mesh with the distributor shaft.

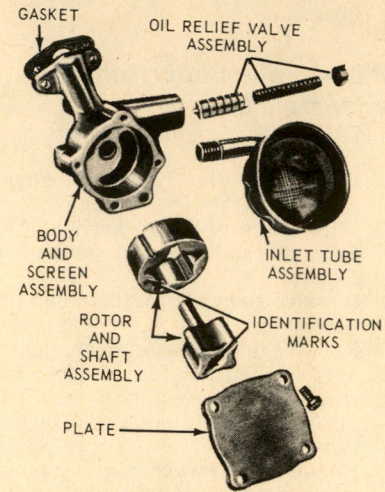

351M, 400 V8 oil pump
(© Ford Motor Co)

7. Torque the oil pump attaching bolts to 12-15 ft. lbs. on the six cylinder engines, 22-32 ft. lbs. on the 302 and 351W V8, 20-35 ft. lbs. on the 351C, 351M and 400 V8, and 20-25 ft. lbs. on the 429, and 460 V8.
8. Clean and install the inlet tube and screen assembly.
9. Install the oil pan as under Oil Pan Removal and Installation.

Rear Main Bearing Oil Seal Replacement

NOTE: *The rear oil seal installed in these engines is a rubber type seal.*
1. Remove the oil pan and oil pump if required.
2. Loosen all main bearing cap bolts, lowering the crankshaft slightly but not more than 1/32 in.
3. Remove the rear main bearing cap, and remove the upper and lower halves of the seal. On the block half of the seal, use a seal removing tool or insert a small metal screw into the end of the seal with which to draw it out.
4. Clean the seal grooves with solvent and dip the replacement seal in clean engine oil.
5. Install the upper seal half in its groove in the block with the lip toward the front of the engine by rotating it on the seal journal of the crankshaft until approximately 3/8 in. protrudes below the parting surface.
6. Tighten the other main bearing caps and torque to specification.
7. Install the lower seal half in the rear main bearing cap with the lip to the front and approximately 3/8

INSTALL SEAL WITH LIP TOWARDS FRONT OF ENGINE

FRONT OF ENGINE

3/8"

SEAL HALVES TO PROTRUDE BEYOND PARTING FACES
THIS DISTANCE TO ALLOW FOR CAP TO BLOCK ALIGNMENT

3/8"

REAR FACE OF REAR MAIN
BEARING CAP AND CYLINDER BLOCK

VIEW LOOKING AT PARTING FACE
OF SPLIT, LIP-TYPE CRANKSHAFT SEAL

Installing split-lip type rear main oil seal (© Ford Motor Co)

in. of the seal protruding to mate with the upper seal.

8. Install the rear main bearing cap and torque.
9. Dip the side seals in engine oil and install them. Tap the seals in the last half inch if necessary. Do not cut the protruding ends of the seals.

AUTOMATIC TRANSMISSION

Transmissions may be identified by the code on the vehicle certification label. The codes are listed at the beginning of this car section.

C4 pan gasket

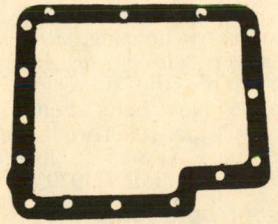

C6 transmission pan gasket shape

FMX pan gasket

Shift Linkage Adjustment

1. With the engine off, loosen the clamp at the shift lever so the shift rod is free to slide.

    On models with a shift cable, remove the nut from the transmission manual lever and disconnect the cable from the transmission.
2. Position the selector lever in D position tightly against the D stop.
3. Shift the lever at the transmission into D position.

NOTE: *D position is second from the rear.*

4. Tighten the clamp and nut.

Neutral Start Switch Adjustment

Models with a column shift lever are not equipped with a neutral start switch. Instead, an ignition lock cylinder-to-shift lever interlock prevents these models from being started in any gear other than Park or Neutral.

Downshift Linkage Adjustment

1. Disconnect the downshift lever return spring.
2. Hold the throttle shaft lever wide open, and hold the downshift rod against through detent stop.
3. Adjust the downshift screw to provide 0.050-0.070 in. clearance between the screw and the throttle shaft lever on 1972 models and 0.010-0.080 in. on 1973 and later models. On the 240 cu. in. engine, tighten the locknut.
4. Connect the downshift lever return spring.

C4 Band Adjustment

INTERMEDIATE BAND

1. Clean all the dirt from the adjusting screw and remove and discard the locknut.
2. Install a new locknut on the adjusting screw. Using a torque wrench, tighten the adjusting screw to 10 ft. lbs.
3. Back off the adjusting screw *exactly 1-3/4 turns.*
4. Hold the adjusting screw steady and tighten the locknut.

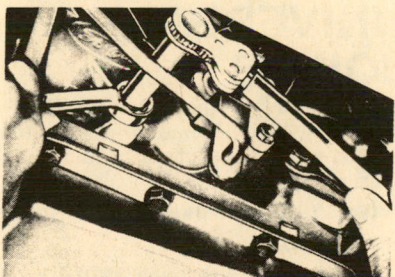

Adjusting intermediate band, C4 and C6 (© Ford Motor Co)

LOW-REVERSE BAND

1. Clean all the dirt from around the band adjusting screw, and remove and discard the locknut.
2. Install a new locknut on the adjusting screw. Using a torque wrench,

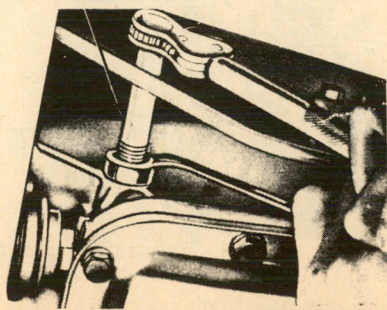

Adjusting low-reverse band, C4 transmission (© Ford Motor Co)

tighten the adjusting screw to 10 ft. lbs.
3. Back off the adjusting screw *exactly three full turns.*
4. Hold the adjusting screw steady and tighten the locknut.

C6 Intermediate Band Adjustment

1. Raise the car on a hoist or place it on jack stands.
2. Clean the threads of the intermediate band adjusting screw.
3. Remove and discard the adjustment screw locknut. Loosely install a new locknut.
4. Tighten the adjusting screw to 10 ft. lbs. and back the screw off *exactly 1-1/2 turns.* Tighten the adjusting screw locknut.

FMX, MX, and CW Band Adjustment

FRONT BAND

1. Drain the transmission fluid and remove the pan, fluid filter screen, and clip.
2. Clean the pan and filter screen and remove the old gasket.
3. Loosen the front servo adjusting screw locknut.
4. Pull back the actuating rod and insert a 1/4 in. spacer bar between the adjusting screw and the servo piston stem. Tighten the adjusting screw to 10 in. lbs. torque. Remove the spacer bar and tighten the adjusting screw an additional 3/4 turn. Hold the adjusting screw and tighten the locknut securely (20-25 ft. lbs.).
5. Install the transmission fluid filter screen and clip. Install the pan with a new pan gasket.

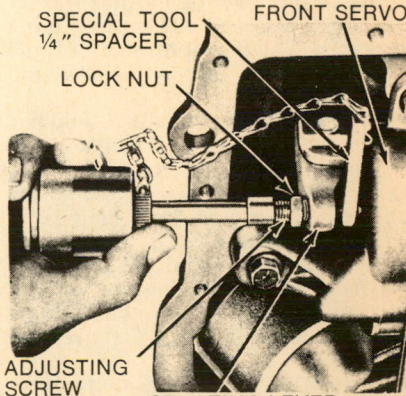

SPECIAL TOOL 1/4″ SPACER — FRONT SERVO
LOCK NUT
ADJUSTING SCREW
ACTUATING LEVER

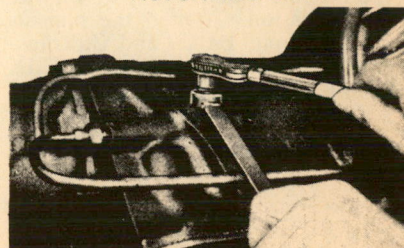

Adjusting front and rear bands, FMX (© Ford Motor Co)

6. Refill the transmission to the mark on the dipstick. Start the engine, run for a few minutes, shift the selector lever through all positions, and place it in Park. Recheck the fluid level and add fluid if necessary.

REAR BAND

1. Locate the external rear band adjusting screw on the transmission case, clean all dirt from the threads, and coat the threads with light oil.

NOTE: *The adjusting screw is on the upper right side of the transmission case. Access is often through a hole in the front floor to the right of center under the carpet.*

2. Loosen the locknut on the rear band external adjusting screw.
3. Using a torque wrench, tighten the adjusting screw to 10 ft. lbs. torque. If the adjusting screw is tighter than 10 ft. lbs. torque, loosen the adjusting screw and retighten to the proper torque.
4. Back off the adjusting screw *exactly 1-1/2 turns.* Hold the adjusting screw steady while tightening the locknut to the proper torque (35-40 ft. lbs.).

Pan Replacement, Fluid Change

1. Raise the car on a hoist or jack stands.
2. Place a drain pan under the transmission pan.

NOTE: *On some pan-filled models of the C4 transmission, the fluid is drained by disconnecting the filler tube from the transmission fluid pan.*

3. Loosen the pan attaching bolts to allow the fluid to drain.
4. When the fluid has stopped draining to the level of the pan flange, remove the pan bolts starting at the rear and along both sides of the pan, allowing the pan to drop and drain gradually.
5. When all the transmission fluid has drained, remove the pan and the fluid filter and clean them.

NOTE: *The oil filter screen and gasket retain the throttle pressure limit valve and spring on the C4. These parts will drop out when the screen and gasket are removed. The valve is installed with the large end toward the valve body in the transmission; the spring fits over the valve stem.*

6. Install the fluid filter screen, a new pan gasket, and the pan on the transmission. Tighten the pan attaching bolts on C4 and C6 transmissions to 12-16 ft lbs. On FMX and CW transmissions, tighten the pan attaching bolts to 10–13 ft lbs.

NOTE: *Beginning 1977, the C6 automatic transmission uses special fluid, ESP-M2C138-CJ. All other transmissions use type F automatic transmission fluid.*

7. Install three quarts of transmission fluid through the filler tube. If the filler tube was removed to drain the

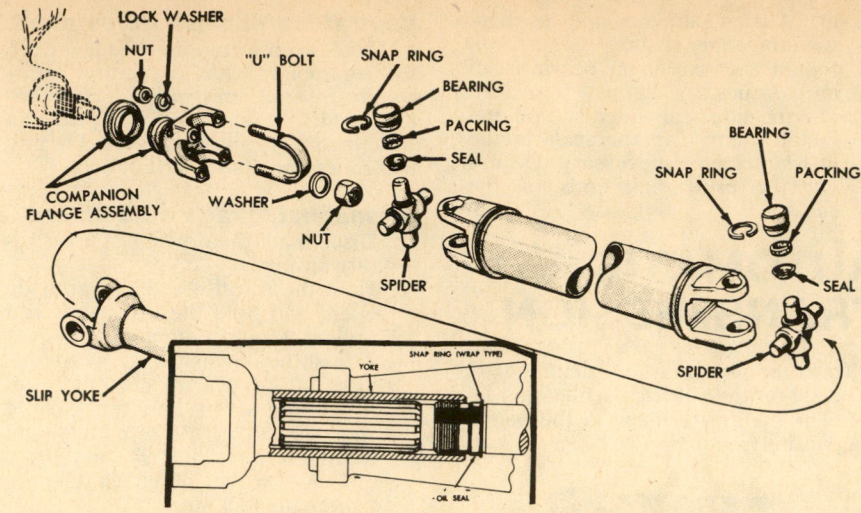

Driveshaft and universal joint (© Ford Motor Co)

transmission, install the filler tube using a new O-ring.

8. Start and run the engine for a few minutes at low idle speed and then at the fast idle speed (about 1,200 rpm) until the normal operating temperature is reached. Do not race the engine.
9. Move the selector lever through all gear positions and place it at the Park position. Check the fluid level, and add fluid until the level is between the Add and Full marks on the dipstick. Do not overfill the transmission.

UNIVERSAL JOINTS

The universal joints on all Fords, Mercurys, and Thunderbirds in this section are of the cross- and needle-bearing-type.

Driveshaft Removal and Installation

All driveshafts through 1978 are retained to the differential pinion flange by U-bolts. 1979 models are attached by a circular coupling flange.

1. Matchmark the position of the driveshaft and differential flange. The

parts must be reassembled in their original locations to maintain driveline balance.

2. Unbolt the U-bolts or coupling flange bolts and allow the driveshaft to drop down.
3. Pull the driveshaft rearward until the slip yoke clears the transmission extension housing. Plug the transmission opening to prevent leakage.
4. To install, lubricate the splines on the slip yoke and install into the extension housing. Line up the marks made during disassembly. Assemble the driveshaft to the flange. New bolts should be used on 1979 models. Torque the attaching bolts to 8-15 ft. lbs. through 1978, 70-90 ft. lbs. 1979.

U-Joint Replacement

Complete U-joint replacement procedures are given in the Capri section.

JACKING, HOISTING

1. Jack the car at the front spring seats of the lower control arms, and at the rear axle housing close to the differential case.

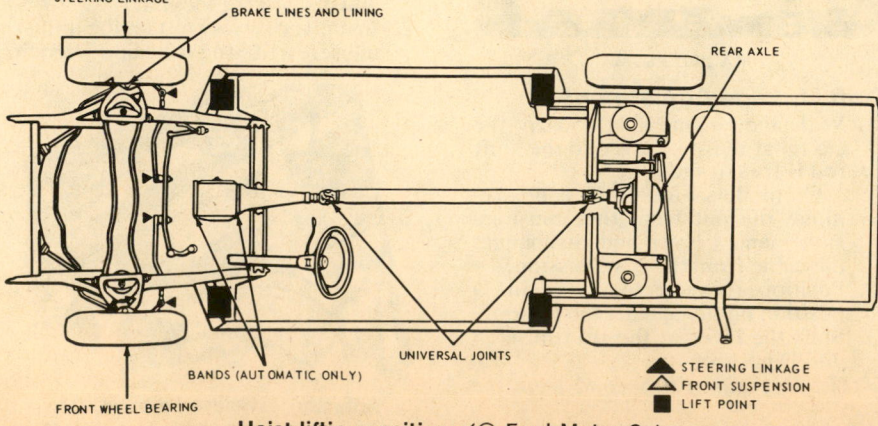

Hoist lifting positions (© Ford Motor Co)

2. To lift at the frame, use adapters so that contact will be made at the points shown. Adapters should support at least 12 sq. in.

REAR AXLE

Two basic types of rear axles are used; a removable differential carrier type and an integral carrier type which occurs in three variations; a standard type, a light duty (WER) version, and a WGX version used on all 1979 models. All WER and WGX types use C-locks on the inside end of the axle shaft to retain it, while removable carrier axles have no C-locks. To properly identify a C-lock axle, drain the lubricant, remove the rear cover and look for the C-lock on the end of the axle shaft in the differential side gear bore. All Traction-Lok (limited slip) axles are of the removable carrier type. The axle type and ratio are stamped on a plate attached to a rear housing cover bolt. If the second letter of the axle model code is F, it is a Traction-Lok axle. Always refer to the axle tag code and ratio when ordering parts.

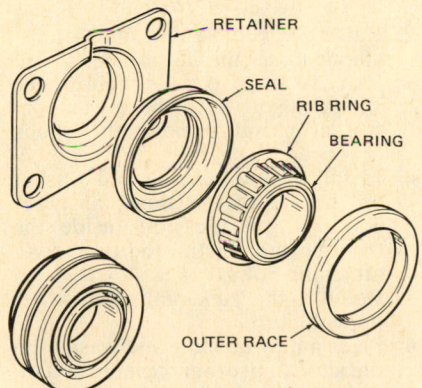

Tapered bearing and retainer–removable carrier axle (© Ford Motor Co)

Axle Shaft, Bearing and Seal Removal and Installation
EXCEPT C-LOCK TYPE

NOTE: *Bearings must be pressed on and off the shaft with an arbor press. Unless you have access to one, it is inadvisable to attempt any repair work on the axle shaft bearing assemblies.*

1. Remove the wheel, tire, and brake drum. With disc brakes, remove the caliper, retainer nuts, and rotor. New anchor plate bolts will be needed for reassembly.
2. Remove the nuts holding the retainer plate to the backing plate, or axle shaft retainer bolts from the housing. Disconnect the brake line with drum brakes.
3. Remove the retainer and install nuts, finger-tight, to prevent the brake backing plate from being dislodged.
4. Pull out the axle shaft and bearing assembly, using a slide hammer.

On models with a tapered roller bearing, the tapered cup will normally remain in the axle housing when the shaft is removed. The cup must be removed from the housing to prevent seal damage when the shaft is reinstalled. The cup can be removed with a slide hammer and an expanding puller.

NOTE: *If end-play is found to be excessive, the bearing should be replaced. Shimming the bearing is not recommended as this ignores end-play of the bearing itself and could result in improper seating of the bearing.*

5. Using a chisel, nick the bearing retainer in 3 or 4 places. The retainer does not have to be cut, but merely collapsed sufficiently to allow the bearing retainer to be slid from the shaft. On Fords and Mercurys, first drill a 1/4 in. hole not more than 5/16 in. deep in the ring surface.

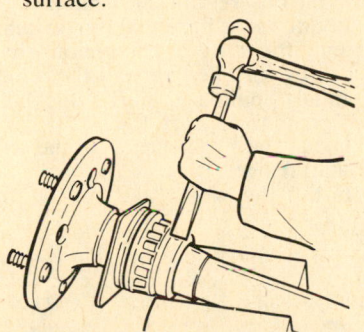

Axle shaft bearing retainer removal —removable carrier axle (© Ford Motor Co.)

6. Press off the bearing and install the new one by pressing it into position. With tapered bearings, place the lubricated seal and bearing on the axle shaft (cup rib ring facing the flange). Make sure that the seal is the correct length. Disc brake seal rims are black, drum brake seal rims are grey. Press the bearing and seal onto the shaft.
7. Press on the new retainer.

NOTE: *Do not attempt to press the bearing and the retainer on at the same time.*

8. On ball bearing models, to replace the seal: remove the seal from the housing with an expanding cone type puller and a slide hammer. The seal must be placed whenever the shaft is removed. Wipe a small amount of sealer onto the outer edge of the new seal before installation; do not put sealer on the sealing lip. Press the seal into the housing with a seal installation tool.
9. Assemble the shaft and bearing in the housing, being sure that the bearing is seated properly in the housing. On ball bearing models, be careful not to damage the seal with the shaft. With tapered bearings, first install the tapered cup on the bearing, and lubricate the outer

diameter of the cup and the seal with axle lube. Then install the shaft and bearing assembly into the housing.
10. Install the retainer, drum or rotor and caliper, wheel and tire. Bleed the brakes.

C-LOCK TYPE

1. Jack up and support the rear of the car.
2. Remove the wheels and tires from the brake drums.
3. Place a drain pan under the housing and drain the lubricant by loosening the housing cover.
4. Remove the nuts securing the brake drums to the axle shaft flanges and remove the drums.
5. Remove the housing cover and gasket, if used.
6. Position jackstands under the rear frame member and lower the axle housing. This is done to give easy access to the inside of the differential.
7. Working through the opening in the differential case, remove the side gear pinion shaft lockbolt and the side gear pinion shaft.

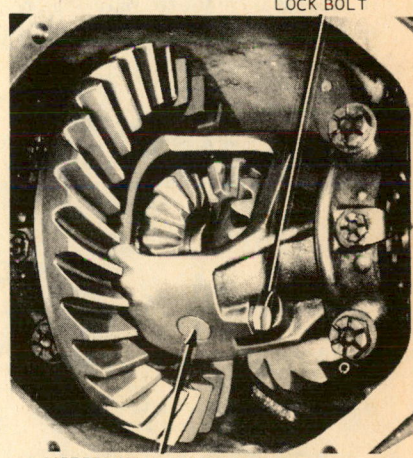

Removing the differential pinion shaft lockbolt—WER axle (© Ford Motor Co.)

8. Push the axle shafts inward and remove the C-locks from the inner end of the axle shafts. Temporarily replace the shaft and lockbolt to retain the differential gears in position.

Removing the axle shaft C-locks—WER axle (© Ford Motor Co.)

9. Remove the axle shafts with a slide hammer. Be sure the seal is not damaged by the splines on the axle shaft.

10. Remove the bearing and oil seal from the housing. Both the seal and bearing can be removed with a slide hammer. Two types of bearings are used on some axles, one requiring a press fit and the other a loose fit. A loose fitting bearing does not necessarily indicate excessive wear.

11. Inspect the axle shaft housing and axle shafts for burrs or other irregularities. Replace any worn or damaged parts. A light yellow color on the bearing journal of the axle shaft is normal, and does not require replacement of the axle shaft. Slight pitting and wear is also normal.

12. Lightly coat the wheel bearing rollers with axle lubricant. Install the bearings in the axle housing until the bearing seats firmly against the shoulder.

13. Wipe all lubricant from the oil seal bore, before installing the seal.

14. Inspect the original seals for wear. If necessary, these may be replaced with new seals, which are prepacked with lubricant and do not require soaking.

15. Install the oil seal.

--- CAUTION ---

Installation of the seal without the proper tool can cause distortion and seal leakage. Oil seals for the right-side are marked with green stripes and the word RIGHT. Seals for the left-side are marked yellow with the word LEFT. Do not interchange seals from side to side.

16. Remove the lockbolt and pinion shaft. Carefully slide the axle shafts into place. Be careful that you do not damage the seal with the splined end of the axle shaft. Engage the splined end of the shaft with the differential side gears.

17. Install the axle shaft C-locks on the inner end of the axle shafts and seat the C-locks in the counterbore of the differential side gears.

18. Rotate the differential pinion gears until the differential pinion shaft can be installed. Install the differential pinion shaft lockbolt. Tighten to 15-22 ft. lbs.

19. Install the brake drum on the axle shaft flange.

20. Install the wheel and tire on the brake drum and tighten the attaching nuts.

21. Clean the gasket surface of the rear housing and install a new cover gasket and the housing cover. WGX covers do not use a gasket. On these models, apply a bead of silicone sealer on the gasket surface. The bead should run inside of the bolt holes.

22. Raise the rear axle so that it is in the running position. Add the amount of specified lubricant to bring the lubricant level to 1/2 in. below the filler hole on WER axles, or 1-1/4 in. below on the WGX.

FRONT SUSPENSION

Shock Absorber Replacement

NOTE: *To purge air from the shock absorber before installation, extend and invert it. Compress the shock and return to its upright position. Repeat this operation several times. Do not extend the shock absorber while it is inverted.*

1. Remove the nut, washer, and bushing from the upper end of the shock absorber.

2. Raise the vehicle and install jackstands under the frame rails.

3. Remove the two bolts securing the shock absorber to the lower control arm and remove the shock absorber.

4. Install a new bushing and washer on the top of the shock absorber and position the unit inside the front spring. Install the two lower attaching bolts.

5. Remove the jackstands and lower the vehicle.

6. Place a new bushing and washer on the shock absorber top stud and install the attaching nut.

Coil Spring and Lower Control Arm Removal and Installation

1. Raise the car and support with stands placed back of the lower arms.

2. If necessary for clearance or access and equipped with drum brakes, remove the wheel and brake drum as an assembly. Remove the brake backing plate attaching bolts and remove the backing plate from the spindle. Wire the assembly back out of the way.

3. If necessary for clearance or access and equipped with disc brakes, remove the wheel from the hub. Remove two bolts and washers that hold the caliper and brake hose bracket to the spindle. Remove the caliper from the rotor and wire it back out of the way. Then, remove the hub and rotor from the spindle.

4. Disconnect the lower end of the shock absorber and push it up to the retracted position.

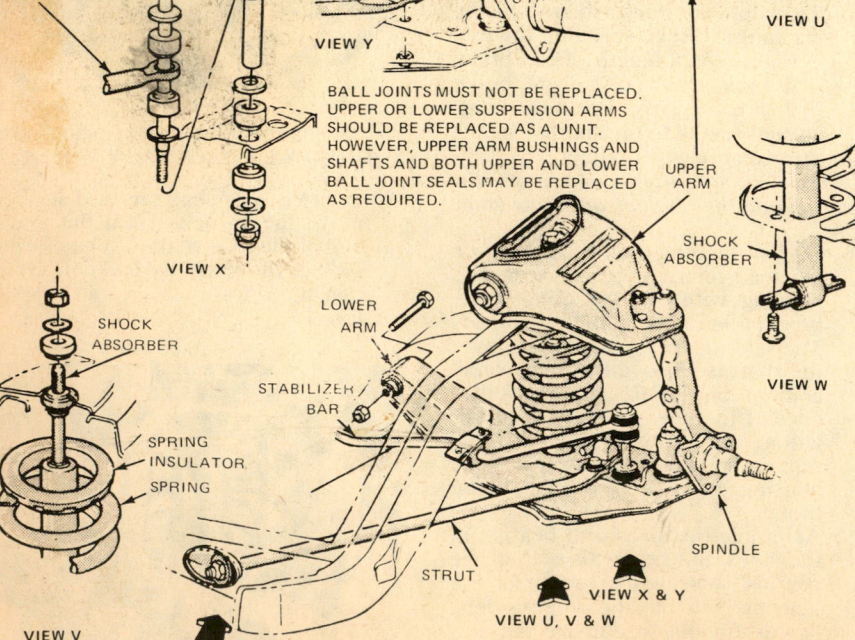

Typical front suspension through 1978; 1976 shown (© Ford Motor Co)

BALL JOINTS MUST NOT BE REPLACED. UPPER OR LOWER SUSPENSION ARMS SHOULD BE REPLACED AS A UNIT. HOWEVER, UPPER ARM BUSHINGS AND SHAFTS AND BOTH UPPER AND LOWER BALL JOINT SEALS MAY BE REPLACED AS REQUIRED.

5. Disconnect the stabilizer bar link from the lower arm.
6. Remove the cotter pins from the upper and lower ball joint stud nuts.
7. Remove the two bolts and nuts holding the strut to the lower arm (through 1978 only).
8. Loosen the lower ball joint stud nut two turns. Do not remove this nut.
9. Install a ball joint removal tool between the upper and lower ball joint studs.
10. Expand the tool until it exerts considerable pressure on the studs. Tap the spindle near the lower stud with a hammer to loosen the stud in the spindle. Do not loosen the stud with tool pressure only.
11. Position a floor jack under the lower arm and remove the lower ball joint stud nut.
12. Install a spring compressor. Lower the floor jack and remove the spring and insulator.
13. Remove the control arm to cross-member attaching parts, and remove the arm from the car.
14. Reverse the procedure to install. If the lower control arm was replaced because of damage, check the front end alignment.

LOWER BALL JOINT

Inspection

THROUGH 1978

1. Raise the vehicle by placing a floor jack under the lower arm; or, raise the vehicle on a hoist and place a jack stand under the lower arm and lower the vehicle onto it to remove the preload from the lower ball joint.
2. Adjust the wheel bearings.
3. Have an assistant grasp the wheel top and bottom and apply alternate in and out pressure to the top and bottom of the wheel.
4. Radial play of 1/4 in. is acceptable measured at the inside of the wheel adjacent to the lower arm.

NOTE: *This radial play is multiplied at the outer circumference of the tire and should be measured only at the inside of the wheel.*

1979

Lower ball joints have built-in wear indicators. See the Capri Section under Fairmont, Zephyr, Mustang, and Capri Lower Ball Joint Inspection for the proper procedure. Note that this procedure does not apply to the upper ball joint.

Replacement

NOTE: *Ford Motor Company recommends replacement of the control arm and ball joint as an assembly, rather than replacement of the ball joint only. However, aftermarket replacement parts are available.*

1. Raise the vehicle on a hoist and al-

low the front wheels to fall to their full down position.
2. Drill a 1/8 in. hole completely through each ball joint attaching rivet.
3. Use a 3/8 in. drill in the pilot hole to drill off the heads of the rivets.
4. Drive the rivets from the lower arm.
5. Place a jack under the lower arm and lower the vehicle about 6 in.
6. Remove the lower ball joint stud cotter pin and attaching nut.
7. Using a ball joint stud removal tool, loosen the ball joint from the spindle and remove the ball joint from the lower arm.
8. Clean all metal burrs from the lower arm and install the new ball joint, using the service part nuts and bolts to attach the ball joint to the lower arm. Do not attempt to rerivet the ball joint once it has been removed.
9. Check the front end alignment.

UPPER BALL JOINT

Inspection

1. Raise the vehicle by placing a floor jack under the lower arm. Do not allow the lower arm to hang freely with the vehicle on a hoist or bumper jack.
2. Have an assistant grasp the bottom of the tire and move the wheel in and out.
3. As the wheel is being moved, observe the upper control arm where the spindle attaches to it. Any movement between the upper part of the spindle and the upper ball joint indicates a bad ball joint which must be replaced.

NOTE: *During this check the lower ball joint will be unloaded and may move; this is normal and not an indication of a bad ball joint. Also, do not mistake a loose wheel bearing for a defective ball joint.*

Replacement

NOTE: *Ford Motor Company recommends replacement of control arm and ball joint as an assembly, rather than replacement of the ball joint only. However, aftermarket replacement parts are available.*

1. Raise the vehicle on a hoist and allow the front wheels to fall to their full down position.

2. Drill a 1/8 in. hole completely through each ball joint attaching rivet.
3. Using a large chisel, cut off the head of each rivet and drive them from the upper arm.
4. Place a jack under the lower arm and lower the vehicle about 6 in.
5. Remove the cotter pin and attaching nut from the ball joint stud.
6. Using a suitable tool, loosen the ball joint stud from the spindle and remove the ball joint from the upper arm.
7. Clean all metal burrs from the upper arm and install the new ball joint, using the service part nuts and bolts to attach the ball joint to the upper arm. Do not attempt to rerivet the ball joint once it has been removed.
8. Check end alignment.

Upper Control Arm
Replacement

1. Remove the wheel. Raise the car and support the frame with stands placed just behind the lower arm pivot (rear pivot on 1979 models).
2. Remove the cotter pin from the upper ball joint stud nut. Loosen the nut a few turns but do not remove.
3. Install a ball joint removal tool between the upper and lower ball joint studs. Expand the tool until it places the upper stud under compression. Tap the spindle near the stud with a hammer to loosen the stud.
4. Remove the tool. Raise the lower arm with a jack until pressure is relieved from the upper stud. Remove the upper stud nut.
5. Remove the upper shaft attaching bolts and the upper arm.
6. To install, position the arm to the frame, install the attaching nuts, and torque to 120-140 ft. lbs. Connect the upper stud to the spindle. Install the attaching nut, and tighten to 75 ft. lbs., then continue to tighten until the cotter pin holes align. Install a new cotter pin. Install the wheel, adjust the wheel bearings, and lower the car. Caster, camber, and toe must be adjusted after installation.

Wheel Bearing Adjustment

1. Raise the front of the vehicle.

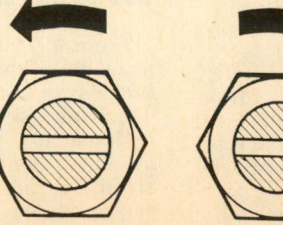
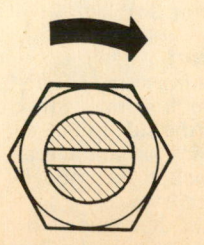
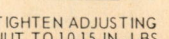
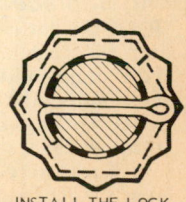

WITH WHEEL ROTATING, TORQUE ADJUSTING NUT, TO 17-25 FT. LBS. | BACK ADJUSTING NUT OFF 1/2 TURN | TIGHTEN ADJUSTING NUT TO 10-15 IN.-LBS. | INSTALL THE LOCK AND A NEW COTTER PIN

Front wheel bearing adjustment (© Ford Motor Co)

2. Remove the wheel cover and grease cap.
3. Remove the cotter pin and nut lock.
4. Back off the adjusting nut and re-tighten the nut to 17-25 ft. lbs. Back off the adjusting nut again 1/2 turn. Retighten the nut to 10-15 in. lbs. Install the nut lock so that the castellations are aligned with the cotter pin hole. Install the cotter pin and bend the ends around the castellations of the nut lock to prevent interference with the radio static collector in the grease cap.
5. Install the grease cap and wheel cover.
6. Lower the vehicle.

REAR SUSPENSION

The rear suspension through 1978 is a coil-link design. Large, low-rate coil springs are mounted between rear axle pads and frame supports. Parallel lower arms extend forward of the spring seats to rubber frame anchor to accommodate driving and braking forces. A third link is mounted between the axle and the frame to control torque reaction forces from the rear wheels.

Lateral (side sway) motion of the rear axle is controlled by a rubber bushed rear track bar, linked laterally between the axle and frame.

The 1979 rear suspension is a four-link coil spring design. The coil springs are mounted between the top of the axle and the frame pads, providing room for vertical placement of the shock absorbers in front of the axle. Two lower arms mount to the axle forward of the outer ends, while the two shorter upper arms mount near the top center of the axle, with an included angle of 90°.

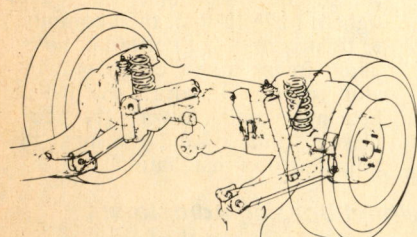

1979 Ford and Mercury rear suspension (© Ford Motor Co)

Spring Replacement
1. Place the car on a hoist and lift under the rear axle housing. Place jack stands under the side rails.
2. Disconnect the track bar at the rear axle housing bracket on models through 1978.
3. On Ford/Mercury, disconnect the rear of the front-to-rear brake line from the rear brake hose at the No. 4 crossmember bracket. Remove the clip.

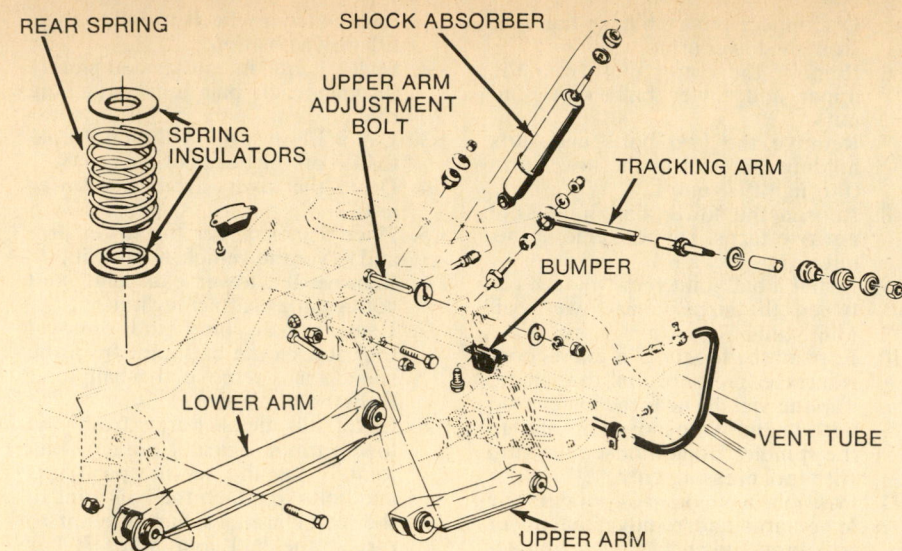

Ford and Mercury rear suspension through 1978; Thunderbird through 1976 similar (© Ford Motor Co.)

4. Disconnect the rear shock absorbers from the rear axle housing brackets.
5. Disconnect the hose from the axle housing vent.
6. Install a spring compressor.
7. Lower the hoist with the axle housing until the coil springs are released.
8. Remove the spring lower retainer with bolt, nut, washer and insulator.
9. Remove the spring with the large rubber insulator pads from car.
10. Install in reverse of above. Bleed the brakes after installation of the brake hose.

Shock Absorber Replacement
Rear shock absorbers on all Fords are straddle-mounted and are held to rubber bushings at both the top and bottom connections. Simply remove the nuts from the top and bottom of the shock absorber and lift the shock absorber off the car.
NOTE: *To purge air from the shock absorber before installation, extend and invert it. Compress the shock and return to its upright position. Repeat this operation several times. Do not extend the shock absorber while it is inverted.*

BRAKES

From 1975 to 1978, these cars are available with a new four-wheel disc brake system combined with the Sure-Track (anti-skid) system. In addition, a hydraulically assisted Hydro-Boost system is available on some models instead of a vacuum assist brake system.

The Hydro-Boost system uses the power steering pump to pressurize the hydraulic system and is connected to the pump by means of normal power steering hydraulic hoses. The decision to use hydraulic assist instead of vacuum assist was made in order to conserve engine vacuum for emission control equipment and other vacuum assisted power accessories. The rear brake caliper on models with four-wheel disc brakes is of single-piston, sliding caliper design. The parking brake design marks a departure from former practice as the parking brake cable acts directly on the brake pads bringing them into contact with the brake rotor (disc). No auxiliary parking brake drum assemblies are required with this arrangement.
NOTE: *Procedure for brake shoe or pad replacement and adjustment as well as wheel and master cylinder overhaul, and brake bleeding can be found in the Unit Repair Section.*

Master Cylinder Replacement
STANDARD BRAKES
1. Working under the dash, disconnect the master cylinder pushrod form the brake pedal. The pushrod cannot be removed from the master cylinder.
2. Disconnect the stoplight switch wires and remove the switch from the brake pedal, using care not to damage the switch.
3. Disconnect the brake lines from the master cylinder.
4. Remove the attaching screws from the firewall and remove the master cylinder from the car.
5. Reinstall in reverse order, leaving the brake line fittings loose at the master cylinder.
6. Fill the master cylinder, and with the brake lines loose, slowly bleed the air from the master cylinder using the foot pedal.

POWER BRAKES (VACUUM ASSIST)
1. Disconnect the brake lines from the master cylinder.

2. Remove the two nuts and lock-washers that attach the master cylinder to the brake booster.
3. Remove the master cylinder from the booster.
4. Reverse above procedure to reinstall.
5. Fill master cylinder and bleed entire brake system.
6. Refill master cylinder.

Brake Vacuum Booster Removal and Installation

1. Working from inside the car, beneath the instrument panel, remove the booster pushrod from the brake pedal.
2. Disconnect the stop light switch wires and remove the switch from the brake pedal. Use care not to damage the switch during removal.
3. Raise the hood and remove the master cylinder from the booster without disconnecting the brake lines. Carefully position the master cylinder out of the way, being careful not to kink the brake lines.
4. Remove the manifold vacuum hose from the booster.
5. Remove the booster to firewall attaching bolts and remove the booster from the car.
6. Reverse the above procedure to reinstall.

Hydro-Boost Accumulator Removal and Installation

1. Open the hood and remove the 2 nuts attaching the master cylinder to the brake booster.
2. Remove the master cylinder from the Hydro-Boost accumulator.
3. Set the master cylinder aside without disturbing the hydraulic lines.
4. Disconnect the pressure, steering and return lines from the accumulator.
5. Plug the lines and ports.
6. Working below the dash, disconnect the Hydro-Boost pushrod from the brake pedal. To do this, disconnect the stoplight switch at the connector. Remove the hairpin retainer. Slide the stoplight switch from the brake pedal pin far enough to clear the switch outer pin hole. Remove the switch from the pin.
7. Loosen the Hydro-Boost attaching nuts and remove the pushrod, washers and bushing from the brake pedal pin.
8. Remove the accumulator.
9. Installation is the reverse of removal. Leave the Hydro-Boost mounting nuts loose until the pushrod and stoplight switch are connected to the brake pedal. After installation, remove the coil wire from the distributor. Fill the power steering reservoir, and while cranking the engine, pump the brake pedal. Do not move the steering wheel until all the air has been pumped out of the system.

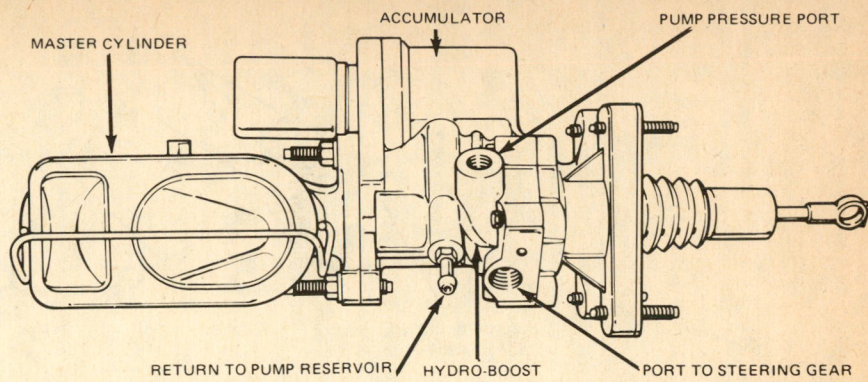

Hydro-Boost accumulator and master cylinder (© Ford Motor Co)

Check the power steering fluid level, install the coil wire, start the engine and pump the brakes while steering from lock to lock. Check for leaks.

Parking Brake Adjustment
REAR DRUM BRAKES

1. Raise the vehicle on an axle hoist with the transmission in Neutral and the parking brake fully released.
2. Tighten the adjusting nut against the cable equalizer until the rear brakes drag when the wheels are turned.
3. Loosen up on the adjustment nut until the brakes are fully released.
4. Tighten the locknut (if used).

REAR DISC BRAKES

1. Be sure the parking brake is fully released.
2. Place the transmission in Neutral and raise the vehicle on an axle hoist.
3. Tighten the adjuster nut until the levers on the calipers just begin to move. Loosen the nut just enough to obtain full return to the stop position.
4. Check the operation. Attempt to pull the parking brake levers rearward. If they can be pulled rearward, the parking brake is too tight.

STEERING

Power Steering Pump Removal and Installation

1. Drain the fluid from the pump reservoir by disconnecting the fluid return hose at the pump. Then, disconnect the pressure hose from the pump.
2. Remove the mounting bolts from the front of the pump. On eight cylinder engines, there is a nut on the rear of the pump that must be removed. After removal, move the pump inward to loosen the belt tension and remove the belt from the pulley. Then, remove the pump from the car.

3. To reinstall the pump, position on mounting bracket and loosely install the mounting bolts and nuts. Put the drive belt over the pulley and move the pump outward against the belt until the proper belt tension is obtained.
4. Tighten the mounting bolts and nuts.
5. Disconnect the coil wire from the distributor. Fill the steering reservoir with fluid. Crank the engine and add fluid until the level stabilizes.
6. Raise the front of the car until the wheels are clear of the floor. Crank the engine and rotate the steering from lock to lock. Recheck the fluid level and add, if necessary.
7. Connect the coil wire. Start the engine, allow it to idle for a few minutes, and rotate the steering from lock to lock. Shut off the engine, lower the car, and recheck the level, adding if necessary.

Steering Wheel Removal and Installation

1. Disconnect the negative battery cable.
2. Remove the horn ring or cap by pushing it down and rotating it counterclockwise. Remove the retaining screws (from the underside of the steering wheel) and the crash pad. With speed control, the switches simply snap into plastic retainers inside the crash pad. Disconnect the horn and speed control wires.
3. Remove and discard the steering wheel nut. Install a steering wheel puller on the end of the shaft and remove the wheel.

— CAUTION —

The use of a knock-off type steering wheel puller or the use of a hammer on the steering shaft will damage the column bearing and collapsible column.

4. Lubricate the steering shaft bushing with white grease. Transfer all serviceable parts to the new steering wheel.
5. With the front wheels pointing

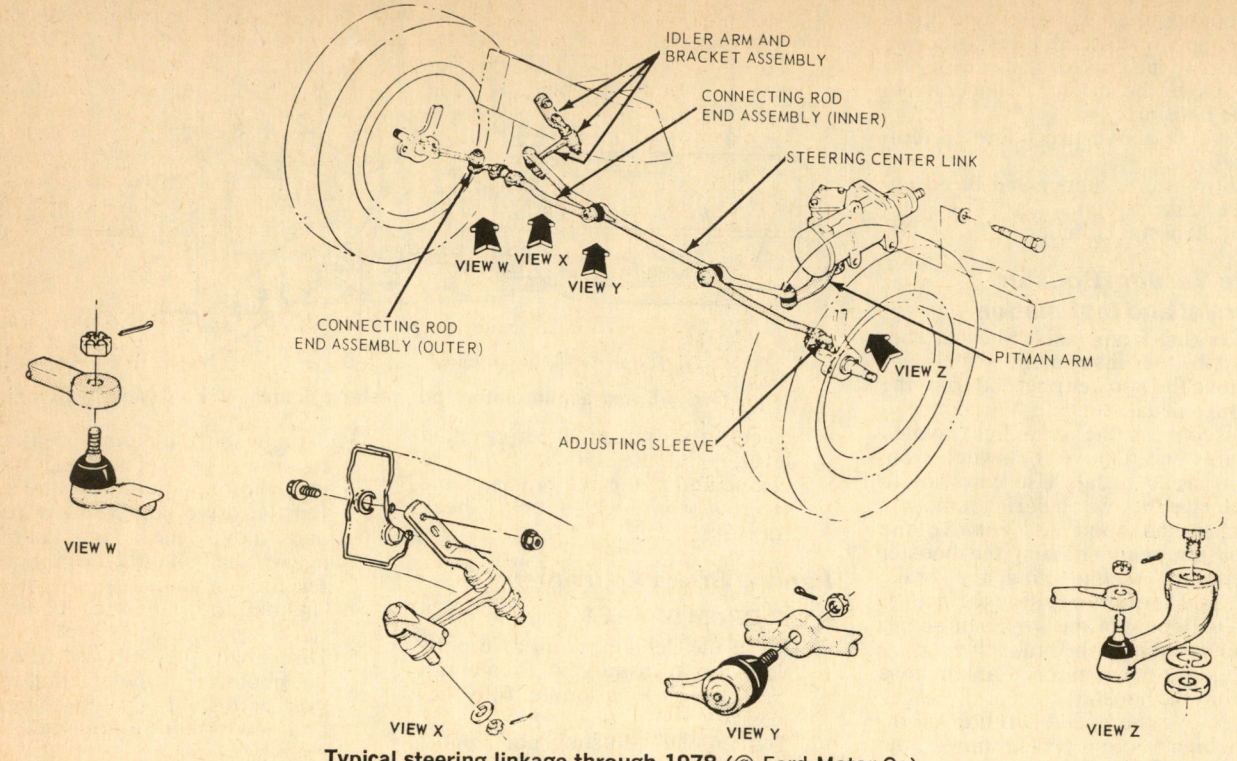

Typical steering linkage through 1978 (© Ford Motor Co)

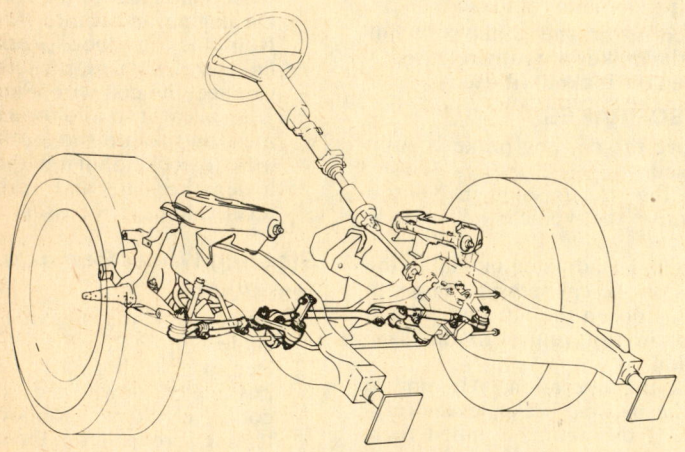

1979 Ford and Mercury steering linkage (© Ford Motor Co.)

straight-ahead, and with the alignment marks on steering wheel and the steering shaft lined up, install the steering wheel and a new locknut. Torque the nut to 30-40 ft. lbs.

6. Connect the horn and speed control wires and install the horn ring or cap. Install the crash pad and retaining screws.

7. Connect the negative battery cable.

Turn Signal Switch Replacement

1. Disconnect the negative battery cable.

2. Remove the steering wheel as outlined in the Steering Wheel Removal and Installation section.

3. Unscrew the turn signal lever from the side of the column. Remove the emergency flasher retainer and knob, if so equipped.

4. Locate and remove the finish cover on the steering column and disconnect the wiring connector plugs.

5. With a tilt steering column, it is necessary to separate the wires from the connector plug in order to remove the switch and wires. First note the location and color code of each wire, prior to removal. Remove the plastic cover from the wiring harness. Attach a piece of heavy cord to the switch wires to pull them down through the column during installation.

6. Remove the retaining clips and screws from the turn signal switch

and lift the switch and wire assembly from the top of the column.

7. Transfer the ground brush located in the turn signal switch cancelling cam to the new switch assembly on cars with speed control.

8. Tape the ends of the new switch wires together and transfer the pull cord to these wires.

9. Pull the wires down through the column with the cord and attach

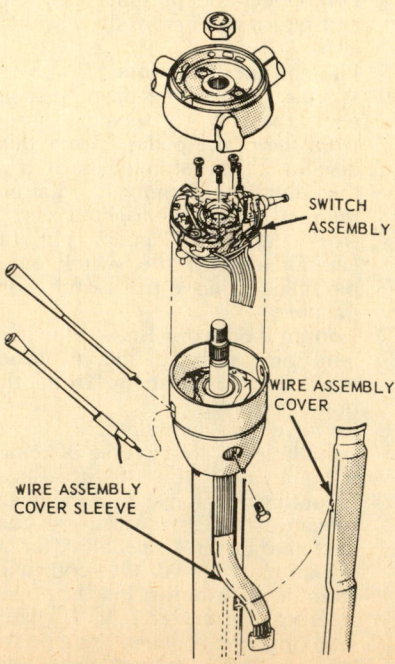

Turn signal switch—fixed column (© Ford Motor Co)

the new switch to the column hub.
10. If the switch wires were separated from the connector plug, press the wires into their proper location. Connect the wiring connector plugs and install the finish cover on the column.
11. Install the turn signal lever. Install the emergency flasher retainer and knob, if so equipped.
12. Install the steering wheel as outlined in the Steering Wheel Removal and Installation section.
13. Connect the negative battery cable and test the operation of the turn signals, horn, emergency flashers, and speed control, if so equipped.

Ignition Lock Cylinder Replacement

1. Disconnect the negative battery cable.
2. With a fixed steering column, remove the steering wheel trim pad and the steering wheel. Insert a stiff wire into the hole in the lock cylinder housing. With a tilt wheel, this hole is on the outside of the steering column near the emergency flasher button; it is not necessary to remove the steering wheel.
3. Place the gear shift lever in Park and turn the ignition key to the ON position.
4. Depress the wire and remove the lock cylinder and wire.
5. Insert the new cylinder into the housing and turn to the OFF position. This will lock the cylinder into position.
6. Reinstall the steering wheel and pad if removed.
7. Connect the negative battery cable.

Ignition Switch Replacement

1. Disconnect the negative battery cable.
2. Remove the shrouding from the steering column, and detach and lower the steering column from the brake support bracket.
3. Disconnect the switch wiring at the multiple plug.
4. Remove the two nuts that retain the switch to the steering column.
5. With column mounted gearshift lever, detach the switch plunger from the switch actuator rod and remove the switch. With console mounted gearshift lever, remove the pin connecting the plunger to the actuator and remove the switch.
6. To re-install the switch, place both the lock mechanism at the top of the column and the switch itself in lock position for correct adjustment. To hold the column in the lock position, place the shift lever in PARK and turn to LOCK and

remove the key. New switches are held in the LOCK position by plastic shipping pins. To pin used switches, pull the switch plunger out as far as it will go and push it back into the first detent. Insert a 3/32 in. diameter wire in the locking hole in the top of the switch.
7. Connect the switch plunger to the switch actuator rod.
8. Position the switch on the column and install the attaching nuts. Do not tighten them.
9. Move the switch up and down to locate mid-position of rod lash, and then tighten the nuts.
10. Remove the locking pin or wire.
11. Attach the steering column to the brake support bracket and install the shrouding.

INSTRUMENT PANEL

Speedometer Cable Replacement

The speedometer cable is attached to the speedometer housing by a tensioned arm, which locks into a groove on the speedometer housing. To release the cable, depress the flat portion of the tensioned arm to disengage it from the groove, and pull the cable away from the speedometer housing.

Headlight Switch Replacement
EXCEPT THUNDERBIRD THROUGH 1976

1. Disconnect the negative battery cable. Remove the knob from the washer switch.
2. On Ford and Mercury, remove the instrument panel pad, and instrument cluster. On 1972 Mercurys, remove the instrument panel pad only.
3. Pull the headlight switch control knob to the full ON position and press the release knob on the switch. With the knob depressed, pull the knob and shaft from the switch.
4. Remove the wire connector from the back of the switch and, if equipped with headlight doors, remove the vacuum hoses.

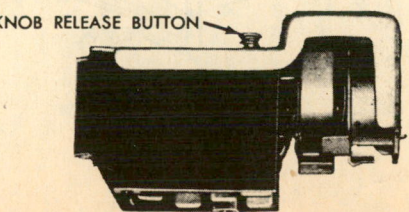

KNOB RELEASE BUTTON

Typical headlight switch
(© Ford Motor Co)

5. Remove the bezel retaining nut and remove the switch from the dash. On 1972 Fords, the switch is attached to the dash with three screws instead of a bezel nut.
6. Reverse the above procedure to reinstall. When installing the headlight switch control knob and shaft, turn the shaft in the switch until a distinct click is heard, locking the shaft in place.

THUNDERBIRD THROUGH 1976

1. Disconnect the negative battery cable.
2. Remove the cluster trim panel.
3. Remove the headlight switch mounting plate.
4. Remove the bezel nut and disconnect the multiple connector.
5. If equipped, remove the vacuum lines.
6. Remove the switch.
7. Reverse the above procedure to install.

WINDSHIELD WIPERS

Wiper Blade Replacement

Three wiper blade attaching methods are used. One type has a tab extending from the blade saddle. Press down on the arm and depress the tab while pulling the blade from the arm. The second type has a tab under the blade saddle that must be depressed while pulling the blade from the arm. The third type is attached to the arm side pin by a spring clip in the blade saddle. To release, insert a tool into the release opening of the blade saddle and depress, while pulling the blade from the arm.

The arm can be disengaged from the pivot by moving the release latch away from the arm, and pulling the arm away from the pivot.

Motor Removal and Installation

1. Disconnect the negative battery cable.
2. Remove the wiper arm and blade assemblies from the pivot shafts.
3. Remove the left side cowl grille.
4. Disconnect the wiper links at the wiper output pin by removing the retaining clip.
5. Disconnect the wire leads from the motor.
6. Remove the motor attaching bolts from under the instrument panel and remove the motor.
7. Reverse the procedure to install.

NOTE: *Before installing the wiper arms and blades, operate the wiper motor to ensure the pivot shafts are in the park position when the arms and blades are installed.*

RADIO

Weak radio reception may be corrected by trimming the radio antenna. The trimmer screw is located at the right rear or the front of the set. Tune the radio to a weak station near 1600 KC on the AM band, and adjust the trimmer screw to obtain the maximum volume. Optimum FM reception can be obtained by extending the antenna to a height of 31 inches.

Removal and Installation

FORD AND MERCURY

1. Disconnect the battery ground cable.
2. Remove the radio knobs, the screws that attach the bezel to the instrument panel, and remove the bezel.
3. Remove the radio mounting plate attaching screws, and disengage the radio by pulling it from the lower rear support bracket.
4. Disconnect all the leads from the radio.
5. Remove the radio mounting plate and the rear upper support; remove the radio from the instrument panel.
6. Reverse the procedure to install.

THUNDERBIRD THROUGH 1976

1. Disconnect the negative battery cable.

2. Remove the knobs from the radio shafts.
3. Remove the radio shaft nuts and the rear support attaching screw.
4. Disconnect the power lead, speaker wires and antenna lead, and remove the radio.
5. Remove the 2 screws attaching the Twilight Sentinel amplifier. Lower the amplifier.
6. Remove the air conditioning duct from beneath the radio.
7. Disconnect the radio rear support.
8. Reverse the procedure to install.

HEATER

VEHICLES WITHOUT AIR CONDITIONING

Heater Core Removal and Installation

FORD AND MERCURY

1. Partially drain the cooling system.
2. Remove the heater hoses at the core.
3. Remove the retaining screws, core cover and seal from the case.
4. Remove the core from the case.
5. Install, applying a thin coat of silicone to the pads.

THUNDERBIRD THROUGH 1976

1. Drain the coolant and disconnect

the hoses from the heater core.
2. Remove the glove box and the heater air outlet register.
3. Remove the mounting screw and disconnect the temperature cable at the blend door crank arm.
4. Remove the blue and red vacuum hoses from the high-low door vacuum motor, the yellow hose from the panel-defrost door motor, and the brown hose at the tee connector to the temperature bypass door motor.
5. Disconnect the wiring connector from the resistor.
6. Remove the 10 retaining screws and the rear half of the plenum case.
7. Remove the heater core tube support bracket mounting nut.
8. Reverse the procedure to install, taking care to reseal the plenum case halves.

Blower Motor Removal and Installation

THUNDERBIRD THROUGH 1976

1. Remove the glovebox and recirc-air register and duct assembly.
2. Remove the two blower lower housing retaining screws.
3. Disconnect the white hose from the outside recirc-air door vacuum motor, and remove the vacuum motor from the blower lower hous-

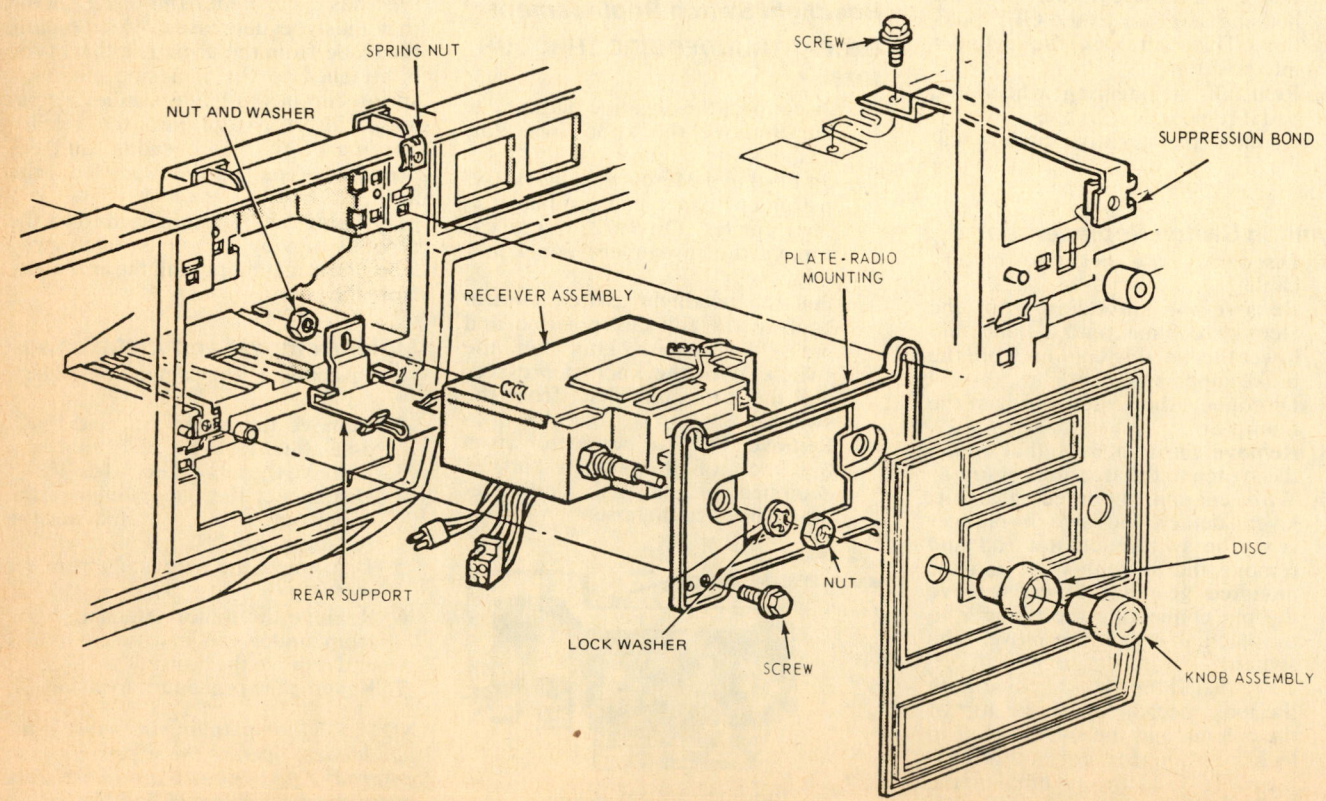

Ford and Mercury radio installation—1978 shown, other years similar (© Ford Motor Co.)

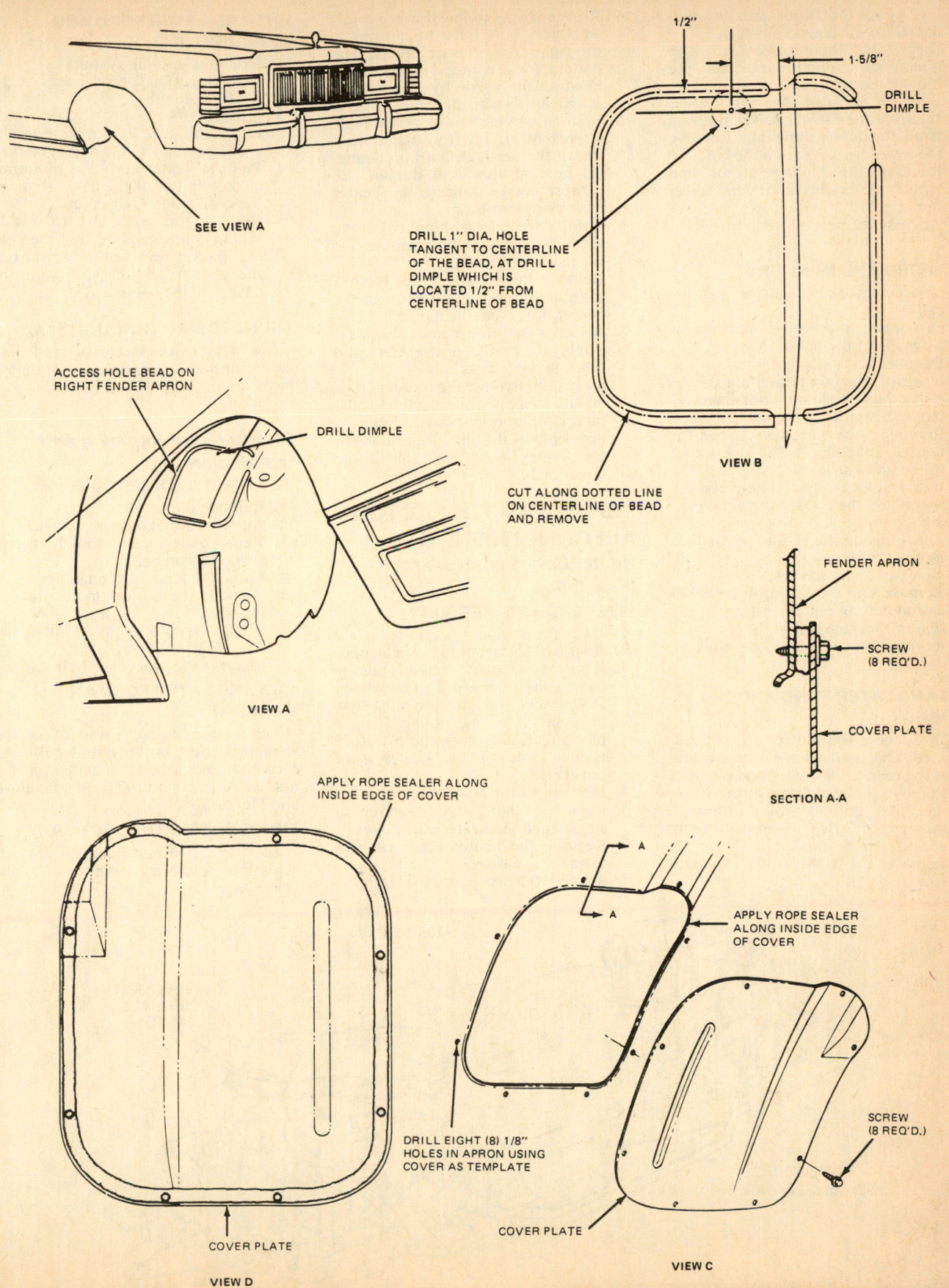

SEE VIEW A

1/2"

1-5/8"

DRILL DIMPLE

DRILL 1" DIA. HOLE TANGENT TO CENTERLINE OF THE BEAD, AT DRILL DIMPLE WHICH IS LOCATED 1/2" FROM CENTERLINE OF BEAD

ACCESS HOLE BEAD ON RIGHT FENDER APRON

DRILL DIMPLE

VIEW B

CUT ALONG DOTTED LINE ON CENTERLINE OF BEAD AND REMOVE

VIEW A

FENDER APRON

SCREW (8 REQ'D.)

COVER PLATE

SECTION A-A

APPLY ROPE SEALER ALONG INSIDE EDGE OF COVER

A

A

APPLY ROPE SEALER ALONG INSIDE EDGE OF COVER

DRILL EIGHT (8) 1/8" HOLES IN APRON USING COVER AS TEMPLATE

SCREW (8 REQ'D.)

COVER PLATE

COVER PLATE

VIEW D

VIEW C

Blower motor access hole (© Ford Motor Co.)

ing. Leave the motor actuator connected to the door crank arm.

4. Disconnect the orange lead wire and black ground wire from the blower motor.
5. Remove the six flange screws and separate the blower lower housing from the upper housing. Remove the lower housing from the car.
6. Remove the blower motor and wheel assembly from the lower housing.
7. Reverse the procedure to install.

1972 FORD AND MERCURY

1. Disconnect the negative battery cable.
2. Disconnect the blower motor wire leads under the hood.
3. Remove any parts mounted on the inside of the right fender apron.
4. Raise the vehicle on a hoist and remove the right front wheel.
5. Remove the fender apron-to-fender attaching bolts and lower the fender apron.
6. Insert a block of wood between the apron and the fender to gain working space.
7. Reach inside the fender apron and remove the blower motor mounting plate attaching screws.
8. Remove the blower motor, wheel and mounting plate from inside the fender as an assembly.
9. Reverse the procedure to install.

1973 AND LATER FORD AND MERCURY

1. Disconnect the blower motor lead wire. This is an orange wire located at the rear of the right hood hinge.
2. Remove the mounting screw from the black ground wire located at the upper cowl. Remove both wires from the clip.
3. Remove the right front tire and wheel.

4. In order to get to the blower motor, an access hole must be cut out in the right front fender apron. The pattern for this hole has been outlined on the apron by the factory. It appears as a beaded line.
5. A small indentation or drill dimple is present 1/2 in. from the centerline of the bead. Drill a 1 in. diameter hole at this drill dimple. Be careful not to damage the heater case by overdrilling.
6. Using sheet metal snips, cut along the bead to create the opening. Do not use a saber saw.
7. Remove the blower motor mounting plate screws and disconnect the cooler tube from the motor.
8. Remove the motor and wheel assembly from the heater case and through the access hole.
9. To install, reverse the removal procedure. Apply rope sealer to the motor mounting plate. Obtain a cover plate, drill 8, 1/8 in. holes in the fender apron and install the cover plate.

VEHICLES WITH FACTORY AIR CONDITIONING

Heater Core Removal and Installation

1972 FORD AND MERCURY

1. Drain the cooling system.
2. Remove the carburetor air cleaner.
3. Remove the two screws retaining the vacuum manifold to the dash. Disconnect the vacuum hoses as necessary, taking note of their placement, and move the manifold to one side of the heater core cover.
4. Disconnect the heater hoses.
5. Remove the seven attaching screws and the heater core cover.
6. Remove the heater core and pad from the housing.
7. Reverse the procedure to install.

1973 AND LATER FORD AND MERCURY

1. Drain the cooling system.
2. Disconnect the heater hoses at the heater core tubes.
3. Remove the seven screws which retain the core cover plate to the core housing and lift off the plate.
4. Pull the heater core and mounting gasket up out of the case. Remove the core mounting gasket.
5. Reverse the procedure to install, taking care to ensure that the core and gasket seat firmly forward of the core retention spring in the case. Fill the cooling system.

THUNDERBIRD THROUGH 1976

See Heater Core Removal and Installation for non-air conditioned Thunderbirds.

Blower Motor Removal and Installation

1972 FORD AND MERCURY

1. Remove the battery.
2. Remove the right front wheel.
3. Remove the vacuum tank bolts and fender apron bolts.
4. Move the fender apron inboard.
5. Remove the blower motor attaching screws and vent hose.
6. Pry upward on the hood hinge and remove the blower.
7. Reverse the procedure to install.

1973 AND LATER FORD AND MERCURY

For air-conditioned cars, follow the same procedure outlined under Blower Motor Removal and Installation for non-air conditioned 1973 and later Ford and Mercury.

THUNDERBIRD THROUGH 1976

See Blower Motor Removal and Installation for non-air conditioned Thunderbirds.

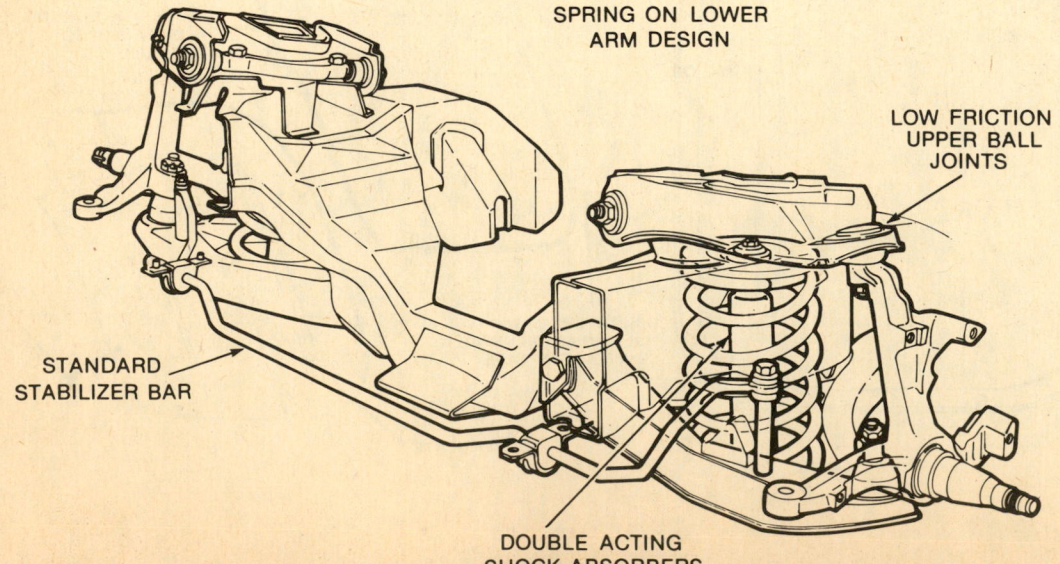

SPRING ON LOWER ARM DESIGN

LOW FRICTION UPPER BALL JOINTS

STANDARD STABILIZER BAR

DOUBLE ACTING SHOCK ABSORBERS

1979 Ford and Mercury front suspension (© Ford Motor Co.)

Lincoln Continental · Mark IV · Mark V

Index

Lincoln Continental • Mark IV • Mark V

YEAR IDENTIFICATION

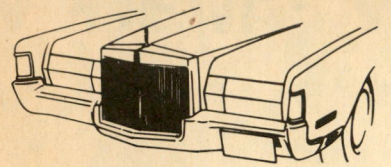

1972 Continental Mark IV

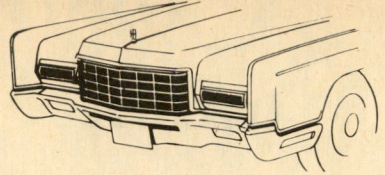

1972 Continental

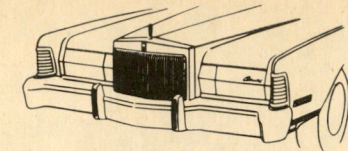

1973 Continental Mark IV

1973 Continental

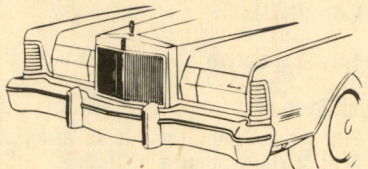

1974 Continental Mark IV

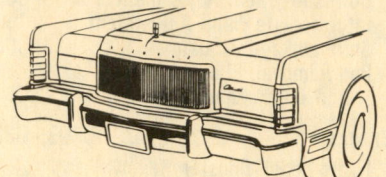

1974 Continental

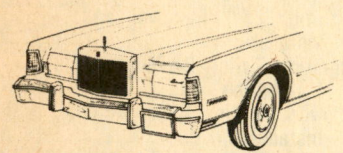

1975 Continental Mark IV

1975 Continental

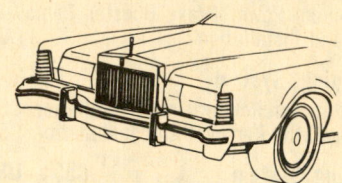

1976 Continental Mark IV

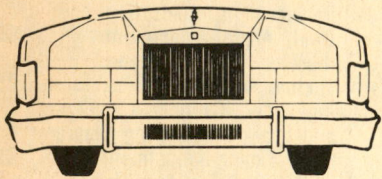

1977 Lincoln Continental

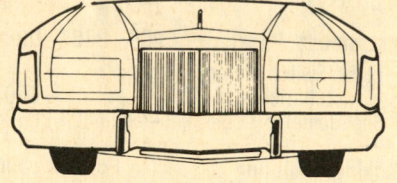

1977 Continental Mark V

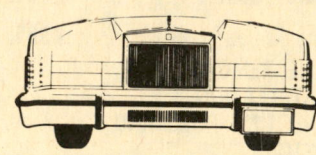

1978 Lincoln Continental

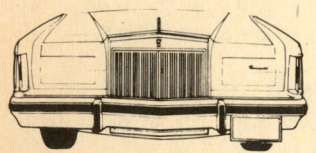

1978 Continental Mark V

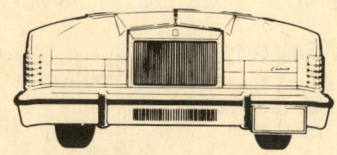

1979 Lincoln Continental

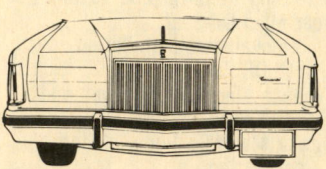

1979 Continental Mark V

ENGINE IDENTIFICATION

The engine code designation is the 5th digit of the vehicle identification number (V.I.N.) The V.I.N. is stamped on a plate located at the left side of the instrument panel visible through the windshield.

Disp	Bbl	'72	'73	'74	'75	'76	'77	'78	'79
8-Cylinder Models									
400	2						S*	S*	S
460	4	A	A	A	A	A	A	A	A

* A in Canada

GENERAL ENGINE SPECIFICATIONS

Year	Engine No. Cyl. Displacement Cu. In.	Carburetor Type	Horsepower @ rpm ■	Torque @ rpm (ft lbs) ■	Bore X Stroke (in.)	Compression Ratio	Oil Pressure @ 2000 rpm
'72	8-460	4 bbl	224 @ 4400	357 @ 2800	4.362 x 3.850	8.50:1	35-75
	8-460 Mark IV	4 bbl	212 @ 4400	342 @ 2800	4.362 x 3.850	8.50:1	35-75
'73	8-460 Continental	4 bbl	224 @ 4400	357 @ 2800	4.362 x 3.850	8.5:1	35-65
	8-460 Mark IV	4 bbl	212 @ 4400	342 @ 2800	4.362 x 3.850	8.5:1	35-65
'74	8-460 Continental	4 bbl	215 @ 4000	350 @ 2600	4.362 x 3.850	8.5:1	35-65
	8-460 Mark IV	4 bbl	220 @ 4000	350 @ 2600	4.362 x 3.850	8.5:1	35-65
'75	8-460 Continental	4 bbl	206 @ 4000①	357 @ 2600②	4.362 x 3.850	8.0:1	35-65
	8-460 Mark IV	4 bbl	194 @ 4000①	347 @ 2600②	4.362 x 3.850	8.0:1	35-65
'76	8-460	4 bbl	202 @ 3800	352 @ 1600	4.362 x 3.850	8.0:1	35-65
'77	8-400	2 bbl	181 @ 4000	331 @ 1600	4.000 x 4.000	8.0:1	45-75
	8-400 Calif.	2 bbl	179 @ 4000	329 @ 1600	4.000 x 4.000	8.0:1	45-75
	8-460 All	4 bbl	208 @ 4000	356 @ 2000	4.362 x 3.850	8.0:1	35-65
'78-	8-400	2 bbl	166 @ 3800	319 @ 1800	4.000 x 4.000	8.0:1	50-75
'79	8-460	4 bbl	210 @ 4200	357 @ 2200	4.362 x 3.850	8.0:1	35-65

■ Horsepower and torque are SAE net figures. They are measured at the rear of the transmission with all accessories installed and operating. Since the figures vary when a given engine is installed in different models, some are representative rather than exact.

① 223 @ 4000—California
② 366 @ 2600—California

TUNE-UP SPECIFICATIONS

Year	Engine No. Cyl. Displacement (cu in.)	hp	SPARK PLUGS Orig. Type ●	SPARK PLUGS Gap (in.)	DISTRIBUTOR Point Dwell (deg)	DISTRIBUTOR Point Gap (in.)	IGNITION TIMING (deg) ▲ Man Trans	IGNITION TIMING (deg) ▲ ● Auto Trans	VALVES Intake Opens ■ (deg)	Fuel Pump Pressure (psi)	IDLE SPEED (rpm) ▲ ● Man Trans	IDLE SPEED (rpm) ▲ ● Auto Trans
'72	8-460	224	ARF-42	.034	26-30	.017	—	10B(6B)	16	5-7	—	625/500②
'73	8-460	224	ARF-22	.034	26-30	.017	—	6B	16	5-7	—	625/500②
'74-'75	8-460 Mark IV	220	ARF-52	.044	Electronic		—	14B	8	6-7	—	650/500②
	8-460	215	ARF-52	.044	Electronic		—	14B	8	6-7	—	650/500②
'76	8-460	202	ARF-52	.044	Electronic		—	8B(14B)	8	6-7	—	650/600②
	8-460 Mark IV	202	ARF-52	.044	Electronic		—	10B	8	6-7	—	650/600②

TUNE-UP SPECIFICATIONS

Year	ENGINE No. Cyl Displacement (cu in.)	hp	SPARK PLUGS Orig. Type ●	SPARK PLUGS Gap (in.)	DISTRIBUTOR Point Dwell (deg)	DISTRIBUTOR Point Gap (in.)	IGNITION TIMING (deg) ▲ Man Trans	IGNITION TIMING (deg) ▲ ● Auto Trans	VALVES Intake Opens ■ (deg)	Fuel Pump Pressure (psi)	IDLE SPEED (rpm) ▲ ● Man Trans	IDLE SPEED (rpm) ▲ ● Auto Trans
'77	8-400	All	ARF-52 (ARF-52-6)	.050(.060)	Electronic		—	8B	17	6.5-7.5	—	650(625)
	8-460	All	ARF-52 (ARF-52-6)	.050(.060)	Electronic		—	16B	8	7.2-8.2	—	650
'78	8-400	All	ARF-52	.050	Electronic		—	13B(16B)	17	6.5-7.5	—	575(600)
	8-460	All	ARF-52	.050	Electronic		—	16B①	8	7.2-8.2	—	580
'79	All				See Underhood Specifications Sticker							

▲ See text for procedure
● Figure in parentheses indicates California engine
■ All figures Before Top Dead Center
① 10B on engines built after July 15, 1977
② First figure is for idle speed with solenoid energized and automatic transmission in Drive, while second figure is for idle speed with solenoid disconnected and automatic transmission in Neutral

B Before Top Dead Center
— Not applicable

NOTE: The underhood specifications sticker often reflects tune-up specification changes made in production. Sticker figures must be used if they disagree with those in this chart.

FIRING ORDER

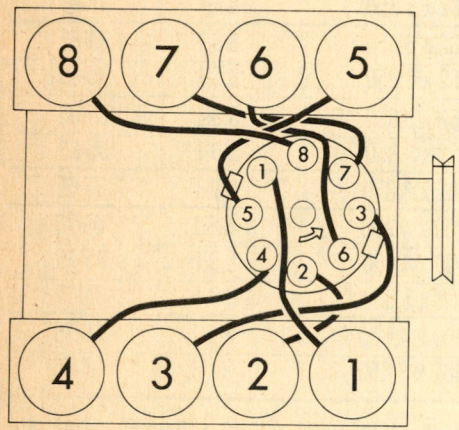

FORD MOTOR CO. 460 V8 (through 1974)
Engine firing order: 1-5-4-2-6-3-7-8
Distributor rotation: counterclockwise

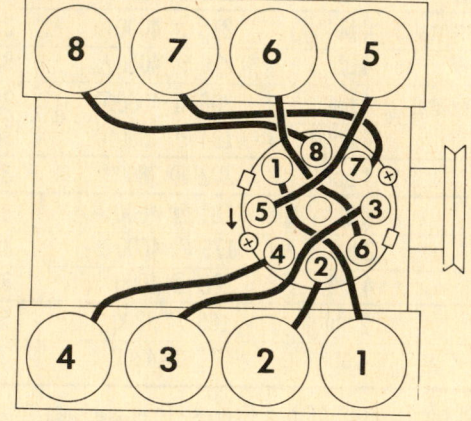

FORD MOTOR CO. 460 V8 (1975 and later)
Engine firing order: 1-5-4-2-6-3-7-8
Distributor rotation: counterclockwise

(Squares are position of latches on 1975-76 models; circles are position of latches on 1977 and later models.)

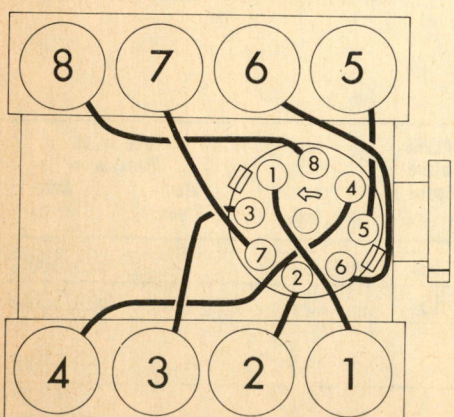

FORD MOTOR CO. 400 V8 (through 1974)
Engine firing order: 1-3-7-2-6-5-4-8
Distributor rotation: counterclockwise

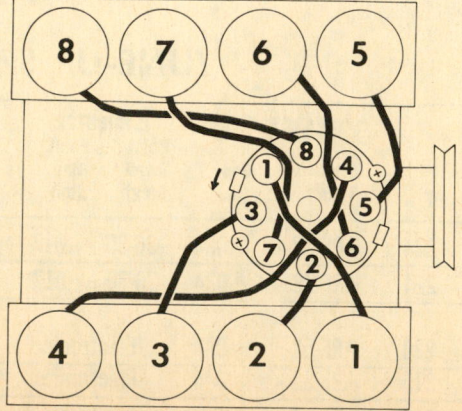

FORD MOTOR CO. 400 V8 (1975 and later)
Engine firing order: 1-3-7-2-6-5-4-8
Distributor rotation: counterclockwise

(Squares are position of latches on 1975-76 models; circles are position of latches on 1977 and later models.)

VALVE SPECIFICATIONS

Year	Engine No. Cyl. Displacement (cu in.)	Seat Angle (deg)	Face Angle (deg)	Spring Test Pressure (lbs @ in.)	Spring Installed Height (in.)	STEM TO GUIDE Clearance (in.) Intake	Exhaust	STEM Diameter (in.) Intake	Exhaust
'72	8-460	45	46	80 @ 1.81	1 13/16	.0010-.0027	.0010-.0027	.3420	.3420
'73	8-460	45	44	170 @ 1.39	1 13/16	.0010-.0027	.0010-.0027	.3420	.3420
'74-'79	8-460	45	44	80 @ 1.81	1 13/16	.0010-.0027	.0010-.0027	.3420	.3420
'77-'79	8-400	45	44	80 @ 1.82①	1 13/16	.0010-.0027	.0015-.0032	.3420	.3414

① exhaust—83 @ 1.68 starting 1978

CAPACITIES

Year	ENGINE No. Cyl. Displacement (cu. in.)	Model	Engine Crankcase Add 1 Qt For New Filter	TRANSMISSION Pts To Refill After Draining Manual 3-Speed	4-Speed	Automatic	Drive Axle (pts)	Gasoline Tank (gals)	COOLING SYSTEM (qts) With Heater	With A/C
'72	8-460	All	4	—	—	6	5	23	19.4	19.4
'73	8-460	Continental	4	—	—	6	5	22	19.5	19.5
	8-460	Mark IV	4	—	—	6	5	22.5	19.5	19.5
'74	8-460	Continental	4	—	—	6	5	22	21.5	21.5
	8-460	Mark IV	4	—	—	6	5	26.5	21.5	21.5
'75-'76	8-460	Continental	4	—	—	6	5	24.2	19.7	19.7
	8-460	Mark IV	4	—	—	6	5	26.5	20.5	20.5
'77	8-400	Continental	4	—	—	6	5	24.2	17.2	17.2
	8-400	Mark V	4	—	—	6	5	26	17.2	17.2
	8-460	Continental	4	—	—	6	5	24.2	18.5	18.5
	8-460	Mark V	4	—	—	6	5	26	18.5	18.5
'78-'79	8-400	Continental	4	—	—	6	5	24.2	16.9	16.9
	8-400	Mark V	4	—	—	6	5	25	16.9	16.9
	8-460	Continental	4	—	—	6	5	24.2	18.6	18.6
	8-460	Mark V	4	—	—	6	5	25	18.7	18.7

— Not applicable

TORQUE SPECIFICATIONS
All readings in ft lbs

Year	Engine Displacement (cu in.)	Cylinder Head Bolts	Rod Bearing Bolts	Main Bearing Bolts	Crankshaft Bolt	Flywheel to Crankshaft Bolts	MANIFOLD Intake	Exhaust
'72-'79	8-460	130-140①	40-45	95-105	70-90	75-85	22-32	28-33
'77-'79	8-400	95-105②	40-45	95-105	70-90	75-85	③	18-24

① In three steps:
Step 1—70-80
Step 2—100-110
Step 3—130-140

② In two steps:
Step 1: 75
Step 2: 95-105

③ 5/16 in. bolt: 19-25
3/8 in. bolt: 22-32

CRANKSHAFT AND CONNECTING ROD SPECIFICATIONS

All measurements are given in in.

Year	Engine Displacement (cu in.)	CRANKSHAFT				CONNECTING ROD		
		Main Brg. Journal Dia	Main Brg. Oil Clearance	Shaft End-Play	Thrust on No.	Journal Diameter	Oil Clearance	Side Clearance
'72-'76	8-460	2.9994-3.0002	.0005-.0025	.004-.008	3	2.4992-2.5000	.0008-.0026	.010-.020
'77-'79	8-460	2.9994-3.0002	.0008-.0015	.004-.008	3	2.4992-2.5000	.0008-.0015	.010-.020
'77-'79	8-400	2.9994-3.0002	.0008-.0015	.004-.008	3	2.3103-2.3111	.0008-.0015	.010-.020

RING GAP

All measurements are given in inches

Year	Engine No. Cyl. Displacement (cu in.)	Top Compression	Bottom Compression		Year	Engine	Oil Control
'72-'79	8-400, 460	.010-.020	.010-.020		'72-'79	8-400, 460	.015-.055

RING SIDE CLEARANCE

All measurements are given in inches

Year	Engine	Top Compression	Bottom Compression		Year	Engine	Oil Control
'72-'79	8-460	.0025-.0045	.0025-.0045		'72-'79	8-400, 460	Snug
'77-'79	8-400	.0020-.0040	.0020-.0040				

PISTON CLEARANCE

Year	Engine	Piston to bore clearance (in.)
'72-'73	8-460	.0014-.0022
'74	8-460	.0022-.0030
'75-'79	8-400, 460	.0014-.0022

WHEEL ALIGNMENT SPECIFICATIONS

Year	Model	CASTER		CAMBER		Toe-in (in.)	Steering Axis Inclin. (deg)	WHEEL PIVOT RATIO (deg)	
		Range (deg)	Pref Setting (deg)	Range (deg)	Pref Setting (deg)			Inner Wheel	Outer Wheel
'72	Continental	½N to 2½P	1½P	½N to 1½P	½P	0 to ¼	7¾	20	18⁷/₁₆
'72-'74	Mark IV	0 to 2P	1P	¼N to 1¼P	½P	¹/₁₆ to ⁵/₁₆	7¾	20	17¾
'73-'74	Continental	½N to 2½P	1P	¼N to 1¼P	½P	0 to ¼	9½	20	17¾①
'75-'77	Mark IV, V	¼P-2¾P	2P	②	③	¹/₁₆-⁵/₁₆	7¾	20	18.09
'78-'79	Mark V	3¼P-4¾P	4P	②	③	¹/₁₆-⁵/₁₆	9½	20	18.09
'75-'79	Continental	1¼P-2¾P	2P	②	③	0-¼	9½	20	18.16

N Negative   P Positive
① 18½° in 1974

② Left: ¼N to 1¼P; Right: ½ N to 1 P
③ Left—½P; Right—¼P

NOTE: For coverage of the Lincoln Versailles, see the Capri and Comet Car section.

CHARGING SYSTEM

Information on alternator and regulator troubleshooting is in the Unit Repair Section under Charging and Starting Systems.

Alternator Removal and Installation

1. Disconnect the negative battery cable.
2. Loosen the alternator mounting bolts, remove the alternator to adjusting arm bolt and remove the belt.
3. Remove the alternator mounting bolt and spacer, position the alternator so that the wire connectors can be disconnected and remove the alternator.
4. Reverse the procedure to reinstall, applying pressure only to the front of the alternator housing when tightening the drive belt. Adjust the belt to give a 1/2 in. deflection along its longest straight run.

Regulator Removal and Installation

1. Disconnect the negative battery cable.
2. Remove the regulator mounting screws and wires, then remove the regulator.
3. Some regulator wiring connectors have a snap-lock that can be disengaged by inserting and twisting a wide blade screwdriver.
4. On replacement, make sure that the regulator has a good ground to the body.

STARTING SYSTEM

Models with the 460 engine, through 1977, use a starter which mounts an outboard solenoid. All others use a remote relay to activate an internal positive engagement drive.

Starter Removal and Installation

1. Disconnect the battery ground cable.
2. Raise the car on a hoist.
3. Disconnect the wires at the solenoid terminals or the starter cable from the motor.
4. Loosen the 2 front brace attaching bolts.
5. Remove all other brace attaching bolts and let the brace hang free.
6. Turn the front wheels to full right lock.

7. Remove the bolts securing the steering idler arm to the frame.
8. Unbolt and remove the starter.
9. Installation is the reverse of removal.

Disabling the Seat Belt/Starter Interlock

It is now legal to disable the seat belt/starter interlock system. However the warning light portion of the system must be left operational.

1. Apply the parking brake and remove the ignition key.
2. Open the hood and locate the system emergency override switch and connector. Remove the connector.
3. Cut the white wire(s) with the pink dots (# 33 circuit) and the red wire(s) with the light blue stripe (# 32 circuit).
4. Splice the two (or four) wires together and tape the splice. Use a butt connector if available.

NOTE: *Do not cut and splice the other connector wires. If the red/yellow hash wire is spliced to any of the other wires the car will start in gear.*

5. Install the connector back on the override switch. Close the hood.
6. Apply the parking brake, buckle the seat belt, and turn the key to the ON position. If the starter cranks in ON or any gear selected, the wrong wires have been cut and spliced. Repeat steps 3-6.
7. Unbuckle the belt and try to start the car. If the car doesn't start, repeat steps 3-6. If the car starts, everything is O.K.
8. To stop the warning buzzer from operating, remove it from the connector. Tape the connector to the wiring harness so that it can't rattle.

NO. 640 CIRCUIT—RED/YELLOW HASH

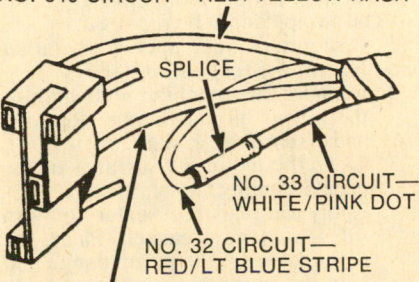

Cut and splice the seat belt/starter interlock wires as shown (© Ford Motor Co)

IGNITION SYSTEM

NOTE: *If the two-piece Dura Spark solid state ignition distributor cap is to be removed, the top part must be removed first, then the rotor, then the bottom of the cap.*

Distributor Removal

The distributor is located at the front of the engine between the cylinder banks.

1. Remove the carburetor air cleaner. With point-type ignition, detach the ignition primary lead and the vacuum advance lead. With solid state ignition, disconnect the distributor wiring connector, detach the vacuum line, and remove and set aside the distributor cap.
2. Carefully mark the position of the rotor in relation to the body of the distributor, and mark the position of the body of the distributor relative to the engine. The marks are made so that the distributor can be reinstalled without having to retime the ignition.
3. Remove the hold-down bolt and lift out the distributor.
4. Installation is the reverse of removal, unless timing has been disturbed. In that case, see "Ignition Retiming."
5. Check the timing setting.

Ignition Timing

All 1974 and later engines have monolithic timing, set at the factory. The monolithic system uses a timing receptacle on the front of the engine which can be connected to digital read-out equipment, which electronically determines timing. Timing can also be adjusted in the conventional way.

1. Locate the timing mark and pointer on the crankshaft damper and the front of the engine. Mark the pointer and timing mark with white chalk. Some 1978 and later engines must have the three pin switch assembly connector disconnected from the ignition module. These have either a barometric pressure switch for high altitude or a distributor modulator switch for economy. See the underhood specifications sticker for details.
2. Install a stroboscopic type timing light and tachometer according to the manufacturer's specifications.
3. Disconnect the vacuum line(s) to the distributor and plug them.
4. Start the engine. Set the idle speed to the figure given on the tune up sticker for timing. If there is no such figure, set the idle speed to the figure given for normal idle.
5. Check the timing mark and pointer alignment with the timing light. The factory allows a tolerance of plus of minus two degrees. To advance the timing, loosen the distributor to block hold-down bolt and turn the distributor clockwise.
6. Tighten the distributor hold-down and check the timing. If necessary, reset the idle speed.

Ignition Retiming

If the timing relationship has been disturbed, retime the ignition as follows: bring No. 1 cylinder up to the firing position. This can be checked by removing the spark plug, placing your thumb in the spark plug hole and then cranking the engine until compression is felt. Now, slowly bring the crankshaft around until the T.D.C. mark on the crankshaft pulley lines up with the pointer. This is the approximate firing position for No. 1 cylinder.

Note the placement of the no. one spark plug wire on the distributor cap. Scribe a mark on the distributor body directly below the no. one spark plug wire. Install the distributor so that the mark that you made is directly beneath the tip of the rotor. Make sure that the distributor shaft is engaged with the oil pump drive. Sometimes it is necessary to crank the engine with the starter to engage the oil pump intermediate shaft. Install the distributor cap and, working counterclockwise, check to make sure that the installation of the spark plug wires corresponds with the firing order of the engine. Check the timing with a timing light.

Contact Point Replacement and Adjustment Through 1973

1. Unsnap the distributor cap retaining clips and position the cap clear of the breaker plate. Remove the rotor by pulling it straight up.
2. Remove the metal point shield, if so equipped.
3. Disconnect the primary lead and condenser wires from the contact point assembly.
4. Remove the contact point and condenser retaining screws. Lift the contact point assembly and condenser from the distributor.
5. Lightly lubricate the distributor cam with heat-resistant lubricant.
6. Place the new contact point assembly and condenser in the distributor. Install, but do not tighten, the retaining screws.
7. Place the ground wire under the contact point assembly screw farthest from the contacts.
8. Turn the engine until the rubbing block on the point assembly is resting on the high point of the distributor cam lobe. Insert a feeler gauge of specified thickness between the contact points and adjust the gap. Tighten the retaining screw and remove the feeler gauge.
9. Connect the primary and condenser wires to the contact point assembly in the same order in which they were removed. On distributors equipped with a metal point shield, the wires should be positioned 180 degrees (180°) from each other before installing the shield.
10. Install the rotor and distributor cap.
11. Check to see that the distributor dwell is within specifications.

SOLID STATE IGNITION

Beginning 1974, Lincolns use a solid state or breakerless ignition system. This system eliminates the contact breaker points, replacing them with a permanent magnet low voltage generator. For more information, see Electronic Ignition in the Unit Repair section.

Tachometer Connection

The coil connector used with solid state ignition is provided with a cavity for connection of a tachometer, so that the connector doesn't have to be removed to check engine rpm.

Install a tach lead with an alligator clip on its end into the cavity marked TACH TEST and connect the other lead to a good ground.

If the coil connector must be removed, pull it out horizontally until it is disengaged from the coil terminal.

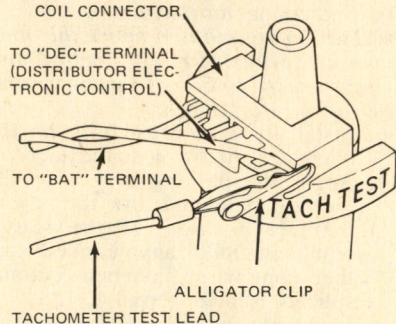

COIL CONNECTOR

TO "DEC" TERMINAL (DISTRIBUTOR ELECTRONIC CONTROL)

TO "BAT" TERMINAL

TACH TEST

ALLIGATOR CLIP

TACHOMETER TEST LEAD

Connecting a tachometer to the electronic ignition coil (© Ford Motor Co)

FUEL SYSTEM

Fuel Pump Replacement

The fuel pump is mounted on the left side of the cylinder front cover.

The pump cannot be repaired.

1. Disconnect the inlet and outlet lines at the fuel pump.
2. Remove the attaching bolts and lift the pump off its mount. Remove and discard the gasket.
3. Clean the mounting surfaces of the pad and pump.
4. Apply oil-resistant sealer to both sides of a new gasket. Place the new gasket on the pump flange and hold the pump against the pad. Be sure that the rocker arm is riding on the camshaft eccentric.
5. Install the bolts and connect the fuel lines.
6. Run the engine and check for leaks.

Fuel Filter Removal and Installation

A separate in-line fuel filter is used. The filter cannot be serviced. Replace it in case of obstruction.

1. Remove the air cleaner.
2. Loosen the hose clamp at the fuel inlet hose connection.

3. Unscrew the filter from the carburetor.
4. Disconnect the filter from the hose and discard the hose clamp.
5. Reverse the above procedure to install, using a new hose clamp. After installation, start the engine and check for fuel leakage.

Idle Speed Adjustment

THROUGH 1973

1. 4300 Carburetor: *Adjust with air cleaner installed.* If it is not possible to adjust carburetor idle speed with the air cleaner installed, the engine idle speed must be rechecked after installing the air cleaner. On models with vacuum controlled heat ducts in the air cleaner, the vacuum line must be plugged if the carburetor is to be adjusted with the air cleaner removed.
2. Run engine at fast idle to equalize operating temperature.
3. Make sure the choke plate is fully released.
4. Turn headlights on high beam.
5. Tape hot idle compensator so that it is fully seated in the closed position.
6. On vehicles equipped with air conditioning, set the idle speed with the air conditioner turned OFF.
7. Remove and plug the vacuum line to the parking brake release, then, set the parking brake and put the transmission in the Drive position.
8. Attach a tachometer of known accuracy to the engine.
9. Adjust the idle speed screw or solenoid to obtain specified rpm. On Carter carburetors, turn the idle speed adjusting screw in to decrease speed and out to increase engine speed. On Autolite carburetors, turn the idle adjusting screw in to increase speed and out to decrease speed. On 1971 carburetors with an electric solenoid, turn the solenoid plunger to the right to increase idle speed and to the left to decrease it. On 1972-73 carburetors with an electric solenoid, turn the adjusting screw in the solenoid mounting bracket to adjust the idle speed.

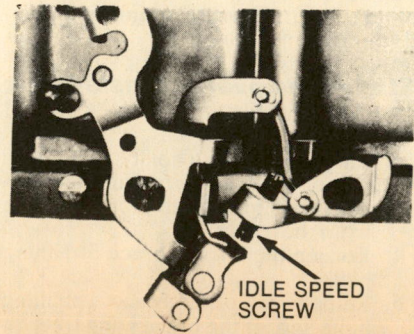

IDLE SPEED SCREW

Autolite carburetor idle speed adjustment (© Ford Motor Co)

NOTE: *There are two engine idle speeds listed for cars with solenoid equipped carburetors. The first or higher speed is adjusted as explained above, the second is adjusted with the solenoid electrical lead disconnected, and the transmission in Park or Neutral, by turning the adjustment screw on the side of the carburetor.*

With the solenoid disconnected, the idle adjusting screw must contact the throttle shaft or the throttle plates may become jammed in the throttle bores of the carburetor when the engine is shut off.

1974

These cars use either the Motorcraft model 4300 4 bbl carburetor or the Carter Thermo-Quad®, which is used only on 1974 California cars.

1. Remove the air cleaner and plug the vacuum line.
2. Set the parking brake.
3. Check the throttle and choke linkage for freedom of movement.
4. Connect a tachometer.
5. Stabilize the engine temperature.
6. Set the ignition timing.
7. Be sure that the choke is fully open.
8. Place automatic transmission in Drive.
9. Turn the solenoid adjusting screw in or out to obtain the higher rpm specified.
10. Disconnect the electrical lead from the throttle solenoid positioner and place the automatic transmission in Neutral.

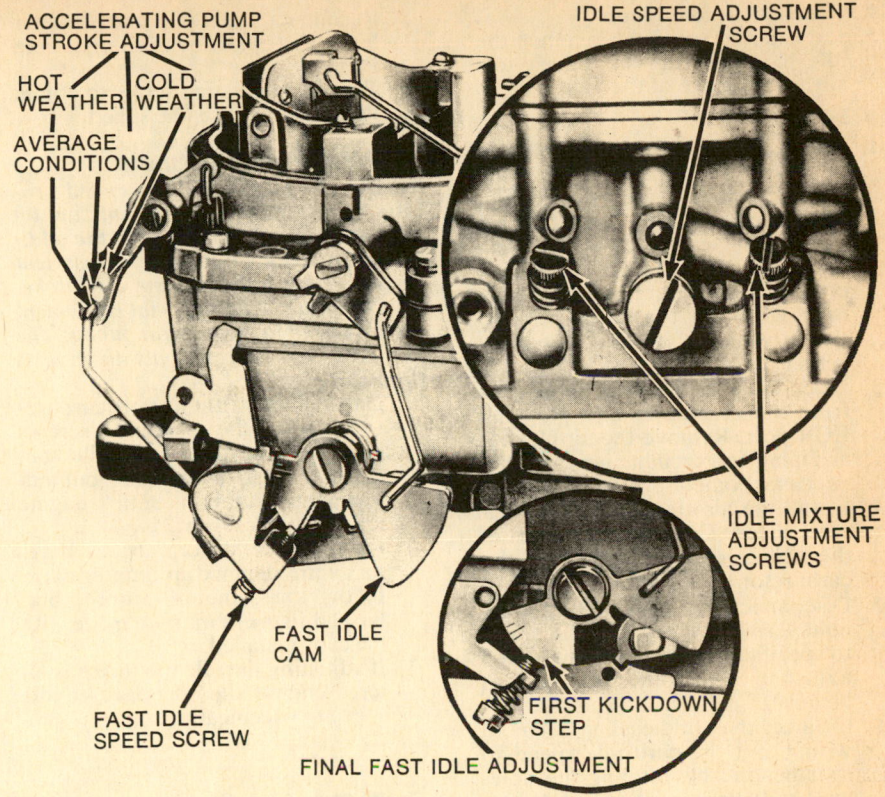

Carter carburetor adjustments
(© Ford Motor Co)

11. Adjust the solenoid off idle speed screw, located on the carburetor body, to obtain the lower specified idle speed.

12. Connect the solenoid wire and allow the plunger to extend.
13. Stop the engine, connect the vacuum line and install the air cleaner.

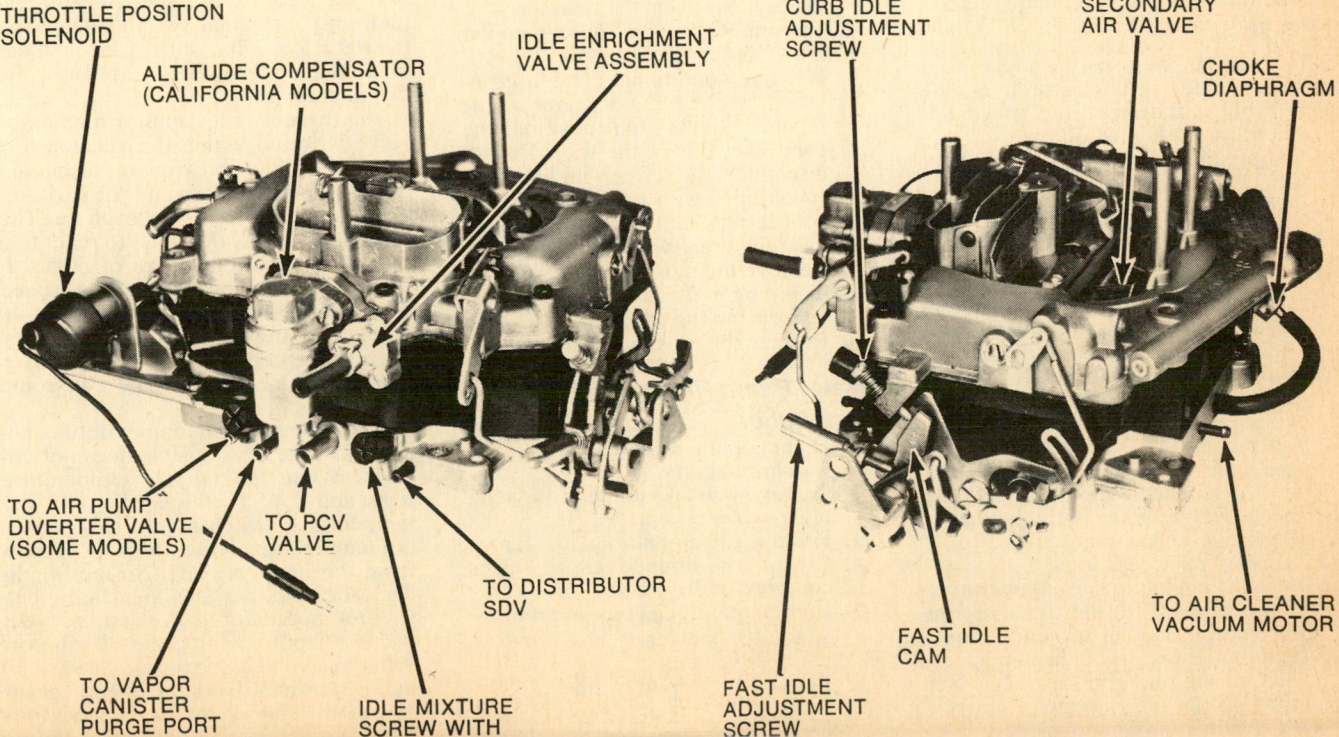

Carter Thermo-Quad® carburetor adjustment points

14. Recheck the idle speed.
15. If it is not as specified, readjust the idle to obtain the smoothest idle within the range of the limiter caps.

1975-76

1. Allow the engine to reach normal operating temperature. Check the timing and adjust it, as necessary.
2. Disconnect and plug the distributor vacuum hoses. Remove the top and center hoses from the CSSA coolant temperature operated vacuum valve (in the heater elbow) and connect the two hoses together.
3. Disconnect the EGR vacuum hoses from the carburetor and plug the EGR port. Remove the air cleaner and plug its vacuum hoses. Connect a tachometer.
4. Install the air cleaner and its vacuum hoses. Connect the hoses to the CSSA vacuum valve and the carburetor EGR port.
5. Disconnect the antidieseling solenoid wiring. Set the low idle speed to specification with the low speed adjusting screw (transmission in Neutral).
6. Connect the antidieseling solenoid wiring. Set the curb idle speed to specification by rotating the solenoid body (transmission in Drive).
7. Shift into Neutral and increase the engine speed for a few seconds.
8. Return the engine speed to idle. Shift into Drive. Recheck the idle speed. Adjust it, if necessary, by repeating steps 5 and 6.
9. Remove the tachometer. Unplug and connect the distributor vacuum hoses.

1977-79

The 400 engine uses the 2150 2 bbl carburetor; the 460 engine uses the 4350 4 bbl carburetor. Idle speed adjustment for both is as follows:

1. Apply the parking brake and block the wheels.
2. Connect a tachometer, following the manufacturer's instructions for use on HEI systems.
3. Remove the air cleaner and plug the vacuum lines on 1977 models only. Leave the air cleaner and lines in place on later models.
4. Remove and plug the EGR vacuum line. On 1978 and later models, disconnect the fuel evaporative canister purge valve vacuum hose from the underhood vacuum hoses. Do not disconnect the hose at the purge valve. Plug both the valve hose and the vacuum source.
5. Turn off all accessories.
6. Run the engine to normal operating temperature with the transmission in Neutral and set the choke linkage on the fast idle cam step specified on the underhood sticker. Set the fast idle screw to the rpm specified on the underhood sticker.
7. Run the engine at 2500 rpm for 15 seconds and recheck fast idle.

8. Reconnect the EGR and canister hoses and place the transmission in Drive.
9. Turn idle adjusting screw to obtain the specified curb idle speed.

Fuel Mixture Adjustment

NOTE: *The factory recommended procedure for adjusting the idle mixture on 1975 and later models requires the addition of an artificial mixture enrichment substance (propane) to the air intake. This method requires special equipment not available to the general public. The following procedures apply to models through 1974.*

1. On engines with Carter carburetors, turn the mixture screws clockwise until engine idle becomes rough, then, back out adjustment screws until engine reaches highest rpm.
2. On Autolite/Motorcraft carburetors with idle mixture limiter caps, follow the same procedure, but, final adjustment must be made with the caps installed.
3. If adjusting the idle mixture has altered engine idle speed, reset idle speed to specification.

COOLING SYSTEM

Radiator Removal and Installation

1. Drain the cooling system.
2. Disconnect the upper and lower radiator hoses from the radiator.
3. Disconnect the transmission cooler lines from the radiator.
4. If the air conditioner condenser attaches to the radiator, remove the retaining bolts and position the condenser out of the way. Do not disconnect the refrigerant lines.
5. If equipped with a fan shroud, disconnect it from the radiator and position it rearward over the fan.
6. Remove the radiator upper support mounting bolts and remove the radiator from the car.
7. Reverse the procedure to install.

Water Pump Removal and Installation

1. Drain cooling system. Remove the fan shroud bolts.
2. Remove bolts retaining fan assembly to water pump.
3. Remove radiator shroud and fan.
4. On air conditioned cars, loosen compressor drive belt.
5. Loosen mounting bolts and remove alternator, power steering and air pump drive belts.
6. Remove water pump pulley.
7. Disconnect radiator lower hose, heater hose, and bypass hose at water pump. Remove any interfering brackets.

8. Remove water pump bolts and remove water pump.
9. Install in reverse order of removal. Adjust belts to give 1/2 in. deflection along the longest straight run.

Thermostat Removal and Installation

1. Drain the radiator so that the coolant level is below the thermostat.
2. Remove the coolant outlet housing retaining bolts, pull the elbow away from the engine, and remove the thermostat and its gasket.
3. Clean the gasket surfaces. Install the thermostat in the block on the 400, and in the intake manifold on the 460. Coat a new gasket with water-resistant sealer, and position the gasket.
4. Position the coolant outlet elbow. Install the retaining bolts.
5. Fill the radiator, install the cap, start the engine, and check the system for leaks.

EMISSION CONTROLS

1972

1972 California cars are equipped with an Electronic Spark Control (ESC) system. This system is composed of an electronic control amplifier, a three-way distributor modulator valve, a speed sensor (found between two sections of the speedometer cable), and a thermal switch (located in the right door pillar of the Lincoln Continental and in the left door pillar of the Continental Mark IV).

The three-way distributor modulator valve is found within the vacuum line connecting the previously discussed ported vacuum switch and the carburetor. It is vented to the atmosphere. The thermal switch is designed to react to a critical temperature range of 50-58° F (outside air temperature). The speed sensor reacts to speeds in excess of 40 mph. The thermal switch dominates over the speed sensor. The impulses from both are fed into the electronic control amplifier.

When the ambient temperature is below 49°F, the ESC system does not operate. When the outside temperature rises above 65°F, the contacts in the temperature switch close. This causes the temperature switch to pass current from the ignition switch to the amplifier. The amplifier then signals the distributor modulator to close and prevent vacuum from reaching the distributor. When the vehicle reaches a speed of 40 mph, the signal from the speed sensor causes the modulator to open and restore normal vacuum advance to the engine. If the engine should overheat at idle, the ported vacuum switch overrides the ESC system and connects intake manifold vacuum to the distributor.

1973

The 1973 emission control system consists of a new Exhaust Gas Recirculation (EGR) system, and a Delayed Vacuum Bypass (DVB) spark advance control system.

The DVB system provides two paths by which distributor vacuum can reach the distributor vacuum advance. The system consists of a spark delay valve, a check valve, a solenoid vacuum valve, and an ambient temperature switch. When the ambient temperature is below 49°F, the temperature switch contacts are open and the vacuum solenoid is open (de-energized). Under these conditions, vacuum will flow from the carburetor, through the open solenoid, and to the distributor. Since the spark delay valve resists the flow of carburetor vacuum, the vacuum will always flow through the vacuum solenoid when it is open, since this is the path of least resistance. When the ambient temperature rises above 60°F, the contacts in the temperature switch (which is located in the door post) close. This passes ignition switch current to the solenoid, energizing the solenoid. This blocks one of the two vacuum paths. All distributor vacuum must now flow through the spark delay valve. When carburetor vacuum rises above a certain level on acceleration, a rubber valve in the spark delay valve blocks vacuum from passing through the valve for from 5 to 30 seconds. After this time delay has elapsed, normal vacuum is supplied to the distributor. When the vacuum solenoid is closed (temperature above 60°), the vacuum line from the solenoid to the distributor is vented to atmosphere. To prevent the vacuum that is passing through the spark delay valve from escaping through the solenoid into the atmosphere, a one-way check valve is installed in the vacuum line from the solenoid to the distributor.

The EGR system consists of a control valve, a temperature-controlled vacuum switch, and a special carburetor mounting spacer. A hole that is drilled in the carburetor flange on the intake manifold passes exhaust gases from the manifold crossover passage into the carburetor spacer. A plunger which is attached to the EGR valve normally prevents the exhaust gases from entering the engine. When the engine coolant temperature reaches 125°F, the EGR vacuum valve opens and connects carburetor vacuum to the EGR valve. Under high carburetor vacuum conditions, the EGR valve opens and recirculates exhaust gases into the engine. This lowers peak combustion temperature and reduces oxides of nitrogen.

The spark delay is connected into the distributor vacuum line and closes on hard acceleration to prevent carburetor vacuum from reaching the distributor. After a predetermined number of seconds, the spark delay valve opens and carburetor vacuum is again connected to the distributor.

To meet the standards of the revised California emission controls, all California engines for 1974 are equipped with the Ford Thermactor system, Exhaust Gas Recirculation (EGR) and the Ford Improved Combustion (IMCO) system.

The Thermactor system keeps hydrocarbon and carbon monoxide emissions at the required level, while the EGR and IMCO systems are designed to reduce oxides of nitrogen.

On models made after 15 March 1973, the ambient temperature controls were removed from the DVB and EGR systems.

1974

The EGR-CSC system regulates distributor spark advance and EGR valve operation, according to coolant temperature, by sequentially switching vacuum sources. The major components are:

a. 95°F EGR-PVS valve,
b. spark delay valve (SDV), and
c. a vacuum check valve.

When coolant temperature is below 85°F, the EGR-PVS valve admits carburetor EGR port vacuum (at about 2500 rpm) directly to the distributor advance diaphragm through a one-way check valve. At the same time, the EGR-PVS valve shuts off carburetor EGR vacuum to the EGR valve and transmission diaphragm.

When coolant temperature is above 95°F, the EGR-PVS valve is actuated and admits carburetor EGR vacuum to the EGR valve and transmission instead of the distributor. At temperatures between 82° and 95°F, the EGR-PVS valve may be open, closed, or in midposition.

The CTAV system (Cold Temperature Actuated Vacuum) consists of an ambient temperature switch, a 3-way vacuum switch, an inline vacuum bleed and a relay. The system is used to more accurately match spark advance to engine requirements in cold ambient temperature conditions. When ambient air temperatures are below 49°F, spark port vacuum is selected for distributor modulation. When ambient temperatures reach 65°F, the system selects EGR vacuum. In between, the system selects either port, depending on the cycle it is in.

1975-79

Lincoln uses catalytic converters on all models starting 1975. To supply air to the converter, the air injection (Thermactor) system has been modified considerably for the first time since its introduction. For information concerning both air injection changes and catalytic converters, see Emission Control Systems in the Unit Repair Section.

A cold start spark advance (CSSA) system has been added to improve cold engine operation. When the coolant temperature is below 125° F, manifold vacuum is routed to the distributor vacuum unit. Above 125° F, carburetor ported vacuum is routed to the distributor through a spark delay valve and coolant temperature operated vacuum valve (PVS).

Another aid to cold engine operation is a cold weather modulator, which is added to the heated air intake system. When the ambient temperature is below 55° F and the engine is cold, the cold weather modulator prevents the door in the air cleaner snorkle from opening to the fresh air position under hard acceleration. Above 55° F, the door works the same as in other years; i.e., opening under hard acceleration or when the engine has reached normal operating temperatures.

All engines have spacer entry EGR valves. The EGR valve is mounted on a spacer which is located beneath the carburetor. This replaces the "floor entry" system used on some 1974 engines.

An electric choke was added in 1975 to open the throttle plates sooner in temperatures above 60° F. At temperatures lower than 60° F, there is no current supplied to the choke, and normal thermostatic choke action occurs. At temperatures above 60°, current is supplied and the throttle plates are opened within 1-1/2 minutes.

Positive crankcase ventilation (PCV) and evaporative emission control systems are carryovers from previous years.

For system checks and adjustments, see Emission Control Systems in the Unit Repair Section.

ENGINE

The 460 cu. in. engine has canted valves, individual bolt mounted rocker arms, semi-hemispherical combustion chambers, tunnel ports, and a block split at the crankshaft centerline. Through 1976, this engine was used exclusively; in 1977, a 400 cubic inch engine was introduced. The 400 cu. in. engine is the same one found in other full size Ford and Mercury products. **NOTE: Only service procedures for the 460 engine are given in this section. See the Ford, Mercury, Thunderbird section for 400 engine procedures.**

ENGINE REMOVAL

Engine Removal and Installation is for the engine only, without the transmission attached.
1. Raise the hood, and cover or mask all parts of the car that could be scratched during Removal and Installation procedures.
2. Set the parking brake and raise the

car. Put stands beneath the underbody front crossmember.

3. Drain the engine cooling system and the engine oil pan.

4. Scribe the hinge outline on the underside of the hood. Remove the hood.

5. Remove the crankcase vent filter hose from the air cleaner. Remove the carburetor air cleaner and air inlet duct assembly. Disconnect the battery ground.

6. Remove both engine radiator hoses.

7. Disconnect heater hoses at intake manifold and water pump. Disconnect power brake and power booster line from the intake manifold connection and position it to one side.

8. Disconnect heater vacuum hose from the intake manifold.

9. Disconnect automatic transmission vacuum line at the intake manifold. Disconnect all vacuum lines at the rear of the manifold.

10. Remove transmission tube slotted bracket from the right rear exhaust manifold mounting stud.

11. Disconnect battery ground strap at cylinder block.

12. Disconnect primary wires at the coil. Disconnect wires from temperature-sending unit and the fast idle solenoid.

13. Disconnect wire from oil pressure-sending unit. Detach wiring loom from valve rocker arm cover and position it out of the way.

14. Disconnect transmission fluid lines at the radiator. Remove transmission fluid filter from underbody side member (if car is so equipped).

15. Remove fuel hose mounting bracket from radiator. Remove the radiator. Remove heat shield from fuel pump.

16. On air-conditioned cars, remove fan drive clutch to water pump pulley retaining bolts. Remove fan drive clutch, fan and compressor pulley from the car as a unit.

17. Remove fan blade and spacer assembly from water pump pulley.

18. On vehicles equipped with air conditioning, disconnect the compressor electrical lead and remove the compressor mounting bracket attaching bolts. Remove the compressor from the engine and position it out of the way without disconnecting the refrigerant lines.

— CAUTION —

If the compressor refrigerant lines do not have enough slack to position the compressor out of the way without disconnecting the refrigerant lines, the air conditioning system will have to be evacuated by a trained air conditioning serviceman. Under no circumstances should an untrained person attempt to disconnect the air conditioning refrigerant lines.

19. Remove the alternator mounting bolts and position the alternator out of the way without disconnecting the wires.

20. Disconnect the transmission and accelerator linkage at the bellcrank. Secure the linkage to the firewall for engine clearance purposes. Disconnect speed control cable.

21. Remove access cover from the converter housing. Remove underbody splash shield at lower front of transmission.

22. Remove resonator inlet pipes from the exhaust manifolds.

23. Remove the power steering pump mounting bracket from the engine and position the pump and bracket out of the way.

24. Remove the nuts and washers that hold the engine front support insulators to the underbody side members.

25. Remove the starter attaching bolts. Remove the starter.

26. Detach the oil cooler inlet and outlet transfer line retaining clip from the cylinder block. Remove the block-to-converter housing supports. Remove the converter access plate.

27. Remove the flywheel to converter retaining nuts.

28. Remove lower converter housing to cylinder block retaining bolts.

29. Install a transmission support under the transmission.

30. Remove the upper converter housing to cylinder block retaining bolts.

31. Attach engine lifting eyes to the manifolds.

32. Install lifting sling and attach to chain hoist. With plenty of help, carefully raise and remove engine from car. Check to make sure that everything is disconnected from the engine before lifting the engine.

33. Install by reversing removal procedure. Torque the converter bolts to 20-30 ft. lbs., and the transmission to engine bolts to 40-50 ft. lbs.

MANIFOLDS

Intake Manifold Removal and Installation

1. Drain the cooling system.

2. Disconnect the upper radiator hose from the thermostat housing and the bypass hose from the intake manifold.

3. Remove the air cleaner and ducts from the engine.

4. Disconnect the spark plug wires from the spark plugs and remove the distributor cap and wires from the engine as an assembly. Mark the position of the distributor rotor in relation to the intake manifold, remove the primary wire from the coil and the distributor hold-down bolt, then, remove the distributor from the engine. Detach the dis-

tributor wire connector with solid state ignition.

5. Remove all vacuum lines from the intake manifold and the wire from the temperature sending unit. Remove the PCV valve and hoses.

6. Disconnect all fuel and vacuum lines from the carburetor.

7. Remove all carburetor and kickdown linkage that attaches to the intake manifold. Remove the air injection supply tubes and check valve at the rear of the cylinder heads. Remove the coil and bracket.

8. Remove the manifold attaching bolts and remove the manifold. If it is necessary to pry the manifold to loosen it from the engine, use care not to damage any gasket sealing surfaces.

9. Clean all gasket surfaces.

10. Apply a 1/8 in. diameter bead of silicone rubber sealer in and along the joint, the full width of the cylinder block mounting surface. Do this in all four corners.

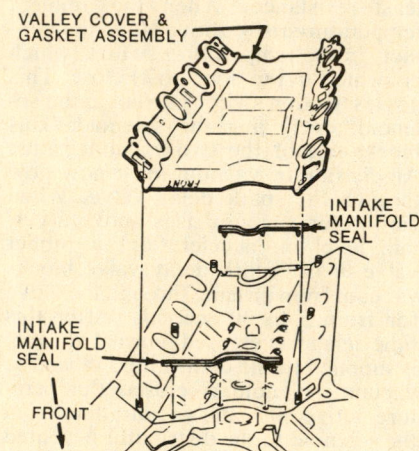

Installing 460 engine intake manifold gasket and seals (© Ford Motor Co.)

11. Install the head to manifold gaskets and the manifold gasket assembly, along with the front and rear manifold to block seals. Apply a bead of sealer at the outer end of each manifold seal.

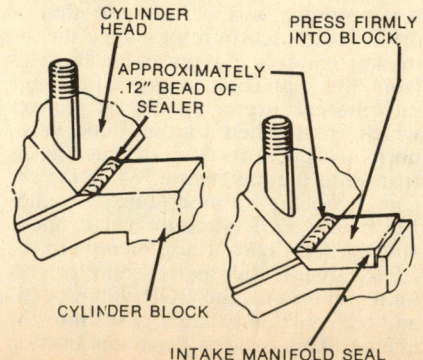

Applying silicone sealant to the cylinder block and intake manifold seals on the 460 engine (© Ford Motor Co.)

12. Lower the manifold into place. Run a finger around the edge of the manifold to make sure the seals are still in place, especially in the back.
13. Tighten the manifold bolts and nuts to the specified torque, in the sequence shown. Replace all components removed, and fill the cooling system. Check the torques after the engine has warmed up to normal operating temperature.

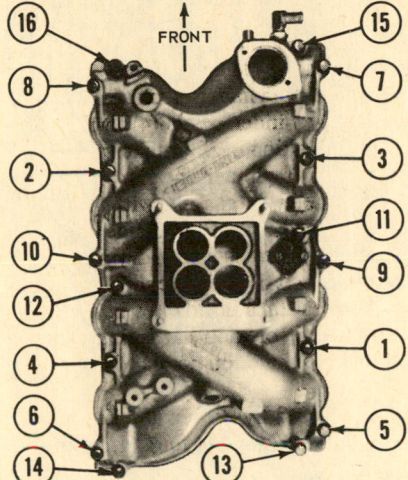

Intake manifold torque sequence
(© Ford Motor Co)

Exhaust Manifold Removal and Installation

1. Remove air cleaner and warm air duct assembly to remove right exhaust manifold.
2. Disconnect manifolds at exhaust pipe or catalyst.
3. Remove retaining bolts and washers, and remove manifolds and spark plug heat shields and lifting brackets.
4. Clean the mating surfaces and apply a light film of graphite grease as a sealant.
5. Position the heat shields and manifolds on the engine. Install the bolts and washers, starting at the fourth bolt hole from the front. On the right manifold, install the air intake heat shield studs at the first and sixth bolt holes from the front. Put the lifting brackets under the bolts at the third exhaust port from the front.
6. Torque the bolts, working from the center to both ends.
7. Replace all other items removed.

VALVE SYSTEM

Valve Guides

These engines use integral valve guides. Lincoln offers valves with oversize stems for worn guides. To fit these, enlarge valve guide bores with valve guide reamers to an oversize that cleans up wear. As an alternative, some local automotive machine shops will fit replacement guides that use standard stem valves.

Rocker Arm Assembly Removal and Installation

These rocker arms are of the pedestal-mounted-type and are removable, one at a time.

1. Remove the PCV valve and hose from valve rocker arm cover. Remove air cleaner and duct assembly. If removing an arm assembly from the left side, take off oil filler cap and air supply hose from valve rocker cover.
2. Disconnect plug wires at spark plugs. Twist, then pull, on molded cap of wire only. Do not pull the wire. Remove wires from bracket on the valve rocker arm covers and pull wires out of the way.
3. Remove rocker arm covers.
4. Remove rocker arm bolt, oil deflector, fulcrum seat, and rocker arm.
5. Apply white grease to top of valve stem.
6. Apply white grease to the folcrum seat and socket.
7. Install each rocker arm, folcrum seat, oil deflector, and bolt. Torque each bolt to 18-25 ft. lbs. To prevent bending pushrods or rocker arms, it is best to tighten the bolts in this sequence: Set no. 1 cylinder on TDC of the compression stroke and tighten intakes no. 1,7,8 and exhausts no. 1,5,4. Turn the crankshaft 180 degrees clockwise and tighten intakes no. 4,5 and exhausts no. 2,6. Turn the crankshaft 270 degrees more and tighten intakes no. 2,3,6 and exhausts no. 3,7,8. Using this sequence, each rocker arm bolt is tightened with its valve closed.

NOTE: *Be sure that the fulcrum seat base is in its cylinder head slot before tightening the bolt.*

8. Clean rocker arm covers and cylinder head gasket surfaces.
9. Apply oil-resistant sealer to one side of new cover gaskets. Apply cemented side of gaskets in rim of covers.
10. Position covers on cylinder heads. Install and tighten the cover bolts.
11. Route spark plug wires in brackets on valve rocker covers. Reconnect plug wires.
12. Install heater tube assembly, if disconnected, and fill cooling system.
13. On the right rocker arm cover, install the PCV valve and hose.
14. Install air cleaner and duct. On the left rocker arm cover, install oil filler cap and air supply hose.

CYLINDER HEAD

Removal and Installation

1. Remove the intake manifold/carburetor assembly. See Intake Manifold section.
2. Disconnect the exhaust pipe or catalytic converter pipe from the exhaust manifold.

Chilton's TIME SAVER

The following is a method for replacing valve springs, oil seals or spring retainers without removing the cylinder head.

1. Purchase an air chuck with a spark plug hole adapter.
2. Remove the valve rocker cover. Remove the rocker arm from the valve to be worked on.
3. Remove the spark plug from the cylinder to be worked on.
4. Turn the crankshaft to bring the piston of this cylinder down, away from possible contact with the valve head. Sharply tap the valve retainer to loosen the valve lock.
5. Then turn the crankshaft to bring the piston in this cylinder to the Exact Top of its Compression Stroke.
6. Screw the air chuck fitting into the spark plug hole.
7. Hook up an air hose to the chuck and turn on the pressure (about 200 psi).
8. With a strong and constant supply of air holding the valve closed, compress the valve spring and remove the lock and retainer.

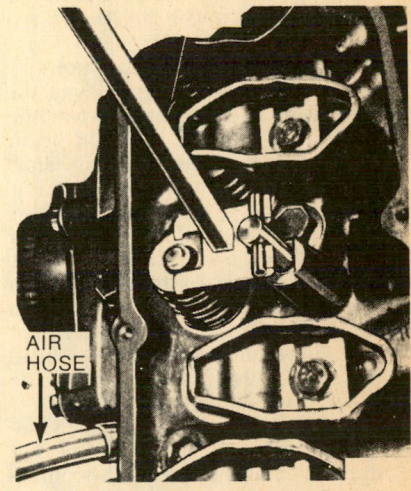

Compressing valve spring
(© Ford Motor Co.)

9. Make the necessary replacements and reassemble.
NOTE: It is important that the operation be performed exactly as stated, in this order. The piston in the cylinder must be on exact top-center to prevent air pressure from turning the crankshaft.

3. Loosen the A/C compressor drive-belt if necessary.
4. Loosen the alternator bolts and remove the alternator/air pump bracket from the cylinder head.

5. Set the A/C compressor out of the way without disconnecting its lines. See Intake Manifold for the specific procedure. Remove the compressor support bracket-to-water pump nuts. Remove the upper compressor bracket from the cylinder head.

6. If not equipped with A/C, remove the power steering pump bracket from the head. Position the pump and bracket out of the way without disconnecting the power steering lines.

7. Remove the valve covers and rocker assemblies, as detailed earlier. Remove the rockers in sequence and number them to aid in correct installation.

8. Remove the head bolts. Lift the heads and exhaust manifolds off as assemblies.

NOTE: *If necessary, pry the forward corners of the heads at the bosses provided on the block, in order to loosen the head gasket. Be careful not to damage the machined surfaces. Discard the gaskets.*

9. If the head is to be machined or disassembled, separate the exhaust manifolds from it.

Installation is as follows:

1. Clean the head, intake manifold, rocker cover, and block gasket surfaces.

2. If the exhaust manifolds were separated from the head, apply graphite grease around the port areas on the manifolds and head. Install the manifold and gasket.

3. Place long cylinder head bolts in the two rear lower bolt holes of the left head. Place a long bolt in the rear lower hole on the right head. Secure the bolts with rubber bands to aid in installation.

4. Fit new head gaskets over the dowels on the block. Do not use sealer on the head gasket surfaces.

5. Lower the head on the block. Align the exhaust manifold studs with the exhaust or converter pipe.

6. Install the remaining cylinder head bolts. The long bolts go in the lower row of holes.

7. Tighten the bolts in proper sequence in three stages, to the figures given in the Torque Specifications chart.

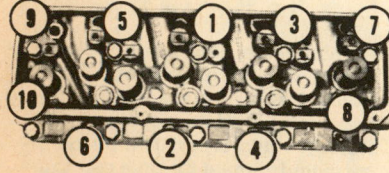

Cylinder head torque sequence
(© Ford Motor Co)

8. Install the push rod and valve rocker assemblies in their original positions as detailed earlier.

9. The remainder of the cylinder head installation procedure is the reverse of removal.

TIMING CASE COVER, CHAIN AND SPROCKETS

Removal and Installation

The front cover oil seal should be replaced whenever the cover is removed.

1. Drain cooling system.
2. Drain crankcase.
3. Remove fan blades from water pump shaft.
4. Remove radiator (fan) shroud.
5. Disconnect all radiator hoses at engine. Disconnect transmission cooler lines.
6. Remove radiator.
7. Loosen alternator and air pump. Loosen air conditioner idler pulley. Remove drive belts with water pump pulley.
8. Remove and set aside air conditioner compressor (do not open compressor lines.)
9. Remove crankshaft pulley attaching bolt and washer. Remove damper and remove Woodruff key from crankshaft.
10. If necessary, disconnect power steering pressure line at pump. Drain fluid.
11. Remove steering pump.
12. Loosen by-pass hose at water pump. Disconnect heater hose at pump.
13. Disconnect and plug fuel inlet line at fuel pump. Disconnect fuel line at carburetor fuel pump. Remove fuel pump.
14. Remove front cover-to-block and oil pan-to-cover attaching bolts. Use a thin bladed knife to cut off the oil pan gasket flush with the engine block, before separating the front cover from the block. Remove front cover and water pump as an assembly. Discard gasket.
15. If a new front cover is to be installed, change the water pump at this time.
16. Check timing chain deflection, at this time, by rotating crankshaft enough to take up the slack on one side of the chain. Establish a reference mark on the block and measure from this point to the chain. Turn the crankshaft the other way to loosen the side of the chain being measured. Pull the chain out with your fingers and measure again. The difference in measurements should not exceed 1/2 in. If it is more than 1/2 in., replace chain and both sprockets.
17. If chain and sprockets are being removed, crank the engine until timing marks on the sprockets are aligned at their closest points on a center line with crankshaft and camshaft centers.
18. Remove camshaft sprocket capscrew, washer, and fuel pump eccentric. Slide off timing chain, sprockets and chain as an assembly.
19. Replace the cover seal, as explained later.

On installation:

1. Install chain and sprockets as an assembly with sprocket timing marks directly toward each other and on a centerline with the crankshaft and camshaft.

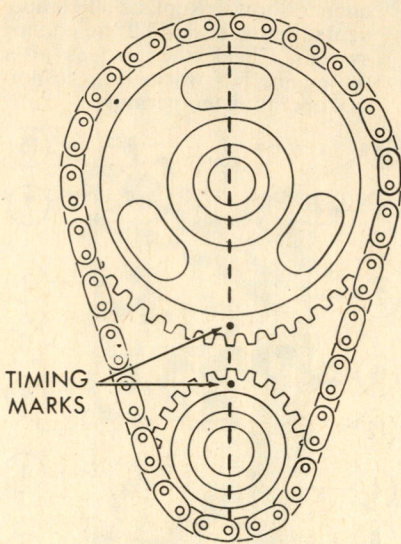

Valve timing alignment marks

2. Install fuel pump eccentric, washer, and attaching cap screw. Torque camshaft sprocket attaching screw to 40-45 ft lbs. Lubricate chain and sprockets with engine oil.

3. Coat the exposed gasket surface of the oil pan with sealer. Cut and position part of a new pan gasket, using sealer at the corners. After cleaning mating surfaces, coat the areas with oil-resistant sealer and position gasket on cylinder block.

4. Position cover over crankshaft and slide cover on against cylinder block. Coat cover retaining screws with oil-resistant sealer and install screws. Torque attaching screws to 10-13 ft lbs.

5. Install power steering pump (if removed).

6. Apply white grease to the front of the crankshaft. Install crankshaft damper Woodruff key and press on crankshaft damper. Do not hammer damper into place. Install damper retainer screw and washer. Tighten to the specified torque.

7. Coat new fuel pump gasket with oil-resistant sealer and place on fuel pump. Install fuel pump. Connect fuel lines to fuel pump.

8. Install air-conditioner compressor and water pump.

9. Install water pump pulley and all drive belts.

10. Position radiator to lower support, position upper support to radiator retaining bolts. Connect all coolant hoses. Connect transmission fluid cooler lines.

11. Place fan assembly inside radiator shroud and set in position on water pump hub. Install shroud to radia-

tor screws and tighten. Insert and tighten fan attaching screws.

12. Adjust belt tension. Tighten alternator and air pump retaining bolts and compressor idler pulley.

13. Fill cooling system. Fill crankcase.

14. Run engine at fast idle and check for coolant and oil leaks. Set ignition timing.

Oil Seal Removal and Installation

The front cover oil seal should be replaced whenever the cover is removed.

1. Drive the old oil seal out with a punch.
2. Clean out the oil seal recess.
3. Coat a new oil seal with grease.
4. Install the new seal in the cover. Be sure that the seal spring is in the correct position.

Camshaft Removal and Installation

1. Remove the hood assembly. If the hood is properly aligned, index the hinges to the hood prior to removing the hood, in order to simplify installation.
2. Remove the intake manifold, referring to the procedure under Intake Manifold Removal and Installation.
3. Remove the distributor and the valve covers.
4. Back off the rocker arm bolts, turn the rocker arms sideways, and remove the push rods and lifters. Keep them in order. Remove the valve lifters with a magnet. Keep them clean and in order.
5. Remove the timing chain and camshaft sprocket.
6. Remove the radiator. Remove the grille.
7. If the car is equipped with an air conditioner, cover the left front fender, lift the condenser out of the engine compartment with the lines still attached, and rest it on the covered fender.
8. Remove the camshaft thrust plate bolts and plate. Remove the camshaft from the front of the cylinder block, taking care not to damage any of the camshaft bearing surfaces.
9. Lubricate the camshaft journals with engine oil. Use engine assembly lubricant on the lobes. Install the camshaft in the engine, using care to prevent damage to the camshaft bearings. Care should also be exercised to see that the rear camshaft bearing plug does not become dislodged in the process of installing the camshaft. Check camshaft end play with a dial indicator. It should be 0.001-0.006 in. Adjust by replacing the thrust plate. On assembly, lubricate the lifters and their bores with thick oil. Use engine assembly lubricant or white grease on the pushrod and valve ends.

PISTONS AND CONNECTING RODS

These assemblies are installed with the notch or arrow in the piston crown facing forward and the matched, numbered side of the rod facing the outside of the block.

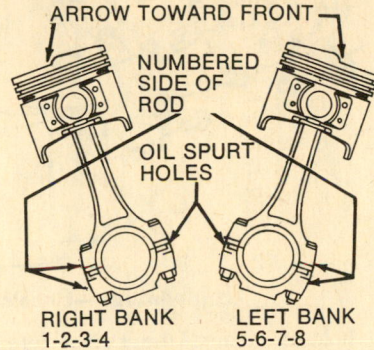

ARROW TOWARD FRONT

NUMBERED SIDE OF ROD

OIL SPURT HOLES

RIGHT BANK 1-2-3-4   LEFT BANK 5-6-7-8

Correct piston and rod positions for 460 engines

ENGINE LUBRICATION

Oil Pan Removal and Installation

1. Disconnect the negative battery cable.
2. Disconnect the fan shroud from the radiator and position it rearward over the fan.
3. Drain the crankcase and remove the oil filter. Remove the X-brace below the pan on the Mark V.
4. On Mark III and Mark IV models, disconnect the transmission cooler lines from the radiator. Remove the bolt that attaches the cooler line bracket to the cylinder block.
5. Remove the end attachments of the front stabilizer bar and rotate the ends downward.
6. Remove the starter attaching bolts.
7. Remove the engine mount to chassis attaching bolts and raise the front of the engine about 3 inches.

8. Place blocks of wood between the mounts and the chassis.
9. Remove the converter housing to engine block support bracket bolts and remove the brackets.
10. Remove the oil pan attaching bolts and remove the pan from the engine. On Mark III and IV models, it will be necessary to move the cooler lines out of position to remove the pan.
11. Clean all gasket mounting surfaces. Coat the block gasket surfaces with gasket cement. Stick the pan gaskets to the block. Position the pan front seal on the front cover. Be sure the tabs are over the oil pan gasket. Position the pan rear seal on the rear main bearing cap. Be sure the tabs are over the pan gasket. Tighten the pan bolts from the center out.
12. The rest of the job is the reverse of removal.

Oil Pump Removal and Installation

1. Remove the oil pan, referring to the procedure for Oil Pan Removal and Installation.
2. Remove the oil pump mounting bolts and remove the pump from the cylinder block.
3. Prime the oil pump by filling the inlet port with clean engine oil. Rotate the pump shaft so that the oil is evenly distributed within the pump body.
4. Install distributor intermediate shaft within the oil pump rotor shaft. Apply oil-resistant sealer to the new oil pump mounting gasket and install the gasket on the oil pump.
5. Insert the intermediate shaft into the distributor shaft hex bore. Make sure that the intermediate shaft is properly seated. Do not attempt to force the pump into position if it does not seat readily, as

INSTALL SEAL WITH LIP TOWARDS FRONT OF ENGINE

FRONT OF ENGINE

3/8"

SEAL HALVES TO PROTRUDE BEYOND PARTING FACES THIS DISTANCE TO ALLOW FOR CAP TO BLOCK ALIGNMENT.

3/8"

REAR FACE OF REAR MAIN BEARING CAP AND CYLINDER BLOCK

VIEW—LOOKING AT PARTING FACE OF SPLIT LIP TYPE CRANKSHAFT SEAL

Rear main seal installation (© Ford Motor Co)

the intermediate shaft hex may be misaligned with the distribtor shaft. To align, rotate the intermediate shaft until it can be seated. Secure the oil pump to the cylinder block and torque the screws to 20-25 ft lbs. As you secure the oil pump, make certain that the gasket is properly installed; leakage resulting from improper gasket installation could cause loss of oil pressure and subsequent engine damage.

6. Install the oil pan and its related parts.

Rear Main Bearing Oil Seal Removal and Installation

See the Ford section for this procedure.

AUTOMATIC TRANSMISSION

All Lincolns and Continentals use a Ford C6 automatic transmission. This heavy-duty three-speed unit is capable of providing automatic upshifts and downshifts through the three forward gear ratios, in addition to offering manual selection of first and second gears.

Only one band—the intermediate band—is used in this transmission. This band, along with the forward clutch, is used to obtain the intermediate gear. The adjustment of this band is the only adjustment required for the C6 transmission.

Shift Linkage Adjustment

1. With the engine off, place the selector lever against the stop in the D position. Weight the lever to

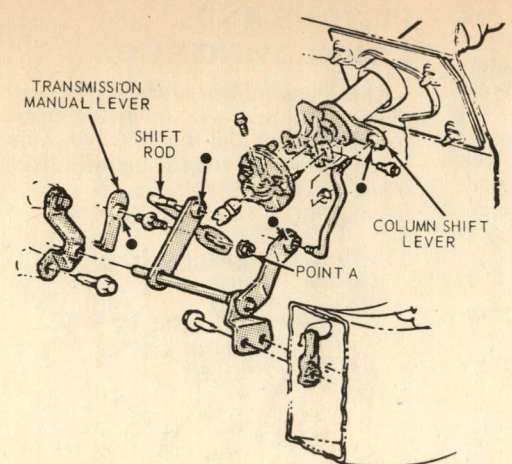
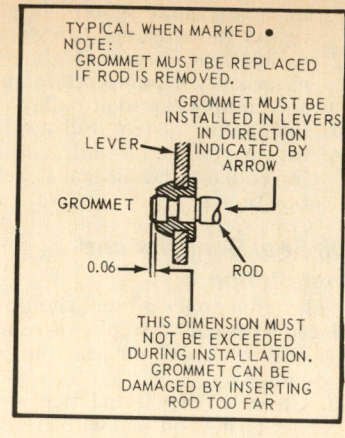

Shift linkage—Lincoln Continental (© Ford Motor Co)

hold it against the Drive detent stop. Raise the car, and remove linkage splash shield, if any.
2. Disconnect the adjustable link from the cable end at the transmission on the Mark IV and V. On the Continental, loosen the adjusting nut on the linkage.
3. Be sure the transmission shift lever is fully engaged in Drive, the second detent position from full counterclockwise.
4. Tighten the adjustment.
5. Check selector lever through all positions to secure correct adjustment.

Downshift Rod Adjustment

1. Remove the air cleaner for access.
2. Hold the carburetor linkage at the wide open throttle position. Hold the transmission downshift rod down against the stop.

3. Adjust the downshift rod adjusting screw to get the correct clearance between the screw and the throttle arm. It should be 0.050-0.070 in. for 1972, and 0.010-0.080 in. for 1973 and later.
4. Replace the air cleaner.

Intermediate Band Adjustment

1. Raise the car on a hoist or place it on jack stands.
2. Clean threads of the intermediate band adjusting screw.
3. Remove the old locknut and install a new one.
4. Tighten the adjusting screw to 10 ft lbs, and back the screw off exactly 1½ turns. Tighten the adjusting screw locknut.

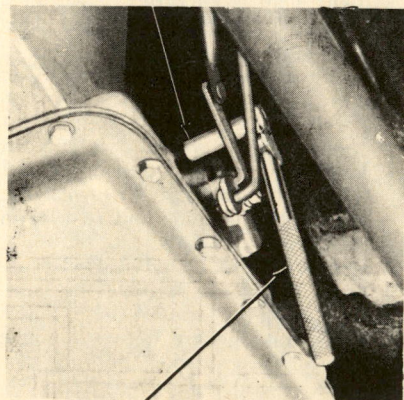

Intermediate band adjustment
(© Ford Motor Co)

Pan Removal, Fluid and Filter Change

1. Raise the vehicle and support it securely. Place a container beneath the transmission.
2. Loosen the transmission pan bolts and allow the fluid to drain into the container. When the fluid has drained to the transmission pan flange level, remove the bolts, working from the rear, to allow the fluid to drain slowly.
3. Remove the pan and clean it. Discard the gasket.

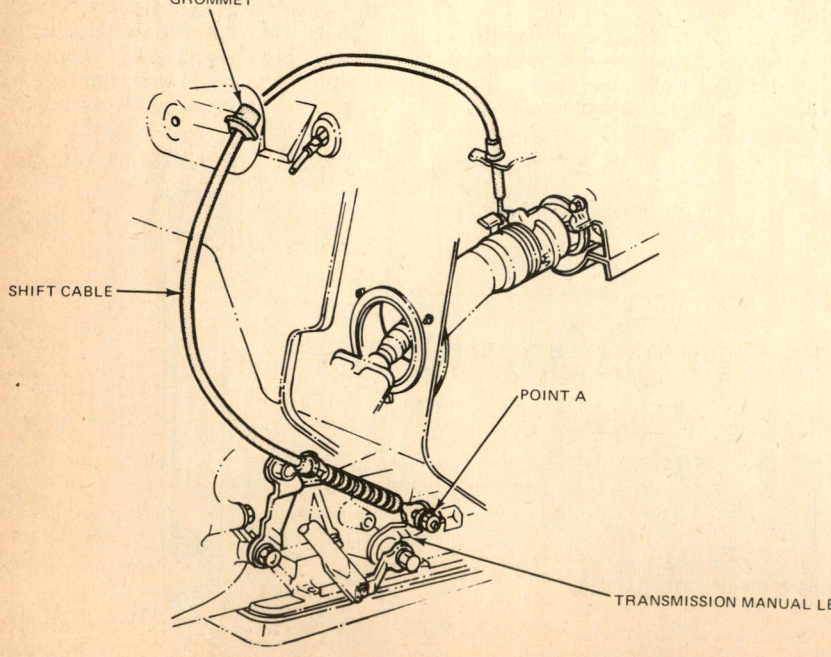

Shift linkage—Mark IV and V (© Ford Motor Co)

4. Clean the filter screen.
5. Place a new gasket on the pan. Install the pan.
6. Add three quarts of fluid through the filler tube. Through 1976 use Type F, for 1977 and later use Type CJ.
7. Run the engine, move the selector lever through all gear ranges. Check the fluid level; add fluid as necessary.

U-JOINTS

The Mark IV and V use a driveshaft with a conventional, or single cardan, universal joint at each end. The Continental uses a driveshaft with double cardan, or constant velocity, universal joints at each end. The double cardan joint can transmit power at greater U-joint angles, with less vibration, than can the single cardan joint. This is especially desirable with longer wheelbase vehicles.

Driveshaft Removal and Installation
1. Matchmark the rear driveshaft yoke and the rear axle drive pinion flange.
2. On Mark IV and V, disconnect the rear U-joint from the rear axle flange. Tape on the loose bearing caps so they don't fall off.
3. On Continental, disconnect the driveshaft from the circular rear axle flange.
4. Pull the driveshaft to the rear until it is free of the transmission.
5. Plug or cap the rear of the transmission to prevent leakage.
6. Grease the transmission yoke spline. Install the yoke on the transmission output shaft. Be careful not to let the yoke assembly bottom heavily on the output shaft.
7. Align the matchmarks at the rear.
8. On the Mark IV and V, install the U-bolts and nuts holding the u-joint to the rear axle flange. Tighten the nuts to 8-15 ft. lbs.
9. On the Continental, install the bolts and nuts, and torque to 70-90 ft. lbs.

U-Joint Overhaul
MARK IV AND V
This procedure is covered for all Ford Motor Company products in the Bobcat car section.

CONTINENTAL THROUGH 1977
These cars use the Dana design double cardan joint.
1. Matchmark all the spiders, yokes, and major components, so that proper balance will be maintained after reassembly.
2. Remove the snap-rings holding the bearings in the front of the center yoke.

Details of the Continental driveshaft and double cardan U-joints through 1977 (© Ford Motor Co.)

3. Use a clamp or vise and a suitable size socket to push in on one bearing until the opposite one sticks out about 3/8 in.
4. Hold the protruding bearing in a vise and drive the center yoke free.
5. Remove the two bearings.
6. Repeat Steps 3 through 5 to remove the other two bearings. Remove the spider from the center yoke.
7. Pull the centering socket yoke off the center stud. Remove the rubber seal.
8. Press the bearing out of the driveshaft yoke until the inside of the center yoke almost contacts the slinger ring at the front of the yoke.
9. Hold the protruding bearing in a vise and drive the center yoke free. Remove the opposite bearing.
10. Remove the center yoke from the spider. Remove the spider from the driveshaft yoke.
11. Clean all parts in solvent. Repair kits are available, containing all the parts that usually wear.
On assembly:
12. Position the spider in the driveshaft yoke. Assemble the needle bearings into the cups, using grease to hold them in place. Grease the spider bearing journals. Make sure the spider bosses or lubrication plugs will be in the original locations. Press in the bearing cups and install the snap-rings.
13. Position the center yoke over the spider ends and press in the bearing cups. Install the snap-rings.
14. Install a new seal on the centering ball stud. Place the centering socket yoke on the stud.
15. Place the front spider in the center yoke. Proceed as in Step 12.
16. Apply pressure on the centering socket yoke to install the last bearing cup.
17. Remove the plug, if any, from spi-

der and grease the U-joints. Replace the plugs.

1978 AND LATER CONTINENTAL
These cars use double cardan joints with a removable centering ball. Original equipment bearing caps are retained by molded plastic retainers which shear off on disassembly. Do not take one of these joints apart unless a repair kit is on hand.
1. Matchmark all the yokes to retain original balance on reassembly.
2. Use the procedure for Continental Through 1977, Steps 3 through 5, to remove the bearings.
3. Remove all the remains of the plastic retaining rings from the yoke grooves. It helps to use a small punch through the injection holes.
4. There is a special centering ball remover tool which may be used to pull off the centering ball. Once the ball is removed, the seal can be pried out to remove the washers, spring, and three ball seats. If the ball seat insert bushing is worn, replace the flange yoke.

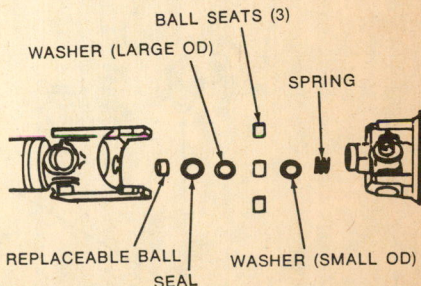

Details of the double cardan U-joint centering ball replaceable components used on Continental starting 1978 (© Ford Motor Co.)

5. Using the special grease supplied in the ball seat repair kit, lubricate all the parts and insert them into

the ball seat cavity: spring, washer (small), three ball seats, large washer, and seal. Lubricate the seal lip and install the seal flush into the flange yoke with the sealing lip inward. Press the ball into place.

6. Use the procedure for Continental Through 1977, Steps 12 and 13, to install the bearing cups and snaprings. If there is any binding, rap the yoke ears slightly with a hammer to relieve it.

JACKING AND HOISTING

See the Ford section for jacking and hoisting instructions.

REAR AXLE

These cars all use a Ford Motor Company removable carrier rear axle, which does not use C-locks to retain the axle shafts. For axle shaft, bearing, and seal removal and installation, see the Ford car section.

FRONT SUSPENSION

All models have a front suspension system in which the coil springs are supported on the lower control arm. Each side of this independent front suspension uses two ball joints—upper and lower. Shock absorbers are positioned within the coil springs and are affixed to the lower suspension member and the top of the spring tower.

See the Ford section for all service procedures.

REAR SUSPENSION

The rear suspension is the coil spring type. The Continental rear axle is lo-cated by two lower control arms between the axle and frame, one upper control arm between the axle and frame through 1976, two upper control arms starting 1977, and a track bar linked laterally between the axle and frame. The Mark IV and V use two upper and two lower control arms and a stabilizer bar.

Spring Removal and Installation

1. Place car on hoist and lift under rear axle housing. Place jack stands under frame side rails.
2. Disconnect rear shock absorbers from the rear axle housing brackets.
3. On Continental, disconnect the rear of the front-to-back brake tube at the No. 4 crossmember bracket. Remove the clip.
4. Lower hoist with axle housing until coil springs are released.
5. Remove spring and insulator.
6. Position the spring with an insulator between the upper end of the frame and the spring seat.
7. Raise the axle housing and connect the shock absorbers.

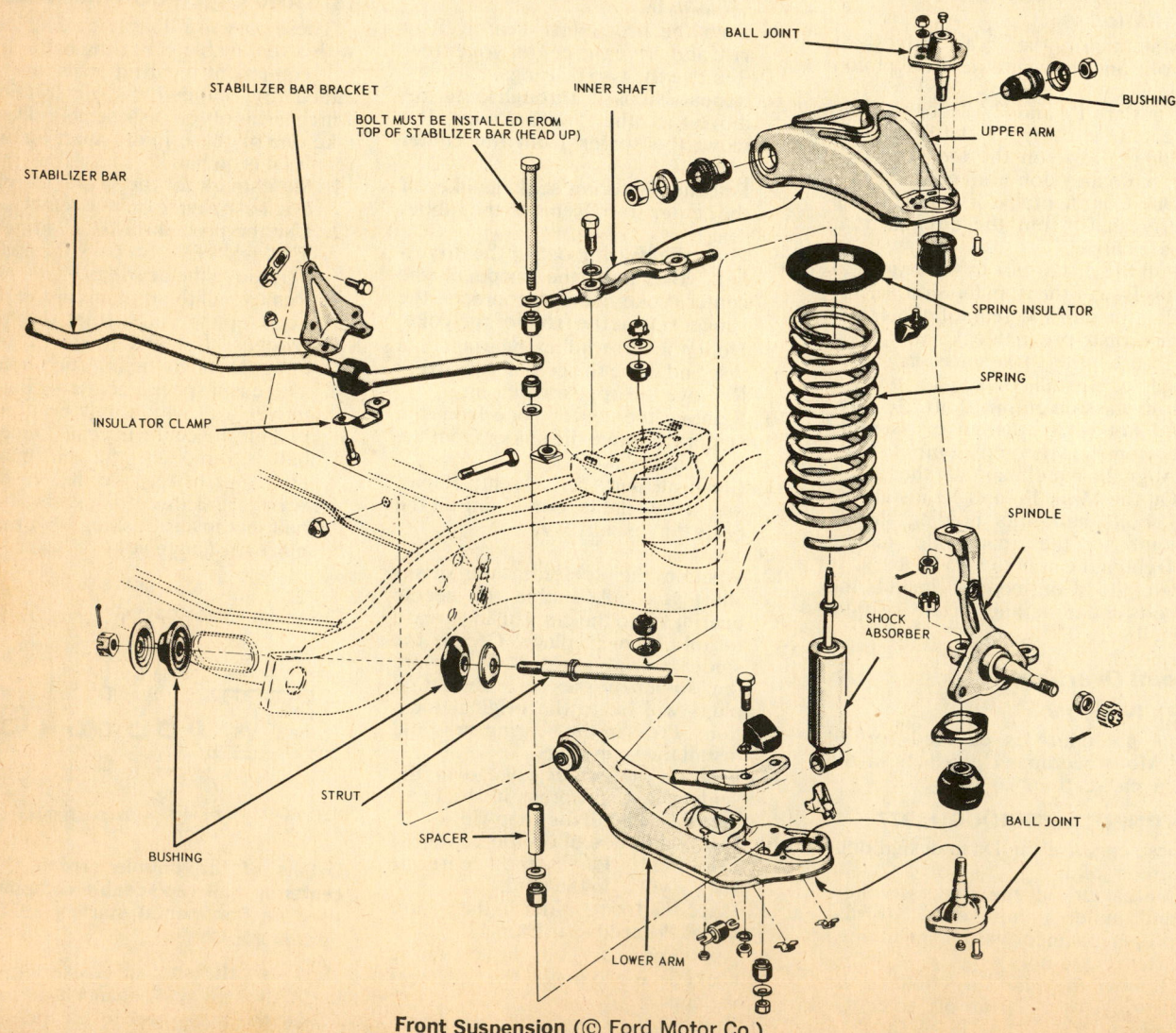

Front Suspension (© Ford Motor Co.)

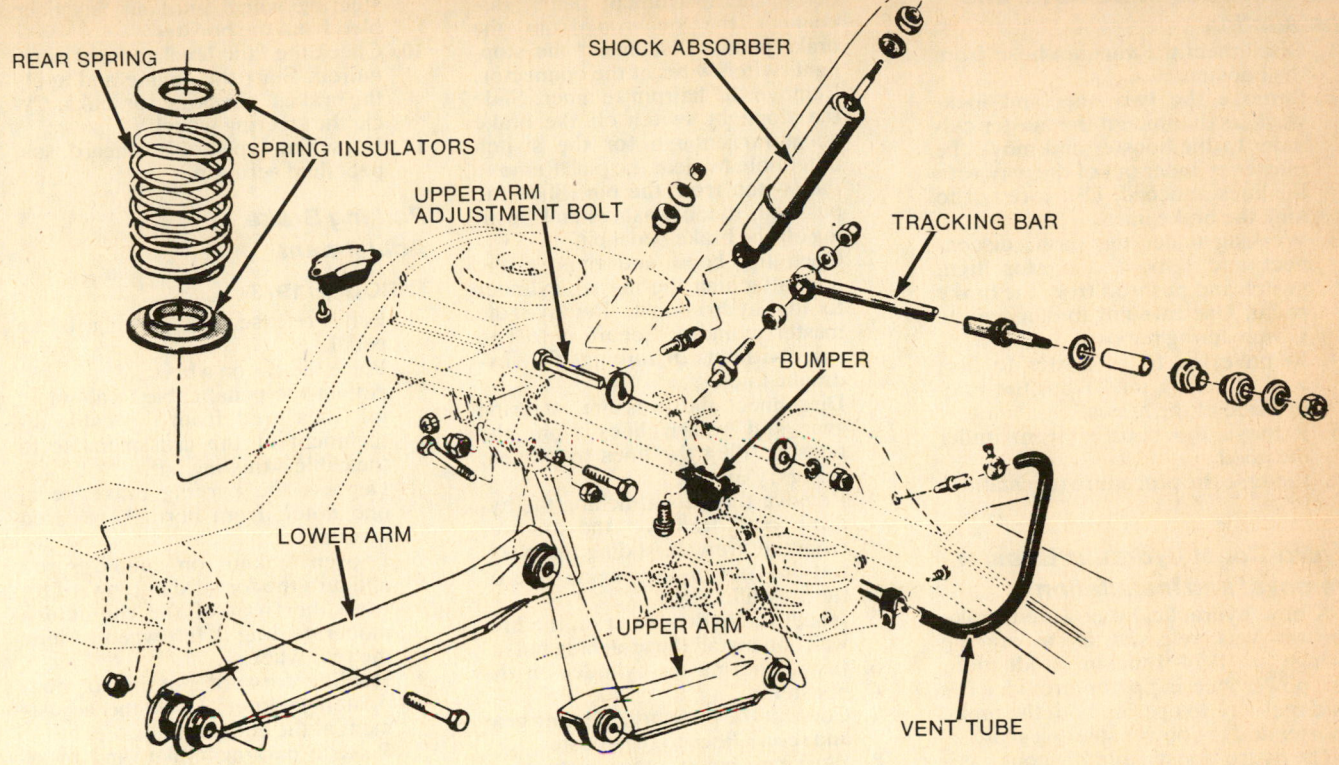

Rear suspension (© Ford Motor Co)

8. Replace the brake hose and bleed the brakes.

Shock Absorber Removal and Installation

1. Raise the vehicle.
2. Remove the shock absorber attaching nut, washer, and insulator from the upper stud at the upper side of the spring upper seat. Compress the shock absorber to clear the hole in the spring seat and remove the inner insulator and washer from the upper attaching stud.
3. Remove the self-locking attaching unit and disconnect the shock absorber lower stud from the mounting bracket on the rear axle housing.
4. Remove the shock absorber from the car.
5. Reverse the procedure to install the new shock absorber.

NOTE: *Purge new shocks of air by repeatedly extending them in their normal position and compressing them while inverted.*

BRAKES

Master Cylinder Removal and Installation

1. Disconnect the brake lines from the master cylinder.
2. Remove the two nuts and lockwashers that attach the master cylinder to the brake booster.
3. Slide the master cylinder forward until it clears the booster pushrod,

then remove the master cylinder from the car.
4. Reverse the procedure to install; but leave the brake lines loose on the master cylinder.
5. Fill the master cylinder with fluid and, using the foot pedal, slowly

bleed the air from the master cylinder.
6. Tighten the brake lines, fill the master cylinder, then, bleed the brake system at the front and then the rear wheels.
7. Refill master cylinder.

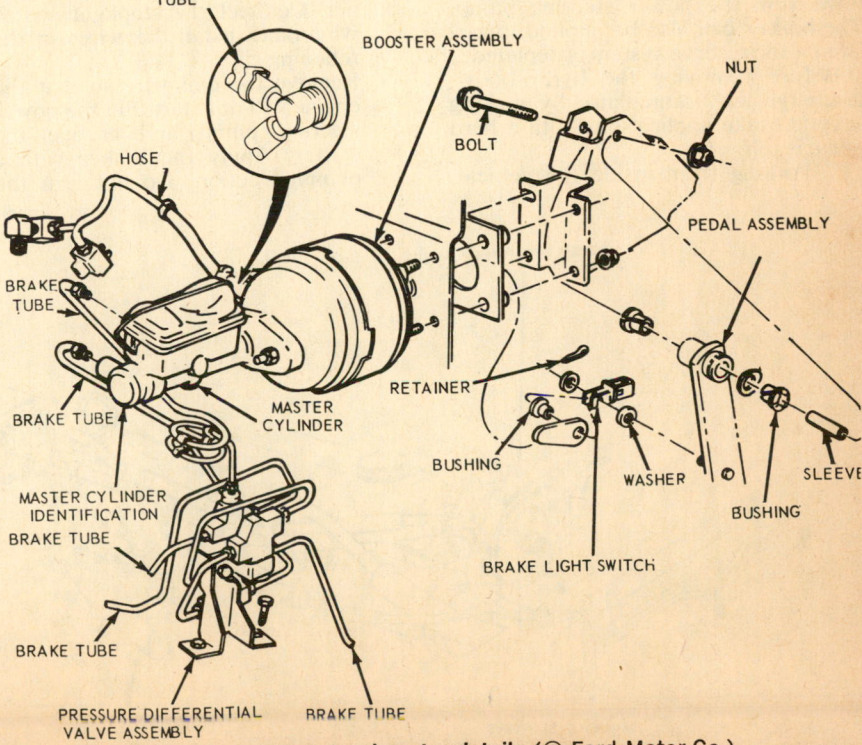

Brake pedal and vacuum booster details (© Ford Motor Co.)

Vacuum Booster Removal and Installation

1. Disconnect the vacuum hose from the booster.
2. Remove the two nuts and lockwashers that mount the master cylinder to the booster and move the master cylinder out of the way with the lines attached. Use care not to kink the brake lines.
3. Working under the dash, disconnect and remove the stop light switch and pushrod from the brake pedal. Use care not to damage the switch during removal.
4. Remove the four booster to firewall attaching nuts from the interior side of the firewall.
5. Remove the booster from under the hood.
6. Reverse the procedure to install.

Hydro-Boost Hydraulic Booster Removal and Installation

A new hydraulically powered brake booster was released as a running change in 1974 Lincoln production. The power steering pump provides the fluid pressure to operate both the brake booster and the power steering gear.

The hydro-boost assembly contains a valve which controls pump pressure while braking, a lever to control the position of the valve and a boost piston to provide the force to operate a conventional master cylinder attached to the front of the booster. The hydro-boost also has a reserve system, designed to store sufficient pressurized fluid to provide at least 2 brake applications in the event of insufficient fluid flow from the power steering pump. The brakes can also be applied unassisted if the reserve system is depleted.

Before removing the hydro-boost, discharge the accumulator by making several brake applications until a hard pedal is felt.

1. Working from inside the vehicle, below the instrument panel, disconnect the pushrod from the brake pedal. Disconnect the stoplight switch wires at the connector. Remove the hairpin retainer. Slide the stoplight switch off the brake pedal far enough for the switch outer hole to clear the pin. Remove the switch from the pin. Slide the pushrod, nylon washers and bushing off the brake pedal pin.
2. Open the hood and remove the nuts attaching the master cylinder to the hydro-boost. Remove the master cylinder. Secure it to one side without disturbing the hydraulic lines.
3. Disconnect the pressure, steering gear and return lines from the booster. Plug the lines to prevent the entry of dirt.
4. Remove the nuts attaching the hydro-boost. Remove the booster from the firewall, sliding the pushrod link out of the engine side of the firewall.
5. Install the hydro-boost on the firewall and install the attaching nuts.
6. Install the master cylinder on the booster.
7. Connect the pressure, steering gear and return lines to the booster.
8. Working below the instrument panel, install the nylon washer, booster pushrod and bushing on the brake pedal pin. Install the switch so that it straddles the pushrod with the switch slot on the pedal pin and the switch outer hole just clearing the pin. Slide the switch completely onto the pin and install the nylon washer. Attach these parts with the hairpin retainer. Connect the stoplight switch wires and install the wires in the retaining clip.
9. Remove the coil wire so that the engine will not start. Fill the power steering pump and engage the starter. Apply the brakes with a pumping action. Do not turn the steering wheel until air has been bled from the booster.
10. Check the fluid level and add as required. Start the engine and apply the brakes, checking for leaks. Cycle the steering wheel.
11. If a whine type noise is heard, suspect fluid aeration.

Parking Brake Adjustment

THROUGH 1973

1. Fully release the parking brake pedal.
2. Raise the car on a hoist.
3. Adjust the pedal cable to about 10 in., measured from the cable attachment at the crossmember to the cable adjusting nut.
4. Depress the parking brake pedal one notch from normal, released position.
5. Loosen locknut on equalizer rod and turn the forward nut inward toward the front of the car until a moderate drag is felt when turning the rear wheels.
6. Holding forward nut in position, tighten locknut. Lock the adjustment at the equalizer.
7. Release parking brake, and make sure that the brake shoes return to the fully released position.

1974 AND LATER REAR DRUM

1. Make sure that the parking brake is fully released.
2. Place the transmission in Neutral.
3. Raise the vehicle on an axle-type hoist.
4. Tighten the adjusting nut against the cable equalizer or cable adjusting rod to cause rear wheel brake drag. Loosen the adjusting nut until the rear brakes are fully released. There should be no brake drag. Tighten the locknut.
5. Lower the vehicle and check the operation of the parking brake.

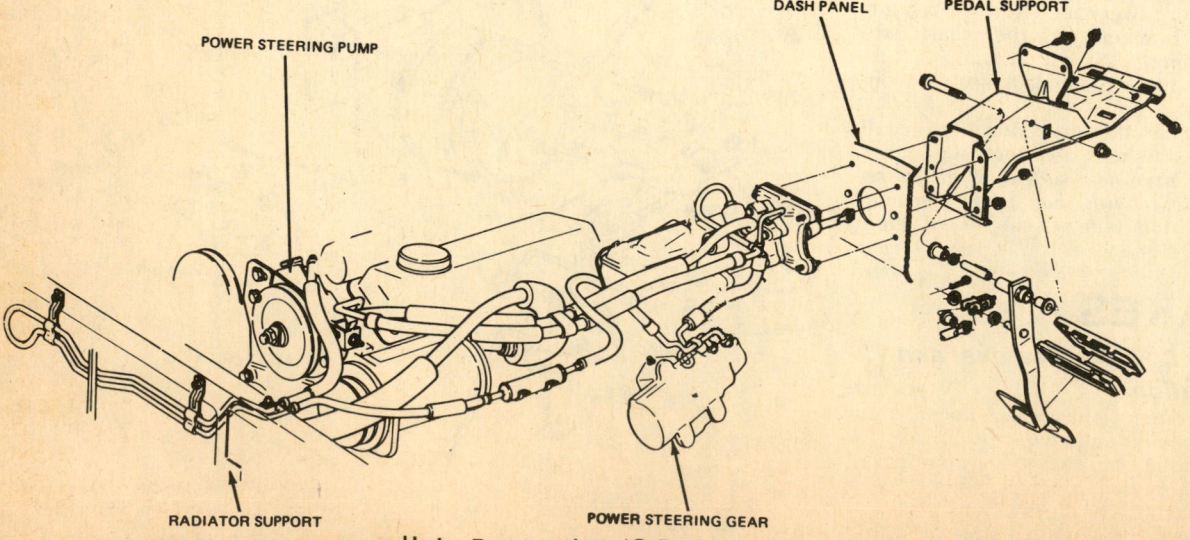

Hydro-Boost system (© Ford Motor Co)

1974 AND LATER REAR DISC

1. Fully release the parking brake. Place the transmission selector in Neutral.
2. Raise the vehicle on an axle-type hoist.
3. Tighten the adjusting nut until the levers on the caliper just start to move.
4. Loosen the adjusting nut just enough to obtain complete return of the levers to the stop position.
5. Apply and release the parking brakes. Check the caliper levers to see if they are at full stop, by trying to pull them rearward. Check that a 1/4 in. drill bit can be freely inserted past the side of the lever into the hole in the caliper housing.
6. If the levers can be moved rearward or the drill bit won't fit, the adjustment is too tight. Repeat the adjustment.

STEERING

Steering Wheel Removal and Installation

1. Disconnect the negative battery cable.
2. If the vehicle is equipped with a horn ring, remove it by rotating it counterclockwise. If equipped with a steering wheel crash pad, remove the retaining screws from the underside of the steering wheel and then remove the crash pad. Disconnect the horn and speed control (if so equipped) wires from the inside of the steering wheel center.
3. Remove the steering wheel nut, install a steering wheel puller on the end of the shaft, and remove the steering wheel.

--- CAUTION ---

The use of a knockoff type steering wheel puller and a hammer is inadvisable, as they may damage the steering column bearing or (in the case of the collapsible-type steering wheel) the column itself.

4. With the front wheels positioned straight ahead, line up the marks on the steering wheel and column and install the steering wheel and the locknut. Tighten the nut to 30-40 ft. lbs.
5. Connect the horn and speed control wires and install the horn ring and the crashpad and retaining screws.
6. Connect the negative battery cable.

Turn Signal Switch Removal and Installation

1. Disconnect the negative battery cable.
2. Remove the steering wheel as outlined in the Steering Wheel Removal and Installation section.
3. Unscrew the turn signal lever from

the side of the column. Remove the emergency flasher retainer and knob.
4. Locate and remove the finish cover on the steering column and disconnect the wiring connector plugs.
5. On all models with a tilt steering column, it is necessary to separate the wires from the connector plug in order to remove the switch and wires. First note the location and color code of each wire, prior to removal. Remove the plastic cover from the wiring harness. Attach a piece of heavy cord to the switch wires to pull them down through the column during installation.
6. Remove the retaining clips and screws from the turn signal switch and lift the switch and wire assembly from the top of the column.
7. Tape the ends of the new switch wires together and transfer the pull cord to these wires.
8. Pull the wires down through the columns with the cord and attach the new switch to the column hub.
9. If the switch wires were separated from the connector plug, press the wires into their proper location. Connect the wiring connector plugs and install the finish cover on the column.
10. Install the turn signal lever. Install the emergency flasher retainer and knob, if so equipped.
11. Install the steering wheel as outlined in the Steering Wheel Removal and Installation section.
12. Connect the negative battery cable and test the operation of the turn signals, horn, emergency flashers, and speed control, if so equipped.

Power Steering Pump Removal and Installation

See the Ford section for all procedures.

Tie-Rod Removal and Installation

1. Raise the front of the vehicle and install jackstands.
2. Remove the cotter pin and nut from the tie-rod end ball stud.
3. Loosen the tie-rod sleeve clamp bolts. Remove the tie-rod end from the center link with a puller.
4. Separate the tie-rod end from the sleeve, counting the number of turns required.

Discard all of the tie-rod end assembly parts which were removed from the sleeve. Use all new parts when the tie-rod ends are replaced.

Installation is as follows:

1. Thread a new tie-rod end into the sleeve. Turn it in the same number of turns required to remove the old one. Don't tighten the sleeve clamp bolts yet.
2. Install a new seal (if used) on the tie-rod end ball stud.
3. Install the stud and nut. Tighten to 43-47 ft lbs. Continue tightening the nut until the next slot aligns with the hole in the stud. Secure with a new cotter pin.
4. Check the toe-in and adjust it as necessary.
5. Loosen the sleeve clamps. Oil the clamps, bolts, sleeve, and nuts.
6. Tighten the clamp nuts.

Ignition Lock Cylinder, Ignition Switch Removal and Installation

See the Ford Section.

INSTRUMENT PANEL

Light Switch Replacement

CONTINENTAL WITHOUT HEADLAMP DELAY SYSTEM

1. Disconnect battery.

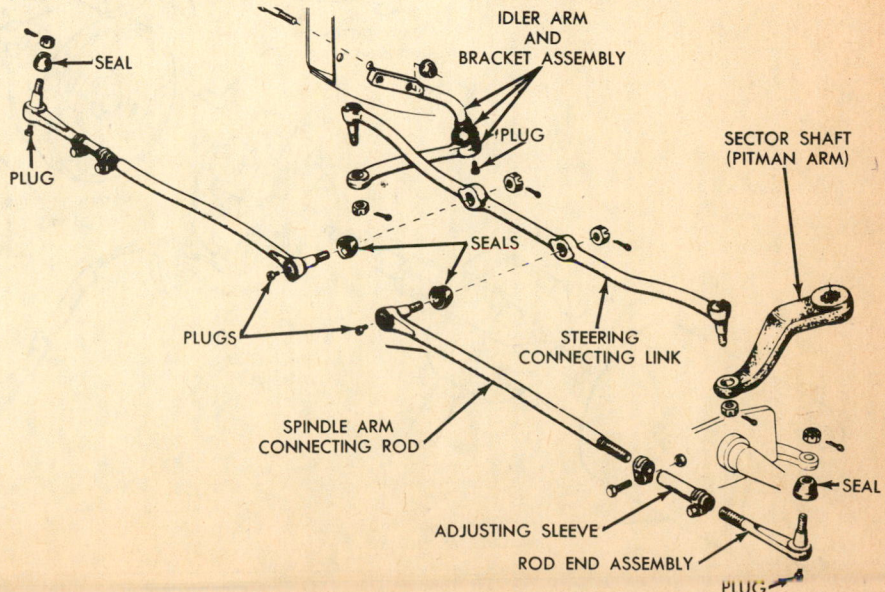

Disassembled view of typical steering linkage (© Ford Motor Co)

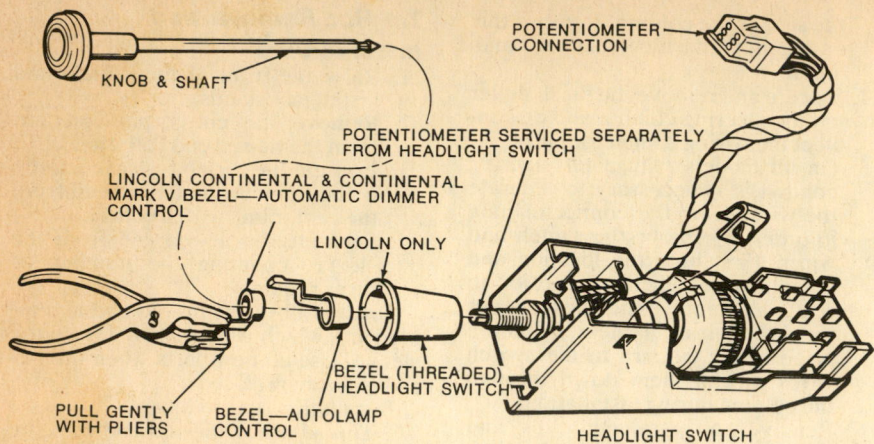

Details of the headlight switch used with the Autolamp headlamp delay system (© Ford Motor Co.)

2. Remove knob and shaft by pressing release knob button on switch housing behind the instrument panel with knob in full on position.
3. Remove moulding nut from switch.
4. Remove the wiring connector from switch.
5. Reverse the procedure for installation.

MARK IV AND V WITHOUT HEADLAMP DELAY SYSTEM

1. Remove the instrument cluster trim panel.
2. Remove the lighting switch mounting plate.
3. Remove the bezel nut and disconnect the multiple connector.
4. Remove the vacuum lines and the switch.
5. Reverse the procedure to install.

CONTINENTAL, MARK IV, MARK V WITH HEADLAMP DELAY SYSTEM

This system, called Autolamp, keeps the headlights on for a preselected period of time after the ignition is turned off. It was first available in 1974.

1. Disconnect the battery ground cable.
2. Remove the switch knob and shaft.
3. Carefully pull the two control bezels out with pliers. There will be only one bezel if the car doesn't have automatic dimmer control.
4. Unscrew the threaded headlight switch bezel. On Continental, remove the screw at the rear corner of the bracket. On Mark IV and V, remove the cluster opening finish panel.
5. On Mark IV and V, remove the four screws from the bracket on the front of the switch.
6. Disconnect the wires and remove the switch. Note their locations and detach any vacuum lines. Remove the bracket from the switch on the Mk IV and V.
7. Reverse the procedure for installation.

Speedometer Cable Removal and Installation

1. Reach up behind the speedometer and depress the quick release tab while pulling back on the cable.
2. Pull the cable out, through the firewall.

NOTE: *Models with speed sensor have upper and lower cables.*

3. If the core is broken, raise and support the car and disconnect the cable from the transmission by removing the bolt holding the clip to the transmission. Remove the cable and driven gear. Take the clip off to separate the driven gear from the cable.

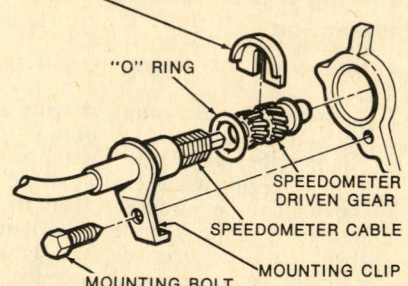

Speedometer cable at the transmission (© Ford Motor Co.)

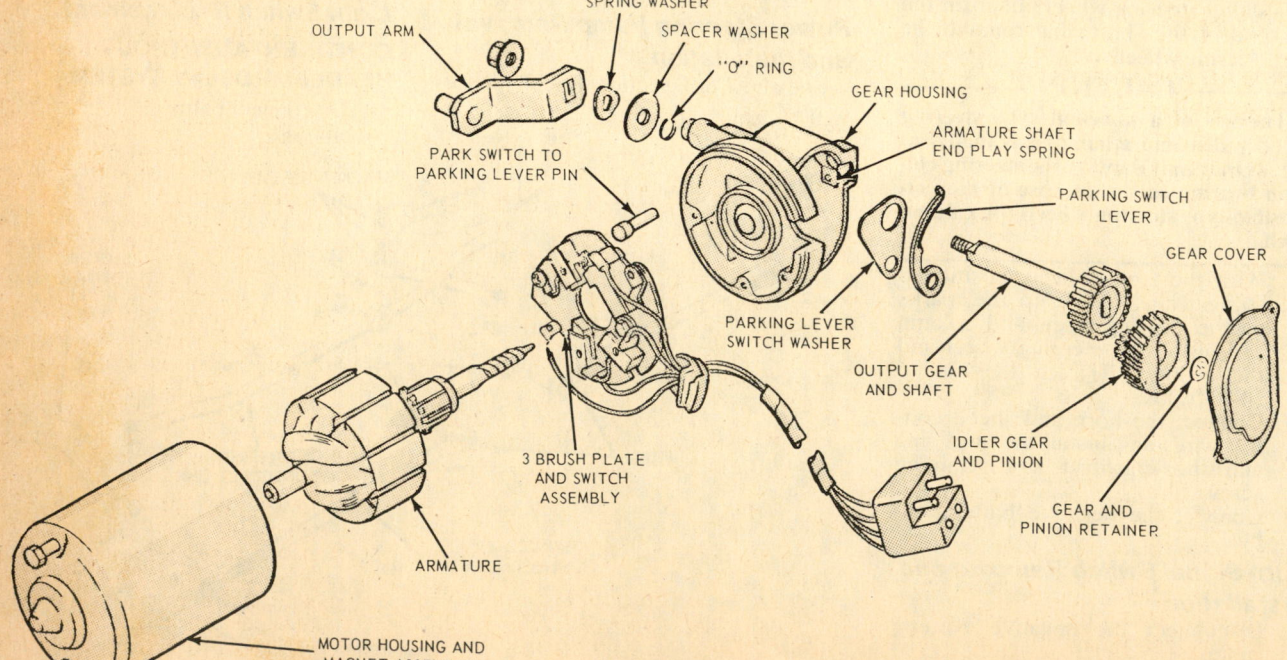

Wiper motor details (© Ford Motor Co.)

4. Remove the core from the cable.
5. Installation is the reverse of removal. Lubricate the core with speedometer cable lubricant before installing it in the casing.

WINDSHIELD WIPERS

Motor Removal and Installation

1. Disconnect battery.
2. Remove wiper arm and blade assemblies from pivot shafts.
3. Remove left cowl screen for access.
4. Disconnect linkage drive arm from motor output arm crank pin by removing retaining clip.
5. Disconnect two push on wire connectors from the motor.
6. Remove three bolts that retain motor and remove.
7. Reverse procedure to install. Be sure that output arm is in Park.

Blade Removal and Installation

Wiper blades are supplied by either Trico or Anco. They come in two attachment types: Bayonet and Side Pin. To remove a Trico bayonet type, depress the tab and pull the blade from the arm. To remove an Anco bayonet type, press inward on the button and remove the blade from the arm. To remove a Trico side pin type, depress the spring clip with a screwdriver and release the blade.

RADIO

Removal and Installation

1972 CONTINENTAL

1. Disconnect battery.
2. Remove map light assembly.
3. Remove lower instrument panel pad.
4. Remove glove box, open ashtray, and leave it open.
5. Remove glove box switch.
6. Through glove box opening remove two nuts retaining radio finish panel to instrument panel.
7. Remove two screws at top of finish panel. Position panel out and disconnect cigar lighter and light from right panel.
8. Through glove box opening remove nut from lower right corner of center finish panel.
9. Remove radio top support nut and three mounting screws. Pull radio out. Disconnect power leads and antenna cable. Remove radio.
10. Reverse procedure to install.

1973-77 CONTINENTAL

1. Disconnect the battery ground cable.
2. Remove the radio knobs.

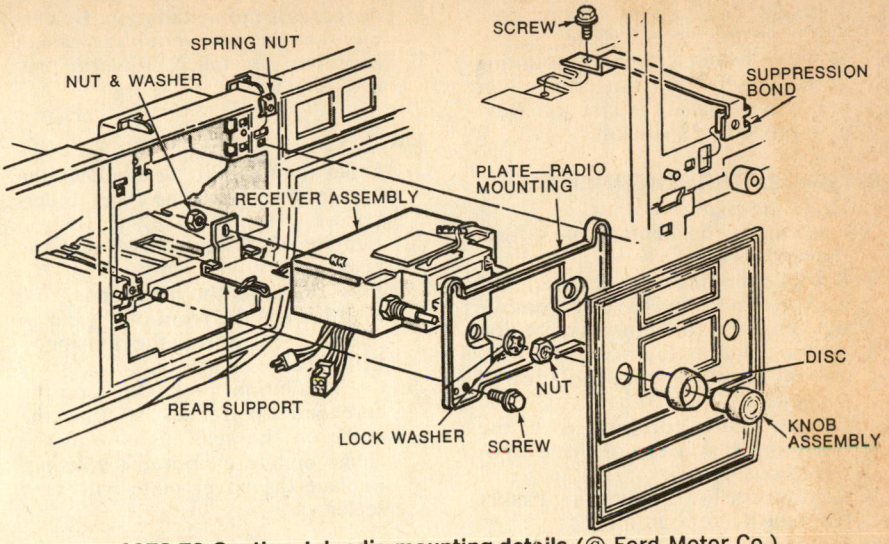

1978-79 Continental radio mounting details (© Ford Motor Co.)

3. Remove and disconnect the map light. It is held by three screws.
4. Remove the steering column shroud, ashtray door pad, and instrument cluster panel pad. Open the glove box.
5. Remove the center register applique. It is held by three screws and two nuts.
6. Detach the lighter and glove box light connectors.
7. Remove the nut holding the radio bracket-to-instrument panel tab. Remove the three screws holding the bracket to the panel.
8. Pull the radio out and disconnect the power, speaker, and antenna leads.
9. Remove the nuts and washers from the control shafts to remove the mounting plate. The rear mounting bracket is held on with one nut.
10. Reverse the procedure for installation.

1978-79 CONTINENTAL

1. Disconnect the battery ground cable.
2. Remove the knobs. Remove the screws holding the radio bezel plate to the instrument panel. Remove the screws holding the radio mounting plate.
3. Detach the radio from the lower rear support bracket.
4. Disconnect the power, antenna, and speaker leads.
5. Remove the mounting plate and rear upper support from the radio.
6. Reverse the procedure for installation.

MARK IV AND V

1. Disconnect the negative battery cable.
2. Pull the radio control knobs off the radio shafts. Disconnect and lower the Twilight Sentinel amplifier, if any.
3. Remove the nuts from both radio control shafts. Disconnect the air conditioning duct under the radio.

4. Remove the radio rear support to panel attaching screw. On some 1976 and later models, this screw was replaced with a rivet. In order to remove the rivet you must drill it out with a 1/4 in. drill bit. When you replace the radio, replace the rivet with a 1/4 in. nut and bolt.
5. Disconnect the radio power wires. Disconnect the speaker wires at the connectors.
6. Disconnect the antenna lead and remove the radio.
7. Reverse the procedure to install.

HEATER

Heater Core Removal

CONTINENTAL THROUGH 1973

1. Drain engine coolant.
2. Disconnect vacuum junction valve from dash panel and move valve and vacuum hoses away from case.
3. Disconnect speed control servo and bracket assembly, if so equipped, from dash panel and move it away from case.
4. Disconnect multiple connector from blower resistor and remove harness from clip on case.
5. Disconnect heater hoses from heater case and remove hose support clamp from case. Move hoses and water valve away from case.
6. Remove seven case cover to case flange attaching screws and wire harness clip.
7. Remove six cover to back plate stud nuts.
8. Remove one upper case to dash panel mounting screw.
9. Remove two case to dash panel mounting stud nuts, one on inboard mounting flange and one below case on lower flange.
10. Carefully move heater core assembly forward to clear mounting studs and lift up and out of vehicle.
11. Remove two spring clips from core tubes on front of core cover.

12. Remove three screws from core end plate and remove plate.
13. Remove heater core and mounting gasket assembly from core cover and remove gasket from core. Reverse procedure to install.

1974 AND LATER CONTINENTAL
1. Drain the engine coolant.
2. Disconnect the heater hoses from the heater core.
3. Remove the heater core cover and gasket. You may have to remove the engine vacuum distribution center and electrical harness ground terminal from the firewall for access.
4. Lift the heater core and lower the mounting gasket out of the evaporator housing.
5. Remove the lower mounting gasket from the heater core.
6. Installation is the reverse of removal.

MARK IV
1. Drain the engine coolant and disconnect the heater hoses from the heater core.
2. Remove the glove box.
3. Remove the heater air outlet register from the plenum assembly. It is held in position by two snap-rings.
4. Remove the temperature control cable assembly mounting screw, and disconnect the end of the cable from the blend door crank arm by removing the spring nut.
5. Remove the blue and red vacuum hoses from the high-low door vacuum motor, and the brown hose at the in-line tee connector to the temperature bypass door motor.
6. Disconnect the wire connector from the resistor.
7. Remove 10 screws from around the flange of the plenum case and remove the rear case half of the plenum.
8. Remove the mounting nut from the heater core tube support bracket.
9. Reinstall in the reverse procedure. To provide a positive seal between the front and rear case halves, apply body sealer around the case

flanges prior to installation. Be certain that the core mounting gasket is properly installed. Reverse procedure to install.

MARK V
1. Drain the coolant. Disconnect the heater hoses from the core, underhood.
2. Remove the four screws and the heater core cover plate.
3. Press down on the heater core and tip it toward the front of the car to release the seal from the housing.
4. Lift the core up and out.
5. On installation, press down on the core and tip it back so that the notch on the seal aligns with the flange on the evaporator housing. Replace the cover plate with new sealer.

Blower Motor Removal
CONTINENTAL
1. Remove hood.
2. Remove right hood hinge and right fender inner support brace as an assembly.
3. Disconnect blower motor air cooling tube from motor.
4. Disconnect motor lead wire from harness and ground wire from firewall.
5. Disconnect rear section of right front fender panel apron from fender around wheel opening and remove two lower fender to cowl mounting screws.
6. Separate fender apron from fender wheel opening so that apron can be pushed downward away from blower motor.
7. Remove four blower motor plate screws. Move motor and wheel forward out of blower scroll and remove assembly through opening while applying pressure to fender apron to enlarge opening at hinge area. Reverse procedure to install.

MARK IV
1. Remove the glove box for access.
2. Remove the recirculation air regis-

ter and duct assembly from the blower assembly.
3. Remove the two screws that attach the blower lower housing to the dash panel.
4. Disconnect the white hose from the outside-recirc air door vacuum motor and remove the vacuum motor from the blower lower housing. It is held in place by two screws. Leave the motor actuator connected to the door crank arm.
5. Disconnect the orange blower motor lead wire from the harness connector, and disconnect the black motor ground wire.
6. Remove the six upper-to-lower blower housing flange screws.
7. Separate the blower lower housing and motor assembly from the upper housing and remove it from beneath the instrument panel.
8. Remove the blower motor and wheel assembly from the lower housing. It is held by four screws.
9. The upper flange of the recirc duct is retained to the blower upper housing with two S-clips that remained on the housing during removal. Be certain that the duct is properly installed in the two clips during reinstallation. Reverse procedure to install.

MARK V
1. Remove the instrument panel pad and the glovebox.
2. Remove the side cowl trim panel. Remove the instrument panel attachment on the right side.
3. Remove the blower housing to firewall nut in the engine compartment. Remove the blower housing to firewall nut in the passenger compartment.
4. Remove the blower housing mounting bracket and cowl top inner screw.
5. Disconnect the white air door vacuum motor hose.
6. Disconnect the blower motor wire plug and the ground wire screw.
7. Remove the blower assembly.
8. Reverse the procedure for installation.

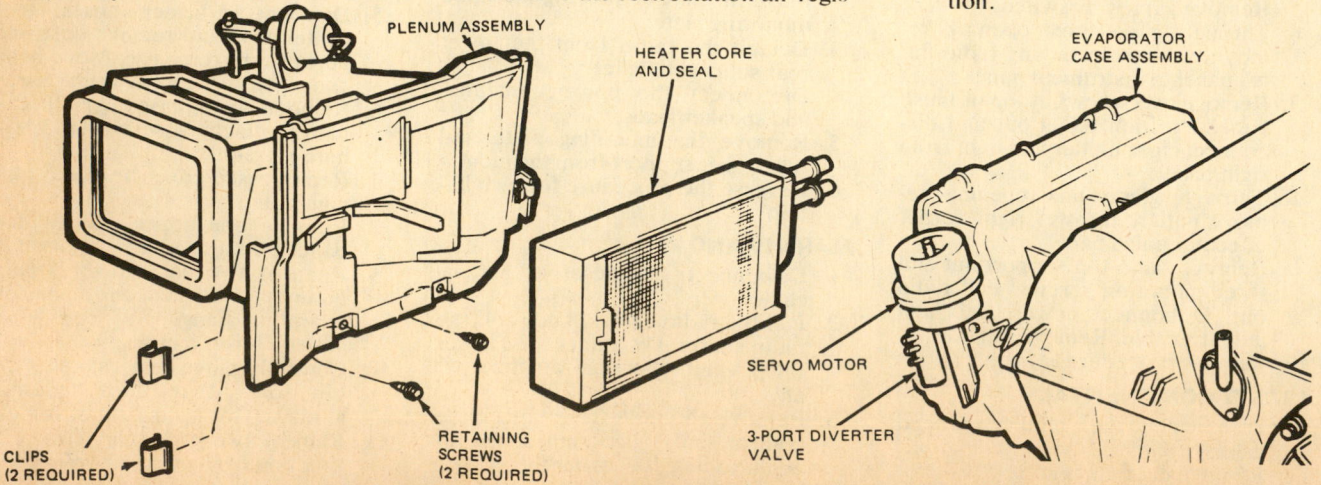

CLIPS (2 REQUIRED)   PLENUM ASSEMBLY   RETAINING SCREWS (2 REQUIRED)   HEATER CORE AND SEAL   SERVO MOTOR   3-PORT DIVERTER VALVE   EVAPORATOR CASE ASSEMBLY

1974-78 Continental heater core assembly (© Ford Motor Co.)

Index

Monza & Vega

1972

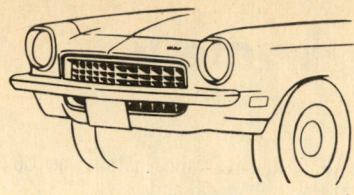

1973

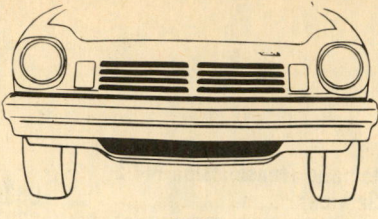

1974

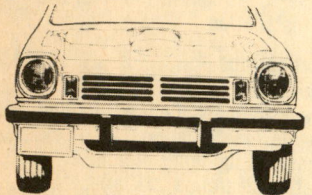

1975 Vega

1975 Monza 2 + 2

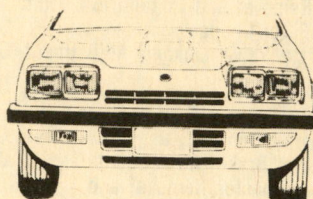

1975 Monza Town Coupe

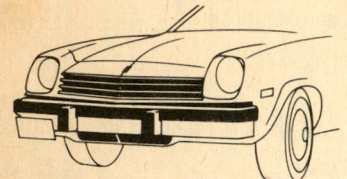

1976 Vega

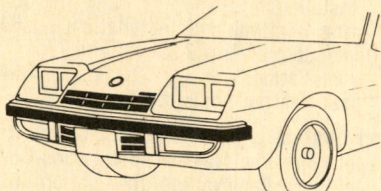

1976 Monza 2 + 2

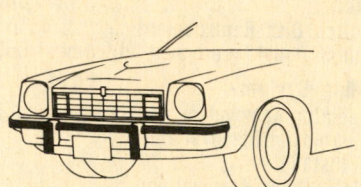

1976 Monza Town Coupe

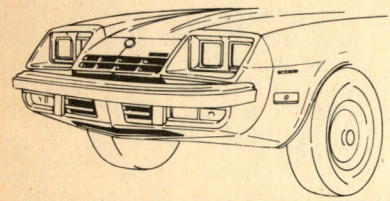

1977 Monza

1977 Vega

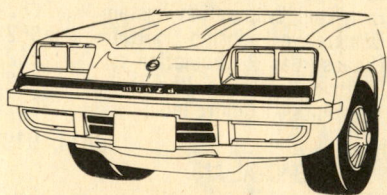

1978 Monza

1978 Monza Town Coupe

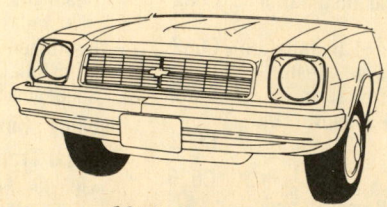

1979 Monza

ENGINE IDENTIFICATION

The engine identification code is the fifth digit of the Vehicle Identification Number, stamped on a plate located on the upper left corner of the instrument panel pad, visible through the windshield.

No. Cyls. Cu. In. Displ.	Manuf.	Carb. bbl	'72	'73	'74	'75	'76	'77	'78	'79
4-122 Cosworth	Chev.	EFI				0	0			
4-140	Chev.	1	A	A	A	A	A			
4-140	Chev.	2	B	B	B	B	B	B		
4-151	Pont.	2							V	V
6-196	Buick	2							C	C
6-231	Buick	2							A	A
8-262	Chev.	2				G	G			
8-305	Chev.	2					Q	U	U	U
8-350 Calif.	Chev.	2				H				

EFI: electronic fuel injection

GENERAL ENGINE SPECIFICATIONS

Year	Engine No. Cyl. Displacement (Cu. In.)	Carburetor Type	Horsepower @ rpm ■	Torque @ rpm (ft lbs) ■	Bore X Stroke (in.)	Compression Ratio	Oil Pressure @ 2000 rpm
'72	4-140	1 bbl	80 @ 4400	121 @ 2800	3.501 x 3.625	8.0:1	40
	4-140	2 bbl	90 @ 4800	121 @ 3200	3.501 x 3.625	8.0:1	40
'73	4-140	1 bbl	72 @ 4400	100 @ 2000	3.501 x 3.625	8.0:1	40
	4-140	2 bbl	85 @ 4800	115 @ 2400	3.501 x 3.625	8.0:1	40
'74	4-140	1 bbl	75 @ 4400	115 @ 2400	3.501 x 3.625	8.0:1	40
	4-140	2 bbl	85 @ 4400	122 @ 2400	3.501 x 3.625	8.0:1	40
'75	4-122	EFI	110 @ 5600	107 @ 4800	3.501 x 3.625	8.0:1	40
	4-140	1 bbl	78 @ 4200	120 @ 2000	3.501 x 3.160	8.5:1	40
	4-140	2 bbl	87 @ 4400	122 @ 2800	3.501 x 3.625	8.0:1	40
	4-140 Calif.	2 bbl	80 @ 4400	116 @ 2800	3.501 x 3.625	8.0:1	40
	8-262	2 bbl	110 @ 3600	200 @ 2000	3.671 x 3.100	8.5:1	32-40
	8-350 Calif.	2 bbl	125 @ 3600	235 @ 2000	4.000 x 3.480	8.5:1	32-40
'76	4-122	EFI	110 @ 5600	107 @ 4800	3.501 x 3.160	8.0:1	27-41
	4-140	1 bbl	70 @ 4400	107 @ 2400	3.501 x 3.625	8.0:1	27-41
	4-140	2 bbl	84 @ 4400	113 @ 3200	3.501 x 3.625	8.0:1	27-41
	8-262	2 bbl	110 @ 3600	195 @ 2000	3.671 x 3.100	8.5:1	32-40
	8-305	2 bbl	140 @ 3800	245 @ 2000	3.736 x 3.480	8.5:1	32-40
'77	4-140	2 bbl	84 @ 4400	117 @ 2400	3.501 x 3.625	8.0:1	27-41
	8-305	2 bbl	145 @ 3800	245 @ 2400	3.736 x 3.480	8.5:1	32-40
	8-305 Calif.	2 bbl	135 @ 3800	240 @ 2000	3.736 x 3.480	8.5:1	32-40
'78-'79	4-151 Pont.	2 bbl	85 @ 4400	123 @ 2800	4.000 x 3.000	8.3:1	36-41
	6-196 Buick	2 bbl	90 @ 3600	165 @ 2000	3.500 x 3.400	8.0:1	37
	6-231 Buick	2 bbl	105 @ 3400	185 @ 2000	3.800 x 3.400	8.0:1	37
	8-305 Chev.	2 bbl	145 @ 3800	245 @ 2400	3.736 x 3.480	8.4:1	32-40

■ Horsepower and torque are SAE net figures. They are measured at the rear of the transmission with all accessories installed and operating. Since the figures vary when a given engine is installed in different models, some are representative rather than exact.

EFI—Electronic Fuel Injection

Monza & Vega

TUNE-UP SPECIFICATIONS

	ENGINE		SPARK PLUGS		DISTRIBUTOR		IGNITION TIMING (deg) ▲		VALVES	Fuel Pump Pressure (psi)	IDLE SPEED (rpm) ▲ ●	
Year	No. Cyl Displacement	hp (cu in.)	Orig. Type	Gap (in.)	Point Dwell (deg)	Point Gap (in.)	Man Trans	● Auto Trans	Intake Opens ■ (deg) ●		Man Trans	Auto Trans
'72	4-140①	1 bbl	R42TS	.035	31-34	.019	6B	6B(4B)	22(28)	3-4½	700	700②/550
	4-140①	2 bbl	R42TS	.035	31-34	.019	8B	8B	28	3-4½	700	700②/550
'73	4-140①	1 bbl	R42TS	.035	31-34	.019	8B	8B	22	3-4½	1000/450	750/450
	4-140①	2 bbl	R42TS	.035	31-34	.019	10B	12B	28	3-4½	1200/450	750②/450
'74	4-140①	1 bbl	R42TS	.035	31-34	.019	10B(8B)	12B(8B)	22	3-4½	1000/700	750/550
	4-140①	2 bbl	R42TS	.035	31-34	.019	10B(8B)	12B(8B)	28	3-4½	1200/700	750②/500
'75	4-122③	EFI	R43TSX	.060	Electronic		12B	——	38	40	800	——
	4-140①	1 bbl	R43TSX	.060	Electronic		8B	10B	22	3-4½	1200/700	700/550
	4-140①	2 bbl	R43TSX	.060	Electronic		10B	12B	28	3-4½	1200/700	750/600
	8-262	2 bbl	R-44TX	.060	Electronic		8B	8B	26	7-8½	800	600
	8-350	2 bbl	R-44TX	.060	Electronic		——	6B	28	7-8½	——	600
'76	4-122③	EFI	R-43LTS	.035	Electronic		12B	——	38	40	600	——
	4-140	1 bbl	R-43TS	.035④	Electronic		8B	10B	34	3-4½	700⑤	750
	4-140	2 bbl	R-43TS	.035④	Electronic		10B	12B	34	3-4½	700	750
	8-262	2 bbl	R-45TS	.045	Electronic		6B	8B(TDC)	26	3-4½	800	600
	8-305	2 bbl	R-45TS	.045	Electronic		——	8B(TDC)	28	3-4½	——	600
'77	4-140	2 bbl	R-43TS	.035	Electronic		TDC(2B)	2B(TDC)	34	3-4½	700(800)	650⑥
	8-305	2 bbl	R-45TS	.045	Electronic		8B	8B(6B)	28	3-4½	600	500⑦
'78	4-151 Pont.	2 bbl	R-43TSX	.060	Electronic		14B	14B⑧	33	4-5.5	1000/500	650/500⑨
	6-196 Buick	2 bbl	R-46TSX	.060	Electronic		15B	15B	17	5-6	800	600
	6-231 Buick	2 bbl	R-46TSX	.060	Electronic		15B	15B	17	5-6	800	600
	8-305 Chev.	2 bbl	R-45TS	.045	Electronic		4B	6B⑩	28	4-5	600	500⑪
'79	4-151 Pont.	2 bbl	R-43TSX	.060	Electronic		⑫	⑫	33	4-5.5	⑫	⑫
	6-196 Buick	2 bbl	R-46TSX	.060	Electronic		15B	15B	16	4-5.75	⑫	⑫
	6-231 Buick	2 bbl	R-46TSX	.060	Electronic		15B	15B	16	4-5.75	⑫	⑫
	8-305 Chev.	2 bbl	R-45TS	.045	Electronic		4B	4B	28	7.5-9	⑫	⑫

▲ See text for procedure
● Figure in parentheses indicates California engine
■ All figures Before Top Dead Center
* Where two figures are separated by a slash, the first figure is for idle speed with solenoid connected, while the second is for idle speed with solenoid disconnected

NOTE: The underhood specifications sticker often reflects tune-up specification changes made in production. Sticker figures must be used if they disagree with those in this chart.

B Before Top Dead Center
—— Not applicable

① Adjust mechanical valve lifter clearance to .015 in. for intake, and to .030 in. for exhaust with engine cold
② For air-conditioned vehicles, adjust idle speed to 800 rpm with A/C on
③ Adjust valve clearance to 0.014 in. (intake and exhaust) with engine cold
④ .045 in. for Monza
⑤ 750 rpm for Monza
⑥ 700 rpm for high altitude
⑦ 800 rpm for high altitude
⑧ California engines without EGR valve: 12B
⑨ with air conditioning: 850/650
⑩ High Altitude: 8B
⑪ High Altitude: 600
⑫ See Underhood Sticker

NOTE: Most 1979 GM carburetors have idle mixture screws concealed by staked-in plugs. These are not meant to be removed, except at carburetor overhaul.

FIRING ORDER

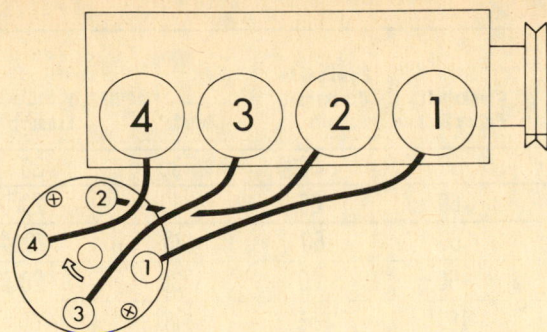

GM (Chevrolet) 140 (2300 cc) 4-cyl.
(through 1974)
Engine firing order: 1-3-4-2
Distributor rotation: clockwise

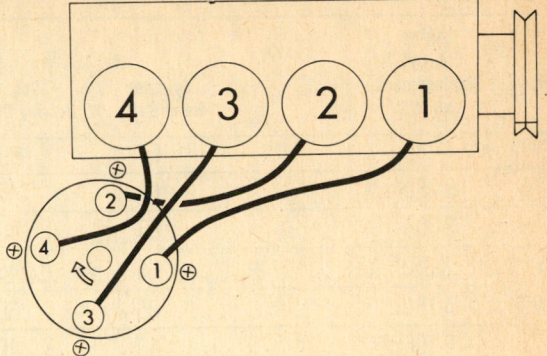

GM (Chevrolet) 140 (2300 cc) 4-cyl.
(1975 and later)
Engine firing order: 1-3-4-2
Distributor rotation: clockwise

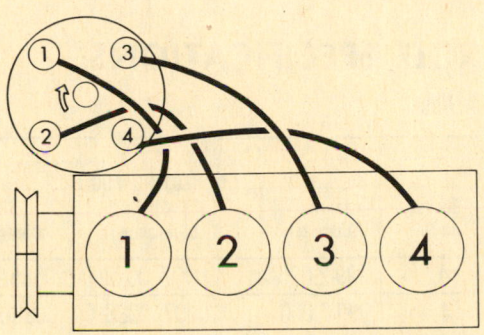

GM (Chevrolet) Cosworth Vega 122 4-cyl.
Engine firing order: 1-3-4-2
Distributor rotation: clockwise

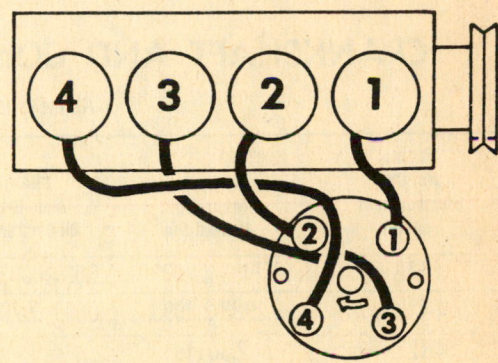

GM (Pontiac) 151 4-cyl. (1977 and later)
Engine firing order: 1-3-4-2
Distributor rotation: clockwise

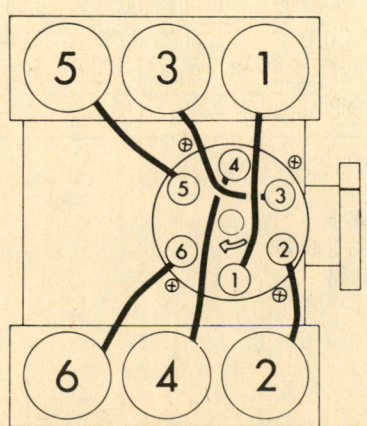

GM (Buick) 196, 231 V6
Engine firing order: 1-6-5-4-3-2
Distributor rotation: clockwise

V6 harmonic balancers have two timing marks: one is 1/8 in. wide, and one is 1/16 in. wide. Use the 1/16 in. mark for timing with a hand held light. The 1/8 in. mark is used only with a magnetic timing pick-up probe.

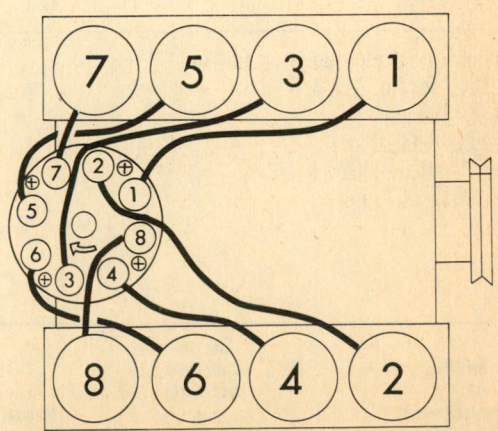

GM (Chevrolet) 262, 305, 350 V8 (1975 and later)
Engine firing order: 1-8-4-3-6-5-7-2
Distributor rotation: clockwise

TORQUE SPECIFICATIONS

All readings in ft lbs

Year	Engine No. Cyl. Displacement (cu in.)	Cylinder Head Bolts	Rod Bearing Bolts	Main Bearing Bolts	Crankshaft Pulley Bolt	Flywheel to Crankshaft Bolts	MANIFOLD Intake	MANIFOLD Exhaust
'72-'77	4-140	60	35	65	80	60②	30	30
'75-'76	8-262	65	45	70	60	60	30	20①
'76-'79	8-305	65	45	80	60	60	30	20①
'75	8-350	65	45	75	60	60	30	20①
'78-'79	4-151	95	30	65	160	55	③	③
'78-'79	6-196, 231	80	40	100	225	60	45	25

① Inside bolts—30 ft. lbs
② '76 and later—65 ft. lbs
③ Bolt—40; Nut—30

CRANKSHAFT AND CONNECTING ROD SPECIFICATIONS

All measurements are given in inches

Year	Engine No. Cyl. Displacement (cu in.)	CRANKSHAFT Main Brg. Journal Dia	CRANKSHAFT Main Brg. Oil Clearance	Shaft End-Play	Thrust on No.	CONNECTING ROD Journal Diameter	CONNECTING ROD Oil Clearance	CONNECTING ROD Side Clearance
'72	4-140	2.2983-2.2993	.0029-.0003	.002-.008	4	1.999-2.000	.0007-.0027①	.0085-.0135
'73-'74	4-140	2.2983-2.2993	.0003-.0020②	.002-.007	4	1.999-2.000	.0007-.0038①	.0085-.0135
'75-'76	4-122	2.3011	⑤	.002-.008	4	1.999-2.000	.0007-.0027	.0009-.0013
'75-'77	4-140	2.3004	.0003-.0029	.002-.008	4	1.999-2.000	.0007-.0027	.0009-.0013
'75-'76	8-262	2.4502③	④	.002-.007	5	2.098-2.099	.0013-.0035	.008-.014
'76-'77	8-305	2.4502③	④	.002-.007	5	2.098-2.099	.0013-.0035	.008-.014
'75	8-350	2.4502③	④	.002-.007	5	2.098-2.099	.0013-.0035	.006-.016
'78-'79	4-151	2.3000	.0002-.0022	.0035-.0085	5	2.0000	.0005-.0026	.006-.022
'78-'79	6-196, 231	2.4995	.0003-.0017	.004-.008	2	2.2487-2.2495	.0005-.0026	.006-.027
'78-'79	8-305	⑥	④	.002-.006	5	2.0988-2.0998	.0013-.0035	.008-.014

① Maximum service clearance = .004 in.
② .0003-.0027 for No. 2, 3, 4, 5
③ No. 5-2.4508 in.
④ No. 1—.0008-.0020 in.
  No. 2, 3, 4—.0011-.0023 in.
  No. 5—.0017-.0033 in.

⑤ No. 1, 2, 3, 5—.0008-.0034
  No. 4—.0002-.0029
⑥ No. 1: 2.4484-2.4493
  Nos. 2, 3, 4: 2.4481-2.4490
  No. 5: 2.4479-2.4488

CAPACITIES

Year	ENGINE No. Cyl. Displacement (cu. in.)	Engine Crankcase Add 1 Qt For New Filter	TRANSMISSION Pts To Refill After Draining Manual 3-Speed	TRANSMISSION 4/5-Speed	TRANSMISSION Automatic ●	Drive Axle (pts)	Gasoline Tank (gals)	COOLING SYSTEM (qts) With Heater	COOLING SYSTEM (qts) With A/C
'72	4-140	3	2.4	3	6①	2.8	11	6.5	6.5
'73	4-140	3	3	3	6②	2.8	11	8.6	9.0
'74	4-140	3	3	3	8	2.8	16	8.6	9.0

CAPACITIES

Year	ENGINE No. Cyl. Displacement (cu. in.)	Engine Crankcase Add 1 Qt For New Filter	TRANSMISSION Pts To Refill After Draining — Manual 3-Speed	4/5-Speed	Automatic ●	Drive Axle (pts)	Gasoline Tank (gals)	COOLING SYSTEM (qts) With Heater	With A/C
'75-'73	4-140, 4-122	3.5	3	3③	8	2.8	16⑤	8.0④	8.0④
	V8-262, 305, 350	4.0	—	3③	8	2.8	18.5	18.0	18.0
'78	4-151	3	—	3③	6	2.8	18.5⑥	10.8	10.8
	6-196	4	—	3③	6	2.8	18.5⑥	11.6	11.6
	6-231	4	—	3③	6	2.8	18.5⑥	11.6	11.6
	8-305	4	—	3③	6	2.8	18.5⑥	16.2	16.2
'79	4-151	3	—	3.5③	7	3.5	18.5⑥	10.8	10.8
	6-196	4	—	3.5③	7	3.5	18.5⑥	11.6	11.6
	6-231	4	—	3.5③	7	3.5	18.5⑥	11.6	11.6
	8-305	4	—	3.5	7	3.5	18.5⑥	16.2	16.2

- ● Specifications do not include torque converter
- ① 5 pts with Turbo Hydra-Matic
- ② 8 pts with Turbo Hydra-Matic
- — Not Applicable
- ③ 5-speed uses Dexron® II automatic transmission fluid
- ④ 6.8 qts—4-122
- ⑤ 18.5 gals—Monza 4-140
- ⑥ Station Wagon and Monza S" Hatchback: 15.0

VALVE SPECIFICATIONS

Year	Engine No. Cyl. Displacement (cu in.)	Seat Angle (deg)	Face Angle (deg)	Spring Test Pressure (lbs @ in.)	Spring Installed Height (in.)	STEM TO GUIDE Clearance (in.) Intake	Exhaust	STEM Diameter (in.) Intake	Exhaust
'75-'76	4-122	46	45	45 @ 1.30	1.30	.0010-.0027	.0010-.0027	.2791	.2791
'72-'77	4-140	46	45	75 @ 1.75	1 ¾	.0010-.0027	.0010-.0027	.3414	.3414
'75-'76	8-262	46	45	80 @ 1.70①	1.70②	.0010-.0027	.0010-.0027	.3414	.3414
'76-'79	8-305	46	45	80 @ 1.70①	1.70②	.0010-.0027	.0010-.0027	.3414	.3414
'75	8-350	46	45	80 @ 1.70①	1.70②	.0010-.0027	.0010-.0027	.3414	.3414
'78-'79	4-151	46	45	84 @ 1.66	1.69	.0010-.0027	.0010-.0027③	.3400	.3400
'78-'79	6-196, 231	45	45	168 @ 1.327	1.727	.0015-.0032	.0015-.0032	.3408	.3408

- ① Exhaust—80 @ 1.61
- ② Exhaust—1.61
- ③ Figure given is at top of stem; bottom of stem: .0020-.0037

RING GAP

All measurements are given in inches

Year	Engine	Top Compression	Bottom Compression
'72-'77	4-140, 4-122	.015-.025	.009-.019
'75	8-262	.010-.020	.013-.025
'75	8-350	.010-.020	.010-.020
'76	8-262	.010-.020	.010-.020
'76-'79	8-305	.010-.020	.010-.025
'78	4-151	.010-.020	.010-.020
'78	6-196, 231	.010-.020	.010-.020
'79	4-151	.015-.026	.009-.019
'79	6-196, 231	.013-.023	.013-.023

Year	Engine	Oil Control
'72-'77	4-140, 4-122	.010-.030
'75-'76	8-262	.010-.025
'75	8-350	.015-.055
'76-'78	8-305	.015-.055
'78	4-151	.015-.035
'78-'79	6-196, 231	.015-.035
'79	4-151	.015-.055
'79	8-305	.010-.035

RING SIDE CLEARANCE

All measurements are given in inches

Year	Engine	Top Compression	Bottom Compression
'72-'77	4-140	.0012-.0027	.0012-.0027
'75-'76	8-262	.0012-.0032	.0012-.0027
'75	8-350	.0012-.0032	.0012-.0027
'76-'79	8-305	.0012-.0032	.0012-.0032
'78-'79	4-151	.0015-.0035	.0015-.0035
'78-'79	6-196, 231	.003-.005	.003-.005

Year	Engine	Oil Control
'72-'77	4-140	.000-.005
'75-'76	8-262	.000-.005
'75	8-350	.000-.005
'76-'77	8-305	.000-.001
'78-'79	4-151	.0015-.0035
'78-'79	8-305	.002-.007
'78-'79	6-196, 231	.0035 Max.

PISTON CLEARANCE

Year	Engine	Piston to Bore Clearance (in.)
'75-'76	4-122	.0020-.0030②
'72-'77	4-140	.0018-.0028①
'75-'76	8-262	.0008-.0018②
'75	8-350	.0007-.0017
'76-'79	8-305	.0007-.0017
'78-'79	4-151	.0025-.0033
'78-'79	6-196, 231	.0008-.0020

① Measured 1.50 in. from top of piston
② Measured 1.75 in. from top of piston

WHEEL ALIGNMENT SPECIFICATIONS

Year	Model	CASTER Range (deg)	CASTER Pref Setting (deg)	CAMBER Range (deg)	CAMBER Pref Setting (deg)	Toe-in (in.)	Steering Axis Inclin. (deg)
'72-'73	All	1¼N to ¼N	¾N	¼N to ¾P	¼P	³⁄₁₆ to ⁵⁄₁₆	8.55
'74	All	1¾N to ¼P	¾N	¾N to 1¼P	¼P	³⁄₁₆ to ⁵⁄₁₆	8.55
'75-'77	All	1¼N to ¼N	¾N	¼N to ¾P	¼P	0 to ⅛①	8.55
'78	All	⅓N to 1⅓N	⅘N	⅓N to ⁷⁄₁₀P	⅕P	0 to ⅛①	8.55
'79	All	⅓N to 1⅓N	⅘N	⁷⁄₁₀N to ³⁄₁₀P	⅕N	.13-.25②	8.55

— Not specified
① Toe-out
② degrees

CHARGING SYSTEM

A 10-SI Series Delcotron alternator is used. This unit features a non-adjustable, integral solid-state regulator mounted inside the slipring end frame. Testing procedures for the integrated charging system are found in the Unit Repair Section.

Alternator Removal and Installation

1. Disconnect the battery.
2. Disconnect the alternator wiring.
3. Remove the alternator brace bolt and V-belt.
4. Remove the pivot mount bolt and the alternator.
5. Installation is the reverse of the removal procedure.
6. Adjust the belt to have 1/4 to 1/2 inch play on the longest span of the belt. If a tensioning gauge is available, adjust the belt to 80 lbs.

STARTING SYSTEM

The starter is a solenoid actuated Delco-Remy unit similar to other Chevrolet starters; beginning 1975, the starter has no R terminal. The HEI system does not use the solenoid to coil wire. See the Unit Repair Section for testing procedures.

Starter Removal and Installation

1. Disconnect the battery ground cable and all the wiring at the solenoid terminals. Install each nut on the terminal from which it was removed, as these nuts are not interchangeable.
2. Loosen the front starter bracket and remove the two mounting bolts.
3. Remove the front bracket bolt and rotate the bracket out of the way.
4. Remove the starter from the car, lowering the front end first.
5. To install, reverse the removal procedure. Tighten the mounting bolts, and then install the brace.

Disabling the Seat Belt/Starter Interlock System

Since the requirement for the interlock system was dropped during the 1975 model year, those systems installed on cars built earlier may now be legally disabled. The seat belt warning light is still required.

1. Disconnect the negative battery cable.
2. Locate the interlock harness connector with orange, yellow and green leads under the left side of the instrument panel on or near the fuse block. 1974 Vegas have the connector under the parking brake cable cover.
3. Cut and tape the ends of the green wire on the body side of the connector.
4. Remove the buzzer from the fuse block or connector.

IGNITION SYSTEM

The 140 cu. in. distributor is mounted in the cylinder head at the rear of the engine and is driven by the camshaft. An unusual feature of this unit is a cup, mounted at the lower end of the driveshaft. This cup is under full engine oil pressure when the engine is running, acting as a vibration damper to reduce driveshaft oscillations. If this cup is not installed after the distributor has been disassembled, engine oil pressure will be lost.

The V8 distributor is mounted at the rear of the engine, gear driven off the camshaft.

The V6 distributor is camshaft driven, and mounted at the front of the engine.

The 151 cu. in. distributor is mounted at the front right side of the engine.

Electronic ignition is standard equipment on all 1975 and later models, eliminating the need for point replacement. Two types of HEI distributors are used. V8 distributors combine all ignition components in one unit. The coil is in the distributor cap and connects directly to the rotor. The inline engine distributor has an externally mounted coil.

Timing Light Connections—HEI System

Timing light connections should be made in parallel using an adapter at the distributor No. 1 terminal.

Tachometer Connections—HEI System

There is a TACH terminal on the V6 and V8 distributor cap and on the 4 cylinder coil. Connect the tachometer to this terminal and ground.

----- CAUTION -----
Grounding the tach terminal could damage the HEI ignition module.

Distributor Removal

1. Release the cap hold-down screws and remove the cap. On electronic ignition, disconnect the wiring harness connectors at the side of the cap and remove the cap.
2. Disconnect the vacuum line and the primary lead.
3. Mark the distributor housing and the engine in line with the rotor centerline with chalk.
4. Remove the hold-down clamp and distributor.

NOTE: *Avoid turning the engine while the distributor is removed.*

Distributor Installation

1. Turn the rotor approximately 1/8 turn clockwise past the alignment mark.
2. Push the distributor into position, moving the rotor to mesh the gears.
3. Install the clamp bolt.
4. Connect the vacuum line and the primary lead.
5. Install the cap and adjust the timing.

Distributor Installation—Engine Disturbed

1. Remove No. 1 spark plug and place a finger over the plug hole. Remove the center coil wire and crank the engine until compression is felt in No. 1 cylinder. Rotate the engine until the timing pointer is aligned with the proper mark.
2. Install the distributor with the vac-

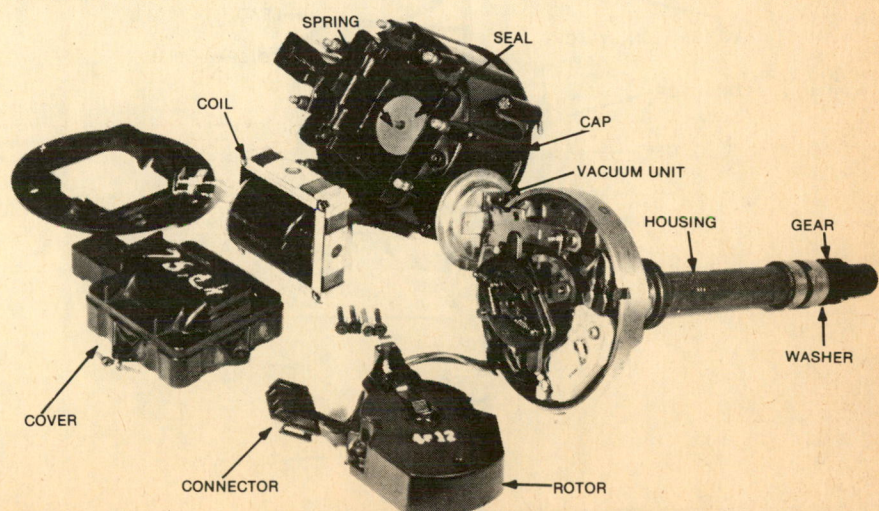

V8 HEI distributor

uum advance pointing toward the front of the engine and the punch-marks on the drive gear in line with the No. 1 cap tower.

3. Install the hold-down clamp and rotate the distributor slightly so that the points are just open. Tighten the clamp bolt.
4. Install the rotor, cap and vacuum line.
5. Connect the primary lead.
6. Check and adjust the ignition timing.

Point Adjustment

Inspect the points for alignment and pitting. If necessary, clean the points with a point file. All the roughness need not be removed. To set the gap, rotate the crankshaft until one of the distributor cam lobes is directly opposite the rubbing block of the point arm (gap at maximum separation). Measure the gap, and if it is not within specifications, loosen the contact point assembly attaching screw and move the assembly to obtain the specified gap. This is done by inserting a screwdriver in the slot formed by the contact points and the breaker plate and levering the points as required. Tighten the attaching screw.

Check the dwell angle. Check the ignition timing, adjusting it if necessary.

Ignition Timing

The timing marks are on a plate mounted on the front of the block and the timing notch is on the crankshaft pulley.

Distributor alignment—OHC 4 cylinder
(© Chevrolet Div., G.M. Corp)

Timing is set as follows:
1. Bring the engine to normal operating temperature, shut the engine off, and connect a timing light to No. 1 spark plug or No. 1 plug tower on HEI. Clean the timing plate and mark the notch in the pulley with chalk.
2. Disconnect and plug the vacuum line to the distributor.
3. See the underhood sticker for the latest certified information on preparing the engine for ignition timing.

4. Set the idle speed to specifications, following the procedure outlined in the Fuel System section.
5. Aim the timing light at the timing marks. If the notch does not align with the correct value on the scale, loosen the distributor clamp locknut and slowly turn the distributor to adjust.
6. Tighten the clamp locknut. Adjust the carburetor idle speed screw to give the specified idle speed with the solenoid disconnected.
7. Reconnect the idle stop solenoid lead. Increase the engine speed to allow the solenoid to extend and then adjust the solenoid plunger screw to obtain the idle speed specified with the solenoid connected.
8. Shut the engine off and connect the vacuum and evaporative emission line.

FUEL SYSTEM

The Rochester MV and 2GC, and the Holley 5210-C carburetors were used on the 4-140. The Holley 5210-C and 6510-C are used on the 4-151. The Rochester 2GE is used on the 6-196 and 6-231. The Rochester 2GC is used on the 8-305 and 8-350.

The electric fuel pump is an integral part of the fuel tank unit assembly, which includes the fuel gauge metering unit. The fuel pump is energized by the ignition switch when the key is in the start or on position. After the engine starts, the pump receives current through the oil pressure safety switch as long as there is approximately 2 psi oil pressure.

Fuel Pump Removal and Installation

1. Disconnect the battery ground cable and siphon the fuel from the tank.

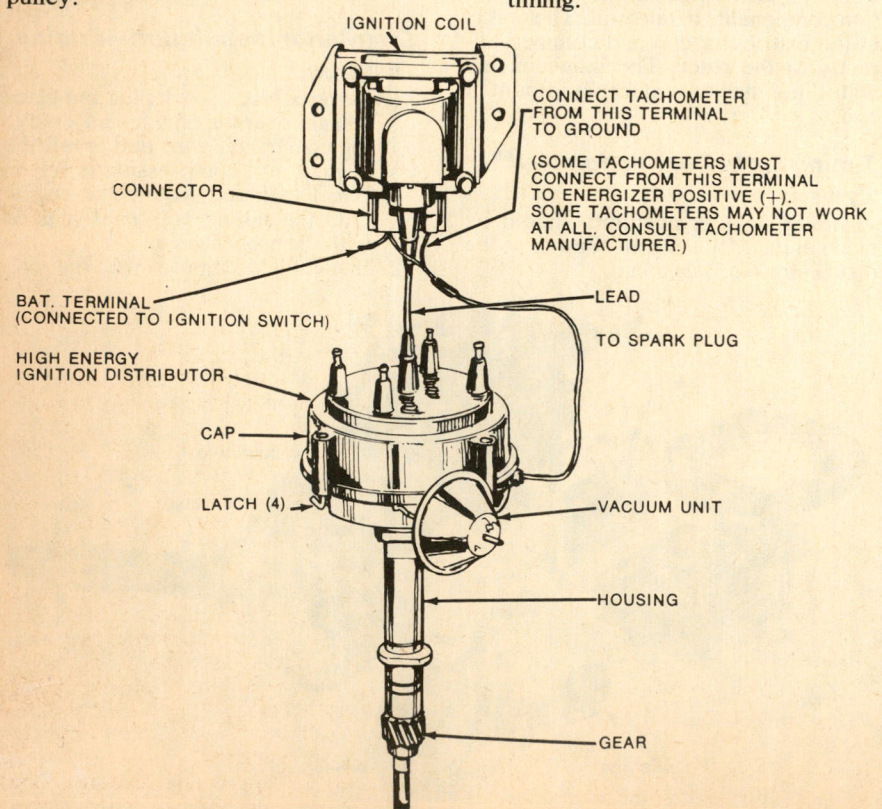

4-cylinder HEI distributor (© Chevrolet Div., G.M. Corp)

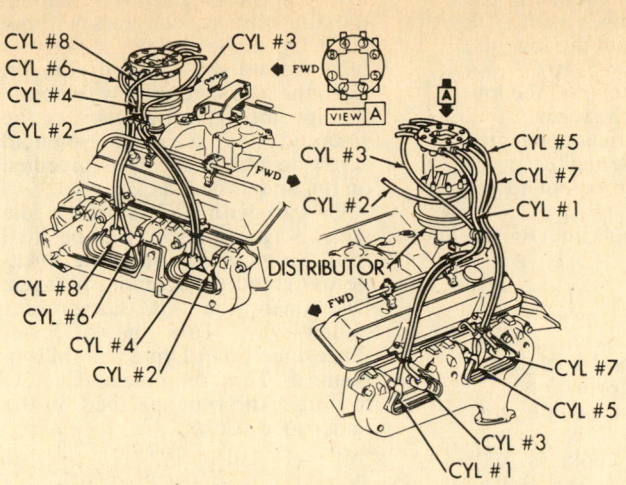

V8 HEI ignition wiring (© Chevrolet Div., G.M. Corp)

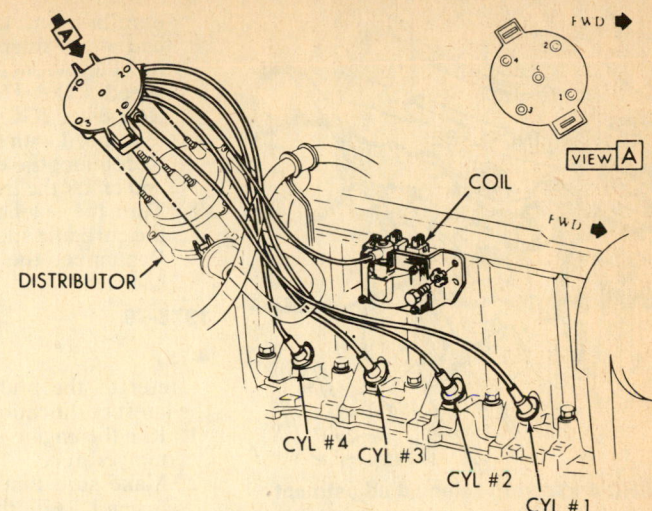

OHC 4-cylinder HEI ignition wiring (© Chevrolet Div., G.M. Corp)

2. Disconnect the gauge sending-unit and pump wires at the rear harness connector.
3. Raise the car. Disconnect the fuel line at the gauge connection.
4. Disconnect the tank vent line to the vapor separator, which is mounted in the tank.
5. Disconnect the gauge wire ground screw from the floorpan.
6. Remove the tank strap bolts and, very carefully, lower the tank.
7. Use the special wrench, or a suitable substitute, to unscrew the retaining cam ring. Do not strike any part of the tank with a metal tool, such as a hammer; there is a danger of explosion from sparks.
8. Remove the gauge sending-unit and fuel pump assembly.
9. Remove the flat wire conductor from the plastic clip on the fuel tube.
10. While squeezing the clamp, pull the pump straight back 1/2 in. for access to the terminals. Remove the two nuts, lockwashers, and wires from the pump.
11. Squeeze the clamp and pull the pump straight back to completely remove it from the sending unit.

----- CAUTION -----

Be careful not to bend the circular support bracket.

12. Slide the replacement pump through the circular support bracket until it rests against the rubber coupling. Be sure that the rubber isolator and saran strainer, supplied in the service package, are attached to the pump.
13. Attach the two pump terminals, using lockwashers and nuts. Be sure that the flat conductor is attached to the terminal farthest away from the float arm.
14. Squeeze the clamp and push the pump into the rubber coupling.
15. Replace the flat wire conductor in the plastic clip on the fuel tube.
16. Install the pump and gauge unit into the tank opening. Tighten the cam ring.
17. Install the fuel tank using a reverse of the removal procedure.

Fuel Filter Removal and Installation

Both paper and bronze filters are used, depending on the carburetor model.

1. Disconnect the fuel line at the intake fuel filter nut on the carburetor.
2. Remove the intake fuel filter nut.
3. Remove the filter element and spring.
4. Install the element spring and element. Bronze filters are installed with the conical section facing out and with a gasket between the filter element and the fuel intake nut.
5. Install the nut using a new gasket and tighten. Do not overtighten this nut, as it is easily stripped.
6. Install fuel line and tighten the connector.

Idle Speed Adjustment

1972

1. The engine must be at normal operating temperature and the air cleaner in place. Air conditioning should be on in 1971 models; off in later models.
2. Detach the fuel tank line from the top of the evaporative emission canister.
3. Disconnect the distributor vacuum line and plug the carburetor hose.
4. Disconnect the electrical connector at the idle stop solenoid on the carburetor.
5. Start the engine and adjust the carburetor idle speed screw to obtain the idle speed specified in the Tune-Up Specifications Chart (for speed with the solenoid disconnected).
6. Reconnect the idle stop solenoid electrical lead. Speed up the engine to allow the solenoid plunger to extend, then adjust the solenoid plunger screw to obtain the idle speed specified in the Tune-Up Specifications Chart (for speed with the solenoid connected).
7. Stop the engine and reconnect the vacuum line and the evaporative emission canister line.

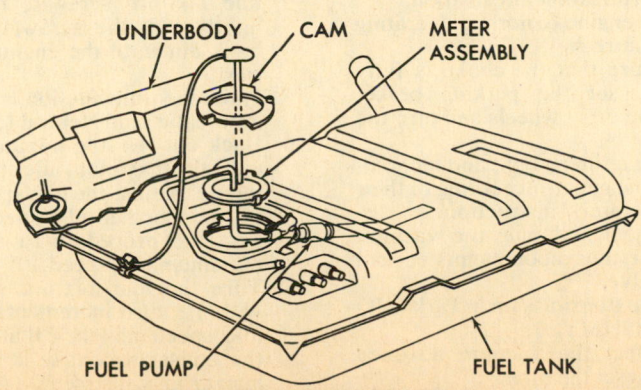

Fuel pump installation (typical)
(© Chevrolet Div., G.M. Corp)

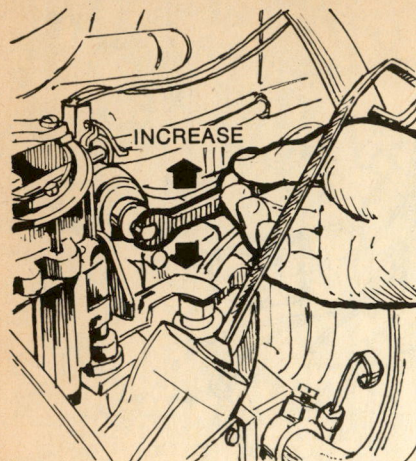

OHC 4 idle stop solenoid adjustment

1973-74

Follow Steps 1 through 4 of the 1972 procedure, then proceed as follows.

Rochester MV 1 bbl

1. Start the engine and, using a 1/8 in. allen wrench, adjust the idle speed to the figure given in the Tune-Up Specifications Chart (for speed with the solenoid disconnected).
2. Check the dwell and ignition timing. Check the idle speed again.
3. Reconnect the electrical wire to the solenoid.
4. Adjust the idle speed (for speed with solenoid connected) by turning the body of the solenoid itself.

Holley 5210-C 2 bbl

1. Start the engine and adjust the idle speed screw for the speed listed in the Tune-Up Specifications Chart (speed with solenoid disconnected).
2. Check the dwell and ignition timing. Check the idle speed again.
3. Reconnect the electrical wire to the solenoid.
4. Adjust the screw on the throttle lever (not the same screw as Step 1). Set the idle speed to the figure given in the Tune-Up Specifications Chart (for speed with the solenoid connected).

1975-77

1. The engine should be at normal operating temperature, air cleaner ON, choke open and the air conditioner OFF.
2. Set the parking brake.
3. Disconnect the fuel tank hose from the vapor canister.
4. Disconnect and plug the vacuum hose. Check and adjust the timing. Reconnect the vacuum hose on Rochester 1MV and 2GC carburetors.
5. Disconnect the electrical connector at the idle stop solenoid.
6. Place automatic transmissions in Drive and manual transmissions in Neutral. On Rochester 1MV car-

buretors, turn the hex screw in the end of the solenoid body with a 1/8 in. allen wrench to set the low idle speed. On Holley 5210-C and Rochester 2GC models, set the low idle speed with the idle screw.
7. Reconnect the electrical connector and crack the throttle slightly.
8. Turn the solenoid in or out to set the curb idle speed.
9. Reconnect the vapor line to the canister.

1978-79

4-151

Refer to the underhood sticker for the latest certification information.
1. Run the engine to normal operating temperature.
2. Make sure that the choke is fully opened, set the parking brake, block the drive wheels and turn the air conditioning off.
3. Connect a timing light and tachometer to the engine according to their manufacturers' instructions.
4. Disconnect and plug the PCV hose at the vapor canister. Disconnect and plug the vacuum advance hose at the distributor.
5. Place the transmission in Drive (AT) or Neutral (MT).
6. Check and adjust timing.
7. Connect the vacuum advance line.
8. On manual transmission cars without A/C: Turn the idle speed screw to achieve the specified rpm. On automatic transmission cars or manual transmission cars with A/C: Turn the idle speed screw to obtain the specified rpm. Disconnect the wire at the wide open throttle A/C override switch. The switch is located on the accelerator linkage bracket. Turn the A/C on. Momentarily open the throttle to extend the solenoid plunger. Adjust the solenoid screw to the rpm specified on the underhood sticker. Connect the override switch and turn the A/C off.
9. Connect all hoses and remove the timing light and tachometer.

6-196, 231, V8-305

Refer to the underhood sticker for the latest certification information.
1. Run the engine to normal operating temperature.
2. Make sure that the choke is fully opened, set the parking brake, block the drive wheels and turn the A/C off.
3. Connect a timing light and tachometer to the engine according to their manufacturers' instructions.
4. Disconnect and plug the vacuum hoses at the vapor cannister and EGR valve.
5. Place the transmission in Park (AT) or Neutral (MT).
6. Disconnect the vacuum advance hose and set the timing.
7. On manual transmission without A/C: Adjust the idle speed screw

to obtain the specified rpm. On automatic transmission cars without A/C: Open the throttle slightly to fully extend the solenoid plunger. Turn the idle speed screw to obtain the specified rpm. Disconnect the solenoid and turn the solenoid screw to obtain the rpm specified on the underhood sticker.

On cars with A/C: Turn the idle speed screw to obtain the specified rpm. Momentarily open the throttle to extend the solenoid plunger. Disconnect the A/C compressor clutch wire. Turn the A/C on. Place the AT in Drive, the MT in Neutral. Turn the solenoid screw to obtain the rpm specified on the underhood sticker.

Idle Mixture Adjustment

THROUGH 1974

The idle mixture screw/s are preset at the factory to insure the lowest possible level of exhaust emissions, and should not be removed unless to perform an overhaul, or the replacement of a throttle body.

To reset the idle mixture, turn the idle mixture screw/s to lightly bottom them, and then turn the screw/s out four complete turns. Adjust the idle stop solenoid to 20 rpm above the idle speed specifications for automatic transmission and 30 rpm above for manual transmission. Adjust the idle mixture screw/s to obtain a 20 to 30 rpm drop of the engine idle speed. Install new limiter caps on the idle mixture adjusting screw/s.

1975-77

1. Have the engine at normal operating temperature and remove the air cleaner for access to the carburetor, if necessary, but leave the vacuum lines connected.
2. Disconnect and plug other vacuum lines as directed by the information on the emission control label under the engine hood.
3. Connect a tachometer to the engine, set the parking brake, and block the drive wheels.
4. Remove the plastic cap/s from the idle mixture screw/s, turn in to lightly seat the screw/s and then back out until the engine will just run.
5. Place the transmission in Drive for automatic, and Neutral for manual.
6. Back out the idle mixture screw/s until the maximum idle speed is obtained. Adjust the idle speed screw to the specified idle speed and repeat the procedure to obtain the maximum idle speed.
7. Turn the idle mixture screw/s in with 1/8 turn increments until the idle speed matches that listed on the emission control label for the lean drop adjustment.
8. Reset the idle speed to specifications and reinstall the air cleaner

and all vacuum hoses. Recheck the idle speed.

1978-79

Changes in the mixture system have made the adjustment of the air/fuel mixture impossible without a propane enrichment system not available to the general public. Of itself, backing out the mixture screw will have little or no effect.

COOLING SYSTEM

The intake manifold is water heated to provide an even intake temperature. All models built after March 1973 have a radiator drain petcock. The 1972 models have neither a block drain plug nor a radiator petcock. To drain the cooling system on these models, either the lower radiator hose must be removed or the coolant must be siphoned out. V8s have block drains.

Starting 1973, all models are equipped with a coolant recovery system reservoir. A translucent plastic reservoir allows for hot coolant expansion. When the engine cools, coolant is drawn into the radiator by vacuum. Additional coolant should be added to the reservoir, not the radiator.

Beginning 1976, the Monza with V8 engine and air conditioning has an auxiliary fan installed forward of the radiator. The fan is operated by a thermostatic switch located on the right rear side of the cylinder head. If engine temperature exceeds approximately 235°F, the switch will close to operate the fan.

Radiator Removal and Installation

1. Drain the radiator.
2. On models with the heavy duty radiator, remove the fan shroud.
3. Disconnect the intake and outlet hoses.
4. Remove the two screws which secure the fan guard to the radiator support, then remove the support and the two radiator pads.

NOTE: *On vehicles with the heavy duty radiator, remove the two upper brackets (instead of the single support).*

5. Lift the radiator up and out of the lower brackets.
6. To install, reverse the removal procedure.

Water Pump Removal and Installation

4-140

The pump bearings are permanently lubricated during manufacture and do not require periodic maintenance other than keeping the air vent (top of housing) and drain holes (bottom of housing) free of dirt and grease.

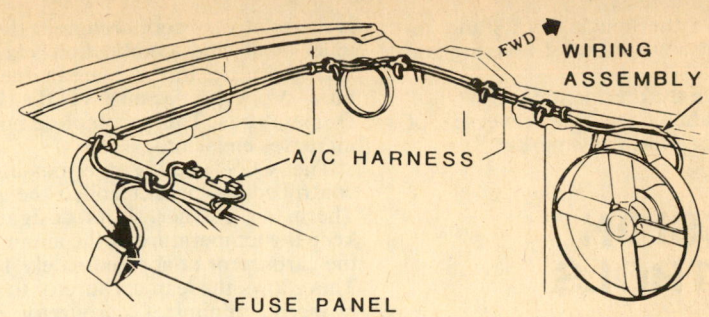

Auxiliary cooling fan-Monza V8 with air conditioning (© Chevrolet Div. G.M. Corp.)

The pump components cannot be serviced separately and, in the event of pump failure, the complete assembly must be replaced as a unit, as follows:

1. Raise and support the hood.
2. Disconnect the negative battery cable.
3. Remove the fan.
4. Loosen, but do not remove, the two lower timing belt cover retaining screws. The holes in the cover are slotted so that the cover is easily removed.
5. Remove the two upper timing belt cover retaining screws and remove the cover.
6. Drain the coolant.
7. Loosen the water pump bolts to relieve the tension on the timing belt.
8. Remove the hoses from the water pump.
9. Remove the water pump bolts, pump and gasket.
10. Thoroughly clean the old gasket material from the pump and block.
11. To install, position the water pump on the block using a new gasket and loosely install the water pump bolts. Make sure that the V grooves of the belt are aligned with the grooves in the water pump.

NOTE: *Use an anti-seize compound on the water pump bolt threads.*

12. A special tool is available to adjust the timing belt. It fits into the round hole in the square lug to the upper right (facing) of the water pump and bears against the pump housing midway between the bolt holes. If this tool is available, apply 15 ft lbs of torque against the water pump (and belt). If the tool is not available, apply a force to the pump in a similar manner. Tighten the pump bolts to 15 ft lbs.
13. Install the radiator and heater hoses to the pump.
14. Install the timing belt cover, lowering the cover lower screw slots over the screws. Loosely tighten the screws against the cover.
15. Install the two upper timing cover screws, then tighten the upper and lower screws to 50 in lbs.
16. Install the fan, tightening the bolts to 20 ft lbs.
17. Fill the cooling system, connect the battery negative cable, start the engine and check for leaks.

4-151, V6 & V8

1. Drain the coolant from the radiator.
2. Loosen the fan pulley bolts.
3. If necessary, remove the alternator with the drive belt and brackets.
4. If necessary, remove the air pump with the drive belt and brackets.
5. Disconnect the lower radiator hose and the heater hose at the water pump.
6. Remove the fan and pulley.
7. Remove the pump-to-cylinder block and power steering-to-pump bolts and remove the water pump and old gasket.
8. Installation is the reverse of removal. Use a new gasket coated with sealer. Adjust the alternator and air pump drive belt tension. Fill the cooling system, run the engine and check for leaks.

Thermostat Removal and Installation

The 4-140 and 4-151 thermostat is located in a housing at the cylinder head water outlet adjacent to the intake manifold. On the V6 and V8 engines, the thermostat is in the water outlet housing in the front of the intake manifold.

4-140

1. Drain the cooling system.
2. Disconnect the upper radiator hose at the engine.
3. On models with the alternator attached to the water outlet, remove the retaining bolt, and position the alternator out of the way.
4. Unbolt the housing and remove the housing, gasket, and thermostat.
5. Replace the thermostat and housing, using a new gasket.
6. Install the alternator retaining bolt in the water outlet housing. (Use sealant on the bolt threads). Install the alternator drive belt and adjust as outlined in the Charging System Section.
7. Replace the radiator hose, fill the cooling system, start the engine, and check for leaks.

4-151, V6 & V8

1. Drain the coolant to a level below that of the water outlet housing.
2. Remove the radiator upper hose.

3. Remove the housing bolts and remove the water outlet housing and gasket.
4. Remove the thermostat.
5. Installation is the reverse of removal. Use a new gasket.

EMISSION CONTROLS

POSITIVE CRANKCASE VENTILATION

All models use the Positive Crankcase Ventilation System (PCV).

Some unburned fuel and combustion products leak past the rings during combustion. These gases travel into the crankcase where, if they are not removed, they will combine with the oil to form sludge and also build excessive pressure inside the crankcase. The PCV system removes these gases from the crankcase and routes them to the intake manifold where they are combined with the air/fuel mixture and reburned in the combustion chamber.

The crankcase gases are drawn from the crankcase by intake manifold vacuum. There is a PCV valve in the line between the crankcase and the intake manifold which regulates the flow of the gases.

EVAPORATIVE EMISSION CONTROL

The Evaporative Emission Control system (EEC) is used on all models. This system limits the amount of gasoline vapor discharged into the air from the gas tank and carburetor. The fuel tank has a nonvented cap. As vapors are generated in the fuel tank, they flow through a liquid vapor separator to a canister where they are stored. Vapors generated by the carburetor after the engine is turned off are also routed to this canister. From the canister, the vapors are routed back to the carburetor where they are burned when the engine is started.

CONTROLLED COMBUSTION SYSTEM

The Controlled Combustion System (CCS) is used on all models. Essentially the CCS increases combustion efficiency through carburetor and distributor calibrations and by increasing engine operating temperatures.

Carburetors are calibrated leaner and initial ignition timing is retarded. The vacuum advance curve is also altered to decrease emissions.

The CCS also incorporates a higher engine operation temperature. A 195° thermostat is used. Engines that run hotter provide more complete vaporation of fuel and reduce quench area in the combustion chamber. Quench area

is the relatively cool area near the cylinder wall and combustion chamber surfaces. Fuel in these areas does not burn properly because of the lower temperatures. This incomplete burning increases emissions.

The CCS uses a thermostatically controlled air cleaner called the Auto-Therm air cleaner. It is designed to keep the temperature of the air entering the carburetor at approximately 100°F. This allows the lean carburetor to work properly, minimizes carburetor icing, and improves engine warm-up characteristics. A sensor unit located on the clean air side of the air filter senses the temperature of the air passing over it and regulates the vacuum supplied to a vacuum diaphragm in the inlet tube of the air cleaner. The colder the air, the greater the amount of vacuum supplied to the vacuum diaphragm. The vacuum diaphragm, depending on the vacuum supplied to it, opens or closes a damper door in the inlet tube of the air cleaner. If the door is open it allows air from the engine compartment to go to the carburetor. If the door is closed, air flows from the heat stove located on the exhaust manifold into the carburetor. In this way, heated air is supplied to the carburetor during cold days and when first starting the engine and warming it up.

AIR INJECTION REACTOR SYSTEM

AIR is used on all 1972 models except non-California cars with single-barrel carburetors. 1975 California cars with the 140 cu. in. engine, Cosworth Vega, and Monza V8 also use an air

pump. 1976 49 states 1 bbl four cylinder engines and California 2 bbl four cylinder engines also have air injection. Both 1977 engines use air injection. California V6 and V8 engines for 1978 use AIR.

The Air Injection Reactor (AIR) system was used to treat exhaust emissions. It consists of an air pump, a diverter valve, and tubes and hoses used to inject the air into the exhaust manifolds. The pump, driven by the engine, compresses air which is routed to the exhaust port of each cylinder. The air provides oxygen to further burn any unburned gases that are left over from the combustion process.

The diverter valve closes during engine overrun and deceleration and dumps the output from the air pump to the atmosphere. This prevents backfire due to air being injected when an overly rich mixture is present in the exhaust port.

TRANSMISSION CONTROLLED SPARK SYSTEM

The Transmission Controlled Spark (TCS) is used on all 1972 models and on all 1973 1 bbl engines with manual transmission. It is also used on all 1973-74 cars built for California with manual transmission and the Cosworth Vega. 1976 1 bbl four cylinder engines with manual transmission also have TCS.

The TCS system is used to prevent vacuum advance when the transmission is in low forward gears. The TCS system consists of a temperature-sen-

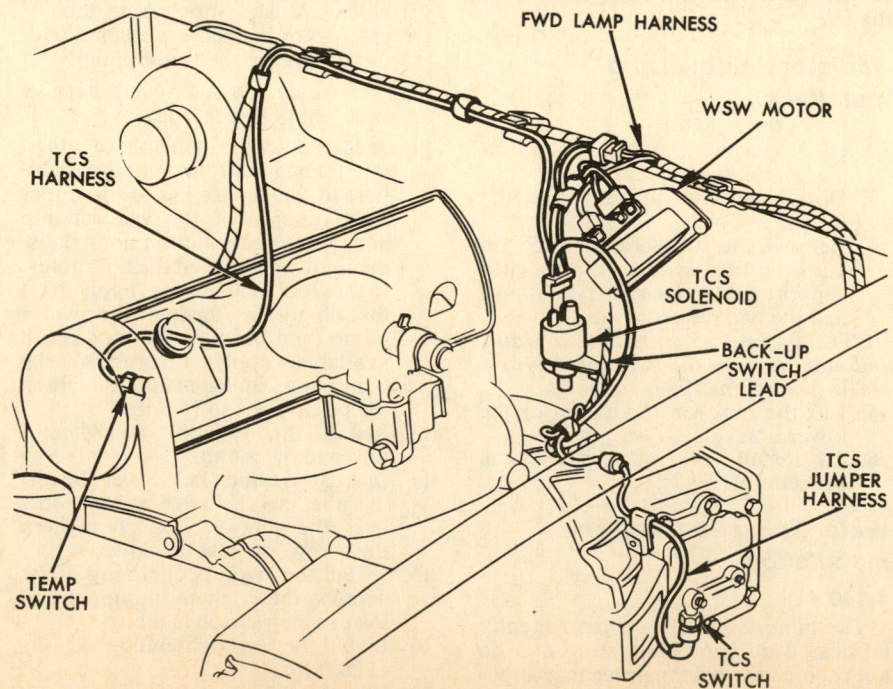

1973-76 TCS electrical components—4 cylinder
(© Chevrolet Div., G.M. Corp)

sing switch, a transmission switch, an idle stop solenoid, and a vacuum advance solenoid.

On 1972 cars, the vacuum advance solenoid is normally open, providing full vacuum to the distributor. When the vacuum advance solenoid is energized, the vacuum to the distributor is turned off and the advance unit is vented to the atmosphere.

The transmission switch is located on the transmission and senses when the transmission is in one of the lower gears. When in a lower gear, the switch activates the vacuum advance solenoid, shutting off vacuum advance. There is also an engine-temperature-sensing switch which overrides the transmission switch. It will allow vacuum advance in the lower gears when engine temperature is below 82° F. There is always vacuum advance in high gear and reverse.

On 1972 California models equipped with an automatic transmission, the transmission switch is a dummy switch and will not energize the solenoid. These engines have vacuum advance only when engine temperature is below 82° F.

An idle stop solenoid is used to prevent afterrun when the ignition is turned off. Afterrun is caused by the higher operating temperatures of today's engines and the wider throttle plate openings necessary for emission controls. The loss of spark from turning off the ignition is usually sufficient to stop the engine. However, if the engine has high enough cylinder temperatures, enough air-fuel mixture can pass the wide throttle plate opening and be ignited without the spark plug and the engine will continue to run even after the key is turned off. The idle solenoid is attached to the carburetor to solve

this problem. The solenoid has an adjustable plunger and is electrically operated. When the ignition is turned on, the plunger is extended and contacts the carburetor throttle lever, opening the throttle plate wide enough for the engine to idle properly. When the ignition is turned off, the plunger retracts and the throttle lever falls back on the lever stop. When the throttle lever is on its stop the throttle plate opening is very small and will not allow enough air-fuel mixture to pass to run the engine with the ignition off.

On 1973-74 and 1976 cars, the vacuum advance solenoid is normally closed, when (de-energized), venting the vacuum advance circuit to the atmosphere and shutting off vacuum to the distributor advance unit.

When the key is turned on, the idle stop solenoid is energized, the plunger extends to touch the throttle lever and maintains idle speed. As long as the engine temperature remains below 93°F, the vacuum advance solenoid is energized and the distributor receives a vacuum supply. The vacuum advance unit functions to give good start-up and drive-away characteristics. When the engine temperature reaches approximately 93°F, the temperature switch breaks the circuit, causing the vacuum advance solenoid to de-energize and cut off the vacuum supply. When the engine overheats, the temperature switch completes the circuit to activate the instrument panel warning lamp. Under normal driving conditions, the transmission switch controls the vacuum advance solenoid. In the lower gears, the switch is open and the solenoid de-energized. In high gear, the switch is closed and energizes the solenoid to open the vacuum port to the distributor and permits the advance

unit to function. The idle stop solenoid operates as before.

EXHAUST GAS RECIRCULATION

Exhaust Gas Recirculation (EGR) is used beginning 1973 on all models.

EGR is used to reduce oxides of nitrogen (NOx) that are formed at high operating temperatures.

EGR operates by introducing small amounts of relatively inert exhaust gas into the intake manifold, lowering the peak combustion temperature. The amount of exhaust gas introduced is regulated by the EGR valve. The EGR valve is vacuum modulated. The vacuum to operate the valve is supplied by an orifice just above the throttle valve in the carburetor.

When there is a high vacuum during heavy acceleration, the valve opens to allow exhaust gas into the intake manifold. At idle or cruising speeds the valve is closed and no exhaust gas is introduced into the intake manifold.

CATALYTIC CONVERTER SYSTEM

The 1975 and later Vega and Monza are equipped with catalytic converters nationwide. A major benefit from the catalytic converter is a large reduction in pollutants, while allowing carburetor settings that provide smoother power, and more spark advance for increased fuel economy and better overall performance.

NOTE: *Unleaded fuel must be used with catalytic converters.*

In addition to the catalytic converters, a restricted fuel inlet is used, which will only accept the smaller fuel nozzles used to dispense unleaded fuel.

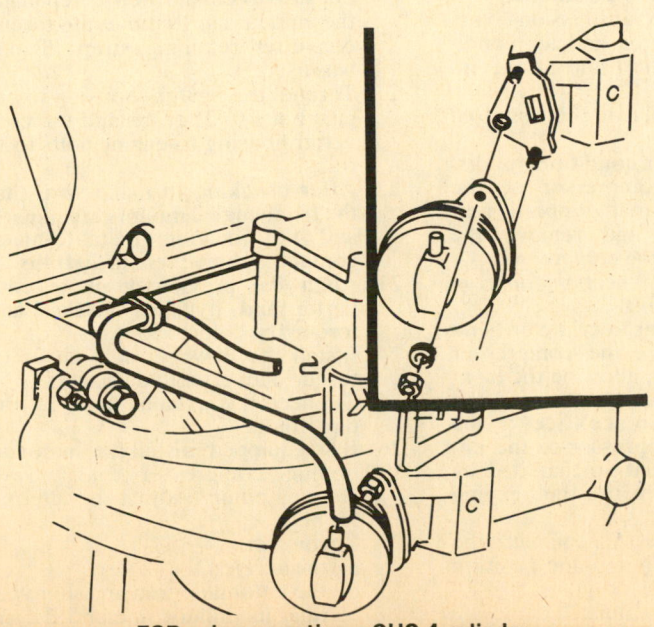

EGR valve mounting—OHC 4 cylinder
(© Chevrolet Div., G.M. Corp)

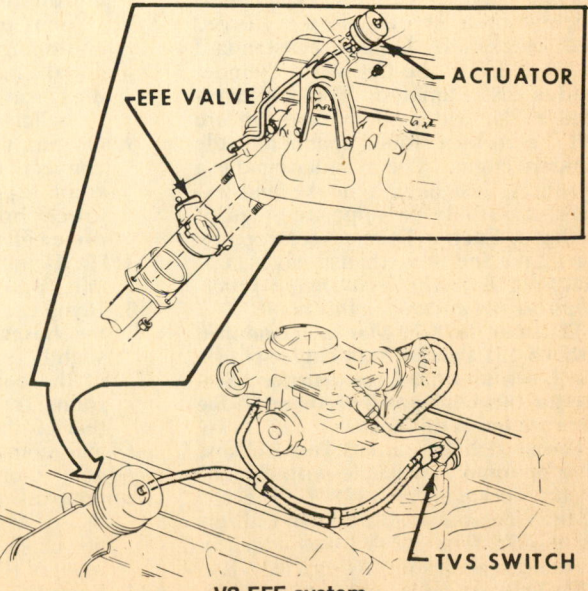

V8 EFE system
(© Chevrolet Div., G.M. Corp)

EARLY FUEL EVAPORATION (EFE)

Early Fuel Evaporation is used on all V8 models and all 1977-79 models. The system consists of an EFE valve at the exhaust manifold flange, an actuator and a thermal vacuum switch (TVS). The TVS is mounted in the water outlet housing and directly controls vacuum in response to coolant temperatures.

The actuator closes the EFE valve when coolant temperatures are below 180°F, routing hot gases to the base of the carburetor. When coolant temperatures reach 180°F, vacuum to the actuator is cut off releasing an internal spring in the actuator and opening the EFE valve.

For further information concerning emission controls, consult the Emission Control Systems Unit Repair Section.

ENGINE

The standard 4 cylinder Vega and 1975-77 Monza engine is a single over-heard camshaft, four cylinder design using a die cast alumnium cylinder block and a cast iron cylinder head. The iron-plated aluminum pistons ride directly on honed and electrochemically treated aluminum bores. The cylinder block is cast of an alloy containing silicon which, after suitable etching, provides a bore surface for the pistons and rings.

The valve train is completely contained in the head, with a straightline vertical valve configuration. The camshaft is driven by a timing belt which in turn is driven from a front crankshaft pulley.

The limited production 1975-76 Cosworth Vega uses the basic Vega engine block with a shorter stroke, forged steel crankshaft. Unlike the standard cast iron head, the Cosworth cylinder head is cast aluminum. The dual overhead cams, water pump, and fan are belt driven in a similar manner to the standard engine. The cylinder head is a crossflow design with intake and exhaust manifolds on opposite sides of the head. Each cylinder is serviced by two intake and two exhaust valves.

NOTE: *Cosworth Vega engine procedures are not covered in this book.*

NOTE: The 1978-79 Monza is equipped with a 4-151 Pontiac built engine of cast iron block and head construction. Service for this engine will be found in the Astre section of this book.

The Monza 2 + 2 and Town Coupe were optionally available with the 262 cu. in. V8 engine in 1975-76. The 350 cu. in. V8 was available only in California in 1975. The 305 V8 was added in 1976 and replaces the 262 cu. in. V8 in 1977. This engine is very similar in design to other small block Chevrolet engines.

NOTE: In 1978 the Buick built V6-196 and 231 engines are offered as options on Monza. Service for these engines may be found in the Apollo section of this book.

NOTE: *The use of anti-seize compound is recommended on all bolts installed in aluminum engine blocks.*

Engine Removal and Installation

4-140

1. Raise and support the hood.
2. Disconnect the battery cables.
3. Drain the cooling system and disconnect the hoses at the radiator.
4. Disconnect the heater hoses at the water pump and at the heat inlet (bottom hose).
5. Disconnect the following emission hoses:
   a. PCV at the cam cover.
   b. The canister vacuum hose at the carburetor.
   c. PCV vacuum hose at the intake manifold.
   d. Bowl vent at the carburetor.
   e. TCS at the rear of the carburetor.
6. Remove the radiator shroud, radiator, fan, fan spacer and air cleaner.
7. Disconnect the follwing electrical leads:
   a. Alternator.
   b. Ignition coil.
   c. Starter solenoid.
   d. Oil pressure sending unit.
   e. Temperature sending unit.
   f. TCS switch at the transmission.
   g. TCS solenoid on the firewall.
   h. Ground strap at the firewall.
8. Disconnect:
   a. Powerglide throttle valve linkage or Turbo Hydra-Matic detent cable.
   b. Fuel line at the rubber hose, rearward of the carburetor.
   c. Automatic transmission vacuum modulator and air conditioning vacuum line at the intake manifold.
   d. Throttle cable at the manifold bellcrank.
9. On cars with air conditioning, disconnect the compressor at the front support, rear support, rear lower bracket and remove the drive belt from the compressor.

NOTE: *Do not disconnect any air conditioning lines or fittings.*

10. Being careful not to crimp or bend the hoses, move the compressor slightly forward, allowing the front of the compressor to rest on the frame forward brace. Secure the rear of the compressor to the engine compartment so that it does not interfere with the engine removal.
11. If so equipped, disconnect the power steering pump and position it out of the way.
12. Raise the car on a hoist.
13. Disconnect the exhaust pipe at the exhaust manifold.
14. Remove the engine flywheel lower cover or the torque converter underpan.
15. On vehicles equipped with automatic transmission:
    a. Mark the converter-to-fly-wheel relationship for reassembly.
    b. Remove the converter to flywheel retaining bolts and install a coverter safety strap, to keep the converter from falling out.
    c. Remove the converter housing to engine retaining bolts.
    d. Loosen the engine front mount retaining bolts at the frame attachment and lower the vehicle on the hoist.
    e. Install a floor jack under the transmission and an engine lifting adapter to raise the engine slightly from its mounts.
    f. Remove the engine front mount retaining bolts.
    g. Remove the engine from the vehicle. Pull the engine forward enough to clear the transmission while slowly lifting the engine.
16. On vehicles with manual transmission:
    a. Remove the flywheel housing to engine retaining bolts.
    b. Proceed with Step 15 above, parts d, e, f, and g.

To install engine:
17. Install two guide pins into the upper bolt holes in the engine block. Guide pins can be fabricated by cutting the heads off two 3/8 in. bolts and sawing screwdriver slots into them.
18. Lower the engine into place, aligning the engine with the transmission.
19. Install the front mount bolts handtight.
20. Install the converter or clutch housing-to-engine bolts, replacing the guide pins. Remove the torque converter retaining strap, if one was used.
21. Torque the clutch housing-to-engine bolts to 25 ft lbs and the converter housing-to-engine bolts to 35 ft lbs.
22. After checking to make sure that the front engine mounts are aligned and not making metal-to-metal contact, tighten them to 20 ft lbs.
23. Align the previously made converter and flywheel marks, and torque the bolts to 35 ft lbs.
24. Install the flywheel dust cover or torque converter underpan.
25. Connect the exhaust pipe at the manifold.
26. If so equipped, install the air conditioning compressor and power steering pump. Adjust the alternator belt.
27. Reconnect:
    a. the accelerator cable,
    b. the automatic transmission vacuum modulator line and the air conditioning vacuum line,
    c. the fuel line, and

d. the Powerglide transmission throttle valve linkage or the Turbo Hydra-Matic detent cable.

28. Attach the following electrical connections:
    a. alternator
    b. coil
    c. starter solenoid
    d. oil pressure switch
    e. temperature switch
    f. TCS transmission switch
    g. TCS solenoid
    h. engine ground strap

29. Replace the air cleaner and install these hoses:
    a. vent tube at the air cleaner base
    b. carburetor bowl vent
    c. PCV vacuum line
    d. vacuum canister hose

30. Install the radiator, radiator panel or shroud, spacer, and fan.

31. Connect the heater and radiator hoses. Fill the cooling system.

32. Connect the battery cables. Start the engine and check for leaks.

V8

1. Raise and support the hood.
2. Disconnect the battery cables.
3. Raise and support the car.
4. Drain the coolant, engine and transmission.
5. Disconnect the exhaust pipes at the manifold.
6. Remove the flywheel or converter underpan.
7. On automatic transmissions, remove the converter-to-flywheel retaining bolts and install a converter retaining strap.
8. Remove the accessible converter housing or flywheel housing-to-engine bolts.
9. Remove the transmission cooler lines from the retaining clips on the side of the engine.
10. Remove the engine front mounting bolts at the frame brackets and lower the car.
11. Remove the radiator panel or shroud.
12. Remove the radiator and fan.
13. Disconnect the heater hose from the water pump and manifold.
14. Remove the air cleaner.
15. Disconnect the electrical leads from:
    • alternator
    • distributor
    • starter solenoid
    • oil pressure switch
    • engine temperature switch
    • temperature gauge switch
    • choke secondary pull-off solenoid
16. Unclip the wiring harness from the rocker cover and position it out of the way.
17. Disconnect the automatic transmission vacuum modulator and air conditioning vacuum line from the manifold.
18. Disconnect the rubber fuel line at the rear of the engine.

19. Disconnect the following:
    • canister vacuum hose at the carburetor
    • accelerator at the carburetor and manifold bracket
    • air conditioning blower delay lead at the rear of the engine.
20. On air conditioned cars, remove the compressor from its mount. Do not disconnect any fittings. Secure the compressor to the fender.
21. Disconnect the power steering pump and lay it aside.
22. Install a floor jack under the transmission.
23. Install a hoist on the engine and raise the engine slightly to take the weight off the engine mounts. Remove the remaining engine to transmission bolts.
24. Remove the engine from the car.
    To install the engine:
25. Install transmission - to - engine guide pins, made from 3/8 in. bolts with the heads cut off, into the engine.
26. Install the engine, aligning the engine with the transmission housing.
27. Align the engine mounts with the frame brackets and lower the engine onto the brackets. Loosely install the engine mount bolts.
28. Remove the guide pins and install the engine-to-housing bolts. Remove the lifting equipment.
29. Remove the support from the transmission and raise and support the car.
30. Remove the converter retaining strap and install and tighten the engine-to-housing bolts.
31. Tighten the engine front mount bolts.
32. Install the converter to the flywheel.
33. Install the flywheel cover or converter underpan.
34. Install the transmission cooler lines in the clips on the side of the block.
35. Connect the exhaust pipe at the manifold and lower the car.
36. Install the air conditioning compressor and power steering pump. Adjust the drive belts.

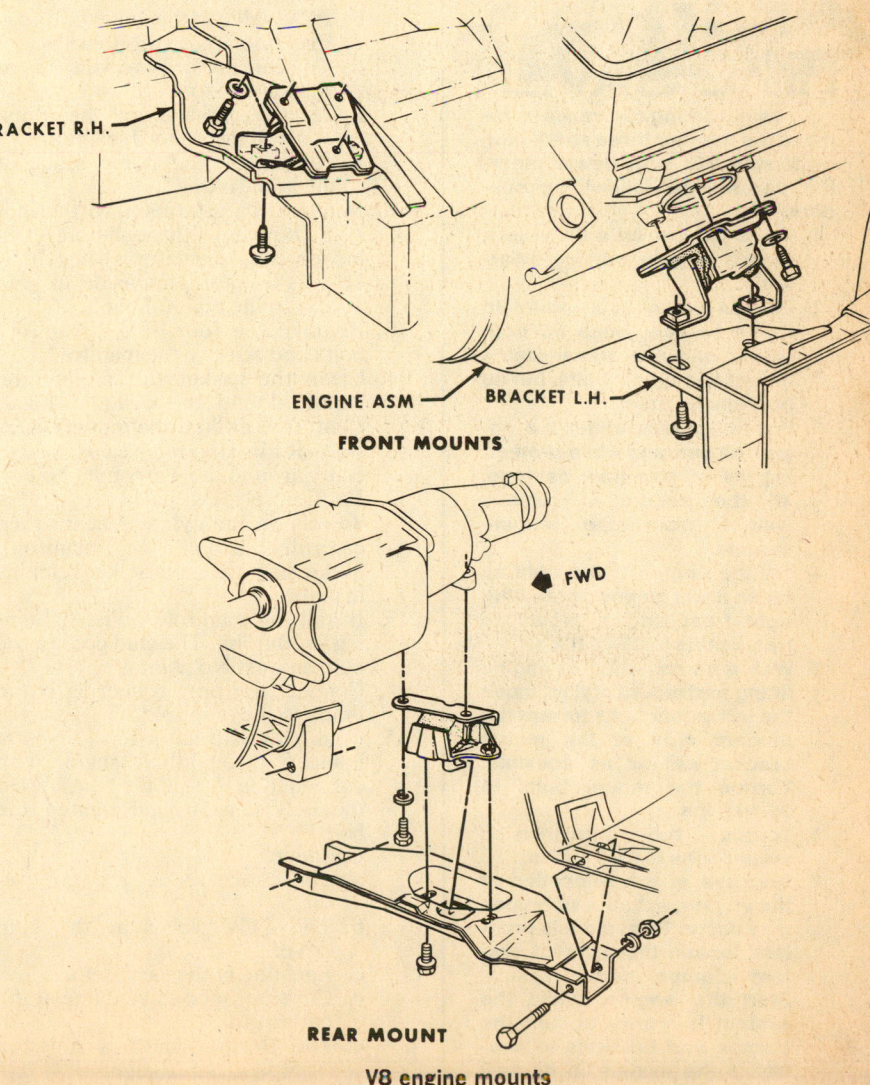

BRACKET R.H.

ENGINE ASM   BRACKET L.H.

FRONT MOUNTS

FWD

REAR MOUNT

V8 engine mounts
(© Chevrolet Div., G.M. Corp)

37. Connect the following:
    - canister vacuum hose to carburetor
    - Accelerator cable at carburetor and manifold bracket
    - air conditioning blower delay lead at side of engine
    - Fuel line to rubber hose at rear of engine
    - air conditioning vacuum line.
38. Install the electrical harness in the clip in the rocker cover and connect the following:
    - alternator
    - distributor
    - starter solenoid
    - oil pressure switch
    - engine temperature switch
    - temperature gauge switch
    - choke secondary pull-off solenoid.
39. Connect the heater hose at the water pump and at the manifold.
40. Install the radiator, fan, radiator panel or shroud, fill the cooling system, add engine oil and fill the transmission.

TIME SAVER

To gain working clearance to remove the number three spark plug on Monza V8s with power steering, perform the following procedure.

1. Raise the car on a lift or jack stands to gain working clearance.
2. Loosen the engine mount to frame bracket bolts on both sides, and the transmission mount to support bolts, but do not remove them.
3. Position a jack under the engine oil pan and while protecting the oil pan from damage, lift the engine to remove weight from the engine mounts.
4. Pry the engine to the right as far as it will go and tighten the right front engine mount to frame bolts to 35-40 ft lbs.
5. With a combination of engine lifting and mount prying, move the left mount bolts toward the inboard side of the mount bracket as far as possible. Torque the mount bolts to 35-40 ft lbs.
6. Torque the transmission mount bolts to 21-31 ft lbs.
7. Because of the relocation of the engine, exhaust vibrations may occur. To avoid this problem, loosen the exhaust system clamps and brackets. Start the engine. While the system is warm, tighten the clamps and brackets to neutralize the system in its new location.

41. Install the air cleaner.
42. Connect the battery cables, start the engine and check for leaks.

MANIFOLDS

Intake Manifold Removal and Installation

4-140

1. Raise and support the hood.
2. Disconnect the negative battery cable.
3. Drain the cooling system.
4. Remove the EGR tube retaining clamps from both the intake and exhaust manifolds. Remove the EGR tube by carefully driving it off.
5. Disconnect the heater hose at the fitting on the intake manifold.
6. Disconnect the air cleaner vent tube from the valve cover, then remove the air cleaner.
7. Remove the air cleaner silencer.
8. Disconnect:
    a. The choke rod at the carburetor.
    b. PCV valve at the valve cover.
    c. Fuel line at the carburetor.
    d. The carburetor bowl vent line at the carburetor.
    e. Throttle linkage and the transmission throttle valve linkage.
    f. Power steering pump brace at the manifold.
9. Remove the alternator to thermostat housing through-bolt and loosen the alternator swivel bolt. Move the alternator aside to gain access to the manifold bolt.
10. Remove the four intake manifold bolts and remove the manifold.
11. Clean the gasket surfaces on the manifold and the cylinder head. Coat the gasket mating surfaces with RTV silicone sealant especially around the water inlet hole.
12. Position a new gasket over the dowels on the cylinder head, then carefully install the manifold. Make sure that the gasket remains in place.
13. Install the manifold bolts, tightening to 30 ft lbs. The stud goes in the hole nearest No. 3 intake port.
14. Connect the power steering pump brace to the manifold.
15. Coat the alternator-to-thermostat housing through-bolt shank with chassis lube. Install the bolt, adjust the belt tension and tighten the bolt.
16. Connect:
    a. The choke rod at the carburetor.
    b. The PCV valve at the cam cover.
    c. Fuel line at the carburetor.
    d. Carburetor bowl vent line at the carburetor.
    e. The throttle and transmission throttle valve linkage.
    f. Vacuum connections at the carburetor.

17. Install the air cleaner silencer and secure it to the heat stove tube.
18. Install the air cleaner. Connect the vent tube to the valve cover.
19. Connect the heater hose to the intake manifold fitting and fill the cooling system.
20. Raise the car. Install the EGR tube on the intake and exhaust manifolds.
21. Install the EGR tube retaining clamps. Lower the car.
22. Connect the negative battery cable and start the engine. Check for leaks and adjust the carburetor.

V8

1. Remove the air cleaner.
2. Drain the radiator.
3. Disconnect:
    a. Battery cables at the battery.
    b. Upper radiator and heater hoses at the manifold.
    c. Crankcase ventilation hoses as required.
    d. Fuel line at the rubber hose.
    e. Accelerator linkage at the pedal lever.
    f. Vacuum hose at the distributor.
    g. Power brake hose at the accelerator bracket.
    h. Ignition coil and temperature sending switch wires.
    i. Air diverter valve line.
    j. Choke pull-off lead.
    k. Air conditioning bracket or power steering brace.
    l. Choke hot and cold air pipes.
4. Remove the distributor cap and scribe the rotor position relative to distributor body.
5. Remove the distributor.
6. If applicable, remove the Delcotron upper bracket.
7. Remove the air pump.
8. Remove the manifold to head attaching bolts, then remove the manifold and carburetor as an assembly.
9. If the manifold is to be replaced, transfer the carburetor (and mounting studs), and other applicable equipment to the new manifold.
10. Before installing the manifold, thoroughly clean the gasket and seal surfaces of the cylinder heads and manifold.
11. Install the manifold end seals, folding the tabs if applicable, and the manifold/head gaskets, using a sealing compound around the water passages. Make sure the gaskets are firmly cemented in place before installing the manifold.
12. When installing the manifold, care should be taken not to dislocate the end seals. it is helpful to use a pilot in the distributor opening. Tighten the manifold bolts to the proper torque in the sequence illustrated.
13. Install the distributor with the rotor in its original location as indicated by the scribe line. If the engine has been disturbed, refer to Distributor Removal and Installation.

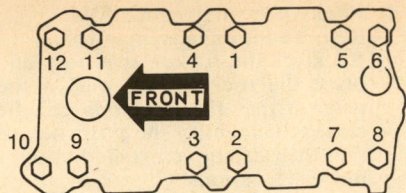

Intake manifold torque sequence—V8

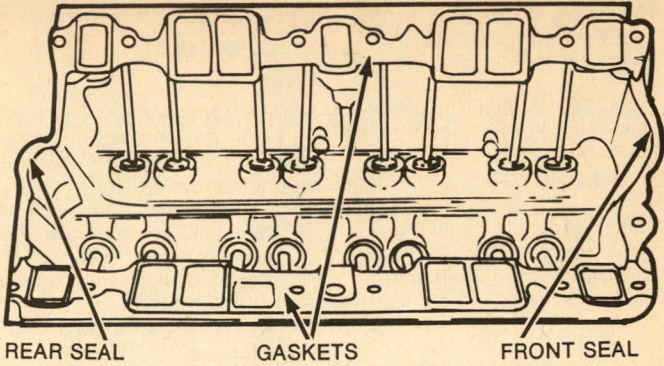

REAR SEAL   GASKETS   FRONT SEAL

V8 intake manifold gasket and seals
(© Chevrolet Div., G.M. Corp)

14. If applicable, install the Delcotron upper bracket and adjust the belt tension.
15. Install the air pump. Adjust all drive belts.
16. Connect all components disconnected in Step 3 above.
17. Fill the cooling system, start the engine, check for leaks and adjust the ignition timing and carburetor idle speed and mixture.

Exhaust Manifold Removal and Installation

4-140

1. From under the car, disconnect the exhaust pipe from the manifold.
2. Remove the intake manifold as described above.
3. Disconnect the oil dipstick bracket at the exhaust manifold.
4. Remove the exhaust manifold bolts, then remove the manifold and carburetor heater assembly.
5. Install the carburetor heater assembly on the new manifold.
6. Install the exhaust manifold and manifold bolts (loosely). The upper bolts are shorter.
7. Tighten the manifold bolts to 30 ft lbs.
8. Connect the exhaust pipe to the manifold.
9. Connect the oil dipstick bracket to the exhaust manifold.
10. Install the intake manifold.

V8 RIGHT SIDE

1. Disconnect the negative battery cable.
2. On air conditioned cars, remove the emission vapor canister. Without disconnecting any lines, remove the air conditioning compressor and place it out of the way.
3. Raise the car and disconnect the exhaust pipe from the manifold. Remove the engine mount-to-frame bolts and slide the engine to the left.
4. Lower the car and disconnect the spark plug wires and temperature sender wire. Remove the alternator and alternator bracket from the exhaust manifold.
5. Remove No. 6 and 8 spark plugs and the six manifold attaching bolts. Remove the spark plug shields from the brackets and bend the brackets upward.
6. Remove the exhaust manifold and EFE valve as an assembly.
7. Installation is the reverse of removal. On installation, be sure to

clean the mating surfaces of the manifold and cylinder head, adjust belt tension where necessary, and align the engine.

V8 LEFT SIDE

1. Disconnect the negative battery cable.
2. Raise the car and disconnect the exhaust pipe from the manifold.
3. Remove the engine mount-to-frame bolts and slide the engine to the right.
4. Remove the two rear manifold bolts, then raise the engine and place a 6 in. piece of 2 x 4 wood block under the left engine mount.
5. Lower the car, remove the air cleaner and dipstick tube bracket nut, and move the dipstick tube aside.
6. Remove the remaining attaching bolts and remove the manifold.
7. To install, clean the mating surfaces of the manifold and cylinder head, install the manifold and the front four attaching bolts, and start the two rear bolts.
8. Install the dipstick tube bracket and air cleaner. Raise the car and remove the block from under the left engine mount.
9. Tighten the two rear manifold attaching bolts and connect the exhaust pipe to the manifold. Align and install the engine mount-to-frame bolts.
10. Lower the car and connect the negative battery cable.

VALVE SYSTEM

The 4-140 cylinder valve train is an overhead camshaft operating mechanical valve tappets (hydraulic starting 1976). The 262, 305, and 350 cu. in. V8s use a single camshaft operating hydraulic lifters.

Valve Lash Adjustment

4 CYLINDER THROUGH 1975

1. Mark the locations of No. 1 and 4 spark plug wires on the side of the distributor with chalk. (Refer to the firing order illustration.)
2. Remove the distributor cap, air

cleaner, and valve cover. Discard the old gasket and thoroughly clean the gasket surfaces.
3. Turn the engine until the rotor points to the No. 1 position and the points are open. The No. 1 intake and exhaust, No. 2 intake and No. 3 exhaust valves are adjusted at this position. The intake valve is the front valve for each cylinder, and the exhaust valve is the rear one.

FRONT | I E I E I E I E |

OHC 4 cylinder valve arrangement

4. Insert the correct size feeler gauge between the camshaft lobe and the valve tappet. If the clearance is between 0.014 and 0.017 in. for intakes or 0.029 and 0.032 in. for exhausts, no adjustment is necessary. This is due to the fact that the adjusting mechanism only allows adjustments in increments of 0.003 in.
5. If lash is 0.003 in. or more out of adjustment, insert a 1/8 in. allen wrench into the tappet adjusting screw and turn it one full turn. Turning clockwise tightens; turning counterclockwise loosens.
6. Check the lash again and adjust further if necessary. Always turn

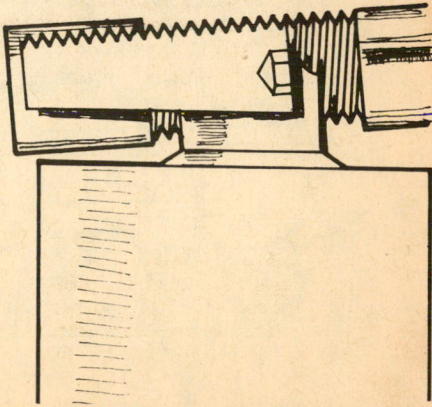

Valve tappet and adjusting screw assembly—OHC 4-cylinder
(© Chevrolet Div., G.M. Corp)

the adjuster screw one full turn. You can feel the flat spot by pressing down on the tappet while adjusting.

7. Turn the engine so that the rotor points to No. 4. Adjust No. 2 exhaust, No. 3 intake, and No. 4 intake and exhaust valves in this position.

8. Replace the valve cover using a new gasket coated with gasket cement, air cleaner, and distributor cap.

V8

V8 engines require no periodic valve adjustment. For initial adjustment procedures after overhaul of cylinder head or removal of valve train, see the Camaro section.

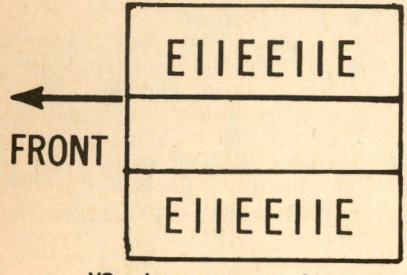

V8 valve arrangement

Valve Guides

4-140

Valves with oversize stems are available in three sizes: 0.003 in. o/s, 0.015 in. o/s and 0.030 in o/s.

V8

Valve guides are integral with the cylinder head. Valve guide bores may be reamed to accommodate oversize valve stems or the guides may be knurled (if wear permits) to allow the retention of standard size valves.

Cylinder Head Removal and Installation

4-140

NOTE: *Cylinder head gasket removal and installation does not require separating the intake and exhaust manifolds from the cylinder head.*

1. Remove the timing belt cover and camshaft cover. Drain the cooling system.
2. Remove the timing belt and camshaft sprocket.
3. Remove the intake and exhaust manifolds.
4. Disconnect the water hose at the thermostat housing (outlet).
5. Remove the cylinder head bolts, then the head and gasket.

NOTE: *If the head sticks, bump the starter a few times to loosen it with compression. Do not insert any tools between the head and block to pry them apart.*

6. Using a new gasket (smooth side up), carefully position the cylinder head on the block.
7. Install the cylinder head bolts finger-tight. Use an anti-seize compound on the threads. Install the lifting bracket under the second head bolt from the front on the spark plug side. The 6-3/8 in. bolts are installed on the manifold side and the 5-5/8 in. bolts are installed on the spark plug side.
8. Tighten the head bolts to 60 ft lbs (in steps), using the illustration.
9. Connect the water hose to the thermostat housing.
10. Install the intake and exhaust manifolds.
11. Install the timing belt and sprocket.
12. Install the front cover and camshaft cover.

V8

1. Drain the coolant.

2. Remove the intake manifold.
3. Remove the exhaust manifolds.
4. Back off the rocker arm nuts and pivot the rocker arms out of the way so that the pushrods can be removed. Identify the pushrods so that they can be reinstalled in their original locations.
5. Remove the cylinder head bolts and cylinder heads.
6. Install using new gaskets. The head gasket is installed with the bead up.

NOTE: *Coat a steel gasket on both sides with sealer. If a steel/asbestos gasket is used, do not apply sealer. Clean the bolt threads, apply sealing compound and install the bolts finger tight.*

7. Tighten the head bolts a little at a time in the sequence illustrated.

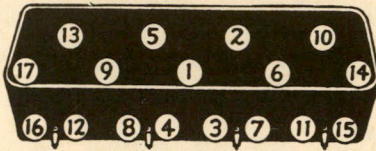

V8 cylinder head torque sequence

8. Install the exhaust and intake manifolds as described previously.
9. Adjust the valves as explained in the Camaro section. Fill the cooling system.

V8 Rocker Arm Removal and Installation

Rocker arms are removed by removing the adjusting nut. Be sure to adjust valve lash after replacing rocker arms.

Rocker arm studs that have damaged threads or are loose in the cylinder heads may be replaced with new studs available in 0.003 in. and 0.013 in. oversize or the bores may be tapped and screw-in replacement studs used. Do not attempt to install an oversize stud without reaming the stud bore. Studs are press-fit. Lubricate the press-fit area of the stud with hypoid axle lubricant.

NOTE: *If engine is equipped with the AIR exhaust emission control system, the interfering components of the system must be removed. Disconnect the lines at the air injection nozzles in the exhaust manifolds.*

TIMING COVER, BELT OR CHAIN, AND CAMSHAFT

Front Cover Removal and Installation

4-140

1. Raise and support the hood.
2. Disconnect the negative battery cable.
3. Remove the fan and spacer.
4. Loosen the two lower cover retaining screws.
5. Remove the two top retaining screws and remove the cover, lift-

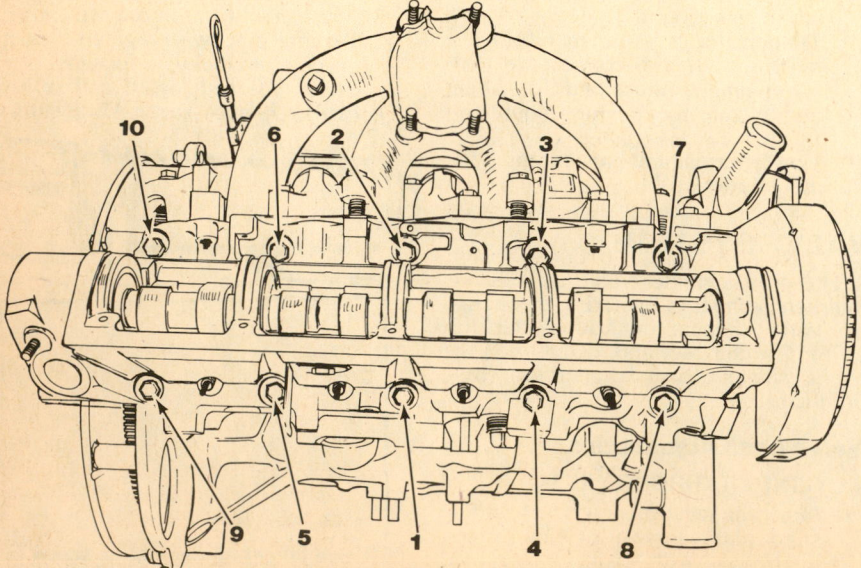

OHC 4 cylinder head torque sequence (© Chevrolet Div., G.M. Corp)

ing it until the slots clear the lower screws.

6. To install, position the cover, lowering it until the slots are over the lower screws. Loosely install the lower screws.
7. Install the upper screws, then tighten all four screws to 50 in lbs.
8. Install the spacer and fan, tightening the bolts to 20 ft lbs.
9. Connect the battery cable and remove the bolt from the hood hold-open link.

V8

NOTE: *The timing case cover oil seal may be replaced without removing the case cover.*

After gaining access to the oil seal, pry the old seal out of the cover with a screwdriver. Then, lubricate the new seal and drive it into place with a seal installer tool.

1. Remove the fan belt, fan, and pulley.
2. Remove the radiator and shroud.
3. Remove the accessory drive pulley and the torsional damper retaining bolt.
4. Remove the damper from the crankshaft.
5. Remove the water pump.
6. Remove the front cover bolts and remove the front cover and gasket.
7. Clean the gasket mating surfaces.
8. Remove any oil pan gasket material that may still be adhering to the oil pan-engine block joint face.
9. Apply 1/8 in. bead of silicone sealant or the equivalent to the joint formed by the oil pan and cylinder block, as well as to the entire oil pan front lip.
10. Coat the cover gasket with gasket sealer and install it on the front cover.
11. Loosely install the front cover on the block. Install the 4 top bolts loosely (about 3 turns). Install two 1/4-20x1/2 in. screws in the hole at each side of the front cover and apply a bead of sealant on the bottom of the seal and install it on the cover.
12. Tighten the screws evenly while aligning the dowel pins and holes in the front cover.
13. Remove the 1/4-20x1/2 in. screws and install the rest of the cover screws.
14. Further installation is the reverse of removal. Refill the engine with oil.

4-140 Timing Belt and Sprocket Removal and Installation

NOTE: *This entire procedure is not necessary to remove only the camshaft sprocket. This can be done simply by removing the upper timing belt cover bolts and pulling the cover forward. Remove the cam sprocket and timing belt. Install the sprocket and belt as un assembly, and reinstall the timing belt*

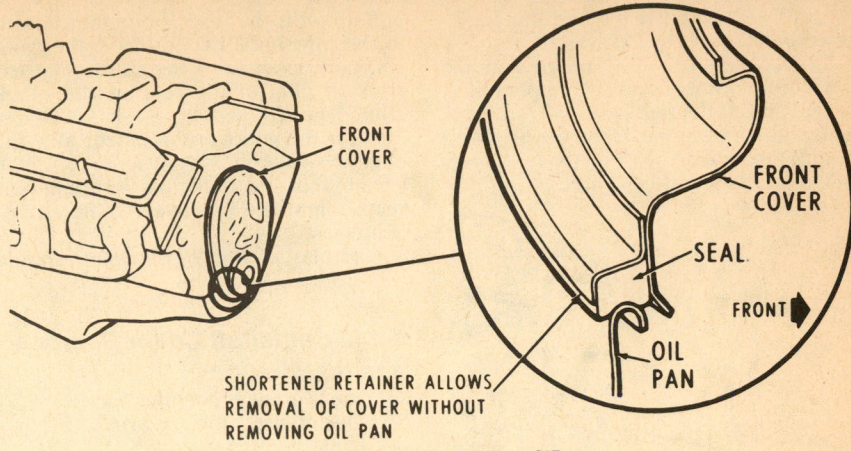

Oil seal installation—V8
(© Chevrolet Div., G.M. Corp)

cover. It is not necessary to adjust the timing belt tension.

1. Raise and support the hood.
2. Disconnect the negative battery cable.
3. Loosen the air conditioner and alternator as necessary and remove the drive belts.
4. Remove the crankshaft pulley and four pulley-to-sprocket bolts. Remove the pulley and damper or washer as applicable.

NOTE: *It is not necessary to remove the pulley if only the camshaft sprocket is being removed.*

5. Drain the engine coolant and loosen the water pump bolts to relieve the tension on the timing belt.
6. Remove the timing belt lower cover.
7. Remove the timing belt.
8. Align one of the holes in the camshaft timing sprocket with the bolt head behind the sprocket. Using a socket on the bolt head to keep the sprocket from rotating, remove the sprocket retaining bolt and washer.
9. Remove the camshaft sprocket.
10. The camshaft sprocket may be removed.
11. Pull the crankshaft sprocket with an installation tool. Make sure that the timing mark is facing out and that the key is installed.
12. To install the camshaft sprocket, align the dowel in the camshaft with the locating hole in the end of the camshaft.
13. Install the sprocket retaining bolt, tightening to 80 ft lbs.
14. Align the timing mark on the camshaft sprocket with the notch on the timing belt upper cover and the crankshaft sprocket timing mark with the cast rib on the oil pump cover.
15. Install the timing belt on the crankshaft sprocket, then with the back of the belt positioned in the water pump track, install the belt on the camshaft sprocket. Make sure that both sprockets maintain their indexed positions.

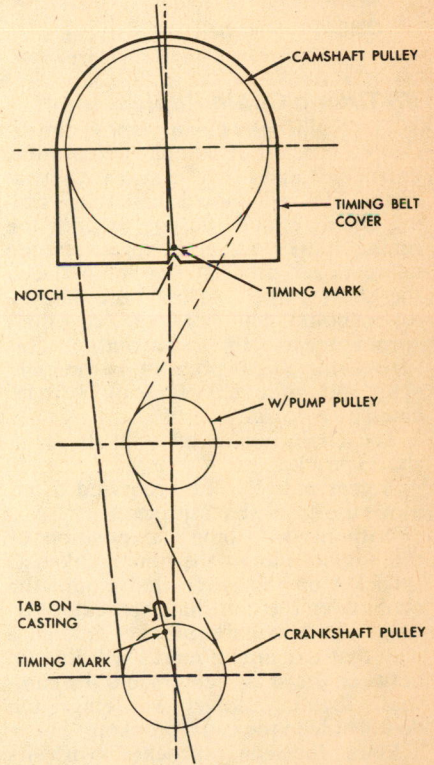

OHC 4 timing sprocket alignment marks
(© Chevrolet Div., G.M. Corp)

16. Install the lower timing belt cover, using anti-seize compound on the threads of the bolts and tightening them to 50 in lbs.
17. Adjust the timing belt tension as described under Water Pump Removal and Installation, Steps 11 and 12.
18. Fill the cooling system.
19. Install the accessory drive pulley to the crankshaft sprocket, aligning the tang on the pulley with the keyway on the crankshaft. Install the damper locating dowel in the locating hole of the sprocket.
20. Loosely install the four sprocket bolts, then install the crankshaft (center) bolt. Tighten the crank-

shaft bolt to 80 ft lbs and the four sprocket bolts to 15 ft lbs.

21. Install the alternator and air conditioning compressor as applicable and adjust the belts.
22. Install the engine front cover, fan and fan spacer.
23. Connect the battery cable.

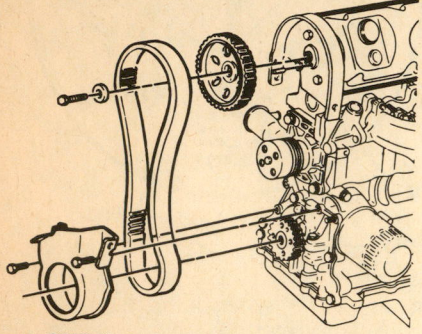

OHC 4 timing belt and sprockets
(© Chevrolet Div., G.M. Corp)

V8 Timing Chain Replacement

To replace the chain, remove the radiator core, water pump, the harmonic balancer, and the crankcase front cover. This will allow access to the timing chain. Crank the engine until the timing marks on both sprockets are nearest each other and in line between the shaft centers. Then take out the three bolts that hold the camshaft sprocket to the camshaft. This sprocket is a light press fit on the camshaft and will come off easily. It is located by a dowel.

The chain comes off with the camshaft sprocket.

A gear puller will be required to remove the crankshaft sprocket.

Without disturbing the position of the engine, mount the new crankshaft sprocket on the shaft, and mount the chain over the camshaft sprocket. Arrange the camshaft sprocket in such a way that the timing marks will line up between the shaft centers and the camshaft locating dowel will enter the dowel hole in the cam sprocket.

Place the cam sprocket, with its chain mounted over it, in position and

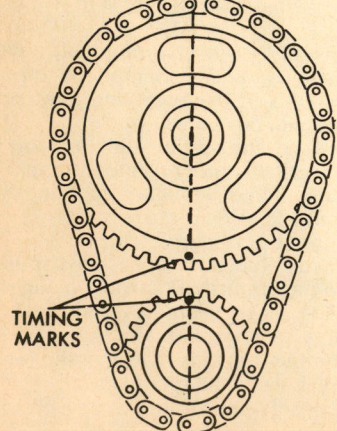

V8 timing mark alignment

pull up with the three bolts that hold it to the camshaft sprocket onto the shaft. Do not drive the camshaft sprocket onto the shaft. The expansion plug at the rear of the block could be dislodged.

After the gears are in place, turn the engine two full revolutions to make certain that the timing marks are in correct alignment between the shaft centers.

End-play of the V8 camshaft should be zero.

4-140 Camshaft Cover Removal and Installation

1. Raise and support the hood.
2. Disconnect the negative battery cable.
3. Remove the air cleaner and the vent tube (at cam cover).
4. Remove the PCV valve from the cam cover.
5. Remove the cam cover screws and the cover.
6. To install, reverse the procedure. Always use a new gasket coated with gasket cement. The oil filler cap is at the forward end of the cover. Tighten the cam cover screws to 35 in lbs.

Camshaft Removal and Installation

4-140

NOTE: *A special valve tappet depressing tool is necessary for camshaft removal.*

1. Remove the hood.
2. Remove the camshaft timing sprocket.
3. Remove the three screws securing the camshaft seal and retainer assembly and timing cover to the cylinder head.
4. Inspect the seal, prying it out and replacing it if necessary.
5. Remove the camshaft cover.
6. Disconnect the fuel line at the carburetor.
7. Remove:
   a. Idle solenoid from its bracket.
   b. The choke coil, cover and rod assembly.
   c. Ignition distributor.
8. Raise the vehicle on a hoist, disconnect the front engine mounts at the body attachment, raise the front of the engine and install wood blocks, about 1-1/2 in. thick, between the engine mounts and the body.
9. Install camshaft removal tool on the cylinder head to hold down the lifters so that the camshaft may be removed.
   a. Position the tool so that the attaching holes are aligned with the lower cam cover bolt holes and the tappet levers of the tool are aligned to depress both valves of each cylinder.
   b. Back off the bolts in the bottom of the tool so that they are not

contacting the bosses beneath the tool.
   c. Install the tool attaching bolts, tightening them securely.
   d. Tighten the bolts in the bottom of the tool until they just touch the bosses of the cylinder head. Before depressing the tappets, rotate the crankshaft pulley timing mark 90° clockwise from the timing mark on the tab. This assures that the pistons are not at TDC and will prevent valve-to-piston contact.
   e. Grease the ball end of the lever depressing bolts and tighten the bolts to depress the tappets.

NOTE: *Torque the lever bolts to 10 ft lbs. If more tightening is required, check to see that the tool is properly installed, then proceed cautiously to prevent damaging the depressing lever.*

10. Slide the camshaft forward until it clears the head.

NOTE: *The camshaft bearings may be removed. It is not necessary to remove the camshaft end plug. Gently tap out the bearings, starting at the forward end. Tap out the rear bearing slowly into the distributor housing, being careful not to unseat the end plug. Crush the rear bearing to remove it from the distributor housing. Install, starting with the rear bearing. The oil holes in the bearings must align with the oil holes in the case. On the first two bearings the oil holes are at 11 o'clock (as seen from the front of the engine) and the oil groove in the number one bearing toward the front of the engine.*

11. Install the camshaft with the journals seated in the bores.
12. With the car up on a hoist, raise the front of the engine and remove the wood blocks from the engine mounts.
13. Install the front engine mounts, then lower the vehicle.
14. Using a new gasket, install the timing belt upper cover and retainer plate and seal assembly. Tighten the retaining bolts to 15 ft lbs.
15. Using a dial indicator, measure the camshaft end-play. If it is not 0.004-0.012 in., select a camshaft retainer (according to cam locator thickness) which will provide more or less end-play as required.
16. Remove the tappet depressing tool by first releasing the tappet depressing lever bolts, and then removing the tool attaching bolts.
17. Install:
   a. Camshaft timing sprocket.
   b. The timing belt.
   c. Front engine cover.
   d. Distributor.
18. Adjust the valve tappets.
19. Install the camshaft cover.
20. Install and adjust the carburetor choke coil, cover and rod assembly.
21. Connect the carburetor fuel line.
22. Install the idle solenoid to the bracket.

23. Check and adjust the ignition timing.

V8
1. Drain the cooling system and remove the radiator. Remove the hood.
2. Remove the water pump and the timing case cover.
3. Turn the crankshaft until the timing marks on the camshaft and crankshaft sprockets are aligned.
4. Remove the valve covers and loosen each rocker arm nut enough to turn the rocker to the side and remove the pushrods. Keep the pushrods in order when they are removed from the engine.
5. Remove the distributor cap and mark the position of the rotor relative to the distributor body and the position of the distributor body relative to the engine. Remove the distributor.
6. Remove the intake manifold, then remove the valve lifters from the engine. Keep the lifters in order when they are removed from the engine.
7. Remove the fuel pump.
8. Remove the timing chain and sprockets from the engine.
9. Install two 5/16 in.-18x4 bolts in the holes in the front of the cam and carefully slide it out of the engine.

NOTE: *On some engine and model combinations it will be necessary to disconnect the motor mounts and jack up the front of the engine or remove the grille from the car in order to gain adequate clearance in front of the engine to get the camshaft out of the engine.*

10. Installation is the reverse of removal.

PISTON & ROD INSTALLATION

NOTE: *4-140 oversize pistons were not supplied initially, since there was no mechanical means available for duplicating the cylinder bore electrochemical etching process. A mechanical honing process has been perfected and oversize pistons are now available.*

The F on the 4 cylinder piston must face toward the front of the engine. On V8s, install the piston with the tang on the connecting rod bearing on the side away from the camshaft. Be sure that the pistons and rods are installed in their original locations.

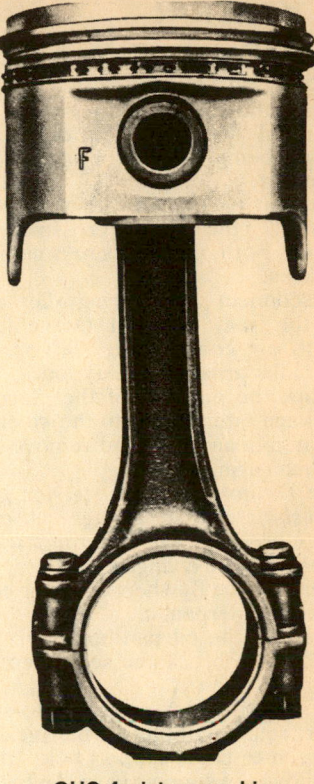

OHC 4 piston marking
(© Chevrolet Div., G.M. Corp)

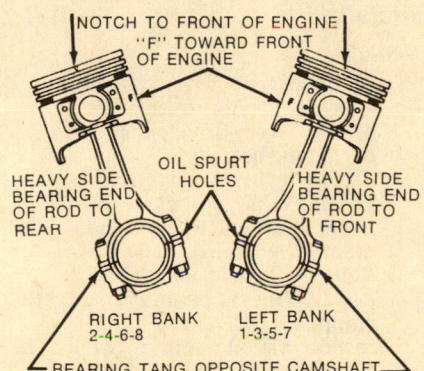

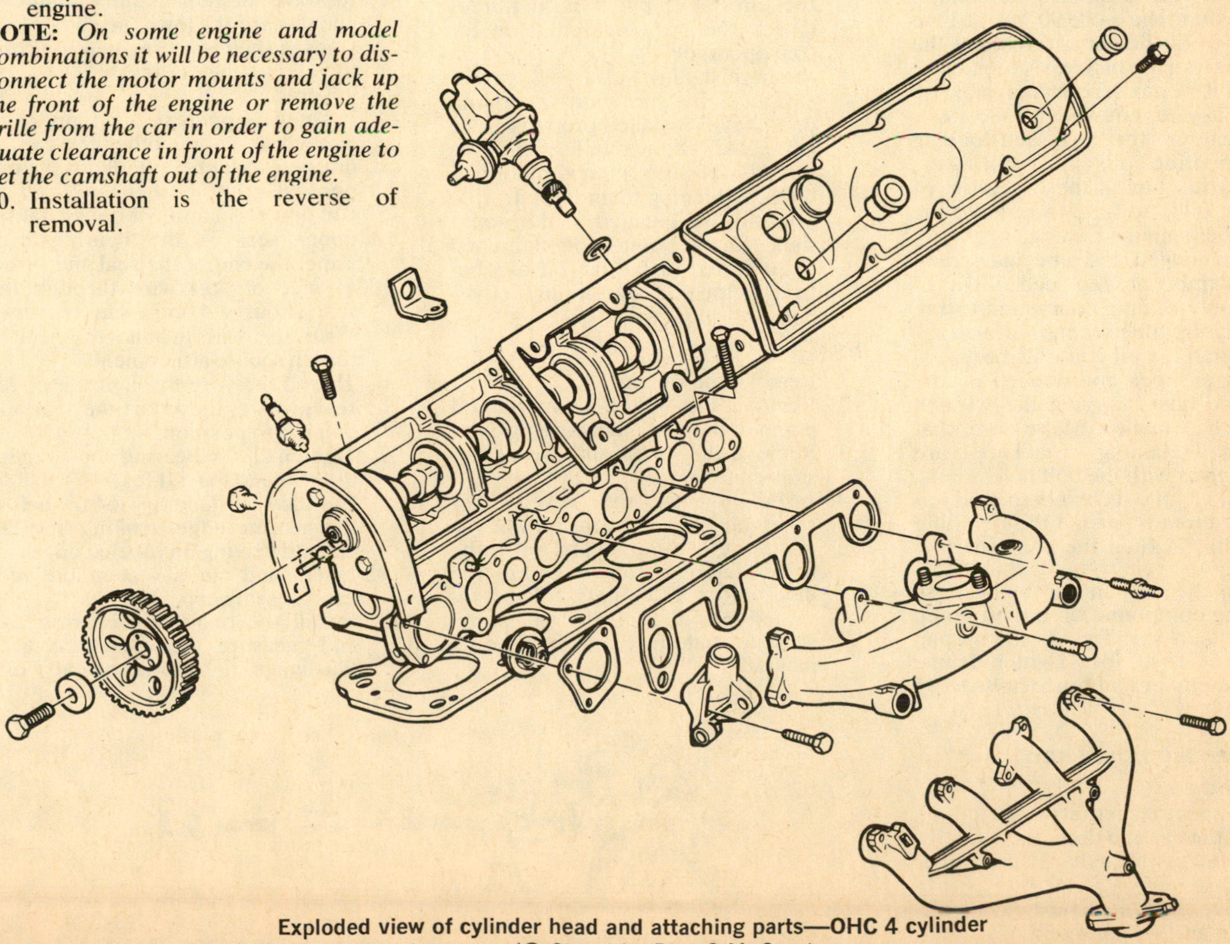

Piston-to-rod relationship—V8

Exploded view of cylinder head and attaching parts—OHC 4 cylinder
(© Chevrolet Div., G.M. Corp)

LUBRICATION

4-140 Oil Pan and Baffle Removal and Installation

1. Raise the vehicle and drain the engine oil. Raise the front of the engine, being careful not to distort the pan.
2. Support the engine with a jack and remove the frame crossmember and both front crossmember braces.
3. Disconnect the steering idler arm at the frame side rail. On vehicles with air conditioning, disconnect the idler arm at the relay rod.
4. Mark the position of the steering linkage pitman arm to the steering gear pitman shaft and remove the pitman arm.

NOTE: *Do not rotate the steering gear pitman shaft while the linkage is disconnected, because the steering wheel alignment will be changed.*

5. Remove the flywheel cover or converter underpan.
6. Remove the oil pan bolts, tap the oil pan to break the seal, then remove the pan.
7. Remove the pick-up screen-to-support retaining bolt and the pick-up screen-to-baffle support bolts, then remove the support from the baffle.
8. Remove the bolt which secures the oil drain back tube to the baffle, then rotate the baffle 90° toward the left side of the car and remove the baffle from the pick-up screen.
9. The oil pump screen and pick up tube may be removed as follows:
   a. Remove the two self-locking mounting bolts (in block).
   b. Lightly tap on the U section of the pick-up tube to remove the tube from the casting.
   c. If damaged, the tube and screen assembly are replaced as a unit.
   d. Apply sealing compound to the pick-up tube sealing surface.
   e. Install the tube into its bore, using an open end wrench on the tube boss, tapping the wrench with a mallet. Make sure that the retaining brackets are aligned with the bolt holes.
   f. Using anti-seize compound on the threads, install the retaining bolts. Tighten the bolts to 25 ft lbs.
10. Install the oil pan and baffle. Use sealing compound on the oil pump gasket surface. Tighten the oil pan bolts to 15 ft lbs. Tighten frame crossmember and brace bolts to 35 ft lbs.

V8 Oil Pan Removal and Installation

1. Disconnect the battery.
2. Raise the car and drain the oil.
3. Disconnect the exhaust crossover pipe.
4. Remove the converter housing underpan and splash shield
5. Scribe marks on each side of the frame crossmember and support the engine. Remove the frame crossmember.
6. Disconnect the steering idler arm at the frame side rail.
7. Disconnect the starter brace and remove the starter.
8. Remove the oil pan bolts and remove the oil pan.
9. Installation is the reverse of removal. Use new gaskets with sealer as a retainer and be sure to match the scribe marks when installing the crossmember. Fill the engine with oil.

Oil Pump Removal and Installation

4-140

1. Remove:
   a. Front engine cover.
   b. Accessory drive pulley.
   c. Timing belt.
   d. Timing belt lower cover.
   e. Crankshaft sprocket.
2. Raise the vehicle on a hoist and drain the engine oil.
3. Remove the oil pan and baffle.
4. Remove the oil pump bolts and the pump.
5. Inspect the oil pump for wear. The pump gears and body are not serviced separately. Replacement of the entire oil pump is required. Check the pressure regulator for free operation.
6. When installing, clean all gasket surfaces. Be sure that the pump drive key is installed properly. Use anti-seize compound on the threads of the pump mounting bolts, tightening them to 15 ft. lbs. The stud is installed in the upper right (facing pump) and tightened to 30 ft lbs. Install the oil pan before tightening the timing cover bolts.

V8

1. Remove the oil pan.
2. Remove the bolt holding the oil pump to the rear main bearing cap.
3. Remove the pump and the extension shaft.
4. Installation is the reverse of removal. Align the slot on the top of the extension shaft with the drive tang on the lower end of the distributor driveshaft. The installed position of the oil pump screen should be parallel to the oil pan rails.

Priming the Oil Pump

To prime the oil pump, fill the gear cavity with engine oil. Do not use grease.

4-140 Oil Pump (Front Cover) Seal Removal and Installation

1. Remove the following:
   a. Engine front cover.
   b. Accessory drive pulley.
   c. Timing belt.
   d. Timing belt lower cover.
   e. Crankshaft timing sprocket.
2. Pry out the old seal, being careful not to damage the housing seal surfaces.
3. Coat the lips of the new seal with oil and apply sealing compound to the outside diameter of the seal.
4. Install the seal with the closed end outward.
5. Install all components removed in Step 1 above.

Rear Main Oil Seal Removal and Installation

4-140

NOTE: *This repair can be made without removing the engine, but the transmission must be removed so that the crankshaft can be lowered.*

1. Remove the oil pan and baffle.
2. Remove the rear main bearing cap and discard the lower seal.
3. Loosen the remaining bearing caps to allow the crankshaft to be lowered.
4. Push the upper seal on one end enough so that the other end can be grasped with pliers. Pull out the upper seal.
5. Cut and form a new braided fabric upper seal in the bearing cap. Taper the end of the seal and insert a piece of soft wire through the seal about 1/4 in. from the end. Wrap the wire around the seal to form a secure attachment.
6. Thread the wire through the upper seal groove, then start the seal and pull it into position.
7. Tighten all the bearing caps except the rear cap to 65 ft lbs.
8. Cut the seal flush to 1/64 in. below the bearing edge, making a clean cut and leaving no raveled edges.
9. Install and cut a seal in the rear main bearing cap.
10. Install the rear main bearing cap and measure the clearance with Plastigage, tightening the cap bolts

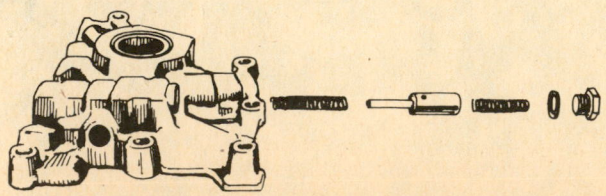

Oil pump pressure regulator (OHC 4 cylinder)

to 65 ft lbs. If the bearing clearance is within specifications, the seal is properly seated.

11. Install the bearing cap, tightening to the specified torque.
12. Install rear main bearing cap side sealant. This is available in a kit, complete with plunger applicator, from Chevrolet. Force the compound firmly into place to ensure that there are no air bubbles.
13. Install the oil pan and baffle.

V8

The rear main bearing seal may be replaced without removing the crankshaft. Seals should only be replaced as a pair. Fabrication of a seal installation tool will prevent damaging the bead on the cylinder block. The seal lips should face the front of the engine when properly installed.

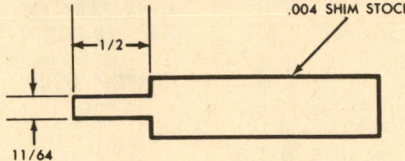

Oil seal installation tool
(© Chevrolet Div., G.M. Corp)

1. Remove the oil pan and pump, and remove the rear main bearing cap.
2. Pry the lower seal out of the bearing cap with a screwdriver, being careful not to gouge the cap surface.
3. Remove the upper seal by lightly tapping on one end with a brass pin punch until the other end can be grasped and pulled out with pliers.
4. Clean the bearing cap, cylinder block, and crankshaft mating surfaces with solvent. Inspect all these surfaces for gouges, nicks, and burrs.
5. Apply light engine oil to the seal lips and bead, but keep the seal ends clean.
6. Insert the tip of the installation tool between the crankshaft and the seal seat of the cylinder block. Place the seal between the tip of the tool and the crankshaft, so that the bead contacts the tip of the tool.
7. Be sure that the seal lip is facing the front of the engine, and work the seal around the crankshaft, using the installation tool to protect the seal from the corner of the cylinder block.

NOTE: *Do not remove the tool until the opposite end of the seal is flush with the cylinder block surface.*

8. Remove the installation tool, being careful not to pull the seal out at the same time.
9. Using the same procedure, install the lower seal into the bearing cap. Use your finger and thumb to lever the seal into the cap.
10. Apply sealer to the cylinder block only where the cap mates to the

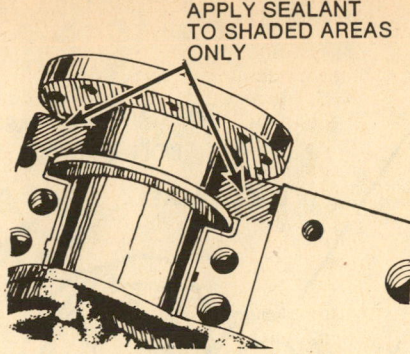

APPLY SEALANT TO SHADED AREAS ONLY

Sealant application—V8

surface. Do not apply sealer to the seal ends.
11. Install the rear cap and torque the bolts to specifications. Install the oil pan and pump.

CLUTCH

The clutch assembly consists of a driven plate, a pressure plate, and a release bearing, and is connected to the clutch pedal by a cable.

Clutch Pedal Free Travel Adjustment

1. Remove the ball stud cap and loosen the locknut on the ball stud end, located to the right of the transmission, on the clutch housing.
2. Adjust the ball stud to obtain 1/8 inch clearance between the release bearing face and the pressure plate release fingers.
3. Tighten the ball stud locknut to 25 ft lbs, being careful not to change the adjustment, and install the ball stud cap.
4. Pull the cable at the clutch fork until the clutch pedal is firmly against the rubber bumper.
5. Push the clutch fork forward until the release bearing contacts the pressure plate fingers, and screw

the pin on the cable forward until it contacts the fork. Turn the pin 1/4 turn clockwise, and seat the pin in its seat on the clutch fork.
6. Attach the cable return spring and install the clutch fork cover.
7. Check the clutch pedal free play. This procedure should provide .90 ± .25 inch lash at the clutch pedal.

NOTE: *When the adjustment of the ball stud and the cable have been completed, verify the clearance between the pressure plate fingers and the release bearing. The release bearing should not be in constant contact with the pressure plate fingers.*

Clutch Disc Removal and Installation

1. Raise the vehicle on a hoist.
2. Remove the transmission as outlined in this section.
3. Remove the clutch fork cover, then disconnect the clutch return spring and control cable from the clutch fork.
4. Remove the input shaft oil seal from the clutch release bearing sleeve.
5. Remove the flywheel housing lower cover.
6. Remove the flywheel housing from the engine.
7. To remove the release bearing from the clutch fork and sleeve, slide the lever off the ball stud against the spring action. If necessary to replace the ball stud, remove the cap, locknut and stud from the housing.
8. If assembly marks on the clutch assembly and flywheel are not distinguishable, remark with paint or center-punch.
9. Loosen the clutch cover to flywheel attaching bolts one turn at a time until the spring pressure is released, to avoid bending the clutch cover flange.
10. Support the pressure plate and cover assembly then remove the bolts and clutch assembly.

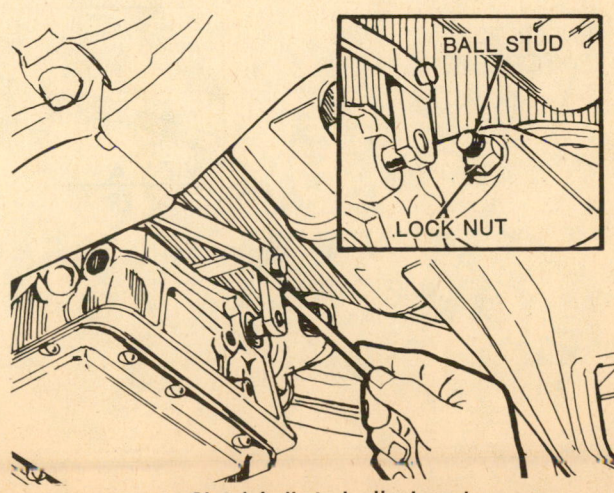

Clutch ball stud adjustment

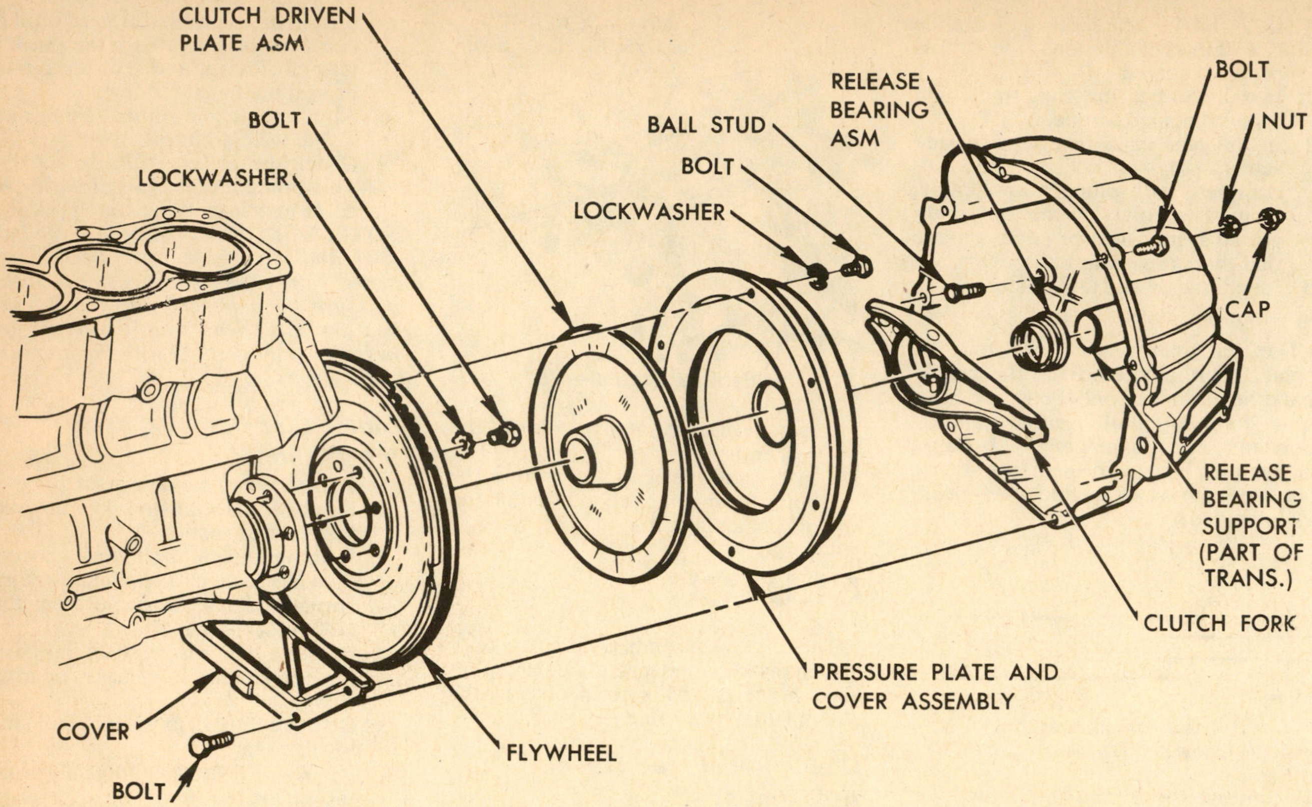

CLUTCH DRIVEN PLATE ASM

BOLT

LOCKWASHER

BALL STUD

BOLT

LOCKWASHER

RELEASE BEARING ASM

BOLT

NUT

CAP

RELEASE BEARING SUPPORT (PART OF TRANS.)

CLUTCH FORK

PRESSURE PLATE AND COVER ASSEMBLY

COVER

BOLT

FLYWHEEL

Exploded view of clutch components (© Chevrolet Div., G.M. Corp)

— **CAUTION** —
Do not disassemble the clutch cover, spring and pressure plate for repair. If defective replace the complete assembly.

11. Index the alignment marks on the clutch assembly and the flywheel. Place the driven plate with the long end of the splined end facing forward, the plate damper springs facing the pressure plate, and insert a dummy input shaft through the cover and the driven plate.

12. Position the complete assembly against the flywheel and insert the dummy shaft into the pilot bearing in the crankshaft.

13. Index the alignment marks and install clutch cover to flywheel bolts finger-tight.

— **CAUTION** —
Tighten all bolts evenly and gradually until tight to avoid possible clutch distortion.

14. Lubricate the clutch fork ball socket and the fingers at the release bearing with a high melting point grease such as graphite grease.

15. Lubricate the recess on the inside of the throwout bearing collar and the fork groove with a light coat of graphite grease. Install the fork in the housing but not on the stud.

16. Install, the bearing on the sleeve, then position the clutch fork over the bearing in the housing and slide the fork onto the ball stud.

17. Install the flywheel housing and the lower cover. Tighten the bolts.

18. Install the transmission as outlined previously.

19. Adjust the clutch as previously outlined.

20. Lower and remove the vehicle from the hoist.

MANUAL TRANSMISSION

The Opel-made transmissions used in 1972 were replaced with Saginaw three and four-speed units in 1973. These are fully synchronized and are similar to those used throughout the Chevrolet line.

A five-speed Borg-Warner T-50 transmission is optional on 1975 and later models. Fourth gear is direct drive with fifth gear an overdrive. The transmission is shifted by a single shift rail enclosed within the transmission.

In 1976-77, the 70 mm four-speed transmission was used on base models. This light weight transmission is also used in the Chevette. Gear shifting is done by an internal shifter shaft.

In 1978, the Saginaw four-speed, now called the 76MM, was reinstated as the standard four-speed.

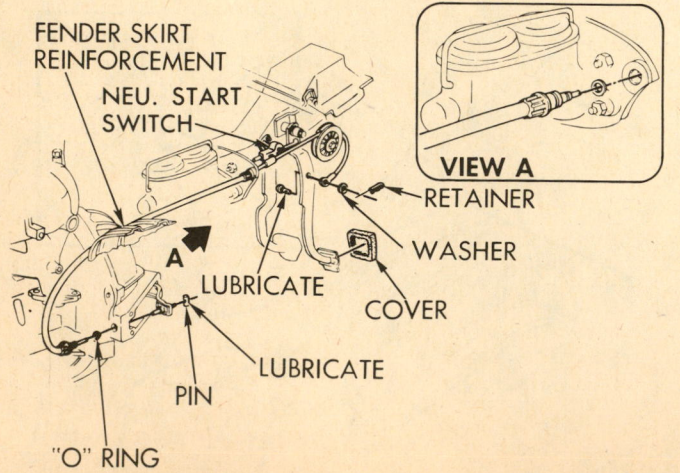

FENDER SKIRT REINFORCEMENT

NEU. START SWITCH

VIEW A

RETAINER

WASHER

COVER

LUBRICATE

LUBRICATE

PIN

"O" RING

Clutch control cable (© Chevrolet Div., G.M. Corp)

Linkage Adjustment

1972 FOUR-SPEED

The reverse gearshift blocker adjustment can only be made on the four-speed transmission. This adjustment is made at the selector shaft on the left side of the transmission.

1. Shift into second gear.
2. Adjust the selector ring so that the shift lever finger ball has equal clearance on both sides in the intermediate lever hole.
3. Back off the selector ring a quarter turn and tighten the locknut.

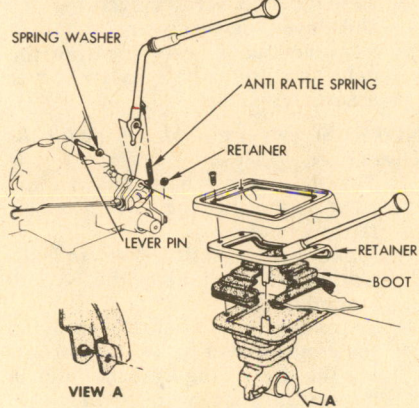

1972 shift control lever (© Chevrolet Div. G.M. Corp.)

1973 AND LATER SAGINAW THREE AND FOUR-SPEED

1. Turn the ignition switch to Off and place the shift lever in Neutral.
2. Raise the car.
3. Loosen the lock nuts on the control rods. Position the transmission side cover levers in their neutral detents.
4. With the floor shift lever in Neutral, align the shifter levers and insert a gauge pin into the levers and bracket.
5. Tighten the First/Reverse (First/Second on four-speed) control rod lock nut against its swivel.
6. Tighten the Second/Third (Third/Fourth on four-speed) control rod lock nut against its swivel.
7. On four-speeds, tighten the Reverse control rod lock nut against its swivel.
8. Remove the gauge pin and check shifter operation.

Transmission Removal and Installation

1972

1. Place the transmission shift lever in Neutral and pull the boot up.
2. Unhook the antirattle coil spring. Remove the shift finger (lower end of the lever) pin retaining clip and pin. Remove shift lever.
3. Raise the vehicle and drain the lubricant from transmission.
4. Remove the driveshaft assembly.

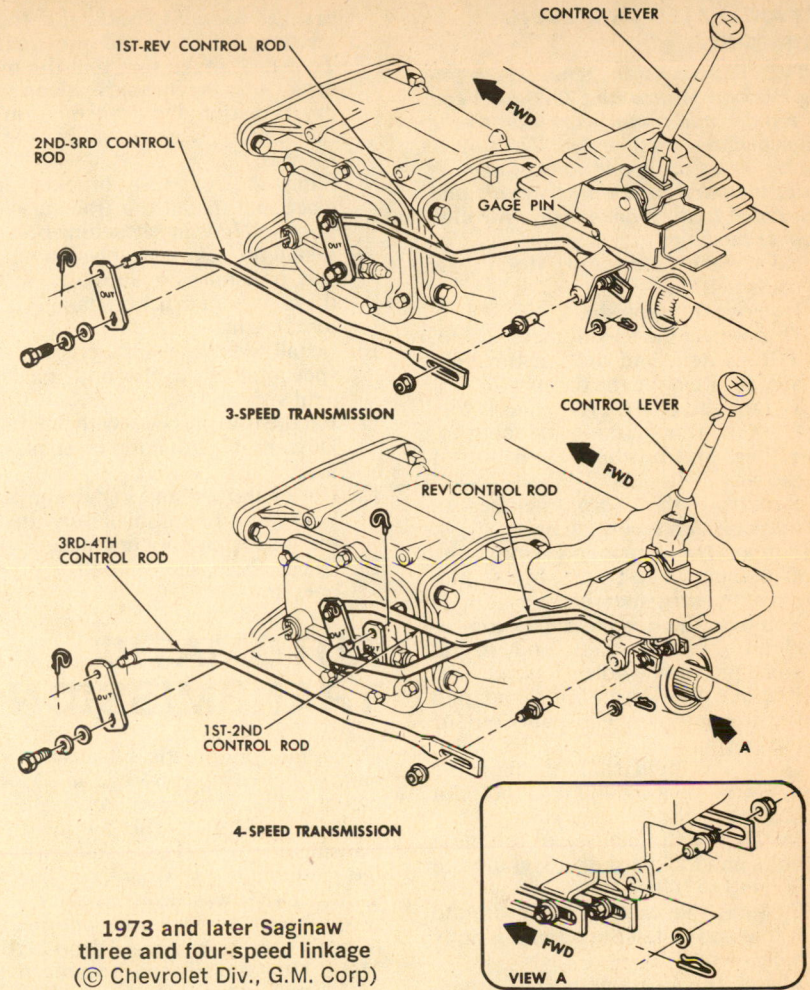

1973 and later Saginaw three and four-speed linkage (© Chevrolet Div., G.M. Corp)

5. Disconnect the speedometer cable, TCS switch and back-up lamp switch.
6. Remove the crossmember-to-transmission mount bolts.
7. Support the engine with an appropriate jack stand and remove the crossmember-to-frame bolts. Remove the crossmember from the vehicle.
8. Remove the transmission to clutch housing upper retaining bolts and install guide pins in the holes.
9. Remove the lower bolts, then slide the transmission rearward and remove it from the vehicle.

NOTE: *Inspect the throwout bearing support gasket located beneath the lip of the support. If defective, replace the gasket before installing the transmission.*

10. Lightly lubricate the inside diameter of the clutch drive gear seal and install the seal on the drive gear.
11. Position a new gasket to the face of the clutch housing. The gasket can be temporarily retained by a small amount of grease.
12. Position the transmission to clutch housing and slide forward, piloting the clutch gear in to the pilot bearing.

NOTE: *Make certain the main drive gear splines are clean and dry.*

13. Install the transmission-to-clutch housing retaining bolts and lockwashers.
14. Position the crossmember to the frame and loosely install the retaining bolts. Install the crossmember-to-transmission mount bolts. Tighten all retaining bolts to specifications. Remove the engine support.

——— CAUTION ———

Check the position of the engine in the front mounts and align as required.

15. Connect the speedometer cable, back-up lamp switch and TCS switch.
16. Install the driveshaft assembly.
17. Fill the transmission to proper level. Lower the vehicle.
18. Lubricate the shift finger bolt and spherical end of the shaft. Install the shift lever in the shift housing and install the bolt. Secure it with a retaining clip.
19. Install the shift lever spring. Position the shift lever boot and bezel to the floor pan. Install the retaining screws.
20. Check the operation of the transmission.

1973 AND LATER THREE AND FOUR-SPEED

NOTE: *Transmission removal beginning 1975 on Monza and 1976 on Vega will require additional work due to the torque arm rear suspension. The torque arm serves as an upper control arm, is rigidly mounted to the differential, and is mounted to the transmission through a rubber bushing.*

1. Raise the car and drain the transmission.
2. Remove the driveshaft.
3. Disconnect the speedometer cable, TCS switch, and the backup light switch. Remove the damper.
4. Detach the control rods and levers from the transmission, tie them together, and position them out of the way.
5. Remove the crossmember-to-transmission mounting bolts.
6. Support the engine and remove the crossmember-to-frame bolts. Remove the crossmember.
7. Remove the top transmission-to-clutch housing bolts and install guide pins in the holes.
8. Remove the lower bolts and pull the transmission back and out of the car.
9. Guide the input shaft through the throwout bearing and into the pilot bearing.
10. Install the transmission retaining bolts and lockwashers. Tighten the bolts to 40 ft lbs.
11. Position the crossmember on the frame and install the retaining bolts hand-tight.
12. Install the crossmember-to-transmission bolts and then tighten all bolts to 28 ft lbs.
13. Remove the engine support.
14. Install the transmission control rods to the shifter. Adjust the linkage as previously outlined.
15. Connect the speedometer cable, TCS switch, and back-up light switch.
16. Install the driveshaft.
17. Fill the transmission to the level of the filler plug.
18. Lower the car and check the transmission operation.

FIVE-SPEED

1. Remove the shift lever boot bezel and slide the shift boot upward on the shift lever.
2. Remove the foam insulator over the shift lever bolts. Remove the four shift lever bolts and remove the shift lever.
3. Raise the car and remove the driveshaft.
4. Remove the damper assembly, converter bracket, and torque arm bracket. Disconnect the speedometer cable and back-up light switch.
5. Support the transmission with a jack and remove the transmission support.
6. Remove the transmission-to-clutch housing bolts and slide the exhaust

bracket forward. Slide the transmission to the rear and remove it.

7. To install, make sure that the main drive gear splines are clean and dry. Position the transmission to the clutch housing and slide it forward.
8. Slide the exhaust bracket into place and install the transmission-to-clutch housing attaching bolts.
9. Install the rear transmission mount and transmission support. Install the converter bracket, damper, and torque arm.
10. Install the driveshaft, connect the speedometer cable and back-up light switch.
11. Fill the transmission with 3 pints of Dexron® II automatic transmission fluid.
12. Lower the car and install the shift lever and foam insulator. Install the shift lever boot and bezel.
13. Check the transmission for proper operation.

AUTOMATIC TRANSMISSION

Several automatic transmissions have been available in Vega and Monza models. The aluminum Powerglide is the two-speed unit. The Torque Drive transmission is a Powerglide without the automatic shifting mechanism. Torque Drive was dropped after 1972, while Powerglide was discontinued in mid-1973. A three-speed Turbo Hydra-Matic 350 transmission became available in 1972. Beginning February 1973, a Turbo Hydra-Matic 250 was introduced to replace the 350. The 250 is similar to the 350, except that the intermediate clutch assembly has been replaced by an externally adjustable intermediate band assembly. The 250 can be identified by the band adjusting screw and locknut on the right side of the case. Starting 1976, a new three-speed transmission is offered: Turbo Hydra-Matic 200. The light weight Turbo Hydra-Matic 200 transmission can sometimes be identified by the

word METRIC stamped into the bottom of the fluid pan. The 200 has 10 pan bolts; the 350 has 13.

Neutral Safety Switch Adjustment

1. Remove four screws securing the floor console.
2. Disconnect the electrical plugs on the back-up, neutral start, and seat belt buzzer (1973 and later) contacts of the neutral safety switch.
3. Place the shift lever in Neutral.
4. Remove two screws securing the shift indicator plate.
5. Remove two screws securing the shift lever curved cover.
6. Remove two screws securing the neutral start switch to the lever assembly.

NOTE: *Screws are hidden beneath the lever cover.*

7. Tilt the switch assembly to the right as you lift the switch out of the lever hole.
8. Make sure the shift lever is in Neutral before installing the switch assembly.
9. Assemble the switch assembly to the control lever bracket by inserting the drive tang into the hole in the neutral start switch lever.

NOTE: *When installing the same neutral switch, align the contact support slot with the service adjustment hole in the switch and insert a 3/32 in. drill to hold the switch in neutral. Remove the drill after the switch is fastened to the shift lever mounting bracket.*

10. Tighten two mounting screws securing the switch assembly to the lever bracket.
11. Install the curved shift lever cover and secure it with two screws.
12. Install the shift indicator plate and attach it with two screws.
13. Moving the control lever out of Neutral will shear the plastic switch locating pin.
14. Plug the electrical connectors into the switch assembly; apply the parking brake and start the vehicle—check for starting in Neutral and Park only. Also check for the back-up lamps being on in Reverse.
15. Turn off the ignition and install the console cover securing it with four screws.

Shift Linkage Adjustment
POWERGLIDE, TORQUE DRIVE

This adjustment gives about 0.05 in. overtravel in each gear shift position to provide full engagement.

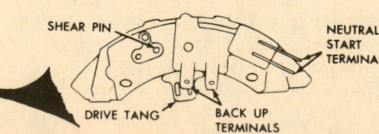

1972 neutral safety switch adjustment—1973 and later switches have two additional terminals for the seat belt alarm (© Chevrolet Div. G.M. Corp.)

1. Loosen the two shift rod adjusting nuts at the swivel. The swivel is attached to the floorshift lever lower lever.
2. Turn the shift lever on the transmission all the way clockwise. This is the Park detent position. Turn the lever counterclockwise two detents to the neutral detent position.
3. Make sure that the floorshift is in the neutral position.
4. Push forward lightly on the floorshift assembly lower lever until the floorshift lever can be felt against its neutral detent. Hold the lower lever in place.
5. Hold a 0.073 in. thick spacer in front of the swivel. Tighten the front adjusting nut to clamp the spacer between the nut and swivel.
6. Pull out the spacer and lightly pull back on the floorshift assembly lower lever. Tighten the rear adjusting nut.

1972 TURBO HYDRA-MATIC

Use the Powerglide and Torque Drive procedure, substituting the following steps:

4. Pull back lightly on the floorshift assembly lower lever until the floorshift lever can be felt to be against its neutral detent. Hold the lower lever in place.
5. Hold a 0.073 in. thick spacer between the nut and swivel.
6. Pull the spacer out and pull lightly forward on the floorshift assembly lower lever. Tighten the front adjusting nut.

NOTE: *Late 1972 models and all 1973 and later models are equipped with slotted control rods. Adjustment of this linkage is given later.*

1973 AND LATER TURBO HYDRA-MATIC 350

1. Loosen the nut and swivel at the transmission lever.
2. Set the transmission lever in Neutral by moving it counterclockwise to the L1 detent and then clockwise three detent positions to Neutral.
3. Position the shift lever in the Neutral notch of the detent plate.
4. Place the flat of the swivel into the slot of the control rod. Install the washer and cotter pin.
5. Tighten the locknut. Adjust the neutral safety switch, if necessary.

1976-79 TURBO HYDRA-MATIC 200

1. Place the shifter in Neutral.
2. Place the transmission lever in Neutral by moving it clockwise as far as it will go, then counterclockwise two detent positions.
3. Insert the pin and lock on the fork. Adjust the shift rod until the hole in the rods lines up with the shifter pin. Install the rod on the pin.

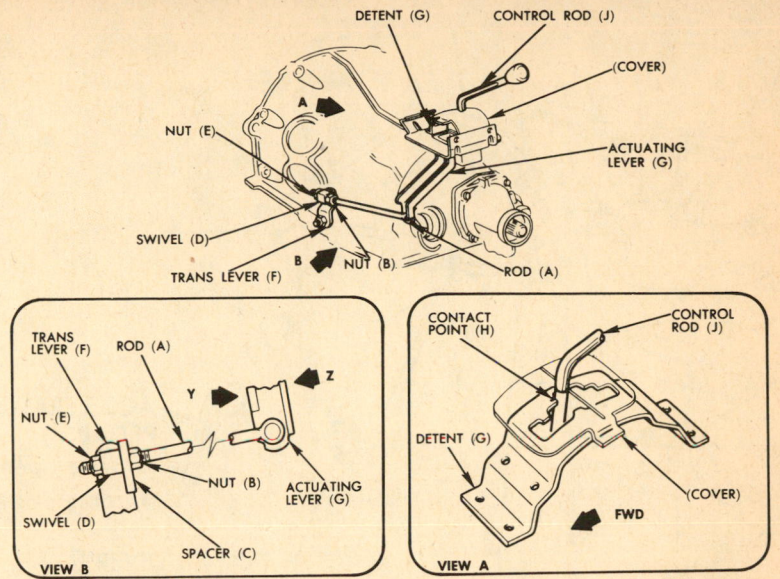

1972 Turbo Hydra-Matic 350 linkage adjustment (© Chevrolet Div., G.M. Corp)

Powerglide Throttle Valve Linkage Adjustment

1. Hold the accelerator pedal all the way down.
2. Unclip and detach the rear end of the throttle valve control rod (horizontal rod).
3. The bellcrank lever stud should be all the way forward in the slot at the front of the throttle valve control rod.
4. Hold the lever at the transmission against its internal stop.
5. If the rear end of the throttle valve control rod does not align with the hole in the lever, pull out the retaining clip from the sleeve in the center of the rod. Adjust the sleeve to lengthen or shorten the rod.

NOTE: *The sleeve is adjustable one turn at a time.*

6. Install the throttle valve control rod in the lever hole and attach the clip.

Turbo Hydra-Matic Downshift Cable (Throttle Valve Cable) Adjustment

1. Remove the air cleaner.
2. Insert a screwdriver on each side of the snap-lock on the bracket at the front of the transmission and pry up to release the lock.
3. Compress the lock tabs and disconnect the snap-lock assembly from the bracket.
4. Position the carburetor lever in the wide open throttle position.
5. Hold the carburetor lever in position and push the snap-lock on the cable down until the top is flush with the cable.

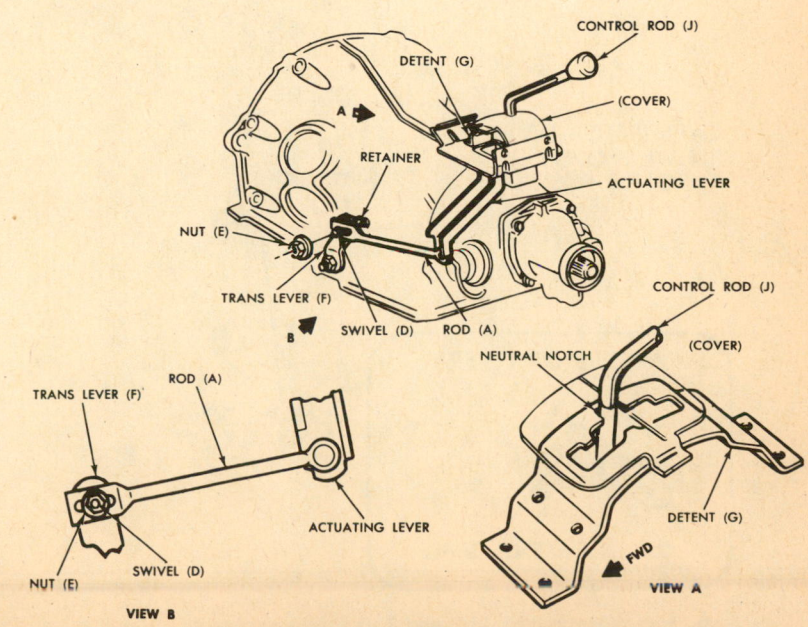

1973 and later Turbo Hydra-Matic linkage (© Chevrolet Div. G.M. Corp.)

Monza & Vega

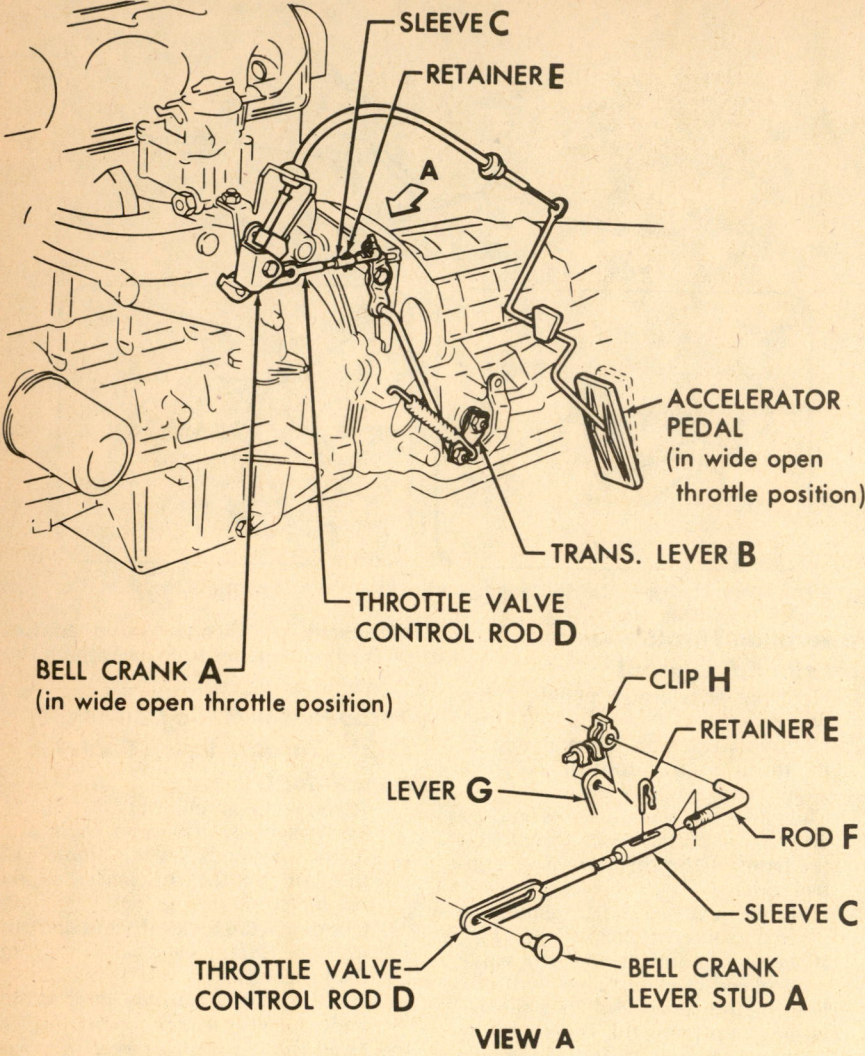

Powerglide throttle valve linkage adjustment (© Chevrolet Div., G.M. Corp)

Labels in upper figure:
- SLEEVE **C**
- RETAINER **E**
- A
- ACCELERATOR PEDAL (in wide open throttle position)
- TRANS. LEVER **B**
- THROTTLE VALVE CONTROL ROD **D**
- BELL CRANK **A** (in wide open throttle position)

Labels in VIEW A:
- CLIP **H**
- RETAINER **E**
- LEVER **G**
- ROD **F**
- SLEEVE **C**
- THROTTLE VALVE CONTROL ROD **D**
- BELL CRANK LEVER STUD **A**

VIEW A

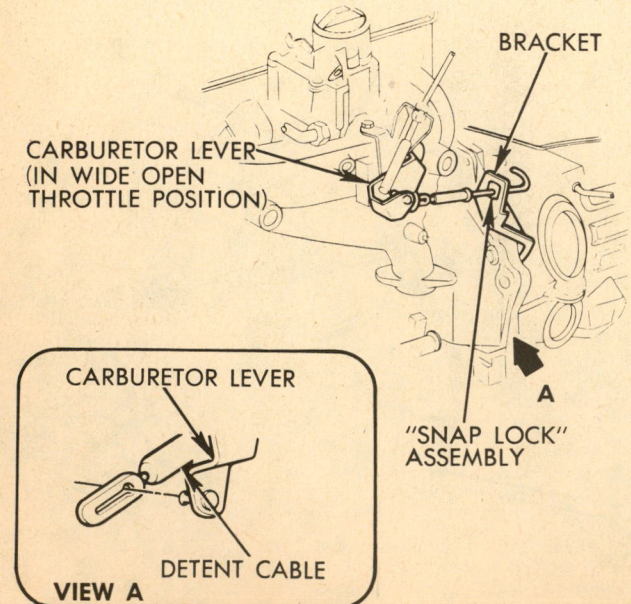

Turbo Hydra-Matic 200, 250 and 350 detent cable adjustment
(© Chevrolet Div., G.M. Corp)

Labels:
- CARBURETOR LEVER (IN WIDE OPEN THROTTLE POSITION)
- BRACKET
- "SNAP LOCK" ASSEMBLY
- A
- CARBURETOR LEVER
- DETENT CABLE
- **VIEW A**

NOTE: *The cable should not be lubricated.*
6. Install the air cleaner.

Powerglide, Torque Drive Low Band Adjustment
1. Position the shift lever in Neutral.
2. Remove the protective cap from the adjusting screw.
3. Loosen the locknut 1/4 turn and hold it with a wrench during the entire adjusting procedure.
4. Tighten the adjusting nut to 70 in lbs, using a 7/32 in. allen wrench.
5. Back off the adjusting nut exactly three turns for a band used less than 6,000 miles. Back off exactly four turns for a band used 6,000 miles or more.
6. Torque the locknut to 15 ft lbs and replace the cap.

Turbo Hydra-Matic 250 Intermediate Band Adjustment
1. Position the shift lever in Neutral.
2. Loosen the locknut and tighten the adjusting screw to 30 in lbs.
3. Back the screw out three turns and then tighten the locknut to 15 ft lbs.

Pan Removal and Installation, Fluid and Filter Change
The fluid should be drained with the transmission warm.
1. Support the transmission at the vibration damper. If necessary, remove the crossmember.
2. Prepare a large pan to catch the transmission fluid.
3. Loosen all the pan screws, then pull one corner down to drain most of the fluid.
4. Remove the pan screws and empty out the pan. The pan can be cleaned out with solvent but it must be dried thoroughly before replacement. Be very careful not to leave any lint or threads from rags in the pan.
5. Remove the filter or strainer retaining bolt (two on Turbo Hydra-Matic 200, 250, and 350). A reuseable strainer is used on two-speed transmissions and the Turbo Hydra-Matic 200 and 250. The strainer may be cleaned in solvent and air-dried thoroughly. Filters are to be replaced. Use a new gasket on all other models.
6. Install the new filter or cleaned strainer.
7. Install the pan with a new gasket. Tighten the bolts evenly (12 ft lbs) in a criss-cross pattern.
8. Replace the crossmembers if removed.
9. Add DEXRON® or Dexron® II transmission fluid through the dipstick tube. Add 6 pints for Turbo Hydra-Matic 200; 5 pints for Turbo Hyrda-Matic 250; and 3 pints for the 350, Torque Drive, and Powerglide.

10. Start the engine and let it idle. Do not race the engine. Shift through all the indicator positions, holding the brakes. Check the fluid level with the engine idling in Park. The level should be between the two dimples on the dipstick, about 1/4 in. below the ADD mark. Add fluid as necessary.

11. Check the fluid level after the car has been driven enough to thoroughly warm up the transmission. The level should be at the FULL mark on the dipstick. If the transmission is overfilled, the excess must be drained off. Overfilling causes aerated fluid, resulting in transmission slippage and probable damage.

U-JOINTS

Driveshaft Removal and Installation

1. Raise and support the car. Mark the relationship of the shaft to the companion flange and disconnect the rear universal joint by removing the trunnion bearing U-bolts. Tape the bearing cups to the trunnion to prevent losing the bearing rollers.

2. Withdraw the driveshaft front yoke from the transmission by moving the shaft rearward and passing it under the axle housing. Cover the transmission opening to prevent fluid or oil loss.

3. Inspect the yoke seal in the transmission extension, replace if necessary.

4. Insert the driveshaft front yoke into transmission extension, making sure that the output shaft splines mate with the driveshaft yoke splines.

5. Align the driveshaft with the companion flange using the reference marks established in the removal procedure. Remove the tape from the U-joint, install the U-bolts to the rear axle flange, and torque them to 15 ft lbs.

Universal Joint Overhaul

1. Remove the driveshaft and matchmark the front yoke to the drive shaft.

2. Remove the snap-rings from the yoke.

3. Using an arbor press or a vise, and suitably sized sockets, press on the trunnion (spider) until the bearing cap is almost out. Grasp the cap in the vise and work it out of the yoke. Repeat the procedure for the remaining bearing caps.

4. Pack the bearings in grease and fill the grease reservoir in the trunnion. Do not over-fill.

5. To install, position the trunnion in the yoke and partially install one bearing cap. Start the trunnion in

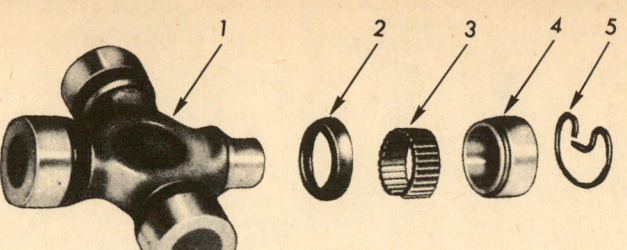

Exploded view of universal joint (© Chevrolet Div., G.M. Corp)

1. Trunnion
2. Seal
3. Bearing
4. Cap
5. Snap ring

the bearing cap and partially install the other cap. Align the trunnion with the other caps and press into place.

6. If necessary, repeat Step 5 above for the other yoke.

7. Install the snap-rings, and install the driveshaft.

REAR AXLE

Vega and Monza axles are the Chevrolet C-lock type with C-locks retaining the axle shafts. All axles are hypoid type, semi-floating with an integral gear carrier and a removable cover plate.

Vega and Monza models use either a 6-1/2 in. or 7-1/2 in. diameter ring gear.

Axle Shaft Removal and Installation

1. Raise and support the car.
2. Remove the wheel and brake drum.
3. Clean all dirt from the carrier area.
4. Drain the lubricant from the carrier by removing the cover.
5. Remove the differential pinion shaft lockscrew and remove the differential pinion shaft.

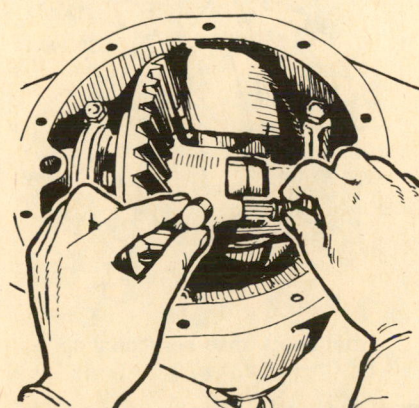

Removing or installing the differential pinion shaft lockpin

6. Push the flanged end of the shaft toward the center of the car and remove the C-lock from the groove in the axle shaft.

7. Pull the axle shaft from the housing. Be careful not to damage the oil seal.

8. Slide the axle shaft into place.

9. Be sure that the splines on the axle

shaft engage with the splines in the differential side gears. Be sure the oil seal is not damaged.

10. Install the axle shaft C-lock. Push the shaft outward so that the C-lock seats in the counter-bore of the differential side gear.

11. Install the differential pinion shaft and lockscrew.

12. Further installation is the reverse of removal. Fill the axle with fresh lubricant.

Oil Seal/Axle Bearing Replacement

1. Remove the axle shaft.

2. If replacing the seal only, insert the button end of the axle shaft behind the steel case of the oil seal and pry the seal out of the bore.

3. When removing the bearings, use a slide hammer with care.

4. Lubricate a new bearing with hypoid axle lubricant, and install it with a driver.

5. Lubricate the cavity between the seal lips with high melting point wheel bearing grease and install the seal in the axle housing until it is flush with the end of the housing.

6. Install the axle shaft.

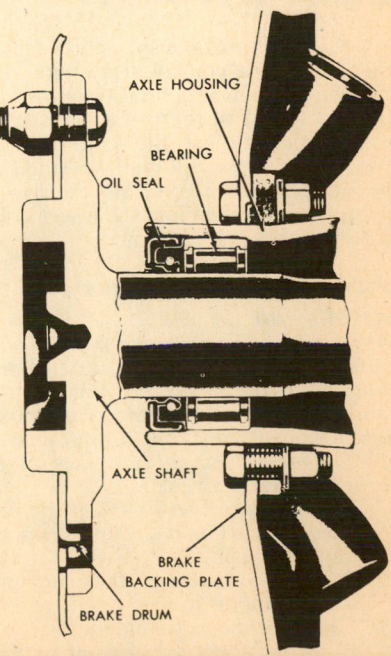

AXLE HOUSING

BEARING

OIL SEAL

AXLE SHAFT

BRAKE BACKING PLATE

BRAKE DRUM

Axle shaft bearing and seal (© Chevrolet Div., G.M. Corp)

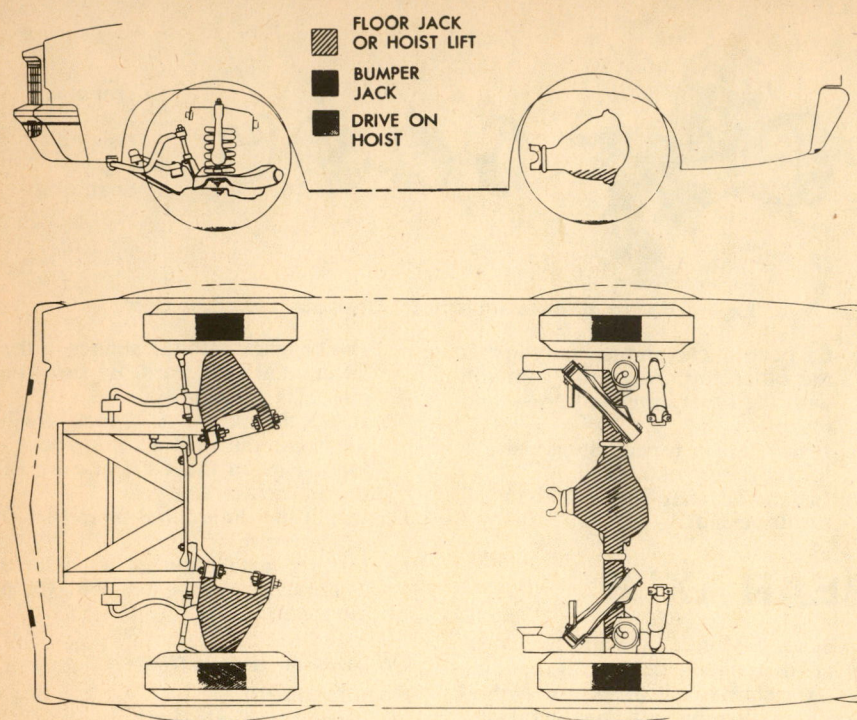

FLOOR JACK
OR HOIST LIFT

BUMPER
JACK

DRIVE ON
HOIST

Lift points (© Chevrolet Div., G.M. Corp)

JACKING, HOISTING

The illustration shows the correct jacking and hoist lifting positions.

FRONT SUSPENSION

Vega and Monza suspension utilizes unequal length control arms with coil springs. The lower control arm bolts to the front end sheet metal with cam bolts which adjust the camber and caster. The upper ball joint is riveted to the upper control arm and the lower ball joint is pressed into the lower control arm.

Shock Absorber Removal and Installation

NOTE: *To purge air from the shock absorber before installation, extend the shock fully and invert it. Compress the shock, and return it to its upright position. Repeat this operation several times. Do not extend the shock absorber while it is inverted.*

1. Pry out the access plug in the engine compartment so that the upper mount is visible.
2. Raise the front of the car and safely support it.
3. Turn the wheels for clearance.
4. Hold the upper shock stud with a wrench. Loosen and remove the locknut.

5. Unbolt the lower end and pull the shock down and out.
6. Place the lower retainer and rubber grommet on the shock stud.
7. Put the shock in place and tighten the lower bolts. Torque to 20 ft lbs.
8. Place the upper grommet, retainer, and nut on the shock stud.
9. Hold the stud with a wrench and tighten the nut. Torque to 120 in lbs.

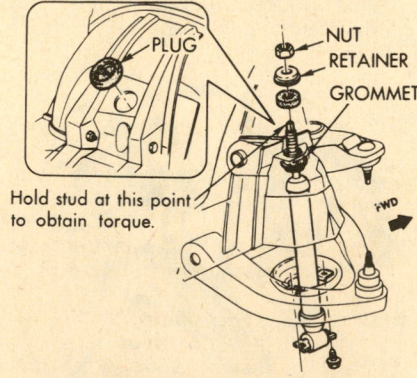

PLUG

NUT
RETAINER
GROMMET

Hold stud at this point to obtain torque.

FWD

Front shock absorber mounting (© Chevrolet Div., G.M. Corp)

Ball Joint Inspection

THROUGH 1974

1. Raise the front of the car and support it under the lower control arm. Make sure that the wheel bearings are properly adjusted before making this check.
2. Turn the wheels straight ahead.
3. Grasp and shake the wheel from side to side, horizontally. If there is noticeable looseness, the tie-rod ends are worn.

4. Grasp the top and bottom of the tire and rock it by pushing in on the top and pulling out on the bottom, then pulling out on the top and pushing in on the bottom. 1/4 in. play indicates worn ball joints.

1975 AND LATER

The lower ball joints incorporate wear indicators. They can be inspected visually; when the 1/2 in. diameter grease fitting is flush with, or inside the cover surface, replace the ball joint. Inspect the grease fitting with the car supported on its wheels so that the lower ball joint is in a loaded condition. Normal protrusion of the grease fitting is .050 in. beyond the cover surface.

Ball joint tightness can also be checked using the preceding procedure.

Ball Joint Removal and Installation

UPPER

1. Jack up the front of the car and support it under the crossmember braces. Remove the wheel.
2. Place a hydraulic jack under the lower control arm.
3. Remove the cotter pin from the ball joint stud. Loosen, but do not remove the nut.
4. The stud may now be pressed out upward. There is a special tool available to do this.
5. Remove the ball joint by grinding off the rivets, or removing the heads of the rivets with a chisel.
6. Bolt the new ball joint on, using the nuts and bolts supplied with the replacement joint.
7. Install the stud to the steering knuckle and torque the nut to 30 ft lbs. If the cotter pin hole does not align, tighten the nut 1/2 of a turn further to line it up. Install a new cotter pin.
8. Install the wheel and lower the car.

LOWER

1. Repeat steps one through three of the upper ball joint procedure.
2. The stud may now be pressed out downward. A special tool is available for this purpose.
3. The old joint must be pressed out of the control arm. A tool is available for this operation.
4. Press in the new joint, positioning it so that the grease bleed vent in the rubber boot is facing inward.
5. Install a lubrication fitting in the new joint.
6. Install the stud to the steering knuckle and torque the nut to 60 ft lbs. If the cotter pin hole does not align, tighten it 1/6 of a turn further. Do not loosen the nut to install the cotter pin.
7. Install the wheel and lower the car.

Spring Removal and Installation

1. Raise the front of the car and support it with jackstands placed un-

der the front crossmember braces.

2. Remove the wheel, shock absorbers, and stabilizer bar.
3. Support the lower control arm outer end with a hydraulic floor jack and a block of wood.
4. Securely fasten the spring to the lower control arm with a heavy chain.
5. To detach the tie rod, remove the cotter pin and nut, and tap on the steering arm (not the tie-rod end) with a hammer. Hold another hammer behind the steering arm to take the force of the tapping. The tie rod should then fall free.
6. Remove the lower ball joint stud from the steering knuckle as described in the Lower Ball Joint Removal and Installation procedure.
7. Very cautiously lower the jack until the spring is fully expanded.
8. Place the spring in its pads on the lower control arm and shock tower. Spring insulators are used on 1976 and later models. On these models, make sure that the insulator is indexed with its closed end located at the high point in the spring seat. Secure the spring with a safety chain as in Step 4.
9. Carefully raise the jack.
10. Place the lower ball joint stud in the steering knuckle. Torque the stud nut to 60 ft lbs. If the cotter pin does not align, tighten it further 1/6 of a turn and insert a new cotter pin.
11. Install the tie-rod end to the steering arm. Torque the nut to 35 ft lbs. If the cotter pin hole does not align, tighten further up to a maximum of 50 ft lbs. Insert a new cotter pin.
12. Replace the shock absorber as described in Shock Absorber Removal and Installation. Do not attach the top end of the shock at this point.
13. Install the stabilizer bar. Tighten the bracket bolts to 30 ft lbs and the control arm bolts to 10 ft lbs.
14. Replace the wheel and lower the car. Install the upper end of the shock absorber.

Lower Control Arm Removal and Installation

1. Raise the front of the car.
2. Remove shock absorber as previously outlined.
3. Remove ball stud from steering knuckle.
4. Remove coil spring using the preceding procedure.
5. Remove the inner pivot cam nuts and bolts.

NOTE: *Mark the position of the cam bolts before loosening nuts. This step will aid in assembly.*

6. Remove the control arm.
7. Install the control arm.

NOTE: *Be sure that the control arm bushings have the metal caps installed.*

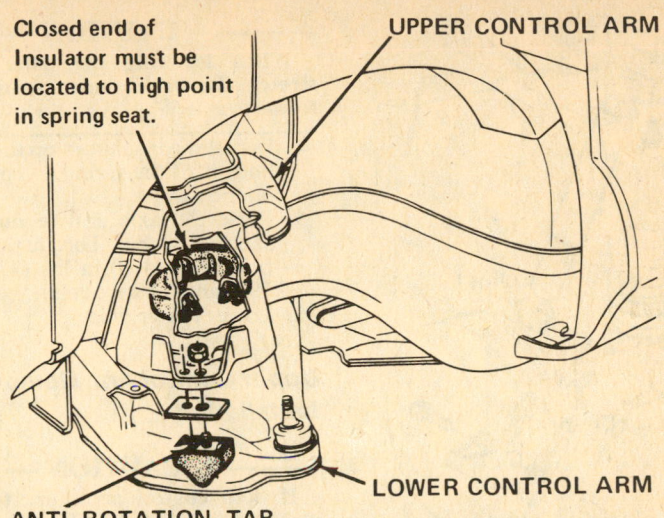

Closed end of Insulator must be located to high point in spring seat.

UPPER CONTROL ARM

LOWER CONTROL ARM

ANTI-ROTATION TAB

Position spring insulators as shown—1976 and later models
(© Chevrolet Div., G.M. Corp)

8. Install the cam bolts through the control arm bushings.

NOTE: *The front cam bolt (camber) must be installed with the head toward the front of the vehicle and the rear cam bolt (caster) must be installed with the head toward the rear of the vehicle.*

9. Install the inner cams to the cam bolt.
10. Install the lockwasher and nut. Torque the nut to 49 ft lbs.
11. Align the cam bolts with the marks made before removal.
12. Install the coil spring.
13. Install the shock absorber.
14. Lower vehicle to the floor.
15. Check front alignment.

Upper Control Arm Removal and Installation

1. Raise the vehicle on a hoist and remove the wheel.
2. Support the lower control arm with a floor jack.
3. Remove the upper ball stud nut and remove the ball stud from the steering knuckle.
4. Remove the control arm pivot bolts and remove the control arm from the vehicle.
5. Install the upper control arm to the vehicle at the inner pivot.

NOTE: *The inner pivot bolts must be installed with the bolt heads to the front (on the front bushing) and to the rear, (on the rear bushing).*

6. Install the inner pivot nuts.
7. Position the control arm in a horizontal plane and tighten the inner pivot nuts to 48 ft lbs.
8. Install the ball stud to the steering knuckle. Torque the nut to 30 ft lbs and install a cotter pin.
9. Install the tire and wheel assembly and lower the vehicle.

Wheel Bearing Adjustment

1. Jack up the front of the car and support it with jackstands.

2. Remove the dust cap with a pair of slip-joint pliers.
3. Remove and discard the cotter pin. Loosen the spindle nut. Tighten it snugly to seat the bearings, and then loosen the nut again.
4. Rotate the wheel and tighten the spindle nut to 12 ft lbs which is roughly equivalent to finger tightness.
5. Back the nut off one flat and insert a new cotter pin. If the hole does not line up, back the nut off 1/2 flat or less to align the hole.
6. Check that the wheel turns freely, and then lock the cotter pin.
7. Bearing end-play should be between 0.001 and 0.008 in. (1971-73) or 0.001-0.005 in. (1974 and later). Tap the dust cap back on and lower the car.

REAR SUSPENSION

Vegas through 1975 use a coil spring rear suspension with upper and lower control arms.

A new torque arm rear suspension is used on 1975 and later Monza models and 1976 and later Vegas using lower control arms and a track bar to control lateral movement. A torque arm is used to control rear axle wind-up. A stabilizer bar is standard and the upper control arms have been eliminated.

Shock Absorber Removal and Installation

NOTE: *To purge air from the shock absorber before installation, extend the shock fully and invert it. Compress the shock, and return it to its upright position. Repeat this operation several times. Do not extend the shock absorber while it is inverted.*

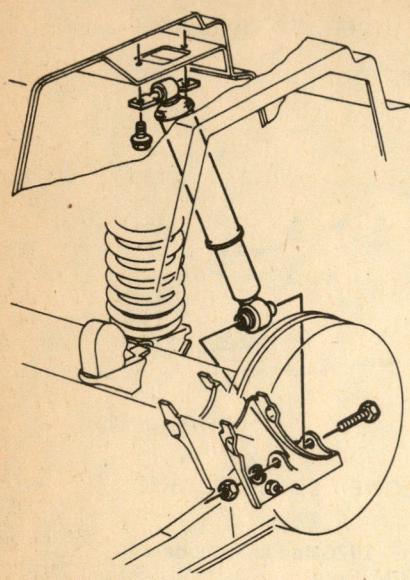

Rear shock absorber mounting
(© Chevrolet Div., G.M. Corp)

1. Raise the vehicle and support the rear axle.
2. Remove the upper attaching bolts and lower through-bolt.
3. Remove the shock absorber.
4. Install the retainer and the rubber grommet onto the shock.
5. Place the shock absorber into the installed position and install the upper retaining bolts. Torque to 18 ft lbs.
6. Coat the through-bolt shank with chassis lube and install it and a rubber grommet on each side of the shock eye. Torque the nut to 80 in lbs (42 ft lbs—1974 and later models).
7. Lower the car.

Rear Spring Removal and Installation

1. Raise the vehicle and support the rear axle, with a hydraulic jack.
2. Disconnect the shock absorber lower bolt, only on one side at a time.
3. Lower the axle and remove the spring and spring insulators.

— CAUTION —

When lowering the axle, do not stretch the brake hose running from frame to axle.

---

4. Install the insulators on the top and bottom of the spring and position it on the axle.
5. Raise the axle and reconnect the shock absorber. Torque the bottom bolt nuts to 80 in lbs (42 ft lbs—1974 and later models).
6. Lower the vehicle.

Upper Control Arm Removal and Installation

— CAUTION —

If both control arms are to be replaced, remove and replace one control arm at a time to prevent the axle from rolling or slipping sideways.

---

1. Raise the vehicle on a hoist and support the rear axle.
2. Remove the control arm front and rear bolts and remove the arm.
3. Press out the bushing.
4. Before the bushing installation, observe that the holes in the control arm have different diameters.
5. Install the small end of the bushing in the largest hole.
6. Press the bushing into the control arm until the bushing flange seats on the control arm.
7. Install the control arm front and rear attaching bolts. Torque to 60 ft lbs.
NOTE: *Car must be at curb height when tightening pivot bolts.*
8. Remove the support from the axle.
9. Lower the vehicle and remove from the hoist.

Lower Control Arm Removal and Installation

— CAUTION —

If both control arms are to be replaced, remove and replace one control arm at a time to prevent the axle from rolling or slipping sideways.

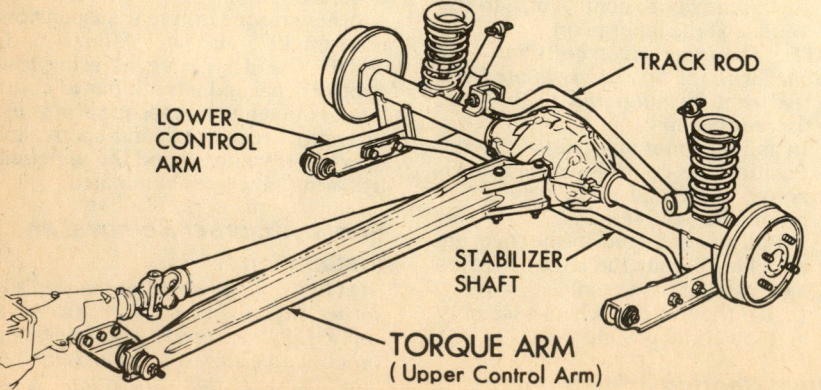

Monza, 1976 and later Vega rear suspension
(© Chevrolet Div., G.M. Corp)

1. Raise the vehicle on a hoist.
2. Support the rear axle.
3. Disconnect the stabilizer bar if so equipped.
4. Remove the control arm front and rear attaching bolts and remove the control arm.
5. Replacement of these bushings is the same procedure as that described for the Upper Control Arm.
6. Place the control arm into position and install the front and rear bolts. Torque to 80 ft lbs with the weight of the car on the suspension.
7. Attach the stabilizer bar and the restraint cable, if so equipped.
8. Remove the support from the axle.
9. Lower the vehicle.

BRAKES

Front disc brakes are standard equipment on all models, with power brakes available beginning 1975. The disc is 10 in. in diameter and 0.5 in. thick. 1976 and later Monza models use a vented disc which is 0.88 in. thick. Hub and disc are one-piece and the assembly is mounted to a one-piece steering knuckle and steering arm. The disc caliper design is similar to the single-piston Delco-Moraine disc brake used on other Chevrolet vehicles.

Rear brakes are drum-type, 9 in. in diameter. Unlike most other brake designs, the rear brakes on 1972-75 models are not automatically adjusted when the brakes are applied, but are adjusted when the parking brake is applied. For this reason, consistent parking in gear without using the parking brake is not recommended. Starting 1976, 9.5 in. diameter self-adjusting rear drum brakes are used on all Vega and Monza models. Adjustment occurs automatically when the brakes are applied during a reverse stop.

The tandem master cylinder pushrod is not adjustable, thus eliminating a pedal free travel adjustment.

Both front and rear hydraulic systems are routed to and from a distribution valve. Any significant change in the pressure difference between the front and rear systems moves a piston which activates a warning light switch, indicating pressure failure in one of the systems.

Master Cylinder Removal and Installation

1. On non-power brakes, disconnect the master cylinder from the brake pedal by detaching the clip and pin.
2. Disconnect the two hydraulic lines at the master cylinder, plugging or covering the ends of the lines.
3. Remove the master cylinder attaching nuts and remove the master cylinder.
4. Reverse the removal procedure to install. Torque the mounting nuts to 24 ft lbs.

5. Bleed the hydraulic system.

Power Booster Removal and Installation

1. Remove the vacuum hose from the check valve.
2. Remove the master cylinder-to-power booster nuts.
3. Remove the brake line distribution and switch mounting bolt from the fender skirt.
4. Pull forward on the master cylinder until the cylinder clears the power booster.
5. Carefully remove the master cylinder with the brake lines attached and set the master cylinder aside. Support the cylinder so that there is no stress on the brake lines. The master cylinder should be moved the minimum distance necessary.
6. Unbolt the power booster from the firewall.
7. Remove the brake pedal pushrod from the pedal pin.
8. Remove the power brake booster.
9. Installation is the reverse of removal. Be sure the brake lines are properly routed to provide sufficient clearance.

Parking Brake Adjustment

1. Raise and support the rear of the car.
2. Apply the parking brake one notch from the fully released position.

NOTE: *On 1977-79 models, it may be necessary to remove the driveshaft to gain access to the parking brake equalizer.*

3. Loosen the adjusting locknut and tighten the adjusting nut until a slight drag is felt when the rear wheels are rotated.
4. Tighten the locknut securely.
5. The rear wheels should rotate freely when the parking brake is fully released.
6. Lower the vehicle.

STEERING

Tie Rod Removal and Installation

1. Place the vehicle on a hoist.
2. Remove the cotter pins from the ball studs and remove the special nuts.
3. To remove the outer ball stud, tap on the steering arm at the tie rod end with a hammer while using a heavy hammer or similar tool as a backing.
4. Remove the inner ball stud from the relay rod using the same procedure as described in Step 3.
5. To remove the tie rod ends from the tie rod, loosen the clamp bolts and unscrew the end assemblies.
6. If the tie rod ends were removed, lubricate the tie rod threads with chassis lube and install the ends on

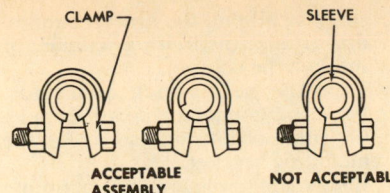

Tie-rod clamp installation
(© Chevrolet Div., G.M. Corp)

the tie rod making sure that both ends are threaded an equal distance from the tie rod.

7. Make sure that the threads on the ball studs and in the ball stud nuts are perfectly clean and smooth. Check the condition of the ball stud seals; replace if necessary.

NOTE: *If threads are not clean and smooth, the ball studs may turn in the tie rod ends when attempting to tighten nut.*

8. Install the ball studs in the steering arms and the relay rod.
9. Install the ball stud nut, tighten and install new cotter pins. Lubricate the tie rod ends.
10. Remove the vehicle from the hoist.
11. Adjust toe-in.

Steering Wheel Removal and Installation

STANDARD WHEEL

1. Disconnect the battery ground cable.
2. Remove the two screws from the back of the wheel, allowing the shroud (horn actuator bar) to be removed.
3. Set the wheel straight ahead. Mark the relationship of the wheel to the shaft and remove the snap-ring (1975 and later) and nut.
4. Remove the steering wheel with a puller, using the two threaded holes in the wheel.
5. Install the wheel, aligning the previously made marks. Make sure that the turn signal switch is in the neutral position. Torque the nut to 30 ft lbs.
6. Make sure that the lower horn insulator, eyelet, and spring are in place.
7. Position the shroud, seating the pin on the right side of the wheel in the hole in the shroud.
8. Replace the two screws in the rear of the wheel. Connect the battery cable.

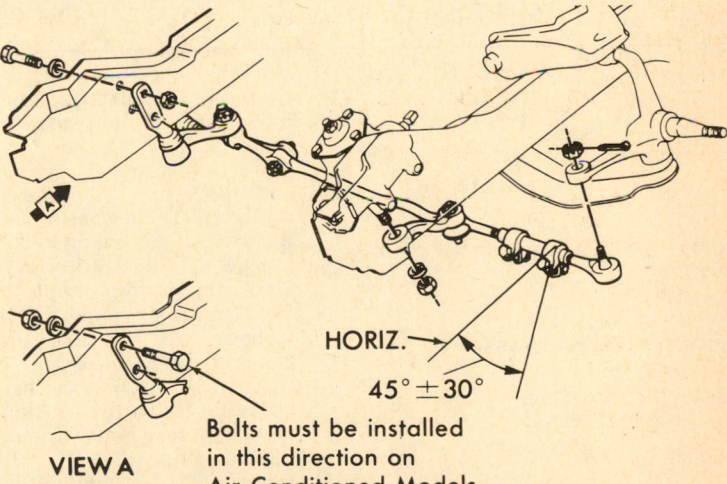

Steering linkage (© Chevrolet Div., G.M. Corp)

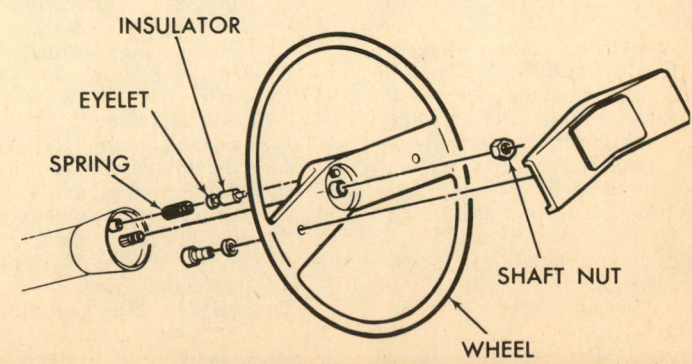

Standard steering wheel assembly—1975 and later models have a snap-ring in front of the nut (© Chevrolet Div., G.M. Corp)

GT AND SPORT WHEEL

1. Disconnect the battery ground cable.
2. Pry off the horn button. Set the wheel in the straight ahead position.
3. Mark the relationship of the wheel to the shaft.
4. Remove the three screws and the upper horn insulator, receiver, and round belleville spring. Remove the snap-ring (1975 and later) and nut.
5. Remove the steering wheel with a puller, utilizing the two threaded holes in the wheel.
6. Replace the wheel, aligning the marks previously made. Make sure that the turn signal switch is in the neutral position. Torque the nut to 30 ft lbs.
7. Make sure that the lower horn insulator, eyelet, and spring are in place.
8. Install the belleville spring, receiver, upper horn insulator, and three screws.
9. Install the horn button and connect the battery cable.

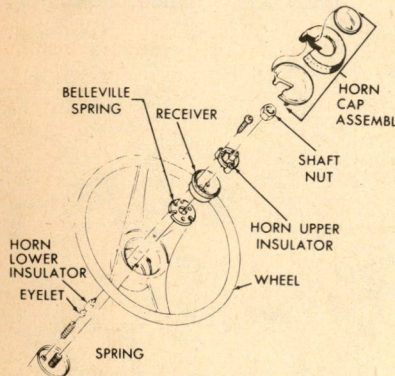

Optional steering wheel assembly —1975 and later models have a snap-ring in front of the nut (© Chevrolet Div., G.M. Corp)

Turn Signal Switch Removal and Installation

STANDARD COLUMN

1. Remove the steering wheel as outlined above.
2. Loosen the three captive screws and lift the cover off the shaft.
3. The lockplate must be depressed with a special tool. Depress the lockplate and remove the wire snap-ring from the shaft.
4. Remove the cancelling cam, upper bearing pre-load spring, and thrust washer from the shaft.
5. Remove the turn signal lever screw and the lever.
6. Push the hazard knob in and unscrew it.
7. Unplug the switch connector from the column and wrap the upper part of the connector with tape.
8. Remove the three switch mounting screws and pull the switch straight up. Guide the wiring connector through the column.
9. Tape the new switch connector. Feed the connector down through the column housing and under the mounting bracket.
10. Install the three switch mounting screws.
11. Replace the hazard flasher knob and the turn signal lever. The turn signal switch should be in Neutral and the hazard flasher knob out.
12. Place the thrust washer, upper bearing preload spring, and cancelling cam on the shaft.
13. Place the lockplate and a new snap-ring on the shaft. Press the lockplate down as in Step three and install the new snap-ring.
14. Replace the cover and its three screws.
15. Install the steering wheel.

TILT COLUMN

1. Remove the steering wheel.
2. Remove the cover from the steering shaft. The screws have plastic retainers on the back of the cover. It is not necessary to completely remove the screws.
3. Remove the turn signal lever screw and lever.
4. Push the hazard warning knob in and remove the knob.
5. Depress the shaft lockplate and remove the retaining snap-ring. Remove the lockplate.
6. Slide the turn signal cancelling cam and upper bearing preload spring off the end of the shaft.
7. Remove the column mounting bracket and gently lower the column. Support the column.
8. Remove the signal switch wire protective cover and strip the wires from the protector. Do not damage the wires. Disconnect the switch connector from the bracket. Tape the wires close to the connectors to facilitate removal.
9. Remove the switch mounting screws and pull the switch straight up, guiding the wiring harness through the column.
10. Tape a new turn signal switch wiring harness and connector and feed the harness through the housing. Push the hazard warning switch in to aid in installation.
11. Reinstall the protective signal switch wire cover.
12. Install the column bracket and raise the column into position.
13. Install the mounting screws and clip the connector to the bracket on the steering column jacket.
14. Install the hazard warning knob and turn signal lever.
15. Be sure the switch is in the neutral position and the hazard warning knob is out. Slide the upper bearing preload spring and cancelling cam onto the shaft.
16. Install the lockplate on the end of the shaft. Compress the lockplate and install a new snap-ring.
17. Reinstall the cover on the end of the shaft.
18. Install the steering wheel.

Ignition Switch Removal and Installation

The ignition switch is mounted on top of the column jacket under the dashboard, completely inaccessible unless the steering column is lowered. The energy-absorbing column is fragile when disconnected and should not be subjected to any shock or excess pressure. Since the column will distort under its own weight, make sure that it is fully supported along its entire length while it is disconnected from the dashboard.

1. Disconnect the battery ground cable.
2. Remove the steering wheel.
3. On manual steering columns, remove the pot joint coupling clamp bolt.
4. On power steering columns, remove the flexible coupling pinch bolt.
5. Move the front seat back out of the way.
6. Remove the three floor pan bracket screws.
7. Remove the two column-to-instrument panel nuts and carefully lower the column far enough to allow the harness plugs to be disconnected.
8. Disconnect the turn signal and ignition switch harnesses.
9. Place the ignition switch in LOCK position.
10. Remove the two switch screws and the switch assembly.
11. When installing, make sure that the switch is in LOCK position.
12. Install the rod to the switch and the switch to the column. Do not use mounting screws longer than the original ones because they could interfere with the ability of the column to collapse.

NOTE: *The following is a mandatory column installation procedure, and must be followed exactly to prevent severe column damage.*

13. On power steering models, place the pot joint clamp over the lower end of the pot joint and assemble the intermediate shaft assembly (pot joint, intermediate shaft and flex coupling) to the steering gear stub shaft, aligning the flat on the stub shaft with the flat in the pot joint.
14. Position the column in the vehicle.
15. On manual steering models, place the pot joint clamp over the lower end of the pot joint and assemble the pot joint to the steering gear wormshaft with the flat in the pot joint. On power steering models, align the steering shaft flat with the flat in the flex coupling. When the

shaft is bottomed against the coupling reinforcement, install and tighten bolt to 30 ft lbs.
16. Connect the turn signal and ignition switch wiring harnesses.
17. Loosely install the steering column bracket to instrument panel stud nuts.
18. Align the pot joint clamp with the groove across the end of the pot joint. Install bolt and nut, tightening nut to 55 ft lbs.

NOTE: *The bolt must pass through the shaft undercut.*
19. With the vehicle on the ground, tighten instrument panel nuts to 19 ft lbs.
20. Slide the toe plate down the column to the floorboard and install the three screws.

NOTE: *On power steering models, alignment flange on the toe plate must be engaged with the front of the toe pan before driving screws. On manual steering models, no side load is allowed during installation of the attaching screws. A side load could cause misalignment.*
21. On manual steering models: remove the alignment spacers. The minimum allowable clearance between the O.D. of the steering shaft and the I.D. of the column jacket lower plastic bushing after installation is 0.18 in.
22. Install the steering wheel.
23. Connect the battery ground cable.

Ignition Lock Cylinder Removal and Installation

Through Mid-1978
1. Place the lock cylinder in the On position.
2. Remove the turn signal switch and steering wheel as previously described.
3. Insert a thin-bladed screwdriver into the rectangular slot inside the column housing. Keep the screwdriver to the right side of the slot and break the housing casting flash loose. Depress the spring latch at the lower end of the lock cylinder. The lock cylinder can be removed with the latch depressed.
4. Place the key part way into the new lock cylinder assembly. If the key is in all the way, the sleeve assembly cannot be installed. Place the wave washer and antitheft ring onto the cylinder.
5. Make sure that the plastic keeper in the sleeve assembly is protruding. Align the lock cylinder lock bolt, the antitheft ring tab, and the slot in the sleeve.
6. Push the sleeve onto the cylinder. Push the key all the way in and rotate the cylinder clockwise.
7. Clamp the tabs of the lock in a padded vise.
8. Place the adapter ring on the cylinder with the serrations out. The adapter ring tab should be against

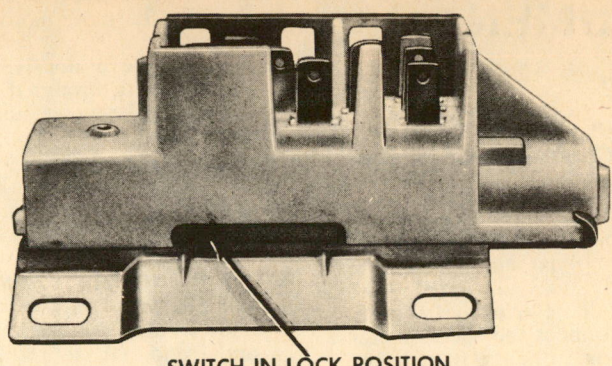

SWITCH IN LOCK POSITION
Ignition switch in lock (© Chevrolet Div., G.M. Corp)

the step in the sleeve. The key must be free to rotate 120°.
9. Tap the adapter into place so that the cylinder extends through it about 1/16 in.
10. Use a small, flat-tipped punch, at least 1/8 in. in diameter, to stake the cylinder over the adapter ring in four places just outside the four dimples.
11. Check the lock for proper operation.
12. Hold the sleeve and turn the tabs clockwise against the stop. Insert the assembly into the housing, aligning the key on the sleeve with the slot in the housing bore.
13. Hold a 0.070 in. drill bit between the lock rim and the housing. Turn the cylinder counterclockwise while pushing in lightly.
14. When the cylinder is felt to go into place, push the cylinder in until the retainer pops into place, securing the cylinder.
15. Remove the drill. Check the operation of the lock.
16. Install the turn signal switch and the steering wheel.

Mid-1978 through 1979
1. Place the lock in the Run position.
2. Remove the lock plate, turn signal switch and buzzer switch.
3. Remove the screw and lock cylinder.

──────── CAUTION ────────

If the screw is dropped on removal, it could fall into the column, requiring complete disassembly to retrieve the screw.

4. Rotate the cylinder clockwise to align the cylinder key with the keyway in the housing.
5. Push the lock all the way in.
6. Install the screw. Tighten the screw to 14 in.lb. for adjustable columns and 25 in.lb. for standard columns.

Power Steering Pump Removal and Installation

THROUGH 1974
1. Disconnect the fluid hoses from the pump or steering gear. Cap or tape

the hose ends to avoid fluid loss.
2. Loosen the pump and remove the drive belt.
3. Remove the drive pulley attaching nut and remove the pulley from the shaft with a puller. Do not hammer on the shaft.
4. Remove the loosened bolts and lift the power steering pump from the brackets.
5. Install the pump in the reverse order of removal. Use the pulley nut to pull the pulley onto the pump shaft.
6. Bleed the power steering system.

1975 AND LATER
1. Remove the battery from the vehicle.
2. Remove the retainers from the pump adjusting bracket. Remove the pump to brace attaching nuts and washers, and the belt.
3. Remove the pump from the remaining engine brackets by moving the pump outward and lifting upward.
4. Lay the pump on the battery box. The pump pulley can be removed with a puller.
5. To remove the pump from the vehicle, remove the adjusting bracket from the pump and disconnect the pressure hoses from the steering gear or the pump.
6. Reinstall the pump in the reverse order of removal. Adjust the drive belt and fill the reservoir.

Power Steering System Bleeding
1. Start the engine and run for a few seconds. Stop the engine and add fluid to refill the reservoir. Repeat this procedure until the level stays constant.
2. Raise the front wheels from the floor and turn the wheels left and right, lightly contacting the steering stops, while the engine speed is approximately 1500 rpm.
3. Lower the car and turn the wheels left and right to the stops. Recheck the fluid level.

NOTE: *The specified fluid is Dexron® II automatic transmission fluid.*

INSTRUMENT PANEL

Speedometer Cable and Instrument Cluster Removal and Replacement

The speedometer and the instruments are removed from the front of the panel by removing the bezel and the lens.

Lift the speedometer away from the panel and disconnect the speedometer cable and wiring from the rear of the cluster. The cable core can then be removed with the aid of a pair of needle nose pliers. If the cable core is broken, it may be necessary to remove the broken piece from the transmission end of the cable.

All of the indicator bulbs are of the quarter twist type and are removed from the rear of the instrument cluster.

Headlight Switch Removal and Installation

1. Disconnect the battery ground cable.
2. Pull the light switch to ON position.
3. Reach up under the instrument panel and depress the switch retainer button while pulling on the knob.
4. Remove the knob and shaft, then remove the ferrule nut with a large screwdriver.
5. Disconnect the multi-contact connector, prying gently with a small screwdriver.
6. Connect the new switch and reverse the removal procedure to complete the replacement.

WINDSHIELD WIPERS

Wiper Blade Removal and Installation

Three methods of blade attachment may be used. If there is a small tab on top of the blade, depress it and slide the blade off. If there is a small spring visible in the top of the blade, insert a screwdriver in the opening, press down and slide the blade off. If there is a clip on the underside of the arm, press down on the clip and slide the blade off.

Motor Removal and Installation

1. Raise the hood.
2. Reaching through cowl opening, loosen the two transmission drive link attaching nuts to the motor crankarm.
3. Remove the transmission drive link from the motor crankarm.
4. Disconnect the wiring, and washer hoses.
5. Remove the three motor attaching screws.
6. Remove the motor while guiding the crankarm through the hole.
7. To install, reverse the removal procedure.

RADIO

Antenna Trimmer Adjustment

1. Remove the right knob and bezel, and locate the trimmer screw above and to the left of the shaft.
2. Temporarily reinstall the knob and tune the radio to a weak station near 1400 KC on the AM dial. Remove the knob.
3. Adjust the trimmer screw until the maximum volume has been reached.
4. Replace the knob and bezel on the radio shaft.

Removal and Installation

VEGA

1. Remove the battery ground cable.
2. Remove the knobs, controls, washers and nuts from the radio bushings.
3. Disconnect the antenna lead, power connector, and speaker connectors from the rear of the receiver.
4. Remove the two screws securing the radio mounting bracket to the instrument panel lower reinforcement and lift out the radio receiver.
5. To install, reverse the removal procedure.

1975 MONZA

1. Disconnect the battery ground cable.
2. Remove the clock set stem knob and instrument panel bezel.
3. Remove the glove compartment.
4. Remove the radio knobs and nuts.
5. Remove the instrument panel pad.
6. Remove the lower screws from the radio mounting bracket.
7. On air conditioned cars, remove the left lap cooler and duct.
8. Remove the steering column mounting bracket and lower and support the steering column.
9. Remove the three screws from the top of the instrument cluster.
10. Remove the 3 bolts from the reinforcement on the instrument panel carrier.
11. Disconnect the speedometer drive cable from the speedometer head.
12. Pull the instrument panel slightly forward and disconnect the electrical and antenna leads.
13. Remove the radio from the instrument panel.
14. Installation is the reverse of removal.

1976 AND LATER MONZA

1. Disconnect the negative battery cable.
2. Remove the knobs, bezels, nuts, and washers from the radio control shafts.
3. Remove the two screws attaching the radio to the instrument panel reinforcement.
4. With mounts still attached, lower the radio and disconnect the electrical leads.
5. Installation is the reverse of removal.

HEATER

Blower Motor Removal and Installation

1. Disconnect the battery ground cable.
2. On 1976 and later models, remove the coolant recovery tank attaching screws and move the tank aside; draining the tank is unnecessary.
3. Disconnect the blower motor lead wire. Disconnect the motor cooling tube on air-conditioned models.
4. Scribe the blower motor flange to case position.
5. Remove the blower to case attaching screws and remove the blower wheel and motor assembly. Pry the flange gently if the sealer is retaining the assembly.
6. Remove the blower wheel retaining nut and separate the motor and wheel.
7. To install, reverse Steps 1-5, lining up the match-marks on the motor flange and case which were made at removal.

NOTE: *Assemble the blower wheel to the motor with the open end of the blower away from the motor. Reseal the motor flange, if necessary.*

Heater Core Removal and Installation

WITHOUT AIR CONDITIONING

1. Disconnect the battery ground cable.
2. Disconnect the blower motor lead wire.
3. Place a pan under the vehicle. Disconnect the heater hoses at the core connections and secure the ends of the hoses in a raised position.
4. Remove the coil bracket to firewall stud nut and move the coil out of the way.
5. Remove the blower intake to firewall screws and nuts and remove the blower intake, blower motor and wheel as an assembly.
6. Remove the core retaining strap screws and remove the core from the vehicle.
7. To install, reverse Steps 1-6.

NOTE: *Be sure that the blower intake sealer is intact, replace if necessary.*

VEGA AND 1975 MONZA WITH AIR CONDITIONING

1. Disconnect the battery ground cable.
2. Disconnect the heater hoses at the core and plug them.
3. Remove the firewall selector stud nuts.
4. Disconnect the left-side flexible dash outlet hose from the center distributor duct.
5. Remove the right-side dash outlet assembly.
6. Remove the instrument bezel and center outlet as an assembly.
7. Remove the ash tray and retainer.
8. Remove the radio as previously outlined.
9. Remove the control - to - dash screws and lower the control assembly.
10. Remove the cigarette lighter. Remove the screw retaining the right side of the dash reinforcement.
11. Pry out the center duct-to-dash clip. Remove the center duct-to-selector duct screws and remove the center duct. Turn the duct clockwise and pull down and to the left to remove.
12. Remove the defroster duct-to-selector duct screw. Remove the remaining selector duct-to-dash screws and pull the duct back far enough to allow the electrical and vacuum lines to be disconnected.
13. Disconnect the lines and the control cable and remove the selector duct assembly.

14. Pry off the temperature door bell-crank, being careful not to bend the arm or damage the selector case.
15. Remove the temperature door. Remove the backing plate and temperature door cable retainer screws.
16. Remove the heater core and backing plate as an assembly. Remove the core retaining straps and withdraw the core.
17. Reverse the removal procedure to install the core.

1976-77 MONZA WITH AIR CONDITIONING

1. Disconnect the negative battery cable.
2. Remove the floor outlet duct. Remove the glove box and door.
3. Remove the right and left-side dash outlets by prying them out with a putty knife or similar tool.
4. Remove the instrument panel pad. Disconnect the vacuum hoses at the valves on the left end of the heater-evaporator.
5. Remove the insulation tray below the instrument cluster. Loosen the console and slide it rearward.
6. Lower the steering column by removing the attaching nuts. Rest the steering column on the driver's seat.
7. Remove the instrument panel-to-dash attaching screws, place a protective cover over the steering column, and lower the instrument panel onto the steering column.

Disconnect the speedometer cable, radio electrical leads, and control head connectors.
8. As an assembly, remove the right-side instrument panel and lap cooler. Remove the modular duct-to-heater-evaporator screw and remove the modular duct.
9. Disconnect the temperature door bowden cable and wiring harness.
10. Remove the heater hoses at the core tubes and place the hoses upright. Plug the core tubes to prevent coolant spillage on heater-evaporator removal.
11. Remove the three heater case stud nuts. Remove the heater core case-to-evaporator case attaching screws.
12. Drive in the case studs to remove them from the firewall and remove the heater core case.
13. Remove the heater core-to-case screws and remove the heater core.
14. Installation is the reverse of removal.

1978- 79 MONZA "S" HATCHBACK AND STATION WAGON WITH AIR CONDITIONING

1. Disconnect the battery ground.
2. Disconnect the hoses at the core tubes and place in raised position.
3. Remove the nuts from the selector duct studs in the engine compartment.
4. Remove the glove box and door.
5. Remove the right outlet to instru-

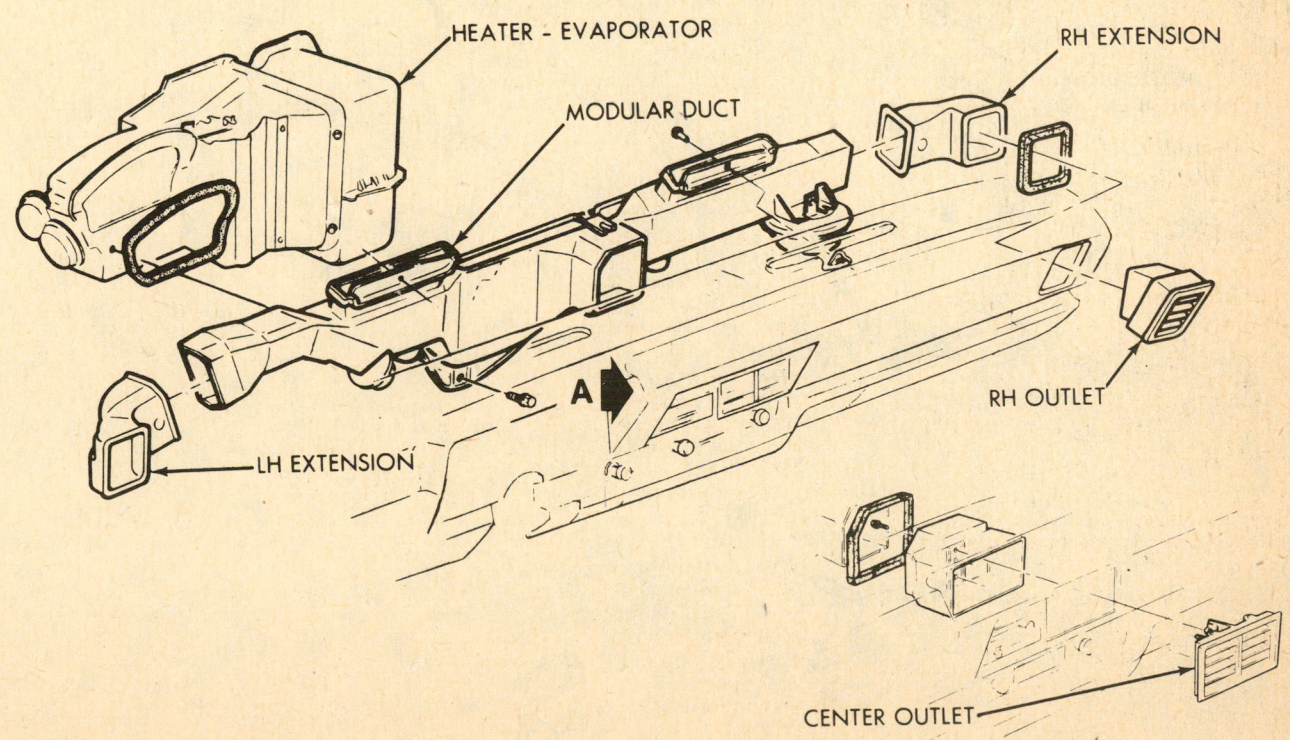

HEATER - EVAPORATOR

MODULAR DUCT

RH EXTENSION

RH OUTLET

LH EXTENSION

A

CENTER OUTLET

VIEW A

A/C Air Distribution Ducts (© Chevrolet Div., G.M. Corp.)

ment panel screws and remove the outlet and hose.

6. Remove the intermediate duct leading to the left outlet.

7. Lower the steering column as described in Ignition Switch Removal and Installation.

8. Remove the instrument panel bezel. Remove the ashtray and retainer.

9. Remove the screws securing the A/C control head to the instrument panel.

10. Disconnect the radio leads and antenna wire.

11. Remove the instrument cluster screws and allow the entire cluster, including the radio, to rest on the steering column.

12. Disconnect the speedometer cable and remove the A/C control head.

13. Remove the center duct screws, then slide it first to the left, then to the right then remove it.

14. Remove the defroster duct and remaining selector ducts.

15. Disconnect all electrical and vacuum lines from the evaporator.

16. Disconnect the temperature door cables.

17. Pry off or punch out the temperature door bell crank.

18. Remove the temperature door.

19. Remove the screws securing the temperature door cable retainer and backing plate.

20. Remove the heater core and backing plate assembly and remove the straps from the core.

21. Installation is the reverse of removal. When installing the ducts, make sure the firewall seals are positioned correctly. When installing the cluster, position the A/C control head and connect the speedometer cable before the cluster is secured. Adjust the temperature door at the selector duct attachment. With the temperature lever and door in the Off position, tighten the cable attaching screw.

1978-79 MONZA (EXCEPT MONZA "S" AND STATION WAGON) WITH AIR CONDITIONING

1. Disconnect the battery ground.
2. Remove the floor outlet duct.
3. Remove the glove box and door.
4. Remove the left and right dash outlets.
5. Remove the instrument panel pad.
6. Disconnect the vacuum hoses and electrical wires from the heater-evaporator case.

7. Remove the insulation tray below the instrument cluster and loosen the console and slide it rearward.

8. Lower the steering column assembly, following the instructions in Ignition Switch Removal and Installation.

9. Remove the instrument panel attaching screws and allow the instrument panel to rest on the steering column.

10. Disconnect the speedometer cable, radio wiring and control head wiring.

11. Remove the right side instrument panel and lap duct.

12. Remove the modular duct from the case.

13. Disconnect the temperature door cable and the wiring harness.

14. Remove the heater hoses from the core tubes and position them upright to avoid coolant loss.

15. Remove the three heater case stud nuts.

16. Remove the heater core case-to-evaporator core case screws.

17. Hammer on the studs, carefully, to break loose the heater core case.

18. Unbolt the core from the case.

19. Installation is the reverse of removal. Replace any damaged sealer.

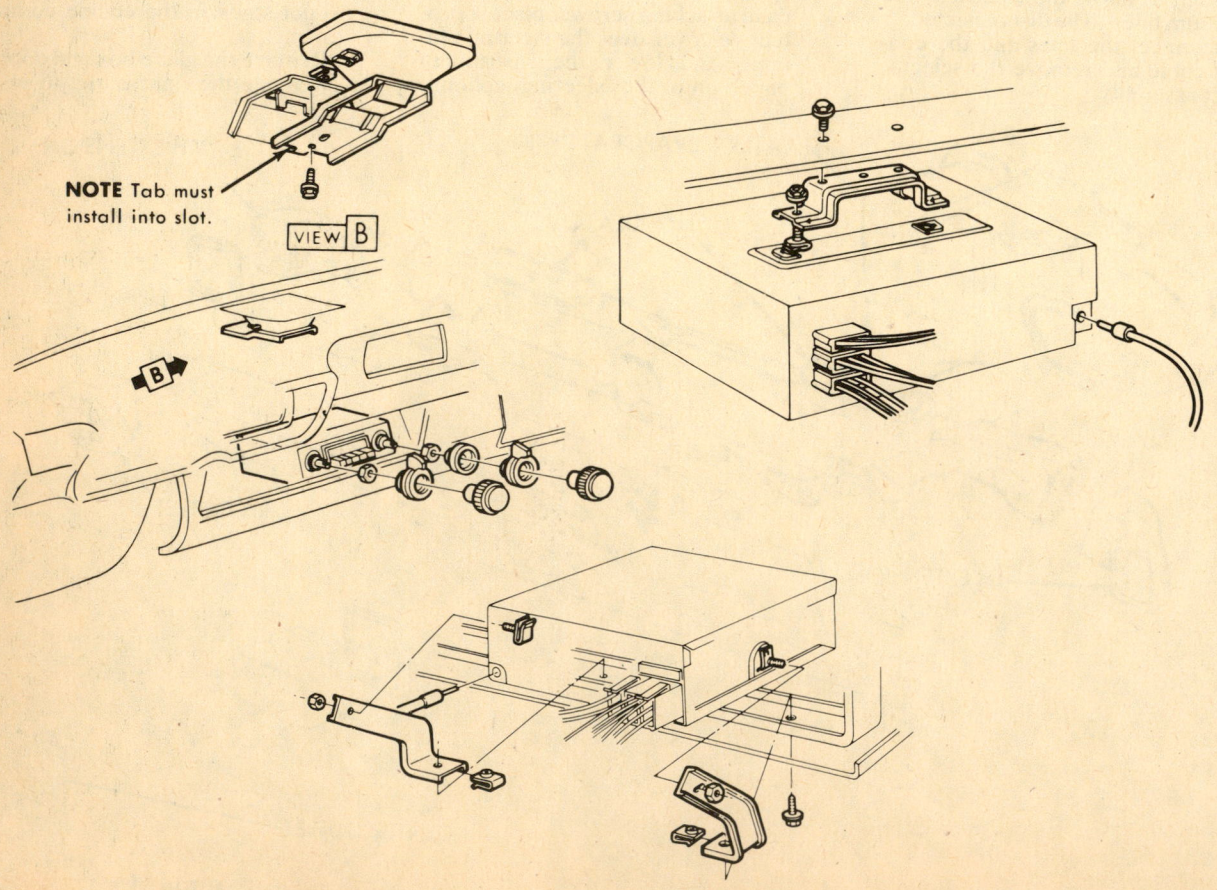

NOTE Tab must install into slot.

VIEW B

1976 and later Monza radio mounting details (© Chevrolet Div., G.M. Corp.)

Index

Oldsmobile • Cutlass • Omega • Starfire

YEAR IDENTIFICATION

1972 Delta 88

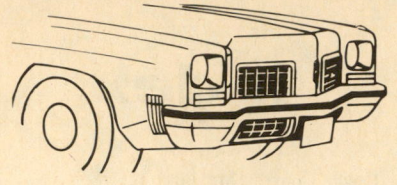

1972 98

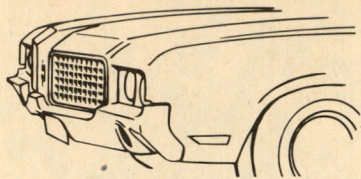

1972 Cutlass Supreme

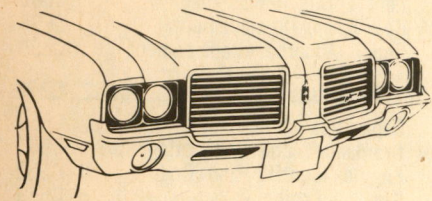

1972 Cutlass S

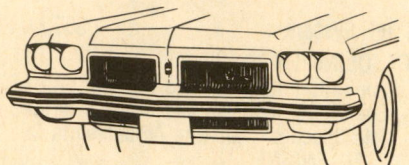

1973 Delta 88

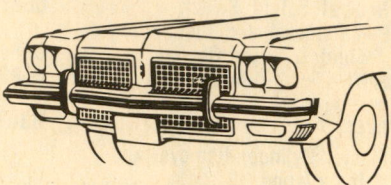

1973 98

1973 Cutlass Supreme

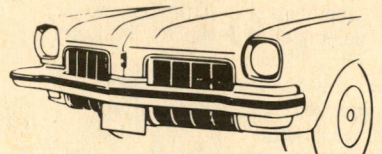

1973 Cutlass S

1973 Omega

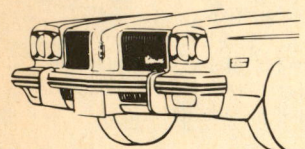

1974 Delta 88

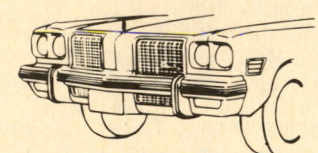

1974 98

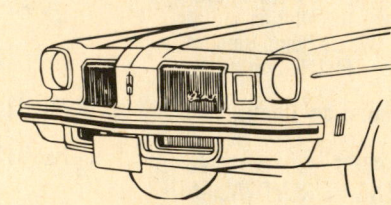

1974 Cutlass

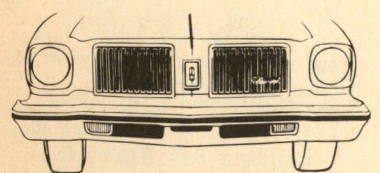

1974 Omega

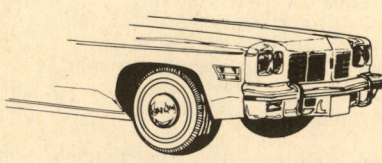

1975 Delta 88

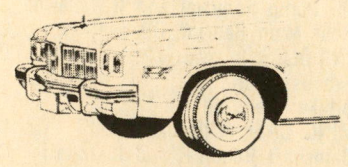

1975 98

1975 Cutlass S

1975 Omega

1975 Starfire

YEAR IDENTIFICATION

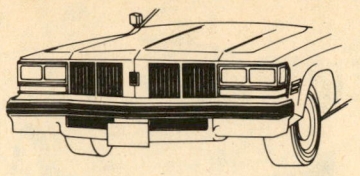

1975 Delta 88

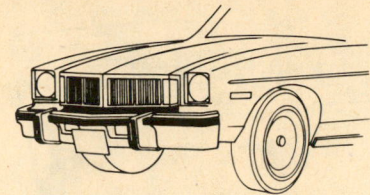

1976 Omega Brougham

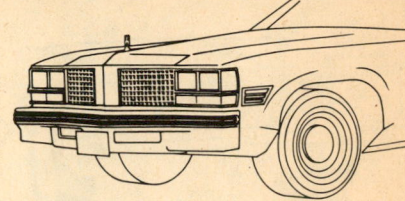

1976 98 Regency Sedan

1976 Starfire

1976 Cutlass

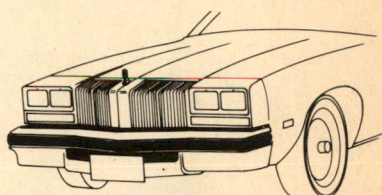

1976 Cutlass S

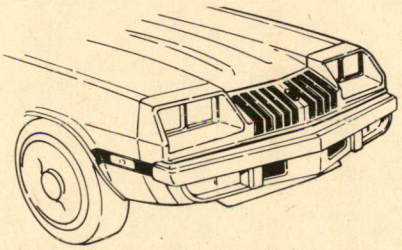

1977 Starfire

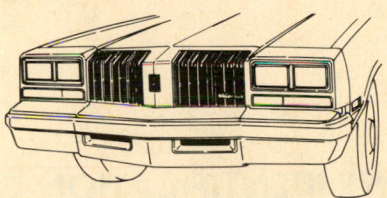

1977 Cutlass S

1977 Cutlass Supreme

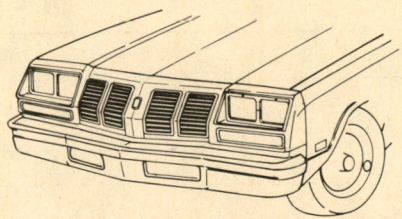

1977 4-4-2

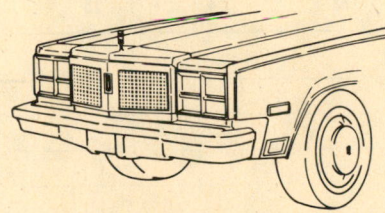

1977 98

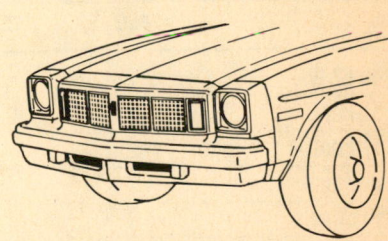

1977 Omega

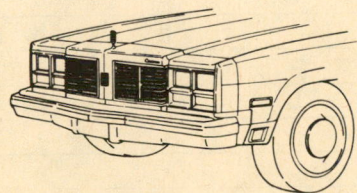

1977 Delta 88

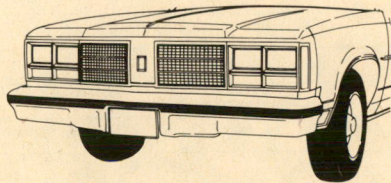

1978 Delta 88

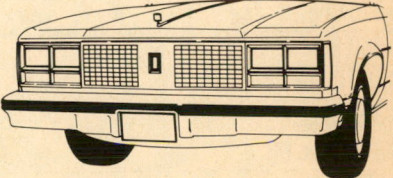

1978 98

1978 Omega

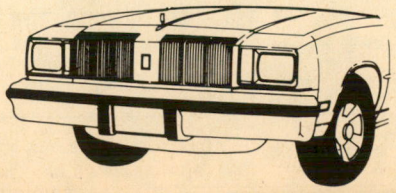

1978 Cutlass

1978 Starfire

YEAR IDENTIFICATION

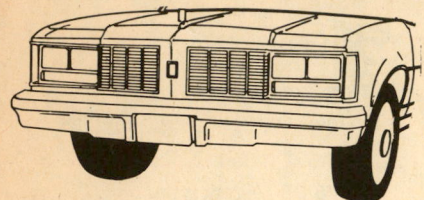

1979 Delta 88

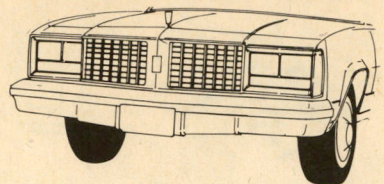

1979 98

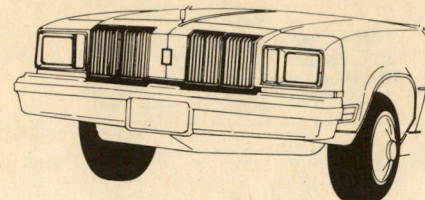

1979 Cutlass

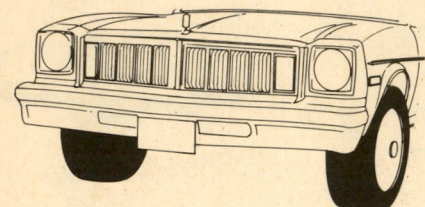

1979 Omega

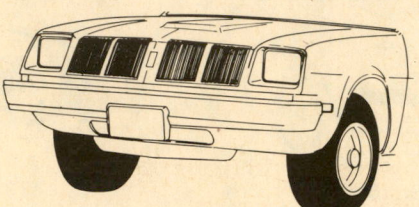

1979 Starfire

ENGINE IDENTIFICATION CODE

Identification is by the 5th digit of the VIN code located on the upper left top of the instrument panel pad.

Displ.	Bbl.	'72	'73	'74	'75	'76	'77	'78	'79
4-140 Chev.	2					B	B		
4-151 Pont.	2							V	V
4-151 Pont.	2							1	I
6-231 Buick	2				C	C	C	A	A
6-250 Chev.	1		D	D	D	D			
8-260 Olds.	2				F	F	F	F	F
8-260 Olds.	Diesel								
8-305 Chev.	2						U	U	G
8-305 Chev.	4							H	H
8-350 Buick	4				J	J		X	
8-350 Chev.	4						L	L	L
8-350 Olds.	2	H	H			H			
8-350 Olds. DE	2	J							
8-350 Olds.	4	K	K	K	K	R	R	R	R
8-350 Olds. DE	4	M	M	M					
8-350 Olds.	Diesel							N	N
8-403 Olds.	4						K	K	K
8-455 Olds.	4	T	T	T	T	T			
8-455 Olds.	4	U	U	U	U				
8-455 Olds.	4	V	V						
8-455 Olds.	4	X							

DE: Dual Exhaust

GENERAL ENGINE SPECIFICATIONS

Year	Engine No. Cyl. Displacement (cu. in.)	Carburetor Type	Horsepower @ rpm ■	Torque @ rpm (ft lbs) ■	Bore X Stroke (in.)	Compression Ratio	Oil Pressure @ 2000 rpm
'72	8-350	2 bbl	160 @ 4000	275 @ 2400	4.057 x 3.385	8.50:1	30-45
	8-350①	2 bbl	175 @ 4000	295 @ 2600	4.057 x 3.385	8.50:1	30-45
	8-350	4 bbl	180 @ 4000	275 @ 2800	4.057 x 3.385	8.50:1	30-45
	8-350①	4 bbl	200 @ 4400	300 @ 3200	4.057 x 3.385	8.50:1	30-45
	8-455	4 bbl	225 @ 3600	360 @ 2600	4.126 x 4.250	8.50:1	30-50
	8-455①	4 bbl	250 @ 4200	370 @ 2800	4.126 x 4.250	8.50:1	30-50
	8-455	4 bbl	270 @ 4400	370 @ 3200	4.126 x 4.250	8.50:1	30-50
	8-455	4 bbl	300 @ 4700	410 @ 3200	4.126 x 4.250	8.50:1	30-50
'73	6-250	1 bbl	100 @ 3600	175 @ 1600	3.875 x 3.530	8.50:1	30-45
	8-350	2 bbl	160 @ 3800	275 @ 2400	4.057 x 3.385	8.50:1	30-45
	8-350	4 bbl	180 @ 3800	275 @ 2800	4.057 x 3.385	8.50:1	30-45
	8-455	4 bbl	225 @ 3600	360 @ 2600	4.126 x 4.250	8.50:1	30-50
	8-455	4 bbl	250 @ 4000	370 @ 2800	4.126 x 4.250	8.50:1	30-50
'74	6-250	1 bbl	100 @ 3600	175 @ 1600	3.875 x 3.530	8.00:1	30-45
	8-350	4 bbl	160 @ 3800	275 @ 2400	4.057 x 3.385	8.50:1	30-45
	8-350	4 bbl	180 @ 3800	275 @ 2800	4.057 x 3.385	8.50:1	30-45
	8-350①	4 bbl	200 @ 4200	300 @ 3200	4.057 x 3.385	8.50:1	30-45
	8-455	4 bbl	210 @ 3600	350 @ 2400	4.126 x 4.250	8.50:1	30-50
	8-455①	4 bbl	230 @ 4000	370 @ 2800	4.126 x 4.250	8.50:1	30-50
'75	6-231 Buick	2 bbl	110 @ 4000	175 @ 2000	3.800 x 3.400	8.00:1	37②
	6-250 Chev.	1 bbl	100 @ 3600	175 @ 1600	3.875 x 3.530	8.50:1	36-41
	8-260 Olds.	2 bbl	110 @ 3400	205 @ 1600	3.500 x 3.385	8.50:1	30-45
	8-350 Buick	2 bbl	145 @ 3200	270 @ 2000	3.800 x 3.850	8.00:1	37②
	8-350 Buick	4 bbl	165 @ 3800	260 @ 2200	3.800 x 3.850	8.00:1	37②
	8-350 Olds.	4 bbl	160 @ 3800	275 @ 2400	4.057 x 3.385	8.50:1	30-45
	8-455 Olds.	4 bbl	190 @ 3400	350 @ 2400	4.126 x 4.250	8.50:1	30-45
'76	4-140 Chev.	2 bbl	85 @ 4400	122 @ 2400	3.500 x 3.625	8.00:1	40
	6-231 Buick	2 bbl	105 @ 3400	185 @ 2000	3.800 x 3.400	8.00:1	37②
	6-250 Chev.	1 bbl	105 @ 3800	185 @ 1200	3.875 x 3.530	8.25:1	36-41
	8-260 Olds.	2 bbl	110 @ 3400	205 @ 1600	3.500 x 3.385	8.00:1	30-45
	8-350 Buick	2 bbl	140 @ 3200	280 @ 1800	3.800 x 3.850	8.00:1	37②
	8-350 Buick	4 bbl	155 @ 3400	280 @ 1800	3.800 x 3.850	8.00:1	37②
	8-350 Olds.	4 bbl	170 @ 3800	275 @ 2400	4.057 x 3.385	8.50:1	30-45
	8-455 Olds.	4 bbl	190 @ 3400	350 @ 2000	4.126 x 4.250	8.50:1	30-45
'77	4-140 Chev.	2 bbl	84 @ 4400	117 @ 2400	3.500 x 3.625	8.0:1	40
	4-151 Pont.	2 bbl	88 @ 4400	128 @ 2400	4.000 x 3.000	8.3:1	40
	6-231 Buick	2 bbl	105 @ 3400	185 @ 2000	3.800 x 3.400	8.0:1	37
	8-260 Olds.	2 bbl	110 @ 3400	205 @ 1800	3.500 x 3.385	7.5:1	40
	8-305 Chev.	2 bbl	145 @ 3800	245 @ 2400	3.736 x 3.480	8.5:1	40
	8-350 Olds.	4 bbl	170 @ 3800	275 @ 2000	4.057 x 3.385	22.5:1	30-45
	8-350 Chev.	4 bbl	170 @ 3800	270 @ 2400	4.057 x 3.385	8.0:1	40
	8-350 Olds.	Diesel	135 @ 2800	285 @ 1800	4.000 x 3.480	8.5:1	40
	8-403 Olds.	4 bbl	185 @ 3600	320 @ 2200	4.351 x 3.385	8.0:1	40
'78	4-151 Pont.	2 bbl	90 @ 4400	130 @ 2400	4.000 x 3.000	8.3:1	40
	6-231 Buick	2 bbl	105 @ 3400	185 @ 2000	3.800 x 3.400	8.0:1	37

GENERAL ENGINE SPECIFICATIONS

Year	Engine No. Cyl. Displacement (cu. in.)	Carburetor Type	Horsepower @ rpm ■	Torque @ rpm ■ (ft lbs) ■	Bore X Stroke (in.)	Compression Ratio	Oil Pressure @ 2000 rpm
'78	8-260 Olds.	2 bbl	110 @ 3400	205 @ 1800	3.500 x 3.385	7.5:1	40
	8-305 Chev.	2 bbl	145 @ 3800	245 @ 2400	3.736 x 3.480	8.5:1	40
	8-305 Chev.	4 bbl	160 @ 4000	265 @ 2200	3.736 x 3.480	8.5:1	40
	8-350 Buick	4 bbl	170 @ 3400	280 @ 1800	3.800 x 3.850	8.0:1	40
	8-350 Chev.	4 bbl	170 @ 3800	270 @ 2400	4.000 x 3.480	8.5:1	40
	8-350 Olds.	4 bbl	170 @ 3800	275 @ 2000	4.057 x 3.385	8.0:1	40
	8-350 Olds.	Diesel	120 @ 3600	220 @ 1800	4.057 x 3.385	22.0:1	40
	8-403 Olds.	4 bbl	185 @ 3600	320 @ 2200	4.351 x 3.385	8.0:1	40
'79	4-151 Pont.	2 bbl	85 @ 4400	123 @ 2800	4.000 x 3.000	8.3:1	40
	6-231 Buick	2 bbl	115 @ 3800	190 @ 2000	3.800 x 3.400	8.0:1	37
	8-260 Olds.	2 bbl	110 @ 3400	205 @ 1800	3.500 x 3.385	7.5:1	40
	8-260 Olds.	Diesel	90 @ 3600	170 @ 2200	3.500 x 3.385	22.5:1	40
	8-305 Chev.	2 bbl	145 @ 3800	245 @ 2400	3.736 x 3.480	8.5:1	40
	8-305 Chev.	4 bbl	160 @ 4000	235 @ 2400	3.736 x 3.480	8.5:1	40
	8-350 Chev.	4 bbl	160 @ 3800	260 @ 2400	4.000 x 3.480	8.5:1	40
	8-350 Olds.	4 bbl	170 @ 3800	275 @ 2000	4.057 x 3.385	8.0:1	40
	8-350 Olds.	Diesel	120 @ 3600	220 @ 2200	4.057 x 3.385	22.5:1	40
	8-403 Olds.	4 bbl	185 @ 3600	320 @ 2200	4.351 x 3.385	8.0:1	40

■ Horsepower and torque are SAE net figures. They are measured at the rear of the transmission with all accessories installed and operating. Since the figures vary when a given engine is installed in different models, some are representative rather than exact.

① Dual exhaust
② @ 2500 rpm

Oldsmobile 88, 98 TUNE-UP SPECIFICATIONS

When analyzing compression test results, look for uniformity among cylinders rather than specific pressures.

Year	Engine No. Cyl Displacement (cu in.)	hp	SPARK PLUGS Orig. Type	Gap (in.)	DISTRIBUTOR Point Dwell (deg)	Point Gap (in.)	IGNITION TIMING (deg) ▲ Man Trans *	Auto Trans	VALVES Intake Opens ■ (deg)	Fuel Pump Pressure (psi)	IDLE SPEED (rpm) ▲ Man Trans ●	Auto Trans
'72	8-350	160	R-46S	.040	28-32	.016	—	8B	16	5½-6½	—	650/600
	8-350	180	R-46S	.040	28-32	.016	—	12B	22	5½-6½	—	600
	8-455	225	R-46S	.040	28-32	.016	—	8B	20	5½-6½	—	650/600
'73	8-350	160	R-46S	.040	30	.016	—	12B	16	5½-6½	—	700/550
	8-455	225	R-46S	.040	30	.016	—	8B	20	5½-6½	—	650/550
'74	8-350	180	R-46S	.040	30	.016	—	12B	16	5½-6½	—	650/550
	8-455	210	R-46S	.040	30	.016	—	8B	20	5½-6½	—	650/550
	8-455	230	R-46SX	.080	Electronic		—	8B	20	5½-6½	—	650/550
'75	8-350	170	R-46SX	.080	Electronic		—	20B	16	5½-6½	—	650/550
	8-455	190	R-46SX	.080	Electronic		—	16B	20	5½-6½	—	650/550
'76	8-350	170	R-46SX	.080	Electronic		—	20B	16	5½-6½	—	650②/550(600)
	8-455	190	R-46SX	.080	Electronic		—	16B①	20	5½-6½	—	650②/550(600)
'77	6-231 Buick	105	R-46TSX	.060③	Electronic		—	12B	17	6-7	—	670/600
	8-260 Olds.	110	R-46SZ	.060	Electronic		—	16B @ 1100	14	6-7	—	650/550
	8-350 Chev.	170	R-45TS	.045	Electronic		—	8B	28	7-9	—	650/500

Oldsmobile 88, 98   TUNE-UP SPECIFICATIONS

When analyzing compression test results, look for uniformity among cylinders rather than specific pressures.

Year	ENGINE No. Cyl Displacement (cu in.)	hp	SPARK PLUGS Orig. Type	Gap (in.)	DISTRIBUTOR Point Dwell (deg)	Point Gap (in.)	IGNITION TIMING (deg) ▲ Man Trans *	Auto Trans	VALVES Intake Opens ■ (deg)	Fuel Pump Pressure (psi)	IDLE SPEED (rpm) ▲ Man Trans	Auto Trans
'77	8-350 Olds.	170	R-46SZ	.060	Electronic		—	@ 1100 20B④	16	6-7	—	650/550⑤
	8-403 Olds.	185	R-46SZ	.060	Electronic		—	20B @ 1100	16	6-7	—	650/550⑤
'78	6-231 Buick	105	R-46TSX	.060	Electronic		—	15B	17	6-7	—	600
	8-260 Olds.	110	R-46SZ	.060	Electronic		—	20B @ 1100	14	6-7	—	500
	8-350 Buick	170	R-46TSX	.060	Electronic		—	15B	19	6-7	—	550
	8-350 Olds.	170	R-46SZ	.060	Electronic		—	20B @ 1100	16	6-7	—	650⑥
	8-350 Olds. Diesel	—	—	—	—		—	5B⑨	16	6-7⑩	—	575
	8-403 Olds.	185	R-46SZ	.060	Electronic		—	18B⑦ @ 1100	16	6-7	—	550⑧
'79	6-231 Buick	115	R-46TSX	.060	Electronic		—	12B	16	5.5-6.5	—	550
	8-260 Olds.	110	R-46SZ	.080	Electronic		—	18B	14	5.5-6.5	—	550
	8-305 Chev.	145	R-45TS	.045	Electronic		—	@ 1100 8B	28	5.5-6.5	—	550
	8-350 Olds.	170	R-46SZ	.080	Electronic		—	20B	16	5.5-6.5	—	550
	8-350 Olds. Diesel	—	—	—	—		—	@ 1100 5B⑨	16	6.0-7.0⑩	—	600
	8-403 Olds.	185	R-46SZ	.080	Electronic		—	24B(20B) @ 1100	16	5.5-6.5	—	550

① 18B with 2.4:1 axle ratio in 98
② A/C on and compressor clutch wires disconnected
③ .040 with R-46TS
④ Calif. 88 Sedan: 18B
⑤ High Altitude: 700/600
⑥ High Altitude: 700
⑦ 88 sta. wgn.: 20B 1100
⑧ High Altitude: 600
⑨ Static
⑩ Injector opening pressure: 1800 psi.
▲ See text for procedure
■ All figures are in degrees Before Top Dead Center

* Set V8 timing through 1974 at 1100 rpm without A/C and at 850 rpm with A/C. See sticker for timing rpm on later models.
● Figures in parentheses apply to California engines. Where two idle speed figures appear separated by a slash, the first is idle speed with solenoid energized, the second is idle speed with solenoid disconnected.
B   Before Top Dead Center
—   Not applicable
NOTE: The underhood specifications sticker often reflects tune-up specification changes made in production. Sticker figures must be used if they disagree with those in this chart.

NOTE: Most 1979 GM carburetors have idle mixture screws concealed by staked-in plugs. These are not meant to be removed, except at carburetor overhaul.

Cutlass, Omega, Starfire,   TUNE-UP SPECIFICATIONS

When analyzing compression test results, look for uniformity among cylinders rather than specific pressures.

Year	ENGINE No. Cyl Displacement (cu in.)	hp	SPARK PLUGS Orig. Type	Gap (in.)	DISTRIBUTOR Point Dwell (deg)	Point Gap (in.)	IGNITION TIMING (deg) ▲ Man ●	Trans * Auto ● Trans	VALVES Intake Opens ■ (deg) ●	Fuel Pump Pressure (psi)	IDLE SPEED (rpm) ▲ Man Trans ●	Auto Trans
'72	8-350	160	R-46S	.040	28-32	.016	8B	8B(6B)	16(22)	5½-6½	750	650/550
	8-350	180	R-46S	.040	28-32	.016	8B	12B	16(22)	5½-6½	750	600
	8-455	250	R-46S	.040	28-32	.016	10B	8B	30⑦	5½-6½	750	600
	8 455	270	R 46S	.040	28-32	.016	10B	8B	30⑦	5½-6½	750	600
	8-455	300	R-45S	.040	28-32	.016	12B	10B	56	5½-6½	750	650

Cutlass, Omega, Starfire,

TUNE-UP SPECIFICATIONS (cont'd)

When analyzing compression test results, look for uniformity among cylinders rather than specific pressures.

Year	ENGINE No. Cyl Displacement (cu in.)	hp	SPARK PLUGS Orig. Type	Gap (in.)	DISTRIBUTOR Point Dwell (deg)	Point Gap (in.)	IGNITION TIMING (deg) ▲ Man ●	Auto Trans * ●	VALVES Intake Opens ■ (deg) ●	Fuel Pump Pressure (psi)	IDLE SPEED (rpm) ▲ Man Trans ●	Auto Trans ●
'73	6-250	100	R-46T	.035	33	.019	6B	6B	16	4-5	700/450	600/450
	8-350	160	R-46S	.040	30	.016	—	14B	22	5½-6½	—	650/550
	8-350	180	R-46S	.040	30	.016	—	12B	22	5½-6½	—	650/550
	8-350	180	R-45S	.040	30	.016	—	12B	22	5½-6½	1000/600	—
	8-455	225	R-45S	.040	30	.016	10B	8B	28	5½-6½	1000/750	650/550
'77	4-140 Chev.	84	R-43TS	.035	Electronic		10B	12B	34	3-4½	1250/700⑰	850/650⑰
	6-231 Buick	105	R-46TSX	.060③	Electronic		12B	12B	17	3-4½⑤	800/600	800/600
	8-260 Olds.	110	R-46SZ	.060	Electronic		16B① @ 1100	16B① @ 1100	14	5-6	750	650/550
	8-305 Chev.	145	R-45TS	.045	Electronic		8B	8B	28	7-9	700/500	700/500
	8-350 Olds.	170	R-46SZ	.060	Electronic		—	20B⑫ @ 1100	16	6-7	—	700/600⑬
	8-350 Chev.	170	R-45TS	.045	Electronic		—	8B⑭	28	7-9	—	650/500⑮
	8-403 Olds.	185	R-46SZ	.060	Electronic		—	20B⑯ @ 1100	16	6-7	—	④
'78	4-151 Pont.	90	R-43TSX	.060	Electronic		14B	14B	33	4-5	②	⑥
	6-231 Buick	105	R-46TSX	.060	Electronic		15B	15B	17	5-6	⑧	600
	8-260 Olds.	110	R-46SZ	.060	Electronic		18B @ 1100	20B㉑ @ 1100	14	5-6	800	500⑳
	8-305 Chev.	145	R-45TS	.045	Electronic		4B	⑱	28	7-9	600	500⑲
	8-305 Chev.	160	R-45TS	.045	Electronic		—	4B	28	7-9	—	500
	8-350 Chev.	170	R-45TS	.045	Electronic		—	8B	28	7-9	—	600(500)
'79	4-151 Pont.	85	R-44TSX	.060	Electronic		14B	14B(12B)	33	4.0-5.5	1000	650
	6-231 Olds.	115	R-46TSX	.060	Electronic		15B	15B	16	5.0-6.0	800	600
	8-260 Olds.	110	R-46SZ	.080	Electronic		18B @ 1100	20B @ 1100	14	5.0-6.0	800	500
	8-260 Olds.	Diesel	—	—			—	5B㉓	14	6.0-7.0㉒	—	600
	8-305 Chev.	145	R-45TS	.045	Electronic		4B	8B	28	5.0-6.0	800	600
	8-305 Chev.	160	R-44TS	.045	Electronic		—	8B	28	5.0-6.0	—	600
	8-350 Chev.	160	R-45TS	.045	Electronic		—	8B	28	5.0-6.0	—	600
	8-350 Olds.	170	R-46SZ	.080	Electronic		—	20B @ 1100	16	5.5-6.5	—	550
	8-350 Olds.	Diesel	—	—	—		—	5B㉓	16	6.0-7.0㉒	—	600
	8-403 Olds.	185	R-46SZ	.080	Electronic		—	24B(20B) @ 1100	16	5.5-6.5	—	550

▲ See text for procedure

■ All figures Before Top Dead Center

● Figure in parentheses indicates California engine. Where two idle speed figures appear separated by a slash, the second is with the idle speed solenoid disconnected.

* Set V8 timing through 1974 at 1100 rpm without A/C and at 850 rpm with A/C. See sticker for timing rpm on later models.

① Cutlass sedan: 18B Omega: 20B

② without A/C: 1000/500 with A/C: 1200/1000

③ .040 in. with R-46TS

④ Cutlass exc. high altitude: 650/550, all high altitude: 700/600

⑤ Figure shown is for starfire. All others: 5½-6½

⑥ without A/C: 650/500 with A/C: 850/650

⑦ Figure is 44 degrees for manual transmission

⑧ MT: 49 states Cutlass except sta. wgn., 49 states Omega, and California Starfire—800 All others—600

⑨ 14B—Omega, California

⑩ A/C on and compressor clutch wires disconnected

⑪ 22B with 2.4:1 axle

⑫ Omega: 18B
⑬ Omega: 650/550
⑭ California Omega: 6B
⑮ High Altitude Omega: 650/600
⑯ Cutlass Wgn: 22B
⑰ High Altitude: MT-1250/800
AT-850/700
⑱ 49 states: 4B
Calif.: 6B
High Altitude: 8B
⑲ High Altitude: 600
⑳ High Altitude Cutlass,

except Sta. Wgn.: 550
㉑ Calif. Cutlass, except
Sta. Wgn.: 18B @ 1100
㉒ Nozzle opening pressure: 1800 psi
㉓ Static
B Before Top Dead Center
TDC Top Dead Center
— Not applicable
N.A. Not Available
NOTE: The underhood specifications sticker often reflects tune-up specification changes made in production. Sticker figures must be used if they disagree with those in this chart.

FIRING ORDER

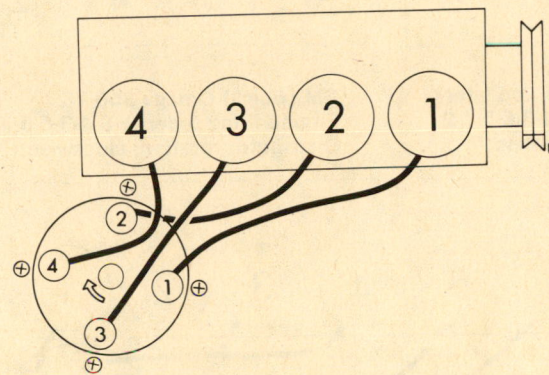

**GM (Chevrolet) 140 (2300 cc) 4-cyl.
(1975 and later)**
Engine firing order: 1-3-4-2
Distributor rotation: clockwise

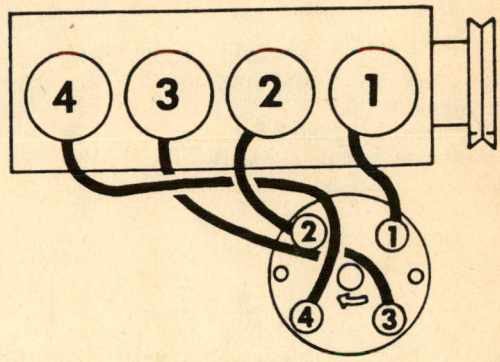

GM (Pontiac) 151 4-cyl. (1977 and later)
Engine firing order: 1-3-4-2
Distributor rotation: clockwise

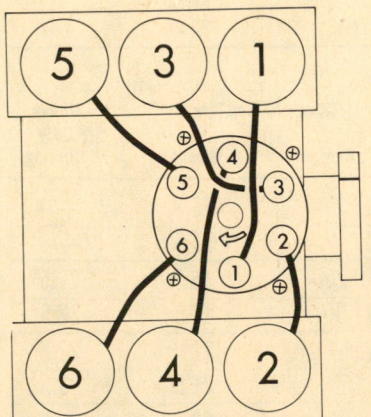

GM (Buick) 196, 231 V6
Engine firing order: 1-6-5-4-3-2
Distributor rotation: clockwise

V6 harmonic balancers have two timing marks: one is 1/8 in. wide, and one is 1/16 in. wide. Use the 1/16 in. mark for timing with a hand held light. The 1/8 in. mark is used only with a magnetic timing pick-up probe.

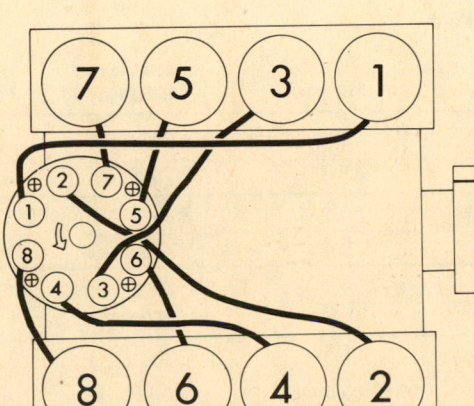

GM (Oldsmobile) 260 V8
Engine firing order: 1-8-4-3-6-5-7-2
Distributor rotation: counterclockwise

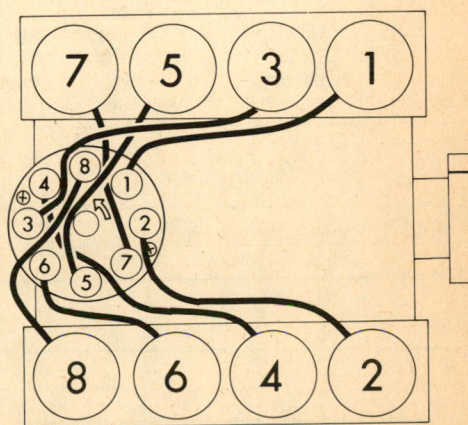

**GM (Oldsmobile) 350, 455 V8
(through 1974 w/point type ignition)**
Engine firing order: 1-8-4-3-6-5-7-2
Distributor rotation: counterclockwise

Oldsmobile • Cutlass • Omega • Starfire

FIRING ORDER

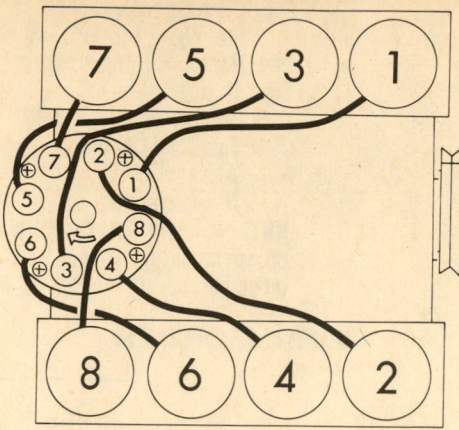

GM (Oldsmobile) 350, 403, 455 V8
(1975 and later w/H.E.I.)
Engine firing order: 1-8-4-3-6-5-7-2
Distributor rotation: counterclockwise

GM (Chevrolet) V8 (1975 and later)
Engine firing order: 1-8-4-3-6-5-7-2
Distributor rotation: clockwise

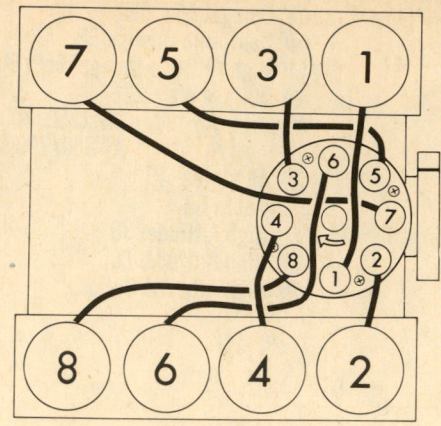

GM (Buick) Omega 350 V8
Engine firing order: 1-8-4-3-6-5-7-2
Distributor rotation: clockwise

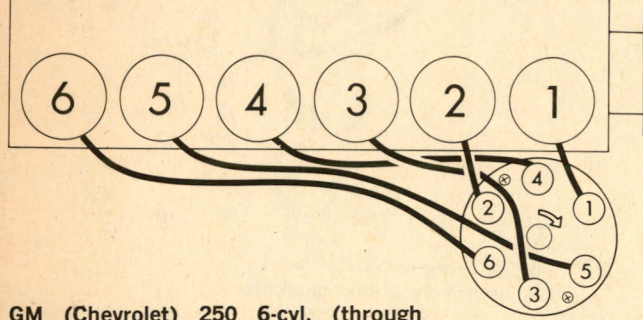

GM (Chevrolet) 250 6-cyl. (through 1974)
Engine firing order: 1-5-3-6-2-4
Distributor rotation: clockwise

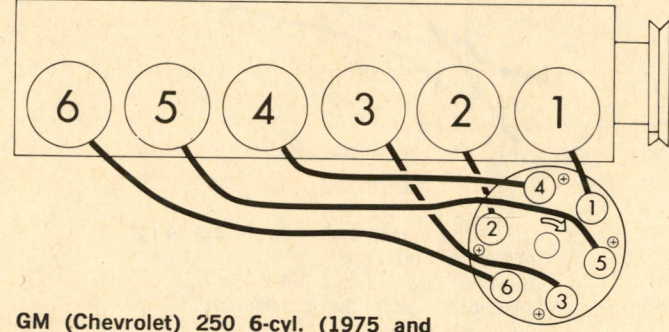

GM (Chevrolet) 250 6-cyl. (1975 and later)
Engine firing order: 1-5-3-6-2-4
Distributor rotation: clockwise

Oldsmobile 88, 98   CAPACITIES

Year	ENGINE No. Cyl. Displacement (Cu. In.)	Engine Crankcase Add 1 Qt For New Filter*	TRANSMISSION Pts To Refill After Draining Automatic	Drive Axle (pts)	Gasoline Tank (gals)	COOLING SYSTEM (qts)		Heavy Duty Cooling
						With Heater	With A/C	
'72	8-350	4	6	4.3	24②	16.2	16.7	——
	8-455	4	6	5.4	24②	17	17.5	——
'73	8-350	4	6	4.3	26	16.2④	16.2	21.5
	8-455	4	6	5.4	26③	17.0⑤	17.5	22.5
'74	8-350	4	6	4.3	26	21⑤	21	22.5
	8-455	4	6	5.5	26③	21⑥	21.5	23.5
'75	8-350	4	6	5.5	26	20⑤	20	22.5
	8-455	4	6	5.5	26③	21⑥	21.5	23.5
'76	8-350, 403	4	6	5.4	26③	20	22.5	22.5
	8-455	4	6	5.4	26③	21⑥	21.5	23.5
'77	6-231 Buick	4	6	4.25	21.0	12.7	12.8	——
	8-260 Olds.	4	6	4.25	21.0	16.9	17.0	——
	8-350 Chev.	4	6	4.25	21.0	16.0	16.7	——
	8-350 (Olds.) 88	4	6	4.25	21.0	14.6	15.3	——
	8-350 (Olds.) 98	4	6	4.25	24.5	14.6	15.3	——
	8-403 Olds.	4	6	4.25	24.5	15.7	16.4	——

Oldsmobile 88, 98 — CAPACITIES

Year	ENGINE No. Cyl. Displacement (Cu. In.)	Engine Crankcase Add 1 Qt For New Filter*	TRANSMISSION Pts To Refill After Draining Automatic	Drive Axle (pts)	Gasoline Tank (gals)	COOLING SYSTEM (qts) With Heater	With A/C	Heavy Duty Cooling
'78	6-231 Buick	4	6	④	25.25	12.25	12.25	12.25
	8-260 Olds.	4	6	④	22.25③	16.25	16.25	16.75
	8-350 Buick	4	6	④	22.25③	14.5	14.5	15.5
	8-350 Olds.	4	6	④	⑤	14.5	14.5	15.5
	8-350 Diesel	7⑥	6	④	22.0	18.0	18.0	18.0
	8-403 Olds.	4	6	④	⑤	15.75	16.5	16.5
'79	6-231 Buick	4	6	4.25	25.0	13.3	13.3	——
	8-260 Olds.	4	6	4.25	25.0	16.4	16.2	——
	8-305 Chev.	4	6	4.25	25.0	15.5	15.8	——
	8-350 Olds.	4	6	4.25	21.0③	14.6	15.3	——
	8-350 Diesel	7.5	6	4.25	23.0	18.0	17.9	——
	8-403 Olds.	4	6	4.25	25.0③	15.7	16.4	——

- • Specifications do not include torque converter
- ② 23 gals on station wagon
- ③ 22 gals on station wagon
- ④ 7.5 inch ring gear: 3.5
  8.5 and 8.75 inch ring gear: 4.25
- ⑤ 88 Sedan and Calif. Coupe: 21.0
  All others: 25.25
- ⑥ Includes mandatory filter change
- —— Not applicable

Cutlass, Omega, Starfire — CAPACITIES

Year	ENGINE No. Cyl. Displacement (Cu. In.)	Engine Crankcase Add 1 Qt For New Filter*	TRANSMISSION Pts To Refill After Draining 3 sp	4sp/5sp	Automatic	Drive Axle (pts)	Gasoline Tank (gals)	COOLING SYSTEM (qts) With Heater	With A/C	Heavy Duty Cooling
'72	8-350	4	3.5	2.25	6	4.25①	20②	15.2	15.7	——
	8-455	4	——	——	6	4.25①	23	17	17.5	——
'73	6-250	4	3.5	——	6	4.25	21	12.5	——	——
	8-350	4	3.5	2.25	6	4.25①⑤	22④	15.9	⑥	21.0
	8-455	4	——	2.25	6	4.25①⑤	22	17.0	18	22
'74	6-250	4	3.5		6	4.25	21	15.5	——	——
	8-350	4			6	4.25⑤	22④	20.0⑨	20.0⑩	——
	8-455	4			6	5.50	22	21.0	21.5	23.5
'77	4-140, 151	3.5		3.0	6	4.25	18.5	8.1	9.3	——
	6-231 Starfire	4		3.0	6	4.25	18.5	11.8	12.2	——
	6-231 Omega	4	3.0	——	6	4.0	21.0	12.7	12.8	——
	6-231 Cutlass	4	——	3.0	6	4.25	22.0	12.7	12.8	——
	8-260 Omega	4	3.0	——	6	4.0	21.0	16.9	17.0	——
	8-260 Cutlass	4	——	3.0	6	4.25	22.0	16.9	17.0	——
	8-305 Omega	4	3.0	——	6	4.0	21.0	15.8	16.1	——
	8-350 (Chev.) Omega	4			6	4.25	21.0	16.0	16.7	——
	8-350 (Olds.) Omega	4			6	4.25	21.0	14.6	15.3	——
	8-350 (Olds.) Cutlass	4			6	4.25	22.0	14.6	15.3	——
	8-403 Cutlass	4			6	4.25	24.5/22	15.7	16.4	——

Cutlass, Omega, Starfire

CAPACITIES

Year	ENGINE No. Cyl. Displacement (Cu. In.)	Engine Crankcase Add 1 Qt For New Filter*	3 sp	TRANSMISSION Pts To Refill After Draining 4sp/5sp	Automatic	Drive Axle (pts)	Gasoline Tank (gals)	COOLING SYSTEM (qts) With Heater	With A/C	Heavy Duty Cooling
'75	6-231	4	——	2.5	6	2.75	18.5	13.3	13.8㉑	——
	6-250	4	3.5		6	4.25	22④	17.0⑬	17.0⑩	——
	8-260	4	3.5		6	4.25	22④	23.5⑨	23.5⑩	23.5
	8-350	4	——		6	4.25⑤	22④	20.0⑨	22.5⑩	
	8-455	4	——		6	5.50	22	21.0	21.5	23.5
'76	4-140	3½	——	2.5⑭	6	2.75	18.5	8.5	——	——
	6-231	4	——	3⑭	6	3.5	18.5	13.5	14	
	6-250 Omega	4	3.5		6	3.5	21	15.5	16.5	
	6-250 Cutlass	4	3.5	3.5	6	4.25	22	17	17	
	8-260 Omega	4	——	3.5	6	3.5	21	23	23.5	
	8-260 Cutlass	4	——		6	4.25	22	23.5	26	
	8-350 Omega	4	——		6	3.5	21	21.5	22	
	8-350, 403	4	——		6	4.25⑤	22	20	22.5	
	8-455	4	——		6	5.4	22	21.0	21.5	23.5
'78	4-151 Pont.	3	——	3.5	6	3.5	18.5	11.0	11.5	——
	6-231 Buick⑦	4	3.5	3.5	6	③	20.75	12.75	12.75	12.75
	6-231 Buick⑧	4	3.5	3.5	6	3.5	18.0⑪	12.0	12.0	12.0
	6-231 Buick⑮	4	——	3.5	6	3.5	18.5	11.75	12.25	
	8-260 Olds.	4	——	3.5	6	3.5	18.0⑪	16.25	16.25	16.75
	8-305 Chev.⑦	4	——	3.5	6	③	20.75	15.75	16.0	16.75
	8-305 Chev.⑧	4	——	3.5	6	3.5	18.0⑪	15.5	15.5	16.25
	8-305 Chev.⑮	4	——	3.5	6	3.5	18.5	16.25	16.25	——
	8-350 Chev.⑦	4	——	——	6	③	20.75	16.0	16.75	16.75
	8-350 Chev.⑧	4	——	——	6	3.5	18.0⑪	15.5	16.25	16.25
'79	4-151 Pont.	3	——	3.0	6	4.25	18.5	11.0	11.5	——
	6-231 Buick⑮	4	——	3.0	6	4.25	18.5	11.8	12.2	——
	6-231 Buick⑦	4	3.5	3.0	6	4.25	21.0	12.8	12.7	——
	6-231 Buick⑧	4	——	3.0	6	3.5	18.2	13.3	13.3	——
	8-260 Olds.⑧	4	——	3.0	6	3.5	18.2	16.6	16.2	17.0
	8-305 Chev.⑮	4	——	3.0	6	4.25	18.5	16.2	16.2	
	8-305 Chev.⑦	4	3.0	——	6	4.25	21.0	15.8	16.1	
	8-305 Chev.⑧	4	——	3.0	6	3.5	18.2	15.5	15.5	
	8-350 Chev.⑦	4	——	——	6	4.25	21.0	15.8	16.1	
	8-350 Olds.⑧	4	——	——	6	3.5	18.2	14.6	14.4	15.3
	8-350 Diesel	7.5	——	——	6	3.5	18.2	18.0	17.9	——

- • Specifications do not include torque converter
- * Add ½ qt. on 4-140
- ① Limited slip differential—5.4 pts
- ② Station wagon 23 gals
- ③ 7.5 inch ring gear: 3.5
  8.5 inch ring gear: 4.25 (Omega only)
- ④ Omega 21 gals
- ⑤ Vista Cruiser—5.5 pts
- ⑥ Omega—16.5 qts
  Cutlass—16 qts
- ⑦ Omega
- ⑧ Cutlass
- ⑨ Omega—18.5 qts
- ⑩ Omega—19.5 qts
- ⑪ Stawgn.: 18.25
- ⑫ California—14.25 qts
- ⑬ Omega—15.5 qts
- ⑭ 3 pts with 70 mm 4-speed, 3½ with 5-speed
- ⑮ Starfire
- —— Not applicable

VALVE SPECIFICATIONS

Year	Engine No. Cyl. Displacement (cu in.)	Seat Angle (deg)	Face Angle (deg)	Spring Test Pressure (lbs @ in.)	Spring Installed Height (in.)	STEM TO GUIDE Clearance (in.) Intake	Exhaust	STEM Diameter (in.) Intake	Exhaust
'72	8-350	⑥	⑦	187 @ 1.27	1 21/32	.0010-.0027	.0015-.0032	.3429	.3424
	8-350 Calif.	45	46	198 @ 1.23	1 21/32	.0010-.0027	.0015-.0032	.3429	.3424
	8-455 98	⑥	46	187 @ 1.27	1 21/32	.0010-.0027	.0015-.0032	.3429	.3424
	8-455	①	④	206 @ 1.19	1 21/32	.0010-.0027	.0015-.0032	.3429	.3424
'73	6-250	46	45	186 @ 1.27	1 21/32	.0010-.0027	.0010-.0027	.3413	.3413
	8-350	②	⑩	187 @ 1.27	1 21/32	.0010-.0027	.0015-.0032	.3429	.3424
	8-455	②	⑩	187 @ 1.27	1 21/32	.0010-.0027	.0015-.0032	.3429	.3424
	8-455 Cutlass M.T.	⑧	⑨	206 @ 1.19	1 21/32	.0010-.0027	.0015-.0032	.3429	.3424
'74	6-250	46	45	186 @ 1.27	1 21/32	.0010-.0027	.0015-.0032	.3413	.3413
	8-350	②	⑩	187 @ 1.27	1 21/32	.0010-.0027	.0015-.0032	.3429	.3424
	8-455	②	⑩	187 @ 1.27	1 21/32	.0010-.0027	.0015-.0032	.3429	.3424
'75	6-231	45	45	168 @ 1.33	1 46/64	.0015-.0035	.0015-.0032	.3407	.3407
	6-250	46	45	186 @ 1.27	1 21/32	.0010-.0027	.0015-.0032	.3413	.3413
	8-260	②	⑩	187 @ 1.27	1 21/32	.0010-.0027	.0015-.0032	.3427	.3424
	8-350 Omega	45	46	180 @ 1.34③	1 46/64	.0015-.0035	.0015-.0032	.3725	.3728
	8-350	②	⑩	187 @ 1.27	1 21/32	.0010-.0027	.0015-.0032	.3429	.3424
	8-455	②	⑩	187 @ 1.27	1 21/32	.0010-.0027	.0015-.0032	.3429	.3424
'76	4-140	46	45	190 @ 1.31	1 3/4	.0010-.0030	.0010-.0040	.3414	.3414
	6-231	45	45	168 @ 1.33	1 46/64	.0015-.0032	.0015-.0032	.3408	.3408
	6-250	46	45	175 @ 1.26	1 21/32	.0010-.0027	.0015-.0032	.3413	.3413
	8-260	②	⑩	187 @ 1.27	1 46/64	.0010-.0027	.0015-.0032	.3428	.3423
	8-350 Omega	45	45	180 @ 1.34③	1 46/64	.0015-.0035	.0015-.0032	.3725	.3726
	8-350, 403	②	⑩	187 @ 1.27	1 21/32	.0010-.0027	.0015-.0032	.3429	.3424
	8-455	②	⑩	187 @ 1.27	1 21/32	.0010-.0027	.0015-.0032	.3429	.3424
'77	4-140 Chev.	46	45	190 @ 1.310	1 3/4	.0010-.0030	.0010-.0040	.3414	.3414
	4-151 Pont.	46	45	177 @ 1.250	1 43/64	.0010-.0027	.0010-.0027	.3422	.3422
	6-231 Buick	45	45	168 @ 1.327	1 46/64	.0015-.0032	.0015-.0032	.3409	.3409
	8-260 Olds.	②	⑩	187 @ 1.270	1 43/64	.0010-.0027	.0015-.0032	.3429	.3427
	8-305 Chev.	46	45	200 @ 1.250	1 45/64	.0010-.0037	.0010-.0037	.3414	.3414
	8-350 Chev.	46	45	200 @ 1.250	1 45/64	.0010-.0037	.0010-.0037	.3414	.3414
	8-350 Olds.	②	⑩	187 @ 1.270	1 43/64	.0010-.0027	.0015-.0032	.3429	.3427
	8-350 Olds Diesel	②	⑩	151 @ 1.300	1 21/32	.0010-.0027	.0015-.0032	.3429	.3424
	8-403 Olds.	②	⑩	187 @ 1.270	1 43/64	.0010-.0027	.0015-.0032	.3429	.3427
'78-'79	4-151 Pont.	46	45	82 @ 1.660	1 43/64	.0010-.0027	.0010-.0027	.3400	.3400
	6-231 Buick	45	45	168 @ 1.327	1 47/64	.0015-.0032	.0015-.0032	.3405-.3412	.3405-.3412
	8-260 Olds.	2	19	187 @ 1.270	1 47/64	.0010-.0027	.0015-.0032	.3425-.3432	.3420-.3427
	8-305 Chev.	46	45	200 @ 1.160	⑤	.0010-.0037	.0010-.0037	.3414	.3414
	8-350 Buick	45	45	180 @ 1.340	1 47/64	.0015-.0035	.0015-.0032	.3720-.3730	.3723-.3730
	8-350 Chev.	46	45	200 @ 1.160	⑤	.0010-.0037	.0010-.0037	.3414	.3414
	8-350 Olds.	②	⑩	187 @ 1.270	1 47/64	.0010-.0027	.0015-.0032	.3425-.3432	.3420-.3427
	8-350 Diesel	②	⑩	151 @ 1.300	1 47/64	.0010-.0027	.0015-.0032	.3425-.3432	.3420-.3427
	8-403 Olds.	②	⑩	187 @ 1.270	1 47/64	.0010-.0027	.0015-.0032	.3425-.3432	.3420-.3427

① Intake 30°, exhaust 45°
② Intake 45°, exhaust 31°
③ Exhaust 177 @ 1.45
④ Intake 30°, exhaust 46°
⑤ intake: 1 23/32
  exhaust: 1 19/32
⑥ Intake 45°, exhaust 30°
⑦ Intake 46°, exhaust 30°
⑧ Intake 31°, exhaust 45°
⑨ Intake 30°, exhaust 44°
⑩ Intake 44°, exhaust 30°

Oldsmobile • Cutlass • Omega • Starfire

TORQUE SPECIFICATIONS

All readings in ft lbs

Year	Engine	Cylinder Head Bolts	Rod Bearing Bolts	Main Bearing Bolts	Crankshaft Bolt	Flywheel to Crankshaft Bolts	MANIFOLD Intake	MANIFOLD Exhaust
'72-'74	6-250	95	35	65	Press fit	60	25	30
	8-All	85	42	120②	160 min	③	40	25
'75	6-231	75	40	115	140 min	55	45	25
	6-250	95	35	65	Press fit	60	①	④
	8-350 Omega	80	40	115	140 min	60	45	28
	8-260, 350, 455	85	42	120②	200-310	③	40	25
'76	4-140	60	35	120②	160 min	60	30	30
	6-231	80	40	115	175	60	45	25
	6-250	95	35	65	Press fit	60	①	④
	8-350 Omega	80	40	115	175	60	45	25
	8-260, 350, 403, 455	85	42	120②	200-310	③	40	25
'77	4-140 Chev.	60	35	65	80	60	30	30
	4-151 Pont.	95	30	65	160	55	⑤	⑤
	6-231 Buick	80	40	115	175	60	45	25
	8-260 Olds.	85	42	②	200-310	③	40	25
	8-305, 350 Chev.	65	45	70	60	60	30	20
	8-350 Olds Diesel	130	42	120	200-300	60	40	25
	8-350, 403 Olds.	130	42	②	200-310	③	40	25
'78-'79	4-151 Pont.	95	30	65	160	55	40	30
	6-231 Buick	80	40	100	225	60	45	25
	8-260 Olds.	85	42	②	200-310	③	40	25
	8-305 Chev.	65	45	70	60	60	30	20
	8-350 Buick	80	40	100	225	60	45	25
	8-350 Chev.	65	45	70	60	60	30	20
	8-350 Olds.	130	42	②	200-310	60	40	25
	8-350 Diesel	130	42	120	200-310	60	40	25
	8-403 Olds.	130	42	②	200-310	60	40	25

① Intake manifold integral with cylinder head
② 80 on No. 1-4, 120 on No. 5
③ A.T. 60 ft lbs.; M.T. 90 ft lbs.
④ Inner bolts—30 ft lbs.; outer bolts—20 ft lbs. minimum
⑤ Manifold-to-manifold: 40,

manifold-to-head nut: 30,
manifold-to-head bolt: 40

RING GAP

All measurements are given in inches

Year	Engine	Top Compression	Bottom Compression
'72-'79	8-350, 403, 455 Olds.	.010-.023	.010-.023
'73-'76	6-250 Chev.	.010-.020	.010-.020
'75-'79	6-231, 8-350 Buick	.010-.020	.010-.020
'76-'77	4-140 Chev.	.015-.026	.009-.020
'77-'79	8-305, 350 Chev.	.010-.030	.010-.035
'78-'79	4-151 Pont.	.010-.020	.010-.020
'78-'79	8-350 Olds Diesel	.015-.025	.015-.025

Year	Engine	Oil Control
'72-'79	6-250 Chev., 8-260, 350, 403, 455 Olds.	.015-.055
'75-'79	6-231, 8-350 Buick	.015-.035
'76-'77	4-140 Chev.	.010-.031
'77-'79	8-305, 350 Chev.	.015-.065
'78-'79	4-151 Pont.	.015-.055
'78-'79	8-350 Olds. Diesel	.015-.055

CRANKSHAFT AND CONNECTING ROD SPECIFICATIONS

All measurements are given in inches

Year	Engine No. Cyl. Displacement (cu in.)	CRANKSHAFT Main Brg. Journal Dia	Main Brg. Oil Clearance	Shaft End-Play	Thrust on No.	Journal Diameter	CONNECTING ROD Oil Clearance	Side Clearance
'72-'73	6-250	2.3004	.0003-.0029	.002-.006	7	1.999-2.000	.0007-.0027	.007-.016
	8-350	2.4990	.0005-.0021④	.004-.008	3	2.1238-2.1248	.0004-.0033	.006-.020
	8-455	2.9998	.0005-.0021②	.004-.008	3	2.4988-2.4998	.0004-.0033	.006-.020⑤
'74	6-250	2.2988	.0035⑧	.002-.006	7	1.999-2.000	.0035	.009-.014
	8-350	2.4990⑨	.0005-.0021④	.004-.008	3	2.1238-2.1248	.0004-.0033	.006-.020
	8-455	2.9998	.0005-.0021②	.004-.008	3	2.4988-2.4998	.0004-.0033	.006-.020
'75-'76	4-140	2.2980	.0035⑧	.002-.007	4	1.9990	.0040 max	.008-.014
	6-231	2.4995	.0004-.0015	.004-.008	2	2.0000	.0005-.0026	.006-.027
	6-250	2.2988	.0035⑧	.002-.006	7	1.999-2.000	.0035	.009-.014
	8-260	2.4990⑨	.0005-.0021④	.004-.008	3	2.1238-2.1248	.0004-.0033	.006-.020
	8-350 Omega	3.0000	.0004-.0015	.003-.009	3	1.9991-2.000	.0005-.0026	.006-.027
	8-350, 403	2.4990⑨	.0005-.0021④	.004-.008	3	2.1238-2.1248	.0004-.0033	.006-.020
	8-455	2.9998	.0005-.0021②	.004-.008	3	2.4988-2.4998	.0004-.0033	.006-.020
'77	4-140 Chev.	2.2980	.0035⑧	.002-.007	4	1.9990	.0040 max	.008-.0135
	4-151 Pont.	2.2988	.0002-.0022	.0015-.0085	5	2.0000	.0005-.0026	.006-.022
	6-231 Buick	2.4995	.0004-.0015	.004-.008	2	1.9960	.0005	.006-.027
	8-260 Olds.	2.4990⑨	.0005-.0021	.004-.014	3	2.21243	.0004-.0033	.006-.020
	8-305, 350 Chev.	⑥	.0035 max ⑦	.002-.006	3	2.1995	.0035 max	.008-.014
	8-350, 403 Olds.	2.4990⑨	.0005-.0021	.004-.014	3	2.21243	.0004-.0033	.006-.020
'78-'79	4-151 Pont.	2.2983-2.2993	.0002-.0022	.0015-.0085	5	2.0000	.0005-.0026	.006-.022
	6-231 Buick	2.4995	.0003-.0017	.004-.008	2	2.2487-2.2495	.0005-.0026	.006-.027
	8-260 Olds.	2.4985-2.4995③	.0005-.0021④	.0035-.0135	3	2.1238-2.1248	.0004-.0033	.006-.020
	8-305 Chev.	⑥	.0035 max ⑦	.002-.006	3	2.1990-2.2000	.0035 max	.008-.014
	8-350 Buick	3.0000	.0004-.0015	.003-.009	3	1.9910-2.0000	.0005-.0026	.006-.027
	8-350 Chev.	⑥	.0035 max ⑦	.002-.006	3	2.1990-2.2000	.0035 max	.008-.014
	8-350 Olds.	2.4985-2.4995③	.0005-.0021④	.0035-.0135	3	2.1238-2.1248	.0004-.0033	.006-.020
	8-350 Diesel	2.9993-3.0003	.0005-.0021④	.0035-.0135	3	2.1238-2.1248	.0005-.0026	.006-.020
	8-403 Olds.	2.4985-2.4995③	.0005-.0021④	.0035-.0135	3	2.1238-2.1248	.0004-.0033	.006-.020

② No. 5—.0020-.0034
③ #1: 2.4988-2.4998
④ #5: .0015-.0031
⑤ W-30—.002-.021
⑥ #1: 2.4484-2.4493 #2,3,4: 2.4481-2.4490 #5: 2.4479-2.4488
⑦ #1 .0020 max
⑨ No. 1—2.4993 in.

RING SIDE CLEARANCE

All measurements are given in inches

Year	Engine	Top Compression	Bottom Compression
'72-'79	8-260, 350, 403, 455 Olds.	.0020-.0040	.0020-.0040
'73-'76	6-250 Chev.	.0012-.0027	.0012-.0032
'75-'79	6-231, 8-350 Buick	.0015-.0050	.0015-.0050
'76-'77	4-140 Chev.	.0010-.0030	.0010-.0030
'77-'79	8-305, 350 Chev.	.0012-.0042	.0012-.0042
'78-'79	4-151 Pont.	.0015-.0035	.0015-.0035
'78-'79	8-350 Olds. Diesel	.005-.007	.0018-.0038

Year	Engine	Oil Control
'72-'76	6-250 Chev.	.000-.005
'72-'79	8-260, 350, 403 Olds.	.0006-.0096
'72-'76	8-455 Olds.	.0021-.0031
'75-'79	6-231, 8-350 Buick	.0035-.0095
'76-'77	4-140 Chev.	.0010-.0060
'77-'79	8-305, 350 Chev.	.002-.008
'78-'79	4-151 Pont.	.0015-.0035
'78-'79	8-350 Olds. Diesel	.0010-.0050

PISTON CLEARANCE

Year	Engine	Piston-to-Bore Clearance (in.)
'72-'74	6-250 Chev.	.0025 max
	8-350, 455 Olds.	.0010-.0020①
'75-'79	6-231, 8-350 Buick	.0013-.0035②
'75-'77	4-140 Chev.	.0050 max
'75-'76	6-250 Chev.	.0025 max
'75-'79	8-260 Olds.	.0010-.0020

Year	Engine	Piston-to-Bore Clearance (in.)
'75-'79	8-350, 403 Olds.	.0010-.0020
'75-'76	8-455 Olds.	.0010-.0020
'77-'79	8-305, 350 Chev.	.0027 Max
'78-'79	4-151 Pont.	.0025-.0033
'78-'79	8-350 Olds Diesel	.005-.006

① 1972 W-30 455—.0025-.0035 in.
② At bottom of skirt

WHEEL ALIGNMENT SPECIFICATIONS

Year	Model	CASTER Range (deg)	Pref Setting (deg)	CAMBER Range (deg)	Pref Setting (deg)	Toe-in (in.)	Steering Axis Inclin. (deg)	WHEEL PIVOT RATIO (deg) Inner Wheel	Outer Wheel
'72	Cutlass	¾N to 1¾N	1¼N	¾N to ¾P*	¼P*	1/16N to 1/16P	8	20	19②
	88 & 98	½P to 1½P	1P	¾N to ¾P*	¼P*	1/16N to 1/16P	9.6	20	18½
'73	Omega	½N to 1½P	½P	½N to 1P	½P	1/16 to 5/16	9	—	—
	Cutlass	¾N to 1¾N	1¼N	⑤	⑤	1/16	10½	20	19②
	88 & 98	0 to 2P	1P	¾N to ¾P*	¼P*	1/16 to 1/16	9½	20	18½
'74	Omega	½N to 1½P	½P	½N to 1P	¼P	1/16 to 5/16	9	—	—
	Cutlass	1N to 1P	0	⑥	⑥	0 to ⅛	10½	20	19②
	Cutlass Salon	1P to 3P	2P	⑥	⑥	0 to ⅛	10½	20	19②
	88, 98	0 to 2P	1P	⑥	⑥	1/16 to 3/16	9½	20	18½
'75-'76	Starfire	1¾N to ¼P	¾N	½N to 1P	¼P	0 to ⅛	9	—	—
	Omega	0 to 2P⑧	1P⑦	0 to 1½P	¾P	0 to ⅛	10½	—	—
	Cutlass	1P to 3P	2P	⑨	⑩	0 to ⅛	10½	20	19②
	88, 98	½P to 2½P	1½P	⑨	⑩	0 to ⅛	10½	20	18½
'77	Starfire	1¼N to ¼N	¾N	¼N to ¾P	¼P	0 to ⅛	9	—	—
	Omega	½P to 1½P	1P	¼P to 1¼P	¾P	0 to ⅛	10½	—	—
	Cutlass	1½P to 2½P	2P	⑪	⑫	0 to ⅛	10½	—	—
	88, 98	2½P to 3½P	3P	¼P to 1¼P	¾P	1/16 to 3/16	10½	—	—
'78	Starfire	⅓N to 1⅓N	⅘N	⅓N to 7/10P	⅕P	0 to ⅛	—	—	—
	Omega pwr. str.	½P to 1½P	1P	⅓P to 1⅓P	⅘P	1/16 to 3/16	—	—	—
	man. str.	½N to 1½N	1N	⅓P to 1⅓P	⅘P	1/16 to 3/16	—	—	—
	Cutlass pwr. str.	2½P to 3½P	3P	0 to 1P	½P	1/16 to 3/16	—	—	—
	man. str.	½P to 1½P	1P	0 to 1P	½P	1/16 to 3/16	—	—	—
	88-98	2½P to 3½P	3P	⅓P to 1⅓P	⅘P	1/16 to 3/16	—	—	—
'79	Starfire	⅓N to 1⅓N	⅘N	⅓N to 7/10P	⅕P	0 to ⅛	—	—	—
	Omega Man. Str.	0 to 2N	1N	0 to 1½P	¾P	1/16 out to 3/16	10.35	—	—
	Pwr. Str.	0 to 2P	1P	0 to 1½P	¾P	1/16 out to 3/16	10.35	—	—
	Cutlass	½P to 1½P	1P	0 to 1P	½P	.05-.15⑬	6.98	—	—
	88-98	2½P to 3½P	3P	⅓P to 1⅓P	⅘P	.06-.18⑬	10.35	—	—

* Left side camber to be ½° more positive than right side
① Power steering—¾N
② Power steering—18
④ 17 7/10 for power steering
⑤ 1°P—LH; ½°N—RH: ± ¾°
⑥ IP ± ½—LH; ½P ± ½—RH

⑦ 1N with manual steering
⑧ 2N to 0 with manual steering
⑨ ¼P to 1¾P—LH, ¼N to 1¼P—RH
⑩ 1P—LH, ½P—RH
⑪ LH: ½P to 1½P

RH: 0 to 1P
⑫ LH: 1P
⑬ degrees
RH: ½P
—Not specified
N Negative   P Positive

CHARGING SYSTEM

The Delco SI alternator with integral, non-adjustable regulator is standard on all models. The alternator has integral capacitors to supress radio interference.

In the diesel engine models, a single, standard Delcotron supplies two parallel-connected 12 volt batteries. The two batteries are needed to cope with the load imposed by the eight glow plugs and the larger starter. There are no special switches or relays in the charging system.

See Charging and Starting Systems in the Unit Repair Section for charging system test procedures.

Alternator Removal and Installation
NOTE: *Before removing the alternator, disconnect the battery ground cable.*
1. Disconnect the wiring from the alternator.
2. Remove the mounting bolt, adjusting bolt, and drive belt.
3. Lift out the alternator.
4. To install, reverse the removal procedure, connect the battery ground cable and tighten the alternator belt. Determine belt tension at a point halfway between the pulleys by pressing on the belt with moderate thumb pressure. If the distance between the pulleys (measured at the pulley center) is 13-16 in., the belt should deflect 1/2 in. at the halfway point or 1/4 in. if the distance is 7-10 in.

Regulator Removal and Installation
This is a completely sealed unit that cannot be adjusted or disassembled.

STARTING SYSTEM

See Charging and Starting Systems in the Unit Repair Section for starter motor service procedures.

The diesel engine starter is of conventional design, but somewhat larger and with a greater output to turn the engine at 100 rpm for starting. The diesel's 22.5:1 compression ratio makes this necessary. A 12 volt heater in each combustion chamber is used to heat the chamber prior to starting. These heaters are called glow plugs. When the key is turned to the RUN position, prior to start, they turn on and remain on a short time. They automatically turn off.

Starter Removal and Installation
EXCEPT V6
1. Disconnect battery and carefully raise the car.
2. Remove upper support attaching bolts.
3. Remove the V8 flywheel housing cover.
4. Remove two starter mounting bolts.
5. Lower starter, disconnect wiring, and remove starter. If equipped with dual exhausts, it may be necessary to remove the lefthand exhaust pipe, except on Chevrolet V8 engines.
6. Install by reversing the procedure.

V6 WITH AUTOMATIC TRANSMISSION
1. Disconnect the battery and raise the car.
2. Disconnect and plug the fluid cooler lines from the transmission.
3. Remove the upper support bolts.
4. Take off the flywheel housing cover.
5. Unfasten the two starter securing bolts and lower the starter.
6. Disconnect the wiring after noting its position for installation.
7. Starter installation is the reverse of removal.

V6 WITH MANUAL TRANSMISSION
1. Disconnect the battery ground cable. Raise and support the front of the car.
2. Unbolt the front crossmember from the body and from the braces. Loosen the brace bolts so that the braces hang down. Remove the crossmember.
3. Unbolt and lower the starter. Disconnect the wiring.
4. Reverse the procedure for installation.

Disabling the Seat Belt/Starter Interlock and Buzzer
The seat belt/starter interlock was used only on early production 1975s. It is now legal to disable the seat belt/starter interlock, but *not* the warning light. To do this, proceed as follows:
1. Disconnect the negative (−) battery cable.
2. Locate the interlock harness connector, which is on or near the fuse block. The connector has orange, yellow, and green leads running to it.
3. Cut and tape the green lead on the body harness side of the interlock connector.
4. a. On Cutlass, 88, and 98 without low coolant warning and heavy duty cooling: disconnect the buzzer or beeper from the fuse panel and remove it.
   b. On Cutlass, 88, and 98 with low coolant warning and heavy duty cooling: cut the yellow wire behind the connector and tape its ends.
   c. On Omega and Starfire: remove the buzzer from its connector on the wiring harness.
5. Check the battery cable.
6. Check system operation by starting the car with the seat belt unfastened.

IGNITION SYSTEM

A high energy ignition (HEI) system was offered as an option on some engines in 1974 and made standard equipment beginning 1975. The HEI distributor replaces the points and condenser with a timing wheel, magnetic pick-up, and control module. On V6 and V8 engines, the coil is built into the distributor cap; on inline engines, the coil is mounted separately. For further description, as well as service procedures for HEI, see the Electronic Ignition unit repair section.

Unlike the gasoline engine, which is a spark-ignition design, the diesel engine is a compression-ignition type. When air is compressed to an extreme, high temperatures are produced. At the moment of extreme compression a small quantity of fuel is sprayed, under high pressure, into the compression chambers. The temperature of compression ignites the tiny fuel droplets. A temperature of about 1750°F is needed for the fuel ignition. The use of glow plugs is necessitated because the combustion chambers are cold prior to an initial start-up and the first few revolutions of the engine would not produce sufficiently high combustion chamber temperatures for fuel ignition. The glow plugs warm the chambers for a few seconds, bringing them up to the required temperatures to aid in starting.

Distributor Removal
1. Remove distributor cap, primary (or feed) wire and vacuum line at the distributor. On inline engines, disconnect the feed wire from the coil.
2. Scribe a mark on the distributor body, locating the position of the rotor, and scribe another mark on the distributor body and engine block, showing the position of the body in the block.
3. Remove the hold-down screw and lift the distributor out of the block.
NOTE: *Do not crank the engine with the distributor removed; this will change the timing.*

Distributor Installation
If engine has *not* been disturbed (cranked) after removing the distributor, perform the following procedure for installation:
1. Turn the rotor until it is about 1/8 turn past the locating mark previously made on the distributor housing.
2. Push the distributor down into the block. It may be necessary to turn the rotor slightly until the shaft en-

gages in the block. The mark on the distributor housing must line up with the mark made on the engine block.

3. Tighten the hold-down bolt until it is snug and then connect the vacuum advance line.
4. Connect the primary wire to the coil or, on HEI, connect the feed wire and install the distributor cap.
5. Check the timing and adjust it as necessary. Tighten the holddown bolt.

If engine has been disturbed (cranked) after removing distributor, perform the following procedure for installation:

1. Crank the engine until no. one piston is at the top of its compression stroke. The compression stroke can be determined by removing the spark plug from the no. one cylinder and placing your thumb over the hole while an assistant slowly cranks the engine. Crank until compression is felt at the hole and then continue cranking slowly until the timing mark on the crankshaft pulley lines up with the 0° timing mark.
2. Position the distributor in the block but do not allow it to engage with its drive gear. Observe the position of the vacuum control unit on the

distributor. If the distributor is located correctly, the vacuum unit will be positioned normally so that the vacuum hose can be easily connected to it.

3. Position the distributor rotor so that it is positioned between terminals 1 & 8 on V8s; 1 & 6 on V6s and 1 & 5 on inline sixes.
4. Install the distributor, making sure the distributor shaft engages the oil pump shaft, thereby allowing the distributor to fully contact the engine block.
5. Install the hold-down clamp and tighten the bolt until it is snug.
6. Turn the distributor slightly until the points just open, then tighten the bolt.
7. Install the distributor cap.
8. Attach all wires and the vacuum advance hose.
9. Check the timing and adjust it as necessary.

Contact Point Replacement Through 1974

V8

1. Remove the distributor cap and rotor.
2. V8 distributors were equipped with a two-piece metal shield to suppress radio static. Remove the two

attaching screws and the shield.
3. Remove the two wiring terminals from the retainer.
4. Remove the mounting screws and lift out the contact points and condenser.
5. Install the new contact points and condenser and tighten the mounting screws.
6. Install the primary and condenser wire terminals in the retainer. If the replacement point set has a snap-lock type retainer, the terminals can be pushed in to provide plenty of clearance between the shield (if so equipped) and the terminals to prevent accidental short circuiting. If the contact points have a screw type retainer, insufficient clearance may exist between the terminals and the shield, possibly causing a short circuit. To prevent this possibility, insert terminals in the retainer and bend them slightly toward the distributor cam. Make sure the wiring does not interfere with the other components.
7. Inspect the cam lubricator wick and replace or rotate it if it is worn out or dry. Using a feeler gauge, check and adjust the point gap.
8. If so equipped, install the two-piece shield and tighten the mounting screws.
9. Install the rotor, making sure that the round peg goes in the round hold and the square peg into the square hole.
10. Install the distributor cap.
11. Set the points to specifications with a dwell meter while the engine is running.

INLINE 6

1. Remove the distributor cap retaining screws and lift off the distributor cap. Remove the rotor.
2. Disconnect the primary and condenser leads from the quick-disconnect terminal.
3. Remove the attaching screw and lift the contact point set from the distributor.
4. Withdraw the condenser retaining screw and remove the condenser.
5. Install the new condenser and tighten its retaining screw.
6. Install the new point set but do not fully tighten its attaching screw.
7. Connect the condenser and primary leads to the quick-disconnect terminal.
8. If necessary, align the contacts by, bending the stationary contact bracket only. Never bend the movable contact arm to correct alignment.
9. Attach a remote starter switch to the electrical system. Crank the engine, rotating the distributor cam until the rubbing block of the movable contact arm rests on a peak of the cam lobe. It is also possible to turn the engine manually.
10. Insert the proper thickness feeler

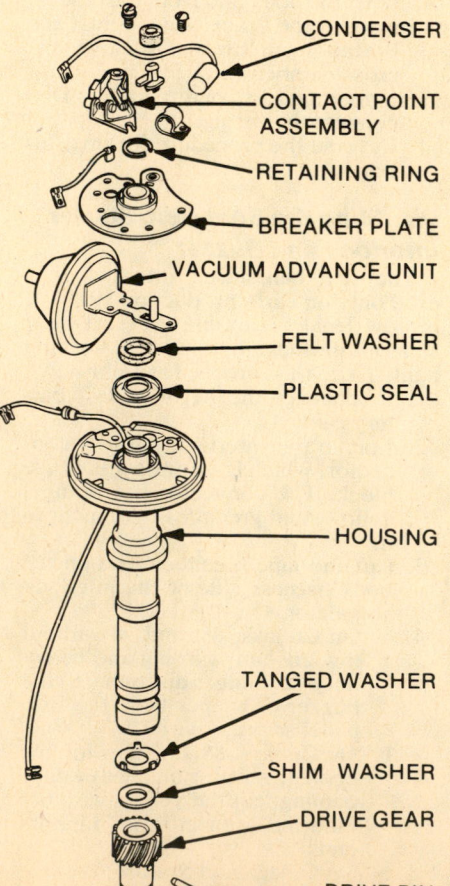

CAP

ROTOR

RADIO FREQUENCY INTERFERENCE SHIELD

WEIGHT SPRINGS

MAINSHAFT

ADVANCE WEIGHTS

CAM WEIGHT BASE ASSEMBLY

CONDENSER

CONTACT POINT ASSEMBLY

RETAINING RING

BREAKER PLATE

VACUUM ADVANCE UNIT

FELT WASHER

PLASTIC SEAL

HOUSING

TANGED WASHER

SHIM WASHER

DRIVE GEAR

DRIVE PIN

Distributor details, externally adjusted type—V8
(© Oldsmobile Div, G. M. Corp)

gauge between the contact points. If necessary, increase or decrease the gap by inserting a screwdriver in the "V" notch of the stationary contact base and using the screwdriver to move the stationary contact.

11. Tighten the point set attaching screw and recheck the gap setting.
12. Install the new rotor and replace the distributor cap. Check the point dwell and the ignition timing.

Ignition Timing

1. Disconnect the vacuum advance hose from the distributor and plug it.
2. Remove the air cleaner and tape over the vacuum hose fitting.
3. Connect the tachometer and adjust the engine speed to specifications.
4. Connect a timing light, loosen the distributor mounting bolt, and turn the distributor until the specified timing is obtained.
5. Tighten the mounting bolt and recheck timing to see if it changed during tightening.
6. Unplug the vacuum advance hose and connect it to the distributor.
7. Remove the tape from the vacuum hose fitting and install and connect the hose, if so equipped.
8. Install the V6 and V8 air cleaner.

NOTE: *Late 1976 and all 1977 and later V6 engine harmonic balancers have two timing marks, one measuring 1/8 in. wide and one measuring the normal 1/16 in. wide. The smaller mark is used for setting the timing with a hand held timing light. The 1/8 in. wide mark will be used in 1977 and later and is required when using magnetic timing equipment. All 1977 and later engines have a mounting bracket on the front cover which will accept a magnetic timing pickup probe.*

Timing Light and Tachometer Hook-Up for HEI

1. Use an adapter between the No. 1 spark plug and No. 1 spark plug lead, when connecting a timing light. Connect the timing light to the adapter; DO NOT pierce the spark plug lead. Because of the higher voltage used in the HEI system, any break in the insulation will cause electricity to jump to the nearest ground, making the No. 1 plug misfire.
2. The tachometer terminal is next to the ignition switch connector on the cap of V6 and V8 distributors or next to the ignition switch connector on the coil on inline six engines.
3. Most new tachometers can be used. Tachometers without a relay can't be used. Check the tach's instructions if you aren't sure. If you don't have the instructions, hook up the tach and check the readings on both the high and low rpm

BATTERY TERMINAL CONNECTED TO IGNITION SWITCH

TACHOMETER TERMINAL

GROUND TERMINAL

C-TERMINAL
CONNECT TACHOMETER FROM THIS TERMINAL TO GROUND (SOME TACHOMETERS MUST CONNECT FROM THIS TERMINAL TO ENERGIZER POSITIVE +. CONSULT TACHOMETER MANUFACTURER.)

B+ TERMINAL

CONNECTOR

LATCH (4)

HEI distributor connections

scales. If they agree, the tach is OK; if they don't use another tach.
4. There is no way of adjusting dwell, since this is controlled by the electronic module.
5. If you want to crank the engine without starting it, disconnect the ignition switch wire at the distributor cap (V8 or V6) or at the coil (inline engines).

Tachometer Hook-Up—Diesel Engine

A magnetic pickup tachometer is necessary because of the lack of an ignition system. The tachometer probe is inserted into the hole in the timing indicator.

FUEL SYSTEM

See Gauges and Indicators in the Unit Repair Section for a discussion of fuel gauge operation.

The fuel system is the heart of the diesel engine. The main components are the injection pump, injection lines and fuel injectors. The fuel injection pump is a small, high pressure rotary pump which delivers a small, metered amount of fuel to the injection nozzles at the proper time. The high pressure lines are all of equal length to avoid differences in timing. The nozzles project into the combustion chambers and spray/atomize the fuel entering the chambers. A small, low pressure trans-

fer pump is employed in the inlet line to the injection pump to keep the injection pump supplied. Engine rpm is controlled by a rotary fuel metering valve operated by the accelerator linkage. A fuel filter is located between the transfer pump and the injection pump.

GASOLINE ENGINES

Fuel Pump Removal and Installation

1. Disconnect the fuel lines.
2. Remove the two mounting bolts.
3. Remove the pump and gasket.
Installation is the reverse of removal.

Fuel Filter Removal and Installation

All carburetors have a fuel filter in the carburetor body. To replace the filter element, remove the fuel inlet line, then remove the inlet fitting and pull out the filter element. Be careful when tightening the brass fitting because the threads are easily stripped.

Idle Speed and Mixture Adjustments

1973-76 1 BBL
NOTE: *1971 and some later models are equipped with a CEC solenoid. This solenoid does not function as an idle speed solenoid and it should not be adjusted during a routine carburetor adjustment.*

1. Run the engine to the normal operating temperature, making sure that the choke is fully open.
2. Set the parking brake and block the drive wheels.
3. Disconnect the fuel tank hose from the vapor canister and the EGR valve hose.
4. Disconnect the distributor vacuum hoses from the CEC solenoid and plug the hose leading to the carburetor.
5. Set the dwell and timing.
6. Turn off the air conditioner and place automatic transmissions in Drive and manual transmissions in Neutral.
7. Connect a tachometer to the engine.
8. Turn the *throttle* stop solenoid plunger inward or outward to obtain the higher of the two idle speeds listed in the specifications tables by turning the large hex nut. On later models, adjustment is made by turning the entire solenoid. Disconnect the lead wire from the solenoid and insert a 1/8 in. allen wrench into the end of the solenoid to obtain the lower of the two idle speeds listed. On models with an automatic transmission, this shut-off speed adjustment should be made with the transmission in Park.
9. Idle mixture is set by increasing the idle speed to about 100 rpm over that specified, cutting the tab off the limiter cap, and turning the mixture screw counterclockwise until the maximum possible speed is reached. The idle speed should then be reset to 100 rpm over that specified. Turn the mixture screw clockwise until the idle speed drops down to the normal specified idle speed.

2 BBL AND 4 BBL THROUGH 1974

NOTE: *Adjust with the air cleaner removed.*
1. Warm up engine and leave it running.
2. Remove air cleaner, disconnect air cleaner hose at the intake manifold and plug the fitting.
3. Make sure the choke is open and the air conditioner is off. Set the parking brake and block the drive wheels.
4. Disconnect the hoses from the vapor canister and the EGR valve, depending on equipment. Plug the hoses, except on 1972 models which are equipped with 4 bbl carburetors. On 1973-75 4 bbl models, plug the hoses.
5. Disconnect the distributor vacuum hose at the distributor and plug the hose.
6. Set the dwell and timing.
7. On models without a throttle solenoid or vacuum actuator, turn the idle speed adjusting screw inward or outward to obtain the idle speed listed in the specifications.

8. On models with a throttle solenoid or vacuum actuator, turn the solenoid plunger inward or outward to obtain the higher of the two idle speeds listed in the tune-up specifications. After this adjustment has been made, disconnect the electric lead from the solenoid or the vacuum hose from the vacuum actuator. Plug the vacuum hose after disconnecting it. On models with an automatic transmission, place the transmission in Park. Adjust the throttle stop screw to obtain an idle speed which corresponds with the lower of the two idle speeds listed in the specifications.

NOTE: *Idle mixture screws have been preset at the factory and capped. Remove the caps only in the case of major overhaul, throttle body removal or when all other possible causes of poor idle condition have been thoroughly checked.*

9. To adjust the idle mixture, stop the engine, connect a CO (carbon monoxide) meter to the exhaust system and turn the idle mixture screws until they are lightly seated. Back out the idle mixture screws 6 full turns, then start engine and adjust the screws equally to obtain a good idle at the specified rpm with a maximum CO reading of 0.3 percent on the 1972-73 models, 0.3 percent on the 1972-73 4 barrel and 0.2 percent on 1974 models. Temporarily install the air cleaner and check that the CO concentration does not exceed the specified level, readjusting idle mixture screws if necessary.
10. Install new idler limiter caps.
11. Reinstall and reconnect everything which was removed or disconnected in Steps 1 through 5.

1975-76 IDLE SPEED—2 BBL AND 4 BBL

1. Run the engine until it reaches normal operating temperature.
2. Remove the air cleaner and disconnect its vacuum hose from the intake manifold. Plug the manifold fitting. Disconnect and plug the evaporative emission hose at the air cleaner.
3. Make sure that the choke is opened and that the A/C is turned off. Apply the parking brake and block the drive wheels.
4. Disconnect and plug the vapor canister and EGR valve vacuum lines.
5. Adjust the timing to specifications.
6. Adjust the curb idle by doing the following:
   a. 231 V6—(vacuum line connected to the distributor) adjust the anti-dieseling solenoid (energized) screw to the specified idle rpm.
   b. 260 V8—(vacuum line connected to the distributor; except California with A/T) adjust the curb idle screw to obtain speci-

fied rpm. On cars with manual transmissions, depress the dashpot and turn it to obtain 0.040 in clearance between its stem and the throttle lever.
   c. Omega (Buick) 350 V8—(vacuum line connected to the distributor) adjust the curb idle screw to the specified rpm. Adjust the dashpot, on California cars, by turning it toward the throttle lever until it just touches it, then 2-1/2 more turns toward the lever.
   d. 350 V8 (Olds) and 455 V8—(distributor vacuum line disconnected and plugged) turn the curb idle screw to obtain specified rpm.
7. On 231 V6 engines, adjust the anti-dieseling solenoid in Neutral (MT) or Drive (AT) with the solenoid wiring disconnected, to the lower of the two idle speed figures in the Tune-Up Specifications chart.
8. On 260, 350 (Olds) and 455 V8s, adjust the idle speed-up solenoid, on cars with air conditioning, as follows:
   a. Turn the A/C on.
   b. Disconnect the compressor wiring at the compressor.
   c. Place the transmission in Drive, with the parking brake applied and the drive wheels blocked.
   d. Adjust the idle speed to 650 rpm.
   e. Reconnect the compressor wiring.
9. Install the air cleaner and all vacuum hoses that were disconnected. Remove the tachometer and the timing light.

1975-76 IDLE MIXTURE—2 BBL AND 4 BBL

Idle mixture is preset at the factory and should not normally require adjustment. However, in cases of high idle emissions, carburetor overhaul, or poor idle quality (which can't be traced to other causes), it is possible to remove the limiter caps and adjust the mixture.

2 bbl—231 V6, 350 V8 (Buick) Omega

1. Allow the engine to reach normal operating temperature. Apply the parking brake, block the drive wheels, and place the transmission in Neutral (M/T) or Drive (A/T).
2. Disconnect the vapor canister hose at the air cleaner. Disconnect and plug the EGR valve and distributor vacuum unit.
3. Adjust the idle rpm to specifications.
4. Cut the tabs off the limiter caps.
5. Turn the mixture screws outward equally until maximum rpm is obtained. If a speed of at least 80 rpm above curb idle can't be obtained, reset the idle speed screw until it can. If the mixture screws aren't balanced or if the carburetor was overhauled, seat the mixture

screws *lightly* and back each out 5 full turns.

6. Turn the mixture screws back in, equally, until the specified idle speed is obtained.

7. Disconnect the tachometer and reconnect all vacuum lines.

2 bbl—260 V8

1. Allow the engine to reach normal operating temperature. Remove the air cleaner, disconnect the air cleaner vacuum hose from the manifold, and plug the fitting.

5. Disconnect the EGR valve vacuum hose from the carburetor. Leave the distributor vacuum hose connected.

NOTE: *On cars with manual transmissions the distributor vacuum hose comes from the same carburetor port. Disconnect the EGR hose while leaving the distributor vacuum hoses connected. On California cars the distributor has no vacuum hose.*

6. Connect a timing light and set the timing to specifications.

7. Remove the limiter caps. Back each mixture screw out as follows:
Manual transmission—6 turns
Automatic transmission—5 turns.

8. Set the engine idle to the following initial specifications:
Manual transmission—1075 rpm
Automatic (in Drive)—610 rpm
California Automatic (in Drive)—700 rpm.

9. Turn each mixture screw 1/2-turn at-a-time until the specified curb idle speed is reached.

10. Adjust the A/C idle speed-up solenoid, if so equipped, and the throttle closing dashpot, as outlined under 1975-76 Idle Speed 2 bbl and 4 bbl.

11. Connect all vacuum hoses which were removed and install the air cleaner. Disconnect the timing light and tach.

4 bbl—350 V8 and 455 V8

1. Allow the engine to reach normal operating temperature. Remove the air cleaner; disconnect and plug its vacuum hoses.

2. Make sure that the choke is opened and the A/C turned off. Apply the parking brake and block the drive wheels.

3. Disconnect the vacuum hoses from the EGR valve and vapor canister. Don't disconnect the distributor hose.

4. Break the tabs off the idle mixture screws.

5. Connect a tachometer. Connect a vacuum gauge to the intake manifold.

6. Turn the idle mixture screws out equally until the idle speed will go no higher. Note the vacuum gauge reading.

NOTE: *If the carburetor has been overhauled or if the mixture screws aren't balanced, lightly seat both screws and*

then turn each out 3 full turns (4 full turns—California).

7. Set the idle speed to 580 rpm (625 rpm—California).

8. Adjust the idle speed to specifications by turning the mixture screws in equally. The vacuum gauge reading should not drop more than 2 in. Hg from the figure obtained in step 6. If it does, repeat the procedure.

9. On California cars, check the CO level with an accurate CO meter. The level should be less than 0.5%. If not, repeat the procedure.

10. Install the air cleaner and connect all vacuum hoses.

1977 IDLE SPEED

6-231, 8-305

1. Set the parking brake and block the wheels.

2. Run the engine to normal operating temperature, and disconnect and plug the vacuum advance hose. On 231, disconnect and plug the air cleaner and EGR vacuum hoses.

3. Check timing.

4. With the choke open, the A/C off and the air cleaner installed, set the idle speed to the specifications shown in the tune-up chart at the front of this section.

5. Reconnect all hoses.

8-260

1. Set the parking brake and block the wheels.

2. Run the engine to normal operating temperature, remove the air cleaner and disconnect and plug the vacuum hose.

3. Turn the A/C off.

4. Disconnect and plug the vapor cannister hose.

5. Disconnect and plug the EGR hose.

6. Check the timing.

7. Set the idle speed screw and the idle speed solenoid to obtain the figures shown in the tune-up chart at the front of this section.

260 V8 antidieseling solenoid

8-350, 403

1. Set the parking brake and block the wheels.

2. Run the engine to normal operating temperature.

3. Turn the A/C off.

4. Disconnect and plug the cannister and EGR hoses at the carburetor.

5. Check the timing. Disconnect the idle speed solenoid.

6. Adjust the idle speed screw to give the low figure shown in the tune-up chart at the front of this section. Connect the idle speed solenoid.

7. Adjust the idle speed solenoid to give the high figure shown in the tune-up chart at the front of this section.

8. Connect all hoses.

1977 IDLE MIXTURE ADJUSTMENT

1. Set the parking brake and block the wheels.

2. Remove the air cleaner, but keep the vacuum hoses connected. On cars with level control, disconnect and plug the compressor vacuum hoses.

3. Disconnect and plug any other hoses listed on the underhood sticker.

4. Run the engine to normal operating temperature; A/C off.

5. Connect an accurate tachometer.

6. Disconnect the vacuum advance and check the timing. Reconnect the advance hose.

7. Remove the limiter caps from the mixture screws.

8. Lightly seat both screws, then back each out equally, just enough so that the engine will run.

9. Place the transmission in Drive (AT) or Neutral (MT).

10. Back each screw out 1/8 turn at a time until the maximum idle speed is recorded, then set the idle speed screw to this rpm:
231 exc. Cal. and High Alt.: AT-640; MT-860
231 Cal. & High Alt.: AT-610; MT-810
305: AT-530; MT-650
260: AT-610; MT-1075
350 Chev. exc. Cal. & High Alt.: 550
350 Chev. Cal. & High Alt.: 650
350 Olds and 403 exc. Cal. & High Alt.: 580
350 Olds and 403 Cal.: 575
350 Olds and 403 High Alt.: 625

11. Turn each screw in 1/8 turn at a time until idle speed reaches:
231 exc. Cal. & High Alt.: AT-600; MT-800
231 Cal. and High Alt.: AT-600; MT-800
305: AT-500; MT-600
260: AT-550; MT-750
350 Chev. exc. Cal. & High Alt.: 500
350 Chev. Cal. & High Alt.: 600
350 Olds and 403 exc. High Alt.: 550
350 Olds and 403 High Alt.: 600

12. If necessary, reset idle to specifications.

13. Reconnect all equipment.

1978-79 IDLE SPEED ADJUSTMENT

5210-C 2-bbl Carburetor

1. Run the engine to normal operating temperature. Make sure that the choke is fully opened. Turn the air conditioning Off and connect a tachometer and timing light to the engine.
2. Set the parking brake and block the drive wheels.
3. Disconnect and plug the PCV hose at the vapor canister. Disconnect and plug the vacuum advance hose at the distributor.
4. Place the transmission in Drive (AT) or Neutral (MT).
5. Check, and if necessary, adjust the timing.
6. Reconnect the vacuum advance hose.
7. Manual transmission without air conditioning: turn the idle screw to obtain the specified rpm.
8. Automatic transmission and/or cars with air conditioning: turn the idle screw to obtain the specified rpm, then disconnect the wire from the air conditioning override switch located on the accelerator linkage bracket. Turn the A/C On. Momentarily open the throttle to extend the solenoid plunger. Adjust the solenoid screw to obtain the rpm specified on the underhood sticker. Reconnect the override switch and turn the A/C Off.
9. Connect the PCV hose and remove the tachometer and timing light.

6510-C 2-bbl Carburetor

1. Run the engine to normal operating temperature. Turn the air conditioning Off and connect a tachometer and timing light to the engine.
2. Set the parking brake and block the drive wheels.
3. Disconnect and plug the PCV hose at the vapor canister.
4. Disconnect and plug the vacuum advance hose at the distributor.
5. Place the transmission in Drive (AT) or Neutral (MT). Check, and if necessary, adjust the timing.
6. Connect the vacuum advance hose.
7. Manual transmission, without A/C: turn the idle speed screw to obtain the specified rpm. Manual transmission with A/C or automatic transmission with or without A/C: Turn the idle speed screw to obtain the specified rpm. Disconnect the wire at the wide open throttle switch located on the accelerator linkage. Set the A/C to On. Momentarily open the throttle to extend the solenoid plunger. Adjust the solenoid screw to obtain the solenoid idle speed specified on the underhood sticker.
8. Connect the PCV hose and remove the tachometer and timing light.

2GC, 2GE 2-bbl Carburetors

1. Run the engine to normal operating temperature. Make sure that the choke is fully opened, turn the A/C Off and connect a tachometer and timing light to the engine according to the manufacturers' instructions.
2. Set the parking brake and block the drive wheels.
3. Disconnect and plug the vacuum hoses at the vapor canister and EGR valve.
4. Place the transmission in Park (AT) or Neutral (MT).
5. Disconnect and plug the vacuum advance hose at the distributor.
6. Check, and if necessary, adjust the timing.
7. Connect the vacuum advance hose.
8. Cars with manual transmission, without A/C: turn the idle speed screw to obtain the specified rpm. Cars with automatic transmission, without A/C: open the throttle momentarily to extend the solenoid plunger. Turn the solenoid screw to adjust the speed to the curb idle rpm listed on the underhood sticker. Turn the idle speed screw to the specified rpm.
   Cars with A/C: Turn idle speed screw to obtain the specified rpm. Disconnect the A/C compressor clutch wire. Turn the A/C On. Open the throttle momentarily to extend the solenoid plunger. Turn the solenoid screw to obtain the rpm specified on the underhood sticker. Connect the compressor clutch wire.
9. Connect all hoses. Remove the tachometer and timing light.

M2MC-210 2-bbl Carburetor

1. Run the engine to normal operating temperature.
2. Disconnect the A/C compressor clutch wire, turn the A/C Off, make sure that the choke is fully opened, place the manual transmission in Neutral, and the automatic transmission in Drive. Set the parking brake and block the drive wheels.
3. Disconnect and plug the vacuum advance hose at the distributor.
4. Check and adjust the timing.
5. Connect the vacuum advance hose.
6. Disconnect the purge hose at the vapor canister.
7. Cars without A/C: turn the idle speed screw to obtain the specified rpm. Cars with A/C: turn the idle speed screw to obtain the specified rpm, turn the A/C On, open throttle momentarily to extend the solenoid plunger and set the solenoid screw to obtain the rpm specified on the underhood sticker. Turn the A/C Off.
8. Connect all hoses and remove the tachometer and timing light. Connect the compressor clutch wire.

M4MC 4-bbl Carburetor

1. Run the engine to normal operating temperature.
2. Make sure that the choke is fully opened, turn the A/C Off and connect a tachometer and timing light to the engine according to the manufacturers' instructions. Set the parking brake and block the drive wheels.
3. Disconnect the purge hose at the vapor canister.
4. Disconnect and plug the EGR vacuum hose at the EGR valve. On 350 engines, plug the purge hose at the canister.
5. Place the transmission in Park.
6. Disconnect and plug the vacuum advance line at the distributor.
7. Check and adjust the timing.
8. Connect the vacuum advance line.
9. Place the transmission in Drive.
10. On cars without A/C: adjust the idle speed screw to obtain the specified rpm. On cars with A/C: disconnect the compressor clutch wire. Open the throttle momentarily to extend the solenoid plunger. Turn the A/C ON and adjust the solenoid screw to obtain the rpm specified on the underhood sticker. Connect the compressor clutch wire and turn the A/C Off.
11. Connect all hoses and remove the tachometer and timing light.

1978-79 IDLE MIXTURE ADJUSTMENT

Changes in the idle system have made impossible the adjustment of the fuel mixture without the aid of a propane enrichment system not available to the general public. Backing out the mixture screw, of itself, will have little or no effect on the mixture.

DIESEL ENGINE

Fuel Supply Pump Removal and Installation

The fuel supply pump is serviced in the same manner as the fuel pump on the gasoline engine.

Fuel Filter Removal and Installation

NOTE: *The fuel filter is a square assembly located at the back of the engine above the intake manifold. To remove the filter, disconnect the fuel lines. Install the lines to the new filter. Start the engine and check for leaks.*

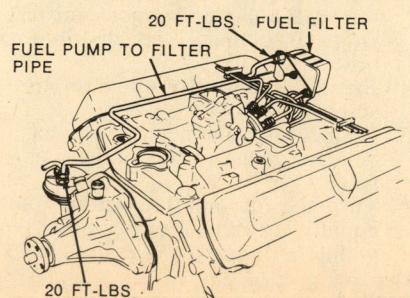

Fuel filter and lines (© Oldsmobile Div., G.M. Corp.)

Fuel Injection Pump Removal and Installation

1. Remove the air cleaner.
2. Remove the filters and pipes from the valve covers and air crossover.
3. Remove the air crossover and cap the intake manifold with screened covers (tool J-26996-1).
4. Disconnect the throttle rod and return spring.
5. Remove the bellcrank.
6. Remove the throttle and transmission cables from the intake manifold brackets.
7. Disconnect the fuel lines from the filter and remove the filter.

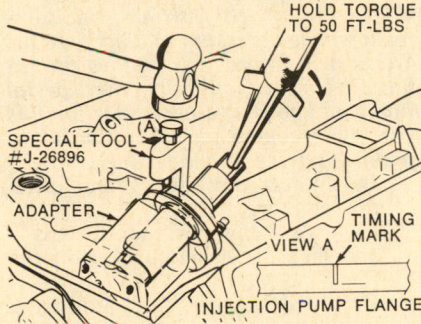

Marking Injection pump adapter (© Oldsmobile Div., G.M. Corp.)

8. Disconnect the fuel inlet line at the pump.
9. Remove the rear A/C compressor brace and remove the fuel line.
10. Disconnect the fuel return line from the injection pump.
11. Remove the clamps and pull the fuel return lines from each injection nozzle.
12. Using two wrenches, disconnect the high pressure lines at the nozzles.
13. Remove the three injection pump retaining nuts with tool J-26987 or its equivalent.
14. Remove the pump and cap all lines and nozzles.

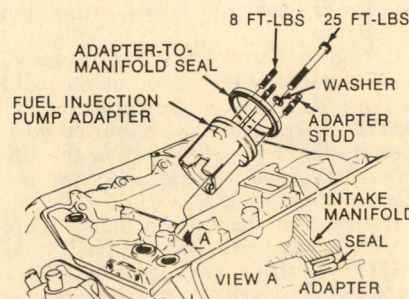

Injection pump adapter bolts (© Oldsmobile Div., G.M. Corp.)

To install:
15. Remove the protective caps.
16. Line up the offset tang on the pump driveshaft with the pump driven gear and install the pump.
17. Install, but do not tighten the pump retaining nuts.
18. Connect the high pressure lines at the nozzles.

19. Using two wrenches, torque the high pressure line nuts to 25 ft. lbs.
20. Connect the fuel return lines to the nozzles and pump.
21. Align the timing mark on the injection pump with the line on the timing mark adaptor and torque the mounting nuts to 35 ft. lbs.

NOTE: *A 3/4 in. open end wrench on the boss at the front of the injection pump will aid in rotating the pump to align the marks.*

22. Adjust the throttle rod:
    a. remove the clip from the cruise control rod and remove the rod from the bellcrank.
    b. loosen the locknut on the throttle rod a few turns, then shorten the rod several turns.
    c. rotate the bellcrank to the full throttle stop, then lengthen the throttle rod until the injection pump lever contacts the injection pump full throttle stop, then release the bellcrank.

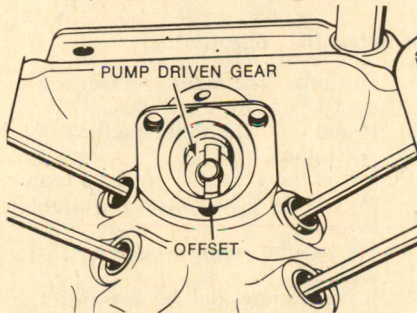

Offset on pump driven gear (© Oldsmobile Div., G.M. Corp.)

    d. tighten the throttle rod locknut.
23. Install the fuel inlet line between the transfer pump and the filter.
24. Install the rear A/C compressor brace.
25. Install the bellcrank and clip.
26. Connect the throttle rod and return spring.
27. Adjust the transmission cable:
    a. push the snap-lock to the disengaged position.
    b. rotate the injection pump lever to the full throttle stop and hold it there.

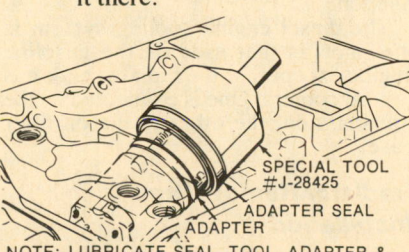

NOTE: LUBRICATE SEAL, TOOL, ADAPTER & MANIFOLD

Installing adapter seal (© Oldsmobile Div., G.M. Corp.)

    c. push in the snap-lock until it is flush.
    d. release the injection pump lever.
28. Start the engine and check for fuel leaks.

29. Remove the screened covers and install the air crossover.
30. Install the tubes in the air flow control valve in the air crossover and install the ventilation filters in the valve covers.
31. Install the air cleaner.

Slow Idle Speed Adjustment

1. Run the engine to normal operating temperature.
2. Insert the probe of a magnetic pickup tachometer into the timing indicator hole.

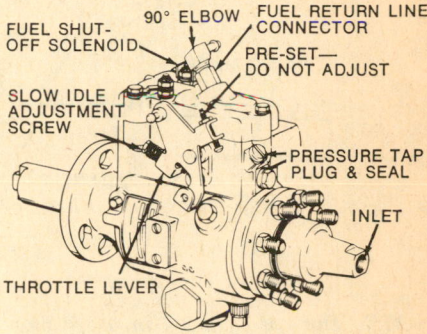

Injection pump slow idle screw (© Oldsmobile Div., G.M. Corp.)

3. Set the parking brake and block the drive wheels.
4. Place the transmission in Drive and turn the A/C Off.
5. Turn the slow idle screw on the injection pump to obtain 575 rpm.

Fast Idle Solenoid Adjustment

1. Set the parking brake and block the drive wheels.
2. Run the engine to normal operating temperature.
3. Place the transmission in Drive, disconnect the compressor clutch wire and turn the A/C On. On cars without A/C, disconnect the solenoid wire, and connect a jumper wire to the solenoid terminals, ground and a 12 volt source.
4. Adjust the fast idle solenoid plunger to obtain 650 rpm.

Cruise Control Servo Relay Rod Adjustment

1. Turn the engine Off.
2. Adjust the rod to minimum slack then put the clip in the first free hole closest to the bellcrank, but within the servo bail.

Injection Timing Adjustment

For the engine to be properly timed, the lines on the top of the injection pump adapter and the flange of the injection pump must be aligned.
1. The engine must be off for reset.
2. Loosen the three pump retaining nuts with tool J-26987 or its equivalent.
3. Align the timing marks and torque the pump retaining nuts to 35 ft. lbs.

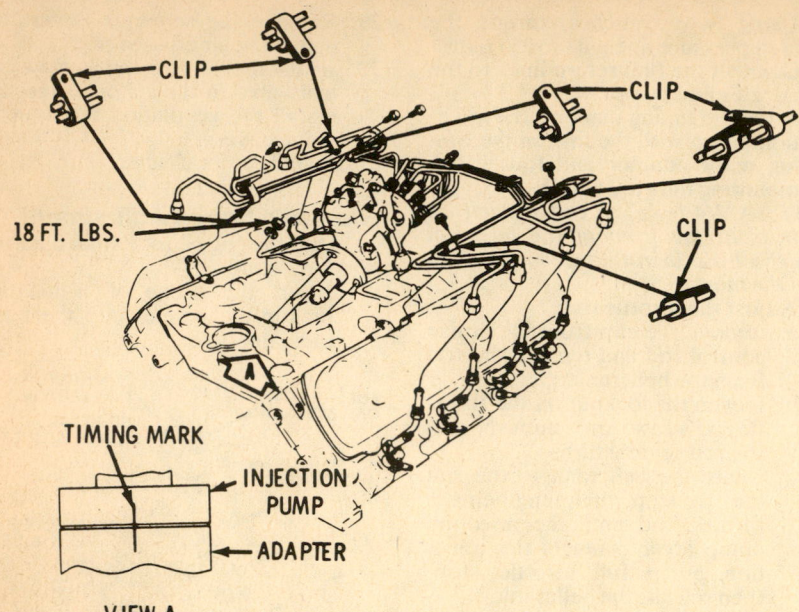

Injector Timing and Marks (© Oldsmobile Div., G.M. Corp.)

NOTE: *The use of a 3/4 in. open end wrench on the boss at the front of the pump will aid in rotating the pump to align the marks.*

4. Adjust the throttle rod. (See Fuel Injection Pump Removal and Installation, Step 22.)

Injection Nozzle Removal and Installation

(LINES REMOVED)

1. Remove the fuel return line from the nozzle.
2. Remove the nozzle hold-down clamp and spacer using tool J-26952.
3. Cap the high pressure line and nozzle tip.

NOTE: *The nozzle tip is highly susceptible to damage and must be protected at all times.*

4. If an old nozzle is to be reinstalled, a new compression seal and carbon stop seal must be installed after removal of the used seals.
5. Remove the caps and install the nozzle, spacer and clamp. Torque to 25 ft. lbs.
6. Replace return line and check for leaks.

Injection Pump Adapter, Adapter Seal, and New Adapter Timing Mark Removal and Installation

1. Remove injection pump and lines as describe earlier.
2. Remove the injection pump adapter.
3. Remove the seal from the adapter.
4. File the timing mark from the adapter.
5. Position the engine at TDC of No. 1 cylinder. Align the mark on the balancer with the zero mark on the

indicator. The index is offset to the right when No. 1 is at TDC.
6. Install, but do not tighten the injection pump.
7. Install the new seal on the adapter using tool J-28425, or its equivalent.
8. Torque the adapter bolts to 25 ft. lbs.
9. Install timing tool J-26896 into the injection pump adapter. Torque the tool, toward No. 1 cylinder, to 50 ft. lbs. Mark the injection pump adapter. Remove the tool.
10. Install the injection pump.

COOLING SYSTEM

Detailed information on cooling system capacity is in the Capacities table. Information on the water temperature light or gauge is in the Unit Repair Section.

The diesel engine cooling system is the same as that used on the gasoline engine except that the radiator tank has two oil coolers. One is connected to the transmission, the other to the oil filter base.

Radiator Removal and Installation

EXCEPT 1975 AND LATER OMEGA

1. Drain the cooling system.
2. Remove the upper radiator baffle and slide the shroud back over the fan.
3. Unfasten the upper and lower hoses from the radiator.
4. Disconnect the overflow hose or the optional coolant recovery system hose.

5. On models equipped with an automatic transmission, disconnect and cap the lines which run to the fluid cooler.
6. Unfasten the radiator's securing bolts and move the radiator upward to disengage it from its supports. Remove the radiator from the car.

NOTE: *It may be necessary to rotate the fan blades in order to keep them out of the way.*

7. Installation is the reverse of removal. Refill the cooling system.

1975 AND LATER OMEGA

NOTE: *On models with air conditioning, it will be necessary to discharge the A/C system in order to remove the radiator. Unless you have the special tools and knowledge necessary for this task, it is recommended that it be left to qualified service personnel only.*

1. Disconnect the battery and drain the radiator.
2. Remove the upper radiator baffle and slide the shroud back over the fan.
3. On models with an automatic transmission, disconnect and cap the fluid cooler lines.
4. Remove the upper and lower radiator hoses. Disconnect the coolant recovery system hose.
5. On models with A/C, discharge the system. To gain working clearance, disconnect the upper A/C condenser line. See the note at the beginning of this procedure.
6. Unfasten its mounting bolts and lift the radiator out of the car.
7. Installation is the reverse of removal. Check the coolant and transmission fluid levels.

Water Pump Removal and Installation

1. Drain the cooling system.
2. Unfasten the heater, bypass, and lower radiator hoses from the pump.
3. Loosen the drive belts. Remove the fan and pulley, complete with the fan clutch, if so equipped.

NOTE: *Keep the fan in an upright position during removal to prevent the silicone fluid from leaking out of the fan clutch.*

4. Unfasten the bolts which secure the water pump and remove it.

NOTE: *On six-cylinder engines, pull the pump straight out, to prevent impeller damage.*

Installation is as follows:
1. Apply a thin coating of sealer to the pump housing gasket mounting surface.
2. Place a *new* gasket on the housing.
3. Install the pump assembly. Lightly oil the self-tapping bolts and tighten them to 13 ft. lbs.
4. Torque the 5/16 in. bolts to 10 ft. lbs.
5. Install the fan assembly and tighten

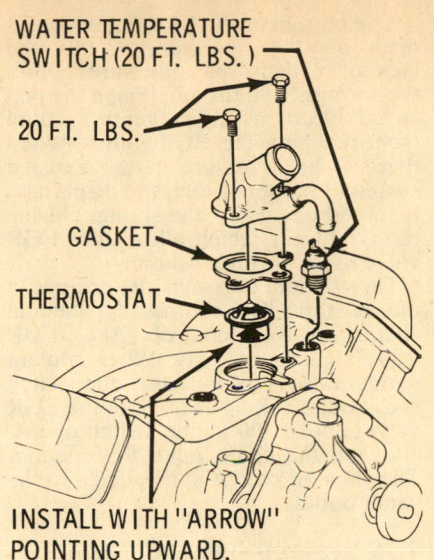

WATER TEMPERATURE
SWITCH (20 FT. LBS.)

20 FT. LBS.

GASKET

THERMOSTAT

INSTALL WITH "ARROW"
POINTING UPWARD.

Typical thermostat installation
(© Oldsmobile Div., GM Corp.)

the bolts which secure it to the pump.
6. Install the drive belts and adjust their tension.
7. Refill the cooling system.

Thermostat Replacement

1. Remove the hoses from the thermostat housing.
2. Remove the bolts, water outlet, and gasket from the thermostat housing.
3. Install the new thermostat and gasket in the engine. The thermostat may be etched with the word front; if so, front must face the radiator.
4. Connect the hoses and refill the cooling system.

EMISSION CONTROLS

NOTE: *See Emission Control Systems in the Unit Repair Section, for testing and adjustment of the various system components.*

Limiter Caps

Beginning 1971, limiter caps (plastic caps) were placed over the idle mixture screws on the carburetor. Mixture is pre-set at the factory.

Transmission-Controlled Spark (TCS)

TCS consists of a temperature switch (6 cyl only), a solenoid valve, and a transmission switch. This system allows vacuum-controlled spark advance to the distributor only when the transmission is in high gear or when a six-cylinder's engine temperature is below 85°F or above 220°F. A vacuum line runs from the carburetor to the TCS solenoid (mounted on the intake

manifold) and on to the vacuum advance unit on the distributor. A pressure-sensitive switch is located on the side of the transmission case (automatic transmission) and is electrically connected to the TCS solenoid at the intake manifold.

When the transmission is in any other gear than high gear, the transmission switch is closed and the circuit to the TCS solenoid is complete. This causes the solenoid to close and prevents carburetor vacuum from reaching the distributor. When the transmission enters high gear, hydraulic pressure opens the transmission switch, and the circuit to the solenoid opens. This permits carburetor vacuum to pass to the distributor and advance the spark. On six-cylinder engines, the temperature sending switch is electrically connected to the solenoid through a relay. At engine temperatures below 85° F or above 220° F, this switch opens up and stops current from reaching the solenoid, thereby permitting vacuum to pass through to the distributor and advancing the spark. The system used on models that are equipped with a manual transmission is identical, except that the transmission switch is manually actuated by the transmission linkage.

Evaporative Control System

The system consists of a special fuel tank, a liquid/vapor separator, a carbon canister, and a special gas cap. A gas tank baffle limits tank capacity by 1 gal to provide room for expansion of fuel. The liquid/vapor separator is mounted to the underbody near the tank. Its purpose is to separate the liquid fuel from the vapors.

A vapor line connects to the separator output and runs to the front of the car where it attaches to a carbon-filled canister mounted on the front fender inner panel. Fuel vapors from the separator are stored here and then withdrawn by manifold vacuum through a hose to the intake manifold where they are reburned.

─── CAUTION ───

The pressure/vacuum cap used with this system cannot be replaced by a cap of any other design.

1972

1972 cars contain the same emission control equipment as 1971 cars with the following exceptions:

Transmission-Controlled Spark Solenoid

For 1972, this switch is used only on Cutlass models equipped with 350 cu in. two-barrel engines and no air conditioning. On all other models equipped with TCS, the vacuum cut-off solenoid is contained in the distributor vacuum control switch.

Idle Solenoid

The two-barrel and four-barrel carburetors are now equipped with an idle solenoid or a vacuum actuator. Both controls help to create a higher idle speed as a means of reducing emissions.

1973

Exhaust Gas Recirculation

All 1973 models are equipped with Exhaust Gas Recirculation (EGR). This system routes a portion of the engine exhaust gases back into the engine to dilute the incoming air/fuel mixture. By reducing the amount of combustible material in the combustion chamber, peak combustion temperature and the corresponding formation of oxides of Nitrogen (NOx) are lowered.

An internal intake manifold passage conducts gases from the intake manifold crossover passage to the air/fuel passages in the manifold on V8 engines. In 6-cylinder engines, a drilled hole passes the exhaust gases to the intake manifold. The EGR control valve is attached to the intake manifold and normally blocks the exhaust gases from entering the engine. The EGR valve contains a spring-loaded diaphragm which is controlled by carburetor vacuum. On V8s, the EGR valve vacuum hose contains a low-temperature cut-off valve which blocks carburetor vacuum from the control valve until the ambient temperature around the intake manifold has reached 50-60°F. The black and white plastic cut-off valve must always be installed with the side marked EGR facing the EGR valve.

Models equipped with a 350 2 bbl engine use the same port on the carburetor as a source for both EGR and distributor vacuum.

V8s made on or after 15 March 1973 have a black plastic cover over the EGR low temperature cut-off valve, so that the valve is dependent upon engine, rather than air, temperature.

Thermal Vacuum Switch

All V8 engines are equipped with a Termal Vacuum Switch (TVS). Vacuum hoses from the carburetor, intake manifold, and distributor connect to this switch which is controlled by engine coolant temperature. During normal engine operation, vacuum from the carburetor passes through the TVS to the distributor. If the engine should overheat while idling, the TVS connects intake manifold vacuum to the distributor which helps to lower the coolant temperature.

On models equipped with a 350 2-bbl engine, the intake manifold vacuum hose to the TVS contains a vacuum reducing valve. The purpose of this valve is to limit the amount of vacuum supplied to the distributor by the intake manifold to 9 in. Hg. This valve is required on this engine because of the fact that the distributor and EGR valve

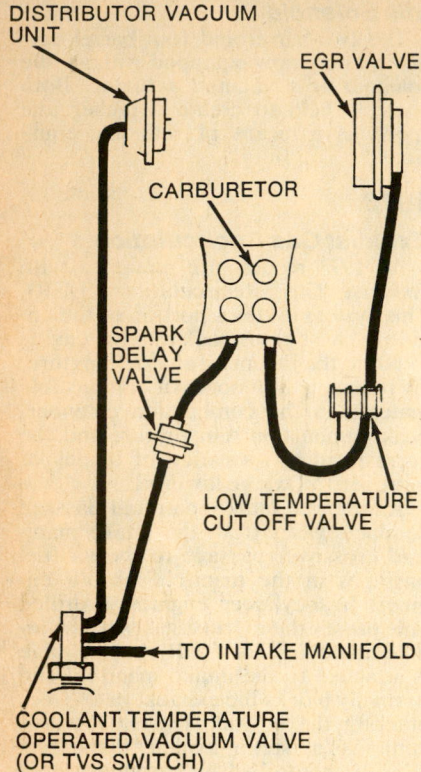

DISTRIBUTOR VACUUM UNIT

EGR VALVE

CARBURETOR

SPARK DELAY VALVE

LOW TEMPERATURE CUT OFF VALVE

TO INTAKE MANIFOLD

COOLANT TEMPERATURE OPERATED VACUUM VALVE (OR TVS SWITCH)

1973 350 4 bbl and 455 V8 emission controls

normally share the same vacuum port on the carburetor. Since the vacuum from this source is divided between two sources, the distributor is calibrated to operate on a maximum of about 7 in. Hg.

Thermal Check and Delay Valve

All 350 and 455 cu. in. 4 bbl carburetor engines, except for the 350 engine equipped with manual transmission, have a thermal check and delay valve. This valve is in the vacuum line which runs between the carburetor spark port and the TVS.

When the underhood (or engine block) temperature is below 50°F full carburetor-ported vacuum is supplied to the distributor vacuum unit. Above 50°F, the valve blocks full vacuum for up to 40 seconds.

If ported vacuum drops, the valve opens, causing the distributor vacuum advance to be retarded. As vacuum increases, the valve closes, blocking full vacuum again.

Cars made from 15 March 1973 have a cover over the valve so that it is more dependent upon engine block temperature.

Air Injection Reactor

All six cylinder engines are equipped with Air Injection Reactor (AIR). A belt-driven air pump supplies air to an injection manifold which has a nozzle positioned behind each exhaust valve. Injection of air at this point causes combustion of any unburned hydrocarbons in the exhaust manifold rather

than allowing them to escape into the atmosphere. An antibackfire (diverter) valve controls the flow of air from the pump to prevent backfires resulting from an overly rich mixture under closed throttle conditions. A check valve functions to prevent hot exhaust gas backflow into the pump and hoses in case of pump failure or when the antibackfire valve is working.

Combined Emission Controls

All Omegas equipped with a six-cylinder engine and a manual transmission are equipped with a CEC valve. This system is basically a Transmission Controlled Spark (TCS) system. The CEC solenoid is mounted on the side of the carburetor and the carburetor vacuum line to the distributor passes through it. This switch, which is normally closed, is energized to allow vacuum advance only under the following conditions: when engine coolant temperature is below 93°F, for a period of 20 seconds after the engine is started, or when the transmission is in third gear. When any of the above conditions exist, a complete circuit is made from the ignition switch through either the temperature switch, time-delay relay, or transmission switch to the CEC solenoid. This energizes the solenoid and causes its plunger to extend, uncovering the carburetor vacuum port to the distributor and raising the idle speed of the engine.

1974
Exhaust Gas Recirculation

The 1974 exhaust gas recirculation (EGR) system remains basically the same as that used on cars made after 15 March 1973 (see above). However, a backpressure transducer valve (BPV) has been added to the EGR system used on V8 engines which are sold in California.

The bottom of the BPV diaphragm is open to exhaust pressure. At idle, the lack of exhaust backpressure allows the spring above the diaphragm to open an air bleed, which prevents vacuum from reaching the EGR valve. When there is backpressure in the exhaust system, i.e., above idle, the diaphragm is forced up against the spring, closing the air bleed, which allows the EGR valve to get normal vacuum.

On 1974 inline six-cylinder engines, a thermostatically controlled vacuum switch (valve) controls the EGR valve's vacuum supply. When coolant temperature is below 100°F, the switch is closed, blocking vacuum to the EGR valve; above 100°F, the switch opens, allowing the EGR valve to function. The vacuum switch is threaded into the water outlet.

TCS System—Inline 6 Engine

The transmission controlled spark system, used on Omega models with six cylinder engines and manual transmissions, is similar to the CEC system used in 1973.

The only difference is that the CEC solenoid has been replaced by a vacuum advance solenoid, which is attached to the coil bracket.

The transmission switch, temperature switch, and time-delay relay remain as before.

Distributor Vacuum Valve

A distributor vacuum valve (DVV) is used on all 350 and 455 cu in. engines sold in California and on some of the 455 cu. in. engines which are sold nationally.

The DVV switches the distributor vacuum advance unit's vacuum source from the carburetor spark port to the EGR port. Below 7 in. Hg, the vacuum unit operates from the spark port. Above 7 in. Hg, the vacuum supply is

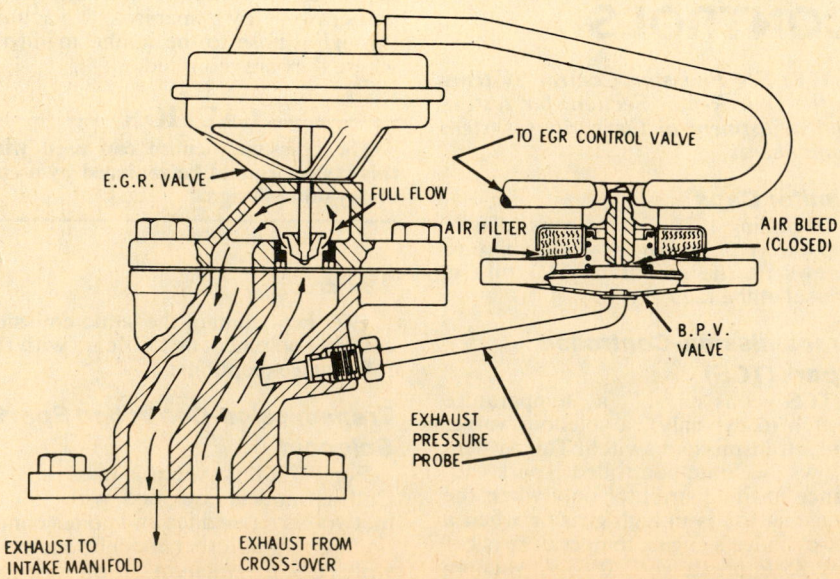

E.G.R. VALVE

FULL FLOW

TO EGR CONTROL VALVE

AIR FILTER

AIR BLEED (CLOSED)

B.P.V. VALVE

EXHAUST PRESSURE PROBE

EXHAUST TO INTAKE MANIFOLD

EXHAUST FROM CROSS-OVER

1974-75 EGR valve with backpressure transducer valve (BPV) is used on California V8s

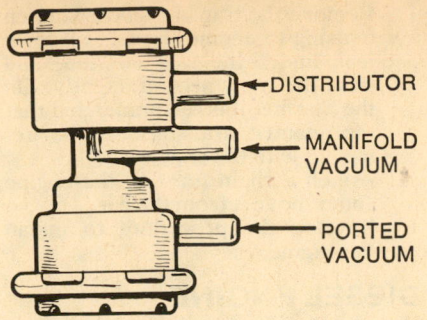

The distributor vacuum valve (DVV) is used on some V8s in 1974-75

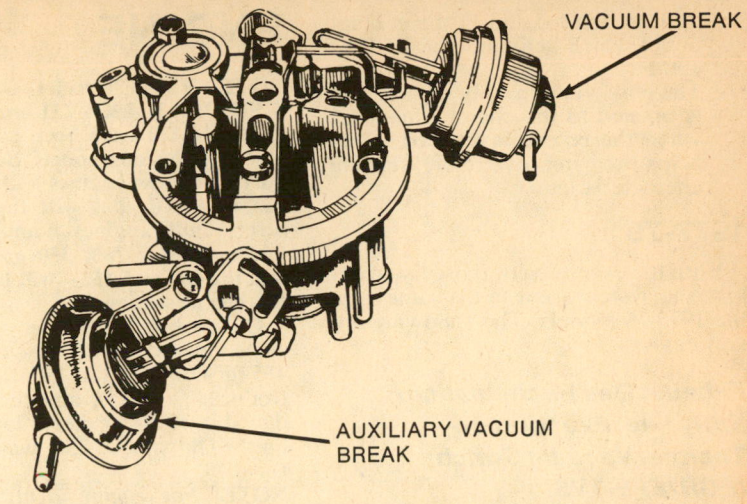

Some 1975-76 carburetors have two choke vacuum breaks

switched by the DVV from the spark port to the EGR port.

Other Emission Control Systems

The rest of the emission control systems used on 1974 Oldsmobile V8 engines remain the same as those described for 1973.

1975-76

Catalytic Converter

All Oldsmobiles use catalytic converters to reduce hydrocarbon/carbon monoxide (HC/CO) emissions. See the Emission Control Unit Repair section for details.

Early Fuel Evaporation (EFE)

The early fuel evaporation (EFE) system is basically a vacuum-operated heat riser valve.

When the engine is cold, the EFE valve is closed by a vacuum motor, forcing the exhaust gases up around a plate underneath the carburetor, which heats the incoming mixture to aid in quicker warm-ups.

When the engine is warm, the vacuum for the EFE vacuum motor is blocked off, and spring tension pulls the heat valve to the opened position.

Vacuum to the EFE vacuum motor is controlled by either a coolant temperature operated vacuum valve, or by an oil temperature sensor and solenoid, depending upon engine application.

EFE is not used on all engines.

Dual Vacuum Break Choke

A dual vacuum break choke is used on inline six and 4 bbl V8 engines.

The secondary vacuum break pulls the choke to almost wide-open position, once the engine has reached a specified temperature. Vacuum to the secondary break is controlled by a coolant temperature operated vacuum valve (V8) or by a solenoid and electrical thermoswitch on inline sixes.

When the coolant temperature is below the specified level, vacuum is blocked to the secondary choke break. As soon as the specified temperature is reached, vacuum is sent to the break, which, in turn, opens the choke plate.

Thermostatic Air Cleaner Thermal Valve

The thermostatic air cleaner (TAC) thermal valve is located on the air cleaner housing. When the engine is cold, the valve restricts the vacuum supplied to the air cleaner door vacuum motor which slows the operation of the door down. Under wide-open throttle conditions, the door does not jump to the full cold air position, thus eliminating the flat spot during cold engine acceleration.

At normal operating temperatures, the thermal valve opens and the air cleaner vacuum motor is allowed to operate in the usual manner.

Temperature Compensated Spark Advance

All V6 engines and most V8s have a temperature compensated spark advance to improve cold engine operation, and fuel economy.

When the engine is below a specified temperature, a coolant temperature operated vacuum valve supplies full manifold vacuum to the distributor vacuum advance unit.

When the coolant goes above the specified temperature, the vacuum valve switches the direct manifold vacuum supply off. This leaves only a manifold vacuum line which has a spark delay valve in it running to the distributor; reducing the amount of vacuum advance at normal operating temperature.

Other Emission Control Systems

Most of the other emission control systems remain as they were in 1974, except for the following changes:

1. Air injection (AIR) is used on some engines.
2. Transmission controlled spark (TCS) is not used.
3. The EGR temperature valve and its cover have been moved to above the water pump on some V8s. Some engines have a thermal vac-

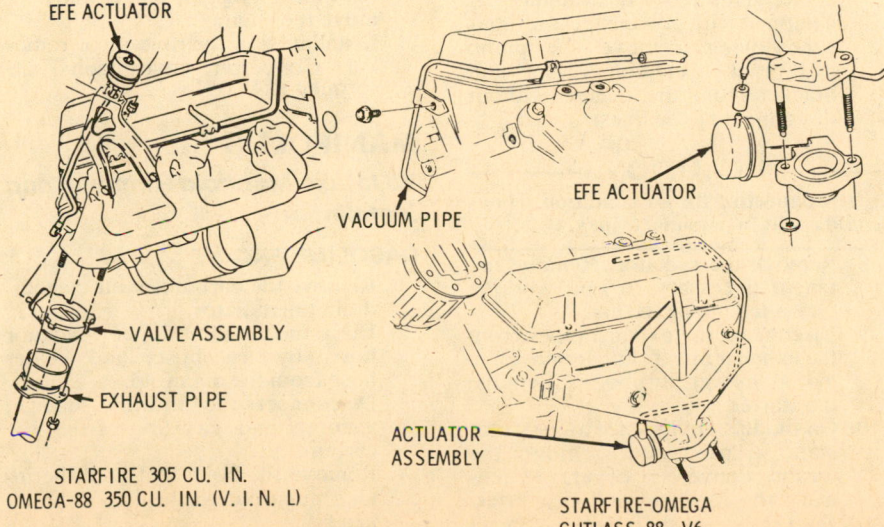

Early fuel evaporation (EFE) valve and vacuum motor

uum switch located in the coolant outlet which activates the EGR at 100°F.

4. The bowl vent on 4 bbl carburetors is opened to the charcoal canister when the engine is shut off. This helps to improve hot starting characteristics.

1977-79

With the exception of those listed below, the systems remain the same as in the 1975-76 models. The following are new devices:

Exhaust Gas Recirculation/ Early Fuel Evaporation— Thermal Vacuum Switch (EGR/EFE-TVS)

This switch advances the timing when the coolant temperature reaches 220°F at idle. The system is used exclusively on the V6.

Distributor Vacuum Delay Valve

This valve delays vacuum from the carburetor for up to thirty seconds at temperatures below 220°F.

Vacuum Reducer Valve

The VRV reduces vacuum in the manifold by 1.5 in. when coolant temperature exceeds 220°F. This prevents detonation.

Early Fuel Evaporation Check Valve

This valve is used in the vacuum line from the carburetor to the EFE-TVS switch on Chevrolet 350 engines, to hold the highest vacuum reached until the TVS switch acts.

Spark Advance Vacuum Modulator

This device is a dual diaphragm regulating valve with ports to the distributor, manifold and ported vacuum, which controls vacuum to the distributor, when both manifold and ported vacuum are below 7 in., or when manifold vacuum increases but ported vacuum stays below 7 in., or when both rise above 7 in.

Electronic Spark Timing Coolant Temperature Sensor

This is an electronic device which regulates spark advance according to engine temperature. It is used on some engines and is located at the top front of the block. It also operates the HOT light.

Electronic Fuel Control

The EFC system was introduced on 4-151 engines made for sale in California. The essential parts are an exhaust gas oxygen sensor, an electronic control unit, a vacuum modulator, a controlled mixture carburetor and a Phase II catalytic converter.

ENGINE

NOTE: The Chevrolet 6-250, 4-140, 8-305, 350; Buick 6-231 and 8-350; and Pontiac 4-151 have been used by Oldsmobile in various models. Service procedures for these engines will be found in car sections dealing with their manufacturer. Only engines manufactured by Oldsmobile—8-260, 350 gas and diesel and the 403 and 455—will be covered in this engine section.

Oldsmobile V8 engines are all of the same block design. These are, the 350, 455 (discontinued in 1976), the 260 (introduced in 1975), and the 403 (introduced in 1977). A diesel 350 V8, based on the Oldsmobile 350, was introduced for 1978.

NOTE: For engine identification, see the engine identification code chart at the beginning of this section.

GASOLINE ENGINE REMOVAL

1. Disconnect the negative battery cable. Remove the air cleaner assembly and heat pipe.
2. Scribe the outline of the hood hinges on the hood and remove the hood.
3. Drain the cooling system and disconnect the radiator and heater hoses from the engine.
4. Disconnect the engine ground strap from the cylinder head. Remove the fan shroud.
5. Disconnect and tag all vacuum lines and electrical leads from the engine.
6. Disconnect the throttle linkage. Disconnect the fuel line from the fuel pump. Remove the clutch equalizer on manual transmission cars.
7. If the car is equipped with an automatic transmission, disconnect the cooler lines from the radiator. If equipped with power steering or air conditioning, remove the pump and bracket or compressor and bracket from the engine without disconnecting the lines.

——— CAUTION ———
Disconnecting the air conditioner lines could result in personal injury.

8. Remove the radiator. Remove the fan, if necessary to gain working clearance. Raise the car.
9. Disconnect the exhaust pipes from the exhaust manifolds. Remove the motor mount thrubolts. Remove the starter.
10. On models equipped with an automatic transmission, remove the torque converter cover. Matchmark the flywheel and converter. Turn the crankshaft pulley to gain access to the three torque converter-to-flywheel attaching bolts and remove the bolts.

11. Remove the transmission or clutch housing-to-engine bolts, place a jack under the transmission, and raise the transmission slightly. On the Starfire, it is recommended that the manual transmission be removed with the engine.
12. Attach a chain hoist to the engine and remove it from the car.
13. Reverse the procedure to install the engine.

DIESEL ENGINE REMOVAL

1. Drain the cooling system.
2. Remove the air cleaner.
3. Mark the hood-to-hinge position and remove the hood.
4. Disconnect the ground cables from the batteries.
5. Disconnect the ground wires at the fender panels and the ground strap at the cowl.
6. Disconnect the radiator hoses, cooler lines, heater hoses, vacuum hoses, power steering pump hoses, air conditioning compressor (hoses attached), fuel inlet hose and all attached wiring.
7. Remove the bellcrank clip.
8. Disconnect the throttle and transmission cables.
9. Remove the radiator.
10. Raise and support the car.
11. Disconnect the exhaust pipes at the manifold.
12. Remove the torque converter cover and the three bolts holding the converter to the flywheel.
13. Remove the engine mount bolts.
14. Remove the three, right side, transmission-to-engine bolts. Remove the starter.
15. Lower the car and attach a hoist to the engine.
16. Slightly raise the transmission with a jack.
17. Remove the three left side transmission-to-engine bolts and remove the engine.
18. Installation is the reverse of removal. Converter cover bolts are torqued to 40 ft. lbs.

MANIFOLDS

V8 Intake Manifold Removal and Installation

GASOLINE ENGINE

1. Remove the carburetor air cleaner, drain the radiator.
2. Disconnect the upper radiator hose, by-pass hose, and heater hose from the manifold.
3. Disconnect the throttle linkage, vacuum and gas lines from the carburetor.
4. Remove the bolts that hold the intake manifold to the two cylinder heads.
5. The coil can be left on the intake manifold if the wires are disconnected through 1974.

6. Remove the generator and air conditioning compressor brackets if necessary.

— CAUTION —

Do not disconnect the A/C lines. Personal injury could result.

7. Disconnect the temperature gauge wire.

NOTE: *On the 455 cu. in. engine it will be necessary to remove the oil filler tube.*

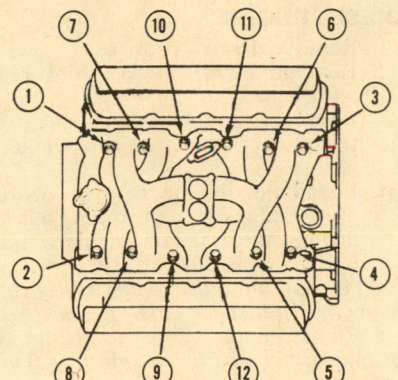

Intake manifold bolt tightening sequence. (© Oldsmobile Div., G.M. Corp.)

8. Install in the reverse order of removal, tightening all bolts first to 15 ft. lbs., then to the figure specified in the torque chart, in the sequence illustrated. Coat all gasket surfaces with sealer.

DIESEL ENGINE

NOTE: If the intake manifold is removed, it will be necessary to remove, disassemble, drain, then reassemble the valve lifters. Special tools are required which are not available to the general public.

V8 Exhaust Manifold Removal and Installation

GASOLINE ENGINE

1. Disconnect the negative battery cable and remove the air cleaner.
2. Remove the bolts from the exhaust manifold flanges on both sides and take off the crossover pipe.
3. On the right side, remove alternator and bracket.
4. Remove the hot air pipe and shroud if so equipped.
5. Disconnect the exhaust pipe from the manifold.
6. Remove the bolts that hold the exhaust manifold to the cylinder head and lift off the exhaust manifolds.
7. On some models with the 455 cu. in. engine, the starter will have to be removed to work on the left-hand exhaust manifold. On air-conditioned models with the 455 cu. in. and 350 cu. in. engines, the front wheel will have to be re-

moved in order to gain access to the right-hand manifold through the opening in the fender inner panel. When installing, tighten the manifold-to-head attaching bolts to 25 ft. lbs. on models through 1973, tightening those in the center first. On 1974 and later engines, tighten the bolts to the following specifications:

> 5/16 in.—25 ft. lbs.
> 3/8 in.—35 ft. lbs.
> 7/16 in.—50 ft. lbs.

DIESEL ENGINE—LEFT SIDE

1. Remove the air cleaner.
2. Remove the alternator lower bracket.
3. Raise and support the car.
4. Remove the crossover pipe.
5. Lower the car.
6. Remove the exhaust manifold.
7. Installation is the reverse of removal.

DIESEL ENGINE—RIGHT SIDE

1. Raise and support the car.
2. Remove the crossover pipe.
3. Disconnect the exhaust pipe.
4. Remove the right front wheel.
5. Remove the exhaust manifold from under the car.
6. Installation is the reverse of removal.

VALVE SYSTEM

Hydraulic lifters are used on all engines. Valve guides are not replaceable, but may be reamed oversize. Occasionally a valve guide bore will be oversize as manufactured. These are marked on the inboard side of the cylinder heads on the machined surface just above the intake manifold.

V8 Rocker Arm Replacement

GASOLINE ENGINE

Remove the valve covers. Remove the two bolts that attach the rocker arm pivot to the cylinder head. Remove the rocker arms in pairs. Install the rocker arms for each cylinder only when the lifters are off the cam lobe and the valves are closed. Lubricate all pivot and rocker arm wear points with white grease. Torque the hardened flanged retaining bolts to 25 ft. lbs.

DIESEL ENGINE

NOTE: If the rocker arms are removed, the lifters will have to be removed, disassembled, drained, then reassembled. Special tools are required which are not available to the general public.

V8 Valve Adjustment

These valves cannot be adjusted. If there is excessive clearance in the valve train, look for worn pushrods, rocker arms, valve springs, or collapsed or stuck valve lifters.

CYLINDER HEAD

V8 Cylinder Head Removal and Installation

— CAUTION —

Do not disconnect the A/C lines. Severe personal injury could result.

GASOLINE ENGINE

1. Drain the cooling system.
2. Remove the intake manifold and carburetor as an assembly.
3. Remove exhaust manifolds.
4. Loosen or remove any accessory brackets which interfere.
5. Remove the valve cover. Loosen any accessory brackets which are in the way.
6. Remove rocker arm bolts, pivots, rocker arms and pushrods. Scribe the pivots and identify the rocker arms and pushrods so that they may be installed in their original locations.

NOTE: *On some models equipped with a 455 cu. in. engine and air conditioning, disconnect the tight motor mount and jack up the right front corner of the engine to remove the No. 8 pushrod. When these models are also equipped with power brakes, it is necessary to disconnect the booster and turn it sideways to remove the No. 7 pushrod.*

7. Remove cylinder head bolts and cylinder head(s).

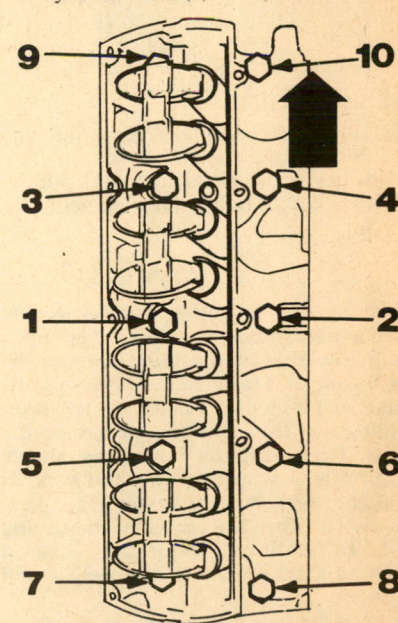

Head bolt torque sequence. (© Oldsmobile Div., G.M. Corp.)

8. Install in the reverse order of removal. It is recommended that the head gasket be coated on both sides with sealer. Dip head bolts in oil before installing. Tighten all head bolts in the correct sequence to 60-70 ft. lbs., then again in sequence to the specified torque. See

Specifications at the beginning of this section for correct head bolt torque. Retorque the bolts after engine is warmed up.

DIESEL ENGINE

NOTE: *If the cylinder heads are removed, it will be necessary to remove, disassemble, drain, then reassemble the valve lifters. Special tools are required which are not available to the general public.*

TIMING CASE AND CAMSHAFT

V8 Front Cover Removal and Installation

GASOLINE ENGINE

1. Drain the coolant. Remove the fan blades and pulley.
2. Remove the vibration damper and crankshaft pulley.
3. Remove the front cover attaching bolts and remove the cover, timing indicator and water pump from the front of the engine.
4. Install in the reverse order of removal using a new gasket with sealing compound. Tighten self-tapping water pump attaching screws to 13 ft. lbs., 5/16 in. front cover attaching bolts to 25 ft. lbs. and the four bottom bolts (cover plate) to 35 ft. lbs. Torque the pulley hub bolt to 160 ft. lbs., crankshaft pulley bolts to 20 ft. lbs. (10 ft. lbs. for 1972 and later), and fan bolts to 20 ft. lbs.

DIESEL ENGINE

1. Drain the cooling system and disconnect the radiator hoses.
2. Remove all belts, fan and pulley, crankshaft pulley and balancer, using a balancer puller.

----- CAUTION -----

The use of any other type of puller, such as a universal claw type which pulls on the outside of the hub, can destroy the balancer. The outside ring of the balancer is bonded in rubber to the hub. Pulling on the outside will break the bond. The timing mark is on the outside ring. If it is suspected that the bond is broken, check that the center of the keyway is 16° from the center of the timing slot. In addition, there are chiseled aligning marks between the weight and the hub.

3. Unbolt and remove the cover, timing indicator and water pump.
4. It may be necessary to grind a flat on the cover for gripping purposes.
5. Grind a chamfer on one end of each dowel pin.
6. Cut the excess material from the front end of the oil pan gasket on each side of the block.
7. Clean the block, oil pan and front cover mating surfaces with solvent.

8. Trim about 1/8 in. off each end of a new front pan seal.
9. Install a new front cover gasket on the block and a new seal in the front cover.
10. Apply sealer to the gasket around the coolant holes.
11. Apply sealer to the block at the junction of the pan and front cover.
12. Place the cover on the block and press down to compress the seal. Rotate the cover left and right and guide the pan seal into the cavity using a small screwdriver.
13. Apply a lubricant, compatible with rubber, on the balancer seal surface.
14. Install the balancer and bolt. Torque the bolt to 200-300 ft. lbs.
15. Install all other parts in reverse of removal.

V8 Timing Chain Replacement and Valve Timing

GASOLINE ENGINE

1. Remove the timing case cover and take off the camshaft gear.

NOTE: *the fuel pump operating cam is bolted to the front of the camshaft sprocket and the sprocket is located on the camshaft by means of a dowel.*

2. Remove the oil slinger, timing chain, and the camshaft sprocket. If the crankshaft sprocket is to be replaced, remove it also at this time.

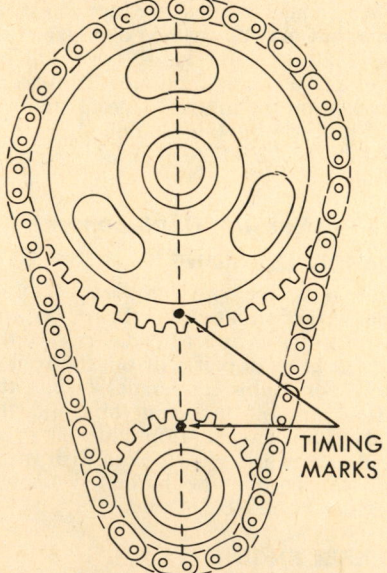

Timing marks. (© Oldsmobile Div., G.M. Corp.)

3. Reinstall the crankshaft sprocket being careful to start it with the keyway in perfect alignment since it is rather difficult to correct for misalignment after the gear has been started on the shaft. Turn the timing mark on the crankshaft gear until it points directly toward the center of the camshaft. Mount the

timing chain over the camshaft gear and start the camshaft gear up on to its shaft with the timing marks as close as possible to each other and in line between the shaft centers. Rotate the camshaft to align the shaft with the new gear.

4. A dowel pin is used for alignment. Secure the camshaft gear and check to see that the mark on the crankshaft sprocket and the mark on the camshaft sprocket are as described above.

DIESEL ENGINE

1. Remove the front cover.
2. Remove the oil slinger, crank gear and chain.
3. Remove the fuel pump eccentric from the crankshaft if replacement is necessary.
4. Installation is the reverse of removal. Make sure the timing marks line up. When the timing marks line up, No. 6 piston is at TDC.

NOTE: *Any time the timing chain and gears are replaced it will be necessary to retime the engine. Refer to the paragraph on Diesel Engine Injection Timing.*

V8 Camshaft Removal and Installation

GASOLINE ENGINE

1. Disconnect the battery.
2. Drain and remove the radiator.
3. Disconnect the fuel line at the fuel pump.
4. Disconnect the throttle cable.
5. Remove the alternator belt, loosen the alternator bolts, and move the alternator to one side.
6. Remove the power steering pump from its brackets and move it out of the way.
7. Remove the air conditioning compressor from its brackets and move the compressor out of the way without disconnecting the lines.
8. Disconnect the hoses from the water pump.
9. Disconnect the electrical and vacuum connections.
10. Mark the distributor as to location in the block. Remove the distributor.
11. Raise the car and drain the oil pan.
12. Remove the exhaust crossover pipe and starter motor.
13. Disconnect the exhaust pipe at the manifold.
14. Remove the harmonic balancer and pulley.
15. Support the engine and remove the front motor mounts.
16. Remove the flywheel inspection cover.
17. Remove the engine oil pan.
18. Support the engine by placing wooden blocks between the exhaust manifolds and the front crossmember.
19. Remove the engine front cover.
20. Remove the valve covers.

21. Remove the intake manifold, oil filler pipe, and temperature sending switch.
22. Mark the lifters, pushrods, and rocker arms as to location so that they may be installed in the same position. Remove these parts.
23. If the car is equipped with air conditioning, remove the condenser attaching bolts and move the condenser to one side.

NOTE: *Do not remove the A/C lines from the condenser.*

24. Remove the fuel pump eccentric, camshaft gear, oil slinger, and timing chain.
25. Carefully remove the camshaft from the engine.
26. Inspect the shaft for signs of excessive wear or damage.
27. Liberally coat camshaft and bearings with heavy engine oil or engine assembly lubricant and insert them into the engine.
28. Align the timing marks on the camshaft and crankshaft gears. See Timing Chain Replacement and Valve Timing for details.
29. Install the distributor using the locating marks made during removal. If any problems are encountered, see Distributor Installation in the Ignition Section.
30. To install, reverse the removal procedure but pay attention to the following points:
    a. Install the timing indicator before installing the power steering pump bracket.
    b. Install the flywheel inspection cover after installing the starter.
    c. Replace the engine oil and radiator coolant.

DIESEL ENGINE

NOTE: Camshaft removal requires the removal, disassembly, draining and reassembly of the lifters. Special tools are required which are not available to the general public.

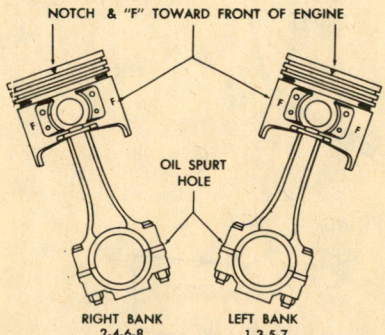

NOTCH & "F" TOWARD FRONT OF ENGINE

OIL SPURT HOLE

RIGHT BANK 2-4-6-8   LEFT BANK 1-3-5-7

Piston and rod assembly—V8

ENGINE LUBRICATION

Oil Pan Removal and Installation
ALL GASOLINE ENGINES EXCEPT 1972 8-455 CUTLASS

1. Disconnect the negative battery cable and remove the dipstick.
2. On 88 and 98 models, remove the upper radiator support and fan shroud attaching screws.
3. Raise the car on a hoist and drain the crankcase.
4. On Cutlass, 442 and Vista Cruiser models, disconnect the exhaust pipe from the right exhaust manifold. On 88 and 98 models lower the relay rod by disconnecting the idler arm or pitman arm.
5. Disconnect the engine mounts and carefully jack the front of the engine up as far as possible. The special lifting tool bolts to the front of the block.
6. Remove crossover pipe and starter.
7. Remove oil pan attaching bolts, rotate the crankshaft until the No. 1 crankshaft throw is up, then remove the oil pan.
8. When installing, apply sealer to both sides of pan gasket and install on block. Install the front and rear (rubber) seals. Install the pan, tightening 5/16 in. bolts to 15 ft. lbs. and 1/4 in. bolts to 10 ft. lbs.
9. Reverse Steps 1 through 6 to complete installation.

1972 455 V8 CUTLASS

1. Disconnect the negative battery cable and disconnect the fan shroud.
2. Raise the car on a hoist and drain the crankcase.
3. Remove the driveshaft.
4. Disconnect the exhaust pipe and starter.
5. Install a rear engine support bar and remove the flywheel housing inspection cover.
6. Disconnect modulator line, speedometer cable, fluid cooler lines, solenoid wire and linkage.
7. Remove transmission crossmember, transmission and flywheel.
8. Raise the front of the engine.
9. Remove the right engine mount and raise the engine 2 in. Install a wedge block.
10. Loosen the left engine mount-to-block bolts enough to allow for the removal of the oil pan bolts.
11. Remove the oil pan bolts, free the pan from the block and disconnect the oil pump.
12. Remove the oil pan and pump.
13. To install, clean all gasket surfaces and apply sealer to both sides of the pan gaskets. Install the gaskets on the block.
14. Install front and rear (rubber) seals.
15. Hold the oil pan in approximate position and install the oil pump, tightening bolts to 35 ft. lbs.
16. Install the oil pan, tightening 5/16 in. bolts to 15 ft. lbs. and 1/4 in. bolts to 10 ft. lbs.
17. Install the flywheel.
18. Remove the wedge block and tighten engine mount to engine block bolts to 50 ft. lbs.

19. Remove front engine support tool and install the transmission.
20. Install transmission crossmember and remove the rear engine support tool.
21. Connect modulator lines, speedometer cable, oil cooler lines, solenoid wire and linkage.
22. Connect the starter and exhaust pipe.
23. Install the driveshaft.
24. Lower car and fill the crankcase.
25. Connect the fan shroud and connect the battery negative cable.

DIESEL ENGINE

1. Remove the vacuum pump and drive (with A/C) or the oil pump drive (wo A/C).
2. Disconnect the batteries and remove the dipstick.
3. Remove the upper radiator support and fan shroud.
4. Raise and support the car. Drain the oil.
5. Remove the flywheel cover.
6. Disconnect the exhaust and crossover pipes.
7. Remove the oil cooler lines at the filter base.
8. Remove the starter assembly. Support the engine with a jack.
9. Remove the engine mounts from the block.
10. Raise the front of the engine and remove the oil pan.
11. Installation is the reverse of removal.

Oil Pump Removal and Installation

GASOLINE AND DIESEL

The oil pump is mounted to the bottom of the block and is accessible only by removing the oil pan.

On V8 engines, including diesel, remove the oil pan, then unbolt and remove the oil pump and screen as an assembly. On the OHV 6 the pickup tube has a bolt-attached bracket.

Rear Main Bearing Oil Seal Replacement

GASOLINE AND DIESEL

The crankshaft need not be removed to replace the rear main bearing upper oil seal.

1. Drain the crankcase and remove the oil pan and rear main bearing cap.
2. Using a blunt-ended tool, drive the upper seal into its groove on each side until it is tightly packed. This is usually 1/4-3/4 in.
3. Cut pieces of new seal 1/16 in. longer than required to fill the grooves and install, packing into place.
4. Carefully trim any protruding seal, being sure not to scratch or damage the bearing surface.
5. Install a new seal in the bearing cap and install cap, tightening bolts to 120 ft. lbs. Install the oil pan.

CLUTCH

Clutch Pedal Adjustment

1972

The clutch pedal should be adjusted so that there is 3/4 to 1 in. free-play at the clutch pedal before the throwout bearing engages the clutch fingers. This adjustment is made under the car at the adjustable clutch rod just in front of the throwout fork. Loosen the jam nut and turn the adjusting screw until the desired clearance is obtained, then tighten the jam nut.

1973 AND LATER—OMEGA, CUTLASS

The clutch pedal free-play should be adjusted to the following specifications, which are measured from the center of the clutch pedal pad:
   1972-77 Cutlass—3/4-1-1/4 in.
   1978-79 Cutlass 11/16-5/8 in.
   1973-79 Omega—7/8-1-1/2 in.
To adjust free-play, proceed in the following manner:
1. Loosen the locknut on the push rod swivel.
2. Detach the pedal return spring.
3. Turn the equalizer assembly until the clutch pedal seats against the rubber bumper on the dash brace.
4. Push the outer end of the clutch fork rearward, so that the throwout bearing just contacts the clutch plate.
5. Remove the retaining clip from the lower push rod swivel and install the swivel in the *upper* gauge hole. Install the retaining clip.
6. Lengthen the push rod until there is no lash.
7. Remove the retaining clip and reinstall the swivel in the *lower* hole on the equalizer lever.
8. Tighten the locknut against the swivel. Be sure that the rod length remains unchanged.
9. Install the pedal return spring and check pedal free-play.

1975 STARFIRE

Adjustment for normal clutch wear is accomplished by turning the clutch fork ball stud counterclockwise to give 11/16 to 1-1/8 in. lash at clutch pedal.
1. Remove the ball stud cap and loosen the locknut on ball stud end located to the right of the transmission on the clutch housing.
2. Adjust the ball stud to obtain 11/16 to 1-1/8 in. free travel.
3. Tighten the locknut to 30 ft lbs being careful not to change adjustment and install ball stud cap.
4. Check the operation of clutch.

1976 AND LATER STARFIRE

1. Remove the clutch fork return spring.
2. Loosen the cable end nut (pin).
3. Push the clutch fork forward until the throwout bearing can be felt to contact the release fingers, while pulling on the end of the clutch cable so that the pedal arm is up against the rubber stop. Tighten the cable end nut (pin) until it touches the fork. Tighten it another quarter turn so that it can drop into the fork groove.
4. Replace the return spring. Pedal play should now be 11/16-1-1/8 in.

Clutch Replacement

OMEGA AND CUTLASS

1. Remove the transmission.
2. Detach the clutch return spring and clutch release rod assembly.
3. Remove the throwout bearing.
4. Without removing the starter from the engine, remove the flywheel housing.
NOTE: *The release yoke, boot and ball stud will remain in the housing.*
5. Scribe a mark opposite the X mark on the flywheel cover.
6. Loosen the pressure plate evenly, one turn at a time.
   Clutch installation is performed in the following order:

─────── CAUTION ───────

Do not lubricate the splines as the lubricant will be forced on to the damper, resulting in clutch rattle.

1. Install the clutch disc/cover assembly and finger-tighten its securing bolts.
NOTE: *Align the mark made during removal with the X mark on the flywheel cover.*
2. Use a clutch arbor or an old input shaft to align the disc by inserting it through the disc and into the pilot bearing.
3. Tighten every other bolt until the cover assembly is within 1/4 in. the of flywheel.
4. Repeat step 3 for the three remaining bolts.
5. Tighten the first three bolts to 30 ft. lb. and then tighten the remaining three bolts to the same figure.
6. Remove the arbor. Lubricate the inside groove of the throwout bearing and the release yoke ball stud with wheel bearing grease.
7. Install the throwout bearing.
8. Install the flywheel housing and the transmission. Adjust clutch free-play as outlined above.

STARFIRE

1. Raise vehicle on hoist.
2. Remove transmission as outlined in this section.
3. Remove clutch fork cover then disconnect clutch return spring and control cable from clutch fork.
4. Remove flywheel housing lower cover.
5. Remove flywheel housing from engine.
6. To remove the release bearing from clutch fork and sleeve, slide lever off ball stud against spring action. If necessary to replace ball stud, remove cap, locknut and stud from housing.
7. If assembly marks on clutch assembly and flywheel are not visible remark with paint or center-punch.
8. Loosen clutch cover-to-flywheel attaching bolts one turn at a time until spring pressure is released, to avoid bending clutch cover flange.
9. Support the pressure plate and cover assembly then remove the bolts and clutch assembly.

─────── CAUTION ───────

Do not disassemble the clutch cover, spring and pressure plate for repair. If defective replace complete assembly.

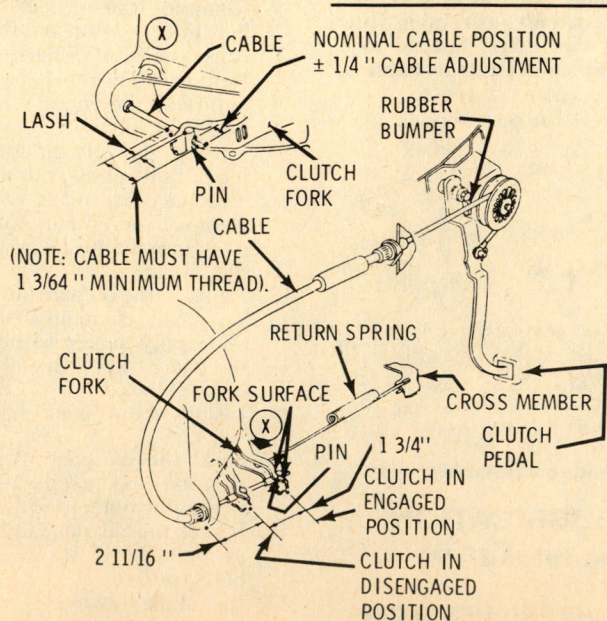

Starfire clutch cable installation and adjustment
(© Oldsmobile Div., GM Corp.)

10. Index alignment marks on clutch assembly and flywheel. Place driven plate on pressure plate with long end of splined end facing forward, damper springs inside pressure plate, and insert a dummy clutch gear shaft through the cover and driven plate.
11. Position the complete assembly against the flywheel and insert the dummy shaft into the pilot bearing in the crankshaft.
12. Index the alignment marks and install clutch cover to flywheel bolts finger-tight.

─────── CAUTION ───────

Tighten all bolts evenly and gradually until tight to avoid possible clutch distortion. Torque bolts 18 ft lbs and remove dummy shaft.

13. Lubricate the clutch fork ball socket and the fingers at the release bearing with a high melting point grease such as graphite grease.
14. Lubricate the recess on the inside of the throwout bearing collar and the fork groove with a light coat of graphite grease. Install fork in housing but not on stud.
15. Install bearing on sleeve, then position clutch fork over bearing in housing and slide fork onto ball stud.
16. Install flywheel housing and lower cover. Tighten bolts to 30 ft. lbs.
17. Install transmission as outlined.
18. Adjust clutch as previously outlined.
19. Lower and remove vehicle from hoist.

MANUAL TRANSMISSION

The 3-speed transmission is the Saginaw unit. The standard 4-speed transmission in all models is the Saginaw unit. The optional heavy-duty 4-speed offered in the Cutlass through 1973 is the Muncie transmission. On the Saginaw, all three shift rods go to levers on the side cover, while on the Muncie, one rod (reverse) goes to a lever on the case extension housing. Some Starfires with the 4 cylinder engine use the GM 70 mm 4-speed transmission. The 5-speed transmission is the Warner T-50 unit. There is no shift linkage adjustment necessary or possible on the GM 70 mm 4-speed or the Warner T-50 5-speed.

See the Capacities Table at the beginning of this section for manual transmission refill capacities. For manual transmission overhaul procedures, see the Unit Repair Section.

Transmission Removal and Installation
1. Disconnect throttle linkage and raise car. If applicable, disconnect T.C.S. switch.
2. Remove driveshaft.
3. Support the rear of the engine. Remove the catalytic converter and/or brackets, if they are in the way.
4. On console equipped floorshifts, disconnect shifter assembly at transmission, allowing this unit to remain in car. On regular floorshifts, remove floor pan seal. Insert a feeler gauge between the shift lever and its point of attachment. This will release a pin allowing the lever to be removed. Remove the 5-speed shift lever. Remove the shifter with transmission.
5. Disconnect parking brake cables and remove the cross member. Remove the Starfire torque arm.
6. Disconnect speedometer cable and back-up light switch.
7. Remove transmission upper and lower bolts.

─────── CAUTION ───────

During removal, use aligning studs to support the transmission, otherwise distortion of the clutch driven plate will result.

8. Slide transmission rearward and remove. On models equipped with dual exhaust, it may be necessary to disconnect left exhaust pipe at the manifold.
9. Install by reversing the procedure. Observe the following torque figures:

Transmission to Clutch Housing	53 ft. lb.
Crossmember to Frame exc. Starfire	25 ft. lb.
Crossmember to Frame Starfire	43 ft. lb.
Crossmember to Transmission	35 ft. lb.
U-Joint Strap bolt	15 ft. lb.
Torque Arm Bracket	30 ft. lb.
Torque Arm to Differential	113 ft. lb.

Shift Linkage Adjustment
COLUMN SHIFT THROUGH 1977
1. With the transmission in reverse loosen the swivel bolts on the shift rods at the transmission.
2. Check that the shift rods move freely in the swivels, then push up on the reverse shift rod until the detent in the column is felt and tighten the swivel bolt for the first-reverse rod.
3. With transmission in neutral, insert a 3/16 in. rod through the second-third shift lever and into the alignment hole. Tighten the swivel bolt for the second-third shift lever.
4. Lower the car and check the shift operation.
5. Place transmission in Reverse and the ignition in LOCK position. Check that the key can be removed, the wheel not turned and the transmission will not shift out of Reverse.
6. Turn the ignition to RUN position and place the transmission in second gear. Check that the ignition key cannot be removed and that the steering wheel will turn.

CUTLASS 3- AND 4-SPEED FLOORSHIFT THROUGH 1977
The linkage adjustment procedure is the same as that described for the column shift type, with the exception that the shift levers are aligned with a 1/4 in. rod.

OMEGA 3-SPEED FLOORSHIFT THROUGH 1977
1. Place the shift lever in Neutral.
2. Loosen the swivel nuts on the shift rods and detach the rods from the shifter assembly.
3. Insert a 1/4 in. pin in the locating gauge hole on the shifter.
4. Adjust the swivel so that free pin length is obtained.
5. Tighten the swivel nuts and attach the shift rods back to the shifter.
6. Position the shift lever in Reverse and turn the ignition key to LOCK.

Cutaway of the five-speed transmission, available in the 1979 Cutlass with the new 260 V8 Diesel.

7. Loosen the equalizer clamp screw and pull the backdrive rod down lightly against the stop.
8. Tighten the clamp screw.
9. Perform steps 5-6 of the Column Shift adjustment.

STARFIRE 4-SPEED FLOORSHIFT THROUGH 1977 (SAGINAW TRANSMISSION)

1. Turn the ignition switch to Off and place the shift lever in Neutral.
2. Loosen the locknuts on the control rods. Position the transmission side cover levers in their neutral detents.
3. With the floor shift lever in Neutral, align the shifter levers and insert a gauge pin into the levers and bracket.
4. Tighten the First/Second control rod locknut against its swivel.
5. Tighten the Third/Fourth control rod locknut against its swivel.
6. Tighten the Reverse control rod locknut against its swivel.
7. Remove the gauge pin and check shifter operation.

3-SPEED LINKAGE ADJUSTMENT 1978-79

Cutlass

1. Turn the ignition switch to Off.
2. Raise and support the car.
3. Remove the retainer from the shift rods.
4. Place the transmission levers in neutral.
5. Align the control levers and place a 1/4 inch gauge pin into the levers and brackets, with the shift handle in neutral.
6. Loosen the nuts on the shift rods and adjust the trunnion and pin assembly on First/Reverse, then tighten the nuts and install the shift rod and retainer.
7. Loosen the shift rod nut and adjust the trunnion and pin assembly on Second/Third, then tighten the nuts and install the shift rod and retainer.
8. Remove the gauge pin from the control lever assembly and check the operation of the control lever. Readjust as required.
9. Lower the car.

Omega

1. Place the transmission in reverse and raise and support the car.
2. Loosen the swivel bolts on the shift rods at the transmission. Make certain the rods are free to move in the swivels.
3. While holding the relay rod in position in the First/Reverse lever, push up on the reverse shift rod until the detent in the column is felt and tighten the swivel bolt for the First/Reverse rod.
4. Position the transmission in Neutral and insert a 3/16 inch rod through the Second/Third shift lever and into the alignment hole.

Tighten the swivel bolt.
5. Lower the car and check the shift operation with the engine off. Start the engine and recheck the operation.
6. Place the transmission in Reverse and the ignition in Lock. Make sure the key can be removed. The transmission should not shift out of Reverse.
7. Turn the ignition to Run and place the transmission in second. Make sure the key cannot be removed and the steering wheel will turn.

1978-79 4-SPEED LINKAGE ADJUSTMENT

1. Turn the ignition switch to the Off position.
2. Raise and support the car.
3. Loosen the lock nuts at the swivels on the shift rods.
4. Set the transmission levers in Neutral.
5. Place the shifter in Neutral.
6. Align the control levers and place a 1/4 inch gauge pin into the levers and bracket.
7. Torque the First/Second shift rod nut to 10 ft. lb.
8. Torque the Third/Fourth shift rod nut to 10 ft. lb.
9. Tighten the reverse nut to 10 ft. lb.
10. Remove the gauge pin, check the operation of the levers and lower the car.

AUTOMATIC TRANSMISSION

All Oldsmobile models use the Turbo Hydra-Matic automatic transmission.

The transmissions can be identified visually: The 200, 250, 350, and 375B have a square or oblong pan with the right rear corner cut off; the 375 and 400 have an irregular pan shape. Some 200s have the word METRIC embossed in the pan. The 200 has ten pan bolts; the 350 and 375B have thirteen. The 250 has an intermediate band adjusting screw on the right side of the case. The 200, 250, 350, and 375B have a downshift cable between the carburetor linkage and the transmission; the 375 and 400 have an electrical downshift switch on the accelerator pedal linkage.

Shift Linkage Adjustment

COLUMN SHIFT

1. Put the column shift lever in Neutral.
2. Loosen the adjusting clamp on the linkage to the transmission.
3. Hold the column shift lever against the stop, but don't raise the lever.
4. Tighten the clamp screw after making sure that the lever on the transmission is engaged in the detent.
5. Check that the key cannot be removed and the steering wheel is not locked with the key in Run and the transmission in Reverse. Check that the key can be removed and the steering wheel and transmission linkage is locked, when the key is in Lock and the transmission in Park.

FLOORSHIFT

The 1975 Starfire uses a rod operated linkage, which is adjusted at the bottom of the shifter. All other models use a cable linkage, adjusted at the transmission.

1. Set the Starfire floorshift lever in

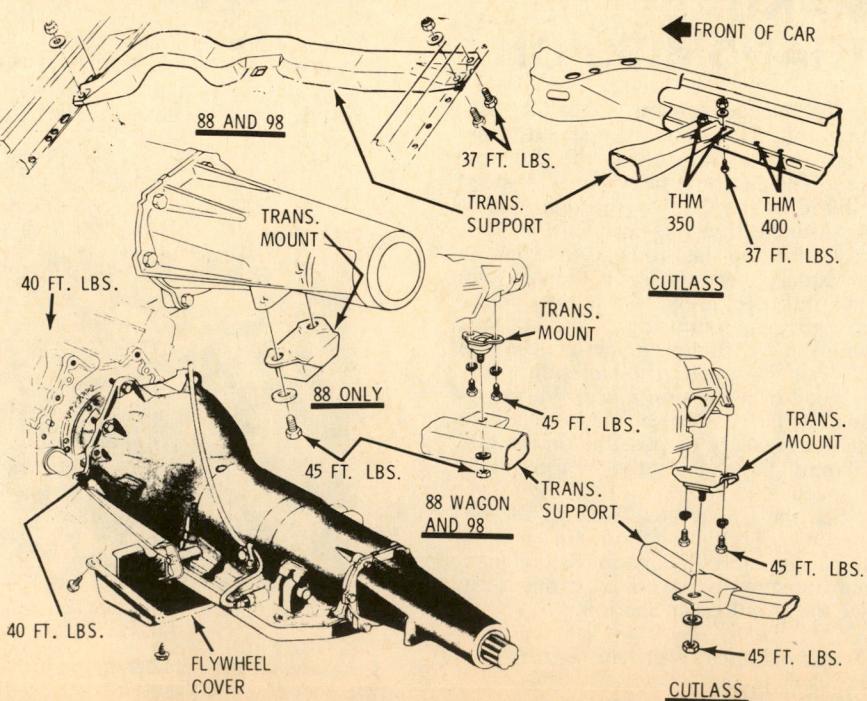

88 AND 98
37 FT. LBS.
TRANS. SUPPORT
FRONT OF CAR
THM 350   THM 400
37 FT. LBS.
CUTLASS
40 FT. LBS.
TRANS. MOUNT
88 ONLY
TRANS. MOUNT
45 FT. LBS.
45 FT. LBS.
88 WAGON AND 98
TRANS. SUPPORT
TRANS. MOUNT
45 FT. LBS.
40 FT. LBS.
FLYWHEEL COVER
45 FT. LBS.
CUTLASS

Transmission attachment (© Oldsmobile Div, G.M. Corp)

Neutral. Set all other models in Park, with the key in Lock.

2. Loosen the adjusting clamp on the linkage.
3. Make sure that the lever on the transmission is engaged in the detent.
4. Tighten the clamp screw.
5. Check that the key cannot be removed and the steering wheel is not locked with the key in Run and the transmission in Reverse. Check that the key can be removed and the steering wheel and transmission linkage is locked, when the key is in Lock and the transmission in Park.

Neutral Safety Switch

1. Place the gear selector in the appropriate range:
   Column—Neutral (N)
   Console—Park (P)
   Starfire Console—Neutral (N)
2. Loosen the switch securing screws.

NOTE: *Remove the center console first, if necessary.*

3. Fit a 0.090 in. gauge pin into the outer hole on the switch cover.
4. Move the switch until the gauge pin drops into the alignment hole on the inner slide. Tighten the switch securing screws; then remove the gauge pin.

Downshift Linkage Adjustment

TURBO HYDRA-MATIC 200, 250, 350, 375B

The downshift cable on all except Cutlass-size body cars is adjusted by removing the spring horseshoe clip holding the outer cable on the engine bracket, holding the carburetor wide open with the engine off, and replacing the clip. On Cutlass-size body cars, the adjustment is made by pulling on the

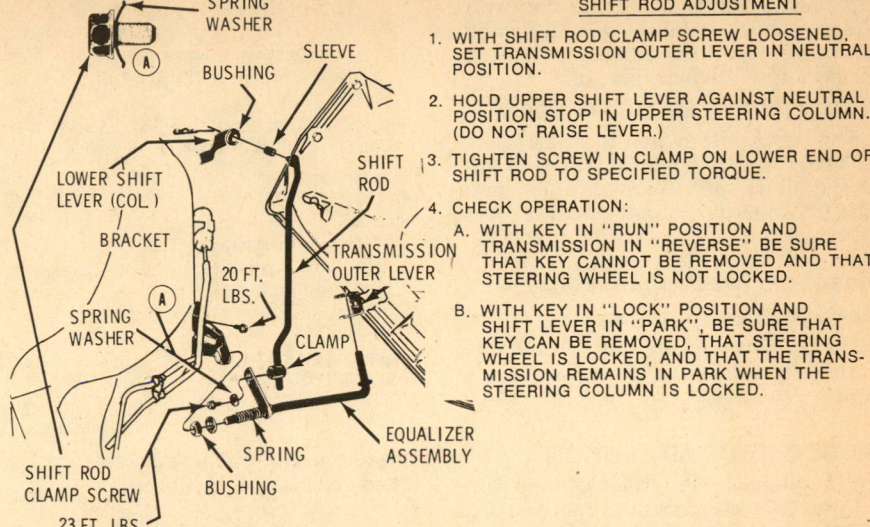

SHIFT ROD ADJUSTMENT

1. WITH SHIFT ROD CLAMP SCREW LOOSENED, SET TRANSMISSION OUTER LEVER IN NEUTRAL POSITION.
2. HOLD UPPER SHIFT LEVER AGAINST NEUTRAL POSITION STOP IN UPPER STEERING COLUMN. (DO NOT RAISE LEVER.)
3. TIGHTEN SCREW IN CLAMP ON LOWER END OF SHIFT ROD TO SPECIFIED TORQUE.
4. CHECK OPERATION:
   A. WITH KEY IN "RUN" POSITION AND TRANSMISSION IN "REVERSE" BE SURE THAT KEY CANNOT BE REMOVED AND THAT STEERING WHEEL IS NOT LOCKED.
   B. WITH KEY IN "LOCK" POSITION AND SHIFT LEVER IN "PARK", BE SURE THAT KEY CAN BE REMOVED, THAT STEERING WHEEL IS LOCKED, AND THAT THE TRANSMISSION REMAINS IN PARK WHEN THE STEERING COLUMN IS LOCKED.

Column shift linkage adjustment through 1976 (© Oldsmobile Div., G.M. Corp.)

ADJUSTMENT PROCEDURE

1. POSITION SHIFT LEVER
   A. NEUTRAL (COLUMN SHIFT - A.T.)
   B. PARK (CONSOLE SHIFT - A.T.)
2. LOOSEN SWITCH ATTACHING SCREWS
3. INSTALL THE .090" GAUGE PIN INTO THE OUTER HOLE IN THE SWITCH COVER.
4. ROTATE SWITCH UNTIL THE PIN GOES INTO THE ALIGNMENT HOLE IN THE INNER PLASTIC SLIDE.
5. TIGHTEN THE SWITCH TO COLUMN ATTACHING SCREWS AND REMOVE GAUGE PIN.
6. APPLY BRAKES FIRMLY AND CHECK TO MAKE SURE STARTER WILL NOT WORK IN ANY SHIFT LEVER POSITION EXCEPT NEUTRAL AND PARK.

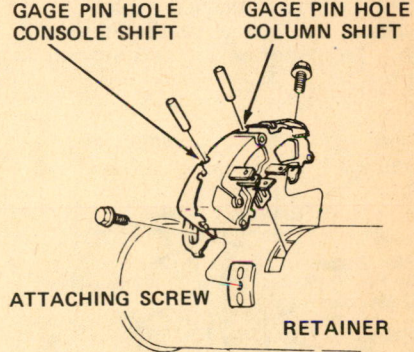

IMPORTANT: EXTREME CARE MUST BE TAKEN NOT TO OVERTORQUE THE ATTACHING SCREWS (20 INCH LBS. MAX.) IF THE RETAINER STRIPS IT MUST BE REPLACED.

Neutral safety switch adjustment (© Oldsmobile Div, G.M. Corp)

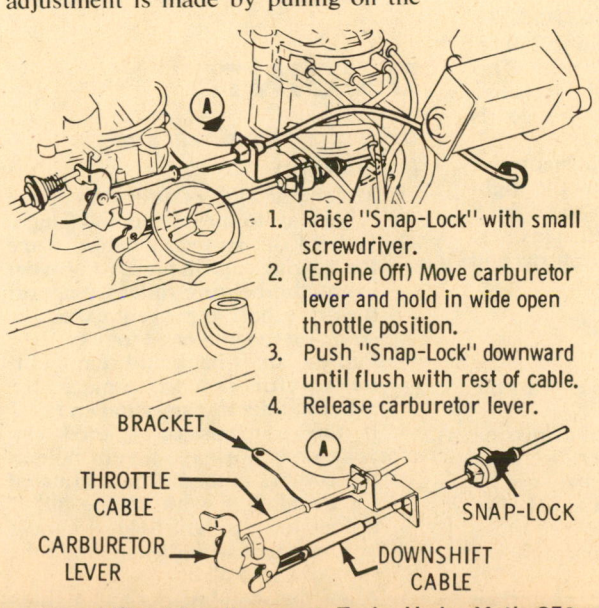

1. Raise "Snap-Lock" with small screwdriver.
2. (Engine Off) Move carburetor lever and hold in wide open throttle position.
3. Push "Snap-Lock" downward until flush with rest of cable.
4. Release carburetor lever.

Downshift cable adjustment, Turbo Hydra-Matic 350 —Omega V8 (© Oldsmobile Div., GM Corp.)

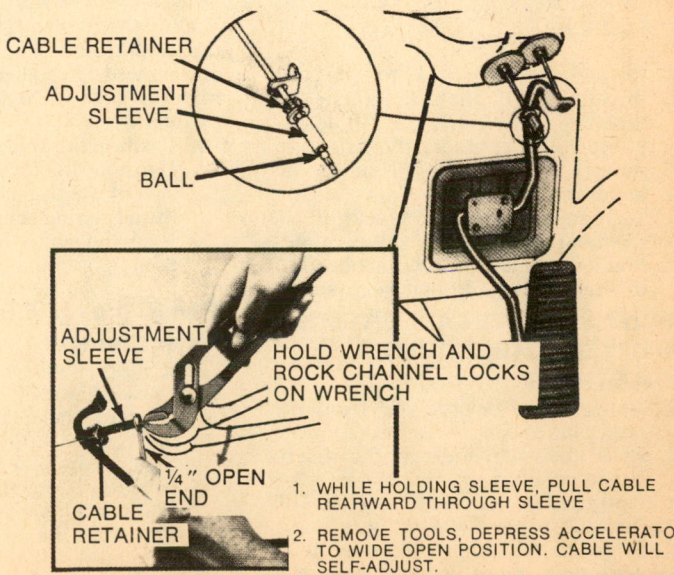

1. WHILE HOLDING SLEEVE, PULL CABLE REARWARD THROUGH SLEEVE.
2. REMOVE TOOLS, DEPRESS ACCELERATOR TO WIDE OPEN POSITION. CABLE WILL SELF-ADJUST.

Downshift cable adjustment, Turbo Hydra-Matic 350—Cutlass V8 (© Oldsmobile Div., G.M. Corp.)

end of the cable inside the car with pliers, while holding the adjusting sleeve in place, then floorboarding the accelerator with the engine off.

TURBO HYDRA-MATIC 375, 400

The downshift switch is adjusted by pushing the switch plunger forward until it is flush with the switch housing, then floorboarding the accelerator with the engine off.

Diesel Engine Transmission Linkage Adjustments

NOTE: *Before making any linkage adjustments, check, and if necessary, adjust the timing.*

THROTTLE ROD ADJUSTMENT

1. If equipped with cruise control, remove the clip from the control rod, then remove the rod from the bellcrank.
2. Remove the throttle valve cable (THM200) or detent cable (THM350) from the bellcrank.
3. Loosen the locknut on the throttle rod, then shorten the rod several turns.

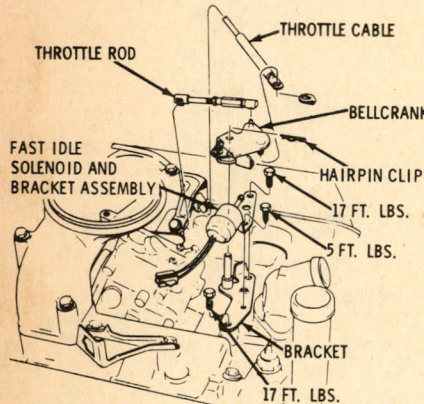

Throttle Linkage (© Oldsmobile Div., G.M. Corp.)

4. Rotate the bellcrank to the full throttle stop, then lengthen the throttle rod until the injection pump lever contacts the injection pump full throttle stop. Release the bellcrank.
5. Tighten the throttle rod locknut.
6. Connect the throttle valve or detent cable and cruise control rod to the bellcrank. Adjust if necessary.

THROTTLE VALVE CABLE (THM200) OR DETENT CABLE (THM350 ADJUSTMENT

1. Remove the throttle rod from the bellcrank.
2. Push the snap lock to the disengaged position.
3. Rotate the bellcrank to the full throttle stop and hold it there.
4. Push in the snap lock until it is flush with the cable end fitting. Release the bellcrank.
5. Reconnect the throttle rod.

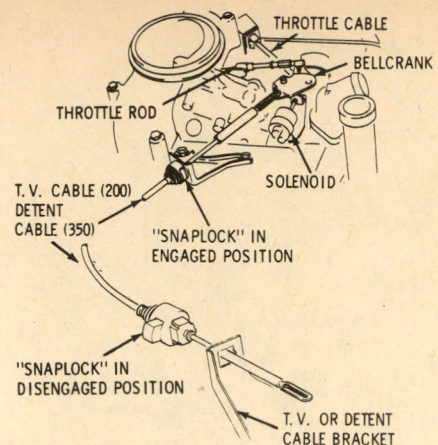

Throttle valve cable adjustment (© Oldsmobile Div., G.M. Corp.)

TRANSMISSION VACUUM VALVE ADJUSTMENT

1. Remove the throttle rod from the bellcrank.
2. Loosen the transmission vacuum valve attaching bolts just enough to disengage the valve from the injection pump shaft.
3. Hold the injection pump lever against the full throttle stop.
4. Rotate the valve to the full throttle position then insert a .090 inch pin to hold the valve in the full throttle position.
5. Rotate the assembly clockwise untill the injection pump lever is contacted.
6. While holding the assembly in contact with the lever, tighten the two bolts holding the vacuum valve to the pump, remove the pin and release the lever, and reconnect the throttle rod to the bellcrank.

Turbo Hydra-Matic 250 Intermediate Band Adjustment

Only the Turbo Hydra-Matic 250 requires periodic band adjustment. This adjustment is required at fluid change intervals, or whenever slippage is evident.

1. Position the shift lever in Neutral.
2. Loosen the locknut on the right side of the transmission and tighten the adjusting screw to 30 in lbs.
3. Back the screw out three turns and then tighten the locknut.

Pan Removal, Fluid and Filter Change

The fluid should be drained with the transmission warm.

1. Support the Starfire transmission at the vibration damper. Remove the crossmember. This may not be necessary on the Turbo Hydra-Matic 200.
2. Prepare a large pan to catch the transmission fluid.
3. Loosen all the pan screws, then pull one corner down to drain most of the fluid.

4. Remove the pan screws and empty out the pan. The pan can be cleaned out with solvent but it must be dried thoroughly before replacement. Be very careful not to leave any lint or threads from rags in the pan.
5. Remove the filter or strainer retaining bolt (two on Turbo Hydra-Matic 250, 350 and 375B). A reuseable strainer is used on the Turbo Hydra-Matic 200 and 250. The strainer may be cleaned in solvent and air-dried thoroughly. Filters are to be replaced.
6. Assemble a new O-ring and filter to the intake pipe on the Turbo Hydra-Matic 375 and 400. Use a new gasket on all other models.
7. Install the new filter or cleaned strainer.
8. Install the pan with a new gasket. Tighten the bolts evenly (12 ft. lbs.) in a criss-cross pattern.
9. Replace the Starfire crossmember.
10. Add DEXRON or DEXRON II transmission fluid through the dipstick tube. Add 4 qts for Turbo Hydra-Matic 250, 3 for all others.
11. Start the engine and let it idle. Do not race the engine. Shift through all the indicator positions, holding the brakes. Check the fluid level with the engine idling in Park. The level should be between the two dimples on the dipstick, about 1/4 in. below the ADD mark. Add fluid as necessary.
12. Check the fluid level after the car has been driven enough to thoroughly warm up the transmission. The level should be at the FULL mark on the dipstick. If the transmission is overfilled, the excess must be drained off. Overfilling causes aerated fluid, resulting in transmission slippage and probable damage.

U-JOINTS

Driveshaft Removal and Installation

1. Matchmark the relationship of the driveshaft to the differential flange.
2. Unbold the straps or flange. Tape the bearing caps in place to prevent losing the bearing rollers. Support the driveshaft to prevent excessive strain on the universal joints.
3. Pull the shaft back and remove it. Be careful not to damage the splines at the transmission end.
4. If the transmission splined slip yoke does not have a vent hole at the center, it should be lubricated for installation with engine oil. If it does have a vent hole, it should be lubricated with grease. Slide the slip yoke into place.
5. Align the matchmarks and tighten the bolts. Strap bolts should be tightened to 14 ft. lbs. through 1974

and 20 ft. lbs. for 1975 and later. Flange bolts should be tightened to 75 ft. lbs. through 1974 and 95 ft. lbs. for 1975 and later.

Universal Joint Overhaul

NOTE: *Some Omegas have a Spicer U-joint which will require removal of the retaining ring from the outer part of the yoke before bearing removal.*

1. If a press is not available, clamp the flange in a vise and, using a socket, press a bearing cap most of the way out of the flange.
2. Grasp the cap with pliers and remove it from the flange.
3. Press the remaining cap out of the flange.
4. On pressing out the caps, plastic retainers will be sheared. Prior to assembly make certain that all remnants are removed.
5. Thoroughly lubricate all parts.
6. Install the new spider in the flange and hand start one new cap. Using a 1-1/8 in. socket on the cap press the cap into the flange and over the spider using a strong vise. Be careful to avoid dropping any needle bearings.
7. Install the opposite cap in a similar manner.

Constant Velocity Joint Overhaul

NOTE: *CV joint overhaul requires a press. The job should not be attempted without one.*

1. Support the drive shaft in a horizontal position in line with the base plate of the press. The bearing cups should be removed in the order indicated.
2. Mark all yokes before disassembly.
3. Place the rear ear of the coupling yoke over a 1-1/8 in. socket. Place a cross press on the bearing cups in the flanged yoke. Press the bearing cup out of the coupling yoke ear. If the cup is not completely removed, insert a spacer and complete the removal.
4. Rotate the shaft 180°. Shear the opposite plastic retainer and press out the cup.
5. Disengage the trunnions of the spider, still attached to the flanged yoke, from the coupling yoke, and pull the flanged yoke and spider from the center ball on the ball support tube yoke.

NOTE: *Prior to 1973, the centering ball was not replaceable.*

6. Pry the seal from the ball cavity, remove the washers, spring and three shoes.

NOTE: *The joint between the shaft and coupling yoke can be serviced without disassembly of the joint between the coupling yoke and flanged yoke.*

7. To install, insert one bearing cup part way into one ear of the ball

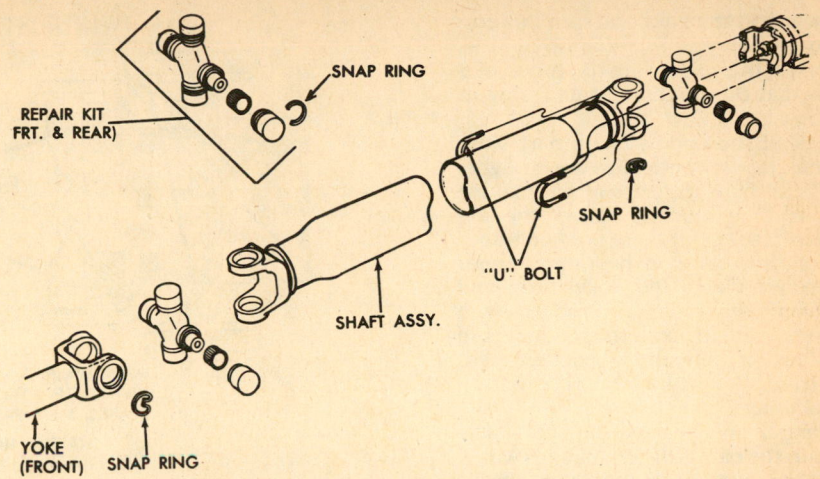

Typical driveshaft assembly (© Oldsmobile Div., G.M. Corp.)

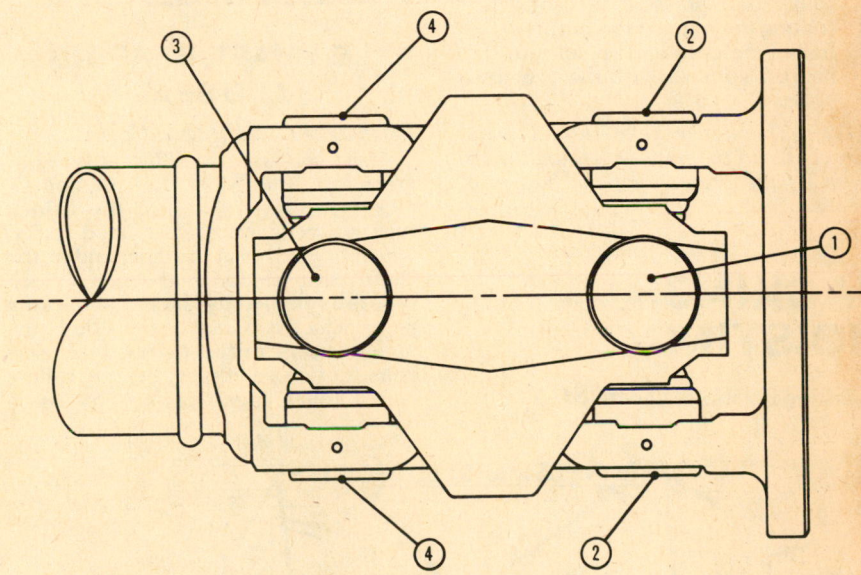

C.V. Joint disassembly sequence (© Oldsmobile Div., G.M. Corp.)

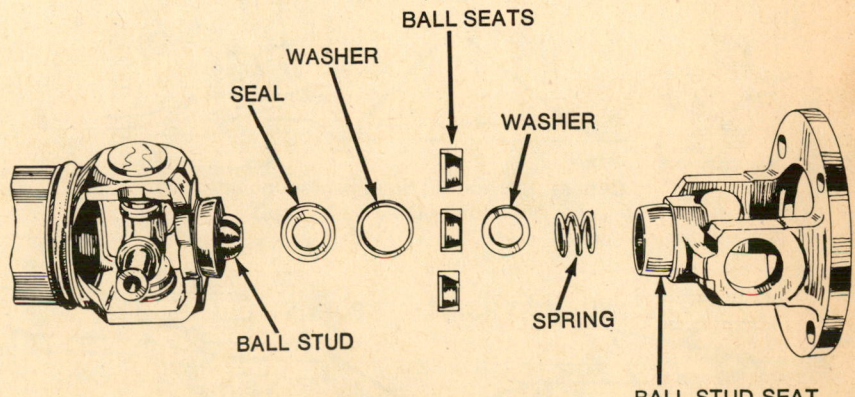

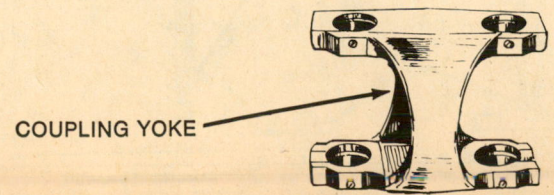

Constant velocity joint

support tube yoke and turn this cup to the bottom.

8. Insert the spider into the tube yoke so that the trunnion seats freely in the cup.

9. Install the opposite cup part way, making sure both cups are straight.

10. Press cups into position making sure they squarely engage the spider. Back off if there is a hang-up.

11. As soon as one bearing retainer groove clears the yoke, stop and install the retainer. Proceed with the other side until the retainer is in place. If difficulty is encountered, strike the yoke sharply with a hammer.

12. Install one bearing cup part way into the ear of the coupling yoke.

13. Make sure that alignment marks are matched.

14. Engage the coupling yoke over the spider and press in the cups, installing the retainers as before.

15. Install the cups and spider into the flanged yoke as with the previous yoke.

NOTE: *The flange yoke should snap over center to the right or left and up or down by the pressure of the ball seat spring.*

JACKING, HOISTING

Lifting Points are illustrated.

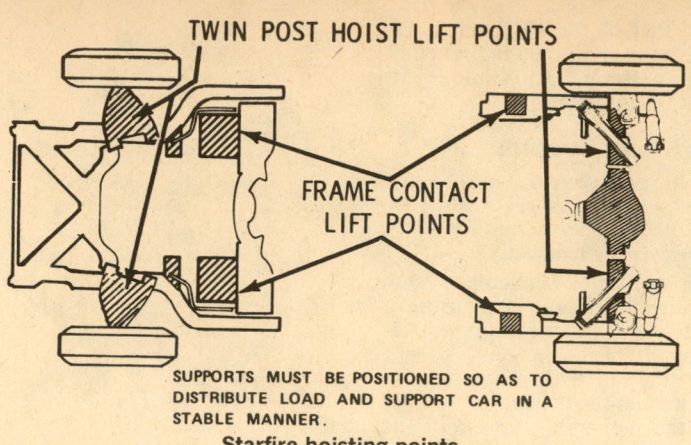

SUPPORTS MUST BE POSITIONED SO AS TO DISTRIBUTE LOAD AND SUPPORT CAR IN A STABLE MANNER.

Starfire hoisting points
(© Oldsmobile Div., GM Corp.)

REAR AXLE

AXLE, SHAFT, BEARING AND SEAL

Removal and Installation

These cars use two different types of drive axle, the C-lock and the non C-lock type. Axle shafts in the C-lock type are retained by C-shaped locks, which fit grooves at the inner end of the shaft. Axle shafts in the non C-lock type are retained by the brake backing plate, which is bolted to the axle housing. Bearings in the C-lock type axle consist of an outer race, bearing rollers and a roller cage, retained by snap-rings. The non C-lock type axle uses a unit roller bearing (inner race, rollers and outer race), which is pressed onto the shaft up to a shoulder. When servicing axles, it is imperative to determine the type.

NOTE: *All Starfires and Omegas use the C-lock axles. Other models may use either kind.*

NON C-LOCK TYPE

————— CAUTION —————

Before attempting any service to the drive axle or axle shafts, remove the axle carrier cover and visually determine if the axle shafts are retained by C-shaped locks at the inner end, or by the brake backing plate at the outer end. If the shafts are not retained by C-locks, proceed as follows.

Design allows for maximum axle shaft end-play of 0.022 in., which can be measured with a dial indicator. If end-play is found to be excessive, the bearing should be replaced. Shimming the bearing is not recommended as this ignores end-play of the bearing itself and could result in improper seating of the bearing.

1. Remove the wheel, tire and brake drum.

2. Remove the nuts holding the retainer plate to the backing plate. Disconnect the brake line.

3. Remove the retainer and install nuts, fingertight, to prevent the brake backing plate from being dislodged.

4. Pull out the axle shaft and bearing assembly, using a slide hammer.

5. Using a chisel, nick the bearing retainer in three or four places. The retainer does not have to be cut, merely collapsed sufficiently, to allow the bearing retainer to be slid from the shaft.

6. Press off the bearing and install the new one by pressing it into position.

7. Press on the new retainer.

NOTE: *Do not attempt to press the bearing and the retainer on at the same time.*

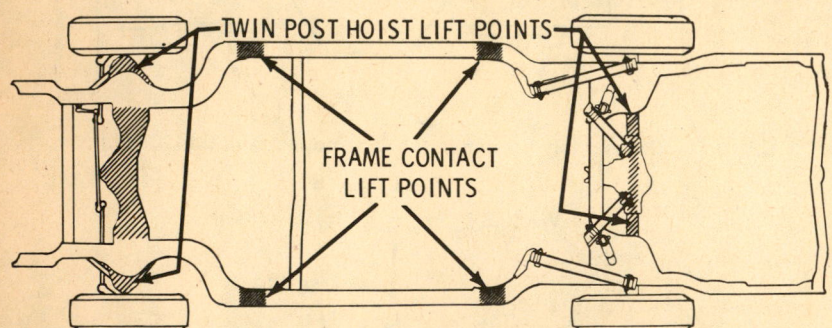

Cutlass, 88, and 98 hoist contact points
(© Oldsmobile Div., G.M. Corp.)

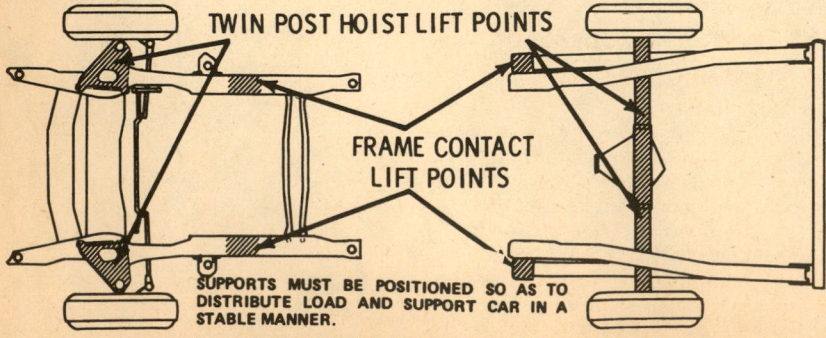

SUPPORTS MUST BE POSITIONED SO AS TO DISTRIBUTE LOAD AND SUPPORT CAR IN A STABLE MANNER.

Omega hoisting points (© Oldsmobile Div, G.M. Corp)

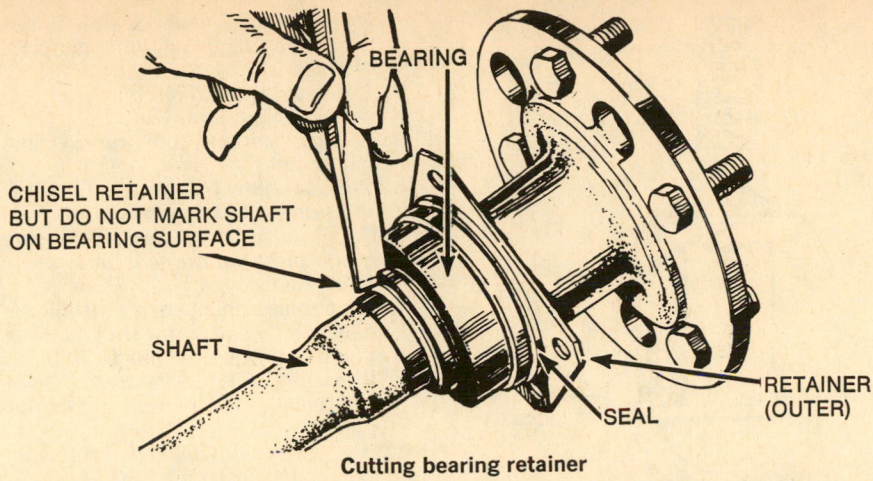

CHISEL RETAINER
BUT DO NOT MARK SHAFT
ON BEARING SURFACE

BEARING

SHAFT

SEAL

RETAINER
(OUTER)

Cutting bearing retainer

8. Assemble the shaft and bearing in the housing, being sure that the bearing is seated properly in the housing.
9. Install the retainer, drum, wheel and tire. Bleed the brakes.

C-LOCK TYPE

——— CAUTION ———

Before attempting any service to the drive axle or axle shafts, remove the carrier cover and visually determine if the axle shaft(s) are retained by C-shaped locks at the inner ends or by a brake backing plate at the outer end. If they are retained by C-shaped locks, proceed as follows.

1. Raise the vehicle and remove the wheels.
2. The differential cover has already been removed (see Caution above). Remove the differential pinion shaft lockscrew and the differential pinion shaft.
3. Push the flanged end of the axle shaft toward the center of the vehicle and remove the C-lock from the end of the shaft.
4. Remove the axle shaft from the housing, being careful not to damage the oil seal.
5. Remove the oil seal by inserting the button end of the axle shaft behind the steel case of the oil seal. Pry the seal loose from the bore.
6. Seat the legs of the bearing puller behind the bearing. Seat a washer against the bearing and hold it in place with a nut. Use a slide hammer to pull the bearing.
7. Pack the cavity between the seal lips with wheel bearing lubricant and lubricate a new wheel bearing with same.
8. Use a suitable driver and install the bearing until it bottoms against the tube. Install the oil seal.
9. Slide the axle shaft into place. Be sure that the splines on the shaft do not damage the oil seal. Make sure that the splines engage the differential side gear.
10. Install the axle shaft C-lock on the inner end of the axle shaft and push the shaft outward so that the C-lock seats in the differential side gear counterbore.
11. Position the differential pinion shaft through the case and pinions, aligning the hole in the case with the hole for the lockscrew.
12. Install the pinion shaft lockscrew.
13. Use a new gasket and install the carrier cover. Be sure that the gasket surfaces are clean before installing the gasket and cover.
14. Fill the axle with lubricant to the bottom of the filler hole.
15. Install the brake drum and wheels and lower the car. Check for leaks and road test the car.

FRONT SUSPENSION

Shock Absorber Replacement

1. Remove the two bolts and lockwashers securing the shock to the lower control arm.
2. Remove the upper nut, retainer, and grommet from the shock.

NOTE: *On Starfires, remove the access plug from the inner fender panel first.*

3. To install, reverse the removal procedure.

NOTE: *Purge new shock absorbers of air by repeatedly extending in their normal position and compressing while inverted.*

Lower Ball Joint Inspection

CUTLASS THROUGH 1973, 1972 88 AND 98

1. Jack up the car and place floor stands under the left and right control arms as near as possible to the lower ball joints. Make sure the car sits steadily on the floor stands.
2. Position a dial indicator so that its button contacts the inside lip of the wheel rim.
3. Place a 2 x 4 (about 6 in. tall) vertically between the lower control arm and the steering knuckle. Insert a pry bar between the wood and the steering knuckle nut and pry gently up and down. The dial indicator reading must not exceed .125 in. and there should be no deflection on the 88 and 98 models. Repeat this procedure for the other side.
4. After completing this vertical check, remove the wood block and reposition the dial indicator button to contact the outer lip of the wheel rim.
5. Push in on the top of the tire while pulling out on the bottom and observe the dial indicator reading. Reverse this push-pull procedure and check the reading. This procedure (horizontal check) enables you to check both upper and lower ball joints. The gauge reading should not exceed .125 in.
6. Do the same on the other side.

1973-74 OMEGA

NOTE: *The lower ball joint used on the Omega is not internally preloaded but rather, is seated by the car's weight. Therefore, some looseness may be apparent when the lower control arm is raised with a jack; this looseness does not necessarily mean that the joint is defective or worn.*

1. Use a jack placed underneath the lower control arm to support vehicle weight.
2. Measure the distance between the grease fitting and the threaded stud.
3. Raise the tire by means of a lever, to seat the ball stud, and measure the distance again.
4. If the difference between the two measurements is greater than 1/16 in., the ball joint is worn and should be replaced.
5. Shake the wheel and observe the end of the stud or the nut on the knuckle boss for *excessive* looseness. Replace any parts which are defective.

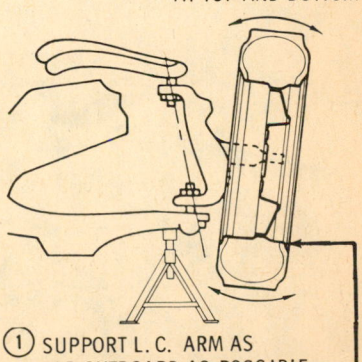

③ ROCK WHEEL IN AND OUT AT TOP AND BOTTOM

① SUPPORT L.C. ARM AS FAR OUTBOARD AS POSSIBLE.

② POSITION DIAL INDICATOR TO CHECK MOVEMENT AT THIS POINT

Ball joint horizontal check
(© Oldsmobile Div, G.M. Corp)

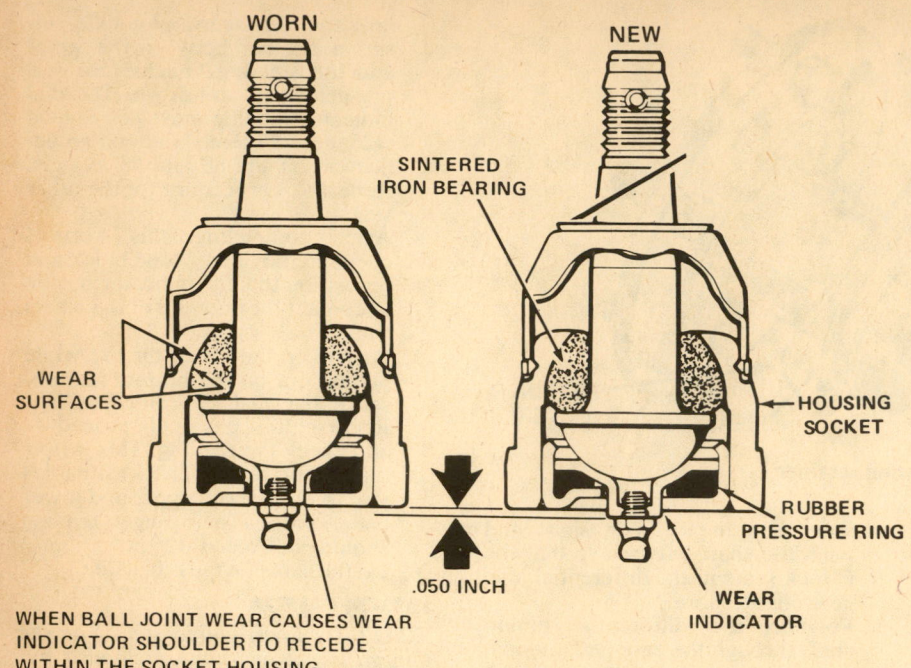

1973 and later Oldsmobile ball joint wear indicator

WHEN BALL JOINT WEAR CAUSES WEAR INDICATOR SHOULDER TO RECEDE WITHIN THE SOCKET HOUSING REPLACEMENT IS REQUIRED

1973-74 88 AND 98, 1974 CUTLASS AND ALL 1975 AND LATER MODELS

These lower ball joints contain a visual wear indicator. The lower ball joint grease plug screws into the wear indicator which protrudes from the bottom of the ball joint housing. As long as the wear indicator extends out of the ball joint housing, the ball joint is not worn. If the tip of the wear indicator is parallel with, or recessed into the ball joint housing, the ball joint is defective.

Lower Ball Joint Removal and Installation

1. Raise car and support the frame with floor stands.
2. Remove the tire and wheel.
3. Place a floor jack under the control arm spring seat.

CAUTION

Leave the jack under the spring seat during removal and installation, in order to keep the spring and control arm positioned.

4. Remove the cotter pin from the ball joint stud and, using a ball joint stud removal tool, separate the ball joint from the steering knuckle.
5. Raise the control arm to relieve tension and remove the stud nut.
6. If the backing plate blocks removal of the ball joint, loosen the backing plate bolts to obtain the necessary clearance.
7. Hold the brake assembly out of

way by placing a wooden block between the frame and the upper control arm.
8. Using a screwdriver or chisel, remove the ball joint seal.
9. Using a suitable tool, remove the ball joint.
10. Press in a new ball joint until it bottoms on the lower control arm.

NOTE: *On disc brake cars, make sure the grease purge on the seal faces away from the brakes.*

11. On Cutlass and Omega install the ball joint stud into the steering knuckle, torque the nut to 70 ft lbs (through 1973) or 95 ft lbs (1974 and later), and install the cotter pin.

NOTE: *Always advance the ball stud nut to align the cotter pin hole.*

12. On 88 and 98, reassemble the suspension and torque the ball joint stud nut to 90 ft lbs (through 1974) or to 105 ft lbs (1975 and later). Install the cotter pin and bend it to the side of the nut. On the Starfire tighten the nut to 65 ft lbs.
13. If applicable, tighten the backing plate bolts.
14. Install the ball joint fitting and lube until grease appears at the seal.
15. Install the tire and wheel assembly.

Upper Ball Joint Inspection

To inspect the upper ball joints, follow Steps 1 and 4-6 of the Cutlass through 1973, 1972 88 and 98 lower ball joint inspection procedure.

Upper Ball Joint Removal and Installation

1. Raise the front of car and place floor stands under the lower control arm between the spring seats and the ball joints.

CAUTION

Leave the jack under the spring seat during removal and installation, in order to keep the spring and control arm positioned.

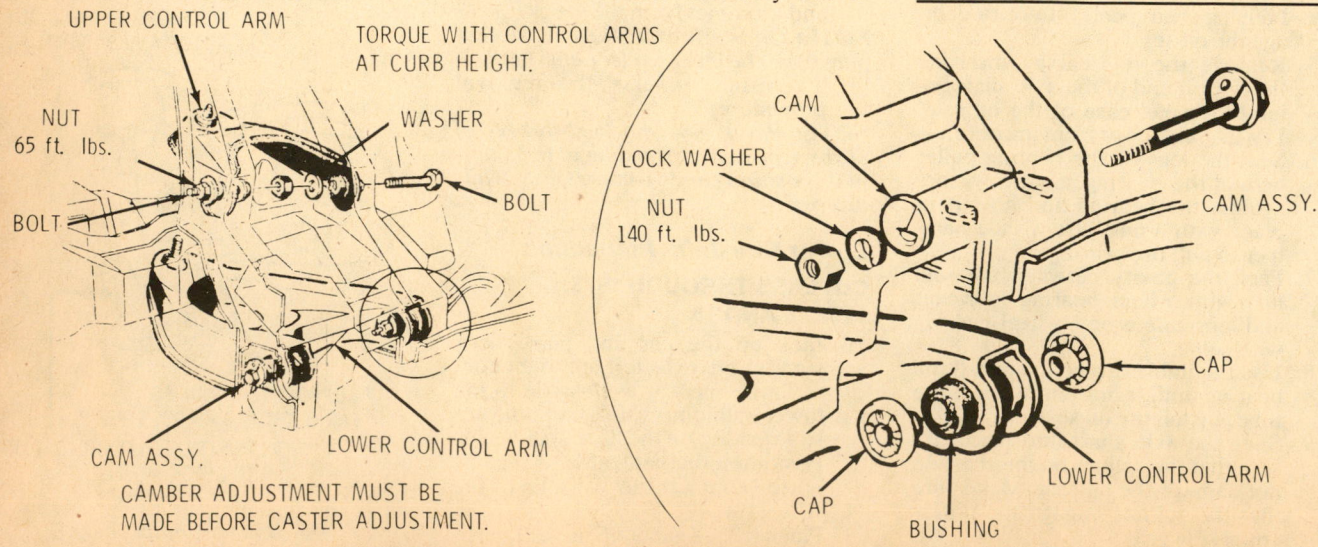

Starfire front suspension (© Oldsmobile Div., GM Corp.)

2. Remove the wheel.
3. Remove the cotter pin from the upper ball joint stud and loosen the upper ball joint nut.
4. Using a ball joint remover tool, break the stud loose and remove the nut and pull the stud out of the knuckle. Support the steering knuckle to prevent damage to the brake line.
5. Using a 1/8 in. diameter drill bit, drill into each of the four rivet heads a depth of 1/4 in.
6. Drill off the rivet heads with a 1/2 in. diameter bit.
7. Punch out the rivets and remove the ball joint.
8. To install, place the new ball joint in the upper control arm and secure it with four bolts and nuts. Tighten the nuts to 8 ft. lbs.
9. Connect the ball joint to steering knuckle. Torque the nut to 40 ft. lbs. minimum (through 1974) or to 70 ft. lbs. (1975 and later). On Starfires, 35 ft. lbs. (min).

NOTE: *When replacing ball joints, use only high-quality replacement parts and bolts and nuts specified to be strong enough to endure the stress. Always advance the ball stud nut to align the cotter pin hole.*

10. Install the grease fitting and lubricate until grease appears at the seal.
11. Install the speedometer cable (if so equipped) and the wheel.

Upper Control Arm Removal and Installation

1. Raise car and place stands under frame.
2. Remove tire and wheel.
3. Place floor jack under lower control arm spring seat.

CAUTION

Leave the jack under the spring seat during removal and installation, in order to keep the spring and control arm positioned.

4. Remove ball joint stud from steering knuckle, by removing cotter pin and nut and pressing joint loose from knuckle. Support hub assembly to prevent damage to the brake line.
5. Loosen the pivot shaft-to-frame nuts and remove the alignment shims. Support hub assembly and remove upper arms by sliding shaft off end of bolts. On Starfires, remove the pivot bolts and remove the control arm from the car; there are no shims.

NOTE: *Mark or locate alignment shims for easier reassembly.*

6. It is necessary to remove upper control arm attaching bolts to gain clearance to remove arm assembly.
7. Remove control arm from car.
8. To reinstall, position bolts loosely in frame and install pivot shaft on bolts.

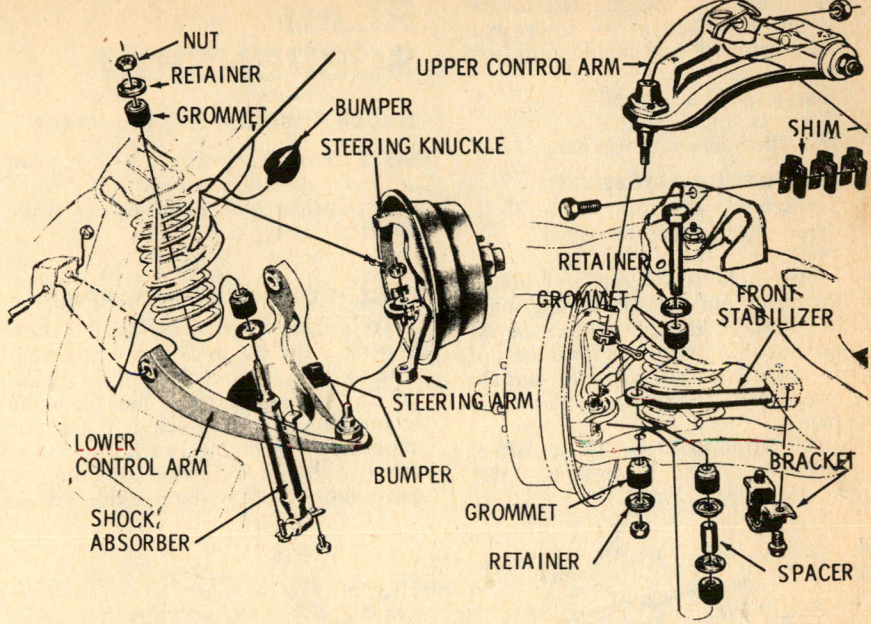

Front suspension—88 and 98 (© Oldsmobile Div, G.M. Corp)

9. Install lock washers and nuts and with brass drift, drive attaching bolts into frame.
10. Install alignment shims (except Starfire) placing them in position from which they were removed. Torque nuts, 80 ft. lbs. for all models except 1972 Cutlass. Torque to 50 ft. lbs. for 1972 Cutlass. Torque to 65 ft. lbs. on Starfire.
11. Connect ball joint stud and torque to specifications.
12. Install wheel and tire and lower car to floor.

Lower Control Arm and/or Spring Removal and Installation

1. Raise front of car and support by stands under frame.
2. Remove tire and wheel.
3. Disconnect stabilizer link from lower arm, if so equipped.

4. Remove shock absorber.
5. Place floor jack under lower arm, between spring and seat and ball joint. Using a spring compressor, compress spring.
6. Disconnect lower control arm ball joint from knuckle.
7. Slowly lower floor jack until spring is fully extended and remove spring.
8. To reinstall, tape insulator to top of spring.
9. While holding spring and insulator against pilot in front cross bar, tilt spring so it will pivot in lower arm. Rotate spring so bottom coil will index with edge of hole in arm spring seat. Spring should not cover any portion of hole.
10. With floor jack positioned between seat and ball joint, raise arm until ball joint is tight in knuckle. Install

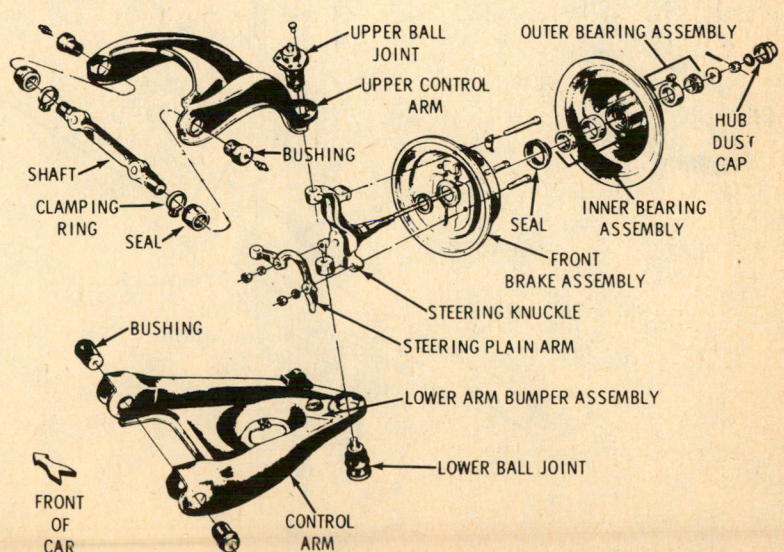

Front suspension, Cutlass (Omega similar) (© Oldsmobile Div., G.M. Corp.)

ball joint nut and tighten to the torque specified in the lower ball joint removal and installation procedure.

11. Install shock absorber.
12. Connect stabilizer link.
13. Install wheel and lower car.

Wheel Bearing Adjustment

1. Tighten the adjusting nut to 30 ft. lbs., while turning the wheel.
2. Back off on the nut 1/2 turn.
3. Finger-tighten the nut and install the cotter pin or the retaining ring.

NOTE: *If the cotter pin cannot be installed, back off on the nut until the slot aligns with the serrations on the nut. Do not back off on the nut more than 1/24 of a turn.*

4. Once adjusted, the front wheel bearings should have 0.001-0.008 in. end-play.

REAR SUSPENSION

Shock Absorber Replacement

NOTE: *Purge new shock absorbers of air by repeatedly extending in their normal position and compressing while inverted.*

EXCEPT OMEGA AND STARFIRE

To replace the rear shock absorber, first raise the car and support the rear axle to prevent stretching of the brake hose. Then remove the nut from the lower end of the shock and tap the shock free from the bracket. To disconnect the shock at the top, remove the bolt or bolts and remove the shock.

OMEGA AND STARFIRE

1. Raise the vehicle and support the rear axle housing.
2. Remove the lower shock mounting bolt from the shock absorber eye.
3. Unfasten the upper mounting bracket bolts and remove the shock.
4. Installation is the reverse of removal, except that the upper attaching bolts should remain loose while the lower (eye) is being tightened.

Coil Spring Replacement

1. Raise the rear axle housing on a floor jack and raise and support the rear frame on jackstands.
2. Disconnect the bottom shock absorber mounts.
3. Disconnect the brake line.
4. Detach the upper suspension arms at the axle housing. Lower the axle housing until the springs are completely extended.
5. Remove the springs. Reverse the procedure for installation. Torque the upper suspension arms to 70 ft. lb. with the car resting on the wheels.

NOTE: *If a spring compressor is used, the suspension arms need not be detached.*

Leaf Spring Replacement

88 WAGON THROUGH 1977

1. Lift the rear of the car by the axle housing and support the car on floor stands.
2. Loosen the tailpipe and resonator if you are removing the right-side spring.
3. Remove the lower shock absorber nut and move the shock out of the way.
4. Relax the springs by lowering the lift or jack. Leave the jack under the housing for support.
5. Remove the bolts and shackles from the rear of the spring.
6. Remove the U-bolt attaching nuts.
7. Remove ONLY the nut from the front spring attachment and, while holding the spring up, remove the bolt from the front of the spring and remove the spring.
8. Remove the insulators and shim from the spring.
9. To install, reverse the removal procedure.

OMEGA

1. Raise the rear of the car on stands.
2. Support the rear axle to take its weight off the springs.
3. Disconnect the bottom of the shock absorber.
4. Loosen the front spring eye bolt.
5. Unbolt the spring front bracket from the underbody.
6. Lower the axle slightly and remove the front bracket from the spring.
7. Pry the parking brake cable out of its retainer bracket on the axle spring mounting plate.

Coil spring rear suspension—except Starfire   (© Oldsmobile Div., GM Corp.)

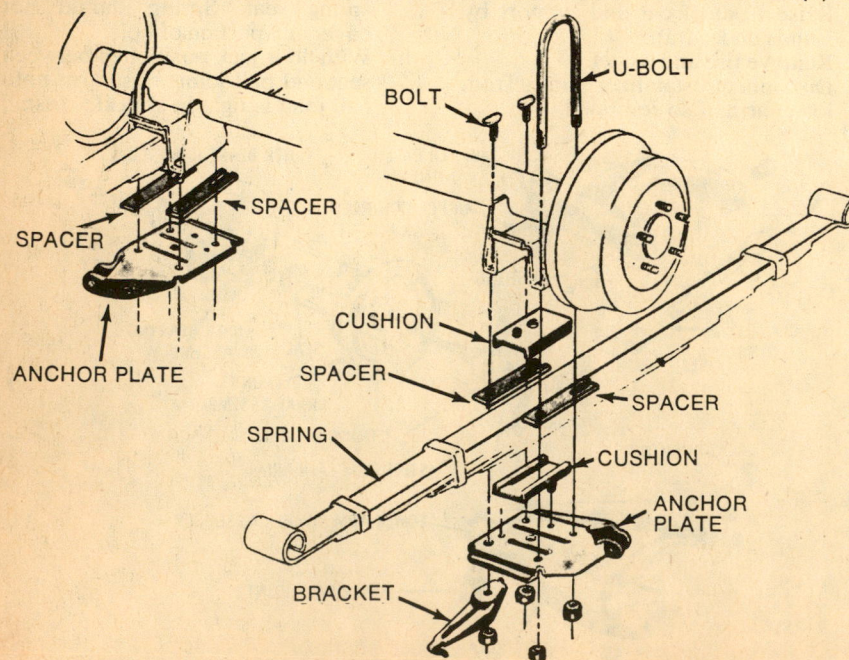

Omega leaf spring rear suspension—Custom Cruiser similar
(© Oldsmobile Div, G.M. Corp)

8. Unbolt the spring from the axle.
9. Remove the spring plate and cushion between the axle and the spring.
10. Remove the lower bolt from the rear spring shackle. Lower the spring.
11. On installation, attach the front bracket to the spring eye. The head of the bolt should be toward the center of the car.
12. Assemble the shackle loosely to the rear spring eye.
13. Raise the rear end of spring and install the lower shackle bolt loosely, making sure that the parking brake cable goes under the spring.
14. Raise the front end of the spring and loosely attach the front bracket to the underbody. Make sure that the bracket tab goes into its slot.
15. Make sure that the upper and lower spring cushions are aligned properly. The upper one has locating ribs and the lower one, a locating dowel.
16. Install the spring lower mounting plate over the locating dowel and loosely install the nuts. Don't forget the parking brake cable bracket.
17. Attach the bottom of the shock absorber.
18. Attach the parking brake cable to the bracket on the lower spring plate.
19. Let the vehicle weight down on the springs. Tighten all the bolts. Torques are: rear shackle bolts—40-60 ft. lbs., front bracket screws—25-35 ft. lbs., front eye bolt—65-80 ft. lbs., and axle bolts—35-50 ft. lbs.

BRAKES

Information on brake adjustments, lining replacement, bleeding procedure, master and wheel cylinder overhaul is in the Unit Repair Section.

Parking Brake Adjustment
1. Apply the parking brake exactly one click on Starfire, two clicks on 1978-79 cars except Starfire, two clicks on 1972-77 Omega and three clicks on 1972-77 cars except Omega and Starfire.
2. Loosen the locknut at the rear of the equalizer adjusting nut. On all except Starfire, tighten the adjusting nut until the rear wheels can barely be turned backward (using two hands) but lock up when moved forward. Tighten the nut against the adjusting nut. On Starfire, tighten the adjuster until a slight drag is felt at the rear wheels.
3. With the parking brake disengaged the rear wheels should turn freely in either direction with no brake drag.

A brake pad with a warning indicator that squeals when the pad is worn to service limits is used on all 1974 and later models with disc brakes

Master Cylinder Removal and Installation
NOTE: *Be sure that the area where the master cylinder is mounted is clean, before beginning removal.*
1. Disconnect and cap or plug hydraulic lines.
2. If there is no power booster unit, remove the pushrod-to-pedal clevis pin.
3. Remove the attaching bolts and master cylinder.
4. Install in the reverse order of removal. Fill with fluid and bleed.

Power Brake Unit Removal and Installation

1972-75
The master cylinder and power booster are removed as a unit. Disconnect vacuum and hydraulic lines. Disconnect the pushrod from the brake pedal. Remove the vacuum unit mounting stud nuts and remove the assembly. Install in the reverse order of removal, tightening the mounting nuts to 28 ft. lbs. Fill the master cylinder reservoir with fluid.

1976-79
1. Remove the two nuts holding the master cylinder to the power unit. Position the master cylinder out of the way. It is not necessary to disconnect the brake lines. On Starfire also remove the distribution pipe and switch mounting bolt before moving the master cylinder.
2. Disconnect the vacuum hose from the vacuum check valve on the front housing. Plug the hose. On Diesel engined cars, disconnect the three hydraulic lines from the power cylinder. Plug the lines immediately.
3. Loosen the four nuts that hold the

power unit to the firewall.
4. Disconnect the pushrod from the brake pedal.
5. Remove the four mounting nuts and lift the power unit off the studs.
6. Installation is the reverse of removal. Torque the mounting studs to 24 ft. lb. On Diesel engined models, refill the power steering reservoir. See Power Steering Pump Removal and Installation for system bleeding.

STEERING

— CAUTION —
Some 1974-76 models have the A.C.R.S. system (air bags). Special servicing information and safety precautions for these cars are given in the Buick car section.

Tie Rod End Removal
1. Raise and support the car.
2. Remove the cotter pins from the ball studs and remove the castellated nuts.
3. Disconnect the tie rod end from the steering arm or knuckle with a ball joint separator.
4. Remove the inner ball stud from the intermediate rod with a puller. Mark the tie rod end position before removal.
5. Loosen the clamp bolts and unscrew the ends from the adjuster tubes. If a force of more than 7 ft. lb. is required to remove the ends after breakaway, the fasteners should be replaced.
6. Clean and inspect all parts. When installing, run the tie rod end to the position marked. Torque the ball stud nuts to 40 ft. lbs.

Steering Wheel Removal and Installation

EXCEPT TILT AND TELESCOPE MODELS
1. Disconnect the battery ground cable.
2. Remove the round center cap horn button by pulling out. If the center horn bar has screws at the back of the wheel spokes, remove them and lift it off. If there are no screws, pull down and out on the horn bar to remove.
3. Detach the horn contact wire.
4. Remove the shaft spring clip on 1975 and later models.
5. Remove the steering wheel nut. If there are no alignment marks, make some.
6. Remove the steering wheel with a puller.
7. Align the marks on replacement. Torque the nut to 35 ft. lbs.

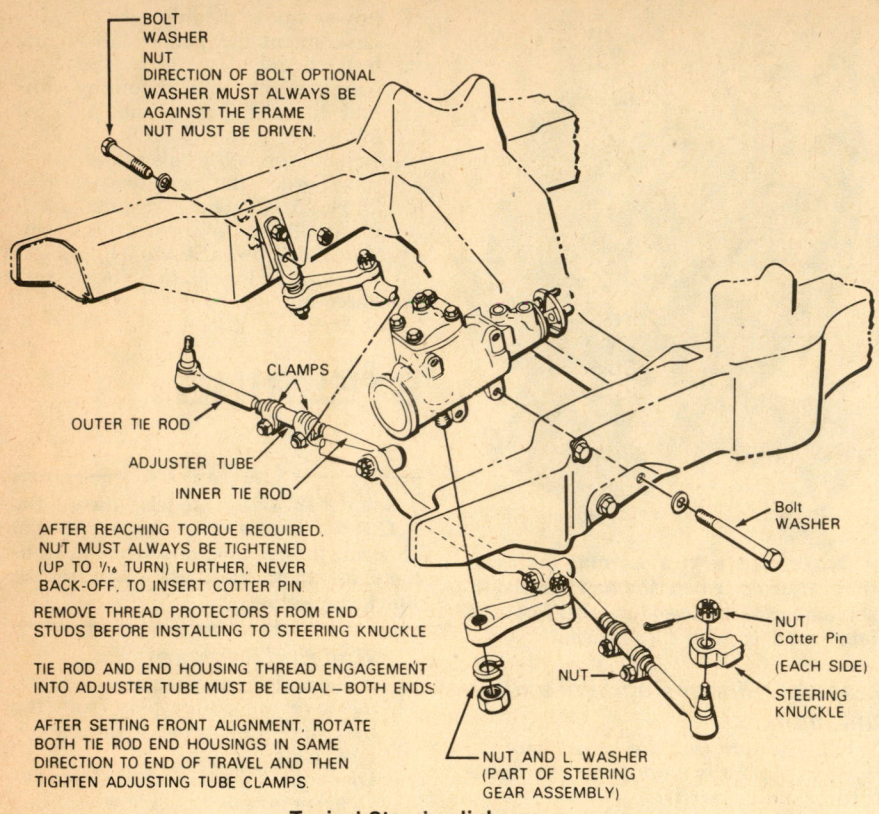

BOLT
WASHER
NUT
DIRECTION OF BOLT OPTIONAL
WASHER MUST ALWAYS BE
AGAINST THE FRAME
NUT MUST BE DRIVEN.

CLAMPS

OUTER TIE ROD

ADJUSTER TUBE

INNER TIE ROD

AFTER REACHING TORQUE REQUIRED,
NUT MUST ALWAYS BE TIGHTENED
(UP TO 1/16 TURN) FURTHER, NEVER
BACK-OFF, TO INSERT COTTER PIN.

REMOVE THREAD PROTECTORS FROM END
STUDS BEFORE INSTALLING TO STEERING KNUCKLE.

TIE ROD AND END HOUSING THREAD ENGAGEMENT
INTO ADJUSTER TUBE MUST BE EQUAL—BOTH ENDS.

AFTER SETTING FRONT ALIGNMENT, ROTATE
BOTH TIE ROD END HOUSINGS IN SAME
DIRECTION TO END OF TRAVEL AND THEN
TIGHTEN ADJUSTING TUBE CLAMPS.

Bolt
WASHER

NUT
Cotter Pin
(EACH SIDE)

STEERING
KNUCKLE

NUT

NUT AND L. WASHER
(PART OF STEERING
GEAR ASSEMBLY)

Typical Steering linkage
(© Oldsmobile Div., GM Corp.)

--- CAUTION ---

Do not hammer on the steering shaft. The energy-absorbing column will be damaged and require replacement.

TILT AND TELESCOPE MODELS

1. Disconnect the battery ground.
2. Remove the three pad attaching screws, lift off the pad assembly and disconnect the horn wire.
3. Push the locking lever counterclockwise to full release.
4. Mark the plate assembly where the two attaching screws attach the plate assembly to the locking lever and remove the two screws.
5. Unscrew and remove the plate assembly. Remove the steering wheel nut.
6. Using a puller, remove the steering wheel.
7. Install a 5/16 in. × 18 set screw into the upper shaft at the full extended position and lock.
8. Install the steering wheel, aligning the scribe mark on the hub with the slash mark on the end of the shaft.

Make sure that the attached end of the upper horn contact assembly is seated flush against the top of the horn contact assembly.

9. Install the steering wheel nut and torque to 30 ft. lb. The remainder of the installation is the reverse of removal. Remove the set screw after steering wheel installation.

Turn Signal Switch Replacement
EXCEPT TILT AND TELESCOPIC COLUMN

1. Disconnect the battery.
2. Remove the steering wheel.
3. Remove the cover from the shaft. Plastic keepers under the cover are not necessary for installation.
4. Depress the lockplate and remove the snap-ring from the shaft.
5. Remove the lockplate and cancelling cam.
6. Remove the upper bearing preload spring.
7. Remove the turn signal lever.
8. Remove the four-way flasher knob.
9. Remove the three screws from the switch.
10. Disconnect the turn signal connector from the wiring harness.

NOTE: *On 1975 and later models, it will be necessary to perform Steps 10 through 13 of Turn Signal Switch Replacement/Tilt and Telescope Column, before proceeding with the next step.*

11. Tape the turn signal wires at the connector and carefully remove the turn signal switch, wiring, and protector from the column as a unit.
12. To install, reverse the removal procedure using a new shaft snap-ring. When replacing screws (especially cover screws), make sure they are of the same size.

TILT AND TELESCOPIC COLUMN

1. Disconnect negative battery cable.
2. Remove the steering wheel.

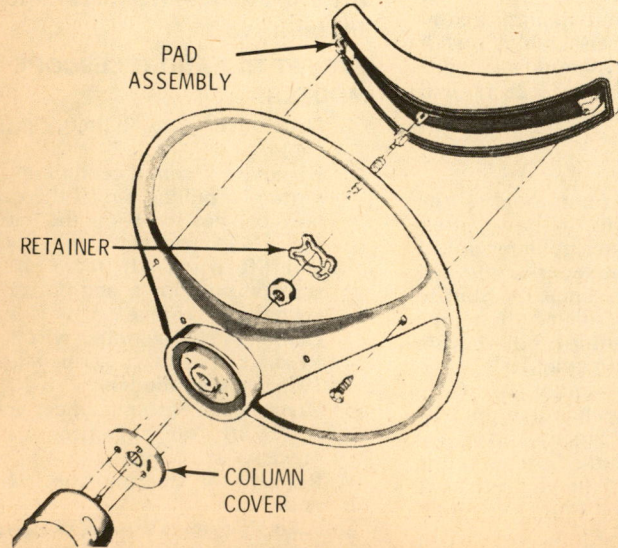

PAD
ASSEMBLY

RETAINER

COLUMN
COVER

Standard steering wheel (© Oldsmobile Div., G.M. Corp.)

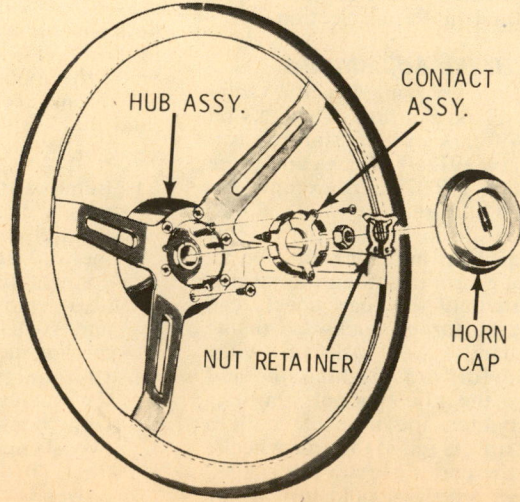

HUB ASSY.

CONTACT
ASSY.

NUT RETAINER

HORN
CAP

Sport steering wheel
(© Oldsmobile Div., G.M. Corp.)

3. Remove the screws and lift the cover from the shaft. Plastic keepers are not necessary for installation.
4. Compress the lockplate and pry the snap-ring from shaft.
5. Remove the lockplate and cancelling cam.
6. Remove the upper bearing preload spring.
7. Remove the turn signal lever and the four-way flasher knob.
8. Lift up on the tilt lever and position the housing in its central position.
9. Remove the switch attaching screws.
10. Remove the lower trim cap from the instrument panel and disconnect the turn signal connector from the harness.
11. Remove the four bolts securing the bracket assembly to the jacket.
12. On cars (except Starfire) with automatic transmission, loosen the screw holding the shift indicator needle and disconnect the clip from the link.
13. Remove the two nuts from the column support bracket while holding the column in position. Remove the bracket assembly and wire protector from the wiring, then loosely install the bracket-to-support column.
14. Tape the turn signal wires at the connector to keep them flat and parallel.
15. Carefully remove the turn signal switch and wiring from the column.
16. To install, reverse the removal procedure, making sure that screws of the same size are used.

Power Steering Pump Removal and Installation
1. Remove the drive belt.
2. Use a puller to remove the pump pulley.
3. Detach and cap the hoses.
4. Remove the pump and mounting bracket.
5. Reverse the procedure for installation. Bleed the system of air by turning the wheels from side to side without hitting the stops, with the wheels off the floor and the engine running.

Ignition Switch and/or Lock Cylinder Replacement

IGNITION SWITCH
1. Disconnect negative battery cable.
2. Place ignition in Off-Unlocked, or Acc (tilt wheel).
3. Remove toe pan cover (if applicable) and loosen toe clamp bolts.
4. Remove lower instrument panel trim and toe pan trim panel.
5. Remove automatic transmission shift indicator needle.
6. Remove steering column instrument panel bracket and let steering wheel rest on the driver's seat.

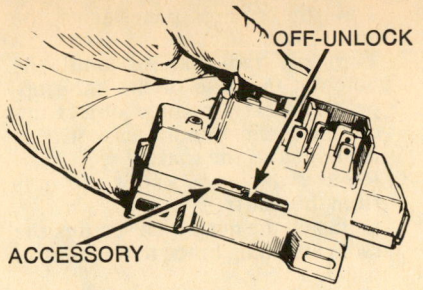

MOVE SWITCH SLIDER TO EXTREME LEFT (ACCESSORY) POSITION THEN MOVE SLIDER TO DETENTS TO THE RIGHT OF "OFF-UNLOCK"

Ignition switch in Off-Unlocked position

7. Remove two switch attaching screws and lift switch off actuator rod.
8. Disconnect wiring.
9. To install, check that lock cylinder is still in Off-Unlocked or Acc (tilt wheel), and move sliding portion of switch until switch hole is positioned correctly. Hold the switch in this position with a 0.090 in. pin.
10. Connect the wiring to the switch.
11. Position switch over actuator rod, install attaching screws and remove the 0.090 in. pin.
12. Reverse Steps 1 through 6 to complete installation.

LOCK CYLINDER
1. Disconnect the negative battery cable.
2. Remove the steering wheel. See the special procedure for cars equipped with air bags.
3. On models equipped with a tilt and travel steering column, pry up the three tabs on the plastic lock cover.
4. On models with a standard or tilt column remove the three screws that attach the lock cover and remove it. The plastic keepers on the underside of the cover can be discarded after the cover is removed.
5. Depress the steering wheel lock plate and pry the snap-ring from the steering shaft.
6. Remove the lock plate, cancelling cam, and upper bearing spring.
7. Position the turn signal lever in the right turn position and unscrew the turn signal lever.
8. Push the hazard warning knob in and unscrew the knob.
9. Remove the turn signal switch retaining screws and pull the switch up out of the way.
10. Turn the key to the Run position.
11. Insert a long thin screwdriver into the slot in the upper bearing housing and depress the release tab while pulling the cylinder from the column.
12. Insert the new lock cylinder into the column after aligning the key on the cylinder with the keyway in the column.

13. Press inward on the cylinder while turning it clockwise.
14. Reverse the procedure to complete installation.

INSTRUMENT PANEL

Headlight Switch Replacement

ALL CUTLASS AND OMEGA; 88 AND 98 THROUGH 1973
1. Disconnect the battery.
2. On 88 and 98 models through 1973 and 1973 and later Cutlass models with air conditioning remove the left-hand control panel from the dash. On 1973 and later Cutlass without air conditioning, remove the column trim cover.
3. Pull the switch to ON position, then depress the spring-loaded button on the switch body and pull knob out of the switch.
4. Remove the escutcheon.
5. Remove the switch from behind the panel and disconnect the multiple connector.
6. Install in the reverse order of the above procedure.

STARFIRE
1. Disconnect the negative (—) battery lead.
2. Remove the left-hand bottom air conditioning outlet or panel lower insulator as necessary.
3. Working underneath the dash, depress the switch shaft retainer. Remove the shaft and knob assembly.
4. Unfasten the switch bezel nut and remove the switch.
5. Disconnect the switch multiconnector by prying it with a small screwdriver at the side of the switch.
6. Installation is the reverse of removal.

1974 AND LATER 88 AND 98
1. Disconnect the negative (—) battery lead.
2. Remove the heater/AC control assembly from the panel, but don't disconnect its leads and vacuum lines.
3. Remove the bezel nut from the switch.
4. Pull the switch out through the heater/AC control opening.
5. Disconnect the wiring and remove the switch.
  Installation is the reverse of removal.

Speedometer Cable Removal and Installation
   The speedometer cable is retained at the rear of the speedometer head by a quick release clip. To remove the cable, reach up behind the speedometer and depress the clip while pushing in, then pulling back on the cable. The ca-

ble may then be pulled from the firewall and into the engine compartment. Raise the car and support it on stands. Disconnect the cable from the transmission and remove the core. When replacing the core, coat all but the top 1/3 with speedometer cable lubricant. Cable replacement is the reverse of removal.

WINDSHIELD WIPERS

Motor Removal and Installation

1. Remove the cowl screen or grille.
2. Loosen the linkage drive link-to-crankarm attaching nuts, and remove the link from the arm.
3. Disconnect the wiring and washer hoses.
4. Remove the three motor attaching screws, guide the crankarm through the hole in the dash, and remove the motor.
5. Reverse the steps to install.

Wiper Blade Replacement

Depending on model and availability, one of three methods is used:
  a. a tab on the arm saddle is depressed.
  b. a spring type blade clip is depressed.
  c. a coil spring retainer is depressed with a screwdriver.

RADIO

Removal and Installation

1972 CUTLASS

1. Disconnect battery.
2. If equipped with air conditioning, remove cool air manifold if necessary.
3. Remove defroster manifold if necessary.
4. Remove radio knobs, washers or rear speaker control.
5. Remove radio attaching nuts and escutcheons.
6. Disconnect all wiring and antenna lead-in.
7. Remove radio support bracket attaching screw(s), if applicable.
8. Remove radio from rear of instrument panel.
9. Install by reversing removal procedure.

88 AND 98 THROUGH 1973

1. Disconnect the negative battery cable.
2. Unfasten the nut which secures the radio to its mounting brace.
3. Detach the speaker and antenna leads from the radio.
4. Unfasten the radio ground strap screw.
5. Use a thin-bladed screwdriver to carefully pry out the map and flood light lens assembly.
6. Unfasten the four right-hand control panel securing screws. With-

draw the control panel from the dash.
7. Turn the radio knobs until the notch at the base of the knob appears. Insert a pointed object under the retainer and release it. Pull the knobs off the shafts.
8. Remove the inside knobs and nuts from the shafts.
9. Unfasten the nut which secures the radio attaching brace to the control panel.
10. Installation is the reverse of removal.

1973 AND LATER CUTLASS

1. Detach the cable from the negative battery terminal.
2. Remove the four screws which secure the steering column cover and separate it from the instrument panel.
3. Pull the knobs off the radio.
4. Unfasten the nuts from the front of the radio.
5. Remove its four retaining screws and then gently pull the right-hand control panel up and out.
6. Unfasten the radio support bracket screw.
7. Remove the four ashtray housing screws and take the housing off the tie-bar.
8. Disconnect the antenna and speaker wiring from the radio.
9. Remove the radio from behind the control panel.
10. Installation is the reverse of removal.

1974 AND LATER 88 AND 98

1. Disconnect the negative (−) cable from the battery. Remove the lower trim panel on 1976 models, and the right trim panel on 1977 and later models.
2. Detach the wiring harness and antenna lead from the radio.
3. On 1974-75 models, unfasten the throttle cable and remove the accelerator linkage, complete with support bracket.
4. Remove the screw which secures the radio bracket to the tie-bar.
5. Pull the knobs off the shafts and unfasten the securing nuts from the shafts.
6. Lower the radio and remove it from behind the dash panel.
7. Installation is the reverse of removal.

1975 STARFIRE

1. Disconnect the battery.
2. Remove the clock set knob.
3. Remove the screws securing the instrument cluster bezel and remove the bezel.
4. Remove the glove compartment.
5. Remove the screws securing the instrument panel crash pad and remove the pad.
6. Pull the knobs off the radio shafts and unfasten the shaft retaining nuts.
7. Remove the two bottom screws from the radio bracket.

8. On models with A/C, remove the left lap cooler and duct.
9. Remove the two steering column bracket nuts and lower the column so that it rests on the driver's seat. Remove the screw which secures the cluster to the carrier, from the steering column bracket.
10. Unfasten the instrument cluster screws, wiring, speedometer cable, and pull the cluster out toward the driver's seat.
11. Remove the lower radio support-to-dash screw.
12. Working through the cluster opening, remove the radio leads and antenna cable.
13. Remove the radio.
14. Installation is the reverse of removal.

1976 AND LATER STARFIRE

1. Disconnect the battery ground cable.
2. Pull off the knobs and bezels.
3. Remove the shaft nuts and washers.
4. Remove the panel lower insulator assembly.
5. Detach the antenna lead from the back of the radio.
6. Remove the heater outlet duct on air conditioned cars.
7. Remove the two screws holding the radio to the panel brace.
8. Lower the radio, detach the speaker and power leads, and remove the mounts from the radio.
9. Reverse the procedure for installation.

OMEGA

1. Disconnect the battery.
2. Remove the knobs, washers, trim plate and nuts.
3. Disconnect the wiring.
4. Remove the radio.
5. Installation is the reverse of removal.

HEATER

Blower Motor and Heater Core Removal and Installation without Air Conditioning

OMEGA

To remove the heater case and core, remove the glovebox. Disconnect the wiring, vacuum lines and defroster hoses from the heater case. Drain the radiator enough so that the heater hoses can be disconnected. Remove the blower assembly attaching screws and remove the heater case from inside the car. Remove the heater core from the case. Install in the reverse of the removal procedure.

To remove the blower motor, disconnect the blower feed wire. Remove the fender filler panel bolts and move the filler panel forward and inward. Remove the blower assembly attaching nuts and screws. Push the heater case studs back so that they do not protrude through the firewall. Push down on the inner fender panel and remove the blower assembly. Remove the blower motor attaching screws and remove the blower. When installing, use a bead of sealer around the heater inlet.

88 AND 98 THROUGH 1976

To remove the heater case and core, disconnect the battery and remove the four heater case to firewall attaching nuts. Drain the radiator enough so that the heater hoses may be disconnected. Disconnect the control cables and vacuum hose. Remove the defroster duct and case attaching screw and the right half of the right hand dash trim panel. Remove the heater case from the car. The heater core may now be removed from the case. Install in reverse order of removal.

To remove the blower motor on models through 1974, disconnect the battery and remove the right front wheel. Remove the canister or battery. Remove the three filler plate to radiator support screws, the filler plate to wheelhouse attaching screws and the filler plate. Remove the blower attaching screws and the connector. Remove the blower. Installation is the reverse of the removal procedure.

To remove the blower motor on 1975 and later models, cut a flap through the inner fender for access. Seal the flap securely after installation.

1977 AND LATER 88 & 98

1. Disconnect the battery ground.
2. Disconnect the blower wiring.
3. Unbolt (6 bolts) the motor and remove it from the case.
4. Disconnect the heater core ground strap.
5. Drain the cooling system and disconnect both core hoses.
6. Remove the seven case-to-plenum screws and remove the case.
7. Remove the core shroud and lift out the core.
8. Installation is the reverse of removal. Replace any sealer damaged during removal.

CUTLASS

To remove the heater blower and inlet assembly, remove the right front fender filler panel. Disconnect the blower motor wiring. Remove the attaching nuts and screws and remove the heater assembly. The blower motor may be removed from the inlet assembly by removing the attaching screws. Installation is the reverse of the removal procedure.

To remove the core from the heater case, drain the radiator, disconnect the heater hoses and remove the attaching nuts. On 1972 models to gain access to the lower nut it will be necessary to disconnect the right fender at the bottom and wedge it away from the body. Disconnect the wiring and the three control cables and remove the case assembly from the firewall. Remove the

core retainer and core. Install in reverse of the above procedure.

STARFIRE

NOTE: *To remove only the blower motor, perform Steps 1 through 4. Skip Step 3.*

1. Disconnect the battery ground cable.
2. Disconnect the blower motor lead wire.
3. Place a pan under the vehicle. Disconnect the heater hoses at the core connections and secure the ends of the hoses in a raised position.
4. Remove the blower intake to firewall screws and nuts and remove the blower intake, blower motor and wheel as an assembly.
5. Remove the core retaining strap screws and remove the core from the vehicle.
6. To install, reverse removal.

NOTE: *Be sure that the blower intake sealer is intact, replace if necessary.*

Blower Motor Removal and Installation with Air Conditioning

88 AND 98 THROUGH 1974

1. Raise the car and remove the right front wheel and tire.
2. Remove the charcoal canister.
3. Unfasten the bolts which attach the radiator supports to the filler panel.
4. Remove the wheel arch securing bolts.
5. Take the right-hand wheel arch filler panel off.
6. Unfasten the blower motor mounting screws, remove the motor and disconnect its wiring.
7. Installation is the reverse of removal.

1975-76 88 AND 98

1. Remove the right front wheel.
2. Cut a flap for access through the inner fender.
3. Remove the blower motor mounting screws and remove the motor.
4. Reverse the procedure for installation. Seal the flap securely.

1977 AND LATER 88 & 98

The blower motor is mounted in the upper evaporator and blower case, by 6 screws (7 with noise suppressor). Disconnect the electrical connectors and remove the screws. Lift the blower straight up to remove.

OMEGA

The blower motor removal procedure for A/C equipped Omega models is similar to that for those models without A/C, except that the fender fill panel must be unbolted and moved forward and inward.

CUTLASS

NOTE: *On 1972 models it is necessary to remove the fender fill panel.*

1. Disconnect the battery ground.
2. Disconnect the blower wiring.
3. Unbolt and remove the motor.
4. Installation is the reverse of removal. Replace any damaged sealer.

1975-76 STARFIRE

NOTE: *This procedure requires discharging and charging the A/C system. Do not attempt it unless you have the special tools and knowledge necessary to perform this task.*

1. Disconnect the battery.
2. Disconnect the blower relay.
3. Carefully discharge the refrigerant from the system. There may be enough clearance to get the blower motor by the A/C line on 1976 and later models. If so, discharging is not necessary.
4. Disconnect the O-ring and the A/C lines.
5. Remove the screws securing the blower motor. Remove the motor.
6. Installation is the reverse of removal. Apply a bead of sealer to the flange before installing the blower motor. Recharge the A/C system.

1977 AND LATER STARFIRE

1. Disconnect the battery ground.
2. Disconnect the relay.
3. Unbolt and remove the blower motor.
4. Reverse for installation. Replace any damaged sealer.

Heater Core Removal and Installation with Air Conditioning

88 AND 98 THROUGH 1973

1. Working inside the car, remove the air distribution hoses from the heater box. Hoses are sometimes held in place by staples. There are also tabs that snap into holes in the end of the hoses.
2. Remove the manifold from the front of the heater box. It is held in place by two screws and a tab.
3. Disconnect the wiring, vacuum hoses, and cables.
4. Disconnect the defroster manifold from the top of the heater box.
5. Working from outside the car, drain the radiator and disconnect the heater hoses.
6. Remove the heater box stud nuts and remove the heater box from the firewall.
7. Remove the heater core from the heater box.
8. Reverse the steps to install.

1974-76 88 AND 98

1. Drain the radiator.
2. Remove the heater case securing nuts. Disconnect the heater hoses.
3. Remove the instrument panel trim pad.
4. Remove the heater case-to-firewall bolts from inside the car.

5. Remove the bottom air duct.
6. Remove the instrument panel crash pad. Unfasten the leads from the clock and glovebox light.
7. Remove the upper right-hand trim panel.
8. Separate the air distribution manifold and defroster duct from the heater case.
9. Remove the lower dash trim panel.
10. Lift out the heater case and disconnect the hoses and cables from it.
11. Remove the core from the case.
12. Installation is the reverse of removal.

1977 AND LATER 88 & 98
1. Disconnect the battery ground.
2. Disconnect the blower wiring.
3. Remove the thermostatic switch and diagnostic connector.
4. Remove the right end of the hood seal and the air inlet screen screws.
5. Remove the 5 case - to - firewall screws at the top, 9 upper case-to-lower case screws at the flange and two more at the plenum.
6. Lift the upper case straight up and off.
7. Disconnect and lift out the heater core.
8. Installation is the reverse of removal. Replace any damaged sealer.

CUTLASS THROUGH 1976
1. Working inside the car, remove the defroster adapter from the upper right side of the heater box.
2. Remove the manifold attached to the front of the heater box. It is secured by two screws and a metal tab. Remove the glovebox, first, if necessary.
3. Disconnect the vacuum hoses, cables, and wiring.
4. Working outside the car, drain the radiator and disconnect the heater hoses from the heater core.
5. Remove the nuts from the heater box studs and remove the heater box.
6. Remove the heater core from the heater box.
7. Reverse the steps to install.

1977 CUTLASS
1. Disconnect the battery ground.
2. Drain the cooling system.
3. Remove the glovebox and the center A/C manifold.
4. Remove the radio and the lower defroster duct bolt.
5. Disconnect the vacuum hoses and the temperature cable.
6. Disconnect the heater hoses and remove the heater-to-firewall attaching bolt inside the car and four nuts in the engine compartment.
7. Remove the heater case and separate the halves.
8. Lift out the core.
9. Installation is the reverse of removal. Replace any damaged sealer.

1978-79 CUTLASS
1. Drain the cooling system.

2. Disconnect the hoses at the core pipes.
3. Remove the retaining bracket and ground strap.
4. Remove the module rubber seal.
5. Remove the module screen.
6. Remove the right windshield wiper arm.
7. Remove the diagonal connector, high blower relay and thermostatic switch mounting screws.
8. Disconnect all electrical connections at the module.
9. Remove the module top cover.
10. Lift out the core.
11. Installation is the reverse of removal. Replace all insulation.

OMEGA
1. Disconnect the battery and drain the cooling system.
2. Detach the upper heater hose at the core tube.
3. Remove all accessible heater core and case securing nuts.
4. Unfasten the right-hand front fender filler panel bolts and lower the panel, in order to gain access to the lower heater hose clamp.
5. Unfasten the hose clamp and detach the hose from the lower heater core tube.
6. Unfasten the lower nut which secures the right-hand heater case/core assembly.
7. Plug both of the core tubes to prevent coolant from leaking.
8. Remove the glovebox and its door.
9. Take the vacuum diaphragm assembly off the right-hand kick-panel.
10. Remove the outlet from the bottom of the heater case.
11. Separate the cold air duct from the heater case.
12. Unfasten the screws which secure the extension to the heater case. Remove the extension from the case.
13. Detach the cables and the wiring from the case. Remove the core and case as an assembly.
14. Remove the core from the case.
15. Installation is the reverse of removal.

1975 STARFIRE
NOTE: *This procedure requires discharging and charging the A/C system. Do not attempt it unless you have the special tools and knowledge necessary to perform this task.*
1. Disconnect the battery.
2. Remove the glovebox.
3. Remove the right-hand air outlet duct.
4. Remove the instrument cluster bezel and the instrument panel crash pad.
5. Remove the left-hand air outlet deflector and feed duct.
6. Remove its retaining screws and lower the steering column so that it rests on the driver's seat.
9. Unfasten the instrument cluster screws, leads, speedometer cable,

and remove the cluster. Remove the radio.
10. Remove the defroster and center distribution ducts.
11. Carefully discharge the refrigerant from the system.
12. Place a container beneath them and then remove the heater hoses from the core pipes. Plug the hoses.
13. Clean the external surfaces and fittings of the VIR assembly.
14. Disconnect the compressor intake line, oil bleed line, and condenser outlet line. Plug all open connections.
15. Loosen the evaporator intake and outlet connections. Remove the VIR mounting clamp screw and remove the clamp. Slide the VIR off the evaporator outlet line and then off the intake line. Remove and throw all the old O-rings away. Plug all open connections.
16. Remove the heater distributor/case stud-to-firewall nuts. Remove the distributor/case assembly, after disconnecting all electrical leads and vacuum hoses from it.
17. Separate the heater case from the distributor and the core from the case.
18. Installation is the reverse of removal. Charge the A/C system and add coolant, as required.

1976 AND LATER STARFIRE
1. Disconnect the battery ground cable.
2. Remove the three nuts from the engine compartment side of the cover plate.
3. Disconnect the heater hoses and fasten them in a raised position to prevent coolant loss. Plug the core tubes.
4. Remove the heater floor outlet.
5. Remove the glove box and door.
6. Remove the right and left instrument panel outlets.
7. Unscrew and move the console back.
8. Remove the instrument panel pad. Remove the column nuts and let the wheel rest on the seat. Remove the instrument panel screws and lower the panel onto the steering column.
9. Remove the right instrument panel and lower outlet as an assembly.
10. Disconnect the vacuum hoses at the left end of the heater case.
11. Remove the modular duct to heater case screw and the two heater case to evaporator case screws. Pry off the retaining clips at the defroster outlets and move the duct back.
12. Pull the heater case away from the firewall until the core tubes clear, then disconnect the temperature cable.
13. Remove the core to case screws and remove the core.
14. Reverse the procedure for installation. Torque the steering column nuts to 25 ft lbs.

Oldsmobile Toronado

YEAR IDENTIFICATION

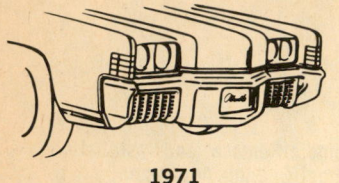
1971

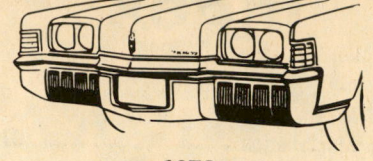
1972

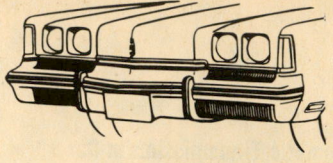
1973

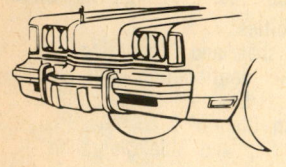
1974

1975

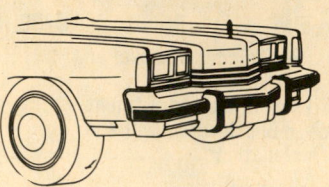
1976

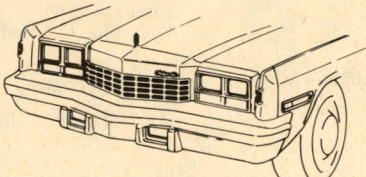
1977

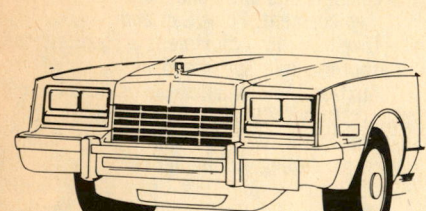
1978

1979

ENGINE IDENTIFICATION CODE

The following are VIN codes for Engine identification. The engine code is the fifth digit of the Vehicle Identification Number (VIN) located on a tag on the upper left corner of the instrument panel pad, visible through the windshield.

Disp	Bbl	'72	'73	'74	'75	'76	'77	'78	'79
8-350	4 turbo								
8-350	Diesel								N
8-403	4						K	K	
8-455	4	W	W	W	W	S			

GENERAL ENGINE SPECIFICATIONS

Year	Engine No. Cyl. Displacement Cu. In.	Carburetor Type	Horsepower @ rpm ■	Torque @ rpm (ft lbs) ■	Bore X Stroke (in.)	Compression Ratio	Oil Pressure @ 1500 rpm
'72	8-455	4 bbl	265 @ 4200	375 @ 2800	4.126 x 4.250	8.50:1	38
'73	8-455	4 bbl	250 @ 4000	375 @ 2800	4.126 x 4.250	8.50:1	38
'74	8-455	4 bbl	230 @ 3800	370 @ 2800	4.126 x 4.250	8.50:1	38
'75-'76	8-455	4 bbl	215 @ 3600	370 @ 2400	4.126 x 4.250	8.50:1	38
'77	8-403	4 bbl	200 @ 3600	330 @ 2400	4.351 x 3.385	8.0:1	38
'78	8-403	4 bbl	185 @ 3600	320 @ 2400	4.351 x 3.385	8.0:1	38
'79	8-350 Turbo	4 bbl	N.A.	N.A.	4.057 x 3.385	8.0:1	38
	8-350 Diesel		N.A.	N.A.	4.057 x 3.385	22.5:1	38

■ Beginning 1972, horsepower and torque are SAE net figures. They are measured at the rear of the transmission with all accessories installed and operating. Since the figures vary when a given engine is installed in different models, some are representative rather than exact.
N.A. Not available

TUNE-UP SPECIFICATIONS

When analyzing compression test results, look for uniformity among cylinders rather than specific pressures.

ENGINE		SPARK PLUGS		DISTRIBUTOR		IGNITION TIMING (deg) ▲ * Auto Trans	VALVES Intake Opens (deg) ●	Fuel Pump Pressure (psi)	IDLE SPEED (rpm) ▲ ● Auto Trans
Year	No. Cyl Displacement (cu in.)	Orig. Type	Gap (in.)	Point Dwell (deg)	Point Gap (in.)				
'72	8-455	46S	.040	28-32	.016	8B	20B	5½-6½	650/550
'73	8-455	R46S	.040	30	.016	8B	20B	5½-6½	650/550
'74	8-455	R46S	.040	30	.016	10B	20B	5½-6½	650/550
'74	8-455	R46SX	.080	Electronic		10B	20B	5½-6½	650/550
'75	8-455	R46SX	.080	Electronic		12B	20B	5½-6½	650/550 (650/600)②
'76	8-455	R46SX	.080	Electronic		14B(12B)	20B	5½-6½	650/550 (650/600)②
'77	8-403	R46SZ	.080	Electronic		24B(20B) @ 1100	16B	5½-6½	650/550(600)
'78	8-403	R-46SZ	.060	Electronic		20B(22B) @ 1100	16B	5.5-6.5	650/550(600)
'79	8-350	R-46SZ	.060	Electronic		③	16B	5.5-6.5	③

* Set timing with carburetor adjusted to 1100 rpm, unless sticker specifies otherwise.

▲ See text for procedure

● Where two figures appear separated by a slash, the first is idle speed with solenoid energized, the second is idle speed with solenoid disconnected. Figure in parentheses indicates California engine.

① Not used

② Solenoid energized (higher) idle speed is set with A/C on and compressor clutch wires disconnected.

③ See Underhood Sticker

B Before Top Dead Center

NOTE: Most 1979 GM carburetors have idle mixture screws concealed by staked-in plugs. These are not meant to be removed, except at carburetor overhaul.

FIRING ORDER

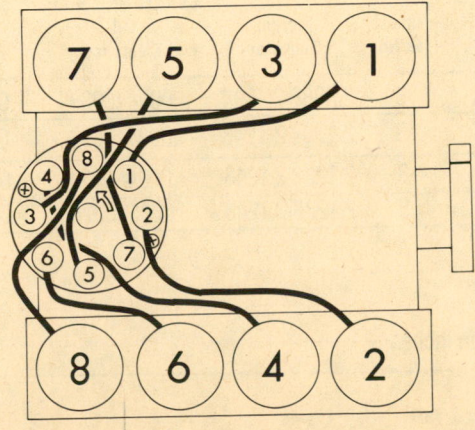

GM (Oldsmobile) 455 V8 (through 1974 w/point-type ignition)
Engine firing order: 1-8-4-3-6-5-7-2
Distributor rotation: counterclockwise

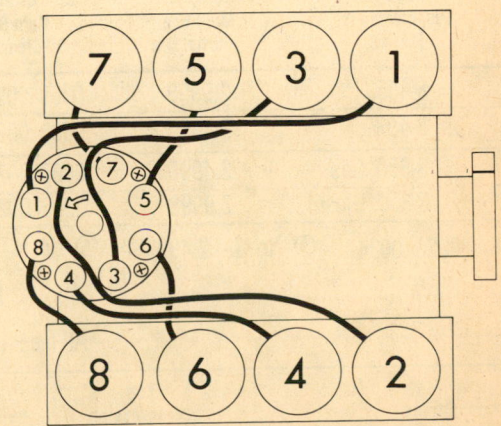

GM (Oldsmobile) 403, 455 V8 (1974 and later w/HEI)
Engine firing order: 1-8-4-3-6-5-7-2
Distributor rotation: counterclockwise

CAPACITIES

Year	ENGINE No. Cyl. Displacement (cu. in.)	Engine Crankcase Add 1 Qt For New Filter	TRANSMISSION Pts to Refill After Draining Automatic •	Drive Axle (pts)	Gasoline Tank (gals)	COOLING SYSTEM (qts) With Heater	With A/C	With Heavy Duty
'72	8-455	5	8	4	25	19.5	20	——
'73	8-455	5	8	4	26	19.5	20	——
'74	8-455	5	8	4	26	21	21.5	
'75-'76	8-455	5	8	4	26	21.5	21.5	
'77	8-403	4	8	4	26	17.2	17.2	
'78	8-403	4.75	8	4	26	17.5	17.5	17.25
'79	8-350 Gasoline	4	10	—	20	14.9	15.6	——
	8-350 Diesel	7.5	10	—	20	18.4	18.4	——

• Does not include torque converter

VALVE SPECIFICATIONS

Year	Engine No. Cyl. Displacement (cu in.)	Seat Angle (deg)	Face Angle (deg)	Spring Test Pressure (lbs @ in.)	Spring Installed Height (in.)	STEM TO GUIDE Clearance (in.) Intake	Exhaust	STEM Diameter (in.) Intake	Exhaust
'72	8-455	45	46	197 @ 1.23	1 $21/32$	.0010-.0027	.0015-.0032	.3429	.3424
'73	8-455	45	46	197 @ 1.23	1 $21/32$	.0010-.0027	.0015-.0032	.3429	.3424
'74	8-455	45	46	197 @ 1.23	1 $21/32$	.0010-.0027	.0015-.0032	.3429	.3424
'75-'76	8-455	45①	44①	187 @ 1.27	1 $39/64$	.0010-.0027	.0015-.0032	.3429	.3424
'77	8-403	45①	44①	187 @ 1.27	1 $43/64$	.0010-.0027	.0015-.0032	.3429	.3424
'78	8-403	45①	44①	187 @ 1.27	1 $43/64$	.0010-.0027	.0015-.0032	.3429	.3424
'79	8-350 Gasoline	45①	46①	187 @ 1.27	1 $43/64$	.0010-.0027	.0015-.0032	.3429	.3424
	8-350 Diesel	45①	46①	152 @ 1.295	1 $43/64$	.0010-.0027	.0015-.0032	.3429	.3424

① Exhaust valve seat 31°   Exhaust valve face 30°

CRANKSHAFT AND CONNECTING ROD SPECIFICATIONS

All measurements are given in inches

Year	Engine No. Cyl. Displacement (cu in.)	CRANKSHAFT Main Brg. Journal Dia	Main Brg. Oil Clearance	Shaft End-Play	Thrust on No.	CONNECTING ROD Journal Diameter	Oil Clearance	Side Clearance
'72-'76	8-455	2.9998	.0005-.0021①	.004-.008	3	2.4988-2.4998	.0004-.0033	.006-.020
'77-'78	8-403	2.4990②	.0005-.0021③	.004-.014	3	2.1238-2.1248	.0004-.0033	.006-.020
'79	8-350 Gas.	2.4990②	.0005-.0021③	.004-.014	3	2.1238-2.1248	.0004-.0033	.006-.020
	8-350 Diesel	2.9998	.0005-.0021③	.004-.014	3	2.1238-2.1248	.0005-.0026	.006-.020

① No. 5—.0020-.0034   ② No. 1—2.4993   ③ No. 5—.0015-.0031

RING GAP

All measurements are given in inches

Year	Engine	Top Compression	Bottom Compression
'72-'76	8-455	.010-.023	.010-.023
'77-'78	8-403	.010-.023	.010-.023
'79	8-350 Gas.	.010-.020	.010-.020
'79	8-350 Diesel	.015-.025	.015-.025

Year	Engine	Oil Control
'72-'76	8-455	.015-.055
'77-'78	8-403	.015-.055
'79	8-350 Gas.	.015-.055
'79	8-350 Diesel	.015-.055

RING SIDE CLEARANCE

All measurements are given in inches

Year	Engine	Top Compression	Bottom Compression
'72-'76	8-455	.0020-.0040	.0020-.0040
'77-'78	8-403	.0020-.0040	.0020-.0040
'79	8-350 Gas.	.0020-.0040	.0020-.0040
'79	8-350 Diesel	.0050-.0070	.0018-.0038

Year	Engine	Oil Control
'72-'76	8-455	.0021-.0031
'77-'78	8-403	.0006-.0096
'79	8-350 Gas.	.0006-.0096
'79	8-350 Diesel	None

PISTON CLEARANCE

Year	Engine	Piston-to-bore Clearance (in.)
'72-'76	8-455	.001-.002
'77-'78	8-403	.001-.002
'79	8-350 Gas.	.00075-.00175
'79	8-350 Diesel	.005-.006

TORQUE SPECIFICATIONS

All readings in ft lbs

Year	Engine No. Cyl. Displacement (cu in.)	Cylinder Head Bolts	Bearing Bolts Rod	Bearing Bolts Main	Crankshaft Bolt	Flywheel to Crankshaft Bolts	MANIFOLD Intake	MANIFOLD Exhaust
'72-'74	8-455	80	42	120	160	60	35	25
'75-'76	8-455	85	42	120	200-310	60	40	25
'77-'78	8-403	130②	42	80①	200-310	60	40	25
'79	8-350 Gas.	130	42	80①	310	60	40	25
'79	8-350 Diesel	130	42	120	310	60	40	25

① 120 on no. 5
② Bolts must be oiled

WHEEL ALIGNMENT SPECIFICATIONS

Year	CASTER Range (deg)	CASTER Pref Setting (deg)	CAMBER Range (deg)	CAMBER Pref Setting (deg)	Toe-in (in.)	Steering Axis Inclin. (deg)	WHEEL PIVOT RATIO (deg) Inner Wheel	WHEEL PIVOT RATIO (deg) Outer Wheel
'72-'74	1½N to 2½N	2N	¼N to ¾P① ¾N to ¼P②	¼P① ¼N②	0 ± 1/16	11	—	—
'75-'76	1N to 1P	0	¼N to ¾P① ¾N to ¼P②	¼P① ¼N②	0 ± 1/16	11	—	—
'77	½N to ½P	0	¼N to ¾P① ¾N to ¼P②	¼P① ¼P②	0 ± 1/16	11	—	—
'78	½N to ½P	0	1/5N to 4/5P① 4/5N to 1/5P②	1/3P 1/3N	0 ± 1/16	11	—	—
'79	2P to 3P	2½P	½N to ½P	0	0 ± 1/16	11	—	—

N Negative   P Positive

① Left side
② Right side

— Not specified

NOTE: Service procedures for the Charging System, Starting System, Ignition System, Fuel System, Cooling System, and Emission Controls on the Toronado can be found in the Oldsmobile section.

IGNITION SYSTEM

Distributor Removal and Installation 1977 and Later

See the Oldsmobile section for earlier models.

1. Remove spark plug cables and wire connectors from cap.
2. Remove the cap.
3. Crank the engine until the rotor points toward the rear of the engine and the No. 1 piston is almost at TDC.
4. Turn the engine until the crankshaft pulley timing mark is at 0. (The white mark on the side of the rotor will be aligned with the white pointer in the distributor.)
5. Remove the distributor clamp and pull the distributor from the block.
6. When installing, make sure that the timing marks are aligned at 0 and the rotor and pointer marks are aligned.

For all other 1977 and later timing and distributor service procedures, see the Emission Control Systems and Electronic Ignition Unit Repair Sections.

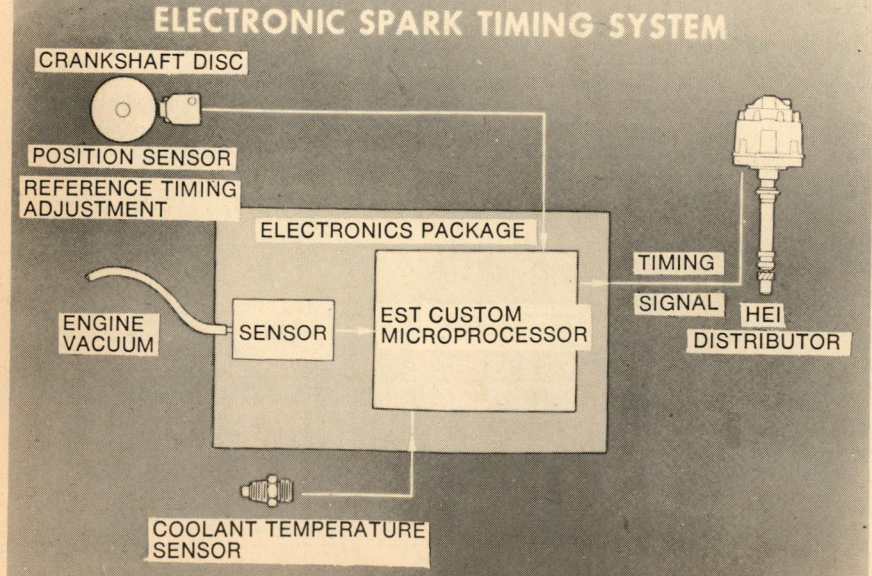

Electronic spark timing control system used on 403 V8 (© Oldsmobile Div., GM Corp)

ENGINE

NOTE: Any engine procedures not given here are the same as those in the Oldsmobile section.

ENGINE REMOVAL AND INSTALLATION

1. Drain radiator.
2. Remove hood, marking hinge for reassembly.
3. If equipped with a fan shroud, unhook the strap and remove the clips holding the seal to the venturi ring. Move the seal toward the radiator.
4. Disconnect battery.
5. Disconnect radiator hoses and cooler lines, heater hoses, vacuum hoses, engine to body ground strap, fuel hose from fuel pump,

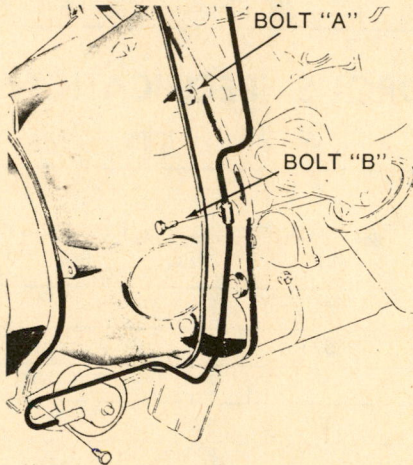

Transmission to engine attachment
(© Oldsmobile Div., G.M. Corp)

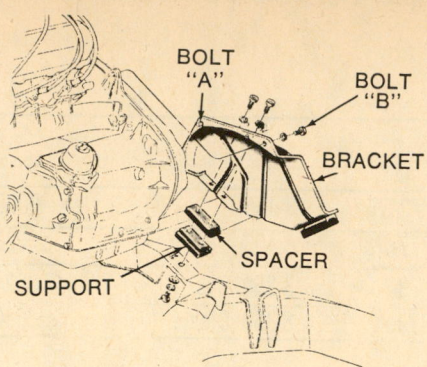

Engine mount attachment
(© Oldsmobile Div., G.M. Corp)

wiring and accelerator cable. Remove the air cleaner, hot air pipe, air conditioner compressor and power steering pump without disconnecting lines and set them aside.

6. Remove coil, throttle control switch bracket, radiator support and radiator.
7. Raise the car.
8. Disconnect exhaust pipes at manifold. Loosen, but do not remove, upper left flywheel cover attaching bolt (this will require $2^{3}/_{8}$ in. × 12 in. and $1^{3}/_{8}$ in. × 6 in. extensions with a $7/_{16}$ in. socket.
9. Disconnect wires and remove starter.
10. Remove torque converter cover and remove three bolts securing the converter to flywheel. Scribe marks on converter and flywheel for reassembly.
11. Support the final drive assembly.
12. Remove two attaching bolts from right output shaft support bracket and one through bolt attaching final drive to engine block on the left side. Scribe around the washers for correct reassembly.
13. Remove engine mount to crossmember nuts and front engine mount nuts. Remove the lower right engine-to-transmission attaching bolt.
14. Lower the car.
15. Support the final drive assembly with a chain stretched under and across the final drive assembly and attached to holes in the frame members.
16. Support engine by using a lifting fixture.
17. Remove five remaining transmission-to-engine bolts.
18. Lift the engine from the car.

—————— CAUTION ——————
If car is to be moved, install converter holding tool.

19. To install, reverse removal procedure.

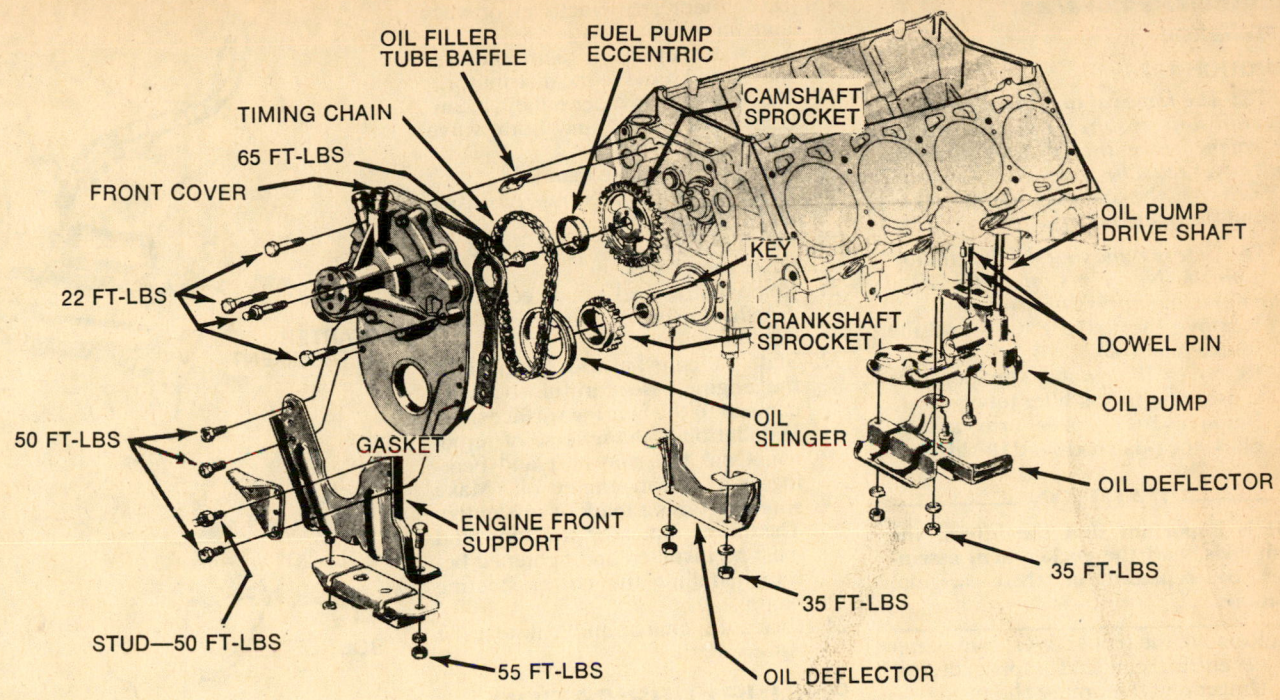

OIL FILLER TUBE BAFFLE

FUEL PUMP ECCENTRIC

TIMING CHAIN

CAMSHAFT SPROCKET

65 FT-LBS

FRONT COVER

OIL PUMP DRIVE SHAFT

22 FT-LBS

KEY

CRANKSHAFT SPROCKET

DOWEL PIN

OIL PUMP

50 FT-LBS

GASKET

OIL SLINGER

OIL DEFLECTOR

ENGINE FRONT SUPPORT

35 FT-LBS

STUD—50 FT-LBS

35 FT-LBS

55 FT-LBS

OIL DEFLECTOR

Front cover components (© Oldsmobile Div., G.M. Corp)

MANIFOLDS

Exhaust Manifold Removal and Installation

LEFT SIDE

1. Remove the air cleaner and the carburetor heat shroud on the manifold.
2. Remove the lower alternator bracket; raise the front of the car and support it securely.
3. Remove the exhaust pipe.
4. Lower the car and remove the manifold attaching bolts. Remove the manifold from above.
5. To install, reverse the removal procedure using the correct torque for the manifold attaching bolts.

RIGHT SIDE

1. Raise the car and support it securely.
2. Remove the exhaust pipe and the right front wheel.
3. Remove the attaching bolts and lower the manifold down and out from under the vehicle.
4. To install, reverse the removal procedure.

TIMING COVER, CHAIN, AND CAMSHAFT

Timing Cover Removal and Installation

In order to remove the front cover, on models through 1976, the engine must be removed from the car.

1. Drain the cooling system. Discon-

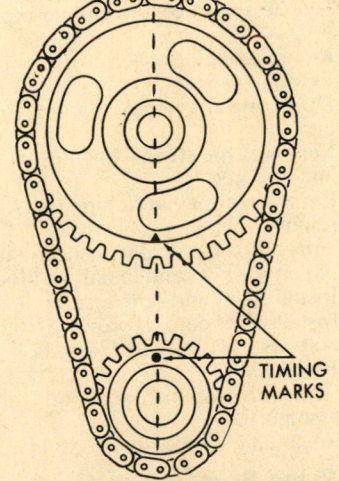

TIMING MARKS

Timing chain alignment

nect the upper and lower radiator, heater and bypass hoses.
2. Remove the radiator, belts, fan and fan pulley, crankshaft pulley and the harmonic balancer.
3. Remove the engine, on models through 1976.
4. Remove the timing cover attaching bolts and pull off the cover. Also, remove the timing pointer and the water pump.
5. Before assembly, remove all old gaskets and install a new timing cover gasket.
6. Position the front cover, timing pointer and the water pump.
7. Lubricate the attaching bolts and install.
8. Install the harmonic balancer on

the crankshaft after lubrication. Replace the engine.
9. Connect all cooling hoses.
10. Install the crankshaft pulley.
11. Install the fan and the fan pulley.
12. Install the drive belts and adjust.
13. Fill the crankcase and the radiator.
14. Run the engine and check for leaks.

Timing Chain Removal and Installation

NOTE: *Models through 1976 require that the engine be removed before performing the chain removal procedure.*

1. Remove the front engine cover.
2. Remove the fuel pump eccentric, oil slinger, cam sprocket and timing chain.

NOTE: *It is necessary to use a puller to remove the crankshaft sprocket.*

4. To install, align the camshaft and crankshaft sprockets. The camshaft sprocket aligning mark must be in the 6 o'clock position while the crankshaft sprocket must be in the 12 o'clock position.

NOTE: *This alignment brings No. 6 cylinder to top dead center. Turn the crankshaft one full turn to bring No. 1 to top dead center.*

5. Position the fuel pump eccentric with the flat side against the gear. Using a brass hammer, place the key against the gear until it bottoms.
6. Install the oil slinger. Replace the cover.

Camshaft Removal and Installation

THROUGH 1976

NOTE: *The removal and installation of the camshaft requires the removal of the engine since the oil pan and the front cover must be removed.*

1. Remove the oil pan, front cover and the distributor.

NOTE: *Before removing the distributor, position the No. 1 piston at top dead center of its compression stroke.*

2. Remove the valve covers and the intake manifold.
3. Remove the water temperature sensor and the oil filler tube.
4. Remove the rocker arm assemblies, the push rods and the lifters.

— CAUTION —

It is important that the lifters, the push rods, and the rocker arm assemblies be replaced in their original positions.

5. Remove the front cover, fuel pump eccentric, camshaft sprocket, oil slinger and the timing chain.
6. Remove the camshaft by carefully sliding it from the front of the engine. Use caution not to damage the camshaft bearings during this procedure. Keep the camshaft parallel with the crankshaft as it is removed.
7. Before installing the camshaft, coat both the cam lobes and the bearings with camshaft grease. Install the camshaft and align the timing marks on the camshaft and crankshaft sprockets as outlined in the Timing Chain Removal and Installation section.
8. Install the distributor.
9. Reverse the removal procedure to complete the installation.

1977 AND LATER

NOTE: *This procedure requires discharge of the A/C system. This should be performed only by a qualified service person.*

1. Disconnect the battery.
2. Drain the coolant.
3. Remove the upper radiator baffle.
4. Disconnect the upper radiator hose and hose support.
5. Disconnect the transmission cooler lines at the radiator.
6. Remove the fan shroud.
7. Remove the radiator.
8. Disconnect the fuel line at the pump.
9. Remove the air cleaner and disconnect the throttle cable.
10. Remove the alternator belt.
11. Unbolt and move the alternator out of the way.
12. Remove the power steering pump.
13. Unbolt and position the A/C compressor out of the way. Do not disconnect the refrigerant lines.
14. Disconnect the thermostat bypass hose at the pump.

15. Disconnect any electrical or vacuum lines in the way.
16. See the section on distributor removal and remove the distributor.
17. Remove the balancer pulley, balancer, front cover and both valve covers.
18. Remove the intake manifold.
19. Remove the rocker arms, pushrods and lifters.
20. Discharge the A/C system and remove the condenser.
21. Remove the fuel pump eccentric, camshaft gear, oil slinger and timing chain.
22. Slide the camshaft out the front of the engine. Be careful to avoid damage to the bearing surfaces.
23. Installation is the reverse of removal. Coat the camshaft and bearings with clean engine oil. Make sure the timing marks are aligned. The timing indicator attaching stud must be installed and tightened before installing the power steering pump.
24. Evacuate, charge and leak test the A/C system.

ENGINE LUBRICATION

Oil Pan Removal and Installation

The engine must be removed from the vehicle in order to remove the oil pan.

1. Remove engine assembly.
2. Remove dipstick.
3. Drain oil and remove filter assembly.
4. Remove the front engine mount and bracket.
5. Remove oil pan attaching bolts and remove oil pan.
6. Apply a good sealer to both sides of pan gaskets and install on block.
7. Install front and rear seal.
8. Install the pan. Torque 5/16 in. bolts to 15 ft lbs and 1/4 in. bolts to 10 ft lbs.
9. Reinstall mount and oil filter assembly.
10. Reinstall engine and fill crankcase.

Oil Pump Removal and Installation

Remove the oil pan. Remove the oil baffle. Remove the oil pump to rear main bearing cap attaching bolts, then remove the pump and drive shaft extension.

Rear Main Bearing Oil Seal Replacement

See Oil Pan Removal and Installation. Remove the oil pan and rear main bearing cap. Using a blunt-ended tool, drive the upper seal into its groove on each side until it is tightly packed. This is usually 1/4—3/4 in. Cut pieces of the old bearing cap seal 1/16 in. longer than the distance each side of the upper seal was compressed. Install these pieces into each side of the upper seal seat, packing them into place. Carefully trim

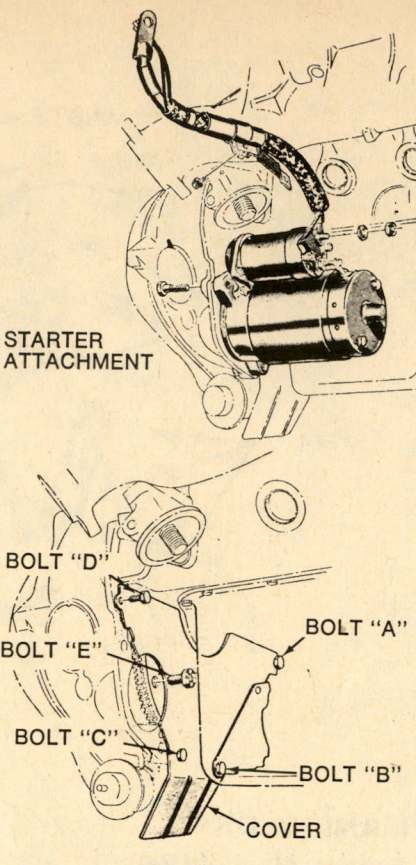

STARTER ATTACHMENT

BOLT "D"
BOLT "E"
BOLT "C"
BOLT "A"
BOLT "B"
COVER

Transmission to converter attachment
(© Oldsmobile Div., G.M. Corp)

any protruding seal, being sure not to scratch or damage the bearing surface. Install a new seal in the bearing cap and install the cap, tightening bolts to the specified torque. Install the oil pan.

AUTOMATIC TRANSMISSION

The Toronado uses a Turbo Hydra-Matic 425 automatic transmission. This is the Turbo Hydra-Matic 400 used in the larger Oldsmobiles, adapted to the front-drive car.

All Turbo Hydra-Matic 425 in-car service procedures are the same as those given for the Turbo Hydra-Matic 400 in the Oldsmobile car section. Only the fluid refill capacity is different.

DIFFERENTIAL

Removal and Installation

1. Disconnect battery.
2. See illustration. Remove bolts A, B, and C. Nut D must be removed with a special wrench.

NOTE: *It may be necessary to remove the transmission filler tube to gain clearance.*

3. Hoist the car. If a two post hoist is used, the car must be supported with floor stands at the front frame rails and the front post lowered.
4. Disconnect right and left drive axles from the output shafts.
5. Remove engine oil filter.
6. Disconnect brace from final drive, then disconnect right-hand output shaft assembly from engine.
7. Remove output shaft assembly from final drive.
8. See illustration. Remove bolt X and loosen bolts Y and Z.
9. Remove final drive cover and allow lubricant to drain.
10. Position transmission lift with adapter for final drive. Install an anchor bolt through final drive housing and lift pad.
11. See illustration. Remove bolts E, F, and G, and nut from H.
12. Move transmission lift toward front of car to disengage final drive splines from transmission. Some transmission fluid will be lost.
13. Lower transmission lift and remove final drive from lift.
14. Using a 9/16 in. socket, remove the left output shaft retainer bolt, then pull output shaft from final drive.
15. Remove transmission to final drive gasket.
16. On installation, apply special seal lubricant to both output shaft seals.
17. Install the left output shaft into the final drive. Retain with bolt and torque to 40 ft. lbs., (45 ft. lbs.—1975 and later).
18. Position final drive on transmission lift and install an anchor bolt through the housing and lift pad.
19. Apply a thin film of special seal lubricant on the transmission side of the new final drive to transmission gasket. Then position gasket on the transmission.
20. Raise the transmission lift. Align the two bolt studs D and H on the transmission with their mating holes in the final drive. Move final drive until it mates with the transmission.

NOTE: *It may be necessary to rotate the left output shaft to align the splines on the final drive with the splines of the transmission output shaft.*

21. Install bolts E, F, and G and nut H finger tight.
22. Install bolt X and torque to 75 ft. lbs. (100 ft. lbs.—1974) (110 ft. lbs. —1975 and later). Tighten and torque bolts Y and Z to 50 ft. lbs. (55 ft. lbs.—1975 and later).
23. Loosen and remove lift from final drive.
24. Position a new cover gasket on the final drive, then install cover. Torque cover bolts to 30 ft. lbs.
25. Install right output shaft into final drive, indexing splines of output shaft with splines of final drive. Install mounting bracket and brace bolts and tighten.

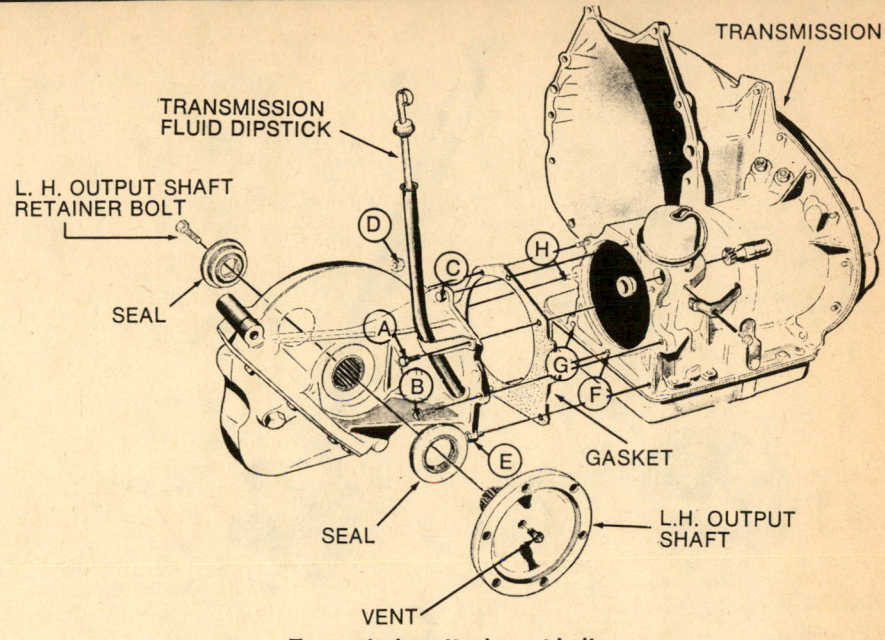

Transmission attachment bolts
(© Oldsmobile Div., G.M. Corp)

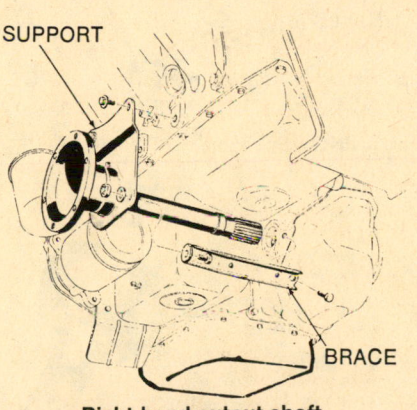

Right-hand output shaft
(© Oldsmobile Div., G.M. Corp)

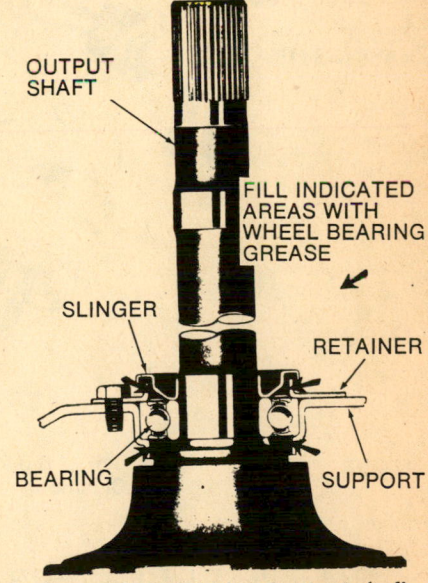

Assembly of right-hand output shaft
(© Oldsmobile Div., G.M. Corp)

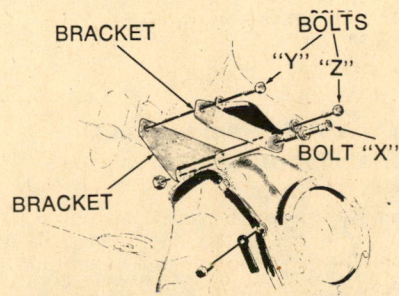

Disconnecting final drive from engine
(© Oldsmobile Div., G.M. Corp)

26. Connect drive axles to output shafts using new bolts. Tighten the bolts to 75 ft. lbs.
27. Install oil filter.
28. Raise hoist, remove studs and lower car.
29. If filler tube was removed, attach a new O-ring and install filler tube.
30. Install bolts A, B, and C and nut D. Torque all final drive to transmission bolts to 25 ft. lbs. (50 ft. lbs.—1974 and later). Torque nuts to

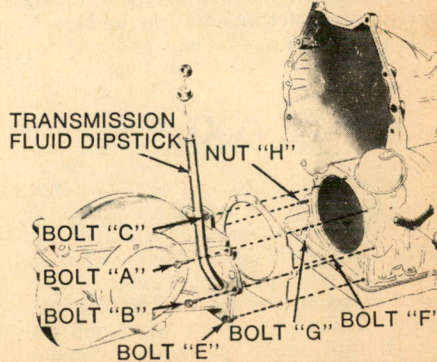

Transmission-to-final drive attachment
(© Oldsmobile Div., G.M. Corp)

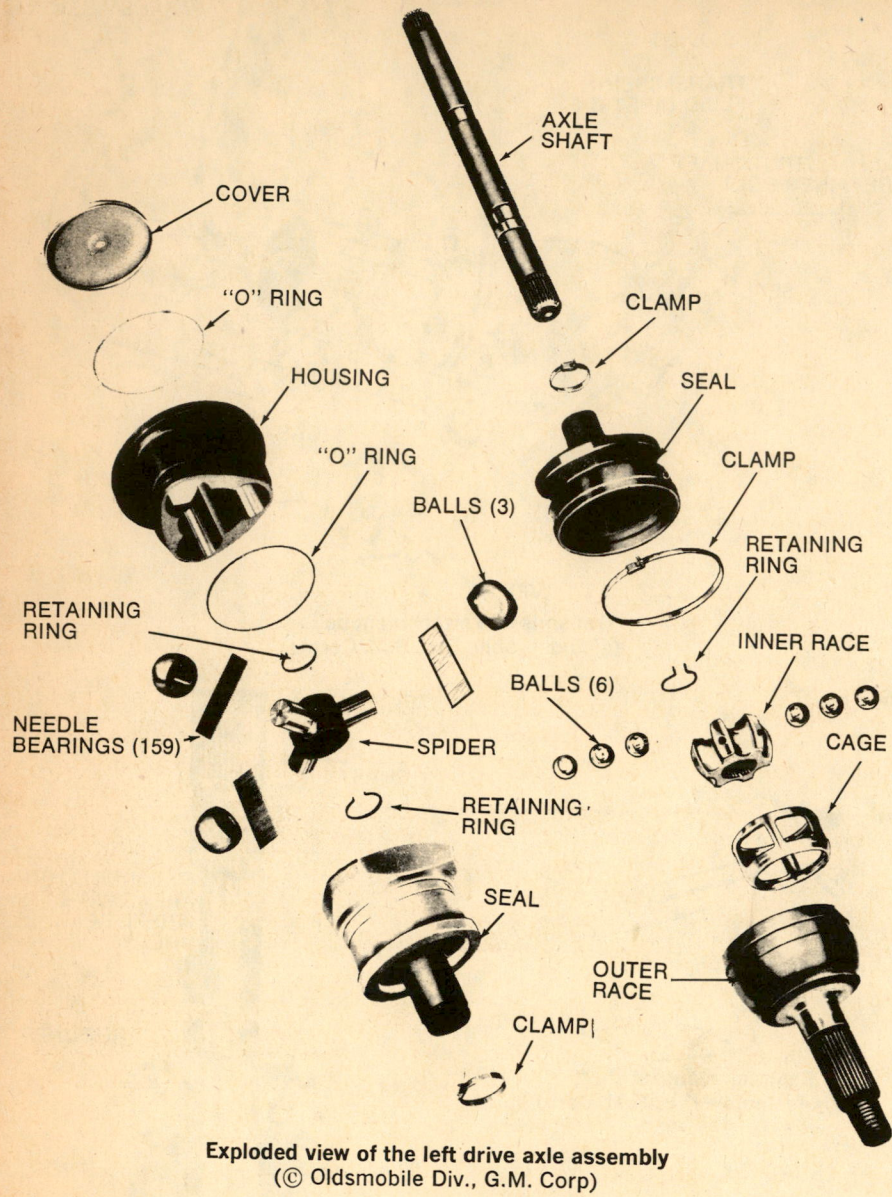

COVER

"O" RING

HOUSING

"O" RING

RETAINING RING

NEEDLE BEARINGS (159)

SPIDER

RETAINING RING

SEAL

CLAMP

AXLE SHAFT

CLAMP

SEAL

CLAMP

RETAINING RING

BALLS (3)

BALLS (6)

INNER RACE

CAGE

OUTER RACE

Exploded view of the left drive axle assembly
(© Oldsmobile Div., G.M. Corp)

CAUTION

Care must be exercised so that constant velocity joints do not turn to full extremes, and that seals are not damaged against shock absorber or stabilizer bar.

8. Carefully place righthand drive axle assembly into lower control arm and enter outer race splines into knuckle.
9. Lubricate final drive output shaft seal, with special seal lubricant.
10. Install right-hand output shaft into final drive and attach the support bolts to engine and brakes. Torque the bolts to 55 ft.lbs.
11. Move right-hand drive axle assembly toward front of car and align with right-hand output shaft. Install attaching bolts and torque to 75 ft. lbs.
12. Install oil filter.
13. Install washer and nut on drive axle. Torque to 140 ft. lbs. (200 ft. lbs.—1975 and later), then insert cotter pin.
14. Remove floor stands and lower hoist.
15. Check engine oil level.

LEFT SIDE

1. Hoist car under lower control arms.
2. Remove wheel. Remove disc.
3. Remove drive axle cotter pin, nut and washer.
4. Remove tie-rod end cotter pin and nut.
5. Remove the tie-rod end from the knuckle with a puller.
6. Remove bolts from drive axle assembly and left output shaft. Insert a spacer between the axle shaft and lower control arm.
7. Remove upper control arm ball joint cotter pin and nut.
8. Using hammer and brass drift, drive on knuckle until upper ball joint stud is free.
9. Using puller, remove lower ball joint from knuckle. Care must be exercised so that ball joint does not damage drive axle seal.
10. Remove knuckle and support, so that brake hose is not damaged.
11. Carefully guide drive axle assembly outboard.

NOTE: *Care must be exercised so that constant velocity joints do not turn to full extremes and that seals are not damaged against shock absorber or stabilizer bar.*

12. Carefully guide left-hand drive axle assembly onto lower control arm and into position on spacer.
13. Insert lower control ball joint stud into knuckle and attach nut. Do not torque.
14. Center left-hand drive axle assembly in opening of knuckle and insert upper ball joint stud.
15. Place brake hose clip over upper ball joint stud and install nut. Do not torque.

about 25 ft. lbs. (50 ft. lbs.—1974 and later).
31. Connect battery.
32. Fill final drive.
33. Check engine oil level. Start engine and check transmission fluid level.
34. Check for any oil leaks.

DRIVE AXLES

Drive axles are flexible assemblies and consist of an axle shaft with an inner and outer constant velocity joint. The right axle shaft has a torsional damper mounted in the center. The inner constant velocity joint has complete flexibility, plus inward and outward movement. The outer constant velocity joint has complete flexibility but doesn't allow for inward and outward movement.

Drive Axle Removal and Installation

RIGHT SIDE

1. Hoist car under lower control arms.
2. Remove drive axle cotter pin, nut and washer.
3. Remove oil filter.
4. Remove inner constant velocity joint attaching bolts.
5. Push inner constant velocity joint outward enough to disengage the right-hand final drive output shaft, then move rearward.
6. Remove right-hand output shaft bracket bolts to engine and final drive.
7. Remove right-hand output shaft and drive axle assembly.

16. Insert tie-rod end stud into knuckle and attach nut. Torque to 35 ft. lbs. on models through 1974 and 40 ft. lbs. on 1975 and later models. Install cotter pin and crimp.
17. Align inner constant velocity joint with output shaft and install attaching bolts. Torque to 65 ft. lbs. (75 ft. lbs.—1975 and later).
18. Torque upper and lower ball joint stud nuts to 50 ft. lbs. upper—60 ft. lbs. lower (95 ft. lbs.—1975 and later). Install cotter pins and crimp.

NOTE: *Upper ball joint cotter pin must be crimped toward upper control arm to prevent interference with outer constant velocity joint seal.*

19. Install drive axle washer and nut. Torque to 150 ft. lbs. on models through 1974 and 200 ft. lbs. on 1975 and later models. Install cotter pin and crimp.
20. Install wheel.
21. Remove floor stands and lower hoist.
22. Check camber, caster and toe-in and adjust if necessary. Refer to Front End Alignment specifications.

FRONT SUSPENSION

The front suspension consists of control arms, stabilizer bar, shock absorbers and a right and left torsion bar. Torsion bars are used in place of conventional coil springs. The front end of the torsion bar is attached to the lower control arm. The rear of torsion bar is mounted into an adjustable arm at the torsion bar crossmember. The ride height of the car is controlled by this adjustment. See the Unit Repair Section for front end height adjustments and alignment.

Wheel Hub Removal and Installation

1. Remove drive axle cotter pin, nut and washer. Remove the brake disc.
2. Position access slot in hub assembly so each of the attaching bolts can be removed.
3. Install a front hub puller and slide hammer.
4. Remove hub assembly.
5. To install, reverse removal procedure. Tighten the axle nut to 140 ft lbs.

NOTE: *O.D. of bearing must be lubricated with E.P. chassis lubricant. Use care when installing hub assembly over drive axle splines.*

Brake Disc Removal and Installation

1. Siphon off about two-thirds of the fluid in the front reservoir of the master cylinder. Do not empty the

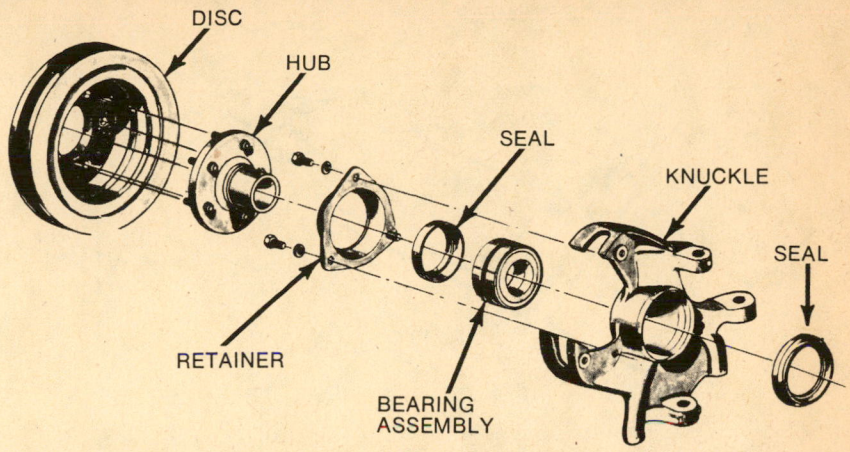

DISC HUB SEAL KNUCKLE SEAL RETAINER BEARING ASSEMBLY

Exploded view of the hub assembly
(© Oldsmobile Div., G.M. Corp)

reservoir or it will be necessary to bleed the system.
2. Hoist the car and remove the wheel.
3. Position piston compressor tool on the caliper and tighten the screw until the piston bottoms and the shoes are backed off the disc.
4. Remove the two caliper to knuckle attaching bolts and carefully lift the caliper from the disc. Support it so that the hose is not kinked or stretched.
5. Mark the hub and disc so that they will be correctly positioned when installed, then pull evenly on the disc to remove.
6. To install, reverse the above procedure. Make sure that the disc is positioned according to the marks made during removal. Tighten the caliper attaching bolts to 35 ft. lbs. Fill the front reservoir of the master cylinder with new fluid and check the action of the brakes.

Torsion Bar Removal and Installation

1. Raise the car and support the frame.
2. Disconnect the parking brake cable at the equalizer and pull it through the support.
3. Install a torsion bar remover tool, remove the torsion bar adjusting bolt and nut, noting the number of turns to remove, and relax the torsion bar. Do the same on the other torsion bar.
4. Remove the bolts and retainer from the torsion bar crossmember. Move the crossmember back until the bars are free and the adjusting arms can be removed. You may have to slide the torsion bars forward.
5. Disconnect the exhaust system hangers.
6. Reverse the procedure for installation.

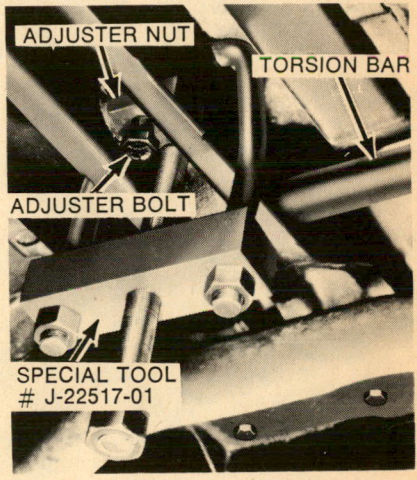

ADJUSTER NUT · TORSION BAR · ADJUSTER BOLT · SPECIAL TOOL # J-22517-01

Torsion bar removal
(© Oldsmobile Div., GM Corp)

Upper Control Arm and Ball Joint Removal and Installation

NOTE: *The upper control arm is serviced as an assembly, less bushings.*

1. Hoist car under lower control arm and remove wheel.
2. Remove upper shock attaching bolt.
3. Remove cotter pin and nut on upper ball joint.
4. Disconnect brake hose clamp from ball joint stud.
5. Separate upper ball joint stud from steering knuckle.
6. Remove upper control arm cam assemblies and remove control arm from car by guiding shock absorber through access hole in arm.
7. Guide upper control arm over shock absorber and install bushing ends into frame horns.
8. Install cam assemblies.
9. Install ball joint stud into knuckle.
10. Install brake hose clip onto ball joint stud.
11. Install ball joint nut. Torque to 50

Oldsmobile Toronado

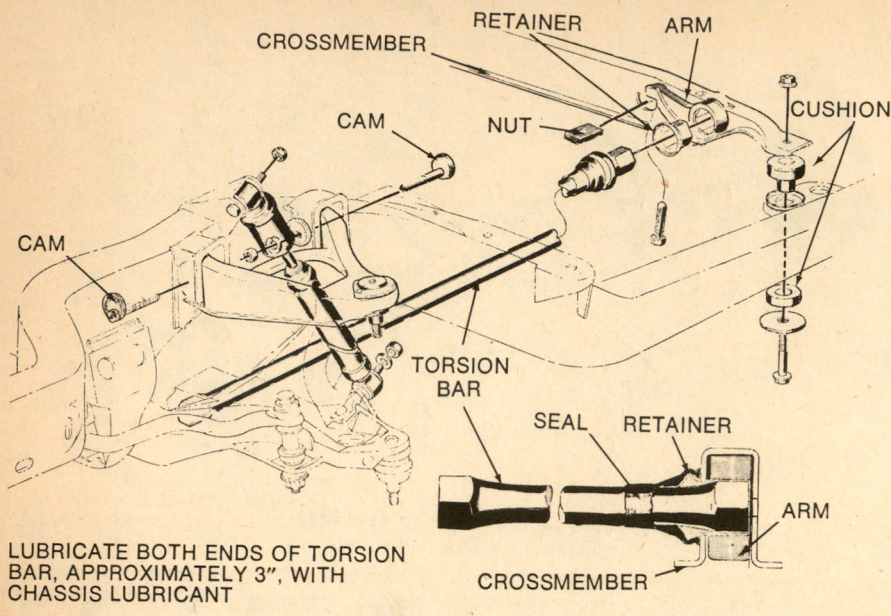

CROSSMEMBER

RETAINER ARM

CAM

NUT

CUSHION

CAM

TORSION BAR

SEAL RETAINER

ARM

CROSSMEMBER

LUBRICATE BOTH ENDS OF TORSION BAR, APPROXIMATELY 3", WITH CHASSIS LUBRICANT

Front suspension
(© Oldsmobile Div., G.M. Corp)

LOWER CONTROL ARM

STABILIZER SHAFT

BUSHING
SPACER
BRACKET
RETAINER
NUT
GROMMET

Lower control arm and related components (© Oldsmobile Div., G.M. Corp)

ft. lbs. (60 ft. lbs.—1975 and later) and insert cotter pin and crimp.

NOTE: *Cotter pin must be crimped toward upper control arm to prevent interference with outer constant velocity joint seal.*

12. Install upper shock attaching bolt and nut. Torque to 90 ft. lbs.
13. Install wheel.
14. Lower hoist.
15. Check camber, caster and toe-in, and adjust if necessary.

Lower Control Arm Removal and Installation

1. Hoist car and support at lift points. Remove wheel assembly.
2. Place torsion bar remover and installer over crossmember so that center screw is seated in dimple of torsion adjusting arm.
3. Remove torsion bar adjusting bolt and nut, counting the number of turns necessary.

NOTE: *This number of turns will be used when installing, to obtain initial ride height.*

4. Turn center screw of tool until torsion bar is completely relaxed.

5. Disconnect shock absorber and stabilizer link from lower control arm.
6. Remove drive axle nut. Remove the bolt and nut from the front of the frame brace. Loosen the rear bolt and move the brace out.
7. Remove cotter pin and nut from lower ball joint stud.
8. Remove ball joint stud from knuckle, using puller.
9. Push drive axle in and pull knuckle outward to gain clearance, then remove lower control arm from knuckle and torsion bar.
10. Install by reversing removal procedure. Check and adjust ride height if necessary.

Ball Joint Check

1. Raise the car and position floor stands under the left and right lower control arm, as near as possible to each lower ball joint. Car must be stable and should not rock on floor stands.
2. Position dial indicator to register vertical movement at wheel hub.

3. Place a pry bar between the lower control arm and the outer race of the constant velocity joint and pry down on the bar. Care must be used so that the drive axle seal is not damaged. The vertical reading must not exceed .125 in.

Lower Ball Joint Removal and Installation

1. Remove the steering knuckle.
2. Drill the top rivet head off.
3. Drill the side rivets just deep enough to remove the rivet head.
4. Using a hammer and punch, drive the rivets out of the control arm.
5. Install service ball joint into control arm and torque bolts and nut. Side bolts are torqued to 25 ft. lbs. while the upper nut is tightened to 45 ft. lbs. Stake the upper nut.
6. Install knuckle.
7. Check the nut to drive axle outer joint clearance. If necessary, grind a maximum of 1/16 in. from the nut.

REAR SUSPENSION

Some models through 1976 are equipped with True-Track Braking (JL9 option). This is an electrically controlled rear brake equalizing system. The wheel speed sensors are mounted under the spindles, each with a driveshaft which runs through the spindle to attach to the grease cap. Care must be taken when removing the rear spindle or the rear assembly not to break the sensor wiring or damage the sensor wiring.

All models have a straight tubular axle housing.

Spindle Removal and Installation

1. Support the rear of the car with stands.
2. Remove the wheel, drum and hub assembly.
3. Disconnect the brake line fitting at the wheel cylinder.

1979 Toronado front (left) and rear (right) wheel bearings require no service or adjustment, and are replaced as a unit. The same system is used on the 1979 Eldorado and Riviera.

4. If equipped with JL9, disconnect the wiring at the sensor.

5. Remove the four spindle attaching bolts and tie the backing plate out of the way.

6. Pull the spindle with a slide hammer.

7. To install, reverse the removal procedure. Install spindle with the keyway up, tightening the four bolts progressively one turn at a time. Adjust the rear wheel bearing.

Rear Wheel Bearing Adjustment

For the rear wheel tapered roller bearings to be correctly adjusted, the following precautions should be taken:

1. The cones must be a slip fit on the spindle.

2. Inside of cones should be lubricated to make sure the cone creeps on the spindle.

3. Spindle nut must be a free-running fit on the threads.

4. Adjustment of rear wheel bearings should be made by continuously revolving the wheel while torquing the nut as follows:
   A. Torque adjusting nut to 25-30 ft. lbs. to seat all components thoroughly.
   B. Back off nut one-half turn, then retighten finger tight.
   C. If unable to insert cotter pin at this position, back off to nearest castellation.
   D. End-play should be 0.001-0.005 in.

Coil Spring Removal and Installation

1. With the car supported with floor stands, position a hoist under the tube assembly and raise it enough to relieve the tension on the shock absorber.

2. Disconnect the shock absorbers at the tube assembly.

3. Carefully lower the tube assembly until the springs are fully extended.

——— CAUTION ———

Do not stretch the brake hydraulic hose.

NOTE: *For 1973 and later models, the factory recommends that a spring compressor be used to compress the spring for removal and installation.*

4. Remove the springs and insulators.

5. When installing, place the insulator on top of the spring and install the spring. The top end of the spring should point to the right side of the car.

6. Hoist the tube assembly and connect the shock absorber.

BRAKES

Brake adjustment, brake lining replacement, hydraulic cylinder overhaul

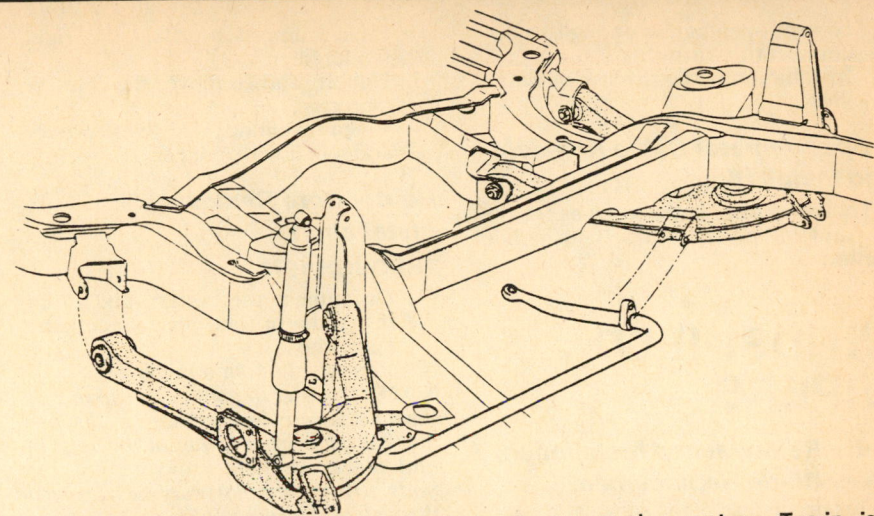

1979 Oldsmobile Toronado independent rear suspension system. Toe-in is adjusted at the inner pivot of the control arm. The rear (and front) wheel bearings require no service or adjustment, and are replaced as a unit. This system is also used on the 1979 Eldorado and Riviera.

and bleeding procedures can be found in the Unit Repair Section.

Parking Brake Adjustment

1. Depress the parking brake pedal exactly three clicks on models through 1977; 2 clicks on 1978-79 models.

2. Tighten the adjusting nut at the cable equalizer until the left rear wheel can just be turned rearward using 2 hands, but is locked in forward rotation.

3. With the parking brake off, the rear wheels should rotate freely in either direction with no drag.

Master Cylinder Removal and Installation

1. Disconnect and plug hydraulic lines, and drain the cylinder.

2. Remove the attaching nuts and remove the master cylinder from the power unit.

Power Booster Removal and Installation

1. From inside the car, detach the brake pushrod from the brake pedal.

2. Detach the vacuum hose at the vacuum cylinder and disconnect the hydraulic line from the front of the slave cylinder.

3. Remove the four nuts that hold the vacuum unit up to the toeboard and remove the unit.

4. Install in reverse order of removal. Bleed system.

STEERING

——— CAUTION ———

Some 1974-76 models may have A.C.R.S. (air bags). See the Buick section for special precautions and procedures.

All steering system procedures are the same as those given in the Oldsmobile section for 88 and 98 models.

INSTRUMENT PANEL

Headlight Switch Replacement

THROUGH 1973

The left hand control panel must be removed in order to remove the headlight switch.

1. Disconnect the battery.

2. Pry the floor lamp lens and lamp assembly out with a thin screwdriver.

3. Remove the screws from the left side of the lower steering trim and from the left hand trim panel.

4. Remove the nut and screw from the temperature cable on the bottom of the air conditioner or heater control.

5. Remove the ground wire attaching screw from the left hand panel lower brace.

6. Remove the four control panel attaching screws and remove the panel.

7. Remove the multiple connector from the headlight switch.

8. Pull the switch to ON position and push in on the small button on the switch, then pull the switch knob and shaft from the switch.

10. Install in reverse order of removal.

1974-76

This procedure is the same as for the 88 and 98, given in the Oldsmobile section.

1977 AND LATER

1. Disconnect the battery ground.

2. Remove the A/C control, but do not disconnect the hoses or wires.

3. Remove the collar from the headlamp switch with a pair of needle-nose pliers.

4. Pull the switch through the A/C

control opening far enough to disconnect the wiring.

5. Installation is the reverse of removal.

Speedometer Cable Removal and Installation

This procedure is the same as for the 88, and 98 given in the Oldsmobile section.

WINDSHIELD WIPERS

Motor Removal and Installation, Wiper Blade Replacement

This procedure is the same as for the 88 and 98, given in the Oldsmobile section.

RADIO

Removal and Installation

This procedure is the same as for the 88 and 98, given in the Oldsmobile section.

HEATER

Blower Motor Removal and Installation

THROUGH 1974

1. Remove the right front fender filler panel.
2. Disconnect the blower electrical wiring.
3. Remove the five nuts and two screws which secure the inlet assembly to the dash.
4. Remove the inlet assembly and the blower motor. The fan may be removed from the shaft by releasing the nut and lockwasher.
5. To install, reverse the removal procedure.

1975-76

This procedure is the same as that given for the 88 and 98 in the Oldsmobile section.

1977 AND LATER

1. Raise and support the car; remove the right front wheel.
2. Cut along the inside of the rectan-

gular stamped bead on the right fender filler.
3. Unbolt and remove the blower motor.
4. When installing, fold the flap over and seal it with a sealer.

Heater Core Removal and Installation

THROUGH 1973

1. Disconnect the battery and drain the radiator and disconnect the heater hoses.
2. Remove the four attaching nuts.
NOTE: *In order to gain access to one of the nuts, it may be necessary to disconnect the right front fender at the bottom and block the fender away from the body so that the nut may be removed through the opening.*
3. Disconnect the wiring, the three control cables, and the defroster duct.
4. Disconnect the right half of the right trim panel. If equipped with air conditioning, remove the instrument panel tie bar.
5. The case assembly may be removed from under the dash. The core may be separated from the case if it is defective.

1974-76

This procedure is the same as that given for the 88 and 98 in the Oldsmobile section.

1977

1. Drain the cooling system.
2. Remove the four heater case attachment nuts.
3. Remove the instrument panel trim cover.
4. Remove the two heater case-to-cowl bolts from inside the car.
5. Remove the lower air duct.
6. Remove the instrument panel pad:
   a. disconnect the battery ground.
   b. remove the courtesy lamps.
   c. carefully pry the speakers from the clips.
   d. remove one screw from each speaker hole.
   e. remove one screw from the left lower outside edge of the instrument panel pad and two screws from the cluster.
   f. open the glovebox and remove one screw from the lower right corner of the glovebox and two screws from the upper edge of the glovebox.
   g. grasp the front center edge of

the pad and pull to release the clips at the windshield edge.
7. Disconnect the wiring from the clock and glovebox.
8. Remove the right upper trim panel.
9. Remove the manifold from the heater case.
10. Disconnect the defroster duct from the case.
11. Remove the lower trim panel:
    a. remove the right side screw.
    b. grip the cover with both hands and carefully pull it from the panel.
    c. remove the left side screw.
    d. slide the steering column collar out of the way.
    e. carefully pull the cover from the panel.
    f. disconnect the lower A/C outlet hoses.
    g. remove the cigarette lighter.
    h. disconnect the parking brake cable.
    i. remove the two lower trim panel-to-tie bar screws.
    j. remove the eight trim panel-to-center tie bar screws.
    k. disconnect the ash tray lamp.
    l. remove the trim panel.
12. Remove the heater case.
13. Separate the case halves and remove the core.
14. Installation is the reverse of removal. Replace any damaged sealer.

1978-79

1. Drain the cooling system.
2. Remove the four heater case attaching nuts.
3. Disconnect the hoses at the core tubes.
4. Remove the instrument panel trim cover.
5. Remove the two heater case-to-cowl bolts located inside the car.
6. Remove the lower air duct.
7. Remove the instrument panel pad.
8. Disconnect the wires at the glove box and clock.
9. Remove the right upper trim panel.
10. Remove the manifold from the heater case.
11. Disconnect the defroster duct from the heater case.
12. Disconnect the lower trim panel.
13. Remove the heater case and disconnect the mode door hoses and temperature control cable from the case. Lift the heater core from the case.
14. Installation is the reverse of removal.

Index

YEAR IDENTIFICATION

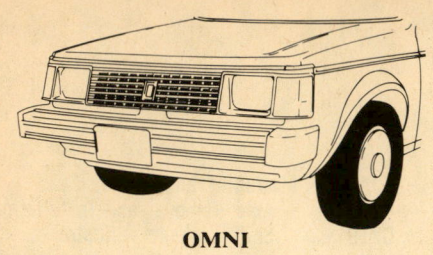

OMNI

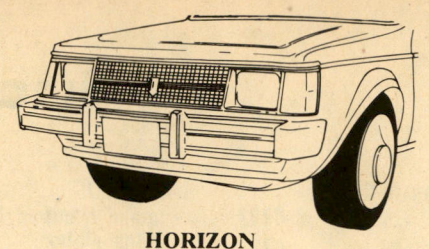

HORIZON

ENGINE IDENTIFICATION

The engine that the factory installed in the car can be identified by the fifth digit of the Vehicle Identification Number, as explained under Engine Code. The engine itself can be identified by the engine serial number. The cubic inch displacement is given by either the second, third, and fourth, or the third, fourth, and fifth digits of the engine serial number, depending on the year and engine.

ENGINE CODE

Displacement	Carb. No. bbl.	HP	'78	'79
104.7	2	75	A	A

Horsepower is SAE net, measured at the output end of the transmission, with all accessories installed and operating. The figure will vary from model to model and is, therefore, intended to be representative rather than exact.

GENERAL ENGINE SPECIFICATIONS

Year	Engine No. Cyl. Displ. Cu. In.	Carb. Type	Horsepower at RPM ■	Torque (ftlb.) at RPM ■	Bore X Stroke (In.)	Compression Ratio	Oil Pressure (psi) at 2000 rpm
'78-'79	4-104.7	2 bbl.	75 @ 5600	90 @ 3200	3.13 x 3.40	8.2:1	60-90

■ Horsepower and torque are SAE net, with all accessories installed and operating. Figure may vary from model-to-model and is intended to be representative rather than exact.

TUNE-UP SPECIFICATIONS

Year	No. Cyl. Displ. Cu. In.	h.p.	Spark Plugs Orig. Type	Gap (in.)	Ignition Timing (deg.) ▲ Man. Trans.	Auto Trans.	Intake Valve Opens (deg.) ■	Fuel Pump Pressure (psi)	Idle Speed (rpm) ▲ Man. Trans.	Auto. Trans.	Valve Lash (in.) ▲ Intake	Exhaust
'78	4-104.7	75	RN-12Y	.035	15B	15B	23	4.5-6	900	900	.008-.012H	.016-.020H
'79	4-104.7	75	RN-12Y	.035	15B	15B	14	4.4-5.8	900	900	.008-.012H	.016-.020H

▲ See text for procedure.
■ Before top dead center

FIRING ORDER

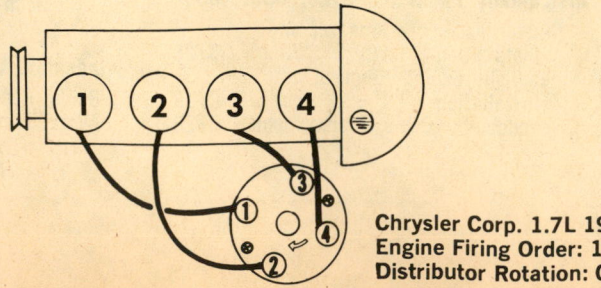

Chrysler Corp. 1.7L 1978 and later
Engine Firing Order: 1-3-4-2
Distributor Rotation: Clockwise

CAPACITIES

Year	Engine	Crankcase incl. Filter	Pints to refill after draining Manual	Pints to refill after draining Automatic	Final Drive (pts.)	Drive Axle (pts.)	Fuel Tank (gal.)	Cooling System (qts.) with Heater	Cooling System (qts.) with A/C
'78	4-104.7	4	2.64	6.2	2	2.8	13	6.5	8.0
'79	4-104.7	4	2.64	6.2	2	2.8	13	6.0	6.0

VALVE SPECIFICATIONS

Year	Engine	Seat Angle (deg.)	Face Angle (deg.)	Spring Test Pressure (lb in.)	Spring Installed Height (in.)	Stem-to-Guide Clearance (in.) Intake	Stem-to-Guide Clearance (in.) Exhaust	Stem Diameter (in.) Intake	Stem Diameter (in.) Exhaust
'78-'79	4-104.7	45	①	②	③	.001-.003	.002-.003	.3130-.3140	.3120-.3130

① Intake: 45°33′
   Exhaust: 43°33′

② outer: 101 @ .878
   inner: 49 @ .720

③ outer: 1.28
   inner: 1.13

TORQUE SPECIFICATIONS
(ft lbs.)

Year	Engine	Cylinder Head Bolts	Connecting Rod Bearing Bolts	Main Bearing Bolts	Crankshaft Bolt	Flywheel to Crankshaft Bolts	Camshaft Cap Bolts
'78-'79	4-104.7	60①	25	47	58	55②	14

① plus ¼ turn more
② 50 with auto. trans.

CRANKSHAFT AND CONNECTING ROD SPECIFICATIONS
(all specifications in inches)

Year	Engine	Main Brg. Journal Dia.	Main Brg. Oil Clearance	Crankshaft End Play	Thrust on No.	Connecting Rod Journal Dia.	Rod Bearing Oil Clearance	Rod Bearing Side Clearance
'78-'79	4-104.7	2.124-2.128	.0010-.0030	.003-.007	3	1.809-1.813	.0011-.0034	.015

PISTON, RING AND PIN SPECIFICATIONS
(all specifications in inches)

Year	Engine	Piston Clearance	Ring Gap Top Compression	Ring Gap Bottom Compression	Ring Gap Oil Control	Ring Side Clearance Top Compression	Ring Side Clearance Bottom Compression	Ring Side Clearance Oil Control	Pin Clearance In Piston
'78-'79	4-104.7	.0011-.027	.012-.018	.012-.018	.010-.016	.0008-.0020	.0008-.0020	.0008-.0020	.00004-.00035

WHEEL ALIGNMENT SPECIFICATIONS
(caster is not adjustable)

Year	Camber Range (deg.)	Camber Preferred	Toe-in (in.)	Steering Axis Inclination (deg.)
'78	¼N to ¾P	5/16P	⅛ out to 0	13.363
'79	⅕N to ⅘P	⅓P	⅖ out to ⅕ in	13.363

CHARGING SYSTEM

A conventional alternator is used. It has six built-in rectifiers which convert AC current to DC current. Current at the output terminal is DC. The main components of the alternator are: the rotor, stator, rectifiers, end shields and the drive pulley.

The electronic voltage regulator is a device which regulates the vehicle electrical system voltage by limiting the output voltage that is generated by the alternator. This is accomplished by controlling the amount of current that is allowed to pass through the alternator field windings. The regulator has no moving parts and requires no adjustment.

Alternator Removal and Installation

1. Disconnect the battery ground cable.
2. Remove the wires from the alternator.
3. Support the alternator, remove the mounting bolts and lift out the unit.
4. Reverse the procedure for installation.

Regulator Removal and Installation

1. Disconnect the battery ground cable.
2. Remove the wires from the regulator.
3. Remove the two sheet metal screws securing the regulator to the right side fender skirt.
4. Installation is the reverse of removal.

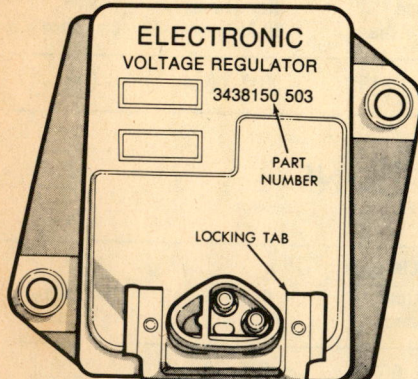

Voltage regulator (© Chrysler Corp.)

STARTING SYSTEM

The starter is an overrunning clutch drive type with a solenoid mounted on the starter motor. Four different starters are used on Omni/Horizon models. Two are built by Nippondenso and two

by Bosch. Removal and installation procedures are the same for all units.

Removal and Installation

1. Disconnect the battery ground cable.
2. Remove the wires from the starter and solenoid.
3. Support the starter, remove the bolts and lift the unit out from the flywheel housing.
4. Installation is the reverse of removal.

IGNITION SYSTEM

Omni/Horizon is equipped with a Lean Burn system. This consists of a spark control "computer", various engine sensors and a specially calibrated carburetor. The function of the system is to help the engine burn an unusually lean fuel/air mixture. The Lean Burn System is fully covered in the Emission Control Section of this book. Electronic ignition is used, thus eliminating the point/condenser system. Also eliminated are most routine adjustments.

Main components of the ignition system are the distributor, coil, ballast resistor, spark plug cables and spark plugs.

Distributor Removal

1. Disconnect the distributor pickup lead wire at the harness connector.
2. Remove the distributor cap.
3. Rotate the engine crankshaft until the rotor is pointing toward the cylinder block. Make a mark on the block at this point for installation reference.
4. Remove the distributor holddown screw.
5. Carefully lift the distributor from the engine. The shaft will rotate slightly as the distributor is removed.

Distributor Installation

1. If the engine has been cranked over while the distributor was removed, rotate the crankshaft until the number one piston is at TDC on the compression stroke. This will be indicated by the O mark on the flywheel aligning with the pointer on the clutch housing. Position the rotor just ahead of the # 1 terminal of the cap and lower the distributor into the engine. With the distributor fully seated, the rotor should be directly under the # 1 terminal.
2. If the engine was not disturbed while the distributor was out, lower the distributor into the engine, engaging the gears and making sure that the gasket is properly seated in the block. The rotor should line up with the mark made before removal.

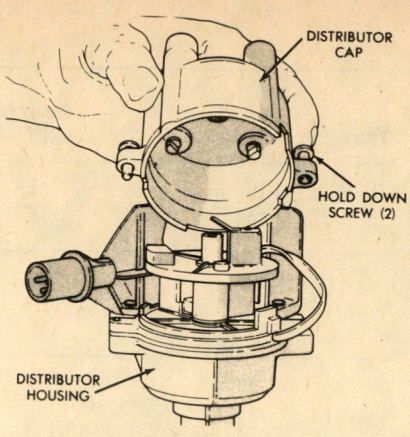

Distributor (© Chrysler Corp.)

3. Tighten the holddown screw and connect the wires.
4. Check and adjust, if necessary, the ignition timing.

Idle Speed Adjustment and Tachometer Hookup

1. Connect the red lead of the test tachometer to the negative primary terminal of the coil and the black lead to a good ground.
2. Turn the selector switch to the appropriate cylinder position and read the idle on the 1000 rpm scale, if so equipped.
3. With the engine at normal operating temperature momentarily open the throttle to check for binding in the linkage. Make sure that the idle screw is against its stop.
4. Adjust the idle speed to specifications. If the engine is equipped with an idle solenoid, the solenoid must be energized and the adjusting screw must be resting on the solenoid plunger.

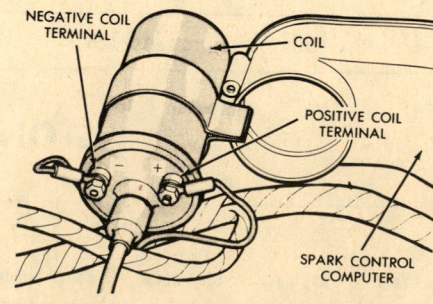

Ignition coil (© Chrysler Corp.)

Ignition Timing

1. Connect a timing light according to the manufacturer's instructions.
2. Run the engine to normal operating temperature.
3. Make sure the idle speed is correct.
4. Loosen the distributor holddown screw just enough so that the distributor can be rotated.
5. Remove the timing hole access cover and aim the timing light at the hole in the clutch housing. Carefully rotate the distributor un-

til the 15 degree mark is aligned with the pointer on the flywheel housing.

6. Tighten the distributor and recheck the timing.
7. Check, and if necessary adjust, the idle speed.

FUEL SYSTEM

The fuel system consists of the fuel tank, fuel pump, fuel filter, carburetor, fuel lines and vacuum lines.

Fuel Pump Removal and Installation

A mechanical fuel pump is located on the left side of the engine. To remove the pump, disconnect the fuel and vapor lines and remove the attaching bolts. Installation is the reverse of removal. Always use a new gasket when installing the pump and make certain the gasket surfaces are clean.

Fuel Filter Removal and Installation

Two filters are used in this system. One is part of the fuel pickup in the fuel tank. The other is a sealed paper unit located in the carburetor inlet. The tank unit does not usually need replacing, but can be replaced if necessary. The carburetor filter should be replaced periodically. Chrysler recommends every 6 months or 7500 miles. To replace the inlet filter, place a rag or container under the inlet and disconnect the fuel line. Unscrew the inlet fitting. The filter has a spring behind it so take care not to lose it. Replacement is the reverse of removal.

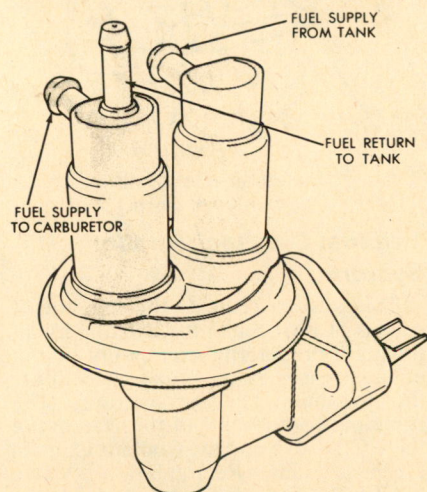

Fuel pump (© Chrysler Corp.)

Idle Speed and Mixture Adjustment

Chrysler recommends the use of a propane enrichment procedure to adjust the mixture. The equipment needed for this procedure is not readily available to the general public. An alternate method recommended by Chrysler is with the use of an exhaust gas analyzer. If this equipment is not available, and a mixture adjustment must be performed, follow this procedure:

1. Run engine to normal operating temperature.
2. Place the transmission in Neutral (MT) or Drive (AT), turn off the lights and air conditioning and make certain that the electric cooling fan is operating.
3. Disconnect the EGR vacuum line, disconnect the distributor electrical advance connector, and ground the carburetor idle stop switch (if equipped with a jumper wire).
4. Connect tachometer according to the manufacturer's specifications.
5. Adjust the idle screw to achieve the curb idle figure listed on the underhood sticker.
6. Back out the mixture screw to achieve the fastest possible idle.
7. Adjust the idle screw to the specified curb idlespeed.

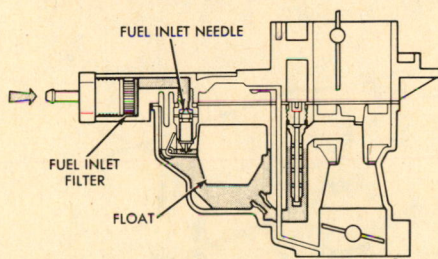

Fuel inlet system (© Chrysler Corp.)

Fast Idle Adjustment

1. Remove the top of the air cleaner.
2. Disconnect and plug the EGR vacuum line.
3. Plug any open vacuum lines, which were connected to the air cleaner.
4. Do not disconnect the vacuum line to the spark control computer. Instead, use a jumper wire to ground the idle stop switch. The air conditioning should be off.
5. Disconnect the engine cooling fan at the radiator and complete the circuit at the plug with a jumper wire to energize the fan.
6. Set the brake, place the transmission in Neutral (MT) or Drive (AT) and position the first step of the fast idle cam under the adjusting screw.
7. Connect a tachometer according to the manufacturer's specifications.
8. Start the engine and observe the idle speed. With the choke fully open, the speed should remain steady. If it gradually increases, the idle stop switch is not properly grounded.
9. Turn the adjusting screw to give 1100 rpm.
10. Operate the throttle linkage a few times and return the screw to the first cam step to recheck rpm.

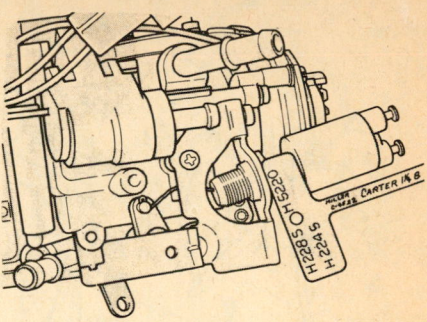

Throttle position transducer adjustment (© Chrysler Corp.)

Throttle Position Transducer Adjustment

1. Disconnect the wiring from transducer.
2. Loosen the locknut and turn the transducer until a gap of 35/64 inch is obtained between the transducer and the mounting bracket.
3. Tighten the locknut.

COOLING SYSTEM

The cooling system consists of a radiator, overflow tank, water pump, thermostat, coolant temperature switch, electric fan and radiator fan switch. The use of an electric fan is necessitated by the transversely mounted engine. A radiator bypass system is used for faster warmup.

Radiator Removal and Installation

1. Move the temperature selector to full on.
2. Open the radiator drain cock.
3. When the coolant reserve tank is empty, remove the radiator cap.
4. Remove the hoses.
5. Remove the upper and lower mounting brackets.
6. Remove the shroud.
7. Remove the fan motor attaching bolts.
8. Remove the top radiator attaching bolts.
9. Remove the bottom radiator attaching bolts.
10. Lift radiator from engine compartment.
11. Installation is the reverse of removal.

Water Pump Removal and Installation

1. Drain the cooling system.
2. Remove the drive belts.
3. Remove the water pump pulley.
4. Unbolt the compressor and/or air pump brackets from the water pump and secure them out of the way.
5. Position the bypass hose lower

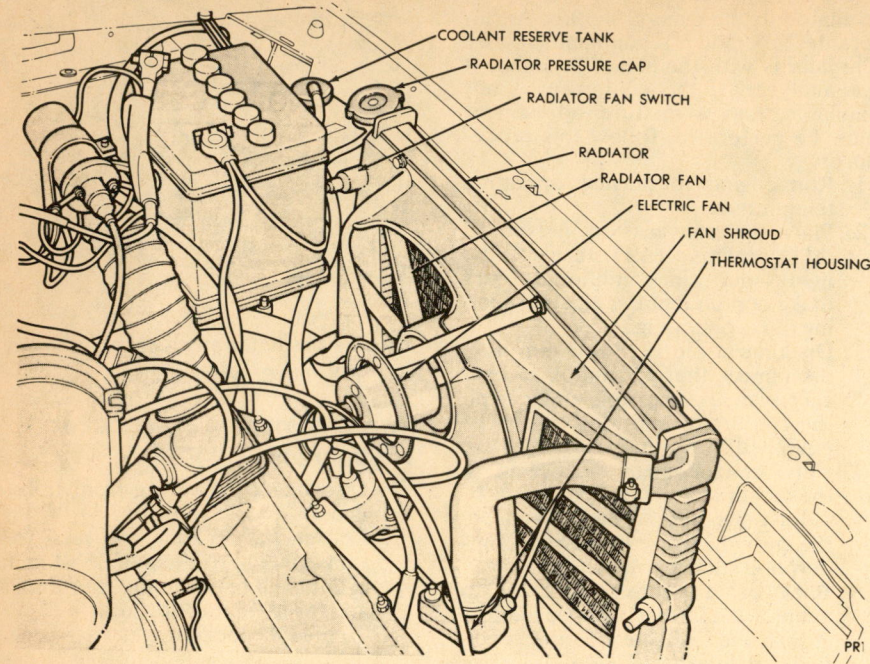

Cooling system (© Chrysler Corp.)

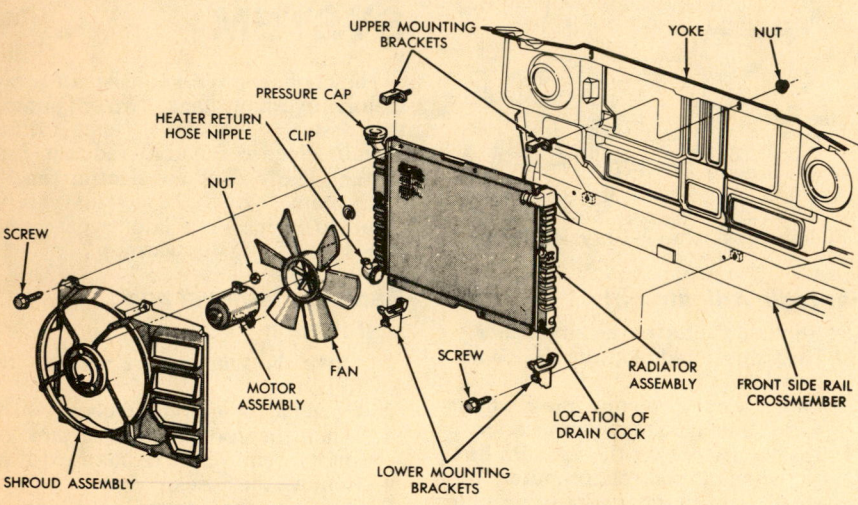

Radiator assembly (© Chrysler Corp.)

clamp in the center of the hose and disconnect the heater hose.

6. Unbolt and remove the water pump. Discard the gasket and clean the gasket surfaces.

7. Installation is the reverse of removal. Torque the water pump bolts to 25 ft. lbs., the alternator adjusting bolt to 30-50 ft. lbs.; the pulley bolts to 85-125 in. lbs.

Thermostat Removal and Installation

1. Drain the cooling system to a level below the thermostat.
2. Remove the hoses from the thermostat housing.
3. Remove the thermostat housing.
4. Remove the thermostat and discard the gasket. Clean the gasket surfaces thoroughly.

5. Using a new gasket, position the thermostat and install the housing and bolts. Make sure that the thermostat is seated properly.
6. Refill the cooling system.

EMISSION CONTROL SYSTEMS

Several different systems are used on each car. Most require no service and those which may require service also require sophisticated equipment for testing purposes. Service procedures are not included, therefore. Following is a brief description of each system.

Catalytic Converter

Two catalysts are used on each car: A small one located just after the exhaust manifold and a larger one located under the car body. Catalysts promote complete oxidation of exhaust gases through the effect of a platinum coated mass in the catalyst shell. Two things act to destroy the catalyst, functionally: excessive heat and leaded gas. Excessive heat during misfiring and prolonged testing with the ignition system in any way altered is the most common occurence. Test procedures should be accomplished as quickly as possible, and the car should not be driven when misfiring is noted.

Heated Air Inlet System

All engines are equipped with a vacuum device located in the carburetor air cleaner air intake. A small door is operated by a vacuum diaphragm and a thermostatic spring. When the air temperature outside is 40°F or lower, the door will block off air entering from outside and allow air channelled from the exhaust manifold area to enter the intake. This air is heated by the hot manifold. At 65°F or above, the door fully blocks off the heated air. At temperatures in between, the door is operated in intermediate positions. During acceleration the door is controlled by engine vacuum to allow the maximum amount of air to enter the carburetor.

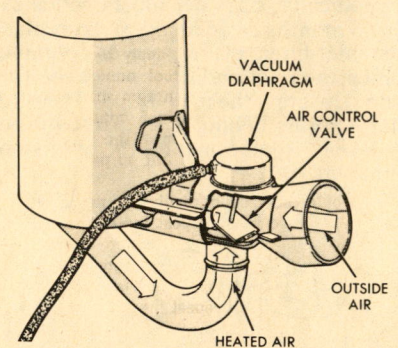

Heated air inlet system
(© Chrysler Corp.)

Exhaust Gas Recirculation System

This system reduces the amount of oxides of nitrogen in the exhaust by allowing a predetermined amount of hot exhaust gases to recirculate and dilute the incoming fuel/air mixture. The principal components of the system are the EGR valve and the Coolant Control Exhaust Gas Recirculation Valve (CCEGR). The former is located in the intake manifold and directly regulates the flow of exhaust gases into the intake. The latter is located in the thermostat housing and overrides the EGR valve when coolant temperature is below 125°F.

Air Injection System

This system is used on all California

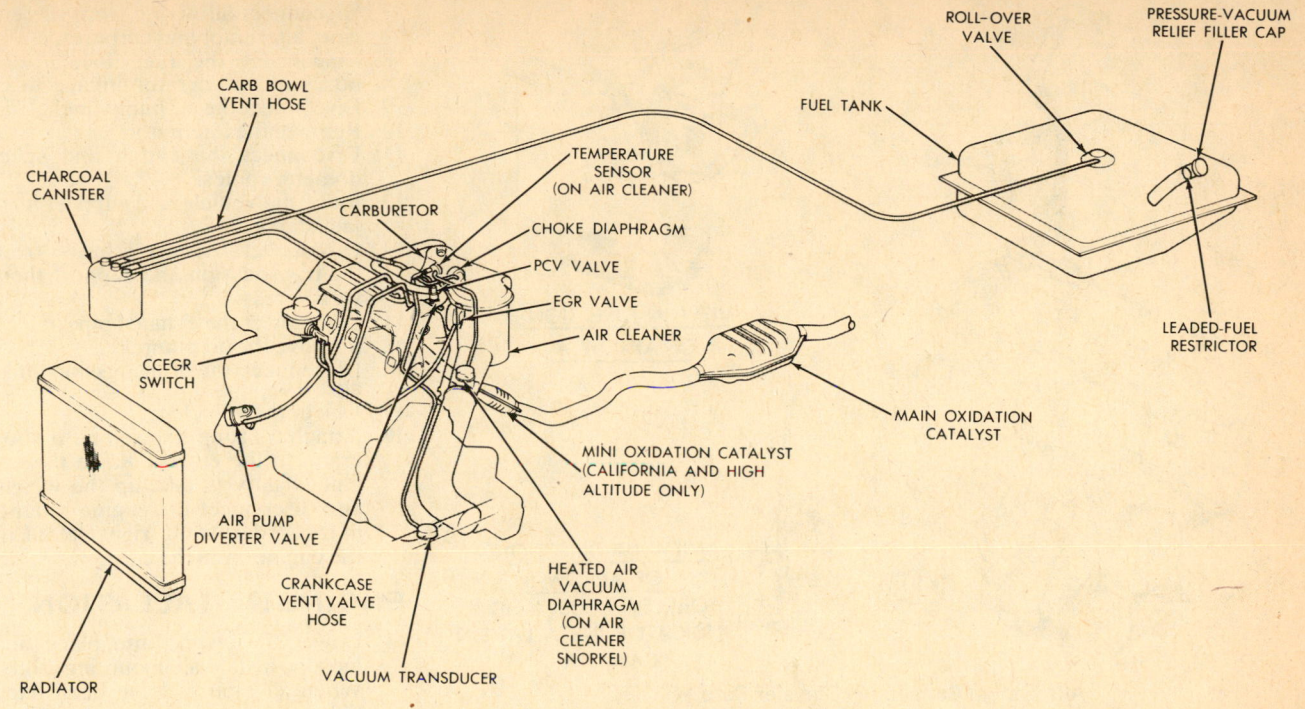

Emission control system (© Chrysler Corp.)

and Canada cars and all other cars built through January 10, 1978. Its job is to reduce carbon monoxide and hydrocarbons to required levels. The system adds a controlled amount of air to exhaust gases, via an air pump and induction tubes, causing oxidation of the gases. The California and other American cars, introduce air into the base of the exhaust manifold. The Canadian system introduces air through the head at the exhaust port. The system is composed of an air pump, a combination diverter/pressure-relief valve, hoses, a check valve to protect the hoses from exhaust gas, and an injection tube.

NOTE: *The system is not noiseless. A certain squeal is present in pump operation.*

Air Aspirator System

All models built after January 10, 1978, except California cars, will have an aspirator valve. This valve utilizes

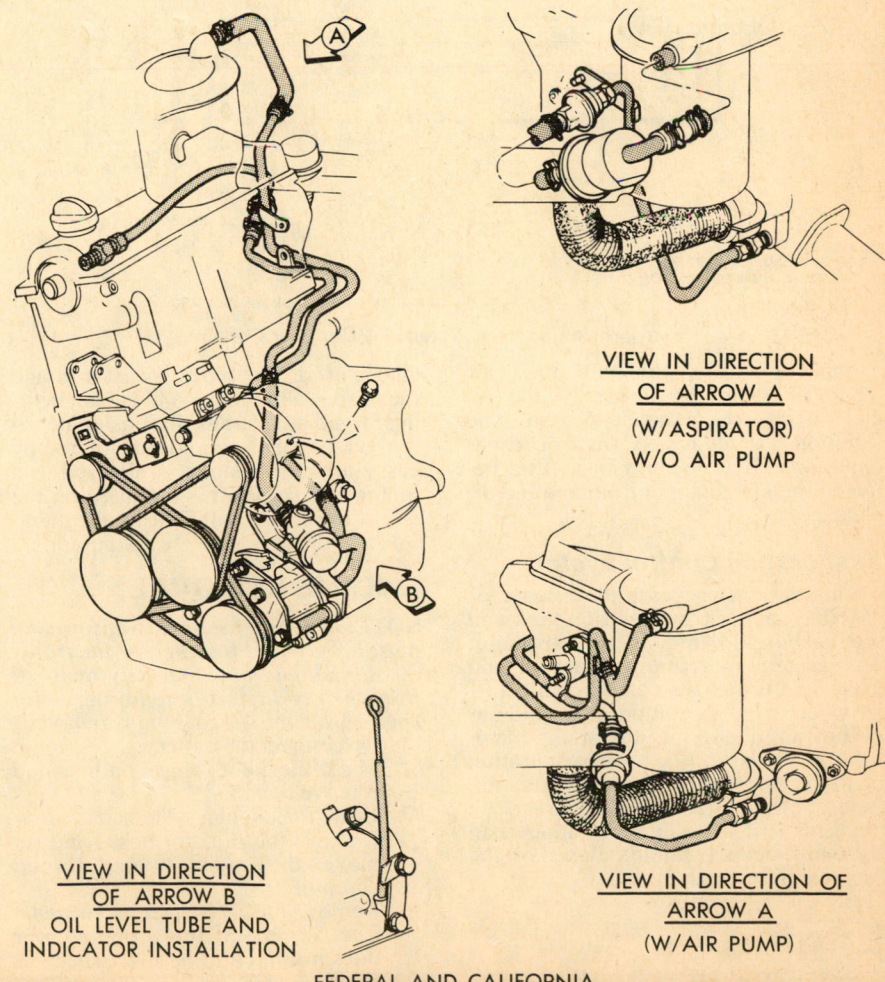

VIEW IN DIRECTION OF ARROW A
(W/ASPIRATOR)
W/O AIR PUMP

VIEW IN DIRECTION OF ARROW B
OIL LEVEL TUBE AND INDICATOR INSTALLATION

VIEW IN DIRECTION OF ARROW A
(W/AIR PUMP)

FEDERAL AND CALIFORNIA

AIR system-Federal and California (© Chrysler Corp.)

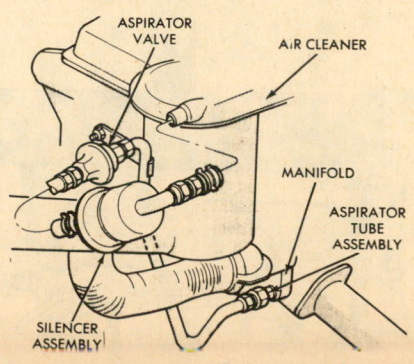

Aspirator system (© Chrysler Corp.)

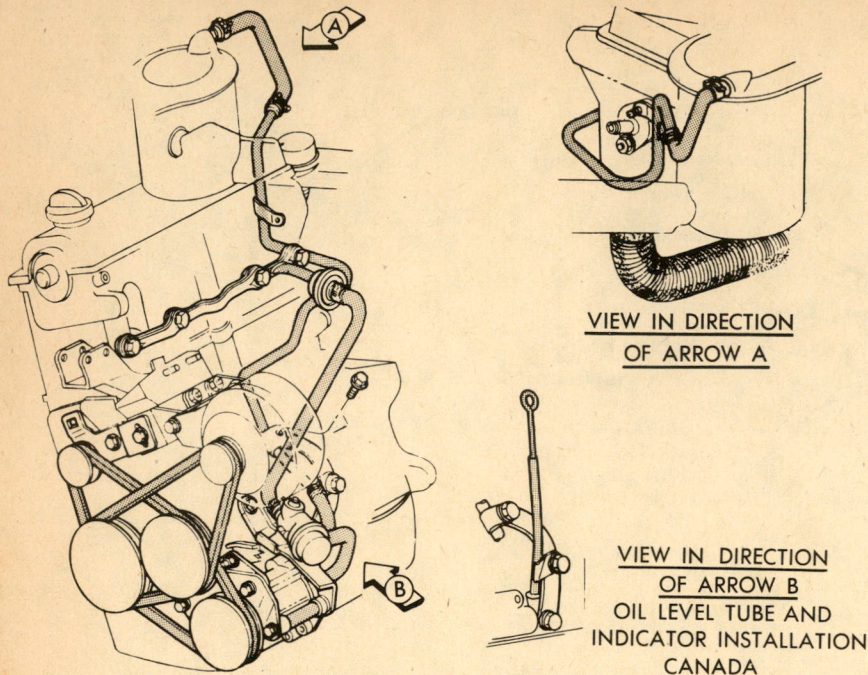

VIEW IN DIRECTION OF ARROW A

VIEW IN DIRECTION OF ARROW B
OIL LEVEL TUBE AND INDICATOR INSTALLATION CANADA

AIR system-Canada (© Chrysler Corp.)

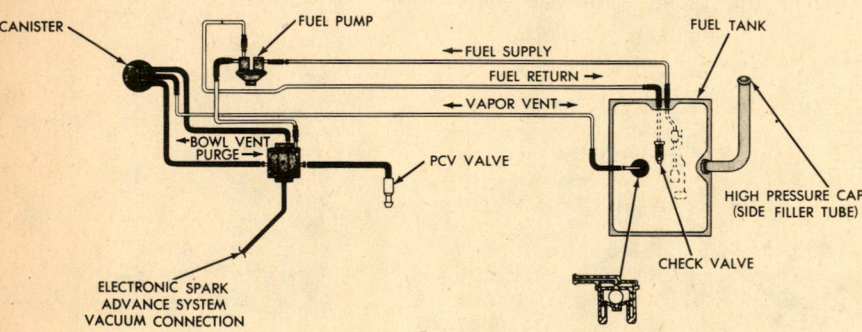

Evaporation control system (© Chrysler Corp.)

exhaust pressure pulsation to draw clean air from the inside of the air cleaner into the exhaust system. The function is to reduce HC (hydrocarbon) emissions. It is located in a tube between the exhaust manifold and the air cleaner.

Evaporation Control System

This system prevents the release of gasoline vapors from the fuel tank and the carburetor into the atmosphere. The system is vacuum operated and draws the fumes into a charcoal canister where they are temporarily held until they are drawn into the intake manifold for burning. For proper operation of the system and to prevent gas tank failure, the lines should never be plugged, and no other cap other than the one specified should be used on the fuel tank filler neck.

Engine

A 104.7 cu.in. (1.7L) displacement, four cylinder, overhead camshaft en-gine is used. The block is cast iron and the head is aluminum. A five main bearing forged steel crankshaft using no vibration damper is employed, rotated by cast aluminum pistons. A sintered iron timing belt sprocket is mounted on the end of the crankshaft. The intake manifold and oil filter base are aluminum.

ENGINE REMOVAL

NOTE: *The engine and transmission must be removed together, or the transmission should be completely removed from the car first. The following is for engine/transmission assembly removal.*

1. Disconnect the battery.
2. Mark the hood hinge outline and remove the hood.
3. Drain the cooling system.
4. Remove the radiator hoses and remove the radiator and shroud assembly.
5. Remove the air cleaner and hoses.
6. The air conditioning compressor does not have to be disconnected. Remove it from its bracket and position it out of the way. Securing it with wire is the best method.

7. Disconnect all wiring from the engine, alternator and carburetor.
8. Disconnect the fuel line, heater hoses and accelerator linkage.
9. Disconnect the air pump lines.
10. Remove the alternator.
11. Disconnect the clutch and speedometer cables.
12. Raise the vehicle and support it on jackstands.
13. Disconnect the driveshafts from the transmission and support them with wires.
14. Disconnect the exhaust pipe.
15. Remove the air pump.
16. Disconnect the transmission linkage.
17. Lower the vehicle.
18. Attach a lifting fixture and a shop crane to the engine. Raise the engine slightly to take up the weight and disconnect the engine mounts in this order: front, right, left. Lift the engine from the car.

ENGINE INSTALLATION

1. Lower the engine into place and loosely install all mounting bolts. When all mounts have been hand tightened, torque each to 40 ft. lbs.
2. Remove the lifting fixture and raise the vehicle, supporting it on jackstands.
3. Connect the driveshafts. Torque the bolts to 35 ft.lbs.
4. Connect the transmission linkage, install the air pump, connect the exhaust pipe and lower the vehicle.
5. Connect the clutch and speedometer cables.
6. Install the alternator.
7. Install the air pump lines.
8. Connect the fuel line, heater hoses and accelerator linkage.
9. Connect all wiring.
10. Mount the air conditioning compressor.
11. Install the air cleaner.
12. Install the radiator and hoses.
13. Fill the cooling system.
14. Install the hood.
15. Connect the battery.
16. Start the engine and run it to normal operating temperature.
17. Check the timing and adjust if necessary. Adjust the carburetor idle speed and mixture, and the transmission linkage.

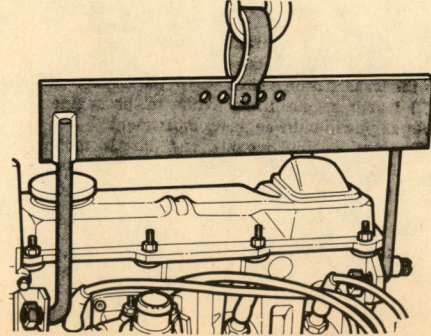

Lifting fixture (© Chrysler Corp.)

MANIFOLDS
Intake Manifold Removal and Installation

1. Remove the air cleaner and hoses.
2. Remove all wiring and any hoses connected to the carburetor and manifold.
3. Disconnect the accelerator linkage.
4. Remove the intake-to-exhaust manifold bolts.
5. Remove the manifold-to-head bolts and lift out the intake manifold.
6. Clean all gasket surfaces and, using new gaskets, install the manifold.
7. Connect all hoses and wires, and install the air cleaner.
8. Connect the accelerator linkage.

Exhaust Manifold Removal and Installation

1. Follow the intake manifold removal procedures above.
2. Disconnect the exhaust pipe.
3. Unbolt and remove the exhaust manifold.
4. Clean the gasket surfaces, and using a new gasket, install the manifold.

VALVE SYSTEM
Valve Adjustment

Valve adjustment is not required as a matter of routine maintenance. It is, however, necessary to check the valve clearance after head repairs. Adjusting clearance is a matter of substituting discs located in the top of the cam follower. The discs are available in .05mm increments from 3.00mm to 4.25mm. One disc is located in each follower. A special tool is required for disc removal and installation. Cold clearance should be .15-.25mm (.006-.010in.) intake and .35-.45mm (.014-.018in.) exhaust; warm clearance is .20-.30mm (.008-.012in.) intake and .40-.50mm (.016-.020in.) exhaust.

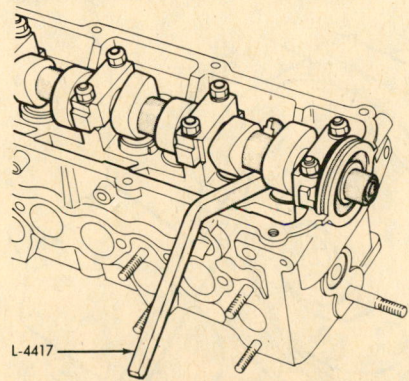

Adjusting valve clearance
(© Chrysler Corp.)
L-4417

CYLINDER HEAD
Cylinder Head Removal and Installation

1. Disconnect the battery

2. Drain the cooling system.
3. Remove the air cleaner assembly.
4. Disconnect all lines, hoses and wires from the head, manifold and carburetor.
5. Disconnect the accelerator linkage.
6. Remove the distributor cap.
7. Disconnect the exhaust pipe.
8. Remove the carburetor.
9. Remove the intake and exhaust manifolds.
10. Remove the upper portion of the front cover.
11. Turn the engine by hand until all gear timing marks are aligned.
12. Loosen the drive belt tensioner and slip the belt off the camshaft gear.

NOTE: *The camshaft timing mark is on the back of the gear and is properly positioned when it is in line with the left corner of the camshaft cover at the head.*

13. If equipped with air conditioning, remove the compressor from the mounting brackets and support it out of the way with wires. Remove the mounting brackets from the head.
14. Remove the valve cover, gaskets and seals.
15. Remove head bolts in reverse order of the tightening sequence.
16. Lift off the head and discard the gasket.
17. Installation is the reverse of removal. Make certain all gasket surfaces are thoroughly cleaned and are free of deep nicks or scratches. Always use new gaskets and seals. Never reuse a gasket or seal, even if it looks good. When positioning the head on the block, insert bolts 8 and 10 (see illustration) to align the head. Tighten bolts in the order shown in the illustration. Bolts should be tightened to 30 ft.lbs. in rotation, then tightened to 60 ft.lbs. When all bolts are at 60 ft.lbs., tighten each 1/4 turn more in sequence. Make sure all timing marks are aligned before installing the drive belt. The drive belt is correctly tensioned when it can be twisted 90° with the thumb and index finger midway between the camshaft and intermediate shaft.

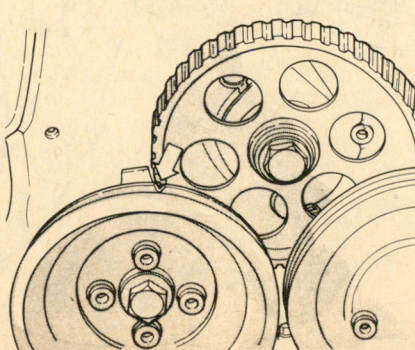

Crankshaft and intermediate gear alignment (© Chrysler Corp.)

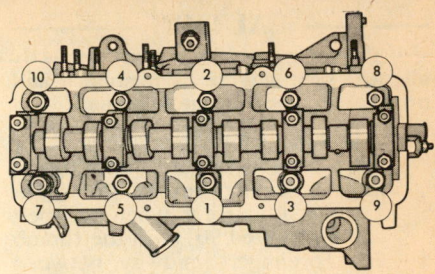

Head bolt sequence (© Chrysler Corp.)

TIMING COVER, BELT AND CAMSHAFT
Timing Cover Removal and Installation

1. Loosen the alternator mounting bolts, pivot the alternator and remove the drive belt.
2. Do the same thing with the air conditioning compressor.
3. Remove the cover retaining nuts, washers and spacers.
4. Remove the cover.
5. Installation is the reverse of removal.

Timing Belt Removal and Installation

1. Remove the timing belt cover.
2. While holding the large hex on the tension pulley, loosen the pulley nut.
3. Remove the belt from the tensioner.
4. Slide the belt off the three toothed pulleys.
5. Using the larger bolt on the crankshaft pulley, turn the engine until the # 1 cylinder is at TDC of the compression stroke. At this point the valves for the # 1 cylinder will be closed and the timing mark will be aligned with the pointer on the flywheel housing. Make sure that the timing mark on the rear face of the camshaft pulley is aligned with the lower left corner of the valve cover.
6. Check that the V-notch in the crankshaft pulley aligns with the dot mark on the intermediate shaft.

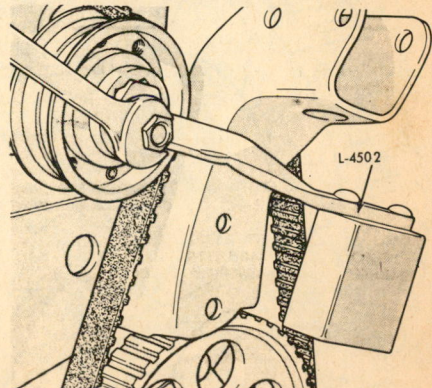

L-4502

Adjusting drive belt tension
(© Chrysler Corp.)

CAUTION

If the timing marks are not perfectly aligned, poor engine performance and probable engine damage will result!

7. Install the belt on the pulleys.
8. Adjust the tensioner by turning the large tensioner hex to the right. Tension is correct when the belt can be twisted 90° with the thumb and forefinger, midway between the camshaft and intermediate pulleys.
9. Tighten the tensioner locknut to 32 ft.lb.
10. Install the timing belt cover and check the ignition timing.

Camshaft Removal and Installation

1. Remove the timing belt cover.
2. Remove the timing belt.
3. Remove the air cleaner assembly.
4. Remove the valve cover.
5. Remove the Nos. 1, 3, and 5 camshaft bearing caps.
6. Loosen caps 2 and 4 diagonally and in increments.
7. Lift the camshaft out.
8. Lubricate the camshaft journals and lobes with engine assembly lubricant and position it in the head.
9. Install a new oil seal.
10. Install the Nos. 1, 3, 5 bearing caps and torque the nuts to 14 ft.lbs.
11. Install the Nos. 2 and 4 caps and diagonally torque the nuts to 14 ft.lbs.
12. Position a dial indicator so that the feeler touches the front end of the camshaft. Check for end play. Play should not exceed .006 in.
13. Place a new seal on the # 1 bearing cap. If necessary, replace the end plug in the head.
14. Follow the procedures under Timing Belt Removal and Installation for belt installation and timing.
15. Check the valve clearance and ignition timing.

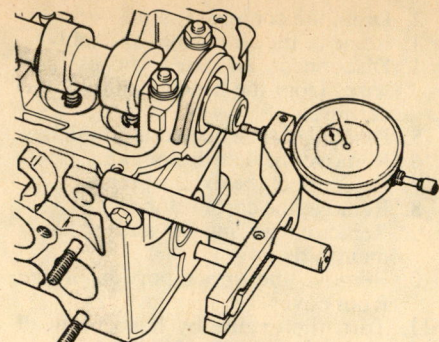

Checking camshaft end-play
(© Chrysler Corp.)

PISTONS AND CONNECTING RODS

The piston crown is marked with an arrow which must point toward the drive belt end of the engine when installed. The connecting rod and cap are marked with rectangular forge marks which must be mated when assembled and which must be on the intermediate shaft side of the engine when installed.

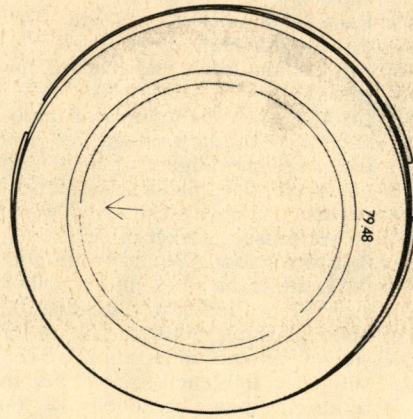

Piston is installed with the arrow facing the timing gear end of the engine
(© Chrysler Corp.)

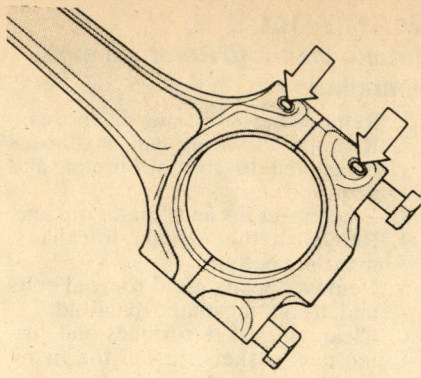

Matching connecting rod with cap
(© Chrysler Corp.)

LUBRICATION

Lubrication is conventional with a gear type pump driven off the intermediate shaft. A pressure relief valve prevents extreme pressure from building up in the system.

Oil Pan Removal and Installation

1. Drain the oil pan.
2. Support the pan and remove the attaching bolts.
3. Lower the pan and discard the gaskets.
4. Clean all gasket surfaces thoroughly and install the pan using gasket sealer and a new gasket.
5. Torque the pan bolts to 7 ft. lbs.
6. Refill the pan, start the engine, and check for leaks.

Oil Pump Removal and Installation

1. Remove the oil pan.
2. Remove the two pump mounting bolts.
3. Pull the oil pump down and out of the engine.
4. Installation is the reverse of remo-

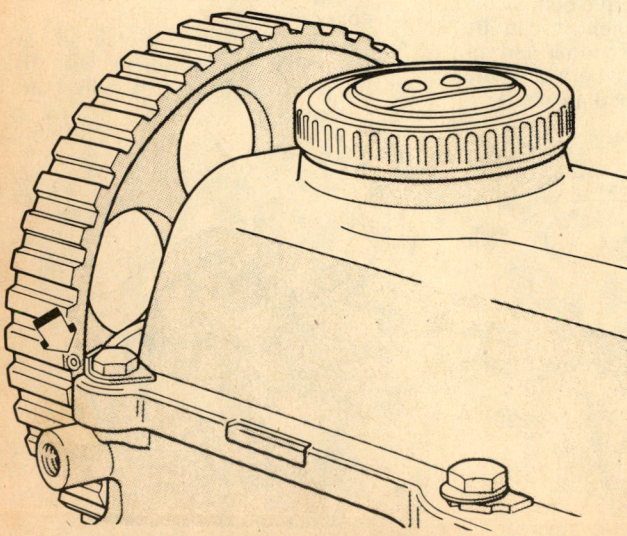

Camshaft gear positioning (© Chrysler Corp.)

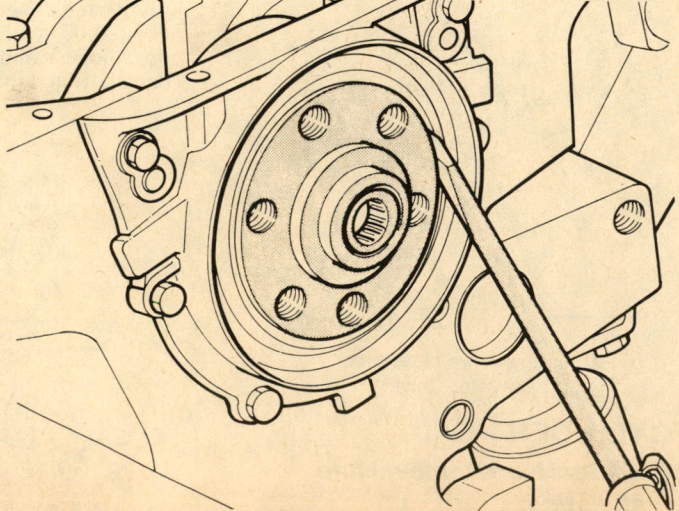

Removing rear main seal (© Chrysler Corp.)

val. Torque pump mounting bolts to 14 ft. lbs.

Rear Main Seal Removal and Installation

The rear main seal is located in a housing on the rear of the block. To replace the seal it is necessary to remove the engine.

1. Remove the transmission and flywheel.

— CAUTION —

Before removing the transmission, align the dimple on the flywheel with the pointer on the flywheel housing. The transmission will not mate with the engine during installation unless this alignment is observed.

2. Very carefully, pry the old seal out of the support ring with a screwdriver.
3. Coat the new seal with clean engine oil and press it into place with a flat piece of metal. Take great care not to scratch the seal or crankshaft.
4. Install the flywheel and transmission.

CLUTCH

The clutch is a single dry disc unit, with no adjustment for wear provided in the clutch itself. Adjustment is made through an adjustable sleeve in the pedal linkage.

Clutch Disc Replacement

NOTE: *Chrysler recommends the use of special tool L-4533 for disc alignment.*

1. Remove the transmission as described earlier.
2. Loosen the flywheel-to-pressure plate bolts diagonally, one or two turns at a time to avoid warpage.
3. Remove the flywheel and clutch disc from the pressure plate.
4. Remove the retaining ring and release plate.
5. Diagonally loosen the pressure plate-to-crankshaft bolts. Mark all parts for reassembly.
6. Remove the bolts, spacer and pressure plate.
7. The flywheel and pressure plate surfaces should be cleaned thoroughly with fine sandpaper.
8. Align marks and install the pressure plate, spacer and bolts. Coat the bolts with thread compound and torque them to 55 ft. lbs.
9. Install the release plate and retaining ring.
10. Using special tool L-4533 or its equivalent, install the clutch disc and flywheel on the pressure plate.

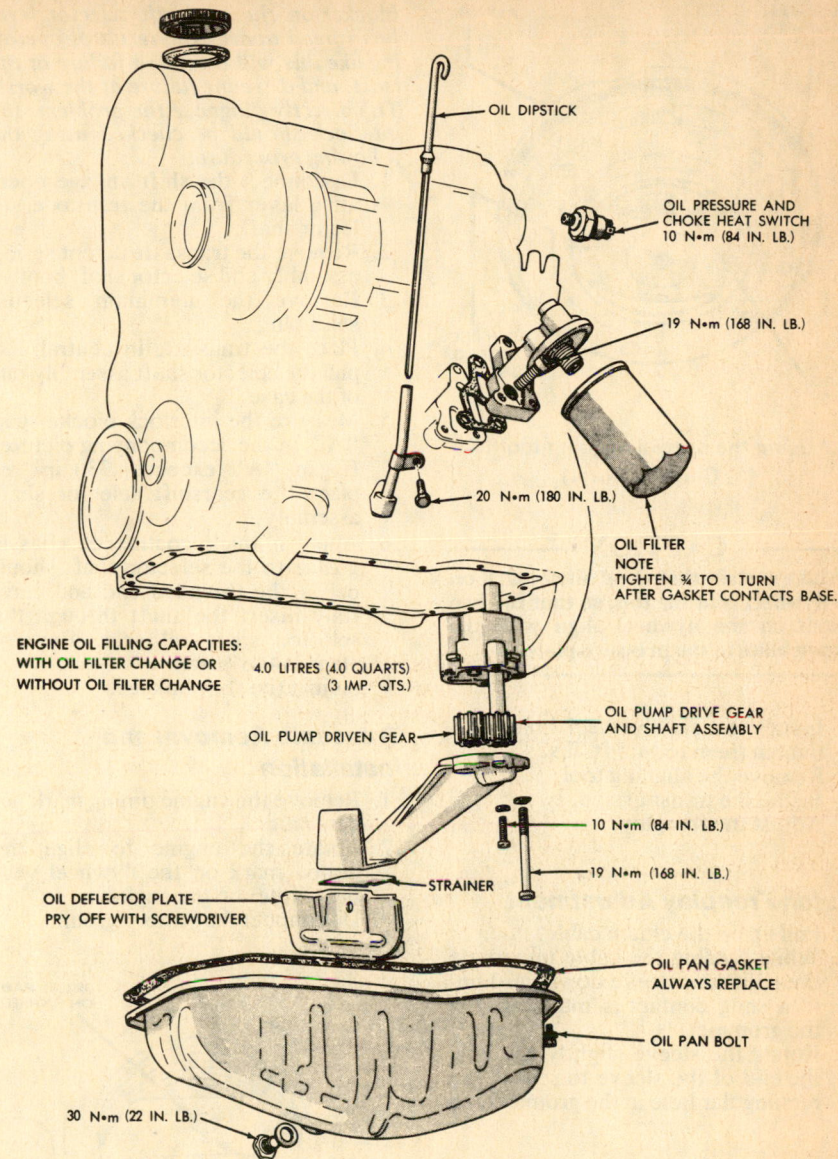

Lubrication system (© Chrysler Corp.)

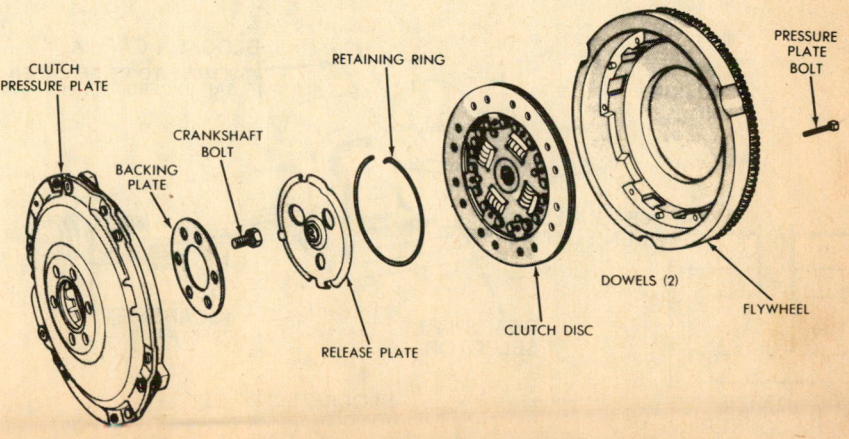

Clutch assembly (© Chrysler Corp.)

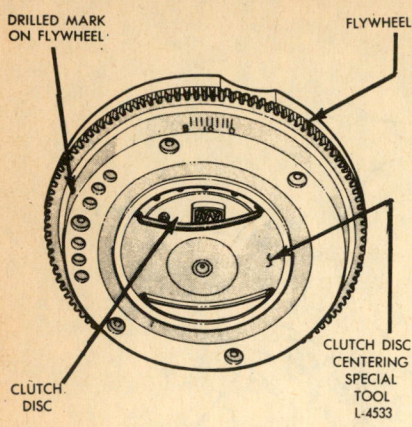

Using the special aligning tool
(© Chrysler Corp.)

CAUTION

Make certain that the drilled mark on the flywheel is at the top, so that the two dowels on the flywheel align with the proper holes in the pressure plate.

11. Install the six flywheel bolts and tighten them to 14.5 ft. lbs.
12. Remove the aligning tool.
13. Install the transmission.
14. Adjust the freeplay.

Clutch Freeplay Adjustment

1. Pull up on the clutch cable.
2. While holding the cable up, rotate the adjusting sleeve downward until a snug contact is made against the grommet.
3. Rotate the sleeve slightly to allow the end of the sleeve to seat in the rectangular hole in the grommet.

MANUAL TRANSMISSION

NOTE: *It is possible for the manual transaxle to become locked in two gears at once. This will occur if the interlock*

blocker on the gearshift selector lever has spread apart. The result of operating like this will be clutch failure at the least, and driveline failure at the worst. To correctly diagnose the problem, the interlock should be checked using the following procedure:

1. Disconnect the shift linkage operating lever from the transaxle selector shaft.
2. Remove the transaxle detent spring assembly and selector shaft boot.
3. Remove the aluminum selector shaft plug.
4. Place the transaxle in neutral and pull the selector shaft assembly out of the case.
5. Measure the interlock blocker gap "A", in the accompanying picture. If gap "A" exceeds .330 in. replace the gearshift selector shaft assembly.
6. Apply a thick coating of chassis grease to the selector shaft shoulder at the threaded end and carefully insert the shaft through the selector shaft oil seal. Reverse steps 1-4 to install.
7. Adjust the shift linkage.

Transaxle Removal and Installation

1. Remove the engine timing mark access plug.
2. Rotate the engine to align the drilled mark on the flywheel with the pointer on the engine.
3. Disconnect the battery ground.

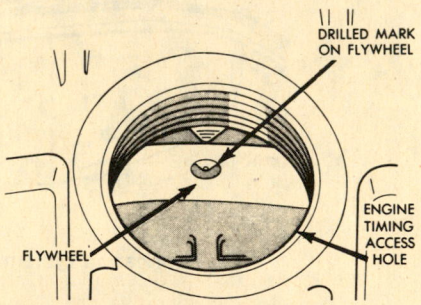

Drilled mark on flywheel
(© Chrysler Corp.)

4. Disconnect the shift linkage rods.
5. Disconnect the starter and ground wires.
6. Disconnect the backup light switch wire.
7. Remove the starter.
8. Disconnect the clutch cable.
9. Disconnect the speedometer cable.
10. Support the weight of the engine from above, preferably with a shop hoist or the fabricated holding fixture.
11. Raise and support the vehicle.
12. Disconnect the drive shafts and support them out of the way.
13. Remove the left splash shield.
14. Drain the transaxle.
15. Unbolt the left engine mount.
16. Remove the transaxle-to-engine bolts.
17. Slide the transaxle to the left until the mainshaft clears, then, carefully lower it from the car.
18. Installation is the reverse of removal.
19. Adjust the clutch cable.
20. Adjust the shift linkage.
21. Fill the transaxle.

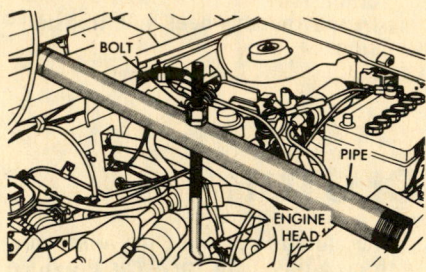

Engine support fixture
(© Chrysler Corp.)

Shift Linkage Adjustment

1. Place the transmission in neutral at the 3-4 position.
2. Loosen the shift tube clamp.
3. Place a 1/2 inch spacer between the shift tube flange and the yoke at the shift base.

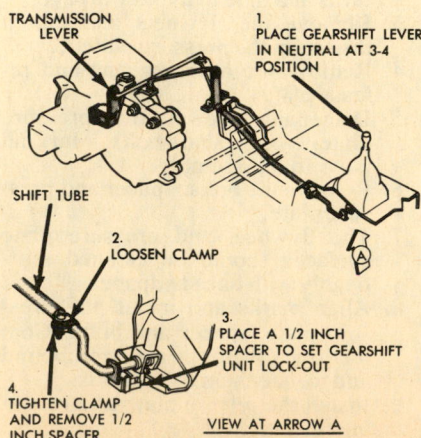

Shift linkage adjustment
(© Chrysler Corp.)

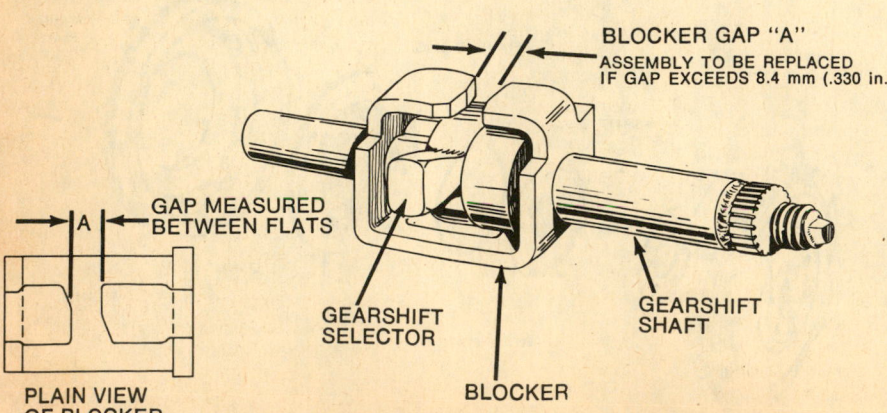

Checking the interlock blocker for failure

4. Tighten the shift tube clamp and remove the spacer.

AUTOMATIC TRANSMISSION

The automatic transaxle combines a torque converter, fully automatic 3-speed transmission, final drive gearing and differential into a compact front wheel drive system. Officially, it is designated the A-404 Torqueflite Automatic Transaxle.

Shift Linkage Adjustment

NOTE: *When it is necessary to disconnect the linkage cable from the lever, which uses plastic grommets as retainers, the grommets should be replaced.*

1. Make sure that the adjustable swivel block is free to slide on the shift cable.
2. Place the shift lever in Park.
3. With the linkage assembled, and the swivel lock bolt loose, move the shift on the transaxle all the way to the rear detent.
4. Tighten the adjuster swivel lock bolt to 8 ft. lb.
5. Check the linkage action.

Throttle Cable Adjustment

1. Adjust the idle speed as previously described.
2. Run the engine to normal operating temperature.
3. Loosen the adjustment bracket lock screw.
4. Make sure the adjustment bracket is free to slide in its slot.
5. Hold the transmission lever firmly rearward against its internal stop and tighten the adjustment bracket lock screw to 9 ft. lb.
6. Test the cable operation.

Band Adjustments

FRONT (KICKDOWN) BAND

Chrysler recommends that the band be adjusted at each fluid change. The adjusting screw is located on the left side of the case.

1. Loosen the lock nut and back off the nut about five full turns.
2. Tighten the band adjusting screw to 72 inch pounds.
3. Back off the adjusting screw exactly 2.5 turns.
4. Hold the adjusting screw and tighten the locknut to 35 ft. lb.

Neutral Start Switch Adjustment

The neutral start circuit is the center contact of the three-terminal switch located in the transmission case.

1. Remove the wiring connector and test for continuity between the center pin and the case. Continuity should exist only in Park and Neutral.
2. Remove the switch and check that the operating lever fingers are centered in the switch opening.
3. Install the switch and a new seal and tighten to 24 ft. lb. Retest with a lamp.
4. Replace the lost transmission fluid.
5. If shift linkage adjustment is correct and the switch still malfunctions, replace the switch.

Pan Removal and Installation, Fluid and Filter Change

NOTE: *RTV silicone sealer is used in place of a pan gasket.*

Chrysler recommends no fluid or filter changes during the normal service life of the car. Severe usage requires a fluid and filter change every 15,000 miles. Severe usage is defined as:
   a. more than 50% heavy city traffic during 90°F weather.
   b. police, taxi or commercial operation or trailer towing.

When changing the fluid, only Dexron or Dexron II fluid should be used. A filter change should be performed at every fluid change.

1. Raise the vehicle and support it on jackstands.
2. Place a large container under the pan, loosen the pan bolts and tap at one corner to break it loose. Drain the fluid.
3. When the fluid is drained remove the pan bolts.
4. Remove the retaining screws and replace the filter. Tighten the screws to 35 inch pounds.
5. Clean the fluid pan, peel off the old RTV silicone sealer and install the pan, using a 1/8 inch bead of new RTV sealer. Always run the sealer bead inside the bolt holes. Tighten the pan bolts to 10-12 ft. lb.
6. Pour four quarts of Dexron or Dexron II fluid through the filler tube.
7. Start the engine and idle it for at least 2 minutes. Set the parking brake and move the selector through each position, ending in Park.
8. Add sufficient fluid to bring the level to the FULL mark on the dipstick. The level should be checked in Park, with the engine idling at normal operating temperature.

CONSTANT VELOCITY JOINTS

The driveshaft assemblies are three piece units. Each driveshaft has an inner sliding constant velocity (Tripode) joint bolted to the transaxle, and an outer constant velocity (Rzeppa) joint with a stub shaft splined into the hub. The connecting shafts for the C/V joints are unequal in length and construction. The left side is a short solid shaft and the right is longer and tubular.

Driveshaft Removal and Installation—Manual Transmission

1. With the vehicle on the floor and the brakes applied, loosen the hub nut.

NOTE: *The hub and driveshafts are splined together and retained by the hub nut which is torqued to 200 ft. lbs.*

2. Raise and support the vehicle and remove the hub nut and washer.
3. Disconnect the lower control arm ball joint stud nut from the steering knuckle.

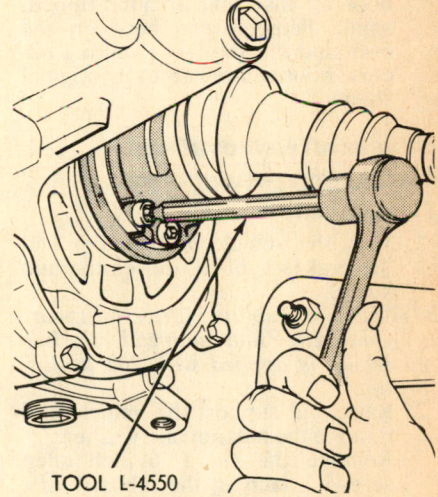

TOOL L-4550
Removing Allen head screws
(© Chrysler Corp.)

4. Remove the six 5/16 inch Allen-head screws which secure the CV joint to the transmission flange.
5. Holding the CV housing, push the outer joint and knuckle assembly outward while disengaging the inner housing from the flange face. Quickly turn the open end of the joint upward to retain as much lubricant as possible, then carefully pull the outer joint spline out of the hub. Cover the joint with a clean towel to prevent dirt contamination.
6. Before installation, make sure that any lost lubricant is replaced. The only lubricant specified is Chrysler part number 4131389. No other lubricant of any type is to be used, as premature failure of the joint will result.
7. Clean the joint body and mating flange face.
8. Install the outer joint splined shaft

into the hub. Do not secure with the nut and washer.

9. Early production vehicles were built with a cover plate between the hub and flange face. This cover is not necessary and should be discarded.

10. Position the inner joint in the transmission drive flange and secure it with six *new* screws. Torque the screws to 37-40 ft. lb.

11. Connect the lower control arm to the knuckle.

12. Install the outer joint and secure it with a *new* nut and washer. Torque the nut with the car on the ground and the brake set. Torque is 200 ft. lb.

13. Stake the new nut to the joint spindle using a tool having a radiused end of .063 inch and approximately 7/16 inch wide. A sharp chisel should not be used since the collar will probably be split.

14. After attaching the driveshaft, if the inboard boot appears to be collapsed or deformed, vent the inner boot by inserting a round-tipped, small diameter rod between the boot and the shaft. As venting occurs, boot will return to its original shape.

Driveshaft Removal and Installation—Automatic Transmission

1. With the vehicle on the floor and the brakes applied, loosen the hub nut.

NOTE: *The hub and driveshafts are splined together and retained by the hub nut which is applied with 200 ft. lbs. torque.*

2. Raise and support the vehicle and remove the hub nut and washer.

3. Remove the six 5/16 inch allen screws attaching the inboard C/V joint to the drive flange.

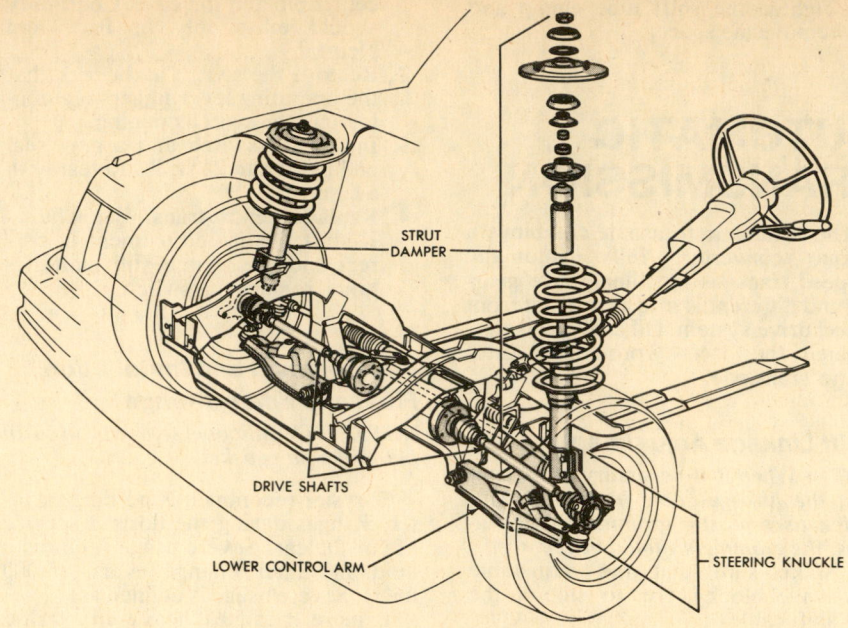

Front suspension (© Chrysler Corp.)

----- CAUTION -----

Do not support and move the vehicle on the wheels with the driveshaft removed; the steering knuckle bearing will be damaged.

4. Install the splined outer shaft into the splined hub and position the inboard C/V joint flange into the transaxle drive flange.

5. Install the allen head screws and tighten to 35 ft. lbs.

6. Install the washer and hub nut. Chrysler recommends the use of a new hub nut. Tighten the nut and lower the vehicle. With the vehicle on the floor and the brakes applied, tighten the nut to 200 ft. lbs. Stake the nut with a sharp chisel.

NOTE: *If the original nut is reused, it must be staked in a different position.*

JACKING AND HOISTING

The illustration shows the correct jacking and hoist lifting positions.

FRONT SUSPENSION

A MacPherson Type front suspension, with vertical shock absorbers attached to the upper fender reinforcement and the steering knuckle, is used. Lower control arms, attached inboard to a cross-member and outboard to the steering knuckle through a ball joint, provide lower steering knuckle position. During steering maneuvers, the upper strut and steering knuckle turn as an assembly.

Strut Removal and Installation

1. Raise and support the vehicle.
2. Remove the wheel.
3. **NOTE:** *If the original strut is to be assembled to the original knuckle, mark the cam adjusting bolt. Remove the cam adjusting bolt, through bolt and brake hose bracket retaining screw.*
4. Remove the strut mounting screws and remove the strut.
5. Installation is the reverse of removal. Torque the strut mounting screws to 27 ft. lbs.; the brake hose bracket screw to 10 ft. lbs.; the cam bolt to 85 ft. lbs., and the wheel nuts to 80 ft. lbs.

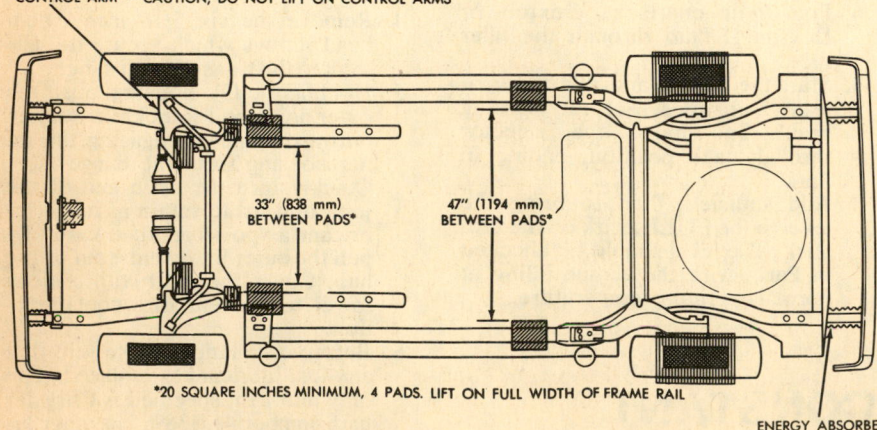

CONTROL ARM — CAUTION; DO NOT LIFT ON CONTROL ARMS

33" (838 mm) BETWEEN PADS*

47" (1194 mm) BETWEEN PADS*

ENERGY ABSORBER

*20 SQUARE INCHES MINIMUM, 4 PADS. LIFT ON FULL WIDTH OF FRAME RAIL

TWIN POST LIFT POINTS
FRAME CONTACT OR FLOOR JACK
DRIVE ON HOIST
O SCISSORS JACK (EMERGENCY) LOCATIONS
LIFTING, JACKING SUPPORT LOCATIONS

Jacking and hoisting instructions (© Chrysler Corp.)

Lower Ball Joint Replacement

The lower ball joints are permanently lubricated, operate with no free play, and are riveted in place. The rivets must be drilled out and replaced with special bolts.

NOTE: *to avoid damage to the control arm surface adjacent to the ball joint during drilling, the use of a center punch and a drill press are strongly recommended.*

1. Remove the lower control arm.
2. Position the assembly with the ball joint up.
3. Center punch the rivets on the ball joint housing side.
4. Using a drill press with a 1/4 inch bit, drill out the center of the rivet.
5. Using a 1/2 inch bit, drill the center of the rivet until the bit makes contact with the ball joint housing.
6. Using a 3/8 inch bit, drill the center of the rivet. Remove the remainder of the rivet with a punch.
7. Position the new ball joint on the control arm and tighten the bolts to 60 ft. lbs.
8. Install the control arm and tighten the ball joint clamp bolt to 50 ft. lbs.; the pivot bolt to 105 ft. lbs. and the stub strut to 70 ft. lbs.

Spring Removal and Installation

1. Remove the struts.
2. Compress the spring, using a reliable coil spring compressor.
3. Hold the strut rod and remove the rod nut.
4. Remove the retainers and bushings.
5. Remove the spring.

NOTE: *Springs are not interchangeable from side to side.*

--- CAUTION ---

When removing the spring from the compressor, open the compressor evenly and not more than 9-1/4 inches.

6. Assembly is the reverse of disassembly.

NOTE: *Torque rod nut to 55 ft. lbs. before removing the spring compressor.*

Lower Control Arm Removal and Installation

1. Raise and support the vehicle.
2. Remove the front inner pivot through bolt, the rear stub strut nut, retainer and bushing, and the ball joint-to-steering knuckle clamp bolt.
3. Separate the ball joint stud from the steering knuckle by prying between the ball stud retainer on the knuckle and the lower control arm.

--- CAUTION ---

Pulling the steering knuckle out from the vehicle after releasing it from the ball joint can separate the inner C/V joint.

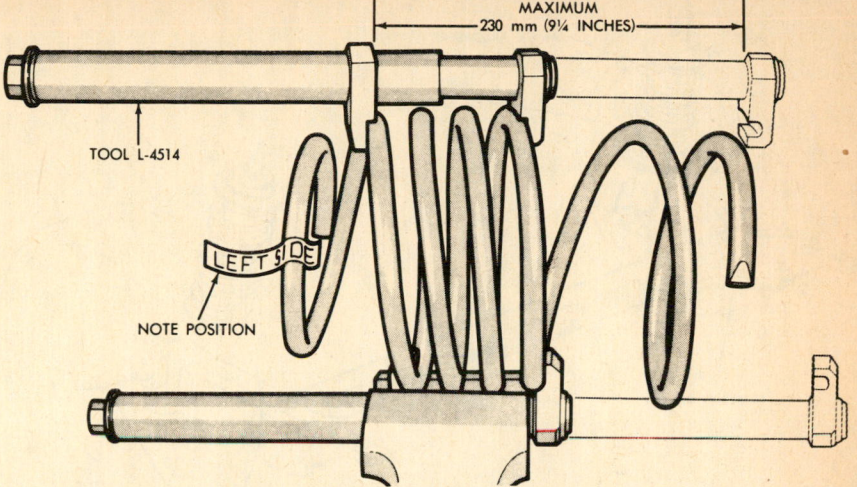

Compressing the spring (© Chrysler Corp.)

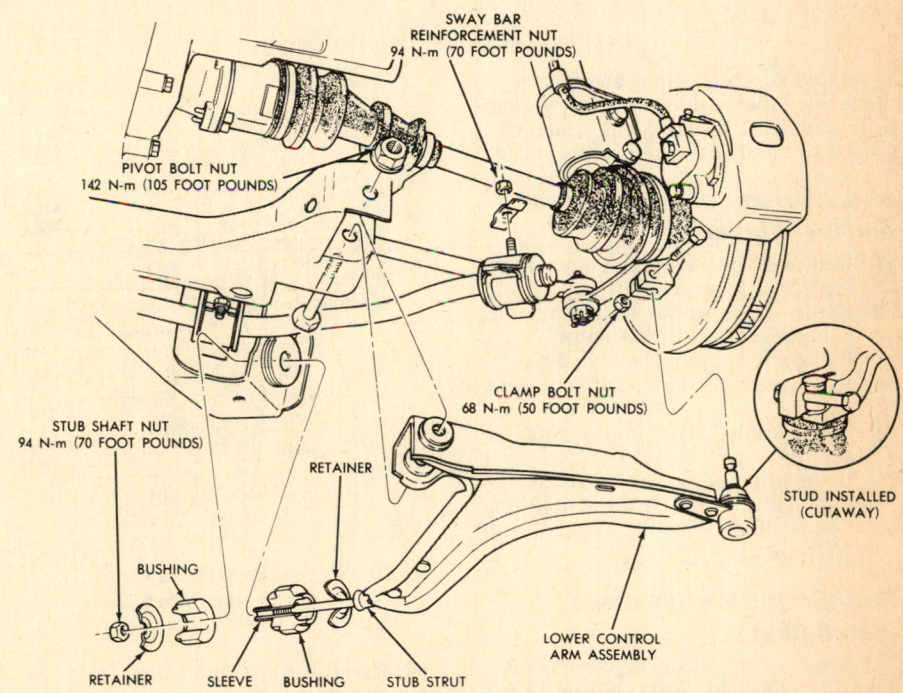

Lower control arm (© Chrysler Corp.)

4. Remove the sway bar-to-control arm nut and reinforcement and rotate the control arm over the sway bar. Remove the rear stub strut bushing, sleeve and retainer.

NOTE: *The substitution of fasteners other than those of the grade originally used is not recommended.*

5. Install the retainer, bushing and sleeve on the stub strut.
6. Position the control arm over the sway bar and install the rear stub strut and front pivot into the crossmember.
7. Install the front pivot bolt and loosely install the nut.
8. Install the stub strut bushing and retainer and loosely assemble the nut.
9. Position the sway bar bracket and stud through the control arm and install the retainer and nut. Tighten the nut to 10 ft. lb.
10. Install the ball joint stud into the steering knuckle and install the clamp bolt. Torque the clamp bolt to 50 ft. lb.

REAR SUSPENSION

A trailing, independent arm assembly, with integral sway bar is used. The wheel spindles are attached to two trailing arms which extend rearward from mounting points on the body where they are attached with shock absorbing, oval bushings. A crossmember

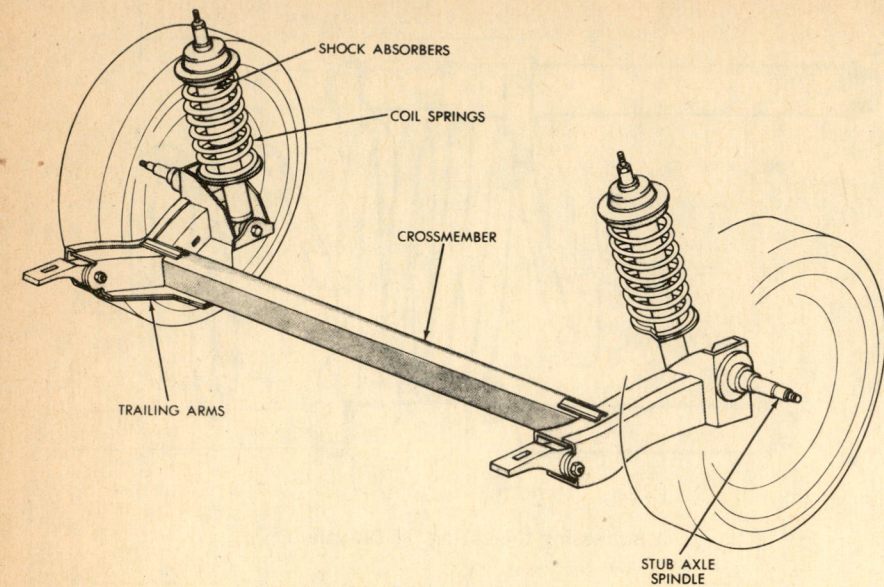

Rear suspension (© Chrysler Corp.)

is welded to the trailing arms, just to the rear of the bushings. A coil spring, over shock absorber strut assembly, similar to the front suspension, is used.

Shock Absorber Strut Removal and Installation

1. Remove the protective cap from the upper mounting nut.
2. Remove the upper mounting nut, isolator retainer and isolator.
3. Raise and support the vehicle.
4. Remove the lower strut mounting bolt.
5. Remove the strut and spring assembly.
6. Installation is the reverse of removal. Torque the lower mounting bolt to 40 ft. lbs.; the upper nut to 20 ft. lbs.

Rear Spring Removal and Installation

The use of a coil spring compressor, such as Chrysler part # L-4514, is necessary.

1. Remove the strut and spring assembly as described earlier.
2. Install the spring compressor on the spring and place it in a vise.

— CAUTION —

Always grip 4 or 5 coils and never extend the retractors beyond 9 1/4 inches.

3. Tighten the retractors evenly until pressure is removed from the upper spring seat.
4. Loosen the retaining nut.

— CAUTION —

Be very careful when loosening the retaining nut. If the spring is not properly compressed, serious injury could result.

5. Remove the lower isolator, pushrod sleeve, and upper spring seat.

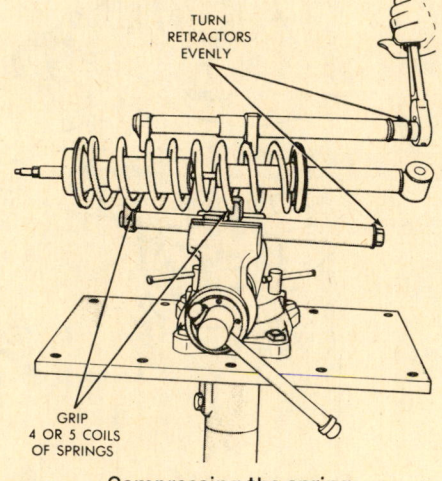

Compressing the spring
(© Chrysler Corp.)

6. Carefully slip the strut from the spring.
7. Remove the rebound bumper and dust shield from the strut.
8. Remove the lower spring seat.
9. Carefully and evenly, remove the compressor from the spring.
10. Install the compressor on the spring, gripping four or five coils.
11. Compress the spring.
12. Install the lower spring seat, dust shield and rebound bumper on the strut.
13. Slip the unit inside the coil spring and install the upper spring seat.
14. Make sure that the level surfaces on the seats are in position with the spring.
15. Install the sleeve on the pushrod and install the retaining nut. Torque the nut to 20 ft. lbs.
16. Install the lower isolator.
17. Install the strut and spring assembly.

BRAKES

A conventional front disc/rear drum setup is used. The front discs are single piston caliper types; the rear drums are activated by a conventional top mounted wheel cylinder. Disc brakes require no adjustments, the drum brakes are self adjusting by means of the parking brake cable. The only variances in the system from those found on the majority of vehicles are that the system is diagonally balanced, that is, the front left and right rear are on one system and the front right and left rear on the other. No proportioning valve is used. Power brakes are optional.

Master Cylinder Removal and Installation

WITH POWER BRAKES

1. Disconnect the primary and secondary brake lines from the master cylinder. Plug the openings.
2. Remove the nuts attaching the cylinder to the power brake booster.
3. Slide the master cylinder straight out, away from the booster.
4. Position the master cylinder over the studs on the booster, align the pushrod with the master cylinder piston and tighten the nuts to 16 ft. lbs.
5. Connect the brake lines.
6. Bleed the brakes.

WITH NON-POWER BRAKES

1. Disconnect the primary and secondary brake lines and install plugs in the master cylinder openings.
2. Disconnect the stoplight switch mounting bracket from under the instrument panel.
3. Pull the brake pedal backward to disengage the pushrod from the master cylinder piston.

NOTE: *This will destroy the grommet.*

4. Remove the master cylinder-to-firewall nuts.
5. Slide the master cylinder out and away from the firewall. Be sure to remove all pieces of the broken grommet.
6. Install the boot on the pushrod.
7. Install a new grommet on the pushrod.
8. Apply a soap and water solution to the grommet and slide it firmly into position in the primary piston socket. Move the pushrod from side to side to make sure it's seated.
9. From the engine side, press the pushrod through the master cylinder mounting plate and align the mounting studs with the holes in the cylinder.
10. Install the nuts and torque them to 16 ft. lbs.
11. From under the instrument panel, place the pushrod on the pin on the pedal and install a new retaining clip.

12. Install the brake lines on the master cylinder.
13. Bleed the system.

Power Booster Removal and Installation

1. Remove the master cylinder; it can be pulled far enough out of the way to allow booster removal without disconnecting the brake lines.
2. Disconnect the vacuum hose from the booster.
3. Under the instrument panel, pry the retainer clip center tang over the end of the brake pedal pin and pull the retainer clip from the pin. Discard the clip.
4. Remove the four booster attaching nuts.
5. Remove the booster from the vehicle.
6. Position the booster on the firewall.
7. Torque the nuts to 20 ft. lbs.
8. Carefully position the master cylinder on the booster.
9. Install the mounting nuts and torque them to 18 ft. lbs.
11. Connect the vacuum hose to the booster.
11. Coat the bearing surface of the pedal pin with chassis lube.
12. Connect the pushrod to the pedal pin and install a new clip.
13. Check the stoplight operation. With vacuum applied to the power brake unit and pressure applied to the pedal, the master cylinder should vent (force a jet of fluid through the front chamber vent port).

Parking Brake Adjustment

1. Fully release the parking brake.
2. Locate the cable connector at the rear suspension crossmember and thoroughly clean the assembly.
3. Loosen the adjusting nut until there is slack in the cable.
4. Insert a thin screwdriver through the slot in the brake backing plate and rotate the starwheel so there is light shoe-to-drum contact.
5. Back off the starwheel to allow free drum rotation.
6. Tighten the cable adjusting nut until a slight drag is felt at the wheels.
7. Loosen the cable adjusting nut until both rear wheels turn freely.
8. Back off the nut two full turns.
9. Apply and release the parking brake several times to make sure that free rotation exists at the wheels.

Steering

The manual steering system consists of a tube which contains the toothed rack, a pinion, the rack slipper, and the rack slipper spring. Steering effort is transmitted to the steering arms by the tie rods which are coupled to the ends of the rack, and the tie rod ends. The connection between the ends of the rack and the tie rod is protected by a bellows type oil seal which retains the gear lubricant.

The power steering system consists of four major parts: the power gear, power steering pump, pressure hose and the return hose. As with the manual system, the turning of the steering wheel is converted into linear travel through the meshing of the helical pinion teeth with the rack teeth. Power assist is provided by an open center, rotary type, three-way control valve which directs fluid to either side of the rack control piston.

Tie Rod End Replacement

1. Loosen the jam nut which connects the tie rod end to the knuckle. Mark the tie rod position on the threads.
2. Using a ball joint separator, remove the tie rod end from the knuckle.
3. Install a new tie rod end in reverse of removal. Torque the end nut to 50 ft. lbs.; the locknut to 65 ft. lbs.
4. Check alignment.

Power Steering Pump Removal and Installation

1. Disconnect the power steering hoses from the pump.
2. Remove the adjusting bolt and slip off the belt.
3. Support the pump, remove the mounting bolts and lift out the pump.
4. Installation is the reverse of removal. Adjust the belt so that there is about 1/2 inch of deflection midway along its longest straight run.

Steering Wheel Removal and Installation

1. Remove the horn button and horn switch.
2. Remove the steering wheel nut.
3. Using a steering wheel puller, remove the steering wheel.
4. Align the master serration in the wheel hub with the missing tooth on the shaft. Torque the shaft nut to 60 ft. lbs.

5. Replace the horn switch and button.

Turn Signal Switch Removal and Installation

1. Disconnect the electrical connector at column.
2. Remove the steering wheel as described earlier.
3. Remove the lower column cover.
4. Remove the wash/wipe switch.
5. Remove the wiring clip and the three screws securing the turn signal switch.
6. Installation is the reverse of removal.

Ignition and Steering Lock Removal and Installation

1. Remove the steering wheel.
2. Remove the upper and lower column covers.
3. Using a hacksaw blade, cut the upper 1/4 inch from the key cylinder retainer pin boss.
4. Using a drift, drive the roll pin from the housing and remove the key cylinder.
5. Insert the new cylinder into the housing, making sure that it en-

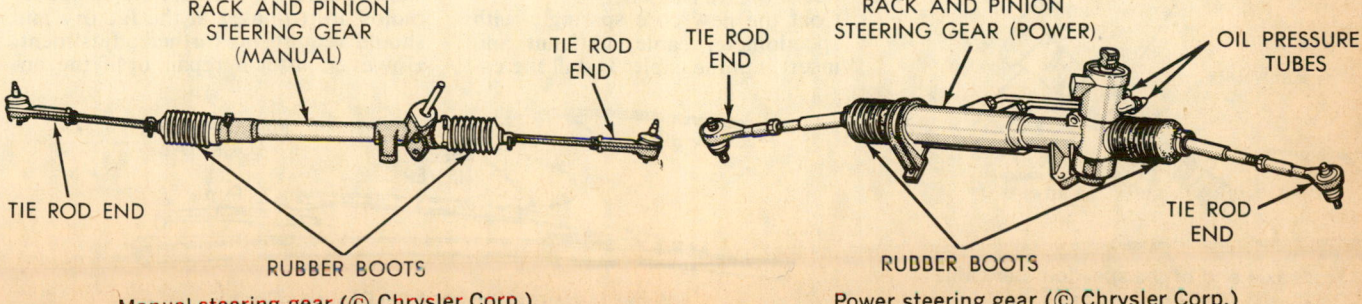

Manual steering gear (© Chrysler Corp.)   Power steering gear (© Chrysler Corp.)

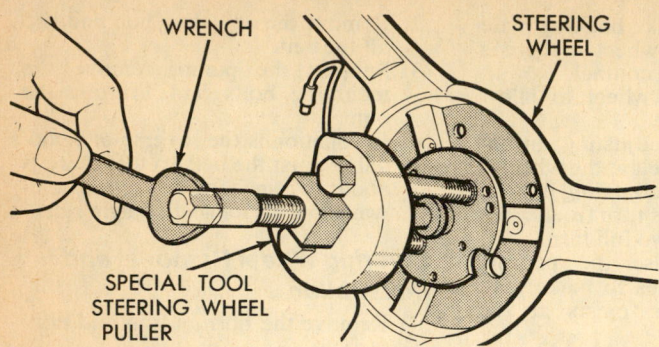

Steering wheel removal (© Chrysler Corp.)

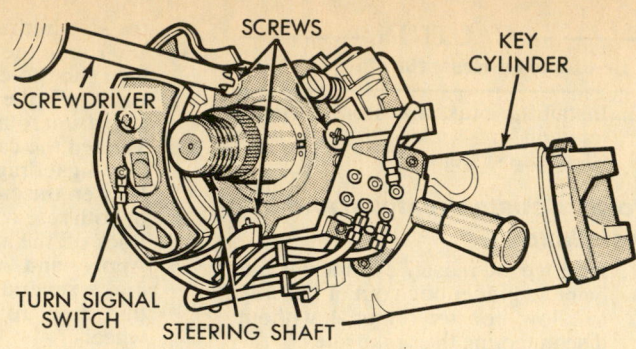

Turn signal switch removal (© Chrysler Corp.)

gages the lug on the ignition switch driver. Install the roll pin.

Ignition Switch Removal and Installation

1. Remove the connector from the switch.
2. Place the key in the LOCK position.
3. Remove the key.
4. Remove the two mounting screws from the switch and allow the switch and pushrod to drop below the jacket.
5. Rotate the switch 90 degrees to permit removal of the switch from the pushrod.
6. To install the switch, position the switch in LOCK (second detent from the top).
7. Place the switch at right angles to the column and insert the pushrod.
8. Align the switch on the bracket and install the screws.
9. With a light rearward load on the switch, tighten the screws. Check for proper operation.

Instrument Panel

The fuel, temperature and oil pressure gauges work on the constant voltage principle through a common voltage limiter which pulses to provide intermittent current to the gauge system.

Cluster Assembly Removal and Installation

1. Remove the two lens assembly

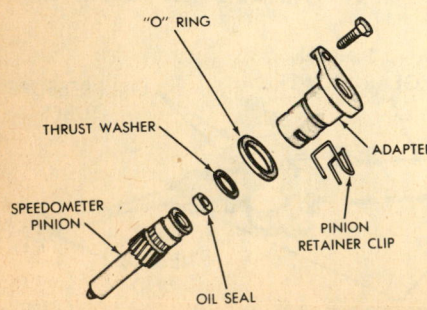

Transaxle end of the speedometer cable (© Chrysler Corp.)

lower attaching retaining springs by pulling rearward with a pliers.
2. Allow the lens assembly to drop as it is pulled rearward.
3. Remove the speedometer assembly (two screws).
4. Remove the two wiring harness connectors.
5. Remove the two cluster attaching screws.
6. Pull the two upper spring retainers away from the panel.
7. If equipped with a clock, reach behind the panel and disconnect the wires.
8. Remove the cluster assembly.
9. Installation is the reverse of removal.

Headlight Switch Removal and Installation

1. Disconnect the battery ground.
2. Pull the headlight knob from the switch.
3. Unscrew the collar from the instrument panel side of the switch.
4. Push the switch through the panel and let it drop; disconnect the wires.
5. Installation is the reverse of removal.

Speedometer Cable Replacement

1. Reach under the instrument panel and depress the spring clip retaining the cable to the speedometer head. Pull the cable back and away from the head.
2. If the core is broken, raise and support the vehicle and remove the cable retaining screw from the cable bracket. Carefully slide the cable out of the transaxle.
3. Coat the new core sparingly with speedometer cable lubricant and insert it in the cable. Install the ca-

ble at the transaxle, lower the car and install the cable at the speedometer head.

Windshield Wipers

Motor Removal and Installation

1. Disconnect the linkage from the motor crank arm.
2. Remove the wiper motor plastic cover.
3. Disconnect the wiring harness from the motor.
4. Remove the three mounting bolts from the motor bracket and remove the motor.
5. Installation is the reverse of removal.

Wiper Blade Replacement

1. Lift the wiper arm away from the glass.
2. Depress the release lever on the bridge and remove the blade assembly from the arm.
3. Lift the tab and pinch the end bridge to release it from the center bridge.
4. Slide the end bridge from the blade element and the element from the opposite end bridge.
5. Assembly is the reverse of removal. Make sure that the element locking tabs are securely locked in position.

Radio

AM, AM/FM monaural, or AM/FM stereo multiplex units are available. All radios are trimmed at the factory and should require no further adjustment. However, after a repair or if the an-

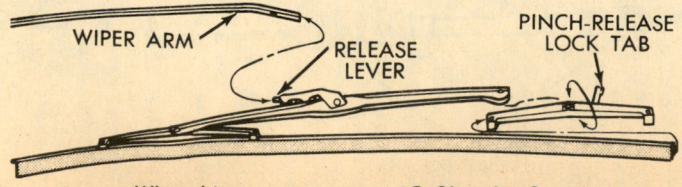

Wiper blade replacement (© Chrysler Corp.)

tenna trim is to be verified, proceed as follows:

1. Turn radio on.
2. Manually tune the radio to a weak station between 1400 and 1600 KHz on AM.
3. Increase the volume and set the tone control to full treble (clockwise).
4. Viewing the radio from the front, the trimmer control is a slot-head located at the rear of the right side. Adjust it carefully by turning it back and forth with a screwdriver until maximum loudness is achieved.

Radio Removal and Installation

1. Remove the seven bezel attaching screws and open the glove compartment.
2. Remove the bezel, guiding the right end around the glove compartment and away from the panel.
3. Disconnect the radio ground strap and remove the two radio mounting screws.
4. Pull the radio from the panel and disconnect the wiring and antenna lead.
5. Installation is the reverse of removal.

HEATER

Heater Assembly Removal and Installation—without Air Conditioning

1. Disconnect the battery and drain the cooling system.
2. Remove the center outside air floor vent housing.
3. Remove the ash tray.
4. Remove the two defroster duct adapter screws. The left one is reached through the ash tray opening.
5. Remove the defrost duct adapter and push the flexible hose up out of the way.
6. Disconnect the temperature control cable.
7. Disconnect the blower motor wiring connector.
8. Disconnect the hoses from the heater core and plug the core openings.
9. Remove the two nuts retaining the heater unit to the firewall.
10. Remove the glove compartment and door.
11. Remove the screw attaching the heater brace bracket to the instrument panel.
12. Remove the heater assembly support strap nut. Disconnect the strap from the plenum stud and lower the heater from the instrument panel.
13. Disconnect the control cable and remove the unit from the car.

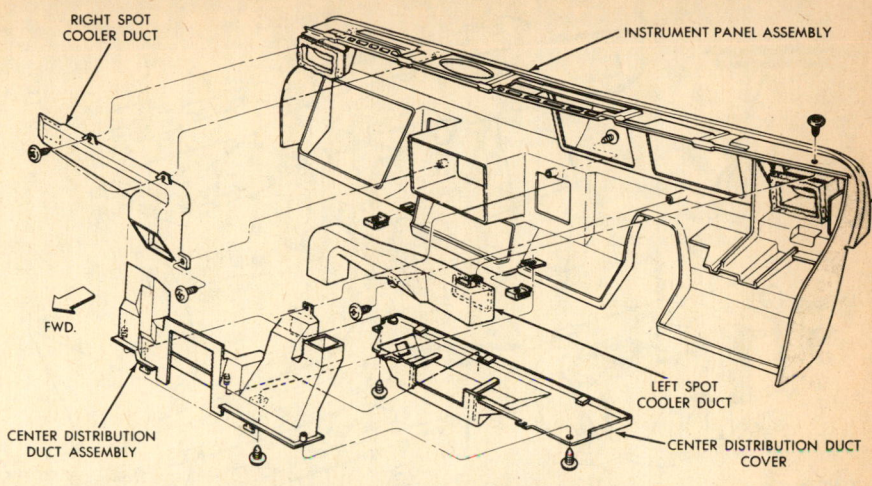

Air Conditioning ducts (© Chrysler Corp.)

14. Connect the control cable and raise the unit into position so that the core tubes and mounting studs fit through their holes in the firewall.
15. Install the support strap and hand tighten the nut.
16. Install and tighten the two heater-to-firewall nuts.
17. Unplug and connect the core tubes.
18. Install the defroster duct adaptor.
19. Install the ash tray.
20. Install the center outside air floor vent housing.
21. Install the glove compartment.
22. Refill the cooling system.

Blower Motor Removal and Installation—without Air Conditioning

The blower motor is located under the instrument panel on the left side of the heater assembly.

1. Disconnect the motor wiring.
2. Remove the left outlet duct.
3. Remove the four motor retaining screws and remove the motor.
4. Installation is the reverse of removal.

Heater Core Removal and Installation—without Air Conditioning

1. Remove the heater assembly as described earlier.

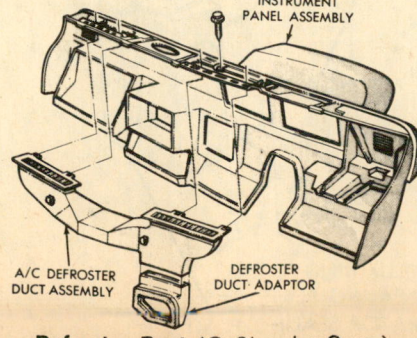

Defroster Duct (© Chrysler Corp.)

2. Remove the left outlet duct.
3. Remove the blower motor.
4. Remove the defroster duct adapter.
5. Remove the outside air and defroster door cover.
6. Remove the defroster door.
7. Remove the defroster door control rod.
8. Remove the core cover.
9. Lift the core from the unit.
10. Installation is the reverse of removal.

Blower Motor Removal and Installation—Air Conditioned Cars

1. Disconnect the battery ground.
2. Remove the three screws securing the glovebox to the instrument panel.
3. Disconnect the wiring from the blower and case.
4. Remove the blower vent tube from the case.
5. Loosen the recirculating door from its bracket and remove the actuator from the housing. Leave the vacuum lines attached.
6. Remove the seven screws attaching the recirculating housing to the A/C unit and remove the housing.
7. Remove the three mounting flange nuts and washers.
8. Remove the blower motor from the unit.
9. Installation is the reverse of removal. Replace any damaged sealer.

Heater Core Removal and Installation—Air Conditioned Cars

Removal of the Heater-Evaporator Unit is required for core removal. Two people will be required to perform the operation. Discharge, evacuation and recharge and leak testing of the refrigerant system is necessary. This work should be performed only by a trained technician. Have the system discharged before attempting removal.

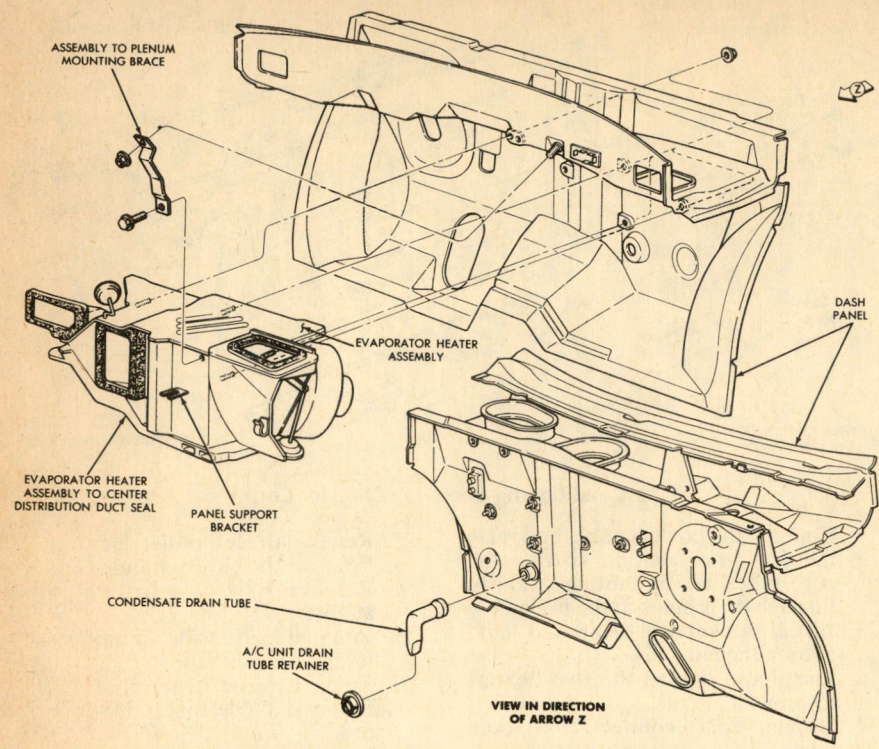

Evaporator-Heater Assembly (© Chrysler Corp.)

During installation, a small can of refrigerant oil will be necessary.

1. Disconnect the battery ground.
2. Drain the coolant.
3. Disconnect the temperature door cable from the heater-evaporator unit.
4. Disconnect the temperature door cable from the retaining clips.
5. Remove the glovebox.
6. Disconnect the vacuum harness from the control head.
7. Disconnect the blower motor lead and anti-diesel relay wire.
8. Remove the seven screws fastening the right trim bezel to the instrument panel. Starting at the right side, swing the bezel clear and remove it.
9. Remove the three screws on the bottom of the center distribution duct cover and slide the cover rearward and remove it.
10. Remove the center distribution duct.
11. Remove the defroster duct adaptor.
12. Remove the H-type expansion valve, located on the right side of the firewall:
    a. remove the 5/16in. bolt in the center of the plumbing sealing plate.
    b. carefully pull the refrigerant lines toward the front of the car, taking care to avoid scratching the valve sealing surfaces.
    c. remove the two 1/4-20 Allen-head capscrews and remove the valve.

13. Cap the pipe openings at once. Wrap the valve in a plastic bag.
14. Disconnect the hoses from the core tubes.
15. Disconnect the vacuum lines at the intake manifold and water valve.
16. Remove the unit-to-firewall retaining nuts.
17. Remove the panel support bracket.
18. Remove the right cowl lower panel.
19. Remove the instrument panel pivot bracket screw from the right side.
20. Remove the screws securing the lower instrument panel at the steering column.
21. Pull back the carpet from under the unit as far as possible.
22. Remove the nut from the evaporator-heater unit-to-plenum mounting brace and blower motor ground cable. While supporting the unit, remove the brace from its stud.
23. Lift the unit, pulling it rearward to allow clearance. These operations may require two people.
24. Slowly lower the unit taking care to keep the studs from hanging-up on the insulation.
25. When the unit reaches the floor, slide it rearward until it is out from under the instrument panel.
26. Remove the unit from the car.
27. Place the unit on a workbench. On the inside-the-car-side, remove the 1/4-20 nut from the mode door actuator on the top cover and the two retaining clips from the front edge of the cover. To remove the mode door actuator, remove the two screws securing it to the cover.
28. Remove the fifteen screws attaching the cover to the assembly and lift off the cover. Lift the mode door out of the unit.
29. Remove the screw from the core retaining bracket and lift out the core.
    To install:
30. Place the core in the unit and install the bracket.
31. Install the actuator arm.

CAUTION

When installing the unit in the car, care must be taken that the vacuum lines to the engine compartment do not hang-up on the accelerator or become trapped between the unit and the firewall. If this happens, kinked lines will result and the unit will have to be removed to free them. Proper routing of these lines will require two people. The portion of the vacuum harness which is routed through the steering column support MUST be positioned BEFORE the distribution housing is installed. The harness MUST be routed ABOVE the temperature control cable.

32. Place the unit on the floor as far under the panel as possible.
33. Raise the unit carefully, at the same time pull the lower instru-

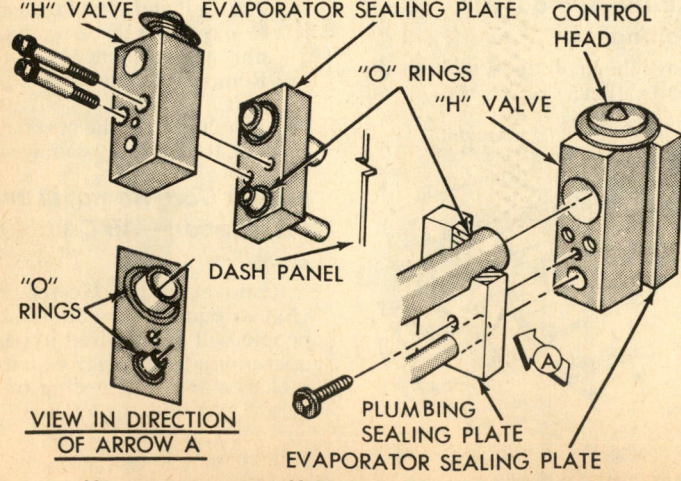

H-type Expansion Valve (© Chrysler Corp.)

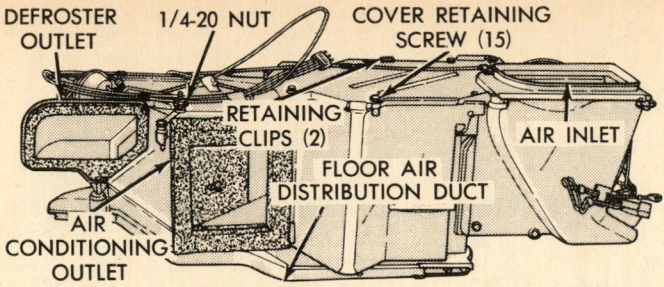

DEFROSTER OUTLET 1/4-20 NUT COVER RETAINING SCREW (15)

RETAINING CLIPS (2)

AIR INLET

FLOOR AIR DISTRIBUTION DUCT

AIR CONDITIONING OUTLET

Heater-Evaporator Unit Positioned for Disassembly
(© Chrysler Corp.)

ment panel rearward as far as possible.

34. Position the unit in place and attach the brace to the stud.

35. Install the lower ground cable and attach the nut.

36. Install and tighten the unit-to-firewall nuts.

37. Reposition the carpet and install, but do not tighten the right instrument panel pivot bracket screw.

38. Place a piece of sheet metal or thin cardboard against the evaporator-heater assembly to center the assembly duct seal.

39. Position the center distributor duct in place making sure that the upper left tab comes in through the left center A/C outlet opening and that each air take-off is properly inserted in its respective outlet.

NOTE: *Make sure that the radio wiring connector does not interfere with the duct.*

40. Install and tighten the screw securing the upper left tab of the center air distribution duct to the instrument panel.

41. Remove the sheet metal or cardboard from between the unit and the duct.

NOTE: *Make sure that the unit seal is properly aligned with the duct opening.*

42. Install and tighten the two lower screws fastening the center distribution duct to the instrument panel.

43. Install and tighten the screws securing the lower instrument panel at the steering column.

44. Install and tighten the nut securing the instrument panel to the support bracket.

45. Make sure that the seal on the unit is properly aligned and seated against the distribution duct assembly.

46. Tighten the instrument panel pivot

bracket screw and install the right cowl lower trim.

47. Slide the distributor duct cover assembly onto the center distribution duct so that the notches lock into the tabs and the tabs slide over the rear and side ledges of the center duct assembly.

48. Install the three screws securing the ducting.

49. Install the right trim bezel.

50. Connect the vacuum harness to the control head.

51. Connect the blower lead and the anti-diesel wire.

52. Install the glovebox.

53. Connect the temperature door cable.

54. Install new O-rings on the evaporator plate and the plumbing plate. Coat the new O-rings with clean refrigerant oil.

55. Place the H-valve against the evaporator sealing plate surface and install the two 1/4-20NC through-bolts. Torque to 6-10 ft. lb.

56. Carefully hold the refrigerant line connector against the valve and install the 5/16-18-NC bolt. Torque to 14-20 ft. lb.

57. Install the heater hoses at the core tubes.

58. Connect the vacuum lines at the manifold and water valve.

59. Install the condensate drain tube.

60. Have the system evacuated, charged and leak tested by a trained technician.

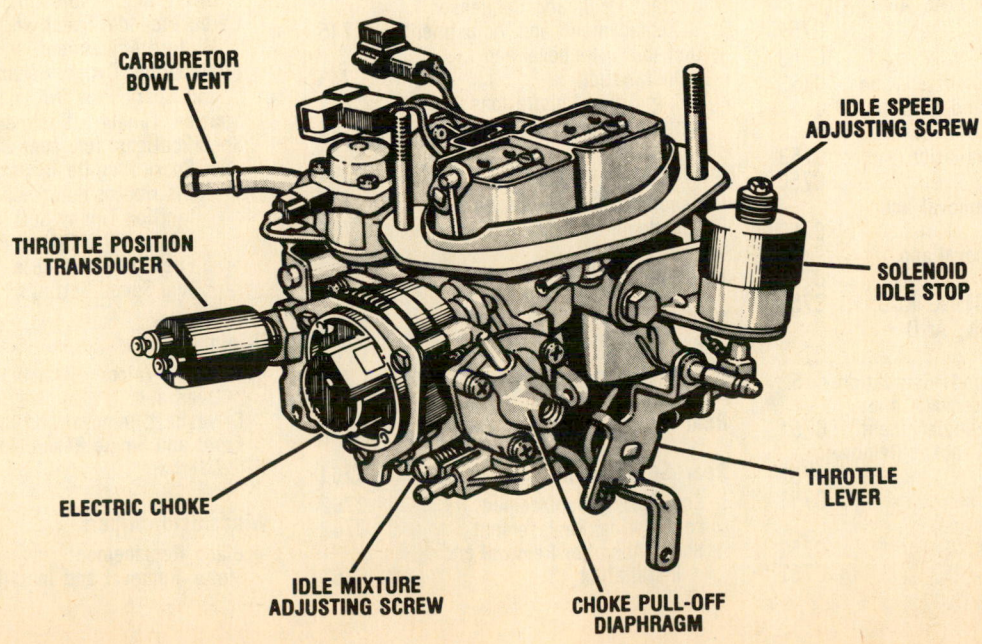

CARBURETOR BOWL VENT

IDLE SPEED ADJUSTING SCREW

THROTTLE POSITION TRANSDUCER

SOLENOID IDLE STOP

ELECTRIC CHOKE

THROTTLE LEVER

IDLE MIXTURE ADJUSTING SCREW

CHOKE PULL-OFF DIAPHRAGM

Details of the staged two-barrel carburetor (© Chrysler Corp.)

Pontiac & Grand Prix

Index

YEAR IDENTIFICATION

1972 Pontiac

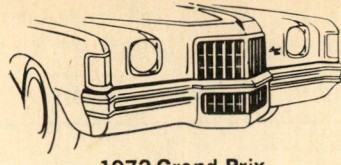

1972 Grand Prix

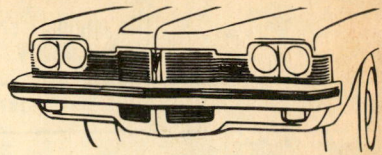

1973 Catalina

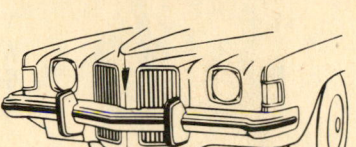

1973 Grand Prix

1974 Catalina

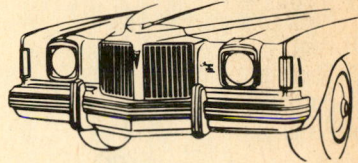

1974 Grand Prix

1974 Grand Ville

1975 Grand Prix

1975 Grandville Brougham, Grand Safari

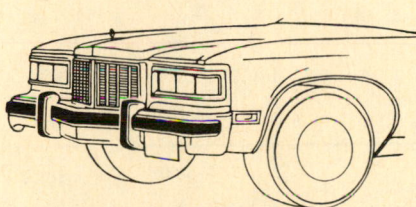

1976 Bonneville Brougham

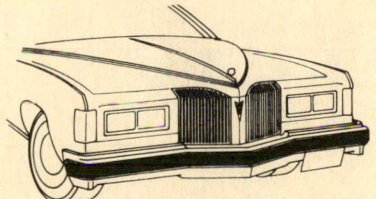

1976 Grand Prix

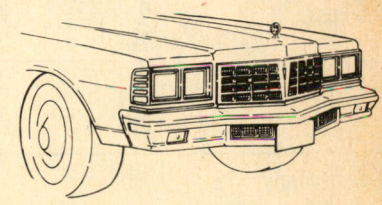

1977 Bonneville Brougham

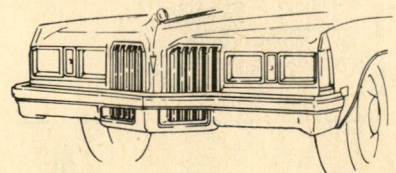

1977 Catalina

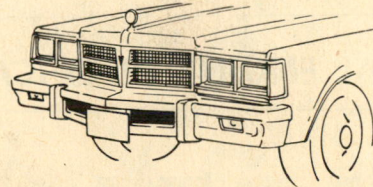

1977 Grand Prix

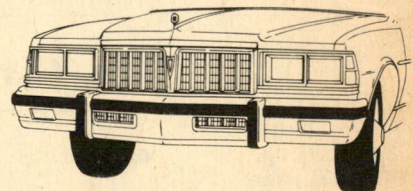

1978 Bonneville

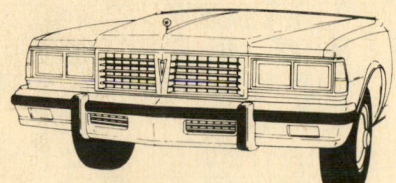

1978 Catalina

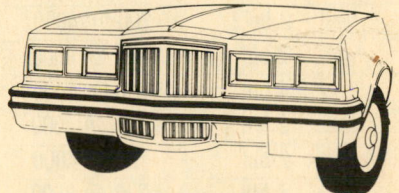

1978 Grand Prix

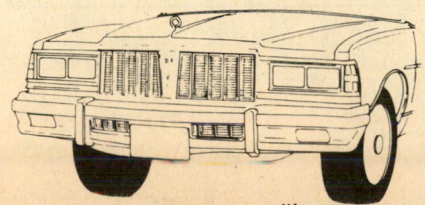

1979 Bonneville

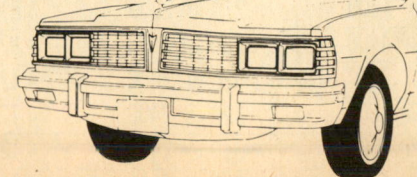

1979 Catalina

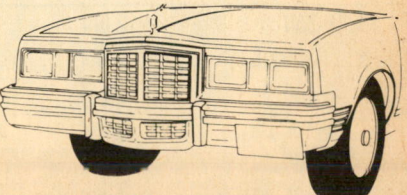

1979 Grand Prix

ENGINE IDENTIFICATION

The engine identification code is the fifth digit of the vehicle identification number (V.I.N.). The V.I.N. is on a plate, visible through the left side of the windshield.

Disp.	Bbl.	1972	1973	1974	1975	1976	1977	1978	1979
6 Cylinder Models									
231 Buick	2						C	A	A
8 Cylinder Models									
301 Pont.	2						Y	Y	Y
301 Pont.	4							W	W
305 Chev.	2						U	U	G
350 Buick	4							X	X
350 Pont.	2					H			
	2HP	M	M			M			
	2DE	N	N						
350 Pont.									
	4					J	P		
	4HP					E			
350 Olds.	4						R	R	R
400 Pont.	2	R	R		R	R			
	2	P	P	P					
400 Pont.	4	S	S	S	S	S	Z	Z	
	4DE	T	T	T					
403 Olds.	4						K	K	K
455 Pont.	2	V							
	2DE	U							
455 Pont.	4	W	W	W	W	W			
	4DE	Y	Y	Y					
	4DE	X	X	X					

SD Super Duty
DE With dual exhaust
HO—High Output
HP—High Performance

GENERAL ENGINE SPECIFICATIONS

Year	Engine No. Cyl. Displacement (cu In.)	Carburetor Type	Horsepower @ rpm ■	Torque @ rpm (ft lbs) ■	Bore X Stroke (in.)	Compression Ratio	Oil Pressure @ 2000 rpm
'72	8-400	2 bbl	175 @ 4000	310 @ 2400	4.1212 x 3.750	8.2:1	35
	8-400 DE	2 bbl	200 @ 4000	325 @ 2400	4.1212 x 3.750	8.2:1	35
	8-400	2 bbl	200 @ 4000	295 @ 2800	4.1212 x 3.750	8.2:1	35
	8-400 DE	4 bbl	250 @ 4400	325 @ 3200	4.1212 x 3.750	8.2:1	35
	8-455	2 bbl	185 @ 4000	350 @ 2000	4.1522 x 4.210	8.2:1	35
	8-455 DE	2 bbl	200 @ 4000	370 @ 2000	4.1522 x 4.210	8.2:1	35
	8-455	4 bbl	220 @ 3600	350 @ 2400	4.1522 x 4.210	8.2:1	35
	8-455 DE	4 bbl	250 @ 3600	370 @ 2400	4.1522 x 4.210	8.2:1	35
'73	8-350	2 bbl	150 @ 4000	270 @ 2000	3.8762 x 3.750	7.6:1	55-60①
	8-350 DE	2 bbl	175 @ 4400	280 @ 2400	3.8762 x 3.750	7.6:1	55-60①
	8-400	2 bbl	170 @ 3600	320 @ 2000	4.1212 x 3.750	8.0:1	55-60①
	8-400 DE	2 bbl	185 @ 4000	320 @ 2400	4.1212 x 3.750	8.0:1	55-60①
	8-400	4 bbl	200 @ 4000	310 @ 2400	4.1212 x 3.750	8.0:1	55-60①
	8-400 DE	4 bbl	230 @ 4400	325 @ 3200	4.1212 x 3.750	8.0:1	55-60①

GENERAL ENGINE SPECIFICATIONS

Year	Engine No. Cyl. Displacement (Cu. In.)	Carburetor Type	Horsepower @ rpm ■	Torque @ rpm (ft lbs) ■	Bore X Stroke (In.)	Compression Ratio	Oil Pressure @ 2000 rpm
'73	8-455	4 bbl	215 @ 3600	350 @ 2400	4.1522 x 4.210	8.0:1	55-60①
	8-455 DE	4 bbl	250 @ 4000	370 @ 2800	4.1522 x 4.210	8.0:1	55-60①
	8-455 S.D. DE	4 bbl	290 @ 4000	390 @ 3600	4.1522 x 4.210	8.4:1	75-80①
'74	8-400	2 bbl	175 @ 3600	315 @ 2000	4.1212 x 3.750	8.0:1	55-60①
	8-400	4 bbl	200 @ 4000	320 @ 2400	4.1212 x 3.750	8.0:1	55-60①
	8-400 DE	4 bbl	225 @ 4400	330 @ 2800	4.1212 x 3.750	8.0:1	55-60①
	8-455	4 bbl	215 @ 3600	355 @ 2400	4.1522 x 4.210	8.0:1	55-60①
	8-455 DE	4 bbl	250 @ 4000	380 @ 2800	4.1522 x 4.210	8.0:1	55-60①
'75	8-400	2 bbl	170 @ 3600	315 @ 2000	4.1212 x 3.750	7.6:1	55-60①
	8-400	4 bbl	185 @ 4000	320 @ 2400	4.1212 x 3.750	7.6:1	55-60①
	8-455	4 bbl	200 @ 3600	355 @ 2400	4.1522 x 4.210	7.6:1	55-60①
'76	8-350	2 bbl	155 @ 4000	280 @ 2000	3.8750 x 3.530	7.6:1	55-60①
	8-350	4 bbl	175 @ 4000	280 @ 2000	3.8750 x 3.530	7.6:1	55-60①
	8-400	2 bbl	170 @ 4000	305 @ 2000	4.1212 x 3.750	7.6:1	55-60①
	8-400	4 bbl	185 @ 3600	310 @ 1600	4.1212 x 3.750	7.6:1	55-60①
	8-455	4 bbl	200 @ 3500	330 @ 2000	4.1522 x 4.210	7.6:1	55-60①
'77	6-231 Buick	2 bbl	105 @ 3200	185 @ 2000	3.8000 x 3.4000	8.0:1	37②
	8-301 Pont.	2 bbl	135 @ 4000	250 @ 1600	4.0000 x 3.0000	8.2:1	35-40①
	8-305 Chev.	2 bbl	145 @ 3800	245 @ 2400	3.7360 x 3.4800	8.5:1	36-41
	8-350 Pont.	4 bbl	170 @ 4000	280 @ 1800	3.8762 x 3.7500	7.6:1	55-60①
	8-350 Olds.	4 bbl	170 @ 3800	275 @ 2000	4.0570 x 3.3850	8.0:1	30-45③
	8-400 Pont.	4 bbl	180 @ 3600	325 @ 1600	4.1212 x 3.7500	7.6:1	55-60①
	8-403 Olds.	4 bbl	185 @ 3600	330 @ 2400	4.3510 x 3.3850	8.0:1	30-45
'78	6-231 Buick	2 bbl	105 @ 3200	185 @ 2000	3.800 x 3.400	8.0:1	37②
	8-301 Pont.	2 bbl	135 @ 4000	250 @ 1600	4.000 x 3.000	8.2:1	35-40①
	8-301 Pont.	4 bbl	145 @ 4000	275 @ 1800	4.000 x 3.000	8.2:1	35-40①
	8-305 Chev.	2 bbl	130 @ 3600	260 @ 1800	3.736 x 3.480	8.5:1	36-41
	8-350 Buick	4 bbl	165 @ 4000	290 @ 1600	3.800 x 3.850	8.0:1	37①
	8-350 Olds.	4 bbl	160 @ 4000	280 @ 1600	4.057 x 3.385	7.9:1	30-45③
	8-400 Pont.	4 bbl	180 @ 3600	325 @ 1600	4.121 x 3.750	7.7:1	55-60①
	8-403 Olds.	4 bbl	185 @ 3600	330 @ 2400	4.351 x 3.385	8.0:1	30-45
'79	6-231 Buick	2 bbl	115 @ 3200	185 @ 2000	3.800 x 3.400	8.0:1	37②
	8-301 Pont.	2 bbl	140 @ 3600	235 @ 2000	4.000 x 3.000	8.1:1	40①
	8-301 Pont.	4 bbl	150 @ 4000	240 @ 2000	4.000 x 3.000	8.1:1	40①
	8-305 Chev.	4 bbl	160 @ 3800	265 @ 2400	3.736 x 3.480	8.5:1	40
	8-350 Buick	4 bbl	155 @ 3400	280 @ 1800	3.800 x 3.850	8.0:1	37①
	8-350 Olds.	4 bbl	170 @ 3800	275 @ 2000	4.057 x 3.385	7.9:1	40③
	8-403 Olds.	4 bbl	185 @ 3600	320 @ 2000	4.351 x 3.385	7.9:1	40③

■ Horsepower and torque are SAE net figures. They are measured at the rear of the transmission with all accessories installed and operating. Since the figures vary when a given engine is installed in different models, some are representative rather than exact.

HO High output
DE Dual exhaust
S.D. Super Duty
① Above 2600 rpm
② At 2400 rpm
③ At 1500 rpm

Pontiac & Grand Prix

TUNE-UP SPECIFICATIONS

When analyzing compression test results, look for uniformity among cylinders rather than specific pressures.

Year	No. Cyl Displacement (cu in.)	hp	Orig. Type ●	Gap (in.)	Point Dwell (deg)	Point Gap (in.)	Man Trans ●	Auto Trans	Intake Opens ■ (deg)	Fuel Pump Pressure (psi)	Man Trans	Auto Trans
'72	8-400	175	R-46TS	.035	28-32	.016	—	10B	26	5-6½	—	625
	8-400	200	R-45TS	.035	28-32	.016	8B	10B	23	5-6½	1000/600	700/500
	8-400	250	R-45TS	.035	28-32	.016	10B	10B	23	5-6½	1000/600	700/500
	8-455	185	R-45TS	.035	28-32	.016	—	10B	30	5-6½	—	625
	8-455	200	R-45TS	.035	28-32	.016	—	10B	23	5-6½	—	625
	8-455	220	R-45TS	.035	28-32	.016	—	10B	23	5-6½	—	650/500
	8-455	250	R-45TS	.035	28-32	.016	—	10B	23	5-6½	—	650/500
'73	8-350	150	R-46TS	.040	28-32	.016	—	12B	26/30	5-6½	—	650
	8-350	175	R-46TS	.040	28-32	.016	—	12B	26/30	5-6½	—	650
	8-400	170	R-46TS	.040	28-32	.016	—	12B	26	5-6½	—	650
	8-400	185	R-46TS	.040	28-32	.016	—	12B	26	5-6½	—	650
	8-400	200	R-45TS	.040	28-32	.016	—	12B	26	5-6½	—	650
	8-400	230	R-45TS	.040	28-32	.016	—	12B	26	5-6½	—	650
	8-455	215	R-45TS	.040	28-32	.016	—	12B	23	5-6½	—	650
	8-455	250	R-45TS	.040	28-32	.016	—	12B	23	5-6½	—	650
	8-455 S.D.	290	R-45TS	.040	28-32	.016	—	12B	42	5-6½	—	750/500
'74	8-400 2 bbl	175	R-46TS	.040	29-31	.016	—	12B (10)	26	5-6½	—	650 (625)
	8-400 4 bbl	All	R-45TS	.040	29-31	.016	—	12B (10)	30	5-6½	—	650 (625)
	8-455 4 bbl	All	R-45TS	.040	29-31	.016	—	12B (10)	23	5-6½	—	650 (625)
'75	8-400 2 bbl	All	R-46TSX	.060	Electronic		—	16B	26	5-6½	—	650
	8-400 4 bbl	All	R-45TSX	.060	Electronic		—	16B (12)	30	5-6½	—	650
	8-455	All	R-45TSX	.060	Electronic		—	16B (10)	23	5-6½	—	650 (625)
'76	8-350	155	R-46TSX	.060	Electronic		—	16B	22	7-8½	—	550
	8-350	175	R-46TSX	.060	Electronic		—	16B	26	7-8½	—	600
	8-400	170	R-46TSX	.060	Electronic		—	16B	26	7-8½	—	550
	8-400	185	R-45TSX	.060	Electronic		—	16B	30	7-8½	—	575
	8-455	200	R-45TSX	.060	Electronic		—	16B	33	7-8½	—	550 (600)
'77	6-231 Buick	105	R-46TSX (R-45TSX)	.060	Electronic		—	12B	17	4¼-5¾	—	600
	8-301 Pont.	135	R-46TSX	.060	Electronic		—	12B	27	7-8½	—	550,650②
	8-305 Chev.	145	R-45TS	.045	Electronic		—	8B(6B)	28	3-4½	—	500
	8-350 Pont.	170	R-45TSX	.060	Electronic		—	16B	29	7-8½	—	575,650②
	8-350 Olds.	170	R-46SX (R-46SZ)	.080	Electronic		—	20B@ 1100	16	5½-6½	—	600,550②
	8-400 Pont.	180	R-45TSX	.060	Electronic		—	16B	29	7-8½	—	575,600②
	8-403 Olds.	185	R-46SX (R-46SZ)	.080	Electronic		—	20B@ 1100	16	6-7½	—	600,550②
'78	6-231 Buick	105	R-46TSX	.060	Electronic		15B	15B	17	4.5-5.74	800	600
	8-301 Pont.	All	R-46TSX⑤	.060	Electronic		—	12B	27	7-8.5	—	550
	8-305 Chev.	130	R-45TS	.045	Electronic		—	8B(6B)	28	3-4.5	—	600 (500)
	8-350 Buick	170	R-46TSX	.060	Electronic		—	15B	16	4.5-5.5	—	550
	8-350 Olds.	170	R-46SZ	.060	Electronic		—	20B@ 1100	17	5.5-6.5	—	550
	8-400 Pont.	180	R-45TSX	.060	Electronic		—	16B	29	7-8.5	—	575
	8-403 Pont.	185	R-46SZ	.060	Electronic		—	20B@ 1100	16	6-7.5	—	600 (550)

TUNE-UP SPECIFICATIONS

When analyzing compression test results, look for uniformity among cylinders rather than specific pressures.

	ENGINE		SPARK PLUGS			DISTRIBUTOR		IGNITION TIMING (deg) ▲		VALVES Intake Opens ■ (deg)	Fuel Pump Pressure (psi)	IDLE SPEED ● (rpm) ▲	
Year	No. Cyl Displacement (cu in.)	hp	Orig. Type	●	Gap (in.)	Point Dwell (deg)	Point Gap (in.)	Man Trans ●	Auto Trans			Man Trans	Auto Trans
'79	6-231 Buick	115	R-45TSX		.060	Electronic		15B	15B	16	4.5-5.5	800	600
	8-301 Pont.	140	R-46TSX		.060	Electronic		—	12B	16	7.0-8.5	—	550
	8-301 Pont.	150	R-45TSX		.060	Electronic		—	12B	16⑥	7.0-8.5	—	500
	8-305 Chev.	160	R-45TS		.045	Electronic		—	8B(6B)	28	4.5-5.5	—	550
	8-350 Buick	155	R-46TSX		.060	Electronic		—	15B	16	4.5-5.5	—	550
	8-350 Olds.	170	R-46SZ		.080	Electronic		—	20B@ 1100	16	5.5-6.5	—	550
	8-403 Olds.	185	R-46SZ		.080	Electronic		—	24B(20B) @ 1100	16	5.5-6.5	—	550

▲ See text for procedure
● Figure in parentheses indicates California engine. Where two idle speeds appear separated by a slash, the second is with the solenoid disconnected.
■ All figures are in degrees Before Top Dead Center. Where two figures appear, the first represents timing with manual transmission, the second with automatic transmission.
① Not used
② Second figure is for air conditioned cars; to be set with A/C on
③ Not used
④ Not used

⑤ with 4 bbl: R-45TSX
⑥ High performance: 27
B Before Top Dead Center
— Not applicable
S.D. Super Duty
NOTE: The underhood specifications sticker often reflects tune-up specification changes made in production. Sticker figures must be used if they disagree with those in this chart.

NOTE: Most 1979 GM carburetors have idle mixture screws concealed by staked-in plugs. These are not meant to be removed, except at carburetor overhaul.

FIRING ORDER

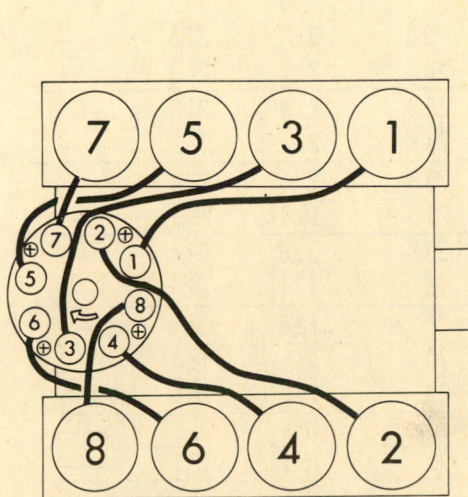

GM (Chevrolet) 305 V8
Engine firing order: 1-8-4-3-6-5-7-2
Distributor rotation: clockwise

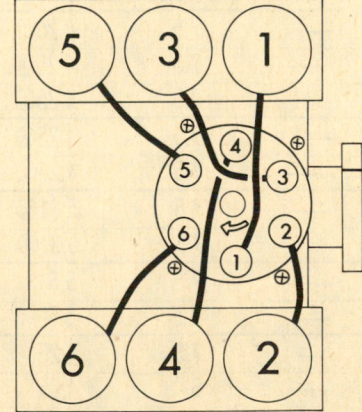

GM (Buick) 231 V6
Engine firing order: 1-6-5-4-3-2
Distributor rotation: clockwise

V6 harmonic balancers have two timing marks: one is 1/8 in. wide, and one is 1/16 in. wide. Use the 1/16 in. mark for timing with a hand held light. The 1/8 in. mark is used only with a magnetic timing pick-up probe.

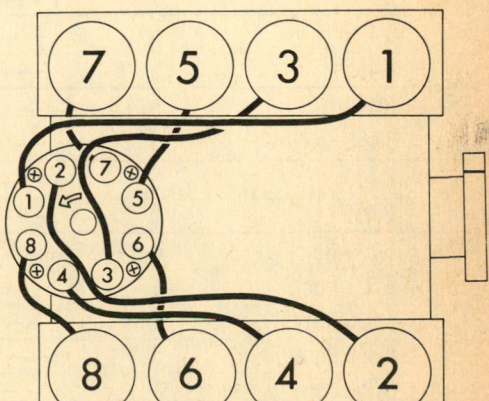

GM (Pontiac) 301, 400 V8 1975-79
Engine firing order: 1-8-4-3-6-5-7-2
Distributor rotation: clockwise

Pontiac & Grand Prix

FIRING ORDER

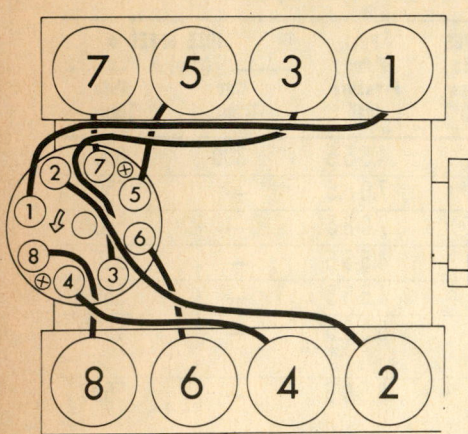

GM (Pontiac) 350, 400, 455 (through 1974)
Engine firing order: 1-8-4-3-6-5-7-2
Distributor rotation: counterclockwise

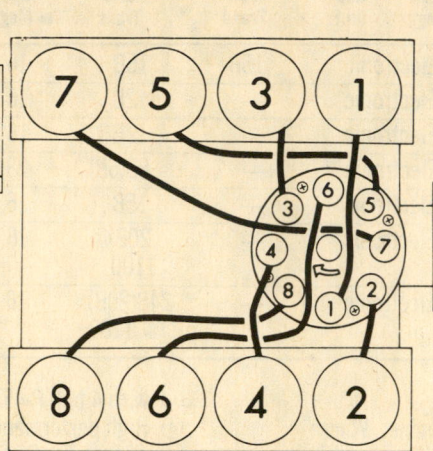

GM(Buick) 350 V8 1978-79
Engine firing order: 1-8-4-3-6-5-7-2
Distributor rotation: clockwise

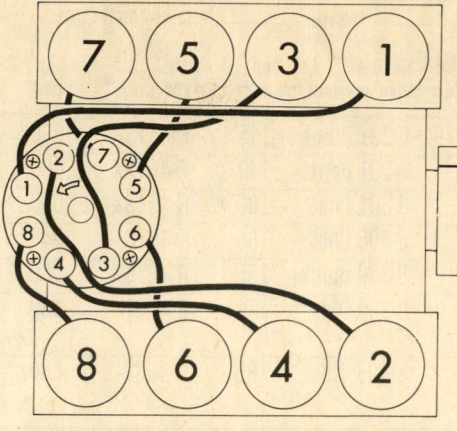

GM (Oldsmobile) 350, 403 V8 (1975 and later)
Engine firing order: 1-8-4-3-6-5-7-2
Distributor rotation: counterclockwise

Pontiac
CAPACITIES

Year	ENGINE No. Cyl. Displacement (Cu. In.)	Engine Crankcase Add 1 Qt For New Filter	TRANSMISSION Pts To Refill After Draining			Drive Axle (pts)	Gasoline Tank (gals) ▲	COOLING SYSTEM (qts)		With Super Cooling
			3-Speed	4-Speed	Automatic ●			With Heater	With A/C	
'72	8-400	5	—	—	7.5	5.5	25	18.6	19.6	—
	8-455	5	—	—	7.5	5.5	25	17.9	19	—
'73	8-350	5	—	—	7.5	4.25①	25.8	21.9	23.3	—
	8-400	5	—	—	7.5	4.25①	25.8	21.9	24.3	—
	8-455	5	—	—	7.5	4.25①	25.8	21.2	22.2	—
'74	8-400	5	—	—	7.5	4.25①	25.8	21.9	24.3	—
	8-455	5	—	—	7.5	4.25①	25.8	21.2	22.2	—
'75	8-400	5	—	—	7.5	5.31②	25.8	21.6	22.4	—
	8-455	5	—	—	7.5	5.31②	25.8	19.8	22.3	—
'76	8-400	5	—	—	7.5	5.5	25.8	21.6	22.4	—
	8-455	5	—	—	7.5	5.5	25.8	22.1	22.1	—
'77	6-231 Buick	4	—	—	7.5	4.25	20	12.8	12.8	—
	8-301 Pont.	5	—	—	6	4.25	20	18.6	18.6	—
	8-305 Chev.	4	—	—	6	3.5	21	16.6	16.6	—
	8-350 Pont.	5	—	—	6	3.5	20	19.8	21	—
	8-350 Olds.	4	—	—	6	3.5	20	15.1	15.1	—
	8-400 Pont.	5	—	—	7.5	4.25	21	19.8	21	—
	8-403 Olds.	4	—	—	7.5	4.25	24.5	16.1	16.1	—
'78	6-231 Buick	4	—	—	③	④	21	14.2	14.1	14.1
	8-301 Pont.	5	—	—	③	④	21	20.2	20.1	20.8
	8-350 Buick Sedan	5	—	—	7.5	④	21	16.6	18.5	19.2
	Sta. Wgn.	5	—	—	7.5	5.4	22	18.6	19.1	19.1
	8-350 Olds.	4	—	—	7.5	④	21	16.5	16.5	16.4
	8-400 Pont.	5	—	—	7.5	④	21	26.3	20.3	20.3

Pontiac — CAPACITIES

Year	ENGINE No. Cyl. Displacement (Cu. In.)	Engine Crankcase Add 1 Qt For New Filter	TRANSMISSION Pts To Refill After Draining Manual 3-Speed	4-Speed	Automatic ●	Drive Axle (pts)	Gasoline Tank (gals) ▲	COOLING SYSTEM (qts) With Heater	With A/C	With Super Cooling
'78	8-403 Olds.	4	—	—	7.5	④	21	17.7	23.0	23.0
'79	6-231 Buick	4	—	—	6	3.5	21	12.1	12.8	—
	8-301 Pont.	5	—	—	6	3.5⑤	21	19.8	20.9	—
	8-350 Buick	5	—	—	6	3.5⑤	21	18.6	19.1	19.1
	8-350 Olds.	4	—	—	6	3.5⑤	21	16.5	16.5	—
	8-403 Olds.	4	—	—	6	3.5⑤	21	16.5	16.5	16.5

① 5 pts with 8.875 in. ring gear
② 4.25 pts with 8.50 in. ring gear
③ Turbo Hydra-Matic 200: 6.0
   Turbo Hydra-Matic 350: 7.5
④ with 8.5 in. ring gear: 4.25
   with 8.75 in. ring gear: 5.4
⑤ Sta. Wgn.: 4.25

● Specifications do not include torque converter
— Not applicable
▲ Station wagon fuel tank (gals)
   '72   23
   '73-'76, '78-'79   22
   '77   22.5

Grand Prix — CAPACITIES

Year	ENGINE No. Cyl. Displacement (Cu. In.)	Engine Crankcase Add 1 Qt For New Filter	TRANSMISSION Pts To Refill After Draining Manual 3-Speed	4-Speed	Automatic ●	Drive Axle (pts)	Gasoline Tank (gals)	COOLING SYSTEM (qts) With Heater	With A/C	With Super Cooling
'72	8-400	5	—	—	7.5	3①	26	18.7	19.7	—
	8-455	5	—	—	7.5	3①	26	18.1	19.2	—
'73	8-400	5	—	—	7.5	4.25	25	23.1	22.9	—
	8-455	5	—	—	7.5	4.25	25	21.3	22.5	—
'74	8-400	5	—	—	7.5	4.25	25	23.1	22.9	—
	8-455	5	—	—	7.5	4.25	25	21.3	22.5	—
'75	8-400	5	—	—	7.5	5.31	25	21.6	24.0	—
	8-455	5	—	—	7.5	5.31	25	20.2	22.2	—
'76	8-350	5	—	—	7.5	3②	25	21.6	22	—
	8-400	5	—	—	7.5	3②	25	22.2	22.2	—
	8-455	5	—	—	7.5	3②	25	22.2	22.2	—
'77	8-301 Pont.	5	—	—	7.5	4.25	25	20.5	20.5	—
	8-350 Pont.	5	—	—	7.5	4.25	25	21.6	22.1	—
	8-350 Olds.	4	—	—	7.5	4.25	25	17	17	—
	8-400 Pont.	5	—	—	7.5	4.25	25	21.6	22.1	—
	8-403 Olds.	4	—	—	7.5	4.25	25	19.0	18.2	—
'78	6-231 Buick	4	—	—	7.5	3.5	18.1	14.3	14.2	14.2
	8-301 Pont.	5	—	—	③	3.5	18.1	20.3	20.2	20.9
	8-305 Chev.	4	—	—	③	3.5	18.1	17.7	17.4	18.1
'79	6-231 Buick	4	3.5	—	6	3.4	18.2	13.6	13.6	—
	8-301 Pont.	5	—	3.5	6	3.4	18.2	21.8	21.8	—
	8-305 Chev.	4	3.5	—	6	3.4	18.2	16.1	16.1	—

● Specifications do not include torque converter
① 5 pts with 8.875 in. ring gear
— Not applicable or specified

② 4.9 with optional axle
③ with Turbo Hydra-Matic 200: 6.0
   with Turbo Hydra-Matic 350: 7.5

TORQUE SPECIFICATIONS

All readings in ft lbs

Year	Engine No. Cyl. Displacement (cu. in.)	Cylinder Head Bolts	Rod Bearing Bolts	Main Bearing Bolts	Crankshaft Bolt	Flywheel to Crankshaft Bolts	MANIFOLD Intake	MANIFOLD Exhaust
'72-'76	All	95	43②	100①	160	95	40	30
'77	6-231 Buick	80	40	100	175 min	60	45	25
	8-301 Pont.	85	30	70③	160	95	35	40
	8-305 Chev.	65	45	70	60	60	30	20
	8-350, 400 Pont.	100	40	100①	160	95	35	40
	8-350, 403 Olds.	130	42	80①	200 min	60	40	25
'78-'79	6-231 Buick	80	40	100	225	60	45	25
	8-301 Pont.	95	30	100	160	95	35	40
	8-305 Chev.	65	45	70	60	60	30	20
	8-350 Buick	80	40	100	225	60	45	25
	8-350 Olds.	130	42	80①	220	60	40	25
	8-400 Pont.	95	40	120	160	95	35	40
	8-403 Olds.	130	42	80①	220	60	40	25

① Rear main—120   ② 63 ft lbs on 455 S.D. engine   ③ Rear Main—100

CRANKSHAFT AND CONNECTING ROD SPECIFICATIONS

All measurements are given in inches

Year	Engine No. Cyl. Displacement (cu in.)	CRANKSHAFT Main Brg. Journal Dia	CRANKSHAFT Main Brg. Oil Clearance	CRANKSHAFT Shaft End-Play	Thrust on No.	CONNECTING ROD Journal Diameter	CONNECTING ROD Oil Clearance	CONNECTING ROD Side Clearance*
'72-'75	8-400	3.000	.0002-.0017	.0030-.0090	4	2.250	.0005-.0025	.012-.017
	8-455	3.250	.0005-.0021	.0030-.0090	4	2.250	.0010-.0031	.012-.017
'75	8-455 S.D.	3.250	.0010-.0026	.0030-.0090	4	2.250	.0015-.0031	.019-.027
'76	8-350, 400	3.000	.0002-.0017	.0030-.0090	4	2.250	.0005-.0025	.012-.017
	8-455	3.250	.0005-.0021	.0030-.0090	4	2.250	.0005-.0025	.012-.017
'77	6-231 Buick	2.500	.0004-.0015	.004-.008	2	2.000	.0005-.0026	.006-.022
	8-301 Pont.	3.000	.0002-.0020	.004-.008	2	2.250	.0005-.0026	.006-.022
	8-305 Chev.	2.448	.0035②	.002-.006	5	2.200	.0035	.008-.014
	8-350, 400 Pont.	3.000	.0002-.0017	.0035-.0085	4	2.250	.0005-.0026	.002-.017
	8-350, 403 Olds.	2.500	.0005-.0021③	.0035-.0085	3	2.124	.0005-.0026	.006-.020
'78-'79	6-231 Buick	2.4995-2.5000	.0003-.0017	.003-.009	2	2.2487-2.2495	.0005-.0026	.006-.027
	8-301 Pont.	3.0000	.0002-.0020	.003-.009	4	2.2500	.0005-.0025	.006-.022
	8-305 Chev.	2.4480-2.4502④	⑤	.002-.007	5	2.0990-2.1000	.0013-.0035	.006-.016
	8-350 Buick	3.0000-3.0005	.0004-.0015	.003-.009	3	1.9910-2.0000	.0005-.0026	.006-.027
	8-350 Olds.	2.4985-2.4995⑥	.0005-.0021③	.0035-.0135	3	2.1238-2.1248	.0005-.0026	.006-.020
	8-400 Pont.	3.0000	.0002-.0020	.003-.009	4	2.2500	.0005-.0025	.006-.022
	8-403 Olds.	2.4985-2.4995⑥	.0005-.0021③	.0035-.0135	3	2.1238-2.1248	.0005-.0026	.006-.020

* Total for two rods
① Not used
② No. 1—.002 Max.
③ No. 5—.0015-.0031
④ #5: 2.4481-2.4508

⑤ #1: .0008-.0020
   #2: .0011-.0023
   #3: .0017-.0033
⑥ #1: 2.4988-2.4998

VALVE SPECIFICATIONS

Year	Engine No. Cyl. Displacement (cu in.)	Seat Angle (deg) ■	Face Angle (deg) ●	Spring Test Pressure▲ (lbs @ in.)	Spring Installed Height (in.)	STEM TO GUIDE Clearance (in.) Intake	Exhaust	STEM Diameter (In.) Intake	Exhaust
'72	8-400 2 bbl	45	44	61 @ 1.59	1 19/32	.0016-.0033	.0021-.0038	.3416	.3411
	8-400 4 bbl	30	29	65 @ 1.57	1 9/16	.0016-.0033	.0021-.0038	.3416	.3411
	8-455 2 bbl	45	44	61 @ 1.59	1 19/32	.0016-.0033	.0021-.0038	.3416	.3411
	8-455 4 bbl	30	29	65 @ 1.57	1 9/16	.0016-.0033	.0021-.0038	.3416	.3411
'73	8-350	45	44	61 @ 1.59	1 19/32	.0016-.0033	.0021-.0038	.3416	.3411
	8-400 2 bbl	45	44	61 @ 1.59	1 19/32	.0016-.0033	.0021-.0038	.3416	.3411
	8-400 4 bbl	30	29	65 @ 1.57	1 9/16	.0016-.0033	.0021-.0038	.3416	.3411
	8-455 2 bbl	45	44	61 @ 1.59	1 19/32	.0016-.0033	.0021-.0038	.3416	.3411
	8-455 4 bbl	30	29	65 @ 1.57	1 9/16	.0016-.0033	.0021-.0038	.3416	.3411
	8-455 S.D.	45	44	70 @ 1.82	1 9/16	.0016-.0033	.0021-.0038	.3416	.3416
'74	8-400	30	29	65 @ 1.57	1 9/16	.0016-.0033	.0021-.0038	.3416	.3411
	8-455 2 bbl	45	44	61 @ 1.59	1 19/32	.0016-.0033	.0021-.0038	.3416	.3411
	8-455 4 bbl	30	29	65 @ 1.57	1 9/16	.0016-.0033	.0021-.0038	.3416	.3411
'75	8-400 2 bbl	45	44	65 @ 1.57	1 9/16	.0016-.0033	.0021-.0038	.3416	.3411
	8-400 4 bbl	45	44	65 @ 1.57	1 19/32	.0016-.0033	.0021-.0038	.3416	.3411
	8-455	45	44	65 @ 1.57	1 9/16	.0016-.0033	.0021-.0038	.3416	.3411
'76	8-350	30	29	66 @ 1.56	1 19/32	.0016-.0033	.0021-.0038	.3416	.3411
	8-400 2 bbl	30	29	70 @ 1.54	1 19/32	.0016-.0033	.0021-.0038	.3416	.3411
	8-400 4 bbl	30	29	70 @ 1.54	1 9/16	.0016-.0033	.0021-.0038	.3416	.3411
	8-455	30	29	65 @ 1.57	1 9/16	.0016-.0033	.0021-.0038	.3416	.3411
'77	6-231 Buick	45	45	164 @ 1.34④	1 47/64	.0015-.0035	.0015-.0032	.3407	.3407
	8-301 Pont.	46	45	166 @ 1.30	1 21/32	.0010-.0027	.0010-.0027	.3422	.3422
	8-305 Chev.	46	45	206 @ 1.25	1 23/32	.0010-.0037	.0010-.0037	.3410	.3410
	8-350 Olds.	45②	44③	180 @ 1.34	1 47/64	.0010-.0027	.0015-.0032	.3425	.3420
	8-350 Pont.	30	29	131 @ 1.19	1 19/32	.0016-.0033	.0021-.0038	.3416	.3411
	8-400 Pont.	30	29	131 @ 1.19	1 19/32	.0016-.0033	.0021-.0038	.3416	.3411
	8-403 Olds.	45②	44③	180 @ 1.34	1 47/64	.0010-.0027	.0015-.0032	.3425	.3420
'78-'79	6-231 Buick	45	45	182 @ 1.34	1 47/64	.0015-.0032	.0015-.0032	.3402-.3412	.3405-.3412
	8-301 Pont.	46	45	165 @ 1.29	1 2/3	.0010-.0027	.0010-.0027⑤	.3425	.3425
	8-305 Chev.	46	45	190 @ 1.16	1 23/32	.0010-.0037	.0010-.0047	.3410	.3410
	8-350 Buick	45	45	180 @ 1.34	1 47/64	.0015-.0032	.0015-.0035	.3720-.3730	.3723-.3730
	8-350 Olds.	45②	46③	190 @ 1.27	1 47/64	.0010-.0027	.0015-.0032	.3425-.3432	.3420-.3427
	8-400 Pont.	30	29	135 @ 1.18	1 27/50	.0016-.0033	.0021-.0038	.3425	.3425
	8-403 Olds.	45②	46③	190 @ 1.27	1 47/64	.0010-.0027	.0015-.0032	.3425-.3432	.3420-.3427

■ Intake valve seat angles are shown. All exhaust valve seat angles are 45° unless otherwise indicated.

● Intake valve face angles are shown. All exhaust valve face angles are 44° unless otherwise indicated.

① Not used
② Exhaust 31
③ Exhaust 30
④ Exhaust—182 @ 1.34
⑤ clearance at bottom of guide: .0020-.0037
HO High output
S.D. Super Duty

▲INNER SPRING TEST PRESSURE

'72	8-400 2 bbl	33 @ 1.55			8-455	37 @ 1.53
	8-400 4 bbl	37 @ 1.53		'75-'76	8-350	33 @ 1.55
'73	8-350	33 @ 1.55			8-400	41 @ 1.50
	8-400 2 bbl	33 @ 1.55			8-455	36 @ 1.53
	8-400 4 bbl	37 @ 1.53		'77	8-350 Pont.	39 @ 1.51①
	8-455	37 @ 1.53			8-400 Pont.	39 @ 1.51①
	8-455 S.D.	40 @ 1.75		'78-'79	8-400	97 @ 1.14
'74	8-400 2 bbl	33 @ 1.55				
	8-400 4 bbl	37 @ 1.53				

① Exhaust—40 @ 1.51

PISTON CLEARANCE

Year	Engine No. Cyl. Displacement (cu. in.)	Clearance (in.) Piston-to-Bore
'72	8-350	.0025-.0033
	8-400	.0025-.0033
	8-455	.0025-.0033
	8-400 Ram Air	.0055-.0061
'73	8-350	.0029-.0037
	8-400	.0029-.0037
	8-455	.0025-.0033
	8-455 S.D.	.0060-.0068
'74-'77	6-231 Buick	.0008-.0014
	8-305 Chev.	.0027 Max.
	8-301, 350, 400 Pont.	.0029-.0037
	8-350, 403 Olds.	.0008-.0018
	8-455 Pont.	.0021-.0029
'78-'79	6-231, 8-350 Buick	.0008-.0020
'78	8-305 Chev.	0.007-.0027
'78-'79	8-301, 400 Pont.	.0025-.0033
	8-350, 403 Olds.	.0010-.0020
'79	8-305 Chev.	.0017-.0042

RING GAP

All measurements are given in inches

Year	Engine No. Cyl. Displacement (cu. in.)	Compression Top	Compression Bottom		Year	Engine No. Cyl. Displacement (cu. in.)	Oil Control
'72-'76	8-350, 400, 455 Pont.	.010-.030	.010-.030		'72-'76	8-350, 400, 455 Pont.	.015-.055
'77	6-231 Buick	.015-.023	.015-.023		'77-'79	6-231, 8-350 Buick	.015-.035
'77-'78	8-305 Chev.	.010-.035	.010-.035		'77-'78	8-305 Chev.	.015-.065
'77-'78	8-301, 350, 400 Pont.	.010-.020	.010-.020			8-301, 350, 400 Pont.	.015-.035
'77-'79	8-350, 403 Olds	.010-.020	.010-.020			8-350 Olds.	.015-.035
'78-'79	6-231, 8-350 Buick	.010-.020	.010-.020			8-403 Olds.	.015-.055
'79	8-301 Pont.	.014-.023	.014-.023		'79	8-305 Chev.	.010-.035
'79	8-305 Chev.	.010-.020	.010-.025				

RING SIDE CLEARANCE

All measurements are given in inches

Year	Engine No. Cyl. Displacement (cu. in.)	Top Compression	Bottom Compression	Year	Engine No. Cyl. Displacement (cu. in.)	Oil Control
'72-'77	8-301, 350, 400, 455 Pont.	.0015-.0050	.0015-.0050	'72-'77	8-301, 350, 400, 455 Pont.	.0015-.0050
'77-'79	6-231, 8-350 Buick	.0030-.0050	.0030-.0050	'77-'79	6-231, 8-350 Buick	.0035 max
	8-305 Chev.	.0012-.0042	.0012-.0042		8-305 Chev.	.0020-.0080
	8-350, 403 Olds	.0020-.0040	.0020-.0040		8-350, 403 Olds	.0006-.0096
'78-'79	8-301, 400 Pont.	.0015-.0035	.0015-.0035	'78-'79	8-301, 400 Pont.	.0015-.0035

WHEEL ALIGNMENT SPECIFICATIONS

Year	Model	CASTER Range (deg)	Pref Setting (deg)	CAMBER Range (deg)	Pref Setting (deg)	Toe-in (in.)	Steering Axis Inclin. (deg.)	WHEEL PIVOT RATIO (deg) Inner Wheel	Outer Wheel
'72	Grand Prix	1N to 2N	1½N	¼N to ¾P	¼P	0 to ⅛	9	20	18
	Catalina, Grand Ville & Bonneville	1N to 2N	1½N	¼N to ¾P	¼P	0 to ⅛	8½	20	18
'73-'74	Grand Prix	2½P to 3½P	3P	½P to 1½P (LH)	1P	0 to ⅛	10½	20	18¹³⁄₁₆ (LH)
				0 to 1P (RH)	½P				19³⁄₁₆ (RH)
'73-'74	Pontiac	½P to 1½P	1P	½P to 1½P (LH)	1P	0 to ⅛	10½	20	18½
				0 to 1P (RH)	½P				
'75-'76	Grand Prix	2½P to 3½P	3P	½P to 1½P (LH)	1P	0 to ⅛	10⅓	—	—
				0 to 1P (RH)	½P				
'75-'76	Pontiac	1P to 2P	1½P	½P to 1P (LH)	1P	0 to ⅛	10⅓	—	—
				0 to 1P (RH)	½P				
'77	Pontiac	2½P to 3½P	3P	0 to 1½	¾P	⅛ to ¼	10⅓		
'77	Grand Prix	2½P to 3½P	5P	½P to 1½P(LH)	1P	0 to ⅛	10⅓	—	—
				0 to 1P (RH)	½P				
'78-'79	Pontiac	2½P to 3½P	3P	⅓P to 1⅓P	⅘P	¹⁄₁₆ to ³⁄₁₆	—	—	—
'78-'79	Grand Prix Man. Str.	½P to 1½P	1P	0 to 1P	½P	¹⁄₁₆ to ³⁄₁₆	—	—	—
	Pwr. Str.	2½P to 3½P	3P	0 to 1P	½P	¹⁄₁₆ to ³⁄₁₆	—	—	—

— Not specified
N Negative   P Positive
LH lefthand side   RH righthand side

CHARGING SYSTEM

An SI series Delcotron alternator is used on all models. This unit has a non-adjustable, integral solid-state regulator.

Testing procedures for the charging system are in the Charging and Starting Systems Unit Repair Section.

Alternator Removal and Installation

1. Disconnect the battery cables.
2. Remove the alternator wires or connector.
3. Loosen the adjusting bolts.
4. Remove the V-belt and through-bolt.
5. Remove the alternator.
6. To install, reverse the removal procedure. Adjust the belt tension so that the longest span of belt between pulleys can be depressed about 1/2 in. in the middle by moderate thumb pressure.

--- CAUTION ---

Pull out on the alternator by hand to avoid damage to the housing and over-tightening, which could damage the bearings.

7. Tighten first the adjuster bolt, then the pivot bolt.

STARTING SYSTEM

A detailed discussion of starters can be found in the Unit Repair Section under Charging and Starting Systems.

Starter Removal and Installation

1. Disconnect the positive cable from the battery.
2. Raise the front of the car and support on stands.
3. Pull the cable and wire loom down to hang free.
4. Disconnect the brace.

5. Remove the mounting screws and the starter motor with the cable and solenoid wires.
6. Remove the wires from the starter.
7. To reinstall, reverse the procedure, first installing the wires to the solenoid.

Disabling the Seat Belt/Starter Interlock System

Since the requirement for the interlock system was dropped during the 1975 model year, those systems installed on cars built earlier may now be legally disabled. The seat belt warning light is still required.

1. Disconnect the negative battery cable.

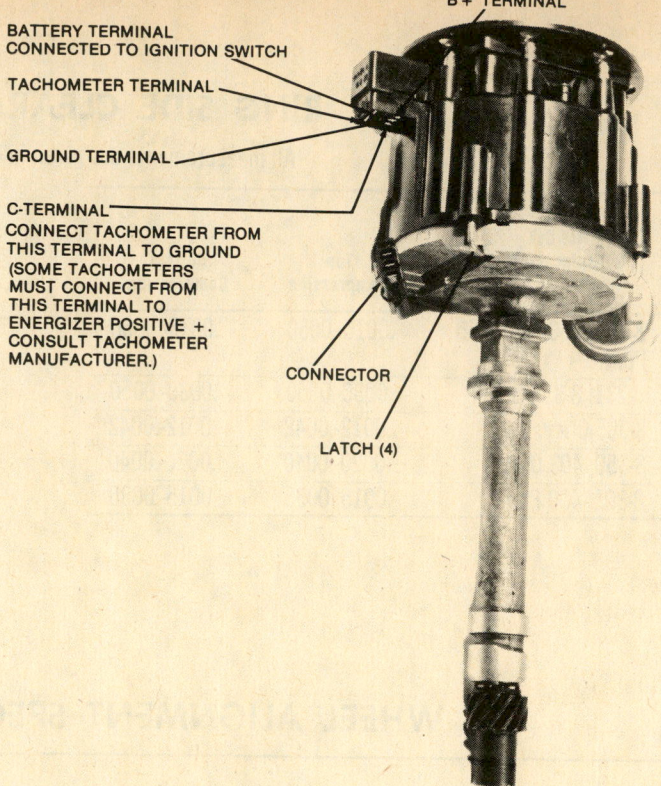

BATTERY TERMINAL CONNECTED TO IGNITION SWITCH

TACHOMETER TERMINAL

GROUND TERMINAL

C-TERMINAL CONNECT TACHOMETER FROM THIS TERMINAL TO GROUND (SOME TACHOMETERS MUST CONNECT FROM THIS TERMINAL TO ENERGIZER POSITIVE +. CONSULT TACHOMETER MANUFACTURER.)

B+ TERMINAL

CONNECTOR

LATCH (4)

High Energy Ignition system distributor

2. Locate the interlock harness connector under the left side of the instrument panel on or near the fuse block.
3. Cut and tape the ends of the green wire on the body side of the connector.
4. Remove the buzzer from the fuse block or connector.

IGNITION SYSTEM

Distributors through 1973 have a Radio Frequency Interference Shield covering the breaker plate assembly. The shield must be removed to install points or condenser, but dwell angle may be set through an opening in the shield. A unitized point and condenser set was introduced in 1974. It was installed as original equipment in some cases. The shield isn't required when the unitized point and condenser set is used.

A unitized electronic ignition system is optional on 1972-74 models having the 455 four-barrel V8.

Starting 1975, Pontiac is using High Energy Electronic ignition on all models. It is also used in place of the unitized system on some 1974 models. It is triggered by a magnetic pulse, and transistor controlled. There is a capacitor in the distributor for radio noise suppression.

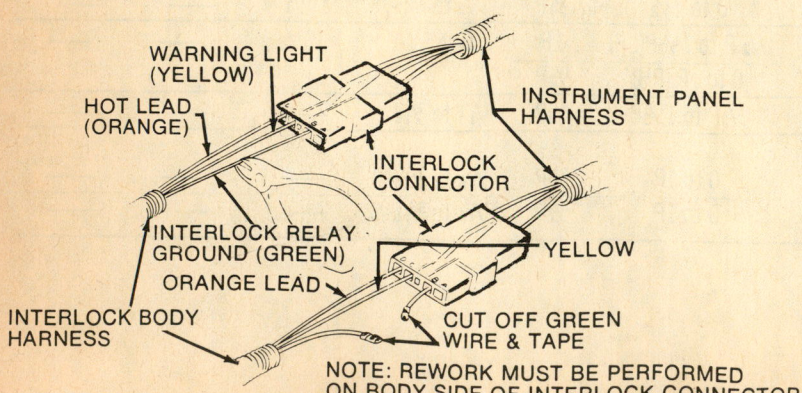

WARNING LIGHT (YELLOW)

HOT LEAD (ORANGE)

INSTRUMENT PANEL HARNESS

INTERLOCK CONNECTOR

INTERLOCK RELAY GROUND (GREEN)

ORANGE LEAD

YELLOW

INTERLOCK BODY HARNESS

CUT OFF GREEN WIRE & TAPE

NOTE: REWORK MUST BE PERFORMED ON BODY SIDE OF INTERLOCK CONNECTOR.

Disabling the seat belt interlock system
(© Pontiac Div., G.M. Corp)

This system may not be compatible with all tachometers, so check the instruction sheet for the tachometer before attempting to hook it up to a car with electronic ignition. There is a terminal on the distributor which is marked TACH; connect a tachometer from this terminal to a suitable ground. Some tachometers may connect from this terminal to the battery positive terminal.

Troubleshooting of the Ignition System can be found in the Unit Repair Section under Electronic Ignition Systems.

Distributor Removal and Installation

1. Disconnect the coil wire connector. On HEI systems, disconnect the ignition switch battery feed wire from the distributor cap.
2. Remove the distributor cap.
3. Crank the engine so that the rotor points to No. 1 cylinder plug tower and the timing mark on the crankshaft pulley are indexed with the pointer.

NOTE: *Observe the position of the rotor and make marks on the distributor housing and on the block that line up with tip of the rotor. Make sure these marks line up upon reassembly.*

4. Remove the distributor vacuum line.
5. Remove the distributor hold-down bolt and clamp. Do not disturb the engine after the distributor has been removed.
6. Lift the distributor out of its bore. Notice the slight rotation of the rotor as the distributor is removed from the block.
7. Installation procedure is the reverse of the removal procedure. However, before inserting the distributor into the block, the rotor should be moved slightly to one side. This is necessary because of the helical cut of the gears. As the distributor seats in its bore, the rotor will rotate slightly so that the reference marks will once again be in line. Retime the engine with a timing light.

Installation If Engine Has Been Disturbed

1. With no. 1 piston on the compression stroke, rotate the crankshaft until the pulley timing mark indexes with the stationary mark at TDC.
2. Replace the distributor to block gasket.
3. Install the distributor in the block. The rotor should point toward the contact in the cap for no. 1 cylinder. Move the rotor slightly to the side because as the distributor is pressed into its bore it will rotate a small amount.
4. Install the distributor clamp and clamp bolt.

5. Install the vacuum line, rotor, cap, and coil wire.
6. Retime the engine with a timing light.

Ignition Timing

NOTE: *Two timing marks may be found on 1976 and later V6 engines. The smaller 1/16 in. groove is used with a hand-held timing light. The second groove is used with magnetic timing equipment.*

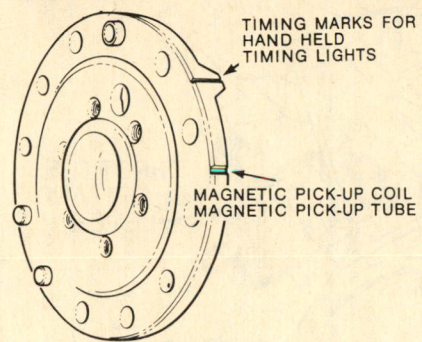

TIMING MARKS FOR HAND HELD TIMING LIGHTS

MAGNETIC PICK-UP COIL
MAGNETIC PICK-UP TUBE

V6 ignition timing mark—1976 and later
(© Pontiac Div., G.M. Corp)

Timing marks are located on the front engine cover and on the harmonic balancer or pulley.

1. Disconnect and plug the distributor vacuum advance hose.
2. Make sure the dwell is adjusted.

NOTE: *It may be necessary to put a small amount of white paint or chalk on the timing marks to make them more visible.*

3. Connect a timing light to no. 1 spark plug.
4. Loosen the distributor clamp.
5. Start the engine and rotate the distributor until the correct marks line up. Tighten the distributor clamp and recheck the timing.
6. Reconnect the vacuum hose.

Contact Point and Condenser Replacement and Adjustment

1. Remove the distributor cap and the rotor.
2. Remove the R.F.I. shield, if so equipped.
3. Remove the screws holding the points in place.
4. Remove the condenser lead and primary lead from the points. Loosen the clamp and slide the condenser out.
5. Install a new set of points and tighten the attaching screws. Adjust the point gap if the point set isn't preset. Install the condenser.
6. Connect the condenser and primary leads, to the points.
7. Apply a very small amount of grease to the breaker cam.
8. Install the R.F.I. shield; the half covering the points should be installed first. You don't need the shield if the unitized point and condenser set is being used.

9. Install the rotor and distributor cap.
10. Set the dwell with the engine running.

FUEL SYSTEM

A non-repairable fuel pump is used. Information on the fuel gauge will be found in the Unit Repair Section.

Fuel Pump Removal and Installation

1. Disconnect the input and output lines from the fuel pump.
2. Remove the bolts which hold the fuel pump and lift off the pump and gasket.

NOTE: *On some models equipped with power steering it is possible, but somewhat difficult, to reach the mounting bolts with the steering pump in place. It may help to slack off on the power steering pump, remove its mounting bolts and, with it still connected to its lines, lift it up out of the way.*

3. Reverse the procedure for installation.

Fuel Filter Replacement

1. Disconnect the fuel line connection at the inlet of the carburetor.
2. Remove the inlet fuel filter nut from the carburetor using a box wrench.
3. Remove the filter element and spring.
4. The element should allow air to pass freely.
5. Install the element spring and a new element into the carburetor. Bronze elements are installed with the small section of the cone facing outward.
6. Install a new gasket on the fitting nut and install the nut.
7. Install the fuel line and tighten securely. Start the engine and check for leaks.

Idle Speed and Mixture Adjustments

1972

Adjust with air cleaner installed.
A Combination Emission Control (C.E.C.) valve is energized through the transmission switch to increase idle speed under conditions of high gear deceleration and to provide full vacuum spark advance during high gear operation. The valve is de-energized at curb idle and in the lower gears to prevent carburetor vacuum from reaching the distributor and advancing ignition timing under these conditions, the result of which is lower exhaust emission. *The valve need not be adjusted unless the solenoid or throttle body is removed, or the carburetor overhauled.*

1. Disconnect the carburetor EVAP hose from the vapor storage canister.

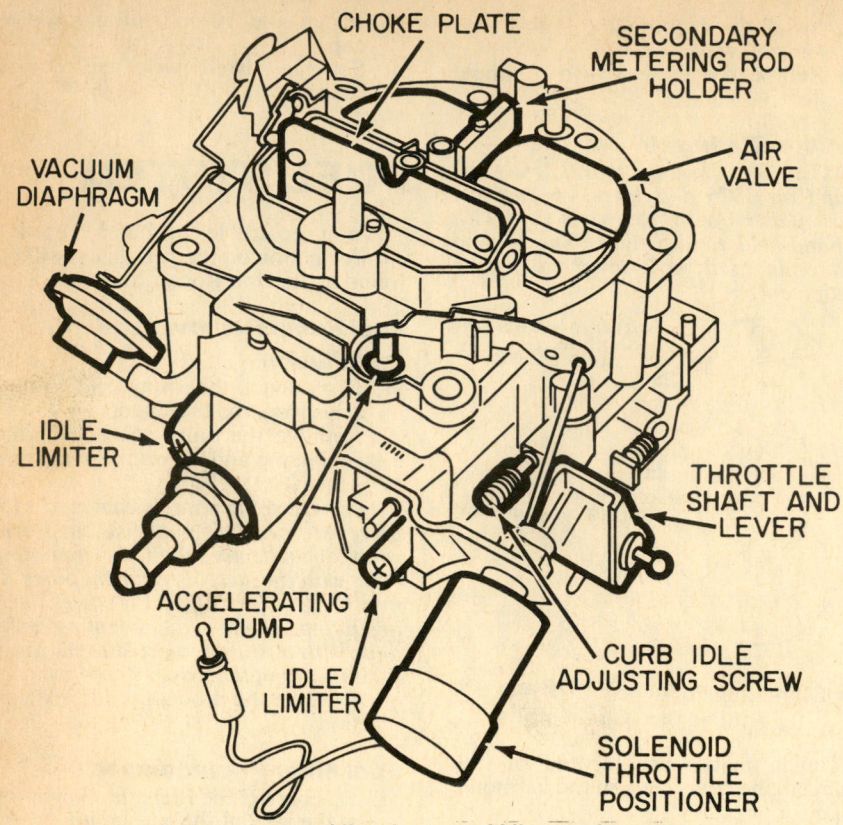

4 bbl carburetor idle mixture and idle speed screws

Labels on diagram:
- CHOKE PLATE
- SECONDARY METERING ROD HOLDER
- AIR VALVE
- VACUUM DIAPHRAGM
- IDLE LIMITER
- ACCELERATING PUMP
- IDLE LIMITER
- THROTTLE SHAFT AND LEVER
- CURB IDLE ADJUSTING SCREW
- SOLENOID THROTTLE POSITIONER

2. Disconnect and plug the carburetor-to-vacuum (distributor vacuum) solenoid hose at the solenoid. Disconnect the throttle solenoid wire on 4 bbl manual transmission engines.
3. Set the dwell and timing (in that order) at specified idle speed.
4. Adjust the carburetor speed screw to obtain specified idle speed, automatic in Drive, manual in Neutral.
5. On 4 bbl manual transmission models, reconnect the throttle solenoid wire, manually extend the solenoid screw and adjust to specified idle rpm.
6. Place automatic in Park, manual in Neutral and check the fast idle speed with the screw on the top step of the cam. Adjust the fast idle screw to obtain 1,700 rpm.

NOTE: *2 bbl carburetors are not adjustable for fast idle.*

7. Reconnect the distributor vacuum and vapor storage hoses.

If the carburetor has been overhauled, or the plastic locks removed from the mixture screws, the following procedure must be used to adjust idle speed and mixture.

1. Turn in the mixture screws until lightly seated, then back out 3-1/2 turns.
2. Start the engine and adjust the carburetor idle speed screw to obtain a speed 25 rpm above the specified idle (automatic), 75 rpm higher for 2 bbl V8 (manual), or 100 rpm higher for 4 bbl V8 (manual).

3. Turn the mixture screws in equally until the specified idle speed is obtained. At this point a CO meter should be employed to adjust the mixture. A reading of 0.2% or less must be maintained.
4. Shut off the engine and install new limiter caps, with tabs against the full rich stops.
5. Adjust the fast idle speed, as described previously.

1973-74
Idle Speed

1. Disconnect and plug the carburetor hose from the vapor canister.
2. Disconnect and plug the distributor and EGR valve vacuum hoses. Plug any open vacuum tubes on the carburetor.
3. Check the dwell and timing.
4. Disconnect the idle stop solenoid wire.
5. Adjust the carburetor idle speed screw to the low rpm specified in the Tune-Up Specifications chart.
6. Reconnect the solenoid wire and adjust the solenoid plunger screw to obtain the specified idle speed.

NOTE: *You might have to work the throttle linkage by hand first, since the solenoid isn't always powerful enough to move it.*

7. On four-barrel carburetors, check the fast idle speed with the fast idle speed screw on the top step of the fast idle cam. Adjust the speed by turning the fast idle screw. Fast idle speed is 1,500 rpm for all engines.

NOTE: *The fast idle speed screw is not the same one used in Step 5. You can't make this adjustment on two-barrel carburetors.*

Idle Mixture

1. Set the parking brake and block the wheels.
2. Disconnect and plug the carburetor hose from the vapor canister in the engine compartment. Disconnect and plug the distributor vacuum hose.
3. If the idle mixture limiter caps are intact and a CO meter is available, attempt to obtain an idle setting of 0.2% CO by adjusting the mixture screws. If this doesn't work, remove the caps and proceed to the next step.

NOTE: *The engine must be at normal operating temperature.*

4. Remove the idle mixture limiter caps. If you have a CO meter, adjust the mixture screws equally to get a reading of 0.2% CO.
5. Run the screws in until they are lightly seated, then back them out six turns for 1973 and seven for 1974.
6. Turn the air conditioner off, place the automatic transmission in Drive (block the wheels), place the manual transmission in Neutral, leave the air cleaner off and plug the air cleaner manifold vacuum fitting. Adjust the idle speed screw or the idle stop solenoid to obtain the following temporary idle speed.

Engine	Year	rpm
All	1973	700
8-400, 2 bbl	1974	720
8-400, 2 bbl, Calif.	1974	690
8-400, 4 bbl	1974	720
8-400, 4 bbl, Calif.	1974	685
8-455, 4 bbl	1974	680
8-455, 4 bbl, Calif.	1974	675

7. Turn the mixture screws in equally to get the highest idle speed. Then set the speed back to that listed in Step 6.
8. Turn the mixture screws in equally until the engine speed drops to the normal idle speed given in the Tune-Up Specifications chart.
9. Install the air cleaner. If the idle speed changes, adjust the mixture screws slightly to compensate.

1975-76

1. The adjustment must be made with the engine at normal operating temperature, with the air conditioner off, and the air cleaner removed. The air cleaner vacuum fitting in the manifold should be plugged. Automatic transmissions should be in Drive and manual transmissions in neutral.
2. Set the parking brake and block the wheels.

3. On all models, disconnect and plug the hose going to the carburetor from the vapor cannister. On 1975 350 V8 2 bbl, detach and plug the distributor vacuum hose to block vacuum advance. Disconnect and plug the EGR hose to the carburetor at the EGR valve end.

4. Use pliers to break off the plastic idle mixture screw limiter caps. Turn in the mixture screws until they seat lightly, then back them out five turns.

5. Adjust the idle speed screw or idle solenoid screw to get the before lean drop idle speed listed on the underhood specifications sticker. The tachometer hookup for the HEI ignition system is covered earlier under Ignition System.

6. Adjust the mixture screws equally (quarter-turn increments are recommended) to obtain the highest possible idle speed. Check the adjustment by shifting into Neutral, running the engine at 2,000 rpm for 5-10 seconds, returning to idle, shifting back into Drive, and letting the speed stabilize for 10 seconds.

7. Return the idle speed to that set in Step 5.

8. Repeat Steps 6 and 7, until no further speed increase is possible.

9. Turn in the mixture screws equally until the normal idle speed is reached.

10. Place the automatic transmission in Park and the manual in neutral. Check the tune-up sticker and adjust the fast idle with the fast idle speed screw. If there is no speed shown, you do not have to adjust the fast idle. For 4MC carburetors, adjust with the fast idle speed screw on the high step of the cam.

11. If there is an idle speed-up solenoid, place the transmission in Drive, disconnect the terminal connector at the air conditioner compressor clutch and adjust the solenoid to give 675 RPM; when finished, reconnect the terminal connector.

12. If there is a dashpot, adjust it so that at idle, there is .040 in. clearance between the tip of the plunger (compressed) and the throttle lever.

13. Replace and connect the air cleaner. Use the mixture screws to make any slight idle speed correction necessary.

14. Replace the distributor and canister hoses.

1977

1. Have the engine at normal operating temperature, the parking brake set, the drive wheels blocked, and the air conditioning off.

2. Remove the air cleaner if necessary, to gain access to the carburetor adjusting screws, but leave the vacuum hoses connected.

3. Disconnect and plug other vacuum

hoses as directed by the information on the underhood emission control label.

4. Disconnect and plug the vacuum advance hose. Adjust the ignition timing if necessary. Reconnect the vacuum advance hose when completed.

5. Remove the limiter caps from the idle screws, and lightly seat the screws. Back the screws out from their seats equally, so that the engine will run.

6. Place the transmission in Drive, with automatic, and in neutral with manual transmission.

7. Back out each screw until the maximum idle speed is obtained. Adjust the idle speed screw until the idle speed matches the specifications listed in Column A.

	A	B
6-231 Buick	640	600
6-231 Buick H, C	610	600
8-301 Pont.	590	550
8-305 Chev.	530	500
8-350 Pont.	600	575
8-350 Olds. H	625	600
8-350 Olds. C	575	550
8-350 Olds.	580	550
8-400 Pont.	615	575
8-403 Olds.	580	550
8-403 Olds. H	625	600
8-403 Olds. C	575	550

C—California
H—High Altitude

8. Turn each screw in with 1/8 turn increments until the idle speed corresponds with the idle speed listed in column B.

9. Install new limiter caps, and reset the idle speed to the specifications listed on the Emission control label.

10. Adjust the fast idle as indicated on the emission control label.

11. Reinstall the air cleaner and the vacuum lines. Recheck the engine idle and adjust as necessary.

1978-79
Idle Speed Adjustment

V6-231, V8-305 WITH 2GC OR 2GE CARBURETOR

1. Set the parking brake and block the wheels.

2. Connect a tachometer to the engine according to the manufacturer's instructions.

3. Turn the air conditioning OFF and disconnect and plug the vacuum hoses at the vapor cansiter and EGR valve.

4. Run the engine to normal operating temperature. Make certain that the choke is fully opened.

5. With the transmission in Park (AT) or Neutral (MT), disconnect the vacuum hose at the distributor and plug it. Set the ignition timing.

6. Unplug and connect the distributor vacuum hose.

7. Adjust the idle speed to specifications by turning the idle adjusting screw.

8. Reconnect the canister and EGR hoses, and remove the tachometer.

V8-301 WITH M2MC-210 CARBURETOR

1. Set the parking brake and block the wheels. Disconnect the air conditioning compressor and turn the air conditioning OFF.

2. Disconnect and plug the vacuum advance hose at the distributor.

3. Start the engine and run it to normal operating temperature. Make certain that the choke is fully opened. Place the transmission in Drive (AT) or neutral (MT).

4. Connect a tachometer to the engine according to the manufacturer's instructions.

5. Set the ignition timing.

6. Unplug and connect the distributor vacuum hose.

7. Disconnect the purge hose at the canister.

*E.G.R. (EXHAUST GAS RECIRCULATION)

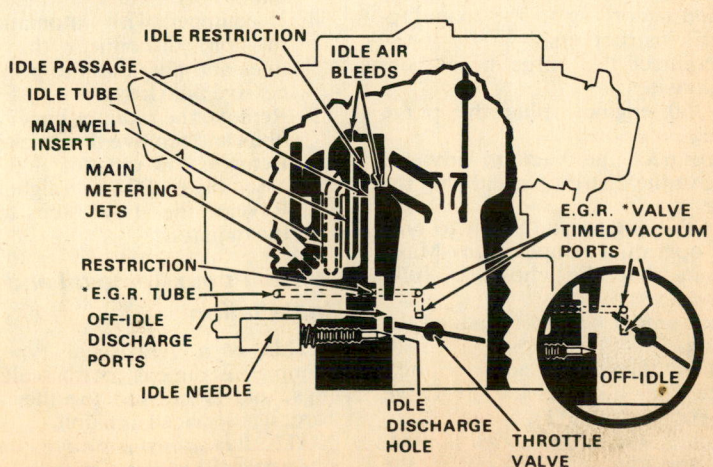

Idle system: 2GC except California and High Altitude

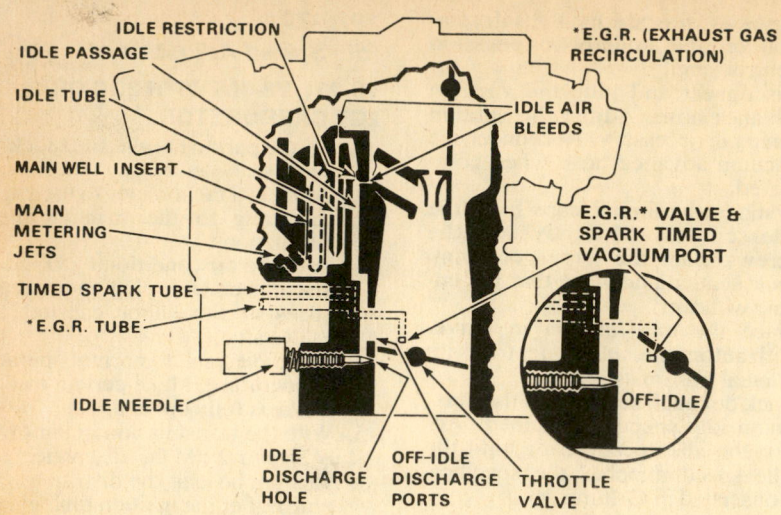

IDLE RESTRICTION
IDLE PASSAGE
IDLE TUBE
MAIN WELL INSERT
MAIN METERING JETS
TIMED SPARK TUBE
*E.G.R. TUBE
IDLE NEEDLE

*E.G.R. (EXHAUST GAS RECIRCULATION)
IDLE AIR BLEEDS
E.G.R.* VALVE & SPARK TIMED VACUUM PORT
OFF-IDLE

IDLE DISCHARGE HOLE
OFF-IDLE DISCHARGE PORTS
THROTTLE VALVE

Idle system: 2GC California and High Altitude

8. On cars with air conditioning: turn the idle speed screw to obtain the specified rpm. Turn the air conditioning ON. Open the throttle momentarily to extend the solenoid plunger. Turn the solenoid to obtain the rpm specified on the underhood sticker. Turn the A/C OFF.

On cars without air conditioning: Turn the idle speed screw to the specified rpm.

9. Stop the engine and reconnect the clutch wire. Remove the tachometer.

V8-301, 350, 400, 403 WITH M4MC CARBURETOR

NOTE: *The 301 is equipped with a hot idle compensator valve. The inlet for this valve is located on top of the air horn. To insure proper idle adjustment, this valve must be closed. Check this by holding a finger over the inlet. If no drop in rpm is noted, the valve is closed. If the valve is open, plug the inlet.*

1. Set the parking brake, block the wheels, turn the air conditioning OFF, connect a tachometer to the engine according to the manufacturer's instructions.
2. Disconnect the purge hose from the cansiter.
3. On 350 engines, plug the purge hose.
4. Disconnect the vacuum advance hose at the distributor and plug the hose.
5. Start the engine and run it to normal operating temperature. Make certain that the choke is fully opened.
6. Check, and if necessary, adjust the timing.
7. Connect the vacuum advance line.
8. Place the transmission in Drive (AT) or neutral (MT).
9. On cars without air conditioning: turn the idle screw to obtain the specified rpm.
On cars with air conditioning:

Disconnect the compressor clutch wire. Turn the A/C ON. Open the throttle momentarily to extend the solenoid plunger. Turn the solenoid to obtain the rpm listed on the underhood sticker. Connect the A/C clutch and turn the A/C OFF.

10. Reconnect all hoses and remove the tachometer.

1978-79 Idle Mixture Adjustment

Modifications to these carburetors prevent the adjustment of fuel mixture without the use of a special propane enrichment system, not available to the general public. Backing out the mixture screw will have little or no effect at all.

COOLING SYSTEM

Radiator Removal and Installation

1. Drain the radiator.
2. On Grand Prix, remove the fan.
3. Disconnect the upper and lower radiator hoses.
4. If equipped with automatic transmission, disconnect the cooling lines and plug them to prevent excessive fluid loss.
5. Remove the radiator upper bracket bolts and remove the bracket.
6. Remove the radiator and shroud assembly by lifting straight up.
7. Reverse the above steps to install the radiator.

Water Pump Removal and Installation

This is a centrifugal type water pump. It is die cast, with sealed bearings, and is pressed together. Therefore, it is serviced as a unit.

NOTE: *It is sometimes more convenient to remove the radiator than to leave it in place. This depends on the working space available and the options on the*

car such as air conditioning and power steering.

1. Disconnect the battery and drain the radiator.
2. Loosen the alternator and remove the fan belt.
3. Remove the power steering and air conditioning belts, if so equipped.
4. Remove the fan and water pump pulley.
5. Remove the front alternator bracket.
6. Remove the heater hose and radiator hose at the pump.
7. Remove the water pump retaining bolts and remove the pump.
8. Install the pump by reversing above steps. Make sure the gasket surfaces are clean and smooth. Always use a gasket sealer on both sides of the gasket. Torque the retaining bolts to 15 ft. lbs.

NOTE: *If a belt tensioning gauge is available, adjust the belts to 100 to 130 lbs. tension on new belts and to 70 lbs. on used belts. If the gauge is not available, adjust the belts so that a 1/4 to 1/2 inch deflection can be made on the longest span of the belt, under moderate thumb pressure.*

Thermostat Replacement

1. Drain the coolant to below the thermostat level.
2. Disconnect the upper hose and remove the water outlet assembly.
3. Replace by reversing the above steps. Clean the gasket surfaces and use a gasket sealer and a new gasket. Torque attaching bolts to 30 ft. lbs.
4. Refill the cooling system.

EMISSION CONTROLS

There are three types of emissions to be controlled: crankcase emissions, carburetor and gas tank vapor emissions, and exhaust emissions. See the Unit Repair Section for troubleshooting and repair information.

1972

All models use the new Speed Control Spark System, (S.C.S.).

Every engine and transmission combination uses the Auto-therm air cleaner, P.C.V. system, and the evaporation control system.

The S.C.S. system uses a solenoid valve in the vacuum line running between the carburetor and the distributor. This valve is the same as the Transmission Controlled Spark Valve used earlier. The difference in this system is that the valve is regulated by vehicle speed using a speed control spark switch, instead of by a transmission switch. The S.C.S. solenoid valve is energized below 38 mph in any gear, under normal operating temperature, allowing no vacuum advance. Above

38 mph, in any gear, or any time engine temperature is higher or lower than normal operating temperature, the solenoid valve is de-energized allowing full vacuum advance to the distributor.

Normally S.C.S. engine operating temperatures range from 95° to 230°. An engine temperature sensing switch is located in the head and de-energizes the solenoid until operating temperature is reached regardless of vehicle speed.

1973

The Controlled Combustion System (C.C.S.) is standard on all engines. The Air Injection Reactor (A.I.R.) is used on all 350 engines with manual transmissions and 350/400 California engines. A combination of the Transmission Controlled Spark and Exhaust Gas Re-Circulation (E.G.R.) is found on all V8 engines.

E.G.R. is a system used to reduce oxides of nitrogen (NOx) emissions. It functions by allowing a small amount of exhaust gas into the air fuel mixture in the intake manifold, under certain conditions.

The EGR-TCS system consists of a temperature switch which senses when the engine temperature is under 71° or over 230°, a second temperature switch sensing engine temperature between 140° and 230°, an EGR solenoid, a vacuum advance solenoid, a transmission switch, and a time delay relay.

The under 71° and over 230° switch is mounted on the left cylinder head. The 140° to 230° switch is mounted in the right cylinder head. The time delay relay is mounted on the vacuum advance solenoid.

The 71° to 230° switch grounds the circuit for the solenoids below 71° and above 230°. The 140° switch passes current to the transmission switch when engine temperature is between 140° and 230°. The transmission switch then grounds the circuit for the solenoids in first gear only. Between 71° and 140° the temperature switches are both open and the solenoids are in the normal positions.

The vacuum advance solenoid is normally closed, allowing no vacuum advance. The EGR solenoid is normally open, allowing exhaust gas recirculation.

Below 71° there is a complete circuit and both solenoids are energized, allowing vacuum advance and cutting off EGR.

From 71° to 140° there is an open circuit, the solenoids return to their normal positions and vacuum advance is cut off and EGR is allowed.

From 140° to 230°, in first gear, there is an open circuit and the solenoids are in their normal positions. The time delay relay maintains the open circuit for 33 to 55 seconds after the transmission shifts into second gear. However, after the time delay in second and third gear, the solenoids are energized to allow vacuum advance and cut off EGR.

Over 235° the solenoids are energized, vacuum advance occurs and there is no EGR.

A mid-year redesign of the emission control system was necessitated by newly-announced Federal standards. On cars equipped with A.I.R., air is not supplied to Nos. 3 and 6 cylinders. This is done by internal changes in the cylinder heads. Mid-year A.I.R. cylinder heads can usually be identified by the absence of a drilled passage and a metal sealing ball at the Nos. 3 and 6 cylinder locations.

The new engines have a relocated vacuum source for the air cleaner. Vacuum is supplied through a tee in the hose feeding vacuum to the distributor vacuum spark thermal valve.

The mid-year EGR system operates basically on the same principle as the 1973 system, except for two major differences:

1. The EGR and TCS systems now work completely independent of each other.
2. A new EGR thermal vacuum valve is used to sense the temperature of the intake manifold coolant. Below 95°F, no EGR; above 95°F, ported EGR.

In the TCS system, full vacuum advance is provided below 62°F. When the temperature rises above 62°F, the distributor vacuum spark thermal valve closes and from this point on the distributor solenoid must be energized to get vacuum advance. The upper temperature limit for vacuum advance cut-in is now 240°F.

The Start-Up Relay Switch gives full advance in any gear for 20 seconds after all engine starts. After the 20 seconds has elapsed, the switch breaks ground and the distributor solenoid is de-energized, shutting off the vacuum advance.

1974

The A.I.R. system is carried over from 1973 and is used on all 400 cu. in. 2 bbl California engines.

The EGR/TCS system is once again together, as in early 1973 systems, and consists of a thermal vacuum valve, vacuum advance solenoid, EGR valve, hot coolant switch, cold feed switch and a time-delay relay for engine starting. The system is found on all V8s.

On the EGR/TCS system, the distributor spark-EGR thermal vacuum valve senses the temperature of the air/fuel mixture inside the intake manifold. Below 62°F, EGR is off and full vacuum advance is provided. When the temperature rises above 62°F, EGR is on (operated by a port above the throttle blade, so that it only comes on above idle). From this point on the distributor vacuum advance solenoid must be energized by the other components and switches to provide vacuum advance.

When the cylinder head metal temperature goes above 125°, 140°, 155°F (depending on use), the cold feed switch closes. This sends the 12V current to the TCS switch. The TCS switch provides a ground only when the transmission shifts into high gear. There is no time delay after shifting into high gear.

Any time the coolant temperature goes over 240°F, the hot coolant switch provides a ground for the distributor solenoid. Since the hot coolant switch will ground whether the TCS switch does or not, vacuum advance will be supplied to the distributor in any gear when the coolant temperature reaches 240°F or above.

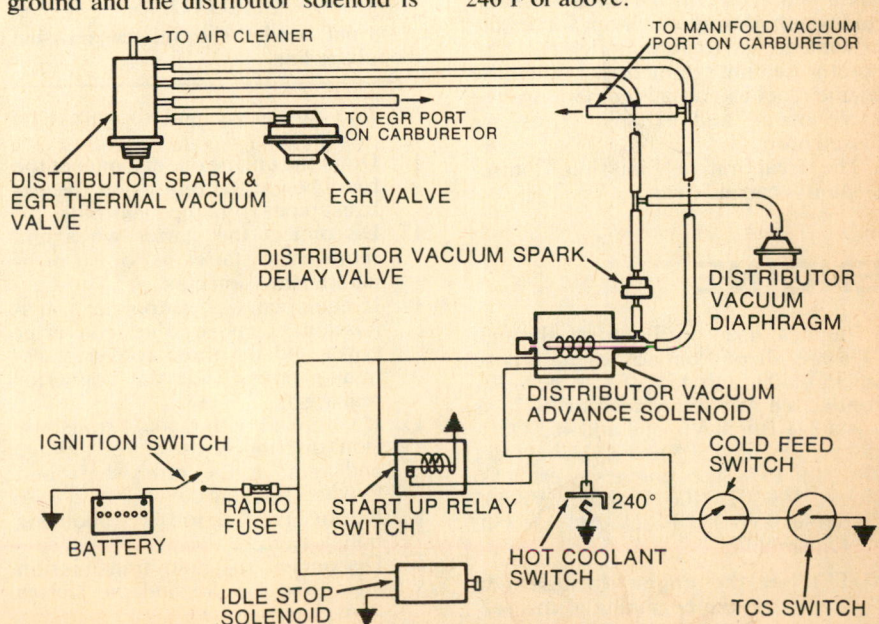

1974 emission control system—schematic diagram
(© Pontiac Div., G.M. Corp)

There is a distributor vacuum spark delay valve on some models, between the distributor solenoid and the distributor acting as a restrictor on vacuum supplied to the distributor. This merely slows down the rate vacuum is initially supplied to the distributor. Full vacuum is eventually supplied.

The function of the start-up relay switch is identical to late 1973.

1975-77

The Controlled Combustion System (C.C.S.) is continued on all non-California engines.

The Air Injection Reactor (A.I.R.), or air pump system is continued in some applications.

E.G.R. (Exhaust Gas Recirculation) is used with the exhaust gas introduced into the intake mixture in the intake manifold and modulated by an exhaust backpressure modulating valve.

A hot air choke is used to provide quick response to engine warmup.

All models have high energy ignition (H.E.I.) to prevent any possible catalyst damage caused by ignition miss. Refer to the Electronic Ignition Unit Repair Section for details.

Oxidizing catalytic converters are used on all models to control hydrocarbons and carbon monoxide. Refer to the Emission Control Unit Repair Section for details on this system.

To maintain a controlled temperature of air, a Thermostatic Air Cleaner, (TAC), is used on all engines to mix pre-heated and non pre-heated air before entering the carburetor. The pre-heating of the air allows leaner carburetor and choke calibrations, resulting in lower emission levels, while maintaining good driveability.

The Early Fuel Evaporation System has a heat valve in the exhaust manifold which, during warm-up, forces the exhaust gases to flow under the carburetor heating the mixture. When the engine reaches normal temperature the valve opens and exhaust gases are routed normally.

The Evaporative Emission Control System is carried over.

ENGINE

Engines used in Pontiacs through 1976 are all of Pontiac design. These are 350, 400, and 455 V8s. A new 301 Pontiac V8 was introduced in 1977, as was a 231 Buick V6, 350 and 403 Oldsmobile V8s, and 305 and 350 Chevrolet V8s. In 1978 the engines were: V6 Buick, V8-301, 400 Pontiac, V8-305 Chevrolet, V8-350 Buick and V8-350, 403 Oldsmobile.

NOTE: See the Engine Identification Code chart at the beginning of this section to identify the engine you are working on. Only procedures for Pontiac V8s are given in this section. For service pro- cedures on other engines, see the car section for that engine's manufacturer.

ENGINE REMOVAL AND INSTALLATION

1. Disconnect the battery cables and remove the battery.
2. Drain the cooling system.
3. Scribe alignment marks around the hood hinges and remove the hood.
4. Disconnect the engine wiring and all ground straps. Disconnect the thermal feed switch from the left rear cylinder head on all 1973 and later cars.
5. Remove the air cleaner and fan shroud, then disconnect the radiator and heater hoses.
6. Remove the radiator.
7. Remove the power steering pump and A/C compressor from the brackets and swing the units aside without disconnecting the hoses.

— CAUTION —

If the compressor refrigerant lines do not have enough slack to position the compressor out of the way without disconnecting the refrigerant lines, the air conditioning system will have to be removed by air-conditioning specialist. Under no conditions should an untrained person attempt to disconnect the air conditioning refrigerant lines. These lines contain pressurized Freon, which can be extremely dangerous.

8. Remove the fan and fan pulley.
9. Disconnect the accelerator linkage or cable and remove the bracket.
10. Disconnect the transmission vacuum modulator line (automatic) and the power brake vacuum line.

— CAUTION —

Do not bend the metal transmission modulator line.

11. Jack up the car and support it on axle stands.
12. Drain the engine oil, disconnect the fuel lines at the pump and the exhaust pipes from the manifolds.
13. Disconnect the starter wires and remove the starter motor on manual transmission cars.
14. If equipped with automatic transmission: remove the converter cover and the three converter retaining bolts. Slide the converter rearward.
15. If equipped with manual transmission: disconnect the clutch linkage and remove the cross-shaft and flywheel housing cover.
16. Remove the four lower bellhousing bolts—two per side.
17. Disconnect the auto transmission filler tube support and the starter wire shield.
18. Remove the two front motor mount bolts, then lower the car to the floor.

19. Support the auto transmission with a wood-padded jack, then remove the two remaining bell-housing bolts from above.
20. Jack up the auto transmission slightly, attach a chain hoist and remove the engine.
21. To install, reverse the removal procedure. Note that there are dowel pins in the block that have matching holes in the bell-housing. These dowel pins must be in almost perfect alignment with their holes before the engine and bell-housing will go together. Do not lower the engine completely while the jack is supporting the transmission.

MANIFOLDS

Exhaust Manifold Removal and Installation

Tab locks are used on the front and rear pairs of bolts on each exhaust manifold. When removing the bolts, straighten the tabs from beneath the car using a long handled screw driver. When installing the tab locks, bend the tabs against the sides of the bolt, not over the top of the bolt.

LEFT MANIFOLD

1. If the car is equipped with power steering, disconnect the power steering pump but leave it attached to its hoses and pull it up out of the way.
2. Remove the alternator belt, the alternator and the mounting bracket as an assembly.
3. From underneath the vehicle, disconnect the exhaust crossover pipe flange.
4. If the car is equipped with power brakes, the rear bolts of the manifold are difficult to reach but they can be removed with a box wrench.
5. Remove the bolts that hold the manifold to the left cylinder head and take off the manifold.

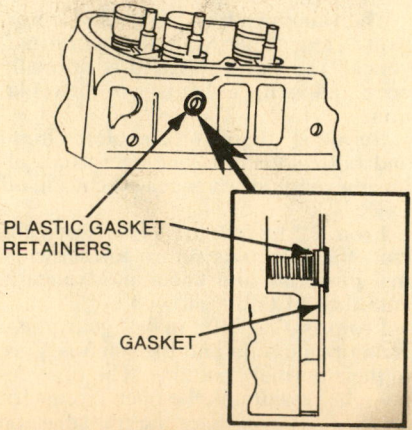

PLASTIC GASKET RETAINERS

GASKET

Plastic manifold gasket retainers used on Pontiac V8s
(© Pontiac Div, G.M. Corp)

RIGHT MANIFOLD

From underneath the vehicle, disconnect the upper flange from the right manifold. This is the upper flange where the cross manifold, exhaust pipe and right manifold join.

From underneath the vehicle, remove the bolts that hold the manifold to the head on the back two flanges. The front flange can be removed from the top of the car with a box wrench.

Intake Manifold Removal and Installation

1. Drain the coolant from the petcocks on the radiator and on each side of the block. Remove the EGR valve where necessary before removing the manifold.

NOTE: *Most of the coolant can be drained from the block through the radiator drain by raising the rear end of the car approximately 15-18 in. off floor.*

2. Remove the air cleaner.
3. Remove the water outlet fitting bolts and position the fitting out of the way, leaving radiator hose attached.
4. Disconnect the heater hose from the fitting.
5. Disconnect the electrical wires and vacuum hoses from all emission switches and solenoids.
6. Remove the spark plug wire brackets from the manifold.
7. On cars equipped with power brakes, remove the power brake vacuum pipe from the carburetor.
8. Disconnect the distributor to carburetor vacuum hoses.
9. Disconnect the fuel line connecting the carburetor and fuel pump.
10. Disconnect the crankcase vent hose from the intake manifold.
11. Disconnect the throttle rod from the carburetor.
12. Remove the screws retaining the throttle control bracket assembly.
13. Remove the intake manifold retaining bolts and nuts, and remove the manifold and gaskets. Make sure that the O-ring seal between the intake manifold and timing chain cover is retained and installed during assembly.
14. Reverse the procedure to install. Use plastic gasket retainers to prevent the manifold gaskets from slipping out of place.

VALVE SYSTEM

All Pontiac design V8 engines use a ball pivot type valve train and non-adjustable hydraulic valve lifters.

Rocker Arm Removal and Installation

1. Remove the valve covers.
2. Remove the rocker arm nut and rocker arm ball.
3. Lift the rocker arm off the rocker arm stud. Always keep the rocker

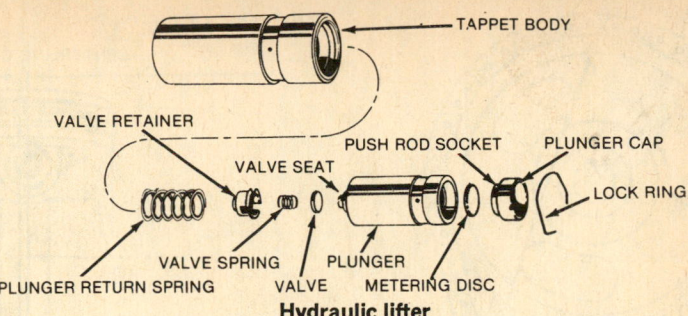

Hydraulic lifter

arm assemblies together and assemble them on the same stud.
4. Remove the pushrod from its bore. Make sure the rods are returned to their original bore, with the same end in the block.
5. Reverse the removal procedure to install the rocker arms. Tighten the ball retaining nuts to 20 ft. lbs.

Valve Guides

Pontiac engines have integral valve guides. Pontiac offers valves with oversize stems for worn guides (0.001, 0.003 and 0.005 in. being available for most engines). To fit these, enlarge valve guide bores with valve guide reamers to an oversize that cleans up wear.

As an alternate procedure, some local automotive machine shops fit replacement guides that use standard stem valves.

CYLINDER HEAD

Cylinder Head Removal and Installation

1. Drain the cooling system including the block. Remove the intake manifold, valley cover, and rocker arm cover.
2. Loosen all rocker arm retaining nuts and pivot rockers off the pushrods.
3. Remove the pushrods and place in order. The pushrods must be replaced in the same position with the same end in the block.
4. On all but the left head of the 455 S.D. engine, remove the exhaust pipe-to-manifold attaching bolts. In order to remove the left head of the 455 S.D., it is necessary to remove the exhaust manifold attaching nuts and drop the manifold. Remove the inner panel of the

carburetor heat stove from the two center cylinder head bolts.
5. Remove the battery ground strap and engine ground strap on the left head; engine ground strap and automatic transmission filler tube bracket on the right head.
6. Remove the cylinder head bolts and head, with the exhaust manifold attached.

NOTE: *Left head must be maneuvered to clear the power steering and power brake units.*

7. Check the head surface for straightness, then place a new head gasket on the block.

NOTE: *Bolts are of three different lengths. When they are properly installed, they will project an equal distance from the head, before tightening.*

8. Install all the bolts and tighten evenly to the specified torque. Tighten to specifications in three stages.

--- CAUTION ---

On the 301 V8 engine, coat all rocker stud lower threads, the cylinder head bolt threads, and the underside of the bolt head with thread sealer.

9. Install the pushrods in their original positions.
10. Position the rocker arms over the pushrods. Tighten the rocker arm ball retaining nut to 20 ft. lbs.
11. Replace the rocker arm cover.
12. Replace the valley cover.
13. Replace the ground straps, oil filler tube bracket, intake manifold.
14. Install the exhaust pipe flange nuts. On 455 S.D. engine, install the left exhaust manifold, with a new gasket.

TIMING COVER, CHAIN, AND CAMSHAFT

Timing Case Cover Removal and Installation, Seal Replacement

1. Drain the radiator and the cylinder block.
2. Loosen the alternator adjusting bolts.
3. Remove the fan, fan pulley, accessory drive belts, and water pump.
4. Disconnect the radiator hoses.
5. Remove the fuel pump.

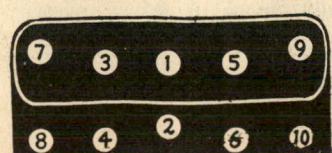

Pontiac 301, 350, 400, 455 V8 cylinder head tightening sequence

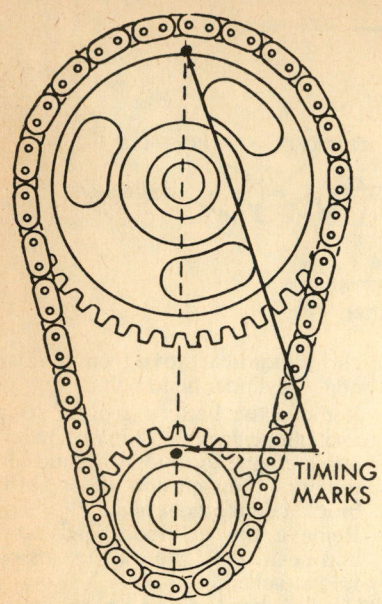

Pontiac 301, 350, 400, 455 V8 valve timing marks (© Pontiac Div., G.M.Corp)

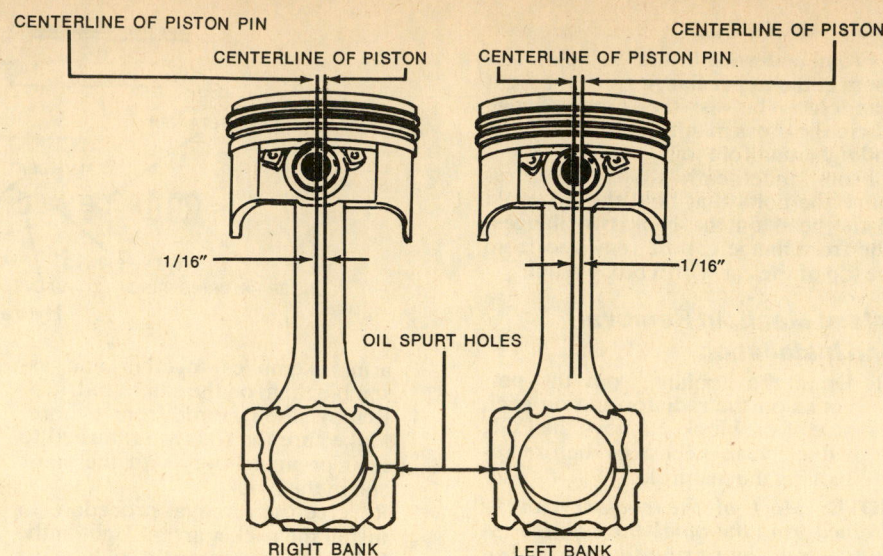

Pontiac 301, 350, 400, 455 V8 piston and rod assembly

6. Remove the harmonic balancer bolt and washer.
7. Remove harmonic balancer.

NOTE: *Do not pry on rubber-mounted balancers. If only the seal is to be replaced, proceed to Step 12.*

8. Remove the front four oil pan to timing cover bolts.
9. Remove the timing cover bolts and nuts and cover to intake manifold bolt.
10. Pull the cover forward and remove.
11. Remove the O-ring from the recess in the intake manifold, then clean all the gasket surfaces.
12. To replace the seal, pry it out of the cover using a screwdriver. Install the new seal with the lip inward.

NOTE: *The seal can be replaced with the cover installed.*

13. To install, reverse the removal procedure, making sure all gaskets are replaced. Tighten the four oil pan bolts to 12 ft. lbs., and the fan pulley bolts to 20 ft. lbs.

Timing Chain and Sprocket Removal and Installation

1. Remove the timing case cover and fuel pump cam.
2. Turn the crank and camshaft (if the chain is broken) until the two timing marks are in line.
3. Using a puller, draw the sprocket off the front of the crankshaft.
4. Install the chain and sprockets with the timing marks aligned.
5. Secure the camshaft sprocket in position, with pump cam in place.

NOTE: *When reassembling the timing case cover, extra care should be taken to make sure that the oil seal between the bottom of the timing case cover and the front of the oil pan is still a good one. Plenty of gasket cement should be*

used, at this point, to prevent oil leaks.

Camshaft Removal and Installation

1. Drain the cooling system and remove the air cleaner.
2. Disconnect all water hoses, vacuum lines and spark plug wires.
3. Disconnect the accelerator linkage, temperature gauge wire, and fuel lines. Remove the radiator.
4. Remove the hood latch brace.
5. Remove the PCV hose, then remove the rocker covers. Remove the water pump.

NOTE: *On air-conditioned models, remove the alternator and bracket.*

6. Remove the distributor, then remove the intake manifold.
7. Remove the valve tappet cover.
8. Loosen the rocker arm nuts and pivot the rockers out of the way.
9. Remove the pushrods and lifters (keep them in proper order).
10. Remove the harmonic balancer, fuel pump, and four oil pan to timing cover bolts.
11. Remove the timing cover and gasket, then remove the fuel pump eccentric and bushing.
12. Align the timing marks, then remove the timing chain and sprockets.
13. Remove the camshaft thrust plate.
14. Remove the camshaft by pulling straight forward, being careful not to damage the cam bearings in the process.

NOTE: *It may be necessary to jack up the engine slightly to gain clearance, especially if motor mounts are worn.*

15. Install the new camshaft, with lobes and journals coated with heavy (SAE 50-60) oil, into the engine, being careful not to damage cam bearings.

NOTE: *Most specialty cams come with a special break-in lubricant for the lobes and journals; if such lubricant is available, use it instead of heavy oil.*

16. Install the camshaft thrust plate and tighten the bolts to 20 ft. lbs.
17. To install, reverse steps 1-12, tightening the sprocket bolts to 40 ft. lbs., the timing cover bolts and nuts to 30 ft. lbs., and the oil pan bolts to 12 ft. lbs.

PISTON AND CONNECTING ROD

The letter F, or the notch in the edge of the piston, goes to the front of the

Piston and rod assembly

engine in all cases. The oil spurt holes on the connecting rod lower ends must face the camshaft. Some 1973, and all 1974 and later, engines don't have these holes. These connecting rods have three dimples on one side of the rod and a single dimple on the connecting rod cap. The dimples must face to the rear on the right bank, and forward on the left.

LUBRICATION

Oil Pan Removal and Installation

1. Disconnect the battery cables.
2. Remove the fan shroud and the power steering belt, then tilt the steering pump upward.
3. Remove the fan and pulley.
4. Disconnect the engine ground straps. Drain the radiator.
5. On A/C cars, remove the compressor from the brackets and swing aside without disconnecting hoses.
6. Check all wiring, fuel lines and hoses for clearance, and disconnect the thermal feed switch from the left rear cylinder head, on 1973 and later models, as the engine must be raised. Disconnect the radiator hose at the water pump.
7. Jack up the car and drain the engine oil.
8. Disconnect the steering idler arm from the frame and remove the Pitman arm from the steering box on Grand Prix.
9. Remove the exhaust crossover pipe on single-exhaust cars; disconnect the manifold flanges on dual-exhaust cars. Wire the pipes out of the way to gain working room.
10. Remove the flywheel housing cover, starter motor and motor bracket.
11. Attach a hoist to the front of the engine.
12. Support the engine on a hoist and remove the front motor mount bolts and mounts.
13. Loosen the rear motor mount at

transmission or, better still, remove it entirely and allow the extension housing to rest on the crossmember.
14. Remove the oil pan bolts, then raise the engine straight up about 4½ in. until the top of the transmission is hitting the floor pan. On some models, it also helps to move the engine forward about 1½ in.
15. Rotate the oil pan forward to clear the oil pump, then remove the oil pan.
16. Place wood blocks between the engine and motor mount brackets for safety.
17. To install, reverse the removal procedure. Clean all gasket surfaces thoroughly. Use gasket cement and a new gasket.

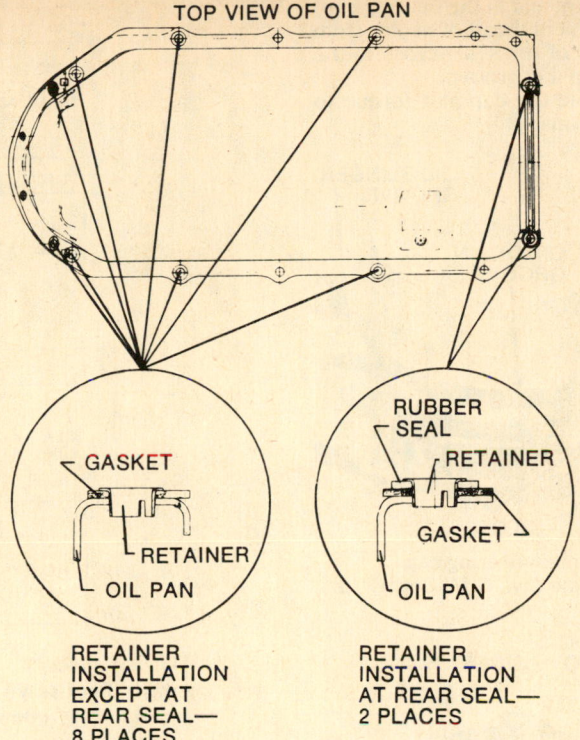

1972 and later Pontiac V8 oil pan gasket installation
(© Pontiac Div., G.M. Corp)

Rear Main Bearing Oil Seal Replacement

1. Remove the oil pan, baffle, and oil pump.
2. Remove the rear main bearing cap.
3. Make a seal tool.
4. Insert the tool against one end of the oil seal in the block and drive the seal gently into the groove ¾ in. Repeat on the other end of the seal.
5. Form a new seal in the cap. Cut four pieces ⅜ in. long from this seal.
6. Work two of the pieces into each of the gaps which have been made at the end of the seal in the block. Do not cut off any material to make them fit.

Front oil pan gasket overlapping side gaskets (© Pontiac Div, G.M. Corp)

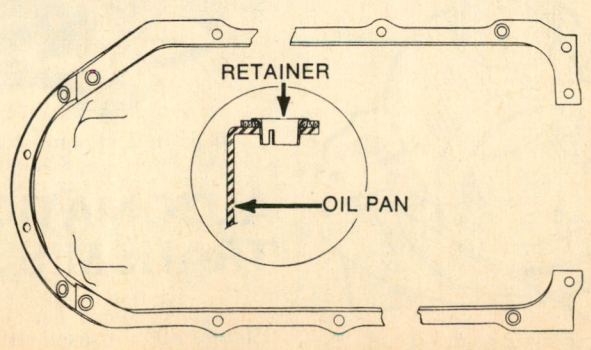

Oil pan gasket retainers
(© Pontiac Div., G.M. Corp)

7. Form a new seal in the bearing cap.
8. Apply a ¹/₁₆ in. bead of sealer from the center of the seal across to the external gasket groove.
9. Reassemble the cap and torque to specifications.

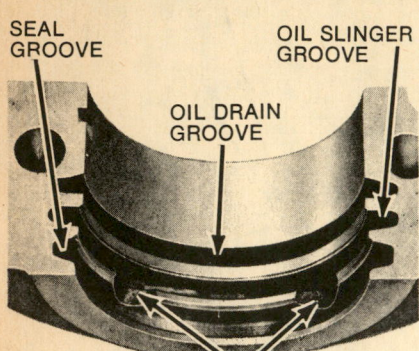

SEAL GROOVE
OIL SLINGER GROOVE
OIL DRAIN GROOVE
SLOTS

Rear main bearing cap
(© Pontiac Div., G.M. Corp)

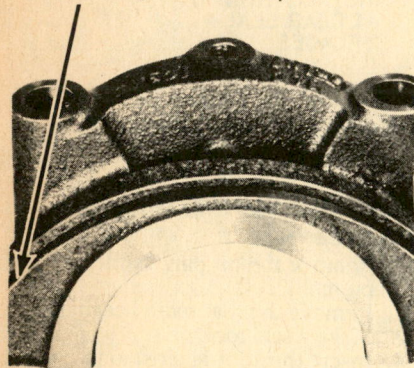

CEMENT GROOVE
1″ TO 1¼″ (BOTH SIDES)

Rear main bearing oil seal positioned in bearing cap (© Pontiac Div, G.M. Corp)

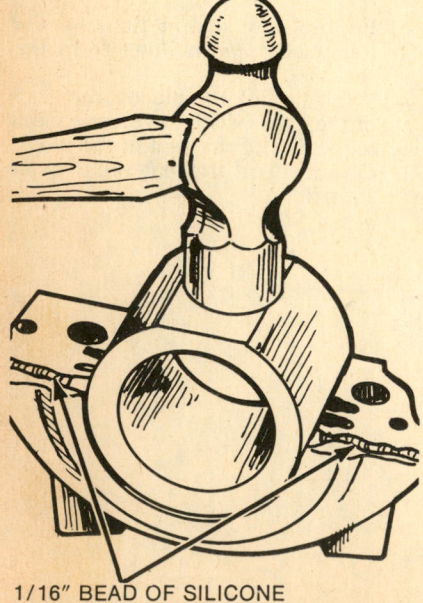

1/16″ BEAD OF SILICONE RUBBER SEALER

Forming a new crankshaft seal

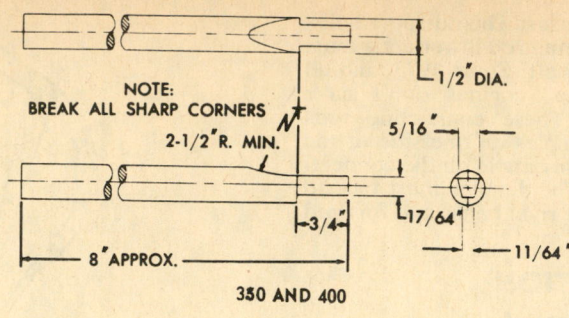

NOTE: BREAK ALL SHARP CORNERS
2-1/2″ R. MIN.
1/2″ DIA.
5/16″
17/64″
3/4″
8″ APPROX.
11/64″

350 AND 400

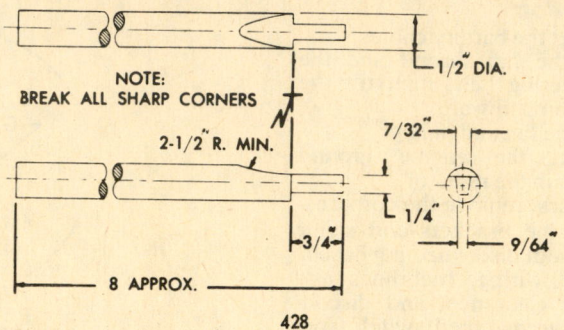

NOTE: BREAK ALL SHARP CORNERS
2-1/2″ R. MIN.
1/2″ DIA.
7/32″
1/4″
3/4″
8 APPROX.
9/64″

428

Pontiac V8 upper rear main bearing seal tool—the lower one is for 455, upper for 301, 350, and 400
(© Pontiac Div., G.M. Corp)

Oil Pump Removal and Installation

1. Remove the oil pan.
2. Remove the oil pump attaching screws, and carefully lower the pump, while removing the pump drive shaft.
3. Prime the pump by filling the gear cavity with petroleum jelly or oil. Never use grease.
4. Reinstall the pump by reversing the order of removal.

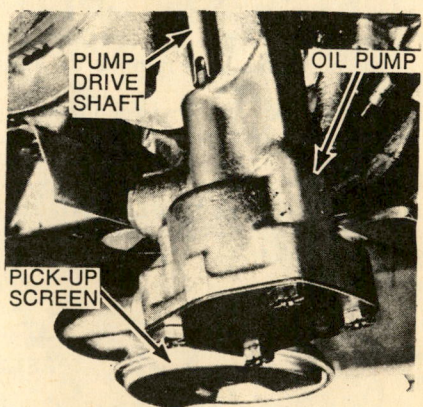

PUMP DRIVE SHAFT
OIL PUMP
PICK-UP SCREEN

Oil pump and pump drive shaft
(© Pontiac Div, G.M. Corp)

AUTOMATIC TRANSMISSION

The three speed Turbo Hydra-Matic 350 and 400 are used with all engines through 1976. The Turbo Hydra-Matic 400 was used on all models, 1972-76. Starting 1977, the Turbo Hydra-Matic 200 and 350 were used; the 400 was no longer available.

The transmissions can be identified visually: The 200 and 350 have a downshift cable between the accelerator linkage and the transmission; the 400 has an electrical downshift switch on the accelerator pedal linkage. The 200 has a pan with ten bolts; the 350 has thirteen. Sometimes the word METRIC is embossed on the 200 pan. The 200 and 350 pan is rectangular or square, with the right rear corner cut off; the 400 pan has an irregular shape.

Throttle Valve Adjustment

1978-79 CARS WITH TURBO HYDRA-MATIC 200

1. Disengage the snap lock so that the cable is free to slide through the lock ring.
2. With the cable installed in the support and attached to the transmission and carburetor lever, move the carburetor lever to the wide open throttle position.
3. Push the snap lock flush and return the carburetor lever to the closed position.

Shift Linkage Adjustment

COLUMN SHIFT

1. Loosen the screw on the adjusting swivel clamp.
2. Place the gearshift lever in Park (Neutral starting 1976) and lock the ignition.
3. Place the transmission shift lever in the Park detent (Neutral starting 1976).
4. Push up on the gearshift control

rod until the lash is taken up in the steering column lock mechanism, then tighten the screw on the swivel clamp.

FLOORSHIFT

1. Disconnect the shift cable from the transmission shift lever by removing the nut from the pin.
2. Adjust the column lock (as in Step 4 of column shift adjustment).
3. Unlock the ignition and rotate the transmission shift lever into Neutral (Park starting 1976).
4. Place console lever in Neutral (Park starting 1976) and move against the forward stop.
5. Assemble the shift cable and pin to the transmission shift lever so that no binding exists, then tighten the nut.

Turbo Hydra-Matic 200 and 350 Downshift Cable Adjustment

1. Disengage the snap lock from the throttle control bracket at the carburetor end of the cable.
2. Move the carburetor lever to the wide open position.
3. Push the snap lock flush into the throttle control bracket and return the carburetor lever to the closed position.

— CAUTION —

Be sure to hold the adjusting screw locknut 1/4 turn loose during the adjusting procedure.

4. Tighten the adjusting screw to 70 in. lbs. and then back off exactly four complete turns for a band with 6,000 miles or more of use; three turns for a band with less than 6,000 miles of use.
5. Tighten the locknut, and install the protective cap.

Neutral Safety/Backup Light Switch Adjustment

NOTE: *This procedure applies to all switches with an adjusting pin hole in the back.*

1. Place the shift lever in Neutral. 1972 floorshift models must be in Park.
2. Loosen the switch mounting screws.
3. Move the switch until you can insert a 0.092 in. (1972-76) or a 0.090 in. (1977 and later) diameter adjusting pin into the hole in the back of the switch about ³⁄₈ in.
4. Tighten the screws and remove the pin.

— CAUTION —

These screws are easily overtightened and stripped. Extreme care must be taken. Maximum torque is 20 *inch* lbs. If the retainer strips it must be replaced.

5. Step on the brake pedal and check

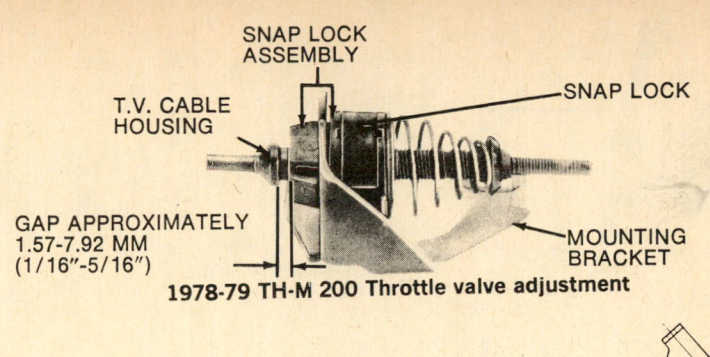

1978-79 TH-M 200 Throttle valve adjustment

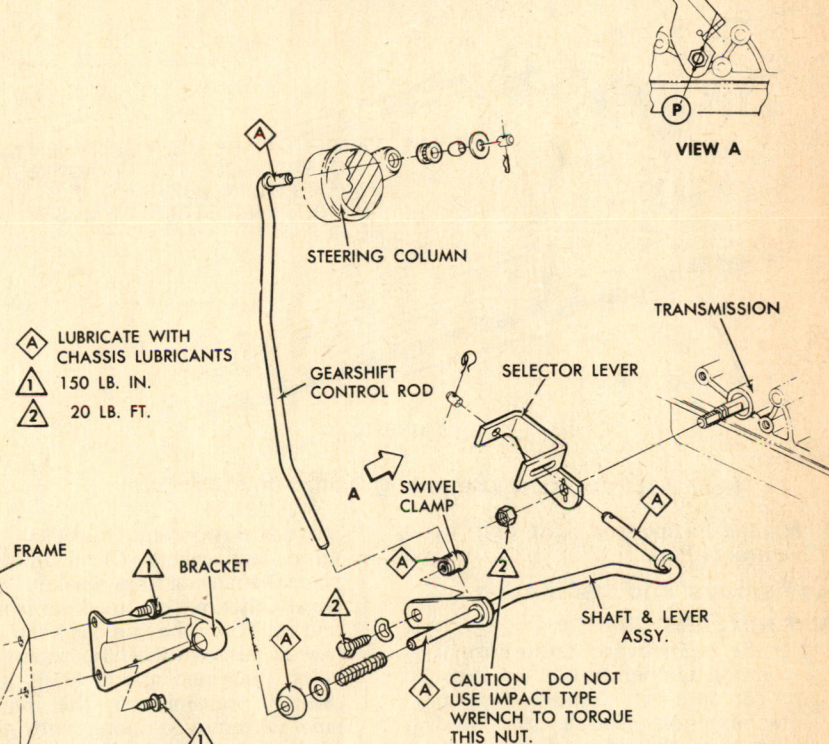

Automatic shift linkage adjustment—column shift (© Pontiac Div., G.M. Corp)

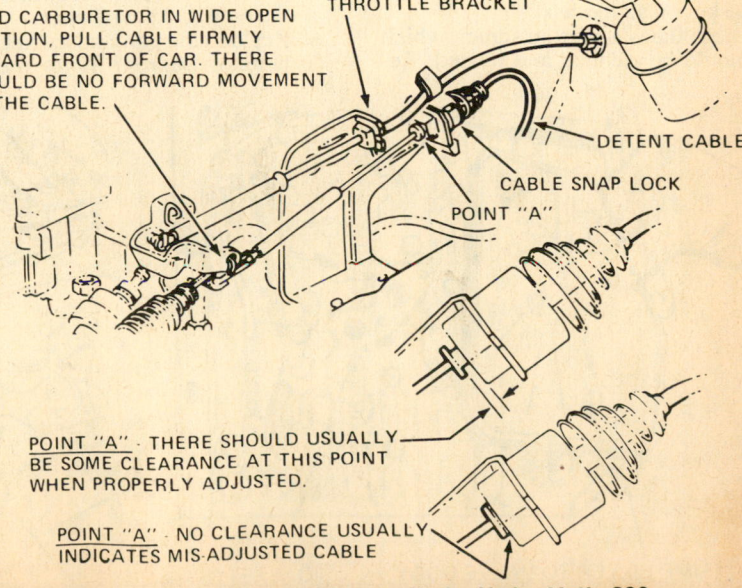

Typical downshift cable adjustment—Turbo Hydra-Matic 200 (© Pontiac Div., G.M. Corp)

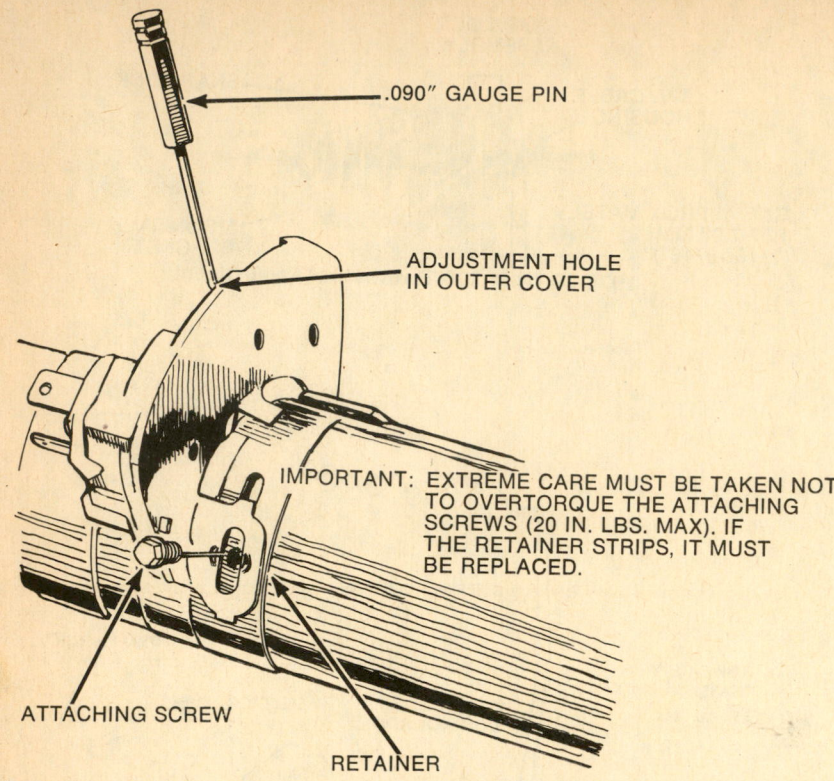

.090" GAUGE PIN

ADJUSTMENT HOLE IN OUTER COVER

IMPORTANT: EXTREME CARE MUST BE TAKEN NOT TO OVERTORQUE THE ATTACHING SCREWS (20 IN. LBS. MAX). IF THE RETAINER STRIPS, IT MUST BE REPLACED.

ATTACHING SCREW

RETAINER

Neutral start switch adjustment (© Pontiac Div., G.M. Corp)

that the engine will start only in Neutral or Park.

Pan Removal and Installation, Fluid and Filter Change

1. Let the engine warm up to normal operating temperature, then raise the car on a lift. Remove the pan attaching bolts and let the fluid drain over the edge of the pan, being careful not to let the hot fluid spill.
2. Remove the pan. Discard the pan gasket on all models.
3. The 200 has a suction screen which should be cleaned and reused. Re-move the two retaining bolts, the screen and gasket. Clean and re-place them using a new gasket.
4. On all other models, the filter is not reused. When the pan has been re-moved, remove the filter retaining bolts, filter and gasket (350). On the 400 transmission, the intake pipe is removed along with the transmission and the O ring gasket discarded.
5. Make sure all the old gasket mate-rial has been removed, then install the new gasket and filter.
6. Replace the pan and gasket. Add 6 pints of Dexron® II for the 200, 3 pints for 350, and 7 pints for the 400.
7. Start the car in Park with the park-ing brake on and let it idle. Shift through all the indicator positions and back to Park. The fluid level should be between the two dimples on the dipstick, about 1/4 in. below the ADD mark. Be very cautious not to overfill. Check the level again after the transmission is thor-oughly warm. The level should then be at FULL HOT.

U-JOINTS

Two basic designs are used; one is a typical solid shaft with two joints. A constant velocity joint is used at the rear on all Pontiac models through 1976 except the Grand Prix and station wagons.

There are two types of cross-and-bearing U-joints. One type is held with a C-shaped lock ring; the other is held with a lock plate.

Driveshaft Removal and Installation

1. Mark the driveshaft rear yoke and the differential flange to assure cor-rect alignment upon reassembly.
2. Remove the bolts and straps (or four bolts on double cardan U-joint) from the differential flange. If the bearing cups are loose, tape them together so the needle rollers don't fall out.
3. Remove the driveshaft assembly by first sliding the driveshaft for-ward to disengage the differential flange, then sliding the shaft down-ward and rearward to disengage the front splined yoke from the transmission output shaft.
4. Installation is the reversal of remo-val. Be sure to align the match mark made before disassembly.

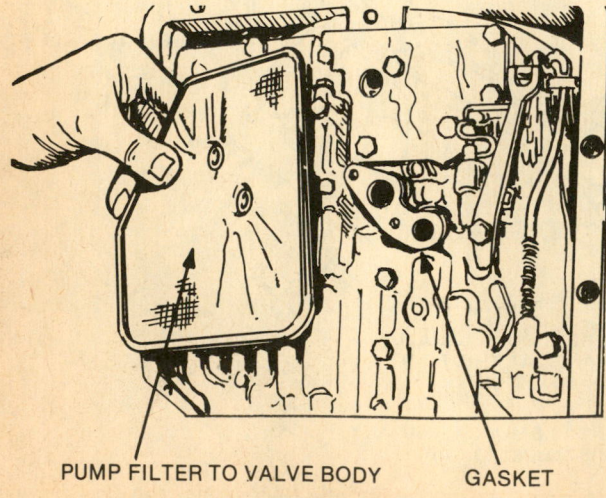

PUMP FILTER TO VALVE BODY

GASKET

Removing the Turbo Hydra-Matic 350 transmission filter

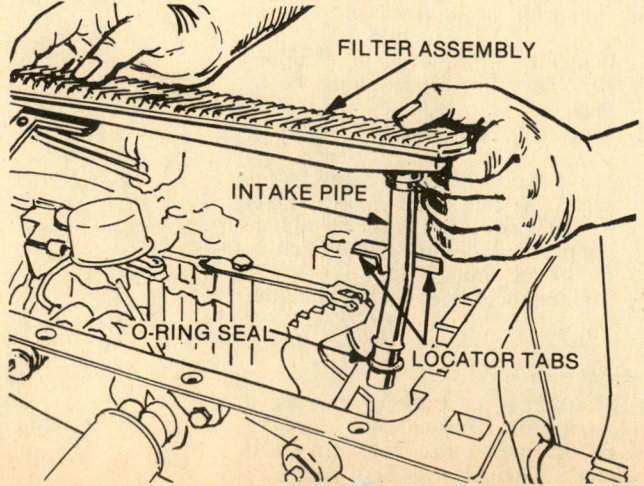

FILTER ASSEMBLY

INTAKE PIPE

O-RING SEAL

LOCATOR TABS

Removing the filter, intake pipe and O ring on Turbo Hydra-Matic 400 transmission

Front and Single Rear U-Joint Overhaul

1. Remove the driveshaft.

NOTE: *The universal may have snap-rings that are used to retain the bearing cups in the yokes. These snap-rings may be located at the outside of each yoke or in a groove at the base or open end of each bearing cap. In both cases, there are four snaprings for each universal joint and they must be removed before proceeding further.*

2. Support the splined yoke (front universal) or the journal (rear universal) in such a manner that will allow the fixed yoke on the driveshaft to be moved. Support the opposite end so that the driveshaft will be in a horizontal position.

3. Using a piece of pipe or similar tool with a large enough diameter, apply force to the fixed yoke until the bearing is almost completely pushed out of the yoke and into the pipe. Remove the bearing completely by inserting a spacer between the seal and the bearing cup and finish pressing the bearing out of its yoke, or by tapping around the circumference of the exposed portion of the bearing with a punch and small hammer.

NOTE: *The plastic which retains factory-installed bearings will be sheared when the bearing cup is pressed out. Be sure to remove the remains of the plas-*

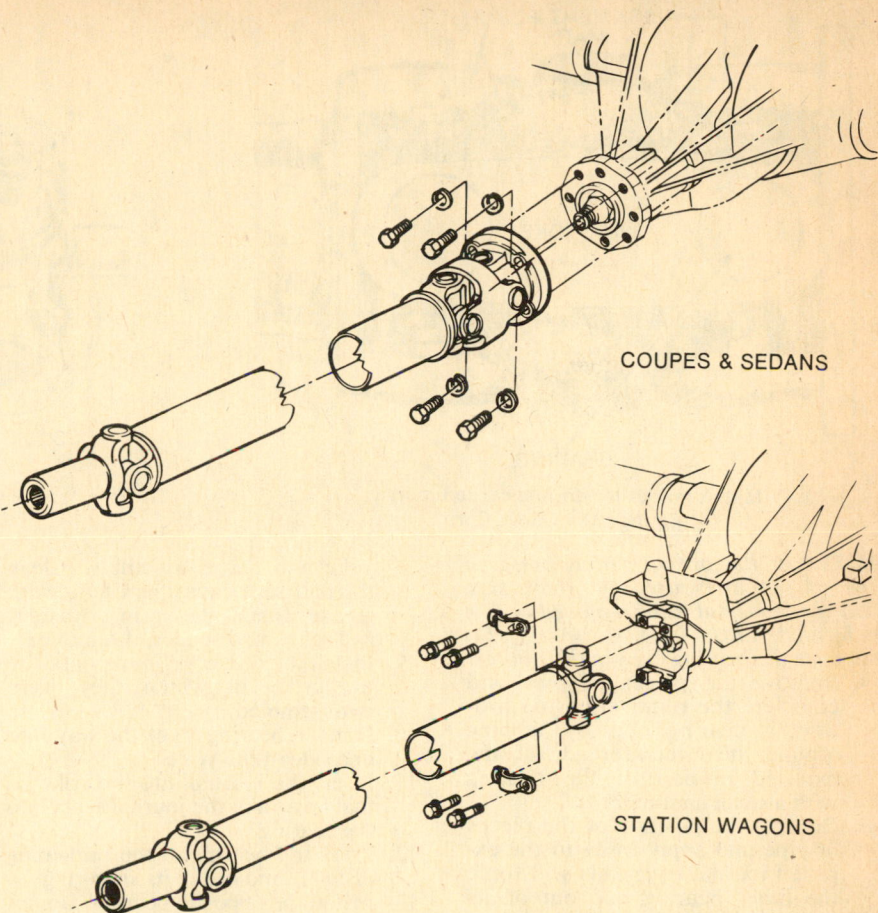

COUPES & SEDANS

STATION WAGONS

U-joint and driveshaft construction through 1976, Grand Prix is similar to station wagon (© Pontiac Div., G.M. Corp)

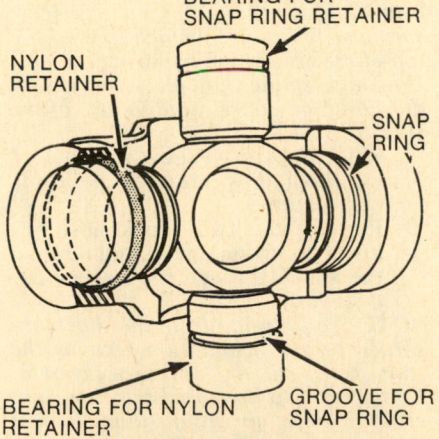

BEARING FOR SNAP RING RETAINER

NYLON RETAINER

SNAP RING

BEARING FOR NYLON RETAINER

GROOVE FOR SNAP RING

U-joint locking methods
(© Pontiac Div., G.M. Corp)

tic retainer from the ears of the yoke. It is easier to remove the remains if a small pin or punch is first driven through the injection holes in the yoke. Failure to remove all of the plastic may prevent the bearing cups from being pressed into place and the bearing retainers from being properly seated.

4. Remove the rest of the bearings following the same procedure.

On installation:

1. Install a bearing $1/4$ of the way into one side of the splined yoke (front universal) or fixed yoke (rear universal).

2. Insert the journal into the yoke so that an arm of the journal seats into the bearing.

3. Press the bearing in the remaining distance and snap the bearing retainer into place.

4. Install the opposite bearing. Do not allow the bearing rollers to jam. Continually check for free movement of the journal in the bearings as they are pressed into the yoke.

5. Install the rest of the bearings in the same manner.

Constant-Velocity Rear U-Joint Overhaul

1. Using a punch, mark the link yoke and the adjoining yokes before dis-

assembly to ensure proper reassembly and driveshaft balance.

NOTE: *It is easier to remove the universal joint bearings from the flange yoke first. The first pair of flange yoke universal joint bearings to be removed is the pair in the link yoke.*

2. With the driveshaft in a horizontal position, solidly support the link yoke (a $1^7/8$ in. pipe will do).

3. Apply force to the bearing cup on the opposite side with a $1^1/8$ in. pipe or a socket the size of the bearing cup. Use a vise or press to apply force. Force the cup inward as far as possible.

Installing snap-ring retainer
(© Pontiac Div., G.M. Corp)

Journal installation
(© Pontiac Div., G.M. Corp)

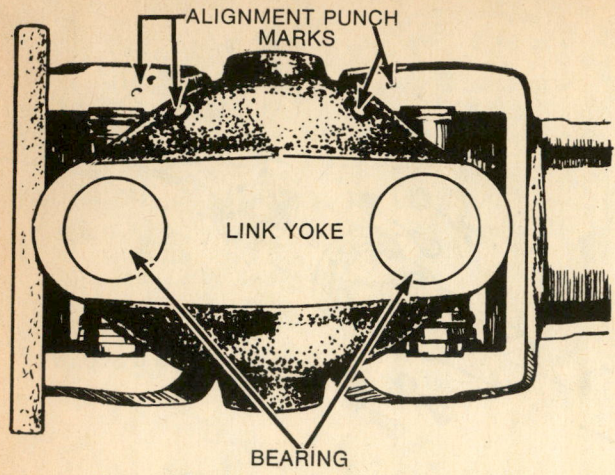

Match marks for double cardan joint
(© Pontiac Div., G.M. Corp)

ALIGNMENT PUNCH MARKS

LINK YOKE

BEARING

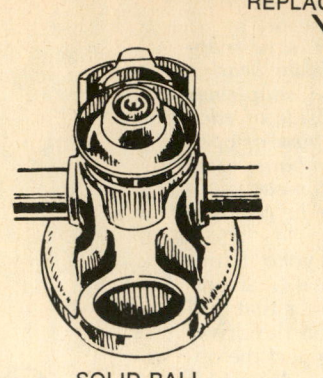 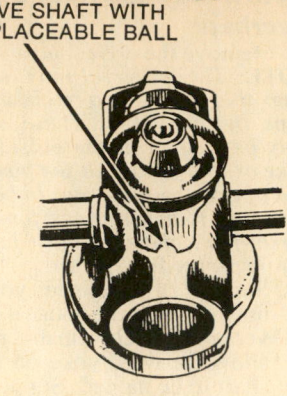

THIS NOTCH IDENTIFIES DRIVE SHAFT WITH REPLACEABLE BALL

SOLID BALL   REPLACEABLE BALL

Solid and replaceable U-joint balls
(© Pontiac Div., G.M. Corp)

NOTE: *In the absence of a press, a heavy vise may be used, but make sure that the universal to be removed is at a right angle to the jaws of the vise. Do not cock the bearing cups in their bores.*

4. Remove the pieces of pipe and complete the removal of the protruding bearing cup by tapping around the circumference of the exposed portion of the bearing with a small hammer.
5. Reverse the position of the pieces of pipe and apply force to the exposed journal end. This will force the other bearing cup out of its bore and allow removal of the flange.

NOTE: *There is a ball joint located between the two universals. The ball portion of this joint is on the inner end of the flange yoke. Prior to 1973, the ball was not replaceable. Beginning 1973, the ball, as well as the ball seat parts, is replaceable. Care must be taken not to damage the ball. The ball portion of this joint is on the driveshaft. To remove the seat, pry the seal out with a screwdriver.*

6. To remove the journal from the flange, use steps two through five.
7. Remove the universal joint bearings from the driveshaft using the steps from two through five. The first pair of bearing caps that should be removed is the pair in the link yoke.
8. Examine the ball stud seat and ball stud for scores or wear. Worn seats can be replaced with a kit. A worn ball, however, requires the replacement of the entire shaft

yoke and flange assembly. Clean the ball seat cavity and fill it with grease. Install the spring, washer, ball seats, and spacer, if removed.

9. Install the universal joints opposite the order in which they were disassembled.
10. Install a bearing ¼ of the way into one side of the yoke.
11. Insert the journal into the yoke so that an arm of the journal seats into the bearing.
12. Press the bearing in the remaining distance and install its snap-ring.
13. Install the opposite bearing. Do not allow the bearing rollers to jam. Continually check for free movement of the journal in the bearings as they are pressed into the yoke.
14. Install the rest of the bearings in the same manner.

REAR AXLE

For axle shaft, bearing, and seal removal and installation procedures, refer to the Astre section.

JACKING, HOISTING

Jack the car at the front spring seats of the lower control arms and, at the rear, at the axle housing.

When using a frame lift, use the side rails at the points shown on the dia-

gram. Be sure that the adapters are properly supporting these designated areas.

FRONT SUSPENSION

Shock Absorber Replacement

1. Remove the nut, retainer and grommet which attach the upper end of the shock absorber to the frame bracket.

NOTE: *The shock absorber stud may turn while loosening the nut. If necessary, use pliers or a wrench to hold the top of the stud while removing the nut. Do not grasp the shaft as any marks on the shaft will cause rapid failure of the shock.*

2. Raise the car to allow removal of the shock down through the lower control arm.
3. Remove the two shock absorber lower attaching screws and remove the shock through the lower control arm.

NOTE: *To purge air from the shock absorber before installation, extend the shock to its extreme and then invert it. Compress it to its closed position, and return it to its upright position. Repeat this operation several times. Do not extend the shock absorber while it is inverted.*

4. Reverse the steps to install. Make sure all grommets and washers are in the correct position. Tighten the stud nut to 10 ft. lbs.

Ball Joint Inspection

1972

NOTE: *Before performing this inspection, make sure the wheel bearings are adjusted correctly and that the A-arm bushings are in good condition.*

1. Jack the car up under the front lower control arm at the spring seat.
2. Raise the car until there is 1-2 in. of clearance under the wheel.

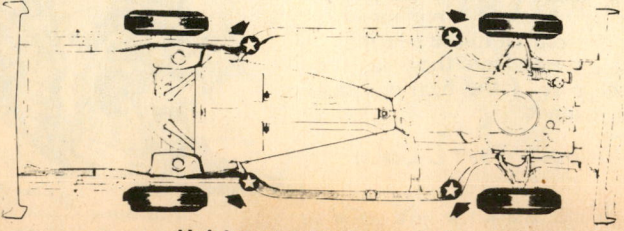

Hoist contact lifting points

3. Insert a bar under the wheel and pry upward. If the wheel raises more than $1/8$ in. the ball joints are worn. Determine if the upper or lower ball joint is worn by visual inspection while prying on the wheel.

NOTE: *Due to the distribution of forces in the suspension, the lower ball joint is usually the defective joint.*

1973 AND LATER

Beginning 1973, lower ball joints contain a visual wear indicator. The lower ball joint grease plug screws into the wear indicator which protrudes from the bottom of the ball joint housing. As long as the wear indicator extends out of the ball joint housing, the ball joint is not worn. If the tip of the wear indicator is parallel with, or recessed into the ball joint housing, the ball joint is defective.

Ball Joint Replacement

The service joint comes with specially hardened bolts and nuts that replace the rivets. It is extremely important that only these special fasteners are installed—standard bolts are not strong enough for this application. Tighten service bolts to 9 ft. lbs. for upper joints, 16 ft. lbs. for lower joints.

All models have their lower ball joints pressed into the control arms. The entire control arm can be removed and the joint pressed out using a large bench vise, or the old joint can be pressed from the arm while in the car using a screw-type remover. The new joint must be pressed into place, in any case, to avoid damage.

Upper Ball Joint Replacement

1. Raise the car and support the lower control arm.
2. Remove the ball joint stud nut and cotter pin. Using a ball joint removing tool, break the taper holding the steering knuckle to the ball joint stud and move the steering knuckle out of the way.
3. Remove the rivets securing the ball joint to the control arm by chiseling or drilling the rivet heads and drive out the rivets with a punch.
4. Remove the ball joint from the control arm.
5. Install the new ball joint assembly using the special bolts supplied with the ball joint. Torque to 9 ft. lbs.
6. Insert the ball stud in the steering knuckle and tighten the nut to 40 ft. lbs. (1972-74), 50 ft. lbs. (1975-77) or 64 ft. lbs. (1978 and later). Insert a new cotter pin.
7. Install the wheel and tire.
8. Lower the car.

NOTE: *It may be necessary to adjust the wheel alignment after installing a new ball joint.*

Lower Ball Joint Replacement

1. Raise the car under the lower control arm.

2. Remove the hub and backing plate or, if equipped with disc brakes, the rotor and caliper assembly, remove the stud nut and cotter pin.
3. Remove the ball joint stud from the steering knuckle using a ball joint removal tool.
4. Pry the ball joint seal and retainer off the joint.
5. Press the ball joint out of the lower control arm. This is a very heavy press fit.
6. Press, do not hammer, a new ball joint into place and reverse steps 1 to 4 to install. Torque the stud nut to 84 ft. lbs. Tighten the nut no more than $1/16$ turn to insert cotter pin.

NOTE: *The bleed vent in the rubber boot of the new ball joint must face inward.*

Spring Removal and Installation

1. Jack up the car and support it on jack stands at the frame side rails.
2. Remove the shock absorber.
3. Disconnect the stabilizer bar at the lower control arm.
4. Support the lower control arm with a hydraulic floor jack, then remove the two inner control arm to front crossmember bolts.
5. Carefully lower the control arm, allowing the spring to relax.
6. Reach in and remove spring.
7. To install, reverse the removal procedure. Tighten the pivot bolts to:
   1972-74—110 ft. lbs.
   1975-77—120 ft. lbs.
   1978 and later—124 ft. lbs.
   Fasteners must be tightened with the car resting on the wheels. Torque the stabilizer bar to 26 ft.

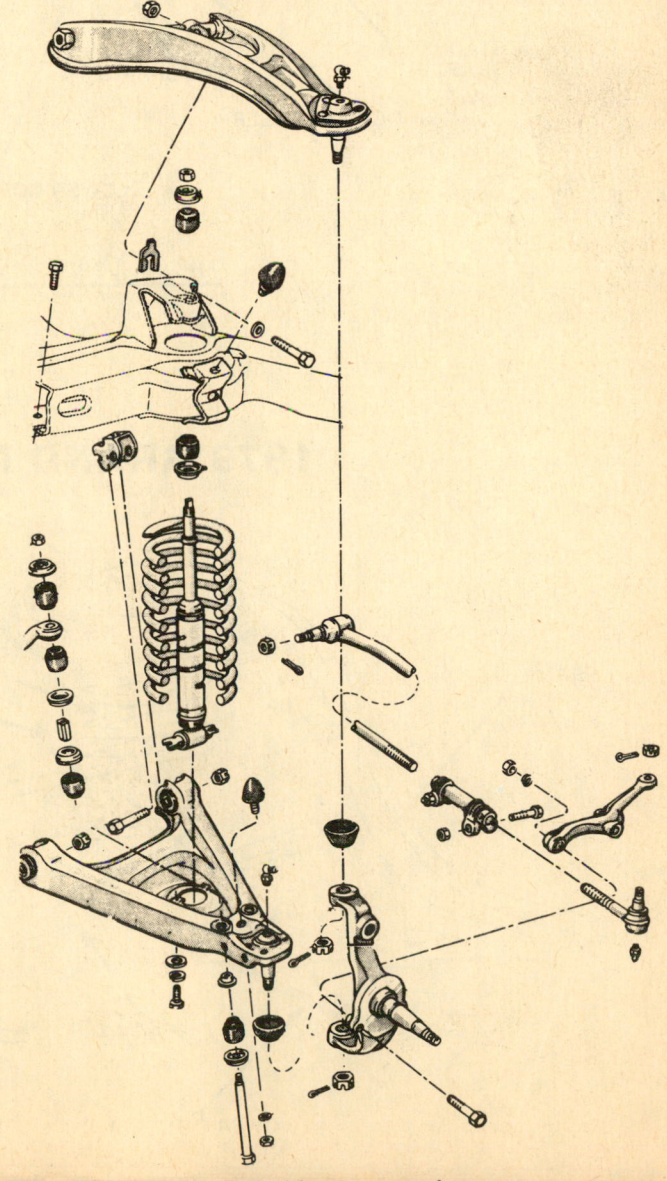

Typical front suspension
(© Pontiac Div., G.M. Corp)

1979 GRAND PRIX

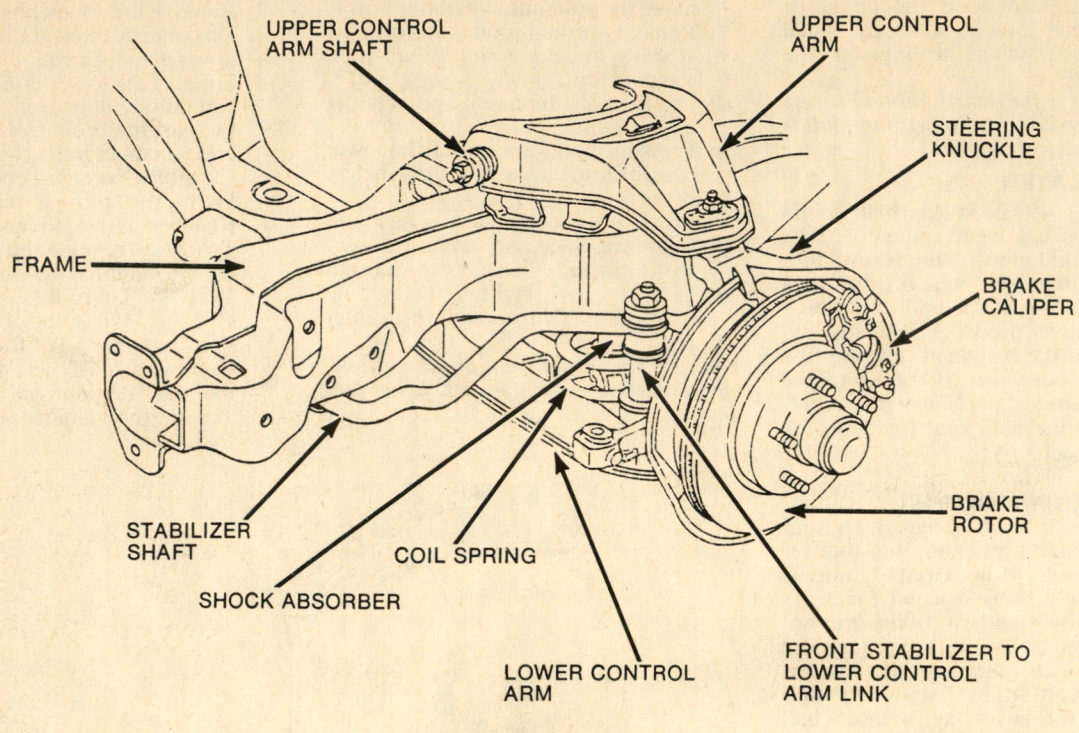

UPPER CONTROL
ARM SHAFT

UPPER CONTROL
ARM

STEERING
KNUCKLE

FRAME

BRAKE
CALIPER

STABILIZER
SHAFT

SHOCK ABSORBER

COIL SPRING

BRAKE
ROTOR

LOWER CONTROL
ARM

FRONT STABILIZER TO
LOWER CONTROL
ARM LINK

FRONT SUSPENSION

1979 GRAND PRIX

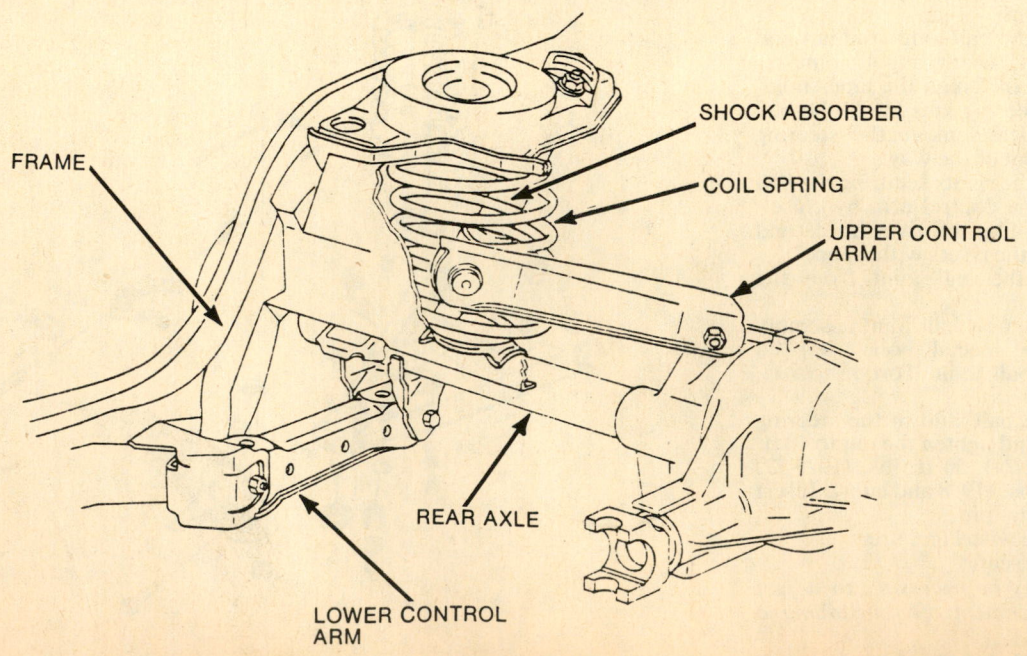

FRAME

SHOCK ABSORBER

COIL SPRING

UPPER CONTROL
ARM

REAR AXLE

LOWER CONTROL
ARM

REAR SUSPENSION

lbs.; the shock absorber upper and lower nuts to 20 ft. lbs.

Upper Control Arm Removal and Installation

1. Raise the vehicle and support it on jack stands under the lower control arm.
2. Remove the wheels.
3. Using a ball joint remover, separate the upper control arm ball stud from the steering knuckle.
4. Remove the two nuts securing the upper control arm to the frame bracket. Tape or wire the shims together and mark them for reinstallation.

NOTE: *In some cases it will be necessary to remove the upper control arm attaching bolts to allow clearance to remove the arm. The bolts are splined into the frame. Remove them as follows:*

    a. Tap down gently on the bolt head with a brass drift.
    b. Gently pry up on the bolt with a box wrench.
    c. Remove the nut, and, using a pry bar and blocks of wood, pry the bolt from the frame.

5. When installing, always use new attaching bolts of the same grade quality, if the originals were removed. Position the new bolts in the frame loosely, install the cross shaft and pull the new bolts up with free-running nuts. Remove the free-running nuts and install locknuts.
6. Install the shim packs and tighten the nuts. Tighten the inner nut first.

Proper torque is 70 ft. lbs. for Grand Prix; 74 ft. lbs. for full-size.

7. Install the ball joint stud, torque the nut to 64 ft. lbs. and install the cotter pin.

NOTE: *When installing the cotter pin, advance the nut 1/16 turn, maximum to align cotter pin hole. Never back-off the nut.*

8. Install the wheel, lower the car and torque the control arm shaft nuts to 64 ft. lbs.

Lower Control Arm Removal and Installation

1. Remove the spring as described earlier.
2. Remove the ball joint from the steering knuckle as described earlier.
3. Remove the control arm from the car.
4. Insert the lower control arm ball stud into the knuckle, install the nut, torque to 83 ft. lbs. and insert the cotter pin. Advance the nut to align the pin holes.
5. Install the spring as described earlier.
6. Lower the vehicle and torque the nuts to 110-124 ft. lbs. for all except 1978 and later Grand Prix, and 70 ft. lbs. for 1978 and later Grand Prix.

Wheel Bearing Adjustment

1. Lift the wheel off the ground by jacking under the lower control arm.
2. Remove the dust cap from the hub.
3. Remove the cotter pin and discard.
4. Snug up the spindle nut to seat the bearings (12 ft. lbs.). Then back off the nut 1/4-1/2 turn.
5. Retighten the nut by hand until it is finger-tight.
6. Loosen the nut until the nearest hole in the spindle lines up with a slot in the spindle nut, and insert a new cotter pin. When the bearing is properly adjusted there will be 0.001-0.005 in. endplay.

NOTE: *Under no circumstances is the final bearing nut adjustment to be even finger-tight.*

7. Replace the dust cover and lower the car.

REAR SUSPENSION

Shock Absorber Replacement

1. Raise the car at the axle housing. Remove the wheel on station wagons.
2. Remove the nut, retainer, and grommet, or nut, and lock washer, which attach the lower end of the shock absorber to its mounting.
3. Remove the two shock absorber upper attaching screws and remove the shock absorber.

NOTE: *To purge air from the shock absorber before installation, extend the shock to its extreme and then invert it.*

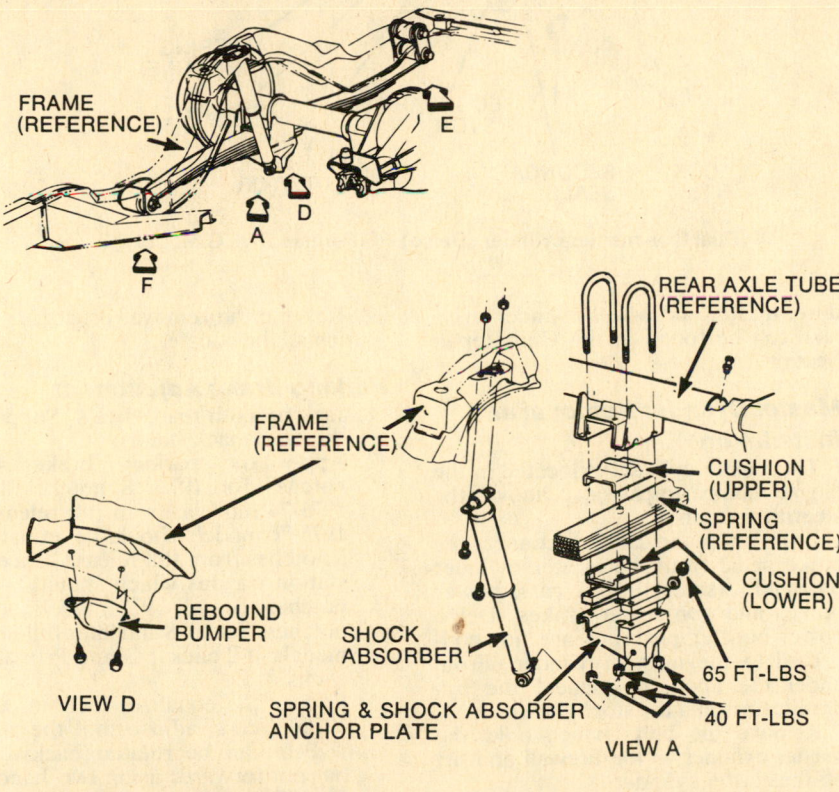

VIEW D — REBOUND BUMPER — FRAME (REFERENCE)

SHOCK ABSORBER — SPRING & SHOCK ABSORBER ANCHOR PLATE

FRAME (REFERENCE) — REAR AXLE TUBE (REFERENCE) — CUSHION (UPPER) — SPRING (REFERENCE) — CUSHION (LOWER) — 65 FT-LBS — 40 FT-LBS — VIEW A

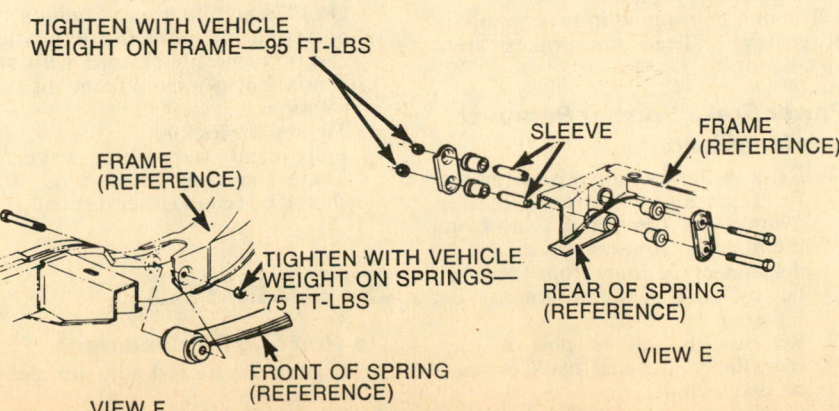

TIGHTEN WITH VEHICLE WEIGHT ON FRAME—95 FT-LBS

FRAME (REFERENCE) — SLEEVE — FRAME (REFERENCE)

TIGHTEN WITH VEHICLE WEIGHT ON SPRINGS—75 FT-LBS — REAR OF SPRING (REFERENCE) — VIEW E

FRONT OF SPRING (REFERENCE) — VIEW F

Pontiac station wagon leaf spring rear suspension through 1976
(© Pontiac Div., G.M. Corp)

Compress it to its closed position, and return it to its upright position. Repeat this operation several times. Do not extend the shock absorber while it is inverted.

4. Reverse the removal procedures to install.

Leaf Spring Replacement, Station Wagon through 1976

1. Jack up the car at the axle housing. Make sure you don't crush the exhaust pipe.
2. Support the car at both frame side rails, using axle stands.
3. Remove the nut and lockwasher from the lower shock stud.
4. Move the shock out of the way.
5. Remove the spring anchor plate nuts, then remove the anchor plate and cushion.
6. Jack the axle housing up and remove the upper cushion.
7. Loosen the upper and lower spring shackle nuts.
8. Loosen the front spring eye bolt.
9. Remove the front eye bolt and carefully lower the spring.
10. Support the spring and remove the lower shackle pin.
11. Remove the spring.
12. To install, reverse the removal procedure. Tighten the front eye bolt to 80 ft. lbs., shackle nuts to 95 ft. lbs., anchor plate nuts to 40 ft. lbs., and lower shock nut to 65 ft. lbs.

Coil Spring Replacement

1. Raise the rear of the car. Place jackstands under the frame side rails.
2. Remove the clip attaching the brake hose to the rear crossmember on Pontiacs. On Grand Prix through 1976, remove the clip and disconnect the brake hose.
3. Support the rear axle housing with a floor jack. On 1973 and later Grand Prix, make sure to support the nose of the axle housing.
4. Disconnect the bottom of the shock absorbers.
5. On 1973 and later Grand Prix, and 1977 and later Pontiac, disconnect the upper control arms at the axle. Disconnect the stabilizer bar, if equipped.
6. Carefully lower the rear axle until the springs are fully extended.
7. Remove the springs.
8. On the installation, make sure that the end of the bottom spring coil is to the rear of the car. The brake system will have to be bled of air on Grand Prix through 1976. Torque the upper control arm-to-axle nuts to 92 ft. lbs. with the car resting on the wheels.

BRAKES

Information on brake adjustment, lining replacement, bleeding proce-

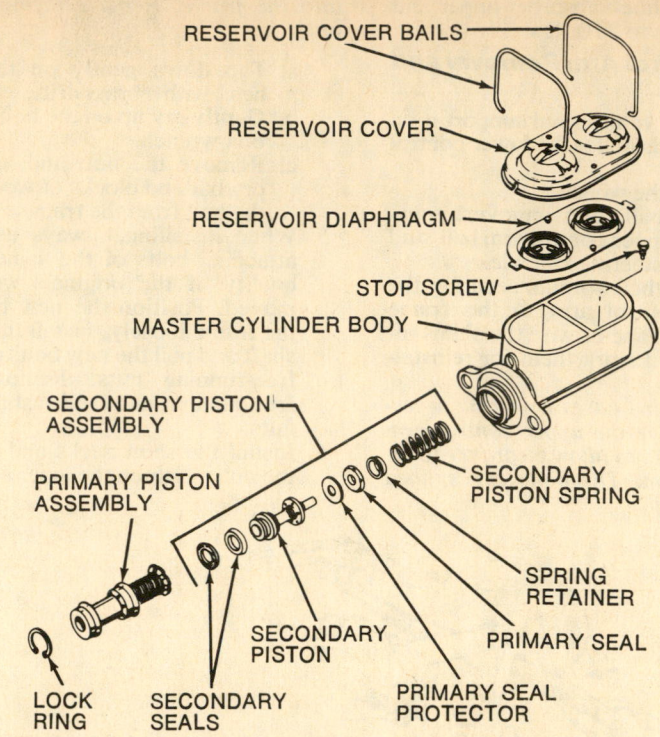

Dual type master cylinder (Delco) (© Pontiac Div., G.M. Corp)

dure, master and wheel cylinder overhaul can be found in the Unit Repair Section.

Master Cylinder Removal and Installation

The master cylinder is located in the engine compartment just above the steering column.

From under the dash, disconnect the brake pedal from the master cylinder on Bendix (some 1972-77 cars) power brakes and non-power brakes. Delco power booster pushrods are not connected to the master cylinder. From under the hood, disconnect the hydraulic lines and the stoplight wire.

Remove the bolts which hold the master cylinder to the firewall and lift off the master cylinder.

The unit is installed in reverse order of removal. Bleed the brakes after installation.

Power Brake Booster Removal and Installation

1. Remove the vacuum hose from the front housing. Remove the master cylinder and position it away from the booster. It is not necessary to disconnect the lines from the master cylinder if it is not to be repaired.
2. Remove the clevis pin retainer from the brake pedal inside the car, on Bendix units.
3. Remove the nuts from the vacuum cylinder studs under the dash and remove the vacuum power section.

4. Reverse the removal procedure to install the booster.

Parking Brake Adjustment

1. Jack up both rear wheels. Support the car on jack stands.
2. Apply the parking brake 4-8 notches for 1972, 8 notches for 1973-74 models, from full release. 1975-76 models should be adjusted 3 notches from full release, except station wagons which should be 6 notches. Set all 1977 models at 6 notches. Set 1978 and later full-size models at 2 clicks; Grand Prix at 6 clicks.
3. Loosen the equalizer locknut. On 1972-77 cars, adjust until the rear wheels can be rotated backward but not forward, using two hands. On 1978 and later cars, tighten the adjusting nut until the left wheel can be turned backward with two hands, but is locked from forward rotation.
4. Tighten the locknut.
5. Fully release the parking brake and rotate the rear wheels; no drag should be felt in either direction.

STEERING

Tie-Rod End Replacement

1. Loosen the tie-rod adjuster sleeve clamp nuts.
2. Remove the tie-rod stud nut cotter pin and nut.

NOTE: *If the torque required to remove*

the nuts and bolts exceeds 7 ft. lbs., it's best to discard them and use new fasteners of equal grade quality.

3. Remove the tie-rod stud from the steering arm or intermediate rod. This is a taper fit. Removal is accomplished by using a ball joint removal tool.
4. Untread the tie rod from the adjuster sleeve. Outer tie rods have right-hand threads and inner tie rods have left-hand threads. Count the number of turns the tie rod must be rotated to remove it from the adjusting sleeve. This will allow a reasonably accurate toe-in realignment upon reassembly.
5. Reverse the removal procedures to install. Clean rust and dirt from the threads. Check the alignment and adjust if necessary.

Power Steering Pump Removal and Installation

1. Disconnect the hoses at the pump. Plug the lines and the pump to prevent loss of fluid.
2. Remove the drive pulley attaching nut.
3. Loosen the bracket-to-pump mounting bolts and remove the drive belt.
4. Slide the pulley from the shaft. Do not hammer on the pulley.
5. Remove the bracket-to-pump mounting bolts and remove the pump.
6. Reverse the removal steps to install.
7. Fill the reservoir and start the engine. Allow the engine to run for a few seconds, and then stop it and recheck the fluid level.
8. Bleed the system by turning the steering wheel to the right and left, without hitting the stops, a number

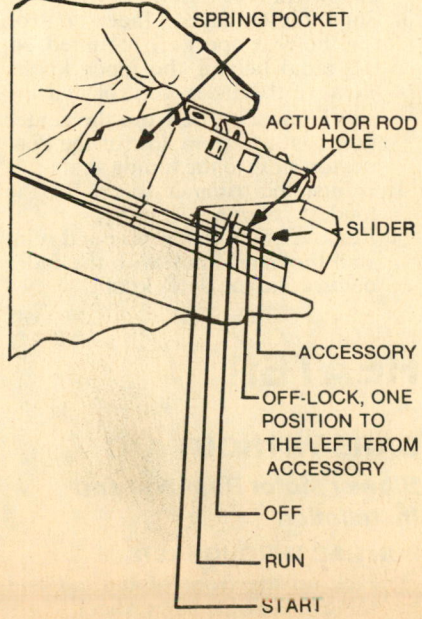

Installing ignition switch

SPRING POCKET
ACTUATOR ROD HOLE
SLIDER
ACCESSORY
OFF-LOCK, ONE POSITION TO THE LEFT FROM ACCESSORY
OFF
RUN
START

of times, to eliminate the air from the fluid.
9. Return the wheels to the center position. Stop the engine and recheck the fluid level.

NOTE: *On some engines, the power steering pump is located low and behind the drive belt. Do not attempt to check the fluid level with the engine running or personal injury can result.*

Steering Wheel Removal and Installation

1. On deluxe models, remove the screws holding the trim cover to the wheel or, if equipped with a horn button, lift the button off.
2. Remove the steering wheel snapring and nut from the steering shaft.
3. Position the wheels in the straight-ahead position and make match marks on the steering shaft and steering wheel.
4. Using a puller, remove the steering wheel.

—————— CAUTION ——————

Don't pound on the steering wheel or the steering shaft. The collapsible column could be damaged enough to require replacement.

5. Disconnect the horn wire insulator by rotating the insulator counterclockwise to unlock position and then pull up.
6. Reverse the removal procedures to install. Make sure the match marks are lined up when installing the wheel. Tighten the nut to 30 ft. lbs. on 1972-77 models; 35 ft. lbs. on 1978 and later models.

Turn Signal Switch Replacement

1. Remove the steering wheel.
2. Loosen the three cover screws and lift cover off the shaft. Do not remove the screws completely.
3. Depress the lockplate downward and remove the snap-ring.
4. Slide the upper bearing spring and turn signal cam off the shaft. Remove the thrust washer.
5. Remove the turn signal lever screw (1972-76) or snap ring (1977 and later) and lever. On models with column mounted dimmer switch, remove the actuator arm, then turn the signal switch.
6. Push the hazard warning switch in and remove the knob.
7. Lower the steering column (on models through 1974) and disconnect the switch wiring.
   On tilt columns, lift up on the tilt lever and center the housing.

—————— CAUTION ——————

The steering column must be supported at all times to prevent damage.

8. Remove the turn signal switch mounting screws and pull the switch straight up with the wire protector and remove it from the housing. On tilt columns, the wiring is held by brackets inside the lower column cover.
9. Reverse the removal procedures to install.

Ignition Switch Replacement

1. Disconnect the battery.
2. Loosen the toe pan screws on the steering column.
3. Remove the column to instrument panel trim plates and attaching nuts.
4. Lower the column and disconnect the switch wire connectors.

—————— CAUTION ——————

The steering column must be supported at all times to prevent damage.

5. Remove the switch attaching screws and remove the switch.
6. To replace, move the key lock to the LOCK position.
7. Move the actuator rod hole in the switch to the LOCK position.
8. Install the switch with the rod in the hole.
9. Position and reassemble the steering column in reverse of the disassembly procedure.

SWITCH ADJUSTMENT— STANDARD COLUMN

1. Place the switch in the OFF position.
2. Position the switch on the column, then move the slider to the extreme left (toward the wheel).
3. Move the slider back two positions to the right of ACCESSORY position.
4. Place the key in any run position and shift the transmission into any position but Park for automatics. Put it in Reverse for manual.
5. Position the lock toward ACCESSORY with a light finger pressure and secure the switch.

SWITCH ADJUSTMENT— TILT COLUMN

1. Place the key in ACCESSORY position; leave the key in the lock.
2. Loosen the switch mounting screws.
3. Push the switch upward toward the wheel to make certain it is in ACCESSORY detent.
4. Hold the key in full counter clockwise ACCESSORY position and tighten the switch mounting screws.
5. The switch is properly adjusted if: it will go into ACCESSORY position, the key can be removed when in lock, and the switch will go into START position.

Lock Cylinder Replacement

1. Remove the steering wheel.

2. Pull the turn signal switch up far enough to allow access to the spring latch slot.
3. Place the key in RUN position, insert a thin screwdriver into the slot next to the switch mounting screw boss and depress the spring latch.

NOTE: *There is a casting flash over this slot if the lock has not been removed before. It is sometimes necessary to use substantial force to remove it. Be careful not to damage anything beneath the flash when penetrating the slot.*

4. Remove the lock from housing.
5. To install, first hold the lock cylinder sleeve and rotate the knob clockwise against the stop.

--- CAUTION ---

If the lock cylinder is forced beyond its normal latched position, complete disassembly of the upper bearing assembly will be necessary to free it.

6. On models through 1974, lay a 1/16 in. drill on the housing surface next to the housing bore.
7. Insert the cylinder into the housing bore, aligning the keyway, and push in to the abutment.
8. Rotate the knob counterclockwise, pushing in slightly, until the cylinder mates with the sector.
9. Push in until the spring latch pops into the groove, then remove the drill.

INSTRUMENT PANEL

Speedometer Cable Removal and Installation

1. Remove the lower A/C duct, or lower instrument panel trimplate, if necessary, to gain access.
2. Disconnect the speedometer cable casing from the speedometer head by depressing the retainer spring and pulling the cable casing away from the speedometer.
   If the cable is broken, raise and support the car, disconnect the cable at the transmission and pull the core from the cable.
3. Remove the cable from the casing

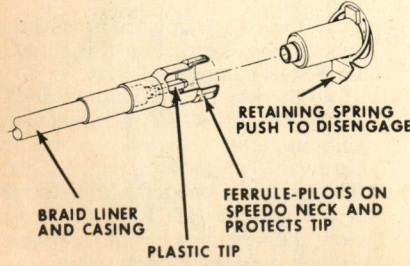

RETAINING SPRING PUSH TO DISENGAGE

FERRULE-PILOTS ON SPEEDO NECK AND PROTECTS TIP

BRAID LINER AND CASING

PLASTIC TIP

Speedometer cable attachment at the speedometer head
(© Pontiac Div., G.M. Corp)

for service or replacement.
4. Install the casing in the reverse order of removal. Coat the new core, liberally, with speedometer cable lubricant.

Headlight Switch Replacement

1. Disconnect the battery. Pull the knob all the way out. From under dash depress button on switch and remove knob and shaft.
2. Remove the retaining nut.
3. Remove the wire connector from the switch and remove the switch.
4. Reverse the procedure to install.

WINDSHIELD WIPERS

Wiper Blade Removal and Installation

Any one of three methods of blade attachment may be used. If there is a small tab on top of the blade, depress it and slide the blade off. If there is a small spring visible in the top of the blade, insert a screwdriver in the opening and press down and slide the blade off. If there is a clip on the underside of the arm, press down on the clip and slide the blade off.

Motor Removal and Installation

1. Disconnect the electrical and the hose connections at wiper.
2. Disconnect the wiper crank from the wiper linkage, through the cowl opening.
3. Remove the wiper motor mounting screws, then remove the motor from the firewall.
4. Install by reversing the removal procedure. Motor must be in the park position.

RADIO

Removal and Installation

PONTIAC THROUGH 1976

1. Disconnect the battery, then remove the radio knobs and hex nuts.
2. Remove the upper and lower instrument panel trim plates and the lower front radio bracket.
3. Remove the glove box and disconnect the radio connections.
4. Loosen the side brace screw and slide the radio toward the front seat.
5. To install, reverse the removal procedure.

1977 AND LATER PONTIAC

1. Disconnect the battery ground cable.
2. Remove the upper trimplate. Remove the radio trimplate by removing the two top screws, the ashtray assembly, disconnecting the

lighter, and removing the ashtray bracket.
3. Remove the two radio screws.
4. Remove the radio through the instrument panel and detach all connectors.
5. Reverse the procedure for installation.

1972 GRAND PRIX

1. Disconnect the battery and remove the lower A/C duct.
2. Remove the control knobs and hex nuts, then remove the support bracket bolt.
3. Disconnect the electrical leads and remove the radio.
4. To install, reverse the removal procedure.

1973 AND LATER GRAND PRIX

1. Disconnect the battery.
2. Remove the knobs, bezels, and right-hand hex nut from the radio. On 1978 and later models, remove the upper and lower instrument panel trimplates.
3. Remove the four retaining screws and the radio trim plate.
4. Remove the two side (one front beginning 1974) retaining screws and the radio mounting bracket retaining screw (below radio). On 1978 and later models, open the glove box and loosen the rear nut at the right side of the radio.
5. Remove the radio and bracket as an assembly; disconnect the radio connections and antenna lead-in while the radio is pulled out.
6. Reverse the steps to install.

Trimming the Radio Antenna

The antenna trimmer adjustment matches the antenna to the radio.
1. Tune the radio to a weak station near 1400 KC on the AM band.
2. Remove the right inner and outer knobs from the radio.
3. Some radios have a fader control for the rear speaker, mounted on the radio behind the inner knob. Remove the fader control and insert a jumper wire from the center hole to the bottom hole of the connector, next to the tuning shaft.
4. Adjust the trimmer screw for the loudest volume.
5. Remove the jumper wire and reinstall the inner knob with the fader control and the outer knob.

HEATER

CARS WITHOUT A/C

Blower Motor Removal and Installation

PONTIAC THROUGH 1976

1. Jack up the front of the car and remove the right front wheel.
2. Cut an access hole along the

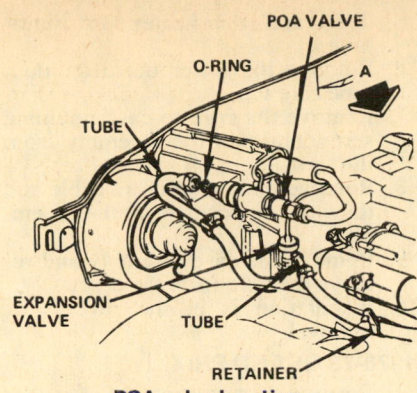

POA valve location
(© Pontiac Div., G.M. Corp)

stamped outline on the right fender skirt, using an air chisel.
3. Disconnect the blower power wire.
4. Remove the blower.
5. To install, reverse the removal procedure, covering the access hole with a metal plate secured with sealer and sheet metal screws.

GRAND PRIX THROUGH 1976
1. Disconnect the power wire.
2. Remove the motor retaining screws.
3. Remove the motor.
4. To install, reverse the removal procedure.

1977 AND LATER PONTIAC AND GRAND PRIX
1. Disconnect the electrical connections from the blower motor.
2. Remove the blower motor flange screws and remove the motor assembly from the heater case.
3. The installation is in the reverse of the removal procedure.

Heater Core Removal and Installation

PONTIAC AND GRAND PRIX THROUGH 1976
1. Drain the radiator.

2. Disconnect the heater hoses at the air inlet assembly.
NOTE: *The water pump hose goes to the right-hand heater core pipe, the other hose (from rear of right cylinder head) goes to the left-hand heater core pipe.*
3. Remove the nuts from the core studs on the firewall (under hood). Remove the glove compartment.
4. From inside the car, remove the defroster nozzle retaining screw from the heater case and pull the heater assembly from the firewall.
5. Disconnect the control cables, vacuum hoses and wires, then remove the heater assembly.
6. Remove the core.
7. To install, reverse the removal procedure, making sure the core is properly sealed during installation.

1977 AND LATER PONTIAC
1. Drain the cooling system.
2. Remove the heater hoses from the core tubes.
3. Disconnect the electrical connections.
4. Remove the front module cover screws, and remove the module assembly.
5. Remove the heater core from the module.
6. Reverse the procedure to install the heater core. Use a strip caulk type sealer when installing the module to the firewall.

1977 GRAND PRIX
1. Disconnect the battery.
2. Drain the cooling system, disconnect the heater hoses, and plug the core tubes.
3. Remove the screws and nuts from the heater module on the engine side.
4. Remove the glove box to gain access to, and remove, the defroster duct screw, and the control cables.
5. Loosen the sealer and remove the case assembly and core from inside the vehicle.

6. The installation is the reverse of removal. Use a strip caulk type sealer when installing the case assembly to the firewall.

1978-79 GRAND PRIX
1. Disconnect the hoses at the core tubes and position them vertically to prevent coolant loss.
2. Remove the core cover from the module.
3. Remove the core bracket and ground screw.
4. Lift out the core.
5. Installation is the reverse of removal. Replace any damaged sealer.

CARS WITH A/C

Blower Motor Removal and Installation

PONTIAC AND GRAND PRIX THROUGH 1976
This procedure is the same as for cars without air conditioning.

1973 GRAND PRIX W/O V.I.R.
On some 1973 Grand Prix models without the V.I.R. (Valves In Receiver) system, removal and replacement of the blower motor may be hindered by the position of the POA (evaporator pressure regulator valve) valve-to-compressor tube. If this tube is positioned so that the blower motor cannot be removed:
1. Disconnect the blower motor feed wire and cooling tube.
2. Remove the six blower retaining screws.
3. Loosen the fitting on the POA valve-to-compressor tube at the POA valve just enough to allow the tube to be turned (approx. $1/4$ to $1/2$ turn).

--------- CAUTION ---------
This procedure should be done only by a trained air-conditioning specialist.

4. Reposition the lower portion of the tube to allow clearance when removing the blower motor. Retighten the fitting.
5. Remove the blower motor and impeller.
6. To install, reverse the removal procedure.

1977 AND LATER PONTIAC AND GRAND PRIX
1. Disconnect the blower motor cooling tube.
2. Disconnect the electrical connections.
3. Remove the motor flange screws, loosen the seal and remove the blower motor assembly from the A/C module.
4. The installation is the reverse.
NOTE: *The blower is mounted horizontally on the Grand Prix, and vertically on the Pontiac.*

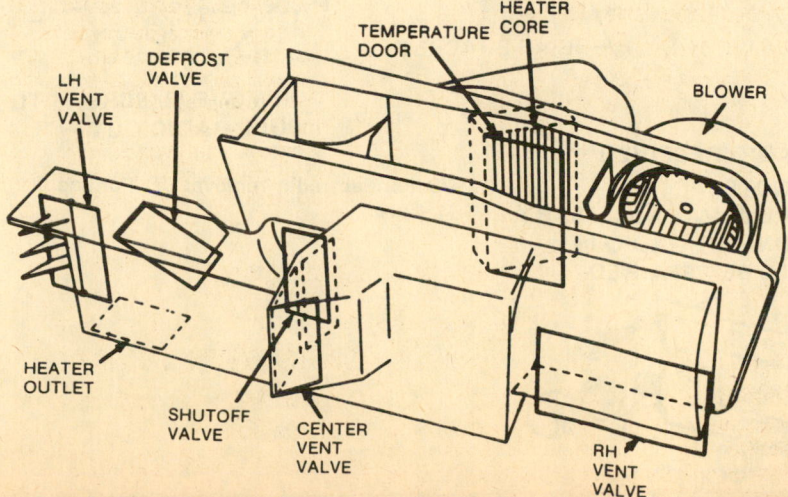

Full size 1977 Pontiacs use a new modular heater/air conditioning system to make service easier (© Pontiac Div., G.M. Corp.)

Pontiac & Grand Prix

Heater Core Removal and Installation

GRAND PRIX THROUGH 1976

1. Drain the radiator.
2. Disconnect the heater hoses.
3. Remove the retaining nuts from the core case studs on the engine side of the firewall.
4. Remove the glove box.
5. Remove the defroster duct retaining screw from the heater case and pull the heater assembly from the firewall.
6. Disconnect the heater control cables and wires.
7. Remove the core tube seal and core assembly retaining strips and remove the core.
8. Reverse the steps to install.

PONTIAC THROUGH 1976

1. Drain the coolant.
2. Disconnect the hoses from the heater core. Plug the tubes to prevent damage to the carpeting on removal.
3. Remove the three nuts and one screw holding the core and case assembly in place.
4. Remove the glove box and upper and lower instrument panel trim plates.
5. Remove the radio.
6. Remove the cold air duct.
7. Remove the heater outlet duct.
8. Remove the screw holding the defroster duct to the heater case.

9. Disconnect the vacuum hoses from the diaphragm, and the A/C temperature cable at the heater case.
10. Remove the core from the case, after removing the 3 retaining screws.
11. Reverse the steps to reinstall the heater core.

1977 AND LATER PONTIAC

1. Drain the cooling system.
2. Disconnect the heater hoses.
3. Remove the retaining bracket and the ground strap.
4. Disconnect the module rubber seal and module screen.
5. Remove the right windshield wiper arm.
6. Remove the diaphragm connections, the hi-blower relay, the thermal switch mounting screws, and all the electrical connections from the module top.
7. Remove the module top cover and remove the core.
8. Installation is the reverse of removal. Apply a strip caulk type sealer when installing the module top.

1977 GRAND PRIX

1. Drain the cooling system.
2. Remove the heater hoses and plug the core tubes.
3. Remove the core stud nuts retaining the case to the firewall.
4. Remove the blower motor resistor to gain access to the upper retaining nut inside the evaporator case.
5. Remove the glove box, the cold air

duct, and the heater distributor tube.
6. Remove the lower defroster duct tube screw.
7. Remove the core to case retaining screw and pull the assembly from the cowl.
8. Remove the temperature cable and the vacuum hoses from the assembly.
9. Remove the case assembly and remove the core from the case.
10. Installation is in the reverse of removal.

1978-79 GRAND PRIX

1. Position the wipers in the UP position.
2. Disconnect and unplug the heater hoses.
3. Remove the module top cover seals.
4. Remove the module top screens.
5. Disconnect all electrical connectors.
6. Move the lower windshield reverse molding out of the way.
7. Remove the cowl brackets.
8. Tape a strip of wood to the lower edge of the windshield glass, to protect the glass.
9. Remove the top cover screws.
10. Cut the sealing material along the cowl with a knife.
11. Pry the cover off from the side, not from the top.
12. Remove the core and seal.
    Installation is the reverse of removal. Use all new sealing material.

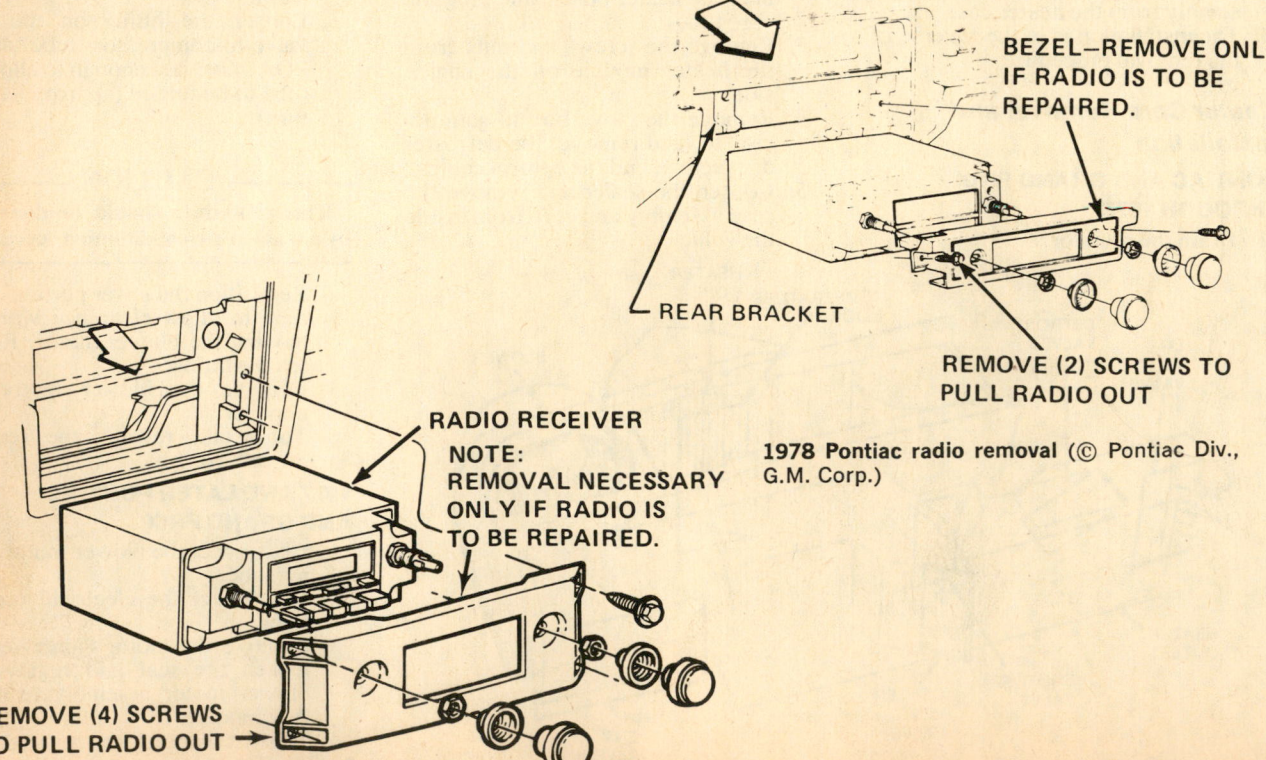

BEZEL—REMOVE ONLY IF RADIO IS TO BE REPAIRED.

REAR BRACKET

REMOVE (2) SCREWS TO PULL RADIO OUT

RADIO RECEIVER
NOTE:
REMOVAL NECESSARY ONLY IF RADIO IS TO BE REPAIRED.

REMOVE (4) SCREWS TO PULL RADIO OUT →

1978 Pontiac radio removal (© Pontiac Div., G.M. Corp.)

1978 Grand Prix radio removal (© Pontiac Div., G.M. Corp.)

UNIT REPAIR SECTION

Charging and Starting ——————
Systems

Index

Testing the Battery

Selection of Battery

The modern car battery is a 12-volt lead-acid unit having a particular ampere hours capacity, depending upon the required work load (radio, air conditioning, electric windows, tailgate, etc.).

Batteries come in different sizes and shapes as specified by the car manufacturer and are matched to the car's electrical needs.

The prime purpose of the battery is to supply a source of energy for cranking the car engine. It also provides the necessary power for the ignition system. A battery can, for a limited time, supply adequate current to satisfy electrical demands during periods when requirements exceed alternator output.

Replacing a Battery

The most convenient and popular way to store new batteries is in a dry state. They are charged at the time of installation.

Before deciding on a particular battery, consider some of the essentials that may put the replacement battery in a different category from the unit originally supplied with the vehicle. When the original battery wears out, resistance in the wiring circuits is probably much increased, and the starter may be less efficient, along with the ignition system. There is also the likelihood that electrical accessories have been added.

All of the above reasons are justification for choosing a battery of greater capacity than the one supplied by the manufacturer.

Preparation

After the electrical needs have been considered, and a selection made, place the new battery on a bench or work table. Never activate a battery installed in the car. Remove vent caps from all the cells.

Fill each cell carefully, using sulfuric acid and distilled water (electrolyte) at a strength of 1.250-1.265 specific gravity to about $3/8$ in. above the top of the separators, or to indicated level mark.

Place a battery type thermometer in one of the center cells. Check specific gravity of the electrolyte with a battery hydrometer. The battery temperature must be above 80°F. and specific gravity must be above 1.250 prior to installing the battery.

In charging 12-volt batteries, set charging rate at 35 amperes until electrolyte has reached 80° F. and electrolyte gravity is 1.250 or higher. Lower charging rates also may be used to obtain 80° F. and 1.250 specific gravity. When charging, do not allow electrolyte temperature to exceed 125° F. Normally, 10-15 minutes charging will be sufficient; however, in colder climates a little longer is O.K.

When the battery is removed from the charger, top up if necessary, with electrolyte, and replace the vent plugs.

When installing, make sure that both ends of the battery cables are clean and securely tightened, observing correct polarity.

Start engine and make sure that the alternator is charging with lights and all accessories on.

--------- CAUTION ---------

Be careful not to install the battery with cables reversed. Reversed polarity can destroy an alternator and regulator in a very short time.

--------- CAUTION ---------

Because electrolyte is extremely corrosive to metals and many other materials, do not pour into sinks or drains. If battery acid is spilled on battery during filling or charging, or on bench or clothing, immediately flush it off with generous amounts of water and baking soda or ammonia.

Battery Troubles—Causes

1. Battery too small for the job (accessories, etc.).
2. Tired battery (worn out).
3. Corroded battery connections.
4. Alternator not charging.
5. Alternator charging rate too low.
6. Regulator defective.
7. Regulator out of adjustment.
8. Regulator has poor ground.
9. Alternator inoperative.
10. Loose alternator drive belt.
11. Constant drain of current due to short circuit.

Battery Troubles— Corrections

1. Battery capacity may be less than requirements demand. Additional accessories, too frequent use of starter, low operational speeds, require a greater source of electrical supply. Install a larger capacity battery.
2. Either age or abuse is the usual cause of a tired battery. No amount of charging will offer more than temporary relief. Install a new battery of proper capacity if plates are sulfated.
3. Corroded battery posts and connections result from the chemical reaction between dissimilar metals and battery electrolyte. Excessive corrosion at a battery post is usually an indication of the failure of a seal between the t or other plastic material, install cable clamp and tighten.
4. Alternator not charging can be caused by a defective alternator or other system component. Check entire charging system and correct the fault.
5. Low charging rate may be caused by a loose drive belt, loose or poor battery post connections, high resistance in charging circuit or a poor or improperly adjusted regulator.
6. Regulator may be defective because of burned points in the regulator or any open circuit in the control system.
7. Regulator out of adjustment.
8. Regulator has poor ground.
9. The alternator may be inoperative because of damaged diodes, poor internal connections, open, grounded, or shorted field circuit, grounded or shorted stator windings.
10. A loose drive belt will cause low, or partial charging. Correct by adjusting drive belt.
11. A constant drain of current from the battery may be caused by frayed insulation on any live wire in the electrical system. This can cause a short circuit. There is also the possibility of a light (in the trunk, glove box, under the hood, etc.) or other electric accessory remaining on after the ignition is turned off. To correct the situation:

First, with a sensitive ammeter, determine whether or not there is a current drain by opening the circuit at either battery post connection, hooking the ammeter in series, and checking for current drain.

Second, if the meter registers a drain, isolate the leak by reconnecting the battery, then, one by one, check each circuit at the fuse block. This is a tedious but unavoidable procedure and consists of removing each fuse and testing that circuit with the prods of an ammeter (in series). The circuit which activates the meter is the guilty one; identify the trouble spot by elimination. Correct the trouble by correcting the short or replacing the switch or other electrical component.

In the event that the fuse block test does not indicate the trouble, check the circuits which are protected with circuit breakers, (headlamps, parking lamps, seat and window controls, etc.).

Specific Gravity Test— Hydrometer

Before attempting any electrical checks, it is important to check the condition of the battery.

While not technically exact, a practical measurement of the chemical condition of the battery is indicated by measuring the specific gravity of the acid (electrolyte) contained in each cell. The electrolyte in a fully charged battery is usually between 1.260 and 1.280 times as heavy as pure water at the same temperature (80°F.). Variations in the specific gravity readings for a fully charged battery may differ. Therefore, it is most important that all battery cells produce an equal reading.

As a battery discharges, a chemical change takes place within each cell. The sulfate factor of the electrolyte combines chemically with the battery plates, reducing the weight of the electrolyte. A reading of the specific gravity of the acid, or electrolyte, of any partially charged battery, will therefore be less than that taken in a fully charged one.

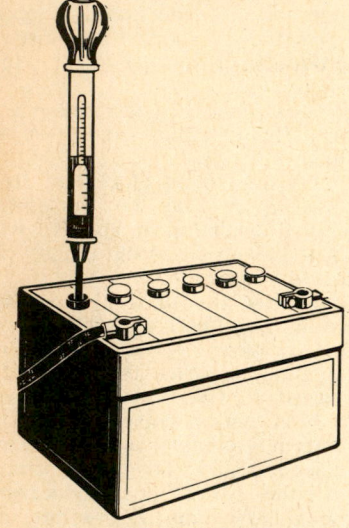

Testing battery specific gravity

The hydrometer is the instrument in general use for determining the specific gravity of liquids. The battery hydrometer is readily available from many sources, including local auto replacement parts stores. The following chart gives an indication of specific gravity value, related to battery charge condition. If, after charging, the specific gravity between any two cells varies more than 50 points (.050), the battery is probably bad.

Specific Gravity Reading	Charged Condition
1.260-1.280	Fully charged
1.230-1.250	Three-quarter charged
1.200-1.220	One-half charged
1.170-1.190	One-quarter charged
1.140-1.160	Just about flat
1.110-1.130	All the way down

Testing Battery Polarity

Battery polarity is very important. Permanent damage to the diodes of alternators will result from reversing polarity.

To determine battery polarity, turn the voltmeter selector to the high read-

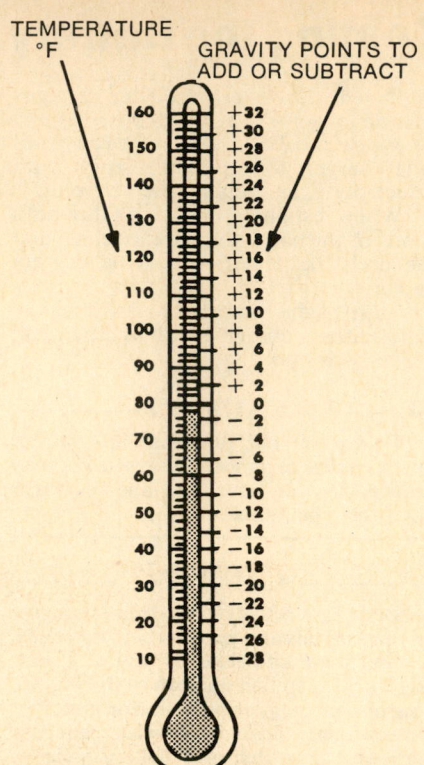

Hydrometer temperature correction chart
(© Chrysler Corp)

ing scale. Connect voltmeter leads to the battery posts. If the gauge needle moves in the correct direction, the positive lead of the meter is on the positive (+) post of the battery. If the gauge needle moves in the wrong direction, polarity is reversed.

Testing the Delco "Sealed Top" Battery

Some GM cars come equipped with a "sealed top" battery which does not require the usual maintenance. Because the battery has a greater amount of electrolyte and a reduced need for water, the top of the battery has no filler caps and is sealed. A small vent is provided at one edge of the battery top.

There are two types of sealed batteries used: one has a charge indicator eye and the other does not. Both types may be tested in the following manner:
1. Check the condition of the battery case. If the case is damaged so that loss of electrolyte is possible, the battery must be replaced.
2. If the battery has a charge indicator eye, check the following:

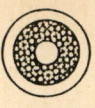

DARKENED INDICATOR WITH GREEN DOT —FULL CHARGE

DARKENED INDICATOR NO GREEN DOT —NEEDS CHARGING

LIGHTENED INDICATOR —REPLACE BATTERY

Delco sealed battery indicator conditions
(© G.M. Corp.)

a. If the eye is dark, the battery has enough electrolyte. If the eye is light, the electrolyte level is too low and the battery must be replaced.
b. If a green dot appears in the middle of the eye, the battery is sufficiently charged; go on to Step 4. If there is no green dot visible, charge the battery as in Step 3.
3. Charge the battery if there is no green dot visible in the eye, or if it is the type without an eye, at the following rates:

Amps	Time
75	40 min
50	1 hr
25	2 hr
10	5 hr

--- CAUTION ---

Do not charge the battery for more than 50 ampere-hours. If the green dot appears or electrolyte squirts out of the vent, stop the charge and go on with Step 4.

4. Either disconnect the high-tension coil wire or the engine harness (electronic ignition) and crank the starter motor for 15 seconds, to remove the surface charge.
5. Connect a voltmeter and a 230 amp load across the battery terminals.
6. Take a voltmeter reading after the load has been connected for 15 seconds, then disconnect the load.
7. Consult the following chart. If the battery voltage is that specified (or more) for the given ambient temperature, the battery is good. If the voltage falls below that specified, then the battery is bad and must be replaced.

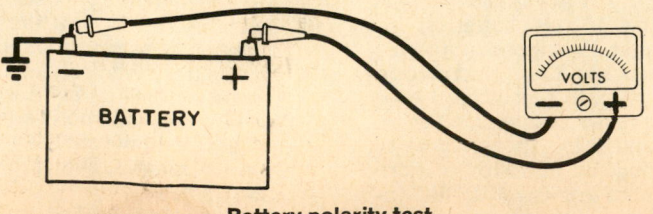

Battery polarity test

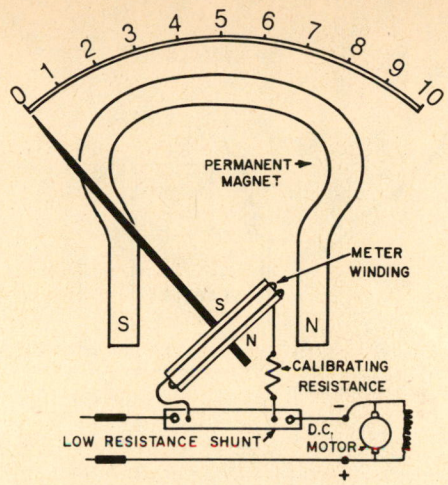

Ohmmeter circuit

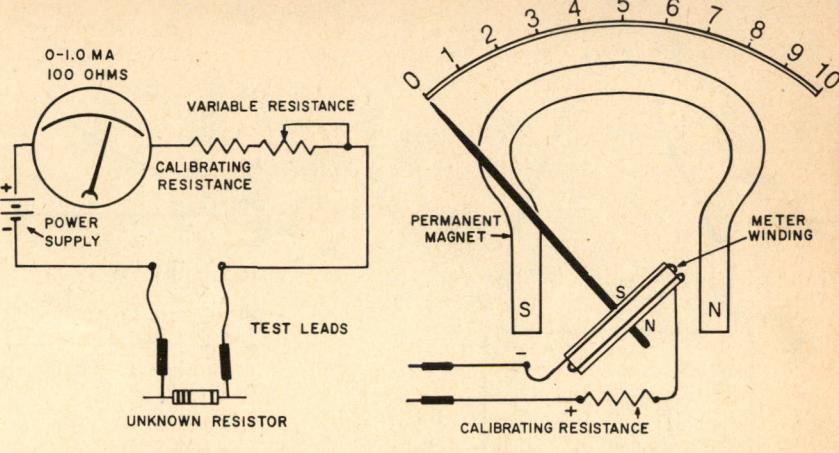

Ammeter circuit

Voltmeter circuit

Ambient Temperature (°F)	Minimum Voltage
70 (or above)	9.6
60	9.5
50	9.4
40	9.3
30	9.1
20	8.9
10	8.7
0	8.5

Know Your Instruments

OHMMETER

An ohmmeter is used to measure electrical resistance in a unit or circuit. The ohmmeter has a self-contained power supply. In use, it is connected across (or in parallel with) the terminals of the unit being tested.

AMMETER

An ammeter is used to measure current (amount of electricity) flowing through a unit, or circuit. Ammeters are always connected in the line (in series) with the unit or circuit being tested.

Delco sealed top battery
(© G.M. Corp.)

VOLTMETER

A voltmeter is used to measure voltage (electrical pressure) pushing the current through a unit, or circuit. The meter is connected across the terminals of the unit being tested. The meter reading will be the difference in pressure (voltage drop) between the two sides of the unit.

TESTING THE STARTER MOTOR

Testing the Starter Circuit

The starter circuit should be divided and tested in four separate phases:
1. Cranking voltage check.
2. Amperage draw.
3. Voltage drop—grounded side.
4. Voltage drop—battery side.

NOTE: *The battery must be in good condition for this test to have significance. To accurately check battery condition, use equipment designed to measure its capacity under a load. Instructions accompanying the equipment should be followed.*

CRANKING VOLTAGE

Turn voltmeter selector to the 16-20 volt scale.

Connect voltmeter leads to the battery posts (observe polarity and reverse meter leads if necessary). Remove the high tension wire from the distributor cap and ground it to prevent starting. Now, turn the key. Observe both voltmeter reading and cranking speed. The cranking speed should be even, and at a satisfactory rate of speed, with a voltmeter reading of at least 9.6 volts.

AMPERAGE DRAW

The amount of current the starter motor draws is usually (but not always) associated with the mechanical problems involved in cranking the engine. (Mechanical trouble in the engine, frozen or worn starter parts, misa-

ligned starter or starter components, etc.) Because starter motor amperage draw is directly influenced by anything restricting the free turning of the engine, or starter, it is important that the engine and all components be at operating temperatures.

To measure starter current draw, remove the high tension wire from the center of the distributor cap and ground it.

NOTE: *On cars with electronic ignition, disconnect the control box from the distributor (harness).*

A very simple and inexpensive starter current indicator is available at auto parts stores. This indicator is an induction type gauge and shows, with-

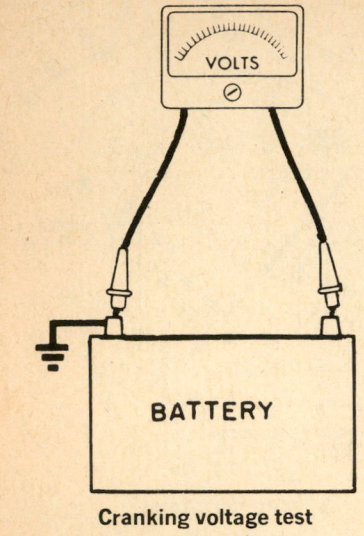

Cranking voltage test

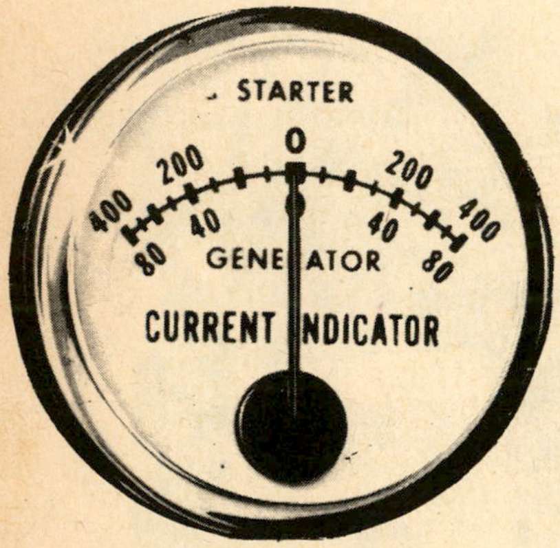

Starter current indicator

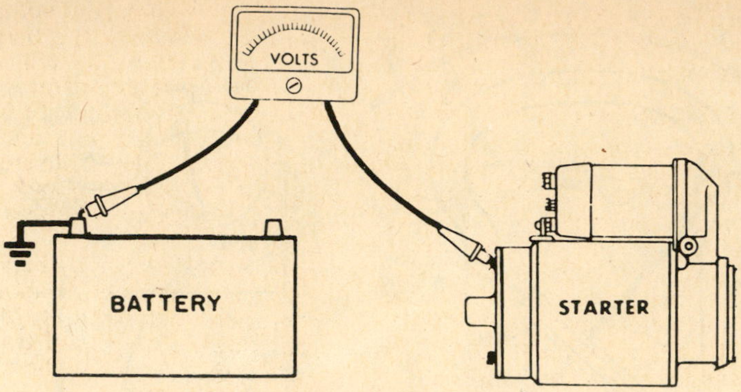

Typical Delco Remy hook-up

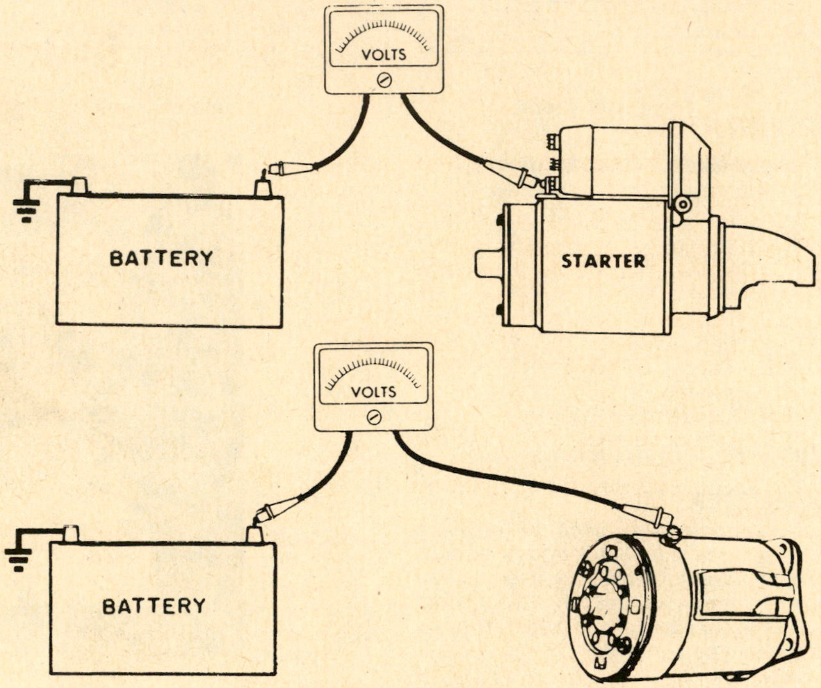

Typical Ford hook-ups

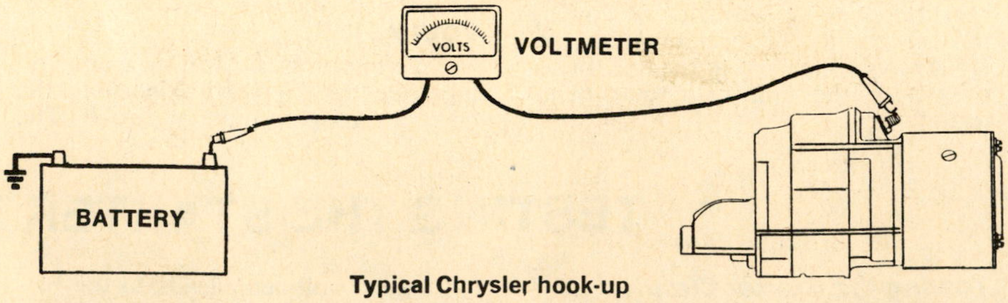

VOLTMETER

Typical Chrysler hook-up

out disconnecting any wires, starter current draw.

Place the yoke of the meter directly over the insulated starter supply cable (cable must be straight for a minimum of 2 in.). Close the starter switch for about 20 seconds, watch the meter dial and record the average reading. If the indicator swings in the wrong direction, reverse the position of the meter. On 12-volt systems, normal draw for small to medium size engines is 75 to 112 amperes. Larger and high compression engines may draw as much as 200 amperes.

More accurate but complex equipment is available from many name brand manufacturers. This equipment consists of a combination voltmeter, ammeter, and carbon pile rheostat. When using this equipment, follow the equipment manufacturer's procedures and recommendations.

High amperage and lazy performance would suggest an excessively tight engine, friction in the starter or starter drive, grounded starter field or armature.

Normal amperage and lazy performance suggest high resistance, or possibly poor connections somewhere in the starter circuit.

Low amperage and lazy or no performance suggest battery condition

poor, bad cables or connections along the line.

VOLTAGE DROP— GROUNDED SIDE

With a voltmeter on the 3 volt scale, without disconnecting any wires, connect negative test lead of the voltmeter to a prod secured in the grounded battery post. The positive test lead is connected to a cleaned, bare metal portion of the starter motor housing. Close the starter switch and note the voltmeter reading. If the reading is the same as battery reading, the ground circuit is open somewhere between the battery and the starter. In many cases the read-

ing will be very small. The reading shown will indicate voltage drop (loss) between battery ground post and starter housing. The drop should not exceed 0.2 volt. If the voltage drop is above the specified amount, the next step is to isolate and correct the cause. It can be a bad cable or connection anywhere in the battery-to-starter ground circuit. A check of this type should progress along the various points of possible trouble, between the battery ground post and the starter motor housing, until the trouble spot has been located.

NOTE: *Due to the design of the Chrys-*

ler reduction gear starter, testing is limited to measuring voltage drop to starter cable connection.

VOLTAGE DROP—BATTERY SIDE

Bad starter cranking may result from poor connections or faulty components of the battery or hot phase of the starter motor circuit. To check this phase of the circuit, without disconnecting any wires, connect one lead of a voltmeter to a prod secured in the hot post of the battery and the other voltmeter lead to the field terminal of the starting motor. The meter should be set to the 16-20 volt scale. Before closing the starter switch, the voltmeter reading will be that of the battery. After closing the starter switch, change the selector on the voltmeter to the 3-volt scale. With a jumper wire between the relay battery terminal and the relay starter switch terminal, crank the engine. If the starting motor cranks the engine, the relay (solenoid) is operating.

While the engine is being cranked, watch the voltmeter. It should not register more than 0.5 volt. If more than this, check each part of the circuit for voltage drop to isolate the trouble (high resistance).

Without disturbing the voltmeter-to-battery hook-up, move the free voltmeter lead to the battery terminal of the relay (solenoid), and crank the engine. The voltmeter should show no more than 0.1 volt.

If this reading is correct, move the same voltmeter lead to the starting motor terminal of the relay (solenoid). While the engine is being cranked, the voltmeter should show no more than 0.3 volt. If it does, the trouble lies in the relay.

If the reading is correct, the trouble is in the cable or connections between the relay and the starting motor.

Starter Motor and System Service

DIAGNOSIS

Starter Won't Crank the Engine

1. Dead battery.
2. Open starter circuit, such as:
   A. Broken or loose battery cables.
   B. Inoperative starter motor solenoid
   C. Broken or loose wire from ignition switch to solenoid.
   D. Poor solenoid or starter ground.
   E. Bad ignition switch.
   F. Defective seat belt interlock system—1974-75 cars only.
3. Defective starter internal circuit, such as:
   A. Dirty or burnt commutator.
   B. Stuck, worn or broken brushes.
   C. Open or shorted armature.
   D. Open or grounded fields.
4. Starter motor mechanical faults, such as:
   A. Jammed armature end bearings.
   B. Bad bearing, allowing armature to rub fields.
   C. Bent shaft.
   D. Broken starter housing.
   E. Bad starter drive mechanism.
   F. Bad starter drive or flywheel-driven gear.
5. Engine hard or impossible to crank, such as:
   A. Hydrostatic lock, water in combustion chamber.
   B. Crankshaft seizing in bearings.
   C. Piston or ring seizing.
   D. Bent or broken connecting rod.
   E. Seizing of connecting rod bearing.
   F. Flywheel jammed or broken.

Starter Spins Free, Won't Engage

1. Sticking or broken drive mechanism.

SOLENOIDS WITHOUT RELAYS

This type of starter solenoid is always mounted on the starter. Makes

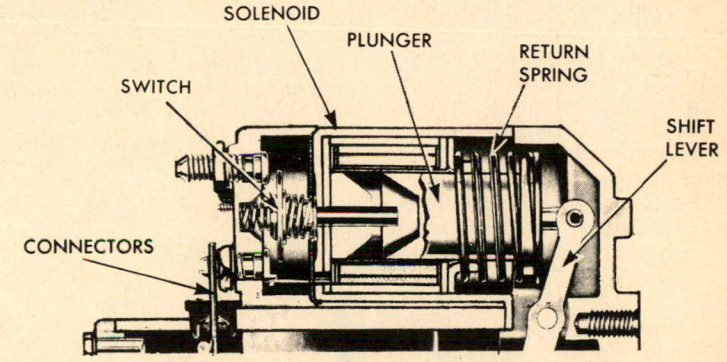

Starter solenoid mounted on starter motor

electrical contact for the starter and pulls the starter and drive clutch into mesh with flywheel. The Chrysler reduction gear starter has this solenoid embodied in the starter housing.

There is only one control terminal on the solenoid.

The ignition by-pass terminal is usually marked R or IGN, if it is used.

SOLENOIDS WITH SEPARATE RELAYS

The solenoid itself is always mounted on the starter. In addition to making contact for the starter, it also pulls the starter drive clutch gear into mesh with flywheel. A single control terminal is used on the solenoid itself. The relay is usually found mounted to the inner fender panel or on the firewall.

SOLENOIDS WITH BUILT-IN RELAYS

These units are always mounted the starter and are connected, through link-

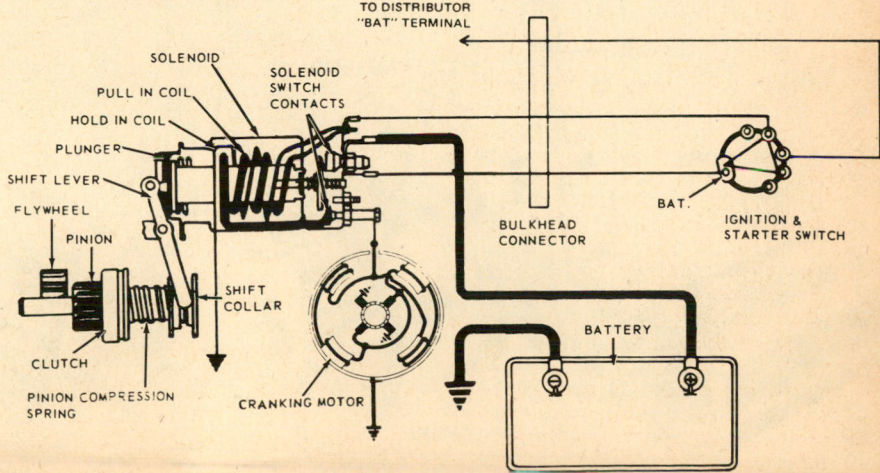

G.M. starter circuit (© G.M. Corp)

Charging and Starting Systems

age, to the starter drive clutch. The relay portion is built into and integral with the solenoid assembly.

NEUTRAL SAFETY SWITCHES

The purpose of the neutral safety switch is to prevent the starter from cranking the engine except when the transmission is in Neutral or Park.

NOTE: *All Ford Motor Co. cars and Cadillacs starting 1974 with a column mounted automatic transmission selector and steering column lock do not have a neutral safety switch; instead the key can only be turned to the "START" position when the selector is in Park or Neutral.*

On some cars, the neutral safety switch is located on the transmission. It serves to ground the solenoid or magnetic switch, whichever is used.

On other cars the neutral safety switch is located either at the bottom of the steering column, where it contacts the shift mechanism, on the steering column, underneath the dash, or on the shift linkage (console).

NOTE: *Recent cars with manual transmissions have a safety switch mounted* on the clutch linkage to prevent starter operation unless the pedal is depressed.

On most cars, the neutral safety switch and the back-up light switch are combined into a single switch mechanism.

See the car sections for specific details.

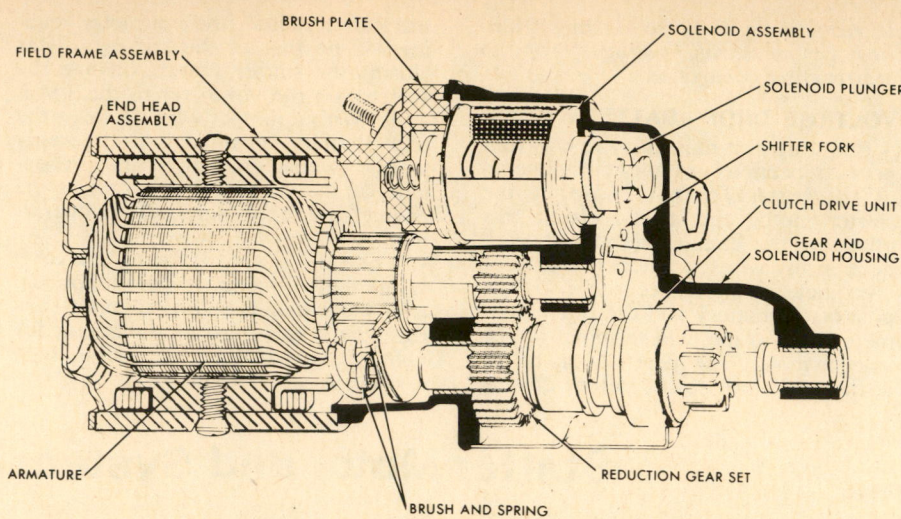

Reduction gear starter motor (© Chrysler Corp)

Troubleshooting Neutral Safety Switches—Quick Test

If the starter fails to function and the neutral safety switch is to be checked, a jumper can be placed across its terminals. If the starter then functions the safety switch is defective.

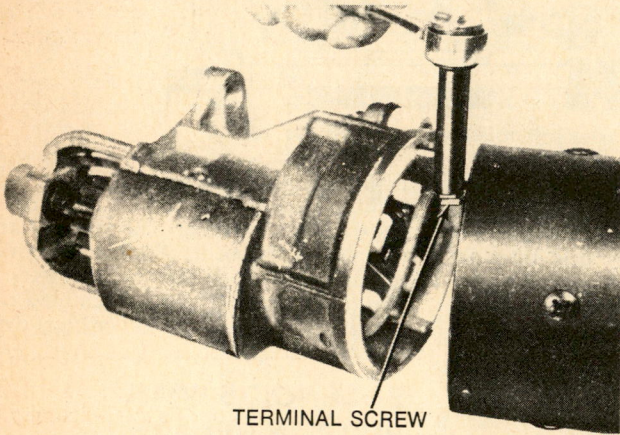

Removing terminal screw—reduction gear motor
(© Chrysler Corp)

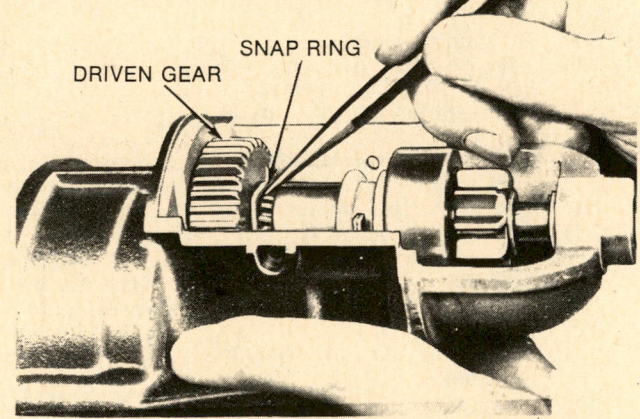

Removing drive gear snap-ring—reduction gear motor
(© Chrysler Corp)

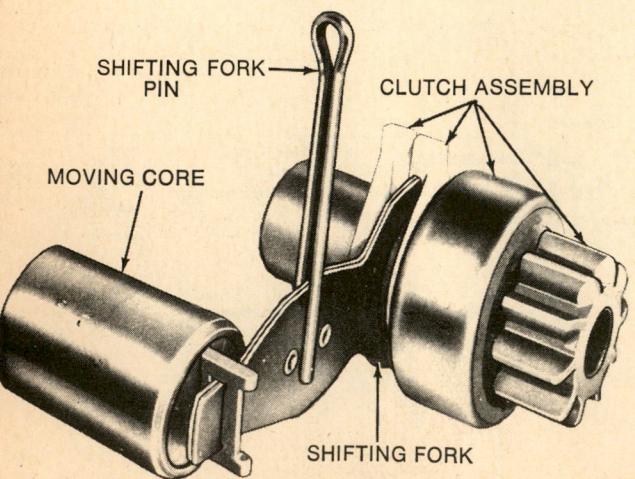

Shift fork and clutch arrangement—reduction gear motor
(© Chrysler Corp)

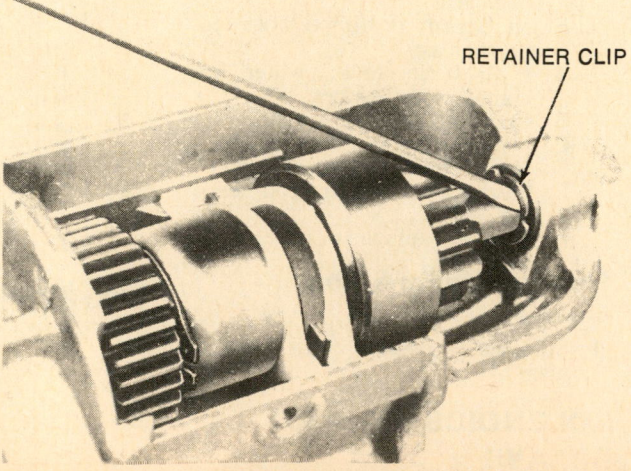

Removing retainer ring—reduction gear motor
(© Chrysler Corp)

In the case of neutral safety switches with one wire, this wire must be grounded for testing purposes. If the starter works with the wire grounded, the switch is defective.

Neutral Safety Switch—Back-up Light Switch

When the neutral safety switch is built in combination with the back-up light switch, the easiest way to tell which terminals are for the back-up lights is to take a jumper and cross every pair of wires. The pair of wires which light the back-up lamps should be ignored when testing the neutral safety switch. Once the back-up light wires have been located, jump the other pair of wires to test the neutral safety switch. If the starter functions only when the jumper is placed across these two wires, the neutral safety switch is defective or requires adjustment.

REDUCTION-GEAR STARTER MOTOR

(Chrysler Corporation)

The housing is die-cast aluminum. A 3.5 to 1 reduction, combined with the starter to ring gear ratio, results in a total gear reduction of about 45 to 1.
NOTE: *The high-pitched sound is caused by the higher starter speed.*

The positive shift solenoid is enclosed in the starter housing and is energized through the ignition switch. When ignition switch is turned to start, the solenoid plunger engages drive gear through a shifting fork. At the completion of travel, the plunger closes a switch to revolve the starter.

An overrunning clutch prevents motor damage if key is held on after engine starts.

No lubrication is required due to Oilite bearings.

1975 and later Chrysler Corporation cars with large V-8s (360 cu. in. and up) and some sixes use a larger reduction gear starter motor. It is similar to the previous models but is more powerful and has a 2:1 gear reduction rather than 3.5:1. The clutch drive unit in the new starter has been enlarged to handle the increased load as have the rest of the components. While the new starter is outwardly similar to the old one, parts are not interchangeable; however removal, installation, disassembly and assembly procedures are unchanged.

Disassembly

1. Support assembly in a vise equipped with soft jaws. Do not clamp. Care must be used not to distort or damage the die cast aluminum.
2. Remove the thru-bolts and the end housing.
3. Carefully pull the armature up and out of the gear housing, and the starter frame and field assembly.

4. Pull the field frame assembly out enough to get at the terminal screw. Remove the screw.
5. Remove the field frame assembly.
6. Remove the nuts holding the solenoid and brush holder plate to the gear housing. Remove the solenoid and brush plate.
7. Remove the nut, washer, and sealing washer from the solenoid brush terminal.
8. Unwind the solenoid lead wire from the brush terminal. Remove the screws and remove the solenoid from the brush plate. Remove the nut and battery terminal from the brush plate.
9. Remove the solenoid contact and plunger assembly, and the return spring.
10. Remove the gear housing dust cover. Remove the driven gear retainer clip.
NOTE: *The retainer is under tension; cover it with a cloth before removal to prevent loss.*
11. Remove the pinion shaft C-clip at the end of the housing. Push the pinion shaft in and remove the clutch assembly. Remove the driven gear and the washer.
12. Remove the retainer pin to remove the shifting fork.

Replacement of Brushes

1. Brushes that are worn more than one-half the length of new brushes, or are oil-soaked, should be replaced.
2. When resoldering the shunt field and solenoid lead, make a strong, low-resistance connection using a high-temperature solder and resin flux. Do not use acid or acid-core solder. Do not break the shunt field wire units when removing and installing the brushes.
3. Brush spring tension should be 32-36 ounces.

Starter Clutch and Pinion Gear Inspection

1. Do not immerse the starter clutch unit in a cleaning solvent. The outside of the clutch and pinion must be cleaned with a cloth so as not to

wash the lubricant from the inside of the clutch.
2. Rotate the pinion. The pinion gear should rotate smoothly and in one direction only. If the starter clutch unit does not function properly, or if the pinion is worn, chipped, or burred, replace the starter clutch unit.

Assembly

1. The shifter fork consists of two spring steel plates held together by two rivets. Before assembling the starter, check the plates for side movement. After lubricating between the plates with a small amount of SAE 10 engine oil, they should have about 1/16 in. side movement to insure proper pinion gear engagement.
2. Position the shift fork in the drive housing and install the shifting fork retainer pin. One tip of the pin should be straight and the other bent at a 15 degree angle away from the housing. The fork and retainer pin should operate freely after bending the tip of the pin.
3. Install the solenoid moving core and engage the shifting fork.
4. Place the pinion shaft into the drive housing and install the friction washer and drive gear.
5. Install the clutch and pinion assembly, thrust washer, and retaining washer.
6. Engage the shifting fork with the clutch actuators.

——— CAUTION ———

The friction washer must be positioned on the shoulder of the splines of the pinion shaft before the driven gear is positioned.

7. Install the driven gear snap ring.
8. Install the pinion shaft retaining ring.
9. The starter solenoid return spring can now be inserted in the movable core.
10. Install the solenoid contact plunger assembly into the solenoid.
11. Assemble the battery terminal stud in the brush holder.

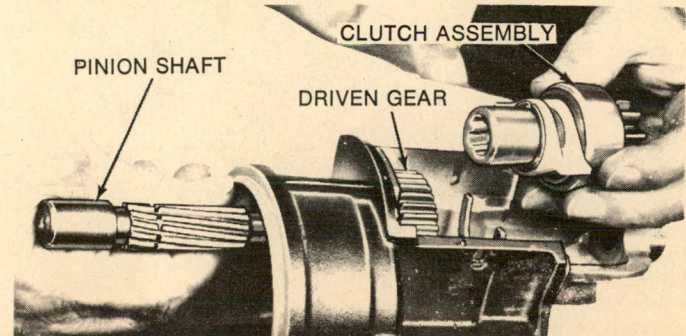

Removing clutch assembly—reduction gear motor
(© Chrysler Corp)

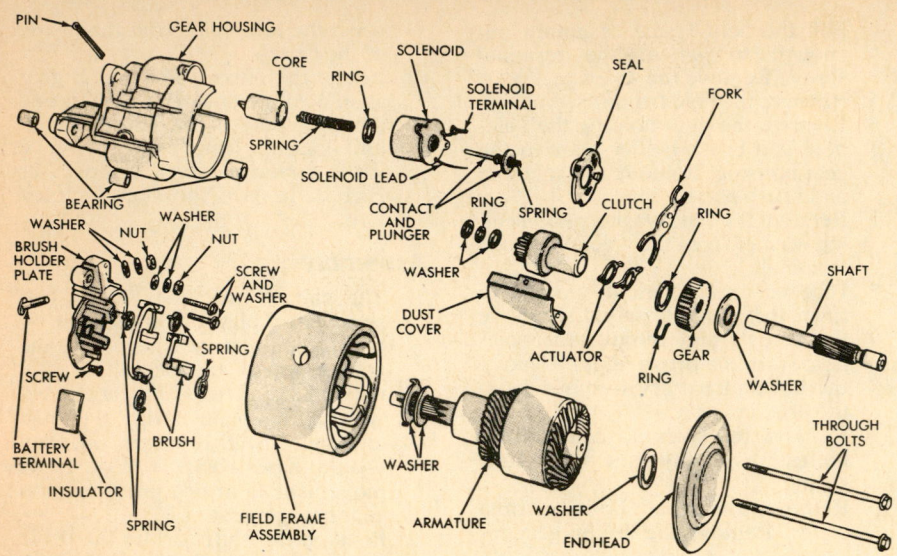

Reduction gear motor—exploded view (© Chrysler Corp)

12. Position the seal on the brush holder plate.
13. Run the solenoid lead wire through the hole in the brush holder and attach the solenoid stud, insulating washer, flat washer, and nut.
14. Wrap the solenoid lead wire tightly around the brush terminal post and solder it.
15. Fix the brush holder to the solenoid attaching screws.
16. Gently lower the solenoid coil and brush plate into the gear housing.
17. Position the brush plate assembly into the starter gear housing, install the nuts, and tighten.
18. Position the brushes with the armature thrust washer.
19. Install the brush terminal screw.
20. Position the field frame on the gear housing and start the armature into the housing, carefully engaging the splines on the shaft with the reduction gear by rotating the armature.
21. Install the thrust washer on the armature shaft.
22. Replace the starter end housing and starter through bolts; tighten securely.

DIRECT DRIVE STARTER MOTOR

(Chrysler Corporation)

NOTE: *The direct drive starter was last used in 1973.*

Disassembly

1. Remove through bolts and tap commutator end head from frame.
2. Remove thrust washers from armature shaft.
3. Lift brush holder springs and remove brushes from holders.
4. Remove brush holder plate.
5. Disconnect the field coil wires at the solenoid connector, and remove the solenoid screws.
6. Remove solenoid and boot.
7. Drive out shift fork pivot pin.
8. Remove drive end pinion housing and spacer washer.

9. Remove shift fork from starter drive.
10. Slide overrunning clutch pinion gear toward commutator, drive stop retainer toward clutch pinion gear and remove the now-exposed snap-ring.
11. Remove overrunning clutch drive from armature shaft.
12. If field coils are good, stop disassembly at this point. If field coils must be replaced, remove ground brushes terminal screw and remove brushes, terminal and shunt wire. Remove pole shoe screws, using a ratchet-type impact driver and special wide screwdriver blade, then remove field coils.
13. Replacement of the brushes, inspection of the starter clutch and pinion, and inspection of the commutator procedures are the same as the reduction-gear starter procedures.

Assembly

1. Install field coils into frame, if removed.

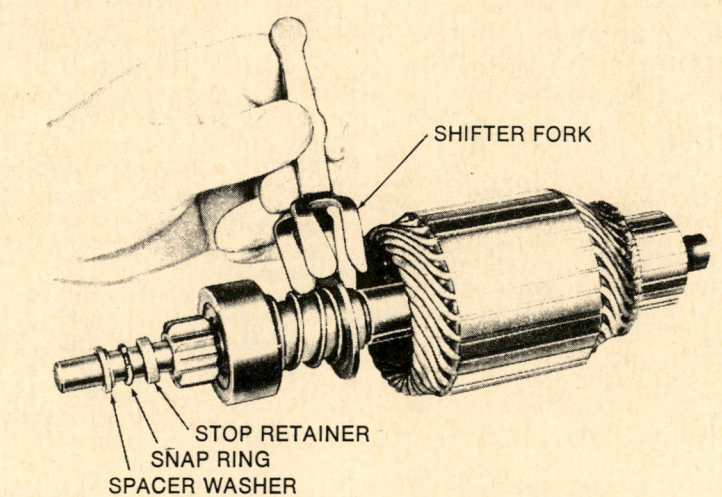

Removing shift fork—direct drive motor
(© Chrysler Corp)

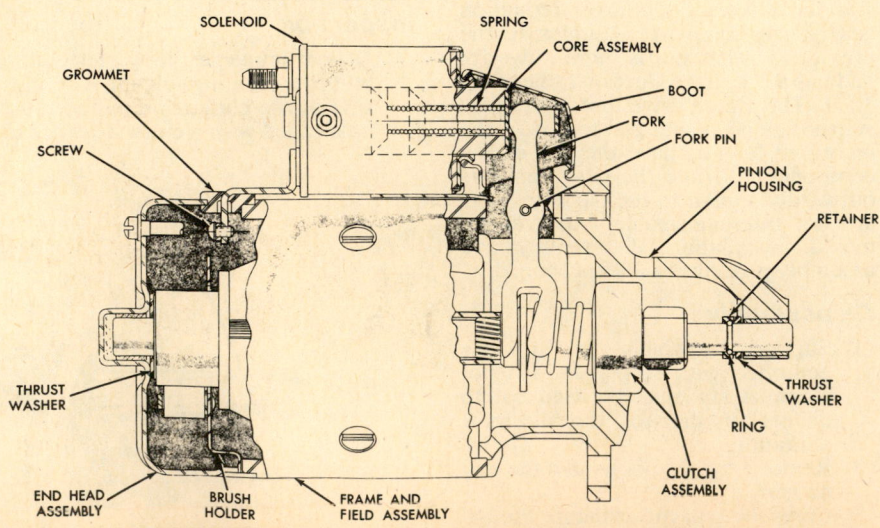

Chrysler direct drive starter motor (© Chrysler Corp)

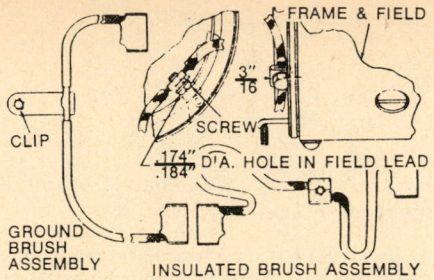

Brush lead arrangement—Chrysler direct drive motor (© Chrysler Corp)

2. Lubricate armature shaft and splines with engine oil.
3. Install starter drive, stop retainer, lock ring and spacer washer.
4. Install shift fork, with *narrow* leg of fork toward commutator.
5. Install pinion housing onto armature shaft, indexing shift fork with slot in housing.
6. Install shift fork pivot pin.
7. With clutch drive, shift fork, and pinion housing assembled onto the armature, slide armature into frame until pinion housing indexes with slot.
8. Install solenoid and boot, tightening bolts to 60-70 in. lbs.
9. Connect field coil wires to solenoid connector, making sure they do not touch frame.
10. Install brush holder plate, indexing tang in frame hole.
11. Place brushes in holders, making sure field coil wires do not interfere.
12. Install thrust washers on commutator end of armature shaft to obtain a maximum of 0.010 in. end-play.
13. Install commutator end head and through bolts. Tighten bolts to 40-50 in. lbs.
14. Measure drive gear pinion clear-

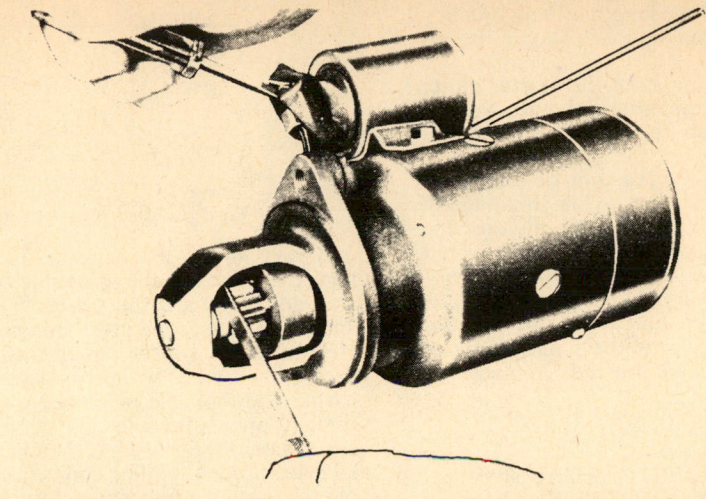

Checking drive pinion clearance—direct drive motor (© Chrysler Corp)

ance; it should be 1/8 in. Adjust by moving solenoid fore and aft as required.

NIPPONDENSO OR BOSCH STARTER MOTOR
(Chrysler Corporation)

Either a Nippondenso or Bosch starter may be used in the Omni and Horizon. Service procedures are the same for both types. The starter drive is an overrunning clutch with a solenoid on the motor.

Disassembly

1. Disconnect the field coil wire from the solenoid terminal.
2. Remove the solenoid mounting screws and work the solenoid off the shift fork.

3. On Nippondenso units, remove the bearing cover, armature shaft lock, washer, spring, and seal.
4. On Bosch units, remove the bearing cover, armature shaft lock, and shim.
5. Remove the two through-bolts and the commutator end frame cover.
6. Remove the two brushes and the brush holder.
7. Slide the field frame off over the armature.
8. Take out the shift lever pivot bolt.
9. Take off the rubber gasket and metal plate.
10. Remove the armature assembly and shift lever from the drive end housing.
11. Press the stop collar off the snap ring. Remove the snap ring, stop collar, and clutch.

Inspection and Service

1. Brushes that are worn more than

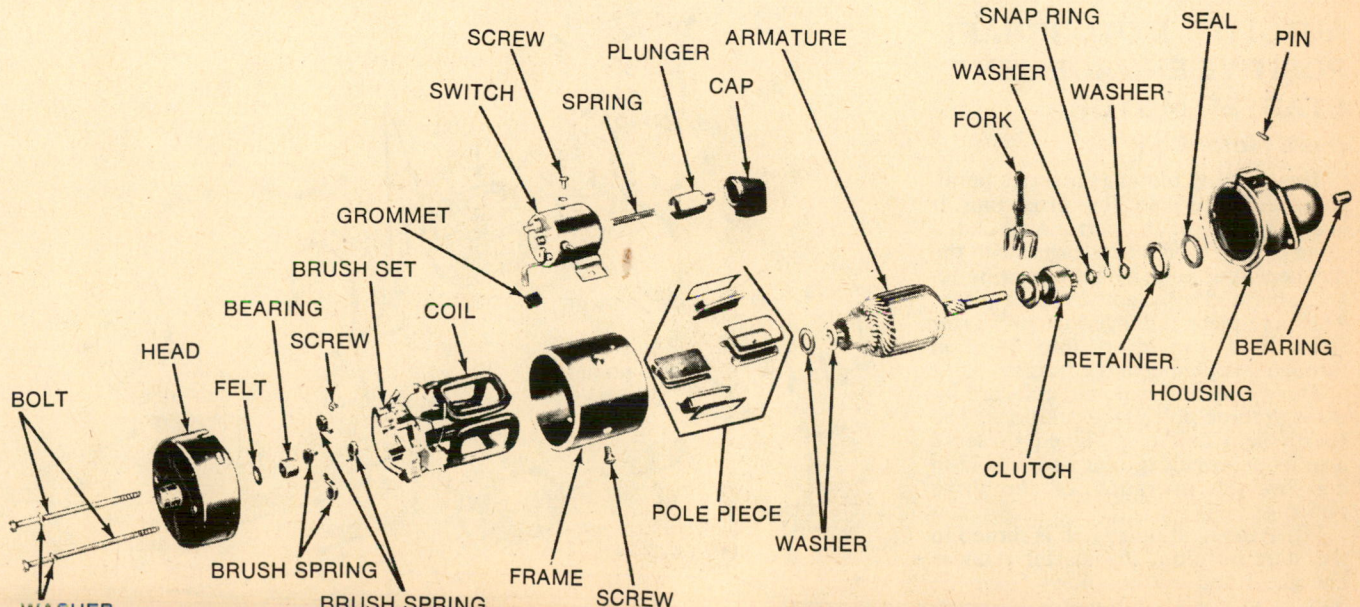

Chrysler direct drive motor—exploded view (© Chrysler Corp)

one-half the length of new brushes, or are oil-soaked, should be replaced.

2. Do not immerse the starter clutch unit in cleaning solvent. Solvent will wash the lubricant from the clutch.

3. Place the drive unit on the armature shaft and, while holding the armature, rotate the pinion. The drive pinion should rotate smoothly in one direction only. The pinion may not rotate easily. If the clutch unit does not function properly, or if the pinion is worn, chipped, or burred, replace the unit.

Assembly

1. Lubricate the armature shaft and splines with SAE 10-W or 30 oil.
2. Install the clutch, stop collar, and lock ring on the armature.
3. Place the armature assembly and shift fork in the drive end housing. Install the shift lever pivot bolt.
4. Install the rubber gasket and metal plate.
5. Slide the field frame into position. Install the brush holder and brushes.
6. Position the commutator end frame cover and install the through bolts.
7. On Nippondenso units, install the seal, spring, washer, armature shaft lock, and bearing cover.
8. On Bosch units, install the shim and armature shaft lock. Check that end play is 0.05-0.3 mm (0.002-0.012 in.). Install the bearing cover.
9. Assemble the solenoid to the shift fork and install the mounting screws.
10. Connect the field coil wire to the solenoid.

AUTOLITE/MOTORCRAFT POSITIVE ENGAGEMENT STARTER MOTOR
(Ford Motor Co.)

This starting motor is a series-parallel wound, four pole, four brush unit. It is equipped with an overrunning clutch drive pinion, which is engaged with the flywheel ring gear by an actuating lever, operated by a movable pole piece. This pole piece is hinged to the starter frame and can drop into position through an opening in the frame.

Three conventional field coils are located at three pole piece positions. The fourth field coil is designed to serve also as an engaging coil and a hold-in coil for the operation of the drive pinion.

When the ignition switch is turned to the start position, the starter relay is energized and current flows from the battery to the starter motor terminal. This prime surge of current first flows through the starter engaging coil, creat-

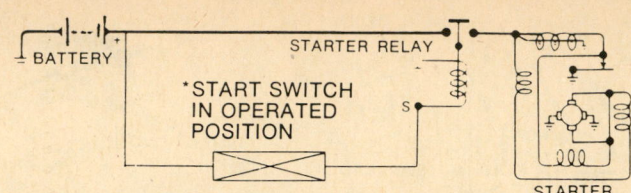

Ford positive engagement starter circuit (© Ford Motor Co.)

ing a very strong magnetic field. This magnetism draws the movable pole piece down toward the starter frame, which then causes the lever attached to it to move the starter pinion into engagement with the flywheel ring gear.

When the movable pole shoe is fully seated, it opens the field coil grounding contacts, and the starter is then in normal operation. A holding coil is used to hold the movable pole shoe in the fully seated position during the engine cranking operation.

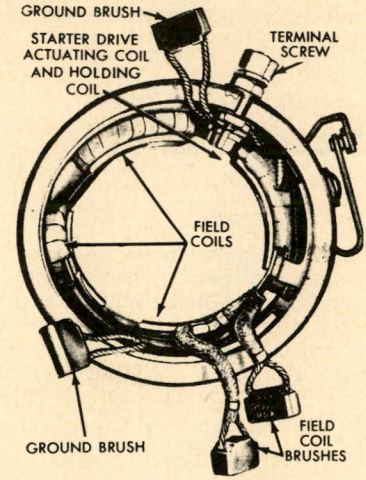

Autolite field coil assembly

Ford Motor Co. automatic transmission models with a floorshift lever have a neutral start switch; column shift models have a mechanical interlock.

This type starter is used on both Ford and American Motors products. There are 4 and 4½ in. diameter versions.

Disassembly

1. Remove brush cover band and starter drive gear actuating lever cover. Observe the brush lead locations for reassembly, then remove the brushes from their holders.

NOTE: *Factory brush length is ½ in.; wear limit is ¼ in.*

2. Remove the through bolts, starter drive gear housing and the drive gear actuating lever return spring.
3. Remove the pivot pin retaining the starter gear actuating lever and remove the lever and the armature.
4. Remove the stop ring retainer. Remove and discard the stop ring holding the drive gear to the armature shaft; then remove the drive gear assembly.
5. Remove the brush end plate.
6. Remove the two screws holding the ground brushes to the frame.
7. On the field coil that operates the starter drive gear actuating lever,

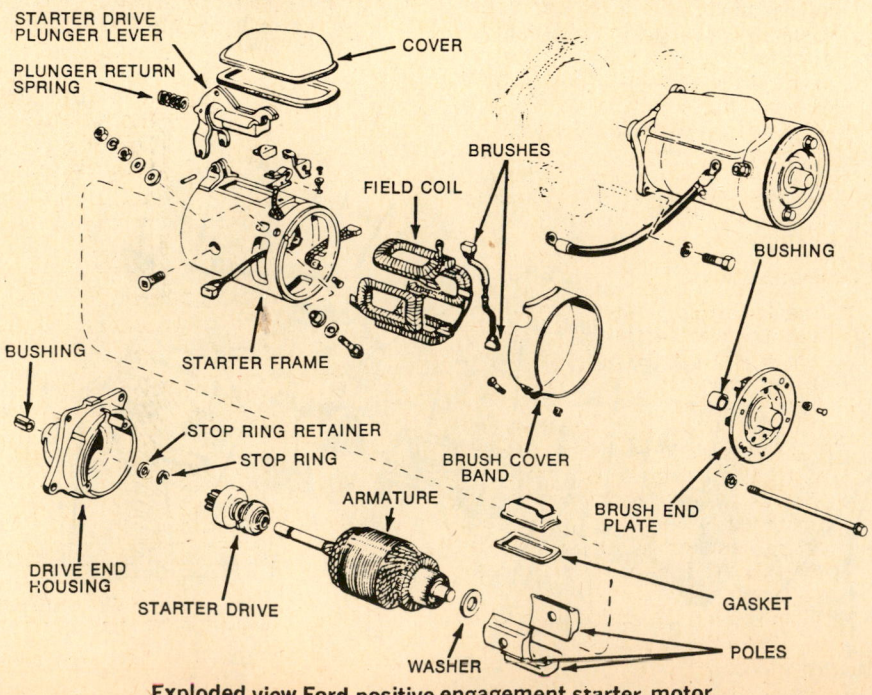

Exploded view Ford positive engagement starter motor
(© Ford Motor Co)

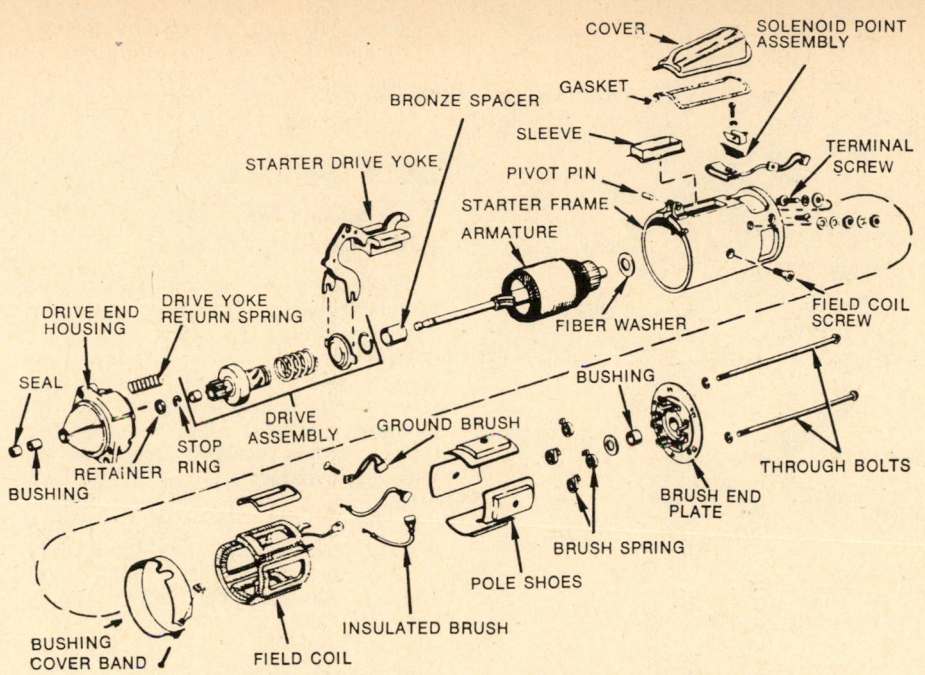

Exploded view AMC positive engagement starter motor
(© American Motors Corp)

bend the tab up on the field retainer and remove the field coil retainer.

8. Remove the three coil retaining screws. Unsolder the field coil leads from the terminal screw, then remove the pole shoes and coils from the frame (use a 300 watt iron).

9. Remove the starter terminal nut, washer, insulator and terminal from the starter frame.

10. Check the commutator for runout. If the commutator is rough, has flat spots, or is more than 0.005 in. out of round, reface the commutator. Clean the grooves in the commutator face.

11. Inspect the armature shaft and the two bearings for scoring and excessive wear. Replace if necessary.

12. Inspect the starter drive. If the gear teeth are pitted, broken, or excessively worn, replace the starter drive.

Assembly

1. Install starter terminal, insulator, washers and retaining nut in the frame. (Be sure to position the slot in the screw perpendicular to the frame end surface.)

2. Position coils and pole pieces, with the coil leads in the terminal screw slot, then install the retaining screws. As the pole screws are tightened, strike the frame several sharp hammer blows to align the pole shoes. Tighten, then stake the screws.

3. Install solenoid coil and retainer and bend the tabs to hold the coils to the frame.

4. Solder the field coils and solenoid wire to the starter terminal, using rosin-core solder and a 300 watt iron.

5. Check for continuity and ground connections in the assembled coils.

6. Position the solenoid coil ground terminal over the nearest ground screw hole.

7. Position the ground brushes to the starter frame and install retaining screws.

8. Position the brush end plate to the frame, with the end plate boss in the frame slot.

9. Lightly Lubriplate the armature shaft splines and install the starter drive gear assembly on the shaft.

Install a new retaining stop ring and stop ring retainer.

10. Postion the fiber thrust washer on the commutator end of the armature shaft, then position the armature in the starter frame.

11. Position the starter drive gear actuating lever to the frame and starter drive assembly, and install the pivot pin.

NOTE: *Fill drive gear housing bore ¼ full of grease.*

12. Position the drive actuating lever return spring and the drive gear housing to the frame, then install and tighten the through bolts. Do not pinch brush leads between brush plate and frame. Be sure that the stop ring retainer is properly seated in the drive housing.

13. Install the brushes in the brush holders and center the brush springs on the brushes.

14. Position the drive gear actuating lever cover on the starter and install the brush cover band with a new gasket.

AUTOLITE/MOTORCRAFT SOLENOID ACTUATED STARTER MOTOR

(Ford Motor Co.)

This starter motor, usually used with 429 and 460 engines through 1977, is a four-brush, four-field, four-pole wound unit. The frame encloses a wound armature, which is supported at the drive end by caged needle bearings and at the commutator end by a sintered copper bushing. The four pole shoes are retained to the frame by one pole screw apiece, and on each pole shoe is wound a ribbon-type field coil connected in series-parallel.

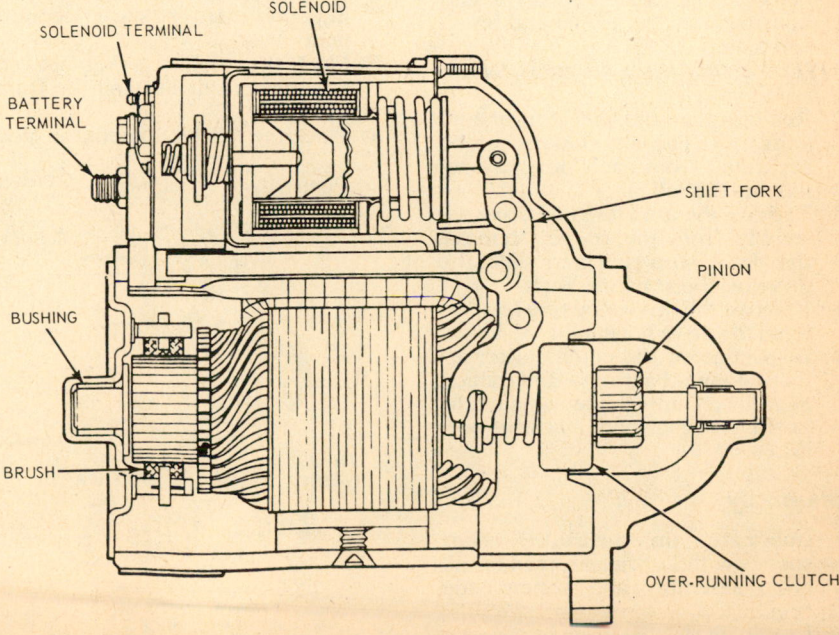

Ford solenoid actuated starter motor (© Ford Motor Co)

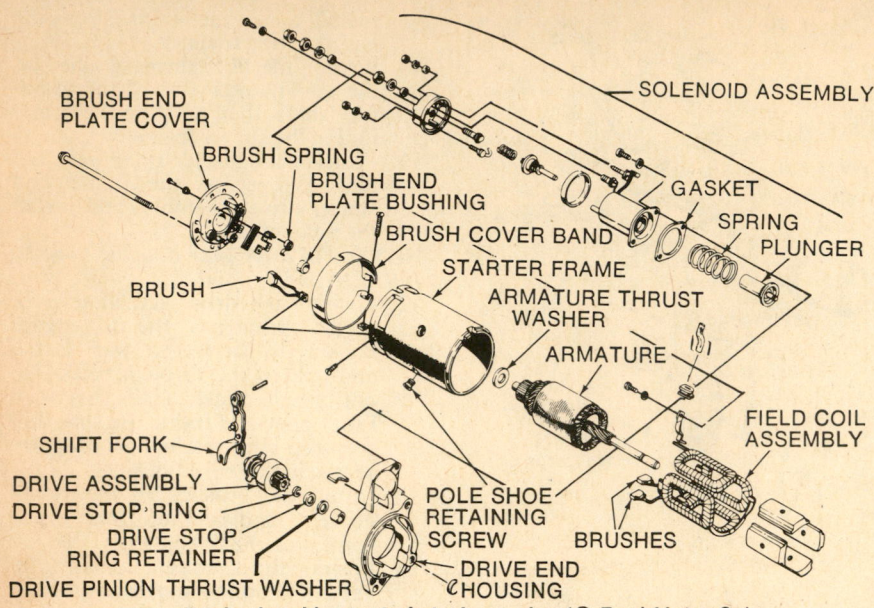

Ford solenoid actuated starter motor (© Ford Motor Co)

The solenoid is mounted to a flange on the starter drive housing, which encloses the entire shift mechanism and solenoid plunger. The solenoid, following standard industry practice, utilizes two windings—a pull-in winding and a hold-in winding.

Disassembly

1. Disconnect the copper strap from the solenoid starter terminal, remove the remaining screws and remove the solenoid.
2. Loosen the retaining screw and slide the brush cover band back far enough to gain access to the brushes.
3. Remove the brushes from their holders, then remove the through bolts and separate the drive end housing from the frame and brush end plate.

NOTE: *Factory brush length is ½ in., wear limit is ¼ in.*

4. Remove the solenoid plunger and shift fork. These two items can be separated from each other by removing the roll pin.
5. Remove the armature and drive assembly from the frame. Remove the drive stop ring and slide the drive off the armature shaft.
6. Remove the drive stop ring retainer from the drive housing.
7. Inspection of the commutator, armature and bearings, and pinion gear procedures is the same as the positive engagement starter procedures.

Assembly

1. Lubricate the armature shaft splines with Lubriplate, then install drive assembly and a new stop ring.
2. Lubricate shift lever pivot pin with Lubriplate, then position solenoid plunger and shift lever assembly in the drive housing.
3. Place a new retainer in the drive housing. Apply a small amount of Lubriplate to the drive end of the armature shaft, then place armature and drive assembly into the drive housing, indexing the shift lever tangs with the drive assembly.
4. Apply a small amount of Lubriplate to the commutator end of the armature shaft, then position the frame and field assembly to the drive housing.
5. Position the brush plate assembly to the frame, making sure it properly indexes. Install through bolts and tighten to 45-85 in. lbs.
6. Install brushes into their holders and make sure leads are not touching any interior starter components.
7. Place the rubber gasket between the solenoid mount and the frame surface.
8. Place the starter solenoid in position with metal gasket and spring, install heat shield (if so equipped) and install solenoid screws.
9. Connect copper strap and install cover band.

DELCO-REMY STARTER MOTOR (General Motors Corp.)

There are many different versions of the Delco-Remy starter, depending upon application. In general, six-cylinder engines use a unit having four field coils in series between the terminal and armature. Standard V8 engines use, depending on displacement, one of three types: one has two field coils in series with the armature and parallel to each other; another has two field coils in parallel between the field terminal and ground, and another has three field coils in series with the armature and one field connected between the motor terminal and ground. Heavy-duty starter motors have series compound windings. On the 1975 and later Delco starter, the terminal that connects the starter solenoid to the ignition coil has been removed as it is unnecessary with the High Energy Ignition System. Starting 1978, a new starter design is used for some smaller engines. It is very similar to previous motors, but has the field coils and pole shoes integral with the motor frame.

In spite of these differences, all Delco-Remy starters are disassembled and assembled in essentially the same manner.

Disassembly

1. Detach the field coil connectors from the motor solenoid terminal.

NOTE: *On models so equipped, remove solenoid mounting screws.*

2. Remove the through bolts.
3. Remove commutator end frame, field frame and armature assembly from drive housing. The diesel starter has an end frame insulator. The diesel armature will remain in

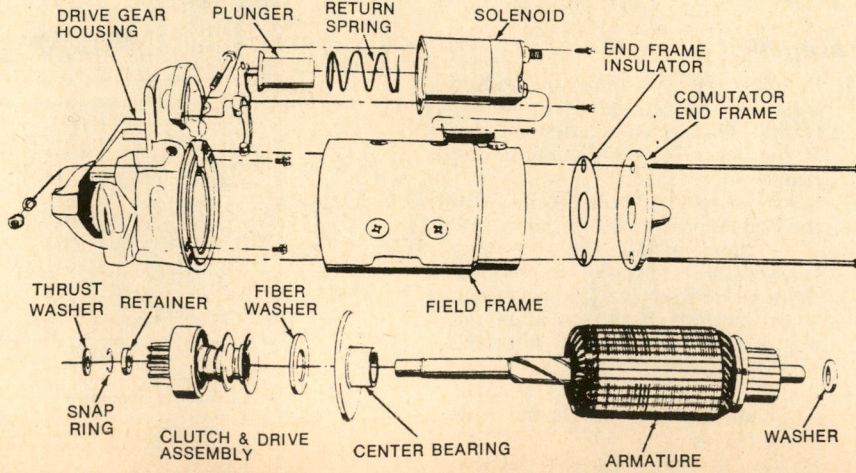

General Motors 350 V8 diesel starter exploded view (© Oldsmobile Div., G.M. Corp.)

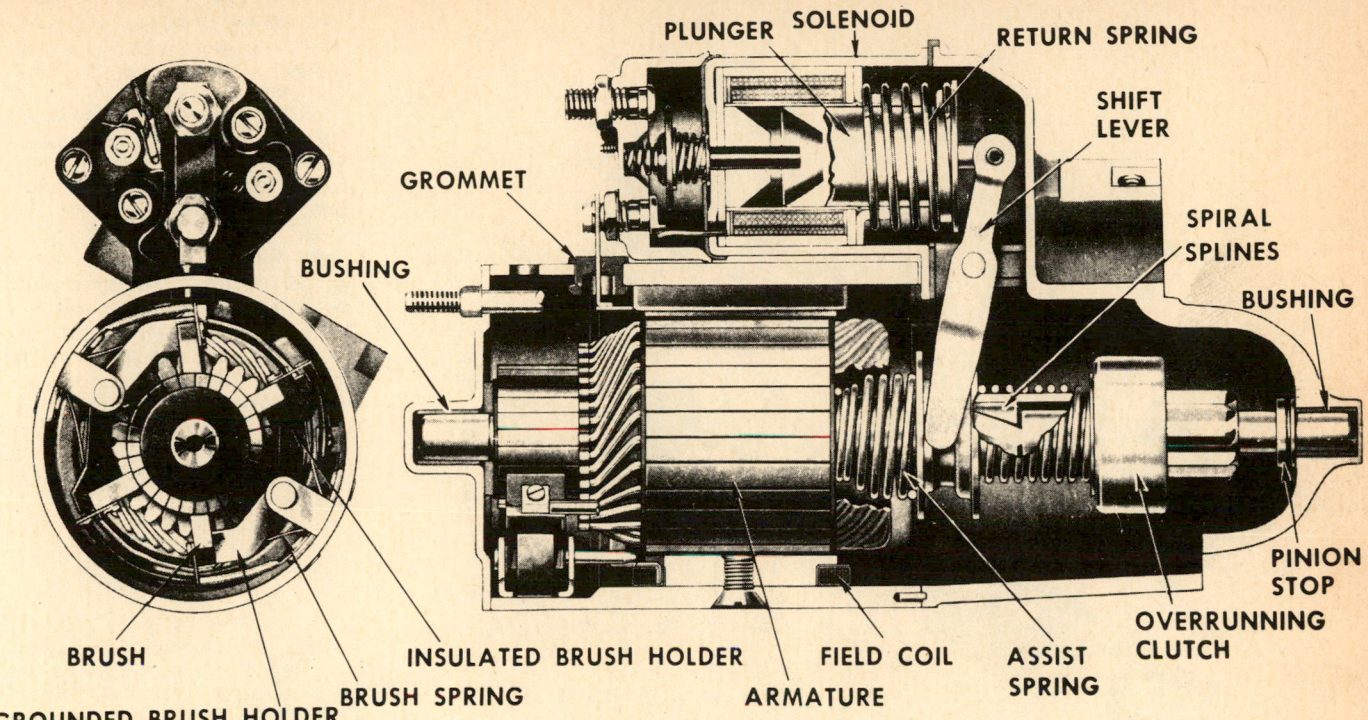

PLUNGER SOLENOID RETURN SPRING

SHIFT LEVER

GROMMET

SPIRAL SPLINES

BUSHING

BUSHING

PINION STOP

OVERRUNNING CLUTCH

BRUSH

INSULATED BRUSH HOLDER

FIELD COIL

ASSIST SPRING

GROUNDED BRUSH HOLDER

BRUSH SPRING

ARMATURE

Typical Delco-Remy starter motor using an assist spring—light duty Chevrolet illustrated
(© Chevrolet Div., G.M. Corp)

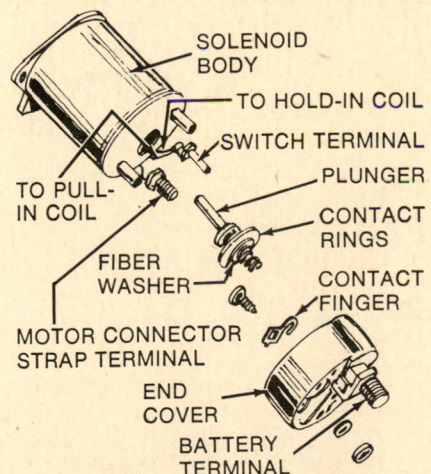

SOLENOID BODY

TO HOLD-IN COIL

SWITCH TERMINAL

PLUNGER

CONTACT RINGS

TO PULL-IN COIL

FIBER WASHER

CONTACT FINGER

MOTOR CONNECTOR STRAP TERMINAL

END COVER

BATTERY TERMINAL

Delco-Remy starter solenoid

the drive end frame. Remove the diesel shift lever pivot bolt and center bearing screws.

4. Remove the overrunning clutch from the armature shaft as follows:
   a. Slide the two-piece thrust collar off the end of the armature shaft.
   b. Slide a standard 1/2 in. pipe coupling or other spacer onto the shaft so that the end of the coupling butts against the edge of the retainer.
   c. Tap the end of the coupling with a hammer, driving retainer towards armature end of snapring.
   d. Remove snap-ring from its groove in the shaft using pliers. Slide retainer and clutch from armature shaft.
5. Disassemble brush assembly from

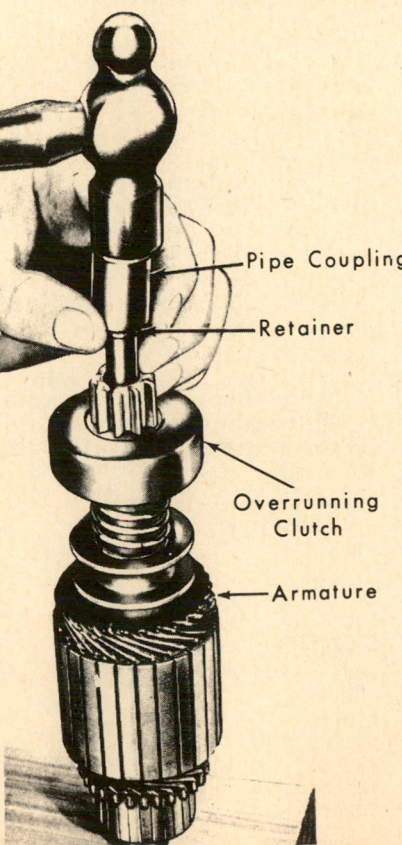

Pipe Coupling

Retainer

Overrunning Clutch

Armature

Driving retainer off snap ring —Delco-Remy motor
(© Chevrolet Div., G.M. Corp)

field frame by releasing the V-spring and removing the support pin. The brush holders, brushes and springs now can be pulled out as a unit and the leads disconnected. On integral frame units, remove the brush holder from the brush support and remove the brush screw.

6. On models so equipped, separate solenoid from lever housing.

Cleaning and Inspection

1. Clean parts with a rag, but do not immerse the parts in a solvent. Immersion in a solvent will dissolve the grease that is packed in the clutch mechanism and damage the armature and field coil insulation.
2. Test overrunning clutch action. The pinion should turn freely in the overrunning direction and must not slip in the cranking direction. Check pinion teeth to see that they have not been chipped, cracked, or excessively worn. Replace the unit if necessary.
3. Inspect the armature commutator. If the commutator is rough or out of round, it should be turned down and undercut.

NOTE: *Undercut the insulation between the commutator bars by 1/32 in. This undercut must be the full width of the insulation and flat at the bottom; a triangular groove will not be satisfactory. Some starter motor models use a*

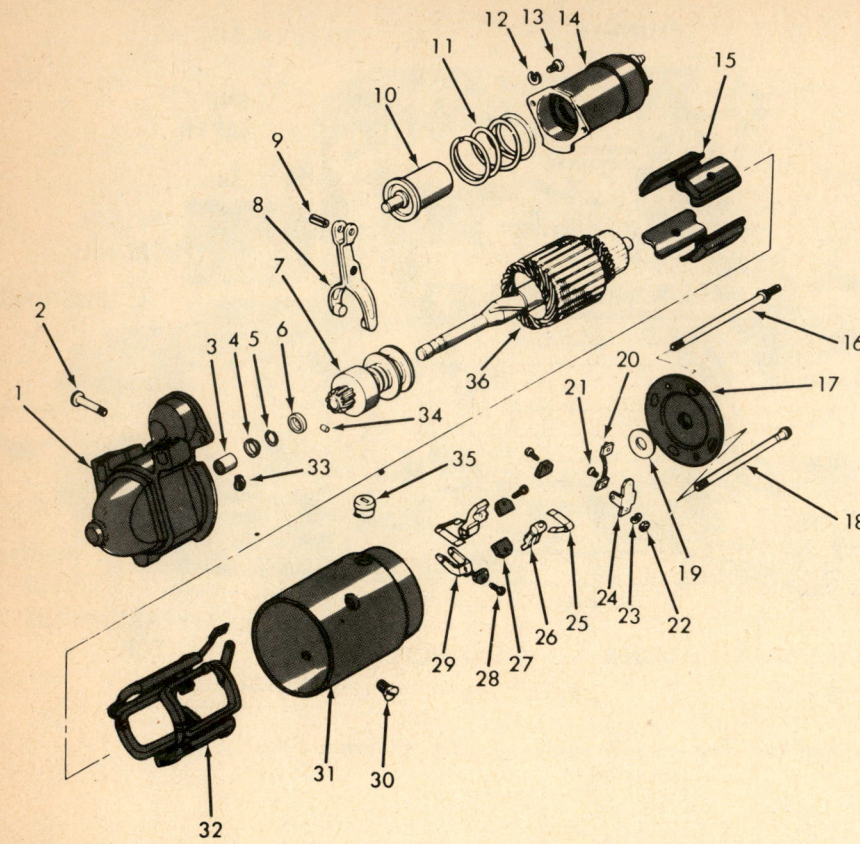

Typical Delco-Remy starter motor exploded view—light duty Chevrolet illustrated
(© Chevrolet Div., G.M. Corp)

1 Starter drive housing	13 Screw	25 Brush spring
2 Shift lever shaft	14 Solenoid switch assembly	26 Brush holder
3 Drive end bushing	15 Pole shoes	27 Brush
4 Drive end washer	16 Through bolt	28 Screw
5 Pinion ring stop	17 End frame	29 Ground brush holder
6 Armature shaft collar	18 Through bolt	30 Screw
7 Starter drive assembly	19 Washer	31 Field frame
8 Shift lever	20 Brush lead	32 Field coil assembly
9 Pin	21 Screw	33 Ring
10 Solenoid plunger	22 Nut	34 Pin
11 Solenoid return spring	23 Washer	35 Field frame grommet
12 Washer	24 Brush support pin	36 Armature

molded armature commutator design and no attempt to undercut the insulation should be made or serious damage may result to the commutator.

Assembly

1. Install brushes into holders. Install solenoid, if so equipped.
2. Assemble insulated and grounded brush holder together using the V-spring and position the assembled unit on the support pin. Push holders and spring to bottom of support and rotate spring to engage the slot in support. Attach ground wire to grounded brush and field lead wire to insulated brush, then repeat for other brush sets.
3. Assemble overrunning clutch to armature shaft as follows:
   a. Lubricate drive end of shaft with silicone lubricant.
   b. Slide clutch assembly onto shaft with pinion outward. On diesel starter, install center

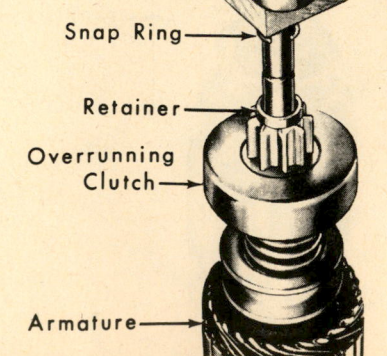

Forcing snap ring over armature shaft—Delco-Remy motor
(© Chevrolet Div., G.M. Corp)

bearing and fiber washer first.
   c. Slide retainer onto shaft with cupped surface facing away from pinion.
   d. Stand armature up on a wood surface, commutator downwards. Position snap-ring on upper end of shaft and drive it onto shaft with a small block of wood and a hammer. Slide snap-ring into groove.
   e. Install thrust collar onto shaft with shoulder next to snap-ring.
   f. With retainer on one side of snap-ring and thrust collar on the other side, squeeze together with two sets of pliers until ring seats in retainer. On models without thrust collar use a washer. Remember to remove washer before continuing.

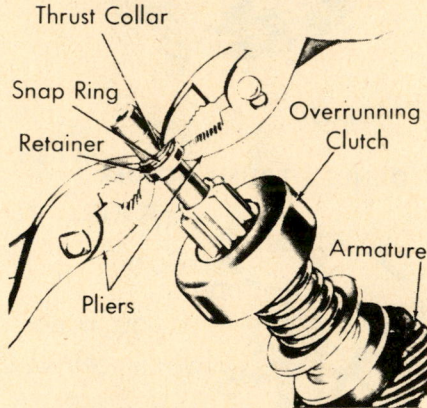

Forcing snap ring into retainer—Delco-Remy motor
(© Chevrolet Div., G.M. Corp)

4. Lubricate drive end bushing with silicone lubricant, then slide armature and clutch assembly into place, at the same time engaging shift lever with clutch. On non-integral starters, the shift lever may be installed in the drive gear housing first. Install the center bearing screws and shift lever pivot bolt on the diesel starter.
5. Position field frame over armature and apply sealer (silicone) between frame and solenoid case. Position frame against drive housing, making sure brushes are not damaged in the process.
6. Lubricate commutator end bushing with silicone lubricant, place a washer on the armature shaft and slide commutator end frame onto shaft. Install through bolts and tighten. On the diesel starter, install the insulator, then the end frame.
7. Reconnect field coil connector/s to the solenoid motor terminal. Install solenoid mounting screws, if so equipped.
8. Check pinion clearance; it should be 0.010-0.140 in. with the pinion in cranking position on all models.

Alternator System Service

PRELIMINARY CHARGING SYSTEM INSPECTION

NOTE: *Before performing any tests on the charging system, these precautions should be taken to ensure the accuracy of the tests in this section.*

1. Check the condition of the alternator belt and tighten it if necessary.
2. Clean the battery cable connections at the battery. Make sure that the connections between the battery wires and the battery clamps are good. Reconnect the negative terminal only, and proceed to the next step.
3. With the key off, insert a test light between the positive terminal on the battery and the disconnected positive battery terminal clamp. If the test light comes on, there is a short in the electrical system of the car. The short has to be repaired before proceeding. if the light fails to glow, reconnect the clamp and proceed to the next step.

NOTE: *Alternators with transistorized regulators sometimes draw a slight current even when the key is turned off. To properly check these systems for a short, the regulator must be disconnected. Also, on cars equipped with an electric clock, disconnect the lead wire from the clock.*

4. Check the charging system wiring for breaks or shorts.
5. Check the battery to make sure that it is fully charged and in good condition.

CHRYSLER ISOLATED FIELD ALTERNATOR (ELECTRONIC REGULATOR)

The Chrysler isolated field alternator derives its name from its construction. Both of the brushes are insulated from ground and there is no heat sink connection, thereby isolating the internal field.

Troubleshooting

NOTE: *See the "Preliminary Charging System Inspection" section before proceeding further. Make sure that the continuous running ventilation blower, if equipped, is disconnected. This blower will run with the key turned on even if the blower controls are off unless disconnected.*

Fusible Links

Chrysler Corporation cars have fusible links connected to the starter relay.

Charging Circuit Resistance Test

NOTE: *The following test requires the*

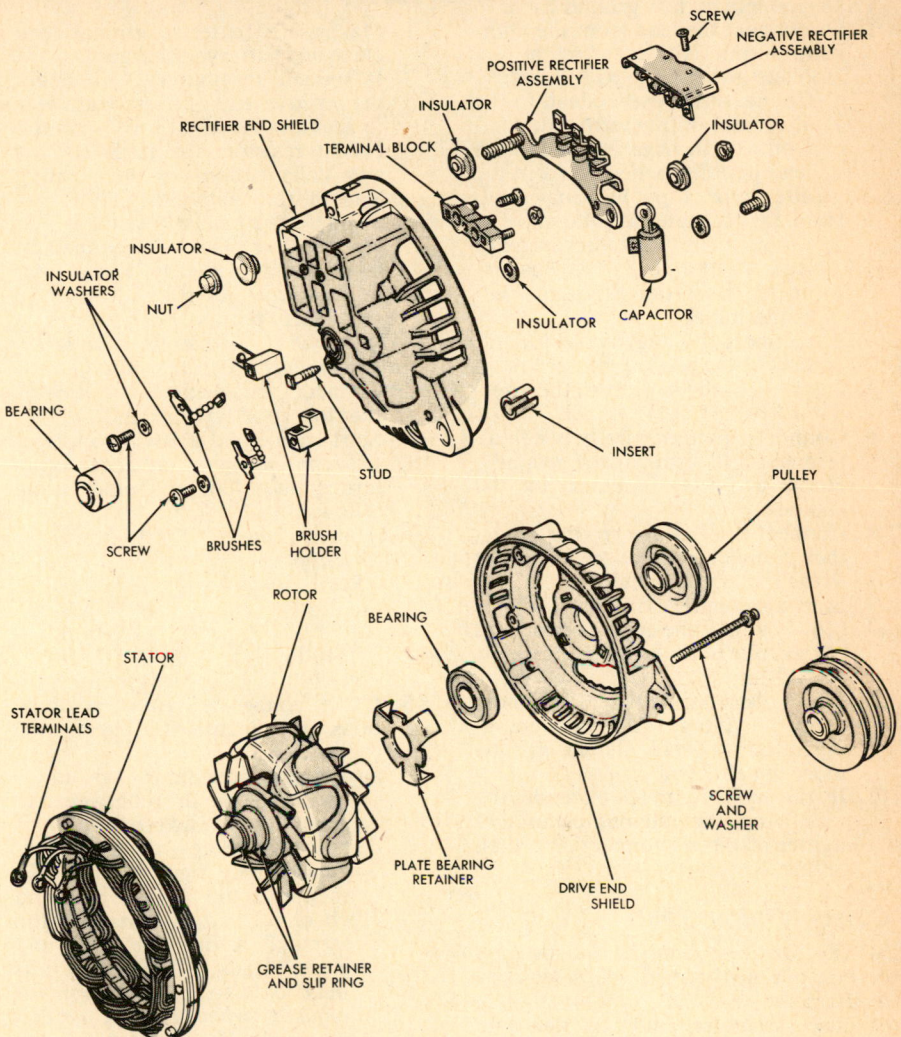

Chrysler alternator assembly—1972-75 (© Chrysler Corp.)

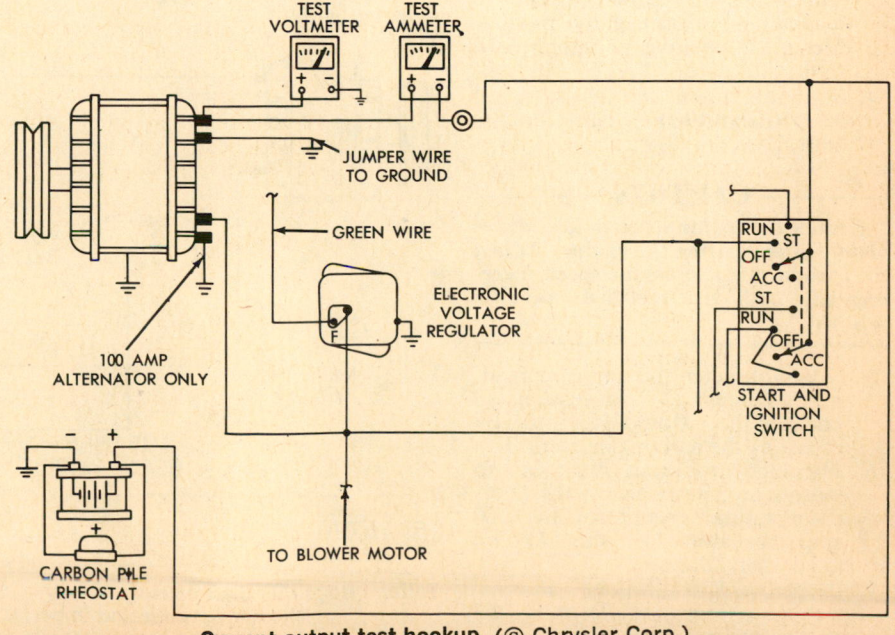

Current output test hookup (© Chrysler Corp.)

use of a carbon pile rheostat, a voltmeter, and an ammeter.

1. Disconnect battery ground cable.
2. Disconnect the lead from the alternator output (BATT.) terminal.
3. Hook up an ammeter as follows:
   a. Connect the positive lead to the alternator output terminal.
   b. Connect the negative lead to the lead just disconnected from the alternator output terminal.
4. Hook up voltmeter as follows:
   a. Connect the positive voltmeter lead to the lead just disconnected from the alternator output terminal.
   b. Connect the negative voltmeter lead to the positive battery post.
5. Disconnect the lead from the alternator field (FLD.) terminal.
6. Connect a jumper wire between alternator field terminal and ground.
7. Hook up a tachometer to the engine.
8. Connect the battery ground cable, then connect a carbon pile rheostat to the battery terminals.
9. Start the engine and allow to idle.
10. Slowly adjust the engine speed and carbon pile until the ammeter registers 20 amps.
11. The voltmeter reading will now show the voltage drop in the charging circuit. There should not be more than 0.7 volt drop.
12. If the voltage drop exceeds 0.7 volt, stop the engine, clean and tighten all circuit connections, then repeat the test.

Current Output Test

NOTE: *This test requires the use of a carbon pile rheostat, a voltmeter, and an ammeter.*

1. The ammeter and carbon pile hookup should remain the same as for the circuit resistance test.
2. Connect the voltmeter negative lead to the battery negative post.
3. Move the positive voltmeter lead to the alternator "BATT" post.
4. Start the engine and adjust speed to 1250 rpm; 900 rpm for the 100 amp alternator.

--- **CAUTION** ---

Reduce the engine speed to idle immediately after starting the engine. Adjust the carbon pile and engine speed incrementally until the specified speed is reached.

5. Note voltmeter and ammeter readings. Maintain a 15 volt reading (13 volts for the 100 amp alternator) by adjusting the carbon pile control.
6. The current output must be no more than 3 amps below the alternator rating, except for the 100 amp alternator which should be no lower than 72 amps.
7. If below specifications, internal trouble is indicated. Remove the alternator for further testing.

Electronic Voltage Regulator Test

1. Make sure battery terminals are clean and battery is charged.
2. In models through 1974, connect the positive lead of a test voltmeter to ignition Terminal No. 1 of the ballast resistor. On 1975-76 Dart and Valiant, connect the positive lead of the voltmeter to the terminal on the ballast resistor which has a blue or black wire connected to it. On all other 1975 and later models, connect the voltmeter to the battery positive post.

NOTE: *Don't remove the connector from the ballast resistor terminal.*

3. Connect the negative voltmeter lead to a good *body* ground.
4. Start engine and allow it to idle at 1250 rpm, all lights and accessories turned off. Voltage should be as follows:

Ambient Temp. 1/4 in. from Regulator	Voltage
−20°F.	14.9-15.9
80°F.	13.9-14.6
140°F.	13.3-13.9
over 140°F.	less than 13.6

5. If the voltage is *below* specifications or fluctuates, check the following:
   a. Voltage regulator ground—check voltage drop between regulator cover and ground.
   b. Harness wiring—disconnect regulator plug (ign. switch off), then turn on ign. switch and check for battery voltage at the terminal having the blue and green leads. *Wiring harness must be disconnected from the regulator when checking individual leads.* If no voltage is present in either lead, the problem is in the car wiring or alternator field.

c. Field-loads relay on 1975-76 models except Dart and Valiant—the test follows.
6. If Step 5 tests showed on malfunctions, install a new regulator and repeat Step 4.
7. If voltage is *above* specifications (Step 4), or fluctuates, check the following:
   a. Ground between regulator and body, and between body and engine.
   b. Ignition switch circuit between switch and regulator.
8. If voltage is still more than 1/2 volt above specifications, install a new regulator and repeat Step 4.

Field-Loads Relay Test

On all 1975-76 Chrysler Corporation cars except Dart and Valiant, the charging system wiring circuit was redesigned to protect the battery from overcharging by the addition of an ignition switch operated field-loads relay. This unit reduces voltage drop between charging system components, making the regulator more sensitive to battery requirements and decreasing the possibility of overcharging. The relay is only used in 1975-76.

1. Disconnect the wiring harness connector at the voltage regulator. Ground the negative lead of the voltmeter.
2. Turn the ignition switch on but don't start the engine.
3. Measure the voltage at the terminals of the disconnected wiring harness connector with the positive lead of the voltmeter. Voltage here should be the same as at the battery.
4. If there is battery voltage at the terminals, the unit is working properly.
5. If battery voltage is not obtained, check all wiring and connections

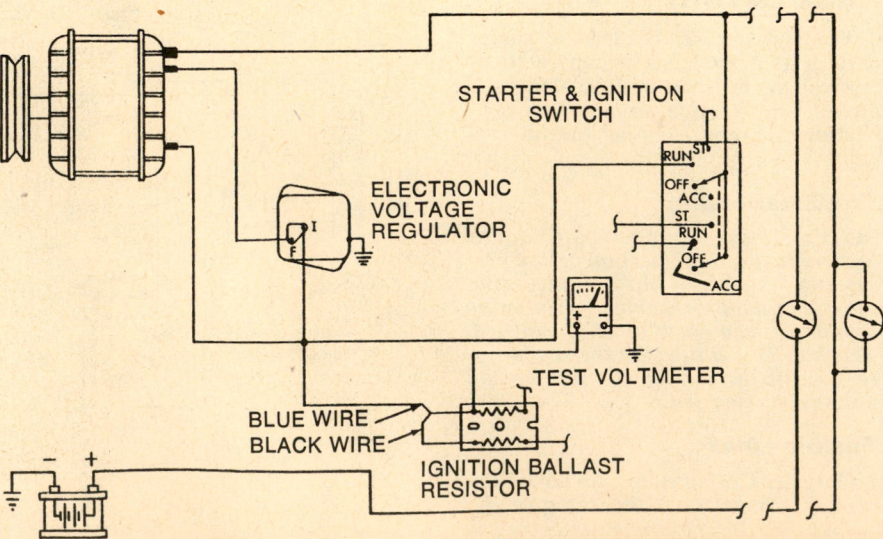

Voltage Regulator Test hook-up through 1974; right ammeter gauge for Monaco, Fury, Chrysler and Imperial, left for all other models
(© Chrysler Corp)

for damage. If they are alright, the unit must be replaced.

DELCOTRON 5.5 SERIES 1D AND 6.2 SERIES 2D

(General Motors Corporation)

The Delcotron continuous output AC generator consists of two major parts—the stator and the rotor. The stator is composed of many turns of wire on the inside of a laminated core that is attached to the generator frame. The rotor is mounted on bearings at each end. Two brushes carry current through slip rings to the field coils, which are wound on the rotor shaft.

The 5.5 Series 1D Delcotron is similar in operation to the 6.2 Series 2D perforated stator Delcotron. Where differences exist, the two units are mentioned separately.

Six diodes, mounted on internal heat sinks, change the AC current output into DC current. This current is controlled by the regulator. The regulator is a double-contact unit combined with a field relay or a triple-contact unit containing an indicator lamp relay as well as the field relay and voltage relay. Transistor regulators were also used in production intermittently.

On high-output Delcotron units, the regulator incorporates a field discharge diode.

These alternators were last used in 1972. Starting 1973, the Delco 10-SI became the standard GM alternator.

Troubleshooting

NOTE: *See the "Preliminary Charging System Inspection" section before proceeding further. Make sure that the con-* *tinous running blower, if equipped, is disconnected. This blower will run with the key on even if the blower control is off.*

Indicator Light Circuit Check:

Check the indicator light for normal operation:

Ignition Switch Condition	Light Condition	Engine Condition
Off	Off	Stopped
On	On	Stopped
On	Off	Running

If the alternator light is operating properly, proceed to the next section. If one of the following conditions exists, proceed as directed:

A. *Ignition Switch off, light stays on*: Disconnect leads from number 1 and 2 terminals. If the light remains on, there is a short between these two leads. If the lamp goes out, replace the rectifier bridge.

B. *Ignition switch on, light off, engine not running*: This condition can be caused by the defects listed in A., by reversal of number 1 and 2 leads at the alternator, or by an open circuit. If the circuit is open proceed as follows:

1. Connect a voltmeter from no. 2 alternator terminal to ground. If a reading is obtained, proceed to the next step. If a zero reading is obtained, repair the circuit between no. 2 terminal and the battery. If the light comes on, no further testing is necessary.
2. With the ignition switch on and with no. 1 and 2 terminals disconnected at the alternator, momen-

tarily ground no. 1 terminal lead.

———— CAUTION ————
Do not ground no. 2 Lead.

If the light still doesn't light, check for a blown fuse or fusible link, burned out bulb, defective bulb socket, or an open no. 1 lead circuit between generator and ignition switch.

3. If the lamp lights, remove the ground at no. 1 terminal, and with no. 1 and 2 terminals connected to the alternator, insert a screwdriver into the test hole at the back of the alternator to ground the winding.
4. If the light does not come on, check the connection between the wiring harness and no. 1 terminal of the alternator. If the connection is alright, disassemble the alternator and check the brushes, slip rings, and field winding.
5. If a light now comes on, and a reading was obtained in step 1, replace the regulator.

C. *Switch on, Light on, Engine Running.* The causes for this condition are covered in Charging System Tests, Low Charging Rate.

Fusible Links

There are four fusible links on all GM cars.

1. The 14 gauge wire that runs from the junction block to the positive battery terminal serves as a fusible link.
2. There is a second link in the circuit between the horn relay and the ignition switch.
3. A third link is in the wire running to the No. 3 voltage regulator ter-

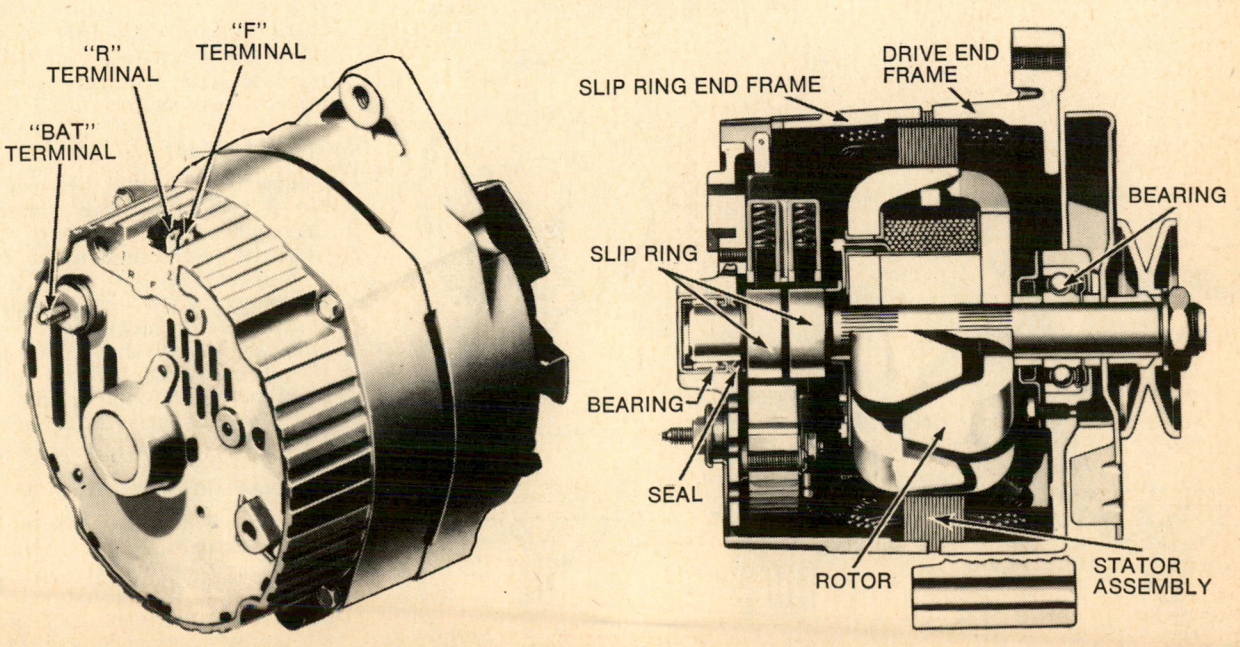

Model 1 D Delcotron alternator (© G.M. Corp.)

minal. It's purpose is to protect the regulator contacts and the alternator field circuit.

4. The fourth link is connected between the main junction block and the horn relay.

These links must be inspected before proceeding with troubleshooting.

Charging System Operation

NOTE: *If the current indicator is to give an accurate reading, the battery cables must be the same gauge and length as the original equipment.*

1. With the engine running and all electrical systems turned off, place a current indicator over the positive battery cable.
2. If a charge of about 5 amps is recorded, the charging system is working. If a draw of about 5 amps is recorded, the system is not working. The needle moves toward the battery when a charge condition is indicated, and away from the battery when a draw condition is indicated. If a draw is indicated, proceed with further testing. If an excessive charge (10-15 amps) is indicated, check for an overcharge, caused by a faulty regulator.

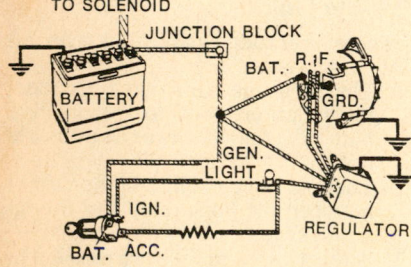

Typical Delcotron circuit diagram
(© Chevrolet Div., G.M. Corp)

Indicator Light Circuit Testing

The indicator light is important in AC charging systems, for it provides initial field excitation current to the alternator. The light goes out when the field relay closes, which applies battery current to both sides of the bulb. If the light does not go on when key is turned, the bulb could be faulty, there could be an open circuit in the wiring or a positive diode in the alternator could be shorted to ground.

1. Disconnect plug from regulator and connect a test light between terminal No. 4 (in plug) and ground. Turn on ignition switch and observe the light. If light does not go on, check bulb socket or wiring between switch and regulator plug. If light goes on, check regulator, wiring between regulator F terminal and alternator, or Delcotron itself.
2. Disconnect jumper wire at ground end and reconnect to F terminal in plug. Turn on ignition for a second and note light. If light goes on, problem is in regulator. If light does not go on, problem is in wire between F terminals (regulator and alternator.)
3. Disconnect light at plug F terminal and reconnect the free end to F terminal at alternator. Turn on ignition switch for a second and note light. If light goes on, the problem is an open circuit in the wire connecting the regulator and alternator F terminals. If light does not go on, the alternator field windings are defective.

   If the indicator light does not extinguish when engine is started, check for a loose drive belt, faulty field relay, faulty alternator, open parallel resistance wire (usually

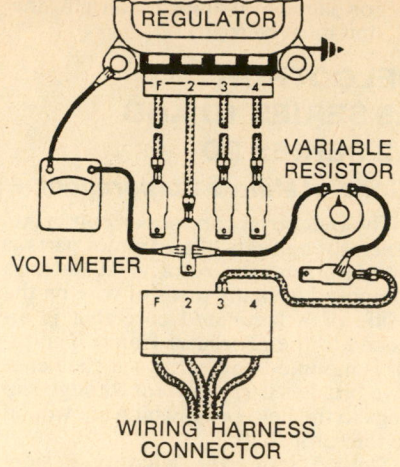

Testing field relay closing voltage
(© Chevrolet Div., G.M. Corp)

shows up at idle). If the light stays on with the key turned off, an alternator positive diode is shorted to ground.

Isolation Test

1. Disconnect the wiring harness from the voltage regulator. With a jumper wire connect the F wire to the no. 3 wire in the wire harness plug.
2. Connect a voltmeter across the battery terminals, the positive voltmeter lead to the positive battery terminal, and the negative lead to the negative terminal. Record the reading.
3. Start the engine. Do not race the engine.
4. Gradually raise engine speed to 1500-2000 rpm. The reading on the voltmeter should increase one to two volts over the initial reading. If there is no increase in the reading, repair the alternator. If there is an increase in the voltmeter reading, replace the regulator.

Field Relay Test

1. Connect a voltmeter between the No. 2 terminal and the ground on the regulator.
2. Start the engine and run at about 1500-2000 RPM.
3. If voltmeter reads zero, check circuit connecting regulator terminal No. 2 and Delcotron R terminal.
4. If voltage exceeds closing voltage (field relay), and light remains on, field relay is faulty and must be checked.

Field Relay Adjustment

1. Connect a voltmeter between No. 2 regulator terminal and ground.
2. To adjust, connect a 50 ohm rheostat between wiring harness terminal No. 3 and regulator terminal No. 2 after disconnecting the spade lug on the end of the No. 2 regulator terminal wire. Connect a volt-

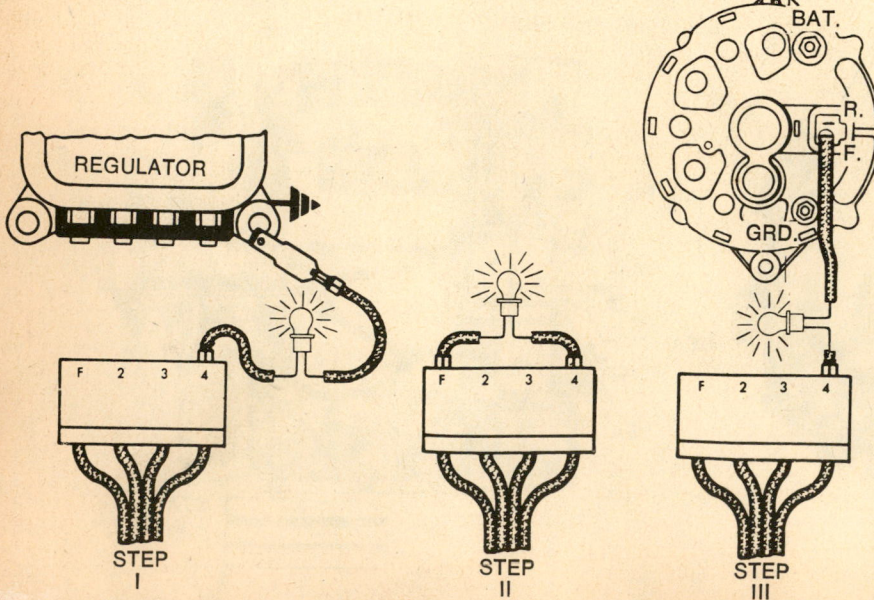

Initial field excitation circuit test hook-ups (© Chevrolet Div., G.M. Corp)

meter between regulator terminal No. 2 and ground, then turn the resistor to "open" position, turn off ignition switch and slowly decrease resistance until relay closes (noting voltage at this point). Voltage can be adjusted by bending heel iron.

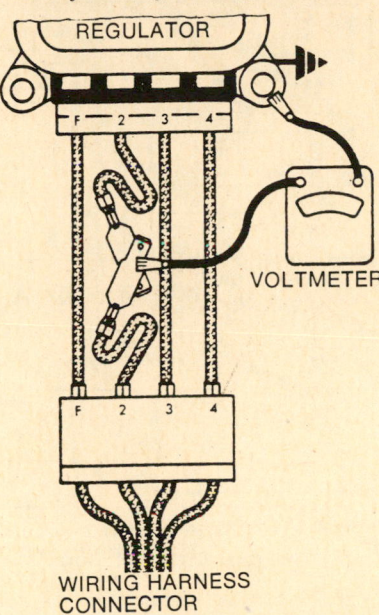

Testing field relay
(© Chevrolet Div., G.M. Corp)

Field Circuit Resistance Testing

The resistance wire is an integral part of the ignition wiring harness. The wire cannot be soldered; and connections must be made using crimp-type connectors. Resistance is 10 ohms, $6\frac{1}{4}$ watts.

1. Connect a voltmeter between the wiring harness terminal No. 4 and ground.
2. Turn on ignition switch, needle must indicate or resistor is open.

Delcotron Current Output Test

NOTE: *Disconnect battery ground ca-*

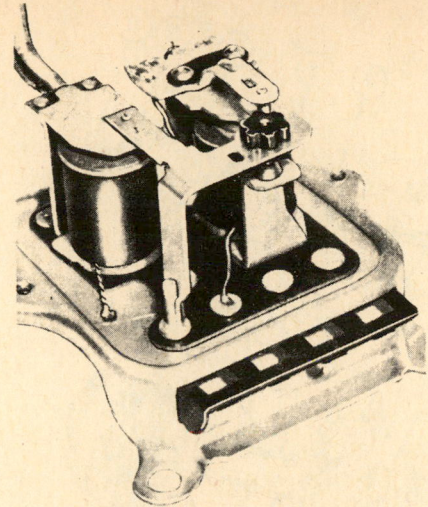

Adjusting field relay closing voltage
(© Chevrolet Div., G.M. Corp)

ble while making test connections, then reconnect cable after completing Step 5. Disconnect battery ground cable again before removing test set-up. This test yields the same information as the isolation test but requires the use of an ammeter and a carbon pile.

1. Disconnect lead from BAT. terminal of Delcotron.
2. Hook an ammeter to the lead just disconnected, and to the BAT. terminal of the Delcotron.
3. Hook up the voltmeter leads to the BAT. terminal and a good ground on the alternator.
4. Disconnect the lead from the FR. terminal of the Delcotron.
5. Hook up a jumper wire between BAT. and F terminals of the Delcotron.
6. With a carbon pile load control hooked up to the battery posts, start the engine and set engine to 1,500 rpm, while adjusting carbon pile to obtain 14 volts. With a 6.2 in. alternator, only 600-800 rpm is required.

─── CAUTION ───

Be careful not to exceed the recommended regulator voltage setting. This is controlled by the carbon pile load.

---

7. Ammeter should read within 10% of rated output, as stamped on frame of each unit.

DELCOTRON 10-SI
(General Motors Corp.)

This system is an integrated AC generating system containing a built-in voltage regulator.

The regulator is mounted inside the slip ring end frame. All regulator components are enclosed in an epoxy molding, and the regulator cannot be adjusted. Rotor and stator tests are the same as for the 5.5 Delcotron, covered previously.

This alternator became standard equipment on all GM cars in 1973, and is also used in some American Motors cars starting 1975. Starting 1976, it is used only on four and six cylinder AMC cars.

Troubleshooting

NOTE: *See the "Preliminary Charging System Inspection" section before proceeding further. Make sure that the continuous running blower, if equipped is disconnected. This blower will run with the key on even if the blower control is off, unless disconnected.*

Charging System Test—Low Charging Rate

1. After battery condition, drive belt tension, and wiring terminals and connections have been checked, charge the battery fully and perform the following test:
2. Connect a test voltmeter between the alternator BAT. terminal and ground, ignition switch on. Connect the voltmeter in turn to alternator terminals No. 1 and No. 2 the

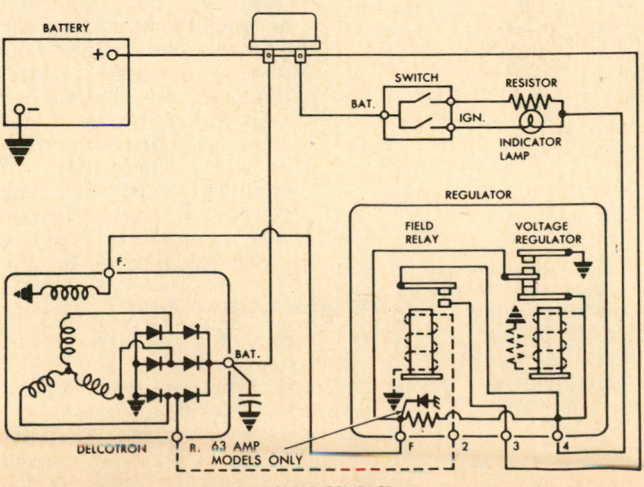

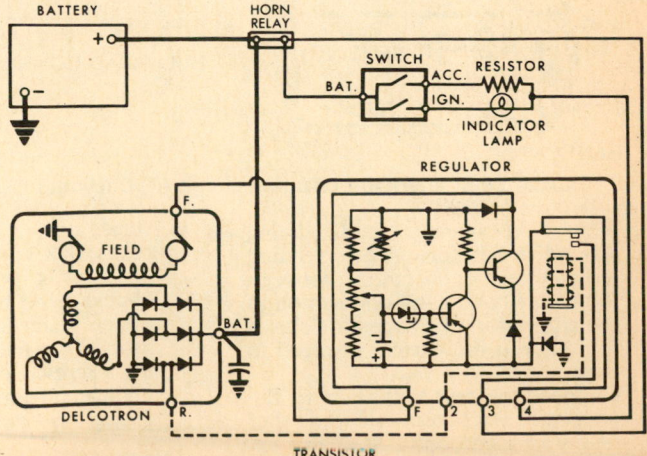

Voltage regulator circuit diagrams (© Chevrolet Div., G.M. Corp)

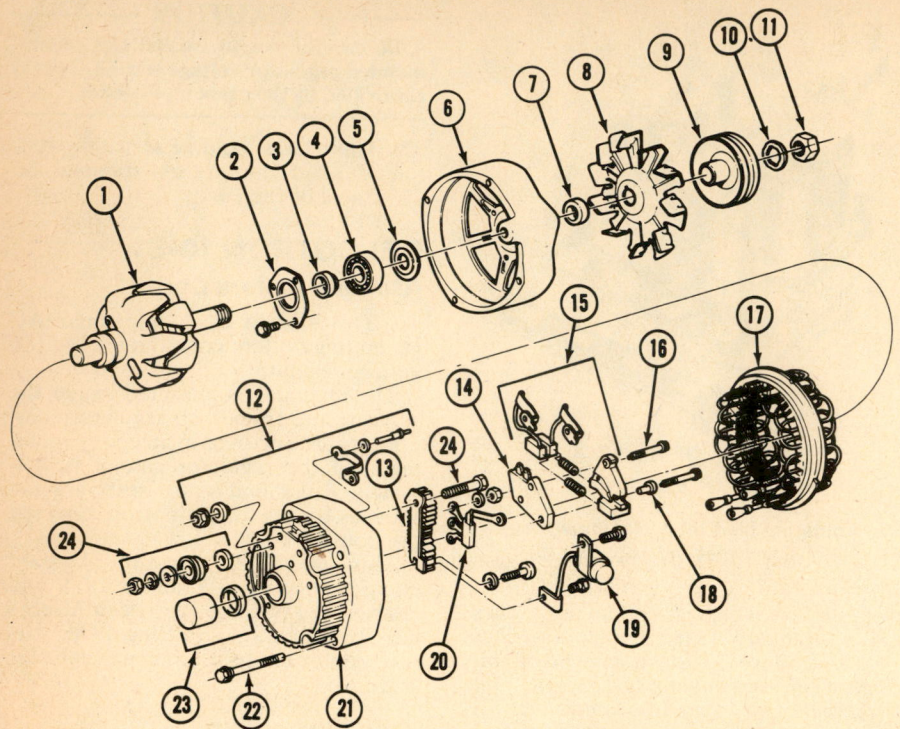

Delcotron 10SI alternator—exploded view (© American Motors Corp.)

1 Rotor
2 Front bearing retainer
3 Inner collar
4 Bearing
5 Washer
6 Front housing
7 Outer collar
8 Fan
9 Pulley
10 Lockwasher
11 Pulley nut
12 Terminal assembly
13 Rectifier bridge
14 Regulator
15 Brush assembly
16 Screw
17 Stator
18 Insulating washer
19 Capacitor
20 Diode trio
21 Rear housing
22 Through bolt
23 Bearing and seal assembly
24 Terminal assembly

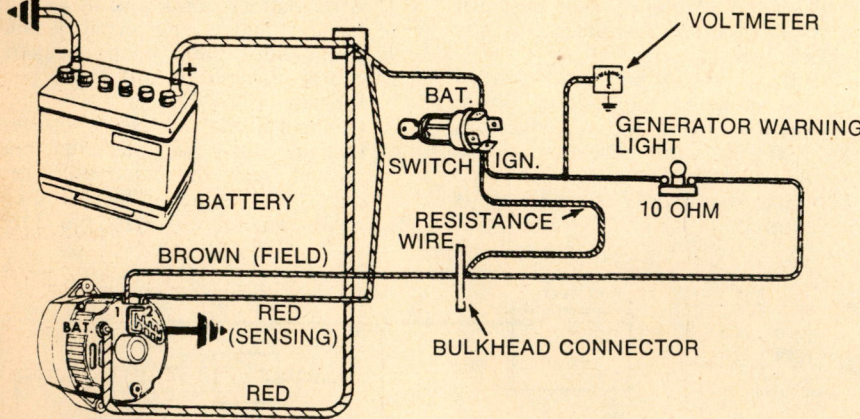

Typical 10-SI alternator charging circuit (© Chevrolet Div., G.M. Corp.)

other voltmeter lead being grounded as before. A zero reading indicates an open circuit between the battery and each connection at the alternator. If this test discloses no faults in the wiring, proceed to Step 3.

3. Connect the test voltmeter to the alternator BAT. terminal (the other test lead to ground), start the engine and run at 1,500-2,000 rpm with all lights and electrical acces-

sories turned on. If the voltmeter reads 12.8 volts or greater, the alternator is good and no further checks need be made. If the voltmeter reads less than 12.8 volts, ground the field winding by inserting a screwdriver into the test hole in the end frame.

CAUTION

Do not force tab more than 3/4 in. into end frame.

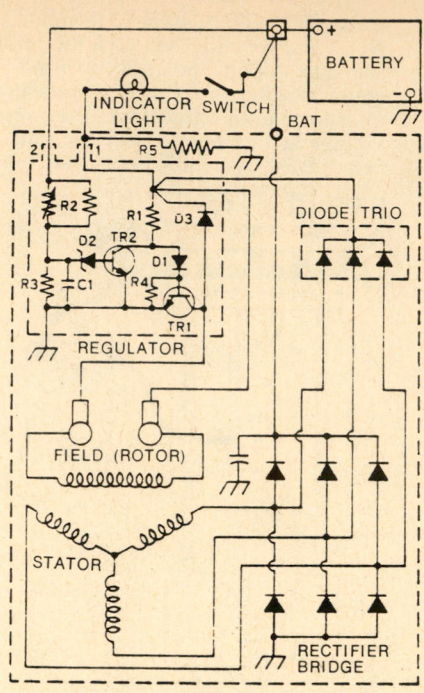

Typical 10-SI charging system circuitry
(© Chevrolet Div., G.M. Corp.)

a. If voltage increases to 13 volts or more, the regulator unit is defective.
b. If voltage does not increase significantly, alternator is defective.

Charging System Test—High Charging Rate

1. With the battery fully charged, connect a voltmeter between alternator terminal between alternator terminal no. 2 and ground. If the reading is zero, no. 2 circuit from the battery is open.
2. If no. 2 circuit is OK, but an obvious overcharging condition still exits, proceed as follows:
   a. Remove the alternator and separate the end frames.
   b. Connect a low-range ohmmeter between the brush lead clip and the end frame, then reverse the lead connections. If both readings are zero, either the brush lead clip is grounded or the regulator is defective. A grounded brush lead clip can be due to a damaged insulating sleeve or omission of the insulating washer.

Alternator Output Test

1. Disconnect the battery ground cable.
2. Disconnect the wire from the battery terminal on the alternator.
3. Connect your ammeter black (negative) lead to the wire removed in step 2, and the ammeter red (positive) lead to the battery terminal on the alternator.

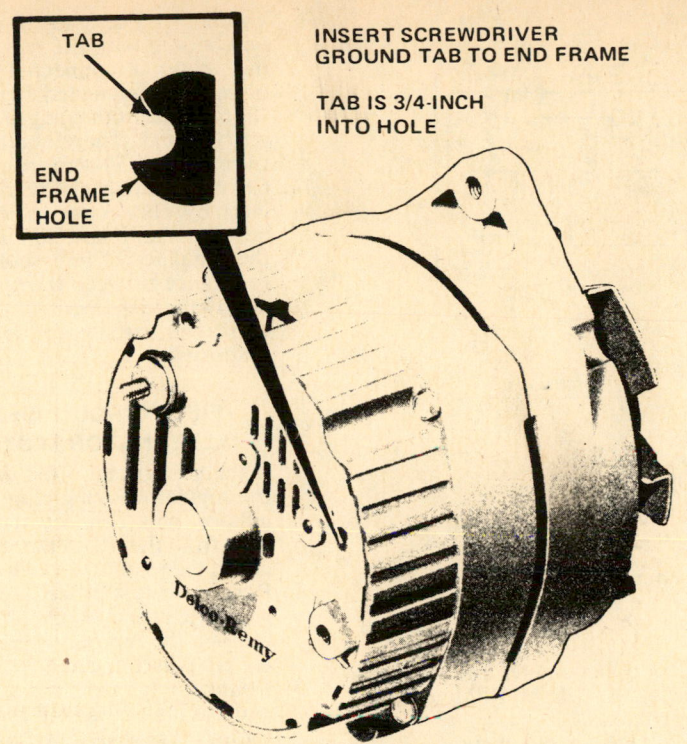

10-SI Delcotron end view
(© Chevrolet Div., G.M. Corp)

AUTOLITE/MOTORCRAFT ALTERNATOR WITH EXTERNAL REGULATOR
(Ford Motor Co.)

The Autolite/Motorcraft charging system is a negative ground system. It includes an alternator, an electromechanical or transistorized regulator, a charge indicator, and a storage battery.

— CAUTION —

Some 1974-76 Continental Mark IVs and Thunderbirds may have two alternators. The second alternator is a high voltage (120 volt) unit which is used to operate a special heated windshield and rear window. This alternator and its wiring are completely isolated from the regular charging system, and all of its connections are marked with warning tags. DO NOT attempt to service the alternator or its wiring and DO NOT confuse its wiring with that of the regular charging system. This system can produce a severe electrical shock.

4. Reconnect the battery ground cable and turn on all electrical accessories. If the battery is fully charged, bump the starter a few times to discharge it partially.
5. Start the engine and run it to obtain a maximum current reading on the ammeter.
6. If the current is within 10 amps of the rated output of the alternator, the alternator is working properly;

if the current is not within 10 amps, insert a screwdriver in the test hole in the end frame and use it to ground the tab in the test hole against the side of the hole.
7. If the current is now within 10 amps of the rated output, remove the alternator and have the voltage regulator replaced; if it is still below 10 amps of rated output, remove the alternator and have it tested further.

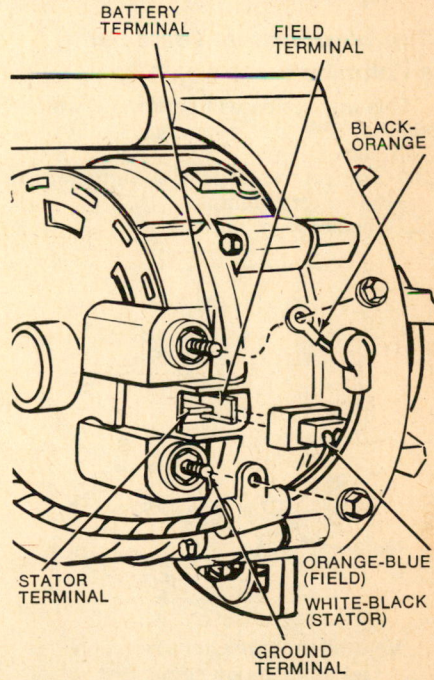

Wiring connections—Ford side terminal alternator   (© Ford Motor Co)

Ford alternators with external voltage regulators are available in two different types, rear terminal and side terminal. Both types provide the same function, the only difference aside from terminal mounting, is in the internal wiring. Ford alternators are also used in American Motors V8 cars starting 1976. All procedures are the same for both alternators, regardless of application.

Troubleshooting

NOTE: *See the "Preliminary Charging*

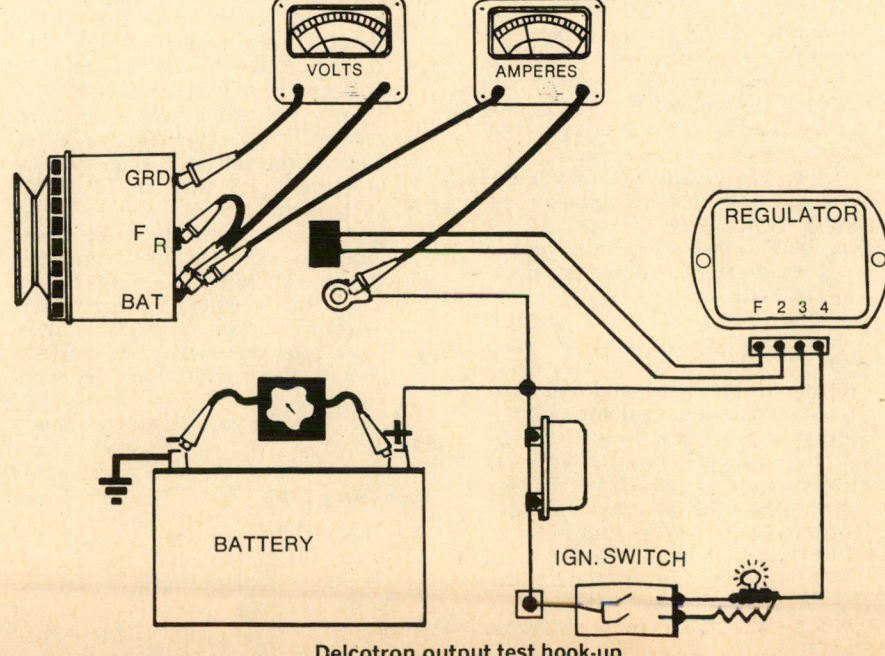

Delcotron output test hook-up

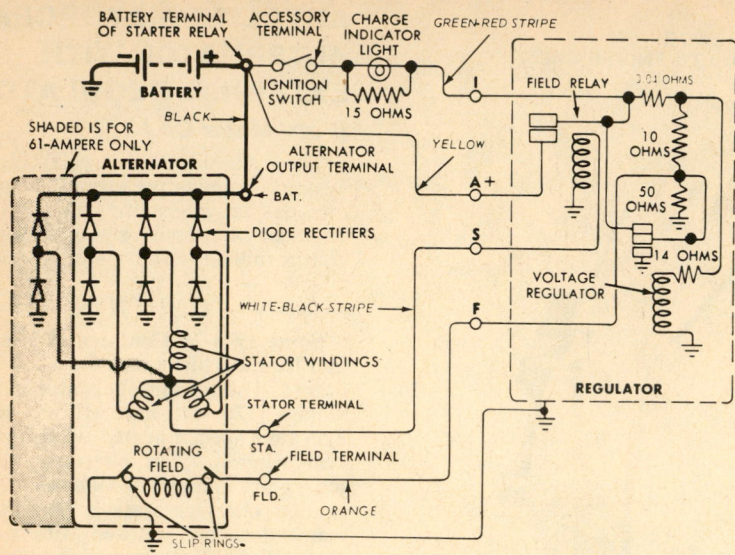

Charging system schematic with electro-mechanical regulator
and charging light
(© Ford Motor Co)

*System Inspection'' section before pro-
ceeding further.*

Charging System Tests Using a Voltmeter

This test series will determine which
element of the charging system is
malfunctioning.

1. Connect the leads of a voltmeter to
   the battery clamps.
2. Check the voltage.

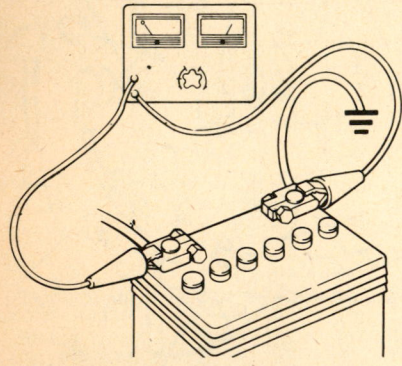

**Voltmeter connections isolation
test and ignition circuit test**
(© Ford Motor Co)

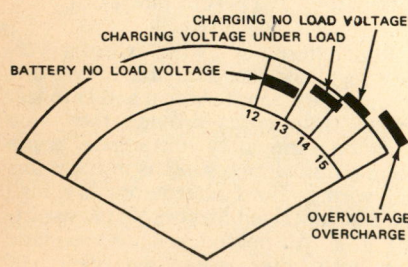

**VOLTMETER TEST
TYPICAL VOLTAGE BANDS SHOWN**

Voltmeter readings isolation test
(© Ford Motor Co)

3. Connect a tachometer and run the
   engine at about 1,500 RPM with no
   electrical load.
4. The voltage should increase 1 V
   but should not be more than 2 V
   above the previously recorded
   voltage.
5. With the engine running, turn on
   the heater and/or air conditioner
   blower motor (high speed) and the
   headlights (high beam).
6. Increase the engine speed to 2000
   RPM.
7. The voltmeter should now indicate
   a minimum of 0.5 V above the first
   recorded battery volage.
8. If the voltmeter indicates more
   than 2 volts above the battery voltage, stop the engine and check the
   regulator and alternator ground
   connections. Clean and tighten
   these connections and repeat the
   test.
9. If the overvoltage condition still
   exists, disconnect the wiring plug
   from the regulator and repeat the
   test.
10. If the overvoltage condition ceases
    replace or adjust the voltage regu-
    lator and repeat the test. If the
    problem is in the regulator, replac-
    ing or adjusting it should provide a
    normal reading.
11. If overvoltage still exists with the
    regulator plug disconnected, repair
    the short in the wiring harness be-
    tween the alternator and regulator;
    then replace the regulator and wir-
    ing plug and repeat the test.
12. If the voltmeter reading does not
    increase 0.5 V check for battery
    voltage at the alternator battery
    terminal and the regulator plug 'A'
    terminal. If there is no voltage, re-
    pair the wiring and repeat the test.
13. If the voltage does not increase by
    0.5 V, the field circuit must be
    checked to determine if it is

grounding. The field circuit should
be checked with the regulator wiring plug disconnected and an
ohmmeter connected between the
'F' terminal of the plug and the battery ground. There should be between 4 and 250 ohms resistance.
14. Check for an open wire in the regu-
    lator by connecting an ohmmeter
    between the 'I' and 'F' terminals of
    the regulator. There should be no
    resistance between the two termin-
    als. If there is about 10 ohms, the
    connector wire inside the regulator
    is shorted.

FIELD CIRCUIT AND ALTERNATOR TESTS

1. If the field circuit is ok, disconnect
   the regulator wiring plug at the regulator and connect the jumper
   wire from the 'A' to the 'F' terminals on the plug.
2. Repeat the test procedure. If there
   is still a problem (under voltage),
   remove the jumper wire and leave
   the plug disconnected.
3. Connect a jumper wire to the FLD
   and BAT terminals on the alternator and repeat the test. If the tests
   are now satisfactory, repair the
   wiring harness between the alternator and regulator. If there is no
   defect in the harness, prelace the
   alternator, and repeat the test.

DIODE TESTS ON CAR

1. Disconnect the electric choke and
   voltage regulator plug.
2. Connect a jumper between the 'A'
   and 'F' terminals of the plug; connect a voltmeter to the battery
   clamps, start the engine and let it
   run at idle.
3. Read and record the voltmeter
   reading; move the voltmeter lead
   to the 'S' terminal in the wiring
   harness and note the reading.
4. If the voltmeter reads 1/2 of battery
   voltage, the diodes are ok.
5. If the voltmeter reads approximately 1.5 V, the alternator has a
   shorted negative diode, or a
   grounded stator winding.
6. If the voltmeter reads about 1.5 V
   less than battery voltage, the alternator has a shorted positive diode.
7. If the voltmeter reads 1.0-1.5 V
   less than 1/2 battery voltage, there
   is an open positive diode; if it is
   1.0-1.5 V more than 1/2 battery
   charge, there is an open negative
   diode.

After the test is complete, reconnect
the choke.

Fusible Links

1. Check the fusible link located between the starter relay and the alternator. Replace the link if it is
   burned or open.
2. Ford, Mercury, Torino, Montego,
   Maverick, Comet, Bobcat, and

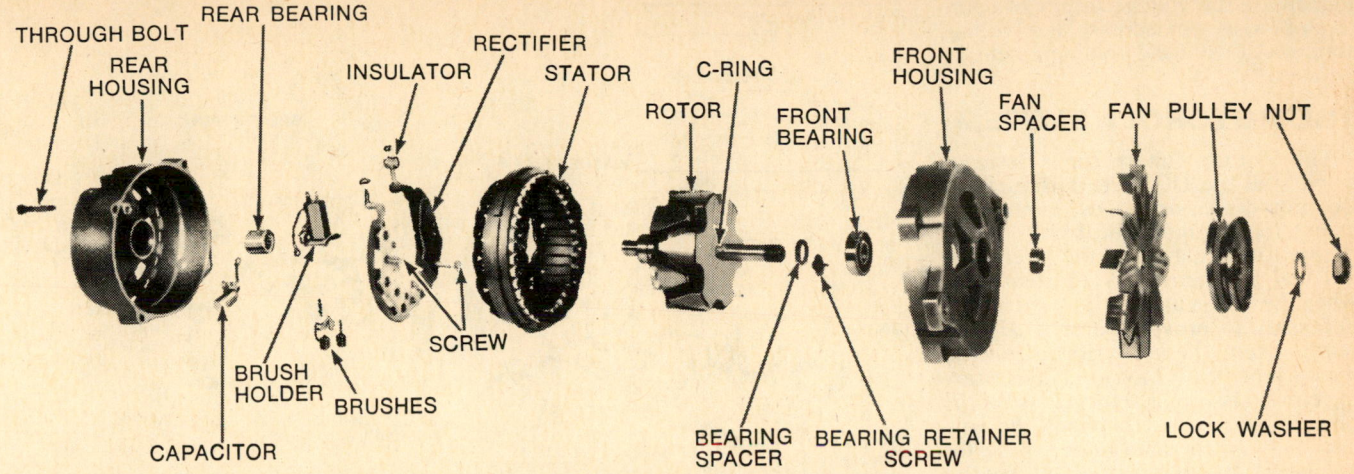

Ford side terminal alternator—exploded view (© Ford Motor Co)

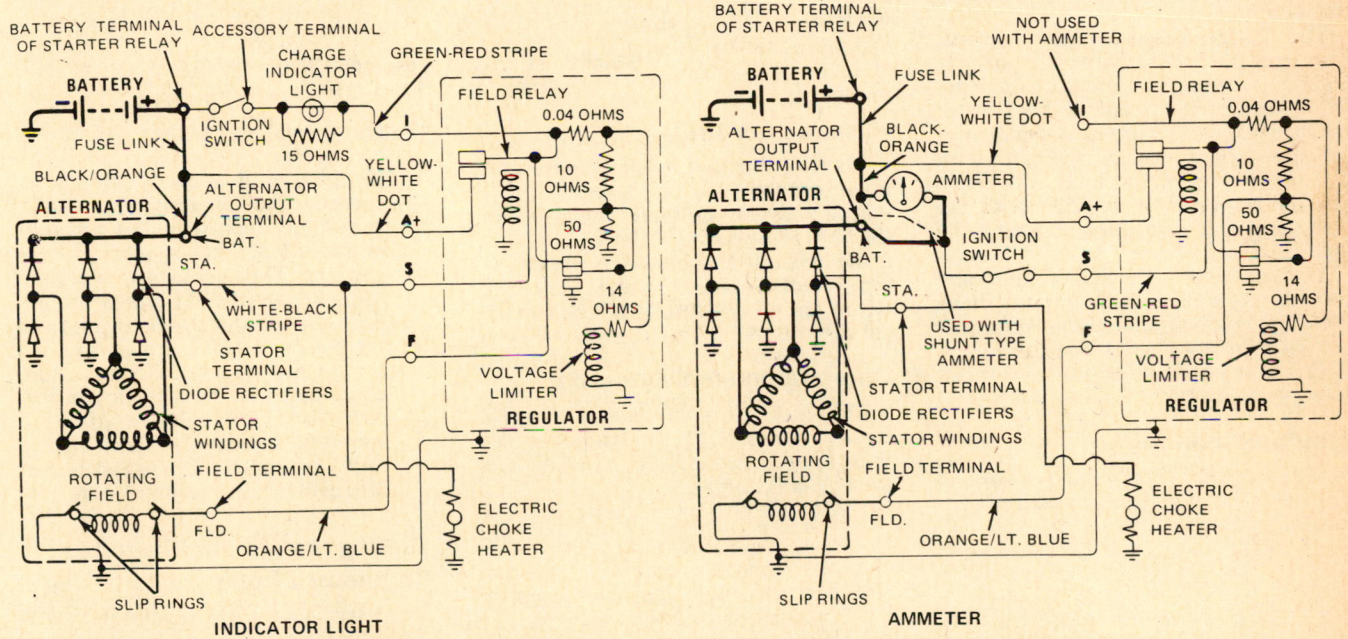

INDICATOR LIGHT

AMMETER

Charging circuit—Ford 90 amp side terminal alternator (© Ford Motor Co)

Pinto all have two fusible links between the starter relay and the alternator. Be sure to check both of them for damage.

Voltage Regulator Adjustments

Ford alternators with external voltage regulators can use either an electromechanical regulator or a transistorized voltage regulator. The electromechanical regulator is not adjustable, and has to be replaced as a unit when faulty; the transistorized voltage regulator is adjustable by means of a screw located in the transistor circuit board. The cover of the electromechanical regulator is held in place by non-removable rivets, while the transistorized regulator cover is held on by Phillips head screws.

To adjust, remove the cover of the regulator, and using a fiber or plastic rod, turn the adjusting screw clockwise

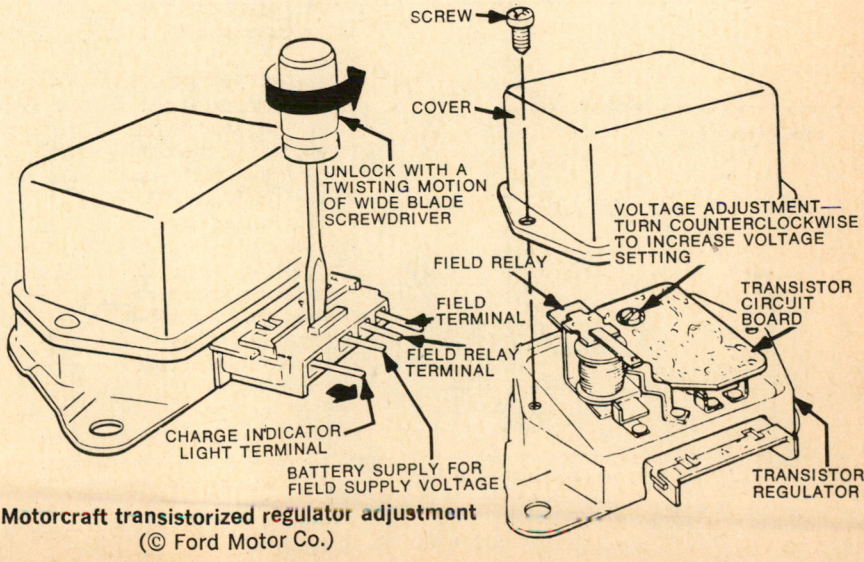

Motorcraft transistorized regulator adjustment (© Ford Motor Co.)

to increase the voltage setting or counterclockwise to decrease the voltage setting. Adjust in 0.2 volt increments.

THE MOTOROLA SYSTEM

The Motorola alternator is designed to pass all the DC current through an isolation diode, or diodes, mounted in an external aluminum heat sink.

Due to the nature of the alternator, residual magnetism is at near zero when the unit is at rest. It is, therefore, necessary to provide some small current to excite the field prior to generating current. With Motorola, this priming current is supplied by means of a 75 ohm resistance unit between the ignition coil and the alternator (inside the regulator). It is quite important that this resistance unit be checked and found satisfactory before proceeding with subsequent tests.

The charge indicator light on some cars operates in the same way as this resistor by furnishing the necessary initial field starting current. If this resistor circuit is open (a burned out indicator lamp) on some models, the alternator will not function. On later models, a resistor is placed in parallel with the bulb to provide excitation current if the bulb burns out.

The regulator is a sealed unit and should require no adjustment. It is therefore, recommended that nonfunctioning regulators be replaced.

This unit was last used on American Motors cars in 1975.

Troubleshooting

NOTE: *See the "Preliminary Charging System Inspection" section before proceeding further.*

Motorola alternator—exploded view
(© American Motors Corp)

Fusible Link Test

There are many fuse links in the car, however, the fuse link located in the wiring between the battery terminal of the horn relay to the main wire harness is the only one that concerns the charging system. This link protects the entire wiring harness. If it fails, all the electrical systems will fail to function.

Charging System Operation

NOTE: *If the current indicator is to give an accurate reading, the battery cables must be of the same gauge and length as the original equipment.*

1. With the engine running and all electrical systems off, place a current indicator over the positive battery cable.
2. If a charge of about 5 amps is recorded, the charging system is working. If a draw of about 5 amps is recorded, the system is not working. The needle moves toward the battery when a charge condition is indicated, and away from the battery when a draw condition is indicated. If a draw is indicated, continue to the next testing procedure. If an overcharge of 10-15 amps is indicated, check for a faulty regulator, or a bad ground at the regulator or the alternator.

Testing the Ignition Switch to Regulator Circuit

1. Disconnect the regulator wires from the regulator.
2. Turn the key. Using a test light or voltmeter, check for current between the voltage supply wire and ground. This wire is usually orange and has another wire connected to it, usually blue or orange with a tracer.
3. If current is present, this part of the system is OK. If no voltage is present, check for broken or shorted wiring, a bad indicator bulb, a bad fuse in the fuse panel, or a bad connection at the ignition switch or on the battery side of the starter relay.

Isolation Test

This test determines whether the regulator or the alternator is faulty, after the rest of the circuit is found to be in good working order.

1. Disconnect the regulator wiring harness from the regulator.
2. Connect a jumper wire from the voltage supply wire from the bat-

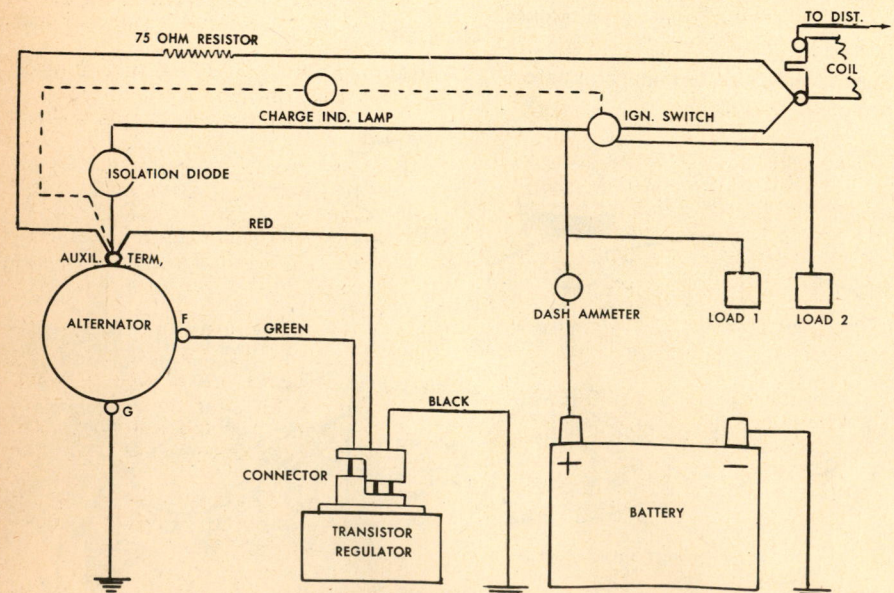

Typical Motorola alternator system charging circuit
(© American Motors Corp)

tery, orange, to the field wire for the alternator, green.

3. Connect a voltmeter to the battery. The positive voltmeter lead goes to the positive terminal and the negative lead to the negative terminal. Record the reading on the voltmeter.
4. Turn off all of the electrical systems and start the engine. Do not race the engine.
5. Gradually increase engine speed to 1500-2000 rpm. The voltmeter reading should increase above the previously recorded battery voltage reading by at least one to two volts. If there is no increase, the alternator is not working correctly. If there is an increase the voltage regulator needs to be replaced.

Field Current Draw Test

1. With battery disconnected, disconnect the wires from the alternator output terminal and the alternator field terminal.
2. With a field rheostat in the open position, connect its leads to the disconnected alternator output wire and to the positive lead of the test ammeter.
3. Connect the negative ammeter lead to the alternator field terminal.
4. Connect the positive voltmeter lead to the alternator field terminal.
5. Connect the negative voltmeter lead to the alternator ground terminal.
6. Reconnect the battery.
7. Start and run the engine at fast idle.
8. Adjust field rheostat to closed position, then note the voltmeter and ammeter readings.
9. Adjust field rheostat control to the open position.
10. Compare the readings obtained in Step 8 with manufacturers' specifications.
11. If readings are zero, there is an indication of trouble in the field coil, or the connections between field coil and slip ring.
12. If readings are low, there is probable trouble in the slip rings or brushes.
13. If readings are high, the field coil is probably shorted.
14. If readings are normal, on an alternator which failed to produce its rated output, the probable cause lies in the stator or diodes. Replace the alternator in this case.

Alternator Output Test (Alternator In Car)

1. Connect a voltmeter to the battery.
2. Start the engine and turn the lights on low beam.
3. Run the engine at 1000 RPM and observe the voltage reading for two minutes. If the voltage remains above 13 V, the alternator and regulator are ok. If not, proceed to

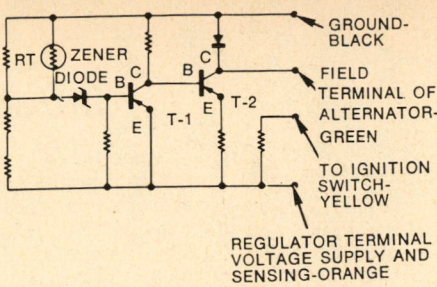

Voltage regulator circuit. RT is a thermistor that regulates voltage according to temperature
(© American Motors Corp)

the Regulator Bypass Test to determine which component is at fault.

Field Draw (Amperage) Test

This test determines if there is an open or short circuit in the alternator brush circuit.
1. Disconnect the voltage regulator.
2. Connect an ammeter between the positive battery post and the green wire leading to the insulated brush terminal of the alternator. Ground the black wire.
3. Turn the alternator rotor slowly by hand. The ammeter should indicate between $1\frac{1}{2}$ and 3 amperes. If the reading varies, the slip rings require cleaning. If the amperage is too high, remove the brush assembly and do continuity and isolation tests on it. Check the rotor field windings if the field draw is too low or high after testing the brush assembly and cleaning the slip rings.

Alternator Output (Regulator Bypass) Test

This test will determine whether the alternator or voltage regulator is at fault for a no or low charge condition.
1. Disconnect the voltage regulator and perform the Field Draw Test. After completing it, disconnect the ammeter.
2. Connect the voltmeter to the battery and start the engine and run it at idle.
3. Connect an ammeter between the battery positive post and the insulated brush on the alternator.
4. Observe the voltage reading while slowly increasing the engine RPM. If 16 volts can be obtained, the alternator is not bad. Do not exceed sixteen volts or component damage may occur. It may take a few minutes for a dead battery to achieve a reading of 16 volts.
5. If the reading does not reach 16 volts then the fault is in the alternator.

Diode Trio Test (on car)

This test will check the field diode assembly for marginal defects which may not affect alternator performance

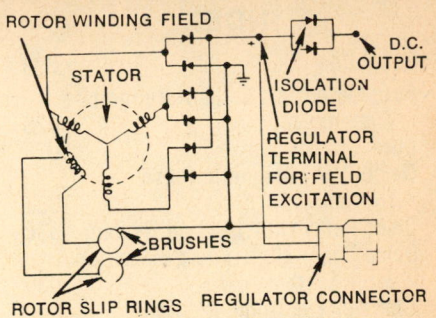

Alternator circuit—40 and 55 amp models
(© American Motors Corp)

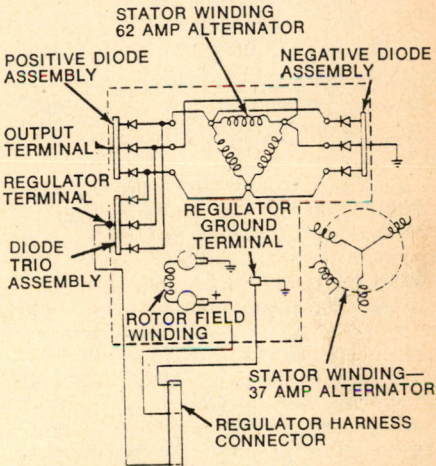

Alternator circuit—62 and 37 amp models
(© AMC)

but may cause the dash indicator light to glow.
1. Do the Regulator Bypass Test. If 16 volts can not be obtained from the alternator, this test's results will not be valid.
2. Start and idle the engine. Connect a voltmeter to the alternator (if no reading is obtained, switch the test leads).
3. Turn on the lights and blower (heater) unit and let them operate for about 2 minutes, then turn them off.
4. Check the meter reading. A good diode will read from zero to 0.2 volts. A reading above this indicates that the diodes are deteriorating. It is not necessary to replace them until the reading is above 0.6 volts.
5. If the meter pulsates, either the diode trio, the positive diode, or the soldered connections between them is beginning to break down. In either case the alternator will have to be disassembled and the diode tested.
6. If the reading is over 0.6 V. but the alternator output is alright, remove the diode trio for a bench test.
7. If the reading is less than 0.6 V. and the diode trio appears to be functioning properly, and the indicator light still glows, check the wiring connections for corrosion.

Electronic Ignition Systems

INDEX

The Ford-Motorcraft Solid-State Ignition System is a pulse triggered, breakerless, transistor controlled ignition system available on some late model 1973 460 V8 Lincolns; all 1974 models sold in the 49 states with a 400 or 460 V8; all 1974 six-cylinder and V8 models sold in California; and is standard equipment on all May 1974 and later Ford Motor Company models. The system utilizes most of the standard ignition components, but substitutes an amplifier module and magnetic pickup assembly for the conventional ignition contact points.

DURA SPARK

Starting 1977, the system was improved and renamed Dura Spark. There are two versions, in 1977: the higher output Dura Spark I for all California engines except the 2300 four, and Dura Spark II for all others. In 1978, only California cars with the 302 V8 (except the Versailles) have Dura Spark I. All other cars have Dura Spark II. The Versailles uses a modified Dura Spark II system which connects to its EEC system. Details on EEC can be found in the Emission Controls Unit Repair Section. The Dura Spark system is easily recognized by a two-piece, flat-topped distributor cap. Dura Spark II is very similar in design to the 1976 electronic system; the ballast resistor is changed from 1.35 to 1.10 ohms to boost output. Dura Spark I uses an all-new control module to sense current flow through the coil, adjusting "dwell" or coil on time for maximum spark intensity. If the module senses that the ignition switch is on but the distributor is not turning, it will turn the coil current off.

In 1978 some models have a special Dura Spark Dual Mode Timing ignition module. This module is equipped with either an altitude senser or an economy modulator. These systems modify the ignition timing to suit conditions. All other functions of the module remain the same. These modules can be identified easily; they have three connectors instead of the usual two.

Introduction

Since these systems do not contain ignition points which wear, ignition performance does not deteriorate with mileage. This, plus the fact that these systems can usually fire a fouled plug, helps to keep down exhaust emissions after a car leaves the factory. All 1973 and later Chrysler Corporation cars and all 1975 and later domestic cars have electronic ignition as standard equipment.

FORD-MOTORCRAFT SOLID-STATE IGNITION SYSTEM

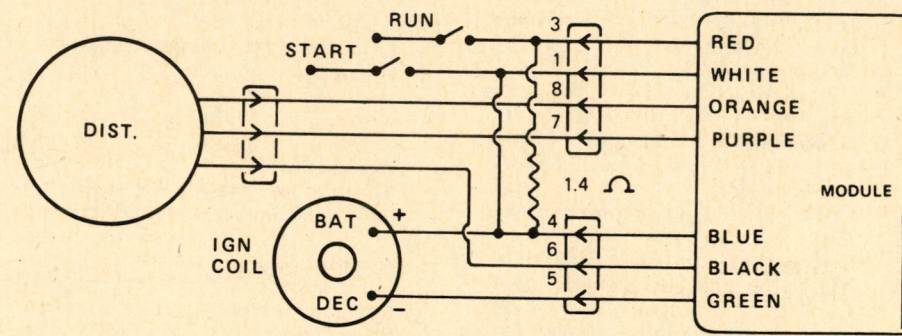

Electronic module schematic—solid-state ignition
(© Ford Motor Co)

Operation

With the ignition switch "on," the primary circuit is on and the ignition coil is energized. When the armature

IGNITION SWITCH

TERMINAL CONNECTOR

PRIMARY RESISTANCE WIRE

QUICK DISCONNECT

OIL FILLED COIL

SPARK PLUG

STARTER RELAY

AMPLIFIER MODULE

BREAKERLESS DISTRIBUTOR

BATTERY

CONNECTOR

━━━ PRIMARY CIRCUIT
▪▪▪▪ SECONDARY CIRCUIT

Ford-Motorcraft Solid-State Ignition System —basic wiring
(© Ford Motor Co)

"spokes" approach the magnetic pickup coil assembly, they induce a voltage which tells the amplifier to turn the coil primary current off. A timing circuit in the amplifier module will turn the current on again after the coil field has collapsed. When the current is "on," it flows from the battery through the ignition switch, the primary windings of the ignition coil, and through the amplifier module circuits to ground. When the current is off, the magnetic field built up in the ignition coil is allowed to collapse, inducing a high voltage into the secondary windings of the coil. High voltage is produced each time the field is thus built up and collapsed.

The high voltage flows through the coil high tension lead to the distributor cap where the rotor distributes it to one of the spark plug terminals in the distributor cap. This process is repeated for every power stroke of the engine.

Ignition system troubles are caused by a failure in the primary and/or the secondary circuit; incorrect ignition timing; or incorrect distributor advance. Circuit failures may be caused by shorts, corroded or dirty terminals, loose connections, defective wire insulation, cracked distributor cap or rotor, defective pick-up coil assembly or amplifier module, defective distributor points or fouled spark plugs.

If an engine starting or operating trouble is attributed to the ignition system, start the engine and verify the complaint. On engines that will not start, be sure that there is gasoline in the fuel tank and that fuel is reaching the carburetor. Then locate the ignition system problem by an oscilloscope test or by a spark intensity test.

Primary Circuit Testing

A breakdown or energy loss in the primary circuit can be caused by: defective primary wiring, loose or corroded connections, inoperative or defective magnetic pick-up coil assembly, or defective amplifier module.

A complete test of the primary circuit consists of checking the circuits in the ignition coil, the magnetic pick-up coil assembly and the amplifier module. Wiring harness checks will be included as a part of basic component circuit tests.

Always inspect connectors for dirt, corrosion or poor fit before assuming you have spotted a possible problem.

Troubleshooting

Make sure that the battery is fully charged before beginning tests. Perform a Spark Intensity Test.

NOTE: *On engines with a catalytic converter, no spark plug should be disconnected for more than 30 seconds to prevent fouling the converter.*
*Certain cylinders must not be disconnected while performing a spark inten-*sity test:
Nos. 1 or 8 on V8
Nos. 3 or 5 on inline 6
Nos. 1 or 4 on V6
Nos. 1 or 3 on inline 4.

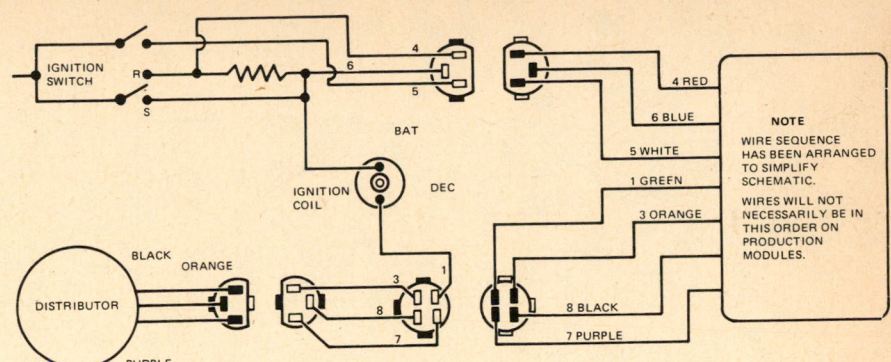

Electronic module schematic—solid-state ignition, 1975
(© Ford Motor Co.)

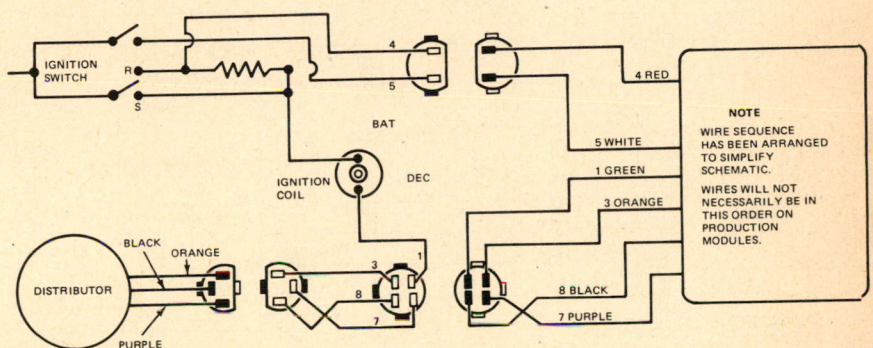

Electronic module schematic—solid-state ignition, 1976 and later
(© Ford Motor Co.)

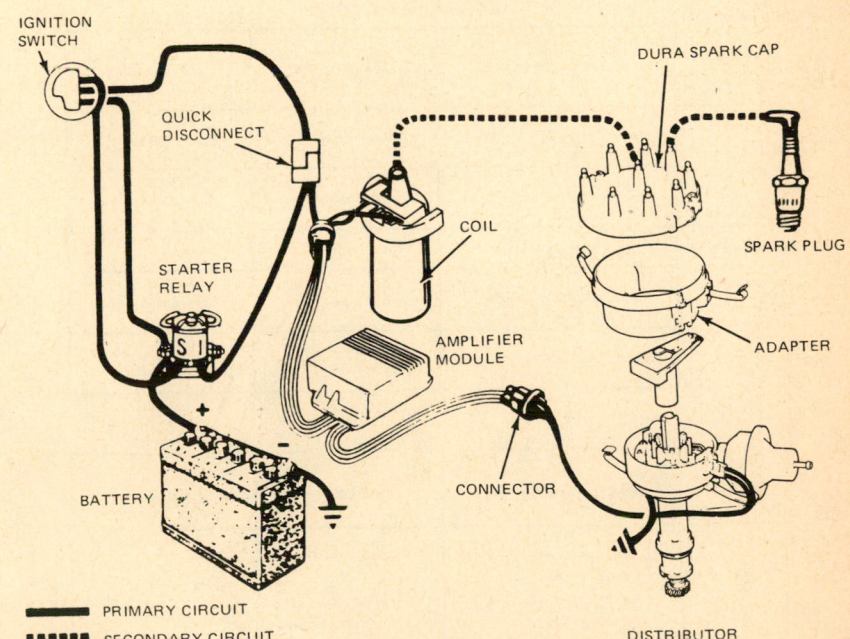

Dura Spark system basic wiring
(© Ford Motor Co.)

— **CAUTION** —

With Dura Spark II and the 1973-76 system, the amplifier module and coil are on whenever the ignition switch is on.

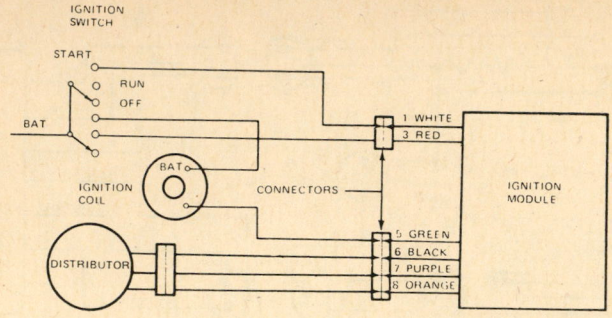

Electronic module schematic—Dura Spark I
(© Ford Motor Co.)

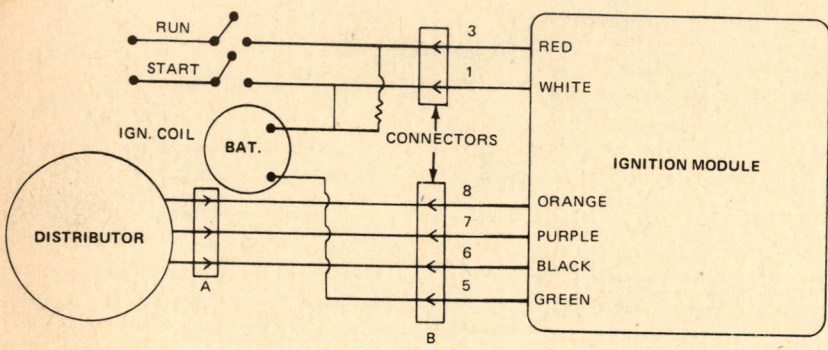

Electronic module schematic—Dura Spark II
(© Ford Motor Co.)

TROUBLE ISOLATION TESTS

	TEST VOLTAGE BETWEEN	SHOULD BE	IF NOT, CONDUCT
KEY ON	Pin # 3 and Engine Ground	Battery Voltage	Module Bias Test
	Pin # 5 and Engine Ground	Battery Voltage	Battery Source Test
CRANKING	Pin # 1 and Engine Ground	8 to 12 volts	Cranking Test
	Pin # 5 and Engine Ground	8 to 12 volts	Starting Circuit Test
	Pin # 7 and Pin # 8	½ volt A.C. or D.C. volt wiggle	Distributor Hardware Test

	TEST RESISTANCE BETWEEN	SHOULD BE	IF NOT, CONDUCT
KEY OFF	Pin # 7 and Pin # 8	400 to 800 ohms	Magnetic Pick-up (Stator) Test
	Pin # 6 and Engine Ground	0 ohms	
	Pin # 7 and Engine Ground	more than 70,000 ohms	
	Pin # 8 and Engine Ground	more than 70,000 ohms	
	Pin # 3 and Coil Tower	7000 to 13000 ohms	Coil Test
	Pin # 5 and Pin # 4	1.0 to 2.0 ohms	
	Pin # 5 and Engine Ground	more than 10.0 ohms	Short Test
	Pin # 3 and Pin # 4	1.0 to 2.0 ohms	Resistance Wire

Ford-Motorcraft Solid-State Ignition System diagnosis through 1974
(© Ford Motor Co)

Before troubleshooting the Dura Spark I system, make an Ignition Module Shut-Down Test as described later.

The first trouble isolation test will be conducted on the harness terminals, with the electronic module disconnected from the circuit. The pin or socket numbers shown in the schematic correspond to those shown in the diagnosis tables through 1977 only.

Make the following tests using a sensitive volt-ohmmeter. These tests will direct you to the proper follow-up test to determine the actual problem.

If the circuit checks good at all these test points, connect a known good electronic module in place of the vehicle module and again perform the spark intensity test. If the substitution corrects the malfunction again reconnect the vehicle module and perform the spark intensity test. If the malfunction still exists, the problem is in the module and it must be replaced. If the problem is gone, it may be in the wiring connectors.

If the substitute module does not correct the problem, reconnect the original module and make repairs elsewhere in the system.

DURA SPARK I IGNITION MODULE SHUT-DOWN TEST

1. Make sure that the module and coil connectors are tight.
2. Connect a voltmeter across the coil primary terminals. Set the meter on the 10 V scale. It should read 0.
3. Turn the ignition switch on and watch the meter.
4. If the meter momentarily shows a reading, then goes back to 0, the shut-down circuit is working. You can go on to the system diagnosis tests.
5. If the voltage reads between 4 and 12 volts, try another module and repeat the test.
6. If there was no reading at all, go on to the system diagnosis tests.

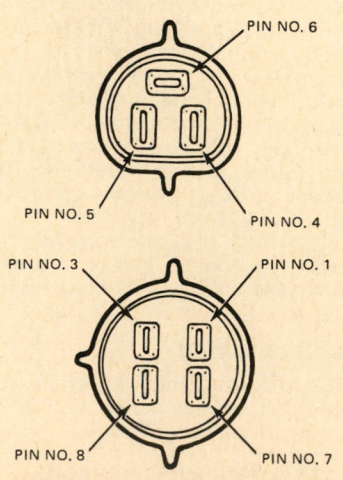

Electronic module connectors— —harness side through 1974
(© Ford Motor Co)

MODULE BIAS TEST

Measure the voltage at the indicated point to engine ground with the ignition key "on." If the voltage observed is less than battery voltage, repair the voltage feed wiring to the module.

BATTERY SOURCE TEST

1. Connect the voltmeter leads from the battery terminal at the coil to engine ground, without disconnecting the coil from the circuit.
2. Install a jumper wire from the other terminal of the coil to a good engine ground.
3. Turn the lights and all accessories off.
4. Turn the ignition switch "on."
5. If the voltmeter reading is between 4.9 and 7.9 volts, the primary circuit from the battery is satisfactory. The reading should be 11.0-14.0 Volts for Dura Spark I.
6. If the voltmeter reading is less check the following:
   a. The primary wiring for worn insulation, broken strands, and loose or corroded terminals.
   b. The resistance wiring for defects (except on Dura Spark I).
7. If the voltmeter reading is greater, the resistance wire should be replaced after verifying a defect (except on Dura Spark I).

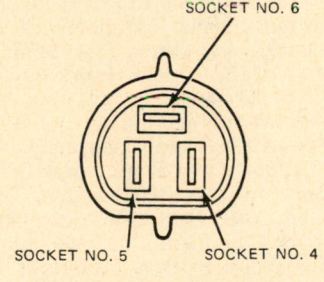

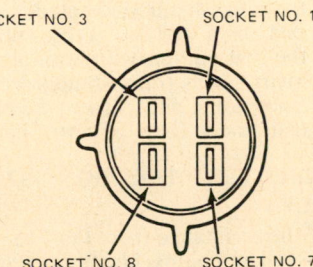

Electronic module connectors—harness side, 1975-77 (© Ford Motor Co.)

CRANKING TEST

Measure the voltage at the indicated point to engine ground with the engine cranking. If the voltage observed is not 8 to 12 volts, repair the voltage feed to the module.

STARTING CIRCUIT TEST

This test maybe used through 1977. Do not perform this on 1978 and later models. If the reading is not between 8 and 12 volts on models through 1974 the ignition by-pass circuit is open or

	TEST VOLTAGE BETWEEN	SHOULD BE	IF NOT, CONDUCT
KEY ON	Socket # 4 and Engine Ground	Battery Voltage ± 0.1 Volt	Module Bias Test
	Socket # 1 and Engine Ground	Battery Voltage ± 0.1 Volt	Battery Source Test
CRANKING	Socket # 5 and Engine Ground	8 to 12 volts	Cranking Test
	Jumper # 1 to # 8 Read # 6	more than 6 volts	Starting Circuit Test
	Socket # 7 and # 3	1/2 volt minimum A.C. or any D.C. volt wiggle	Distributor Hardware Test

	TEST VOLTAGE BETWEEN	SHOULD BE	IF NOT, CONDUCT
KEY OFF	Socket # 7 and # 3 Socket # 8 and Engine Ground Socket # 7 and Engine Ground Socket # 3 and Engine Ground	400 to 800 ohms 0 ohms more than 70,000 ohms	Magnetic Pick-up (Stator) Test
	Socket # 4 and Coil Tower Socket # 1 and Pin # 6	7000 to 13000 ohms 1.0 to 2.0 ohms	Coil Test
	Socket # 1 and Engine Ground	more than 4.0 ohms	Short Test
	Socket # 4 and # 6	1.0 to 2.0 ohms	Resistance Wire Test

Ford-Motorcraft Solid-State ignition system diagnosis, 1975 (© Ford Motor Co.)

	TEST VOLTAGE BETWEEN	SHOULD BE	IF NOT, CONDUCT
KEY ON	Socket No. 4 and Engine Ground	Battery Voltage ± 0.1 Volt	Battery Source Test
	Socket No. 1 and Engine Ground	Battery Voltage ± 0.1 Volt	Battery Source Test
CRANKING	Socket No. 5 and Engine Ground	8 to 12 volts	Check Supply Circuit (starting) through Ignition Switch
	Jumper No. 1 to No. 8 Read No. 6	more than 6 volts	Starting Circuit Test
	Pin No. 3 and Pin No. 8	1/2 volt minimum A.C. or any D.C. volt wiggle	Distributor Hardware Test

	TEST VOLTAGE BETWEEN	SHOULD BE	IF NOT, CONDUCT
KEY OFF	Socket No. 8 and No. 3 Socket No. 7 and Engine Ground Socket No. 8 and Engine Ground Socket No. 3 and Engine Ground	400 to 800 ohms 0 ohms more than 70,000 ohms more than 70,000 ohms	Magnetic Pick-up (Stator) Test
	Socket No. 4 and Coil Tower	7000 to 13,000 ohms	Coil Test
	Socket No. 1 and Engine Ground	more than 4.0 ohms	Short Test

Ford-Motorcraft Solid-State ignition system diagnosis, 1976 and later (© Ford Motor Co.)

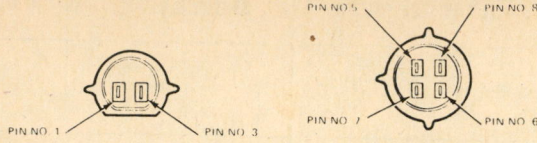

Dura Spark I electronic module connectors—harness side through 1977 (© Ford Motor Co.)

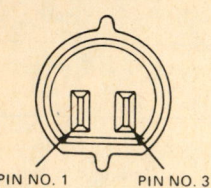
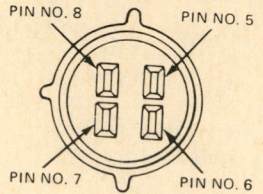

Dura Spark II electronic module connectors—harness side through 1977 (© Ford Motor Co.)

	Test Voltage Between	Should Be	If Not, Conduct
KEY ON	Pin #3 and Engine Ground	Battery Voltage ± 0.1 volts	Module Bias Test
	Pin #5 and Engine Ground	Battery Voltage ± 0.1 volts	Battery Source Test
CRANKING	Pin #1 and Engine Ground	8 to 12 volts	Cranking Test
	Jumper #5 to #6 – Read Coil "Bat" Term. & Engine Ground**	More than 6 volts	Starting Circuit Test
	Pin #7 and Pin #8	1/2 volt minimum wiggle	Distributor Hardware Test

	Test Resistance Between	Should Be	If Not, Conduct**
KEY OFF	Pin #7 and Pin #8 Pin #6 and Engine Ground Pin #7 and Engine Ground Pin #8 and Engine Ground	400 to 800 ohms 0 ohms More than 70,000 ohms More than 70,000 ohms	Magnetic Pick-up (Stator) Test
	Pin #3 and Coil Tower	7,000 to 13,000 ohms	Coil Test
	Pin #5 and Coil "Bat" Term.	1.0 to 2.0 ohms Dura Spark II 0.5 to 1.5 ohms Dura Spark I	
	Pin #5 and Engine Ground	More than 4 ohms	Short Test
	Pin #3 and Coil "Bat" Term. (Except Dura Dura Spark I)	0.7 to 1.7 ohms Dura Spark II	Resistance Wire Test

**Test duration shall be less than 30 seconds (Dura Spark I)

Dura Spark ignition system diagnosis through 1977 (© Ford Motor Co.)

grounded from either the starter solenoid or the ignition switch to Pin 5. On 1975 and later models, the switch bypass circuit is open or grounded from either the starter solenoid or the switch to no. 5, if the reading is under 6 volts. Check the primary connections at the coil.

DISTRIBUTOR HARDWARE TEST

1. Disconnect the three-wire weatherproof connector at the distributor pigtail.
2. Connect a D.C. voltmeter on a 2.5 volt scale to the two parallel blades. With the engine cranking, the meter needle should oscillate.

3. Remove the distributor cap and check for visual damage or misassembly.

NOTE: *To remove the two-piece Dura Spark distributor cap, take off the top portion, then the rotor, then the bottom adaptor portion.*

a. Sintered iron armature (4, 6 or 8-toothed wheel) must be tight on the sleeve, and the roll pin aligning the armature must be in position.
b. Sintered iron stator must not be broken.
c. Armature must rotate when the engine is cranked.

4. If the hardware is alright, but the meter doesn't oscillate, replace the magnetic pick-up assembly.

MAGNETIC PICK-UP TESTS THROUGH 1977 ONLY

1. Resistance of pick-up coil measured between two parallel pins in the distributor connector must be 400-800 ohms.
2. Resistance between the third blade (ground) and the distributor body must be zero ohms.
3. Resistance between either parallel blade and engine ground must be greater than 70,000 ohms.
4. If any test fails, the distributor stator assembly is defective and must be replaced.
5. If the above readings are not the same as measured in the original test, check for a defective harness. If the readings are the same, proceed.
6. If these tests check alright, the signal generator portion of the distributor is working properly.

IGNITION COIL TEST

The ignition coil must be diagnosed separately from the rest of the ignition system.

1. Primary resistance must be 0.5-1.5 ohms for Dura Spark I through 1977, and 0.71-0.77 ohms 1978 and later. It must measure 1.0-2.0 ohms for Dura Spark II through 1977 and the 1973-76 system. For 1978 and later Dura Spark II, it must be 1.13-1.23 ohms.
2. Secondary resistance must be 7,000-13,000 ohms through 1977. 1978 and later Dura Spark I systems must read 7350-8250 ohms, while the 1978 and later Dura Spark II figure is 7700-9300 ohms.
3. If resistance tests are alright, but the coil is still suspected, test the coil on a coil tester by following the test equipment manufacturer's instructions for a standard coil. If the reading differs from the original test, check for a defective harness.

SHORT TEST THROUGH 1977 ONLY

If the resistance from Pin 5 to ground is less than 4 ohms, check for a short to ground at the ignition coil or in the wiring to the coil.

RESISTANCE WIRE TEST

Replace the resistance wire if it doesn't show a resistance of 1.0-2.0 ohms for the 1973-76 system, 0.7-1.7 for Dura Spark II through 1977, and 1.05-1.15 ohms 1978 and later. The resistance wire isn't used on Dura Spark I.

SPARK PLUG WIRE RESISTANCE

Resistance on these wires must not exceed 5,000 ohms per inch. To properly measure this, remove the wires from the plugs, and remove the distributor cap. Measure the resistance through the distributor cap at that end. Do not pierce any ignition wire for any reason. Measure only from the two ends.

NOTE: *Silicone grease must be reapplied to the spark plug wires whenever they are removed:*

When removing the wires from the spark plugs, a special tool such as the one pictured should be used. Do not pull on the wires. Grasp and twist the boot to remove the wire.

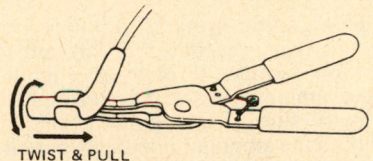

TWIST & PULL

Special tool for removing spark plug wires (© Ford Motor Co)

Whenever the high tension wires are removed from the plugs, coil, or distributor, silicone grease must be applied to the boot before reconnection. Use a clean small screwdriver blade to coat the entire interior surface with Ford silicone grease D7AZ-19A331-A, Dow. Corning # 111, or General Electric G-627.

Adjustments

The air gap between the armature and magnetic pick-up coil in the distributor is not adjustable, nor are there any adjustments for the amplifier module. Inoperative components are simply replaced. Any attempt to connect components outside the vehicle may result in component failure.

Component Replacement

MAGNETIC PICK-UP ASSEMBLY REMOVAL AND INSTALLATION

1. Remove the distributor cap and rotor and disconnect the distributor harness plug.

NOTE: *To remove the two-piece Dura Spark distributor cap, take off the top portion, then the rotor, then the bottom adaptor.*

2. Using a small gear puller or two screwdrivers, lift or pry the armature from the advance plate sleeve. Remove the roll pin.
3. Remove the large wire retaining clip from the base plate annular groove.
4. Remove the snap-ring which secures the vacuum advance link to the pick-up assembly.

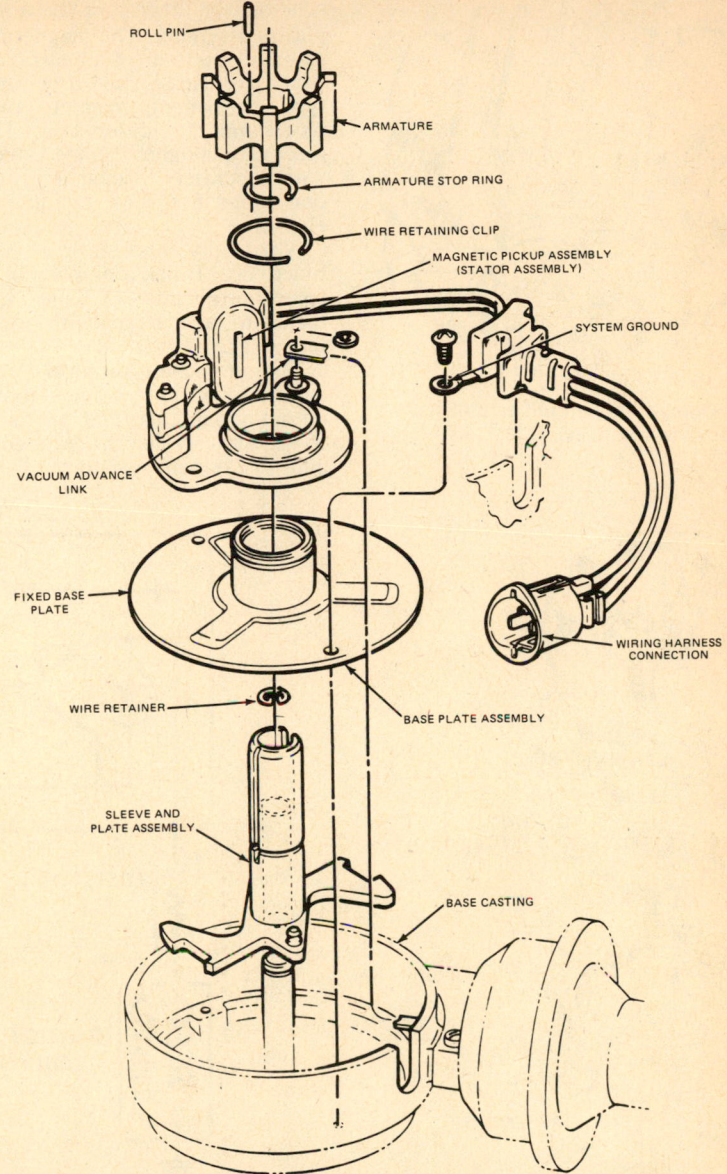

Ford-Motorcraft Solid-State Ignition distributor disassembled
(© Ford Motor Co)

5. Remove the magnetic pick-up assembly ground screw and lift the assembly from the distributor.
6. Lift the vacuum advance arm off the post on the pick-up assembly and move it out against the distributor housing.
7. Place the new pick-up assembly in position over the fixed base plate and slide the wiring in position through the slot in the side of the distributor housing.
8. Install the fine wire snap-ring securing the pick-up assembly to the fixed base plate.
9. Position the vacuum advance arm over the post on the pick-up assembly and install the snap-ring.
10. Install the grounding screw through the tab on the wiring harness and into the fixed base plate.
11. Install the armature on the advance plate sleeve making sure that the roll pin is engaged in the matching slots.
12. Install the distributor rotor cap.
13. Connect the distributor wiring plug to the vehicle harness.

DELCO-REMY MAGNETIC PULSE SYSTEM

Components

The Delco-Remy magnetic pulse, fully transistorized ignition system uses a magnetic pulse distributor having no breaker points. This system switches power electronically rather than with ignition contact points. Instead of the familiar cam and breaker plate assembly, this distributor uses a

Electronic Ignition Systems

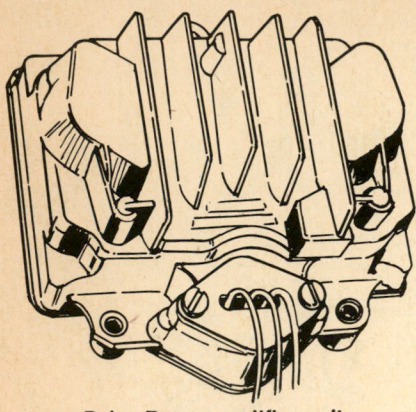

Delco-Remy amplifier unit
(© Chevrolet Div., G.M. Corp)

rotating iron timer core and a magnetic pickup assembly. The magnetic pickup assembly consists of a bearing plate on which are sandwiched a ceramic ring-type permanent magnet, two pole pieces and a pick-up coil. The pole pieces are doughnut shaped steel plates with accurately spaced internal teeth, one tooth for each cylinder of the engine.

A critically important part is the iron timer core. It has a number of equally spaced projections or vanes and is attached to, and rotates with, the distributor shaft.

The transistor control unit, the switchbox of the system, is mounted in an aluminum case and contains three transistors, a zener diode, a condenser and five small resistors. The zener diode is a circuit protection device. Remaining components control and switch ignition-coil current electronically; there are no moving parts in the control unit.

The ignition coil is of standard design except for a special winding. The external primary resistor is a ceramic type, similar to those used on various conventional systems.

The system was last used in 1972.

Operation

The ignition primary circuit is connected from the battery, through the ignition switch, through the ignition pulse amplifier assembly, through the primary side of the ignition coil, and back to the amplifier housing where it is grounded externally. The secondary

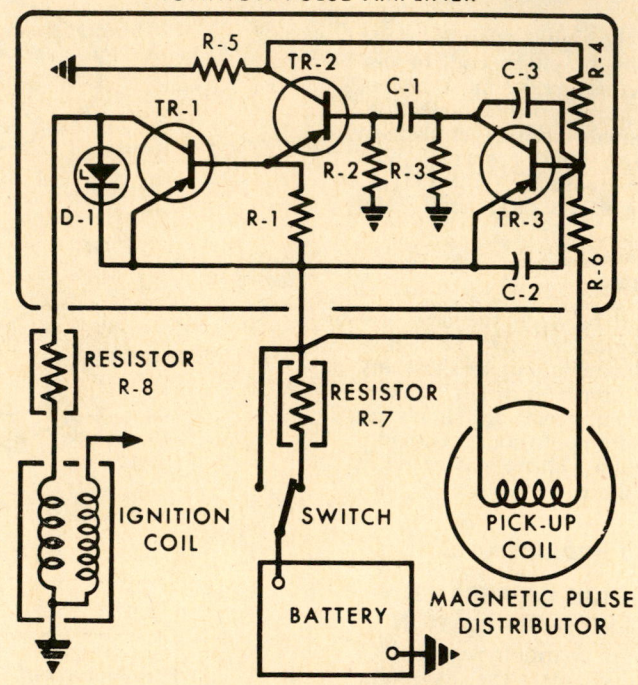

Delco-Remy amplifier schematic
(© Chevrolet Div., G.M. Corp)

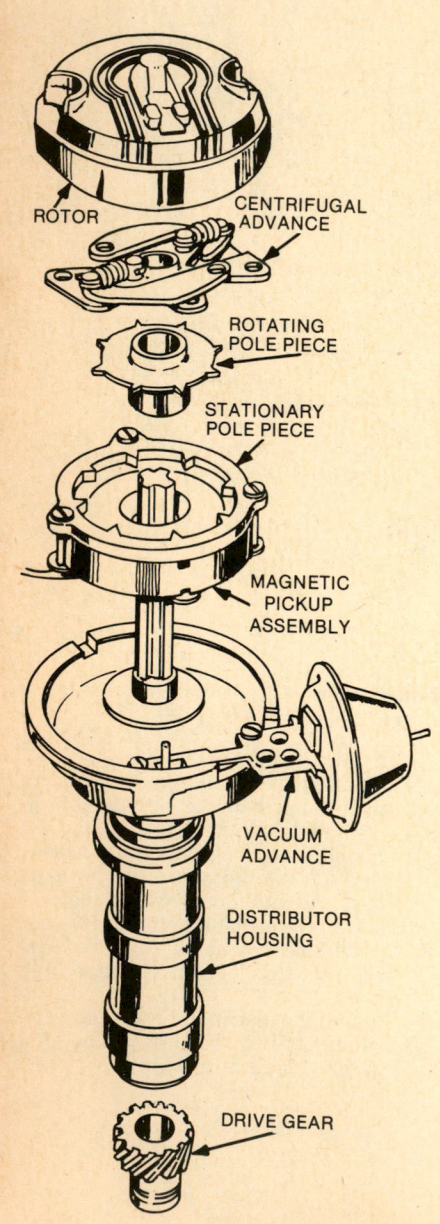

Delco-Remy pulse distributor exploded view (© Chevrolet Div., G.M. Corp)

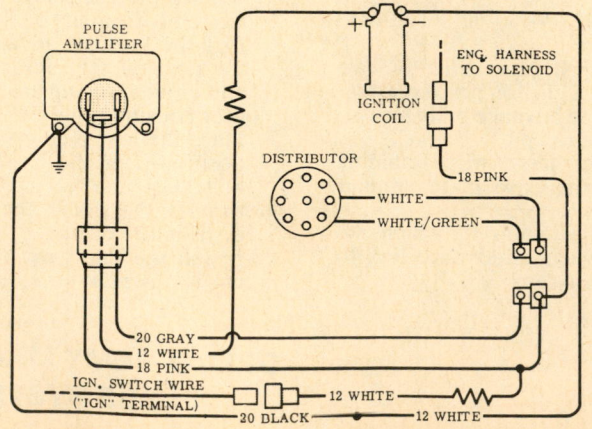

Delco-Remy circuit diagram
(© Chevrolet Div., G.M. Corp)

circuit is the same as in conventional ignition systems: the secondary side of the coil, the coil wire to the distributor, the rotor, the spark plug wires and the spark plugs.

The magnetic pulse distributor is also connected to the ignition pulse amplifier. As the distributor shaft rotates, the distributor rotating pole piece turns inside the stationary pole piece, the eight teeth on the rotating pole piece align with the eight teeth on the stationary pole piece eight times during each distributor revolution (two crankshaft revolutions since the distributor runs at one-half crankshaft speed). As the rotating pole piece teeth move close to, and align with, the teeth on the stationary pole piece, the magnetic rotating pole piece induces voltage into the magnetic pole piece through the stationary pole piece. This voltage pulse is sent to the ignition pulse amplifier from the magnetic pole piece. When the pulse enters the amplifier, it signals the ignition pulse amplifier to interrupt the ignition primary circuit. This causes the primary circuit to collapse and begins the induction of the magnetic lines of force from the primary side of the coil into the secondary side of the coil. This induction provides the required voltage to fire the spark plugs.

The advantages of this system are that the transistors in the ignition pulse amplifier can make and break the primary ignition circuit much faster than conventional ignition points, and

higher primary voltage can be utilized since this system can be made to handle higher voltage without adverse effects, whereas ignition breaker points cannot. The shorter switching time of this system allows longer coil primary circuit saturation time and longer induction time when the primary circuit collapses. This increased time allows the primary circuit to build up more current and the secondary circuit to discharge more current.

Troubleshooting

CAUTIONS

1. Don't use 18 volts or 24 volts for emergency starting.
2. Never crank engine with coil high-tension lead or more than three spark plug leads disconnected.
3. Don't short circuit between coil and positive terminal and ground.
4. On any repair that necessitates replacement of control unit or ignition resistor, perform complete charging system check before releasing the unit. Basic cause of trouble may be high or uncontrolled charging rate.

ENGINE SURGE OR INTERMITTENT MISS

Since there are so many possible causes for this problem, all other possible defects must be ruled out before the specialized components of the

electronic ignition system are judged defective.

As a general rule, a miss or surge that is caused by an ignition problem will be much more pronounced than a similar problem that is caused by carburetion. Also, carburetion is usually affected by temperature more than the ignition system is. A carburetor or intake manifold vacuum leak is often compensated for by the choke when the engine is cold. When the engine warms up and the choke is released, the engine surge will show up.

If the ignition system is found to be the source of the problem, first check all connections in the system to make sure that they are *clean and tight*. Check the coil and spark plug high-tension wires with an ohmmeter to be sure they have the correct resistance. Check the inside and outside of the distributor cap and the tower on the ignition coil for cracks which would allow the high voltage intended for the spark plugs to short to ground.

If none of the above checks uncovers a defective component, the distributor pick-up coil leads may be reversed in the connector, or the pick-up coil itself may have an intermittent open.

ENGINE WILL NOT START OR IS HARD TO START

1. Disconnect a spark plug wire from one spark plug and hold the wire ¼ in. from a good ground with a pair of insulated pliers.

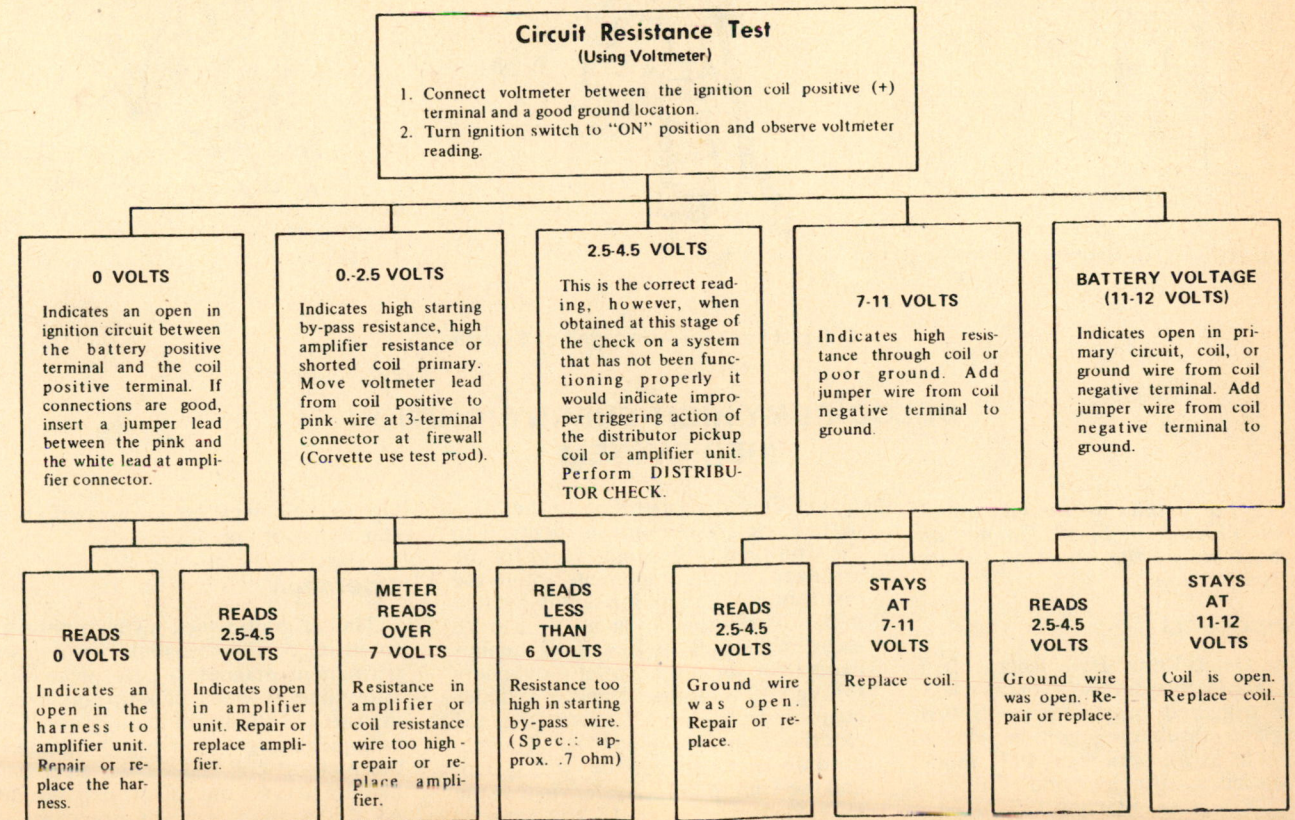

Magnetic Pulse System (© Chevrolet Div., G.M. Corp)

2. Crank the engine over and observe whether a spark jumps from the plug wire to ground.

3. *If spark occurs*, the problem is not in the ignition system.

4. *If spark does not occur*, reconnect the spark plug wire that was disconnected and connect a tachometer between the positive (+) coil primary terminal and the pink wire in the three-wire connector to the ignition pulse amplifier.

5. Crank the engine over and observe the tachometer.

6. *If the tachometer needle deflects* while cranking the engine, perform

"Ignition Distributor Test" to locate the problem.

7. *If the tachometer needle does not deflect* while cranking the engine, perform "Circuit Resistance Test" to pinpoint the problem.

CIRCUIT RESISTANCE TEST
IGNITION DISTRIBUTOR CHECK

1. Disconnect the distributor leads from the engine wiring harness.
2. Connect the two leads of an ohmmeter to the distributor leads at the connector.
3. Rotate the magnetic pick-up assembly in the distributor through

full vacuum advance travel and read the ohmmeter. If the reading is not within a range of 500-700 ohms, replace the magnetic pick-up assembly.

4. If the reading is within the 500-700 ohms range, disconnect one ohmmeter lead from the distributor connector and connect it to a good ground. If the reading is less than infinity (needle moves to end of scale), replace the magnetic pick-up assembly.

5. If the reading is infinite, and there was no spark when the spark plug wire was disconnected from the plug, the amplifier is defective.

DELCO-REMY UNIT IGNITION SYSTEM

This system is almost identical to the Delco-Remy Magnetic Pulse System. The ignition primary circuit passes through the electronic module (called the ignition pulse amplifier in Delco-

Remy system) and is interrupted when a signal is sent to the control module from the distributor. The main difference between the two systems is that, in the Unitized System, the ignition coil

and control module are attached to the distributor body, making a compact, one-piece ignition system. It is optional equipment on some 1972-74 model Pontiacs with V8 engines.

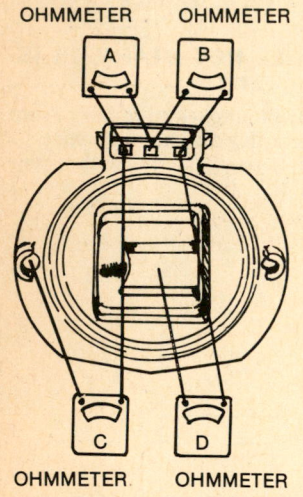

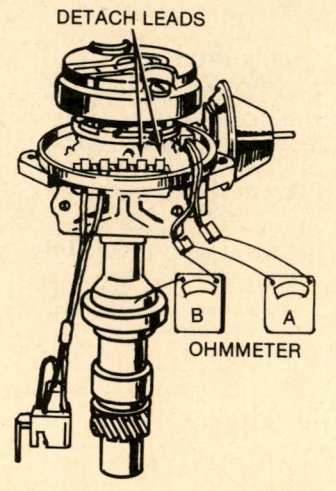

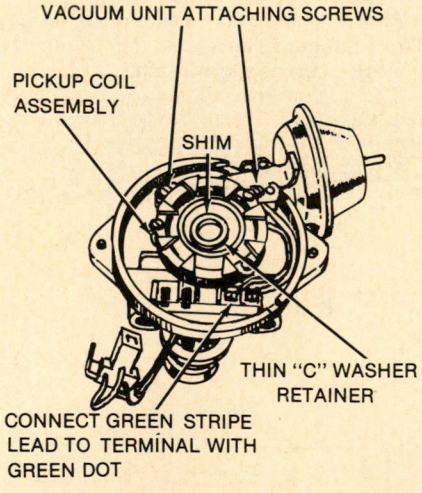

Coil test hook-up—Unit Ignition System

DELCO-REMY HIGH ENERGY IGNITION (HEI) SYSTEM

NOTE: *For details on the Oldsmobile Tornado Electronic Spark Timing Control System, see the Emission Control Systems Section.*

Components

The Delco-Remy High Energy Ignition (HEI) System is a breakerless, pulse triggered, transistor controlled, inductive discharge ignition system available as an option on 1974 model Oldsmobiles, Buicks, and Cadillacs with V8 engines. Starting 1975, HEI is used on all GM passenger car engines as standard equipment.

It is similar in operation to the Magnetic Pulse System and is identical to the Unit Ignition System except for the arrangement of components within the distributor. The ignition coil is located in the distributor cap on all V6 and V8 engines through 1977, and all engines except for some Chevrolet 4 cylinders through 1978. Inline 4 and 6 cylinder engines, through 1977 mount the coil externally on the engine block. The major difference between the HEI System and the Unit Ignition System is that the HEI System is a full 12 volt system, while the Unit Ignition System incorporates a resistance wire to limit the vol-

tage to the coil except during periods of starter motor operation.

Operation

The magnetic pick-up assembly located inside the distributor contains a permanent magnet, a pole piece with internal teeth, and a pick-up coil. When the teeth of the rotating timer core and pole piece align, an induced voltage in the pick-up coil signals the electronic module to open the coil primary circuit. As the primary current decreases, a high voltage is induced in the secondary windings of the ignition coil, direct-

UNIT IGNITION SYSTEM TROUBLE SHOOTING

Insure that black and pink leads are connected as shown in Fig. 1. Tighten both bolts, Fig. 1. Loose bolts may cause poor performance and radio interference.

ON THE VEHICLE

ON THE BENCH

ENGINE WILL NOT RUN

1. Check ignition switch connector, Fig. 1.
2. Connect voltmeter from ignition switch connector to ground.
3. Turn on ignition switch.
4. If reading is zero, circuit is open between connector and ignition switch. Repair if needed.
5. If reading is battery voltage, hold one spark lead with insulating pliers about 1/4 in. from dry area of engine block while cranking engine.

If sparking occurs, trouble most likely is not ignition. Check fuel system.

ENGINE WILL START BUT NOT RUN, AND ENGINE MISS OR SURGE.

1. Insure that fuel system is satisfactory.
2. Check spark plug leads for arcing or leakage to ground.
3. Check spark plugs.

If no defects are found, follow procedure under "On the Bench" with Unit Ignition System initially either on or off the vehicle.

If no spark, follow procedure under "On the Bench," with Unit Ignition System initially either on or off the engine.

ON THE BENCH

1. Disassemble unit (Fig. 2).
2. Inspect coil, eight inserts, shell and rotor for arc-over or leakage.

1. Connect ohmmeter, Fig. 3.
2. Parts A and B each should be practically zero. If infinite on either reading, replace coil.
3. Part C should be 6000-9000 ohms. If outside range, replace coil.
4. Part D should be infinite. If not, replace coil.

1. Connect test stand vacuum source to vacuum unit.
2. Connect ohmmeter Parts A and B, Fig. 4.
3. Observe ohmmeter throughout vacuum range.
4. If Part A reads less than 650 ohms, or more than 850 ohms at any time, replace pickup coil, per Step 7 below.
5. If Part B reads other than infinite at any time, replace pickup coil, per step 7 below.
6. If vacuum unit is inoperative, replace per Step 7 below.
7. Remove unit from engine, drive pin from gear, remove rotor and shaft assembly from housing, remove shim and then "C" washer to replace pickup coil or vacuum unit (Fig. 5).

If no defects have been found, remove two attaching screws and replace module.

Fig. 1

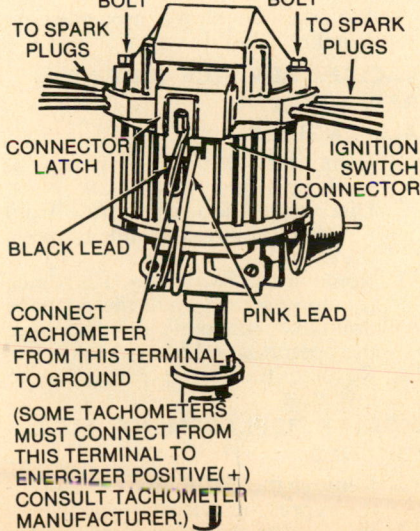

Unit Ignition System test hook-up
(© Pontiac Div., G.M. Corp)

Fig. 2

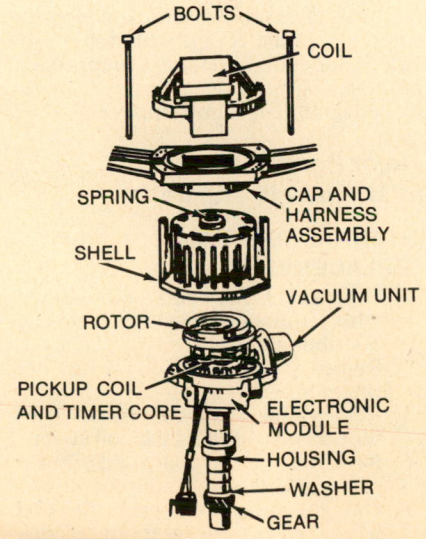

Unit Ignition System exploded view
(© Pontiac Div., G.M. Corp)

Electronic Ignition Systems

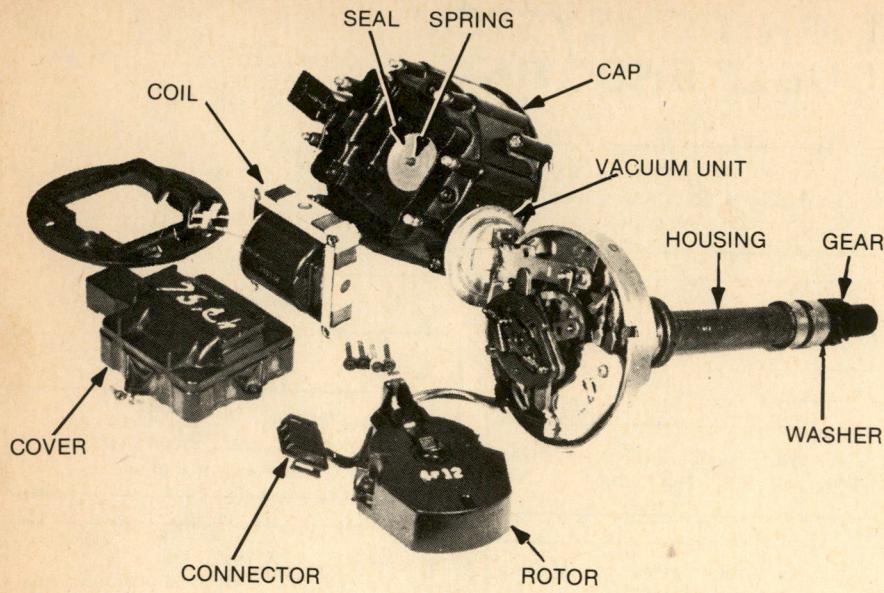

HEI distributor internal parts, V6 and V8

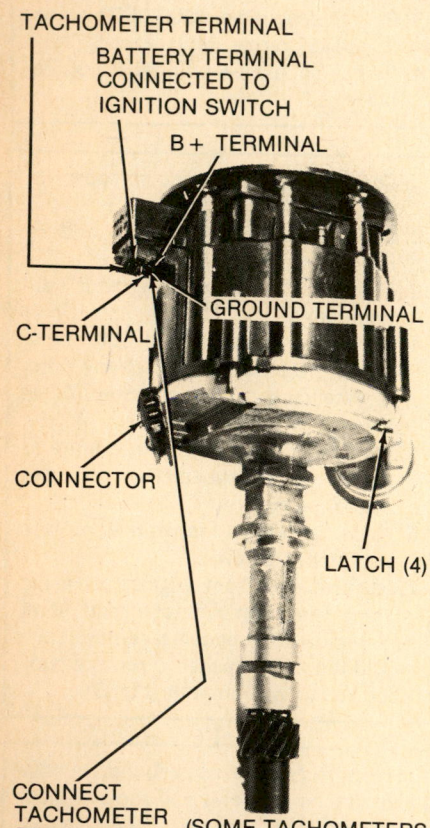

TACHOMETER TERMINAL

BATTERY TERMINAL CONNECTED TO IGNITION SWITCH

B + TERMINAL

C-TERMINAL

GROUND TERMINAL

CONNECTOR

LATCH (4)

CONNECT TACHOMETER FROM THIS TERMINAL TO GROUND

(SOME TACHOMETERS MUST CONNECT FROM THIS TERMINAL TO ENERGIZER POSITIVE +. CONSULT TACHOMETER MANUFACTURER.)

High Energy Ignition System distributor, V6 and V8

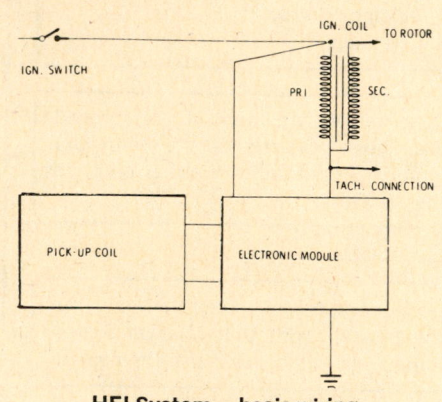

HEI System—basic wiring
(© Oldsmobile Div., G.M. Corp)

The HEI System features a longer spark duration which is instrumental in firing lean and EGR diluted fuel/air mixtures. The condenser (capacitor) located within the HEI distributor is provided for noise (static) suppression purposes only and is not a regularly replaced igniton system component.

Major Repair Operations (distributor in engine)

INTERNAL IGNITION COIL REPLACEMENT

1. Disconnect the feed and module wire terminal connectors from the distributor cap.
2. Remove the ignition wire set retainer.
3. Remove the 4 coil cover-to-distributor cap screws and the coil cover.
4. Remove the 4 coil-to-distributor cap screws.
5. Using a blunt drift, press the coil wire spade terminals up out of distributor cap.
6. Lift the coil up out of the distributor cap.
7. Remove and clean the coil spring,

rubber seal washer and coil cavity of the distributor cap.
8. Coat the rubber seal with a dielectric lubricant furnished in the replacement ignition coil package through 1977.
9. Reverse the above procedures to install.

EXTERNAL IGNITION COIL REPLACEMENT

1. Remove the ignition switch-to-coil lead from the coil.
2. Unfasten the distributor leads from the coil.
3. Remove the screws which secure the coil to the engine and lift it off.

Installation is the reverse of removal.

DISTRIBUTOR CAP REPLACEMENT, ALL ENGINES

1. Remove the feed and module wire terminal connectors from the distributor cap.
2. Remove the retainer and spark plug wires from the cap.
3. Depress and release the 4 distributor cap-to-housing retainers and lift off the cap assembly.
4. If the cap has an internal coil, remove the coil from the old cap and install into the new cap.
5. Using a new distributor cap, reverse the above procedures to assemble being sure to clean and lubricate the rubber seal washer with dielectric lubricant.

ROTOR REPLACEMENT, ALL ENGINES

1. Disconnect the feed and module wire connectors from the distributor.
2. Depress and release the 4 distributor cap to housing retainers and lift off the cap assembly.
3. Remove the two rotor attaching screws and rotor.
4. Reverse the above procedure to install.

VACUUM ADVANCE UNIT REPLACEMENT, ALL ENGINES

1. Remove the distributor cap and rotor as previously described.
2. Disconnect the vacuum hose from the vacuum advance unit. Remove the module.
3. Remove the two vacuum advance retaining screws, pull the advance unit outward, rotate and disengage the operating rod from its tang.
4. Reverse the above procedure to install.

MODULE REPLACEMENT, ALL ENGINES

1. Remove the distributor cap and rotor as previously described.
2. Disconnect the harness connector and pick-up coil spade connectors from the module (note their positions).

ing a spark through the rotor and high voltage leads to fire the spark plugs. The dwell period is automatically controlled by the electronic module and is increased with increasing engine rpm.

3. Remove the two screws and module from the distributor housing.
4. Coat the bottom of the new module with dielectric lubricant.

NOTE: *The lubricant is required for proper module cooling.*

Reverse the above procedure to install. Be sure that the leads are installed correctly.

FIGURE A

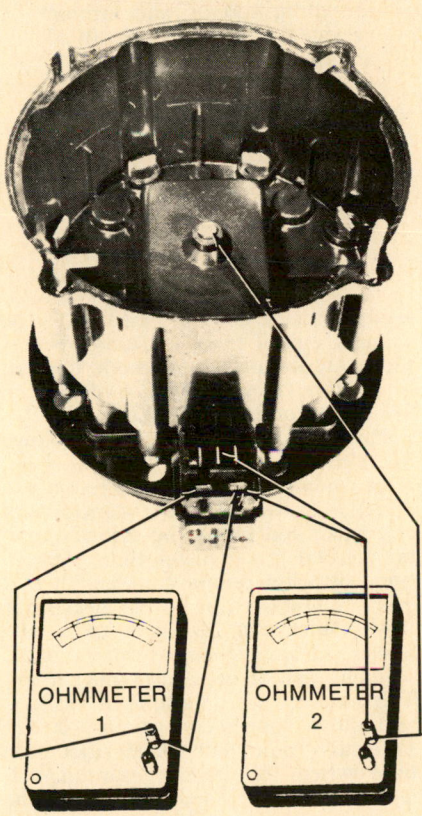

Replace coil only if both readings in Step 2 are infinite

DISTRIBUTOR REMOVAL, ALL ENGINES

1. Disconnect the ground cable from the battery.
2. Disconnect the feed and module terminal connectors from the distributor cap. (Don't use a screwdriver).
3. Disconnect the hose at the vacuum advance.
4. Depress and release the 4 distributor cap-to-housing retainers and lift off the cap assembly.
5. Using crayon or chalk, make locating marks on the rotor and module and on the distributor housing and engine for installation purposes.
6. Loosen and remove the distributor clamp bolt and clamp, and lift distributor out of the engine. Noting the relative position of the rotor and module alignment marks, make a second mark on the rotor to align it with the one mark on the module.

HIGH ENERGY IGNITION DIAGNOSIS

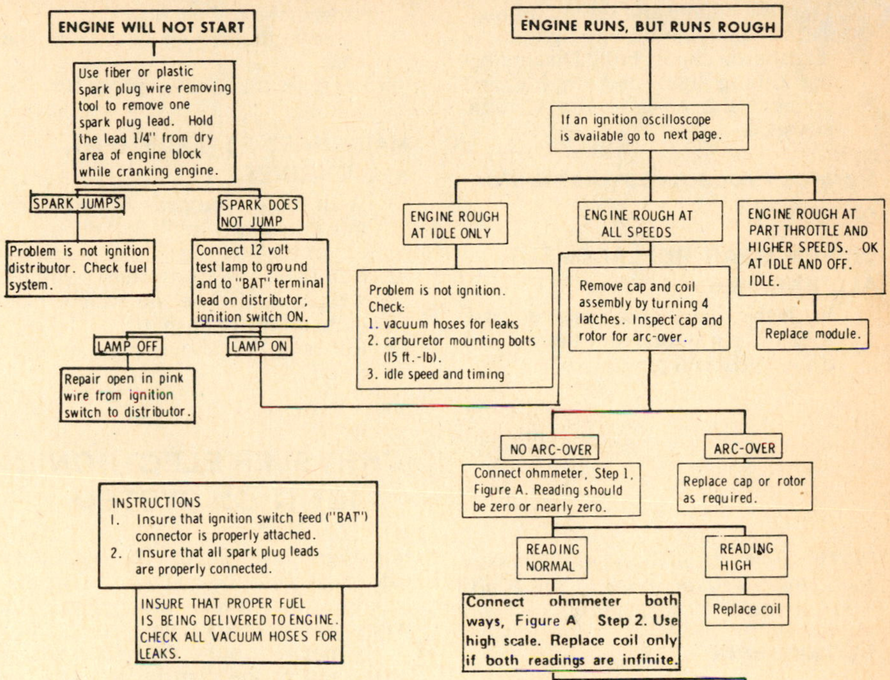

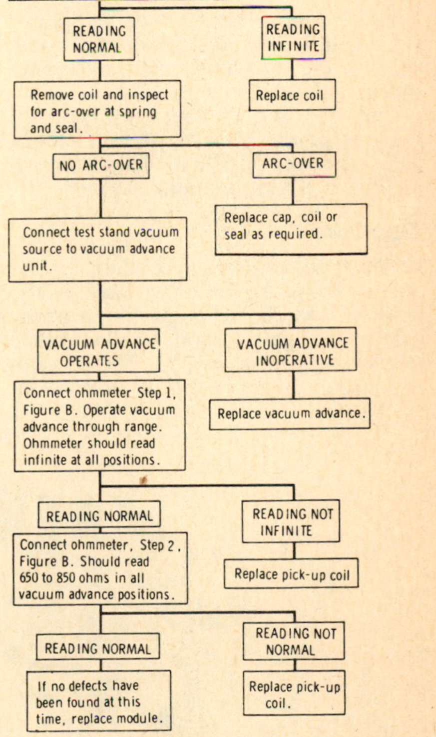

ENGINE WILL NOT START

Use fiber or plastic spark plug wire removing tool to remove one spark plug lead. Hold the lead 1/4" from dry area of engine block while cranking engine.

SPARK JUMPS

Problem is not ignition distributor. Check fuel system.

SPARK DOES NOT JUMP

Connect 12 volt test lamp to ground and to "BAT" terminal lead on distributor, ignition switch ON.

LAMP OFF

Repair open in pink wire from ignition switch to distributor.

LAMP ON

ENGINE RUNS, BUT RUNS ROUGH

If an ignition oscilloscope is available go to next page.

ENGINE ROUGH AT IDLE ONLY

Problem is not ignition. Check:
1. vacuum hoses for leaks
2. carburetor mounting bolts (15 ft.-lb)
3. idle speed and timing

ENGINE ROUGH AT ALL SPEEDS

Remove cap and coil assembly by turning 4 latches. Inspect cap and rotor for arc-over.

ENGINE ROUGH AT PART THROTTLE AND HIGHER SPEEDS. OK AT IDLE AND OFF. IDLE.

Replace module.

NO ARC-OVER

Connect ohmmeter, Step 1, Figure A. Reading should be zero or nearly zero.

ARC-OVER

Replace cap or rotor as required.

READING NORMAL

Connect ohmmeter both ways, Figure A, Step 2. Use high scale. Replace coil only if both readings are infinite.

READING HIGH

Replace coil

READING NORMAL

Remove coil and inspect for arc-over at spring and seal.

READING INFINITE

Replace coil

NO ARC-OVER

Connect test stand vacuum source to vacuum advance unit.

ARC-OVER

Replace cap, coil or seal as required.

VACUUM ADVANCE OPERATES

Connect ohmmeter Step 1, Figure B. Operate vacuum advance through range. Ohmmeter should read infinite at all positions.

VACUUM ADVANCE INOPERATIVE

Replace vacuum advance.

READING NORMAL

Connect ohmmeter, Step 2, Figure B. Should read 650 to 850 ohms in all vacuum advance positions.

READING NOT INFINITE

Replace pick-up coil

READING NORMAL

If no defects have been found at this time, replace module.

READING NOT NORMAL

Replace pick-up coil.

INSTRUCTIONS
1. Insure that ignition switch feed ("BAT") connector is properly attached.
2. Insure that all spark plug leads are properly connected.

INSURE THAT PROPER FUEL IS BEING DELIVERED TO ENGINE. CHECK ALL VACUUM HOSES FOR LEAKS.

FIGURE B

DETACH LEADS FROM MODULE

OHMMETER 2   OHMMETER 1

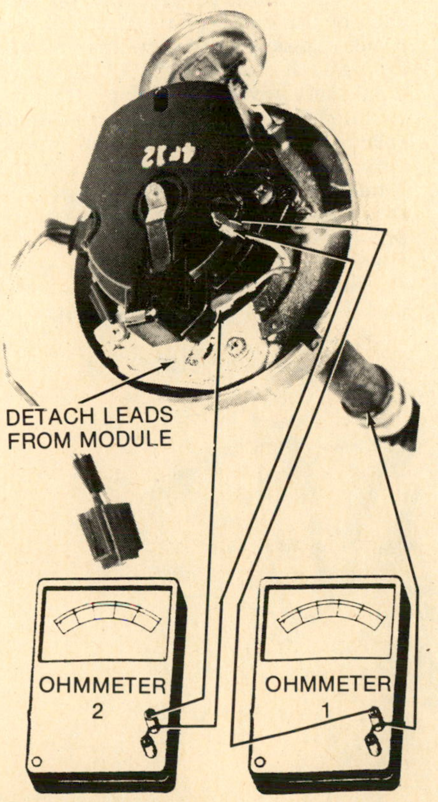

DISTRIBUTOR INSTALLATION, ALL ENGINES

1. With a new O-ring on the distributor housing and the second mark on the rotor aligned with the mark on the module, install the distributor, taking care to align the mark on the housing with the one on the engine. It may be necessary to lift the distributor and turn the rotor slightly to align the gears and the oil pump driveshaft.
2. With the respective marks aligned, install the clamp and bolt finger-tight.
3. Install and secure the distributor cap.
4. Connect the feed and module connectors to the distributor cap.
5. Connect a timing light to the engine and plug the vacuum hose.

6. Connect the ground cable to the battery.
7. Start the engine and set the timing.
8. Turn the engine off and tighten the distributor clamp bolt. Disconnect the timing light and unplug and connect the hose to the vacuum advance.

Service Procedures (distributor removed)

DRIVEN GEAR REPLACEMENT, ALL ENGINES

1. With the distributor removed, use a ⅛ in. pin punch and tap out the driven gear roll pin.

2. Hold the rotor end of shaft and rotate the driven gear to shear any burrs in the roll pin hole.
3. Remove the driven gear from the shaft.
4. Reverse the above procedure to install.

MAINSHAFT REPLACEMENT, ALL ENGINES

1. With the driven gear and rotor removed, gently pull the mainshaft out of the housing.
2. Remove the advance springs, weights and slide the weight base plate off the mainshaft.
3. Reverse the above procedure to install.

POLE PIECE, MAGNET OR PICKUP COIL REPLACEMENT, ALL ENGINES

The pole piece, magnet, and pickup coil are serviced as an assembly.
1. With the mainshaft out of its housing, remove the thin "C" washer on top of the pickup coil assembly, remove the pickup coil leads from the module, and remove the pickup coil as an assembly. Do not remove the three screws and attempt to service the parts individually. They are aligned at the factory.
2. Reverse the removal procedure to install. Note the alignment marks when the drive gear is reinstalled.

CHRYSLER ELECTRONIC IGNITION SYSTEM

NOTE: *For details on the Chrysler Lean Burn system, refer to the Emission Control Systems Section.*

Components

This system consists of a special pulse-sending distributor, an electronic control unit, a two-element ballast resistor, and a special ignition coil.

The distributor does not contain breaker points or a condenser, these parts being replaced by a distributor reluctor and a pick-up unit.

Operation

The ignition primary circuit is connected from the battery, through the ignition switch, through the primary side of the ignition coil, to the control unit where it is grounded. The secondary circuit is the same as in conventional ignition systems: the secondary side of the coil, the coil wire to the distributor, the rotor, the spark plug wires, and the spark plugs.

The magnetic pulse distributor is also connected to the control unit. As the distributor shaft rotates, the distributor reluctor turns past the pick-up unit. As the reluctor turns past the pick-up unit, each of the eight (or six) teeth on the reluctor pass near the pick-up unit once during each distributor revolution (two crankshaft revolutions since the distributor runs at one-half crankshaft speed). As the reluctor teeth move close to the pick-up unit, the magnetic rotating reluctor induces voltage into the magnetic pick-up unit. This voltage pulse is sent to the ignition control unit from the magnetic pick-up unit. When the pulse enters the control unit, it signals the control unit to interrupt the ig-

nition primary circuit. This causes the primary circuit to collapse and begins the induction of the magnetic lines of force from the primary side of the coil into the secondary side of the coil. This induction provides the required voltage to fire the spark plugs.

The advantages of this system are that the transitors in the control unit can make and break the primary ignition circuit much faster than conventional ignition points can, and higher primary voltage can be utilized, since this system can be made to handle higher voltage without adverse effects, whereas ignition breaker points cannot. The quicker switching time of this system allows longer coil primary circuit saturation time and longer induction time when the primary circuit collapses. This increased time allows the primary circuit to build up more current and the secondary circuit to discharge more current.

System Test

A voltmeter with a 20,000 ohm/volt rating and a 1½ volt battery powered ohmmeter are required. Car battery voltage must be at least 12 volts.
1. Remove the wiring plug from the control unit.

--- **CAUTION** ---

Make sure the ignition switch is off when removing or replacing the control unit connector.

2. Turn the ignition switch on.
3. Ground the negative voltmeter lead.
4. Connect the voltmeter positive lead to the harness connector cavity No. 1 (shown on the schematic). Voltage should be within 1 volt of battery voltage with all accessories off. If not, check the circuit through to the battery.
5. Connect the voltmeter positive lead to cavity No. 2. Voltage

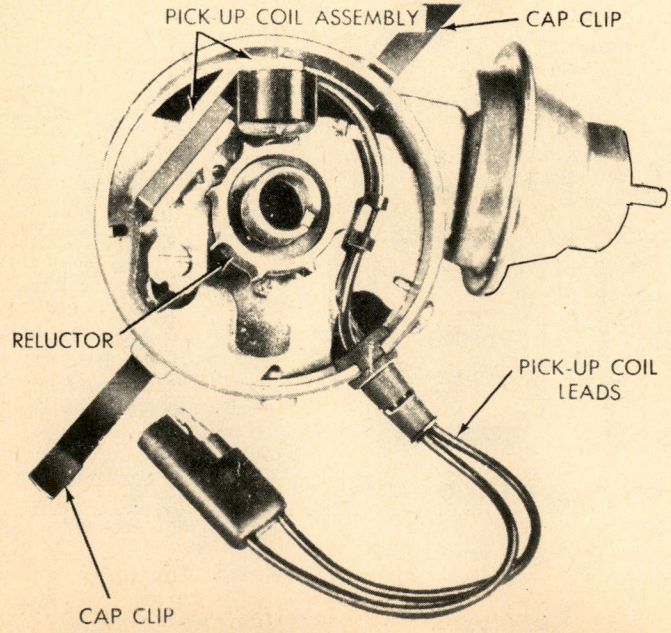

PICK-UP COIL ASSEMBLY — CAP CLIP

RELUCTOR

PICK-UP COIL LEADS

CAP CLIP

Chrysler electronic ignition distributor (© Chrysler Corp.)

should be within 1 volt of battery voltage with all accessories off. If not, check the circuit through to the battery.

6. Connect the voltmeter positive lead to cavity No. 3. Voltage should be within 1 volt of battery voltage with all accessories off. If not, check the circuit through to the battery.

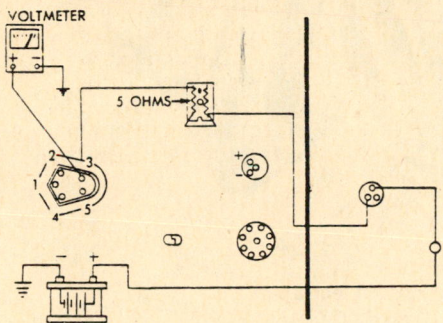

Circuit to be checked out if voltage at plug cavity No. 3 is not within 1 volt of battery voltage (© Chrysler Corp.)

7. Turn the ignition switch off.
8. Connect the ohmmeter leads to cavities No. 4 and 5. The resistance should be 150-900 ohms. If it isn't, detach the dual lead connector from the distributor. Check the resistance at the dual lead connector. If it still isn't within the range, replace the distributor pick-up coil.

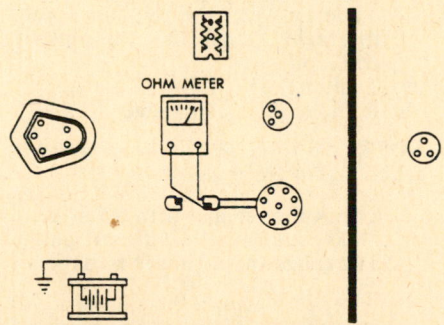

Checking the resistance at the dual lead connector (© Chrysler Corp.)

9. Connect one ohmmeter lead to a ground and the other to either distributor connector. If the ohmmeter shows a reading, replace the distributor pick-up coil.
10. Connect one ohmmeter lead to a ground and the other to the control unit pin No. 5. The ohmmeter should show continuity. If not, remove and remount the control unit and check again. Replace the control unit if no continuity can be established.
11. Make sure the ignition switch is off and replace the control unit connector plug and the distributor plug.
12. Check the air gap adjustment, as shown later.

TROUBLESHOOTING CHRYSLER ELECTRONIC IGNITION

Condition	Possible Cause	Correction
ENGINE WILL NOT START (Fuel and carburetion known to be OK)	a) Dual Ballast	Check resistance of each section: Compensating resistance: .50-.60 ohms @ 70°-80°F Auxiliary Ballast: 4.75-5.75 ohms Replace if faulty. Check wire positions.
	b) Faulty Ignition Coil	Check for carbonized tower. Check primary and secondary resistances: Primary: 1.41-1.79 ohms @ 70°-80°F Secondary: 9,200-11,700 ohms @ 70°-80°F Check in coil tester.
	c) Faulty Pickup or Improper Pickup Air Gap	Check pickup coil resistance: 400-600 ohms Check pickup gap: .010 in. feeler gauge should not slip between pickup coil core and an aligned reluctor blade. No evidence of pickup core striking reluctor blades should be visible. To reset gap, tighten pickup adjustment screw with a .008 in. feeler gauge held between pickup core and an aligned reluctor blade. After resetting gap, run distributor on test stand and apply vacuum advance, making sure that the pickup core does not strike the reluctor blades.
	d) Faulty Wiring	Visually inspect wiring for brittle insulation. Inspect connectors. Molded connectors should be inspected for rubber inside female terminals.
	e) Faulty Control Unit	Replace if all of the above checks are negative. Whenever the control unit or dual ballast is replaced, make sure the dual ballast wires are correctly inserted in the keyed molded connector.
ENGINE SURGES SEVERELY (Not Lean Carburetor)	a) Wiring	Inspect for loose connection and/or broken conductors in harness.
	b) Faulty Pickup Leads	Disconnect vacuum advance. If surging stops, replace pickup.
	c) Ignition Coil	Check for intermittent primary.
ENGINE MISSES (Carburetion OK)	a) Spark Plugs	Check plugs. Clean and regap if necessary.
	b) Secondary Cable	Check cables with an ohmmeter, or observe secondary circuit performance with an oscilloscope.
	c) Ignition Coil	Check for carbonized tower. Check in coil tester.
	d) Wiring	Check for loose or dirty connections.
	e) Faulty Pickup Lead	Disconnect vacuum advance. If miss stops, replace pickup.
	f) Control Unit	Replace if the above checks are negative.

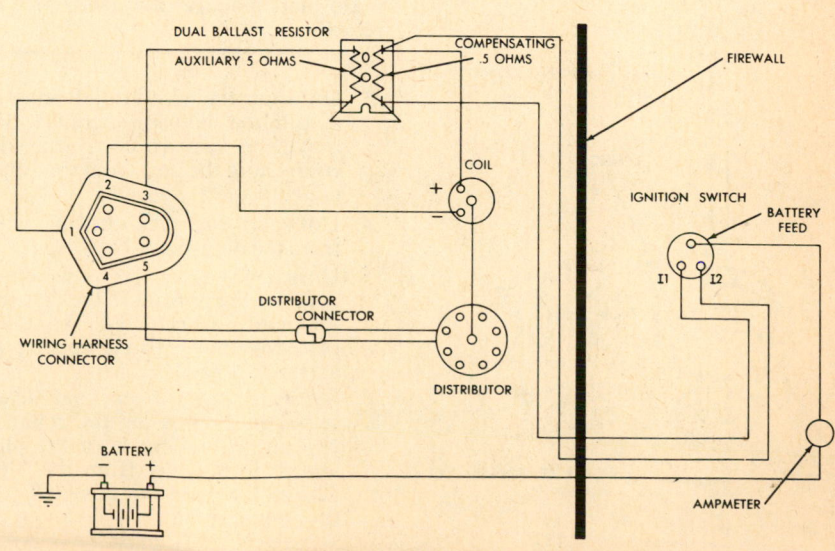

Chrysler corporation electronic ignition system schematic (© Chrysler Corp.)

13. Remove the center wire from the distributor cap. Very cautiously, using insulated pliers and a very heavy glove, hold the cable about ³/₁₆ in. from the engine block and have the starter operated. If there is no spark, replace the control unit. Try the test again. If there is still no spark, replace the coil.

Pick-Up Coil Replacement

1972-74

1. Remove the distributor.
2. Remove the pick-up coil mounting screw.
3. Remove the wires from the retainers on the upper plate and distributor housing.

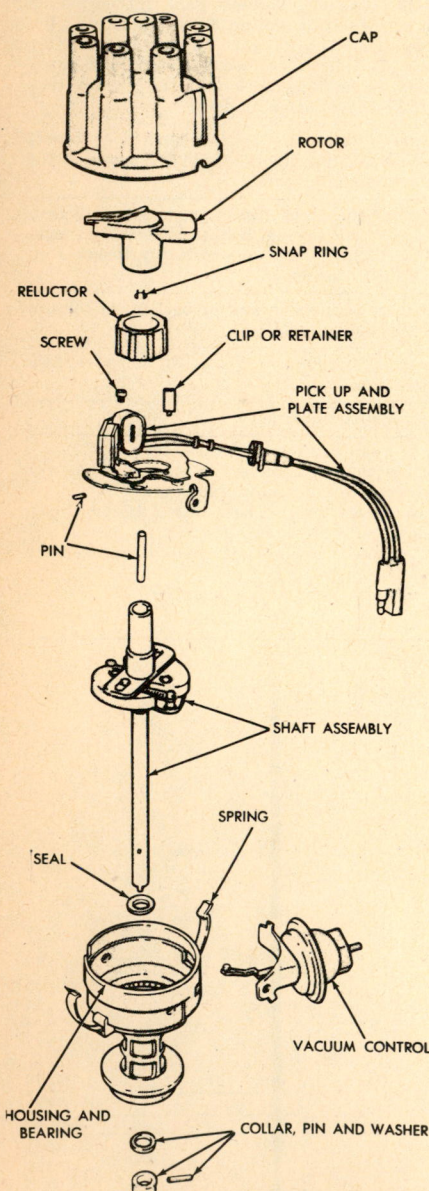

Chrysler Electronic Ignition distributor disassembled—V8
(© Chrysler Corp)

CAP
ROTOR
SNAP RING
RELUCTOR
SCREW
CLIP OR RETAINER
PICK UP AND PLATE ASSEMBLY
PIN
SHAFT ASSEMBLY
SPRING
SEAL
VACUUM CONTROL
HOUSING AND BEARING
COLLAR, PIN AND WASHER

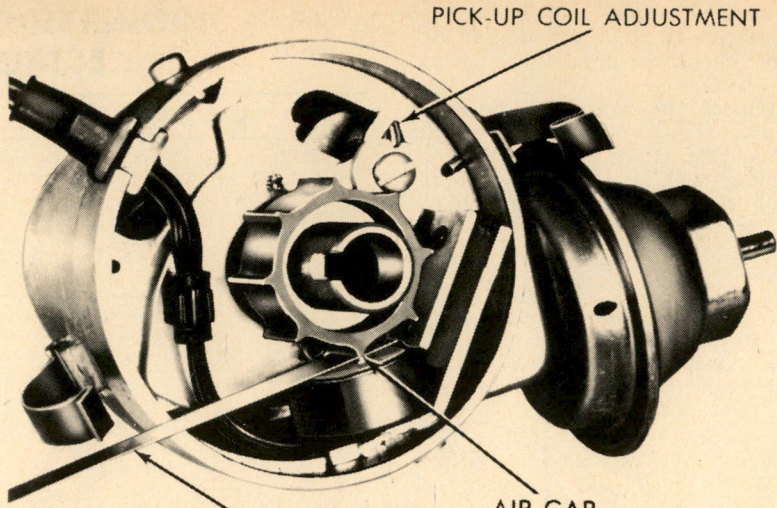

PICK-UP COIL ADJUSTMENT
NON-MAGNETIC FEELER GAUGE
AIR GAP

Air gap adjustment—Chrysler Electronic Ignition distributor (© Chrysler Corp)

4. Remove pick-up coil from the upper plate.
5. Position the pick-up coil on the pivot of the upper plate and install the mounting screw. Do not tighten.
6. Insert the wires into the appropriate retainers in the distributor.
7. Install the distributor.
8. Set the air gap.

1975 AND LATER

1. Remove the distributor from the engine.
2. Using two small pry-bars or screwdrivers (maximum ⁷/₁₆ in. wide), pry the reluctor off the shaft from the bottom.

— CAUTION —

Do not damage the teeth on the reluctor.

3. Unfasten the vacuum advance-to-distributor housing screws. Remove the vacuum unit, after disconnecting the arm from the upper plate.
4. Unfasten the pick-up coil wires from the distributor housing.
5. Unfasten the two screws which secure the lower plate to the distributor housing. Lift out the lower plate together with the upper plate and pick-up coil.
6. Separate the upper and lower plates by depressing the retaining clip on the underside of the plate and slide it away from the stud. The pick-up coil will come off with the upper plate; they cannot be separated; they must be serviced as an assembly.

   Installation is the reverse of removal. Place a small amount of distributor grease on the support pins on the lower plate.

Air Gap Adjustment

1. Align one reluctor tooth with the pick-up coil tooth.
2. Loosen the pick-up coil hold-down screw.
3. Insert a 0.008 in. (0.006 starting 1977) nonmagnetic feeler gauge between the reluctor tooth and the pick-up coil tooth.
4. Adjust the air gap so that contact is made between the reluctor tooth, the feeler gauge, and the pick-up coil tooth.
5. Tighten the hold-down screw.
6. Remove the feeler gauge.

NOTE: *No force should be required in removing the feeler gauge.*

7. Check the air gap with a 0.010 in. (0.008 starting 1977) feeler gauge. The gauge should not fit into the air gap.

— CAUTION —

DO NOT FORCE THE FEELER GAUGE INTO THE AIR GAP.

NOTE: *Lean burn engines through 1977 (first generation system) have two pick-up air gaps. The gap is .008 in. for start, and .012 in. for run. The second generation system has only one distributor pick-up.*

8. Apply vacuum to the vacuum unit and rotate the governor shaft. The pick-up pole should not hit the reluctor teeth. The gap was not properly adjusted if any hitting occurs. If hitting occurs on only one side of the reluctor, the distributor shaft is probably bent, and the governor and shaft assembly should be replaced.

CHRYSLER CORPORATION OMNI/ HORIZON HALL EFFECT ELECTRONIC IGNITION

The Omni/Horizon Hall Effect electronic ignition is used in conjunction with the Chrysler Lean Burn System (covered in the Emission Controls Unit Repair Section). It consists of a sealed Spark Control Computer, five engine sensors (vacuum transducer, coolant switch, Hall Effect pickup assembly, throttle position transducer, and carburetor switch), coil, spark plugs, ballast resistor, and the various wires needed to connect the components.

The distributor contains the Hall Effect pickup assembly which replaces the breaker points assembly in conventional systems. The pickup assembly supplies the computer with information on engine speed and crankshaft position, and is only one of five signals which the computer uses as input to determine ignition timing. The Hall Effect is a shift in magnetic field, caused, in this installation, when one of the rotor blades passes between the two arms of the sensor.

Operation

There are essentially two modes of operation of the Spark Control com-

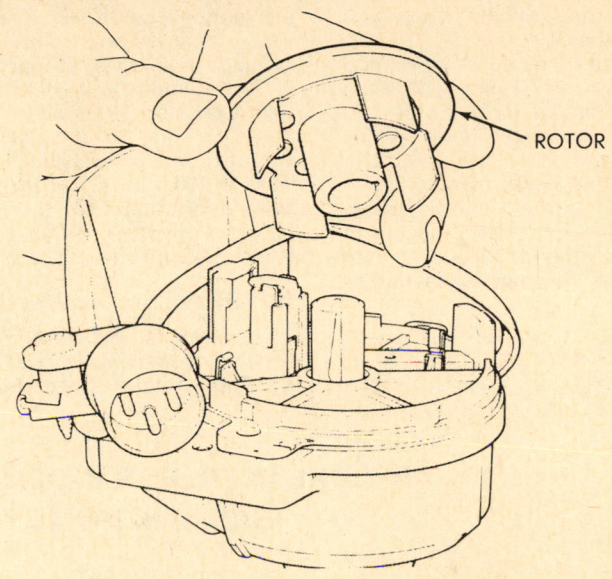

Hall Effect rotor removal (© Chrysler Corp)

puter: the start mode and the run mode. The start mode is only used during engine cranking. During cranking only the Hall Effect pickup signals the computer. These signals are interpreted to provide a fixed number of degrees of spark advance. The computer shuts off coil primary current in accordance with the pickup signals. As in conventional ignition systems, primary current shutdown causes secondary field collapse,

and the high voltage is sent from the coil to the distributor, which then sends it to the spark plug.

After the engine starts, and during normal engine operation, the computer functions in the run mode. In this mode the Hall Effect pickup serves as only one of the five signals to the computer. It is a reference signal of maximum possible spark advance. The computer then determines, from information pro-

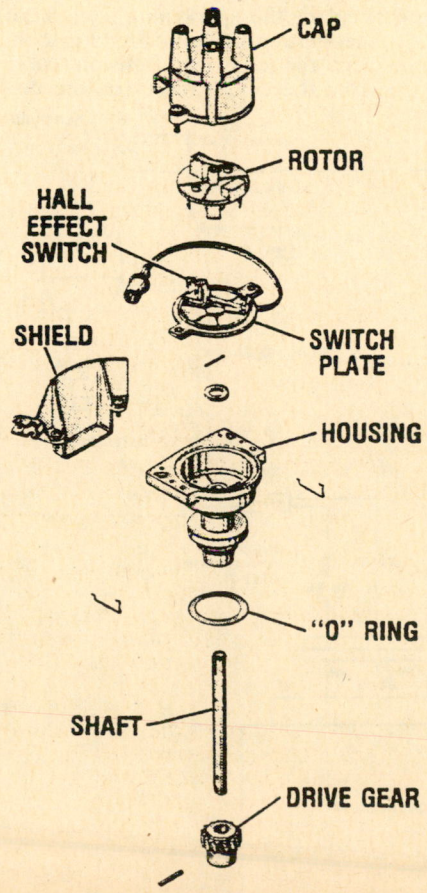

Hall Effect distributor—exploded view
(© Chrysler Corp)

CAP
ROTOR
HALL EFFECT SWITCH
SHIELD
SWITCH PLATE
HOUSING
"O" RING
SHAFT
DRIVE GEAR

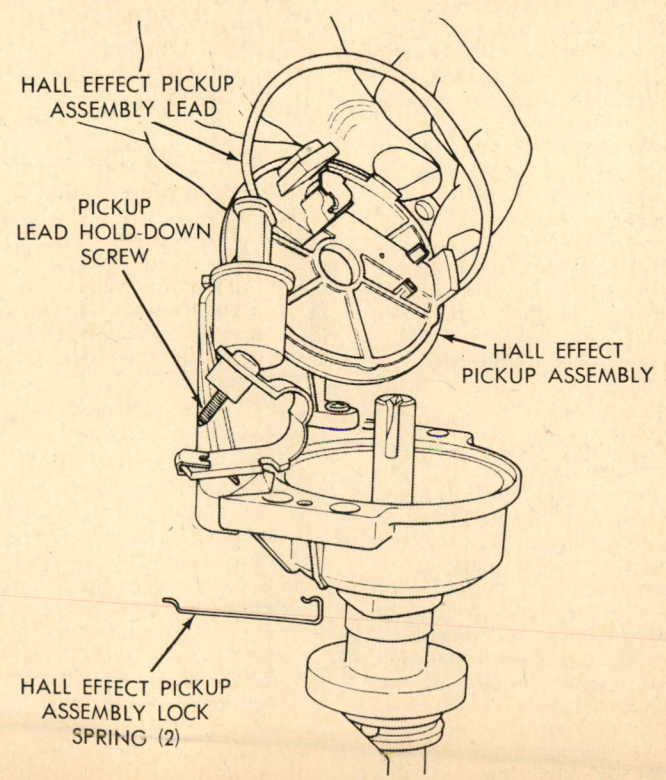

HALL EFFECT PICKUP ASSEMBLY LEAD
PICKUP LEAD HOLD-DOWN SCREW
HALL EFFECT PICKUP ASSEMBLY
HALL EFFECT PICKUP ASSEMBLY LOCK SPRING (2)

Hall Effect pickup installation (© Chrysler Corp)

vided by the other four sensors, how much of this advance is necessary, and shuts down the primary current accordingly to fire the spark plug at the exact moment when this advance (crankshaft position) is reached.

There is a third mode of operation which only becomes functional when the computer fails. This is the limp-in mode. This mode functions on signals from the pickup only, and results in very poor engine performance. However, it does allow the car to be driven to a repair shop. If a failure occurs in the pickup assembly or the start mode of the computer, the engine will neither start nor run.

System Tests

All system tests are covered in the Emission Control Systems Unit Repair Section under "Chrysler Corporation Lean Burn System".

The ignition coil can be tested on a conventional coil tester. The ballast resistor, mounted on the firewall, must be included in all tests. Primary resistance at 70°F should be 1.60-1.79 ohms for the Chrysler Prestolite coil, and 1.41-1.62 ohms for the Chrysler Essex coil. Secondary resistance should be 9400-11,700 ohms for the Prestolite, 8000-11,200 ohms for the Essex. The ballast resistor should measure 0.50-0.60 ohms resistance at 70°F.

Hall Effect Pickup Replacement

1. Loosen the distributor cap retaining screws and remove the cap.
2. Pull straight up on the rotor and remove it from the shaft.
3. Disconnect the pickup assembly lead.
4. Remove the pickup lead hold down screw.
5. Remove the pickup assembly lock springs and lift off the pickup.
6. Install the new pickup assembly onto the distributor housing and fasten it into place with the lock springs.
7. Fasten the pickup lead to the housing with the hold down screw.
8. Reconnect the lead to the harness.
9. Press the rotor back into place on the shaft. Do not wipe off the silicone grease on the metal portion of the rotor.
10. Replace the distributor cap and tighten the retaining screws.

AMC BREAKERLESS INDUCTIVE DISCHARGE (BID) IGNITION SYSTEM

Components

The AMC breakerless inductive discharge (BID) ignition system consists of five components:
Control unit
Coil
Breakerless distributor
Ignition cables
Spark plugs

The control unit is a solid-state, epoxy-sealed module with waterproof connectors. The control unit has a built-in current regulator, so no separate ballast resistor or resistance wire is needed in the primary circuit. Battery voltage is supplied to the ignition coil positive (+) terminal when the ignition key is turned to the "ON" or "START" position; low voltage coil primary current is also supplied by the control unit.

In place of the points, cam, and condensor, the distributor has a sensor and trigger wheel. The sensor is a small coil which generates an electromagnetic field when excited by the oscillator in the control unit.

This system was last used in 1977.

Operation

When the ignition switch is turned on, the control unit is activated. The control unit the sends an oscillating signal to the sensor which causes the sensor to generate a magnetic field. When one of the trigger wheel teeth enters this field, the strength of the oscillation in the sensor is reduced. Once the strength drops to a predetermined level, a demodulator circuit operates the control unit's switching transistor. The switching transistor is wired in series with the coil primary circuit; it switches the circuit off inducing high voltage in the coil secondary winding when it gets the demodulator signal.

From this point on, tthe BID ignition system works in the same manner as a conventional ignition system.

System Test

1. Check all the BID ignition system electrical connections.
2. Disconnect a spark plug lead from the spark plug.
3. Using insulated pliers and a heavy glove, hold the end of the lead 1/2 in. away from a ground. Crank the engine. If there is a spark, the trouble is not in the ignition system. Check the distributor cap, rotor, and wires.
4. Replace the spark plug lead. Turn the ignition switch off and disconnect the coil high tension cable from the center tower on the dis-

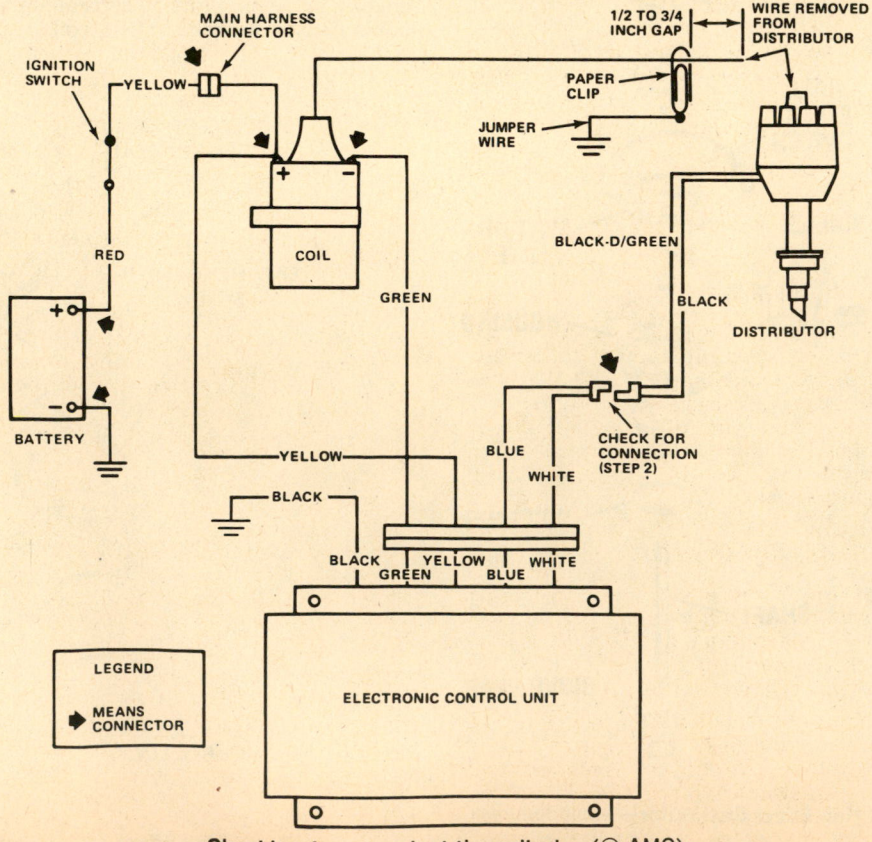

Checking for a spark at the coil wire (© AMC)

tributor cap. Place a paper clip around the cable 1/2-3/4 in. from the metal end. Ground the paper clip to the engine. Crank the engine. If there is no spark, the distributor cap or rotor may be at fault.

5. Turn the ignition switch off and replace the coil wire. Make the spark test of Step 3 again. If there is no spark, check the coil high tension wire with an ohmmeter. It should show 5-10,000 ohms resistance. If not replace it and repeat the spark test.

6. Detach the distributor sensor lead wire plug. Check the wire connector by trying a no. 16 (0.177 in.) drill bit for a snug fit in the female terminals. Apply a light coat of Silicone Dielectric Compound or its equivalent to the male terminals. Fill the female cavities 1/4 full. Reconnect the plug.

7. Repeat the test of Step 4.

8. If there was a spark in Step 7, detach the sensor lead plug and try a replacement sensor. Try the test again. If there is a spark, the sensor was defective.

9. Connect a voltmeter between the coil positive terminal and an engine ground. With the ignition switch on, the voltmeter should read battery voltage. If it is lower, there is a high resistance between the battery (through the ignition switch) and the coil.

10. Connect the voltmeter between the coil negative terminal and an engine ground. With the ignition switch on, the voltage should be 5-8. If not, replace the coil. If you get a battery voltage reading, crank the engine slightly to move the trigger wheel tooth away from the sensor; voltage should drop to 5-8.

11. Check the sensor resistance by connecting an ohmmeter to its leads. Resistance should be 1.6-2.4 ohms.

Coil Testing

Test the coil with a conventional coil checker or an ohmmeter. Primary resistance should be 1.25-1.40 ohms and secondary resistance should be 9-12 kilo-ohms. The open output circuit should be more than 20 kilovolts. Replace the coil if it doesn't meet specifications.

Distributor Overhaul

NOTE: *If you must remove the sensor from the distributor for any reason, it will be necessary to have the special sensor positioning gauge in order to align it properly during installation.*

1. Scribe matchmarks on the distributor housing, rotor, and engine block. Disconnect the leads and vacuum lines from the distributor. Remove the distributor. Unless the cap is to be replaced, leave it con-

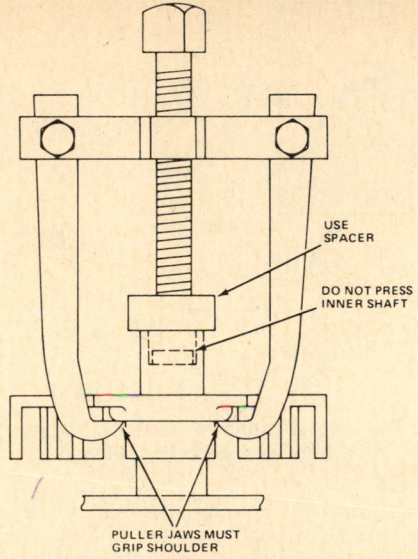

Removing the trigger wheel (Ⓒ AMC)

nected to the spark plug cables and position it out of the way.

2. Remove the rotor and dust cap.

3. Place a small gear puller over the trigger wheel, so that its jaws grip the inner shoulders of the wheel and not its arms. Place a thick washer between the gear puller and the distributor shaft to act as a spacer; do not press against the smaller inner shaft.

4. Loosen the sensor hold-down screw with a small pair of needle-nosed pliers; it has a tamper-proof head. Pull the sensor lead grommet out of the distributor body and pull out the leads from around the spring pivot pin.

5. Release the sensor securing spring by lifting it. Make sure that it clears the leads. Slide the sensor off the bracket. *Remember, a special gauge is required for sensor installation.*

6. Remove the vacuum advance unit securing screw. Slide the vacuum unit out of the distributor. Remove it only if it is to be replaced.

7. Clean the vacuum unit and sensor brackets. Lubrication of these parts is not necessary.

BID distributor assembly is as follows:

1. Install the vacuum unit, if it was removed.

2. Assemble the sensor, sensor guide, flat washer, and retaining screw. Tighten the screw only far enough to keep the assembly together; don't allow the screw to project below the bottom of the sensor.

NOTE: *Replacement sensors come with a slotted-head screw to aid in assembly. If the original sensor is being used, replace the tamper-proof screw with a conventional one. Use the original washer.*

3. Secure the sensor on the vacuum advance unit bracket, making sure

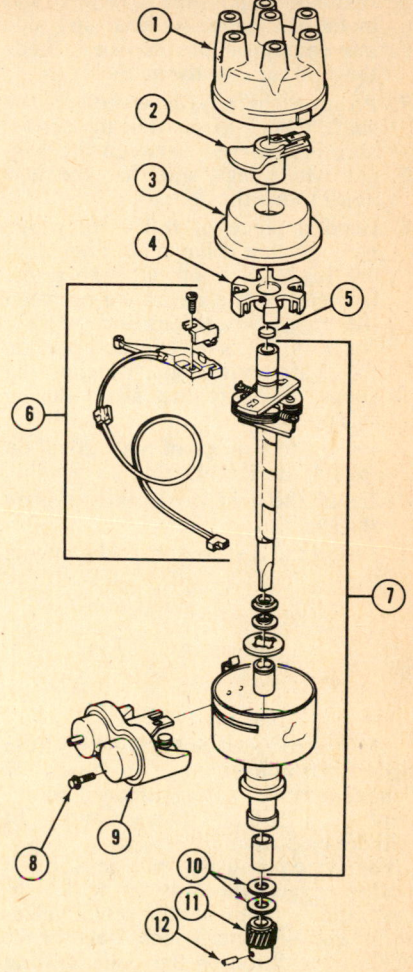

BID distributor components (Ⓒ AMC)

1 Cap
2 Rotor
3 Dust shield
4 Trigger wheel
5 Felt lubricator
6 Sensor assembly
7 Distributor body
8 Vacuum unit screw
9 Vacuum advance unit
10 Shim
11 Drive gear
12 Pin

that the tip of the sensor is placed in the notch on the summing bar.

4. Position the spring on the sensor and route the leads around the spring pivot pin. Fit the sensor lead grommet into the slot on the distributor body. Be sure that the lead can't get caught in the trigger wheel.

5. Place the special sensor positioning gauge over the distributor shaft, so that the flat on the shaft is against the large notch on the gauge. Move the sensor until the sensor core fits into the small notch on the gauge. Tighten the sensor securing screw with the gauge in place (through the round hold in the gauge).

6. It should be possible to remove and install the gauge without any side movement of the sensor. Check this and remove the gauge.

7. Position the trigger wheel on the shaft. Check to see that the sensor core is centered between the trigger wheel legs and that the legs don't touch the core.

8. Bend a piece of 0.050 in. gauge wire, so that it has a 90° angle and one leg 1/2 in. long. Use the gauge to measure the clearance between the trigger wheel legs and the sensor boss. Press the trigger wheel on the shaft until it just touches the gauge. Support the shaft during this operation.

9. Place 3 to 5 drops of SAE 20 oil on the felt lubricator wick.

10. Install the dust shield and rotor on the shaft.

11. Install the distributor on the engine

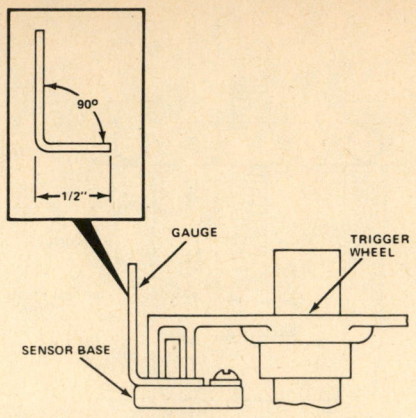

Fabricate a gauge to measure trigger wheel clearance (© AMC)

using the matchmarks made during removal and adjust the timing. Use a new distributor mounting gasket.

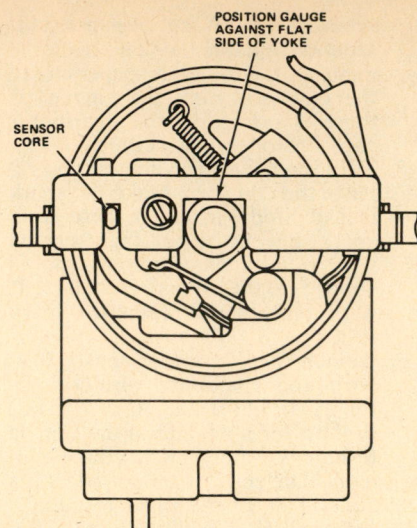

Using the special gauge to align the sensor coil (© AMC)

AMC SOLID STATE IGNITION (SSI) SYSTEM

AMC introduced Solid State Ignition (SSI) as a running change on some 1977 Canadian models. It is standard equipment on all 1978 and later six and eight cylinder engines.

The system consists of a sensor and toothed trigger wheel inside the distributor, and a permanently sealed electronic control unit which determines dwell, in addition to the coil, ignition wires, and spark plugs.

The trigger wheel rotates on the distributor shaft. As one of its teeth nears

the sensor magnet, the magnetic field shifts toward the tooth. When the tooth and sensor are aligned, the magnetic field is shifted to its maximum, signaling the electronic control unit to switch off the coil primary current. This starts an electronic timer inside the control unit, which allows the primary current to remain off only long enough for the spark plug to fire. The timer adjusts the amount of time primary current is off according to conditions, thus automatically adjusting dwell. There is also a

special circuit within the control unit to detect and ignore spurious signals. Spark timing is adjusted by both mechanical (centrifugal) and vacuum advance.

A wire of 1.35 ohms resistance is spliced into the ignition feed to reduce voltage to the coil during running conditions. The resistance wire is bypassed when the engine is being started so that full battery voltage may be supplied to the coil. Bypass is accomplished by the I-terminal on the solenoid.

Secondary Circuit Test

1. Disconnect the coil wire from the center of the distributor cap.

NOTE: *Twist the rubber boot slightly in either direction, then grasp the boot and pull straight up. Do not pull on the wire, and do not use pliers.*

Hold the wire 1/2 in. from a ground with a pair of insulated pliers and a heavy glove. As the engine is cranked, watch for a spark.

2. If a spark appears, reconnect the coil wire. Remove the wire from one spark plug, and test for a spark as above.

— **CAUTION** —

Do not remove the spark plug wires from cylinders 3 or 5 on a 6 cylinder engine, or cylinders 3 or 4 on a V8 when performing this test, as sensor damage could occur.

If a spark occurs, the problem is in the fuel system or ignition timing. If no spark occurs, check for a defective rotor, cap, or spark plug wires.

3. If no spark occurs from the coil wire in Step 2, test the coil wire

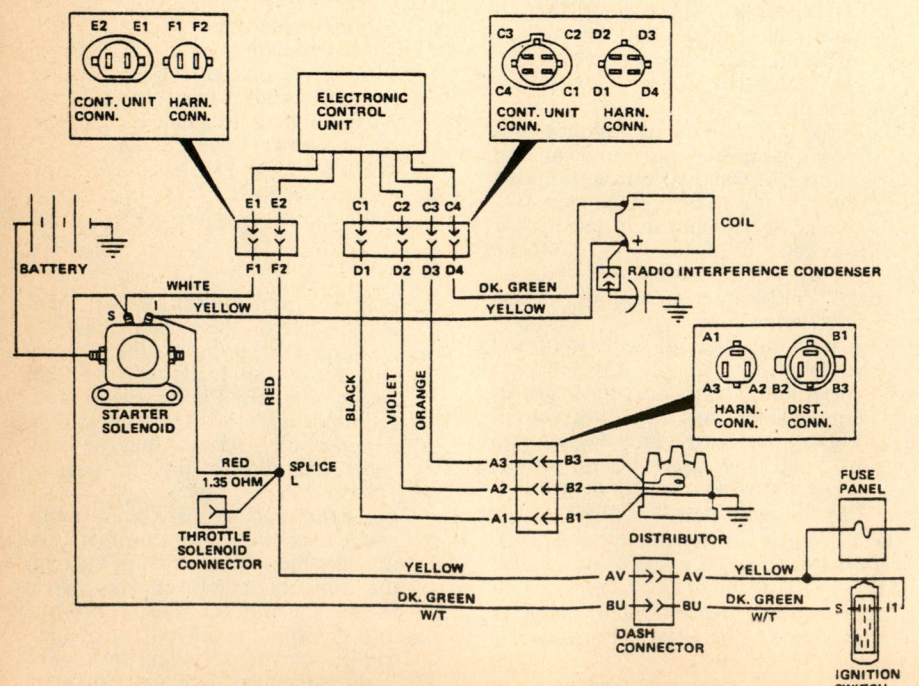

SSI system schematic (© AMC)

resistance with an ohmmeter. It must not exceed 10,000 ohms.

Coil Primary Circuit Test

1. Turn the ignition On. Connect a voltmeter to the coil positive (+) terminal and a ground. If the voltage is 5.5-6.5 volts, go to Step 2. If above 7 volts, go to Step 4. If below 5.5 volts, disconnect the condenser lead and measure. If the voltage is now 5.5-6.5 volts, replace the condenser. If not, go to Step 6.
2. With the voltmeter connected as in Step 1, read the voltage with the engine cranking. If battery voltage is indicated, the circuit is okay. If not, go to Step 3.
3. Check for a short or open in the solenoid I-terminal wire. Check the solenoid for proper operation.
4. Disconnect the wire from the solenoid I-terminal, with the ignition On and the voltmeter connected as in Step 1. If the voltage drops to 5.5-6.5 volts, replace the solenoid. If not, connect a jumper between the coil negative (−) terminal and a ground. If the voltage drops to 5.5-6.5 volts, go to Step 5. If not, repair the resistance wire.
5. Check for continuity between the coil-terminal and D4 and D1 to ground. If the continuity is okay, replace the control unit. If not, check for an open wire and go to Step 2.
6. Turn ignition Off. Connect an ohmmeter between the + coil terminal and dash connector AV. If above 1.40 ohms, repair the resistance wire.
7. With the ignition Off, connect the ohmmeter between connector AV and ignition switch terminal 11. If less than 0.1 ohm, replace the ignition switch or repair the wire, whichever is the cause. If above 0.1 ohm, check connections, and check for defective wiring.

Coil Test

1. Check the coil for cracks, carbon tracks, etc., and replace as necessary.
2. Connect an ohmmeter across the coil + and − terminals, with the coil connector removed. If 1.13-1.23 ohms / 75°F, go to Step 3. If not, replace the coil.
3. Measure the resistance across the coil center tower and either the + or − terminal. If 7700-9300 ohms, the coil is okay. If not, replace.

Control Unit and Sensor Test

1. With the ignition On, remove the coil high tension wire from the distributor cap and hold 1/2 in. from ground with insulated pliers. Disconnect the 4 wire connector at the control unit. If a spark occurs (normal), go to Step 2. If not, go to Step 5.

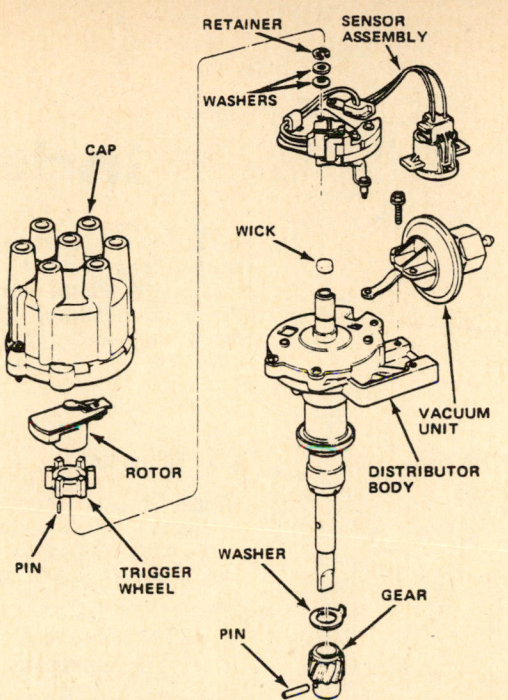

Six cylinder SSI distributor—V8 similar (© AMC)

2. Connect an ohmmeter to D2 and D3. If the resistance is 400-800 ohms (normal), go to Step 6. If not, go to Step 3.
3. Disconnect and reconnect the 3 wire connector at distributor. If the reading is now 400-800 ohms, go to Step 6. If not, disconnect the 3 wire connector and go to Step 4.
4. Connect the ohmmeter across B2 and B3. If 400-800 ohms, repair the harness between the 3 wire and 4

CONNECT OHMMETER TO B2 AND B3

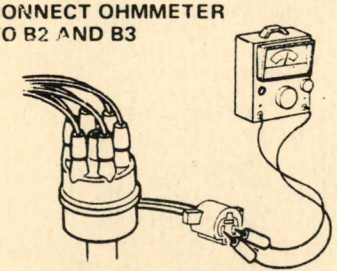

Step 4 of the control unit and sensor test (© AMC)

wire connectors. If not, replace the sensor.
5. Connect the ohmmeter between D1 and the battery negative terminal. If the reading is 0 (0.002 or less), go to Step 2. If above 0.002 ohms, there is a bad ground in the cable or at the distributor. Repair the ground and retest.
6. Connect a voltmeter across D2 and D3. Crank the engine. If the needle fluctuates, the system is okay. If not, either the trigger wheel is defective, or the distributor is not turning. Repair or replace as required.

Ignition Feed to Control Unit Test

NOTE: *Do not perform this test without first performing the Coil Primary Circuit Test.*

1. With the ignition On, unplug the 2 wire connector at the module. Connect a voltmeter between F2 and ground. If the reading is battery voltage, replace the control unit and go to Step 3. If not, go to Step 2.
2. Repair the cause of the voltage reduction: either the ignition switch or a corroded dash connector. Check for a spark at the coil wire. If okay, stop. If not, replace the control unit and check for proper operation.
3. Reconnect the 2 wire connector at the control unit, and unplug the 4 wire connector at the control unit. Connect an ammeter between C1 and ground. If it reads 0.9-1.1 amps, the system is okay. If not, replace the module.

DISCONNECT 4-WIRE CONNECTOR AT CONTROL UNIT

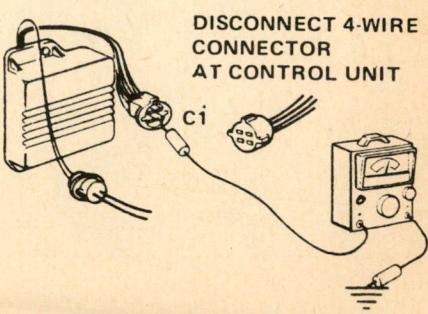

Step 3 of the ignition feed to control unit test (© AMC)

Carburetors

Index

NOTE: *New model year carburetor specifications are not released by the manufacturers until well after the press date for this manual. These will be included in the next edition.*

CARBURETOR FUNCTIONS, PRINCIPLES, AND CIRCUITS

FUNCTIONS

Gasoline is the source of fuel for power in the automobile engine and the carburetor is the mechanism which automatically mixes liquid fuel with air in the correct proportions to provide the desired power output from the engine. The carburetor performs this function by metering, atomizing, and mixing fuel with air flowing through the engine.

A carburetor also regulates the volume of air-to-fuel mixture which enters the engine. It is the carburetor's regulation of the mixture flow which gives the operator control of the engine speed.

Metering

The automotive internal combustion engine operates efficiently within a relatively small range of air-to-fuel ratios. It is the function of the carburetor to meter the fuel in exact proportions to the air flowing into the engine, so that the optimum ratio of air-to-fuel is maintained under all operating conditions. Regulations governing exhaust gas emissions have made the proper metering of fuel by the carburetor an increasingly important factor. Too rich a mixture will result in poor economy and increased emissions, while too lean a mixture will result in loss of power and generally poor performance.

Carburetors are matched to engines so that metering can be accomplished by using carefully calibrated metering jets which allow fuel to enter the engine at a rate proportional to the engine's ability to draw air.

Atomization

The liquid fuel must be broken up into small particles so that it will more readily mix with air and vaporize. The more contact the fuel has with the air, the better the vaporization. Atomization can be accomplished in two ways: air may be drawn into a stream of fuel which will cause a turbulence and break the solid stream of fuel into smaller particles; or a nozzle can be positioned at the point of highest air velocity in the carburetor and the fuel will be torn into a fine spray as it enters the air stream.

Distribution

The carburetor is the primary device involved in the distribution of fuel to the engine. The more efficiently fuel and air are combined in the carburetor, the smoother the flow of vaporized mixture through the intake manifold to each combustion chamber. Hence, the importance of the carburetor in fuel distribution.

PRINCIPLES

Vacuum

All carburetors operate on the basic principle of pressure difference. Any pressure less than atmospheric pressure is considered vacuum or a low pressure area. In the engine, as the piston moves down on the intake stroke with the intake valve open, a partial vacuum is created in the intake manifold. The farther the piston travels downward, the greater the vacuum created in the manifold. As vacuum increases in the manifold, a difference in pressure occurs between the carburetor and cylinder. The carburetor is positioned in such a way that the high pressure above it, and the vacuum or low pressure beneath it, causes air to be drawn through it. Fuel and air always move from high to low pressure areas.

Venturi Principle

To obtain greater pressure drop at the tip of the fuel nozzle so that fuel will flow, the principle of increasing the air velocity to create a low pressure area is used. The device used to increase the velocity of the air flowing through the carburetor is called a venturi. A venturi is a specially designed restriction placed in the air flow. In order for the air to pass through the restriction, it must accelerate causing a pressure drop or vacuum as it passes.

CARBURETOR CIRCUITS

Float Circuit

The float circuit includes the float, float bowl, and a needle valve and seat. This circuit controls the amount of gas allowed to flow into the carburetor.

As the fuel level rises, it causes the float to rise which pushes the needle valve into its seat. As soon as the valve and seat make contact, the flow of gas is cut off from the fuel inlet. When the level of fuel drops, the float sinks and releases the needle valve from its seat

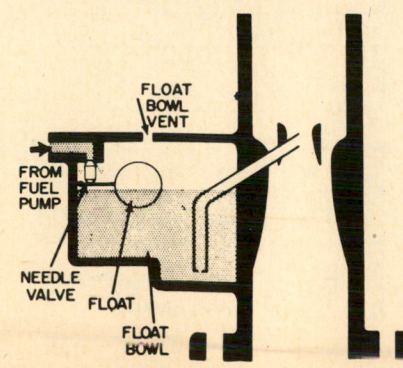

Float circuit
(© United Delco Div., G.M. Corp)

which allows the gas to flow in. In actual operation, the fuel is maintained at practically a constant level. The float tends to hold the needle valve partly closed so that the incoming fuel just balances the fuel being withdrawn.

Idle and Low Speed Circuit

When the throttle is closed or only slightly opened, the air speed is low and practically no vacuum develops in the venturi. This means that the fuel nozzle will not feed. Thus, the carburetor must have another circuit to supply fuel during operation with a closed or slightly opened throttle.

This circuit is called the idle and low speed circuit. It consists of passages in which air and gas can flow beneath the throttle plate. With the throttle plate closed, there is high vacuum from the intake manifold. Atmospheric pressure pushes the air/fuel mixture through the passages of the idle and low speed circuit and past the tapered point of the idle adjustment screw, which regulates engine idle mixture volume.

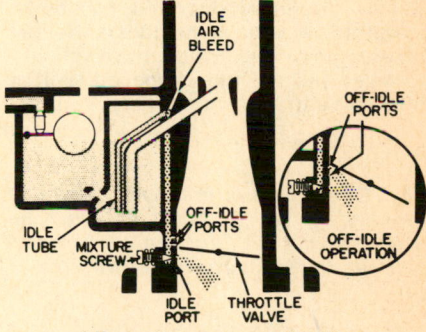

Idle and low speed circuit
(© United Delco Div., G.M. Corp)

High Speed Partial Load Circuit

When the throttle plate is opened sufficiently, there is little difference in vacuum between the upper and lower part of the air horn. Thus, little air/fuel mixture will discharge from the low speed and idle circuit. However, under this condition enough air is moving through the air horn to produce vacuum in the venturi to cause the main nozzle or high speed nozzle to discharge fuel. The circuit from the float bowl to the main nozzle is called the high speed partial load circuit. A nearly constant air/fuel ratio is maintained by this circuit from part to full-throttle.

High Speed Full Power Circuit

For high-speed, full-power, wide open throttle operation, the air/fuel mixture must be enriched; this is done either mechanically or by intake manifold vacuum.

Full Power Circuit (Mechanical)

This circuit includes a metering rod

jet and a metering rod. The rod has two steps of different diameters and is attached to the throttle linkage.

When the throttle is wide open, the metering rod is lifted bringing the smaller diameter of the rod into the jet. When the throttle is partly closed, the larger diameter of the metering rod is in the jet. This restricts fuel flow to the main nozzle but adequate amounts of fuel do flow for part-throttle operation.

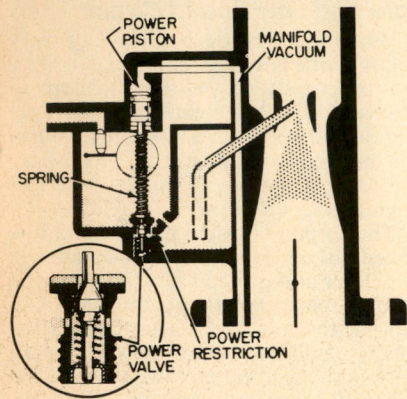

Power circuit
(© United Delco Div., G.M. Corp)

Full Power Circuit (Vacuum)

This circuit is operated by intake manifold vacuum. It includes a vacuum diaphragm or piston linked to a valve.

When the throttle is opened so that intake manifold vacuum is reduced, the spring raises the diaphragm or piston. This allows more fuel to flow in, either by lifting a metering rod or by opening a power valve.

Accelerator Pump Circuit

For acceleration, the carburetor must deliver additional fuel. A sudden inrush of air is caused by rapid acceleration or applying full throttle.

When the throttle is opened, the pump lever pushes the plunger down and this forces fuel to flow through the accelerator pump circuit and out the pump jet. This fuel enters the air passage through the carburetor to supply additional fuel demands.

Choke

When starting an engine, it is necessary to increase the amount of fuel delivered to the intake manifold. This increase is controlled by the choke.

The choke consists of a valve in the top of the air horn controlled mechanically by an automatic device. When the choke valve is closed, only a small amount of air can get past it. When the engine is cranked, a fairly high vacuum develops in the air horn. This vacuum causes the main nozzle to discharge a heavy stream of fuel. The quantity delivered is sufficient to produce the correct air/fuel mixture needed for starting the engine. The choke is released either manually or by heat from the engine.

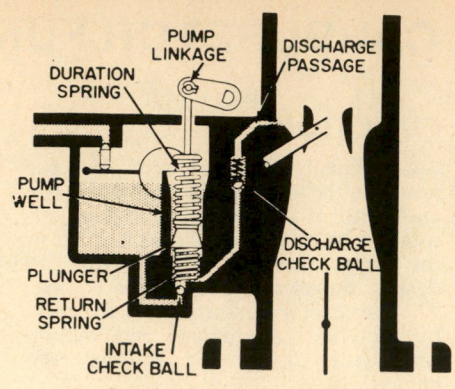

Accelerator pump circuit
(© United Delco Div., G.M. Corp)

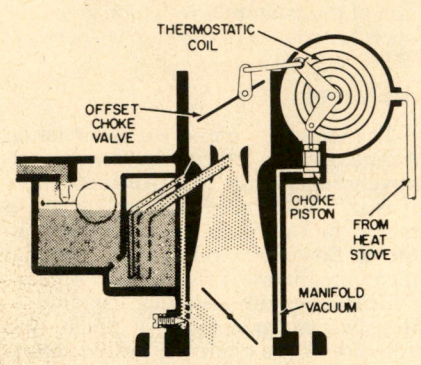

Choke system
(© United Delco Div., G.M. Corp)

NOTE: *Carburetor problems cannot be isolated effectively unless all other engine systems are functioning correctly and the engine is properly tuned.*

TROUBLESHOOTING

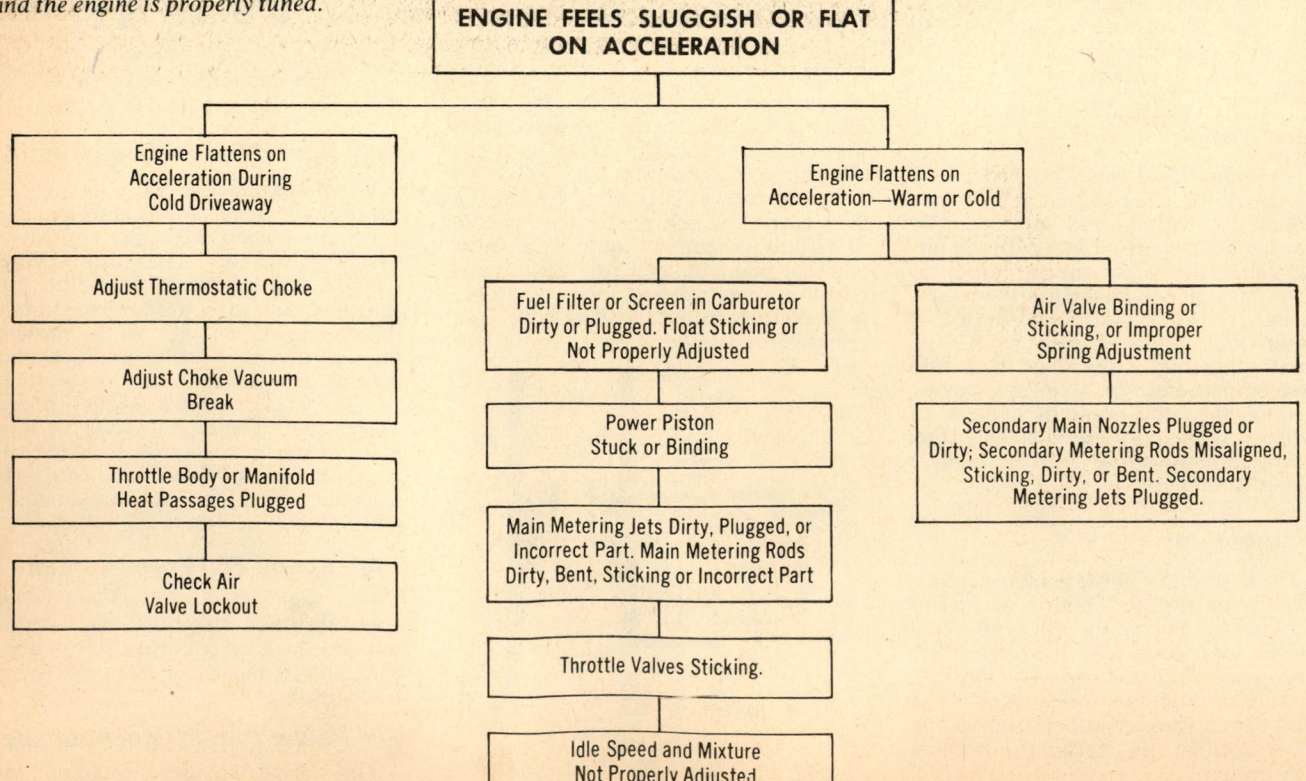

ENGINE FEELS SLUGGISH OR FLAT ON ACCELERATION

Engine Flattens on Acceleration During Cold Driveaway
- Adjust Thermostatic Choke
- Adjust Choke Vacuum Break
- Throttle Body or Manifold Heat Passages Plugged
- Check Air Valve Lockout

Engine Flattens on Acceleration—Warm or Cold

- Fuel Filter or Screen in Carburetor Dirty or Plugged. Float Sticking or Not Properly Adjusted
- Power Piston Stuck or Binding
- Main Metering Jets Dirty, Plugged, or Incorrect Part. Main Metering Rods Dirty, Bent, Sticking or Incorrect Part
- Throttle Valves Sticking.
- Idle Speed and Mixture Not Properly Adjusted

- Air Valve Binding or Sticking, or Improper Spring Adjustment
- Secondary Main Nozzles Plugged or Dirty; Secondary Metering Rods Misaligned, Sticking, Dirty, or Bent. Secondary Metering Jets Plugged.

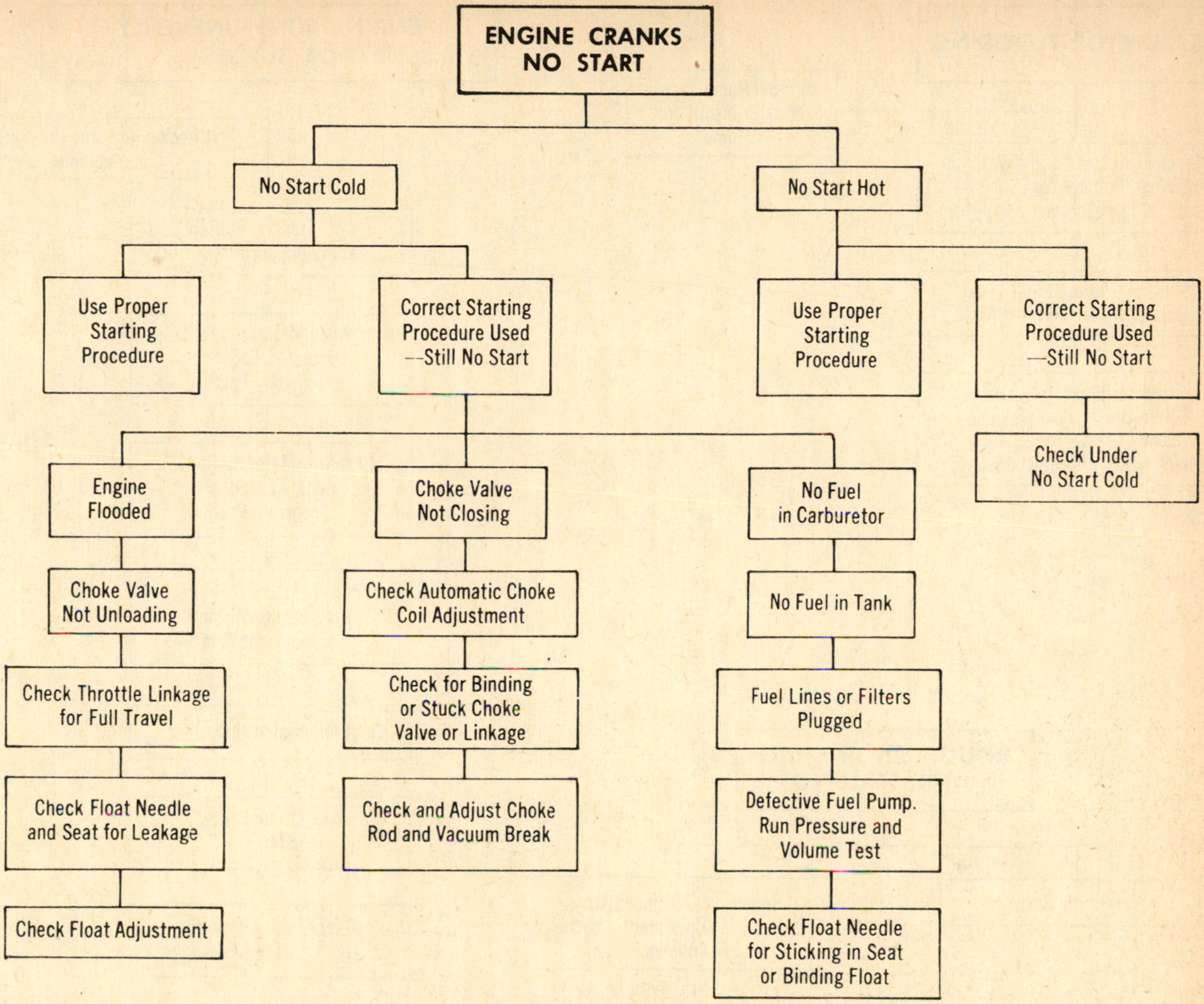

```
                        ┌─────────────────┐
                        │  ENGINE CRANKS  │
                        │    NO START     │
                        └─────────────────┘
              ┌──────────────────┴──────────────────┐
      ┌───────────────┐                      ┌───────────────┐
      │ No Start Cold │                      │ No Start Hot  │
      └───────────────┘                      └───────────────┘
```

No Start Cold		No Start Hot	
Use Proper Starting Procedure	Correct Starting Procedure Used —Still No Start	Use Proper Starting Procedure	Correct Starting Procedure Used —Still No Start

Under "Correct Starting Procedure Used —Still No Start" (No Start Hot): **Check Under No Start Cold**

Engine Flooded	Choke Valve Not Closing	No Fuel in Carburetor
Choke Valve Not Unloading	Check Automatic Choke Coil Adjustment	No Fuel in Tank
Check Throttle Linkage for Full Travel	Check for Binding or Stuck Choke Valve or Linkage	Fuel Lines or Filters Plugged
Check Float Needle and Seat for Leakage	Check and Adjust Choke Rod and Vacuum Break	Defective Fuel Pump. Run Pressure and Volume Test
Check Float Adjustment		Check Float Needle for Sticking in Seat or Binding Float

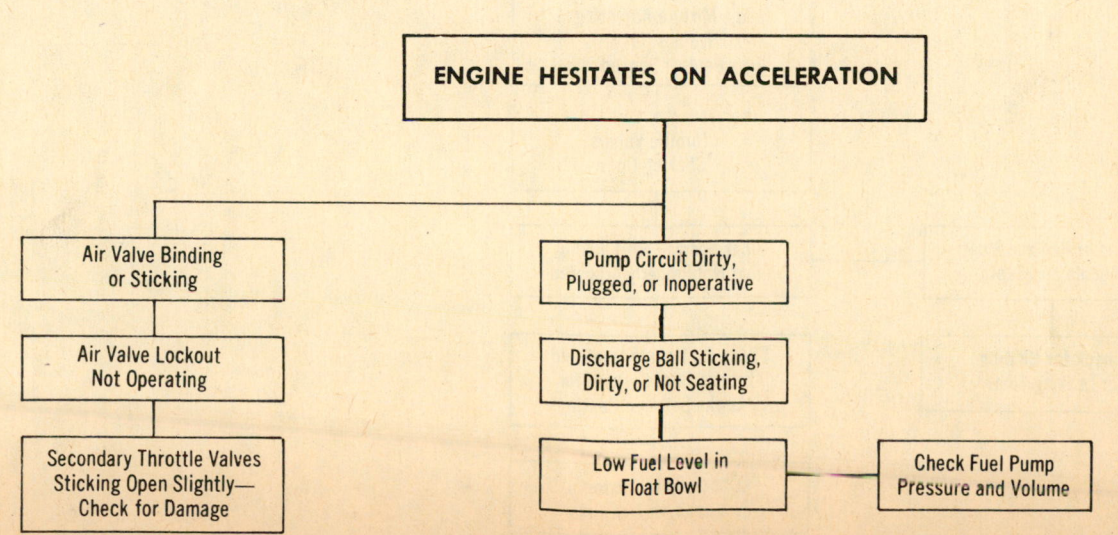

ENGINE HESITATES ON ACCELERATION

Air Valve Binding or Sticking	Pump Circuit Dirty, Plugged, or Inoperative
Air Valve Lockout Not Operating	Discharge Ball Sticking, Dirty, or Not Seating
Secondary Throttle Valves Sticking Open Slightly— Check for Damage	Low Fuel Level in Float Bowl — Check Fuel Pump Pressure and Volume

Carburetors

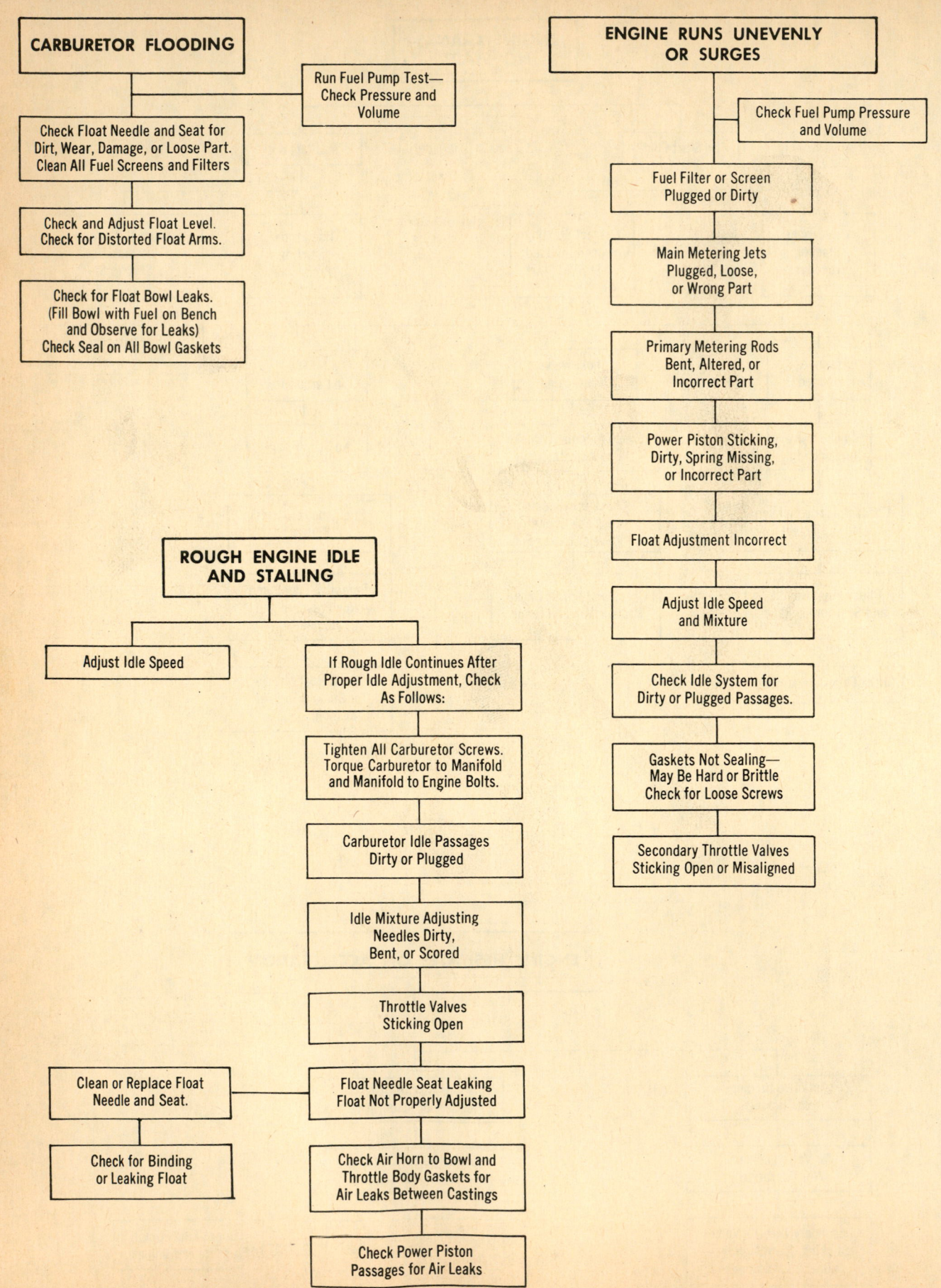

CARBURETOR FLOODING

Run Fuel Pump Test—
Check Pressure and
Volume

Check Float Needle and Seat for
Dirt, Wear, Damage, or Loose Part.
Clean All Fuel Screens and Filters

Check and Adjust Float Level.
Check for Distorted Float Arms.

Check for Float Bowl Leaks.
(Fill Bowl with Fuel on Bench
and Observe for Leaks)
Check Seal on All Bowl Gaskets

**ROUGH ENGINE IDLE
AND STALLING**

Adjust Idle Speed

If Rough Idle Continues After
Proper Idle Adjustment, Check
As Follows:

Tighten All Carburetor Screws.
Torque Carburetor to Manifold
and Manifold to Engine Bolts.

Carburetor Idle Passages
Dirty or Plugged

Idle Mixture Adjusting
Needles Dirty,
Bent, or Scored

Throttle Valves
Sticking Open

Clean or Replace Float
Needle and Seat.

Float Needle Seat Leaking
Float Not Properly Adjusted

Check for Binding
or Leaking Float

Check Air Horn to Bowl and
Throttle Body Gaskets for
Air Leaks Between Castings

Check Power Piston
Passages for Air Leaks

**ENGINE RUNS UNEVENLY
OR SURGES**

Check Fuel Pump Pressure
and Volume

Fuel Filter or Screen
Plugged or Dirty

Main Metering Jets
Plugged, Loose,
or Wrong Part

Primary Metering Rods
Bent, Altered, or
Incorrect Part

Power Piston Sticking,
Dirty, Spring Missing,
or Incorrect Part

Float Adjustment Incorrect

Adjust Idle Speed
and Mixture

Check Idle System for
Dirty or Plugged Passages.

Gaskets Not Sealing—
May Be Hard or Brittle
Check for Loose Screws

Secondary Throttle Valves
Sticking Open or Misaligned

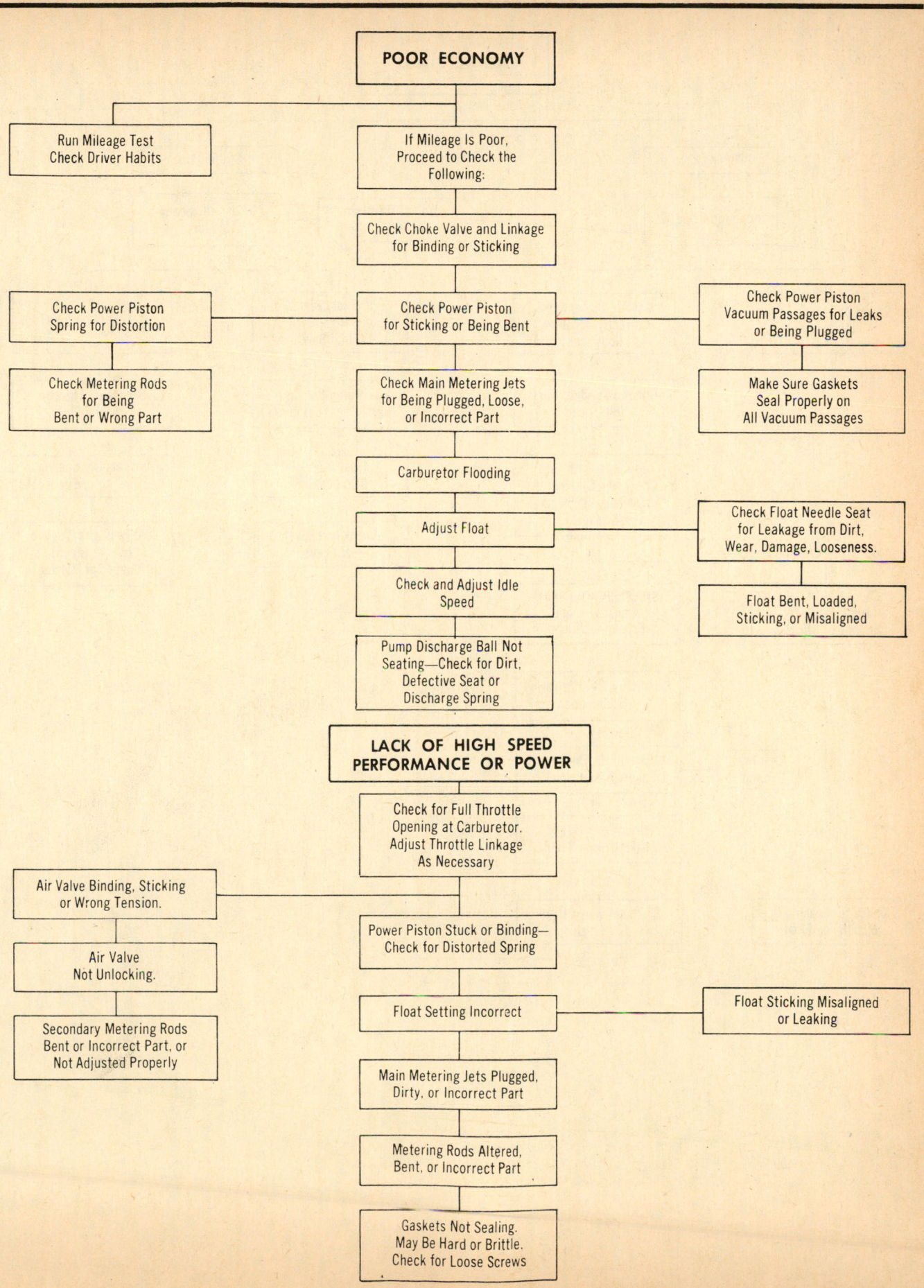

POOR ECONOMY

Run Mileage Test
Check Driver Habits

If Mileage Is Poor,
Proceed to Check the
Following:

Check Choke Valve and Linkage
for Binding or Sticking

Check Power Piston
Spring for Distortion

Check Power Piston
for Sticking or Being Bent

Check Power Piston
Vacuum Passages for Leaks
or Being Plugged

Check Metering Rods
for Being
Bent or Wrong Part

Check Main Metering Jets
for Being Plugged, Loose,
or Incorrect Part

Make Sure Gaskets
Seal Properly on
All Vacuum Passages

Carburetor Flooding

Adjust Float

Check Float Needle Seat
for Leakage from Dirt,
Wear, Damage, Looseness.

Check and Adjust Idle
Speed

Float Bent, Loaded,
Sticking, or Misaligned

Pump Discharge Ball Not
Seating—Check for Dirt,
Defective Seat or
Discharge Spring

**LACK OF HIGH SPEED
PERFORMANCE OR POWER**

Check for Full Throttle
Opening at Carburetor.
Adjust Throttle Linkage
As Necessary

Air Valve Binding, Sticking
or Wrong Tension.

Power Piston Stuck or Binding—
Check for Distorted Spring

Air Valve
Not Unlocking.

Float Setting Incorrect

Float Sticking Misaligned
or Leaking

Secondary Metering Rods
Bent or Incorrect Part, or
Not Adjusted Properly

Main Metering Jets Plugged,
Dirty, or Incorrect Part

Metering Rods Altered,
Bent, or Incorrect Part

Gaskets Not Sealing.
May Be Hard or Brittle.
Check for Loose Screws

Carburetors

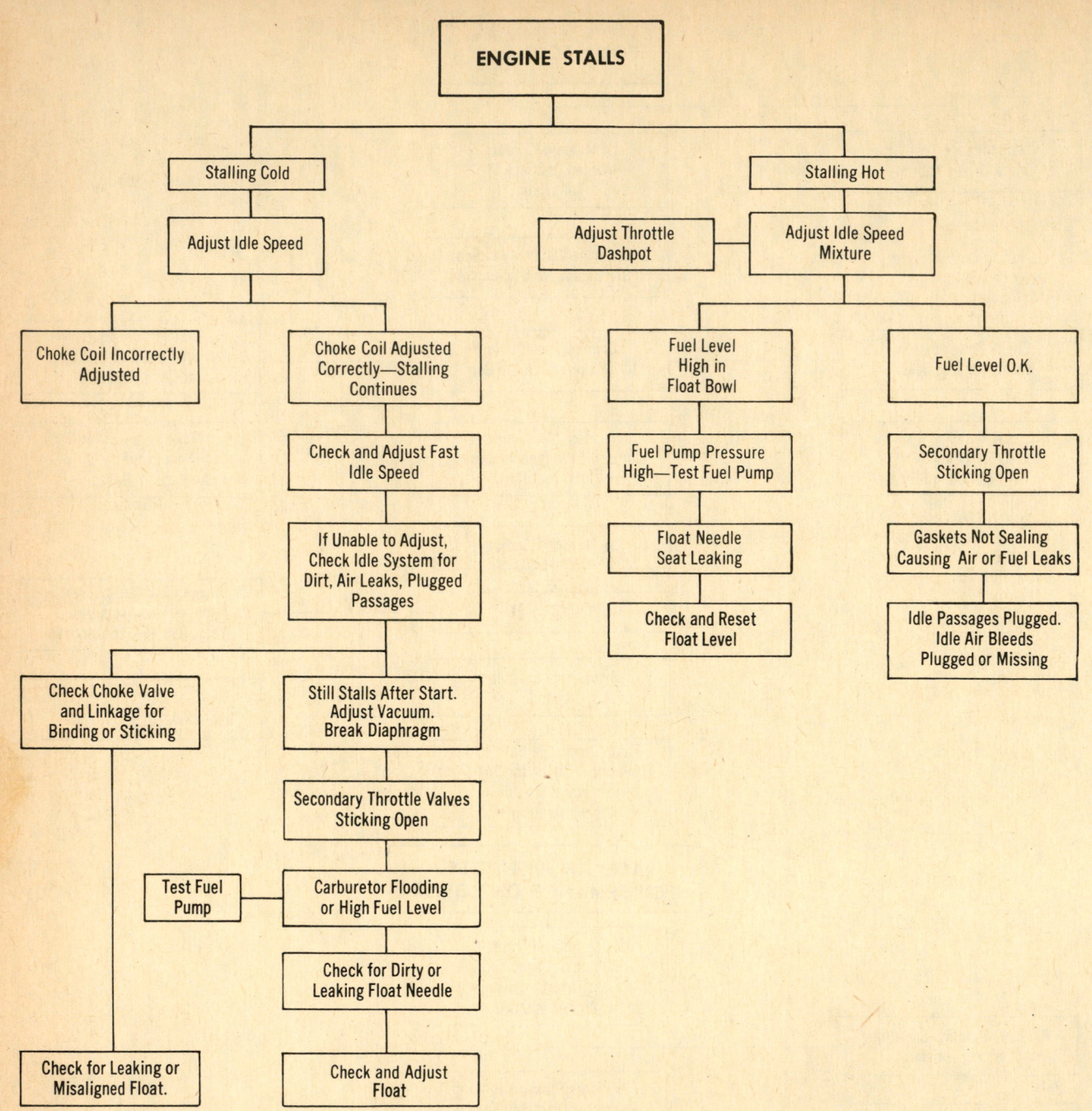

```
                        ┌──────────────────────┐
                        │   ENGINE  STALLS     │
                        └──────────────────────┘
                ┌──────────────────┴──────────────────┐
        ┌───────────────┐                      ┌───────────────┐
        │ Stalling Cold │                      │ Stalling Hot  │
        └───────────────┘                      └───────────────┘
        ┌──────────────────┐      ┌──────────────────┐  ┌──────────────────┐
        │ Adjust Idle Speed│      │ Adjust Throttle  │──│ Adjust Idle Speed│
        └──────────────────┘      │ Dashpot          │  │ Mixture          │
                                  └──────────────────┘  └──────────────────┘
```

Stalling Cold → Adjust Idle Speed

- Choke Coil Incorrectly Adjusted
- Choke Coil Adjusted Correctly—Stalling Continues
  - Check and Adjust Fast Idle Speed
  - If Unable to Adjust, Check Idle System for Dirt, Air Leaks, Plugged Passages
    - Check Choke Valve and Linkage for Binding or Sticking
      - Check for Leaking or Misaligned Float.
    - Still Stalls After Start. Adjust Vacuum. Break Diaphragm
      - Secondary Throttle Valves Sticking Open
      - Carburetor Flooding or High Fuel Level — Test Fuel Pump
      - Check for Dirty or Leaking Float Needle
      - Check and Adjust Float

Stalling Hot → Adjust Idle Speed Mixture

- Fuel Level High in Float Bowl
  - Fuel Pump Pressure High—Test Fuel Pump
  - Float Needle Seat Leaking
  - Check and Reset Float Level
- Fuel Level O.K.
  - Secondary Throttle Sticking Open
  - Gaskets Not Sealing Causing Air or Fuel Leaks
  - Idle Passages Plugged. Idle Air Bleeds Plugged or Missing

CARTER CARBURETORS

MODEL BBD

The BBD carburetor is a two barrel unit. It is equipped with a dashpot on some applications.

Vacuum Step-Up Piston Adjustment

This adjustment applies only to 1974 and later models.
1. Remove the dust cover.
2. Be sure not to disturb the adjusting screw on top of the piston. If it is disturbed, reset the gap at the top of the piston to 0.035-0.040 in.
3. Back off the curb idle adjustment until the throttle valves are completely closed. Count the number of turns so that the screw can later be returned to the original position.
4. Fully depress the step-up piston while holding moderate pressure on the rod lifter tab and loosen and tighten the rod lifter lockscrew.
5. Release the piston and rod lifter; return the curb idle screw to its original position.
6. Replace the dust cover, unless the accelerator pump is to be adjusted.

Accelerator Pump Adjustment

1974 AND LATER
1. Back off the idle adjusting screw. Open the choke valve so that the

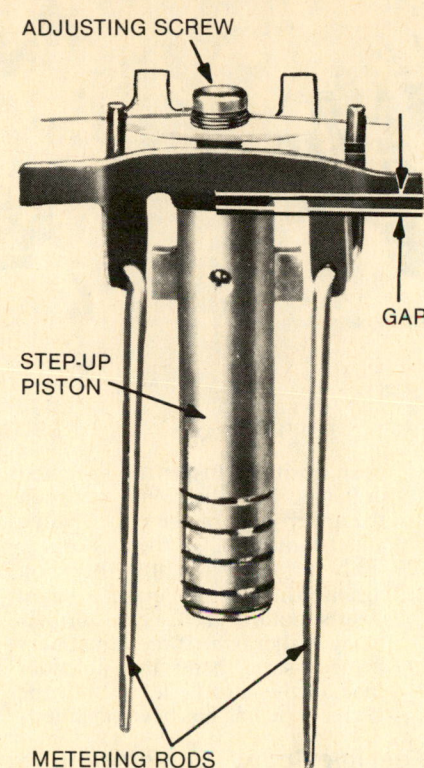

ADJUSTING SCREW

GAP

STEP-UP PISTON

METERING RODS

BBD vacuum step-up piston and metering rod assembly (© AMC)

fast idle cam allows the throttle valves to close. Be sure that the accelerator pump "S" link is in the outer hole of the pump arm if there are two holes.
2. Turn the idle adjusting screw in two complete turns after it contacts the stop.
3. Remove the dust cover. With the throttle valves closed tightly, measure the distance between the top of the air horn and the top of the pump plunger shaft. If the dimension is not as specified, loosen the pump arm adjusting lockscrew (near the plunger shaft) and rotate the sleeve to obtain the correct dimension.

Fast Idle Cam Position Adjustment

1. With the fast idle speed adjusting screw contacting the second highest speed step on the fast idle cam, move the choke valve toward the closed position with light pressure on the choke shaft lever. On AMC, loosen the choke cover and turn 1/4 turn rich.
2. Insert the specified drill (refer to Specifications), between the top of the choke valve and the wall of the air horn. An adjustment will be necessary if a slight drag is not ob-

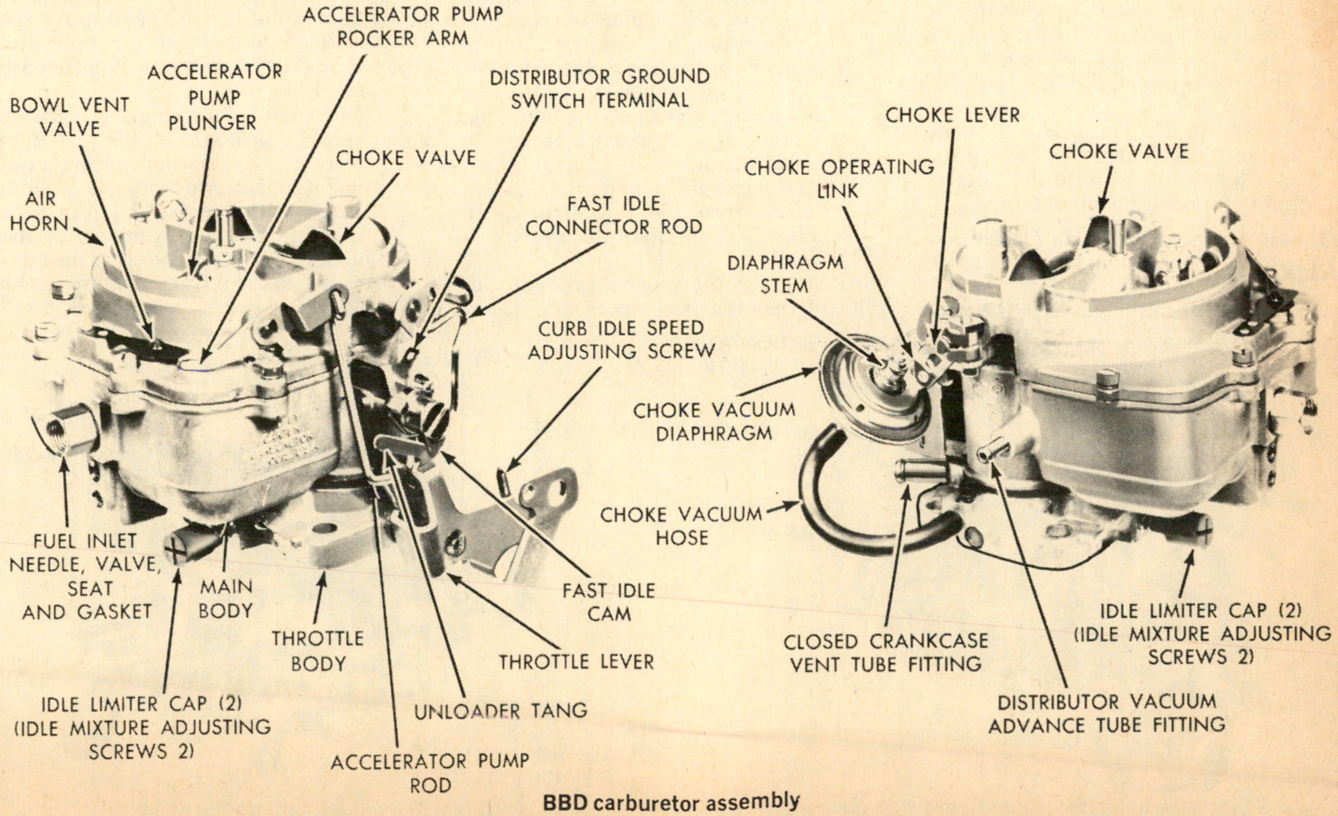

ACCELERATOR PUMP ROCKER ARM

DISTRIBUTOR GROUND SWITCH TERMINAL

BOWL VENT VALVE

ACCELERATOR PUMP PLUNGER

CHOKE VALVE

CHOKE LEVER

CHOKE VALVE

AIR HORN

CHOKE OPERATING LINK

FAST IDLE CONNECTOR ROD

DIAPHRAGM STEM

CURB IDLE SPEED ADJUSTING SCREW

CHOKE VACUUM DIAPHRAGM

CHOKE VACUUM HOSE

FUEL INLET NEEDLE, VALVE, SEAT AND GASKET

MAIN BODY

THROTTLE BODY

FAST IDLE CAM

THROTTLE LEVER

CLOSED CRANKCASE VENT TUBE FITTING

IDLE LIMITER CAP (2) (IDLE MIXTURE ADJUSTING SCREWS 2)

IDLE LIMITER CAP (2) (IDLE MIXTURE ADJUSTING SCREWS 2)

UNLOADER TANG

ACCELERATOR PUMP ROD

DISTRIBUTOR VACUUM ADVANCE TUBE FITTING

BBD carburetor assembly

Carter Carburetors

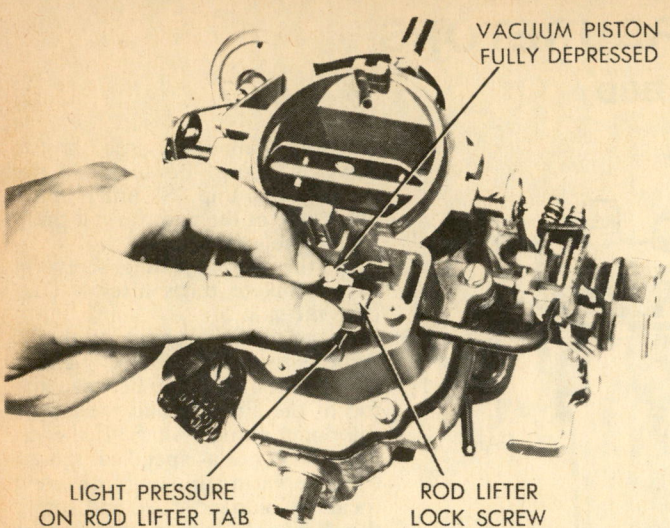

VACUUM PISTON FULLY DEPRESSED

LIGHT PRESSURE ON ROD LIFTER TAB

ROD LIFTER LOCK SCREW

BBD vacuum step-up piston adjustment (© Chrysler Corp.)

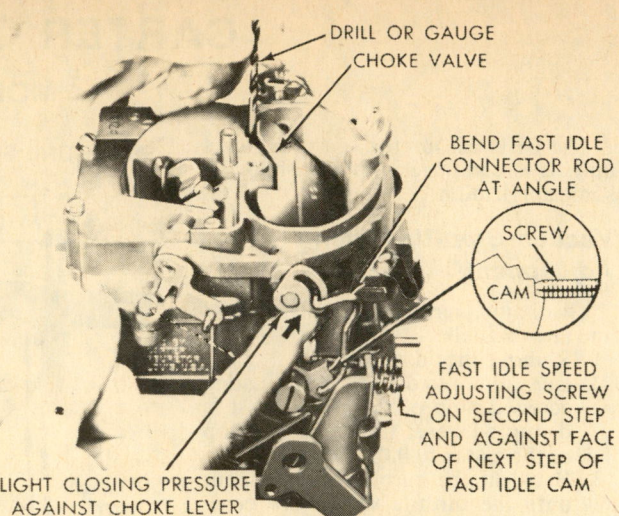

DRILL OR GAUGE CHOKE VALVE

BEND FAST IDLE CONNECTOR ROD AT ANGLE

SCREW

CAM

FAST IDLE SPEED ADJUSTING SCREW ON SECOND STEP AND AGAINST FACE OF NEXT STEP OF FAST IDLE CAM

LIGHT CLOSING PRESSURE AGAINST CHOKE LEVER

BBD fast idle cam position adjustment

tained as the drill is being removed.
3. If an adjustment is required, bend the fast idle connector rod at the angle.

Accelerator Pump & Bowl Vent
THROUGH 1973

1. Back off the idle speed adjusting screw to completely close the throttle valves. Open the choke valve so that the fast idle cam allows the throttle valves to seat in the bores.
2. Be sure that the accelerator pump operating rod is in the medium stroke hole in the throttle lever.
3. Close the throttle valves tightly. Measure the distance between the air cleaner gasket surface and the top of the accelerator pump rod. This measurement should be .200 in.
4. To adjust the pump travel, bend the accelerator pump operating rod at a lower angle, until the correct pump travel has been obtained.

Choke Unloader (Wide Open Kick)

1. Hold the throttle valves in the wide

open position. Insert the specified drill (see Specifications) between the upper edge of the choke valve and the inner wall of the air horn.
2. With a finger lightly pressing against the control lever, a slight drag should be felt as the drill is being withdrawn. If an adjustment is necessary, bend the unloader tang on the throttle lever until the correct opening has been obtained.

Fast Idle Speed (On Vehicle)

1. On 1974 and later Chrysler products, disconnect and plug the connections for the heated air control, EGR, and OSAC valve or distributor. With the engine off and the transmission in Park or Neutral position, open the throttle slightly.
2. Close the choke valve until the fast idle screw can be positioned on the second highest speed step of the fast idle cam.
3. Start the engine and let the idle stabilize. Turn the fast idle speed screw in or out to obtain the specified speed.
4. Stopping the engine between adjustments is not necessary. How-

ever, reposition the fast idle speed screw on the cam after each speed adjustment to provide the correct throttle closing torque.

Vacuum Kick (Initial Choke Valve Clearance) Adjustment
CHRYSLER PRODUCTS

1. If the adjustment is to be made with the engine running, disconnect the fast idle linkage to allow the choke to close to the kick position with engine at curb idle. If an auxiliary vacuum source is to be used, as recommended for 1977 and later, open the throttle valves (engine not running) and move the choke to the closed position. Release the throttle first, then release the choke.
2. When using an auxiliary vacuum source, disconnect the vacuum hose from the carburetor and connect it to the hose from the vacuum supply with a small length of tube to act as a fitting. Removal of the hose from the diaphragm may require sufficient force to damage the system. Apply a vacuum of 10 (15

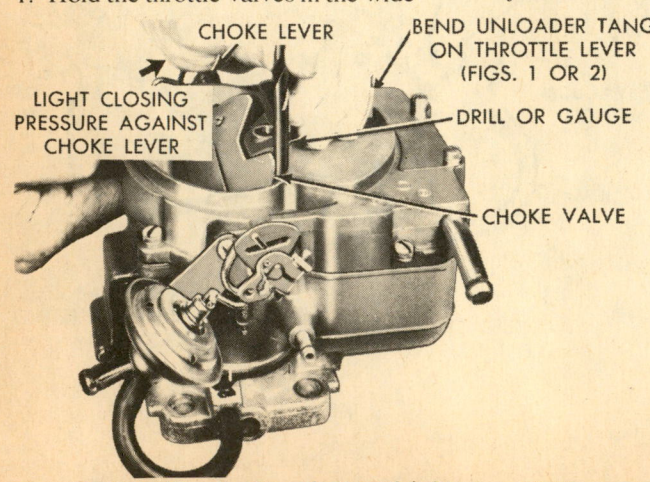

CHOKE LEVER

BEND UNLOADER TANG ON THROTTLE LEVER (FIGS. 1 OR 2)

LIGHT CLOSING PRESSURE AGAINST CHOKE LEVER

DRILL OR GAUGE

CHOKE VALVE

BBD choke unloader adjustment (wide open kick)

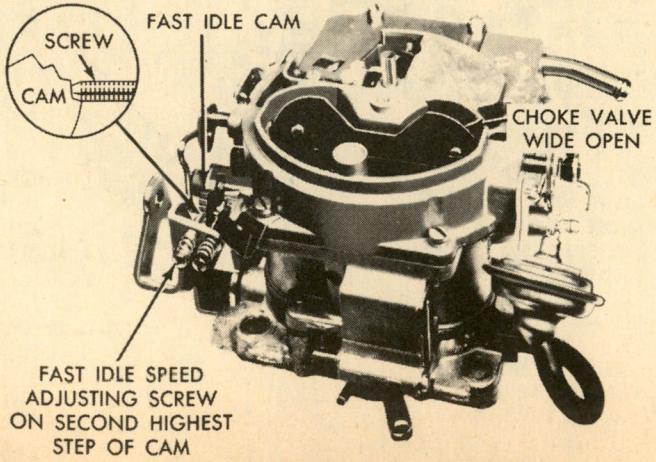

SCREW

CAM

FAST IDLE CAM

CHOKE VALVE WIDE OPEN

FAST IDLE SPEED ADJUSTING SCREW ON SECOND HIGHEST STEP OF CAM

BBD fast idle adjustment on the vehicle

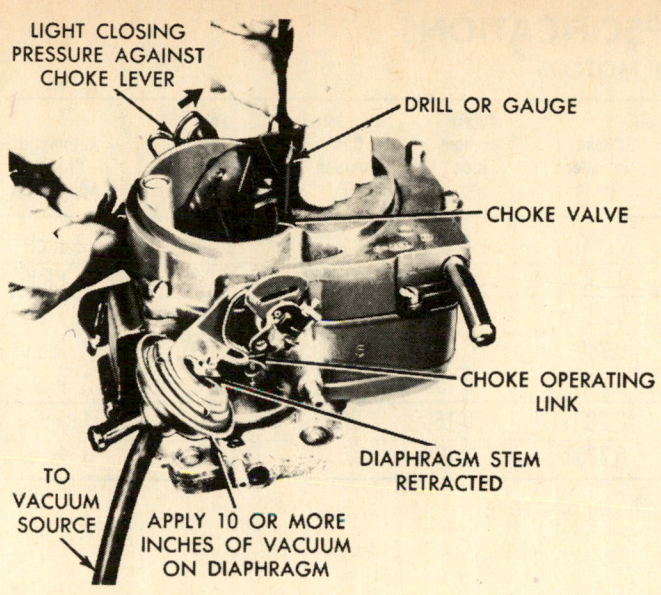

LIGHT CLOSING
PRESSURE AGAINST
CHOKE LEVER

DRILL OR GAUGE

CHOKE VALVE

CHOKE OPERATING
LINK

DIAPHRAGM STEM
RETRACTED

TO
VACUUM
SOURCE

APPLY 10 OR MORE
INCHES OF VACUUM
ON DIAPHRAGM

BBD vacuum kick adjustment

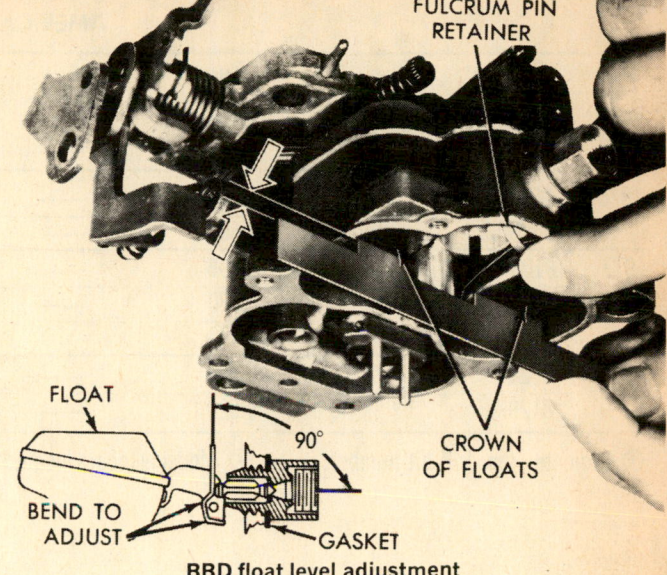

FLOAT
FULCRUM PIN
RETAINER

FLOAT

90°

CROWN
OF FLOATS

BEND TO
ADJUST

GASKET

BBD float level adjustment

beginning 1973) or more in. of mercury.

3. Insert the specified drill (refer to Specifications) between the top of the choke valve and the wall of the air horn. Apply sufficient closing pressure on the lever to which the choke rod attaches to provide a minimum choke valve opening without distortion of the diaphragm link. Note that the cylindrical stem of the diaphragm will extend as the internal spring is compressed. This spring must be fully compressed for proper measurement of the vacuum kick adjustment.

4. An adjustment will be necessary if a slight drag is not obtained as the drill is being removed. Shorten or lengthen the diaphragm link to obtain the correct choke opening. Length changes should be made carefully by bending (opening or closing) the U-bend provided in the diaphragm link.

⎯⎯ CAUTION ⎯⎯
Do not apply twisting or bending force to the diaphragm.

5. Reinstall the vacuum hose on the correct carburetor fitting. Return the fast idle linkage to its original condition if it was disturbed, as suggested in Step 1.

6. Make the following check: With no vacuum applied to the diaphragm, the choke valve should move freely between the open and closed positions. If its movement is not free, examine the linkage for misalignment or interference caused by the bending operation. Repeat the adjustment if necessary to provide proper link operation.

AMC PRODUCTS
This adjustment is called Initial Choke Valve Clearance Adjustment on AMC products.

1. Remove the choke cover.
2. Apply a vacuum of at least 19 inches of mercury to pull the diaphragm in against the stop.
3. Open the throttle valve slightly to place the fast idle screw on the high step of the cam.
4. Hold the choke coil tang in the closed position. Measure the clearance between the choke plate upper edge and the air horn wall.
5. Adjust the clearance by bending the diaphragm connector link at the angle.

Float Level
CHRYSLER PRODUCTS
1. Invert the carburetor so that the weight of the floats is the only force on the needle and seat.
2. Use a T-scale to check the float level. Measure from the surface of the fuel bowl to the crown of each float at center.
3. To adjust, hold the floats on the bottom of the bowl and bend the float lip to give the specified dimension.

AMERICAN MOTORS PRODUCTS
1. Remove the air horn.
2. Hold the float lip gently against the needle to raise the float.
3. Place a straightedge across the float bowl to measure the float level at the top of the float.
4. To adjust, bend the float lip, being careful not to exert pressure on the synthetic needle tip.

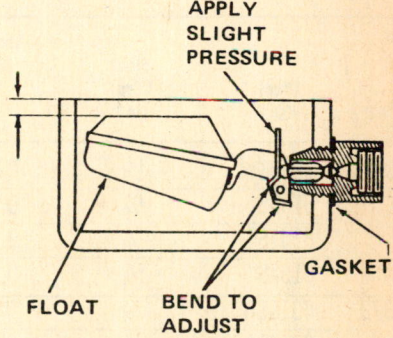

APPLY
SLIGHT
PRESSURE

GASKET

FLOAT

BEND TO
ADJUST

BBD float level adjustment for AMC products (© AMC)

Dashpot Adjustment
1976 AMERICAN MOTORS PRODUCTS
1. Make sure that the idle speed adjustment is correct.
2. Hold the dashpot plunger in against the stop.
3. Measure the clearance between the plunger and the throttle lever with the throttle in idle position. It should be .104 in.
4. Adjust by turning the dashpot.

CHRYSLER PRODUCTS
The dashpot is used on manual transmission models only.
1. Make sure that the curb idle speed is correctly adjusted.
2. Start the engine. Position the throttle lever so that the actuating tab is just contacting the dashpot plunger stem. Let the engine speed stabilize for 30 seconds.
3. The speed should be 2500 rpm for 1973 and later models, 2000 through 1972.
4. Adjust the setting by loosening the locknut and moving the dashpot.

Carter Carburetors

CARTER BBD SPECIFICATIONS
AMERICAN MOTORS

Year	Model ④	Float Level (in.)	Accelerator Pump Travel (in.)	Bowl Vent (in.)	Choke Unloader (in.)	Choke Vacuum Kick ①	Fast Idle Cam Position ①	Fast Idle Speed (rpm)	Automatic Choke Adjustment
1976	8067	¼	0.500	——	0.250	0.128	0.095	1700	2 Rich
	8073	¼	0.500	——	0.250	0.128	0.095	1700	1 Rich
1977	8103	¼	0.496	——	0.280	0.150	0.120	1600	1 Rich
	8104	¼	0.520	——	0.280	0.128	0.095	1500	1 Rich
	8117	¼	0.480	——	0.280	0.152	0.112	1600	1 Rich
1978	8128	¼	0.496	——	0.280	0.150	0.110	1600	Index
	8129	¼	0.520	——	0.280	0.128	0.095	1500	1 Rich

① Indicates the drill bit number.   ④ Model numbers located on the tag or casting

CHRYSLER PRODUCTS

Year	Model ④	Float Level (in.)	Accelerator Pump Travel (in.)	Bowl Vent (in.)	Choke Unloader (in.)	Choke Vacuum Kick ①	Fast Idle Cam Position ①	Fast Idle Speed (rpm)	Automatic Choke Adjustment
1972	6149S	¼	0.225③	¹⁵⁄₆₄	¼	25	41	1700	Fixed
	6150S	¼	0.225③	¹⁵⁄₆₄	¼	25	41	1900	Fixed
	6151S	¼	0.225③	¹⁵⁄₆₄	¼	25	41	1800	Fixed
	6152S	¼	0.225③	¹⁵⁄₆₄	¼	25	41	2000	Fixed
1973	6316SA	¼	0.242③	——	¼	24	41	1700	Fixed
	6317SA	¼	0.242③	——	¼	30	41	1700	Fixed
	6343SA	¼	0.242③	——	¼	24	41	1700	Fixed
	6344SA	¼	0.242③	——	¼	24	41	1700	Fixed
1974	6464S	¼	0.500③	——	.325	25	41	1700	Fixed
	6465S	¼	0.500③	——	.325	35	41	1500	Fixed
	6466S	¼	0.500③	——	.325	25	41	1700	Fixed
	6467S	¼	0.500③	——	.325	35	41	1500	Fixed
1975	8000S	¼	0.500③	——	0.280	0.130	0.070	1500	Fixed
	8064S	¼	0.500③	——	0.310	0.070	0.070	1500	Fixed
	8001S	¼	0.500③	——	0.310	0.110	0.070	1500	Fixed
	8003S	¼	0.500③	——	0.310	0.110	0.070	1500	Fixed
	8066S	¼	0.500③	——	0.280	0.130	0.070	1500	Fixed
	8062S	¼	0.500③	——	0.310	0.110	0.070	1500	Fixed
1976	8071S	¼	0.500③	——	0.280	0.130	0.070	1500	Fixed
	8069S	¼	0.500③	——	0.310	0.070	0.070	1200	Fixed
	8070S	¼	0.500③	——	0.310	0.110	0.070	1500	Fixed
	8077S, 8099S	¼	0.500③	——	0.280	0.110	0.070	1250	Fixed
	8072S	¼	0.500③	——	0.310	0.070	0.070	1500	Fixed
1977	8087S	¼	0.469③	——	0.280	0.100	0.070	1600	Fixed
	8089S	¼	0.469③	——	0.280	0.130	0.070	1600	Fixed
	8090S	¼	0.469③	——	0.280	0.130	0.070	1700	Fixed
	8127S	¼	0.469③	——	0.280	0.110	0.070	1500	Fixed
	8093S	¼	0.469③	——	0.310	0.130	0.070	1400	Fixed

CHRYSLER PRODUCTS

Year	Model ④	Float Level (in.)	Accelerator Pump Travel (in.)	Bowl Vent (in.)	Choke Unloader (in.)	Choke Vacuum Kick	Fast Idle Cam Position ①	Fast Idle Speed (rpm)	Automatic Choke Adjustment
1977	8094S	¼	0.469③	——	0.310	0.070	0.070	1400	Fixed
	8096S	¼	0.469③	——	0.310	0.110	0.070	1500	Fixed
	8126S	¼	0.469③	——	0.310	0.110	0.070	1500	Fixed
1978	8136S	¼	0.500③	0.080	0.280	0.110	0.070	1500	Fixed
	8137S	¼	0.500③	0.080	0.280	0.100	0.070	1600	Fixed
	8177S	¼	0.500③	0.080	0.280	0.100	0.070	1600	Fixed
	8175S	¼	0.500③	0.080	0.280	0.160	0.070	1400	Fixed
	8143S	¼	0.500③	0.080	0.280	0.150	0.070	1500	Fixed

① Indicates the drill bit number.   ③ At idle   ④ Model numbers located on the tag or casting

MODEL YF, YFA

The YF carburetor is a single barrel downdraft carburetor with a diaphragm type accelerator pump and diaphragm operated metering rods.

Float Adjustment

1. Invert the air horn assembly and check the clearance from the top of the float to the surface of the air horn with a T-scale. The air horn should be held at eye level when gauging and the float arm should be resting on the needle pin.
2. Do not exert pressure on the needle valve when measuring or adjusting the float. Bend the float arm as necessary to adjust the float level.

--- CAUTION ---

Do not bend the tab at the end of the float arm as it prevents the float from striking the bottom of the fuel bowl when empty and keeps the needle in place.

Metering Rod Adjustment

1. Remove the air horn. Back out the idle speed adjusting screw until the throttle plate is seated fully in its bore.
2. Press down on the upper end of the diaphragm shaft until the diaphragm bottoms in the vacuum chamber.
3. The metering rod should contact

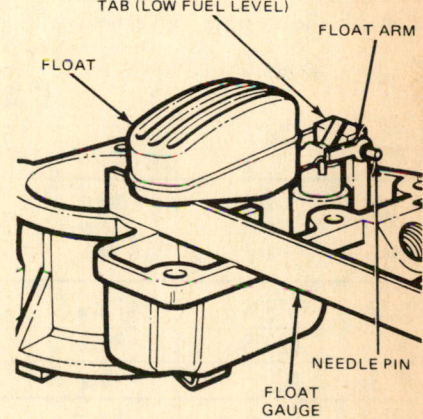

YFA float level adjustment

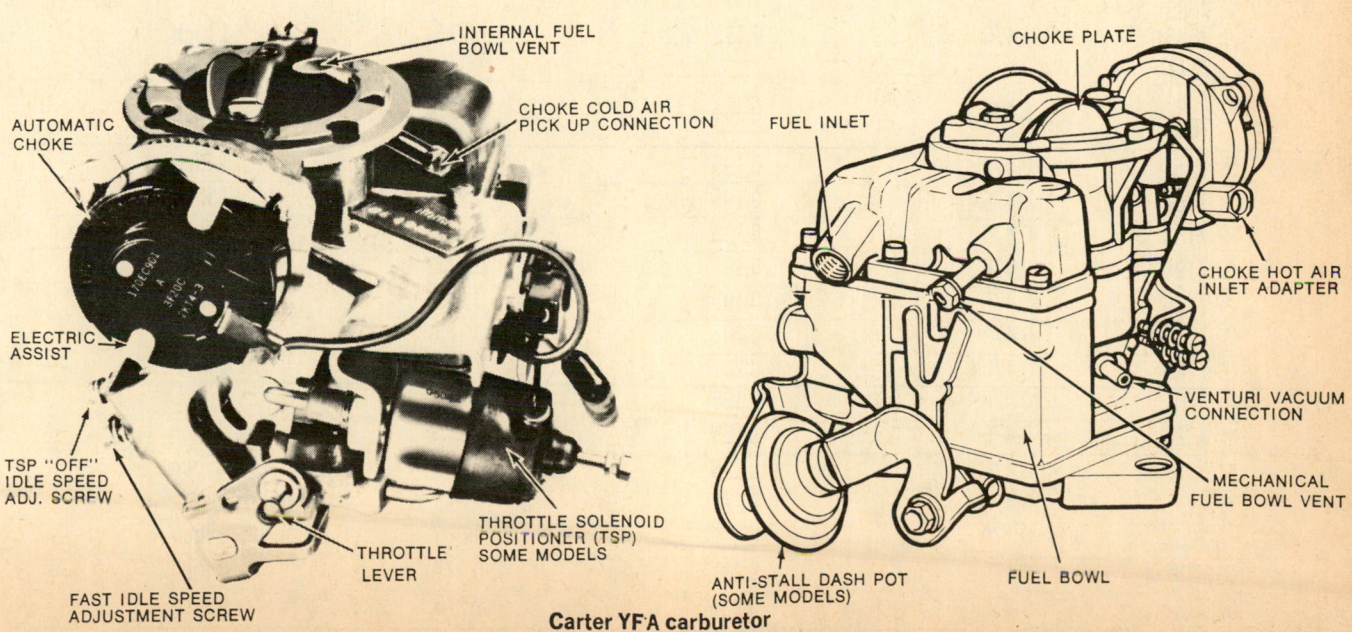

Carter YF-A carburetor

the bottom of the metering rod well and lifter link at the outer end nearest the springs and at the supporting link.

4. On models not equipped with an adjusting screw, adjust by bending the lip of the metering rod arm to which the metering rod is attached.

5. On models with an adjusting screw, turn the screw until the metering rod just bottoms in the body casting. For final adjustment, turn the screw one additional turn clockwise.

Fast Idle Cam Adjustment

1. Put the fast idle screw on the second step of the fast idle cam against the shoulder of the high step.
2. Adjust by bending the choke plate connecting rod to obtain the specified clearance between the lower edge of the choke plate and the air horn wall.

Choke Unloader Adjustment

1. With the throttle valve held wide

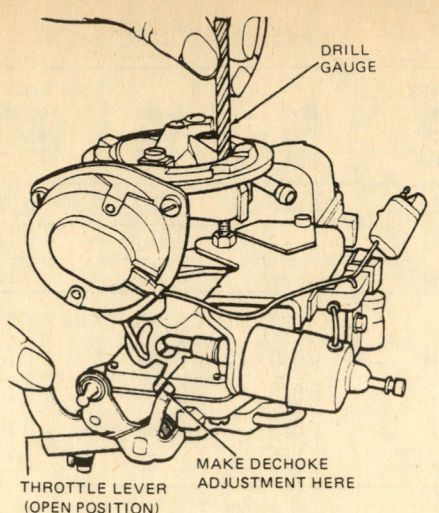

YF A choke unloader adjustment

open and the choke valve held in the closed position, bend the unloader tang on the throttle lever to obtain the specified clearance between the lower edge of the choke valve and the air horn wall.

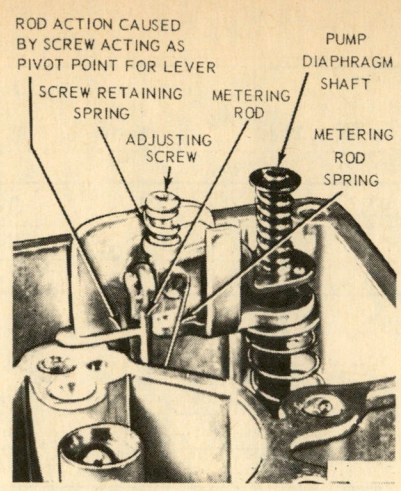

YF A metering rod adjustment

Automatic Choke Adjustment

1. Loosen the choke cover retaining screws.
2. Turn the choke cover so that the index mark on the cover lines up with the specified mark on the choke housing.

CARTER YF, YFA SPECIFICATIONS

AMERICAN MOTORS

Year	Model ①	Float Level (in.)	Fast Idle Cam (in.)	Unloader (in.)	Choke
1972	6199S	29/64	1600 RPM	0.300	Index
	6200S	29/64	1600 RPM	0.300	Index
1973	All	29/64	Index mark	0.275	1 Rich
1974	All	0.476	0.190	0.275	1 Rich
1975	All	0.476	0.190	0.275	1 Rich
1976	7083, 7085, 7112	0.476	0.185	0.275	1 Rich
	7084, 7086	0.476	0.185	0.275	2 Rich
1977	7151	0.476	0.195	0.275	1 Rich
	7152	0.476	0.195	0.275	1 Rich
	7153	0.476	0.195	0.275	Index
	7195	0.476	0.195	0.275	1 Rich
	7223	0.476	0.195	0.275	Index
	7111	0.476	0.201	0.275	2 Rich
	7189	0.476	0.201	0.275	1 Rich
1978	7201	0.476	0.195	0.275	Index
	7228	0.476	0.195	0.275	1 Rich
	7229	0.476	0.195	0.275	1 Rich
	7235	0.476	0.195	0.275	Index
	7267	0.476	0.195	0.275	1 Rich
	7232	0.476	0.201	0.275	2 Rich
	7233	0.476	0.201	0.275	1 Rich

FORD MOTOR CO.

Year	Model ①	Float Level (in.)	Fast Idle Cam (in.)	Unloader (in.)	Choke
1972	D2DF-AA	3/8	0.105	0.280	Index
	D2DF-BA	3/8	0.170	0.250	Index
	D2DF-CA	3/8	0.170	0.250	Index
	D2DF-DA	3/8	0.140	0.250	1 Rich
	D2DF-EA	3/8	0.140	0.250	1 Rich
	D2AF-JA	3/8	0.220	0.250	1 Lean
1973	D3DF-AA	3/8	0.170	0.250	Index
	D3DF-CA	3/8	0.140	0.250	1 Rich
1974	D4DE-JA	3/8	0.140	0.250	1 Rich
	D4DE-JB	3/8	0.140	0.250	Index
	D4DE-ABA	3/8	0.170	0.250	Index
	D4DE-KA	3/8	0.140	0.250	1 Rich
	D4DE-KB	3/8	0.140	0.250	Index
	D4DE-EA	3/8	0.140	0.250	Index
1975	D5DE-EA	3/8	0.140	0.250	2 Rich
	D5DE-MA	3/8	0.140	0.250	2 Rich
	D5DE-ZA	3/8	0.140	0.250	2 Rich
	D5DE-DA	3/8	0.140	0.250	2 Rich
	D5DE-GA	3/8	0.140	0.250	2 Rich
1976	D6BE-AA	25/32	0.140	0.250	1 Rich
	D6BE-BB	25/32	0.140	0.250	2 Rich
	D5DE-DB	25/32	0.140	0.250	2 Rich
	D5DE-MB	25/32	0.140	0.250	2 Rich
	D6DE-AB	25/32	0.140	0.250	Index
	D6DE-BB	25/32	0.140	0.250	Index
1977-78	D7BE-AA,AB,BA	25/32	0.140	0.250	Index
	D7BE-FA,HB, GB,GC	25/32	0.140	0.250	2 Rich
	D7BE-NA,DA	25/32	0.140	0.250	1 Rich

① Model number located on the tag or casting

The Carter RBS is a single barrel carburetor made from an aluminum casting. It is equipped with a vacuum piston automatic choke. The 1973 and later models use an EGR (Exhaust Gas Recirculation) system.

Float Level Adjustment

1. After removing the bowl and the bowl gasket, invert the carburetor so that only the weight of the float is pressing down on the needle and seat assembly.
2. Measure the vertical distance from the casting to the projections at the outer ends of the float.
3. Measure both ends of the float and, if adjustment is necessary, it can be done by holding the lip end of

MODEL RBS

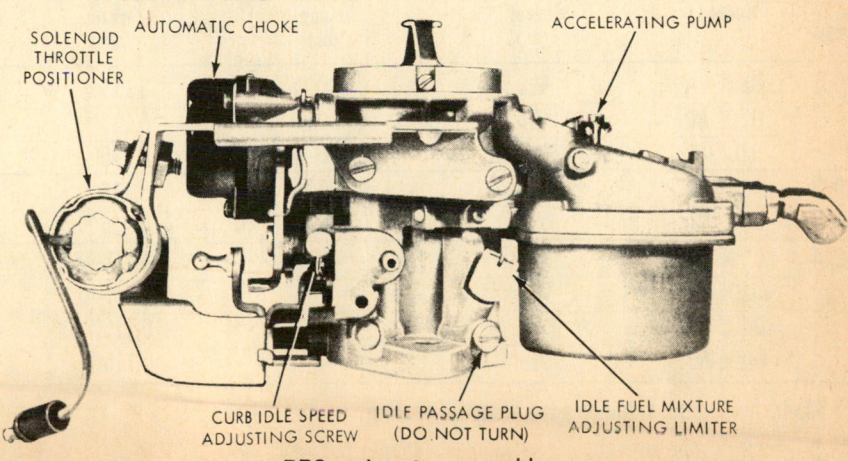

RBS carburetor assembly

Carter Carburetors

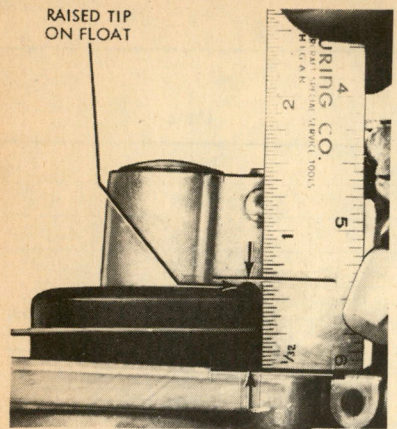

RBS float level adjustment

RBS accelerator pump adjustment

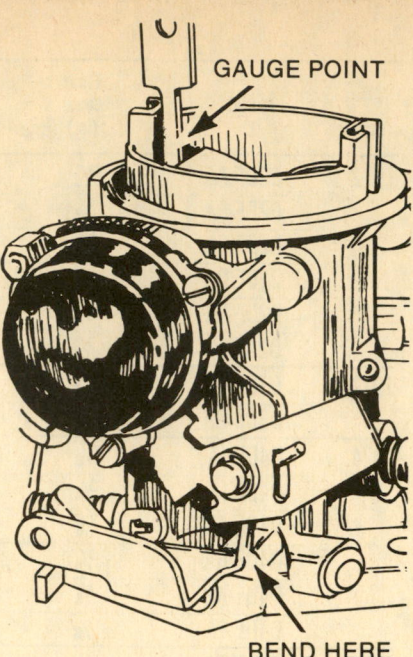

BEND HERE

RBS choke unloader adjustment

the float bracket with needle nose pliers and bending the float bracket at its narrowest point.

Float Drop Adjustment

With the air horn upright and the float hanging free, measure the vertical distance from the main body casting surface of the fuel bowl to the outer ends of the float on the top side. Adjust by bending the tab at the end of the float arm. The proper setting is 1.250 in.

Accelerator Pump Adjustment

NOTE: *The accelerator pump adjustment must be made before adjusting the bowl vent or the choke unloader.*

The pump stroke is measured as the difference in height between the measured height with the throttle valve fully closed and fully open. To adjust, open or close the pump connector link at the offset portion.

Fast Idle Cam Adjustment

Place the fast idle screw on the second step of the fast idle cam and against the shoulder of the high step. Specified clearance should exist between the lower edge of the choke valve and the air horn wall. If adjustment is needed, bend the choke plate connecting rod.

Choke Unloader Adjustment

With the throttle valve wide open, the clearance between the upper edge of the valve and the inner air horn wall should be to specification. If it is not, adjust by bending the tang on the throttle lever.

Fast Idle Speed Adjustment

1. Revolve the fast idle cam until the tang on the throttle lever is aligned with the mark on the cam.
2. Proper clearance should exist between the throttle valve and the carburetor bore on the idle port side.

3. If adjustment is required, close the choke valve fully and put the fast idle connector rod against the end of the slot in the cam. Bend the connector rod at the offset portion to align the marks.

Automatic Choke Adjustment

1. Loosen the choke cover retaining screws.
2. Turn the choke cover so that the index mark on the cover lines up with the specified mark on the choke housing.

CARTER RBS SPECIFICATIONS

FORD MOTOR CO.

Year	Model ①	Float Level (in.)	Accelerator Pump (in.)	Fast Idle (rpm)	Fast Idle Throttle Plate (in.)	Choke Unloader (in.)	Choke
1972	D2OF-LA	9/16	0.400③	0.115②	——	0.250	Index
	D2OF-MA	9/16	0.400③	0.115②	——	0.250	1 Rich
	D2OF-SA	9/16	0.400③	0.115②	——	0.250	1 Rich
1973	D3OF-BA	9/16	0.420③	0.115②	——	0.250	Index
	D3OF-CA	9/16	0.400③	0.115②	——	0.250	Index
1974	D4DE-BB	9/16	——	0.115②	——	0.250	Index
	D4DE-SB	9/16	——	0.115②	——	0.250	Index
	D4DE-AAA	9/16	——	0.115②	——	0.250	1 Lean
	D4DE-AB	9/16	——	0.115②	——	0.250	Index

① Model numbers located on a tag or on the casting
② At kickdown
③ Closed throttle.

MODEL WGD

This carburetor is used on 1972 Pontiacs. It carries model number 6311S.

Float Adjustment

1. With the air horn inverted, check to see that the float is parallel with the outer edge of the air horn casting.
2. Adjust by bending the float arm. Next, place the gauge between the air horn and the center of the float. The distance should be ⁵⁄₁₆ in.
3. Adjust the float level by bending the float arm until the float touches the gauge. The float should not have excessive clearance at the hinge pin and must operate freely.

NOTE: *When adjusting the float, care must be exercised to avoid pressing the flared tip needle into the needle seats as a false setting will result. Allow only the float weight to seat the needle when gauging.*

Pump Adjustment

1. Back out the throttle stop screw.
2. Turn the fast idle cam to "hot" position and fully close the throttle valves.
3. Place a ¼ in. gauge or a similar straightedge across the dust cover boss. The dust cover boss should be parallel with the top surface of the pump arm.

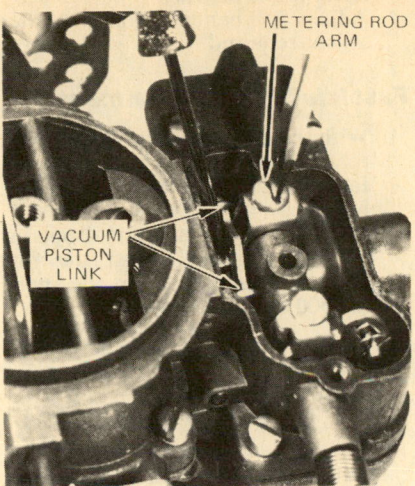

WGD metering rod adjustment

4. Adjust by bending the pump rod at the offset.

Metering Rod Adjustment

NOTE: *This adjustment should be made after the pump adjustment. No metering rod gauges are necessary.*

1. Back out the throttle screw and fully close the throttle valves. Press down on the vacuum piston link until the metering rods bottom.
2. While holding the rods down and

WGD fast idle cam adjustment

the metering arm tongue against the lip of the vacuum piston link, carefully tighten the metering arm set screw.

Fast Idle Cam Adjustment

1. Open the throttle to clear the fast idle cam and close the choke valve.
2. With the choke valve held fully closed and the stop on the fast idle cam against the casting, there should be 0.005 in. minimum clear-

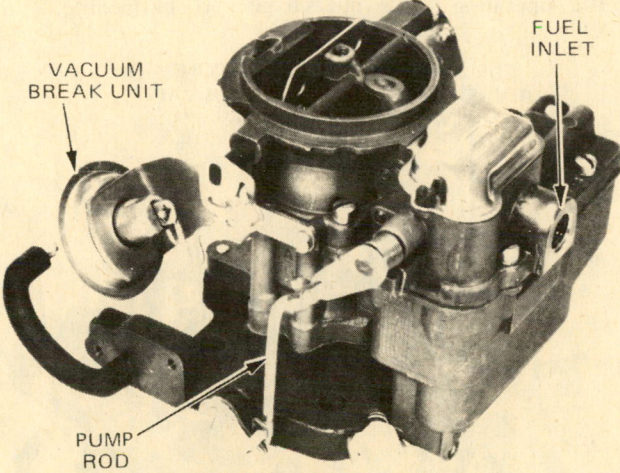

WGD carburetor assembly

WGD float level adjustment

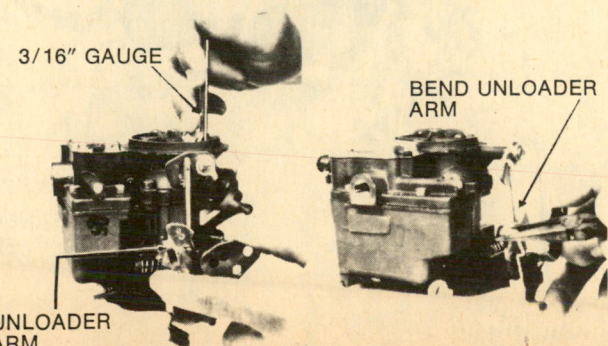

WGD choke unloader adjustment

WGD pump adjustment

Carter Carburetors

ance between the inner and outer choke levers.

3. Adjust by bending the outer lever lug as required.

NOTE: *With the choke fully closed, the tang on the fast idle cam must clear the stop on the throttle body flange.*

Unloader Adjustment

1. Hold the choke closed lightly.
2. Fully open the throttle, forcing the choke valve open.
3. Check the clearance between the upper edge of the choke valve and

the wall of the air horn. The clearance should be $3/16$ in.

4. Adjust by bending the unloader arm as required.

Fast Idle Speed Adjustment

1. With the carburetor on the engine, rotate the fast idle cam until the fast idle tang contacts the cam's high step.
2. With the engine at normal operating temperature, adjust the fast idle tang to obtain an engine speed of 1500 rpm.

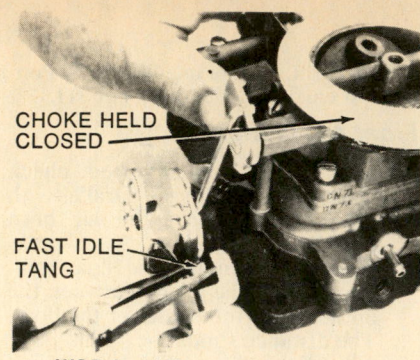

CHOKE HELD CLOSED

FAST IDLE TANG

WGD fast idle speed adjustment

MODEL TQ

The TQ (Thermo-Quad) has a fuel bowl made of phenolic resin. This acts as a heat insulator. Fuel is kept 20 degrees cooler than in metal carburetors. It also has a suspended design metering system which aids in cooling. All the calibration points are in the upper aluminum casting or air horn and are in effect suspended in the cavities in the main body.

Float Adjustment

1. With the bowl cover inverted, the gasket installed, and the floats resting on the seated needle, the dimension of each float from the bot-

tom side of the float to the cover gasket should be as shown in the specifications chart.

2. To adjust, bend the float lever.

Secondary Throttle Linkage

1. Block the choke valve in the wide open position and invert the carburetor.
2. Slowly open the primary throttle valves until the secondary valves start to open. Measure between the lower edge of the primary valve and its bore.
3. If it is necessary to adjust, bend the secondary throttle operating

rod at the lower angle until the correct dimension is obtained.

Secondary Air Valve Opening

1. With the air valve in the closed position, the opening along the air valve at its long side must be at its maximum and parallel with the air horn gasket surface.
2. With the air valve wide open, the opening of the air valve at the short side and the air horn must match the dimensions in the Specifications Charts. The corner of the air valve is notched for adjustment. Bend the corner with a pair of pliers to give proper opening.

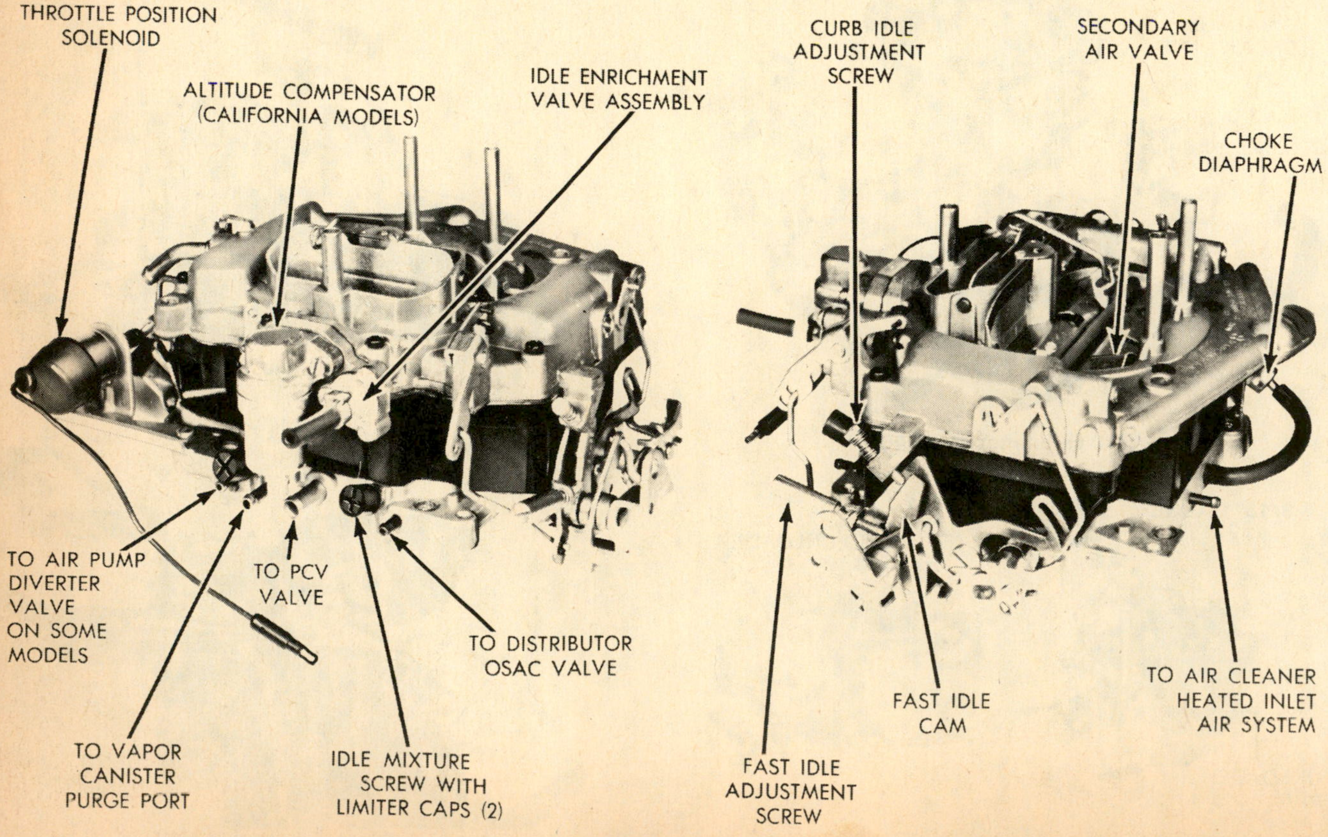

THROTTLE POSITION SOLENOID

ALTITUDE COMPENSATOR (CALIFORNIA MODELS)

IDLE ENRICHMENT VALVE ASSEMBLY

CURB IDLE ADJUSTMENT SCREW

SECONDARY AIR VALVE

CHOKE DIAPHRAGM

TO AIR PUMP DIVERTER VALVE ON SOME MODELS

TO PCV VALVE

TO DISTRIBUTOR OSAC VALVE

TO VAPOR CANISTER PURGE PORT

IDLE MIXTURE SCREW WITH LIMITER CAPS (2)

FAST IDLE ADJUSTMENT SCREW

FAST IDLE CAM

TO AIR CLEANER HEATED INLET AIR SYSTEM

TQ carburetor assembly

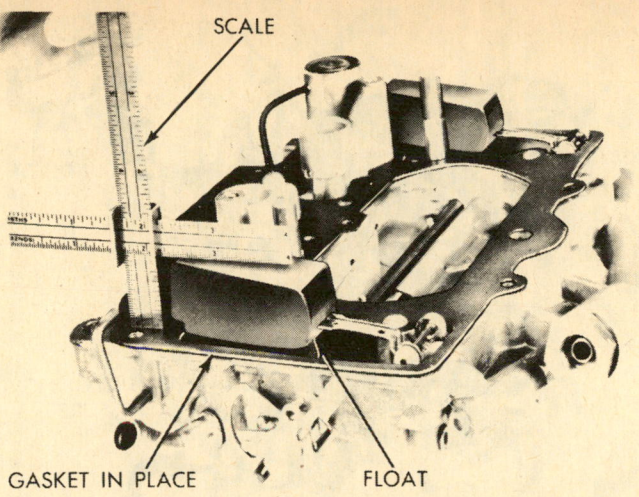

TQ float adjustment

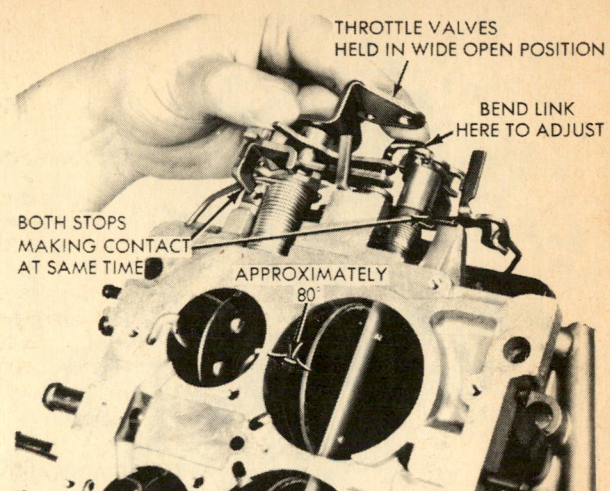

TQ secondary throttle adjustment

Accelerator Pump Adjustment

THROUGH 1975

1. Move the choke valve wide open to release the fast idle cam.
2. Back off the idle speed adjusting screw until the throttle valves are seated in the bores.
3. Be sure that the throttle connector rod is in the center (three holes) or the inner (two holes) hole of the pump arm.
4. Close the throttle valve tightly and measure the distance between the top of the bowl cover and the end of the plunger shaft. The dimension should be as shown in the Specifications Chart.
5. Bend the throttle connector rod at the lower angle to adjust.

1976 AND LATER

1. Make sure the throttle connector rod is in the correct hole of the pump arm.

2. Measure the height of the accelerator pump plunger at curb idle. The ignition switch must be on if there is a idle stop solenoid.
3. Adjust plunger height by bending the throttle connector rod.

Choke Control Lever

1. Disconnect the diaphragm rod.
2. Close the choke by pushing on the choke lever with the throttle partly open.
3. Measure the vertical distance from the top of the rod hole in the control lever down to the carburetor base. The dimension should be as shown in the Specifications Chart.
4. To adjust, bend the link which connects the two choke shafts.

Choke Vacuum Kick Adjustment

NOTE: *The test can be made on or off the vehicle.*
1. If the adjustment is to be made

with the engine running, back off the fast idle speed screw until the choke can be closed to the kick position with the engine at curb idle. (Note the number of screw turns required so that the fast idle can be returned to the original adjustment.)
2. If an auxiliary vacuum scource is to be used, as recommended for 1977 and later open the throttle valve (engine not running) and move the choke to the closed position. Release the throttle first, then release the choke.

When using an auxiliary vacuum source, disconnect the vacuum hose from the carburetor and connect it to the hose from the vacuum supply with a small length of tube to act as a fitting. Removal of the hose from the diaphragm may require sufficient force to bend the bracket. Apply a vacuum of 15 or more in. of mercury.

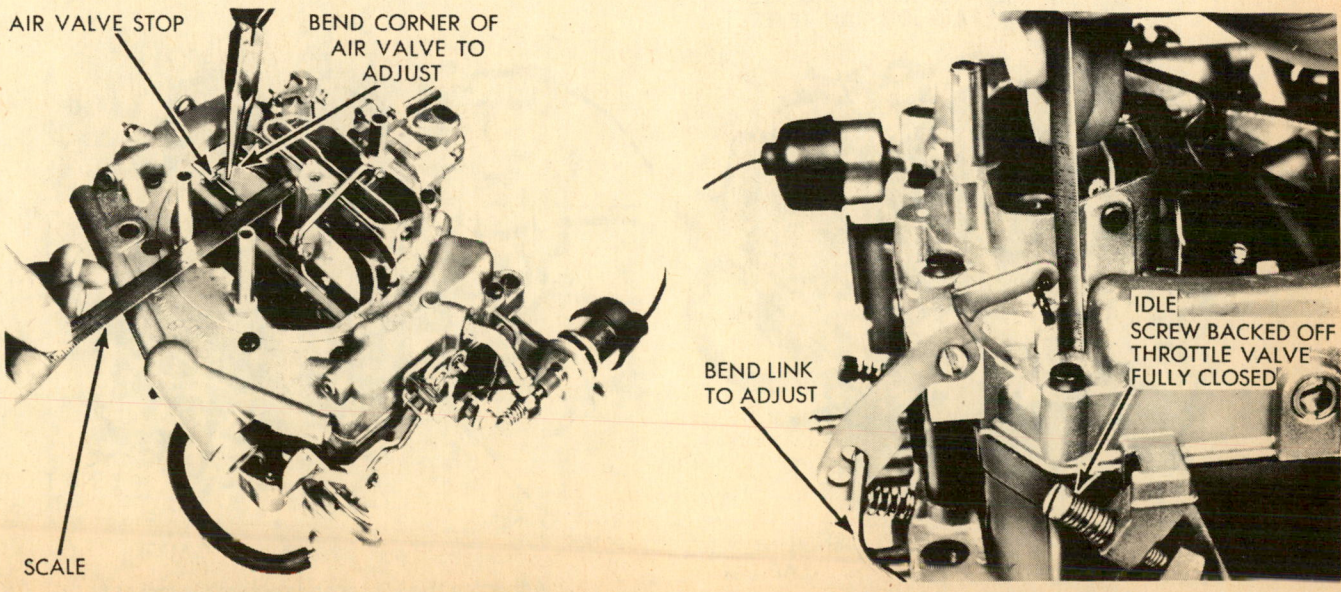

TQ secondary air valve adjustment

TQ accelerator pump adjustment

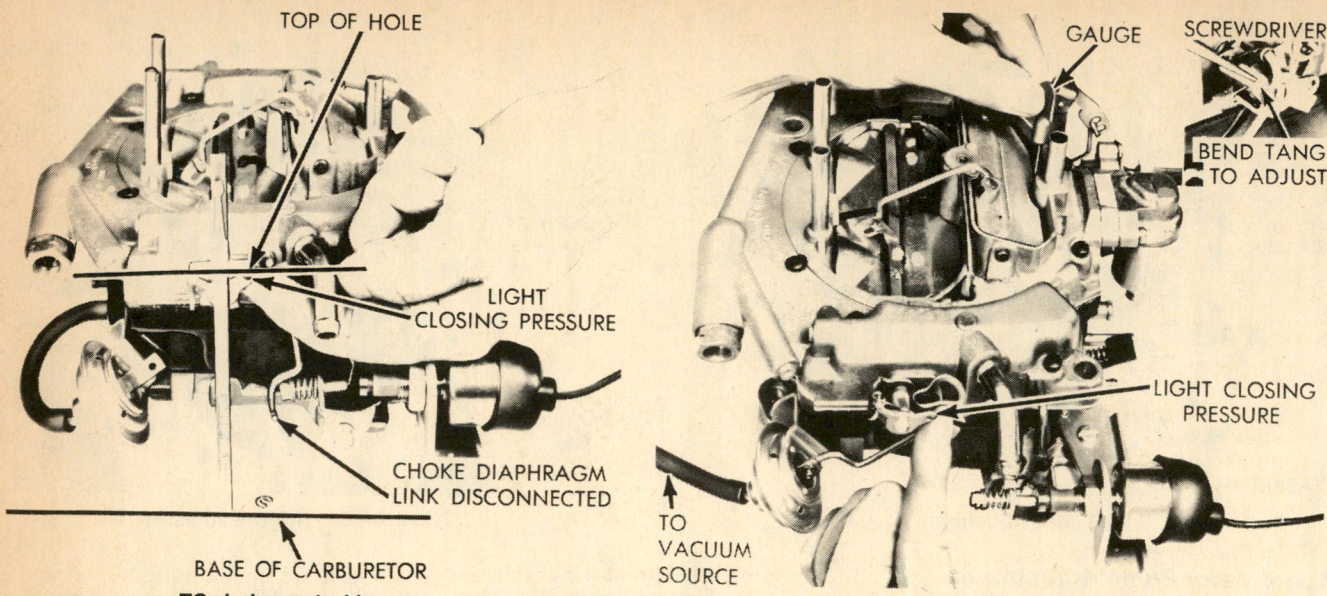

TOP OF HOLE

LIGHT
CLOSING PRESSURE

CHOKE DIAPHRAGM
LINK DISCONNECTED

BASE OF CARBURETOR

TQ choke control lever

GAUGE

SCREWDRIVER

BEND TANG
TO ADJUST

LIGHT CLOSING
PRESSURE

TO
VACUUM
SOURCE

TQ vacuum kick adjustment

3. Insert the specified drill between the long side, lower edge, of the choke valve and the air horn wall.
4. Apply sufficient pressure on the choke control lever to provide a minimum choke valve opening. The spring connecting the control lever to the adjustment lever must be fully extended for proper adjustment.
5. Bend the tang to change contact with the end of the diaphragm rod. Do not adjust the diaphragm rod. A slight drag should be felt as the drill is being removed.

Fast Idle Cam Linkage

1. With the fast screw on the second fastest step of the cam against the shoulder of the first step, there should be 0.110 in. (.100 beginning 1974) between the air horn wall and edge of the choke valve.
2. To adjust, bend the fast idle connector rod at the lower angle.

Secondary Throttle Lockout

1. Move the choke control lever to the open choke position.
2. Measure the clearance between the lockout lever and the stop.
3. Bend the tang on the fast idle control lever to provide the proper clearance. The reading should be 0.010 to 0.030 for models through 1972, and 0.060 to 0.090 in. beginning 1973.

Bowl Vent Valve Adjustment

1. Remove the bowl vent valve checking hole plug in the bowl cover.

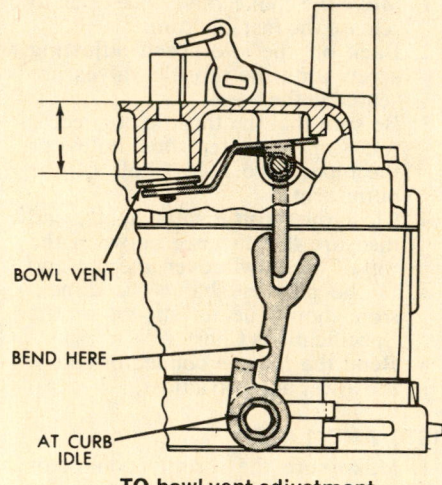

BOWL VENT

BEND HERE

AT CURB
IDLE

TQ bowl vent adjustment

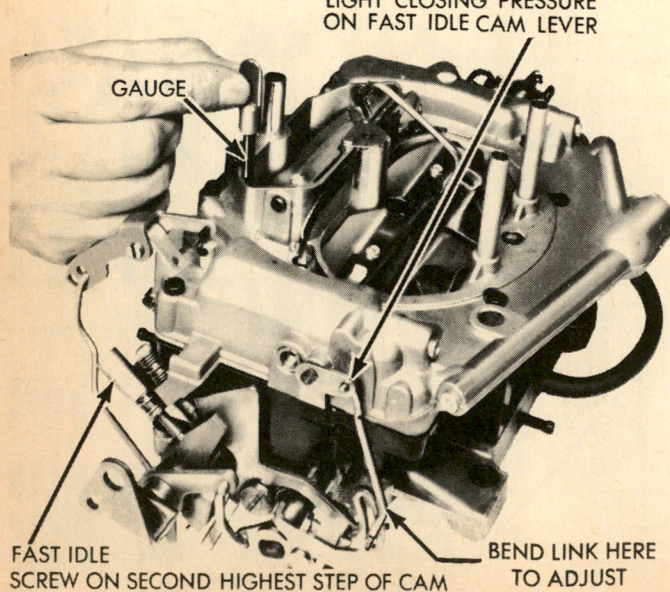

LIGHT CLOSING PRESSURE
ON FAST IDLE CAM LEVER

GAUGE

FAST IDLE
SCREW ON SECOND HIGHEST STEP OF CAM

BEND LINK HERE
TO ADJUST

TQ adjusting fast idle cam linkage

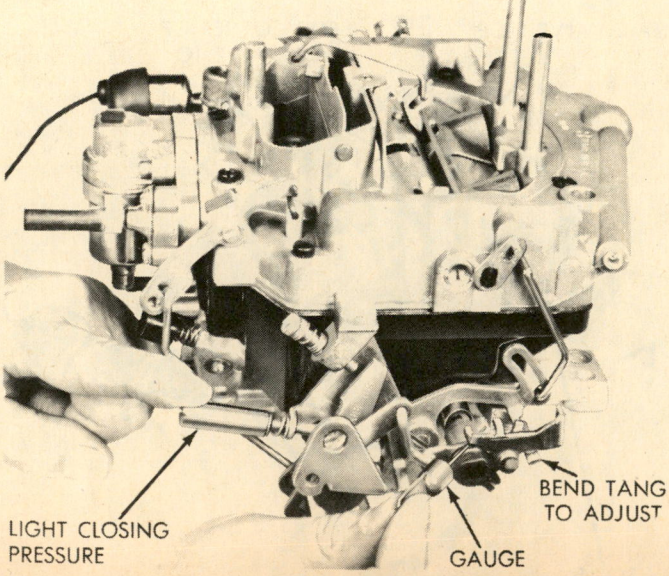

LIGHT CLOSING
PRESSURE

GAUGE

BEND TANG
TO ADJUST

Adjusting the TQ secondary throttle lockout

2. With the throttle valve in the idle position insert a narrow ruler down through the hole.
3. Allow the ruler to rest lightly on the top of the valve. Measure from the top of the valve to the top of the bowl cover at the opening. The correct dimension should be $^{13}/_{16}$ in.
4. Bend the bowl vent operating lever at the notch to adjust.
5. Install a new plug.

Fast Idle Speed Cam

1. Disconnect and plug the heated air, EGR, OSAC valve, or distributor connections on 1974 and later models. With lean burn, do not disconnect the spark control computer hose. Use a jumper wire to ground the carburetor idle stop switch. With the engine off and the transmission in Park or Neutral, open the throttle slightly.
2. Close the choke valve until the fast idle screw can be positioned on the second step of the cam against the shoulder of the first step.
3. Start the engine and adjust the screw to obtain the specified fast idle speed.

FAST IDLE SCREW ON SECOND STEP AGAINST SHOULDER OF FIRST STEP

TQ fast idle cam adjustment

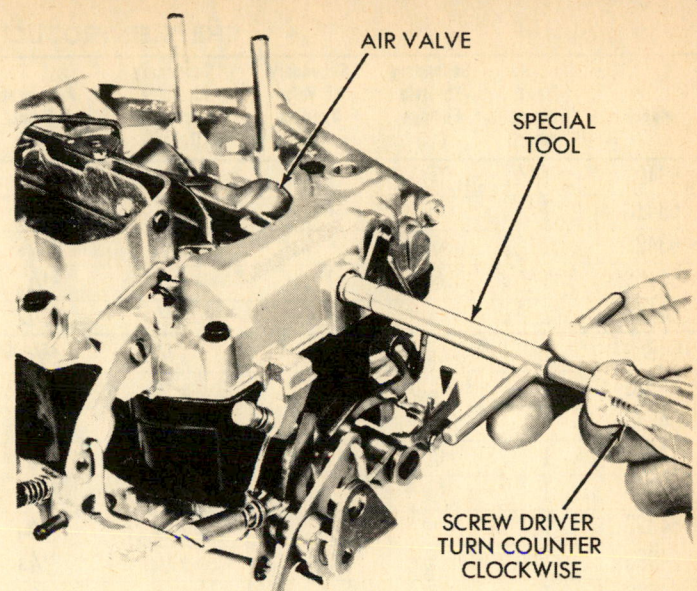

AIR VALVE

SPECIAL TOOL

SCREW DRIVER TURN COUNTER CLOCKWISE

TQ air valve spring tension adjustment

Choke Unloader Adjustment

1. Hold the throttle valves in the wide open position and insert the specified drill between the bottom of the choke valve and inner wall of the air horn.
2. With a finger pressing lightly against the choke control lever, a slight drag should be felt as the drill is being withdrawn.
3. To adjust, bend the tang on the fast idle lever.

Secondary Air Valve Spring Tension

1. Loosen the air valve lock plug and allow the air valve to position itself in the wide open position.

CAUTION

Hold the adjustment plug with a screwdriver when loosening the lock plug. If you don't, the spring may snap out of position and require carburetor disassembly to retrieve it.

2. With a long screwdriver that will enter the center of tool C-4152 positioned on the air valve adjustment plug, turn the plug counterclockwise until the air valve contacts the stop lightly, then tighten the specified amount.
3. Hold the adjustment plug with the screwdriver and tighten the lock plug with the tool. Make sure the adjustment does not move and that the air valve moves freely.

CARTER TQ SPECIFICATIONS

CHRYSLER PRODUCTS

Year	Model ①	Float Setting (in.)	Secondary Throttle Linkage (in.)	Secondary Air Valve Opening (in.)	Secondary Air Valve Spring (turns)	Accelerator Pump (in.)	Choke Control Lever (in.)	Choke Unloader (in.)	Vacuum Kick (in.)	Fast Idle Speed (rpm)
1972	6090S	1	②	$^{31}/_{64}$	1	$^{31}/_{64}$	$3 \, ^3/_8$	0.190	28	1900
	6138S	1	②	$^{29}/_{64}$	1	$^9/_{16}$	$3 \, ^3/_8$	0.190	21	1900
	6139S	1	②	$^{29}/_{64}$	1	$^{31}/_{64}$	$3 \, ^3/_8$	0.190	28	1900
	6140S	1	②	$^{31}/_{64}$	1	$^9/_{16}$	$3 \, ^3/_8$	0.190	21	1900
	6165S	1	②	$^{31}/_{64}$	1	$^9/_{16}$	$3 \, ^3/_8$	0.190	21	2000
	6166S	1	②	$^{31}/_{64}$	1	$^{31}/_{64}$	$3 \, ^3/_8$	0.190	28	2100
1973	6318S	$1 \, ^1/_{16}$	②	$^{29}/_{64}$	$1 \, ^1/_4$	$^{35}/_{64}$	$3 \, ^3/_8$	0.190	21	1300
	6319S	$1 \, ^1/_{16}$	②	$^{29}/_{64}$	$1 \, ^1/_4$	$^{31}/_{64}$	$3 \, ^3/_8$	0.190	21	1800
	6320S	$1 \, ^1/_{16}$	②	$^{31}/_{64}$	$1 \, ^1/_4$	$^{35}/_{64}$	$3 \, ^3/_8$	0.190	21	1300
	6321S	$1 \, ^1/_{16}$	②	$^{31}/_{64}$	$1 \, ^1/_4$	$^{31}/_{64}$	$3 \, ^3/_8$	0.190	21	1800
	6322S	$1 \, ^1/_{16}$	②	$^{31}/_{64}$	$1 \, ^1/_4$	$^{31}/_{64}$	$3 \, ^3/_8$	0.190	21	1700
	6324S	$1 \, ^1/_{16}$	②	$^{31}/_{64}$	$1 \, ^1/_4$	$^{31}/_{64}$	$3 \, ^3/_8$	0.190	21	1800
	6339S	$1 \, ^1/_{16}$	②	$^{29}/_{64}$	$1 \, ^1/_4$	$^{35}/_{64}$	$3 \, ^3/_8$	0.190	21	1700

Carter Carburetors

CHRYSLER PRODUCTS

Year	Model ①	Float Setting (in.)	Secondary Throttle Linkage (in.)	Secondary Air Valve Opening (in.)	Secondary Air Valve Spring (turns)	Accelerator Pump (in.)	Choke Control Lever (in.)	Choke Unloader (in.)	Vacuum Kick (in.)	Fast Idle Speed (rpm)
1973	6340S	1 1/16	②	29/64	1 1/4	31/64	3 3/8	0.190	21	1800
	6341S	1 1/16	②	29/64	1 1/4	35/64	3 3/8	0.190	21	1700
	6342S	1 1/16	②	29/64	1 1/4	31/64	3 3/8	0.190	21	1700
	6410S	1 1/16	②	31/64	1 1/4	31/64	3 3/8	0.190	21	1700
	6411S	1 1/16	②	31/64	1 1/4	31/64	3 3/8	0.190	21	1700
1974	6488S	1	②	1/2	1 1/4	35/64	3 3/8	.310	21	1800
	6452S	1	②	1/2	1 1/4	35/64	3 3/8	.310	4	1900
	6453S	1	②	1/2	1 1/4	31/64	3 3/8	.310	21	1900
	6454S	1	②	1/2	1 1/4	35/64	3 3/8	.310	4	1900
	6455S	1	②	1/2	1 1/4	31/64	3 3/8	.310	21	1900
	6489S	1	②	1/2	1 1/4	31/64	3 3/8	.310	21	2000
	6496S	1	②	1/2	1 1/4	31/64	3 3/8	.310	21	2000
	6456S	1	②	1/2	1 1/4	35/64	3 3/8	.310	4	1700
	6457S	1	②	1/2	1 1/4	31/64	3 3/8	.310	21	1800
	6459	1	②	1/2	1 1/4	31/64	3 3/8	.310	21	1800
	6460S	1	②	1/2	1 1/4	31/64	3 3/8	.310	21	1700
	6461S	1	②	1/2	1 1/4	31/64	3 3/8	.310	21	1700
	6462S	1	②	1/2	1 1/4	31/64	3 3/8	.310	21	1700
	6463S	1	②	1/2	1 1/4	31/64	3 3/8	.310	21	1700
1975	9004S	29/32	②	1/2	1 1/4	35/64	3 3/8	0.310	0.100	1600
	9002S	29/32	②	1/2	1 1/4	35/64	3 3/8	0.310	0.100	1600
	9046S	29/32	②	1/2	1 1/4	35/64	3 3/8	0.310	0.100	1800
	9008S	29/32	②	1/2	1 1/4	35/64	3 3/8	0.310	0.100	1800
	9053S	29/32	②	1/2	1 1/4	35/64	3 3/8	0.310	0.100	1800
	9009S	29/32	②	1/2	1 1/4	35/64	3 3/8	0.310	0.100	1600
	9010S	29/32	②	1/2	1 1/4	35/64	3 3/8	0.310	0.100	1600
	9011S	29/32	②	1/2	1 1/4	35/64	3 3/8	0.310	0.100	1600
	9012S	29/32	②	1/2	1 1/4	35/64	3 3/8	0.310	0.100	1800
1976	9002S	29/32	②	33/64	1 1/4	33/64	3 3/8	0.310	0.100	1700
	9055S	29/32	②	33/64	1 1/4	33/64	3 3/8	0.310	0.100	1700
	9074S	29/32	②	33/64	1 1/4	33/64	3 3/8	0.310	0.100	1600
	9057S	29/32	②	33/64	1 1/4	33/64	3 3/8	0.310	0.100	1600
	9054S	29/32	②	33/64	1 1/4	33/64	3 3/8	0.310	0.100	1800
	9058S	29/32	②	33/64	1 1/4	31/64	3 3/8	0.310	0.100	1600
	9059S	29/32	②	33/64	1 1/4	31/64	3 3/8	0.310	0.100	1600
	9066S	29/32	②	33/64	1 1/4	33/64	3 3/8	0.310	0.100	1600
	9062S	29/32	②	33/64	1 1/4	33/64	3 3/8	0.310	0.100	1600
	9052S	29/32	②	33/64	1 1/4	33/64	3 3/8	0.310	0.100	1600
1977	9076S	27/32	②	1/2	1 1/2	33/64	3 3/8	0.310	0.150	1700
	9077S	27/32	②	31/64	1 1/2	33/64	3 3/8	0.310	0.100	1400
	9078S	27/32	②	1/2	1 1/4	33/64	3 3/8	0.310	0.100	1400
	9080S	27/32	②	1/2	1 1/4	33/64	3 3/8	0.310	0.100	1200
	9081S	27/32	②	1/2	1 1/4	33/64	3 3/8	0.310	0.100	1600
	9093S	27/32	②	17/32	1 1/4	33/64	3 3/8	0.310	0.150	1500
	9101S	27/32	②	1/2	1 1/4	33/64	3 3/8	0.310	0.100	1600
1978	9147S	29/32	②	1/2	1 1/2	31/64	3 3/8	0.310	0.100	1600
	9137S	29/32	②	1/2	1 1/2	31/64	3 3/8	0.310	0.100	1600

CHRYSLER PRODUCTS

Year	Model ①	Float Setting (in.)	Secondary Throttle Linkage (in.)	Secondary Air Valve Opening (in.)	Secondary Air Valve Spring (turns)	Accelerator Pump (in.)	Choke Control Lever (in.)	Choke Unloader (in.)	Vacuum Kick (in.)	Fast Idle Speed (rpm)
1978	9134S	29/32	②	1/2	1 1/2	31/64	3⅜	0.310	0.100	1500
	9104S	29/32	②	1/2	1 1/2	31/64	3⅜	0.310	0.150	1500
	9140S	29/32	②	1/2	1 1/2	33/64	3⅜	0.310	0.150	1500
	9108S	27/32	②	1/2	1 1/2	33/64	3⅜	0.310	0.100	1400
	9109S	27/32	②	1/2	1 1/2	33/64	3⅜	0.310	0.100	1400
	9110S	27/32	②	1/2	1 1/2	33/64	3⅜	0.310	0.100	1600
	9111S	27/32	②	1/2	1 1/2	33/64	3⅜	0.310	0.100	1400
	9112S	29/32	②	1/2	1 1/2	33/64	3⅜	0.310	0.100	1200
	9148S	29/32	②	1/2	1 1/2	33/64	3⅜	0.310	0.100	1600

① Model numbers located on the tag or on the casting
② Adjust link so primary and secondary stops both contact at same time

NOTE: All choke settings are fixed.

Ford, Autolite, Motorcraft Carburetors

MODEL 1250

The model 1250 is a single barrel downdraft carburetor designed for use on the 1600 cc Pinto engine. It is equipped with a diaphragm type accelerator pump and a water heated thermostatic choke.

Choke Plate Pulldown

1. Remove the thermostatic spring and the water housing.
2. Push in on the vacuum piston until the vacuum inner bleed slot is fully exposed.
3. Take a length of 0.040 in. wire and insert it into this slot. Raise the piston to trap the wire.
4. Partially open the throttle valve so that the choke plate may be moved toward the closed position.
5. Close the choke plate until its movement is stopped.
6. Check the clearance between the bottom of the choke plate and the inside wall of the carburetor body.
7. If the specified clearance is not present, bend the extension of the choke thermostat lever to adjust it.

Dechoke

1. Open the throttle valve fully and measure the clearance between the bottom of the choke plate and the carburetor body.
2. If adjustment is necessary, bend the tang on the fast idle cam.

Accelerator Pump Stroke

1. Back out the throttle stop screw so that the throttle plate may be fully closed.
2. Depress the plunger of the accelerator pump diaphragm and check

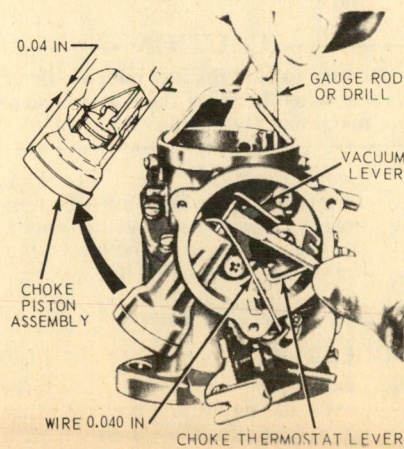

Choke plate pulldown adjustment
(© Ford Motor Co)

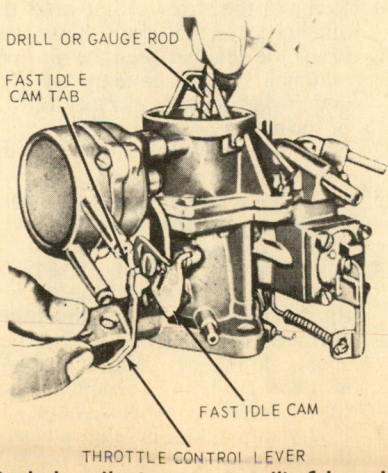

Dechoke adjustment—Autolite 1 barrel
(© Ford Motor Co)

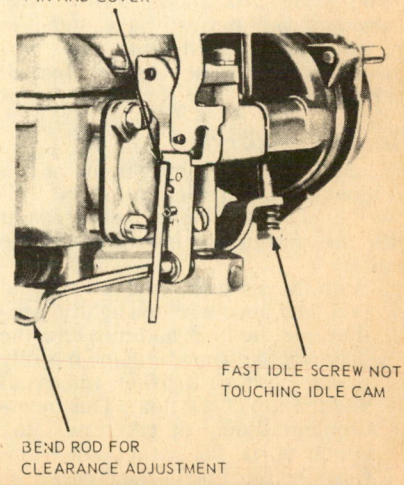

WITH THROTTLE PLATE FULLY CLOSED, INSERT A *Gauge* THAT EQUALS THE SPECIFIED CLEARANCE BETWEEN THE PIN AND COVER

Accelerator pump adjustment
(© Ford Motor Co)

the clearance between the operating lever and the plunger with the proper gauge.

3. To adjust, bend the gooseneck of the pump push rod. Closing the gooseneck will lengthen the stroke and expanding it will shorten the stroke.

4. Reset the throttle valve stop screw.

Fast Idle

1. After adjusting the choke plate pulldown, hold the choke plate in the closed position.
2. Make sure the fast idle tab is on the second step of the fast idle cam.
3. Install the thermostatic spring and water housing. Locate the spring in the center slot and accurately align the marks on the housing.
4. Connect a tachometer to the engine.
5. Run the engine until the normal operating temperature is reached.
6. Put the fast idle tab on the second step of the fast idle cam and check engine speed. If adjustment is needed, bend the tab which contacts the fast idle cam.

Float Level

1. Disconnect all connections to the carburetor upper body including the fule line, decel valve hose, choke fast idle pivot screw, and the thermostatic housing. Remove the upper carburetor body.
2. With the upper carburetor body held so that the float hangs down, measure the distance from the bottom of the float to the upper body gasket. To adjust, bend the tab which contacts the needle valve and seat assembly.
3. Invert the carburetor so that the float rests on the carburetor body. Again measure the distance from

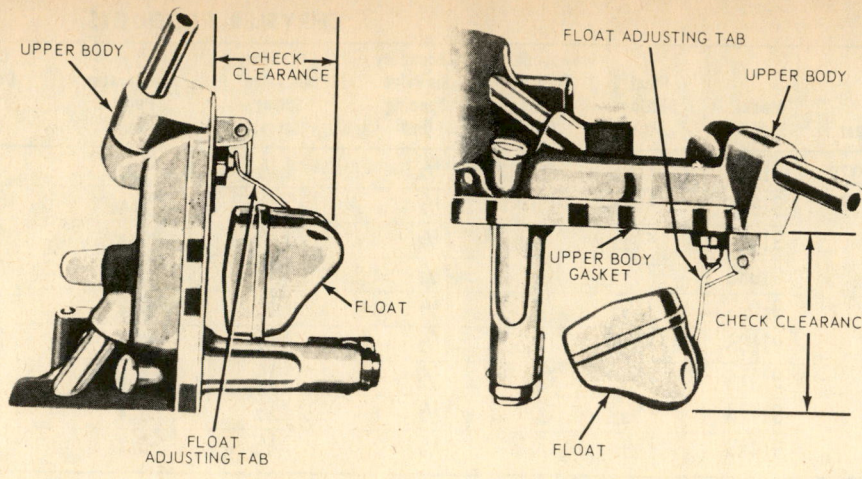

Adjusting float level—Model 1250
(© Ford Motor Co)

the bottom of the float to the body gasket. Adjust by bending the tab which rests on the needle valve housing.

Vent Valve Adjustment

1. Adjust the vent valve only after the accelerator pump has been properly adjusted.

2. Set the linkage in the hot idle position.
3. The groove in the vent valve should now be even with the open end of the vent.
4. Bend the arm on the vent valve actuating lever to align the groove with the edge of the bore.

FORD, AUTOLITE, MOTORCRAFT MODEL 1250 SPECIFICATIONS

Pinto

Year	(9510)* Carburetor Identification	Float Level (in.)	Pump (in.)	Fast Idle (rpm)	Choke Plate Pulldown (in.)	Dechoke (in.)	Choke Setting
1972	721F-KFA	②	0.070	1700	0.075	0.210	Index
1973	731F-KAA	②	0.085	—	0.075	—	Index

* Basic carburetor number ② Body vertical—1.200

MODELS 2100, 2150

The Model 2100 and 2150 two barrel carburetor are basically the same in construction. Adjustments are performed in the same manner for all carburetors.

Float Level (Dry)

The dry float level measurement is a preliminary check and must be followed by a wet float level measurement with the carburetor mounted on the engine.

1. With the air horn removed and the fuel inlet needle seated lightly, gently raise the float and measure the distance between the main body gasket surface (gasket removed) and the top of the float. This measurement should be taken near the center of the float at a point 1/8 in. from the free end of the float.
2. If necessary, bend the float tab to obtain the correct level.

Float Level (Wet)

1. Remove the screws that hold the air horn to the main body and break the seal between the air horn and main body. Leave the air horn and gasket loosely in place on top of the main body.
2. Start the engine and allow it to idle for at least three minutes.
3. After the engine has idled long enough to stabilize the fuel level, remove the air horn assembly.
4. With the engine idling, use a T-scale to measure the distance from the top of the fuel bowl machined surface to the surface of the fuel. The scale must be held at least 1/– in. away from any vertical surface to ensure proper measurement.
5. If any adjustment is required, stop the engine to avoid a fire from fuel spraying on the engine.
6. Bend the float tab upward to raise

the level and downward to lower the level.

— CAUTION —

Be sure to hold the fuel inlet needle off its seat when bending the float tab so as not to damage the Vitron® tip.

7. Each time the float level is changed, the air horn must be temporarily positioned and the engine started to stabilize the fuel level before again checking it.

Choke Plate Pulldown

MODEL 2100

1. Loosen the screws on the choke cover and rotate the cover 1/4 turn counterclockwise (rich), then tighten the screws.
2. Operate the throttle to allow full closing of the choke plate.

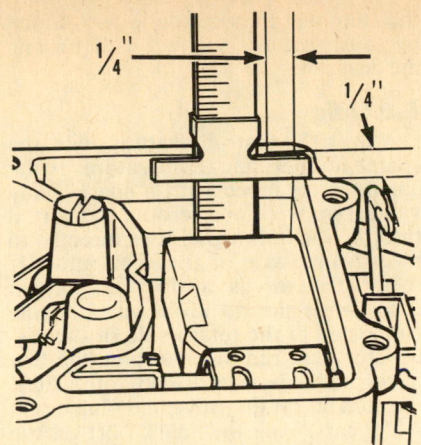

Fuel level measurement (wet)
(© Ford Motor Co)

3. Press down on the choke modulator arm until the choke modulator diaphragm is bottomed and then measure the distance from the lower edge of the choke plate to the inside air horn wall.
4. Adjustment is achieved by turning the diaphragm stop screw on the underside of the air horn.
5. Turn the screw clockwise to decrease clearance and counterclockwise to increase clearance.

NOTE: *Do not reset the choke cover until the fast idle cam adjustment is made.*

AMC MODEL 2100

1. Loosen the choke cover screws and rotate the cover ¼ turn counterclockwise (rich).
2. Disconnect the choke heat inlet tube. Set the fast idle speed screw on the second step of the fast idle cam.
3. Start the engine without moving the throttle linkage. Turn the fast idle cam lever adjusting screw out three turns.
4. Check the clearance between the lower edge of the choke valve and the air horn wall.
5. Adjust by twisting the modulator arm. Be very careful not to damage the nylon modulator piston rod.
6. Stop the engine and connect the heat tube.
7. Make the fast idle cam adjustment before resetting the choke cover.

MODEL 2150

1. Remove the air cleaner assembly.
2. Set the throttle on the top step of the fast idle cam.
3. Noting the position of the choke housing cap, loosen the retaining screws and rotate the cap 90 degrees in the rich (closing) direction.
4. Activate the pull-down motor by manually forcing the pull-down control diaphragm link in the direction of applied vacuum or by applying vacuum to the external vacuum tube.
5. Using a drill gauge of the specified diameter, measure the clearance

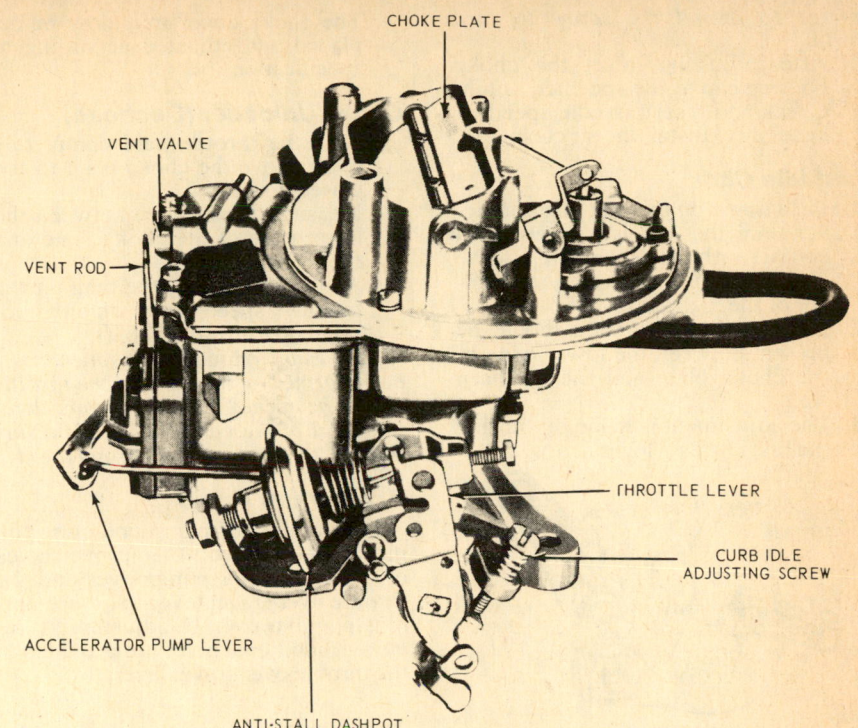

Model 2100 two barrel carburetor
(© Ford Motor Co)

between the choke plate and the center of the air horn wall nearest the fuel bowl.
6. To adjust, reset the diaphragm stop on the end of the choke pull-down diaphragm.

NOTE: *Loctite® was applied to the adjusting screw during manufacture and this will have to be loosened before the adjustment can be made. Heat the area around the screw with an electric soldering gun until the Loctite® softens*

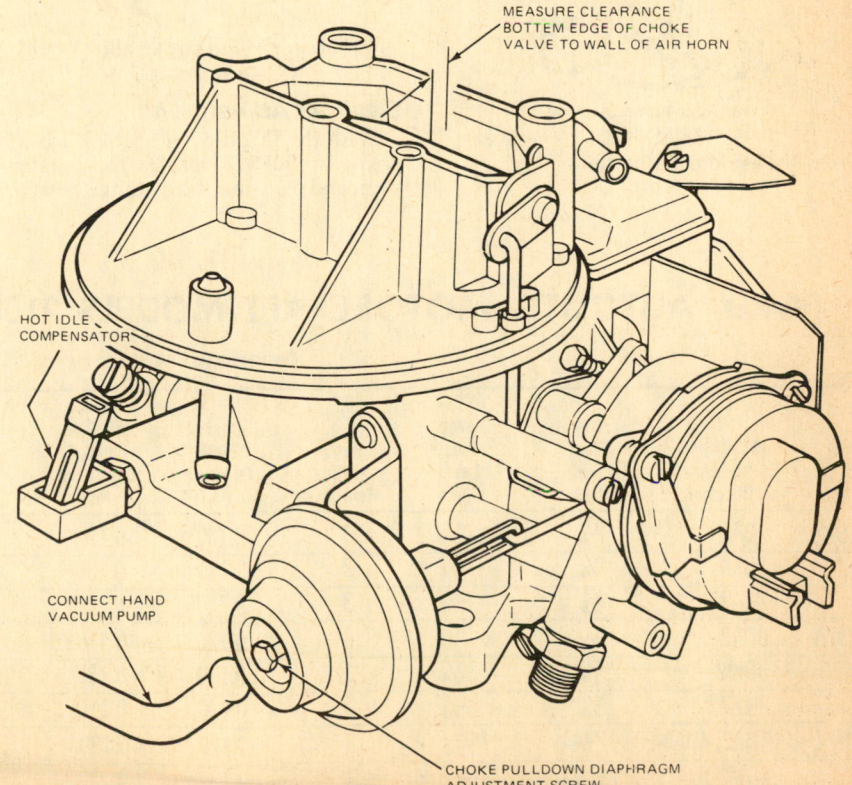

Adjusting choke plate pulldown (© Ford Motor Co)

enough to permit the screw to turn freely.

7. After adjusting, reset the choke housing cap to the specified notch. Check and reset fast idle speed, if necessary. Install the air cleaner.

Fast Idle Cam

1. Push down on the fast idle cam lever until the fast idle screw is in contact with the second step of the fast idle cam and against the shoulder of the high step.
2. The specified clearance should be present between the lower edge of the choke plate and the air horn wall.
3. The adjustment is made by turning the fast idle cam lever screw.

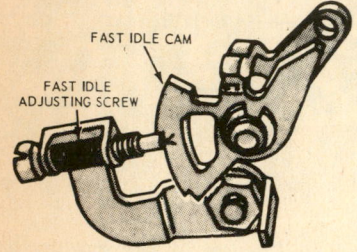

CONVENTIONAL ONE - PIECE FAST IDLE LEVER

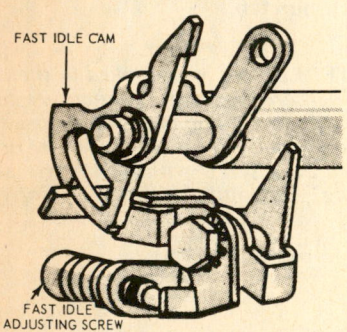

TWO - PIECE FAST IDLE LEVER
FOR 351-C ENGINE

Fast idle adjustment
(© Ford Motor Co)

4. The choke cover may now be replaced and adjusted according to specification.

Choke Unloader (Dechoke)

1. With the throttle held completely open, move the choke plate to the closed position.
2. Measure the distance between the lower edge of the choke plate and the air horn wall.
3. Adjust by bending the tang on the fast idle speed lever which is located on the throttle shaft.

NOTE: *Final unloader adjustment must be performed on the car and the throttle should be opened by using the accelerator pedal of the car. This is to be sure that full throttle operation is achieved.*

Accelerator Pump

The accelerator pump operating rod must be positioned in the proper holes of the accelerator pump lever and the throttle over-travel lever to assure correct pump travel. If adjusting is required, additional holes are provided in the throttle over-travel lever.

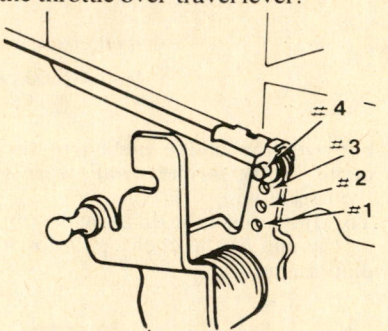

Accelerator pump stroke adjustment
(© Ford Motor Co)

Dashpot Adjustment

With the throttle set at the curb idle position, fully depress the dashpot stem and measure the distance between

the stem and the throttle lever. Adjust by loosening the locknut and turning the dashpot.

Fast Idle

Adjust the fast idle setting with the engine at operating temperature. If the engine is equipped with a spark delay valve, remove it and reroute the partial throttle vacuum signal line directly to the advance side of the distributor. If the distributor is a dual diaphragm type, leave the manifold vacuum line connected to the retard side of the distributor, and remove and plug the line to the advance side. Remove the EGR vacuum line at the valve and plug it. On AMC cars, plug the spark port on the carburetor. The fast idle screw should be resting against the second step of the fast idle cam on all except those 1975 and later models used with a 302 cu. in. engine. These have the screw set on the high step of the fast idle cam. Adjust the fast idle speed by turning the fast idle screw.

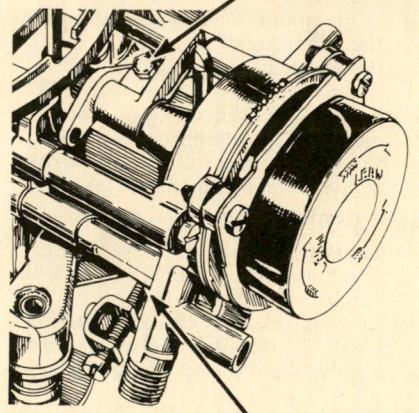

FAST IDLE CAM LEVER SCREW

SECOND STEP OF CAM

2100, 2150 fast idle cam linkage adjustment

FORD, AUTOLITE, MOTORCRAFT MODELS 2100, 2150 SPECIFICATIONS

American Motors

Year	(9510)* Carburetor Identification	Dry Float Level (in.)	Wet Float Level (in.)	Pump Setting Hole #①	Choke Plate Pulldown (in.)	Fast Idle Cam Linkage Clearance (in.)	Fast Idle (rpm)	Dechoke (in)	Choke Setting	Dashpot (in.)
1972	2DA2	3/8	3/4	3	0.130	0.120	1600	0.200	2 Rich	9/64
	2DM2	3/8	3/4	3	0.140	0.130	1600	0.200	1 Rich	7/64
	2RA2	3/8	3/4	3	0.130	0.120	1600	0.200	2 Rich	—
1973	3DA2	3/8	3/4	3	0.120	0.110	1600	0.250	2 Rich	—
	3DM2	3/8	3/4	3	0.130	0.130	1600	0.250	1 Rich	9/64
	3RA2	3/8	3/4	3	0.120	0.110	1600	0.250	2 Rich	—
1974	4DA2, 4DA2-E	25/64	25/32	3	0.140	0.130	1600	0.250	1 Rich	—
	4DM2	25/64	25/32	3	0.130	0.130	1600	0.250	2 Rich	9/64
	4RA2, 4RAC2	25/64	25/32	3	0.140	0.130	1600	0.250	1 Rich	—

AMERICAN MOTORS

Year	(9510)* Carburetor Identification	Dry Float Level (in.)	Wet Float Level (in.)	Pump Setting Hole #①	Choke Plate Pulldown (in.)	Fast Idle Cam Linkage Clearance (in.)	Fast Idle (rpm)	Dechoke (in)	Choke Setting	Dashpot (in.)
1975	5DA2	13/32	3/4	3	0.140	0.130	1600	0.250	1 Rich	——
	5DMS	13/32	3/4	3	0.130	0.130	1600	0.250	2 Rich	3/32
	5RAS	13/32	3/4	3	0.140	0.130	1600	0.250	1 Rich	
1976	6DA2	13/32	3/4	3	0.140	0.130	1600	0.250	1 Rich	——
	6DM2	35/64	15/16	3	0.130	0.120	1600	0.250	2 Rich	——
	6RA2	13/32	3/4	3	0.140	0.130	1600	0.250	1 Rich	——
1977	7RA2	5/16	0.780	3	0.136	0.126	1600	0.250	1 Rich	——
	7RA2C	5/16	0.780	3	0.130	0.120	1800⑥	0.250	1 Rich	
	7DA2	5/16	0.780	3	0.136	0.126	1600	0.250	Index	——
	7RA2A	5/16	0.780	3	0.104	0.089	1800	0.250	1 Rich	——
1978	8DA2	0.555	0.780	3	0.136	0.126	1600	0.250	Index	
	8RA2	0.555	0.780	3	0.136	0.126	1600	0.250	1 Rich	
	8RA2C	0.555	0.780	3	0.136	0.120	1800	0.250	1 Rich	
	8RA2A	0.555	0.780	3	0.089	0.078	1800	0.170	2 Rich	
	8DA2A	0.555	0.930	3	0.089	0.078	1600	0.170	2 Rich	

Ford Products

Year	(9510)* Carburetor Identification	Dry Float Level (in.)	Wet Float Level (in.)	Pump Setting Hole #①	Choke Plate Pulldown (in.)	Fast Idle Cam Linkage Clearance (in.)	Fast Idle (rpm)	Dechoke (in)	Choke Setting	Dashpot (in.)
1972	D2AF-FB	7/16	13/16	3	0.140	0.130	1500	0.030	Index	1/8
	D2AF-GB	7/16	13/16	3	0.140	0.130	1500	0.030	Index	1/8
	D2AF-HA	7/16	13/16	2	0.150	0.130	1400	0.060	1 Rich	1/8
	D2GF-AA	7/16	13/16	2	0.150	0.130	1400	0.060	1 Rich	1/8
	D2GF-BA	7/16	13/16	2	0.150	0.130	1400	0.060	1 Rich	——
	D2MF-FB	7/16	13/16	4	0.180	0.150	1500	0.060	1 Rich	——
	D2OF-KA	7/16	13/16	2	0.150	0.130	1400	0.060	1 Rich	——
	D2OF-VB	7/16	13/16	3	0.190	0.160	1400	0.030	2 Rich	——
	D2WF-CA	7/16	13/16	3	0.190	0.160	1400	0.030	2 Rich	——
	D2ZF-FA	7/16	13/16	2	0.150	0.130	1400	0.060	1 Rich	——
	D2ZF-LA	7/16	13/16	3	0.240	0.210	1500	0.030	1 Rich	——
1973	D3AF-CE	7/16	13/16	3	②	②	1500	②	1 Rich	——
	D3AF-DC	7/16	13/16	3	②	②	1500	②	3 Rich	——
	D3GF-AF	7/16	13/16	2	②	②	1400	②	3 Rich	——
	D3GF-BB	7/16	13/16	2	②	②	1250	②	3 Rich	——
	D3ZF-EA	7/16	13/16	2	②	②	1400	②	1 Rich	——
	D3AF-KA	7/16	13/16	3	②	②	1500	②	3 Rich	——
	D3MF-AE	7/16	13/16	3	②	②	1500	②	3 Rich	——
	D3MF-BA	7/16	13/16	3	②	②	1500	②	3 Rich	——
	D3AF-NA	7/16	13/16	3	②	②	1500	②	1 Rich	——
	D3AF-JA	7/16	13/16	3	②	②	1500	②	1 Rich	——
	D3AF-XA	7/16	13/16	3	②	②	1500	②	3 Rich	——
	D3DF-EA	7/16	13/16	2	②	②	1400	②	3 Rich	——
	D3OF-EA	7/16	13/16	2	②	②	1400	②	3 Rich	——

Ford • Autolite • Motorcraft Carburetors

Ford Products

Year	(9510)* Carburetor Identification	Dry Float Level (in.)	Wet Float Level (in.)	Pump Setting Hole #①	Choke Plate Pulldown (in.)	Fast Idle Cam Linkage Clearance (in.)	Fast Idle (rpm)	Dechoke (in)	Choke Setting	Dashpot (in.)
1973	D3AF-ABA	7/16	13/16	2	②	②	1400	②	3 Rich	——
	D30F-JA	7/16	13/16	2	②	②	1500	②	3 Rich	——
	D3MF-DA	7/16	13/16	3	②	②	1500	②	3 Rich	——
	D3MF-EA	7/16	13/16	3	②	②	1500	②	3 Rich	——
	D3AF-RA	7/16	13/16	2	②	②	1500	②	1 Rich	——
	D3AF-RB	7/16	13/16	2	②	②	1500	②	3 Rich	——
	D3AF-CE	7/16	13/16	3	②	②	1500	②	1 Rich	——
	D3MF-GA	7/16	13/16	3	②	②	1500	②	3 Rich	——
	D3AF-PA	7/16	13/16	3	②	②	1500	②	3 Rich	——
	D3ZF-FA	7/16	13/16	3	②	②	1500	②	3 Rich	——
1974	D4AE-DA	7/16	13/16	2	②	②	1500	②	1 Rich	——
	D4AE-EA	7/16	13/16	2	②	②	1500	②	3 Rich	——
	D4AE-FA	7/16	13/16	3	②	②	1500	②	3 Rich	——
	D4AE-GA	7/16	13/16	3	②	②	1500	②	3 Rich	——
	D4DE-LA	7/16	13/16	2	②	②	1500	②	3 Rich	——
	D4DE-RB	7/16	13/16	2	②	②	1500	②	3 Rich	——
	D40E-FA	7/16	13/16	2	②	②	1500	②	3 Rich	——
	D4AE-HB	7/16	13/16	3	②	②	1500	②	3 Rich	——
	D4DE-NB	7/16	13/16	2	②	②	1500	②	3 Rich	——
	D4DE-PA	7/16	13/16	2	②	②	1500	②	3 Rich	——
	D40E-CA	7/16	13/16	2	②	②	1500	②	3 Rich	——
	D4ME-BA	7/16	13/16	3	②	②	1500	②	3 Rich	——
	D4ME-CA	7/16	13/16	3	②	②	1500	②	3 Rich	——
1975	D5ZE-AC	3/8	3/4	2	0.145	②	1500	②	2 Rich	——
	D5ZE-BC	3/8	3/4	2	0.145	②	1500	②	2 Rich	——
	D5ZE-CC	3/8	3/4	3	0.145	②	1500	②	2 Rich	——
	D5ZE-DC	3/8	3/4	2	0.145	②	1500	②	2 Rich	——
	D5DE-AA	7/16	13/16	2	0.140	②	1500	②	3 Rich	——
	D5DE-BA	7/16	13/16	2	0.140	②	1500	②	3 Rich	——
	D5DE-JA	7/16	13/16	2	0.140	②	1500	②	3 Rich	——
	D5ZE-JA	7/16	13/16	2	0.140	②	1500	②	3 Rich	——
	D50E-AA	7/16	13/16	2	0.140	②	1500	②	3 Rich	——
	D50E-DA	7/16	13/16	2	0.140	②	1500	②	3 Rich	——
	D5DE-HA	7/16	13/16	3	0.140	②	1500	②	3 Rich	——
	D5DE-UA	7/16	13/16	2	0.140	②	1500	②	3 Rich	——
	D50E-BA	7/16	13/16	3	0.125	②	1500	②	3 Rich	——
	D50E-CA	7/16	13/16	3	0.125	②	1500	②	3 Rich	——
	D50E-GA	7/16	13/16	2	0.125	②	1500	②	3 Rich	——
	D5AE-AA	7/16	13/16	3	0.125	②	1500	②	3 Rich	——
	D5AE-EA	7/16	13/16	3	0.125	②	1500	②	3 Rich	——
	D5ME-BA	7/16	13/16	2	0.125	②	1500	②	3 Rich	——
	D5ME-FA	7/16	13/16	2	0.125	②	1500	②	3 Rich	——
1976	D5ZE-BE	3/8	3/4	2	0.105	②	1600③	②	3 Rich	——
	D6ZE-AA	3/8	3/4	2	0.100	②	1600③	②	3 Rich	——
	D6ZE-BA	3/8	3/4	2	0.100	②	1600③	②	3 Rich	——
	D6ZE-CA	13/32	3/4	2	0.110	②	1600③	②	3 Rich	——

Ford Products

Year	(9510)* Carburetor Identification	Dry Float Level (in.)	Wet Float Level (in.)	Pump Setting Hole # ①	Choke Plate Pulldown (in.)	Fast Idle Cam Linkage Clearance (in.)	Fast Idle (rpm)	Dechoke (in)	Choke Setting	Dashpot (in.)
1976	D6ZE-DA	3/8	3/4	3	0.110	②	1600③	②	3 Rich	——
	D5DE-AEA	7/16	13/16	2	0.160	②	2000④	②	3 Rich	——
	D5DE-AFA	7/16	13/16	2	0.160	②	2000④	②	3 Rich	——
	D5WE-FA	7/16	13/16	2	0.160	②	2000④	②	3 Rich	——
	D6ZE-JA	7/16	13/16	2	0.160	②	2000④	②	3 Rich	——
	D6OE-AA	7/16	13/16	3	0.160	②	2000④	②	3 Rich	——
	D6OE-BA	7/16	13/16	3	0.160	②	2000④	②	3 Rich	——
	D6OE-CA	7/16	13/16	3	0.160	②	2000④	②	3 Rich	——
	D6WE-AA	7/16	13/16	2	0.160	②	1350⑤	②	3 Rich	——
	D6WE-BA	7/16	13/16	2	0.160	②	1350⑤	②	3 Rich	——
	D6AE-HA	7/16	13/16	2	0.160	②	1350⑤	②	3 Rich	——
	D6ME-AA	7/16	13/16	2	0.160	②	1350⑤	②	3 Rich	——
1977-78	D7YE-AA	0.375	0.750	3	0.122	0.142	1600	—	2 Rich	——
	D7YE-BA	0.375	0.750	3	0.122	0.142	1700	—	Index	——
	D7YE-EA	0.375	0.750	3	0.122	0.142	1600	—	2 Rich	——
	D7BE-JA	0.438	0.813	2	0.147	0.167	2100	—	1 Rich	——
	D7BE-LA	0.438	0.813	2	0.147	0.167	2100	—	1 Rich	——
	D7BE-MA	0.438	0.813	2	0.147	0.167	2000	—	1 Rich	——
	D7BE-PA	0.438	0.813	2	0.147	0.167	2100	—	1 Rich	——
	D7BE-YA	0.438	0.813	2	0.147	0.167	2100	—	1 Rich	——
	D7DE-KA	0.438	0.813	2	0.147	0.167	2100	—	1 Rich	——
	D7DE-LA	0.438	0.813	2	0.147	0.167	2000	—	1 Rich	——
	D7WE-EA	0.438	0.813	2	0.147	0.167	2100	—	1 Rich	——
	D7WE-EB	0.438	0.813	2	0.147	0.167	2100	—	1 Rich	——
	D7AE-ADA	0.438	0.813	3	0.179	0.189	1400	—	2 Rich	——
	D7AE-AHA	0.438	0.813	3	0.179	0.189	1400	—	Index	——
	D7AE-CA	0.438	0.813	3	0.179	0.189	1400	—	Index	——
	D7AE-DA	0.438	0.813	3	0.179	0.189	1350	—	Index	——
	D7DE-RA	0.438	0.813	3	0.179	0.189	1400	—	3 Rich	——
	D7DE-RB	0.438	0.813	3	0.179	0.189	1400	—	3 Rich	——
	D7OE-CA	0.750	0.750	3	0.167	0.187	1350	—	2 Rich	——
	D7OE-LA	0.750	0.750	3	0.167	0.187	2000	—	2 Rich	——
	D7OE-NA	0.750	0.750	3	0.167	0.187	1350	—	2 Rich	——
	D7OE-RA	0.750	0.750	3	0.167	0.187	1350	—	2 Rich	——
	D7AE-ACA	0.438	0.813	2	0.156	0.170	1350	—	Index	——
	D7AE-AKA	0.438	0.813	3	0.179	0.189	1400	—	Index	——
	D7AE-GA	0.438	0.813	3	0.179	0.189	1350	—	Index	——
	D7OE-HA	0.438	0.813	3	0.185	0.205	1350	—	2 Rich	——
	D7OE-HB	0.438	0.813	3	0.185	0.205	1350	—	Index	——
	D7OE-MA	0.438	0.813	3	0.185	0.205	1400	—	Index	——
	D7OE-TA	0.438	0.813	3	0.185	0.205	1350	—	2 Rich	——

* Basic carburetor number for Ford products
① With link in inboard hole of pump lever
② Electric choke; see pulldown procedure in text
③ Figure given is for manual transmission; for automatics add 100 RPM.
④ Figure given is for 49 states Granada and Monarch; for Calif. Granada and Monarch and all Torino, Montego and Cougar models, figure is 1400 RPM.
⑤ Figure given is for 49 states model; Calif. specification is 1150 RPM.
⑥ 1600 with 360V8

MODEL 2700 VV

The 2700 VV carburetor is a two barrel unit, used on some California V8s. The area of the venturi varies with engine speed and load, unlike conventional fixed venturi carburetors. Fuel flow is controlled by metering rods. The variable venturi valve and the metering rods are controlled by vacuum and throttle position. Since the variable venturi keeps air speed constant, separate idle, and enrichment systems are not needed.

Float Level Adjustment

1. Remove and invert the upper part of the carburetor, with the gasket in place.
2. Measure the vertical distance between the carburetor body, outside the gasket, and the bottom of the float.

3. To adjust, bend the float operating lever that contacts the needle valve. Make sure that the float remains parallel to the gasket surface.

Float Drop Adjustment

1. Remove and hold upright the upper part of the carburetor.
2. Measure the vertical distance between the carburetor body, outside the gasket, and the bottom of the float.
3. Adjust by bending the stop tab on the float lever that contacts the hinge pin.

Fast Idle Speed Adjustment

1. With the engine warmed up and idling, place the fast idle lever on the step of the fast idle cam speci-

fied on the engine compartment sticker or in the specifications chart. Disconnect and plug the EGR vacuum line.
2. Make sure the high speed cam positioner lever is disengaged.
3. Turn the fast idle speed screw to adjust to the specified speed.

Fast Idle Cam Adjustment

1. Loosen the choke coil cap.
2. Place the fast idle lever in the corner of the specified step of the fast idle cam (the highest step is first) with the high speed cam positioner retracted.
3. If the adjustment is being made with the carburetor removed, hold the throttle lightly closed with a rubber band.
4. Turn the choke coil cap clockwise until the lever contacts the fast idle cam adjusting screw.
5. Turn the fast idle cam adjusting screw until the index mark on the cap lines up with the specified mark on the casting.
6. Tighten the choke coil cap.

Cold Enrichment Metering Rod Adjustment

A dial indicator is required for this adjustment.
1. Remove the choke coil cap.
2. Attach a weight to the choke coil mechanism to seat the cold enrichment rod.
3. Install and zero a dial indicator with the tip on top of the enrichment rod. Raise and release the weight to zero the dial indicator.
4. With the choke coil cover at the index position, the dial indicator should read the specified dimension. Turn the adjusting nut to correct.
5. Correct the choke cap setting.

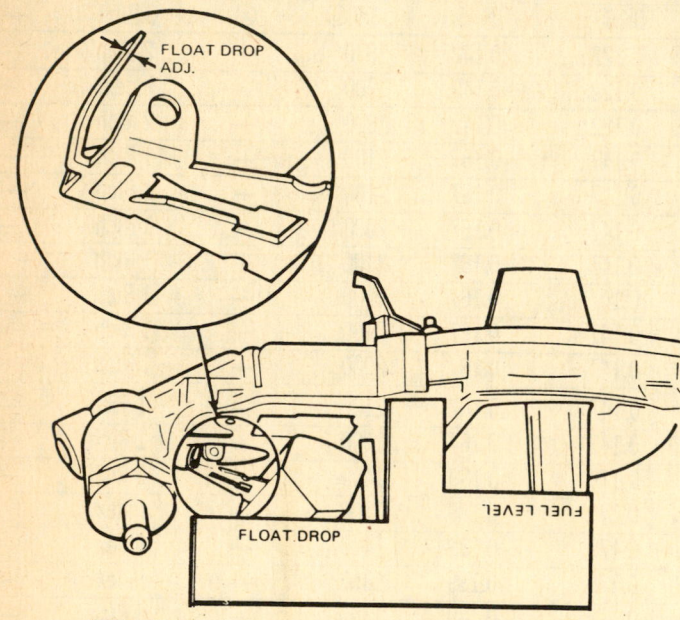

2700 VV float drop adjustment (© Ford Motor Co.)

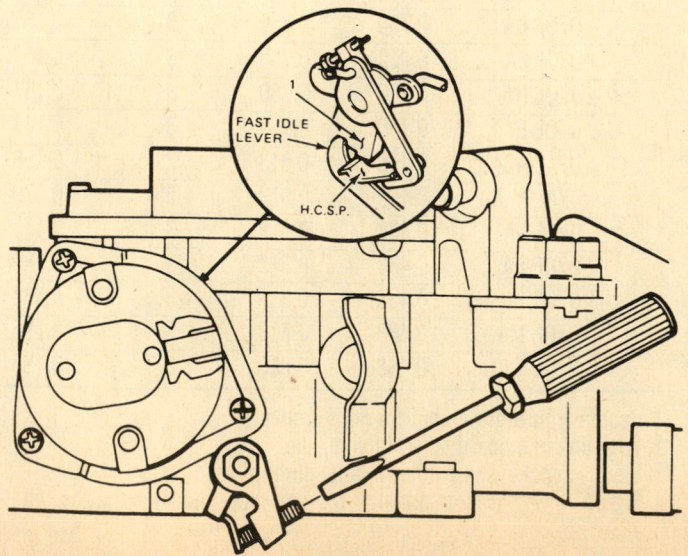

2700 VV float level adjustment (© Ford Motor Co.)

2700 VV fast idle speed adjustment (© Ford Motor Co.)

Control Vacuum Adjustment

1. Make sure the idle speed is correct.
2. Using a $5/32$ in. Allen wrench, turn the venturi valve diaphragm adjusting screw clockwise until the valve is firmly closed.
3. Connect a vacuum gauge to the vacuum tap on the venturi valve cover.
4. Idle the engine and use a $1/8$ in Allen wrench to turn the venturi bypass adjusting screw to the specified vacuum setting. You may have to correct the idle speed.
5. Turn the venturi valve diaphragm adjusting screw counterclockwise until the vacuum drops to the specified setting. You will have to work the throttle to get the vacuum to drop.
6. Reset the idle speed.

Internal Vent Adjustment

This adjustment is required whenever the idle speed adjustment is changed.
1. Make sure the idle speed is correct.
2. Place a 0.010 in. feeler gauge between the accelerator pump stem and the operating link.
3. Turn the nylon adjusting nut until there is a slight drag on the gauge.

Venturi Valve Limiter Adjustment

1. Remove the carburetor. Take off the venturi valve cover and the two rollers.
2. Use a center punch to loosen the expansion plug at the rear of the carburetor main body on the throttle side. Remove it.
3. Use an Allen wrench to remove the venturi valve wide open stop screw.
4. Hold the throttle wide open.
5. Apply a light closing pressure on the venturi valve and check the gap between the valve and the air horn wall. To adjust, move the venturi valve to the wide open position and insert an Allen wrench into the stop screw hole. Turn clockwise to increase the gap. Remove the wrench and check the gap again.

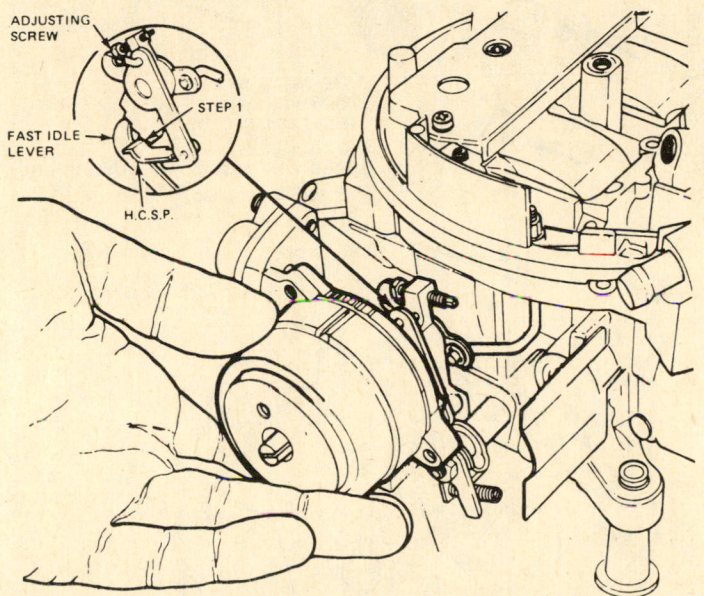

2700 VV fast idle cam adjustment (© Ford Motor Co.)

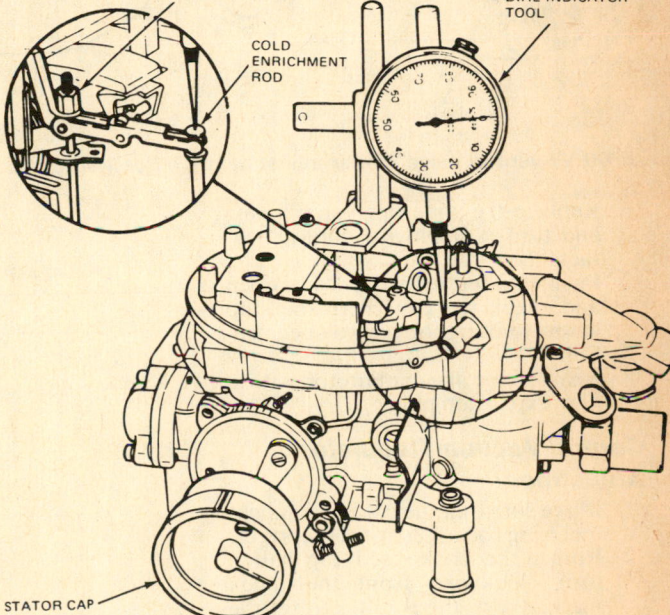

2700 VV cold enrichment metering rod adjustment
(© Ford Motor Co.)

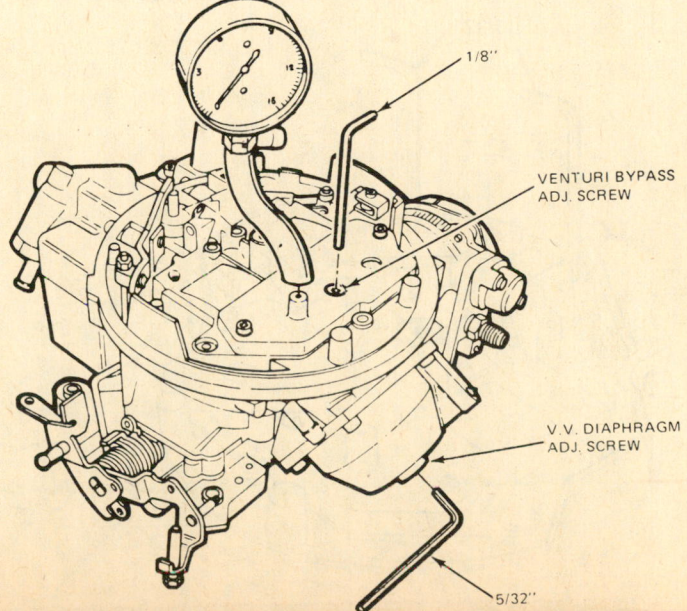

2700 VV control vacuum adjustment (© Ford Motor Co.)

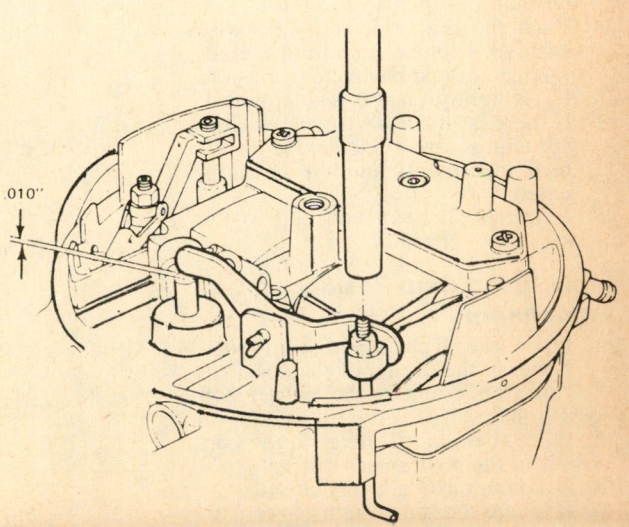

2700 VV internal vent adjustment (© Ford Motor Co.)

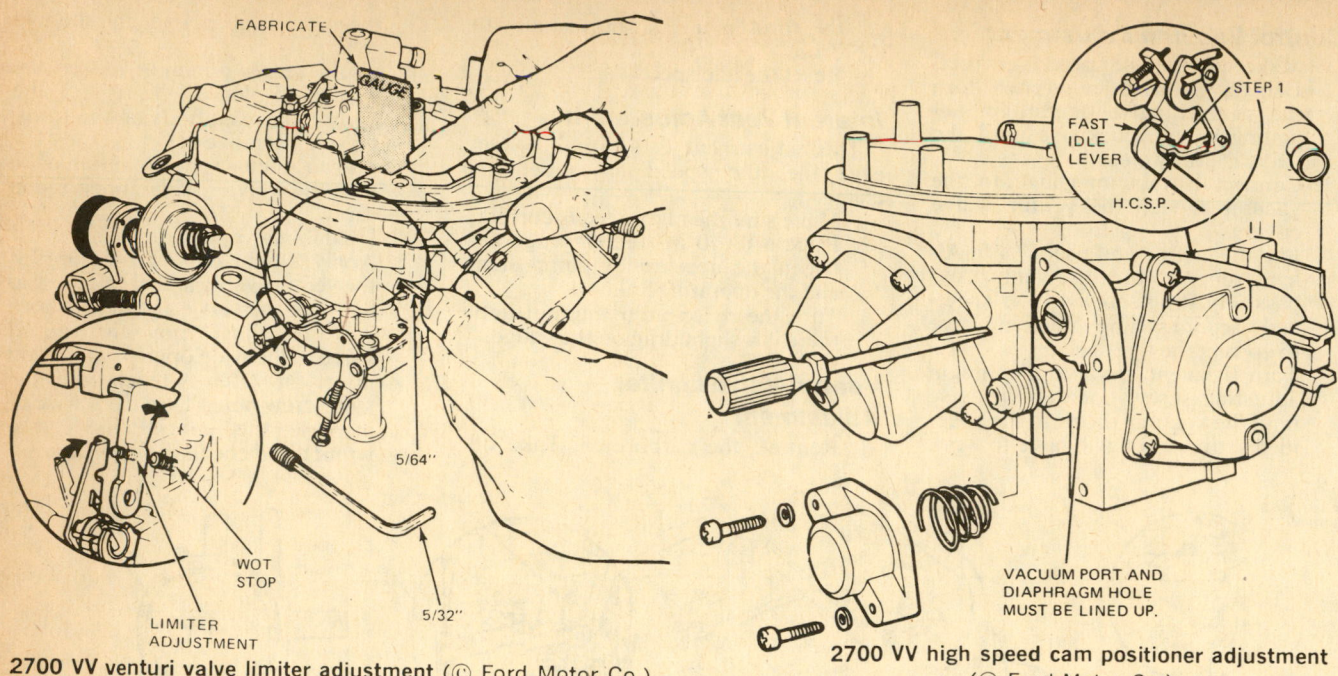

2700 VV venturi valve limiter adjustment (© Ford Motor Co.)

2700 VV high speed cam positioner adjustment
(© Ford Motor Co.)

6. Replace the wide open stop screw and turn it clockwise until it contacts the valve.
7. Push the venturi valve wide open and check the gap. Turn the stop screw to bring the gap to specifications.
8. Reassemble the carburetor with a new expansion plug.

Control Vacuum Regulator Adjustment

1. Make sure that the cold enrichment metering rod adjustment is correct.
2. Rotate the choke coil cap half a turn clockwise from the index mark. Work the throttle to set the fast idle cam.
3. Press down lightly on the regulator rod. If there is no down travel, turn the adjusting screw counterclockwise until some travel is felt.
4. Turn the regulator rod clockwise with an Allen wrench until the adjusting nut just begins to rise.
5. Press lightly on the regulator rod. If there is any down travel, turn the adjusting screw clockwise in $1/4$ turn increments until it is eliminated.
6. Return the choke coil cap to the specified setting.

High Speed Cam Positioner Adjustment

1. Place the high speed cam positioner in the corner of the specified cam step, counting the highest step as the first.
2. Place the fast idle lever in the corner of the positioner.
3. Hold the throttle firmly closed.
4. Remove the diaphragm cover. Adjust the diaphragm assembly clock-

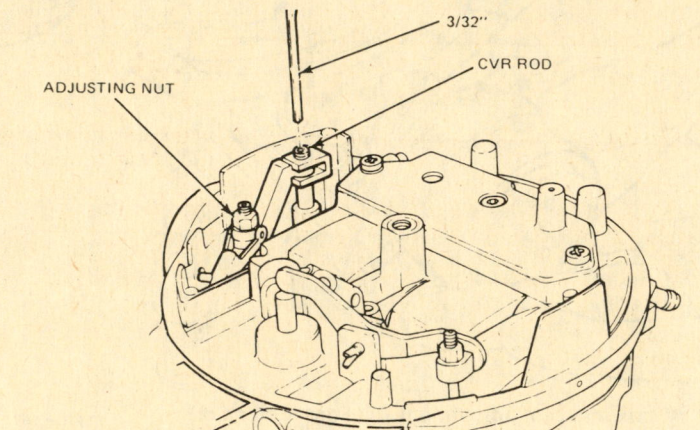

2700 VV control vacuum regulator adjustment (© Ford Motor Co.)

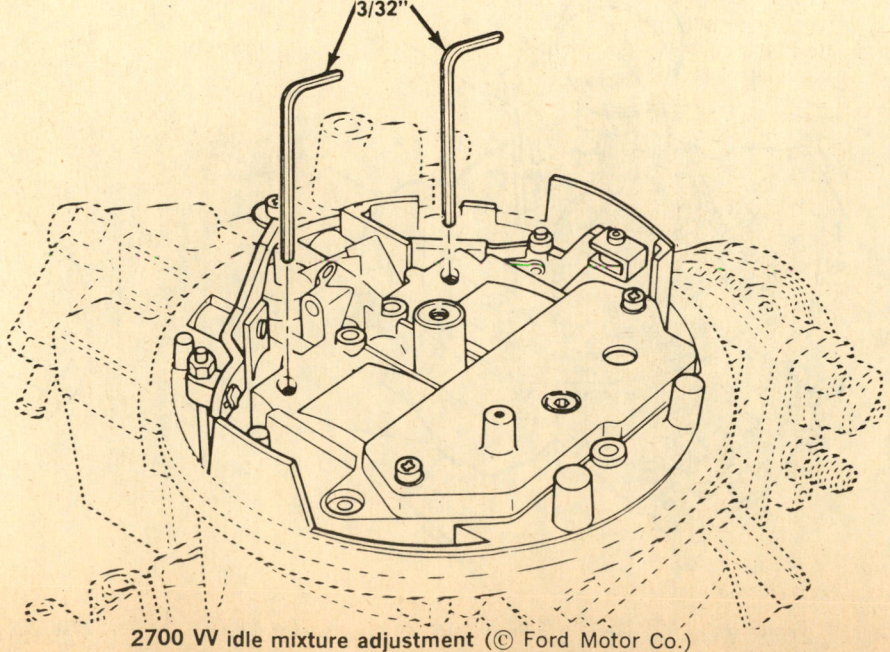

2700 VV idle mixture adjustment (© Ford Motor Co.)

wise until it lightly bottoms. Turn it counterclockwise ½ to 1½ turns until the vacuum port and diaphragm hole line up.

5. Replace the cover.

Idle Mixture Adjustment

The results of this adjustment should be checked with an emissions tester, to make sure that emission limits are not exceeded.

1. Remove the air cleaner cover only.
2. Use a ³/₃₂ in. Allen wrench to adjust the mixture for each barrel by turning the air adjusting screw. Turn clockwise to richen.

Motorcraft Model 2700 VV Specifications

Ford Products

Year	Model	Float Level (in.)	Float Drop (in.)	Fast Idle Cam Setting (notches)	Cold Enrichment Metering Rod (in.)	Control Vacuum (in. H₂0)	Venturi Valve Limiter (in.)	Choke Cap Setting (notches)
1977-78	Pinto, Bobcat	1³/₆₄	1¹⁵/₃₂	4 Rich/2nd step	.125	5.0	1³/₃₂	Index
	All other	1³/₆₄	1¹⁵/₃₂	1 Rich/3rd step	.125	5.0	6¹/₆₄	Index

MODEL 5200

The 5200 carburetor is a two-stage, two-venturi carburetor in which the secondary venturi is the larger. The secondary system is mechanically operated. It is used with 2000, 2300 and 2800 cc engines.

Fast Idle Cam

1. Insert a ⁵/₃₂ in. drill between the lower edge of the choke plate and the air horn wall.
2. With the fast idle screw held on the second step of the fast idle cam, measure the clearance between the tang of the choke lever and the arm on the fast idle cam.
3. Bend the choke lever tang to adjust it if it is not up to specification.

2. Pull the water cover and the thermostatic spring cover assembly out of the way.
3. Set the fast idle cam on the high step.
4. Push the diaphragm stem against its stop and insert the specified gauge between the lower edge of

the choke valve and the air horn wall.
5. Apply sufficient pressure to the upper edge of the choke valve to take up any slack in the choke linkage.
6. Turn the adjusting screw in or out to adjust the choke plate-to-air horn clearance.

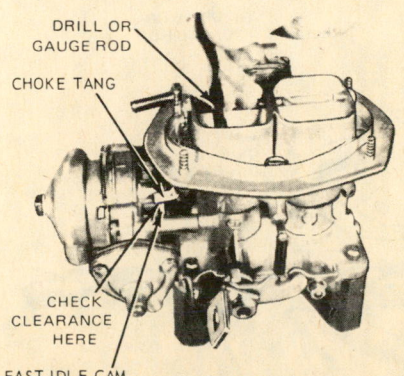

Fast idle cam adjustment
(© Ford Motor Co)

Choke Plate Pulldown

1. Remove the choke thermostatic spring cover.

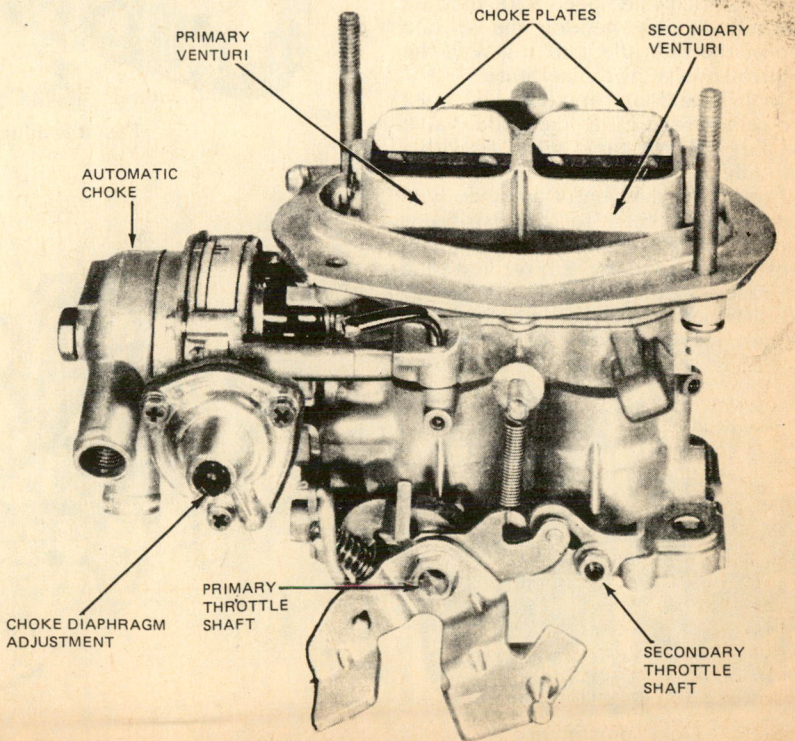

Model 5200 carburetor (© Ford Motor Co)

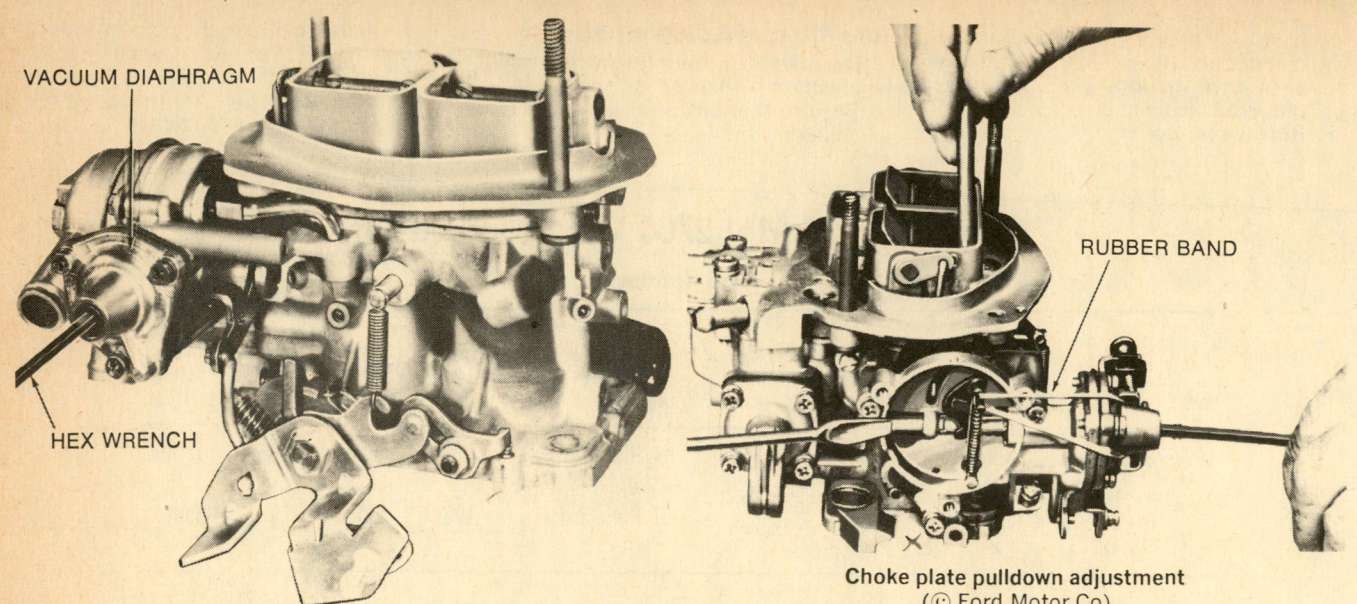

VACUUM DIAPHRAGM

HEX WRENCH

Dechoke adjustment (© Ford Motor Co)

RUBBER BAND

Choke plate pulldown adjustment
(© Ford Motor Co)

Dechoke (Unloader) Adjustment

1. Hold the throttle in the wide open position.
2. Remove any slack from the choke linkage by applying pressure to the upper edge of the choke valve.
3. Measure the distance from the lower edge of the choke valve to the air horn wall.
4. Make adjustments by bending the tab on the fast idle lever where it touches the fast idle cam.

Fast Idle Speed

Set the fast idle speed with the fast idle screw positioned on the second step of the fast idle cam and with the engine at operating temperature.

On 1975 and later models, you must also remove the EGR line at the valve and plug it. If the car is equipped with a spark delay valve, remove the valve and route the distributor advance vacuum signal directly to the distributor advance diaphragm. On all manual transmission models, remove and plug the vacuum line to the distributor. If the distributor also has a retard diaphragm, leave the hose connected to it

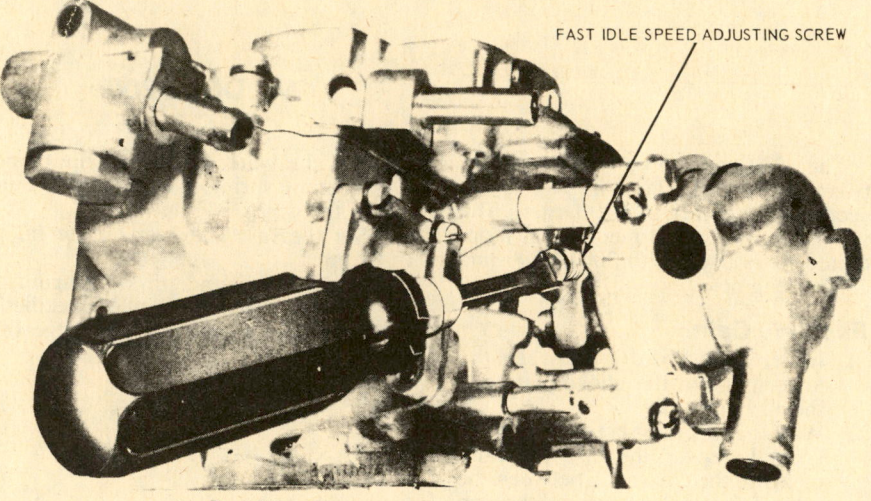

FAST IDLE SPEED ADJUSTING SCREW

Fast idle adjustment (© Ford Motor Co)

FLOAT

DRILL OR GAUGE ROD

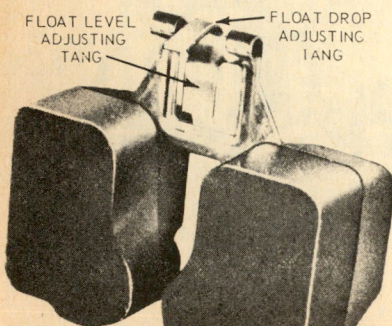

FLOAT LEVEL ADJUSTING TANG

FLOAT DROP ADJUSTING TANG

Float adjustment
(© Ford Motor Co)

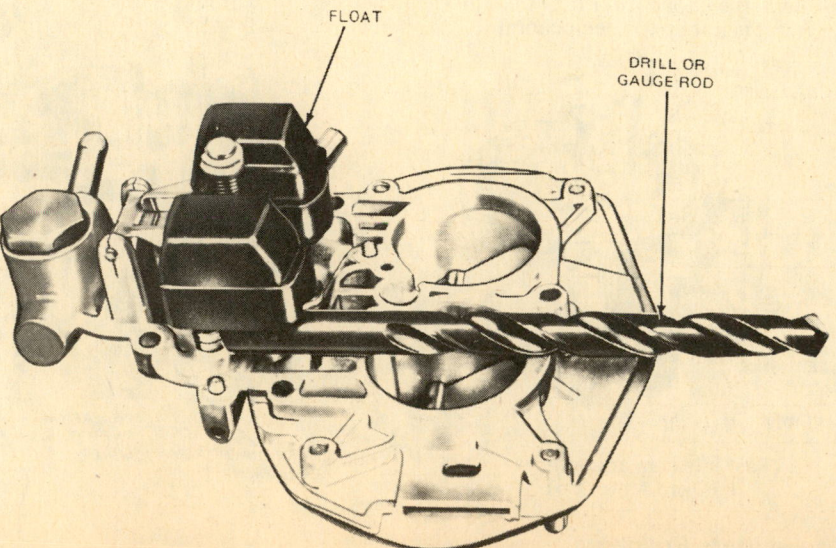

Checking float level
(© Ford Motor Co)

alone. If the engine has a deceleration valve, remove this hose at the carburetor and plug it. Finally, if the car has air conditioning it must be off before adjusting the fast idle.

Float Level Adjustment

With the bowl cover held upside down and the float tang resting lightly on the spring loaded fuel inlet needle, measure the clearance between the edge of the float and the bowl cover. To adjust the level, bend the float tang up or down as required. Adjust both floats equally.

Secondary Throttle Stop Screw

1. Turn the secondary throttle stop screw counterclockwise until the secondary throttle plate seats in its bore.
2. Turn the screw clockwise until it touches the tab on the secondary throttle lever.
3. Add 1/4 turn clockwise for four-cylinder engines and 3/4 turn for V6 engines through 1976 and the stop is adjusted.

FORD, AUTOLITE, MOTORCRAFT MODEL 5200 SPECIFICATIONS

Ford Products

Year	(9510)* Carburetor Identification①	Dry Float Level (in.)	Pump Hole Setting	Choke Plate Pulldown (in.)	Fast Idle Cam Linkage (in.)	Fast Idle (rpm)	Dechoke (in.)	Choke Setting	Dashpot (in.)
1972	D22F-AB	0.420	3	0.236	0.156	1800	0.256	1 Lean	——
	D22F-BB	0.420	2	0.236	0.079	1600	0.256	1 Lean	——
	D22F-CB	0.420	3	0.236	0.156	1800	0.256	1 Lean	——
	D22F-DB	0.420	2	0.236	0.079	1600	0.256	1 Lean	——
	D22F-EA	0.420	3	0.236	0.156	1800	0.256	Index	——
	D22F-GA	0.420	3	0.236	0.156	1800	0.256	Index	——
1973	D32F-CA	0.420	2	0.158	0.158	1800	0.256	Index	——
	D32F-BD	0.420	2	0.158	0.118	1600	0.256	1 Lean	——
1974	D42E-AA	0.460	2	0.280	0.158	1800	0.255	Index	——
	D42E-BA	0.460	2	0.280	0.158	1800	0.255	1 Rich	——
	D42F-EA	0.460	2	0.236	0.158	1800	0.255	Index	——
	D42F-GA	0.460	2	0.236	0.158	1800	0.255	Index	——
	D4ZE-CA	0.430	2	0.195	0.195	1800	0.256	1 Rich	——
	D4ZE-BC	0.430	2	0.195	0.195	1800	0.255	1 Rich	——
	D4ZE-DC	0.430	2	0.195	0.195	1800	0.255	1 Rich	——
	D42E-EB	0.460	2	0.158	0.158	1800	0.255	Index	——
	D42E-CD	0.460	2	0.280	0.158	1800	0.255	Index	——
	D42E-AC	0.460	2	0.280	0.158	1800	0.255	Index	——
	D42E-KA	0.460	2	0.280	0.158	1800	0.255	1 Rich	——
1975	D52E-AA	0.460	2	0.200	0.100	1800	0.260	1 Lean	——
	D52E-BA	0.460	2	0.200	0.100	1800	0.260	1 Lean	——
	D52E-CA	0.460	2	0.200	0.100	1800	0.260	1 Lean	——
	D52E-DB	0.460	2	0.200	0.100	1800	0.260	1 Lean	——
	D5ZE-EA	0.460	2	0.200	0.100	1800	0.260	1 Lean	——
	D5ZE-FA	0.460	2	0.200	0.100	1800	0.260	1 Lean	——
	D5ZE-GA	0.460	2	0.200	0.100	1800	0.260	1 Lean	——
	D5ZE-HB	0.460	2	0.200	0.100	1800	0.260	1 Lean	——
1976	D6EE-BA	0.460	2	0.200	0.100	1500①	0.260	1 Lean	——
	D6EE-CA	0.460	2	0.270	0.160	1500①	0.260	1 Lean	——
	D6EE-DA	0.460	2	0.200	0.100	1500①	0.260	1 Lean	——
	D6ZE-EA	0.460	2	0.270	0.160	1500①	0.260	1 Lean	——
1977-78	D7EE-AAA	0.453	2	0.200	0.120	2000	0.180	Index	——
	D7EE-AB	0.453	2	0.240	0.120	1800	0.240	2 Rich	——
	D7EE-BDA	0.453	2	0.280	0.120	1500	0.240	2 Rich	——
	D7EE-BGA	0.453	2	0.240	0.120	1500	0.240	Index	——
	D7FF-BHA	0.453	2	0.240	0.120	1500	0.240	Index	——
	D7EE-BLA	0.453	2	0.240	0.120	2000	0.240	Index	——

Ford • Autolite • Motorcraft Carburetors

Ford Products

Year	(9510)* Carburetor Identification①	Dry Float Level (in.)	Pump Hole Setting	Choke Plate Pulldown (in.)	Fast Idle Cam Linkage (in.)	Fast Idle (rpm)	Dechoke (in.)	Choke Setting	Dashpot (in.)
1977-78	D7EE-BMA	0.453	2	0.240	0.120	2000	0.240	Index	——
	D7EE-DA	0.453	2	0.240	0.120	1500	0.240	2 Rich	——
	D7EE-EA	0.453	2	0.240	0.120	2000	0.240	Index	——
	D7EE-FA	0.453	2	0.240	0.120	1800	0.240	Index	——
	D7EE-GA	0.453	2	0.200	0.120	2000	0.200	Index	——
	D7EE-HA	0.453	2	0.240	0.120	1500	0.240	2 Rich	——
	D7EE-JA	0.453	2	0.240	0.120	2000	0.240	Index	——
	D7EE-KB	0.453	2	0.240	0.120	1800	0.240	2 Rich	——
	D7EE-LA	0.453	2	0.240	0.120	1800	0.240	Index	——
	D7EE-SA	0.453	2	0.240	0.120	1800	0.240	2 Rich	——
	D7EE-TA	0.453	2	0.240	0.120	1800	0.240	2 Rich	——
	D7EE-UA	0.453	2	0.240	0.120	1800	0.240	Index	——
	D7EE-VA	0.453	2	0.240	0.120	1800	0.240	Index	——

* Basic carburetor number
① Figure given is for all manual transmissions; for automatic trans. the figures are: (49 states) 2000 RPM; (Calif.) 1800 RPM.

MODEL 4300, 4350

The model 4300 and 4350 4 barrel carburetor is composed of three main assemblies: the air horn, the main body, and the throttle body. The air horn assembly serves as the fuel bowl cover as well as the housing for the choke valve and shaft. It contains the accelerator pump linkage, fuel inlet seat, float and lever, booster venturi, and internal fuel bowl vents.

The main body houses the fuel metering passages, accelerator pump mechanism, and the power valve.

The throttle body contains the primary and secondary throttle valves and shafts, the curb idle adjusting screw, the fast idle adjusting screw, the idle mixture adjusting screws, and the automatic choke assembly.

Float Adjustment

1. Adjustments to the fuel level are best made with the carburetor removed from the engine and the carburetor cleaned upon disassembly.
2. Invert the air horn assembly and remove the gasket from the surface.
3. Use a T-scale to measure the distance from the floats to the air horn casting. Position the scale horizontally over the flat surface of both floats at the free ends and parallel to the air horn casting. Hold the lower end of the vertical scale in full contact with the smooth surface of the air horn.

——— CAUTION ———
The end of the vertical scale must not come into contact with any gasket sealing ridges while measuring the float level.

4. The free end of each float should just touch the horizontal scale, if one float is lower than the other; twist the float and lever assembly slightly to correct.
5. Adjust the float level by bending the tab which contacts the needle and seat assembly.

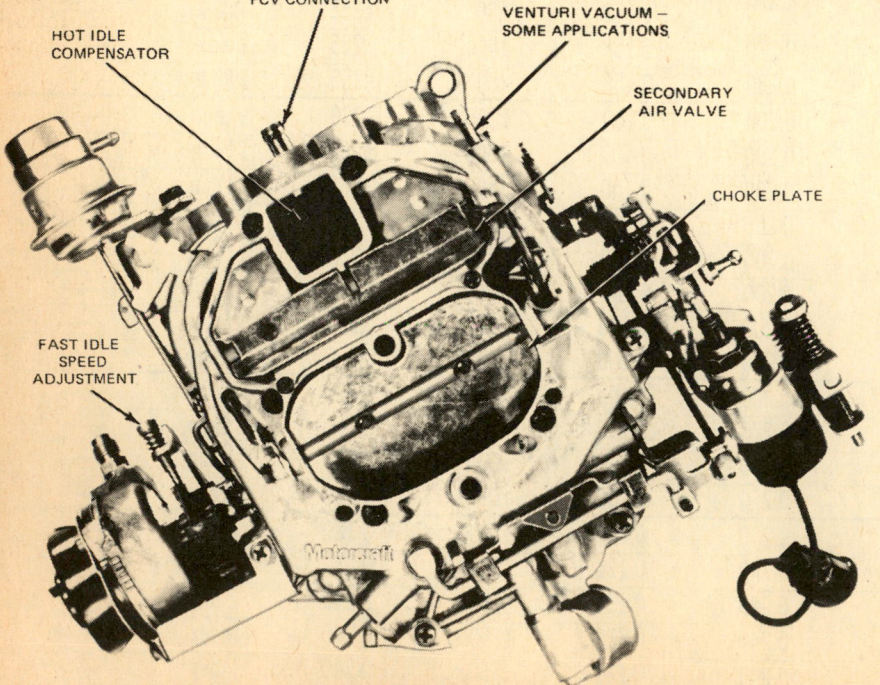

PCV CONNECTION
VENTURI VACUUM – SOME APPLICATIONS
HOT IDLE COMPENSATOR
SECONDARY AIR VALVE
CHOKE PLATE
FAST IDLE SPEED ADJUSTMENT

Top view—Model 4300 carburetor
(© Ford Motor Co)

NOTE: *The illustrations in this section show an alternate method of adjusting the floats on the model 4300 carburetor.*

The procedure includes the fabrication of a gauge and a bending device. After fabricating the gauge, it is possible to adjust it to the specified dimensions and insert it into the air horn outboard holes. Both pontoons should just touch the gauge.

A float tab bending tool is also shown and may be used in the following manner.

To raise the float: insert the open end of the bending tool to the RIGHT side of the float lever tab and between the needle and float hinge. Raise the float lever off of the needle and bend the tab downward.

To lower the float: insert the bending tool to the LEFT side of the float lever tab between the needle and float hinge, support the float lever, and bend the tab upward.

Choke Plate Pulldown

1. Remove the air cleaner and choke thermostatic spring housing.
2. Bend a wire gauge (0.036 in. diameter) at a 90 degree angle about 1/8 in. from one end.
3. Block the throttle open so that the fast idle screw does not contact the fast idle cam.
4. Insert the bent end of the wire gauge between the lower edge of the piston slot and the upper edge of the right hand slot in the choke housing.
5. Pull the choke piston lever counterclockwise until the gauge is snug in the piston slot. Hold the wire in place by exerting light pressure in a rearward direction on the choke piston lever. Check the distance from the lower edge of the choke valve to the air horn wall.
6. Adjustment is done by loosening the hex head screw (left-hand thread) on the choke valve shaft and prying the link away from the shaft. Use a drill gauge 0.010 in. under the specified clearance between the lower edge of the choke valve and the air horn wall. Hold the choke valve against the gauge and maintain a light rearward pressure on the choke lever.
7. With the choke piston snug against the 0.036 in. wire and the choke valve against the drill, tighten the hex screw on the choke valve shaft. The use of a gauge 0.010 in. undersize compensates for tolerance in the linkage.
8. Use the correct size gauge for final measurement.
9. Replace the housing on the thermostatic spring.

Delayed Choke Pulldown

The 4350 is also equipped with a vacuum-diaphragm operated delayed choke pulldown that opens the choke

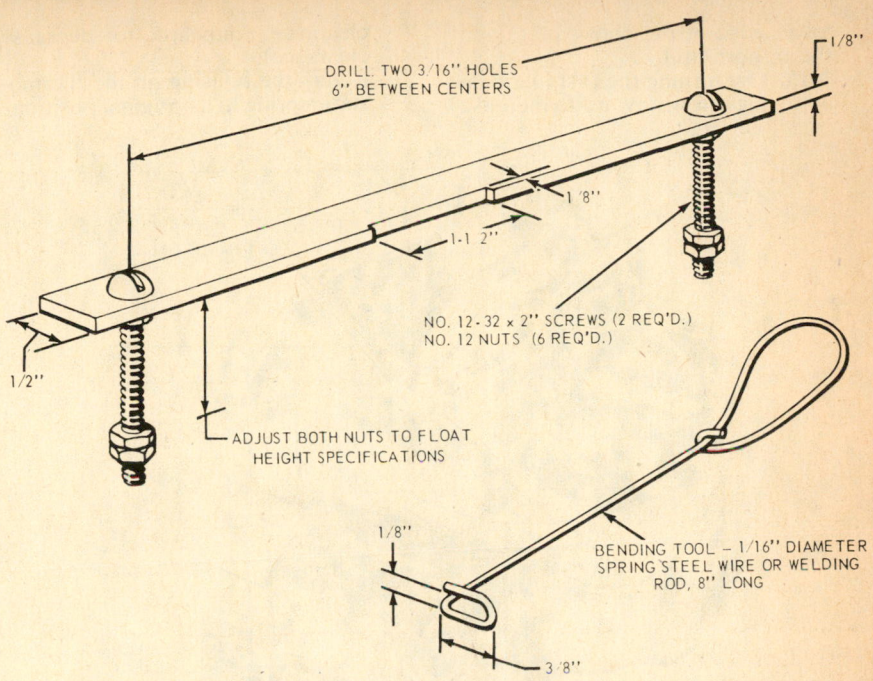

DRILL TWO 3/16" HOLES
6" BETWEEN CENTERS

NO. 12-32 x 2" SCREWS (2 REQ'D.)
NO. 12 NUTS (6 REQ'D.)

ADJUST BOTH NUTS TO FLOAT HEIGHT SPECIFICATIONS

BENDING TOOL — 1/16" DIAMETER SPRING STEEL WIRE OR WELDING ROD, 8" LONG

Construction of float level gauge and float arm bending tool
(© Ford Motor Co)

to a wider setting after about 6-18 seconds of engine operation.

1. With the throttle set on the fast idle cam, note the position of the index marks on the cap. Loosen the retaining screws and rotate the cap ninety degrees (1/4 turn), in the closing (rich) direction.
2. Disconnect the vacuum supply hose from the port on the delayed choke pulldown diaphragm assembly. After removing the filter cap, place a piece of tape over the purge hole, and apply vacuum to the port.
3. Measure the dimension at the lower edge of the choke plate at the center of the air horn. To adjust

this figure, turn the stop screw on the delayed choke pulldown diaphragm.

Fast Idle Cam Adjustment

1. Loosen the screws on the choke thermostatic spring cover and rotate the housing 1/4 turn counter clockwise. Tighten the screws.
2. Open the throttle and allow the choke valve to close completely.
3. Push down on the fast idle cam counterweight until the fast idle screw is in contact with the second step of the dam and against the high step.
4. Measure the clearance between the

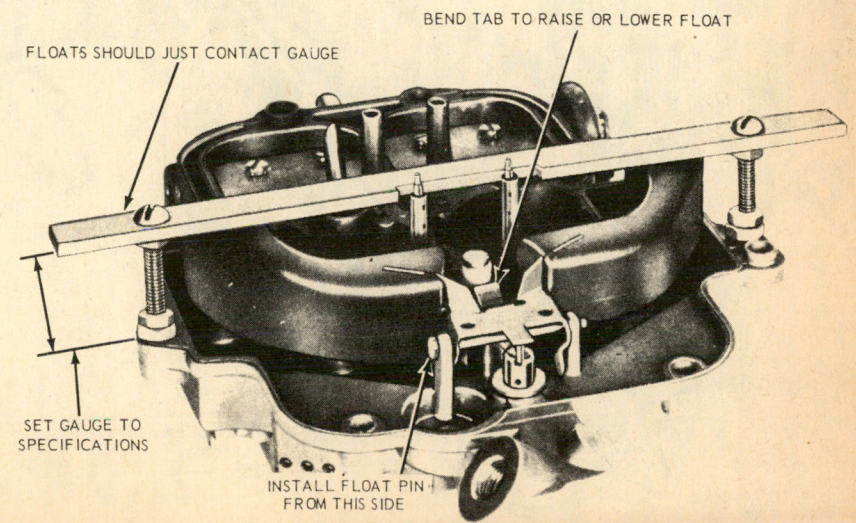

BEND TAB TO RAISE OR LOWER FLOAT

FLOATS SHOULD JUST CONTACT GAUGE

SET GAUGE TO SPECIFICATIONS

INSTALL FLOAT PIN FROM THIS SIDE

Measuring float level
(© Ford Motor Co)

Ford • Autolite • Motorcraft Carburetors

lower edge of the choke plate and the air horn wall.
5. Adjust by turning the fast idle cam adjusting screw (inward to increase

clearance, outward to decrease clearance).
6. Return the housing on the thermostatic spring to its original position.

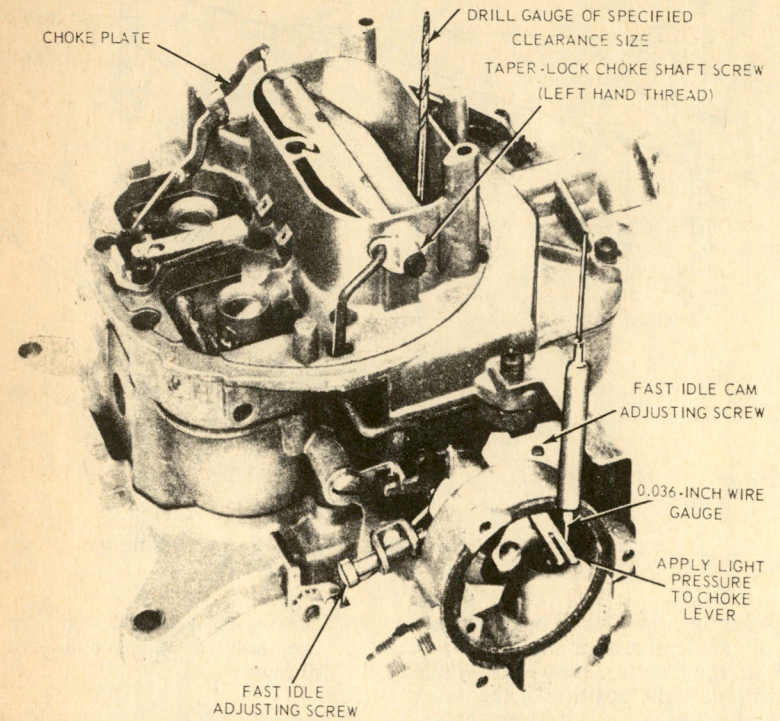

Choke plate pulldown and fast idle cam adjustment
(© Ford Motor Co)

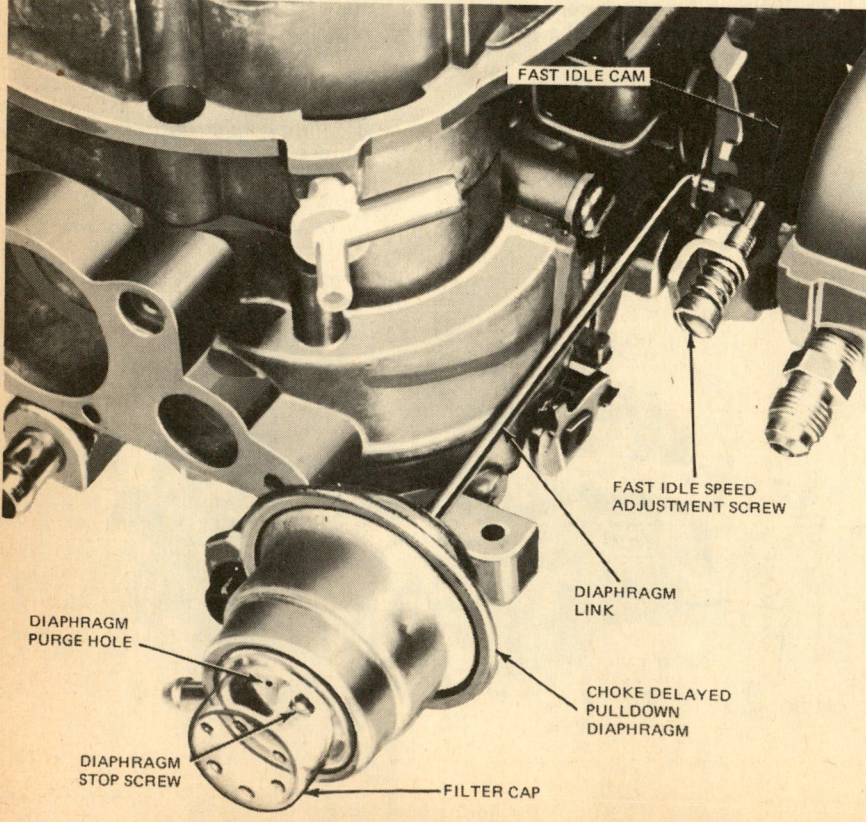

Motorcraft 4350 delayed choke assembly (© Ford Motor Co.)

Choke Unloader (Dechoke) Adjustment

1. Open the throttle fully and hold it in this position.
2. Rotate the choke plate toward the closed position until the pawl on the fast idle speed lever contacts the fast idle cam.
3. Check the clearance between the lower edge of the choke plate and the air horn wall.
4. Adjust by bending the pawl on the fast idle speed lever forward to increase the clearance and backward to decrease the clearance.

Accelerator Pump Stroke Adjustment

MODEL 4300 THROUGH 1974

The accelerator pump should not need adjustment as its stroke is preset in compliance with exhaust emission control standards. If for any reason the stroke must be altered, it may be done by repositioning the external link in the desired holes.

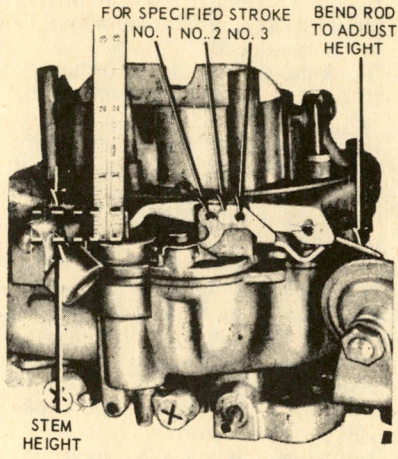

Accelerator pump adjustment
(© Ford Motor Co)

MODEL 4350 BEGINNING 1975

The accelerator pump adjustment is preset at the factory for reduced exhaust emissions. Adjustment is provided only for different engine installations. The adjustment is internal, with

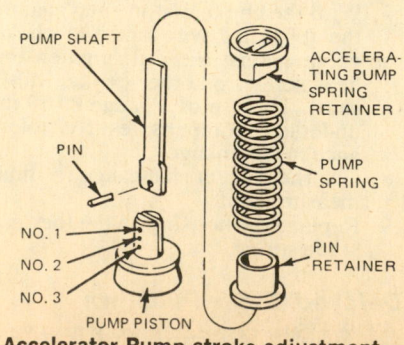

Accelerator Pump stroke adjustment—
—Motorcraft 4350-4V

three piston-to-shaft pin positions in the pump piston.

To check that the shaft pin is located in the specified piston hole, remove the carburetor air horn and invert it. Disconnect the accelerator pump from the operating arm by pressing downward on the spring and sliding the arm out of the pump shaft slot. Disassemble the spring and nylon keeper retaining the adjustment pin. If the pin is not in its specified hole, remove it, reposition the shaft to the correct hole in the piston assembly and reinstall the pin. Then, slide the nylon retainer over the pin and position the spring on the shaft. Finally, compress the spring on the pump arm and install the pump on the pump arm. **NOTE:** *Under no circumstances should you adjust the stroke of the accelerator pump by turning the vacuum limiter lever adjusting nut. This adjustment is* *preset at the factory and modification could result in poor cold driveability.*

Fast Idle Speed

The fast idle speed is adjusted with the engine at operating temperature and the fast idle screw on the second step of the fast idle cam. Adjust by turning the fast idle screw in or out as required.

On AMC cars, disconnect and plug the vacuum line at the EGR valve, and remove the electrical connector from the TCS valve. On Ford cars, first remove and plug the distributor vacuum lines. Remove the top and center CSSA system PVS switch hoses (located in the heater elbow) and connect them together. Remove the EGR hose from the carburetor port and plug the port. When the fast idle speed is set, reconnect those hoses removed previously.

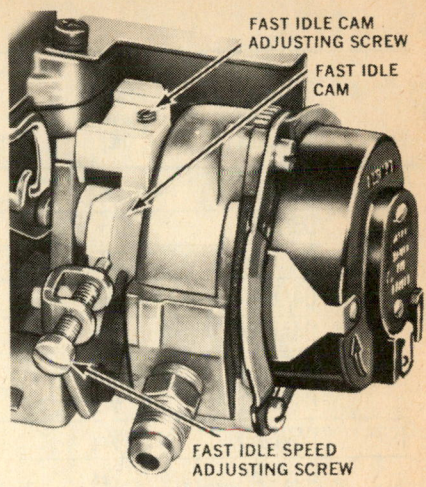

Fast idle adjustment
(© Ford Motor Co)

FORD, AUTOLITE, MOTORCRAFT MODELS 4300, 4350 SPECIFICATIONS

American Motors

Year	(9510)* Carburetor Identification ①	Dry Float Level (in.)	Pump Hole Setting	Choke Plate Pulldown (in.)	Fast Idle Cam Linkage (in.)	Fast Idle (rpm)	Dechoke (in.)	Choke Setting	Dashpot (in.)
1972	2RA4	13/16	Center	0.190	0.190	1600	0.300	1 Rich	9/64
	2TA4	13/16	Center	0.190	0.190	1600	0.300	1 Rich	9/64
	2TM4	13/16	Center	0.190	0.190	1600	0.300	1 Rich	9/64
1973	3TA4	13/16	Center	0.190	0.160	1600	0.275	2 Rich	9/64
	3TA4 (Police)	15/16	Center	0.190	0.160	1600	0.275	2 Rich	9/64
	3TM4	13/16	Center	0.190	0.160	1600	0.275	2 Rich	9/64
1974	4TA4, 4TM4	13/16	Center	0.170	0.160	1600	0.325	2 Rich	9/64
1975	5TA4	0.90	Lower	0.140	0.160	1600	0.325	2 Rich	—
1976	6TA4	0.090	Lower	0.130	0.135	1600	0.325	2 Rich	—

Ford Products

Year	(9510)* Carburetor Identification	Dry Float Level (in.)	Pump Hole Setting	Choke Plate Pulldown (in.)	Fast Idle Cam Linkage (in.)	Fast Idle (rpm)	Dechoke (in.)	Choke Setting	Dashpot
1972	D2AF-AA	49/64	1	0.220	0.200	1350	—	2 Rich	—
	D2AF-LA	49/64	1	0.215	0.190	1900	—	2 Rich	—
	D2SF-AA	49/64	1	0.220	0.200	1350	—	2 Rich	—
	D2SF-BA	49/64	1	0.220	0.200	1350	—	2 Rich	—
	D2VF-AA	49/64	1	0.230	0.200	1250	—	Index	—
	D2VF-BA	49/64	1	0.230	0.200	1250	—	Index	—
	D2ZF-AA	13/16	1	0.200	0.180	1200	—	Index	—
	D2ZF-BB	13/16	1	0.200	0.200	1200	—	Index	—
	D2ZF-DA	13/16	1	0.200	0.200	1200	—	Index	—
	D2ZF-GA	13/16	1	0.200	0.180	1200	—	Index	—
1973	D3VF-DA	0.76	1	0.210	0.190	1350	—	Index	—
	D3ZF-AC	0.82	1	0.180	0.180	1300	—	Index	—
	D3ZF-BC	0.82	1	0.170	0.170	1300	—	INR	—

Ford Products

Year	(9510)* Carburetor Identification	Dry Float Level (in.)	Pump Hole Setting	Choke Plate Pulldown (in.)	Fast Idle Cam Linkage (in.)	Fast Idle (rpm)	Dechoke (in.)	Choke Setting	Dashpot
1973	D3ZF-DC	0.82	1	0.180	0.180	1300	——	Index	——
	D3AF-HA	0.76	1	0.210	0.200	1350	——	Index	——
	D3AF-EB	0.88	1	0.200	0.200	1900	——	Index	——
1974	D4AE-AA	¾	1	0.230	0.200	1900	——	Index	——
	D4AE-NA, D4VE-AB	¾	1	0.220	0.200	1250	——	Index	——
	D4TE-ATA	13/16	1	0.220	0.180	1250	——	Index	——
	D40E-AA	13/16	1	0.180	0.180	1800	——	Index	——
1975	D5VE-AD	15/16	1	②	0.160	1600	0.300	2 Rich	——
	D5VE-BA	15/16	1	②	0.160	1600	0.300	2 Rich	——
	D5AE-CA	31/32	1	②	0.160	1600	0.300	2 Rich	——
	D5AE-DA	31/32	1	②	0.160	1600	0.300	2 Rich	——
1976	D6AE-CA	1.00	2	0.140③	0.140	1350	0.300	2 Rich	——
	D6AE-FA	1.00	2	0.140③	0.140	1350	0.300	2 Rich	——
	D6AE-DA	1.00	2	0.160④	0.160	1350	0.300	2 Rich	——
1977-78	D7AE-AAA	1.00	2	0.140	0.140	1350	0.300	Index	——
	D7AE-ANA	1.00	2	0.140	0.140	1350	0.300	Index	——
	D7AE-ZA	1.00	2	0.140	0.140	1350	0.300	Index	——
	D7PE-AA	1.00	2	0.140	0.140	1350	0.300	Index	——
	D7VE-KA	1.00	2	0.140	0.140	1350	0.300	2 Lean	——
	D7VE-SA	1.00	2	0.140	0.140	1350	0.300	Index	——

* Basic carburetor number for Ford products.

① The identification tag is on the bowl cover.

② Initial—0.160 in.
Delayed—0.190 in.

③ Initial Figure given; delayed—0.190

④ Initial Figure given; delayed—0.210

HOLLEY CARBURETORS

MODEL 1920

On these units, the choke valve in the carburetor bore is connected to a well-type automatic choke.

The accelerator pump is a diaphragm, spring-driven type operated by a lever connected to the throttle shaft.

A two-stage power valve, mounted in the metering body and actuated by manifold vacuum, delivers additional fuel for full power and high speed operation.

This carburetor is used on Chrysler Corporation six-cylinder engines, through 1973.

Float Level Adjustment

NOTE: *Do not allow the float tab to contact the float needle head during the* *adjustment procedure as the rubber tip of the needle can be compressed, giving a false reading.*

UNITS THROUGH 1972

1. With the carburetor inverted, slide the special float gauge into position and test the setting on the "touch" leg of the gauge. The float should just touch the gauge.
2. Reverse the gauge and test the "no touch" leg. The float should just clear the gauge.
3. To adjust, bend the float tab which touches the head of the fuel inlet needle, using needle nose pliers.
4. This adjustment corresponds to a wet fuel level of 27/32 in., measured through the economizer opening from the top of the bowl.

1973 UNITS

1. With the carburetor inverted, measure from the top of the float to the upper wall of the main body with the gauge against the cast rib, approximately 2 in. from the float hinge pin.
2. Be sure that the gauge is parallel with the top of the float. Refer to the Specifications Chart for the proper dry float setting.
3. Adjust by bending the float tab which touches the head of the fuel needle using needle nosed pliers.

Float Bowl Vent Valve Adjustment

1. With the throttle valve closed, the bowl vent should be adjusted so

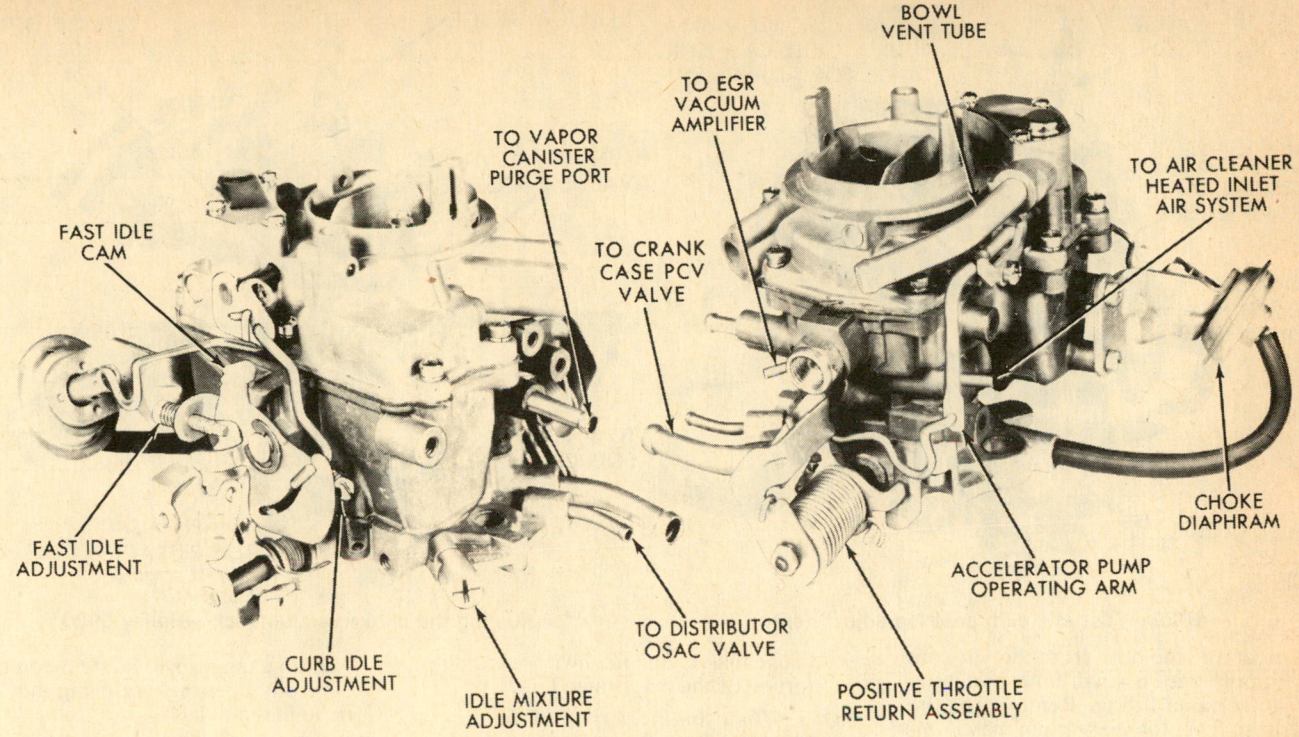

BOWL VENT TUBE

TO EGR VACUUM AMPLIFIER

TO VAPOR CANISTER PURGE PORT

TO AIR CLEANER HEATED INLET AIR SYSTEM

FAST IDLE CAM

TO CRANK CASE PCV VALVE

CHOKE DIAPHRAM

FAST IDLE ADJUSTMENT

ACCELERATOR PUMP OPERATING ARM

CURB IDLE ADJUSTMENT

TO DISTRIBUTOR OSAC VALVE

IDLE MIXTURE ADJUSTMENT

POSITIVE THROTTLE RETURN ASSEMBLY

Carburetor assembly—Holley 1920

that the shank of a drill of the size listed in the Specifications Chart can be inserted between the bowl vent stem and the bowl vent rod.
2. Adjust by bending the bowl vent operating lever up or down as required.
3. Be sure that the vent rod does not bind in the guide after adjusting.

Fast Idle Cam Position and Choke Unloader Adjustment

1. With the fast idle speed adjusting screw contacting the second highest step on the fast idle cam, move the choke valve toward the closed

position with light pressure on the choke shaft lever.
2. Insert the specified gauge between the top of the choke valve and the wall of the air horn. Refer to the Specifications Chart.
3. Adjust by bending the fast idle link at the lower angle, until the correct valve opening has been obtained.
NOTE: *When the correct fast idle cam position adjustment has been made, the choke unloader (wide open kick) adjustment has also been obtained. No further adjustment is required.*

Choke Vacuum Kick

NOTE: *The test can be made on or off the vehicle.*

1. If adjustments are to be made with the engine running, back off the fast idle speed screw until the choke can be closed to the kick position with the engine at curb idle.
2. Note the number of screw turns required so that fast idle can be returned to its original adjustment.
3. If an auxiliary vacuum source is to be used, open the throttle valve (engine not running) and move the choke to the closed position. Release the throttle first, then release the choke.

When using an auxiliary vacuum source, disconnect the vacuum hose from the carburetor and con-

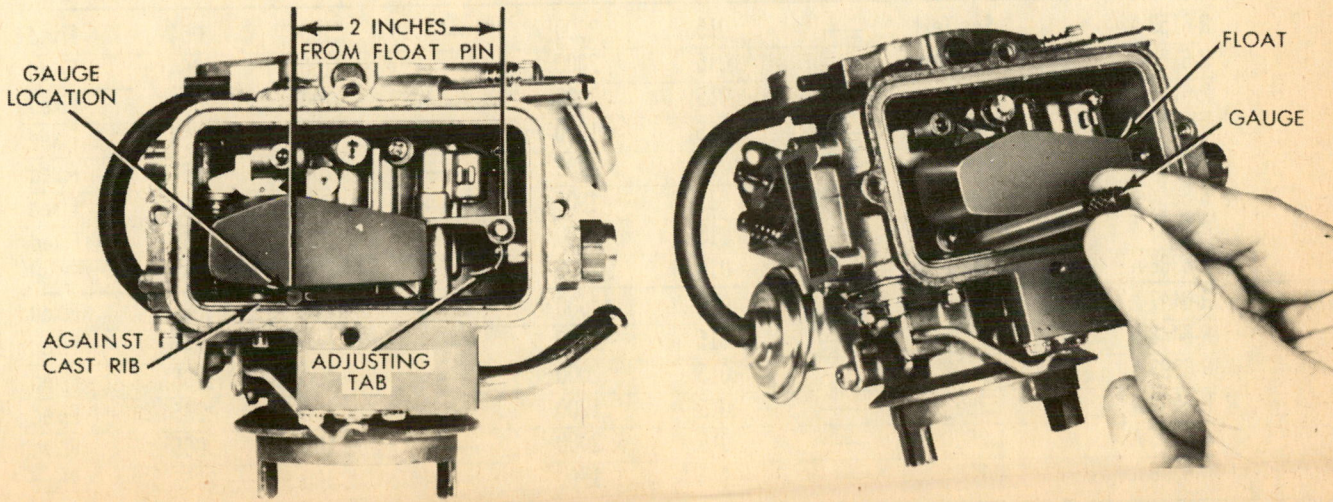

GAUGE LOCATION

2 INCHES FROM FLOAT PIN

FLOAT

GAUGE

AGAINST CAST RIB

ADJUSTING TAB

Adjusting the float level—Holley 1920

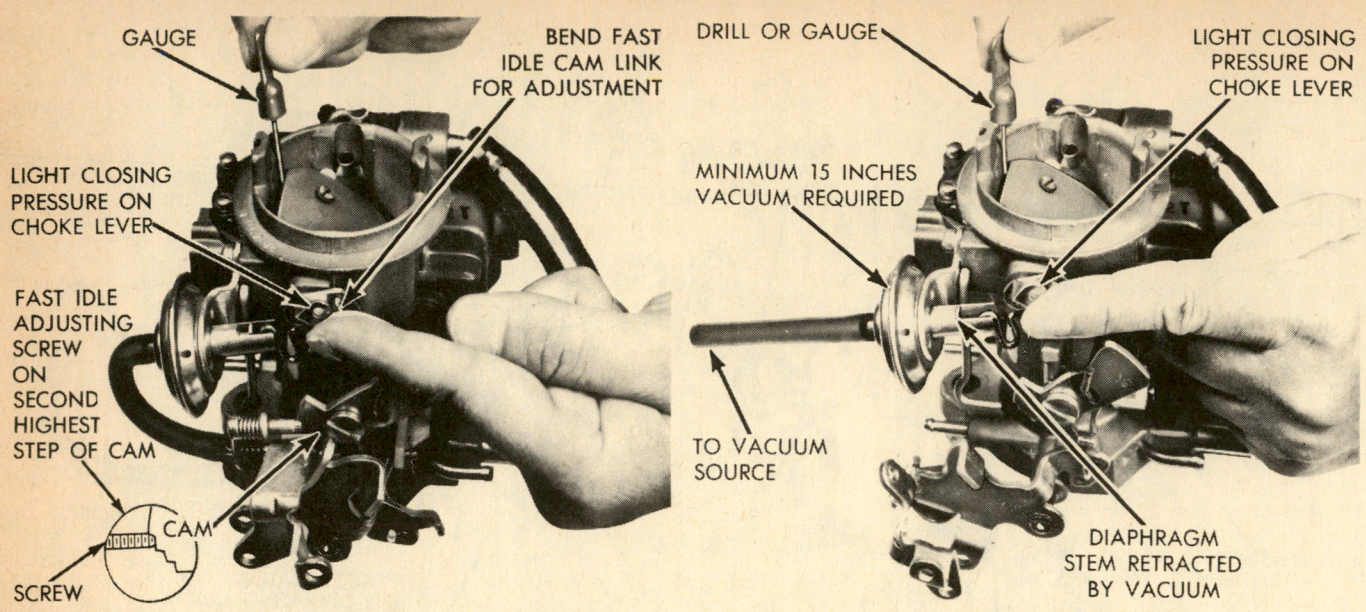

1920—Fast idle cam position adjustment   **Adjusting the choke vacuum kick—Holley 1920**

nect it to the hose from the vacuum supply with a small length of tube to act as a fitting. Removal of the hose from the diaphragm may damage the system. Apply a vacuum of 15 or more in. of mercury.

4. Insert the gauge between the top of the choke valve and the wall of the air horn. Refer to the Specifications Chart.

5. Apply sufficient closing pressure on the lever to which the choke rod attaches to provide a minimum

choke valve opening without distortion of the diaphragm link.

NOTE: *The cylindrical stem of the diaphragm extends as the internal spring is compressed. This spring must be fully compressed for proper measurement of the vacuum kick adjustment.*

6. Adjustment is necessary if a slight drag is not obtained when removing the gauge. Shorten or lengthen the diaphragm link to obtain the correct choke valve opening.

Length changes should be made by carefully opening or closing the U-bend in the link.

NOTE: *Do not apply a twisting or bending force to the diaphragm.*

7. After completion of adjustment, reinstall the vacuum hose onto the correct carburetor fitting.

8. Return the fast idle screw to its original location if disturbed. Make the following check. With no vacuum applied to the diaphragm, the

Holley Carburetor Specifications Model 1920

Chrysler Corporation

Year	Carb. Part No. ⑦	Float Level (in.)	Accelerator Pump Adjustment (in.)	Bowl Vent Clearance (in.)	Fast Idle (rpm)	Choke Unloader Clearance (in.)	Vacuum Kick (in.)	Fast Idle Cam Position (in.)	Choke
1972	R-6153-A	See Text	——	.015	2000	——	.100	.064	Fixed
	R-6154-A	See Text	——	.015	2000	——	.100	.064	Fixed
	R-6155-A	See Text	——	.015	2000	——	.100	.064	Fixed
	R-6156-A	See Text	——	.015	1900	——	.100	.064	Fixed
	R-6363-A	See Text	——	.015	2000	——	.100	.064	Fixed
	R-6364-A	See Text	——	.015	1900	——	.100	.064	Fixed
	R-6365-A	See Text	——	.015	2000	——	.100	.064	Fixed
	R-6366-A	See Text	——	.015	2000	——	.100	.064	Fixed
1973	R-6447-A	.260	——	.015	2000	——	.100	.065	Fixed
	R-6448-A	.260	——	.015	1700	——	.080	.045	Fixed
	R-6593-A	.260	——	.015	2000	——	.100	.065	Fixed
	R-6594-A	.260	——	.015	1700	——	.100	.065	Fixed
	R-6595-A	.260	——	.015	2000	——	.100	.065	Fixed
	R-6596-A	.260	——	.015	1700	——	.100	.065	Fixed

— Not Applicable

choke valve should move freely between the open and closed positions. If the movement is not free, examine the linkage for misalignment or interferences caused by the bending operation.

Well-type Automatic Choke

1. To function properly, it is important that all parts be clean and move freely. Other than an occasional cleaning, the choke requires no attention. However, it is important that the choke control unit work freely in the well and at the choke shaft.
2. Move the choke rod up and down to check for free movement on the pivot. If the unit binds, a new choke unit should be installed.

NOTE: *This type of choke is serviced only as a unit. Do not attempt to repair or change the setting.*

When installing the choke unit, be certain that the coil housing does not contact the sides of the well in the exhaust manifold. Any contact at this point will affect choke operation. Do not lubricate any parts of the choke or the control unit. This causes an accumulation of dirt which will result in binding of the mechanism.

MODEL 1945

The model 1945 carburetor is a concentric downdraft single barrel carburetor with an internal float bowl which completely surrounds the venturi. The unit uses dual nitrophyl floats which permit operation at extreme angles. It is used on 1974 and later Chrysler Corporation six-cylinder engines.

Float Adjustment

1. Remove the float bowl cover and invert the bowl. Hold the retaining spring in place.
2. Place a straightedge across the surface of the bowl. It should just clear the toes of the floats by the specified measurement.
3. If the adjustment is necessary, bend the float tang to obtain the correct adjustment.

Fast Idle Adjustment

1. Remove the air cleaner and disconnect the vacuum lines to the heated air control and the OSAC (Orifice Spark Advance Control) valve. If there is no OSAC valve, disconnect the hose to the distributor and the EGR hose. Cap all carburetor vacuum fittings.
2. With the engine off, transmission in Neutral and the parking brake set, open the throttle and close the choke.
3. Close the throttle. This will place the fast idle speed screw on the highest step.

4. Move the fast idle cam until the screw drops to the second highest speed step.
5. Start the engine and stabilize the engine speed. Rotate the fast idle speed screw to obtain the specified setting. See Specifications Chart.

Choke Unloader Adjustment

1. Hold the throttle valves wide-open and insert the specified gauge between the upper edge of the choke valve and the inner wall of the air horn.
2. Place slight pressure against the control lever and attempt to remove the gauge. There should be a slight drag as the gauge is being withdrawn. If adjustment is necessary, bend the unloader tang on the throttle lever until the correct opening has been obtained.

Choke Vacuum Kick Adjustment

1. With the engine running, back off the fast idle screw to allow the choke to close to the kick position with the engine at curb idle. Note the number of turns. If the adjustment is made with the engine stopped as recommended for 1977 and later, open the throttle and move the choke to the closed position. Release the throttle first and then the choke.

2. If an auxiliary vacuum source is used, disconnect the vacuum hose from the carburetor and connect it to the hose from the vacuum supply with an extra length of tube. Apply a vacuum of 15 or more in. of mercury.
3. Insert the correct gauge (see Specifications Chart) between the choke valve upper edge and the wall of the air horn. Close and hold the choke rod lever with light pressure. The cylindrical stem of the diaphragm will extend as the internal spring is compressed. This spring must be fully compressed for proper measurement of the vacuum kick.
4. If adjustment is necessary, shorten or lengthen the diaphragm link to obtain the correct opening.

——— CAUTION ———
Do not twist or bend the diaphragm.

5. Install the vacuum hose on the correct carburetor fitting and connect the fast idle linkage.
6. Check the operation in the following manner. With vacuum applied to the diaphragm, the choke valve should move freely between the open and closed positions. If there is binding, examine the linkage for misalignment or interference caused by bending.

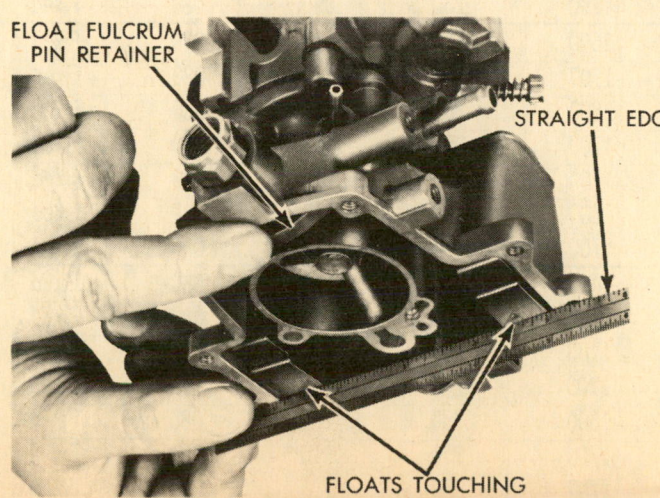

FLOAT FULCRUM PIN RETAINER

STRAIGHT EDGE

FLOATS TOUCHING

Checking the float adjustment—Holley 1945

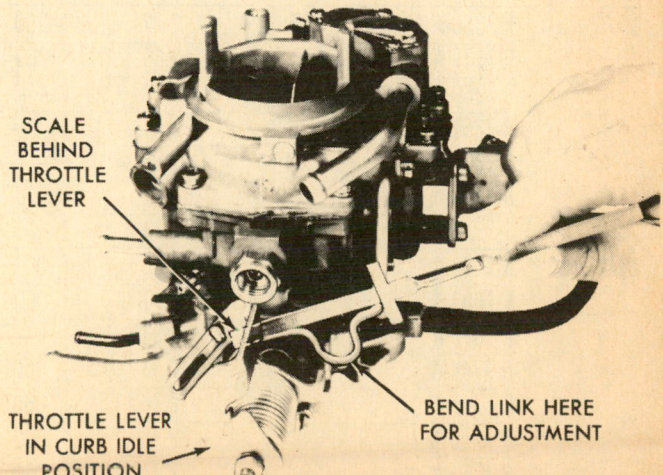

SCALE BEHIND THROTTLE LEVER

THROTTLE LEVER IN CURB IDLE POSITION

BEND LINK HERE FOR ADJUSTMENT

Choke unloader adjustment—Holley 1945

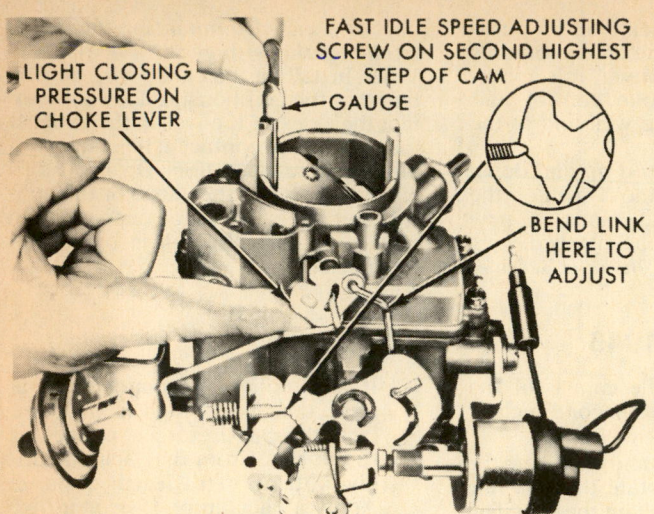

Checking the fast idle adjustment—Holley 1945

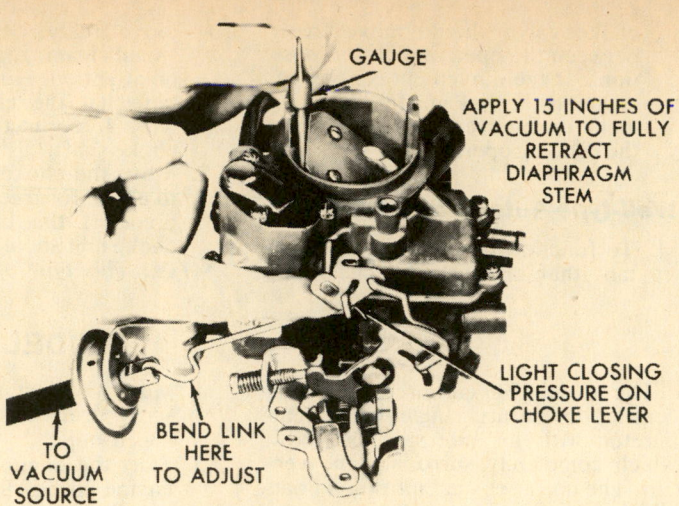

Choke vacuum kick adjustment—Holley 1945

Model 1945

Chrysler Corporation

Year	Carb. Part No. ②	Float Level (in.)	Accelerator Pump Adjustment (in.)	Bowl Vent Clearance (in.)	Fast Idle (rpm)	Choke Unloader Clearance (in.)	Vacuum Kick (in.)	Fast Idle Cam Position (in.)	Choke
1974	R-6721-A	.046	.680	——	1600	.250	.140	.080	Fixed
	R-6722-A	.046	.810	——	1800	.250	.090	.080	Fixed
	R-6723-A	.046	.680	——	1600	.250	.140	.080	Fixed
	R-6724-A	.046	.750	——	1800	.250	.080	.080	Fixed
	R-6725-A	.046	.750	——	1600	.250	.140	.080	Fixed
	R-6726-A	.046	.750	——	1800	.250	.090	.080	Fixed
1975	R-7329-A	.046	2.22	——	1700	.250	.130	.080	Fixed
	R-7017-A	.046	2.22	——	1600	.250	.130	.080	Fixed
	R-7018-A	.046	2.33	——	1700	.250	.090	.080	Fixed
	R-7019-A	.046	2.22	——	1600	.250	.130	.080	Fixed
	R-7020-A	.046	2.33	——	1700	.250	.090	.080	Fixed
	R-7029-A	.046	2.22	——	1600	.250	.130	.080	Fixed
	R-7210-A	.046	2.33	——	1700	.250	.090	.080	Fixed
1976	R-7356-A	①	2.22	.060	1600	.250	.110	.080	Fixed
	R-7357-A	①	2.65	.060	1700	.250	.100	.080	Fixed
	R-7360-A	①	2.22	——	1600	.250	.110	.080	Fixed
	R-7361-A	.046	2.65	——	1700	.250	.100	.080	Fixed
	R-7363-A	.046	2.65	——	1700	.250	.100	.080	Fixed
	R-7823-A	①	2.22	.070	1600	.250	.110	.080	Fixed
	R-7824-A	①	2.33	.105	1700	.250	.100	.080	Fixed
1977	R-7632-A	①	2.22	.060	1400	.250	.110	.080	Fixed
	R-7633-A	①	2.33	.060	1700	.250	.110	.080	Fixed
	R-7635-A	①	2.33	——	1700	.250	.110	.080	Fixed
	R-7744-A	①	2.33	.060	1700	.250	.130	.080	Fixed
	R-7745-A	①	2.22	.060	1600	.250	.150	.080	Fixed
	R-7746-A	①	2.33	.060	1700	.250	.110	.080	Fixed
	R-7764-A	①	2.22	.060	1700	.250	.110	.080	Fixed
	R-7765-A	①	2.33	.060	1700	.250	.110	.080	Fixed

Chrysler Corporation

Year	Carb. Part No. ②	Float Level (in.)	Accelerator Pump Adjustment (in.)	Bowl Vent Clearance (in.)	Fast Idle (rpm)	Choke Unloader Clearance (in.)	Vacuum Kick (in.)	Fast Idle Cam Position (in.)	Choke
1978	R-7988-A	①	2.22	.062	1400	.250	.110	.080	Fixed
	R-7989-A	①	2.33	.062	1600	.250	.110	.080	Fixed
	R-8008-A	①	2.33	.062	1700	.250	.110	.080	Fixed
	R-8010-A	①	2.33	.062	1500	.250	.130	.080	Fixed
	R-8394-A	①	2.33	.062	1700	.250	.110	.080	Fixed

① Flush with the top of the bowl cover gasket, plus or minus 1/32
② Located on a tag attached to the carburetor.

MODEL 1946

This unit is a one barrel, altitude compensating model used on 1978 Fairmont and Zephyr cars with automatic transmission and 200 cid, 6-cylinder engines.

Fast Idle Cam Position Adjustment

1. Position the fast idle adjusting screw on the second highest step of the fast idle cam.
2. Lightly move the choke plate toward the closed position.
3. Check the fast idle cam setting by placing either an .080 in. gauge, or a # 46 drill bit between the upper edge of the choke plate and the air horn wall.
4. If the setting is not as specified, bend the fast idle cam link.

Fast Idle Adjustment

1. Remove the spark delay valve, if so equipped, and route the distrib-utor vacuum hose directly to the advance side of the distributor.
2. Trace the EGR signal vacuum hose from the EGR valve to the carburetor. If an EGR/PVS valve or cold weather modulator is located in the hose, disconnect the EGR hose at the EGR valve and plug the hose. If not equipped with EGR/PVS or a cold weather modulator, do not detach the hose.
3. Run the engine to normal operating temperature. With the choke plate fully open and the transmission in neutral (MT) or park (AT), place the fast idle screw on the next to the highest step of the fast idle cam. Allow the engine speed to stabilize and adjust the speed to the fast idle speed specification found on the underhood sticker.
4. Run the engine at 2500 rpm for about 15 seconds and recheck the fast idle speed.
5. When the speed is properly ad-justed, turn off the engine and re-route the vacuum lines.

Accelerator Pump Stroke

The accelerator pump stroke is preset at the factory and should not be adjusted to improve driveability.

Dechoke Adjustment

1. With the engine off, hold the throttle in the wide open position.
2. Insert a .250 in. gauge between the upper edge of the choke plate and the wall of the air horn.
3. With a slight pressure against the choke shaft a slight drag should be felt when the gauge is withdrawn.
4. To adjust, bend the unloader tab on the throttle lever until the correct opening is obtained.

Choke Pulldown

1. Set the fast idle screw on the highest step of the fast idle cam.

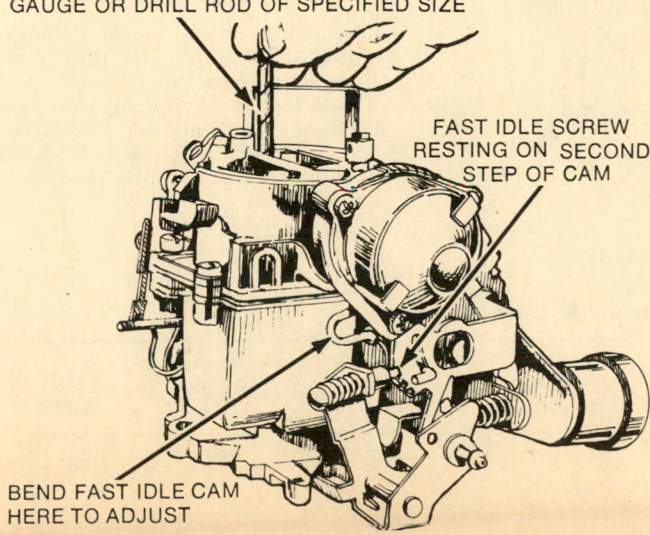

GAUGE OR DRILL ROD OF SPECIFIED SIZE

FAST IDLE SCREW RESTING ON SECOND STEP OF CAM

BEND FAST IDLE CAM HERE TO ADJUST

Fast idle cam position adjustment

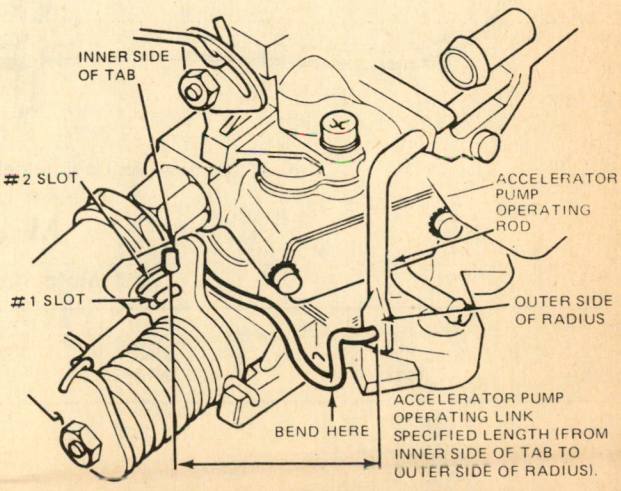

INNER SIDE OF TAB

#2 SLOT

#1 SLOT

ACCELERATOR PUMP OPERATING ROD

OUTER SIDE OF RADIUS

BEND HERE

ACCELERATOR PUMP OPERATING LINK SPECIFIED LENGTH (FROM INNER SIDE OF TAB TO OUTER SIDE OF RADIUS).

Accelerator pump adjustment

Holley Carburetors

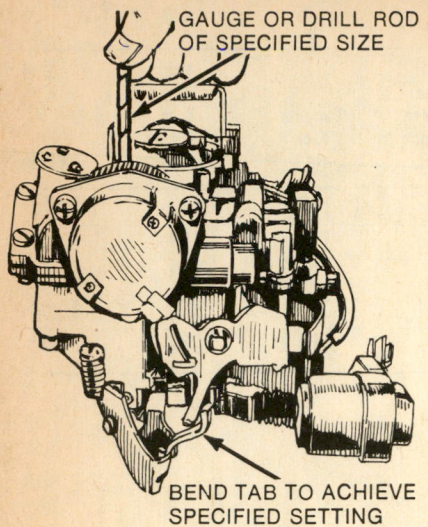

GAUGE OR DRILL ROD OF SPECIFIED SIZE

BEND TAB TO ACHIEVE SPECIFIED SETTING

Dechoke adjustment

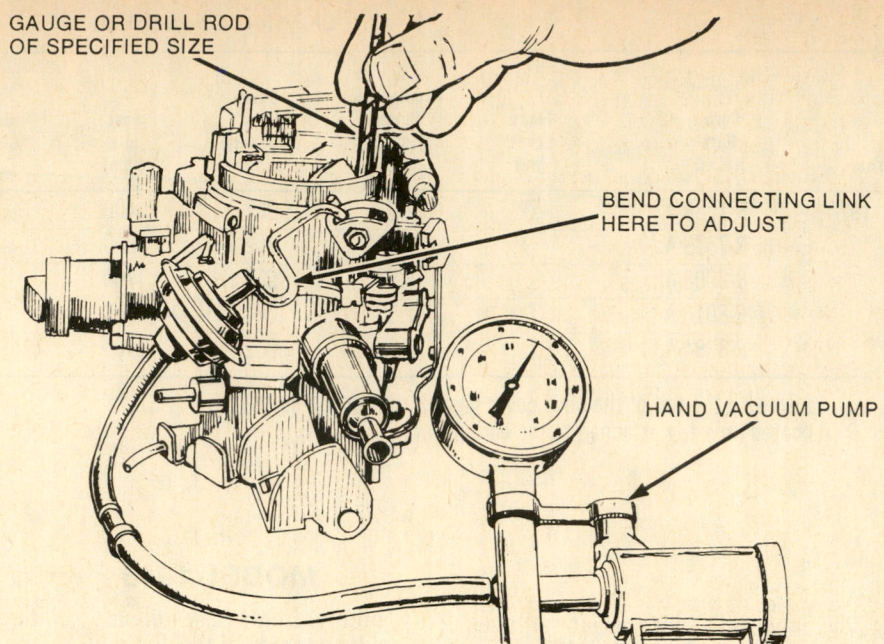

GAUGE OR DRILL ROD OF SPECIFIED SIZE

BEND CONNECTING LINK HERE TO ADJUST

HAND VACUUM PUMP

Choke pulldown adjustment

2. Cool the choke housing until the plate is fully closed.
3. Mark the choke setting for later resetting.
4. Loosen the screws and rotate the choke cap 90° in the rich (closed) direction. Tighten the screws.
5. Activate the pulldown diaphragm by applying vacuum to the external tube.

6. Make sure that the pulldown diaphragm is fully retracted.
7. If the motor does not fully retract with vacuum, test it for leakage. Replace it if it leaks.

8. Insert a .026 in. gauge, or a #71 drill bit between the upper edge of the choke plate and the air horn wall.
9. To adjust, bend the pulldown linkage as required.

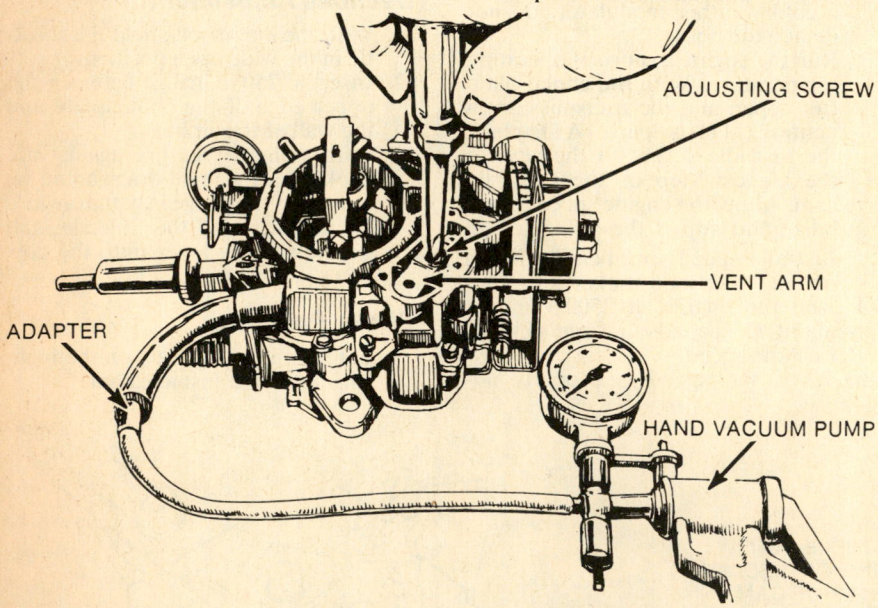

ADJUSTING SCREW

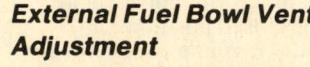

VENT ARM

ADAPTER

HAND VACUUM PUMP

External fuel bowl vent adjustment

External Fuel Bowl Vent Adjustment

1. Disconnect the canister vent hose from the fuel bowl vent.
2. Attach a hand operated vacuum pump to the vent tube using a 3/8 in. adapter.
3. Remove the vent cover and gasket and vent spring.
4. The adjusting screw is located on the nylon arm. Turn it clockwise until no more than 1/8 in. of threads is visible above the vent arm.
5. Operate the hand vacuum pump and turn the screw 1/8 turn at a time counterclockwise, until vacuum is registered on the gauge. Release the vacuum and turn the screw 1/2 turn clockwise. Disconnect the pump and replace the vent cover.

Model 1946

Ford Motor Co. Fairmont & Zephyr

Year	Part Number	Float Setting	Choke Pulldown (in.)	Fast Idle Cam Slot	Accelerator Pump Stroke Slot	Fast Idle Clearance (in.)	Choke Setting
1978	D8BZ-9510R D8BZ-9510AA D8BZ-9510U D8BZ-9510A	see text	.026	#2	#2	.080	Fixed

Float Level

1. Remove the air horn, place a finger over the hinge pin retainer. and catch the accelerator pump ball when the main body is inverted.

2. Lay a straight edge across the housing under the floats. The lowest point of the floats should just touch the straight edge.

3. If necessary, bend the tang on the float arm.

4. Turn the main body back and check the float alignment. No binding should exist through the float movement range.

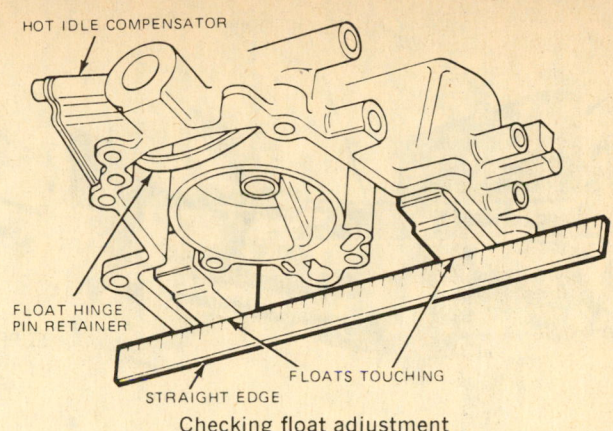

Checking float adjustment

MODEL 2210

This carburetor is a two-barrel unit but can be considered as two carburetors built side by side into one unit, utilizing the same fuel and air inlets. Each throat of the carburetor has its own throttle valve and main metering systems and are supplemented by the float, accelerating, idle, and power systems.

The 1971 version is equipped with a hot idle compensator valve which is a thermostatically operated air bleed to relieve an over-rich condition at idle. There is a bowl vent valve tube which works in conjunction with the vent valve. In 1973, an extra port for use with the (EGR) Exhaust Gas Recirculation system was added.

This carburetor is used on some 1971 383 and all 1972-73 400 two-barrel Chrysler Corporation engines.

Float Adjustment

1. Invert the air horn so that the weight of the float only is forcing the needle against the seat.

2. Measure the clearance between the top of the float and the float stop.

3. Be sure the drill gauge is perfectly level when measuring. Adjust by bending the float lip toward or away from the needle, using a narrow blade screwdriver, until the correct clearance of the setting has been obtained.

Float Drop Adjustment

1. Check the float drop by holding the air horn in an upright position.

2. The bottom edge of the float should be parallel to the underside surface of the air horn.

3. Adjust by bending the tang on the float arm.

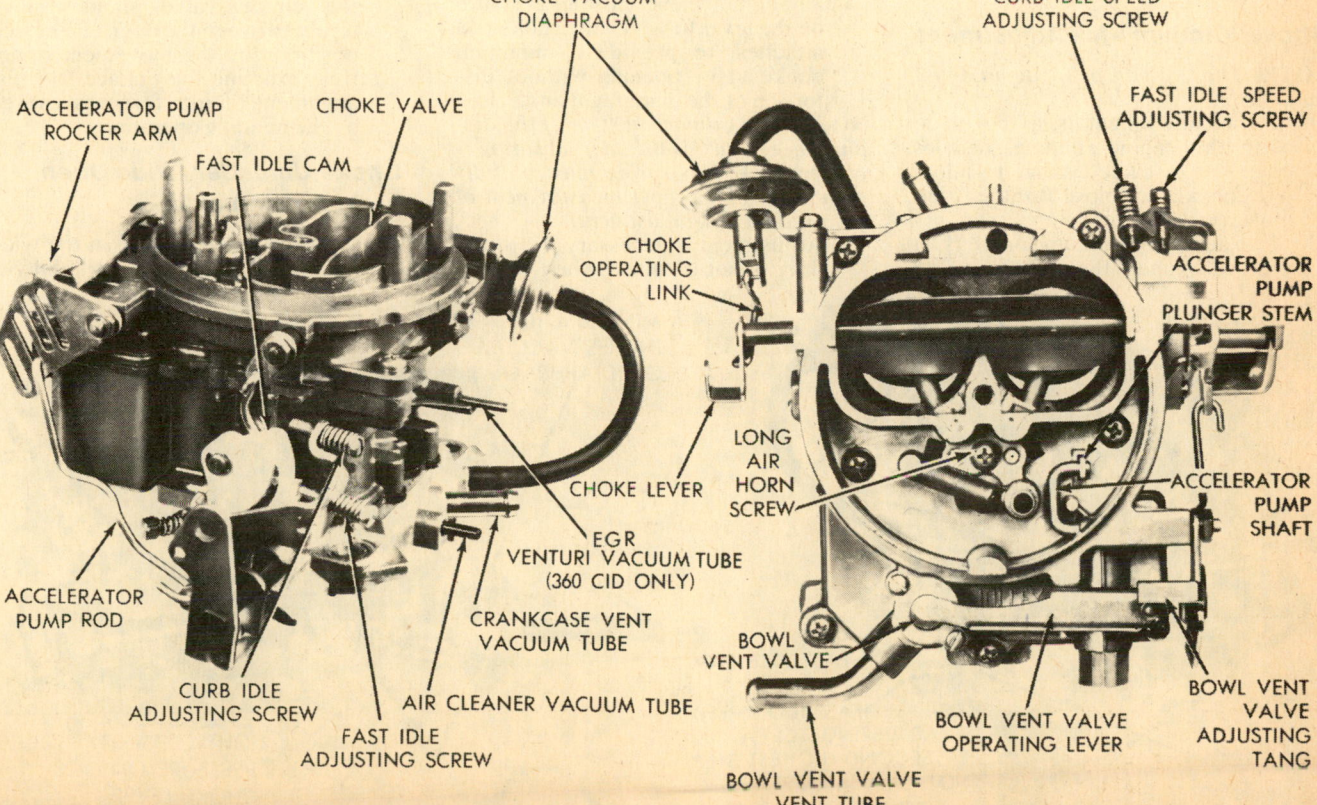

Carburetor assembly—Holley 2210

Holley Carburetors

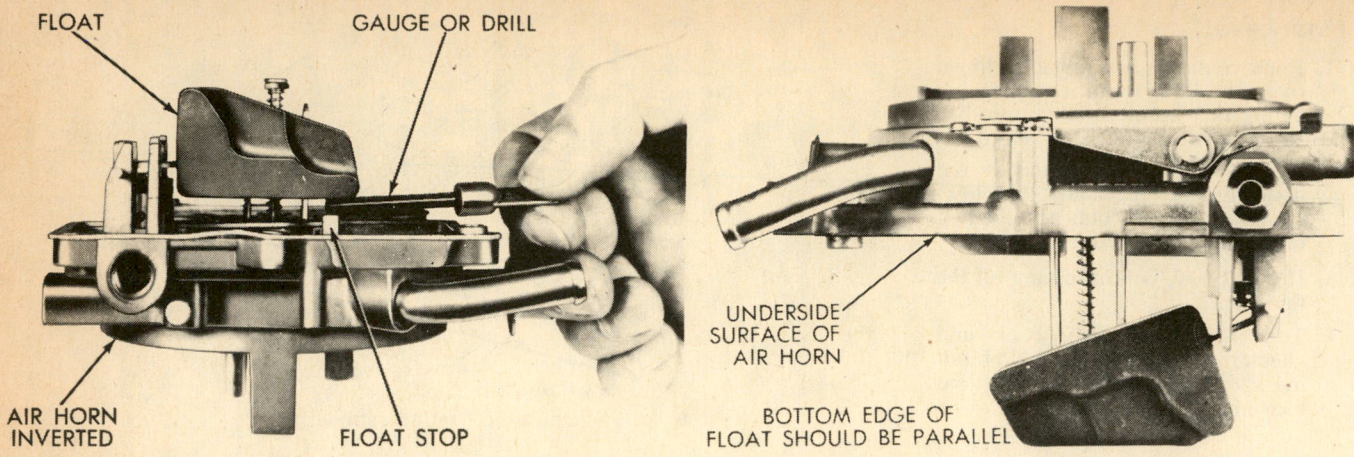

Checking the float adjustment—Holley 2210

FLOAT
GAUGE OR DRILL
AIR HORN INVERTED
FLOAT STOP

UNDERSIDE SURFACE OF AIR HORN
BOTTOM EDGE OF FLOAT SHOULD BE PARALLEL

Checking the float drop—Holley 2210

Fast Idle Cam Position Adjustment

1. With the fast idle speed adjustment screw contacting the second highest step on the fast idle cam, move the choke valve toward the closed position with light pressure on the choke shaft lever.
2. Insert the specified gauge between the top of the choke valve and the wall of the air horn. Refer to the Specifications Chart.
3. An adjustment will be necessary if a slight drag is not obtained as the drill shank is being removed.
4. Adjust by bending the fast idle link at the angle.

Choke Vacuum Kick Adjustment

NOTE: *The test can be made on or off the vehicle.*
1. If the adjustment is to be made with the engine running, disconnect the fast idle linkage to allow the choke to close to the kick position.
2. If an auxiliary vacuum source is to be used, open the throttle valve

(engine not running) and move the choke to the closed position. Release the throttle first, then release the choke.
When using an auxiliary vacuum source, disconnect the vacuum hose from the carburetor and connect it to the hose from the vacuum supply with a small length of tube to act as a fitting. Removal of the hose from the diaphragm may require forces which could damage the system. Apply a vacuum of 10 or more in. of mercury.
3. Insert the gauge between the top of the choke valve and the wall of the air horn. Refer to the Specifications Chart.
4. Apply sufficient closing pressure on the lever to which the choke rod attaches, to provide a minimum choke valve opening without distortion of the diaphragm link.

NOTE: *The cylindrical stem of the diaphragm extends as the internal spring is compressed. This spring must be fully compressed for proper measurement of the vacuum kick adjustment.*
5. Adjustment is necessary if a slight drag is not obtained when remov-

ing the gauge. Shorten or lengthen the diaphragm link to obtain the correct choke valve opening. Length changes should be made by carefully opening or closing the U-bend provided in the link. Improper bending causes contact between the U-section and the diaphragm assembly.

NOTE: *Do not apply a twisting or bending force to diaphragm.*
6. After completing adjustments, reinstall the vacuum hose on the correct carburetor fitting.
7. Return the fast idle linkage to its original location if it was disturbed. Make the following check. With no vacuum applied to the diaphragm, the choke valve should move freely between the open and closed positions. If the movement is not free, examine the linkage for misalignment or interferences caused by the bending operation.

Choke Unloader (Wide Open Kick) Adjustment

1. With the throttle valve in the wide open position, insert a drill bit be-

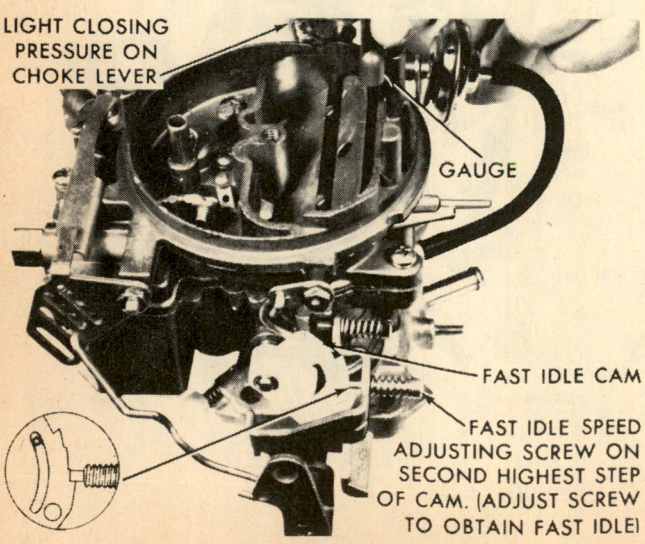

LIGHT CLOSING PRESSURE ON CHOKE LEVER
GAUGE
FAST IDLE CAM
FAST IDLE SPEED ADJUSTING SCREW ON SECOND HIGHEST STEP OF CAM. (ADJUST SCREW TO OBTAIN FAST IDLE)

2210—Fast idle cam position adjustment

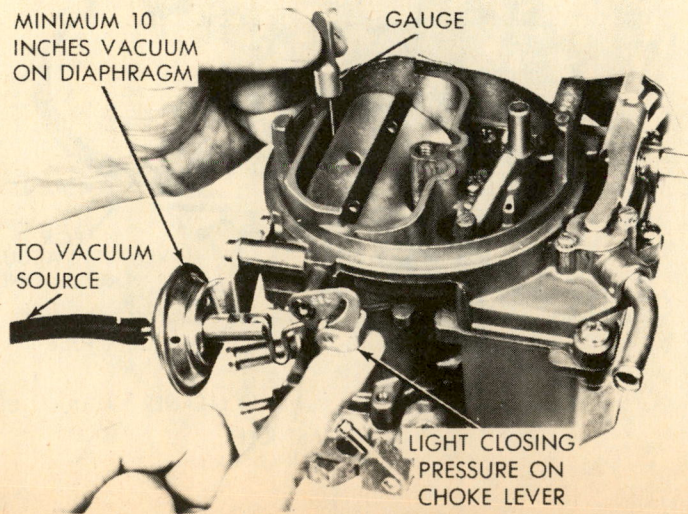

MINIMUM 10 INCHES VACUUM ON DIAPHRAGM
GAUGE
TO VACUUM SOURCE
LIGHT CLOSING PRESSURE ON CHOKE LEVER

2210—Vacuum kick adjustment

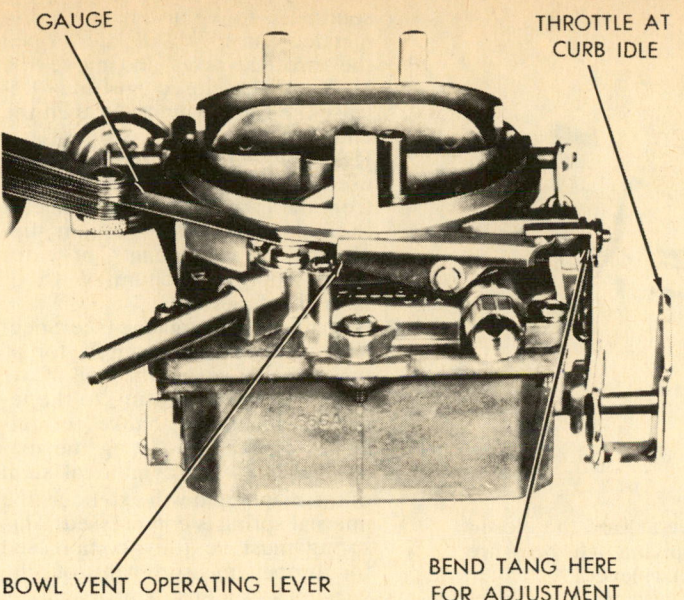

GAUGE

THROTTLE AT CURB IDLE

BOWL VENT OPERATING LEVER

BEND TANG HERE FOR ADJUSTMENT

2210—Choke unloader adjustment

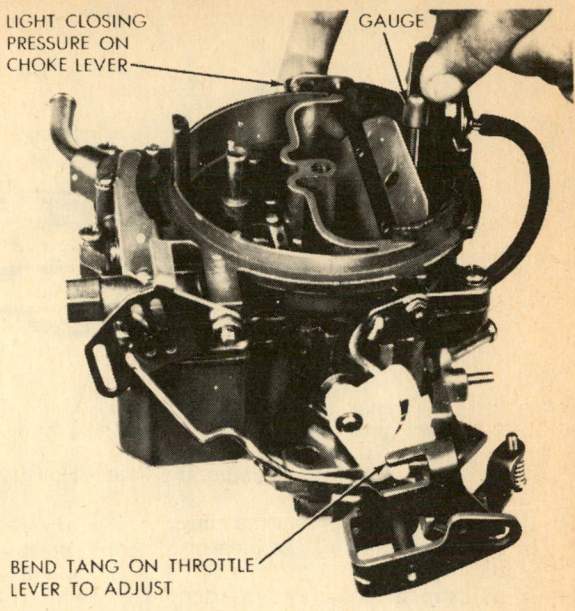

LIGHT CLOSING PRESSURE ON CHOKE LEVER

GAUGE

BEND TANG ON THROTTLE LEVER TO ADJUST

2210—Bowl vent valve adjustment

tween the upper edge of the choke valve and the inner wall of the air horn. Refer to the Specifications Chart.
2. With a finger lightly pressing against the shaft lever, a slight drag should be felt as the drill is being withdrawn.
3. Adjust by bending the unloader tang on the throttle lever until the correct opening has been obtained.

Accelerator Pump Adjustment

1. Back off the curb idle speed adjust-

ing screw.
2. Open the choke valve so that the fast idle cam allows the throttle valves to be completely seated in the bores.
3. Be sure that the pump connector rod is installed in the correct slot of the accelerator pump rocker arm. The slot for manual transmissions is next to the retaining nut.
4. Close the throttle valves tightly. Measure the distance between the top of the air horn and the end of the plunger shaft. Refer to the Specifications Chart.

5. Adjust by bending the pump operating rod at the loop of the rod.

Bowl Vent Valve Clearance Adjustment

1. With the throttle valves at curb idle, it should be possible to insert a gauge between the bowl vent valve plunger stem and the operating rod. Refer to the Specifications Chart.
2. Adjust by bending the tang on the pump lever to change the arc of contact with the throttle lever.

Model 2210
Chrysler Corporation

Year	Carb.★ Part No.	Float Level (in.)	Accelerator Pump Adjustment (in.)	Bowl Vent Clearance (in.)	Fast Idle (rpm)	Choke Unloader Clearance (in.)	Vacuum Kick (in.)	Fast Idle Cam Position (in.)	Choke
1972	R-6162-A	.180	.285	.015	1900	.170	.100	.064	Fixed
	R-6164-A	.180	.250	.015	2000	.170	.100	.064	Fixed
	R-6368-A	.180	.285	.015	1900	.170	.100	.110	Fixed
	R-6370-A	.180	.285	.015	2000	.170	.100	.110	Fixed
1973	R-6452-A	.180	.250	.015	1900	.170	.150	.110	Fixed
	R-6454-A	.180	.250	.015	1800	.170	.150	.110	Fixed
	R-6472-A	.180	.250	.015	1800	.170	.150	.110	Fixed
	R-6575-A	.180	.250	.015	1900	.170	.150	.110	Fixed

★ Located on a tag attached to the carburetor

MODEL 2245

The model 2245 carburetor is a two barrel unit used on 1974 and later Chrysler products with 360 or 400 cubic inch engines.

Float Adjustment

1. Invert the air horn so that the weight of the float is forcing the metering needle against its seat.

2. Measure the distance between the top of the float and the float stop. The clearance should be the same as given in the Specifications

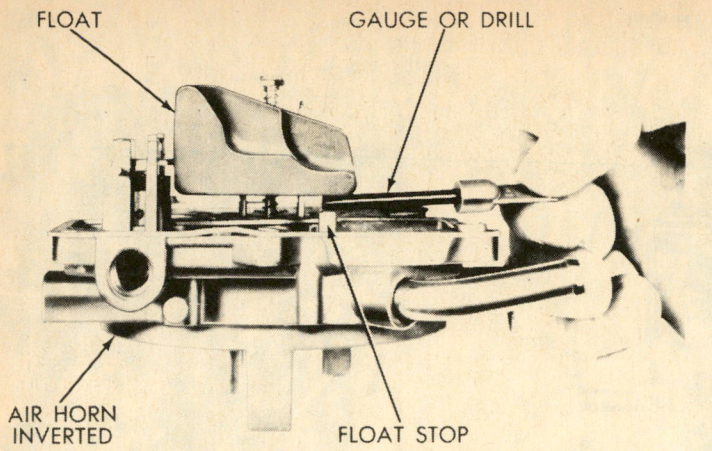

FLOAT   GAUGE OR DRILL

AIR HORN
INVERTED

FLOAT STOP

Adjusting the float—Holley 2245

Chart. Make certain that the gauge is level when making the measurement.

3. If adjustment is necessary, bend the float adjusting tab toward or away from the needle until the correct clearance is obtained. A narrow-bladed screwdriver may be used to bend the tab.

4. Check the float drop by holding the air horn upright. The bottom edge of the float should be parallel to the underside of the air horn. If an adjustment is necessary, bend the tang on the float arm.

Fast Idle Cam Position Adjustment

1. Position the fast idle speed adjusting screw on the second highest notch on the fast idle cam. Move the choke valve toward the closed position by applying light pressure on the choke shaft lever.

2. Insert the correct gauge (see Specifications Chart) between the top of the choke valve and the wall of the air horn. An adjustment will be necessary if there is not a slight drag when the gauge is removed.

3. If an adjustment is necessary, bend the fast idle connector rod at the angle.

Vacuum Kick Adjustment

1. The adjustment must be made with some type of vacuum source. If the adjustment is made with the engine running, disconnect the fast idle linkage to allow the choke to close to the kick position with the engine at curb idle. If an auxiliary vacuum source is to be used as recommended for 1977 and later, open the throttle valves and move the choke to the closed position. Release the throttle first and then the choke.

2. If an auxiliary vacuum source is used, disconnect the vacuum hose from the carburetor and connect it to the hose from the vacuum supply with a small length of extra hose. Apply a vacuum of 15 or more in. of mercury.

3. Insert the correct gauge (see Specifications Chart) between the top of the choke valve and the wall of the air horn. Apply pressure to the lever to which the choke rod attaches without distorting the diaphragm link. The cylindrical stem of the diaphragm will extend as the internal spring is compressed. This spring must be fully compressed for proper measurement of the vacuum kick adjustment.

4. If a slight drag is not felt when the gauge is removed, adjustment is necessary. Adjust the diaphragm link to obtain the correct choke valve opening. Adjustments can be made by carefully opening or closing the U-bend in the link.

--- **CAUTION** ---

Do not twist or bend the diaphragm.

5. Connect the vacuum hose to the correct carburetor fitting. Replace the linkage.

6. Make the following check. With vacuum applied to the diaphragm, the choke valve should move

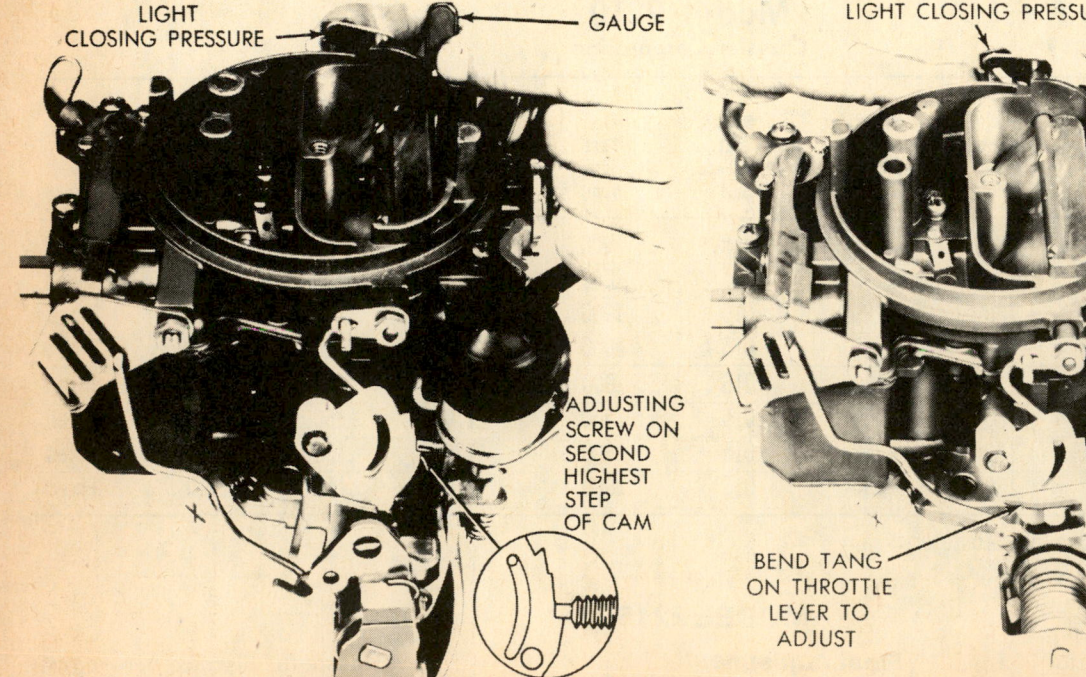

LIGHT CLOSING PRESSURE   GAUGE

ADJUSTING SCREW ON SECOND HIGHEST STEP OF CAM

LIGHT CLOSING PRESSURE   GAUGE

THROTTLE IN WIDE OPEN POSITION

BEND TANG ON THROTTLE LEVER TO ADJUST

Adjusting the fast idle cam—Holley 2245   Adjusting the choke unloader—Holley 2245

freely between open and closed positions. If the movement is not free, examine the linkage for misalignment or interference caused by the bending operation.

Choke Unloader (Wide Open Kick) Adjustment

1. Place the throttle valves in the wide-open position and insert the proper gauge (see Specifications Chart) between the upper edge of the choke valve and the inner wall of the air horn.
2. While holding pressure on the choke lever, a slight drag should be felt as the gauge is removed.
3. If an adjustment is necessary, bend the unloader tang on the throttle lever until the correct opening has been obtained.

Accelerator Pump Adjustment

THROUGH 1975

1. Back off the curb idle adjusting screw and open the choke valve so that the fast idle cam allows the throttle valves to be completely seated in their bores.

NOTE: *Make certain that the pump connector rod is placed in the correct slot of the Aaccelerator pump rocker arm. On manual transmission models, it is the first slot next to the retaining nut.*

2. Close the throttle valves and measure the distance from the top of the air horn to the end of the plunger shaft. See Specifications Chart.
3. If adjustment is needed, bend the pump operating rod at its loop until

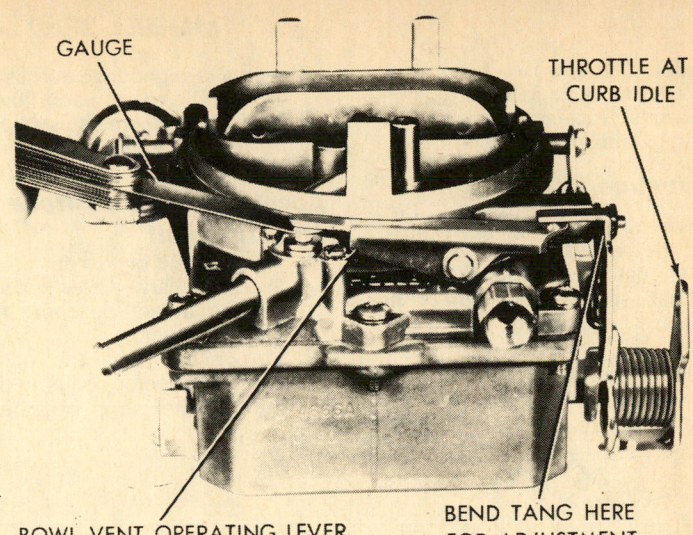

Adjusting the bowl vent clearance—Holley 2245

the correct setting has been obtained.

1976-77

1. Make sure that the pump connector rod is in the first slot next to the retaining nut of the pump arm on 360 engines, and in the second slot for the 400.
2. Measure the drop of the pump plunger between curb idle and wide open throttle.
3. Adjust the travel by bending the operating rod.

1978 AND LATER

1. Hold the throttle valves in the wide open position.
2. Lightly press a finger against the

control lever to move the choke valve toward the closed position.
3. Insert a .170 inch gauge between the top of the choke valve and the air horn wall at the throttle lever side.
4. Adjust by bending the tang on the throttle lever.

Bowl Vent Valve Clearance

1. With the throttle valves set at curb idle, insert the specified gauge between the bowl vent valve plunger stem and the operating rod.
2. If the gauge does not fit, bend the tang on the pump lever until the correct clearance has been obtained.

Model 2245

Chrysler Corporation

Year	Carb.★ Part No.	Float Level (in.)	Accelerator Pump Adjustment (in.)	Bowl Vent Clearance (in.)	Fast Idle (rpm)	Choke Unloader Clearance (in.)	Vacuum Kick (in.)	Fast Idle Cam Position (in.)	Choke
1974	R-6731-A	.180	.255	.015	1800	.170	.150	.110	Fixed
	R-6990-A	.180	.255	.015	1600	.170	.150	.110	Fixed
	R-7139-A	.180	.255	.015	1600	.170	.150	.110	Fixed
1975	R-7226-A	.190	.250	.015	1600	.170	.150	.110	Fixed
	R-7211-A	.190	.250	.015	1600	.170	.150	.110	Fixed
	R-7027-A	.190	.250	.015	1600	.170	.150	.110	Fixed
1976	R-7364-A	.190	.265	.025	1600	.170	.150	.110	Fixed
	R-7366-A	.190	.265	.025	1600	.170	.150	.110	Fixed
1977	R-7671-A	.190	.265	.025	1700	.170	.110	.110	Fixed
1978	R-7991-A	.188	.265	.025	1600	.170	.110	.110	Fixed
	R-8326-A	.188	.265	.025	1600	.170	.110	.110	Fixed

★ Located on a tag attached to the carburetor.

MODEL 2280

The model 2280 is a two barrel unit used on 1978 and later 318 cid engines with automatic transmission in all states except California.

Float Adjustment

1. Remove the carburetor air horn.
2. Invert the carburetor body, taking care to catch the pump intake check ball, so that the weight of the floats only, is forcing the needle against the seat. Hold a finger against the hinge pin retainer to fully seat the float in the float pin cradle.

3. Lay a straight edge across the float bowl. The toe of each float should be 5/16 in. from the straight edge. If necessary, bend the float tang to adjust.

Accelerator Pump Stroke Measurement

1. Remove the bowl vent cover plate and vent valve lever spring. Take care to avoid loosening the vent valve retainer.
2. Make sure that the accelerator pump connector rod is in the inner hole of the pump operating lever

and the throttle is at curb idle.
3. Place a straight edge on the bowl vent cover surface of the air horn, over the accelerator pump lever.
4. The lever surface should be flush with the air horn. If not, adjust it by bending the pump connector rod at the 90 degree bend.

NOTE: *If this adjustment is changed, both the bowl vent and the mechanical power valve adjustments must be reset.*

Choke Unloader Adjustment

1. Hold the throttle valves in the wide open position.

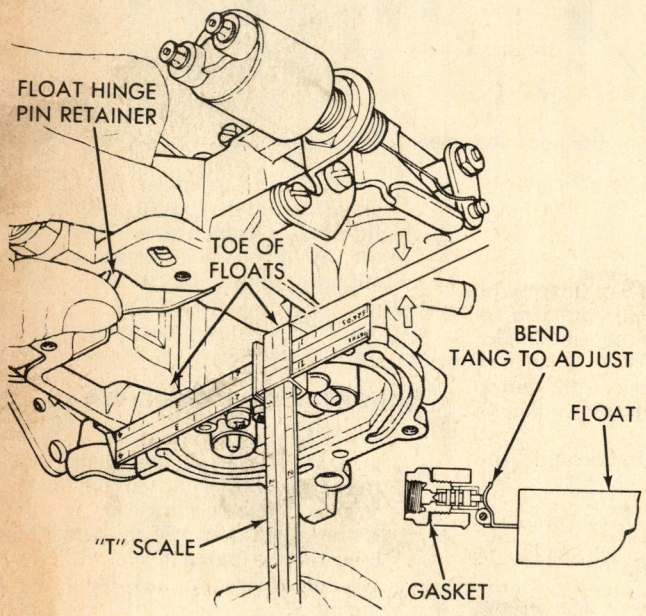

FLOAT HINGE PIN RETAINER

TOE OF FLOATS

BEND TANG TO ADJUST

FLOAT

"T" SCALE

GASKET

Float setting adjustment

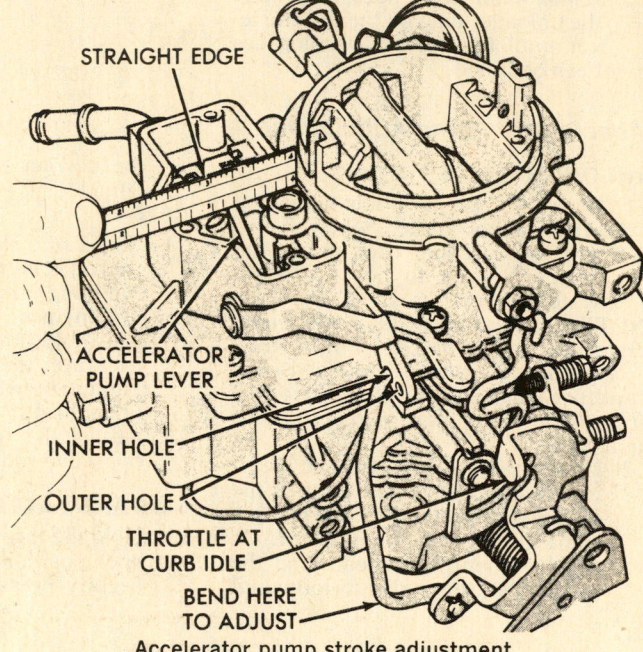

STRAIGHT EDGE

ACCELERATOR PUMP LEVER

INNER HOLE

OUTER HOLE

THROTTLE AT CURB IDLE

BEND HERE TO ADJUST

Accelerator pump stroke adjustment

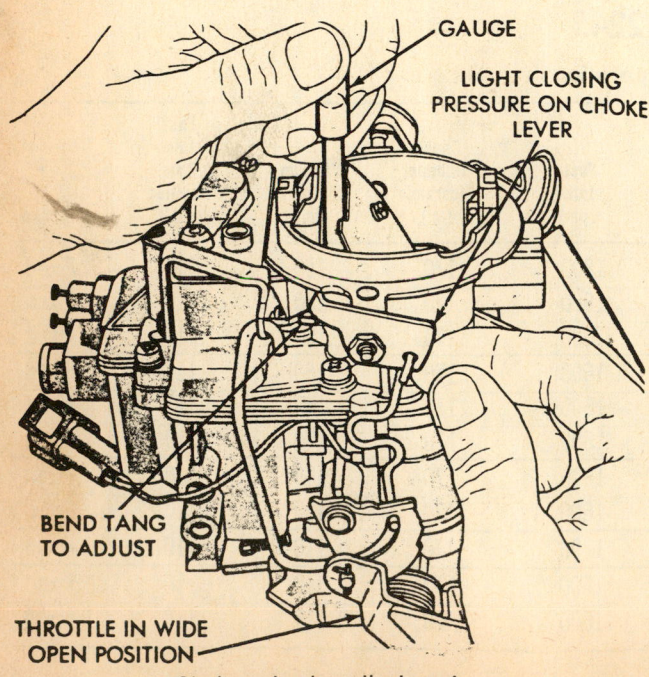

GAUGE

LIGHT CLOSING PRESSURE ON CHOKE LEVER

BEND TANG TO ADJUST

THROTTLE IN WIDE OPEN POSITION

Choke unloader adjustment

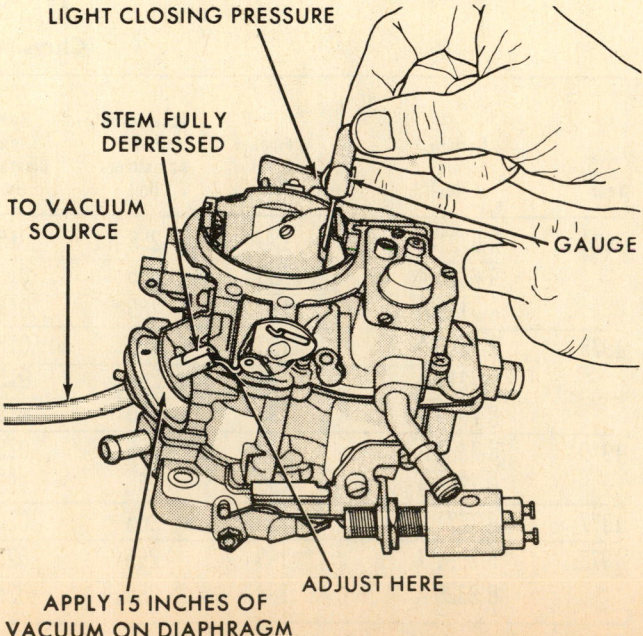

LIGHT CLOSING PRESSURE

STEM FULLY DEPRESSED

TO VACUUM SOURCE

GAUGE

ADJUST HERE

APPLY 15 INCHES OF VACUUM ON DIAPHRAGM

Choke vacuum kick adjustment

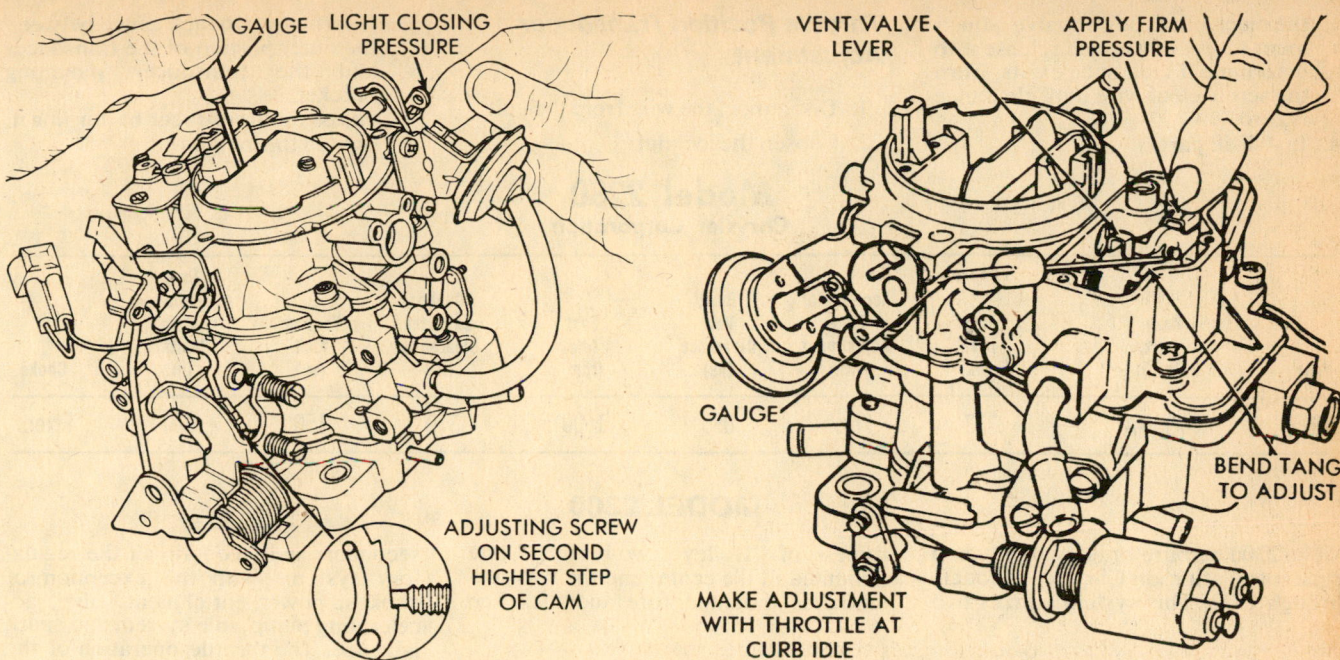

Fast idle cam position adjustment

Bowl vent valve adjustment

2. Lightly press a finger against the control lever to move the choke valve toward the closed position.
3. Insert a .310 inch gauge between the top of the choke valve and the air horn wall.
4. Adjust, if necessary, by bending the tang on the accelerator pump lever.

Choke Vacuum Kick Adjustment

1. Open the throttle, close the choke, then close the throttle to trap the fast idle can at the closed choke position.
2. Disconnect the vacuum hose from the carburetor and connect it to an auxiliary vacuum source with a length of hose. Apply at least 15 in. Hg.
3. Completely compress the choke lever spring in the diaphragm stem without distorting the linkage.
4. Insert a .150 inch gauge between the top of the choke valve and the air horn wall.
5. Adjust by bending the diaphragm

link. Check for free movement. Replace the vacuum hose.

Fast Idle Cam Position Adjustment

1. Position the adjusting screw on the second highest step of the fast idle cam.
2. Move the choke towards the closed position with light finger pressure.
3. Insert a .070 inch gauge between the choke valve and the air horn wall.
4. Adjust by opening or closing the U-bend in the fast idle connector link.

Bowl Vent Valve Adjustment

1. Remove the bowl vent cover and

vent valve lever spring. Take care to avoid disturbing the lever retainer.
2. With the throttle at curb idle, press firmly down on the vent valve lever where the spring seats.
3. Insert a .030 inch gauge between the vent valve tang and the lever.
4. Adjust by bending the end of the vent valve lever up or down.

Mechanical Power Valve Adjustment

1. Remove the bowl vent cover plate, vent valve lever, spring and retainer. Remove the lever pivot pin.
2. Hold the throttle in the wide open position.
3. Using a 5/64 in. allen wrench, press

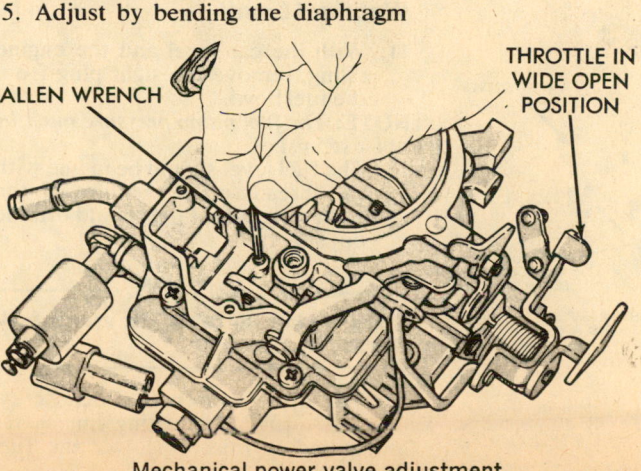

Mechanical power valve adjustment

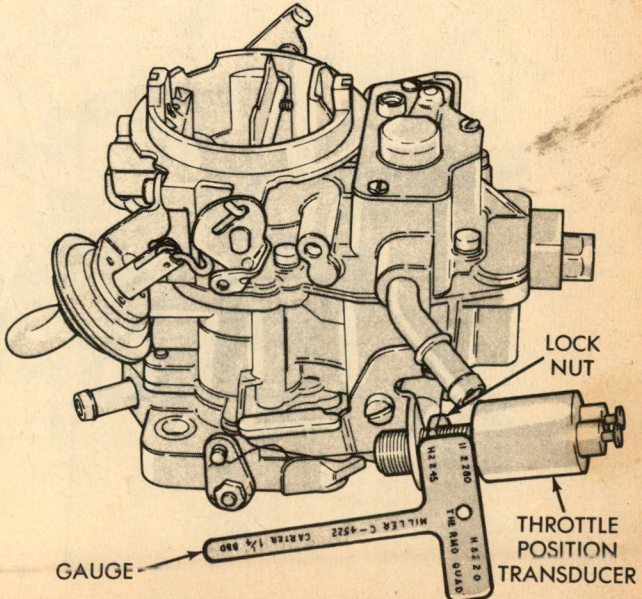

Throttle position transducer adjustment

Holley Carburetors

the mechanical power valve adjustment screw down, and release it to determine if clearance exists. Turn the screw clockwise until clearance is zero.

4. Install all parts.

Throttle Position Transducer Adjustment

1. Disconnect the wire from the unit.
2. Loosen the locknut.
3. Insert an 11/16 inch gauge between the outer portion of the transducer and the transducer mounting bracket.
4. Adjust the transducer by turning it.
5. Tighten the locknut.

Model 2280
Chrysler Corporation

Year	Carb. Part No. ⑦	Float Level (in.)	Accelerator Pump Adjustment (in.)	Bowl Vent Clearance (in.)	Fast Idle (rpm)	Choke Unloader Clearance (in.)	Vacuum Kick (in.)	Fast Idle Cam Position (in.)	Choke
1978	R-7990-A	.313	Flush	.030	1600	.310	.150	.070	Fixed

MODEL 2300

The 2300 carburetor is used only in a triple installation on Chrysler products through 1972. This system utilizes two types of Holley two-barrels, one mounted in the center and the two secondaries mounted fore and aft. The secondary units contain all the regulatory systems with the exception of chokes, power enrichment valve, accelerating pump, idle system and spark advance. The throttle operation of the primary carburetor is conventional whereas the secondary units are equipped with throttle control vacuum diaphragms for the purpose of opening the secondary throttles which close mechanically. The choke used only on the primary unit is controlled by a temperature sensing choke coil mounted on the intake manifold, over the exhaust crossover passage.

The only adjustments required on the secondary units are the float level and the wet fuel level. All other adjustments are made on the primary unit.

Float Adjustment

1. Make a preliminary float adjustment by inverting the fuel bowl and turning the adjustable needle and seat until the float is centered in the bowl.
2. Do not fully tighten the lock screw. Snug the screw to temporarily retain adjustment.

NOTE: *Final adjustment of the float is made on the vehicle.*

Wet Fuel Level

1. With the car level and the engine idling, remove the sight plug from the fuel bowl.

NOTE: *The fuel pump pressure must be at least 5 psi.*

2. The fuel level should be in line with the threads at the bottom of the sight plug hole. Fuel should dribble out slowly.

CAUTION
Use a cloth to catch the excess fuel. Discard it safely.

---

3. To adjust, loosen the lock screw and turn the adjusting nut as required to raise or lower the fuel level.

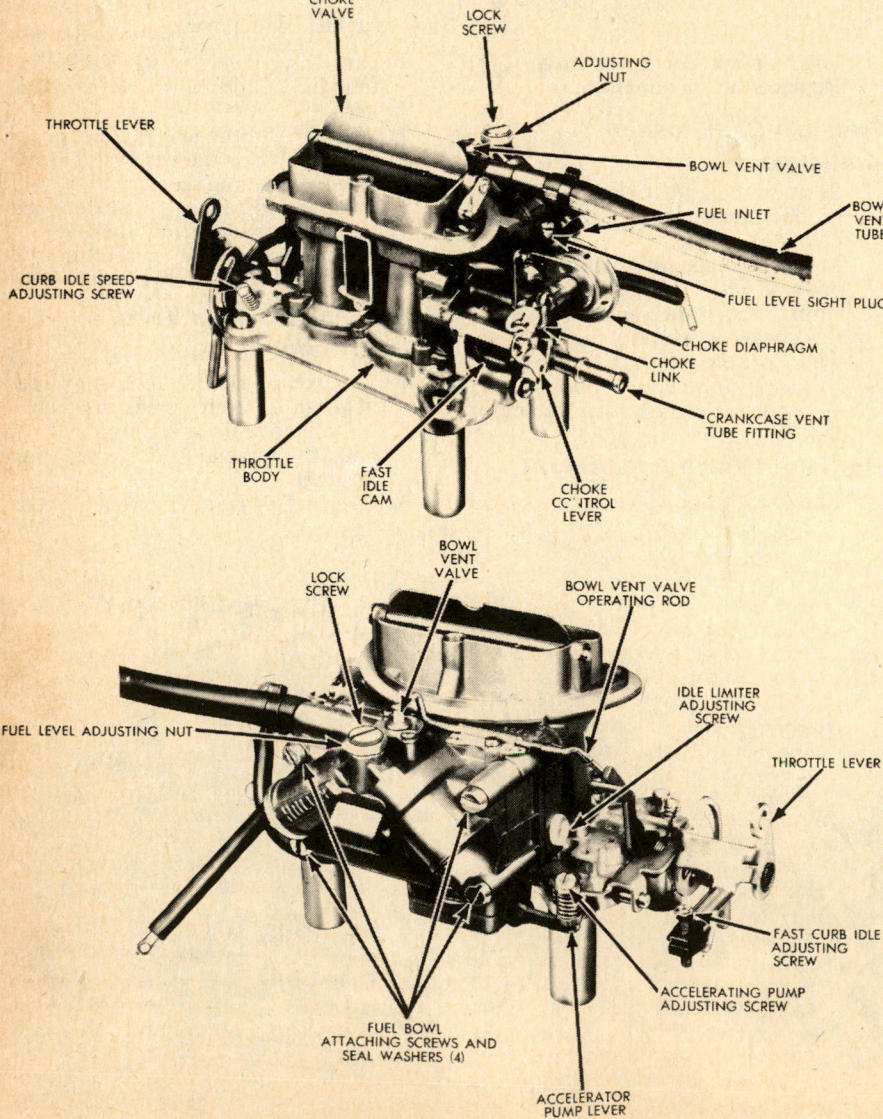

Carburetor assembly—Holley 2300

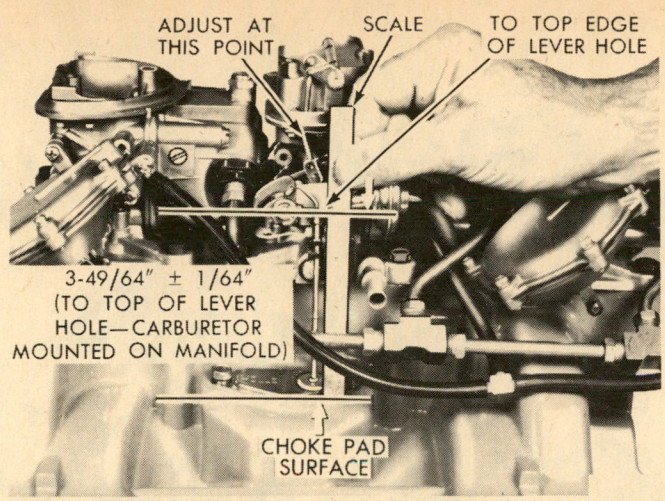

ADJUST AT THIS POINT   SCALE   TO TOP EDGE OF LEVER HOLE

3-49/64" ± 1/64"
(TO TOP OF LEVER
HOLE—CARBURETOR
MOUNTED ON MANIFOLD)

CHOKE PAD SURFACE

Adjusting the 2300 choke control lever

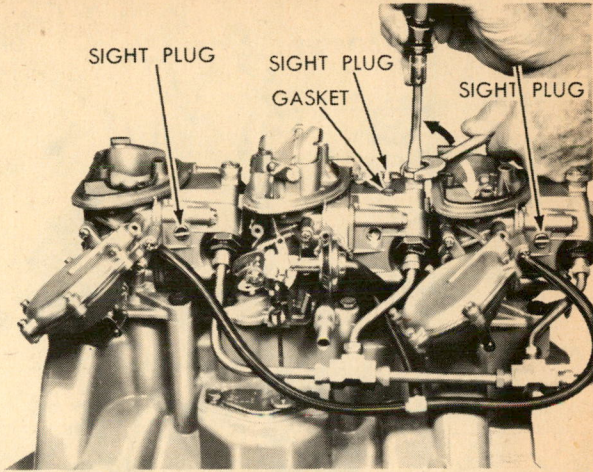

SIGHT PLUG   SIGHT PLUG   SIGHT PLUG
GASKET

Adjusting 2300 fuel level on vehicle

Automatic Choke Control Lever Setting

Adjustment of the choke control lever is necessary to provide the correct relationship between the choke valve, the thermostatic coil spring, and the fast idle cam. It should be checked and adjusted (if necessary), as preparation of the choke system linkage before making the Vacuum Kick, Cam Position, or Unloader adjustment. These three adjustments must be made after adjustment of the choke control lever.

NOTE: *Improper bending of the choke rod will result in binding.*

1. Open the throttle to mid-position; close the choke valve by applying slight pressure on the choke control lever.
2. The top of choke rod hole in the control lever should be $3^{49/64}$ in. above the choke pad with the carburetor on the engine, or $1^{23/32}$ in. above the carburetor base with the carburetor on a bench.
3. Adjust by bending the choke shaft rod.

Fast Idle Cam Position Adjustment

1. With the fast idle speed adjusting screw contacting the second highest step on the fast idle cam, move the choke valve toward the closed position with light pressure on the choke control lever.
2. Insert the specified gauge between the top of the choke valve and the wall of the air horn. Refer to the Specifications Chart.
3. An adjustment will be necessary if a slight drag is not obtained as the drill shank is being removed.
4. Adjust by bending the cam position adjusting tang.

Choke Unloader Adjustment (Wide Open Kick)

1. Hold the throttle valves in the wide-open position.
2. Insert the specified drill between the upper edge of the choke valve and the inner wall of the air horn. Refer to the Specifications Chart.
3. With a finger lightly pressing against the choke control lever, a slight drag should be felt as the drill is being withdrawn.
4. Adjust by bending the unloader tang until the correct opening has been obtained.

Choke Vacuum Kick Adjustment

NOTE: *The test can be made on or off the vehicle.*

1. If adjustment is to be made with the engine running, position the fast idle tang (cam position adjustment) to allow the choke to close to the kick position.
2. If an auxiliary vacuum source is to be used, open the throttle valve (engine not running) and move the choke to the closed position. Release the throttle first, then release the choke.
   When using an auxiliary vacuum source, disconnect the vacuum hose from the carburetor and connect it to the hose from the vacuum supply with a small length of tube to act as a fitting. Removal of the hose from the diaphragm may require forces which damage the diaphragm. Apply a vacuum of 10 or more in. of mercury.
3. Insert the gauge between the top of the choke valve and the wall of the air horn. Refer to the Specifications Chart.
4. Apply sufficient closing pressure on the lever to which the choke rod attaches to provide a minimum choke valve opening without distortion of the diaphragm link.

NOTE: *The cylindrical stem of the diaphragm extends as the internal spring is compressed for proper measurement of the vacuum kick adjustment.*

5. Adjustment is necessary if a slight drag is not obtained when removing the gauge. Shorten or lengthen the diaphragm link to obtain the correct choke valve opening. Length changes should be made by carefully opening or closing the U-bend provided in the link. Improper bending causes contact between the U-section and the diaphragm assembly.

NOTE: *Do not apply a twisting or bending force to the diaphragm.*

6. After completion of adjustment, reinstall the vacuum hose onto the correct carburetor fitting.
7. Return the fast idle screw to its original location if it was disturbed. Make the following check. With no vacuum applied to the diaphragm, the choke valve should move freely between the open and closed positions. If the movement is not free, examine the linkage for misalignment or interferences caused by the bending operation.

Fast Idle Speed Adjustment (On Vehicle)

1. Open the throttle slightly with the engine off. Close the choke valve until the fast idle screw tang can be positioned on the second highest-speed step of the fast idle cam.
2. Start the engine and determine the stabilized speed.
3. Bend the fast idle tang by use of a screwdriver placed in the tang slot to secure the specified speed. Refer to the Specifications Chart.

NOTE: *Bend it only in a direction perpendicular to the contact surface of the cam. Movement in any other direction changes the cam position adjustment. Bend it only when the tang is clear of the cam. Stopping the engine between adjustments is not necessary. However, reposition the fast idle tang on the cam after each speed adjustment to provide correct throttle closing torque.*

Holley Carburetors

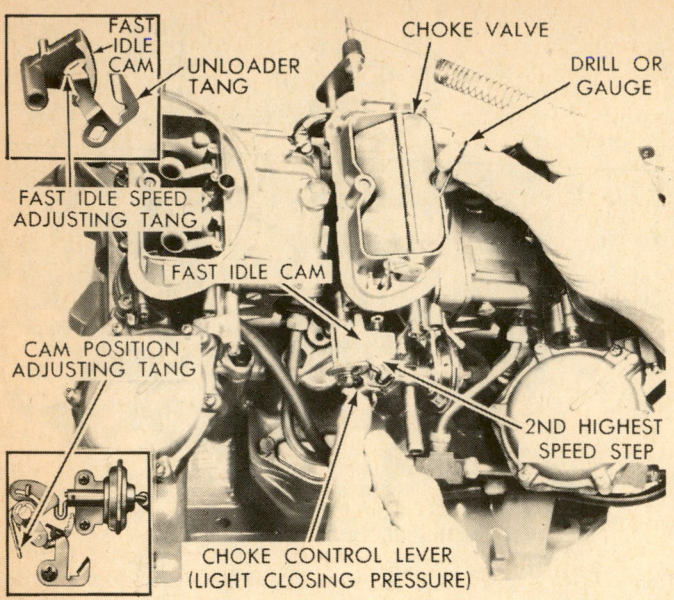

FAST IDLE CAM

UNLOADER TANG

FAST IDLE SPEED ADJUSTING TANG

FAST IDLE CAM

CAM POSITION ADJUSTING TANG

CHOKE VALVE

DRILL OR GAUGE

2ND HIGHEST SPEED STEP

CHOKE CONTROL LEVER (LIGHT CLOSING PRESSURE)

2300—Fast idle cam position adjustment, Chrysler

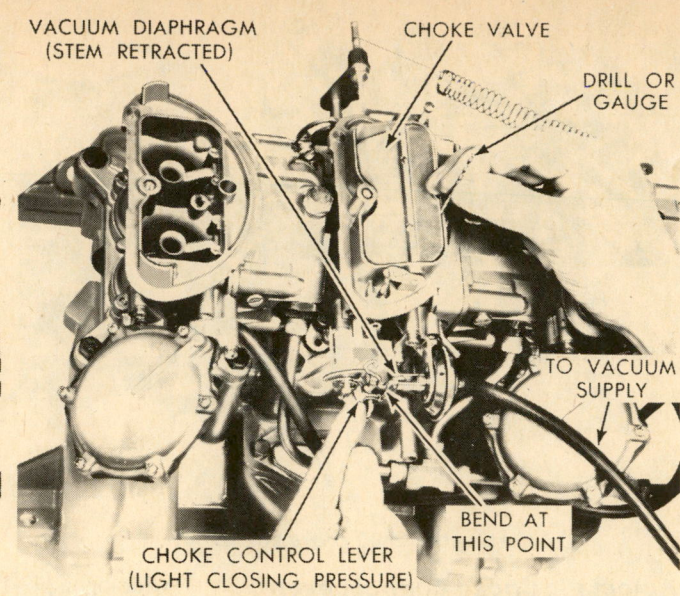

VACUUM DIAPHRAGM (STEM RETRACTED)

CHOKE VALVE

DRILL OR GAUGE

TO VACUUM SUPPLY

BEND AT THIS POINT

CHOKE CONTROL LEVER (LIGHT CLOSING PRESSURE)

2300—Choke vacuum kick adjustment, Chrysler

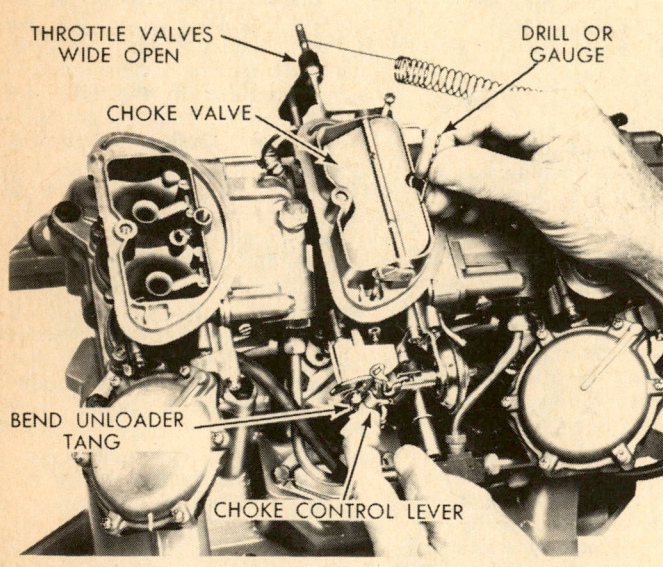

THROTTLE VALVES WIDE OPEN

CHOKE VALVE

DRILL OR GAUGE

BEND UNLOADER TANG

CHOKE CONTROL LEVER

2300—Choke unloader adjustment—wide open kick, Chrysler

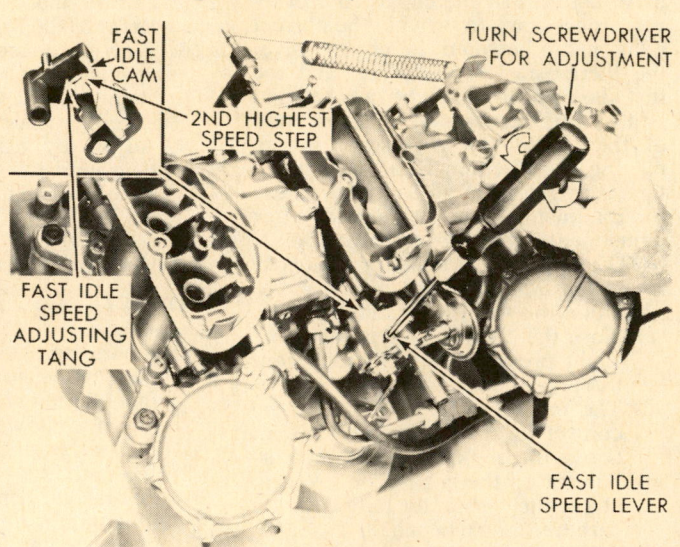

FAST IDLE CAM

2ND HIGHEST SPEED STEP

TURN SCREWDRIVER FOR ADJUSTMENT

FAST IDLE SPEED ADJUSTING TANG

FAST IDLE SPEED LEVER

2300—Fast idle speed adjustment on the vehicle

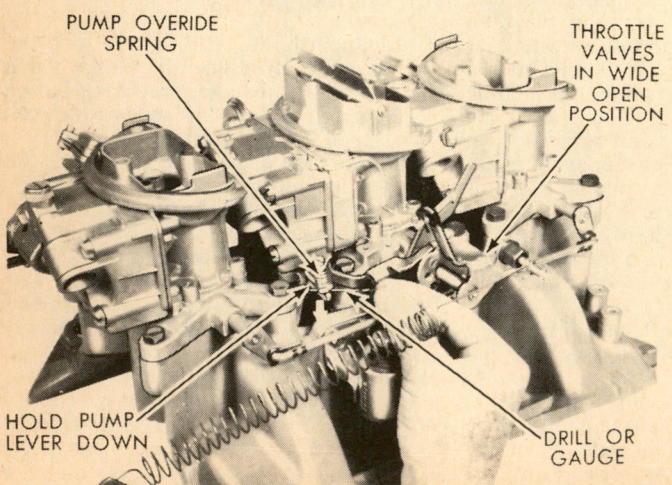

PUMP OVERIDE SPRING

THROTTLE VALVES IN WIDE OPEN POSITION

HOLD PUMP LEVER DOWN

DRILL OR GAUGE

Checking the 2300 accelerator pump lever adjustment, Chrysler

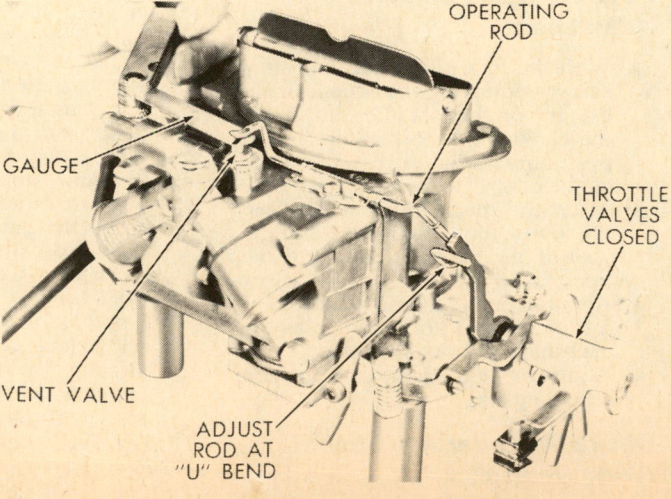

OPERATING ROD

GAUGE

THROTTLE VALVES CLOSED

VENT VALVE

ADJUST ROD AT "U" BEND

Checking the 2300 bowl vent valve adjustment

Accelerator Pump Adjustment

1. With the throttle lever in the wide open position and the pump lever fully compressed (down), measure the clearance between the spring adjusting nut and the arm of the pump lever. Refer to Specifications Chart. It should be a minimum of 0.015 in. and a maximum of 0.063 in.

2. Adjust by turning the nut or screw as required while holding the opposite end. (The pump operating lever is not threaded.) There should be no free movement of the pump lever when the throttle is at curb idle.

Bowl Vent Valve Adjustment

1. With the throttle valves at fast curb idle, insert the drill gauge between the bowl vent valve and the bowl vent rod with the fast curb idle speed properly set. Refer to the Specifications Chart.

2. Adjust by bending the rod to change the arc of contact with the throttle lever, until the correct clearance has been obtained.

Model 2300
Chrysler Corporation

Year	Carb. Part No. ②	Float Level (in.)	Accelerator Pump Adustment (in.)	Bowl Clearance Vent (in.)	Fast Idle (rpm)	Choke Unloader Clearance (in.)	Vacuum Kick (in.)	Fast Idle Cam Position (in.)	Choke
1972	R-6404-A	①	.015-.063	.015	1800	.150	.070	.060	Fixed

① Invert the bowl and set the float for a preliminary adjustment; then set wet level to the bottom of the sight plug opening.

② Located on a tag attached to the carburetor

MODEL 5210-C

The Holley 5210-C is a progressive two barrel carburetor with a new automatic choke system which is activated by a water heated thermostatic coil. An electrically heated choke is used on the Pontiac 151 four. It also has an exhaust gas recirculation system with the valve located in the intake manifold. It is used on General Motors and 1977-78 AMC four-cylinder engines.

Float Level

1. With the carburetor air horn inverted, and the float tang resting lightly on the inlet needle, insert the specified gauge between the air horn and the float.
2. Bend the float tang if an adjustment is needed.

Float Drop

1. With the air horn right side up,

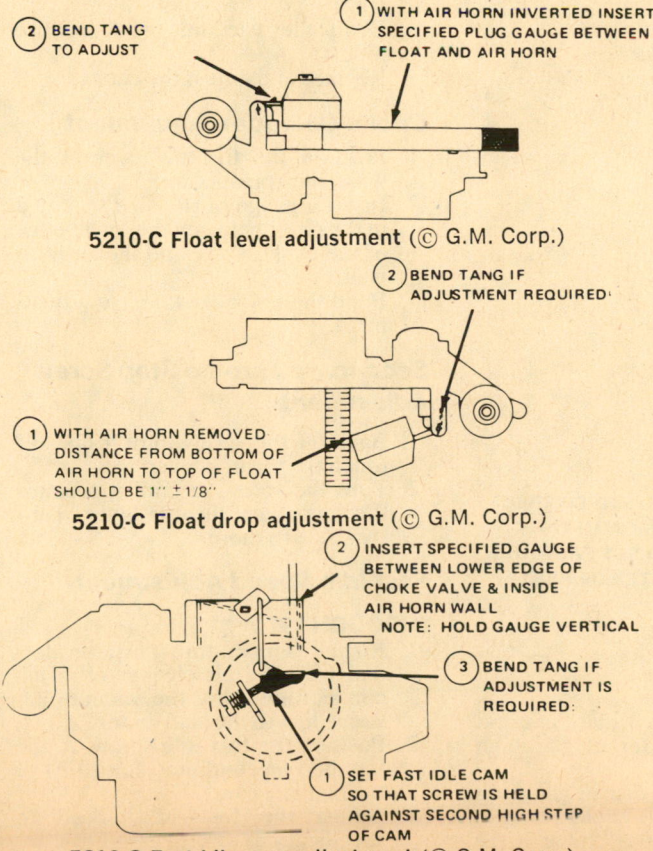

5210-C Float level adjustment (© G.M. Corp.)

5210-C Float drop adjustment (© G.M. Corp.)

5210-C Fast idle cam adjustment (© G.M. Corp.)

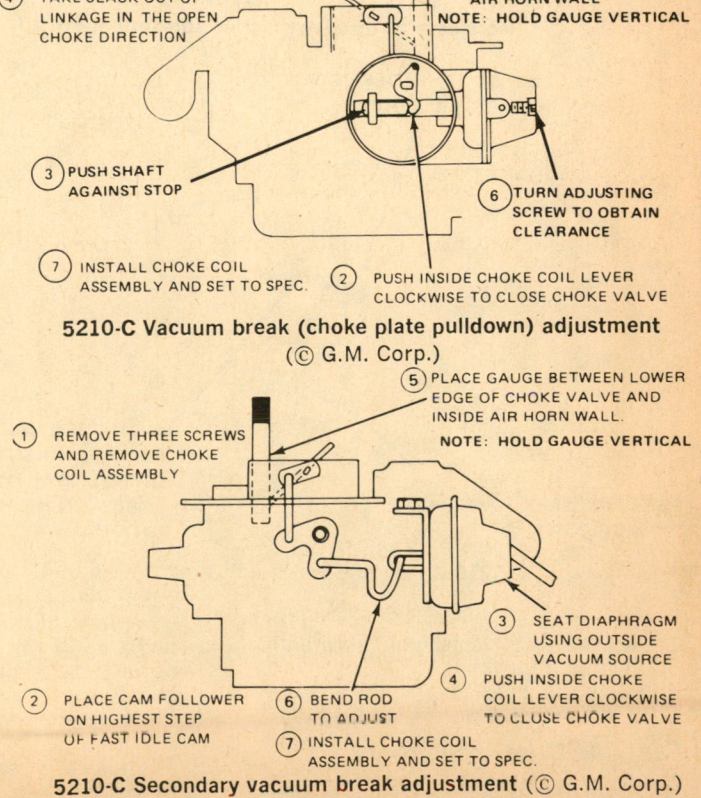

5210-C Vacuum break (choke plate pulldown) adjustment (© G.M. Corp.)

5210-C Secondary vacuum break adjustment (© G.M. Corp.)

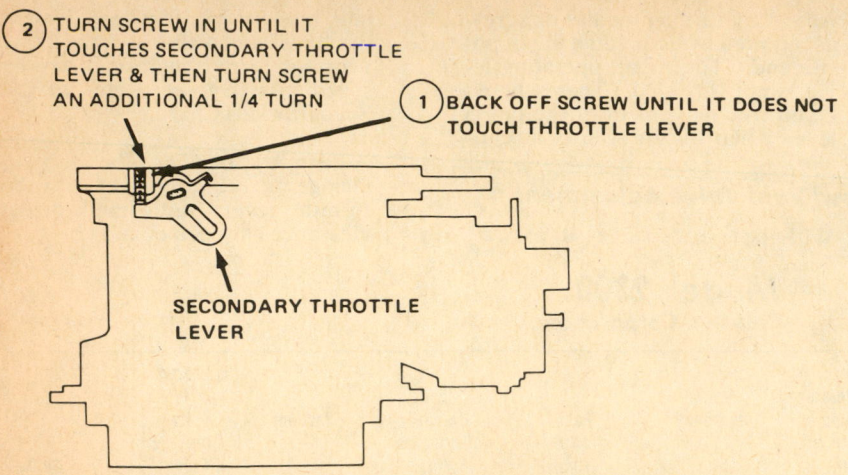

5210-C Choke unloader adjustment (© G.M. Corp.)

2 TURN SCREW IN UNTIL IT TOUCHES SECONDARY THROTTLE LEVER & THEN TURN SCREW AN ADDITIONAL 1/4 TURN

1 BACK OFF SCREW UNTIL IT DOES NOT TOUCH THROTTLE LEVER

SECONDARY THROTTLE LEVER

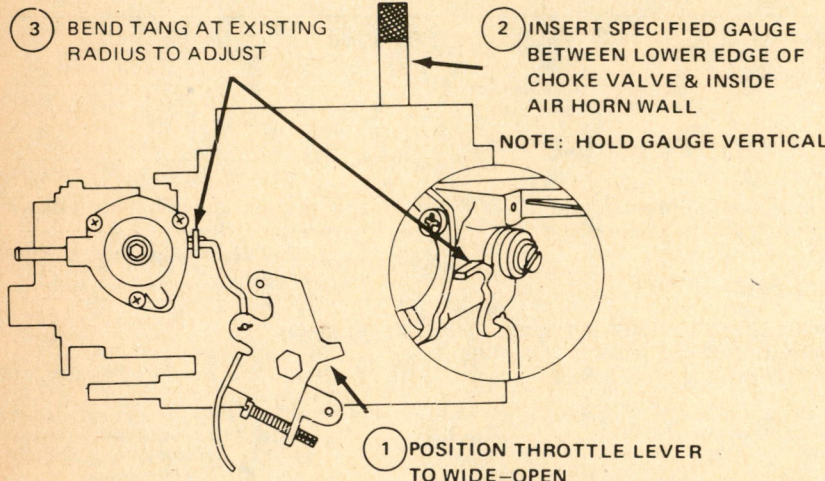

3 BEND TANG AT EXISTING RADIUS TO ADJUST

2 INSERT SPECIFIED GAUGE BETWEEN LOWER EDGE OF CHOKE VALVE & INSIDE AIR HORN WALL

NOTE: HOLD GAUGE VERTICAL

1 POSITION THROTTLE LEVER TO WIDE–OPEN

5210-C Secondary throttle stop screw adjustment (© G.M. Corp.)

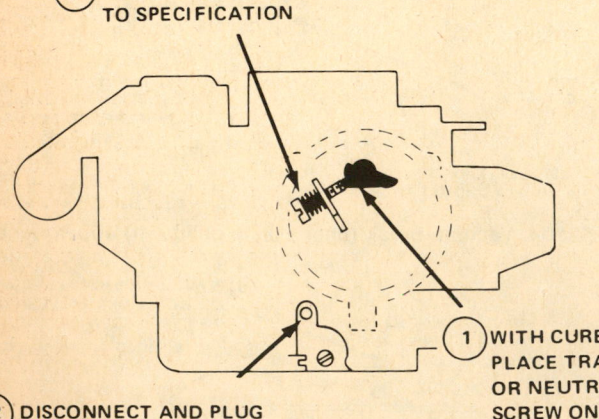

3 ADJUST FAST IDLE SCREW TO SPECIFICATION

2 DISCONNECT AND PLUG EGR PORT

1 WITH CURB IDLE SPEED CORRECT, PLACE TRANSMISSION IN PARK OR NEUTRAL AND SET FAST IDLE SCREW ON HIGH STEP OF FAST IDLE CAM

5210-C Fast idle speed adjustment (© G.M. Corp.)

measure between the air horn and the top of the float.
2. Bend the float tang if an adjustment is needed.

Fast Idle Cam Adjustment

1. Place the fast idle screw on the sec-ond step of the fast idle cam and against the shoulder of the high step.
2. Place the specified drill or gauge on the down side of the choke plate.
3. To adjust, bend the choke lever tang.

Choke Plate Pulldown (Vacuum Break) Adjustment

1. Remove the three hex headed screws and ring which retain the choke cover.

CAUTION

Do not remove the choke water housing screw if adjusting on the car. Pull the choke water housing and bimetal cover assembly back out of the way.

2. Push the diaphragm shaft against the stop. Push the coil lever clockwise.
3. Insert the specified size gauge on the down side of the primary choke plate.
4. Take the slack out of the linkage and turn the adjusting screw with a $5/32$ in. Allen wrench.

Secondary Vacuum Break Adjustment

1. Remove the three screws and the choke coil assembly.
2. Place the cam follower on the highest step of the fast idle cam.
3. Seat the diaphragm by applying an outside source of vacuum.
4. Push the inside choke coil lever counterclockwise through 1977; clockwise for 1978 and later, to close the choke valve.
5. Place a gauge of the size specified in the chart between the lower edge of the choke valve and the air horn wall.
6. Bend the vacuum break rod to adjust.
7. Replace and adjust the choke.

Choke Unloader Adjustment

1. Position the throttle lever at the wide open position.
2. Insert a gauge of the size specified in the chart between the lower edge of the choke valve and the air horn wall.
3. Bend the unloader tang for adjustment.

Secondary Throttle Stop Screw Adjustment

1. Back off the screw until it doesn't touch the throttle lever.
2. Turn the screw in until it touches the secondary throttle lever. Turn it in $1/4$ turn more.

Fast Idle Speed Adjustment

THROUGH 1975

1. Engine temperature must be normal with the air cleaner off. Disconnect and plug the vacuum advance line to the distributor.
2. Position the fast idle screw on the top step (second step for 1975) of the fast idle cam.
3. Adjust the fast idle speed to specifications.
4. Adjustments are made by turning

Holley Carburetors

the fast idle screw in or out.

1976 AND LATER
1. The engine must be at normal operating temperature with the air cleaner off.
2. With the engine running, position the fast idle screw on the high step of the cam. Plug the EGR Port on the carburetor.
3. Adjust the speed by turning the fast idle screw.

Model 5210-C

AMC OHC 4 Cylinder

Year	Carb. Part No. ① ②	Float Level (Dry) (in.)	Float Drop (in.)	Pump Position	Fast Idle Cam (in.)	Choke Plate Pulldown* (in.)	Secondary Vacuum Break (in.)	Fast Idle Setting (rpm)	Choke Unloader (in.)	Choke Setting
1977	7711	0.420	—	—	0.140	0.246	——	1600	0.300	1 Rich
	7712	0.420	—	—	0.140	0.246	——	1600	0.300	1 Rich
	7799	0.420	—	—	0.135	0.215	——	1600	0.300	Index
	7846	0.420	—	—	0.101	0.204	——	1600	0.300	1 Rich
1978	8163	.420	—	—	.193	.191	——	1800	.300	1 NR
	8164	.420	—	—	.204	.202	——	1800	.300	1 NR
	8165	.420	—	—	.177	.180	——	1800	.300	Index

CHEVROLET Monza, Vega

Year	Carb. Part No.	Float Level (Dry)	Float Drop	Pump Position	Fast Idle Cam	Choke Plate Pulldown*	Secondary Vacuum Break	Fast Idle Setting	Choke Unloader	Choke Setting
1973	R-6477A	0.420	1	#3	0.140	0.300	——	2000	——	1 Rich
	R-6478A	0.420	1	#2	0.140	0.300	——	2200	——	2 Rich
	R-6580A	0.420	1	#2	0.140	0.300	——	2200	——	2 Rich
	R-6581A	0.420	1	#3	0.140	0.300	——	2000	——	1 Rich
1974	338179	0.420	1	#3	0.140	0.300	——	2000⑥	——	2½ Rich
	338181	0.420	1	#3	0.140	0.300	——	2000⑥	——	2½ Rich
	338168	0.420	1	#2	0.140	0.300	——	2200⑥	——	3½ Rich
	338170	0.420	1	#2	0.140	0.300	——	2200⑥	——	3½ Rich
1975	348659, 348663,	0.420	1	#2	0.110	0.325	——	1600⑥	——	3 Rich
	348661, 348665	0.420	1	#2	0.110	0.275	——	1600⑥	——	3 Rich
	348660, 348664	0.420	1	#2	0.110	0.300	——	1600⑥	——	4 Rich
	348662, 348666	0.420	1	#2	0.110	0.275	——	1600⑥	——	4 Rich
1976	366829, 366831	0.420	1	#3	0.320	0.313	——	2200	0.375	2 Rich
	366833, 366841	0.420	1	#3	0.320	0.268	——	2200	0.375	2 Rich
	366830, 366832	0.420	1	#2	0.320	0.288	——	2200	0.375	3 Rich
	366834, 366840	0.420	1	#2	0.320	0.268	——	2200	0.375	3 Rich
1977	458103, 458105	0.420	1	#2	0.120	0.250	——	2500	0.350	3 Rich
	458107, 458109	0.420	1	#2	0.120	0.275	——	2500	0.400	3 Rich
	458102, 458104	0.420	1	#1	0.085	0.250	——	2500	0.350	3 Rich
	458106, 458108	0.420	1	#1	0.120	0.275	——	2500	0.400	3 Rich
	458110, 458112	0.420	1	#1	0.120	0.300	——	2500	0.400	3 Rich
1978	see notes	.520	1	—	.150	⑦	.400	⑩	.350	⑧

Oldsmobile Starfire

Year	Carb. Part No.	Float Level (Dry)	Float Drop	Pump Position	Fast Idle Cam	Choke Plate Pulldown*	Secondary Vacuum Break	Fast Idle Setting	Choke Unloader	Choke Setting
1976	Manual	0.420	1	#3	0.320	0.313③	——	2200	0.375	2 Rich
	Automatic	0.420	1	#2	0.320	0.288③	——	2200	0.375	3 Rich
1977	458102, 458104	0.420	1	④	0.085	0.250	0.400	2500	0.350	3 Rich
	458103, 458105	0.420	1	④	0.120	0.250	0.400	2500	0.350	3 Rich
	458106, 458107, 458108, 458109	0.420	1	④	0.120	0.275	0.400	2500	0.400	3 Rich
	458110, 458112	0.420	1	④	0.120	0.300	0.400	2500	0.400	3 Rich
1978	see notes	.520	1	—	.150	⑨		⑩	.350	⑪

U105

Holley Carburetors

Pontiac Astre, Sunbird, Ventura

Year	Carb. Part No. ① ②	Float Level (Dry) (in.)	Float Drop (in.)	Pump Position	Fast Idle Cam (in.)	Choke Plate Pulldown* (in.)	Secondary Vacuum Break (in.)	Fast Idle Setting (rpm)	Choke Unloader (in.)	Choke Setting
1975	Manual	0.420	1	#3	0.140	0.300	——	2000⑥	——	2½ Rich
	Automatic	0.420	1	#2	0.140	0.400	——	2200⑥	——	3½ Rich
1976	Manual	0.410	1	#3	0.420	0.313③	——	2200⑥	0.375	2 Rich
	Automatic	0.410	1	#2	0.320	0.288③	——	2200⑥	0.375	3 Rich
1977	458102, 458103, 458104, 458105	0.420	1	④	0.085	0.250		2500	0.350	3 Rich
	458107, 458109	0.420	1	④	0.125	0.275	0.400	2500	0.350	3 Rich
	458110, 458112	0.420	1	④	0.120	0.300	0.400	2500	0.350	3 Rich
1978	see notes	.520	1	—	.150	⑫	——	⑬	.350	⑭

① Located on tag attached to the carburetor, or on the casting or choke plate
② Beginning 1974, GM identification numbers are used in place of the Holley numbers
③ 0.268 in California
④ #1 manual, #2 automatic
⑤ Not used
⑥ With no vacuum to the distributor
* Vacuum break initial choke valve clearance on AMC
⑦ Part #10001048, 10001050: .300
    #10001047, 10001049, 10001052, 10001054: .325
⑧ Part #10001047, 10001049: 1 Rich
    #10001048, 10001050, 10001052, 10001054: 2 Rich

⑨ Part #10001047, 10001049: .325
    #10004048, 10004049: .300
⑩ Part #10001047, 10001049: 2200
    #10004048, 10004049: 2400
⑪ Part #10001047, 10001049: 1 Rich
    #10004048, 10004049: 2 Rich
⑫ Part #10001047, 10001049: .325
    #10004048, 10004049: .300
⑬ Part #10001047, 10001049: 2200
    #10004048, 10004049: 2400
⑭ Part #10001047, 10001049: 1 Rich
    #10004048, 10004049: 2 Rich

MODEL 5220

This is a staged two barrel unit used on Omni/Horizon cars with manual transmission.

Float Setting Adjustment

1. Remove and invert the air horn.
2. Insert a .480 inch gauge between the air horn and float.
3. If necessary, bend the tang on the float arm to adjust.

Vacuum Kick Adjustment

1. Open the throttle, close the choke, then close the throttle to trap the fast idle system at the closed choke position.
2. Disconnect the vacuum hose to the carburetor and connect it to an auxiliary vacuum source.
3. Apply at least 15 inches Hg. vacuum to the unit.
4. Apply sufficient force to close the choke valve without distorting the linkage.
5. Insert a .070 inch gauge between the top of the choke plate and the air horn wall.
6. Adjust by rotating the allen screw in the center diaphragm housing.

7. Replace the vacuum hose.

Throttle Position Transducer Adjustment

1. Disconnect the wire from the transducer.

2. Loosen the locknut.
3. Place an 11/16 inch gauge between the outer portion of the transducer and the mounting bracket.
4. To adjust the gap, turn the transducer.
5. Tighten the locknut.

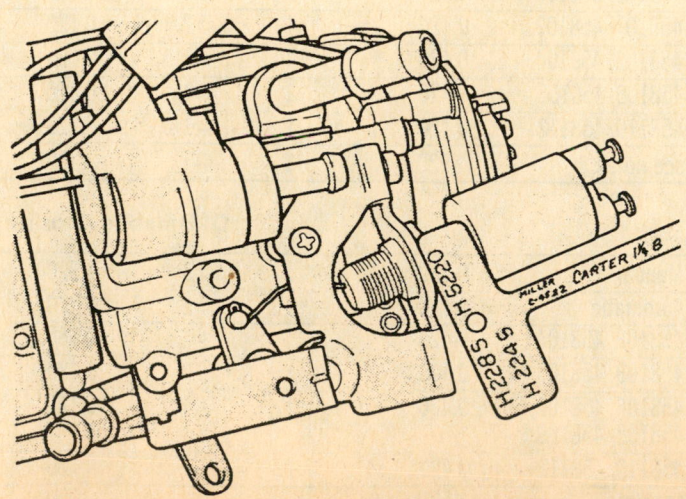

Throttle position transducer adjustment

Model 5220

Chrysler Corporation

Year	Carb. Part No.	Accelerator Pump	Dry Float Level (in.)	Vacuum Kick (in.)	Curb Idle RPM (w/fan)	Fast Idle RPM (w/fan)	Throttle Position Transducer (in.)	Throttle Stop Speed RPM	Choke
1978	R-8376A, 8378A, 8384A, 8439A, 8441A, 8505A, 8507A	#2 hole	.480	.070	900	1100	.547	700	2 NR

MODEL 6500

This is a Holley-Weber Unit used on 1978 Pinto and Bobcat models with the 2.3L engine. It is available only in California. With the exception of an externally variable fuel metering system in place of the fuel enrichment valve, it is identical to the 1977 model Motorcraft 5200. For all adjustments, refer to this listing in the Motorcraft section of Carburetor Unit Repair.

MODEL 6510-C

The 6510-C is used on subcompact GM cars with the 4-151 engine. It is available only in California.

This is a staged, two barrel unit which incorporates a feedback air/fuel

MODEL 6500, 6510-C

metering system. The system uses five new and additional components.
   a. oxygen sensor
   b. electrical control unit
   c. vacuum modulator
   d. feedback diaphragm and idle needle
   e. main feedback idle system

Vacuum Break Adjustment

1. Remove the choke coil assembly.
2. Push the choke coil lever clockwise to close the choke valve.
3. Push the choke shaft against its stop.
4. Take the slack out of the linkage, in the open direction.
5. Insert a .325 inch gauge between the lower edge of the choke plate

and the air horn wall. Turn the adjusting screw on the diaphragm housing to adjust.

Fast Idle Cam Adjustment

1. Set the fast idle cam so that the screw is on the second highest step of the fast idle cam.
2. Insert a .150 inch gauge between the lower edge of the choke valve and the air horn wall.
3. Bend the tang on the arm to adjust.

Unloader Adjustment

1. Place the throttle in the wide open position.
2. Insert a .350 inch gauge between

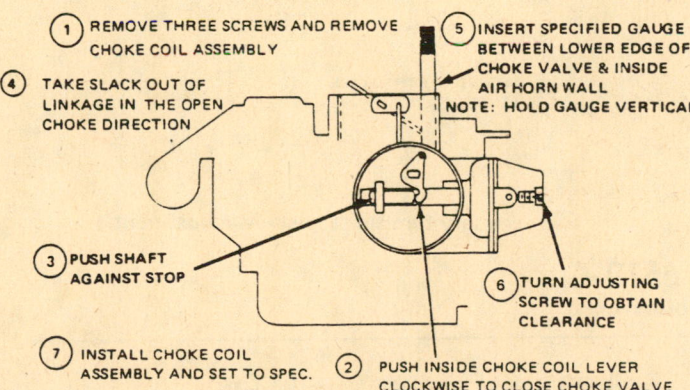

Vacuum break adjustment

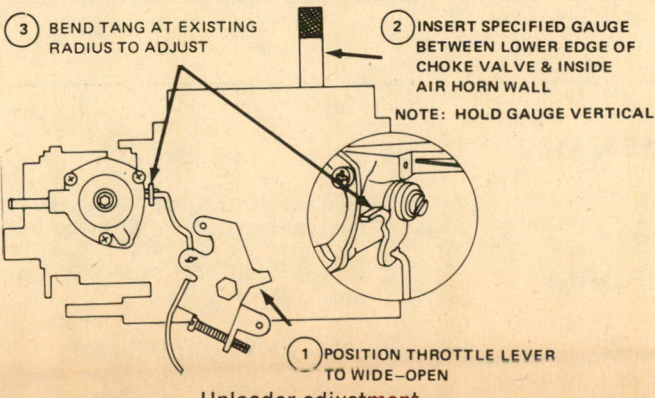

Unloader adjustment

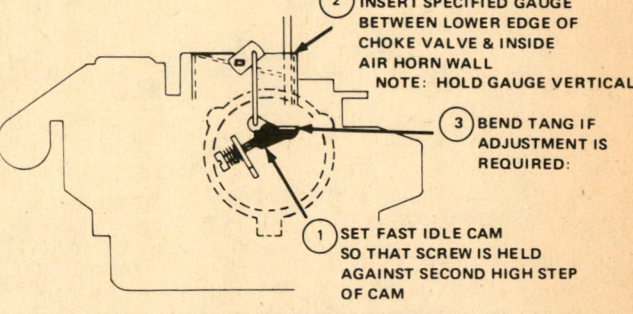

Fast idle cam adjustment

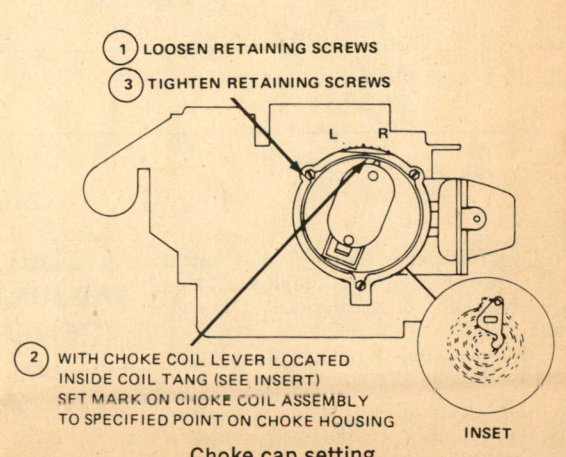

Choke cap setting

Holley Carburetors

the lower edge of the choke valve and the air horn wall.

3. Bend the tang on the choke arm to adjust.

Choke Cap Setting

1. Loosen the retaining screws.
2. Make sure that the choke coil lever is located inside the coil tang.
3. Turn the cap to give a 1 notch rich setting.
4. Tighten the retaining screws.

Fast Idle Adjustment

1. With the curb idle speed correct,

place the fast idle screw on the highest cam step and adjust to 2400 rpm.

NOTE: *The EGR line must be disconnected and plugged.*

Float Level Adjustment

1. Remove and invert the air horn.
2. Place a .520 inch gauge between the air horn and the float.
3. If necessary, bend the float arm tang to adjust.

Float Drop Setting

1. Hold the air horn right side up. The

distance between the bottom of the air horn and the top of the float should be 1 inch.

2. If necessary, bend the tang on the side of the float arm support, to adjust.

Secondary Throttle Stop Screw Adjustment

1. Back off the screw until it does not touch the lever.
2. Turn the screw in until it touches the lever, then turn it and additional 1/4 turn.

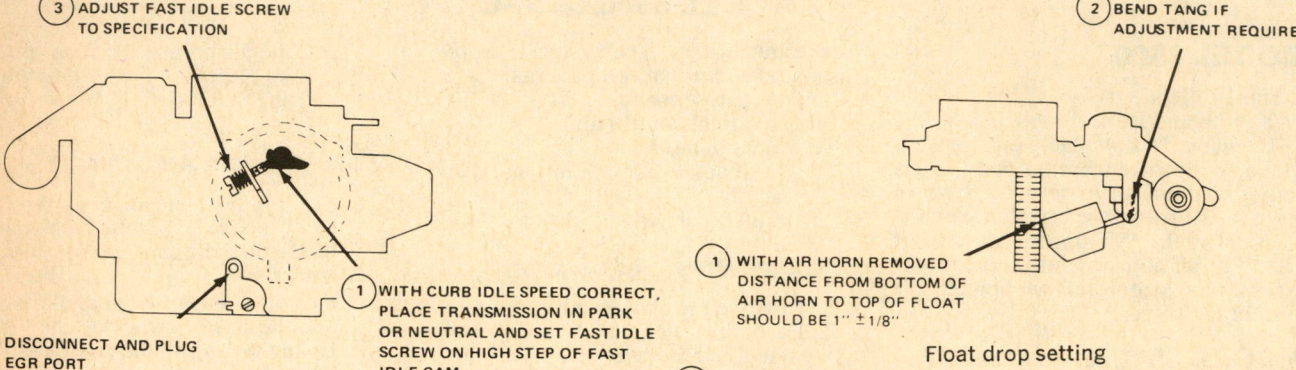

Fast idle cam adjustment

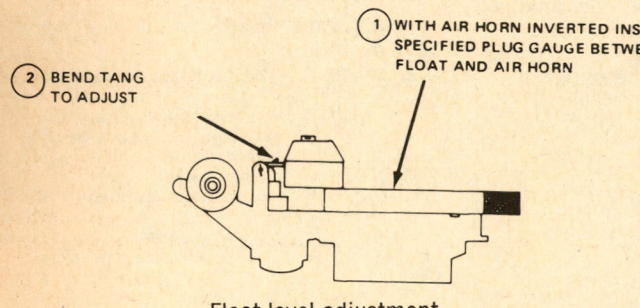

Float level adjustment

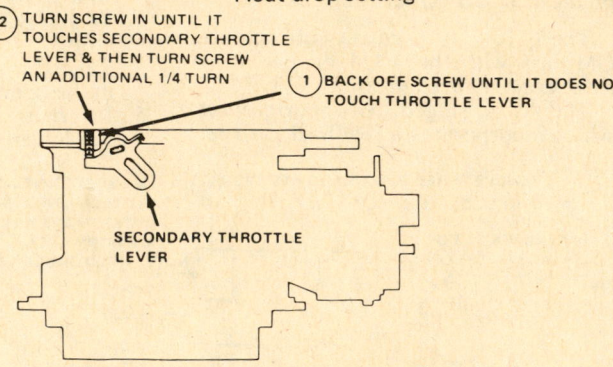

Float drop setting

Secondary throttle stop screw adjustment

Model 6510-C
General Motors Corp.

Year	Part Number	Vacuum Break Adjustment (in.)	Fast Idle Cam Adjustment (in.)	Unloader Adjustment (in.)	Fast Idle Adjustment (rpm)	Float Level Adjustment (in.)	Choke Setting
1978	10001056, 10001058	.250	.150	.350	2400	.520	1 Rich

MODEL 4150, 4160

The 4150 and 4160 are four barrel carburetors which contain all the basic systems in the primary sides. The secondary sides of these units contain a fuel transfer and bypass system which richens the mixture when needed.

Some 4150 models have a central fuel inlet whereas other units have a side inlet.

MODEL 4150 ADJUSTMENTS (GENERAL MOTORS)

Float Adjustment

1. A preliminary float adjustment can be made by inverting the primary fuel bowl and turning the adjust-

able needle seat until the top of the float is the specified distance from the top of the fuel bowl.

2. Repeat Step 1 for the secondary float.

Air Vent Valve Adjustment

1. Back off the idle speed screw until the throttle valves are fully closed.

4150—Air vent valve adjustment, GM

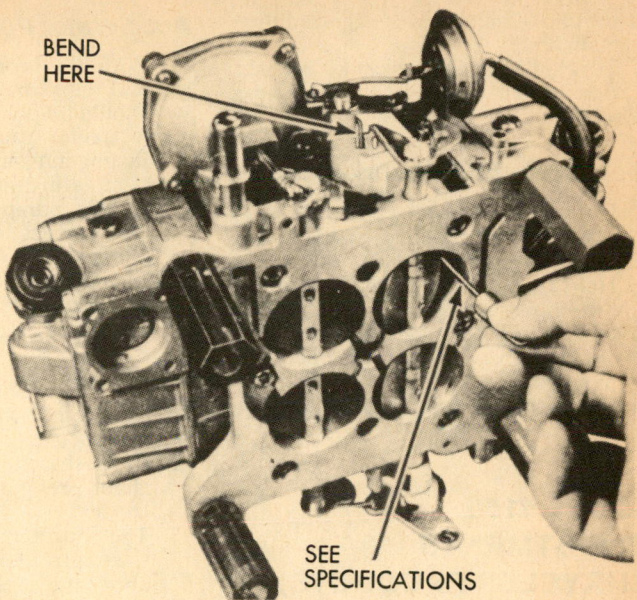

4150—Fast idle cam adjustment, GM

2. Check the clearance between the choke valve and the seat.
3. Bend the air valve rod to adjust.
4. Turn the idle screw in until contact is made with the throttle lever, then turn the screw in 1½ additional turns for preliminary idle speed adjustments.

Secondary Throttle Valve Stop Screw

1. Back off the adjustment screw until the throttle plates are fully closed.
2. Turn the adjustment screw until it just touches the throttle lever and then make ½ turn more to position the valves.

Fast Idle Cam Adjustment

1. Open the throttle slightly, close the choke plate, and position the fast idle lever against the top step of the fast idle cam.
2. Adjust the fast idle to give the 0.025 in. opening on the throttle plates on the idle transfer slot side of the carburetor.
3. Bend the fast idle lever to adjust.

Accelerator Pump Adjustment

1. Hold the throttle lever in the wide-open position with a rubber band; hold the pump lever fully pressed down; then measure the clearance between the spring adjusting nut and the arm of the pump lever.
2. Clearance should be 0.015 in.; adjust by turning the nut or screw as required while holding the opposite end.
3. After the adjustment is made, rotate the throttle lever to fully closed and partly open again. Any movement of the throttle lever should be noticed at the operating lever spring end, indicating the correct pump tip-in.

Choke Unloader Adjustment

1. Hold the throttle lever in the wide-open position with a rubber band.
2. Hold the choke valve toward the closed position against the unloader tang of the throttle shaft, then measure the opening between

4150—Accelerator Pump adjustment, GM

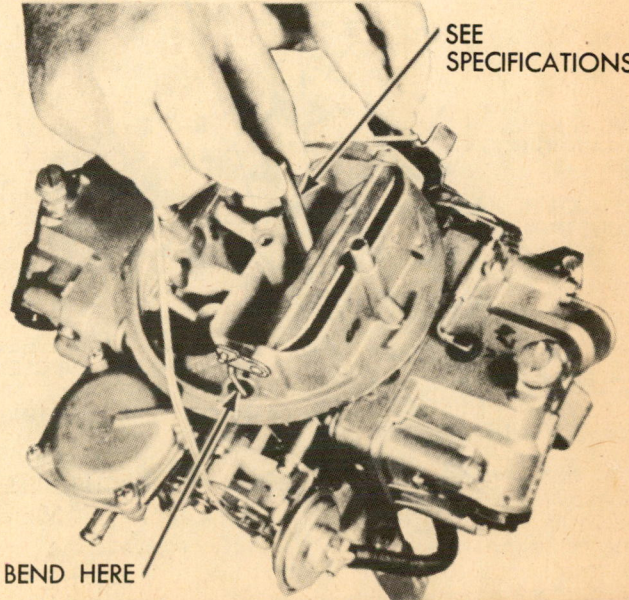

4150—Choke unloader adjustment, GM

the choke valve lower edge and the main body.

3. To adjust, bend the choke rod at the offset end. Recheck after adjusting.

Vacuum Break Adjustment

1. Hold the choke valve closed with a rubber band attached to the linkage.
2. Hold the vacuum break in against the stop.
3. Measure the distance between the choke valve lower edge and the main body.
4. Bend the vacuum break link to adjust.

MODEL 4160 ADJUSTMENTS (CHRYSLER PRODUCTS)

Bowl Vent Valve Adjustment

1. With the throttle valves at curb idle, it should be possible to insert a 0.015 in. gauge between the bowl vent valve plunger stem and the operating rod.
2. If an adjustment is necessary, bend the rod to change the arc of contact with the throttle lever until the correct clearance has been obtained.

Accelerator Pump Adjustment

1. With the throttle valves open wide and the pump lever held down, it should be possible to insert a 0.015 in. feeler gauge between the adjusting nut and the lever.
2. If an adjustment is necessary, adjust the pump override screw until the correct clearance has been obtained.
3. There must be no free movement of the pump lever when the throttle is at curb idle.

Choke Lever Adjustment

1. Open the throttle to the mid position.
2. Close the choke valve by exerting slight pressure on the choke control lever.
3. The top of the choke rod hole in the control lever should be $2^3/_4$ in. above the choke assembly with the carburetor on the engine. With the carburetor on the bench, the measurement should be $1^9/_{16}$ in. above the carburetor base.
4. To adjust, bend the choke shaft rod at the top bend.

CAUTION

Improper bending will cause binding of the rod. Check for free movement between the open and closed position.

Choke Unloader Adjustment (Wide Open Kick)

1. Adjust the choke control lever.
2. Hold the throttle valves in the wide-open position. Insert the specified drill between the upper edge of the choke valve and the inner wall of the air horn.
3. With a finger pressed against the choke control lever, a slight drag should be felt as the drill is being withdrawn. If an adjustment is to be made, bend the flat tang that contacts the bottom of the fast idle cam until the correct opening has been obtained.

Fast Idle Speed Adjustment

1. With the engine off and the transmission in Neutral, open the throttle slightly.
2. Close the choke valve until the fast idle screw tang can be positioned on the second highest step of the fast idle cam.
3. Start the engine and determine the stabilized speed. Bend the fast idle tang by use of a screwdriver placed in the tang slot to secure the specified speed.
4. Reposition the fast idle tang on the cam after each speed adjustment, to provide the correct throttle closing torque.

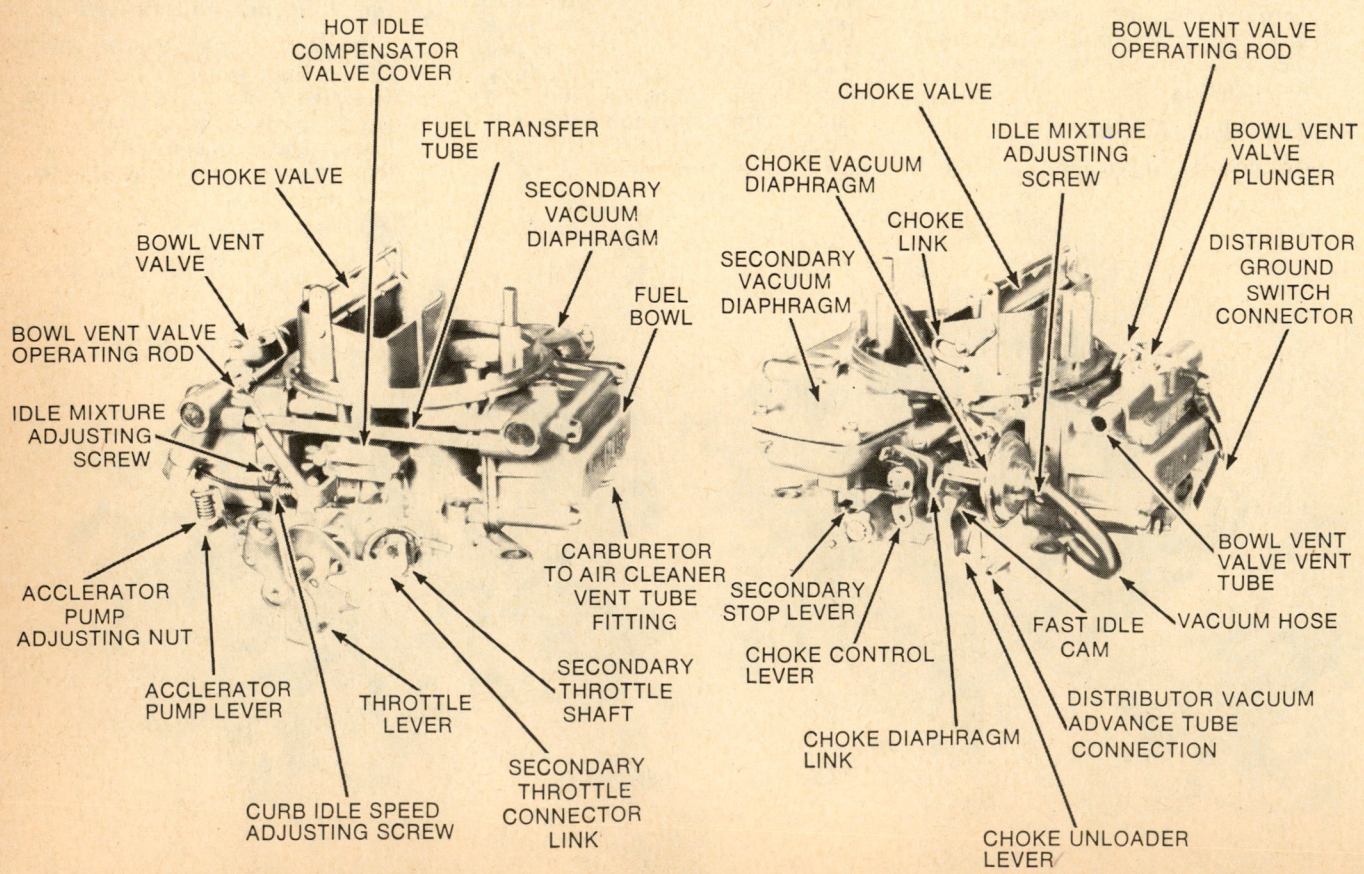

Carburetor assembly—Holley 4160

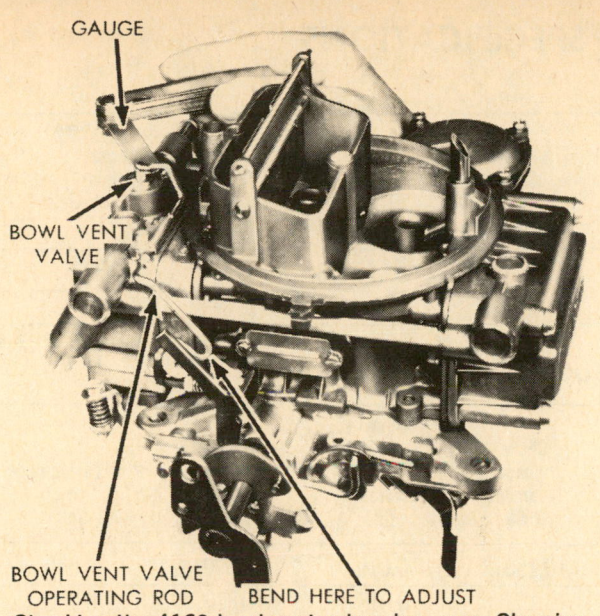

GAUGE

BOWL VENT VALVE

BOWL VENT VALVE OPERATING ROD

BEND HERE TO ADJUST

Checking the 4160 bowl vent valve clearance, Chrysler

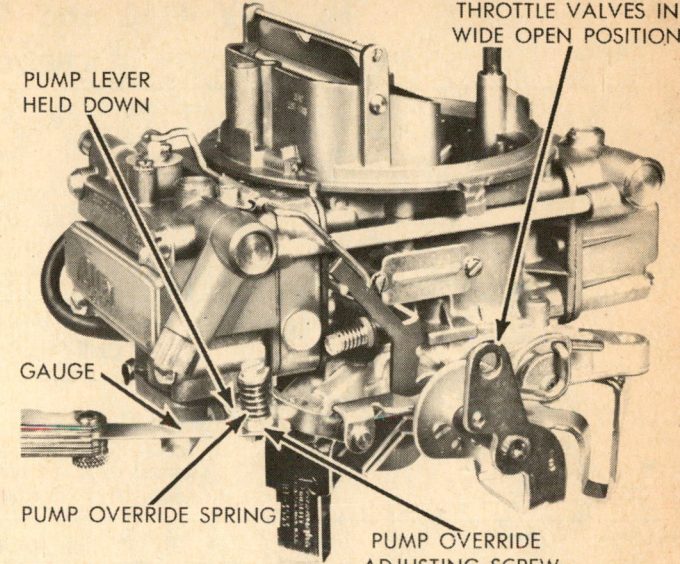

THROTTLE VALVES IN WIDE OPEN POSITION

PUMP LEVER HELD DOWN

GAUGE

PUMP OVERRIDE SPRING

PUMP OVERRIDE ADJUSTING SCREW

Checking 4160 accelerator pump lever clearance, Chrysler

CAUTION

Bend only in a direction perpendicular to the contact surface of the cam. Movement in any other direction will change the cam position adjustment described earlier.

Fast Idle Cam Position Adjustment

1. Adjust the choke control lever.
2. With the fast idle speed adjusting tang contacting the second highest speed step on the fast idle cam, move the choke valve toward the closed position with light pressure on the choke control lever.
3. Insert a 0.060 in. drill bit between the choke valve and the wall of the air horn. An adjustment will be necessary if a slight drag is not ob-

tained as the drill is being removed.
4. To adjust, bend the adjusting tang until the correct choke valve opening has been obtained.

Vacuum Kick Adjustment

1. Start the engine and position the fast idle tang to allow choke closure to the kick position.
2. Insert the specified drill between the choke valve and the wall of the air horn. Apply sufficient closing pressure on the lever to which the choke rod attaches to provide a minimum choke valve opening without distortion of the diaphragm link.

NOTE: *The cylindrical stem of the diaphragm will extend as an internal spring is compressed. This spring must be fully compressed for proper measurement of the vacuum link adjustment.*

3. An adjustment will be necessary if a slight drag is not obtained as the drill is being removed. Shorten or lengthen the diaphragm link to obtain the correct choke opening. Length changes should be made by carefully opening or closing the bend provided in the diaphragm link.

CAUTION

Do not apply twisting or bending force to the diaphragm.

---

4. With no vacuum applied to the diaphragm, the choke valve should move freely between the open and closed positions. If the movement is not free, examine the linkage for misalignment or interference caused by the bending operation. Repeat the adjustment if necessary to provide the proper link operation.

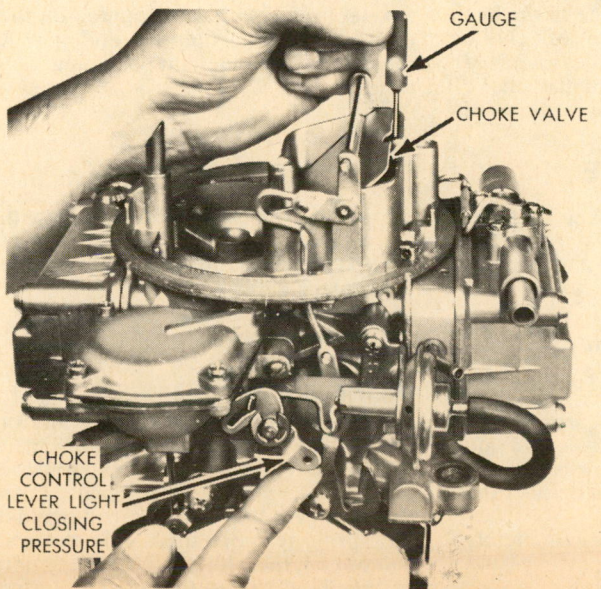

GAUGE

CHOKE VALVE

CHOKE CONTROL LEVER LIGHT CLOSING PRESSURE

4160 Choke unloader adjustment, Chrysler

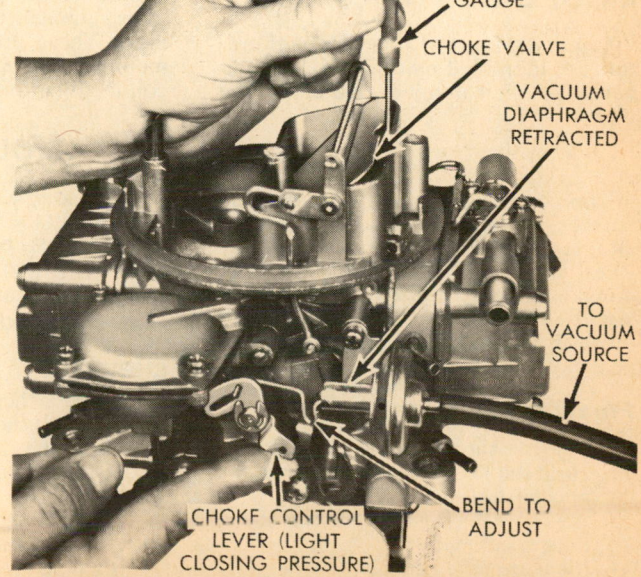

GAUGE

CHOKE VALVE

VACUUM DIAPHRAGM RETRACTED

TO VACUUM SOURCE

CHOKE CONTROL LEVER (LIGHT CLOSING PRESSURE)

BEND TO ADJUST

4160—Vacuum kick adjustment, Chrysler

HOLLEY 4150 and 4160 SPECIFICATIONS

CHEVROLET

Year	Carb. Part No. ①	Float Level (Dry) (in.)	Accelerator Pump Lever Adjustment (in.)	Choke Setting (in.)	Choke Unloader Clearance (in.)	Fast Idle On Car (rpm)	Choke Vacuum Break (in.)
1972	R6238-A	⑩	0.015	1.320⑪	0.350	2350	0.350
	R6239-A	⑩	0.015	1.320⑪	0.350	2350	0.350

CHRYSLER PRODUCTS

Year	Carburetor Part No. ①	Float Level (Dry) (in.)	Minimum Pump Clearance (in.)	Choke Setting	Choke Unloader Clearance (in.)	Bowl Vent Valve Clearance (in.)	Fast Idle Speed (rpm)	Vacuum Kick (in.)
1972	R-6160-A	⑫	0.015	Fixed	0.150	0.015	1600	0.080
	R-6252-A	⑫	0.015	Fixed	0.150	0.015	1800	0.140
	R-6253-A	⑫	0.015	Fixed	0.150	0.015	1600	0.080
	R-6254-A	⑫	0.015	Fixed	0.150	0.015	1800	0.140
	R-6255-A	⑫	0.015	Fixed	0.150	0.015	1600	0.080
	R-6256-A	⑫	0.015	Fixed	0.150	0.015	2000	0.140
	R-6257-A	⑫	0.015	Fixed	0.150	0.015	1800	0.080
	R-6290-A	⑫	0.015	Fixed	0.150	0.015	1500	0.080

① Located on tag attached to carburetor, or on the casting or choke plate
② Not used
③ Not used
④ Not used
⑤ Not used
⑥ Not used
⑦ Not used
⑧ Not used
⑨ Not used
⑩ Float centered in bowl
⑪ Bottom of throttle body to center of hole in operating lever
⑫ Primary 0.110 in., secondary 0.204 in.

ROCHESTER CARBURETORS

MODEL IDENTIFICATION

General Motors Rochester carburetors are identified by their model number. The first number indicates the number of barrels, while one of the last letters indicates the type of choke used. These are V for the manifold mounted choke coil, C for the choke coil mounted on the carburetor, and E for electric choke, also mounted on the carburetor. Model numbers ending in A indicate an altitude-compensating carburetor.

MODEL 1ME

This is a new Rochester Monojet carburetor, designed for use on the Chevette. It is also used on Chevrolet inline sixes, starting 1977. It is a single bore downdraft unit. Some models have a hot idle compensator. The 1ME has an integral automatic choke system with an electrically heated choke coil.

Float Level Adjustment

1. Remove the top of the carburetor.
2. Hold the float retaining pin in place and push down on the float arm at the outer end against the top of the float needle valve.
3. Measure the distance from the bump on the top of the float, at the end to the bowl gasket surface, without the gasket.
4. To adjust, bend the float arm at the point where it joins the float.

Metering Rod Adjustment

CHEVETTE

1. Remove the top of the carburetor.
2. Back out the idle stop solenoid and rotate the fast idle cam so that the fast idle screw does not contact the cam.
3. With the throttle valve completely closed, make sure the power piston is all the way up.
4. Insert the specified size gauge between the bowl gasket surface with no gasket and the lower surface of the metering rod holder, next to the metering rod.
5. To adjust, carefully bend the metering rod holder.

INLINE SIXES

1. Remove the top of the carburetor and the gasket.
2. Remove the metering rod. Hold the throttle valve wide open. Push down on the metering rod against spring tension, then slide the rod out of the slot in the holder and remove it from the main metering jet.

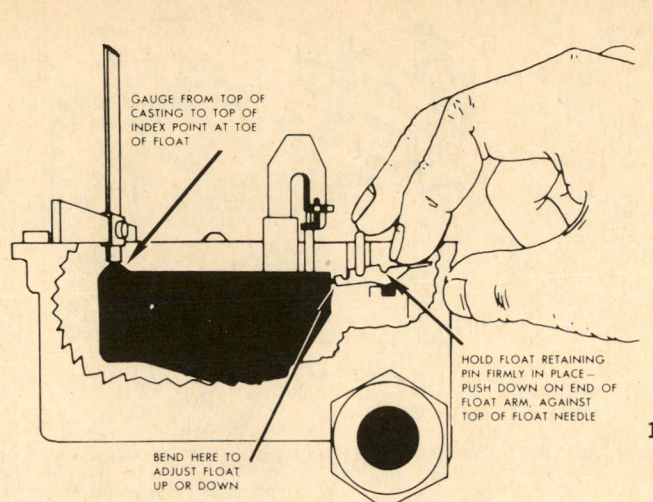

GAUGE FROM TOP OF CASTING TO TOP OF INDEX POINT AT TOE OF FLOAT

HOLD FLOAT RETAINING PIN FIRMLY IN PLACE — PUSH DOWN ON END OF FLOAT ARM, AGAINST TOP OF FLOAT NEEDLE

BEND HERE TO ADJUST FLOAT UP OR DOWN

1ME Float level adjustment (© Chevrolet Div., G.M. Corp.)

③ TURN FAST IDLE SCREW IN OR OUT TO OBTAIN SPECIFIED FAST IDLE R.P.M. — SEE DECAL

② PLACE FAST IDLE SCREW ON HIGHEST STEP OF FAST IDLE CAM

① ADJUST CURB IDLE SPEED — SEE DECAL

1ME Fast idle speed adjustment (© Chevrolet Div., G.M. Corp.)

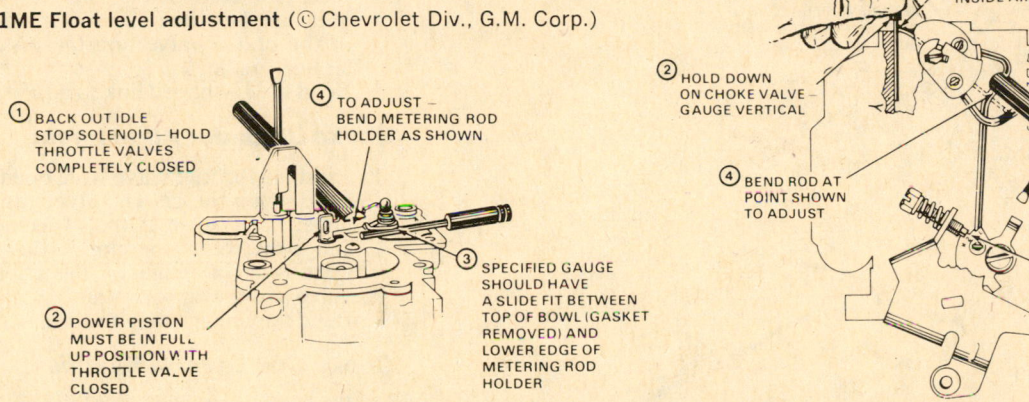

① BACK OUT IDLE STOP SOLENOID — HOLD THROTTLE VALVES COMPLETELY CLOSED

④ TO ADJUST — BEND METERING ROD HOLDER AS SHOWN

② POWER PISTON MUST BE IN FULL UP POSITION WITH THROTTLE VALVE CLOSED

③ SPECIFIED GAUGE SHOULD HAVE A SLIDE FIT BETWEEN TOP OF BOWL (GASKET REMOVED) AND LOWER EDGE OF METERING ROD HOLDER

1ME Metering rod adjustment (© Chevrolet Div., G.M. Corp.)

⑤ GAUGE BETWEEN UPPER EDGE OF CHOKE VALVE (AT CENTER) AND INSIDE AIRHORN WALL

② HOLD DOWN ON CHOKE VALVE — GAUGE VERTICAL

④ BEND ROD AT POINT SHOWN TO ADJUST

WITH FAST IDLE ADJUSTMENT MADE, FAST IDLE SCREW MUST BE HELD FIRMLY ON SECOND STEP OF FAST IDLE CAM AGAINST HIGHEST STEP

1ME Fast idle cam adjustment (© Chevrolet Div., G.M. Corp.)

3. Back out the idle stop solenoid and hold the throttle valve completely closed.
4. Hold the power piston down and swing the metering rod holder over the flat surface of the bowl casting next to the carburetor bore. The gauge should be a slide fit between the rod holder and the flat surface.
5. Adjust by carefully bending the metering rod holder.

Fast Idle Speed Adjustment

NOTE: *This adjustment is not possible on some California and high altitude carburetors. It should not be done on carburetors with an idle dashpot.*
1. The engine should be at normal temperature with the air cleaner in place. Disconnect and plug EGR valve vacuum line.
2. Make sure that the curb idle speed is as specified.
3. Place the fast idle screw or cam follower on the highest cam step with the engine running.
4. Adjust the fast idle speed screw to the correct fast idle speed. If there is no screw, adjust by bending the tang.

Fast Idle Cam Adjustment

1. Hold the fast idle speed screw on the second cam step against the shoulder of the high step.
2. Hold the choke valve closed with a finger.
3. Insert the specified gauge between the center upper (lower starting 1978) edge of the choke valve and the airhorn wall.

4. Bend the linkage rod at the upper angle to adjust.

Vacuum Break Adjustment

1976

1. Place the fast idle speed screw on the highest cam step.
2. Tape over the bleed hole in the diaphragm unit. Apply suction by mouth to seat the diaphragm.

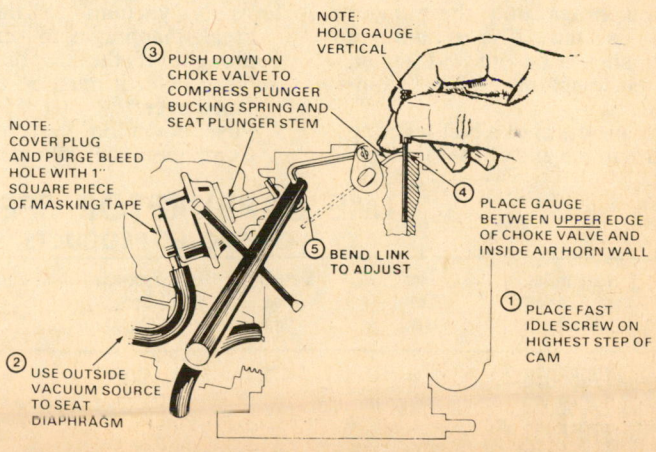

NOTE: HOLD GAUGE VERTICAL

③ PUSH DOWN ON CHOKE VALVE TO COMPRESS PLUNGER BUCKING SPRING AND SEAT PLUNGER STEM

NOTE: COVER PLUG AND PURGE BLEED HOLE WITH 1" SQUARE PIECE OF MASKING TAPE

④ PLACE GAUGE BETWEEN UPPER EDGE OF CHOKE VALVE AND INSIDE AIR HORN WALL

⑤ BEND LINK TO ADJUST

② USE OUTSIDE VACUUM SOURCE TO SEAT DIAPHRAGM

① PLACE FAST IDLE SCREW ON HIGHEST STEP OF CAM

1ME Vacuum break adjustment (© Chevrolet Div., G.M. Corp.)

Rochester Carburetors

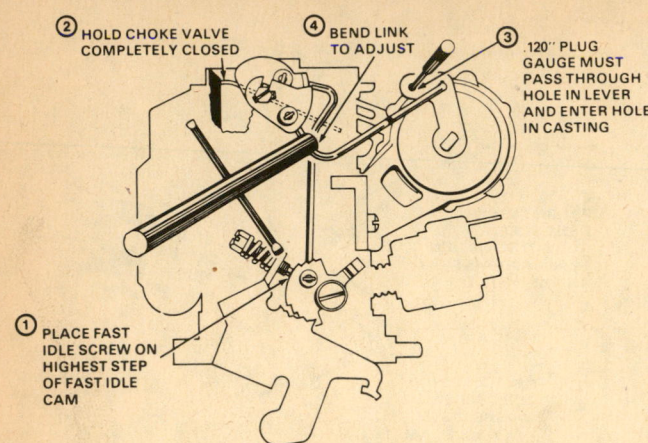

1ME Choke coil lever adjustment (© Chevrolet Div., G.M. Corp.)

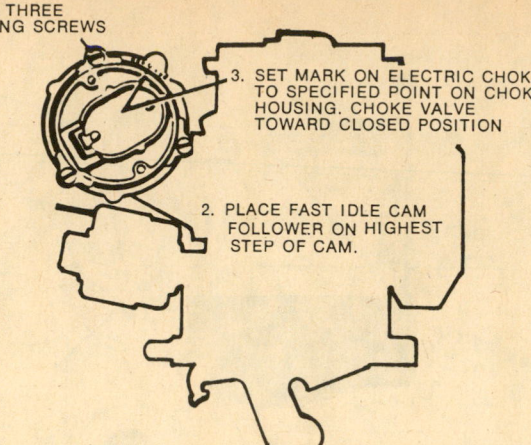

1ME Electric choke adjustment (© Chevrolet Div., G.M. Corp.)

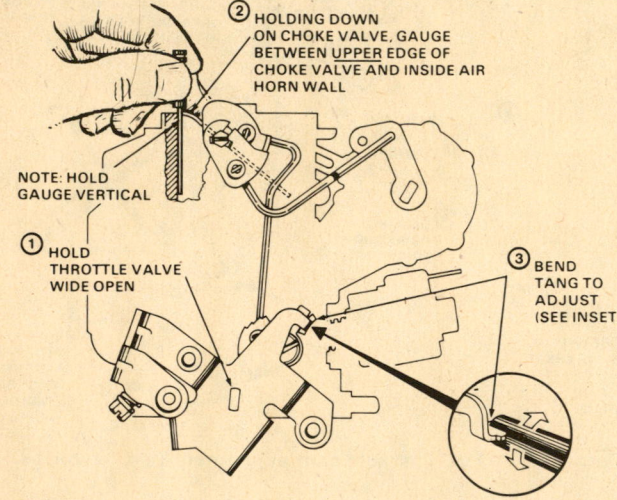

1ME Choke unloader adjustment (© Chevrolet Div., G.M. Corp.)

3. Push down on the choke valve with a finger.
4. Insert the gauge between the upper edge of the choke valve and the air-horn wall.
5. Bend the link to adjust.

1977
1. Place the fast idle screw on the high step of the cam.
2. Apply vacuum to the vacuum break diaphragm until the plunger is fully seated. The diaphragm plunger should be out and seated with the bucking spring compressed.
3. Push up on the choke coil lever so the rod is in the end of the slot.

4. Insert the specified drill bit between the upper center edge of the choke valve and the air horn wall.
5. Bend the rod to adjust.
6. Check the fast idle cam (choke rod) adjustment.

1978
1. Place the fast idle screw or cam follower on the high step of the cam.
2. Apply vacuum to the vacuum break diaphragm to seat the diaphragm. If the diaphragm has a bleed hole, it must be temporarily taped over.
3. Push down on the choke valve. Compress the plunger bucking spring and seat the plunger stem on models so equipped.
4. Measure between the lower edge of the choke valve and the inside air horn wall.
5. Bend the U-shaped link to adjust.

Choke Unloader Adjustment

1. Hold the throttle valve wide open.
2. Hold down the choke valve with a finger and insert the specified gauge between the upper (lower starting 1978) edge of the choke valve and the airhorn wall.
3. Bend the linkage tang to adjust.

Choke Coil Lever Adjustment

1. Place the fast idle speed screw or cam follower on the highest cam step.
2. Hold the choke valve closed.
3. Insert a 0.120 in. gauge through the hole in the arm on the choke housing and into the hole in the casting.
4. Bend the link to adjust.

Electric Choke Adjustment

1. Place the fast idle cam follower on the high step.
2. Loosen the three retaining screws and rotate the cover counterclockwise until the choke valve just closes.
3. Align the index mark on the cover with the specified housing mark.
4. Tighten the three screws.
NOTE: *Failure of the electric choke heater circuit will cause the oil pressure light to go on.*

1ME CARBURETOR SPECIFICATIONS
CHEVROLET PRODUCTS, CHEVETTE

Year	Carburetor Identification① Number	Float Level (in.)	Metering Rod (in.)	Fast Idle Speed (rpm)	Fast Idle Cam (in.)	Vacuum Break (in.)	Choke Unloader (in.)	Choke Setting (notches)
1976	17056036, 17056030, 17056031, 17056037	5/32	0.072	2000②	0.065	0.070	0.165	3 Rich

CHEVROLET PRODUCTS, CHEVETTE

Year	Carburetor Identification① Number	Float Level (in.)	Metering Rod (in.)	Fast Idle Speed (rpm)	Fast Idle Cam (in.)	Vacuum Break (in.)	Choke Unloader (in.)	Choke Setting (notches)
	17056032, 17056034, 17056033, 17056035	5/32	0.073	2000③	0.045	0.070	0.200	3 Rich
	17056330, 17056331	5/32	0.072	2000	0.065	0.070	0.165	3 Rich
	17056332, 17056333, 17056334	5/32	0.073	2000	0.045	0.070	0.200	3 Rich
	17056335	5/32	0.073	2000	0.045	0.120	0.200	3 Rich
1977	17057016	3/8	0.070	2000	0.095	0.125	0.325	1 Lean
	17057013, 17057015	3/8	0.070	2000	0.100	0.125	0.325	1 Rich
	17057018	3/8	0.070	2000	0.085	0.120	0.325	1 Rich
	17057014, 17057020	3/8	0.070	2000	0.085	0.120	0.120	2 Rich
	17057310, 17057312	3/8	0.070	1800	0.100	0.100	0.110	Index
	17057314, 17057318	3/8	0.070	1800	0.100	0.110	0.110	Index
	17057042, 17057044, 17047045, 17057332, 17057334, 17057335	5/32	0.080	2300	0.050	0.080	0.200	2 Rich
	17057030, 17057031, 17057032, 17057034, 17057035	5/32	0.080	2300	0.050	0.080	0.200	3 Rich
1978	17058013	3/8	0.080	2000	0.180	0.200	0.500	Index
	17058014	5/16	0.100	2100	0.180	0.200	0.500	Index
	17058020	5/16	0.100	2100	0.180	0.200	0.500	Index
	17058314	3/8	0.100	2000	0.190	0.245	0.400	Index
	17058031	5/32	0.080	2400	0.105	0.150	0.500	2 Rich
	17058032	5/32	0.080	2400	0.080	0.130	0.500	3 Rich
	17058033	5/32	0.080	2400	0.080	0.130	0.500	2 Rich
	17058034	5/32	0.080	2400	0.080	0.130	0.500	3 Rich
	17058035	5/32	0.080	2300	0.080	0.130	0.500	3 Rich
	17058036	5/32	0.080	2400	0.080	0.130	0.500	3 Rich
	17058037	5/32	0.080	2400	0.080	0.130	0.500	2 Rich
	17058038	5/32	0.080	2400	0.080	0.130	0.500	3 Rich
	17058042	5/32	0.080	2400	0.080	0.160	0.500	2 Rich
	17058044	5/32	0.080	2400	0.080	0.160	0.500	2 Rich
	17058045	5/32	0.080	2300	0.080	0.160	0.500	2 Rich
	17058332	5/32	0.080	2400	0.080	0.160	0.500	2 Rich
	17058334	5/32	0.080	2400	0.080	0.160	0.500	2 Rich
	17058335	5/32	0.080	2300	0.080	0.160	0.500	2 Rich

① Stamped on float bowl, next to fuel inlet nut ③ 2200 rpm for the last two numbers

② 2200 rpm for the first two numbers

Rochester Carburetors

MODEL MV, 1 MV

The model MV carburetor is a single bore, down-draft carburetor with an aluminum throttle body, automatic choke, internally balanced venting, and a hot idle compensating system for cars equipped with automatic transmissions. Newer models are also equipped with Combination Emission Control valves (C.E.C.) and an Exhaust Gas Recirculation (EGR) system. An electrically operated idle stop solenoid replaces the idle stop screw of older models.

The MV carburetor is used on General Motors inline four and six cylinder cars through 1976.

Fast Idle Speed Adjustment

NOTE: *The fast idle adjustment must be made with the transmission in Neutral.*

1. Disconnect and plug the distributor vacuum line on 1976 models. Position the fast idle lever on the high step of the fast idle cam.

2. Be sure that the choke is properly adjusted and in the wide open position with the engine warm.
3. Bend the fast idle lever until the specified speed is obtained.

Choke Rod (fast idle cam) Adjustment

NOTE: *Adjust the fast idle before making choke rod adjustments.*

1. Place the fast idle cam follower on the second step of the fast idle cam and hold it firmly against the rise to the high step.
2. Rotate the choke valve in the direction of a closed choke by applying force to the choke coil lever.
3. Bend the choke rod to give the specified opening between the lower edge (upper edge for 1976) of the choke valve and the inside air horn wall.

NOTE: *Measurement must be made at the center of the choke valve.*

Choke Vacuum Break Adjustment

The adjustment of the vacuum break diaphragm unit insures correct choke valve opening after engine starting.

1. Remove the air cleaner on vehicles with Therm AC air cleaner; plug the sensor's vacuum take off port.
2. Using an external vacuum source, apply vacuum to the vacuum break diaphragm until the plunger is fully seated.
3. When the plunger is seated, push the choke valve toward the closed position.
4. Holding the choke valve in this position, place the specified gauge between the lower edge (upper edge for 1976) of the choke valve and the air horn wall.
5. If the measurement is not correct, bend the vacuum break rod.

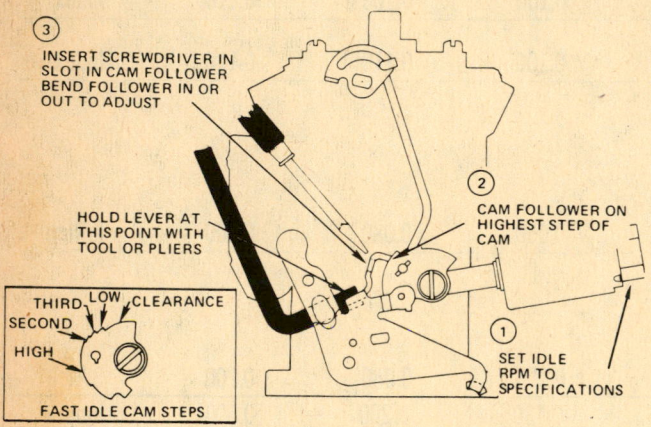

Fast Idle Adjustment
(© Chevrolet Div., G.M. Corp)

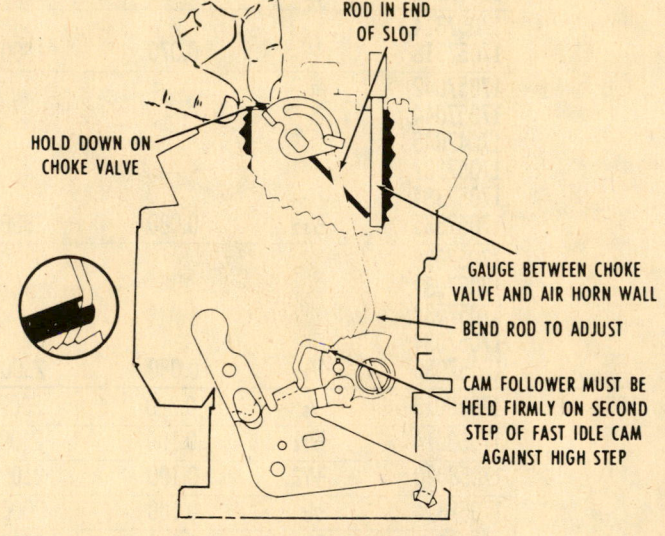

Fast Idle Cam Adjustment through 1975
(© Chevrolet Div., G.M. Corp)

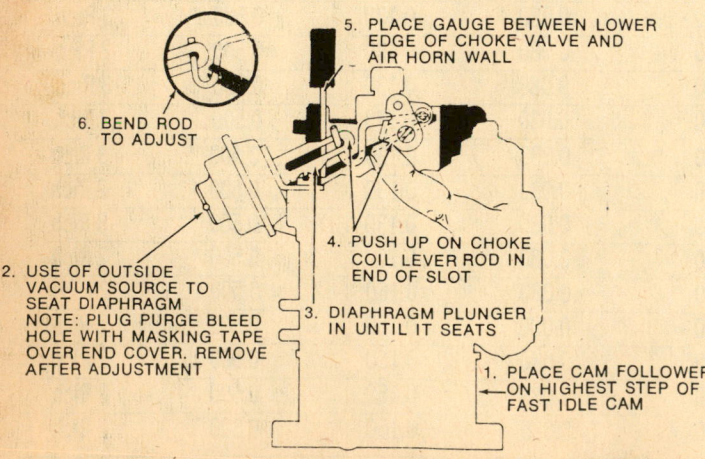

Primary vacuum break adjustment, beginning 1975
(© Chevrolet Div., G.M. Corp.)

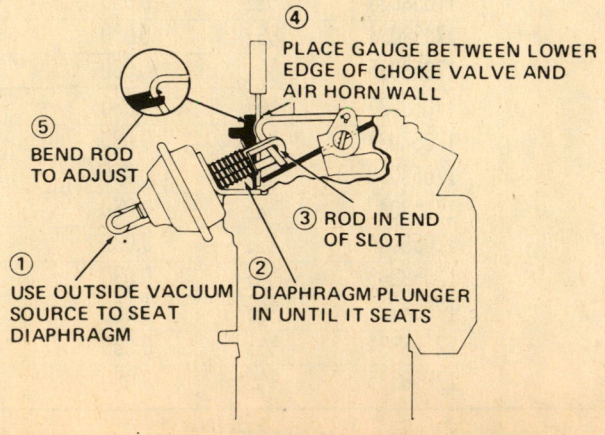

Vacuum Break Adjustment through 1975
(© Chevrolet Div., G.M. Corp)

Choke Auxiliary Vacuum Break Adjustment (beginning 1975)

This adjustment is required in addition to the preceding vacuum break adjustment, beginning 1975.

1. Using an external source of vacuum, apply vacuum to the auxiliary vacuum break diaphram until the plunger is seated fully.
2. Place the cam follower on the highest step of the fast idle cam.
3. With the diaphragm seated, insert the specified gauge between the upper edge of the choke valve and the inner air horn wall.
4. To adjust the clearance, bend the link between the vacuum break and the choke lever.

NOTE: *The auxiliary vacuum break diaphragm is on the same side of the carburetor as the throttle stop solenoid.*

Choke Unloader Adjustment

1. Apply pressure to the choke valve and hold it in the closed position.
2. Open the throttle valve to the wide open position.
3. Check the dimension between the lower edge (upper edge for 1976) of the choke plate and the air horn wall; if adjustment is needed, bend the unloader tang on the throttle lever.

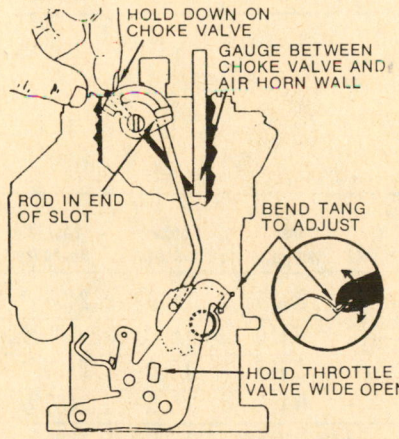

Adjusting Choke Unloader
(© Chevrolet Div., G.M. Corp)

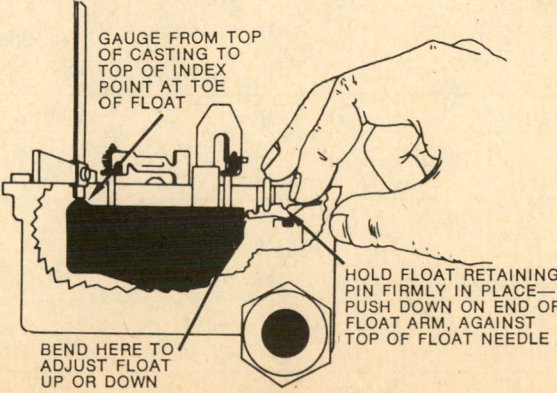

HOLD DOWN ON CHOKE VALVE
GAUGE BETWEEN CHOKE VALVE AND AIR HORN WALL
ROD IN END OF SLOT
BEND TANG TO ADJUST
HOLD THROTTLE VALVE WIDE OPEN

GAUGE FROM TOP OF CASTING TO TOP OF INDEX POINT AT TOE OF FLOAT
HOLD FLOAT RETAINING PIN FIRMLY IN PLACE—PUSH DOWN ON END OF FLOAT ARM, AGAINST TOP OF FLOAT NEEDLE
BEND HERE TO ADJUST FLOAT UP OR DOWN

Float Level
(© Pontiac Div., G.M. Corp)

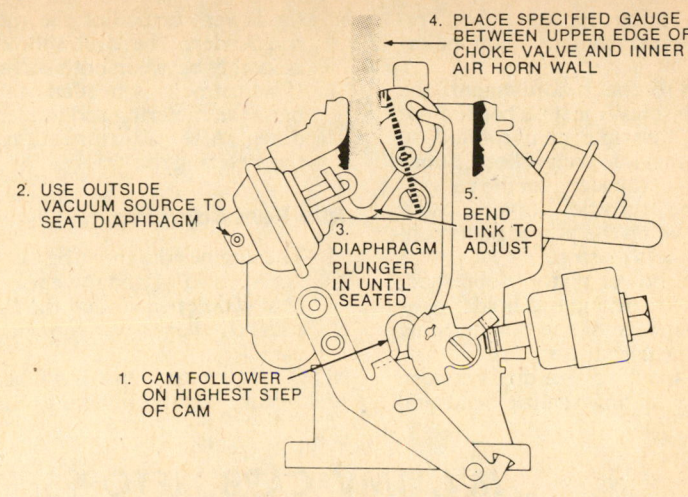

4. PLACE SPECIFIED GAUGE BETWEEN UPPER EDGE OF CHOKE VALVE AND INNER AIR HORN WALL
2. USE OUTSIDE VACUUM SOURCE TO SEAT DIAPHRAGM
3. DIAPHRAGM PLUNGER IN UNTIL SEATED
5. BEND LINK TO ADJUST
1. CAM FOLLOWER ON HIGHEST STEP OF CAM

Auxiliary vacuum break adjustment, beginning 1975

(© Chevrolet Div., G.M. Corp.)

Choke Coil Rod Adjustment

1. Disconnect the thermostatic coil rod from the upper choke lever and hold the choke valve closed.

BOTTOM OF ROD SHOULD BE EVEN WITH TOP OF LEVER
PULL UP ON ROD TO END OF TRAVEL
CHOKE VALVE COMPLETELY CLOSED
BEND ROD TO ADJUST

Choke coil rod adjustment
(© Chevrolet Div., G.M. Corp.)

2. Push down on the coil rod to the end of its travel.
3. The top of the rod should be even with the bottom hole in the choke lever.
4. To make adjustments, bend the rod.

Float Adjustment

1. Hold the float retainer in place and the float arm against the top of the float needle by pushing down on the float arm at the outer end toward the float bowl casting.
2. Using an adjustable T scale, measure the distance from the toe of the float to the float bowl gasket surface.

NOTE: *The float bowl gasket should be removed and the gauge held on the index point on the float for accurate measurement.*

3. Adjust the float level by bending the float arm up or down at the float arm junction.

Metering Rod Adjustment

1. Hold the throttle valve wide open and push down on the metering rod

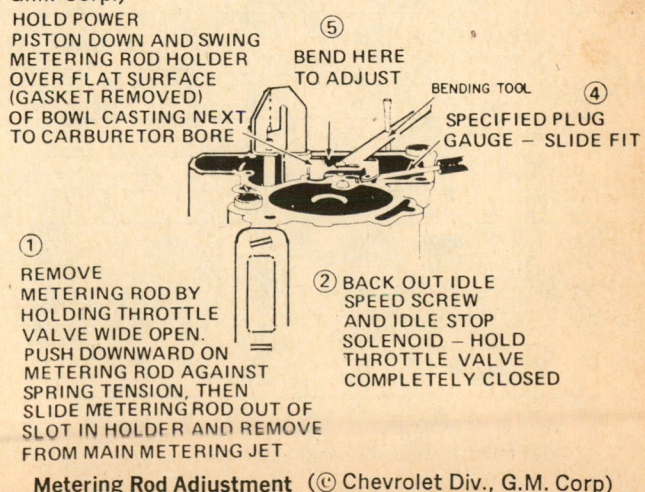

HOLD POWER PISTON DOWN AND SWING METERING ROD HOLDER OVER FLAT SURFACE (GASKET REMOVED) OF BOWL CASTING NEXT TO CARBURETOR BORE
⑤ BEND HERE TO ADJUST
BENDING TOOL
④ SPECIFIED PLUG GAUGE – SLIDE FIT
① REMOVE METERING ROD BY HOLDING THROTTLE VALVE WIDE OPEN. PUSH DOWNWARD ON METERING ROD AGAINST SPRING TENSION, THEN SLIDE METERING ROD OUT OF SLOT IN HOLDER AND REMOVE FROM MAIN METERING JET
② BACK OUT IDLE SPEED SCREW AND IDLE STOP SOLENOID – HOLD THROTTLE VALVE COMPLETELY CLOSED

Metering Rod Adjustment (© Chevrolet Div., G.M. Corp)

against spring tension, then remove the rod from the main metering jet.

2. In order to check adjustment, the slow idle screw must be backed out and the fast idle cam rotated so that the fast idle cam follower does not contact the steps on the cam.

3. With the throttle valve closed, push down on the power piston until it contacts its stop.

4. With the power piston depressed, swing the metering rod holder over the flat surface of the bowl casting next to the carburetor bore.

5. Insert a specified size drill between the bowl casting sealing bead and

the lower surface of the metering rod holder. The drill should slide smoothly between both surfaces.

6. If adjustment is needed, carefully bend the metering rod holder up or down. After adjustment, reinstall the metering rod.

Idle Vent Adjustment

1. The engine idle must be set at the specified RPM and the choke valve held wide open so that the fast idle cam follower is not contacting the cam.

NOTE: *If the carburetor is off the car, a preliminary idle setting can be made by*

turning the idle speed screw in 1½ turns from the closed throttle valve position.

2. With the throttle stop screw held against the idle stop screw, the idle vent valve should be open to specification. To check, a drill of specified size may be inserted between the top of the air horn casting and the bottom surface of the valve.

3. If adjustment is necessary, turn the slotted vent valve head with a screwdriver. Turning the head clockwise increases the clearance.

NOTE: *On models equipped with an idle stop solenoid, the solenoid must be activated when checking and adjusting the valve.*

MV, 1MV CARBURETOR SPECIFICATIONS

BUICK

Year	Carburetor Identification①	Float Level (in.)	Metering Rod (in.)	Pump Rod	Idle Vent (in.)	Vacuum Break (in.)	Auxiliary Vacuum Break (in.)	Fast Idle Off Car (in.)	Choke Rod (in.)	Choke Unloader (in.)	Fast Idle Speed (rpm)
1974	Automatic	¼	0.080	——	——	0.300	——	——	0.245	0.500	1800②
	Manual	¼	0.080	——	——	0.350	——	——	0.275	0.500	1800②
1975	7045012	¹¹/₃₂	0.080	——	——	0.200	0.215	——	0.160	0.275	1700②
	7045013	¹¹/₃₂	0.080	——	——	0.350	0.312	——	0.275	0.275	1800②
	7045314	¹¹/₃₂	0.080	——	——	0.275	0.312	——	0.230	0.275	1700②

① The Carburetor identification number is stamped on the float bowl, next to the fuel inlet nut.

② In Neutral or Park

CHEVROLET

Year	Carburetor Identification①	Float Level (in.)	Metering Rod (in.)	Pump Rod	Idle Vent (in.)	Vacuum Break (in.)	Auxiliary Vacuum Break (in.)	Fast Idle Off Car (in.)	Choke Rod (in.)	Choke Unloader (in.)	Fast Idle Speed (rpm)
1972	7042014	¼	0.080	——	——	0.190	——	——	0.125	0.500	2400②
	7042017	¼	0.078	——	——	0.225	——	——	0.150	0.500	2400②
	7042984	¼	0.078	——	——	0.190	——	——	0.125	0.500	2400②
	7042987	¼	0.076	——	——	0.225	——	——	0.150	0.500	2400②
1973	7043014	¼	0.080	——	——	0.300	——	——	0.245	0.500	1800②
	7043017	¼	0.080	——	——	0.350	——	——	0.275	0.500	1800②
1974	7044014	³/₁₀	0.079	——	——	0.275	——	——	0.230	0.500	1800②③
	7044017	³/₁₀	0.072	——	——	0.350	——	——	0.275	0.500	1800②③
	7044314	³/₁₀	0.073	——	——	0.300	——	——	0.245	0.500	1800②③
1975	7045013	¹¹/₃₂	0.080	——	——	0.200	0.215	——	0.160	0.215	1800④
	7045012	¹¹/₃₂	0.080	——	——	0.350	0.312	——	0.275	0.275	1800④
	7045314	¹¹/₃₂	0.080	——	——	0.275	0.312	——	0.230	0.275	1800④
1976	17056012	¹¹/₃₂	0.084	——	——	0.140	0.265	——	0.100	0.260	2200⑤
	17066013	¹¹/₃₂	0.082	——	——	0.140	0.325	——	0.140	0.260	2100
	17056016	¹¹/₃₂	0.080	——	——	0.140	WFO	——	0.115	0.260	2200⑤
	17056018	¹¹/₃₂	0.084	——	——	0.140	0.265	——	0.100	0.260	2200⑤
	17056314	¹¹/₃₂	0.083	——	——	0.150	0.325	——	0.135	0.260	1700

① The carburetor identification number is stamped on the float bowl, next to the fuel inlet nut.

② High step of cam.

③ Without vacuum advance.

④ 1700 rpm with automatic transmission in neutral.

⑤ 2100 rpm with integral intake manifold.

CHEVROLET VEGA, MONZA

Year	Carburetor Identification①	Float Level (in.)	Metering Rod (in.)	Pump Rod (in.)	Vacuum Break (in.)	Auxiliary Vacuum Break (in.)	Fast Idle Off Car (in.)	Choke Rod (in.)	Choke Unloader (in.)	Fast Idle Speed (rpm)
1972	Manual	1/8	——	——	0.200	——	0.110	0.130	0.375	2400②
	Automatic	1/16	——	——	0.120	——	0.110	0.070	0.375	2800②
1973	Manual	0.06	——	——	0.140	——	——	0.110	0.375	2000③
	Automatic	0.06	——	——	0.120	——	——	0.085	0.375	2200③
1974	Manual	0.06	——	——	0.130	——	——	0.080	0.375	2000③
	Automatic	0.06	——	——	0.130	——	——	0.080	0.375	2200③
1975	Manual	1/8	——	——	0.100	0.450	——	0.080	0.375	2000
	Automatic	1/8	——	——	0.100	0.450	——	0.080	0.375	2000
1976	Manual	1/8	——	——	0.060	0.450	——	0.045	0.215	1200
	Automatic	1/8	——	——	0.060	0.450	——	0.045	0.215	750

① The carburetor identification number is stamped on the float bowl, next to the fuel inlet nut.

② TCS disconnected for full vacuum advance.
③ No vacuum to distributor.

OLDSMOBILE

Year	Carburetor Identification①	Float Level (in.)	Metering Rod (in.)	Pump Rod	Idle Vent (in.)	Vacuum Break (in.)	Auxiliary Vacuum Break (in.)	Fast Idle Off Car (in.)	Choke Rod (in.)	Choke Unloader (in.)	Fast Idle Speed (rpm)
1973-74	Manual	1/4	0.080	——	——	0.350	——	——	0.275	0.500	②
	Automatic	1/4	0.080	——	——	0.300	——	——	0.245	0.500	②
1975	Manual	11/32	0.080	——	——	0.350	0.312	——	0.275	0.275	1800②
	Automatic	11/32	0.080	——	——	0.200	0.215	——	0.160	0.275	1800②
1976	4-140 Man.	1/8	——	——	——	0.055	0.450	——	0.045	0.215	——
	4-140 Auto.	1/8	——	——	——	0.060	0.450	——	0.045	0.215	——
	6-250 Man.	11/32	——	——	——	0.165	0.320	——	0.140	0.265	——
	6-250 Auto.	11/32	——	——	——	0.140	0.265	——	0.100	0.265	——
	6-250 Calif.	11/32	——	——	——	0.150	0.260	——	0.135	0.265	——

① The carburetor identification number is stamped on the float bowl, next to the fuel inlet nut.

② Preset
③ Low step of cam.

PONTIAC

Year	Carburetor Identification①	Float Level (in.)	Metering Rod (in.)	Pump Rod	Idle Vent (in.)	Vacuum Break (in.)	Auxiliary Vacuum Break (in.)	Fast Idle Off Car (in.)	Choke Rod (in.)	Choke Unloader (in.)	Fast Idle Speed (rpm)
1972	7042014	1/4	0.080	——	——	0.200	——	——	0.160	0.500	2400②
	7042017	1/4	0.080	——	——	0.230	——	——	0.180	0.500	2400②
	7042984	1/4	0.080	——	——	0.200	——	——	0.160	0.500	2400②
	7042987	1/4	0.080	——	——	0.230	——	——	0.180	0.500	2400②
1973	7043014	1/4	0.080	——	——	0.300	——	——	0.245	0.500	2400②
	7043017	3/4	0.080	——	——	0.350	——	——	0.275	0.500	2400②
1974	7044041	0.354	0.079	——	——	0.275	——	——	0.230	0.500	1800②
	7044017	0.354	0.072	——	——	0.350	——	——	0.275	0.500	1800②
	7044314	0.354	0.073	——	——	0.300	——	——	0.245	0.500	1800②
1975	7045012	11/32	0.080	——	——	0.200	0.215	——	0.160	0.275	1800②
	7045013	11/32	0.080	——	——	0.350	0.312	——	0.275	0.275	1800②
	7045014	11/32	0.080	——	——	0.257	0.312	——	0.230	0.275	1800②
	Astre Man.	1/8	——	——	——	0.130	——	——	0.080	0.375	2000③
	Astre Auto.	1/8	——	——	——	0.130	——	——	0.080	0.375	2000③

Rochester Carburetors

PONTIAC

Year	Carburetor Identification①	Float Level (in.)	Metering Rod (in.)	Pump Rod	Idle Vent (in.)	Vacuum Break (in.)	Auxiliary Vacuum Break (in.)	Fast Idle Off Car (in.)	Choke Rod (in.)	Choke Unloader (in.)	Fast Idle Speed (rpm)
1976	4-140 Man.	⅛	——	——	——	0.055	0.450	——	0.045	0.215	——
	4-140 Auto.	⅛	——	——	——	0.060	0.450	——	0.045	0.215	——
	6-250 Man.	¹¹⁄₃₂	——	——	——	0.165	0.320	——	0.140	0.265	——
	6-250 Auto	¹¹⁄₃₂	——	——	——	0.140	0.265	——	0.100	0.265	——
	6-250 Calif.	¹¹⁄₃₂	——	——	——	0.150	0.260	——	0.135	0.265	——

① The carburetor identification number is stamped on the float bowl, next to the fuel inlet nut.

② High step of cam.

③ No vacuum to distributor.

MODEL 2GC, 2GV, 2GE

This two barrel carburetor is used on General Motors cars. The newer carburetors use a plastic float and a longer needle and seat to provide better fuel control. See the beginning of the Rochester section for an explanation of the type designations.

Fast Idle Speed Adjustment

1. Except on some Oldsmobile cars, the fast idle is set automatically

when the curb idle and mixture is set.
2. Some Oldsmobile 2GC carburetors have a screw to adjust the fast idle.

Choke Rod (fast idle cam)

1. Turn in the idle cam stop screw, if any, until it just contacts the bottom step of the fast idle cam. Then turn the screw one full turn.
2. Place the idle screw on the second

step of the fast idle cam against the shoulder of the high step.
3. Hold the choke valve closed and check the clearance between the upper edge of the choke valve and the air horn wall.
4. Adjust the clearance by bending the tang on the choke lever.

2GC, 2GE Intermediate Choke Rod (Choke Coil Lever) Adjustment, Beginning 1975

1. Remove the thermostatic cover coil, gasket, and inside baffle plate assembly.
2. Place the idle speed screw on the highest step of the fast idle cam.
3. Close the choke valve by pushing up on the intermediate choke lever.
4. The edge of the coil lever inside the choke housing must line up with the edge of a 0.120 in. drill bit inserted into the hole inside the choke housing.
5. Adjust by bending the intermediate choke rod at the first bend from the bottom of the rod.

Vacuum Break Adjustment

1. Remove the air cleaner. Vehicles with a Therm AC air cleaner should have the sensor's vacuum take-off port plugged.
2. Using an external vacuum source, apply vacuum to the vacuum break

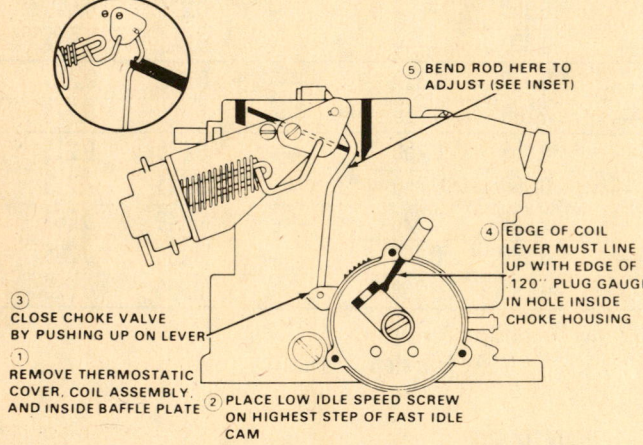

Intermediate choke rod adjustment, beginning 1975

(© Chevrolet Div., G.M. Corp.)

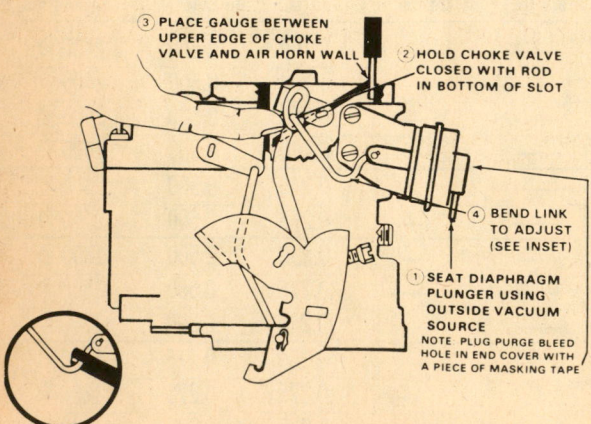

Primary vacuum break adjustment, beginning 1975

(© Buick Div., G.M. Corp.)

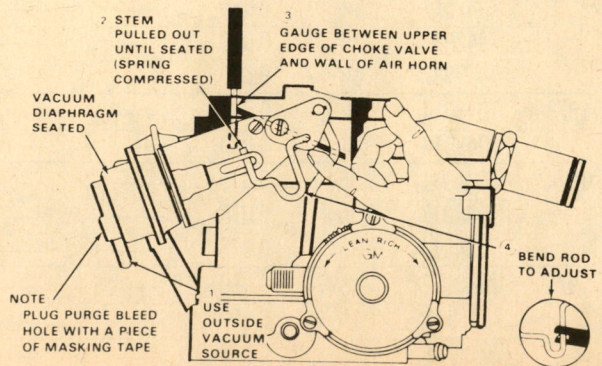

Auxiliary vacuum break adjustment, beginning 1975

(© Buick Div., G.M. Corp.)

diaphragm until the plunger is fully seated. If the diaphragm has a bleed hole, tape it over.

3. When the plunger is seated, push the choke valve toward the closed position. For 1975-76 models, place the idle speed screw on the high step of the fast idle cam.
4. Holding the choke valve in the closed position, place the specified size gauge between the upper (lower, through 1974) edge of the choke valve and the air horn wall.
5. If the measurement is not correct, bend the vacuum break rod.

Auxiliary Vacuum Break, Beginning 1975

1. Seat the auxiliary vacuum diaphragm by applying an outside source of vacuum. Tape over the vacuum bleed hole so the vacuum will not bleed down.
2. Place the idle speed screw on the high step of the fast idle cam.
3. Hold the choke toward the closed choke position.
4. Measure the distance between the upper edge of the choke valve and the air horn wall.
5. Adjust by bending the auxiliary vacuum break rod at the bottom of the U-shaped bend. Remove the piece of tape from the auxiliary vacuum diaphragm.

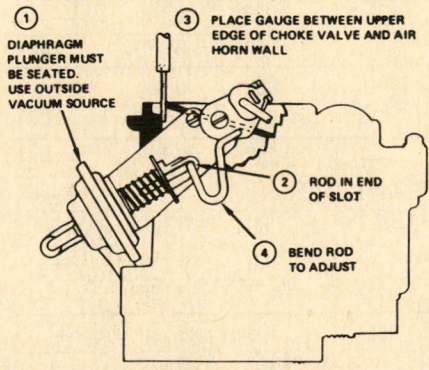

Vacuum Break Adjustment
(© Chevrolet Div., G.M. Corp)

Choke Unloader Adjustment

1. Hold the throttle valves wide open.
2. Close the choke valve.
3. Bend the unloader tang to obtain the proper clearance between the upper edge of the choke valve and air horn wall.

2GV Choke Coil Rod Adjustment

1. Hold the choke valve completely open.
2. Disconnect the coil rod from the upper lever and push down on the rod to the end of its travel.
3. When the rod is all the way down, the top of the rod should line up with the bottom of the slotted hole on the choke valve linkage.
4. Adjust by bending the lever.

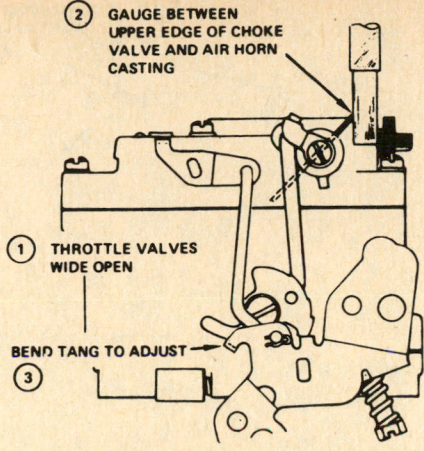

Choke Unloader Adjustment
(© Chevrolet Div., G.M. Corp)

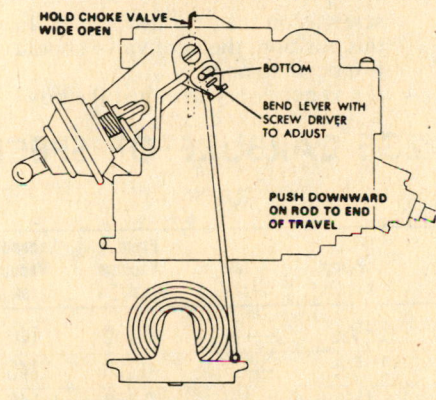

Choke Coil Rod Adjustment
(© Chevrolet Div., G.M. Corp)

Float Level

With the air horn assembly upside down, measure the distance from the air horn gasket to the lip at the toe of the float. Bend the float arm to adjust to specifications.

Float Drop

Holding the air horn assembly upright, measure the distance from the gasket to the lip or notch at the toe of the float. If correction is necessary, bend the float tang at the rear, next to the needle and seat.

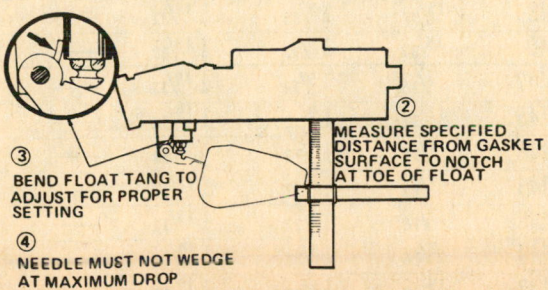

Float Drop, Plastic Float

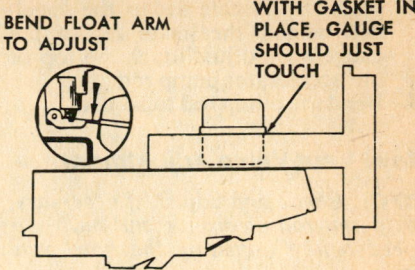

Float Level Measurement, Metal Float

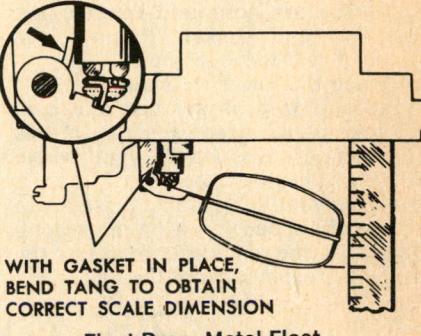

Float Drop, Metal Float

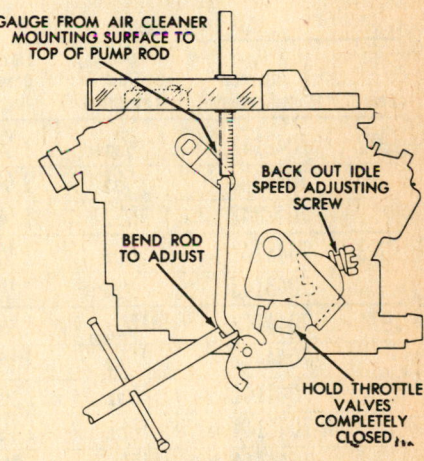

Accelerator Pump Rod
(© Dodge Div., Chrysler Corp)

Accelerator Pump Rod

1. Back out the idle speed screw and completely close the throttle valves.
2. Place the pump gauge across the air horn ring.

Rochester Carburetors

3. With the T-scale set to the specified height, the lower leg of the gauge should just touch the top of the accelerator pump rod.
4. Bend the pump rod to adjust.

Bowl Vent Valve Adjustment

NOTE: *Check and adjust, if necessary, the pump rod clearance and curb idle speed before adjusting the bowl vent valve.*

1. Remove the two bowl vent valve cover attaching screws in the top of the air horn and remove the cover and gasket. Remove the bowl vent valve spring.
2. Place the idle speed screw on the second step of the fast idle cam next to the highest step. In this position, the bowl vent valve should just be closed.
3. If the vent valve is just closed with the idle speed screw on the second step of the fast idle cam, rotate the fast idle cam so that the idle speed

screw is on the next lower step. In this position, the vent valve should just begin to open.
4. If it is necessary to adjust the bowl

vent valve, turn the adjustment screw in the top of the valve, to obtain the conditions mentioned in Steps 2 and 3.

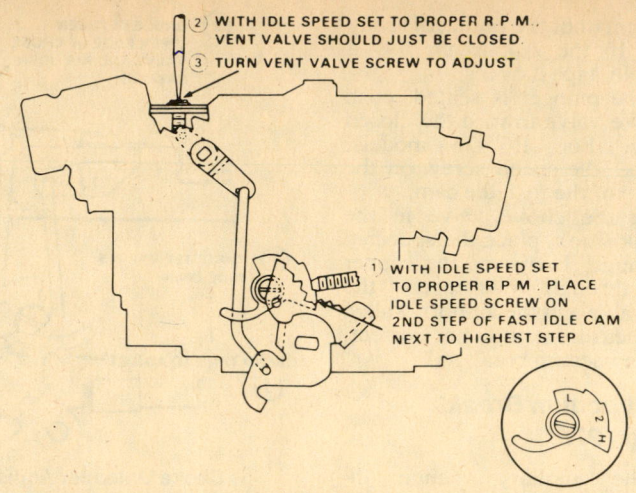

② WITH IDLE SPEED SET TO PROPER R P M. VENT VALVE SHOULD JUST BE CLOSED.
③ TURN VENT VALVE SCREW TO ADJUST
① WITH IDLE SPEED SET TO PROPER R P M. PLACE IDLE SPEED SCREW ON 2ND STEP OF FAST IDLE CAM NEXT TO HIGHEST STEP

Bowl vent valve adjustment (© Buick Div., G.M. Corp.)

2GC, 2GV, 2GE CARBURETOR SPECIFICATIONS

BUICK

Year	Carburetor Identification①	Float Level (in.)	Float Drop (in.)	Pump Rod (in.)	Idle Vent (in.)	Primary Vacuum Break (in.)	Secondary Vacuum Break (in.)	Automatic Choke (notches)	Choke Rod (in.)	Choke Unloader (in.)	Fast Idle Speed (rpm)
1972	7042142	15/32	1 7/8	1 15/32	——	0.150	0.140	——	0.080	0.180	——
	7042143	15/32	1 7/8	1 15/32	——	0.160	0.140	——	0.080	0.180	——
	7042842	15/32	1 7/8	1 15/32	——	0.150	0.140	——	0.080	0.180	——
1973	7043142	15/32	1 9/32	1 15/32	——	0.140	0.120	——	0.080	0.180	——
	7043143	15/32	1 9/32	1 15/32	——	0.150	0.120	——	0.080	0.200	——
1974	7044142	15/32	1 9/32	1 15/32	——	0.140	0.120	——	0.080	0.180	——
	7044442	15/32	1 9/32	1 15/32	——	0.140	0.120	——	0.080	0.180	——
	7044141	15/32	1 9/32	1 15/32	——	0.160	0.120	——	0.080	0.180	——
	7044144	15/32	1 9/32	1 15/32	——	0.140	0.120	——	0.080	0.180	——
	7044444	15/32	1 9/32	1 15/32	——	0.140	0.120	——	0.080	0.180	——
1975	7045145	15/32	1 9/32	1 15/32	——	0.120	0.120	Index	0.080	0.120	——
	7045146	15/32	1 9/32	1 15/32	——	0.120	0.120	——	0.080	0.120	——
	7045147	15/32	1 9/32	1 15/32	——	0.120	0.120	1 Lean	0.080	0.120	——
	7045148	15/32	1 9/32	1 15/32	——	0.120	0.120	1 Rich	0.080	0.120	——
	7045149	15/32	1 9/32	1 15/32	——	0.120	0.120	1 Rich	0.080	0.120	——
	7045446	15/32	1 9/32	1 15/32	——	0.120	0.120	——	0.080	0.120	——
	7045448	15/32	1 9/32	1 15/32	——	0.120	0.120	Index	0.080	0.120	——
	7045449	15/32	1 9/32	1 15/32	——	0.120	0.120	1 Lean	0.080	0.120	——
	7045143	15/32	1 9/32	1 15/32	——	0.140	0.120	1 Rich	0.080	0.140	——
	7045140	15/32	1 9/32	1 15/32	——	0.140	0.120	1 Rich	0.080	0.140	——
1976	17056447	7/16	1 9/32	1 19/32	——	0.130	0.100	1 Rich	0.080	0.140	——
	17056145	13/32	1 9/32	1 19/32②	——	0.110	0.100	1 Rich	0.080	0.140	——
	17056148	7/16	1 9/32	1 19/32	——	0.120	0.100	1 Rich	0.080	0.140	——
	17056149	7/16	1 9/32	1 19/32	——	0.120	0.100	1 Rich	0.800	0.140	——
	17056448	7/16	1 9/32	1 19/32	——	0.130	0.110	1 Rich	0.080	0.140	——
	17056449	7/16	1 9/32	1 19/32	——	0.130	0.110	1 Rich	0.080	0.140	——
	17056143	15/32	1 9/32	1 19/32	——	0.140	0.100	1 Rich	0.080	0.180	——
	17056140	15/32	1 9/32	1 19/32	——	0.140	0.100	1 Rich	0.080	0.180	——

BUICK

Year	Carburetor Identification①	Float Level (in.)	Float Drop (in.)	Pump Rod (in.)	Idle Vent (in.)	Primary Vacuum Break (in.)	Secondary Vacuum Break (in.)	Automatic Choke (notches)	Choke Rod (in.)	Choke Unloader (in.)	Fast Idle Speed (rpm)
1977	17057140	¹⁵/₃₂	1 ⁵/₃₂	1 ⁹/₁₆	——	0.140	0.100	1 Rich	0.080	0.180	——
	17057141, 17057145, 17057147	⁷/₁₆	1 ⁵/₃₂	1 ½	——	0.110	0.040	1 Rich	0.080	0.140	——
	17057143, 17075144	⁷/₁₆	1 ⁵/₃₂	1 ¹⁷/₃₂	——	0.130	0.100	1 Rich	0.080	0.140	——
	17057146, 17057148	⁷/₁₆	1 ⁵/₃₂	1 ¹⁷/₃₂	——	0.110	0.040	1 Rich	0.080	0.140	——
	17057445	⁷/₁₆	1 ⁵/₃₂	1 ½	——	0.140	0.100	1 Rich	0.080	0.140	——
	17057446, 17057448	⁷/₁₆	1 ⁵/₃₂	1 ½	——	0.130	0.110	1 Rich	0.080	0.140	——
	17057447	⁷/₁₆	1 ⁵/₃₂	1 ½	——	0.130	0.100	1 Rich	0.080	0.140	——
1978	17058104	¹⁵/₃₂	1 ⁹/₃₂	1 ²¹/₃₂	——	0.160	——	Index	0.260	0.325	——
	17058105	¹⁵/₃₂	1 ⁹/₃₂	1 ²¹/₃₂	——	0.160	——	Index	0.260	0.325	——
	17058108	¹⁹/₃₂	1 ⁹/₃₂	1 ²¹/₃₂	——	0.160	——	Index	0.260	0.325	——
	17058110	¹⁹/₃₂	1 ⁹/₃₂	1 ²¹/₃₂	——	0.160	——	Index	0.260	0.325	——
	17058112	¹⁹/₃₂	1 ⁹/₃₂	1 ²¹/₃₂	——	0.160	——	Index	0.260	0.325	——
	17058114	¹⁹/₃₂	1 ⁹/₃₂	1 ²¹/₃₂	——	0.160	——	Index	0.260	0.325	——
	17058126	¹⁹/₃₂	1 ⁹/₃₂	1 ¹⁷/₃₂	——	0.150	——	Index	0.260	0.325	——
	17058128	¹⁹/₃₂	1 ⁹/₃₂	1 ¹⁷/₃₂	——	0.150	——	Index	0.260	0.325	——
	17058404	½	1 ⁹/₃₂	1 ²¹/₃₂	——	0.160	——	½ Lean	0.260	0.325	——
	17058405	½	1 ⁹/₃₂	1 ²¹/₃₂	——	0.160	——	½ Lean	0.260	0.325	——
	17058408	²¹/₃₂	1 ⁹/₃₂	1 ²¹/₃₂	——	0.160	——	½ Lean	0.260	0.325	——
	17058410	²¹/₃₂	1 ⁹/₃₂	1 ²¹/₃₂	——	0.160	——	½ Lean	0.260	0.325	——
	17058412	²¹/₃₂	1 ⁹/₃₂	1 ²¹/₃₂	——	0.160	——	½ Lean	0.260	0.325	——
	17058414	²¹/₃₂	1 ⁹/₃₂	1 ²¹/₃₂	——	0.160	——	½ Lean	0.260	0.325	——
	17058140	⁷/₁₆	1 ⁵/₃₂	1 ¹⁹/₃₂	——	0.070	0.110	1 Rich	0.080	0.140	——
	17058143	⁷/₁₆	1 ⁵/₃₂	1 ⁹/₁₆	——	0.080	0.110	1 Rich	0.080	0.140	——
	17058144	⁷/₁₆	1 ⁵/₃₂	1 ⁵/₈	——	0.060	0.110	1 Rich	0.080	0.140	——
	17058145	⁷/₁₆	1 ⁵/₃₂	1 ¹⁹/₃₂	——	0.060	0.110	1 Rich	0.080	0.160	——
	17058148	⁷/₁₆	1 ⁵/₃₂	1 ¹⁹/₃₂	——	0.080	0.110	1 Rich	0.080	0.150	——
	17058149	⁷/₁₆	1 ⁵/₃₂	1 ¹⁹/₃₂	——	0.080	0.110	1 Rich	0.080	0.150	——
	17058141	⁷/₁₆	1 ⁵/₃₂	1 ¹⁹/₃₂	——	0.100	0.140	1 Rich	0.080	0.140	——
	17058147	⁷/₁₆	1 ⁵/₃₂	1 ¹⁹/₃₂	——	0.100	0.140	1 Rich	0.080	0.140	——
	17058182	⁷/₁₆	1 ⁵/₃₂	1 ¹⁹/₃₂	——	0.080	0.110	1 Rich	0.080	0.140	——
	17058183	⁷/₁₆	1 ⁵/₃₂	1 ¹⁹/₃₂	——	0.080	0.110	1 Rich	0.080	0.140	——
	17058444	⁷/₁₆	1 ⁵/₃₂	1 ¹⁹/₃₂	——	0.100	0.140	1 Rich	0.080	0.140	——
	17058446	⁷/₁₆	1 ⁵/₃₂	1 ¹⁹/₃₂	——	0.110	0.130	1 Rich	0.080	0.140	——
	17058447	⁷/₁₆	1 ⁵/₃₂	1 ¹⁹/₃₂	——	0.110	0.150	1 Rich	0.080	0.140	——
	17058448	⁷/₁₆	1 ⁵/₃₂	1 ⁹/₁₆	——	0.100	0.140	1 Rich	0.080	0.140	——
	17058185	⁷/₁₆	1 ⁵/₃₂	1 ¹⁹/₃₂	——	0.050	0.110	1 Rich	0.080	0.140	——
	17058187	⁷/₁₆	1 ⁵/₃₂	1 ¹⁹/₃₂	——	0.050	0.110	1 Rich	0.080	0.140	——
	17058189	⁷/₁₆	1 ⁵/₃₂	1 ¹⁹/₃₂	——	0.080	0.110	1 Rich	0.080	0.140	——
	17058188	⁷/₁₆	1 ⁵/₃₂	1 ⁵/₈	——	0.050	0.120	1 Rich	0.080	0.140	——

① The carburetor identification number is stamped on the float bowl, next to the fuel inlet nut.
② 1¾ in. on Skyhawk.

CHEVROLET

Year	Carburetor Identification①	Float Level (in.)	Float Drop (in.)	Pump Rod (in.)	Idle Vent (in.)	Primary Vacuum Break (in.)	Secondary Vacuum Break (in.)	Automatic Choke (notches)	Choke Rod (in.)	Choke Unloader (in.)	Fast Idle Speed (rpm)
1972	7042111	$^{23}/_{32}$	1 $^9/_{32}$	1 $^1/_2$	——	0.180	——	——	0.100	0.325	——
	7042113	$^{23}/_{32}$	1 $^9/_{32}$	1 $^1/_2$	——	0.180	——	——	0.100	0.325	——
	7042831	$^{23}/_{32}$	1 $^9/_{32}$	1 $^1/_2$	——	0.180	——	——	0.100	0.325	——
	7042833	$^{23}/_{32}$	1 $^9/_{32}$	1 $^1/_2$	——	0.180	——	——	0.100	0.325	——
	7042112	$^{23}/_{32}$	1 $^9/_{32}$	1 $^1/_2$	——	0.170	——	——	0.100	0.325	——
	7042114	$^{23}/_{32}$	1 $^9/_{32}$	1 $^1/_2$	——	0.170	——	——	0.100	0.325	——
	7042118	$^{23}/_{32}$	1 $^9/_{32}$	1 $^1/_2$	——	0.190	——	——	0.100	0.325	——
	7042832	$^{23}/_{32}$	1 $^9/_{32}$	1 $^1/_2$	——	0.170	——	——	0.100	0.325	——
	7042834	$^{23}/_{32}$	1 $^9/_{32}$	1 $^1/_2$	——	0.170	——	——	0.100	0.325	——
	7042838	$^{23}/_{32}$	1 $^9/_{32}$	1 $^1/_2$	——	0.190	——	——	0.100	0.325	——
	7042100	$^{25}/_{32}$	1 $^{31}/_{32}$	1 $^5/_{16}$	——	0.080	——	——	0.040	0.215	——
	7042820	$^{25}/_{32}$	1 $^{31}/_{32}$	1 $^5/_{16}$	——	0.080	——	——	0.040	0.215	——
	7042101	$^{25}/_{32}$	1 $^{31}/_{32}$	1 $^5/_{16}$	——	0.110	——	——	0.075	0.215	——
	7042821	$^{25}/_{32}$	1 $^{31}/_{32}$	1 $^5/_{16}$	——	0.110	——	——	0.075	0.215	——
1973	7043100	$^{21}/_{32}$	1 $^9/_{32}$	1 $^5/_{16}$	——	0.080	——	——	0.150	0.215	——
	7043101	$^{21}/_{32}$	1 $^9/_{32}$	1 $^5/_{16}$	——	0.080	——	——	0.150	0.215	——
	7043120	$^{21}/_{32}$	1 $^9/_{32}$	1 $^5/_{16}$	——	0.080	——	——	0.150	0.215	——
	7043105	$^{21}/_{32}$	1 $^9/_{32}$	1 $^5/_{16}$	——	0.080	——	——	0.150	0.215	——
	7043114	$^{19}/_{32}$	1 $^9/_{32}$	1 $^7/_{16}$	——	0.130	——	——	0.245	0.325	——
	7043113	$^{19}/_{32}$	1 $^9/_{32}$	1 $^7/_{16}$	——	0.140	——	——	0.200	0.250	——
	7043112	$^{19}/_{32}$	1 $^9/_{32}$	1 $^7/_{16}$	——	0.130	——	——	0.245	0.325	——
	7043111	$^{19}/_{32}$	1 $^9/_{32}$	1 $^7/_{16}$	——	0.140	——	——	0.200	0.250	——
	7043118	$^{19}/_{32}$	1 $^9/_{32}$	1 $^7/_{16}$	——	0.130	——	——	0.245	0.325	——
1974	7044111	$^{19}/_{32}$	1 $^9/_{32}$	1 $^9/_{32}$	——	0.140	——	——	0.200	0.250	1600②
	7044112	$^{19}/_{32}$	1 $^9/_{32}$	1 $^3/_{16}$	——	0.130	——	——	0.245	0.325	1600②
	7044113	$^{19}/_{32}$	1 $^9/_{32}$	1 $^9/_{32}$	——	0.140	——	——	0.200	0.250	1600②
	7044114	$^{19}/_{32}$	1 $^9/_{32}$	1 $^3/_{16}$	——	0.130	——	——	0.245	0.325	1600②
	7044115	$^{19}/_{32}$	1 $^9/_{32}$	1 $^9/_{32}$	——	0.140	——	——	0.200	0.250	1600②
	7044116	$^{19}/_{32}$	1 $^9/_{32}$	1 $^3/_{16}$	——	0.130	——	——	0.245	0.325	1600②
	7044118	$^{19}/_{32}$	1 $^9/_{32}$	1 $^3/_{16}$	——	0.130	——	——	0.245	0.325	1600②
	7044123	$^{19}/_{32}$	1 $^9/_{32}$	1 $^9/_{32}$	——	0.140	——	——	0.200	0.250	1600②
	7044124	$^{19}/_{32}$	1 $^9/_{32}$	1 $^3/_{16}$	——	0.130	——	——	0.245	0.325	1600②
1975	7045105	$^{19}/_{32}$	1 $^7/_{32}$	1 $^{19}/_{32}$	——	0.130	——	——	0.375	0.350	——
	7045106	$^{19}/_{32}$	1 $^7/_{32}$	1 $^{19}/_{32}$	——	0.130	——	——	0.380	0.350	——
	7045111	$^{21}/_{32}$	$^{31}/_{32}$	1 $^5/_8$	——	0.130	——	——	0.400	0.350	——
	7045112	$^{21}/_{32}$	$^{31}/_{32}$	1 $^5/_8$	——	0.130	——	——	0.400	0.350	——
	7045114	$^{21}/_{32}$	$^{31}/_{32}$	1 $^5/_8$	——	0.130	——	——	0.400	0.350	——
	7045115	$^{21}/_{32}$	$^{31}/_{32}$	1 $^5/_8$	——	0.130	——	——	0.400	0.350	——
	7045123	$^{21}/_{32}$	$^{31}/_{32}$	1 $^5/_8$	——	0.130	——	——	0.400	0.350	——
	7045124	$^{21}/_{32}$	$^{31}/_{32}$	1 $^5/_8$	——	0.130	——	——	0.400	0.350	——
	7045405	$^{21}/_{32}$	1 $^7/_{32}$	1 $^{19}/_{32}$	——	0.130	——	——	0.380	0.350	——
	7045406	$^{21}/_{32}$	1 $^7/_{32}$	1 $^{19}/_{32}$	——	0.130	——	——	0.380	0.350	——
1976	17056108	$^9/_{16}$	1 $^9/_{32}$	1 $^{21}/_{32}$	——	0.140	——	Index	0.260	0.325	——
	17056110	$^9/_{16}$	1 $^9/_{32}$	1 $^{21}/_{32}$	——	0.140	——	Index	0.260	0.325	——
	17056111	$^9/_{16}$	1 $^9/_{32}$	1 $^{21}/_{32}$	——	0.140	——	Index	0.260	0.325	——
	17056112	$^9/_{16}$	1 $^9/_{32}$	1 $^{21}/_{32}$	——	0.140	——	Index	0.260	0.325	——
	17056113	$^9/_{16}$	1 $^9/_{32}$	1 $^{21}/_{32}$	——	0.140	——	Index	0.260	0.325	——
	17056114	$^{21}/_{32}$	$^{31}/_{32}$	1 $^{11}/_{16}$	——	0.130	——	1 Rich	0.260	0.325	——

CHEVROLET

Year	Carburetor Identification①	Float Level (in.)	Float Drop (in.)	Pump Rod (in.)	Idle Vent (in.)	Primary Vacuum Break (in.)	Secondary Vacuum Break (in.)	Automatic Choke (notches)	Choke Rod (in.)	Choke Unloader (in.)	Fast Idle Speed (rpm)
1976	17056430	9/16	1 9/32	1 21/32	——	0.140	——	Index	0.260	0.325	——
	17056432	9/16	1 9/32	1 21/32	——	0.140	——	Index	0.260	0.325	——
1977	17057108, 17057110, 17057111, 17057112, 17057113, 17057114, 17057121, 17057123	19/32	1 9/32	1 21/32	——	0.160	——	Index	0.260	0.325	——
	17057408, 17057410, 17057412, 17057414	21/32	1 9/32	1 21/32	——	0.160	——	½ Lean	0.260	0.325	——
1978	17058102	15/32	1 9/32	1 17/32	——	0.150	——	Index	0.260	0.325	——
	17058103	15/32	1 9/32	1 17/32	——	0.150	——	Index	0.260	0.325	——
	17058104	15/32	1 9/32	1 21/32	——	0.160	——	Index	0.260	0.325	——
	17058107	15/32	1 9/32	1 17/32	——	0.160	——	Index	0.260	0.325	——
	17058109	15/32	1 9/32	1 17/32	——	0.160	——	Index	0.260	0.325	——
	17058404	½	1 9/32	1 21/32	——	0.160	——	½ Lean	0.260	0.325	——
	17058405	½	1 9/32	1 21/32	——	0.160	——	Index	0.260	0.325	——
	17058447	7/16	1 5/32	1 5/8	——	0.110	0.150	1 Rich	0.080	0.140	——
	17058143	7/16	1 5/32	1 5/8	——	0.040	0.110	1 Rich	0.080	0.140	——
	17058147	7/16	1 5/32	1 5/8	——	0.100	0.140	1 Rich	0.080	0.140	——
	17058144	7/16	1 5/32	1 5/8	——	0.060	0.110	1 Rich	0.080	0.140	——

① The carburetor identification number is stamped on the float bowl, next to the fuel inlet nut.
② This setting is with the low idle at 500 rpm with the clutch fan disengaged.

CHEVROLET VEGA, MONZA

Year	Carburetor Identification①	Float Level (in.)	Float Drop (in.)	Pump Rod (in.)	Idle Vent (in.)	Primary Vacuum Break (in.)	Secondary Vacuum Break (in.)	Automatic Choke (notches)	Choke Rod (in.)	Choke Unloader (in.)	Fast Idle Speed (rpm)
1972	Manual	19/32	1 7/8	1 1/16	——	0.100	——	——	0.080	0.215	2400②
	Automatic	19/32	1 7/8	1 1/16	——	0.085	——	——	0.060	0.215	2800②
1975	7045101, 7045105	19/32	1 7/32	1 19/32	——	0.130	——	Index	0.375	0.350	——
	7045401, 7045405	21/32	1 7/32	1 19/32	——	0.130	——	Index	0.380	0.350	——
	7045102, 7045106	19/32	1 7/32	1 19/32	——	0.130	——	Index	0.375	0.350	——
	7045406	21/32	1 7/32	1 19/32	——	0.130	——	Index	0.380	0.350	——
1976	17056101	17/32	1 9/32	1 5/8	——	0.130	——	Index	0.260	0.325	——
	17056102	17/32	1 9/32	1 5/8	——	0.130	——	Index	0.260	0.325	——
	17056104	17/32	1 5/32	1 5/8	——	0.140	——	Index	0.260	0.325	——
	17056404	9/16	1 3/16	1 21/32	——	0.140	——	Index	0.260	0.325	——
1977	17057104, 17057105	½	1 9/32	1 21/32	——	0.150	——	Index	0.260	0.325	——
	17057107,										

Rochester Carburetors

CHEVROLET VEGA, MONZA

Year	Carburetor Identification①	Float Level (in.)	Float Drop (in.)	Pump Rod (in.)	Idle Vent (in.)	Primary Vacuum Break (in.)	Secondary Vacuum Break (in.)	Automatic Choke (notches)	Choke Rod (in.)	Choke Unloader (in.)	Fast Idle Speed (rpm)
1977	17057109	½	1 9/32	1 21/32	—	0.160	—	Index	0.260	0.325	—
	17057404, 17057405	½	1 9/32	1 21/32	—	0.160	—	½ Lean	0.260	0.325	—
1978	17058102	15/32	1 9/32	1 17/32	—	0.150	—	Index	0.260	0.325	—
	17058103	15/32	1 9/32	1 17/32	—	0.150	—	Index	0.260	0.325	—
	17058104	15/32	1 9/32	1 21/32	—	0.160	—	Index	0.260	0.325	—
	17058107	15/32	1 9/32	1 17/32	—	0.160	—	Index	0.260	0.325	—
	17058109	15/32	1 9/32	1 17/32	—	0.160	—	Index	0.260	0.325	—
	17058404	½	1 9/32	1 21/32	—	0.160	—	½ Lean	0.260	0.325	—
	17058405	½	1 9/32	1 21/32	—	0.160	—	Index	0.260	0.325	—
	17058447	7/16	1 5/32	1 5/8	—	0.110	0.150	1 Rich	0.080	0.140	—
	17058143	7/16	1 5/32	1 5/8	—	0.040	0.110	1 Rich	0.080	0.140	—
	17058147	7/16	1 5/32	1 5/8	—	0.100	0.140	1 Rich	0.080	0.140	—
	17058144	7/16	1 5/32	1 5/8	—	0.060	0.110	1 Rich	0.080	0.140	—

① The carburetor identification number is stamped on the float bowl, next to the fuel inlet nut.
② TCS disconnected for full vacuum advance.

OLDSMOBILE

Year	Carburetor Identification①	Float Level (in.)	Float Drop (in.)	Pump Rod (in.)	Idle Vent (in.)	Primary Vacuum Break (in.)	Secondary Vacuum Break (in.)	Automatic Choke (notches)	Choke Rod (in.)	Choke Unloader (in.)	Fast Idle Speed (rpm)
1972	7042155	17/32	1 3/8	1 3/8	—	0.200	—	1 Lean	0.160	0.170	—
	7042156	17/32	1 3/8	1 3/8	—	0.200	—	Index	0.160	0.170	—
1973	All	15/32	1 9/32	1 11/32	—	0.200	—	Index	0.160	0.250	—
1975	7045143	15/32	1 9/32	1 19/32	—	0.140	0.120	1 Rich	0.080	0.080	Preset
	7045147	7/16	1 9/32	1 19/32	—	0.120	0.120	1 Lean	0.080	0.140	1800②
	7045149	7/16	1 9/32	1 19/32	—	0.120	0.120	1 Rich	0.080	0.140	1800②
	7045160	9/16	1 7/32	1 11/32	—	0.145	0.265	1 Rich	0.085	0.180	Preset
	7045161	9/16	1 7/32	1 11/32	—	0.145	0.265	1 Rich	0.085	0.180	Preset
	7045449	7/16	1 9/32	1 19/32	—	0.120	0.120	1 Lean	0.080	0.140	Preset
1976	17056143	15/32	1 5/32	1 11/32	—	0.140	0.100	1 Rich	0.080	0.180	—
	17056145	7/16	1 5/32	1 19/32	—	0.110	0.100	1 Rich	0.080	0.140	—
	17056149	7/16	1 5/32	1 19/32	—	0.120	0.100	1 Rich	0.080	0.140	—
	17056447	7/16	1 5/32	1 19/32	—	0.130	0.110	1 Rich	0.080	0.140	—
	17056449	7/16	1 5/32	1 19/32	—	0.130	0.110	1 Rich	0.080	0.140	—
1977	17057145, 17057146, 17057148	7/16	1 5/32	1 19/32	—	0.110	0.090	1 Rich	0.080	0.140	—
	17057143, 17057144, 17057447	7/16	1 5/32	1 19/32	—	0.130	0.100	1 Rich	0.080	0.140	—
	17057445	7/16	1 5/32	1 19/32	—	0.140	0.110	1 Lean	0.080	0.140	—
	17057446, 17057448	7/16	1 5/32	1 19/32	—	0.130	0.110	1 Rich	0.080	0.140	—
	17057104, 17057105	7/16	1 9/32	1 21/32	—	—	0.130	Index	0.260	0.325	—
	17057107, 17057109	7/16	1 9/32	1 5/8	—	—	0.130	Index	0.260	0.325	—

OLDSMOBILE

Year	Carburetor Identification①	Float Level (in.)	Float Drop (in.)	Pump Rod (in.)	Idle Vent (in.)	Primary Vacuum Break (in.)	Secondary Vacuum Break (in.)	Automatic Choke (notches)	Choke Rod (in.)	Choke Unloader (in.)	Fast Idle Speed (rpm)
1977	17057112, 17057114	$^{19}/_{32}$	$1\,^9/_{32}$	$1\,^{21}/_{32}$	——	——	0.130	Index	0.260	0.325	——
	17057113, 17057123	$^{19}/_{32}$	$1\,^9/_{32}$	$1\,^5/_8$	——	——	0.130	Index	0.260	0.325	——
	17057404	$^1/_2$	$1\,^9/_{32}$	$1\,^{21}/_{32}$	——	——	0.140	1 Lean	0.260	0.325	——
	17057405	$^1/_2$	$1\,^9/_{32}$	$1\,^5/_8$	——	——	0.140	1 Lean	0.260	0.325	——
1978	17058102	$^{15}/_{32}$	$1\,^9/_{32}$	$1\,^{17}/_{32}$	——	0.130	——	Index	0.260	0.325	——
	17058103	$^{15}/_{32}$	$1\,^9/_{32}$	$1\,^{17}/_{32}$	——	0.130	——	Index	0.260	0.325	——
	17058104	$^{15}/_{32}$	$1\,^9/_{32}$	$1\,^{21}/_{32}$	——	0.130	——	Index	0.260	0.325	——
	17058105	$^{15}/_{32}$	$1\,^9/_{32}$	$1\,^{21}/_{32}$	——	0.130	——	Index	0.260	0.325	——
	17058107	$^{15}/_{32}$	$1\,^9/_{32}$	$1\,^{17}/_{32}$	——	0.130	——	Index	0.260	0.325	——
	17058108	$^{19}/_{32}$	$1\,^9/_{32}$	$1\,^{21}/_{32}$	——	0.130	——	Index	0.260	0.325	——
	17058109	$^{15}/_{32}$	$1\,^9/_{32}$	$1\,^{17}/_{32}$	——	0.130	——	Index	0.260	0.325	——
	17058110	$^{19}/_{32}$	$1\,^9/_{32}$	$1\,^{21}/_{32}$	——	0.130	——	Index	0.260	0.325	——
	17058111	$^{19}/_{32}$	$1\,^9/_{32}$	$1\,^{17}/_{32}$	——	0.130	——	Index	0.260	0.325	——
	17058113	$^{19}/_{32}$	$1\,^9/_{32}$	$1\,^{17}/_{32}$	——	0.130	——	Index	0.260	0.325	——
	17058121	$^{19}/_{32}$	$1\,^9/_{32}$	$1\,^{17}/_{32}$	——	0.130	——	Index	0.260	0.325	——
	17058123	$^{19}/_{32}$	$1\,^9/_{32}$	$1\,^{17}/_{32}$	——	0.130	——	Index	0.260	0.325	——
	17058126	$^{19}/_{32}$	$1\,^9/_{32}$	$1\,^{17}/_{32}$	——	0.130	——	Index	0.260	0.325	——
	17058128	$^{19}/_{32}$	$1\,^9/_{32}$	$1\,^{17}/_{32}$	——	0.130	——	Index	0.260	0.325	——
	17058140	$^7/_{16}$	$1\,^5/_{32}$	$1\,^{19}/_{32}$	——	0.070	0.110	1 Rich	0.080	0.140	——
	17058145	$^7/_{16}$	$1\,^5/_{32}$	$1\,^{19}/_{32}$	——	0.060	0.110	1 Rich	0.080	0.160	——
	17058147	$^7/_{16}$	$1\,^5/_{32}$	$1\,^{19}/_{32}$	——	0.100	0.140	1 Rich	0.080	0.140	——
	17058182	$^7/_{16}$	$1\,^5/_{32}$	$1\,^{19}/_{32}$	——	0.080	0.110	1 Rich	0.080	0.140	——
	17058183	$^7/_{16}$	$1\,^5/_{32}$	$1\,^{19}/_{32}$	——	0.080	0.110	1 Rich	0.080	0.140	——
	17058185	$^7/_{16}$	$1\,^5/_{32}$	$1\,^{19}/_{32}$	——	0.050	0.110	1 Rich	0.080	0.140	——
	17058187	$^7/_{16}$	$1\,^5/_{32}$	$1\,^{19}/_{32}$	——	0.080	0.110	1 Rich	0.080	0.140	——
	17058189	$^7/_{16}$	$1\,^5/_{32}$	$1\,^{19}/_{32}$	——	0.080	0.110	1 Rich	0.080	0.140	——
	17058404	$^1/_2$	$1\,^9/_{32}$	$1\,^{21}/_{32}$	——	0.140	——	$^1/_2$ Lean	0.260	0.325	——
	17058405	$^1/_2$	$1\,^9/_{32}$	$1\,^{21}/_{32}$	——	0.140	——	$^1/_2$ Lean	0.260	0.325	——
	17058408	$^{21}/_{32}$	$1\,^9/_{32}$	$1\,^{21}/_{32}$	——	0.140	——	$^1/_2$ Lean	0.260	0.325	——
	17058410	$^{21}/_{32}$	$1\,^9/_{32}$	$1\,^{21}/_{32}$	——	0.140	——	$^1/_2$ Lean	0.260	0.325	——
	17058444	$^7/_{16}$	$1\,^5/_{32}$	$1\,^{19}/_{32}$	——	0.100	0.140	1 Rich	0.080	0.140	——
	17058446	$^7/_{16}$	$1\,^5/_{32}$	$1\,^{19}/_{32}$	——	0.110	0.130	1 Rich	0.080	0.140	——
	17058447	$^7/_{16}$	$1\,^5/_{32}$	$1\,^{19}/_{32}$	——	0.110	0.150	1 Rich	0.080	0.140	——
	17058448	$^7/_{16}$	$1\,^5/_{32}$	$1\,^9/_{16}$	——	0.100	0.140	1 Rich	0.080	0.140	——

① The carburetor identification number is stamped on the float bowl, next to the fuel inlet nut.

② In Park
③ In Neutral

PONTIAC

Year	Carburetor Identification①	Float Level (in.)	Float Drop (in.)	Pump Rod (in.)	Idle Vent (in.)	Primary Vacuum Break (in.)	Secondary Vacuum Break (in.)	Automatic Choke (notches)	Choke Rod (in.)	Choke Unloader (in.)	Fast Idle Speed (rpm)
1972	7042060	$^5/_8$	$1\,^9/_{32}$	$1\,^{11}/_{32}$	——	0.122	——	——	0.085	0.180	——
	7042061	$^5/_8$	$1\,^9/_{32}$	$1\,^{11}/_{32}$	——	0.122	——	——	0.085	0.180	——
	7042062	$^9/_{16}$	$1\,^9/_{32}$	$1\,^{11}/_{32}$	——	0.105	——	——	0.085	0.180	——
	7042064	$^5/_8$	$1\,^9/_{32}$	$1\,^{11}/_{32}$	——	0.150	——	——	0.085	0.180	——
	7042100	$^{25}/_{32}$	$1\,^{31}/_{32}$	$1\,^5/_{16}$	——	0.080	——	——	0.040	0.215	——
	7042101	$^{25}/_{32}$	$1\,^{31}/_{32}$	$1\,^5/_{16}$	——	0.100	——	——	0.075	0.215	——

Rochester Carburetors

Year	Carburetor Identification①	Float Level (in.)	Float Drop (in.)	Pump Rod (in.)	Idle Vent (in.)	Primary Vacuum Break (in.)	Secondary Vacuum Break (in.)	Automatic Choke (notches)	Choke Rod (in.)	Choke Unloader (in.)	Fast Idle Speed (rpm)
1973	7043062	$^{21}/_{32}$	$1\,^9/_{32}$	$1\,^5/_{16}$	——	0.167	——	——	0.085	0.180	——
	7043063	$^{21}/_{32}$	$1\,^9/_{32}$	$1\,^5/_{16}$	——	0.167	——	——	0.085	0.180	
	7043071	$^{23}/_{32}$	$1\,^9/_{32}$	$1\,^5/_{16}$	——	0.195	——	——	0.085	0.180	
	7043072	$^{23}/_{32}$	$1\,^9/_{32}$	$1\,^5/_{16}$	——	0.167	——	——	0.085	0.180	
	7043060	$^{21}/_{32}$	$1\,^9/_{32}$	$1\,^5/_{16}$	——	0.157	——	——	0.085	0.180	
	7043061	$^{21}/_{32}$	$1\,^9/_{32}$	$1\,^5/_{16}$	——	0.157	——	——	0.085	0.180	
	7043066	$^{21}/_{32}$	$1\,^9/_{32}$	$1\,^5/_{16}$	——	0.180	——	——	0.085	0.180	
	7043067	$^{21}/_{32}$	$1\,^9/_{32}$	$1\,^5/_{16}$	——	0.180	——	——	0.085	0.180	
	7043070	$^{23}/_{32}$	$1\,^9/_{32}$	$1\,^5/_{16}$	——	0.157	——	——	0.085	0.180	
1974	7043060	0.670	$1\,^3/_4$	$1\,^5/_{16}$	——	0.157	——	1 Lean	0.085	0.180	——
	7043062	0.670	$1\,^3/_4$	$1\,^5/_{16}$	——	0.167	——	1 Lean	0.085	0.180	
	7043070	0.670	$1\,^3/_4$	$1\,^5/_{16}$	——	0.157	——	1 Lean	0.085	0.180	
	7043071	0.670	$1\,^3/_4$	$1\,^5/_{16}$	——	0.195	——	1 Lean	0.085	0.180	
	7043072	0.670	$1\,^3/_4$	$1\,^5/_{16}$	——	0.167	——	1 Lean	0.085	0.180	
	7044063	0.670	$1\,^3/_4$	$1\,^5/_{16}$	——	0.157	——	1 Lean	0.085	0.180	
	7044066	0.670	$1\,^3/_4$	$1\,^5/_{16}$	——	0.177	——	1 Lean	0.085	0.180	
	7044067	0.670	$1\,^3/_4$	$1\,^5/_{16}$	——	0.177	——	1 Lean	0.085	0.180	
1975	7045160	$^9/_{16}$	$1\,^7/_{32}$	$1\,^3/_4$	0.025	0.145	0.265	1 Rich	0.085	0.180	
	7045162	$^9/_{16}$	$1\,^7/_{32}$	$1\,^{13}/_{16}$	0.025	0.145	0.260	1 Rich	0.085	0.180	
	7045171	$^9/_{16}$	$1\,^7/_{32}$	$1\,^{13}/_{16}$	0.025	0.145	0.260	1 Rich	0.085	0.180	
	7045143	$^{15}/_{32}$	$1\,^7/_{32}$	$1\,^{13}/_{16}$	0.025	0.140	0.120	1 Rich	0.080	0.180	
1976	6-231 Man.	$^7/_{16}$	$1\,^9/_{32}$	$1\,^{19}/_{32}$	——	0.110	0.100	1 Rich	0.080	0.140	
	6-231 Auto.	$^7/_{16}$	$1\,^9/_{32}$	$1\,^{19}/_{32}$	——	0.120	0.100	1 Rich	0.080	0.140	
	6-231 Calif.	$^7/_{16}$	$1\,^9/_{32}$	$1\,^{19}/_{32}$	——	0.130	0.110	1 Rich	0.080	0.140	
	8-350 Ventura	$^{15}/_{32}$	$1\,^9/_{32}$	$1\,^{11}/_{32}$	——	0.140	0.100	1 Rich	0.080	0.180	
	8-350, 400 Auto.	$^9/_{16}$	$1\,^9/_{32}$	$1\,^{11}/_{32}$	——	0.165	0.285	1 Rich	0.085	0.180	
1977	17057141, 17057147	$^7/_{16}$	$1\,^5/_{32}$	$1\,^5/_8$	——	0.110	0.090	1 Rich	0.080	0.140	——
	17057143, 17057144	$^7/_{16}$	$1\,^5/_{32}$	$1\,^{19}/_{32}$	——	0.130	0.100	1 Rich	0.080	0.140	——
	17057145	$^7/_{16}$	$1\,^5/_{32}$	$1\,^{19}/_{32}$	——	0.110	0.090	1 Rich	0.080	0.140	——
	17057446, 17057448	$^7/_{16}$	$1\,^5/_{32}$	$1\,^{19}/_{32}$	——	0.130	0.110	1 Rich	0.080	0.140	——
	17057447	$^7/_{16}$	$1\,^5/_{32}$	$1\,^{19}/_{32}$	——	0.130	0.100	1 Rich	0.080	0.140	——
	17057148	$^7/_{16}$	$1\,^5/_{32}$	$1\,^9/_{16}$	——	0.110	0.090	1 Rich	0.080	0.140	——
	17057149	$^7/_{16}$	$1\,^5/_{32}$	$1\,^9/_{16}$	——	0.110	0.040	1 Lean	0.080	0.140	——
	17057445	$^7/_{16}$	$1\,^5/_{32}$	$1\,^9/_{16}$	——	0.140	0.110	1 Lean	0.080	0.140	——
1978	17058102	$^{19}/_{32}$	$1\,^9/_{32}$	$1\,^{17}/_{32}$	——	0.130	——	Index	0.260	0.325	——
	17058103	$^{19}/_{32}$	$1\,^9/_{32}$	$1\,^{17}/_{32}$	——	0.130	——	Index	0.260	0.325	——
	17058108	$^{19}/_{32}$	$1\,^9/_{32}$	$1\,^{21}/_{32}$	——	0.130	——	Index	0.260	0.325	——
	17058110	$^{19}/_{32}$	$1\,^9/_{32}$	$1\,^{21}/_{32}$	——	0.130	——	Index	0.260	0.325	——
	17058111	$^{19}/_{32}$	$1\,^9/_{32}$	$1\,^5/_8$	——	0.130	——	Index	0.260	0.325	——
	17058112	$^{19}/_{32}$	$1\,^9/_{32}$	$1\,^{21}/_{32}$	——	0.130	——	Index	0.260	0.325	——
	17058113	$^{19}/_{32}$	$1\,^9/_{32}$	$1\,^5/_8$	——	0.130	——	Index	0.260	0.325	——
	17058114	$^{19}/_{32}$	$1\,^9/_{32}$	$1\,^{21}/_{32}$	——	0.130	——	Index	0.260	0.325	——
	17058121	$^{19}/_{32}$	$1\,^9/_{32}$	$1\,^5/_8$	——	0.130	——	Index	0.260	0.325	——
	17058123	$^{19}/_{32}$	$1\,^9/_{32}$	$1\,^5/_8$	——	0.130	——	Index	0.260	0.325	——

PONTIAC

Year	Carburetor Identification①	Float Level (in.)	Float Drop (in.)	Pump Rod (in.)	Idle Vent (in.)	Primary Vacuum Break (in.)	Secondary Vacuum Break (in.)	Automatic Choke (notches)	Choke Rod (in.)	Choke Unloader (in.)	Fast Idle Speed (rpm)
1978	17058126	$^{19}/_{32}$	$1\,^9/_{32}$	$1\,^{17}/_{32}$	——	0.130	——	Index	0.260	0.325	——
	17058128	$^{19}/_{32}$	$1\,^9/_{32}$	$1\,^{17}/_{32}$	——	0.130	——	Index	0.260	0.325	——
	17058145	$^7/_{16}$	$1\,^5/_{32}$	$1\,^5/_8$	——	0.110	0.110	1 Lean	0.080	0.160	
	17058147	$^7/_{16}$	$1\,^5/_{32}$	$1\,^5/_8$	——	0.140	0.140	1 Rich	0.080	0.140	
	17058182	$^7/_{16}$	$1\,^5/_{32}$	$1\,^5/_8$	——	0.110	0.110	1 Rich	0.080	0.140	
	17058183	$^7/_{16}$	$1\,^5/_{32}$	$1\,^5/_8$	——	0.110	0.110	1 Rich	0.080	0.140	
	17058185	$^7/_{16}$	$1\,^5/_{32}$	$1\,^{19}/_{32}$	——	0.110	0.110	1 Rich	0.080	0.140	
	17058187	$^7/_{16}$	$1\,^5/_{32}$	$1\,^{19}/_{32}$	——	0.110	0.110	1 Rich	0.080	0.140	
	17058189	$^7/_{16}$	$1\,^5/_{32}$	$1\,^{19}/_{32}$	——	0.110	0.110	1 Rich	0.080	0.140	
	17058408	$^{21}/_{32}$	$1\,^9/_{32}$	$1\,^{21}/_{32}$	——	0.140	0.140	½ Lean	0.260	0.325	
	17058410	$^{21}/_{32}$	$1\,^9/_{32}$	$1\,^{21}/_{32}$	——	0.140	0.140	½ Lean	0.260	0.325	
	17058412	$^{21}/_{32}$	$1\,^9/_{32}$	$1\,^{21}/_{32}$	——	0.140	0.140	½ Lean	0.260	0.325	
	17058414	$^{21}/_{32}$	$1\,^9/_{32}$	$1\,^{21}/_{32}$	——	0.140	0.140	½ Lean	0.260	0.325	
	17058444	$^7/_{16}$	$1\,^5/_{32}$	$1\,^5/_8$	——	0.140	0.140	1 Rich	0.080	0.140	
	17058446	$^7/_{16}$	$1\,^5/_{32}$	$1\,^5/_8$	——	0.140	0.140	1 Rich	0.080	0.140	
	17058447	$^7/_{16}$	$1\,^5/_{32}$	$1\,^5/_8$	——	0.150	0.150	1 Rich	0.080	0.140	
	17058448	$^7/_{16}$	$1\,^5/_{32}$	$1\,^5/_8$	——	0.140	0.140	1 Rich	0.080	0.140	

① The carburetor identification number is stamped on the float bowl, next to the fuel inlet nut.

MODEL 2MC, M2MC, M2ME

The Rochester model 2MC carburetor is a two-barrel single stage carburetor which incorporates the design features of the primary side of the Rochester Quadrajet four-barrel carburetor. It is used on small displacement V8s. The M2MC version with front and rear vacuum break diaphragms, was introduced in 1977 on the 301 V8.

Fast Idle Speed

1. Place the fast idle lever on the high step of the fast idle cam.
2. Turn the fast idle screw out until the throttle valves are closed.
3. Turn the screw in to contact the lever, then turn it in three more turns. Check this preliminary setting against the sticker figure.

Fast Idle Cam (Choke Rod) Adjustment

1. Adjust the fast idle speed.
2. Place the cam follower lever on the second step of the fast idle cam, holding it firmly against the rise of the high step.
3. Close the choke valve by pushing upward on the choke coil lever inside the choke housing.
4. Gauge between the upper edge of the choke valve and the inside of the air horn wall.

5. Bend the tang on the fast idle cam to adjust.

Pump Adjustment

1. With the fast idle cam follower off the steps of the fast idle cam, back out the idle speed screw until the throttle valves are completely closed.
2. Place the pump rod in the proper hole of the lever.
3. Measure from the top of the choke valve wall, next to the vent stack, to the top of the pump stem.
4. Bend the pump lever to adjust.

Choke Coil Lever Adjustment

1. Remove the choke cover and thermostatic coil from the choke housing.
2. Push up on the coil tang (counterclockwise) until the choke valve is closed. The top of the choke rod should be at the bottom of the slot in the choke valve lever. Place the fast idle cam follower on the high step of the cam.
3. Insert a 0.120 in. plug gauge in the hole in the choke housing.
4. The lower edge of the choke coil lever should just contact the side

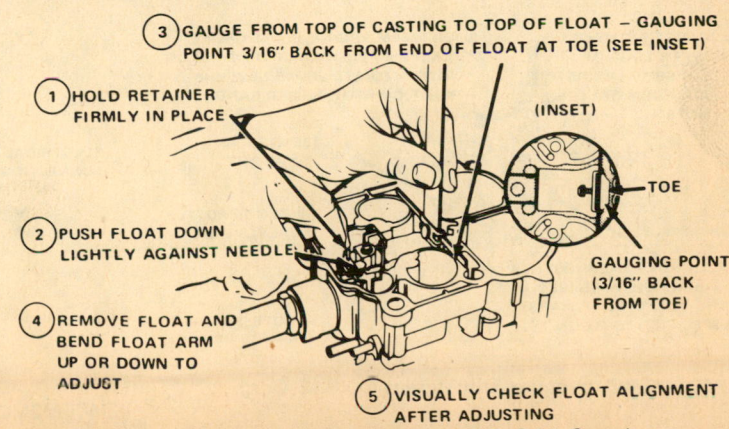

2MC, M2MC float level adjustment (© G.M. Corp.)

Rochester Carburetors

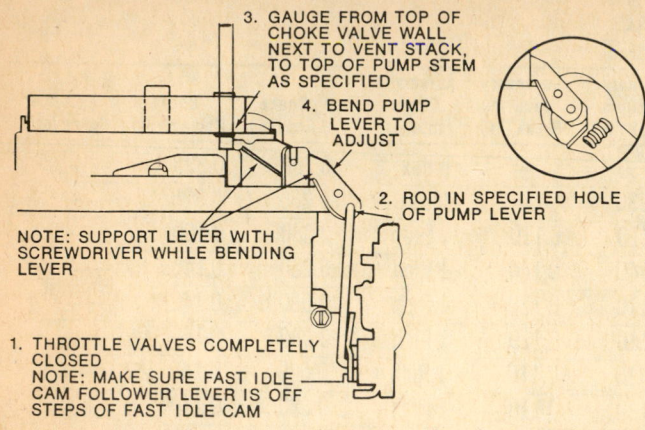

3. GAUGE FROM TOP OF CHOKE VALVE WALL NEXT TO VENT STACK, TO TOP OF PUMP STEM AS SPECIFIED

4. BEND PUMP LEVER TO ADJUST

2. ROD IN SPECIFIED HOLE OF PUMP LEVER

NOTE: SUPPORT LEVER WITH SCREWDRIVER WHILE BENDING LEVER

1. THROTTLE VALVES COMPLETELY CLOSED
NOTE: MAKE SURE FAST IDLE CAM FOLLOWER LEVER IS OFF STEPS OF FAST IDLE CAM

Pump adjustment (© Buick Div., G.M. Corp.)

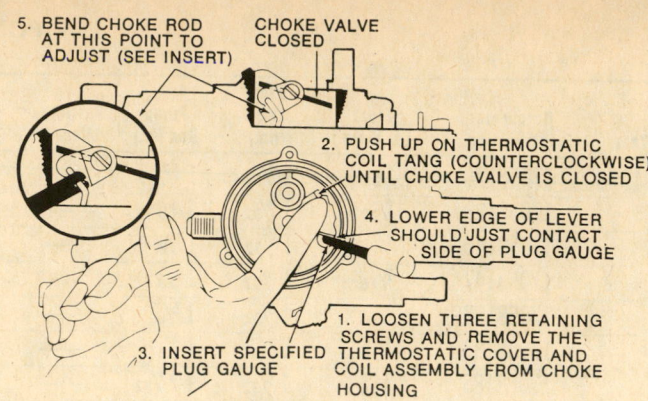

5. BEND CHOKE ROD AT THIS POINT TO ADJUST (SEE INSERT)

CHOKE VALVE CLOSED

2. PUSH UP ON THERMOSTATIC COIL TANG (COUNTERCLOCKWISE) UNTIL CHOKE VALVE IS CLOSED

4. LOWER EDGE OF LEVER SHOULD JUST CONTACT SIDE OF PLUG GAUGE

3. INSERT SPECIFIED PLUG GAUGE

1. LOOSEN THREE RETAINING SCREWS AND REMOVE THE THERMOSTATIC COVER AND COIL ASSEMBLY FROM CHOKE HOUSING

Choke coil lever adjustment (© Buick Div., G.M. Corp.)

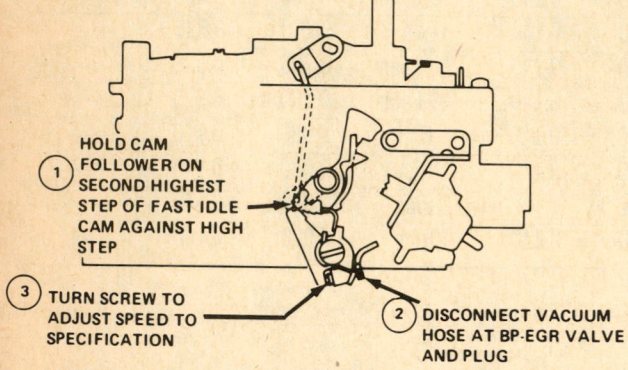

① HOLD CAM FOLLOWER ON SECOND HIGHEST STEP OF FAST IDLE CAM AGAINST HIGH STEP

③ TURN SCREW TO ADJUST SPEED TO SPECIFICATION

② DISCONNECT VACUUM HOSE AT BP-EGR VALVE AND PLUG

M2MC fast idle speed adjustment (© G.M. Corp.)

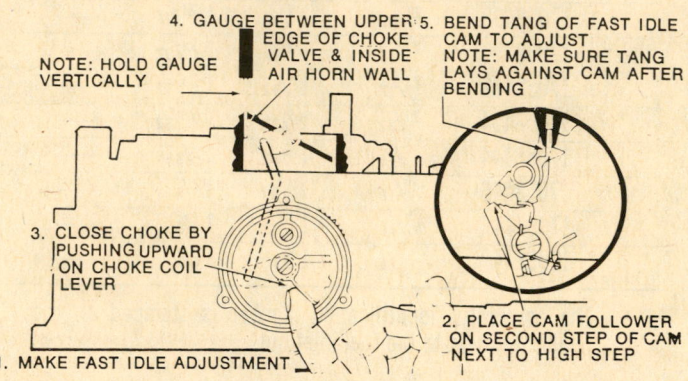

4. GAUGE BETWEEN UPPER EDGE OF CHOKE VALVE & INSIDE AIR HORN WALL

NOTE: HOLD GAUGE VERTICALLY

5. BEND TANG OF FAST IDLE CAM TO ADJUST
NOTE: MAKE SURE TANG LAYS AGAINST CAM AFTER BENDING

3. CLOSE CHOKE BY PUSHING UPWARD ON CHOKE COIL LEVER

2. PLACE CAM FOLLOWER ON SECOND STEP OF CAM NEXT TO HIGH STEP

1. MAKE FAST IDLE ADJUSTMENT

Fast idle cam (choke rod) adjustment (© Buick Div., G.M. Corp.)

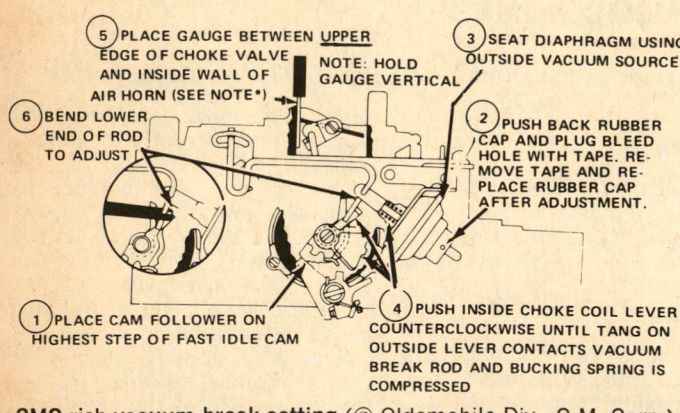

⑤ PLACE GAUGE BETWEEN UPPER EDGE OF CHOKE VALVE AND INSIDE WALL OF AIR HORN (SEE NOTE*)

⑥ BEND LOWER END OF ROD TO ADJUST

NOTE: HOLD GAUGE VERTICAL

③ SEAT DIAPHRAGM USING OUTSIDE VACUUM SOURCE

② PUSH BACK RUBBER CAP AND PLUG BLEED HOLE WITH TAPE. REMOVE TAPE AND REPLACE RUBBER CAP AFTER ADJUSTMENT.

① PLACE CAM FOLLOWER ON HIGHEST STEP OF FAST IDLE CAM

④ PUSH INSIDE CHOKE COIL LEVER COUNTERCLOCKWISE UNTIL TANG ON OUTSIDE LEVER CONTACTS VACUUM BREAK ROD AND BUCKING SPRING IS COMPRESSED

2MC rich vacuum break setting (© Oldsmobile Div., G.M. Corp.)

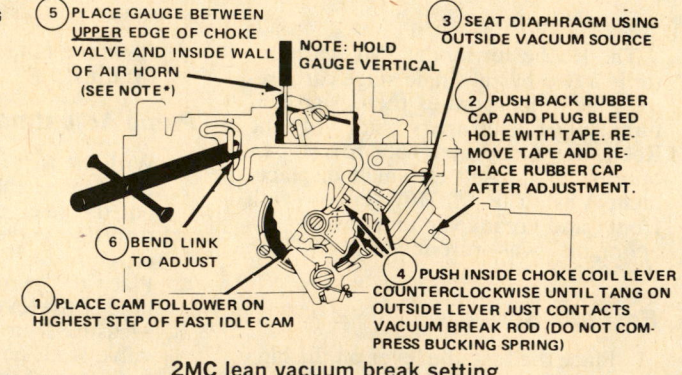

⑤ PLACE GAUGE BETWEEN UPPER EDGE OF CHOKE VALVE AND INSIDE WALL OF AIR HORN (SEE NOTE*)

NOTE: HOLD GAUGE VERTICAL

③ SEAT DIAPHRAGM USING OUTSIDE VACUUM SOURCE

② PUSH BACK RUBBER CAP AND PLUG BLEED HOLE WITH TAPE. REMOVE TAPE AND REPLACE RUBBER CAP AFTER ADJUSTMENT.

⑥ BEND LINK TO ADJUST

① PLACE CAM FOLLOWER ON HIGHEST STEP OF FAST IDLE CAM

④ PUSH INSIDE CHOKE COIL LEVER COUNTERCLOCKWISE UNTIL TANG ON OUTSIDE LEVER JUST CONTACTS VACUUM BREAK ROD (DO NOT COMPRESS BUCKING SPRING)

2MC lean vacuum break setting (© Oldsmobile Div., G.M. Corp.)

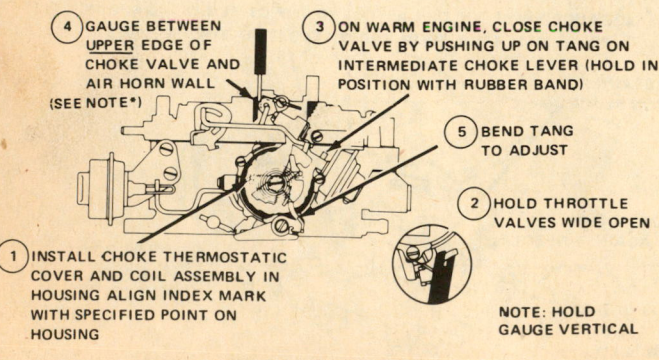

④ GAUGE BETWEEN UPPER EDGE OF CHOKE VALVE AND AIR HORN WALL (SEE NOTE*)

③ ON WARM ENGINE, CLOSE CHOKE VALVE BY PUSHING UP ON TANG ON INTERMEDIATE CHOKE LEVER (HOLD IN POSITION WITH RUBBER BAND)

⑤ BEND TANG TO ADJUST

② HOLD THROTTLE VALVES WIDE OPEN

① INSTALL CHOKE THERMOSTATIC COVER AND COIL ASSEMBLY IN HOUSING ALIGN INDEX MARK WITH SPECIFIED POINT ON HOUSING

NOTE: HOLD GAUGE VERTICAL

2MC, M2MC unloader adjustment (© G.M. Corp.)

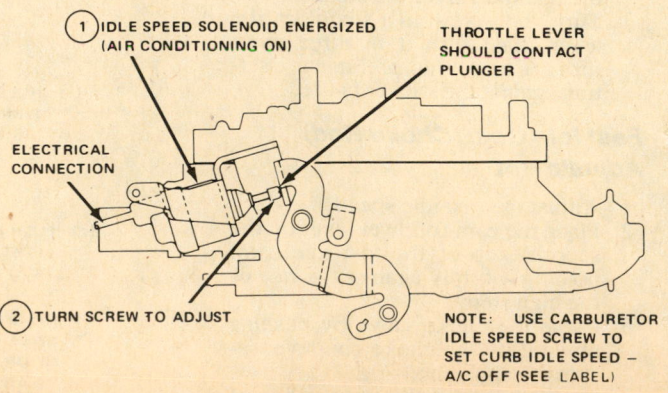

① IDLE SPEED SOLENOID ENERGIZED (AIR CONDITIONING ON)

THROTTLE LEVER SHOULD CONTACT PLUNGER

ELECTRICAL CONNECTION

② TURN SCREW TO ADJUST

NOTE: USE CARBURETOR IDLE SPEED SCREW TO SET CURB IDLE SPEED — A/C OFF (SEE LABEL)

2MC, M2MC air conditioning idle speed-up solenoid adjustment (© Oldsmobile Div., G.M. Corp.)

of the plug gauge.
5. Bend the choke rod to adjust.

2MC Lean/Rich Vacuum Break Adjustment

1. Place the cam follower on the highest step of the fast idle cam.
2. Seat the vacuum break diaphragm by using an outside vacuum source. Tape over the bleed hole, if any, under the rubber cover on the diaphragm.
3. Remove the choke cover and thermostatic coil and push up on the coil lever inside the choke housing until the tang on the vacuum break lever contacts the tang on the vacuum break plunger stem. Do not compress the bucking spring for lean adjustment. Compress the bucking spring for rich adjustment.
4. With the choke rod in the bottom of the slot in the choke lever, gauge between the upper edge of the choke valve and the inside wall of the air horn.
5. Bend the link rod at the vacuum

break plunger stem to adjust the rich setting. Bend the link rod at the opposite end from the diaphragm to adjust the lean setting.

M2MC Front/Rear Vacuum Break Adjustment

1. Seat the front diaphragm, using an outside vacuum source. If there is an air bleed hole on the diaphragm, tape it over.
2. Remove the choke cover and coil. Rotate the inside coil lever counterclockwise.
3. Check that the specified gap is present between the top of the choke valve and the air horn wall.
4. Turn the front vacuum break adjusting screw to adjust.
5. To adjust the rear vacuum break diaphragm, perform Steps 1-3 on the rear diaphragm, but make sure that the plunger bucking spring is compressed and seated in Step 2. Adjust by bending the link at the bend nearest the diaphragm.

Unloader Adjustment

1. With the choke valve completely closed, hold the throttle valves wide open.
2. Measure between the upper edge of the choke valve and air horn wall.
3. Bend the tang on the fast idle lever to obtain the proper measurement.

Air Conditioning Idle Speed-Up Solenoid Adjustment

1. With the engine at normal operating temperature and the air conditioning turned on but the compressor clutch lead disconnected, the solenoid should be electrically energized (plunger stem extended).
2. Adjust the plunger screw to obtain the specified idle speed.
3. Turn off the air conditioner. The solenoid plunger should move away from the tang on the throttle lever.
4. Adjust the curb idle speed with the idle speed screw, if necessary.

2MC, M2MC, M2ME CARBURETOR SPECIFICATIONS

BUICK

Year	Carburetor Identification①	Float Level (in.)	Choke Rod (in.)	Choke Unloader (in.)	Vacuum Break Lean or Front (in.)	Vacuum Break Rich or Rear (in.)	Pump Rod (in.)	Choke Coil Lever (in.)	Automatic Choke (notches)
1975	7045156	5/32	0.130	0.285	0.235	0.150	9/32②	0.120	1 Rich
	7045248	5/32	0.130	0.285	0.235	0.150	9/32②	0.120	1 Rich
	7045358	3/16	0.130	0.285	0.300	0.150	5/16③	0.120	1 Rich
	7045354	3/16	0.130	0.285	0.300	0.150	5/16③	0.120	1 Rich
1976	17056156	1/8	0.105	0.210	0.175	0.110	9/32②	0.120	1 Rich
	17056158	1/8	0.105	0.210	0.175	0.110	9/32②	0.120	1 Rich
	17056458	1/8	0.105	0.210	0.175	0.110	3/16③	0.120	1 Rich
	17056454	1/8	0.105	0.210	0.175	0.110	3/16③	0.120	1 Rich
1977	17057172	11/32	0.075	0.240	0.135	0.240	3/8③	0.120	2 Rich
	17057173	11/32	0.075	0.240	0.165	0.240	3/8③	0.120	2 Rich
1978	17058160	11/32	0.133	0.220	0.149	0.227	1/4③	0.120	2 Lean
	17058192	1/4	0.074	0.350	0.117	0.103	9/32②	0.120	1 Rich
	17058496	1/4	0.077	0.243	0.136	0.211	3/8③	0.120	1 Rich

CHEVROLET

Year	Carburetor Identification①	Float Level (in.)	Choke Rod (in.)	Choke Unloader (in.)	Vacuum Break Lean or Front (in.)	Vacuum Break Rich or Rear (in.)	Pump Rod (in.)	Choke Coil Lever (in.)	Automatic Choke (notches)
1978	All	1/4	0.314	0.314	0.136	——	9/32②	0.120	Index

Rochester Carburetors

Year	Carburetor Identification①	Float Level (in.)	Choke Rod (in.)	Choke Unloader (in.)	Vacuum Break Lean or Front (in.)	Vacuum Break Rich or Rear (in.)	Pump Rod (in.)	Choke Coil Lever (in.)	Automatic Choke (notches)
1975	7045297	3/16	0.130	0.300	0.300	0.150	9/32②	0.120	1 Rich
	7045354	3/16	0.130	0.300	0.300	0.150	5/16③	0.120	1 Rich
	7045358	3/16	0.130	0.300	0.300	0.150	5/16③	0.120	1 Rich
	7045156	5/32	0.130	0.300	0.300	0.150	9/32②	0.120	1 Rich
	7045598	5/32	0.130	0.300	0.300	0.150	3/16②	0.120	Index
	7045298	5/32	0.130	0.300	0.300	0.150	3/16②	0.120	1 Rich
	7045356	5/32	0.130	0.300	0.300	0.150	3/16②	0.120	Index
1976	17056156	1/8	0.105	0.210	0.175	0.110	9/32②	0.120	1 Rich
	17056157	1/8	0.105	0.210	0.175	0.110	3/16③	0.120	1 Rich
	17056158	1/8	0.105	0.210	0.175	0.110	9/32②	0.120	1 Rich
	17056454	1/8	0.105	0.210	0.210	0.110	3/16③	0.120	1 Rich
	17056455	1/8	0.120	0.210	0.210	0.130	9/32②	0.120	1 Rich
	17056456	1/8	0.105	0.210	0.210	0.110	3/16③	0.120	Index
	17056457	1/8	0.105	0.210	0.245	0.110	3/16③	0.120	Index
	17056458	1/8	0.105	0.210	0.210	0.110	3/16③	0.120	1 Rich
	17056459	1/8	0.105	0.210	0.210	0.110	3/16③	0.120	Index
1977	17057150, 17057151	1/8	0.085	0.190	0.160	0.090	11/32③	0.120	2 Rich
	17057157	1/8	0.090	0.190	0.190	0.100	3/8③	0.120	1 Rich
	17057156, 17057158	1/8	0.085	0.190	0.160	0.090	11/32③	0.120	1 Rich
1978	17058150	3/8	0.065	0.203	0.203	0.133	1/4②	0.120	2 Rich
	17058151	3/8	0.065	0.203	0.229	0.133	11/32③	0.120	2 Rich
	17058152	3/8	0.065	0.203	0.203	0.133	1/4②	0.120	2 Rich
	17058154	3/8	0.065	0.203	0.146	0.245	11/32③	0.120	2 Rich
	17058155	3/8	0.065	0.203	0.146	0.245	11/32③	0.120	2 Rich
	17058156	3/8	0.065	0.203	0.229	0.133	11/32③	0.120	2 Rich
	17058158	3/8	0.065	0.203	0.229	0.133	11/32③	0.120	2 Rich
	17058450	3/8	0.065	0.203	0.146	0.289	11/32③	0.120	2 Rich

Year	Carburetor Identification①	Float Level (in.)	Choke Rod (in.)	Choke Unloader (in.)	Vacuum Break Lean or Front (in.)	Vacuum Break Rich or Rear (in.)	Pump Rod (in.)	Choke Coil Lever (in.)	Automatic Choke (notches)
1975	7045156	5/32	0.130	0.275	0.230	0.150	9/32②	0.120	1 Rich
	7045297	3/16	0.130	0.275	0.275	0.180	9/32②	0.120	1 Rich
	7045298	5/32	0.130	0.275	0.275	0.150	9/32②	0.120	1 Rich
	7045598	5/32	0.160	0.275	0.230	0.150	9/32②	0.120	1 Rich
	7045356	5/32	0.160	0.275	0.275	0.180	9/32②	0.120	1 Rich
1976	8-260 Man.	1/8	0.105	0.210	0.175	0.110	3/16③	0.120	1 Rich
	8-260 Auto.	1/8	0.105	0.210	0.175	0.110	9/32②	0.120	1 Rich
	8-260 Calif.	1/8	0.105	0.210	0.210	0.110	3/16③	0.120	1 Rich④
1977	17057172	11/32	0.075	0.240	0.135	0.240	3/8③	0.120	2 Rich
	17057173	11/32	0.075	0.240	0.165	0.240	3/8③	0.120	2 Rich
1978	17058160	11/32	0.126	0.203	0.142	0.195	1/4②	0.120	2 Rich

① The carburetor identification number is stamped on the float bowl, next to the fuel inlet nut.

② Inner hole
③ Outer hole
④ Index on LeMans

QUADRAJET

The Rochester Quadrajet carburetor is a two stage, four-barrel downdraft carburetor. It has been built in many variations designated as 4MC, M4MC, M4MCA, M4ME, M4MEA, and 4MV. See the beginning of the Rochester section for an explanation of these designations.

The primary side of the carburetor is equipped with two primary bores and a triple venturi with plain tube nozzles. During off idle and part throttle operation, the fuel is metered through tapered metering rods operating in specially designed jets positioned by a manifold vacuum responsive piston.

The secondary side of the carburetor contains two secondary bores. An air valve is used on the secondary side for metering control and supplements the primary bore.

The secondary air valve operates tapered metering rods which regulate the fuel in constant proportion to the air being supplied.

Fast Idle Speed

1. Position the fast idle lever on the high step of the fast idle cam, the second step on the 1974 454 cu. in. engine—only.
2. Be sure that the choke is wide open and the engine warm. Plug the EGR vacuum hose. Disconnect the vacuum hose to the front vacuum break unit, if there are two.
3. Make a preliminary adjustment by turning the fast idle screw out until the throttle valves are closed, then screwing it in three turns after it contacts the lever.
4. Use the fast idle screw to adjust the fast idle to the speed, and under the conditions, specified on the engine compartment sticker or in the specifications chart.

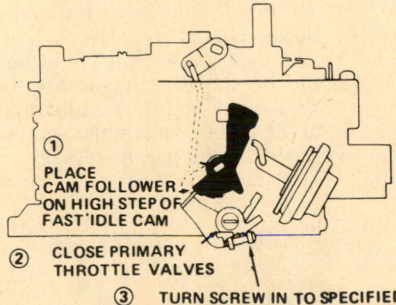

Fast Idle Adjustment
(© Chevrolet Div., G.M. Corp)

Choke Rod (Fast idle cam)

1. Adjust the fast idle and place the cam follower on the second step of the fast idle cam.
2. Close the choke valve by exerting counterclockwise pressure on the external choke lever. On 1975 and later models, remove the coil as-

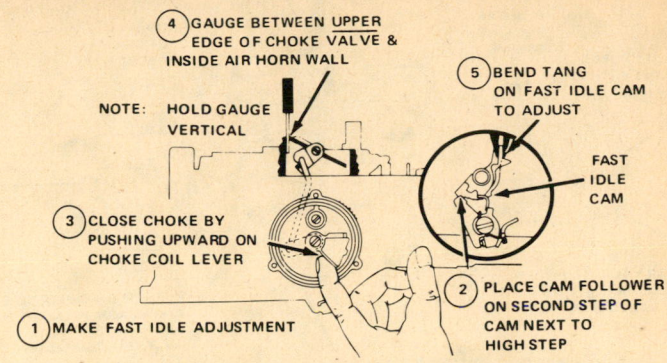

Quadrajet choke rod (fast idle cam) adjustment
(© G.M. Corp.)

sembly from the choke housing and push upon the choke coil lever.

3. Insert a gauge of the proper size between the lower (upper beginning 1975) edge of the choke valve and the inside air horn wall.
4. To adjust models through 1974, bend the choke rod. To adjust 1975 and later models, bend the tang on the fast idle cam. Be sure that the tang rests against the cam after bending.

Primary Vacuum Break (Through 1974)

1. Fully seat the vacuum break diaphragm using an outside vacuum source.
2. Open the throttle valve enough to allow the fast idle cam follower to clear the fast idle cam.
3. The end of the vacuum break rod should be at the outer end of the slot in the vacuum break diaphragm plunger.
4. The specified clearance should register from the lower end of the choke valve to the inside air horn wall.
5. If the clearance is not correct, bend the vacuum break link at the point shown in the illustration.

Primary (Front) Vacuum Break Adjustment (Beginning 1975)

1. Loosen the three retaining screws and remove the thermostatic cover and coil assembly from the choke housing.
2. Place the cam follower lever on the highest step of the fast idle cam through 1977.
3. Seat the front vacuum diaphragm using an outside vacuum source. If there is a diaphragm unit bleed hole, tape it over.
4. Push up on the inside choke coil lever until the tang on the vacuum break lever contacts the tang on the vacuum break plunger.
5. Place the proper size gauge between the upper edge of the choke valve and the inside of the air horn wall.
6. To adjust, turn the adjustment screw on the vacuum break plunger lever.
7. Install the vacuum hose to the vacuum break unit.

Secondary Vacuum Break (Through 1974)

1. Using an outside vacuum source,

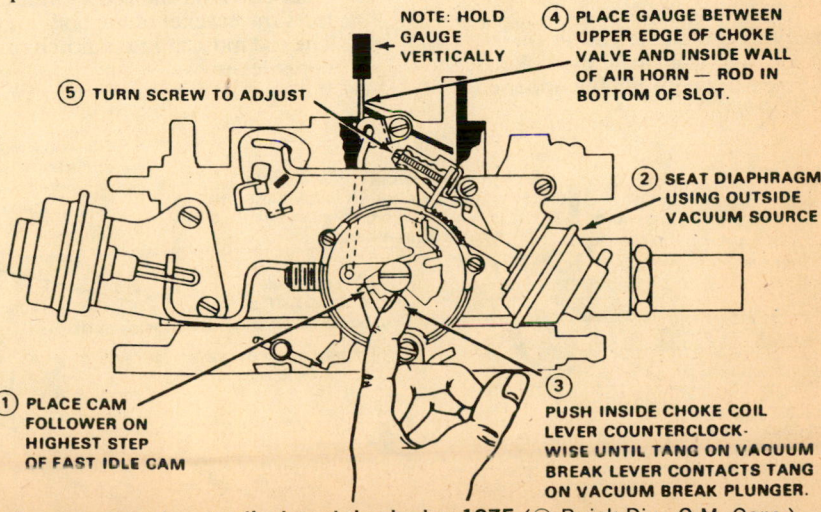

Front vacuum break adjustment, beginning 1975 (© Buick Div., G.M. Corp.)

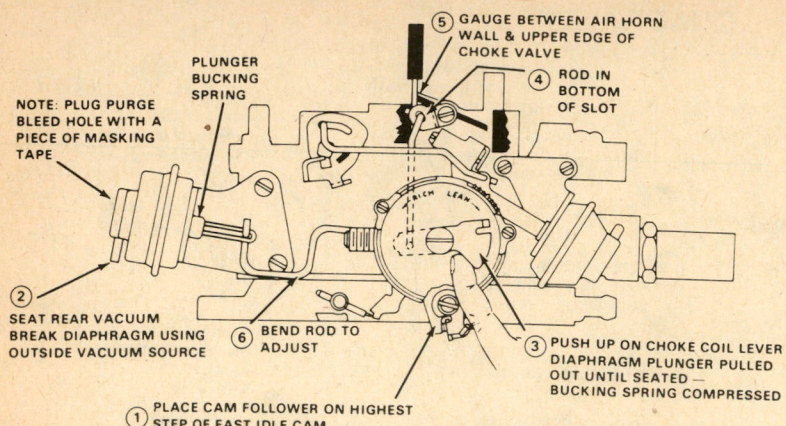

Rear vacuum break adjustment, beginning 1975 (except 454 cu in.)
(© Buick Div., G.M. Corp.)

seat the auxiliary vacuum break diaphragm plunger.
2. Rotate the choke lever in the closed position until the spring loaded diaphragm plunger is fully extended.
3. Holding the choke valve closed, check the distance between the lower edge of the choke valve and the air horn wall.
4. To adjust to specifications, bend the vacuum break link.

Secondary (Rear) Vacuum Break Adjustment (Beginning 1975)

1. Remove the thermostatic cover and coil assembly from the choke housing.
2. Place the cam follower on the highest step of the fast idle cam through 1977.
3. Tape over the bleed hole in the rear vacuum break diaphragm and seat the diaphragm using an outside vacuum source. Make sure the diaphragm plunger bucking spring, if any, is compressed.
4. Close the choke by pushing up on the choke coil lever inside the choke housing.
5. With the choke rod in the bottom of the slot in the choke lever, measure between the upper edge of

the choke valve and the air horn wall with a wire type gauge.
NOTE: *On 1975 454 cu. in. engines only, the choke valve should be held wide open.*
6. To adjust, bend the vacuum break rod at the first bend near the diaphragm.
7. Remove the tape covering the bleed hole of the diaphragm and connect the vacuum hose.

Choke Unloader

1. Push up on the vacuum break lever to close the choke valve, and fully open the throttle valves.
2. Measure the distance from the lower (upper beginning 1975) edge of the choke valve to the air horn wall.
3. To adjust, bend the tang on the fast idle lever.

4MV Choke Coil Rod

1. Close the choke valve by rotating the choke coil lever counterclockwise.
2. Disconnect the thermostatic coil rod from the upper lever.
3. Push down on the rod until it contacts the bracket of the coil.
4. The rod must fit in the notch of the upper lever.
5. If it does not, it must be bent on the

curved portion just below the upper lever.

MC, ME Choke Coil Lever Adjustment

1. Remove the choke cover and thermostatic coil from the choke housing. Place the fast idle cam follower on the high step.
2. Push up on the coil tang (counterclockwise) until the choke valve is closed. The top of the choke rod should be at the bottom of the slot in the choke valve lever.
3. Insert a 0.120 in. drill bit in the hole in the choke housing.
4. The lower edge of the choke coil lever should just contact the side of the plug gauge.
5. Bend the choke rod at the top angle to adjust.

Secondary Closing Adjustment

This adjustment assures proper closing of the secondary throttle plates.
1. Set the slow idle as per instructions in the appropriate car section. Make sure that the fast idle cam follower is not resting on the fast idle cam and the choke valve is wide open.
2. There should be 0.020 in. clearance between the secondary throttle actuating rod and the front of the slot on the secondary throttle lever with the closing tang on the throttle lever resting against the actuating lever.
3. Bend the secondary closing tang on the primary throttle actuating rod or lever to adjust.

Secondary Opening Adjustment

1. Open the primary throttle valves until the actuating link contacts the upper tang on the secondary lever.
2. With two point linkage, the bottom of the link should be in the center of the secondary lever slot.
3. With three point linkage, there should be 0.070 in. clearance between the link and the middle tang.
4. Bend the upper tang on the secondary lever to adjust as necessary.

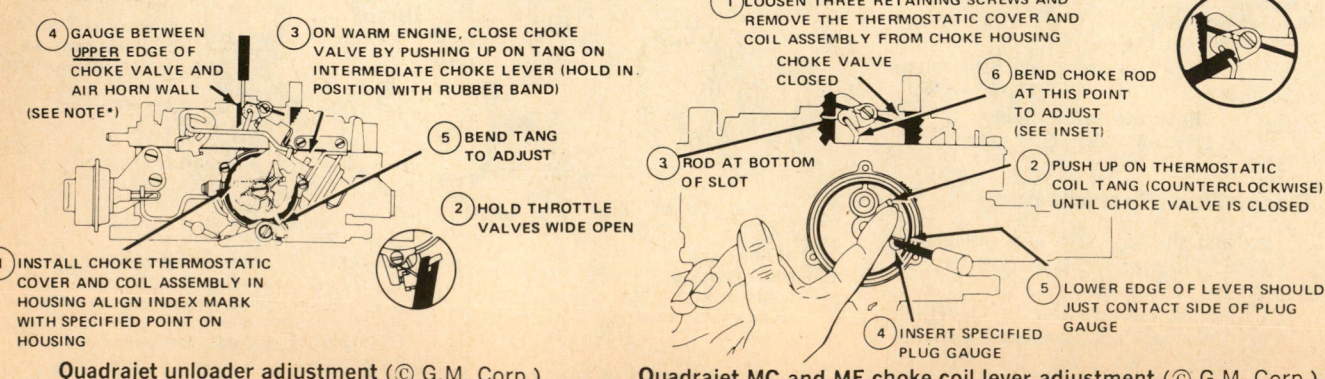

Quadrajet unloader adjustment (© G.M. Corp.)

Quadrajet MC and ME choke coil lever adjustment (© G.M. Corp.)

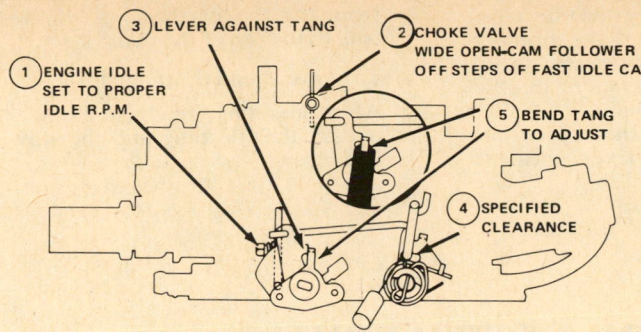

Quadrajet Secondary closing adjustment (© G.M. Corp.)

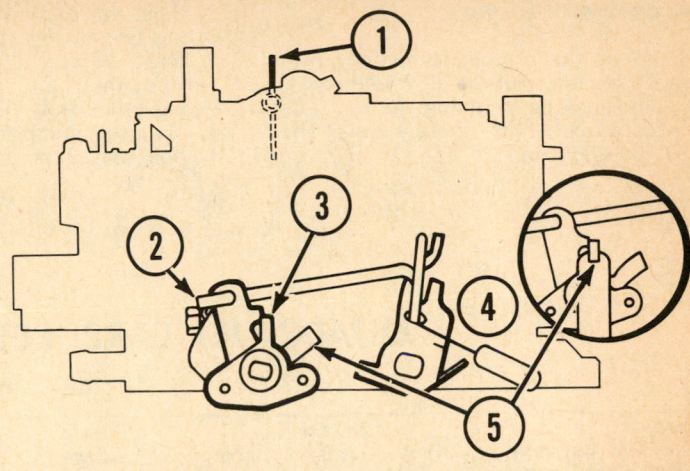

Secondary Closing Adjustments

1—Choke fully open and fast idle cam follower off steps of fast idle cam.
2—Slow idle set properly.
3—Make sure throttle lever tang is against secondary throttle rod operating lever as shown in 3.
4—Gauge between rod and end of slot as shown in 4.
5—To adjust, open throttle slightly and bend tang.

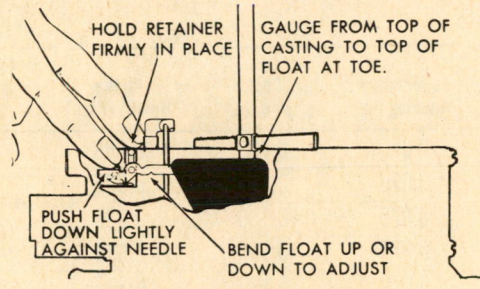

Adjusting Float Level
(© Pontiac Div., G.M. Corp)

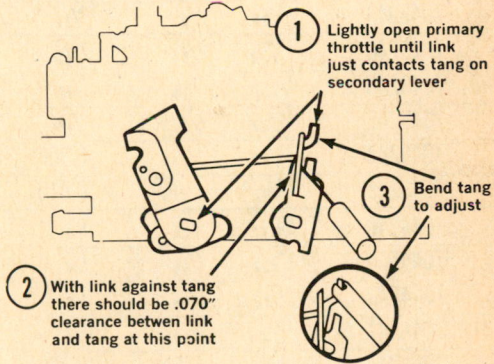

Secondary Opening Adjustments
(© Oldsmobile Div., G.M. Corp)

Air Valve Spring Setting (© Pontiac Div., G.M. Corp)

Air Valve Spring Adjustment

To adjust the air valve spring wind-up, loosen the Allen head lockscrew and turn the adjusting screw counter-clockwise to remove all spring tension. With the air valve closed, turn the adjusting screw clockwise the specified number of turns after the torsion spring contacts the pin on the shaft. Hold the adjusting screw in this position and tighten the lockscrew.

Float Level

With the air horn assembly removed, measure the distance from the air horn gasket surface (gasket removed) to the top of the float at the toe ($1/16$ in. back from the toe on 1975 models; $3/16$ in. back on 1976 and later models).
NOTE: *Make sure the retaining pin is firmly held in place and that the tang of the float is firmly against the needle and seat assembly.*

Bend the float arm to adjust.

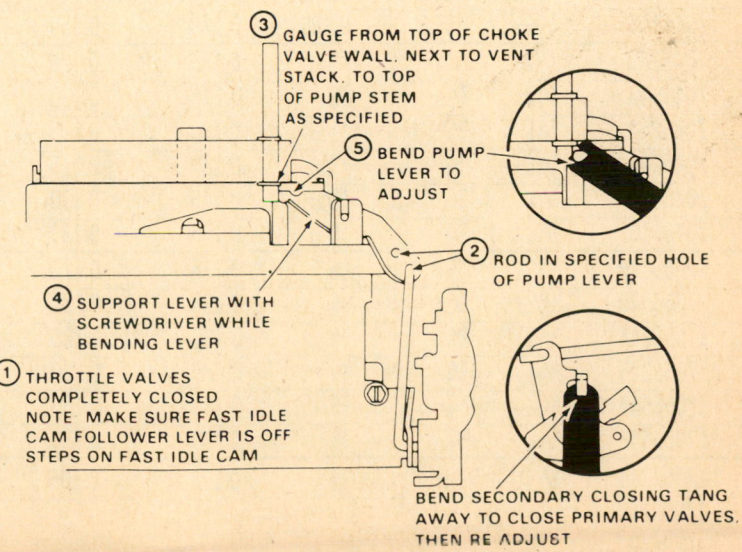

Accelerator Pump Rod Adjustment
(© Pontiac Div., G.M. Corp)

Rochester Carburetors

Accelerator Pump

1. Close the primary throttle valves by backing out the slow idle screw and making sure that the fast idle cam follower is off the steps of the fast idle cam.

2. Bend the secondary throttle closing tang away from the primary throttle lever, if necessary, to insure that the primary throttle valves are fully closed.

3. With the pump in the appropriate hole in the pump lever, measure from the top of the choke valve wall to the top of the pump stem.

4. To adjust, bend the pump lever.

5. After adjusting, readjust the secondary throttle tang and the slow idle screw.

QUADRAJET CARBURETOR SPECIFICATIONS

BUICK

Year	Carburetor Identification①	Float Level (in.)	Air Valve Spring (turn)	Pump Rod (in.)	Primary Vacuum Break (in.)	Secondary Vacuum Break (in.)	Secondary Opening (in.)	Choke Rod (in.)	Choke Unloader (in.)	Fast Idle Speed④ (rpm)
1972	7042240	3/8	1/2	1/4	0.180	——	0.070	0.130	0.335	700
	7042242	3/8	1/2	1/4	0.200	——	0.070	0.130	0.335	700
	7042243	13/32	1/2	1/4	0.215	——	0.070	0.130	0.335	920
	7042244	15/32	1/2	9/32	0.170	——	0.070	0.130	0.335	700
	7042245	15/32	1/2	9/32	0.170	——	0.070	0.130	0.335	820
	7042940	3/8	1/2	1/4	0.180	——	0.070	0.130	0.335	700
	7042942	3/8	1/2	1/4	0.200	——	0.070	0.130	0.335	700
	7042944	15/32	1/2	9/32	0.170	——	0.070	0.130	0.335	700
1973	7043240	13/32	7/16	7/16	0.215		0.070	0.130	0.335	700
	7043243	13/32	7/16	7/16	0.215		0.070	0.130	0.335	920
	7043242	13/32	7/16	7/16	0.200		0.070	0.130	0.335	920/700③
	7043244	15/32	11/16	0.306	0.170		0.070	0.130	0.335	700
	7043245	15/32	11/16	0.410	0.170		0.070	0.130	0.335	820
1974	7044240	13/32	7/16	1/4	0.215	0.160	0.070	0.130	0.335	700
	7044540	13/32	7/16	1/4	0.215	0.160	0.070	0.130	0.335	700
	7044242	13/32	7/16	1/4	0.200	0.180	0.070	0.130	0.335	700
	7044241	13/32	7/16	1/4	0.215	0.160	0.070	0.130	0.335	700
	7044244	15/32	11/16	0.306	0.170	0.150	0.070	0.130	0.335	700
	7044544	15/32	11/16	0.306	0.170	0.150	0.070	0.130	0.335	700
	7044546	15/32	11/16	0.306	0.170	0.150	0.070	0.130	0.335	700
	7044246	15/32	11/16	0.306	0.170	0.150	0.070	0.130	0.335	700
1975	7045240	7/16	7/16	9/32	0.135	0.120	②	0.095	0.240	1800
	7045548	7/16	7/16	9/32	0.135	0.120	②	0.095	0.240	1800
	7045244	5/16	3/4	15/32	0.130	0.115	②	0.095	0.240	1800
	7045246	5/16	3/4	15/32	0.130	0.115	②	0.095	0.240	1800
	7045544	5/16	3/4	15/32	0.145	0.130	②	0.095	0.240	1800
	7045546	5/16	3/4	15/32	0.145	0.130	②	0.095	0.240	1800
1976	17056240	15/32	7/16	3/8	0.135	0.120	②	0.095	0.250	1800
	17056540	15/32	7/16	3/8	0.135	0.120	②	0.095	0.250	1800
	17056244	5/16	3/4	3/8	0.130	0.120	②	0.095	0.250	1800
	17056246	5/16	3/4	3/8	0.130	0.120	②	0.095	0.250	1800
	17056544	5/16	3/4	3/8	0.130	0.130	②	0.095	0.250	1800
	17056546	5/16	3/4	3/8	0.130	0.130	②	0.095	0.250	1800
1977	17057241	5/16	3/4	3/8	0.120	0.105	②	0.095	0.240	⑤
	17057250, 17057253, 17057255, 17057256	13/32	1/2	9/32	0.120	0.170	②	0.095	0.205	⑤

BUICK

Year	Carburetor Identification①	Float Level (in.)	Air Valve Spring (turn)	Pump Rod (in.)	Primary Vacuum Break (in.)	Secondary Vacuum Break (in.)	Secondary Opening (in.)	Choke Rod (in.)	Choke Unloader (in.)	Fast Idle Speed④ (rpm)
1977	17057258	13/32	1/2	9/32	0.125	0.215	②	0.095	0.205	⑤
	17057550, 17057553	13/32	1/2	9/32	0.125	0.215	②	0.095	0.200	⑤
1978	17058240	7/32	3/4	9/32	0.117	0.117	②	0.074	0.243	⑤
	17058241	5/16	3/4	3/8	0.120	0.103	②	0.096	0.243	⑤
	17058250	13/32	1/2	9/32	0.129	0.183	②	0.096	0.220	⑤
	17058253	13/32	1/2	9/32	0.129	0.183	②	0.096	0.220	⑤
	17058254	15/32	1/2	9/32	0.136	——	②	0.103	0.220	⑤
	17058257	13/32	1/2	9/32	0.136	0.231	②	0.103	0.220	⑤
	17058258	13/32	1/2	9/32	0.136	0.231	②	0.103	0.220	⑤
	17058259	13/32	1/2	9/32	0.136	0.231	②	0.103	0.220	⑤
	17058582	15/32	7/8	9/32	0.179	——	②	0.314	0.277	⑤
	17058584	15/32	7/8	9/32	0.179	——	②	0.314	0.277	⑤
	17058282	15/32	7/8	9/32	0.157	——	②	0.314	0.277	⑤
	17058284	15/32	7/8	9/32	0.157	——	②	0.314	0.277	⑤
	17058228	15/32	1	9/32	0.179	——	②	0.314	0.277	⑤
	17058502	15/32	7/8	9/32	0.164	——	②	0.314	0.277	⑤
	17058504	15/32	7/8	9/32	0.164	——	②	0.314	0.277	⑤
	17058202	15/32	7/8	9/32	0.157	——	②	0.314	0.277	⑤
	17058204	15/32	7/8	9/32	0.157	——	②	0.314	0.277	⑤
	17058540	7/32	3/4	9/32	0.117	0.117	②	0.074	0.243	⑤
	17058550	13/32	1/2	9/32	0.136	0.231	②	0.103	0.220	⑤
	17058553	15/32	1/2	9/32	0.129	0.231	②	0.096	0.220	⑤
	17058559	15/32	1/2	9/32	0.136	——	②	0.096	0.231	⑤

① The carburetor identification number is stamped on the float bowl, near the secondary throttle lever.
② No measurement necessary on two point linkage; see text
③ Manual/Automatic
④ On low step of cam, automatic in Drive through 1974; on high step of cam, automatic in Park starting 1975.
⑤ 3 turns after contacting lever for preliminary setting

CADILLAC

Year	Carburetor Identification①	Float Level (in.)	Air Valve Spring (turn)	Pump Rod (in.)	Primary Vacuum Break (in.)	Secondary Vacuum Break (in.)	Secondary Opening (in.)	Choke Rod (in.)	Choke Unloader (in.)	Fast Idle Speed② (rpm)
1972	7047231	15/64	1/2	11/32	0.140	——	③	0.090	0.312	——
	7047232	23/64	1/2	11/32	0.140	——	③	0.090	0.312	——
1973	7047331	1/4	1/2	11/32	0.200	——	③	0.090	0.015	——
	7047332	23/64	1/2	11/32	0.205	——	③	0.090	0.015	——
1974	7044230	1/4	3/8	1/4	0.185	——	③	0.110	0.312	1200-1500
	7044232	23/64	1/2	1/4	0.200	——	③	0.110	0.312	1200-1500
	7044530	1/4	3/8	1/4	0.185	——	③	0.110	0.312	1200-1500
	7044532	23/64	1/2	1/4	0.200	——	③	0.110	0.312	1200-1500
	7044234	1/4	7/16	11/32	0.185	——	③	0.110	0.312	1200-1500
	7044235	23/64	9/16	11/32	0.200	——	③	0.110	0.312	1200-1500
	7044233	19/64	3/8	11/32	0.185	——	③	0.110	0.312	1200-1500

Rochester Carburetors

CADILLAC

Year	Carburetor Identification①	Float Level (in.)	Air Valve Spring (turn)	Pump Rod (in.)	Primary Vacuum Break (in.)	Secondary Vacuum Break (in.)	Secondary Opening (in.)	Choke Rod (in.)	Choke Unloader (in.)	Fast Idle Speed② (rpm)
1975	7045230	15/32	7/16	3/8	0.160	0.130	③	0.080	0.215	1200-1250
	7045530	15/32	1/2	3/8	0.230	0.230	③	0.080	0.215	1200-1250
1976	7056232	13/32	3/8	3/8	0.160	0.160	③	0.080	0.230	1400
	7056230	13/32	3/8	3/8	0.160	0.160	③	0.080	0.230	1400
	7056530	7/16	3/8	9/32	0.160	0.160	③	0.080	0.230	1400
1977	17057232, 17057233	13/32	1/2	3/8	0.140	0.140	③	0.080	0.230	1400
	17057230	13/32	1/2	7/16	0.140	0.140	③	0.080	0.230	1400
	17057231	17/32	1/2	3/8	0.140	0.140	③	0.080	0.230	1400
	17057530	13/32	1/2	7/16	0.150	0.150	③	0.080	0.230	1500
1978	17058230	13/32	1/2	3/8	0.150	0.165	③	0.080	0.230	1500
	All others	13/32	1/2	3/8	0.140	0.250	③	0.080	0.230	1400

① The carburetor identification number is stamped on the float bowl, near the secondary throttle lever.
② On second step of cam.
③ No measurement necessary on two point linkage; see text.

CHEVROLET

Year	Carburetor Identification①	Float Level (in.)	Air Valve Spring (turn)	Pump Rod (in.)	Primary Vacuum Break (in.)	Secondary Vacuum Break (in.)	Secondary Opening (in.)	Choke Rod (in.)	Choke Unloader (in.)	Fast Idle Speed② (rpm)
1972	7042220	1/4	7/16	3/8	0.250	——	⑤	0.100	0.450	——
	7042216	1/4	7/16	3/8	0.250	——	⑤	0.100	0.450	——
	7042215	1/4	7/16	3/8	0.250	——	⑤	0.100	0.450	——
	7042217	1/4	7/16	3/8	0.250	——	⑤	0.100	0.450	——
	7042202	1/4	1/2	3/8	0.215	——	⑤	0.100	0.450	——
	7042203	1/4	1/2	3/8	0.215	——	⑤	0.100	0.450	——
	7042902	1/4	1/2	3/8	0.215	——	⑤	0.100	0.450	——
	7042903	1/4	1/2	3/8	0.215	——	⑤	0.100	0.450	——
1973	7043202	7/32	1/2	13/32	0.250	——	⑤	0.430	0.450	——
	7043203	7/32	1/2	13/32	0.250	——	⑤	0.430	0.450	——
	7043212	7/32	1	13/32	0.250	——	⑤	0.430	0.450	——
	7043213	7/32	1	13/32	0.250	——	⑤	0.430	0.450	——
	7043200	1/4	11/16	13/32	0.250	——	⑤	0.430	0.450	——
	7043201	1/4	11/16	13/32	0.250	——	⑤	0.430	0.450	——
1974	7044202	1/4	7/8	13/32②	0.230	——	⑤	0.430	0.450	1600③-1300④
	7044203	1/4	7/8	13/32②	0.230	——	⑤	0.430	0.450	1600③-1300④
	7044206	1/4	7/8	13/32②	0.230	——	⑤	0.430	0.450	1600③-1300④
	7044207	1/4	7/8	13/32②	0.230	——	⑤	0.430	0.450	1600③-1300④
	7044223	3/8	7/16	13/32②	0.220	——	⑤	0.430	0.450	1600③-1300④
	7044201	3/8	7/16	13/32②	0.250	——	⑤	0.430	0.450	1600③-1300④
	7044500	3/8	7/16	13/32②	0.250	——	⑤	0.430	0.450	1600③-1300④
	7044208	1/4	1	13/32②	0.230	——	⑤	0.430	0.450	1600③-1300④
	7044209	1/4	1	13/32②	0.230	——	⑤	0.430	0.450	1600③-1300④
	7044210	1/4	1	13/32②	0.230	——	⑤	0.430	0.450	1600③-1300④
	7044211	1/4	1	13/32②	0.230	——	⑤	0.430	0.450	1600③-1300④
	7044502	1/4	7/8	13/32②	0.230	——	⑤	0.430	0.450	1600③-1300④

CHEVROLET

Year	Carburetor Identification[1]	Float Level (in.)	Air Valve Spring (turn)	Pump Rod (in.)	Primary Vacuum Break (in.)	Secondary Vacuum Break (in.)	Secondary Opening (in.)	Choke Rod (in.)	Choke Unloader (in.)	Fast Idle Speed[2] (rpm)
1974	7044503	1/4	7/8	13/32[2]	0.230	——	[5]	0.430	0.450	1600[3]-1300[4]
	7044506	1/4	7/8	13/32[2]	0.230	——	[5]	0.430	0.450	1600[3]-1300[4]
	7044507	1/4	7/8	13/32[2]	0.230	——	[5]	0.430	0.450	1600[3]-1300[4]
	7044221	3/8	7/16	13/32	0.250	——	[5]	0.430	0.450	1600[3]-1300[4]
	7044225	3/8	7/16	13/32	0.220	——	[5]	0.430	0.450	1600[3]-1300[4]
	7044226	1/4	3/4	13/32	0.230	——	[5]	0.430	0.450	1600[3]-1300[4]
	7044505	3/8	7/16	13/32	0.250	——	[5]	0.430	0.450	1600[3]-1300[4]
	7044526	1/4	3/4	13/32	0.230	——	[5]	0.430	0.450	1600[3]-1300[4]
1975	7045200	17/32	9/16	0.275	0.200	0.550	[5]	0.300	0.325	1000
	7045202	15/32	7/8	0.275	0.180	0.170	[5]	0.300	0.325	1600
	7045203	15/32	7/8	0.275	0.180	0.170	[5]	0.300	0.325	1600
	7045206	15/32	7/8	0.275	0.180	0.170	[5]	0.300	0.325	1600
	7045207	15/32	7/8	0.275	0.180	0.170	[5]	0.300	0.325	1600
	7045208	15/32	7/8	0.275	0.180	0.170	[5]	0.300	0.325	1600
	7045209	15/32	7/8	0.275	0.180	0.170	[5]	0.300	0.325	1600
	7045210	15/32	7/8	0.275	0.180	0.170	[5]	0.300	0.325	1600
	7045211	15/32	7/8	0.275	0.180	0.170	[5]	0.300	0.325	1600
	7045222	15/32	7/8	0.275	0.180	0.170	[5]	0.300	0.325	1600
	7045223	15/32	7/8	0.275	0.180	0.170	[5]	0.300	0.325	1600
	7045224	15/32	3/4	0.275	0.180	0.170	[5]	0.325	0.325	1600
	7045228	15/32	3/4	0.275	0.180	0.170	[5]	0.325	0.325	1600
	7045502	15/32	7/8	0.275	0.180	0.170	[5]	0.300	0.325	1600
	7045503	15/32	7/8	0.275	0.180	0.170	[5]	0.300	0.325	1600
	7045504	15/32	7/8	0.275	0.180	0.170	[5]	0.300	0.325	1600
	7045506	15/32	7/8	0.275	0.180	0.170	[5]	0.300	0.325	1600
	7044507	15/32	7/8	0.275	0.180	0.170	[5]	0.300	0.325	1600
1976	17056202	13/32	7/8	9/32	0.185	——	[5]	0.325	0.325	1600
	17056203	13/32	7/8	9/32	0.170	——	[5]	0.325	0.325	1600
	17056206	13/32	7/8	9/32	0.185	——	[5]	0.325	0.325	1600
	17056207	13/32	7/8	9/32	0.170	——	[5]	0.325	0.325	1600
	17056210	13/32	1.0	9/32	0.185	——	[5]	0.325	0.325	1600
	17056211	13/32	3/4	9/32	0.185	——	[5]	0.325	0.325	1600
	17056228	13/32	7/8	9/32	0.185	——	[5]	0.325	0.325	1600
	17056502	13/32	7/8	9/32	0.185	——	[5]	0.325	0.325	1600
	17056506	13/32	3/4	9/32	0.185	——	[5]	0.325	0.325	1600
	17056528	13/32	7/8	9/32	0.185	——	[5]	0.325	0.325	1600
	17056200	13/32	7/8	9/32	0.240	0.160	[5]	0.190	0.270	1600
1977	17057202, 17057204	15/32	7/8	15/32	0.180	——	[5]	0.325	0.280	1600
	17057203	15/32	7/8	15/32	0.180	——	[5]	0.325	0.280	1300
	17057502, 17057504	15/32	7/8	15/32	0.165	——	[5]	0.325	0.280	1600
	17057210, 17057510, 17057528	15/32	1	15/32	0.180	——	[5]	0.325	0.280	1600
	17057211	15/32	1	15/32	0.180	——	[5]	0.325	0.280	1300
	17057228	13/32	1	15/32	0.180	——	[5]	0.325	0.280	1600
	17057582, 17057584	15/32	7/8	13/32	0.180	——	[6]	0.325	0.280	1600

Rochester Carburetors

CHEVROLET

Year	Carburetor Identification[1]	Float Level (in.)	Air Valve Spring (turn)	Pump Rod (in.)	Primary Vacuum Break (in.)	Secondary Vacuum Break (in.)	Secondary Opening (in.)	Choke Rod (in.)	Choke Unloader (in.)	Fast Idle Speed[2] (rpm)
1978	17058202	$^{15}/_{32}$	$^{7}/_{8}$	$^{9}/_{32}$	0.179	——	[2]	0.314	0.277	[5]
	17058203	$^{15}/_{32}$	$^{7}/_{8}$	$^{9}/_{32}$	0.179	——	[2]	0.314	0.277	[5]
	17058204	$^{15}/_{32}$	$^{7}/_{8}$	$^{9}/_{32}$	0.179	——	[2]	0.314	0.277	[5]
	17058210	$^{15}/_{32}$	$^{1}/_{2}$	$^{9}/_{32}$	0.203	——	[2]	0.314	0.277	[5]
	17058211	$^{15}/_{32}$	$^{1}/_{2}$	$^{9}/_{32}$	0.203	——	[2]	0.314	0.277	[5]
	17058228	$^{15}/_{32}$	$^{7}/_{8}$	$^{9}/_{32}$	0.203	——	[2]	0.314	0.277	[5]
	17058502	$^{15}/_{32}$	$^{7}/_{8}$	$^{9}/_{32}$	0.187	——	[2]	0.314	0.277	[5]
	17058504	$^{15}/_{32}$	$^{7}/_{8}$	$^{9}/_{32}$	0.187	——	[2]	0.314	0.277	[5]
	17058582	$^{15}/_{32}$	$^{7}/_{8}$	$^{9}/_{32}$	0.203	——	[2]	0.314	0.277	[5]
	17058584	$^{15}/_{32}$	$^{7}/_{8}$	$^{9}/_{32}$	0.203	——	[2]	0.314	0.277	[5]

[1] The carburetor identification number is stamped on the float bowl, near the secondary throttle lever.

[2] Without vacuum advance.

[3] With automatic transmission; vacuum advance connected and EGR disconnected and the throttle positioned on the high step of cam.

[4] With manual transmission; without vacuum advance and the throttle positioned on the high step of cam.

[5] No measurement necessary on two point linkage; see text.

OLDSMOBILE

Year	Carburetor Identification[1]	Float Level (in.)	Air Valve Spring (turn)	Pump Rod (in.)	Primary Vacuum Break (in.)	Secondary Vacuum Break (in.)	Secondary Opening (in.)	Choke Rod (in.)	Choke Unloader (in.)	Fast Idle Speed[2] (rpm)
1972	7042250	$^{1}/_{4}$	$^{1}/_{2}$	$^{3}/_{8}$	0.230	——	0.070	0.120	0.200	——
	7042251	$^{1}/_{4}$	$^{3}/_{4}$	$^{3}/_{8}$	0.215	——	0.070	0.120	0.200	——
	7042252	$^{1}/_{4}$	$^{3}/_{4}$	$^{3}/_{8}$	0.215	——	0.070	0.120	0.200	——
	7042953	$^{1}/_{4}$	$^{3}/_{4}$	$^{3}/_{8}$	0.215	——	0.070	0.120	0.200	——
1973	7043256	$^{1}/_{4}$	$^{3}/_{4}$	——	0.200	——	0.070	0.120	0.300	——
	7043257	$^{1}/_{4}$	$^{1}/_{2}$	——	0.200	——	0.070	0.120	0.300	——
	7043255	$^{1}/_{4}$	$^{3}/_{4}$	——	0.200	——	0.070	0.120	0.300	——
	7043251	$^{1}/_{4}$	$^{3}/_{4}$	——	0.200	——	0.070	0.120	0.300	——
	7043253	$^{1}/_{4}$	$^{3}/_{4}$	——	0.275	——	0.070	0.120	0.300	——
	7043252	$^{1}/_{4}$	$^{3}/_{4}$	——	0.200	——	0.070	0.120	0.300	——
	7043259	$^{1}/_{4}$	$^{3}/_{4}$	——	0.215	——	0.070	0.120	0.300	——
1974	7043250	$^{1}/_{4}$	$^{1}/_{2}$	$^{3}/_{8}$	0.200	——	0.070	0.120	0.300	1000[2]
	7043251	$^{1}/_{4}$	$^{3}/_{4}$	$^{3}/_{8}$	0.200	——	0.070	0.120	0.300	1000[2]
	7043252	$^{1}/_{4}$	$^{3}/_{4}$	$^{3}/_{8}$	0.200	——	0.070	0.120	0.300	1000[2]
	7043254	$^{1}/_{4}$	$^{3}/_{4}$	$^{3}/_{8}$	0.275	——	0.070	0.120	0.300	1000[2]
	7043255	$^{1}/_{4}$	$^{1}/_{2}$	$^{3}/_{8}$	0.200	——	0.070	0.120	0.300	1000[2]
	7043256	$^{1}/_{4}$	$^{1}/_{2}$	$^{3}/_{8}$	0.200	——	0.070	0.120	0.300	1000[2]
	7043259	$^{1}/_{4}$	$^{3}/_{4}$	$^{3}/_{8}$	0.215	——	0.070	0.120	0.300	1000[2]
	7043282	$^{1}/_{4}$	$^{3}/_{4}$	$^{3}/_{8}$	0.215	——	0.070	0.120	0.300	1000[2]
	7044557	$^{1}/_{4}$	$^{3}/_{4}$	$^{3}/_{8}$	0.200	——	0.070	0.120	0.300	1000[2]
	7044558	$^{1}/_{4}$	$^{3}/_{4}$	$^{3}/_{8}$	0.200	——	0.070	0.120	0.300	1000[2]
	7044559	$^{1}/_{4}$	$^{3}/_{4}$	$^{3}/_{8}$	0.275	——	0.070	0.120	0.300	1000[2]
1975	7045183	$^{3}/_{8}$	$^{1}/_{2}$	$^{9}/_{32}$	0.190	0.140	[4]	0.135	0.235	[3]
	7045250	$^{3}/_{8}$	$^{1}/_{2}$	$^{9}/_{32}$	0.250	0.180	[4]	0.170	0.300	[3]
	7045483	$^{3}/_{8}$	$^{1}/_{2}$	$^{9}/_{32}$	0.275	0.180	[4]	0.135	0.235	[3]
	7045550	$^{3}/_{8}$	$^{1}/_{2}$	$^{9}/_{32}$	0.275	0.180	[4]	0.135	0.235	[3]
	7045264	$^{17}/_{32}$	$^{1}/_{2}$	$^{9}/_{32}$	0.150	0.260	[4]	0.130	0.235	[3]

OLDSMOBILE

Year	Carburetor Identification①	Float Level (in.)	Air Valve Spring (turn)	Pump Rod (in.)	Primary Vacuum Break (in.)	Secondary Vacuum Break (in.)	Secondary Opening (in.)	Choke Rod (in.)	Choke Unloader (in.)	Fast Idle Speed② (rpm)
1975	7045184	3/8	3/4	9/32	0.190	0.140	④	0.135	0.235	③
	7045185	3/8	3/4	9/32	0.275	0.140	④	0.135	0.235	③
	7045251	3/8	3/4	9/32	0.190	0.140	④	0.135	0.235	③
	7045484	3/8	3/4	9/32	0.190	0.140	④	0.135	0.235	③
	7045485	3/8	3/4	9/32	0.190	0.180	④	0.160	0.235	③
	7045551	3/8	3/4	9/32	0.190	0.140	④	0.135	0.235	③
	7045246	5/16	3/4	3/8	0.130	0.115	④	0.095	0.240	③
	7045546	5/16	3/4	3/8	0.145	0.130	④	0.095	0.240	③
1976	17056246	5/16	3/4	3/8	0.130	0.120	④	0.095	0.250	——
	17056250	13/32	1/2	9/32	0.190	0.140	④	0.130	0.230	——
	17056251	13/32	3/4	9/32	0.190	0.140	④	0.130	0.230	——
	17056252	13/32	3/4	9/32	0.190	0.140	④	0.130	0.230	——
	17056253	13/32	1/2	9/32	0.190	0.140	④	0.130	0.230	——
	17056255	13/32	3/4	9/32	0.190	0.140	④	0.130	0.230	——
	17056256	13/32	3/4	9/32	0.190	0.140	④	0.130	0.230	——
	17056257	13/32	3/4	9/32	0.190	0.140	④	0.130	0.230	——
	17056258	13/32	1/2	9/32	0.190	0.140	④	0.130	0.230	——
	17056259	13/32	1/2	9/32	0.190	0.140	④	0.130	0.230	——
	17056546	5/16	3/4	3/8	0.130	0.130	④	0.095	0.250	——
	17056550	13/32	1/2	9/32	0.190	0.140	④	0.130	0.230	——
	17056551	13/32	3/4	9/32	0.190	0.140	④	0.130	0.230	——
	17056552	13/32	3/4	9/32	0.200	0.140	④	0.130	0.230	——
	17056553	13/32	1/2	9/32	0.190	0.140	④	0.130	0.230	——
	17056556	13/32	3/4	9/32	0.190	0.140	④	0.130	0.230	——
1977	17057250, 17057252, 17057253, 17057255, 17057256	13/32	1/2	9/32	0.135	0.180	④	0.100	0.220	⑤
	17057257, 17057258, 17057550, 17057552, 17057553	13/32	1/2	9/32	0.135	0.225	④	0.100	0.220	⑤
	17057202, 17057204	15/32	7/8	9/32	0.160	——	④	0.325	0.280	⑤
	17057502, 17057504 17057582, 17057584	15/32	7/8	9/32	0.175	——	④	0.325	0.280	⑤
1978	17058202	15/32	7/8	9/32	0.157	——	④	0.314	0.277	⑤
	17058204	15/32	7/8	9/32	0.157	——	④	0.314	0.277	⑤
	17058250	13/32	1/2	9/32	0.129	0.183	④	0.096	0.220	⑤
	17058253	13/32	1/2	9/32	0.129	0.183	④	0.096	0.220	⑤
	17058257	13/32	1/2	9/32	0.136	0.230	④	0.103	0.220	⑤
	17058258	13/32	1/2	9/32	0.136	0.230	④	0.103	0.220	⑤
	17058259	13/32	1/2	9/32	0.136	0.183	④	0.103	0.220	⑤
	17058502	15/32	7/8	9/32	0.164	——	④	0.314	0.277	⑤
	17058504	15/32	7/8	9/32	0.164	——	④	0.314	0.277	⑤
	17058553	13/32	1/2	9/32	0.136	0.230	④	0.103	0.220	⑤

Rochester Carburetors

OLDSMOBILE

Year	Carburetor Identification①	Float Level (in.)	Air Valve Spring (turn)	Pump Rod (in.)	Primary Vacuum Break (in.)	Secondary Vacuum Break (in.)	Secondary Opening (in.)	Choke Rod (in.)	Choke Unloader (in.)	Fast Idle Speed② (rpm)
1978	17058555	13/32	1/2	9/32	0.136	0.230	④	0.103	0.220	⑤
	17058582	15/32	7/8	9/32	0.179	——	④	0.314	0.277	⑤
	17058584	15/32	7/8	9/32	0.179	——	④	0.314	0.277	⑤

① The carburetor identification number is stamped on the float bowl, next to the secondary throttle lever.
② On low step.
③ 1800 rpm on Omega and 400 cu. in. engines with the cam follower on the highest step of the fast idle cam; 900 rpm on all others with the fast idle cam follower on the lowest step of the fast idle cam.
④ No measurement necessary on two point linkage; see text.
⑤ 3 turns after contacting lever for preliminary setting.

PONTIAC

Year	Carburetor Identification①	Float Level (in.)	Air Valve Spring (turn)	Pump Rod (in.)	Primary Vacuum Break (in.)	Secondary Vacuum Break (in.)	Secondary Opening (in.)	Choke Rod (in.)	Choke Unloader (in.)	Fast Idle Speed② (rpm)
1972	7042262	1/4	7/16	13/32	0.290	——	0.070	0.100	——	——
	7042263	1/4	11/16	13/32	0.290	——	0.070	0.100	——	——
	7042264	1/4	5/8	13/32	0.290	——	0.070	0.100	——	——
	7042270	1/4	7/16	7/16	0.290	——	0.070	0.100	——	——
	7042273	1/4	7/16	7/16	0.290	——	0.070	0.100	——	——
1973	7043263	13/32	5/8	13/32	0.290	——	0.070	0.100	——	——
	7043264	13/32	1/2	13/32	0.290	——	0.070	0.100	——	——
	7043274	13/32	9/16	13/32	0.290	——	0.070	0.100	——	——
	7043262	13/32	3/8	13/32	0.290	——	0.070	0.100	——	——
	7043265	13/32	9/16	13/32	0.290	——	0.070	0.100	——	——
	7043272	13/32	3/8	13/32	0.290	——	0.070	0.100	——	——
1974	7043263	25/64	5/8	0.410	0.290	——	0.070	0.205	0.310	1500
	7044262	25/64	3/8	0.410	0.260	——	0.070	0.205	0.310	1500
	7044266	25/64	1/2	0.410	0.260	——	0.070	0.205	0.310	1500
	7044267	25/64	3/8	0.410	0.260	——	0.070	0.205	0.310	1500
	7044268	25/64	1/2	0.410	0.260	——	0.070	0.205	0.310	1500
	7044269	25/64	1/2	0.410	0.290	——	0.070	0.205	0.310	1500
	7044270	25/64	3/4	0.410	0.290	——	0.070	0.205	0.310	2000
	7044272	25/64	3/8	0.315	0.290	——	0.070	0.205	0.310	1500
	7044273	25/64	3/4	0.410	0.290	——	0.070	0.205	0.310	2000
	7044274	25/64	9/16	0.315	0.290	——	0.070	0.205	0.310	1500
	7044560	25/64	3/8	0.410	0.260	——	0.070	0.205	0.310	1500
	7044568	25/64	1/2	0.410	0.260	——	0.070	0.205	0.310	1500
1975	7045246	5/16	1/2	15/32	0.130	0.115	②	0.095	0.240	1800
	7045546	5/16	1/2	15/32	0.145	0.130	②	0.095	0.240	1800
	7045263	1/2	1/2	9/32	0.150	0.260	②	0.130	0.230	1800
	7045264	1/2	1/2	9/32	0.150	0.260	②	0.130	0.230	1800
	7045268	1/2	3/8	9/32	0.150	0.260	②	0.130	0.230	1800
	7045269	1/2	3/8	9/32	0.160	0.265	②	0.130	0.230	1800
	7045274	1/2	1/2	9/32	0.150	0.260	②	0.130	0.230	1800
	7045260	1/2	1/2	9/32	0.150	0.260	②	0.130	0.230	1800

Rochester Carburetors

1. Choke shaft and lever assembly
2. Roll pin, air valve lockout lever
3. Lever, air valve lockout
4. Clip, choke rod (upper)
5. Choke valve
6. Screw, choke valve (2)
7. Screw, air horn (long)
8. Secondary metering rod holder and screw
9. Screw, air horn (short)
10. Screw, air horn (countersunk) (2)
11. Roll pin, dash pot lever
12. Dash pot actuating
13. Clip, air valve rod
14. Rod, air valve
15. Lever, idle vent valve
16. Lever, pump actuating
17. Roll pin, pump lever
18. Screw, idle vent valve
19. Idle vent valve
20. Idle vent valve (thermostatic type)
21. Air horn assembly
22. Metering rod, secondary (2)
23. Dashpot assembly (early)
24. Pump assembly
25. Spring, pump return
26. gasket, air horn
27. Float assembly
28. Hinge pin, float assembly
29. Spring, primary metering rod retainer
30. Insert, float bowl
31. Screw, idle compensator cover (2)
32. Cover, idle compensator
33. Idle compensator assembly
34. Seal, idle compensator
35. Choke rod
36. Baffle, secondary bores
37. Lever, choke rod (lower end)
38. Primary metering rod (2)
39. Main metering jet, primary (2)
40. Power piston assembly
41. Spring, power piston
42. Retainer, pump discharge ball
43. Ball, pump discharge
44. Pull clip float needle (early)
45. Screw, float needle diaphragm retainer (early)
46. Retainer, float needle assembly (early)
47. Float needle and diaphrgm assy. (early)
48. Needle and seat assembly (standard)
49. Float bowl assembly
50. Screw, vacuum break control
51. Hose, vacuum control
52. Vacuum break control assembly
53. Rod, vacuum break control
54. Clip, vacuum break rod
55. Vacuum diaphragm assembly
56. Fast idle cam
57. Lever, secondary lockout
58. Filter nut, fuel inlet
59. Gasket, filter nut
60. Gasket, fuel filter
61. Filter, fuel inlet
62. Spring, filter relief
63. Spring, idle adjusting screw
64. Screw, idle adjusting
65. Gasket, throttle body to bowl
66. Throttle body assembly

67. Fast idle lever
68. Screw, cam and fast idle lever
69. Spring, cam and fast idle lever
70. Spring, fast idle screw
71. Screw, fast idle adjusting
72. Fast idle cam follower lever
73. Spring, idle mixture needle (2)

74. Idle mixture needle (2)
75. Screw, throttle body to bowl
76. Throttle lever, primary
77. Screw, throttle lever attaching
78. Clip, pump rod
79. Pump rod

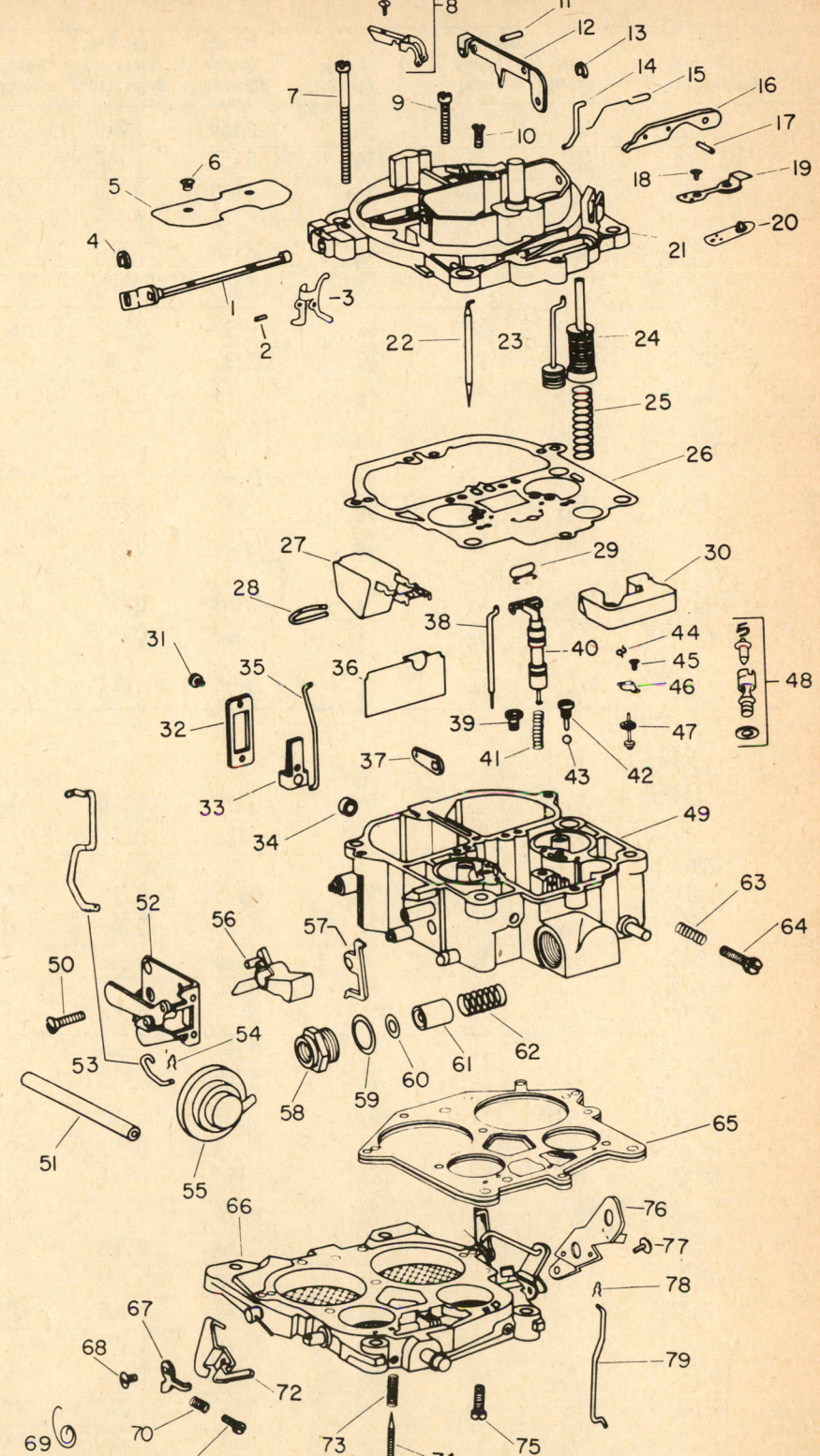

Exploded view, Typical Rochester 4MV Carburetor
(© Rochester Products Div., G.M. Corp.)

Rochester Carburetors

Year	Carburetor Identification①	Float Level (in.)	Air Valve Spring (turn)	Pump Rod (in.)	Primary Vacuum Break (in.)	Secondary Vacuum Break (in.)	Secondary Opening (in.)	Choke Rod (in.)	Choke Unloader (in.)	Fast Idle Speed② (rpm)
1975	7045262	1/2	1/2	9/32	0.150	0.260	②	0.130	0.230	1800
	7045266	1/2	1/2	9/32	0.150	0.260	②	0.130	0.230	1800
	7045562	1/2	1/2	9/32	0.150	0.260	②	0.130	0.230	1800
	7045564	1/2	1/2	9/32	0.150	0.260	②	0.130	0.230	1800
	7045568	1/2	1/2	9/32	0.150	0.260	②	0.130	0.230	1800
	7045566	1/2	1/2	9/32	0.150	0.260	②	0.130	0.230	1800
1976	7045246	5/16	3/4	3/8	0.130	0.120	②	0.095	0.250	1800
	7045546	5/16	3/4	3/8	0.130	0.130	②	0.095	0.250	1800
	7045268	17/32	1/2	3/8	0.160	0.250	②	0.125	0.230	1800
	7045264, 7045274, 7045266	17/32	1/2	3/8	0.160	0.250	②	0.125	0.230	1800
	7045263	17/32	5/8	3/8	0.170	0.250	②	0.125	0.230	1800
	7045564	17/32	1/2	3/8	0.150	0.260	②	0.130	0.230	1800
	7045260, 7045262	17/32	1/2	3/8	0.160	0.250	②	0.125	0.230	1800
	8-455 Man.	17/32	1/2	3/8	0.160	0.250	②	0.125	0.230	1800
	7045562, 7045566	17/32	1/2	3/8	0.170	0.250	②	0.120	0.230	1800
1977	17057250, 17057253, 17057255, 17057256	13/32	1/2	9/32	0.120	0.170	②	0.095	0.205	900
	17057258	13/32	1/2	9/32	0.125	0.215	②	0.095	0.205	1000
	17057550, 17057553	13/32	1/2	9/32	0.125	0.215	②	0.095	0.200	1000
	17057262	17/32	1/2	3/8	0.150	0.240	②	0.130	0.220	1800
	17057263	17/32	5/8	3/8	0.165	0.240	②	0.130	0.220	1800
	17057266, 17057274	17/32	1/2	3/8	0.150	0.240	②	0.130	0.220	1800
1978	17058202	15/32	——	9/32	0.157	——	②	0.314	0.277	③
	17058204	15/32	——	9/32	0.157	——	②	0.314	0.277	③
	17058241	5/16	3/4	3/8	0.117	0.103	②	0.096	0.243	③
	17058250	13/32	1/2	9/32	0.119	0.167	②	0.088	0.203	③
	17058253	13/32	1/2	9/32	0.119	0.167	②	0.088	0.203	③
	17058258	13/32	1/2	9/32	0.126	0.212	②	0.092	0.203	③
	17058263	17/32	5/8	3/8	0.164	0.260	②	0.129	0.220	③
	17058264	17/32	1/2	3/8	0.149	0.260	②	0.129	0.220	③
	17058266	17/32	1/2	3/8	0.149	0.260	②	0.129	0.220	③
	17058272	15/32	5/8	3/8	0.126	0.195	②	0.071	0.222	③
	17058274	17/32	1/2	3/8	0.149	0.260	②	0.129	0.220	③
1978	17058276	17/32	1/2	3/8	0.149	0.260	②	0.129	0.220	③
	17058278	17/32	1/2	3/8	0.149	0.260	②	0.129	0.220	③
	17058502	15/32	——	9/32	0.164	——	②	0.314	0.277	③
	17058504	15/32	——	9/32	0.164	——	②	0.314	0.277	③
	17058553	13/32	1/2	9/32	0.126	0.212	②	0.092	0.203	③
	17058582	15/32	7/8	9/32	0.179	——	②	0.314	0.277	③
	17058584	15/32	7/8	9/32	0.179	——	②	0.314	0.277	③

① The carburetor identification number is stamped on the float bowl, near the secondary throttle lever.

② No measurement necessary on two point linkage; see text.

③ 1 1/2 turns after contacting lever for preliminary setting

Index

Emission Control Systems

Cars that do not have emission controls pollute the air because they allow chemical compounds to escape from the engine crankcase, from the exhaust, and from evaporation of fuel out of the tank and carburetor. Emission controls consist of: 1. changes in engine design, 2. calibration, or 3. add-on devices, that either reduce or eliminate the amount of harmful chemicals that escape from the car.

Changes in engine design consist mostly of refinements in combustion chamber shape, or variations in bore and stroke to produce ideal surface-to-volume ratios. If the amount of surface in the combustion chamber is kept to a minimum, the emissions will be reduced because there is less chance for gasoline to cling to the surface without burning. The unburned gasoline is swept out the exhaust and causes high hydrocarbon emissions from the tailpipe. Reducing compression ratios is another design change that lowers the heat of the burning mixture and cuts down on NOx (oxides of nitrogen) emissions.

Engine calibration has a big effect on emissions out the tailpipe. The calibra-

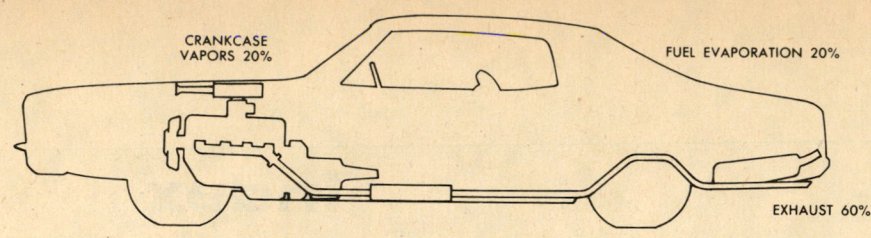

Automotive air pollutants

tion consists of spark timing, fuel mixture, choke setting, idle speed, and spark plug gap. Calibrations are not a service problem as long as the engine is adjusted to the factory specifications, which are either on a sticker in the engine compartment, or in manuals such as this. Engines must be adjusted to these factory specifications, or emissions will be high. It is common knowledge that adjustments outside of the specifications will make many (but not all) engines run better. The days when we could adjust engines for best performance are gone. Now we must adjust for lowest emissions, which means

going strictly by the factory specifications.

The biggest problems in servicing are the add-on devices for emission control. They are classified as Crankcase controls, Evaporation controls, or Exhaust controls. Crankcase and evaporation controls are simple in design, with few variations. But exhaust controls include air cleaner devices, exhaust gas recirculation, air injection systems, carburetor devices, and a tremendous number of vacuum spark advance devices. Following is a description of each group of controls and how they work to reduce emissions.

Crankcase Controls

The first emission control was the positive crankcase ventilation (PCV) system, which appeared on new domestic cars in the early 1960s. Ventilation of a crankcase is necessary because of the compression blow-by past the piston rings. This blowby is mostly unburned gasoline. If allowed to stay in the crankcase, it dilutes the oil and increases engine wear. Before PCV systems, the crankcase was vented through a road draft tube. The suction of airflow past the end of the tube drew out the crankcase fumes and fresh air entered through the oil breather cap. When the car was moving, there was a continuous flow of fresh air through the crankcase.

The PCV system accomplishes the

same thing, but it uses engine vacuum instead of the road draft to draw out the crankcase fumes. The crankcase or the rocker arm cover is connected by a hose to engine vacuum at the intake manifold or carburetor. When the engine is running, the crankcase fumes are drawn into the engine and burned in the combustion chamber. Fresh air enters the crankcase through the oil filler cap on the open system. When the oil filler cap is connected to the air cleaner, it is known as a closed system.

At wide open throttle, there is little vacuum in the engine, so the PCV system doesn't pull any fumes out of the crankcase. On the open system the fumes go out through the oil filler cap into the atmosphere at wide open throt-

tle. On the closed system the fumes go into the air cleaner, where they are drawn into the engine by the rush of air through the cleaner, so they end up being burned in the engine anyway.

Because the hose connection from the crankcase to the intake manifold acts like a vacuum leak, there has to be some kind of control to limit the air flow. The PCV valve is the control. It can be an actual valve, with an internal plunger, or a simple orifice without any moving parts. In the plunger types, a spring moves the plunger against engine vacuum, allowing less flow at high vacuum and more flow at low vacuum. If there is an intake manifold cough back or spit back, the plunger moves to close the PCV valve and prevent a

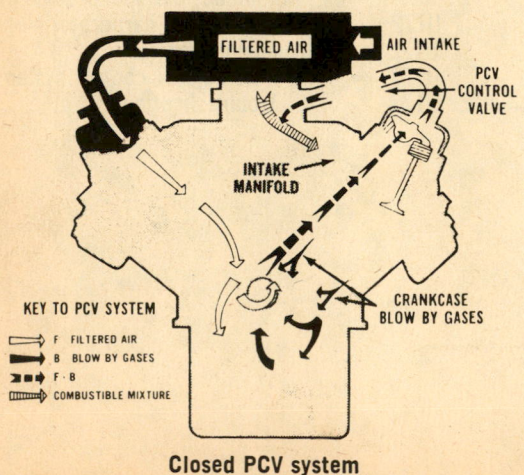

Closed PCV system

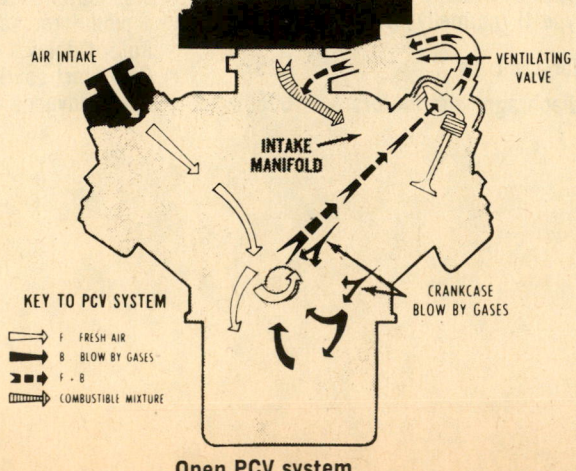

Open PCV system

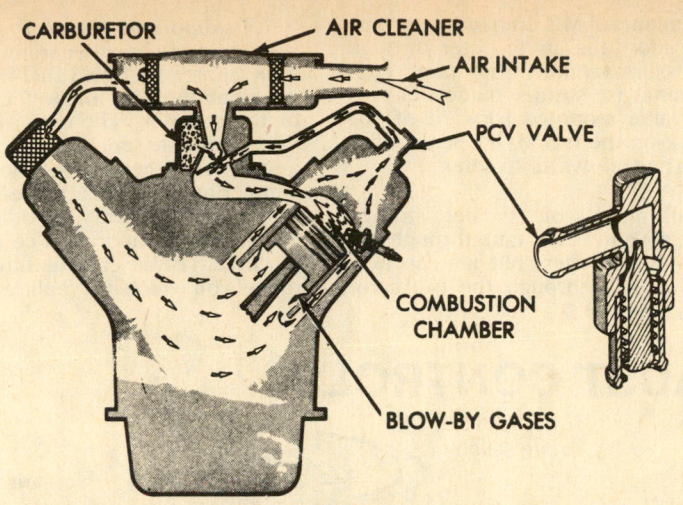

Positive crankcase ventilation system (© Chrysler Corp.)

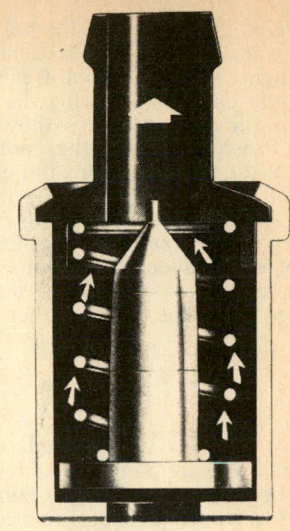

PCV valve

crankcase explosion.

Originally all the PCV systems used a simple hose from the rocker cover to the intake manifold or carburetor, with the PCV valve mounted at one end of the hose. Fresh air always entered through the oil filler cap, whether it connected to the air cleaner or not. On later models, the plumbing is not as simple, but the principle is still the same. Fresh air enters the air cleaner and goes through a hose to the crankcase or rocker cover. The fumes exit the crankcase and enter the intake manifold, either through a hose or some other type of connection, usually with a PCV valve controlling the flow.

Most systems use some kind of PCV filter, usually mounted at the end of the hose in the air cleaner. The filter keeps dust from entering the crankcase, and also prevents oil fumes from ruining the air cleaner element.

Testing Crankcase Controls

Checking crankcase vacuum is the most effective way to test any PCV system. If there is vacuum in the crankcase, then the major part of the system has to be working.

Inspect the system to find out where the fresh air enters the engine. This is usually through a hose attached to the air cleaner, but it may be through the oil filler cap on some models. If the fresh air entry is separate from the oil filler cap, remove the hose and plug it so fresh air cannot enter the crankcase. If the fresh air entry is through the oil filler cap, simply remove the cap.

On all models, use a piece of paper or a PCV tester to measure the crankcase vacuum at the oil filler cap, with the cap removed, and the engine idling in Park or Neutral. It may take a few seconds for the vacuum to build up enough to suck the piece of paper against the oil filler hole. If the vacuum does not build up, check to be sure you have plugged the fresh air entry. An alternate method on some cars is to use the piece of paper or PCV tester on the end of the fresh air entry hose. When you do it that way, the oil filler cap must be the solid type and you must leave it in place.

If there is no crankcase vacuum, pull the PCV valve from the crankcase and hold your finger over the end of it. You should feel full manifold vacuum with

the engine idling. If not, the valve is plugged or there is an obstruction in a hose or passageway. On some designs the valve may be screwed into its mounting, with a hose leading to the rocker cover or crankcase. If the valve has good suction, but there is no crankcase vacuum, check the hose to be sure it is open. PCV valves that are restricted or plugged must be replaced, unless they are the type that will come apart for cleaning. Lack of crankcase vacuum can also be caused by vacuum leaks at rocker cover, oil pan, or other engine gaskets. Usually, tightening the bolts will stop the leak.

In some extreme cases, usually on high mileage engines, the PCV system is in good shape, but the blowby past the rings is so much that the system can't handle it, and the engine will blow smoke out the oil filler hole. Switching to a PCV valve with a higher flow may temporarily correct the problem, but the only good solution is to do a ring job on the engine.

After checking crankcase vacuum, always check the condition of the fresh air filter and hose, to be sure they are clean and not clogged.

Evaporation Controls

Most evaporation fuel losses come from the fuel tank. On an uncontrolled car the vapors go out through the tank vent, which may be in several places at the top of the tank, or in the cap. There are also some losses through the bowl vent on the carburetor, but these are minor compared to the tank.

Evaporation controls are made up of hoses which allow the tank and carburetor vapors to go either to the engine crankcase or to a canister filled with charcoal. When the engine is running, vacuum from the PCV system cleans the vapors out of the crankcase.

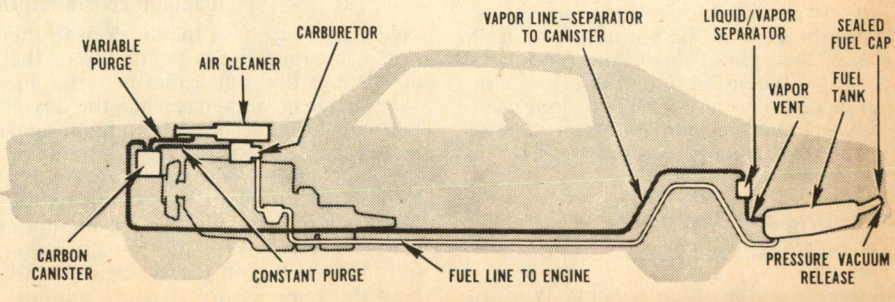

Evaporation control system

If a charcoal canister is used, a hose to the intake manifold or carburetor base allows engine vacuum to pull fresh air through the canister, drawing the vapors into the engine where they are burned. Fresh air enters the canister through a filter, which keeps the charcoal clean.

When the engine is running, air must enter the tank to replace the fuel that is used up and prevent a vacuum. On Chrysler crankcase storage systems, this air enters through a breather cap on the engine. AMC crankcase storage models allow the air to enter through the pressure-vacuum fuel tank cap. Ford crankcase storage models have a 3-way valve mounted forward of the fuel tank on the frame. It opens under vacuum and allows air to enter

On all makes of canister storage models, air enters the tank through the filter in the canister, but air can also enter the tank through the pressure-vacuum tank cap.

All evaporation control systems use some sort of vapor separator at the fuel tank to prevent liquid fuel from traveling along the vent line to the crankcase or the canister. The early models had very elaborate separators mounted separately from the tank, but now they are simpler and usually attached to the top of the tank. The only periodic servicing required on evaporation controls is replacement of the canister filter on those models on which it is replaceable.

EXHAUST CONTROLS

Exhaust controls vary considerably in design. There are almost 60 different systems or devices used on the domestic makes to control exhaust emissions. Following are basic descriptions of the common systems.

THERMOSTATIC AIR CLEANER

Fresh air supplied to the air cleaner comes either from the normal snorkle, or from a tube connected to an exhaust manifold stove. A door in the snorkle regulates the source of incoming air so that a warm engine always takes in warm air, approximately 100°F. The snorkle door may be controlled by a thermostatic spring or expansion bulb, or it may be vacuum operated. The vacuum operated designs use a thermostatic bimetal switch inside the air cleaner that bleeds off vacuum as the engine warms up, and regulates the position of the air door. On all late model cars, the snorkle is connected to a long tube so it takes in cooler air from outside the engine compartment. In hot climates the cool air tube is necessary because underhood air can easily reach 200°F.

Vacuum operated air doors are all designed so that the air cleaner takes in cold air when there is no vacuum. This means that an air door in the hot air position will switch to the cold position at wide open throttle because of the loss of manifold vacuum. The sudden switching of the door from hot to cold may cause a stumble or misfire in the engine, so some designs include a modulator valve mounted on the side of the air cleaner to block the vacuum and hold the door in the hot air position. A small thermostat inside the modulator opens it when the underhood temperatures reach normal. Other designs use a delay valve that allows the air door to move to the cold position slowly, to prevent stumble.

Testing Air Cleaners, Non-Vacuum Type

To test the non-vacuum type of heated air cleaner found on some Ford Motor Co. and American Motors Corp. engines, start with an engine that is

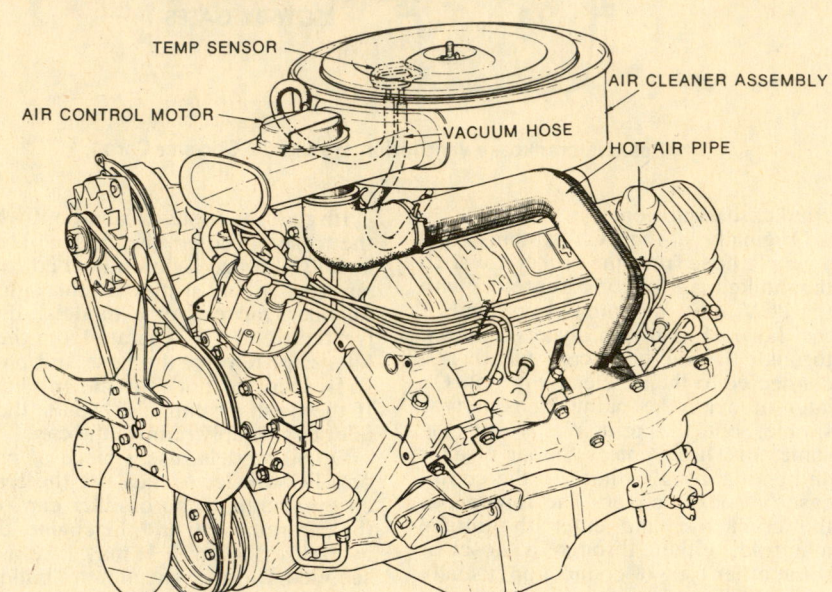

A typical heated air cleaner system, with the hot air pipe connected to the left exhaust manifold (© G.M. Corp.)

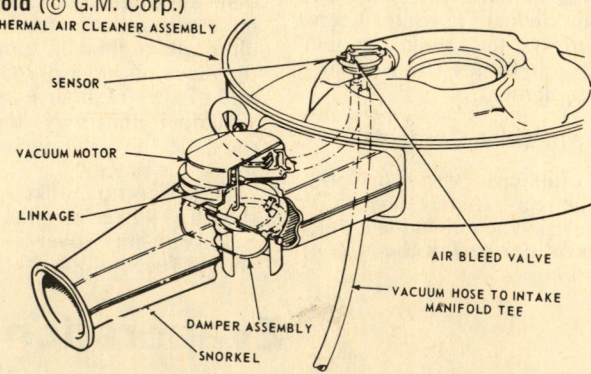

Vacuum controlled thermostatic air cleaner.

cold enough to have the air door in the hot air position. Remove the top of the air cleaner and put a thermometer inside the cleaner, then replace the cover without the nuts. Start the engine and watch the air door through the end of the air cleaner. You may have to remove some air ducting to be able to see the air door. As soon as the air door starts to move from the hot air position, lift the top off the air cleaner and read the temperature. If the temperature is between 130 and 150°F, the thermostat is working correctly. If not, replace the thermostat.

--- CAUTION ---

Do not replace the thermostat if the temperature is off by only a few degrees. It must be considerably out of specification, or perhaps not opening at all, to affect the running of the car.

Testing Air Cleaners, Vacuum Type

To test the vacuum type of heated air cleaner, inspect the air door with the engine off. It should be in the cold air position. Start the engine. If the engine

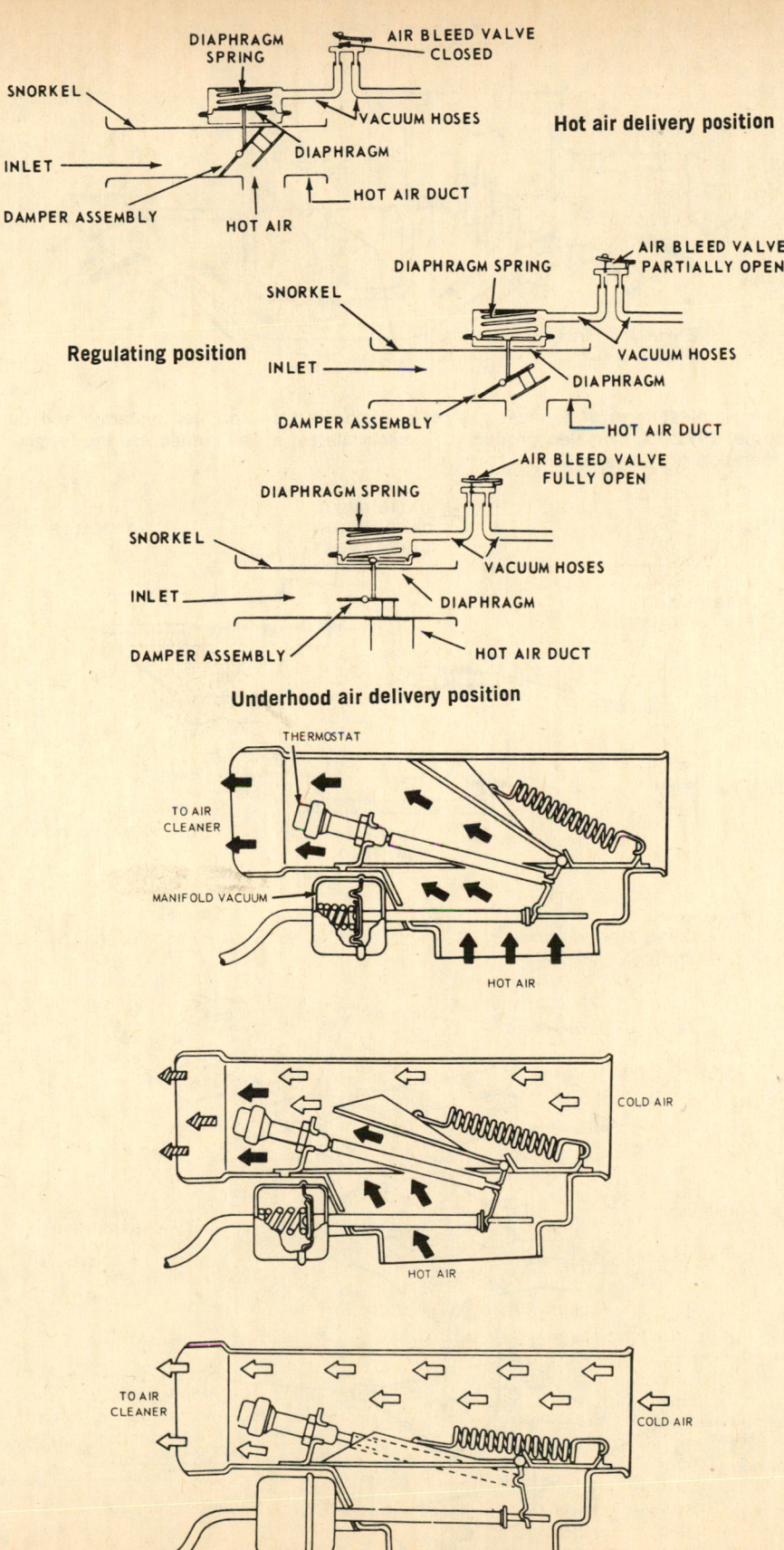

Hot air delivery position

Regulating position

Underhood air delivery position

Ford used a non vacuum temperature control on their heated air cleaner for many years. This particular model shown has a vacuum override which opens the door during cold acceleration. (© Ford Motor Co.)

is cold, the air door should move to the hot air position. As the engine warms up, the air door should move to a mid position, depending on the outside air temperature.

If the outside air is extremely cold, the air door may stay in the hot air position indefinitely. On a warm day, after the engine warms up the air door should move to the cold air position. If it doesn't, the temperature sensor inside the air cleaner might be faulty, or the air door itself might be hanging up. Check the air door by running a hose from manifold vacuum to the vacuum motor. Connect and disconnect the hose to see if the air door moves freely. If the air door is free, check out the hoses for leaks or blockage. If the hoses are okay, the trouble must be in the temperature sensor, and it should be replaced.

Both General Motors and Ford use a modulator in the air cleaner vacuum line on some engines. The modulator mounts on the side of the air cleaner and has two hose connections, one to the air cleaner temperature sensor, and the other to the vacuum motor. Below 50-80°F. the modulator is a one-way check valve, which allows vacuum to move the air door to the hot air position, but traps the vacuum so the door will not jump back to the cold air position during acceleration. This prevents a stumble.

After the modulator warms up, the check valve unseats so that the vacuum can pass freely in either direction, and the air door then operates normally. The connections for the modulator are important. The connection in the center goes to the vacuum motor, and the connection on the edge goes to the vacuum source, which is the temperature sensor.

To test the modulator on a cold engine, apply enough vacuum to the edge port to move the air door to the hot position. Then remove the hose from the port, and the air door should stay in the hot position. Make the same test when the engine is warmed up, and the air door should move to the cold position when you pull off the hose.

EXHAUST GAS RECIRCULATION

NOx (oxides of nitrogen) is a tailpipe emission caused by the oxidation of nitrogen in the combustion chamber. When the peak combustion temperatures go over 2500°F. NOx is formed in excessive amounts. To keep the combustion temperatures down, exhaust gas is recirculated on most 1972 and later cars. Recirculation is accomplished by allowing intake manifold vacuum to draw exhaust gas into the intake manifold. Usually, an EGR (exhaust gas recirculation) valve is used to control the flow of exhaust gas, but some of the early systems had simple orifices that were open at all times.

Emission Control Systems

Ford cold weather modulator is mounted in the air cleaner.

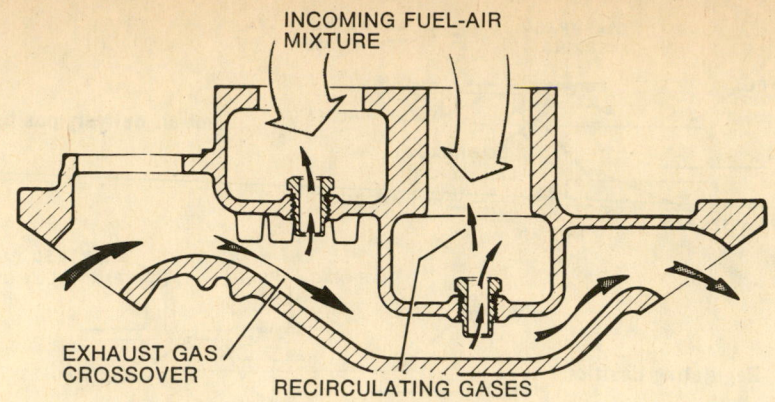

The simplest form of exhaust gas recirculation is this floor jet system, used on some 1972-73 Chrysler products. It recirculates at all times during engine operation (© Chrysler Corp.)

The first Chrysler Corporation cars equipped with EGR used the Floor Jet system. Directly under the primary barrels of the carburetor were stainless steel jets screwed into holes drilled from the floor of the intake manifold into the exhaust crossover passage. The floor jets were open at all times, continuously allowing a small amount of exhaust gas to be drawn into the intake manifold and be recirculated. There is nothing on the outside of the engine to indicate that the floor jets are installed, but if you open the throttle and choke with the engine dead, you can see the jets by looking down through the carburetor throats with a flashlight.

Other systems use an EGR valve to control the flow of exhaust gas into the intake manifold. All EGR valves look alike, and are operated by vacuum.

When the vacuum is off, the valve is closed. Several different types of controls are used to turn the vacuum to the EGR valve on and off. Most of them have to do with engine temperature, as described later.

Ported vacuum EGR systems are the simplest. When the EGR valve hose is connected to the base of the carburetor, without a separate amplifier, the system is operated by ported vacuum. The hose may not run directly from the EGR valve to the carburetor, but may go through a temperature control valve of some sort. In a ported vacuum system, the vacuum to operate the EGR valve is taken from a port that is above the throttle plate at idle, and thus not subject to vacuum. Because there is no vacuum, the spring in the EGR valve closes it, and the exhaust gas does not recirculate. As the throttle is opened, the port is exposed to vacuum, and the EGR valve opens.

Venturi vacuum systems, with an amplifier, are the most complicated,

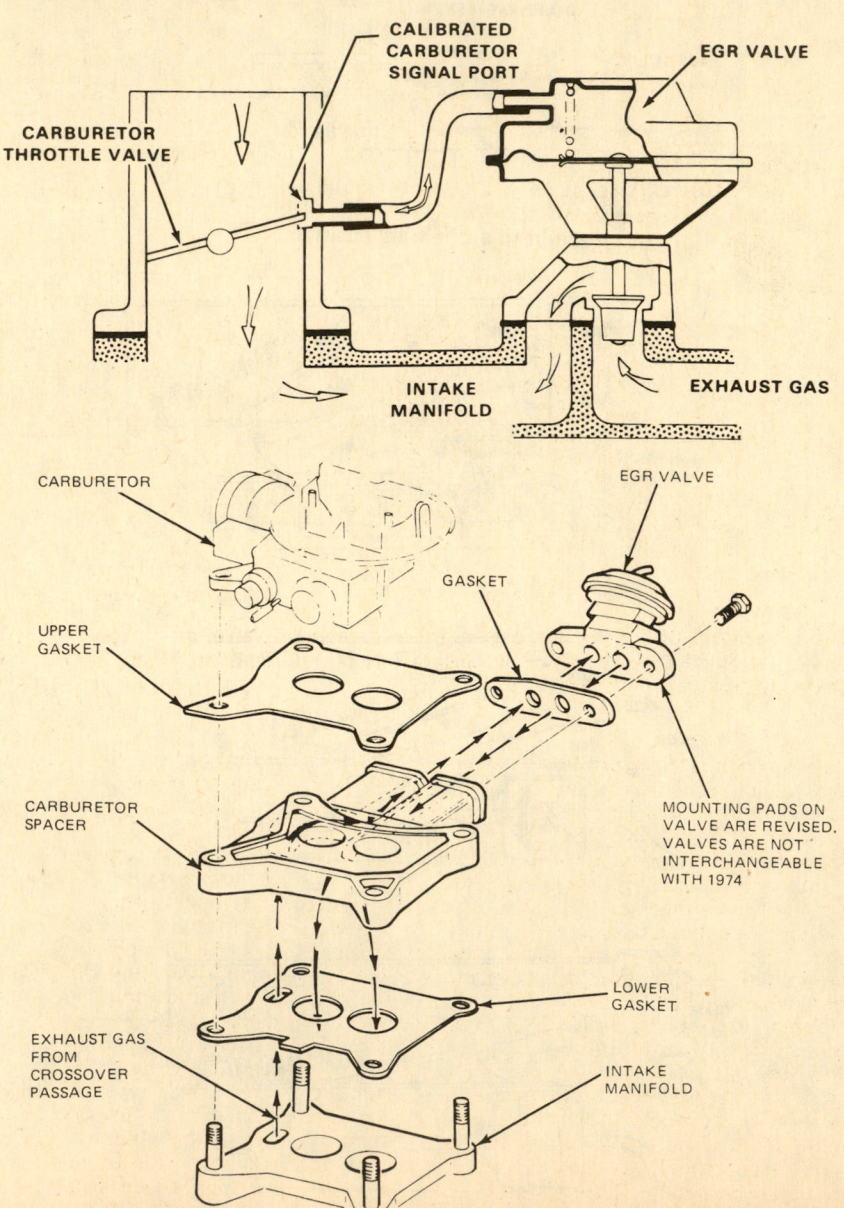

Most cars use an EGR system with a valve and a ported vacuum signal, as shown here. Some cars use the venturi vacuum with a separate amplifier to operate the valve. (© Chrysler Corp.)

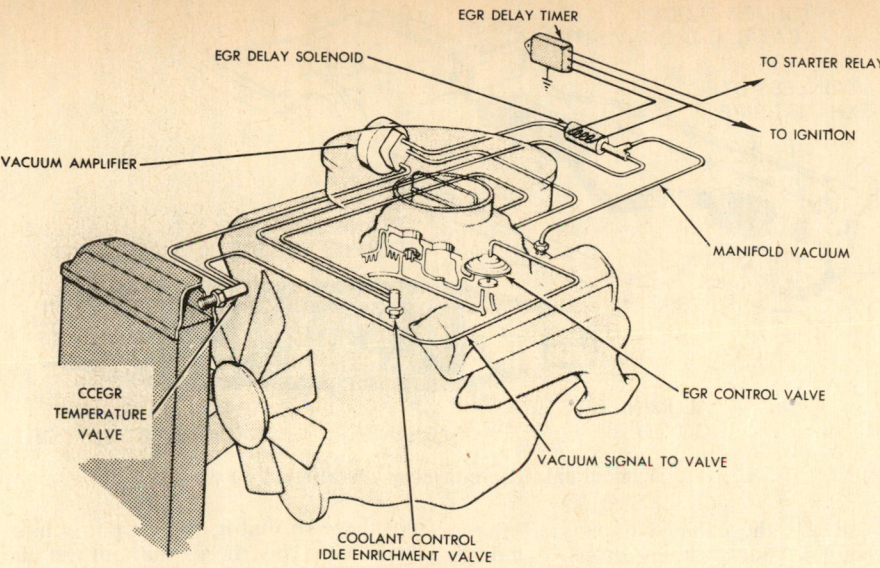

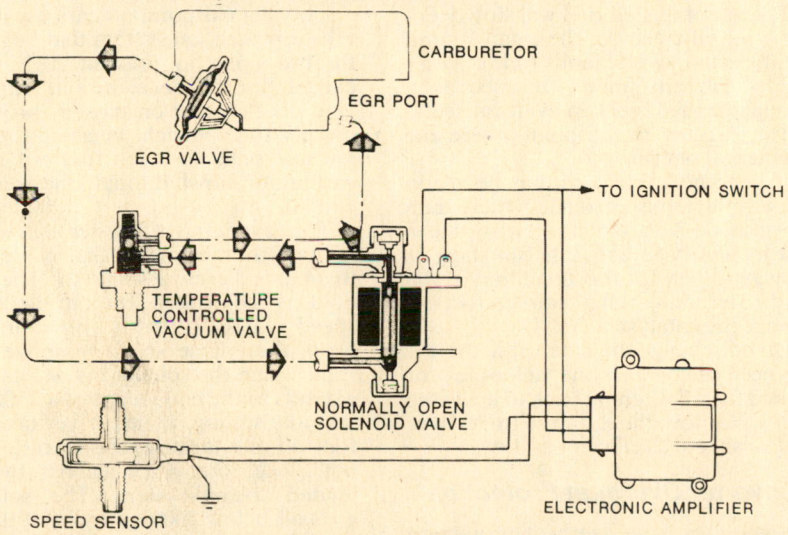

Venturi vacuum exhaust gas recirculation

The sub system uses an electronic amplifier, a solenoid valve, and a speed sensor to cut off the EGR vacuum above approximately 65 mph on some Ford Motor Company products. (© Ford Motor Co.)

because of the number of hoses. Manifold vacuum is connected to the amplifier by a hose, and then connects to the EGR valve. The amplifier also connects to venturi vacuum. At idle there is no venturi vacuum, but above idle the air moves through the carburetor venturi fast enough to create a vacuum. This slight amount of vacuum opens the amplifier, which then allows manifold vacuum to open the EGR valve.

Temperature controls for EGR systems come in many different designs. They are all made so that the EGR valve stays closed when the engine or the outside air is cold. After the engine or the outside air warms up, the temperature control allows the EGR valve to operate normally. Before March 15, 1973, many EGR systems used a temperature control that was sensitive to outside air temperature. Even with a

fully warmed up engine, the EGR system would stay off if the outside temperature was cold enough. On cars made after March 15, 1973, the temperature controls were all sensitive to engine coolant temperature, or engine compartment temperature.

Some Ford Motor Co. models shut off the EGR above 65 mph with a complicated system consisting of a speed sensor, an electronic amplifier, and a vacuum solenoid. The speed sensor, in the speedometer cable behind the instrument panel, sends a signal to the amplifier, which is above the glove box. The amplifier then turns off a vacuum solenoid in the engine compartment and vacuum to the EGR valve is blocked. The high speed EGR cutoff was widely used in 1973, but only on police interceptor models in 1974, and dropped after that.

Testing EGR Systems

Testing of EGR systems should verify that the EGR valve is closed at idle, open above idle, and that the exhaust gas is actually recirculating. If the EGR valve sticks open at idle, the engine will run very rough, or may not even start. If this happens the valve should be removed and cleaned, or replaced. To check for valve opening above idle, check with a mirror or your fingers to see if the diaphragm or stem moves when the engine is at a fast idle in Park or Neutral. If the diaphragm does not move when the throttle is opened, there is either a problem with vacuum, or the valve is stuck closed. With a vacuum gauge hooked up to the EGR port, you should see vacuum on the gauge when the throttle is opened. EGR valves should not leak when tested with a hand vacuum pump. If they do they must be replaced.

To find out if the exhaust gas is actually recirculating, use a hand vacuum pump or mouth suction through a hose to open the EGR valve with the engine idling. If the engine runs rough or dies, you know the exhaust gas is recirculating. If the engine does not run rough, make a second test at 2500 rpm. Opening the EGR valve at that rpm should cause a change in engine speed. If it does, you know the exhaust gas is recirculating. To make the 2500 rpm test, remove and plug the hose from the EGR port. Attach your suction hose to the EGR valve before running the engine at 2500 rpm. Simply pulling off the EGR hose at 2500 rpm is not a valid test, because the extra air entering the engine through the hose could cause a speed change all by itself. On most engines you won't have to go this far, because opening the EGR valve at idle will prove that the exhaust is recirculating.

If the exhaust is not recirculating, it means that a passageway or the valve itself is clogged up. The only way to fix it is to scrape out the clogging as best you can, or replace the clogged part.

Many 1977 and later EGR valves have a back pressure sensor built into the valve. This sensor is a pressure operated bleed that disables the EGR valve and keeps it closed when there is no exhaust pressure. This type of valve cannot be tested with a hand vacuum pump with the engine off because the bleed is open. The only practical way to test these new valves is by substitution of a known good valve. If a valve is not available, the suspected valve can be removed, and the mounting holes temporarily taped shut. If this corrects the problem, then a new valve should be installed.

Chrysler Corp. EGR Reminder Light

NOTE: *This light is designed to remind the driver that regularly scheduled ser-*

vice is due; it does not mean that the EGR system is not working properly. It is found on some 1975 and 1976 models.

1. After checking the EGR system for proper operation, slide the rubber boot on the EGR reminder odometer on the speedometer cable up, out of the way,
2. Reset the odometer with a small screwdriver.
3. Slide the boot back down over the odometer. The light will come on again when the next 15,000 mile check-up is due.

CATALYTIC CONVERTERS

A catalytic converter is a chamber in the exhaust system that contains a catalyst. When hydrocarbons or carbon monoxide pass over the catalyst they react with the oxygen in the exhaust and are converted into harmless water and carbon dioxide. The catalyst inside the converter is made in two forms. General Motors and American Motors use the pellet form, in which loose pellets are packed into the converter and can be emptied out and changed, if necessary. Ford and Chrysler use the honeycomb catalyst, which is built into the converter shell and is not replaceable. On Ford and Chrysler products the entire converter must be replaced if it goes bad.

There is no way to test a converter in the field to see if it is actually working. Tailpipe readings may be used to set carburetor idle mixtures, when the car maker requires it, but taking a tailpipe reading to determine if the converter is working is not possible.

The one field check that is recommended in all cases is to inspect for mechanical damage. If a converter gets overheated, the catalyst can melt and block the exhaust. Pellets or pieces of the catalyst may even come flying out the tailpipe while the engine is running. If this happens, the pellets or the entire converter must be changed.

Checking for a melted converter that restricts the exhaust can be done with a vacuum gauge connected to the engine. Run the engine at about 2500 rpm in Park or Neutral. If the vacuum reading

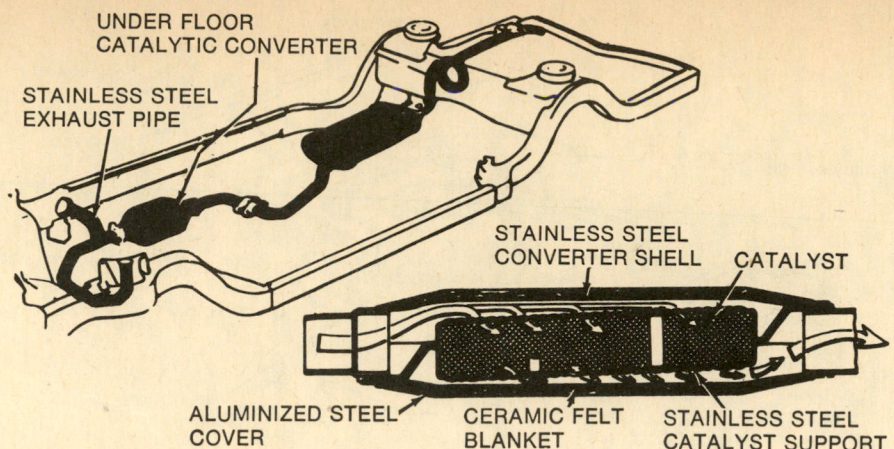

Typical catalytic converter installation

is steady, the exhaust is okay. If the vacuum reading slowly drops, it indicates a buildup of pressure in the exhaust.

The use of leaded fuel will slowly destroy the efficiency of the catalyst until finally, after several tanks full, it won't do its job any more. If used long enough, leaded fuel can even cause catalyst plugging to the point where the engine will not run.

If you know that a car has been run on several tanks of leaded fuel, then you can be sure that the catalyst has lost its ability to convert. But there is no way to test for this condition in the field. The only thing you can do is change the catalyst.

Do not change the catalyst if the car has been run on only one tank or less of leaded fuel. Switching back to lead free fuel will allow the catalyst to recover and be almost as efficient as it was.

Converter Overheat Protection

Some cars have overheat protection systems for the converter. Ford Motor Co. sometimes uses a heat sensitive switch mounted in the floorpan above the converter. The switch turns a vacuum solenoid on and off to control the vacuum to the air pump bypass valve. When the vacuum is shut off the bypass valve dumps the pump air into the at-

mosphere so that it doesn't pump into the exhaust any more. Without the air in the exhaust, the converter can't convert, and it cools down.

Chrysler Corporation cars use an overheat protection system that holds the throttle open to prevent high speed closed throttle deceleration. Any engine decelerating on closed throttle is usually running rich, because the high vacuum pulls so much fuel out of the carburetor bowl through the idle circuit.

To prevent this, Chrysler uses a solenoid on the carburetor that is identical to an anti-dieseling solenoid. The solenoid is controlled by an electronic speed switch so that it only comes on when the engine speed is above 2000 rpm. When the solenoid is on, its stem extends to the equivalent of a 1500 rpm fast idle setting. If the driver takes his foot off the throttle, the throttle does not close, but rests against the extended solenoid stem. The solenoid goes off below 2000 rpm so that the engine doesn't run away with the car in traffic.

To test the system put the transmission in Park or Neutral and operate the throttle from under the hood. Slowly increase the engine speed until it is above 2000 rpm. The solenoid stem should extend. As the speed drops below 2000 rpm, the stem should retract.

To determine if the car is equipped with the system, look for the speed switch on the right fender panel. Some cars may not have the overheat protection system, but do have an anti-dieseling solenoid on the carburetor. The anti-dieseling solenoid is easily identified because it is energized whenever the ignition switch is on.

VACUUM OPERATED EXHAUST HEAT RISER VALVES

Exhaust heat riser valves have been used for many years to force part of the engine exhaust through a passageway under the intake manifold and preheat

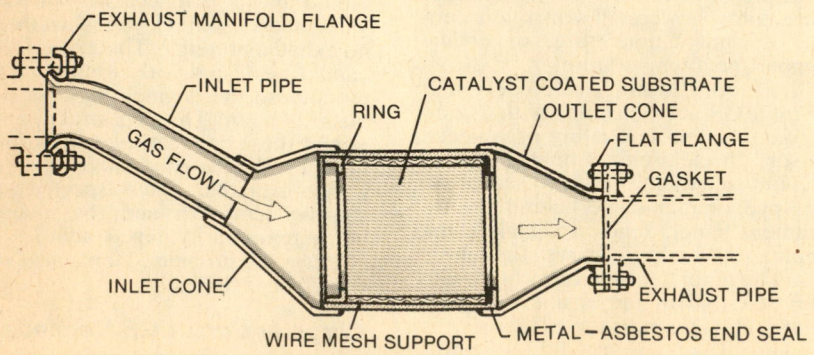

Cross section of typical catalytic converter

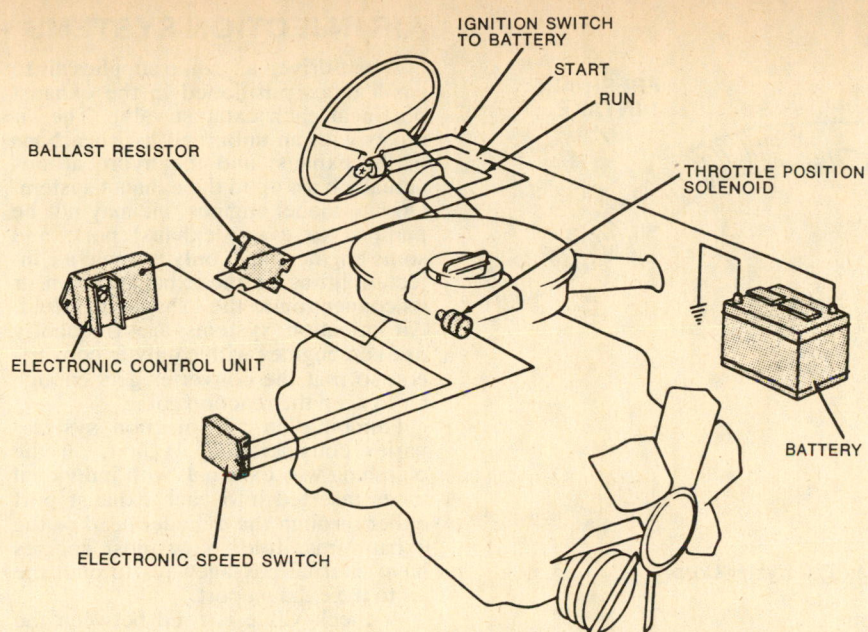

Catalyst overheat protection system (© Chrysler Corp.)

the fuel mixture. The heat valve was spring loaded into the closed position, but heat would make the spring relax so that during high speed operation or after warmup the exhaust would push it open.

Now, many engines use vacuum operated heat valves, controlled by a vacuum switch that is sensitive to engine temperature. Ford calls their system simply a vacuum operated exhaust heat valve. General Motors refers to theirs as Early Fuel Evaporation, and Chrysler calls theirs a Power Heat Control Valve.

On all these systems, manifold vacuum is used to close the valve, and force the exhaust gases through the crossover passage in the intake manifold. All the systems have some kind of temperature valve that shuts the vacuum off when the engine warms up.

Both Chrysler and Ford products use a simple coolant temperature-sensitive vacuum switch mounted on the intake

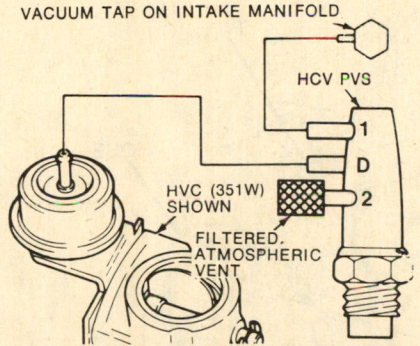

Vacuum exhaust heat valve system. HVC means Heat Control Valve. (© Ford Motor Co.)

manifold coolant passage. The Chrysler switch has two hose connections. It actually does triple duty because it also controls the vacuum supply to the idle enrichment system and the air switching valve.

Ford's vacuum switch has three hose connections, but one of them is a vent with a filter to keep the dirt out.

General Motors cars use either a coolant vacuum switch, or a vacuum solenoid connected to an oil temperature switch. The coolant vacuum switch has two hose connections and a vent when it controls the heat valve only. When it is tied into other emission control systems, it can have as many as five hose connections, and a vent. Many General Motors cars also have a check valve in the hose so that vacuum will be trapped in the heat valve actuator when the engine is accelerated. This keeps the heat valve in the closed position and prevents a rattle.

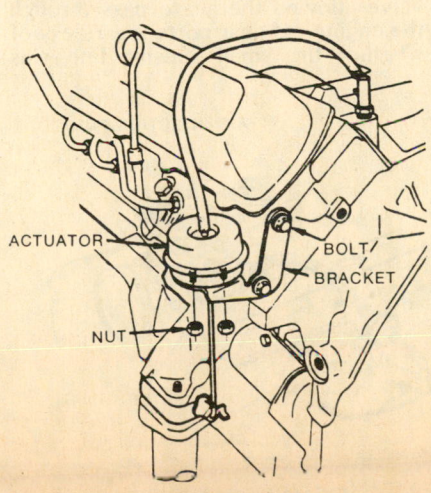

EFE valve

Testing Vacuum Operated Exhaust Heat Riser Valves

Testing the vacuum operated heat riser valve is a matter of making sure it closes and opens freely. You can move it by hand to see if it works, on a warm engine. On a cold engine, the valve should be closed, and disconnecting the hose should allow it to open. On a cold engine, there should be vacuum at the vacuum actuator, and on a warm engine the vacuum should be shut off.

AIR ASPIRATOR SYSTEM

1977 and later Chrysler Corporation cars which use this system have done away with the air pump. The complete air aspirator system consists of a hose from the clean side of the air cleaner, the aspirator valve mounted on top of the engine, and a tube connecting the valve with the exhaust manifold. The suction in the exhaust draws in air through the air cleaner and this extra air helps the catalytic converter burn up the pollutants. The aspirator valve is similar to the check valve used with all air pump systems. It keeps the exhaust from flowing back into the air cleaner, but allows clean air to go into the exhaust.

Testing The Air Aspirator System

Testing the air aspirator valve is done by disconnecting the hose from the air cleaner and checking for slight suction at idle with a piece of paper over the end of the valve. Speeding the engine up slightly will show if the valve is leaking. Exhaust should not come out of the valve. Vibration of the valve diaphragm is normal, due to exhaust impulses.

PULSE AIR INJECTION

This system is used on 1977 and later Chevette 1600cc 4-cylinder engines, and on Vega, Astre, Sunbird, Monza 140 cu. in. 4 cylinder engines. It is not used on the 151 cu. in. engine in the 1978 and later models. The system is similar to Chrysler's Air Aspirator (see earlier). A hose from the clean side of the air cleaner connects to the pulse air valve. Four tubes connect the pulse air valve to each cylinder's exhaust port. Suction in the exhaust draws fresh air from the air cleaner into the exhaust, and the air helps the catalytic converter burn up the pollutants. The pulse air valve consists of four check valves built into a housing. It allows each exhaust port to suck in fresh air independently of the other ports. The check valves only open when there is suction in the exhaust. If there is any back pressure, the check valves close to prevent exhaust flow back into the air cleaner. On some applications the pulse air valve is connected to only

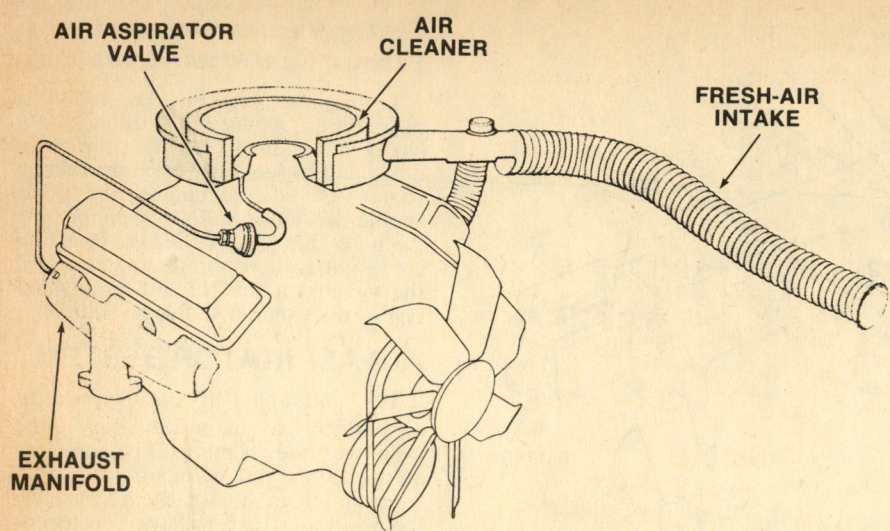

Chrysler Air Aspirator system (© Chrysler Corp.)

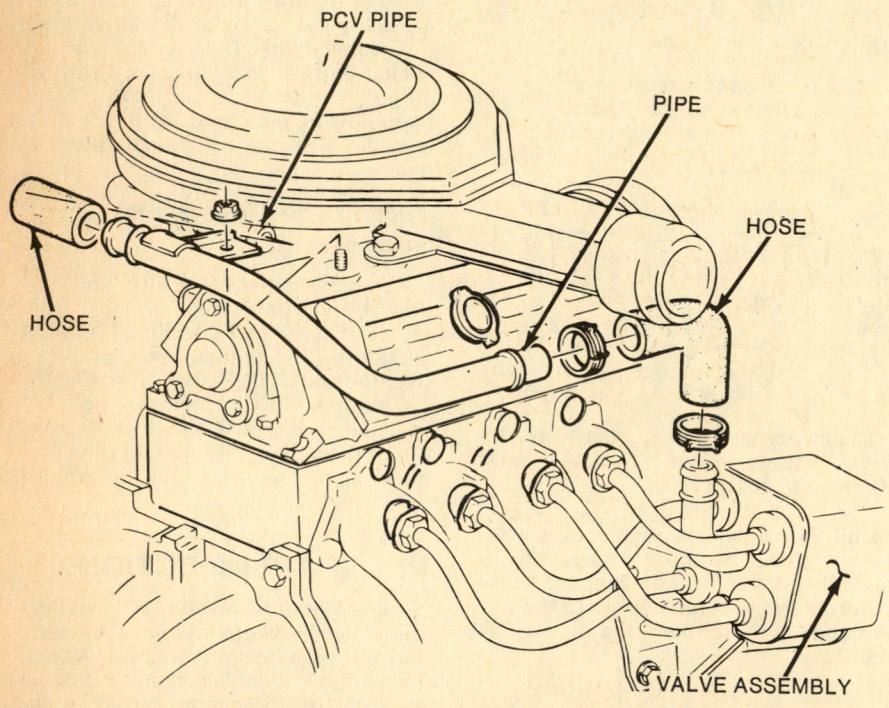

Chevette Pulse Air pipe and hose (© G.M. Corp.)

three of the four exhaust ports on a 4-cylinder engine.

Testing Pulse Air Injection

To test the pulse air valve, remove the rubber hose from the valve and run the engine at idle. You should notice a slight pulsation of the valves, drawing air into the exhaust. With the engine off, use a vacuum pump to apply 15 in. Hg. vacuum. The vacuum will slowly bleed off, but as long as it takes more than two seconds to fall from 15 in. to 5 in. Hg. the valve is okay. If the vacuum falls off faster than that, the valve is leaking and must be replaced.

AIR INJECTION SYSTEMS

A belt-driven air pump supplies air to small tubes positioned in the exhaust port near each exhaust valve. The air mixes with an unburned hydrocarbons in the exhaust and the hydrocarbons actually burn up in the exhaust system. On late model engines, air may not be pumped to every exhaust port, and some engines have only a single air injection fitting on the exhaust pipe near its connection to the exhaust manifold. Air injection systems are frequently used on engines with catalytic converters, so that the converter gets enough air to keep the reaction going.

Plumbing on air injection systems varies considerably. At first, all the plumbing was external, with individual tubes inserted into each exhaust port either through the cylinder head or the exhaust manifold. Now most engines have internal passageways to duct the air to the exhaust port.

A check valve is used between the pump and the exhaust port nozzle to keep hot exhaust gases from traveling up the plumbing and destroying the pump. Some V8s and V6s use two check valves.

An anti-backfire valve, also called bypass valve or diverter valve, is used between the pump and the check valve. Usually, the diverter valve is mounted on the pump or near it. A small sensing hose connects the diverter valve to intake manifold vacuum. When the vacuum rises during deceleration, the diverter valve opens, and sends the pump air into the atmosphere. This prevents the over-rich deceleration mixture in the exhaust system from exploding or backfiring out the tailpipe.

In 1975, some cars started using a diverter valve that looks similar to the old Ford valve (made by Carter Carburetor), but has the small hose connection on the end instead of the side. The older Ford Motor Co. diverter valve was normally in the running position, but the new one is normally in the dump position. In other words, the old valve allowed the air to pass through the engine exhaust ports regardless of whether the small sensing line was

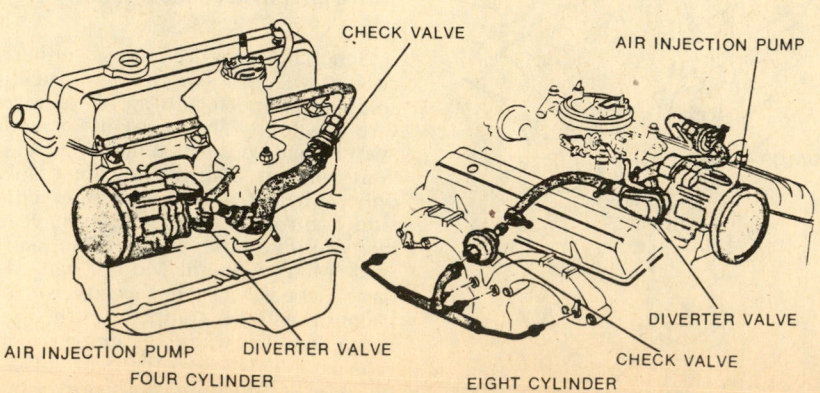

Chevrolet air pump system (© G.M. Corp.)

FOUR CYLINDER

EIGHT CYLINDER

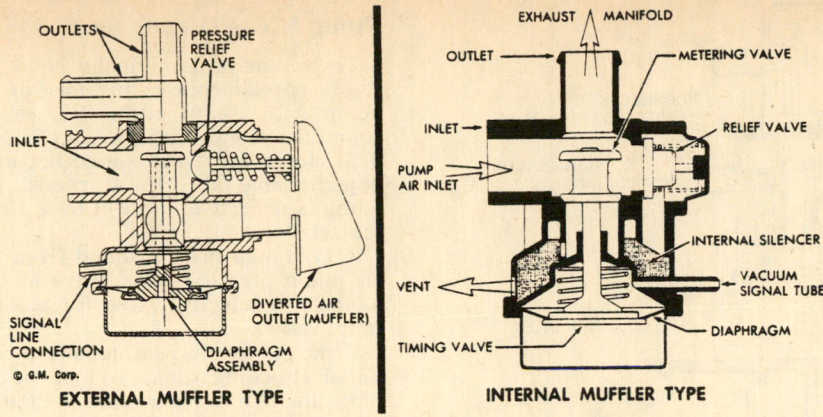

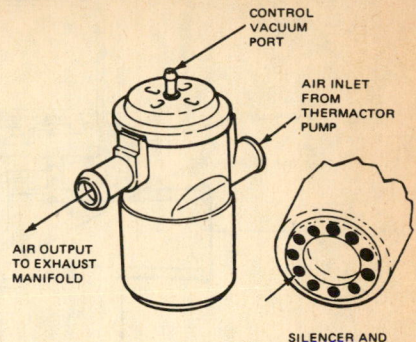

General Motors Diverter Valves (© G.M. Corp.)

Catalyst cars use a different air bypass valve, with small hose connecting to the end. (© Ford Motor Co.)

hooked up. The new valve, being normally in the dump position, must have the small sensing line hooked up to manifold vacuum, which pulls the valve mechanism from the dump position into the normal running position.

Unfortunately, the new style valve will not go into the dump position automatically during deceleration. To get the valve to dump, a vacuum differential valve (VDV) is connected in the sensing line. Manifold vacuum goes through the VDV and then to the diverter valve. When the manifold vacuum increases during deceleration, the VDV closes the sensing line. This shuts off the vacuum to the diverter valve, and the valve goes into the dump position.

A further refinement of this, in 1976, is to connect the sensing line to ported (above the throttle plates) vacuum instead of manifold vacuum, and eliminate the VDV. In this situation, the diverter valve only receives vacuum above idle, because the vacuum port in the carburetor throat is above the throt-

tle plate at idle. So whenever the engine idles, the diverter valve goes to the dump position. It also dumps during deceleration, because the throttle at that time is in the idle position.

Some systems have a delay valve, similar to a spark delay valve, in the sensing hose. This delays for a few seconds the drop in vacuum when the throttle closes, so that the air is not dumped every time the driver takes his foot off the throttle in traffic.

Temperature controls are also used in the sensing hose hookup. Usually, the temperature valve shuts the vacuum off when the engine is cold, so that the pump air doesn't go to the engine exhaust ports until the engine warms up.

Some cars have a temperature sensor mounted under the car above the catalytic converter. If the converter overheats, the sensor turns off a solenoid which shuts off the air to the diverter valve. The diverter valve then goes to the dump position, shutting off the air to the exhaust to keep the converter

from melting or burning up.

1976 and later Ford Motor Company 4-cylinder, V6, and some inline 6 engines use a unique air bypass valve, with two small sensing hoses connected to it. Each of the hoses connects to one side of a diaphragm in the valve. The hose on the body of the valve connects to manifold vacuum, and the hose closer to the end connects to a separate on-off valve.

The diaphragm has a small hole so that the vacuum or pressure on each side will equalize. As long as the end chamber is sealed by the separate valve being closed, nothing happens, and the air flows through the bypass valve on the way to the exhaust ports. But if the separate valve is opened, it admits atmospheric pressure to one side of the diaphragm, and the vacuum on the other side moves the bypass valve to the dump position, exhausting the pump air into the atmosphere.

Two types of separate valves are used, one of them an electric solenoid operated valve, and the other a vacuum-operated valve. The electric solenoid is controlled by a Thermo Actuated Valve (TAV) in the air cleaner. When the engine is cold, the TAV closes, which energizes the solenoid. Atmospheric pressure then enters the upper chamber on the bypass valve and it goes to the dump position. When the engine warms up, the TAV opens, shuts off the solenoid, and the bypass valve goes into the normal running position.

On some California engines the solenoid is connected so that manifold vacuum passes through the solenoid to get to the bypass valve. A small filter-vent is placed over the end of the nozzle on the end cap of the bypass valve. With the same electrical hookup, this setup has the same action as that described earlier.

The vacuum operated valve, which takes the place of the solenoid on V6 and some inline 6 engines, is connected to ported (above the throttle plates) carburetor vacuum. It is called the Idle Vacuum Valve. At idle, there is no ported vacuum, and the idle vacuum

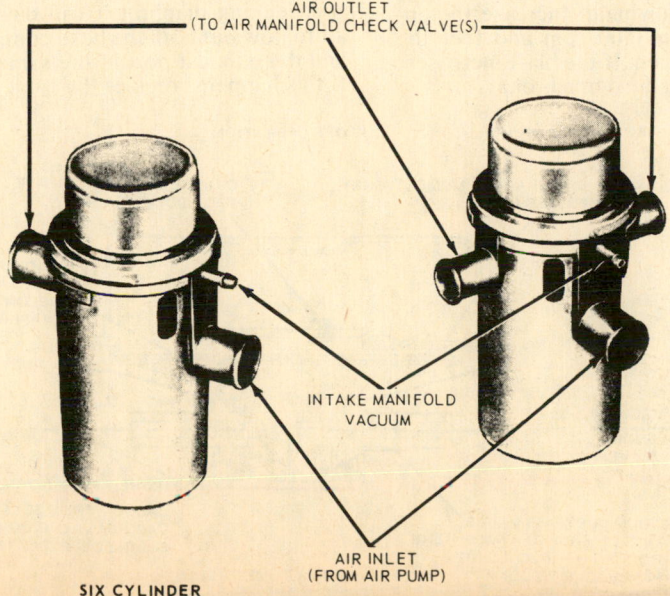

These bypass valves have internal cotton silencers (© Ford Motor Co.)

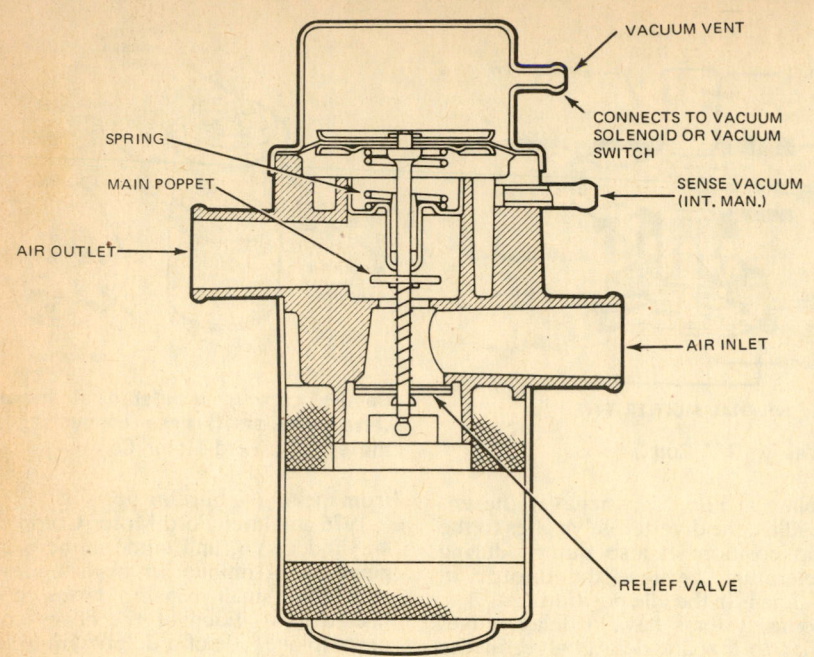

Vacuum differential valve-VDV

Pump Noise Diagnosis

The air pump is normally noisy; as engine speed increases, the noise of the pump will rise in pitch. The rolling sound the pump bearings make is normal. However, if this sound becomes objectionable at certain speeds, the pump is defective and will have to be replaced.

A continual hissing sound from the air pump pressure relief valve at idle indicates a defective valve. Replace the relief valve.

If the pump rear bearing fails, a continual knocking sound will be heard. Since the rear bearing is not separately replaceable, the pump will have to be replaced as an assembly.

Anti-backfire Valve Tests

Detach the hose, which runs from the bypass valve to the check valve.

Connect a tachometer to the engine. With the engine running at normal idle speed, check to see that air is flowing from the bypass valve hose connection.

Speed the engine up, so that it is running at 1,500-2,000 rpm. Allow the throttle to snap shut. The flow of air from the bypass valve at the check valve hose connection should stop momentarily and air should then flow from the exhaust port on the valve body or the silencer assembly.

Let the throttle snap shut several times. If the flow of air is not diverted into the atmosphere from the valve exhaust port or if it fails to stop flowing from the hose connection, check the vacuum lines and connections. If these are tight, either the bypass valve or one of the accessory valves in the small sensing hose is defective and must be replaced.

A leaking diaphragm will cause the air to flow out both the hose connection and the exhaust port at the same time. If this happens, replace the valve.

valve opens, which causes the bypass valve to go to the dump position. Above idle, the idle vacuum valve closes, and the bypass valve goes into the running position. A temperature control, a delay valve, and a vacuum reservoir all control the ported vacuum supply to the idle vacuum valve.

Air Pump Tests

--- CAUTION ---

Do not hammer on, pry or bend the pump housing while tightening the drive belt or testing the pump.

Before proceeding with the tests, check the pump drive belt tension.

If the belt squeals when the engine is running, the pump may be dragging or seized. Remove the belt and turn the pump by hand to check for seizure. Disregard any chirping, squealing, or rolling sounds from inside the pump when turning it by hand, as these are normal.

Check the hoses and connections for leaks. Hissing or a blast of air is indicative of a leak. Soapy water, applied lightly around the area in question, is a good method for detecting leaks.

To test air output, disconnect the air hose from the pump wherever it is convenient. If you disconnect it from one check valve on a V8 or V6, the other hose should also be disconnected and plugged for the test. Run the engine at idle and feel the blast of air from the hose with your hand. Increase the engine speed to 1500 rpm and feel the blast of air again. If the blast increases, and is steady, the pump is okay.

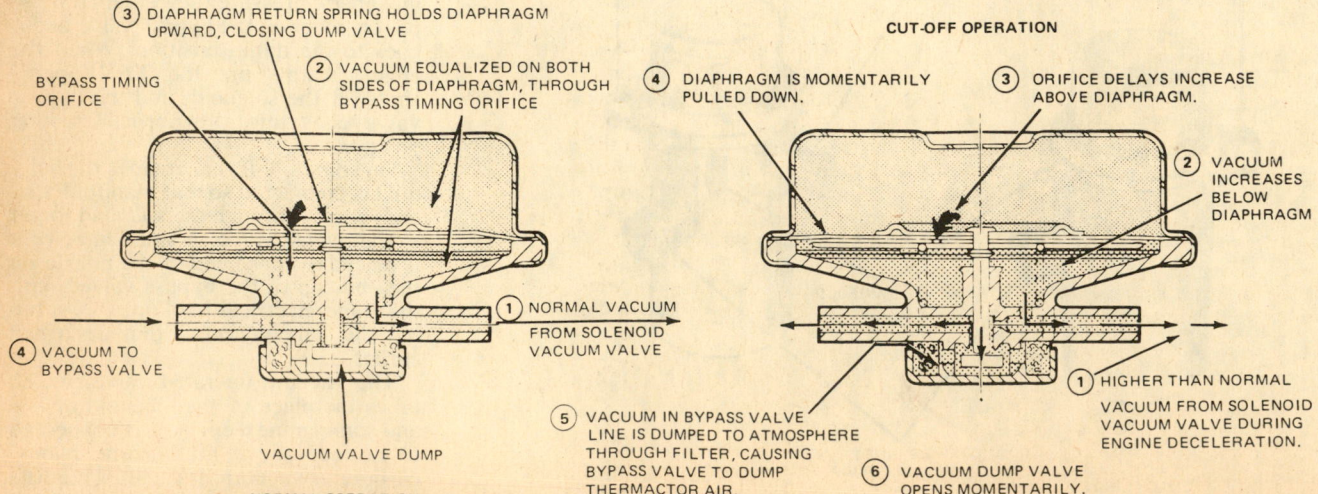

Timed air bypass valve with integral vacuum differential function (© Ford Motor Co.)

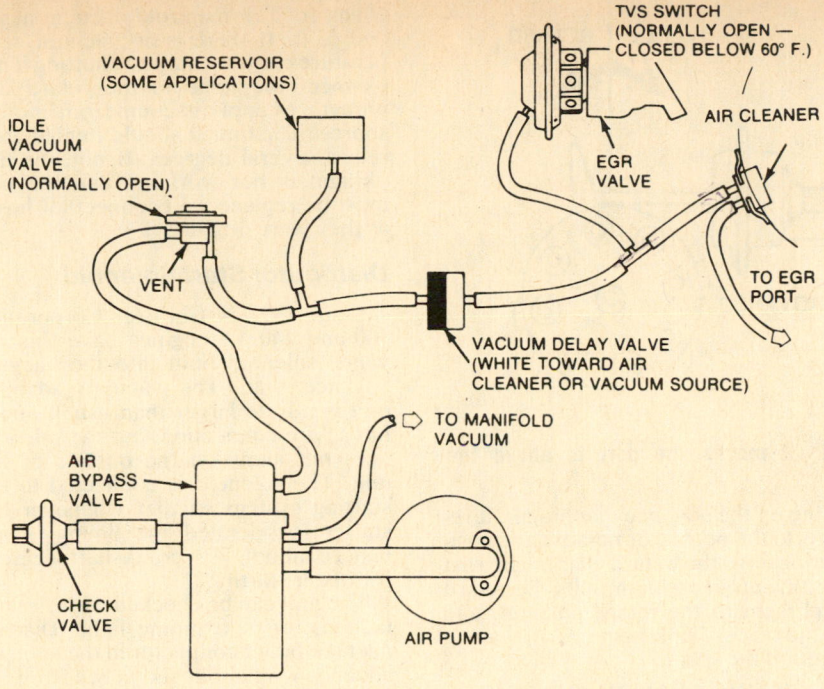

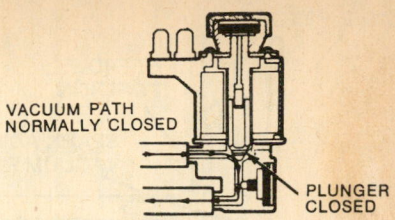

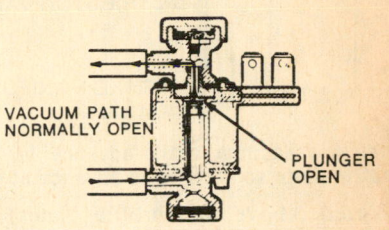

VACUUM PATH NORMALLY CLOSED — PLUNGER CLOSED

SOLENOID VACUUM VALVE FOR NORMALLY CLOSED (TYPE 1) SYSTEMS

VACUUM PATH NORMALLY OPEN — PLUNGER OPEN

SOLENOID VACUUM VALVE FOR NORMALLY OPEN (TYPE 2) SYSTEM

Air pump system using a timed air by-pass valve vacuum vent

Normally closed and normally open solenoids. Notice the open space between the hose connections on the normally open model

Late model systems should stop flowing at idle, as described earlier. If not, the bypass valve or accessory valve is defective.

Check Valve Test

Remove the hose from the check valve. With the engine running at 1500 rpm in Park or Neutral, hold the back of your hand near the check valve to test for exhaust gas leakage. If the valve leaks, it must be replaced.
NOTE: *Vibration and flutter of the valve at idle is a normal condition caused by exhaust pulsations. It does not mean that the valve is defective.*

Vacuum Differential Valve Test

Disconnect the small sensing hose at the bypass valve and connect a vacuum gauge to the hose. With the engine idling in Park or Neutral, the gauge should read full manifold vacuum.

Run the engine at a steady 2500 rpm in Park or Neutral, and release the throttle. As the engine decelerates, the vacuum gauge should drop close to zero, then return to full manifold vacuum as the engine speed drops to idle. If not, the VDV is defective and must be replaced.
NOTE: *The small hose nozzle should be connected to manifold vacuum.*

Solenoid Vacuum Valve Tests (Ford Products)

Solenoid vacuum valves used with the air injection system on 1975 and later Ford products are of two types, normally closed and normally open. On the normally closed type, applying electric current to the terminals will open the vacuum valve. On the normally open type, applying current will close the valve. The closed valve has both hose connections at the bottom end, and the manifold vacuum connects to the bottom nozzle, furthest from the electrical connector. The open valve has the connection separated, with one at the top and the other at the bottom. Manifold vacuum connects to the top nozzle, nearest the electric connector.

TYPE I (NORMALLY CLOSED)

With the engine idling in Park or Neutral, detach the vacuum supply hose from the solenoid bottom nozzle. Vacuum should be felt at the end of the hose with your finger. If not, check the hose and source of vacuum. When vacuum is good at the hose, reconnect it to the solenoid bottom nozzle.

Disconnect the other hose from the solenoid and connect a vacuum gauge to the solenoid. Disconnect the elec-
tricity from the solenoid. With the engine idling, there should be no reading on the gauge. Connect one terminal of the solenoid to the battery positive post, and the other terminal to ground. The vacuum gauge should read full manifold vacuum. Disconnect the battery hookup. The vacuum gauge should drop to zero. If the solenoid does not operate correctly, replace it.

TYPE II (NORMALLY OPEN)

With the engine idling in Park or Neutral, detach the vacuum supply hose from the solenoid upper nozzle. Vacuum should be felt at the end of the hose with your finger. If not, check the hose and source of vacuum. When vacuum is good at the hose, reconnect it to the solenoid bottom nozzle.

Disconnect the other hose from the solenoid and connect a vacuum gauge to the solenoid. Disconnect the electricity from the solenoid. With the engine idling, full manifold vacuum should appear on the gauge. Connect one terminal of the solenoid to the battery positive post and the other terminal to ground. The vacuum gauge should drop to zero. Disconnect the battery hookup, and full manifold vacuum should appear on the gauge.

If the solenoid does not operate correctly, replace it.

Distributor Controls

All distributor controls act in some way to change or eliminate vacuum advance during certain operating conditions. Usually, the control cuts down
on the amount of vacuum advance, in effect retarding the spark, so that the exhaust will get hotter and burn up hydrocarbon and carbon monoxide emissions before they go out the tailpipe.

The distributor vacuum advance unit might be connected, according to factory design, to either manifold vacuum

Emission Control Systems

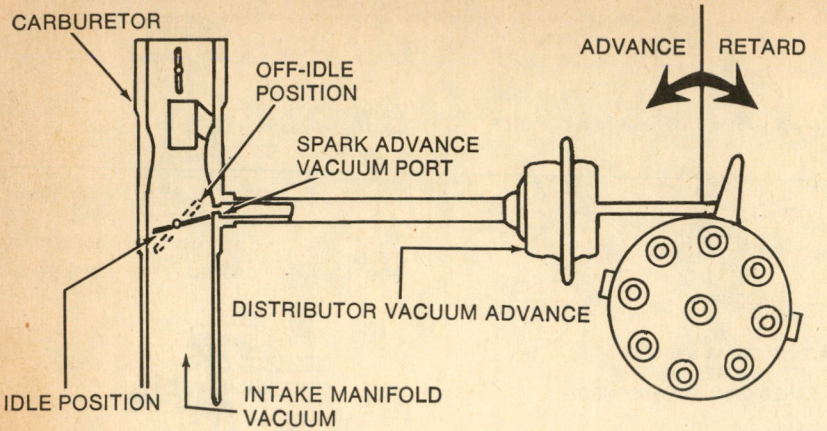

When the vacuum spark advance is "ported" it means the port is above the throttle plate so there is no advance at idle

or ported (above the throttle plates) carburetor vacuum. Either way, the vacuum spark advance curve is approximately the same for all running conditions above idle. At idle, however, the manifold vacuum hookup results in full advance, while the ported hookup gives zero advance. If the hoses are hooked up the wrong way, the addition or lack of advance will affect idle speed, requiring a readjustment of the throttle position to bring the idle speed back to specifications. When this is done, emissions will usually be high, so it is important to keep the hoses hooked up correctly.

Dual Diaphragm Distributors

These distributors have two hose connections, one in the normal position, and the other closer to the distributor body. The hose fitting next to the body is for the retard diaphragm, and is connected to manifold vacuum. The retard diaphragm affects the spark only at idle, when there is no vacuum on the advance diaphragm. In effect, the retard diaphragm provides a movable resting place for the advance diaphragm. When ported vacuum is not

acting on the advance diaphragm, it returns to the neutral or no-advance position against the retard diaphragm. At idle, manifold vacuum pulls the retard diaphragm to the retard position, and the advance diaphragm follows along to retard the spark.

TESTING DUAL DIAPHRAGM DISTRIBUTORS

To test a dual diaphragm distributor, connect a timing light to the engine. Remove the retard hose from the distributor and plug the hose. With the engine running, increase the speed to a fast idle and watch the timing marks. The timing should advance. If not, either the vacuum unit is faulty, the vacuum port is plugged, or there is a temperature control device that is shutting off the vacuum. Apply hand pump or mouth suction vacuum to the advance diaphragm and the timing should advance. If not, the distributor must be disassembled and repaired. Failure to advance could be caused by a faulty diaphragm or a sticking advance plate.

Remove the advance hose from the vacuum unit and read the timing at normal idle speed. Remove the plug that was inserted in the retard hose, and

check for full manifold vacuum at the end of it. If there is no vacuum, temperature controls may be shutting it off. Connect the hose to the retard diaphragm, or apply vacuum from another source. The timing should immediately retard several degrees. If not, the diaphragm is not working, and the unit must be replaced. Reconnect all hoses as they were originally.

Distributor Start Solenoid

Some 1972-74 Chrysler Corporation 400 and 440 V8 engines have this advance solenoid built into the vacuum advance unit. The vacuum advance unit is a little larger than usual, and it has a wire connection, but the solenoid does not show on the outside of the unit. The solenoid is connected to the starting system so that whenever the starter is operated the timing is advanced about 7½ crankshaft degrees for faster starting.

The unit can be checked with either a tachometer or a timing light. Disconnect the bullet connector in the vacuum advance wire about six inches from the unit. Hook up a tachometer or a timing light. Then, with the engine idling, connect a long jumper wire from the battery positive post to the end of the wire from the vacuum unit. The engine speed should increase about 50 rpm or more. If using a timing light, you should see about 7½ degrees more advance.

CAUTION

Do not leave the jumper connected for more than 30 seconds, or the solenoid might overheat.

The solenoid is not repairable. The entire vacuum unit must be replaced if the solenoid doesn't work.

Distributor Vacuum Deceleration Valve

First used on Chrysler Corporation engines as part of the original Clean Air Package, this valve was later used on AMC, Ford, and Pontiac engines. It was commonly known as a spark valve. Its purpose is to advance the spark during deceleration, by sending full manifold vacuum to the vacuum advance unit. At all other times the vacuum advance unit receives ported (above the throttle plates) carburetor vacuum.

Three checks should be made on the valve: the amount of vacuum at the distributor, any valve leaks, and the adjustment. To check the amount of vacuum at the distributor, use a T-fitting and a short length of vacuum hose to connect a vacuum gauge into the distributor vacuum line near the distributor. At idle, with the engine fully warmed up, the vacuum on the gauge should be less than 1 Hg. If the gauge shows more than 1 Hg, the idle speed is too fast, or the valve is leaking. To

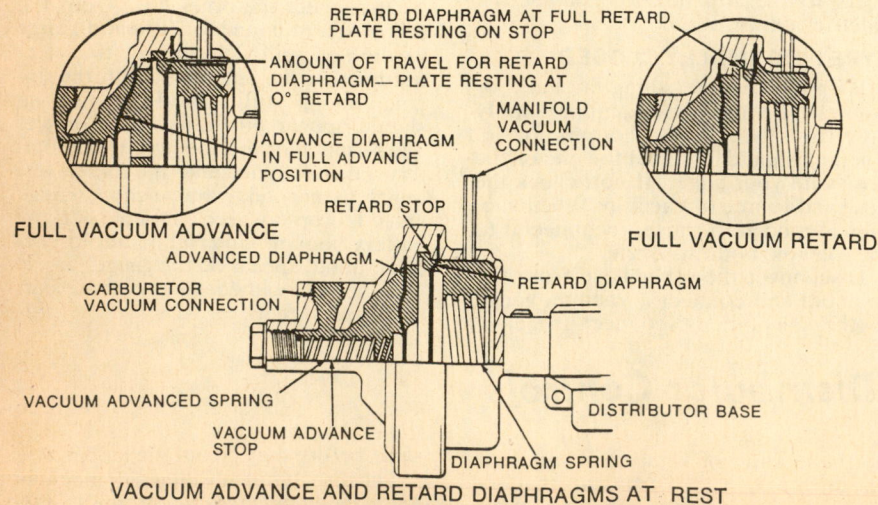

Operation of the dual diaphragm vacuum advance (© Ford Motor Co.)

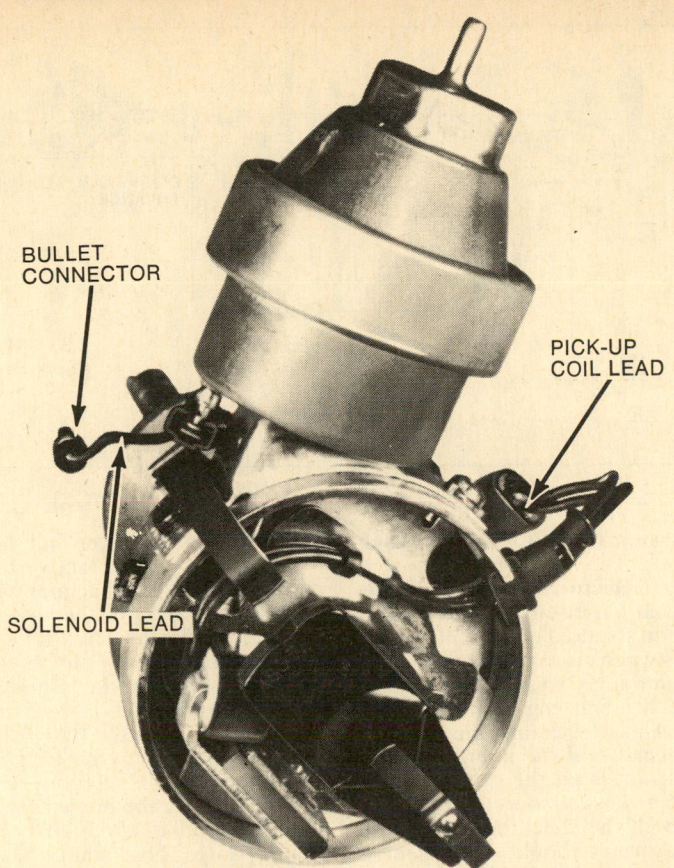

BULLET CONNECTOR

PICK-UP COIL LEAD

SOLENOID LEAD

Distributor start solenoid used on Electronic distributor
(© Chrysler Corp.)

check for a leak, remove the large manifold vacuum hose on the side of the valve. If the vacuum drops, the valve is leaking and must be replaced. If the vacuum stays high, reduce the engine idle speed so that the port in the carburetor is covered.

To check the valve adjustment, connect the manifold vacuum hose and run the engine at 2000 rpm for 5 seconds. Then release the throttle. The distributor vacuum should go over 16 in. Hg. and stay there for about one second. Within about three seconds after you release the throttle, the distributor vacuum should drop to below 6 in. Hg. If

the carburetor is equipped with a dashpot to make the throttle close slowly, the time may be about one second longer. If the time is too long, remove the cover on the valve and turn the screw clockwise to reduce the time. To increase the time, turn the screw counterclockwise. If the valve will not adjust properly, it must be replaced, and the new valve adjusted to specifications.

Spark Delay Valve

This small valve is connected between the carburetor and the distributor vacuum advance, so that the ported

(above the throttle plates) vacuum to the distributor must pass through the valve. A restriction in the valve delays the vacuum applied to the vacuum advance unit so that the advance comes in slowly. When there is no vacuum at the carburetor port, as during idle or wide open throttle, a check valve inside the spark delay valve opens and dumps the vacuum so that the vacuum advance unit returns to the no-advance position without any delay.

Ford Products use spark delay valves with one side black and the other colored. The colored side indicates the amount of delay, which can be from one to 28 seconds. The valve should always be installed with the black side toward the source of vacuum, and the colored side toward the distributor.

General Motors spark delay valves are a different shape than Ford, and are marked on both sides with the names of the components they connect to. Usually, they are marked CARB on one side, and either TVS or DIST on the other. Of course, the CARB side must be connected to the carburetor port.

Spark delay valves can be tested for correct operation and leaks with a source of vacuum such as a hand vacuum pump or a running engine, and a vacuum gauge. Connect the vacuum gauge to the distributor side of the valve, and the vacuum source to the other side. The gauge should rise slowly until it reads the amount of vacuum available. The time to rise to the maximum reading should be from one to 28 seconds. If the vacuum gauge does not read anything, the valve is plugged. If the vacuum reads instantly, without any delay, the valve is open. In either case, the spark delay valve must be replaced. To test the check valve part of the spark delay valve, remove the vacuum source and the vacuum gauge should drop instantly to zero without any delay. If there is any delay, the spark delay valve is defective and must be replaced.

Distributor Vacuum Vent Valve

Some 1977 and later Ford engines have a distributor vacuum vent valve to prevent fuel from flowing to the distributor through the vacuum line, and to act as a delay valve. Vacuum spark advance is delayed during acceleration by this valve. It also eliminates vacuum advance during heavy acceleration, deceleration, and idle by venting the spark port vacuum to the atmosphere.

The valve can be tested with an external vacuum source, a length of vacuum hose, and a vacuum gauge. Apply 10 in. Hg. of vacuum to the "VAC" side of the valve. This is the side with the code number. Connect a 24 in. length of hose to the gauge; connect the other end to the other side of the vent valve. Observe the time in seconds for the gauge to register 8 in. Hg., while

TO CARBURETOR → TO DISTRIBUTOR

TO MANIFOLD

VACUUM UNIT

VACUUM UNIT COVER

ADJUSTING SCREW

Distributor vacuum control valve sometimes called a spark valve (© Chrysler Corp.)

applying a constant 10 in. Hg. If the code number on the valve is 20, it should take 16-36 seconds. If the code number is 40, it should take 28-67 seconds. Be careful when making this test not to allow oil or dirt to enter the valve. No repairs are possible to the valve. It must be replaced if found defective.

Delay Vacuum Bypass

This system, used on Ford Products in 1973 only, bypasses the spark delay valve below an ambient temperature of 49-65°F. so that the vacuum advance unit receives ported carburetor vacuum without any delay. Above 49-65°F. the ported vacuum must pass through the spark delay valve.

The system consists of an ambient temperature switch mounted in the front door hinge post (either side), a vacuum solenoid mounted on the engine near the distributor, a check valve, a spark delay valve, and the connecting hoses and wires.

To test for correct operation, disconnect the hose from the distributor vacuum advance and set the throttle so the engine runs at approximately 1500 rpm with the transmission in Park or Neutral. Connect a vacuum gauge to the hose and see if the vacuum rises slowly to about 5 in. Hg. If the vacuum gauge shows a few inches of vacuum immediately, without a slow rise, it means the system is in the bypass mode, or the system is not working right. To be sure the system is not in the bypass mode, warm the temperature switch in the door hinge post with a hot cloth, and make the test again. The bypass system will not affect the maximum amount of vacuum on the gauge, only the rate of rise. Each time you test it you must disconnect and reconnect the vacuum gauge to check the rate of rise.

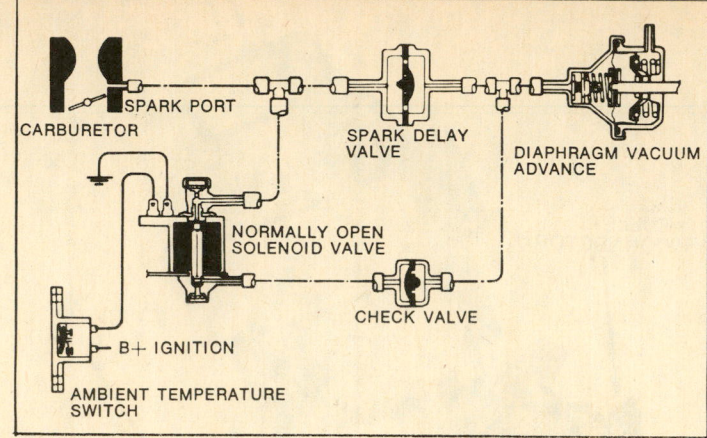

Ford Delay Vacuum By-pass system (© Ford Motor Co.)

If the system doesn't work, test each component. The temperature switch should be electrically open below 49-65°F. and closed above that figure. The vacuum solenoid is normally open, and closes when current is applied. Use only a continuous source of vacuum, such as a running engine, to test the solenoid. A hand vacuum pump cannot be used because of the internal bleed. The black nozzle on the solenoid connects to the vacuum source. The black sides of both the check valve and the spark delay valve should be connected to the vacuum source. When testing the check valve, vacuum applied to the white side should hold and not leak down. Vacuum applied to the black side should not build up at all. Repairs are not possible on any of the components. They must be replaced when they wear out.

Thermal Check and Delay Valve

This is a spark delay valve with a built-in temperature control. Below 50°F. the valve is open and the distributor receives ported (above the throttle plates) carburetor vacuum without any delay. Above 50°F. the valve closes to a small orifice so that it takes about 40 seconds at part throttle before the distributor gets all of the ported vacuum.

To test the valve, connect a hand vacuum pump to the CARB nozzle and a vacuum gauge to the TVS nozzle. Be sure the valve is at room temperature (68°F.). Work the pump rapidly to create a vacuum of about 20 in. Hg. on the pump gauge. The vacuum gauge should lag behind. When you stop pumping, the pump gauge should drop slightly, and in a few seconds should read the same as the vacuum gauge. If not, the valve is defective and must be replaced. When the valve is cold, it is open, and vacuum should pass freely through so that both gauges register the same with no lag.

Transmission Controlled Spark

This system is used widely on General Motors cars, but variations of it are also found on American Motors, Chrysler Corporation, and Ford Motor Company cars. The object of transmission controlled spark is to eliminate vacuum spark advance in the lower gears. Once the transmission gets into high gear, vacuum spark advance is allowed for better gas mileage and part throttle response. Because each of the car maker's systems are different, we will describe them separately.

AMERICAN MOTORS

Manual transmission cars produced before March 15, 1973 eliminate vacuum advance in the lower gears when the air temperature at the front of the car is below 63° F. If the temperature is above 63°F. vacuum advance is allowed in all gears.

The vacuum supply to the distributor vacuum advance unit is controlled by a solenoid vacuum valve mounted on the top of the engine. This valve receives current whenever the ignition switch is on, and is grounded to complete the circuit through a solenoid control switch

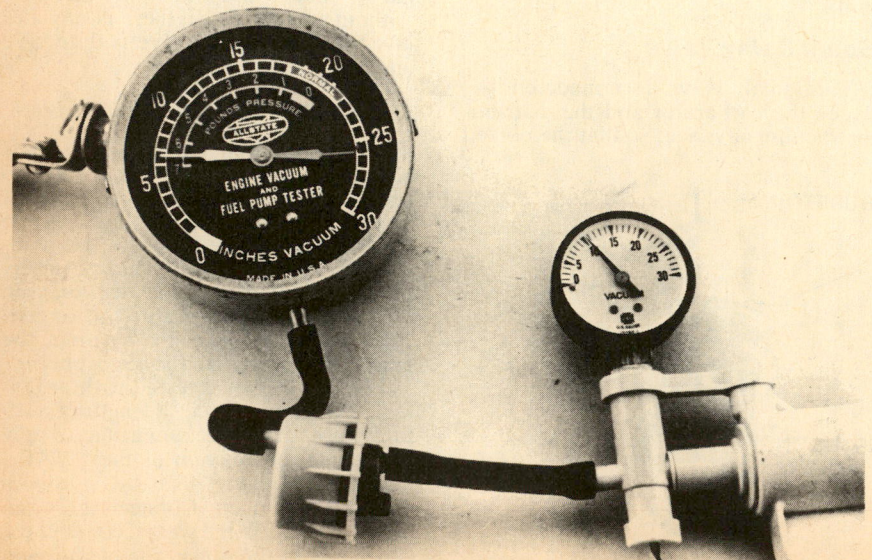

Testing the thermal check and delay valve is easy with a hand vacuum pump. Notice the difference in the readings on the two vacuum gauges.

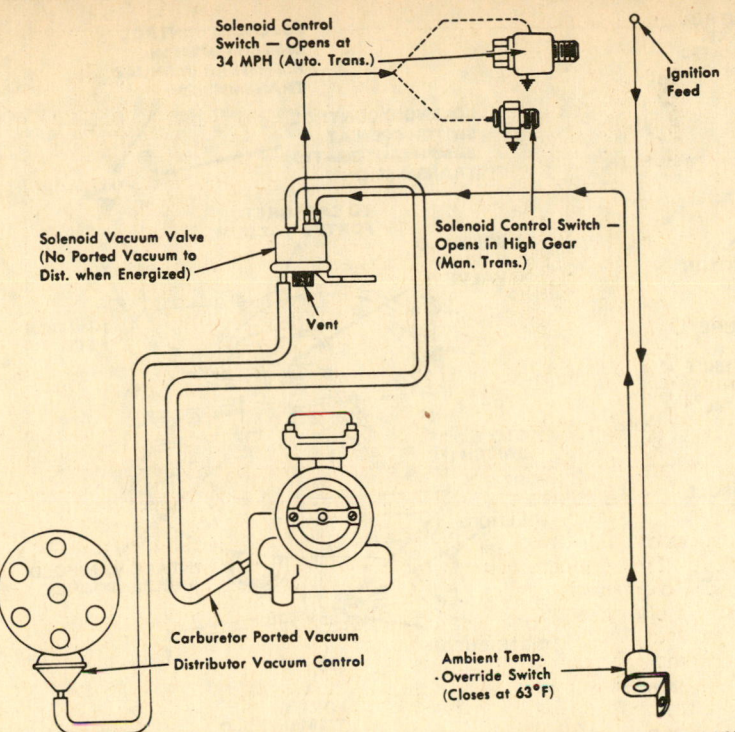

Solenoid Control Switch — Opens at 34 MPH (Auto. Trans.)

Ignition Feed

Solenoid Vacuum Valve (No Ported Vacuum to Dist. when Energized)

Vent

Solenoid Control Switch — Opens in High Gear (Man. Trans.)

Carburetor Ported Vacuum

Distributor Vacuum Control

Ambient Temp. Override Switch (Closes at 63°F)

1973 AMC six cylinder TCS system used before March 15. (© AMC)

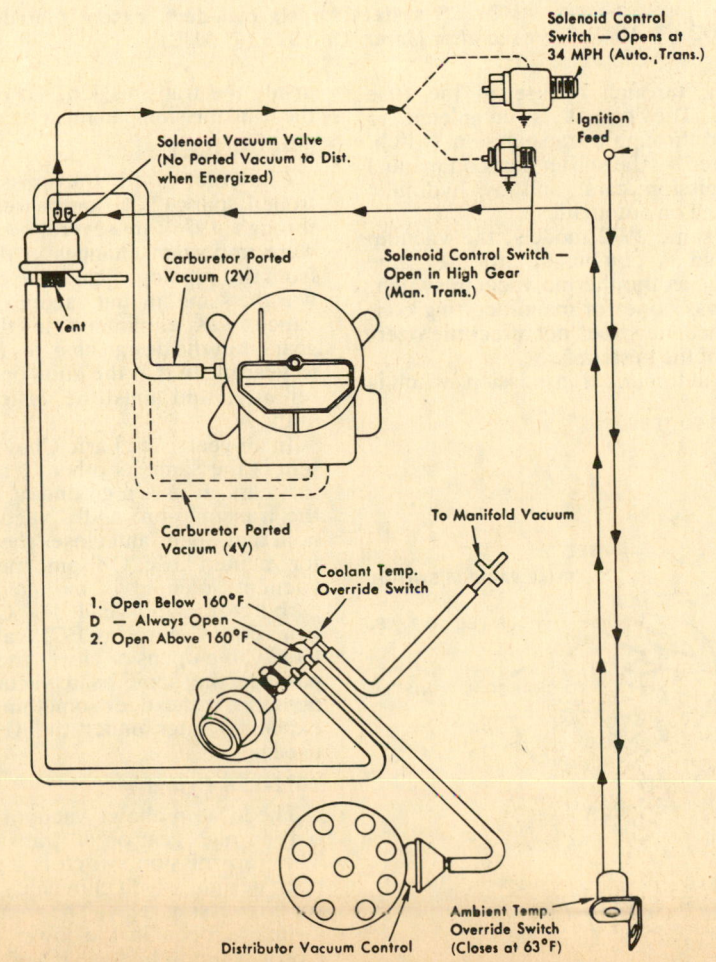

Solenoid Control Switch — Opens at 34 MPH (Auto. Trans.)

Ignition Feed

Solenoid Vacuum Valve (No Ported Vacuum to Dist. when Energized)

Vent

Carburetor Ported Vacuum (2V)

Solenoid Control Switch — Open in High Gear (Man. Trans.)

Carburetor Ported Vacuum (4V)

To Manifold Vacuum

Coolant Temp. Override Switch

1. Open Below 160°F
D — Always Open
2. Open Above 160°F

Distributor Vacuum Control

Ambient Temp. Override Switch (Closes at 63°F)

1973 AMC V8 TCS system used before March 15 (© AMC)

on the transmission. The solenoid vacuum valve is normally open, but is held closed in the lower gears by the completed circuit through the transmission switch, which is normally closed. When the transmission is shifted into high gear, the shifter shaft opens the transmission switch, which breaks the circuit and allows the solenoid vacuum valve to open for normal vacuum advance. The temperature switch at the front of the car is in series between the ignition switch and the solenoid vacuum valve. Below 63°F. the temperature switch opens, and prevents the solenoid vacuum valve from closing in the lower gears.

Manual transmission cars after March 15, 1973 use the same system, except that the temperature switch is not used.

Automatic transmission cars built before March 15, 1973 eliminate vacuum advance below 34 mph when the air temperature at the front of the car is below 63°F. If the temperature is above 63°F. vacuum advance is allowed at all speeds. The same solenoid vacuum valve is used, as on the manual transmission cars, but it is connected to a solenoid control switch on the transmission where the speedometer cable connects. The operation of the solenoid vacuum valve and solenoid control switch are the same as on the manual transmission cars, except that the solenoid control switch is sensitive to speed instead of gear position.

After March 15, 1973, the solenoid control switch on automatic transmission cars was moved up to the top of the engine and made sensitive to governor hydraulic pressure only. A hydraulic line from the transmission conducts governor pressure to the switch. In the top center of the switch is a small Allen screw that is used to adjust the switching point to exactly 34 mph. The temperature switch is not used after March 15, 1973.

To test the system, connect a vacuum gauge to the distributor vacuum hose, using enough additional hose to come out from under the hood and through the side window into the car, so that the vacuum gauge can be seen while driving. Then drive the car to test the system. On a manual transmission car, you should see vacuum on the gauge in high gear only. On an automatic, you should see vacuum above approximately 34 mph only. On cars with temperature control, the temperature must be above 63°F. Because the distributor runs on ported vacuum, you must have the throttle open a little to get vacuum. Also, you must slow down to approximately 25 mph before the solenoid vacuum valve will close. This means that once you have gone above 34 mph, you will continue to see vacuum on the gauge when the throttle is open, as long as the car does not go below the speed that closes the solenoid. If the system does not work cor-

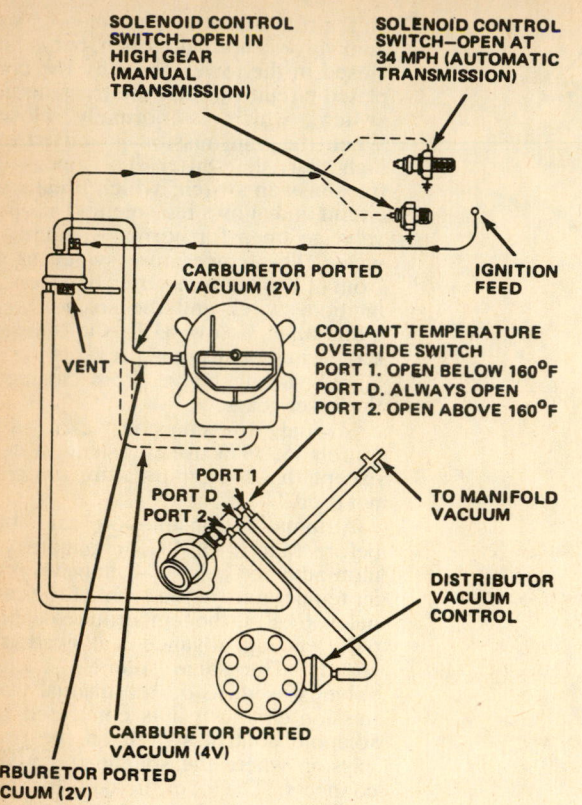

AMC TCS system for V8—used after March 15, 1973 (© AMC)

AMC TCS system for six cylinders, except Matador 258—used after March 15, 1973 (© AMC)

rectly, check out the individual units or the hose connections.

BUICK V8

Ported vacuum advance is allowed in High gear on 3-speed manual and all automatic transmission cars. 4-speed manual transmission cars allow vacuum advance only in 4th gear. Vacuum to the distributor vacuum advance unit is controlled by a vacuum solenoid that is normally open. The solenoid receives its current from the ignition switch, through a fuse in the fuse block. The circuit is completed to ground through a transmission switch, operated by the shifter shaft on manual transmission cars, and by hydraulic pressure on automatics.

On some 1972 models, the vacuum solenoid is combined into the same housing as the thermo-vacuum switch. This was done for manufacturing convenience, and does not affect the operation of the system.

The automatic transmission switch is inside the transmission. To replace it, the transmission pan must be removed.

CHEVROLET

Chevrolet used transmission controlled spark (TCS) on passenger cars through 1974. In several years there were important changes in the design from the previous year. The end result was the same, in that vacuum spark advance was eliminated in the lower gears, but the design changes from year to year mean that the units operate differently, and must be tested differently.

In all years, the basic Chevrolet system is the same as other General Motors cars. It uses a grounding switch at the transmission, and a vacuum solenoid that opens and closes the distributor vacuum hose. On some models, the vacuum solenoid is mounted on the carburetor and is called a Combined Emission Control (CEC) valve. The CEC valve opens or closes the vacuum passage the same as a vacuum solenoid, but it also does something else, as explained later under the years it is used.

1972-73 6-Cylinder

The system allows vacuum advance only in high gear on all transmissions. The transmission switch is a normally open design, which eliminates the need for a reversing relay. The transmission switch is open in the lower gears. It closes when in high gear, and turns on the CEC valve. The time relay turns on the CEC valve for 20 seconds after the

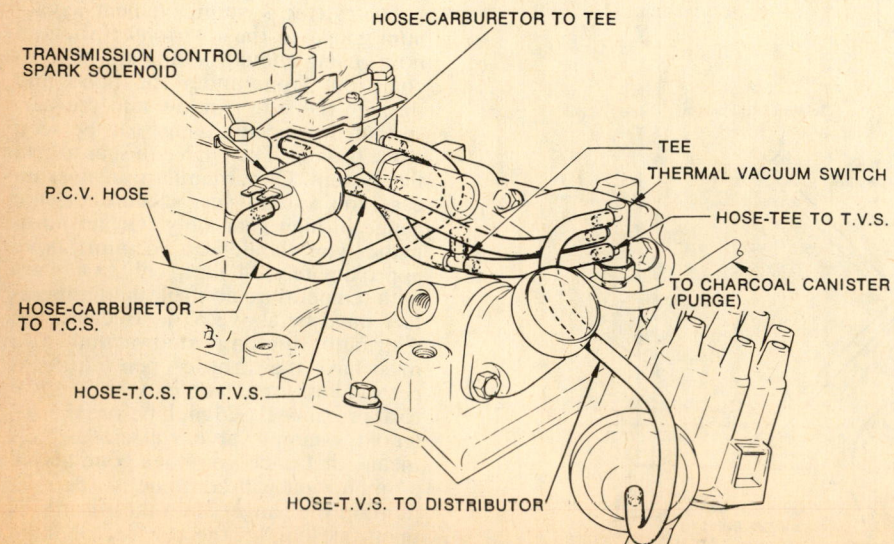

GM TCS system installation (© G.M. Corp.)

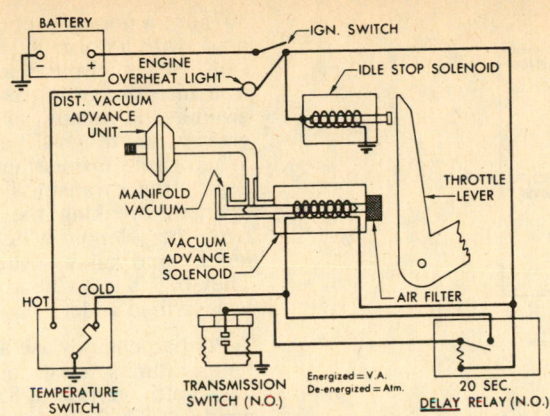

1972 Chevrolet 307, 350, 400 V8 TCS system, engine off. (© G.M. Corp.)

ignition switch is turned on. The relay has a different part number from earlier models, and is wired differently.

Cold override temperature control switching temperature is 82°F. for 1972, and 93°F. for 1973. Six-cylinder engines also have an idle stop solenoid mounted next to the CEC valve. It is important that you don't confuse the two. The CEC valve has vacuum hoses connected to it.

1974 6-Cylinder

The CEC valve is discontinued for 1974, and a vacuum solenoid is used instead. This is a normally closed solenoid, mounted on the side of the engine at the coil mounting bolt. Other than the CEC valve action, operation of the 1974 6-cylinder system is the same as in 1973.

1972 V8

The CEC valve is not used. Vacuum advance is turned on and off by a vacuum solenoid with normally closed design. New for 1972 is a delay relay, that keeps the vacuum solenoid off for 20

seconds after shifting into high gear. The delay relay is used only on 307, 350, and 400 V8s. The cold override switch turns on the vacuum solenoid below 82°F. coolant temperature. The cold override switch is built into the sending unit that operates the red HOT light on the dash. In Corvettes, the cold override and a hot override operating at 232°F. are built into the same sending unit. The sending unit for the Corvette temperature gauge is separate.

1973-74 V8

There is no CEC valve. The delay relay is eliminated, and a time relay is used. The time relay turns on the vacuum solenoid to give vacuum advance for about 20 seconds every time the ignition switch is turned on. Because all 1973-74 V8 engines with TCS operate the distributor vacuum advance on full manifold vacuum, turning on the solenoid gives a faster idle. The vacuum solenoid is a normally closed design, used with a normally open transmission switch.

VEGA, ASTRE, MONZA, SUNBIRD, STARFIRE OHC 4-CYLINDER

The 1972 models use a normally open vacuum solenoid, with a normally closed transmission switch. In the lower gears the transmission switch is closed, which grounds the vacuum solenoid and energizes it, shutting off vacuum advance. When an automatic or 3-speed manual transmission shifts into high, or a 4-speed manual shifts into 3rd and 4th, the transmission switch is opened, breaking the ground circuit from the solenoid, which opens the solenoid and allows vacuum advance.

1972 automatic transmission cars sold in California have all the equipment described above, but the transmission is rigged so the switch never opens. The solenoid stays energized whenever the ignition switch is on, and cancels the vacuum advance at all times, except when the cold override is working.

All models have a cold temperature override switch built into the sending unit for the HOT light. When engine coolant is below 82°F. the switch grounds a TCS relay on the firewall. The relay then opens a pair of points and de-energizes the vacuum solenoid, which allows vacuum advance.

On 1973 and later models the system is basically the same, but the action of the solenoid and transmission switch have been reversed. Now the vacuum solenoid is normally closed, and the transmission switch is normally open. When the transmission is in the lower gears the transmission switch is open, which keeps the solenoid de-energized and it stays closed, blocking vacuum advance. In high gear (also in 3rd on 4-speed manual) the transmission switch closes, grounding the vacuum solenoid and making it open, which allows vacuum advance.

The change in the system also eliminates the relay for cold override. Now the cold override sending unit grounds the vacuum solenoid directly below 93°F. allowing vacuum advance in all gears. The special lockout on 1972 California cars is not used in 1973 or later years.

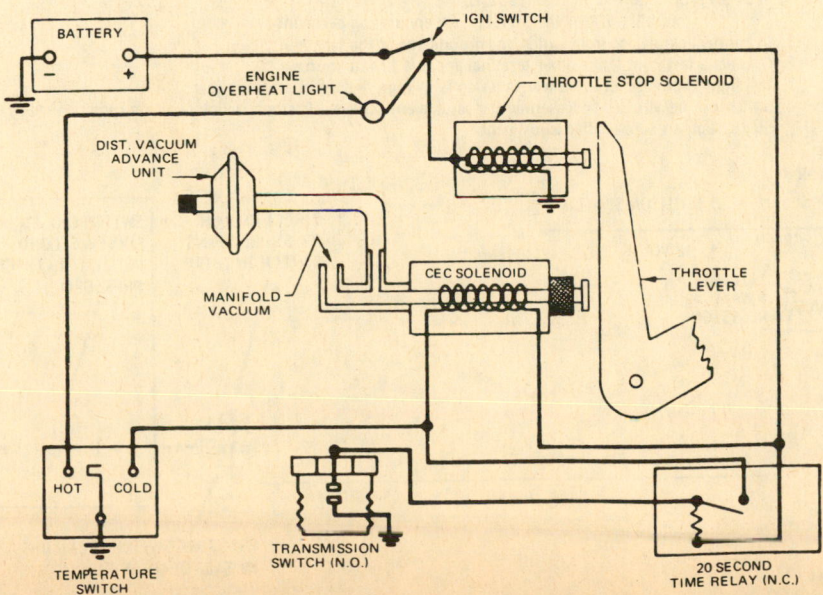

1973-74 Chevrolet TCS system without the reversing relay (© G.M. Corp.)

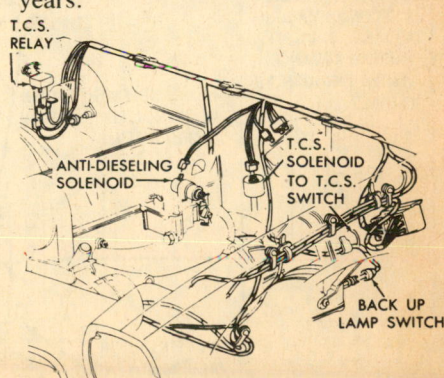

1972 Chevrolet Vega TCS system wiring (© G.M. Corp.)

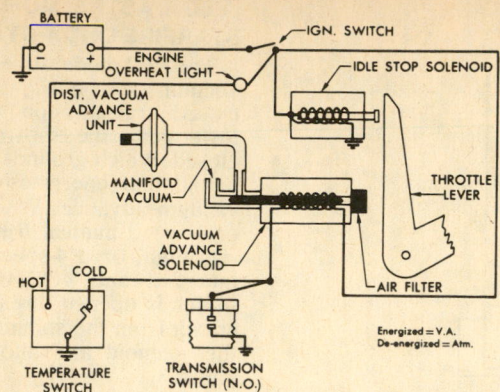

1973-76 Chevrolet Vega TCS system, engine off (© G.M. Corp.)

OLDSMOBILE V8

All Oldsmobile V8s use a normally open vacuum solenoid, teamed with a transmission switch that is normally closed. In the lower gears the transmission switch is closed, which grounds the vacuum solenoid and energizes it, shutting off vacuum advance. When the transmission goes into high gear, the transmission switch is opened, breaking the ground circuit from the solenoid, which opens the solenoid and allows vacuum advance. 1972 cars use the combined vacuum solenoid and thermo-vacuum switch, but the operation of the system is the same. Oldsmobile V8s do not use any temperature control in the TCS system.

PONTIAC V8

Pontiac V8s through 1972 (except the 307) use a normally open vacuum solenoid, with a normally closed transmission switch. In the lower gears the transmission switch is closed, which grounds the vacuum solenoid and energizes it, shutting off vacuum advance. When the transmission goes into high gear, the transmission switch is opened, breaking the ground circuit from the solenoid which opens the solenoid and allows vacuum advance. The 307 V8 is a Chevrolet engine, and is described under Chevrolet TCS.

Pontiac engines use a three-terminal temperature sending unit that combines TCS cold override at 85-95°F., hot override at 220-230°F., and operation of the HOT light. The sending unit is not a ground, as in other TCS systems, but is in series in the hot lead, between the ignition switch and the vacuum solenoid. When the cold or hot override operate, they break the hot circuit to the vacuum solenoid.

1973 Pontiac V8s use a special system, unlike any other General Motors car. Cars produced before March 15, 1973 deny vacuum advance in low gear, but allow vacuum advance about 40

V8 TRANSMISSION CONTROLLED SPARK (TCS)
Vacuum and Electrical Circuits

AUTOMATIC TRANSMISSIONS - CONTROLLED BY DIRECT CLUTCH PRESSURE

MANUAL TRANSMISSIONS - CONTROLLED BY SHIFT LEVER POSITION

TO TEST SOLENOID
1. Disconnect hoses and electrical connector.
2. Connect a hose to the distributor vacuum port on the solenoid and blow into it.
3. Air should come out the vacuum port that was connected to the carburetor.
4. Plugging this port should shut off air through the solenoid.
5. Connect a jumper from one terminal to ground. Connect the other terminal to 12 volts.
6. Air should now come out the vent port. Plugging the vent port should shut off air flow through the solenoid.

TO TEST SWITCH (AUTOMATIC TRANSMISSIONS)
1. Disconnect connector from side of transmission.
2. Connect test light from T.C.S. switch terminal to 12 volt source. ➡
3. Test light should be off when transmission is in reverse (engine running) and on when transmission is in drive.

TO TEST SWITCH (MANUAL TRANSMISSION)
   SINGLE TERMINAL SWITCH (On side of transmission)
1. Disconnect connector from switch on side of transmission.
2. Connect test light from T.C.S. switch terminal to 12 volt source.
3. Test light should be off when transmission is in high and on in all lower gears.

TO TEST SWITCH (MANUAL TRANSMISSION)
   DOUBLE TERMINAL SWITCH (in engine compartment)
1. Disconnect connector from switch and ground one of the terminals.
2. Connect a test light to the other terminal and to a 12 volt source.
3. Test light should be off when transmission is in high and on in all lower gears.
4. Switch can be adjusted by loosening the adjustment screws. Position switch to obtain condition stated in Step 3, tighten screws after adjustment.

> **Important**
> Test lamp must not be larger than an 1893 glove box lamp bulb. Larger bulbs using more than .8 amps will damage the switch contacts.

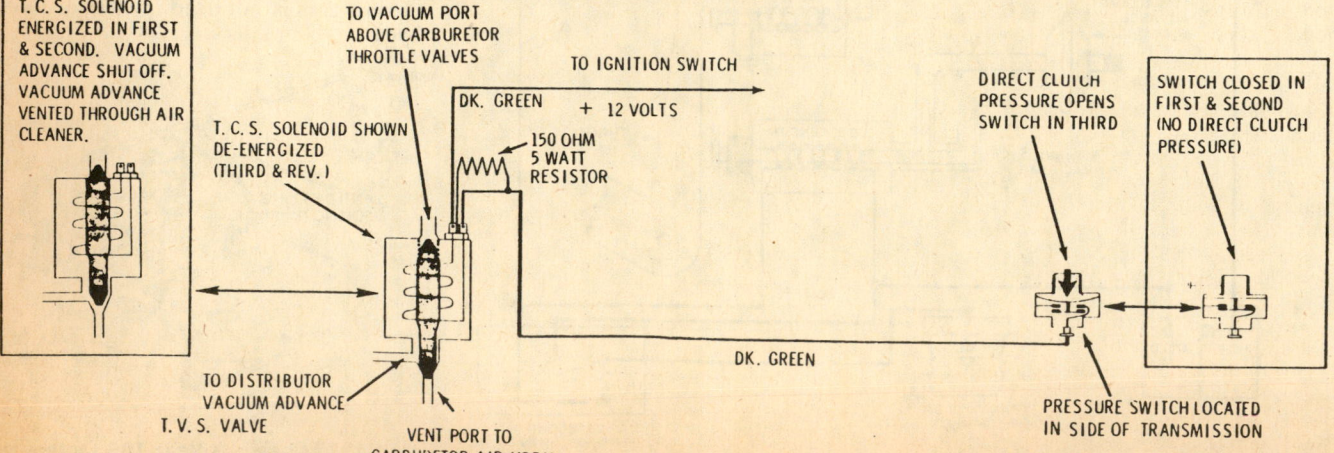

Oldsmobile TCS system—V8 engines (© G.M. Corp.)

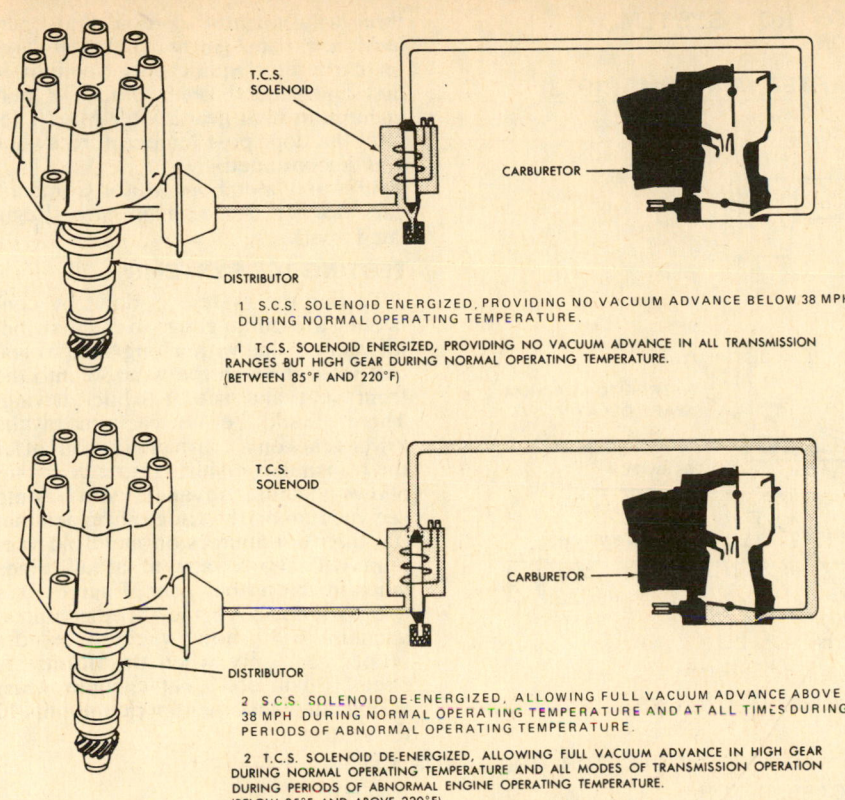

1 S.C.S. SOLENOID ENERGIZED, PROVIDING NO VACUUM ADVANCE BELOW 38 MPH DURING NORMAL OPERATING TEMPERATURE.

1 T.C.S. SOLENOID ENERGIZED, PROVIDING NO VACUUM ADVANCE IN ALL TRANSMISSION RANGES BUT HIGH GEAR DURING NORMAL OPERATING TEMPERATURE. (BETWEEN 85°F AND 220°F).

2 S.C.S. SOLENOID DE-ENERGIZED, ALLOWING FULL VACUUM ADVANCE ABOVE 38 MPH DURING NORMAL OPERATING TEMPERATURE AND AT ALL TIMES DURING PERIODS OF ABNORMAL OPERATING TEMPERATURE.

2 T.C.S. SOLENOID DE-ENERGIZED, ALLOWING FULL VACUUM ADVANCE IN HIGH GEAR DURING NORMAL OPERATING TEMPERATURE AND ALL MODES OF TRANSMISSION OPERATION DURING PERIODS OF ABNORMAL ENGINE OPERATING TEMPERATURE. (BELOW 85°F AND ABOVE 220°F)

1972 Pontiac V8 (except 307) TCS vacuum solenoid operation. Note that manifold vacuum comes from underneath the throttle valve (© G.M. Corp.)

seconds after the transmission shifts into second gear. Vacuum advance is controlled by a normally closed vacuum solenoid, with a normally open transmission switch. However, two other units, a time delay relay and a thermal delay switch, are in series between the vacuum solenoid and the transmission switch, and both of them must be closed before the transmission switch can complete the ground circuit to energize the vacuum solenoid. The transmission switch closes in second gear and stays closed in high. The thermal delay switch closes when the cylinder head metal gets up to operating temperature. This takes a little bit longer than warming up the coolant. The delay relay closes 30 or 50 seconds after it is grounded through both the thermal delay switch and the transmission switch. At the end of the delay time period, vacuum advance is allowed. If the transmission goes out of second or high gear the timing starts all over again when the transmission goes back into second or high, and 30 or 50 seconds later vacuum advance is allowed.

A cold-hot override switch allows vacuum advance in all gears below 71°F. or above 235°F. coolant temperature. Also tied into this sytem is an exhaust gas recirculation vacuum solenoid, which comes on at the same time as the vacuum advance solenoid. Cars produced after March 15, 1973

allow vacuum advance only in high gear. The vacuum advance unit receives vacuum from two sources. One is a spark thermal valve that opens below 62°F. air-fuel mixture temperature.

The other source is a vacuum solenoid mounted on the engine and connected to ported (above the throttle plates) vacuum on manual transmission engines, or manifold vacuum on automatic transmission engines. The hose from the spark thermal valve connects to the vacuum solenoid, but the solenoid does not shut off that vacuum. When the spark thermal valve is open, the vacuum it supplies goes through the solenoid, passing alongside the internal plunger and on to the vacuum advance. Another hose connection to the vacuum solenoid supplies vacuum that is actually turned on and off by the solenoid plunger.

The vacuum solenoid is a normally closed design, and it is connected to ground through a cold feed switch and a transmission switch. The cold feed switch is at the rear of the left cylinder head. It closes only when the engine is warm. Since the cold feed switch and the transmission switch are connected in series, both of them must be closed to allow vacuum advance.

A start-up relay on the firewall also supplies a ground for the vacuum solenoid during the first 20 seconds after the ignition switch is turned on, to give better performance. A hot coolant switch also provides a ground for the vacuum solenoid whenever the engine coolant temperature goes over 240°F. to provide better cooling. None of the TCS controls are used to operate the exhaust gas recirculation system.

1974 V8s combine the two thermal vacuum valves from 1973 and call the combination the Distributor Spark-EGR Thermal Vacuum Valve. It is mounted on the intake manifold in

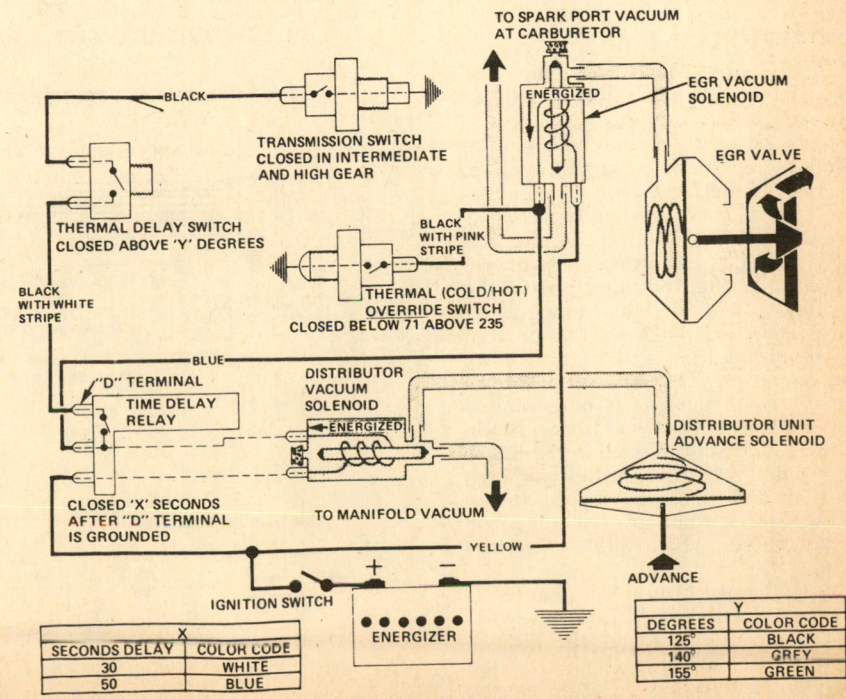

SECONDS DELAY	COLOR CODE
30	WHITE
50	BLUE

DEGREES	COLOR CODE
125°	BLACK
140°	GREY
155°	GREEN

Early 1973 Pontiac TCS-EGR system (© G.M. Corp.)

PONTIAC'S EMISSIONS CONTROL SYSTEM
- PARTS LOCATION -
1973 LATE PRODUCTION (ON OR AFTER MARCH 15, 1973)

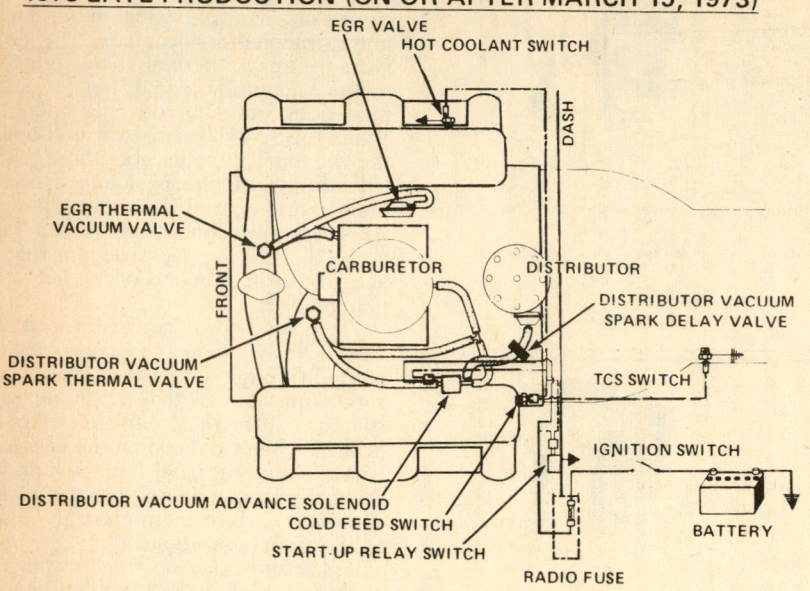

Late 1973 Pontiac TCS-EGR systems (© G.M. Corp.)

three-way vacuum solenoid that operates the exhaust gas recirculation valve on carburetor spark port vacuum in first and second gear, and EGR port vacuum in high gear. After March 15, 1973 the door post temperature switch was discontinued.

1974 and later Ford Motor Company cars do not use Transmission Regulated Spark.

TESTING TCS SYSTEMS

Testing the system is done by connecting a vacuum gauge to the distributor vacuum line with a long hose so you can put it through the window into the front seat and see it while driving. There should be no vacuum in the lower gears on a warm engine, but after the transmission shifts into a gear that allows vacuum advance, you should see vacuum on the gauge. Engines that run their distributors on manifold vacuum will show vacuum at all times when in the proper gear. Engines that use ported (above the throttle plates) vacuum will show vacuum in the proper gear only when the throttle is open. If you don't get vacuum when you should, test the individual units in the system.

front of the caruburetor and connected with hoses to both the TCS and EGR systems. Below an air-fuel temperature of 62°F the valve is open and allows vacuum advance. Above 62°F the valve is closed and the vacuum advance gets its vacuum through the TCS vacuum solenoid, which is open only in high gear. The vacuum solenoid, a normally closed design, is grounded through a transmission switch that closes only in high gear. The cold feed switch and start up relay are used the same as in 1973.

FORD MOTOR COMPANY

The 1972 Ford Motor Company system is called Transmission Regulated Spark. Vacuum advance is allowed only in high gear. The vacuum is controlled by a solenoid vacuum valve, sometimes called a Distributor Modulator Valve. The vacuum valve receives current from the ignition switch, but this current passes through a temperature switch in the front door post of the car. Below 49-65°F. the temperature switch is open, blocking the current and preventing the vacuum valve from being energized. The vacuum valve is a normally open design. It is grounded through a normally closed transmission switch, which stays closed in the lower gears. When the transmission is in high gear, the transmission switch opens, breaking the circuit and opening the vacuum valve, which allows vacuum advance.

The 1973 Ford Motor Company system is called TRS+1. As far as the vacuum advance is concerned, the TRS+1 does exactly the same thing that the 1972 TRS system does. The difference is that the temperature switch and transmission switch also operate a

Ford transmission controlled spark system (© Ford Motor Co.)

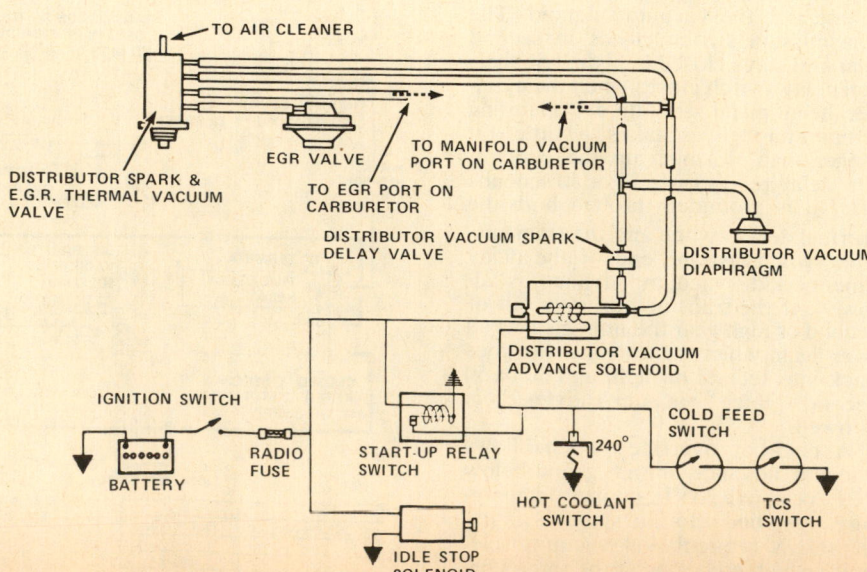

1974 Pontiac V8 engine TCS system wiring (© G.M. Corp.)

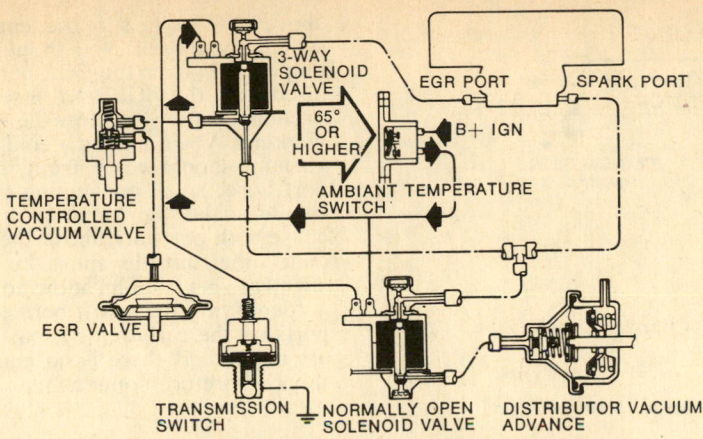

Ford transmission Regulated Spark Plus 1 system. At 65 degrees or higher the temperature switch is closed, allowing the ignition switch to energize the three- way vacuum solenoid (© Ford Motor Co.)

Vacuum solenoids can be tested by disconnecting all wiring and connecting hot and ground wires to the solenoid terminals, to make it open or close. You should be able to blow through the solenoid when it is open, but not when it's closed. Because solenoids exist in both normally open and normally closed designs, it is important to use the right solenoid. If the wrong solenoid is used, the system will work backwards, giving advance in the lower gears but not in high. The same goes for the transmission switch, which exists in both normally open and normally closed designs. The term "normally open" means that the solenoid or switch is open when it is not energized or activated. In the case of a vacuum solenoid, normally open means that if you were holding the solenoid in your hand without any wires connected to it, the vacuum passages would be open, allowing vacuum to pass. In the case of a transmission switch, the term "normally open" refers to the electrical path, which is "open" or "off" so that it will not conduct electricity. Nor-

mally closed, of course, means that the electric contacts are closed so that the current can pass. But normally closed on a vacuum solenoid means that the vacuum passage is blocked so the vacuum can't get through.

All electrical switches should be tested with a penlight-powered test light. Testing with a car battery and a light bulb is dangerous, because you might put so much current through the switch that it burns up.

Unless you are familiar with handling small electrical probes, relays should be tested by elimination. Test everything else first, and if the system still doesn't work, it must be the relay. It's not that relays can't be tested, but they are expensive, and one small slip with a hot wire can burn up $20 in parts.

Chrysler Corporation NOx Control System

Chrysler Corporation's NOx Control

System is actually a form of transmission controlled spark.

1972 manual transmission cars use a simple system that cancels vacuum advance in the lower gears. A normally open vacuum solenoid is used, with a normally closed transmission switch. In the lower gears the transmission switch is closed, which completes the ground circuit from the solenoid and keeps the solenoid energized to cancel vacuum advance. In high gear the transmission switch opens, breaking the ground circuit and allowing the vacuum solenoid to open.

The 1972 automatic transmission cars have a control unit without the vacuum switch. The vacuum advance is cancelled whenever the air temperature is over 70°F. and the car speed is below 30 mph.

All Chrysler vacuum solenoids are normally open, and all transmission switches are normally closed. The vacuum switch and the speed switch are both normally open.

Speed Controlled Spark

American Motors cars used a type of speed controlled spark, but they called it transmission controlled spark, so it is covered under that heading. The system that is called Speed Controlled Spark was used one year only, in 1972, on Cadillac and Pontiac. A vacuum solenoid is used, connected to a speed switch in the speedometer cable. Below approximately 35 mph the speed switch is closed, which grounds and energizes the vacuum solenoid and blocks the vacuum to the distributor advance unit. When the car speed goes over approximately 35 mph, the speed switch opens, breaking the circuit and allowing vacuum advance. The vacuum solenoid is a normally open design, and the speed switch is normally closed.

The Pontiac system has an additional unit, a cold-hot temperature override

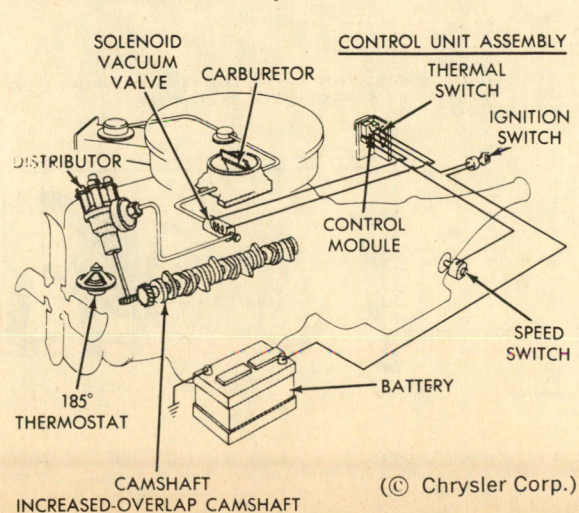

1972 Chrysler NOx system—automatic transmission

(© Chrysler Corp.).

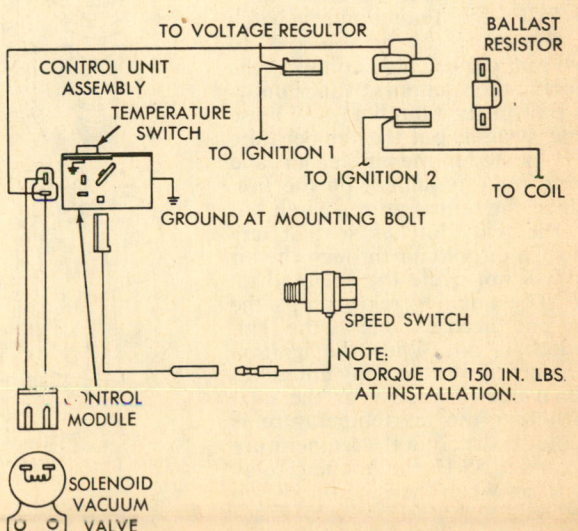

1972 Chrysler NOx system schematic—automatic transmission (© Chrysler Corp.)

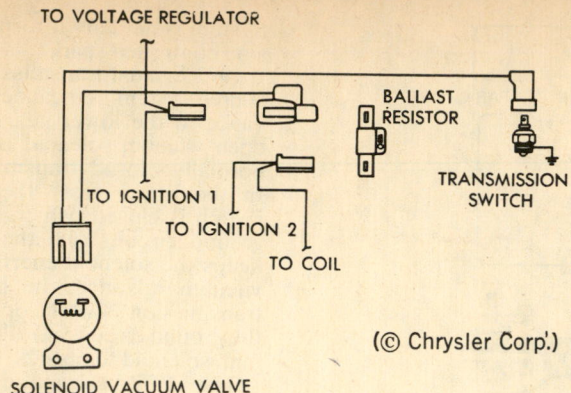

1972 Chrysler NOx system schematic—manual transmission

(© Chrysler Corp.)

switch. This switch is built into the same sending unit that operates the red HOT light. It has three terminals. Current to operate the vacuum solenoid runs through the override switch. Below approximately 90°F. or above 225°F. coolant temperature, the override switch opens the circuit between the ignition switch and the vacuum solenoid, which turns off the solenoid and allows vacuum advance.

Temperature Activated Vacuum (TAV) and Cold Temperature Activated Vacuum (CTAV) Systems

This system, used only on Ford 6-cylinder engines, switches the vacuum source back and forth between the carburetor spark port and EGR port, according to the air temperature. A 3-nozzle vacuum solenoid is used, connected to a temperature switch located in the front door post on cars built before March 15, 1973. Below approximately 55°F. outside air temperature, the temperature switch is open, and the solenoid is not energized. In this position, the solenoid connects the spark port to the vacuum advance unit. Above 55°F. the temperature switch closes, and energizes the solenoid. In this position, the solenoid connects the EGR port to the vacuum advance unit.

Cars built after March 15, 1973 use the same system, but the temperature switch is located in the air cleaner, and a latching relay is added, on the firewall. Once the temperature switch has closed, the relay latches so that any sudden rush of cold air through the air cleaner will not cycle the solenoid on and off. The latching relay keeps the solenoid energized as long as the ignition switch is on. When the ignition switch is turned off, the relay unlatches and the system is ready for the next start, whether the air temperature is hot or cold. If the air at the temperature switch is over 55°F. the latching relay will come on when the ignition switch is turned on.

Test the system with a vacuum gauge connected to the vacuum advance hose at the distributor. With the temperature

above 65°F. (to be sure the temperature switch has closed) you should be getting vacuum from the EGR port. If you disconnect the EGR port hose and the vacuum drops, you know the system is working. When making a cold test, the vacuum should come from the spark port hose, so disconnecting that hose should make the vacuum drop. Because both ports are above the throttle plate, the throttle must be opened slightly to get vacuum at the hose.

Identifying the spark port and EGR ports on the carburetor is easy if they are marked. If there is no marking on the carburetor, connect two vacuum

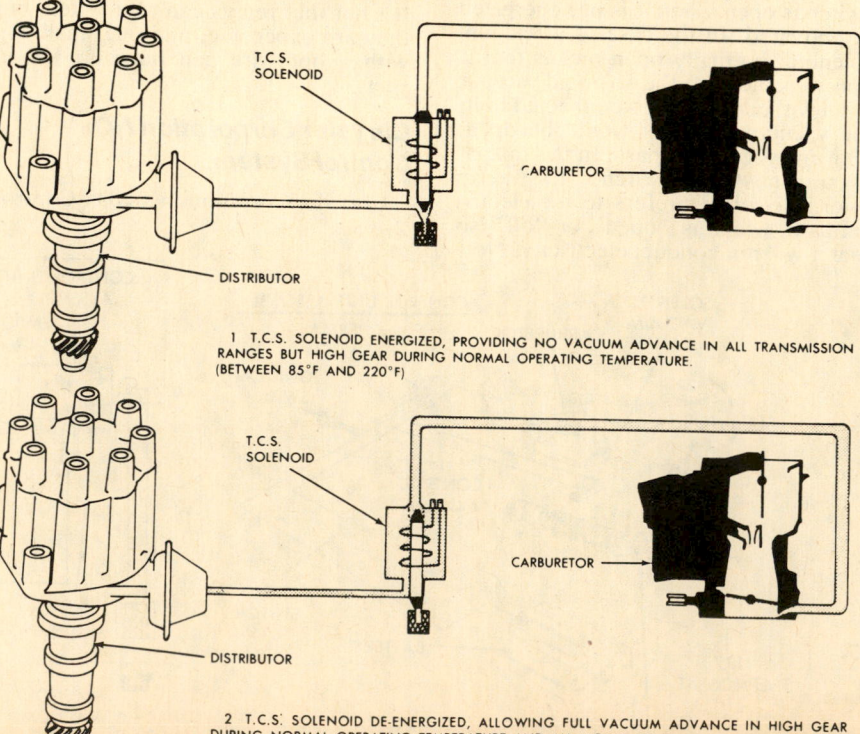

1972 Cadillac speed controlled spark system. (© G.M. Corp.)

1 T.C.S. SOLENOID ENERGIZED, PROVIDING NO VACUUM ADVANCE IN ALL TRANSMISSION RANGES BUT HIGH GEAR DURING NORMAL OPERATING TEMPERATURE. (BETWEEN 85°F AND 220°F)

2 T.C.S. SOLENOID DE-ENERGIZED, ALLOWING FULL VACUUM ADVANCE IN HIGH GEAR DURING NORMAL OPERATING TEMPERATURE AND ALL MODES OF TRANSMISSION OPERATION DURING PERIODS OF ABNORMAL ENGINE OPERATING TEMPERATURE. (BELOW 85°F AND ABOVE 220°F)

1972 Pontiac speed controlled spark solenoid operation (© G.M. Corp.)

gauges, one to each port. At idle you should not have any vacuum. If you do see vacuum, it usually means the engine is idling too fast. Close the throttle slightly to slow down the idle and the vacuum should drop to almost zero.

When you open the throttle, you will see vacuum on one gauge before the other. The gauge that gets vacuum first is connected to the spark port.

Orifice Spark Advance Control (OSAC)

This is strictly a Chrysler Corporation system, used on several years and models. In effect, it is simply a mechanism that delays the application of vacuum to the distributor vacuum advance unit. When the throttle is opened, the carburetor port is exposed to vacuum. This vacuum goes through a hose to the OSAC valve, and then to the distributor vacuum advance. The OSAC valve is sometimes mounted on the firewall, and sometimes on the air cleaner. In-

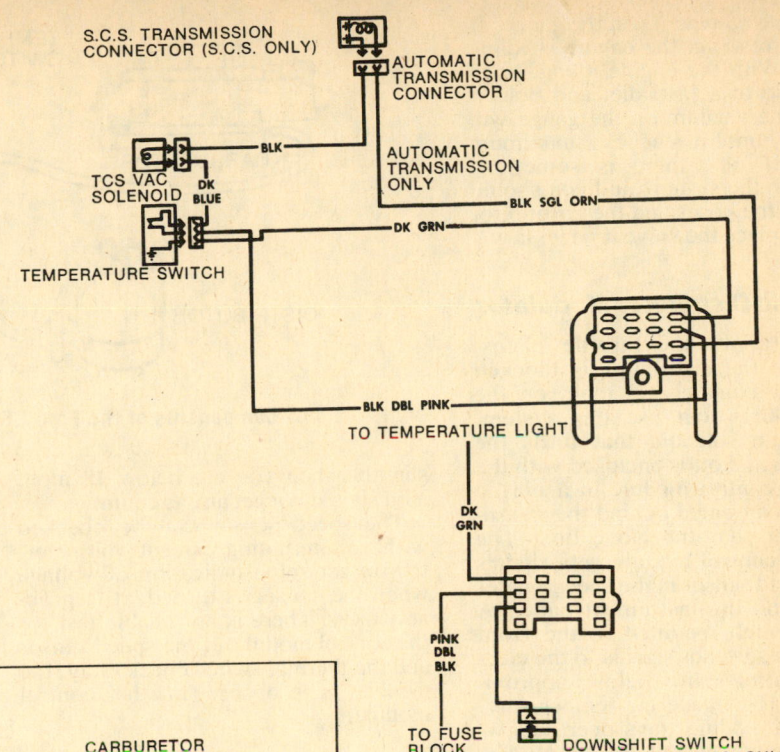

1972 Pontiac SCS system schematic
(© G.M. Corp.)

side the OSAC valve is a calibrated orifice that delays the vacuum as much as 27 seconds, depending on the calibration of the valve.

Some OSAC valves have temperature control that senses the temperature inside the air cleaner or inside the plenum chamber behind the firewall, depending on where the valve is mounted. If the valve contains temperature control, it will be wide open below 60°F. bypassing the orifice and allowing vacuum advance without any delay. Above 60°F. the bypass closes and the delay takes over.

To test the valve, just connect a vacuum gauge to the DIST connection on the valve. With the engine idling, you

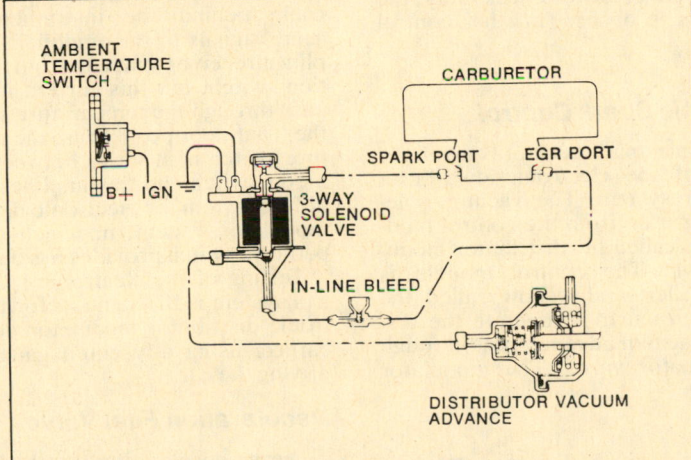

Early 1973 Ford Temperature Activated Vacuum system
(© Ford Motor Co.)

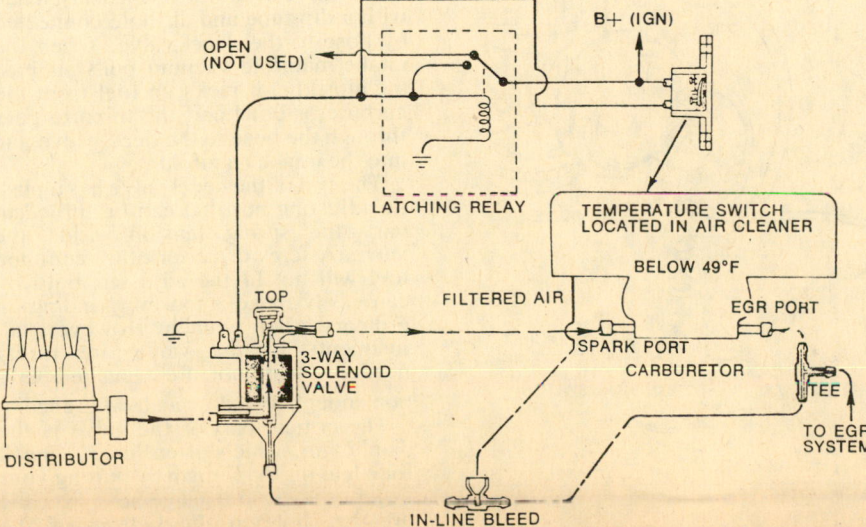

Ford cold temperature activated vacuum system (after March 15, 1973) (© Ford Motor Co.)

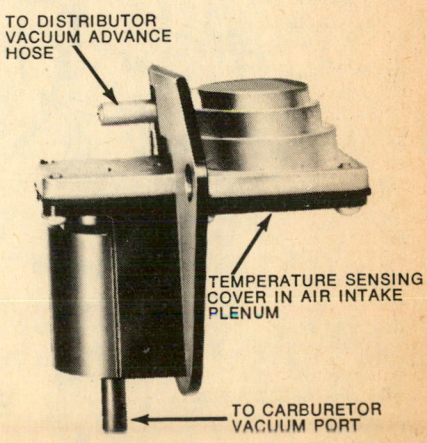

Chrysler orifice spark advance control (OSAC) valve (© Chrysler Corp.)

should have no reading on the gauge. If there is a reading, the engine is idling too fast. With the engine idling, open the throttle to a fast idle, and hold it steady. The vacuum on the gauge will rise slowly until it reaches a maximum reading. If not, there is something wrong with the system, and you should check out the hoses and the carburetor port, or replace the valve if necessary.

Electronic Distributor Modulator

Ported (above the throttle plates) vacuum to the distributor is blocked below approximately 25 mph, on the Ford products that use this system. The vacuum solenoid that turns the vacuum on and off is enclosed with the electronic control module in a plastic box that is mounted behind the instrument panel near the glove box. The electronic control module gets signals from a speed sensor in the speedometer cable behind the instrument panel. A thermal switch mounted in the front door post also sends signals to the electronic control unit. Below approximately 68°F. outside air temperature, the control module stays open, allowing vacuum advance at all speeds. The thermal switch itself is electrically closed at low temperature, and open at high temperature.

To test the system, disconnect the vacuum hose at the distributor and connect a vacuum gauge to the hose. Position the gauge so you can see it while driving the car. Above approximately 25 mph you should get vacuum on the gauge. When decelerating, the vacuum is shut off at approximately 18 mph. Check this by opening the throttle

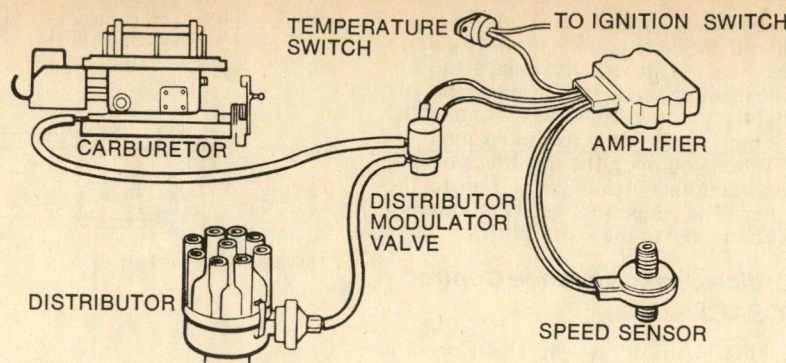

Components of the Ford ESC system (© Ford Motor Co.)

slightly when you are below 18 mph. You should not get any vacuum.

The speed sensor can be checked with an alternating current voltmeter. If you get some indication of voltage when the sensor is turned, it is probably okay. There is no reliable test for the control module. If the speed sensor and the thermal switch check okay, the trouble is probably in the control module.

Electronic Spark Control

Electronic spark control is a refined version of the electronic distributor modulator system. The vacuum solenoid is separate from the control module, and is called the distributor modulator valve. The control module is much smaller, and is now called the amplifier. Vacuum to operate the distributor vacuum advance runs through the modulator valve. The modulator

valve is closed at low speeds, and opens at 25-40 mph, depending on the car. The speed at which vacuum is allowed depends on the amplifier, which is available in several settings, each a different color. The amplifier is mounted behind the instrument panel near the glove box.

A speed sensor in the speedometer cable behind the instrument panel sends signals to the amplifier. The amplifier receives current from the ignition switch, but this current must first pass through the temperature switch in the front door post. Thus, the temperature switch is in series between the ignition switch and the amplifier. This is different from the electronic distributor modulator system, in which the temperature switch provides a ground.

Testing of the electronic spark control system is the same as for the electronic distributor modulator described earlier, using a vacuum gauge while driving the car.

Deceleration Fuel Valve

During deceleration, the high intake manifold vacuum opens the decel valve on the intake manifold and pulls in an air-fuel mixture from the carburetor. The Pinto carburetor is specially made with a dip tube and air hole connected by hose to the decel valve. When the intake manifold vacuum pulls air past the dip tube, it picks up fuel from the carburetor bowl and the mixture goes through the hose to the decel valve and into the intake manifold.

The end of the decel valve has a plastic adjusting nut that can be turned to vary the spring tension inside the valve. A screwdriver or other common tool will not fit the adjuster, but you can easily make a tool by grinding an ordinary Allen wrench. However, adjustments to the valve are rarely needed, and do not affect engine operation enough to make much difference.

The critical part of the valve is the diaphragm, which often leaks. Check for a leaking diaphragm by putting your finger or a vacuum gauge hose over the breather hole in the bottom of the valve. If you feel any vacuum or get any reading on a gauge with the engine

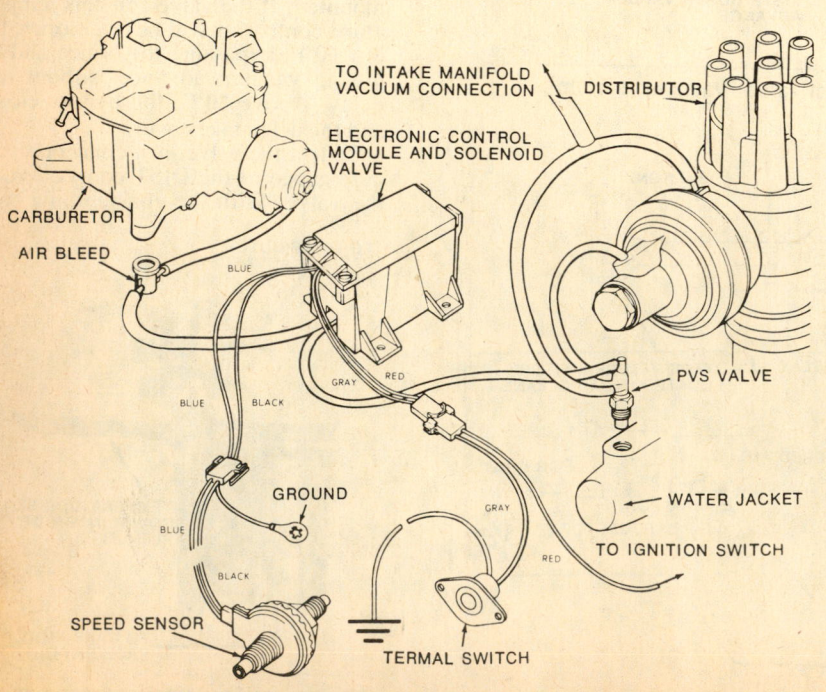

Ford electronic distributor modulator system (© Ford Motor Co.)

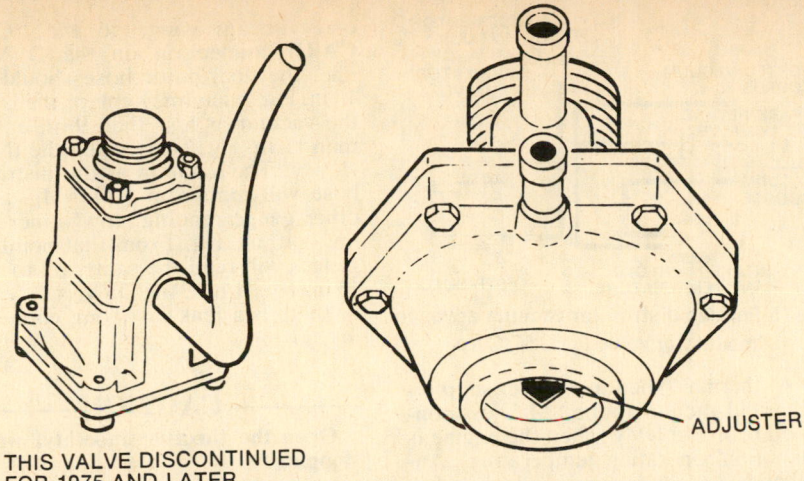

THIS VALVE DISCONTINUED
FOR 1975 AND LATER

THE TYPE USED IN 1975 AND LATER
IS ADJUSTABLE

ADJUSTER

The two types of Ford fuel decel valves (© Ford Motor Co.)

idling, the diaphragm is leaking and must be replaced. A repair kit is available, or you can replace the entire valve.

Vacuum Reducer Valve

Inserted between the manifold vacuum source and the distributor, this valve reduces the vacuum acting on the advance diaphragm by about 3 in. Hg. This valve is always used on a system that includes a distributor thermal vacuum switch. The vacuum advance unit operates on ported (above the throttle plates) vacuum, except when the engine overheats above 225°F. This opens the thermal vacuum switch and sends full manifold vacuum through the vacuum reducer valve to the advance unit. Thus, the vacuum reducer valve is only operating when the engine is overheated.

To test the valve, connect a vacuum gauge to the TVS nozzle, and a hand vacuum pump to the MAN nozzle. When you pump up 15 in. Hg. vacuum on the hand pump, the vacuum on the separate gauge should be 3 to 4 in. Hg. lower. Both gauges should hold the vacuum without leakdown. If not, the

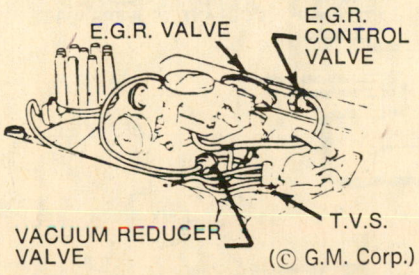

E.G.R. VALVE
E.G.R. CONTROL VALVE
VACUUM REDUCER VALVE
T.V.S.
(© G.M. Corp.)

Vacuum reducer valve. The valve has one port on the manifold side and two ports on the DTVS side of the valve; the center port is open to vent at the carburetor air horn, the outboard port to the "MT" port of the DTVS (distributor thermal vacuum switch).

valve is defective and must be replaced.

Distributor Vacuum Valve

There are several double-headed valves that look the same. The only way to tell them apart is by the part number on the valve. The valve used by Oldsmobile in 1974 only is part number 416972. It has three hose connections, to the EGR port, the spark port, and the distributor vacuum advance. The vacuum advance unit runs on spark port vacuum up to approximately 8 in. Hg. The valve then switches so the vacuum advance runs on EGR port vacuum.

To test the valve, disconnect the distributor vacuum hose and connect a vacuum gauge to the hose. Use a T-fitting and a short length of hose to connect a second vacuum gauge to the hose at the carburetor EGR port. With the engine idling, gradually open the

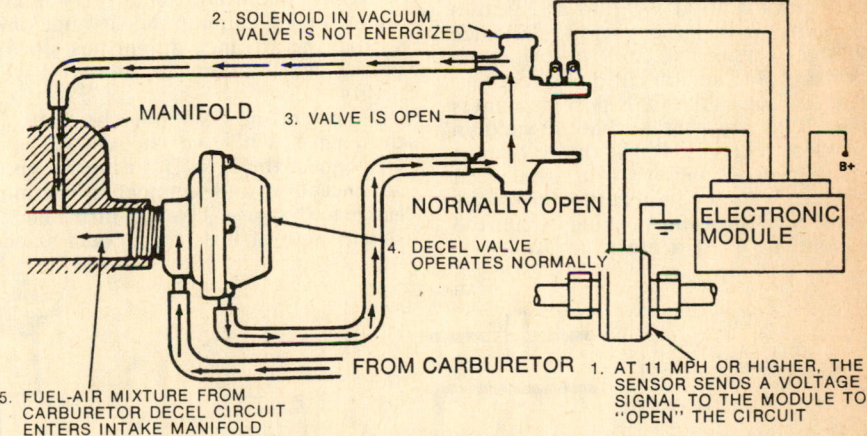

2. SOLENOID IN VACUUM VALVE IS NOT ENERGIZED
MANIFOLD
3. VALVE IS OPEN
NORMALLY OPEN
ELECTRONIC MODULE
B+
4. DECEL VALVE OPERATES NORMALLY
FROM CARBURETOR
1. AT 11 MPH OR HIGHER, THE SENSOR SENDS A VOLTAGE SIGNAL TO THE MODULE TO "OPEN" THE CIRCUIT
5. FUEL-AIR MIXTURE FROM CARBURETOR DECEL CIRCUIT ENTERS INTAKE MANIFOLD

1975-76 Ford speed modulated fuel decel valve (© Ford Motor Co.)

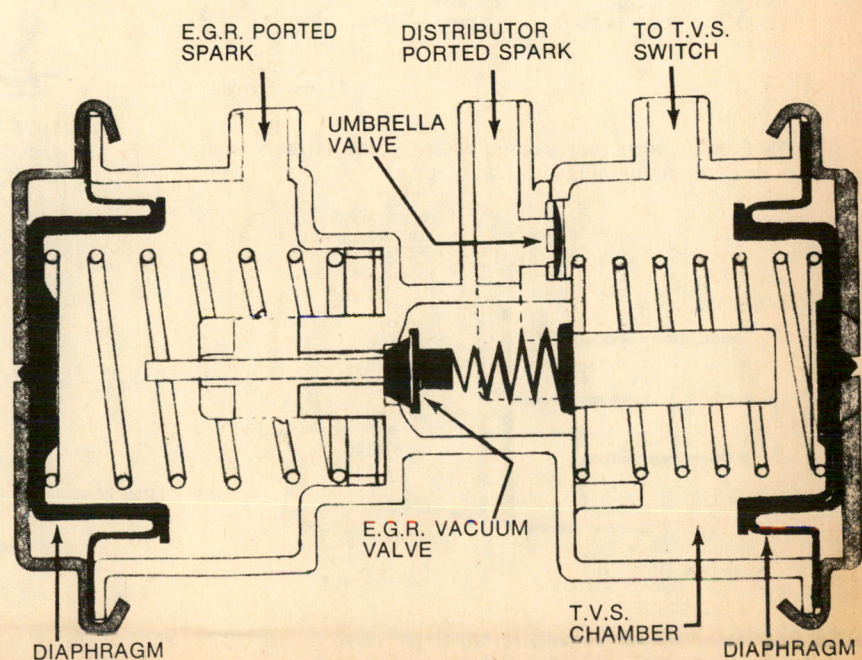

E.G.R. PORTED SPARK
DISTRIBUTOR PORTED SPARK
TO T.V.S. SWITCH
UMBRELLA VALVE
E.G.R. VACUUM VALVE
T.V.S. CHAMBER
DIAPHRAGM
DIAPHRAGM

1974 Oldsmobile Distributor vacuum valve (© G.M. Corp.)

Emission Control Systems

throttle while you watch the gauges. The gauge at the distributor will rise to about 8 in. Hg. Then the EGR port gauge will come up quickly to the same reading. From that point, additional throttle opening will give the same reading on both gauges. If the valve doesn't work that way, either a hose is blocked or incorrectly hooked up, or the DVV is defective.

Distributor Vacuum Advance Modulator Valve

Pontiac uses this DVV valve on some 1975 455 V8s. The valve looks the same as the one used by Oldsmobile in 1974, but is different. The valve has three hose connections, marked "C" for carburetor EGR port, "M" for manifold vacuum, and "D" for distributor vacuum advance. A thermal vacuum valve and a retard delay valve are also connected to the DVV with hoses.

The DVV switches back and forth between manifold vacuum and ported vacuum so that the vacuum advance unit gets either full EGR port vacuum or manifold vacuum cut down to 10 in. Hg. As long as the EGR port vacuum is over 10 in. Hg. that is what the vacuum advance receives. But if the EGR port vacuum drops below 10 in. Hg. as at idle or wide open throttle, then the valve switches and provides manifold vacuum up to 10 in. Hg.

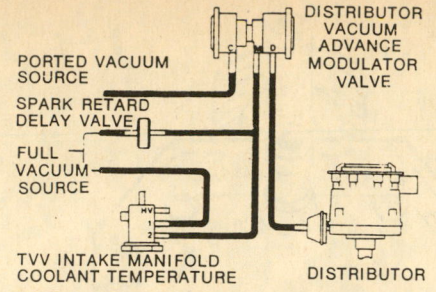

1975 Pontiac distributor vacuum advance modulator valve (© G.M. Corp.)

A thermal vacuum valve supplies manifold vacuum to the "M" hose connection on the DVV when the engine is at normal operating temperature. Another hose supplies manifold vacuum through a spark retard delay valve. When the engine is cold, the thermal vacuum valve closes, leaving the hose with the retard delay valve the only source for manifold vacuum. The delay valve traps vacuum in the advance unit so that the advance diminishes slowly during acceleration, for better driveability.

Testing of the DVV must be done on the engine, with two vacuum gauges. Disconnect the hose from the vacuum advance unit and connect a vacuum gauge to the hose. Use a T-fitting and a short length of hose to connect a sec-

ond vacuum gauge to the "C" or CARB connection on the DVV. At idle, the distributor hose should have 10 in. Hg. vacuum. Replace the DVV if the vacuum is less than 9 in. or more than 11 in. Hg. Next, open the throttle slowly. The vacuum at the distributor hose will remain at 10 in. Hg. as the other gauge reading slowly increases, up to 10 in. Hg. From that point both gauges will read the same, up to about 15 in. Hg. If not, the DVV is defective, or there is a leak or wrong connection in a hose.

— CAUTION —

Open the throttle smoothly, without stopping.

Retard Delay Valve

When the throttle is suddenly opened, engine vacuum drops immediately, and this causes the vacuum advance to move quickly from the advance position to the neutral or no-advance position. A retard delay valve is a restriction with a one-way check valve. It allows the vacuum to act on the vacuum advance unit normally, but when the vacuum drops, the delay valve traps the vacuum in the advance unit and lets it out slowly. It takes sev-

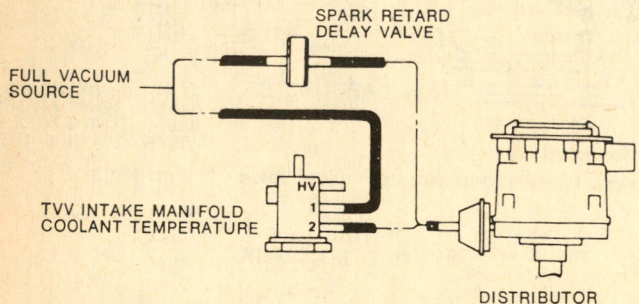

1975 Pontiac with four second retard delay valve in operation on cold engine only (© G.M. Corp.)

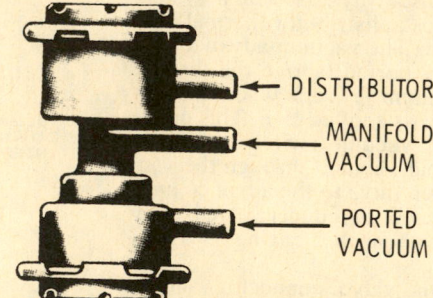

1976-77 Oldsmobile spark advance vacuum modulator (© Oldsmobile Div. G.M. Corp.)

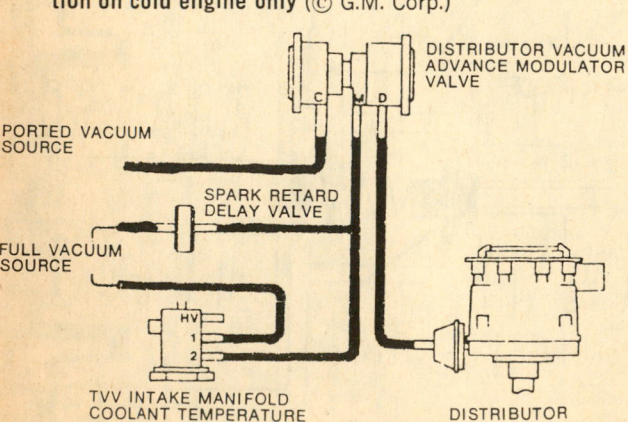

1975 Pontiac with four second retard delay valve in operation on cold engines only. When the engine is warm, vacuum advance passes through the modulator valve. (© G.M. Corp.)

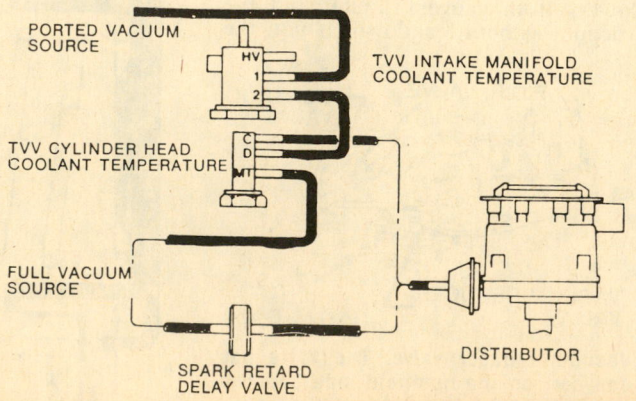

1975 Pontiac with full vacuum advance and four second retard delay when engine is cold. When the engine is warm, the source is ported vacuum with hot coolant override protection.

eral seconds for the advance unit to return to the neutral position.

Some cars have the retard delay valve hooked up so that it only operates when the engine is cold. At normal operating temperature the delay is bypassed.

Testing of the delay valve can be done with a hand vacuum pump. Connect the pump to the MAN side of the valve, or the side that connects to the vacuum source on the engine. Connect a separate vacuum gauge to the other side of the valve. When the hand pump is operated, the vacuum will rise on both the pump gauge and the separate gauge equally. When the release is pulled, the pump gauge will drop to zero immediately, but the separate gauge will take several seconds to drop to zero. If it doesn't work that way, the delay valve is defective, and must be replaced.

Cold Start Spark Advance

A coolant sensitive vacuum switch (PVS) is combined with a delay valve (Distributor Retard Control Valve) to provide retard delay when the engine coolant is below 128°F. Ths hose routing is set up so that the vacuum advance unit operates on manifold vacuum through the retard delay valve when the engine is cold, and on ported vacuum through a spark delay valve when the engine is warm. The system also has an overheat PVS that switches the vacuum advance over to manifold vacuum (through the spark delay valve) when the engine coolant gets over 235°F.

Testing the spark delay valve is covered in this section under Spark Delay Valve. Testing for the Distributor Retard Control Valve is the same as for the Retard Delay Valve in this section.

When the 128° PVS is cold, connection No. 2 is blocked and D and 1 are connected. When it is over 128°F. No. 1 is blocked and D and 2 are connected.

Spark Advance Vacuum Modulator

Used only on the 260 V8, which is an Oldsmobile engine, but appears in other GM cars, the SAVM is a double-headed valve that looks like the valve used by Pontiac in 1975, and Oldsmobile in 1974. This valve is not the same. It has part No. 553952. The three hoses are connected to the vacuum advance unit, manifold vacuum, and ported vacuum. The SAVM switches back and forth between manifold vacuum and ported (above the throttle plates) vacuum so that the vacuum advance unit gets either ported vacuum or manifold vacuum reduced to 7 in. Hg. As long as the ported vacuum is over 7 in. Hg. that is what the vacuum advance receives. But if the ported vacuum drops below 7 in. Hg. as at wide open throttle or idle, then the valve switches and provides

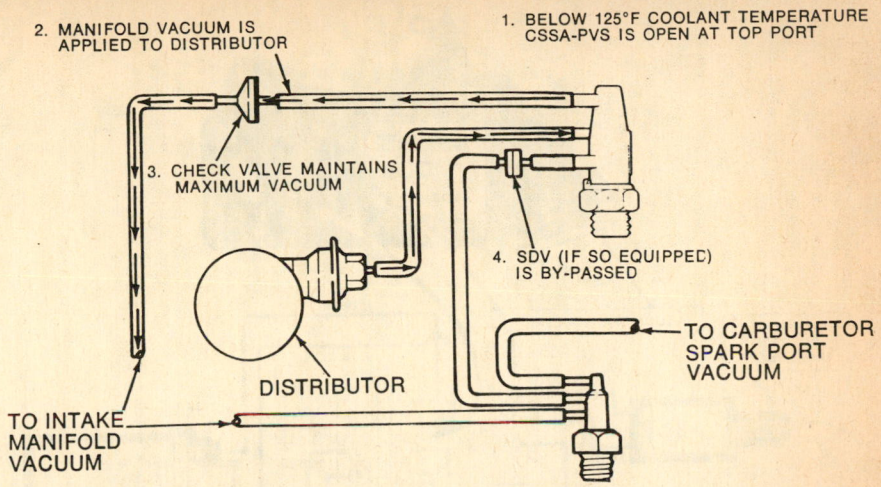

1975-76 Ford cold start spark advance system (CSSA) (© Ford Motor Co.)

manifold vacuum up to 7 in. Hg.

To test the SAVM, connect a vacuum gauge to the "distributor" connection, and a hand vacuum pump to the "intake manifold" connection. Slowly pump up the vacuum. The reading on the separate gauge should equal the pump vacuum up to 7 in. Hg. As the pump goes on up to 15 in. Hg. or more, the gauge should stay at 7 in. Hg.

For the second test, switch the hand pump to the connection marked "carburetor" but leave the separate gauge on "distributor," and plug the manifold vacuum connection. Slowly pump up vacuum. The separate gauge should stay at zero until the pump output reaches 7 in. Hg. At that point the separate gauge should show the same vacuum as the pump, and it should continue to show the same vacuum as the pump output rises to 15 in. Hg. and beyond.

For the third test, switch the hoses so the vacuum pump is connected to "distributor" and the separate gauge connected to "carburetor," with the manifold vacuum connection plugged. Pump up several inches of vacuum. The separate gauge should stay at zero. If not, the SAVM is leaking, and must be replaced.

The SAVM must pass all three tests. If it fails any one, it must be replaced.

Chrysler Corporation Lean Burn System

This system, introduced in 1976, is based on the principle that lower NOx emissions would occur if the air/fuel ratio inside the cylinder area was raised from its current point (15.5:1) to a much leaner point (18:1). In order to make the engine workable, a solution to the problems of carburetion and timing had to be found, since a lean running engine is not the most efficient in terms of driveability. Chrysler adapted a conventional Thermo-Quad carburetor, and later a two barrel unit, to handle the added air coming in, but the real

advance of the system is the Spark Control Computer. Since a lean burning engine demands precise ignition timing, additional spark control was needed for the distributor. The computer supplies this control by providing an infinitely variable advance curve. Input data is fed instantaneously to the computer by a series of sensors located in the engine compartment which monitor timing, water temperature, air temperature, throttle position, idle/off-idle operation, and intake manifold vacuum. The program schedule module of the Spark Control Computer receives the information from the sensors, processes it, and then directs the ignition control module to advance or retard the timing as necessary. This whole process is going on continuously as the engine is running, taking only a thousandth of a second to complete a circuit from sensor to distributor. The components of the system are as follows: Modified carburetor; Spark Control Computer, consisting of two interacting modules, the Program Schedule Module which is responsible for translating input data, and the Ignition Control Module which transmits data to the distributor to advance or retard the timing.

The start pick-up sensor, located inside the distributor, supplies a signal to the computer providing a fixed timing point that is only used for starting the car. It also has a back-up function of taking over engine timing in case the run pick-up fails. Since the timing in this pick-up is fixed at one point, the car will be able to run but not very well. The run pick-up sensor, also located in the distributor, provides timing data to the computer once the engine is running. It also monitors engine speed, and helps the computer decide when the piston is reaching the top of its compression stroke. Starting 1978, the system is simplified to use only one distributor pick-up. This pick-up provides the basic timing signal to the computer for both the start and the run modes.

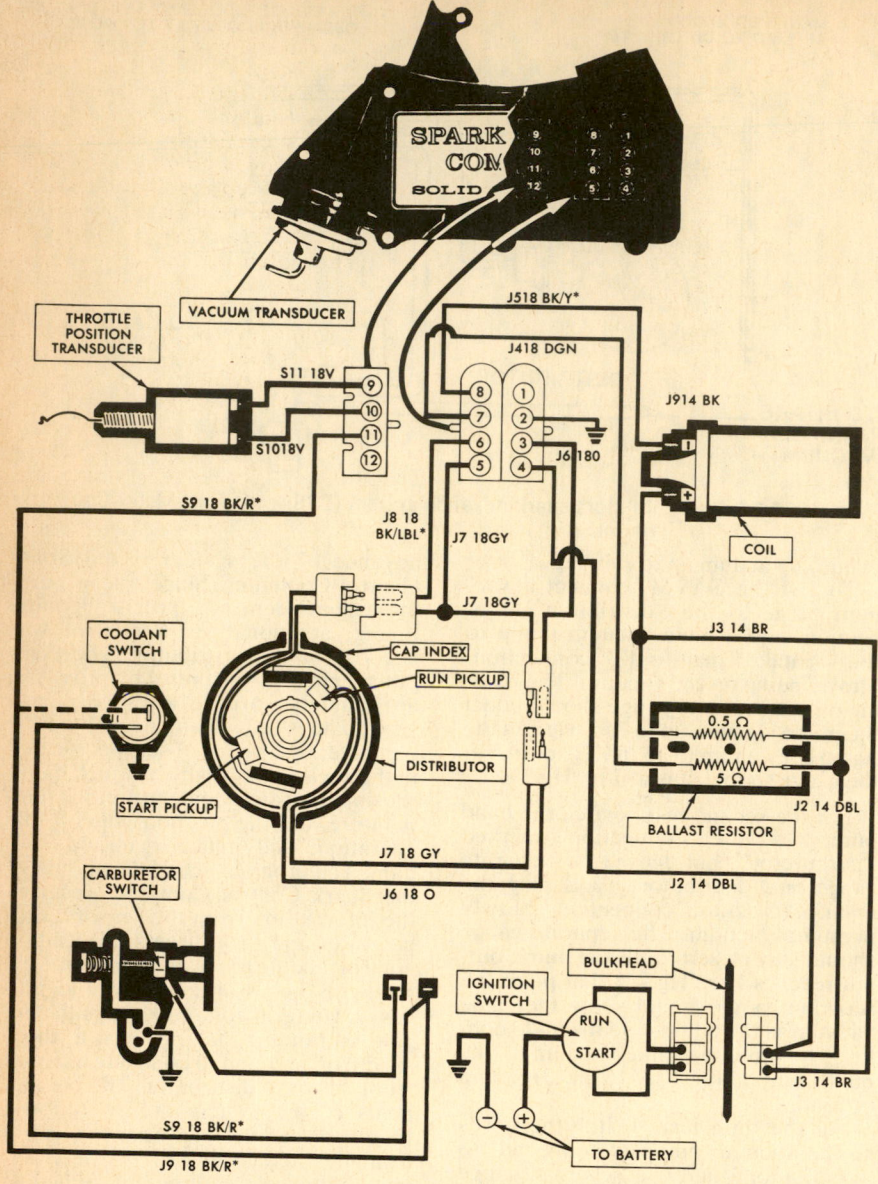

Lean Burn System wiring schematic, 1977 and earlier (© Chrysler Corp.)

The coolant temperature sensor, located on the water pump housing, informs the computer when the coolant temperature is below 150°. The air temperature sensor, inside the computer itself, monitors the temperature of the air coming in the air cleaner. The air temperature sensor is only used through 1977.

The throttle position transducer, located on the carburetor, monitors the position and rate of change of the throttle plates. When the throttle plates start to open and as they continue to open toward full throttle, more and more spark advance is called for by the computer. If the throttle plates are opened quickly, even more spark advance is given for about one second. The amount of maximum advance is determined by the temperature of the air coming into the air cleaner through

1977. Less advance under acceleration will be given if the air entering the air cleaner is hot, while more advance will be given if the air is cold.

The carburetor switch sensor, located on the end of the idle stop solenoid, tells the computer if the engine is at idle or off-idle.

The vacuum transducer, located on the computer, monitors the amount of intake manifold vacuum; the more vacuum, the more spark advance to the distributor. In order to obtain this spark advance in the distributor, the carburetor switch sensor has to remain open for a specified amount of time, during which time the advance will slowly build up to the amount indicated as necessary by the vacuum transducer. If the carburetor switch should close during that time, the advance to the distributor will be cancelled. From

here the computer will start with an advance countdown if the carburetor switch is reopened within a certain amount of time. The advance will continue from a point decided by the computer. If the switch is reopened after the computer has counted down to "no advance," the vacuum advance process must start over again.

OPERATION

When you turn the ignition key on, the start pick-up sends its signal to the computer, which relays back information for more spark advance during cranking. As soon as the engine starts, the run pick-up takes over, and receives more advance for about one minute. This advance is slowly eliminated during the one minute warm up period. While the engine is cold, (coolant temperature below 150° as monitored by the coolant temperature sensor), no more advance will be given to the distributor until it reaches normal operating temperature. At this point, normal operation of the system will begin.

In 1978 and later models, there is only one pick-up coil. The computer functions on two modes: the start mode and the run mode. These modes are equivalent in function to the two pick-up coils used earlier.

In normal operation, the basic timing information is related by the run pick-up to the computer along with input signals from all the other sensors. From this data, the computer determines the maximum allowable advance or retard to be sent to the distributor for any situation.

If either the run pick-up or the computer should fail, the back up system of the start pick-up takes over. This supplies a fixed timing signal to the distributor which allows the car to be driven until it can be repaired. In this mode, very poor fuel economy and performance will be experienced. If the start pick-up or the ignition control module section of the computer should fail, the car will not start or run. Since the 1978 and later models, including the Omni/Horizon, have only one pick-up, if that pick-up coil or the start mode of the computer should fail, the engine will not start or run.

EQUIPMENT

Some of the procedures in this section refer to an adjustable timing light. This is also known as a spark advance tester, i.e., a device that will measure how much spark advance is present going from one point, a base figure, to another. Since precise timing is very important to the Lean Burn System, do not attempt to perform any of the tests calling for an adjustable timing light without one.

TROUBLESHOOTING

1. Remove the coil wire from the distributor cap and hold it cautiously about ¼ in. away from an engine

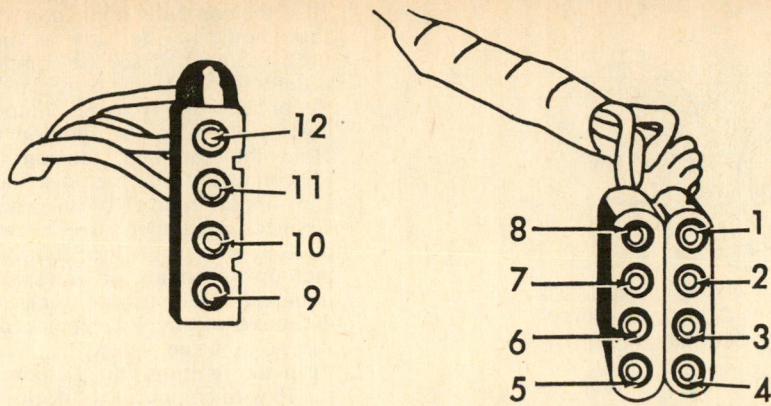

Single and dual connectors at the Spark Control Computer, through 1977 (© Chrysler Corp.)

ground, then have someone crank the engine while you check for spark.

2. If you have a good spark, slowly move the coil wire away from the engine and check for arcing at the coil while cranking.

3. If you have good spark and it is not arcing at the coil, check the rest of the parts of the ignition system.

ENGINE NOT RUNNING—WILL NOT START

ALL EXCEPT OMNI/HORIZON

This test is for the start pick-up in 1977 and earlier models, and the entire pick-up assembly in all 1978 and later models except the Omni/Horizon.

1. Check the battery specific gravity; it must be at least 1.220 to deliver the necessary voltage to fire the plugs.

2. Remove the terminal connector from the coolant switch, and put a piece of paper or plastic between the curb idle adjusting screw and the carburetor switch.

3. Connect the negative lead of a voltmeter to a good engine ground, turn the ignition switch to the "run" position and measure the voltage at the carburetor switch terminal. If you receive a reading of more than five but less than 10 volts, go on to Step 7. If the vol-

tage is more than 10, check for continuity between terminal 2 of the dual connector through 1977, or terminal 10 for 1978 and later, and a ground.

4. If the voltage was less than 5, turn the ignition switch "off" and disconnect the double terminal connector from the bottom of the Spark Control Computer. Turn the ignition switch back to the "run" position and measure the voltage at terminal number 4 1977 and earlier, number 2 1978 and later; if the voltage is not within 1 volt of the voltage you received in Step 1, check the wiring between the terminal and the ignition switch. If the voltage is correct, go on to the next step.

5. Turn the ignition switch "off" and disconnect the single connector from the bottom of the Spark Control Computer through 1977. Use the double connector on 1978 and later models. Using an ohmmeter, check for continuity between terminal 11 1977 and earlier, number 7 1978 and later, and the carburetor switch terminal. There should be continuity. If not, check the wiring.

6. For 1977 and earlier models, if continuity was found or established in Step 5, but the engine won't start,

replace the Spark Control Computer. If it still won't start, go on to the next step.

For 1978 and later models, if there is continuity in Step 5, next check for continuity between terminal 10 and a ground. If continuity exists, replace the computer. If not, check the wires for opens or poor connections, and only proceed to Step 7 if the engine still won't start.

7. For 1977 and earlier models, turn the ignition switch to the run position. Check for voltage at terminals 7 and 8 of the double connector. If you received voltage within 1 volt of that recorded in Step 1, proceed to the next step. If you did not on terminal 7, check the wiring between it and the ignition switch and check the 5 ohm side of the ballast resistor. If you did not on terminal 8, check the wiring, and the primary windings of the coil and the 1/2 ohm side of the ballast resistor.

For 1978 and later, touch the positive voltmeter lead to terminal 1, the negative lead to a ground. It should measure, within one volt, battery voltage as measured in Step 1. If so, go to Step 8. If not, check the wiring and connections between the connector and the ignition switch.

8. Turn the ignition switch "off" and with an ohmmeter, measure resistance between terminals 5 and 6 of the dual connector through 1977, or terminals 5 and 9, 1978 and later. If you do not receive a reading of 150-900 ohms disconnect the pick-up leads at the distributor. On 1977 and earlier systems, be sure you have disconnected the start pick-up. Measure the resistance going into the distributor. If you get a reading of 150-900 ohms here, the wiring between the terminals and the distributor is faulty. If you still do not get a reading between 150-900 ohms, replace the pickup. If you received the proper reading when you initially checked the terminals, proceed to the next step.

9. Connect one lead of an ohmmeter to a good engine ground and with the other lead, check the continuity of both pick-up leads going into the distributor. If there is not continuity, go on to the next step. If you do get a reading, replace the pickup. Be sure that you are working on the start pick-up on 1977 and earlier models.

10. Remove the distributor cap and check the air gap of the pick-up coil. Adjust if necessary and proceed to the next step.

11. Replace the distributor cap, and start the engine. If it still will not start, replace the Spark Control Computer. If the engine still does not work, put the old one back and retrace your steps paying close at-

SPARK CONTROL COMPUTER

10-WIRE HARNESS CONNECTOR

1978 and later 10 terminal harness (© Chrysler Corp.)

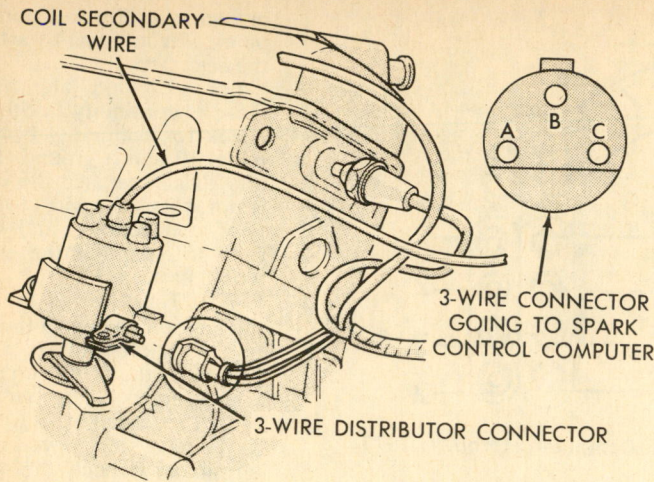

COIL SECONDARY WIRE

3-WIRE CONNECTOR GOING TO SPARK CONTROL COMPUTER

3-WIRE DISTRIBUTOR CONNECTOR

Omni/Horizon distributor pick-up coil connector (© Chrysler Corp.)

tention to any wiring which may be shorted.

OMNI/HORIZON

1. Before performing this test, be sure the "Troubleshooting" test has been performed. Measure the battery specific gravity; it must be at least 1.220, temperature corrected. Measure the battery voltage and make a note of it.
2. Disconnect the thin wire from the negative coil terminal.
3. Remove the coil high tension lead at the distributor cap.
4. Turn the ignition On. While holding the coil high tension lead 1/4 in. from a ground, connect a jumper wire from the negative coil terminal to a ground. A spark should be obtained from the high tension lead.
5. If there is no spark, use a voltmeter to test for at least 9 volts at the positive coil terminal (ignition On). If so, the coil must be replaced. If less than 9 volts is obtained, check the ballast resistor, wiring, and

connections. If the car still won't start, proceed to Step 6.

6. If there was a spark in Step 4, turn the ignition Off, reconnect the wire to the negative coil terminal, and disconnect the distributor pick-up coil connector.
7. Turn the ignition On, and measure voltage between pin B of the pick-up coil connector on the spark control computer side, and a good engine ground. Voltage should be the same as the battery voltage measured in Step 1. If so, go to Step 11. If not, go to the next Step.
8. Turn the ignition Off and disconnect the 10 terminal connector at the spark control computer.
9. Check for continuity between pin B of the pick-up coil connector on the computer side, and terminal 3 of the computer connector. If there is no continuity, the wire must be replaced. If continuity exists, go to the next step.
10. With the ignition On, connect a voltmeter between terminals 2 and

10 of the computer connector. Voltage should be the same as measured in Step 1. If so, the computer is defective and must be replaced.
11. Reconnect the 10 wire computer connector. Turn the ignition On. Hold the coil high tension lead (disconnected at the distributor cap) about 1/4 in. from a ground. Connect a jumper wire between pins A and C of the distributor pick-up coil connector. If a spark is obtained, the distributor pick-up is defective and must be replaced. If not, go to the next step.
12. Turn the ignition Off. Disconnect the 10 wire computer connector.
13. Check for continuity between pin C of the distributor connector and terminal 9 of the computer connector. Also check for continuity between pin A of the distributor connector and terminal 5 of the computer connector. If continuity exists, the computer is defective and must be replaced. If not, the wires are damaged. Repair them and recheck, starting at Step 11.

ENGINE RUNNING BADLY

(Run Pick-Up Tests)

These tests are for 1977 and earlier systems with two pick-ups only.

1. Start the engine and let it run for a couple of minutes. Disconnect the distributor start pick-up lead. If the engine still runs, leave this test and go on to the Start Timer Advance Test. If the engine stops, proceed to step 2.
2. Reconnect the start pick-up, turn the ignition switch off and disconnect the dual connector from the bottom of the computer.
3. Using an ohmmeter, measure the resistance between terminals 3 and 5 of the dual connector. Resistance should be 150-900 ohms. If it is, proceed to the next step. If not, disconnect the run pick-up leads

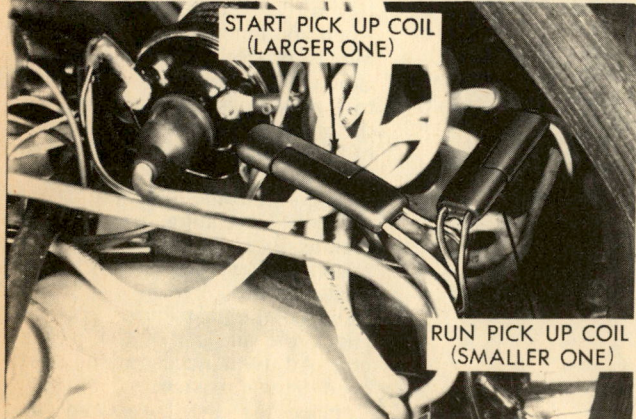

START PICK UP COIL (LARGER ONE)

RUN PICK UP COIL (SMALLER ONE)

Distributor pick-up connector identification, 1977 and earlier. 1978 and later models, except the Omni/Horizon, have one of these connectors (© Chrysler Corp.)

CHECK RESISTANCE BETWEEN TERMINALS

Checking the 'run' pick-up at the distributor leads, 1977 and earlier (© Chrysler Corp.)

from the distributor. Measure the resistance going into the distributor. If the resistance is now between 150-900 ohms, there is bad wiring between terminals 3 and 5 of the double connector plug and the distributor connector terminal. If the resistance is still not within 150-900 ohms, replace the run pickup and try to start the engine. If the engine still fails to start, go on to step 4.

4. Disconnect the run pick-up coil from the distributor. Use an ohmmeter to check for continuity at each of the leads going into the distributor. If there is continuity shown, replace the pick-up coil and repeat Step 1. If you do not get a reading of continuity, proceed to the next step.
5. Remove the distributor cap, check the gap of the run pick-up and adjust it if necessary.
6. Reinstall the distributor cap, check the wiring and try to start the car. If it does not start, replace the Spark Control Computer and try again. If it still does not start repeat the test paying close attention to all wiring connections.

START TIMER ADVANCE TEST
1977 AND EARLIER

1. Hook up an *adjustable* timing light to the engine.
2. Have an assistant start the engine, place his foot firmly on the brake, then open and close the throttle and place the transmission in Drive.
3. Locate the timing signal immediately after the transmission is put in drive. The meter on the timing light should show about 5-9° advance over basic timing. This advance should slowly decrease to the basic timing after about one minute. If it did not increase the 5-9°, or return after one minute, replace the Spark Control Computer. If it did operate properly, proceed to the next test.

1978 AND LATER

1. Connect an adjustable timing light.
2. Connect a jumper wire from the carburetor switch to a ground.
3. Start the engine and immediately adjust the timing light so that the basic timing light is seen on the timing plate of the engine. The meter (on the timing light) should show an 8° advance on all engines. Continue to observe the mark for 90 seconds, adjusting the light as necessary. The additional advance will slowly decrease to the basic timing signal over a period of about one minute. If not, replace the Spark Control Computer and recheck. If it is ok, go on to the next test.

THROTTLE ADVANCE TEST
Before performing this test, the

throttle position transducer must be adjusted. The adjustments are as follows:

1977 AND EARLIER

1. The air temperature sensor inside the Spark Control Computer must be cool (below 135°). If the engine is at operating temperature, either turn it off and let it cool down or remove the top of the air cleaner and inject a spray coolant into the computer over the air temperature sensor for about 15 seconds. If steps 2-5 take longer than 3-4 minutes, recool the sensor.
2. Start the engine and wait about 90 seconds, then connect a jumper wire between the carburetor switch terminal and a ground.
3. Disconnect the electrical connector from the transducer and check the timing, adjusting if necessary. Reconnect the electrical connector to the transducer and recheck the timing.
4. If the timing is more advanced than specified on the tune-up decal, loosen the transducer lock nut and turn the transducer clockwise until it comes within limits, then turn it an additional ½ turn clockwise and tighten the locknut.
5. If the timing is at the specified limits, loosen the locknut and turn the transducer counterclockwise until the timing just begins to advance. At that point, turn the transducer ½ turn clockwise and tighten the locknut. Go to step 6 of this procedure.

1978 AND LATER

1. Disconnect the throttle position transducer wiring.
2. Loosen the locknut.
3. Place the Chrysler special tool # C-4522 between the outer body of the transducer and its mounting bracket.
4. Adjust the transducer for a clearance fit by rotating the body.
5. Retighten the locknut. Go on to Step 6 of this procedure.

6. Turn the ignition switch off and disconnect the single connector computer.
7. With an ohmmeter, measure the resistance between terminals 9 and 10 of the single connector through 1977, and terminals 8 and 9, 1978 and later. The measured resistance should be between 50-90 ohms. If it is, reconnect it and go on to the next step. If not, remove the connector from the throttle position transducer and measure the resistance at the transducer terminals. If you now get a reading of 50-90 ohms, check the wiring between the connector terminals and the transducer terminals. If you do not get the 50-90 reading, replace the transducer and proceed to the next step.
8. Perform this step on 1977 and earlier models only. Reconnect the wiring and turn the switch to the run position without starting the engine. Hook up a voltmeter, negative lead to an engine ground, and touch the positive lead to one terminal of the transducer while opening and closing the throttle all the way. Do the same thing to the other terminal of the transducer. Both terminals should show a 0.5-2 volt change when opening and closing the throttle. If not proceed to the next step.
9. Position the throttle linkage on the fast idle cam and ground the carb switch with a jumper wire. Disconnect the wiring connector from the transducer and connect it to a transducer that you know is good.
10. Move the core of the transducer all the way in, start the engine, wait about 90 seconds and then move the core out about an inch.
11. Adjust the timing light so that it registers the basic timing. The timing light meter should show the additional amount of advance as given on the tune-up sticker in the engine compartment. If it is within

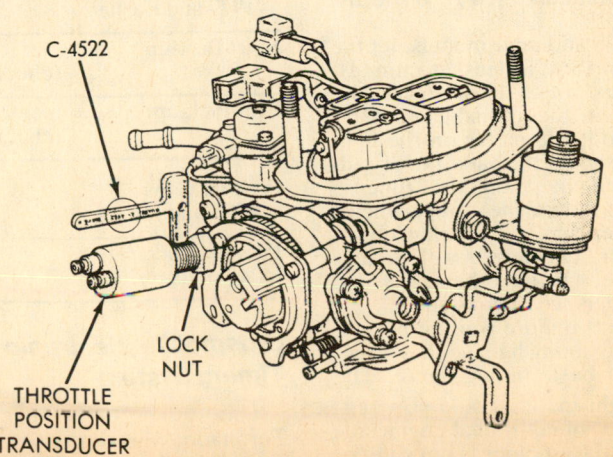

C-4522

LOCK NUT

THROTTLE POSITION TRANSDUCER

1978 and later throttle transducer adjustment (© Chrysler Corp.)

the specifications, move the core back into the transducer, and the timing should go back to the original position. If the timing did advance and return, go on the next step on 1977 and earlier models only. If it did not advance and/or return, replace the Spark Control Computer and try this test over again. If it still fails, replace the transducer.

12. On 1977 and earlier models, reset the timing light meter, and have an assistant move the transducer core in and out 5-6 times quickly. The timing should advance 7-12° for about a second and then return to the base figure. If it did not, replace the Spark Control Computer; if you did not get the 0.5-2 volt change in reading in step 8, replace the transducer.

13. Remove the test transducer (from step 9) and reconnect all wiring.

VACUUM ADVANCE TEST (VACUUM TRANSDUCER)

1. Hook up an adjustable timing light.
2. Start the engine and let it warm up; make sure the transmission is in Neutral and the parking brake is on.
3. Place a small piece of plastic or paper between the carburetor switch and the curb idle adjusting screw (on the Omni/Horizon, between the carburetor switch and throttle lever); if the screw is not touching the switch make sure the fast idle cam is not on or binding; the linkage is not binding, or the throttle stop screw is not overadjusted. Adjust the timing light for the basic timing figure. On 1977 and earlier models, the meter of the timing light should show 2-5° of advance with a minimum of 16 in. of vacuum at the vacuum transducer (checked with a vacuum gauge). If this advance is not present, replace the Spark Control Computer and try the test again. If the advance is present, let the engine run for about 9 minutes then go on to the next step.

On 1978 and later models, let the engine run for at least 9 minutes, and check for at least 16 in. Hg. vacuum at the transducer. After this period, the meter on the light should show the additional advance indicated on the tune-up sticker in the engine compartment. If not, replace the Spark Control Computer. On the Omni/Horizon, stop here. On all other 1978 and later models, go on to Step 5.

4. After the 9 minute waiting period, adjust the timing light so that it registers the basic timing figure. The timing light meter should now register 32-35° of additional engine advance. If the advance is not shown, replace the Spark Control Computer and repeat the test; if it is

shown, proceed to Step 5.

5. Remove the insulator (paper or plastic) that was installed in Step 3; the timing should return to its base setting. If it does not, make sure the curb idle adjusting screw is not touching the carburetor switch. If that is alright, turn the engine off and check the wire between terminal 11 of the single connector (from the bottom of the Spark Control Computer) through 1977, or terminal 7 on 1978 and later cars, and the carburetor switch terminal for a bad connection. If it turns out alright, and the timing still will not return to its base setting, replace the Spark Control Computer.

COOLANT SWITCH TEST

1. Connect one lead of the ohmmeter to a good engine ground, the other to the black wire with a tracer in it.
2. If the engine is cold (below 150°) there should be continuity in the switch. With the thermostat open, and the engine warmed up, there should be no continuity. If either of the conditions in this step are not met, replace the switch.

REMOVAL AND OVERHAUL

None of the components of the Lean Burn System (except the carburetor) may be taken apart and repaired. When a part is known to be bad, it should be replaced.

The Spark Control Computer is held on by mounting screws inside the air cleaner on all models except the Omni/Horizon. On those models only, first remove the battery, then disconnect the 10 terminal connector and the air duct from the computer. Next remove the vacuum line from the transducer. Remove the three screws securing the computer to the left front fender, and remove the computer. To remove the Throttle Position Transducer, loosen the locknut and unscrew it from the mounting bracket, then unsnap the core from the carburetor linkage.

Pick-up Gaps
—1977 and Earlier

Start Pick-up	(set to)	0.008
	(check)	0.010
Run Pick-up	(set to)	0.012
	(check at)	0.014

Pick-up Gaps
—1978 and Later

| Pick-up Coil to Reluctor | 0.006 |

Oldsmobile Electronic Spark Timing System

This system, introduced on the 1977 Toronado, varies the ignition timing electronically. In 1977, the system is triggered by crankshaft position and speed, rather than by the distributor,

for greater accuracy. The main system components are an electronic controller under the glove box, a pulse generator disc on the front of the crankshaft which aligns with a crankshaft sensor on the engine block, and a special HEI distributor. The distributor has no mechanical or vacuum advance equipment, nor does it have a magneitc pickup coil and pole piece. Timing is not adjusted by moving the distributor, but by moving the adjuster bolt on the crankshaft sensor.

The 1978 and later system eliminates the crankshaft sensor and disc. Timing inputs are received from the distributor, which contains the HEI rotor, terminal, and pole piece, and a special pick-up coil and harness. The distributor has no vacuum or centrifugal advance equipment. Timing in this system is adjusted conventionally, by turning the distributor.

The controller receives electronic inputs (from the crankshaft sensor in 1977, and from the distributor in later years) on engine speed and crankshaft position and from a coolant temperature sensor which varies in resistance with temperature. It also receives direct inputs from engine vacuum and atmospheric (underhood) pressure. An instrument panel "Check Ignition" light warns of controller failure. The light will also come on whenever the reference timing connector is grounded, or under low system voltage.

TIMING ADJUSTMENT—1977

1. Make sure the distributor is correctly aligned. With the timing mark aligned with the O (TDC) mark on the timing tab, the white mark on the side of the distributor rotor should be aligned with the white pointer in the distributor. The rotor will be pointing toward the rear of the engine. Adjust by loosening the holddown clamp and moving the distributor.

———— CAUTION ————

Detach the ignition feed wire (black/pink stripe) from the distributor to prevent arcing when making adjustments.

2. Find the timing connector (purple wire), taped to the controller wire harness. Ground it. The "Check Ignition" light will go on.
3. The timing should be at 20 degrees at idle. Check with a timing light.
4. To adjust, stop the engine, loosen the two crankshaft sensor clamp bolts, and turn the adjuster bolt. Turn clockwise to advance, about one turn per degree.
5. Check the timing again. Stop the engine, tighten the clamp bolts, and remove the ground connection from the timing connector.

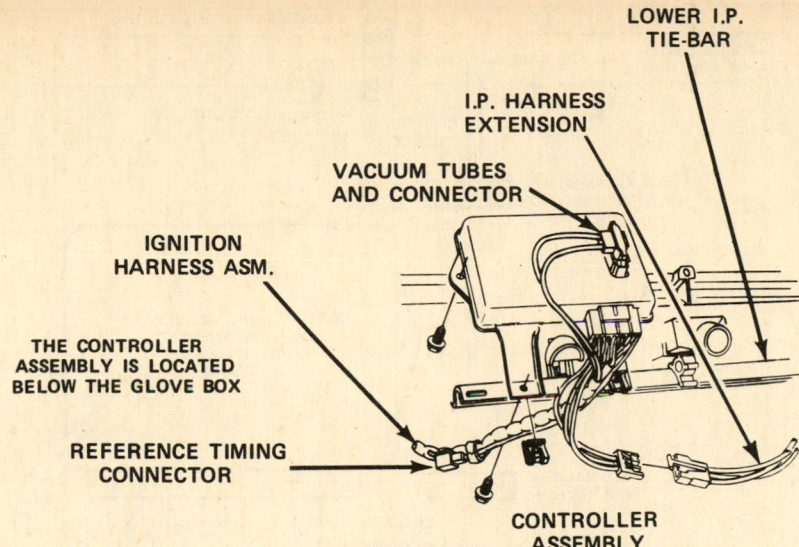

The reference timing connector must be grounded to adjust the basic timing
(© Oldsmobile Div., G.M. Corp.)

TIMING ADJUSTMENT—1978 AND LATER

1. Ground the reference timing connector (purple wire) with a jumper wire.
2. Connect a timing light and a tachometer, and start the engine. The "Check Ignition" light should be on. If not, check the connector ground.
3. Timing should be 20° @ 1100 rpm for 49 States cars, and 22° @ 1100 rpm for California cars.
4. To adjust the timing, loosen the distributor clamp bolt and turn it clockwise to advance, counterclockwise to retard. After adjustment, tighten the clamp bolt and recheck the timing. Remove the jumper wire.

TROUBLESHOOTING—1977

Engine Won't Start

1. Check that battery voltage is 12 volts or more.
2. Check the fuse in the fuse panel. If it is blown, detach the 3 wire connector near the controller. Replace the fuse and turn the ignition on. If the fuse again blows, repair the short in the pink double black wire from the fuse panel to the connector. If the new fuse doesn't blow, repair the short in the red wire from the crankshaft sensor to the connector.
3. If the fuse was ok in Step 2, cautiously check the spark at one of the plugs.
4. If there is a good spark in Step 3, check the timing as detailed earlier. The problem is probably not in the ignition system.
5. If there was no spark in Step 3, check the crankshaft disc and sensor for damage. Check that the sensor is aligned with the disc and

that there is 0.045-0.055 in. gap between the disc and sensor. Check the ground screw (black wire) at the distributor.
6. Turn the ignition key to Run. Check for battery voltage at the ignition wire connector at the distributor (black with pink stripe). If voltage is low, check the wire from distributor to ignition switch and the switch.
7. Check for battery voltage at terminal J2 (pink and red wires) in the connector at the control box. If voltage is less, check the pink wire from the connector at the controller to the 3 wire connector near the controller. Also check the pink double black stripe wire through the instrument panel harness to the fuse panel. Turn the ignition switch Off.

8. Check the tan wire in the 2 wire connector near the distributor, but don't disconnect it. Voltage should be 0.5-2 volts while operating the starter.
9. If all the voltages in Steps 6-8 were ok, the problem is in the distributor cap, rotor, coil, and module.
10. If the voltage was not correct in Step 8, check at terminal C (tan wire) in the connector at the controller. This reading should be 0.5-2 volts while cranking. If it is, check the tan wire from the controller to the 2 wire connector near the distributor. If it isn't, check the voltage at terminal D (light blue wire) in the connector at the controller while cranking. Then disconnect the crankshaft sensor and check the voltage again. If the voltages aren't the same (0.5-2 volts different), replace the controller.
11. If the voltages taken in step 10 are the same, turn the ignition key to Run and check the voltage at the 12 volt terminal and at the shield terminal in the crankshaft sensor connector. You should get 11 volts or more at the 12 volt terminal and 0 at the shield terminal. If the voltages aren't right, replace the harness.
12. If the voltage readings taken in Step 11 are correct, turn the ignition switch to Run and check the voltage at the connector 8-10 volt terminals. If you get 8-10 volts, replace the crankshaft sensor. If not, check the voltage at the controller connector with the key in run. You should get 8-10 volts at terminal D (light blue wire) and terminal E (purple wire).
13. If you got 8-10 volts in Step 12, replace the harness. If you didn't, replace the controller.

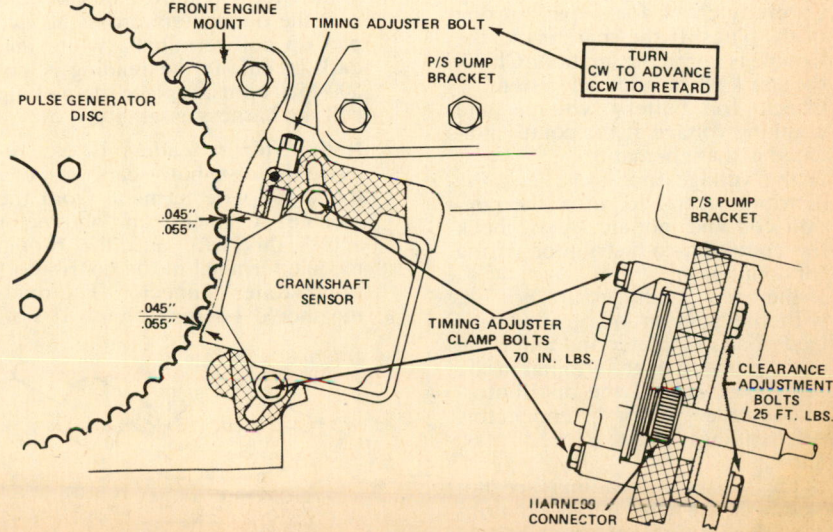

Timing and sensor clearance adjuster bolts
(© Oldsmobile Div., G.M. Corp.)

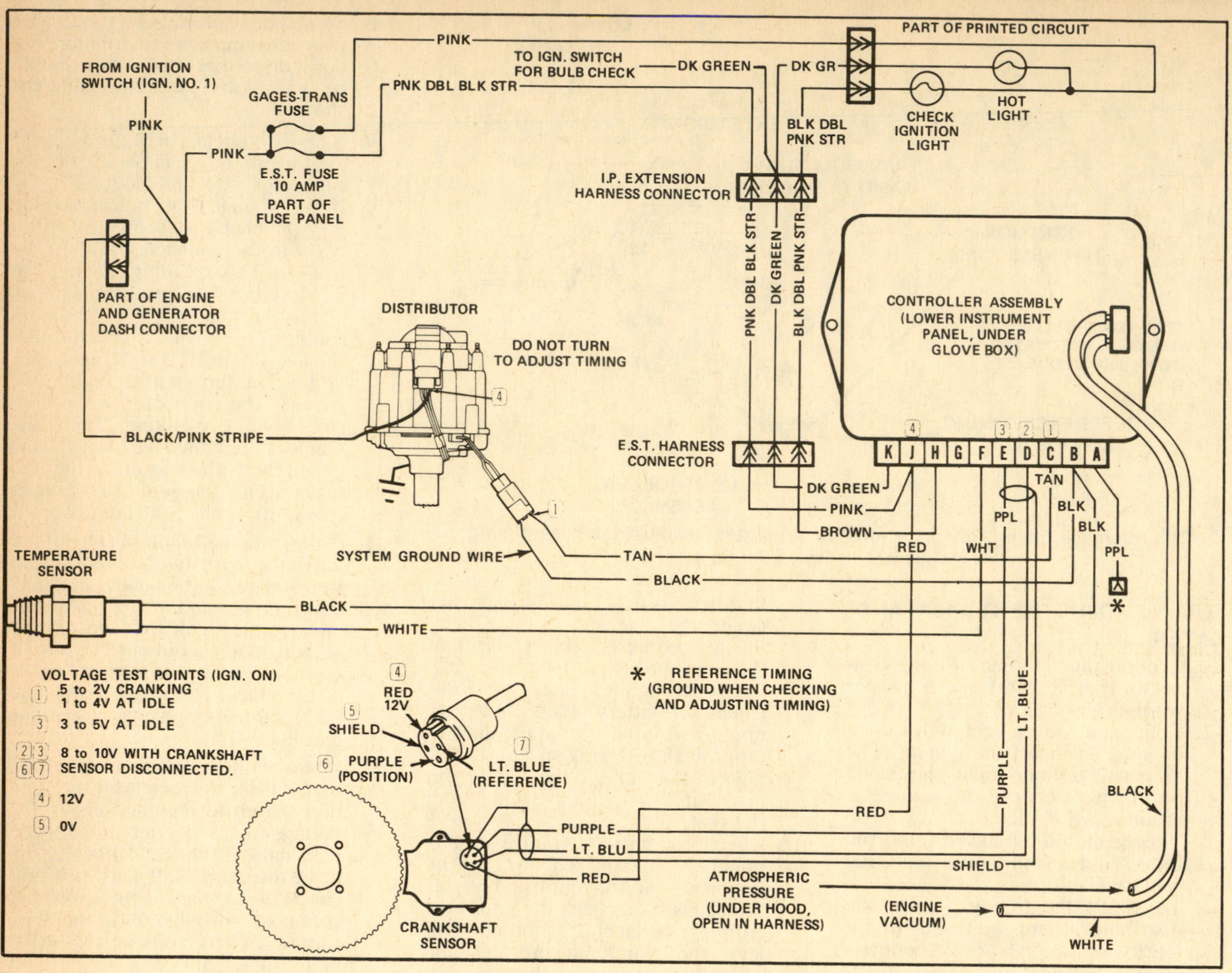

PART OF PRINTED CIRCUIT

PINK

TO IGN. SWITCH FOR BULB CHECK — DK GREEN — DK GR

FROM IGNITION SWITCH (IGN. NO. 1)

GAGES-TRANS FUSE

PNK DBL BLK STR

PINK

CHECK IGNITION LIGHT

HOT LIGHT

BLK DBL PNK STR

PINK

E.S.T. FUSE 10 AMP PART OF FUSE PANEL

I.P. EXTENSION HARNESS CONNECTOR

DISTRIBUTOR

CONTROLLER ASSEMBLY (LOWER INSTRUMENT PANEL, UNDER GLOVE BOX)

PART OF ENGINE AND GENERATOR DASH CONNECTOR

DO NOT TURN TO ADJUST TIMING

PNK DBL BLK STR

DK GREEN

BLK DBL PNK STR

BLACK/PINK STRIPE

E.S.T. HARNESS CONNECTOR

K J H G F E D C B A

TAN

DK GREEN

PINK

BROWN

PPL

BLK

BLK

TEMPERATURE SENSOR

SYSTEM GROUND WIRE

TAN

RED

WHT

PPL

BLACK

BLACK

WHITE

VOLTAGE TEST POINTS (IGN. ON)
1. .5 to 2V CRANKING
1 to 4V AT IDLE
3. 3 to 5V AT IDLE
2 3 8 to 10V WITH CRANKSHAFT
6 7 SENSOR DISCONNECTED.
4. 12V
5. 0V

RED 12V

SHIELD

PURPLE (POSITION)

LT. BLUE (REFERENCE)

* REFERENCE TIMING (GROUND WHEN CHECKING AND ADJUSTING TIMING)

PURPLE

LT. BLUE

BLACK

CRANKSHAFT SENSOR

PURPLE

LT. BLU

RED

RED

SHIELD

ATMOSPHERIC PRESSURE (UNDER HOOD, OPEN IN HARNESS)

(ENGINE VACUUM)

WHITE

Oldsmobile Electronic Spark Timing system schematic, 1977 only (© Oldsmobile Div., G.M. Corp.)

TROUBLESHOOTING—1978 AND LATER

1. Carefully check for a spark at one of the plugs. If the spark is ok, the trouble is not in the ignition. Check the spark plugs, and fuel system.
2. Check for battery voltage and cranking voltage at the points indicated in the schematic.
3. If the voltages are ok, check the distributor cap and rotor, the ignition coil and module. Also check the controller-to-distributor wiring for continuity.
4. If the Step 2 voltages are not ok, with the ignition off ground one lead of an ohmmeter and touch the other probe to each terminal in the distributor half of the distributor-to-controller harness connector. All readings must exceed 1000 ohms.
5. If the resistance readings are not ok, check the wires into the distributor for shorts. If the module (brown) reading was bad, and the wire is ok, test the module. Re-

place the pick-up coil and harness if the module checks ok.
6. If the Step 4 readings are ok, connect the ohmmeter across the two pick-up coil terminals (white and dark green). If the reading is not 500-1500 ohms, replace the pick-up coil and harness assembly.
7. If the Step 6 reading is ok, remove the distributor cap. Remove the single wire terminal from the module. Connect an ohmmeter across this wire and the brown module terminal in the distributor-to-controller connector. The reading should be zero ohms. If not,

replace the pick-up coil and harness.
8. If the Step 7 reading is ok, use a jumper wire to ground the module wire removed in Step 7. Reconnect the distributor harness connector.

Remove the 6 wire connector from the controller. Connect an ohmmeter across terminals E (white) and C (dark green) in the harness connector. Resistance should be 500-1500 ohms. If not, replace the harness. Connect one ohmmeter lead to a ground, and the other to terminal J (brown); zero resistance should be measured. If not, replace the harness.
9. If all Step 8 readings are ok, check to make sure the controller is grounded. If so, be sure the ignition is off, and replace the controller. Do not turn on the ignition again until the controller is properly grounded.

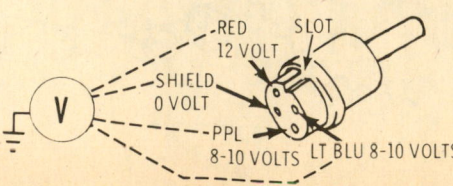

RED 12 VOLT

SLOT

SHIELD 0 VOLT

V

PPL 8-10 VOLTS

LT BLU 8-10 VOLTS

Crankshaft sensor connector terminals (© Oldsmobile Div., G.M. Corp.)

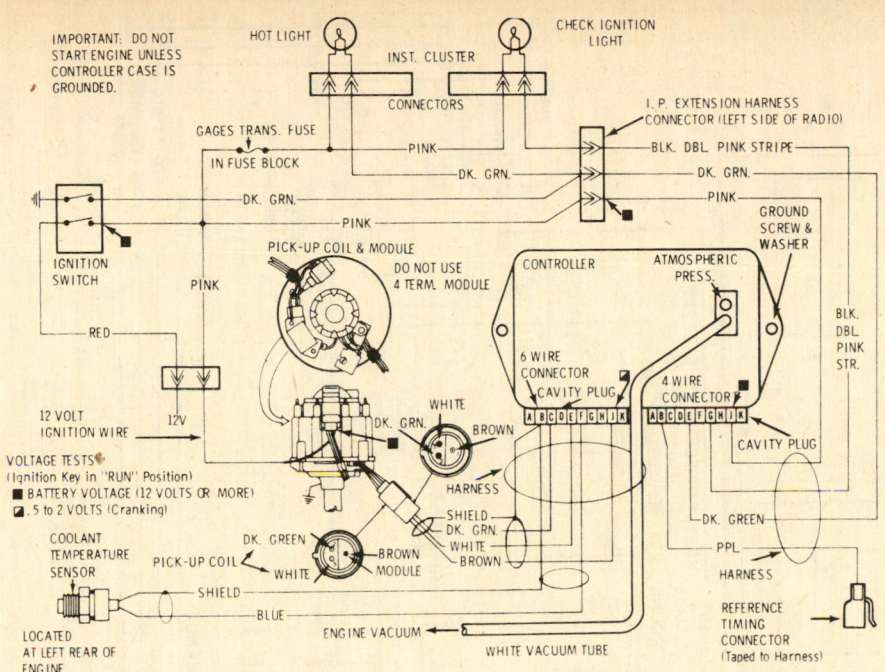

IMPORTANT: DO NOT START ENGINE UNLESS CONTROLLER CASE IS GROUNDED.

HOT LIGHT
CHECK IGNITION LIGHT

INST. CLUSTER
CONNECTORS

I. P. EXTENSION HARNESS CONNECTOR (LEFT SIDE OF RADIO)

GAGES TRANS. FUSE IN FUSE BLOCK

PINK
BLK. DBL. PINK STRIPE

DK. GRN.
DK. GRN.

DK. GRN.
PINK

IGNITION SWITCH

PINK

PICK-UP COIL & MODULE
DO NOT USE 4 TERM. MODULE

CONTROLLER
ATMOSPHERIC PRESS.

GROUND SCREW & WASHER

RED

6 WIRE CONNECTOR
CAVITY PLUG
A B C D E F G H J K

4 WIRE CONNECTOR
A B C D E F G H J K

BLK. DBL. PINK STR.

12 VOLT IGNITION WIRE

12V

CAVITY PLUG

VOLTAGE TESTS
(Ignition Key in "RUN" Position)
■ BATTERY VOLTAGE (12 VOLTS OR MORE)
▨ .5 to 2 VOLTS (Cranking)

WHITE
BROWN

DK. GRN.

DK. GREEN

COOLANT TEMPERATURE SENSOR

PICK-UP COIL

HARNESS

DK. GREEN

PPL

SHIELD
DK. GRN.
WHITE
BROWN

HARNESS

DK. GREEN
BROWN
MODULE

WHITE

SHIELD

BLUE

ENGINE VACUUM

WHITE VACUUM TUBE

REFERENCE TIMING CONNECTOR
(Taped to Harness)

LOCATED AT LEFT REAR OF ENGINE

Oldsmobile Electronic Spark Timing schematic, 1978 and later (© Oldsmobile Div., G.M. Corp.)

Electronic Engine Control System

Ford's EEC system was introduced in 1978, on the Versailles. Designed to precisely control ignition timing, EGR and Thermactor (air pump) flow, the system consists of an Electronic Control Assembly (ECA), seven monitoring sensors, a Dura Spark II ignition module and coil, a special distributor assembly, and an EGR system designed to operate on air pressure.

The ECA is a solid state micro computer, consisting of a processor assembly and a calibration assembly. The processor continuously receives inputs from the seven sensors, which it converts to usable information for the calculating section of the computer. It also performs ignition timing, Thermactor and EGR flow calculations, processes the information and sends out signals to the ignition module and control solenoids to adjust the timing and flow of the systems accordingly. The calibration assembly contains the memory and programming for the processor.

Processor inputs come from sensors monitoring manifold pressure, barometric pressure, engine coolant temperature, inlet air temperature, crankshaft position, throttle position, and EGR valve position.

The manifold absolute pressure sensor determines changes in intake manifold pressure (barometric pressure minus manifold vacuum) which result from changes in engine load and speed, or in atmospheric pressure. Its signal is used by the ECA to set part throttle spark advance and EGR flow rate.

Barometric pressure is monitored by a sensor mounted on the firewall. Measurements taken are converted into a useable electrical signal. The ECA uses this reference for altitude-dependent EGR flow requirements.

Engine coolant temperature is measured at the rear of the intake manifold by a sensor consisting of a brass housing containing a thermistor (resistance decreases as temperature rises). When reference voltage (about 9 volts, supplied by the processor to all sensors) is applied to the sensor, the resistance can be measured by the resulting voltage drop. Resistance is then interpreted as coolant temperature by the ECA. This sensor replaces both the PVS and EGR PVS in conventional systems. EGR flow is cut off by the ECA when a predetermined temperature value is reached. The ECA will also advance initial ignition timing to increase idle speed if the coolant over-

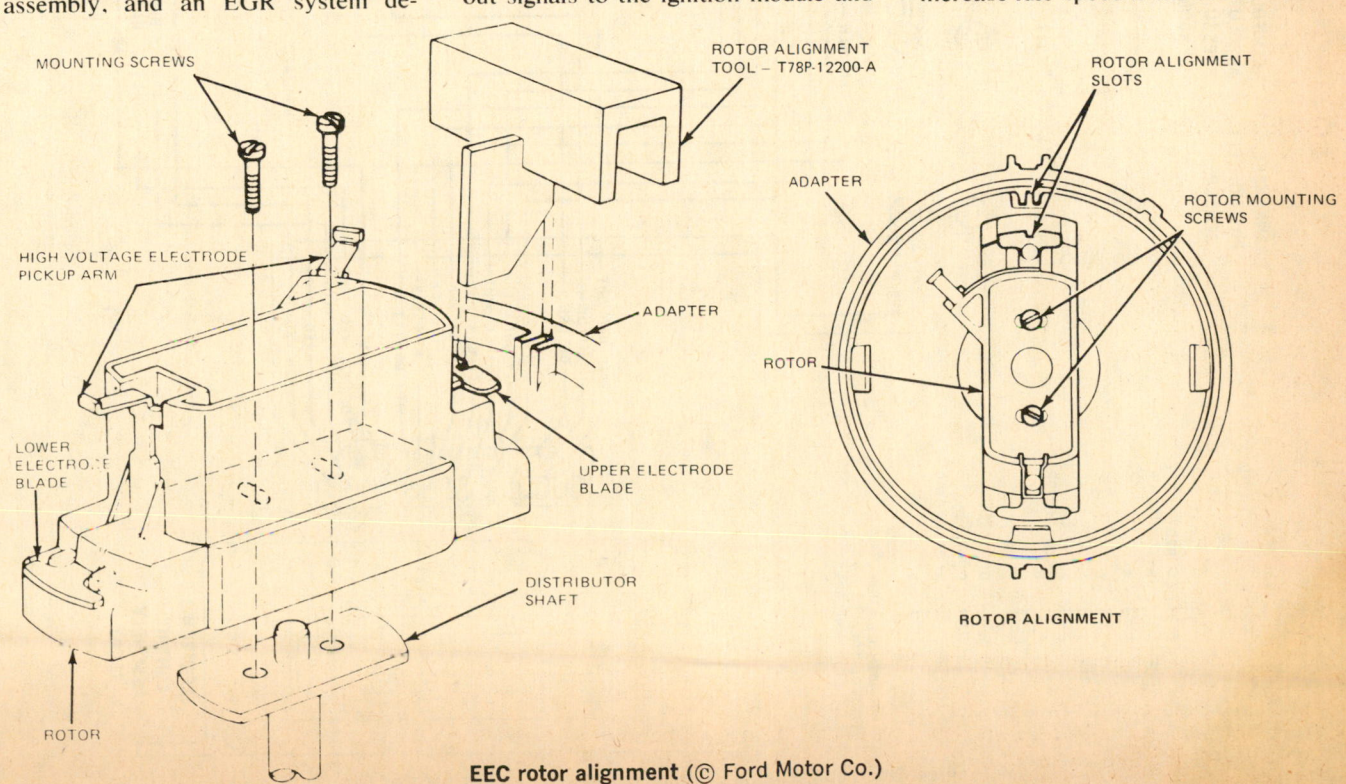

MOUNTING SCREWS

ROTOR ALIGNMENT TOOL – T78P-12200-A

ROTOR ALIGNMENT SLOTS

ADAPTER

ROTOR ALIGNMENT SLOTS

ROTOR MOUNTING SCREWS

HIGH VOLTAGE ELECTRODE PICKUP ARM

ADAPTER

ROTOR

LOWER ELECTRODE BLADE

UPPER ELECTRODE BLADE

DISTRIBUTOR SHAFT

ROTOR

ROTOR ALIGNMENT

EEC rotor alignment (© Ford Motor Co.)

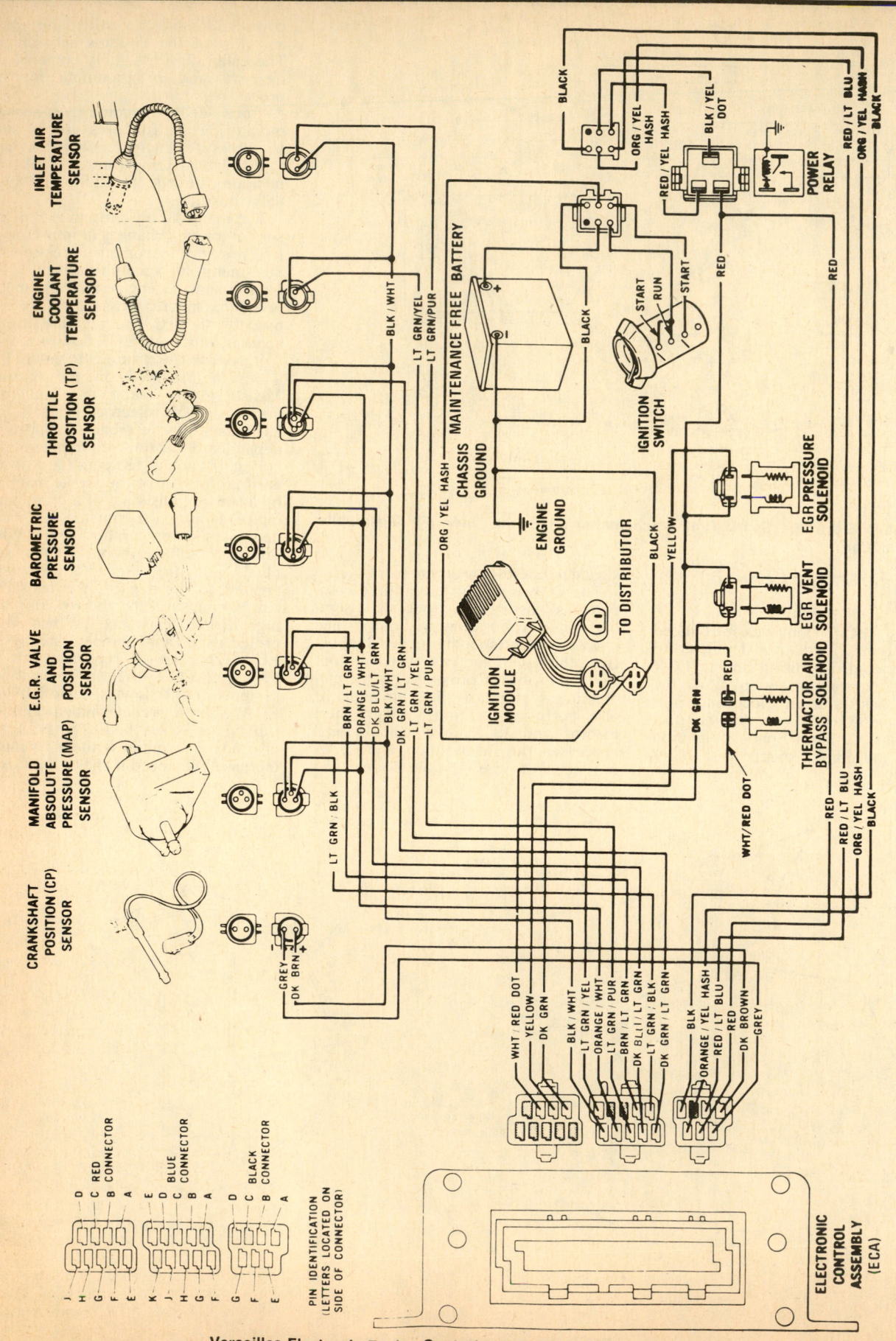

Versailles Electronic Engine Control schematic (© Ford Motor Co.)

heats due to prolonged idle. A faster idle speed increases coolant and radiator air flow.

Inlet air temperature is measured by a sensor mounted in the air cleaner. It functions in the same way as the coolant sensor. The ECA uses its signal for proper spark advance and Thermactor flow. At high inlet temperatures (above 90°F) the ECA modifies timing advance to prevent spark knock.

The crankshaft is fitted with a four-lobed powdered metal pulse ring, positioned 10° BTDC. Its position is constantly monitored by the crankshaft position sensor. Signals are sent to the ECA describing both the position of the crankshaft at any given moment, and the frequency of the pulses (engine rpm). These signals are used to determine optimum ignition timing advance. If either the sensor or wiring is broken, the ECA will not receive a signal, and thus be unable to send any signal to the ignition module. This will prevent the engine from starting.

The throttle position sensor is a rheostat connected to the throttle plate shaft. Changes in throttle plate angle change the resistance value of the reference voltage supplied by the processor. Signals are interpreted in one of three ways by the ECA:

Closed throttle (idle or deceleration)
Part throttle (cruise)
Full throttle (maximum acceleration)

A position sensor is built into the EGR valve. The ECA uses its signal to determine EGR valve position. The valve and position sensor are replaced as a unit, should either fail.

Because of the complicated nature of this system, special diagnostic tools are necessary for troubleshooting. Any troubleshooting without these tools must be limited to mechanical checks of connectors and wiring.

The distributor is locked in place during engine manufacture; no rotational adjustment is possible for initial ignition timing, since all timing is controlled by the ECA. There are no me-chanical advance mechanisms or adjustments under the rotor, thus there is no need to remove it except for replacement.

ROTOR REMOVAL AND INSTALLATION

A special rotor alignment tool is essential for this job.

1. Remove the distributor cap by releasing the two spring clips. If any spark plug wires must be removed, note that their order on the cap is not the same as the engine firing order. The inner ring of numbers on the cap is for the Versailles. It reads 1-2-7-5-6-8-4-3. The engine firing order is 1-5-4-2-6-3-7-8.

NOTE: *Do not remove any of the silicone grease from the distributor cap electrodes. It turns brown with age but this does not affect its performance.*

2. Rotate the crankshaft to align the distributor rotor upper blade, which is slotted, with the slot in the distributor adapter, which is an integral part of the distributor. Use the rotor alignment tool to ensure that the rotor is properly positioned before disassembly.

3. If the rotor or adapter is damaged so that alignment with the tool is impossible, position the crankshaft with the No. 1 piston at compression TDC. This is done by aligning the zero mark on the crankshaft damper with the front cover timing pointer.

4. Remove the rotor alignment tool. Use a magnetic screwdriver to remove the two screws securing the rotor. Remove the rotor.

CAUTION

Do not rotate the crankshaft with the rotor removed.

5. Before installing the new rotor, the lower electrode blades must be coated with silicone grease. The coating should be 1/16 in. thick on all sides outboard of the plastic.

6. Place the new rotor on the distributor shaft with the upper blade slot pointing to the slot in the distributor adapter. Install the two retaining screws, but do not tighten them.

7. Position the rotor alignment tool in place. Be sure its blade engages both the rotor and the adapter notches.

8. Tighten the rotor retaining screws. Remove the alignment tool and reinstall the distributor cap. If any wires were removed from the cap, their ends should be coated with the special grease mentioned in Step 5 before installation.

Electronic Spark Selection

Electronic Spark Selection is used on 1978 and later Cadillac Sevilles. The system advances or retards ignition timing according to conditions. Timing is retarded during starting to reduce the load on the starter. By delaying ignition until the piston is nearly at TDC, the piston is not forced downward prematurely. Timing is also retarded on California cars when coolant temperature is below 130°F. This reduces catalyst warm-up time. Spark timing is advanced during high engine vacuum/high engine rpm conditions (highway cruise) to increase efficiency and fuel economy.

Components used in addition to the G.M. HEI system are an electronic decoder and a five-pin distributor module. The HEI pick-up coil sends its signal to the decoder to provide engine speed and ignition timing information. The decoder signal sends its information on through the five-pin connector. The signal either delays or does not delay coil primary current shut down. Coolant temperature on California Sevilles is sensed at the EGR solenoid. This system is not serviceable without special diagnostic tools.

Carburetor Controls

Carburetors on emission controlled cars have always been calibrated for a lean mixture, so you could say that the entire carburetor is an emission control device. We won't go into the details of carburetor calibration here. What we want to cover are the devices, both on and off the carburetor, that work with it for emission control.

Electric Choke

A non-electric choke uses a "stove" on the exhaust manifold or a well on the intake manifold to provide heat. When the well is used, the choke coil is surrounded by the warm intake manifold, heated by the exhaust crossover passage. When the stove is used, the choke housing is connected to engine vacuum, and a long tube pulls the heated air from the stove into the choke housing to heat up the choke coil and cause the choke to open as the engine warms up. When an electric choke is used, it can be in addition to all the above, or it can be the only source of choke heat, depending on the design.

The electric choke has a small heater next to the choke coil. This heater receives its current from different sources, depending on the car maker.

Ford Motor Company and American Motors chokes are powered from the alternator "center tap," which produces about 7 volts. As the alternator is only putting out voltage when the engine is running, the electric choke is automatically shut off when the engine is off. It is important that the choke is connected only to the special "center tap" provided on the alternator. The description "center tap" refers to the construction of the alternator wiring, and not to the location of the connection.

Inside the Ford 4-bbl. choke cover is a thermostatic switch that turns on the heating element at approximately 80°F. Above that, the element stays on as long as the engine is running. The 80°F. figure was selected because the engine is warm enough at that temperature to keep running without the choke. When the heater comes on, the choke opens very quickly. When the engine is shut off and cools down, the choke switch

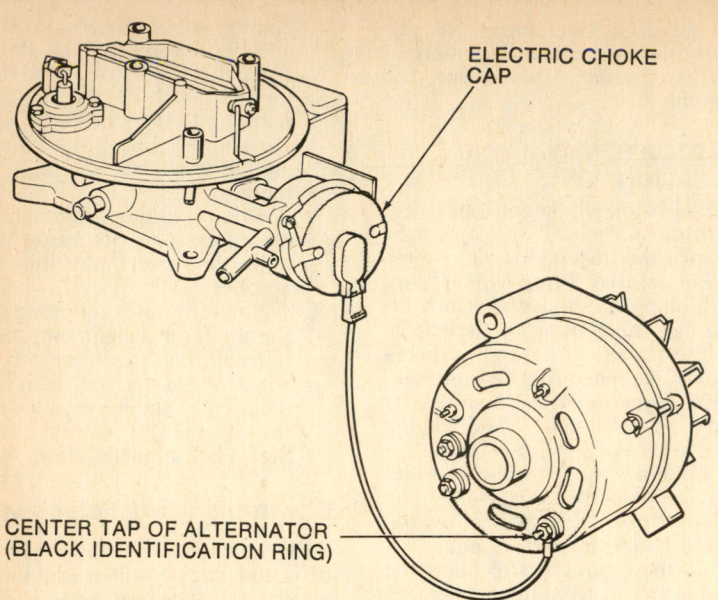

ELECTRIC CHOKE CAP

CENTER TAP OF ALTERNATOR (BLACK IDENTIFICATION RING)

Ford electric choke system (© Ford Motor Co.)

may stay on to as low at 65°F. at the choke housing. On a warm restart, where the choke switch was still on, the heating element would heat up the choke and open it shortly after the engine started.

It isn't necessary to check the exact switching temperature of the choke housing. Just be sure that the switch is open when the engine is cold, and closed when it is warm. The switch can be tested with a penlight-powered test light, between the choke terminal and ground, with the wire from the alternator disconnected.

Ford 4-cylinder engines use a similar choke without the bimetal switch. The heating element is on whenever the engine is running.

Chrysler Corporation vehicles with an electric choke use a well type choke, which receives heat both from the intake manifold and the electric choke heater. A separate choke control unit is mounted on top of the intake manifold and connected to the heater with a wire. This wire disconnects at the choke control unit only, not at the heater.

Choke control units may be single and double stage. The double stage is recognized by the external resistor alongside the unit. The single stage unit turns on the choke heater at approximately 60°F. and off at 110°F. The double stage unit keeps the heater on below 60°F. but the current runs through the resistor. At approximately 60°F. the resistor is taken out of the circuit and the heater gets full current. At 110°F. the control unit turns the heater off.

Testing can be done with a non-powered test light on the choke terminal to find out if the heater is on or off. The ignition switch must be on. If the light glows, you know the control unit is on.

On two-stage units, the light will glow dimly when the resistor is in the circuit, and brightly when the resistor is out. The current to the control unit comes from the ignition switch, and there is no fuse.

Cadillac, Chevrolet, and Chevette use an electric choke that is mounted on the carburetor. The choke has a dual element behind the coil spring. Whenever the engine is running, the choke heater is in operation. Below 50-70°F. a bimetal snap disc in the choke cover turns off the large section of the heating element so that only the small section gives off heat. Above 50-70°F. the disc switches on the large heating element for faster choke opening.

Current to the choke is controlled by a three-terminal oil pressure switch. One of the terminals is a ground for the red oil pressure light on the instrument panel. The other two terminals are a switch in series between the ignition

switch and the choke heater. Oil pressure operates the switch so that the choke gets current only when the engine is running. The circuit is fused through the backup light or transmission fuse in the fuse block.

NOTE: *Failure of the choke heater circuit will cause the oil pressure light to go on.*

Staged Choke Pulldown

Ford Motor Company 2-bbl. and 4-bbl. V8 carburetors have a vacuum diaphragm housing and bracket mounted on the carburetor base on the choke housing side of the carburetor. The housing is connected by a hose to intake manifold vacuum. On the opposite end of the housing a pull rod connects to the choke linkage. Inside the housing are two chambers, one for vacuum and one filled with silicone fluid. The two chambers are separated by an orifice. When the engine starts, manifold vacuum in the vacuum chamber pulls the fluid through the orifice and slowly creates a vacuum in the second chamber. The vacuum in the second chamber slowly pulls the choke open. The length of time to pull the choke open is controlled by the size of the orifice, and varies from approximately 15 to 60 seconds.

Below 60°F. a bimetal valve in the vacuum end of the housing shuts off the vacuum so the unit does not work. On both 2-bbl. and 4-bbl. carburetors,

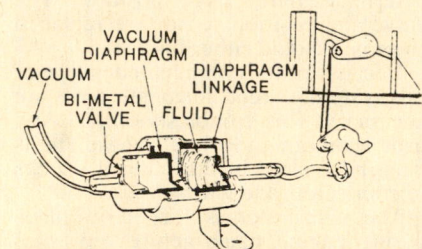

VACUUM DIAPHRAGM
VACUUM
BI-METAL VALVE
DIAPHRAGM LINKAGE
FLUID

Ford staged choke construction
(© Ford Motor Co.)

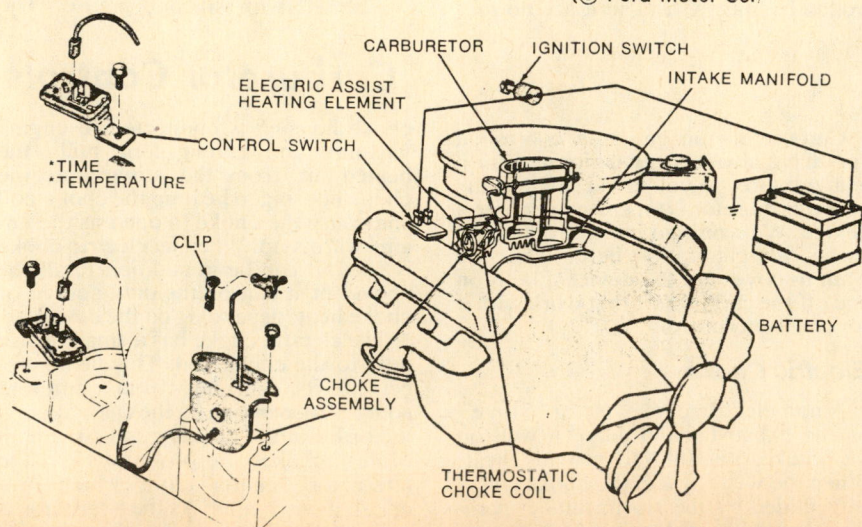

TIME TEMPERATURE
ELECTRIC ASSIST HEATING ELEMENT
CONTROL SWITCH
CLIP
CARBURETOR
IGNITION SWITCH
INTAKE MANIFOLD
BATTERY
CHOKE ASSEMBLY
THERMOSTATIC CHOKE COIL

1973 Chrysler Corporation electric choke system. (© Chrysler Corp.)

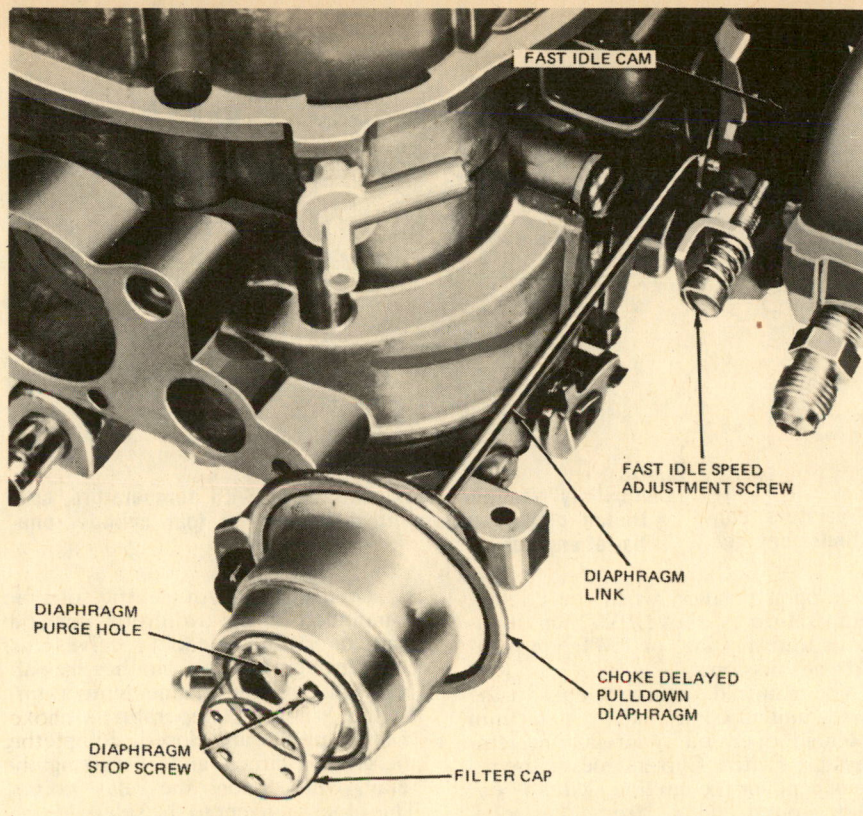

Motorcraft 4350 delayed choke assembly (© Ford Motor Co.)

the staged pulldown is in addition to the normal pulldown that opens the choke partway as soon as the engine starts.

The staged choke pulldown was used only in 1972, on all V8 carburetors.

To test the pulldown, have the engine running at idle, and disconnect the hose. Plug the hose with your finger so the engine doesn't die, and wait for the pull rod to extend all the way. Then hook up the hose and see how long it takes for the rod to pull into the housing. If the rod doesn't pull in at all, or pulls in immediately, without any delay, the unit should be replaced.

Delayed Choke Pulldown

Some 1974 Ford Motor Company 460 V8s used a Carter Thermo-Quad 4-bbl. carburetor with delayed choke pulldown. The normal choke diaphragm is on the same side of the carburetor as the choke housing. It opens the choke part way as soon as the engine starts. On the opposite side of the carburetor from the choke housing is the delayed pulldown diaphragm. It is connected to manifold vacuum, but a restriction inside the diaphragm housing delays the movement of the pulldown for three to ten seconds. The delayed pulldown not only opens the choke further than the initial pulldown, but also pulls the throttle off the top step of the fast idle cam onto the second step.

The pulldown diaphragm can be checked by connecting it to vacuum of a running engine, or by disconnecting

and reconnecting its hose on a running engine to see how long it takes to make a full stroke. It should take approximately three to ten seconds to make a stroke. If not, it should be replaced.

1975 and later Ford-Motorcraft 4300 4-bbl. carburetors also use a delayed pulldown system. When the engine starts, a vacuum piston inside the choke housing opens the choke partway. About 6 to 18 seconds later, the delayed pulldown located on the carburetor in front of the choke housing pulls the choke open further, and also

pulls the fast idle cam to a lower step. This gives more precise choking, and slows the engine down to prevent damage to the catalytic converter from overly long fast idle.

The pulldown diaphragm housing has an internal restriction in the vacuum passage. It receives full manifold vacuum when the engine starts, but the restriction delays the stroke of the pull rod, giving the engine a few seconds to warm up before it opens the choke and slows down the fast idle.

The action of the pulldown diaphragm can be checked on a running engine by disconnecting the hose, waiting until the pull rod extends, and then connecting the hose again. The pull rod should take several seconds to stroke back into the housing. If not, the unit should be replaced.

Fast Idle Pulloff

1976 Chevrolet 454 V8s use an electric choke 4-bbl. carburetor with an extra vacuum diaphragm on the front. The diaphragm is connected by a hose to the same thermal vacuum switch that controls the Early Fuel Evaporation actuator. Below 150°F. coolant temperature, the vacuum is shut off. Above that temperature the TVS opens the passage and allows vacuum to operate the diaphragm, which then pulls the throttle off the high step of the fast idle cam onto the next lower step. Reducing the idle this way prevents damage to the catalytic converter if the car is left to warm up unattended.

Testing the vacuum diaphragm can be done with a hand vacuum pump. The pull rod should make a full stroke, and the diaphragm should hold vacuum without leaking.

Temperature Controlled Choke Vacuum Break

1975 and later General Motors

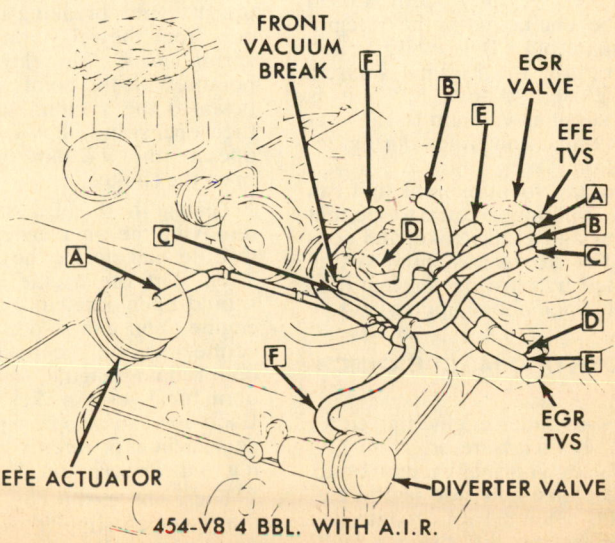

1976 Chevrolet fast idle pulloff (© G.M. Corp.)

Emission Control Systems

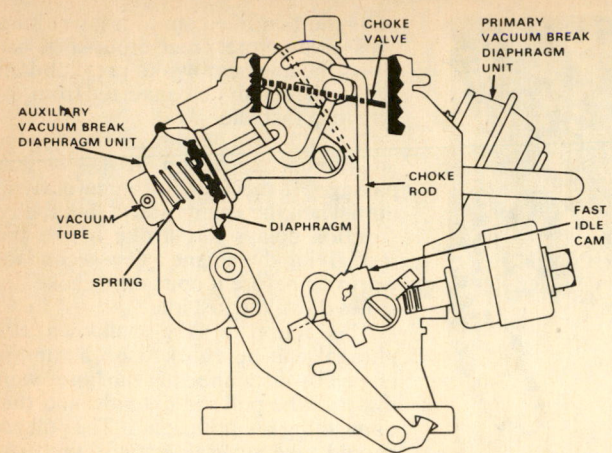

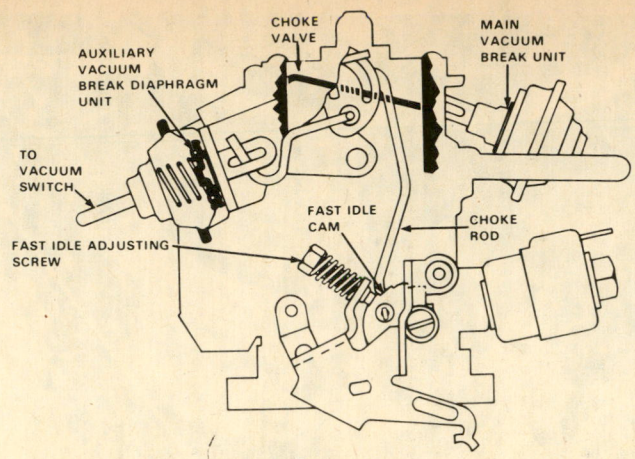

Auxiliary vacuum break unit used with temperature controlled choke vacuum break system on six cylinder engines.

Auxiliary vacuum break unit used with temperature controlled choke vacuum break system on four cylinder one-barrel engines

(Buick, Chevrolet, Oldsmobile, Pontiac) passenger cars use this system on 6-cylinder inline and 140 cubic inch OHC 4-cylinder engines. The system uses an extra vacuum break diaphragm or electric solenoid to open the choke as the engine warms up. There are three different carburetors used on these two engines, and each carburetor uses a slightly different system.

6-CYLINDER ENGINES

The normal vacuum break unit is on the choke coil side of the carburetor. It opens the choke partway as soon as the engine starts. The temperature controlled vacuum break is on the throttle lever side of the carburetor. It opens the choke to an almost wide open position whenever the engine is running, and the coolant temperature is above 80°F. Manifold vacuum comes through a hose from a thermal vacuum switch on the right front of the cylinder head. Above the switch is a manifold vacuum fitting screwed into the intake manifold part of the head. (This system is used only on the engine with the integral head and manifold.) Below 80°F. coolant temperature, the thermal vacuum switch is closed. Above 80°F. it is open, and supplies vacuum to the vacuum break unit at all times during engine operation.

Testing of the vacuum break unit can be done by applying vacuum to see that it moves through a full stroke, and does not leak. The thermal vacuum switch can be tested by blowing through it to see that it is open above approximately 80°F.

4-CYLINDER OHC 140 CUBIC INCH ENGINES

The 140 4-cylinder engine has either a 1-bbl. or 2-bbl. carburetor. The 1-bbl. carburetor uses a normal vacuum break unit on the choke-coil side of the carburetor, and a temperature controlled vacuum break on the throttle lever side. It opens the choke to a nearly

wide open position when the coolant temperature is above 93°F. on automatic transmission, or 120°F. on manual transmission.

The manifold vacuum supply to the break unit is controlled by a vacuum solenoid, operated by a relay and temperature switch. Current goes to the relay whenever the ignition switch is on. The ground circuit from the relay grounds at the same sending unit that turns on the red HOT light. The sending unit has two terminals, one for the relay and another for the HOT light. The relay also connects to the vacuum solenoid, supplying current to operate the solenoid.

The relay points are normally closed. When the temperature switch is cold, it closes and provides a ground for the relay. This completed circuit causes the relay points to open, blocking any current flow to the vacuum solenoid, which stays closed so no vacuum can pass.

When the temperature switch warms up, it opens, breaking the ground circuit from the relay, and allowing the spring inside the relay to close the points. With the points closed, current flows to the vacuum solenoid, which then opens and allows the vacuum to operate the vacuum break unit and open the choke.

Testing the 1-bbl. system is done by removing the air cleaner, opening the throttle, and closing the choke by hand. Then start the engine and the choke should open immediately on a warm engine. You can also check it by disconnecting and reconnecting the hose on a running engine, to see if the vacuum break unit makes a full stroke. Each unit can also be tested to see if it gets vacuum or electric current according to the description above.

The 2-bbl. carburetor uses a system that is much simpler because no vacuum is used. We continue to call it a vacuum break, but actually the whole

system is electric. An electric solenoid is mounted on the carburetor near the cam cover. The solenoid receives current through a relay on the firewall, controlled by the engine temperature switch. When the temperature switch is cold its points are closed, completing the ground circuit and energizing the relay, which opens the relay points. This blocks current to the solenoid.

As the coolant temperature goes over 93°F. on automatic transmission, or 120°F. on manual, the temperature switch opens, de-energizing the relay and allowing the relay points to close. Current then flows to the solenoid, which opens the choke.

Testing the electric 2-bbl. system should be done by closing the choke and then starting the engine to see if the solenoid opens it. The solenoid itself can be tested with a hot wire from the battery. When energized, the solenoid stem should stay in when you push it in, and you should not be able to pull it out with your fingers. When de-energized, you should be able to move the stem in and out.

Idle Enrichment System

Some Chrysler Corporation automatic transmission cars, 1975 and later, have an idle enrichment valve built into the carburetor. The valve opens or closes a passageway that admits extra air to the idle system. When the valve is open, the idle mixture is lean from the excess air. When the valve is closed, the idle mixture is rich, because the air is shut off. The valve is turned on and off by manifold vacuum, connected by a hose.

All cars have a coolant temperature control valve called a Coolant Control Idle Enrichment valve. This is a mechanical valve, mounted on a coolant passage and connected by hoses between the manifold vacuum source and the idle enrichment valve. When the engine is cold, the valve is open, allow-

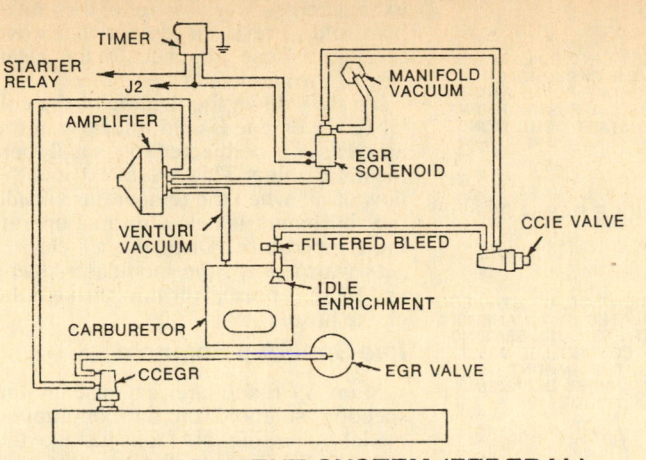

IDLE ENRICHMENT SYSTEM (FEDERAL)

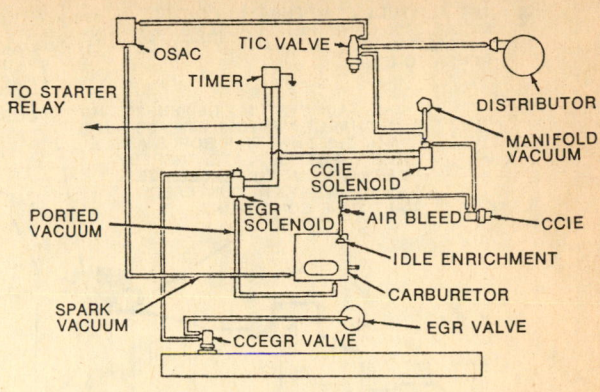

IDLE ENRICHMENT SYSTEM (FEDERAL)

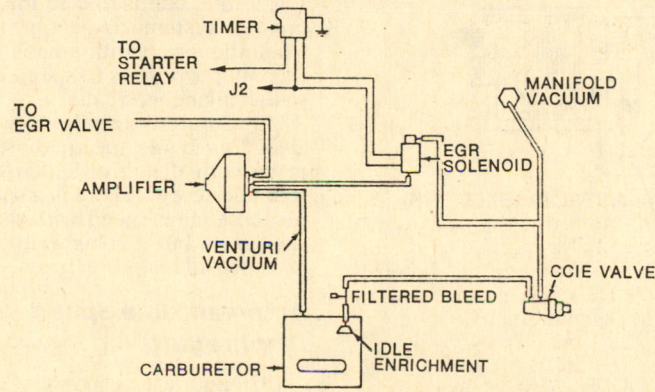

IDLE ENRICHMENT SYSTEM (CALIFORNIA)

ing vacuum to operate the idle enrichment valve and richen the idle. When the engine warms up, the valve closes, and stops the idle enrichment.

Some engines also have a vacuum solenoid connected to the same timer that provides EGR delay. On most engines the solenoid has three hose connections, one to manifold vacuum, one to the idle enrichment valve, and the third to the EGR amplifier. When the solenoid is not energized, it allows vacuum to go to the EGR valve, but blocks the vacuum to the idle enrichment valve. When energized, the vacuum to the EGR amplifier is blocked, but the vacuum passes to the idle enrichment valve. The timer energizes the solenoid during the first 35 or 60 seconds, depending on the car model. This means that when the engine is cold, the idle is enriched during the first 35 or 60 seconds of engine operation.

One engine, the 49-State 318 V8 with catalytic converter, uses two separate solenoids, one for EGR and one for Idle enrichment, but the working of the system is the same.

Next to the idle enrichment valve, inserted in the hose, is a small air bleed. It lets a constant small supply of air into the hose to keep it purged of fuel vapor.

Testing the system can be done on a cold engine by disconnecting the hose at the carburetor and connecting a vacuum gauge to the hose. Start the engine and note the length of time that vacuum appears on the gauge. At the end of the timed period, the gauge should drop to zero. Allow the engine to warm up to operating temperature and make the test again. This time you should not see any vacuum on the gauge, because the CCIE valve should be closed. If your car does not have a timer, you will see vacuum for several minutes after a cold start, until the engine warms up.

To check the effect of the idle enrichment, use a hand vacuum pump on the idle enrichment valve on the carburetor. With vacuum applied, the valve will be closed, richening the idle, and changing the idle speed. Release the vacuum and the speed should go back where it was. If there is no speed change, either the valve is not working, or a carburetor passage is blocked with dirt. The valve should also hold vacuum without leaking down.

Altitude Compensation

Air at high altitude is much thinner than at sea level, so engines run rich. To keep the mixture correct, and prevent rich running that causes high emissions, many 1976 and later 4-bbl. carburetors have an altitude compensation system.

Carter Thermo-Quad four-barrel carburetor with altitude compensation, as used on Chrysler Corporation cars.

Emission Control Systems

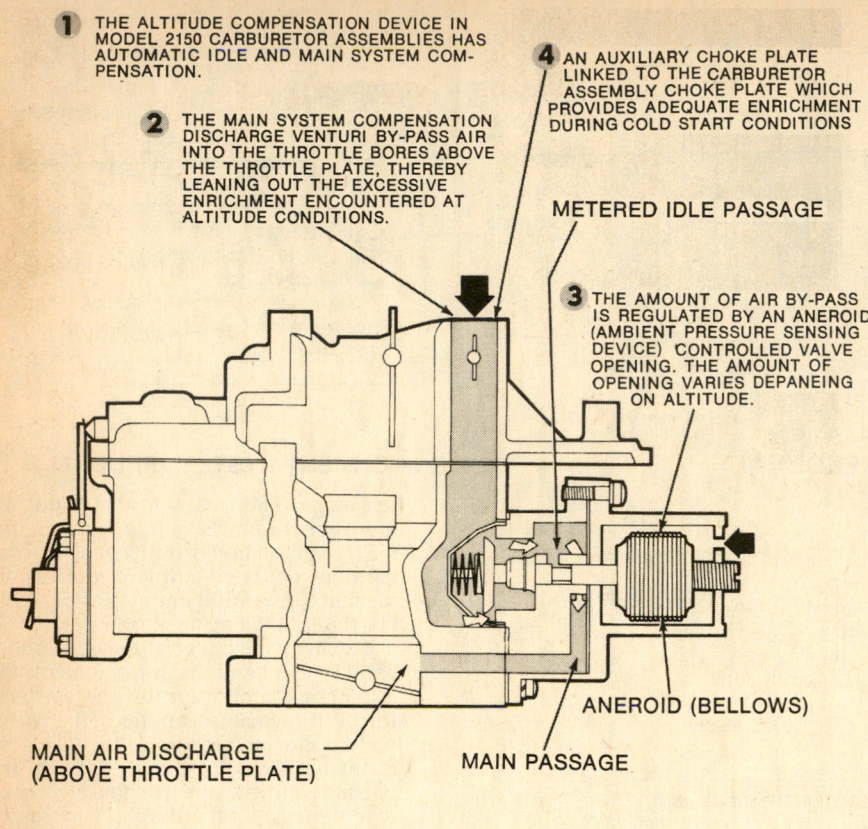

1. THE ALTITUDE COMPENSATION DEVICE IN MODEL 2150 CARBURETOR ASSEMBLIES HAS AUTOMATIC IDLE AND MAIN SYSTEM COMPENSATION.

2. THE MAIN SYSTEM COMPENSATION DISCHARGE VENTURI BY-PASS AIR INTO THE THROTTLE BORES ABOVE THE THROTTLE PLATE, THEREBY LEANING OUT THE EXCESSIVE ENRICHMENT ENCOUNTERED AT ALTITUDE CONDITIONS.

4. AN AUXILIARY CHOKE PLATE LINKED TO THE CARBURETOR ASSEMBLY CHOKE PLATE WHICH PROVIDES ADEQUATE ENRICHMENT DURING COLD START CONDITIONS

METERED IDLE PASSAGE

3. THE AMOUNT OF AIR BY-PASS IS REGULATED BY AN ANEROID (AMBIENT PRESSURE SENSING DEVICE) CONTROLLED VALVE OPENING. THE AMOUNT OF OPENING VARIES DEPANEING ON ALTITUDE.

MAIN AIR DISCHARGE (ABOVE THROTTLE PLATE)

MAIN PASSAGE

ANEROID (BELLOWS)

CODE
- ☐ MAIN AIR
- ■ AIR PRESSURE

Motorcraft two-barrel and four-barrel altitude compensation device.

The heart of an altitude compensation system is a sealed bellows chamber, called an aneroid. The aneroid is sealed at sea level, and expands at high altitude. This expansion is used to open or close a passageway and lean out the mixture. The Carter Thermo-Quad, used on Chrysler Corporation products, and the Ford-Motorcraft 4300 4-bbl. use an aneroid that opens an air passage to lean the mixture. The Thermo-Quad bleeds this air into the main metering system, while the Ford 4300 bleeds the air into the main venturi.

The General Motors Rochester 4-bbl. uses an aneroid that works with the fuel metering adjustable part throttle feature. The adjustable part throttle fuel feed is adjusted at the factory to give the right fuel mixture at sea level. When the aneroid expands at high altitude, it shuts off the adjustable fuel passage to lean the mixture.

Choke Air Modulator

1975 and later Buick-built engines (sometimes used in other GM division cars) have a choke coil that is mounted on the carburetor. The coil housing receives heated air from a stove on the exhaust crossover passage in the intake manifold. Fresh air enters the stove through a hose attached to the clean side of the air cleaner.

To slow down the heating of the coil when the engine is cold, the hose at the air cleaner is connected to a small thermostatic valve. This valve restricts the flow of air when the temperature inside the air cleaner is below normal operating temperature. Once the air cleaner gets warmed up, the modulator opens and there is normal air flow through the choke hose.

Idle Speedup Solenoid

Many 1976 and later cars use an idle speedup solenoid on air conditioned models. The solenoid looks just like the old anti-dieseling or idle stop solenoid. The difference is that the idle speedup solenoid is connected to the air conditioning system and only comes on when the air conditioning is turned on. Its only purpose is to speed up the idle so the engine won't die.

On carburetors equipped with the solenoid, curb idle speed adjustments are made with the throttle screw, not the solenoid screw. There is a specification for the engine speed with the solenoid energized, but it is higher than the normal curb idle.

Automatic Idle Speed Diaphragm

1976 and later Chrysler Corporation 6-cylinder engines with a 1-bbl. carburetor use a special diaphragm or dashpot on some models. The stem of the dashpot touches the throttle lever.

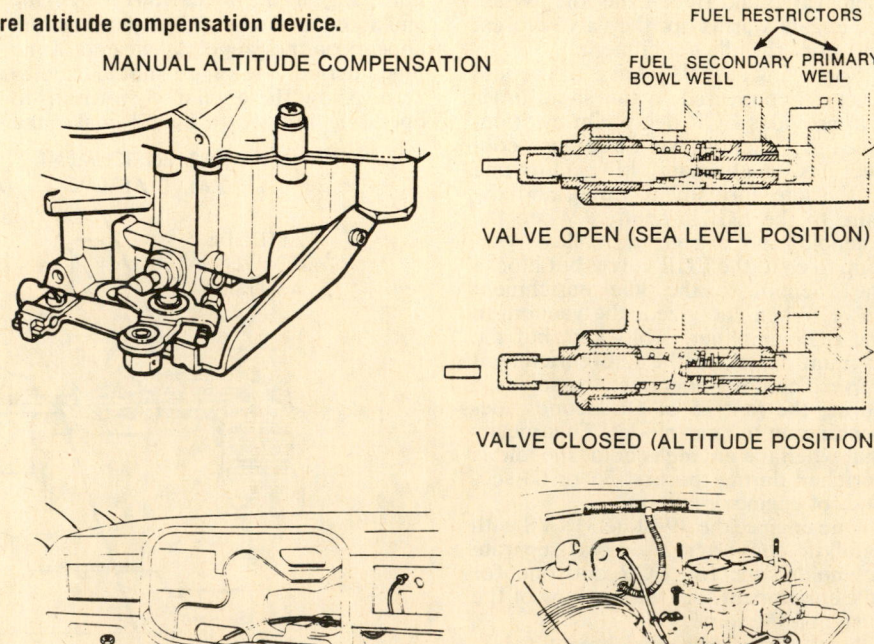

MANUAL ALTITUDE COMPENSATION

FUEL RESTRICTORS

FUEL SECONDARY PRIMARY
BOWL WELL WELL

VALVE OPEN (SEA LEVEL POSITION)

VALVE CLOSED (ALTITUDE POSITION)

ALTITUDE CONTROL ASSEMBLY

Motorcraft 2300 four cylinder manual altitude control

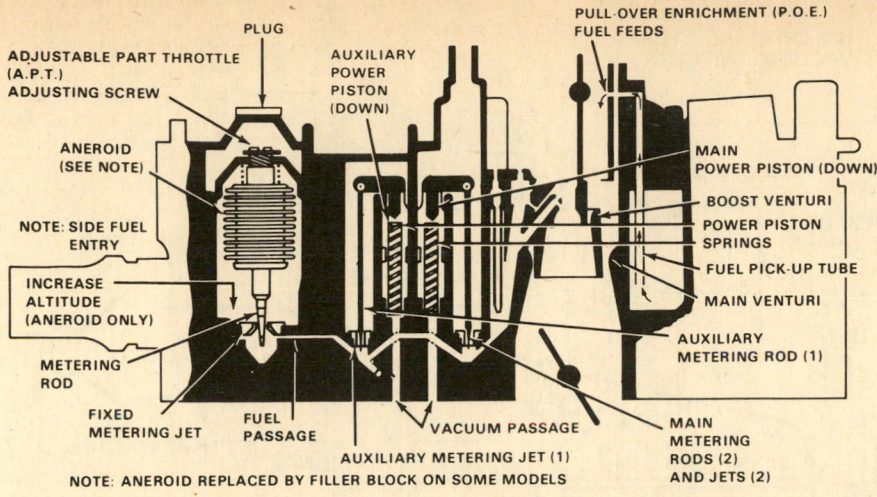

Rochester four barrel carburetor with altitude compensation as used on General Motors cars.

The dashpot is connected to manifold vacuum, which compresses a spring inside the dashpot housing. If the load on the engine is changed by turning the air conditioner on or shifting into DRIVE, the vacuum will drop, and the dashpot spring will open the throttle to bring the speed back up to what it was. Theoretically, whatever load is put on the engine will be balanced by the dashpot, and the idle speed will remain constant.

On 1976 models, the diaphragm was not adjustable, but the throttle speed screw actually rested against the diaphragm stem. In 1977 models this was changed so that the throttle speed screw is separate, and the diaphragm stem pushes against the throttle lever. The 1977 dashpot has a threaded housing and locknut.

To adjust the 1977 dashpot, start the engine in Neutral and position the throttle lever so the actuating tab on the lever is touching the stem of the dashpot, but not depressing it. Wait 30 seconds to allow the engine to settle down, but keep the throttle so it is just touching the stem. In that position, the engine speed should be 2500 rpm. If not, move the throttle so the speed is 2500, and adjust the dashpot by loosening the locknut and turning the housing so the stem just touches the throttle lever.

Ford Feedback Carburetor Electronic Engine Control

This system, first used on 1978 Pinto and Bobcat models sold in California with the 2.3 liter four cylinder engine, actually consists of three subsystems: a two part catalytic converter, a Thermactor (air pump) system, and an electronically controlled feedback carburetor.

The converter consists of two catalytic converters in one shell. The front section is designed to control all three engine emissions (Nox, HC, and CO). The rear section acts only on HC and CO. There is a space between the two sections which serves as a mixing chamber. Air is pumped into this area by the Thermactor system to assist in the oxidation of HC and CO.

The Thermactor system is the same as that found on conventional Ford models, with the addition of a second air control valve and a second exhaust check valve.

An electronically controlled feedback carburetor is used to precisely calibrate fuel metering. The air/fuel ratio is externally controlled and variable. It is adjusted according to conditions by the Electronic Control Unit (ECU). There are two modes of operation: closed loop control and open loop control. Under closed loop operation, each component in the chain is sensitive to the signals sent by the other components. This means that the carburetor mixture is being controlled by the vacuum regulator/solenoid, which is adjusted by the ECU, which is receiving signals from the oxygen sensor in the exhaust manifold, which is measuring a mixture determined by the carburetor, and so on. In this case, the feedback loop is complete. Under open loop operation, the carburetor air/fuel mixture is controlled directly by the ECU according to a predetermined setting. Open loop operation takes place when the coolant temperature is below 125°F, or when the throttle is closed, during idle or deceleration.

The ECU receives signals from the exhaust gas oxygen sensor, the throttle angle vacuum switch, and the cold temperature vacuum switch, analyzes them, and sends out commands to the vacuum solenoid/regulator, which in turn adjusts, by means of vacuum, the height of the carburetor fuel metering rod. In this way, the fuel mixture is adjusted according to conditions. The ECU also varies the transition time from rich to lean (and vice versa) according to engine rpm. The rpm signal is taken from the coil connector TACH terminal.

Electronic Fuel Control System

Similar in both principle and hardware to the Ford Feedback Carburetor System, the G.M. Electronic Fuel Control System is first used in 1978 on the

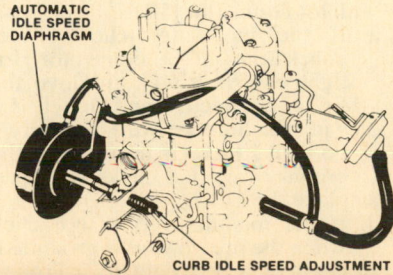

1976 Chrysler six cylinder automatic idle speed diaphragm (© Chrysler Corp.)

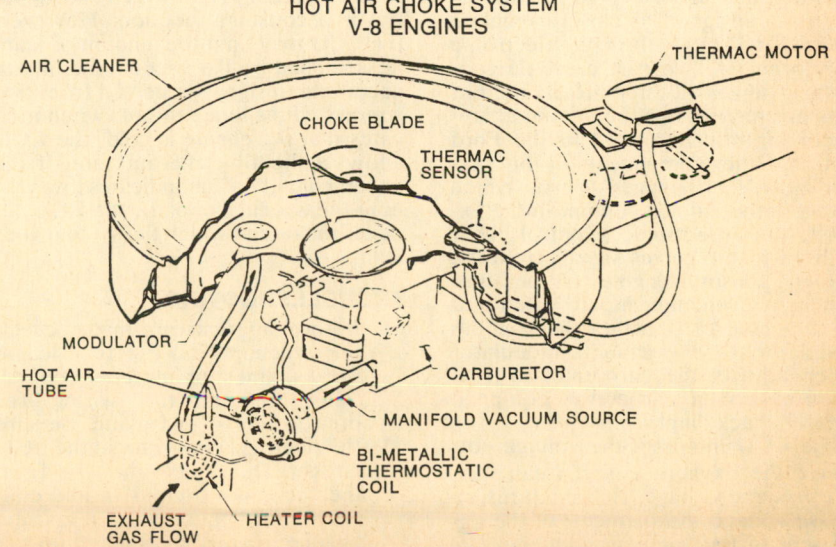

Choke hot air modulator system-1975 and later G.M. (© G.M. Corp.)

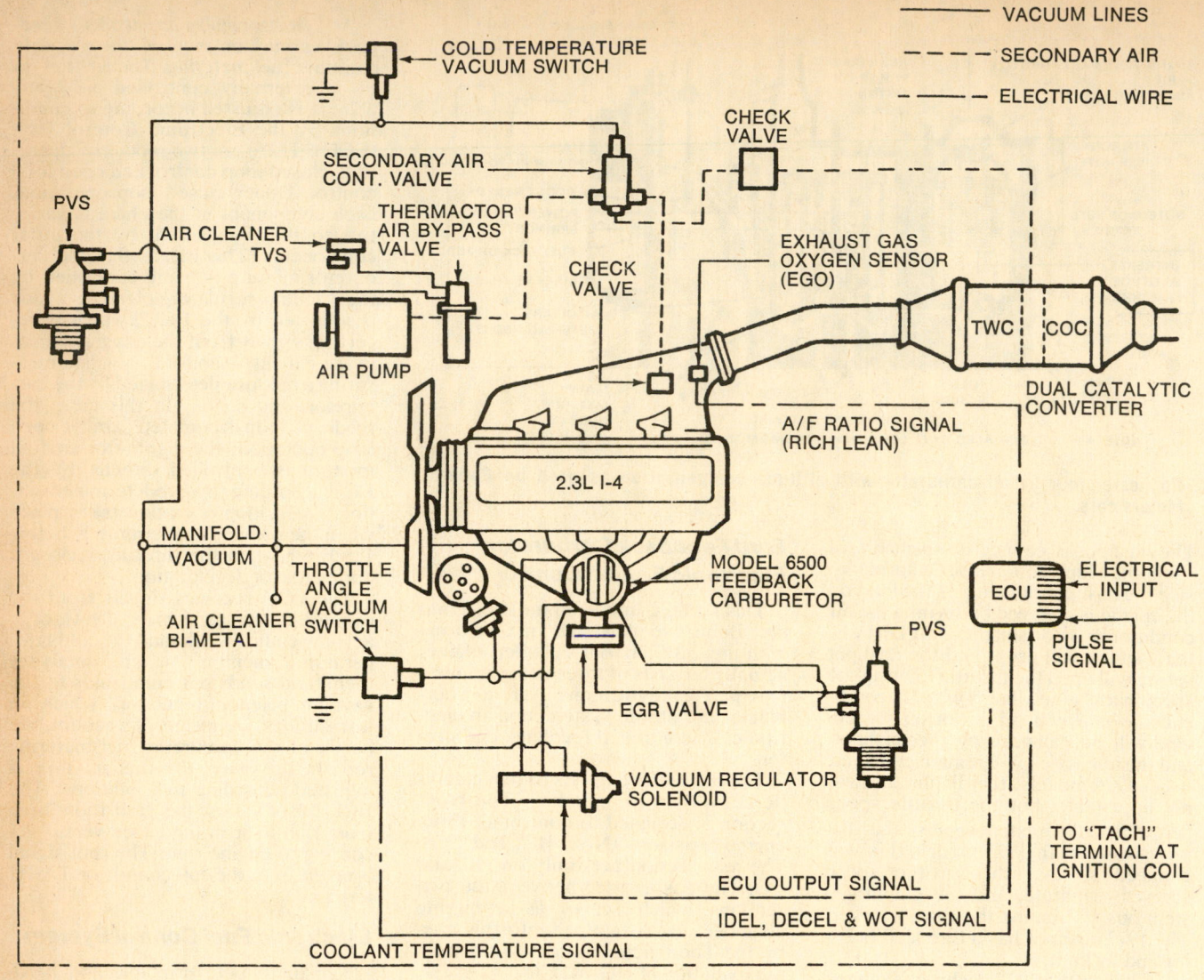

Ford Feedback Carburetor Electronic Engine Control schematic (© Ford Motor Co.)

Pontiac 151 cubic inch (2.5 liter) four cylinder engine installed in Sunbirds, Starfires, and Monzas sold in California. It is designed to closely regulate the air/fuel ratio through electronic monitoring. A two part catalytic converter oxidizes all three pollutants, but does not have either the mixing chamber or air injection used in the Ford system. Other components in this system include an oxygen sensor which monitors the oxygen content in the exhaust, an Electronic Control Unit (ECU) which receives signals from the oxygen sensor, engine temperature switch, and vacuum input switch and sends a control signal to the vacuum modulator, the vacuum modulator which adjusts the carburetor air/fuel mixture, and a carburetor equipped with feedback diaphragms.

The ECU monitors the voltage output of the oxygen sensor. Lean mixtures reduce voltage, rich mixtures increase voltage. Adjustments of the signal sent to the vacuum modulator are made by the ECU according to the oxygen sensor output. Unlike the Ford system, there is no open loop or closed loop operation. The oxygen sensor input is a constant function. However, the ECU may limit the amount of leanness applied by the vacuum modulator according to signals received from two sources. If the temperature switch indicates that the engine is cold, the ECU allows a slightly richer mixture. If the vacuum input switch indicates low vacuum (heavy engine load), the ECU reduces the rate at which the system goes lean.

TROUBLESHOOTING

1. Before any tests are made, check the vacuum hoses for leaks, breaks, kinks, or improper connections. Inspect the wiring for breaks, shorts, or fraying. Be sure the electrical connector at the ECU is tight. Disconnect the wire from the vacuum switch (3B), and connect a test light between it and the positive battery terminal. Run the engine at 1500 rpm, with the trans-

mission in Neutral. The test light should go on and off as the vacuum hose is removed and replaced at the switch. If not, replace the switch.
2. Turn the ignition switch to run (engine off).
3. The vacuum modulator should emit a steady clicking sound. If so, go to Step 4. If not, ground one end of a jumper wire to a ground, the other to the brown wire in the modulator connector (5B).
   a. If the modulator clicks once, check the ECU connector for tightness. If it's ok, remove the ECU connector and touch 5A with the jumper wire. If there's no click, there is an open in the brown wire. If it clicks once, replace the ECU.
   b. If the modulator does not click when the brown wire is grounded, connect a test light to a ground and the pink wire at the modulator (1D). If the test light goes on, replace the modulator. If not,

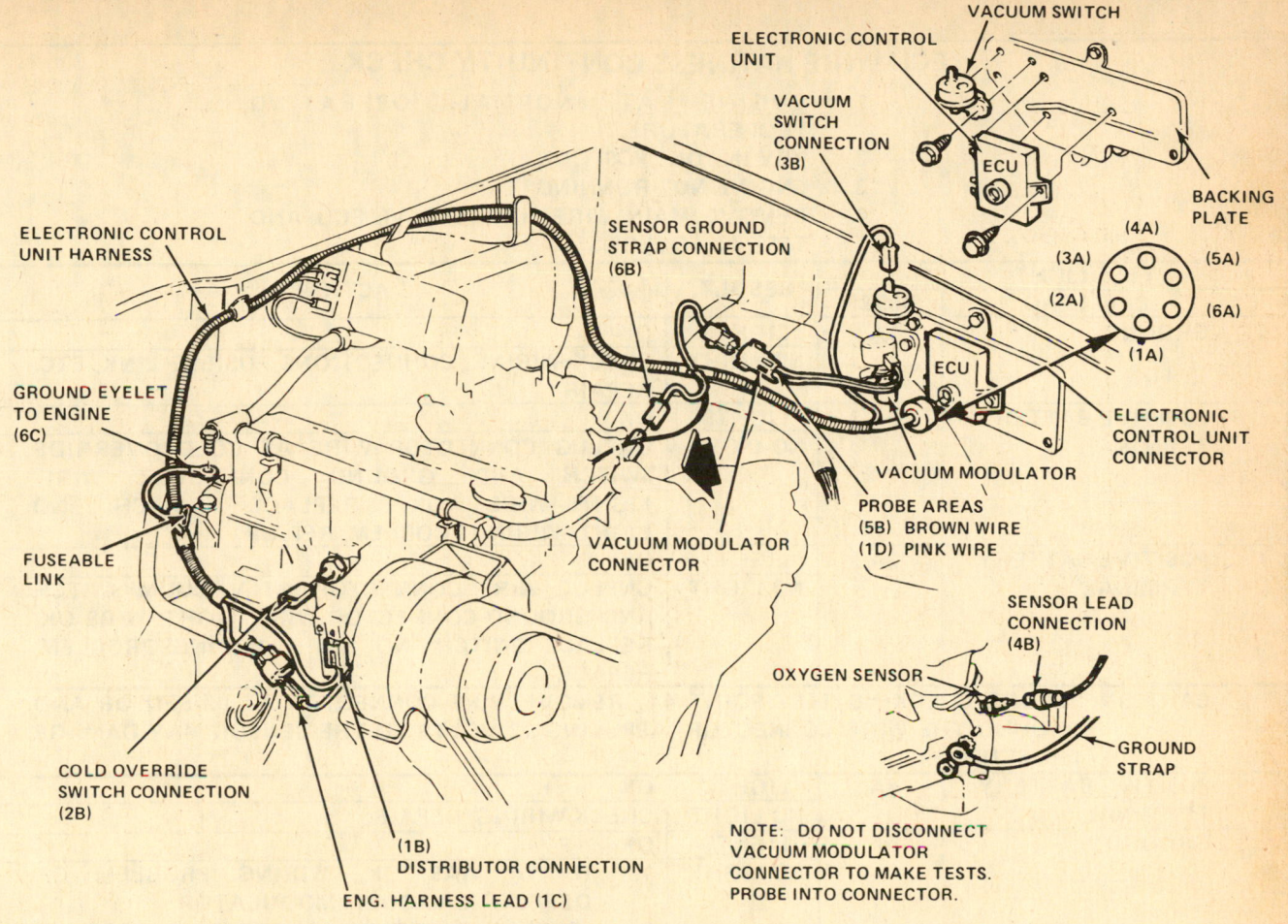

ELECTRONIC CONTROL UNIT

VACUUM SWITCH

VACUUM SWITCH CONNECTION (3B)

SENSOR GROUND STRAP CONNECTION (6B)

ELECTRONIC CONTROL UNIT HARNESS

GROUND EYELET TO ENGINE (6C)

FUSEABLE LINK

COLD OVERRIDE SWITCH CONNECTION (2B)

VACUUM MODULATOR CONNECTOR

(1B) DISTRIBUTOR CONNECTION

ENG. HARNESS LEAD (1C)

ECU

BACKING PLATE

(4A)
(3A)   (5A)
(2A)   (6A)
(1A)

ELECTRONIC CONTROL UNIT CONNECTOR

VACUUM MODULATOR

PROBE AREAS
(5B) BROWN WIRE
(1D) PINK WIRE

SENSOR LEAD CONNECTION (4B)

OXYGEN SENSOR

GROUND STRAP

NOTE: DO NOT DISCONNECT VACUUM MODULATOR CONNECTOR TO MAKE TESTS. PROBE INTO CONNECTOR.

Electronic Fuel Control system components and test connections (© Oldsmobile Div., G.M. Corp.)

there is an open in the pink wire.
4. If a clicking sound is heard, use a T-fitting to attach a vacuum gauge between the center port of the vacuum modulator and the carburetor. Start the engine, allow it to reach operating temperature, and let the engine idle. Automatic transmission should be in Drive (front wheels blocked, parking brake on), manual in Neutral.
  a. If the gauge reads above 7 in. Hg., replace the vacuum modulator.
  b. If the gauge reads 2-4 in. Hg., shift the transmission to Neutral or Park, with an automatic, and increase the engine speed to 3500 rpm. If the reading is still 2-4 in., the system is ok; either the ignition or fuel supply is faulty. If it reads below 2-4 in., the carburetor is faulty.
  c. If the gauge reads below 2-4 in., shift to Neutral or Park, with automatic transmission, and increase the engine speed to 3500 rpm. If it now reads 2-4 in., adjust the idle speed to read 2-4 in. at normal idle, according to the emission sticker in the engine compartment. If the reading is

still below that figure, go to the next Step.

5. Remove the oxygen sensor wire (4B).
  a. If the vacuum gauge reads above 1 in. Hg., disconnect the modulator connector. If the vacuum falls below 1 in., replace the ECU. If it stays above 1 in., replace the vacuum modulator.
  b. If it reads below 1 in., connect a jumper wire from the positive battery terminal to the oxygen sensor terminal (4B). Go to the next Step.

6. If the gauge reads below 4 in., go to Step 7. If it reads 4-7 in., leave the jumper connected, and disconnect the vacuum hose at the center port of the modulator. Set the fast idle screw on the high step of the cam and note the engine rpm. Reconnect the hose and note the rpm.
  a. If the engine speed drops 50 rpm or more when the hose is reconnected, replace the oxygen sensor.
  b. If it drops less than 50 rpm, the problem is in the carburetor.

7. If after Step 5b the gauge still reads below 4 in., remove the jumper wire and reconnect the oxygen sensor wire. Ground the jumper wire and connect the other end to the brown wire at the modulator connector (5B).

  a. If the gauge reads 4-7 in., go to the next Step.
  b. If the gauge reads below 4 in., remove and plug the modulator vacuum hose from the carburetor. If the reading is still below 4 in., replace the modulator. If it is above 4 in., the problem is in the carburetor.

8. If the gauge reads 4-7 in. in Step 7a, remove the jumper wire at the modulator, and ground the engine temperature switch wire (2B).

  a. If the vacuum gauge reads 4-7 in., replace the temperature switch.
  b. If it reads under 4 in., go to the ECU Wiring Harness Continuity Check. If after the check the reading is still below 4 in., repair the ECU harness. If not, replace the ECU.

ECU WIRE HARNESS CONTINUITY CHECK

1. ENGINE AT NORMAL OPERATING TEMPERATURE.
2. KEY IN "ON" POSITION.
3. ENGINE NOT RUNNING.
4. REMOVE MAIN WIRE HARNESS AT ECU AND TEST AS FOLLOWS.

TEST LIGHT			
CLIP LEAD	PROBE	RESULT	ACTION
GROUND	1A	LIGHTS	OK
		NO LIGHT	CHECK WIRING, CONNECTIONS FUSIBLE LINK, ETC. REPAIR
POSITIVE BATTERY TERMINAL	2A	LIGHTS	OK
		NO LIGHT	UNPLUG CONNECTOR WIRE AT COLD OVERRIDE SWITCH AND GROUND CONNECTOR WIRE. LIGHTS—WIRE OK, REPLACE SWITCH. NO LIGHT—WIRING PROBLEM, REPAIR.
POSITIVE BATTERY TERMINAL	3A	LIGHTS	OK
		NO LIGHT	UNPLUG WIRE CONNECTOR AT VACUUM SWITCH AND GROUND CONNECTOR WIRE. LIGHT—WIRE OK, REPLACE SWITCH. NO LIGHT—WIRING PROBLEM, REPAIR.
CAUTION: BEFORE CHECKING TEST POINT 4A, REMOVE WIRE CONNECTOR AT O_2 SENSOR AND GROUND THE WIRE CONNECTOR. APPLYING 12 VOLTS TO THE SENSOR MAY DAMAGE THE SENSOR.			
POSITIVE BATTERY TERMINAL	4A	LIGHTS	OK
		NO LIGHT	CHECK WIRING, REPAIR.
GROUND	5A	LIGHTS	OK
		NO LIGHT	1. IF 1A WAS OK, WIRING PROBLEM OR DEFECTIVE VACUUM MODULATOR. 2. IF 1A WAS NOT OK, CORRECT 1A PROBLEM AND THEN RECHECK 5A.
POSITIVE BATTERY TERMINAL	6A	LIGHTS	OK
		NO LIGHT	CHECK WIRING, GROUND EYELET AT ENGINE BLOCK, REPAIR.

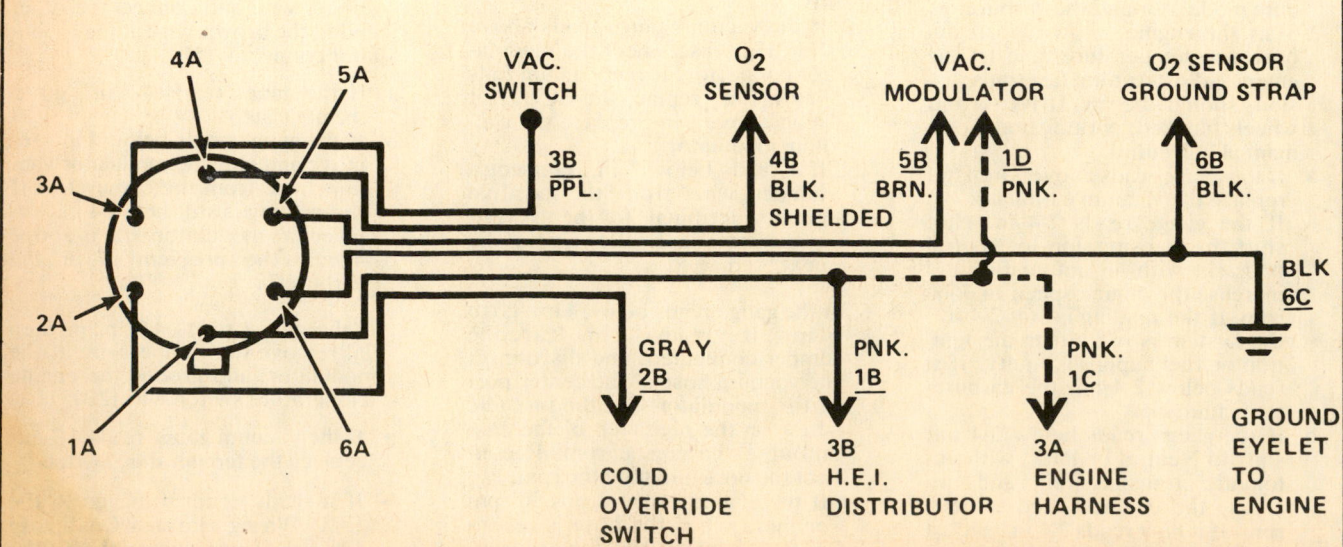

Engine Troubleshooting

INDEX

Group		Topic
1	*	Battery
2	*	Cranking system
3	*	Primary electrical system
4	*	Secondary electrical system
5	*	Fuel system
6	*	Engine compression
7	**	Engine vacuum
8	**	Secondary electrical system
9	**	Valve train
10	**	Exhaust system
11	**	Cooling system
12	**	Engine lubrication

*—The engine need not be running.   **—The engine must be running.

General Diagnosis

PROBLEM: Symptom	Begin diagnosis at Section Two, Number ———
Engine won't start:	
Starter doesn't turn	1.1, 2.1
Starter turns, engine doesn't	2.1
Starter turns engine very slowly	1.1, 2.4
Starter turns engine normally	3.1, 4.1
Starter turns engine very quickly	6.1
Engine fires intermittently	4.1
Engine fires consistently	5.1, 6.1
Engine runs poorly:	
Hard starting	3.1, 4.1, 5.1, 8.1
Rough idle	4.1, 5.1, 8.1
Stalling	3.1, 4.1, 5.1, 8.1
Engine dies at high speeds	4.1, 5.1
Hesitation (on acceleration from standing stop)	5.1, 8.1
Poor pickup	4.1, 5.1, 8.1
Lack of power	3.1, 4.1, 5.1, 8.1
Backfire through the carburetor	4.1, 8.1, 9.1
Backfire through the exhaust	4.1, 8.1, 9.1
Blue exhaust gases	6.1, 7.1
Black exhaust gases	5.1
Running on (after the ignition is shut off)	3.1, 8.1
Susceptible to moisture	4.1
Engine misfires under load	4.1, 7.1, 8.4, 9.1
Engine misfires at speed	4.1, 8.4
Engine misfires at idle	3.1, 4.1, 5.1, 7.1, 8.4

PROBLEM: Symptom	Probable Cause
Engine noises: ①	
Metallic grind while starting	Starter drive not engaging completely
Constant grind or rumble	*Starter drive not releasing, worn main bearings
Constant knock	Worn connecting rod bearings
Knock under load	Fuel octane too low, worn connecting rod bearings
Double knock	Loose piston pin
Metallic tap	*Collapsed or sticky valve lifter, excessive valve clearance, excessive end play in a rotating shaft
Scrape	*Fan belt contacting a stationary surface
Tick while starting	S.U. electric fuel pump (normal), starter brushes
Constant tick	*Generator brushes, shreaded fan belt
Squeal	*Improperly tensioned fan belt
Hiss or roar	*Steam escaping through a leak in the cooling system or the radiator overflow vent
Whistle	*Vacuum leak
Wheeze	Loose or cracked spark plug

The following section is designed to aid in the rapid diagnosis of engine problems. The systematic format is used to diagnose problems ranging from engine starting difficulties to the need for engine overhaul. It is assumed that the user is equipped with basic hand tools and test equipment (tach-dwell meter, timing light, voltmeter, and ohmmeter).

Troubleshooting is divided into two sections. The first, *General Diagnosis*, is used to locate the problem area. In the second, *Specific Diagnosis*, the problem is systematically evaluated.

SPECIFIC DIAGNOSIS

This section is arranged so that following each test, instructions are given to proceed to another, until a problem is diagnosed.

①—It is extremely difficult to evaluate vehicle noises. While the above are general definitions of engine noises, those starred (*) should be considered as possibly originating elsewhere in the car. To aid diagnosis, the following list considers other potential sources of these sounds.

Metallic grind:
Throwout bearing; transmission gears, bearings, or synchronizers; differential bearings, gears; something metallic in contact with brake drum or disc.

Metallic tap:
U-joints; fan-to-radiator (or shroud) contact.

Scrape:
Brake shoe or pad dragging; tire to body contact; suspension contacting undercarriage or exhaust; something non-metallic contacting brake shoe or drum.

Tick:
Transmission gears; differential gears; lack of radio suppression; resonant vibration of body panels; windshield wiper motor or transmission; heater motor and blower.

Squeal:
Brake shoe or pad not fully releasing; tires (excessive wear, uneven wear, improper inflation); front or rear wheel alignment (most commonly due to improper toe-in).

Hiss or whistle:
Wind leaks (body or window); heater motor and blower fan.

Roar:
Wheel bearings; wind leaks (body and window).

SAMPLE SECTION

Test and Procedure	Results and Indications	Proceed to
4.1—Check for spark: Hold each spark plug wire approximately ¹/₄″ from ground with gloves or a heavy, dry rag. Crank the engine and observe the spark.	If no spark is evident:	**4.2**
	If spark is good in some cases:	**4.3**
	If spark is good in all cases:	**4.6**

DIAGNOSIS

Test and Procedure	Results and Indications	Proceed to
1.1—Inspect the battery visually for case condition (corrosion, cracks) and water level.	If case is cracked, replace battery:	**1.4**
	If the case is intact, remove corrosion with a solution of baking soda and water (CAUTION: *do not get the solution into the battery*), and fill with water:	**1.2**
1.2—Check the battery cable connections: Insert a screwdriver between the battery post and the cable clamp. Turn the headlights on high beam, and observe them as the screwdriver is gently twisted to ensure good metal to metal contact.	If the lights brighten, remove and clean the clamp and post; coat the post with petroleum jelly, install and tighten the clamp:	**1.4**
	If no improvement is noted:	**1.3**

Testing battery cable connections using a screwdriver

Test and Procedure	Results and Indications	Proceed to
1.3—Test the state of charge of the battery using an individual cell tester or hydrometer.	If indicated, charge the battery. NOTE: *If no obvious reason exists for the low state of charge (i.e., battery age, prolonged storage), the charging system should be tested:*	**1.4**

Spec. Grav. Reading	Charged Condition
1.260-1.280	Fully Charged
1.230-1.250	Three Quarter Charged
1.200-1.220	One Half Charged
1.170-1.190	One Quarter Charged
1.140-1.160	Just About Flat
1.110-1.130	All The Way Down

SPECIFIC GRAVITY CORRECTION

+120	+.016
	+.012 ADD
+100	+.008 TO READING
	+.004
+80	NO CORRECTION
	−.004
+60	−.008
	−.012
+40	−.016
	−.020
+20	−.024 SUBTRACT FROM READING
	−.028
0	−.032
	−.036
−20	−.040

ELECTROLITE TEMPERATURE (°F)

The effect of temperature on the specific gravity of battery electrolyte

Test and Procedure	Results and Indications	Proceed to
1.4—Visually inspect battery cables for cracking, bad connection to ground, or bad connection to starter.	If necessary, tighten connections or replace the cables:	**2.1**

Tests in Group 2 are performed with coil high tension lead disconnected to prevent accidental starting.

Test and Procedure	Results and Indications	Proceed to
2.1—Test the starter motor and solenoid: Connect a jumper from the battery post of the solenoid (or relay) to the ignition switch post of the solenoid (or relay).	If starter turns the engine normally:	**2.2**
	If the starter buzzes, or turns the engine very slowly:	**2.4**
	If no response, replace the solenoid (or relay).	**3.1**
	If the starter turns, but the engine doesn't, ensure that the flywheel ring gear is intact. If the gear is undamaged, replace the starter drive.	**3.1**
2.2—Determine whether ignition override switches are functioning properly (clutch start switch, neutral safety switch), by connecting a jumper across the switch(es), and turning the ignition switch to "start".	If starter operates, adjust or replace switch:	**3.1**
	If the starter doesn't operate:	**2.3**

Test and Procedure	Results and Indications	Proceed to
2.3—Check the ignition switch "start" position: Connect a 12V test lamp between the starter post of the solenoid (or relay) and ground. Turn the ignition switch to the "start" position, and jiggle the key.	If the lamp doesn't light when the switch is turned, check the ignition switch for loose connections, cracked insulation, or broken wires. Repair or replace as necessary:	3.1
	If the lamp flickers when the key is jiggled, replace the ignition switch.	3.3

Checking the ignition switch "start" position

Test and Procedure	Results and Indications	Proceed to
2.4—Remove and bench test the starter.	If the starter does not meet specifications, repair or replace as needed:	3.1
	If the starter is operating properly:	2.5
2.5—Determine whether the engine can turn freely: Remove the spark plugs, and check for water in the cylinders. Check for water on the dipstick, or oil in the radiator. Attempt to turn the engine using an 18″ flex drive and socket on the crankshaft pulley nut or bolt.	If the engine will turn freely only with the spark plugs out, and hydrostatic lock (water in the cylinders) is ruled out, check valve timing:	9.2
	If engine will not turn freely, and it is known that the clutch and transmission are free, the engine must be disassembled for further evaluation.	
3.1—Check the ignition switch "on" position: Connect a jumper wire between the distributor side of the coil and ground, and a 12V test lamp between the switch side of the coil and ground. Remove the high tension lead from the coil. Turn the ignition switch on and jiggle the key.	If the lamp lights:	3.2
	If the lamp flickers when the key is jiggled, replace the ignition switch:	3.3
	If the lamp doesn't light, check for loose or open connections. If none are found, remove the ignition switch and check for continuity. If the switch is faulty, replace it:	

Checking the ignition switch "on" position

Test and Procedure	Results and Indications	Proceed to
3.2—Check the ballast resistor or resistance wire, if used, for an open circuit, using an ohmmeter.	Replace the resistor or the resistance wire if the resistance is zero.	3.3
3.3—Visually inspect the breaker points for burning, pitting, or excessive wear. Gray coloring of the point contact surfaces is normal. Rotate the crankshaft until the contact heel rests on a high point of the distributor cam, and adjust the point gap to specifications. On electronic ignitions with adjustable pick-up coils, use non-magnetic feeler gauges to check the air gap. Make sure the timing rotor is tight on the shaft, and rotates when engine is cranked.	If the breaker points are intact, clean the contact surfaces with fine emery cloth, and adjust the point gap to specifications. If pitted or worn, replace the points and condenser, and adjust the gap to specifications: NOTE: *Always lubricate the distributor cam according to manufacturer's recommendations when servicing the breaker points.* Set gap to specifications. Repair as necessary.	3.4 3.4 3.4

Engine Troubleshooting

Test and Procedure	Results and Indications	Proceed to
3.4—Connect a dwell meter between the distributor primary lead and ground. Crank the engine and observe the point dwell angle. On electronic ignitions test the pick-up coil according to the manufacturer's specifications. 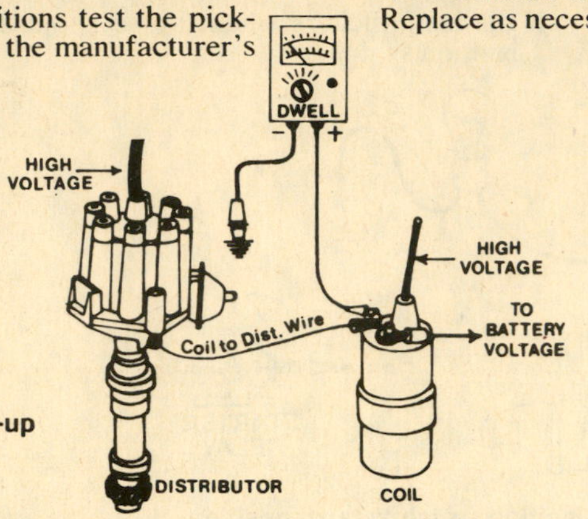	If necessary, adjust the point dwell angle: NOTE: *Increasing the point gap decreases the dwell angle, and vice-versa.* If dwell meter shows little or no reading: Replace as necessary. 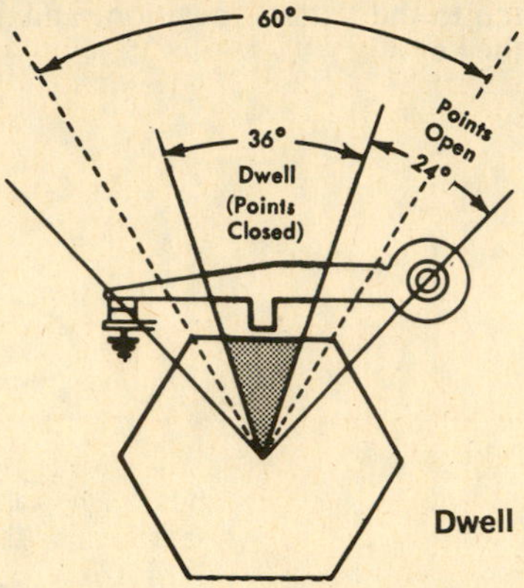	3.6 3.5 3.6

HIGH VOLTAGE

DWELL

Coil to Dist. Wire

HIGH VOLTAGE

TO BATTERY VOLTAGE

Dwell meter hook-up

DISTRIBUTOR   **COIL**

60°

36° Dwell (Points Closed)

Points Open

24°

Dwell angle

Test and Procedure	Results and Indications	Proceed to
3.5—Check the condenser for short: Connect an ohmmeter across the condenser body and the pigtail lead.	If any reading other than infinite resistance is noted, replace the condenser:	3.6

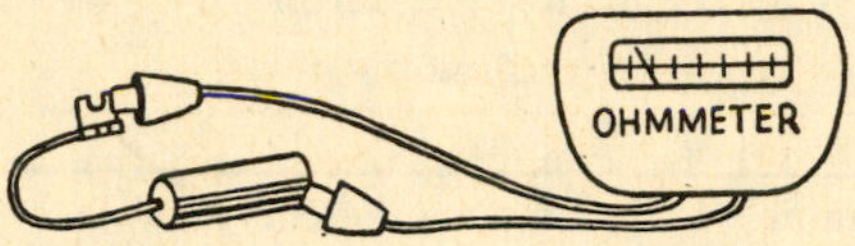

Checking the condenser for short

OHMMETER

Test and Procedure	Results and Indications	Proceed to
3.6—Test the coil primary resistance: Connect an ohmmeter across the coil primary terminals, and read the resistance on the low scale. Note whether an external ballast resistor or resistance wire is utilized. NOTE: *On HEI systems with an integral coil, connect the ohmeter to the TACH and BAT terminals of the distributor cap.*	Coils utilizing ballast resistors or resistance wires should have approximately 1.0-2.0 ohms resistance; coils with internal resistors should have approximately 4.0 ohms resistance. If values far from the above are noted, replace the coil: NOTE: *HEI coils must measure less than 1.0 ohm.*	4.1
4.1—Check for spark: Hold each spark plug wire approximately ¼" from ground with gloves or a heavy, dry rag. Crank the engine, and observe the spark. NOTE: *On some electronic ignitions, this test must not be performed on certain cylinders.*	If no spark is evident: If spark is good in some cylinders: If spark is good in all cylinders:	4.2 4.3 4.6
4.2—Check for spark at the coil high tension lead: Remove the coil high tension lead from the distributor and position it approximately ¼" from ground. Crank the engine and observe spark. CAUTION: *This test should not be performed on cars equipped with transistorized ignition.*	If the spark is good and consistent: If the spark is good but intermittent, test the primary electrical system starting at 3.3: If the spark is weak or non-existent, replace the coil high tension lead, clean and tighten all connections and retest. If no improvement is noted:	4.3 3.3 4.4
4.3—Visually inspect the distributor cap and rotor for burned or corroded contacts, cracks, carbon tracks, or moisture. Also check the fit of the rotor on the distributor shaft (where applicable). If silicone grease is used on the contacts, check for correct application.	If moisture is present, dry thoroughly, and retest per 4.1: If burned or excessively corroded contacts, cracks, or carbon tracks are noted, replace the defective part(s) and retest per 4.1: If the rotor and cap appear intact, or are only slightly corroded, clean the contacts thoroughly (including the cap towers and spark plug wire ends) and retest per 4.1: If the spark is good in all cases: If the spark is poor in all cases:	4.1 4.1 4.6 4.5

Test and Procedure	Results and Indications	Proceed to
4.4—Check the coil secondary resistance: Connect an ohmmeter across the distributor side of the coil and the coil tower. Measure between the rotor button in the distributor cap and the TACH or BAT terminal with HEI. Read the resistance on the high scale of the ohmmeter.	The resistance of a satisfactory coil should be between 4K ohms and 12K ohms (6K -30K ohms with HEI). If the resistance is considerably higher (i.e., 40K ohms) replace the coil, and retest per 4.1: NOTE: *This does not apply to high performance coils.*	**4.1**

Testing the coil secondary resistance

Test and Procedure	Results and Indications	Proceed to
4.5—Visually inspect the spark plug wires for cracking or brittleness. Ensure that no two wires are positioned so as to cause induction firing (adjacent and parallel). Remove each wire, one by one, and check resistance with an ohmmeter. NOTE: *Do not pierce wires with a probe to check; measure from end to end.*	Replace any cracked or brittle wires. If any of the wires are defective, replace the entire set. Replace any wires with excessive resistance (over 8000 ohms per foot for suppression wire), and separate any wires that might cause induction firing. NOTE: *Allowable resistance for Dura Spark wires is 5000 ohms per inch.*	**4.6**
4.6—Remove the spark plugs, noting the cylinders from which they were removed, and evaluate according to the chart below.	See below.	**See below.**

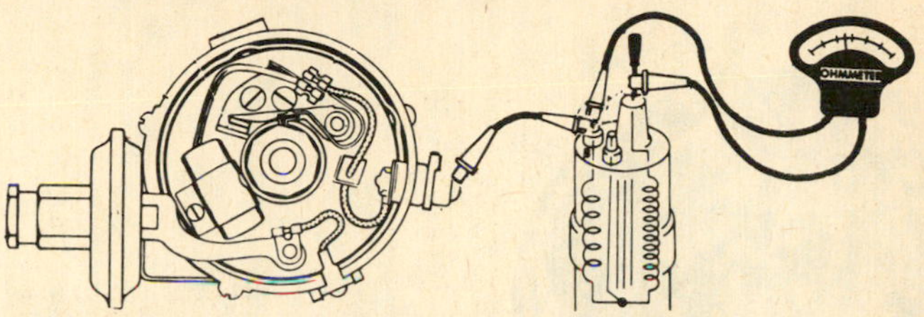

Condition	Cause	Remedy	Proceed/to
Electrodes eroded, light brown deposits. 	Normal wear. Normal wear is indicated by approximately .001″ wear per 1000 miles.	Clean and regap the spark plug if wear is not excessive: Replace the spark plug if excessively worn:	**4.7**
Carbon fouling (black, dry, fluffy deposits).	If present on one or two plugs: Faulty high tension lead(s). Burnt or sticking valve(s).	Test the high tension leads: Check the valve train: (Clean and regap the plugs in either case.)	**4.5** **9.1**
	If present on most or all plugs: Overly rich fuel mixture, due to restricted air filter, improper carburetor adjustment, improper choke or heat riser adjustment or operation.	Check the fuel system:	**5.1**

Test and Procedure	Results and Indications		Proceed to
Oil fouling (wet black deposits)	Worn engine components. NOTE: *Oil fouling may occur in new or recently rebuilt engines until broken in.*	Check engine vacuum and compression: Replace with new spark plug.	**6.1**

Lead fouling (gray, black, red, green, tan, or yellow deposits, which appear glazed or cinderlike).	Combustion by-products.	Clean and regap the plugs: (Use plugs of a different heat range if the problem recurs.)	**4.7**

Gap bridging (deposits lodged between the electrodes).	Incomplete combustion, or transfer of deposits from the combustion chamber.	Replace the spark plugs.

Test and Procedure	Results and Indications		Proceed to
Overheating (burnt electrodes, and extremely white insulator with small black spots).	Ignition timing advanced too far.	Adjust timing to specifications:	8.2
	Overly lean fuel mixture.	Check the fuel system:	5.1
	Spark plugs not seated properly.	Clean spark plug seat and install a new gasket washer: (Replace the spark plugs in all cases.)	4.7
Pre-ignition (melted or severely burned electrodes, blistered or cracked insulators, or metallic deposits on the insulator).	Incorrect spark plug heat range.	Replace with plugs of the proper heat range:	4.7
	Ignition timing advanced too far.	Adjust timing to specifications:	8.2
	Spark plugs not being cooled efficiently.	Clean the spark plug seat, and check the cooling system:	11.1
	Fuel mixture too lean	Check the fuel system:	5.1
	Poor compression.	Check compression:	6.1
	Fuel grade too low.	Use higher octane fuel:	4.7
4.7—Determine the static ignition timing: Using the flywheel or crankshaft pulley timing marks as a guide, locate top dead center on the *compression* stroke of the No. 1 cylinder. Remove the distributor cap.	Adjust the distributor so that the rotor points toward the No. 1 tower in the distributor cap, when the points are just opening on conventional ignitions, or when a trigger wheel spoke is aligned with the pick-up coil on electronic ignitions:		4.8
4.8—Check coil polarity: Connect a voltmeter negative lead to the coil high tension lead, and the positive lead to ground (NOTE: *reverse the hook-up for positive ground cars*). Crank the engine momentarily.	If the voltmeter reads up-scale, the polarity is correct:		5.1
	If the voltmeter reads down-scale, reverse the coil polarity (switch the primary leads):		5.1
5.1—Determine that the air filter is functioning efficiently: Hold paper elements up to a strong light, and attempt to see light through the filter.	Clean permanent air filters in solvent (or manufacturer's recommendation), and allow to dry. Replace paper elements through which light cannot be seen:		5.2

Checking coil polarity

Engine Troubleshooting

Test and Procedure	Results and Indications	Proceed to
5.2—Determine whether a flooding condition exists: Flooding is identified by a strong gasoline odor, and excessive gasoline present in the throttle bore(s) of the carburetor.	If flooding is not evident:	5.3
	If flooding is evident, permit the gasoline to dry for a few moments and restart.	
	If flooding doesn't recur:	5.6
	If flooding is persistant:	5.5
5.3—Check that fuel is reaching the carburetor: Detach the fuel line at the carburetor inlet. Hold the end of the line in a cup (not styrofoam), and crank the engine.	If fuel flows smoothly:	5.6
	If fuel doesn't flow (NOTE: *Make sure that there is fuel in the tank*), or flows erratically:	5.4
5.4—Test the fuel pump: Disconnect all fuel lines from the fuel pump. Hold a finger over the input fitting, crank the engine (with electric pump, turn the ignition or pump on), and feel for suction.	If suction is evident, blow out the fuel line to the tank with low pressure compressed air until bubbling is heard from the fuel filler neck. Also blow out the carburetor fuel line (both ends disconnected):	5.6
	If no suction is evident, replace or repair the fuel pump: NOTE: *Repeated oil fouling of the spark plugs, or a no-start condition, could be the result of a ruptured vacuum booster pump diaphragm, through which oil or gasoline is being drawn into the intake manifold (where applicable).*	5.6
5.5—Check the needle and seat: Tap the carburetor in the area of the needle and seat.	If flooding stops, a gasoline additive (e.g., Gumout) will often cure the problem:	5.6
	If flooding continues, check the fuel pump for excessive pressure at the caruburetor (according to specifications). If the pressure is normal, the needle and seat must be removed and checked, and/or the float level adjusted:	5.6
5.6—Test the accelerator pump by looking into the throttle bores while operating the throttle.	If the accelerator pump appears to be operating normally:	5.7
	If the accelerator pump is not operating, the pump must be reconditioned. Where possible, service the pump with the carburetor(s) installed on the engine. If necessary, remove the carburetor. Prior to removal:	5.7
5.7—Determine whether the carburetor main fuel system is functioning: Spray a commercial starting fluid into the carburetor while attempting to start the engine.	If the engine starts, runs for a few seconds, and dies:	5.8
	If the engine doesn't start:	6.1
5.8—Uncommon fuel system malfunctions: See below:	If the problem is solved:	6.1
	If the problem remains, remove and recondition the carburetor.	

Condition	Indication	Test	Usual Weather Conditions	Remedy
Vapor lock	Car will not restart shortly after running.	Cool the components of the fuel system until the engine starts.	Hot to very hot	Ensure that the exhaust manifold heat control valve is operating. Check with the vehicle manufacturer for the recommended solution to vapor lock on the model in question.
Carburetor icing	Car will not idle, stalls at low speeds.	Visually inspect the throttle plate area of the throttle bores for frost.	High humidity, 32-40 F.	Ensure that the exhaust manifold heat control valve is operating, and that the intake manifold heat riser is not blocked.
Water in the fuel	Engine sputters and stalls; may not start.	Pump a small amount of fuel into a glass jar. Allow to stand, and inspect for droplets or a layer of water.	High humidity, extreme temperature changes.	For droplets, use one or two cans of commercial gas dryer (Dry Gas) For a layer of water, the tank must be drained, and the fuel lines blown out with compressed air.

Test and Procedure	Results and Indications	Proceed to
6.1—Test engine compression: Remove all spark plugs. Insert a compression gauge into a spark plug port, crank the engine to obtain the maximum reading, and record.	If compression is within limits on all cylinders:	7.1
	If guage reading is extremely low on all cylinders:	6.2
	If gauge reading is low on one or two cylinders: (If gauge readings are identical and low on two or more adjacent cylinders, the head gasket must be replaced.)	6.2

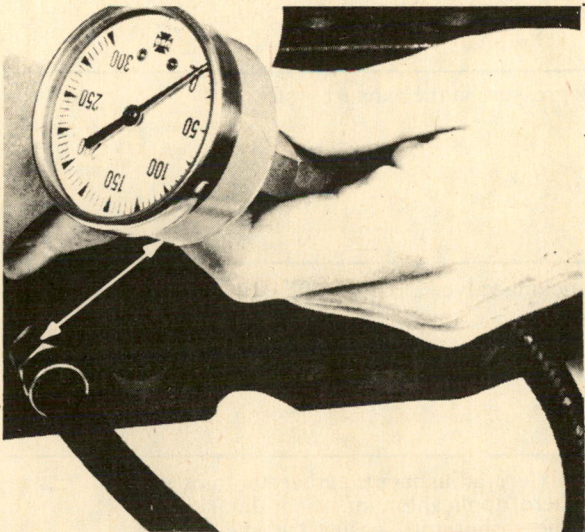

Testing compression

Maxi. Press. Lbs. Sq. In.	Min. Press. Lbs. Sq. In.	Maxi. Press. Lbs. Sq. In.	Min. Press. Lbs. Sq. In.	Max. Press. Lbs. Sq. In.	Min. Press. Lbs. Sq. In.	Max. Press. Lbs. Sq. In.	Min. Press. Lbs. Sq. In.
134	101	162	121	188	141	214	160
136	102	164	123	190	142	216	162
138	104	166	124	192	144	218	163
140	105	168	126	194	145	220	165
142	107	170	127	196	147	222	166
146	110	172	129	198	148	224	168
148	111	174	131	200	150	226	169
150	113	176	132	202	151	228	171
152	114	178	133	204	153	230	172
154	115	180	135	206	154	232	174
156	117	182	136	208	156	234	175
158	118	184	138	210	157	236	177
160	120	186	140	212	158	238	178

Compression pressure limits

Test and Procedure	Results and Indications	Proceed to
6.2—Test engine compression (wet): Squirt approximately 30 cc. of engine oil into each cylinder, and retest per 6.1.	If the readings improve, worn or cracked rings or broken pistons are indicated:	
	If the readings do not improve, burned or excessively carboned valves or a jumped timing chain are indicated: NOTE: A jumped timing chain is often indicated by difficult cranking.	7.1
7.1—Perform a vacuum check of the engine: Attach a vacuum gauge to the intake manifold beyond the throttle plate. Start the engine, and observe the action of the needle over the range of engine speeds.	See below.	See below

Engine Troubleshooting

	Reading	Indications	Proceed to
	Steady, from 17-22 in. Hg.	Normal.	**8.1**
	Low and steady.	Late ignition or valve timing, or low compression:	**6.1**
	Very low.	Vacuum leak:	
	Needle fluctuates as engine speed increases.	Ignition miss, blown cylinder head gasket, leaking valve or weak valve spring:	**6.1, 8.3**
	Gradual drop in reading at idle.	Excessive back pressure in the exhaust system:	**10.1**
	Intermittent fluctuation at idle.	Ignition miss, sticking valve:	**8.3, 9.1**
	Drifting needle.	Improper idle mixture adjustment, carburetors not synchronized (where applicable), or minor intake leak. Synchronize the carburetors, adjust the idle, and retest. If the condition persists:	**7.2**
	High and steady.	Early ignition timing:	**8.2**

7.2—Attach a vacuum gauge per 7.1, and test for an intake manifold leak. Squirt a small amount of oil around the intake manifold gaskets, carburetor gaskets, plugs and fittings. Obsserve the action of the vacuum gauge.

If the reading improves, replace the indicated gasket, or seal the indicated fitting or plug: **8.1**

If the reading remains low: **7.3**

Reading	Indications	Proceed to
7.3—Test all vacuum hoses and accessories for leaks as described in 7.2. Also check the carburetor body (dashpots, automatic choke mechanism, throttle shafts) for leaks in the same manner.	If the reading improves, service or replace the offending part(s): If the reading remains low:	8.1 6.1
8.1—Check the point dwell angle: Connect a dwell meter between the distributor primary wire and ground. Start the engine, and observe the dwell angle from idle to 3000 rpm.	If necessary, adjust the dwell angle. NOTE: *Increasing the point gap reduces the dwell angle and vice-versa.* If the dwell angle moves outside specifications as engine speed increases, the distributor should be removed and checked for cam accuracy, shaft endplay and concentricity, bushing wear, and adequate point arm tension (NOTE: *Most of these items may be checked with the distributor installed in the engine, using an oscilloscope):*	8.2
8.2—Connect a timing light (per manufacturer's recommendation) and check the dynamic ignition timing. Disconnect and plug the vacuum hose(s) to the distributor if specified, start the engine, and observe the timing marks at the specified engine speed.	If the timing is not correct, adjust to specifications by rotating the distributor in the engine: (Advance timing by rotating distributor opposite normal direction of rotor rotation, retard timing by rotating distributor in same direction as rotor rotation.)	8.3
8.3—Check the operation of the distributor advance mechanism(s): To test the mechanical advance, disconnect the vacuum advance, and observe the timing marks with a timing light as the engine speed is increased from idle. If the mark moves smoothly, without hesitation, it may be assumed that the mechanical advance is functioning properly. To test vacuum advance and/or retard systems, alternately crimp and release the vacuum line, and observe the timing mark for movement. If movement is noted, the system is operating.	If the systems are functioning: If the systems are not functioning, remove the distributor, and test on a distributor tester:	8.4 8.4
8.4—Locate an ignition miss: With the engine running, remove each spark plug wire, one by one, until one is found that doesn't cause the engine to roughen and slow down. NOTE: *Certain cylinders must not be disconnected on some electronic ignitions.*	When the missing cylinder is identified:	4.1
9.1—Evaluate the valve train: Remove the valve cover, and ensure that the valves are adjusted to specifications. A mechanic's stethoscope may be used to aid in the diagnosis of the valve train. By pushing the probe on or near push rods or rockers, valve noise often can be isolated. A timing light also may be used to diagnose valve problems. Connect the light according to manufacturer's recommendations, and start the engine. Vary the firing moment of the light by increasing the engine speed (and therefore the ignition advance), and moving the trigger from cylinder to cylinder. Observe the movement of each valve.	See below	See below

Engine Troubleshooting

Observation	Probable Cause	Remedy	Proceed to
Metallic tap heard through the stethoscope.	Sticking hydraulic lifter or excessive valve clearance.	Adjust valve. If tap persists, remove and replace the lifter:	10.0
Metallic tap through the stethoscope, able to push the rocker arm (lifter side) down by hand.	Collapsed valve lifter.	Remove and replace the lifter:	10.1
Erratic, irregular motion of the valve stem.*	Sticking valve, burned valve.	Recondition the valve and/or valve guide:	Next Chapter-ter
Eccentric motion of the pushrod at the rocker arm.*	Bent pushrod.	Replace the pushrod:	10.1
Valve retainer bounces as the valve closes.*	Weak valve spring or damper.	Remove and test the spring and damper. Replace if necessary:	10.1

*—When observed with a timing light.

Test and Procedure	Results and Indications	Proceed to
9.2—Check the valve timing: Locate top dead center of the No. 1 piston, and install a degree wheel or tape on the crankshaft pulley or damper with zero corresponding to an index mark on the engine. Rotate the crankshaft in its direction of rotation, and observe the opening of the No. 1 cylinder intake valve. The opening should correspond with the correct mark on the degree wheel according to specifications.	If the timing is not correct, the timing cover must be removed for further investigation:	
10.1—Determine whether the exhaust manifold heat control valve is operating: Operate the valve by hand to determine whether it is free to move. If the valve is free, run the engine to operating temperature and observe the action of the valve, to ensure that it is opening.	If the valve sticks, spray it with a suitable solvent, open and close the valve to free it, and retest. If the valve functions properly: If the valve does not free, or does not operate, replace the valve:	10.2 10.2
10.2—Ensure that there are no exhaust restrictions: Visually inspect the exhaust system for kinks, dents, or crushing. Also note that gases are flowing freely from the tailpipe at all engine speeds, indicating no restriction in the muffler or resonator.	Replace any damaged portion of the system:	11.1
11.1—Visually inspect the fan belt for glazing, cracks, and fraying, and replace if necessary. Tighten the belt so that the longest span has approximately 1/2″ play at its midpoint under thumb pressure.	Replace or tighten the fan belt as necessary:	11.2

Checking the fan belt tension
(© Outboard Marine Corp.)

Test and Procedure	Results and Indications	Proceed to
11.2—Check the fluid level of the cooling system.	If full or slightly low, fill as necessary:	**11.5**
	If extremely low:	**11.3**
11.3—Visually inspect the external portions of the cooling system (radiator, radiator hoses, thermostat elbow, water pump seals, heater hoses, etc.) for leaks. If none are found, pressurize the cooling system to 14-15 psi.	If cooling system holds the pressure:	**11.5**
	If cooling system loses pressure rapidly, reinspect external parts of the system for leaks under pressure. If none are found, check dipstick for coolant in crankcase. If no coolant is present, but pressure loss continues:	**11.4**
	If coolant is evident in crankcase, remove cylinder head(s), and check gasket(s). If gaskets are intact, block and cylinder heads(s) should be checked for cracks or holes.	
	If the gasket(s) is blown, replace, and purge the crankcase of coolant:	**12.6**
	NOTE: *Occasionally, due to atmospheric and driving conditions, condensation of water can occur in the crankcase. This causes the oil to appear milky white. To remedy, run the engine until hot, and change the oil and oil filter.*	
11.4—Check for combustion leaks into the cooling system: Pressurize the cooling system as above. Start the engine, and observe the pressure gauge. If the needle fluctuates, remove each spark plug wire, one by one, noting which cylinder(s) reduce or eliminate the fluctuation. NOTE: *Cetain cylinders must not be disconnected on some electronic ignitions.*	Cylinders which reduce or eliminate the fluctuation, when the spark plug wire is removed, are leaking into the cooling system. Replace the head gasket on the affected cylinder bank(s).	

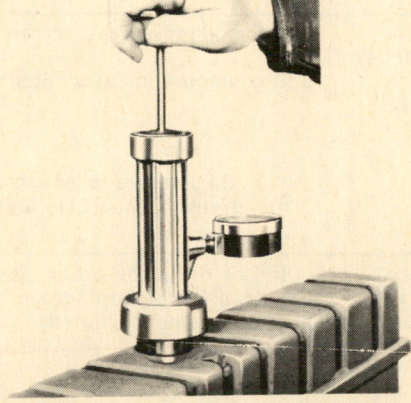

Radiator pressure tester

Test and Procedure	Results and Indications	Proceed to
11.6—Test the thermostat: Start the engine cold, remove the radiator cap, and insert a thermometer into the radiator. Allow the engine to idle. After a short while, there will be a sudden, rapid increase in coolant temperature. The temperature at which this sharp rise stops is the thermostat opening temperature.	If the thermostat opens at or about the specified temperature:	**11.7**
	If the temperature doesn't increase: (If the temperature increases slowly and gradually, replace the thermostat.)	**11.7**
11.5—Check the radiator pressure cap: Attach a radiator pressure tester to the radiator cap (wet the seal prior to installation). Quickly pump up the pressure, noting the point at which the cap releases.	If the cap releases within ± 1 psi of the specified rating, it is operating properly:	**11.6**
	If the cap releases at more than ± 1 psi of the specified rating. It should be replaced:	**11.6**

Engine Troubleshooting

Test and Procedure	*Results and Indications*	*Proceed to*

PRESSURE CAP   ADAPTER   TOOL

Testing the radiator pressure cap

11.7—Check the water pump: Remove the thermostat elbow and the thermostat, disconnect the coil high tension lead (to prevent starting), and crank the engine momentarily.	If coolant flows, replace the thermostat and retest per 11.6:	**11.6**
	If coolant doesn't flow, reverse flush the cooling system to alleviate any blockage that might exist. If system is not blocked, and coolant will not flow, recondition the water pump.	
12.1—Check the oil pressure gauge or warning light: If the gauge shows low pressure, or the light is on, for no obvious reason, remove the oil pressure sender. Install an accurate oil pressure gauge and run the engine momentarily.	If oil pressure builds normally, run engine for a few moments to determine that it is functioning normally, and replace the sender.	
	If the pressure remains low:	**12.2**
	If the pressure surges:	**12.3**
	If the oil pressure is zero:	**12.3**
12.2—Visually inspect the oil: If the oil is watery or very thin, milky, or foamy, replace the oil and oil filter.	If the oil is normal:	**12.3**
	If after replacing oil the pressure remains low:	**12.3**
	If after replacing oil the pressure becomes normal:	
12.3—Inspect the oil pressure relief valve and spring, to ensure that it is not sticking or stuck. Remove and thoroughly clean the valve, spring, and the valve body.	If the oil pressure improves:	
	If no improvement is noted:	**12.4**

Oil pressure relief valve
(© British Leyland Motors)

12.4—Check to ensure that the oil pump is not cavitating (sucking air instead of oil): See that the crankcase is neither over nor underfull, and that the pickup in the sump is in the proper position and free from sludge.	Fill or drain the crankcase to the proper capacity, and clean the pickup screen in solvent if necessary. If no improvement is noted:	**12.5**
12.5—Inspect the oil pump drive and the oil pump:	If the pump drive or the oil pump appear to be defective, service as necessary and retest per 12.1:	**12.1**
	If the pump drive and pump appear to be operating normally, the engine should be disassembled to determine where blockage exists.	
12.6—Purge the engine of ethylene glycol coolant: Completely drain the crankcase and the oil filter. Obtain a commercial solvent, designated for this purpose, and follow the instructions precisely. Following this, install a new oil filter and refill the crankcase with the proper viscosity oil. The next oil and filter change should follow shortly thereafter (1000 miles).		

Engine Rebuilding

This section describes, in detail, the procedures involved in rebuilding a typical engine. The procedures specifically refer to an inline engine, however, they are basically identical to those used in rebuilding engines of nearly all design and configurations. Procedures for servicing atypical engines (i.e., horizontally opposed) are described in the appropriate section, although in most cases, cylinder head reconditioning procedures described in this chapter will apply.

The section is divided into two sections. The first, Cylinder Head Reconditioning, assumes that the cylinder head is removed from the engine, all manifolds are removed, and the cylinder head is on a workbench. The camshaft should be removed from overhead cam cylinder heads. The second section, Cylinder Block Reconditioning, covers the block, pistons, connecting rods and crankshaft. It is assumed that the engine is mounted on a work stand, and the cylinder head and all accessories are removed.

Procedures are identified as follows:

Unmarked—Basic procedures that must be performed in order to successfully complete the rebuilding process.

Starred (*)—Procedures that should be performed to ensure maximum performance and engine life.

Double starred (**)—Procedures that may be performed to increase engine performance and reliability. These procedures are usually reserved for extremely heavy-duty or competition usage.

In many cases, a choice of methods is also provided. Methods are identified in the same manner as procedures. The choice of method for a procedure is at the discretion of the user.

The tools required for the basic rebuilding procedure should, with minor exceptions, be those included in a mechanic's tool kit. An accurate torque wrench, and a dial indicator (reading in thousandths) mounted on a universal base should be available. Bolts and nuts with no torque specification should be tightened according to size (see chart). Special tools, where required, all are readily available from the major tool suppliers. The services of a competent automotive machine shop must also be readily available.

When assembling the engine, any parts that will be in frictional contact must be pre-lubricated, to provide protection on initial start-up. Any product specifically formulated for this purpose may be used.

NOTE: *Do not use engine oil.* Where semi-permanent (locked but removable) installation of bolts or nuts is desired, threads should be cleaned and coated with a non-hardening sealant.

Studs may be permanently installed using a non-hardening sealant.

Aluminum has become increasingly popular for use in engines, due to its low weight and excellent heat transfer characteristics. The following precautions must be observed when handling aluminum engine parts:

—Never hot-tank aluminum parts.

—Remove all aluminum parts (identification tags, etc.) from engine parts before hot-tanking (otherwise they will be removed during the process).

—Always coat threads lightly with engine oil or anti-seize compounds before installation, to prevent seizure.

—Never over-torque bolts or spark plugs in aluminum threads. Should stripping occur, threads can be restored according to the following procedure, using Heli-Coil thread inserts:

Tap drill the hole with the stripped threads to the specified size (see chart). Using the specified tap (NOTE: *Heli-Coil tap sizes refer to the size thread being replaced, rather than the actual tap size*), tap the hole for the Heli-Coil. Place the insert on the proper installation tool (see chart). Apply pressure on the insert while winding it clockwise into the hole, until the top of the insert is one turn below the surface. Remove the installation tool, and break the installation tang from the bottom of the insert by moving it up and down. If the Heli-Coil must be removed, tap the removal tool firmly into the hole, so that it engages the top thread, and turn the tool counter-clockwise to extract the insert.

There are also several other types of thread repair devices available. Snapped bolts or studs may be removed, using a stud extractor (unthreaded) or Vise-Grip pliers (threaded). Penetrating oil (e.g., Liquid Wrench) will often aid in breaking frozen threads. In cases where the stud or bolt is flush with, or below the surface, proceed as follows:

Drill a hole in the broken stud or bolt, approximately 1/2 its diameter. Select a screw extractor (e.g., Easy-Out) of the proper size, and tap it into the stud or bolt. Turn the extractor counterclockwise to remove the stud or bolt.

TORQUE (ft lbs)*

U.S.

Bolt Diameter (inches)	Bolt Grade (SAE)				Wrench Size (inches)	
	1 and 2	5	6	8	Bolt	Nut
1/4	5	7	10	10.5	3/8	7/16
5/16	9	14	19	22	1/2	9/16
3/8	15	25	34	37	9/16	5/8
7/16	24	40	55	60	5/8	3/4
1/2	37	60	85	92	3/4	13/16
9/16	53	88	120	132	7/8	7/8
5/8	74	120	167	180	15/16	1
3/4	120	200	280	296	1-1/8	1-1/8
7/8	190	302	440	473	1-5/16	1-5/16
1	282	466	660	714	1-1/2	1-1/2

Metric

Bolt Diameter (mm)	Bolt Grade				Wrench Size (mm) Bolt and Nut
	5D	8G	10K	12K	
6	5	6	8	10	10
8	10	16	22	27	14
10	19	31	40	49	17
12	34	54	70	86	19
14	55	89	117	137	22
16	83	132	175	208	24
18	111	182	236	283	27
22	182	284	394	464	32
24	261	419	570	689	36

* Torque values are for lightly oiled bolts. CAUTION: Bolts threaded into aluminum require much less torque.

Engine Rebuilding

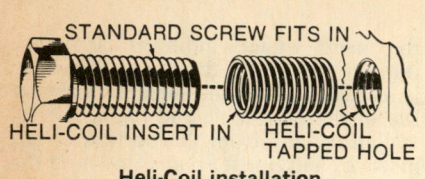

Heli-Coil installation
(© Chrysler Corp.)

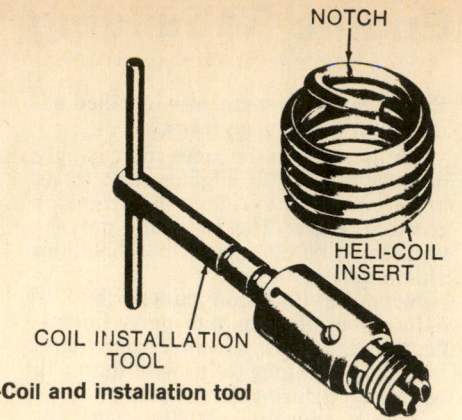

Heli-Coil and installation tool

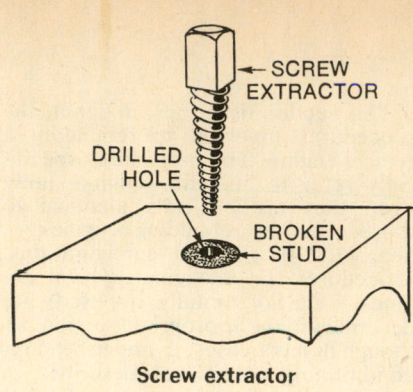

Screw extractor

Heli-Coil Insert			Drill	Tap	Insert. Tool	Extracting Tool
Thread Size	Part No.	Insert Length (In.)	Size	Part No.	Part No.	Part No.
1/2 -20	1185-4	3/8	17/64 (.266)	4 CPB	528-4N	1227-6
5/16-18	1185-5	15/32	Q (.332)	5 CPB	528-5N	1227-6
3/8 -16	1185-6	9/16	X (.397)	6 CPB	528-6N	1227-6
7/16-14	1185-7	21/32	29/64 (.453)	7 CPB	528-7N	1227-16
1/2 -13	1185-8	3/4	33/64 (.516)	8 CPB	528-8N	1227-16

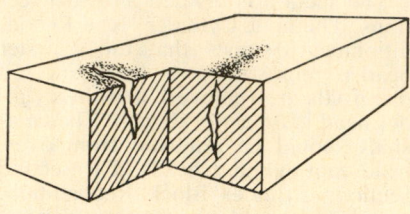

Magnaflux indication of cracks

Magnaflux and Zyglo are inspection techniques used to locate material flaws, such as stress cracks. Magnafluxing coats the part with fine magnetic particles, and subjects the part to a magnetic field. Cracks cause breaks in the magnetic field, which are outlined by the particles. Since Magnaflux is a magnetic process, it is applicable only to ferrous materials. The Zyglo process coats the material with a fluorescent dye penetrant, and then subjects it to blacklight inspection, under which cracks glow brightly. Parts made of any material may be tested using Zyglo. While Magnaflux and Zyglo are excellent for general inspection, and locating hidden defects, specific checks of suspected cracks may be made at lower cost and more readily using spot check dye. The dye is sprayed onto the suspected area, wiped off, and the area is then sprayed with a developer. Cracks then will show up brightly. Spot check dyes will only indicate surface cracks; therefore, structural cracks below the surface may escape detection. When questionable, the part should be tested using Magnaflux or Zyglo.

CYLINDER HEAD RECONDITIONING

Procedure	Method
Identify the valves:	Invert the cylinder head, and number the valve faces front to rear, using a permanent felt-tip marker.

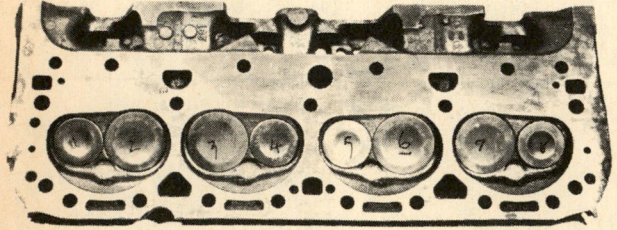

Valve identification

Procedure	Method
Remove the rocker arms:	Remove the rocker arms with shaft(s) or balls and nuts. Wire the sets of rockers, balls and nuts together, and identify according to the corresponding valve.
Remove the valves and springs:	Using an appropriate valve spring compressor (depending on the configuration of the cylinder head), compress the valve springs. Lift out the keepers with needlenose pliers, release the compressor, and remove the valve, spring, and spring retainer.

CYLINDER HEAD RECONDITIONING

Procedure	*Method*

Check the valve stem-to-guide clearance:

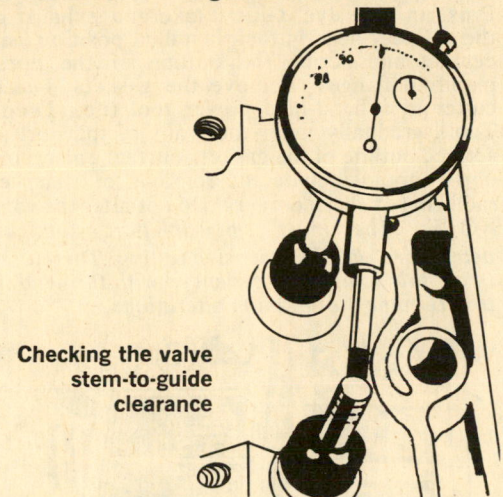

Checking the valve stem-to-guide clearance

Clean the valve stem with lacquer thinner or a similar solvent to remove all gum and varnish. Clean the valve guides using solvent and an expanding wire-type valve guide cleaner. Mount a dial indicator so that the stem is at 90° to the valve stem, as close to the valve guide as possible. Move the valve off its seat, and measure the valve guide-to-stem clearance by moving the stem back and forth to actuate the dial indicator. Measure the valve stems using a micrometer, and compare to specifications, to determine whether stem or guide wear is responsible for excessive clearance.

De-carbon the cylinder head and valves:

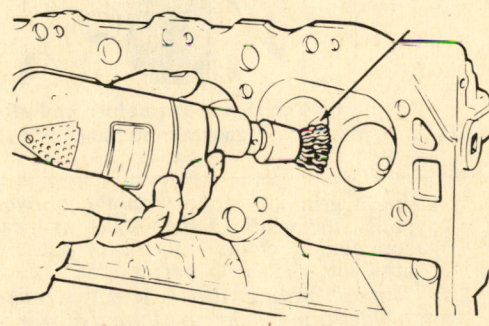

Removing carbon from the cylinder head

Chip carbon away from the valve heads, combustion chambers, and ports, using a chisel made of hardwood. Remove the remaining deposits with a stiff wire brush. NOTE: *Ensure that the deposits are actually removed, rather than burnished.*

Hot-tank the cylinder head:

Have the cylinder head hot-tanked to remove grease, corrosion, and scale from the water passages. NOTE: *In the case of overhead cam cylinder heads, consult the operator to determine whether the camshaft bearings will be damaged by the caustic solution.*

Degrease the remaining cylinder head parts:

Using solvent (i.e., Gunk), clean the rockers, rocker shaft(s) (where applicable), rocker balls and nuts, springs, spring retainers, and keepers. Do not remove the protective coating from the springs.

Check the cylinder head for warpage:

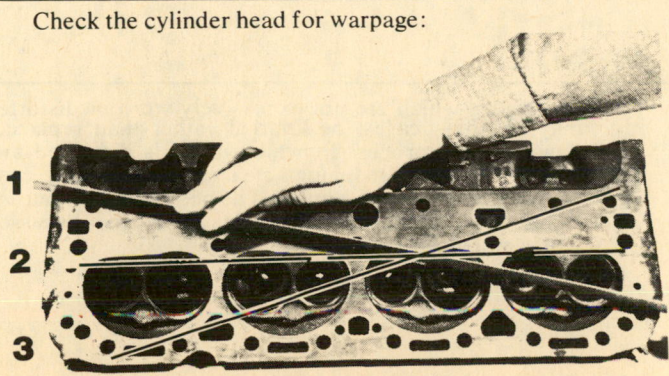

1 & 3 CHECK DIAGONALLY
2 CHECK ACROSS CENTER

Place a straight-edge across the gasket surface of the cylinder head. Using feeler gauges, determine the clearance at the center of the straight-edge. Measure across both diagonals, along the longitudinal centerline, and across the cylinder head at several points. If warpage exceeds .003″ in a 6″ span, or .006″ over the total length, the cylinder head must be resurfaced. NOTE: *If warpage exceeds the manufacturers maximum tolerance for material removal, the cylinder head must be replaced.* When milling the cylinder heads of V-type engines, the intake manifold mounting position is altered, and must be corrected by milling the manifold flange a proportionate amount.

Checking the cylinder head for warpage

Engine Rebuilding

CYLINDER HEAD RECONDITIONING

Procedure	Method

** Porting and gasket matching:

** Coat the manifold flanges of the cylinder head with Prussian blue dye. Glue intake and exhaust gaskets to the cylinder head in their installed position using rubber cement and scribe the outline of the ports on the manifold flanges. Remove the gaskets. Using a small cutter in a hand-held power tool (i.e., Dremel Moto-Tool), gradually taper the walls of the port out to the scribed outline of the gasket. Further enlargement f the ports should include the removal of sharp edges and radiusing of sharp corners. Do not alter the valve guides. NOTE: *The most efficient port configuration is determined only by extensive testing. Therefore, it is best to consult someone experienced with the head in question to determine the optimum alterations.*

Marking the cylinder head for gasket matching

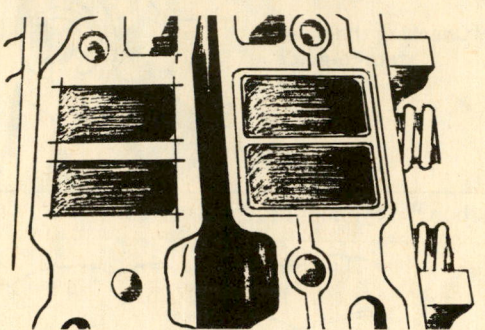

Port configuration before and after gasket matching

** Polish the ports:

** Using a grinding stone with the above mentioned tool, polish the walls of the intake and exhaust ports, and combustion chamber. Use progressively finer stones until all surface imperfections are removed. NOTE: *Through testing, it has been determined that a smooth surface is more effective than a mirror polished surface in intake ports, and vice-versa in exhaust ports.*

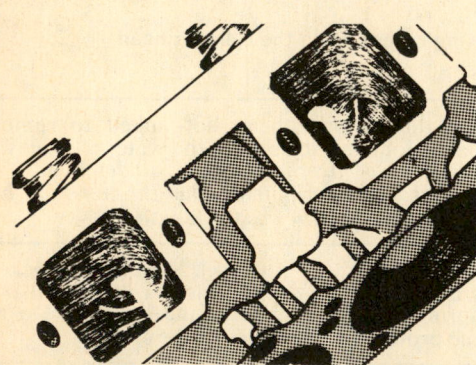

Relieved and polished ports

* Knurling the valve guides:

* Valve guides which are not excessively worn or distorted may, in some cases, be knurled rather than replaced. Knurling is a process in which metal is displaced and raised, thereby reducing clearance. Knurling also provides excellent oil control. The possibility of knurling rather than replacing valve guides should be discussed with a machinist.

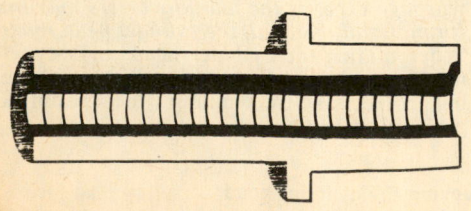

Cut-away view of a knurled valve guide

CYLINDER HEAD RECONDITIONING

Procedure	Method

Replacing the valve guides: NOTE: *Valve guides should only be replaced if damaged or if an oversize valve stem is not available.*

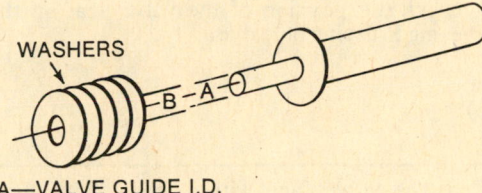

A—VALVE GUIDE I.D.
B—LARGER THAN THE
VALVE GUIDE O.D.

Valve guide removal tool

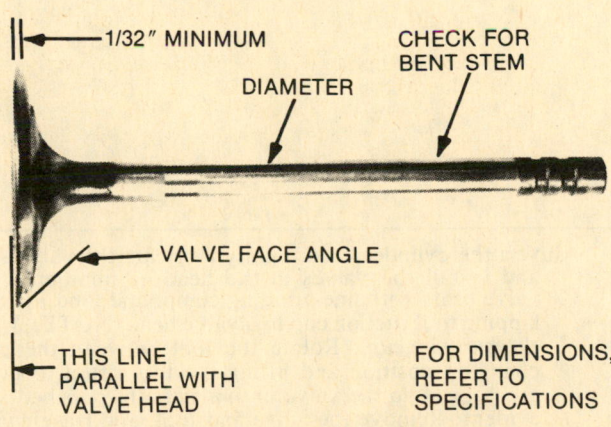

WASHERS

A—VALVE GUIDE I.D.
B—LARGER THAN THE
VALVE GUIDE O.D.

Valve guide installation tool (with washers used during installation)

Depending on the type of cylinder head, valve guides may be pressed, hammered, or shrunk in. In cases where the guides are shrunk into the head, replacement should be left to an equipped machine shop. In other cases, the guides are replaced as follows: Press or tap the valve guides out of the head using a stepped drift (see illustration). Determine the height above the boss that the guide must extend, and obtain a stack of washers, their I.D. similar to the guide's O.D., of that height. Place the stack of washers on the guide, and insert the guide into the boss. NOTE: *Valve guides are often tapered or beveled for installation.* Using the stepped installation tool (see illustration), press or tap the guides into position. Ream the guides according to the size of the valve stem.

Replacing valve seat inserts:

Replacement of valve seat inserts which are worn beyond resurfacing or broken, if feasible, must be done by a machine shop.

Resurfacing (grinding) the valve face:

1/32″ MINIMUM

DIAMETER

CHECK FOR BENT STEM

VALVE FACE ANGLE

THIS LINE PARALLEL WITH VALVE HEAD

FOR DIMENSIONS, REFER TO SPECIFICATIONS

Critical valve dimensions

Using a valve grinder, resurface the valves according to specifications. CAUTION: *Valve face angle is not always identical to valve seat angle.* A minimum margin of 1/32″ should remain after grinding the valve. The valve stem top should also be squared and resurfaced, by placing the stem in the V-block of the grinder, and turning it while pressing lightly against the grinding wheel.

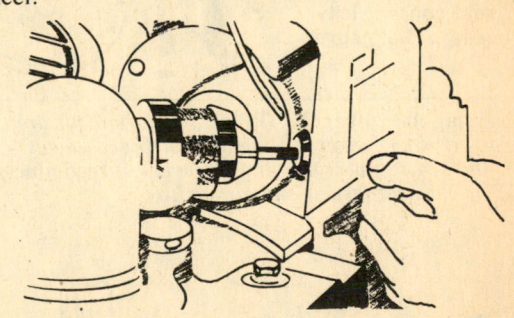

Grinding a valve

* Resurfacing the valve seats using a grinder:

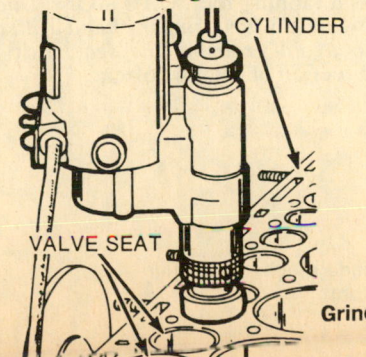

CYLINDER

VALVE SEAT

Grinding a valve seat

Select a pilot of the correct size, and a coarse stone of the correct seat angle. Lubricate the pilot if necessary, and install the tool in the valve guide. Move the stone on and off the seat at approximately two cycles per second, until all flaws are removed from the seat. Install a fine stone, and finish the seat. Center and narrow the seat using correction stones, as described above.

Engine Rebuilding

CYLINDER HEAD RECONDITIONING

Procedure	Method

Procedure

Resurfacing the valve seats using reamers:

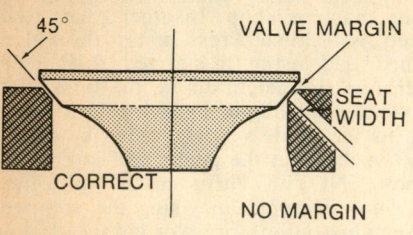

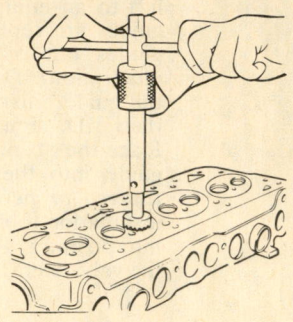

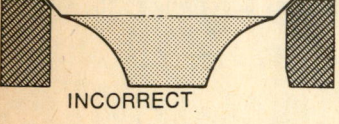

Valve seat width and centering

Reaming the valve seat (© Outboard Marine Corp)

Method

Select a reamer of the correct seat angle, slightly larger than the diameter of the valve seat, and assemble it with a pilot of the correct size. Install the pilot into the valve guide, and using steady pressure, turn the reamer clockwise. CAUTION: *Do not turn the reamer counterclockwise.* Remove only as much material as necessary to clean the seat. Check the concentricity of the seat (see below). If the dye method is not used, coat the valve face with Prussian blue dye, install and rotate it on the valve seat. Using the dye marked area as a centering guide, center and narrow the valve seat to specifications with correction cutters. NOTE: *When no specifications are available, minimum seat width for exhaust valves should be 5/64", intake valves 1/16".* After making correction cuts, check the position of the valve seat on the valve face using Prussian blue dye.

Checking the valve seat concentricity:

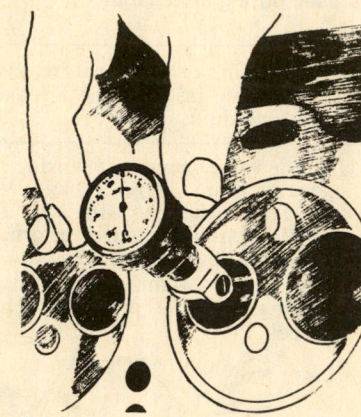

Checking the valve seat concentricity using a dial gauge

Coat the valve face with Prussian blue dye, install the valve, and rotate it on the valve seat. If the entire seat becomes coated, and the valve is known to be concentric, the seat is concentric.

---

* Install the dial gauge pilot into the guide, and rest of the arm on the valve seat. Zero the gauge, and rotate the arm around the seat. Run-out should not exceed .002".

---

* Lapping the valves: NOTE: *Valve lapping is done to ensure efficient sealing of resurfaced valves and seats. Valve lapping alone is not recommended for use as a resurfacing procedure.*

Hand lapping the valves

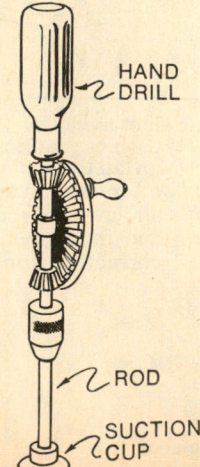

HAND DRILL

ROD

SUCTION CUP

Home made mechanical valve lapping tool

* Invert the cylinder head, lightly lubricate the valve stems, and install the valves in the head as numbered. Coat valve seats with fine grinding compound, and attach the lapping tool suction cup to a valve head (NOTE: *Moisten the suction cup*). Rotate the tool between the palms, changing position and lifting the tool often to prevent grooving. Lap the valve until a smooth, polished seat is evident. Remove the valve and tool, and rinse away all traces of grinding compound.

** Fasten a suction cup to a piece of drill rod, and mount the rod in a hand drill. Proceed as above, using the hand drill as a lapping tool. CAUTION: *Due to the higher speeds involved when using the hand drill, care must be exercised to avoid grooving the seat.* Lift the tool and change direction of rotation often.

CYLINDER HEAD RECONDITIONING

Procedure	Method

Check the valve springs:

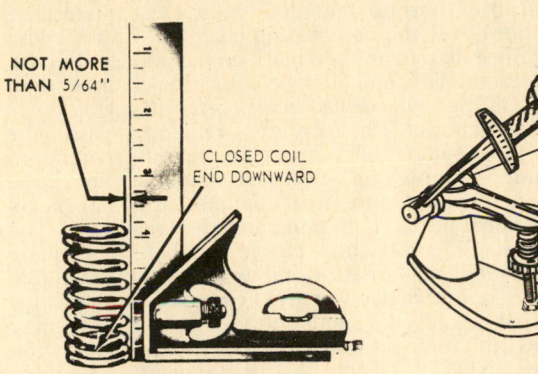

Place the spring on a flat surface next to a square. Measure the height of the spring, and rotate it against the edge of the square to measure distortion. If spring height varies (by comparison) by more than $1/16''$ or if distortion exceeds $1/16''$, replace the spring.

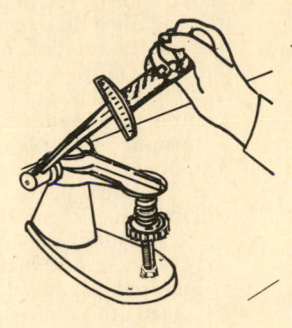

** In addition to evaluating the spring as above, test the spring pressure at the installed and compressed (installed height minus valve lift) height using a valve spring tester. Springs used on small displacement engines (up to 3 liters) should be ∓ 1 lb. of all other springs in either position. A tolerance of ∓ 5 lbs. is permissible on larger engines.

Checking the valve spring
free length and squareness

(© Outboard Marine Corp.)

* Install valve stem seals:

RETAINER
SPRING
VALVE
SEAL

* Due to the pressure differential that exists at the ends of the intake valve guides (atmospheric pressure above, manifold vacuum below), oil is drawn through the valve guides into the intake port. This has been alleviated somewhat since the addition of positive crankcase ventilation, which lowers the pressure above the guides. Several types of valve stem seals are available to reduce blow-by. Certain seals simply slip over the stem and guide boss, while others require that the boss be machined. Recently, Teflon guide seals have become popular. Consult a parts supplier or machinist concerning availability and suggested usages. NOTE: *When installing seals, ensure that a small amount of oil is able to pass the seal to lubricate the valve guides; otherwise, excessive wear may result.*

Valve stem seal
installation

Install the valves:

Lubricate the valve stems, and install the valves in the cylinder head as numbered. Lubricate and position the seals (if used, see above) and the valve springs. Install the spring retainers, compress the springs, and insert the keys using needlenose pliers or a tool designed for this purpose. NOTE: *Retain the keys with wheel bearing grease during installation.*

Checking valve spring installed height:

Measure the distance between the spring pad and the lower edge of the spring retainer, and compare to specifications. If the installed height is incorrect, add shim washers between the spring pad and the spring. CAUTION: *Use only washers designed for this purpose.*

GRIND OUT THIS PORTION

Valve spring installed
height dimension
(© Porsche)

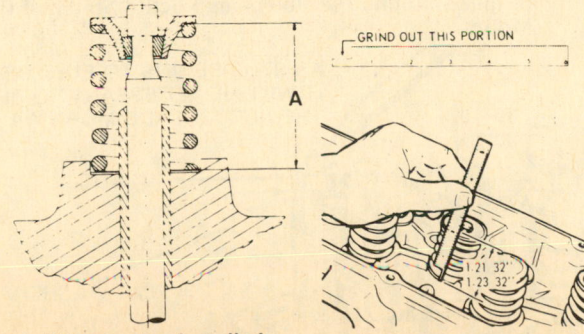

Measuring valve spring
Installed height (© Outboard Marine Corp.)

CYLINDER HEAD RECONDITIONING

Procedure	Method

** CC'ing the combustion chambers:

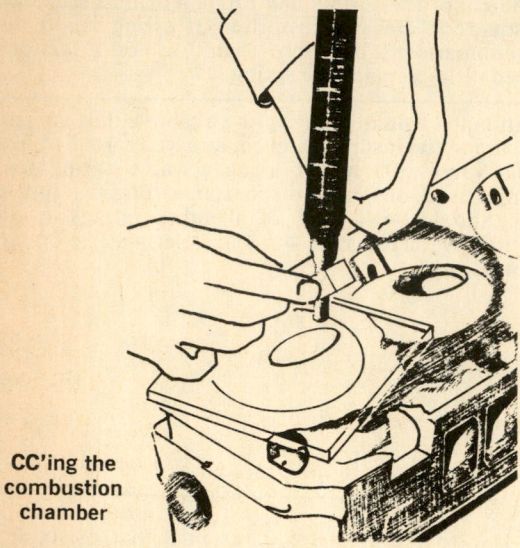

CC'ing the combustion chamber

** Invert the cylinder head and place a bead of sealer around a combustion chamber. Install an apparatus designed for this purpose (burette mounted on a clear plate; see illustration) over the combustion chamber, and fill with the specified fluid to an even mark on the burette. Record the burette reading, and fill the combustion chamber with fluid. (NOTE: *A hole drilled in the plate will permit air to escape*). Subtract the burette reading, with the combustion chamber filled, from the previous reading, to determine combustion chamber volume in cc's. Duplicate this procedure in all combustion chambers on the cylinder head, and compare the readings. The volume of all combustion chambers should be made equal to that of the largest. Combustion chamber volume may be increased in two ways. When only a small change is required (usually), a small cutter or coarse stone may be used to remove material from the combustion chamber. NOTE: *Check volume frequently.* Remove material over a wide area, so as not to change the configuration of the combustion chamber. When a larger change is required, the valve seat may be sunk (lowered into the head). NOTE: *When altering valve seat, remember to compensate for the change in spring installed height.*

Inspect the rocker arms, balls, studs, and nuts (where applicable):

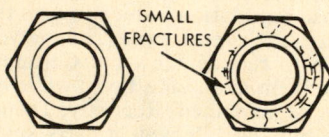

SMALL FRACTURES

Stress cracks in rocker nuts
(© Ford Motor Co.)

Visually inspect the rocker arms, balls, studs, and nuts for cracks, galling, burning, scoring, or wear. If all parts are intact, liberally lubricate the rocker arms and balls, and install them on the cylinder head. If wear is noted on a rocker arm at the point of valve contact, grind it smooth and square, removing as little material as possible. Replace the rocker arm if excessively worn. If a rocker stud shows signs of wear, it must be replaced (see below). If a rocker nut shows stress cracks, replace it. If an exhaust ball is galled or burned, substitute the intake ball from the same cylinder (if it is intact), and install a new intake ball. NOTE: *Avoid using new rocker balls on exhaust valves.*

Replacing rocker studs:

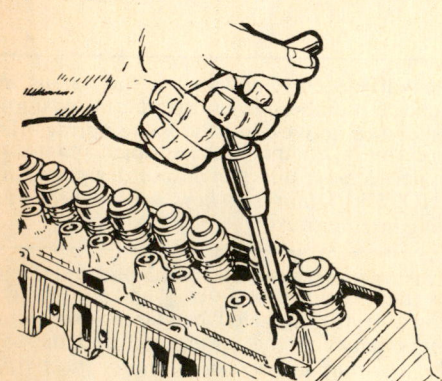

Reaming the stud bore for oversize rocker studs

In order to remove a threaded stud, lock two nuts on the stud, and unscrew the stud using the lower nut. Coat the lower threads of the new stud with Loctite, and install.

Two alternative methods are available for replacing pressed in studs. Remove the damaged stud using a stack of washers and a nut (see illustration). In the first, the boss is reamed .005-.006" oversize, and an oversize stud pressed in. Control the stud extension over the boss using washers, in the same manner as valve guides. Before installing the stud, coat it with white lead and grease. To retain the stud more positively drill a hole through the stud and boss, and install a roll pin. In the second method, the boss is tapped, and a threaded stud installed. Retain the stud using Loctite Stud and Bearing Mount.

Extracting a pressed in rocker stud

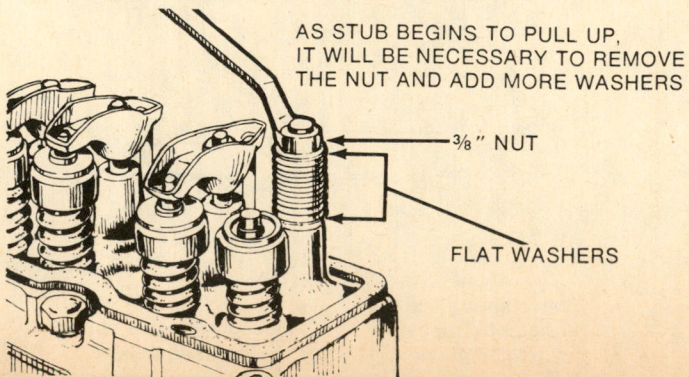

AS STUB BEGINS TO PULL UP, IT WILL BE NECESSARY TO REMOVE THE NUT AND ADD MORE WASHERS

⅜" NUT

FLAT WASHERS

CYLINDER HEAD RECONDITIONING

Procedure	Method

Inspect the rocker shaft(s) and rocker arms (where applicable):

Remove rocker arms, springs and washers from rocker shaft. NOTE: *Lay out parts in the order they are removed.* Inspect rocker arms for pitting or wear on the valve contact point, or excessive bushing wear. Bushings need only be replaced if wear is excessive, because the rocker arm normally contacts the shaft at one point only. Grind the valve contact point of rocker arm smooth if necessary, removing as little material as possible. If excessive material must be removed to smooth and square the arm, it should be replaced. Clean out all oil holes and passages in rocker shaft. If shaft is grooved or worn, replace it. Lubricate and assemble the rocker shaft.

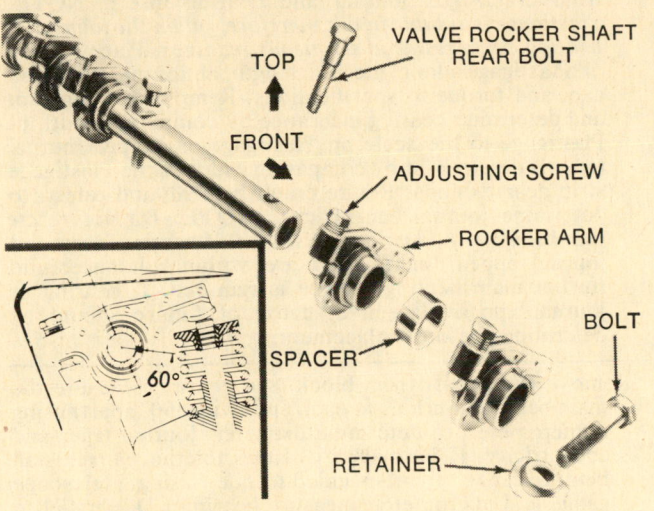

Disassembled rocker shaft parts arranged for inspection

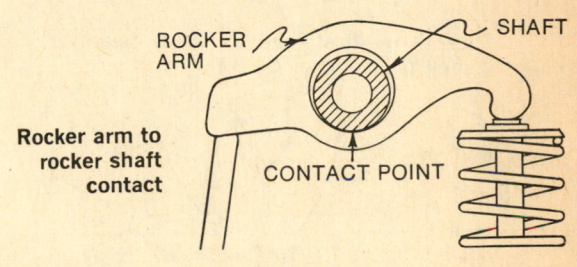

Rocker arm to rocker shaft contact

Inspect the camshaft bushings and the camshaft (overhead cam engines):

See next section.

Inspect the pushrods:

Remove the pushrods, and, if hollow, clean out the oil passages using fine wire. Roll each pushrod over a piece of clean glass. If a distinct clicking sound is heard as the pushrod rolls, the rod is bent, and must be replaced.

* The length of all pushrods must be equal. Measure the length of the pushrods, compare to specifications, and replace as necessary.

Inspect the valve lifters:

Remove lifters from their bores, and remove gum and varnish, using solvent. Clean walls of lifter bores. Check lifters for concave wear as illustrated. If face is worn concave, replace lifter, and carefully inspect the camshaft. Lightly lubricate lifter and insert it into its bore. If play is excessive, an oversize lifter must be installed (where possible). Consult a machinist concerning feasibility. If play is satisfactory, remove, lubricate, and reinstall the lifter.

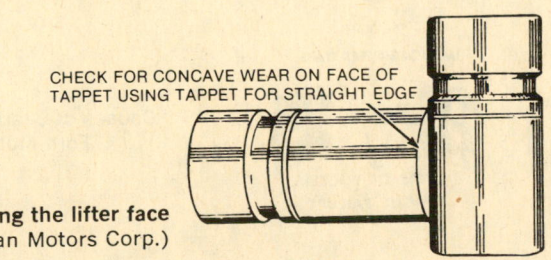

CHECK FOR CONCAVE WEAR ON FACE OF TAPPET USING TAPPET FOR STRAIGHT EDGE

Checking the lifter face
(© American Motors Corp.)

* Testing hydraulic lifter leak down:

Submerge lifter in a container of kerosene. Chuck a used pushrod or its equivalent into a drill press. Position container of kerosene so pushrod acts on the lifter plunger. Pump lifter with the drill press, until resistance increases. Pump several more times to bleed any air out of lifter. Apply very firm, constant pressure to the lifter, and observe rate at which fluid bleeds out of lifter. If the fluid bleeds very quickly (less than 15 seconds), lifter is defective. If the time exceeds 60 seconds, lifter is sticking. In either case, recondition or replace lifter. If lifter is operating properly (leak down time 15-60 seconds), lubricate and install it.

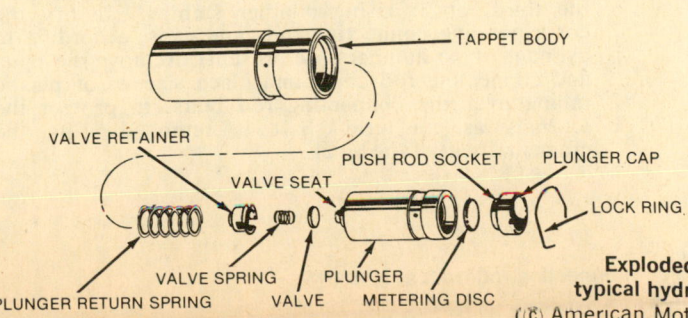

Exploded view of a typical hydraulic lifter
(© American Motors Corp.)

CYLINDER BLOCK RECONDITIONING

Procedure	*Method*

Checking the main bearing clearance:

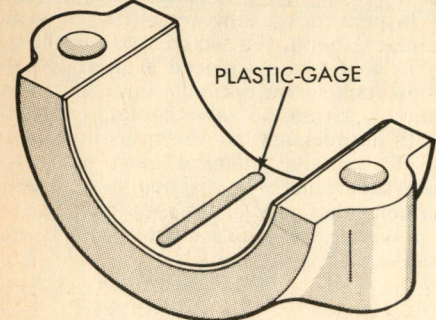

Installing Plastigage on lower bearing shell (© Chrysler Corp.)

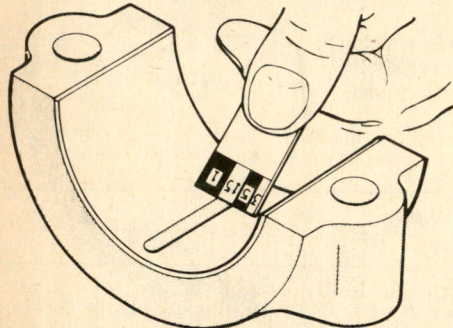

Measuring Plastigage to determine bearing clearance (© Chrysler Corp.)

Invert engine, and remove cap from the bearing to be checked. Using a clean, dry rag, thoroughly clean all oil from crankshaft journal and bearing insert. NOTE: *Plastigage is soluble in oil; therefore, oil on the journal or bearing could result in erroneous readings.* Place a piece of Plastigage along the full length of journal, reinstall cap, and torque to specifications. Remove bearing cap, and determine bearing clearance by comparing width of Plastigage to the scale on Plastigage envelope. Journal taper is determined by comparing width of the Plastigage strip near its ends. Rotate crankshaft 90° and retest, to determine journal eccentricity. NOTE: *Do not rotate crankshaft with Plastigage installed.* If bearing insert and journal appear intact, and are within tolerances, no further main bearing service is required. If bearing or journal appear defective, cause of failure should be determined before replacement.

* Remove crankshaft from block (see below). Measure the main bearing journals at each end twice (90° apart) using a micrometer, to determine diameter, journal taper and eccentricity. If journals are within tolerances, reinstall bearing caps at their specified torque. Using a telescope gauge and micrometer, measure bearing I.D. parallel to piston axis and at 30° on each side of piston axis. Subtract journal O.D. from bearing I.D. to determine oil clearance. If crankshaft journals appear defective, or do not meet tolerances, there is no need to measure bearings; for the crankshaft will require grinding and/or undersize bearings will be required. If bearing appears defective, cause for failure should be determined prior to replacement.

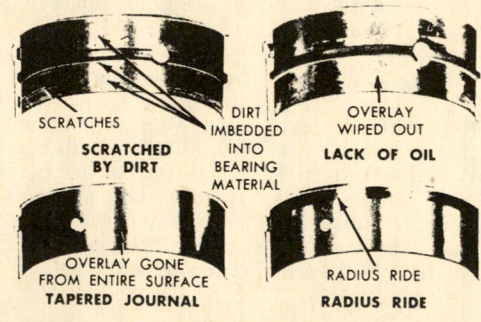

SCRATCHES — DIRT IMBEDDED INTO BEARING MATERIAL
SCRATCHED BY DIRT

OVERLAY WIPED OUT
LACK OF OIL

BRIGHT (POLISHED) SECTIONS
IMPROPER SEATING

OVERLAY GONE FROM ENTIRE SURFACE
TAPERED JOURNAL

RADIUS RIDE
RADIUS RIDE

CRATERS OR POCKETS
FATIGUE FAILURE

Causes of bearing failure (© Ford Motor Co.)

Removing the crankshaft:

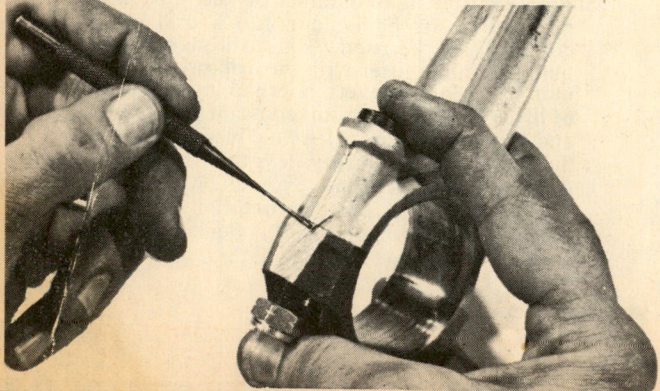

Connecting rod matching marks

Using a punch, mark the corresponding main bearing caps and saddles according to position (i.e., one punch on the front main cap and saddle, two on the second, three on the third, etc.). Using number stamps, identify the corresponding connecting rods and caps, according to cylinder (if no numbers are present). Remove the main and connecting rod caps, and place sleeves of plastic tubing over the connecting rod bolts, to protect the journals as the crankshaft is removed. Lift the crankshaft out of the block.

CYLINDER BLOCK RECONDITIONING

Procedure	Method
Checking the connecting rod bearing clearance:	Connecting rod bearing clearance is checked in the same manner as main bearing clearance, using Plastigage. Before removing the crankshaft, connecting rod side clearance also should be measured and recorded.
	* Checking connecting rod bearing clearance, using a micrometer, is identical to checking main bearing clearance. If no other service is required, the piston and rod assemblies need not be removed.
Remove the ridge from the top of the cylinder:	In order to facilitate removal of the piston and connecting rod, the ridge at the top of the cylinder (unworn area; see illustration) must be removed. Place the piston at the bottom of the bore, and cover it with a rag. Cut the ridge away using a ridge reamer, exercising extreme care to avoid cutting too deeply. Remove the rag, and remove cuttings that remain on the piston. CAUTION: *If the ridge is not removed, and new rings are installed, damage to rings will result.*

RIDGE CAUSED BY CYLINDER WEAR

CYLINDER WALL
TOP OF PISTON

Cylinder bore ridge
(© Pontiac Div. G.M. Corp.)

Procedure	Method
Removing the piston and connecting rod:	Invert the engine, and push the pistons and connecting rods out of the cylinders. If necessary, tap the connecting rod boss with a wooden hammer handle, to force the piston out. CAUTION: *Do not attempt to force the piston past the cylinder ridge* (see above).

Removing the piston

Procedure	Method
Service the crankshaft:	Ensure that all oil holes and passages in the crankshaft are open and free of sludge. If necessary, have the crankshaft ground to the largest possible undersize.
	** Have the crankshaft Magnafluxed, to locate stress cracks. Consult a machinist concerning additional service procedures, such as surface hardening (e.g., nitriding, Tuftriding) to improve wear characteristics, cross drilling and chamfering the oil holes to improve lubrication, and balancing.
Removing freeze plugs:	Drill a hole in the center of the freeze plugs, and pry them out using a screwdriver or drift.
Remove the oil gallery plugs:	Threaded plugs should be removed using an appropriate (usually square) wrench. To remove soft, pressed in plugs, drill a hole in the plug, and thread in a sheet metal screw. Pull the plug out by the screw using pliers.
Hot-tank the block:	Have the block hot-tanked to remove grease, corrosion, and scale from the water jackets. NOTE: *Consult the operator to determine whether the camshaft bearings will be damaged during the hot-tank process.*

CYLINDER BLOCK RECONDITIONING

Procedure	Method
Check the block for cracks:	Visually inspect the block for cracks or chips. The most common locations are as follows: Adjacent to freeze plugs. Between the cylinders and water jackets. Adjacent to the main bearing saddles. At the extreme bottom of the cylinders. Check only suspected cracks using spot check dye (see introduction). If a crack is located, consult a machinist concerning possible repairs.
	** Magnaflux the block to locate hidden cracks. If cracks are located, consult a machinist about feasibility of repair.
Install the oil gallery plugs and freeze plugs:	Coat freeze plugs with sealer and tap into position using a piece of pipe, slightly smaller than the plug, as a driver. To ensure retention, stake the edges of the plugs. Coat threaded oil gallery plugs with sealer and install. Drive replacement soft plugs into block using a large drift as a driver.
	* Rather than reinstalling lead plugs, drill and tap the holes, and install threaded plugs.
Check the bore diameter and surface:	Visually inspect the cylinder bores for roughness, scoring, or scuffing. If evident, the cylinder bore must be bored or honed oversize to eliminate imperfections, and the smallest possible oversize piston used. The new pistons should be given to the machinist with the block, so that the cylinders can be bored or honed exactly to the piston size (plus clearance). If no flaws are evident, measure the bore diameter using a telescope gauge and micrometer, or dial guage, parallel and perpendicular to the engine centerline, at the top (below the ridge) and bottom of the bore. Subtract the bottom measurements from the top to determine taper, and the parallel to the centerline measurements from the perpendicular measurements to determine eccentricity. If the measurements are not within specifications, the cylinder must be bored or honed, and an oversize piston installed. If the measurements are within specifications the cylinder may be used as is, with only finish honing (see below). NOTE: *Prior to submitting the block for boring, perform the following operation(s).*

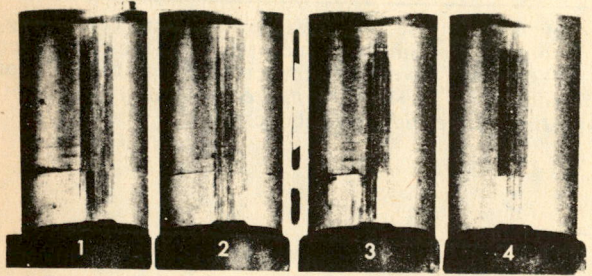

1, 2, 3 Piston skirt seizure resulted in this pattern. Engine must be rebored

4. Piston skirt and oil ring seizure caused this damage. Engine must be rebored

Cylinder wall damage (© Daimler-Benz A.G.)

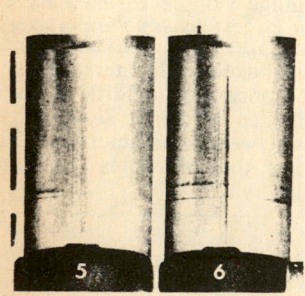

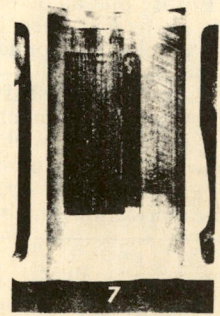

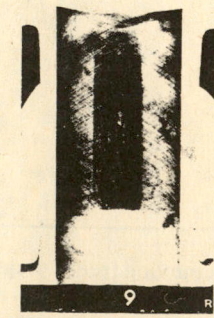

5, 6 Score marks caused by a split piston skirt. Damage is not serious enough to warrant reboring

7. Ring seized longitudinally, causing a score mark 1 3/16" wide, on the land side of the piston groove. The honing pattern is destroyed and the cylinder must be rebored

8. Result of oil ring seizure. Engine must be rebored

9. Oil ring seizure here was not serious enough to warrant reboring. The honing marks are still visible

Cylinder wall damage
(© Daimler-Benz A.G.)

CYLINDER BLOCK RECONDITIONING

Procedure	Method

Check the bore diameter and surface:

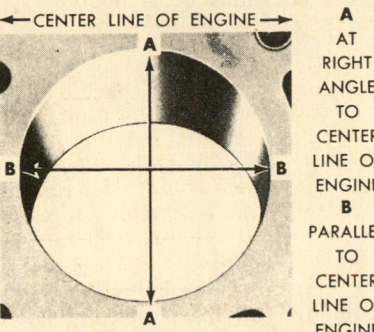

A AT RIGHT ANGLE TO CENTER LINE OF ENGINE

B PARALLEL TO CENTER LINE OF ENGINE

Cylinder bore measuring positions
(ⓒ Ford Motor Co.)

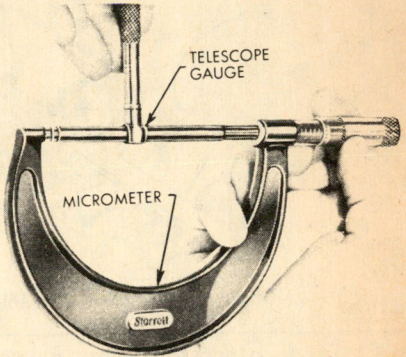

TELESCOPE GAUGE 90° FROM PISTON PIN

TELESCOPE GAUGE

MICROMETER

Measuring the cylinder bore with a telescope gauge
(ⓒ Buick Div. G.M. Corp.)

Determining the cylinder bore by measuring the telescope gauge with a micrometer
(ⓒ Buick Div. G.M. Corp.)

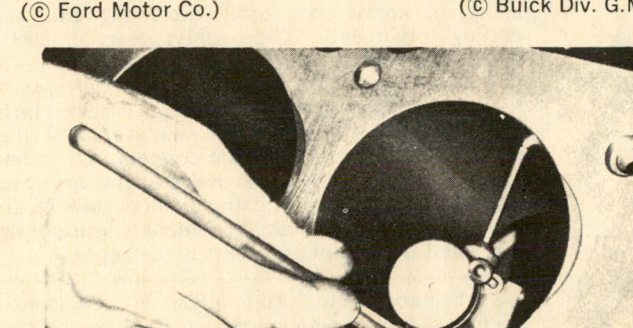

Measuring the cylinder bore with a dial gauge
(ⓒ Chevrolet Div. G.M. Corp.)

Check the block deck for warpage:

Using a straightedge and feeler gauges, check the block deck for warpage in the same manner that the cylinder head is checked (see Cylinder Head Reconditioning). If warpage exceeds specifications, have the deck resurfaced. NOTE: *In certain cases a specification for total material removal (Cylinder head and block deck) is provided. This specification must not be exceeded.*

* Check the deck height:

The deck height is the distance from the crankshaft centerline to the block deck. To measure, invert the engine, and install the crankshaft, retaining it with the center main cap. Measure the distance from the crankshaft journal to the block deck, parallel to the cylinder centerline. Measure the diameter of the end (front and rear) main journals, parallel to the centerline of the cylinders, divide the diameter in half, and subtract it from the previous measurement. The results of the front and rear measurements should be identical. If the difference exceeds .005″, the deck height should be corrected. NOTE: *Block deck height and warpage should be corrected at the same time.*

CYLINDER BLOCK RECONDITIONING

Procedure	*Method*

Check the cylinder block bearing alignment:

Remove the upper bearing inserts. Place a straightedge in the bearing saddles along the centerline of the crankshaft. If clearance exists between the straightedge and the center saddle, the block must be alignbored.

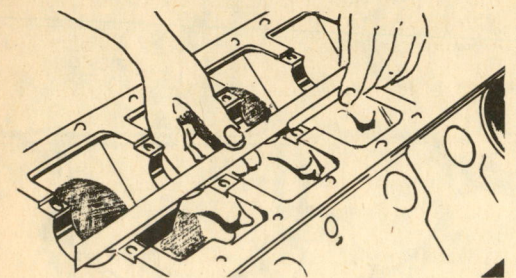

Checking main bearing saddle alignment

Clean and inspect the pistons and connecting rods:

Using a ring expander, remove the rings from the piston. Remove the retaining rings (if so equipped) and remove piston pin. NOTE: *If the piston pin must be pressed out, determine the proper method and use the proper tools; otherwise the piston will distort.* Clean the ring grooves using an appropriate tool, exercising care to avoid cutting too deeply. Thoroughly clean all carbon and varnish from the piston with solvent. CAUTION: *Do not use a wire brush or caustic solvent on pistons.* Inspect the pistons for scuffing, scoring, cracks, pitting, or excessive ring groove wear. If wear is evident, the piston must be replaced. Check the connecting rod length by measuring the rod from the inside of the large end to the inside of the small end using calipers (see illustration). All connecting rods should be equal length. Replace any rod that differs from the others in the engine.

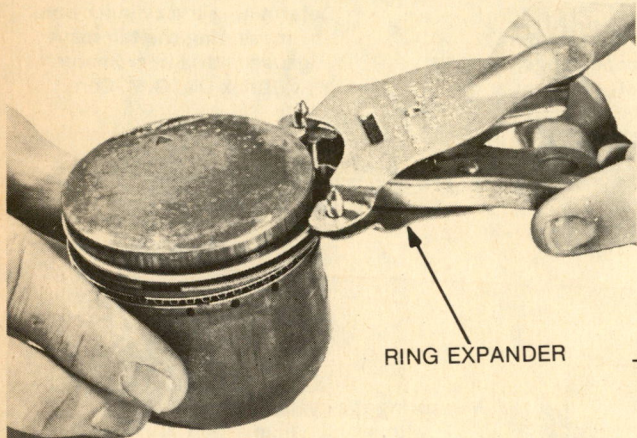

RING EXPANDER

* Have the connecting rod alignment checked in an alignment fixture by a machinist. Replace any twisted or bent rods.

* Magnaflux the connecting rods to locate stress cracks. If cracks are found, replace the connecting rod.

Removing the piston rings

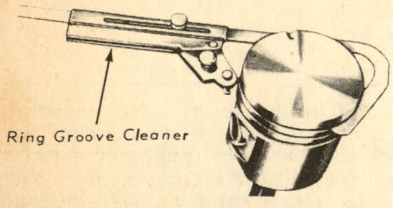

Ring Groove Cleaner

Cleaning the piston ring grooves
(© Ford Motor Co.)

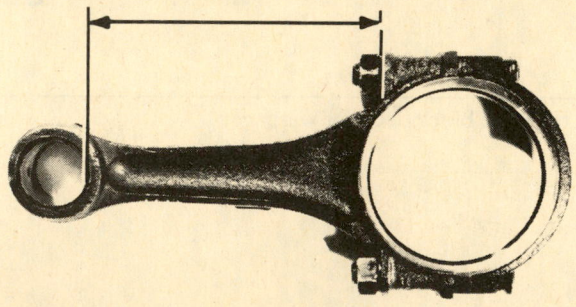

Connecting rod length checking dimension

Fit the pistons to the cylinders:

Using a telescope gauge and micrometer, or a dial gauge, measure the cylinder bore diameter perpendicular to the piston pin, $2\frac{1}{2}''$ below the deck. Measure the piston perpendicular to its pin on the skirt. The difference between the two measurements is the piston clearance. If the clearance is within specifications or slightly below (after boring or honing), finish honing is all that is required. If the clearance is excessive, try to obtain a slightly larger piston to bring clearance within specifications. Where this is not possible, obtain the first oversize piston, and hone (or if necessary, bore) the cylinder to size.

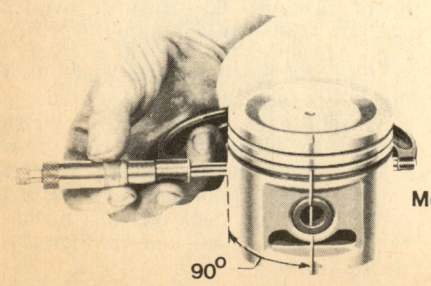

90°

Measuring the piston for fitting
(© Buick Div. G.M. Corp.)

CYLINDER BLOCK RECONDITIONING

Procedure	Method

Assemble the pistons and connecting rods:

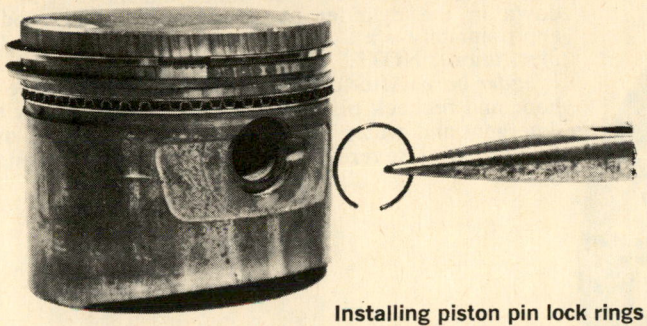

Installing piston pin lock rings

Inspect piston pin, connecting rod small end bushing, and piston bore for galling, scoring, or excessive wear. If evident, replace defective part(s). Measure the I.D. of the piston boss and connecting rod small end, and the O.D. of the piston pin. If within specifications, assemble piston pin and rod. CAUTION: *If piston pin must be pressed in, determine the proper method and use the proper tools; otherwise the piston will distort.* Install the lock rings; ensure that they seat properly. If the parts are not within specifications, determine the service method for the type of engine. In some cases, piston and pin are serviced as an assembly when either is defective. Others specify reaming the piston and connecting rods for an oversize pin. If the connecting rod bushing is worn, it may in many cases be replaced. Reaming the piston and replacing the rod bushing are machine shop operations.

Clean and inspect the camshaft:

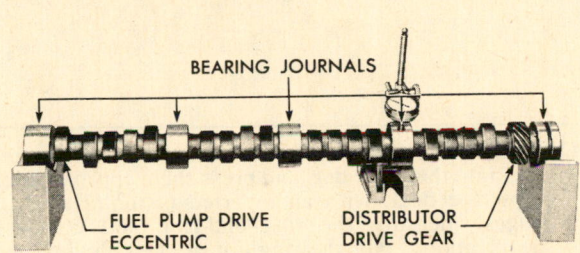

BEARING JOURNALS

FUEL PUMP DRIVE ECCENTRIC

DISTRIBUTOR DRIVE GEAR

Checking the camshaft for straightness
(© Chevrolet Motor Div. G.M. Corp.)

Degrease the camshaft, using solvent, and clean out all oil holes. Visually inspect cam lobes and bearing journals for excessive wear. If a lobe is questionable, check all lobes as indicated below. If a journal or lobe is worn, the camshaft must be reground or replaced. NOTE: *If a journal is worn, there is a good chance that the bushings are worn.* If lobes and journals appear intact, place the front and rear journals in V-blocks, and rest a dial indicator on the center journal. Rotate the camshaft to check straightness. If deviation exceeds .001″, replace the camshaft.

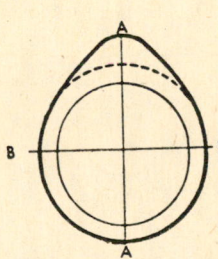

Camshaft lobe measurement
(© Ford Motor Co.)

* Check the camshaft lobes with a micrometer, by measuring the lobes from the nose to base and again at 90° (see illustration). The lift is determined by subtracting the second measurement from the first. If all exhaust lobes and all intake lobes are not identical, the camshaft must be reground or replaced.

Replace the camshaft bearings:

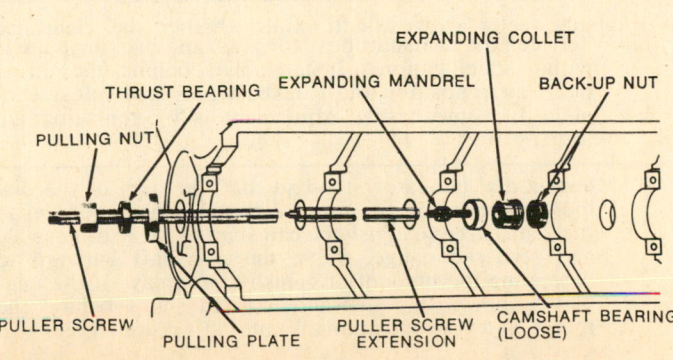

EXPANDING COLLET

THRUST BEARING   EXPANDING MANDREL   BACK-UP NUT

PULLING NUT

PULLER SCREW   PULLING PLATE   PULLER SCREW EXTENSION   CAMSHAFT BEARING (LOOSE)

Camshaft removal and installation tool (typical)
(© Ford Motor Co.)

If excessive wear is indicated, or if the engine is being completely rebuilt, camshaft bearings should be replaced as follows: Drive the camshaft rear plug from the block. Assemble the removal puller with its shoulder on the bearing to be removed. Gradually tighten the puller nut until bearing is removed. Remove remaining bearings, leaving the front and rear for last. To remove front and rear bearings, reverse position of the tool, so as to pull the bearings in toward the center of the block. Leave the tool in this position, pilot the new front and rear bearings on the installer, and pull them into position: Return the tool to its original position and pull remaining bearings into position. NOTE: *Ensure that oil holes align when installing bearings.* Replace camshaft rear plug, and stake it into position to aid retention.

CYLINDER BLOCK RECONDITIONING

Procedure	*Method*

Finish hone the cylinders:

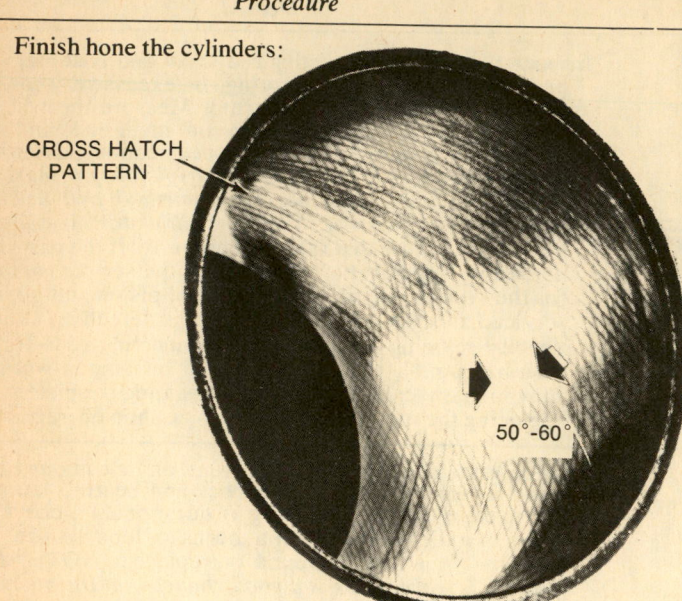

CROSS HATCH
PATTERN

50°-60°

Finish honed cylinder
(© Chrysler Corp.)

Chuck a flexible drive hone into a power drill, and insert it into the cylinder. Start the hone, and move it up and down in the cylinder at a rate which will produce approximately a 60° cross-hatch pattern (see illustration). NOTE: *Do not extend the hone below the cylinder bore.* After developing the pattern, remove the hone and recheck piston fit. Wash the cylinders with a detergent and water solution to remove abrasive dust, dry, and wipe several times with a rag soaked in engine oil.

Check piston ring end-gap:

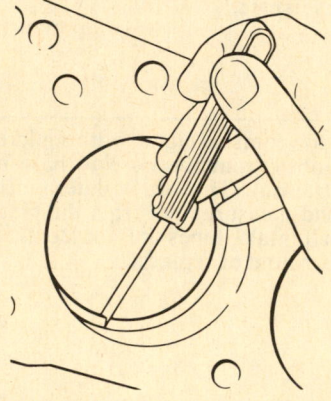

Checking ring end-gap
(© Outboard Marine Corp.)

Compress the piston rings to be used in a cylinder, one at a time, into that cylinder, and press them approximately 1" below the deck with an inverted piston. Using feeler gauges, measure the ring end-gap, and compare to specifications. Pull the ring out of the cylinder and file the ends with a fine file to obtain proper clearance. CAUTION: *If inadequate ring end-gap is utilized, ring breakage will result.*

Install the camshaft:

Liberally lubricate the camshaft lobes and journals, and slide the camshaft into the block. CAUTION: *Exercise extreme care to avoid damaging the bearings when inserting the camshaft.* Install and tighten the camshaft thrust plate retaining bolts.

Check camshaft end-play:

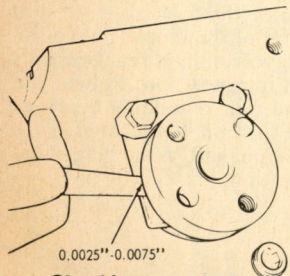

0.0025"-0.0075"
**Checking camshaft
end-play with a
feeler gauge**

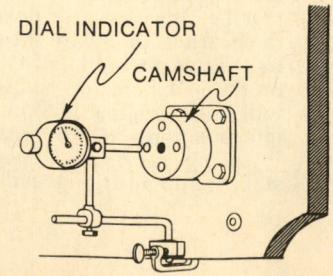

DIAL INDICATOR

CAMSHAFT

**Checking camshaft end-play with a
dial indicator**

(© Outboard Marine Corp.)

Using feeler gauges, determine whether the clearance between the camshaft boss (or gear) and backing plate is within specifications. Install shims behind the thrust plate, or reposition the camshaft gear and retest end-play. In some cases, adjustment is by replacing the thrust plate.

---

* Mount a dial indicator stand so that the stem of the dial indicator rests on the nose of the camshaft, parallel to the camshaft axis. Push the camshaft as far in as possible and zero the gauge. Move the camshaft outward to determine the amount of camshaft endplay. If the end-play is not within tolerance, install shims behind the thrust plate, or reposition the camshaft gear and retest.

CYLINDER BLOCK RECONDITIONING

Procedure	Method

Install the piston rings:

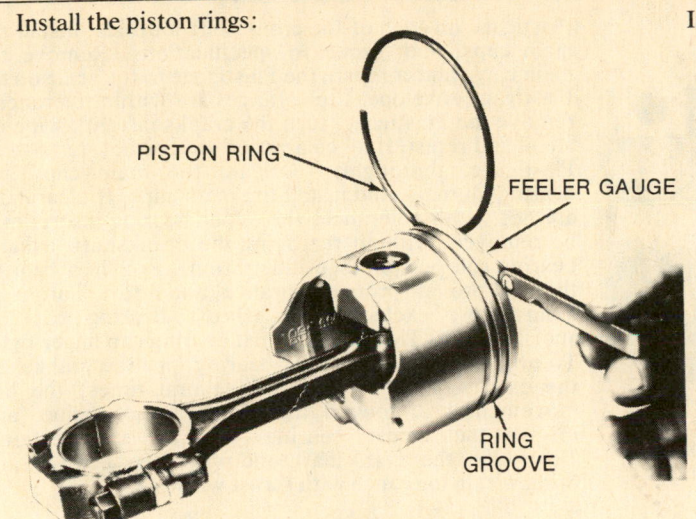

PISTON RING

FEELER GAUGE

RING GROOVE

Inspect the ring grooves in the piston for excessive wear or taper. If necessary, recut the groove(s) for use with an overwidth ring or a standard ring and spacer. If the groove is worn uniformly, overwidth rings, or standard rings and spacers may be installed without recutting. Roll the outside of the ring around the groove to check for burrs or deposits. If any are found, remove with a fine file. Hold the ring in the groove, and measure side clearance. If necessary, correct as indicated above. NOTE: *Always install any additional spacers above the piston ring.* The ring groove must be deep enough to allow the ring to seat below the lands (see illustration). In many cases, a "go-no-go" depth gauge will be provided with the piston rings. Shallow grooves may be corrected by recutting, while deep grooves require some type of filler or expander behind the piston. Consult the piston ring supplier concerning the suggested method. Install the rings on the piston, lowest ring first, using a ring expander. NOTE: *Position the ring markings as specified by the manufacturer (see car section).*

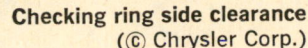

Checking ring side clearance
(© Chrysler Corp.)

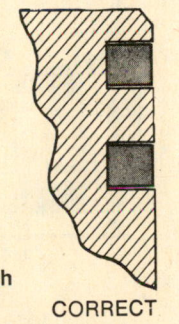 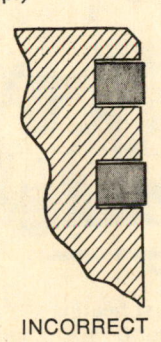

Piston groove depth

CORRECT   INCORRECT

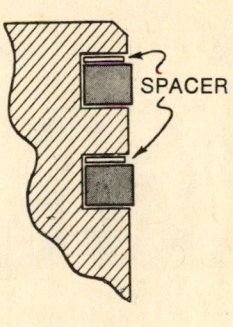

SPACER

Correct ring spacer installation

Install the rear main seal (where applicable):

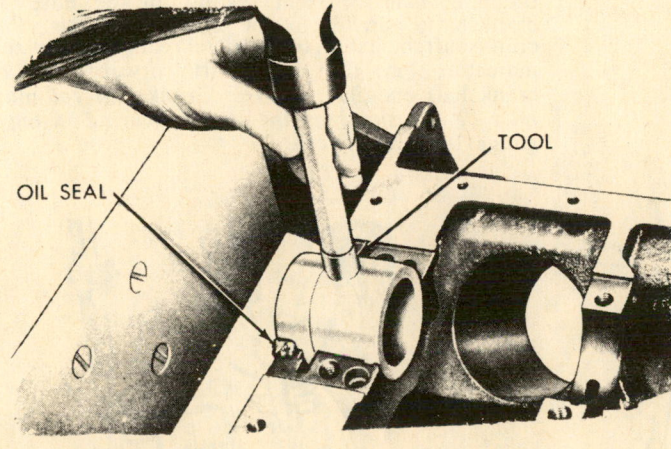

OIL SEAL

TOOL

Seating the rear main seal

Position the block with the bearing saddles facing upward. Lay the rear main seal in its groove and press it lightly into its seat. Place a piece of pipe the same diameter as the crankshaft journal into the saddle, and firmly seat the seal. Hold the pipe in position, and trim the ends of the seal flush if required.

Install the crankshaft:

Thoroughly clean the main bearing saddles and caps. Place the upper halves of the bearing inserts on the saddles and press into position. NOTE: *Ensure that the oil holes align.* Press the corresponding bearing inserts into the main bearing caps. Lubricate the upper main bearings, and lay the crankshaft in position. Place a strip of

CYLINDER BLOCK RECONDITIONING

Procedure	Method

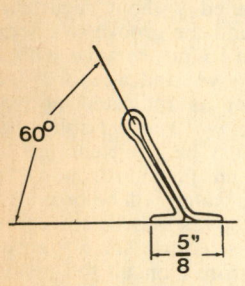

Home made bearing roll-out pin
(© Pontiac Div. G.M. Corp.)

INSTALLING BEARING SHELL

REMOVING BEARING SHELL

Removal and installation of upper bearing insert using a roll-out pin
(© Buick Div. G.M. Corp.)

Plastigage on each of the crankshaft journals, install the main caps, and torque to specifications. Remove the main caps, and compare the Plastigage to the scale on the Plastigage envelope. If clearances are within tolerances, remove the Plastigage, turn the crankshaft 90°, wipe off all oil and retest. If all clearances are correct, remove all Plastigage, thoroughly lubricate the main caps and bearing journals, and install the main caps. If clearances are not within tolerance, the upper bearing inserts may be removed, without removing the crankshaft, using a bearing roll out pin (see illustration). Roll in a bearing that will provide proper clearance, and retest. Torque all main caps, excluding the thrust bearing cap, to specifications. Tighten the thrust bearing cap finger tight. To properly align the thrust bearing, pry the crankshaft the extent of its axial travel several times, the last movement held toward the front of the engine, and torque the thrust bearing cap to specifications. Determine the crankshaft end-play (see below), and bring within tolerance with thrust washers.

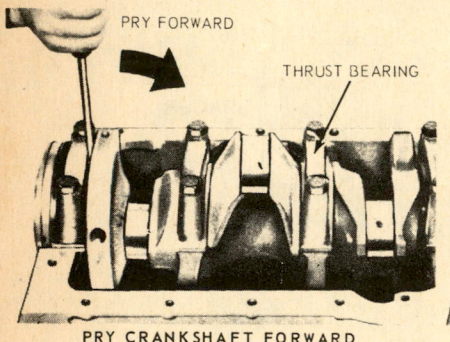

PRY FORWARD

THRUST BEARING

PRY CRANKSHAFT FORWARD

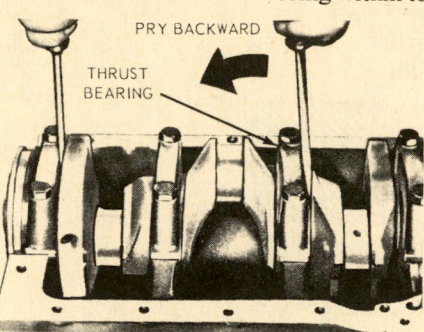

PRY BACKWARD

THRUST BEARING

PRY CAP BACKWARD

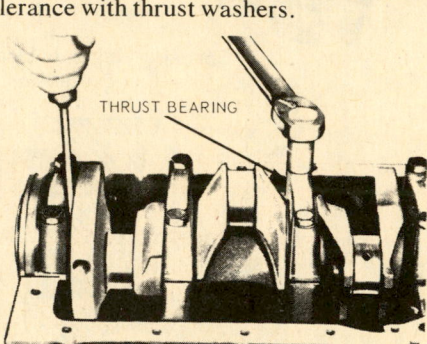

THRUST BEARING

TIGHTEN CAP

Aligning the thrust bearing
(© Ford Motor Co.)

Measure crankshaft end-play:

Mount a dial indicator stand on the front of the block, with the dial indicator stem resting on the nose of the crankshaft, parallel to the crankshaft axis. Pry the crankshaft the extent of its travel rearward, and zero the indicator. Pry the crankshaft forward and record crankshaft end-play. NOTE: *Crankshaft end-play also may be measured at the thrust bearing, using feeler gauges* (see illustration).

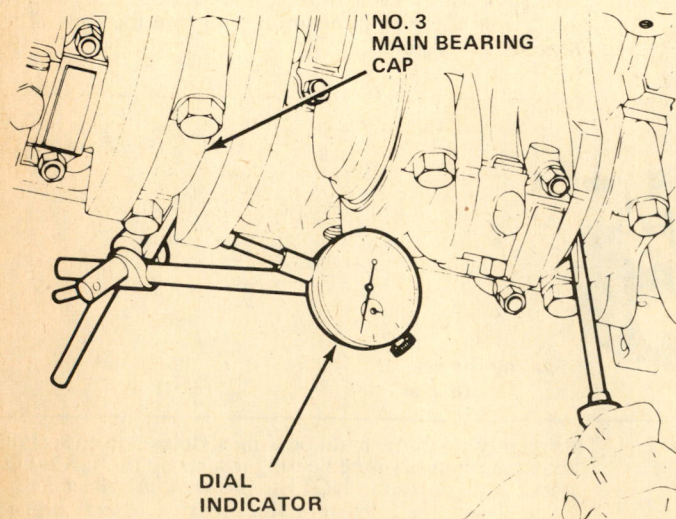

NO. 3 MAIN BEARING CAP

DIAL INDICATOR

Checking crankshaft end-play with a dial indicator

Checking crankshaft end-play with a feeler gauge

CYLINDER BLOCK RECONDITIONING

Procedure	Method

Install the pistons:

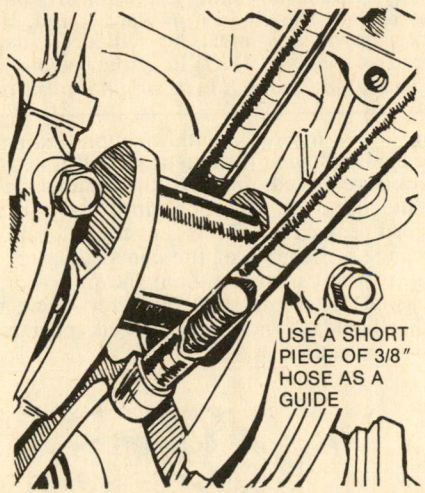

USE A SHORT PIECE OF 3/8″ HOSE AS A GUIDE

Tubing used as guide when installing a piston

Installing a piston

Press the upper connecting rod bearing halves into the connecting rods, and the lower halves into the connecting rod caps. Position the piston ring gaps according to specifications (see car section), and lubricate the pistons. Install a ring compresser on a piston, and press two long (8″) pieces of plastic tubing over the rod bolts. Using the tubes as a guide, press the pistons into the bores and onto the crankshaft with a wooden hammer handle. After seating the rod on the crankshaft journal, remove the tubes and install the cap finger tight. Install the remaining pistons in the same manner. Invert the engine and check the bearing clearance at two points (90° apart) on each journal with Plastigage. NOTE: *Do not turn the crankshaft with Plastigage installed.* If clearance is within tolerances, remove *all* Plastigage, thoroughly lubricate the journals, and torque the rod caps to specifications. If clearance is not within specifications, install different thickness bearing inserts and recheck. CAUTION: *Never shim or file the connecting rods or caps.* Always install plastic tube sleeves over the rod bolts when the caps are not installed, to protect the crankshaft journals.

Check connecting rod side clearance:

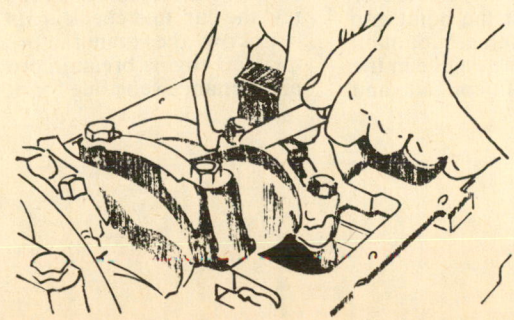

Checking connecting rod side clearance

Determine the clearance between the sides of the connecting rods and the crankshaft, using feeler gauges. If clearance is below the minimum tolerance, the rod may be machined to provide adequate clearance. If clearance is excessive, substitute an unworn rod, and recheck. If clearance is still outside specficiations, the crankshaft must be welded and reground, or replaced.

CYLINDER BLOCK RECONDITIONING

Procedure	Method
Inspect the timing chain:	Visually inspect the timing chain for broken or loose links, and replace the chain if any are found. If the chain will flex sideways, it must be replaced. Install the timing chain as specified. NOTE: *If the original timing chain is to be reused, install it in its original position.*
Check timing gear backlash and runout:	Mount a dial indicator with its stem resting on a tooth of the camshaft gear (as illustrated). Rotate the gear until all slack is removed, and zero the indicator. Rotate the gear in the opposite direction until slack is removed, and record gear backlash. Mount the indicator with its stem resting on the edge of the camshaft gear, parallel to the axis of the camshaft. Zero the indicator, and turn the camshaft gear one full turn, recording the runout. If either backlash or runout exceed specifications, replace the worn gear(s).

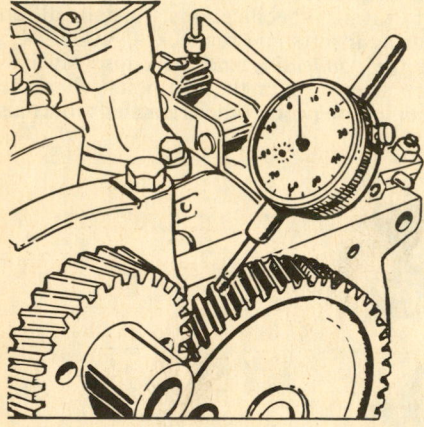

Checking camshaft gear backlash

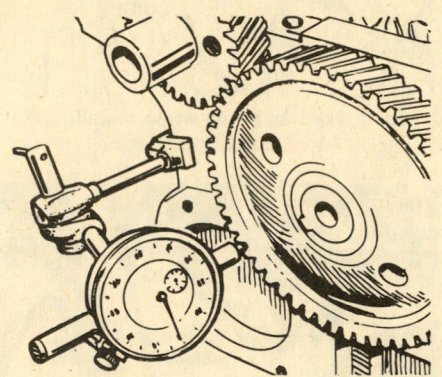

Checking camshaft gear runout

Completing the Rebuilding Process

Following the above procedures, complete the rebuilding process as follows:

Fill the oil pump with oil, to prevent cavitating (sucking air) on initial engine start up. Install the oil pump and the pickup tube on the engine. Coat the oil pan gasket as necessary, and install the gasket and the oil pan. Mount the flywheel and the crankshaft vibration damper or pulley on the crankshaft. NOTE: *Always use new bolts when installing the flywheel.* Inspect the clutch shaft pilot bushing in the crankshaft. If the bushing is excessively worn, remove it with an expanding puller and a slide hammer, and tap a new bushing into place.

Position the engine, cylinder head side up. Lubricate the lifters, and install them into their bores. Install the cylinder head, and torque it as specified in the car section. Insert the pushrods (where applicable), and install the rocker shaft(s) (if so equipped) or position the rocker arms on the pushrods. If solid lifters are utilized, adjust the valves to the "cold" specifications.

Mount the intake and exhaust manifolds, the carburetor(s), the distributor and spark plugs. Adjust the point gap and the static ignition timing. Mount all accessories and install the engine in the car. Fill the radiator with coolant, and the crankcase with high quality engine

Break-in Procedure

Start the engine, and allow it to run at low speed for a few minutes, while checking for leaks. Stop the engine, check the oil level, and fill as necessary. Restart the engine, and fill the cooling system to capactiy. Check the point dwell angle and adjust the ignition timing and the valves. Run the engine at low to medium speed (800-2500 rpm) for approximately ½ hour, and retorque the cylinder head bolts. Road test the car, and check again for leaks.

Follow the manufacturer's recommended engine break-in procedure and maintenance schedule for new engines.

Index

Applicability Chart

| Model | Year | TYPE | |
		3-Spd	4/5 Spd
American Motors	1972	16, 17	18
	1973-74	16	18
	1975-76	4, 16, 19	
	1977-79	4	7, 21
Apollo, Skylark	1973-79	10	
Barracuda, Challenger	1972	1, 2	3
	1973-74	1	3
Buick Special, Century, Skylark, Regal, GS	1972	10	11
	1973-79	10	
Camaro	1972-73	9, 10	11, 12
	1974	9, 10	11, 12, 18
	1975-77	10	12, 18
	1978-79	10	12
Chevelle, Malibu	1972-74	9, 10	11, 12
	1975-77	10	
	1978-79	10	12
Chevette	1976-79		15
Chevrolet	1972-73	9, 10	
Comet, Maverick	1972-77	4	
Corvette	1972-73		11, 12
	1974		11, 12, 18
	1975-76		12, 18
	1977-79		18
Cougar	1972-73	4	8
Dart, Demon, Aspen, Volare, Valiant, Duster	1972-74	1, 2	3
	1975-79	1, 4	3
Dodge, Coronet, Charger, Plymouth, Belvedere, Satellite, Fury	1972	1, 2	3
	1973-74	1	3
	1975-79	1, 4	3
Diplomat, Le Baron	1978-79		3
Fairmont, Zephyr	1978-79	4	5
Ford, Mercury, Montego, Mustang, Torino	1972-75	4	8
Firebird	1972-73	9, 10	11, 12
	1974	9, 10	11, 12, 18
	1975-79	10	12, 18

Applicability Chart

Make	Model	TYPE 3-Spd	TYPE 4/5 Spd
Granada, Monarch	1975-76	4	
	1977	4	8
	1978-79		8
Grand Prix	1978-79	10	
Monte Carlo	1972-74	9	
	1978-79	10	12
Monza, Skyhawk, Starfire, Sunbird	1975-79	10	12, 15, 20
Mustang II	1974-79		7
Nova	1972-74	9, 10	11, 12
	1975-79	10	12
Oldsmobile Cutlass, 4-4-2	1972-73	10	11
	1974-79	10	20
Omega	1973-79	10	20
Omni, Horizon	1978-79		22
Pinto, Bobcat	1972-73 1600cc		6
	1972-79		5
Tempest, GTO, LeMans	1972-74	9, 10	11, 12
Vega, Cosworth Vega, Astre	1972	13	14
	1973-75	10	12
	1976-77	10	15, 20
Ventura, Phoenix	1972-79	10	12, 20

Type Numbers Refer to Sections in Text
See Car Sections for Visual Transmission Model Identification

Section Page Numbers

Transmission	Type	Page No.
Diagnosis		U229
How to Identify a Transmission		U229
Chrysler Corporation		
A-230 Fully Synchronized Chrysler 3-Speed	1	U230
A-390 Fully Synchronized Chrysler 3-Speed	4	U240
A-903, A-250 Chrysler 3-Speed	2	U232
A-833 Chrysler 4-Speed and Overdrive-4	3	U234
A-412 4-Speed Chrysler Transaxle	22	U281
Ford Motor Company		
3.03 Fully Synchronized Ford 3-Speed	4	U240
Ford German 4-Speed, 71WG, 72WG, 75WT, 77ET, 78E	5	U243
Ford British 4-Speed, 71WG, 72WG	6	U246
Ford RAD 4-Speed	7	U248
Ford 4-Speed, 4-Speed Overdrive	8	U251

Transmission	Type	Page No.
General Motors Corporation		
Muncie Fully Synchronized 3-Speed	9	U254
Saginaw Fully Synchronized 3-Speed	10	U256
Muncie 4-Speed	11	U258
Saginaw 4-Speed	12	U260
Vega 3-Speed	13	U260
Vega 4-Speed	14	U264
70 mm. 4-Speed	15	U266
Warner Gear, American Motors		
Warner T-14, T-15 Fully Synchronized 3-Speed	16	U268
Warner T-96 3-Speed	17	U270
AMC 150T Fully Synchronized 3-Speed	4	U240
Warner T-10 4-Speed	18	U271
AMC Overdrive	19	U273
Warner T-50 5-Speed	20	U276
Warner SR4 4-Speed	7	U248
AMC HR1 4-Speed	21	U279

Manual Transmissions

DIAGNOSIS

Jumping out of High Gear

1. Misalignment of transmission case or clutch housing.
2. Worn pilot bearing in crankshaft.
3. Bent transmission shaft.
4. Worn high speed sliding gear.
5. Worn teeth in clutch shaft.
6. Insufficient spring tension on shifter rail plunger.
7. Bent or loose shifter fork.
8. End-play in clutch shaft.
9. Gears not engaging completely.
10. Loose or worn bearings on clutch shaft or mainshaft.

Sticking in High Gear

1. Clutch not releasing fully.
2. Burred or battered teeth on clutch shaft.
3. Burred or battered transmission main-shaft.
4. Frozen synchronizing clutch.
5. Stuck shifter rail plunger.
6. Gearshift lever twisting and binding shifter rail.
7. Battered teeth on high speed sliding gear or on sleeve.
8. Lack of lubrication.
9. Improper lubrication.
10. Corroded transmission parts.
11. Defective mainshaft pilot bearing.

Jumping out of Second Gear

1. Insufficient spring tension on shifter rail plunger.
2. Bent or loose shifter fork.
3. Gears not engaging completely.
4. End-play in transmission main-shaft.
5. Loose transmission gear bearing.
6. Defective mainshaft pilot bearing.
7. Bent transmission shaft.
8. Worn teeth on second speed sliding gear or sleeve.
9. Loose or worn bearings on transmission mainshaft.
10. End-play in countershaft.

Sticking in Second Gear

1. Clutch not releasing fully.

2. Burred or battered teeth on sliding sleeve.
3. Burred or battered transmission main-shaft.
4. Frozen synchronizing clutch.
5. Stuck shifter rail plunger.
6. Gearshift lever twisting and binding shifter rail.
7. Lack of lubrication.
8. Second speed transmission gear bearings locked will give same effect as gears stuck in second.
9. Improper lubrication.
10. Corroded transmission parts.

Jumping out of Low Gear

1. Gears not engaging completely
2. Bent or loose shifter fork.
3. End-play in transmission main-shaft.
4. End-play countershaft.
5. Loose or worn bearings on transmission mainshaft.
6. Loose or worn bearings in countershaft.
7. Defective mainshaft pilot bearing.

Sticking in Low Gear

1. Clutch not releasing fully.
2. Burred or battered transmission main-shaft.
3. Stuck shifter rail plunger.
4. Gearshift lever twisting and binding shifter rail.
5. Lack of lubrication.
6. Improper lubrication.
7. Corroded transmission parts.

Jumping out of Reverse Gear

1. Insufficient spring tension on shifter rail plunger.
2. Bent or loose shifter fork.
3. Badly worn gear teeth.
4. Gears not engaging completely.
5. End-play in transmission main-shaft.
6. Idler gear bushings loose or worn.
7. Loose or worn bearings on transmission mainshaft.
8. Defective mainshaft pilot bearing.

Sticking in Reverse Gear

1. Clutch not releasing fully.
2. Burred or battered transmission main-shaft.
3. Stuck shifter rail plunger.
4. Gearshift lever twisting and binding shifter rail.
5. Lack of lubrication.
6. Improper lubrication.
7. Corroded transmission parts.

Failure of Gears to Synchronize

1. Binding pilot bearing on mainshaft, will synchronize in high gear only.
2. Clutch not releasing fully.
3. Detent springs weak or broken.
4. Weak or broken springs under balls in sliding gear sleeve.
5. Binding bearing on clutch shaft.
6. Binding countershaft.
7. Binding pilot bearing in crankshaft.
8. Badly worn gear teeth.
9. Scored or worn cones.
10. Improper lubrication.
11. Constant mesh gear not turning freely on transmission mainshaft. Will synchronize in that gear only.

Gears Spinning When Shifting into Gear from Neutral

1. Clutch not releasing fully.
2. In some cases an extremely light lubricant in transmission will cause gears to continue to spin for a short time after clutch is released.
3. Binding pilot bearing in crankshaft.

--- CAUTION ---

Care must be exercised during the disassembly and assembly of manual transmissions due to the usage of metric nuts and bolts. The proper wrenches and sockets should be used to avoid damage to the transmission and fasteners. Do not attempt to interchange metric threaded fasteners with U.S. Fine or Standard fasteners as damage can result.

How to Identify a Transmission

First, find the make and year of car in the Applicability Chart. Look in the appropriate column, 3-Speed or 4/5-Speed, to find which transmissions may have been used in that car. Next, go to the Section Page Numbers listing and note the page numbers of the overhaul sections for the possible transmission. Check the application listing at the start of each transmission overhaul section to narrow the possibilities down further. An explanation of how to visually identify each individual transmission is in each car section under Manual Transmission.

TYPE-1
A-230 FULLY SYNCHRONIZED
CHRYSLER 3-SPEED

Application
Aspen, 1976-79
Barracuda, 1972-74
Challenger, 1972-74
Charger, 1972-74
Dart, 1972-76
Dodge, 1972-79
Plymouth, 1972-79
Valiant, 1972-76
Volare, 1976-79

DISASSEMBLY

Shift Housing and Mechanism

1. Shift to second gear.
2. Unbolt and remove side cover with shift mechanism.
   If shaft O-ring seals need replacement:
3. Pull shaft forks out of shafts.
4. Remove nuts and operating levers from shafts.
5. Deburr shafts. Remove shafts.

Drive Pinion Retainer and Extension Housing

1. Unbolt pinion bearing retainer from front of transmission case. Remove retainer and gasket. Pry off retainer oil seal.
   For clearance:
2. With a brass drift, tap drive pinion as far forward as possible. Rotate cut away part of second gear next to countershaft gear. Shift second-third synchronizer sleeve forward.
3. Remove speedometer pinion adapter retainer. Work adapter and pinion out of extension housing.
4. Unbolt extension housing. Break

housing loose with plastic hammer and carefully remove.

Idler Gear and Mainshaft

1. Insert dummy shaft in case to push reverse idler shaft and key out of case.
2. Remove dummy shaft and idler gear together to prevent losing rollers.
3. Remove both tanged idler gear thrust washers.
4. Remove mainshaft assembly through rear of case.

Countershaft Gear and Drive Pinion

1. Using a mallet and dummy shaft, tap the countershaft rearward enough to remove key. Drive countershaft out of case, maintaining contact between countershaft and dummy shaft so that washers will not drop out.
2. Lower countershaft gear to bottom of case.
3. Remove snap-ring from pinion bearing outer race (outside front of case).
4. Drive pinion shaft into case with plastic hammer. Remove assembly through rear of case.
5. If bearing is to be replaced, remove snap-ring and press off bearing.
6. Lift countershaft gear and dummy shaft out through rear of case.

Mainshaft

1. Remove snap-ring from front end of mainshaft along with second gear stop ring. Remove the synchronizer and second gear from mainshaft.

2. Spread snap-ring in mainshaft bearing retainer. Slide retainer back off the bearing race.
3. Remove snap-ring at rear of mainshaft. Support front side of reverse gear. Press bearing off mainshaft. Be careful not to let parts drop when bearing clears shaft.
4. Remove from press. Remove mainshaft bearing and reverse gear from shaft.
5. Remove snap-ring from rear of shaft. Slide first-reverse synchronizer assembly off splines and remove rearward. Remove stop-ring and first gear through the rear.

ASSEMBLY

Countershaft Gear

1. Slide dummy shaft into countershaft gear.
2. Slide one roller thrust washer over dummy shaft and into gear, followed by 22 greased rollers.
3. Repeat Step 2, adding one roller thrust washer on end.
4. Repeat steps 2 and 3 at other end of countershaft gear. There is a total of 88 rollers and 6 thrust washers.
5. Place greased front thrust washer on dummy shaft against gear with tangs forward.
6. Grease rear thrust washer and stick it in place in the case, with tangs rearward. Place countershaft gear assembly in bottom of transmission case until drive pinion is installed.

Pinion Gear

1. Press new bearing on pinion shaft with snap-ring groove forward. Install new snap-ring.

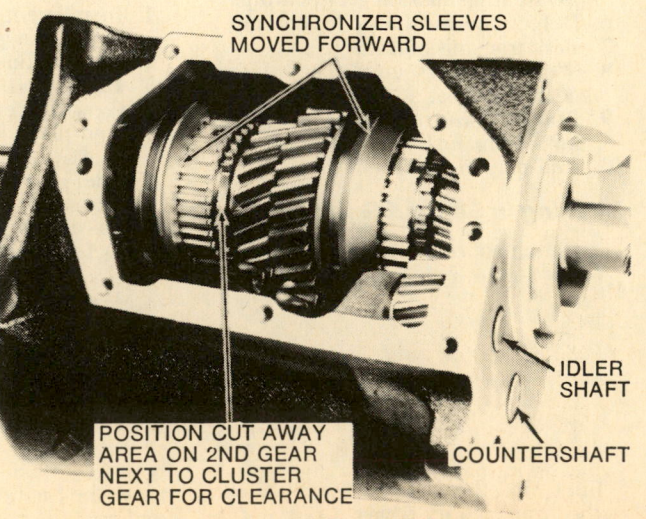

TYPICAL SHIFT LEVER

SPEEDOMETER DRIVE ASSEMBLY

BACK-UP LIGHT SWITCH

DRIVE PINION RETAINER

FILL PLUG

IDENTIFICATION NUMBER PAD

DRAIN PLUG

Side views of A-230 transmission
(© Chrysler Corp)

SYNCHRONIZER SLEEVES MOVED FORWARD

IDLER SHAFT

COUNTERSHAFT

POSITION CUT AWAY AREA ON 2ND GEAR NEXT TO CLUSTER GEAR FOR CLEARANCE

Positioning second gear and shift sleeves for clearance
(© Chrysler Corp)

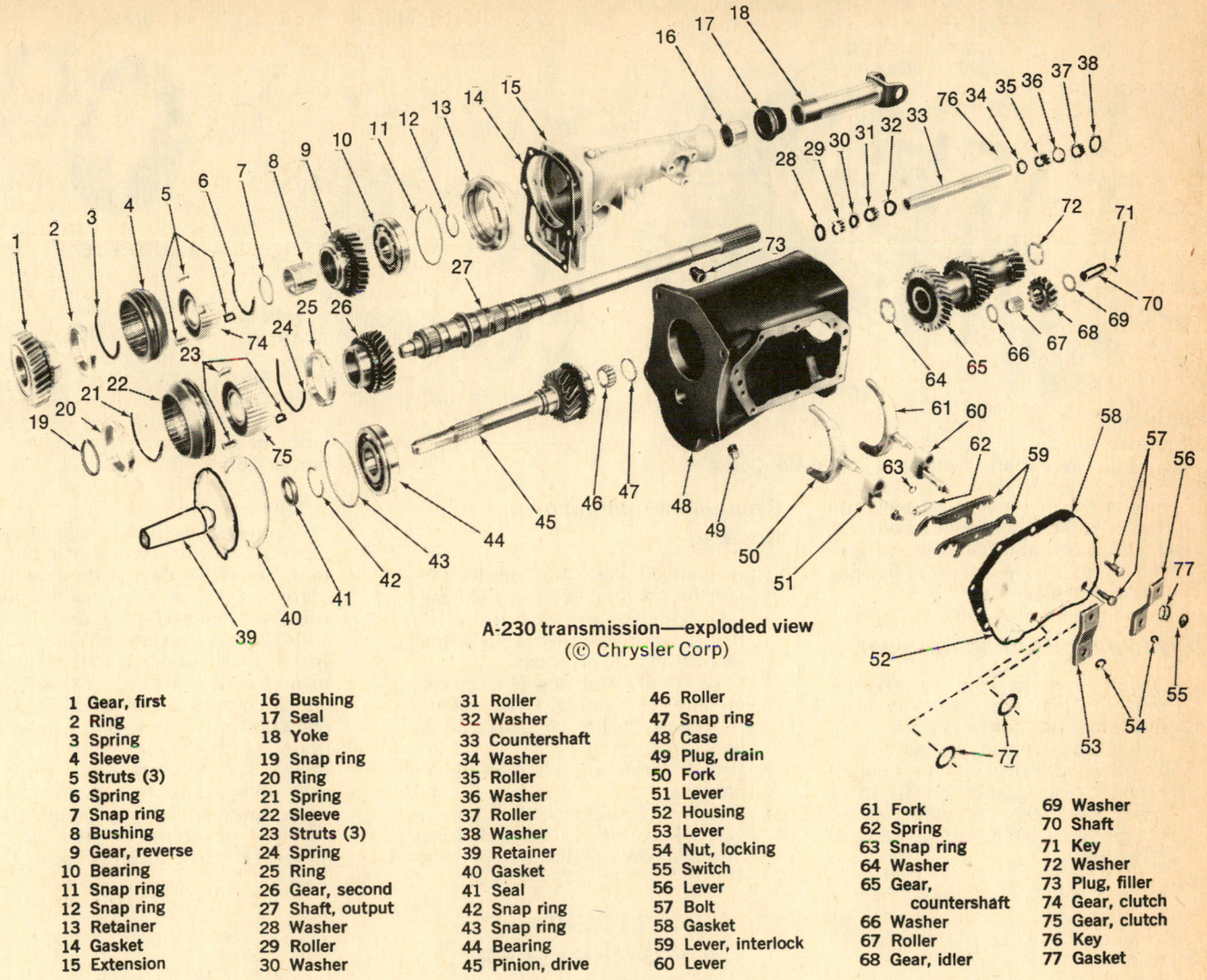

A-230 transmission—exploded view
(© Chrysler Corp)

1 Gear, first	16 Bushing	31 Roller	46 Roller		61 Fork	69 Washer
2 Ring	17 Seal	32 Washer	47 Snap ring		62 Spring	70 Shaft
3 Spring	18 Yoke	33 Countershaft	48 Case		63 Snap ring	71 Key
4 Sleeve	19 Snap ring	34 Washer	49 Plug, drain		64 Washer	72 Washer
5 Struts (3)	20 Ring	35 Roller	50 Fork		65 Gear,	73 Plug, filler
6 Spring	21 Spring	36 Washer	51 Lever		countershaft	74 Gear, clutch
7 Snap ring	22 Sleeve	37 Roller	52 Housing		66 Washer	75 Gear, clutch
8 Bushing	23 Struts (3)	38 Washer	53 Lever		67 Roller	76 Key
9 Gear, reverse	24 Spring	39 Retainer	54 Nut, locking		68 Gear, idler	77 Gasket
10 Bearing	25 Ring	40 Gasket	55 Switch			
11 Snap ring	26 Gear, second	41 Seal	56 Lever			
12 Snap ring	27 Shaft, output	42 Snap ring	57 Bolt			
13 Retainer	28 Washer	43 Snap ring	58 Gasket			
14 Gasket	29 Roller	44 Bearing	59 Lever, interlock			
15 Extension	30 Washer	45 Pinion, drive	60 Lever			

2. Install 15 rollers and retaining ring in drive pinion gear.

3. Install drive pinion and bearing assembly into case.

4. Install the countershaft gear assembly by positioning it and thrust washers so countershaft can be tapped into position. Be careful to keep the countershaft against the dummy shaft to keep parts from falling between them. Install key in countershaft.

5. Tap drive pinion forward for clearance.

Mainshaft

1. Place a stop-ring flat on the bench. Place a clutch gear and a sleeve on top. Drop the struts in their slots and snap in a strut spring placing the tang inside one strut. Turn the assembly over and install second strut spring, tang in a different strut.

2. Slide first gear and stop-ring over rear of mainshaft and against thrust flange between first and second gears on shaft.

3. Slide first-reverse synchronizer assembly over rear of mainshaft, indexing hub slots to first gear stop-ring lugs.

4. Install first-reverse synchronizer clutch gear snap-ring on mainshaft.

5. Slide reverse gear and mainshaft bearing into place. Press bearing on shaft, supporting inner race of bearing. Be sure snap-ring groove on outer race is forward.

6. Install bearing retaining snap-ring on mainshaft. Spread snap-ring in retainer groove and slide it over the bearing. Seat ring in groove. This snap-ring is selected for minimum end play. There are several thicknesses available.

7. Place second gear over front of mainshaft with thrust surface against flange.

8. Install stop-ring and second-third synchronizer assembly against second gear. Install second-third synchronizer clutch gear snap-ring on shaft.

9. Move second-third synchronizer sleeve forward as far as possible. Install front stop-ring, inside the sleeve with lugs indexed to struts.

Coat the stop-ring with grease to hold it in position.

10. Rotate cut-out on second gear toward countershaft gear to provide clearance.

11. Insert mainshaft assembly into case. Tilt assembly to clear cluster gears and insert pilot rollers in drive pinion gear. If assembly is correct, the bearing retainer will bottom to the case without force. If not, check for a misplaced strut, pinion roller, or stop-ring.

Reverse Idler Gear

1. Place dummy shaft into idler gear. Insert 22 greased rollers.

2. Position reverse idler thrust washers in case with grease.

3. Position idler gear and dummy shaft in case. Install idler shaft and key.

Extension Housing

1. Remove extension housing yoke seal. Drive bushing out from inside housing.

2. Align oil hole in bushing with oil

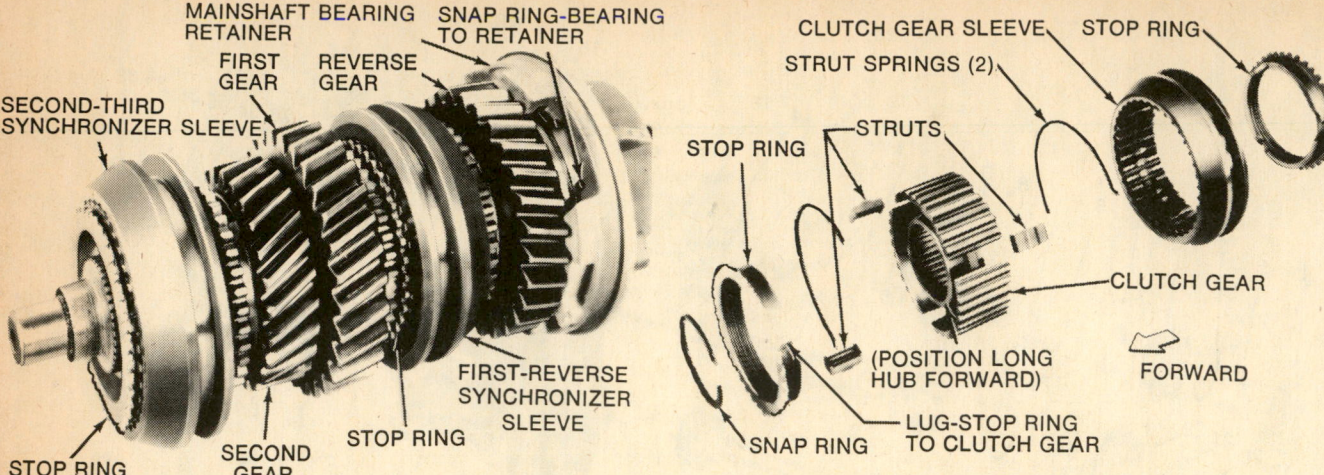

Mainshaft assembly (© Chrysler Corp)

Details of second-third synchronizer (© Chrysler Corp)

slot in housing. Drive bushing into place. Drive new seal into housing.
3. Install extension housing and gasket to hold mainshaft and bearing retainer in place.

Drive Pinion Bearing Retainer

1. Install outer snap-ring on drive pinion bearing. Tap assembly back until snap-ring contacts case.
2. Install a new seal in retainer bore.
3. Position main drive pinion bearing retainer and gasket on front of case. Coat threads with sealing compound, install bolts, torque to 30 ft. lbs.

Gearshift Mechanism and Housing

1. If removed, place two interlock levers on pivot pin with spring hangers offset toward each other, so that spring installs in a straight line. Place E-clip on pivot pin.
2. Grease and install new O-ring seals on both shift shafts. Grease housing bores. Push each shaft into its bore.
3. Install spring on interlock lever hangers.
4. Rotate each shift shaft fork bore to vertical position. Install shift forks through bores and under both interlock levers.
5. Position second-third synchronizer sleeve to rear, in second gear position. Position first-reverse synchronizer sleeve to middle of travel, in neutral position. Place shift forks in the same positions.
6. Install gasket and gearshift mechanism. The bolt with the extra long shoulder must be installed at the center rear of the case. Torque bolts to 15 ft. lbs.
7. Install speedometer drive pinion gear and adapter. Range number on adapter, which represents the number of teeth on the gear, should be in 6 o'clock position.

TYPE-2
A-903 CHRYSLER
3-SPEED

Application (6 cylinder)
Charger/Coronet, 1972
Barracuda, 1972

Dart, 1972
Dodge, 1972
Belvedere/Satellite, 1972

Plymouth, 1972
Valiant, 1972

A-250 CHRYSLER
3-SPEED

Application (6 cylinder)
Dart, 1973-74
Valiant, 1973-74

DISASSEMBLY

1. Remove output shaft yoke.
2. Remove the bolts that attach the extension housing to the transmission case. Remove the housing.
3. Remove extension housing oil seal.
4. Remove the transmission case cover. Measure synchronizer float with feeler gauges on A-903 models. This measurement is taken between the end of a synchronizer pin and the opposite synchronizer

outer ring. This measurement should be .060-.117 in.
5. Remove the attaching bolts and remove the main drive pinion bearing retainer. Then grasp the pinion shaft and pull the assembly out of the case.

── CAUTION ──

Be careful not to bind the inner synchronizer ring on the drive pinion clutch teeth.

6. Remove the snap-ring that locks the main drive pinion bearing onto the pinion shaft. Remove the bearing washer, press the shaft out of

the bearing and remove the oil slinger.
7. Remove the snap-ring from the pilot bearing in the end of the drive pinion and remove the 14 rollers.
8. With the transmission in reverse, remove the outer center bearing snap-ring, then partially remove the mainshaft.
9. Cock the mainshaft, then remove the clutch sleeve, the outer synchronizer rings, the front inner ring and the second-third shift box.
10. Remove clutch gear retaining snap ring and slide the clutch gear off the end of the mainshaft.
11. Slide the second-speed gear, stopring and synchronizer spring off

the mainshaft.

12. Remove the low and reverse sliding gear and shift fork, as the mainshaft is completely withdrawn from the case.
13. Check cluster gear end-play. End-play should be .005-.022 in. This measurement will determine thrust washer thickness at reassembly.
14. Drive the countershaft rearward, removing key, and out of the case.
15. Lift the gear cluster and thrust washers out of the case. Remove the needle bearings (22 each end), and spacer from the cluster.
16. Drive the reverse idler shaft toward the rear and out of the case. Remove key.
17. Lift the reverse idler gear, thrust washers and 22 needle bearings out of the case.
18. Remove gearshift operating levers from their respective shafts. On an A-250 transmission, remove the tapered pins retaining the shift shafts to the case with a hammer and an $1/8$ in. punch. Drive out the front pin to the front and the rear pin to the rear.
19. Drive out tapered retaining pin from either of the two lever shafts, then withdraw the shaft from inside the transmission case. (The detent balls are springloaded, as the shaft is being withdrawn, the balls will fall to the bottom of the case.)
20. Remove the interlock sleeve, spring, pin and both balls from the case. Drive out the remaining tapered pin, then slide the lever shaft out of the transmission.
21. Remove the lever shaft seals and discard them.

ASSEMBLY

1. Install two new shift lever shaft seals in the case.
2. Carefully insert low and reverse lever shaft into the rear of the case, through the seal and into position. Lock with a tapered pin. Turn lever until the center detent is in line with the interlock bore.
3. Slide the interlock sleeve in its bore in the case, followed by one of the interlock balls. Then, install interlock spring and pin.
4. Place the remaining interlock ball on top of the interlock spring.
5. Depress the interlock ball and at the same time install the second and high lever shaft into the fully seated position, with the center detent aligned with the detent ball. Secure the shaft with the remaining tapered pin.
6. Install the operating levers and secure to the shafts with nuts. Torque the nuts to 18 ft. lbs.

Countershaft (Cluster) Gear

1. Slide the dummy shaft and tubular spacer into the bore of the counter-gear.
2. Grease and install 22 bearing rollers into each end of the counter-gear bore in the area around the arbor. Install the bearing retaining rings at each end of the gear, covering the bearings. If countershaft gear end-play measured over .022 in. at disassembly, install new thrust washers.
3. Install a thrust washer at each end of the countergear and over the arbor. Install the countergear assembly in the case, making sure the tabs on the thrust washers slide into the grooves in the case.

Reverse Idler Gear

1. Coat the bore of the reverse idler gear with grease, then slide dummy shaft into the bore, then install 22 bearing rollers in the bore and around the dummy shaft.
2. Install a new thrust washer at each end of the gear and over the arbor.
3. With the beveled end of the teeth forward, slide the gear into position in the case. Install the reverse idler shaft in its bore in the rear of the case. Install Woodruff key and align with the keyway in the case.
4. Align the idler gear with the shaft, then drive the shaft into the case and gear until the key seats in recess.

Mainshaft

1. Install rear bearing on mainshaft and install selective fit snap-ring.
2. Hold low and reverse sliding gear in position with shift fork. Insert mainshaft with rear bearing through rear of case and into the sliding gear. Both shift forks are offset toward rear of the case.
3. Place synchronizer spreader ring, and then rear stop ring, on synchronizer splines of second speed gear. Install second speed gear on mainshaft, with shims if required. Shims should be installed to correct excessive synchronizer float. If synchronizer float is below minimum, as measured on disassembly, shorten all six synchronizer pins.
4. Install synchronizer clutch gear on mainshaft. Install snap-ring.
5. Install second and direct fork in lever shaft with offset toward rear of transmission. Hold synchronizer clutch gear sleeve and two outer rings together, with pins in holes in clutch gear sleeve. Engage second and direct fork with clutch gear sleeve.
6. While holding synchronizer parts and fork in position, slide mainshaft forward, starting synchronizer clutch gear into clutch gear sleeve and mainshaft rear bearing into the case bore. Synchronizer parts must be correctly positioned before mainshaft is positioned.
7. While holding synchronizer parts in position, tap mainshaft forward

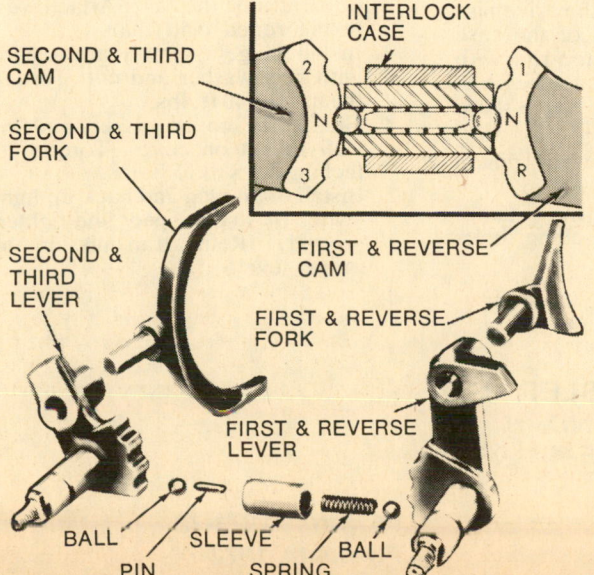

Shift forks and levers

INTERLOCK CASE

SECOND & THIRD CAM
SECOND & THIRD FORK
SECOND & THIRD LEVER
FIRST & REVERSE CAM
FIRST & REVERSE FORK
FIRST & REVERSE LEVER
BALL
PIN
SLEEVE
SPRING
BALL

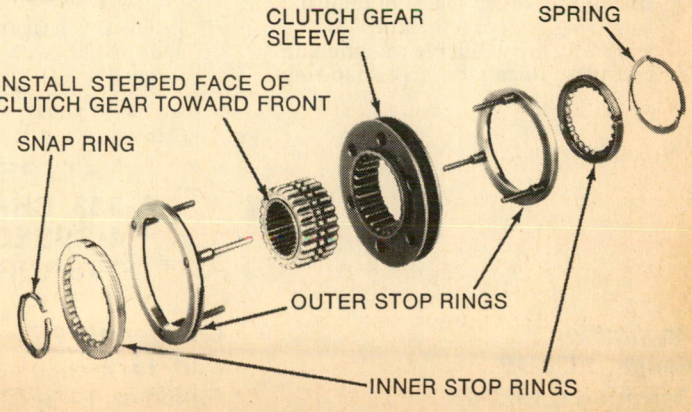

Synchronizer assembly

CLUTCH GEAR SLEEVE
SPRING
INSTALL STEPPED FACE OF CLUTCH GEAR TOWARD FRONT
SNAP RING
OUTER STOP RINGS
INNER STOP RINGS

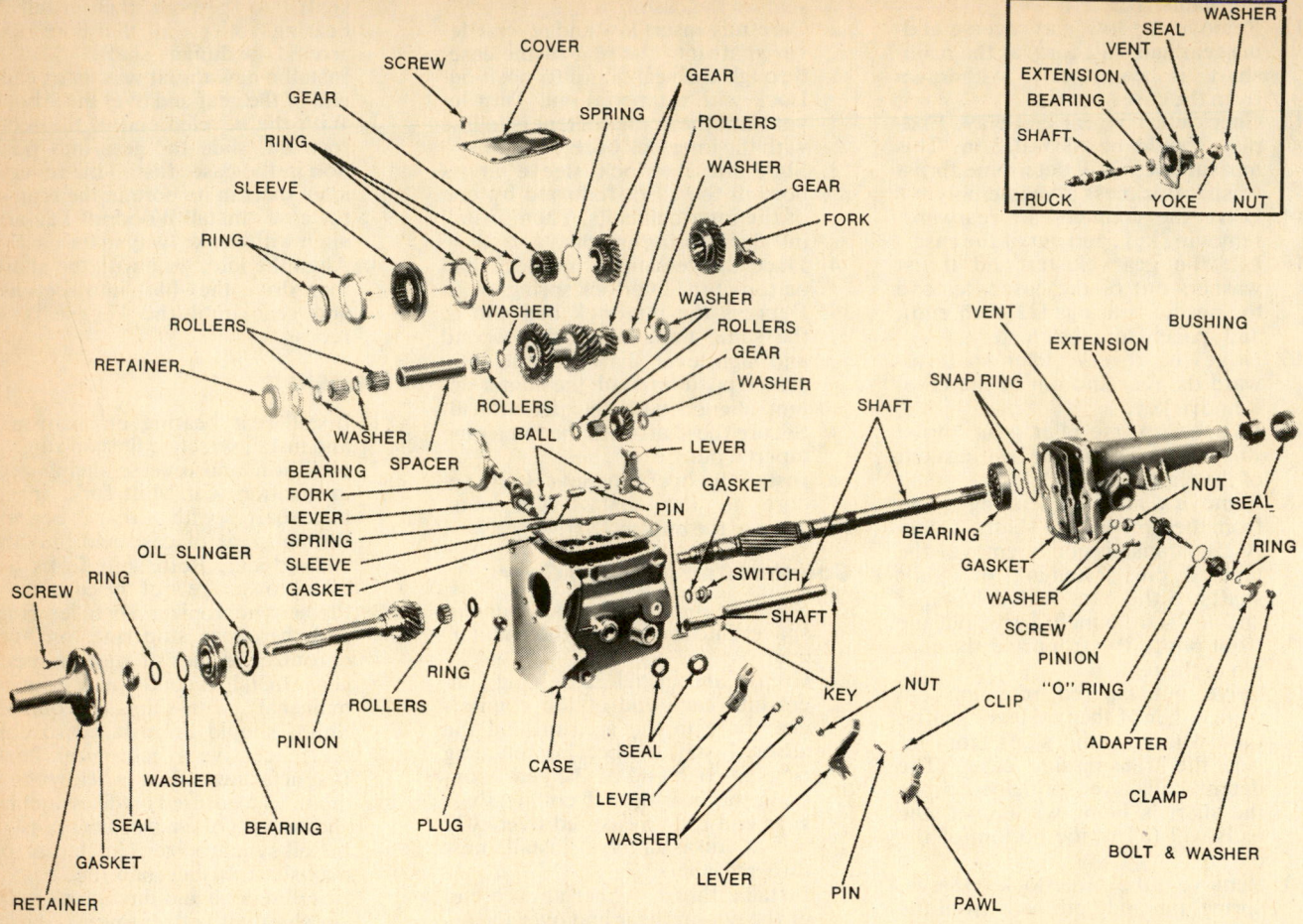

A-903, A-250 Chrysler transmission

until rear bearing bottoms in the case bore.

8. Install mainshaft rear bearing selective fit snap-ring into groove in case bore.

Drive Pinion (Clutch Shaft)

1. Slide the oil slinger over the pinion shaft and down against the gear.
2. Slide the bearing over the pinion shaft (ring groove away from the gear), then press to a firm seat against the oil slinger and gear.
3. Install the keyed washer, then the snap-ring. Four thicknesses of snap-ring are available to eliminate end-play. Install the large snap-ring

onto the race of the ball bearing.

4. Install 14 greased bearing rollers in the bore of the pinion shaft gear. Install bearing roller retaining ring in the pinion gear bore.
5. Install third gear outer stop-ring and third gear inner stop-ring onto the mainshaft. Guide the drive pinion through the front of the case and engage the inner stop-ring with the clutch teeth, then seat the bearing so the large snap-ring is hard against the case.
6. Install a new seal in the pinion bearing retainer.
7. Install the gasket on the retainer and install with attaching bolts torqued to 30 ft. lbs.

Extension Housing

1. Install a new rear mainshaft bushing, and a new oil seal.
2. Protect the oil seal with thimble-type seal protector, and with gasket attached, slide the extension housing over the mainshaft and down against the case. Attach with bolts torqued to 50 ft. lbs.
3. Install flange assembly and secure with new washer and nut. Torque the nut to 140 ft. lbs.
4. Grease the cover gasket, and install gasket on cover. Torque attaching bolts to 12 ft. lbs.
5. Install drain plug and back-up light switch (if so equipped) and tighten securely. Refill transmission to proper level.

TYPE-3
A-833 CHRYSLER
4-SPEED AND
OVERDRIVE-4

Application		
Aspen, 1976-79	Charger, 1972-74	Le Baron, 1978-79
Barracuda, 1972-74	Dart, 1972-76	Plymouth, 1972-74
Challenger, 1972-74	Diplomat, 1978-79	Valiant, 1972-76
	Dodge, 1972-74	Volare, 1976-79

This unit is used by several Chrysler Corporation cars and varies somewhat with car application. However, illustrations and repair procedures may be considered as typical. Starting 1976, there is an overdrive four speed available as an option on some models. This transmission is similar in design to the A-833 Chrysler four speed but repair procedures are different.

DISASSEMBLY

NOTE: *Steps 1-11 apply to both 4-Speed and Overdrive-4.*

1. If available, mount transmission in a repair stand.
2. Disconnect gearshift control rods from the shift control levers and the transmission operating levers.
3. Remove the two gearshift control housing mounting bolts.
4. Remove gearshift control housing from the transmission extension housing or mounting bracket (if so equipped).
5. Remove the gearshift control housing mounting bracket bolts, then, remove the bracket (if so equipped).
6. Remove back-up light switch (if so equipped).
7. Remove output companion flange nut and washer, if used, then pull the flange from the mainshaft (output shaft).
8. Remove gearshift housing-to-transmission case attaching bolts.
9. With all levers in the neutral detent position, pull housing out and away from the case.

NOTE: *If first and second, or third and fourth shift forks remain in engagement with the synchronizer sleeves, work the sleeves and remove forks from the case.*

10. Remove nuts, lock washers and flat washers that hold first-second, and third-fourth-speed shift operating levers to the shafts.
11. Disengage shift levers from the flats on the shafts and remove levers. Remove the E-ring on the overdrive four speed.

4-Speed

NOTE: *Steps 12-37 apply only to the 4-Speed; Overdrive-4 disassembly follows.*

12. Remove gearshift lever shafts out of the housing, allowing detent balls to fall free. Remove seals and discard.
13. Slide interlock sleeve, interlock pin and spring from the housing.
14. Remove main drive pinion bearing retainer attaching bolts, then slide retainer and gasket from the main drive shaft. Remove the pinion oil seal.
15. Remove the attaching bolts that hold the tailshaft extension housing to the transmission case.
16. Slide the third-fourth synchronizer sleeve slightly forward, slide the reverse idler gear to the center of

its shaft, then, using a soft hammer, tap rearward on the extension housing. Slide housing and mainshaft assembly out and away from the case.
17. Remove the snap-ring that holds the third-fourth synchronizer clutch gear and sleeve. Then, slide third-fourth synchronizer assembly from the end of the mainshaft.
18. Slide third speed gear and stop-ring from the mainshaft.

NOTE: *Do not separate third-fourth-speed synchronizer clutch gear, sleeve, shift plates or spring unless replacement is required.*

19. With long-nose pliers, compress the snap-ring that retains the mainshaft center bearing in the extension housing.
20. With snap-ring compressed, pull the mainshaft assembly and bearing out of the extension housing.
21. Remove and discard extension housing rear oil seal.
22. Remove rear bearing from the mainshaft by inserting steel plates on the front side of first-speed gear, then, with an arbor press, force the rear bearing from the mainshaft.
23. Remove the snap-ring that holds the mainshaft bearing onto the shaft.
24. Remove mainshaft bearing, retainer ring, first-speed gear, and first-speed stop-ring.
25. Remove the snap-ring that holds the first and second clutch sleeve gear and clutch to the mainshaft.
26. Slide the first and second clutch sleeve gear and clutch from the mainshaft.

NOTE: *Do not dismantle the clutch unless inspection reveals need for parts replacement.*

27. With a feeler gauge, measure countershaft gear end-play. This measurement should be .015-.025 in. If measurement is greater than specified, a new thrust washer of desirable thickness must be installed at assembly.
28. Drive the reverse idler gear shaft, from front to rear, far enough out of the case to permit removal of the reverse idler gear.
29. Remove idler gear shaft from the case, then remove the Woodruff key from the shaft.
30. Remove reverse gearshift lever detent spring retainer, gasket, plug and detent ball spring from the rear of the case.
31. Push the reverse gearshift lever shaft into the case, and remove. Lift the detent ball from the bottom of the case.
32. Remove the shift fork from the shaft and detent plate.
33. Using a countershaft dummy, drive the countershaft from the gear and case, allowing the countergear and dummy assembly to rest on the bottom of the case.

34. Remove the main drive pinion bearing outer snap-ring, then with a soft hammer, drive the main drive pinion into the case and remove.
35. Remove the main drive pinion bearing outer snap-ring, then, with an arbor press, remove the bearing from the main drive pinion. Remove the oil slinger.
36. Lift the countergear cluster from the bottom of the case.
37. Remove the countergear dummy shaft, 76 bearing rollers, thrust washers and tubular spacer from the center of the countergear.

Overdrive-4

1. Remove the bolt and retainer holding the speedometer pinion adapter in the extension housing, then remove the pinion adapter.
2. Remove the bolts attaching the extension housing to the transmission case.
3. Rotate the extension housing on the output shaft to expose the rear of the countershaft. Install one bolt to hold the extension in place.
4. Drill a hole in the countershaft extension plug at the front of the case.
5. Reaching through this hole, push the countershaft to the rear to expose the Woodruff key; when exposed, remove it. Push the countershaft forward against the expansion plug, and using a brass drift, tap the countershaft forward until the expansion plug is removed.
6. Using a countershaft arbor, push the countershaft out the rear of the case, but don't let the countershaft washers fall out of position. Lower the cluster gear to the bottom of the transmission case.
7. Remove the bolt and rotate the extension back to the normal position.
8. Remove the drive pinion attaching bolts and slide the retainer and gasket from the pinion shaft, then pry the pinion or seal from the retainer. When installing the new seal, don't nick or scratch the seal bore in the retainer or the surface on which the seal bottoms.
9. Using a brass drift, tap the pinion and bearing assembly forward and remove through the front of the case.
10. Slide the third and overdrive synchronizer sleeve slightly forward, slide the reverse idler gear to the center of its shaft, and tap the extension housing rearward. Slide the housing and mainshaft assembly out and away from the case.
11. Remove the snap ring holding the third and overdrive synchronizer clutch gear and sleeve assembly to the mainshaft, then remove the synchronizer assembly.

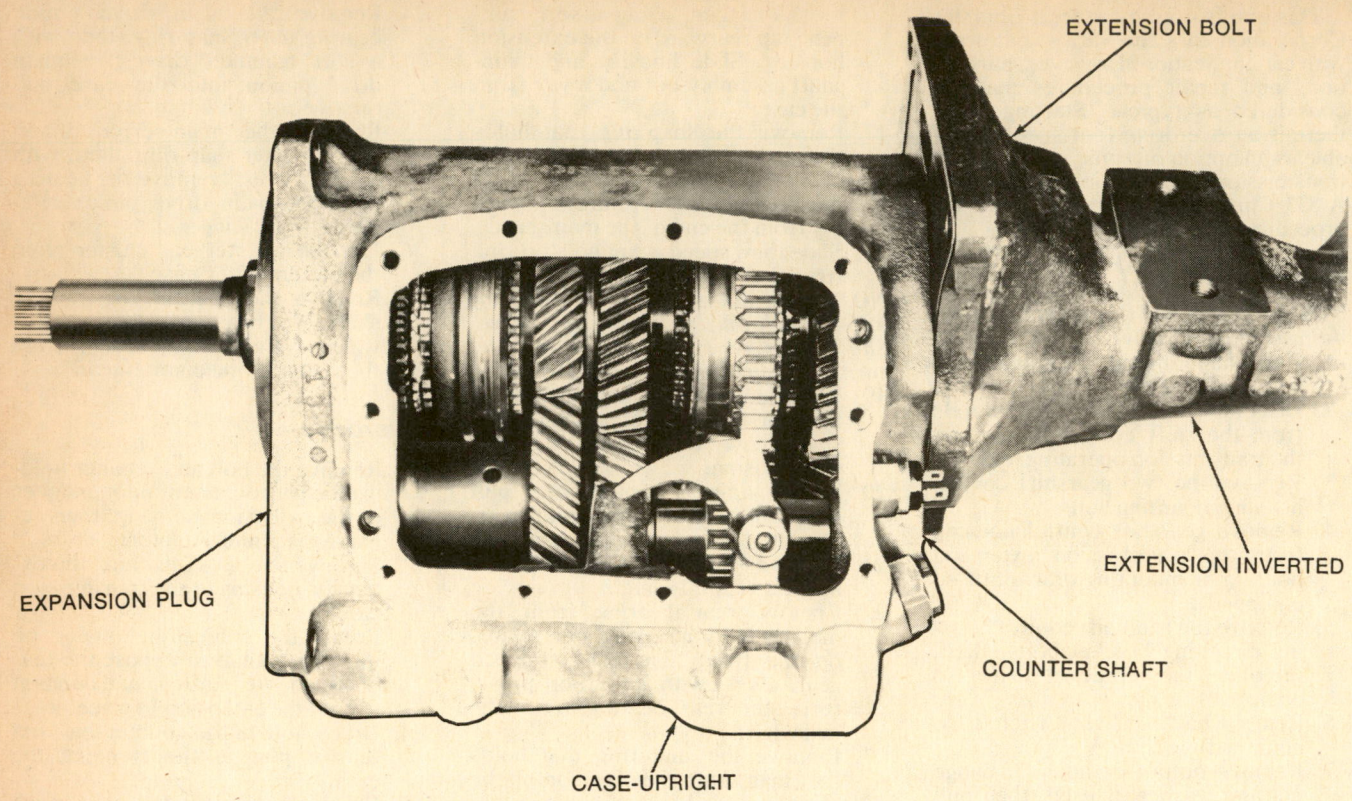

EXTENSION BOLT

EXTENSION INVERTED

COUNTER SHAFT

CASE-UPRIGHT

EXPANSION PLUG

Rotating the extension housing on an Overdrive-4 (© Chrysler Corp.)

12. Slide the overdrive gear and stop ring off the mainshaft. Using pair of long nose pliers, compress the snap ring holding the mainshaft bearing in the extension housing. With it compressed, pull the mainshaft assembly and bearing out of the extension housing.
13. Remove the snap ring holding the mainshaft on the shaft. The bearing is removed by inserting steel plates on the front side of the first speed gear, then pressing the mainshaft through the bearing being careful not to damage the gear teeth.
14. Remove the bearing, retainer ring, first speed gear and stop ring from the shaft.
15. Remove the snap-ring. Remove the first and second clutch gear and sleeve assembly from the mainshaft.
16. Remove the drive pinion bearing inner snap ring, then using an arbor press, remove the bearing. Remove the snap ring and bearing rollers from the cavity in the drive pinion.
17. Remove the countershaft gear from the bottom of the case, then remove the arbor, needle bearings, thrust washers and spacers from the center of the countershaft gear.
18. Remove the reverse gearshift lever detent spring retainer, gasket, plug, and detent ball spring from the rear of the case.
19. The reverse idler gear shaft is a

tight fit in the case and will have to be pressed out.
20. If there is oil leakage visible around the reverse gearshift lever shaft, push the lever shaft in and remove it from the case. Remove the detent ball from the bottom of the transmission case and remove the shift fork from the shaft and detent plate.

ASSEMBLY
4-SPEED
1. Slide the second-speed gear over the mainshaft (synchronizer cone toward rear) and down into position against the shoulder on the shaft.
2. Slide first and second clutch sleeve gear assembly (including second gear stop-ring) over the mainshaft. Be sure shift fork groove is toward the front and down into position against second-speed gear, (stopring must be indexed with the shift plates). Install a new snap-ring to secure.
3. Slide low gear stop-ring over the shaft and down into position and index with the shift plates.
4. Slide first-speed gear, (synchronizer cone toward clutch sleeve gear) over the mainshaft and down into position against the clutch sleeve gear.
5. Install the mainshaft bearing retainer ring, followed by the mainshaft center bearing. Using an arbor or other suitable tool, press the

bearing down into position. Install new snap-ring.
6. Slide the rear bearing over the mainshaft and drive, or press, into position.
7. Install partially assembled mainshaft into the extension housing far enough to engage the retaining ring in the slot in the extension housing. Compress the retaining ring and, at the same time, seat the mainshaft in the extension housing.
8. Slide third-speed gear over the mainshaft, synchronizer cone forward, followed by third gear stopring.
9. Install third and fourth-speed synchronizer clutch gear assembly onto the mainshaft (shift fork groove toward rear) down against third-speed gear. Be sure to index the rear stop-ring with the clutch shift plates.
10. Install retaining snap-ring, then, using heavy grease, position the front stop-ring over the clutch gear, indexing the ring slots with the shift plates.

NOTE: *If above indexing of the stoprings and the positioning of the gears and clutches is ignored at this point, damage will most likely result when mating the extension housing to the transmission case.*
11. Grease the bore of the countergear at each end, then install the roller bearing tubular spacer (centered). Insert the countergear dummy shaft.

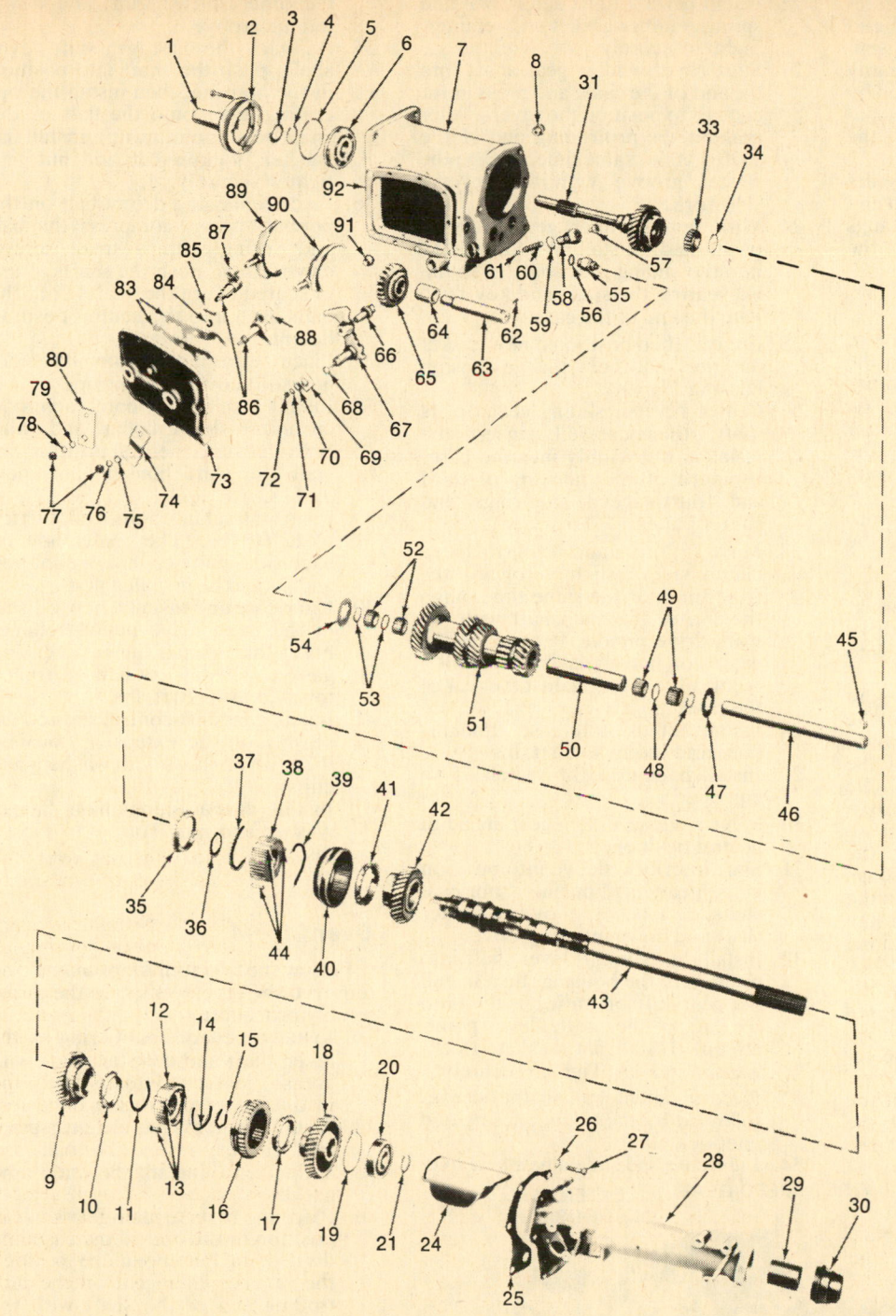

A-833 4-speed transmission disassembled

39 Shift strut spring
40 Clutch sleeve
41 Stop ring
42 3rd speed gear
43 Mainshaft (output)
44 Shift struts (3)
45 Woodruff key
46 Countershaft
47 Gear thrustwasher (1)
48 Needle roller bearing thrustwasher
49 Needle bearing rollers
50 Bearing spacer
51 Countershaft gear (cluster)
52 Needle bearing rollers
53 Needle roller bearing thrustwasher
54 Gear thrustwasher (1)
55 Backup light switch
56 Backup light switch gasket
57 Plug
58 Reverse detent ball spring retainer
59 Gasket
60 Reverse detent ball spring
61 Rerverse detent ball
62 Woodruff key
63 Reverse idler gear shaft
64 Reverse idler gear bushing
65 Reverse idler gear
66 Reverse shifter fork
67 Reverse lever
68 Reverse lever shaft oil seal
69 Reverse operating lever
70 Flatwasher
71 Lockwasher
72 Nut
73 Gearshift control housing
74 1st and 2nd operating lever
75 Flatwasher
76 Lockwasher lever
77 Lever nut
78 Lever lockwasher
79 Lever flatwasher
80 3rd and 4th operating lever
81 Switch
82 Gasket
83 Interlock lever (2)
84 E-ring
85 Spring
86 Oil seal (2)
87 3rd and 4th lever
88 Ist and 2nd lever
89 3rd and 4th speed fork
90 1st and 2nd speed fork
91 Drain plug
92 Shift control housing gasket

1 Bearing retainer
2 Bearing retainer gasket
3 Bearing retainer oil seal
4 Inner bearing snap-ring
5 Outer bearing snap-ring
6 Pinion bearing
7 Transmission case
8 Filler plug
9 2nd speed gear
10 Stop ring
11 Shift strut springs
12 Clutch gear
13 Shift struts (3)
14 Shift strut spring
15 Snap-ring
16 1st and 2nd clutch sleeve gear
17 Stop ring
18 1st speed gear
19 Bearing retainer ring
20 Rear bearing
21 Snap-ring
24 Baffle
25 Case to extension housing gasket
26 Lockwasher
27 Bolt
28 Extension housing
29 Mainshaft yoke bushing
30 Oil seal
31 Main drive pinion
33 Needle bearing rollers
34 Snap-ring
35 Stop ring
36 Snap-ring
37 Shift strut spring
38 Clutch gear

12. Grease each bearing roller, then install 19 bearing rollers at each end of the gear. Now, install a flat spacer onto each end of the dummy shaft and into the gear, followed by 19 more bearing rollers and a spacer ring into each end of the countergear.
13. Grease the tanged thrust washers and install them, one over each end of the dummy shaft, with the tangs toward the case (away from the gear).
14. Lay the countergear assembly into the bottom of the case.
15. To install the main drive pinion, slide the bearing oil slinger over the main drive pinion shaft, then, press the main drive pinion bearing on the pinion shaft. (Be sure the outer snap-ring groove is toward the front). Seat bearing all the way, against shoulder on gear.
16. Install a new inner snap-ring into the bearing retainer groove of the shaft.
17. Now, install the outer snap-ring into the main drive pinion bearing. Then, insert and tap the main drive pinion and bearing assembly into the front of the case.
18. Start the countershaft into its bore at the rear of the case. Raise the countergear cluster assembly until the gear bore is aligned with the countershaft bore in the case. (Be sure the thrust washer tangs are in place in the case recesses.)
19. Press the countershaft into the countergear, washer and bearings assembly while displacing the dummy shaft. Install Woodruff key into countershaft, then continue pressing the countershaft and key into its bore and recess.

NOTE: *Countergear end-play should not exceed .029 in.*

20. Install a new oil seal onto the reverse gearshift lever shaft.
21. Lubricate and carefully install the lever shaft into the bore in the case. Insert reverse fork into the lever.

22. Install reverse shift detent ball and spring retainer gasket and retainer. Tighten securely.
23. Start reverse idler gear shaft into the end of the case, and press in far enough to position the reverse idler gear on the protruding end of the shaft. At the same time, engage the shifter groove with the reverse shift fork.
24. With reverse idler gear properly positioned, install Woodruff key into the sliding gear shaft, then finish seating the shaft and key flush with the end of the case.
25. Grease, then position a new gasket on the end of the extension housing.
26. Center reverse sliding gear on its shaft, then carefully insert the mainshaft assembly into the case. (Be sure of the indexing of third and fourth-speed stop-rings and shifter plates.)
27. Move third and fourth-speed clutch sleeve slightly toward the front, and, at the same time, align the end of the mainshaft with the main drive pinion. Push in on the extension housing assembly until it is entirely seated against the rear of the case.
28. Install extension-to-case attaching bolts and torque to 50 ft. lbs.
29. Install back-up light switch (if so equipped).
30. Move reverse sliding gear ahead to neutral position.
31. Slide interlock sleeve into position in the gearshift housing. Lubricate and slide a new seal over a shifter shaft and down into its groove.
32. Install the gearshift lever shaft into position in the housing, then install the gearshift operating lever onto the flats of the shaft, (lever pointing up). Install flat washer, Lockwasher and nut. Tighten securely.
33. Place a detent ball in the sleeve, followed by the poppet spring and interlock pin.
34. Lubricate and slide a new seal over

the other shifter shaft and down into its groove.
35. As with the first gearshift lever shaft, push the shaft into position in the housing, then install the operating lever onto the flats of the shaft (lever pointing up). Install flat washer, lockwasher and nut and tighten securely.
36. Place remaining detent ball on the poppet spring, compress the ball and spring with a small screwdriver, then, push the shafts in until seated. Turn the shafts until the balls drop into the neutral position detent.
37. Place transmission on its side, gearshift cover opening up.
38. Install a shift fork onto each synchronizer sleeve collar, and, with both sleeves in neutral position, install the shift housing and new gasket.
39. Install attaching bolts and tighten to 12 ft. lbs. (The center bolt on each side of the cover is a pilot bolt and should be installed first).
40. Lubricate and install a new oil seal in the main drive pinion retainer bore, then install the retainer and gasket. Install attaching bolts, torqued to 15-20 ft. lbs.
41. Install gearshift control and rod assembly on the extension housing, then, secure rods with washers and clips.
42. Install output companion flange, washer and nut. Torque to 175 ft. lbs.

Overdrive-4

Follow the first four steps only if you removed the reverse shaft in the disassembly procedure.

1. Install a new oil seal O-ring on the lever shaft and coat the shaft with grease; insert it into its bore and install the reverse fork in the lever.
2. Install the reverse detent spring and gasket; insert the ball and spring and install the plug and gasket.
3. Place the reverse idler gear shaft in position in the end of the case and drive it in far enough to position the reverse idler gear on the protruding end of the shaft with the fork slot toward the rear. While doing this, engage the slot with the reverse shift fork.
4. With the reverse idler gear correctly positioned, drive the reverse gear shaft into the case far enough to install the Woodruff key. Drive the shaft in flush with the end of the transmission case. Install the back-up light switch and gasket.

Overdrive-4 Mainshaft gear identification (© Chrysler Corp.)

Labels: FIRST & SECOND CLUTCH SLEEVE GEAR; FIRST SPEED GEAR; EXTENSION HOUSING; SECOND SPEED GEAR; MAINSHAFT; SNAP RING; STOP RING; THIRD & O/D CLUTCH SLEEVE; STOP RING; OVERDRIVE GEAR

Countershaft Gear and Drive Pinion

5. Coat the inside bore of the counter-

shaft gear with a thin film of grease and install the roller bearing spacer with an arbor, into the gear; center the spacer and arbor.

6. Install the roller bearings and a spacer ring on each end.
7. Replace worn thrust washers; coat the new ones with grease and install them over the arbor with the tang side toward the case boss.
8. Install the countershaft assembly into the case and allow the gear assembly to sit on the bottom of the case so that the thrust washers won't come out of position.
9. Press the drive pinion bearing on the pinion shaft. Make sure the outer snap ring groove is toward the front end and the bearing is seated against the shoulder on the gear.
10. Install a new snap ring on the shaft to hold the bearing in place; make sure the snap ring is seated and that there is minimum end play. There are several snap-ring thicknesses available for adjustment.
11. Place the pinion shaft in a soft-jawed vise and install the roller bearings in the cavity of the shaft. Coat them with grease and install the bearing retaining snap-ring.
12. Install a new oil seal in the bore.

Extension Housing Bushing

13. Remove the yoke seal from the extension housing.
14. Drive out the old bushing and drive in a new one, aligning the oil hole in the bushing with the slot in the housing.
15. Place a new seal in the opening of the extension housing and then drive it into place.

Mainshaft

Assemble the synchronizer as follows:

1. Place a stop ring flat on a bench followed by the clutch gear and sleeve; drop the struts in their slots and snap in a strut spring placing the tang inside one strut. Install the second strut spring tang in a different strut after turning the assembly over.
2. Slide the second speed gear over the mainshaft with the synchronizer cone toward the rear and down against the shoulder on the shaft.
3. Slide the first and second gear synchronizer assembly including stop rings with lugs indexed in the hub slots, over the mainshaft down against the second gear cone and hold it there with a new snap ring. Slide the next snap ring over the shaft and index the lugs into the clutch hub slots.

4. Slide the first speed gear with the synchronizer cone toward the clutch sleeve just installed over the mainshaft and into position against the clutch sleeve gear.
5. Install the mainshaft bearing retaining ring followed by the mainshaft rear bearing; press the bearing down into position and install a new snap ring to secure it. There are several snap-ring thicknesses available for minimum end play.
6. Install the partially assembled mainshaft into the extension housing far enough to engage the bearing retaining ring in the slot in the extension housing. Compress the ring with pliers so that the mainshaft ball bearing can move in and bottom against its thrust shoulder in the extension housing. Release the ring and make sure that it is seated.
7. Slide the overdrive gear over the mainshaft with the synchronizer cone toward the front followed by the gear's snap ring.
8. Install the third-overdrive gear synchronizer clutch gear assembly on the mainshaft against the overdrive gear. Make sure to index the rear stop ring with the clutch gear struts.
9. Install the snap ring and position the front stop ring over the clutch gear again lining up the ring lugs with the struts; coat a new extension gasket with grease and place it in position.
10. Slide the reverse idler gear to the center of its shaft and move the third-overdrive synchronizer as far forward as possible without losing the struts.
11. Insert the mainshaft assembly in the case tilting it as necessary. Place the third-overdrive sleeve in the neutral detent.
12. Rotate the extension on the mainshaft to expose the rear of the countershaft and install one bolt to hold it in position.
13. Install the drive pinion and bearing assembly through the front of the case and position it in the front bore. Install the outer snap ring in the bearing groove and tap lightly into place. If it doesn't bottom easily, check to see if a strut, pinion roller or stop ring is out of position.
14. Turn the transmission upside down while holding the countershaft gear to prevent damage. Then lower the countershaft gear assembly into position making sure that the teeth mesh with the drive pinion gear.
15. Start the countershaft into the bore at the rear of the case and push until it is in about halfway; then install the Woodruff key and push it in until it is flush with the rear of the case.
16. Rotate the extension back to normal position and install the bolts; turn the transmission upright and

install the drive pinion bearing retainer and gasket. Coat the threads with sealing compound and tighten the attaching bolts to 30 ft. lbs.
17. Install a new expansion plug in its bore.

Gearshift Housing and Mechanism

18. Install the interlock levers on the pivot pin and secure with the E-ring. Install the spring with a pair of pliers.
19. Grease and install new O-ring seals on both shift shafts; grease the housing bores and push the shafts through.
20. Install the operating levers and tighten the retaining nuts to 18 ft. lbs.; make sure the third-overdrive lever points down.
21. Rotate each shift shaft fork bore straight up and install the third-overdrive shift fork in its bore and under both interlock levers.
22. Position both synchronizer sleeves in neutral and place the first and second gear shift fork in the groove of the first and second gear synchronizer sleeve. Slide the reverse idler gear to neutral. Turn the transmission on its right side and place the gearshift housing gasket in place holding it there with grease. Install the reverse detent ball and spring into the case bore.
23. As the shift housing is lowered in place, guide the third-overdrive shift fork into its synchronizer groove then lead the shaft of the first and second shift fork into its bore in the first and second shift lever.
24. Raise the interlock lever with a screwdriver to allow the first and second shift fork to slip under the levers. The shift housing will now seat against the case.
25. Install the bolts lightly and shift through all the gears to check for proper operation.
26. The reverse shift lever and the first and second gear shift lever have cam surfaces which mate in reverse position to lock the first and second lever, the fork and synchronizer in the neutral position. To check for proper operation, put the transmission in reverse, and, while turning the input shaft, move the first and second lever in each direction. If it locks up or becomes harder to turn, select a new shift lever size with more or less clearance. If there is too little cam clearance, it will be difficult or impossible to shift into reverse.
27. Grease the reverse shaft, install the operating lever and nut, and install the speedometer drive pinion gear and adapter, making sure the range number is in the straight down position.

TYPE-4
3.03 FULLY SYNCHRONIZED
FORD 3-SPEED

Application
Comet, 1972-77
Cougar, 1972
Fairmont (6 cylinder), 1978-79

Granada, 1975-77
Maverick, 1972-77
Monarch, 1975-77
Montego, 1972-75

Mustang, 1972-73
Torino, 1972-75
Zephyr (6 cylinder), 1978-79

A-390
FULLY SYNCHRONIZED
CHRYSLER 3-SPEED

Application (6 cylinder)
Dart, 1975-76
Dodge, 1975-76
Plymouth, 1975-76
Valiant, 1975-76

AMC 150T
FULLY SYNCHRONIZED
3-SPEED

Application
American Motors, 1975-79

NOTE: *1975 and later versions of this transmission are also identified with the name Tremec. It is built in Mexico and purchased for use by several manufacturers. The service procedures are very similar, regardless of application.*

DISASSEMBLY

1. Drain the lubricant, then remove the cover bolts and the case cover. Late models are drained by removing the lower extension housing bolt.
2. Remove the five attaching screws, then remove the extension housing from the transmission case. Remove a long spring which retains the detent plug in the case. Remove the detent plug with a small magnet.
3. Remove the four attaching screws, then remove the front bearing retainer from the case.
4. Remove the filler plug. Working through the filler plug hole, drive the roll pin out of the case and countershaft with a small punch.
5. With a dummy shaft, push the countershaft out of the rear of the case until the countershaft cluster gear can be lowered to the bottom of the case. Remove the countershaft from the front of the case.
6. Remove the snap-ring. Lift the input gear and shaft from the front of the case. Press the shaft out of the bearing.
7. Remove the snap-ring that holds the speedometer gear onto the shaft. Slide the speedometer gear off the output shaft. Remove the speedometer gear lockball.
8. Remove the snap-ring that holds the output shaft bearing on the

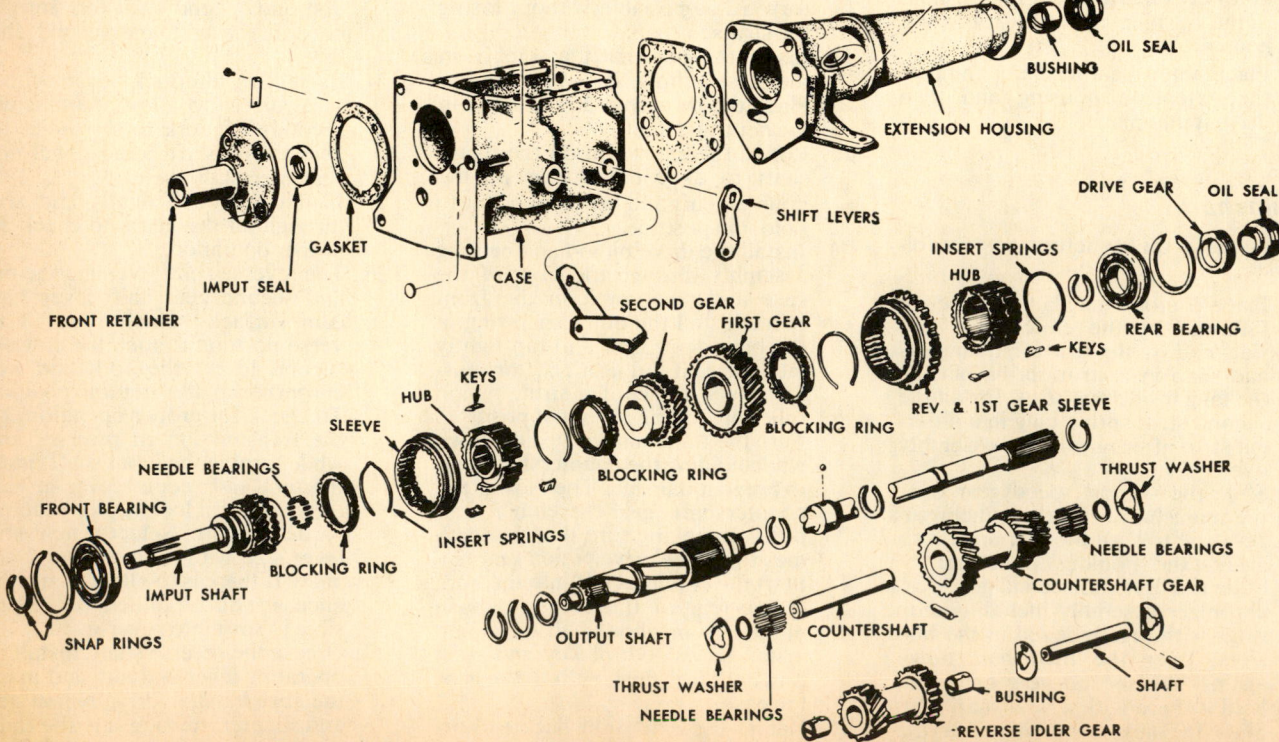

3.03 Ford 3-speed transmission disassembled (© Ford Motor Co)

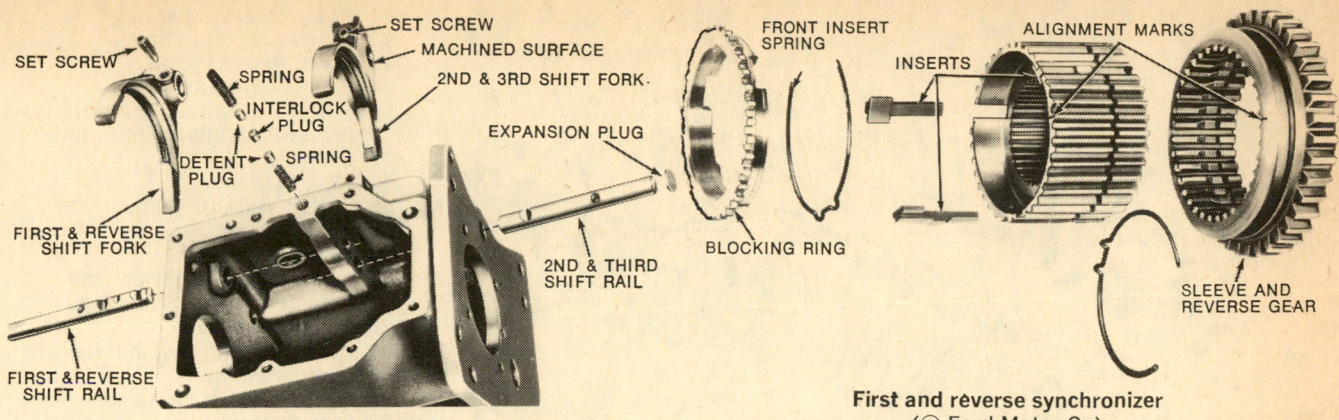

Shift rail and forks

First and reverse synchronizer
(© Ford Motor Co)

shaft. With a puller, remove the bearing from both the case and shaft.

9. Place both shift levers in the neutral position.

10. Remove the set screw that holds the first and reverse shift fork to the shift rail. Slide first and reverse shift rail out through the rear of the case.

11. Rotate the first and reverse shift fork upward, then lift it from the case.

13. Remove the set screw that holds the second and third shift fork to the shift rail. Rotate the shift rail 90°.

13. With a magnet, lift the interlock plug from the case.

14. Tap on the inner end of the second and third shift rail to remove the expansion plug from the front of the case. Remove the shift rail.

NOTE: *On 1972 RAT model transmissions, pull the input gear and shaft forward until the gear contacts the case. On all other models, remove the input gear and shaft through the front of the case.*

15. Rotate the second and third shift fork upward, then lift it from the case.

16. Lift the output shaft out through the top of the case.

17. Working through the front bearing opening, drive the reverse idler shaft out through the rear of the case.

18. Lift the reverse idler gear and two thrust washers from the case.

19. Lift the countershaft gear and thrust washers from the case.

20. Remove the countershaft-to-case retaining pin and any needle bearings which may have fallen into the case.

21. Remove the shift levers and shafts from the case. Discard the O-rings.

22. Remove the snap-ring from the front of the output shaft, then slide the synchronizer and the second-speed gear from the shaft.

23. Remove the next snap-ring and thrust washer from the output shaft, then slide the first gear and blocking ring off the shaft.

24. Remove the next snap-ring from the output shaft, then press off the first-reverse synchronizer hub from the shaft.

25. Remove the dummy shaft, 50 bearing rollers and the two retainer washers from the countershaft gear.

26. Disassemble the synchronizers.

ASSEMBLY

1. Coat the bore in each end of the countershaft gear with grease. Hold the dummy shaft in the gear and install 25 bearing rollers and a retainer washer in each end of the gear. Install the countershaft gear, thrust washers and dummy shaft in the case. End-play is controlled with variable thickness thrust washers to .004-.018 in. Let the gear cluster assembly lie in the bottom of the case.

2. Install the reverse idler gear, thrust washers and shaft in the case. Make sure that the thrust washer with the flat side, is at the web end

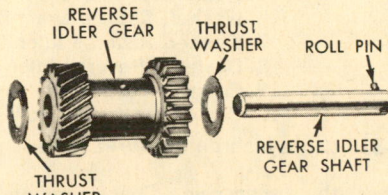

Reverse idler shaft
(© Ford Motor Co)

and that the spur gear is toward the rear of the case. Idler gear end-play should be .004-.018 in.

3. Install an insert spring into the groove of the first and reverse synchronizer hub. Be sure that the spring covers all insert grooves. Start the hub in the sleeve, being sure the alignment marks are properly indexed. Position the three inserts in the hub and be sure the small end is over the spring and that the shoulder is on the inside of the hub. Slide the sleeve and reverse gear onto the hub until the detent is engaged. Install the other insert spring in the front of the hub to hold the inserts against it.

4. Install one insert spring into a groove of the second-third synchronizer hub. With the alignment marks on the hub and sleeve aligned, start the hub into the sleeve. Place the three inserts on top of the retaining spring and push the assembly together. Install the remaining insert spring, so that the spring ends cover the same slots as do the other spring. Do not stagger the springs. Place a synchronizer blocking ring in each end of the synchronizer sleeve.

5. Lubricate the output shaft splines and machined surfaces with transmission lubricant.

6. Press the first and reverse synchronizer hub onto the output shaft, with the teeth end of the gear facing toward the rear end of the shaft. Secure it with the snap-ring.

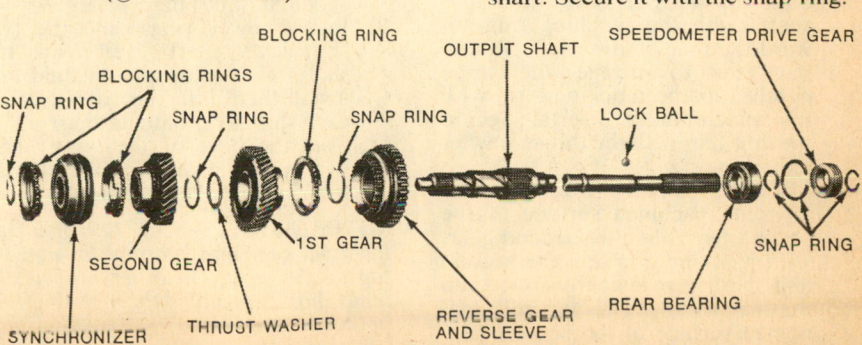

Output shaft (© Ford Motor Co)

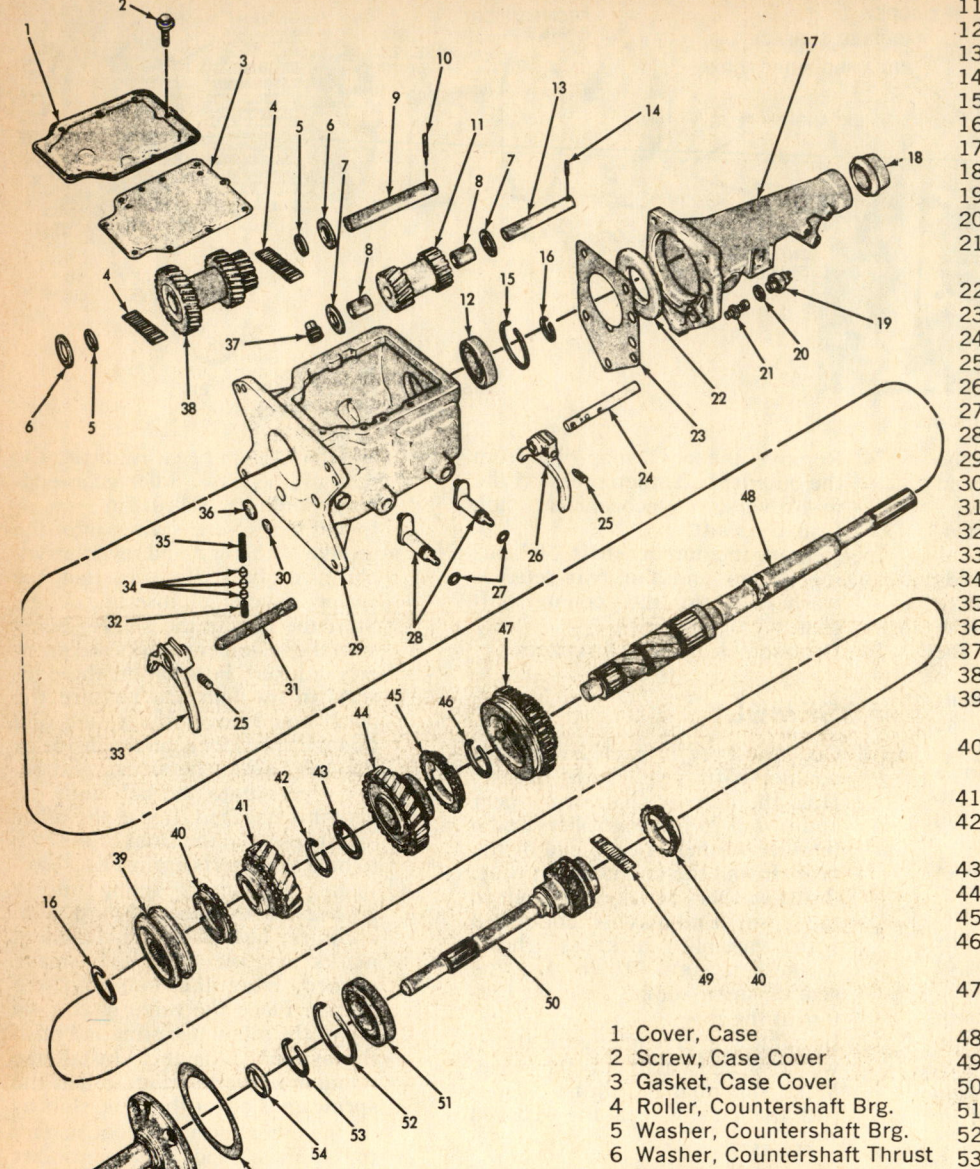

11 Gear, Reverse Idler
12 Bearing, Output Shaft
13 Shaft, Reverse Idler
14 Pin, Reverse Idler Stop
15 Snap Ring, Output Shaft Brg. Outer
16 Snap Ring, Output Shaft, Inner
17 Extension
18 Seal, Extension
19 Switch, Back-Up Lamp
20 Gasket, Back-Up Lamp Switch
21 Screw, Extension
   Lockwasher, Extension Screw
22 Retainer, Output Shaft Brg.
23 Gasket, Extension
24 Rail, Gearshift First and Reverse
25 Screw, Fork Set
26 Fork, Gearshift First and Reverse
27 Seal, Gearshift Lever Shaft Oil
28 Lever, Gearshift
29 Case
30 Plug
31 Rail, Gearshift Second and Third
32 Spring, Gearshift Detent Pin
33 Fork, Gearshift Second and Third
34 Pin, Gearshift Detent
35 Spring, Gearshift Detent Pin
36 Plug
37 Plug, Case Filler
38 Gear, Countershaft
39 Synchronizer Assy., Second and
   Third
40 Ring, Synchronizer Second and
   Third Stop
41 Gear, Second Speed
42 Snap Ring, Low Speed Gear
   Thrust Washer
43 Washer, Low Speed Gear Thrust
44 Gear, Low Speed
45 Ring, Synchronizer Low Stop
46 Snap Ring, Synchronizer Low and
   Reverse Clutch Gear
47 Synchronizer Assy., Low and
   Reverse
48 Shaft, Output
49 Roller, Output Shaft Pilot
50 Shaft, Input
51 Bearing, Input Shaft
52 Snap Ring, Bearing, Outer
53 Snap Ring, Bearing, Inner
54 Seal, Bearing Retainer Oil
55 Gasket, Bearing Retainer
56 Retainer, Bearing
57 Screw, Bearing Retainer

1 Cover, Case
2 Screw, Case Cover
3 Gasket, Case Cover
4 Roller, Countershaft Brg.
5 Washer, Countershaft Brg.
6 Washer, Countershaft Thrust
7 Washer, Reverse Idler Thrust
8 Bushing, Reverse Idler
9 Countershaft
10 Pin, Countershaft Roll

Exploded view of Chrysler A-390 fully synchronized three speed

7. Place the blocking ring on the tapered machined surface of the first gear.
8. Slide the first gear onto the output shaft, with the blocking ring toward the rear of the shaft. Rotate the gear to engage the three notches in the blocking ring with the synchronizer inserts. Secure the first gear with the thrust washer and snap-ring.
9. Slide the blocking ring onto the tapered, machined surface of the second gear. Slide the second gear, with blocking ring and the second and third gear synchronizer, onto the mainshaft. The tapered machined surface of the second gear must be toward the front of the shaft. Secure the synchronizer

with a snap-ring. Check the end play between the synchronizer and snap-ring with a feeler gauge. It should be 0.004 in.
10. Install new O-rings onto the two shift lever shafts. Lubricate the shafts with transmission fluid and install them into the case. Secure each shift lever onto its shaft.
11. Coat the bore of the input shaft with a light coat of grease. Install the 15 bearing rollers into the bore.

NOTE: *On RAT models (1972) install the input gear and bearing through the top of the case. On other models the input shaft is installed through the front of the transmission.*

12. Position the output shaft assembly in the case.

13. Place the second and third-speed shift fork in the synchronizer groove. Rotate the fork into position and install the second and third-speed shift rail. Move the rail inward until the detent plug engages the forward notch (second). Secure the fork to the shaft with a set screw. Move the synchronizer to the neutral position.
14. Install the interlock pin in the case.
15. Place first and reverse shift fork in the groove of the first and reverse synchronizer. Rotate the fork into position and install the first and reverse shift rail. Move the rail inward until the center notch is aligned with the detent bore. Secure the fork to the shaft with a set screw.

16. Install a new expansion plug in the case front.
17. Install the input shaft and gear in the front of the case.
18. Place front bearing retainer (with new gasket in place) on the case with the oil return groove at the bottom. Torque attaching screws to 30 ft. lbs.
19. Install the large snap-ring on the rear bearing. Place the bearing on the output shaft, with the snap-ring end toward the rear of the shaft. Press bearing into place and secure with a snap-ring.
20. Hold the speedometer drive gear lock ball in the detent and slide the speedometer gear into place. Secure the gear with a snap-ring.

21. Lift the countershaft gear cluster up into place, and, by entering the countershaft at the rear of the case, push the dummy shaft out of the gear and transmission case. Before the countershaft is completely in place, align the roll pin hole in the shaft with the hole in the case.

NOTE: *On all eight-cylinder vehicles and Ford six-cylinder models the countershaft is a press fit in the case. On Ford six-cylinder models with RAN transmissions, there is a radial clearance of .020 in. at front bore and .010 in. at rear.*

22. Working through the filler hole, install a roll pin into the case and countershaft.

23. Install filler and drain plugs in the case.
24. Coat a new extension housing gasket with sealer and install it on the case.
25. Apply sealer to attaching screws and secure extension housing to the case by torquing the screws to 42 to 50 ft. lbs.
26. With transmission in gear, pour lubricant over the entire gear train while rotating the input or output shaft.
27. Install the transmission cover, with a new sealer-coated gasket in place, and torque the nine attaching screws to 14-19 ft lbs.
28. Check operation of transmission in all of the gear positions.

TYPE-5
FORD 4-SPEED
(GERMAN DESIGN)
TYPES 71 WG, 72 WG, 75 WT, 77 ET, 78 ET

Application (4 cylinder)
Bobcat, 1976-79
Fairmont, 1978-79
Pinto, 1972-79
Zephyr, 1978-79

NOTE: *Cars equipped with this transmission are identified by a transmission ID code suffix of AA, AD, BA, or AE. The transmission ID code appears on a tag located under the left extension housing-to-case bolt.*

TRANSMISSION DISASSEMBLY

1. Remove the clutch release bearing and lever and detach the clutch housing.
2. Drain the lubricant and remove the cover and gasket from the case.
3. Remove the threaded plug, spring and shift rail detent plunger from the front of the case.
4. Drive the access plug from the rear of the case. Drive the interlock retaining pin from the case and remove the interlock plate.
5. Remove the roll pin from the selector lever arm.
6. Tap the front end of the shift rail, to displace the plug at the rear of the extension housing. Remove the shift rail from the rear of the extension housing.
7. Remove the selector arm and shift forks from the case.
8. Remove the extension housing attaching bolts. Loosen the extension housing and rotate the housing to align the countershaft with the cutaway in the extension housing flange.
9. Drive the countershaft rearward until the shaft clears the front of the case. Install a dummy shaft in

the case and gear until the countershaft gear can be lowered to the bottom of the case. Remove the countershaft.
10. Lift the extension housing and mainshaft from the case as an assembly.
11. Remove the input shaft bearing retainer attaching bolts. Remove the input shaft and bearing retainer from the case as an assembly.
12. Remove the reverse idler gear and shaft from the rear of the case.
13. Remove the bearing retainers, bearings, and dummy shaft from the countershaft gear.
14. Remove the pilot bearing and bear-

ing retainer from the input shaft gear.
15. Do not remove the ball bearing from the input shaft unless replacement is necessary. To remove it, take off the snap-ring and press the bearing off the shaft.
16. Pry the input shaft seal out of the bearing retainer.
17. Lift the fourth gear blocker ring from the front of the output shaft.
18. Remove the snap-ring from the forward end of the output shaft.
19. Support third gear on press plates and place the output shaft and extension housing in a press. Press the output shaft out of the third-

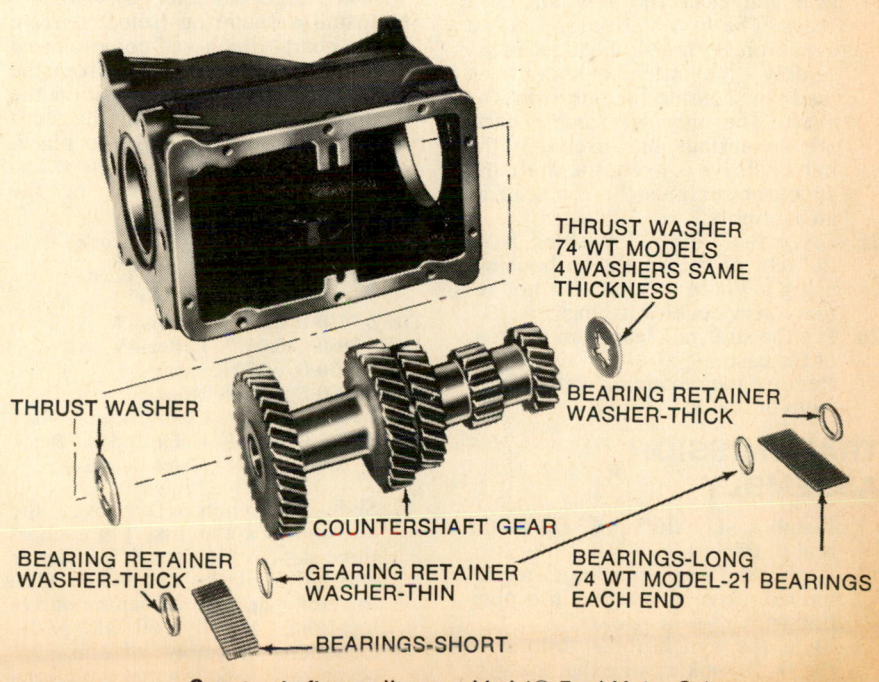

THRUST WASHER
74 WT MODELS
4 WASHERS SAME
THICKNESS

THRUST WASHER

BEARING RETAINER
WASHER-THICK

COUNTERSHAFT GEAR

BEARING RETAINER
WASHER-THICK

GEARING RETAINER
WASHER-THIN

BEARINGS-LONG
74 WT MODEL-21 BEARINGS
EACH END

BEARINGS-SHORT

Countershaft gear disassembled (© Ford Motor Co)

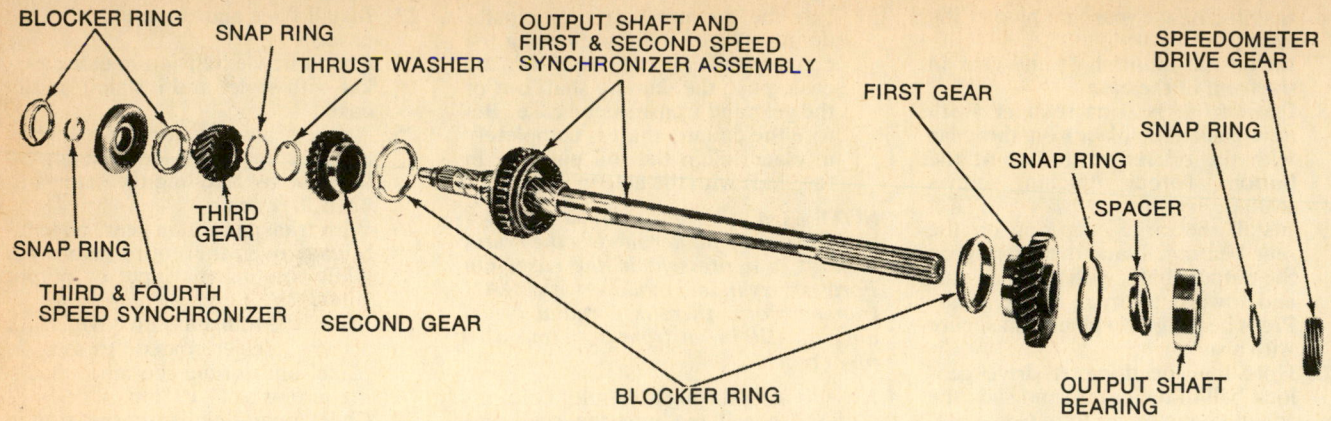

BLOCKER RING

SNAP RING

THRUST WASHER

OUTPUT SHAFT AND
FIRST & SECOND SPEED
SYNCHRONIZER ASSEMBLY

SPEEDOMETER
DRIVE GEAR

FIRST GEAR

SNAP RING

THIRD
GEAR

SNAP RING

SPACER

SNAP RING

THIRD & FOURTH
SPEED SYNCHRONIZER

SECOND GEAR

BLOCKER RING

OUTPUT SHAFT
BEARING

Output shaft disassembled —Types 71WG-AD and 72WG-AE
(© Ford Motor Co)

fourth speed synchronizer and third gear, while supporting the extension housing and output shaft from beneath. Remove the snap-ring and washer and remove second gear and the blocker ring from the output shaft.

NOTE: *On model 77 ET and 78 ET transmissions, a press is not needed to remove the third-fourth speed synchronizer and third gear.*

20. Disassemble the synchronizer assembly by pulling the sleeve from the hub and removing the inserts and spring.
21. Remove the snap-ring which retains the output shaft bearing to the extension housing.
22. Use a plastic hammer and tap the output shaft assembly from the extension housing.
23. Measure or scribe the speedometer gear location on the output shaft and press the gear off.
24. Position press plates behind first gear and place the assembly in a press. The first and second speed synchronizer are serviced as an assembly. No attempt should be made to separate the hub from the shaft. The only serviceable parts are the springs and inserts. If the hub or sleeve is worn, the shaft and synchronizer must be replaced as an assembly.
25. Drive the shift rail bushing from the rear of the extension housing, using a ⁹/₁₆ in. socket. Do not remove serviceable bushings.
26. Pry the shift rail seal from the rear of the case.
27. Remove the remaining shift linkage from the case.

TRANSMISSION ASSEMBLY

1. Install a new shift rail seal in the rear of the case.
2. If the shift rail bushing was removed, drive a new one into position with a ⁹/₁₆ in. socket.
3. Slide the synchronizer hub over the shaft, making sure that the shift fork groove is toward the front of

the shaft. The sleeve and hub are select fit and must be assembled with the etch marks in the same relative locations. Locate an insert in each of three slots in the hub. Oil all parts, and install an insert spring inside the sleeve. The spring tab must locate in a U-section of an insert. Fit the other spring to the opposite face, making sure that the tab locates in the same insert. Both springs should be in the same rotational direction. The tab end of one spring should be aligned with the tab of the spring on the opposite side.

4. Assemble a blocker ring on the first gear side of the first-second synchronizer. Lubricate the cone surface of first gear and all output shaft gear journals, and slide the cone onto the output shaft, so that the cone surface engages the blocker ring.
5. Position the spacer on the output shaft, larger diameter rearward.
6. Install a snap-ring (selected from the chart) which will come closest to removing all end-play from the output shaft bearing. Position the output shaft bearing on the shaft and press the bearing into place. Secure the bearing with the thickest snap-ring that will fit the groove.

Part No.	Thickness	Identification
D1FZ-7030-A	0.0679-	Color Coded— Copper
D1FZ-7030-B	0.0689-	Letter—W
D1FZ-7030-C	0.0699-	Letter—V
D1FZ-7030-D	0.0709-	Letter—U
D1FZ-7030-E	0.0719-	None
D1FZ-7030-F	0.0728-	Color Coded—Blue
D1FZ-7030-G	0.0738-	Color Coded—Black
D1FZ-7030-H	0.0748-	Color Coded— Brown

7. Slide the synchronizer over the hub and locate an insert in each of three slots in the sleeve. The sleeve and hub must be assembled with the etch marks in the same relative locations. Lightly oil all parts. Complete assembly of the synchronizer by following directions in previous Step 3.

8. Position second gear and the blocker ring on the output shaft, dog teeth facing rearward. Install the washer and snap-ring. Position third gear on the output shaft, dog teeth forward. Lubricate the gear cones and assemble a blocker ring on third gear cone.
9. Position the third-fourth synchronizer assembly on the output shaft, hub boss facing forward.
10. Install press plates against the boss on the synchronizer hub.
11. Place the entire unit in a press, extension end up, and press the synchronizer assembly onto the output shaft as far as possible.
12. Retain the third-fourth synchronizer assembly to the output shaft with a snap-ring. Pull up on the synchronizer so that the snap-ring is tight in the groove.
13. Lubricate the gear cone and place the blocker ring on the input shaft gear cone.
14. Press the speedometer drive gear onto the shaft to marked location.

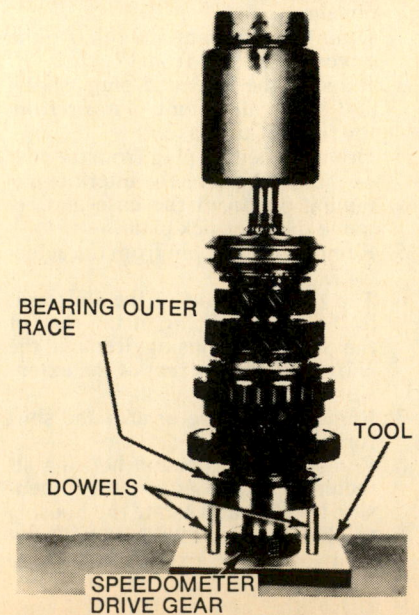

BEARING OUTER RACE

TOOL

DOWELS

SPEEDOMETER DRIVE GEAR

Installing speedometer driven gear
(© Ford Motor Co)

15. Lubricate the bearing bore of the extension housing. Install the output shaft in the housing. It may be necessary to tap the shaft while holding the synchronizer sleeves firmly. Secure the shaft to the housing with the snap-ring previously installed.

16. Press the bearing on the input shaft. The snap-ring groove must be toward the front of the shaft. Use the thickest snap-ring that will fit.

17. Slide the spacer and dummy shaft into the countershaft gear. Position a thin bearing retaining washer on each end of the dummy shaft. Lubricate the roller bearings and load long bearings in the small end of the gear and short bearings in the long end of the gear. 19 needle bearings are used at either end of the gear on 71 WG and 72 WG series transmissions, and 21 needle bearings at either end of the gear on 75 WT, 77 ET, and 78 ET series transmissions. Place a thick retaining washer over each end of the dummy shaft. Grease the thrust washers and place one on each end of the dummy shaft. The tabs must be in the same relative position to engage the slots in the case when the gear is lowered. Loop a piece of rope around each end of the gear and carefully install the gear and rope through the rear of the case. Lower the gear in place.

18. Lubricate the reverse idler gear shaft. Position the selector lever relay on the pivot pin. Secure with a spring clip. Hold the gear in the lever, long hub toward the rear of the case, and slide the reverse idler shaft into place. Seat the shaft in the case with a brass hammer.

19. Install a new seal in the input shaft bearing retainer. Install the input shaft in the case with a new bearing retainer O-ring. Tap on the outer race of the bearing to seat the outer snap-ring.

—— CAUTION ——
Use a soft hammer and do not tap on the input shaft itself.

20. Carefully slide third-fourth synchronizer sleeve into fourth speed position.

21. Place a new gasket on the extension housing.

22. Lubricate and install the input shaft pilot bearing on the shaft. Slide the extension housing and output shaft into place, being careful not to disturb the third-fourth speed synchronizer.

23. Align the cutaway in the extension housing flange with the countershaft bore in the rear of the case.

24. Lift the countershaft gear into place and install the countershaft, making sure that the thrust wash-

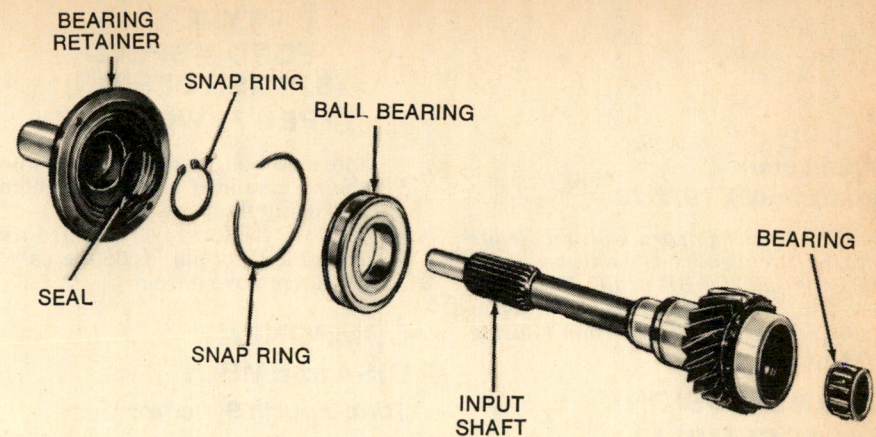

Input shaft disassembled —Types 71WG-AD and 72WG-AE
(© Ford Motor Co)

ers remain in place. The flat on the countershaft should be parallel to the top of the case. Tap the shaft with a brass hammer until the front of the shaft is flush with the case.

25. Rotate the extension housing to align the bolt holes and loosely install the attaching bolts. Make sure that the rail slides freely in its bore. Binding is remedied by slightly rotating the extension housing to free the rail, then pushing the housing into the case. Apply sealer to the attaching bolts and torque to 33-36 ft. lbs. Place the shift forks in the synchronizer sleeves. Install the interlock lever and new retaining pin. Lubricate the shift rail oil seal and slide the shift rail through the extension housing, case and second and first speed shift fork. Position the selector arm on the rail and slide the rail through third and fourth speed shift fork. Slide the shift rail through the front of the case until the center detent bore is aligned with the detent plunger bore. Install a new retaining pin in the selector arm.

26. Install the detent plunger, spring and plug with sealer.

27. Install a new access plug in the rear of the case.

28. Position a new oil seal with tension spring and lip facing in the direction of the case.

29. Drive the seal in until it bottoms.

30. Position a new O-ring in the groove in the case. Position the input shaft bearing retainer with the groove in the retainer aligned with the oil passage in the case. Install the retaining bolts finger-tight.

31. Install the flywheel housing and tighten the retaining bolts and the front bearing retainer attaching bolts. Coat the retainer with grease.

32. Install the clutch release arm and bearing.

33. Install a new extension housing plug, using sealer.

34. Install a new cover gasket and cover, with the vent to the rear. Apply sealer to the left front cover attaching bolt. Torque to 8-10 ft. lbs.

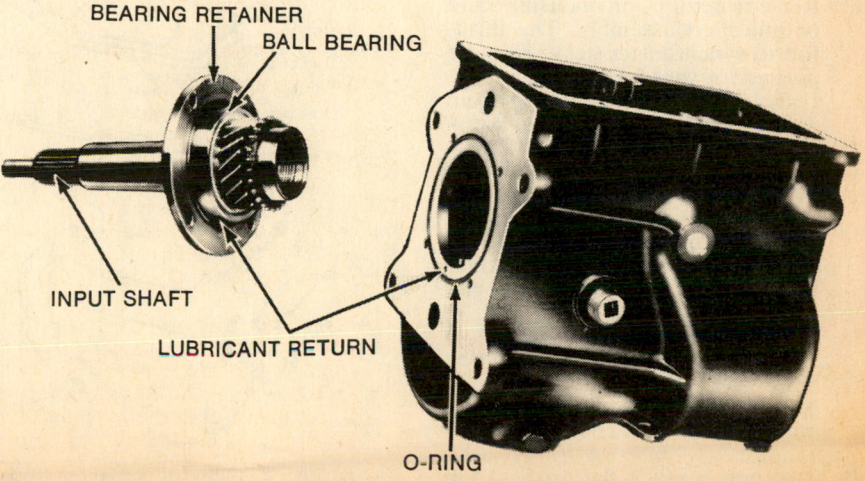

Installing input shaft gear (© Ford Motor Co)

TYPE-6
FORD 4-SPEED
(BRITISH DESIGN)
TYPES 71 WG, 72 WG

Application
Pinto (1600), 1972-73

NOTE: *Cars equipped with this transmission are identified by a transmission ID code suffix of BB or BC. The transmission ID code appears on a tag located under the left extension housing-to-case bolt.*

TRANSMISSION DISASSEMBLY

1. Remove four bolts and top cover plate.
2. Pry plug from rear of extension housing.
3. Remove plunger screw from right side of case.
4. Working through the top cover opening, use a punch to remove the pin securing the shift selector arm to the shift shaft.
5. Pull the shift shaft rearward, being careful not to drop the shift selector arm and the interlock plate.
6. Move the first-second and third-fourth gear synchronizer hubs toward the input shaft bearing.
7. If necessary, remove the shift shaft plunger spring from the case. The plunger screw was removed in Step 3.
8. Remove the pin from the third-fourth shift fork. Remove the fork.
9. Unbolt extension housing from case. With a plastic hammer, tap the extension housing slightly rearward. Rotate the housing until the countershaft lines up with the notch in the housing flange.
10. Tap the countershaft rearward with a brass drift until it is just clear of the front of the case. Push the countershaft out with a dummy shaft. Lower the cluster gear to the bottom of the case.
11. Remove extension housing and output shaft assembly. The third-fourth synchronizer sleeve must be pushed forward for clearance.
12. Unbolt front bearing retainer from case. Remove retainer and gasket.
13. Remove input shaft oil seal.
14. Remove the snap ring around the input shaft bearing. Tap the input shaft gear and bearing assembly out of the transmission with a brass drift. Remove the needle roller bearing from the recess in the end of the input shaft gear.
15. Remove the cluster gear, two thrust washers, and the dummy shaft from the case. Remove 20 needle rollers and a retaining washer from each end of the cluster gear.
16. Assemble a nut, a flat washer, and a sleeve on a $5/6$ in. x 24 UNF

threaded bolt. Screw the bolt into the reverse idler shaft and tighten to pull out the shaft.
17. Remove the low-reverse shift fork from the lever pin inside the case. Do not remove the pin.

COMPONENT DISASSEMBLY
Third-Fourth Synchronizer

1. Remove fourth gear blocking ring from input shaft gear side of assembly.
2. Remove synchronizer hub snapring from forward end of output shaft and discard.
3. Support third gear. Press the output shaft out of the third-fourth gear synchronizer and third gear. Be careful not to drop the output shaft.
4. Pull the sleeve off the hub. Remove the inserts and springs.
5. Check all parts for wear. Synchronizer hub and sleeve should be replaced if worn or damaged.

First-Second Synchronizer

1. Remove plug in extension housing. Remove speedometer driven gear.
2. Remove snap-ring holding output shaft bearing to extension housing. With a plastic hammer, tap output shaft assembly out of housing.
3. Remove snap-ring holding speedometer drive gear. Pull off gear. Remove snap-ring holding output shaft bearing.
4. Support low and reverse sliding gear. Press low and reverse sliding

gear, spacer, and output shaft bearing from the output shaft.
5. Remove snap-ring holding first-second synchronizer assembly to output shaft.
6. Support second gear. Press second gear and first-second synchronizer assembly from output shaft.
7. Dismantle synchronizer assembly. Replace synchronizer hub or sleeve if worn or damaged. The output shaft bearing must be replaced.

Input Shaft and Gear

1. Remove and discard input shaft snap-ring.
2. Press off input shaft bearing.

COMPONENT ASSEMBLY
Third-Fourth Synchronizer

1. Slide gear over hub. Locate an insert in each slot.
2. Install a synchronizer spring inside the sleeve beneath the inserts; the spring tang should fit into an insert. Install the other spring on the opposite side, fitting the tang into the same insert. When viewed from the edge, the springs should run in opposite directions.
3. Place the third gear on the output shaft with the dog teeth forward. Assemble the blocking ring on the third gear cone.
4. Place the synchronizer assembly on the output shaft with the boss forward.
5. Support the hub. Press the hub on the output shaft and install a new snap-ring.

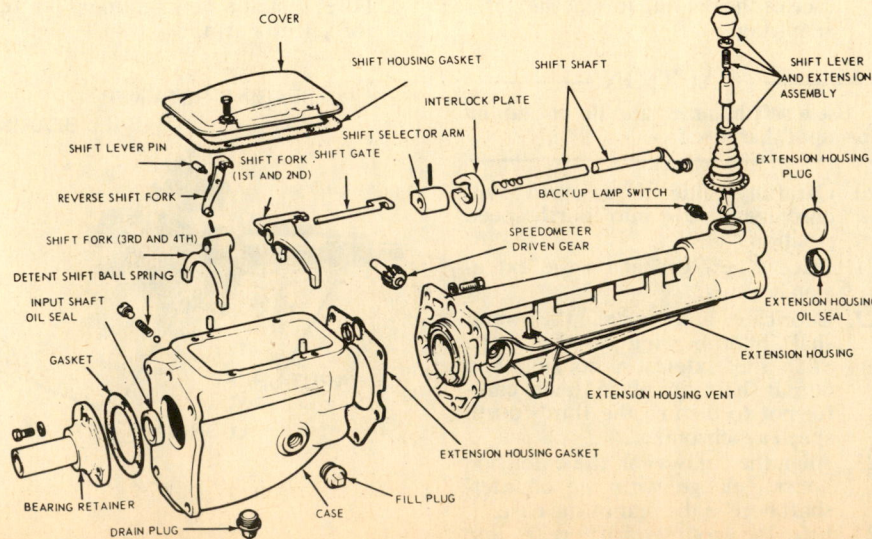

British 4-speed transmission disassembled—Types 71WG-BC and 72WG-BB
© Ford Motor Co

First-Second Synchronizer

1. Install the second gear on the output shaft with the cone and dog teeth to the rear.
2. Slide the synchronizer sleeve over the hub. Place an insert in each of the three slots.
3. Install synchronizer springs as for third-fourth synchronizer assembly.
4. Install a blocking ring to cone on second gear.
5. Install synchronizer assembly on output shaft with the gear teeth on the periphery of the synchronizer sleeve forward. Slide low and reverse sliding gear to the rear of the synchronizer hub.
6. Support the sliding gear. Press synchronizer assembly onto output shaft as far as possible.
7. Secure the synchronizer assembly with snap-ring.
8. Place a blocking ring on first gear side of first-second synchronizer assembly on output shaft. Install first gear, cone side forward.
9. Place the spacer with the larger diameter adjacent to first gear.
10. Select a snap-ring of the proper size to hold the output shaft bearing into the bearing recess with no end float.
11. Position the selected snap-ring loosely on the output shaft next to the spacer.
12. Support the bearing inner race. Press the bearing onto the shaft.
13. Select the thickest snap-ring that fits the groove to hold the bearing to the output shaft.
14. Locate output shaft ball bearing in shaft indent, push speedometer drive gear onto output shaft. Install new snap-ring.
15. Heat the end of the extension housing. Do not use a torch. A pan of hot water is recommended.
16. Install the output shaft into the extension housing. Install the snapring securing the output shaft bearing to the housing.
17. Replace the speedometer driven gear. Install a new plug, using sealer.

Input Shaft and Gear

1. Support the input shaft bearing inner race. Press the bearing onto the shaft.
2. Install the snap-ring securing the bearing to the input shaft.

TRANSMISSION ASSEMBLY

1. Slide the low-reverse lever onto the lever pin inside the case.
2. Push the idler shaft into the case. Place the reverse idler gear on the shaft. Locate the low-reverse lever in the gear groove. Tap the reverse idler shaft into position with a soft hammer.
3. Slide a dummy shaft into the cluster gear. Push a retainer washer into the gear bore. Grease and install 20 needle rollers and the second retaining washer. Install the washers and rollers at the other end of the gear. Grease and install the thrust washers with their convex side into the gear recess.
4. Place the cluster gear in the bottom of the case. Position the thrust washers with the flat upward.
5. Place the input shaft and gear in the case. Using a brass drift, tap

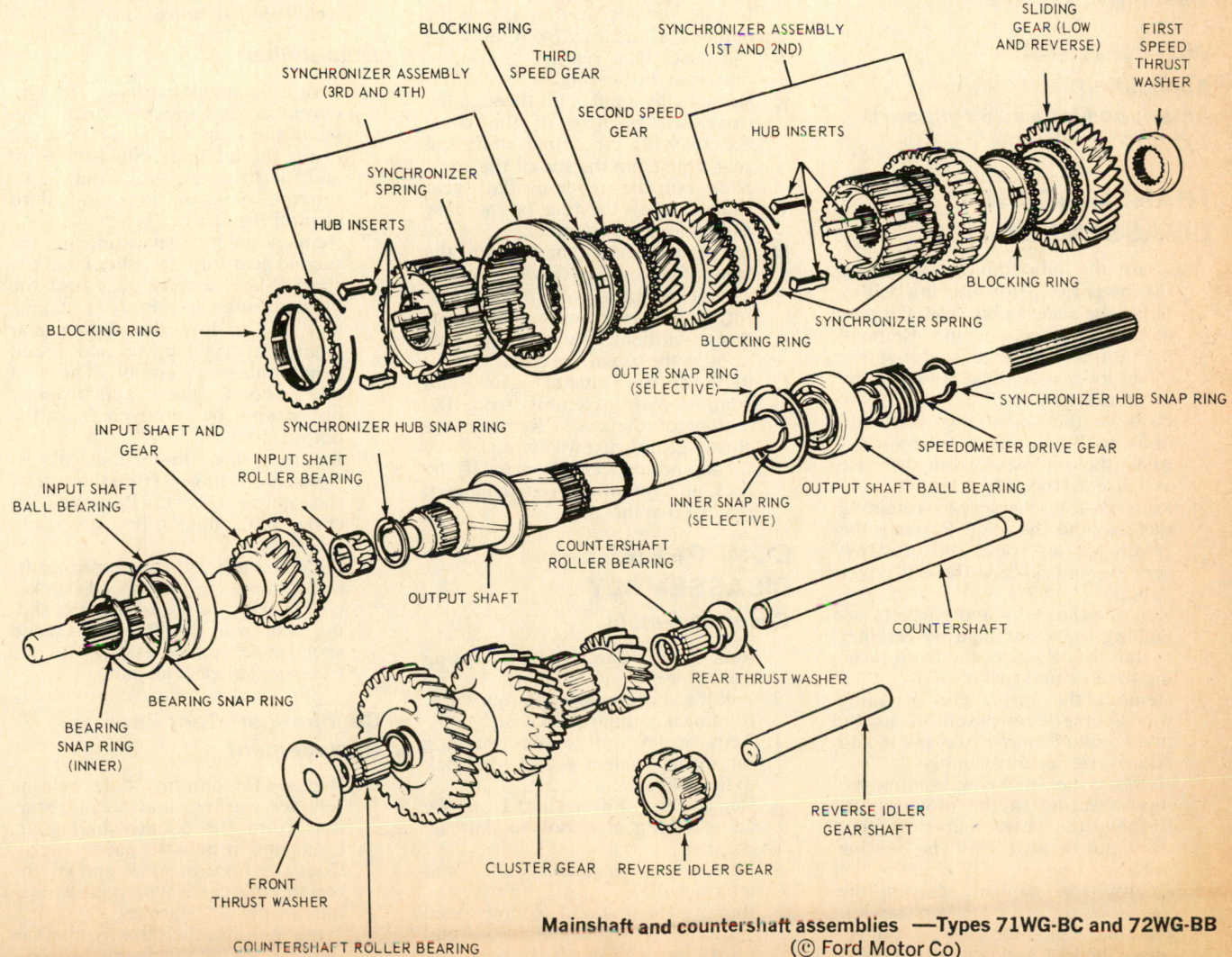

Mainshaft and countershaft assemblies —Types 71WG-BC and 72WG-BB
(© Ford Motor Co)

bearing outer race into place. Be careful not to damage the dog teeth on the input shaft gear with the cluster gear. Install the bearing snap-ring.

6. Place the input shaft needle bearing in the input shaft gear recess.
7. Drive a new oil seal into the input shaft retainer. Cover the input shaft splines. Install a new gasket on the transmission front face. Check that the retainer oil groove is lined up with the oil passage in the case. Coat the bolts with sealer and install them with lock-washers.
8. Locate the fourth gear blocking ring on the input shaft gear cone.
9. Install a new oil seal in the shift shaft aperture. Drive the seal in with a socket.
10. Install a new sealer coated gasket to the extension housing.

11. Pull the third-fourth synchronizer sleeve forward. Slide the extension housing and output shaft into position. Align the cutaway on the extension housing with the countershaft aperture in the rear face of the case.
12. Using loops of cord, lift the cluster gear into mesh with the output and input shaft gears. Take care not to drop the countershaft thrust washers.
13. Tap the countershaft into place, driving out the dummy shaft, ensuring that the lug on the rear of the countershaft fits into the recess on the extension housing flange.
14. Push the extension housing onto the transmission case. Apply sealer to bolts. Torque to 30-35 ft. lbs.
15. Replace both shift forks. Secure third-fourth fork with a new pin.

16. Position shift forks to synchronizer sleeves. Move synchronizer hubs into neutral positions.
17. Grease shift shaft oil seal in rear of case. Slide shift shaft through extension housing. Position shift selector arm and interlock plate so that interlock plate locates in cutouts in shift forks. Pass the shift shaft through the shift selector arm and forks until the pin holes are aligned.
18. Replace the plunger ball and spring. Replace the retaining screw, using sealer.
19. Install the pin through the shift selector arm and shift shaft.
20. Apply sealer to plug. Tap plug into rear of extension housing.
21. Install top cover and gasket.
22. Refill transmission with 2.8 pints SAE 80 oil.

Application
Mustang II, 1974-79

WARNER SR4

Application
American Motors, (6 cylinder), 1977-79

TRANSMISSION DISASSEMBLY

1. Drain the lubricant by removing the lower extension housing bolt.
2. Drive the access plug from the rear of the extension housing. Remove the nut and washer securing the offset lever assembly. Remove the offset lever assembly.
3. Remove the remaining extension housing bolts and washers. Remove the extension from the case and discard the old gasket.
4. Remove the cap screws retaining the cover to the case. Remove the cover, shifter fork, shift rod assembly, and discard the old cover gasket.
5. Remove the bolts and washers attaching the front bearing retainer to the case. Remove the front bearing retainer and gasket.
6. Remove the spring clip retaining the reverse lever assembly to the pivot bolt. Remove the pivot and the reverse lever assembly.
7. Remove the snap-ring holding the input bearing to the input shaft. Remove the outer snap-ring from the input bearing. Pull the bearing out.
8. Remove the snap-ring securing the speedometer drive gear on the output shaft. Slide the gear off and remove the lock ball from the shaft.

TYPE-7
FORD RAD 4-SPEED

9. Remove the snap-ring retaining the output shaft bearing on the shaft. Use the outer snap-ring to pull the output shaft bearing from the shaft and case, then remove the snap-ring from the bearing.
10. Remove the input shaft through the front bearing hole in the case. Carefully lift the output shaft and gear train from the top of the case. Slide out the reverse idler gear shaft through the rear of the case and remove reverse gear.
11. Insert a dummy shaft from the front of the case to drive the countershaft out of the rear of the case. Lift out the countershaft gear, thrust washers, and dummy shaft through the top of the case.
12. Remove the cluster gear and dummy shaft assembly from the bottom of the case. Remove the cluster gear thrust washers.
13. Clean and inspect all parts. If the back-up light switch was damaged, remove it at this time.

COMPONENT DISASSEMBLY
Cover Assembly

1. Remove the detent screw, spring and plunger.
2. Pull the shifter shaft rod rearward, rotating it counterclockwise.
3. Remove the spring pin retaining the manual selector and interlock to the shifter shaft.
4. Remove the shifter shaft from the cover taking care not to damage the seal.
5. Remove the manual selector and interlock plate.
6. Remove the first and second speed shifter fork. Remove the third and fourth speed shifter fork.

7. Clean and inspect all parts. Replace the shifter shaft seal and welch plug, if damaged.

Output Shaft

1. Scribe alignment marks on the synchronizer and blocker rings. Remove the snap-ring from the front of the output shaft. Slide the third and fourth speed synchronizer assembly, blocker rings and third gear off the shaft.
2. Remove the next snap-ring and the second gear thrust washer from the shaft. Slide second gear and the blocker ring off the shaft, taking care not to lose the sliding gear from the first and second speed synchronizer assembly. The first and second speed synchronizer hub cannot be removed from the output shaft.
3. Remove the first gear thrust washer (oil slinger) from the rear of the output shaft. Remove the spring pin retaining first gear onto the shaft.
4. Slide first gear off the output shaft, and remove the first speed blocker ring. Take care not to lose the sliding gear from the first and second speed synchronizer assembly.
5. Clean and inspect all parts.

Countershaft Gear Bearing Replacement

1. Remove the dummy shaft, bearing retainer washers and needle bearings from the countershaft gear. Clean and inspect all parts.
2. Coat the bore at each end of the countershaft gear with grease to retain the needle bearings.
3. While holding the dummy shaft in the gear, install the needle bearings

and retainer washers in each end of the gear.

Input Shaft Bearing Replacement

1. Remove the roller bearings from the input shaft.
2. Remove the snap-ring retaining the input shaft bearing. Press the input shaft out of the bearing. Clean and inspect all parts.
3. Press the input shaft bearing onto the input shaft, making sure that the snap-ring groove faces the front of the shaft. Install a new snap-ring to retain the bearing on the shaft.
4. Lightly coat the bore of the input shaft with grease.

NOTE: *If a thick film of grease, such as wheel bearing grease, is applied to the shaft, the lubrication holes may become clogged, thereby preventing transmission oil from reaching the bearings, possibly resulting in premature bearing failure.*

5. Install the roller bearings in the bore.

Synchronizer Replacement

1. Scribe alignment marks on the hub and sleeve of the synchronizer.
2. Push the synchronizer sleeve from each synchronizer hub.

NOTE: *The first and second speed synchronizer hub cannot be removed from the output shaft.*

3. Separate the inserts and insert springs from the hubs, taking care not to mix the parts of the first and second speed synchronizer with that of the third and fourth speed synchronizer. Clean and inspect all parts.
4. Position the sleeve on the hub, making sure that the alignment marks scribed prior to disassembly are aligned.
5. Position the 3 inserts on the hub.

Install the insert springs, taking care to seat the bent tab in one of the inserts. The springs must face in opposite directions.

COMPONENT ASSEMBLY

Output Shaft

1. Place a blocker ring on the cone of first gear, and slide the gear and ring assembly onto the output shaft. Make sure that the inserts in the synchronizer engage in the blocker ring notches.
2. Install the spring pin retaining first gear to the output shaft.
3. Install a blocker ring on the cone of second gear, and slide the gear and ring assembly onto the output shaft. Make sure that the inserts in the synchronizer engage in the blocker ring notches.
4. Install the second gear thrust washer and new snap-ring on the shaft.
5. Install a blocker ring on the cone of third gear, and slide the gear and ring assembly onto the output shaft. Install the third and fourth speed synchronizer. Make sure that the inserts in the synchronizer engage in the blocker ring notches.
6. Install a new third and fourth gear synchronizer snap-ring.
7. Place the first gear thrust washer (oil slinger) on the shaft and on the spring pin retaining first gear.

—————— CAUTION ——————

The oil grooves must be positioned against the gear.

Cover Assembly

1. Install the third and fourth speed shifter fork into the cover.
2. Install the first and second speed shifter fork into the cover. Lubricate the shifter shaft bore with grease.
3. Install the manual selector arm through the interlock plate, and position the two pieces into the cover, with the wide leg of the in-

terlock plate towards the inside of the transmission case.
4. Align the shifter shaft in the cover, and insert the shaft through the shifter forks and manual selector. Coat the shifter shaft with a light coating of grease. Make sure the detent grooves face the plunger side of the cover.
5. Align the pin holes in the manual selector arm and shifter shaft. Install the spring pin flush with the surface of the selector arm.
6. Install the detent plunger, spring, and plug. Tighten the plug to 8-12 ft. lbs.
7. Check the operation of the shift forks in each gear position.

TRANSMISSION ASSEMBLY

1. Position the reverse idler gear and shaft in place.
2. Coat the surfaces of the countershaft thrust washers with a thin film of grease and position in the case. The plastic washer goes in front, the bronze one at the rear. Position the cluster gear assembly in the bottom of the case.
3. Place the transmission in the vertical position. Align the countershaft gear bore and thrust washers with the bore in the case. Install the countershaft from the rear of the case. Return the transmission to the horizontal position.
4. Position the output shaft assembly into the case through the cover opening. With the snap-ring groove facing rearward, place the rear bearing on the output shaft. Place the transmission in the vertical position and install the bearing. Position the first gear thrust washer on the roll pin carefully, holding it tightly during bearing installation. Install the rear bearing snap-rings.
5. Install the input shaft and blocker ring through the front of the case. Make sure that the blocker ring notches engage the synchronizer insert.
6. Install the front bearing retainer

HUB INSERTS (THIRD & FOURTH)

SYNCHRONIZER SPRINGS

PART OF ASSEMBLY OR ASSEMBLY HUB

HUB INSERTS (FIRST AND SECOND)

RAD synchronizer spring rotation ((c) Ford Motor Co)

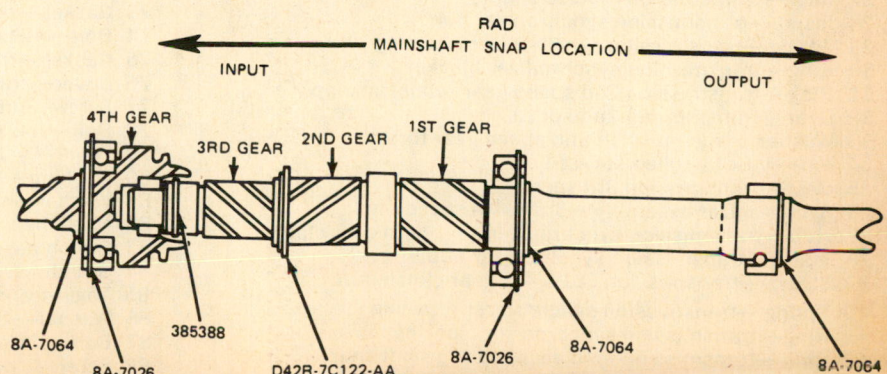

RAD
MAINSHAFT SNAP LOCATION
INPUT   OUTPUT

4TH GEAR   3RD GEAR   2ND GEAR   1ST GEAR

8A-7064   385388   8A-7026   8A-7064   8A-7064
       8A-7026   D42R-7C122-AA

RAD mainshaft snap-ring locations ((c) Ford Motor Co)

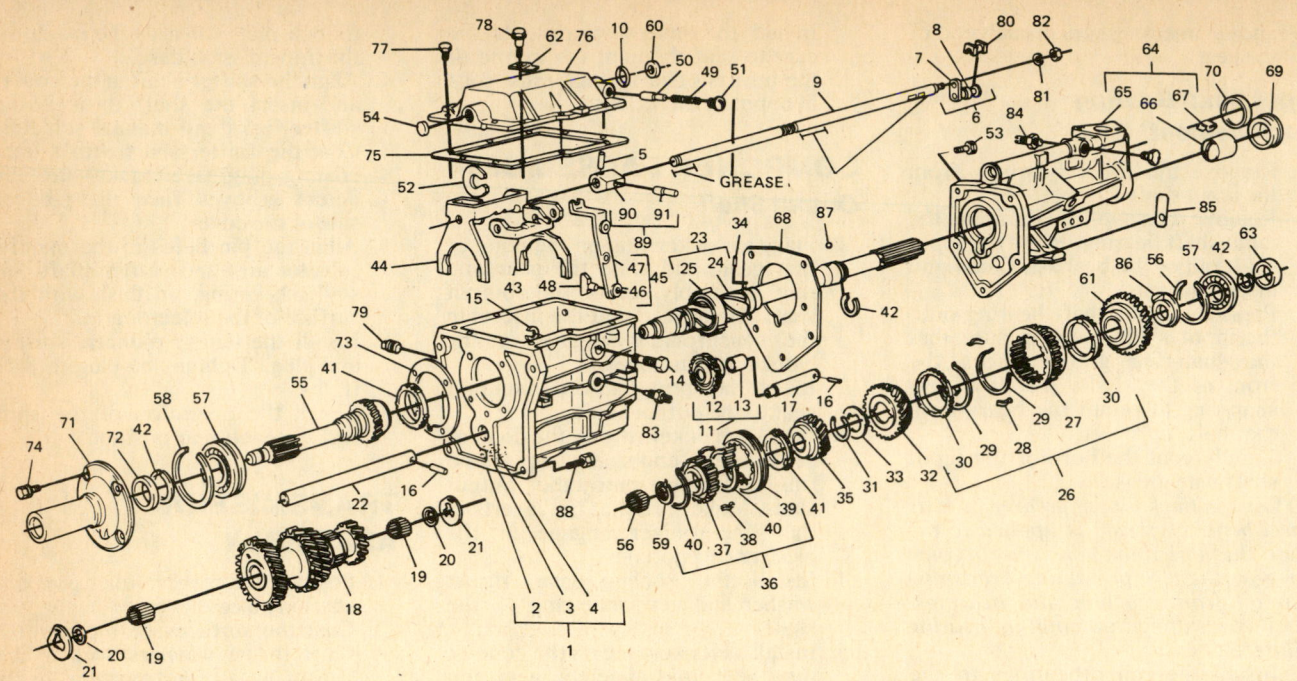

RAD transmission disassembled (© Ford Motor Co)

1 Case assembly—transmission
2 Case—transmission
3 Magnet—transmission case chip
4 Nut spring 9/64
5 Pin—3/16 diameter x 13/16 rolled spring
6 Lever assembly—transmission gearshift shaft offset
7 Lever transmission gearshift shaft offset
8 Pin—transmission gearshift shaft offset lever
9 Shaft—transmission shifter
10 Seal—O-ring
11 Gear & bush assembly—transmission reverse idler sliding
12 Gear—transmission reverse idler sliding
13 Bushing—transmission reverse idler gear
14 Pin—transmission reverse gear selector fork pivot
15 Ring—7/16 retaining
16 Pin—1/4 x 1 spring
17 Shaft—transmission reverse idler gear
18 Gear—transmission countershaft
19 Roller—transmission countershaft bearing
20 Washer—208/.918 flat
21 Washer—transmission countershaft gear thrust
22 Countershaft—transmission
23 Shaft assembly—transmission output
24 Shaft—transmission output
25 Hub—transmission synchronizer 1st & 2nd gear cluster
26 Shaft and gear assembly—transmission output
27 Gear—transmission reverse sliding
28 Insert—transmission synchronizer hub
29 Spring—transmission synchronizer retaining
30 Ring—transmission synchronizer blocking
31 Ring—transmission 2nd speed gear retaining snap
32 Gear—transmission 2nd speed
33 Washer—transmission 2nd speed gear thrust
34 Pin—1/8 x 1/4 rolled spring
35 Gear—transmission 3rd speed
36 Synchronizer assembly—3rd & 4th speed
37 Hub—transmission synchronizer   ; 4th gear clutch
38 Insert—transmission synchronizer hub
39 Sleeve—transmission 3rd & 4th gear clutch hub
40 Spring—transmission synchronizer retaining
41 Ring—transmission synchronizer blocking
42 Ring—transmission m/d gear bearing shaft snap
43 Fork—transmission 1st & 2nd gear shift
44 Fork—transmission 3rd & 4th gear shift
45 Lever assembly—transmission reverse gear shaft relay

46 Retaining—transmission reverse gear shaft relay lever
47 Lever—transmission reverse gear shaft relay
48 Fork—transmission reverse gear shift
49 Spring—transmission shifter interlock
50 Plunger—transmission meshlock
51 Screw—m12 x 10 round head flat
52 Plate—transmission gear selector interlock
53 Screw & washer assembly—m10 x 30 hex head
54 Plug—3/4 diameter welch type
55 Shaft—transmission input
56 Roller—transmission mainshaft bearing
57 Bearing assembly—transmission m/d gear ball
58 Ring—m/d gear bearing retaining snap
59 Ring—1.00 retaining
60 Seal—transmission shift shaft
61 Gear—transmission 1st speed
62 Clip—spark control switch wire retaining
63 Gear—speedometer drive
64 Extension assembly—transmission
65 Extension—transmission
66 Bushing—transmission extension
67 Stop—transmission gear shift lever reverse
68 Gasket—transmission extension
69 Seal assembly—transmission extension oil
70 Plug—transmission extension
71 Retainer—transmission input shaft gear bearing
72 Seal assembly—transmission input shaft oil
73 Gasket—transmission input shaft bearing retainer
74 Bolt—M8 x 20 hex head-lock
75 Gasket—transmission case cover
76 Cover—transmission case
77 Screw—m6 x 20 hex head
78 Bolt—m6 x 32 hex washer HD shoulder
79 Plug—1/2-14 pipe (filler)
80 Bushing—transmission gear shift damper
81 Washer—spring lock
82 Nut—hexagon
83 Switch assembly—back-up lamp
84 Switch assembly—transmission seat belt warning sensor
85 Tag—transmission service identification
86 Washer—transmission 1st gear thrust
87 Ball—.25 diameter
88 Screw & lockwasher assembly—m12 x 40
89 Arm assembly—transmission control selector
90 Arm—transmission control selector
91 Pin—transmission gear shift

using a new gasket. Apply gasket sealer to the bolt threads and tighten to 11-15 ft. lbs.

7. Install the reverse idler gear lever assembly, taking care to insert the fork in the reverse idler gear groove.

8. Apply gasket sealer to the reverse lever pivot bolt threads and install the bolt. Align the lever on the pivot bolt and torque the bolt to 15-25 ft. lbs. Install the reverse lever retaining spring clip to the reverse gear pivot bolt. Tilt the transmission forward and pour a light

coating of gear lube over the gear train.

9. Using a new cover gasket, install the cover assembly. Install the bolts and wiring clips and tighten.

NOTE: *The two shouldered locating bolts must be installed first. Position the shift rail in first or third gear.*

10. Insert the speedometer drive gear lock ball into its hole. While holding the ball, slide the speedometer drive gear into place and secure it with a new snap-ring.

11. Using a new gasket, install the extension housing to the case. Using gasket sealer on the bolts, tighten them to 18-27 ft. lbs. Take care not to damage the extension yoke seal.

12. Install the offset lever assembly onto the shift shaft, securing the assembly with a nut and flat washer. Tighten to 8-12 ft. lbs.

13. Insert the gearshift lever into place. Check its operation in each gear position.

14. Install the access plug into the rear of the extension housing, using a soft mallet.

TYPE-8
FORD 4-SPEED,
4-SPEED OVERDRIVE

Application
Cougar, 1972-73
Granada, 1977-79
Monarch, 1977-79
Montego, 1972-73
Mustang V8, 1972-73
Torino V8, 1972-73

DISASSEMBLY

1. Remove retaining clips and flat washers from the shift rods at the levers.

2. Remove shift linkage control bracket attaching screws and remove shift linkage and control brackets.

3. Remove cover attaching screws. Then lift cover and gasket from the case. Remove the long spring that holds the detent plug in the case. Remove the plug with a magnet.

4. Remove extension housing attaching screws. Then, remove extension housing and gasket.

5. Remove input shaft bearing retainer attaching screws. Then, slide retainer from the input shaft.

6. Working a dummy shaft in from the front of the case, drive the countershaft out the rear of the case. Let the countergear assembly lie in the bottom of the case. Remove the set screw from the first-second shift fork. Slide the first-second shift rail out of the rear of the case. Use a magnet to remove the interlock detent from between the first-second and third-fourth shift rails.

7. Locate first-second-speed gear shift lever in neutral. Locate third fourth-speed gear shift lever in third-speed position.

NOTE: *On overdrive transmissions, locate third-fourth speed gear shift-lever in the fourth speed position.*

8. Remove the lockbolt that holds the third-fourth-speed shift rail detent spring and plug in the left side of

the case. Remove spring and plug with a magnet.

9. Remove the detent mechanism set screw from top of case. Then, remove the detent spring and plug with a small magnet.

10. Remove attaching screw from the third-fourth-speed shift fork. Tap lightly on the inner end of the shift rail to remove the expansion plug from front of case. Then, withdraw the third-fourth-speed shift rail from the front. (Do not lose the interlock pin from rail.)

11. Remove attaching screw from the first and second-speed shift fork. Slide the first-second shift rail from the rear of case.

12. Remove the interlock and detent plugs from the top of the case with a magnet.

13. Remove the snap-ring or disengage retainer that holds the speedometer drive gear to the output shaft, then remove speedometer gear drive ball.

14. Remove the snap-ring used to hold the output shaft bearing to the shaft. Pull out the output shaft bearing.

15. Remove the input shaft bearing snap-rings. Use a press to remove the input shaft bearing. Remove the input shaft and blocking ring from the front of the case.

16. Move output shaft to the right side

of case. Then, maneuver the forks to permit lifting them from the case.

17. Support the thrust washer and first-speed gear to prevent sliding from the shaft, then lift output shaft from the case.

18. Remove reverse gear shift fork attaching screw. Rotate the reverse shift rail 90°, then, slide the shift rail out the rear of the case. Lift out the reverse shift fork.

19. Remove the reverse detent plug and spring from the case with a magnet.

20. Using a dummy shaft, remove the reverse idler shaft from the case.

21. Lift reverse idler gear and thrust washers from the case. Be careful not to drop the bearing rollers or the dummy shaft from the gear.

22. Lift the countergear, thrust washers, rollers and dummy shaft assembly from the case.

23. Remove the next snap-ring from the front of the output shaft. Then, slide the third-fourth synchronizer blocking ring and the third-speed gear from the shaft.

24. Remove the next snap-ring and the second-speed gear thrust washer from the shaft. Slide the second-speed gear and the blocking ring from the shaft.

25. Remove the snap-ring, then slide the first-second synchronizer,

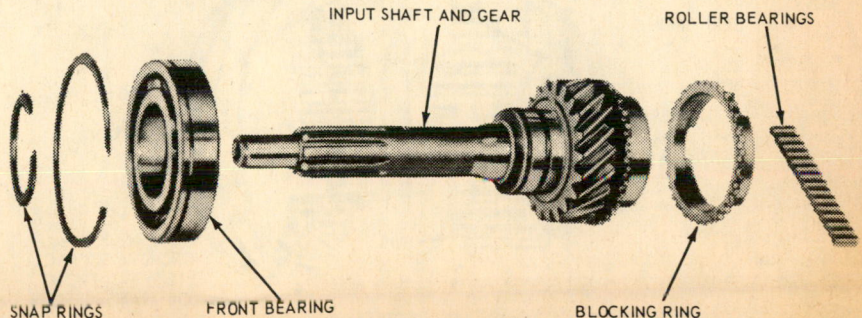

4-Speed overdrive input shaft details (© Ford Motor Co.)

INPUT SHAFT AND GEAR

ROLLER BEARINGS

SNAP RINGS

FRONT BEARING

BLOCKING RING

blocking ring and the first-speed gear from the shaft.

26. Remove the thrust washer from rear of the shaft.

UNIT REPAIRS

Cam and Shaft Seals

1. Remove attaching nut and washers from each shift lever, then remove the three levers.
2. Remove the three cams and shafts from inside the case.
3. Replace the old O-rings with new ones that have been well-lubricated.
4. Slide each cam and shaft into its respective bore in the transmission.
5. Install the levers and secure them with their respective washers and nuts.

Synchronizers

1. Push the synchronizer hub from each synchronizer sleeve.
2. Separate the inserts and springs from the hubs. Do not mix parts of the first-second with parts of third-fourth synchronizers.
3. To assemble, position the hub in the sleeve. Be sure the alignment marks are properly indexed.
4. Place the three inserts into place on the hub. Install the insert springs so that the irregular surface (hump) is seated in one of the inserts. Do not stagger the springs.

Countershaft Gear

1. Dismantle the countershaft gear assembly.
2. Assemble the gear by coating each end of the countershaft gear bore with grease.
3. Install dummy shaft in the gear. Then install 21 bearing rollers and a retainer washer in each end of the gear.

Reverse Idler Gear

1. Dismantle reverse idler gear.
2. Assemble reverse idler gear by coating the bore in each end of reverse idler gear with grease.
3. Hold the dummy shaft in the gear and install the 22 bearing rollers and the retainer washer into each end of the gear.
4. Install the reverse idler sliding gear on the splines of the reverse idler gear. Be sure the shift fork groove is toward the front.

Input Shaft Seal

1. Remove the seal from the input shaft bearing retainer.
2. Coat the sealing surface of a new seal with lubricant, then press the new seal into the input shaft bearing retainer.

ASSEMBLY

1. Grease the countershaft gear thrust surfaces in the case. Then, position a thrust washer at each end of the case.
2. Position the countershaft gear, dummy shaft, and roller bearings in the case.
3. Align the gear bore and thrust washers with the bores in the case. Install the countershaft.
4. With the case in a horizontal position, countershaft gear end-play should be from .004-.018 in. Use thrust washers to obtain play within these limits.
5. After establishing correct endplay, place the dummy shaft in the countershaft gear and allow the gear assembly to remain on the bottom of the case.
6. Grease the reverse idler gear thrust surfaces in the case, and position the two thrust washers.
7. Position the reverse idler gear, sliding gear, dummy, etc. in place. Make sure that the shift fork groove in the sliding gear is toward the front.
8. Align the gear bore and thrust washers with the case bores and install the reverse idler shaft.
9. Reverse idler gear end-play should be .004-.018 in. Use selective thrust washers to obtain play within these limits.
10. Position reverse gear shift rail detent spring and detent plug in the case. Hold the reverse shift fork in place on the reverse idler sliding gear and install the shift rail from the rear of the case. Lock the fork to the rail with the Allen head set screws.
11. Install the first-second synchronizer onto the output shaft. The first and reverse synchronizer hub are a press fit and should be installed with gear teeth facing the rear of the shaft.

NOTE: *On overdrive transmissions, first and reverse synchronizer hub is a slip fit.*

12. Place the blocking ring on second gear. Slide second-speed gear onto the front of the shaft with the synchronizer coned surface toward the rear.
13. Install the second-speed gear thrust washer and snap-ring.
14. Slide the fourth gear onto the shaft with the synchronizer coned surface front.
15. Place a blocking ring on the fourth gear.
16. Slide the third-fourth speed gear synchronizer onto the shaft. Be sure that the inserts in the synchronizer engage the notches in the blocking ring. Install the snap-ring onto the front of the output shaft.
17. Put the blocking ring on the first gear.
18. Slide the first gear onto the rear of the output shaft. Be sure that the inserts engage the notches in the blocking ring and that the shift fork groove is toward the rear.

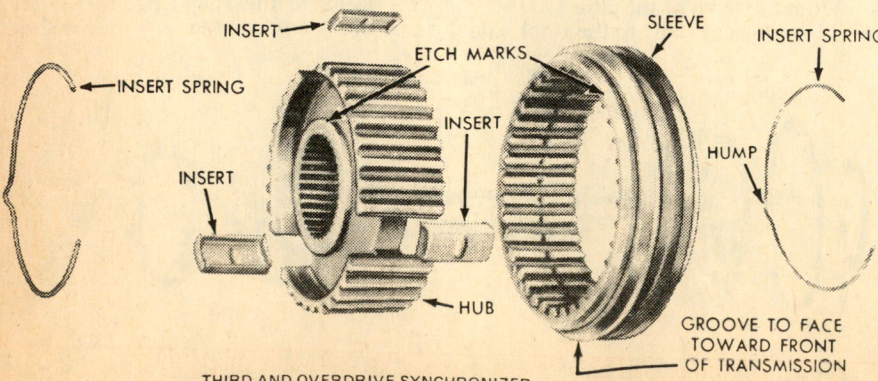

FIRST AND SECOND SPEED SYNCHRONIZER

THIRD AND OVERDRIVE SYNCHRONIZER

4-Speed overdrive synchronizer assembly (© Ford Motor Co.)

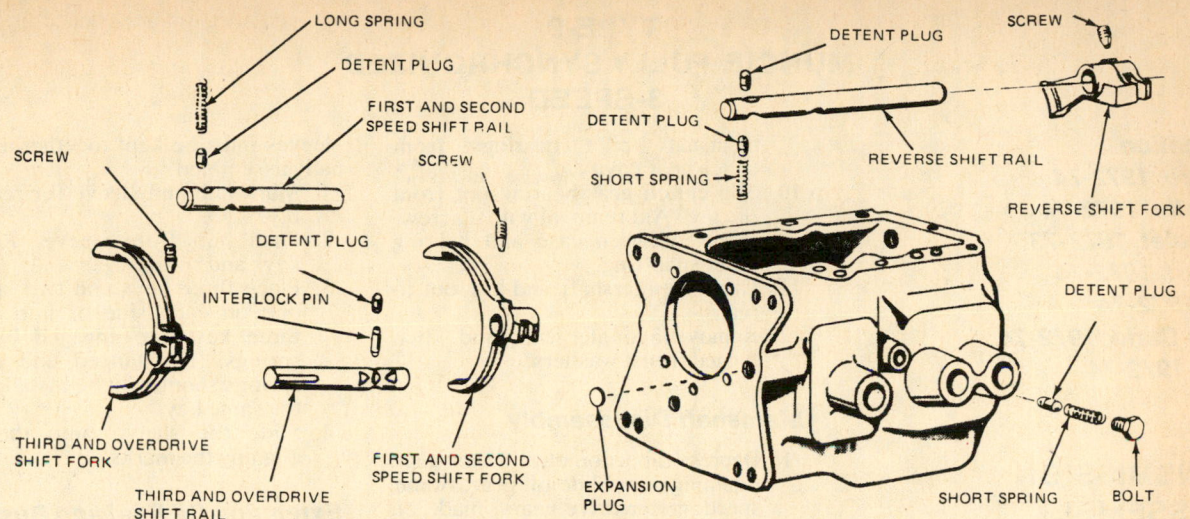

4-Speed overdrive shift rail and fork details (© Ford Motor Co.)

19. Install heavy thrust washer onto the rear of the output shaft.
20. Lower the output shaft assembly into the case.
21. Position the first-second speed shift fork and the third-fourth-speed shift fork in place on their respective gears. Rotate them into place.
22. Place a spring and detent plug in the detent bore. Place the reverse shift rail into neutral position.
23. Coat the third-fourth-speed shift rail interlock pin (tapered ends) with grease, then position it in the shift rail.
24. Align the third-fourth-speed shift fork with the shift rail bores and slide the shift rail into place. Be sure that the three detents are facing the outside of the case. Place the front synchronizer into fourth-speed position and install the set screw into the third-fourth-speed shift fork. Move the synchronizer to neutral position. Install the third-fourth-speed shift rail detent plug, spring and bolt into the left side of the transmission case. Place the detent plug (tapered ends) in the detent bore.
25. Align first-second-speed shift fork with the case bores and slide the shift rail into place. Lock the fork with the set screw.
26. Coat the input gear bore with a small amount of grease. Then install the 15 bearing rollers.
27. Put the blocking ring in the third-fourth synchronizer. Place the input shaft gear in the case. Be sure that the output shaft pilot enters the roller bearing of the input shaft gear.
28. With a new gasket on the input bearing retainer, dip attaching bolts in sealer, install bolts and torque to 30-36 ft. lbs.
29. Press on the output shaft bearing, then install the snap-ring to hold

the bearing.
30. Position the speedometer gear drive ball in the output shaft and slide the speedometer drive gear into place. Secure gear with snap-ring.
31. Align the countershaft gear bore and thrust washers with the bore in the case. Install the countershaft.
32. With a new gasket in place, install and secure the extension housing. Dip the extension housing screws in sealer, then torque screws to 42-50 ft. lbs.
33. Install the filler plug and the drain plug.
34. Pour E.P. gear oil over the entire gear train while rotating the input shaft.

35. Place each shift fork in all positions to make sure they function properly. Install the remaining detent plug in the case, followed by the spring.
36. With a new cover gasket in place, install the cover. Dip attaching screws in sealer, then torque screws to 14-19 ft. lbs.
37. Coat the third-fourth speed shift rail plug bore with sealer. Install a new plug.
38. Secure each shift rod to its respective lever with a spring washer, flat washer and retaining pin.
39. Position the shift linkage control bracket to the extension housing. Install and torque the attaching screws to 12-15 ft. lbs.

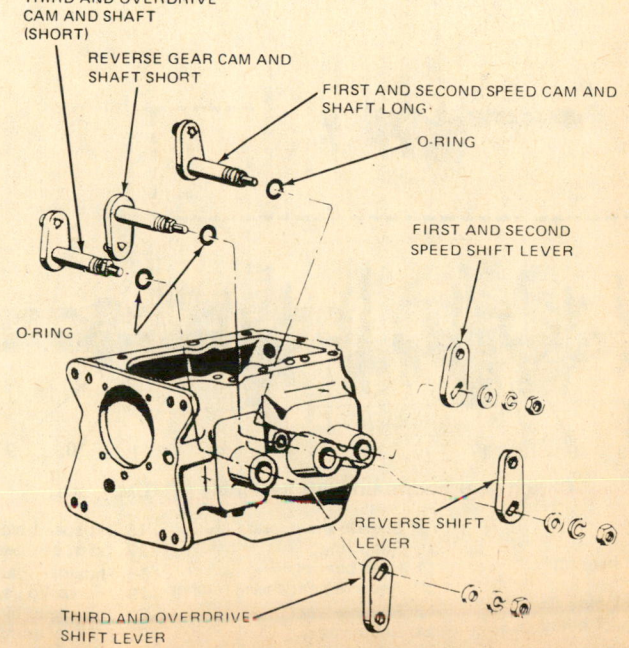

4-Speed overdrive cams and shift levers (© Ford Motor Co.)

TYPE-9
MUNCIE FULLY SYNCHRONIZED
3-SPEED

Application
Camaro, 1972-74
Chevelle, 1972-74
Chevrolet, 1972-73
Firebird, 1972-74
GTO, 1972-74
Monte Carlo, 1972-74
Nova, 1972-74

TRANSMISSION DISASSEMBLY

1. Remove side cover and shift forks.
2. Unbolt extension. Rotate extension to line up groove in extension flange with reverse idler shaft. Drive reverse idler shaft and key out of case with a brass drift.
3. Move second-third synchronizer sleeve forward. Remove extension housing and mainshaft assembly.
4. Remove reverse idler gear from case.
5. Remove third speed blocker ring from clutch gear.
6. Expand snap-ring which retains mainshaft rear bearing. Tap gently on end of mainshaft to remove extension.
7. Remove clutch gear bearing retainer and gasket.
8. Remove snap-ring. Remove clutch gear from inside case by gently tapping on end of clutch gear.
9. Remove oil slinger. Remove 16

mainshaft pilot bearings from clutch gear cavity.
10. Slip clutch gear bearing out front of case. Aid removal with a screwdriver between case and bearing outer snap-ring.
11. Drive countershaft and key out to rear.
12. Remove countergear and two tanged thrust washers.

Mainshaft Disassembly

1. Depress speedometer drive gear retaining clip. Slide off gear. Some speedometer drive gears, made of metal, must be pulled off.
2. Remove rear bearing snap-ring.
3. Support reverse gear and press on rear of mainshaft to remove reverse gear, thrust washer, and rear bearing. Be careful not to cock the bearing on the shaft.
4. Remove first and reverse sliding clutch hub snap-ring.
5. Support first gear. Press on rear of mainshaft to remove clutch assembly, blocker ring, and first gear.
6. Remove second and third speed sliding clutch hub snap-ring.
7. Support second gear. Press on front of mainshaft to remove clutch assembly, second speed blocker ring, and second gear from shaft.

Clutch Keys and Springs

Keys and springs may be replaced if worn or broken, but the hubs and

sleeves must be kept together as originally assembled.
1. Mark hub and sleeve for reassembly.
2. Push hub from sleeve. Remove keys and springs.
3. Place three keys and two springs, one on each side of hub, so all three keys are engaged by both springs. The tanged end of the springs should not be installed into the same key.
4. Slide the sleeve onto the hub, aligning the marks.

Extension Oil Seal and Bushing

1. Remove seal.
2. Using bushing remover and installer, drive bushing into extension housing.
3. Drive new bushing in from rear. Lubricate inside of bushing and seal. Install new oil seal with seal installer.

Clutch Bearing Retainer Oil Seal

1. Pry old seal out.
2. Install new seal using seal installer. Seat seal in bore.

Mainshaft Assembly

1. Turn front of mainshaft up.
2. Install second gear with clutching teeth up; the rear face of the gear butts against the flange on the mainshaft.
3. Install a blocking ring with clutching teeth downward. All three blocking rings are the same.
4. Install second and third synchronizer assembly with fork slot down. Press it onto mainshaft splines. Both synchronizer assemblies are identical but are assembled differently. The second-third speed hub and sleeve is assembled with the sleeve fork slot toward the thrust face of the hub; the first-reverse hub and sleeve, with the fork slot opposite the thrust face. Be sure that the blocker ring notches align with the synchronizer assembly keys.
5. Install synchronizer snap-ring. Both synchronizer snap-rings are the same.
6. Turn rear of shaft up.
7. Install first gear with clutching teeth upward; the front face of the gear butts against the flange on the mainshaft.
8. Install a blocker ring with clutching teeth down.
9. Install first and reverse synchronizer assembly with fork slot up. Press it onto mainshaft splines. Be sure blocker ring notches align

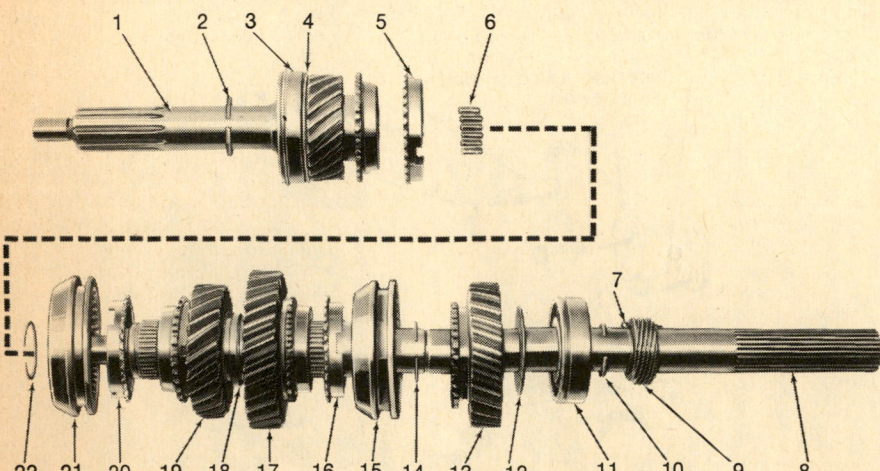

Clutch gear and mainshaft assembly (© G.M. Corp)

1 Clutch gear
2 Snap ring
3 Clutch gear bearing
4 Oil slinger
5 3rd speed blocker ring
6 Mainshaft pilot bearings (16)
7 Retaining clip
8 Mainshaft
9 Speedo drive gear
10 Snap ring
11 Rear bearing
12 Reverse gear thrust washer
13 Reverse gear
14 Snap ring
15 1st speed synchronizer assembly
16 1st speed blocker ring
17 1st speed gear
18 Shoulder (part of mainshaft)
19 2nd speed gear
20 2nd speed blocker ring
21 2-3 synchronizer assembly
22 Snap ring

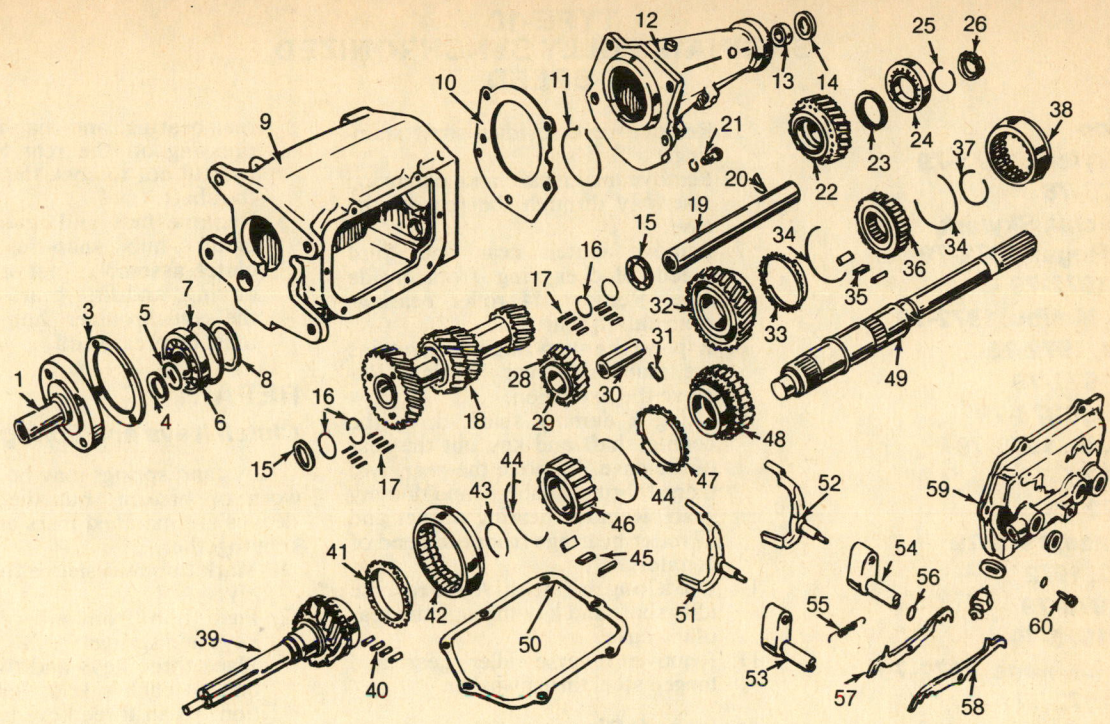

Muncie 3-speed transmission disassembled

1 Bearing retainer	16 Bearing washer	33 1st speed blocker ring	47 2nd speed blocker ring
2 Bolt and lock washer	17 Needle bearings	34 Synchronizer key spring	48 2nd speed gear
3 Gasket	18 Countergear	35 Synchronizer keys	49 Mainshaft
4 Oil seal	19 Countershaft	36 1st and reverse synchronizer	50 Gasket
5 Snap ring (bearing-to-main	20 Woodruff key	hub assembly	51 2nd and 3rd shifter fork
drive gear)	21 Bolt (extension-to-case)	37 Snap ring	52 1st and reverse shifter fork
6 Main drive gear bearing	22 Reverse gear	38 1st and reverse synchronizer	53 2-3 shifter shaft assembly
7 Snap ring bearing	23 Thrust washer	collar	54 1st and reverse shifter
8 Oil slinger	24 Rear bearing	39 Main drive gear	shaft assembly
9 Case	25 Snap ring	40 Pilot bearings	55 Spring
10 Gasket	26 Speedometer drive gear	41 3rd speed blocker ring	56 O-ring seal
11 Snap ring (rear bearing-to-	27 Retainer clip	42 2nd and 3rd synchronizer	57 1st and reverse detent cam
extension)	28 Reverse idler gear	collar	58 2nd and 3rd detent cam
12 Extension	29 Reverse idler bushing	43 Snap ring	59 Side cover
13 Extension bushing	30 Reverse idler shaft	44 Synchronizer key spring	60 Bolt and lock washer
14 Oil seal	31 Woodruff key	45 Synchronizer keys	
15 Thrust washer	32 1st speed gear	46 2nd and 3rd synchronizer hub	

with synchronizer assembly keys and both synchronzier sleeves face front of mainshaft.

10. Install snap-ring.
11. Install reverse gear with clutching teeth down.
12. Install steel reverse gear thrust washer with flats aligned.
13. Press rear ball bearing onto shaft with snap-ring slot down.
14. Install snap-ring.
15. Install speedometer drive gear and retaining clip.

TRANSMISSION ASSEMBLY

1. Place a row of 29 roller bearings, a bearing washer, a second row of 29 bearings, and a second bearing washer at each end of the counter-gear. Hold in place with grease.
2. Place countergear assembly through rear case opening with a tanged thrust washer, tang away from gear, at each end. Install countershaft and key from rear of case. Be sure that thrust washer tangs are aligned with notches in case.
3. Place reverse idler gear in case. Do not install reverse idler shaft yet.
4. Expand snap-ring in extension. Assemble extension over mainshaft and onto rear bearing. Seat snap-ring.
5. Load 16 mainshaft pilot bearings into clutch gear cavity. Assemble third speed blocker ring onto clutch gear clutching surface with teeth toward gear.
6. Place clutch gear assembly, without front bearing, over front of mainshaft. Make sure that blocker ring notches align with keys in second-third synchronizer assembly.
7. Stick gasket onto extension housing with grease. Assemble clutch gear, mainshaft, and extension to case together. Make sure that clutch gear teeth engage teeth of countergear anti-lash plate.
8. Rotate extension housing. Install reverse idler shaft and key.
9. Torque extension bolts to 45 ft. lbs.
10. Install oil slinger with inner lip facing forward. Install front bearing outer snap-ring to bearing. Slide bearing into case bore.
11. Install snap-ring to clutch gear stem. Install bearing retainer and gasket. Torque bolts to 20 ft. lbs. Retainer oil return hole must be at 6 o'clock.
12. Shift both synchronizer sleeves to neutral positions. Install side cover, aligning shifter forks with synchronizer sleeve grooves.
13. Torque side cover bolts to 20 ft. lbs.

TYPE-10
SAGINAW FULLY SYNCHRONIZED
3-SPEED

Application
Apollo, Skylark, 1973-79
Astre, 1973-76
Buick Special, Skylark,
Century, Regal, 1972-79
Camaro, 1972-79
Chevelle, Malibu, 1972-79
Chevrolet, 1972-73
Firebird, 1972-79
Grand Prix, 1978-79
Monte Carlo, 1978-79
Monza, 1976
Nova, 1972-79
Olds Cutlass, 1972-79
Olds 4-4-2, 1972
Omega, 1973-79
Phoenix, 1978-79
Tempest, Le Mans, 1972-79
Ventura, 1972-77
Vega, 1973-76

TRANSMISSION DISASSEMBLY

1. Remove side cover assembly and shift forks.
2. Remove clutch gear bearing retainer.
3. Remove clutch gear bearing to gear stem snap-ring. Pull clutch gear outward until a screwdriver can be inserted between bearing and case. Remove clutch gear bearing.
4. Remove speedometer driven gear and extension bolts.

5. Remove reverse idler shaft snap-ring.
6. Remove mainshaft and extension assembly through the rear of the case.
7. Remove clutch gear and third speed blocker ring from inside case. Remove 14 roller bearings from clutch gear.
8. Expand the snap-ring which retains the mainshaft rear bearing. Remove the extension.
9. Using a dummy shaft, drive the countershaft and key out the rear of the case. Remove the gear, two tanged thrust washers, and dummy shaft. Remove bearing washer and 27 roller bearings from each end of countergear.
10. Use a long drift to drive the reverse idler shaft and key through the rear of the case.
11. Remove reverse idler gear and tanged steel thrust washer.

Mainshaft Disassembly

1. Remove second and third speed sliding clutch hub snap-ring from mainshaft. Remove clutch assembly, second speed blocker ring, and second gear from front of mainshaft.
2. Depress speedometer drive gear retaining clip. Remove gear. Some units have a metal speedometer driver gear which must be pulled off.
3. Remove rear bearing snap-ring.
4. Support reverse gear. Press on rear of mainshaft. Remove reverse gear, thrust washer, spring washer,

rear bearing, and snap-ring. When pressing off the rear bearing, be careful not to cock the bearing on the shaft.
5. Remove first and reverse sliding clutch hub snap-ring. Remove clutch assembly, first speed blocker ring, and first gear. Sometimes the synchronizer hub and gear must be pressed off.

REPAIR
Clutch Keys and Springs

Keys and springs may be replaced if worn or broken, but the hubs and sleeves are matched pairs and must be kept together.
1. Mark hub and sleeve for reassembly.
2. Push hub from sleeve. Remove keys and springs.
3. Place three keys and two springs, one on each side of hub, in position, so all three keys are engaged by both springs. The tanged end of the springs should not be installed into the same key.
4. Slide the sleeve onto the hub, aligning the marks.
NOTE: *A groove around the outside of the synchronizer hub marks the end that must be opposite the fork slot in the sleeve when assembled.*

Extension Oil Seal and Bushing

1. Remove seal.
2. Using bushing remover and installer tool, drive bushing into extension housing.
3. Drive new bushing in from the rear. Lubricate inside of bushing and seal. Install new oil seal with extension seal installer tool or other suitable tool.

Clutch Bearing Retainer Oil Seal

1. Pry old seal out.
2. Install new seal using seal installer. Seat seal in bore.

MAINSHAFT ASSEMBLY

1. Turn front of mainshaft up.
2. Install second gear with clutching teeth up; the rear face of the gear butts against the flange on the mainshaft.
3. Install a blocker ring with clutching teeth down. All three blocker rings are the same.
4. Install second and third speed synchronizer assembly with fork slot down. Press it onto mainshaft splines. Both synchronizer assemblies are the same. Be sure that blocker ring notches align with synchronizer assembly keys.
5. Install synchronizer snap-ring.

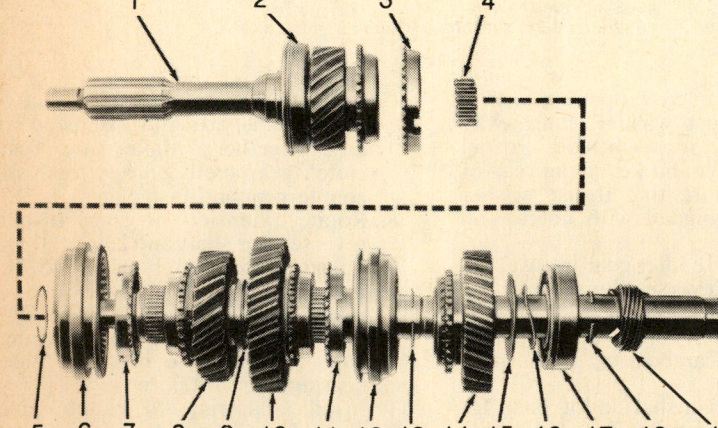

Clutch gear and mainshaft assembly (© G.M. Corp)

1 Clutch gear	8 2nd speed gear
2 Clutch gear bearing	9 Shoulder (part of main shaft)
3 3rd speed blocker ring	10 1st speed gear
4 Mainshaft pilot bearings (14)	11 1st speed blocker ring
5 Snap ring	12 1st speed synchronizer assembly
6 2-3 synchronizer assembly	13 Snap ring
7 2nd speed blocker ring	

14 Reverse gear	
15 Reverse gear thrust washer	
16 Spring washer	
17 Rear bearing	
18 Snap ring	
19 Speedo drive gear and clip	
20 Mainshaft	

Both synchronizer snap-rings are the same.

6. Turn rear of shaft up.
7. Install first gear with clutching teeth up; the front face of the gear butts against the flange on the mainshaft.
8. Install a blocker ring with clutching teeth down.
9. Install first and reverse synchronizer assembly with fork slot down. Press it onto mainshaft splines. Be sure blocker ring notches align with synchronizer assembly keys.
10. Install snap-ring.
11. Install reverse gear with clutching teeth down.
12. Install steel reverse gear thrust washer and spring washer.
13. Press rear ball bearing onto shaft with snap-ring slot down.
14. Install snap-ring.
15. Install speedometer drive gear and

retaining clip. Press on metal speedometer drive gear.

TRANSMISSION ASSEMBLY

1. Using dummy shaft, load a row of 27 roller bearings and a thrust washer at each end of countergear. Hold in place with grease.
2. Place countergear assembly into case through rear. Place a tanged thrust washer, tang away from gear, at each end. Install countershaft and key, making sure that tangs align with notches in case.
3. Install reverse idler gear thrust washer, gear, and shaft with key from rear of case. Be sure thrust washer is between gear and rear of case with tang toward notch in case.

4. Expand snap-ring in extension. Assemble extension over rear of mainshaft and onto rear bearing. Seat snap-ring in rear bearing groove.
5. Install 14 mainshaft pilot bearings into clutch gear cavity. Assemble third speed blocker ring onto clutch gear clutching surface with teeth toward gear.
6. Place clutch gear, pilot bearings, and third speed blocker ring assembly over front of mainshaft assembly. Be sure blocker rings align with keys in second-third synchronizer assembly.
7. Stick extension gasket to case with grease. Install clutch gear, mainshaft, and extension together. Be sure clutch gear engages teeth of countergear anti-lash plate. Torque extension bolts to 45 ft. lbs.
8. Place bearing over stem of clutch

1 Synchronizer retainer ring
2 Synchronizer blocking ring
3 Synchronizer assembly
4 Second speed gear
5 Main shaft
6 Synchronizer assembly
7 Gear assembly
8 Thrust washer
9 Retainer clip

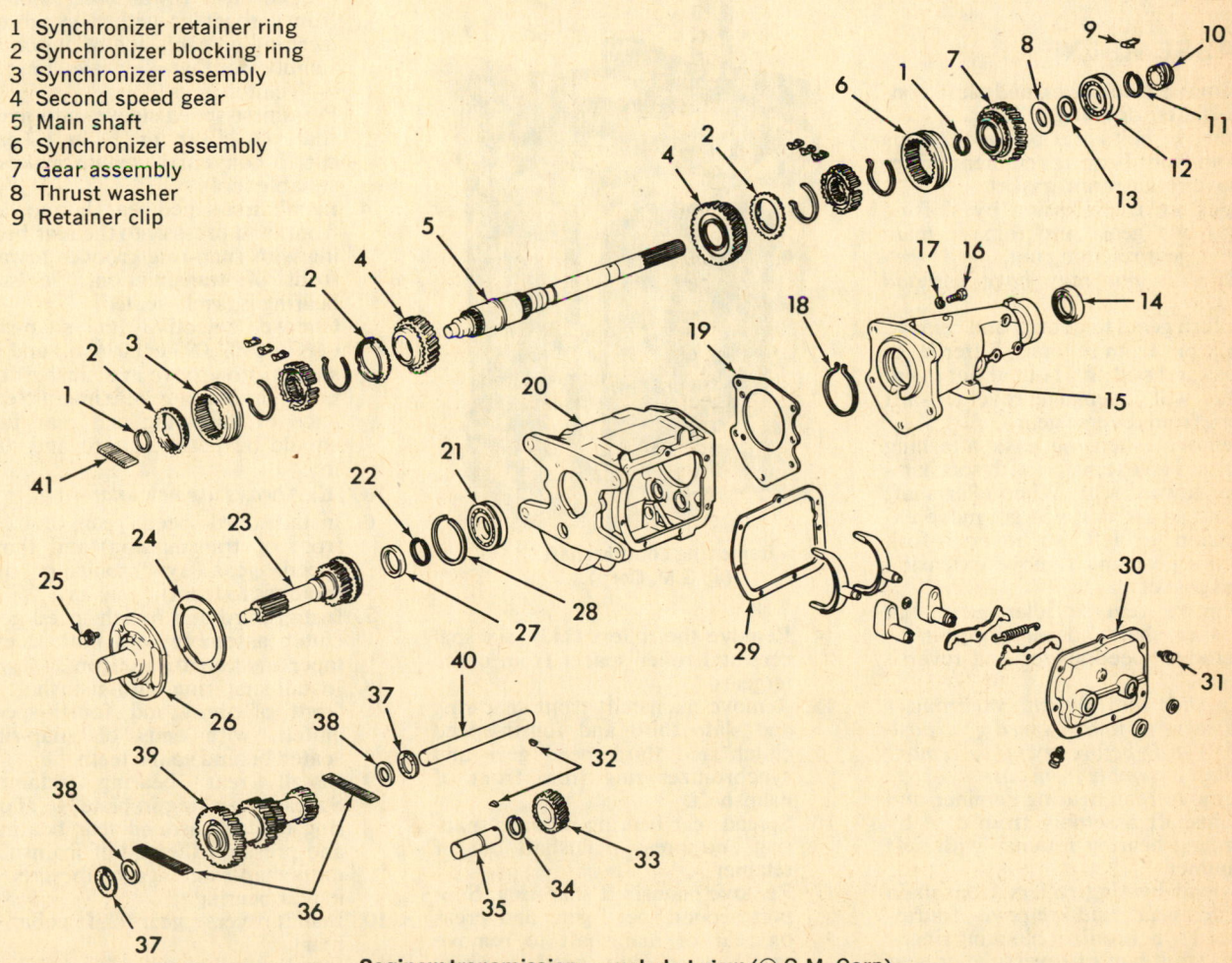

Saginaw transmission—exploded view (© G.M. Corp)

10 Speedometer drive gear	18 Rear bearing location ring	26 Retainer assembly	34 Retaining ring
11 Ring	19 Gasket	27 Ring	35 Shaft
12 Mainshaft bearing	20 Case	28 Clutch gear bearing locating ring	36 Roller
13 Washer	21 Bearing assembly	29 Cover gasket	37 Washer
14 Seal	22 Ring	30 Cover assembly	38 Washer
15 Extension housing	23 Clutch gear	31 Bolt and lockwasher	39 Gear assembly
16 Bolt	24 Gasket	32 Woodruff keys	40 Counter gear shaft
17 Washer	25 Bolt and lockwasher	33 Gear assembly	41 Mainshaft bearing roller

gear and into front case bore. Install front bearing to clutch gear snap-ring.

9. Install clutch gear bearing retainer and gasket. The retainer oil return hole must be at the bottom. Torque retainer bolts to 10 ft. lbs.

10. Install reverse idler gear shaft E-ring.
11. Shift synchronizer sleeves to neu-tral positions. Install cover, gasket, and forks, aligning forks with synchronizer sleeve grooves. Torque side cover bolts to 10 ft. lbs.

12. Install speedometer driven gear.

TYPE-11 MUNCIE 4-SPEED

Removing countershaft
(© G.M. Corp)

Application
Buick Special, GS, 1972
Camaro, 1972-74
Chevelle, 1972-74
Corvette, 1972-74
Firebird, 1972-74
GTO, 1972-74
Nova, 1972-74
Olds Cutlass, 4-4-2, 1972-73
Tempest, 1972-74

DISASSEMBLY

1. Remove side cover and shift controls after draining.
2. Remove bolts and bolt lock strips from front bearing retainer and remove retainer and gasket.
3. Lock up transmission by shifting into two gears and remove main drive gear retaining nut.

NOTE: *This nut may have lefthand threads.*

4. Return gears to neutral and remove lock pin from reverse shifter lever boss and pull shaft out about 1/8 in. This will disengage reverse shift fork from reverse gear.
5. Remove extension case attaching bolts. Tap extension with soft hammer toward rear. When idler shaft is out as far as it will go, move extension to left so reverse fork clears gear and remove extension and gasket.
6. Remove reverse idler gear, flat washer, shaft and roll spring pin.
7. Remove speedometer and reverse gears.

NOTE: *Slide third-fourth synchronizer clutch sleeve to fourth-speed gear position (forward) before trying to remove mainshaft assembly from case.*

8. Remove rear bearing retainer and mainshaft assembly from case by tapping bearing retainer with soft hammer.
9. Unload bearing rollers from main drive gear and remove fourth-speed synchronizer blocking ring.
10. Lift front half of reverse idler gear with tanged thrust washer from case.
11. Press main drive gear down from bearing.
12. Tap front bearing and snap-ring from case.
13. From front of case, press out countershaft. Then, remove the countershaft gear and both tanged washers.

14. Remove the rollers (112), six spacers and roller spacer from countergear.
15. Remove mainshaft front snap-ring and slide third and fourth-speed clutch and third-speed gear and synchronizer ring from front of mainshaft.
16. Spread rear bearing retainer snap-ring and press mainshaft out of retainer.
17. Remove mainshaft snap-ring. Support second-speed gear and press on rear of mainshaft to remove rear bearing, first-speed gear and sleeve, first-speed synchronizing ring, first-second-speed synchronizer clutch, second-speed synchronizer ring and second-speed gear.

After thoroughly cleaning case and all parts, make thorough inspection and replace required parts. In checking bearings do not spin at high speeds, but rather clean and rotate by hand to de-tect roughness and unevenness. Spinning can damage balls and races.

ASSEMBLY
Mainshaft

1. From rear of shaft, assemble second-speed gear (hub of gear toward rear of shaft).
2. Install first-second synchronizer clutch assembly onto mainshaft (sleeve taper toward rear, hub to front); together with a synchronizer ring on each side of clutch assembly so that keyways line up with clutch keys.
3. Press first-speed sleeve onto mainshaft. (A $1\frac{3}{4}$ in. or $1\frac{5}{8}$ in. ID pipe cut to convenient length makes a suitable tool).
4. Install first-speed gear (hub toward front) and press onto the rear bearing with snap-ring grooves toward front of transmission. Be sure bearing is firmly seated.
5. Choose selective fit snap-ring (.087, .090, .093 or .096 in.) and install it into groove in mainshaft behind rear bearing. Maximum clearance of snap-ring and rear face should be between zero and .005 in.

NOTE: *Always use new snap-ring.*

6. Install third-speed gear (hub to front of transmission) and third-speed gear synchronizing ring (notches to front).
7. Install third and fourth-speed gear clutch assembly with both sleeve taper and hub toward front.
8. Install snap-ring onto mainshaft in front of third and fourth-speed clutch, with ends of snap-ring seated behind spline teeth.
9. Install rear bearing retainer. Spread snap-ring in plate, to allow ring to drop around rear bearing, and press on the end of mainshaft until snap-ring engages the groove in rear bearing.
10. Install reverse gear (shift collar to rear).
11. Install speedometer drive gear.

Countergear

1. Install roller spacer into counter-gear.
2. With heavy grease to assist, install a spacer in either end of counter-gear, 28 roller bearings, then a spacer and 28 more rollers. Then, install another spacer. In the other

end of the countergear, do the same.

3. Insert dummy shaft into counter-gear.

Transmission

1. Rest case on side with cover opening toward mechanic. Install countergear tanged thrust washers in place, holding with heavy grease. Make sure tangs are in proper notches.
2. Set countergear in place. Use care not to disturb tanged washers.
3. Position transmission case so that it rests on front face.
4. Lubricate and insert countershaft in rear. Turn countershaft so flat on end of shaft is horizontal and facing bottom of case.

NOTE: *The flat of shaft must be hori-zontal and toward bottom to mate with rear bearing retainer when installed.*

5. Align countergear with shaft in rear and hole in front of case (pushing dummy shaft out front of case) until flat of shaft is flush with rear of case. Be sure thrust washers remain in place.
6. Check end-play in countergear (dial indicator should be used). If end-play is more than .025 in. install new thrust washer.
7. Install cage and 17 roller bearings into main drive gear. Use heavy grease to hold bearings.
8. Install main drive gear with bearings through side opening of case and into position in front bore.
9. Place gasket in position on rear bearing retainer.
10. Install fourth-speed synchronizing

ring onto main drive gear (notches toward rear).
11. Position tanged thrust washer for reverse idler on machined face. Position front of reverse idler gear next to thrust washer (hub facing toward rear of case).

CAUTION

Before attempting to install mainshaft to case, slide the third-fourth synchronizer clutch sleeve forward into fourth-speed detent position.

12. Lower mainshaft assembly into case. Be sure notches on fourth-speed synchronizer ring correspond to keys in clutch assembly.
13. With guide pin in rear bearing retainer aligned with hole in rear of

1	Mainshaft bearing
2	Retaining ring
3	Blocking ring
4	Synchronizer sleeve
5	Synchronizer spring
6	Synchronizer hub
7	Shift plate
8	Synchronizer unit
9	Third speed gear
10	Main shaft
11	Spring
12	Second speed gear
13	Sleeve
14	Synchronizer unit
15	First speed gear
16	Sleeve
17	Locating ring
18	Mainshaft rear housing
19	Bearing retaining ring
20	Reverse gear
21	Speedometer drive gear
22	Bolt
23	Lock
24	Lock

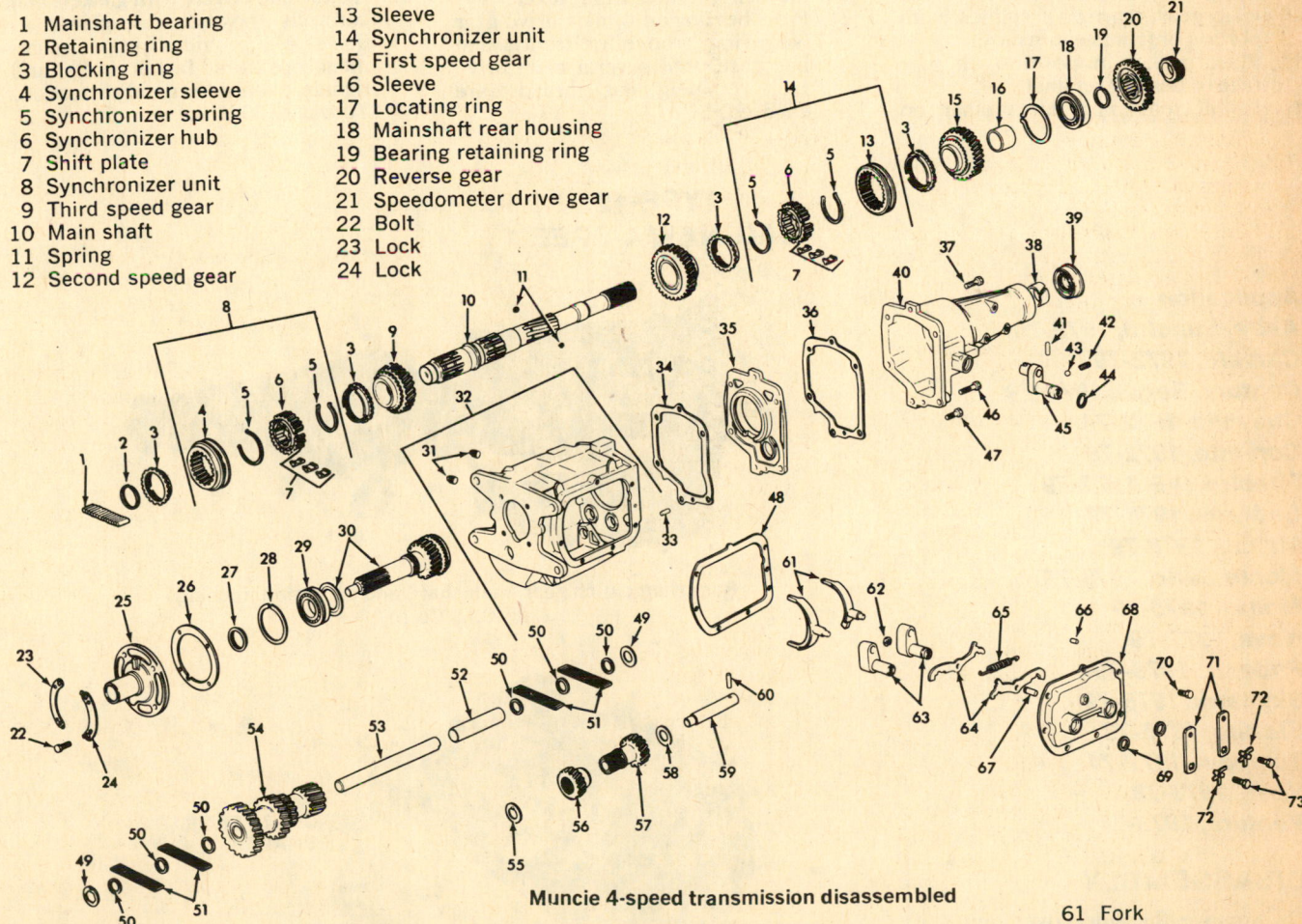

Muncie 4-speed transmission disassembled

25	Bearing retainer
26	Gasket
27	Nut
28	Snap ring
29	Bearing with snap ring
30	Main drive gear
31	Filler plug
32	Case assembly
33	Dowel
34	Gasket
35	Bearing retainer
36	Gasket
37	Bolt
38	Extension bushing
39	Seal assembly
40	Extension assembly
41	Pin
42	Spring
43	Ball
44	Seal
45	Reverse shift fork
46	Bolt
47	Bolt
48	Gasket
49	Washer
50	Washer
51	Roller
52	Spacer with washer
53	Counter shaft
54	Counter shaft gear
55	Washer
56	Reverse idler front gear
57	Reverse idler gear assembly
58	Washer
59	Reverse idler gear shaft
60	Pin
61	Fork
62	Ring
63	Shaft assembly
64	Detent cam
65	Spring
66	Dowel pin
67	Locating pin
68	Cover
69	Shifter shaft seal
70	Bolt
71	Shifter shaft lever
72	Lock
73	Bolt

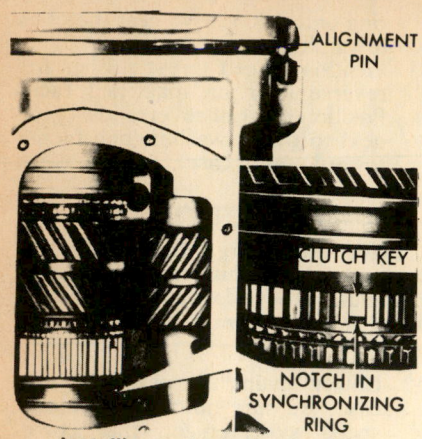

Installing mainshaft assembly
(© G.M. Corp)

case, tap rear bearing retainer into position with soft hammer.

14. From rear of case, insert reverse idler gear, engaging splines with portion of front gear in case.

15. Place gasket in position on rear face of bearing retainer.

16. Install remaining flat washer on reverse idler shaft.

17. Install reverse idler shaft, roll pin, and thrust washer into gears and front boss of case. Make sure to pick up front tanged thrust washer.

18. Pull reverse shifter shaft to left side of extension and rotate shaft to bring reverse shift fork forward in extension (reverse detent position). Start extension onto transmission case, while slowly pushing in on shifter shaft to engage the shift fork with the reverse gear shift collar. Then, pilot the reverse idler shaft into the extension housing, permitting the extension to slide into the transmission case.

19. Install extension and retainer-to-case attaching bolts.

20. Push or pull reverse shifter shaft to line up grooves in the shaft with the holes in the boss and drive in the lockpin. Install shift lever.

21. Press bearing onto main drive gear (snap-ring groove in front), and into case until several main drive gear retaining nut threads are exposed.

22. Lock transmission by shifting into two gears. Install main drive gear retaining nut onto the gear shaft and draw it up tight. Be sure bearing is completely seated against shoulder. Torque retaining nut to 40 ft. lbs. and lock in place by staking into main drive gear shaft hole with punch. Do not damage shaft threads.

23. Install main drive gear bearing retainer, gasket attaching bolts and boltlock retainers. Use a suitable seal on bolts. Tighten to 20 ft. lbs.

24. Shift mainshaft third-fourth sliding clutch sleeve into neutral position and first-second sliding clutch into second gear (forward) detent position. Shift side cover third-fourth shift lever into neutral detent and first-second shift lever into second gear detent position.

25. Install side cover, with gasket, and carefully position in place. A dowel pin provides proper alignment position. Install bolts and tighten evenly to avoid distortion. Torque to 20 ft. lbs.

TYPE-12 SAGINAW 4-SPEED

Removing clutch gear, mainshaft, and extension housing
(© G.M. Corp)

Application
Astre, Sunbird, 1975-79
Camaro, 1972-79
Century, Regal, 1978-79
Chevelle, 1972-74
Corvette, 1972-76
Firebird, (V8) 1972-79
Le Mans, 1978-79
Malibu, 1978-79
Monte Carlo, 1978-79
Monza, 1975-79
Nova, 1972-79
Phoenix, 1978-79
Skyhawk, 1975-79
Starfire, 1975-79
Tempest, 1972-74
Vega, 1973-78
Ventura, 1973-74

DISASSEMBLY

1. Remove the side cover and shift forks after draining the transmission.

2. Remove the clutch gear bearing retainer. Remove the bearing-to-gear stem snap-ring and pull out on the clutch gear until a screwdriver can be inserted between the bearing, large snap-ring, and case to pry the bearing off.

NOTE: *The clutch gear bearing is a slip-fit on the gear and in the case. Removal of the bearing will provide clear-*

Counter gear shaft exposed for removal
(© Chevrolet Div., G.M. Corp)

1 Clip
2 Speedometer drive gear
3 Snap ring
4 Mainshaft rear bearing
5 Washer (wavy)
6 Washer (wavy)
7 First speed gear
8 Blocking ring
9 Retaining ring
10 Synchronizer assembly
11 Spring
12 Synchronizer key
13 Synchronizer hub
15 Second speed gear
16 Main shaft
17 Third speed gear
18 Synchronizer assembly
19 Mainshaft bearing rollers
20 Extension housing oil seal
21 Extension housing
22 Bolt
23 Washer
24 Rear bearing ring
25 Gasket
26 Case assembly
27 Drain plug

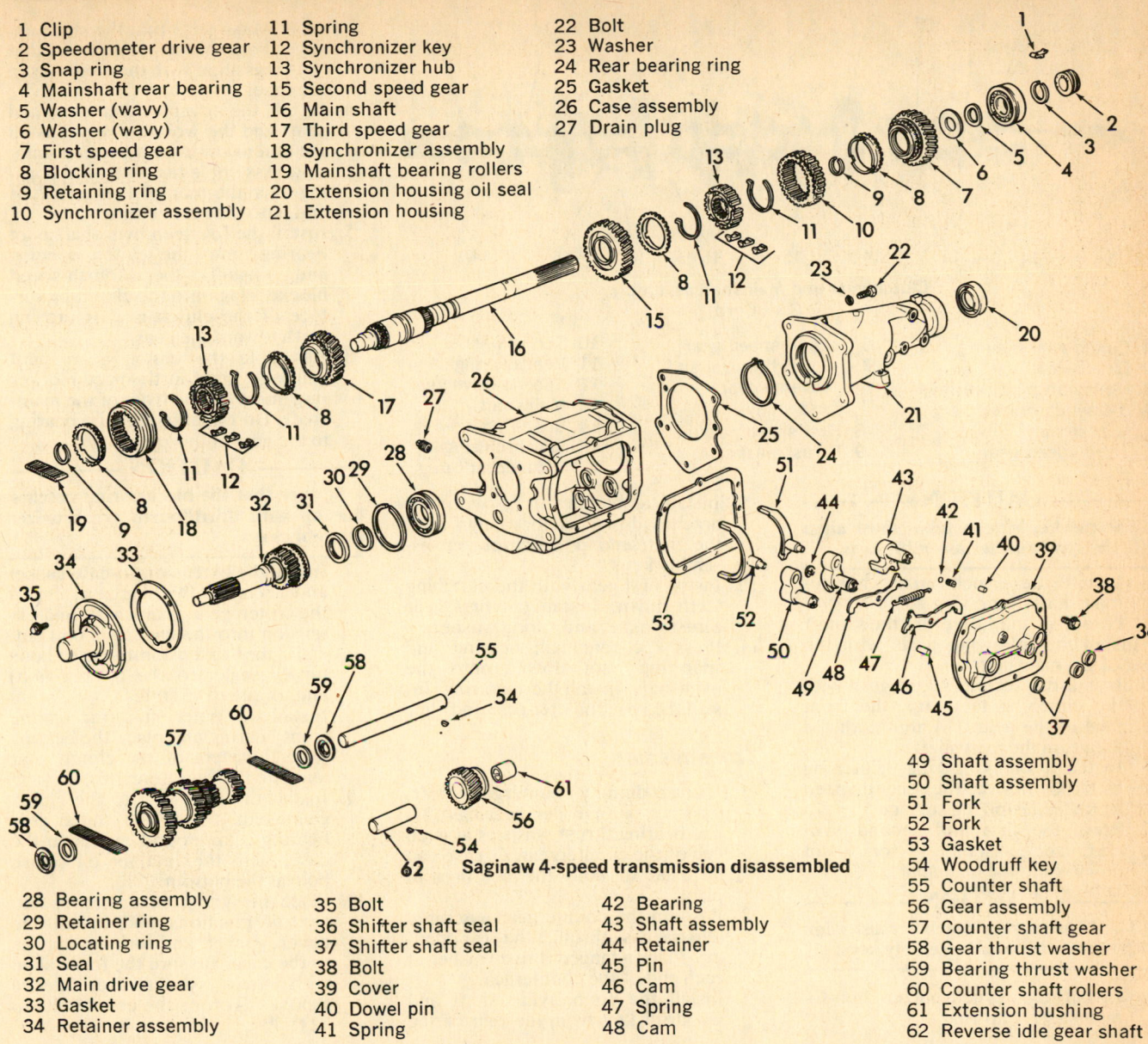

Saginaw 4-speed transmission disassembled

28 Bearing assembly
29 Retainer ring
30 Locating ring
31 Seal
32 Main drive gear
33 Gasket
34 Retainer assembly
35 Bolt
36 Shifter shaft seal
37 Shifter shaft seal
38 Bolt
39 Cover
40 Dowel pin
41 Spring
42 Bearing
43 Shaft assembly
44 Retainer
45 Pin
46 Cam
47 Spring
48 Cam
49 Shaft assembly
50 Shaft assembly
51 Fork
52 Fork
53 Gasket
54 Woodruff key
55 Counter shaft
56 Gear assembly
57 Counter shaft gear
58 Gear thrust washer
59 Bearing thrust washer
60 Counter shaft rollers
61 Extension bushing
62 Reverse idle gear shaft

ance for clutch gear and mainshaft removal.

3. Remove the rear extension attaching bolts and remove the clutch gear, mainshaft, and extension as an assembly.
4. Spread the snap-ring which holds the mainshaft rear bearing and remove the extension case.
5. Remove the countershaft and its woodruff key by driving out of the rear of the case with a pipe or an old countershaft. Remove the countergear assembly and bearings.
6. Using a long drift, drive the reverse idler shaft and woodruff key through the rear of the case.
7. Expand and remove the third and fourth-speed sliding clutch hub snap-ring from the mainshaft. Remove the clutch assembly, third gear blocker ring, and third-speed gear from the front of the mainshaft.

8. Press in the speedometer gear retaining clip and slide the gear off the mainshaft. Remove the rear bearing snap-ring from its groove in the mainshaft.
9. With first gear supported on press plates, press first gear, thrust washer, spring washer, rear bearing, and snap-ring from the rear of the mainshaft.

— CAUTION —

Be careful to center the gear, washers, bearings, and snap-ring when pressing the rear bearing.

10. Expand and remove the first and second sliding clutch hub snap-ring from the mainshaft and remove the clutch assembly, second-speed blocker ring, and second-speed gear from the rear of the mainshaft.

After thoroughly cleaning all parts and the transmission case, inspect and

replace all damaged or worn parts. When checking the bearings, do not spin them at high speeds. Clean and rotate the bearings by hand to detect roughness and unevenness. Spinning can damage balls and races.

ASSEMBLY

Mainshaft

Install the following parts with the front of the mainshaft facing up:

1. Install the third-speed gear with the clutching teeth up; the rear face of the gear will abut with the mainshaft flange.
2. Install a blocking ring, clutching teeth down, over the third-speed gear synchronizing surface.

NOTE: *All four blocker rings are the same.*

3. Press the third and fourth synchronizer assembly, fork slot down, onto the mainshaft splines until it bottoms.

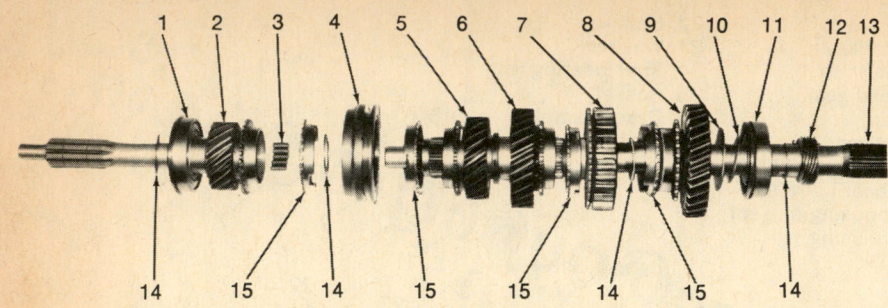

Clutch gear and mainshaft assembly
(© G.M. Corp)

1 Clutch gear bearing
2 Clutch gear
3 Mainshaft pilot bearings
4 3-4 synchronizer assembly
5 Third speed gear
6 Second speed gear
7 1-2 synchronizer and reverse gear assembly
8 First speed gear
9 Thrust washer
10 Spring washer
11 Rear bearing
12 Speedo drive gear
13 Mainshaft
14 Snap-ring
15 Synchronizing "blocker" ring

—————— CAUTION ——————
The blocker ring notches must align with the synchronizer assembly keys.

4. Install the synchronizer hub-to-mainshaft snap-ring. (Both synchronizer snap-rings are the same.) Install the following parts with the rear of the mainshaft up.
5. Install the second-speed gear with the clutching teeth up; the front face of the gear will abut with the flange on the mainshaft.
6. Install a blocking ring, clutching teeth down, over the second-speed gear synchronizing surface.
7. Press the first and second synchronizer assembly, fork slot down, onto the mainshaft.

—————— CAUTION ——————
The blocker ring notches must align with the synchronizer assembly keys.

8. Install the synchronizer hub-to-mainshaft snap-ring.

9. Install a blocker ring with the notches down so they align with the first/second synchronizer assembly keys.
10. Install first gear with the clutching teeth down. Install the first gear thrust washer and spring washer.
11. Press the rear ball bearing and snap-ring, slot down, onto the mainshaft. Install the snap-ring. Install the speedometer gear and clip.

Transmission

1. Using a dummy countergear shaft, load a row of roller bearings (27) and bearing thrust washers at each end of the countergear. Grease can be used to hold the bearings in place.
2. Position the countergear assembly into the case through the rear opening. Place a tanged thrust washer at each end of the countergear.
3. Install the countergear shaft and woodruff key from the rear of the

case. Make sure that the shaft engages both thrust washers and that the tangs align with their notches in the case.
4. Install the reverse idler gear and shaft and the woodruff key. Install the extension-to-rear bearing snapring. Assemble the extension housing over the rear of the mainshaft and onto the rear bearing.
5. Install the fourteen mainshaft pilot bearings into the clutch opening and install the fourth-speed blocker ring onto the clutching surface of the clutch gear (clutching teeth toward the gear.)
6. Assemble the clutch gear, pilot bearings, and fourth-speed blocker ring unit over the front of the mainshaft. Do not assemble the bearing to the gear at this point.

—————— CAUTION ——————
Be sure that the blocker ring notches line up with third/fourth synchronizer assembly keys.

7. Install the extension-to-case gasket and secure it with grease. Insert the clutch gear, mainshaft, and extension into the case as a unit. Install the extension-to-case bolts (apply sealer to the bottom bolt) and torque to 45 ft. lbs.
8. Install the outer snap-ring on the front bearing and place the bearing over the stem of the clutch gear and into the case bore.
9. Install the snap-ring to the clutch gear stem. Install the clutch gear bearing retainer and gasket to the case, with the retainer oil return hole at the bottom.
10. Place the synchronizer sleeves into neutral positions and install the cover, gasket, and fork assemblies to the case. Be sure the forks align with their synchronizer sleeve grooves. Torque the cover bolts to 22 ft. lbs.

TYPE-13
VEGA 3-SPEED

Application
Vega, 1972

TRANSMISSION DISASSEMBLY

1. Remove the shift lever boot. Remove the TCS switch and back-up light switch.
2. Remove the cotter pins from each end of the shift control rod. Remove washers and shift control rod.
3. Remove retaining rings, wave rings, and selector ring from selector shaft. Slide the selector lever and shift idler lever shaft from the intermediate shift lever assembly

while simultaneously removing the selector ring.
4. Remove the transmission case cover and gasket.
5. Invert the transmission to drain the oil.
6. Remove the rear extension attaching bolts and rotate the extension until the countergear shaft is exposed.
7. From the front of the transmission, remove the countergear shaft. Lift the countergear from the case. Do not lose the lockball.
8. Engage second gear to prevent the second-third fork pin from binding against the case. Use a 1/8 in. pin punch to remove all lockpins.
9. Drive the lockpins from both shif-

ter forks. Place the transmission in third gear and be sure that the second-third intermediate lever engages the shifter shaft. This will allow the intermediate levers to pivot as the shifter shaft is removed.
10. Insert a long narrow drift through the bolt hole at the rear of the case and drive the second-third shifter shaft from the case. Remove the fork.
11. Drive the first-reverse shifter shaft from the front of the case and remove the fork from the case.
12. Remove the selector shaft intermediate lever lockpins. Remove the shaft and levers from the case.
13. Remove the snap-ring from the rear bearing retainer groove and

1 Rear extension to case bolts
2 Back-up lamp switch and seal ring
3 Shift idler lever spring
4 Intermediate lever bushing snap-ring
5 Intermediate lever bushing
6 Shift idler lever
7 Rear extension
8 Rear extension gasket
9 Reverse idler gear shaft and lockball
10 Reverse idler gear and bushing assembly
11 2-3 speed shifter shaft
12 2-3 speed shift fork and spiral pin
13 Cotter pin
14 Waved washer
15 Shift selector rod
16 Washer
17 Selector shaft
18 Selector shaft seal
19 2-3 intermediate shift lever and spiral pin
20 1st-reverse intermediate shift lever and spiral pin
21 Cover gasket
22 Cover assembly
23 Cover-to-case screws
23a Clutch drive gear seal
24 Clutch drive gear assembly

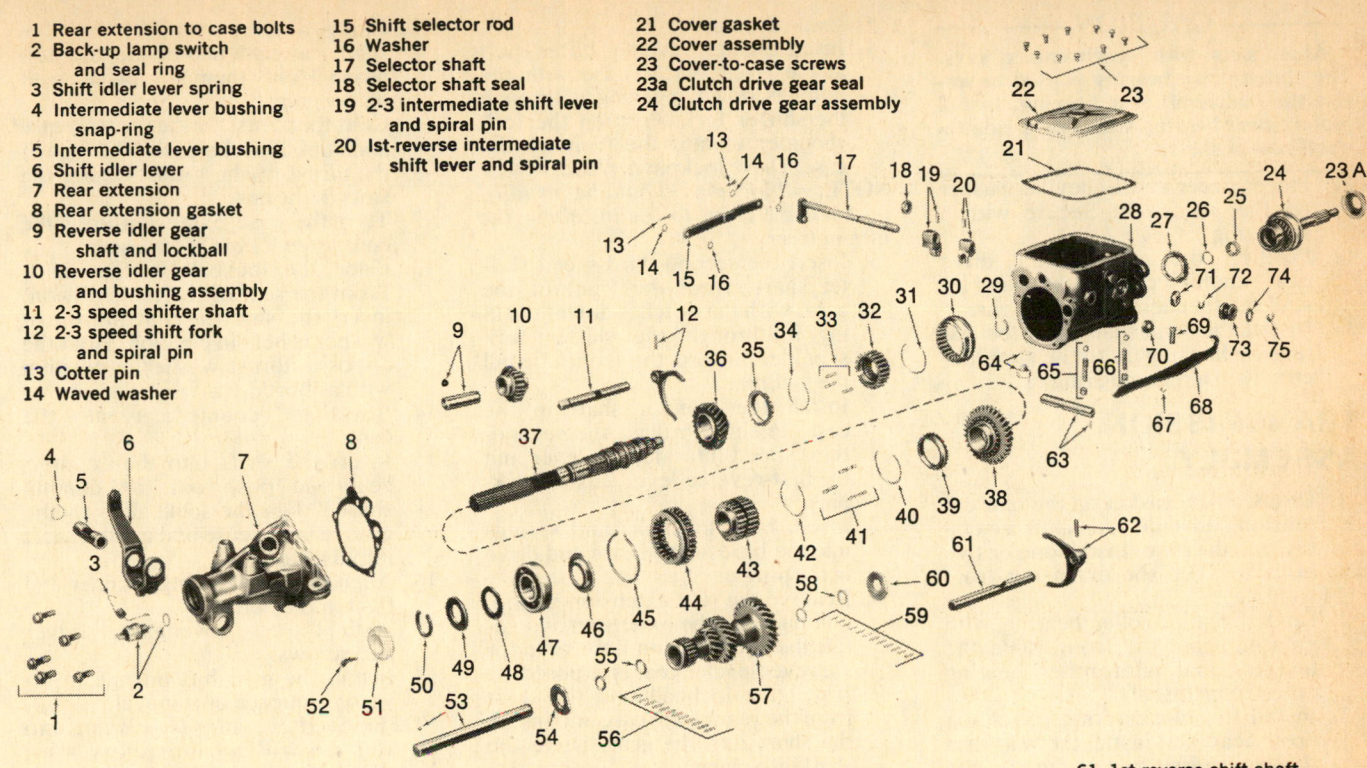

Exploded view (inverted) of Vega 3-speed transmission
(© Chevrolet Div., G.M. Corp)

25 Mainshaft pilot bearing assembly
26 Pilot bearing spacer ring
27 3rd gear synchronizer ring
28 Transmission case
29 2-3 speed synchronizer assembly retaining ring
30 2-3 speed synchronizer sleeve
31 Synchronizer spring
32 2-3 synchronizer hub
33 2-3 synchronizer keys
34 Synchronizer spring
35 2nd gear synchronizer ring
36 2nd speed gear
37 Mainshaft
38 1st speed gear
39 1st speed gear synchronizer ring
40. Synchronizer spring
41 1st-reverse synchronizer keys
42 Synchronizer spring
43 1st-reverse synchronizer hub
44 1st-reverse synchronizer sleeve
45 Rear bearing to extension locking ring
46 1st-reverse key stop-ring
47 Mainshaft rear bearing
48 Rear bearing spacer
49 Belleville washer
50 Rear bearing retaining ring
51 Speedo drive gear
52 Speedo drive clip
53 Countergear shaft and lockball
54 Countergear thrust washer
55 Countergear bearing washer
56 Countergear roller bearings (24)
57 Countergear
58 Countergear bearing washer
59 Countergear roller bearings (24)
60 Countergear thrust washers
61 1st-reverse shift shaft
62 1st-reverse shift fork and spiral pin
63 Intermediate lever shaft and pin
64 TCS switch and gasket
65 2-3 shift detent ball, spring and hole plug
66 1st-reverse shift detent ball, spring and hole plug
67 Pivot pin lockring
68 Shift selector rod
69 Selector lever pivot pin
70 Oil filler plug
71 Selector shaft oil seal
72 Selector shaft lockring
73 Selector shaft ring
74 Belleville washer
75 Selector shaft lockring

slide the rear extension from the mainshaft assembly.

14. Remove the clutch drive gear from the case.

15. Position first-reverse sliding gear to the rear of the hub shaft and remove the mainshaft assembly from the case. Remove the lockpins and detent balls from the bottom of the case.

16. Drive the plugs and springs from the shift rail detent holes.

17. Remove the reverse idler gear and shaft from the case.

Mainshaft Disassembly

NOTE: *The synchronizer hubs and sliding sleeves are a select assembly and kept together as originally assembled. Keys and springs may be replaced.*

1. Remove the snap-ring from in front of the clutch hub.

2. Depress the retaining clip and slide the speedometer drive gear from the shaft.

3. Remove the snap-ring, spacer and Belleville washer from the shaft.

4. Support first gear and press the mainshaft until the bearing and synchronizers are free on the shaft. Remove all loose parts from the shaft.

5. Support second speed gear and press on shaft until second-third synchronizer assembly and second speed gear are free.

Mainshaft Assembly

1. From the front of the mainshaft, install the second speed gear. The gear must turn freely on the shaft.

2. Install the second-third synchronizer onto second speed gear cone.

3. Install front and rear synchronizer key springs into second-third speed synchronizer hubs, so that hooked spring ends are in the same slot and raised ends are against the blocker rings.

4. Install sliding sleeve and keys on clutch hub. Arrows must point to front of shaft.

5. Press second-third speed synchronizer hub onto the mainshaft. Secure with a snap-ring.

6. Install both clutch key springs into first-reverse speed synchronizer hub. Hooks of both springs must rest in the same hub slot and raised spring ends should be positioned opposite each other against the blocker rings.

7. Assemble the sliding gear and keys on hub assembly with longer key flat and fork groove on gear toward the rear of the shaft.

8. From the rear of the mainshaft, slide on first gear. Gear must turn freely.

9. Place first-reverse speed synchronizer ring onto first speed gear cone.

10. Slide the first-reverse synchronizer assembly onto the mainshaft. Slide the stop-ring, rear extension retaining ring and rear bearing onto the shaft. Support the rear bearing inner race and press the components together.

Manual Transmissions

─── CAUTION ───

Align slots with synchronizer keys. The clutch drive bearing is used to service the mainshaft rear bearing. Install replacement bearing with shield side toward rear of shaft.

11. Place spacer and Belleville washer on the mainshaft. Secure with a snap-ring.
12. Position the speedometer drive gear retaining clip on shaft and install the speedometer drive gear.
13. Install the mainshaft into the extension housing up to the stop. Secure with a retaining ring.

TRANSMISSION ASSEMBLY

1. Install a new gasket on the rear extension and slide mainshaft assembly into the case. Install one or two bolts to keep the extension from rotating.
2. Coat the pilot roller bearing with grease. From the front, slide the lockring and pilot roller bearing onto the mainshaft.
3. Install the blocker ring on clutch drive gear, and install the gear into the transmission case, up to the

snap-ring stop.
4. Insert the first-reverse shifter shaft at the front of the case with the notches down, pushing it through the shifter fork. Position the fork shoulder toward the front of the case. Drive lockpin in place.
NOTE: *All lockpins should be installed protruding 1/16 in. to 5/16 in. above the fork or lever.*
5. Insert the second-third speed shifter shaft, from the front of the case, with the notches down, pushing it through the shifter fork shoulder toward the front. Install the lockpin.
6. Install the selector shaft in the case. Push it through the second-third speed intermediate lever and the first-reverse lever. Install lockpins.
7. Install both lockballs and springs into the bores in the case and drive in the plugs.
8. Remove the rear extension bolt(s), pull back on the extension and rotate the extension until the bore for the reverse idler gear is exposed.
9. Install the lockball into the shaft from the rear of the case and install the shaft into the gear. Drive the shaft into place.

10. Using a dummy shaft, install a spacer at each end of the countergear. Hold them in place with heavy grease.
11. Coat the thrust washer with grease and stick it to the case. The lugs of the thrust washers must engage the slots in the case.
12. Turn the case extension until the countergear bore is exposed.
13. Place the lockball in the shaft. From the rear of the transmission, insert the shaft so that the thrust washer is held in position. Hold the opposite thrust washer in position with a short drift.
14. Insert the countergear into the case.
15. Insert the shaft into the countergear and push out the dummy shaft. Align the lockball with the groove in the case and tap the shaft into the case.
16. Align the rear bearing retainer and tighten the bolts.
17. Install the case cover gasket, cover and screws.
18. Install the gearshift linkage in reverse sequence of removal.
NOTE: *Start the idler lever shaft into the shift control simultaneously when installing selector ring.*

TYPE-14 VEGA 4-SPEED

Application
Vega, 1972

TRANSMISSION DISASSEMBLY

1. Follow Steps 1-7 under early Vega 3-Speed transmission for removal of gearshift linkage, case cover and countergear shaft and countergear.
2. Drive out intermediate shift lever pin and remove intermediate lever. Use a 1/8 in. pin punch to drive out all pins.
3. Slide the reverse shaft to rear of the case so that the scallop in the selector shaft will clear the reverse shaft.
4. Shift transmission to neutral. Push in on the selector shaft and turn so that the lockpins are in the vertical position. Drive the lockpin out of the third-fourth speed intermediate lever cam and then from the first-second speed intermediate lever cam. Remove the selector shaft.
5. Pry the selector shaft seal rings out of the case.
6. Remove the lockball plugs with a slide hammer. Remove the thrust springs and balls.
7. Place the transmission in first gear and drive the lockpins out of the shifter forks and selector levers. Remove the first-second lever pin first.

8. From the rear of the transmission drive out the first-second shifter shaft with a brass drift. Remove the fork from the sliding sleeve.
9. Tap the third-fourth shifter shaft rearward until the fork can be removed from the shaft, then drive out the third-fourth shifter shaft through the front of the case.
10. Remove the clutch drive gear from the case.
11. Remove the rear extension and mainshaft from the case.
12. Push the reverse idler gear shaft toward the rear. Be sure that the lockball is not lost, and remove the reverse idler gear and shaft from the case.
13. From the front of the transmission, drive out the reverse shifter shaft with a brass drift. Remove the shifter fork from the case.

Mainshaft Disassembly

1. Remove the snap-ring from the rear bearing retainer groove and remove the mainshaft assembly from the rear bearing retainer.
2. Depress the retaining clip and remove the speedometer driven gear.
3. Remove needle bearing, spacer ring and synchronizer ring. The sliding sleeve, keys and clutch keys can also be removed.
NOTE: *The synchronizer hubs and sliding sleeves are a select assembly and*

should be kept together as originally assembled.

4. Remove the snap-ring from in front of the synchronizer hub.
5. Remove the snap-ring, spacer and Belleville washer from the shaft.
6. Support second gear and press the mainshaft until the bearing and synchronizers are free on the shaft. Remove all loose parts.
7. Remove third speed synchronizer hub snap-ring. Support third gear and press the mainshaft until the synchronizer and third gear are free.

Mainshaft Assembly

1. From the front of the mainshaft, install the third speed gear. Gear must turn freely.
2. Install the third speed synchronizer ring onto the third speed gear cone.
3. Install the rear clutch key spring into the third-fourth speed synchronizer hub so that the hooked spring rests in one of the slots and the raised end is toward the blocker ring.
4. Press the third-fourth speed clutch hub onto the mainshaft.
5. Secure the third-fourth synchronizer hub with a snap-ring.
6. From the rear of the mainshaft slide on the second speed gear. Gear must turn freely.
7. Place the second speed synchron-

1 Intermediate lever bushing
   snap-ring
2 Cotter pin
3 Shift idler lever and spring
4 Intermediate lever bushing
5 Rear extension and
   retaining bolts
6 Rear extension gasket
7 Reverse idler gear shaft
   and lockball
8 Reverse idler gear and
   bushing assembly

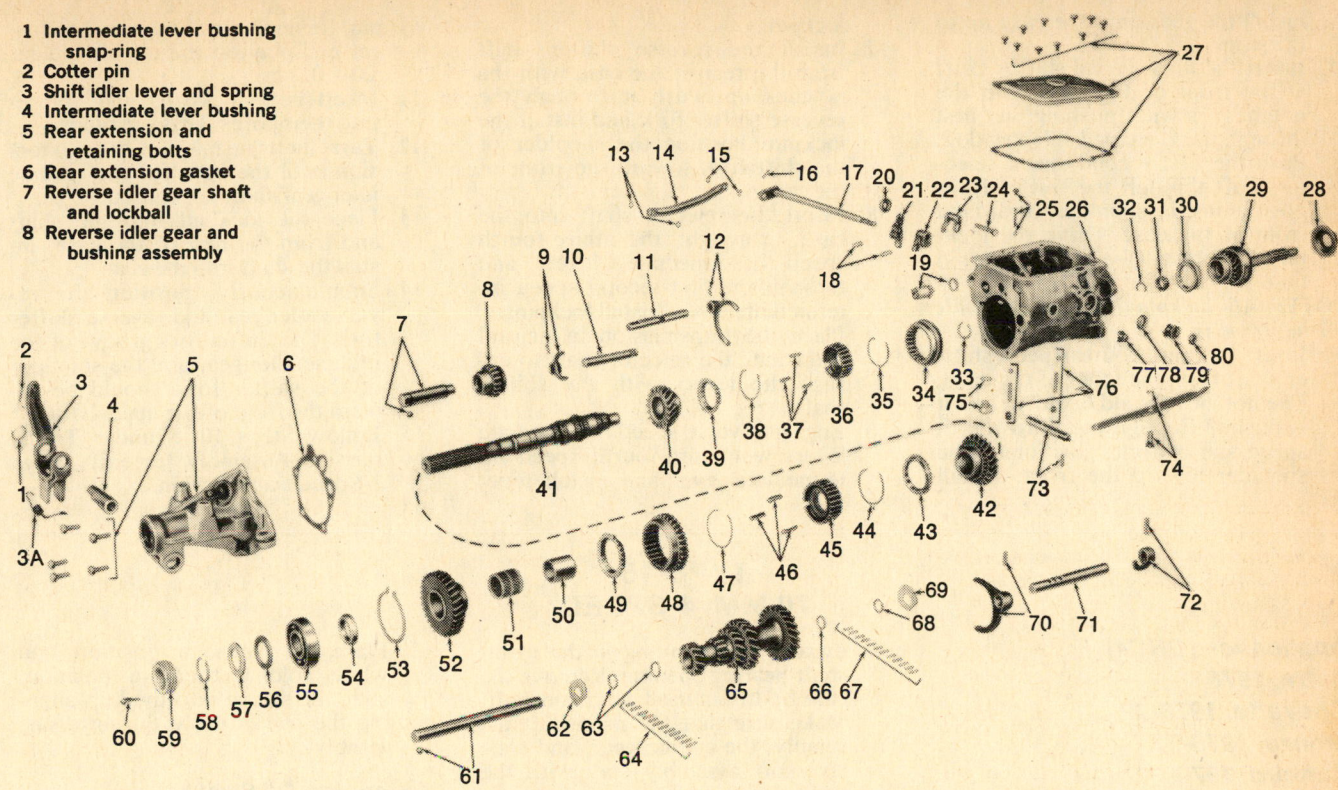

Exploded view (inverted) of Vega 4-speed transmission (© Chevrolet Div., G.M. Corp)

9 Reverse idler gear shift fork and spiral pin	26 Transmission case	45 1st-2nd synchronizer hub	63 Countergear bearing washers
10 Reverse idler gear shifter shaft	27 Cover gasket, cover, and screws	46 1st-2nd synchronizer keys	64 Countergear roller bearings (24)
11 3-4 speed shifter shaft	28 Clutch drive gear to housing seal	47 Synchronizer spring	65 Countergear
12 3-4 speed shift fork and spiral pin	29 Clutch drive gear assembly	48 1st-2nd synchronizer sleeve	66 Countergear bearing washer
13 Washers	30 4th gear synchronizer ring	49 1st speed synchronizer ring	67 Countergear roller bearings (24)
14 Shift control rod	31 Mainshaft pilot bearing assembly	50 1st speed gear bushing	68 Countergear bearing washer
15 Washers	32 Pilot bearing spacer ring	51 1st gear needle bearing assembly	69 Countergear thrust washer
16 Cotter pin	33 3-4 speed synchronizer assembly retaining ring	52 1st speed gear	70 1st-2nd shift fork and spiral pin
17 Selector shaft	34 3-4 speed synchronizer sleeve	53 Rear bearing to extension locking ring	71 1st-2nd shift shaft
18 Spiral pins	35 Synchronizer spring	54 Rear bearing spacer ring (front)	72 1st-2nd selector lever cam and spiral pin
19 Back-up lamp switch and seal ring	36 3-4 synchronizer hub	55 Mainshaft rear bearing	73 Intermediate lever shaft and pin
20 Selector shaft oil seal	37 3-4 synchronizer keys	56 Rear bearing spacer (rear)	74 Shift selector rod, pivot pin and lock ring
21 3rd-4th speed intermediate shifter lever	38 Synchronizer spring	57 Belleville washer	75 TCS switch and gasket
22 1st-2nd intermediate shift lever	39 3rd speed gear synchronizer ring	58 Rear bearing retaining ring (brg.-to-mainshaft)	76 Shifter shaft detent balls, springs and hole plugs
23 Reverse intermediate lever	40 3rd speed gear	59 Speedo drive gear	77 Oil filler plug
24 Reverse intermediate lever pin	41 Mainshaft	60 Speedo drive clip	78 Selector shaft oil seal
25 Reverse shifter shaft detent ball, spring and cap	42 2nd speed gear	61 Countergear shaft and lockball	79 Selector shaft adjusting ring
	43 2nd speed synchronizer ring	62 Countergear thrust washer	80 Selector shaft locknut
	44 Synchronizer spring		

izer ring on the second speed gear cone.

8. Install both synchronizer key springs into the first-second speed synchronizer hub, so that the spring hooks rest in the same hub slot and the other spring ends are positioned opposite each other and toward the blocker rings. Install the sliding gear and keys on the hub.

9. Slide the first-second speed synchronizer hub, needle bearing and inner sleeve onto the mainshaft. Slide the spacer, rear extension retaining ring and rear bearing onto the shaft.

10. Support the rear bearing inner race

and press the components together.

NOTE: *Align the slots in the synchronizer rings with the synchronizer keys.*

11. Install the spacer and Belleville washer on the mainshaft and secure with snap-ring.

NOTE: *The concave side of the Belleville washer should face the bearing.*

12. Position the speedometer gear retaining clip on the shaft and install the gear.

13. Place the mainshaft assembly into the rear bearing retainer up to the stop. Secure with a snap-ring.

14. Assemble the third-fourth speed synchronizer assembly on hub with

the raised end of the key springs toward the blocker ring.

NOTE: *Arrows on the keys point toward the shifter fork groove.*

TRANSMISSION ASSEMBLY

1. Install a new gasket onto the rear extension.

2. Slide the mainshaft assembly into the transmission case.

3. From the front, slide the spacer ring and needle bearing onto the mainshaft. Coat the needle bearing and roller with grease.

4. Install the synchronizer blocker ring on the clutch drive gear and

install the gear onto the case up to the stop.

5. Insert the first-second shifter shaft at the front of the case with the notches down, pushing it first through the L shaped selector dog. Push the first-second speed selector shaft through the shifter fork, positioning the shoulder toward the front of the case. Drive the lockpins in. Install selector dog pin first.

NOTE: *All lockpins should protrude $1/16$ in. to $5/64$ in.*

6. Insert the third-fourth speed shifter shaft from the front of the case. The notches should be down and it is pushed through the third-fourth speed shifter fork, positioning the shoulder toward the front. Install lockpin.

7. Install the reverse shifter shaft from the rear of the case with the notches up. Push it through the reverse shifter fork and install the lockpin. Position the shoulder of the shift fork toward the front of the case.

8. Insert the selector shaft into the case; through the third-fourth speed intermediate lever and through the first-second speed intermediate lever. Install lockpins.

9. Place the transmission in neutral and rotate the selector shaft to engage the levers with the shifter shafts.

10. Engage reverse speed intermediate levers with third-fourth speed intermediate lever and install pivot pin. Reverse speed intermediate lever end-play on the pin should be .004-.012 in.

11. Insert both lockballs and springs into their bores. Drive in plugs.

12. Turn the transmission case extension until the bore for the reverse idler gear shaft is exposed.

13. Place the lockball into the shaft and from the rear of the case, install the shaft into the gear.

14. Simultaneously, position the reverse idler gear and reverse shifter fork. The shifter fork groove of the reverse idler gear and the shoulder of the shifter fork should be toward the front of the mainshaft.

15. Follow Steps 10-18 under Transmission Assembly for early Vega 3-Speed transmission.

TYPE-15
70 MM. 4-SPEED

Application (OHC4)
Astre, 1976
Chevette, 1976-79
Monza, 1976-77
Sunbird, 1976
Starfire, 1976-77
Vega, 1976-77

DISASSEMBLY

1. Place the transmission so that it is resting on the bellhousing.
2. Drive the spring pin from the shifter shaft arm assembly and shifter shaft, then remove the shifter shaft arm assembly.
3. Remove the five bolts holding the extension housing to the transmission case and remove the extension.
4. Press down on the speedometer gear retainer and remove the gear and retainer from the mainshaft.
5. Remove the snap rings from the shifter shaft and remove the reverse shifter shaft cover, shifter shaft detent cap, the spring and ball, and the interlock lock pin.
6. Pull the reverse lever shaft outward to disengage the reverse idler; remove the idler shaft with the gear attached.
7. Remove the snap ring on the reverse gear and reverse countershaft gear; when finished remove the gears.
8. Turn the transmission on its side and remove the clutch gear bearing retainer bolts, the retainer and gasket.
9. Remove the snap-ring holding the clutch gear ball bearing to the bell housing; and then remove the bolts holding the bell housing to the case.
10. Turn the transmission so that it rests on the bell housing again and

expand the snap-ring in the mainshaft bearing opening. Remove the case by lifting it off the mainshaft. Make sure that the mainshaft assembly, the countergear, and shifter shaft assembly stay with the bell housing.

11. Lift the entire mainshaft assembly complete with shifter forks and countergear from the bell housing.

Mainshaft

12. Separate the shift shaft assembly and countergear from the mainshaft.
13. Remove the clutch gear and blocker ring from the mainshaft. When doing this, make sure you don't lose any of the clutch gear roller bearings.
14. Remove the snap ring in front of third-fourth gear synchronizer hub and remove the hub, using an arbor press if necessary.
15. Remove the blocker ring and the third speed gear, then using press plates, remove the ball bearing from the rear of the mainshaft. Remove the remaining parts from the mainshaft keeping them in order for later reassembly.

ASSEMBLY
Synchronizer Keys and Springs

1. The synchronizer hubs and sliding sleeves are an assembly and should be kept together as originally assembled; the keys and springs can be replaced.
2. Mark the position of the hub and sleeve for reassembly.
3. Push the hub from the sliding sleeve; the keys will fall out and the springs can be easily removed.
4. Place the new springs in position with one on each side of the hub so that the three keys are engaged by both springs.

5. Place the keys in position and while holding them in position, slide the sleeve into the hub aligning the marks made during disassembly.

Extension Oil Seal

6. Pry the old seal from rear of the extension, then drive the bushing from the rear of the extension housing.
7. Coat the inside diameter of the seal and bushing with transmission fluid and install them.

Drive Gear Bearing Oil Seal

8. Pry out the old seal, and install a new one making sure that it bottoms properly in its bore.

Mainshaft

9. With the rear of the mainshaft turned up, install the second speed gear with the clutching teeth upward; the rear face of the gear will butt against the flange of the mainshaft.
10. Install a blocker ring with the clutching teeth down over the second speed gear.
11. Install the first and second synchronizer assembly with the fork slot down; press it on the splines on the mainshaft until it bottoms. Make sure the notches of the blocker ring align with the keys of the synchronizer assembly.
12. Install the synchronizer hub to the mainshaft snap-ring, then install a blocker ring with the notches down so that they align with the keys of the first and second gear synchronizer assembly.
13. Install the first speed gear with the clutching teeth down; install the rear ball bearing with the snap-ring groove down and press into place on the mainshaft.

1 Bolt
2 Bearing retainer
3 Seal assembly
4 Gasket
5 Clutch housing
6 Wire assembly
7 Switch assembly (TCS)
8 Gasket assembly
9 Case assembly
10 Spring
11 Cap
12 Ball
13 Gasket
14 Cap
15 Retainer
16 Back-up light switch
17 Plug
18 Cap
19 Bolt
20 Retaining ring
21 Locating ring
22 Bearing assembly
23 Bearing assembly
24 Bolt
25 Main drive gear
26 Bearing rollers
27 Shift fork
28 Pin
29 Bushing
30 Detent lever
31 Shift fork
32 Shift shaft
33 Pin
34 Lock ring
35 Extension assembly
36 Gasket
37 Arm assembly
38 Pin
39 Bushing
40 Seal
41 Reverse shaft and lever
42 Lock ring
43 Clip
44 Retaining ring
45 Synchronizer assembly
46 Mainshaft
47 Second speed gear
48 Synchronizer assembly
49 Synchronizer blocking ring
50 Synchronizer spring
51 Synchronizer key
52 Third speed gear
53 First speed gear
54 Locating ring
55 Mainshaft rear bearing
56 Reverse gear
57 Retaining ring
58 Speedometer drive gear
59 Retainer ring
60 Thrust washer
61 Countershaft gear
62 Locating ring
63 Bearing race
64 Bearing assembly
65 Countershaft reverse gear
66 Reverse idler shaft
67 Retainer ring
68 Thrust washer
69 Reverse idler gear

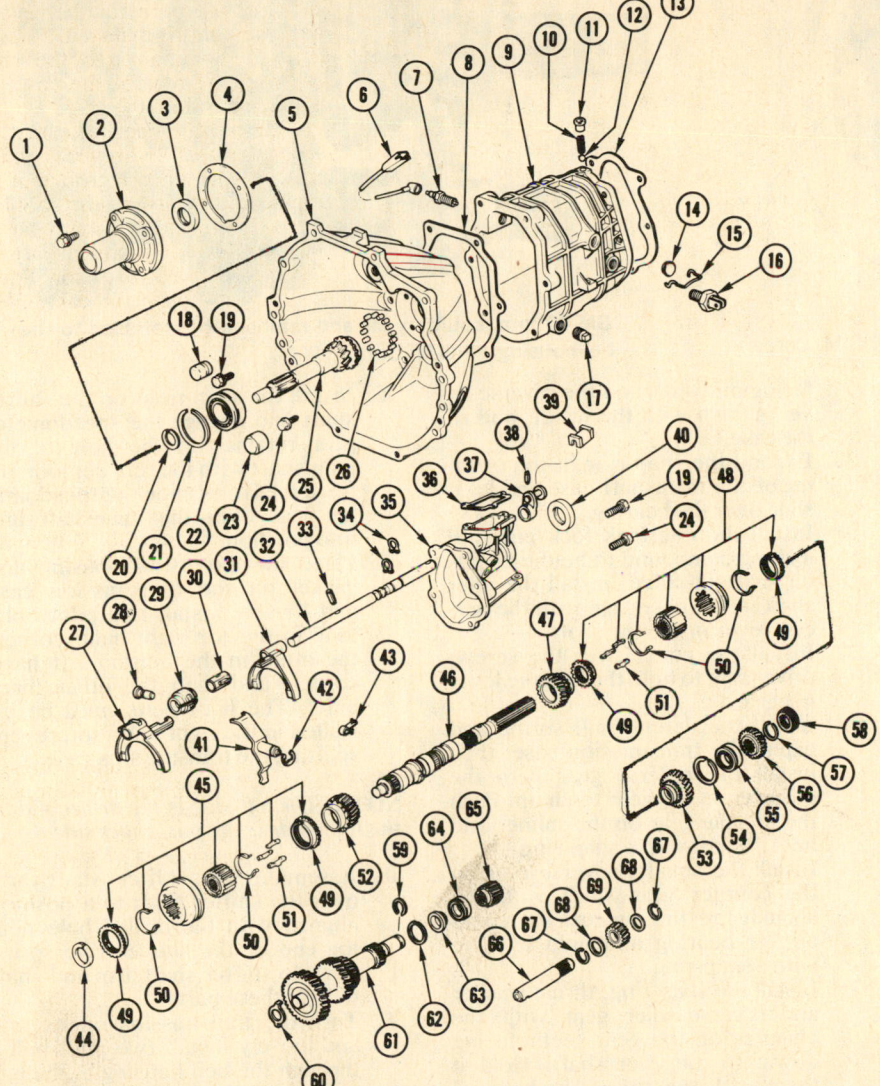

Exploded view of GM 70 mm. transmission (© G.M. Corp.)

14. Turn the mainshaft up and install the third speed gear with the clutching teeth going up; the front face of the gear will butt against the flange on the mainshaft.
15. Install a blocker ring with the clutching teeth down, over the synchronizer surface of the third speed gear.
16. Install the third and fourth gear synchronizer assembly with the fork slot down; make sure the notches of the blocker ring align with the keys of the synchronizer assembly.
17. Install the synchronizer hub to mainshaft snap-ring; install a blocker ring with the notches down so that they align with the keys of the third and fourth gear synchronizer assembly.

Components to Transmission Case

18. Using a press, install the shielded ball bearing to the clutch gear shaft with the snap-ring groove up.
19. Install the snap-ring on the clutch gear shaft; place the pilot bearings into the clutch gear cavity, using heavy grease to hold them in place.
20. Assemble the clutch gear to the mainshaft and then install the detent lever to the shift shaft with the roll pin.
21. Slide the first and second gear shifter so that it engages the detent lever.
22. Assemble the third and fourth gear shifter fork to the detent bushing and slide the assembly on the shift shaft to place it below the first and

second shifter fork arm.
23. Install the shifter assembly to the synchronizer sleeve grooves on the mainshaft.

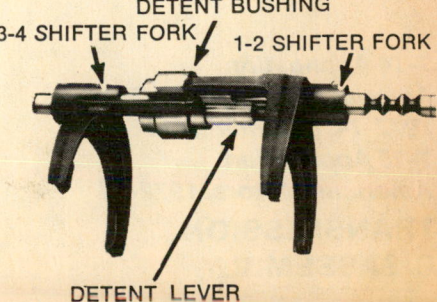

DETENT BUSHING
3-4 SHIFTER FORK   1-2 SHIFTER FORK

DETENT LEVER
GM 70 mm. shift forks assembled
(© G.M. Corp.)

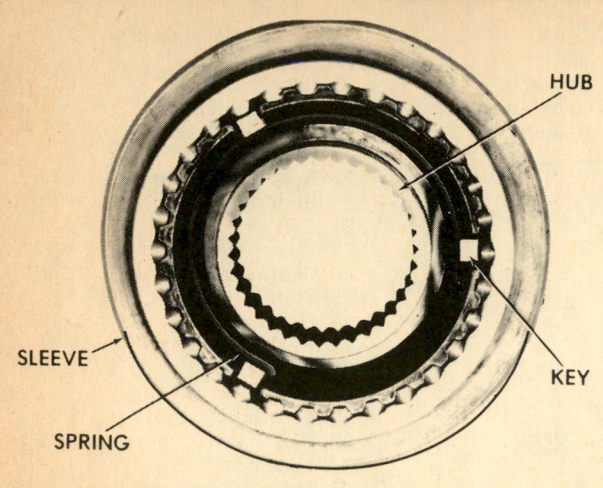

SLEEVE

SPRING

HUB

KEY

GM 70 mm. synchronizer assembly (© G.M. Corp.)

GM 70 mm. countergear and mainshaft assembled to the bellhousing (© G.M. Corp.)

24. With the front of the bell housing resting on wooden blocks, place a thrust washer over the hole for the countergear shaft. The thrust washer must be placed in the holes in the bellhousing.

25. Mesh the countershaft gears to the mainshaft gears and install this into the bellhousing.

26. Turn the bellhousing on its side, and install the snap-ring to the ball bearing on the clutch gear; then install the bearing retainer to the bellhousing. Make sure you use sealant on the four retaining bolts.

27. Turn the bellhousing so that it is resting on the blocks again, and install the reverse lever to the case using grease to hold it in place. When it's installed, the screwdriver slot should be parallel to the front of the case.

28. Install the reverse lever snap ring; install the roller bearing to the countergear opening with the snap ring groove inside of the case.

29. Install the gasket on the bellhousing with rubber cement. Before installing the case, make sure the synchronizers are in the neutral position, the detent bushing slot is

facing outward, and the reverse lever is flush with the inside wall of the case.

30. Expand the snap-ring in the opening of the mainshaft case and let it slide over the bearing.

31. Install the interlock lock pin with locking compound to hold the shifter shaft in place; install the idler shaft so it will engage with the reverse lever inside the shaft.

32. Install the cover over the screwdriver arm to hold the reverse lever in place.

33. Install the detent ball, spring and cap in the transmission case, then install the reverse gear with the chamfer on the gear teeth up. Push the reverse gear on the splines and hold it there with a snap-ring.

34. Install the smaller reverse gear on the counter gear shaft with the shoulder resting against the countergear bearing and hold it there with a snap-ring.

35. Install the snap-ring, thrust washer and reverse idler gear with the chamfer of the gear teeth facing down, to the idler shaft. Hold it there with the thrust washer and snap-ring.

36. Install the snap-rings on the shifter shaft and engage the speedometer gear retainer in the hole in the mainshaft with the retainer loop toward the front; slide the speedometer gear over the mainshaft and into position.

37. Place the extension housing and gasket on the transmission case and loosely install two pilot bolts (one in the top right hand corner; the other in the bottom left hand corner) and then the other three bolts. The pilot bolts *must* be installed in the right holes to prevent splitting the transmission case.

NOTE: *The left side is the driver's side; the right side is the passenger side.*

38. Assemble the shifter shaft arm over the shifter shaft to a position aligned with the drilled hole near the end of the shaft; drive spring pin into shifter shaft arm and shaft to hold these parts.

39. Turn the transmission on its side and loosely install two pilot bolts, through the bell housing in the left top and right bottom holes, and then the four retaining bolts.

TYPE-16
WARNER T-14, T-15
FULLY SYNCHRONIZED
3-SPEED

T-14 Application
American Motors (6 Cyl.)
1972-74, (Gremlin), 1976
T-15 Application
American Motors, 1972-74

TRANSMISSION DISASSEMBLY

1. Remove cover, front bearing cap, gasket, and two front bearing snap rings.

2. Align notch in clutch shaft third gear with countergear. Remove clutch shaft and front bearing. A puller may be needed.

3. Pull off front bearing.

4. Remove extension housing and gasket. Using oil seal remover and slide hammer, remove extension housing oil seal. Remove extension housing bushing. Install new bushing, aligning oil groove with housing slot.

5. Remove snap-ring, speedometer

drive gear, and locating ball.

6. Remove two rear bearing snap-rings and pull off rear bearing.

7. Move mainshaft aside. Remove both shift forks.

8. Push front synchronizer toward rear. Tilt front of mainshaft up and out through top of case.

9. If necessary, remove the transmission controlled spark switch assembly.

10. Drive out roll pins. Push shift shafts into case. Remove shift

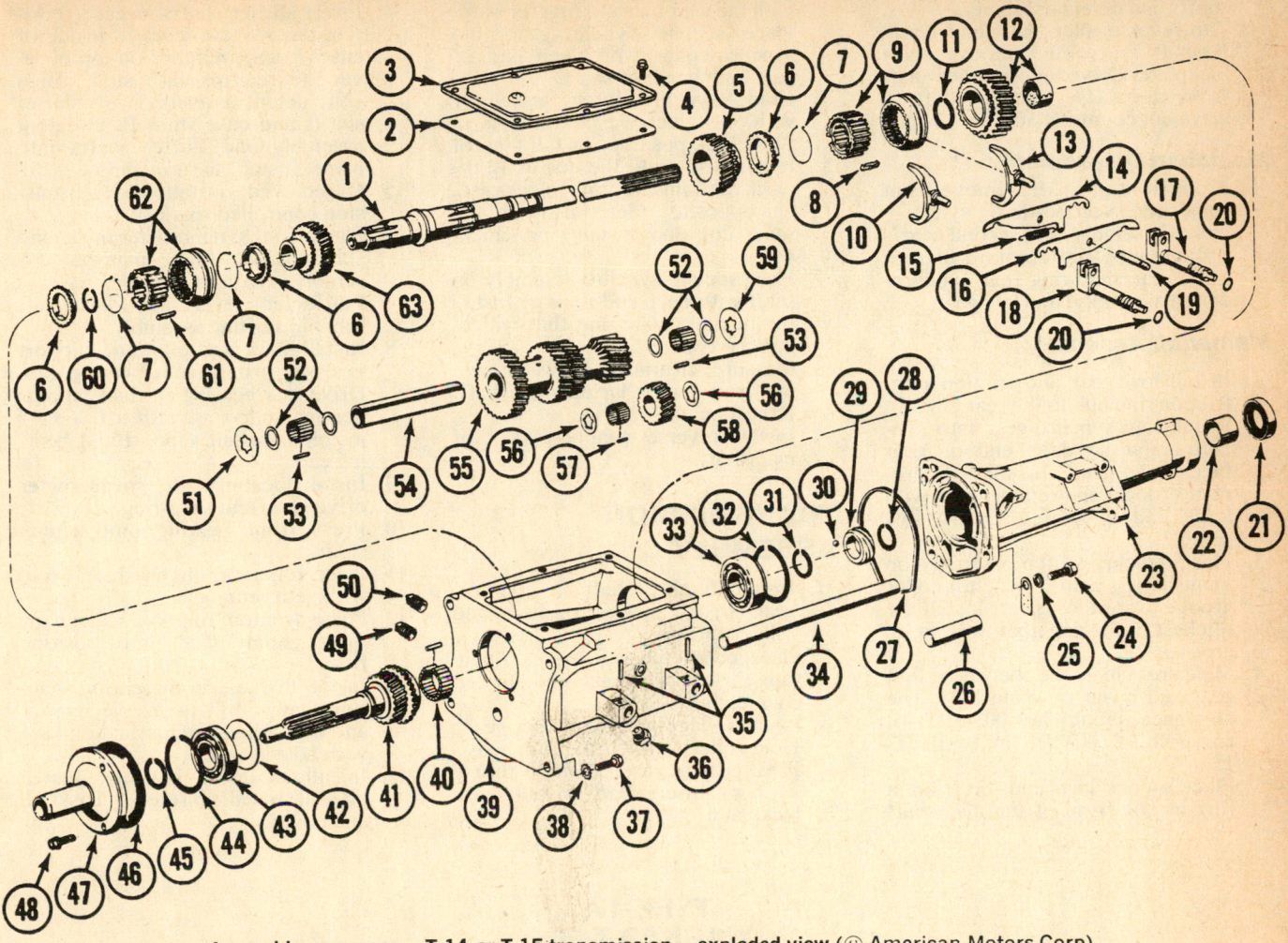

Assembly sequence—T-14 or T-15 transmission—exploded view (© American Motors Corp)

1. Spline Shaft
2. Gasket
3. Case Cover
4. Bolt
5. First Gear
6. Clutch Friction Ring Set
7. Shaft Plate Retaining Spring
8. Clutch Shaft First and Reverse Plate
9. First and Reverse Clutch Assembly
10. Shifter Second and High Fork
11. Clutch First and Reverse Gear Snap Ring
12. Reverse Gear
13. Shifter First and Reverse R Fork
14. Shifter Interlock First and Reverse Lever
15. Speed Finder Interlock Poppet Spring
16. Shifter Interlock Second and Third Lever
17. Shifter Fork First and Reverse Shaft
18. Shifter Fork Second and Third Shaft
19. Shifter Fork Interlock Lever Pivot Pin

20. Shifter Fork Shaft Seal
21. Rear Bearing Cap Oil Seal
22. Rear Bearing Cap Bushing
23. Rear Bearing Cap
24. Bolt
25. Lock Washer
26. Idler Gear Shaft
27. Rear Bearing Cap Gasket
28. Speedometer Drive Gear Ring
29. Speedometer Drive Gear
30. Speedometer Drive Gear Ball
31. Rear Ball Bearing Lockring
32. Rear Ball Bearing Lockring
33. Rear Ball Bearing
34. Countershaft
35. Shifter Fork Retaining Pin
36. Solenoid Control Switch
37. Bolt
38. Lock Washer
39. Case
40. Spline Shaft Pilot Bearing Roller
41. Clutch Shaft
42. Front Ball Bearing Washer
43. Front Ball Bearing
44. Front Ball Bearing Lockring
45. Front Ball Bearing Snap Ring
46. Gasket

47. Front Bearing Cap
48. Bolt
49. Drain Plug
50. Filler Pipe Plug
51. Front Countershaft Gear Thrust Washer
52. Countershaft Gear Bearing Roller Washer
53. Countershaft Gear Bearing Roller
54. Countershaft Gear Roller Bearing Spacer
55. Countershaft Gear
56. Reverse Idler Gear Bearing Roller Washer
57. Reverse Idler Gear Bearing Roller
58. Reverse Idler Gear
59. Rear Countershaft Thrust Washer (Less Lip)
60. Clutch Second and Third Snap Ring
61. Clutch Shaft Second and Third Plate
62. Second and Third Clutch Assembly
63. Second Gear

Manual Transmissions

shafts and detent assembly.

11. Tap reverse idler shaft and countershaft rearward. Remove shaft lockplate. Drive reverse idler shaft from case. Use dummy shaft to drive out countershaft.

Mainshaft Disassembly

1. From front of shaft, remove front snap-ring, second-third synchro-clutch assembly, and second gear.
2. From rear of shaft, remove reverse gear, rear snap-ring rear synchro-clutch assembly, and low gear.

Mainshaft Assembly

1. Install low gear and friction ring; friction ring hub to the rear.
2. Install low synchro-gear into synchro-collar so deep end of gear faces low gear. Install synchro-plates (dogs) and retainer ring with large end of plates toward low gear.
3. Place synchro-clutch assembly on mainshaft with synchro-collar groove toward low gear. Install the thickest snap-ring that will fit in groove.
4. Measure clearance between first gear and collar on mainshaft. The clearance should be .003-.012 in. for the T-14; .003-.014 in. for the T-15.
5. Place second gear and the friction ring on the front of the mainshaft

with the gear hub and ring forward. Place second synchro-gear into synchro-collar with deep end of gear facing rear of shaft.
6. Hold synchro-clutch assembly with one synchro-plate, or dog, in 12 o'clock position. Install tang of retainer ring into the dog at 12 o'clock and install ring clockwise. On opposite side, start with the same dog and install ring clockwise.
7. Place second synchro assembly on shaft with deep end to rear. Install the thickest snap-ring that will fit into the goove.
8. Measure clearance between second gear and collar on mainshaft. It must be .003-.018 in.
9. Install reverse gear on rear of mainshaft.

TRANSMISSION ASSEMBLY

1. Install dummy shaft in countergear. Install spacer washers and roller bearings.
2. Place countergear in case. Align thrust washers at each end. Insert countershaft.
3. Install rollers in reverse idler gear. Hold rollers with petroleum jelly. Place gear in case. Position thrust washers. Insert shaft. Install shaft lockplate.

4. Insert shifter shafts in case. Position low-reverse lever to inside of case. Locate notches on top of levers to rear of case stud. Align shift detent assembly with shifter shafts and case stud. Push detent assembly and shifter shafts into place. Install shaft roll pins.
5. If removed, install the transmission controlled spark switch.
6. Place front synchronizer in second shift position. Place mainshaft assembly in case to one side.
7. Pull detent levers up. Place shift forks in shifting assembly.
8. Install mainshaft pilot end support in case. Install front bearing cap. Drive rear bearing on thickest rear bearing snap-ring with a 1¼ x 17 in. pipe. Install support and bearing cap.
9. Install locating ball, speedometer drive gear, and snap-ring.
10. Press front bearing onto clutch shaft.
11. Place rollers in clutch shaft. Hold with petroleum jelly.
12. Place friction ring on mainshaft. Slide clutch shaft into position from front.
13. Install thickest front bearing snap-ring that will fit in groove, gasket and cap. Align cap lubrication hole with hole in case.
14. Install extension housing. Install oil seal. Install shift lever, gaskets, and cover.

TYPE-17 WARNER T-96 3-SPEED

Application
American Motors (6 Cyl.), 1972

DISASSEMBLY

1. Remove top cover.
2. Remove front bearing cap, clutch shaft snap-ring, and bearing lock-ring.
3. Use a bearing puller and a thrust yoke to remove front bearing.
4. Remove oil slinger.
5. Remove extension housing. Replace rear bearing oil seal and extension housing bushing if necessary.
6. Remove speedometer drive gear snap-ring, drive gear, and retaining ball.
7. Move mainshaft assembly to rear ½ in. Lower front of clutch shaft and raise rear of countergear. Remove clutch shaft.
8. Check 21 roller bearings inside rear of clutch shaft for wear, pitting, or scoring.
9. Remove second-third shifter fork. Tilt mainshaft to remove synchro-clutch snap-ring.

10. Remove synchro-clutch. second gear, and low and reverse gear.
11. Remove low-reverse shifter fork.
12. Remove mainshaft and rear bearing from rear of case. Press rear bearing from shaft.
13. Remove reverse idler shaft and countershaft lockplate.
14. Drive countershaft out to rear with a dummy shaft. Lower dummy shaft and countergear to bottom of case.
15. Drive reverse idler shaft out to rear. Remove gear. Remove countergear.
16. Note position of reverse idler shaft thrust washers; check for wear or damage.
17. Remove outer shift levers and shifter shaft lockpin. Remove shifter shafts from inside case. Remove two interlock ball bearings. Remove interlock sleeve, pin, and spring. Remove shifter shaft O-rings.

ASSEMBLY

1. Install new shift shaft O-rings.
2. Install low-reverse shift shaft inter-

lock sleeve, ball bearing, and spring.
3. Install second-third shift shaft. Place second ball bearing in position.
4. Place shifter mechanism in any gear. With one end of interlock sleeve against shifter shaft quadrant, measure clearance between opposite end of sleeve and the other quadrant. Clearance should be .001-.007 in. Selective lengths of interlock sleeves are available for adjustment. Install lockpins and shift levers.
5. Install dummy shaft in countergear. Install needle bearings, spacer, and washers. Install thrust washers. The bronze front washer must index with the case. Install countergear assembly in bottom of case.
6. Install reverse idler gear with chamfered side of teeth to front. Drive reverse idler shaft in from rear.
7. Drive countershaft into place. Install lockplate.
8. Press rear bearing on mainshaft. Install snap-rings. Place mainshaft

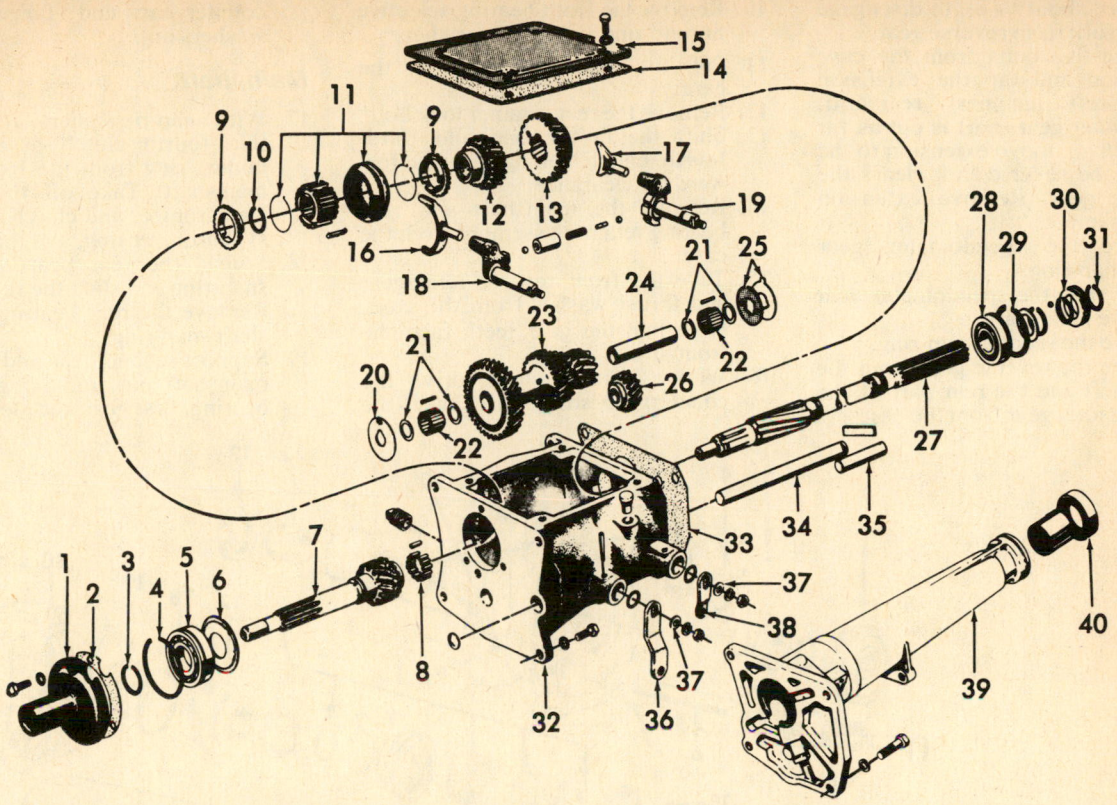

T-96 transmission—exploded view (© American Motors Corp)

1 Bearing cap	11 Synchronizer	21 Bearing washers	31 Snap-ring
2 Gasket	12 Second gear	22 Bearing rollers	32 Case
3 Snap-ring	13 First and reverse gear	23 Countershaft gear	33 Extension gasket
4 Lock ring	14 Cover gasket	24 Countershaft spacer	34 Countershaft
5 Bearing	15 Cover	25 Thrust washer	35 Reverse idler shaft
6 Retaining washer	16 Second and third fork	26 Reverse idler gear	36 Second and third lever
7 Clutch shaft	17 First and reverse fork	27 Mainshaft	37 Shift lever seal
8 Bearing rollers	18 Second and third shaft	28 Rear bearing	38 First and reverse lever
9 Friction ring set	19 First and reverse shaft	29 Lock ring	39 Extension
10 Snap-ring	20 Thrust washer	30 Speedometer drive gear	40 Extension seal

in case.

9. Install shifter forks. Install first-reverse sliding gear, second gear, and synchro-clutch assembly, hub forward.

10. Install thickest mainshaft front snap-ring that will fit in groove.

11. There should be .003-.010 in. clearance between second gear and the mainshaft shoulder, with the synchro-clutch hub pressed against the snap-ring.

12. Hold the 21 clutch shaft bearings in

place with petroleum jelly. Install front friction ring and clutch shaft on mainshaft.

13. Simultaneously install the mainshaft rear bearing, align the shifter forks and gears, and guide the mainshaft into the clutch shaft.

14. Install the thickest rear mainshaft snap-ring that will fit in the groove.

15. Install retaining ball, speedometer drive gear, and snap-ring.

16. Install extension housing with a new oil seal.

17. Place oil slinger on clutch shaft with concave side to rear. Install front bearing using thrust yoke. Install thickest snap-ring that will fit in the groove.

18. Install bearing cap and a new gasket.

19. Check clearance of synchro-clutch friction rings. Both clearances should be .036-.100 in.

20. Check transmission operation in all gears; then install the case cover and gasket.

TYPE-18
WARNER T-10
4-SPEED

Application
American Motors, 1972-74
Camaro, 1974-77
Corvette, 1974-79
Firebird, 1974-79

DISASSEMBLY

Transmission

1. Drain transmission, shift into second gear. Then remove the side cover and shift controls.

2. Remove four bolts from front bearing retainer, then remove retainer and gasket.

3. Remove output shaft companion flange, if any.

4. Drive lockpin up from reverse shifter lever boss, then pull shift-

shaft out about 1/8 in. to disengage shifter fork from reverse gear.
5. Remove five bolts from the case extension and tap the extension (with soft hammer) rearward. When idler gear shaft is out as far as it will go, move extension to the left so the reverse fork clears the reverse gear. Remove extension and gasket.
6. Remove the speedometer gear outer snap-ring.
7. Tap or slide the speedometer gear from the mainshaft.
8. Remove the second snap-ring.
9. Remove the reverse gear from the mainshaft and the rear part of the reverse idler gear from the case.

10. Remove the front bearing selective fit snap-ring and spacer washer.
11. Pull the front bearing from the case.
12. Remove the rear retainer lock bolt.
13. Shift the first-second and third-fourth clutch sliding sleeves forward for clearance.
14. Remove the mainshaft and rear bearing retainer assembly from the case.
15. Take the front reverse idler gear and thrust washer from the case. Note that the gear teeth face the front.
16. With a dummy shaft, drive the countergear shaft out. Take the

countergear and tanged thrust washers out.

Mainshaft

17. With snap-ring pliers, remove the third-fourth clutch assembly retaining ring from the front of the mainshaft. Take off the washer, synchronizer and clutch assembly, synchronizer ring, and third gear.
18. Spread the rear bearing retainer snap-ring and slide the retainer off. Remove the rear bearing to mainshaft snap-ring.
19. Support second gear and press the mainshaft out, removing the rear bearing, first gear and sleeve, first-

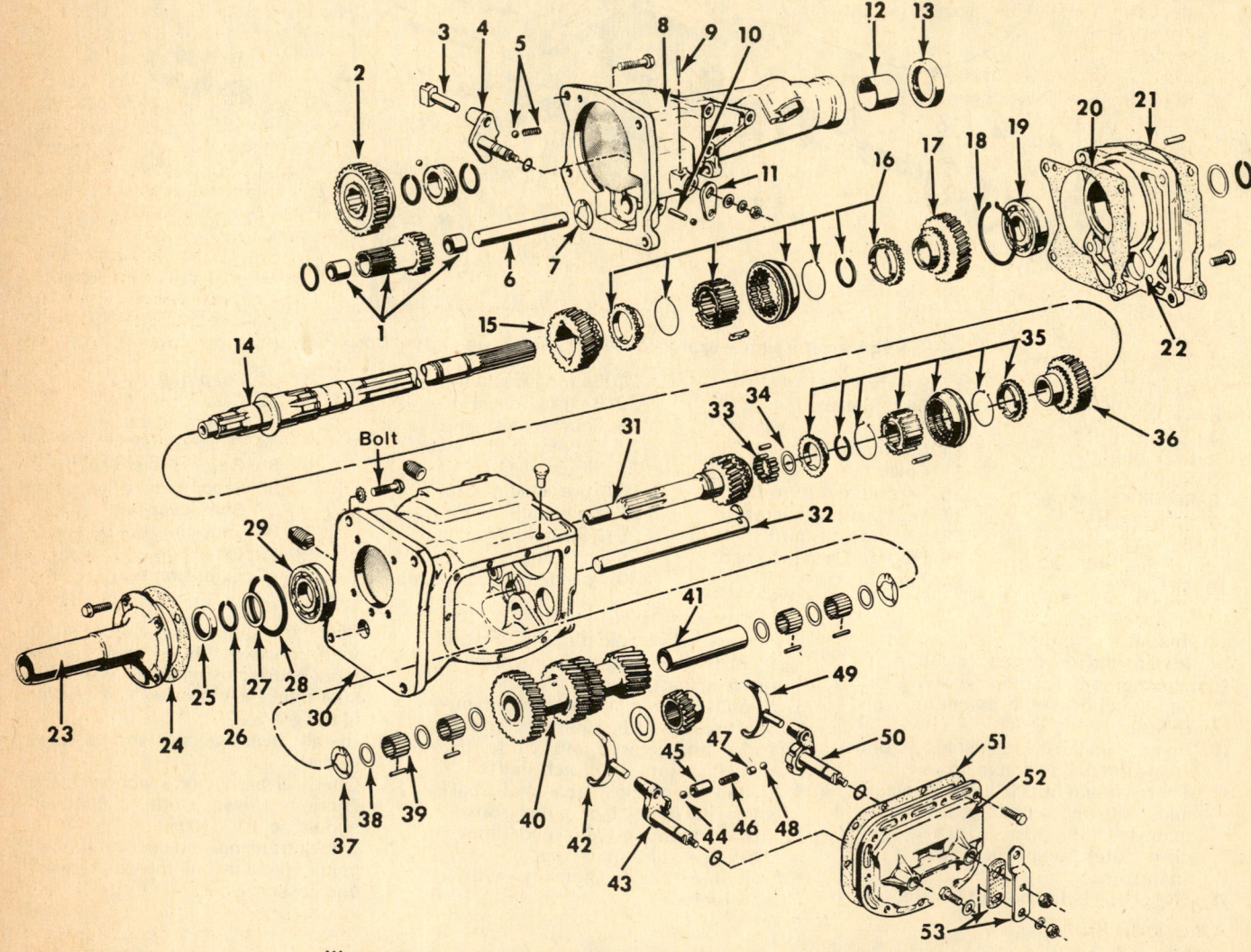

Warner T-10 transmission disassembled (American Motors application)

1 Reverse idler gear
2 Reverse gear
3 Reverse fork
4 Reverse shaft
5 Poppet ball and spring
6 Idler shaft
7 Thrust washer
8 Reverse housing
9 Reverse pin
10 Lock pin
11 Reverse lever
12 Bushing
13 Seal
14 Mainshaft
15 2nd gear
16 Synchro assy
17 1st gear
18 Snap-ring
19 Adapter bearing
20 Adapter
21 Gasket
22 Adapter
23 Front bearing cap
24 Gasket
25 Seal
26 Snap-ring
27 Washer
28 Lock ring
29 Front bearing
30 Case
31 Clutch shaft
32 Countershaft
33 Rollers
34 Roller spacer
35 Synchro assy
36 3rd gear
37 Countergear washer
38 Roller bearing washer
39 Rollers
40 Countergear
41 Spacer
42 3rd-4th fork
43 3rd-4th shaft
44 Poppet ball
45 Interlock sleeve
46 Poppet spring
47 Interlock
48 Poppet ball
49 1st-2nd fork
50 1st-2nd shaft
51 Cover gasket
52 Cover
53 Shift levers

second clutch and synchronizer assembly, and second gear.

ASSEMBLY
Mainshaft

1. From the rear of the shaft, install second gear with the hub to the rear.
2. Install the first-second synchronizer clutch assembly with the sliding clutch sleeve taper to the rear and the hub to the front. Put a synchronizer ring on both sides of the clutch assemblies.
3. Place the first gear sleeve on the shaft. Press the sleeve on until second gear, the clutch assembly, and sleeve bottom against the shoulder of the mainshaft.
4. Install first gear with the hub toward the front and the inner race. Press the rear bearing on with the snap-ring groove to the front.
5. Install the spacer and select the thickest snap-ring that can be fitted into the mainshaft behind the rear bearing.
6. Install third gear with the hub to the front. Install the third gear synchronizing ring with the notches to the front.
7. Install the third-fourth gear clutch assembly with the taper to the front. Make sure that the keys in the hub match the notches in the third gear synchronizing ring.
8. Install the thickest snap-ring that will fit in the mainshaft groove in front of the third-fourth clutch assembly.
9. Put the rear bearing retainer over the end of the shaft. Place the snap-ring in the groove in the rear bearing.
10. Install reverse gear with the shift collar to the rear.
11. Install a snap-ring, the speedometer drive gear, and a snap-ring.

Countergear

1. Install countergear dummy shaft

and tubular roller bearing spacer into the countergear.
2. Using heavy grease to hold the rollers, install 20 bearing rollers in either end of the countergear, two spacers, 20 more rollers, then one spacer. Install the same combination of rollers and spacers in the other end of the countergear.
3. Set the countergear assembly in the bottom of the transmission case, be sure the tanged thrust washers are in their proper position.

Transmission

1. Place the case on its side. Install the countergear tanged washers with the tangs in the thrust face notches, holding them with grease.
2. Install the countergear and dummy shaft. Push the countergear shaft in from the rear, forcing the dummy shaft out the front. Install the shaft key and tap the shaft in until it is flush with the rear face of the case.
3. Install the front reverse idler gear with the teeth forward. Use grease to hold the thrust washer in place.
4. Use heavy grease to hold the 16 roller bearings and the washer in the main drive gear. Mate the main drive gear with the mainshaft. Hold them together by moving the third-fourth clutch sliding sleeve forward.
5. Place a new gasket on the rear of the case. Install the mainshaft and drive gear assembly into the case.
6. Align the rear bearing retainer with the case. Install the locating pin and locking bolt.
7. Put the bearing snap-ring on the front main bearing. Tap the bearing into the case. Install the spacer washer and the thickest snap-ring that can be fitted.
8. Install the front bearing retainer and a gasket. Use a sealer on the bolts.

9. Install the rear reverse idler gear. Engage the splines with the portion of the gear in the case.
10. Slide the reverse gear on the shaft. Install the speedometer gear and the two thickest snap-rings that can be fitted.
11. Install the idler shaft into the extension until the hole in the shaft lines up with the lockpin hole. Drive the lockpin and a sealer coated plug into place.
12. Place the reverse shifter shaft and detent into the extension. Use grease to hold the reverse shift fork in position. Install the shaft O-ring after the shaft is in place.
13. Put the tanged thrust washer on the reverse idler shaft. The tang must be in the notch of the extension housing thrust face.
14. Place the first-second and third-fourth clutch sliding sleeves in the neutral position. Pull the reverse shift shaft partway out and push the reverse shift fork in as far as possible. Start the extension housing onto the mainshaft. At the same time, push in on the shifter shaft to engage the shift fork with the reverse gear collar. When the fork engages, turn the shifter shaft to let the reverse gear go to the rear and the extension housing to fit in place.
15. Install the reverse shift shaft lockpin.
16. Install the extension housing bolts, making sure to use sealer on the upper left-side bolt.
17. Position the first-second clutch sliding sleeve into second gear and the third-fourth clutch sliding sleeve into neutral. Position the forward shift forks in the sliding sleeves.
18. Place the first-second shifter shaft and detent plate into second gear position. Install the slide cover gasket, with sealer.

TYPE-19
AMC OVERDRIVE

Application
American Motors (6 Cyl. Gremlin, Hornet, Pacer), 1975-76

This unit uses an electrical solenoid valve to actuate a hydraulic circuit which engages and disengages a planetary gear system. Overdrive is available only in high gear.

NOTE: *To make removal of the overdrive unit from the transmission easier, drive the car with overdrive engaged, then disengage it with the clutch pedal down. You can drain the transmission*

and overdrive by removing the transmission bottom extension housing bolt.

DISASSEMBLY

1. Use a 1/4 in. thick (or less) open end wrench to remove the solenoid valve.
2. At the front of the unit, remove the self-locking nuts holding the clutch piston apply bars to the thrust bearing cover pins. Discard the nuts; they can't be reused.
3. Remove the nuts and lockwashers from the case studs. Remove the copper gaskets used under the two

top nuts. Separate the main and rear cases.
4. Remove the loose clutch return springs and the clutch brake ring and gaskets from the main case. If the brake ring is stuck, tap it with a plastic hammer; don't pry on it.
5. Remove the main case lower pan, gasket, filter, and pressure plug. A new gasket will be needed.
6. Use a spanner pin tool (one can be fabricated) to unscrew the pressure filter plug and remove the pressure filter and aluminum washer.
Use the spanner tool to unscrew the pump body plug and the non-

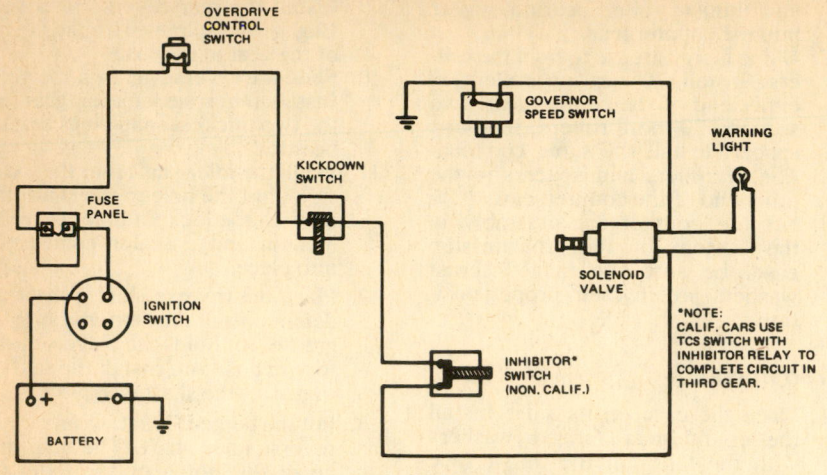

AMC overdrive electrical circuit

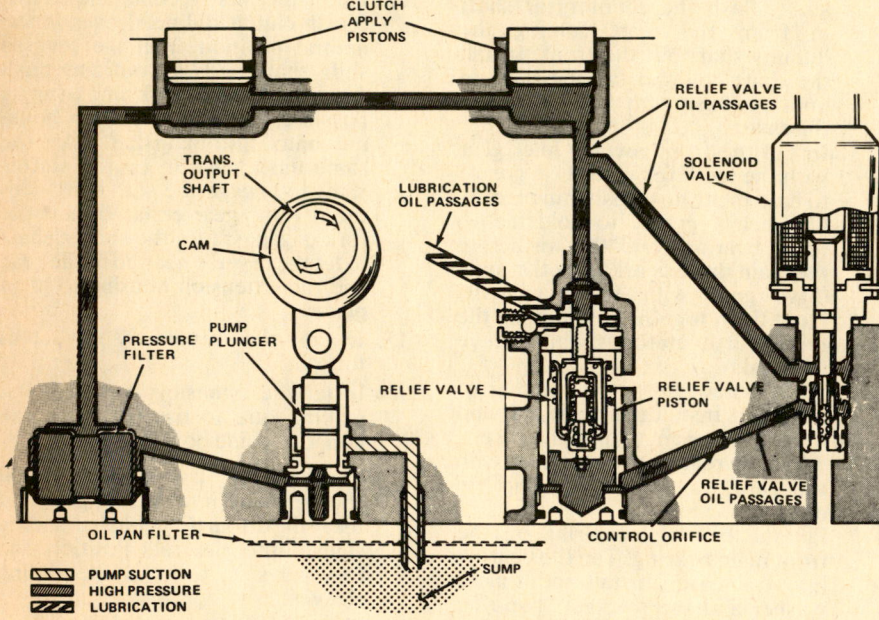

PUMP SUCTION
HIGH PRESSURE
LUBRICATION

AMC overdrive hydraulic circuit, engaged

return valve ball seat spring, check ball, and seat. Remove the O-ring from the plug.

8. Use pliers to carefully take the clutch apply pistons from their bores. Remove the piston O-rings.

NOTE: *Don't remove the lubrication relief valve yet.*

9. Pull the pump body up and slide the plunger out. Remove the body from the case, taking note of the flat side which must align with a lubrication feed hole. Remove the drive cam and key from the pump strap. Don't take apart the pump strap and plunger.

10. Now remove the relief valve piston plug with the spanner tool and take out the piston and spring. Remove the plug O-ring. Don't try to take the spring off the valve piston. Use a magnet or needlenose pliers to remove the relief valve and spring assembly. Don't try to remove the

spring from the valve. A special tool is available to remove the relief valve sleeve and body; it is a hook device that pulls the valve body and sleeve out together. Don't jerk the body and sleeve out; they can easily be damaged. Remove all the valve body, sleeve, and plug O-rings.

11. In the rear case, remove the sliding clutch, sun gear, and thrust bearing cover assembly from the mainshaft annulus gear. Remove the pinion carrier assembly from the gear.

12. Remove the sun gear snap-ring and the sliding clutch ring lock. Push the sun gear out of the hub.

13. Support the thrust bearing cover and gently drive the clutch hub from the bearing.

14. Remove the thrust bearing snap-ring and press the bearing from the cover, using an arbor press. Don't remove the thrust bearing cover

bolts.

15. Remove the overrunning clutch snap-ring and the brass oil slinger.

16. Remove the overrunning clutch. Remove the mainshaft thrust washer from the recess in the annulus gear.

17. Pry the expansion plug out of the rear case. Place the rear case face down on two wood blocks, and using snap-ring pliers through the expansion plug hole, expand the mainshaft bearing snap-ring while tapping the mainshaft out of the case with a mallet.

18. Hold the splined end of the mainshaft and remove the drive gear locknut. Remove the speedometer drive gear tab washer and the gear. Press off the mainshaft bearing.

19. Pry the rear case oil seal out and remove the mainshaft bearing snap-ring. Don't remove the disc washer or rear bushing; the rear case must be replaced if these are damaged.

ASSEMBLY

1. Lubricate the mainshaft bearing with the lubricant to be used in the transmission and overdrive (SAE 80 gear lubricant is recommended). Put the bearing on the mainshaft with the snap-ring groove on the rear. Seat the bearing with a length of pipe.

2. Install the speedometer drive gear with the shoulder side toward the mainshaft bearing. Install a new drive gear washer on top of the gear with the tab in the mainshaft slot and finger tighten the drive gear locknut. Hold the mainshaft splines and torque the locknut to 55 ft. lbs. Bend the washer against the nut in two places.

3. Put a new mainshaft bearing snapring in the groove in the rear case.

4. Place the mainshaft upright and lower the rear case over it. Tap the case with a soft hammer to start the bearing. Expand the snap-ring and tap the case down until the bearing and snap-ring are seated.

5. Lubricate the lip of the new rear case oil seal and install the seal. Install a new expansion plug in the case.

6. Lubricate the mainshaft thrust washer and place it in the recess in the annulus gear.

7. Assemble and lubricate the overrunning clutch. Install it in the bore of the annulus gear. Install the brass oil slinger, shoulder out, and the snap-ring.

8. Lubricate the pinion carrier assembly and install it in the annulus gear.

9. Press the thrust bearing into the thrust bearing cover and install the snap-ring. Lubricate the bearing. Position the bearing and clutch hub. Tap the cover to start the

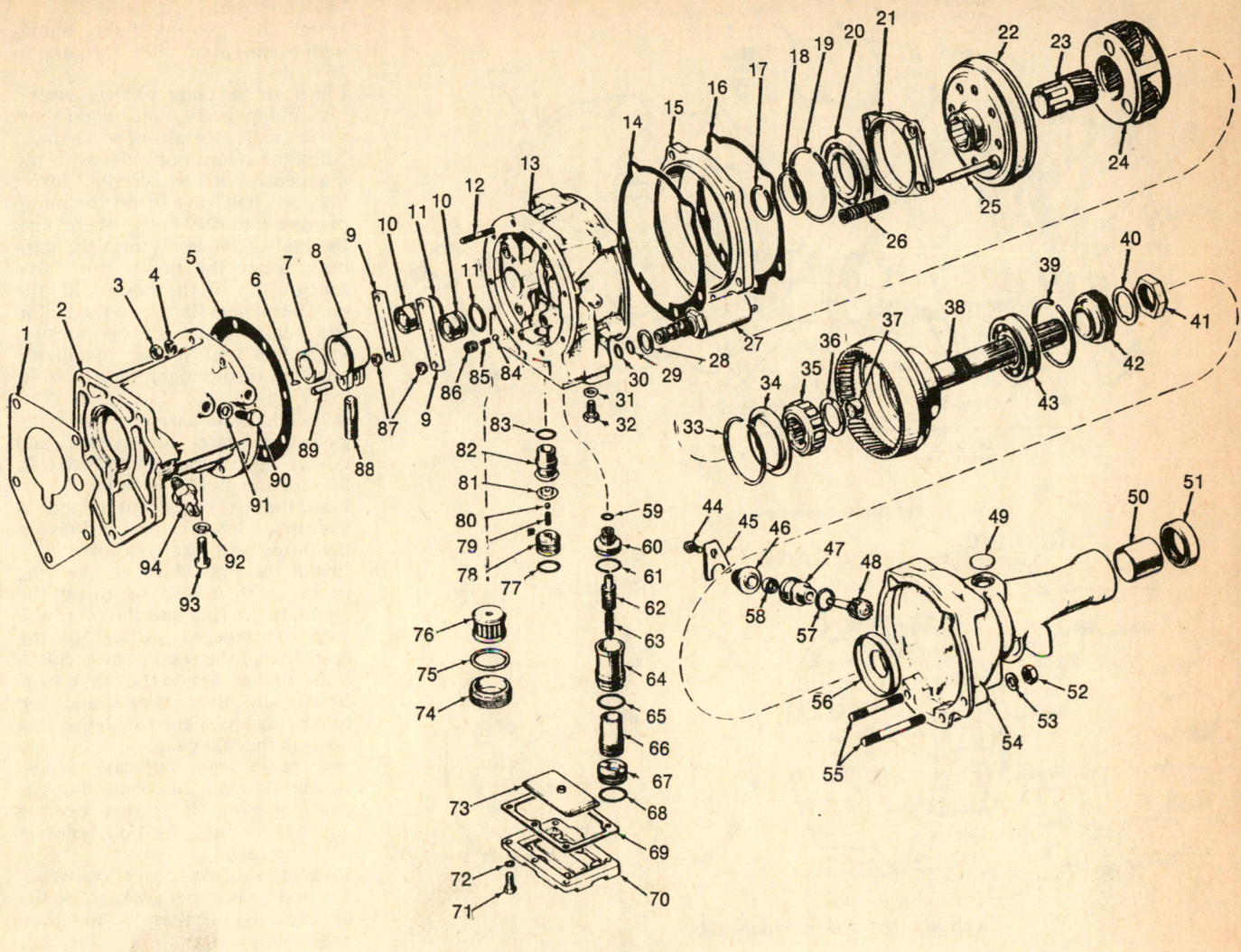

Exploded view, AMC overdrive

1 Gasket Transmission to Adapter
2 Adapter, Transmission
3 Nut, Self Locking, Main Case Stud
4 Washer, Lock
5 Gasket, Main Case to Transmission Adaptor
6 Key, Pump Strap Cam Drive
7 Cam, Pump Strap
8 Strap, Pump
9 Bar, Clutch Piston Apply
10 Piston, Clutch Apply
11 Seal, Clutch Apply Piston O-Ring
12 Stud, Main Case to Transmission Adapter
13 Main Case
14 Gasket, Clutch Brake Ring (front)
15 Brake Ring, Clutch
16 Gasket, Clutch Brake Ring (rear)
17 Ring, Sun Gear Snap
18 Ring Lock, Sliding Clutch
19 Ring, Thrust Bearing Snap
20 Bearing, Thrust
21 Cover, Thrust Bearing
22 Clutch, Sliding
23 Sun Gear
24 Assembly, Pinion Carrier
25 Bolt, Thrust Bearing Cover (4 reqd.)
26 Spring, Clutch Return (4 reqd.)
27 Solenoid Valve
28 Washer, Solenoid Valve
29 Seal, Solenoid Valve O-Ring
30 Seal, Solenoid Valve O-Ring
31 Gasket, Main Case Pressure Plug
32 Plug, Main Case Pressure

33 Ring, Overrunning Clutch Snap
34 Slinger, Overrunning Clutch Oil
35 Assembly, Overrunning Clutch
36 Washer, Mainshaft Thrust
37 Bushing, Mainshaft Support (Included in Mainshaft)
38 Main Shaft and Annulus Gear
39 Ring, Mainshaft Bearing Snap
40 Washer, Speedometer Drive Gear Tab
41 Nut, Speedometer Drive Gear Lock
42 Gear, Speedometer Drive
43 Bearing, Mainshaft
44 Bolt, Speedometer Adapter Clamp
45 Clamp, Speedometer Adapter
46 Adapter, Speedometer to Governor Speed Switch
47 Adapter, Speedometer Driven Gear
48 Gear, Speedometer Driven
49 Plug, Expansion
50 Bushing, Rear Case (included in Case)
51 Seal, Rear Case Oil
52 Nut, Self Locking, Main Case to Rear Case Stud
53 Washer, Lock
54 Rear Case
55 Stud, Main Case to Rear Case
56 Washer, Disc (not removed: included in rear case)
57 Seal, Speedometer Adapter O-Ring
58 Seal, Speedometer Adapter Oil
59 Seal, Relief Valve Body O-Ring (Inner)
60 Body, Relief Valve
61 Seal, Relief Valve Body O-Ring (Outer)
62 Assembly, Relief Valve and Spring
63 Spring, Relief Valve Residual Pressure

64 Sleeve, Relief Valve
65 Seal, Relief Valve Sleeve O-Ring
66 Piston, Relief Valve
67 Plug, Relief Valve Piston
68 Seal, Relief Valve Piston Plug O-Ring
69 Gasket, Oil Pan
70 Oil Pan
71 Bolt, Oil Pan
72 Washer, Lock
73 Filter, Oil Pan
74 Plug, Pressure Filter
75 Washer, Pressure Filter (Aluminum)
76 Filter, Pressure
77 Seal, Pump Body O-Ring
78 Plug, Pump Body
79 Spring, Non-return Valve Ball-seat
80 Ball, Non-return Valve Check
81 Seat, Non-return Valve
82 Body, Pump Plunger
83 Seal, Pump Plunger Body O-Ring
84 Ball, Lubrication Relief Valve Check
85 Spring, Lubrication Relief Valve
86 Plug, Lubrication Relief Valve
87 Nut, Self Locking, Clutch Piston Apply Bar
88 Plunger, Pump
89 Pin, Pump Plunger
90 Bolt, Gearshift Lever Retainer to Adapter
91 Washer, Lock
92 Washer, Lock
93 Bolt, Rear Support Cushion to Adapter
94 Switch, Back-up Light

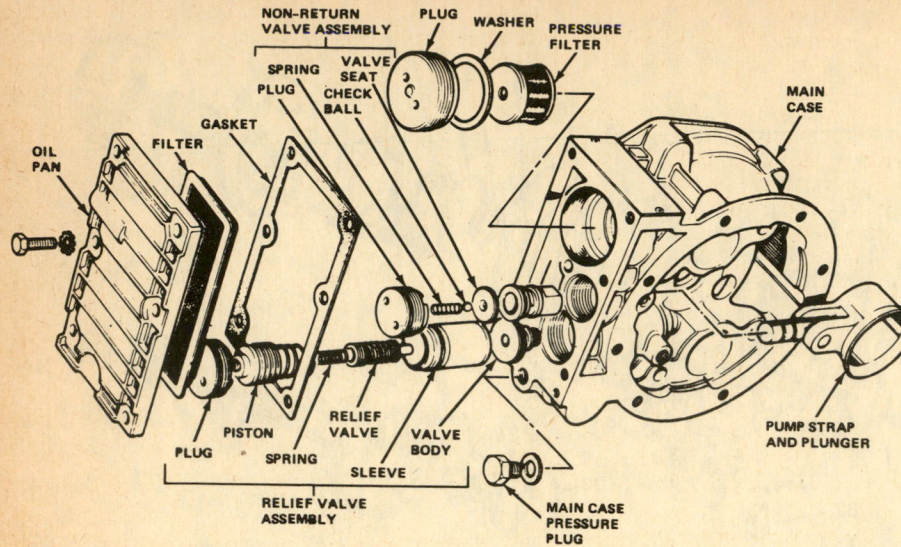

NON-RETURN VALVE ASSEMBLY, PLUG, WASHER, PRESSURE FILTER, SPRING, VALVE SEAT, PLUG, CHECK BALL, GASKET, FILTER, OIL PAN, MAIN CASE, PISTON, PLUG, RELIEF VALVE, SPRING, VALVE BODY, SLEEVE, RELIEF VALVE ASSEMBLY, MAIN CASE PRESSURE PLUG, PUMP STRAP AND PLUNGER

Lower main case details

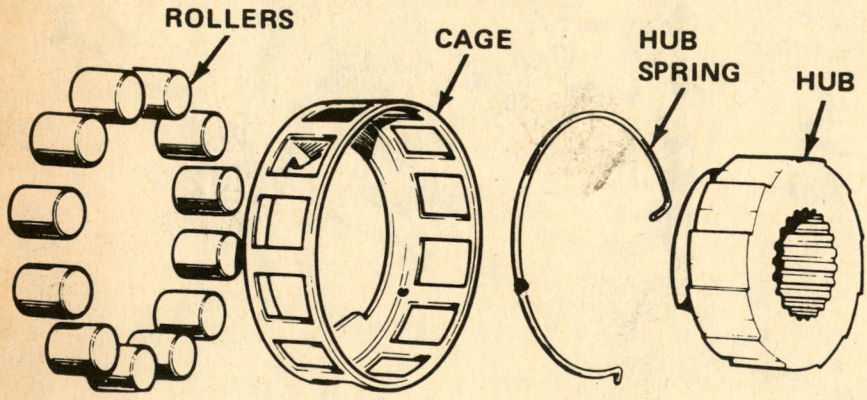

ROLLERS, CAGE, HUB SPRING, HUB

Overrunning clutch components

bearing onto the hub. Turn the assembly over, support the thrust bearing cover, and drive the hub into the bearing.

10. Install the sun gear into the sliding clutch hub. Install the ring lock, sharp edge up, and the snap-ring.

11. Engage the sun gear into the pinion gear and install the sliding clutch assembly onto the mainshaft annulus gear. Make sure the sliding clutch is seated and the gears fully engaged. Turning the shaft will make it easier.

12. Lubricate the clutch apply pistons, install new O-rings, and install the pistons with the counterbored end out.

13. Lubricate the relief valve components and install new O-rings. Insert the relief valve body into the case, align the sleeve hole with the bore oil hole and insert it with the O-ring end up. Push the sleeve firmly into the bore, install the valve and spring assembly in the body, install the residual pressure spring in the valve and spring assembly. Install the piston in the valve sleeve and install the plug,

tightening it to 16 ft. lbs.

14. Install the pressure filter, aluminum washer, and plug, torquing to 16 ft. lbs.

15. Lubricate the pump plunger assembly, pump body, and non-return valve seat. Install new O-rings. Align the pump body flat with the main case bore oil hole and insert the body halfway. Insert the pump plunger into the body, then push the body completely into the case bore. Place the non-return valve seat on top of the body with the check ball seat up. Place the ball in the seat. Install the non-return valve ball seat spring. Install the plug and spring, tightening to 16 ft. lbs.

16. Install the main case pressure plug, gasket, pan filter, new gasket, and cover. Tighten the pan bolts to 6 ft. lbs. and the plug to 16 ft. lbs.

17. Place the rear case front up and install new clutch return springs on the thrust bearing cover bolts.

18. Install the first clutch brake ring gasket on the rear case. Install the clutch brake ring into the rear case with the tapered surface to the rear. Install the second new clutch brake ring gasket on the brake ring. Make sure the gaskets and the brake ring are aligned with the stud holes in the rear case.

19. Use sealer on the case studs. Lower the main case onto the rear case, aligning the thrust bearing cover bolts with the bolt holes in the main case.

20. Install the six nuts, four lockwashers, and two copper gaskets (on the upper studs). Tighten the nuts in a criss-cross pattern to 11 ft. lbs.

21. Install the clutch apply bars on the thrust bearing cover bolts and fasten with new locknuts, tightened to 8 ft. lbs.

22. Install the solenoid valve.

23. Lubricate the new drive cam and install it and the key on the output shaft. Install the snap-ring.

24. Pour about a pint of lubricant in through the access hole in the front of the main case. On installation, tighten the overdrive case to adapter nuts to 18 ft. lbs. Check the lubricant level at the transmission filler plug; the two units have a common lubricant supply.

TYPE-20
WARNER T50
5-SPEED

Application
Astre, 1976-77
Cosworth Vega, 1976
Cutlass, 1976, 1978-79

LeMans (260), 1976
Monza, 1976-79
Omega, 1976, 1978-79
Skyhawk, 1976-79

Starfire, 1976-79
Sunbird, 1976-79
Vega, 1976-77
Ventura, 1976-77

NOTE: *Some small parts may or may not be installed in the transmission being serviced. Some are applicable only to certain car makes and models; some were installed in later production versions. Be sure to note these items during disassembly to avoid confusion later.*

DISASSEMBLY

Drain the unit and remove it from the vehicle.

1. Remove the plug, poppet spring and mesh lock plunger. Remove the selector lever pivot.
2. Drive the spring pin from the shifter head and shift rail. You can leave the pin in place if you aren't disassembling the linkage.
3. Remove the six bolts which retain the transmission case and extension housing to the center support.
4. Slide the case forward from the transmission. Remove the needle thrust bearing and race from the input shaft or case. Remove the lipped thrust washer, if any.
5. Disassembly may be completed on a bench; however, a holding fixture will simplify the job by supporting the transmission.
6. Remove the extension housing by sliding it rearward. The shifter head, shift rail and selector are not fastened to the housing and should not be permitted to drop out and be damaged. The selector lever is held to the shift rail with a retaining clip and pin.

NOTE: *The needle rollers are not always retained in the needle race. Catch loose needles as they fall out during disassembly so that they can be replaced in the mating race during assembly.*

7. Remove the rail selector pin and the rail selector.
8. Press down on the speedometer gear retainer tab and remove the gear and retainer from the output shaft. Later speedometer gears are retained by a snap-ring and ball.
9. Remove the snap-ring, thrust washer, first speed gear, and blocking ring from the output shaft.
10. Remove the snap-ring from behind the synchronizer hub.
11. Move the shift rail to locate the pawl to permit removal of the first and reverse shift link.
12. Slide the first and reverse synchronizer, shift fork, and rail rearward from the transmission. Remove the reverse idler gear from the idler shaft, slide reverse gear off the output shaft.
13. Position the interlock pawl in a position to permit the second and third speed shift link and shift fork to be removed.
14. Position the interlock pawl in an outboard position to permit the fourth and fifth shift fork and link to be removed.
15. Remove the center support from the output shaft and cluster gear.

16. Remove the needle thrust race and bearing from the output shaft or center support. Remove the lipped thrust race, if any.
17. Remove the cluster gear from the remaining gears.
18. Remove the output shaft from the input shaft.
19. The remaining components may be removed one at a time from the output shaft.

Service Hints

1. The second-third synchronizer must be installed with the large chamfer on the outside diameter to the front. If it is not, there will be interference between the sleeve and cluster gear in second gear.

ONE END OF EACH SPRING TO BE ASSEMBLED IN STRUT SLOT AS SHOWN IN OPPOSITE DIRECTION.

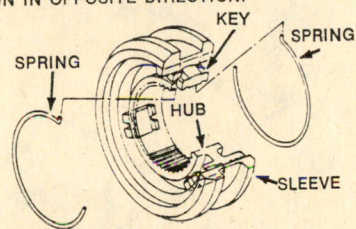

T50 5 speed synchronizer details
(© Pontiac Div., G.M. Corp.)

2. Lack of mainshaft end play can be caused by bearing thrust plates or bearing spacers out of place. The fifth gear roller bearing front spacer can be dislodged and trapped between the fourth-fifth synchronizer hub and mainshaft shoulder.
3. Some transmissions have an anti-rattle plate and spring at the front of the cluster gear. The purpose of this is to lessen gear rattle in neutral with the clutch engaged. In some cases, the anti-rattle plate causes a whine in fourth gear.
4. There are a number of possible causes for hard shifting in this transmission. Check for the shift handle retainer being misaligned. To adjust, loosen the bolts holding the handle and move the rear end of the retainer until shift lever movement is equal in all gears. A hard shift from first to second can be caused by the lower end of the shift lever and the reverse inhibitor cam making contact. Incorrect installation of the interlock pawl retaining plate will cause hard shifting. The inside of the plate should be symmetrical about the interlock pawl and shift link slots. Vague shifting may be caused by side play of the shift lever. This can be the result of a loose roll pin in the upper shift rail at the shifter head. Use of a lubricant other than Dexron II will cause shifting problems, especially when cold.
5. A grind in reverse can be caused by

an improperly functioning reverse inhibitor mechanism or shift lever centering springs.

ASSEMBLY

1. Assemble the third speed gear over the output shaft with the coned end toward the front and against the shaft shoulder.

NOTE: *Synchronizer assemblies are similar except hub splines differ. The hub and sleeve are a selective fit to obtain a free sliding fit with .002 inch maximum backlash. Keep mated parts together to insure correct sliding fit and backlash.*

2. Assemble the blocker rings with the slots aligned with the shift keys of the second-third synchronizer assembly.
3. Assemble the synchronizer and blocker rings, with the chamfer on the sleeve toward the front of the shaft, over the output shaft and position them on the face of the third speed gear.
4. Assemble a snap-ring in the shaft groove ahead of the synchronizer hub.
5. Assemble the second gear, coned end in, against the blocker ring.
6. Assemble a thrust washer on the face of the second speed gear.
7. Assemble a snap-ring in the shaft groove in front of the thrust washer.
8. Assemble the fifth gear over the output shaft against the thrust washer. Assemble one needle spacer over the shaft and into the gear bore. Follow the spacer with a row of needles, a second spacer, a second row of needles, and a third spacer. Use petroleum jelly to retain these parts as they are assembled. One needle space in each row should not be used.
9. Assemble the blocker rings with the slots aligned to the shift keys on the fourth-fifth synchronizer assembly. Install the assembly on the output shaft with the chamfered edge of the sleeve toward the front.
10. Install the needle thrust bearing on the end of the fourth-fifth synchronizer assembly.
11. Assemble 19 needle rollers into the second step of the input shaft bore and carefully lower the shaft with needles over the end of the output shaft. Petroleum jelly or low melting point grease should hold needles in position.
12. Assemble a needle thrust washer and thrust plate over the output shaft against the shaft shoulder. Some models will also have a lipped thrust washer.
13. Install the output shaft, mainshaft, and countergear into the center support
14. Install the reverse gear and bushing assembly over the output shaft and against the center support.

1. Oil seal
2. Bushing
3. Pin
4. Shifter head
5. Threaded plug
6. Poppet spring
7. Mesh lock plunger
8. Breather
9. Selector lever pivot
10. Wiring harness clip*
11. Name plate
12. Back-up light bracket*
13. Cup plug
14. Extension housing
15. Switch
16. 3/8-16 x 3-1/4 hex head bolt
17. Switch
18. Needle bearing
19. Shift Rail
20. Spring pin
21. Rail selector end
22. First & reverse shift fork
23. Shift fork pad
24. First & reverse shift link
25. Gasket
26. 9/16-18 plug
27. Speedometer gear
28. Speedometer gear retaining clip
29. Snap ring
30. Thrust-washer
31. 1st speed gear
32. Snap ring
33. Blocking ring
34. Synchronizer spring
35. Shift plate
36. Clutch hub
37. Clutch sleeve
38. Reverse gear & bushing assembly
39. Bushing
40. Selector arm
41. Spring pin
42. Interlock pawl
43. Selector arm retaining screw
44. 1/4-20 x 3/4 hex head self tapping screw
45. Reverse idler gear & bushing
46. Bushing
47. Spring pin
48. Reverse idler shaft
49. Dowel pin
50. Center support
51. Magnet
52. Needle bearing
53. Shift rail
54. Pin
55. Retaining clip
56. Selector lever
57. Needle bearing
58. Thrust washer
59. Needle thrust bearing
60. Needle thrust race*
61. Output shaft
62. 3rd speed gear
63. Blocking ring
64. Synchronizer spring
65. Synchronizer shift plate
66. Clutch hub
67. Clutch sleeve
68. Snap ring

69. Synchronizer blocking ring
70. 2nd speed gear
71. Thrust washer
72. Snap ring
73. Spacer
74. 5th speed gear
75. 2nd & 3rd shift link
76. 2nd & 3rd shift fork
77. 4th & 5th shift link
78. 4th & 5th shift fork
79. Needle rollers
80. Spacer

81. Synchronizer blocking ring
82. Synchronizer spring
83. Shift plate
84. Clutch hub
85. Clutch sleeve
86. Synchronizer blocking ring
87. Needle thrust bearing
88. Needle rollers
89. Input drive gear
90. Needle thrust plate*
91. Needle thrust bearing
92. Thrust washer
93. Needle bearing

94. Oil seal
95. Cluster gear
96. Spring*
97. Spring pin*
98. Gear damper*
99. Snap ring
100. Thrust washer*
101. Needle bearing
102. 1/2 inch pipe plug
103. Transmission case sleeve
104. Transmission case

* Not used in all transmissions.

Exploded view of the T-50 5-speed (© G.M. Corp.)

15. Install the reverse idler gear and bushing assembly over the reverse idler shaft to mesh with the reverse gear.

16. Put the fourth-fifth shift fork on the fourth-fifth synchronizer sliding sleeve. Locate the interlock pawl to let the shift link be put through the center slot in the center support. Install the fourth-fifth shift link through the slot and engage it with the shift fork.

17. Locate the interlock pawl to let the first-reverse shift link be installed in the inboard slot of the center support. Install the link into the shift fork.

18. If the selector arm was removed, install it over the shift rail, aligning the holes. Drive the spring pin into place.

19. Install the shift rail through the shift fork from front to rear with the notches at the rear.

20. Engage the shift fork with the first-reverse synchronizer sleeve. Slide the synchronizer hub over the output shaft, with the chamfered edge of the sleeve to the front.

21. Guide the shift rail through the interlock pawl, second-third fork, and fourth-fifth fork. Be sure the selector arm is aligned with the notch in the shift link.

22. Install a snap-ring in the output shaft groove. Put a blocker ring

and first gear over the shaft, behind the first-reverse synchronizer assembly. Align the notches in the blocker ring with those in the synchronizer hub.

23. Install a thrust washer and snap-ring behind the first gear.
24. Put the speedometer gear retainer in the hole in the output shaft with the loop forward. Slide on the speedometer gear until the retainer locks it.
25. Slide the rail selector onto the shift rail with the ball inward and drive the spring pin in. Install the selector lever and shift rail into the hole in the extension housing. Install

the shifter head on the rail, but don't put in the pin yet.
26. Put a bead of silicone sealant on the case and extension housing. Make sure the needle rollers in the extension housing stay in place. Install the extension housing over the output shaft and guide the selector lever to engage the rail selector.
27. Install the lipped needle thrust race, if any, needle thrust bearing, and flat race over the input shaft.
28. Bolt the cases to the center support. Torque the bolts to 35 ft. lbs. If there is binding, check to see if a fifth gear spacer might have fallen between the fifth gear and the

synchronizer.
29. Drive the pin into the shifter head and shift rail. Install the mesh lock plunger, spring, and threaded plug. Use thread locking compound on the plug. Align the holes in the selector lever and the extension housing and install the selector lever pivot, tightening to 60 ft. lbs.
30. Fill the transmission with about 3½ pts. of Dexron II automatic transmission fluid.
31. After the transmission is installed, place the transmission and shift lever in neutral. Apply silicone sealant inside the bolt pattern and bolt the shift lever and cover down.

TYPE-21
AMC HR-1
4-SPEED

Application
American Motors OHC
4 cylinder, 1977-79

The HR-1 transmission has an identification tag under the lower left extension housing to transmission case bolt. The entire transmission is metric, except for the filler plug, speedometer gear clamp blot, and crossmember bolts. The lubricant fill capacity is 2.4 pts. of SAE 80W-90, API GL-4 gear lubricant. The filler plug is in the left side of the case; there is no drain plug.

GEARSHIFT LEVER REMOVAL

1. Shift into neutral. Remove the bezel and the inner and outer dust boots.
2. Pull off the E-clip and slide the spring up on the lever.
3. Straighten the locktabs and unscrew the large plastic locknut at the base of the lever.
4. Lift the lever out.
5. Reverse the procedure for installation.

TRANSMISSION DISASSEMBLY
Case

1. Pull the throwout lever straight out of the clutch housing to detach the lever retaining clip from the pivot ball stud. Slide the throwout lever and bearing off the front bearing cap. Unbolt the clutch housing.
2. Remove the vibration damper and transmission mount from the extension housing. Remove the backup light switch.
3. Unbolt and remove the top cover and gasket.
4. At the upper left corner on the left side of the transmission, unscrew the detent plug and remove the de-

tent spring and plunger.
5. Punch out the access plug at the top right rear face of the case. Insert a 5/16 in. diameter rod and drive out the interlock plate retaining pin.
6. Drive out the selector arm roll pin with a 5/32 in. punch.
7. Tap the shift rail back until it pushes out the large plug at the rear of the extension housing and pull it out. Now you can remove the selector arm, interlock plate, and shift forks.

NOTE: *Make a note of the arrangement of the shift mechanism before removing it.*

8. Unbolt and remove the front bearing cap and O-ring. The O-ring and cap oil seal should be replaced.
9. Remove the front bearing retaining and locating snap-rings. Remove the bearing with a puller.
10. Unbolt the extension housing. Tap it with a soft hammer to break it loose. Remove the clutch (input) shaft from the front of the case, and the extension housing and output shaft gear train from the rear of the case.

─────── CAUTION ───────
Don't let the third-fourth synchronizer sleeve separate from the hub.
─────────────────────────

11. Pry the shift rail oil seal out of the case at the top rear.
12. Remove the roller bearing from the inner end of the clutch shaft or from the front end of the mainshaft.
13. Screw a slide hammer into the reverse idler gear shaft and remove it. Remove the reverse idler gear and spacer, noting their positions.
14. Push the countershaft out the back of the case. Use a dummy shaft inserted from the front end of the case to push it out and keep all the

bearings in place.
15. Remove the shift fork from the reverse lever. Remove the spring clip holding the reverse lever on the lever pivot shaft; remove the reverse lever and lever spring.

NOTE: *Make a note of the arrangement of the reverse shift mechanism before removing it.*

16. Remove the countershaft gear along with the dummy shaft. Separate the 38 needle bearings and 4 retainers. Note the location of the bearing retainers; there are thick and thin ones. There are also short and long needle bearings. Remove the countershaft gear thrust washers.

Output Shaft Gear Train

1. Remove the fourth gear blocking ring from the third-fourth synchronizer at the front of the shaft.
2. At the front of the extension housing, compress the snap-ring and slide it forward. Separate the shaft from the extension housing by tapping it out with a soft hammer.
3. Remove the snap-ring at the front of the shaft. It should be replaced.
4. Remove the third-fourth synchronizer. Mark the hub and sleeve for reassembly. Separate the sleeve and hub, remove the synchronizer inserts and springs.
5. Remove third gear and the blocking ring. Remove the second gear snap-ring, take off second gear and the blocking ring.
6. Remove the gear bearing snap-ring toward the speedometer gear.
7. Press off first gear, the first gear spacer, the rear bearing, and the speedometer gear as an assembly.
8. Remove the first gear blocking ring.
9. Mark the first-second synchronizer sleeve and hub for reassembly. Remove the sleeve, inserts, and springs.

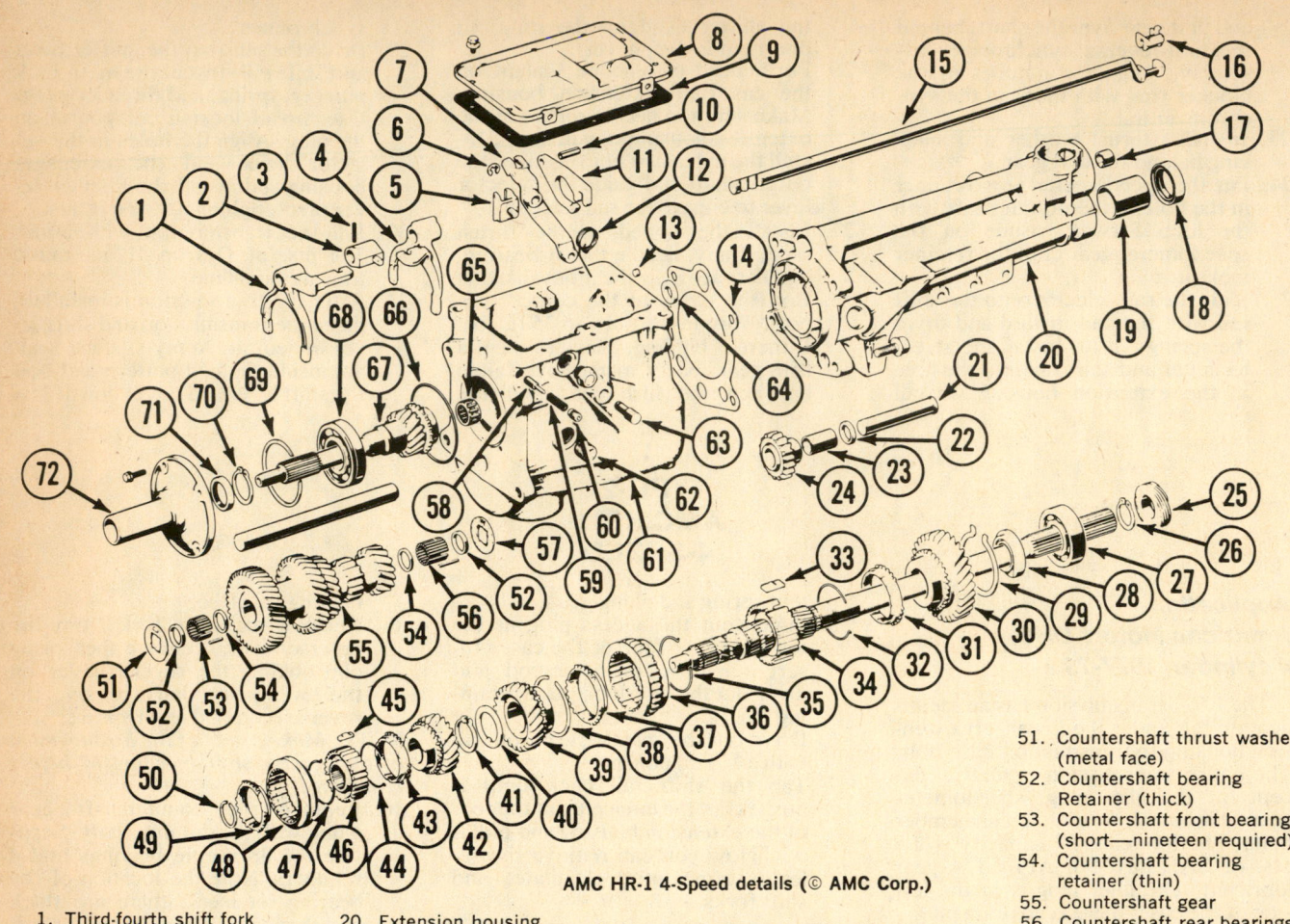

AMC HR-1 4-Speed details (© AMC Corp.)

1. Third-fourth shift fork
2. Selector arm
3. Selector arm roll pin
4. First-second shift fork
5. Reverse level shift fork
6. Reverse lever spring clip
7. Reverse lever
8. Top cover
9. Top cover gasket
10. Interlock plate retaining pin
11. Interlock plate
12. Reverse lever spring
13. Interlock retaining pin access plug
14. Extension housing gasket
15. Shift rail
16. Shift rail insert
17. Shift rail bushing (nylon)
18. Extension housing seal
19. Extension housing bushing (Serviced as a part of housing

20. Extension housing
21. Reverse idler gear shaft
22. Reverse idler gear spacer
23. Reverse idler gear bushing (Serviced as part of gear)
24. Reverse idler gear
25. Speedometer gear
26. Rear bearing snap ring
27. Rear bearing
28. Oil slinger/spacer
29. Output shaft rear snap ring
30. First gear
31. First gear blocking ring
32. First-second synchronizer insert spring
33. First-second synchronizer insert (3)
34. Output shaft and first-second synchronizer hub assembly (Serviced as assembly only)
35. First-second synchronizer insert spring

36. First-second synchronizer sleeve
37. Second gear blocking ring
38. Second gear stop ring (Installed on gear)
39. Second gear
40. Second gear spacer
41. Second gear snap ring
42. Third gear
43. Third gear blocking ring
44. Third-fourth synchronizer insert spring
45. Third-fourth synchronizer insert (3)
46. Third-fourth synchronizer hub
47. Third-fourth synchronizer insert spring
48. Third-fourth synchronizer sleeve
49. Fourth gear blocking ring
50. Output shaft front snap ring

51. Countershaft thrust washer (metal face)
52. Countershaft bearing Retainer (thick)
53. Countershaft front bearings (short—nineteen required)
54. Countershaft bearing retainer (thin)
55. Countershaft gear
56. Countershaft rear bearings (long—nineteen required)
57. Countershaft thrust washer (metal face)
58. Detent plunger
59. Detent spring
60. Detent plug
61. Transmission case
62. Fill plug
63. Reverse level pivot (Serviced as part of case)
64. Shift rail oil seal
65. Clutch shaft roller bearing
66. Front bearing cap O-ring
67. Clutch shaft
68. Front bearing
69. Front bearing locating snap ring
70. Front bearing retaining snap ring
71. Front bearing cap oil seal
72. Front bearing cap

CAUTION

Do not try to remove the first-second synchronizer hub from the shaft.

10. Remove the extension housing oil seal. The best way is to use a slide hammer seal puller.

TRANSMISSION ASSEMBLY

NOTE: *Lubricate all thrust washers, needle and roller bearings, and gear tapered surfaces with petroleum jelly.*

Lubricate all other components with SAE 80W-90 gear lubricant.

Output Shaft Gear Train

1. Seat the rear bearing in the extension housing, using a soft hammer.
2. The output shaft gear snap-ring is available in several sizes; select the thickest one that will fit in the groove in the extension housing, then remove it.
3. Remove the rear bearing from the extension housing, using a long punch or a socket drive extension.

4. Lubricate the output shaft, synchronizers, and gear bores with transmission lubricant; lubricate the tapered blocking ring gear surfaces with petroleum jelly.
5. Install the synchronizer spring and inserts in the first-second hub, install the synchronizer sleeve over the hub and inserts, using the alignment marks made on disassembly. Engage the tang end of each insert spring in the same synchronizer insert, but position them so that the open ends of each spring face away from each other.

6. Install the blocking ring on the tapered surface of second gear; install the ring and gear on the shaft. Make sure the synchronizer inserts engage in the blocking ring notches.
7. Install the second gear thrust washer and snap-ring on the output shaft. Make sure the tabbed end of the snap-ring is seated in the shaft groove. Second gear end play, measured with feeler gauges, must be 0.004-0.014 in. If it is excessive, replace the thrust washer, snap-ring, and gear to correct.
8. Install the first gear blocking ring on the tapered gear surface; install the ring and gear on the shaft. Make sure that the tapered gear surface faces the first-second synchronizer hub and that the synchronizer inserts engage in the blocking ring notches.
9. Put the oil slinger/spacer on the shaft. The grooves must be toward first gear and the flat surface must be away from it.
10. Place the output shaft rear snapring, selected in Step 2, on the shaft over the slinger/spacer and against first gear.
11. Drive or press the rear bearing on the output shaft. Use force only on the inner race. Make sure the bearing seats against the slinger/spacer and that first gear seats in the first-second synchronizer hub.
12. Install the thickest possible rear bearing snap-ring in the shaft groove, making sure it is completely seated.
13. Press the speedometer gear into place. Do not press it down all the way against the bearing; there is a special AMC positioning gauge, J-26832, designed for this job.
14. Install third gear on the output shaft; install the blocking ring on the tapered gear surface.
15. Assemble the third-fourth synchronizer hub, sleeve, inserts, and springs, using the hub to sleeve alignment marks made on disassembly. Engage the tang ends of each insert spring in the same insert, but face the open ends away from each other.
16. Install the third-fourth synchronizer assembly on the output shaft and install the front snap-ring. Check synchronizer end play with feeler gauges; it should be 0.004-0.014 in. If it is excessive, replace the snap-ring, synchronizer

hub, and sleeve to correct.
17. Insert the output shaft and gear train assembly into the extension housing. Tap the front end of the shaft with a soft hammer to seat the rear bearing.
18. Compress the output shaft rear snap-ring and install it in the housing groove. Make sure it is fully seated.

Case

1. Insert the dummy shaft into the countershaft gear. Coat the needle bearings and retainers with petroleum jelly. Install a thin bearing retainer in the needle bearing bores in each end of the gear. Install the long needle bearings in the bore at the rear of the gear. Install the short needle bearings in the bore at the front of the gear. Install a thick bearing retainer in each gear bore over the ends of the needle bearings. Coat the replacement thrust washers with petroleum jelly. Position a thrust washer over the bearing bore at the rear of the countershaft gear. Push the dummy shaft through far enough to hold the washer in place.
2. Align the front thrust washer locating tab with the notch in the case. Place the gear in the case. Push the dummy shaft far forward enough to hold the thrust washer and countershaft gear in place. Stand the front case on its end. Align the locating tab on the rear thrust washer with the notch in the case and install it between the gear and case.
3. Install the countershaft, making sure that the step in the rear end of the shaft is horizontal, with the lower step down.
4. Check the countershaft gear end play with feeler gauges. It should be 0.006-0.018 in. If it is excessive, replace the thrust washers.
5. Install the reverse lever fork in the reverse lever. Install the reverse lever and spring on the pivot shaft in the case and install the spring clip.
6. Place the reverse idler gear and spacer in the case. Make sure the spacer is between the idler gear and the rear of the case. Make sure the reverse lever fork engages the idler gear.
7. Install the reverse idler shaft from the rear of the case. Make sure the reverse lever fork stays engaged with the gear.

8. Use a socket to drive a new shift rail oil seal into the back of the case.
9. Coat the output shaft pilot bearing with petroleum jelly and install it into the clutch (input) shaft bore.
10. Install the blocking ring on the tapered surface of the clutch shaft. Place the shaft in the case.
11. Install a new gasket on the extension housing. Insert the output shaft into the case and install the clutch shaft on the output shaft. Make sure the two shafts are fully engaged.
12. Make sure that the notch in the end of the countershaft is aligned with the extension housing recess. If you don't do this, you will likely crack the case.
13. Coat the extension housing bolts with non-hardening sealer and install them finger tight.
14. Install the front bearing on the clutch shaft and into the the case, driving on the inner race only. Install the front bearing retaining and locating snap-rings.
15. Install the front bearing cap with a new oil seal and O-ring.
16. Install the shift forks in the synchronizer sleeves. Position the interlock plate and its new retaining pin in the case. Lubricate the shift rail with transmission lube and install it into the case through the first-second shift fork and the interlock plate. Place the selector arm on the shift rail and slide it through the third-fourth shift fork and into the front of the case. Install the selector arm roll pin, making sure it is in flush.
17. Install the detent plunger, spring, and plug in the case.
18. Tighten the extension housing bolts to 34 ft. lbs.
19. Install replacement access plugs in the extension housing shift rail bore and in the interlock plate retaiing pin access hole.
20. Install a new extension housing oil seal.
21. Fill the case with SAE 80W-90, API GL-4 lubricant (2.4 pts.) to the edge of the filler plug hole. Install the top cover.
22. Replace the vibration damper and transmission mount on the extension housing.
23. Install the clutch housing, throwout lever, and throwout bearing. Tighten the clutch housing to transmission case bolts to 54 ft. lbs.

TYPE-22
A-412 4-SPEED
CHRYSLER TRANSAXLE

Application
Plymouth Horizon, 1978-79
Dodge Omni, 1978-79

DISASSEMBLY

NOTE: *Final mainshaft adjustment requires a measurement made with a spe-*
cial tool. Check Step 16 of the assembly procedure before disassembly.

1. Remove the clutch pushrod, being careful not to bend it.

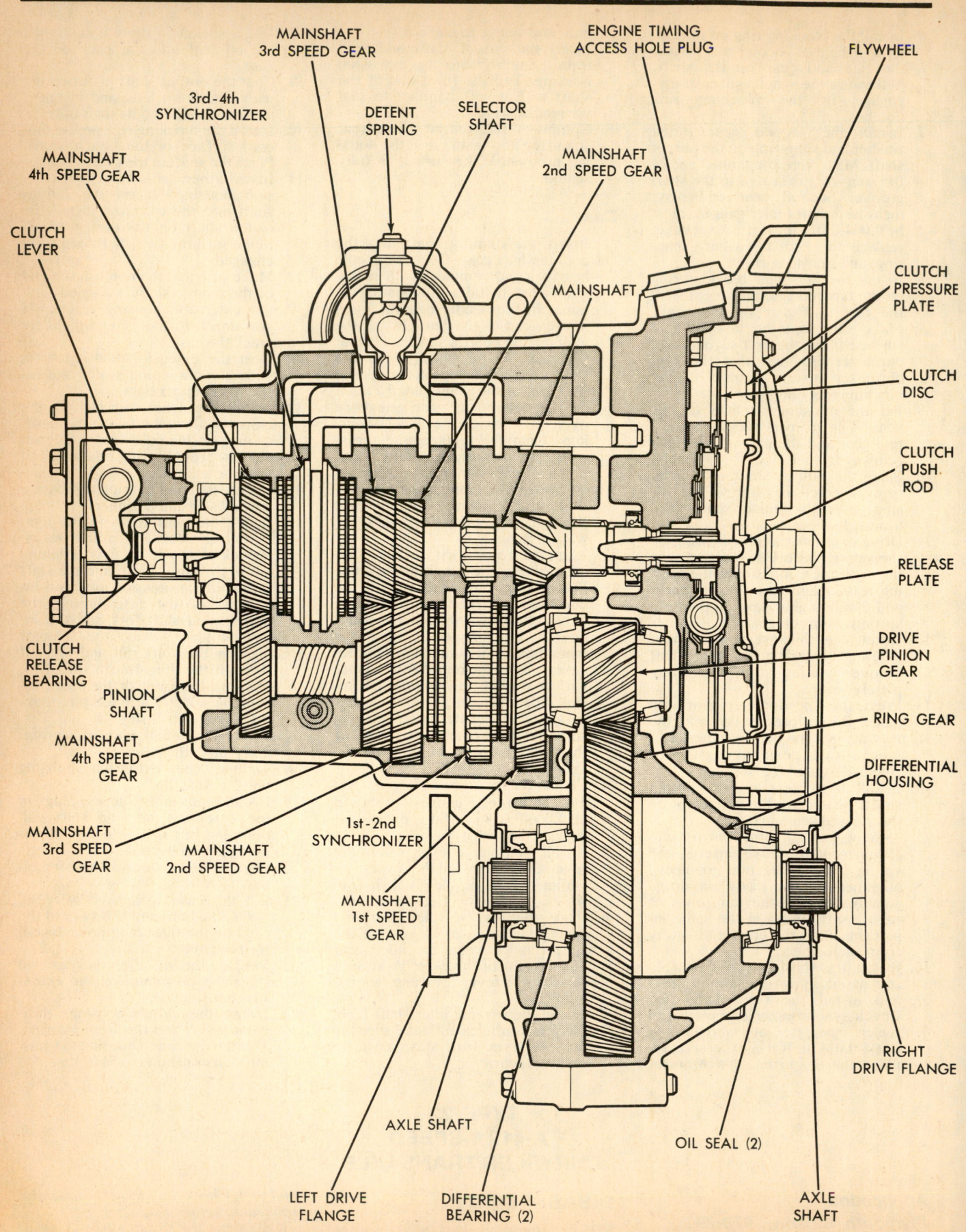

MAINSHAFT 3rd SPEED GEAR

ENGINE TIMING ACCESS HOLE PLUG

FLYWHEEL

3rd-4th SYNCHRONIZER

DETENT SPRING

SELECTOR SHAFT

MAINSHAFT 2nd SPEED GEAR

MAINSHAFT 4th SPEED GEAR

CLUTCH LEVER

MAINSHAFT

CLUTCH PRESSURE PLATE

CLUTCH DISC

CLUTCH PUSH ROD

RELEASE PLATE

CLUTCH RELEASE BEARING

PINION SHAFT

MAINSHAFT 4th SPEED GEAR

DRIVE PINION GEAR

RING GEAR

DIFFERENTIAL HOUSING

MAINSHAFT 3rd SPEED GEAR

MAINSHAFT 2nd SPEED GEAR

1st-2nd SYNCHRONIZER

MAINSHAFT 1st SPEED GEAR

RIGHT DRIVE FLANGE

LEFT DRIVE FLANGE

AXLE SHAFT

DIFFERENTIAL BEARING (2)

OIL SEAL (2)

AXLE SHAFT

Cutaway view of the Chrysler 4-speed transaxle (© Chrysler Corp.)

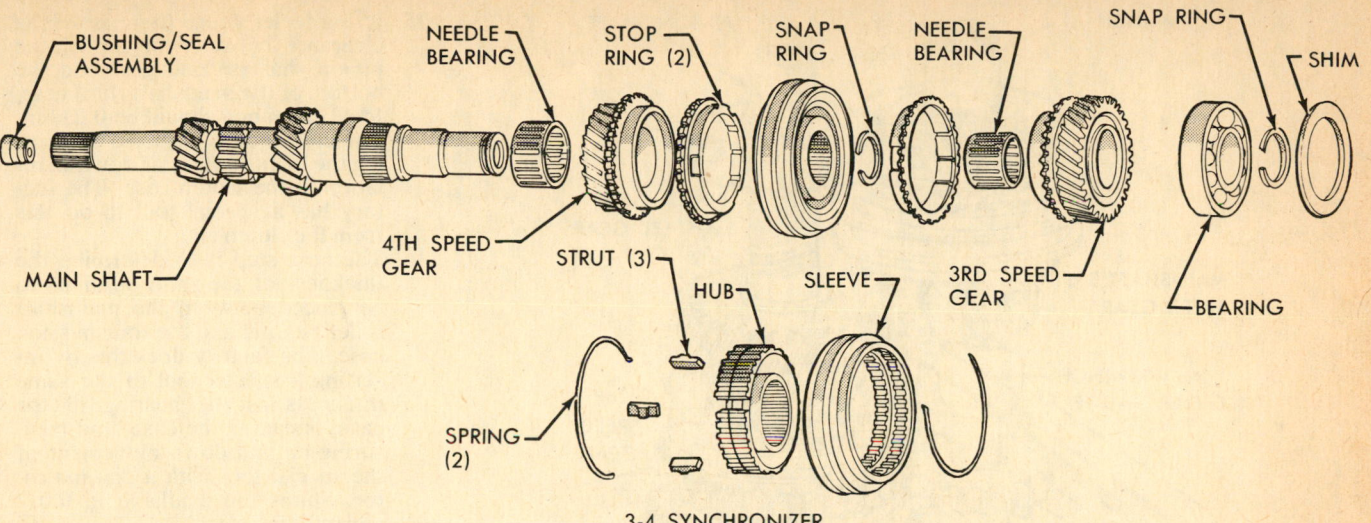

Transaxle mainshaft details (© Chrysler Corp.)

2. Unscrew the selector shaft plug from the case. Remove the detent spring assembly and rubber boot. Tap out the selector shaft and pry out the oil seal.
3. Pry out the two mainshaft bearing retaining nut rubber plugs with a screwdriver.
4. Take off the clutch release bearing end cover by removing the four bolts. Take out the release bearing and plastic sleeve.
5. Use two screwdrivers to push the circlip off the clutch torque shaft. Pull the torque shaft out of the case and remove the pedal return spring and release lever. Pry out the torque shaft oil seal.
6. Remove the three mainshaft bearing retainer nuts. Two of them were under the rubber covers removed earlier and the third is inside the clutch release housing. The three studs and clips will drop into the case.
7. Remove the ten case attaching bolts and four stud nuts. Remove the transmission case. The factory uses a special tool to do this—it pushes against the end of the mainshaft. Make sure to tag all shims for reuse.
8. Remove the two bolts and take out the reverse shift fork and supports.
9. Remove the snap-ring from the end of the pinion shaft.
10. Pull off the bearing and fourth gear from the end of the mainshaft. Take the needle bearing for the fourth gear off, too.
11. Pry off the two shift rail E-clips with a screwdriver. Remove the shift forks assembly.
12. Lift the mainshaft assembly out. It can be fully disassembled by removing snap-rings and components. The clutch pushrod seal and bushing assembly can be driven out of the shaft with a 3/8 in. diameter brass rod. Replace it by driving

with a plastic hammer.
13. Remove the fitted snap-ring from the pinion shaft and lift off the third gear. Lift off the second gear and its needle bearing.
14. Pry or pull out the reverse idler gear shaft.
15. Pull (with a puller) off the first gear and first-second synchronizer assembly from the pinion shaft.
NOTE: *The inner sleeve for second gear and the first gear are removed together.*
16. Take off the first gear needle bearing. Scribe a mark across the first-second synchronizer for reassembly.
17. Remove the four pinion shaft retainer bolts, lift off the retainer, the thrust washer (the flat side goes up), and remove the pinion shaft.

ASSEMBLY

1. Temporarily install the pinion shaft with its bearings and retainer, using a small shim of measured thickness. Bolt down the retainer. Use a dial indicator to measure the up and down end play of the shaft.
NOTE: *Don't turn the shaft while measuring end play; you will get a false reading.*
2. Take the shim used in Step 1 out and reassemble with a new shim chosen to give 0.008 in. preload. Determine the correct size by adding the test shim thickness in Step

1, the measured end play on the shaft, and the preload of 0.008 in. Shims are available in thicknesses from 0.025 in. to 0.055 in.
3. If you have installed new bearings on the pinion shaft, lubricate them with transmission oil, install the shaft, and check the shaft turning torque with a torque wrench. It should be 4.4-13.1 in. lbs. If it isn't, reset the preload.
4. Install the pinion shaft. Place the first gear thrust washer over the shaft with the flat side up (toward the gear). Install the pinion shaft retainer and tighten the bolts to 29 ft. lbs.
5. Install the needle bearing, the first gear, and the first gear synchronizer stop ring over the shaft.
NOTE: *The wear limit for the spacing between the synchronizer teeth on the first gear and those on the stop ring is 0.019 in. There is one tooth missing from the first gear stop ring. First gear will grind if this ring isn't used.*
6. Align the marks on the first-second synchronizer hub and sleeve, made on disassembly. Install the synchronizer, driving it into place.
7. Drive the second gear needle bearing inner race into place over the shaft.
8. Drive the reverse idler gear shaft into place. Make sure that the threaded hole in the top of the shaft is centered pointing out be-

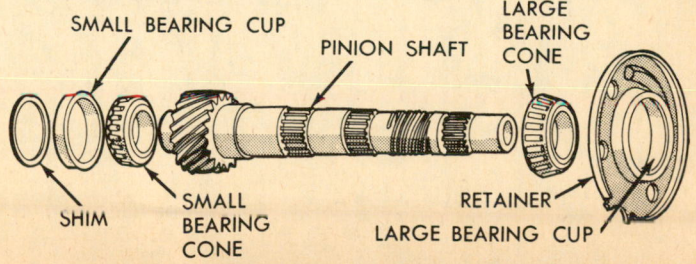

Transaxle pinion shaft details (© Chrysler Corp.)

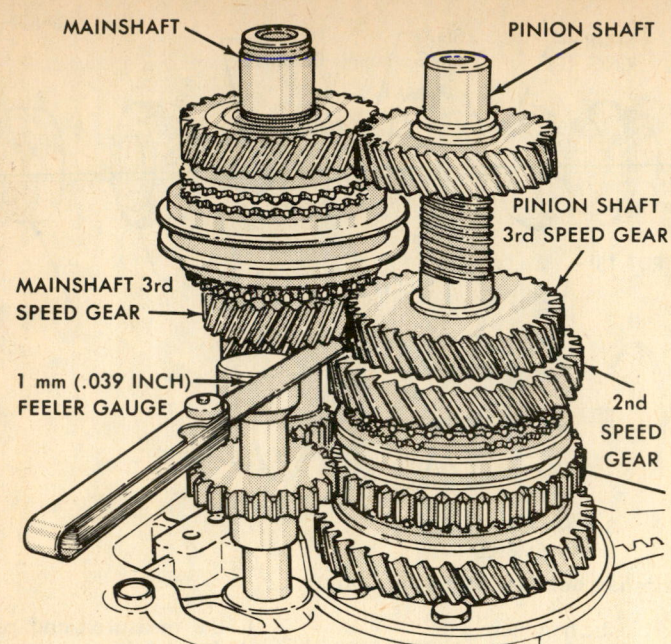

MAINSHAFT

PINION SHAFT

PINION SHAFT 3rd SPEED GEAR

MAINSHAFT 3rd SPEED GEAR

1 mm (.039 INCH) FEELER GAUGE

2nd SPEED GEAR

Measuring gear clearance (© Chrysler Corp.)

tween the two nearest case edge bolt holes.

9. Put the second gear needle bearing over the pinion shaft. Put the second gear stop ring, second gear, and third gear onto the shaft. Make sure that third gear has the thrust face down.

10. Install the snap-ring to hold third gear. Measure end play between third gear and the snap-ring with a feeler gauge; it should be .000-.008 in., as little as possible. Snap-rings are available in thicknesses from

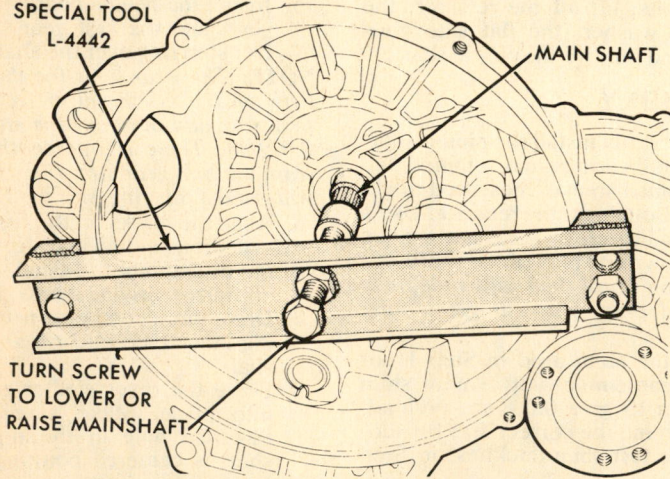

SPECIAL TOOL L-4442

MAIN SHAFT

TURN SCREW TO LOWER OR RAISE MAINSHAFT

Adjusting mainshaft gear clearance (© Chrysler Corp.)

0.098-0.118 in. for adjustment. Replace the snap-ring with the one selected.

11. Install the mainshaft assembly.
12. Install the shift forks assembly and install the E-clips.
13. Install the fourth gear needle bearing over the mainshaft. Put the fourth gear synchronizer stop ring in place. Install the fourth gear and the snap-ring.
14. Install the reverse shift fork and the support brackets, tightening the bolts to 105 in. lbs.

15. Use a feeler gauge to measure the clearance between the top of the pinion shaft second gear and the bottom of the mainshaft third gear. Ideal clearance should be 0.039 in. The clearance is adjusted by forcing the mainshaft up or down in relation to the clutch case. The factory has a special tool to do this from the clutch end.

16. The next step is to determine the thickness of the shim or shims to be placed between the mainshaft roller bearing and the transmission case. The factory does this by inserting a special tool of the same thickness as the bearing in the case, installing the case, and measuring up and down movement of the special tool with a dial indicator. Shims are available in 0.012 and 0.024 in. sizes.

Up and down movement	Shim size needed
0.000-0.018 in.	none
0.019-0.029 in.	0.012 in.
0.030-0.041 in.	0.024 in.
0.042-0.57 in.	0.035 in.

17. After the selected shim is installed behind the bearing, tighten the bearing retainer clamp bolts to 155 in. lbs. Install the transmission case to the clutch housing, using the guide pin for alignment. Tighten the stud nuts and bolts to 250 in. lbs.

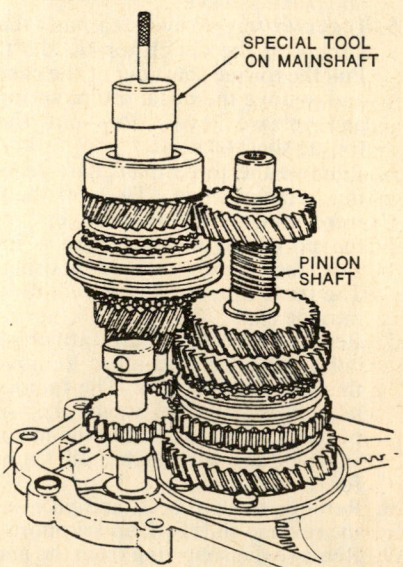

SPECIAL TOOL ON MAINSHAFT

PINION SHAFT

Special tool used to determine mainshaft bearing shim thickness (© Chrysler Corp.)

DRIVE AXLES

The rear axle must transmit power through 90°. To accomplish this, straight cut bevel gears or spiral bevel gears were used. This type of gear is satisfactory for differential side gears, but since the centerline of the gears must intersect, they rapidly became unsuited for ring and pinion gears. The lowering of the driveshaft brought about a variation of the bevel gear, which is called the hypoid gear. This type of gear does not require a meeting of the gear centerlines and can therefore be underslung, relative to the centerline of the ring gear.

Gear Ratios

The drive axle of a vehicle is said to have a certain axle ratio. This number (usually a whole number and a decimal fraction) is actually a comparison of the number of gear teeth on the ring gear and the pinion gear. For example, a 4.11 rear means that theoretically, there are 4.11 teeth on the ring gear and one tooth on the pinion. Actually, on a 4.11 rear, there are 37 teeth on the ring gear and nine teeth on the pinion gear. By dividing the number of teeth on the pinion gear into the number of teeth on the ring gear, the numerical axle ratio (4.11) is obtained. This also provides a good method of ascertaining exactly which axle ratio one is dealing with.

Differential Operation

The differential is an arrangement of gears that permits the rear wheels to turn at different speeds when cornering and divides the torque between the axle shafts. The differential gears are mounted on a pinion shaft and the gears are free to rotate on this shaft. The pinion shaft is fitted in a bore in the differential case and is at right angles to the axle shafts.

Power flow through the differential is as follows. The drive pinion, which is turned by the driveshaft, turns the ring gear. The ring gear, which is bolted to the differential case, rotates the case. The differential pinion forces the pinion gears against the side gears. In cases where both wheels have equal traction, the pinion gears do not rotate on the pinion shaft, because the input force of the pinion gear is divided equally between the two side gears. Consequently the pinion gears revolve with the pinion shaft, although they do not revolve on the pinion shaft itself. The side gears, which are splined to the axle shafts, and meshed with the pinion gears, rotate the axle shafts.

When it becomes necessary to turn a corner, the differential becomes effective and allows the axle shafts to rotate at different speeds. As the inner wheel slows down, the side gear splined to the inner wheel axle shaft also slows down. The pinion gears act as balancing levers by maintaining equal tooth loads to both gears while allowing unequal

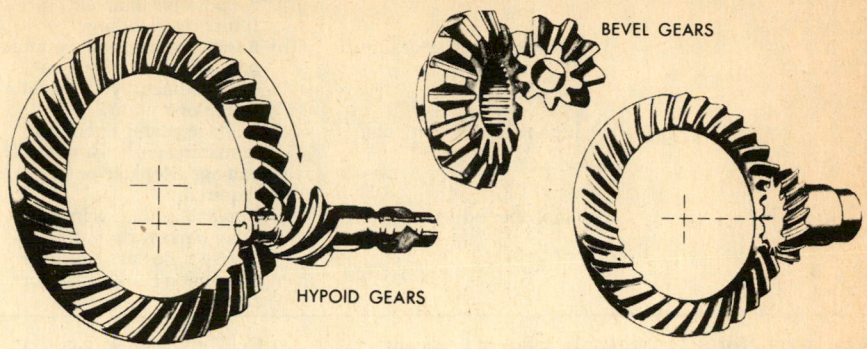

BEVEL GEARS

HYPOID GEARS

SPIRAL BEVEL GEARS

Hypoid gear application
(© Chevrolet Div., G.M. Corp)

Bevel gear application
(© Chevrolet Div., G.M. Corp)

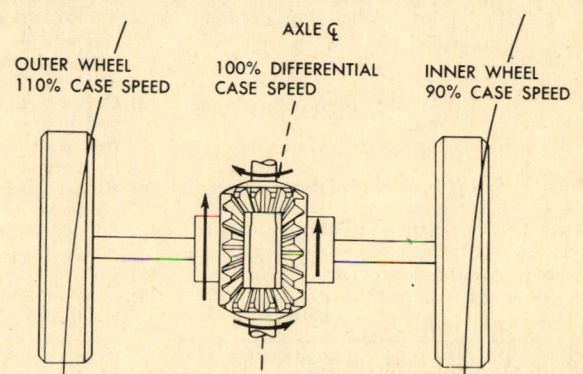

AXLE ℄

OUTER WHEEL 110% CASE SPEED

100% DIFFERENTIAL CASE SPEED

INNER WHEEL 90% CASE SPEED

Differential action during cornering
(© Chevrolet Div., G.M. Corp)

GENERAL DRIVE AXLE DIAGNOSTIC GUIDE

(Also see following text for further differential diagnosis.)

CONDITION	POSSIBLE CAUSE	CORRECTION
REAR WHEEL NOISE	(a) Loose Wheel.	(a) Tighten loose wheel nuts.
	(b) Spalled wheel bearing cup or cone.	(b) Check rear wheel bearings. If spalled or worn, replace.
	(c) Defective or brinelled wheel bearing.	(c) Defective or brinelled bearings must be replaced. Check rear axle shaft end-play.
	(d) Excessive axle shaft end-play.	(d) Readjust axle shaft end-play.
	(e) Bent or sprung axle shaft flange.	(e) Replace bent or sprung axle shaft.
SCORING OF DIFFERENTIAL GEARS AND PINIONS	(a) Insufficient lubrication.	(a) Replace scored gears. Scoring marks on the pressure face of gear teeth or in the bore are caused by instantaneous fusing of the mating surfaces. Scored gears should be replaced. Fill rear axle to required capacity with proper lubricant.
	(b) Improper grade of lubricant.	(b) Replace scored gears. Inspect all gears and bearings for possible damage. Clean and refill axle to required capacity with proper lubricant.
	(c) Excessive spinning of one wheel.	(c) Replace scored gears. Inspect all gears, pinion bores and shaft for scoring, or bearings for possible damage.

TOOTH BREAKAGE (RING GEAR AND PINION)	(a) Overloading.	(a) Replace gears. Examine other gears and bearings for possible damage. Avoid future overloading.	
	(b) Erratic clutch operation.	(b) Replace gears, and examine remaining parts for possible damage. Avoid erratic clutch operation.	
	(c) Ice-spotted pavements.	(c) Replace gears. Examine remaining parts for possible damage. Replace parts as required.	
	(d) Improper adjustment.	(d) Replace gears. Examine other parts for possible damage. Be sure ring gear and pinion backlash is correct.	
REAR AXLE NOISE	(a) Insufficient lubricant.	(a) Refill rear axle with correct amount of the proper lubricant. Also check for leaks and correct as necessary.	
	(b) Improper ring gear and pinion adjustment.	(b) Check ring gear and pinion tooth contact.	
	(c) Unmatched ring gear and pinion.	(c) Remove unmatched ring gear and pinion. Replace with a new matched gear and pinion set.	
	(d) Worn teeth on ring gear or pinion.	(d) Check teeth on ring gear and pinion for contact. If necessary, replace with new matched set.	
	(e) End-play in drive pinion bearings.	(e) Adjust drive pinion bearing preload.	
	(f) Side play in differential bearings.	(f) Adjust differential bearing preload.	
	(g) Incorrect drive gearlash.	(g) Correct drive gear lash.	
	(h) Limited-Slip differential—moan and chatter.	(h) Drain and flush lubricant. Refill with proper lubricant.	
LOSS OF LUBRICANT	(a) Lubricant level too high.	(a) Drain excess lubricant.	
	(b) Worn axle shaft oil seals.	(b) Replace worn oil seals with new ones. Prepare new seals before replacement.	
	(c) Cracked rear axle housing.	(c) Repair or replace housing as required.	
	(d) Worn drive pinion oil seal.	(d) Replace worn drive pinion oil seal with a new one.	
	(e) Scored and worn companion flange.	(e) Replace worn or scored companion flange and oil seal.	
	(f) Clogged vent.	(f) Remove obstructions.	
	(g) Loose carrier housing bolts or housing cover screws.	(g) Tighten bolts or cover screws to specifications and fill to correct level with proper lubricant.	
OVERHEATING OF UNIT	(a) Lubricant level too low.	(a) Refill rear axle.	
	(b) Incorrect grade of lubricant.	(b) Drain, flush and refill rear axle with correct amount of the proper lubricant.	
	(c) Bearings adjusted too tightly.	(c) Readjust bearings.	
	(d) Excessive wear in gears.	(d) Check gears for excessive wear or scoring. Replace as necessary.	
	(e) Insufficient ring gear-to-pinion clearance.	(e) Readjust ring gear and pinion backlash and check gears for possible scoring.	

speeds of rotation at the axle shafts. If the vehicle speed remains constant, and the inner wheel slows down to 90 percent of vehicle speed, the outer wheel will speed up to 110 percent.

Limited-Slip Differential Operation

Limited-slip differentials provide driving force to the wheel with the best traction before the other wheel begins to spin. This is accomplished through clutch plates or cones. The clutch plates or cones are located between the side gears and inner wall of the differential case. When they are squeezed together through spring tension and outward force from the side gears, three reactions occur. Resistance on the side gears causes more torque to be exerted on the clutch packs or clutch cones. Rapid one-wheel spin cannot occur, because the side gear is forced to turn at the same speed as the case. Most important, with the side gear and the differential case turning at the same speed, the other wheel is forced to rotate in the same direction and at the same speed as the differential case. Thus driving force is applied to the wheel with the better traction.

DIFFERENTIAL DIAGNOSIS

The most essential part of rear axle service is proper diagnosis of the problem. Bent or broken axle shafts or broken gears pose little problem, but isolating an axle noise and correctly interpreting the problem can be extremely difficult, even for an experienced mechanic.

Any gear driven unit will produce a certain amount of noise, therefore, a specific diagnosis for each individual unit is the best practice. Acceptable or normal noise can be classified as a slight noise heard only at certain speeds or under unusual conditions. This noise tends to reach a peak at 40-60 mph, depending on the road condition, load, gear ratio and tire size. Frequently, other noises are mistakenly diagnosed as coming from the rear axle. Vehicle noises from tires, transmission, driveshaft, U-joints and front and rear wheel bearings will often be mistaken as emanating from the rear axle. Raising the tire pressure to eliminate tire noise (although this will not silence mud or snow treads), listening for noise at varying speeds and road conditions and listening for noise at drive and coast conditions will aid in diagnosing alleged rear axle noises.

External Noise Elimination

It is advisable to make a thorough road test to determine whether the noise originates in the rear axle or whether it originates from the tires, engine transmission, wheel bearings or road surface. Noise originating from other places cannot be corrected by overhauling the rear axle.

Road Noise

Brick roads or rough surfaced concrete, may cause a noise which can be mistaken as coming from the rear axle. Driving on a different type of road, (smooth asphalt or dirt) will determine whether the road is the cause of the noise. Road noise is usually the same on drive or coast conditions.

Tire Noise

Tire noise can be mistaken as rear axle noises, even though the tires on the front are at fault. Snow tread and mud tread tires or tires worn unevenly will frequently cause vibrations which seem to originate elsewhere; *temporarily, and for test purposes only,* inflate the tires to 40-50 lbs. This will significantly alter the noise produced by the tires, but will not alter noise from the rear axle. Noises from the rear axle will normally cease at speeds below 30 mph on coast, while tire noise will continue at lower tone as car speed is decreased. The rear axle noise will usually change from drive conditions to coast conditions, while tire noise will not. Do not forget to lower the tire pressure to normal after the test is complete.

Engine and Transmission Noise

Engine and transmission noises also seem to originate in the rear axle. Road test the vehicle and determine at which speeds the noise is most pronounced. Stop the car in a quiet place to avoid interfering noises. With the transmission in neutral, run the engine slowly through the engine speeds corresponding to the car speed at which the noise was most noticeable. If a similar noise was produced with the car standing still, the noise is not in the rear axle, but somewhere in the engine or transmission.

Front Wheel Bearing Noise

Front wheel bearing noises, sometimes confused with rear axle noises, will not change when comparing drive and coast conditions. While holding the car speed steady, lightly apply the footbrake. This will often cause wheel bearing noise to lessen, as some of the weight is taken off the bearing. Front wheel bearings are easily checked by jacking up the wheels and spinning the wheels. Shaking the wheels will also determine if the wheel bearings are excessively loose.

Rear Axle Noises

If a logical test of the vehicle shows that the noise is not caused by external items, it can be assumed that the noise originates from the rear axle. The rear axle should be tested on a smooth level road to avoid road noise. It is not advisable to test the axle by jacking up the rear wheels and running the car.

True rear axle noises generally fall into two classes; gear noise and bearing noises, and can be caused by a faulty driveshaft, faulty wheel bearings, worn differential or pinion shaft bearings, U-joint misalignment, worn differential side gears and pinions, or mismatched, improperly adjusted, or scored ring and pinion gears.

REAR WHEEL BEARING NOISE

A rough rear wheel bearing causes a vibration or growl which will continue with the car coasting or in neutral. A brinelled rear wheel bearing will also cause a knock or click approximately every two revolutions of the rear wheel, due to the fact that the bearing rollers do not travel at the same speed as the rear wheel and axle. Jack up the rear wheels and spin the wheel slowly, listening for signs of a rough or brinelled wheel bearing.

DIFFERENTIAL SIDE GEAR AND PINION NOISE

Differential side gears and inions seldom cause noise since their movement is relatively slight on straight ahead driving. Noise produced by these gears will be more noticeable on turns.

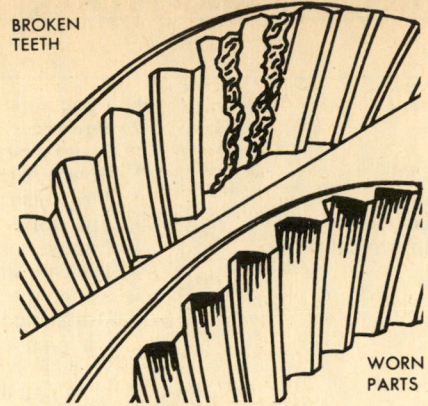

Two types of damage which cause gear noise
(© Chevrolet Div., G.M. Corp)

PINION BEARING NOISE

Pinion bearing failures can be distinguished by their speed of rotation, which is higher than side bearings or axle bearings. Rough or brinelled pinion bearings cause a continuous low pitch whirring or scraping noise beginning at low speeds.

SIDE BEARING NOISE

Side bearings produce a constant rough noise, which is slower than the pinion bearing noise. Side bearing noise may also fluctuate in the above rear wheel bearing test.

GEAR NOISE

Two basic types of gear noise exist. First, is the type produced by bent or broken gear teeth which have been forcibly damaged. The noise from this type of damage is audible over the entire speed range. Scoring or damage to the hypoid gear teeth generally results from insufficient lubricant, improper lubricant, improper breakin, insufficient gear backlash, improper ring and pinion gear alignment or loss of torque on the drive pinion nut. If not corrected, the scoring will lead to eventual erosion or fracture of the gear teeth. Hypoid gear tooth fracture can also be caused by extended overloading of the gear set (fatigue fracture) or by shock overloading (sudden failure). Differential and side gears rarely give trouble, but common causes of differential failure are shock loading, extended overloading and differential pinion seizure at the cross-shaft, resulting from excessive wheel spin and consequent lubricant breakdown.

The second type of gear noise pertains to the mesh pattern between the ring and pinion gears. This type of abnormal gear noise can be recognized as

a cycling pitch or whine audible in either drive, float or coast conditions. Gear noises can be recognized as they tend to peak out in a narrow speed range and remain constant in pitch, whereas bearing noises tend to vary in pitch with vehicle speeds. Noises produced by the ring and pinion gears will generally follow the pattern below.

A. Drive Noise:	Produced under vehicle acceleration.
B. Coast Noise:	Produced while the car coasts with a closed throttle.
C. Float Noise:	Occurs while maintaining constant car speed (just enough to keep speed constant) on a level road.
D. Drive, Coast and Float Noise:	These noises will vary in tone with speed and be very rough or irregular if the differential or pinion shaft bearings are worn.

Bearing Diagnosis

This section will help in the diagnosis of bearing failure and the causes. Bearing diagnosis can be very helpful in determining the cause of rear axle failure.

When disassembling a rear axle, the general condition of all bearings should be noted and classified where possible. Proper recognition of the cause will help in correcting the problem and avoiding a repetition of the failure.

Some of the common causes of bearing failure are:

a. Abuse during assembly or disassembly.
b. Improper assembly methods.
c. Improper or inadequate lubrication.
d. Bearing contact with dirt or water.
e. Wear caused by dirt or metal chips.
f. Corrosion or rust.
g. Seizing due to overloading.
h. Overheating.
i. Frettage of the bearing seats.
j. Brinelling from impact or shock loading.
k. Manufacturing defects.
l. Pitting due to fatigue.

To avoid damage to the bearing from improper handling, it is best to treat a used bearing the same as a new bearing. Always work in a clean area with clean tools. Remove all outside dirt from the housing before exposing a bearing and clean all bearing seats before installing a bearing.

─────────── **CAUTION** ───────────

Never spin a bearing, either by hand or with compressed air, as this will lead to almost certain bearing failure.

Drive Axles

NOISE DIAGNOSIS CHART

PROBLEM	CAUSE
1. Identical noise in Drive or Coast conditions	1. Road noise Tire noise Front wheel bearing noise
2. Noise changes on a different type of road	2. Road noise Tire noise
3. Noise tone lowers as car speed is lowered	3. Tire noise
4. Similar noise is produced with car standing and driving	4. Engine noise Transmission noise
5. Vibration	5. Rough rear wheel bearing Unbalanced or damaged driveshaft Unbalanced tire Worn universal joint in driveshaft Misaligned drive shaft at companion flange Excessive companion flange runout
6. A knock or click approximately every two revolutions of rear wheel	6. Brinelled rear wheel bearing
7. Noise most pronounced on turns	7. Differential side gear and pinion wear or damage
8. A continuous low pitch whirring or scraping noise starting at relatively low speed	8. Damaged or worn pinion bearing
9. Drive noise, coast noise or float noise	9. Damaged or worn ring and pinion gear
10. Clunk on acceleration or deceleration	10. Worn differential cross-shaft in case
11. Clunk on stops	11. Insufficient grease in driveshaft slip yoke
12. Groan in Forward or Reverse	12. Improper differential lubricant
13. Chatter on turns	13. Improper differential lubricant Worn clutch plates
14. Clunk or knock during operation on rough roads.	14. Excessive end-play of axle shafts to differential cross-shaft

LIMITED-SLIP DIFFERENTIAL DIAGNOSIS

Lubrication

The use of proper lubricant is very important in limited-slip type drive axles. The forces applied when cornering tend to apply the clutch pack or clutch cones. The use of the wrong lubricant can cause the clutch surfaces to grab and chatter while turning. Always follow the manufacturer's recommendations regarding drive axle lubrication. When chatter is encountered, the differential lubricant should be drained and refilled with the specified lubricant.

Testing

The clutch operation on all limited-slip type axles can be tested as follows. Refer to the manufacturer in question.

AMERICAN MOTORS "TWIN-GRIP"

1. With the engine off and the transmission in neutral, jack up one rear wheel.
2. Block the other wheel to prevent it from moving.
3. With a socket and torque wrench on the axle shaft nut, turn the raised wheel forward.
4. The torque required to move the wheel should be 70-100 ft lbs for $8\frac{7}{8}$ in. axles or 80-120 ft lbs for $7\frac{9}{16}$ in. axles.
5. A breakaway torque which is less than the specified figure, indicates a need for repair or replacement.

CADILLAC CONTROLLED DIFFERENTIAL

This unit should not be serviced. If a malfunction exists that cannot be cured by changing the fluid, remove the unit and install a new one.

CHRYSLER CORP. SURE-GRIP

1. Place the vehicle on a hoist with the engine off and the automatic transmission in Park (manual transmission in low gear).
2. Attempt to rotate the wheel by hand, by gripping the tire.
3. If it is extremely difficult, if not impossible, to rotate either wheel the Sure-Grip differential can be assumed to be performing satisfactorily.
4. If it is relatively easy to continuously turn either rear wheel, the unit should be removed and replaced.

——————— CAUTION ———————

The Sure-Grip differential is serviced as a unit only. Under no circumstances should the unit be disassembled and reinstalled.

FORD MOTOR COMPANY EQUA-LOK

1. Jack up one rear wheel and remove the wheel cover.
2. Block the other wheel front and rear to prevent the car from moving.
3. Using a 200 ft lbs capacity torque wrench on one of the wheel lug nuts, measure the torque required to continuously rotate the wheel. The breakaway torque reading can be disregarded. The minimum torque to continuously rotate the wheel should be as follows.
All axles except integral carrier type: 75 ft lbs.
Integral carrier type axles: 50 ft lbs.
4. If the minimum torque is not as specified, the differential should be checked for improper assembly.

FORD MOTOR COMPANY TRACTION-LOK

1. Follow the procedure for the Ford Motor Company Equa-Lok rear. The minimum torque to continuously rotate the wheel (disregarding the breakaway torque) should be at least 40 ft lbs.

GENERAL MOTORS CORP. (EXCEPT CADILLAC) POSITRACTION

1. Place the transmission in neutral.
2. Raise one rear wheel off the floor and block the other rear wheel (front and rear) to prevent the car from moving.
3. Install a torque wrench and extension on the lug nut and note the torque required to continuously rotate one rear wheel. Disregard the breakaway torque figure, as this may be a great deal higher.
4. The minimum torque to continuously rotate the rear wheel should be at least 35 ft lbs. If it is not, the rear axle is in need of service.

General Diagnosis

Improper operation of a limited-slip type rear axle is generally indicated by clutch slippage or grabbing, which will sometimes produce a whirring or chatter sound. Occasionally, this condition is induced by improper lubrication. Check the unit for the wrong type of lubricant or lubricant which has broken down or become contaminated. Replace the lubricant with the type specified by the manufacturer.

During normal driving, i.e., straight-ahead driving, both wheels are rotating at equal speeds, and the driving force is distributed equally between both wheels. When cornering, the inside wheel delivers extra driving force, causing slippage in both clutch packs. Therefore, if the wheel rotation of both rear wheels is not equal, the unit will constantly be functioning as if the car were cornering. This will cause constant slippage and lead to eventual failure of the unit. It is important that there be no excessive differences in wheel and tire size, wear pattern, or tire pressures between both rear wheels. Swerving on acceleration is an indication of one or more of the above conditions. Before attempting an overhaul or replacement operation, check both rear wheels for identical tire sizes, tire pressure, tire tread depth, and wear pattern.

DRIVE AXLE DISASSEMBLY ANALYSIS

Testing the Gear Tooth Contact Pattern

Once it has been established that the differential is indeed in need of service, the worst procedure is to simply plunge ahead and remove the differential and disassemble the parts. Prior to disassembly, a tooth contact pattern test should be made. However, it is worthwhile to first know the nomenclature associated with hypoid gear teeth.

The thick end of the tooth is called the heel and the thin end of the tooth is called the toe. The base half of the tooth is called the flank and the other end of the tooth is known as the face. The imaginary line at the halfway point between the face and flank is known as the pitch line. The space between the meshed pinion and ring gear tooth is known as backlash.

A gear tooth contact pattern can be made with the carrier in or out of the housing depending on the type of carrier. On integral carrier models, the lubricant must be drained and the rear cover removed. The ring gear will now be exposed and the test can be made with the carrier still in the housing. On removable carrier models, drain the lubricant and remove the carrier from the housing. The test can be made on the bench.

Unlike simple spur gears, hypoid gear teeth leave a complex pattern on the ring gear. When hypoid gears turn, the line contact between pinion and ring gear teeth has the same wiping motion as with spur gear teeth. Because of the complicated movement of hypoid gear teeth, the contact area takes an oval shape as opposed to the rectangular shape left by spur gear teeth. Actually, the tooth contact test shows where each gear tooth has been wiped by the movement of the contact line, so that you can tell whether the gears are set correctly. With a properly adjusted ring and pinion (with properly adjusted pinion depth and backlash) the tooth contact will be close to center. In this case, the load is borne by the strongest part of the tooth. If the gear setting is off, the contact line may reach any part of the edge of a tooth, and the metal will be overloaded at that point. When overload occurs, rapid deterioration of the gears will follow.

PREPARING THE TEST

Coat the drive gear teeth with a metallic base artists' oil color such as zinc white or titanium white. The tooth coating material must be smooth and firm enough to spread without running. A consistency somewhat like toothpaste works well. If it is necessary to thicken the material, add a small amount of cup grease.

NOTE: *Prussian blue dye does not work well, since the blue tends to smear the pattern.*

Thoroughly clean the ring gear and pinion before applying the testing material. Any gear lube left on the teeth will make the pattern quite unreadable. Coat the drive and coast sides of all the ring gear teeth, but leave the pinion gear teeth clean. Do not apply the coating too thickly as the pattern will be smeared.

Because the axle gears are normally easy to rotate, turning resistance must be applied to produce pressure between the pinion and ring gear teeth to make a legible pattern. On a removable carrier type axle, insert a large screwdriver between the carrier housing and the differential case rim. Apply the load squarely against the case rim while prying out against the upper or lower section of the carrier housing. On integral carrier models, apply the parking brake to a point where it requires approximately 50 ft lbs to turn the pinion with a torque wrench. Since the shape and position of the contact pattern will vary, depending on the load, try to use the same load for each test or the results can be misleading. This is especially true when testing after an overhaul.

Once the gears have a load applied, obtain a tooth contact pattern by rotating the ring gear and pinion one complete turn in each direction. This will produce a constant pattern on the coast and drive side of each tooth. Do not

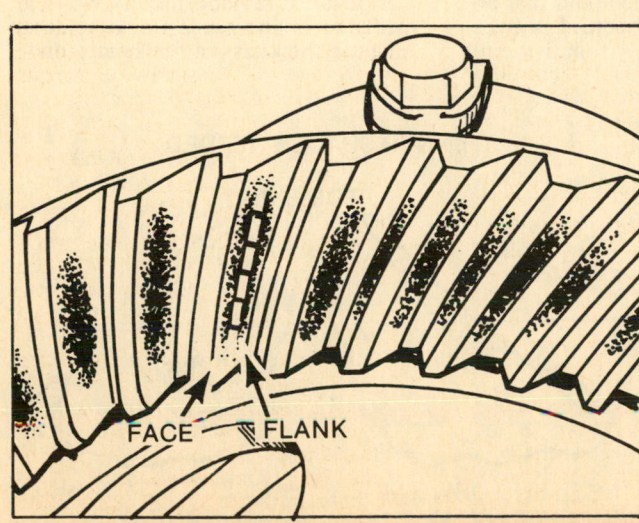

Gear tooth face and flank showing oval gear tooth contact pattern

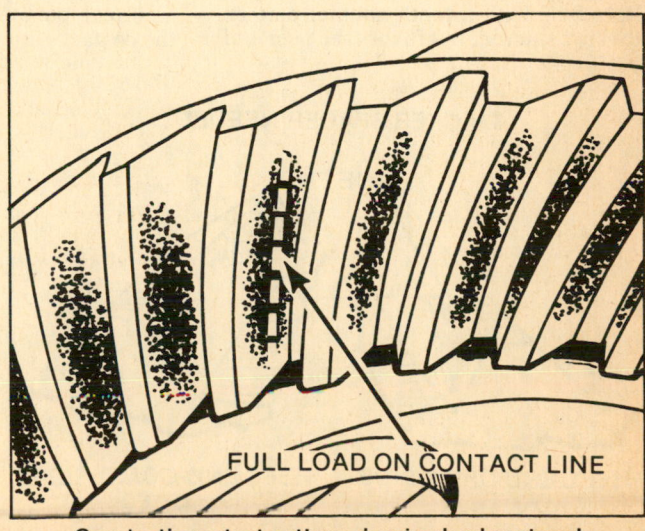

Gear tooth contact pattern showing load centered on gear tooth

Drive Axles

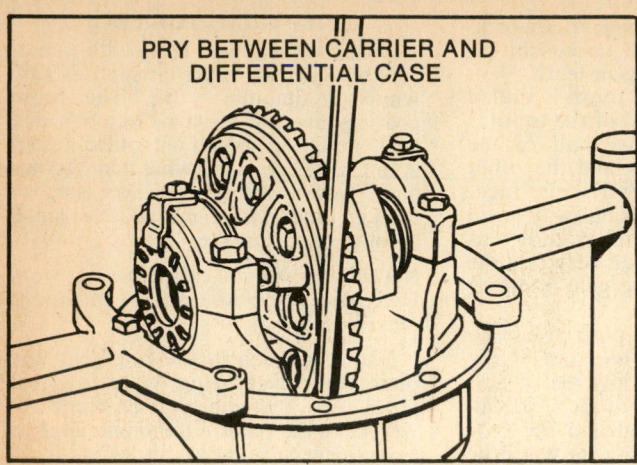

Applying a load to the differential case

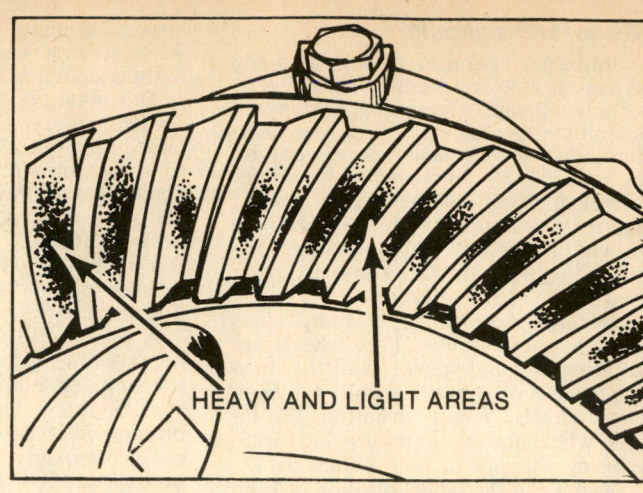

HEAVY AND LIGHT AREAS

Excessive run-out will cause an uneven pattern

rotate the ring gear more than one revolution in each direction as this will tend to obscure the pattern.

NOTE: *If the pattern does not look right on the first try, try again.*

Making a good gear tooth test takes a little practice; so if it is not right, try again.

INTERPRETING GEAR TOOTH CONTACT PATTERNS

The tooth contact pattern should be the same on every tooth. If the pattern shows heavy and light areas on different teeth, check the ring gear and differential case for excessive run-out.

NOTE: *Run-out can be cured in many cases by removing the ring gear from the case, rotating it 90° or 180°, and remounting it.*

Since you can only apply test load pressure to the gears, the contact pattern will be less distinct toward the tooth ends. But, when the ring gear and pinion are under operating loads in the vehicle, the tooth contact area spreads out, especially towards the heel end of the tooth. For this reason, do not try to "get by" with a tooth contact pattern that is centered, but favors the heel end

of the teeth. This will only lead to overloading at the heel ends of the gear teeth. On the other hand, a contact pattern which is reasonably centered, but favors the toe end of the teeth, is acceptable.

Assuming that the tooth contact pattern is even on all teeth, the main problem is to get the most distinct part of the pattern centered on both the drive and coast sides of the ring gear teeth. The contact patterns should be nearly opposite each other on both sides of each tooth. In some cases, the pattern will be centered on the drive side and off center on the coast side, or vice versa. The off center pattern can be moved to a more acceptable position by slightly altering the backlash. This procedure will not seriously affect the other pattern. More often, however, the pattern will be off center on both sides of the teeth. The basic cause of this condition is an improperly adjusted pinion.

ADJUSTING PINION DEPTH

It is necessary to understand that an incorrect pinion depth setting moves the contact pattern away from the cen-

ter on both sides of the tooth in opposite directions. This means that when you install a thicker or thinner washer under the pinion head you bring the pattern into the center of the tooth from opposite ends.

When the contact pattern is high on the heel end of the drive side and low on the toe end of the coast side, a thicker washer is needed to bring the pinion in, toward the center of the drive side. Increasing the thickness of the spacer washer will bring the pattern in, toward the center of the drive gear teeth, and also will move the pattern down from the tooth face. However, this movement is less than the in-or-out movement.

When tooth contact is low on the toe end of the drive side and high on the heel end of the coast side, the pinion must be moved out, by installing a thinner washer under the pinion head. This will move the pattern inward toward the center, and will also result in slight movement of the pattern up from the tooth flank.

A factory service facility will use special tools and gauge blocks to determine the thickness of the spacer under

THICKER SPACER NEEDED

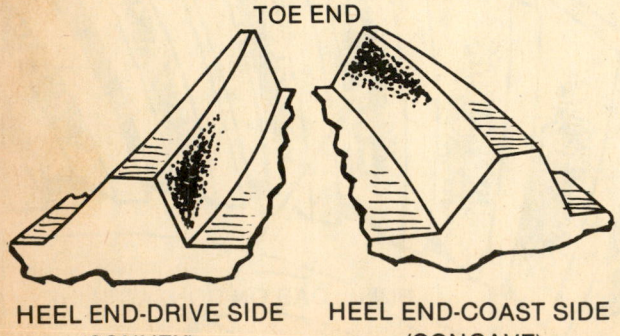

TOE END

HEEL END-DRIVE SIDE (CONVEX)   HEEL END-COAST SIDE (CONCAVE)

Tooth contact patterns high on the tooth side

THINNER SPACER NEEDED

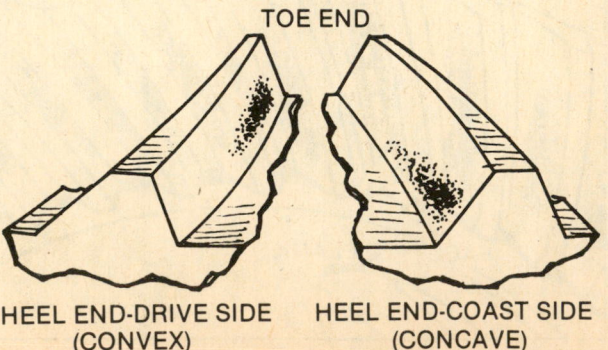

TOE END

HEEL END-DRIVE SIDE (CONVEX)   HEEL END-COAST SIDE (CONCAVE)

Gear contact pattern low on tooth side

PATTERN MOVES TOWARD CENTER AND DOWN

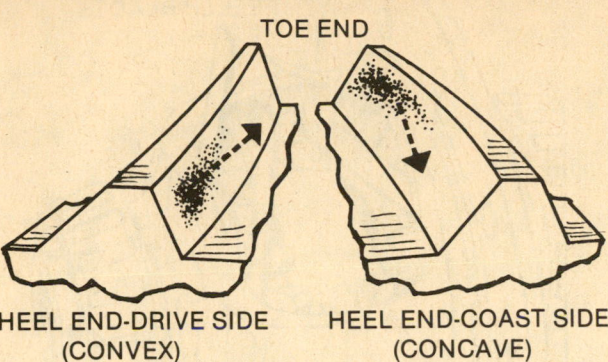

TOE END

HEEL END-DRIVE SIDE (CONVEX) HEEL END-COAST SIDE (CONCAVE)

A thicker spacer moves the pattern in and down

PATTERN MOVES INWARD AND UP

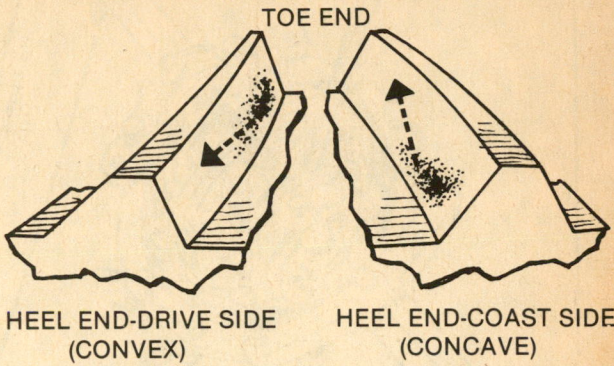

TOE END

HEEL END-DRIVE SIDE (CONVEX) HEEL END-COAST SIDE (CONCAVE)

A thinner spacer will move the pattern up and inward

the pinion head. In the absence of such specialized equipment, the following procedure may be used. Bear in mind that with the "hit-or-miss" method, each time you are wrong with the pinion depth, the unit must be disassembled, the spacer thickness changed, and the unit must be completely set up again.

Gather a handful of spacers to cover any thickness and several collapsible pinion spacers (if the unit uses them). Assemble the unit. If the original gear set is being reused, and the tooth contact pattern is reasonably correct, install a new spacer of the same thickness as the old one. This will provide a reasonable starting point. If the gear contact pattern test indicates a need for movement of the pinion, use a new spacer 0.001-0.002 in. thicker or thinner, depending on the direction the pinion must go. If a new gear set is being used, the thickness of the spacer will have to be determined in the following manner. Compare the markings on the old and new pinion. It will usually be marked with a number preceded by a plus (+) or minus (−) sign. This number indicates the production deviation from the nominal pinion, which are known as "zero pinions." In service, zero pinions are rare. Assume that the old pinion is marked with a plus two (+2). Assume that the new pinion is marked with a +3. By comparing the pinion markings, find the numerical difference between the two pinions, in this case +1. With a micrometer, measure the thickness of the original spacer. We will assume that the old spacer is 0.030 in. thick. If the numerical difference between pinions is a positive number (+1) the spacer should be 0.001 in. thinner than the original spacer, or 0.029 in. total. If the numerical difference is a negative number (say, −1) then the spacer should be increased by 0.001 in., to 0.031 in. total. This will only provide a reasonable beginning point.

It is rare that this method works out the first time. Assemble the pinion, differential, and ring gear with the spacer

One example of pinion markings

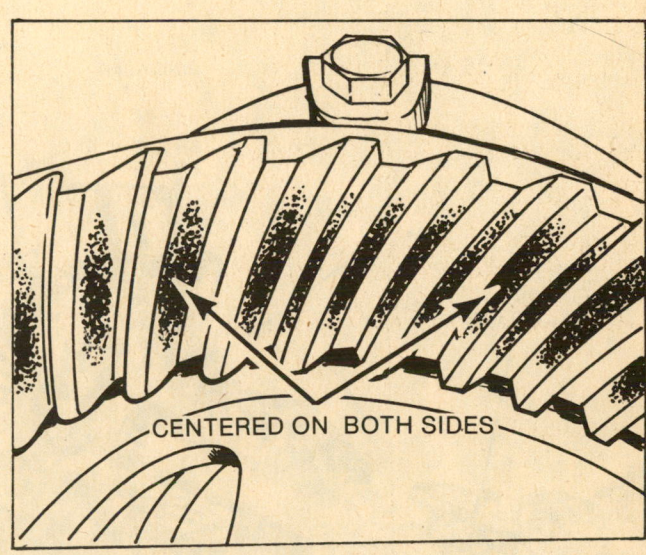

Gear tooth contact pattern showing load centered on gear tooth

of calculated thickness. The side bearing preload, backlash, pinion nut torque, and pinion rotating torque must all be set correctly. Obtain a gear tooth pattern on the ring gear teeth and analyze the results. Small deviations from the acceptable pattern can usually be made by varying the backlash within the limits of specifications. If the gear tooth contact pattern is off, the unit must be disassembled and another spacer installed. This spacer must be of suitable thickness to compensate for the contact pattern test.

NOTE: *Without special tools, there is absolutely no way of determining exactly how much to increase or decrease the thickness of the pinion shim; it must be estimated.*

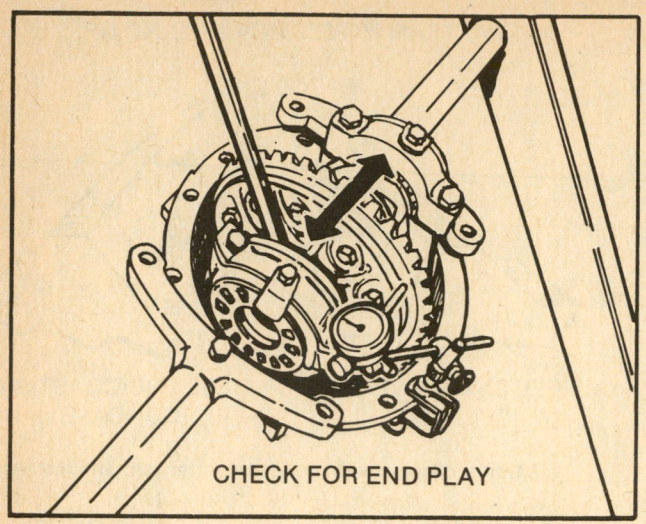

Checking differential bearing end-play

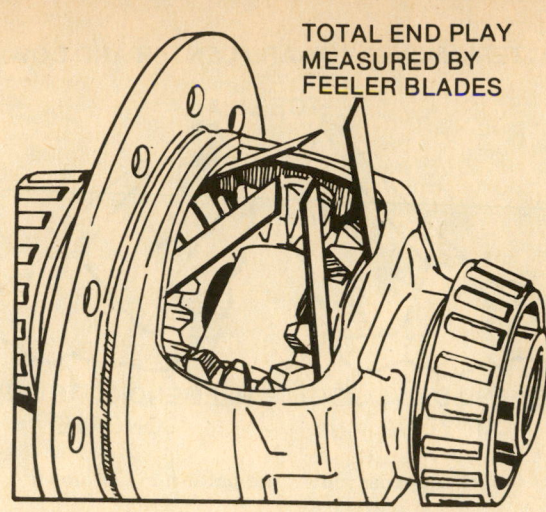

TOTAL END PLAY MEASURED BY FEELER BLADES

Checking total differential end-play

After estimating the thickness of the new shim, assemble the unit again, setting all preloads and backlash. Check the contact pattern again and act accordingly. If the unit uses a collapsible spacer, be sure a new one is installed each time it is disassembled. Crushed spacers can not be used again. It is well to note that the unit may have to be assembled and disassembled several times before an acceptable contact pattern is obtained.

ADJUSTING BACKLASH

The tooth contact pattern can be altered slightly, by varying the backlash adjustment within the limits of the specifications. The backlash adjustment can be used to alter a pattern which is slightly off center on either side of the tooth, but should not be used as a substitute for pinion depth adjustment. This adjustment must always be made after the pinion depth has been adjusted.

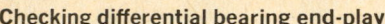

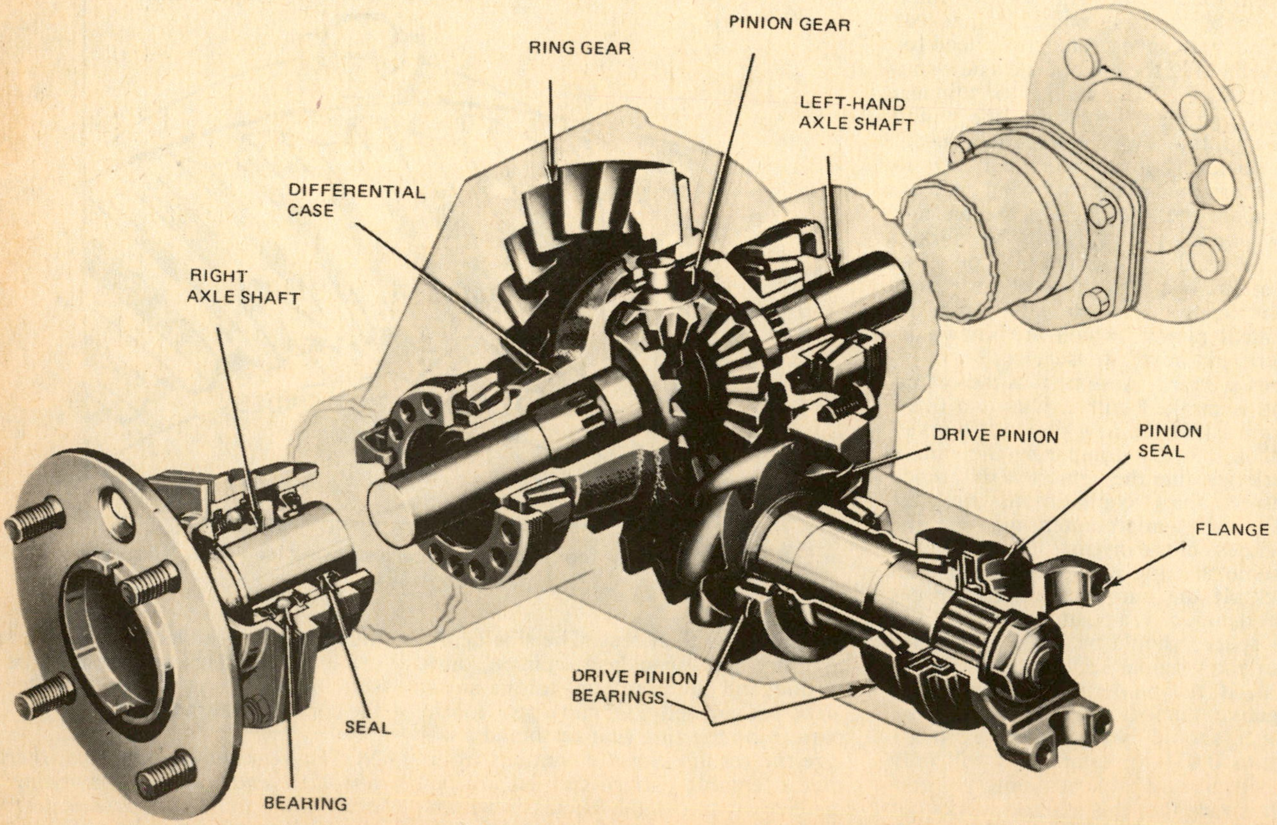

RING GEAR

PINION GEAR

LEFT-HAND AXLE SHAFT

DIFFERENTIAL CASE

RIGHT AXLE SHAFT

DRIVE PINION

PINION SEAL

FLANGE

DRIVE PINION BEARINGS

SEAL

BEARING

Typical differential components (© Ford Motor Co.)

Index

SERVICE PROCEDURE INDEX

Section Numbers Refer to Sections in Text

Manufacturer	Car	Year	Caster, Camber, and Toe-in
American Motors			
American Motors (all except Pacer)		1972-79	3
Pacer		1975-79	9
Chrysler Corporation			
Plymouth Valiant, Duster, Baracuda; Dodge Dart, Demon, Challenger		1972-76	4
Plymouth Volare; Dodge Aspen; Dodge Diplomat; Chrysler LeBaron		1976-79	5
Plymouth Satellite, Road Runner, GTX; Dodge Coronet, Charger		1972	4
Plymouth Satellite, Fury (1975-76 only); Dodge Coronet, Charger, Magnum; Chrysler Cordoba		1973-79	5
Plymouth Fury; Dodge Polara, Monaco		1972-73	4
Plymouth Fury (1974 only), Gran Fury; Dodge Monaco, Gran Monaco, St. Regis		1974-79	5
Chrysler, Chrysler Imperial		1972-73	4
Chrysler (full-size), Imperial		1974-79	5
Ford Motor Company			
Ford Fairmont, Mustang; Mercury Capri, Zephyr		1978-79	8
Ford Pinto, Mustang II; Mercury Bobcat		1972-79	8
Ford Torino, LTD II; Mercury Montego		1972-79	7
Ford Mustang; Mercury Cougar		1972-73	3
Ford Elite; Mercury Cougar		1974-79	7
Ford Maverick; Mercury Comet		1972-77	3
Ford Granada; Mercury Monarch; Lincoln Versailles		1975-79	3
Ford (full-size); Mercury (full-size)		1972-79	7
Ford Thunderbird; Lincoln Mk IV, Mk V		1972-78	7
Lincoln Continental		1972-79	7
General Motors			
Chevrolet Chevette		1976-79	6
Chevrolet Vega, Monza; Pontiac Astre, Sunbird; Oldsmobile Starfire; Buick Skyhawk		1972-79	9
Chevrolet Nova; Pontiac Ventura; Phoenix; Oldsmobile Omega; Buick Apollo		1972-79	1
Chevrolet Chevelle, Malibu, Monte Carlo; Pontiac Le Mans, GTO, Grand Prix; Oldsmobile Cutlass; Buick Skylark, GS, Century, Riviera		1972-79	1
Chevrolet Camaro; Pontiac Firebird		1972-79	1
Chevrolet Corvette		1972-79	1
Chevrolet (full-size)		1972-79	1
Pontiac (full-size); Oldsmobile (full-size); Buick (full-size)		1972-79	1
Oldsmobile Toronado; Cadillac Eldorado		1972-79	10
Cadillac (full-size)		1972-76	2
Cadillac (full-size)		1977-79	1
Cadillac Seville		1976-79	1

Front End Alignment

WHEEL ALIGNMENT

Front wheel alignment is the position of the front wheels relative to each other and to the vehicle. It is determined, and must be maintained to provide safe, accurate steering, directional stability, and minimum tire wear. Many factors are involved in wheel alignment, and adjustments are provided to return those that might change due to normal wear to their original value. The factors which determine wheel alignment are dependent on one another; therefore, when one of the factors is adjusted, the others must be adjusted to compensate.

Descriptions of these factors and their effects on the car are provided below. Adjustment specifications for each model year are given at the beginning of each Car Section.

Camber

Camber angle is the number of degrees that the centerline of the wheel is inclined from the vertical when viewed from the front. A small degree of positive camber reduces loading of the outer wheel bearing, and allows for easier steering.

Caster

Caster angle is the number of degrees that a line drawn through the steering knuckle pivots is inclined from the vertical, toward the front or rear of the car. A small degree of positive caster improves directional stability and decreases susceptibility to cross winds or road surface deviations.

Steering Axis Inclination

Steering axis inclination is the number of degrees that a line drawn through the steering knuckle pivots is inclined to the vertical, when viewed

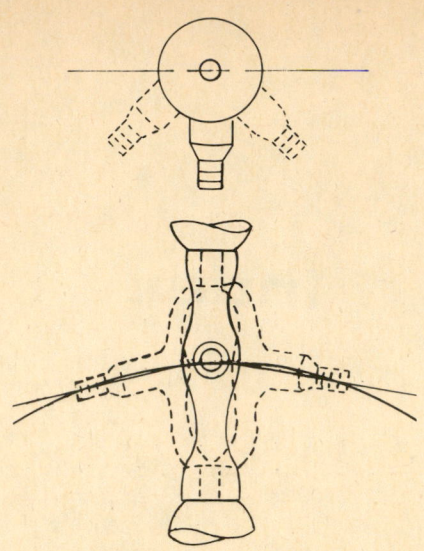

Arc generated by the spindle as the steering knuckle turns

from the front of the car. This, in combination with caster, is responsible for directional stability and self-centering of the steering. As the steering knuckle swings from lock to lock, the spindle generates an arc (see illustration), the high point being the straight ahead position of the wheel. Due to this arc, as the wheel turns, the front of the car is raised. The weight of the car acts against this lift, and attempts to return the spindle to the high point of the arc, resulting in self-centering when the steering wheel is released, and straight line stability.

Included Angle

Included angle is the sum of the camber angle and the steering axis inclination. This angle is determined by the design of the steering knuckle forging

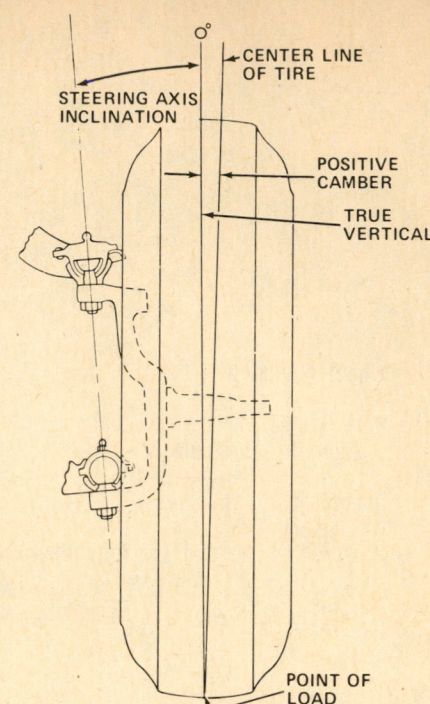

Camber and steering axis inclination angles

and must remain constant. Therefore, if a different camber angle is necessary to make the included angle on both sides identical, a bent spindle or steering knuckle is indicated. When indicated, the damaged suspension member must be replaced, to permit accurate front wheel alignment. Since steering knuckle damage is most commonly due to impact on the lower portion of the wheel (i.e., hitting curb), the side with the greater included angle (camber angle same on each side) will often be found to have a bent spindle.

Toe

Toe is the difference of the distance between the centers of the front and rear of the front wheels, measured at spindle height. It is most commonly measured in inches, but is occasionally referred to as an angle between the wheels. Toe-in indicates that the front of the tires are closer together than the rear; toe-out is the opposite condition. Toe-in compensates for the tendency of the wheels to deflect out while in motion. Due to this tendency, the wheels of a car with properly adjusted toe-in are traveling straight forward when the car itself is moving straight forward, resulting in directional stability and minimum tire wear. Front wheel drive and four wheel drive cars are normally set with toe-out, to compensate for the drive axles' tendency to pull the front wheels together.

Steering wheel spoke misalignment is often an indication of incorrect front end alignment. Care should be exercised when aligning the front end to

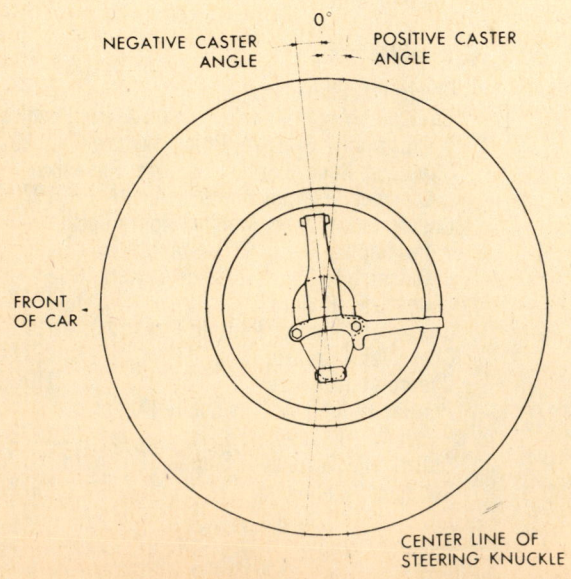

Caster angle

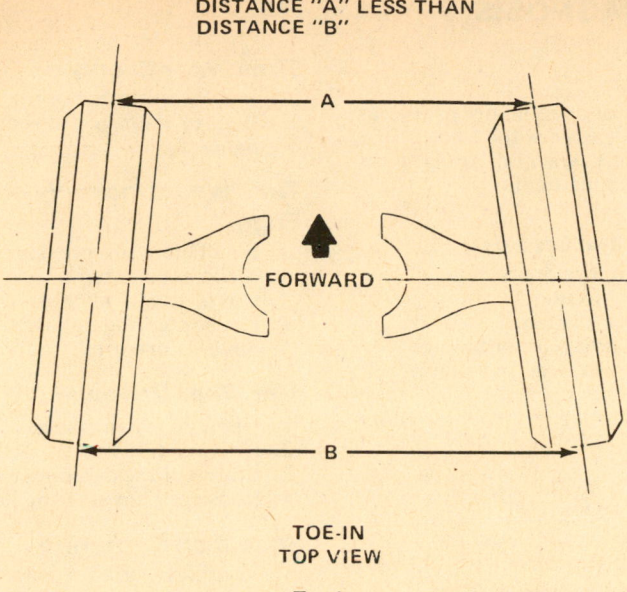

DISTANCE "A" LESS THAN
DISTANCE "B"

A

FORWARD

B

TOE-IN
TOP VIEW

Toe-in

maintain steering wheel spoke position. When adjusting the tie rod ends, adjust each an equal amount (in the opposite direction) to increase or decrease toe. If, following toe adjustment, further adjustments are necessary to center the steering wheel spokes, adjust the tie rod ends an equal amount in the same direction.

Steering Radius

When a car is negotiating a turn, the outer wheel follows the path of a circle of a larger radius than the inner wheel. For this reason, the inner wheel must be steered to a somewhat larger angle than the outer wheel. This value (known as the Ackerman effect) is designed into the steering linkage; therefore, if alignment is adjusted properly, and the steering radius (or toe-out on turns) appears to be incorrect, it is indicated that the steering arms or the linkage is bent.

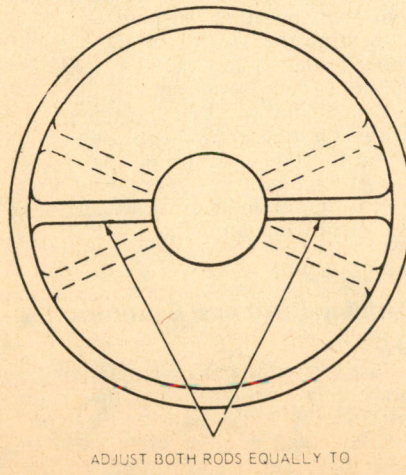

ADJUST BOTH RODS EQUALLY TO

MAINTAIN NORMAL SPOKE POSITION

Steering wheel spoke alignment

Tracking

Tracking is the relationship between the paths traveled by the front and rear wheels when the vehicle is traveling in a straight line. When a car is tracking correctly, the path of the rear wheels will duplicate, or evenly straddle the path of the front wheels. Observing the car from the rear as it is driven away in a straight line will often make incorrect tracking evident.

If incorrect tracking is indicated, check as follows: Drop a plumb line from each lower ball joint, and from a point at each end of the rear axle, and mark the points on the ground with chalk. Measure these points from front to rear and diagonally. If the diagonal measurements are different (a tolerance of +1/4" is acceptable), but the longitudinal measurements are the same, the frame is swayed (diamond shaped). If the diagonal and longitudinal measurements are both different, the rear axle is misaligned. If both diagonal and longitudinal measurements are different, but the car does not appear to be tracking incorrectly, a kneeback condition is indicated. Kneeback implies that one side of the front suspension is bent or pushed back. It is possible to align the front end to specifications, and, if kneeback exists, have very poor handling characteristics.

RIDE HEIGHT ADJUSTMENT

This Adjustment is required before adjusting front end alignment on cars with torsion bar front suspension.
NOTE: *The car must be on a level floor with the gas tank full and the tires properly inflated. There should be no unusual loads in the car.*

Chrysler Corporation

Through 1974

Jounce the car at least five times and allow it to settle.

Find measurement "B" by measuring from the lowest point of the lower ball joint or steering knuckle arm to the floor.

Find measurement "A" by measuring from the lowest point of the torsion bar adjusting blade (between the control arm halves) to the floor on models with the two-piece lower control arm. With the one-piece lower control arm, measure from the lowest point of the torsion bar front anchor at the rear of the lower control arm flange to the floor.

Subtract measurement "B" from measurement "A". The difference is the front end height for that side. Measure the other side in the same way. Check the figures against those given with the Front End Alignment Specifications in the front of the car section. Adjust the height by turning the torsion bar adjusting bolt clockwise to raise, and counterclockwise to lower. The height should not vary more than 1/8 in. from side to side.

1975 and Later

Jounce the car at least five times and allow it to settle.

Find the front end height on models with front to rear torsion bars by measuring from the lowest point of the lower control arm torsion bar anchor, at a point one inch forward of the rear face of the anchor, to the ground. On models with transverse (across the chassis) torsion bars, measure from the lowest point of the lower control arm inner pivot pushing to the floor.

Check the figures against those given with the Front End Alignment Specifications in the front of the car section. Adjust the height by turning the torsion bar adjusting bolt clockwise to raise, and counterclockwise to lower. The height should not vary more than 1/8 in. from side to side.
NOTE: *A change of front tire size can change front end height on these cars.*

Cadillac Eldorado and Oldsmobile Toronado

Front ride height is controlled by the settings of the torsion bar adjusting bolts. The height is adjusted by turning the adjusting bolt clockwise to raise, and counterclockwise to lower. Rear ride height can only be corrected by spring replacement or shimming.

Cadillac Eldorado

Front ride height is measured from the lower edge of the shock absorber dust cover to the centerline of the lower shock mounting bolt. Rear ride height is measured from the top of the axle to the frame.

Front End Alignment

DIAGNOSIS

Hard Ride
1. Excessive tire pressure
2. Shock absorbers malfunctioning
3. Broken spring
4. Worn suspension bushings

Soft Ride
1. Insufficient tire pressure
2. Worn shock absorbers
3. Collapsed or weak spring

Car Veers to One Side
1. Unequal tire pressures
2. Incorrect caster, camber, or toe
3. Unequal spring rates
4. Unequal shock absorber control
5. Incorrect steering axis inclination (bent spindle)
6. Damaged suspension components or bushings
7. Incorrect tracking
8. Dragging brake
9. Grease on brake lining

Wander
1. Incorrect or unequal tire pressures
2. Incorrect caster or toe
3. Excessively worn or damaged suspension components

Hard or Erratic Steering
1. Insufficient tire pressure
2. Lack of lubrication
3. Binding or damaged steering column, steering gear, or linkage
4. Loose power steering pump belt, or poor pump operation
5. Worn or damaged suspension components

Tires Wear in Center
1. Excessive tire pressure

Tires Wear on Both Edges
1. Insufficient tire pressure

Tires Wear Evenly on One Edge
1. Incorrect camber or toe
2. Bent or damaged suspension components

Tires Wear Unevenly on One Edge
1. Insufficient tire pressure
2. Incorrect camber or toe
3. Out of round wheel and/or tire
4. Loose steering linkage
5. Severe cornering

Tire Wear Unequally
1. Unequal tire pressure
2. Unequal tire size
3. Incorrect toe or camber
4. Loose or bent steering linkage

Squeal on Cornering
1. Insufficient tire pressure
2. Incorrect toe or camber
3. Severe cornering

Typical height measuring locations for Chrysler Corp. cars with two-piece lower control arm through 1974 (© Chrysler Corp.)

Ride height specifications are:

1971-73
Front   8 to 8$\frac{1}{4}$ in.
Rear   3$\frac{15}{16}$ to 4$\frac{11}{16}$ in.

1974
Front   8$\frac{3}{16}$ to 8$\frac{7}{16}$ in.
Rear   4$\frac{13}{16}$ to 5$\frac{9}{16}$ in.

1975
Front   8$\frac{1}{4}$ to 8$\frac{1}{2}$ in.
Rear   5$\frac{1}{16}$ to 5$\frac{5}{16}$ in.

1976-78
Front   8$\frac{3}{16}$ to 8$\frac{7}{16}$ in.
Rear   4$\frac{13}{16}$ to 5$\frac{9}{16}$ in.

Oldsmobile Toronado

The front height is measured from the rocker panelmoulding lower edge, 6 inches rearward of the forward edge of the door opening, to the floor. The rear height is measured from the rocker panel moulding lower edge, 60 inches back from the front height measuring point, to the floor.
Ride height specifications are:

1971-74
Front   8$\frac{3}{4}$ in.
Rear   8 in.

1975-78
Front   9 in.
Rear   9$\frac{1}{4}$ in.

CASTER, CAMBER AND TOE ADJUSTMENT

Use the Service Procedure Index at the start of this section to relate these section numbers to makes and models.

Section 1

General Motors Shim Type

Caster and Camber are controlled by shims between the frame bracket and the upper suspension arm pivot shaft.

To adjust caster, remove shims from the front bolt and replace them at the rear bolt, or vice versa. To adjust camber, add or remove the same number of shims from each bolt.

Keep in mind when loosening the bolts that the upper suspension arm is supporting the weight of the vehicle. Loosen the bolts only a sufficient amount to remove the shims.

Adjust toe-in by loosening the clamps on the sleeves at the outer ends of the tie-rod, and turning the sleeves an equal amount in the opposite direction, to maintain steering wheel spoke alignment while adjusting toe-in.

Section 2

Cadillac Strut and Eccentric Type

Caster is adjusted by lengthening or shortening the struts at the frame crossmember. To adjust, turn both nuts an equal number of turns in the same direction. Lengthening the strut increases negative caster. One turn of the nuts changes caster approximately $\frac{1}{2}$°.

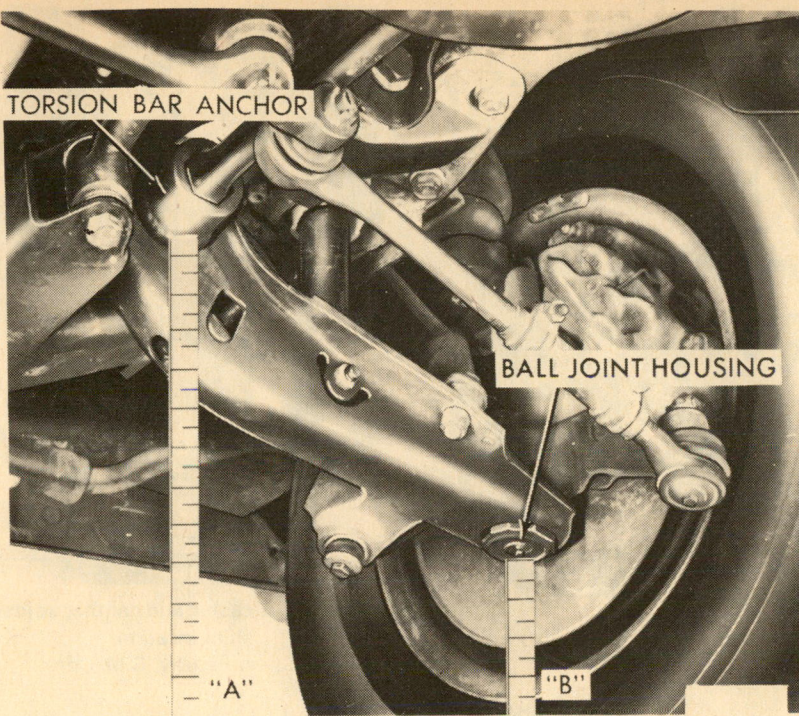

Typical height measuring location for Chrysler Corp. cars with one-piece lower control arm through 1974 (© Chrysler Corp.)

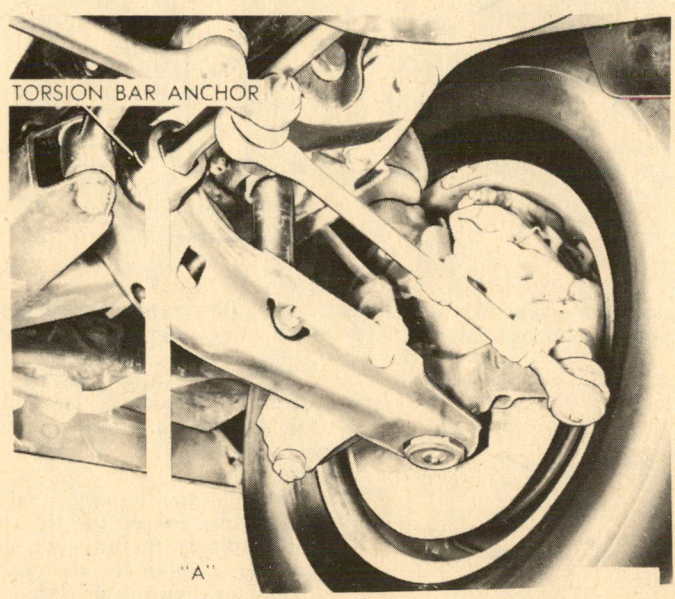

Typical height measuring location for 1975 and later Chrysler Corp. cars with longitudinal torsion bars (© Chrysler Corp.)

Section 3

Ford Motor Co. and AMC Strut and Eccentric Type

Caster is adjusted by lengthening or shortening the struts at the frame crossmember. To adjust, turn both nuts an equal number of turns in the same direction. Caster adjustments should be within 1/4° of the opposing side of the car.

To adjust camber, loosen the lower control arm pivot bolt and rotate the eccentrics.

Adjust toe-in by loosening the clamp bolts, and turning the adjuster sleeves at the outer ends of the tie rod. Turn each sleeve an equal amount in the opposite direction, in order to maintain steering wheel spoke alignment.

Section 4

Chrysler Corp. Eccentric Type

Ride height should be checked before front end alignment. Ride height is not adjustable on the Omni or Horizon.

Caster and camber are controlled by eccentric (cam) bolts; only camber is adjustable on the Omni/Horizon. The

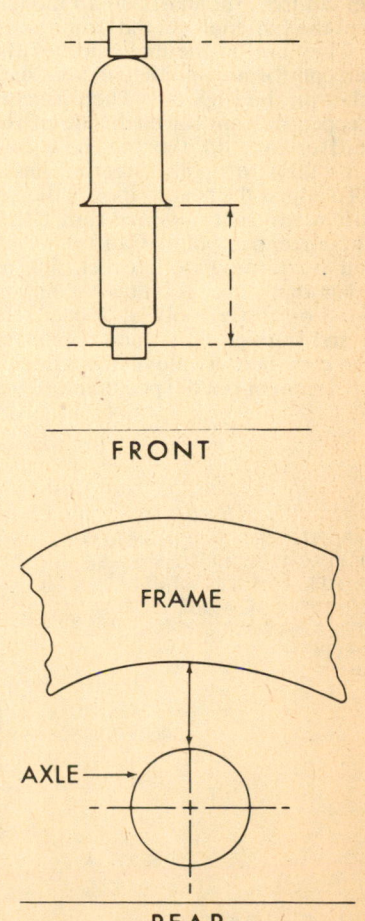

Cadillac Eldorado ride height measuring locations (© Cadillac Div., G.M. Corp.)

Camber is adjusted by turning the camber eccentric located in the steering knuckle upper support. Turning the eccentric changes the camber by moving the steering knuckle in or out.

Loosen the ball joint stud locknut and tap the knuckle to free the eccentric, being careful not to strike the brake line or ball joint seal. Turn the eccentric until camber is within specifica- tions. The stud must be positioned to the rear of the eccentric in order to maintain correct steering geometry. Tighten the ball joint stud nut to 60 ft. lbs.

Adjust toe-in by loosening the clamp bolts, and turning the adjuster sleeves at the outer ends of the tie rod. Turn each sleeve an equal amount in the opposite direction, in order to maintain steering wheel spoke alignment.

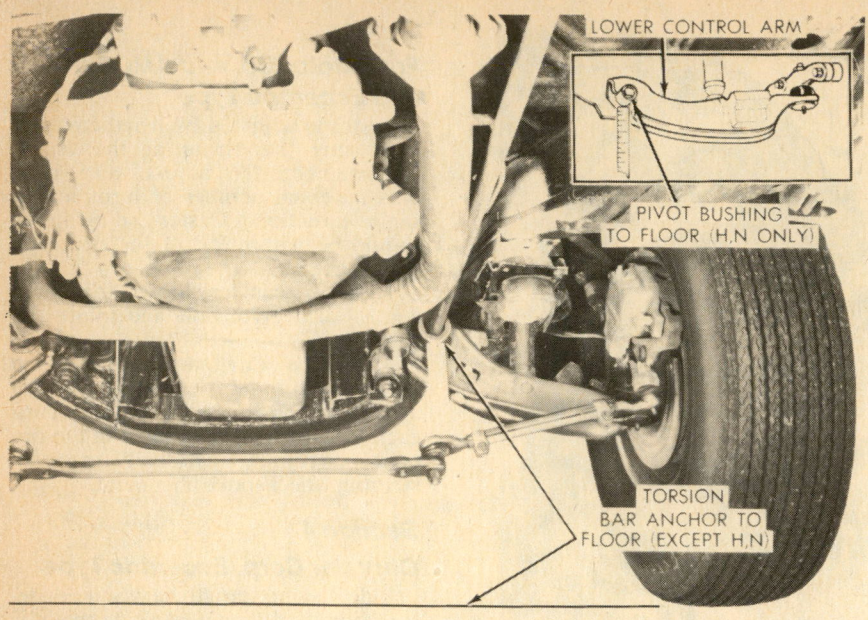

Height measuring location for Chrysler Corp. cars with transverse torsion bars
(© Chrysler Corp.)

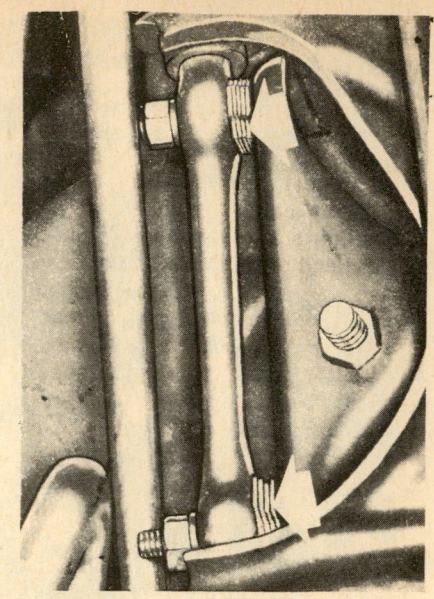

Typical type 1 caster and camber adjusting shim location
(© Chevrolet Div., G.M. Corp.)

cam bolts are located at the ends of the upper control arm shafts on all models except the Imperial and the Omni/Horizon. They are on the underside of the upper control arm pivot bar attaching bracket on the Imperial. There is only one eccentric cam for each side of the Omni/Horizon, on the top bolt connecting the strut to the steering knuckle. To adjust the caster, loosen the eccentric (cam) bolt nuts and turn either of the eccentric bolts. Camber is adjusted by turning both eccentrics an equal amount, except on the Omni/Horizon. For those models, loosen the cam and through bolts, and rotate the upper cam bolt to move the knuckle and wheel in or out to specification. Re-

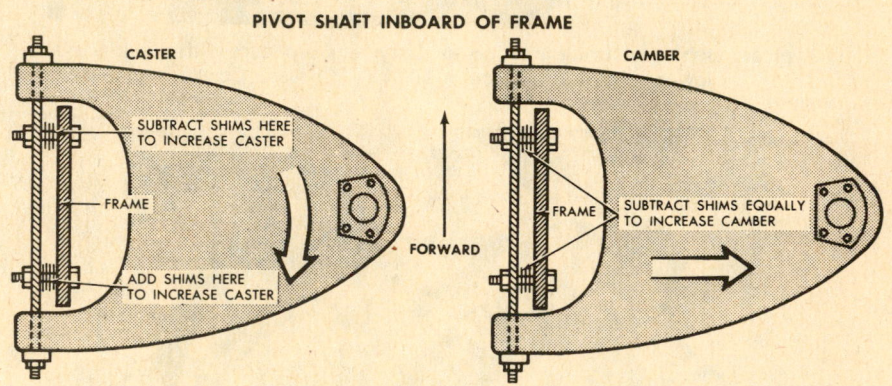

PIVOT SHAFT INBOARD OF FRAME

Typical caster and camber adjustment, type 1 (Reverse the procedure for shims on the opposite side of the frame) (© Chevrolet Div., G.M. Corp.)

check caster after setting camber. Torque the eccentric (cam) bolts to 85 ft lbs on the Omni/Horizon, 160 ft lbs on the Imperial, and 65-70 ft lbs on all others.

To adjust toe-in (toe-out on the Omni/Horizon), loosen the tie rod clamp bolts and turn the adjuster sleeves at the outer ends of the tie rod an equal amount in opposite directions so that steering wheel spoke alignment is maintained.

Section 5

Chrysler Corp. Pivot Bar Type

Ride height should be checked before front end alignment.

Caster and camber are controlled by the positioning of the upper control arm pivot bar adjusting bolts. To adjust caster, loosen one of the pivot bar adjusting bolts or nuts and slide one end of the bar either inboard or outboard in its elongated mounting hole in the cross-member. Camber is adjusted by loosening both the pivot bar adjusting

TO ADJUST FRONT CARRYING HEIGHT RAISE CAR AT FRONT CROSSMEMBER TO RELIEVE STRAIN ON ADJUSTING BOLT. LUBRICATE ADJUSTING BOLT BEFORE ATTEMPTING TO CHANGE CARRYING HEIGHT

MEASURE FROM ROCKER MLDG. TO LEVEL FLOOR AS SHOWN

6" REARWARD OF DOOR OPENING

60"

TORONADO

FRONT   REAR   LEVEL SURFACE

FRONT TO REAR ± 1/2"
SIDE TO SIDE 1/2"
FRONT TO REAR SLOPE +3/4"

MEASURE WITH FULL GAS TANK SEAT REARWARD. TIRE PRESSURE CORRECT. DOOR CLOSED AND TRUNK EMPTY

Oldsmobile Toronado ride height measuring locations
(© Oldsmobile Div., G.M. Corp.)

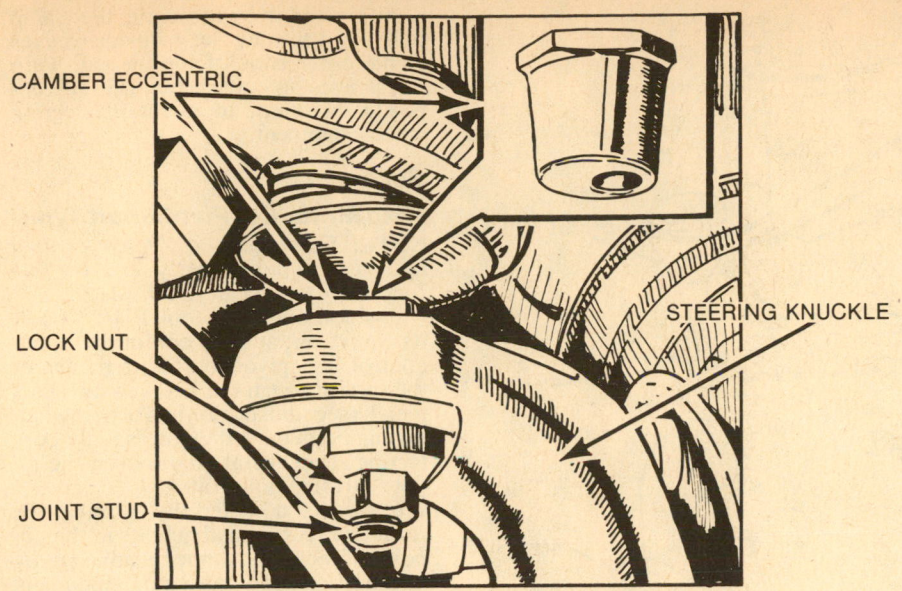

CAMBER ECCENTRIC

LOCK NUT

JOINT STUD

STEERING KNUCKLE

Details of type 2 camber adjustment
(© Cadillac Div, G.M. Corp)

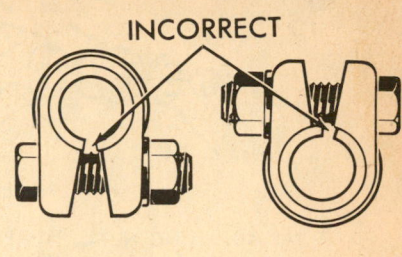

INCORRECT

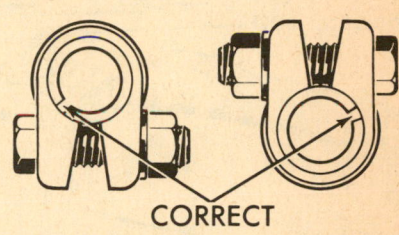

CORRECT

Typical tie rod clamp to sleeve position
(© Cadillac Div, G.M. Corp.)

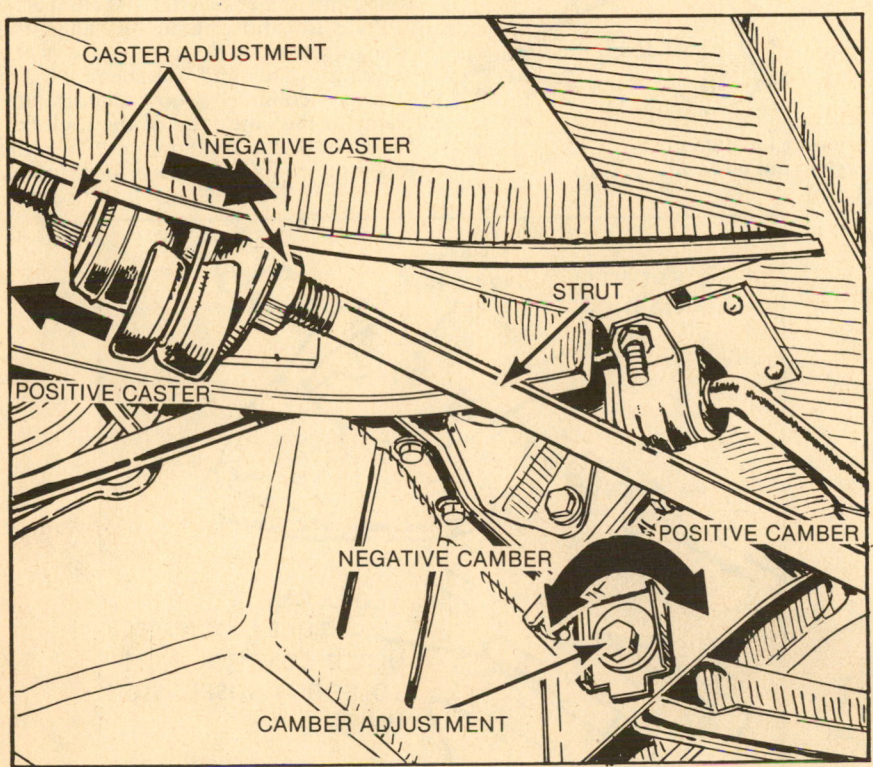

CASTER ADJUSTMENT

NEGATIVE CASTER

STRUT

POSITIVE CASTER

NEGATIVE CAMBER

POSITIVE CAMBER

CAMBER ADJUSTMENT

**Location of caster and camber adjustments
for Type 3**
(© Snap-On Tools Corp)

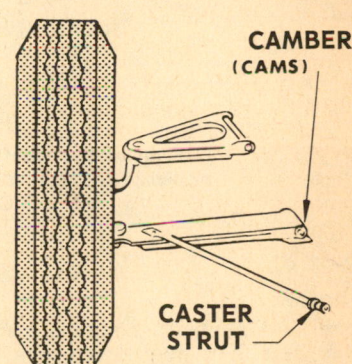

CAMBER
(CAMS)

**CASTER
STRUT**

**Location of caster and camber
adjustments for type 3**
(© Snap-On Tools Corp.)

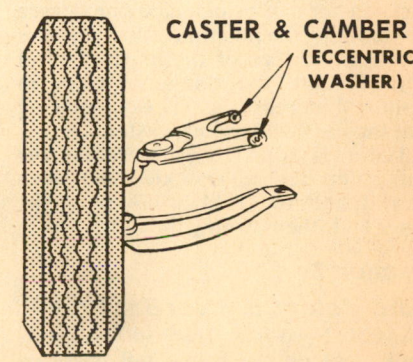

CASTER & CAMBER
(ECCENTRIC
WASHER)

**Location of caster and camber adjustment
for type 4 (except Imperial and Omni/
Horizon)** (© Snap-On Tools Corp.)

Type 5 caster and camber adjusting pry bar
(© Chrysler Corp)

bolts or nuts and sliding both ends of the bar an equal amount.

NOTE: *Chrysler recommends the use of a special pry bar no. C-4196 for the adjusting operation on the upper control arm pivot bar.*

Recheck caster after setting camber.

Torque the pivot bar adjusting bolts or nuts to 160 ft lbs.

To adjust toe-in, loosen the tie rod clamp bolts and turn the adjuster sleeves at the outer ends of the tie rod an equal amount in opposite directions, so that steering wheel spoke alignment is maintained.

Front End Alignment

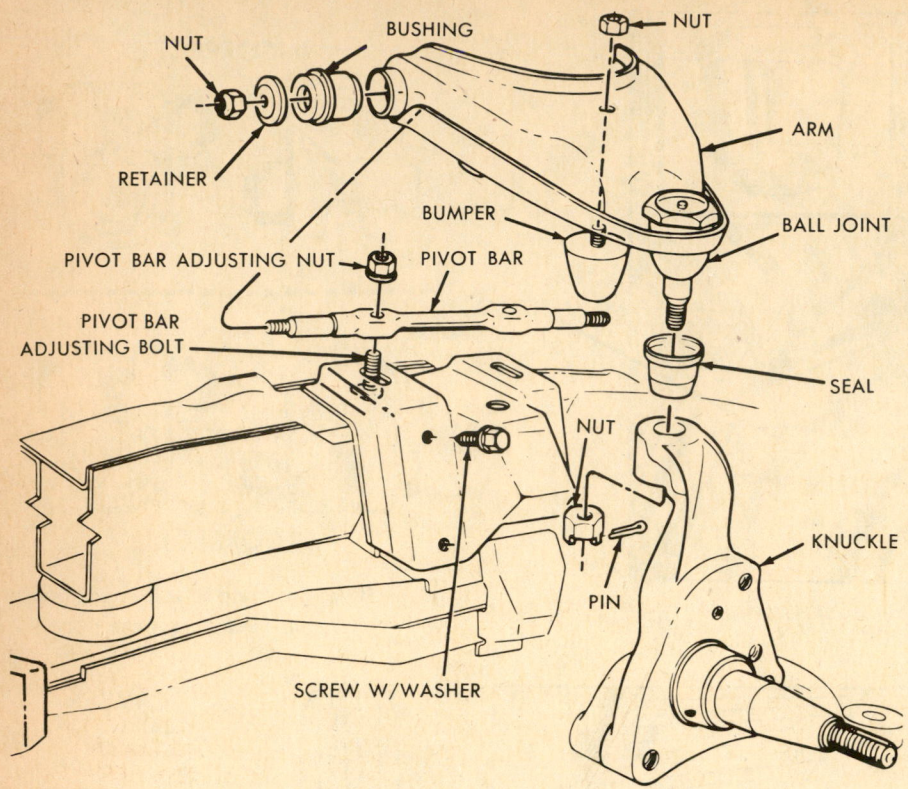

Type 5 upper control arm showing location of
pivot bar and pivot bar adjusting nut and bolt
(© Chrysler Corp)

Adjust toe-in by loosening the clamp bolts, and turning the adjuster sleeves at the outer ends of the tie-rod. Turn the sleeves an equal amount in the opposite direction, to maintain steering wheel alignment.

Section 8
Ford Motor Co. Pivot Shaft Type

NOTE: *Fairmont and Zephyr camber and caster is permanently set at the factory. Only toe-in can be adjusted.*

Position one Ford tool T74P-3000 or its equivalent at each end of the upper control arm, pivot shaft with the leg of the tools through the holes in the sheet metal (see illustration). Turn the adjusting bolts until they are solidly contacting sheet metal, and loosen the pivot shaft retaining bolts.

Caster is adjusted by turning the front and rear adjusting bolts in the opposite direction. Camber is adjusted by turning both bolts an equal amount in the same direction. Following the adjustments, tighten the pivot shaft retaining bolts, remove the adjusting tools, and recheck caster and camber.

Prior to adjusting toe-in, align the straight ahead marks at the base of the steering wheel and the head of the steering column. Loosen both the clamp at the outer end of the rack bellows and the tie rod jam nuts. Turn the inner tie rod shafts to adjust toe-in.

Section 6
Chevette

Caster and camber are not fully adjustable, but they may be corrected. Camber can be increased by approximately one degree by removing the upper ball joint, turning it around, and reinstalling it with the flat on the upper flange on the inboard side of the control arm. Caster can be changed one degree by changing the position of the washers between the legs of the upper control arm. Placing the thinner washer in front will increase caster, while placing it at the back will reduce caster.

Toe-in is adjusted by loosening the nuts at the steering knuckle end of each tie-rod and the rubber cover at the other end, then turning the rod.

Section 7
Ford Motor Co. Pivot Bar Type

Install Ford tool T69P-3000-A or its equivalent on the frame rail, position the hooks around the upper control arm pivot shaft, and tighten the adjusting nuts of the tool slightly. Loosen the pivot shaft retaining bolts to permit adjustment.

To adjust caster, loosen or tighten either the front or rear adjusting nut. After adjusting caster, adjust camber by loosening or tightening both nuts an equal amount. Tighten the shaft retaining bolts to specifications, remove the tool, and recheck the adjustments.

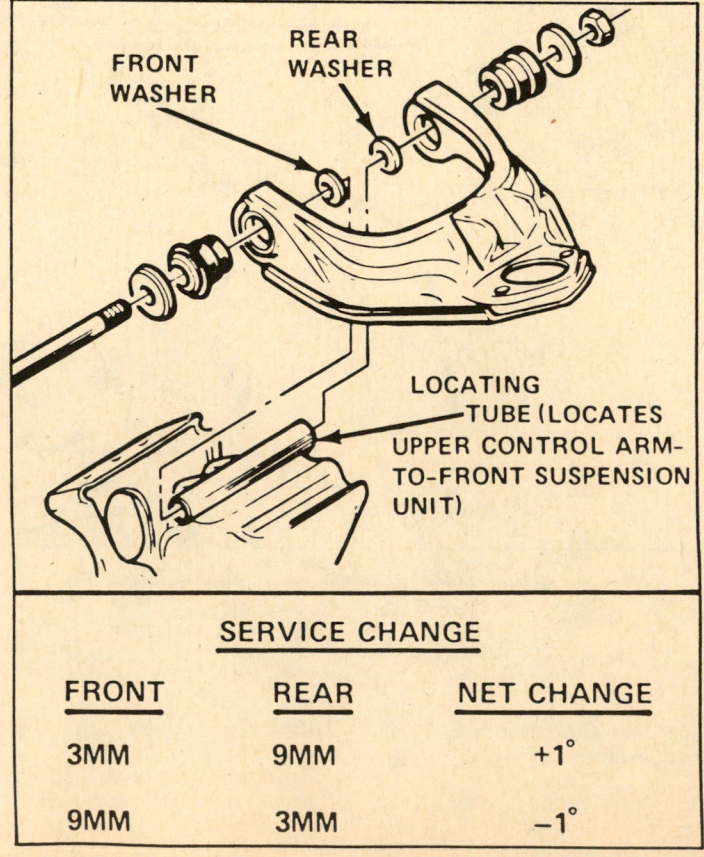

SERVICE CHANGE		
FRONT	REAR	NET CHANGE
3MM	9MM	+1°
9MM	3MM	−1°

Type 6 caster adjustment
(© Chevrolet Div., G.M. Corp.)

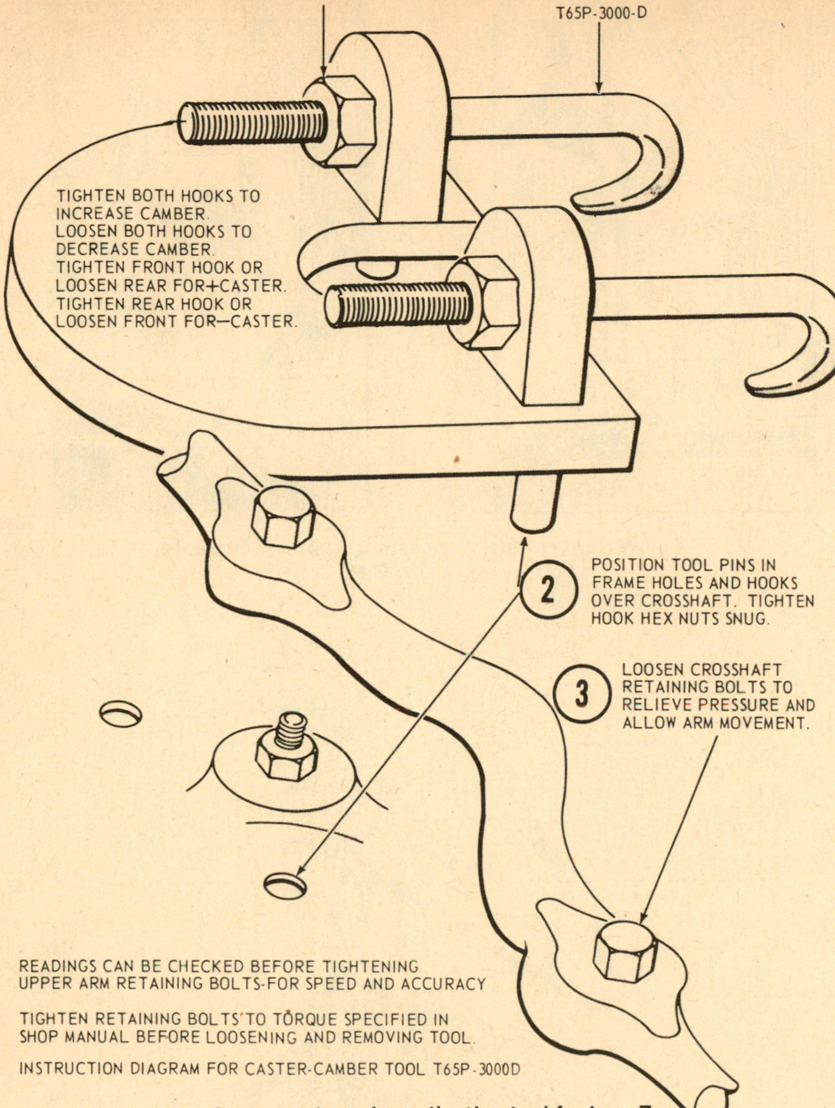

T65P-3000-D

TIGHTEN BOTH HOOKS TO
INCREASE CAMBER.
LOOSEN BOTH HOOKS TO
DECREASE CAMBER.
TIGHTEN FRONT HOOK OR
LOOSEN REAR FOR+CASTER.
TIGHTEN REAR HOOK OR
LOOSEN FRONT FOR—CASTER.

② POSITION TOOL PINS IN
FRAME HOLES AND HOOKS
OVER CROSSHAFT. TIGHTEN
HOOK HEX NUTS SNUG.

③ LOOSEN CROSSHAFT
RETAINING BOLTS TO
RELIEVE PRESSURE AND
ALLOW ARM MOVEMENT.

READINGS CAN BE CHECKED BEFORE TIGHTENING
UPPER ARM RETAINING BOLTS-FOR SPEED AND ACCURACY

TIGHTEN RETAINING BOLTS TO TORQUE SPECIFIED IN
SHOP MANUAL BEFORE LOOSENING AND REMOVING TOOL.

INSTRUCTION DIAGRAM FOR CASTER-CAMBER TOOL T65P-3000D

Caster and camber adjusting tool for type 7
(© Ford Motor Co)

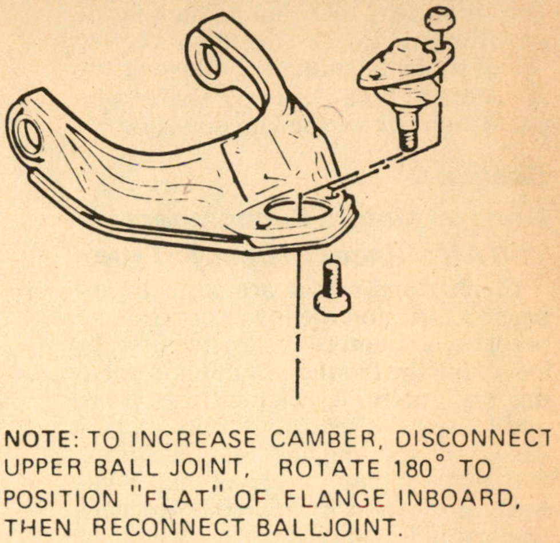

NOTE: TO INCREASE CAMBER, DISCONNECT
UPPER BALL JOINT, ROTATE 180° TO
POSITION "FLAT" OF FLANGE INBOARD,
THEN RECONNECT BALLJOINT.

Type 6 camber adjustment
(© Chevrolet Div., G.M. Corp.)

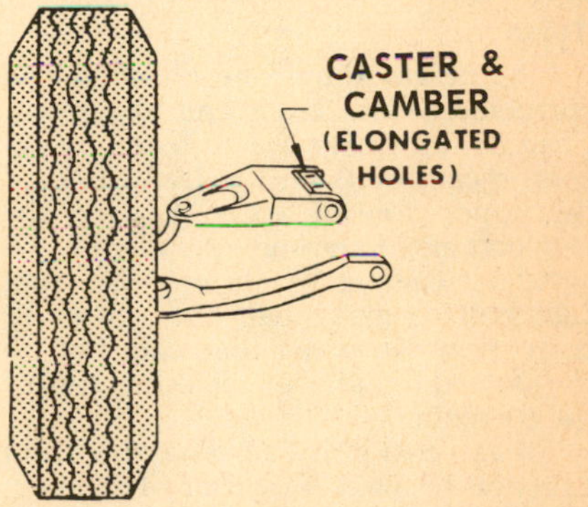

CASTER &
CAMBER
(ELONGATED
HOLES)

**Location of caster and camber adjustments
for type 7**
(© Snap-On Tools Corp)

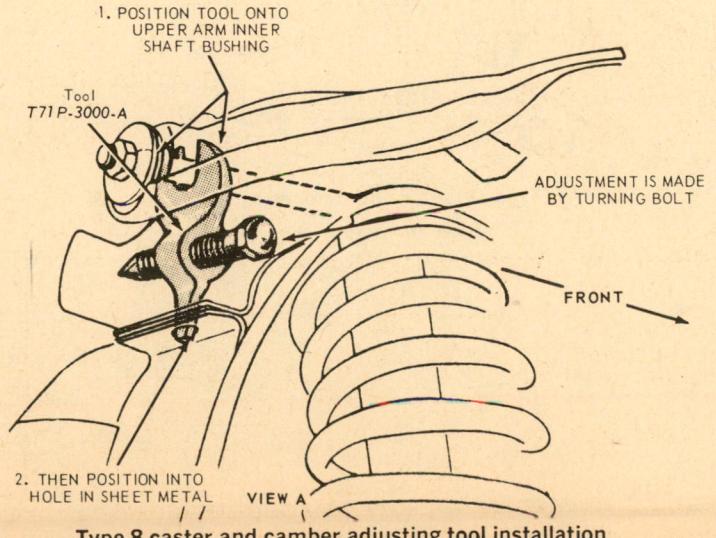

1. POSITION TOOL ONTO
UPPER ARM INNER
SHAFT BUSHING

Tool
T71P-3000-A

ADJUSTMENT IS MADE
BY TURNING BOLT

FRONT

2. THEN POSITION INTO
HOLE IN SHEET METAL   VIEW A

Type 8 caster and camber adjusting tool installation
(© Ford Motor Co)

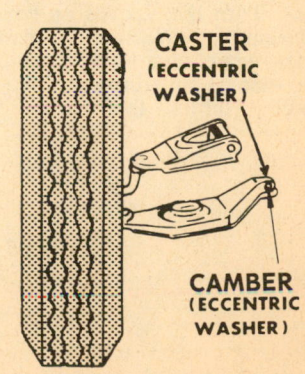

CASTER
(ECCENTRIC
WASHER)

CAMBER
(ECCENTRIC
WASHER)

**Location of caster and camber adjustments
for type 9**
(© Snap-On Tools Corp)

Front End Alignment

Turn the shafts an equal amount in the opposite direction, to maintain steering wheel spoke alignment. Following the adjustment, hold the inner shafts with pliers, and tighten the jam nuts.

Section 9

General Motors Subcompact and AMC Pacer Eccentric Type

Camber and caster are adjusted using eccentrics on the lower control arm pivot bolts. Camber is adjusted first, by loosening the front pivot nut and rotating the eccentric. Tighten the front, and loosen the rear pivot nuts. Adjust caster by rotating the rear eccentric, and tighten the rear pivot nut while holding the bolt in position. Recheck camber and caster.

To adjust toe-in, loosen the clamps on the adjusting sleeves at the outer ends of the tie rod, and turn each sleeve an equal amount in the opposite direction, to maintain steering wheel spoke alignment while adjusting toe-in.

Section 10

General Motors Torsion Bar Type

Ride height should be checked and corrected before front end alignment. Caster and camber are adjusted by eccentric cam bolts on the frame end of the upper control arms. Loosen the cam bolt nuts to permit adjustment.

Adjust camber by turning the front cam bolt to make half the necessary correction. Turn the rear cam bolt in the same direction for the other half of the correction.

Adjust caster by turning the front cam bolt to make a quarter of the necessary correction. Turn the rear cam bolt to bring the camber back to the correct setting. The caster should now be correct.

Tighten the cam bolts to 95 ft lbs, 110 for 1975 and later Toronado. Hold the bolts when tightening the nuts to prevent the settings from changing.

Adjust toe-out by centering the steering wheel, loosening the tie rod sleeve clamps, and turning the adjusting sleeves. Turn the sleeves an equal amount in opposite directions to maintain steering wheel alignment. Position the sleeve clamps up to avoid linkage interference. Tighten the clamps to 22 ft lbs.

Type 9 camber (left) and caster (right) adjustments
(© Chevrolet Div, G.M. Corp)

CASTER AND CAMBER CAMS

Typical caster and camber cam locations, type 10

Index

Brakes

BRAKE DIAGNOSIS CHART

Condition	Mechanical	Hydraulic	Vacuum (Power Unit)
Low pedal (Excessive pedal travel to apply brakes)	FGIMfg	T	k
Spongy Pedal (A springy sensation of pedal upon application)	I	PQU	
Hard Pedal (Excessive pedal pressure needed to stop vehicle)	AFGKVaf	RTUW	cehk
Fading Pedal (A falling away of pedal under steady foot pressure)	I	PQSTW	
Grabbing or Pulling	ADEGHIKL NVXYZa	RW	k
Noise (Squealing, clicking or scraping noise)	FGHILMN		
Chatter or Shudder (May be accompanied by brake roughness or pedal pulsation)	DGILNO		
Dragging Brakes (Slow or incomplete release of brakes)	ABCFGHK LVafg	RUTW	k

D. Wheel bearings loose.
E. Front wheel alignment or uneven tire tread.
F. Brake shoes improperly adjusted. Automatic adjuster parts corroded, distorted or broken.
G. Brake linings or disc pads worn, contaminated or distorted.
H. Shoe return spring weak, broken, improperly installed.
I. Drums cracked, thin (beyond 0.060″ of original specifications), scored, hard spotted, or out of round.

K. Brake support plate ledges rusted or grooved.
L. Support plate loose, worn, or distorted.
M. Disc brake pad "knock back" (loose or worn wheel bearings or steering parts).
N. Caliper not aligned with disc or loose.
O. Disc has excessive lateral runout. Excessively out of parallel.
P. Hydraulic system fluid has air in it, improper quality (low boiling point).

Q. Hoses and lines soft or weak (expanding under pressure).
R. Hoses and lines kinked, collapsed, dented, or clogged.
S. Hoses and lines loosely connected, ruptured, or damaged (causing leakage).
T. Master cylinder primary cup worn or damaged, bore worn, rough, corroded.

U. Master cylinder check valve faulty, or compensator port blocked.
V. Wheel or caliper cylinder pistons frozen or seized.
W. Wheel or caliper cylinder cups swollen, worn or damaged seals; bores rough or corroded.
X Wheel or caliper cylinders mismatched (size).
Y. Check tire pressure.

Z. Rear wheels (both) grabbing. Rear brake line proportioning valve defective—replace.
a. Power unit valve rod linkage binding.
c. Vacuum lines loose, broken, collapsed. Engine vacuum low.
e. Vacuum check valve defective or sticking.
f. Power unit hydraulic pushrod improperly adjusted.
g. Air trapped in hub cavity of master cylinder. Inspect and remove master cylinder boot if installed.
h. Air filter dirty, clogged.
k. Corrosion or lack of lubrication in power cylinder. Control valve, power cylinder, piston or diaphragm defective.

A. Pedal linkage binding. (Check by bleeding one wheel cylinder using light pedal effort. Observe for smooth full travel of pedal)
B. Parking brake cables and linkage sticking, dirty or corroded.
C. Parking brake improperly adjusted (too loose or too tight).

SERVICING DRUM BRAKES

DUO-SERVO BRAKE

Refer to the Drum Brake Application Chart for adjuster applications.

Star and Screw Adjuster

The duo-servo brake, with star and screw type self-adjusters, is used on most late-model American cars. The same basic brake unit has been used on all cars. General Motors cars use a rod-operated lever to turn the star-wheel, while all others use a cable-operated lever. This is the only difference, other than size, among units used on different models.

ADJUSTMENT

1. Remove the access slot plug from

DRUM BRAKE APPLICATION CHART

Car and Years	Brake Type	Self-Adjuster Type
AMERICAN MOTORS 1972-79 all models	Duo-Servor	Star & Screw
CHRYSLER CORP. 1792-79 all models	Duo-Servo	Star & Screw
FORD MOTOR CO. 1972-79 all models	Duo-Servo	Star & Screw
GENERAL MOTORS CORP. 1972-79 all models except below	Duo-Servo	Star & Screw
1972-79 Astre, Monza, Skyhawk, Starfire, Sunbird, Vega	Duo-Servo	Expanding Strut
1976-79 Chevette	Duo-Servo	Pin and Slot

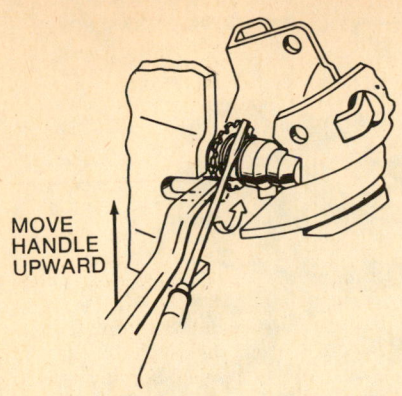

MOVE HANDLE UPWARD

Self-adjuster method. Push the self-adjusting lever out of the way with a small screwdriver or ice pick to back off star wheel.

the backing plate or front of drum on GM cars. On some late-model GM cars, there is no access slot in the backing plate or in the front of the drums. It has been filled in and must be punched out to gain access to the adjuster. Complete the adjustment and cover the hole with a plug to prevent entrance of dirt and water.

2. Using a brake adjusting spoon or screwdriver, pry downward on the end of the tool (starwheel teeth moving up) to tighten the brakes, or upward on the end of the tool (starwheel teeth moving down) to loosen the brakes.

NOTE: *It will be necessary to use a*

small screwdriver to hold the adjusting lever away from the starwheel. Be careful not to bend the adjusting lever.

SHOE GUIDE (ANCHOR PIN) PLATE
WASHER
PARKING BRAKE LINK
ANCHOR PIN
FORWARD
PARKING BRAKE LEVER RETAINING CLIP
SECONDARY SHOE
LINK SPRING
PRIMARY SHOE
SHOE HOLD-DOWN SPRING
PARKING BRAKE LEVER
PARKING BRAKE CABLE HOUSING RETAINER
CABLE HOOK
REAR BRAKE
PARKING BRAKE CABLE AND HOUSING
AUTOMATIC ADJUSTER SPRING

Bendix duo-servo self-adjusting brake—Ford type

PRIMARY RETURN SPRING
SECONDARY RETURN SPRING
ANCHOR PLATE
CABLE GUIDE
SHOE TAB (3)
SHOE RETAINERS, SPRING AND NAIL ASSEMBLIES
ANTI-RATTLE SPRING
STRUT
PARKING BRAKE LEVER
SHOE TO SHOE SPRING
SECONDARY SHOE AND LINING
SUPPORT PLATE
LEVER SPRING
ADJUSTER LEVER
ADJUSTER SCREW ASSEMBLY
OVERLOAD SPRING
LEFT REAR

Bendix duo-servo self-adjusting brake—Chrysler Corp. 11 in. type

3. When the brakes are tight almost to the point of being locked, back off on the starwheel until the wheel is able to rotate freely. The starwheel on each set of brakes (front or rear) must be backed off the same number of turns to prevent brake pull from side to side.

4. When all four brakes are adjusted, check brake pedal travel and then make several stops, while backing the car up, to equalize all the wheels.

TESTING ADJUSTER

1. Raise the vehicle on a hoist, with a helper in the car, to apply the brakes.

2. Loosen the brakes by holding the adjuster lever away from the starwheel and backing off the starwheel approximately 30 notches.

3. Spin the wheel and brake drum in reverse and apply the brakes. The movement of the secondary shoe should pull the adjuster lever up, and when the brakes are released the lever should snap down and turn the starwheel.

4. If the automatic adjuster doesn't work, the drum must be removed and the adjuster components inspected carefully for breakage, wear, or improper installation.

BRAKE SHOE REMOVAL

NOTE: *If you are not thoroughly familiar with the procedures involved in brake replacement, disassemble and as-*

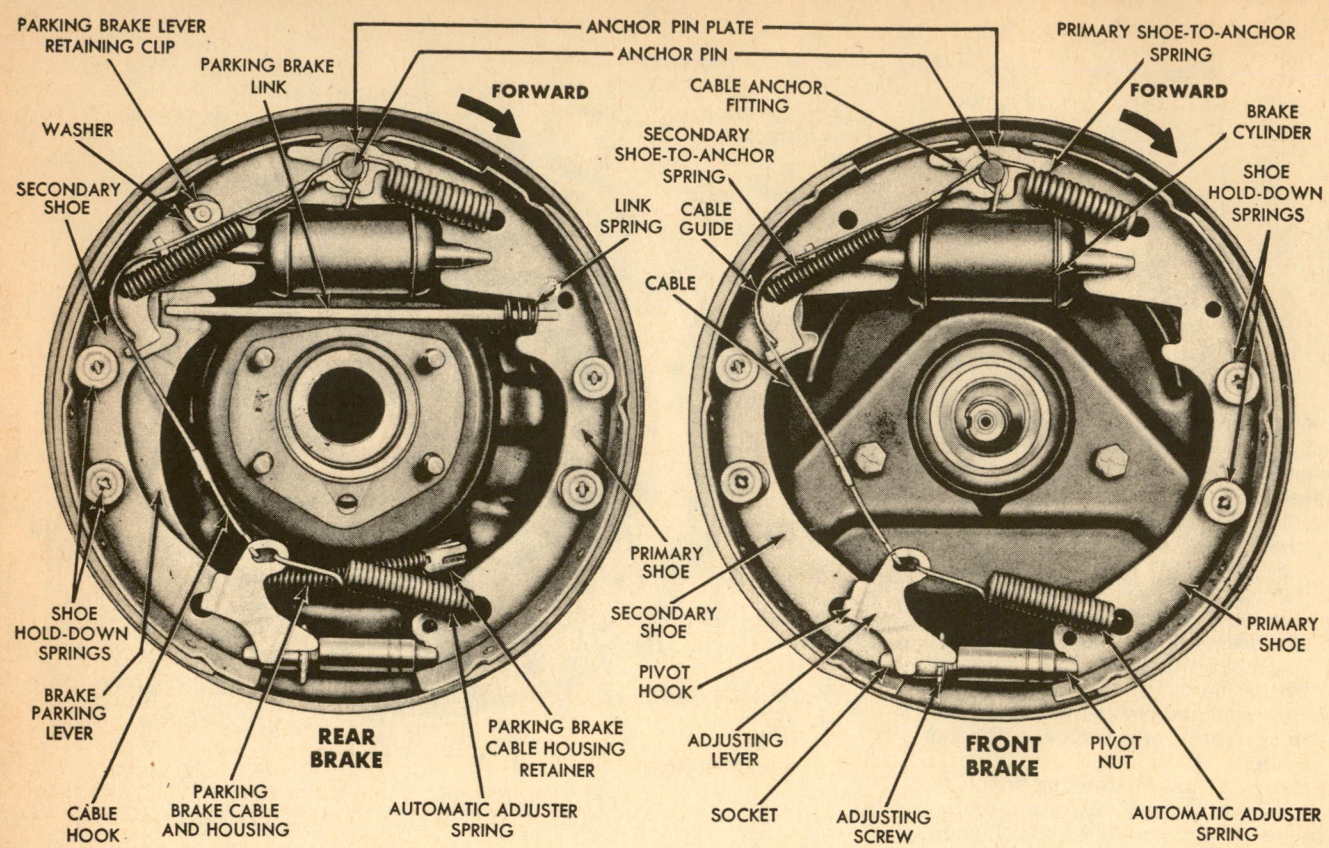

PARKING BRAKE LEVER RETAINING CLIP
PARKING BRAKE LINK
WASHER
SECONDARY SHOE
ANCHOR PIN PLATE
ANCHOR PIN
FORWARD
CABLE ANCHOR FITTING
SECONDARY SHOE-TO-ANCHOR SPRING
LINK SPRING
CABLE GUIDE
CABLE
PRIMARY SHOE-TO-ANCHOR SPRING
FORWARD
BRAKE CYLINDER
SHOE HOLD-DOWN SPRINGS
SHOE HOLD-DOWN SPRINGS
BRAKE PARKING LEVER
CABLE HOOK
PARKING BRAKE CABLE AND HOUSING
REAR BRAKE
PARKING BRAKE CABLE HOUSING RETAINER
AUTOMATIC ADJUSTER SPRING
PRIMARY SHOE
SECONDARY SHOE
PIVOT HOOK
ADJUSTING LEVER
SOCKET
ADJUSTING SCREW
FRONT BRAKE
PIVOT NUT
AUTOMATIC ADJUSTER SPRING
PRIMARY SHOE

Bendix duo-servo self-adjusting brakes

semble one side at a time, leaving the other wheel intact, as a reference.

1. Remove the brake drum.
2. Place the hollow end of a brake spring service tool on the brake shoe anchor pin and twist it to disengage one of the brake retaining springs. Repeat this operation to remove the other spring. On GM cars, grasp the secondary shoe return spring with a pair of pliers and lift upward on the spring to disengage it from the automatic adjuster link.

——— CAUTION ———

Be careful that the springs do not slip off the tool during removal, as the spring could break loose and cause personal injury.

3. Reach behind the brake backing plate and place a finger on the end of one of the brake holddown mounting pins. Using a pair of pliers, grasp the washer on the top of the hold-down spring that corresponds to the pin that you are holding. Push down on the pliers and turn them 90° to align the slot in the washer with the head on the spring mounting pin. Remove the spring and washer and repeat this operation on the holddown spring of the other brake shoe.
4. Step 4 varies according to manufacturer:

On Ford and American Motors cars, place the tip of a screwdriver on the top of the brake adjusting screw and move the screwdriver upward to lift up on the brake adjusting lever. When there is enough slack in the automatic adjuster cable, disconnect the loop on the top of the cable from the anchor. Grasp the top of each brake shoe and move them outward to disengage from the wheel cylinder and parking brake link (if working on rear wheels). When the brake shoes are clear, lift them from the backing plate. Twist the shoes slightly and the automatic adjuster assembly will disassemble itself.

On GM cars, remove the automatic adjuster link. Remove the automatic adjuster lever, pivot, and override spring from the secondary spring as an assembly. Move the top of each brake shoe outward to clear the wheel cylinder pins and parking brake link (rear brakes). Lift the brakes from the backing plate and remove the adjusting screw.

On Chrysler cars, slide the automatic adjuster cable from the anchor pin and disengage it from the adjusting lever. Remove the cable, overload spring, and cable guide. Disconnect the automatic adjuster lever return spring and remove the spring and lever. Move the top of the brake shoes outward to clear

the wheel cylinder pins and parking brake link (rear brakes). Lift the brakes from the backing plate and remove the adjusting screw.

5. If you are working on rear brakes, grasp the end of the brake cable spring with a pair of pliers and, using the brake lever as a fulcrum, pull the end of the spring away from the lever. Disengage the cable from the brake lever.

BRAKE SHOE INSTALLATION

1. If you are working on rear brakes, the brake cable must be connected to the secondary brake shoe before the shoe is installed on the backing plate. To do this, transfer the parking brake lever from the old secondary shoe to the new one. This is accomplished by spreading the bottom of the horseshoe clip and disengaging the lever. Position the lever on the new secondary shoe and install the spring washer and the horseshoe clip. Close the bottom of the clip after installing it. Grasp the metal tip of the parking brake cable with a pair of pliers. Position a pair of side cutters on the end of the cable coil spring and, using the pliers as a fulcrum, pull the coil spring back with the side cutters. Position the cable in the parking brake lever.
2. Apply a light coating of high-temperature grease to the brake shoe contact points on the backing

plate. Position the primary brake shoe on the front of the backing plate and install the hold-down spring and washer over the mounting pin. Install the secondary shoe on the rear of the backing plate.

3. If working on rear brakes, install the parking brake link between the primary brake shoe and the secondary brake shoe.

4. Step 4 varies according to manufacturer:

On Ford and American Motors cars, install the automatic adjuster cable loop end on the anchor pin. Make sure that the crimped side of the loop faces the backing plate.

On GM cars, assemble the automatic adjuster lever, pivot, and override spring and install to the secondary spring as an assembly.

On Chrysler, install the automatic adjuster lever and return spring. Install the adjuster overload spring and cable. One end of the cable engages with the adjusting lever while the other slips over the anchor pin underneath the primary and secondary return springs.

5. Install the return spring in the primary brake shoe and, using the tapered end of a brake spring service tool, slide the top of the spring onto the anchor pin.

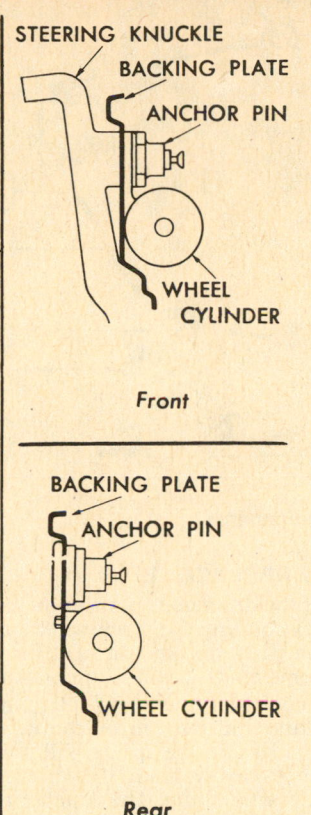

Front

Rear

CAUTION

Be careful to make sure that the spring does not slip off the tool during installation, as the spring could break loose and cause personal injury.

6. Install the automatic adjuster cable guide in the secondary brake shoe, making sure that the flared hole in the cable guide is inside the hole in the brake shoe. Fit the cable into the groove in the top of the cable guide.

7. Install the secondary shoe return spring through the hole in the cable guide and the brake shoe. Using the brake spring tool, slide the top of the spring onto the anchor pin.

8. Clean the threads on the adjusting screw and apply a *light* coating of high-temperature grease to the threads. Screw the adjuster closed, then open it one-half turn.

9. Install the adjusting screw between the brake shoes with the star wheel nearest to the secondary shoe. Make sure that the star wheel is in a position that is accessible from the adjusting slot in the backing plate.

10. Install the short, hooked end of the automatic adjuster spring in the proper hole in the primary brake shoe.

11. Connect the hooked end of the automatic adjuster cable and the free

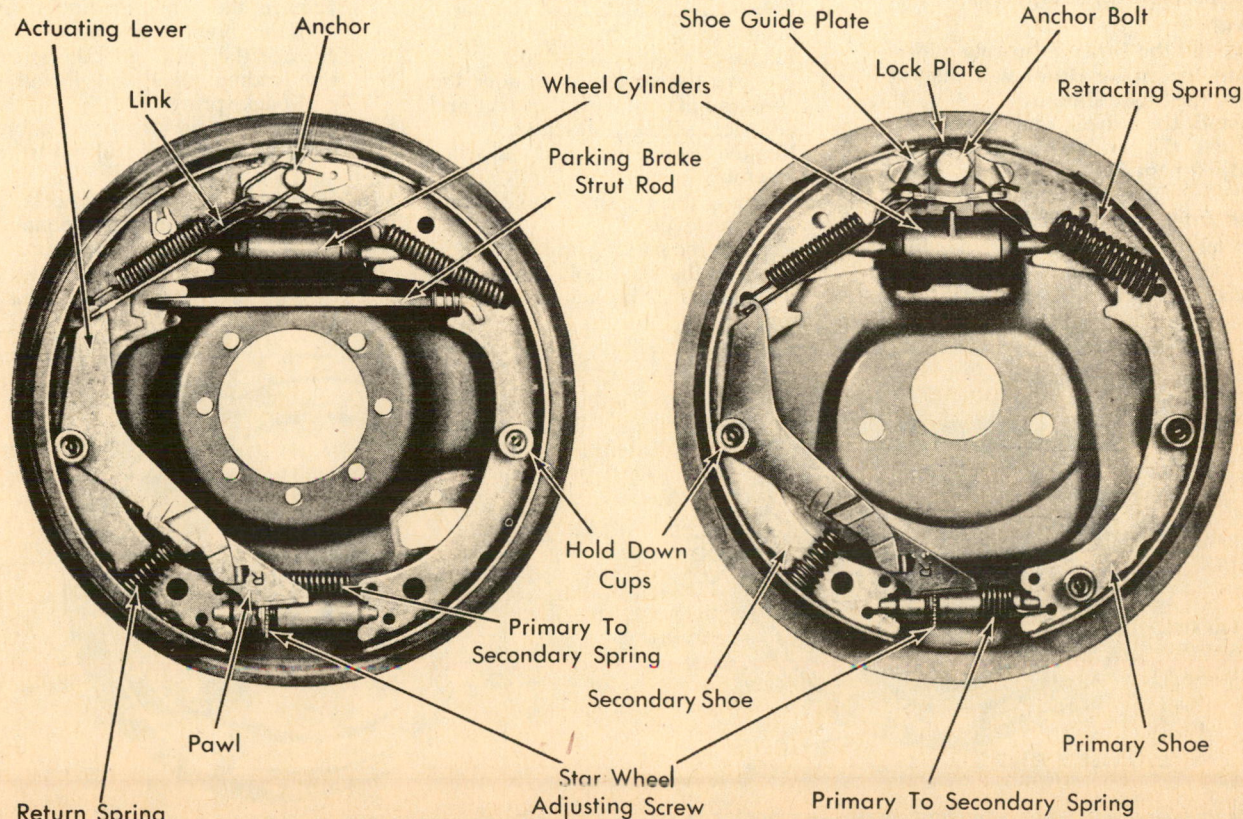

Bendix duo-servo self-adjusting brake—G.M. type

end of the automatic adjuster spring in the slot in the top of the automatic adjuster lever.

12. Pull the automatic adjuster lever (the lever will pull the cable and spring with it) downward and to the left, and engage the pivot hook of the lever in the hole in the secondary brake shoe.

13. Check the entire brake assembly to make sure everything is installed

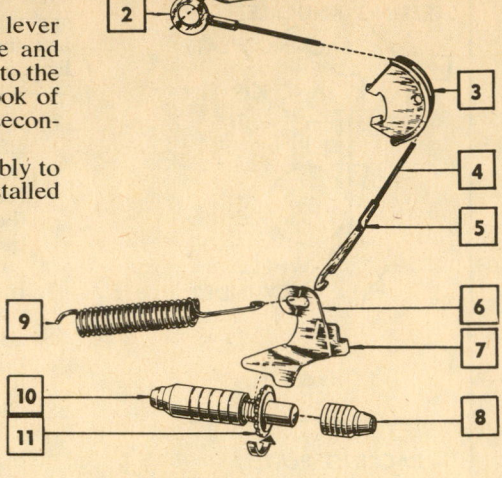

1 Shoe guide plate
2 Cable anchor fitting
3 Cable guide
4 Cable
5 Cable hook
6 Lever
7 Pivot hook
8 Socket
9 Spring—automatic adjuster
10 Pivot nut
11 Adjusting screw

Self-adjusting brake components

properly. Make sure that the shoes engage the wheel cylinder properly and are flush on the anchor pin. Make sure that the automatic adjuster cable is flush on the anchor pin and in the slot on the back of cable guide. Make sure that the adjusting lever rests on the adjusting screw star wheel. Pull upward on the adjusting cable until the adjusting lever is free of the star wheel, then release the cable. The adjusting lever should snap back into place on the adjusting screw star wheel and turn the wheel one tooth.

14. Expand the brake adjusting screw until the brake drum will just fit over the brake shoes.

15. Install the wheel and drum and adjust the brakes. (See "Brake Adjustment.")

Expanding Strut Adjuster

Duo-servo brakes with expanding strut adjusters are used exclusively on GM subcompact cars through 1975.

SHOE REPLACEMENT

1. If the drum does not slip off easily, try rotating the drum while pulling on it. If no amount of effort will remove it, it will be necessary to knock out the metal plug in the drum and push in on the adjuster rod so that the spring will pull the shoes away from the drum. Remove the drum. The adjuster rod is at the 2 o'clock position on the left wheel and at the 10 o'clock position on the right wheel.

2. Release all tension from the parking brake equalizer.

3. Remove the pull-back spring.

4. Remove the shoes from under the clips and lift out with the strut and adjuster assembly attached.

5. Remove the strut and adjuster assembly.

6. Remove the parking brake cable from the lever.

7. Remove the parking brake lever.

8. Remove the shoe hold-down clips only if they are broken or worn.

ADJUSTER DISASSEMBLY

1. Remove the adjuster assembly from the wheel.

2. Separate the rod assembly from the adjuster locks. A special tool is necessary for this job. It is available at most auto parts stores.

3. Slide the rod off from the strut.

ADJUSTER ASSEMBLY

1. Assemble the adjuster lock to the strut, making sure that the index hole in the lock is lined up and seated with the hole in the strut.

2. Slide the rod assembly onto the strut and over the adjuster locks. When properly installed, about 1/2 of the index hole in the adjuster lock should be covered by the rod assembly.

9. Using white grease, lubricate the six contact surfaces on the backing plate. Do not allow any grease to contact the brake linings.

10. Install the parking brake lever to the rear brake shoe and install the parking brake strut and adjuster. The rear shoe can be identified as having a hole for the parking brake lever and one for the adjusting rod.

11. Connect both shoes with the lower spring.

12. Install both shoes with the spring onto the backing plate, placing the spring under the shoe anchor. Position the lever and adjuster assembly.

13. Engage the wheel cylinder links with the shoes.

14. Engage the parking brake strut to the leading shoe and install the pull-back spring.

15. Connect the parking brake cable to its lever, being careful not to activate the adjuster.

16. Install the drums and wheels, and adjust the parking brake equalizer. Lower the vehicle to the floor.

17. Adjust the parking brake and service brake by pulling and releasing

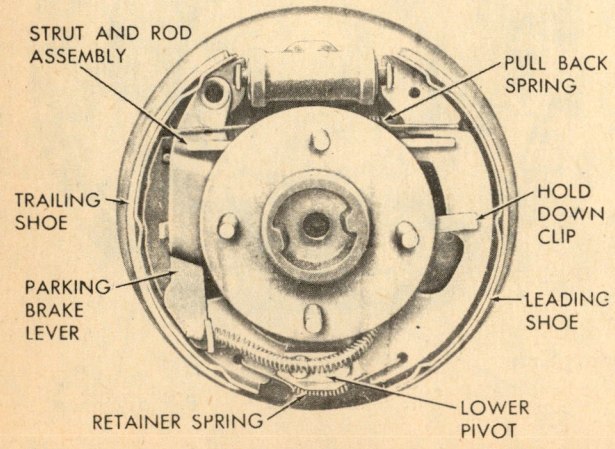

Bendix duo-servo self-adjusting brake—expanding strut type (© Chevrolet Div., G.M. Corp)

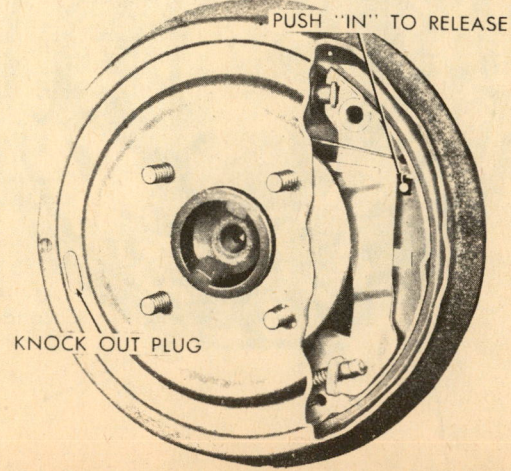

Release adjuster to remove drum on expanding strut rear brakes (© Chevrolet Div., G.M. Corp)

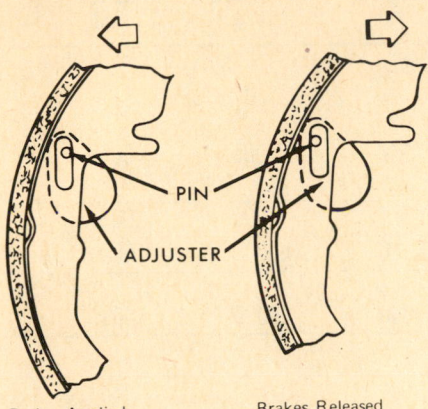

Adjuster remains in new position as brakes are released—shoe travel stops at contact with adjuster pin.

Adjuster is rotated outward by shoe as brakes are applied.

Brakes Applied   Brakes Released

Pin and slot adjuster operation
(© Chevrolet Div., G.M. Corp.)

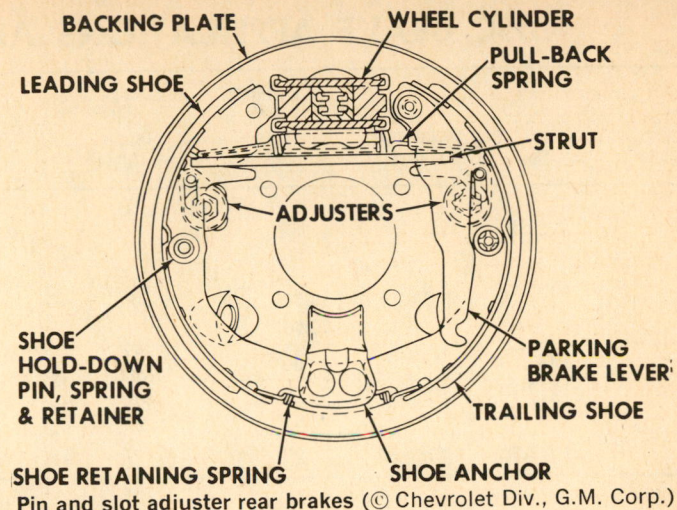

Pin and slot adjuster rear brakes (© Chevrolet Div., G.M. Corp.)

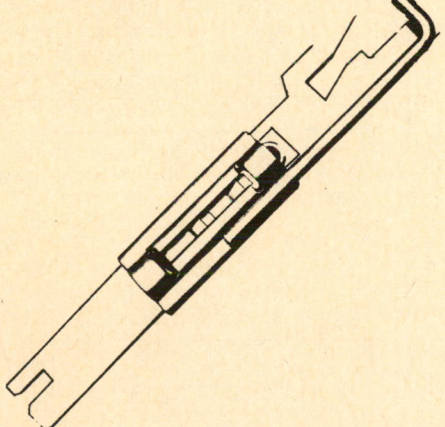

Adjuster properly positioned for installation— expanding strut rear brakes
(© Chevrolet Div., G.M. Corp)

the handle several times.
18. Seal the adjuster hole in the drum with a rubber or plastic replacement plug.

Pin and Slot Adjuster

The duo-servo brake with pin and slot adjusters is a new design for the Chevette.

SHOE REPLACEMENT

1. Remove the brake drum.
2. Loosen the equalizer to let all tension from the parking brake cable.
3. Unhook the parking brake cable from the lever.
4. Use pliers to remove the long shoe pull back spring at the top.
5. Use pliers to remove the shoe hold down springs and retainers from the middle of each shoe.
6. Separate the shoes at the top and remove them.
7. Check that the adjusters work properly; it should take 29-36 ft. lbs torque to turn the adjusters. The adjusters and backing plate must be replaced as an assembly.
8. Lubricate the shoe contact surfaces on the backing plate and all pivot points with brake lubricant. Lubricate the parking brake cable.
9. Lubricate the pivot end of the parking brake lever and attach the lever to the shoe.
10. Connect the shoes at the bottom with the retaining spring.
11. Place the shoes in position and fasten the front shoe with the hold down spring and retainer. Be sure that the adjuster peg is in the shoe slot.
12. Install the parking brake lever to front shoe strut. Fasten down the rear shoe with the hold down spring and retainer. Be sure that the adjuster peg is in the shoe slot.
13. Install the shoe pull back spring.
14. Attach the end of the parking brake cable to the lever.
15. Replace the drum. Adjust the brakes by applying the brake several times until the pedal is firm. Check the fluid level frequently. Adjust the parking brake.

SERVICING FRONT DISC BRAKES

Caliper disc brakes can be divided into three types: the four-piston, fixed-caliper type; the single-piston, floating-caliper type, and the single-piston sliding-caliper type. Refer to the Disc Brake Chart for applications.

In the four piston type (two in each side of the caliper) braking effect is achieved by hydraulically pushing both shoes against the disc sides.

With the single piston floating-caliper type the inboard shoe is pushed hydraulically into contact with the disc, while the reaction force thus generated is used to pull the outboard shoe into frictional contact (made possible by letting the caliper move slightly along the axle centerline).

In the sliding caliper (single piston) type, the caliper assembly slides along

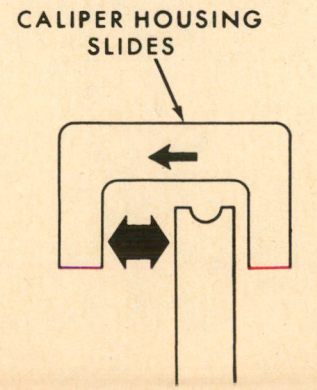

Floating caliper disc brake operation

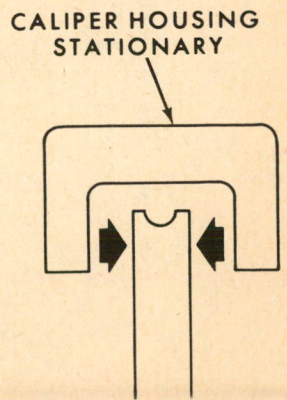

Floating caliper disc brake operation

Disc Brakes

DISC BRAKE APPLICATIONS AND SPECIFICATIONS

Vehicle	Year	Caliper Type	Mounting Bolt Torque (ftlb)	Bridge Bolt Torque (ftlb)	Rotor Original Thickness (in.)	Rotor Minimum Thickness (in.)	Rotor Parallel Variation (in.)	Rotor Maximum Runout (in.)
American Motors								
All	1972-74	Floating	upper 105 lower 85	30-35	1.000	.940	.0005	.005
All	1975-76	Sliding	80	15	1.190	1.120	.0005	.003
Matador	1977-79	Sliding	80	18	1.190	1.120	.0005	.003
All except Matador	1977-79	Sliding	80	18	.880	.810	.0005	.003
Chrysler Corp.								
Omni/Horizon	1978-79	Sliding	95-125	25-40	.500	.455	.0005	.004
Valiant/Dart	1972	Fixed	50-80	70-80	.810	.780	.0005	.0025
Mid-Sized	1972-79	Floating	100	35	1.010	.940	.0005	.0025①
Full-Sized	1972-79	Sliding	100	—	1.250	1.180	.0005	.0025①
Imperial Rear	1974-75	Sliding	—	—	1.000	.940	.0005	.004
Ford Motor Co.								
Mustang, Cougar	1972-73	Floating	upper 120 lower 65	25-35	.935	.875	.0007	.002
Ford, Mercury, Lincoln	1972	Floating	upper 125 lower 105	25-35	1.180	1.120	.0007	.003
Pinto	1972-73	Sliding	—	—	.750	.685	.0007	.003
Montego, Torino	1972-76							
Thunderbird	1972-79							
Ford, Mercury, Lincoln	1974-79							
Elite	1975-76							
Cougar	1974-79							
Mk. IV	1972-77							
Mk. V	1978-79							
LTD II	1977-79	Sliding	—	35	1.180	1.120	.0005②	.003
Pinto	1974-79							
Bobcat	1975-79							
Mustang	1974-79							
Maverick, Comet	1972-77							
Granada, Monarch	1974-79							
Versailles	1977-79							
Fairmont, Zephyr	1978-79	Sliding	—	35	.870	.810	.0005	.003
Ford, Mercury, Lincoln, Mk. V Granada, Monarch, Versailles	All Rear	Sliding	—	35	.945	.895	.0005	.004

DISC BRAKE APPLICATIONS AND SPECIFICATIONS

Vehicle	Year	Caliper Type	Mounting Bolt Torque (ftlb)	Bridge Bolt Torque (ftlb)	Rotor Original Thickness (in.)	Rotor Minimum Thickness (in.)	Rotor Parallel Variation (in.)	Rotor Maximum Runout (in.)
General Motors								
Buick Full-Sized Front or Rear	1972	Sliding	35	—	1.290	1.230	.0005	.004
	1973-74	Sliding	35	—	1.290	1.215	.0005	.004
	1975-77	Sliding	35	—	1.290	1.230	.0005	.004
	1978-79	Sliding	35	—	1.040	.965	.0005	.004
Buick Mid-Sized Front or Rear	1972-79	Sliding	35	—	1.040	.965	.0005	.004
Buick Compact	1975-77	Sliding	35	—	1.040	.980	.0005	.005
Buick Skyhawk	1975	Sliding	—	—	.500	.455	.0005	.005
	1976-79	Sliding	—	—	.880	.815	.0005	.005
Cadillac Front	1972-77	Floating	—	—	1.250	1.220	.0005	.0025
	1978-79	Floating	—	—	1.037	.980	.0005	.005
Rear	1978-79	Floating	—	—	.9744	.910	.0005	.003
Cadillac Eldorado Front or Rear	1972-79	Sliding	—	—	1.210	1.190	.0005	.008
Cadillac Seville Front	1976-79	Sliding	—	—	1.037	.980	.0005	.005
Rear	1976-77	Sliding	—	—	.9744	.905	.0005	.005
Rear	1978-79	Sliding	—	—	.9744	.910	.0005	.003
Chevrolet Full-Sized	1972	Sliding	35	—	1.285	1.230	.0005	.002
	1973-77	Sliding	35	—	1.285	1.230	.0005	.002
Chevrolet Chevelle, Nova Camaro	1972-77	Sliding	35		1.035	.980	.0005	.002
Chevrolet Vega, Monza	1972-75	Sliding	—	—	.500	.470	.0005	.005
	1976-79	Sliding	—	—	.880	.830	.0005	.005
Chevette	1976-79	Sliding	—	—	.500	.390	.0005	.002
Corvette Front or Rear	1972-79	Fixed	Front 130 rear 60	—	1.250	1.230	.0005	.002
Chevrolet All except Chevette, Corvette, Monza	1978-79	Sliding	—	—	1.037	.980	.0005	.005
Oldsmobile 88, 98	1972-74	Sliding	40	—	1.280	1.230	.0005	.005
Oldsmobile Toronado	1972-79	Sliding	40	—	1.205	1.185	.0005	.002
Oldsmobile Mid-Sized	1972-77	Sliding	35	—	1.035	.980	.0005	.004
Oldsmobile Omega	1973-77	Sliding	40	—	1.040	.965	.0005	.005
Oldsmobile Starfire	1975	Sliding	—	—	.500	.400	.0005	.005
	1976-79	Sliding	—	—	.880	.830	.0005	.005

Disc Brakes

DISC BRAKE APPLICATIONS AND SPECIFICATIONS

Vehicle	Year	Caliper Type	Mounting Bolt Torque (ftlb)	Bridge Bolt Torque (ftlb)	Rotor Original Thickness (in.)	Rotor Minimum Thickness (in.)	Rotor Parallel Variation (in.)	Rotor Maximum Runout (in.)
Oldsmobile All except Starfire, Toronado	1978-79	Sliding	40	—	1.040	.980	.0005	.004 .005 StaWgn
Pontiac Full-Sized	1972	Sliding	35	—	1.250	1.230	.0005	.002
	1973-77	Sliding	35	—	1.285	1.215	.0005	.004
Pontiac LeMans, Firebird	1972	Sliding	35	—	1.005	.960	.0007	.004
	1973-77	Sliding	35	—	1.035	.965	.0007	.004
Pontiac Ventura, Phoenix	1972-77	Sliding	35	—	1.035	.965	.0007	.004
Pontiac Astre, Sunbird	1975	Sliding	—	—	.500	.470	.0005	.005
	1976-79	Sliding	—	—	.880	.830	.0005	.005
Pontiac All except Sunbird	1978-79	Sliding	35	—	1.040	.980	.0005	.004

① 1975 and later: .004   ② 1978-79 Lincoln and Mk.V: .00025

the machined surfaces of the anchor plate. A steel key located between the machined surfaces of the caliper and the machined surfaces of the anchor plate is held in place with either a retaining screw or two cotter pins. The caliper is held in place against the anchor plate with one or two support springs.

Inspection

Disc pads (lining and shoe assemblies) should be replaced in axle sets (both wheels) when the lining on any pad is worn to 1/16 in. at any point. *If lining is allowed to wear past 1/16 in. minimum thickness severe damage to disc may result.*

NOTE: *State inspection specifications take precedence over these general recommendations.*

Note that disc pads in floating caliper type brakes may wear at an angle, and measurement should be made at the narrow end of the taper. Tapered linings should be replaced if the taper exceeds 1/8 in. from end to end (the difference between the thickest and thinnest points).

When the caliper is unbolted from the hub do not let it dangle by the brake hose; it can be rested on a suspension member or wired onto the frame. All disc brake systems are inherently self-

─── CAUTION ───

To prevent costly paint damage, remove some brake fluid (don't re-use) from the reservoir and install the reservoir cover before replacing the disc pads. When replacing the pads, the piston is depressed and fluid is forced back through the lines to squirt out of the fluid reservoir.

adjusting and have no provision for manual adjustment.

Servicing the Caliper Assembly

1. Raise the vehicle on a hoist and remove the front wheels.
2. Working on one side at a time only, disconnect the hydraulic inlet line from the caliper and plug the end. Remove the caliper mounting bolts or pins, and shims (if used) and slide the caliper off the disc.
3. Remove the disc pads from the caliper. If the old ones are to be reused, mark them so that they can be reinstalled in their original positions.
4. Open the caliper bleed screw and drain the fluid. Clean the outside of the caliper and mount it in a vise with padded jaws.
5. Remove the bridge bolts, separate the caliper halves, and remove the

─── CAUTION ───

When cleaning any brake components, use only brake fluid or denatured (Isopropyl) alcohol. Never use a mineral-based solvent, such as gasoline or paint thinner, since it will swell and quickly deteriorate rubber parts.

two O-ring seals from the transfer holes.

6. Pry the lip on each piston dust boot from its groove and remove the piston assemblies and springs from the bores. If necessary, air pressure may be used to force the pistons out of the bores, using care to prevent them from popping out of control.
7. Remove the boots and seals from the pistons and clean the pistons in brake fluid. Blow out the caliper passages with an air hose.
8. Inspect the cylinder bores for scoring, pitting, or corrosion. Corrosion is a pitted or rough condition not to be confused with staining. Light rough spots may be removed by rotating crocus cloth, using finger pressure, in the bores. Do not polish with an in and out motion or use any other abrasive.
9. If the pistons are pitted, scored, or worn, they must be replaced. A

corroded or deeply scored caliper should also be replaced.

10. Check the clearance of the pistons in the bores using a feeler gauge. Clearance should be 0.002-0.006 in. If there is excessive clearance the caliper must be replaced.

11. Replace all rubber parts and lubricate with brake fluid. Install the seals and boots in the grooves in each piston. The seal should be installed in the groove closest to the closed end of the piston with the seal lips facing the closed end. The lip on the boot should be facing the seal.

12. Lubricate the piston and bore with brake fluid. Position the piston return spring, large coil first, in the piston bore.

13. Install the piston in the bore, taking great care to avoid damaging the seal lip as it passes the edge of the cylinder bore.

14. Compress the lip on the dust boot into the groove in the caliper. Be sure the boot is fully seated in the groove, as poor sealing will allow contaminants to ruin the bore.

15. Position the O-rings in the cavities around the caliper transfer holes, and fit the caliper halves together. Install the bridge bolts (lubricated with brake fluid) and be sure to torque to specification.

16. Install the disc pads in the caliper and remount the caliper on the hub (see Disc Pad Replacement). Connect the brake line to the caliper and bleed the brakes (see Brake Bleeding). Replace the wheels. Recheck the brake fluid level, check the brake pedal travel, and road test the vehicle.

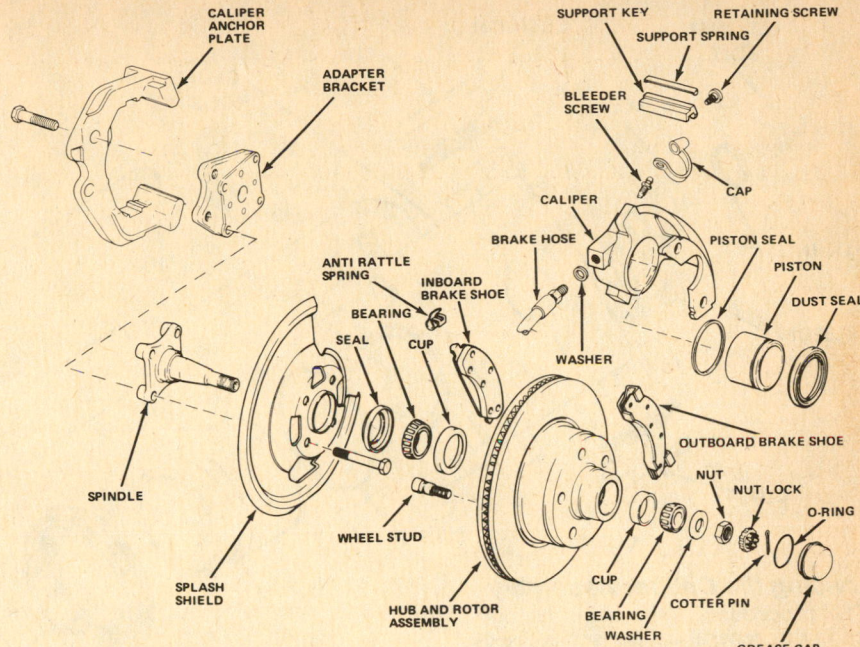

Bendix single piston disc brake (© American Motors Corp.)

BENDIX SINGLE PISTON BRAKE (AMERICAN MOTORS)

Service procedures are the same as outlined under Kelsey-Hayes Single Piston Brake (American Motors).

DELCO-MORAINE 4 PISTON BRAKE
Pad Replacement

1. Raise the car and remove the front wheels.

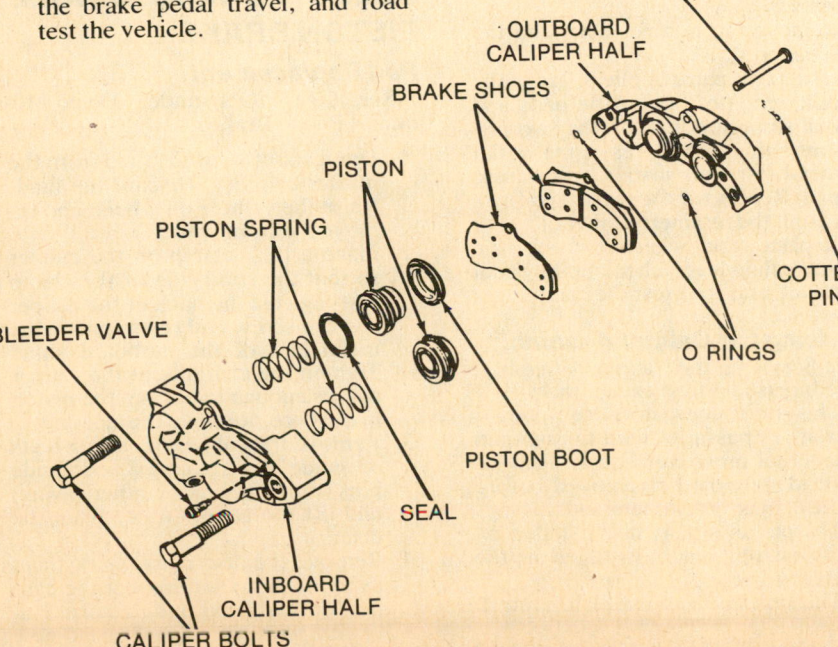

Delco Moraine four piston disc brake (© Chevrolet Div., G.M. Corp)

— CAUTION —

To prevent paint damage from brake fluid, be sure to remove part of brake fluid (don't re-use) from master cylinder and to keep the master cylinder covered. Do not allow cylinder to empty or air will be pumped into system.

2. Remove and discard the cotter pin from the end of the pad retaining pin. Remove the retaining pin or pins. If old pads are to be re-used, mark them so that they can be returned to their original positions.

3. Push one pad back so that it is as far away from the disc as possible. Remove that pad and replace it with a new one. Replace the second pad in the same manner. Pistons are spring loaded so it will be difficult to insert the new pad. To facilitate this job, use a stiff, long-bladed putty knife to hold back the pistons while inserting the new pad. If this fails to work, it may be necessary to release some of the fluid pressure by loosening the bleeder screw. This will require bleeding air from the system later.

NOTE: *Pads are interchangeable from inboard to outboard and right to left on most cars. Corvette pads have offset linings. The end with the most metal is installed toward the front. Shims must be replaced in their exact position.*

4. With new pads in place install the retaining pin and lock it in place with a new cotter pin.

5. Replace the wheels, check the brake fluid level, check brake pedal travel, and road test the car.

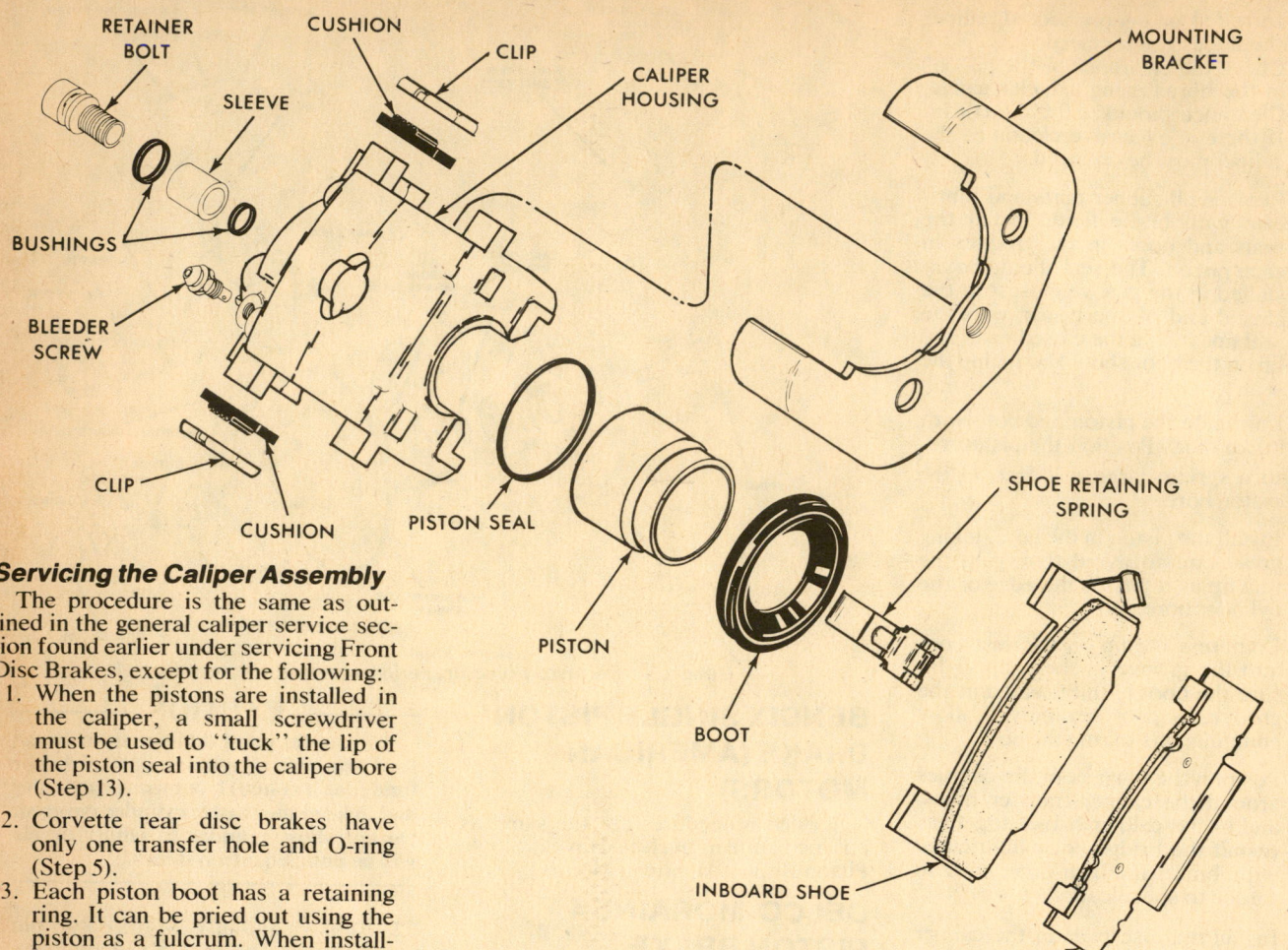

RETAINER BOLT · CUSHION · CLIP · CALIPER HOUSING · MOUNTING BRACKET · SLEEVE · BUSHINGS · BLEEDER SCREW · CLIP · CUSHION · PISTON SEAL · PISTON · BOOT · SHOE RETAINING SPRING · INBOARD SHOE · OUTBOARD SHOE

Delco-Moraine single piston disc brake used on Chevette (© Chevrolet Div., G.M. Corp.)

Servicing the Caliper Assembly

The procedure is the same as outlined in the general caliper service section found earlier under servicing Front Disc Brakes, except for the following:

1. When the pistons are installed in the caliper, a small screwdriver must be used to "tuck" the lip of the piston seal into the caliper bore (Step 13).
2. Corvette rear disc brakes have only one transfer hole and O-ring (Step 5).
3. Each piston boot has a retaining ring. It can be pried out using the piston as a fulcrum. When installing the ring in the piston bore make sure it is seated evenly flush or below the machined face of the caliper (Steps 6 & 13).
4. Piston to bore clearance should be from 0.0045-0.010 in. except Corvette rear which is 0.0035-0.009 in. (Step 10).
5. The piston seal lip faces toward the spring end of the piston, and the fold in the piston boot faces toward the seal (Step 14).
6. Slide the caliper over the disc. A putty knife can be used to hold back the pistons so that the caliper can be completely lowered into position. The caliper should be positioned carefully to avoid tearing the rubber boot on the edge of the disc. Secure the caliper to the mounting bracket and torque to specifications. Install the pads as instructed earlier (Step 16).
7. When the brake hose is connected it should not be twisted or touch other parts at any time during suspension or steering travel (Step 16).

KELSEY-HAYES 4 PISTON BRAKE

Pad Replacement

See CAUTION under Delco-Moraine 4 Piston Brake.

1. Raise the car and remove the front wheels.
2. Remove the retainer bolts and the retainer(s).
3. Using two pairs of pliers, grasp the outer ends of one of the pads and pull straight out. Push the two pistons into their bores using a flat metal bar and install a new disc pad. Repeat for the second pad.
4. Install the retainer(s) and bolts.
5. Replace the wheels, check the brake fluid level, check brake pedal travel, and road test the car.

Servicing the Caliper Assembly

See Servicing the Caliper Assembly. Procedure is identical except that:

1. This unit does not use internal transfer passages with O-rings, an external crossover line is used instead. It must be removed before the caliper is disassembled.
2. The piston seal is not installed on the piston, but is installed in the groove in the piston bore.
3. This unit does not use piston return springs.
4. Caliper is mounted on disc and then pads are installed.

DELCO-MORAINE SINGLE PISTON BRAKE

Pad Replacement

See CAUTION under Delco-Moraine 4 Piston Brake.

1. Drain about ²/₃ of the fluid from the master cylinder. Discard the fluid. Raise the vehicle on a hoist and remove the front wheels.
2. Place a "C" clamp on the caliper so that the solid side of the clamp rests against the back of the caliper and the screw end rests against the metal part of the outboard shoe. Tighten the clamp until the caliper moves enough to bottom the piston in the bore. Remove the clamp.
3. Remove the caliper mounting bolts or guide pin retainers and guide pins (throw the old retainers away) and lift the caliper away from the disc.
4. Remove the disc pads (mark them as to location) and inspect the caliper for fluid leaks and damage. Lubricate with silicon and install new sleeves and bushings in caliper ears.

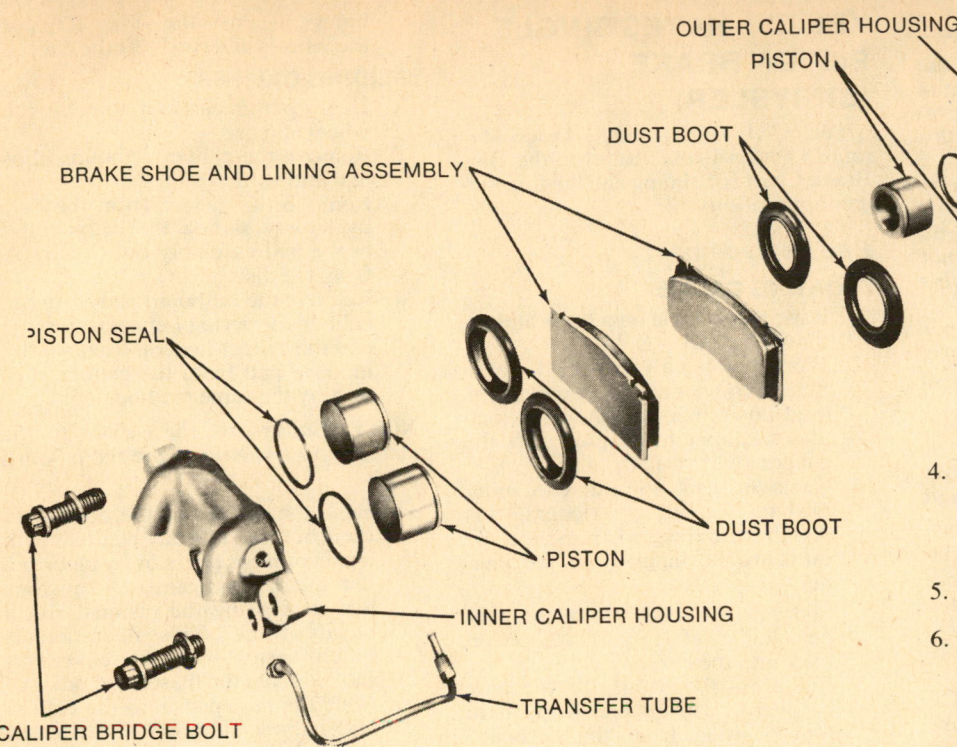

Kelsey-Hayes four piston disc brake (© Chrysler Corp)

5. Place the inboard pad in the caliper so that the bottom edge contacts the piston, and press the pad flat against the piston.

NOTE: *Most cars use a spring to locate the pad. The clip-type spring must be assembled onto the pad before the pad is placed over the piston.*

6. Place the outboard pad in the caliper so that the two ears on the pad fit over the ears on the caliper. Squeeze the ears on the pad tight around the caliper ears with a pair of pliers, except on subcompact cars.
7. Position the caliper assembly onto the disc, align the mounting holes, and make sure that the brake line isn't twisted.
8. Install the mounting bolts (making sure that they pass under the retaining ears on the inboard shoe) and torque to specification. On models with guide pins, install the mounting pins with new retainers.
9. On Chevette, clinch the outboard shoe tabs to the caliper with a pair of channel lock pliers.
10. Check the brake fluid level and pump the brake pedal to seat the linings against the disc. Replace the wheels and road test the car.

Servicing the Caliper Assembly

See CAUTION under Delco-Moraine 4 Piston Brake.
1. Raise the vehicle on a hoist and remove the front wheels.

2. Working on one side at a time only, disconnect the brake hose from the steel brake line and cap the fittings. Remove the U-shaped retainer from the hose fitting (if applicable).
3. Remove the caliper mounting bolts or guide pin retainers and guide pins (throw the old retainers away)
and lift the caliper away from the disc.
4. Clean the holes and the bushing grooves in the caliper ears, and wipe all dirt from the mounting bolts. If the bolts are corroded or damaged they should be replaced.
5. Remove the shoe support springs (if applicable) from the piston.
6. Remove the sleeves from the ears of the caliper with a suitable drift pin. Remove the rubber bushings from the grooves in the caliper ears.
7. Remove the brake hose, drain the brake fluid, and clean the outside of the caliper.
8. Pad the inside of the caliper with towels and direct compressed air into the brake fluid inlet hole to remove the piston.
9. Use a screwdriver to pry the boot out of the caliper. Avoid scratching the bore.

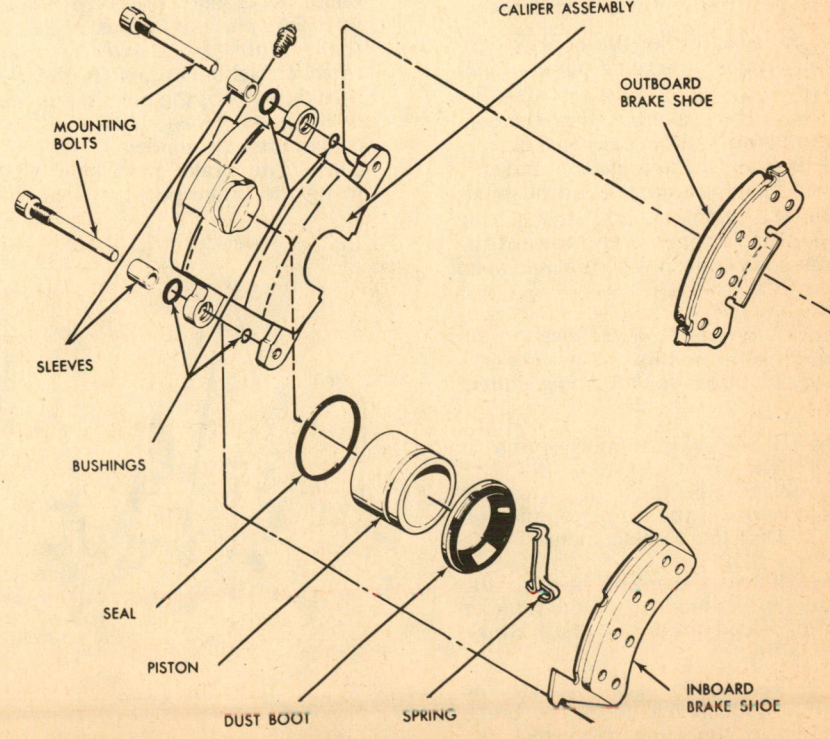

Delco-Moraine single piston disc brake (© Chevrolet Div., G.M. Corp)

— CAUTION —

To prevent damage to the piston use just enough air pressure to ease it out of the bore. Do not attempt to catch or protect the piston with the hand since this may cause serious injury.

---

10. Remove the piston seal from its groove in the caliper bore. *Do not use a metal tool of any type for this operation.*
11. Blow out all passages in the caliper and bleeder valve. Clean the piston and piston bore with fresh brake fluid.
12. Examine the piston for scoring, scratches, or corrosion. If any of these conditions exist the piston must be replaced, as it is plated and cannot be refinished.
13. Examine the bore for the same defects. Light rough spots may be removed by rotating crocus cloth, using finger pressure, in the bore. Do not polish with an in and out motion or use any other abrasive.
14. Lubricate the piston bore and the new rubber parts with fresh brake fluid. Position the seal in the piston bore groove.
15. Lubricate the piston with brake fluid and assemble the boot into the piston groove so that the fold faces the open end of the piston.
16. Insert the piston into the bore, taking care not to unseat the seal.
17. Force the piston to the bottom of the bore. (This will require a force of 50-100 lbs). Seat the boot lip around the caliper counterbore.

    Proper seating of the boot is very important for sealing out contaminants.
18. Install the brake hose into the caliper using a new copper gasket.
19. Lubricate the new sleeves and rubber bushings. Install the bushings in the caliper ears. Install the sleeves so that the end toward the disc pad is flush with the machined surface.

NOTE: *Lubrication of the sleeves and bushings is essential to ensure the proper operation of the sliding caliper design.*

20. Install the shoe support spring (if applicable) in the piston.
21. Install the disc pads in the caliper and remount the caliper on the hub (see Disc Pad Replacement).
22. Reconnect the brake hose to the steel brake line. Install the retainer clip. Bleed the brakes (see Brake Bleeding).
23. Replace the wheels, check the brake fluid level, check the brake pedal travel, and road test the vehicle.

KELSEY-HAYES SINGLE PISTON BRAKE (CHRYSLER)

See CAUTION under Delco-Moraine 4 Piston Brake. Refer to the Disc Brake Chart for sliding and floating caliper applications.

Pad Replacement

FLOATING CALIPER

1. Raise the vehicle on a hoist and remove front wheels.
2. Working on only one brake at a time, remove the caliper guide pins (and positioners, on AMC) which attach caliper to adapter. Lift the caliper away from the disc.
3. Remove (and discard) the inner bushings (and positioners, on AMC) from the guide pins, and the outboard bushings from the caliper.
4. Slide the disc pads out of the caliper, and carefully push the piston back into the bore.
5. Compress the flanges of the new outboard bushings and work them into position from the outboard side of the caliper.
6. Slide the new disc pads into position (outboard pad in the retaining spring) and carefully slide the caliper assembly over the rotor.
7. Compress the flanges of the new inner bushings and install them. Install new positioners on the guide pins with the open ends out on AMC models.
8. Install the guide pins from the inboard side and press in while threading pin into adapter. *Use extreme care to avoid crossing threads.* Tighten to 25-40 ft. lbs. Be sure the tabs of the positioners are over the machined surfaces of the caliper on AMC models.
9. Check the brake fluid level and pump the brake pedal to seat the linings against the disc. Replace the wheels and road test the car.

SLIDING CALIPER

1. Jack up the car and remove the wheel and tire.
2. Remove the caliper retaining clips and anti-rattle springs.
3. Remove the caliper from the disc by slowly sliding the caliper and brake pad assembly out and away from the disc.
4. Remove the outboard pad from the caliper by prying between the pad and the caliper fingers. Remove the inboard pad from the caliper support by the same method.

NOTE: *Safety-wire the caliper to the suspension while removing the inboard pad.*

5. Push the pistons to the bottom of their bores. This may be done with a pair of large pliers or by placing a flat metal bar against the pistons and depressing the pistons with a steady force. This operation is much easier with the cover removed from the master cylinder.
6. Slide the new pads into the caliper and caliper support. The ears of the pad should rest on the bridges of the caliper.

— CAUTION —

No free play should exist between the brake shoe flanges and the caliper fingers. Bend the flanges to eliminate free play.

---

7. Install the caliper on the disc and install the caliper retaining clips and anti-rattle springs. Install the retaining screws. Pump the brake pedal until it is firm.

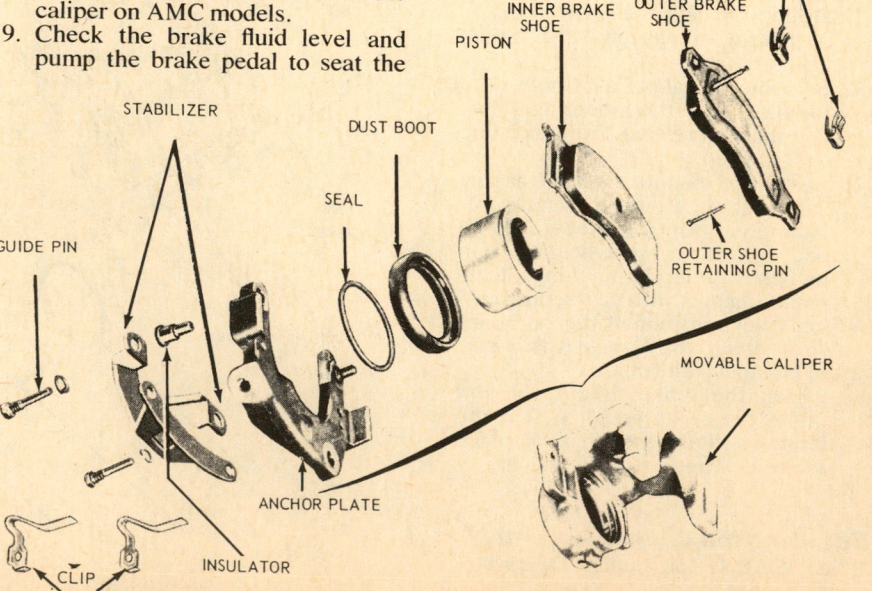

Kelsey-Hayes single piston disc brake—Ford (© Ford Motor Co)

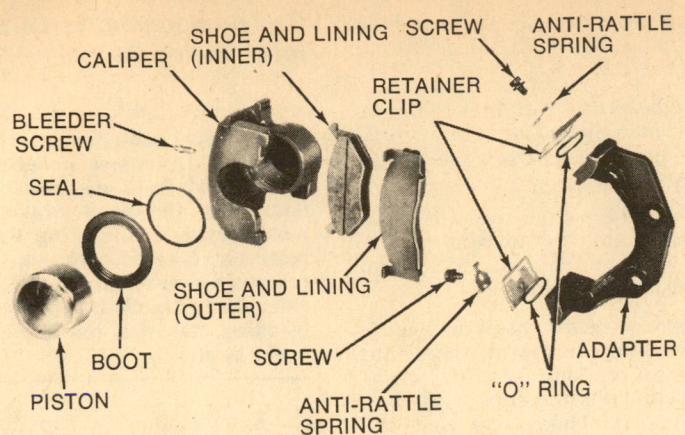

CALIPER

SHOE AND LINING (INNER)

SCREW

ANTI-RATTLE SPRING

RETAINER CLIP

BLEEDER SCREW

SEAL

SHOE AND LINING (OUTER)

SCREW

BOOT

PISTON

ANTI-RATTLE SPRING

"O" RING

ADAPTER

Kelsey-Hayes single piston sliding caliper disc brake—Chrysler (© Chrysler Corp)

Servicing the Caliper Assembly
FLOATING CALIPER

1. Remove the caliper assembly from the car *without* disconnecting the hydraulic line.
2. Support the caliper assembly on the upper control arm and surround it with shop towels to absorb any brake fluid. Slowly depress the brake pedal until the piston is pushed out of its bore.

—— CAUTION ——

Do not use compressed air to force the piston from its bore; injury could result.

3. Disconnect the brake line from the caliper and plug it to prevent fluid loss.
4. Mount the caliper in a soft-jawed vise and clamp lightly. Do not tighten the vise too much or the caliper will become distorted.
5. Work the dust boot out with your fingers.
6. Use a small pointed *wooden* or *plastic* stick to work the piston seal out of the groove in the bore. Discard the seal.

—— CAUTION ——

Using a screwdriver or other metal tool could scratch the piston bore.

7. Using the same wooden or plastic stick, press the outer bushings out of the housing. Discard the old bushings. Remove the inner bush-

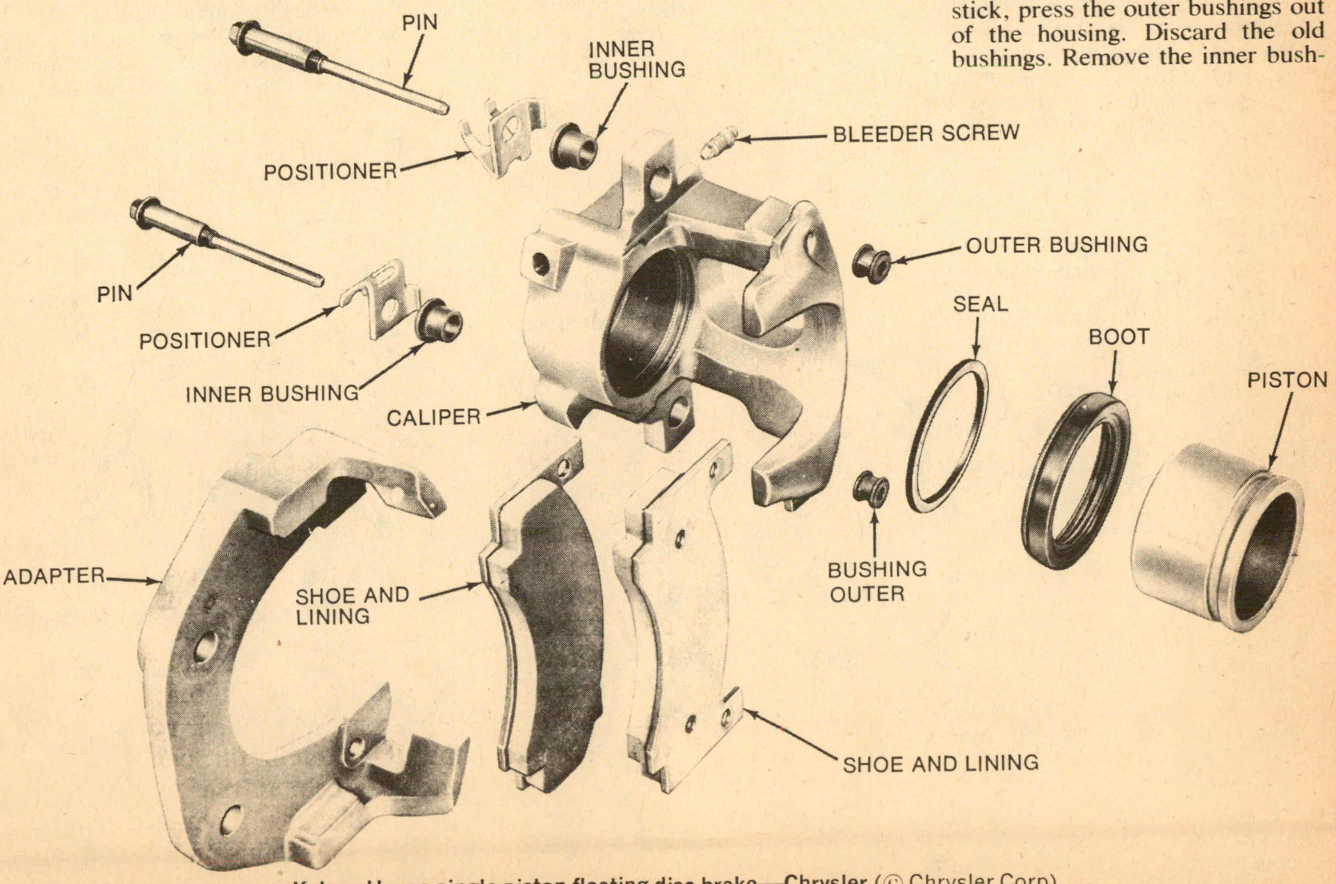

8. Check the fluid level in the master cylinder and add fluid as needed.
9. Install the wheel and tire.

Caliper Removal and Installation

1. Raise the car and support it securely with jackstands.
2. Remove the wheel and tire assembly from the car.
3. Detach the brake hose from the frame mounting bracket. Disconnect the intermediate hose bracket on Volare/Aspen. Plug the brake tube to prevent fluid loss.

4. a. On floating caliper, remove the guide pins (and positioners, on AMC) attaching the caliper to the adapter.
   b. On sliding caliper, remove the screw, clip, and anti-rattle spring attaching the caliper to the adapter.
5. Slide the caliper assembly away from the disc. Hold the outboard pad while doing this so that it can't fall out.
6. Remove the pads if the caliper is being overhauled.
7. Install the calipers. Connect the brake hose and bleed the brake system.

PIN

POSITIONER

PIN

POSITIONER

INNER BUSHING

ADAPTER

SHOE AND LINING

INNER BUSHING

BLEEDER SCREW

OUTER BUSHING

SEAL

BOOT

PISTON

BUSHING OUTER

CALIPER

SHOE AND LINING

Kelsey-Hayes single piston floating disc brake—Chrysler (© Chrysler Corp)

ings in the same manner. Discard them as well.

8. Clean all parts in denatured alcohol or brake fluid. Blow out all bores and passages with compressed air.

9. Inspect the piston and bore for scoring or pitting. Replace the piston if necessary. Bores with light scratches or corrosion may be cleaned with crocus cloth. Bores with deep scratches may be honed if you do not increase the bore diameter more than 0.002 in. Replace the housing if the bore must be enlarged beyond this.

NOTE: *Black stains are caused by piston seals and are harmless.*

10. If the bore had to be honed, clean its grooves with a stiff, non-metallic rotary brush. Clean the bore twice by flushing it out with brake fluid and drying it with a soft, lint-free cloth.

Caliper assembly is as follows:

1. Clamp the caliper in a soft-jawed vise; do not overtighten.

2. Dip a new piston seal in brake fluid or the lubricant supplied with the rebuilding kit. Position the new seal in one area of its groove and gently work it into place with clean fingers, so that it is correctly seated. Do not use an old seal.

3. Coat a new boot with brake fluid or lubricant (as above), leaving a generous amount inside.

4. Insert the boot in the caliper and work it into the groove, using your fingers only. The boot will snap into place once it is correctly positioned. Run your forefinger around the inside of the boot to make sure that it is correctly seated.

5. Install the bleed screw in its hole and plug the fluid inlet on the caliper.

6. Coat the piston with brake fluid or lubricant. Spread the boot with your fingers and work the piston into the boot.

7. Depress the piston; this will force the boot into its groove on the piston. Remove the plug and bottom the piston in the bore.

8. Compress the flanges of new guide pin bushings and work them into place by pressing *in* on the bushings with your fingertips, until they are seated. Make sure that the flanges cover the housing evenly on all sides.

9. Install the caliper on the car as previously outlined.

SLIDING CALIPER

The overhaul procedure for these calipers is identical to that for the floating caliper, except that there are no guide pin bushings to be removed or installed.

KELSEY-HAYES SINGLE PISTON BRAKE (AMERICAN MOTORS)

For disc brake service procedures for AMC models through 1974, see the floating caliper service sections for "Kelsey-Hayes Single Piston Brake (Chrysler)."

Pad Replacement—1975 and later Sliding Caliper

— CAUTION —

To prevent paint damage from leaking brake fluid, remove about 2/3 of the brake fluid from the larger reservoir (supplying the front brakes), in the master cylinder and keep the cylinder reservoir covered. Do not allow the reservoir level to get too low or air will enter the hydraulic system, necessitating bleeding. Do not reuse the removed brake fluid.

1. Remove the hub caps and loosen the front wheel lug nuts slightly. Firmly apply the parking brake and block the rear wheels.

2. Raise the front of the car and install jackstands beneath the front jacking points or lower control arms. Remove the front wheels.

3. Working on only one caliper at a time, bottom the caliper piston in its bore by carefully inserting a screwdriver between the piston and the inboard shoe and prying back on the piston.

NOTE: *Take care not to damage the rubber piston seals. If the piston cannot be bottomed with a screwdriver, a large C-clamp will suffice.*

4. Using a 1/4 in. hex key or allen wrench, remove the caliper support key retaining screw.

5. Remove the caliper support key and support spring using a punch pin and hammer. Lift the caliper

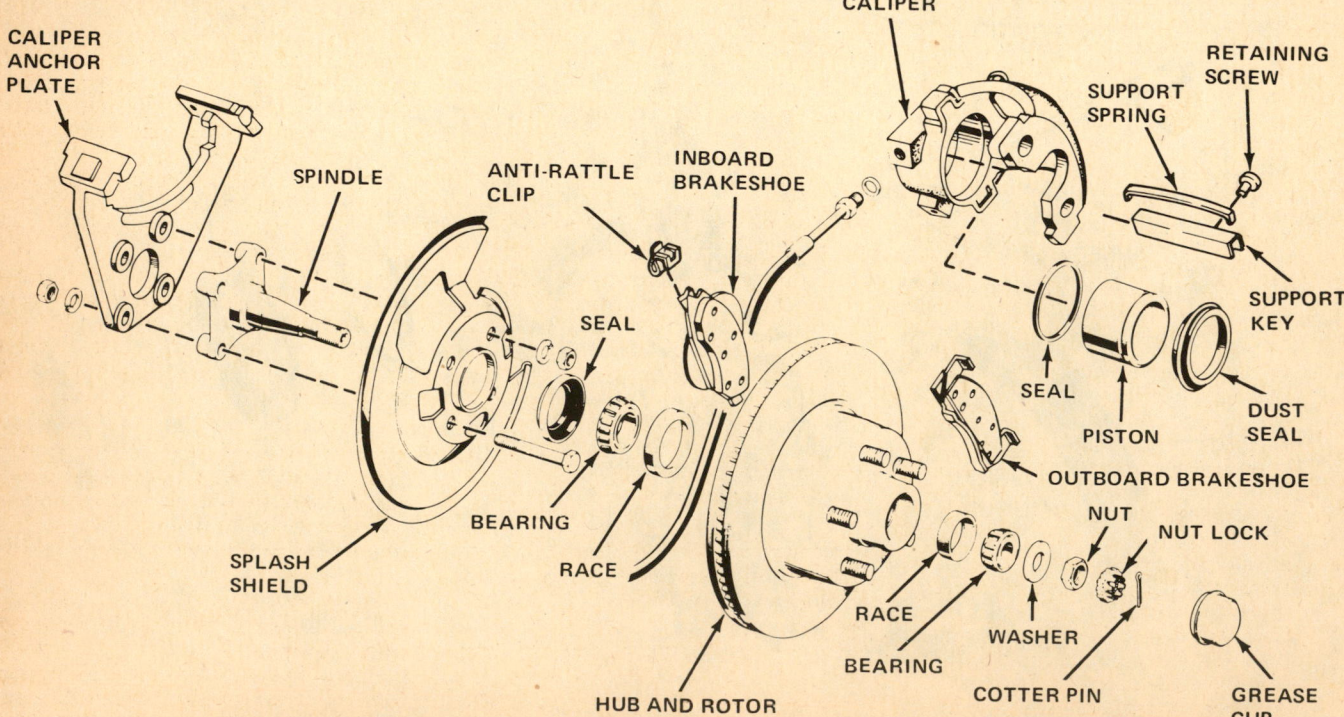

Kelsey-Hayes single piston sliding caliper disc brake—AMC (© American Motors Corp.)

assembly off its anchor plate and over the rotor (disc).

NOTE: *Do not allow the caliper to hang by its flexible brake hose. Use a piece of heavy wire to suspend the caliper from the coil spring until you are ready to reinstall it.*

6. Remove the inboard brake shoe from the anchor plate. Remove the inboard brake shoe anti-rattle spring from the inboard shoe, noting its position for reassembly.
7. Remove the outboard brake shoe from the caliper, rapping lightly

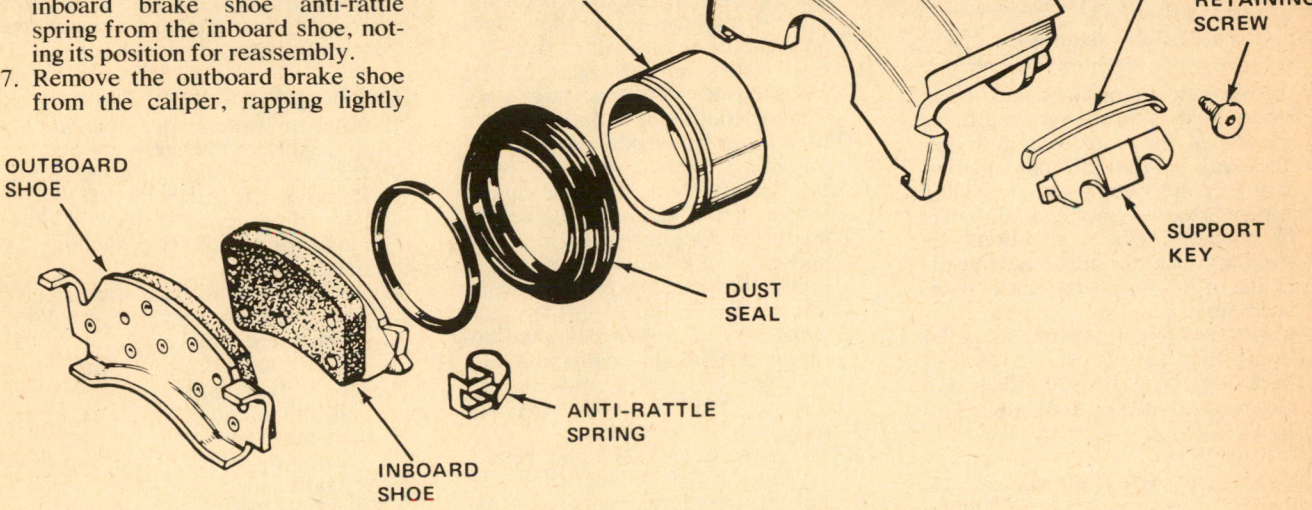

Caliper details—AMC sliding caliper disc brake (© American Motors Corp.)

with a hammer, if necessary, to free it from the caliper.
8. Wipe the inside of the caliper free of all accumulated brake pad dust, road dirt and other foreign material with a clean, dry rag.

NOTE: *Do not blow the caliper clean with compressed air as this may dislodge the rubber dust cover.*

Check the piston seals for evidence of leakage from the piston bore, and overhaul the caliper if necessary. Clean all rust and dirt from the abutment (sliding), surfaces of the caliper and caliper anchor plate using a wire brush and crocus cloth. Then, lightly grease the sliding surfaces with white grease to ensure that the sliding motion of the caliper is not impaired.

9. Install the inboard brake shoe anti-rattle spring on the rear flange of the inboard brake shoe, making sure that the looped section of the clip is facing away from the rotor.
10. Install the assembled inboard brake shoe and anti-rattle spring in the caliper anchor plate, taking care not to dislodge the anti-rattle spring during installation.
11. Install the outboard brake shoe in the caliper, making sure to seat the shoe flange fully, into the outboard arms of the caliper.
12. Install the caliper assembly over the rotor and into position in the anchor plate. Exercise extreme care when installing the caliper not to tear or dislodge the piston dust cover on the inboard brake shoe.
13. Align the caliper assembly with the abutment surfaces of the anchor

plate and insert the caliper support key and support spring between the abutment surfaces at the rearward end of the caliper and anchor plate. Then using a hammer and drift pin, drive the caliper support key and spring into position. Install the support key retaining screw and tighten to 15 ft lbs.
14. Fill the master cylinder reservoir to within 1/4 in. of the rim. Press the brake pedal firmly several times to seat the shoes.
15. Install the wheels and lower the car. Road-test the car after rechecking the fluid level and checking for firm brake pedal.

Servicing the 1975 and Later Sliding Caliper Assembly

1. Remove the caliper as in Steps 1-7 of "Disc Pad Replacement."
2. Place a clean piece of paper on your work area to put the parts of the caliper on while it is being disassembled.
3. Drain the brake fluid from the caliper by opening the bleeder plug.
4. Place the caliper assembly in a vise with padded jaws.

—— **CAUTION** ——
Do not overtighten the vise; too much pressure will cause distortion of the caliper bore.

5. Using compressed air, remove the piston from the caliper bore. Be careful not to damage the piston or the bore. Leave the dust boot in

the caliper groove while the piston is being removed.
6. Take the caliper out of the vise and withdraw the dust boot.
7. Work the piston seal out of its groove in the piston bore with a small, pointed wooden or plastic stick. Do not use a screwdriver or other metallic tool to remove the seal as it could damage the bore. Throw the old seal away.
8. Unscrew the bleeder plug.
9. Clean all of the parts in brake fluid *(do not use solvent)* and wipe them dry with a clean, lint-free cloth. Dry the passages and bores with compressed air.

Check the cylinder bore for scoring, pitting, and/or corrosion. If the caliper bore is deeply scored or corroded, replace the entire caliper.

If it is only lightly scored or stained, polish with crocus cloth. Use finger-pressure to rotate the crocus cloth in the cylinder bore. Any black stains found in the bore are caused by seals and are harmless.

—— **CAUTION** ——
Do not slide the crocus cloth in and out of the bore. Do not use any other type of abrasive material.

Check the piston. If it is pitted, scored, or worn, it should be replaced with a new one.

Check the piston-to-bore clearance with a feeler gauge. It should be 0.002-0.006 in. If it is more than this, replace the caliper assembly.

Disc Brakes

Assembly and installation are as follows:

1. Dip a new piston seal in clean brake fluid. Position the seal in one area of the groove in the cylinder bore and gently work it into place around the groove until it is seated. Be sure that your fingers are clean before touching the seal.

CAUTION

Never reuse an old piston seal.

---

2. Coat a new piston boot with clean brake fluid. Work it into the outer groove of the bore with your fingers until it snaps into place. Don't worry if the boot seems too large for the groove; once seated, it will fit properly. Check the boot, by running your forefinger around the inside of it, to be sure that it is correctly installed.
3. Coat the piston with plenty of brake fluid. Spread the boot with your fingers and insert the piston
4. Depress the piston until it bottoms in the boot.

CAUTION

Apply uniform force to the piston or it will crack.

---

5. Install the caliper assembly as in Steps 9-15 of "Pad Replacement."

KELSEY-HAYES SINGLE PISTON FLOATING CALIPER BRAKE (FORD)
Pad Replacement

FORD, MERCURY, AND LINCOLN THROUGH 1972

1. Check brake fluid level in the large (primary) reservoir of the master cylinder. Remove enough fluid so that this reservoir is only half full. Do not re-use this fluid, throw it away.
2. Remove the wheel and tire assembly.
3. Remove the inboard pad hold down clips.
4. Using a small screwdriver, remove the retaining clips from the outboard pad and remove the pad.
5. Remove the caliper locating pins (2) from the back of the caliper.
6. Remove the upper stabilizer.
7. Remove the caliper assembly from the anchor plate and detach the outboard pad and retaining pins from the caliper.
8. Using a piece of wire, hang the caliper from the upper control arm.
9. Remove the caliper locating pin insulators from the anchor plate.
10. Remove the inboard pad and inspect the disc surfaces for wear.

11. Install the inboard pad to the anchor plate. Insert new locating pin insulators into the anchor plate.
NOTE: *When replacing pads, install new stabilizer, insulators, shoe clips and pins. It may help to wet insulators with water before installing.*
12. Install the inboard pad hold down clips and tighten bolts.
13. The piston must be fully retracted into the cylinder before the caliper and pad assembly will fit over the disc. Retracting the piston can be made easier by fabricating a retracting tool using a bolt, a nut, a used outer brake pad and a retaining spring.
14. Position the tool onto the caliper holding it in place with the retaining spring. Gradually turn in on the bolt pausing to allow the piston to pull in the seal. Make sure the piston is fully bottomed in the cylinder to create proper clearance between the pads. Inspect piston dust boot and replace if cracked. See Servicing the Caliper Assembly for replacement procedures.
15. Install the outer brake pad, retaining pins and new retainer clips.
16. Join the caliper assembly to the anchor plate.
17. Install the stabilizers to caliper.
18. Check the brake fluid level and pump the brake pedal to seat the pads against the disc. Install the wheels and road test the car.

MUSTANG AND COUGAR THROUGH 1973

1. Make sure large master cylinder reservoir is only half full.
2. Remove the front wheel and tire.
3. Disconnect and plug the brake line if necessary.
4. Remove the caliper locating pins and stabilizer bolts.
5. Lift caliper off disc. If working on both wheels, mark calipers right or left.
6. Remove the inboard pad hold down clips and the pin insulators from the anchor plate.
7. Remove the inboard pad.
8. Using a small screwdriver, lift the outer pad retaining clips off the retaining pins. Remove the outer pad.
9. Insert new caliper locating pin insulators in the anchor plate.
10. Install the inboard pad retaining clips.
11. Using a piston retracting tool (see steps 13 & 14 of Disc Pad Replacement for Ford, Mercury, etc.), push the piston completely into its cylinder.
12. Install outer pad and retaining clips.
13. Install the caliper onto the disc being careful not to pinch the piston boot between the inner pad and the piston.

14. Attach a new stabilizer to the caliper with clean locating pins.
15. Attach the stabilizer to the anchor plate.
16. Connect brake hose (if previously disconnected) using new copper washers, one on each side of the hose fitting. Bleed brakes.
17. Check the brake fluid level and pump the brake pedal to seat the pads against the disc. Install the wheels and road test the car.

Servicing the Caliper Assembly

1. Raise the vehicle on a hoist and remove the front wheels.
2. Disconnect and plug the brake line.
3. Remove the lockwires from the two caliper mounting bolts and remove the bolt. Lift the caliper off the disc.
4. Remove and discard the locating pin insulators. Replace all rubber parts at reassembly.
5. Remove the retaining clips with a screwdriver and slide the outboard pad and retaining pins out of the caliper. Remove the inboard pad. Loosen the bleed screw and drain the brake fluid.
6. Remove the two small bolts and caliper stabilizers.
7. Remove the inboard pad retaining clips and bolts.
8. Clean and inspect all parts, and reinstall on anchor plate. Do not tighten stabilizer bolts at this time.
9. Remove the piston by applying compressed air to the fluid inlet hole. Use care to prevent the piston from popping out of control.

CAUTION

Do not attempt to catch the piston with your hand. Use folded towels to cushion it.

---

10. Remove the piston boot. Inspect the piston for scoring, pitting, or corrosion. The piston must be replaced if there is any visible damage or wear.
11. Remove the piston seal from the cylinder bore. *Do not use any metal tools for this operation.*
12. Clean the caliper with fresh brake fluid. Inspect the cylinder bore for damage or wear. Light defects can be removed by rotating crocus cloth around the bore. Do not use any other type of abrasive.
13. Lubricate all new rubber parts in brake fluid. Install the piston seal in the cylinder groove. Install the boot into its piston groove.
14. Install the piston, open end out, into the bore while working the boot around the outside of the piston. Make sure boot lip is seated in the piston groove.
15. Slide the anchor plate assembly onto the caliper housing and reinstall the locating pins. Tighten pins to specification. Tighten stabilizer

anchor plate bolts. Perform Steps 4-8 of Disc Pad Replacement.

16. Connect the brake line and bleed the brakes (see Brake Bleeding).
17. Install the front wheels, recheck the brake fluid level, and road test the car.

FORD SINGLE PISTON SLIDING CALIPER BRAKE

Pad Replacement

ALL MODELS EXCEPT PINTO THROUGH 1973 AND FAIRMONT/ZEPHYR

1. Raise the car, safely support it and remove the tire and wheel assembly.
2. Remove the retaining screw from the caliper retaining key.
3. Using a hammer and drift, remove the caliper retaining key and support spring from the anchor plate. Be careful not to damage key.
4. Push the caliper down against the anchor plate and rotate the upper end off the anchor plate.
5. Remove the inboard pad from the anchor plate. Do not lose the anti-rattle clip. Tap lightly on the outer pad to free it from the caliper. If the original pads are to be reused, mark them as to location for correct installation.
6. Clean all components and inspect for damage, leakage and excessive wear.

NOTE: *If the pads on one wheel are replaced it is necessary to replace those on the other wheel to maintain equal braking action.*

7. When installing new pads, use a 4 in. C-clamp and a block of wood measuring 1³/₄ in. x 1 in. x ³/₄ in. thick. This will aid in seating the piston in its cylinder so that the caliper will fit over the new pads when installed.
8. Install the anti-rattle clip on the lower inboard pad support located on the anchor plate (on the lower end of the inner pad, starting 1974). The loop of the clip must be toward the inside of the plate. Place the inner pad on the anchor plate.
9. Install the outer pad with the upper flanges over the shoulders on the caliper legs. If the old pads are reused, be certain they are installed in their original positions.
10. If previously used, remove the C-clamp from the caliper since the piston will remain seated in its cylinder.
11. Position the caliper assembly lower V-groove on the anchor plate lower abutment surface.
12. Pivot the caliper housing upward toward the disc until the outer edge of the piston dust boot is about ¹/₄ in. from the upper edge of inboard pad.

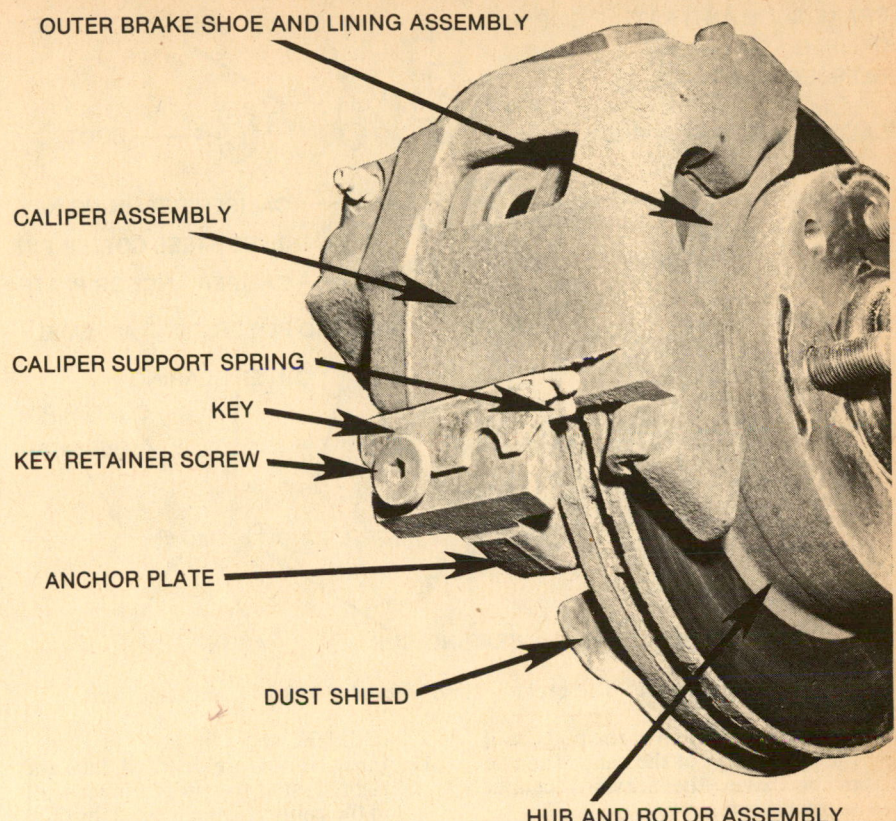

OUTER BRAKE SHOE AND LINING ASSEMBLY

CALIPER ASSEMBLY

CALIPER SUPPORT SPRING

KEY

KEY RETAINER SCREW

ANCHOR PLATE

DUST SHIELD

HUB AND ROTOR ASSEMBLY

Ford Sliding caliper disc brake—all models except Pinto through 1973
(© Ford Motor Co)

13. Place a piece of thin cardboard between the inboard pad and the lower half of the piston dust boot to prevent pinching of the boot when rotating the caliper onto the disc.
14. Continue to rotate the caliper onto the disc until a slight resistance is felt.
15. Gradually remove the cardboard as the caliper rotates onto the disc. Complete the rotation onto the disc and completely remove the cardboard.
16. Slide the caliper up against the upper anchor plate abutment and center it over the lower anchor plate abutment.
17. Install the caliper support spring and key into the opening between the lower end of the caliper and the lower anchor plate abutment. The hole in the slot must be centered over the threaded hole in the anchor plate.
18. Install the key retaining screw and torque to 12-16 ft. lbs.
19. Check the brake fluid level and pump the brake pedal to seat the pads against the disc. Install the wheels and road test the car.

PINTO THROUGH 1973

1. Raise car and support safely. Remove wheel and tire assembly.
2. Remove the two cotter pins from the retaining key.
3. Using a hammer and drift, carefully remove the key.
4. Push in on the caliper assembly and lift it away from the anchor plate.

NOTE: *Do not stretch or twist the brake hose.*

5. Using wire, temporarily suspend the caliper assembly from the upper suspension arms.
6. If brake pads are to be reused, mark them as to correct location.
7. Remove the pads from the anchor plate.
8. Clean the caliper, anchor plate and disc and inspect them for leakage, damage or excessive wear.

NOTE: *If the shoes are replaced on one wheel they must also be replaced on the other wheel to maintain balanced brake action.*

9. When installing new pads, it is necessary to compress the piston in its cylinder to provide enough clearance for the caliper to fit over the pads. To perform this, place a block of wood (1³/₄" x 1" x ³/₄" thick) on the piston and clamp down on it with a 4 in. C-clamp.
10. Place pads and anti-rattle clips in anchor plate.
11. Remove the C-clamp from the piston and remove the wire holding the caliper to the suspension arm.
12. Place the caliper on the anchor plate so that the lower edge of the caliper is on top of the rear caliper support spring.

Disc Brakes

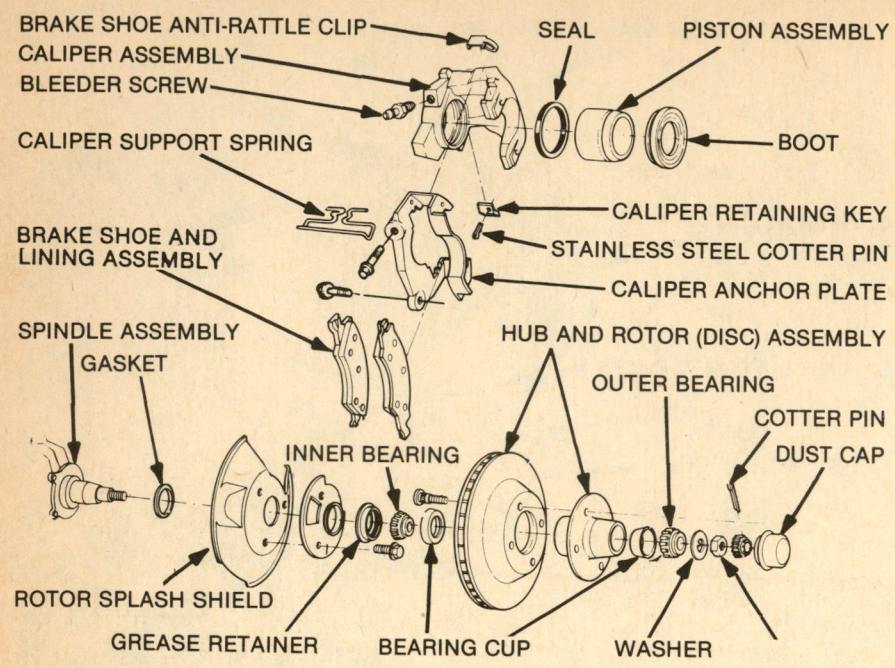

BRAKE SHOE ANTI-RATTLE CLIP
CALIPER ASSEMBLY
BLEEDER SCREW
CALIPER SUPPORT SPRING
BRAKE SHOE AND LINING ASSEMBLY
SPINDLE ASSEMBLY
GASKET
ROTOR SPLASH SHIELD
GREASE RETAINER
BEARING CUP
INNER BEARING
WASHER
SEAL
PISTON ASSEMBLY
BOOT
CALIPER RETAINING KEY
STAINLESS STEEL COTTER PIN
CALIPER ANCHOR PLATE
HUB AND ROTOR (DISC) ASSEMBLY
OUTER BEARING
COTTER PIN
DUST CAP

Ford sliding caliper disc brake—Pinto through 1973 (© Ford Motor Co)

13. Pivot the caliper over the pads until the upper edge of the caliper can be pushed over the forward caliper support spring.
14. Using a heavy screwdriver, hold the caliper over the upper support spring and against the anchor plate. Insert the retaining key.
15. Install two new stainless steel cotter pins in the key.
16. Check the brake fluid level and pump the brake pedal to seat the pads against the disc. Install the wheels and road test the car.

FAIRMONT/ZEPHYR

1. Remove about half of the fluid from the master cylinder reservoir.
2. Loosen the lug nuts and raise and support the vehicle.
3. Remove the front wheel. Be careful to avoid damage to the caliper splash shield or bleed screw.
4. Remove the caliper locating pins. Remove the caliper assembly from the integral spindle anchor plate and rotor. Remove the outer shoe from the caliper.
5. Remove the inner shoe and inspect the rotor surfaces.
6. Secure the caliper assembly with a length of wire.
7. Remove and discard the plastic bushings inside the caliper locating pin insulators.
8. Remove and discard the locating insulators.
9. Using a 4 inch C-clamp and a $2^3/_4$ x 1 x $^1/_4$ in. piece of wood, seat the piston in its bore.
10. Install new insulators and sleeves in the caliper housing. Both insulator flanges must straddle the housing holes and the sleeves must bottom in the insulators as well as

under the upper lip.
11. Inner shoes are marked left and right. Install the proper inner shoe in the caliper. Do not bend the clips too far or they will become distorted.
12. Outer shoes are marked left and right. Install the proper outer shoe making sure that the clip and buttons are properly seated.
13. Refill the master cylinder.
14. Install the wheel, lower the car and test the brakes.

Servicing the Caliper Assembly

ALL MODELS EXCEPT PINTO THROUGH 1973 AND FAIRMONT/ZEPHYR

To service the caliper on these models, follow the instructions listed for the same models under Pad Replacement. The instructions are identical with one exception—caliper service requires you to disconnect and connect the brake hose from the caliper and bleed the brakes. If it is necessary to remove and install piston, follow steps 6-12 of Pinto through 1973.

PINTO THROUGH 1973

1. Raise the car and support safely. Remove the wheel and tire assembly.
2. Disconnect the brake hose from the caliper.
3. Remove the two cotter pins from the retaining key.
4. Using a drift and hammer, remove the retaining key.
5. Press inward on the caliper assembly pad and lift it away from the anchor plate.
6. Remove the piston by applying air pressure to the caliper fluid port.

IMPORTANT: *To prevent piston damage and possible personal injury, place a cloth over the piston before applying air pressure.*

7. If the piston is seized in its cylinder, tap lightly around the piston while applying air pressure.
8. Remove and discard the piston dust boot and seal.
9. Clean (using alcohol) and inspect all parts for damage or excessive wear. Replace the piston if pitted or scored or if the chrome plating is worn off.
10. Lightly coat a new piston seal with clean brake fluid and seat it in the piston groove.
11. Install a new dust boot with its flange in the outer groove of the cylinder.
12. Coat the piston with fluid and install in the cylinder. Spread the dust boot over the piston while inserting it in cylinder and seat it in the piston groove.
13. Place the caliper on the anchor plate so that the lower edge of the caliper can be pushed over the forward caliper support spring.
14. Using a heavy screwdriver, hold the caliper over the upper support spring and against the anchor plate. Insert the retaining key.
15. Install two new stainless steel cotter pins in the key.
16. Connect the brake hose and bleed the brakes.
17. Check the brake fluid lever and pump the brake pedal to seat the pads against the disc.

FAIRMONT/ZEPHYR

1. Loosen the front wheel lug nuts.
2. Raise and support the car.
3. Remove the front wheel taking care to avoid damage to the splash shield and bleeder screw.
4. Loosen the flexible brake hose-to-brake tube fitting at the frame and remove the horseshoe type retaining clip from the hose and bracket. Remove the hose from the bracket and unscrew it from the caliper.
NOTE: *If both calipers are being removed, mark them left and right.*
5. Remove the caliper locating pins.
6. Lift the caliper from the rotor.
7. Place a wadded cloth in front of the piston and apply compressed air at the hose hole.

--- **CAUTION** ---

Never attempt to stop the piston with your hand. The piston can emerge from its bore with considerable force due to built-up air pressure.

8. Remove the dust boot and piston seal.
9. Clean all metal parts in isopropyl alcohol. Dry all parts with compressed air.
10. Coat all parts with clean brake fluid before installing. Make certain that the seal does not become twisted,

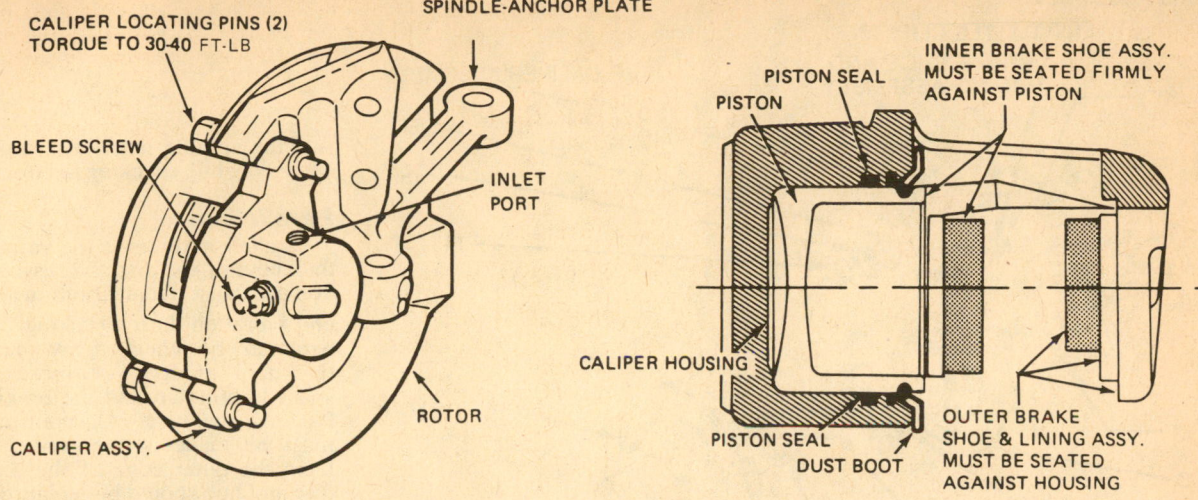

CALIPER LOCATING PINS (2)
TORQUE TO 30-40 FT-LB

SPINDLE-ANCHOR PLATE

BLEED SCREW

INLET PORT

CALIPER ASSY.

ROTOR

CALIPER ASSEMBLY INSTALLED
L.H. SIDE SHOWN

PISTON SEAL

PISTON

INNER BRAKE SHOE ASSY.
MUST BE SEATED FIRMLY
AGAINST PISTON

CALIPER HOUSING

PISTON SEAL

DUST BOOT

OUTER BRAKE
SHOE & LINING ASSY.
MUST BE SEATED
AGAINST HOUSING

CALIPER SECTIONAL VIEW (TYPICAL)

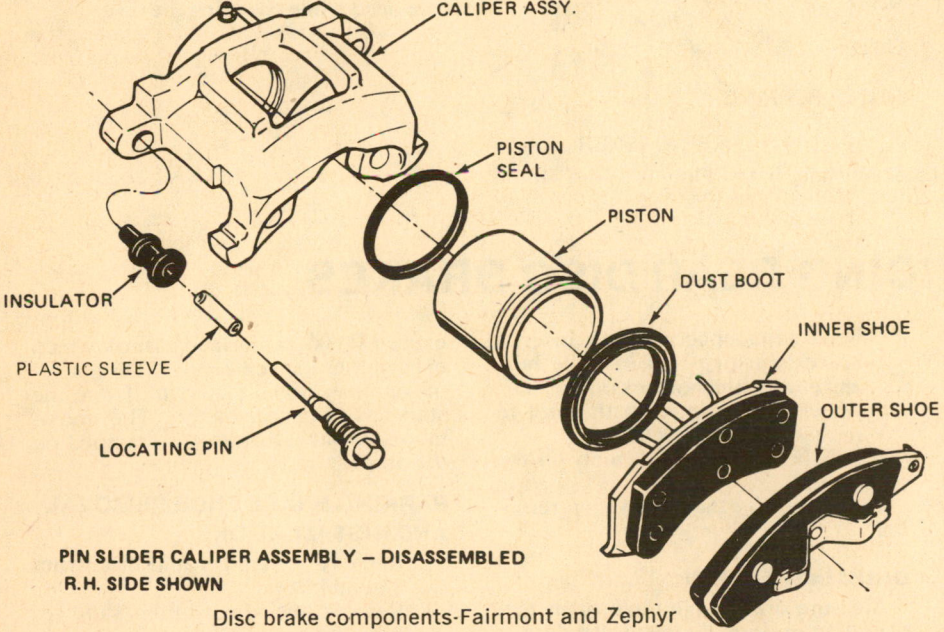

CALIPER ASSY.

PISTON SEAL

PISTON

DUST BOOT

INNER SHOE

OUTER SHOE

INSULATOR

PLASTIC SLEEVE

LOCATING PIN

PIN SLIDER CALIPER ASSEMBLY – DISASSEMBLED
R.H. SIDE SHOWN

Disc brake components-Fairmont and Zephyr

and that it is firmly seated in its groove.

11. Install a new dust boot and insert the piston in its bore. Spread the dust boot over the piston as it's installed.

12. Position the caliper over the rotor with the outer shoe against the rotor braking surface to prevent pinching the boot.

13. Connect the locating pins to the anchor plate and insulators. Be sure the locating pins are free of dirt, grease or oil.

14. Torque the locating pins to 30-40 ft. lbs.

15. Install the flexible hose into the caliper and torque it to 20-30 ft. lbs.

NOTE: *It is not necessary for the hose to be flush with the caliper when tightened; two or three threads may be visible when properly torqued. Do not over-torque.*

16. Connect the upper end of the hose. Tighten the fitting nut to 10-18 ft. lbs.

17. Bleed the system and center the differential valve. Fill the master cylinder.

SERVICING THE DISC— ALL CARS

Disc Replacement

1. Raise the vehicle on a hoist and remove the wheel.

2. Remove the caliper mounting bolts. Slide the caliper away from the disc and suspend it using a wire loop. On some cars, it is advisable to install a cardboard spacer between the pads to prevent the piston from coming out of its cylinder.

3. Remove the wheel bearing nut from the spindle and remove the

outer wheel bearing roller assembly from the hub.

On Ford sliding caliper brakes, remove the wheel bearing adjusting nut and pull the hub and disc assembly outward enough to loosen the washer and outer wheel bearing. Push the assembly back onto the spindle and remove the washer and outer wheel bearing from the spindle.

4. Remove the hub and disc assembly from the spindle.

5. Installation of hub and disc is in reverse order of removal.

NOTE: *The disc is removable from the hub on the Eldorado, Toronado, and Corvette (rear only).*

To separate the rear disc and hub on a Corvette the three hub-to-disc attaching rivets must be drilled out. This can be done with the hub and rotor mounted on the car. It is not necessary to install new rivets when the disc is installed.

Lateral Runout

Lateral runout is the movement of the disc from side to side (wobble) as it rotates. Excessive runout will result in brake chatter, pedal pumping, excessive pedal travel, or vibration during braking.

To check lateral runout:

1. Tighten the spindle nut until there is no end-play in the bearings, just loose enough to allow wheel to turn.

2. Fasten a dial indicator to the suspension so that the point contacts the disc face about 1/2 in. from the outer edge.

3. Set the dial to zero. Turn the disc through one complete revolution and check the indicator as the disc moves.

If the runout is more than the allowable maximum the disc and hub assembly should be replaced. Be sure to read-

Disc Brakes

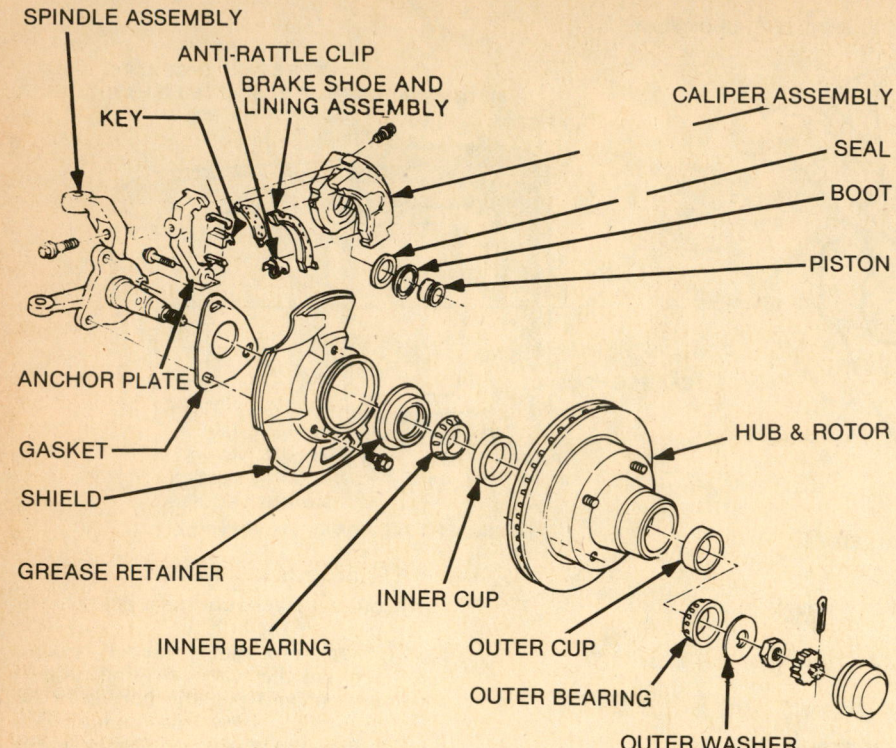

SPINDLE ASSEMBLY
ANTI-RATTLE CLIP
BRAKE SHOE AND LINING ASSEMBLY
KEY
CALIPER ASSEMBLY
SEAL
BOOT
PISTON
ANCHOR PLATE
GASKET
SHIELD
HUB & ROTOR
GREASE RETAINER
INNER CUP
INNER BEARING
OUTER CUP
OUTER BEARING
OUTER WASHER

Front Disc Brake Assembly—1974 and Later Mustang II and Pinto (© Ford Motor Co.)

just the spindle nut if its setting was changed while checking the disc.

Parallelism

Parallelism refers to the variations in thickness of the disc. Excessive variation can cause pedal vibration and front end vibration during braking. Parallelism can be checked by measuring thickness at four or more equally spaced points around the braking surface of the disc. All measurements must be made at the same distance from the outer edge of the disc. The disc and hub should be replaced if variations in thickness exceed specification. Do not forget to adjust the spindle nut to specification if its setting was changed while checking the disc.

SERVICING REAR DISC BRAKES

IMPERIAL

Pad Replacement and Caliper Service

The sliding caliper which is used on the rear of 1974-75 Imperial models is serviced in the same manner as the Kelsey-Hayes sliding caliper which is used on the front. Disc brake pad changing and caliper removal procedures are identical, except that the rear caliper has a dust shield, which must be removed prior to caliper removal.

Parking Brake

The disc used on the rear of 1974-75 Imperial has a 7 in. internal parking brake drum. The brake assembly itself is mounted on the rear axle flange and disc adapter.

See the car section for parking brake adjustment procedures.

REAR DISC/DRUM REMOVAL AND INSTALLATION

1. Remove the caliper assembly. See the procedure for removing the sliding caliper from the front wheels of Chrysler products. Do not disconnect the caliper from the brake lines; safety wire it to the rear spring.
2. Remove the inboard pad.
3. Take the plug out of the parking

brake adjuster access hole. Insert a brake adjusting tool into the hole and engage the notches on the starwheel. Pry down with the tool to release the adjustment.
4. Pull the disc/drum assembly off the studs.

Installation is the reverse of removal.

DRUM INSPECTION

Measure drum runout and diameter. Variation in drum diameter should not

exceed 0.006 in. Reface drums which exceed these specifications. Do not remove more than 0.060 in. from the standard drum diameter. The maximum allowable diameter is stamped on the drum.

PARKING BRAKE SHOE REMOVAL AND INSTALLATION

1. Remove the caliper and disc/drum assembly.
2. Remove the lower brake shoe return spring.

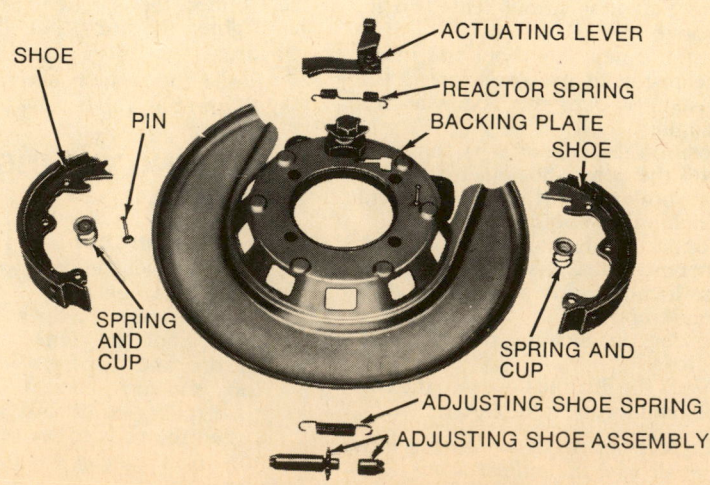

SHOE
PIN
ACTUATING LEVER
REACTOR SPRING
BACKING PLATE
SHOE
SPRING AND CUP
SPRING AND CUP
ADJUSTING SHOE SPRING
ADJUSTING SHOE ASSEMBLY

Rear wheel parking brake components— Corvette (© Chevrolet Div., GM Corp)

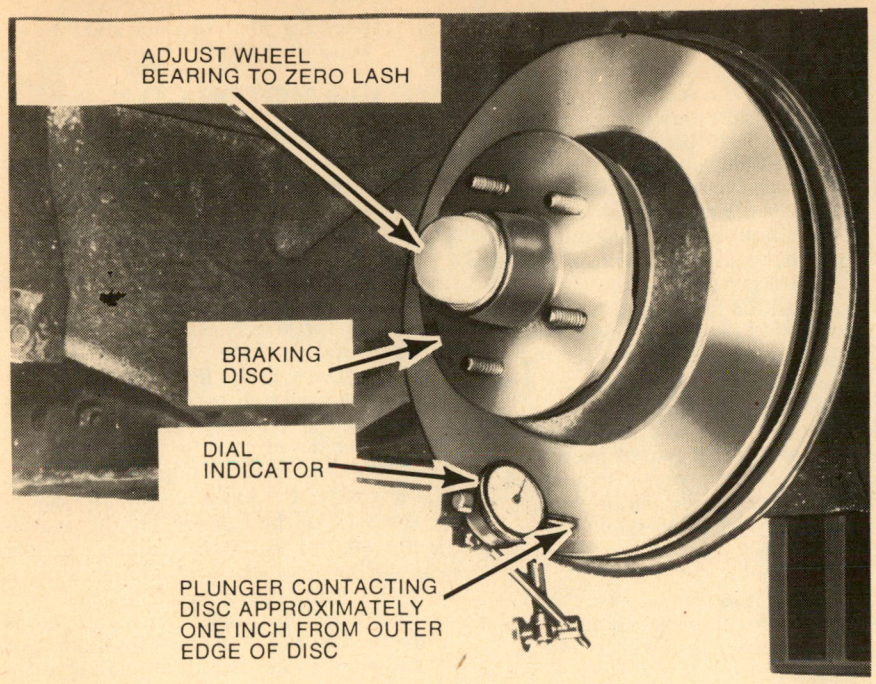

ADJUST WHEEL
BEARING TO ZERO LASH

BRAKING
DISC

DIAL
INDICATOR

PLUNGER CONTACTING
DISC APPROXIMATELY
ONE INCH FROM OUTER
EDGE OF DISC

Checking disc runout
(© Chrysler Corp)

3. Spread the shoes slightly and remove the starwheel adjuster assembly.

4. Remove the upper shoe return spring.

5. Move the shoes off the support and remove the retainers, springs and nails. Remove the shoes.

Installation is as follows:

1. Lubricate the shoe tab contact area on the support plate with special brake grease.

2. Position the shoes on the support plate and install the nails, springs, and retainers.

3. Install the upper shoe return spring.

4. Install the starwheel adjuster. The starwheel goes forward on the left side and rearward in the right side.

5. Install the lower shoe return spring.

6. Install the disc/drum and caliper.

LEVER, CAM AND SHAFT REMOVAL AND INSTALLATION

1. Detach the parking brake cable from the inner operating lever and separate the snap ring retainer from the shaft. Remove the operating lever.

2. Remove the inner shaft snapring and the cam lever. Remove the cam.

3. Pull out the shaft.

Installation is the reverse of removal. Lubricate the shaft with brake grease.

CHEVROLET CORVETTE

Pad Replacement and Caliper Service

The Corvette uses Delco-Moraine four-piston fixed caliper disc brakes on the rear wheels, as well as on the front. Rear disc brake pad replacement and caliper service procedures are the same as those for "Delco-Moraine 4 Piston Brake."

Parking Brakes

The discs used on the rear of the Corvette have integral drums which are used as parking brakes only. See the "Chevrolet-Corvette" section for parking brake adjustment procedures.

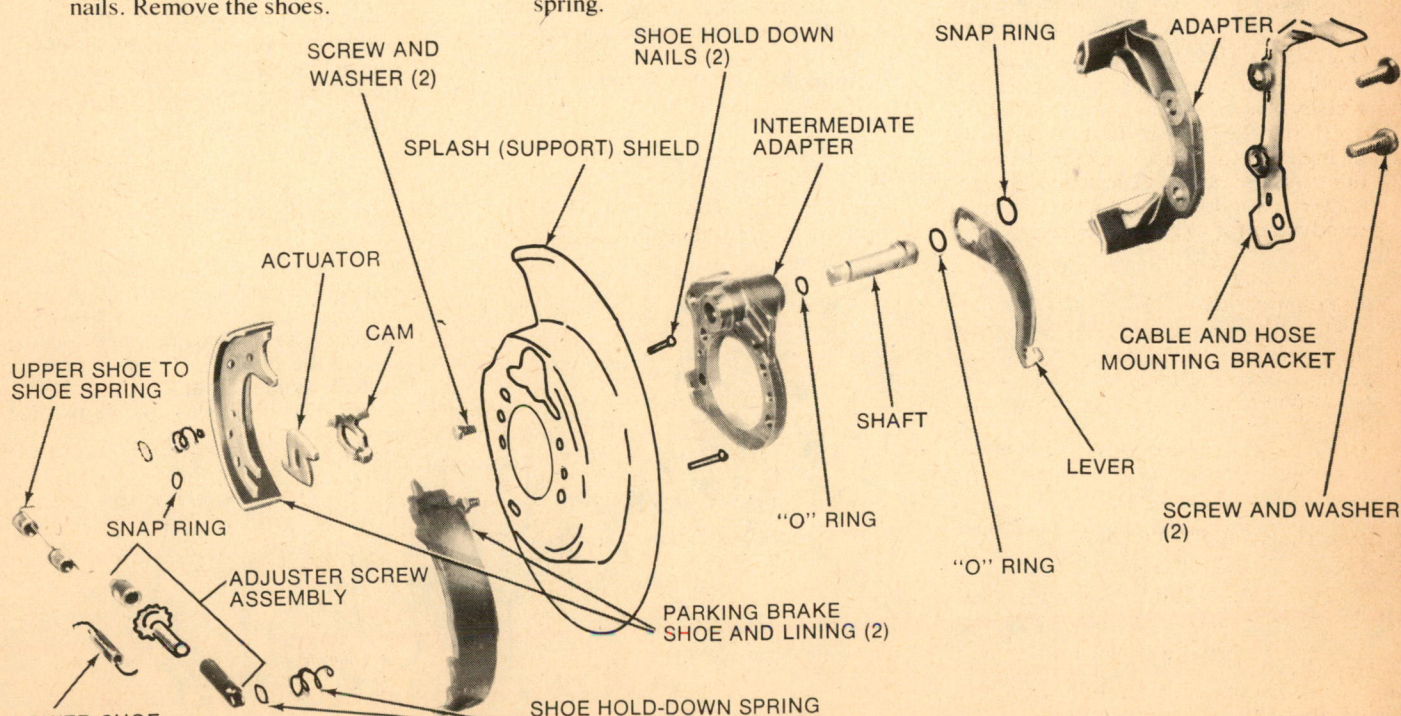

SCREW AND WASHER (2)

SHOE HOLD DOWN NAILS (2)

SNAP RING

ADAPTER

SPLASH (SUPPORT) SHIELD

INTERMEDIATE ADAPTER

ACTUATOR

CAM

UPPER SHOE TO SHOE SPRING

SNAP RING

ADJUSTER SCREW ASSEMBLY

LOWER SHOE TO SHOE SPRING

SHAFT

"O" RING

PARKING BRAKE SHOE AND LINING (2)

SHOE HOLD-DOWN SPRING RETAINER AND SPRING (2)

"O" RING

LEVER

CABLE AND HOSE MOUNTING BRACKET

SCREW AND WASHER (2)

Rear wheel parking brake components—Imperial (© Chrysler Corp)

Disc Brakes

CORVETTE PARKING BRAKE SHOE REMOVAL AND INSTALLATION

1. Jack the car up and remove the rear wheels and tires.
2. Remove the brake caliper from the disc. Do not disconnect the brake line, but remove the line clip from the control arm and hang the caliper above the disc with wire.
3. Drill the disc retaining rivets out and remove the disc from the axle hub. It is not necessary to replace the rivets when the disc is reinstalled.
4. Insert a screwdriver into the adjusting hole and turn the screw several times to expand the shoes.
5. Push the brake shoes forward until the front shoe hold-down spring can be seen through the adjusting hole.
6. Insert a pair of needle-nosed pliers through the hole and grasp the hold-down pin. Depress the spring with a screwdriver inserted from the side and turn the pin 90° to free the spring and retainer. Remove the spring and retainer.
7. Repeat this operation on the rear brake shoe.
8. Retract the shoes by turning the adjuster screw. Pull the shoes from the adjuster and remove the adjuster and spring.
9. Separate the shoes at the anchor pin and lift the shoes up and out of the housing, while allowing the straight part of the return spring to go between the outer tip of the anchor pin and the axle flange plate.
10. Lightly lubricate the backing plate shoe contact surfaces, anchor pin,

and adjusting screw threads.
11. Install the return spring on the replacement shoes and position the shoes on the anchor pin.
12. Install the adjuster spring and adjuster. Turn the adjuster screw to expand the shoes.
13. Turn the axle shaft flange so that the adjustment hole aligns with the front hold-down spring pin.
14. Push the shoe forward and over the hold-down pin.
15. Install the spring and retainer over the hold-down pin and using needle-nosed pliers and a screwdriver as in step 6, depress the spring and twist the pin 90°.
16. Repeat the above step on the rear shoe. Another pair of needle-nosed pliers will have to be utilized to hold the pin in position, as head of this pin is not accessible.
17. Turn the adjuster screw to retract the shoes.
18. Install the brake disc onto the studs, making sure that the adjustment holes in the disc and flange align.
19. Install the caliper.
20. Adjust the parking brake as described above.
21. Install the tire and wheel and lower the car.

BURNISHING NEW PARKING BRAKE LININGS

Perform this procedure after new parking brake shoes have been installed:
1. Adjust the parking brakes.
2. Drive the car at a steady 50 mph and apply the parking brake lever 10 to 12 notches (until a light drag is felt).
3. Hold this speed with the brake ap-

plied for 50-60 seconds and then release the brake.

FORD MOTOR CO.

Starting 1975, rear disc brakes are standard equipment on Continental Mark IV and V models and are optional on Lincoln, Ford, Mercury, Thunderbird, Granada, Monarch, and Versailles.

The rear sliding caliper assembly is similar to the one used on the front, except for the parking brake mechanism and a bigger anti-rattle spring. The parking brake lever on the caliper is cable-operated by depressing (or releasing) the parking brake pedal under the dash panel.

When the pedal is depressed, the cable rotates the parking brake lever (on the back of the caliper) and the operating shaft (inside the caliper). Three steel balls, which are located in pockets on the opposing heads of the shaft and thrust screw, roll between ramps formed in the pockets. The motion of the balls forces the thrust screw away from the shaft which, in turn, forces the piston and pad assembly against the disc to create braking action.

An automatic adjuster in the piston compensates for pad wear by moving the thrust screw.

Pad Replacement

NOTE: *This procedure requires the use of a special service tool.*
1. Raise the car and support it with jackstands. Block the front wheels if they remain on the ground.
2. Remove the wheel and tire.
3. Disconnect the cable from the caliper parking brake lever. Be careful not to kink or cut the cable and return spring.
4. Unfasten the setscrew which secures the caliper key. Use a hammer and soft brass drift (if necessary) to slide the support spring and retaining key out of the anchor plate.
5. Push the caliper against the anchor plate and rotate its upper end away from the plate. If a ridge of rust on the disc prevents caliper removal, scrape the rust away with a putty knife or similar blunt tool.
6. If the disc is scored to the point

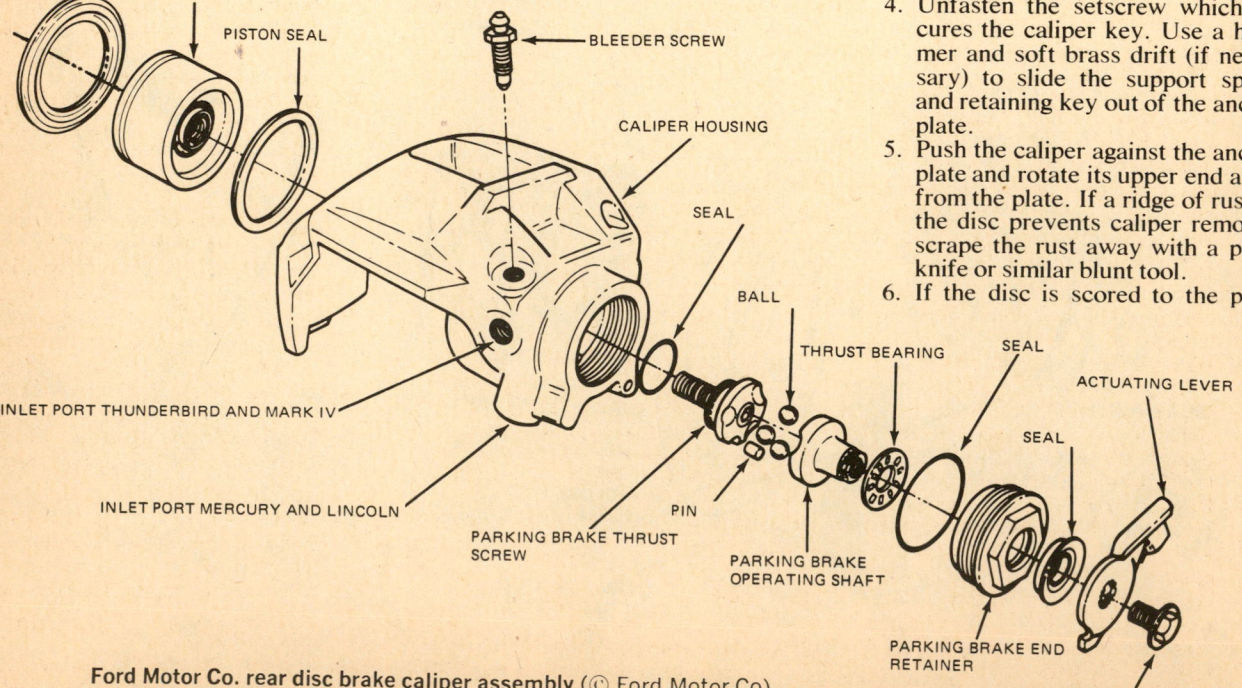

Ford Motor Co. rear disc brake caliper assembly (© Ford Motor Co)

that the caliper still can't be removed, loosen the caliper end retainer ½-turn, after removing the retaining screw and caliper parking brake lever. Also, be sure to matchmark the caliper housing and end retainer to ensure that the retainer is only given ½-turn.

CAUTION

Turning the end retainer more than ½-turn could cause internal fluid leaks in the caliper, which would make caliper rebuilding necessary.

7. Wire the caliper assembly out of the way to avoid stretching or kinking the brake hose.
8. Remove the inner pad assembly from the retaining clip. Tap lightly on the outer pad to free it from the caliper.
9. Mark the pads for proper installation if they are not going to be replaced. Used pads must be returned to the same side from which they were removed.
10. If the pad is worn to within ⅛ in. of the shoe surface, replace all of the pads on both rear brakes. Do not replace just one pad or one set of pads; uneven braking will result.

NOTE: *Pad replacement requires the use of a special tool to bottom the piston in its bore.*

11. Inspect the caliper for leaks. Clean any rust off the caliper and anchor plate sliding surfaces or inner brake pad abutment surfaces on the anchor plate.

Installation is as follows:

1. If the end retainer was loosened in order to remove the caliper, perform the following:
   a. Install the caliper on the anchor plate and secure it with the key, but do not install the pads.
   b. Tighten the retainer end to 75-95 ft. lbs.
   c. Install the caliper parking brake lever with the arm pointing rearward and down. This allows the cable to pass under the axle.
   d. Tighten the lever retaining screw to 16-22 ft. lbs. Check for free rotation of the lever.
   e. Remove the caliper.
2. The following special steps must be performed if new pads are being installed:
   a. Remove the disc and install the caliper less the pads. Use only the key to retain the caliper.
   b. Seat the special tool firmly against the piston by holding the shaft rotating the tool handle.
   c. Loosen the handle ½-turn. Hold the handle and rotate the tool shaft clockwise until the caliper piston bottoms (it will continue to turn after it bottoms).
   d. Rotate the handle until the piston is firmly seated.

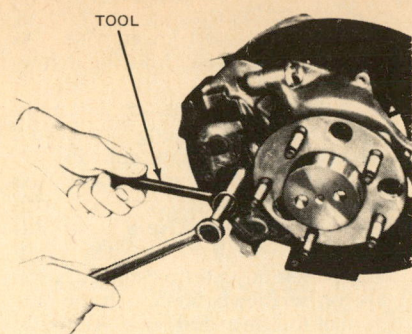

TOOL

Adjusting the rear caliper piston depth with the special tool (© Ford Motor Co)

   e. Remove the caliper and install the disc.
3. Confirm that the brake pad anti-rattle clip is correctly positioned in the lower inner brake pad support, the clip loop should face the inside of the anchor plate.
4. Fit the inner pad assembly on the anchor plate, with the lining facing the disc.
5. Install the outer brake pad with its lower flanges against the caliper leg abutments and its upper flanges against the machined shoulder surfaces.
6. Lubricate the caliper and anchor plate sliding surfaces with special brake lubricant. Keep the lubricant off the pad and disc.
7. Position the caliper housing lower groove against the anchor plate lower abutment surfaces. Rotate the housing until it is completely over the disc. Be careful not to damage the dust boot.
8. Slide the caliper outward until the inner pad is seated firmly against the disc. Measure the outer pad-to-disc clearance. It should be ¹⁄₁₆ in. or less. If it is more, adjust the piston *outward* with the special tool (See step 2). Each ¼-turn of the piston is about ¹⁄₁₆ in. of piston movement.

CAUTION

If piston clearance is more than ¹⁄₁₆ in., the adjuster may pull out of the piston when the service brakes are applied, causing adjuster failure.

9. Center the caliper over the lower anchor plate abutment, while holding it over the upper abutment.
10. Install the retaining spring and key in the keyway and slide them into the opening at the lower end of the caliper and anchor plate abutment. Center the semi-circular slot in the key over the anchor plate setscrew hole. Tighten the setscrew to 12-16 ft. lbs.
11. Attach the parking brake cable to the lower lever end.
12. If the caliper was completely removed (lines disconnected), bleed

the hydraulic system. Run the engine and lightly pump the service brake pedal 40 times; allow one second between brake applications. Check the parking brake for too much travel or too light operating effort. Repeat the pumping and adjust the cable, if necessary.
13. Install the wheel and tire, remove the jackstands and lower the car.
14. Make sure that the service brake pedal feels firm and then road-test the car. Check parking brake operation.

Caliper Removal and Installation

Perform all of the necessary procedures in the disc brake pad removal and installation section, and do the following:

1. Prior to removing the caliper, disconnect the rear brake pipe fitting from the hose end at the frame bracket.
2. Plug the brake pipe.
3. Unfasten the horseshoe clip from the hose fitting and separate the hose from the bracket. On Granadas, Versailles and Monarchs, remove the hose bracket from the spring seat.
4. On Lincoln, Fords, and Mercury models, unscrew the hose fitting from the caliper. On Mark IV, V, Granada, Monarch, Versailles and Thunderbird models, unfasten the hollow retaining nut which secures the fitting to the caliper.

When installing the caliper, perform the following additional steps.

1. On Lincoln, Ford, and Mercury models, put a new gasket on the fitting and screw the fitting into the caliper port; tighten to 20-30 ft. lbs. On Mark IV, V, Granada, Monarch, Versailles and Thunderbird models, put new gaskets on either side of the fitting outlet and insert the hollow securing bolt through the washers and fitting; tighten to 17-20 ft. lbs. On Granada, Versailles and Monarch be sure to fit the hose pin in the hole on the caliper.
2. Fit the upper end of the flexible hose in the bracket and install the horseshoe clip. Do not twist or coil the brake hose; keep the stripe on the hose straight. On Granada Versailles, and Monarch, install the hose bracket on the spring seat.
3. Unplug the pipe. Connect the hose to the pipe and tighten the fitting to 10-15 ft. lbs.
4. Bleed the brake system.

Caliper Overhaul

1. Remove the caliper assembly from the car.
2. Remove the retaining screw, parking brake lever, and caliper end retainer.
3. Pull out the operating shaft, thrust

Disc Brakes

bearing, and balls from the caliper.
4. Using either a magnet or tweezers, extract the thrust screw anti-rotation pin.
5. Using a 1/4 in. Allen key, rotate the thrust screw counterclockwise to remove it.
6. Push the piston/adjuster assembly out of its bore from behind.

NOTE: *A special tool is available to do this. Use care not to scratch the bore or press on the piston adjuster can while removing the piston.*

7. Remove and discard the following:
   a. Piston seal
   b. Boot
   c. Thrust screw O-ring seal
   d. End retainer O-ring
   e. End retainer lip seal
8. Clean all metal parts in isopropyl alcohol. Dry them with compressed air. Be sure that no foreign material remains in the caliper.
9. Inspect the caliper bores. The thrust screw bore must be smooth and show no sign of pitting.
10. If the piston is pitted, scored, or the plating worn off, replace the piston/adjuster as an assembly. The adjuster can should not be loose, high, or damaged; if it is, replace the piston/adjuster assembly. If brake adjustment is incorrect, replace the piston/adjuster assembly.

NOTE: *The piston and the adjuster must be replaced as an assembly. No attempt to repair the adjuster should be made.*

11. If in doubt about adjuster operation; check it as follows:
    a. Install the thrust screw in the piston/adjuster.
    b. Pull the two pieces apart about 1/4 in. and release them.
    c. When the pieces are pulled apart, the brass drive ring should remain stationary, causing the nut to turn.
    d. When the pieces are released, the nut should remain stationary and the drive ring rotate.
    e. Replace the piston/adjuster if it fails to operate in this manner.
12. Inspect all bearing, sliding, rotating and rolling surfaces for wear, pitting or brinnelling. Replace any parts necessary. A polished appearance on ball paths or bearing surfaces is OK, as long as there is no sign of wear into the surface.

Assembly is as follows:
1. Coat a new piston seal with clean brake fluid. Seat the seal in the groove of the bore. Be sure it is not twisted.
2. Seat the flange of a new dust boot squarely in the caliper bore outer groove.
3. Coat the piston/adjuster assembly with clean brake fluid. Spread the dust boot over the piston and install the piston. Seat the dust boot in the piston/adjuster groove.

4. Lay the caliper assembly (rear of bore up) in a soft-jawed vise. Do not tighten the vise; housing distortion will result.
5. Fill the piston/adjuster assembly up to the bottom edge of thrust screw bore with clean brake fluid.
6. Install a new O-ring in the thrust screw groove, after coating it with clean brake fluid. Use a 1/4 in. Allen key to install the thrust screw in the piston adjuster assembly, until its top surface is flush with the bottom of the threaded bore. Align the notches on the thrust screw with those on the caliper housing. Install the anti-rotation pin.
7. Install one ball in each of the three thrust screw pockets. Coat all components of the parking brake mechanism with a liberal amount of silicone grease.
8. Install the parking brake operating shaft over the balls. Coat the thrust bearing with silicone grease and fit it on the shaft.
9. Install a new lip seal and O-ring on the caliper end retainer. Coat both seals with a light film of silicone grease and install the end retainer on the caliper; tighten it to 75-90 ft. lbs. Hold the operating shaft so that it is securely seated against the parking brake mechanism during end retainer installation. If the lip seal is dislocated, reseat it.
10. Install the parking brake lever over its keyed spline, so that it points down and rearward. Torque the lever securing screw to 16-22 ft. lbs. Check the lever for freedom of movement.
11. Support the caliper and bottom the piston with the special tool as in steps 2b through d of the disc brake pad replacement procedure.
12. Install the caliper.

Disc Removal and Installation

1. Remove the caliper assembly and wire it out of the way, unless it is to be serviced. Do not remove the anchor plate.
2. If corrosion makes identification difficult, mark the raised (not the braking) surface of the disc "RIGHT" or "LEFT" prior to removal.
3. Remove the securing nuts and take the disc off the axle shaft.

Installation is as follows:
1. If a new disc is being used, remove its protective coating with carburetor degreaser.
2. Identify the left and right discs before installation. The words "LEFT" and "RIGHT" are cast into the inner surface of the raised section of the disc. This is important, since the cooling vanes cast into the disc must face in the direction of forward rotation.
3. Install the two disc securing nuts.
4. Install the caliper.

CADILLAC AND BUICK

Four-wheel disc brakes became standard equipment on 1976 Cadillac Eldorados; they are optional on Buick Rivieras starting 1977, and on Century and Electra models, except Century station wagons, starting 1978.

Pad Replacement

1. Remove and discard 2/3 of the brake fluid in the rear (forward, on Eldorado) master cylinder reservoir. This will prevent overflow when removing the rear calipers.
2. Raise the car and remove the wheel and tire. Install one wheel lug nut with the flat side toward the rotor to secure the rotor when the caliper is removed.
3. Loosen the tension on the parking brake cable at the equalizer. Remove the cable from the parking brake lever.
4. Remove the return spring, locknut, lever, lever seal, and antifriction washer.

NOTE: *The lever must be held in place while removing the nut.*

5. Clean any dirt from the caliper surface in the area of the lever seal. Using a 7 in. or larger C-clamp with the solid end on the lever stop and screw end on the back of the outboard pad, turn the clamp until the piston bottoms in the caliper.

NOTE: *Do not position the C-clamp on the actuator screw.*

6. Before removing the clamp, lubricate the caliper housing surface (under the lever seal), with silicone.
7. Install the anti-friction washer, lever seal, and lever, using new parts if necessary.

NOTE: *Install the lever on the hex with the arm pointing downward.*

8. Rotate the lever toward the front of the car, hold in this position, install the nut, and torque to 25 ft. lbs. Then rotate the lever back to stop.
9. Install the lever return spring and remove the C-clamp.

NOTE: *Return springs are color coded —red for right-hand caliper, black for left-hand.*

10. Remove the brake line from the caliper and plug the opening.

NOTE: *If the brake line nut is seized, the brass bolt and block on the caliper can be removed with the brake line attached by removing the bolt and block copper washers after removing the caliper mounting bolts. Plug the openings.*

11. Remove the caliper mounting bolts, remove the caliper with the brake pads, then remove the pads.
12. Clean the face of the piston. Inspect the piston and check valve area for fluid leaks evidenced by excessive moisture around boot area. Check the dust boot for cuts,

cracks, or other damage which would affect its sealing ability. Replace if leaks are present.

--- **CAUTION** ---

Do not use compressed air to clean the caliper to avoid the possibility of unseating the dust boot.

13. Check the piston boot seal for leaks. If leaks are present, replace the piston seal and the boot seal.
14. Check for leaks at the threaded end of the actuator screw. If leaks are present, replace the seal. Replace the caliper if the bore is scratched or nicked.
15. Remove and discard the two caliper mounting sleeves and four bushings. Install new bushings and sleeves, using silicone lube.

NOTE: *The sleeves are installed in the inner bushings.*

16. Remove and discard the piston check valve. Install a new piston check valve.

IMPORTANT: *Do not use front brake pads on the rear calipers.*

17. Position a new inboard pad on the piston. The D-shaped tab MUST fit in the indentation present in the piston. Should the piston need rotation, use the special tool.
18. Install the new outboard pad.
19. Remove all dirt from the caliper mounting bolts. Do not use sandpaper or a wire brush as this will damage the plating. Replace the bolts if corroded or damaged.

NOTE: *If the brass bolt and block was removed with the brake line, unplug the fittings and install the bolt and block using two new copper gaskets. Torque the bolt to a maximum of 30 ft. lbs.*

20. Slide the caliper over the rotor and install the mounting bolts. Make sure that all sleeves, bushings, and pins are well lubricated with silicone.

NOTE: *The mounting bolt should go under the inboard shoe ears.*
21. Torque the caliper mounting bolts to 30 ft. lbs.
22. Unplug the fittings and install the brake line tube nut into the caliper. Pump the brake pedal to seat the pad against the rotor.
23. Clinch the upper ear of the outboard pad by placing a 12 in. pliers with one jaw on top of the upper ear and the other jaw in the notch on the bottom of the pad, opposite the upper ear. After clinching there should be no radial clearance between the pad ears and the caliper housing. If any radial clearance exists, repeat the clinching procedure.
24. Connect the parking brake cables and adjust the parking brake.
25. Bleed the rear brake system. After bleeding, apply the service brake several times to ensure adjustment.
26. Remove the one wheel lug nut used to retain the rotor and install the wheel and tire. Lower the car and tighten the wheel lug nuts to 130 ft. lbs.

Caliper Overhaul

Caliper removal is detailed under Pad Replacement.
1. Remove the caliper assembly.
2. Clamp the caliper in a vise.
3. Remove and discard the two mounting sleeves and four bushings.
4. Remove the pads and the lever return spring.
5. Pad the caliper with a shop towel to catch the piston. Move the lever back and forth to move the piston out. If it won't come out, remove the locknut, lever, lever seal, and anti-friction washer. Turn the screw with a 9/16 in. wrench until the piston pops out.
6. Remove the piston assembly and balance spring.

7. Remove the locknut, lever, lever seal, and anti-friction washer if you haven't already.
8. Push the actuator screw out of the housing. Remove the piston seal and boot.
9. Flush the caliper housing with denatured alcohol and blow out the passages.
10. Start assembly by installing the new piston seal. Install the new boot onto the new piston assembly. The seal lip fits into the groove in the piston.

NOTE: *The Eldorado piston assemblies are shorter in piston length and will not interchange with those for other models.*

11. Fit a new thrust washer and seal onto the actuator screw.
12. Position the actuator screw in the piston assembly. Adjuster screws, levers, and caliper castings are marked L and R for left and right.
13. Coat the piston seal with a film of clean brake fluid. Fit the balance spring into the piston assembly spring retainer and start the assembly into the caliper housing.
14. Now the piston must be pushed straight back all the way in the housing. If it isn't forced in straight, the actuator screw seal will be damaged. The piston can be forced in with a clamp.
15. With the piston clamped in place, install the anti-friction washer (coat it with a silicone spray), new lever seal, lever, and locknut. Install the lever away from the stop. Rotate the lever in the apply direction and hold it until the nut is tightened to 25 ft. lbs.
16. Release the clamp and rotate the lever back to the stop.
17. Drive the boot into place until the seal bottoms in the housing.
18. Replace the pads and caliper. Bleed the hydraulic system.

HYDRAULIC CYLINDERS AND VALVES

MASTER CYLINDERS

Dual master cylinders, used on all cars, are actually two single master cylinders operating in the same bore. They are designed so that the front and rear brakes have separate hydraulic systems. Malfunction in either system has no effect on the other system but is immediately evident to the driver because of the additional pedal travel required to actuate the remaining half of the brake system. Service procedure for single master cylinders is identical, except that there is only one piston assembly and no stop screw. Some master cylinders have bleed screws on the outlet flanges and may be bled without disturbing the wheel cylinders.

Servicing Master Cylinders
1. Remove the cylinder from the car and drain the brake fluid.
2. Mount the cylinder in a vise so that the outlets are up and remove the seal from the hub.
3. Remove the stop screw from the bottom of the front reservoir.
4. Remove the snap-ring from the front of the bore and remove the primary piston assembly.
5. Remove the secondary piston assembly using compressed air or a piece of wire. Cover the bore opening with a cloth to prevent damage to the piston.
6. Clean metal parts in brake fluid and discard rubber parts.

7. Inspect the bore for damage or wear, and check pistons for damage and proper clearance in the bore.
8. If the bore is only slightly scored or pitted it may be honed. Always use hones that are in good condition and completely clean the cylinder with brake fluid when honing is completed. If any evidence of contamination exists in the master cylinder the entire hydraulic system should be flushed and refilled with clean brake fluid. Blow out passages with compressed air.
9. Install new secondary seals in the two grooves in the flat end of the front piston. The lips of the seals

Brakes

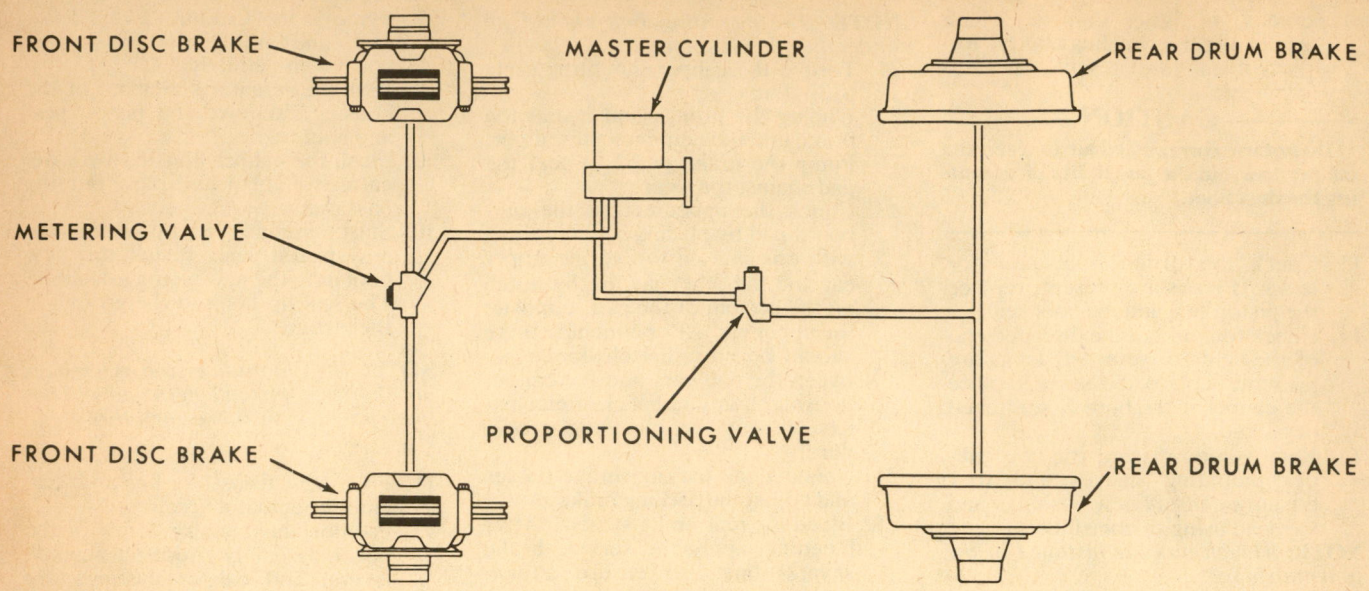

FRONT DISC BRAKE

MASTER CYLINDER

REAR DRUM BRAKE

METERING VALVE

FRONT DISC BRAKE

PROPORTIONING VALVE

REAR DRUM BRAKE

Disc brake hydraulic system

10. Install a new primary seal and the seal protector on opposite end of the front piston with the lips of the seal facing outward.
11. Coat the seals with brake fluid. Install the spring on the front piston with the spring retainer in the primary seal.
12. Insert the piston assembly, spring end first, into the bore and use a wooden rod to seat it.
13. Coat the rear piston seals with brake fluid and install them into the piston grooves with the lips facing the spring end.
14. Assemble the spring onto the piston and install the assembly into the bore spring first. Install the snap-ring.
15. Hold the piston at the bottom of the bore and install the stop screw. Install a new seal on the hub. Bench-bleed the cylinder or install and bleed the cylinder on the car.

WHEEL CYLINDERS

Servicing Wheel Cylinders

1. Raise the vehicle on a hoist and remove the wheel and drum from the brake to be serviced.
2. Remove the brake shoes and clean the backing plate and wheel cylinder.
3. Disconnect the brake line from the brake hose. Remove the brake hose retainer clip at the frame bracket and remove the hose from the wheel cylinder. (On rear brakes it will only be necessary to remove the line from the cylinder.)
4. Remove the cylinder mounting bolts and remove the cylinder.
5. Remove the boots from the cylinder ends and discard. Remove the pistons, remove and discard the

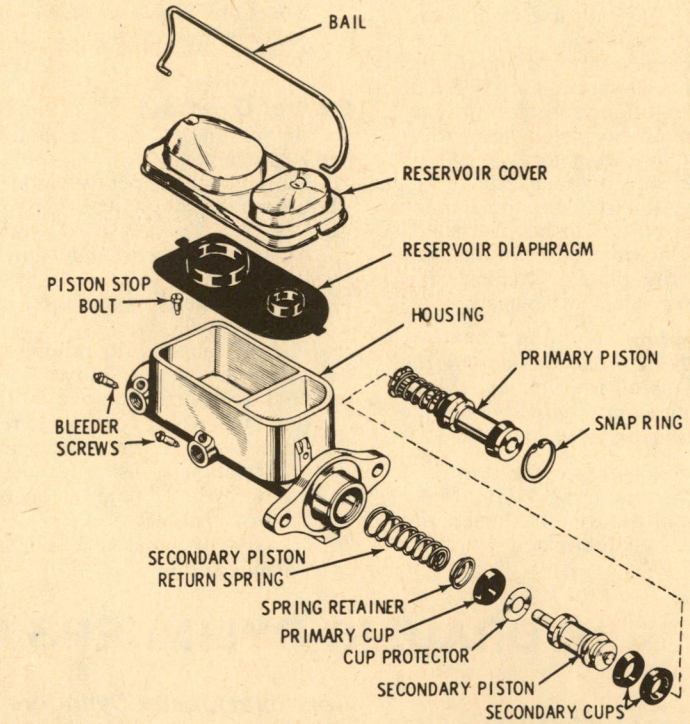

BAIL

RESERVOIR COVER

RESERVOIR DIAPHRAGM

PISTON STOP BOLT

HOUSING

PRIMARY PISTON

SNAP RING

BLEEDER SCREWS

SECONDARY PISTON RETURN SPRING

SPRING RETAINER

PRIMARY CUP

CUP PROTECTOR

SECONDARY PISTON

SECONDARY CUPS

Bendix dual master cylinder
(© Oldsmobile Div., G.M. Corp)

seal cups, and remove the expanders and spring.

6. Inspect the bore and pistons for damage or wear. Damaged pistons should be discarded, as they cannot be reconditioned. Slight bore roughness can be removed using a brake cylinder hone or crocus cloth. (Cloth should be rotated in the bore under finger pressure. Do not slide lengthwise). Use only lint-free cloth for cleaning.

7. Clean the cylinder and internal parts *using only brake fluid or denatured alcohol.*
8. Insert the spring expander assembly. Lubricate all rubber parts using only fresh brake fluid.
9. Install new cups with the seal lips facing inwards.
10. Install the pistons and rubber boots. Install the cylinder on the car in reverse order of removal. Bleed the cylinder (see Brake Bleeding).

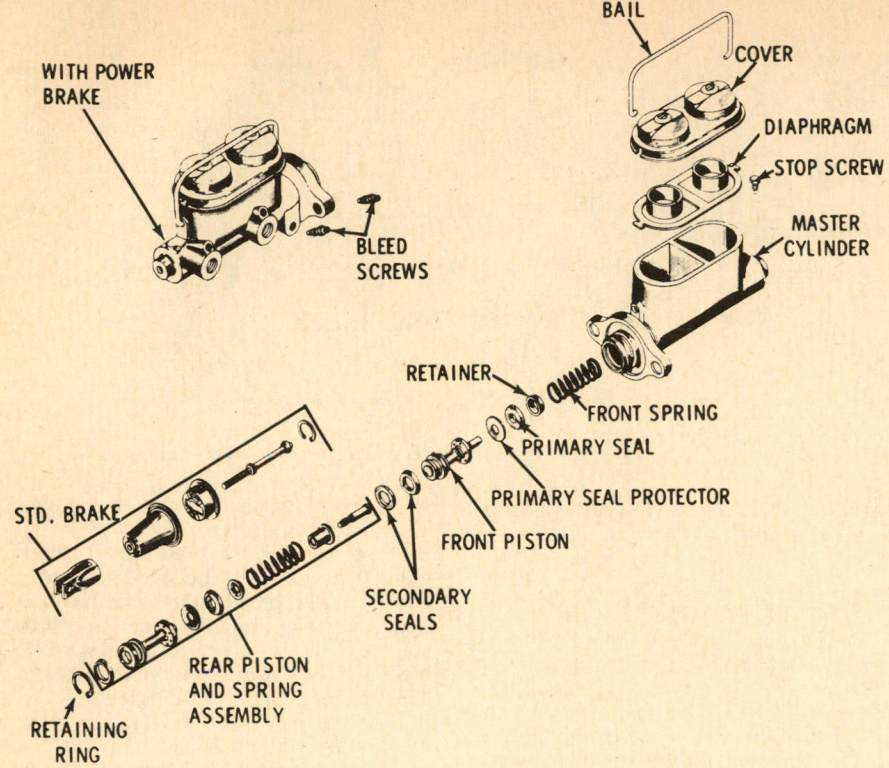

Moraine dual master cylinder (© Oldsmobile Div., G.M. Corp)

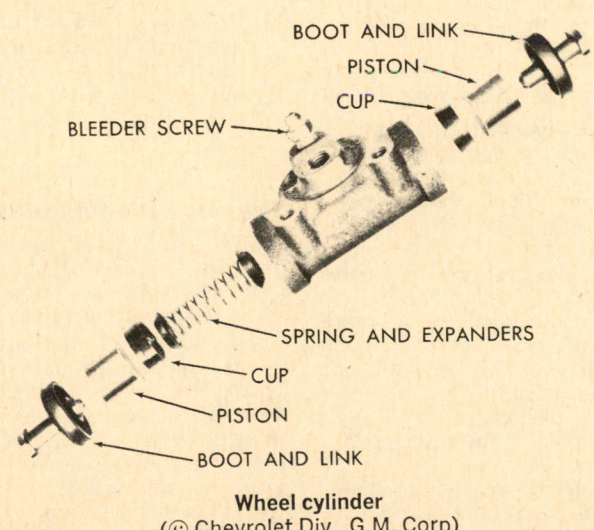

Wheel cylinder
(© Chevrolet Div., G.M. Corp)

PROPORTIONING VALVES

On vehicles equipped with front disc and rear drum (or rear disc) brakes a proportioning valve is an important part of the system. It is installed in the hydraulic line to the rear brakes. Its function is to maintain the correct proportion between line pressures to the front and rear brakes. It prevents early lock-up of rear brakes and provides balanced braking during hard stops. *No attempt at adjustment of this valve should be made, as adjustment is pre-set and tampering will result in uneven braking action.*

To assure correct installation when replacing the valve, the outlet to the rear brakes is stamped with the letter "R". Replacement is a simple job requiring no special instructions.

General Motors and American Motors have a combination valve on their front disc (rear drum) brake cars. This valve combines in one unit, a metering

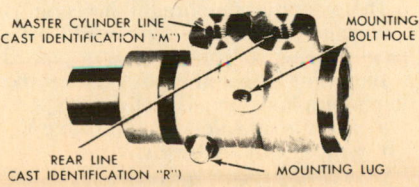

Proportioning valve

valve, a proportioning valve and a pressure differential warning valve. Mounted on top of the unit is an electrical terminal which connects to the brake warning light on the dash. Ford introduced this unit to their cars, in 1972. This unit is not serviceable and must be replaced if faulty.

METERING VALVES

On some vehicles equipped with disc brakes a metering valve is used. This valve is installed in the hydraulic line to the front brakes, and functions to delay pressure buildup to the front brakes on application. It provides balanced braking during mild stops. Its purpose is to reduce front brake pressure until rear brake pressure builds up adequately to overcome the rear brake shoe return springs. In this way disc brake pad life is extended because it prevents the front disc brakes from carrying all or most of the braking load at low operating line pressures.

The metering valve can be checked very simply. With the car stopped, gently apply the brakes. At about one inch of travel a very small change in pedal effort (like a small bump) will be felt if the valve is operating properly. Metering valves are not serviceable, and must be replaced if defective.

PRESSURE DIFFERENTIAL WARNING VALVES

Since the introduction of dual master cylinders to the hydraulic brake system, a pressure differential warning signal has been added. This signal consists of a warning light on the dashboard activated by a differential pressure switch located below the master cylinder. The signal indicates a loss of fluid pressure in either the front or rear brakes, and should warn the driver that a hydraulic failure has occurred.

The pressure differential warning valve is a housing with the brake warning light switch mounted centrally on top. Directly below the switch is a bore containing a piston assembly. The piston assembly is located in the center of the bore and kept in that position by equal fluid pressure on either side. Fluid pressure is provided by two brake lines, one coming from the rear brake system and one from the front brakes. If a leak develops in either system (front or rear), fluid pressure to that side of the piston will decrease or stop causing the piston to move in that direction. The plunger on the end of the switch engages with the piston. When the piston moves off center, the plunger moves and triggers the switch to activate the warning light on the dash.

After repairing and bleeding any part of the hydraulic system the warning light may remain on due to the pressure differential valve remaining in the off-center position. All cars except a few

Brakes

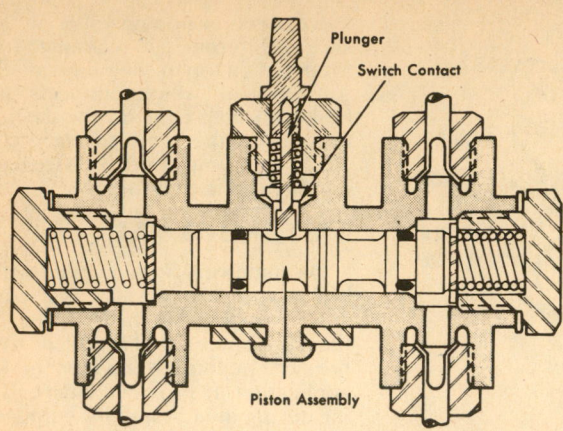
Pressure differential warning valve—ON position

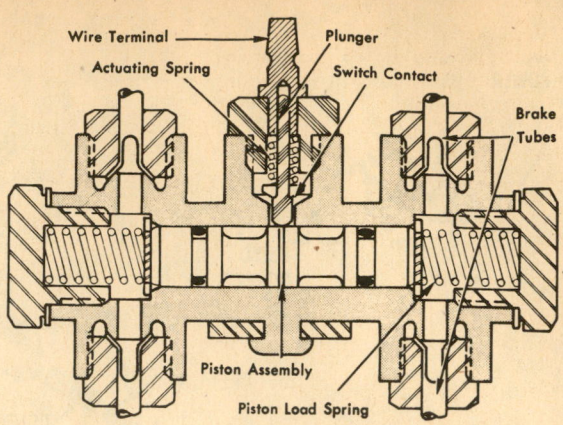
Pressure differential warning valve—OFF position

American Motors models have a self-centering valve. After repairs or bleeding have been performed, center the valve by applying moderate pressure on the brake pedal. This will turn out the light.

NOTE: *Front wheel balancing of cars equipped with disc brakes may also cause a pressure differential in the front branch of the system.*

To centralize the valve on drum only American Motors cars through 1974, perform the following procedure:

1. Before repairing or bleeding the brakes, disconnect the switch terminal wire and remove the nylon switch terminal, contact plunger spring, and nylon plunger with contact.
2. If the light had come on and actuated the valve, spring pressure may hold the plunger. To release the plunger, apply a small amount of brake pedal pressure.

NOTE: *Location of the leak can be determined by the position of the plunger in its bore. The top of the plunger will lean to the side (front or rear) which has the low pressure.*

3. Make the repair and bleed the brakes. Install the spring and plunger in the valve with the contact down.
4. Install the nylon terminal and connect the warning light wire to the terminal.
5. Replace the valve assembly if any fluid leaks from the center terminal opening while removing the terminal.

IMPORTANT: *The switch assembly is non-serviceable, replace if faulty.*

BRAKE BLEEDING

The purpose of bleeding brakes is to expel air trapped in the hydraulic system, and there are two methods of accomplishing this. The quickest and easiest of the two is pressure bleeding, but special pressure equipment is needed to externally pressurize the hydraulic system. The other, more commonly used method is gravity bleeding.

Gravity Bleeding Procedure

NOTE: *When bleeding brakes on American Motors cars through 1974 (drum only), it is necessary to remove warning light switch terminal and plunger. For details, see Pressure Differential Warning Valves.*

1. Clean the bleed screw at each wheel.
2. Attach a small rubber hose to one of the bleed screws and place the end in a container of brake fluid.
3. Top up the master cylinder with brake fluid. (Check often during bleeding). Pump up the brake pedal and hold.
4. Open the bleed screw about one-quarter turn, press the brake pedal to the floor, close the bleed screw and slowly release the pedal. Continue until no more air bubbles are forced from the cylinder on application of the brake pedal.

5. Repeat procedure on remaining wheel cylinders.

Master cylinders equipped with bleed screws may be bled independently. When bleeding the Bendix-type dual master cylinder it is necessary to solidly cap one reservoir section while bleeding the other to prevent pressure loss through the cap vent hole.

Disc brakes may be bled in the same manner as drum brakes, except that:

1. It usually requires a longer time to bleed a disc brake thoroughly.
2. The disc should be rotated to make sure that the piston has returned to the unapplied position when bleeding is completed and the bleed screw closed.

Pressure Bleeding Disc Brakes

NOTE: *See NOTE under Gravity Bleeding Procedure.*

Pressure bleeding disc brakes will close the metering valve and the front brakes will not bleed. For this reason it is necessary to manually hold the metering valve open during pressure bleeding. Never use a block or clamp to hold the valve open, and never force the valve stem beyond its normal position. Two different types of valves are used. The most common type requires the valve stem to be held in while bleeding the brakes, while the second type requires the valve stem to be held out (.060 in. minimum travel). Determine the type of visual inspection.

POWER BRAKES

VACUUM OPERATED BOOSTER

Power brakes operate just as standard brake systems except in the actuation of the master cylinder pistons. A vacuum diaphragm is located on the front of the master cylinder and assists the driver in applying the brakes, reducing both the effort and travel he

must put into moving the brake pedal.

The vacuum diaphragm housing is connected to the intake manifold by a vacuum hose. A check valve is placed at the point where the hose enters the diaphragm housing, so that during periods of low manifold vacuum brake assist vacuum will not be lost.

Depressing the brake pedal closes off the vacuum source and allows atmospheric pressure to enter on one side of

the diaphragm. This causes the master cylinder pistons to move and apply the brakes. When the brake pedal is released, vacuum is applied to both sides of the diaphragm, and return springs return the diaphragm and master cylinder pistons to the released position. If the vacuum fails, the brake pedal rod will butt against the end of the master cylinder actuating rod, and direct mechanical application will occur as the pedal is depressed.

The hydraulic and mechanical problems that apply to conventional brake systems also apply to power brakes, and should be checked for if the tests and chart below do not reveal the problem.

Tests for a system vacuum leak as described below:

1. Operate the engine at idle with the transmission in Neutral without touching the brake pedal for at least one minute.
2. Turn off the engine, and wait one minute.
3. Test for the presence of assist vacuum by depressing the brake pedal and releasing it several times. Light application will produce less and less pedal travel, if vacuum was present. If there is no vacuum, air is leaking into the system somewhere.

Test for system operation as follows:

1. Pump the brake pedal (with engine off) until the supply vacuum is entirely gone.
2. Put a light, steady pressure on the pedal.
3. Start the engine, and operate it at idle with the transmission in Neutral. If the system is operating, the brake pedal should fall toward the floor if constant pressure is maintained on the pedal.

Power brake systems may be tested for hydraulic leaks just as ordinary systems are tested, except that the engine should be idling with the transmission in Neutral throughout the test.

Power Brake Booster
Troubleshooting Chart

The following items are in addition to those listed in the "Brake Diagnosis Chart" at the front of the Hydraulic Brake Section. Check those items first.

HARD PEDAL

1. Faulty vacuum check valve
2. Vacuum hose kinked, collapsed, plugged, leaky, or improperly connected
3. Internal leak in unit
4. Damaged vacuum cylinder
5. Damaged valve plunger
6. Broken or faulty springs
7. Broken plunger stem

GRABBING BRAKES

1. Damaged vacuum cylinder
2. Faulty vacuum check valve
3. Vacuum hose leaky or improperly connected
4. Broken plunger stem

PEDAL GOES TO FLOOR

Generally, when this problem occurs, it is not caused by the power brake booster. In rare cases, a broken plunger stem may be at fault.

Overhaul

Most power brake boosters are serviced by replacement only. In many

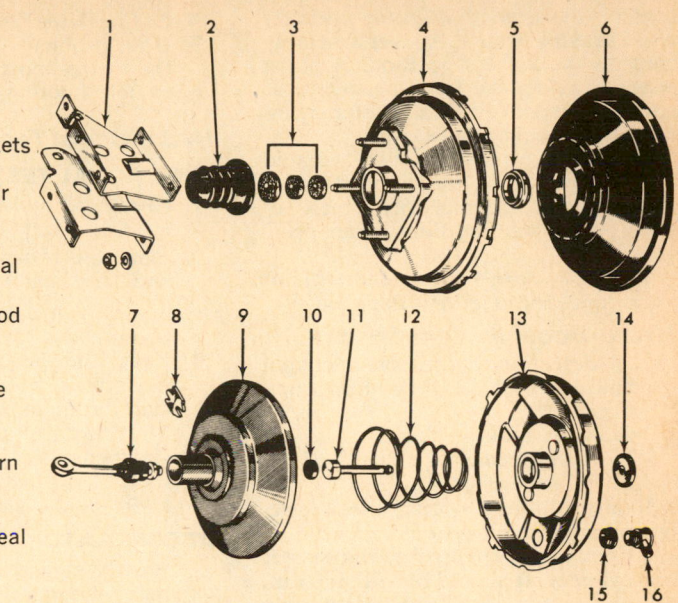

1 Rear housing mounting brackets
2 Pushrod boot
3 Foam and felt air filter-silencers
4 Rear housing
5 Rear housing seal
6 Diaphragm
7 Air valve push rod assembly
8 Air valve lock
9 Diaphragm plate
10 Reaction disc
11 Piston rod
12 Diaphragm return spring
13 Front housing
14 Front housing seal
15 Grommet
16 Check valve

Bendix single diaphragm booster components (© Chevrolet Div., G.M. Corp.)

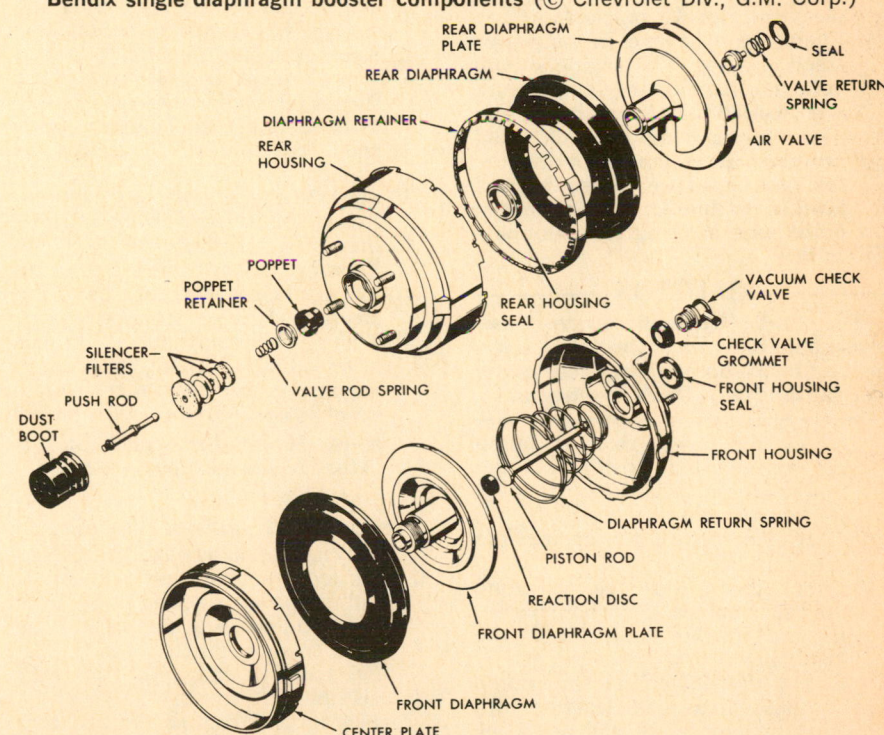

Bendix dual diaphragm booster components (© Chevrolet Div., G.M. Corp.)

cases, repair parts are not available. A good many special tools are required for rebuilding these units. For these reasons, it would be most practical to replace a failed booster with a new or remanufactured unit.

HYDRO-BOOST

Hydro-boost was first offered as a mid-year option on 1974 Continental Mark IV models. Starting 1975, it became standard on all Ford Motor Company cars equipped with four wheel disc brakes.

Beginning 1976, Hydro-boost and four wheel disc brakes were used on the Cadillac Eldorado. The method of operation, maintenance, and testing are the same for both Ford Motor Company cars and Cadillac. Only mounting and hose routings would differ.

Hydro-boost differs from conventional power brake systems, in that it operates from power steering pump fluid pressure, rather than intake manifold vacuum.

The hydro-boost unit contains a spool valve with an open center which controls the strength of pump pressure when braking occurs. A lever assembly controls the valve's position. A boost piston provides the force necessary to operate the conventional master cylinder on the front of the booster.

A reserve of at least two assisted brake applications is supplied by a spring-loaded accumulator, which retains power steering fluid under pressure.

The brakes can be operated without assist, once the reserve is depleted.

Hydro-Boost System Checks

1. A defective hydro-boost cannot cause any of the following conditions:
   a. Noisy brakes
   b. Fading pedal
   c. Pulling brakes

   If any of these occur, check elsewhere in the brake system.
2. Check the fluid level in the master cylinder. It should be within 1/4 in. of the top. It if isn't, add only DOT-3 or DOT-4 brake fluid until the correct level is reached.
3. Check the fluid level in the power steering pump. The engine should be at normal running temperature and stopped. The level should register on the pump dipstick. Add power steering fluid to bring the reservoir level up to the correct level. Low fluid level will result in both poor steering and stopping ability.

CAUTION

The brake hydraulic system uses brake fluid only, while the power steering and hydro-boost systems use power steering fluid only. Don't mix the two.

4. Check the power steering pump belt tension, and inspect all of the power steering/hydro-boost hoses for kinks or leaks.
5. Check and adjust the engine idle speed, as necessary.
6. Check the power steering pump fluid for bubbles. If air bubbles are present in the fluid, bleed the system:
   a. Fill the power steering pump reservoir to specifications with the engine at normal operating temperature.
   b. With the engine running, rotate the steering wheel through its normal travel 3 or 4 times, without holding the wheel against the stops.

c. Check the fluid level again.
7. If the problem still exists, go on to the hydro-boost test sections and troubleshooting chart.

Hydro-Boost Tests
FUNCTIONAL TEST
1. Check the brake system for leaks or low fluid level. Correct as
2. Place the transmission in Neutral and stop the engine. Apply the brakes 4 or 5 times to empty the accumulator.
3. Keep the pedal depressed with moderate (25-30 lbs.) pressure and start the engine.
4. The brake pedal should fall slightly and then push back up against your foot. If no movement is felt, the hydro-boost system is not working.

ACCUMULATOR LEAK TEST
1. Run the engine at normal idle. Turn the steering wheel against one of the stops; hold it there for no longer than 5 seconds. Center the steering wheel and stop the engine.
2. Keep applying the brakes until a "hard" pedal is obtained. There should be a minimum of 2 power assisted brake applications when pedal pressure of 20-25 lbs. is applied.
3. Start the engine and allow it to idle. Rotate the steering wheel against the stop. Listen for a light "hissing" sound; this is the accumulator being charged. Center the steering wheel and stop the engine.
4. Wait one hour and apply the brakes several times without starting the engine. As in step 2, there should be at least two stops with power assist. If not, the accumulator is defective and must be replaced.

Hydro-Boost System Bleeding
The system should be bled whenever the booster is removed and installed.
1. Fill the power steering pump until the fluid level is at the base of the pump reservoir neck. Disconnect the battery lead from the HEI distributor.
2. Jack up the front of the car, turn

the wheels all the way to the left, and crank the engine for a few seconds.
3. Check steering pump fluid level. If necessary, add fluid to the "Add" mark on the dipstick.
4. Lower the car, connect the battery lead, and start the engine. Check fluid level and add fluid to the "Add" mark if necessary.

With the engine running, turn the wheels from side to side to bleed air from the system. Make sure that the fluid level stays above the internal pump casting.
5. The hydro-boost system should now be fully bled. If the fluid is foaming after bleeding, stop the engine, let the system set for one hour, then repeat the second part of Step 4.

The preceding procedure should be effective in removing excess air from the system, however sometimes air may still remain trapped. When this happens the booster may make a "gulping" noise when the brake is applied. Lightly pumping the brake pedal with the engine running should cause this noise to disappear. After the noise stops, check the pump fluid level and add as necessary.

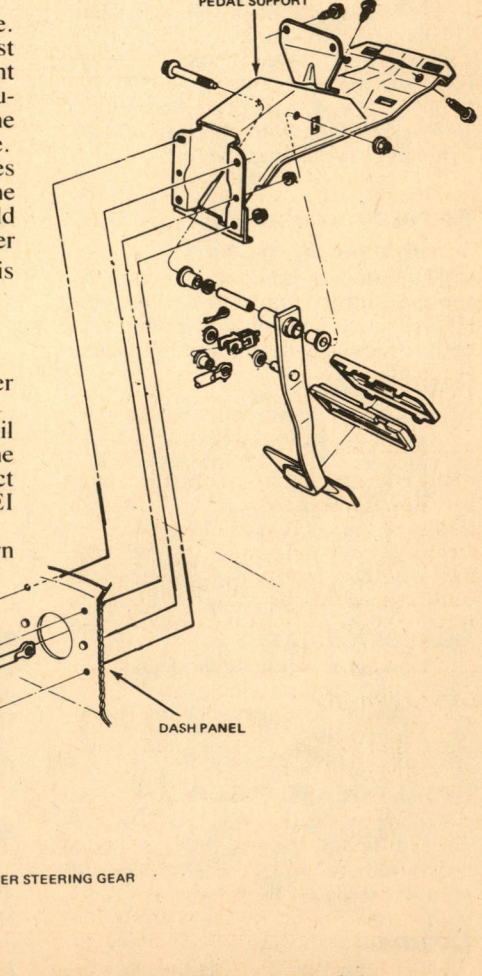

PEDAL SUPPORT

DASH PANEL

POWER STEERING GEAR

RADIATOR SUPPORT

Hydro-boost component and related system locations (© Ford Motor Co)

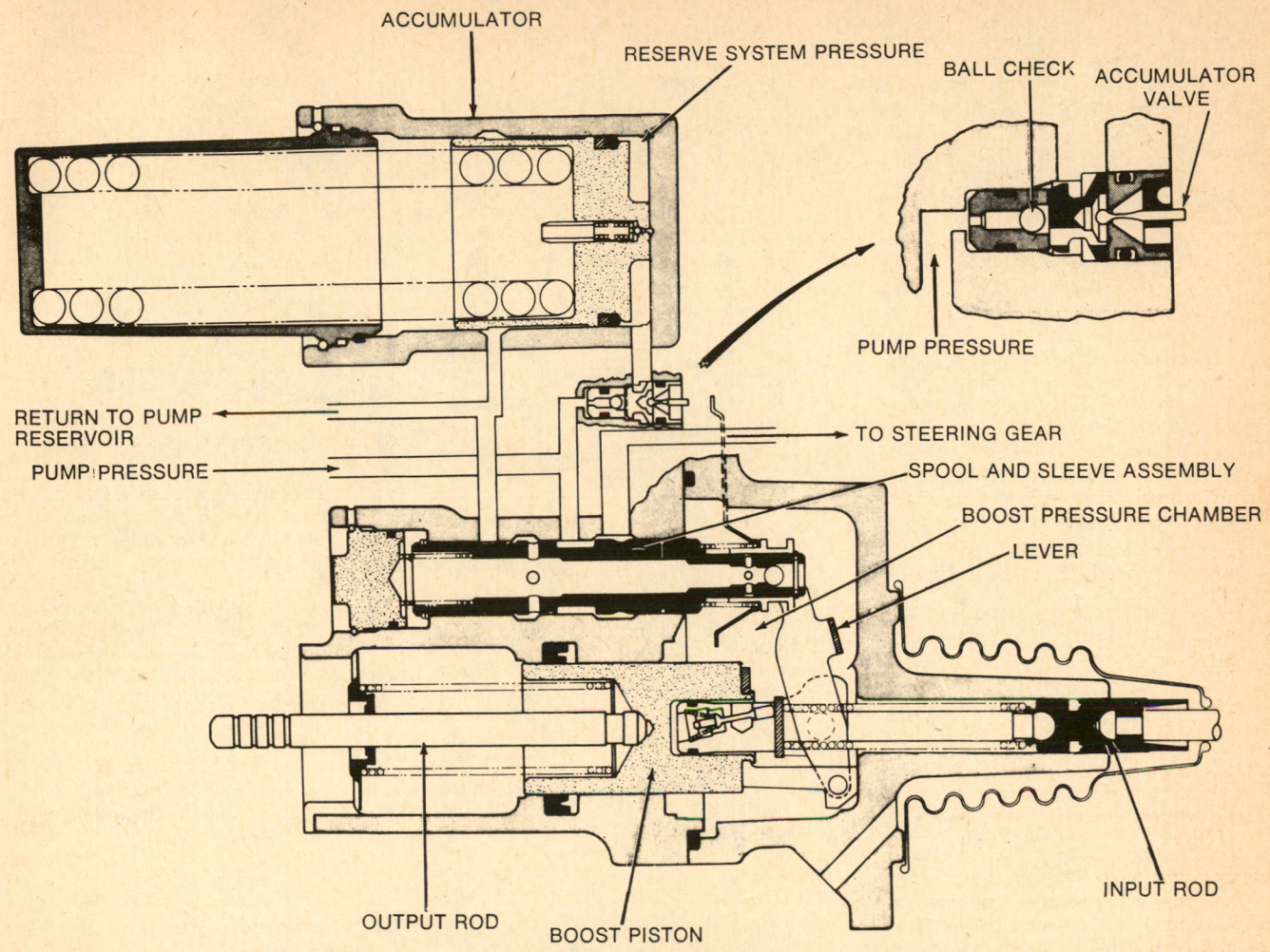

Cutaway view of the hydro-boost power brake unit and accumulator (© Ford Motor Co)

Overhaul

Ford Motor Company services the Hydro-boost unit with a replacement new or rebuilt unit only. No provisions are made for overhaul of the unit. GM Hydro-boost units may be overhauled.

--- **CAUTION** ---

Do not attempt to interchange parts between Hydro-boost units of different makes of cars, because of pressure differentials and differences of the tolerances of the internal parts. Pressure could exceed the normal accumulator release pressure of 1,400 psi, and injury or damage could result.

Disassembly

NOTE: *Have a drain pan ready to catch and discard leaking fluid during disassembly.*

1. Remove the booster assembly from the car.
2. Secure the booster in a vise on a mounting bracket, if possible with the pedal rod down. Pump the pedal rod 4 to 5 times, assuring that accumulator pressure is depleted. Cut the strap securing the accumulator cap.
3. Depress the accumulator spring cap with a 12 in "C" clamp and unseat the retaining ring with a small punch and remove the ring.
4. Release the "C" clamp slowly to relieve spring tension and remove the cap and spring.
5. To remove the piston, pressurize the booster thru the inlet port with air pressure, while the gear and return ports are plugged, and the piston will move out of its bore and can be removed.
6. If air is not available, form a hook from stiff wire and engage the piston in the piston fluid inlet hole. Wrap the wire around a suitable tool and pry against the housing to remove piston. Discard the piston.
7. Remove the accumulator plunger seat and guide assembly, and with a wire hook, remove the spacer-charging orifice and ball assembly and discard.
8. Loosen and remove five special bolts while holding the front housing and carefully lift off the front housing. A Torx socket is required. The spool valve and power piston assembly will remain with the rear cover.
9. Remove the output rod and piston return spring from the power piston assembly and the spool valve spring from the valve. Remove the output rod retainer assembly from the housing.
10. Remove the spool valve and examine for scratches and wear marks. Reuse or replace as necessary.
11. Inspect the power piston for scratches and worn areas. Replace or reuse as necessary. If replacement of the power piston is necessary, snip off the staked end of the connecting pin and remove the pin with a small punch.
12. Clean and flush all parts with clean power steering fluid.

Assembly

1. Lower the new spacer-charging orifice and ball assembly into the accumulator valve bore on the front of the housing.
2. Mount a new "O" ring onto the new accumulator plunger seat and guide the assembly and insert into the valve bore.

3. If a new power piston was needed, install a new pin in the hole to engage the piston connecting bracket to the small yoke in the lever and mushroom the end of the pin to avoid loss.

4. Install a new figure eight seal on the mating face of the rear housing and a new power piston seal in the front housing.

5. Insert the spool valve and spring into the bore while pulling up on the power piston and extending the lever to accept the sleeve on the spool valve. With the lever extended, put the front housing over the rear housing and slide the lever pins into the slot in the sleeve of the spool valve.

6. Lower the front housing down into the rear cover while centering the power piston in the bore.

NOTE: *If a seal protector is not available, extreme care must be exercised in seating the piston to the seal so that the seal lip is not damaged.*

7. Install the five special bolts and torque to 20 ft. lbs. A Torx socket is required.

8. Install the output rod, spring and new spring retainer, securing the retainer by tapping it into place with a 7/8 in. deep well socket and a hammer.

9. Install the new accumulator piston assembly and install the new "O" ring to the accumulator cap. With the 12 in. "C" clamp, depress the cap and spring and install the retaining clip in the bore of the front housing.

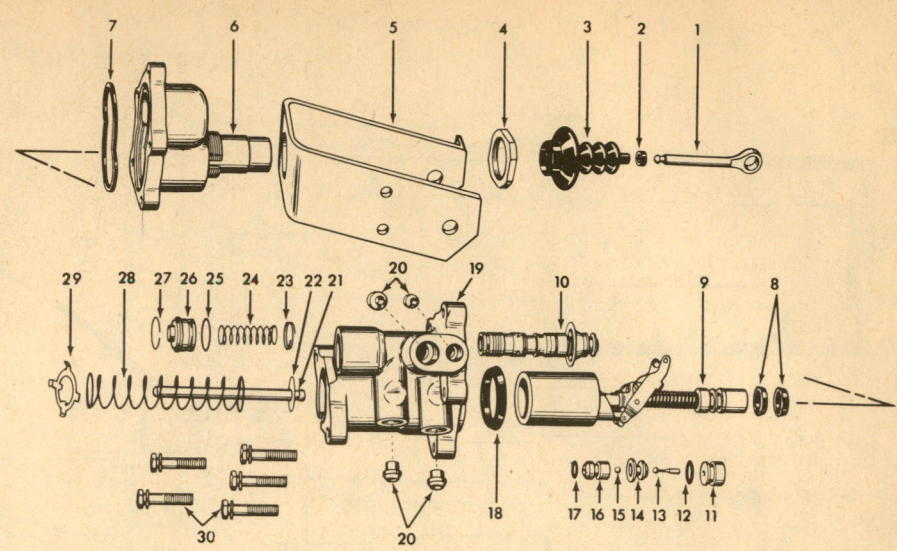

Typical Hydro-boost components, less accumulator assembly
(© Chevrolet Div., G.M. Corp.)

1 Pedal push rod	11 Plunger seat	21 Output push rod
2 Pedal rod retainer	12 "O" ring seal	22 Push rod retainer
3 Boot	13 Plunger	23 Spiral snap ring
4 Bracket nut	14 Spacer	24 Spool spring
5 Linkage bracket	15 Check valve ball	25 Plug "O" ring
6 Booster cover	16 Accumulator check	26 Spool plug
7 Cover to housing seal	valve	27 Snap ring
8 Input rod seals	17 "O" ring seal	28 Piston return spring
9 Input rod and piston	18 Piston seal	29 Spring retainer
assy.	19 Booster housing	30 Housing to cover
10 Spool assembly	20 Tube seat inserts	bolts

10. Install the new strap from the drip pan to the accumulator cap.

11. Install the unit on the car and bleed the system.

Hydro-Boost Troubleshooting Chart

HIGH PEDAL AND STEERING EFFORT (IDLE)
1. Loose/broken power steering pump belt
2. Low power steering fluid level
3. Leaking hoses or fittings
4. Low idle speed
5. Hose restriction
6. Defective power steering pump

HIGH PEDAL EFFORT (IDLE)
1. Binding pedal/linkage
2. Fluid contamination
3. Defective hydro-boost unit

POOR PEDAL RETURN
1. Binding pedal linkage
2. Restricted booster return line
3. Internal return system restriction

PEDAL CHATTER/PULSATION
1. Power steering pump drivebelt slipping
2. Low power steering fluid level
3. Defective power steering pump
4. Defective hydro-boost unit

BRAKES OVERSENSITIVE
1. Binding pedal/linkage
2. Defective hydro-boost unit

NOISE
1. Low power steering fluid level
2. Air in the power steering fluid
3. Loose power steering pump drivebelt
4. Hose restrictions

MANUAL STEERING
GEAR APPLICATION INDEX

Listed below are the different types of steering gear and the make of car in which each is used. Section numbers refer to the text sections that cover that particular type of steering gear.

Gear Type	Section	Make	Year
A	2	Ford Motor Co. and Lincoln-Mercury Division All models except those using type D	1972-79
B	3	General Motors Corp., All models except Chevette	1972-79
		American Motors Corp., All models except Pacer	1972-79
C	4	Chrysler Corp., All except Omni/Horizon	1972-79
D	5	Ford Motor Co., Fairmont, Zephyr, Pinto, Bobcat, Mustang II, 1979 Mustang and Capri	1972-79
E	6	American Motors Pacer	1975-79
F	7	Chevette	1976-79
G	8	Omni, Horizon	1978-79

Gear Types

A Ford steering gear, recirculating ball
B Saginaw steering gear, recirculating ball
C Chrysler steering gear, recirculating ball
D Ford rack and pinion steering gear
E AMC rack and pinion steering gear
F Chevette rack and pinion steering gear
G Chrysler rack and pinion

Section Page Numbers

POWER STEERING
GEAR APPLICATION INDEX

Section Numbers Refer to Sections in Text

Make	Year	Gear Type	Sections
American Motors			
All except Pacer	1972-79	D	2,5
Pacer	1975-79	G	2,11
Chrysler Corporation			
All except Omni/Horizon	1972-79	C	2,6
Omni/Horizon	1978-79	H	10
Ford Motor Company			
Fairmont, Zephyr	1978-79	F	2,8
Maverick, Comet	1972-79	A	2,3
Granada, Monarch	1976-79	A	2,3
Mustang, Cougar	1972-73	D	2,5
Cougar	1974-79	E	2,7
Cougar, 351 V8; Elite	1975-76	D	2,5
Torino, Montego	1972-76	E	2,7
Ford, Mercury, Thunderbird, Lincoln	1972-79	E	2,7
Mustang II, Pinto, Bobcat	1972-79	F	2,8
Mustang, Capri	1979	F	2,8
General Motors			
All except Corvette	1972-79	D	2,5
Corvette	1972-79	B	8,4

Gear Types

A Bendix linkage-type (Ford Non-Integral System)
B Saginaw linkage-type
C Chrysler full-time (constant control type)
D Saginaw rotary-type
E Ford torsion bar (Ford integral system)
F Ford integral rack and pinion
G AMC rack and pinion
H Chrysler rack and pinion

Section Page Numbers

Manual Steering

MANUAL STEERING DIAGNOSIS

Condition	Possible Cause	Correction
Hard steering	(a) Low or uneven tire pressure.	(a) Inflate tires to recommended pressures.
	(b) Insufficient lubricant in the steering gear housing or in steering linkage.	(b) Lubricate as necessary.
	(c) Steering gear shaft adjusted too tight.	(c) Adjust according to instructions.
	(d) Front wheels out of line.	(d) Align the wheels. See the Front Suspension Section.
	(e) Steering column misaligned.	(e) Adjust
Excessive play or looseness in the steering wheel	(a) Steering gear shaft adjusted too loose or badly worn.	(a) Replace worn parts and adjust according to instructions.
	(b) Steering linkage loose or worn.	(b) Replace worn parts.
	(c) Front wheel bearings improperly adjusted.	(c) Adjust according to instructions.
	(d) Steering arm loose on steering gear shaft.	(d) Inspect for damage to the gear shaft and steering arm, replace parts as necessary.
	(e) Steering gear housing attaching bolts loose.	(e) Tighten attaching bolts to specifications.
	(f) Steering arms loose at steering knuckles.	(f) Tighten according to specifications.
	(g) Worn ball joints.	(g) Replace the ball joints as necessary.
	(h) Worm shaft bearing adjustment too loose.	(h) Adjust worm bearing preload according to instructions.

SECTION 1

STEERING GEAR ALIGNMENT

Before any steering gear adjustments are made, it is recommended that the front end of the car be raised and a thorough inspection be made for stiffness or lost motion in the steering gear, steering linkage and front suspension. Worn or damaged parts should be replaced, since a satisfactory adjustment of the steering gear cannot be obtained if bent or badly worn parts exist.

It is also very important that the steering gear be properly aligned in the car. Misalignment of the gear places a stress on the steering worm shaft, therefore a proper adjustment is impossible. To align the steering gear, loosen the mounting bolts to permit the gear to align itself. Check the steering gear mounting seat, and if there is a gap at any of the mounting bolts, proper alignment may be obtained by placing shims where excessive gap appears. Tighten the steering gear bolts. Alignment of the gear in the car is very important and should be done carefully so that a satisfactory, trouble-free gear adjustment may be obtained.

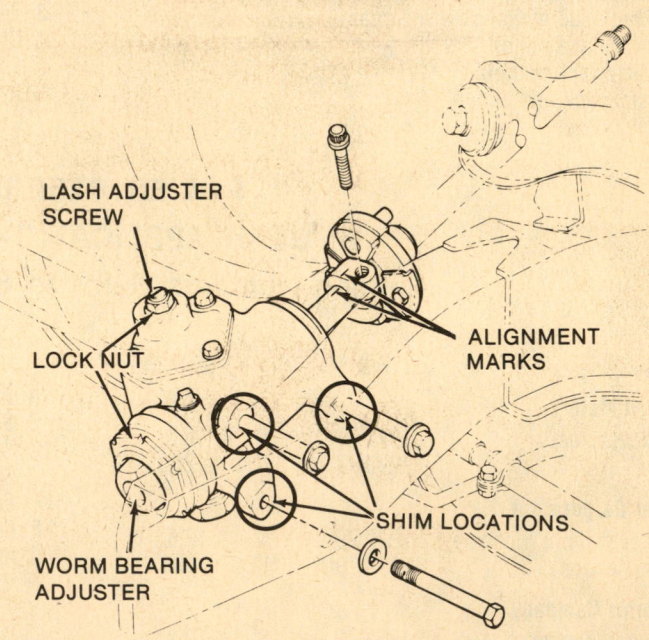

LASH ADJUSTER SCREW

LOCK NUT

ALIGNMENT MARKS

SHIM LOCATIONS

WORM BEARING ADJUSTER

Typical adjustment and shim location (© Chevrolet Div., G.M. Corp.)

SECTION 2

FORD RECIRCULATING BALL TYPE

Steering Worm and Sector Gear Adjustments

The ball nut assembly and the sector gear must be adjusted properly to maintain a minimum amount of steering shaft end-play and a minimum amount of backlash between the sector gear and the ball nut. There are only two adjustments that may be done on this steering gear and they should be done as follows:

1. Disconnect the pitman arm from the steering pitman-to-idler arm rod.

2. Loosen the locknut on the sector shaft adjustment screw and turn the adjusting screw counterclockwise.

3. Measure the worm bearing preload by attaching an in lbs torque wrench to the steering wheel nut.

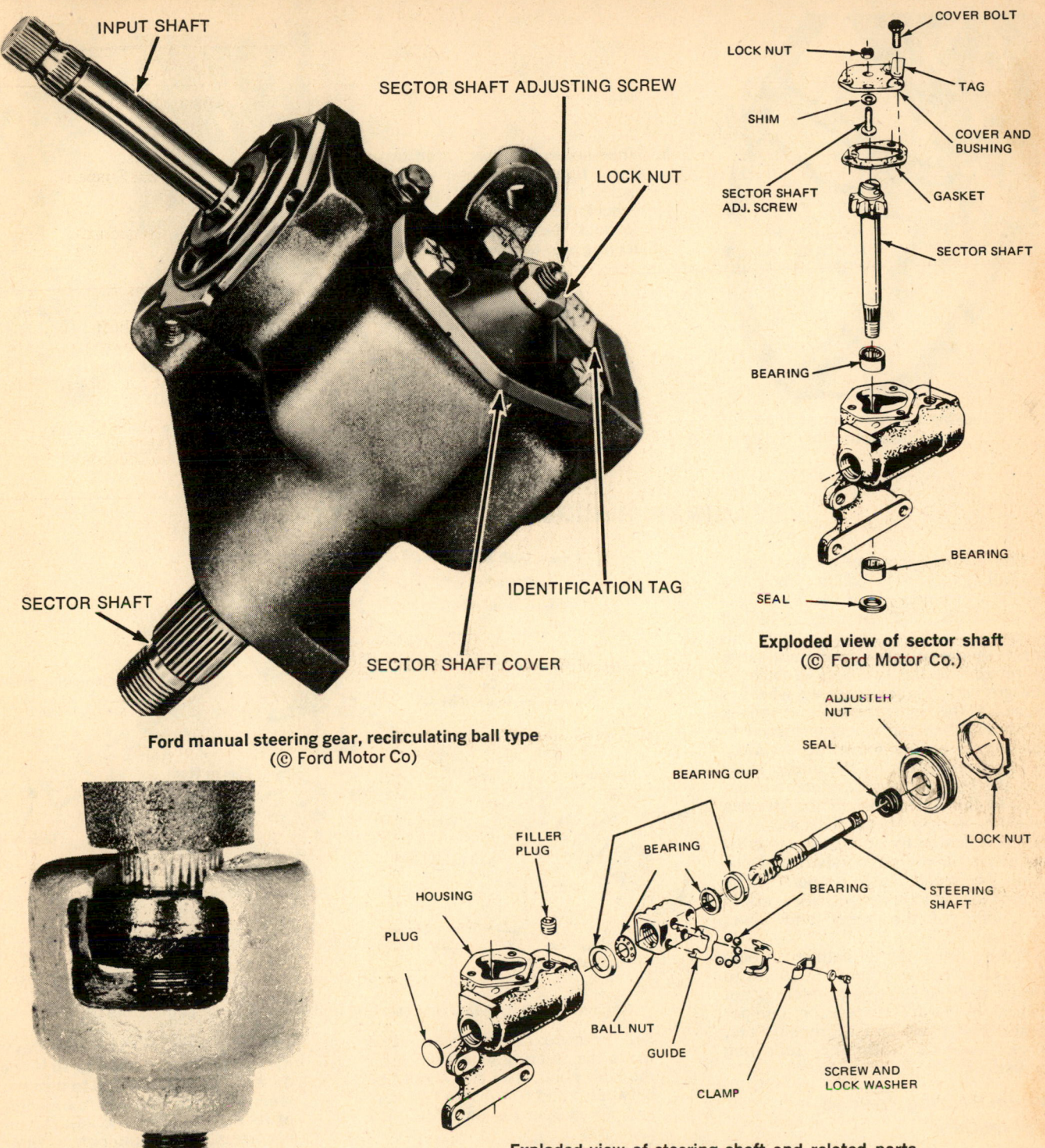

INPUT SHAFT

SECTOR SHAFT ADJUSTING SCREW

LOCK NUT

SECTOR SHAFT

IDENTIFICATION TAG

SECTOR SHAFT COVER

Ford manual steering gear, recirculating ball type
(© Ford Motor Co)

COVER BOLT

LOCK NUT

TAG

SHIM

COVER AND BUSHING

SECTOR SHAFT ADJ. SCREW

GASKET

SECTOR SHAFT

BEARING

BEARING

SEAL

Exploded view of sector shaft
(© Ford Motor Co.)

ADJUSTER NUT

SEAL

BEARING CUP

LOCK NUT

FILLER PLUG

BEARING

BEARING

STEERING SHAFT

HOUSING

PLUG

BALL NUT

GUIDE

SCREW AND LOCK WASHER

CLAMP

Exploded view of steering shaft and related parts
(© Ford Motor Co.)

Removing pitman arm
(© Ford Motor Co)

With the steering wheel off center, note the reading required to rotate input shaft about $1\frac{1}{2}$ turns either side of center. If the torque reading is not about 3-8 in lbs., adjust the gear as given in the next step.

4. Loosen the steering shaft bearing adjuster locknut and tighten or back off the bearing adjusting screw until the preload is within the specified limits.
5. Tighten the steering shaft bearing adjuster locknut to 60-80 ft lbs, and recheck the preload torque.
6. Turn the steering wheel slowly to either stop. Turn *gently* against the stop to avoid possible damage to

the ball return guides. Then rotate the wheel $2\frac{3}{4}$ turns (2 turns with 16:1 ratio) to center the ball nut on Maverick, Comet, Granada, and Monarch; $3\frac{1}{4}$ turns on larger models.
7. Turn the sector adjusting screw clockwise until the proper torque (7-13 in lbs) is obtained that is necessary to rotate the worm gear past its center (high spot).

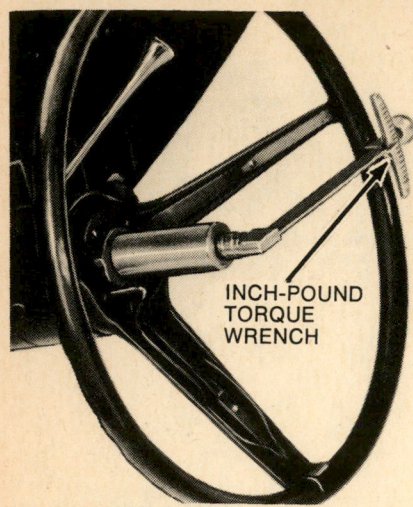

Checking steering gear preload
(© Ford Motor Co)

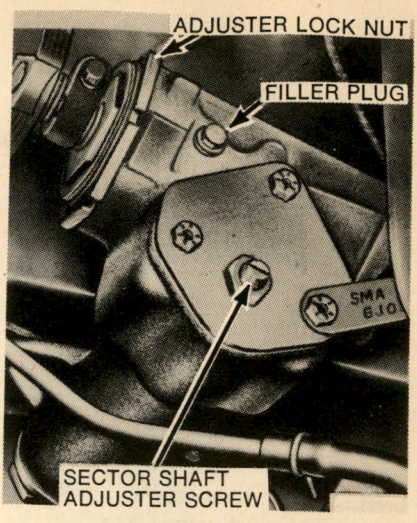

Steering gear adjustments
(© Ford Motor Co)

8. While holding the sector adjusting screw, tighten the sector screw adjusting locknut to 32-40 ft lbs and recheck the backlash adjustment.
9. Connect the pitman arm to the steering arm-to-idler arm rod.

SECTION 3
SAGINAW RECIRCULATING BALL TYPE

The steering gear is of the recirculating ball nut type. The ball nut, mounted on the worm gear, is driven by means of steel balls which circulate in helical grooves in both the worm and nut. Ball return guides attached to the nut serve to recirculate the two sets of balls in the grooves. As the steering wheel is turned to the right, the ball nut moves upward. When the wheel is turned to the left, the ball nut moves downward.

The sector teeth on the pinion shaft and the ball nut are designed so that they fit the tightest when the steering wheel is straight ahead. This mesh action is adjusted by an adjusting screw which moves the pinion shaft endwise until the teeth mesh properly. The worm bearing adjuster provides proper preloading of the upper and lower bearings.

Before doing the adjustment procedures given below, refer to Section 1 to ensure that the steering problem is not caused by faulty suspension components, bad front end alignment, etc. Then, proceed with the following adjustments.

Worm Bearing Preload Adjustment

--------- CAUTION ---------
Do not turn steering wheel hard against stops as damage to ball nut assembly may result. Use a torque wrench calibrated to 50 in lbs or less.

1. Disconnect the steering linkage ball stud from the pitman arm.
2. Loosen the pitman shaft adjusting screw locknut and back off adjusting screw a few turns.
3. Install an in lbs torque wrench to the steering wheel attaching nut

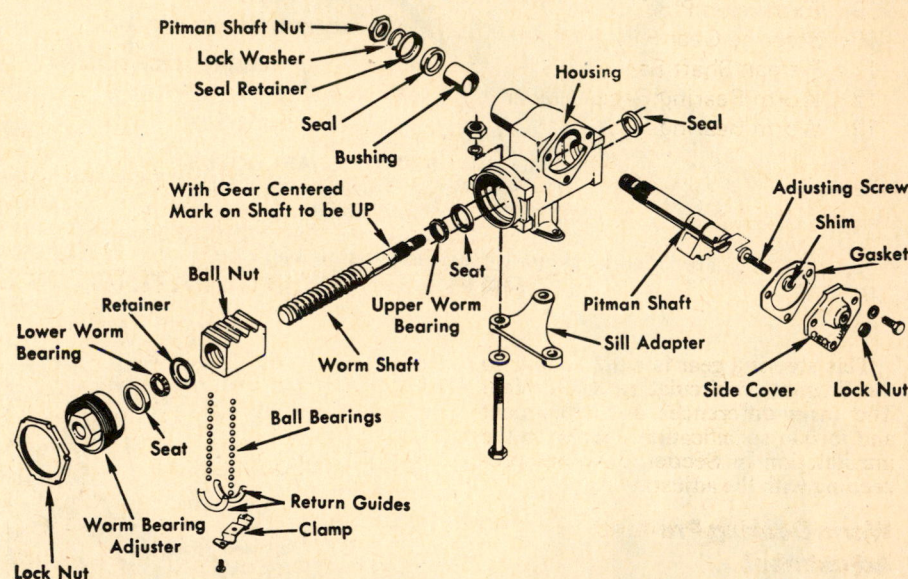

Saginaw steering gear, recirculating ball type (© American Motors Corp)

and measure the pull needed to move the steering wheel when off the high point. The pull should be between 4 and 6 in lbs on GM cars and 5 and 8 in lbs on AMC vehicles.
4. To adjust the worm bearing, loosen the worm bearing adjuster locknut with a brass drift and turn the adjuster screw until the proper pull is

Sector and Ball Nut Backlash Adjustment

1. After the worm bearing preload has been adjusted correctly, loosen the pitman shaft adjusting screw obtained. When adjustment is correct, tighten the adjuster locknut, and recheck with the torque wrench.
locknut and turn the pitman shaft

adjusting screw until a pull of 5 to 9 in lbs on GM cars and 4 to 10 in lbs on AMC cars is required to turn the steering wheel through the center of its travel. When the adjustment is correct, tighten the pitman shaft adjusting screw locknut and recheck the adjustment.
NOTE: *This torque is in addition to Worm bearing preload torque. Total torque required to turn the worm shaft should not exceed 16 in lbs.*
2. Turn the steering wheel to the center of its turning limits (pitman arm disconnected). If the steering wheel is removed, the mark on the steering shaft should be at top center.
3. Connect the ball stud to the pitman arm, tightening the attaching nut to 45-35 ft lbs.

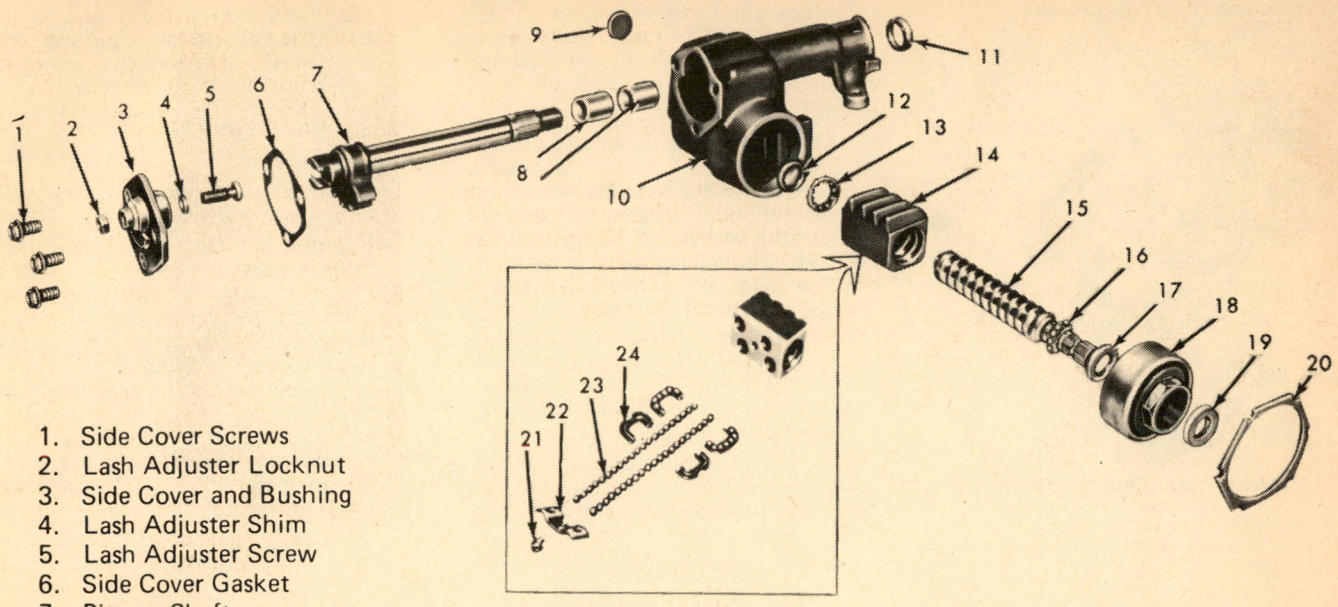

1. Side Cover Screws
2. Lash Adjuster Locknut
3. Side Cover and Bushing
4. Lash Adjuster Shim
5. Lash Adjuster Screw
6. Side Cover Gasket
7. Pitman Shaft
8. Pitman Shaft Bushings

9. Expansion Plug
10. Steering Gear Housing
11. Pitman Shaft Seal
12. Worm Bearing Race—Lower
13. Worm Bearing—Lower

14. Ball Nut
15. Wormshaft
16. Worm Bearing—Upper
17. Worm Bearing Race—Upper
18. Adjuster Plug
19. Wormshaft Seal

20. Adjuster Plug Locknut
21. Clamp Screw
22. Ball Guide Clamp
23. Balls
24. Ball Guides

Corvette steering gear, recirculating ball type (© G.M. Corp)

SECTION 4
CHRYSLER RECIRCULATING BALL TYPE

This steering gear is quite similar to the Saginaw recirculating ball design. The main differences are adjustment and torque specifications. Refer to the introduction in Section 3 before proceeding with the adjustments.

Worm Bearing Pre-load Adjustment

1. Remove the steering gear arm and lockwasher from the sector shaft, using a suitable gear puller.
2. Remove the horn button or horn ring.
3. Loosen the cross-shaft adjusting screw locknut, and back out the adjusting screw about two turns.
4. Turn the steering wheel two complete turns from the straight ahead position, and place an in lb torque wrench on the steering shaft nut.
5. Rotate the steering shaft at least one turn toward the straight ahead position while measuring the torque on the torque wrench. The torque should be between $1\frac{1}{8}$ and $4\frac{1}{2}$ in lbs to move the steering wheel. If torque is not within these limits, loosen the worm shaft bearing adjuster locknut and turn the adjuster clockwise to increase the preload or counterclockwise to de-

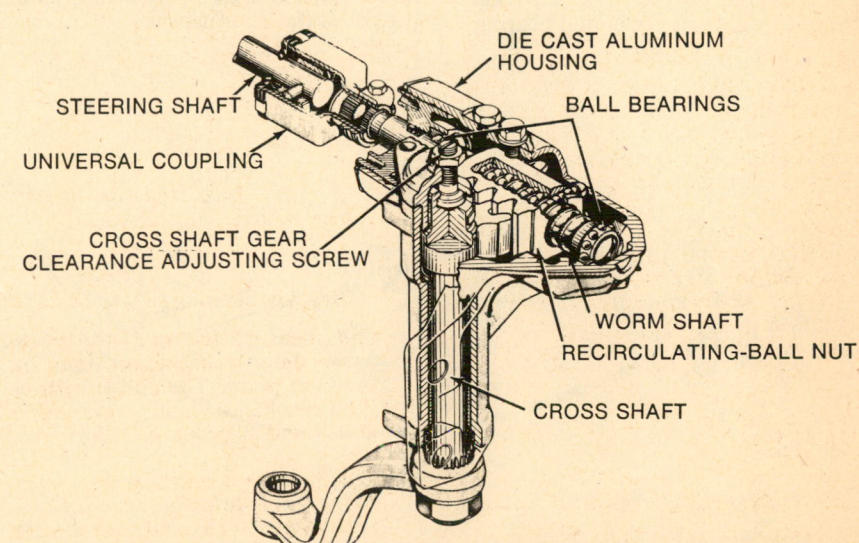

Chrysler steering gear, recirculating ball type
(© Chrysler Corp)

crease the preload. When the preload is correct, hold the adjuster screw steady and tighten the locknut. Recheck preload.

Ball Nut Rack and Sector Mesh Adjustment

NOTE: *This adjustment can be accur-*

ately made only after proper preloading of worm bearing.

1. Turn steering wheel gently from one stop to the other, counting the number of turns. Turn the steering wheel back exactly half way, to the center position.
2. Turn the cross-shaft adjusting

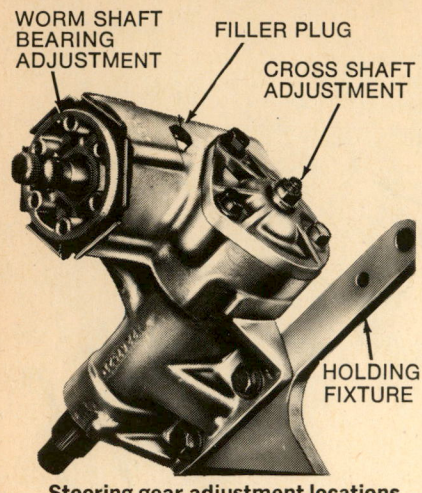

WORM SHAFT BEARING ADJUSTMENT

FILLER PLUG

CROSS SHAFT ADJUSTMENT

HOLDING FIXTURE

Steering gear adjustment locations
(© Chrysler Corp)

screw clockwise to remove all lash between ball nut rack and the sector gear teeth, then tighten adjusting screw locknut to 35 ft lbs.

3. Turn the steering wheel about 1/4 turn away from the center or high spot position. With the torque wrench on the steering wheel nut measure the torque required to turn the steering wheel through the high spot at the center position. The reading should be between 8 and 11 in lbs. This is the total of the worm shaft bearing preload and the ball nut rack and sector gear mesh load. Readjust the cross-shaft adjustment screw if necessary to obtain a correct torque reading.

4. After completing the adjustments, place the front wheels in a straight ahead position, and with the steering wheel and steering gear centered, install the steering arm on cross-shaft. Tighten the steering arm retaining nut to 180 ft lbs.

Cross-Shaft Oil Seal Replacement

1. Remove the steering gear arm retaining nut and lockwasher.
2. Remove seal with a seal puller or other appropriate tool.
3. Place a new oil seal onto the splines of the cross-shaft with the lip of the seal facing the housing.
4. With a seal installer tool or its equivalent, press the seal into the housing.
5. Remove the tool, and install the steering gear arm, lockwasher, and retaining nut. Tighten the nut to 180 ft lbs torque.

SECTION 5
FORD RACK AND PINION TYPE

The steering gear input shaft is connected to the steering shaft. A pinion gear is machined on the input shaft and engages the rack. Rotation of the input shaft pinion causes the rack to move from side to side.

A tie rod is attached at both ends of the rack by a moveable joint. The unit is sealed at each end with a rubber bellows. The steering gear is filled with SAE-90 oil at initial assembly and checking or refilling is not required unless leakage is evident.

Replacement of the inner tie rods, rack, housing, or upper pinion bearing,

necessitates removal of the steering gear assembly.

It is important to remember that when the front wheels are off the ground, the steering wheel should not be moved quickly or forcefully from lock to lock. This could cause a buildup of hydraulic pressure within the assembly which could damage or blow off the bellows.

With the front suspension and linkage in good condition and gear in proper adjustment, there should be no more than 3/8 in. free-play measured at the rim of the steering wheel.

When turning the steering wheel from one stop to the other in a stationary vehicle, there should be no knock produced by the steering gear.

All repair and adjustment procedures require the removal of the rack and pinion gear from the vehicle.

Support Yoke to Rack Adjustment

1. Clean the exterior of the gear thoroughly and place it, using the mounting pads, in a soft-jawed vise, with the yoke cover up.

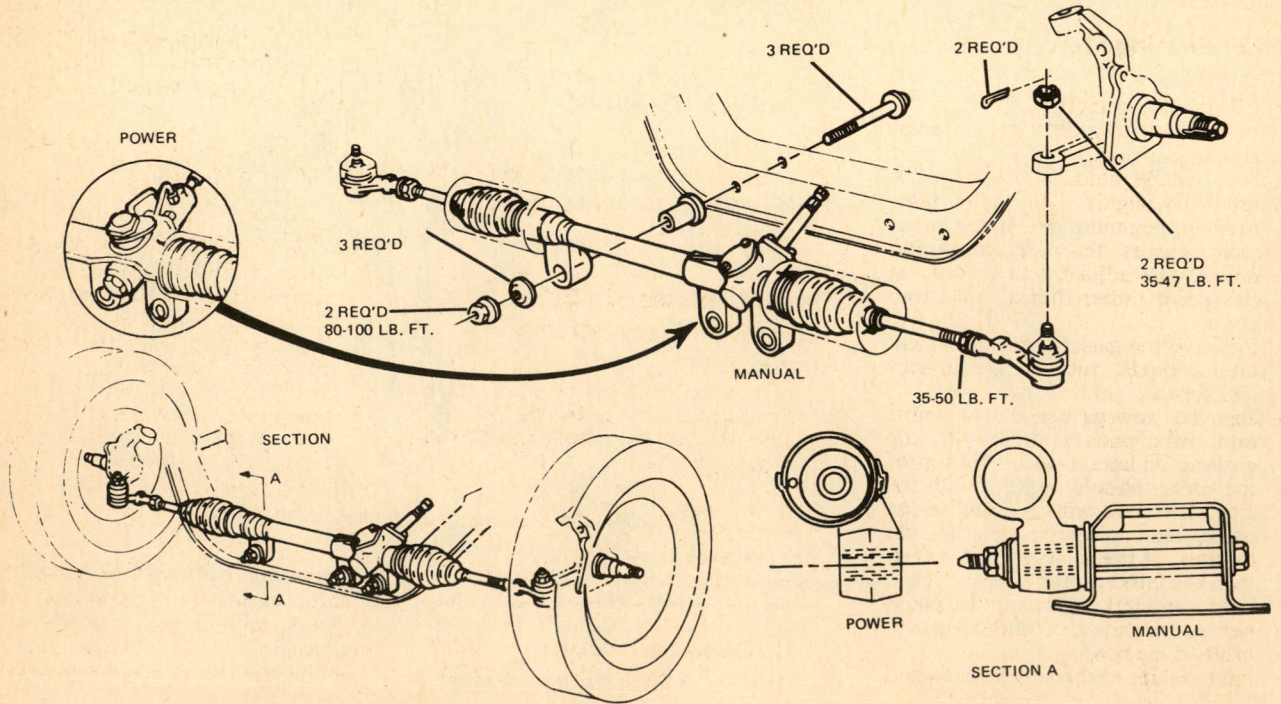

POWER

3 REQ'D

2 REQ'D

3 REQ'D

2 REQ'D
80-100 LB. FT.

2 REQ'D
35-47 LB. FT.

MANUAL

35-50 LB. FT.

SECTION

A

A

POWER

MANUAL

SECTION A

Mustang II rack and pinion steering gear (© Ford Motor Co)

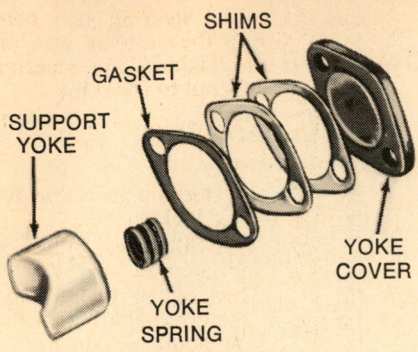

Support yoke assembly
(© Ford Motor Co)

2. Remove the yoke cover, gasket, shims, and yoke spring.
3. Clean the cover and housing flange areas thoroughly.
4. Reinstall the yoke and cover, omitting the gasket, shims, and spring. Tighten the cover bolts lightly, until the cover just touches the yoke.
5. Measure the gap between the cover and the housing flange with a feeler gauge. With the gasket, add selected shims to give a combined shim pack thickness of 0.005-0.006 in. more than the gap.
6. Remove the cover.
7. Assemble the gasket next to the housing flange and then assemble the selected shims, spring, and cover.
8. Add a sealant to cover the bolt threads and torque to 7-10 ft lbs through 1972, and 15-20 ft lbs on later models.
9. Check to see that gear operates smoothly without binding or slackness.

Pinion Bearing Preload Adjustment

1. Loosen the attaching bolts of the yoke cover to relieve spring pressure on the rack.
2. Remove the pinion cover and clean area thoroughly. On some later models, beginning 1974, the input shaft passes through the pinion cover. The adjustment is made at this point rather than at a bottom cover.
3. Remove the gasket and shims. On later models, remove the spacer and shims.
4. Install a new gasket and fit shims until shim pack is flush with the gasket. On later models, the top of the spacer should be flush with the gasket. Check with a straightedge using light pressure. Install the thinnest of the selected shims first, then the 0.093 in. shim and cover.
5. Add one 0.005 in. shim to the pack, next to the pinion cover, in order to preload the bearing.
6. Add sealant to the bolt threads and

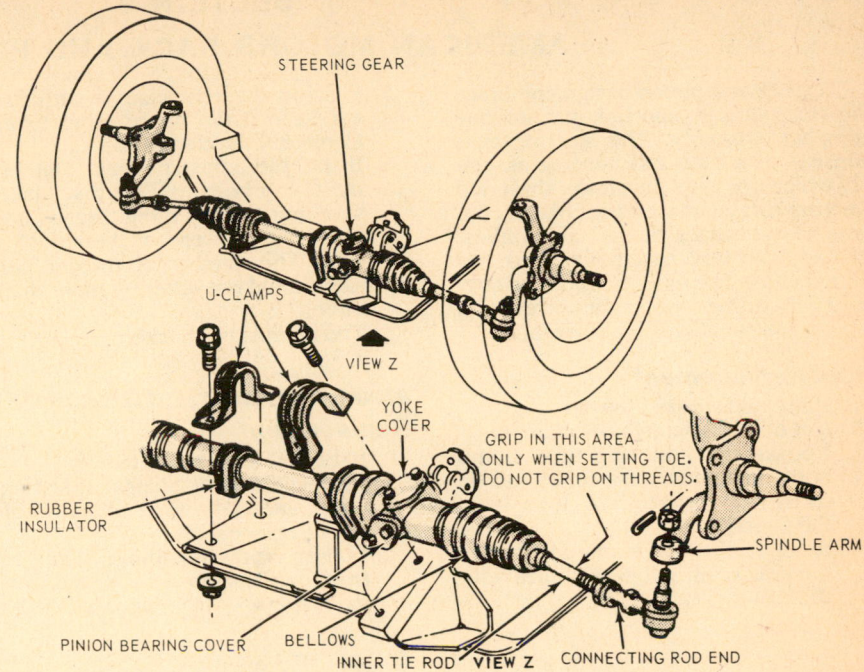

Pinto steering gear assembly, rack and pinion type (© Ford Motor Co)

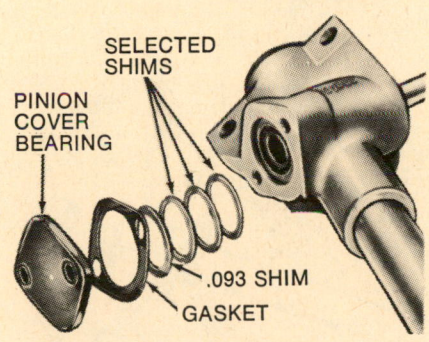

Pinion bearing preload cover and shims
(© Ford Motor Co)

install. Torque to 15-20 ft lbs.
7. Torque yoke cover bolts to 7-10 ft lbs through 1972, and 15-20 ft lbs on later models.

Tie Rod Articulation Effort Adjustment Fairmont and Zephyr Only

1. Install the hook end of a pull scale through the hole in the tie rod end stud. The effort to move the tie rod should be 1-5 lb.

— CAUTION —

Do not damage the tie rod neck when pulling with the scale.

2. If the effort falls outside the range, replace the ball joint/tie rod assem-

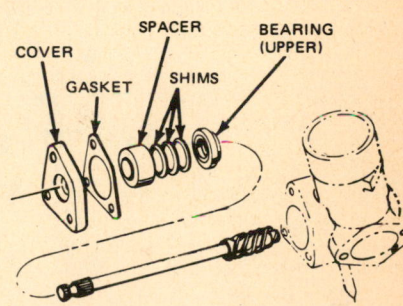

Pinion bearing preload is adjusted at the upper cover on later models
(© Ford Motor Co)

bly. Save the tie rod end for use on the new assembly.

Input Shaft Seal Replacement

1. Clean the area around the input shaft end-seal. Do not scratch or damage the pinion shaft.
2. Pry the pinion seal from its bore.
3. Lubricate the new pinion seal and install it over the shaft.
4. Use a piece of tubing to engage the outer flange of the seal and press or tap the seal into place so it is flush with shoulder of the bore.

— CAUTION —

If the outer edge of the seal is not engaged during assembly, the seal will be damaged.

SECTION 6
AMERICAN MOTORS RACK AND PINION TYPE

The rack and pinion design combines the steering gear and linkage into one compact assembly. The steering gear consists of a tube and housing assembly which contains the pinion shaft and steering rack. The steering linkage consists of two inner tie rod assemblies, two adjuster tube assemblies, and two tie rod ends. The inner tie rods are covered with rubber boots, connected with a pressure-equalizing breather tube.

Boot Replacement

1. Raise and support the car.
2. Cut off the original boot clamps.
3. Loosen the adjusting tube clamp bolts, matchmark the tubes and tie rods, and unscrew the tube from the tie rods.
4. Remove the old boots and install the new ones. Align the holes with the breather tube.

5. Position the boot clamps with the ear ³/₄ in. from the breather tube. Compress the clamps.
6. Install the adjuster tubes. Tighten the clamp bolts to 22 ft lbs. Make sure that at least three threads are visible at each end of the adjuster tube. The number of threads per side should not differ by more than three.
7. Toe-in must be checked.

Mounting Clamp and Grommet Replacement

1. Raise and support the car.
2. Remove the boot clamps, adjusting tubes, and boots as in Steps 1-3 of Boot Replacement.
3. Loosen both mounting clamp to front crossmember bolts, then remove them.

4. Remove the clamps and grommets with a twisting, pulling motion.
5. Install the replacement clamps and grommets, aligning the grommet holes with the breather tube.
6. Install the mounting bolts and tighten them to 50 ft lbs.
7. Replace the boots and adjuster tubes as in Steps 4-7 of Boot Replacement.

Tie Rod End and Adjuster Tube Replacement

1. Raise and support the car.
2. Turn the wheels to the stop in the direction of the tie rod end to be removed. Jack the lower control arm up at least 2 in. Remove the cotter pin and nut at the tie rod end. Remove the tie rod end from

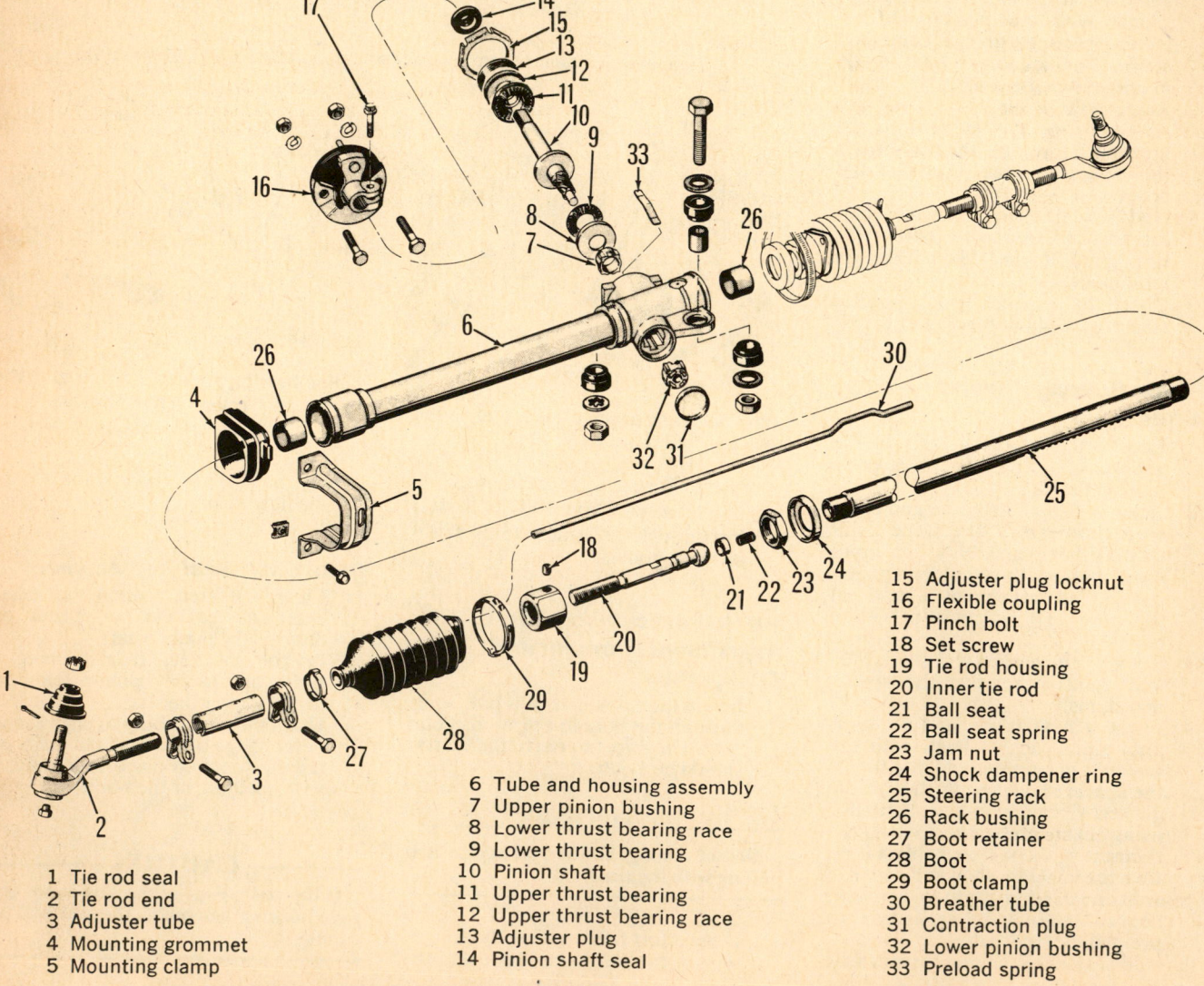

6 Tube and housing assembly
7 Upper pinion bushing
8 Lower thrust bearing race
9 Lower thrust bearing
10 Pinion shaft
11 Upper thrust bearing
12 Upper thrust bearing race
13 Adjuster plug
14 Pinion shaft seal

15 Adjuster plug locknut
16 Flexible coupling
17 Pinch bolt
18 Set screw
19 Tie rod housing
20 Inner tie rod
21 Ball seat
22 Ball seat spring
23 Jam nut
24 Shock dampener ring
25 Steering rack
26 Rack bushing
27 Boot retainer
28 Boot
29 Boot clamp
30 Breather tube
31 Contraction plug
32 Lower pinion bushing
33 Preload spring

1 Tie rod seal
2 Tie rod end
3 Adjuster tube
4 Mounting grommet
5 Mounting clamp

Exploded view of the American Motors Pacer manual rack and pinion steering gear
(© American Motors Corp)

the steering arm using a tie rod end removal tool.

3. Matchmark the positions of the adjusting tubes and tie rod ends.
4. Install the new tie rod ends and adjuster tubes. Torque the clamp bolts to 22 ft lbs and the tie rod end nuts to 50 ft lbs. Replace the cotter pins. Make sure that at least three threads are visible at each end of the adjuster tube. The number of threads per side should not differ by more than three.
5. Toe-in must be checked.

Inner Tie Rod Housing, Tie Rod, Ball Seat, and Spring Replacement

1. Raise and support the car.
2. Disconnect the tie rod ends as in Step 2 of Tie Rod End and Adjuster Tube Replacement.

3. Matchmark the adjuster clamps and inner tie rods. Loosen the clamp bolts and unscrew the adjuster tube and tie rod end from the inner rods.
4. Cut off the large boot clamps and move the boots aside.
5. Slide the plastic shock dampener rings off the jamnuts and loosen the jamnuts.
6. Loosen the setscrews in the tie rod housings. Unscrew the housings from the rack. Remove the inner tie rods, tie rod housings, ball seats, and springs.
7. Use waterproof EP lithium base chassis grease on all the replacement inner tie rod assembly surfaces. Pack the tie rod housing with the grease.
8. Install the ball seat springs and ball seats.

9. Assemble the inner tie rods and housings and install them on the rack. Tighten the tie rod housing to 25 ft lbs while rocking the inner tie rod to prevent grease lock. Back the housing off 1/8 turn; the tie rod should rock and rotate freely in the housing. Tighten the tie rod housing set-screws to 60 in lbs.
10. Hold the tie rod end housings with an end wrench and tighten the jamnuts to 100 ft lbs. Slide the shock dampener rings over the jamnuts.
11. Install the boot and clamps as in Steps 4 and 5 of Boot Replacement.
12. Screw the adjuster tube and tie rod end assembly onto the inner tie rod, aligning the matchmarks.
13. Replace the tie rod ends in the steering arms and torque the nuts to 50 ft lbs. Replace the cotter pins.

SECTION 7

CHEVETTE RACK AND PINION TYPE

The Chevette rack and pinion system incorporates both the steering gear and linkage assembly in one package. The pinion and most of the rack are in an aluminum housing. The pinion is supported by and turns in a sealed ball bearing at the top and a pressed in roller bearing at the bottom.

Wear is compensated for by an adjuster spring which forces the rack against the pinion teeth. The inner tie rod assemblies are threaded and staked to the rack. The unit must be removed from the car to remove the inner tie rod assemblies, which have a spring loaded spherical joint to allow both rocking and rotating movement.

Any service other than replacement of the outer tie rods or the boots requires removal of the unit from the car. Torque for the outer tie rod jam nuts is 50 ft lbs.

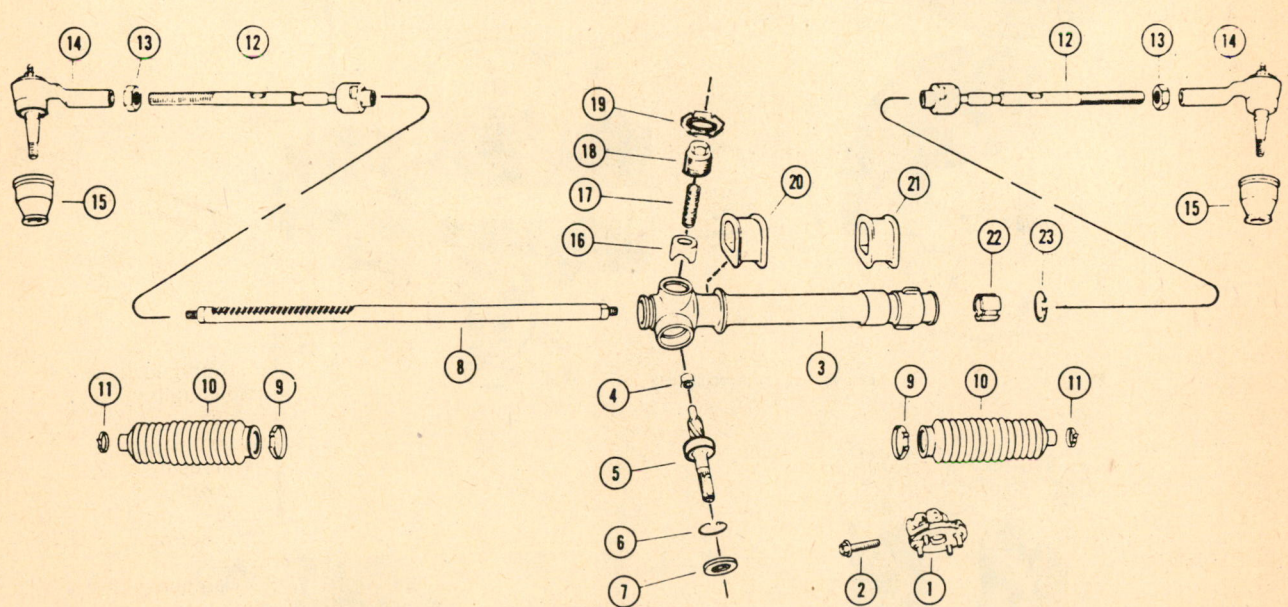

1 Coupling and steering flange assembly	9 Boot clamp	17 Adjuster spring
2 Pinch bolt	10 Boot	18 Adjuster plug
3 Housing assembly	11 Boot clamp	19 Adjuster plug locknut
4 Roller bearing assembly	12 Inner tie rod assembly	20 Left mounting grommet
5 Bearing and pinion assembly	13 Jam nut	21 Right mounting grommet
6 Retaining ring	14 Outer tie rod assembly	22 Rack bushing
7 Steering pinion seal	15 Tie rod seal	23 Retaining ring
8 Steering rack	16 Rack bearing	

Chevette rack and pinion steering (© Chevrolet Div., G.M. Corp.)

Section 8

Chrysler Rack and Pinion

This system is used exclusively on the Omni/Horizon models. It consists of housing which contains a toothed rack, a pinion, the rack slipper and the rack slipper spring. Steering effort is transmitted by the tie rods to the steering arms. The connection between the rack and the tie rod is protected by a bellows type seal which contains the gear lubricant. The gear is permanently lubricated at the factory and cannot be adjusted or serviced.

POWER STEERING

Before investigating any power steering system, first be sure of the general condition of the systems around it. Simple items such as tire pressure, loose belts, or faulty front end parts can have great effect on the function of the power steering system. After a common-sense general inspection has been made, consult Section 1 and proceed from there. Specific listings of make, model and year will be found in the Application Index.

SECTION 1

GENERAL DIAGNOSIS

Hard Steering
1. Improper tire pressure.
2. Loose pump drive belt.
3. Low or incorrect hydraulic fluid.
4. Loose, bent or poorly lubricated front end parts.
5. Improper front end alignment, especially caster.
6. Bind in steering column or mechanism.
7. Air in hydraulic system.
8. Low pump output or leaks in

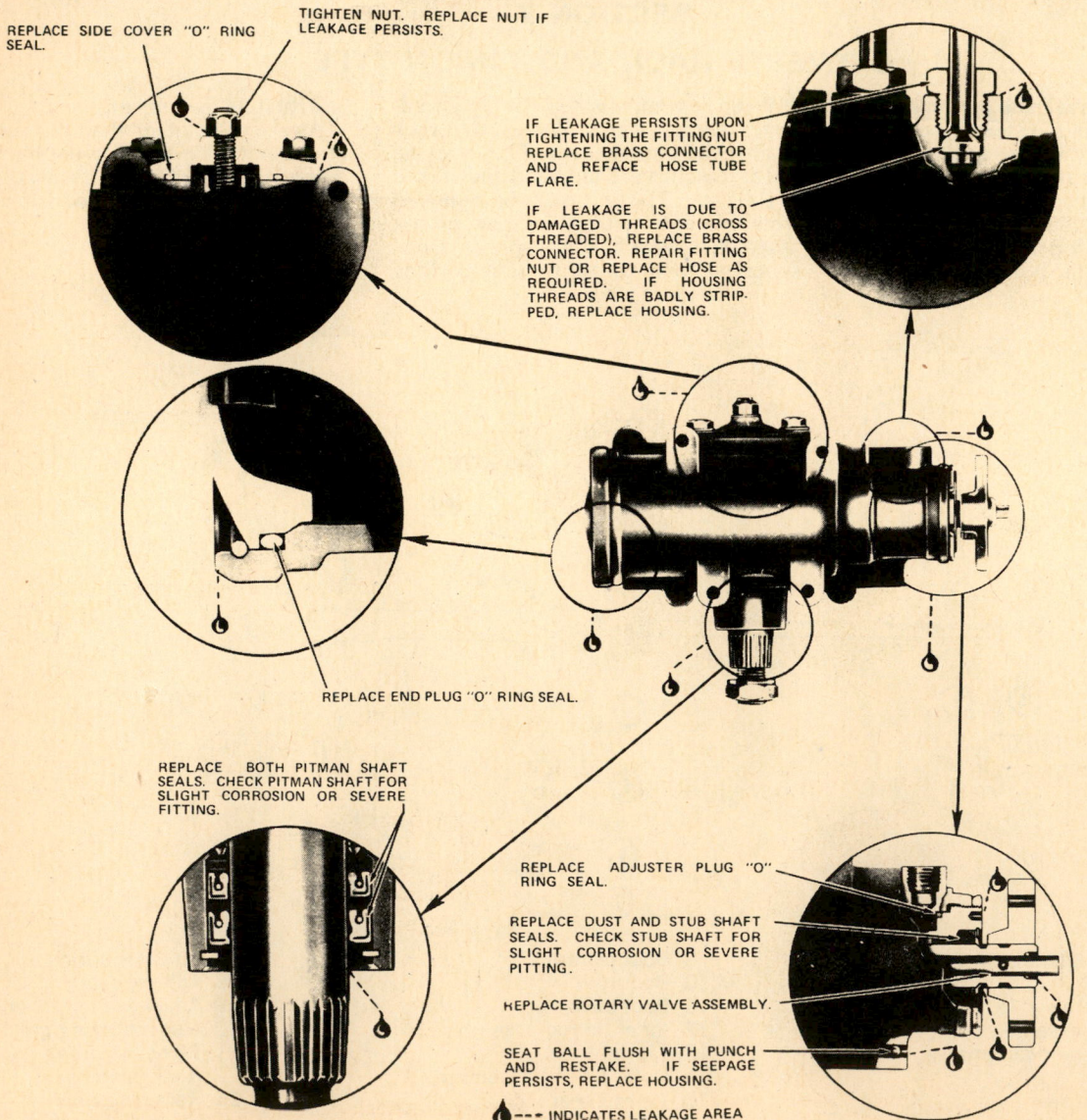

REPLACE SIDE COVER "O" RING SEAL.

TIGHTEN NUT. REPLACE NUT IF LEAKAGE PERSISTS.

IF LEAKAGE PERSISTS UPON TIGHTENING THE FITTING NUT REPLACE BRASS CONNECTOR AND REFACE HOSE TUBE FLARE.

IF LEAKAGE IS DUE TO DAMAGED THREADS (CROSS THREADED), REPLACE BRASS CONNECTOR. REPAIR FITTING NUT OR REPLACE HOSE AS REQUIRED. IF HOUSING THREADS ARE BADLY STRIPPED, REPLACE HOUSING.

REPLACE END PLUG "O" RING SEAL.

REPLACE BOTH PITMAN SHAFT SEALS. CHECK PITMAN SHAFT FOR SLIGHT CORROSION OR SEVERE FITTING.

REPLACE ADJUSTER PLUG "O" RING SEAL.

REPLACE DUST AND STUB SHAFT SEALS. CHECK STUB SHAFT FOR SLIGHT CORROSION OR SEVERE PITTING.

REPLACE ROTARY VALVE ASSEMBLY.

SEAT BALL FLUSH WITH PUNCH AND RESTAKE. IF SEEPAGE PERSISTS, REPLACE HOUSING.

⬤--- INDICATES LEAKAGE AREA

Diagnosis of power steering gear leakage areas (©Pontiac Div., G.M. Corp.)

system.
9. Obstruction in lines.
10. Pump valves sticking or out of adjustment.
11. System leakage

Loose Steering

1. Loose wheel bearings.
2. Faulty shocks.
3. Worn Pitman arm or front end components.
4. Loose steering gear mountings or lingage points.
5. Steering mechanism worn or improperly adjusted.
6. Valve spool improperly adjusted.

Veer or Wander

1. Improper tire pressure.

2. Improper front end alignment.
3. Dragging brakes.
4. Bent frame.
5. Improper rear end alignment.
6. Faulty shocks or springs.
7. Loose or bent front end components.
8. Play in Pitman arm.
9. Loose wheel bearings.
10. Binding Pitman arm.
11. Spool valve sticking or improperly adjusted.

Wheel Oscillation

1. Improper tire pressure.
2. Loose wheel bearings.
3. Improper front end alignment.
4. Bent spindle.
5. Worn, bent or broken front end components.

6. Tires out of round or imbalanced.

Noises

1. Loose belts.
2. Low fluid, air in system.
3. Foreign matter in system.
4. Improper lubrication.
5. Interference or chafing in front end.
6. Steering gear mountings loose.
7. Incorrect adjustment or wear in mechanism.
8. Faulty valves or wear in pump.
9. Growling noise caused by low fluid.

External Leakage

1. Leakage from pump unit.
2. Leakage from steering unit.
3. Leakage from connecting lines.

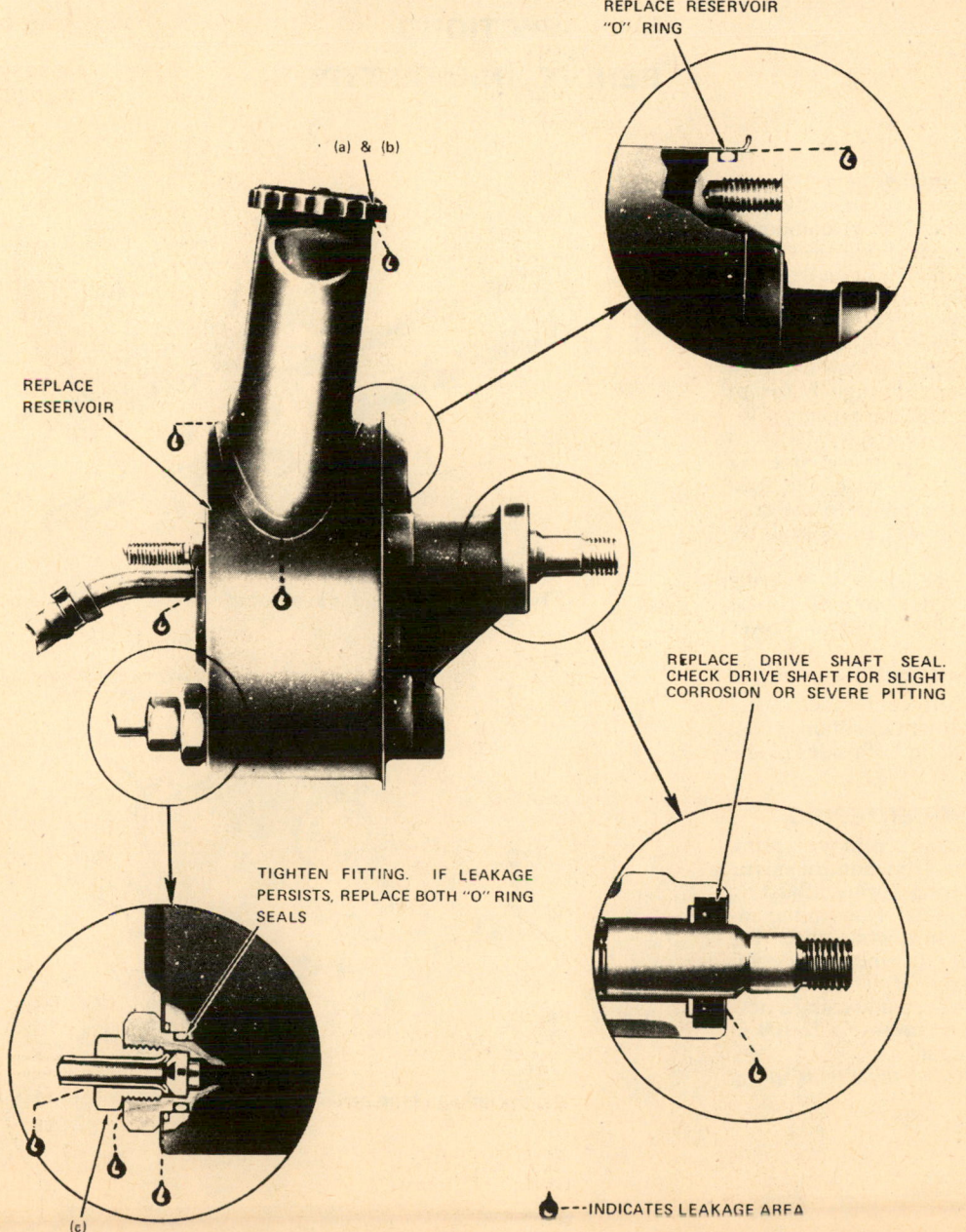

Diagnosis of power steering pump leakage areas (© Pontiac Div., G.M. Corp.)

SECTION 2

PRELIMINARY TESTS

NOTE: *The following tests are generally applicable to most power steering systems.*

Turning Effort

Check the effort required to turn the steering wheel after aligning the front wheels and inflating the tires to the proper pressure.

1. With the vehicle on dry pavement and the front wheels straight ahead, set the parking brake and turn the engine on.

2. After a short warm-up period turn the steering wheel back and forth several times to warm the steering fluid.

3. Attach a spring scale to the steering wheel rim and measure the pull required to turn the steering wheel one complete revolution in each direction.

NOTE: *This test may be done with torque wrench on the steering wheel nut. See the section on Manual Steering for a discussion of this test.*

Checking the Fluid Flow and Pressure Relief Valve in the Pump Assembly

When the wheels are turned hard right or hard left, against the stops, the fluid flow and pressure relief valves come into action. If these valves are working, there should be a slight buzzing noise. Do not hold the wheels in the extreme position for over three or four seconds because, if the pressure relief valve is not working, the pressure could get high enough to damage the system.

SECTION 3

BENDIX LINKAGE-TYPE

The Bendix linkage-type power steering system is a hydraulically controlled linkage-type system composed of an integral pump and fluid reservoir, a control valve, a power cylinder, connecting fluid lines, and the steering linkage. The hydraulic pump, which is driven by a belt turned by the engine, draws fluid from the reservoir and provides fluid pressure through hoses to the control valve and the power cylinder. There is a pressure relief valve to limit the pressures within the steering system to a safe level. After the fluid has passed from the pump to the control valve and the power cylinder, it returns to the reservoir.

The Bendix linkage-type steering system when used in Ford-built cars is called the Ford Non-Integral Power Steering System.

The only adjustment that can be made to the unit is to center the control valve. This adjustment maintains equal hydraulic pressure on both sides of the spool valve.

CONTROL VALVE CENTERING

1. Raise vehicle and remove spring cap and screws from control valve.
2. Torque centering spring adjusting nut to 90-100 in lbs. Loosen the adjusting nut 1/4 turn while observing spool bolt for movement and compensate with nut adjustment.
3. Replace spring cap and using a new gasket, torque screws to 72-100 in lbs and lower car.

NOTE: *Do not start engine with spring cap removed.*

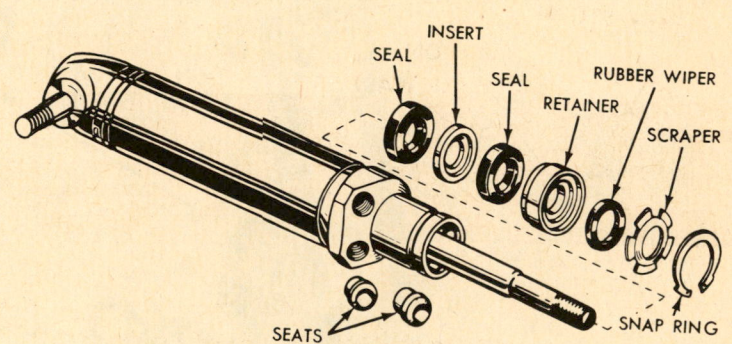

Typical power cylinder seal locations (© Ford Motor Co.)

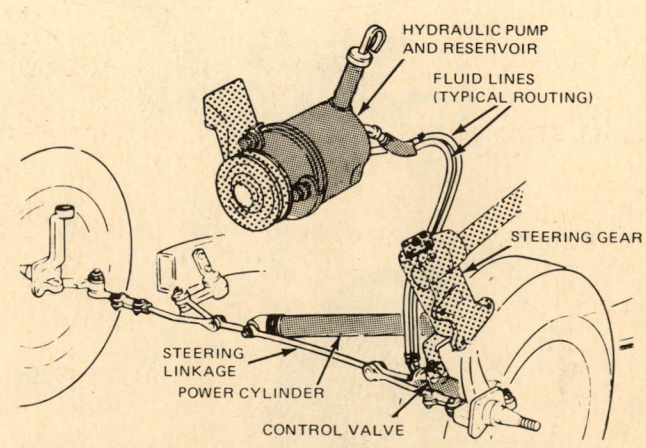

Bendix linkage-type power steering system (© Ford Motor Co)

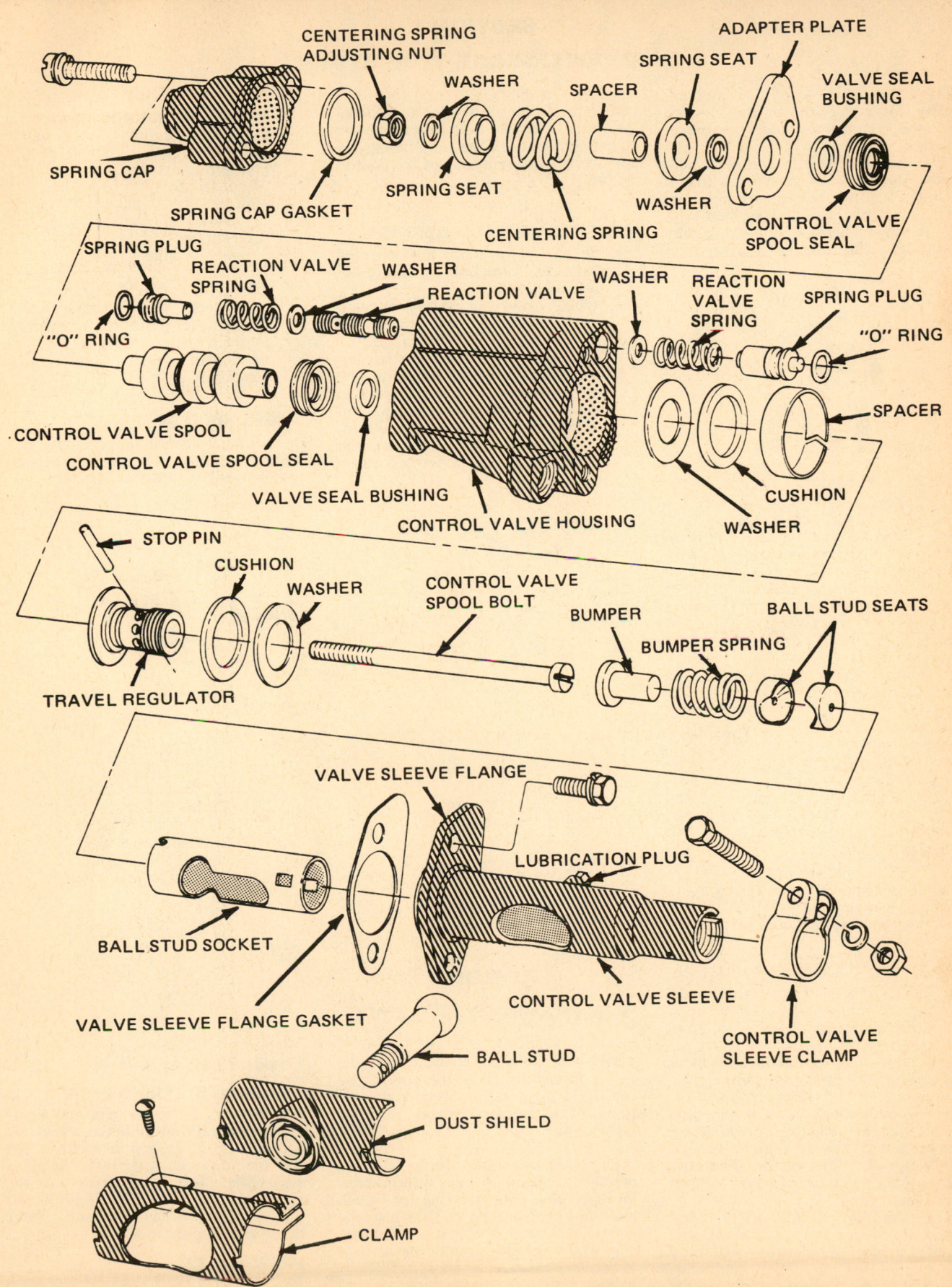

Exploded view of control valve (© Ford Motor Co.)

Power Steering

SECTION 4

SAGINAW LINKAGE-TYPE SYSTEM

The Corvette is the only car which uses the Saginaw linkage type power steering.

The design of this system is similar to the Bendix Linkage-type in that it includes a power piston assembly and control valve assembly mounted with the steering linkage and is hydraulically controlled. The unit is activated by movement of the ball stud at the control valve when the linkage is moved by the steering gear. The only on-car adjustment is the centering of the control valve.

CONTROL VALVE CENTERING

1. Piston rod must be disconnected from the frame bracket before adjustment is made.
2. While observing safety precautions, raise car, start engine and observe piston rod movement.
3. If piston rod remains retracted, remove dust cover and turn adjusting nut clockwise until rod begins to move out. Reverse nut rotation until piston rod begins to move in. Adjust nut exactly $\frac{1}{2}$ rotation needed to change piston rod direction.
4. If piston rod extends when engine is started, adjust nut counter-clockwise until direction of rod changed and adjust nut exactly $\frac{1}{2}$ of needed rotation as in step 3. If control valve is balanced, rod can be moved in and out manually. Stop engine.
5. Connect cylinder rod to frame bracket.
6. While still on lift, restart engine and wheels should remain stationary at center position. If movement is noted, reset adjusting nut until movement is gone. Reinstall dust cover cap.

PRESSURE TEST

To check hydraulic pressure, proceed as outlined in Section 6. Pressure should be 870 to 1000 P.S.I.

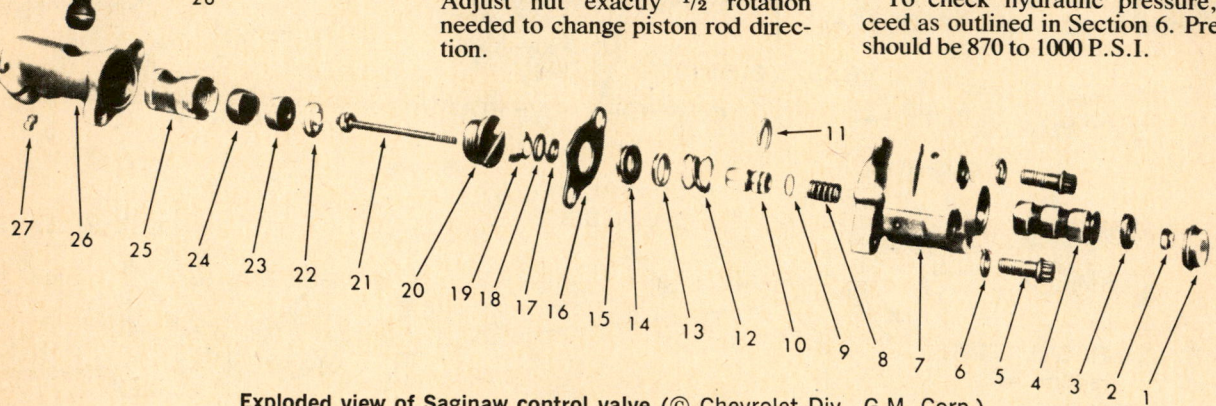

Exploded view of Saginaw control valve (© Chevrolet Div., G.M. Corp.)

1 Dust cover	11 Spring thrust washer	21 Valve shaft
2 Adjusting nut	12 Valve spring	22 Valve seat spring
3 Vee block seal	13 Spring retainer	23 Ball seat
4 Valve spool	14 Annulus seal	24 Ball seat
5 Valve mounting bolts	15 Annulus spacer	25 Sleeve bearing
6 Lock washer	16 Gasket	26 Adapter housing
7 Valve housing	17 Valve shaft washer	27 Lubrication fitting
8 Valve adjustment spring	18 "D" ring seal	28 Ball stud
9 "O" ring seal	19 Plug to sleeve key	29 Seal
10 Valve reaction spool	20 Ball adjuster nut	30 Clamp

SECTION 5

SAGINAW ROTARY-TYPE

The rotary type power steering gear is designed with all components in one housing.

The power cylinder is an integral part of the gear housing. A double-acting piston allows oil pressure to be applied to either side of the piston. The one-piece piston and power rack is meshed to the sector shaft.

The hydraulic control valve is composed of a sleeve and valve spool. The spool is held in the neutral position by the torsion bar and spool actuator. Twisting of the torsion bar moves the valve spool, allowing pressure to be directed to either side of the power piston, depending on the directional rotation of the steering wheel, to give power assist.

On many General Motors cars a modified version of the system provides variable ratio steering for easier and safer control. The steering gear ratio will vary from a high ratio of about 16:1 while steering straight ahead to a lower gear ratio of about 12.4:1 while making a full turn to either side.

Power Steering Unit

CHECKING STEERING EFFORT

Run the engine to attain normal operating temperatures. With the wheels on a dry floor, hook a pull scale to the spoke of the steering wheel at the outer edge. The effort required to turn the steering wheel should be $3\frac{1}{2}$-5 lbs. If the pull is not within these limits, check the hydraulic pressure.

PRESSURE TEST

To check the hydraulic pressure, dis-

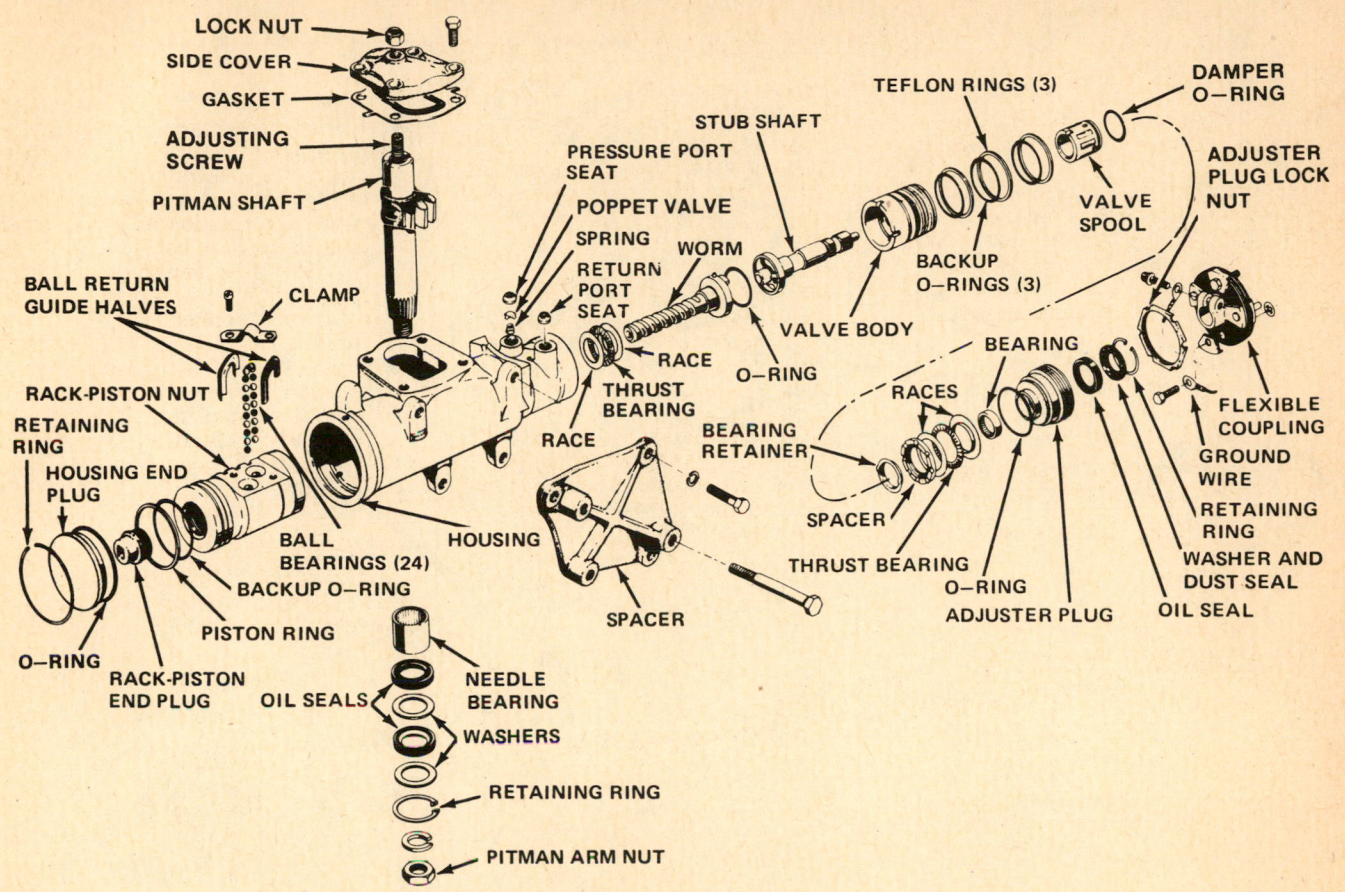

LOCK NUT
SIDE COVER
GASKET
ADJUSTING SCREW
PITMAN SHAFT
BALL RETURN GUIDE HALVES
CLAMP
RACK-PISTON NUT
RETAINING RING
HOUSING END PLUG
O—RING
RACK-PISTON END PLUG
OIL SEALS
BACKUP O—RING
PISTON RING
BALL BEARINGS (24)
HOUSING
NEEDLE BEARING
WASHERS
RETAINING RING
PITMAN ARM NUT
SPACER
RACE
THRUST BEARING
BEARING RETAINER
SPACER
THRUST BEARING
O—RING
ADJUSTER PLUG
PRESSURE PORT SEAT
POPPET VALVE
SPRING
RETURN PORT SEAT
WORM
RACE
STUB SHAFT
VALVE BODY
O—RING
RACES
TEFLON RINGS (3)
BACKUP O—RINGS (3)
VALVE SPOOL
BEARING
DAMPER O—RING
ADJUSTER PLUG LOCK NUT
FLEXIBLE COUPLING
GROUND WIRE
RETAINING RING
WASHER AND DUST SEAL
OIL SEAL

Saginaw rotary gear, exploded view (© American Motors Corp)

connect the pressure hose from the gear. Now connect the pressure gauge between the pressure hose from the pump and the steering gear housing. Fill the fluid reservoir to the proper level. Run the engine and turn the wheel to a full right and a full left turn to the wheel stops to attain normal operating temperatures (150°F-170°F).

Hold the wheel in this position only momentarily.

The initial pressure gauge reading should be 80-125 psi. If the pressure reading is less than the minimum pressure needed for proper operation, check for hose restrictions. Close the valve at the gauge. Do not close the valve for more than 5 seconds. The pressure reading should be within 50 psi of 1350 to 1450 psi, (1200 to 1300 with 6-cylinder engines). If the pressure is 100 psi or more below specifications, the pump is defective and needs repair. If the pressure reading is within

50 psi of the minimum specifications, the pump is normal and needs only an adjustment of the power steering gear or flow control valve.

If the maximum pressure specification still cannot be obtained by turning the steering wheel against the stops momentarily, then the steering gear is leaking internally and must be disassembled and repaired.

WORM BEARING PRELOAD AND SECTOR MESH ADJUSTMENTS

NOTE: *The steering gear must be out of the car to adjust it on 1974 and later models. On earlier models only the over-center preload (sector shaft) can be adjusted with the steering gear in the car.*

Disconnect the Pitman arm from the sector shaft, then completely back off on the sector shaft adjusting screw on the sector shaft cover.

Center the steering on the high point, then attach an in lb torque wrench to

the steering wheel attaching nut. The torque required to keep the wheel moving for one complete turn should be ¹/₂-2 in lbs.

If the torque is not within these limits, loosen the thrust bearing locknut and tighten or back off on the valve sleeve adjuster plug to bring the preload within limits. Tighten the thrust bearing locknut and recheck the preload.

Slowly rotate the steering wheel several times, then center the steering on the high point. Now, turn the sector shaft adjusting screw until a steering shaft torque of 3-6 in lbs more is required to move the worm through the center point. Tighten the sector shaft adjusting screw locknut to 35 ft lbs and recheck the sector mesh adjustment. Total steering gear preload should be 14 in lbs or less.

Install the pitman arm and draw the arm into position with the nut.

SECTION 6

CHRYSLER FULL-TIME (CONSTANT CONTROL TYPE)

The power steering gear system for Chrysler Corporation cars is called the Constant Control type. This system consists of a hydraulic pressure pump, a power steering gear and connecting hoses.

The power steering gear housing contains a gear shaft and sector gear, a power piston with gear teeth milled into the side of the piston which is in constant mesh with the gear shaft sector teeth, a worm shaft which connects the

steering wheel to the power piston through a coupling. The worm shaft is geared to the piston through recirculating ball contact.

A pivot lever is fitted into the spool valve at the upper end and into a drilled

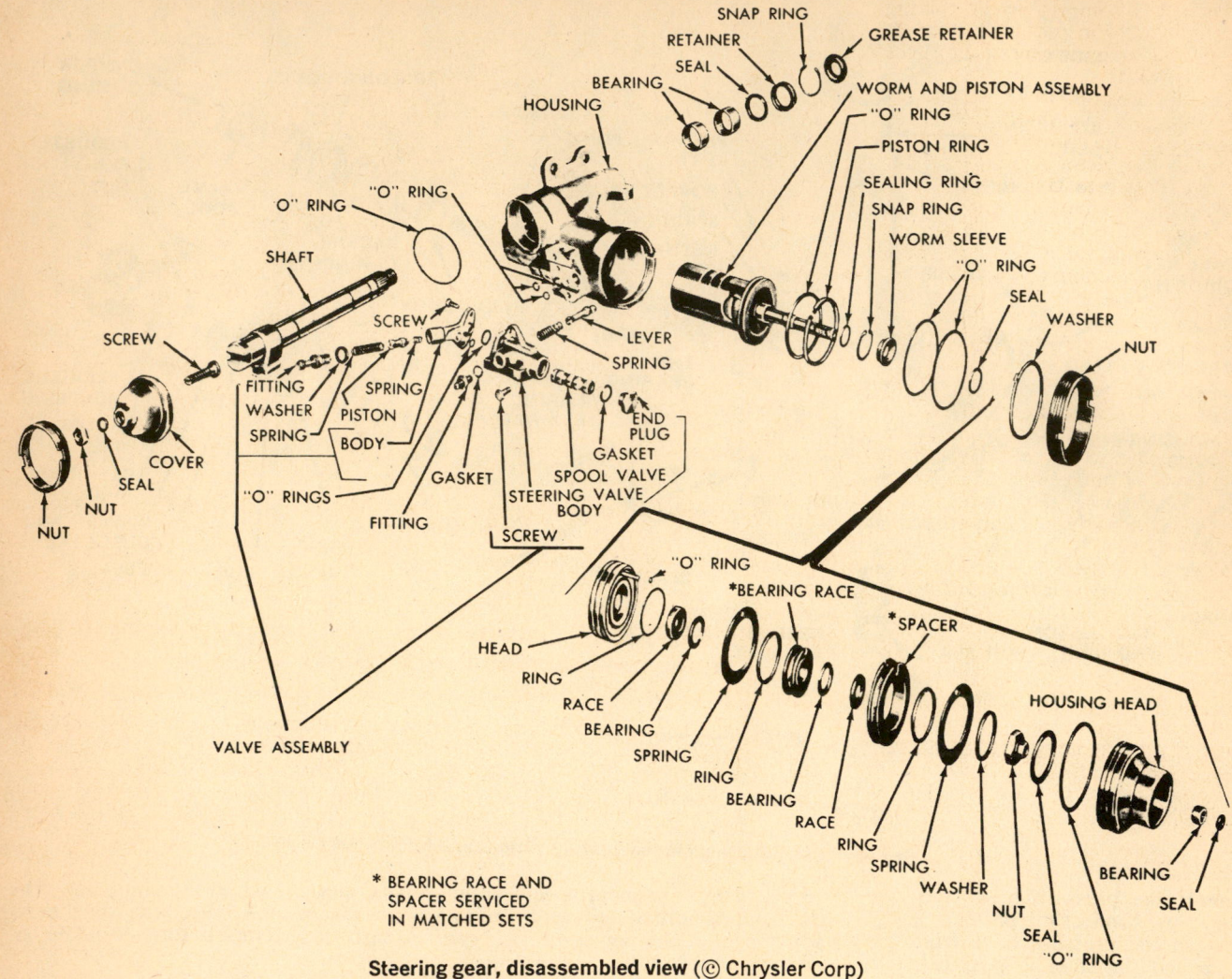

Steering gear, disassembled view (© Chrysler Corp)

hole in the center thrust bearing race at the lower end. The center thrust bearing race is held firmly against the shoulder of the worm shaft by two thrust bearings, bearing races and an adjusting nut. The pivot lever pivots in the spacer which is held in place by the pressure plate.

When the steering wheel is turned to the left the worm shaft moves out of the power piston a few thousandths of an inch, the center thrust bearing race moves the same distance since it is clamped to the worm shaft. The race thus tips the pivot lever and moves the spool valve down, allowing fluid under pressure to flow into the left-turn power chamber and force the power piston down. As the power piston moves, it rotates the cross-shaft sector gear and, through the steering linkage, turns the front wheels.

On a right turn the worm shaft moves into the power piston, the center thrust bearing race thus tips the pivot lever and moves the spool valve up, allowing fluid under pressure to flow into the right power chamber and force the power piston up.

PRESSURE TEST

Connect the pressure test hoses with the pressure gauge installed between the pump and steering gear.

Now, fill the reservoir to the level mark, then start the engine and bleed the system. Allow the engine to idle until the fluid in the reservoir is between 150°F. and 170°F. Now turn the steering wheel to the extreme right and check the pressure reading, then turn to the extreme left and check the reading again. The gauge reading should be equal in each direction. If not, it indicates excessive internal leakage in the unit.

SECTOR SHAFT ADJUSTMENT

1. Disconnect the center link from the steering gear arm.
2. Start the engine and run it at idle speed.
3. Turn the steering wheel lock-to-lock, counting the number of turns. Turn the wheel back 1/2 the total turns.
4. Loosen the sector shaft adjusting screw until backlash is evident in the steering gear arm.

5. Tighten the adjusting screw until the backlash just disappears.
6. Turn the adjusting screw an additional 3/8 to 1/2 turn and tighten the locknut to 28 ft. 1b.

VALVE BODY CENTERING

NOTE: *This procedure may be used to replace the valve body.*

1. Disconnect the high pressure and return hoses at the valve body and support the ends above the reservoir level.
2. Remove the two screws attaching the valve body to the main gear housing.
3. Lift the valve body up and away from the valve lever.
4. Remove the two screws attaching the control valve body to the steering valve body and separate the two bodies.
5. Remove the outlet spring fitting and piston.
6. Carefully shake out the spool valve and check for nicks and scoring.
7. Clean all parts in solvent and blow out all passages with compressed air. Lubricate all parts and pas-

sages with compressed air. During cleaning and inspection, never do anything to remove the sharp edges of the valve.

8. Install the spool valve so that the lever hole is aligned with the lever opening in the valve body.

9. Install the piston, spring and fittings. Torque to 25 ft. lb.

10. Position two new O-rings on the control valve body and attach to the steering valve body. Tighten the two attaching screws to 95 in. lb.

11. Align the lever hole in the valve spool with the lever opening in the valve body.

12. Install the valve body on the gear housing making sure that the valve lever enters the hole in the valve spool and the key section on the bottom of the valve body nests with the keyway in the housing.

13. Install the two screws and tighten to 7 ft. lb.

14. Connect the high pressure and return hoses to the valve body.

15. Start the engine. Turn the steering wheel from lock to lock several times to expel the air. Refill the reservoir.

16. With the steering wheel in the straight ahead center position, start and stop the engine several times, tapping the valve body up or down

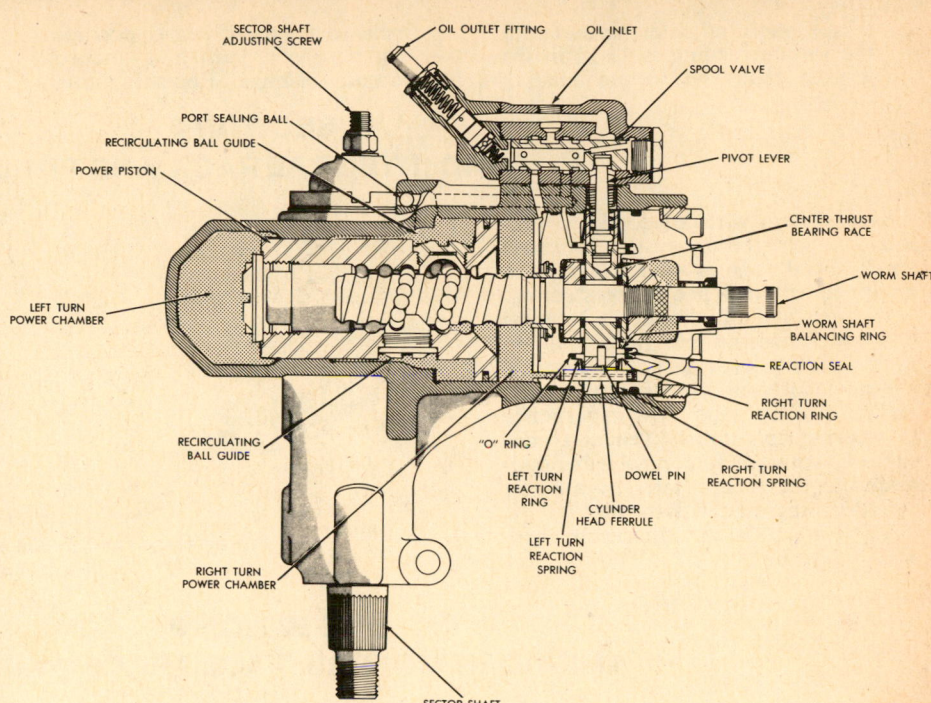

Chrysler power steering gear (© Chrysler Corp)

as required until there is no movement of the steering wheel when the engine is started or stopped.

17. When the valve is centered, tighten the two valve body-to-housing screws to 200 in. lb.

SECTION 7
FORD TORSION BAR (FORD INTEGRAL SYSTEM)

In the Ford integral power steering system, the steering unit is a torsion bar type which is hydraulically assisted. It includes a worm and one piece rack piston which is meshed to the gear teeth on the steering sector shaft. The unit also includes a hydraulic rotary valve sleeve assembly, input shaft and torsion bar assembly which are mounted on the end of the worm shaft and operated by the twisting action of the torsion bar. The combining of the steering gear, the power unit, and the control valve into one unit eliminates the need for all external hoses except the pressure and return hoses from the power steering pump.

The only adjustment that can be made on the car is the center position load to eliminate excessive lash between sector and rack teeth.

1. Disconnect pitman arm and pressure return line. Cycle steering to purge fluid from gear assembly into a clean container.

2. With an in. lbs. torque wrench on the steering wheel nut, turn the steering wheel 45 degrees from the left stop and determine the torque required to rotate shaft 1/8 of a turn from that point.

3. Return steering wheel back to center and rotate wheel back and forth through the center position, and if necessary, loosen lock nut and turn

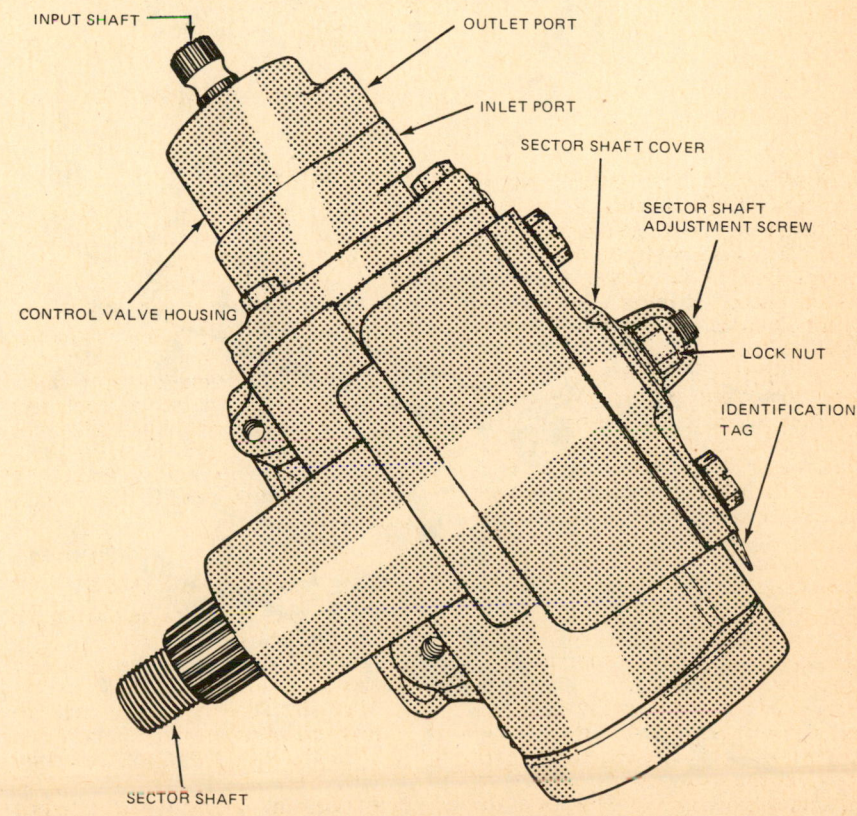

Power steering gear (© Lincoln-Mercury Div., Ford Motor Co)

Power Steering

sector shaft adjuster screw until the torque reading is 11-12 in lbs greater than the torque reading measured at the 45 degree position.

4. Tighten lock nut and recheck torque readings. Replace pitman arm, connect fluid lines, fill reservoir with specified fluid and bleed system.

SECTION 8
FORD INTEGRAL RACK AND PINION

This system was developed to provide a power steering system for those small Ford Motor Company cars equipped with rack and pinion steering.

It consists of a hydraulic mechanical unit which uses an integral piston and rack design to provide power assisted steering. Internal valves both direct and control the pump flow in response to steering conditions. The unit consists of a rotary fluid control valve integrated to the input shaft and a boost cylinder integrated with the rack.

There are no in-car adjustments possible on this unit.

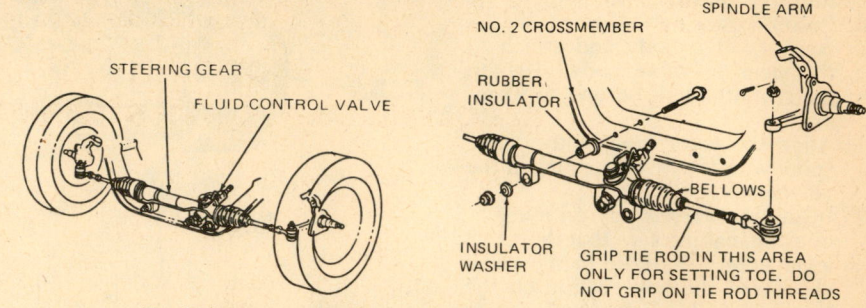

Ford integral rack and pinion steering gear installation
(© Ford Motor Co)

SECTION 9
AMERICAN MOTORS PACER RACK AND PINION

The Pacer rack and pinion power steering system consists of an integral tube and housing assembly which contains the steering rack and piston, the pinion shaft and valve body assembly, and the adjuster plug assembly. In operation, the fluid under pressure from the power steering pump is sent through the inlet hose to the steering gear housing and into the valve body. The valve body then directs the fluid to either side of the power cylinder to provide a power assist for the wheels. There are no in-car adjustments possible on this system.

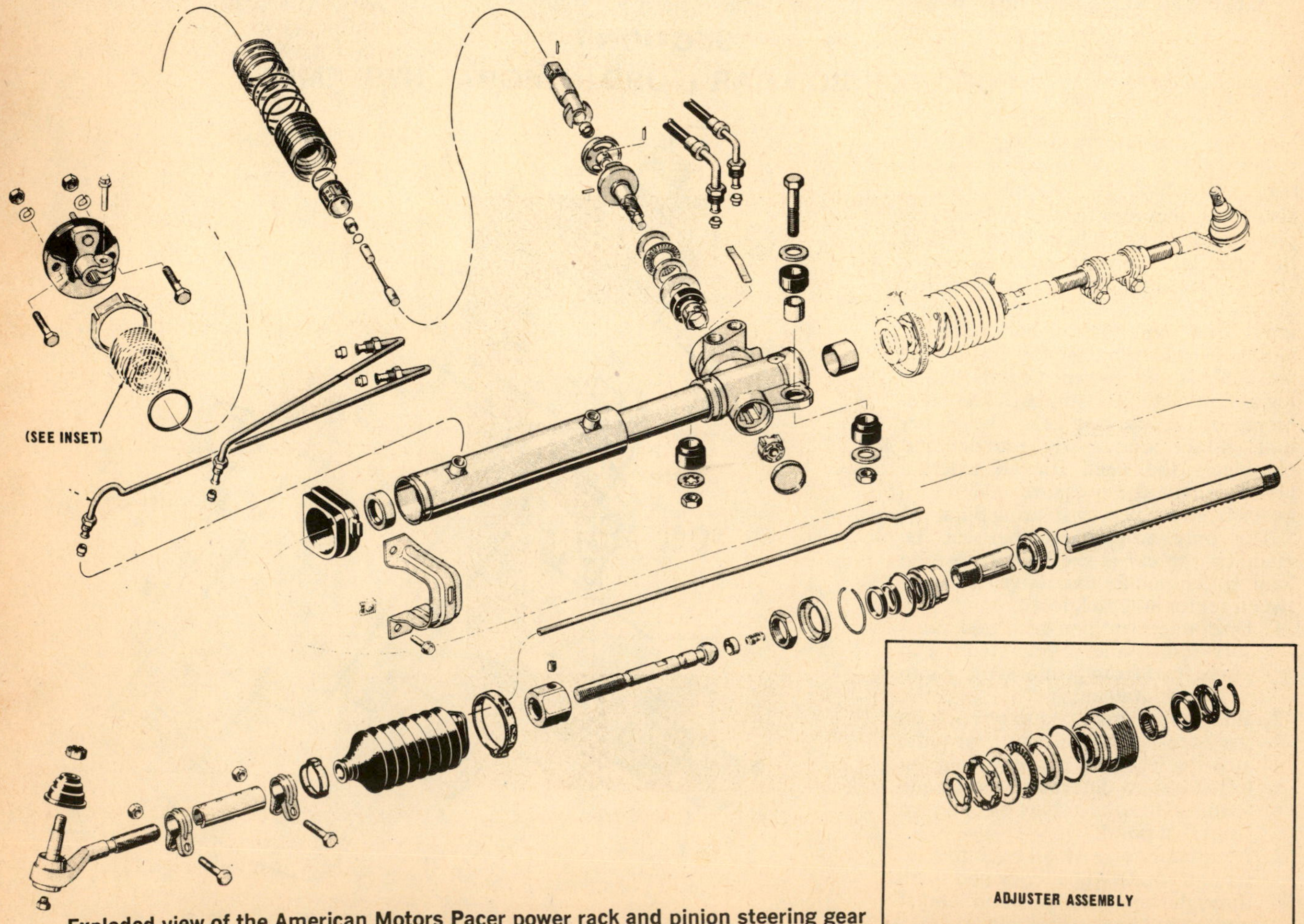

(SEE INSET)

ADJUSTER ASSEMBLY

Exploded view of the American Motors Pacer power rack and pinion steering gear
(© American Motors Corp)

SECTION 10

CHRYSLER RACK AND PINION

This system is used exclusively on the Omni/Horizon models. It consists of four major parts: the power gear, the pump, the pressure hose, and the return hose. Steering wheel motion is converted into linear travel through the meshing of the helical pinion teeth with the rack teeth. Power assist is provided by an open-counter, rotary type three-way control valve which directs oil to either side of the integral rack piston. The rack piston is permanently secured to the rack and is sealed in the gear by the piston ring. No in-car adjustments are possible.

SECTION 11

RECOMMENDED POWER STEERING FLUID

American Motors	AMC power steering fluid, or Dexron II®
Chrysler Corporation	Chrysler power steering fluid, part no. 2084329, or equivalent, automatic transmission fluid not recommended

Ford Motor Co.
1972-77   Ford C1AZ-1958-A or Type "F" ATF
1978-79 All except Lincoln Continental and Mark V   Ford CIAZ-1958 2-A or type "F" ATF

1978-79
Lincoln Continental and Mk. V   Ford D5AZ-14582-A

General Motors	GM power steering fluid, part no. 1050017 or equivalent, or Dexron II®

SECTION 12

STEERING GEAR RATIO

The ratio of a steering system is the relationship of the steering wheel movement to that of the front wheel movement, measured in degrees, that the steering wheel must be turned, to move the front wheels 1 degree. Example; If the ratio is 16.0 to 1, the steering wheel must be turned 16 degrees to move the front wheel 1 degree.

The constant ratio steering maintains the same ratio from center to full right and left turns, while the variable ratio steering varies the ratio beginning approximately 40 degrees from each side of the center steering wheel position to the full right and left turns. The variable ratio steering is accomplished by having a short tooth on each side of a long center tooth on the pitman shaft sector and less depth in the mating gear teeth for the shorter teeth to engage. When making a turn with the shorter teeth engaged, greater movement is accomplished with less steering wheel movement, therefore lowering the steering ratio.

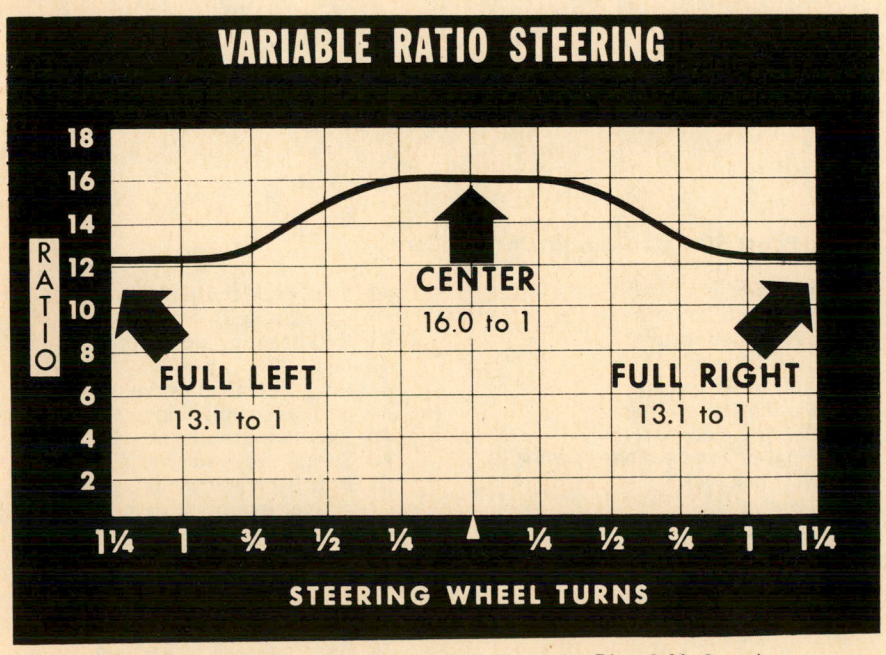

Typical variable steering ratios (© Chevrolet Div.. G.M. Corp.)

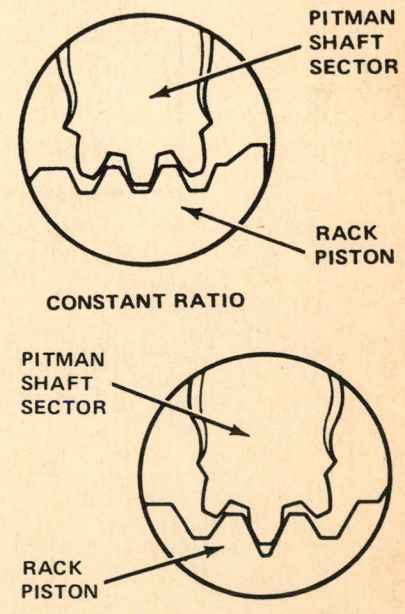

Rack and sector comparison for constant and variable ratio steering
(© American Motors Corp.)

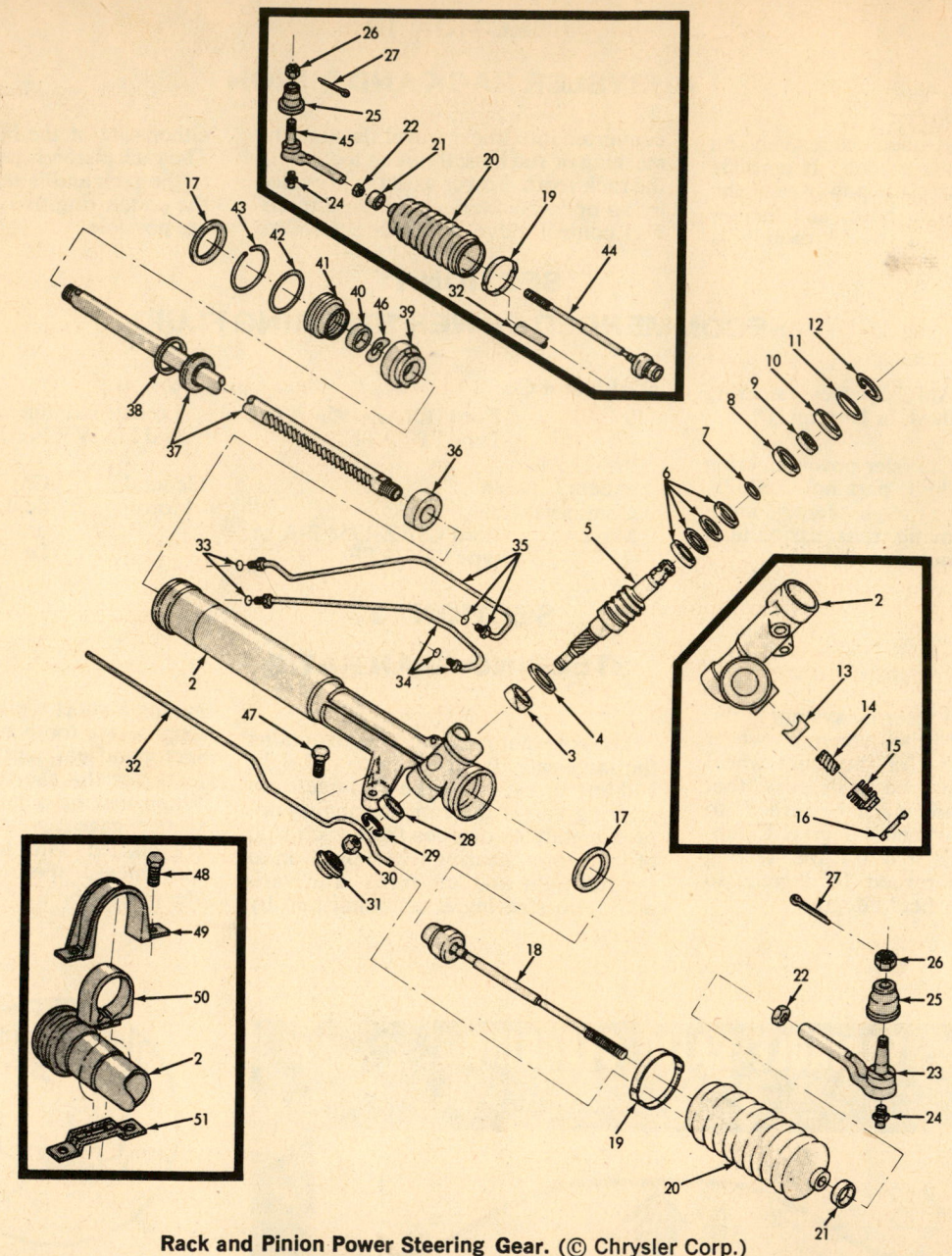

Rack and Pinion Power Steering Gear. (© Chrysler Corp.)

1 Gear assembly
2 Housing assembly
3 Bushing, upper pinion
4 Seal, rack and pinion
5 Pinion, with valve assembly
6 Ring, valve body
7 Ring, spool, shaft retaining
8 Annulus, stub shaft bearing
9 Bearing, needle assembly
10 Seal, stub shaft
11 Seal, stub shaft dust
12 Ring, seal retaining
13 Bearing, rack
14 Spring, adjuster
15 Plug, adjuster
16 Nut, adjuster plug lock
17 Ring, shock dampener
18 Rod assembly, inner tie, left
19 Clamp, boot
20 Boot, rack and pinion
21 Clamp, boot (tie rod end)

22 Nut, hex jam
23 Tie rod, outer, left
24 Fitting, lubrication
25 Seal, tie rod
26 Nut, outer tie rod
27 Pin, cotter
28 Bearing, ball, assembly
29 Ring, pinion bearing retaining
30 Nut, hex lock
31 Cover, dust
32 Tube, breather
33 Seal, cylinder oil line "O" ring
34 Kit, cylinder oil line, left,
      w/ "O" ring seal
35 Kit, cylinder oil line, right
      w/ "O" ring seal
36 Seal, inner rack
37 Rack, assembly piston and
      steering
38 Ring, piston
39 Bulkhead, cylinder inner

40 Seal, rack and pinion
      (bulkhead)
41 Bulkhead, cylinder outer
42 Seal, "O" ring
43 Ring, bulkhead retaining
44 Rod, assembly, inner tie, right
45 Tie rod, outer, right
46 Spring, wave washer
47 Bolt, rack and pinion, steering
      gear mounting, left
48 Bolt, rack and pinion, steering
      gear mounting, right
49 Bracket, rack and pinion
      steering, gear mounting,
      outer
50 Bushing, rack and pinion
      steering gear
51 Bracket, rack and pinion
      steering gear mounting,
      inner

Gauges and Indicators

INDEX

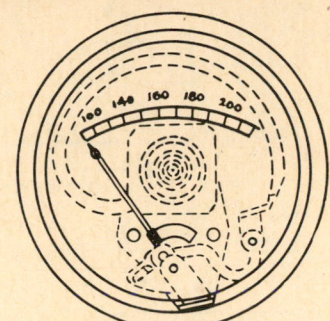

Bourdon tube gauge

There are various systems used to indicate values of heat, pressure, vacuum, current flow, and fuel supply. The following are the more popular systems used.

Bourdon Tube

This gauge consists of a flattened tube that is bent to form a curve. The curve tends to straighten under internal pressure caused by engine oil pressure. The curved tube is geared or linked to an indicator needle which may be read on a calibrated scale.

Bourdon tube oil pressure gauges are used on some Corvettes and the optional instrument panels on some Chevrolet sport models. This type of gauge may be easily distinguished from the electrical type by the small copper or nylon tube running from the gauge to the engine.

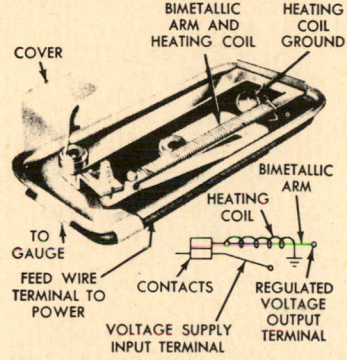

Constant voltage regulator

Bi-Metallic or Thermal

This gauge is activated by the difference in the expansion factors of a bi-metal bar. A sending unit, consisting of a variable resistance conductor, influences current flow to a voltage limiter, or directly to a heating element coiled around a bi-metal bar in the gauge. A bi-metallic gauge pointer will move slowly to its gauging position.

Magnetic

In this system, the indicator needle is moved by changing the balance between the magnetic pull of two coils built in the gauge. When the ignition switch is in the "off" position, the pointer may rest any place on the gauge dial. Balance is controlled by the action of a sending unit or a tank unit containing a rheostat, the value of which varies with temperature, pressure or movement of a float arm. A magnetic gauge will snap to its position when turned on.

Vacuum Gauges

The gauge operates by monitoring engine vacuum. High engine vacuum draws the needle to the high side of the gauge against internal spring tension. As engine vacuum decreases, the spring tension overcomes the vacuum pull and the needle moves to the low side of the gauge.

Warning Lights

This system is quite popular and may be used to indicate heat, low pressure or as a battery discharge indicator. General Motors uses a two-light temperature indicator version of this unit in some models.

SECTION 1
BOURDON TUBE

Oil Pressure

The gauge is the pressure expansion type and is activated by oil pressure developed by the oil pump, acting directly on the mechanism of the gauge. The gauge is connected by a small tube to the main oil passage in the engine oiling system. This design registers the full pressure of the oil pump.

TESTING

A gauge pointer that flutters is usually an indicator that oil has entered the gauge tube. The tube should contain trapped air to cushion the pulsations of the oil pump and relief valve.

Oil can work up into the gauge line as a result of a gauge or tube leak or improper installation. To correct this condition, renew the unit or correct the leak; then, with the gauge line disconnected at both ends, blow the line clear. Connect line at gauge first and then at the engine.

If the gauge reads too low or reads no pressure, test for a possible obstruction by disconnecting the line at the gauge. Hold the end of the line over an empty container, then start the engine. After a few bubbles, oil should flow steadily.

If oil does not flow satisfactorily, first make sure that the oil level is correct and that the oil pump is functioning. Should the engine oil system be operating correctly, the problem is either with the gauge or the line. Check the line for kinks, leaks, or blockage which would prevent oil from reaching the gauge. If the line is unobstructed, remove the gauge unit from the instrument panel. Check to make sure that the hole leading to the Bourdon tube is clear and be sure that the lever linkage and pointer gears operate freely. If none of these points is at fault, the Bourdon tube itself is defective and the gauge must be replaced.

SECTION 2
BI-METAL

The fuel gauge system consists of a sending unit, located in the fuel tank, and a registering unit mounted in the instrument cluster. The sending unit is a rheostat that varies its resistance depending on the amount of fuel in the

Fuel

Bi-metal or thermal type gauges operate on the principle of constant applied voltage and are sensitive only to changes originating at the sending unit.

tank.

TESTING THE DASH GAUGE

To safely test this type of voltage regulated system:

Gauges

1. Have the ignition switch in the "off" position.
2. Connect the terminals of four, series-connected. D-type flashlight batteries (total of six volts) to the terminals of the gauge to be tested. Three volts should cause the gauge to read approximately half-scale.

If the gauge reads half-full and was not working properly before, the sending unit in the tank is probably defective.

If the gauge is inaccurate or does not register, replace it.

If both the fuel gauge and temperature gauge are in error, in the same manner, the constant voltage regulator is probably at fault.

While working under the dash, be careful not to ground any of the gauges. A full flow of current through the regulator to ground is likely to burn out the regulator.

TESTING THE SENDING UNIT

If the dash gauge test shows that unit to be satisfactory, the sending unit or gauge system wiring is faulty. Substitute a jumper wire between the gauge and the tank unit. If the gauge now functions, replace the wire. If the gauge still does not function correctly, replace the tank sending unit.

Oil Pressure

Oil pressure gauges of the bi-metal type operate on the same principle as gas gauges. They are activated by temperature and the difference in the expansion factors of a bi-metal bar.

The pressure sending unit consists of a pressure-activated variable resistor. This sealed unit is usually screwed into the engine oil pressure circuit. As pressure is applied to one side of a diaphragm, linkage advances a contact arm across the coils of a resistor. This action reduces resistance in the gauge circuit, thus increasing current flow and heat to the bi-metal arm in the gauge. The gauge is calibrated to read oil pressure in psi.

Run the engine and have an assistant watch the dash gauge. If the gauge reads zero, turn off the engine and remove the sending unit from the engine block. Restart the engine and allow it to idle for a minute. If there is oil pressure, oil should surge from the sending

Bi-metallic fuel gauge system

unit hole. If no oil flows from the hole, the problem is with the engine lubricating system. If oil flows, the fault lies with the sending unit, the wiring, or the dash gauge.

Check the gauge by grounding the connecting wire for an instant with the ignition switch turned on. A good gauge will go to the top of its scale.

If the gauge did not move when grounded, check the wiring to the dash unit for continuity. If the wiring is not faulty and the gauge doesn't register when grounded, replace the gauge. If the gauge functions when grounded, replace the sending unit.

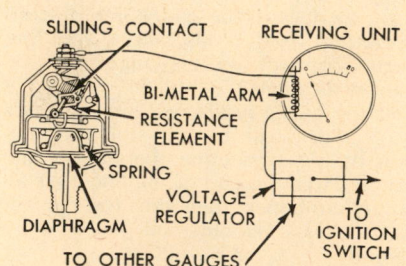

Bi-metallic oil gauge circuit

SECTION 3
MAGNETIC

Fuel

The magnetic fuel gauge consists of two units, the dash unit and the sending unit in the fuel tank. One terminal of the dash unit is connected to the ignition switch so that the system is active only when the ignition is on. With the ignition off, the pointer may come to rest at any position on the dial.

The gauge pointer is moved by vary-

Temperature

The temperature gauge consists of a sending unit, mounted in the cylinder head or block, and a remote resistor unit (temperature gauge) mounted on the instrument panel. The principle of operation is essentially the same as the bi-metallic fuel gauge, the exception being that the resistance of the sending unit is influenced by engine temperature instead of tank fuel level, as with the fuel gauge.

The temperature sending unit is constructed with a coil spring and sensing disc. Current passing through this coil encounters increased resistance, proportional to an increase in temperature. The gauge registers this resistance change and is calibrated to indicate the temperature.

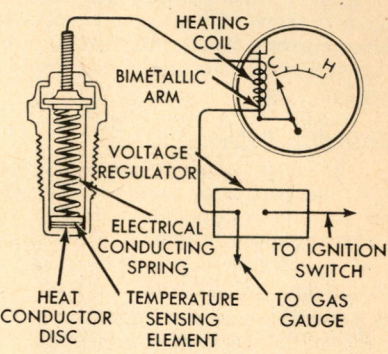

Bi-metallic temperature gauge

TESTING THE DASH GAUGE

Connect four D-cells (total of 6 volts) in series with the dash gauge, with the ignition switched off. A good gauge will register $1/2$ on the scale. Replace the gauge if it does not move.

TESTING THE SENDING UNIT

Bring the engine to normal operating temperature (check with a thermometer). If the gauge doesn't register, disconnect the connecting wire from the engine sending unit and ground the connecting wire for an instant and have an assistant observe the gauge.

If the gauge shows no reading, replace the connecting wire. If the gauge registers when grounded, replace the sending unit.

ing the magnetic pull of two coils in the unit. The magnetic pull is controlled by the action of the tank unit which contains a variable rheostat, the value of which varies with movement of a float and arm.

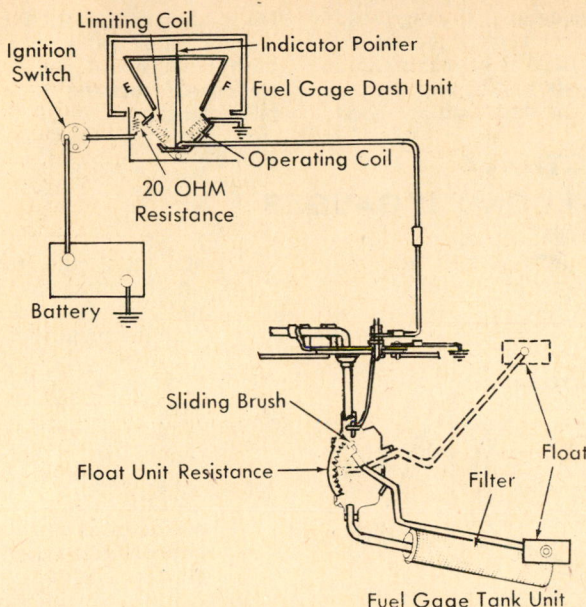

Magnetic fuel gauge circuit

When the ignition switch is on and the tank unit arm is in the full position, the current flow to ground is through the resistor, battery coil and the ground coil. Because the ground coil has more windings than the battery coil, it builds up a stronger magnetic field and the pointer is pulled to the full position.

When the tank unit arm is in the empty position, the current flow is through the resistor, the battery coil and the wire to ground at the tank unit. The pointer is thus pulled to the empty position. The resistor in series with the battery coil balances resistance between the two coils in the dash unit.

TESTING THE DASH GAUGE

Disconnect the wire from the tank unit. Using a tank unit of known accuracy, clip a test wire from the body of the test unit to ground. Clip another test wire from the connector of the test unit to the tank unit wire. With the ignition on, moving the float arm through its entire range should cause the gauge to respond proportionally. If the dash gauge does not correspond to the movement of the test unit and the wiring to the gauge is OK, the dash unit is bad.

TESTING THE TANK UNIT

If tests indicate that the trouble lies in the tank unit, remove the unit and check for mechanical failure. The unit may have either a ruptured or binding float.

An electrical check for circuit continuity may be made throughout the unit's range.

Temperature

The temperature gauge system consists of a magnetic dash unit and a resistance-type sending unit screwed into the water jacket of the cylinder head or the engine block.

The dash unit has two magnetic poles. One of the windings is connected to the ignition switch and ground. This electromagnet exerts a steady pull to hold the gauge pointer to the left or "cold" position when the ignition is on.

The other winding in the dash unit connects to a ground through the engine sending unit. This electromagnet exerts a steady pull on the gauge pointer toward the right, or "hot" side of the gauge. The strength of this pull is dependent upon the current allowed to pass through the engine unit (sending unit) resistor.

The sending unit, located in the engine cooling system, contains a flat disc (thermistor) that changes resistance as its temperature varies.

NOTE: *This sending unit, while similar in appearance, is different and is not interchangeable with the unit used in systems using bi-metal or thermal dash gauges. The resistance of the thermistor disc is maximum when the temperature is cold and minimum when hot. The decrease in resistance allows more current to flow through the electromagnet connected to the engine unit. The resulting* *increase in magnetic pull causes the gauge pointer to move to the right, or "hot" side.*

TESTS

1. Disconnect the wire at the sending unit and turn on the ignition switch. The gauge hand should stay against the cold side stop pin.
2. Ground the wire disconnected from the sending unit. With the ignition switch still on, the gauge hand should swing across the dial to the hot stop pin.

CORRECTIVE MEASURES

If the gauge hand does not stay to the left, either the wire is grounded between the dash unit and the engine unit or the dash unit is defective.

Test further by disconnecting the sending unit wire at the gauge. Turn on the ignition. If the gauge hand stays on the left-hand stop pin, replace the disconnected wire. If the gauge still moves, replace the gauge.

If the gauge hand does not swing across the dial, there is an open circuit in the wire between the sending unit and gauge, the gauge is defective, or current is not reaching the dash gauge.

Test further by grounding the sending unit terminal of the dash gauge and turning on the ignition. If the gauge hand stays on the left-hand stop pin, replace the disconnected wire. If the gauge still moves, replace the gauge.

If the gauge hand does not swing across the dial, there is an open circuit in the wire between the sending unit and gauge, the gauge is defective, or current is not reaching the dash gauge.

Test further by grounding the sending unit terminal of the dash gauge and turning on the ignition. If the gauge hand now moves, replace the disconnected wire. If the gauge hand does not move, connect a test lamp into the circuit. If the test lamp does not light, test the wire between the ignition switch and the dash unit by connecting the lamp to the accessory terminal at the ignition switch and ground. The test lamp should light.

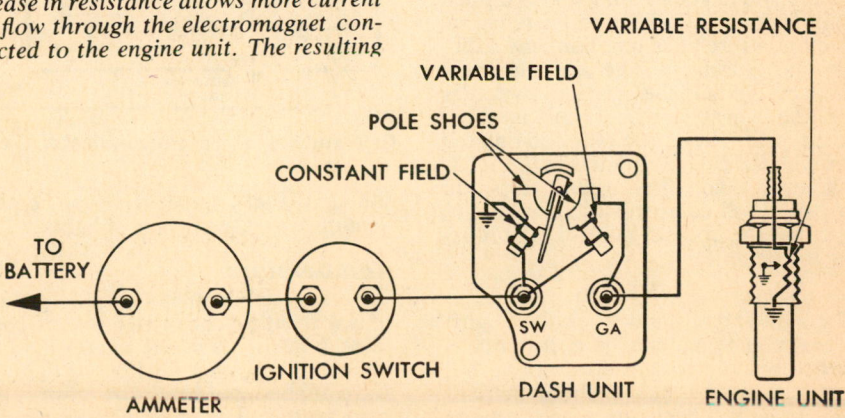

Magnetic temperature gauge

If the gauge hand operates correctly, but the gauge does not indicate temperature correctly, either the sending unit is defective or the dash gauge is out of calibration. Replace sending unit with one of known accuracy. If gauge reading is still incorrect, replace the gauge.

If the gauge hand is at maximum at all times, and tests 1 and 2 indicate that the wiring and the dash unit are good, the sending unit must be replaced.

If the gauge hand will not move, the dash unit is bad, or incorrectly installed. Correct the installation or replace the gauge.

SECTION 4
VACUUM AND ECONOMY GAUGES

The fuel economy gauge indicates engine manifold vacuum, as a function of throttle position and engine load. The face of the gauge dial is divided into three segments; Poor (low vacuum), Good (normal vacuum for cruise), and Decelerate (high vacuum). Although the gauge is not intended as a close tolerance vacuum indicator, it may be assumed that a gauge reading continuously below the Good band (normal cruise or idle) may mean poor engine performance due to improper ignition timing or manifold vacuum leakage.

A manifold vacuum pulsation restrictor is inserted in the vacuum tube at the end closest to the manifold vacuum connection. This enables the inside area of the vacuum hose to serve as a small vacuum reservoir, thereby reducing the manifold vacuum pulsations and to also damp the gauge reading restriction against studden accelerator operation.
NOTE: *Some manufacturers do not use the restrictor in the vacuum line.*

Testing

A standard vacuum system test, using a hand operated vacuum test pump, is conducted as follows:

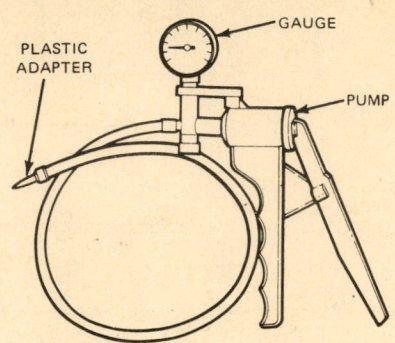

Vacuum hand pump
(© Ford Motor Company)

1. Disconnect the vacuum tube at the manifold vacuum connection.
2. Insert the tester into the end of the vacuum tube and hand pump to approximately 20 inches vacuum. Observe the test gauge for a loss in vacuum.
   a. If the tester vacuum gauge indicates a loss in vacuum, remove the vacuum tube connector from the threaded vacuum connector on the back of the gauge. Apply a short length of teflon tape around the threads of the vacuum connection and rein-

stall the vacuum tube connector on the threaded vacuum connection. Recheck the gauge with the hand vacuum pump. If the tester gauge still indicates a loss in vacuum, replace the gauge assembly.
   b. If the vacuum reading remains steady, the vacuum tube and gauge are OK. Check the end of the tube to be sure the pulsation restrictor is installed; then reconnect the manifold vacuum connection.

Connect the vacuum tube of the test pump directly to the economy gauge tube connector. Pump the tester to approximately 20 inches vacuum and observe the tester gauge for a loss in vacuum.

If the tester gauge indicates a loss in vacuum, replace the economy gauge assembly.

If the tester gauge reading remains steady, the hose to the engine manifold vacuum port must be repaired or replaced.
NOTE: *If a hand operated vacuum pump is not available, the engine can be used as a source of vacuum, with a separate vacuum gauge and attaching tee as testing tools.*

SECTION 5
WARNING LIGHTS

Oil Pressure

The warning or indicator light system supplies the driver with a visual signal of low engine oil pressure. The light usually lights at pressures below 5 psi.

The low pressure warning light is wired in series with an oil pressure sending unit. The sending unit is tapped into the main oil gallery and is sensitive to oil pressure. The unit contains a diaphragm, spring linkage and electrical contacts. When the ignition switch is on, the warning light circuit is energized and the circuit is completed through the closed contacts in the sending unit. When the engine starts, oil pressure will compress the diaphragm, opening the contact points and breaking the circuit.

TESTS

The light should light when the engine is not running and the ignition switch is turned on. If the light does not go on, first substitute a new bulb. If there is still no light, check the wire from the light to the switch. If the wire is not at fault, disconnect the wire at the send-

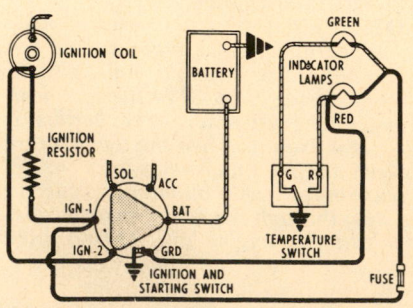

Cold and hot temperature indicator circuit

ing unit and ground it. Replace the sending unit if the light now lights.

Temperature

This system employs a heat sending unit with either one or two sets of contacts. Some systems use a green light to indicate subnormal, and a red light to warn of abnormal heat. The more common system, however, uses a simple make-and-break heat-sensitive sending unit screwed into the engine cooling system, and wired in series with the hot indicator light in the instrument panel.

The two-light system uses a bi-metal element mounted between two signal circuits. Normal operating temperature (somewhere between 120°F. and 250°F.) will cause the bi-metal bar to assume a position of no contact between the low and the high temperature circuit. When the ignition switch is turned on, with a cold engine, the cold (green) circuit is complete. If the engine becomes hot enough to move the bi-metal bar so that it touches the contacts of the hot circuit, the hot (red) light comes on. This hot signal indicates that temperatures are in the area of 250°F. in the sealed cooling system.

TESTS

Use the same testing procedure given for oil pressure.

Charge Indicator

A light is used to indicate general charging system operation. When output is below battery potential, a red light is shown. When output is above battery potential, other factors (wiring, voltage regulator, etc.) being normal, the light is out.

The charge indicator bulb is connected to the charging circuit, obtaining its ground through the voltage regulator. When the output rises above battery potential, the current flow causes the light to go out.

When an alternator is used, it is necessary to supply a small amount of excitation current to the alternator field, due to the small amount of residual magnetism. Current can be supplied from the battery, through the indicator light, and to the regulator terminal on the alternator. This current has a value of about 12 volts at .25 amperes and will cause the indicator light to come on when the ignition switch is turned on. Most systems have a resistor in parallel with the bulb to provide excitation if the bulb burns out and to prevent the light from glowing dimly during normal operation.

When the alternator starts to generate, an output voltage is developed at the regulator terminal. When this voltage exceeds the battery voltage, current will pass from the alternator to the battery and to the system. This current is flowing in the reverse direction of the voltage supplied by the battery. The current flow coming from the alternator exceeds the battery current by a regulated 1 or 2 volts. This is not enough to light the indicator light, therefore, the light will go out when the alternator is supplying sufficient current.

If the alternator output current should drop below battery voltage, current will begin to flow in the opposite direction. If it exceeds 2 or 3 volts, the light will glow indicating that the alternator is not operating properly.

Coolant Level Indicator

Some GM models have a warning light which comes on if the coolant level in the radiator drops below a predetermined level. The coolant level indicator consists of three units; a sending unit which is threaded into the side tank of the radiator, a module which is mounted behind the instrument cluster, and a warning light. As a bulb test, the light is wired so that it comes on when the key is turned to the "START" position.

LIGHT DOESN'T COME ON

Perform the following checks if the warning light won't come on when the key is turned to the "START" position:

1. With the ignition switch in the "ON" position, unfasten the lead from the coolant level sending unit. If the light comes on replace the sending unit.
2. If the light didn't come on in step 1, check the light in the indicator and replace it, if necessary.

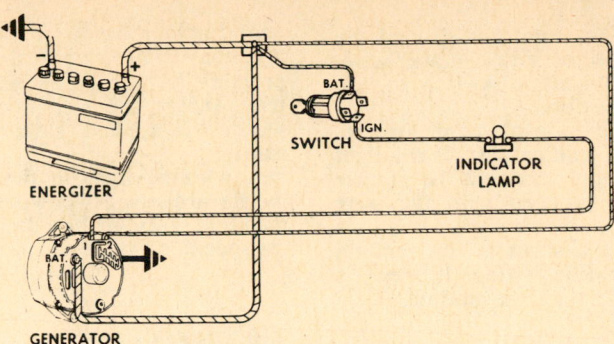

Charging indicator light circuit

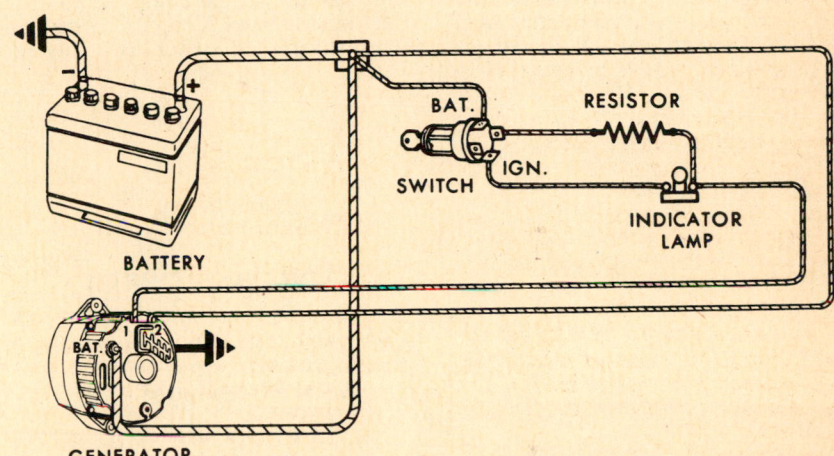

Simplified typical charging system schematic showing the resistor wired in parallel with the charge indicator lamp (© Cadillac Div., G.M. Corp.)

3. If the bulb is OK, check the wiring between the sending unit and module, and then between the module and light. If the wiring is not "open," replace the module.

LIGHT WON'T GO OUT

Perform the following checks if the light won't go out when the coolant is at the specified level:

1. Detach the lead from the coolant

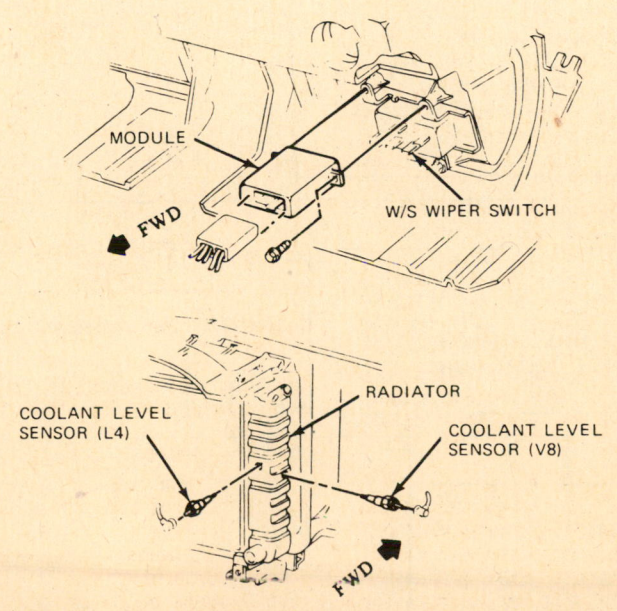

Coolant level sending unit and module (© Chevrolet Div., G.M. Corp.)

level sending unit and ground the lead connector with a jumper wire. Turn the ignition switch to the "ON" position.

2. If the light doesn't come on, replace the sending unit. If the light remains on disconnect the jumper wire and proceed with the next step.

3. Check for a short in the sending unit-to-module wiring. If there is no short, replace the module.

Fuel Economy Warning Light

The fuel economy warning light system consists of a normally closed vacuum switch, an instrument panel warning light, vacuum hose, wire harness, and attaching hardware. Its operation is similar in function to that of the oil pressure (switch type) indicating system, except the switch opens when vacuum is applied, rather than pressure.

A warning light in the instrument panel warns the driver when the engine manifold vacuum has dropped below the specified limit.

Electrical Circuit

The warning light bulb is powered by the ignition switch accessory circuit through the printed circuit board of the instrument panel. The wire harness and normally closed switch assembly provide the ground circuit for the bulb. With the ignition switch ON and the engine not running, the colored light will be illuminated. As the engine is started and the manifold vacuum reaches the specified limit of about 4 to 6 in. of hg., the vacuum switch opens the ground circuit and the warning light will go out.

Testing

If the warning light does not operate with the ignition switch on, (engine not running), or if the warning light remains on after the engine has started, refer to the diagnosis charts for repair procedures.

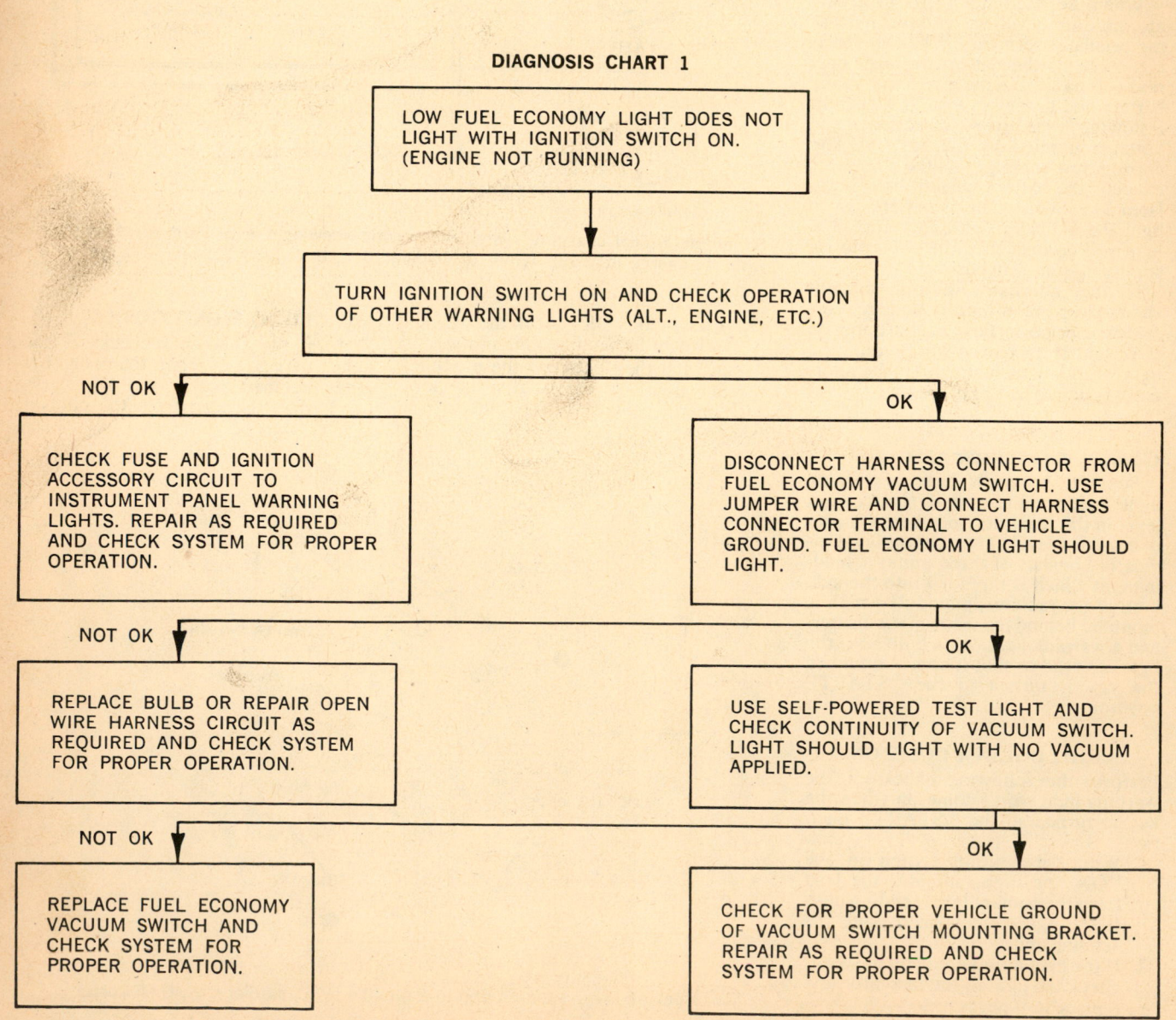

DIAGNOSIS CHART 1

LOW FUEL ECONOMY LIGHT DOES NOT LIGHT WITH IGNITION SWITCH ON. (ENGINE NOT RUNNING)

TURN IGNITION SWITCH ON AND CHECK OPERATION OF OTHER WARNING LIGHTS (ALT., ENGINE, ETC.)

NOT OK — CHECK FUSE AND IGNITION ACCESSORY CIRCUIT TO INSTRUMENT PANEL WARNING LIGHTS. REPAIR AS REQUIRED AND CHECK SYSTEM FOR PROPER OPERATION.

OK — DISCONNECT HARNESS CONNECTOR FROM FUEL ECONOMY VACUUM SWITCH. USE JUMPER WIRE AND CONNECT HARNESS CONNECTOR TERMINAL TO VEHICLE GROUND. FUEL ECONOMY LIGHT SHOULD LIGHT.

NOT OK — REPLACE BULB OR REPAIR OPEN WIRE HARNESS CIRCUIT AS REQUIRED AND CHECK SYSTEM FOR PROPER OPERATION.

OK — USE SELF-POWERED TEST LIGHT AND CHECK CONTINUITY OF VACUUM SWITCH. LIGHT SHOULD LIGHT WITH NO VACUUM APPLIED.

NOT OK — REPLACE FUEL ECONOMY VACUUM SWITCH AND CHECK SYSTEM FOR PROPER OPERATION.

OK — CHECK FOR PROPER VEHICLE GROUND OF VACUUM SWITCH MOUNTING BRACKET. REPAIR AS REQUIRED AND CHECK SYSTEM FOR PROPER OPERATION.

DIAGNOSIS CHART 2

LOW FUEL ECONOMY LIGHT DOES NOT GO OUT WITH ENGINE RUNNING.

START ENGINE. ALLOW TO WARM UP AND RUN AT IDLE. FUEL ECONOMY LIGHT SHOULD BE ON.

IF LOW FUEL ECONOMY LIGHT STAYS ON, DISCONNECT WIRE HARNESS CONNECTOR TO FUEL ECONOMY VACUUM SWITCH. LIGHT SHOULD GO OUT.

NOT OK

CHECK WIRE HARNESS CIRCUIT FOR GROUND OR SHORT. REPAIR AS REQUIRED AND CHECK SYSTEM FOR PROPER OPERATION.

OK

CHECK VACUUM HOSE TO VACUUM SWITCH FOR LEAK. PINCHED OR PLUGGED CONDITION.

NOT OK

REPAIR OR REPLACE VACUUM HOSE AS REQUIRED AND CHECK SYSTEM FOR PROPER OPERATION.

OK

USE HAND VACUUM PUMP AND CHECK VACUUM SWITCH FOR PROPER OPERATION. REPLACE SWITCH, IF REQUIRED, AND CHECK SYSTEM FOR PROPER OPERATION.

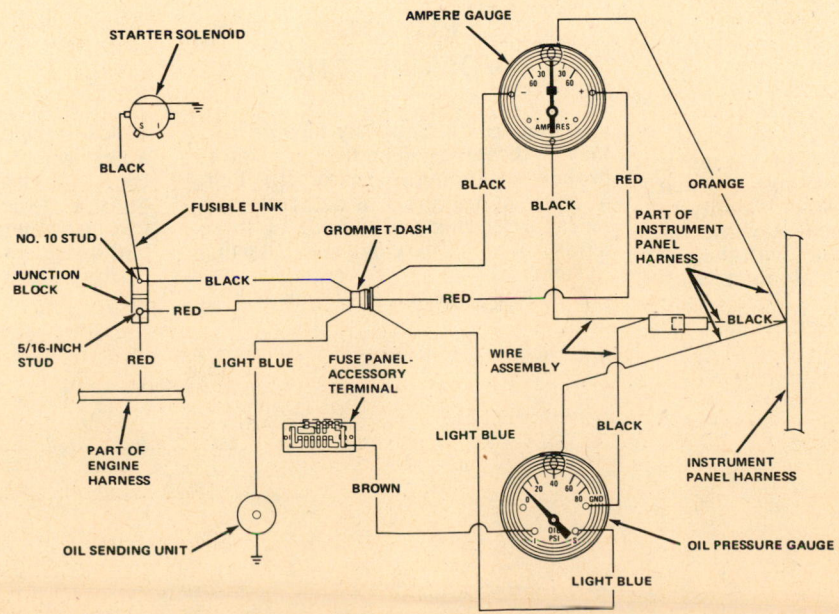

Typical ammeter and oil pressure gauge wiring
(© American Motors Corp.)

SECTION 6
AMMETERS

The automotive ammeter is a gauge or meter used to indicate direction and relative value of current flow. This type of charge indicator is usually equipped with a dampening device to reduce pointer fluctuation during current surge from the voltage regulator. An ammeter is always wired in series with the circuit being monitored.

The meter will show charge when the battery is being charged and discharge when the battery is being discharged. It merely gives an indication of the state of charge of the battery, since it shows a relatively high charging rate when the battery is low, and a low charging rate when the battery is near full charge. An ammeter does not give a complete report of battery condition, whereas a voltmeter does. Just after cranking the engine, the meter will swing toward the charge side for a short time, if lights and accessories are turned off. As the energy spent in cranking is restored to the battery, the pointer will gradually move back toward center but should stay on the charge side. If the battery charge is low, however, the indicator will show a high charging rate for an indeterminate length of time.

The ammeter does not show the charging rate of the alternator.

At speeds above 30-35 mph, with all lights and accessories on, the indicator should show a reading somewhere on the charge side, depending on the state of the battery. Above this speed, the indicator should never show a discharge reading; if it does, the alternator and regulator should be tested. See "Charging and Starting Systems" for troubleshooting.

AMMETER DIAGNOSIS

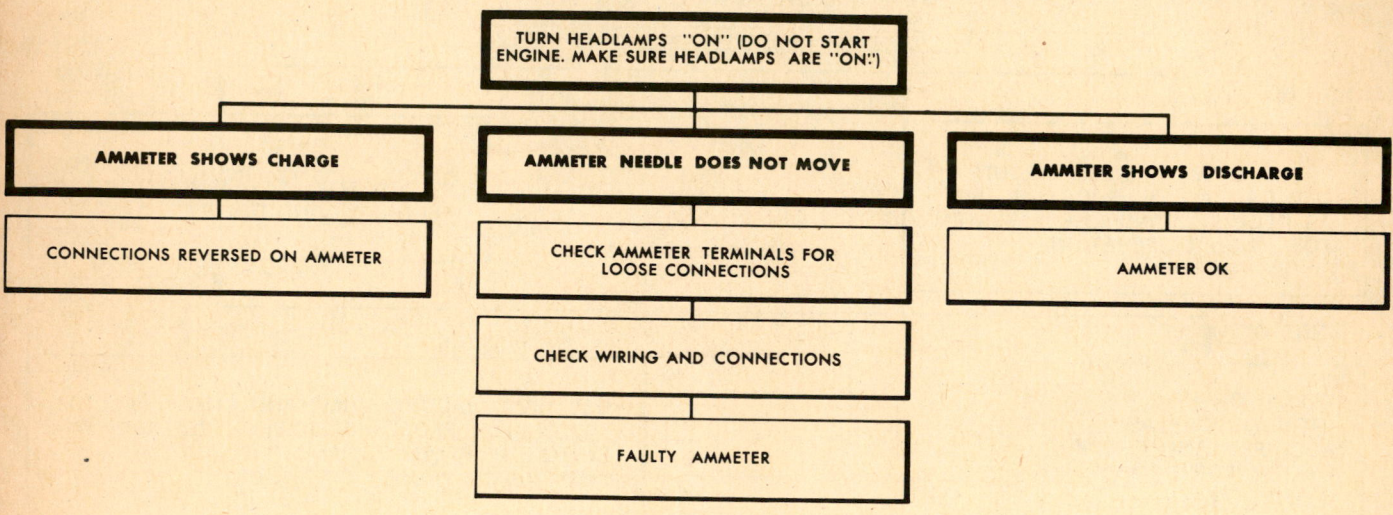

SECTION 7
VOLTMETERS

A voltmeter is used on some cars, instead of an ammeter. The voltmeter indicates regulated voltage, which shows the charging system's ability to keep the battery charged. A voltmeter is always wired in parallel with the circuit being monitored. Voltmeter readings that are continuously high or low, may indicate a defective regulator, broken or slipping alternator drivebelt, a faulty alternator, or a defective battery. For testing and service of these items, see "Charging and Starting Systems."

If a faulty voltmeter is suspected, check the voltage regulator output with a test voltmeter of known accuracy (See "Charging and Starting Systems"). If the voltage indicated on the test instrument is within specifications, and disagrees with the car's voltmeter reading, replace the car's voltmeter.

Diagnostic Charts

STARTING SYSTEM DIAGNOSIS

Problems

● Most probable causes
✔ Possible causes

Causes	Repeated clicking from starter	Cranks very slowly	Starter Spins, but does not turn engine	Starter clunks, but does not turn engine	No sound from starter	Excessive Starter Current draw
Battery Not Fully Charged	●	●		●	●	
Loose Battery Cables	●	●		●	✔	✔
Defective Battery	✔	✔		✔	✔	✔
Shorted or Loose Starter Wire	✔	✔		✔	✔	✔
Defective Solenoid	✔				✔	✔
Engine Overheated		✔		✔		
Low Temperature		●		✔		
Thick Oil		✔		✔		
Internal Engine Malfunction		✔		✔		
Defective Starter		✔		✔		
Defective Starter Drive		✔	●			
Open Circuit in Solenoid Armature, or Field Coils				●		●
Short in Field or Armature Coils				●		●
Neutral Safety Switch Misadjusted					✔	
Fusible Link Melted					✔	
Defective Ignition Switch					✔	
Clutch Switch Misadjusted					✔	

CLUTCH AND MANUAL TRANSMISSION DIAGNOSIS

Problems

● Most probable causes
✔ Possible causes

Causes	Noisy in Forward Speeds	Noisy in Reverse	Noisy in Neutral	Hard Shifting	Jumping Out of Gear	Sticking in Gear	Gears Clash	Locks in Two Gears	Leaks
Low or Wrong Lubricant	✔	✔	✔	✔		✔	✔		✔
Transmission Misaligned or Loose	✔	✔	✔		✔				
Maindrive Gear or Bearing Damaged	●	✔	✔			✔	✔		
Speedometer Drive Noise	✔	✔							
Mainshaft Gears or Bearing Damaged	●	✔	✔			●			
Incorrect End Play on Shafts	✔	✔	✔			✔			
Reverse Idler Gear or Shaft Damaged		●	✔						
Incorrect Clutch Adjustment				●	✔		●	●	
Shift Linkage Misadjusted				●	✔	✔		●	
Bent Shifter Forks or Shafts				✔	✔	✔		✔	
Damaged Synchronizers				✔	✔	✔	●		
Speed Too High on Downshift				●			✔		
Front Main Bearing Damaged	✔	✔	✔		✔				
Bent Output Shaft					✔				
High Idle Speed							✔		
Wait 3-4 Sec. Before Shifting Into a Non-synchronized Gear							●		
Bent Shift Rods								✔	
Overfilled									●
Seals at Covers or Extension Housing Bad									✔
Loose Main Drive Gear Bearing Retainer									✔
Operating Shaft Seals Bad									✔
Worn Extension Housing Bushing									✔

GENERAL MOTORS TURBO HYDRA-MATIC 350 AUTOMATIC TRANSMISSION DIAGNOSIS

Causes

● Most probable causes
✔ Possible causes

Problems	Low oil level/water in oil	Vacuum leak	Modulator and/or valve	Strainer and/or gasket	Governor valve/valve	Valve body gasket/plate	Pressure regulator valve	1-2 shift valve	2-3 shift valve	Manual low-control valve	Detent valve and linkage	Manual valve and linkage	2-3 accumulator	Gasket screen-pressure	Pump gears
Slips in all ranges	✔		✔	✔		✔	✔						✔		✔
Drive slips—no First gear	✔		✔	✔		✔	✔						✔		✔
No 1-2 upshift		✔			✔	✔	✔	✔							
Slips, 1-2 upshift	✔		✔			✔	✔	✔				✔			
Harsh 1-2 upshift		✔	✔				✔								
No 2-3 upshift						✔		✔							
2-3 upshift early or late		✔			✔	✔	✔		✔		✔				
Slips, 2-3 upshift	✔		✔			✔	✔		✔			✔			
No full throttle downshift		✔	✔				✔		✔		✔				
2-3 upshift, full throttle only		✔									✔				
Car drives in Neutral											●				
Slips in Reverse	✔		✔	✔		✔	✔	✔					✔	✔	✔
1-2 or 2-3 shifts noisy	●														
Noisy in all ranges	✔			✔		✔									✔
Spews oil out of the breather	✔			✔											

CHRYSLER TORQUEFLITE AUTOMATIC TRANSMISSION DIAGNOSIS

Causes

✔ Possible causes

Problems	Oil level	Control linkage	Oil pressure check	Kickdown band	Low-reverse band	Improper engine idle	Servo linkage	Accumulator	Valve body assembly	Manual valve lever	Air pressure check	Servo link	Governor	Gear shift cable	Regulator valve	Converter control valve	Strainer	Breather clogged	Cooler or lines
Harsh N to D or N to R shift					✔	✔	✔	✔	✔		✔	✔							
Delayed Shift — N to D	✔				✔						✔								
Runaway on upshift — 2-3 kickdown	✔		✔	✔	✔						✔	✔		✔					
Harsh upshift and 3-2 kickdown			✔	✔	✔						✔	✔		✔					
No upshift	✔		✔	✔							✔	✔	✔	✔	✔				
No kickdown on normal downshift	✔		✔	✔							✔	✔		✔		✔	✔		
Erratic shifts	✔		✔	✔				✔								✔	✔	✔	
Slips in forward drive positions	✔			✔							✔	✔		✔					
Slips in Reverse only				✔			✔		✔			✔		✔					
Slips in all positions	✔			✔								✔		✔			✔		
No drive in any positions	✔			✔								✔	✔	✔				✔	
No drive in forward positions				✔	✔						✔	✔		✔	✔		✔		
No drive in Reverse				✔			✔		✔			✔		✔	✔				
Drives in Neutral											✔	✔				✔			
Drags or locks						✔	✔		✔						✔				
Noises	✔										✔	✔			✔		✔	✔	
Hard to fill or blows out	✔										✔						✔	✔	✔
Transmission overheats	✔					✔	✔				✔				✔	✔		✔	✔

This transmission is used on all Chrysler Corporation cars since 1967 and on American Motors products since 1972.

FORD C-6 AUTOMATIC TRANSMISSION DIAGNOSIS

Causes

● Most probable causes
✔ Possible causes

Problems	Fluid level	Vacuum diaphragm	Manual linkage	Governor	Valve body	Pressure regulator	Intermediate band	Low-reverse clutch	Intermediate clutch	Engine idle speed	Intermediate servo	Downshift linkage	Extension rear oil seal	Perform air pressure check	Perform rear pressure check	Perform pressure check	Engine performance
No drive in D, 2, and 1				✔	✔									✔		✔	
1-2 or 2-3 shift points erratic	✔	✔	✔	✔	✔								✔	✔		✔	
Rough 1-2 upshifts		✔			✔	✔	✔			✔				✔		✔	
Rough 2-3 upshifts		✔			✔	✔	✔			✔				✔		✔	
Dragged out 1-2 shift	✔	✔			✔	✔	✔			✔				✔		✔	
No 1-2 or 2-3 shift		✔		✔	✔	✔	✔			✔		✔		✔		✔	
No 3-1 shift in D				✔	✔												
No forced downshifts		✔			✔							✔					
Runaway engine on 3-2 downshift		✔			✔	✔	✔			✔				✔		✔	
Rough 3-2 or 3-1 shift at closed throttle		✔								✔	✔						
Shifts 1-3 in D		✔		✔	✔			✔		✔							
Creeps excessively										●							
Slips in first gear, D	✔	✔			✔	✔								✔		✔	
Slips in second gear	✔	✔			✔	✔	✔			✔				✔		✔	
Slips or chatters in R	✔	✔			✔	✔		✔						✔		✔	
No drive in D only				✔	✔									✔		✔	
No drive in 2 only	✔			✔	✔					✔				✔		✔	
No drive in 1 only	✔			✔	✔									✔		✔	
No drive in R only	✔			✔	✔			✔						✔		✔	
No drive in any lever position	✔			✔	✔	✔								✔		✔	
Lockup in 2 only									●								
Parking lock broken				✔													
Transmission overheats			✔		✔									✔		✔	
Maximum speed too low																	✔
Transmission noisy in N and P	✔				✔												
Transmission noisy in all gears	✔				✔												
Fluid leak	✔	✔									✔				✔		
Car moves forward in N				✔													

BRAKE DIAGNOSIS

Problems

● Most probable causes
✔ Possible causes

Legend: ● = Most probable causes, ✔ = Possible causes

Causes	Brake Tell-Tale Glows During Stop	Brakes Chatter (Roughness)	Brakes Squeak During Application	Scraping Noise from Brakes	Uneven Braking Action (Front to Rear)	Uneven Braking Action (Pulls to Side)	Brakes Drag	Brakes Slow to Release	Brakes Slow to Respond	Excessive Braking Action	Excessive Brake Pedal Effort	Pedal Travel Gradually Increases	Excessive Brake Pedal Travel
Leaking Brake Line or Connection	●				✔							●	✔
Leaking Wheel Cylinder or Piston Seal	✔					✔				✔		●	✔
Leaking Master Cylinder	✔											●	✔
Restricted Brake Fluid Passage						✔	✔	✔	✔	✔		✔	✔
Air In Brake System	●				✔								●
Contaminated or Improper Brake Fluid	✔						✔	✔	✔				
Faulty Metering Valve (Disc Only)	✔				✔		✔	✔	✔	✔			✔
Sticking Wheel Cylinder or Caliper Pistons					✔	✔	✔				✔		
Improperly Adjusted Master Cylinder Push Rod	✔							●	✔				✔
Leaking Vacuum System									✔		●		
Restricted Air Passage In Power Unit									✔	●	✔		
Improperly Assembled Power Unit								●		✔	✔		
Damaged Power Unit								✔	✔	✔	✔		
Brake Assembly Attachments—Missing or Loose		✔		✔	✔	✔	✔						✔
Brake Pedal Linkage Interference or Binding							●	●	✔		✔		
Worn Out Brake Lining—Replace			✔	✔	✔	✔					✔		
Uneven Brake Lining Wear—Replace	✔			✔	✔	✔							✔
Glazed Brake Lining—Sand Lightly			✔		✔	✔			✔		●		
Incorrect Lining Material—Replace		✔	●		✔				✔	✔	✔		
Contaminated Brake Lining—Replace		✔	✔	✔	●	●			✔	●			
Linings Damaged By Abusive Use—Replace			✔	✔	✔	✔					●	✔	
Excessive Brake Lining Dust—Remove with Air			✔		●	●					●	✔	
Brake Drums or Rotors Heat Spotted or Scored		●	✔		✔	✔					✔		
Out-of-Round or Vibrating Brake Drums		●											
Out-of-Parallel Brake Rotors		●											
Excessive Rotor Run-Out		✔											
Faulty Automatic Adjusters	✔				✔	✔	✔					●	✔
Weak or Incorrect Brake Shoe Return Springs			✔	●	✔	✔	●	✔		✔			
Drums Tapered or Threaded				●									
Incorrect Wheel Cylinder Sizes					✔	✔					✔	✔	
Improperly Adjusted Parking Brake							✔						
Incorrect Front End Alignment						●							
Incorrect Tire Pressure					✔	✔							
Incorrect Wheel Bearing Adjustment		✔		✔									✔
Loose Front Suspension Attachments		✔		●	✔								
Out-of-Balance Wheel Assemblies		●											
Driver Riding Brake Pedal					✔		✔				✔	✔	✔
Faulty Proportioning Valve							✔	✔	✔		✔		
Insufficient Brake Shoe Pad Lubricant			●	●	✔		✔	✔					

DISC BRAKE DIAGNOSIS

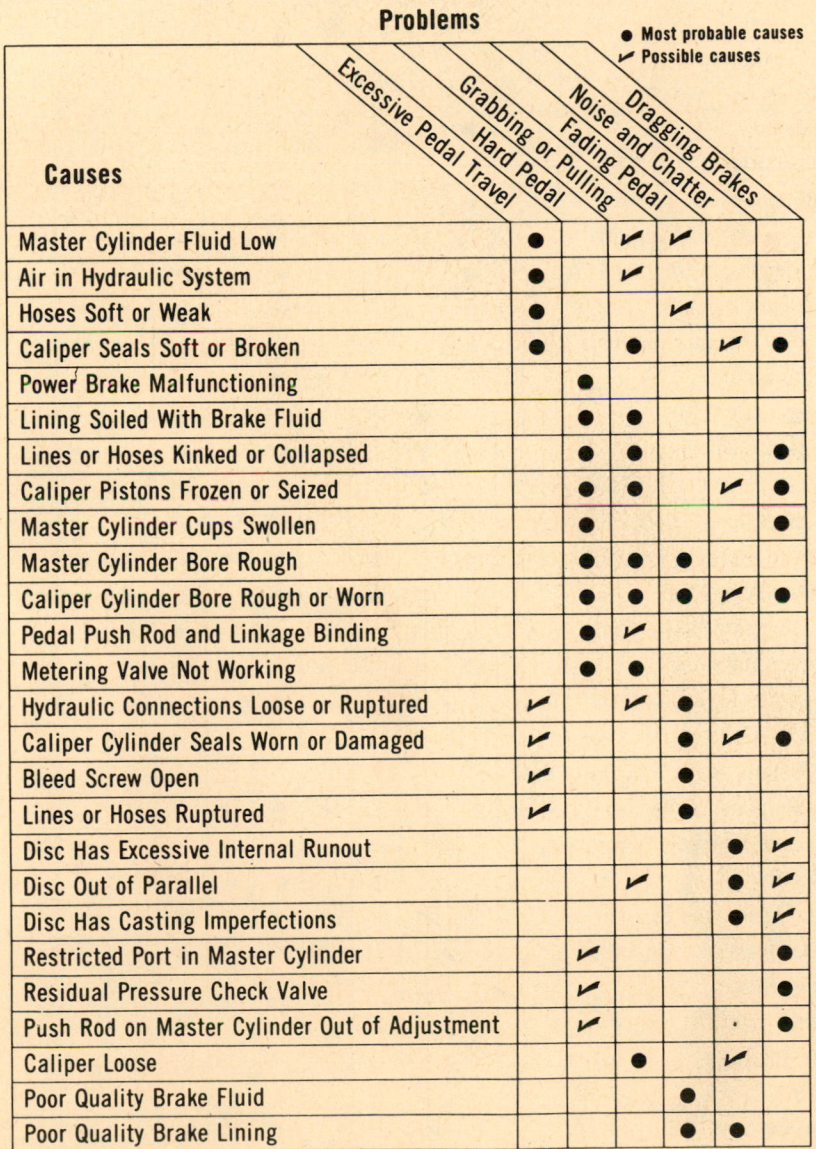

Problems

● Most probable causes
✔ Possible causes

Causes	Excessive Pedal Travel	Hard Pedal	Grabbing or Pulling	Fading Pedal	Noise and Chatter	Dragging Brakes
Master Cylinder Fluid Low	●		✔	✔		
Air in Hydraulic System	●		✔			
Hoses Soft or Weak	●			✔		
Caliper Seals Soft or Broken	●			●	✔	●
Power Brake Malfunctioning		●				
Lining Soiled With Brake Fluid		●	●			
Lines or Hoses Kinked or Collapsed		●	●			●
Caliper Pistons Frozen or Seized		●	●		✔	●
Master Cylinder Cups Swollen		●				●
Master Cylinder Bore Rough		●	●	●		
Caliper Cylinder Bore Rough or Worn		●	●	●	✔	●
Pedal Push Rod and Linkage Binding		●	✔			
Metering Valve Not Working		●	●			
Hydraulic Connections Loose or Ruptured	✔		✔	●		
Caliper Cylinder Seals Worn or Damaged	✔			●	✔	●
Bleed Screw Open	✔			●		
Lines or Hoses Ruptured	✔			●		
Disc Has Excessive Internal Runout					●	✔
Disc Out of Parallel			✔		●	✔
Disc Has Casting Imperfections					●	✔
Restricted Port in Master Cylinder		✔				●
Residual Pressure Check Valve		✔				●
Push Rod on Master Cylinder Out of Adjustment		✔			·	●
Caliper Loose			●		✔	
Poor Quality Brake Fluid				●		
Poor Quality Brake Lining				●	●	

Diagnostic Charts

AIR CONDITIONING DIAGNOSIS

Problems

Legend: ● Most probable causes ↙ Possible causes

Causes	Compressor Discharge Pressure Too High	Compressor Discharge Pressure Too Low	P.O.A. Valve Inlet Pressure Too High	P.O.A. Valve Inlet Pressure Too Low	Nozzle Outlet Temperature Too High	Nozzle Outlet Temperature Too Low	Evaporator Too Warm	Blown Thermal Limiter	Compressor Clutch Slips	Water Blowing Out Discharge Nozzle	Compressor Not Operating	Water Drains Onto Floor
Engine Overheated	●				↙		↙	↙				
Overcharge of Refrigerant or Air in System	●				↙		↙	↙				
Restriction in Condenser	●				↙		↙	↙				
Restriction in Receiver-Dehydrator		●		↙	↙		↙					
Restriction in Any High Pressure Line	●	↙			↙		↙	↙	↙			
Condenser Air Flow Blocked	●				↙		↙	↙	↙			
P.O.A. Valve Inlet Pressure Too High	●											
Insufficient Refrigerant		●		↙	●		●			↙		
Defective Compressor		●	↙		↙			↙	↙	●		
Plug in Refrigerant System	↙	●	↙	↙	↙		↙	↙	↙	↙		
P.O.A. Valve Inlet Pressure Too Low		●				↙	↙			↙		
P.O.A. Valve Stuck Open					↙	↙	↙			↙		
Capillary Tube to Evaporator Tube Contact	↙		●		↙	↙		●	↙			
Expansion Valve Inoperative	↙	↙	●	↙	●		●	↙	●	↙		
Inlet Screen Plugged or Valve Fails		↙		●	↙		↙			↙		
Restriction in System Hoses or Tubes	↙	↙		●	↙	↙	↙	↙	↙	↙		
Poor Seal Evaporator to Evaporator Inlet Case		↙		↙	●							
Poor Seal Evaporator to Heater Case		↙		↙	●							
Defective or Missing Evaporator Drain Hose										●		●
Air Ducts Not Properly Connected		↙		↙	●	↙						
Vacuum Hoses Not Connected Properly					●	↙						
P.O.A. Valve Faulty			●		●	●						
Low Charge or Discharged System		↙	↙	↙	↙		●		↙	↙		
Thermal Limiter Improperly Installed							●			↙		
Thermal Limiter Blown											●	
Faulty Superheat Shut Off Switch							●			↙		
Head Pressure Too High								●				
Pulley Wobbles								●				
Loose Compressor Drive Belt		↙	↙		↙				●		●	
Defective Clutch or Coil		↙	↙		↙				●		●	
Restriction in Suction Line		↙	↙		↙				●	↙		
Defective Suction Throttling Valve		↙	↙	●					↙			
Defective Expansion Valve	↙		●	↙	↙		↙		↙			
Plugged or Kinked Evaporator Drain Hose												●
Broken Compressor Drive Belt											●	
No Power to Clutch							↙				●	
Faulty Switch or Wiring									↙		●	

COOLING SYSTEM DIAGNOSIS

Problems

● Most probable causes
✔ Possible causes

Causes	External Leakage	Internal Leakage	Poor Circulation	Overheating	Overflow Loss	Corrosion	Temp Too Low (Slow Engine Warm Up)	Water Pump Noisy
Hose Leaking	●				●			
Water Pump Leaking	●				●			
Damaged Gasket	●	●			●			
Leaking Heater Core	●				✔			
Cracked Cylinder Block	●	●			✔			
Faulty Pressure Cap	●	●			●	●		
Oil Cooler Fittings Loose	●	●			✔			
Faulty Head Gasket	●	●			✔			
Loose Cylinder Head Bolts	●	●			✔			
Cracked Valve Port			●		✔			
Cracked Cylinder Wall			●		✔			
Leaking Oil Cooler			●					
Low Coolant Level				●	●			
Collapsed Radiator Hose				●	●			
Fan Belt Loose				●	✔			✔
Air Leak Through Bottom Hose			✔	●				
Faulty Thermostat				●	●		●	
Water Pump Impeller Broken				●				●
Restricted Radiator Core				●	●			
Restricted Engine Water Jacket				●				
Incorrect Ignition Timing				●				
Inaccurate Temperature Gauge				●			●	
Excessive Engine Idling				●				
Frozen Coolant				●				
Faulty Vacuum By Pass Valve				✔	●			
Overfilling					●			
Blown Head Gasket	✔				●			
Coolant Foaming					●			
Insufficient Corrosion Inhibitor				✔	✔	●		
Extended Use of Anti-Freeze				✔	✔	●		
High Mineral and Lime Content of Coolant				✔	✔	●		
Faulty Temperature Sending Unit							●	
Faulty Heater Controls				✔			●	
Defective Seal								●
Bearing Corroded								●

FRONT SUSPENSION DIAGNOSIS

Problems

● Most probable causes
✔ Possible causes

Causes	Front Wheel Shimmy	Pull to One Side	Excessive Play in Steering	Wheel Tramp	Excessive Tire Wear	Hard Steering	Front End Wandering	Front End Noise
Out of Balance Tires	●			●		✔		
Worn or Out of Adjustment Wheel Bearings	✔					✔		
Worn Tie Rod Ends	✔							
Worn Ball Joints	✔							
Incorrect Wheel Alignment	●	✔			✔	✔	●	
Incorrect Ride Height	✔							
Low or Uneven Tire Pressures		●			●	●	✔	
Front or Rear Brake Dragging		✔						
Grease or Brake Fluid on Brake Linings		✔						
Broken or Sagging Front Spring		✔				✔	✔	
Incorrect Steering Gear Adjustment			✔					
Worn Front End Parts			●					●
Shock Absorber Inoperative or Loose				✔		✔	✔	✔
Ball Joint Needs Lubrication						✔		✔
Loose Stabilizer Bar								✔
Loose Lugnuts								✔
Loose Brake Parts								✔
Improper Tire Size						✔		
Bent or Worn Steering Linkage						✔	✔	

TIRE WEAR DIAGNOSIS

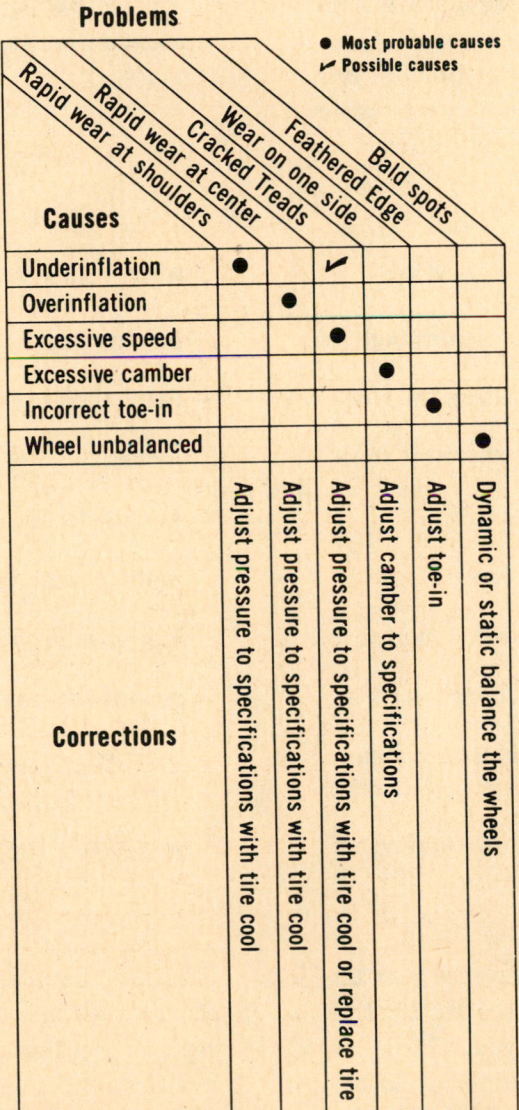

Problems

● Most probable causes
✔ Possible causes

Causes	Rapid wear at shoulders	Rapid wear at center	Cracked Treads	Wear on one side	Feathered Edge	Bald spots
Underinflation	●		✔			
Overinflation		●				
Excessive speed			●			
Excessive camber				●		
Incorrect toe-in					●	
Wheel unbalanced						●
Corrections	Adjust pressure to specifications with tire cool	Adjust pressure to specifications with tire cool	Adjust pressure to specifications with tire cool or replace tire	Adjust camber to specifications	Adjust toe-in	Dynamic or static balance the wheels

SI Metric Tables

The following tables are given in SI (International System) metric units. SI units replace both customary (English) and the older gavimetric units. The use of SI units as a new worldwide standard was set by the International Committee of Weights and Measures in 1960. SI has since been adopted by most countries as their national standard.

These tables are general conversion tables which will allow you to convert customary units, which appear in the text, into SI units.

The following are a list of SI units and the customary units, used in this book, which they replace:

To measure:	Use SI units:	Which replace (customary units):
mass	kilograms (kg)	pounds (lbs)
temperature	Celsius (°C)	Fahrenheit (°F)
length	millimeters (mm)	inches (in.)
force	newtons (N)	pounds force (lbs)
capacities	liters (l)	pints/quarts/gallons (pts/qts/gals)
torque	newton-meters (N·m)	foot pounds (ft lbs)
pressure	kilopascals (kPa)	pounds per square inch (psi)
volume	cubic centimeters (cm^3)	cubic inches (cu in.)
power	kilowatts (kW)	horsepower (hp)

If you have had any prior experience with the metric system, you may have noticed units in this chart which are not familiar to you. This is because, in some cases, SI units differ from the older gravimetric units which they replace. For example, newtons (N) replace kilograms (kg) as a force unit, kilopascals (kPa) replace atmospheres or bars as a unit of pressure, and, although the units are the same, the name Celsius replaces centigrade for temperature measurement.

If you are not using the SI tables, have a look at them anyway; you will be seeing a lot more of them in the future.

ENGLISH TO METRIC CONVERSION: MASS (WEIGHT)

Current **mass** measurement is expressed in pounds and ounces (lbs. & ozs.). The metric unit of mass (or weight) is the kilogram (kg). Even although this table does not show conversion of masses (weights) larger than 15 lbs, it is easy to calculate larger units by following the data immediately below.

To convert ounces (oz.) to grams (g): multiply th number of ozs. by 28
To convert grams (g) to ounces (oz.): multiply the number of grams by .035

To convert pounds (lbs.) to kilograms (kg): multiply the number of lbs. by .45
To convert kilograms (kg) to pounds (lbs.): multiply the number of kilograms by 2.2

lbs	kg	lbs	kg	oz	kg	oz	kg
0.1	0.04	0.9	0.41	0.1	0.003	0.9	0.024
0.2	0.09	1	0.4	0.2	0.005	1	0.03
0.3	0.14	2	0.9	0.3	0.008	2	0.06
0.4	0.18	3	1.4	0.4	0.011	3	0.08
0.5	0.23	4	1.8	0.5	0.014	4	0.11
0.6	0.27	5	2.3	0.6	0.017	5	0.14
0.7	0.32	10	4.5	0.7	0.020	10	0.28
0.8	0.36	15	6.8	0.8	0.023	15	0.42

ENGLISH TO METRIC CONVERSION: TEMPERATURE

To convert Fahrenheit (°F) to Celsius (°C): take number of °F and subtract 32; multiply result by 5; divide result by 9

To convert Celsius (°C) to Fahrenheit (°F): take number of °C and multiply by 9; divide result by 5; add 32 to total

Fahrenheit (F)		Celsius (C)		Fahrenheit (F)		Celsius (C)		Fahrenheit (F)		Celsius (C)	
°F	°C	°C	°F	°F	°C	°C	°F	°F	°C	°C	°F
−40	−40	−38	−36.4	80	26.7	18	64.4	215	101.7	80	176
−35	−37.2	−36	−32.8	85	29.4	20	68	220	104.4	85	185
−30	−34.4	−34	−29.2	90	32.2	22	71.6	225	107.2	90	194
−25	−31.7	−32	−25.6	95	35.0	24	75.2	230	110.0	95	202
−20	−28.9	−30	−22	100	37.8	26	78.8	235	112.8	100	212
−15	−26.1	−28	−18.4	105	40.6	28	82.4	240	115.6	105	221
−10	−23.3	−26	−14.8	110	43.3	30	86	245	118.3	110	230
−5	−20.6	−24	−11.2	115	46.1	32	89.6	250	121.1	115	239
0	−17.8	−22	−7.6	120	48.9	34	93.2	255	123.9	120	248
1	−17.2	−20	−4	125	51.7	36	96.8	260	126.6	125	257
2	−16.7	−18	−0.4	130	54.4	38	100.4	265	129.4	130	266
3	−16.1	−16	3.2	135	57.2	40	104	270	132.2	135	275
4	−15.6	−14	6.8	140	60.0	42	107.6	275	135.0	140	284
5	−15.0	−12	10.4	145	62.8	44	112.2	280	137.8	145	293
10	−12.2	−10	14	150	65.6	46	114.8	285	140.6	150	302
15	−9.4	−8	17.6	155	68.3	48	118.4	290	143.3	155	311
20	−6.7	−6	21.2	160	71.1	50	122	295	146.1	160	320
25	−3.9	−4	24.8	165	73.9	52	125.6	300	148.9	165	329
30	−1.1	−2	28.4	170	76.7	54	129.2	305	151.7	170	338
35	1.7	0	32	175	79.4	56	132.8	310	154.4	175	347
40	4.4	2	35.6	180	82.2	58	136.4	315	157.2	180	356
45	7.2	4	39.2	185	85.0	60	140	320	160.0	185	365
50	10.0	6	42.8	190	87.8	62	143.6	325	162.8	190	374
55	12.8	8	46.4	195	90.6	64	147.2	330	165.6	195	383
60	15.6	10	50	200	93.3	66	150.8	335	168.3	200	392
65	18.3	12	53.6	205	96.1	68	154.4	340	171.1	205	401
70	21.1	14	57.2	210	98.9	70	158	345	173.9	210	410
75	23.9	16	60.8	212	100.0	75	167	350	176.7	215	414

Metric Tables

ENGLISH TO METRIC CONVERSION: LENGTH

To convert inches (ins.) to millimeters (mm): multiply number of inches by 25.4

To convert millimeters (mm) to inches (ins.): multiply number of millimeters by .04

Inches		Decimals	Milli-meters	Inches to millimeters inches	mm	Inches		Decimals	Milli-meters	Inches to millimeters inches	mm
	1/64	0.015625	0.3969	0.0001	0.00254		33/64	0.515625	13.0969	0.6	15.24
1/32		0.03125	0.7937	0.0002	0.00508	17/32		0.53125	13.4937	0.7	17.78
	3/64	0.046875	1.1906	0.0003	0.00762		35/64	0.546875	13.8906	0.8	20.32
1/16		0.0625	1.5875	0.0004	0.01016	9/16		0.5625	14.2875	0.9	22.86
	5/64	0.078125	1.9844	0.0005	0.01270		37/64	0.578125	14.6844	1	25.4
3/32		0.09375	2.3812	0.0006	0.01524	19/32		0.59375	15.0812	2	50.8
	7/64	0.109375	2.7781	0.0007	0.01778		39/64	0.609375	15.4781	3	76.2
1/8		0.125	3.1750	0.0008	0.02032	5/8		0.625	15.8750	4	101.6
	9/64	0.140625	3.5719	0.0009	0.02286		41/64	0.640625	16.2719	5	127.0
5/32		0.15625	3.9687	.001	0.0254	21/32		0.65625	16.6687	6	152.4
	11/64	0.171875	4.3656	0.002	0.0508		43/64	0.671875	17.0656	7	177.8
3/16		0.1875	4.7625	0.003	0.0762	11/16		0.6875	17.4625	8	203.2
	13/64	0.203125	5.1594	0.004	0.1016		45/64	0.703125	17.8594	9	228.6
7/32		0.21875	5.5562	0.005	0.1270	23/32		0.71875	18.2562	10	254.0
	15/64	0.234375	5.9531	0.006	0.1524		47/64	0.734375	18.6531	11	279.4
1/4		0.25	6.3500	0.007	0.1778	3/4		0.75	19.0500	12	304.8
	17/64	0.265625	6.7469	0.008	0.2032		49/64	0.765625	19.4469	13	330.2
9/32		0.28125	7.1437	0.009	0.2286	25/32		0.78125	19.8437	14	355.6
	19/64	0.296875	7.5406	0.01	0.254		51/64	0.796875	20.2406	15	381.0
5/16		0.3125	7.9375	0.02	0.508	13/16		0.8125	20.6375	16	406.4
	21/64	0.328125	8.3344	0.03	0.762		53/64	0.828125	21.0344	17	431.8
11/32		0.34375	8.7312	0.04	1.016	27/32		0.84375	21.4312	18	457.2
	23/64	0.359375	9.1281	0.05	1.270		55/64	0.859375	21.8281	19	482.6
3/8		0.375	9.5250	0.06	1.524	7/8		0.875	22.2250	20	508.0
	25/64	0.390625	9.9219	0.07	1.778		57/64	0.890625	22.6219	21	533.4
13/32		0.40625	10.3187	0.08	2.032	29/32		0.90625	23.0187	22	558.8
	27/64	0.421875	10.7156	0.09	2.286		59/64	0.921875	23.4156	23	584.2
7/16		0.4375	11.1125	0.1	2.54	15/16		0.9375	23.8125	24	609.6
	29/64	0.453125	11.5094	0.2	5.08		61/64	0.953125	24.2094	25	635.0
15/32		0.46875	11.9062	0.3	7.62	31/32		0.96875	24.6062	26	660.4
	31/64	0.484375	12.3031	0.4	10.16		63/64	0.984375	25.0031	27	690.6
1/2		0.5	12.7000	0.5	12.70						

ENGLISH TO METRIC CONVERSION: TORQUE

To convert foot-pounds (ft. lbs.) to Newton-meters: multiply the number of ft. lbs. by 1.3

To convert inch-pounds (in. lbs.) to Newton-meters: multiply the number of in. lbs. by .11

in lbs	N-m	in lbs	N-m	in lbs	N-m	in lbs	N-m	in lbs	N-m	in lbs	N-m
0.1	0.01	1	0.11	10	1.13	19	2.15	28	3.16		
0.2	0.02	2	0.23	11	1.24	20	2.26	29	3.28		
0.3	0.03	3	0.34	12	1.36	21	2.37	30	3.39		
0.4	0.04	4	0.45	13	1.47	22	2.49	31	3.50		
0.5	0.06	5	0.56	14	1.58	23	2.60	32	3.62		
0.6	0.07	6	0.68	15	1.70	24	2.71	33	3.73		
0.7	0.08	7	0.78	16	1.81	25	2.82	34	3.84		
0.8	0.09	8	0.90	17	1.92	26	2.94	35	3.95		
0.9	0.10	9	1.02	18	2.03	27	3.05	36	4.07		

ENGLISH TO METRIC CONVERSION: TORQUE

Torque is now expressed as either foot-pounds (ft./lbs.) or inch-pounds (in./lbs.). The metric measurement unit for torque is the Newton-meter (Nm). This unit—the Nm—will be used for all SI metric torque references, both the present ft./lbs. and in./lbs.

ft lbs	N-m	ft lbs	N-m	ft lbs	N-m	ft lbs	N-m
0.1	0.1	33	44.7	74	100.3	115	155.9
0.2	0.3	34	46.1	75	101.7	116	157.3
0.3	0.4	35	47.4	76	103.0	117	158.6
0.4	0.5	36	48.8	77	104.4	118	160.0
0.5	0.7	37	50.7	78	105.8	119	161.3
0.6	0.8	38	51.5	79	107.1	120	162.7
0.7	1.0	39	52.9	80	108.5	121	164.0
0.8	1.1	40	54.2	81	109.8	122	165.4
0.9	1.2	41	55.6	82	111.2	123	166.8
1	1.3	42	56.9	83	112.5	124	168.1
2	2.7	43	58.3	84	113.9	125	169.5
3	4.1	44	59.7	85	115.2	126	170.8
4	5.4	45	61.0	86	116.6	127	172.2
5	6.8	46	62.4	87	118.0	128	173.5
6	8.1	47	63.7	88	119.3	129	174.9
7	9.5	48	65.1	89	120.7	130	176.2
8	10.8	49	66.4	90	122.0	131	177.6
9	12.2	50	67.8	91	123.4	132	179.0
10	13.6	51	69.2	92	124.7	133	180.3
11	14.9	52	70.5	93	126.1	134	181.7
12	16.3	53	71.9	94	127.4	135	183.0
13	17.6	54	73.2	95	128.8	136	184.4
14	18.9	55	74.6	96	130.2	137	185.7
15	20.3	56	75.9	97	131.5	138	187.1
16	21.7	57	77.3	98	132.9	139	188.5
17	23.0	58	78.6	99	134.2	140	189.8
18	24.4	59	80.0	100	135.6	141	191.2
19	25.8	60	81.4	101	136.9	142	192.5
20	27.1	61	82.7	102	138.3	143	193.9
21	28.5	62	84.1	103	139.6	144	195.2
22	29.8	63	85.4	104	141.0	145	196.6
23	31.2	64	86.8	105	142.4	146	198.0
24	32.5	65	88.1	106	143.7	147	199.3
25	33.9	66	89.5	107	145.1	148	200.7
26	35.2	67	90.8	108	146.4	149	202.0
27	36.6	68	92.2	109	147.8	150	203.4
28	38.0	69	93.6	110	149.1	151	204.7
29	39.3	70	94.9	111	150.5	152	206.1
30	40.7	71	96.3	112	151.8	153	207.4
31	42.0	72	97.6	113	153.2	154	208.8
32	43.4	73	99.0	114	154.6	155	210.2

ENGLISH TO METRIC CONVERSION: FORCE

Force is presently measured in pounds (lbs.). This type of measurement is used to measure spring pressure, specifically how many pounds it takes to compress a spring. Our present force unit (the pound) will be replaced in SI metric measurements by the Newton (N). This term will eventually see use in specifications for electric motor brush spring pressures, valve spring pressures, etc.

To convert pounds (lbs.) to Newton (N): multiply the number of lbs. by 4.45

lbs	N	lbs	N	lbs	N	oz	N
0.01	0.04	21	93.4	59	262.4	1	0.3
0.02	0.09	22	97.9	60	266.9	2	0.6
0.03	0.13	23	102.3	61	271.3	3	0.8
0.04	0.18	24	106.8	62	275.8	4	1.1
0.05	0.22	25	111.2	63	280.2	5	1.4
0.06	0.27	26	115.6	64	284.6	6	1.7
0.07	0.31	27	120.1	65	289.1	7	2.0
0.08	0.36	28	124.6	66	293.6	8	2.2
0.09	0.40	29	129.0	67	298.0	9	2.5
0.1	0.4	30	133.4	68	302.5	10	2.8
0.2	0.9	31	137.9	69	306.9	11	3.1
0.3	1.3	32	142.3	70	311.4	12	3.3
0.4	1.8	33	146.8	71	315.8	13	3.6
0.5	2.2	34	151.2	72	320.3	14	3.9
0.6	2.7	35	155.7	73	324.7	15	4.2
0.7	3.1	36	160.1	74	329.2	16	4.4
0.8	3.6	37	164.6	75	333.6	17	4.7
0.9	4.0	38	169.0	76	338.1	18	5.0
1	4.4	39	173.5	77	342.5	19	5.3
2	8.9	40	177.9	78	347.0	20	5.6
3	13.4	41	182.4	79	351.4	21	5.8
4	17.8	42	186.8	80	355.9	22	6.1
5	22.2	43	191.3	81	360.3	23	6.4
6	26.7	44	195.7	82	364.8	24	6.7
7	31.1	45	200.2	83	369.2	25	7.0
8	35.6	46	204.6	84	373.6	26	7.2
9	40.0	47	209.1	85	378.1	27	7.5
10	44.5	48	213.5	86	382.6	28	7.8
11	48.9	49	218.0	87	387.0	29	8.1
12	53.4	50	224.4	88	391.4	30	8.3
13	57.8	51	226.9	89	395.9	31	8.6
14	62.3	52	231.3	90	400.3	32	8.9
15	66.7	53	235.8	91	404.8	33	9.2
16	71.2	54	240.2	92	409.2	34	9.4
17	75.6	55	244.6	93	413.7	35	9.7
18	80.1	56	249.1	94	418.1	36	10.0
19	84.5	57	253.6	95	422.6	37	10.3
20	89.0	58	258.0	96	427.0	38	10.6

ENGLISH TO METRIC CONVERSION: LIQUID CAPACITY

Liquid or fluid capacity is presently expressed as pints, quarts or gallons, or a combination of all of these. In the metric system the liter (l) will become the basic unit. Fractions of a liter would be expressed as deciliters, centiliters, or most frequently (and commonly) as milliliters.

To convert pints (pts.) to liters (l): multiply the number of pints by .47
To convert liters (l) to pints (pts.): multiply the number of liters by 2.1
To convert quarts (qts.) to liters (l): multiply the number of quarts by .95

To convert liters (l) to quarts (qts.): multiply the number of liters by 1.06
To convert gallons (gals.) to liters (l): multiply the number of gallons by 3.8
To convert liters (l) to gallons (gals.): multiply the number of liters by .26

gals	liters	qts	liters	pts	liters
0.1	0.38	0.1	0.10	0.1	0.05
0.2	0.76	0.2	0.19	0.2	0.10
0.3	1.1	0.3	0.28	0.3	0.14
0.4	1.5	0.4	0.38	0.4	0.19
0.5	1.9	0.5	0.47	0.5	0.24
0.6	2.3	0.6	0.57	0.6	0.28
0.7	2.6	0.7	0.66	0.7	0.33
0.8	3.0	0.8	0.76	0.8	0.38
0.9	3.4	0.9	0.85	0.9	0.43
1	3.8	1	1.0	1	0.5
2	7.6	2	1.9	2	1.0
3	11.4	3	2.8	3	1.4
4	15.1	4	3.8	4	1.9
5	18.9	5	4.7	5	2.4
6	22.7	6	5.7	6	2.8
7	26.5	7	6.6	7	3.3
8	30.3	8	7.6	8	3.8
9	34.1	9	8.5	9	4.3
10	37.8	10	9.5	10	4.7
11	41.6	11	10.4	11	5.2
12	45.4	12	11.4	12	5.7
13	49.2	13	12.3	13	6.2
14	53.0	14	13.2	14	6.6
15	56.8	15	14.2	15	7.1
16	60.6	16	15.1	16	7.6
17	64.3	17	16.1	17	8.0
18	68.1	18	17.0	18	8.5
19	71.9	19	18.0	19	9.0
20	75.7	20	18.9	20	9.5
21	79.5	21	19.9	21	9.9
22	83.2	22	20.8	22	10.4
23	87.0	23	21.8	23	10.9
24	90.8	24	22.7	24	11.4
25	94.6	25	23.6	25	11.8
26	98.4	26	24.6	26	12.3
27	102.2	27	25.5	27	12.8
28	106.0	28	26.5	28	13.2
29	110.0	29	27.4	29	13.7
30	113.5	30	28.4	30	14.2

Metric Tables

ENGLISH TO METRIC CONVERSION: PRESSURE

The basic unit of pressure measurement used today is expressed as pounds per square inch (psi). The metric unit for psi will be the kilopascal (kPa). This will apply to either fluid pressure or air pressure, and will be frequently seen in tire pressure readings, oil pressure specifications, fuel pump pressure, etc.

To convert pounds per square inch (psi) to kilopascals (kPa): multiply the number of psi by 6.89

Psi	kPa	Psi	kPa	Psi	kPa	Psi	kPa
0.1	0.7	37	255.1	82	565.4	127	875.6
0.2	1.4	38	262.0	83	572.3	128	882.5
0.3	2.1	39	268.9	84	579.2	129	889.4
0.4	2.8	40	275.8	85	586.0	130	896.3
0.5	3.4	41	282.7	86	592.9	131	903.2
0.6	4.1	42	289.6	87	599.8	132	910.1
0.7	4.8	43	296.5	88	606.7	133	917.0
0.8	5.5	44	303.4	89	613.6	134	923.9
0.9	6.2	45	310.3	90	620.5	135	930.8
1	6.9	46	317.2	91	627.4	136	937.7
2	13.8	47	324.0	92	634.3	137	944.6
3	20.7	48	331.0	93	641.2	138	951.5
4	27.6	49	337.8	94	648.1	139	958.4
5	34.5	50	344.7	95	655.0	140	965.2
6	41.4	51	351.6	96	661.9	141	972.2
7	48.3	52	358.5	97	668.8	142	979.0
8	55.2	53	365.4	98	675.7	143	985.9
9	62.1	54	372.3	99	682.6	144	992.8
10	69.0	55	379.2	100	689.5	145	999.7
11	75.8	56	386.1	101	696.4	146	1006.6
12	82.7	57	393.0	102	703.3	147	1013.5
13	89.6	58	399.9	103	710.2	148	1020.4
14	96.5	59	406.8	104	717.0	149	1027.3
15	103.4	60	413.7	105	723.9	150	1034.2
16	110.3	61	420.6	106	730.8	151	1041.1
17	117.2	62	427.5	107	737.7	152	1048.0
18	124.1	63	434.4	108	744.6	153	1054.9
19	131.0	64	441.3	109	751.5	154	1061.8
20	137.9	65	448.2	110	758.4	155	1068.7
21	144.8	66	455.0	111	765.3	156	1075.6
22	151.7	67	461.9	112	772.2	157	1082.5
23	158.6	68	468.8	113	779.1	158	1089.4
24	165.5	69	475.7	114	786.0	159	1096.3
25	172.4	70	482.6	115	792.9	160	1103.2
26	179.3	71	489.5	116	799.8	161	1110.0
27	186.2	72	496.4	117	806.7	162	1116.9
28	193.0	73	503.3	118	813.6	163	1123.8
29	200.0	74	510.2	119	820.5	164	1130.7
30	206.8	75	517.1	120	827.4	165	1137.6
31	213.7	76	524.0	121	834.3	166	1144.5
32	220.6	77	530.9	122	841.2	167	1151.4
33	227.5	78	537.8	123	848.0	168	1158.3
34	234.4	79	544.7	124	854.9	169	1165.2
35	241.3	80	551.6	125	861.8	170	1172.1
36	248.2	81	558.5	126	868.7	171	1179.0

ENGLISH TO METRIC CONVERSION: PRESSURE

The basic unit of pressure measurement used today is expressed as pounds per square inch (psi). The metric unit for psi will be the kilopascal (kPa). This will apply to either fluid pressure or air pressure, and will be frequently seen in tire pressure readings, oil pressure specifications, fuel pump pressure, etc.

To convert pounds per square inch (psi) to kilopascals (kPa): multiply the number of psi by 6.89

Psi	kPa	Psi	kPa	Psi	kPa	Psi	kPa
172	1185.9	216	1489.3	260	1792.6	304	2096.0
173	1192.8	217	1496.2	261	1799.5	305	2102.9
174	1199.7	218	1503.1	262	1806.4	306	2109.8
175	1206.6	219	1510.0	263	1813.3	307	2116.7
176	1213.5	220	1516.8	264	1820.2	308	2123.6
177	1220.4	221	1523.7	265	1827.1	309	2130.5
178	1227.3	222	1530.6	266	1834.0	310	2137.4
179	1234.2	223	1537.5	267	1840.9	311	2144.3
180	1241.0	224	1544.4	268	1847.8	312	2151.2
181	1247.9	225	1551.3	269	1854.7	313	2158.1
182	1254.8	226	1558.2	270	1861.6	314	2164.9
183	1261.7	227	1565.1	271	1868.5	315	2171.8
184	1268.6	228	1572.0	272	1875.4	316	2178.7
185	1275.5	229	1578.9	273	1882.3	317	2185.6
186	1282.4	230	1585.8	274	1889.2	318	2192.5
187	1289.3	231	1592.7	275	1896.1	319	2199.4
188	1296.2	232	1599.6	276	1903.0	320	2206.3
189	1303.1	233	1606.5	277	1909.8	321	2213.2
190	1310.0	234	1613.4	278	1916.7	322	2220.1
191	1316.9	235	1620.3	279	1923.6	323	2227.0
192	1323.8	236	1627.2	280	1930.5	324	2233.9
193	1330.7	237	1634.1	281	1937.4	325	2240.8
194	1337.6	238	1641.0	282	1944.3	326	2247.7
195	1344.5	239	1647.8	283	1951.2	327	2254.6
196	1351.4	240	1654.7	284	1958.1	328	2261.5
197	1358.3	241	1661.6	285	1965.0	329	2268.4
198	1365.2	242	1668.5	286	1971.9	330	2275.3
199	1372.0	243	1675.4	287	1978.8	331	2282.2
200	1378.9	244	1682.3	288	1985.7	332	2289.1
201	1385.8	245	1689.2	289	1992.6	333	2295.9
202	1392.7	246	1696.1	290	1999.5	334	2302.8
203	1399.6	247	1703.0	291	2006.4	335	2309.7
204	1406.5	248	1709.9	292	2013.3	336	2316.6
205	1413.4	249	1716.8	293	2020.2	337	2323.5
206	1420.3	250	1723.7	294	2027.1	338	2330.4
207	1427.2	251	1730.6	295	2034.0	339	2337.3
208	1434.1	252	1737.5	296	2040.8	240	2344.2
209	1441.0	253	1744.4	297	2047.7	341	2351.1
210	1447.9	254	1751.3	298	2054.6	342	2358.0
211	1454.8	255	1758.2	299	2061.5	343	2364.9
212	1461.7	256	1765.1	300	2068.4	344	2371.8
213	1468.7	257	1772.0	301	2075.3	345	2378.7
214	1475.5	258	1778.8	302	2082.2	346	2385.6
215	1482.4	259	1785.7	303	2089.1	347	2392.5

Turn Signal Flasher and Fuse Box Location Chart

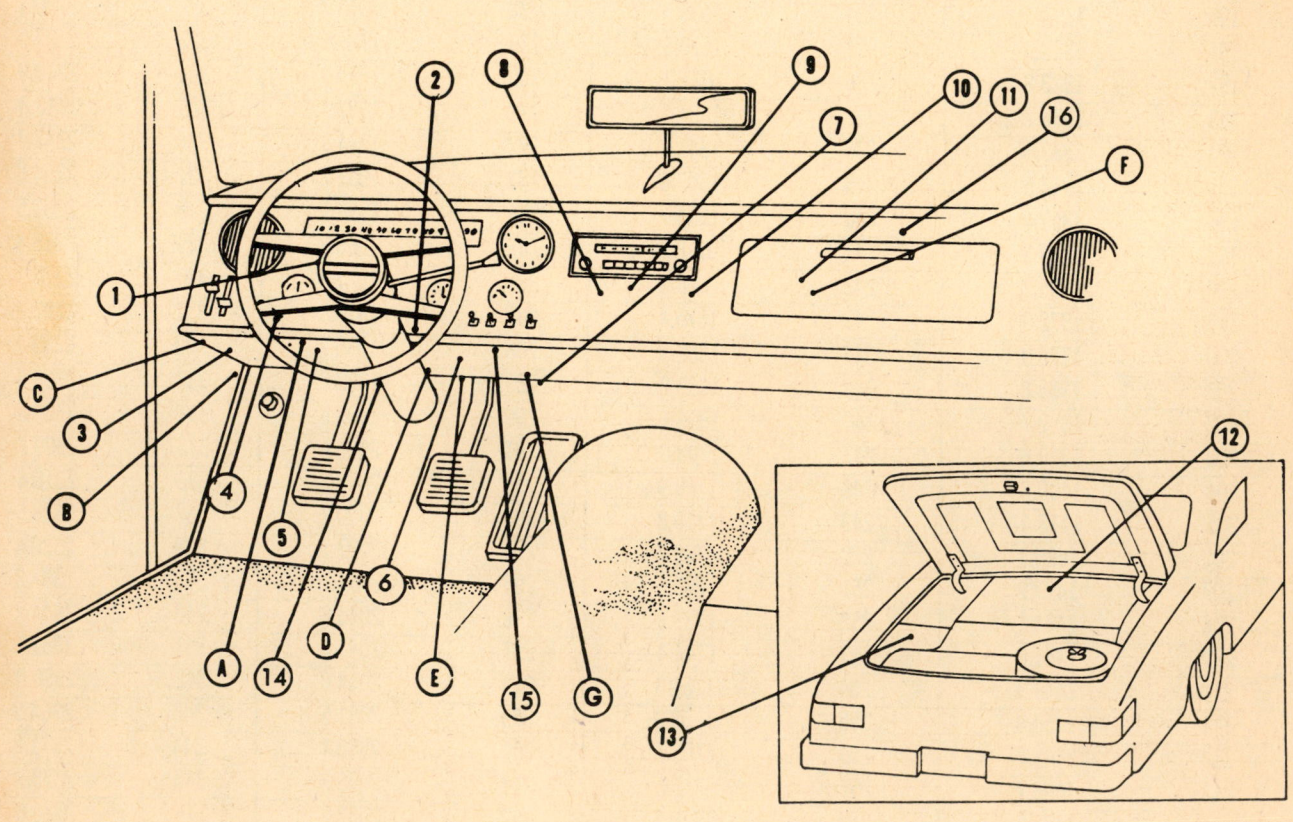

TURN SIGNAL FLASHER, HAZARD WARNING FLASHER, AND FUSE BLOCK LOCATION

	1972 TSF	1972 HWF	1973 TSF	1973 HWF	1974 TSF	1974 HWF	1975 TSF	1975 HWF	1976 TSF	1976 HWF	1977 TSF	1977 HWF	1978-79 TSF	1978-79 HWF	Through 1973 Fuse Block Location	1974 Fuse Block Location	1975-79 Fuse Block Location
American Motors																	
Ambassador	2	3	2	3	2	3	—	—	—	—	—	—	—	—	C	F	—
Concord, Hornet, Gremlin	3	3	3	3	3	2	3	2	3	2	3	6	3	6	C	C	C
Javelin	3	3	3	3	3	3	—	—	—	—	—	—	—	—	C	C	C
Matador	2	3	2	3	2	3	3	1	3	1	3	1	3	1	C	F	F
Pacer	—	—	—	—	—	—	3	5	3	5	3	5	3	5	—	—	F
Chrysler Corporation																	
Barracuda, Challenger	10	6	8	6	6	6	—	—	—	—	—	—	—	—	D,A	G	—
Chrysler	5	5	5	5	5	5	14	5	14	5	14	1	14	1	A	A	A
Cordoba	—	—	—	—	—	—	1	15	1	15	1	15	1	15	—	—	A
Dart, Aspen	10	6	8	6	8	6	5	5	5	5	5	5	5	5	D	D	A
Dodge	5, 10	5	8	6	8	6①	4③	15④	4③	15④	1	15④	1	15④	A	D②	A
Imperial	5	5	5	6	5	5	14	5	—	—	—	—	—	—	F	A	A
Omni, Horizon	—	—	—	—	—	—	—	—	—	—	—	—	3	3	—	—	C
Plymouth	5, 10	5	8	6	8	6①	4③	15④	4③	15④	1	15④	1	15④	A	D②	A
Valiant, Volare, Diplomat, LeBaron	10	6	8	5	8	6	5	5	5	5	5	5	5	5	A	D	A
Ford Motor Company⑤																	
Comet, Maverick	5	5	5	5	5	5	5	3	5	3	5	3	5	3	E	E	E,C
Cougar	8	10	8	10	3	3	3	3	3	3	5	5	5	5	E	C	C,A
Torino, Elite	5	5	5	5	3	3	3	3	3	3	—	—	—	—	E	C	C
Fairmont, Zephyr	—	—	—	—	—	—	—	—	—	—	—	—	16	11	—	—	A
Ford	10	3	3	3	3	3	3	3	3	3	3	3	3	3	E	A	C
Granada, Monarch, Versailles	—	—	—	—	—	—	6	14	6	14	6	14	6	14	—	—	C
Lincoln Continental	3	3	3	3	10	5	10	5	10	5	10	5	10	5	F	A	A
Mark III, IV, V	3	5	3	5	3	5	3	5	3	5	3	5	9	5	F	A	A
Mercury	10	3	3	3	3	3	3	3	3	3	3	3	3	3	E	A	C
Montego	5	5	5	5	3	3	3	3	3	3	—	—	—	—	E	C	C
Mustang	8	10	16	10	—	—	—	—	—	—	—	—	—	—	E	—	—
Mustang II	—	—	—	—	7	7	7	7	7	7	7	7	7	7	—	G	G
Pinto, Bobcat	16	16	16	16	16	16	16	16	16	16	16	16	16	16	E	E	E
Thunderbird, LTD II	3	5	3	5	3	5	3	5	3	5	3	5	5	5	F	A	A
General Motors Corporation⑤																	
Buick	3	3	3	3	3	3	3	3	3	3	3	3	3	3	—	—	B
Buick Apollo, Skylark	—	—	5	3	5	3	3	3	3	3	3	3	3	3	B	B	B
Buick Skylark, Regal, Century	4	3	4	3	14	3	14	3	14	3	14	3	3	3	C	C	B
Buick Skyhawk	—	—	—	—	—	—	3	3	3	3	3	3	3	3	B	B	B
Cadillac, Eldorado	14	3	14	3	14	3	6	3	6	3	5	3	5	3	B	B	B
Cadillac Seville	—	—	—	—	—	—	5	5	5	5	5	5	5	5	—	—	A
Camaro	8	3	8	3	8	3	14	5	14	5	14	5	3	3	A	A	A
Chevelle, Malibu	7	3	4	3	4	3	14	5	14	5	5	5	3	3	A	A	A
Chevette	—	—	—	—	—	—	—	—	6	5	6	5	6	5	—	—	C
Chevrolet	7	3	6	3	6	3	14	5	14	5	5	5	5	5	A	A	A
Nova	7	3	10	3	10	3	14	5	14	5	6	5	6	5	A	A	A
Corvette	11	3	11	3	6	3	14	5	14	5	6	5	6	5	A	A	A
Monza	—	—	—	—	—	—	14	3	14	3	14	3	14	3	—	—	C
Vega	5	3	5	3	5	3	14	3	14	3	14	3	—	—	C	C	C
Oldsmobile	4	3	4	3	5	3	5	5	5	5	5	5	5	5	C	C	A
Oldsmobile Cutlass	4	3	4	3	14	3	14	3	14	3	5	5	3	3	C	C	C
Oldsmobile Omega	—	—	5	3	6	3	6	5	6	5	3	3	3	3	—	—	C
Oldsmobile Starfire	—	—	—	—	—	—	14	3	14	3	3	3	3	3	—	—	C
Oldsmobile Toronado	4	3	4	3	5	3	5	5	5	5	5	5	5	5	C	C	A
Pontiac Astre, Sunbird	—	—	—	—	—	—	14	3	14	3	3	3	3	3	—	—	C
Pontiac	3	3	3	3	3	3	5	3	5	3	3	3	3	3	C	C	B
Firebird	3	3	3	3	3	3	5	3	5	3	5	3	3	3	C	C	B
LeMans, GTO, Grand Am	3	3	3	3	3	3	5	3	5	3	3	3	3	3	C	C	B
Ventura, Phoenix	3	3	3	3	3	3	5	3	5	3	10	3	3	3	C	C	B

①—5 on full size models
②—A on full size models
TSF—Turn Signal Flasher
HWF—Hazard Warning Flasher
③—14 on full size models
④—5 on full size models
⑤—Most hazard warning flashers and some turn signal flashers are mounted on fuse panel.

ANTI-FREEZE INFORMATION

Freezing and Boiling Points of Solutions
According to Percentage of Alcohol or Ethylene Glycol

Freezing Point of Solution	Alcohol Volume %	Alcohol Solution Boils at	Ethylene Glycol Volume %	Ethylene Glycol Solution Boils at
20°F.	12	196°F.	16	216°F.
10°F.	20	189°F.	25	218°F.
0°F.	27	184°F.	33	220°F.
−10°F.	32	181°F.	39	222°F.
−20°F.	38	178°F.	44	224°F.
−30°F.	42	176°F.	48	225°F.

Note: above boiling points are at sea level. For every 1,000 feet of altitude, boiling points are approximately 2°F. lower than those shown. For every pound of pressure exerted by the pressure cap, the boiling points are approximately 3°F. higher than those shown.

To Increase the Freezing Protection of Anti-Freeze Solutions Already Installed

Cooling System Capacity Quarts	Number of Quarts of ETHYLENE GLYCOL Anti-Freeze Required to Increase Protection													
	From +20°F. to					From +10°F. to					From 0°F. to			
	0°	−10°	−20°	−30°	−40°	0°	−10°	−20°	−30°	−40°	−10°	−20°	−30°	−40°
10	1¾	2¼	3	3½	3¾	¾	1½	2¼	2¾	3¼	¾	1½	2	2½
12	2	2¾	3½	4	4½	1	1¾	2½	3¼	3¾	1	1¾	2½	3¼
14	2¼	3¼	4	4¾	5½	1¼	2	3	3¾	4½	1	2	3	3½
16	2½	3½	4½	5¼	6	1¼	2½	3½	4¼	5¼	1¼	2¼	3¼	4
18	3	4	5	6	7	1½	2¾	4	5	5¾	1½	2½	3¾	4¾
20	3¼	4½	5¾	6¾	7½	1¾	3	4¼	5½	6½	1½	2¾	4¼	5¼
22	3½	5	6¼	7¼	8¼	1¾	3¼	4¾	6	7¼	1¾	3¼	4½	5½
24	4	5½	7	8	9	2	3½	5	6½	7½	1¾	3½	5	6
26	4¼	6	7½	8¾	10	2	4	5½	7	8¼	2	3¾	5½	6¾
28	4½	6¼	8	9½	10½	2¼	4¼	6	7½	9	2	4	5¾	7¼
30	5	6¾	8½	10	11½	2½	4½	6½	8	9½	2¼	4¼	6¼	7¾

Test radiator solution with proper hydrometer. Determine from the table the number of quarts of solution to be drawn off from a full cooling system and replace with undiluted anti-freeze, to give the desired increased protection. For example, to increase protection of a 22-quart cooling system containing Ethylene Glycol (permanent type) anti-freeze, from +20°F. to −20°F. will require the replacement of 6¼ quarts of solution with undiluted anti-freeze.

ANTI-FREEZE CHART
Temperatures Shown in Degrees Fahrenheit
+32 is Freezing

Cooling System Capacity Quarts	Quarts of ETHYLENE GLYCOL Needed for Protection to Temperatures Shown Below													
	1	2	3	4	5	6	7	8	9	10	11	12	13	14
10	+24°	+16°	+ 4°	−12°	−34°	−62°								
11	+25	+18	+ 8	− 6	−23	−47					For capacities over 30 quarts di-			
12	+26	+19	+10	0	−15	−34	−57°				vide true capacity by 3. Find quarts			
13	+27	+21	+13	+ 3	− 9	−25	−45				Anti-Freeze for the ⅓ and multiply			
14			+15	+ 6	− 5	−18	−34				by 3 for quarts to add.			
15			+16	+ 8	0	−12	−26							
16			+17	+10	+ 2	− 8	−19	−34	−52°		For capacities under 10 quarts			
17			+18	+12	+ 5	− 4	−14	−27	−42		multiply true capacity by 3.			
18			+19	+14	+ 7	0	−10	−21	−34	−50°	Find quarts Anti-Freeze for the			
19			+20	+15	+ 9	+ 2	− 7	−16	−28	−42	tripled volume and divide by			
20				+16	+10	+ 4	− 3	−12	−22	−34	−48°	3 for quarts to add.		
21				+17	+12	+ 6	0	− 9	−17	−28	−41			
22				+18	+13	+ 8	+ 2	− 6	−14	−23	−34	−47°		
23				+19	+14	+ 9	+ 4	− 3	−10	−19	−29	−40		
24				+19	+15	+10	+ 5	0	− 8	−15	−23	−34	−46°	
25				+20	+16	+12	+ 7	+ 1	− 5	−12	−20	−29	−40	−50°
26					+17	+13	+ 8	+ 3	− 3	− 9	−16	−25	−34	−44
27					+18	+14	+ 9	+ 5	− 1	− 7	−13	−21	−29	−39
28					+18	+15	+10	+ 6	+ 1	− 5	−11	−18	−25	−34
29					+19	+16	+12	+ 7	+ 2	− 3	− 8	−15	−22	−29
30					+20	+17	+13	+ 8	+ 4	− 1	− 6	−12	−18	−25

MECHANICS' DATA

Tap Drill Sizes

National Coarse or U.S.S.

Screw & Tap Size	Threads Per Inch	Use Drill Number
No. 5	40	39
No. 6	32	36
No. 8	32	29
No. 10	24	25
No. 12	24	17
1/4	20	8
5/16	18	F
3/8	16	5/16
7/16	14	U
1/2	13	27/64
9/16	12	31/64
5/8	11	17/32
3/4	10	21/32
7/8	9	49/64
1	8	7/8
1 1/8	7	63/64
1 1/4	7	1 7/64
1 1/2	6	1 11/32

National Fine or S.A.E.

Screw & Tap Size	Threads Per Inch	Use Drill Number
No. 5	44	37
No. 6	40	33
No. 8	36	29
No. 10	32	21
No. 12	28	15
1/4	28	3
5/16	24	1
3/8	24	Q
7/16	20	W
1/2	20	29/64
9/16	18	33/64
5/8	18	37/64
3/4	16	11/16
7/8	14	13/16
1 1/8	12	1 3/64
1 1/4	12	1 11/64
1 1/2	12	1 27/64

Decimal Equivalent Size of the Number Drills

Drill No.	Decimal Equivalent	Drill No.	Decimal Equivalent	Drill No.	Decimal Equivalent
80	.0135	53	.0595	26	.1470
79	.0145	52	.0635	25	.1495
78	.0160	51	.0670	24	.1520
77	.0180	50	.0700	23	.1540
76	.0200	49	.0730	22	.1570
75	.0210	48	.0760	21	.1590
74	.0225	47	.0785	20	.1610
73	.0240	46	.0810	19	.1660
72	.0250	45	.0820	18	.1695
71	.0260	44	.0860	17	.1730
70	.0280	43	.0890	16	.1770
69	.0292	42	.0935	15	.1800
68	.0310	41	.0960	14	.1820
67	.0320	40	.0980	13	.1850
66	.0330	39	.0995	12	.1890
65	.0350	38	.1015	11	.1910
64	.0360	37	.1040	10	.1935
63	.0370	36	.1065	9	.1960
62	.0380	35	.1100	8	.1990
61	.0390	34	.1110	7	.2010
60	.0400	33	.1130	6	.2040
59	.0410	32	.1160	5	.2055
58	.0420	31	.1200	4	.2090
57	.0430	30	.1285	3	.2130
56	.0465	29	.1360	2	.2210
55	.0520	28	.1405	1	.2280
54	.0550	27	.1440		

Decimal Equivalent Size of the Letter Drills

Letter Drill	Decimal Equivalent	Letter Drill	Decimal Equivalent	Letter Drill	Decimal Equivalent
A	.234	J	.277	S	.348
B	.238	K	.281	T	.358
C	.242	L	.290	U	.368
D	.246	M	.295	V	.377
E	.250	N	.302	W	.386
F	.257	O	.316	X	.397
G	.261	P	.323	Y	.404
H	.266	Q	.332	Z	.413
I	.272	R	.339		

Decimal Equivalents of the Common Fractions

Fraction	Decimal	Fraction	Decimal	Fraction	Decimal
1/64	.0156	21/64	.3281	43/64	.6719
1/32	.0313	11/32	.3438	11/16	.6875
3/64	.0469	23/64	.3594	45/64	.7031
1/16	.0625	3/8	.3750	23/32	.7188
5/64	.0781	25/64	.3906	47/64	.7344
3/32	.0938	13/32	.4063	3/4	.7500
7/64	.1094	27/64	.4219	49/64	.7656
1/8	.1250	7/16	.4375	25/32	.7813
9/64	.1406	29/64	.4531	51/64	.7969
5/32	.1563	15/32	.4688	13/16	.8125
11/64	.1719	31/64	.4844	53/64	.8281
3/16	.1875	1/2	.5000	27/32	.8438
13/64	.2031	33/64	.5156	55/64	.8594
7/32	.2188	17/32	.5313	7/8	.8750
15/64	.2344	35/64	.5469	57/64	.8906
1/4	.2500	9/16	.5625	29/32	.9063
17/64	.2656	37/64	.5781	59/64	.9219
9/32	.2813	19/32	.5938	15/16	.9375
19/64	.2969	39/64	.6094	61/64	.9531
5/16	.3125	5/8	.6250	31/32	.9688
		41/64	.6406	63/64	.9844
		21/32	.6563